D1574063

Wörterbücher
Dictionaries
Dictionnaires

HSK 5.3

Handbücher zur Sprach- und Kommunikationswissenschaft

Handbooks of Linguistics and Communication Science

Manuels de linguistique et des sciences de communication

Mitbegründet von
Gerold Ungeheuer

Herausgegeben von / Edited by / Édités par
Hugo Steger
Herbert Ernst Wiegand

Band 5.3

Walter de Gruyter · Berlin · New York
1991

Wörterbücher
Dictionaries
Dictionnaires

Ein internationales Handbuch zur Lexikographie
An International Encyclopedia of Lexicography
Encyclopédie internationale de lexicographie

Edited by / Herausgegeben von / Éditée par
Franz Josef Hausmann · Oskar Reichmann
Herbert Ernst Wiegand · Ladislav Zgusta

Dritter Teilband / Third Volume / Tome Troisième

Walter de Gruyter · Berlin · New York
1991

∞ Gedruckt auf säurefreiem Papier, das die US-ANSI-Norm über Haltbarkeit erfüllt

Die Deutsche Bibliothek — CIP-Einheitsaufnahme

Handbücher zur Sprach- und Kommunikationswissenschaft / mitbegr. von Gerold Ungeheuer. Hrsg. von Hugo Steger; Herbert Ernst Wiegand. — Berlin; New York: de Gruyter.
  Teilw. mit Parallelt.: Handbooks of linguistics and communication science. — Früher hrsg. von Gerold Ungeheuer und Herbert Ernst Wiegand
NE: Ungeheuer, Gerold [Begr.]; Steger, Hugo [Hrsg.]; PT
Bd. 5. Wörterbücher.
  Teilbd. 3 (1991)

Wörterbücher: ein internationales Handbuch zur Lexikographie = Dictionaries / hrsg. von Franz Josef Hausmann ... — Berlin; New York: de Gruyter.
  (Handbücher zur Sprach- und Kommunikationswissenschaft; Bd. 5)
NE: Hausmann, Franz Josef [Hrsg.]; PT
Teilbd. 3 (1991)
  ISBN 3-11-012421-1

© Copyright 1991 by Walter de Gruyter & Co., D-1000 Berlin 30.
Dieses Werk einschließlich aller seiner Teile ist urheberrechtlich geschützt. Jede Verwertung außerhalb der engen Grenzen des Urheberrechtsgesetzes ist ohne Zustimmung des Verlages unzulässig und strafbar. Das gilt insbesondere für Vervielfältigungen, Übersetzungen, Mikroverfilmungen und die Einspeicherung und Verarbeitung in elektronischen Systemen.
Printed in Germany
Satz und Druck: H. Heenemann GmbH & Co, Berlin
Buchbinderische Verarbeitung: Lüderitz & Bauer, Berlin

Inhalt / Contents / Table des matières

Dritter Teilband / Third Volume / Tome Troisième

Kartenverzeichnis / Map Index / Index des cartes géographiques XXV

XXI. Lexikographie der Einzelsprachen V: Weitere europäische und ihnen benachbarte Sprachen
Lexicography of Individual Languages V: Further Languages of Europe and Adjacent Areas
Lexicographie des langues particulières V: Autres langues européennes et langues avoisinantes

220. Karl Horst Schmidt, Altirische Lexikographie 2339
     (Lexicography of Old-Irish · Lexicographie de l'ancien irlandais)

221. Elmar Ternes, Die Lexikographie der neukeltischen Sprachen 2343
     (Lexicography of Contemporary Celtic Languages · Lexicographie des langues celtiques contemporaines)

222. William R. Schmalstieg, Lexicography of the Baltic Languages I: Lithuanian, Old Prussian 2351
     (Die Lexikographie der baltischen Sprachen I: Litauisch und Altpreußisch · Lexicographie des langues baltes I: lituanien et ancien prussien)

223. Wolfgang P. Schmid, Die Lexikographie der baltischen Sprachen II: Lettisch . 2354
     (Lexicography of the Baltic Languages II: Latvian · Lexicographie des langues baltes II: lette)

224. Armin Hetzer, Albanische Lexikographie 2361
     (Albanian Lexicography · Lexicographie albanaise)

225. Gevork Djahukyan, Armenian Lexicography 2367
     (Armenische Lexikographie · Lexicographie arménienne)

226. Miren Azkarate, Basque Lexicography 2371
     (Baskische Lexikographie · Lexicographie basque)

227. Ferenc Bakos, Die Lexikographie der uralischen Sprachen I: Ungarisch . . . 2375
     (Lexicography of the Uralic Languages I: Hungarian · Lexicographie des langues ouraliennes I: hongrois)

228. Jarmo Korhonen/Ingrid Schellbach-Kopra, Die Lexikographie der uralischen Sprachen II: Finnisch 2383
     (Lexicography of the Uralic Languages II: Finnish · Lexicographie des langues ouraliennes II: finnois)

228a. Mikko Korhonen, Die Lexikographie der uralischen Sprachen III: Lappisch . . 2388
     (Lexicography of the Uralic Languages III: Lapp · Lexicographie des langues ouraliennes III: lapon)

229. Alo Raun, Lexicography of the Uralic Languages IV: Estonian and Livonian . . 2392
     (Die Lexikographie der uralischen Sprachen IV: Estnisch und Livisch · Lexicographie des langues ouraliennes IV: estonien et livonien)

230. Daniel Abondolo, Lexicography of the Uralic Languages V: Other Uralic Languages 2395
(Die Lexikographie der uralischen Sprachen V: Sonstige uralische Sprachen · Lexicographie des langues ouraliennes V: autres langues ouraliennes)

231. Andreas Tietze, Die Lexikographie der Turksprachen I: Osmanisch-Türkisch . 2399
(Lexicography of the Turkic Languages I: Osman-Turkish · Lexicographie des langues turques I: osmano-turc)

232. Gerhard Doerfer, Die Lexikographie der Turksprachen II: Sonstige Turksprachen 2407
(Lexicography of the Turkic Languages II: Other Turkic Languages · Lexicographie des langues turques II: autres langues turques)

233. Brian George Hewitt, Lexicography of the Caucasian Languages I: Georgian and Kartvelian 2415
(Die Lexikographie der kaukasischen Sprachen I: Georgisch und Kharthwelsprachen · Lexicographie des langues caucasiennes I: géorgien et kharthvèle)

234. Brian George Hewitt, Lexicography of the Caucasian Languages II: Northwest Caucasian Languages 2418
(Die Lexikographie der kaukasischen Sprachen II: Nordwestkaukasische Sprachen · Lexicographie des langues caucasiennes II: langues caucasiennes du Nord-Ouest)

235. Johanna Nichols, Lexicography of the Caucasian Languages III: Northeast Caucasian Languages 2421
(Die Lexikographie der kaukasischen Sprachen III: Nordostkaukasische Sprachen · Lexicographie des langues caucasiennes III: langues caucasiennes du Nord-Est)

XXII. Lexikographie der Einzelsprachen VI: Die semitohamitischen Sprachen
Lexicography of Individual Languages VI: The Hamito-Semitic Languages
Lexicographie des langues particulières VI: Langues chamito-sémitiques

236. Stanislav Segert/Yona Sabar, Hebrew and Aramaic Lexicography 2424
(Hebräische und aramäische Lexikographie · Lexicographie hébraïque et araméenne)

237. John A. Haywood, Arabic Lexicography 2438
(Arabische Lexikographie · Lexicographie arabe)

238. Wolf Leslau, Lexicography of the Semitic Languages of Ethiopia 2448
(Die Lexikographie der semitischen Sprachen Äthiopiens · Lexicographie des langues sémitiques d'Ethiopie)

239. Abdallah Bounfour, La lexicographie berbère 2455
(Die Lexikographie des Berberischen · Berber Lexicography)

240. Paul Newman/Roxana Ma Newman, Lexicography of the Chadic Languages . 2457
(Die Lexikographie der tschado-hamitischen Sprachen · Lexicographie des langues tchado-chamitiques)

241. Gene Balford Gragg, Lexicography of the Cushitic Languages 2461
(Die Lexikographie der kuschitischen Sprachen · Lexicographie des langues couchitiques)

XXIII. Lexikographie der Einzelsprachen VII: Die iranischen Sprachen
Lexicography of Individual Languages VII: The Iranian Languages
Lexicographie des langues particulières VII: Langues iraniennes

242. Manfred Mayrhofer, Altiranische Lexikographie 2470
(Old Iranian Lexicography · Lexicographie de l'ancien iranien)

243. David Neil MacKenzie, Middle Iranian Lexicography 2473
(Mitteliranische Lexikographie · Lexicographie du moyen iranien)

244. John R. Perry, Modern Iranian Lexicography: Persian/Tajik	2477
(Neuiranische Lexikographie: Farsi/Tadyk · Lexicographie de l'iranien moderne: persan/tadjik)	
245. Sonja Fritz, Die Lexikographie der übrigen neuiranischen Sprachen	2481
(Lexicography of Other Modern Iranian Languages · Lexicographie d'autres langues iraniennes modernes)	

XXIV. Lexikographie der Einzelsprachen VIII: Die Sprachen des indischen Subkontinents
Lexicography of Individual Languages VIII: The Languages of the Indian Subcontinent
Lexicographie des langues particulières VIII: Les langues du sous-continent indien

246. Sumitra M. Katre, Lexicography of Old Indo-Aryan: Vedic and Sanskrit	2487
(Die Lexikographie des Altindoarischen: Vedisch und Sanskrit · Lexicographie de l'ancien indo-aryen: védique et sanskrit)	
247. Elisabeth Strandberg, Lexicography of Middle Indo-Aryan	2497
(Die Lexikographie des Mittelindoarischen · Lexicographie du moyen indo-aryen)	
248. Ram Adhar Singh, Lexicography of New Indo-Aryan	2507
(Die Lexikographie des Neuindoarischen · Lexicographie de l'indo-aryen moderne)	
249. Bhadriraju Krishnamurti, Dravidian Lexicography	2521
(Dravidische Lexikographie · Lexicographie dravidienne)	
250. Norman Zide, Lexicography of Other Languages of the Indian Subcontinent: The Munda Languages	2533
(Die Lexikographie der sonstigen Sprachen des indischen Subkontinents: Die Munda-Sprachen · La lexicographie des autres langues du sous-continent indien: les langues munda)	

XXV. Lexikographie der Einzelsprachen IX: Die tibetobirmanischen Sprachen
Lexicography of Individual Languages IX: The Tibeto-Burman Languages
Lexicographie des langues particulières IX: Les langues tibéto-birmanes

251. Melvyn C. Goldstein, Tibetan Lexicography	2548
(Tibetische Lexikographie · Lexicographie tibétaine)	
252. John Okell, Burmese Lexicography	2550
(Birmanische Lexikographie · Lexicographie birmane)	
253. James A. Matisoff, Lexicography of Other Tibeto-Burman Languages	2555
(Die Lexikographie der sonstigen tibetobirmanischen Sprachen · Lexicographie des autres langues tibéto-birmanes)	

XXVI. Lexikographie der Einzelsprachen X: Die austronesischen Sprachen
Lexicography of Individual Languages X: The Austronesian Languages
Lexicographie des langues particulières X: Les langues austronésiennes

254. John U. Wolff, Javanese Lexicography	2561
(Javanische Lexikographie · Lexicographie javanaise)	
255. John U. Wolff, Lexicography of Indonesian	2563
(Die Lexikographie des Bahasa Indonesia · Lexicographie du Bahasa Indonesia)	
256. John U. Wolff, Lexicography of the Languages of Indonesia Aside From Indonesian and Javanese	2566
(Die Lexikographie der sonstigen Sprachen Indonesiens · Lexicographie des autres langues d'Indonésie)	

257. R. David Paul Zorc, Tagalog Lexicography 2568
     (Tagalische Lexikographie · Lexicographie tagale)
258. R. David Paul Zorc, Lexicography of Other Philippine Languages 2571
     (Die Lexikographie der sonstigen Philippinensprachen · Lexicographie des autres langues philippines)
259. John U. Wolff, Polynesian and Melanesian Lexicography 2573
     (Polynesische und melanesische Lexikographie · Lexicographie polynésienne et mélanésienne)

XXVII. Lexikographie der Einzelsprachen XI: Südostasiatische Sprachen
Lexicography of Individual Languages XI: The Languages of South-East Asia
Lexicographie des langues particulières XI: Langues du Sud-Est asiatique

260. Theraphan L. Thongkum/Pranee Kullavanijaya, Lexicography of the Thai Language 2576
     (Die Lexikographie der Thai-Sprache · Lexicographie de la langue thai)
261. Dinh-Hoa Nguyen, Vietnamese Lexicography 2583
     (Vietnamesische Lexikographie · Lexicographie vietnamienne)
262. David Thomas, Lexicography of Other Southeast Asian Languages 2589
     (Die Lexikographie weiterer Sprachen Südostasiens · La lexicographie d'autres langues du Sud-Est asiatique)

XXVIII. Lexikographie der Einzelsprachen XII: Ostasiatische Sprachen
Lexicography of Individual Languages XII: The Languages of East Asia
Lexicographie des langues particulières XII: Langues est-asiatiques

263. Thomas B. I. Creamer, Chinese Lexicography 2595
     (Chinesische Lexikographie · Lexicographie chinoise)
264. Key P. Yang, Korean Lexicography 2611
     (Koreanische Lexikographie · Lexicographie coréenne)
265. Bruno Lewin, Japanische Lexikographie 2617
     (Japanese Lexicography · Lexicographie japonaise)
266. Michael Weiers, Mongolische Lexikographie 2623
     (Mongolian Lexicography · Lexicographie mongole)

XXIX. Lexikographie der Einzelsprachen XIII: Arktische und pazifische Sprachen
Lexicography of Individual Languages XIII: The Languages of the Arctic and of the Pacific
Lexicographie des langues particulières XIII: Les langues de l'Arctique et de l'Océanie

267. Robert Austerlitz, Lexicography of the Paleosiberian Languages 2627
     (Die Lexikographie der paläosibirischen Sprachen · Lexicographie des langues paléo-sibériennes)
268. Steven A. Jacobson/Lawrence D. Kaplan, Lexicography of the Eskimo-Aleut Languages 2631
     (Die Lexikographie der aleutisch-eskimoischen Sprachen · Lexicographie des langues esquimau-aléoutes)

Inhalt IX

269. Stephen A. Wurm, Lexicography of the Languages of New Guinea 2634
(Die Lexikographie der Sprachen Neuguineas · Lexicographie des langues de Nouvelle-Guinée)

270. Peter Austin, Australian Lexicography 2638
(Australische Lexikographie · Lexicographie australienne)

XXX. Lexikographie der Einzelsprachen XIV: Die Sprachen Schwarzafrikas
Lexicography of Individual Languages XIV: The Languages of Black Africa
Lexicographie des langues particulières XIV: Les langues d'Afrique noire

271. M. Lionel Bender, Lexicography of Nilo-Saharan 2642
(Nilo-saharische Lexikographie · Lexicographie nilo-saharienne)

272. Edgar C. Polomé, Lexicography of the Niger-Kordofanian Languages 2646
(Die Lexikographie der Niger-Kordofan-Sprachen · Lexicographie des langues nigéro-congolaises)

273. Eric P. Hamp, Lexicography of the Khoisan Languages 2649
(Die Lexikographie der Khoisan-Sprachen · Lexicographie des langues Khoin)

XXXI. Lexikographie der Einzelsprachen XV: Die Indianersprachen Amerikas während der Kolonialzeit
Lexicography of Individual Languages XV: The Languages of the American Indians in the Colonial Period
Lexicographie des langues particulières XV: Les langues amérindiennes pendant la période coloniale

274. Frances Karttunen, Nahuatl Lexicography 2657
(Die Lexikographie des Nahuatl · Lexicographie du nahuatl)

275. Norman A. McQuown, Lexikographie der Mayasprachen 2661
(Lexicography of the Mayan Languages · Lexicographie des langues maya)

276. Wolf Dietrich, Die Lexikographie des Tupí-Guaraní 2670
(Lexicography of the Tupi-Guarani · Lexicographie du tupí-guaraní)

277. Bruce Mannheim, Lexicography of Colonial Quechua 2676
(Die Lexikographie des Ketschua · Lexicographie du quechua)

278. Martha J. Hardman-de-Bautista, Aymara Lexicography 2684
(Die Lexikographie des Aymara · Lexicographie de l'aymara)

XXXII. Lexikographie der Einzelsprachen XVI: Die Indianersprachen seit ca. 1800
Lexicography of Individual Languages XVI: The Languages of the American Indians From About 1800 On
Lexicographie des langues particulières XVI: Les langues indiennes d'Amérique depuis env. 1800

279. Richard A. Rhodes, Lexicography of the Languages of the North American Indians 2691
(Die Lexikographie der Indianersprachen Nordamerikas · Lexicographie des langues indiennes d'Amérique du Nord)

280. Doris Bartholomew, Lexicography of the Languages of the Mesoamerican Indians 2697
(Die Lexikographie der Indianersprachen Mesoamerikas · Lexicographie des langues indiennes d'Amérique centrale)

281. Mary Ritchie Key, Lexicography of the Languages of the Indians of the Orinoco and Amazon Area 2700
(Die Lexikographie der Indianersprachen des Orinoco- und Amazonas-Gebietes · Lexicographie des langues indiennes des régions de l'Orénoque et de l'Amazone)

282. Mary Ritchie Key, Lexicography of the Languages of the Andean Indians . . . 2704
(Die Lexikographie der andinen Indianersprachen · Lexicographie des langues indiennes des Andes)

283. Harriet E. Manelis Klein, Lexicography of the Indian Languages of Southern Brazil and the Rio de la Plata Region 2706
(Die Lexikographie der Indianersprachen des südlichen Brasilien und des Rio-de-la-Plata-Raumes · Lexicographie des langues indiennes du Brésil du Sud et du Rio de la Plata)

284. Harriet E. Manelis Klein, Lexicography of the Indian Languages of Southern South America 2708
(Die Lexikographie der Indianersprachen im südlichen Südamerika · Lexicographie des langues indiennes de la partie méridionale de l'Amérique du Sud)

XXXIII. Theorie der zwei- und mehrsprachigen Lexikographie I: Prinzipien und Bauteile
Theory of Bilingual and Multilingual Lexicography I: Principles and Components
Théorie de la lexicographie bilingue et plurilingue I: Principes et éléments

285. Hans-Peder Kromann/Theis Riiber/Poul Rosbach (†), Principles of Bilingual Lexicography 2711
(Prinzipien der zweisprachigen Lexikographie · Principes de la lexicographie bilingue)

286. Franz Josef Hausmann/Reinhold Otto Werner, Spezifische Bauteile und Strukturen zweisprachiger Wörterbücher: eine Übersicht 2729
(Specific Component Parts and Structures of Bilingual Dictionaries: A Survey · Eléments et structures spécifiques du dictionnaire bilingue: vue d'ensemble)

287. Hans-Peder Kromann/Theis Riiber/Poul Rosbach (†), Grammatical Constructions in the Bilingual Dictionary 2770
(Die Konstruktionen im zweisprachigen Wörterbuch · Informations d'ordre syntaxique dans le dictionnaire bilingue)

287 a. Margaret Cop, Collocations in the Bilingual Dictionary 2775
(Die Kollokationen im zweisprachigen Wörterbuch · Les collocations dans le dictionnaire bilingue)

288. Ronald Lötzsch, Die Komposita im zweisprachigen Wörterbuch 2779
(Compounds in the Bilingual Dictionary · Les mots composés dans le dictionnaire bilingue)

289. Jane Rosenkilde Jacobsen/James Manley/Viggo Hjørnager Pedersen, Examples in the Bilingual Dictionary 2782
(Die Beispiele im zweisprachigen Wörterbuch · Les exemples dans le dictionnaire bilingue)

290. Hans Schemann, Die Phraseologie im zweisprachigen Wörterbuch 2789
(Phraseology in the Bilingual Dictionary · La phraséologie dans le dictionnaire bilingue)

291. Franz Josef Hausmann, Die Paradigmatik im zweisprachigen Wörterbuch . . . 2794
(Paradigmatic Information in the Bilingual Dictionary · L'information paradigmatique dans le dictionnaire bilingue)

292. Reinhold Werner, Die Markierungen im zweisprachigen Wörterbuch 2796
(Labels in the Bilingual Dictionary · Les marques d'usage dans le dictionnaire bilingue)

XXXIV. Theorie der zwei- und mehrsprachigen Lexikographie II: Ausgewählte Beschreibungsprobleme
Theory of Bilingual and Multilingual Lexicography II: Selected Problems in Description
Théorie de la lexicographie bilingue et plurilingue II: Problèmes choisis de description

293. Bernard P. F. Al, Dictionnaire bilingue et ordinateur 2804
(Der Computer in der zweisprachigen Lexikographie · The Computer in Bilingual Lexicography)

294. Veronika Schnorr, Problems of Lemmatization in the Bilingual Dictionary . . 2813
(Probleme der Lemmatisierung im zweisprachigen Wörterbuch · Problèmes de la lemmatisation dans le dictionnaire bilingue)

295. Alain Duval, L'équivalence dans le dictionnaire bilingue 2817
(Die Äquivalenz im zweisprachigen Wörterbuch · Equivalence in the Bilingual Dictionary)

296. Ilse Karl, Grammatische und lexikalische Kategorisierung im zweisprachigen Wörterbuch 2824
(Grammatical and Lexical Categorization in the Bilingual Dictionary · Catégories grammaticales et lexicales dans le dictionnaire bilingue)

297. Bernard P. F. Al, L'organisation microstructurelle dans le dictionnaire bilingue . 2828
(Formen von Mikrostrukturen im zweisprachigen Wörterbuch · Forms of Microstructure in the Bilingual Dictionary)

298. Werner Wolski, Formen der Textverdichtung im zweisprachigen Wörterbuch . 2837
(Forms of Textual Compression in the Bilingual Dictionary · Compression du texte dans le dictionnaire bilingue)

299. Reinhard Rudolf Karl Hartmann, Contrastive Linguistics and Bilingual Lexicography 2854
(Kontrastive Linguistik und zweisprachige Lexikographie · Linguistique contrastive et lexicographie bilingue)

300. Josette Rey-Debove, La métalangue dans les dictionnaires bilingues 2859
(Die lexikographische Metasprache im zweisprachigen Wörterbuch · Lexicographical Metalanguage in the Bilingual Dictionary)

301. Alain Rey, Divergences culturelles et dictionnaire bilingue 2865
(Kulturelle Verschiedenheit und zweisprachiges Wörterbuch · Cultural Differences and the Bilingual Dictionary)

302. Annegret Bollée, Problèmes de description lexicographique des langues pidgins et créoles 2870
(Probleme der lexikographischen Beschreibung von Pidgin- und Kreolsprachen · Problems in the Lexicographical Description of Pidgin and Creole Languages)

XXXV. Typologie und ausgewählte Typen der zwei- und mehrsprachigen Lexikographie
Typology and Selected Types of Bilingual and Multilingual Lexicography
Typologie et types choisis de la lexicographie bilingue et plurilingue

303. Franz Josef Hausmann, Typologie der zweisprachigen Spezialwörterbücher . . 2877
(Typology of Specialized Bilingual Dictionaries · Typologie des dictionnaires bilingues spécialisés)

304. Adeline Gorbahn-Orme/Franz Josef Hausmann, The Dictionary of False Friends 2882
(Das Wörterbuch der falschen Freunde · Le dictionnaire de faux amis)

305. Ekkehard Zöfgen, Bilingual Learner's Dictionaries 2888
(Zweisprachige Lernwörterbücher · Les dictionnaires d'apprentissage bilingues)

305 a. Heike Abend, Das Reisewörterbuch 2903
(The Tourist's Dictionary · Le dictionnaire à l'usage des touristes)

306. Günther Haensch, Die mehrsprachigen Wörterbücher und ihre Probleme . . . 2909
(Multilingual Dictionaries and Their Problems · Les dictionnaires multilingues et leurs problèmes)

307. Günther Haensch, Die zweisprachige Fachlexikographie und ihre Probleme . . 2937
(Bilingual Lexicography of Specialized Languages and its Problems · La lexicographie des langues de spécialités et ses problèmes)

XXXVI. Die zweisprachigen Wörterbücher in Geschichte und Gegenwart
Bilingual Dictionaries Past and Present
Les dictionnaires bilingues hier et aujourd'hui

308. Roger Jacob Steiner, Bilingual Lexicography: English-Spanish, Spanish-English   2949
(Die zweisprachige Lexikographie Englisch-Spanisch, Spanisch-Englisch · La lexicographie bilingue anglais-espagnol, espagnol-anglais)

309. Franz Josef Hausmann, La lexicographie bilingue anglais-français, français-anglais 2956
(Die zweisprachige Lexikographie Englisch-Französisch, Französisch-Englisch · Bilingual Lexicography: English-French, French-English)

310. Kurt-Michael Pätzold, Bilingual Lexicography: English-German, German-English 2961
(Die zweisprachige Lexikographie Englisch-Deutsch, Deutsch-Englisch · La lexicographie bilingue anglais-allemand, allemand-anglais)

311. Desmond O'Connor, Bilingual Lexicography English-Italian, Italian-English . 2970
(Die zweisprachige Lexikographie Englisch-Italienisch, Italienisch-Englisch · La lexicographie bilingue anglais-italien, italien-anglais)

312. Robert A. Verdonk, La lexicographie bilingue espagnol-français, français-espagnol 2976
(Die zweisprachige Lexikographie Spanisch-Französisch, Französisch-Spanisch · Bilingual Lexicography: Spanish-English, English-Spanish)

313. Franz Josef Hausmann, Die zweisprachige Lexikographie Spanisch-Deutsch, Deutsch-Spanisch 2987
(Bilingual Lexicography: Spanish-German, German-Spanish · La lexicographie bilingue espagnol-allemand, allemand-espagnol)

314. Annamaria Gallina, La lexicographie bilingue espagnol-italien, italien-espagnol   2991
(Die zweisprachige Lexikographie Spanisch-Italienisch, Italienisch-Spanisch · Bilingual Lexicography: Spanish-Italian, Italian-Spanish)

315. Wolfgang Rettig, Die zweisprachige Lexikographie Französisch-Deutsch, Deutsch-Französisch 2997
(Bilingual Lexicography: French-German, German-French · La lexicographie bilingue français-allemand, allemand-français)

316. Nicole Bingen/Anne-Marie Van Passen, La lexicographie bilingue français-italien, italien-français 3007
(Die zweisprachige Lexikographie Französisch-Italienisch, Italienisch-Französisch · Bilingual Lexicography: French-Italian, Italian-French)

Inhalt XIII

317. Laurent Bray/Maria Luisa Bruna/Franz Josef Hausmann, Die zweisprachige Lexikographie Deutsch-Italienisch, Italienisch-Deutsch 3013
(Bilingual Lexicography: German-Italian, Italian-German · La lexicographie bilingue allemand-italien, italien-allemand)

318. Stefan Ettinger, Die zweisprachige Lexikographie mit Portugiesisch 3020
(Bilingual Lexicography With Portuguese · La lexicographie bilingue avec le portugais)

319. Dietfried Krömer, Die zweisprachige lateinische Lexikographie seit ca. 1700 . . 3030
(Bilingual Lexicography of Latin Since 1700 · La lexicographie bilingue du latin depuis 1700)

320. Noel Edward Osselton, Bilingual Lexicography With Dutch 3034
(Die zweisprachige Lexikographie mit Holländisch · La lexicographie bilingue avec le hollandais)

321. André Kahlmann, La lexicographie bilingue suédois-français, français-suédois . 3040
(Die zweisprachige Lexikographie Schwedisch-Französisch, Französisch-Schwedisch · Bilingual Lexicography: Swedish-French, French-Swedish)

321a. Gustav Korlén, Die zweisprachige Lexikographie Schwedisch-Deutsch, Deutsch-Schwedisch 3043
(Bilingual Lexicography: Swedish-German, German-Swedish · La lexicographie bilingue suédois-allemand, allemand-suédois)

321b. Arne Olofsson, Bilingual Lexicography: Swedish-English, English-Swedish . . 3047
(Die zweisprachige Lexikographie Schwedisch-Englisch, Englisch-Schwedisch · La lexicographie bilingue suédois-anglais, anglais-suédois)

322. Jens Rasmussen, La lexicographie bilingue avec le danois 3051
(Die zweisprachige Lexikographie mit Dänisch · Bilingual Lexicography With Danish)

323. Jan A. Czochralski, Die zweisprachige Lexikographie mit Polnisch 3061
(Bilingual Lexicography With Polish · La lexicographie bilingue avec le polonais)

324. Wolfgang Eismann, Die zweisprachige Lexikographie mit Russisch 3068
(Bilingual Lexicography With Russian · La lexicographie bilingue avec le russe)

325. John A. Haywood, Bilingual Lexicography With Arabic 3086
(Die zweisprachige Lexikographie mit Arabisch · La lexicographie bilingue avec l'arabe)

326. K. Balasubramanian, Bilingual Lexicography on the Indian Subcontinent . . . 3096
(Die zweisprachige Lexikographie des indischen Subkontinents · La lexicographie bilingue du sous-continent indien)

327. Thomas B. I. Creamer, Bilingual Lexicography With Chinese 3107
(Die zweisprachige Lexikographie mit Chinesisch · La lexicographie bilingue avec le chinois)

328. Daisuke Nagashima, Bilingual Lexicography With Japanese 3113
(Die zweisprachige Lexikographie mit Japanisch · La lexicographie bilingue avec le japonais)

XXXVII. Lexikographie von Hilfssprachen und anderen Kommunikationssystemen
Lexicography of Auxiliary Languages and of Other Communication Systems
Lexicographie des langues auxiliaires et d'autres systèmes de communication

329. Reinhard Haupenthal, Lexikographie der Plansprachen 3120
(Lexicography of Auxiliary Languages · La lexicographie des langues auxiliaires internationales)

330. Fritz Haeger (†), Lexikographie der Kurzschriften 3137
(Dictionaries of Shorthand · Dictionnaires de sténographie)

331. Jerome D. Schein, Dictionaries of Deaf Languages 3141
(Lexikographie zur Gehörlosensprache · Lexicographie de la langue des sourds)

332. Hilda Caton, Dictionaries in and of Braille 3145
(Blindenschriftliche Lexikographie · Lexicographie en braille)

333. Joachim Knape, Wörterbücher zu Bildsymbolen 3148
(Dictionaries of Pictorial Symbols · Dictionnaires de symboles)

334. Ladislav Zgusta, Probable Future Developments in Lexicography 3158
(Über die zukünftige Entwicklung der Lexikographie · Quelques réflexions sur l'avenir de la lexicographie)

XXXVIII. Bibliographischer Anhang und Register
Bibliographic Appendix and Indexes
Annexe bibliographique et index

335. Margaret Cop, Bibliography of Dictionary Bibliographies 3168
(Bibliographie der Wörterbuch-Bibliographien · Bibliographie des bibliographies de dictionnaires)

336. F. J. H./O. R./H. E. W./L. Z./unter Mitarbeit von Thorsten Roelcke, Sachregister 3178
(Subject Index · Index des matières)

337. F. J. H./O. R./H. E. W./L. Z./unter Mitarbeit von Jenifer Brundage und Gisela Schmidt, Namenregister 3250
(Index of Names · Index des noms)

Erster Teilband (Übersicht)
First Volume (Overview of Contents)
Tome Premier (articles parus)

I. Lexikographie und Gesellschaft I: Wörterbücher und Öffentlichkeit
Lexicography and Society I: Dictionaries and Their Public
Lexicographie et société I: Les dictionnaires et leur public

1. Franz Josef Hausmann, Die gesellschaftlichen Aufgaben der Lexikographie in Geschichte und Gegenwart 1

2. Franz Josef Hausmann, Das Wörterbuch im Urteil der gebildeten Öffentlichkeit in Deutschland und in den romanischen Ländern 19

3. John Algeo, Dictionaries as Seen by the Educated Public in Great Britain and the USA 28

4. John Algeo, The Image of the Dictionary in the Mass Media: USA 34

5. Laurent Bray, Le dictionnaire dans les mass-médias en France 38

6.	Jean-Claude Boulanger, Lexicographie et politique langagière: l'exemple français des avis officiels	46
7.	Yakov Malkiel, Wörterbücher und Normativität	63
8.	Ladislav Zgusta, The Role of Dictionaries in the Genesis and Development of the Standard	70
9.	Jean-Pierre Beaujot, Dictionnaire et idéologies	79
10.	Janet Whitcut, The Dictionary as a Commodity	88
10a.	Edward Gates, The Training of Lexicographers	94
11.	Franz Josef Hausmann, Dictionary Criminality	97

II. Lexikographie und Gesellschaft II: Wörterbücher und ihre Benutzer
Lexicography and Society II: Dictionaries and Their Users
Lexicographie et société II: Le dictionnaire et ses utilisateurs

12.	Reinhard Rudolf Karl Hartmann, Sociology of the Dictionary User: Hypotheses and Empirical Studies	102
13.	Peter Kühn, Typologie der Wörterbücher nach Benutzungsmöglichkeiten	111
14.	Ulrich Püschel, Wörterbücher und Laienbenutzung	128
15.	Laurent Bray, Consultabilité et lisibilité du dictionnaire: aspects formels	135
16.	Giovanni Nencioni, The Dictionary as an Aid in Belles Lettres	146
17.	Rolf Bergmann, Wörterbücher als Hilfsmittel der philologischen Arbeit	152
18.	Gisela Harras, Wörterbücher als Hilfsmittel der linguistischen Forschung	159
19.	Jochen Hoock, Wörterbücher als Hilfsmittel für den Historiker	163
20.	Juan C. Sager, The Dictionary as an Aid in Terminology	167
21.	Hans J. Vermeer, Wörterbücher als Hilfsmittel für unterschiedliche Typen der Translation	171
22.	Gaston Gross, Le dictionnaire et l'enseignement de la langue maternelle	174
23.	Reinhard Rudolf Karl Hartmann, The Dictionary as an Aid to Foreign-Language Teaching	181
24.	Martha Ripfel, Die normative Wirkung deskriptiver Wörterbücher	189
25.	Henri Béjoint, The Teaching of Dictionary Use: Present State and Future Tasks	208

III. Geschichte und Theorie der Lexikographie: Allgemeine Aspekte
History and Theory of Lexicography: General Aspects
Théorie et histoire de la lexicographie: Aspects généraux

26.	Franz Josef Hausmann, Pour une histoire de la métalexicographie	216
27.	Noel Edward Osselton, The History of Academic Dictionary Criticism With Reference to Major Dictionaries	225
28.	Oskar Reichmann, Geschichte lexikographischer Programme in Deutschland	230
29.	Herbert Ernst Wiegand, Der gegenwärtige Status der Lexikographie und ihr Verhältnis zu anderen Disziplinen	246

30. Luis Fernando Lara, Dictionnaire de langue, encyclopédie et dictionnaire encyclopédique: le sens de leur distinction 280

31. Dirk Geeraerts, Principles of Monolingual Lexicography 287

32. Ladislav Zgusta, The Influence of Scripts and Morphological Language Types on the Structure of Dictionaries 296

33. Josette Rey-Debove, La métalangue lexicographique: formes et fonctions en lexicographie monolingue 305

34. Elisabeth Link/Burkhard Schaeder, Fachsprache der Lexikographie 312

35. Claude Poirier, Les différents supports du dictionnaire: livre, microfiche, dictionnaire électronique 322

IV. Theorie der einsprachigen Lexikographie I: Bauteile und Strukturen von Wörterbüchern
Theory of Monolingual Lexicography I: Components and Structures of Dictionaries
Théorie de la lexicographie monolingue I: Éléments et structures du dictionnaire

36. Franz Josef Hausmann/Herbert Ernst Wiegand, Component Parts and Structures of General Monolingual Dictionaries: A Survey 328

37. Werner Wolski, Das Lemma und die verschiedenen Lemmatypen 360

38. Herbert Ernst Wiegand, Aspekte der Makrostruktur im allgemeinen einsprachigen Wörterbuch: alphabetische Anordnungsformen und ihre Probleme 371

38a. Herbert Ernst Wiegand, Der Begriff der Mikrostruktur: Geschichte, Probleme, Perspektiven 409

39. Herbert Ernst Wiegand, Arten von Mikrostrukturen im allgemeinen einsprachigen Wörterbuch 462

40. Nina Catach, L'orthographe dans le dictionnaire monolingue 501

41. Elmar Ternes, Die phonetischen Angaben im allgemeinen einsprachigen Wörterbuch 508

42. Joachim Mugdan, Information on Inflectional Morphology in the General Monolingual Dictionary 518

43. Patrick Dockar Drysdale, Etymological Information in the General Monolingual Dictionary 525

44. Herbert Ernst Wiegand, Die lexikographische Definition im allgemeinen einsprachigen Wörterbuch 530

45. Anthony Paul Cowie, Information on Syntactic Constructions in the General Monolingual Dictionary 588

46. Harald Burger, Phraseologismen im allgemeinen einsprachigen Wörterbuch . . 593

47. Robert Martin, L'exemple lexicographique dans le dictionnaire monolingue . . 599

47a. Gisela Harras, Zu einer Theorie des lexikographischen Beispiels 607

48. Werner Wolski, Die Synonymie im allgemeinen einsprachigen Wörterbuch . . 614

49. Wolfgang Müller, Die Antonyme im allgemeinen einsprachigen Wörterbuch . . 628

50.	Josette Rey-Debove, Le traitement analogique dans le dictionnaire monolingue	635
51.	Franz Josef Hausmann, Les homonymes et les paronymes dans le dictionnaire monolingue	640
52.	Wolfgang Rettig, Die Wortbildungszusammenhänge im allgemeinen einsprachigen Wörterbuch	642
53.	Franz Josef Hausmann, Die Markierung im allgemeinen einsprachigen Wörterbuch: eine Übersicht	649
54.	Günter Dietrich Schmidt, Diachronische Markierungen im allgemeinen einsprachigen Wörterbuch	657
55.	Hermann Niebaum, Diatopische Markierungen im allgemeinen einsprachigen Wörterbuch	662
56.	Broder Carstensen, Die Markierung von Entlehnungen im allgemeinen einsprachigen Wörterbuch	668
57.	Pierre Corbin, Les marques stylistiques/diastratiques dans le dictionnaire monolingue	673
58.	Hartwig Kalverkämper, Diatechnische Markierungen im allgemeinen einsprachigen Wörterbuch	680
59.	Burkhard Schaeder, Diafrequente Markierungen im allgemeinen einsprachigen Wörterbuch	688
60.	Ulrich Püschel, Evaluative Markierungen im allgemeinen einsprachigen Wörterbuch	693
61.	Michel Glatigny, Les commentaires normatifs dans le dictionnaire monolingue	700
62.	Werner Hupka, Die Bebilderung und sonstige Formen der Veranschaulichung im allgemeinen einsprachigen Wörterbuch	704
63.	Laurent Bray, Les renvois bibliographiques dans le dictionnaire monolingue	726
64.	Joachim Mugdan, Grundzüge der Konzeption einer Wörterbuchgrammatik	732
65.	Dieter Herberg, Wörterbuchvorwörter	749
66.	Betty Kirkpatrick, User's Guides in Dictionaries	754
67.	Margaret Cop, Linguistic and Encyclopedic Information Not Included in the Dictionary Articles	761
67a.	Alan Kirkness, Wörterbuchregister	767

V. Theorie der einsprachigen Lexikographie II: Ausgewählte Beschreibungsprobleme im allgemeinen einsprachigen Wörterbuch
Theory of Monolingual Lexicography II: Selected Problems of Description in the General Monolingual Dictionary
Théorie de la lexicographie monolingue II: Problèmes choisis de la description dans le dictionnaire monolingue

68.	Henning Bergenholtz, Probleme der Selektion im allgemeinen einsprachigen Wörterbuch	772
69.	Ekkehard Zöfgen, Homonymie und Polysemie im allgemeinen einsprachigen Wörterbuch	779

70.	Gerhard Strauß, Angabe traditioneller Wortarten oder Beschreibung nach funktionalen Wortklassen im allgemeinen einsprachigen Wörterbuch?	788
71.	Günther Drosdowski, Die Beschreibung von Metaphern im allgemeinen einsprachigen Wörterbuch	797
72.	Werner Wolski, Die Beschreibung von Modalpartikeln im allgemeinen einsprachigen Wörterbuch	805
73.	Werner Holly, Die Beschreibung sprachhandlungsbezeichnender Ausdrücke im allgemeinen einsprachigen Wörterbuch	814
74.	Armin Burkhardt, Die Beschreibung von Gesprächswörtern im allgemeinen einsprachigen Wörterbuch	822
75.	Peter Kühn, Die Beschreibung von Routineformeln im allgemeinen einsprachigen Wörterbuch	830
76.	Walther Dieckmann, Die Beschreibung der politischen Lexik im allgemeinen einsprachigen Wörterbuch	835
77.	Günter Kempcke, Probleme der Beschreibung fachsprachlicher Lexik im allgemeinen einsprachigen Wörterbuch	842
78.	Ludwig Jäger/Sabine Plum, Probleme der Beschreibung von Gefühlswörtern im allgemeinen einsprachigen Wörterbuch	849
79.	Gottfried Kolde, Probleme der Beschreibung von sog. Heckenausdrücken im allgemeinen einsprachigen Wörterbuch	855
80.	Ewald Lang, Probleme der Beschreibung von Konjunktionen im allgemeinen einsprachigen Wörterbuch	862
81.	Wolfgang Müller, Die Beschreibung von Affixen und Affixoiden im allgemeinen einsprachigen Wörterbuch	869
82.	Peter von Polenz, Funktionsverbgefüge im allgemeinen einsprachigen Wörterbuch	882
83.	Dieter Viehweger (†), Probleme der Beschreibung semantischer Vereinbarkeitsrelationen im allgemeinen einsprachigen Wörterbuch	888
84.	Immo Wegner, Lexikographische Definition und Frame-Theorie im allgemeinen einsprachigen Wörterbuch	893
85.	Fritz Neubauer, Vocabulary Control in the Definitions and Examples of Monolingual Dictionaries	899
86.	Gérard Gorcy, Différenciation des significations dans le dictionnaire monolingue: problèmes et méthodes	905
87.	Reinhold Werner, Probleme der Anordnung der Definitionen im allgemeinen einsprachigen Wörterbuch	917
88.	Josette Rey-Debove, Les systèmes de renvois dans le dictionnaire monolingue	931
89.	Danielle Corbin/Pierre Corbin, Sélection et description des dérivés et composés dans le dictionnaire monolingue	937
90.	Heidrun Gerzymisch-Arbogast, Standardisierte Wörterbuchartikel des allgemeinen einsprachigen Wörterbuches als Texte: Probleme der Kohärenz und der Thema-Rhema-Struktur	946
90a.	Werner Wolski, Formen der Textverdichtung im allgemeinen einsprachigen Wörterbuch	956

VI. Wörterbuchtypen I: Allgemeine Aspekte der Wörterbuchtypologie und allgemeine einsprachige Wörterbücher
Dictionary Types I: General Aspects of Dictionary Typology and Monolingual Dictionaries
Typologie des dictionnaires I: Aspects généraux et types principaux

91.	Franz Josef Hausmann, Wörterbuchtypologie	968
92.	Franz Josef Hausmann, Das Definitionswörterbuch	981
93.	Werner Hupka, Das enzyklopädische Wörterbuch	988

VII. Wörterbuchtypen II: Syntagmatische Spezialwörterbücher
Dictionary Types II: Syntagmatic Dictionaries
Typologie des dictionnaires II: Dictionnaires syntagmatiques

94.	Ekkehard Zöfgen, Das Konstruktionswörterbuch	1000
95.	Franz Josef Hausmann, Le dictionnaire de collocations	1010
96.	Hans Schemann, Das phraseologische Wörterbuch	1019
97.	Wolfgang Mieder, Das Sprichwörterbuch	1033
98.	Franz Josef Hausmann, Das Zitatenwörterbuch	1044
99.	Franz Josef Hausmann, Das Satzwörterbuch	1050
100.	Franz Josef Hausmann, Weitere syntagmatische Spezialwörterbücher	1054

Zweiter Teilband (Übersicht)
Second Volume (Overview of Contents)
Tome Second (articles parus)

Kartenverzeichnis / Map Index / Index des cartes géographiques	XXIV

VIII. Wörterbuchtypen III: Paradigmatische Spezialwörterbücher
Dictionary Types III: Paradigmatic Dictionaries
Typologie des dictionnaires III: Les dictionnaires paradigmatiques

101.	Oskar Reichmann, Das onomasiologische Wörterbuch: Ein Überblick	1057
102.	Franz Josef Hausmann, The Dictionary of Synonyms: Discriminating Synonymy	1067
103.	Franz Josef Hausmann, Das Synonymenwörterbuch: Die kumulative Synonymik	1076
104.	Franz Josef Hausmann, Das Antonymenwörterbuch	1081
105.	Carla Marello, The Thesaurus	1083
106.	Franz Josef Hausmann, Le dictionnaire analogique	1094
107.	Franz Josef Hausmann, Das Umkehrwörterbuch	1100
108.	Werner Scholze-Stubenrecht, Das Bildwörterbuch	1103
109.	Giovanni Meo Zilio, Le dictionnaire de gestes	1112

110.	Franz Josef Hausmann, Das Wörterbuch der Homonyme, Homophone und Paronyme	1120
111.	Nicole Celeyrette-Pietri, Le dictionnaire de rimes	1125
112.	Kurt Gärtner/Peter Kühn, Das rückläufige Wörterbuch	1131
113.	Franz Josef Hausmann, Wörterbücher weiterer ausdrucksseitiger Paradigmen	1144
114.	Gerhard Augst, Das Wortfamilienwörterbuch	1145

IX.	Wörterbuchtypen IV: Spezialwörterbücher zu markierten Lemmata der Standardsprache Dictionary Types IV: Dictionaries Dealing Specifically With Marked Standard Language Entrywords Typologie des dictionnaires IV: Dictionnaires des entrées marquées de la langue standard	
115.	Oskar Reichmann, Wörterbücher archaischer und untergegangener Wörter	1153
116.	Robert Barnhart/Clarence Barnhart, The Dictionary of Neologisms	1159
117.	Wilfried Seibicke, Wörterbücher des landschaftlich markierten Wortschatzes	1166
118.	Alan Kirkness, Das Fremdwörterbuch	1168
119.	Franz Josef Hausmann/Wilfried Seibicke, Das Internationalismenwörterbuch	1179
120.	Franz Josef Hausmann, Das Wörterbuch der Sprechsprache, des Argot und des Slang	1184
121.	Wilfried Seibicke, Das Schimpfwörterbuch	1190
122.	Edgar Radtke, Das Wörterbuch des sexuellen Wortschatzes	1193
123.	Manfred Kaempfert, Das Schlagwörterbuch	1199
124.	Franz Josef Hausmann, Das Wörterbuch der schweren Wörter	1206
125.	Jean-Paul Colin, Le dictionnaire de difficultés	1210

X.	Wörterbuchtypen V: Wörterbücher zu bestimmten weiteren Lemmatypen Dictionary Types V: Dictionaries Dealing With Certain Other Types of Entrywords Typologie des dictionnaires V: Dictionnaires traitant certains autres types d'entrées	
126.	Franz Josef Hausmann/Gerhard Jerabek, Le dictionnaire grammatical	1218
127.	Franz Josef Hausmann, Wortklassenbezogene Wörterbücher	1221
128.	Elisabeth Link, Das Wörterbuch der Wortbildungsmittel	1223
129.	Oskar Reichmann, Erbwortbezogene Wörterbücher im Deutschen	1231
130.	Erwin Reiner, Le dictionnaire de doublets	1241
131.	Franz Josef Hausmann, Das Onomatopöienwörterbuch	1245
132.	Dieter Kremer, Das Wörterbuch der Berufsbezeichnungen	1248
133.	Lothar Voetz, Wörterbücher von Tier- und Pflanzenbezeichnungen	1254

134.	Charles Bernet, Le dictionnaire d'éponymes	1258
135.	Hans-Bernd Menzel, Das Abkürzungswörterbuch	1261

XI. Wörterbuchtypen VI: Namenwörterbücher (unter besonderer Berücksichtigung des Deutschen)
Dictionary Types VI: Onomastic Dictionaries (With Special Reference to German)
Typologie des dictionnaires VI: Dictionnaires de noms propres (référence spéciale à l'allemand)

136.	Wilfried Seibicke, Personennamenwörterbücher	1267
137.	Albrecht Greule, Ortsnamenwörterbücher	1276
138.	Wolfgang P. Schmid, Gewässernamenwörterbücher	1284
139.	Wilfried Seibicke, Weitere Typen des Namenwörterbuchs	1291

XII. Wörterbuchtypen VII: Spezialwörterbücher mit bestimmten Informationstypen
Dictionary Types VII: Dictionaries Offering Specific Types of Information
Typologie des dictionnaires VII: Dictionnaires specialisés donnant certains types d'information

140.	Dieter Nerius, Das Orthographiewörterbuch	1297
141.	Henriette Walter, Le dictionnaire de prononciation	1304
142.	Franz Josef Hausmann, Das Flexionswörterbuch	1311
143.	Willy Martin, The Frequency Dictionary	1314
144.	Yakov Malkiel, Das etymologische Wörterbuch von Informanten- und Korpussprachen	1323
145.	Bernhard Forssman, Das etymologische Wörterbuch rekonstruierter Sprachen	1335
146.	Wilhelm Kesselring, Das chronologische Wörterbuch	1342
147.	Franz Josef Hausmann, Le dictionnaire humoristique	1348

XIII. Wörterbuchtypen VIII: Didaktische Spezialwörterbücher
Dictionary Types VIII: Specialized Teaching Dictionaries
Typologie des dictionnaires VIII: Les dictionnaires pédagogiques

148.	Peter Kühn, Das Grundwortschatzwörterbuch	1353
149.	Franz Josef Hausmann, Das Kinderwörterbuch	1365
150.	René Lagane, Les dictionnaires scolaires: enseignement de la langue maternelle	1368
151.	Thomas Herbst, Dictionaries for Foreign Language Teaching: English	1379
152.	Franz Josef Hausmann, Les dictionnaires pour l'enseignement de la langue étrangère: français	1386

XIV. Wörterbuchtypen IX: Auf die Varietäten der Sprache bezogene Wörterbücher
Dictionary Types IX: Dictionaries Dealing With Language Varieties
Typologie des dictionnaires IX: Dictionnaires traitant différentes variétés de la langue

153.	Oskar Reichmann, Das gesamtsystembezogene Wörterbuch	1391
154.	Oskar Reichmann, Das Sprachstadienwörterbuch I: Deutsch	1416
154a.	Piet van Sterkenburg, Das Sprachstadienwörterbuch II: Niederländisch	1430
155.	Richard W. Bailey, The Period Dictionary III: English	1436
156.	Bodo Müller, Das Sprachstadienwörterbuch IV: Die romanischen Sprachen	1457
157.	Pierre Rézeau, Le dictionnaire dialectal: l'exemple français	1467
158.	Manfred Görlach, The Dictionary of Transplanted Varieties of Languages: English	1475
158a.	Franz Josef Hausmann, Les dictionnaires du français hors de France	1500
159.	Kurt Opitz, The Technical Dictionary for the Expert	1505
160.	Hartwig Kalverkämper, Das Fachwörterbuch für den Laien	1512
161.	Dieter Möhn, Das gruppenbezogene Wörterbuch	1523
162.	Edgar Radtke, Wörterbücher von Geheimsprachen	1532

XV. Wörterbuchtypen X: Auf Texte bezogene Wörterbücher
Dictionary Types X: Dictionaries Dealing With Texts
Typologie des dictionnaires X: Dictionnaires traitant de textes

163.	Oskar Reichmann, Das textsortenbezogene Wörterbuch	1539
164.	Josef Mattausch, Das Autoren-Bedeutungswörterbuch	1549
165.	Suzanne Hanon, La concordance	1562
166.	Paul Sappler, Der Index/Das Belegstellenwörterbuch	1567

XVI. Arbeitsverfahren in der Lexikographie
Procedures in Lexicographical Work
Les méthodes du travail lexicographique

167.	Claude Dubois, Considérations générales sur l'organisation du travail lexicographique	1574
168.	Oskar Reichmann, Formen und Probleme der Datenerhebung I: Synchronische und diachronische historische Wörterbücher	1588
169.	Henning Bergenholtz/Joachim Mugdan, Formen und Probleme der Datenerhebung II: Gegenwartsbezogene synchronische Wörterbücher	1611
170.	Kurt Opitz, Formen und Probleme der Datenerhebung III: Fachwörterbücher	1625
171.	Martha Ripfel, Probleme der Erhebung metalexikographischer Daten	1631
172.	Burkhard Schaeder, Quantitative Datenerhebung	1638

173.	Francis E. Knowles, The Computer in Lexicography	1645
173 a.	Gérard Gorcy, L'informatisation d'un dictionnaire: l'exemple du Trésor de la langue française	1672

XVII. Lexikographie der Einzelsprachen I: Die alten Sprachen des Nahen Ostens und die klassischen Sprachen
Lexicography of Individual Languages I: The Ancient Languages of the Near East and the Classical Languages
Lexicographie des langues particulières I: Les langues anciennes d'Asie mineure et les langues classiques

174.	Jürgen Osing, Ägyptische und koptische Lexikographie	1679
175.	Miguel Civil, Sumerian and Akkadian Lexicography	1682
176.	Annelies Kammenhuber, Hethitische Lexikographie	1686
177.	Stanislav Segert/Françoise Grillot/Volkert Haas/John A. Brinkman, The Lexicography of Other Ancient Languages of the Near East	1690
178.	Ladislav Zgusta/Demetrius J. Georgacas (†), Lexicography of Ancient Greek	1694
179.	Demetrius J. Georgacas (†)/Barbara Georgacas, The Lexicography of Byzantine and Modern Greek	1705
180.	Dietfried Krömer, Lateinische Lexikographie	1713

XVIII. Lexikographie der Einzelsprachen II: Die romanischen Sprachen
Lexicography of Individual Languages II: The Romance Languages
Lexicographie des langues particulières II: Les langues romanes

181.	Dieter Woll, Portugiesische Lexikographie	1723
181 a.	José Luis Pensado, Galician Lexicography	1736
182.	Günther Haensch, Spanische Lexikographie	1738
183.	Günther Schütz, Cuervos Wörterbuch als herausragendes Werk der hispanischen Lexikographie	1767
184.	Günther Haensch, Katalanische Lexikographie	1770
185.	Laurent Bray, La lexicographie française des origines à Littré	1788
186.	Alain Rey, La lexicographie française depuis Littré	1818
187.	Max Pfister, Die italienische Lexikographie von den Anfängen bis 1900	1844
188.	Aldo Duro, La lexicographie italienne du XXe siècle	1863
189.	Paul Miron, Rumänische Lexikographie	1880
190.	Johannes Kramer, Die Lexikographie des Provenzalischen, Rätoromanischen, Sardischen und Dalmatischen	1891
191.	Heinrich Kohring, Judenspanische Lexikographie	1905

XIX. Lexikographie der Einzelsprachen III: Die germanischen Sprachen
Lexicography of Individual Languages III: The Germanic Languages
Lexicographie des langues particulières III: Les langues germaniques

192.	Elfriede Stutz (†), Gotische Lexikographie	1908

193.	Poul Lindegård Hjorth, Danish Lexicography	1913
194.	Dag Gundersen, Norwegian Lexicography	1923
195.	Magnus Pétursson, Inselnordische Lexikographie	1928
196.	Lars Holm/Hans Jonsson, Swedish Lexicography	1933
197.	Noel Edward Osselton, English Lexicography From the Beginning Up To and Including Johnson	1943
198.	John A. Simpson, English Lexicography After Johnson to 1945	1953
199.	Robert Ilson, Present-Day British Lexicography	1967
199a.	Adam Jack Aitken, The Lexicography of Scots	1983
200.	John Algeo, American Lexicography	1987
201.	Hans Heestermans, Niederländische Lexikographie und Lexikographie des Afrikaans	2010
202.	Nils Århammar, Friesische Lexikographie	2022
203.	Klaus Grubmüller, Die deutsche Lexikographie von den Anfängen bis zum Beginn des 17. Jahrhunderts	2037
204.	Peter Kühn/Ulrich Püschel, Die deutsche Lexikographie vom 17. Jahrhundert bis zu den Brüdern Grimm ausschließlich	2049
205.	Peter Kühn/Ulrich Püschel, Die deutsche Lexikographie von den Brüdern Grimm bis Trübner	2078
206.	Herbert Ernst Wiegand, Die deutsche Lexikographie der Gegenwart	2100
207.	Joshua Fishman, The Lexicography of Yiddish	2246

XX.	Lexikographie der Einzelsprachen IV: Die slavischen Sprachen Lexicography of Individual Languages IV: The Slavic Languages Lexicographie des langues particulières IV: Les langues slaves	
208.	Franz Wenzel Mareš, Altkirchenslavische Lexikographie	2255
209.	Stanisław Urbańczyk, Polnische Lexikographie. Polabische Lexikographie	2268
210.	Siegfried Michalk, Sorbische Lexikographie	2274
211.	Alois Jedlička, Tschechische Lexikographie	2278
212.	Ján Horecký, Slowakische Lexikographie	2284
213.	Radoslav Katičić, Serbokroatische Lexikographie	2288
214.	Katja Sturm-Schnabl, Slowenische Lexikographie	2296
215.	Blaže Koneski, Makedonische Lexikographie	2302
216.	Klaus Steinke, Bulgarische Lexikographie	2304
217.	Helmut Jachnow, Russische Lexikographie	2309
218.	Jaroslav B. Rudnyckyj, Ukrainian Lexicography	2329
219.	Peter J. Mayo, Belorussian Lexicography	2335

Kartenverzeichnis / Map Index / Index des cartes géographiques

Karte 221.1: Geographische Verbreitung der neukeltischen Sprachen
(Geographical distribution of contemporary Celtic languages · Extension géographique des langues celtiques contemporaines) 2344

Karte 223.1: Skizze des Gebietes des Estnischen, Lettischen und Litauischen
(Area of the Estonian, Latvian, and Lithuanian · Aire linguistique de l'estonien, du lette et du lituanien) 2358

Karte 224.1: Die Albaner im Kreise ihrer südosteuropäischen Nachbarn
(The Albanians and their Southeast European neighbours · Les Albanais et leurs voisins de l'Europe du sud-est) 2362

Map 226.1: The main dialects of the Basque language: their geographical distribution
(Das Verbreitungsgebiet der hauptsächlichen Dialekte des Baskischen · L'extension géographique des principaux dialectes basques) 2372

Karte 227.1: Das Verbreitungsgebiet des Ungarischen
(Language area of Hungarian · Aire linguistique du hongrois) 2379

Karte 228.1: Siedlungsgebiete der ostsee-finnischen Völker und der Lappen
(The Finnish peoples of the Baltic Sea and the Lapps: settlement areas · Habitat des peuples finnois de la mer baltique et des Lapons) 2383

Karte 228a.1: Das lappische Sprachgebiet
(Lapp language area · Aire linguistique du lapon) 2388

Map 233.1: Current distribution of the indigenous languages of the Caucasus (with detailed reference to the North West and South Caucasian families)
(Gegenwärtiges Verbreitungsgebiet der kaukasischen Sprachen mit besonderer Berücksichtigung der nordwest- und südkaukasischen Sprachfamilien · Extension géographique actuelle des langues indigènes du Caucase avec référence spéciale aux familles de langues du nord-ouest et du sud) 2415

Map 236.1: Geographical Distribution of Hebrew and Aramaic: 1000-600 B. C. and in Modern Times
(Verbreitungsgebiet des Hebräischen und Aramäischen: 1000-600 vor Christus sowie in der Neuzeit · Extension géographique de l'hébreu et de l'araméen: de 1000 à 600 av. J.-C. et aux temps modernes) 2424

Map 236.2: Hebrew and Aramaic in the Late Antiquity
(Hebräisch und Aramäisch in der Spätantike · L'hébreu et l'araméen à la fin de l'antiquité) 2425

Map 237.1: The Arabic-speaking world
(Die arabisch sprechende Welt · Le monde arabophone) 2439

Map 238.1: Languages of Ethiopia
(Die Sprachen Äthiopiens · Les langues de l'Ethiopie) 2448

Map 240.1: Chadic language family
(Die tschado-hamitische Sprachfamilie · Les langues tchado-chamitiques) 2458

Map 241.1: Location of some Cushitic languages
(Lokalisierung der kuschitischen Sprachen · Localisation des langues couchitiques) 2461

Karte 242.1: Verbreitung altiranischer Corpussprachen
(Location of Old Iranian corpus languages · L'extension géographique des langues de corpus de l'ancien iranien) 2470

Map 243.1: Middle Iranian languages
(Mitteliranische Sprachen · Les langues du moyen iranien) 2474

Map 243.2: Languages of the Sogdian diaspora
(Die Sprachen der sogdianischen Diaspora · Les langues de la diaspora sogdienne) 2475

Map 244.1: Area of Persian/Tajik
(Verbreitungsgebiet des Farsi/Tadyk · L'extension géographique du persan/tadjik) 2478

Karte 245.1: Skizze des Verbreitungsgebietes sonstiger neuiranischer Sprachen
(Area of other modern Iranian languages · L'extension géographique d'autres langues iraniennes modernes) 2482

Map 248.1: New Indo-Aryan languages
(Die neuindoarischen Sprachen · Les langues de l'indo-aryen moderne) 2508

Map 249.1: Dravidian languages in South Asia
(Dravidische Sprachen in Südasien · Les langues dravidiennes de l'Asie du sud) 2522

Map 252.1: Area for Burmese lexicography
(Verbreitung des Birmanischen · L'extension géographique du birman) 2551

Map 255.1: Location of selected languages in Malaysia, Indonesia, and Brunei
(Lokalisierung ausgewählter Sprachen in Malaysia, Indonesien und Brunei · Localisation de langues choisies de Malaisie, d'Indonésie et de Brunei) 2564

Map 258.1: Location of other Philippine languages
(Lokalisierung der sonstigen Philippinen-Sprachen · Localisation des autres langues philippines) 2571

Map 261.1: Vietnamese speaking areas
(Vietnamesisch sprechende Gebiete · Aires vietnamophones) 2584

Map 262.1: Smaller languages of Southeast Asia
(Kleinere Sprachen Südostasiens · Les langues mineures du Sud-Est asiatique) 2590

Map 263.1: People's Republic of China: ethnolinguistic distribution
(Die ethnolinguistische Verteilung in der VR China · Répartition ethno-linguistique dans la République Populaire de Chine) 2596

Map 264.1: Korean dialects
(Die koreanischen Dialekte · Les dialectes coréens) 2614

Karte 266.1: Verbreitungsgebiet des Mongolischen
(Mongolian language area · L'extension géographique du mongol) 2624

Map 267.1: Paleosibirian languages
(Die paläosibirischen Sprachen · Les langues paléo-sibériennes) 2627

Map 269.1: Location of the languages referred to in Art. 269 (New Guinea)
(Lokalisierung der Sprachen von Art. 269 · Localisation des langues mentionnées dans l'art. 269) 2635

Map 270.1: Location of the Australian aboriginal languages referred to in Art. 270
(Lokalisierung der australischen Eingeborenensprachen von Art. 270 · Localisation des langues australiennes indigènes mentionnées dans l'art. 270) 2639

Map 272.1: Languages of Africa referred to in Art. 272
(Die in Art. 272 erwähnten Sprachen Afrikas · Les langues africaines mentionnées dans l'art. 272) 2646

Map 274.1: Location of Nahuatl-speaking communities in the 20th Century
(Lokalisierung der Nahuatl sprechenden Gemeinschaften im 20. Jahrhundert · Localisation des communautés parlant le nahuatl au 20ème siècle) 2657

Karte 275.1: Maya-Sprachen Mexikos und Mittelamerikas
(The Mayan languages of Mexico and Central America · Les langues maya du Mexique et d'Amérique centrale) 2662

Karte 276.1: Lokalisierung einiger Tupí-Guaraní-Sprachen
(Location of some Tupi-Guarani languages · Localisation de quelques langues du tupi-guarani) 2671

Map 277.1: Departments in which Southern Peruvian Quechua is spoken today
(Gebiete in denen gegenwärtig südperuanisches Ketschua gesprochen wird · Régions dans lesquelles le quechua sud-péruvien est parlé actuellement) 2677

Map 277.2: The Inca Empire at the time of conquest
(Das Inkareich zur Zeit der Eroberung · L'empire inca à l'époque de la conquête) 2677

Map 278.1: Areas of Jaqi language (Aymara, Jaqaru, and Kawki) in Peru, Bolivia, and Chile
(Verbreitungsgebiete der Jaqi-Sprache [Aymara, Jaqaru und Kawki] in Peru, Bolivien und Chile · L'extension géographique de la langue Jaqi [Aymara, Jaqaru et Kawki] au Pérou, en Bolivie et au Chili) 2685

Map 281.1: Approximate locations of some South American Indian groups
(Ungefähre Lokalisierung einiger südamerikanischer Indianerstämme · Localisation approximative de quelques tribus indiennes d'Amérique du sud) 2701

XXI. Lexikographie der Einzelsprachen V: Weitere europäische und ihnen benachbarte Sprachen
Lexicography of Individual Languages V: Further Languages of Europe and Adjacent Areas
Lexicographie des langues particulières V: Autres langues européennes et langues avoisinantes

220. Altirische Lexikographie

1. Glossen und Glossare in der älteren irischen Überlieferung
2. Zur Bestimmung der altirischen Materialgrundlage
3. Zum Verhältnis von sprachlicher Struktur zu lexikographischer Darstellung im Altirischen
4. Moderne Lexikographie des Altirischen (deskriptiv und etymologisch)
5. Literatur (in Auswahl)

1. Glossen und Glossare in der älteren irischen Überlieferung

Die wichtigste Quelle des Altirischen stellen die in Handschriften aus dem 8. und 9. Jh. überlieferten Glossen dar (Stokes/Strachan 1975; Thurneysen 1975, 4ff.). Sie sind mit Latein durchsetzt und dienen der Erläuterung lateinischer Texte: Paulusbriefe (= *Würzburger Glossen*), Psalmen (= *Mailänder Glossen*), Priscians *Institutio de arte grammatica* (= *St. Galler Glossen*) u. a. Interlinear und marginal in die Handschriften eingefügt, bestehen die Glossen teils aus Übersetzungen einzelner Wörter, häufiger aus „Scholien", die die inhaltlichen Zusammenhänge erklären (Zimmer 1881, 88). — Von den Glossen zu unterscheiden sind die später überlieferten Glossare, darunter besonders die *Sanas Cormaic* [Cormacs Flüstern] des *Cormac Úa Cuilennáin*, Bischof von Cashel, der 901 König von Munster wurde (vgl. Stokes 1862, 1—46; Meyer 1912). Dieses später erweiterte Glossar „etymologisiert irische Wörter und erklärt ungewöhnliche Ausdrücke der Dichter- und Gesetzessprache" (Thurneysen 1980, 20; vgl. auch Bachellery/Lambert 1983, 22). Seine ältesten Handschriftenfragmente sind im Buch von Leinster (12. Jh.) überliefert. Die übrigen Glossare sind jüngeren Datums: O'Malconry 13./14. Jh. (Stokes 1900); O'Davoren 16. Jh. (Stokes 1862, 47—124; Ebel 1873/75; Stokes 1904); O'Clery 17. Jh. (Miller 1879/80; 1881/83). Der Arbeitsprozeß, der zur Anlage alphabetischer Glossare führte, läßt sich aus kleineren Glossensammlungen zu verschiedenen mittelirischen Texten erschließen:

(1) „to extract from a given text the phrase or sentence in which a lemma with an interlinear or a marginal gloss was found, and to put these phrases together in the order in which they follow in the text"; (2) „the lemma with the gloss was taken out of the context and placed at the head, followed by the quotation"; (3) „the lemmata are arranged under the letters of the alphabet" (Meyer 1907, 138; 139; 140).

Daß die größeren Glossare das Ergebnis der Verschmelzung verschiedener kleiner, auf Einzeltexte bezogener Glossare darstellen, erklärt auch die Aufnahme von bis zu sechs homonymen Wörtern in ein Glossar: die uneinheitlichen Bedeutungen spiegeln die voneinander abweichenden Kontexte wieder (Zimmer 1881, 90f.). Ende des 17. Jh. und während des 18. Jh. kommen irisch-englische Glossare auf, indem die vormals irischen Erläuterungen ins Englische übersetzt werden. Als Musterbeispiel für die unkritische Auswertung der Glossare ist O'Reilly (1864) bekannt (Zimmer 1881, 97ff.). Metrisch gebundene Glossare sind vom Beginn des 12. Jh. an belegt. Sie dienen der Interpretation obsoleter oder lateinischer Wörter und der Differenzierung von Synonymen und Homonymen (Stokes 1893).

2. Zur Bestimmung der altirischen Materialgrundlage

Hier müssen zwei Faktoren berücksichtigt werden: (1) Absolute Chronologie der inschriftlichen und handschriftlichen Überlieferung: die bis ins 4. Jh. n. Chr. datierbaren Ogom-Inschriften (Macalister 1945; 1949) und die altirischen Glossen aus dem 8. und 9. Jh. stellen die beiden ältesten geschlossenen Textkorpora dar; (2) Relative Chronologie der bewahrten archaischen Züge in Grammatik und Lexikographie: vor das klassische Altirische der Glossen einzuordnen sind außer dem Ogom-Irischen Archaisches Irisch (6. Jh.) und Frühaltirisch (7. Jh.). Obwohl nur durch mittel- und frühneuirische Handschriften überliefert, hat das in bestimmten Genres (älteste Schicht der Gesetze; Dichtung; Saga-Spruchdichtung) erhaltene Archaische Irisch in Jahrhunderten mündlicher Überlieferung einen altertümlicheren Status bewahrt als das klassische Altirische. Das Frühaltirische hinwiederum verbindet altirisches Überlieferungsdatum mit archaischen Zügen im Lautstand (Binchy 1972, 29—38; Greene 1976; 1977; Schmidt 1982, 64ff.). Die in mittelirischen Handschriften ab dem 12. Jh. auf uns gekommenen Sagen entsprechen nicht selten einem modernisierten Altirisch (Greene 1977, 11).

3. Zum Verhältnis von sprachlicher Struktur zu lexikographischer Darstellung im Altirischen

Die Probleme betreffen vornehmlich Orthographie und Wortbildung. Orthographisch bestehen Unterschiede zwischen den alt- und mittelirischen Handschriften: z. B. **máthir** „Mutter": später **máthair**; **orpe**, **orbe**, **orbbae** „Erbschaft": später **orb(b)a**. Die unterschiedliche Orthographie hat zur Folge, daß die Wörterbücher bzw. sogar die verschiedenen Faszikel eines Wörterbuches keinem einheitlichen Prinzip folgen:

„alors que J. Vendryes, à la suite d'Ascoli, adoptait l'orthographe la plus ancienne (celle des gloses du vieil-irlandais), les *Contributions* ont uniformisé l'orthographe sur celle des documents les plus abondants, qui consistent en manuscrits datant de l'époque du moyen-irlandais ou de l'irlandais moderne" (Bachellery/Lambert 1983, 18).

Eine orthographische Unsicherheit ergibt sich, wenn die Entscheidung über den Akzent als Anzeiger der Vokallänge nicht zu erbringen ist: z. B. „**gábait** (length of vowel doubtful)" (Dictionary 1983, 351). Im Bereich der Wortbildung stehen die Probleme im Zusammenhang mit dem flektierenden Sprachtypus des Altirischen: Suffixableitungen und Komposita können sowohl unter die ihnen zu Grunde liegende lexikographische Basis subsumiert als auch als unabhängige Einheiten zitiert werden: z. B. *sen* „alt" mit Ableitungen wie *sen-argat* „altes Geld", *-ben* „alte Frau", *-fer* „alter Mann" usw. gegenüber **senḟocul** (1*sen* + *focal*) „an old saying, a proverb" (Dictionary 1983, 170f.; 178; das *punctum delens* über dem *f* zeigt Lenierung an). Die unterschiedliche Behandlung der Komposita entspricht in der Regel dem Grad ihrer von der Komposition unabhängigen neuen Begrifflichkeit. Das gleiche Prinzip läßt sich auf Suffixableitungen anwenden:

„On comprendra qu'il n'était pas question de mettre sous la rubrique *ber-* 'porter' ni *birit* 'truie' ni *ambrit* 'stérile', bien éloignés tous deux de leur source; la saine méthode imposait de les traiter comme des mots indépendants" (Lexique 1959, XII).

Bei der Verbalkomposition stellt sich nicht nur die Frage der Anordnung der Lemmata unter *Präverb* bzw. unter *Verbalstamm*. Das Altirische unterscheidet auch zwischen *prototonierten* und *deuterotonierten* Verbalformen, und das prototonierte Verbalnomen kann der deuterotonierten finiten Verbalform gegenüber ein unabhängiges Lemma bilden: z. B. *tóbae* „act of cutting, cutting down, removing" (Dictionary 1983, 594) vs. *do·fuiben* „cuts, cuts off [...]" (Dictionary 1983, 234).

4. Moderne Lexikographie des Altirischen (deskriptiv und etymologisch)

Eine Differenzierung zwischen deskriptiver und etymologischer Lexikographie ist nur bedingt möglich, da die deskriptiven Wörterbücher manchmal etymologische Hinweise enthalten, während das Lexique étymologique auch Textzitaten breiten Raum einräumt. Sieht man ab von den mittelalterlichen Glossaren, so lassen sich die deskriptiven Wörterbücher in drei Gruppen unterteilen: (1) auf Textkorpora bezogene Glossare; (2) Wörterbücher des älteren Irischen; (3) Sachbezogene Wörterbücher. — Die weitgehend auf mittelirische Texte bezogenen Glossare der Gruppe I, Windisch (1880), dazu die Kritik von Zimmer (1881), Atkinson (1887), dazu Stokes (1888—90), Calder (1917) und (1922) u. a. wurden sukzessive durch die 22 Faszikel des Dictionary (1983) ersetzt. — Gruppe II wird eingeleitet durch zwei unvollendet gebliebene Werke: (1) Ascoli (1907), ein nach Wurzeln angeordnetes und sämtliche Belege der altirischen Denkmäler erfassendes Glossar, das auf Wörter mit anlautendem **A E I O U L R S N M G** sowie wenige mit **C** beschränkt ist; (2) Meyer (1906), der **A — DNO** enthält und den Übergang zu dem Dictionary (1983) einleitet. Dessen 22 Faszikel erschienen 1913—75, eingeleitet durch Marstrander, **D — Degóir** (1913), dazu Marstrander (1917—19), und abgeschlossen durch Maura Carney/Máirin O'Daly, **B** (1975). Vier Faszikel, **D — Degóir** (1913), E (1932), dazu Marstrander (1932), **F — Fochraic** (1950), **Fochrotae — Futhu** (1957) waren als Teile eines Dictionary of the Irish Language based mainly on Old and Middle Irish Materials konzipiert; die meisten Lieferungen, beginnend mit **M** (1939) und endend mit **B** (1975), wurden jedoch als Contributions to a Dictionary of the Irish Language publiziert. Die Wissenschaftsgeschichte des Unternehmens, dessen Planung bis ins Jahr 1852 zurückreicht, hat Quin (Dictionary 1983, VI) beschrieben. Die von John O'Donovan (1809—1861) entwickelte Grundkonzeption — Exzerpierung von Texten und älteren Handschriften, Erläuterung der Bedeutung der Wörter durch reichliche Verwendung von Zitaten, Begrenzung der Etymologie auf Lehnwörter und innerirische Ableitungen — wurde bis zum Abschluß des Wörterbuches beibehalten. Ein kleineres deutsch-amerikanisch-irisches Projekt, geplant als Kurzgefaßtes Wörterbuch der alt- und mittelirischen Sprache mit deutscher und englischer Übersetzung, war Hessens Irisches Lexikon (1933—1940), das aber über vier Faszikel, **A — Cennaid, I — Ruud**, nicht hinausgekommen ist. Wertvolle Beiträge zur irischen Lexikographie wurden auch in Stokes/Meyer I, II, III (1900, 1904, 1907) und Meyer (1912—1921) veröffentlicht. — Zu den Wörterbüchern der Gruppe III gehören Indices zur irischen Dichtung, z. B. Thurneysen (1980), und auf Gesetze und Namen bezogene Glossare wie Atkinson (1901), dazu Stokes (1903), Joyce (1887; 1883; 1913), Hogan (1910), O'Brien (1976). — Auch bei der etymologischen Lexikographie lassen sich drei Gruppen unterscheiden: (1) Indices zu historischen Grammatiken und Handbüchern wie Zeuss 1871, dazu Güterbock/Thurneysen 1881 und Hogan 1892, Thurneysen 1975, Pedersen 1976, Lewis/Pedersen 1961. — (2) Etymologische Wörterbücher, unter denen dem Lexique étymologique (1959 ff.) besondere Bedeutung zukommt; vgl. außerdem Stokes/Bezzenberger (1979), Henry (1900), MacBain (1911), Fleuriot (1964), Campanile (1974); Walde/Pokorny (1973), Pokorny (1959/1969). — (3) Auf Lehnwortschichten bezogene Arbeiten. Für das Altirische hat die lateinische Schicht besondere Bedeutung: vgl. Güterbock (1882), Loth (1892), Sarauw (1900), Vendryes (1902), MacNeill (1931), Jackson (1953, 122—148) und letztlich McManus (1983; 1984). Die skandinavischen Lehnwörter haben durch Marstrander (1915) eine zusammenfassende Bearbeitung erfahren.

5. Literatur (in Auswahl)

5.1. Wörterbücher

Ascoli 1907 = Graziadio Isaia Ascoli: Glossario dell'antico Irlandese. In: Archivio Glottologico Italiano 6. Roma. Torino. Firenze 1879 [487 S., abgeschlossen 1907].

Atkinson 1901 = Robert Atkinson: Ancient Laws of Ireland. Vol. VI. Glossary to volumes I—V. Dublin 1901 [792 S.].

Campanile 1974 = Enrico Campanile: Profilo etimologico del Cornico antico. Pisa 1974 [136 S.].

Dictionary 1983 = Dictionary of the Irish Language based mainly on old and middle Irish materials. Compact edition. Dublin, Royal Irish Academy 1983 [VIII, 632 S.].

Fleuriot 1964 = Léon Fleuriot: Dictionnaire des gloses en vieux breton. Paris 1964 [372 S., 8 planches].

Henry 1900 = Victor Henry: Lexique étymologique des termes les plus usuels du breton moderne. Rennes 1900 (Bibliothèque bretonne armoricaine, fasc. 3) [XXIX, 350 S.].

Hessens Irisches Lexikon 1933—1940 = Hessens Irisches Lexikon. Kurzgefaßtes Wörterbuch der alt- und mittelirischen Sprache [...] von Séamus Coamhánach, Rudolf Hertz, Vernam E. Hull, Gustav Lehmacher. Halle/S. 1933—1940 [XXVII, 144, 232 S.].

Hogan 1910 = Edmund Hogan: Onomasticon Goedelicum [...]. An Index, with Identifications, to the Gaelic Names of Places and Tribes. Dublin. London 1910 [XVI, 696 S.].

Joyce 1887; 1883; 1913 = P. W. Joyce: The Origin and History of Irish Names of Places I. II. III. Dublin 1887. 1883. 1913 [XII, 589; VI, 538; X, 598 S.].

Lexique étymologique 1959; 1960; 1974; 1978; 1981; 1987 = Joseph Vendryes: Lexique étymologique de l'Irlandais ancien A, MNOP, RS, TU, B, C. Paris 1959 [XXIV, 106 S.], 1960 [77, 25, 36, 17 S.], 1974 [VIII, 55, 206 S., hrsg. von E. Bachellery], 1978 [VI, 189, 31 S., hrsg. von E. Bachellery/P.-Y. Lambert], 1981 [XIV, 119 S. hrsg. von E. Bachellery/P.-Y. Lambert], 1987 [300 S., hrsg. von E. Bachellery/P.-Y. Lambert].

Loth 1892 = Joseph Loth: Les mots latins dans les langues Brittoniques. Paris 1892 [246 S.].

MacBain 1911 = Alexander MacBain: An Etymological Dictionary of the Gaelic Language. Stirling 1911 [XXXVII, 412 S. First Edition 1896].

Marstrander 1915 = Carl J. S. Marstrander: Bidrag til det norske sprogs historie i Irland. Kristiania 1915 [167 S.].

Meyer 1906 = Kuno Meyer: Contributions to Irish Lexicography. Vol. I, Part I. A-DNO. Halle/S. 1906 [XXXI, 670 S.].

O'Reilly 1864 = Edward O'Reilly: An Irish-English Dictionary [...] with a Supplement [...] by John *O'Donovan*. 2. Aufl. Dublin 1864 [725 S.; 3. Aufl. 1877].

Pokorny 1959, 1969 = Julius Pokorny: Indogermanisches etymologisches Wörterbuch. 2 Bde. Bern. München 1959. 1969 [1183, 495 S.].

Stokes/Bezzenberger 1979 = Whitley Stokes/Adalbert Bezzenberger: Wortschatz der keltischen Spracheinheit. 5., unveränderte Aufl. Göttingen 1979 [337 S.; 4. Aufl. 1894].

Vendryes 1902 = Joseph Vendryes: De hibernicis vocabulis quae a latina lingua originem duxerunt. Paris 1902 [199 S.].

Walde/Pokorny 1973 = Alois Walde: Vergleichendes Wörterbuch der indogermanischen Sprachen. Hrsg. und bearbeitet von Julius Pokorny I. II. III. Photomech. Nachdruck. Göttingen 1973 [877, 716, 269 S.; 1. Aufl. 1930, 1927, 1932].

5.2. Sonstige Literatur

Atkinson 1887 = Robert Atkinson: The Passions and the Homilies from Leabhar Breac; Text, Translation and Glossary (Todd Lecture Series, Vol. II). Dublin 1887 [958 S.].

Bachellery/Lambert 1983 = Édouard Bachellery/Pierre-Yves Lambert: Le Lexique étymologique de l'Irlandais ancien de J. Vendryes. In: Alfred Bammesberger (Hrsg.): Das etymologische Wörterbuch. Fragen der Konzeption und Gestaltung. Regensburg 1983 [17—24].

Binchy 1972 = Daniel A. Binchy: Varia hibernica. In: Herbert Pilch/Joachim Thurow (Hrsg.): Indo-Celtica. Gedächtnisschrift für Alf Sommerfelt. München 1972, 29—41.

Calder 1917 = George Calder: Auraicept na n-Éces, The Scholars' Primer [...] with Introduction, Translation of the Ballymote Text, Notes and Indices. Edinburgh 1917 [LVI, 374 S.].

Calder 1922 = George Calder: Togail na Tebe, The Thebaid of Statius. The Irish Text [...] with Introduction, Translation, Vocabulary and Notes. Cambridge 1922 [XXIII, 431 S.].

de Bernardo Stempel 1987 = Patrizia de Bernardo Stempel: The Reverse Old and Middle Irish Dictionary. In: Celtic Cultures Newsletter 5. Galway 1987, 21—24.

Ebel 1873/75 = Hermann Ebel: Observations sur le glossaire d'O'Davoren. In: Revue Celtique 2. Paris 1873/75, 453—481.

Greene 1976 = David Greene: The Diphthongs of Old Irish. In: Ériu 27. Dublin 1976, 26—45.

Greene 1977 = David Greene: Archaic Irish. In: Karl Horst Schmidt (Hrsg. unter Mitwirkung von Rolf Ködderitzsch): Indogermanisch und Keltisch. Wiesbaden 1977, 11—33.

Güterbock 1882 = Bruno G. Güterbock: Bemerkungen über die lateinischen Lehnwörter im Irischen. Erster Teil: Zur Lautlehre. Diss. Leipzig 1882.

Güterbock/Thurneysen 1881 = Bruno G. Güterbock/Rudolf Thurneysen: Indices glossarum et vocabularum quae in Grammaticae Celticae editione altera explanantur composuerunt B. G. et R. Th. Leipzig 1881.

Hogan 1892 = Edmund Hogan: Supplement to the Index Vocabulorum of Zeuss 'Grammatica Celtica'. Irish Academy. Todd Lecture Series, Vol. IV. Dublin 1892, 267—282.

Jackson 1953 = Kenneth Jackson: Language and History in Early Britain. Edinburgh 1953.

Lewis/Pedersen 1961 = Henry Lewis/Holger Pedersen: A Concise Comparative Celtic Grammar. 3rd edition. Reprinted with corrections and a supplement 1961 [1. Aufl. 1937].

Macalister 1945; 1949 = R. A. S. Macalister: Corpus Inscriptionum Celticarum Vol. I. II. Dublin 1945, 1949.

MacNeill 1931 = Eoin MacNeill: Beginnings of Latin Culture in Ireland. In: Studies. An Irish Quarterly Review Vol. 20. No. 77. Dublin 1931, 39—48, No. 79, 449—460.

Marstrander 1917—19 = Carl J. S. Marstrander: The Dictionary of the Irish Academy. In: Revue Celtique 37. Paris 1917/19, 1—23.

Marstrander 1932 = Carl J. Marstrander: Dictionary of the Irish Language [...]. Fasciculus II: E, edited by Maud Joynt and Eleanor Knott [...]. In: Norsk Tidsskrift for Sprogvidenskap 5. Oslo 1932, 366—371.

McManus 1983 = Damian McManus: A Chronology of the Latin Loan-Words in Early Irish. In: Ériu 34. Dublin 1983, 21—71.

McManus 1984 = Damian McManus: On Final Syllables in the Latin Loan-Words in Early Irish. In: Ériu 35. Dublin 1984, 137—162.

Meyer 1907 = Kuno Meyer: The Sources of some Middle-Irish Glossaries. In: Stokes/Meyer 1907, 138—144.

Meyer 1912 = Kuno Meyer: Sanas Cormaic. An Old-Irish Glossary [...], edited from the copy in the Yellow Book of Lecan. In: Anecdota from Irish Manuscripts, edited by O. J. Bergin, R. I. Best, Kuno Meyer, J. G. O'Keefe, Vol. IV. Halle/S. Dublin 1912.

Meyer 1912—1921 = Kuno Meyer: Zur keltischen Wortkunde § 1—§ 251. Sitzungsberichte d. Königl. Preuß. Akad. d. Wiss., Phil.-Hist. Classe 1914—1919 und in: Zeitschrift für Celtische Philologie 13. Halle/S. 1921, 184—193.

Miller 1879—83 = Arthur W. K. Miller: O'Clery's Irish Glossary. In: Revue Celtique 4. Paris 1879/80, 349—428; 5. Paris 1881/83, 1—69.

O'Brien 1976 = M. A. O'Brien (ed.): Corpus Genealogiarum Hiberniae with an introduction by J. V. Kelleher. Dublin 1976.

O'Riain 1985 = Pa'draig O'Riain (ed.): Corpus Genealogiarum Sanctorum Hiberniae. Dublin 1985.

Pedersen 1976 = Holger Pedersen: Vergleichende Grammatik der keltischen Sprachen I. II. Göttingen 1976 [Nachdruck der 1. Aufl. 1909. 1913].

Sarauw 1900 = Chr. Sarauw: Irske Studier. København 1900.

Schmidt 1982 = Karl Horst Schmidt: Die Würzburger Glossen. In: Zeitschrift für Celtische Philologie 39. Tübingen 1982, 54—77.

Stokes 1862 = Whitley Stokes: Three Irish Glossaries. London. Edinburgh 1862.

Stokes 1888—90 = Whitley Stokes: On Professor Atkinson's edition of the Passions and Homilies in the Lebar Brecc. In: Transactions of the Philological Society. London 1888—90, 203—234; Repr.: Amsterdam 1968.

Stokes 1893 = Whitley Stokes: On the metrical glossaries of the mediaeval Irish. In: Beiträge zur Kunde der indogermanischen Sprachen 19. Göttingen 1893, 1—120.

Stokes 1900 = Whitley Stokes: O'Mulconry's Glossary. In: Stokes/Meyer 1900, 232—324.

Stokes 1903 = Whitley Stokes: A Criticism of Dr. Atkinson's Glossary to Volumes I—V of the Ancient Laws of Ireland. London 1903.

Stokes 1904 = Whitley Stokes: O'Davoren's Glossary. In: Stokes/Meyer 1904, 197—504.

Stokes/Meyer 1900, 1904, 1907 = Whitley Stokes/Kuno Meyer (Hrsg.): Archiv für Celtische Lexikographie I, II, III. Halle/S. 1900, 1904, 1907.

Stokes/Strachan 1975 = Whitley Stokes/John Strachan: Thesaurus Palaeohibernicus. A Collection of Old-Irish Glosses, Scholia, Prose and Verse. 2 vols. with supplement by Whitley Stokes. Dublin 1975 [1. Aufl. 1901; 1903; supplement 1910].

Thurneysen 1975 = Rudolf Thurneysen: A Grammar of Old Irish. Revised and enlarged edition with supplement. Translated from the German by D. A. Binchy and Osborn Bergin. Dublin 1975 [Reprint von 1946].

Thurneysen 1980 = Rudolf Thurneysen: Die irische Helden- und Königssage bis zum 17. Jahrhundert. Hildesheim. New York 1980 [Nachdruck von: Halle/S. 1921].

Windisch 1880 = Ernst Windisch: Irische Texte mit Wörterbuch. Leipzig 1880.

Windisch 1905 = Ernst Windisch: Die altirische Heldensage Táin Bó Cúalnge nach dem Buch von Leinster in Text und Uebersetzung mit einer Einleitung. Leipzig 1905.

Zeuss 1871 = Johann Kaspar Zeuss: Grammatica Celtica [...]. Editio altera curavit H. Ebel. Berlin 1871 [1. Aufl. 1853].

Zimmer 1881 = Heinrich Zimmer: Keltische Studien. Erstes Heft: Irische Texte mit Wörterbuch von E. Windisch. Berlin 1881.

Karl Horst Schmidt, Bonn
(Bundesrepublik Deutschland)

221. Die Lexikographie der neukeltischen Sprachen

1. Genealogische und typologische Gegebenheiten
2. Allgemeine Charakteristik und gemeinsame Probleme
3. Irisch
4. Schottisch-Gälisch
5. Manx
6. Walisisch (Kymrisch)
7. Bretonisch
8. Kornisch
9. Literatur (in Auswahl)

1. Genealogische und typologische Gegebenheiten

Von den sechs neukeltischen Sprachen (vgl. Karte 221.1) sind noch vier Sprachen lebendig: Irisch, Schottisch-Gälisch, Walisisch, Bretonisch. Zwei Sprachen sind ausgestorben: Kornisch (Ende des 18. Jh. ausgestorben) und Manx (letzter Sprecher verstorben 1974). Die neukeltischen Sprachen gliedern sich in zwei Unterfamilien: goidelische Sprachen (Irisch, Schottisch-Gälisch, Manx) und britannische Sprachen (Walisisch, Bretonisch, Kornisch). Diese beiden Gruppen sind genealogisch und typologisch sehr weit voneinander entfernt (cf. Ternes 1978). Die drei goidelischen Sprachen gehen alle auf das (belegte) Altirische zurück. Schottisch-Gälisch und Manx gelten erst ab ca. 15. Jh. als eigenständige Sprachen. Irisch und Schottisch-Gälisch haben eine jeweils auf das Altirische zurückgehende stark historische Orthographie, während Manx eine wesentlich jüngere eigene Orthographietradition besitzt. Die britannischen Sprachen lassen sich nicht auf eine belegte, sondern nur rekonstruierbare Ursprache zurückführen. Walisisch und Bretonisch verwenden jeweils eine unabhängig voneinander entstandene, im Prinzip phonemisch orientierte Orthographie. Die kornische Orthographie gleicht der walisischen. Unabhängig von der Einteilung Goidelisch-Britannisch nimmt

Karte 221.1: Geographische Verbreitung der neukeltischen Sprachen

das Bretonische typologisch eine Sonderstellung ein, da es sich von den Britischen Inseln entfernt hat und von Beginn seiner Geschichte an (ca. 5. Jh.) auf dem europäischen Festland angesiedelt ist (cf. Ternes 1979). Das bedeutet gleichzeitig, daß Bretonisch als einzige Sprache politisch, wirtschaftlich und kulturell französischem Einfluß ausgesetzt ist, während alle anderen Sprachen mit dem Englischen in Kontakt stehen. Daher sind Lehn- und Fremdwörter im Bretonischen überwiegend französischer, in den anderen Sprachen englischer Herkunft.

2. Allgemeine Charakteristik und gemeinsame Probleme

2.1. Sprachstruktur

Eine Besonderheit der keltischen Sprachen stellen die sog. *Anlautmutationen* dar. Dabei handelt es sich um den grammatisch und/oder lexikalisch bedingten Wechsel wortanlautender Konsonantenphoneme, z. B. bret. *penn* 'Kopf' wechselt mit *benn* und *fenn* (cf. Ternes 1977). Außerdem kommt die Präfigierung von Konsonanten vor vokalischem Stammanlaut vor, z. B. ir. *úll* 'Apfel' — pl. *na húlla* 'die Äpfel'. Keltische Wörterbücher verzeichnen in der Regel nur die nicht-mutierten Stammformen, so daß zur Auffindung eines Wortes im Wörterbuch mutationsbedingte Veränderungen rückgän-

gig gemacht werden müssen. Dies setzt die Kenntnis der betreffenden Regeln voraus. In einem fortlaufenden Text ist etwa jedes dritte Wort von einer solchen Veränderung betroffen. Nur Cregeen 1835 (Manx) weicht von der Regel ab, indem er zahlreiche mutierte Einträge aufnimmt und von diesen auf die jeweilige Stammform verweist.

2.2. Idiomatik, Kollokation

Bis in die jüngste Zeit standen die keltischen Sprachen der Entwicklung der sog. SAE-Sprachen *(Standard Average European)* fern. Damit sind idiomatische Wendungen und überhaupt semantisch-syntaktische Verträglichkeiten häufig grundlegend anders als in den geläufigeren europäischen Sprachen. Zweisprachige Wbb. mit reinen Wortentsprechungen (z. B. MacKenzie 1845: Schottisch-Gälisch) sind daher nur von begrenztem Wert. Die folgenden Wörterbücher enthalten verhältnismäßig zahlreiche Wendungen: Dinneen 1904, de Bhaldraithe 1959 (beide Irisch), Dwelly 1920 (Schottisch-Gälisch), Vallée 1931, Helias 1986 (beide Bretonisch). Das fast vollständige Fehlen von Stilwörterbüchern ist in diesem Zusammenhang besonders nachteilig. Eine positive Ausnahme ist Gros 1970—1974 für Bretonisch.

2.3. Zweitsprache

Entsprechend den politischen Verhältnissen sind zweisprachige Wörterbücher des Bretonischen fast ausschließlich mit Französisch kombiniert, die aller anderen Sprachen fast ausschließlich mit Englisch. Seltene Ausnahmen sind z. B. de Hae 1952 (Irisch-Französisch), Delaporte 1979 (Bretonisch-Englisch). Andere Zweitsprachen als Englisch und Französisch kommen nur in ganz speziellen Fällen vor, z. B. Finck 1899 (Wb. eines archaischen irischen Dialekts; Zweitsprache Deutsch). Insbesondere ist festzuhalten, daß es keine zweisprachigen Wörterbücher zweier keltischer Sprachen untereinander gibt.

2.4. Neologismen

Die sozio-kulturellen Bedingungen in den keltischen Ländern während der letzten Jahrhunderte hatten zur Folge, daß die keltischen Sprachen weitgehend auf den Gebrauch in Haus, Hof, Familie und bei der Ausübung traditioneller Berufe (Landwirtschaft, Fischfang u. ä.) eingeschränkt wurden. Daher mangelt es an einem Wortschatz für die Erfordernisse des modernen Lebens in Wissenschaft, Technik, Verwaltung, Erziehung usw. Die keltische Lexikographie verhält sich in dieser Hinsicht konservativ und puristisch. Bis in die 1. Hälfte des 20. Jh. wurde in Wörterbüchern meist überhaupt nur der Wortschatz einer vorindustriellen Gesellschaft verzeichnet. Seitdem werden zunehmend auch Neologismen aufgenommen, überwiegend puristisch aus keltischem Wortmaterial gebildet. Es fehlt jedoch an Institutionen zur Vereinheitlichung und Durchsetzung dieser Bestrebungen. Viele Wörter werden nur von ihren Autoren verwendet. Überhaupt beschränkt sich die Verwendung keltischer Neologismen weitgehend auf akademische Kreise. Das Gros der autochthonen Bevölkerung verwendet englische bzw. französische Wörter (z. B. bret. *oto* 'Auto'), die jedoch im allgemeinen in Wörterbüchern nicht verzeichnet sind. Man möchte den Einfluß des Englischen bzw. des Französischen nicht auch noch in Wörterbüchern kodifizieren und somit sanktionieren. Besonders intensiv wird die Schaffung neuer Terminologien heute für das Walisische betrieben, cf. Williams 1973. Soweit keltisches Material verwendet wird, stammt dieses bei den goidelischen Sprachen aus dem Irischen. Für die britannischen Sprachen kann das Irische kein Vorbild abgeben, da es genealogisch zu weit entfernt ist. Hier hat das Walisische eine gewisse Leitfunktion. Es wäre zu wünschen, daß Neologismen in Wörterbüchern als solche gekennzeichnet würden. Dies ist nur ganz selten der Fall, z. B. in Fournier 1903 (Irisch) durch Asterisk. Auch der Grad der Akzeptation sollte zu erkennen sein, da sich ein Nichteingeweihter durch die Verwendung eines reinen 'Schreibtischworts' leicht der Lächerlichkeit preisgibt.

2.5. Norm

Bis gegen Ende des 19. Jh. gab es große Unsicherheiten auf dem Gebiet der Sprachnormierung. Für den Gebrauch in Wbb.n hat sich heute jedoch bei allen Sprachen eine weitgehend stabile Norm herauskristallisiert. Dies gilt besonders für Orthographie und Morphologie. Dabei sind allerdings Lizenzen bezüglich regional oder dialektal bedingter Sonderformen üblich. Manchmal sind Regionalismen in Wbb.n verzeichnet. Eine wichtige Ausnahme bildet hingegen die Aussprache. Hier existiert für keine Sprache eine verläßliche Norm, wobei die Problematik in jedem Land etwas anders gelagert ist. Daher sind in Wörterbüchern nur selten Ausspracheangaben zu finden. Eigentliche Aussprachewörterbücher gibt es überhaupt nicht. Keltische Wörterbücher repräsentieren fast ausschließlich den *code écrit*. Die Ermittlung der Aussprache ist für Nicht-Fachleute oft sehr schwierig. Dies gilt besonders für Irisch und Schottisch-Gälisch, wo die Kluft zwischen Schreibung und Lautung besonders groß ist. Die Transkriptionen in den wenigen Wörterbüchern mit Ausspracheangaben (z. B. Ó Duirinne/Ó Dálaigh für Irisch, MacLennan 1925 für Schottisch-Gälisch) sind in der Regel so dilettantisch, daß sie fast ohne Wert sind. Brauchbar sind die Ausspracheangaben nur bei Dieckhoff 1932 (Schottisch-Gälisch) und neuerdings Foclóir 1986 (Irisch). Letzteres ist das erste keltische Wb. überhaupt mit IPA-Transkription.

2.6. Allgemeine Wertung, Desiderata

Gemessen an den seit Jahrhunderten andauernden ungünstigen politischen, wirtschaftlichen, sozialen und kulturellen Bedingungen hat die Lexikographie der keltischen Sprachen eine große Zahl von Wörterbüchern, darunter einige wirklich bedeutende Werke, hervorgebracht. Nicht selten sind solche Werke die heroische Unternehmung einer idealistisch gesinnten Einzelpersönlichkeit (z. B. Roparz Hemon für Bretonisch). An Desiderata sind vor allem zu nennen: grammatische Wörterbücher, Stilwörterbücher, Aussprachewörterbücher sowie jede Art von didaktisierten Wbb.n (Grund- und Aufbauwortschatz, Wortschatz nach Sachgruppen u. dgl.).

3. Irisch

Zum Alt- und Mittelirischen sowie zur Etymologie des Irischen, s. Art. 220. Eine vollständige Bibliographie irischer Wörterbücher bis 1971 findet sich in Bibliography 1913, 6 ff., Best 1969, 5 ff. und Baumgarten 1986, 111 ff. Das *Dictionary of the Irish Language* (DIL), welches im Laufe seiner komplizierten Entstehungsgeschichte (1913—1975) mehrfach Herausgeber, Titel und Format wechselte, ist heute am leichtesten in der *Compact Edition* (Inhalt ungekürzt, Format stark verkleinert, nur mit Lupe lesbar) zugänglich: Dictionary 1983 (cf. Art. 220). Es ist ein historisches Wb. mit englischer Übersetzung, zahlreichen Zitaten und Quellenangaben. Die Schreibung der Einträge folgt derjenigen in mittel- und frühneuirischen Mss. und entspricht nicht der heutigen Orthographie. Zur Auffindung der Wörter in ihrer heutigen Form ist daher der neuirische Index von de Bhaldraithe 1981 zu benutzen. — Die irischen Einträge in Wörterbüchern bis ca. 1950 (einschl. jüngerer Nachdrucke) erscheinen meist in *Gaelic type*, einem von den üblichen Lateinbuchstaben abweichenden Duktus. Dies impliziert nicht nur eine andere Form der Buchstaben, sondern wegen teilweise an-

Aṁar, -air, *pl. id.*, aṁra, -raiġ, and aṁranna, *m.*, a mercenary, a recruit, a wild fellow, a glutton, a monster; the aṁar ranked in dignity with the óiġ-tiġearna (*F. F.*); in some folktales, an ogre; a child (*loc.*); fear-a., man servant; ban-a., maid servant; *smt.* abar; aṁaraċ, *id.*
Aṁaraċ, -aiġe, *a.*, stupid; passionate, wild, gluttonous.
Aṁaraċ, -aiġe, *a.*, aggressive, quarrelsome, aiming, hitting; darting, thrusting; ɼo ha., by chance.
Aṁaraim, -mar, *v. tr.*, I hit (*F. F.*); I aim at.
Aṁarán, -áin, *pl. id.*, *m.*, the gannet or solan goose (*Antr.*); a cur dog; a stupid, dull man, a greenhorn.
Aṁarṁar, -aire, *a.*, fierce, wild.
Aṁarós, -óiġe, -ósa, *f.*, a little bitch; a little barker; a foolish or fierce woman.
Aṁaróir, -óra, *m.*, a fierce person or

Textbeispiel 221.1: Wörterbuchausschnitt (aus: Dinneen 1904, new ed. 1927, 39)

derer Schreibkonventionen auch eine etwas abweichende alphabetische Reihenfolge, z. B. **amhas** 'mercenary, Söldner' entspricht in *Gaelic type* (transliteriert) **amhas** (Textbeispiel 221.1). Außerdem ist eine Orthographiereform im Jahre 1948 zu beachten, welche eine gewisse Vereinfachung der stark historischen Orthographie brachte, z. B. alt **bliadhain** vs. neu **bliain** 'Jahr'. — Frühe irisch-englische Wbb. von Bedeutung sind Shaw 1780 (cf. Schottisch-Gälisch), Coneys 1849. Bis ins 20. Jh. besonders weit verbreitet war O'Reilly 1817, new ed. 1864 (trotz der berechtigten Kritik, cf. Art. 220). Es wurde abgelöst durch Dinneen 1904, new ed. 1927 (seitdem immer wieder nachgedruckt, in *Gaelic type*), welches für den älteren rustikalen Wortschatz auch heute noch unentbehrlich ist. Das Standardwerk für den heutigen Wortschatz (einschl. Neologismen) ist Ó Dónaill 1977. An älteren englisch-irischen Wörterbüchern sind zu nennen Foley 1855, Fournier 1903, Lane 1904 (new ed. 1916) und besonders, auch heute noch mit Gewinn zu benutzen, Mc Cionnaith 1935 (auch unter der anglisierten Namensform McKenna verzeichnet). Das maßgebliche Werk ist heute de Bhaldraithe 1959, mit Ergänzungen de Bhaldraithe 1978. Ein einsprachiges Wb. des Irischen existiert nicht, befindet sich aber u. d. T. *Foclóir na Nua-Ghaeilge* [Wb. des Neuirischen] in der Planung.

4. Schottisch-Gälisch

Eine kurze Geschichte der schottisch-gälischen Lexikographie bietet Thomson 1983, 61—63 (von Kenneth D. MacDonald). In demselben Werk finden sich auch Kurzbiographien bedeutender Lexikographen (passim, in alphabetischer Ordnung). Abgesehen von Wortlisten des 17. und 18. Jh. ist das erste größere Wb. Shaw 1780, welches aber gemischt irische und schottisch-gälische Wörter enthält und daher auch unter Irisch verzeichnet ist. Das bedeutendste Werk der frühen Zeit ist das von der *Highland Society of Scotland* herausgegebene *Dictionarium Scoto-Celticum* in drei Sprachen (Gälisch-Englisch-Latein): Highland Society 1828. Diejenigen Wbb., welche im 19. Jh. bis weit ins 20. Jh. hinein für praktische Zwecke die weiteste Verbreitung erfuhren, sind MacAlpine 1832 für Gälisch-Englisch und MacKenzie 1845 für Englisch-Gälisch (beide Werke in zahlreichen Nachdrucken, sowohl getrennt als auch zusammen in einem Band). Dabei ist MacKenzie wegen seiner undifferenzierten Angaben von begrenztem Wert und konnte sich nur mangels besserer Werke für Gälisch als Zielsprache durchsetzen. Zu erwähnen sind weiterhin MacEachen 1842, welches in seiner erweiterten Ausgabe von 1902 zum Schulwörterbuch des 20. Jh. wurde, sowie MacLennan 1925, welches eine Erweiterung und Modernisierung von MacAlpine darstellt. Das bedeutendste Werk des 20. Jh. ist Dwelly 1920 (ursprünglich in Faszikeln 1901—1911). Es enthält einen sehr umfangreichen älteren rustikalen Wortschatz (entsprechend Dinneen für Irisch), präzisiert durch zahlreiche Zeichnungen von Tieren, Pflanzen, Werkzeugen, Geräten u. dgl. von hohem natur- und volkskundlichen Wert, aber keine Neologismen. Seit jüngerem liegt ein neues englisch-gälisches Wb. als Ersatz für MacKenzie vor: Thomson 1981 (teilweise in reformierter Orthographie). An Spezialwörterbüchern sind zu nennen: MacBain 1896 für die Etymologie und Dieckhoff 1932 für die Aussprache (allerdings ohne normative Bedeutung, cf. 2.5.). Ein großes historisches Wb. ist seit 1966 an der Universität Glasgow unter der Herausgeberschaft von Kenneth D. MacDonald in Arbeit (cf. Thomson 1983, 62f.). Wichtigstes Desiderat bleibt im Augenblick ein neues gälisch-englisches Wb. für den modernen Wortschatz.

5. Manx

Die frühesten Wörterbücher des Manx sind Cregeen 1835 (Manx-Englisch) und Kelly 1866 (Manx-Englisch-Manx). Eine kritische Würdigung dieser beiden Werke bietet Thomson 1969, 202ff. Das Manuskript von Kelly ist wesentlich älter als das Publikationsdatum. Daher gehen beide Werke auf eine Zeit zurück (18./19. Jh.), als die Sprache noch einigermaßen intakt war. Dies gilt nicht mehr für die folgenden Werke: Kneen 1938 (mit Ausspracheangaben für Manx) und Fargher 1979 (beide Englisch-Manx). Sie enthalten zahlreiche Neologismen (meist nach irischem oder schottisch-gälischem Vorbild) und repräsentieren daher z. T. eine Art *Neo-Manx*, d. h. eine nach dem Aussterben der Sprache künstlich wiederbelebte Sprachform. Ganz anderer Art ist Broderick 1984: Es enthält ein Verzeichnis der tatsächlich registrierten Wörter und Formen der letzten muttersprachlichen Sprecher (sog. *Late Spoken Manx*). — Ein Glossar der frühesten Prosatexte in Manx (17. Jh.) findet sich bei Thomson 1954—1959.

6. Walisisch (Kymrisch)

Ein bibliographisches Verzeichnis der walisischen Wörterbücher von 1547 bis 1972 findet sich bei Emanuel 1972. Das erste walisische Wb. ist Salesbury 1547, welches für Waliser zum Erlernen des Englischen bestimmt war (mit einer Einleitung zur Aussprache des Englischen). Weitere frühe Werke: Davies 1632 (Walisisch-Latein-Walisisch), Richards 1753, Pughe 1793—1803. Das erste einsprachige Wb. einer keltischen Sprache überhaupt ist Ellis 1868. Bis heute ist Wales das einzige keltische Land mit einer entwickelten einsprachigen Lexikographie. Bemerkenswert ist, daß zweisprachige Wbb. mit der jeweiligen keltischen Sprache als Zielsprache in Wales von Anfang an stärker vertreten sind als in anderen keltischen Ländern. Auch sind Wbb. mit Aussprachenangaben zum *Englischen* (bzw. *Französischen*) nur in Wales zu finden. Eine (populäre) phonetische Transkription der englischen Einträge enthält auch Spurrell 1850. Aus diesem und aus seinem walis.-engl. Pendant (Spurrell 1848) entwickelte sich das bis in die Mitte des 20. Jh. am weitesten verbreitete zweisprachige Wb. (zahlreiche Neuauflagen, beide Teile auch in einem Band). Spätere Bearbeitungen stammen von Anwyl 1914, 1916 (und spätere Auflagen) sowie zuletzt Lewis 1960. Seinen Rang verlor dieses Werk erst durch das Erscheinen von Evans/Thomas 1958 (zahlreiche Neuauflagen), welches heute das meistbenutzte Wb. ist. Es enthält im walis.-engl. Teil (wahrscheinlich in Anlehnung an GPC, s. u.) außer der englischen Übersetzung auch einsprachige walisische Worterklärungen. Der dadurch in Anspruch genommene Platz geht auf Kosten von Wendungen und Kollokationen. Auch reicht der Wortschatz für die verschiedensten Texttypen nicht aus. Ein umfangreicheres rein zweisprachiges walis.-engl. Wb. ist ein Desiderat. Für Neologismen s. Williams 1973. — Seit 1950 erscheint in Lieferungen das umfangreiche *Geiriadur Prifysgol Cymru* (GPC) [Wb. der Universität von Wales]: Geiriadur 1950ff. Es ist im Prinzip ein historisches Wb. mit zahlreichen Quellenangaben und Zitaten, enthält aber auch Etymologien, grammatische Angaben, einsprachige Worterklärungen, englische Übersetzungen, idiomatische Wendungen u. a. Damit ist es wohl das vielseitigste aller keltischen Wörterbücher. Gegenüber dem irischen DIL (Dictionary 1983) hat es den Vorteil der größeren Einheitlichkeit in Konzeption und Ausführung. Für *Mittelwalisisch* gibt es neben dem GPC auch das (leider unvollendete) *Geirfa Barddoniaeth Gynnar Gymraeg* [Vokabular der frühen walisischen Dichtung]: Lloyd-Jones 1931—1963. Erwähnenswert ist das wahrscheinlich einzige Reimwörterbuch für eine keltische Sprache: Morganwg o. J. Walisisch verfügt auch über das einzige rückläufige Wörterbuch: Zimmer 1987. — Schließlich ist auf eine spezifische Lücke hinzuweisen. In Wales herrscht ein Zustand echter *Diglossie: Literary Welsh* vs. *Living Welsh (Cymraeg Byw)*. Alle Wörterbücher beruhen ausschließlich auf *Literary Welsh*. In der Lexikographie spielt *Cymraeg Byw* bisher überhaupt keine Rolle.

7. Bretonisch

Ein bibliographisches Verzeichnis der bretonischen Wörterbücher von den Anfängen bis 1945 findet sich bei Hemon 1947, 153ff. (cf. auch ibd. 74ff.). Das Bretonische weist die mit Abstand komplizierteste sprachpolitische Situation aller keltischen Sprachen auf, was besonders in der Lexikographie zum Ausdruck kommt. Seit dem 17. Jh. bestehen zwei Schriftsprachen nebeneinander: (1) eine Form, die den größeren Teil des Sprachgebiets umfaßt und auf dem Dialekt von Léon beruht (mit den Initialen der beteiligten Dialekte als KLT bezeichnet), (2) eine Form, die auf dem besonders abweichenden Dialekt von Vannes beruht (Vannetais). — Das älteste Wb. ist das *Catholicon* von Lagadeuc 1499 (Bretonisch-Französisch-Latein). Unter den übrigen frühen Werken sind von besonderer Bedeutung: das *Sacré Collège de Jésus* von Maunoir 1659 (das Erscheinen dieses Werkes markiert den Beginn des Neubretonischen), Châlons 1723 (erstes Wb. des Vannetais), Rostrenen 1732 und Le Pelletier 1752. Die heutige Standardsprache für das KLT geht auf die Werke von Le Gonidec 1821, 1847 zurück. In der Folge sind hervorzuheben Troude 1869, 1876 sowie die noch heute verwendeten Ernault 1927 und Vallée 1931, 1948 (alle KLT). Für das Vannetais: Ernault 1904, Guillevic/Le Goff 1924. Seit ca. 1940 ist die sprachpolitische Situation weiter verkompliziert und mit starken politischen Emotionen aufgeladen. Es entstanden zwei neue Orthographien: *Orthographe unifiée* (1941) versuchte, KLT und Vannetais zu vereinigen; dagegen war *orthographe universitaire* (1955) von François Falc'hun explizit gegen dieses Vorhaben gerichtet (cf. Fleuriot 1983). Die Werke von Hemon 1943 (bretonisch-französisch) und Hemon 1950 (französisch-bretonisch) verwenden *orthographe unifiée* und sind — auch ohne politische Implikationen — zu den heute am meisten benutzten Wörterbüchern geworden (zahlreiche jeweils erweiterte Neuauflagen). Dagegen hat *orthographe universitaire* zunächst nur ein kleineres Wb. hervorgebracht: Stéphan-Sèite 1956, neuerdings aber Helîas 1986. Ein neues groß angelegtes französisch-bretonisches Wb. ist Le Dû/Le Berre 1975 ff., ein neues Wb. für Vannetais Herrieu 1981. — Das umfangreichste Werk ist *Geriadur Istorel ar Brezhoneg* (GIB) [Historisches Wb. des Bretonischen] von Hemon 1958—1979, eine unter schwierigsten Bedingungen (im Exil) geleistete *tour de force* eines einzigen Autors. Stilistik: Gros 1970—1974; Etymologie: Ernault 1887, Henry 1900 (veraltet) und Guyonvarc'h 1973 ff. (nur sehr langsam voranschreitend). Wbb. für ältere Sprachzustände: Altbretonisch: Fleuriot 1964 (Neuausgabe Evans/ Fleuriot 1985); Mittelbretonisch: Ernault 1895—1896.

8. Kornisch

Das älteste Dokument ist das *Vocabularium Cornicum* (ca. 1100), eine kornische Version von Ælfrics lateinisch-altenglischem Vokabular, wobei die altenglischen Glossen durch kornische ersetzt sind (s. Graves 1962). Alle anderen Wörterbücher sind erst nach dem Aussterben der Sprache entstanden. Von den älteren Werken beruht Williams 1865 ausschließlich auf originalen Quellen *(Late Cornish),* während Jago 1887 wegen seines Pseudo-Kornisch kritisiert wurde. Die heute verbreiteten Wörterbücher sind Nance 1955 (Kornisch-Englisch) und Nance 1952 (Englisch-Kornisch), beide mit mehreren Neuauflagen. Sie repräsentieren z. T. *Neo-Kornisch* (cf. Manx) mit zahlreichen Neologismen, wobei nach dem Vorbild einer anderen Sprache (meist Walisisch) gebildete Wörter und wiederbelebte alte Wörter als solche gekennzeichnet sind. Zur Etymologie: Campanile 1974, welches über den ausführlichen Index auch für die Etymologie der übrigen britannischen Sprachen benutzt werden kann.

9. Literatur (in Auswahl)

9.1. Wörterbücher

9.1.1. Irisch

de Bhaldraithe 1959 = Tomás de Bhaldraithe (ed.): English-Irish Dictionary. Baile Átha Cliath 1959 [864 S.].

de Bhaldraithe 1978 = Tomás de Bhaldraithe: English-Irish Dictionary. Terminological Additions and Corrections. Baile Átha Cliath 1978 [25 S.].

de Bhaldraithe 1981 = Tomás de Bhaldraithe: Innéacs Nua-Ghaeilge don *Dictionary of the Irish Language.* Baile Átha Cliath 1981 [78 S.].

Coneys 1849 = Thomas de Vere Coneys: Foclóir Gaoidhilge-Sacs-Béarla. An Irish-English Dictionary. Dublin 1849 [382 S.].

Dictionary 1983 = Dictionary of the Irish Language. Based mainly on Old and Middle Irish materials. Compact Edition. Dublin 1983 [632 S., jede Seite 4 verkleinerte Originalseiten].

Dinneen 1904 = Patrick S. Dinneen: Foclóir Gaedhilge agus Béarla. An Irish-English Dictionary. Dublin 1904. New ed. 1927 [1344 S.; repr. 1970].

Finck 1899 = Franz Nikolaus Finck: Die araner mundart. Ein beitrag zur erforschung des westirischen. 2. band. Wörterbuch. Marburg 1899 [349 S.; 1. Bd. Grammatik].

Foclóir 1986 = Foclóir Póca: English-Irish/Irish-English Dictionary. Baile Átha Cliath 1986 [535 S.].

Foley 1855 = Daniel Foley: An English-Irish Dictionary. Dublin 1855 [384 S.].

Fournier 1903 = Edmund E. Fournier: An English-Irish Dictionary and Phrase Book. Dublin 1903. 3rd ed. 1907 [332 S.].

de Hae 1952 = Ristéard de Hae: Foclóir Gaedhilge agus Frainncise. Baile Átha Cliath 1952 [440 S.].

Lane 1904 = T. O'Neill Lane: Lane's English-Irish Dictionary (Foclóir Béarla-Gaedhilge). Dublin. London 1904 [581 S.]. New ed. 1916 [1748 S.].

Mc Cionnaith 1935 = L. Mc Cionnaith: Foclóir Béarla agus Gaedhilge. English-Irish Dictionary. Baile Átha Cliath 1935 [1546 S.].

McKenna 1935 = Mc Cionnaith 1935.

Ó Dónaill 1977 = Niall Ó Dónaill: Foclóir Gaeilge-Béarla. Baile Átha Cliath 1977 [1309 S.].

Ó Duirinne/Ó Dálaigh = Séamus Ó Duirinne and Pádraig Ó Dálaigh: The Educational Pronouncing Dictionary of the Irish Language. Dublin o. J. [1922] [199 S.].

O'Reilly 1817 = Edward O'Reilly: An Irish-English Dictionary. Dublin 1817. New ed. 1864 [725 S.].

Shaw 1780 = William Shaw: A Galic and English Dictionary. An English and Galic Dictionary. 2 Bde. London 1780 [ca. 700 S.].

9.1.2. Schottisch-Gälisch

Dieckhoff 1932 = Henry Cyril Dieckhoff: A Pronouncing Dictionary of Scottish Gaelic. Based on the Glengarry Dialect [...]. Edinburgh. London 1932 [XXXIII, 186 S.].

Dwelly 1920 = Edward Dwelly: The Illustrated Gaelic-English Dictionary. 2nd ed. Glasgow 1920 [1034 S.; 9th ed. 1977].

Highland Society 1828 = Highland Society of Scotland: Dictionarium Scoto-Celticum: A Dictionary of the Gaelic Language. 2 Bde. Edinburgh. London 1828 [776 + 1016 S.].

MacAlpine 1832 = Neil MacAlpine: A Pronouncing Gaelic-English Dictionary. Edinburgh 1832. New ed. Glasgow 1929 [281 S.].

MacBain 1896 = Alexander MacBain: An Etymological Dictionary of the Gaelic Language. Inverness 1896. New ed. Stirling 1911 [412 S.; repr. Glasgow 1982].

MacEachen 1842 = Evan MacEachen: Faclair Gaidhlig is Beurla. Perth 1842. 2nd ed. MacEachen's Gaelic-English Dictionary. Inverness 1902. 5th ed. 1965 [321 S.].

MacKenzie 1845 = John MacKenzie: An English-Gaelic Dictionary. Edinburgh 1845 [265 S.; ursprüngl. Teil II zu MacAlpine 1832, 2nd ed. 1845; auch getrennt publ.; repr. Glasgow 1971].

MacLennan 1925 = Malcolm MacLennan: A Pronouncing and Etymological Dictionary of the Gaelic Language. Gaelic-English, English-Gaelic. Edinburgh 1925 [613 S.; repr. Aberdeen 1979].

Shaw 1780 = [s. Irisch]

Thomson 1981 = Derick S. Thomson: The New English-Gaelic Dictionary. Glasgow 1981 [210 S.].

9.1.3. Manx

Broderick 1984 = George Broderick: A Handbook of Late Spoken Manx. Vol. 2 Dictionary. Tübingen 1984 [523 S.; Vol. 1 Grammar and Texts].

Cregeen 1835 = Archibald Cregeen: A Dictionary of the Manks Language with the Corresponding Words or Explanations in English. Douglas 1835 [188 S.; repr. 1911, 1977].

Fargher 1979 = Douglas C. Fargher: Fargher's English-Manx Dictionary. Douglas 1979 [888 S.].

Kelly 1866 = John Kelly [Juan y Kelly]: Fockleyr Manninagh as Baarlagh. An English and Manx Dictionary. Douglas 1866 [2 Teile in 1 Bd.; zs. 432 S.].

Kneen 1938 = J. J. Kneen: „Mona's Herald" English-Manx Pronouncing Dictionary. Douglas 1938 [96 S.; repr. 1953, 1970].

Thomson 1954—59 = Robert Leith Thomson: A Glossary of Early Manx. In: Zeitschrift für celtische Philologie 24 (1954), 272—307; 25 (1956), 100—140, 264—308; 27 (1958/59), 79—160.

9.1.4. Walisisch

Anwyl 1914 = J. Bodvan Anwyl (ed.): Spurrell's Welsh-English Dictionary. Geiriadur Cymraeg a Saesneg. Carmarthen 1914. 10th ed. 1925 [415 S.].

Anwyl 1916 = J. Bodvan Anwyl (ed.): Spurrell's English-Welsh Dictionary. Geiriadur Saesneg a Chymraeg. Carmarthen 1916. 9th ed. 1926 [390 S.].

Davies 1632 = John Davies: Antiquae linguae Britannicae [...] dictionarium duplex [...] prius, Britannico-Latinum [...] posterius, Latino-Britannicum. Londini 1632 [840 S.].

Ellis 1868 = Robert Ellis: Geiriadur Cymreig Cymraeg. Caernarfon 1868 [300 S.].

Evans/Thomas 1958 = H. Meurig Evans and W. O. Thomas: Y Geiriadur Mawr. The Complete Welsh-English, English-Welsh Dictionary. Llandybie 1958. 8th ed. Abertawe. Llandysul 1978 [492, 367 S.].

Geiriadur 1950ff. = Geiriadur Prifysgol Cymru. A Dictionary of the Welsh Language. Caerdydd 1950ff. [zuletzt Lief. XXXIV, 1985, lledneisiaf — lloerdduw, S. 2135—2198].

Lewis 1960 = Henry Lewis: Collins-Spurrell Welsh Dictionary. London. Glasgow 1960 [317 S.].

Lloyd-Jones 1931—63 = J. Lloyd-Jones: Geirfa Barddoniaeth Gynnar Gymraeg. 2 Bde. Caerdydd 1931—1963 [774 S.; letzter Eintrag: heilic].

Morganwg o. J. = Iolo Morganwg: Geiriadur y Bardd. Caernarfon o. J. [frühes 19. Jh.; 288 S.].

Pughe 1793—1803 = William Owen Pughe: Geiriadur Cymraeg a Saesoneg. A Welsh and English Dictionary. 2 Bde. London 1793—1803. 3rd ed. Geiriadur Cenhedlaethol Cymraeg a Saesneg. A National Dictionary of the Welsh Language. Ed. by Robert John Pryse. 2 Bde. Denbigh 1866—1873 [672 + 638 S.].

Richards 1753 = Thomas Richards: Antiquae linguae Britannicae thesaurus: being a British, or Welsh-English Dictionary. Bristol 1753 [68, 488 S.].

Salesbury 1547 = William Salesbury: A Dictionary in Englyshe and Welshe. London 1547 [164 S.].

Spurrell 1848 = William Spurrell: Geiriadur Cymraeg a Seisoneg. A Dictionary of the Welsh Language with English Synonyms and Explanations. Carmarthen 1848 [304 S.; 6th ed. = Anwyl 1914].

Spurrell 1850 = William Spurrell: An English-Welsh Pronouncing Dictionary. Geiriadur Cynaniaethol Seisoneg a Chymraeg. Carmarthen 1850 [435 S.; 7th ed. = Anwyl 1916].

Williams 1973 = Jac L. Williams (ed.): Geiriadur Termau. Dictionary of Terms. Caerdydd 1973 [544 S.].

Zimmer 1987 = Stefan Zimmer: A Reverse Dictionary of Modern Welsh. Geiriadur Gwrthdroadol Cymraeg Diweddar. Hamburg 1987 [177 S.].

9.1.5. Bretonisch

Châlons 1723 = Pierre de Châlons: Dictionnaire breton-françois du diocèse de Vannes. Vannes 1723. Rééd. par Joseph Loth. Rennes 1895 [115 S.].

Delaporte 1979 = Raymond Delaporte: Elementary Breton-English Dictionary. Cork 1979 [110 S.].

Ernault 1887 = Emile *Ernault:* Dictionnaire étymologique du breton moyen. Nantes 1887. Paris 1888 [218 S.].

Ernault 1895—96 = Emile Ernault: Glossaire moyen-breton. 2ᵉ éd. 2 Bde. Paris 1895—1896 [zs. 833 S.].

Ernault 1904 = Emile Ernault: Dictionnaire breton-français du dialecte de Vannes. Vannes 1904. 2ᵉ éd. 1938 [239 S.].

Ernault 1927 = Emile Ernault: Gériadurig brezoneg-galleg. Vocabulaire breton-français. Saint-Brieuc 1927 [685 S.]. 2ᵉ éd. Brest 1984 [446 S.].

Evans/Fleuriot 1985 = Claude Evans and Léon Fleuriot: A Dictionary of Old Breton. Dictionnaire du vieux breton. Historical and Comparative. In two parts. 2 Bde. Toronto 1985 [zs. 574 S.; Bd. 1 identisch mit Fleuriot 1964].

Fleuriot 1964 = Léon Fleuriot: Dictionnaire des gloses en vieux breton. Paris 1964 [372 S.].

Gros 1970—74 = Jules Gros: Le trésor du breton parlé (Eléments de stylistique trégorroise). Première partie: Le langage figuré. 2ᵉ éd. Saint-Brieuc 1970. Deuxième partie: Dictionnaire breton-français des expressions figurées. Saint-Brieuc 1970. Troisième partie: Le style populaire. Lannion 1974 [253 + 560 + 400 S.].

Guillevic/Le Goff 1924 = A. Guillevic et P. Le Goff: Vocabulaire breton-français et français-breton du dialecte de Vannes. 2ᵉ éd. Vannes 1924 [81, 105 S.].

Guyonvarc'h 1973ff. = Christian-J. Guyonvarc'h: Dictionnaire étymologique du breton ancien, moyen et moderne. Origine et histoire des mots. Rennes 1973 ff. [bisher 480 S.; zuletzt Fasz. 6 alkimiezh — amleal].

Helias 1986 = Per Jakez Helias (dir.): Dictionnaire breton. Breton-français/français-breton. Paris 1986 [816 S.].

Hemon 1943 = Roparz Hemon: Dictionnaire breton-français. Brest 1943 [445 S.]. Spätere Auflagen: Nouveau dictionnaire breton-français. 5ᵉ éd. 1973 [838 S.; 6ᵉ éd. 1978].

Hemon 1950 = Roparz Hemon: Dictionnaire français-breton. La Baule 1950 [spätere Auflagen Brest]. Nouvelle éd. Brest 1974 [420 S.].

Hemon 1958—79 = Roparz Hemon: Geriadur Istorel ar Brezhoneg. Dictionnaire historique du breton. Châteaulin u. a. [Ort mehrfach wechselnd] 1959—1979 [so ab Buchstabe B; Buchstabe A u. d. T. Dafar Geriadur Istorel ar Brezhoneg, o. O. 1958; zs. 204 + 3232 S.].

Henry 1900 = Victor Henry: Lexique étymologique des termes les plus usuels du breton moderne. Rennes 1900 [350 S.].

Herrieu 1981 = Abbé Mériadeg Herrieu: Dictionnaire français-breton. Vannetais. Hennebont 1981 [203 S.].

Lagadeuc 1499 = Jehan Lagadeuc: Catholicon en troys langaiges, scavoir est breton, francoys et latin [...]. Tréguier 1499. Publié et édité avec une introduction par Christian-J. Guyonvarc'h. Rennes 1975 [CLII, 15, 210 S.].

Le Dû/Le Berre 1975ff. = Jean Le Dû/Yves Le Berre: Dictionnaire pratique français-breton. Brest. Rennes 1975ff. [bisher 427 S.; zuletzt Fasz. V Espèce — justice, 1985].

Le Gonidec 1821 = Jean-François Le Gonidec: Dictionnaire celto-breton ou breton-français. Angoulême 1821 [462 S.].

Le Gonidec 1847 = Jean-François Le Gonidec: Dictionnaire français-breton. Saint-Brieuc 1847 [836 S.].

Le Pelletier 1752 = Dom Louis Le Pelletier: Dictionnaire de la langue bretonne. Paris 1752 [927 S.].

Maunoir 1659 = Père J. Maunoir: Le sacré collège de Jésus, [...] où l'on enseigne en langue Armorique les leçons chrestiennes [...], un Dictionnaire, une Grammaire et Syntaxe en même langue. Quimper 1659 [130, 176, 77 S.].

Rostrenen 1732 = Grégoire de Rostrenen: Dictionnaire françois-celtique ou françois-breton. Rennes 1732 [980 S.].

Stéphan-Sèité 1956 = Stéphan-Sèité: Lexique breton-français et français-breton. Geriadurig brezoneg-galleg ha galleg-brezoneg. o. O. [Brest] 1956 [195 S.]. 20ᵉ éd. 1979 [388 S.].

Troude 1869 = A. E. Troude: Nouveau dictionnaire pratique français et breton du dialecte de Léon. Brest 1869 [940 S.].

Troude 1876 = A. E. Troude: Nouveau dictionnaire pratique breton-français du dialecte de Léon. Brest 1876 [824 S.].

Vallée 1931 = François Vallée: Grand dictionnaire français-breton. Avec le concours de E. Ernault et R. Le Roux. Rennes 1931 [814 S.]. Nachdr. [mit Vallée 1948] Gronwel 1980.

Vallée 1948 = François Vallée: Supplément au Grand Dictionnaire français-breton. La Baule 1948 [177 S.].

9.1.6. Kornisch

Campanile 1974 = Enrico Campanile: Profilo etimologico del Cornico antico. Pisa 1974 [136 S.].

Jago 1887 = Frederick W. P. Jago: An English-Cornish Dictionary. London 1887.

Nance 1952 = R. Morton Nance (ed.): An English-Cornish Dictionary. Marazion 1952. Repr. Penzance 1973 [201 S.].

Nance 1955 = R. Morton Nance (ed.): A Cornish-English Dictionary. Marazion 1955. Repr. 1971 [104 S.].

Williams 1865 = Robert Williams: Lexicon Cornu-Britannicum: A Dictionary of the Ancient Cornish Language of Cornwall, [...] with Translations in English. Llandovery. London 1865 [398 S.].

9.2. Sonstige Literatur

Baumgarten 1986 = Rolf Baumgarten: Bibliography of Irish Linguistics and Literature 1942—71. Dublin 1986.

Best 1969 = R. I. Best: Bibliography of Irish Philology and Manuscript Literature. Publications 1913—1941. Dublin 1969.

Bibliography 1913 = Bibliography of Irish Philology and of Printed Irish Literature. Dublin 1913 [von R. I. Best].

Emanuel 1972 = Helen Emanuel: Geiriaduron Cymraeg 1547—1972. In: Studia Celtica 7. 1972, 141—154.

Fleuriot 1983 = Léon Fleuriot: Les réformes du breton. In: István Fodor/Claude Hagège (eds.), Language Reform — La réforme des langues — Sprachreform. Vol. II. Hamburg 1983, 27—47.

Graves 1962 = Eugene Van Tassel Graves: The Old Cornish Vocabulary. Ph. D. Columbia University (New York) 1962.

Hemon 1947 = Roparz Hemon: La langue bretonne et ses combats. La Baule 1947.

Ternes 1977 = Elmar Ternes: Konsonantische Anlautveränderungen in den keltischen und romanischen Sprachen. In: Romanistisches Jahrbuch 28. 1977, 19—53.

Ternes 1978 = Elmar Ternes: Zur inneren Gliederung der keltischen Sprachen. Typologische Unterschiede zwischen den goidelischen und britannischen Sprachen. In: Zeitschrift für Vergleichende Sprachforschung 92. 1978, 195—217.

Ternes 1979 = Elmar Ternes: Die Sonderstellung des Bretonischen innerhalb der keltischen Sprachen. Eine typologische Untersuchung. In: Zeitschrift für celtische Philologie 37. 1979, 214—228.

Thomson 1969 = R. L. Thomson: The Study of Manx Gaelic. Sir John Rhŷs Memorial Lecture. In: Proceedings of the British Academy 55. 1969, 177—210.

Thomson 1983 = Derick S. Thomson (ed.): The Companion to Gaelic Scotland. Oxford 1983.

Elmar Ternes, Hamburg
(Bundesrepublik Deutschland)

222. Lexicography of the Baltic Languages I: Lithuanian, Old Prussian

1. Early Lithuanian Dictionaries
2. Contemporary Lithuanian Dictionaries
3. Old Prussian Lexicography
4. Selected Bibliography

1. Early Lithuanian Dictionaries

The contemporary political borders of the Lithuanian Republic of the USSR correspond quite well to the borders of Lithuanian language usage, the only exceptions being several minor neighboring border dialects spoken in Belorussia and northeastern Poland. Sirvydas 1642, the 3rd edition of the first dictionary in which the Lithuanian language figures, is a Polish-Latin-Lithuanian dictionary designed for use by students and clergy of the Jesuit Academy. The initial pages of the only known copy of the 1st edition are lacking so its date (1620?) is uncertain as is the date of the 2nd edition (1631?) of which there are no extant copies, although there exist copies of the 4th (1677) and 5th (1713). Sirvydas created such neologisms as kokýbė 'quality' (< kóks 'what kind of') and kiekýbė 'quantity' (< kiek 'how many') which have entered into the modern language. Haack, 1730, the first dictionary in Lithuania Minor was designed for theology students at Halle university. Ruigys 1747, the second dictionary in Lithuania Minor, in addition to religious terminology includes works from the folk language. Using the unpublished manuscript of Jakūbas Brodovskis, but basing himself primarily on Ruigys 1747, Milkus 1800 created a more complete dictionary. Nesselmann 1851 also contains words from the living folk language, but lacks the indication for intonation which was not customary for that time. Kurschat 1870—1874 and 1883 have the correct intonations, but as a result of Kurschat's dialect frequently confuse *ė* and *ie* (= standard *ie*) and contain many loan translations based on German. Kurschat 1968 ff. (a nephew) is a second somewhat supplemented edition of Kurschat 1870—1874. Juška 1897 ff. (aided by his brother Jonas) is a dictionary of the living Lithuanian folk language with Russian and Polish definitions. Publication ceased with the appearance of Vol. II, part 1 in 1922.

2. Contemporary Lithuanian Dictionaries

Būga 1924 f. was planned as a dictionary to contain the entire Lithuanian lexical stock, but only reached the second fascicle in 1925.

Words are explained in Lithuanian, but quotations from source material remain in the original language, rather than being translated into Lithuanian and for many words Būga gave the etymology, history and dialectology. After Būga's death (1924) his 600,000 cards lay untouched until 1930 when Juozas Balčikonis was appointed editor of the new Lithuanian dictionary. The new editorial staff decided to omit proper nouns, word etymology and history and to give definitions only in Lithuanian. Nevertheless Balčikonis 1941 and 1947 were adjudged unsatisfactory, and Balčikonis left his post as editor. For the continuance of the dictionary a new set of instructions was introduced, viz., (a) widely used international words were to be included, — (b) illustrative material should first give sentences from contemporary Soviet literature and the press, and only following that should come examples from the folk language, folklore and Old Lithuanian writings, — (c) prefixed verbs are to be alphabetized under the unprefixed verbs, e.g., under the entry *gaūbti* 'to cover' one finds subheadings for *ap-gaūbti* 'to envelope', *į-gaūbti* 'to bend inwards', etc., and similarly all nouns derived from verbs are classified under the unprefixed stem form, — (d) participial adverbs are defined under the verb from which they are derived, — (e) verbal transitivity is marked, — (f) paradigmatic intonational class is given, — (g) parallel forms and dialect forms are given under the entry for the more common form, — (h) an indication of the source of words borrowed from neighboring languages is given, although the origin of international words is not given, — (i) after the individual meaning an attempt is made to give picturesque sentences, frequently with a figurative meaning, — (j) with some words an indication of the historical or stylistic connotation or sphere of usage is given, — (k) quotations are taken from the works of various Lithuanian writers and scientists.

In order to conform with the new editorial instructions new editions of Vol. I and II were issued in 1968 and 1969 respectively. A 2nd supplemented edition of Kruopas 1954, Kruopas 1972, contains about 60,000 entries including the fundamental lexicon of Lithuanian and dialect words such as Samogitian (= Zhemaitish, Low Lithuanian) *buklùs* 'clever' (= standard *gudrùs*), archaisms such as *vētušas* 'old' (= standard *sēnas*), words denoting aspects of former life styles, e.g., *árklas* 'wooden plow', popular scientific terms such as *dalmuō* 'quotient', commonly used international words such as *kombáinas* 'combine', a few borrowings such as *bāzė* 'base', and ethnonyms such as *rùsai* 'Russians', etc. Since the 16th century, and perhaps beginning even before, many German and Slavic loanwords had found their way into the Lithuanian language. Some of these unacceptable foreign words are listed in order to provide the dictionary user with a suitable Lithuanian equivalent, e.g., under *pēčius* (= Slavic *pečь*) the reader is referred to the native word *krósnis* 'stove.'

The most important bilingual dictionary is Senn 1926 ff., the latter volumes of which are more complete as a result of the collaboration of Antanas Salys which began with p. 449 of Vol. II. Entries in this dictionary are characterized as to usage (e.g., dialectal, high style [hochsprachlich], obsolete [between 1800 and 1920], peasant speech, ecclesiastical, sports, contemptuous, vulgar, Old Lithuanian [before Donelaitis], American Lithuanian, etc). A typical entry contains an indication of paradigmatic accentuation, a note on the usage, one or more definitions with several examples of the use of the word in a sentence.

Of the approximately 20 bilingual dictionaries recently published in Lithuania the following are fairly typical.

Piesarskas 1979 containing about 50,000 entries is designed for Lithuanians and all English words are stressed, prepositional government is given, and examples of usage and stylistic characterization help define the function of the word. Laučka 1975 is designed to help people read English belletristic, publicistic and scientific literature. This dictionary contains words of the literary language, neologisms, many fundamental scientific words and Americanisms. Not only is this the most complete English-Lithuanian dictionary to date, but it contains many phraseological units and examples to illustrate the meanings of the words. For example, under the entry **all** we find Lithuanian explanations of such expressions as *all and sundry, beyond all doubt,* etc.

3. Old Prussian Lexicography

In the 13th century the boundaries of the Old Prussian language extended from the lower reaches of the Vistula to the Neman (Nemunas, Memel) according to sources stemming from the Teutonic Knights. Under pressure from the latter the Old Prussian language began to disappear, possibly still being maintained by a few people, however, until the very beginning of the 18th century.

One of the first monuments of Old Prussian, forming a part of the *Codex Neumannianus,* is the *Elbing vocabulary,* the original of which dates from around 1300. This is an 802-word Ordensdeutsch (= East Middle German mixed with Upper and Lower German) — Old Prussian vocabulary in which words are arranged according to related concepts rather than in alphabetical order, e. g., *Jormettan* 'year' etc. Simon Grunau's *Prussian Chronicle* (1517—1526) contains a list of about 100 Old Prussian words apparently in a somewhat distorted form and (in most versions) a German gloss (one version has Latin glosses). All of the earlier grammars of Old Prussian such as Trautmann 1910 contain glossaries of Old Prussian. Mažiulis 1981 contains both a Lithuanian-Old Prussian and a German-Old Prussian glossary. As well as attested Old Prussian words Toporov 1975 ff. gives words reconstructed on the basis of toponymic and onomastic data. The maximal variant of entries of attested words contains the following information. (a) the meaning of the word with an indication of the German gloss (if there is one), — (b) an indication as to where the word occurs in the texts (references are usually to Trautmann 1910), — (c) the accompanying context (in the case of Simon Grunau's and the Elbing vocabularies the context is provided by the preceding and following words in the semantic group), — (d) an indication of the grammatical form, — (e) various conjectures concerning the interpretation of the orthography, — (f) information on the composition of the word, — (g) etymological parallels from other Indo-European languages represented (where possible) in hierarchical order of relevance for the Old Prussian word, — (h) the semantic motivation for the proposed etymology along with typological parallels, — (i) comments on the theme of the word and the corresponding realia, — (j) relevant Old Prussian toponymic and onomastic data, — (k) literature concerning the etymologized word, primarily that appearing after Trautmann 1910, — (l) one or more possible phonemic or phonetic transcriptions of the word.

4. Selected Bibliography

4.1. Dictionaries

Balčikonis 1941 = Juozas Balčikonis, ed.: Lietuvių kalbos žodynas. Kaunas 1941. Vol. I [XXIV, 1008 p.], 1947, Vol. II [XV, 850 p.].

Būga 1924 f. = Kazimieras Būga: Lietuvių kalbos žodynas. Kaunas 1924 f. [CXLIX, 82 p.].

Haack 1730 = Friedrich Wilhelm Haack: Vocabularium Litthvanico-Germanicum et Germanico-Litthvanicum. Halle 1730 [336 p.].

Juška 1897 ff. = Antanas Juška: Litovskij slovar' A. Juškeviča s tolkovaniem slov na russkom i pol'skom jazykax. St. Petersburg 1897 ff. [XXVII, 997 p.].

Kruopas 1954 = Jonas Kruopas: Dabartinės lietuvių kalbos žodynas. Vilnius 1954 [XVI, 990 p. 2nd supplemented ed. 1972; XXIV, 976 p.].

Kruopas 1956 ff. = Jonas Kruopas et al. eds.: Lietuvių kalbos žodynas (Lithuanian Academy dictionary). Vols. III—XIII 1956 ff. Vol. I 1968 [XXXI, 1230 p.], Vol. II 1969 [XIX, 1187 p.].

Kurschat 1870 = Friedrich Kurschat: Wörterbuch der littauischen Sprache. Vol. I 1870 [XX, 723 p.], Vol. II. 1874 [XII, 390 p.] Halle a. S.

Kurschat 1883 = Friedrich Kurschat: Littauisch-deutsches Wörterbuch. Halle a. S. 1883 [XII, 529 p.].

Kurschat 1968 ff. = Alexander Kurschat: Littauisch-deutsches Wörterbuch. Vols. I—IV. Göttingen 1968 ff. [XXXIX, 2778 p.].

Laučka 1975 = Alfonsas Laučka et al.: English-Lithuanian dictionary. Vilnius 1975 [1094 p.].

Lyberis 1971 = Antanas Lyberis: Litovsko-russkij slovar'. Vilnius 1971 [747 p.].

Mažiulis 1966 = Vytautas Mažiulis: Prūsų kalbos paminklai. Vilnius 1966 [254 p.].

Mažiulis 1981 = Vytautas Mažiulis: Prūsų kalbos paminklai II. Vilnius 1981 [396 p.].

Milkus 1800 = Kristijonas Milkus: Littauisch-deutsches und Deutsch-littauisches Wörterbuch. Vols. I—II. Königsberg 1800 [928 p.].

Nesselmann 1851 = Georg Heinrich Ferdinand Nesselmann: Wörterbuch der Littauischen Sprache. Königsberg 1851 [XI, 555 p.].

Piesarskas 1979 = Bronius Piesarskas/Bronius Svecevičius: Lithuanian-English dictionary. Vilnius 1979 [912 p.].

Ruigys 1747 = Pilypas Ruigys: Littauisch-Deutsches und Deutsch-Littauisches Lexikon. Vols. I—II. Königsberg 1747 [616 p.].

Senn 1926 ff. = Alfred Senn/Max Niedermann/Franz Brender/Antanas Salys: Wörterbuch der litauischen Schriftsprache. Vols. I—V. Heidelberg 1926 ff. [XII, 3316 p.].

Sirvydas 1642 = Konstantinas Sirvydas: Dictionarium trium linguarum. 3rd ed. Vilnius 1642 [560 p.] Republished with commentary as Pirmasis lietuvių kalbos žodynas. Vilnius 1979 [900 p.].

4.2. Other Publications

Toporov 1975ff. = Vladimir Toporov: Prusskij jazyk. Vols. I—IV. Moscow 1975ff.

Trautmann 1910 = Reinhold Trautmann: Die altpreussischen Sprachdenkmäler. Göttingen 1910 [Reprt. 1970.].

William R. Schmalstieg,
Pennsylvania State University,
University Park, Pennsylvania (USA)

223. Die Lexikographie der baltischen Sprachen II: Lettisch

1. Die Anfänge der lettischen Lexikographie
2. Die 2. Hälfte des 19. Jahrhunderts
3. Das 20. Jahrhundert
4. Literatur (in Auswahl)

1. Die Anfänge der lettischen Lexikographie

Sieht man von der nicht zu beantwortenden Frage ab, ob sich in dem vom Lübecker Stadtrat 1525 beschlagnahmten, für Riga bestimmten Faß *plenu[m] libris lutterianisz ecia[m] missis in vulgari livonico lettico ac estonico* (vgl. Biezais 1973, 25—31; gegen Johansen 1959, Johansen/v. zur Mühlen 1973, 343) etwa auch grammatische oder lexikalische Schriften befanden, dann beginnt die lettische Lexikographie schwer faßbar noch mit den bisher nicht gefundenen *Nomenclatores* des deutschen Priesters Hartmann Tolgsdorf (1550—1620), sicher aber mit dem Theologen G. Mancelius (1593 bis 1654), der im semgalischen Mežmuiža (Grenzhof, seit 1937 Augstkalne) geboren wurde. Sein Lettus, „Das ist Wortbuch sampt angehengtem täglichen Gebrauch der Lettischen Sprache; Allen und jedem Außheimischen / die in Churland / Semgallen und Lettischem Liefflande bleiben / vnd sich redlich nehren wollen / zu Nutze verfertigt" (1638), soll, wie Titel und Vorwort lehren, den Deutschen, des Lettischen Unkundigen dienen, vor allem aber den Einheimischen die christliche (lutherische) Verkündigung nahe bringen. Das Wörterbuch umfaßt (1.) ein deutsch-lett. im Ganzen alphabetisch geordnetes (Ausnahmen z. B. *bleiben ... außbleiben, wegbleiben ... überbleiben*) Wörterverzeichnis (ca. 6000 Wörter) auf der Grundlage seines Heimatdialekts mit gelegentlicher Angabe dialektaler Abweichungen, (2.) eine thematisch geordnete *Phraseologica Lettica* (beginnend mit: 'von Gott und Geistern' und schließend mit den Zahlwörtern, Cap. 51). Hier werden auch Orts- und Personennamen geboten. Angefügt sind (3.) 10 Gespräche, die Aufschluß über die Umgangssprache jener Zeit geben (Draviņš 1965, 59) und (4.) eine Übersetzung der Sprüche Salomos (bereits 1637 erschienen). Abgesehen von den lateinischen Wörtern sind deutsche und lettische Wörter in der auf niederdeutscher Tradition beruhenden Fraktur-Schrift geschrieben, die bis ins 19. Jh. maßgeblich blieb. Die Schreibung richtet sich

Textbeispiel 223.1: Wörterbuchausschnitt (aus: Mancelius 1638)

nach der Aussprache (phonetisches Prinzip), Kürzen und Längen werden (mit Hilfe von *h*, aber $\bar{\imath}$ = *ie*) unterschieden, offene und geschlossene Aussprache des *e* gelegentlich. Daneben kommen auch etymologische Gesichtspunkte zur Geltung, wenn etwa die Schreibung *kungs* statt *kunx* oder *sirrds* statt *sirrtz* empfohlen wird oder der Genitiv Plur. mit -*o*, der Akkusativ Sing. aber mit -*u* bezeichnet wird (heute beide -*u*). Die Differenzierungen sind nicht konsequent durchgeführt (vgl. Zemzare 1961, 11—63; Roze 1982, 50—55; Ozols 1965, 152—204).

1.1. Der Lettus hat zusammen mit den anderen Schriften des Mancelius in Orthographie, Form und Zielsetzung stark auf die lett. Lexikographie des 17./18. Jh. eingewirkt und dadurch zur Ausbildung der lett. Schriftsprache beigetragen. So haben sowohl die im Druck erschienenen Wörterbücher wie z. B. (a) das *Dictionarium Polono-Latino-Lottavicum* des Jesuiten Georg Elger (1683) (vgl. Zemzare 1961, 64—72) mit ca. 14 000 Stichwörtern, dessen Vorbild allerdings das *Dictionarium trium linguarum* (Polnisch-lateinisch-litauisch) des litauischen Jesuiten Constantin Szyrwid war (Pakalka 1979), (b) das erst 1936 publizierte *Lettisch-deutsche Lexikon* von Johannes Langius aus dem Jahre 1685 mit 7 000 Wörtern (Zemzare 1961, 84—90), (c) das viersprachige (deutsch, lateinisch, polnisch, lettisch) Vokabular von G. Dressel (1688) (Zemzare 1961, 91—93), (d) das deutsch-lettische Wörterbuch von Liborius Depkin (Anfang 18. Jh.), (e) das lettische Wörterbuch von Caspar Elvers (1748) mit etwa 8 000 Wörtern (Zemzare 1961, 103—117), als auch die nur handschriftlich überlieferten Wörterbücher, wie die beiden Abschriften eines Lettisch-Deutschen Wörterbuchs von Christopher Fürecker (2. Hälfte des 17. Jh.) mit ca. 4 000 Wörtern (Zemzare 1961, 73—83) u. a. aus Mancelius geschöpft und im wesentlichen derselben Zielsetzung gedient.

1.2. Als sprachliche Grundlage wurde wie schon bei Mancelius das Mittellettische benutzt. Eine Ausnahme bildet das nur im Manuskript erhaltene *Vocabularium Germanico-Curlandicum* mit etwa 900 Wörtern (Zemzare 1961, 100—102; 379—381; Endzelīns 1971, 456 f.). Das erste Wörterbuch, das auf lettgalischer (ostlettischer) Grundlage aufbaut, ist das *Słownik polsko-łacinsko-łotewski* des litauischen Geistlichen J. Kurminas, Vilna 1858 (Zemzare 1961, 207—211). — Eine gewisse Verselbständigung kündigt sich an mit Gotthard Friedrich Stender's *Entwurf eines Lettischen Lexici* (Braunschweig 1761, 1763) mit zunächst etwa 4 000 Wörtern nebst Sprichwörtern, Rätseln und Hinweisen auf Dialektismen. Die lettischen Wörter werden jetzt in lat. Schrift gesetzt. Man beachte aber, daß die Evangelien und Episteln des G. Elger im Jahre 1672 in gotischer Schrift erschienen sind, während eine erst 1961 von K. Draviņš veröffentlichte, umfangreichere, aus dem Jahre 1640 stammende Handschrift in lateinischen Buchstaben geschrieben ist (Draviņš 1961) [Lateinische Handschrift, gotischer Druck war wohl ein Brauch der Zeit]. Dieser Entwurf geht dann in G. F. Stender's *Lettisches Lexikon* ein (Mitau 1789), das nicht nur von Caspar Elvers und dem inzwischen erschienenen Wörterbuch von Jacob Lange (1772—1777) Gebrauch macht, sondern auch in der Folgezeit vom Sohn Alexander Stender (1820), H. Harder und A. Vellīgs (1828) ergänzt wird, und inzwischen 7 000 Stichwörter im lettisch-deutschen Teil und 14 000 im deutsch-lettischen Teil umfaßt. Es enthält auch eine größere Zahl von Gehöft-Namen, dagegen sind Berg- und Flußnamen selten und dann aus J. Lange übernommen (Zemzare 1961, 124—129, 175—187).

2. Die 2. Hälfte des 19. Jahrhunderts

Einen starken Einschnitt in die bisherige lettische Wörterbuchtradition verursachen die Jungletten *(jaunlatvieši)* in der 2. Hälfte des 19. Jh. Sie versuchen, sich vom deutschen und kirchlichen Einfluß zu lösen und die Pflege der lettischen Literatursprache in den Vordergrund zu stellen. Die Germanismen werden zurückgedrängt, an ihre Stelle treten lettische Neologismen, die mit Hilfe lettischer Wortbildungsmittel griechischen, lateinischen, deutschen, litauischen oder russischen Wörtern nachgebildet sind, oder auch aus der Volkssprache geschöpfte Dialektwörter. Eine führende Rolle spielt dabei die 1862 von K. Valdemārs, K. Barons und J. Alunāns begründete Zeitschrift *Pētersburgas Avīzes* mit ihrer Fremdwörterbeilage (Alunāns 1956, 232 ff.; Zemzare 1961, 215 ff.; Roze 1982, 66 ff.; Brence 1982). Hierher gehören u. a. das auf Betreiben von K. Valdemārs vom (russischen) Ministerium für Volksaufklärung herausgegebene *Russisch-Lettisch-Deutsche Wörterbuch* (Moskau 1872 [50 000 Wörter], kürzere Fassung Jelgava 1890) und das etwa 13 000 Stichwörter umfassende *Lettisch-Rus-*

sisch-Deutsche Wörterbuch (Moskau 1879), die beide für Letten bestimmt sind und zahlreiche Neubildungen enthalten (Zemzare 1961, 218—321). Ein Konkurrenz-Unternehmen dazu stellt das *Lettisch-deutsche Wörterbuch* von J. Neikens, beendet von Bischof Dr. Carl Christian Ulmann, dar (Riga 1872) mit etwa 20 000, im deutsch-lettischen Teil 35 000 Wörtern. Es bietet erstmals — wenn auch unvollständig — Intonationsangaben und macht ebenfalls von den inzwischen sich z. T. einbürgernden Neologismen Gebrauch (Zemzare 1961, 333—343; Roze 1982, 72—75). Ein litauisch-polnisch-lettisch-russisches Wörterbuch und ein lettisch-litauisch-polnisches Wörterbuch werden von den Litauern M. Miežinis und A. Juška (1892, bzw. 1875) herausgegeben (Zemzare 1961, 372—399). In verstärktem Maße beginnt man jetzt, sich auch dem Livischen, dem Lettischen der kurischen Nehrung, einzelnen Dialektgebieten, terminologischen Wörterbüchern und gesonderten Fremdwörtern und Synonymen zuzuwenden.

3. Das 20. Jahrhundert

Nach einer Reihe von Konversations- und zweisprachigen Wörterbüchern von Jēkabs Dravnieks (1858—1927) erreichte die lettische Lexikographie ihren Höhepunkt mit dem von K. Mühlenbach (Kārlis Mīlenbahs, 1853—1916) in den neunziger Jahren des 19. Jh. begonnenen und von Jānis Endzelīns (1873—1961) 1932 abgeschlossenen Lettisch-deutschen Wörterbuch (Mühlenbach/Endzelin 1923—1932). Dem vierbändigen Werk wurden 1934—1946 von Edīte Hauzenberga-Šturma noch zwei Ergänzungsbände hinzugefügt (Endzelīns/Hauzenberga 1934—1946). Es umfaßt auf 5 480 Seiten ca. 120 000 Wörter (Laua 1969, 17 zählt 110 410), die in alphabetischer Reihenfolge in der heute üblichen lettischen Orthographie (Ausnahme *uo* statt *o*) mit Intonationsangaben, historischen Belegen, Kontexten aus Literatur, Folklore, Umgangssprache und etymologischen Angaben aufgeführt werden. Die sog. Internationalismen sind nicht aufgenommen. Dieses als Thesaurus konzipierte, wissenschaftlichen Ansprüchen genügende Werk, das verschiedene Wörterbuchtypen in sich vereinigt, mußte sowohl kleinere, praktischen Zwecken dienende Wörterbücher, als auch eine Reihe von Spezialwörterbüchern nach sich ziehen. Außerdem wurden vor allem nach der Errichtung des selbständigen lettischen Staates (1918) neben dem Deutschen und Russischen auch andere Sprachen für die lexikographische Verarbeitung bedeutsam, vor allem das Englische und Französische. Da man in allen Fällen auf schon vorhandene Sammlungen und Traditionen zurückgreifen konnte, empfiehlt sich eine zeitliche Aufgliederung etwa in die Zeit vor 1940, Kriegszeit und Sowjet-Lettland nicht, wenn sich auch hinsichtlich der Produktivität, der Gewichtung und der Aufnahme von Internationalismen deutliche Unterschiede abzeichnen.

3.1. So dienen *praktischen* Bedürfnissen das von E. Ozoliņš bearbeitete, von J. Endzelīns redigierte *Lettisch-deutsche und deutsch-lettische Wörterbuch,* Riga, 2. Aufl. 1935, die englisch-lettischen Wörterbücher von K. Roze (1931) und E. Turkina (1937) und der letzteren *Lettisch-Englisches Wörterbuch* (1936, ²1962) (Turkina 1962) mit ca. 31 000 Wörtern. Ein *Lettisch-französisches Wörterbuch* entstand 1941. Ein zweibändiges, von der lett. Akademie herausgegebenes und von einem Autorenkollektiv bearbeitetes Russisch-lettisches Wörterbuch erschien 1959, ein weiteres 1980, 1981 (ein einbändiges mit 35 000 Wörtern erschien in 3. Aufl. 1974) (vgl. Roze 1982, 81 f.), ein lett.-deutsches mit ca. 33 000 Wörtern in 2. Auflage 1980 (Bisenieks 1980), ein deutsch-lettisches Wörterbuch in 2. Aufl. mit ca. 52 000 Wörtern 1968 (Granta/Pampe 1968). Dem *Litauisch-lettischen Wörterbuch* (Bojāte/Subatnieks 1964) mit ca. 50 000 Wörtern folgte das *Lettisch-litauische Wörterbuch* (Balkevičius/Kabelka 1977) in Vilnius mit etwa 42 000 Wörtern.

3.2. Mit der zunehmenden Normierung der lettischen Schriftsprache (vgl. Rūķe-Draviņa 1977) wurden nun auch *orthographische* Wörterbücher (zuletzt Ceplītis u. a. 1981) notwendig, besondere *Stil-* oder *phraseologische* Wörterbücher entstanden. Vor dem 2. Weltkriege wurde ein *Englisch-lettisches phraseologisches Wörterbuch* begonnen (vgl. Roze 1982, 81), ein lettisch-russisches erschien 1965 (Caubuliņa u. a. 1965), ein zweibändiges russisch-lettisches 1974 (Bauga u. a. 1974), ein deutsch-lettisches 1980 (Celmrauga u. a. 1980), eine Sammlung idiomatischer Ausdrücke verfaßte V. Rūķe-Draviņa in Stockholm 1974 (Rūķe-Draviņa 1974). — Ein Fremdwörterbuch *(Svešvārdu vārdnīca)* erschien in drei Auflagen (1951, 1969, 1978) (dazu Sehwers 1953). — Ein *Wörterbuch lettischer Synonyme* umfaßte 1964 20 000 Syn-

A

a, Ausruf der Freude, der Angst, des Unwillens, der Zurückweisung: *a, kā es te saimniekuotu* Vēr. I, 399. *a, liec mani mierā! a, ka tevi jupis parautu!*

— **a·a, a·ã** (li. *aà*), 1) Ausruf nach einer genügenden Belehrung: *vai pats mājās? — nê, viņš uz lauka. — aa, tad es viņu dabūšu.* 2) Ausdruck des Selbstbewusstseins: *viņš jau tevi pārspēj. — aa!* Er übertrifft ja dich. — Keine Spur davon!

ab für *ap* infl. EPr. 22. —

ab, oder Kleinschmidt 8, RKr. XIV, 41; *aba,* infl.: *Lementars aba ābece;* [auch *abu*: *sīkus luopus abu jebkuŗu luopu* Glück, II Mos. 22,10. Gleich li., z. B. bei Širvyd, *aba* aus slav. *abo* „oder"].

aba, 1) eben: *aba tālab, tālab aba, tāpēc aba,* eben deswegen; *ap kalnu it kā dūmi kūpuļuoja, — aba tālab kalns dabūjis vārdu* (zilais kalns) LP. VII, 1324. *tas jau aba tas, kas samaitā mūsu krietnākuos nuoduomus. nu ab' tikai apjēdzuos, ka māmiņas man nevaid* BW. 23832. [Wenn dies *aba* alt wäre, so könnte man das *a-* mit dem *a-* von *ai. áha* „gewiss, ja" vergleichen; nun ist aber z. B. *tāpēc aba* gleichbedeutend mit *tā ba pēc* z. B. bei Manzel, und aus *tā-ba* könnte, indem es als *tā-aba* aufgefasst wurde, dies *aba* entnommen sein]. 2) *bet aba* [wohl aus slav. *abo* „etwa"] *nu kāda laba diena zem kunga pātagas dzīvuot?* Purap. 3) *jūs gan iesiet, es aba ne* Wid. [Im letzten Satze geht *aba* über *abar* wohl auf d. *aber* zurück.]

aba-dui für *abi divi,* beide. Kruhten, N.-Bartau; *aba-divi* Ronneb. PS. [Mit diesem *aba-* vgl. weissruss. *обóдва* „beide".]

abaju > abai [auch in Grawendahl], SF. als Sammelzahlwort: [*abaju vāgu* „beide Wagen" N.-Schwnbg.]; *abai slieču pārlūza,* die Sohlen beider Schlitten gingen entzwei, *abai skrituļu,* die Räder beider Wagen BB. XIV, 144. — [Altes Neutrum, gleich apr. *abbaien* und aksl. *oboje* dass.].

abāda, N.-Schwnbg.; *abada (?),* in Grosdohn nach Etn. IV, 17, eine aus eben geschlachtetem Schweinefleisch und Kohl bestehende Speise [s. *apbēdas*].

abâdi, dial. für *abējâdi.* Dond. —

abejâdi C., *abējâdi* PS., auf beiderlei Art; *abējādi slikti,* so oder so ist es schlecht.

abejâds C., *abējâds* PS., beiderlei: *es sēju abējādus miežus, divkanšu un seškanšu,* ich säte beiderlei Gerste, die zwei- und sechszeilige.

abeji C. [und in Saussen], *abēji* PS. (li. *abejì*), 1) beiderlei: *tādēļ gājis ar abejiem ābuoļiem uz savu pilsētu* LP. VI, 602, mit beiderlei Äpfeln, d. h. mit den von beiden Apfelbäumen gepflückten Ä. — *brālis nuorauj nuo abejiem augļiem* LP. VI, 761; *abeju dzimumu bērni.* 2) beide, a) bei plur. t.: *abeji rati jāaizjūdz,* beide Wagen müssen angespannt werden; b) in manchen Gegenden Mittelkurlands und auch in Livland für *abi, abas* gesetzt: *abejās ruokās,* in beiden Händen; *šuo abeju krūmu uogas labas* Grünh. 3) Nom., Akk. Dual.: [*ābeju komanu* (Bersohn)]. *divej krekļu mugurā, abej meļnu nuovalkātu* BW. 20630,5. *cūku gani cūkas zīda, abej ausu turēdami* 29350,1; *mūs muižā divej' vārtu, abej veļnu sargājami* 31417,1. [Wohl, gleich li. *abeja* bei Bezzenberger BGLS. 186 f., altes Neutrum, wie *abaju* oben].

abejpus (ceļa), zu beiden Seiten des Weges MWM. IX, 939; auch *abej pušu, abu pušu, abjupus ceļam, ceļa: veldrē rudzi, veldrē mieži abej pušu* (Var.: *abejpus, abjupus, abu pušu*) *liela ceļa* (Var.: *lielceļam*) BW. 28437.

abejup, nach beiden Seiten hin: *dižņu cirvi tā sniedza tam, — abejup asu* O. V, 235.

abigals [in Nigranden], jemand, der es mit beiden Teilen hält [vgl. li. *abigaliaĩ* „von beiden Enden"]; *abgaļigs,* dass. als Adjektiv.

abi, beide, erstarrter Nom., Akk. Dual. fem. und neutr. (li. *abì,* slav. *обѣ*); jetzt als Nom. Pl. masc. empfunden, und dazu d. Nom. fem. *abas* hinzugebildet; Gen. *abu, abju, abēju, abeju* Bers.,

onyme, 1972 bereits 27 000 (Zemzare 392 f.; Roze 82; Grīnberga u. a. 1964, 1972). Ein vierbändiges *Häufigkeitswörterbuch* (Jakubaite u. a. 1968—1976) wertet nicht nur die schöne Literatur, sondern auch Journale, Zeitschriften und wissenschaftliche Literatur aus. Dazu ist 1976 auch ein rückläufiges Wörterbuch *(Inversā vārdnīca)* (vgl. Soida/Kļaviņa 1970) erschienen. Und schließlich wird jetzt vom Andreja Upīša Valodas un Literatūras Institūts der lettischen Akademie der Wissenschaften ein achtbändiges Wörterbuch der lettischen Literatursprache herausgegeben, von denen 1989 sieben (die Buchstaben A—S umfassend) veröffentlicht sind (Bendiks u. a. 1972 ff.). Dieses auf einen Umfang von etwa 80 000 Wörtern geplante Wörterbuch will die lettische Literatursprache von den 70er Jahren des vorigen Jahrhunderts bis zur Gegenwart umfassen. Ein einbändiges Lettisch-lettisches Wörterbuch (*Latviešu valodas vārdnīca* red. D. Gulevska) wurde 1987 in Riga veröffentlicht.

3.3. Angesichts dieser Spezialisierung liegt es auf der Hand, daß man die auf G. Mancelius (s. 1) zurückgehende Tradition der Berücksichtigung der *lettischen Dialekte* (vgl. Karte 223.1) wieder aufgreift. Erinnert sei an das unveröffentlichte, im Britischen Museum aufbewahrte *Vocabularium Germanico-Curlandicum* aus dem 17. Jh. (Zemzare 1961, 100—102), an das Wörterbuch von J. Kurmins (s. 1.2.), das als erstes lettgalisches Wörterbuch zu gelten hat, oder an die lettischen Sprachreste auf der Kurischen Nehrung von M. J. A. Voelkel (Heidelberg 1879) und an einzelne kleine Sammlungen von Dialektwörtern (Seewald 1863 ff., Endzelīns 1971, 17—30, Zemzare 1961, 391 f.). Einer Anregung von J. Endzelin aus dem Jahre 1953 folgend hatte bereits D. Zemzare in den Jahren 1966—1971 mit der systematischen Sammlung begonnen (Zemzare 1966 ff.). Angestrebt wird ein umfassendes lettisches Dialektwörterbuch, für welches im Institut für lettische Sprache und Literatur der lett. Akademie bereits 800 000 Karteikarten mit Dialektwörtern, lexikalischen Varianten, Wortverbindungen und Phraseologismen vorliegen (Kagaine 1985). Als erstes vollständiges lettisches Dialektwörterbuch kann das dreibändige Werk von F. Kagaine (Kagaine/Raģe 1977—1983) gelten. Ein lettgalisch-russisches Wörterbuch, das in den dreißiger Jahren begonnen wurde, scheint nicht erschienen zu sein (Roze 1982, 81).

3.4. Endlich muß auch noch des lettischen *Spezialwortschatzes* gedacht werden, der quer durch die Dialekte verfolgt wird. Schon Kr. Valdemārs hatte 1881 ein kleines Wörterbuch des Fischereiwesens herausgegeben (Zemzare 1961, 384 f.). Inzwischen verfügt man über eine Sammlung der Fischnamen im Lettischen (Laumane 1973, mit etymologischen Bemerkungen), über ein Lexikon der Handwerksbezeichnungen in einigen süd-lettgalischen Mundarten und ihre Beziehungen zu entsprechenden Bezeichnungen in den slavischen Sprachen (Reķēna 1975). Ein Russisch-Lettisches Polytechnisches Wörterbuch kam 1977 heraus (Roze 1982, 82).

3.5. Einen wichtigen Platz in der sprachhistorischen Untersuchung des Lettischen nehmen die *Eigennamen,* vor allem die *Orts-* und *Gewässernamen* ein. Sie wurden anfangs in die Wörterbücher mit aufgenommen (G. Mancelius, G. F. Stender), von J. Endzelin aber besonderen Sammlungen vorbehalten. Seine Sammlung lettischer Ortsnamen erschien 1922—1925 (Endzelīns 1922—25). Die etymologische Deutung der Gewässernamen folgte 1934 (Endzelīns 1934). Eine Neubear-

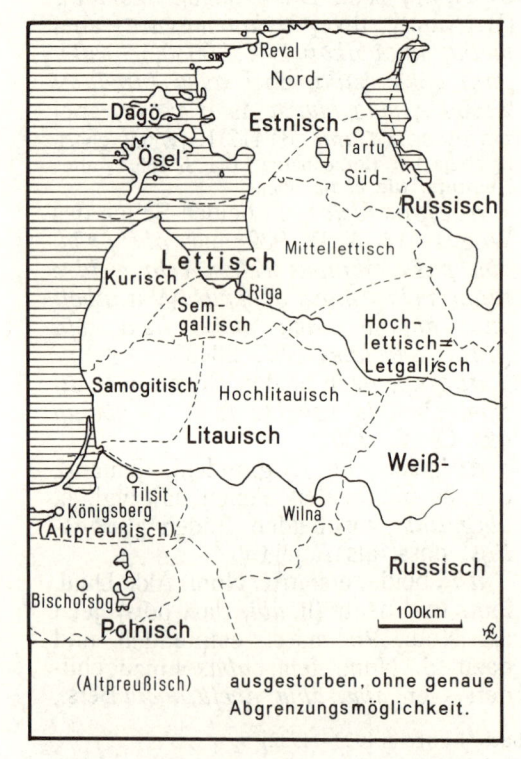

Karte 223.1: Skizze des Gebietes des Estnischen, Lettischen und Litauischen

beitung (Endzelīns 1956/1961) ist bis jetzt nicht zum Abschluß gekommen. Ein reichhaltiges Orts- und Personennamenbuch verfaßte J. Plāķis 1936—1939. Dem Gebiet von Kauguri hat V. Rūķe-Draviņa eine besondere Arbeit gewidmet (Rūķe-Draviņa 1971). Für das kurische Gebiet kann die Untersuchung von V. Kiparsky (1939) mit reichhaltigen historischen Belegen dienen.

3.6. Für die lettischen *Lehnwörter* im Livischen, Finnischen und Slavischen stehen einige alphabetisch geordnete Sammlungen zur Verfügung (Kalima 1936, Suhonen 1973, Laučiūtė 1982).

3.7. Auffallend an der lettischen Lexikographie der jüngsten Zeit ist der Umstand, daß Wörterbücher zu einzelnen Schriftstellern (wie z. B. Rainis) fehlen (Laua 1969, 242). Das Wortregister zum altlettischen G. Elger ist in Stockholm entstanden. Für die Etymologie ist man noch immer auf Mühlenbach/ Endzelin 1923—1932, auf Einzeluntersuchungen und auf das litauische etymologische Wörterbuch von E. Fraenkel angewiesen. — Aus diesem Überblick, der im wesentlichen nur veröffentlichte Wörterbücher (selten nur handschriftlich überlieferte) in Betracht zieht, Einzeluntersuchungen zur lettischen Lexikologie und Lexikographie kaum berücksichtigt, mußte das Lettische im Ausland weitgehend ausgeklammert werden. Dennoch sollte bedacht werden, daß man z. B. dem Lettischen auf der kurischen Nehrung heute nur noch und nicht mehr lange unter Vertriebenen in Deutschland begegnen kann (vgl. Plāķis 1927, Kwauka/Pietsch 1977, Schmid 1989).

3.8. In den Nachkriegsjahren sorgten lettische Emigranten vor allem in Westdeutschland, Dänemark, Schweden und Amerika für Nachdrucke, z. B. des lettischen Wörterbuchs von Mühlenbach/Endzelin (Chicago 1953—1955) (s. 3), des deutsch-lettischen Wörterbuchs von Ozoliņš (Eutin 1964), des lettisch-englischen Wörterbuchs von Turkina (Kopenhagen 1964), des englisch-lettischen von K. Roze (Göppingen 1945, Stockholm 1945) u. a. (s. 3.1). Dazu kommen solche Wörterbücher, die von der neuen Sprachumgebung der Letten herausgefordert wurden wie das lettisch-schwedische Wörterbuch von W. Freij, A. Veinbergs und V. Zante (Stockholm 1952) und das schwedisch-lettische von A. Veinbergs (Stockholm 1949). — Unter den Ortsnamenbüchern (3.5) verdient besondere Hervorhebung die in Amerika entstandene, neue Bearbeitung lettgalischer Ortsnamen von Zeps (1984).

4. Literatur (in Auswahl)

4.1. Wörterbücher

Balkevičius/Kabelka 1977 = J. Balkevičius/J. Kabelka: Latvių kalbų-Lietuvių žodynas. Vilnius 1977 [760 S.].

Bauga u. a. 1974 = A. Bauga/A. Jostsone/L. Tjurina: Krievu-latviešu frazeoloģiskā vārdnīca I, II. Rīgā 1974 [758 + 735 S., Taschenbuchformat].

Bendiks u. a. 1972 ff. = Latviešu literārās valodas vārdnīca. Redakcijas Koleģija: H. Bendiks, L. Ceplītis, R. Grabis, A. Laua, A. Miķelsone, L. Roze, M. Stengrevica, J. Sudrabkalns: I (A), Rīgā 1972 [517 S.], II (B—F) Rīgā 1973 [550 S.], III (G—I), Rīgā 1975 [745 S.], IV (J—L) Rīgā 1980 [759 S.], V (Ļ—N) Rīgā 1984 [770 S.], VI (Ņ—P) Rīgā 1986 [623 S.], VII (S), Rīgā 1989 [600 S.].

Bisenieks 1980 = Latviešu-vācu vārdnīca sastādījis autoru kollektivs, V. Bisenieka un I. Niseloviča redakcijā. Pārstrādāts otrais izdevums. Rīgā 1980 [890 S.].

Bojāte/Subatnieks 1964 = A. Bojāte/V. Subatnieks: Lietuviešu-latviešu vārdnīca redigējis J. Balkevičs. Rīgā 1964 [915 S.].

Caubuliņa u. a. 1965 = D. Caubuliņa/N. Ozoliņa/ A. Plēsuma: Latviešu-krievu frazeoloģiskā vārdnīca. Rīgā 1965 [673 S. Taschenbuchformat].

Celmrauga u. a. 1980 = I. Celmrauga/R. Livšica/ H. Rozenbaha/K. Sējēja/B. Veinerte/E. Pampes redakcijā: Vāculatviešu frazeoloģiskā vārdnīca. Rīgā 1980 [445 S., Taschenbuchformat].

Ceplītis u. a. 1981 = L. Ceplītis/D. Guļevska/A. Mikelsona/T. Porīte: Latviešu valodas pareizrakstības vārdnīca. Rīgā 1981.

Elger 1683 = Dictionarivm Polono-Latino-Lottavicum. Opus posthumum. R. P. Georgii Elger... Vilnae 1683.

Endzelīns 1922—25 = Jānis Endzelīns: Latvijas vietu vārdi. Wiederabdruck in Endzelīns 1971 ff. IV 1, 13—302.

Endzelīns 1934 = Jānis Endzelīns: Die lettländischen Gewässernamen. In: Zeitschrift für slavische Philologie 11. 1934, 112—150. Wiederabdruck in Endzelīns 1971 ff., III 2, 162—194.

Endzelīns 1956/1961 = Jānis Endzelīns: Latvijas PSR vietvārdi I 1 (A—J), Rīgā 1956 [XXII, 425 S.], I 2 (K—O), Rīgā 1961 [XI, 505 S.].

Endzelīns/Hauzenberga 1934—1946 = Jānis Endzelīns/Edīte Hauzenberga: Papildinājumi un labojumi K. Mühlenbacha Latviešu valodas vārdnīcai V, VI. Rīgā 1934—1946. 2. Aufl. V Chicago 1956 [841 S.], VI Chicago 1956 [827 S.].

Granta/Pampe 1968 = K. Granta/E. Pampe: Vācu-latviešu vārdnīca, otrais izdevums (pārstrādāts un papildināts. Rīgā 1968 [1001 S.].

Grīnberga u. a. 1964, 1972 = E. Grīnberga/O. Kalnciems/G. Lukstiņš/J. Ozols: Latviešu valodas sinonimu vārdnīca. Rīgā 1964. 2. Aufl. 1972 [528 S. 671 S.].

Guļevska 1987 = Dainuvīte Guļevska (red.): Latviešu valodas vārdnīca, A—Ž. Rīga 1987 [883 S.].

Jakubaite u. a. 1968—1976 = T. Jakubaite/D. Kristovska/V. Ozola/R. Prūse/N. Sīka: Latviešu valodas biežuma vārdnīca 1—4. Rīgā 1968—1976 [Bd. 1—3 1973 in einem Band 1004 S. Bd. 4: 646 S. Taschenbuchformat].

Kagaine/Rāǵe 1977—1983 = Elga Karlovna Kagaine/Silvia Karlovna Rāǵe: Ērǵemes izloksnes vārdnīca I (A—I), Rīgā 1977 [536 S.], II (J—P), Rīgā 1978 [591 S.], III (P—Z), Rīgā 1983 [800 S.].

Kalima 1936 = Jalo Kalima: Itämeren-suomalaisten kielten baltilaiset lainasanat. Helsinki 1936 [252 S.].

Kwauka/Pietsch 1977 = Paul Kwauka/Richard Pietsch: Kurisches Wörterbuch mit einer Einführung von Prof. Dr. Erich Hofmann. Berlin 1977 [87 S.].

Laučiūtė 1982 = Ju. A. Laučiūtė: Slovar' baltizmov v slavjanskich jazykach. Leningrad 1982 [211 S.].

Laumane 1973 = Benita Edmundovna Laumane: Zivju nosaukumi Latviešu valodā. Rīgā 1973 [307 S.].

Laumane 1987 = Benita Laumane: Zvejvietu nosaukumi Latvijas PSR piekrastē. Rīgā 1987 [171 S.].

Mancelius 1638 = Georgius Mancelius: Lettus. Das ist Wortbuch sampt angehengtem täglichen Gebrauch der Lettischen Sprache [...]. Erster Theil, Riga 1638. Faksimile-Ausgabe bei August Günther, Altlettische Sprachdenkmäler II. Heidelberg 1929, 1—222; Phraseologica Lettica, Das ist: Täglicher Gebrauch der Lettischen Sprache [...] Anderer Theil. ebd. S. 223—414; Die Sprüche Salomonis in die Lettische Sprache gebracht... Riga 1637. ebd. S. 415—518.

Mühlenbach/Endzelin 1923—1932 = Kārlis Mühlenbachs Lettisch-deutsches Wörterbuch redigiert, ergänzt und fortgesetzt von J. Endzelin: Bd. I Riga 1923—1925 [839 S.], II, Riga 1925—1927 [909 S.], III, Riga 1927—1929 [1167 S.], IV, Riga 1929—1932 [895 S.], 2. Aufl. Chicago 1955.

Ozoliņš/Endzelīns 1935 = Lettisch-deutsches und deutsch-lettisches Wörterbuch geordnet von Ed. Ozolin, redigiert von J. Endzelin. 1. Aufl. Riga 1926, 2. Ergänzte Auflage Riga 1935 [Taschenbuchformat, 667 S.].

Pakalka 1979 = Kazys Pakalka: Pirmasis Lietuvių žodynas; Konstantinas Širvydas Dictionarium trium linguarum. Vilnius 1979 [900 S.]. Faksimile-Ausgabe der 3. Aufl. des Wörterbuchs von 1642 (1. Aufl. um 1620).

Plāķis 1936—1939 = J. Plāķis: Latvijas vietu vārdi un latviešu pavārdi: I. Kurzemes vārdi. Rīgā 1936. II. Zemgales vārdi. Rīgā 1939 (Acta Universitatis Latviensis, Filologijas un filosofijas fak. serija IV 1, V 5).

Reķēna 1975 = Antonina Stanislavovna Reķēna: Amatniecības leksika dažās Latgales dienvidu izloksnēs un tās sakari ar atbilstošajiem nosaukumiem slavu valodās. Rīgā 1975 [707 S.].

Rūķe-Draviņa 1974 = Velta Rūķe-Draviņa: Vārds īstā vietā „The Right Word in the Right Place". Stockholm 1974 [338 S.].

Suhonen 1973 = Seppo Suhonen: Die jungen lettischen Lehnwörter im Livischen. (Mémoires de la Société Finno-Ougrienne 154) Helsinki 1973 [250 S.].

Turkina 1962 = E. Turkina: Latviešu-Angļu vārdnīca M. Andersones redakcijā. Rīgā 1962 [776 S.].

Zeps 1984 = Valdis J. Zeps: The Placenames of Latgola (Wisconsin Baltic Studies 1). Madison 1984 [XLVI, 632 S.].

4.2. Sonstige Literatur

Alunāns 1956 = Juris Alunāns: Izlase. Rīgā 1956.

Biezais 1973 = Haralds Biezais: Beiträge zur lettischen Kultur- und Sprachgeschichte. Åbo 1981 (Acta Academiae Aboensis, Ser. A vol. 47,2).

Brence 1982 = M. Brence: Juris Alunāns (1832—1864). In: Latviešu valodas kulturas jautājumi 18. 1982, 41—46.

Draviņš 1961 = Kārlis Draviņš: Evangelien und Episteln ins Lettische übersetzt von Georg Elger. Bd. 1 Texte. Bd. 2 Wortregister. Lund 1961, 1976 (Slaviska Institutionen vid Lunds Universetet, Text-och Materialutgåvor. 1.2.).

Draviņš 1965 = Kārlis Draviņš: Altlettische Schriften und Verfasser I. Lund 1965 (Slaviska Institutionen vid Lunds Universitet, Slaviska och baltiska studier 7).

Endzelīns 1971 = Jānis Endzelīns: Darbu izlase I, Rīgā 1971, II, Rīgā 1974, III 1, Rīgā 1979, III 2, Rīgā 1980, IV 1, Rīgā 1981, IV 2, Rīgā 1982.

Johansen 1959 = P. Johansen: Gedruckte deutsche und undeutsche Messen für Riga 1525. Zeitschrift für Ostforschung 8. 1959, 523—532.

Johansen/v. zur Mühlen 1973 = P. Johansen/Heinz v. zur Mühlen: Deutsch und Undeutsch im mittelalterlichen und frühneuzeitlichen Reval. Köln. Wien 1973.

Kagaine 1985 = Elga Karlovna Kagaine: Apvienotas Latviešu izlokšņu vārdnīcas. Veidošanas problēmas. In: Valodas aktualitātes 1984 (Rīgā 1985), 64—86.

Kiparsky 1939 = Valentin Kiparsky: Die Kurenfrage. Annalis Academiae scientarum Fennicae, Ser. B. Tom. XLII. Helsinki 1939.

Laua 1969 = A. Laua: Latviešu Leksikologija. Rīgā 1969.

Ozols 1965 = Arturs Ozols: Veclatviešu valoda. Rīgā 1965.

Plāķis 1927 = J. Plāķis: Kursenieku valoda. Acta Universitatis Latviensis 16. 1927.

Roze 1982 = Liene Roze: Pasaule vārdnīcas skatijumā. Rīgā 1982.

Rūķe-Draviņa 1971 = Velta Rūķe-Draviņa: Place Names in Kauguri County, Latvija. Stockholm 1971 (Acta Universitatis Stockholmiensis, Stockholm Slavic Studies 6).

Rūķe-Draviņa 1977 = Velta Rūķe-Draviņa: The Standardization Process in Latvian 16th Century to the Present (Acta Universitatis Stockholmiensis, Stockholm Slavic Studies 11), Uppsala 1977.

Schmid 1989 = Wolfgang P. Schmid (Hrsg.): Nehrungskurisch, Sprachhistorische und instrumentalphonetische Studien zu einem aussterbenden Dialekt (Abhandlungen d. Akad. d. Wiss. u. d. Lit. zu Mainz, geistes- u. sozialwiss. Kl. 1989, 2). Wiesbaden 1989.

Seewald 1863ff. = P. Seewald: Einige lettische Ausdrucksformen aus der Privatgut Lindensehen Gemeinde in Kurland. Magazin der lettischen literärischen Gesellschaft 13, 2—3; 14, 1—2; 15, 1—4 (Mitau 1863—1877).

Sehwers 1953 = Johannes Sehwers: Sprachlich-Kulturhistorische Untersuchungen vornehmlich über den deutschen Einfluß im Lettischen. Berlin 1953.

Zemzare 1961 = Daina Zemzare: Latviešu vārdnīcas (līdz 1900. gadam). Rīgā 1961.

Zemzare 1966ff. = Daina Zemzare: Palīgs apvidu vārdu vācējiem 5. 1966 — 14. 1971.

Wolfgang P. Schmid, Göttingen
(Bundesrepublik Deutschland)

224. Albanische Lexikographie

1. Einleitung
2. Wörterverzeichnisse aus der Zeit der Türkenherrschaft
3. Wörterbücher vor 1945
4. Die Entwicklung nach dem 2. Weltkrieg
5. Literatur (in Auswahl)

1. Einleitung

Albanisch ist eine alte Balkansprache, als deren nächste indoeuropäische Verwandte Griechisch und Armenisch gelten. Die Sprache ist erst seit dem Ausgang des Mittelalters schriftlich dokumentiert. Das Siedlungsgebiet (vgl. Karte 224.1) an der Westseite der Balkanhalbinsel umfaßt zwei Dialektgruppen, die ungefähr durch den Fluß Shkumbin, an dem die Stadt Elbasan liegt, getrennt werden. Das nördlich gelegene gegische Gebiet reicht bis nach Jugoslawien hinein; der südliche toskische Dialektbereich ragt an der Küste des Ionischen Meeres bis auf griechisches Staatsgebiet. Von gewisser kulturhistorischer Bedeutung sind albanische Streusiedlungen in Süditalien (Kalabrien, Sizilien) sowie in Attika und einigen vorgelagerten griechischen Inseln. Diese sogenannten albanischen „Kolonien" wurden im 14.—17. Jahrhundert in Besitz genommen und gehören vorwiegend der toskischen Mundartgruppe an. Als Ergebnis eines allmählichen Prozesses hatten die Albaner am Anfang des 20. Jahrhunderts zu etwa 70% den Islam angenommen, was für die wortschatzmäßige Zusammensetzung der Umgangssprache nicht ohne Auswirkungen blieb.

2. Wörterverzeichnisse aus der Zeit der Türkenherrschaft

Das erste erhaltene albanisch-fremdsprachige Wörterverzeichnis stammt vom Kölner Pilger Arnold von Harff (Groote 1860; Hetzer 1981), der um 1496 nach Palästina reiste und in seinem Reisebericht nebst Glossen anderer Sprachen auch ein gegisch-ripuarisches Vokabelverzeichnis überlieferte. Das *Dictionarium Latino-Epiroticum* von Franciscus Blanchus (Frang Bardhi, Rom 1635) wurde zu Zwecken der katholischen Seelsorge im Norden des Landes hergestellt. Es erlebte zwei Nachdrucke im 20. Jahrhundert, die zu wissenschaftlichen Zwecken veranstaltet wurden. Der eigentliche Wörterbuchteil darin umfaßt 188 Seiten à 30 Zeilen. Das erste neugriechisch-albanische Wörterverzeichnis für den Gebrauch bei den Orthodoxen stammt von Theodor Kaballiōtēs (Kavalliotis, Venedig 1770). Es umfaßt nur etwa 1000 Lemmata und ist daher deutlich weniger umfangreich als dasjenige von Blanchus/Bardhi (1635). Als Sammlung des Wortschatzes eines nordosttoskischen Dialekts, der der heutigen Schriftsprache sehr nahe steht, ist es jedoch von besonderer Bedeutung für die Sprachgeschichte und wurde einmal im 18. Jahrhundert (Thunmann 1774) nachgedruckt

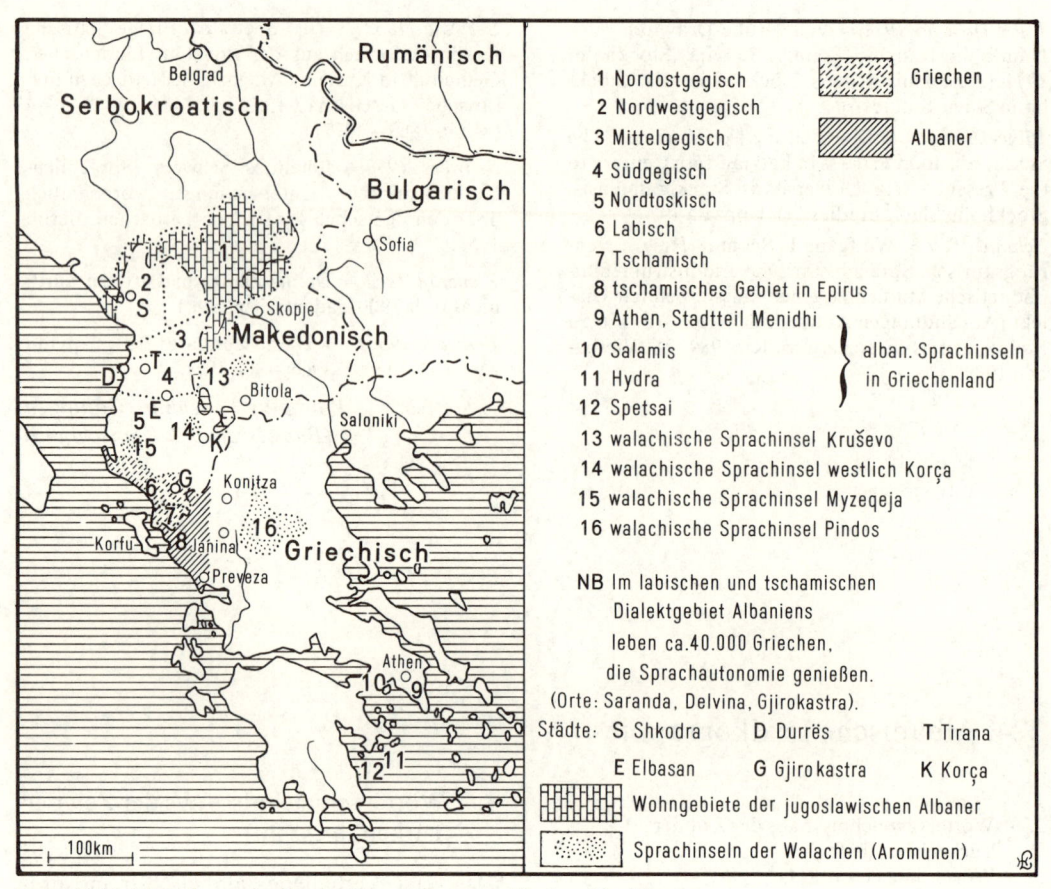

Karte 224.1: Die Albaner im Kreise ihrer südosteuropäischen Nachbarn

und seither dreimal zu wissenschaftlichen Zwecken ediert. Ebenfalls für den Gebrauch in orthodoxen Schulen verfaßt wurde das Glossar von Daniel Moschopolites (Wien 1802), aus dem William Leake 1835 Auszüge mit englischen Äquivalenten veröffentlichte. Wie Kavalliotis geht auch Daniel von der neugriechischen Umgangssprache als Bezugssprache für Albanisch aus. — Je nach Konfession benutzten die Albaner im Buchdruck entweder das lateinische oder das griechische Alphabet mit spezifischen Zusatzzeichen. Da auf britische Initiative hin 1824—1827 in Korfu ein neugriechisch-albanisches Neues Testament in griechischen Buchstaben gedruckt worden war, benutzten ausländische Albanologen bis zur Mitte des 19. Jahrhunderts auch dieses Alphabet zur Wiedergabe des Albanischen. So lehnen sich die albanisch-deutschen Wörterverzeichnisse in den Lehrbüchern von Xylander (1835) und von Hahn (1854) an die von der Bibelgesellschaft benutzte Orthographie unter Zugrun-

delegung neugriechischer Lesegewohnheiten und Ausspracheregeln an. Dozon (1878) benutzt hingegen bereits eine eigene Schreibweise auf Basis des lateinischen Alphabets. Die genannten Werke beziehen sich alle auf toskische (südliche) Mundarten. Trotz eines gewissen internationalen Interesses an der albanischen Sprache erschien dazu im 19. Jahrhundert kein einziges praktisches Wörterbuch in Form einer bibliographisch selbständigen Veröffentlichung. Es ist kennzeichnend für die eher akademische Interessenlage, daß als erstes das Etymologische Wörterbuch von Gustav Meyer (1891) erschien. Das erste deskriptive Wörterbuch, das verschiedene Mundarten berücksichtigte, die Herkunft verzeichnete und die Bedeutung in griechischen Äquivalenten angab, wurde vom langjährigen Übersetzer und Kolporteur der Bibelgesellschaft, Konstantin Kristoforidhi (Χριστοφορίδης, 1827—1895) zusammengestellt. Es erschien jedoch erst 1904 postum in Athen (Christophorides 1904). Im Jahre 1908 folgte ein anonym von der Kulturgesellschaft „Bashkimi" (Vereinigung) in Shkodra (Scùtari) herausgegebenes umfangreiches nordgegisch-italienisches Wörterbuch (Fialuer i Rii 1908).

3. Wörterbücher vor 1945

Alle bisher aufgeführten Glossare und Wörterbücher sind zweisprachig mit Äquivalenten in einer westlichen Bildungssprache. Von praktischem Nutzen sind sie indessen nicht mehr; als Sprachdenkmäler sind einige von ihnen wiederholt bearbeitet und nachgedruckt worden. Die Situation änderte sich grundlegend, als Albanien 1912 die staatliche Unabhängigkeit vom Osmanischen Reich gewonnen hatte. Jetzt bestand Bedarf an praktischen Hilfsmitteln für den Verkehr mit den Einheimischen, zumal später Teile des albanischen Siedlungsgebietes vorübergehend oder auf Dauer von fremden Mächten beansprucht und besetzt wurden. So erschienen handliche Wörterverzeichnisse mit deutscher oder italienischer Bezugssprache. Von dauerhaftem Wert sind jedoch nur die umfangreicheren Ausgaben, die in den dreißiger Jahren erschienen. Von dem Wörterbuch der Freiin von Godin (1930) erschien nur der deutsch-albanische Teil, Nelo Drizari erarbeitete 1934 ein albanisches Wörterbuch mit englischer Bezugssprache. Den Höhepunkt der Lexikographie der Zwischenkriegszeit bildet das monumentale albanisch-italienische Wörterbuch von Leotti (Rom 1937), das sich durch besonders reichhaltige Beispielsätze und phraseologische Angaben auszeichnet. Die genannten Werke sind, da sie mit Ausnahme des Wörterbuchs von Godin (1930) auf dem Toskischen basieren, immer noch von gewissem praktischem Nutzen. Weil es damals keine für das ganze Land verbindliche sprachliche Norm gab, erfassen die Wörterbücher gewöhnlich schwerpunktmäßig den Wortschatz eines der beiden Großdialekte und verzeichnen aus der anderen Traditionslinie nur ergänzendes Material oder lautliche Varianten. Den Versuch, im Rahmen eines einsprachig-erklärenden Wörterbuchs Mundartwortschatz zu dokumentieren, unternahm Gázulli (1941) mit nordgegischem Material. — Zwar erst 1948 veröffentlicht, aber bereits vor dem 2. Weltkrieg zusammengestellt wurde das historische albanisch-englische Wörterbuch von Stuart E. Mann (Mann 1948). Es ist das bisher einzige, das Belegstellen aus dem älteren Schrifttum des 17.—18. Jahrhunderts und aus den Bibelübersetzungen des 19. Jahrhunderts nachweist.

4. Die Entwicklung nach dem 2. Weltkrieg

Zwar einigten sich die Albaner bereits 1908 auf das heute noch gültige Lateinalphabet, aber eine schriftsprachliche Norm im Rahmen des Dialektausgleichs (Byron 1976) wurde erst schrittweise in den sechziger Jahren erarbeitet. 1972 wurde dieses Diskussionsergebnis in einem Abkommen, an dessen Unterzeichnung auch Vertreter der in Jugoslawien lebenden Albaner teilnahmen, gebilligt und wird seither auch von den meisten im Ausland lebenden Albanern befolgt. Unmittelbar nach dem Kriege jedoch war es vordringlich, für alle Kultursachbereiche eine Fachterminologie zu entwickeln. Gleichzeitig wurden zweisprachige Wörterbücher für den praktischen Gebrauch erarbeitet. Auf Grund der politischen Beziehungen genossen Wörterbücher mit den Bezugssprachen Russisch, Bulgarisch, Ungarisch und Serbokroatisch den Vorzug (Kostallari 1954, 1959; Kacori 1960; Tamás 1953, Dančetović 1947; Barić 1950). Das albanisch-deutsche Wörterbuch von Lambertz (1954) basiert in erster Linie auf der nordgegischen Belletristik der Vorkriegszeit und spiegelt nur unzureichend die zum Zeitpunkt des Erscheinens bereits erfolgte Wortschatzentwicklung. An wissenschaftlichen Vorhaben aus der frühen Nachkriegszeit sind zu nennen: ein einsprachig erklärendes Wörterbuch (Fjalor 1954) und Xhuvanis 1961 zum ersten Mal veröffentlichte Bearbeitung von Kristoforidhis Wörterbuch (Textbeispiel 224.1). Çabej veröffentlichte Ergänzungen und Korrekturen zu Meyers Etymologischem Wörterbuch, die jedoch erst seit Mitte der siebziger Jahre gesammelt herausgegeben werden (Çabej 1976; Çabej 1982). Eine Zusammenfassung der etymologischen Forschung versuchte Huld (1984). Das phraseologische Wörterbuch von Gjevori (1972) basiert auf gegischem Material und dokumentiert vornehmlich die Umgangssprache der Kosovaren (in Südserbien); erklärt werden die Eintragungen aber in der modernen Schriftsprache. Eine Fortführung der Arbeit von Gazulli (1941) unternahm Zymberi (1979), indem er seltene Wortschatzelemente namentlich des gegischen Mundartareals nachwies. — Seit der Festlegung einer verbindlichen sprachlichen Norm sind wir im Ausland besser denn je mit Wör-

gojë -a *sh.* goja -të *ef. ὀθ.* = 1) στόμα, 2) dialekti, gjuha = ἡ διάλεκτος, ἡ γλῶσσα, njeri me gojë = që ka gojë = κακόστομος, κακόγλωσσος, mbeti pa gojë = ἔμεινεν ἄναυδος, ἀναπολόγητος, hap gojënë (Përm.) = gromësij

gojë-ambëlë -i -a *mb. ἐπθ.* = γλυκόστομος, εὐπροσήγορος

gojë-artë -i -a *mb. ἐπθ.* = χρυσόστομος

gojë-keq -i -e -ja *mb. ἐπθ.* = κακόστομος

gojë-mbajtunë -i -a (g.) *mb. ἐπθ.* = βραδύγλωσσος, edhe *gjuhë-mbajturë -i -a* (t.)

gojëplot (Bd.) *ndf. ἐπρ.* = ἐλευθεροστόμως, ἀσυστόλως

gojë-sbrazëtë -i -a (për të keq = ἐπί κακοῦ) *mb. ἐπθ.* = κακόστομος

golë -a *sh.* gola -të *ef. ὀθ.* nji si *gojë -a*

gollovexhgë -a (Ber.) *sh.* gollovexhga -të *ef. ὀθ.* = 1) gjithë lëvezhga e arrësë e pathyerë = ὁλόκληρος ὁ φλοιός τοῦ καρυδίου ἄσπαστος, 2) (fig.) rrashta e këthmillit = (μεταφ.) τό ὄστρεον τοῦ κοχλίου, shif *lëvoxhgë -a*

gomar -i (g. t. Bgd.) *sh.* gomarë -të *em. ὀα.* = ὁ ὄνος, edhe *magjar -i*

gomare -ja *sh.* gomare -të *ef. ὀθ.* = ἡ ὄνος, edhe *magjare -ja*

gomarjar -i, gomarjare -ja (t.) *sh.* gomarjarë -të (*m.*), gomarjare -të (*fm.*). *e. ὀ.* = ὁ, ἡ γαϊδουριάρης -σα

gomënë -a *sh.* gomëna -të *ef. ὀθ.* krhs. *pellk -gu* (i lumit)

gongë -a (njeri, kalë, mushkë, dhi a dele) *ef. ὀθ.* = ἀδύνατος, ἄσαρκος

gop -i *em. ὀα.* = bythë -a, pith -dhi = τό αἰδοῖον τῆς γυναικός

göptuer -ori (Shk.) a **goptur -i, goptore -ja** *sh.* goptorë -të (*m.*), goptore -të (*fm.*) *mb. ἐπθ.* = ὁ, ἡ λαίμαργος, edhe *gushpuer -ori, gushpore -ja*

gore -ja (Tir.) *sh.* gore -të *ef. ὀθ.* = ἡ σκύλα, edhe *buçë -a*

gorgë -a *sh.* gorga -të *ef. ὀθ.* = vent si gropë

gorishtë -a ??? (*sh.* gorishta -të) = (χέρσος; μηλόβοτος);

goruc -i *em. ὀα.* = plak i mpshtjellurë nga pleqëria, edhe *kruspull -i* a *kuspull -i*

gorricë -a *sh.* gorrica -të *ef. ὀθ.* = ἀγριοαχλαδιά

gorruzhdë -a (g. Mal.) *ef. ὀθ.* = lug'e madhe që përziejnë qullinë

gostë -a (Shk.) *ef. ὀθ.* edhe:

gosti -a *ef. ὀθ.* = εὐωχία, συμπόσιον

gostis -it -it (g.), **gostit -it -it** (t.) = ἐστιῶ, παραθέτω τράπεζαν

gostitem *fol. pës. ὁ. παθ.* = ἐστιῶμαι

goshdë -a (g.) *sh.* goshdë -të *ef. ὀθ.* = καρφί, ἧλος, shif *peronë -a* — mbërthej me goshdë = καρφώνω

goshdohem *fol. pës. ὁ. παθ.* = καρφώνομαι

goshdoj *fol. vepr. ὁ. ἐν.* = καρφώνω

govatë -a *sh.* govata -të *ef. ὀθ.* = për të larë petkat e për të bartë me të baltë mjeshtërit = σκάφη διά πλύσιμον καί διά πηλόν, δι'ἧς κουβαλοῦσι πηλόν οἱ κτίσται, edhe *magje petëkash, koritë rrobesh*

govoshkë -a (Kav.) *ef. ὀθ.* = 1) arrë fyckë = κούφιον κάρυον, 2) guacë = ὄστρεον

gozhitë -a (Gjir.) *sh.* gozhita -të *ef. ὀθ.* = ἡ καλαμιά τοῦ ἀραβοσίτου, edhe *misërishte -ja, kacarrum -i*

gra -të *sh.* i f. grua πληθ. τῆς λέξ. grua

grabë -a (çam.) *ef. ὀθ.* = i thonë asaj sgauresë që ban lumi ndë trapt duk'e ngranë përmbrenda edhe e ban posi qemer (ὡς θόλον), atje futenë baritë a udhëtarëtë, kur i ze shiu mb'udhë, për me mos ulagë = *streh -i* (Përm.)

Textbeispiel 224.1: Wörterbuchausschnitt (aus: Xhuvani 1961)

terbüchern versorgt, die den neuen Standard widerspiegeln. Andererseits sind einsprachig erklärende Wörterbücher und mehrsprachig normative Fachterminologien veröffentlicht worden. Am umfangreichsten sind die Wörterbücher mit serbokroatischer Bezugssprache (Ndreca 1976; Zajmi 1974; Zajmi 1981). Von hohem Niveau sind jedoch auch die Nachschlagewerke mit englischen, französischen und deutschen Äquivalenten (Kiçi 1969, 1976; Kokona 1977; Bejta 1978; Buchholz 1977; Simoni 1978). 1980 bzw. 1984 erschienen zwei einsprachig erklärende Wörterbücher der Akademie der Wissenschaften (Fjalor i gjuhës 1980; Fjalor i shqipes 1984) und 1985 das Albanische Enzyklopädische Wörterbuch (Fjalori 1985), das neben Appellativa auch in großem Umfang Eigennamen erfaßt, die sich auf Albanien beziehen. Es handelt sich nicht um ein allgemeines Lexikon, sondern um ein Handbuch, in dessen Titel das Beiwort 'Albanisch' die inhaltliche Abgrenzung bezeichnet. Alle drei Veröffentlichungen der Akademie zusammengenommen dokumentieren die lexikalische Norm in einer für den Durchschnittsleser ausreichenden Weise. Ein Nachteil der heute erreichten Lage besteht darin, daß sowohl die Regelwerke, als auch die Sammlungen 'seltener' Wörter den tatsächlichen Wortgebrauch unzureichend widerspiegeln. Namentlich für Jugoslawien, aber auch für Albanien im engeren Sinne gilt, daß in der Umgangssprache den sogenannten „Barbarismen" (Wörtern türkischer, neugriechischer und serbokroatischer Herkunft) eine große Bedeutung zukommt. Allein mit Hilfe der Akademie-Veröffentlichungen ist es nicht möglich, Belletristik und sogenannte Dokumentarliteratur (Memoiren, historische Romane oder gar volkskundlich-historische Abhandlungen) inhaltlich zu erfassen. Daher stellen vor dem 2. Weltkrieg erschienene Wörterbücher immer noch eine willkommene Ergänzung dar. Ein Desideratum wäre die semantische Analyse der im Albanischen reichlich vorhandenen Entlehnungen aus dem Osmanischen, die im allgemeinen lautlich wenig verfremdet übernommen wurden. Das Verzeichnis von Boretzky (1976) gibt jedoch nur unvollkommen Aufschluß über die Bedeutungsunterschiede zwischen Ausgangs- und Zielsprache. — Für die in Albanien lebende griechische Minderheit, die ungefähr 40 000 Seelen umfaßt, wurde das albanisch-neugriechische Wörterbuch von Gjini (1971) herausgegeben. — Ein Rechtschreibungswörterbuch im Umfang von 32 000 Stichwörtern ohne Angabe der Bedeutungen erschien 1976 in Tirana (Fjalori 1976). Wie verlautet, arbeitet die Akademie der Wissenschaften an einer Erfassung des gesamten albanischen Wortschatzes unter Berücksichtigung der Mundarten und der Sprachdenkmäler; mit einer baldigen Veröffentlichung dieses in Karteiform gesammelten Materials ist jedoch nicht zu rechnen. Vorläufig ist die Sprachpflege mit der Durchsetzung des neuen Standards in allen Lebensbereichen befaßt. Dazu gehört auch die Entwicklung der Fachsprachen, deren terminologische Glossare seit Jahren in loser Folge mit französischer und russischer Bezugssprache erscheinen (Fjalor i termave 1976, 1982). Während in einem ersten Schritt der Entwicklung fachsprachlicher Terminologie häufig romanische Wörter in lautlich angepaßter Form übernommen wurden, ist jetzt die Tendenz zur Ersetzung derartiger „internationaler" Wörter durch Neubildungen auf Grundlage des alten Wortschatzfundus zu beobachten.

5. Literatur (in Auswahl)

5.1. Wörterbücher

Bardhi 1635 = Dictionarium Latino-Epiroticum [...] per R. D. Franciscum Blanchum. Romae 1635 [Nachdrucke: Mario Roques: Le Dictionnaire Albanais de 1635. Paris 1932, 60, 16, 224 S.; Engjëll Sedaj: Fjalor latinisht-shqip 1635. Prishtina 1983, 385 S.].

Barić 1950 = Henrik Barić: Rečnik srpskoga ili hrvatskoga i arbanaskoga jezika. 1: A—O. Zagreb 1950 [28, 672 S. nicht mehr erschienen].

Bejta 1978 = Murat Bejta: Fjalor frëngjisht-shqip. Prishtina 1978 [620 S.].

Boretzky 1976 = Norbert Boretzky: Der türkische Einfluß auf das Albanische. 2: Wörterbuch der albanischen Turzismen. Wiesbaden 1976 [224 S.] (Albanische Forschungen, 12).

Buchholz 1977 = Oda Buchholz/Wilfried Fiedler/Gerda Uhlisch: Wörterbuch Albanisch-Deutsch. Leipzig 1977 [739 S.].

Çabej 1976 = Eqrem Çabej: Studime etimologjike në fushë të shqipes. In: Studime gjuhësore. I—II. Prishtina 1976 [389, 507 S.].

Çabej 1982 = Eqrem Çabej: Studime etimologjike në fushë të shqipes. Bd. 1, Tirana 1982, [8, 339 S.], Bd. 2, 1976 [616 S., albanisch und französisch].

Christophorides 1904 = Kōnstantinos Christophoridēs: Lexikon tēs Albanikēs glōssēs. Athen 1904 [Nachdruck siehe Xhuvani 1961].

Cordignano 1938 = Fulvio Cordignano: Dizionario italiano-albanese. Bologna 1968 [757 S., 1. Aufl. Scutari 1938].

Dančetović 1947 = Vojislav Dančetović: Fjalor sërbokroatisht-shqip. Srpskohrvatsko-albanski rečnik. Tirana 1947 [407 S.].

Daniel Moschopolites 1802 = Eisagōgikē didaskalia periechousa Lexikon Tetraglōsson [...] syntetheisa [...] para tou [...] Kyriou Daniēl tou ek Moschopoleōs [...] (Wien) 1802 [92 S., Nachdrucke: siehe Leake 1835; Das Lexikon Tetraglosson des Daniil Moschopolitis. Neu ediert von J. Kristophson, In: Zeitschrift für Balkanologie 10.1974.1, S. 3—128].

Dozon 1878 = A. Dozon: Manuel de la langue chkipe ou Albanaise. Vocabulaire. Paris 1878 [104 S.].

Drizari 1934 = Nelo Drizari: Albanian-English and English-Albanian Dictionary. New York 1934 [3, 313 S., Nachdrucke New York 1957, 1975].

Fialuer i Rii 1908 = Fialuer i Rii i Shcypës. Shkodra 1908 [Nachdruck: Fjalori i „Bashkimit". Prishtina 1978, 16, 538 S.].

Fjalor 1954 = Fjalor i gjuhës shqipe. Tirana 1954 [7, 648 S., Nachdruck Prishtina 1976].

Fjalor i gjuhës 1980 = Fjalor i gjuhës së sotme shqipe. Tirana 1980 [26, 2273 S.].

Fjalor i shqipes 1984 = Fjalor i shqipes së sotme. Tirana 1984 [21, 1515 S.].

Fjalor i termave 1976 = Fjalor i termave të tregtisë së jashtme. Shqip-frëngjisht-rusisht. Tirana 1976 [155 S., Außenhandelsterminologie].

Fjalor i termave 1982 = Fjalor i termave të bibliotekës dhe të bibliografisë. Shqip-frëngjisht-rusisht. Tirana 1982 [127 S., Terminologie des Bibliothekswesens und der Bibliographie].

Fjalori 1976 = Fjalori drejtshkrimor i gjuhës shqipe. Tirana 1976 [761 S.].

Fjalori 1985 = Fjalori enciklopedik shqiptar. Tirana 1985 [15, 1245 S.].

Gazulli 1941 = Nikollë Gazulli: Fjalorth i rí. Tirana 1941 [Nachdruck Prishtina 1968, 528 S.].

Gjevori 1972 = Mehmet Gjevori: Frazeologjizma të gjuhës shqipe. Prishtina 1972 [432 S.].

Gjini 1971 = Niko Gjini: Fjalor shqip-greqisht. Lexiko Albano-Ellēniko. Tirana 1971 [551 S.].

Godin 1930 = Marie Amelie Freiin von Godin: Wörterbuch der albanischen und deutschen Sprache. 1: Deutsch-Albanisch. Leipzig 1930 [419 S.].

von Hahn 1854 = Johann Georg von Hahn: Albanesische Studien. 3: Beiträge zu einem albanesisch-deutschen Lexikon. Jena 1854 [241 S.].

Huld 1984 = Martin E. Huld: Basic Albanian etymologies. Columbus, Ohio 1984 [213 S.].

Kacori 1960 = Thoma Kacori: Bălgarsko-albanski rečnik. Fjalor bulgarisht-shqip. Sofia 1960 [871 S.].

Kavalliotis 1770 = Prōtopeiria para tou sophologiōtatou [...] Theodōrou Anastasiou Kaballiōtou tou Moschopolitou [...] Enetiēsin 1770 [96 S. Nachdrucke: Gustav Meyer: Das griechisch-süd-rumänisch-albanesische Wörterverzeichnis des Kavalliotis. In: Sitzungsberichte der philosophisch-historischen Classe der kaiserlichen Akademie der Wissenschaften (Wien), 132 (1895), 127 S. (Albanesische Studien, IV) — Harald Haarmann: Über die Geschichte und Sprache der Albaner und der Wlachen. Hamburg 1976 [nach Thunmann 1774] (Romanistik in Geschichte und Gegenwart, 4) — Das dreisprachige Wörterverzeichnis von Theodoros Anastasiu Kavalliotis aus Moschopolis [...] Neu bearbeitet [...] von Armin Hetzer. Hamburg 1981, 278 S. (Balkan-Archiv, N.F., Beiheft 1)].

Kiçi 1969 = Gasper Kiçi/Hysni Aliko: Fjalor anglisht-shqip. Roma 1969 [11, 627 S.].

Kiçi 1976 = Gasper Kiçi: Albanian-English Dictionary. Tivoli 1976 [448 S.].

Kokona 1977 = Vedat Kokona: Fjalor shqip-frëngjisht. Tirana 1977 [591 S.].

Kostallari 1954 = Androkli Kostallari: Russko-albanskij slovař. Fjalor rusisht-shqip. Moskau 1954 [636 S., Nachdruck Prishtina 1966].

Kostallari 1959 = Androkli Kostallari: Karmannyj albansko-russkij slovař. Moskau 1959 [428 S., Albanisch-russisches Taschenwörterbuch].

Lacalendola 1932 = Adamo Lacalendola: Dizionario della lingua albanese-tosca. Parte italiano-albanese. Palo de Colle 1932 [155 S.], Parte albanese-italiana. 1936 [179 S.].

Lambertz 1954 = Max Lambertz: Lehrgang des Albanischen. 1: Albanisch-deutsches Wörterbuch. Berlin 1954 [18, 228 S.].

Leotti 1937 = Angelo Leotti: Dizionario albanese-italiano. Roma 1937 [21, 1710 S.].

Mann 1948 = Stuart Edward Mann: An historical Albanian-English Dictionary. 1496—1938. London. New York. Toronto 1948 [9, 601 S.].

Massolini/Buttafava 1979 = C. B. Massolini/U. Buttafava: Vocabolario albanese-italiano. Fjalor shqip-italisht. Roma 1979 [355 S.].

Meyer 1891 = Gustav Meyer: Etymologisches Wörterbuch der albanesischen Sprache. Straßburg 1891 [13, 526 S.] (Sammlung indogermanischer Wörterbücher, 3).

Ndreca 1976 = Mikel Ndreca: Fjalor shqip-serbokroatisht. Prishtina 1976 [48, 377 S.].

Simoni 1978 = Zef Simoni: Fjalor gjermanisht-shqip. Tirana 1978 [9, 564 S.].

Tamás 1953 = Lajos Tamás/István Schütz: Albán-magyar szótár. Budapest 1953 [379 S.].

Weigand 1914 = Gustav Weigand: Albanesisch-deutsches und deutsch-albanesisches Wörterbuch. Leipzig 1914 [179 S.].

Xhuvani 1961 = Aleksandër Xhuvani: Fjalor shqip-greqisht. Lexikon albano-ellēnikon. Tirana 1961 [Nachdruck Prishtina 1977, 397 S.].

Zajmi 1974 = Abdullah Zajmi/Mehdi Bardhi u. a.: Fjalor serbokroatisht-shqip. Prishtina 1974 [1015 S.].

Zajmi 1981 = Abdullah Zajmi/Mehdi Bardhi u. a.: Fjalor shqip-serbokroatisht. Prishtina 1981 [1065 S.].

Zymberi 1979 = Abdullah Zymberi: Fjalorth i fjalëve të rralla. Prishtina 1979 [199 S., Wörterbuch seltener Wörter].

5.2. Sonstige Literatur

Agani 1981 = Hilmi Agani: Fjalori i Kujunxhiçit në dritën e shqipes së Rahovecit e të Gjakovës. Prishtina 1981.

Bibliographie Albanaise = Bibliographie Albanaise. Description raisonnée des ouvrages publiés en albanais ou relatifs à l'Albanie du 15e siècle à l'année 1900 par Émile Legrand. Œuvre posthume complétée par Henri Gûys. Paris. Athen 1912 [Nachdruck Leipzig 1973].

Byron 1976 = Janet Byron: Selection among alternatives in language standardization. The case of Albanian. The Hague 1976 (Contributions to the sociology of language, 12).

Groote 1860 = E. von Groote (Hrsg.): Die Pilgerfahrt des Ritters Arnold von Harff von Cöln durch Italien [...] Köln 1860 [51, 280 S., darin auf S. 65 das erste albanische Wörterverzeichnis].

Hamp 1972 = Eric P. Hamp: Albanian. In: Current trends in linguistics. Vol. 9.: Linguistics in Western Europe. The Hague. Paris 1972, 1626—1692.

Hetzer 1981 = Armin Hetzer: Wie ist Arnold von Harffs Wörterverzeichnis (1496) zu lesen?. In: Balkan-Archiv, N.F., 6.1981, 227—262.

Hetzer 1983 = Armin Hetzer: Neues zu Kavalliotis' „Prōtopeiria". In: Balkan-Archiv, N.F., 8.1983, 95—158.

Hetzer 1984 = Armin Hetzer: Geschichte des Buchhandels in Albanien. Prolegomena zu einer Literatursoziologie. Berlin 1984 (Balkanologische Veröffentlichungen, 10).

Hetzer/Roman 1983 = Armin Hetzer/Viorel Simon Roman: Albanien — Albania. Ein bibliographischer Forschungsbericht. A bibliographic research survey. München. New York. London. Paris 1983 (Bibliographien zur Regionalen Geographie und Landeskunde, 3).

Leake 1835 = William Martin Leake: Travels in Northern Greece. London 1835 [4 Bände].

Thunmann 1774 = Johann Thunmann: Untersuchungen über die Geschichte der östlichen europäischen Völker. I. Theil. Leipzig 1774.

Xylander 1835 = Josef Ritter von Xylander: Die Sprache der Albanesen oder Schkipetaren. Frankfurt a. M. 1835.

Armin Hetzer, Bremen
(Bundesrepublik Deutschland)

225. Armenian Lexicography

1. Glosses and Etymologies
2. Early Dictionaries
3. Early Printed Dictionaries
4. Modern Printed Dictionaries
5. Dictionaries of the Modern Language
6. Selected Bibliography

1. Glosses and Etymologies

In the 5th century, at the dawn of Armenian literature, there were no lexicographical works proper about the Armenian language in existence. However, glosses as well as etymologies of proper names were widespread. This tradition continued into later years.

In the 6th—10th centuries there appeared collections of philosophical terms and their definitions as well as collections of anatomical and other terms. Also from this period a Greek wordlist in Armenian letters and a Latin-Armenian glossary with Latin transcriptions of the Armenian words are preserved. None of these collections or wordlists are alphabetized.

2. Early Dictionaries

In the 11th—16th centuries Armenian lexicography developed, forming an independent branch of culture. Glossaries and dictionaries proper from this period can be distinguished.

The wordlists of dictionaries were partially based on glossaries. The most popular dictionary from this period is the one called "Poetic Words". Containing a great number of words used in Armenian manuscripts, this dictionary has an almost perfect alphabetical order and is based on definite explanatory principles. The dictionary called "Demonstration for Poets" contains large sets of synonyms for poets and rhetoricians. The same aim was pursued in the "Panegyrical Words" which contains stylistically marked words and word combinations. — Other lexicographical works from this period include specialized and terminological dictionaries pertaining to different fields of school education and culture. — Lists of philosophical terms and definitions compiled in the previous period were summed up and included in "Philosophical Definitions". — Lexicographical works of a linguistic nature were presented in a glossary of grammatical terms and an orthographic dictionary aimed at standardizing Armenian orthography (12th century). — A large number of medical terms were presented in specialized dictionaries, the largest ones being those by Amirdovlat Amassiatsi (15th century). His "Useless for Ignorants" is not only a unique medical and pharmacological work, but also a kind of polyglot dictionary which gives equivalents of medical terms in Armenian, Arabic, Greek, Persian, Turkish and Latin. — Besides medical dictionaries, in which foreign words are used to help the reader understand the subject better, dictionaries intended for philological purposes were also compiled during this period. Among the dictionaries of this type are the dictionary of Persian words used by Eghishe (5th century) with Armenian translations, and the Hebrew-Armenian dictionary of biblical proper names. Similar to modern translation dictionaries is the Arabic-Persian-Armenian dictionary (14th century). The Mongolian wordlist by Kirakos Gandzaketsi (13th century) is of considerable scientific interest, being the first written record of Mongolian words. Armenian dictionaries compiled in this period were commonly known by the names "Words" (Bařk[c]), "Explanation of Words" (Lucumn bařic[c]), "Collection of Words" (Hawak[c]umn bařic[c], Gumarumn bařic[c]), etc. Beginning from the 13th century they sometimes appear under the name "Wordbook" (Bařgirk[c]).

3. Early Printed Dictionaries

The first printed dictionaries relating to Armenian were the Armenian-Latin dictionaries compiled in Europe by F. Rivola (1621, 1633) and C. Galanus (1645). In the second half of the 17th century, printed dictionaries compiled by Armenians appeared. The Bible, published in 1666 had as its appendix a concordance compiled by Oskan Erevantsi. In 1635 a Latin-Armenian dictionary by A. Nersesovich was published. The first Armenian explanatory dictionary, published in 1698 by Eremia Meghretsi (8500 entries), was compiled on the basis of medieval manuscript dictionaries, retaining their merits and demerits.

In the 17th century all printed dictionaries related to Armenian were published outside Armenia. In Armenia itself manuscript dictionaries were copied and some new ones were compiled.

4. Modern Printed Dictionaries

Throughout the 18th and up to the last quarter of the 19th century, the old literary language, Grabar, remained the prevailing language of lexicography, though by the second half of the 19th century Ashkharabar had become the only language of literature.

In the 18th century Mkhitar Sebastatsi and his pupils published the "Dictionary of the Armenian Language" (Venice, 1749) which, compared to the dictionary by Eremia, is far richer; it contains illustrations from literature and gives more accurate definitions of the words. The second volume (1769) contains also proper names and Grabar-Ashkharabar, Ashkharabar-Grabar dictionaries. The two-volume "New Dictionary of the Armenian Language" by G. Avetikian, Kh. Syurmelian and M. Avgerian (1836—1837) contains a richer vocabulary of Grabar and has up to this day been the main source for Grabar studies. The authors give Greek and Latin equivalents with philological purposes in view, as well as Turkish translations for Western Armenians. On the basis of this dictionary, in 1846 a handy dictionary was published, the second completed edition of which (Avgerian 1865) contained over 5000 new words. The Armenian-Latin dictionary by M. Ciakciak (1837) comprised almost as rich a Grabar vocabulary as the "New Dictionary".

During this period the study of Ashkharabar vocabulary was just beginning and, naturally, there was no standardization or any clear-cut distinction made between literary and dialectal words. The attempts to compile dictionaries reflecting the vocabulary of the two branches of New Armenian, Eastern and Western, were still not independent of Grabar. In 1869, a large Ashkharabar-Grabar dictionary with over 40 000 entries was published by E. Hyurmuzian. In East Armenia a Grabar-Ashkharabar dictionary containing 12 000 words was published by H. Artsakhetsi in 1830.

Beginning in the 18th century and especially in the 19th century a great number of Armenian bilingual and multilingual dictionaries were published. Among the dictionaries compiled by Eastern Armenians, bilingual dictionaries relating to Russian prevailed, while Western Armenians compiled dictionaries dealing with Turkish, English and French. Up to the last quarter of the 19th century a great number of Russian-Armenian (1788, 1821, 1841, 1854, 1860), Armenian-Russian (1788, 1821, 1841, 1854, 1860), Turkish-Armenian (1794, 1841, 1843, 1864, 1866, 1870), Armenian-Turkish (1838, 1850, 1860), English-Armenian (1803, 1825, 1835, 1840, 1843, 1865), Armenian-English (1825, 1835, 1843, 1866, 1875), French-Armenian (1812, 1840, 1850) and Armenian-French (1817, 1861), as well as Italian-Armenian (1804, 1829, 1846), Armenian-Italian (1837), Persian-Armenian (1826), Greek-Armenian (1848) and Armenian-Greek (1868) dictionaries were published.

During this same period, there also appeared dialectal (1847, 1862, 1870, 1874), reverse (1862), concordance (of the New Testament, 1878), proper name (1714, 1769, 1815, 1839, 1850) and encyclopedic (1749) dictionaries.

5. Dictionaries of the Modern Language

Since the last quarter of the 19th century, Ashkharabar has become the predominant language of Armenian lexicography. The process of standardization of the Ashkharabar vocabulary was for a long time carried out in bilingual dictionaries. Monolingual Ashkharabar dictionaries proper appeared later. Two political events played an essential role in the fate of 20th century Armenian lexicography with opposite results: massacres and deportations of Armenians by the Turkish government in 1915 deprived Western lexicography of its focal point, while due to the foundation of a Soviet State in Eastern Armenia, Eastern lexicography became concentrated in the Armenian SSR.

The first explanatory (monolingual) dictionary of Western literary Armenian was published by S. Gabamadjian in 1892. Its 2nd edition (1910) contains 70 000 entries. The other explanatory dictionaries (Gevorgian 1934, Kerobian 1962) are less valuable. Explanatory dictionaries in Eastern Armenia appeared sometime later. Among them, the following are worth mentioning: 1) the dictionary by S. Malkhassiants (1—4, 1944—1945) containing besides Ashkharabar the vocabulary of Grabar, Middle Armenian and dialects taken from different lexicographical sources (over 120 000 entries); 2) the four-volume dictionary by the Armenian Academy of Sciences including predominantly Eastern Armenian vocabulary (90 000 entries); and 3) E. Aghayan's dictionary (1976) containing more entries (over 135 000) but fewer verbal illustrations.

In the study, planning and standardization of the New Armenian vocabulary a certain role belongs to the dictionaries of synonyms (H. Gayayan 1938; A. Sukiassian 1967), phraseology (ZHLDB 1975), orthography (the largest by H. Barseghian 1973), foreign words and locutions (1902, 1908, 1911, 1912, 1930, 1935, 1951) and particularly the dictionaries of terminology. Terminological dictionaries are both explanatory and bilingual. One of the first works in this field was the botanical dictionary of Gh. Alishan (1895). Owing to the development and standardization of Armenian as the state language the number of these dictionaries is especially great in the Armenian SSR. Each sphere of human life is reflected in corresponding dictionaries, sometimes in several variants with different terminological coverage.

Many general bilingual and multilingual dictionaries are currently being created. Among the dictionaries compiled by Eastern Armenians, dictionaries relating to Russian continue to prevail. The largest Russian-Armenian dictionaries are those compiled by H. Daghbashian (1906), by the Institute of Linguistics (1—4, 1954—1958), and by A. Gharibian (1968); the largest Armenian-Russian dictionaries were compiled by Daghbashian (1911) and by the Institute of Linguistics (1984). Other dictionaries compiled in the Armenian SSR are German-Russian (1976), English-Armenian (1984), Armenian-Kurdish (1939, 1936, 1957), Armenian-Azerbaijani (1978), etc. The Pahlavi-Persian-Armenian-Russian-English dictionary by R. Abrahamian (1965) is intended for scientific purposes.

In Western lexicography, dictionaries relating to French, English and Turkish continue to prevail. While Norayr Buzandatsi chose Grabar as the language of translation for his large French-Armenian dictionary (1884, begun in 1866) and G. Lusignan (1—2, 1900, begun earlier) preserved some Grabarian explanations, the language of translation in all other dictionaries has been Ashkharabar. The first was the French-Armenian dictionary by P. Nuparian (1889, 2nd ed.

1892) followed by more than a dozen others. Since 1887 more than ten Armenian-French dictionaries have been published. The largest English-Armenian dictionaries are those compiled by H. Chagmagchian (1922, 2nd ed. 1953, 3rd ed. 1960) and M. Kouyoumdjian (1961), and the largest Armenian-English dictionary is that compiled by Kouyoumdjian (1950). Among the numerous dictionaries relating to Turkish, the most valuable ones are the Turkish-Armenian-French (1888), Turkish-Armenian (1892), and Armenian-Turkish (1891) dictionaries by M. Abikian. The Turkish-Armenian (1912) and Armenian-Turkish (1907) dictionaries by P. Z. Karapetian should also be mentioned. Other bilingual and multilingual dictionaries are: Arabic-Armenian (1952, 1959, 1960), Armenian-Arabic (1896, 1953, 1954, 1963), Bulgarian-Armenian-Turkish (1904), German-Armenian (1884—1889), Armenian-German (1952), Spanish-Armenian (1955), Italian-Armenian (1908^2, 1922), Armenian-Italian (1922), Greek-Armenian (1930), as well as Latin-Armenian (1893), Armenian-Latin (1887, 2nd ed. 1966) and Esperanto-Armenian (1910, 1912).

Eastern Armenian dictionaries differ considerably from Western Armenian dictionaries in structure and in the way the material is presented: Eastern Armenian dictionaries give more clear-cut definitions of lexical meanings and have a specific system of markings concerning the usage of words; in Western Armenian dictionaries lexical meanings are mainly explained by synonyms, and sometimes antonyms are given. The Western Armenian dictionaries also provide additional information and usually have rich pictorial illustrations.

Among the dictionaries pursuing chiefly linguistic aims, etymological, dialectal, reverse and word-frequency dictionaries should be mentioned.

The best etymological dictionary is the "Armenian Root Dictionary" by H. Adjarian (1—7, 1927—1935, 2nd ed. 1—4, 1971—1979).

The largest collections of dialect words are to be found in "Armenian Words and Idioms" by S. Amatuni (1912), and the "Armenian Provincial Word Dictionary" by H. Adjarian (1913). "The Dictionary of Dialect Words" by the Institute of Linguistics is still being edited.

The first reverse dictionary (for Grabar) was published in 1862.

Reverse dictionaries published later are: for Western Armenian by P. Terzian (1905), Kh. Atanassian (1961); and for Eastern Armenian by V. Grigorian and others (1976).

A word-frequency dictionary was compiled by B. Ghazarian (1982).

The only concordance published in Western Armenian is one of the Bible. The systematic publication of other concordances is being sponsored by the Institute of Linguistics in Yerevan. Since 1963, dozens of concordances of old and middle Armenian authors have been published.

Other lexicographical works which have been compiled are: the "Dictionary of Personal Names" by H. Adjarian (1—5, 1942—1962), encyclopedias, etc.

6. Selected Bibliography

Abikian 1888 = Mihran Abikian: Erek'lezvyan əndarjak baŕaran tačkeren-hayeren-gałłieren (Trilingual Comprehensive Dictionary Turkish-Armenian-French). Constantinople 1888 [1156 p.].

Abikian 1892 = Mihran Abikian: Əndarjak baŕaran hayeren-tačkeren (Comprehensive Dictionary Armenian-Turkish). Constantinople 1892 [671 p.].

Adjarian 1913 = Hrachia Adjarian: Hayeren gavaŕakan baŕaran (Dictionary of Dialect Words). Tbilisi 1913 [1168 p.].

Adjarian 1927—1935 = Hrachia Adjarian: Hayeren armatakan baŕaran (Armenian Root Dictionary). 1—7. Yerevan 1927—1935 [1236 + 1350 + 1492 + 1350 + 1294 + 1631 + 210 = 8563 p.].

Adjarian 1942—1962 = Hrachia Adjarian: Hayoc anjnanunneri baŕaran (Dictionary of Personal Names). 1—5. Yerevan 1942—1962 [647 + 682 + 740 + 685 + 384 = 3138 p.].

Aghayan 1976 = Edward Aghayan: Ardi hayereni bačatrakan baŕaran (Explanatory Dictionary of Modern Armenian). Yerevan 1976 [1631 p.].

Amatuni 1912 = Sahak Amatuni: Hayoc baŕ u ban (Armenian Words and Idioms). Vagharshapat 1912 [727 p.].

Avgerian 1865 = Mkrtich Avgerian: Aŕjeŕn baŕaran haykazean lezui (Handy Dictionary of the Armenian Language). 2nd ed. Venice 1865 [849 p.].

Avetikian 1836—1837 = Gabriel Avetikian/Khachatur Syurmelian/Mkrtich Avgerian: Nor baŕgirk haykazean lezui (New Dictionary of the Armenian Language). 1—2. Venice 1836—1837 [1160 + 1067 + 2227 p.].

Buzandatsi 1884 = Norayr Buzandatsi: Baŕgirk' i gałłieren lezuē i hayerēn (Dictionnaire français-arménien). Constantinople 1884 [1304 p.].

Chagmagchian 1922 = Harutiun Chagmagchian: Əndarjak baŕaran angleren-hayeren (A Comprehensive Dictionary English-Armenian). Boston 1922. 2nd ed. Beyrouth 1952. 3d ed. Beyrouth 1960 [1424 p.].

Ciakciak 1837 = Manvel Ciakciak: Baṙgirk i barbaṙ hay ew italakan (Dizionario armeno-italiano). Venice 1837 [1534 p.].

Daghbashian 1906 = Harutiun Daghbashian: Liakatar baṙaran ṙuserenič hayeren (Russian-Armenian Complete Dictionary). Tbilisi 1906 [1237 p.].

Daghbashian 1911 = Harutiun Daghbashian: Liakatar baṙaran hayerenič ṙuseren (Armenian-Russian Complete Dictionary). Tbilisi 1911 [757 p.].

Eremia 1698 = Eremia Meghretsi: Baṙgirk' hayoc'g (Armenian Dictionary). Leghorn 1698 [344 p.].

Gabamadjian 1892, 1910 = Simon Gabamadjian: Nor baṙgirk hayeren lezvi (New Dictionary of the Armenian Language). Constantinople 1892 [672 p.]. 2nd ed. 1910 [1413 p.].

Hyurmuzian 1869 = Edward Hyurmuzian: Baṙgirk yašxarhabarē i grabar (New Armenian-Old Armenian Dictionary). Venice 1869 [575 p.].

Karapetian 1907 = Petros Zeki Karapetian: Mec baṙaran hayeren-osmaneren (Armenian-Turkish Great Dictionary). Constantinople 1907 [923 p.].

Karapetian 1912 = Petros Zeki Karapetian: Mec baṙaran osmaneren-hayeren (Turkish-Armenian Great Dictionary). Constantinople 1912 [968 p.].

Kouyoumdjian 1950 = Mesrop Kouyoumdjian: Əndarjak baṙaran hayerene-anglieren (A Comprehensive Dictionary Armenian-English). Cairo 1950 [1158 p.].

Kouyoumdjian 1961 = Mesrop Kouyoumdjian: Əndarjak baṙaran anglierene hayeren (A Comprehensive Dictionary English-Armenian). Cairo 1961 [1416 p.].

Lusignan 1900 = Gviton Lusignan: Nor baṙgirk' patkerazard fransahay (Nouveau Dictionnaire illustré Français-Arménien). Paris 1900. 2nd ed. Constantinople 1909—1910 [1074 + 817 = 1891 p.].

Malkhassiants 1944—1945 = Stepan Malkhassiants: Hayeren bačatrakan baṙaran (Armenian Explanatory Dictionary). 1—2. Yerevan 1944—1945 [630 + 512 + 614 + 646 = 2462 p.].

Mkhitar 1749—1769 = Mkhitar Sebastiatsi: Baṙgirk' haykazean lezui (Dictionary of the Armenian Language). 1—2. Venice 1749—1769 [1273 + 2250 = 3523 p.].

Nuparian 1889 = Mesrop Nuparian: Baṙaran franserene hay ašxarhik (Dictionnaire Français-Arménien). Constantinople 1889. 2nd ed. 1892 [1115 p.].

Rivola 1621 = Franchisco Rivola: Baṙgirk hayoč (Dictionarium Armeno-Latinum). Mediolani 1621 [479 p.].

Sukiassian 1967 = Ashot Sukiassian: Hayoč lezvi homanišneri baṙaran (Dictionary of Armenian Synonyms). Yerevan 1967 [683 p.].

ZHLBB = Žamanakakič hayoc' lezvi bac'atrakan baṙaran (Explanatory Dictionary of the Modern Armenian Language). 1—4. Yerevan 1969—1980 [612 + 722 + 582 + 836 = 2752 p.].

ZHLDB = Žamanakakic hayoč lezvi darjvacabanakan baṙaran (Phraseological Dictionary of the Modern Armenian Language). Yerevan 1975 [630 p.].

Gevork Djahukyan, Yerevan (USSR)

226. Basque Lexicography

1. Preliminaries
2. Characteristics of Basque Lexicography
3. Classification of the Dictionaries
4. Selected Bibliography

1. Preliminaries

The Basque language or *euskara* is spoken on both sides of the Pyrenees, in the South-Western area of France and the North-Western area of Spain, by 600.000 or 700.000 of the 3.000.000 inhabitants.

Several factors explain the shrinking of the Basque-speaking area (the space in white on the map 224.1 shows the non-Basque-speaking area) and help one to understand the development of Basque lexicography. (a) Basque literary production started in the XVIth century and has been quite scarce until this century. (b) Basque has been undergoing the process of standardization for the last twenty years. It was only in 1968 that the Royal Academy of the Basque language started to unify the orthography and morphology. (c) The Basque language did not obtain until 1982 the status of official language, and then only for the Basque Autonomous Community which includes the provinces of Guipuzcoa, Biscaye and Alava. The conjunction of the last two factors entails that the Basque language had no presence in the schools; therefore, it did not develop a technical, scientific terminology and the people were not educated in their own tongue.

2. Characteristics of Basque Lexicography

The factors just mentioned in part 1. influenced Basque lexicography in several ways. (a) Scarcity of the number of diction-

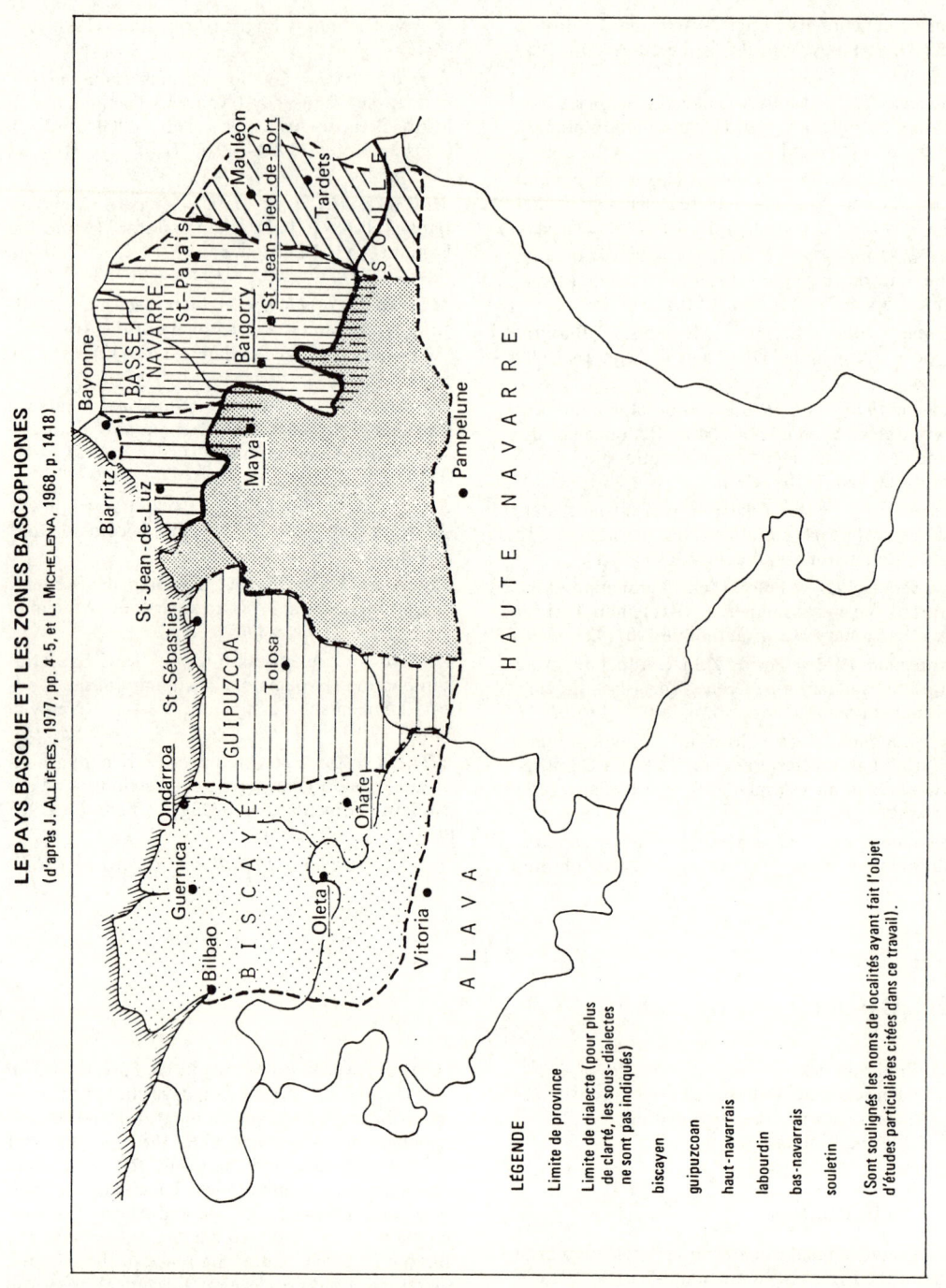

LE PAYS BASQUE ET LES ZONES BASCOPHONES
(d'après J. ALLIÈRES, 1977, pp. 4-5, et L. MICHELENA, 1968, p. 1418)

LÉGENDE

Limite de province

Limite de dialecte (pour plus de clarté, les sous-dialectes ne sont pas indiqués)

biscayen
guipuzcoan
haut-navarrais
labourdin
bas-navarrais
souletin

(Sont soulignés les noms de localités ayant fait l'objet d'études particulières citées dans ce travail).

Map 226.1: The main dialects of the Basque language: their geographical distribution

aries, although their number has increased little in this century. Furthermore some dictionaries have not been published (cf. 3.1.1., 3.1.4) and some have even been lost. Nowadays many scholars choose these unpublished dictionaries as subjects for their research, so they will soon be available accompanied by detailed studies. (b) Lack of monolingual standard dictionaries. Instead the dictionaries compiled have been dialectal, the first standard dictionaries going back to the seventies. And they mainly are bilingual (or trilingual); the first monolingual standard dictionary is being prepared by a board sponsored by the Royal Academy of the Basque language. (c) Lack of technical, scientific terminology and lack of an official body which takes on the task of proposing the necessary neologisms, forcing the lexicographer to fill in on his own these onomasiological gaps or to leave them in his dictionary. Nevertheless, the work of the *Unibertsitate Zerbitzuetarako Euskal Ikastetxea* (= UZEI), a Basque Institute for University Services should be mentioned. UZEI is a private Institute, created in 1978, which, among other services, takes care of coordinating scholars working in each specific field, the production of technical terminology being their goal. The Institute's development of terminology has been severely criticized for having borrowed terms too extensively and for ignoring the semantic values of words already present in the language. (d) Lack of a unified orthography (the main differences lying between the Western dialects, or those spoken in the Spanish territory, and the Eastern dialects, or those spoken in the French territory) entailed that each lexicographer used the system familiar to him. (e) Lack of grammatical information is another shared feature. We shall not mention these last two points when discussing the dictionaries, unless they constitute an exception.

3. Classification of the Dictionaries

A chronological point of view will be adopted when presenting the dictionaries within each major class.

3.1. General Bilingual or Trilingual Dictionaries

(1) Pouvreau (middle of the XVIIth century). This is a Basque-French dictionary, with occasional translations into Spanish, Latin, Italian and even Hebrew, which mainly gives an account of the Eastern dialects. Although many very basic words are missing, it often gives the words in context, carefully indicating the author who used them. Dialectal information, on the other hand, is unusual.

(2a) Larramendi (1745). Despite having chosen Spanish as the source language (with the aim of helping people learn Basque), the *Diccionario Trilingüe del Castellano, Bascuence, y Latín* (= D.T.) can be considered the first attempt at a general, unified (in a certain sense) dictionary. It is general, because it includes all the dialects; thus, among the equivalents of each entry the user finds synonyms and near-synonyms in the other dialects, an attempt to enrich the Basque speaker's vocabulary. It is standard because, aware of the onomasiological gaps in the language and fervent an apologist of his language as Larramendi was, he filled gaps by creating neologisms for and only for the technical and scientific fields. But since he did not mark these neologisms, the genuine Basque words he collected from native speakers and from texts are mixed with borrowings Basque had long before accepted and with his own creations. Found guilty for this reason, the D.T. was rejected by Azkue (1905—06) and his followers, but it is being rehabilitated nowadays. Nevertheless, the D.T. influenced lexicographical and literary production for over a century and a half.

(2b) Larramendi also left an unpublished Basque-Spanish dictionary (cf. Altuna 1967) which seems to be the unfinished version in reverse of his D.T.

(3) Aizkibel (1883). Among the lexicographical works following the trend of Larramendi, Aizkibel's work deserves mention. It is basically a version of the D.T. in reverse, but it is also enriched with other sources (e.g., Pouvreau's dictionary (cf. 3.1.(1)), short vocabularies of some grammars, etc.) and the source to which each entry belongs is carefully marked. The author's attempt at a unified orthography and the marking of the neologisms and the field a word belongs to (including such fields as zoology, agriculture, artillery, navigation, etc.) are worthy of mention. Aizkibel also includes, now and then, verbal paradigms and quotations from literary texts for words which may not be usual.

(4) Harriet (end of the XIXth century). This unpublished Basque-French dictionary is presumably the most complete bilingual dictionary (even more so than Azkue 1905—06) because of its size and because of the number of literary texts the author makes use of, so that several quotations can be found in most entries, besides the information about the literary dialect the entry belongs to, including also some etymologies.

(5) Azkue (1905—06); the great dictionary of this century. This is a dialectal and at the same time a historical dictionary. It largely influenced Basque writers, orators and linguists. By rejecting Larramendi's D.T., for it contained numerous non-specified neologisms, Azkue tried to collect for his dictionary only genuine Basque words, leaving borrowed terms and neologisms aside. This goal compelled him (a) to mark after each entry the dialect and area(s) where the word had

been collected and to use quotations, although not systematically, indicating the author, the title and the page; (b) to differentiate with a double question mark borrowings which, because of their tradition, are to be considered Basque words; and (c) to leave aside, in his search for words with true tradition, the neologisms coined by the purists of his time, who tried to substitute every borrowed term, no matter the date of the borrowing, with genuine Basque terms. Because of his cautiousness despite the overwhelming purist trend of that time and because he collected the largest set of aural and written material ever known, Azkue's *Diccionario Vasco-Español-Francés* is an obligatory reference for any lexicographer.

(6) After the impetus Azkue gave to lexicography, several quite small dictionaries were published. However, two large dictionaries worth mentioning here are:

(6a) Lhande (1926) which only covers the Eastern dialects, giving a deeper insight into them than Azkue, and which uses a broader criterion for the selection of the entries, considering as Basque all words which are really used, no matter whether they are borrowings or not.

(6b) Mugica (1965) and Mugica (1981). This is another large dialectal dictionary mainly based on Azkue which contrasts, especially in the Basque-Spanish version of 1981, with other dictionaries published at that time (cf. 3.1.(7)) in that (a) It does not follow the unified orthography (b) It remains dialectal (c) There is a definite tendency to create Basque neologisms instead of accepting borrowings from other languages to fill in the gaps modern life creates in the language. The lack of a critical criterion for selecting the words to be included in the dictionary is its worst aspect.

(7) Mujika (1977a), Mujika (1977b) and Kintana/Aurre/Badiola et al. (1980) are supposed to be the third important step in the development of Basque lexicography. Although of little interest to the lexicographer, they are the first attempt at a modern, standard, medium sized dictionary, using the unified orthography proposed in 1968 and including an explicit discussion in the foreword of (a) the word forms to be accepted in a standard language; (b) the written form of the borrowings when they do not coincide with the Basque alphabet, and (c) the cultural and technical, but not too specialized, neologisms required by the present everyday life.

However, Mujika (1977a) and Mujika (1977b) are far less trustworthy because of the author's wrongly coined neologisms.

3.2. General Monolingual Dictionaries

(1) Sarasola (1982). This dictionary of frequency is based on a statistical sample collected from the printed material published in the year 1977 and is intended to be a quantitative description of present day written Basque. It is one of the preliminary works leading to a Normative Dictionary of the Basque language.

(2) Sarasola (1984). The first two volumes have appeared of a yet unpublished dictionary which attempts to be a helpful tool for cultivating the standard written language and which is mainly based on the literary tradition from 1750 to 1964. This is also the first dictionary which gives grammatical information about each entry and the date of the first appearance of the word and of its different values (restricted of course to the chosen period). The other big contribution of this dictionary is the discussion and the practical considerations it raises concerning which words should be chosen for the standard lexicon. Using a broad criterion Sarasola accepts all words, provided they have a minimal literary tradition, no matter whether they are dialectal, borrowings or neologisms. In short, this dictionary opens a new era for Basque lexicography and it can be viewed as the starting point of a Dictionary of Authorities.

(3) *Orotariko Euskal Hiztegia*. The General Basque Dictionary would be an approximate translation for the title of this monolingual dictionary which started to be compiled by professors Michelena and Sarasola, and is now being compiled by prof. Sarasola after prof. Michelena's death. Three volumes are already published. It is basically a bank of lexical data structured as a dictionary, taking systematically into account all preceding dictionaries and literary texts from the period 1545—1965. The following information is given in each entry: grammatical and dialectal information, the different meanings the word may have, where it is used, its etymology, and information that other dictionaries have given about it and its literary history.

4. Selected Bibliography

4.1. Dictionaries

Aizkibel 1883 = Jose Francisco Aizkibel: Diccionario Basco Español titulado Euskeratik Erderara biurtzeko itz-tegia. Tolosa 1883 [1257 p.].

Azkue 1905—06 = Resurrección María Azkue: Diccionario Vasco-Español-Francés. Bilbao [Vol. 1 1905, 561 p., Vol. 2 1906, 486 p., 2nd edition 1969, 3rd edition 1984].

Harriet = Maurice Harriet: Dictionnaire Basque-Français, manuscript. Held in Le Pétit-Séminaire de Saint-François-Xavier de Uztaritz. End of the XIXth century [3536 p.].

Kintana/Aurre/Badiola et al. 1980 = Xabier Kintana/Jon Aurre/Rikardo Badiola et al.: Hiztegia 80. Bilbao 1980 [854 p.].

Larramendi 1745 = Manuel Larramendi: Diccionario Trilingüe del Castellano, Bascuence y Latin. San Sebastián 1745 [Vol 1 436 p., Vol 2 392 p.] [Facsimile reprint 1984].

Lhande 1926 = Pierre Lhande: Dictionnaire Basque-Français et Français-Basque. Paris 1926 [1117 p.].

Michelena 1987 = Luis Michelena: Diccionario General Vasco. Orotariko Euskal Hiztegia. Bilbao 1987 [Vol. 1 A-Ama. 902 p., 1989 Vol. 2 Ame-Asd 807 p, Vd. 3 Ase-Bapuru].

Mugica 1965 = Plácido Mugica: Diccionario Castellano-Vasco. Bilbao 1965 [1897 p.].

Mugica 1981 = Plácido Mugica: Diccionario Vasco-Castellano. Bilbao 1981 [2098 p.].

Mujika 1977a = Luix Mari Mujika: Diccionario General y Técnico 1. Castellano-Euskara. Bilbao 1977 [597 p.].

Mujika 1977b = Luix Mari Mujika: Hiztegi Orokor-Teknikoa 2. Euskara-Gaztelera. Bilbao 1977 [618 p.].

Pouvreau = Silvain Pouvreau: Dictionnaire Basque-Français; manuscript. Held in the Bibliothèque Nationale in Paris. XVIIth century.

Sarasola 1982 = Ibon Sarasola: Gaurko Euskara Idatziaren Maiztasun Hiztegia. San Sebastian 1982 [2 Vol. 837 p., 3rd Vol. 146 p.].

Sarasola 1984 = Ibon Sarasola: Hautalanerako Euskal Hiztegia. San Sebastian [Vol. 1: A-aurten, 1984, Vol. 2: Aurtiki-ebaki, 1985. 270 p.].

4.2. Other Publications

Altuna 1967 = Patxi Altuna: Larramendiren iztegi berria. In: Euskera XII. 1967, 139—300.

Miren Azkarate, San Sebastian (Spain)

227. Die Lexikographie der uralischen Sprachen I: Ungarisch

1. Einführung
2. Von den Anfängen bis 1783
3. Die Zeit von 1784 bis 1861
4. Die Zeit von 1862 bis 1944
5. Die Gegenwart
6. Literatur (in Auswahl)

1. Einführung

Das Ungarische gehört zum finnisch-ugrischen Zweig der uralischen Sprachfamilie und ist die Muttersprache von circa 15 Millionen Menschen, die — bei divergierenden politischen und ethnischen Grenzen — vorwiegend im Karpaten-Donaubecken und insbesondere in der Republik Ungarn beheimatet sind. Über eine Million Sprecher des Ungarischen leben als Exilanten in der Diaspora. — Die Ungarn (oder Magyaren) siedelten Ende des 9. Jh. im Karpatenbecken und haben — wenn auch zunächst mit zeitlicher Verzögerung — alle bestimmenden Geistesströmungen der europäischen Kulturgeschichte gestaltend übernommen.

2. Von den Anfängen bis 1783

2.1. Wie bei vielen europäischen Völkern setzte auch bei der ungarischen Nation die Pflege der Grammatik und der Lexikographie mit dem Studium der lateinischen Sprache ein. Abgesehen von einigen Glossen zu lateinischen Predigten, ergänzenden Wörterbucheintragungen und nach Begriffen zusammengestellten Nomenklaturen (wobei nur die Nomenclatura des Balázs Szikszai Fabricius von 1590 (= SzikszF.) eine lateinisch-ungarische Originalquelle darstellt — vgl. die Bemerkungen zum *Régi magyar glosszárium* im Abschnitt 5.2.) sind eigentliche Wörterbücher erst seit der Mitte des 16. Jh. zu verzeichnen. Zunächst erschienen ungarische Äquivalente in etlichen mehrsprachigen Wörterbüchern, von denen das zehnsprachige Wörterbuch des Ambrosius Calepinus (= Cal.) für spätere Lexikographen zu einem wichtigen Quellenwerk wurde. In diesen frühen polyglotten Wörterbüchern mit ungarischem Anteil finden sich auch Ansätze einer lexikographischen Erfassung des Čakavisch-Kroatischen (Verantius 1595), des Slowakischen (Verborum 1648) und des Rumänischen (LexMars.). — Albert Szenci Molnár war ein hervorragender Lexikograph des

17. Jh., der sich die deutsche humanistische Pädagogik und insbesondere Dasypodius zum Vorbild nahm, in seinen Wörterbüchern jedoch zugleich die Ausrichtung an ungarischen Lehrplänen zu erkennen gibt. Der ungarisch-lateinische Teil der ersten Ausgabe seines Wörterbuchs (= MA. 1604), das 1611 auch griechische Äquivalente bietet und 1621 bereits die Ausmaße eines Schulwörterbuchs übertrifft, ist das erste komplette Wörterbuch dieser Art. Im 18. Jh. setzte Ferenc Pápai Páriz das Werk Molnárs durch eine Neubearbeitung fort (= PP.), in der er den lateinisch-ungarischen Teil, dessen Wortgut sich nicht mit dem des ungarisch-lateinischen Teils deckt, der lediglich eine Erweiterung der Vorgaben von Calepinus und Molnár darstellt, ganz überarbeitet hat. Dieses Wörterbuch genoß im 18. Jh. absolute Autorität. — Für Schulzwecke dienten die Vokabulare zum Lehrbuch *Ianua Linguarum* von Comenius (Tsaholci-Bihari 1647, Lexicon ianuale 1652), und die von den Jesuiten auch in Ungarn bevorzugten Wörterbücher von E. Alvarus (1703), Chr. Cellarius (1719 und 1798) und Fr. Wagner (1750 und 1822). Cellarius folgte in seinem Wörterbuch besonders konsequent dem „etymologischen Prinzip", d. h. der Anordnung nach Wortbildung.

2.2. Zu den Wörterbüchern kann man ferner die Sammlungen von Redensarten und Sprichwörtern (Baranyai Decsi 1598, Kis-Viczay 1713) zählen. Als Fachwörterbücher, deren Anzahl in der zweiten Hälfte des 18. Jh. deutlich ansteigt, gelten botanische Nomenklaturen und Sammlungen ärztlicher Terminologie. Zur ganzen Periode s. Melich 1907.

3. Die Zeit von 1784 bis 1861

3.1. Der circa 80 Jahre umfassende Zeitraum von 1784 bis 1861 ist die Blütezeit der ungarischen Lexikographie. Die führende Intelligenz hatte erkannt, daß die Emanzipation und Vervollkommnung der Muttersprache eine wichtige Voraussetzung für die Existenz eines bürgerlichen Nationalstaates ist. Die Lexikographie wurde somit essentieller Teil umfassender politischer Bemühungen. Die Ideologen der ungarischen Aufklärung (Bessenyei, Versegi u. a.) legten dar, daß es unaufschiebbar sei, ein muttersprachliches Großwörterbuch — das für die westeuropäischen Sprachen schon seit Jahrhunderten existierte — zu schaffen. Zu diesem Zweck wurde 1825 die Ungarische Gelehrte Gesellschaft gegründet, an deren verschiedenen lexikographischen Arbeiten auch die führenden Literaten teilnahmen. Während die Erarbeitung des Thesaurus noch auf sich warten ließ, wurde als Markstein das erste ungarische Bedeutungswörterbuch (SzD.) veröffentlicht.

3.2. Im 19. Jh. verliert das Wörterbuch von Páriz seine hegemoniale Stellung und erweist sich trotz verschiedener Überarbeitungen als überholt. Bei der Neuausgabe der Werke von Cellarius und Wagner stützten sich Ézsajás Budai (1798) bzw. F. Versegi (1822) bereits auf Material aus der lebenden Sprache. Das Ungarische überwand damit die Suprematie des Lateinischen, war nicht mehr „dienende Magd" der fremden Sprache. — Die damaligen Lexikographen waren der Meinung, daß dem Wörterbuch eine wichtige gestalterische Rolle bei der Herausbildung einer zeitgemäßen Standardsprache zufalle. Der Aufklärer Versegi wollte anhand des Wortgutes darlegen, wie große Fortschritte das ungarische Bildungswesen bereits gemacht hatte. Ähnliche Ziele bewegten auch József Márton, Honorarprofessor der Wiener Universität, der zwischen 1799 und 1823 ein Dutzend deutsch-ungarischer und ungarisch-deutscher Wörterbücher herausgegeben hat. Obwohl beide Verfasser mit sicherem Urteil aus den gleichen Quellen schöpften, ist der Wortschatz der genannten Wörterbücher nicht identisch, da sie in unterschiedlichem Maße auf Spracherneuerung zielende Neologismen, Regionalismen und wiederbelebte Wörter aus der alten Literatur enthalten. Unter dem Einfluß deutscher Quellen (Adelung, Kirsch, Scheller, Campe) bildeten Versegi und Márton kompositorisch zahlreiche Lehnübersetzungen, die zum Teil Eingang in den ungarischen Sprachschatz fanden. — Einige Forscher trugen umfangreiche, bis zu 80 000 Stichwörter fassende Korpora zusammen (Fábchich 1794, Kresznerics 1831, Kassai 1833, Simai 1833). Trotz der Tendenz zum einsprachigen ungarischen Bedeutungswörterbuch bediente man sich zur Erläuterung weiterhin deutscher und/oder lateinischer Äquivalente. In diesen Wörterbüchern wurden Grundsätze der Bedeutungsgliederung und des davon ausgehenden Artikelaufbaus erarbeitet und durchgesetzt. — Das zweiteilige, von der Akademie herausgegebene *Magyar és német zsebszótár* (= Tzs.), das bis dahin bedeutsamste Werk der ungarischen Lexikographie, umfaßt 75 000 Stichwörter und ist weniger ein einfaches zweisprachiges ungarisch-deutsches Wörterbuch als vielmehr ein Vorläufer des Großwörterbuchs. Seine Bedeutung, die in einer entscheidenden Förderung der Vereinheitlichung des ungarischen Wortschatzes zu sehen ist, wird dadurch ergänzt, daß selbst die bewußt aufgenommenen Neologismen rasche Verbreitung fanden.

3.3. Daneben kam es zur Ausbildung bestimmter Wörterbuchtypen. — Gleichfalls von der Akademie veranstaltet, erschien 1838 das *Magyar Tájszótár* (= Tsz.), das das erste Idiotikon innerhalb der Uralistik ist und unter genauer Provenienzangabe früher und für dieses Wörterbuch neu gesammelte Belege mitteilt. — Eine spezifische Erscheinung des frühen 19. Jh. sind die Neologismenwörterbücher (Kunoss 1834, Királyföldy 1846). — Die Industrialisierung bedingte neben Neubildungen auch ein massenhaftes Eindringen fremden Wortgutes, das einen Bedarf an Fremdwörterbüchern nach sich zog (Kunoss 1835, Forstinger 1854). — Der allgemeine Fortschritt führte auch zur Entwicklung erläuternder und translatorischer Fachwörterbücher, die in großer Anzahl und für die verschiedensten Sparten erschienen. Eine terminologische Vereinheitlichung war das Ziel der 1834 von der Akademie herausgegebenen Sachwörterbücher für Philosophie (PhilMúsz.) und Mathematik (MathMúsz.). In dieser Periode gibt es ferner bereits etymologische Wörterbücher (Leschka 1825, Dankovszky 1833). — Beziehungen zu literarischen Quellen zeigen das Reimwörterbuch von Simai (1809) und die Stilwörterbücher von Szaitz (1788) und Noszkó (1791). — Die Sammlungen von Redensarten und Sprichwörtern bereicherten Szirmay (1804) und Erdélyi (1851).

3.4. Das Spektrum der Wörterbuchtypen wurde außerdem durch pragmatische Wörterbücher erweitert. Der für die ungarische Entwicklung ausschlaggebende deutsche Einfluß findet seinen Niederschlag in der Tatsache, daß in dem hier interessierenden Zeitabschnitt 6 lateinisch-ungarischen Wörterbüchern 40 für das Deutsche gegenüberstehen. Die hervorzuhebenden Hand- und Kleinwörterbücher von Mór Ballagi (1854) hatten zahlreiche Auflagen. Zweisprachige Wörterbücher für das Französische und das Türkische entstanden nun als selbständige Originalwerke. Symptomatisch für diese Periode ist es jedoch, daß von einem englisch-ungarischen Wörterbuch nur die erste Lieferung im Druck erscheinen konnte. Das nach der zweiten Ausgabe von Molnárs Werk (MA. 1611) erste griechische Wörterbuch ist ein weiteres Ergebnis damaliger lexikographischer Arbeit. — In polyglotten Wörterbüchern wurden neben dem Lateinischen, Ungarischen und Deutschen auch das Slowakische (Bernolák 1825) und das Rumänische (Micu-Klein 1806, Bobb 1822, LexBud. 1825) lexikographisch weitergehend erfaßt. — Zur ganzen Periode s. Gáldi 1957.

4. Die Zeit von 1862 bis 1944

4.1. Im Jahre 1862 erschien in sechs Bänden das lange erwartete, 100 000 Stichwörter enthaltende große Wörterbuch der Akademie (CzF.). Die alphabetische Ordnung, die sorgfältige semantische Gliederung der Artikel, reiches phraseologisches Material und zahlreiche Belegstellenzitate weisen seine Anlage als modern aus. Obzwar anachronistische Ansätze der Etymologie und die Aufnahme von Eigennamen Kritik auslösten, gilt dieses Werk als Grundstein der neueren ungarischen Lexikographie. In dem fast gleichzeitig publizierten *A magyar nyelv teljes szótára* (Ballagi 1868) wird auf abstrahierte Wurzeln und Ortsnamen verzichtet. Diese wichtigen, aber bald veralteten Bedeutungswörterbücher konnte das kurzgefaßte Wörterbuch von József Balassa (1940) nicht ersetzen, obwohl es viel zuvor nicht erschlossenes Material enthält.

4.2. Von den historischen Wörterbüchern aus der Zeit der Jahrhundertwende ist das dreibändige *Magyar nyelvtörténeti szótár* (= NySz.) auch heute noch unentbehrlich. In diesem Werk werden genaue Angaben zu den Belegstellen, den Quellen und ihren Kontexten sowie zur ursprünglichen diachronen Bedeutung gemacht. Die Stichwörter sind durch ein eigenes Wörterverzeichnis leicht aufzufinden. Allerdings ist an dem Werk zu kritisieren, daß wichtige Quellen nicht exzerpiert worden sind und die Bearbeitung stellenweise ungenau ist. — Sprachdenkmäler aus Urkunden wurden in *Magyar Oklevélszótár* (= OklSz.) veröffentlicht. — Das Wörterbuch der Spracherneuerung (NyUSz.) gibt außer den Neubildungen selbst auch Umstände und Zeitpunkt ihrer Einführung an. — Mit dem *Magyar-ugor összehasonlító szótár* (= MUSz.) von J. Budenz erreichte die etymologische Forschung in Ungarn europäisches Niveau. Ein von Zoltán Gombocz und J. Melich bearbeitetes etymologisches Wörterbuch (EtSz.) zeichnet sich durch Datenreichtum und durch das übergreifende theoretische Wissen und den kritischen Geist der Bearbeiter aus, deren Perfektionismus das Werk jedoch nur bis zum Buchstaben G fortschreiten ließ. Das 6000 Stichwörter erklärende, primär für das breite Publikum gedachte *Magyar szófejtő szótár* (= SzófSz.) weist ebenfalls viele Etymologien erstmals nach.

4.3. Aufgrund der Begriffsbestimmungen zum und der grundlegenden Typisierung des Dialektwortschatzes (bzw. der Regionalismen) sowie der Auswertung dialektalen Materials ist *Magyar Tájszótár* (= MTsz.) auch in theoretischer Hinsicht bedeutend. Etwa 80 000 seit 1838 gesammelte Belege werden hier mit genauer Orts- und Quellenangabe zitiert. — Das in der Moldau und in den „Sieben Dörfern" (Hétfalu) des Burzenlandes gesprochene, in sich uneinheitliche Dialektgut der Csángós hat Yrjö Wichmann aufgezeichnet (CsángSz.). Das *Szamosháti szótár* (= SzamSz.) stellt mit seiner Aufarbeitung des gesamten Wortschatzes eines Gebiets eine höherstehende Form des regionalen Dialektwörterbuchs dar und hat im folgenden Schule gemacht.

4.4. Weiteren einsprachigen Wörterbuchtypen gehören an: (a) Das erste ungarische Synonymwörterbuch (Póra 1907), das in seiner Anlage Rogets *Thesaurus* folgt, aber nur einen beschränkten Wortschatz bietet und in der Anordnung nicht konsequent verfährt. (b) Wörterverzeichnisse zum Wortschatz einzelner Schriftsteller, von denen lediglich dasjenige in der Mikszáth-Monographie von M. Rubinyi (1910) Erwähnung verdient. (c) Fremdwörterbücher, von denen einige — bei insgesamt steigender Produktion — mehrere Auflagen erreichten (z. B. Babos 1865, Radó 1904, Horovitz 1908). (d) Neuere Sammlungen von Idiotismen und Sprichwörtern (Sirisaka 1890, Margalits 1896).

4.5. In der sich gleichzeitig verstärkt entfaltenden zweisprachigen Lexikographie wächst einerseits die Anzahl der Wörterbücher stark an und andererseits werden viele Sprachen nun erstmals von ungarischer Seite erfaßt: Finnisch, Hebräisch, Russisch, Spanisch, Ukrainisch und Zigeunersprache. Das weiterhin primäre Interesse für das Deutsche zeigt sich darin, daß allein für diese Sprache mehr Wörterbücher herauskommen als für alle übrigen zusammen. Mit der Intensivierung zwischenstaatlicher Beziehungen geht insbesondere ein sprunghafter Anstieg der Erstellung englischer und französischer Wörterbücher einher. Eine über mehrere Jahrhunderte bestehende Lücke wird durch einige italienisch-ungarische Wörterbücher geschlossen. Die Herausgabe rumänischer, serbokroatischer und slowakischer Wörterbücher findet eine bedeutsame Fortsetzung. Nach der Jahrhundertwende erarbeiten B. Kelemen (Deutsch-Ungarisch/Ungarisch-Deutsch) und A. Sauvageot (Französisch-Ungarisch/Ungarisch-Französisch) die ersten zweisprachigen Großwörterbücher. Neu in seiner Art ist H. Schlandts *Deutsch-magyarisches Sprichwörterlexikon* (1913). Zweisprachige Fachwörterbücher, in denen das Ungarische mit verschiedenen Sprachen kombiniert ist (Deutsch, Englisch, Französisch, Italienisch, Russisch), erscheinen in mannigfaltigsten Ausprägungen. — Zur ganzen Periode s. J. Kelemen 1970.

5. Die Gegenwart

5.1. Als kulturpolitische Aufgabe der Lexikographie, die nach dem 2. Weltkrieg einen neuerlichen Aufschwung erfahren hat, galt zunächst die Schaffung eines zeitgemäßen Bedeutungswörterbuchs. Im Institut für Sprachwissenschaft der Akademie wurde 1962 *A magyar nyelv értelmező szótára* (= ÉrtSz.) fertiggestellt. Unter Beachtung der Sprache der Klassiker wird mit 60 000 Stichwörtern bzw. 206 873 Eintragungen im wesentlichen die gegenwärtige Gemeinsprache der gebildeten Schicht vermittelt. (Zu prinzipiellen und praktischen Fragen der Zusammenstellung s. Országh 1960.) Für einen breiteren Benutzerkreis ist das Handwörterbuch *Magyar értelmező kéziszótár* (= ÉKsz.) bestimmt, das in kürzeren Artikeln gedrängtere Erklärungen und eine Reihe von neuen Stichwörtern mit in jüngerer Zeit aufgekommenen Neologismen bietet. — Das *Magyar Szinonimaszótár* (= SzinSz.) stellt Synonyme auf semantischer und stilistischer Ebene einander gegenüber, so daß sich Erläuterungen erübrigen, verzeichnet die Lexeme zum Teil in mehreren Synonymreihen und macht daneben stellenweise auch phrasematische Angaben.

5.2. Das beispiellos reichhaltige Werk *Erdélyi magyar szótörténeti tár* (= SzT.) enthält das Wortmaterial der siebenbürgischen handschriftlichen Quellen vom 13. Jh. an. Mit den bislang erarbeiteten vier Bänden — von jeweils über 1 000 Seiten — ist das Projekt bis zum Anfang des Buchstaben H fortgeschritten. Das *Régi magyar glosszárium* (= RMG.) vereinigt das Material von etwa 50 ungarischen Wörterverzeichnissen aus der Zeit vom 14. bis zum 16. Jh. in einer einzigen alphabetischen Folge. — *A magyar nyelv történeti-etimológiai szótára* (= TESz.) beschränkt sich nicht auf die Etymologie, sondern verfolgt jeweils die gesamte Wortgeschichte und berücksichtigt semantische und kulturgeschichtliche Aspekte in gebührendem Maße. — Die uralischen Elemente des ungarischen Wortschatzes werden — unter Erörterung etwaiger früherer Fehldeutungen — in *A magyar szókészlet finnugor elemei* (= MSzFgrE.) eingehender als zuvor speziell behandelt.

5.3. Von den geplanten vier Bänden des *Új magyar tájszótár* (= ÚMTsz.) sind bisher lediglich die ersten zwei im Druck erschienen. Das komplette Werk soll aus den unterschiedlichsten gedruckten und handschriftlichen Quellen der Jahre 1890 bis 1960 Belege zu rund 120 000 Stichwörtern aufarbeiten. — Unter den fünf regionalen Dialektwörterbüchern hat das der Szegeder Mundart (SzegSz.) die größte Bedeutung. Das südliche Transdanubien ist in dem *Ormánysági szótár* (= OrmSz.), die ungarische Sprachinsel bei Osijek (Jugoslawien) in dem *Szlavóniai (kórogyi) szótár* (= SzlavSz.) dialektologisch bearbeitet. Nur Regionalismen bestimmter Gegenden — so aus Oberwart (Österreich) und Mihályi (Westungarn) — enthalten *Felsőőri tájszótár* von Imre (1973) und *Mihályi tájszótár* von J. Kiss (1979).

5.4. Älterer Tradition folgen: (a) Der orthographische Ratgeber *Helyesírási Kéziszótár* (= HKsz.) mit 130 000 Wörtern und Wendungen. (b) Die Idiomatismensammlung *Magyar szólások és közmondások* (= MSzK.), die ihr wörterbuchartig geordnetes Material in Redensarten und Sprichwörter differen-

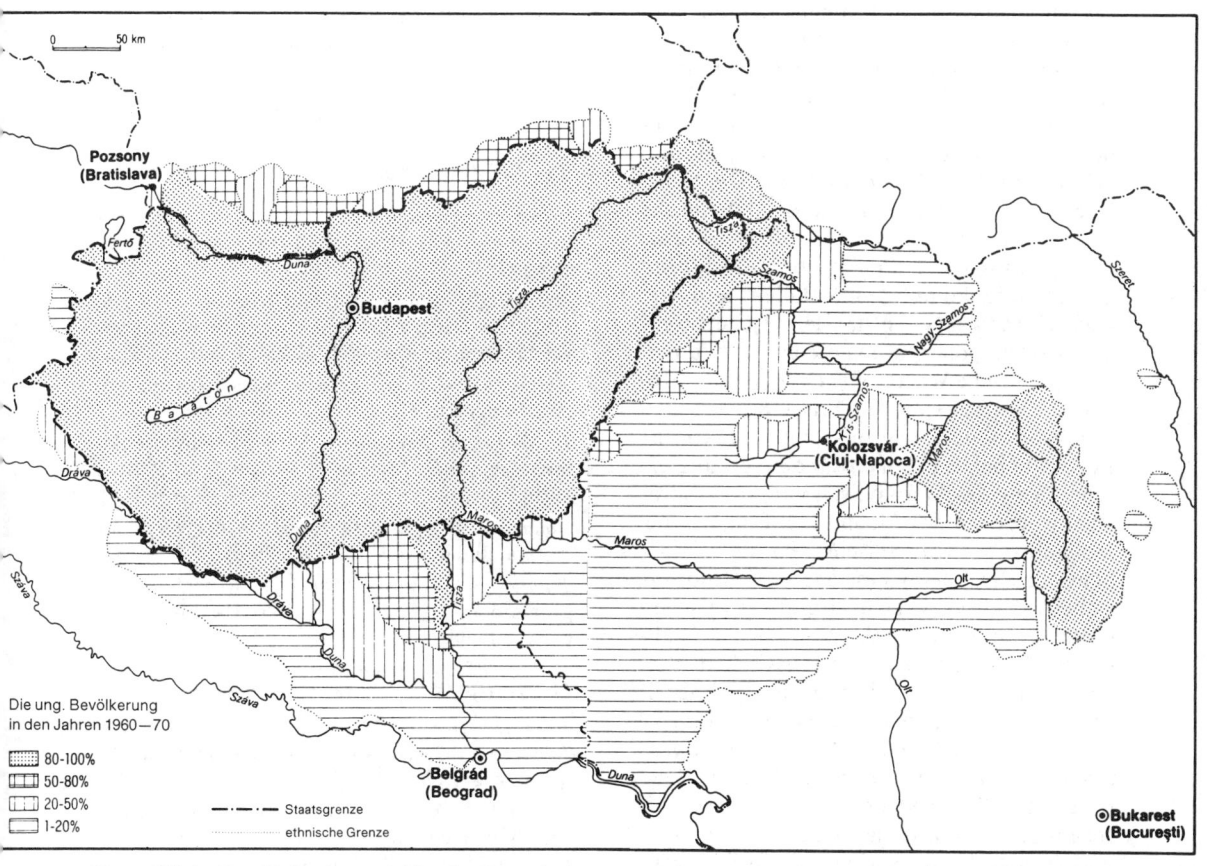

Karte 227.1: Das Verbreitungsgebiet des Ungarischen (aus: Magyar Néprajzi Lexikon III, 1980, 496—497)

ziert. (c) An die Stelle früherer Fremdwörterbücher traten nach 1957 die Klein- und Handwörterbücher von Ferenc Bakos (1957 und 1973).

5.5. Neue Wörterbuchtypen in Ungarn: (a) Als erstes Autorenwörterbuch erfaßt *Petőfi Szótár* (= PetőfiSz.) mit 22 178 Stichwörtern den vollständigen Wortschatz aus Petőfis Gesamtwerk. Die zweite Korpusbearbeitung dieser Art behandelt den dichterischen Wortschatz von Gyula Juhász (JuhászGySz.). (b) Das rückläufige Wörterbuch *A magyar nyelv szóvégmutató szótára* (= VégSz.) wurde bereits maschinell erarbeitet. (c) *Földrajzi nevek etimológiai szótára* (= FNESz.) unterrichtet in 6850 Artikeln (in ca. 13 340 Artikeln in der neuen Fassung) über den Ursprung ungarischer und ausländischer geographischer Namen. (d) Das Aussprachewörterbuch *Idegen nevek kiejtési szótára* von T. Magay (1974) gibt eine vereinfachte phonetische Transkription der verbreitetsten nichtungarischen Eigennamen an.

5.6 Ein bedeutsames Moment der neueren Entwicklung ist der Aufschwung der zweisprachigen Lexikographie. Die Dreigliederung in Groß-, Hand- und Kleinwörterbuch setzt sich bei den größeren Sprachen allmählich durch. Neben der Fertigstellung moderner Großwörterbücher für das Deutsche, Englische, Französische und Italienische wurden wissenschaftlich ebenbürtige Werke zum Russischen herausgegeben. Aufgrund der Kulturabkommen mit Polen und der Tschechoslowakei entstanden tschechisch-ungarische, polnisch-ungarische und ungarisch-polnische Wörterbücher; zu dem in Rumänien erarbeiteten rumänisch-ungarischen Großwörterbuch trugen auch ungarische Fachleute bei. Das Spektrum der von ungarischer Seite lexikographisch erfaßten Sprachen wurde um das Albanische, Bulgarische, Holländische, Koreanische, Portugiesische, Schwedische, Vietnamesische und Hindi erweitert. Die zweisprachigen polytechnischen Großwörterbücher (mit deutschem, englischem, französischem oder russischem Anteil) stellen ein neues Element in der ungarischen Lexikographie dar. Das auf nahezu 70 Bände angewachsene *Műszaki Értelmező Szótár* erklärt die fachspezifischen Ausdrücke und Wortbedeutungen je eines technischen oder wissenschaftlichen Teilbereichs und enthält deren deutsche, englische, französische und russische Entsprechungen. — Zur ganzen Periode s. Bakos 1966.

5.7. Ein Blick auf das Werk von L. Gáldi und L. Országh kann ein repräsentatives Bild der gegenwärtigen ungarischen Lexikographie vermitteln. Außer mit theoretischen Arbeiten zur Methodologie und Geschichte der Lexikographie beschäftigten sich die beiden bereits verstorbenen Gelehrten, Lehrer eines großen Teils der jetzt tätigen ungarischen Lexikographen, mit ein- und zweisprachiger Lexikographie. Die Idee und die Konzeption von *Petőfi Szótár* (5.5.) stammen von Gáldi, die Bearbeitung des siebenbändigen ungarischen Bedeutungswörterbuchs (5.1.) wurde während eines Jahrzehnts von Országh geleitet. Diese Arbeiten hielten sie jedoch nicht davon ab, die Redaktion des englisch-ungarischen und des ungarisch-englischen Wörterbuchs (Országh 1953 und 1960, Neubearbeitungen 1963 und 1976) bzw. — in Zusammenarbeit mit L. Hadrovics — des russisch-ungarischen und des ungarisch-russischen Wörterbuchs (Hadrovics-Gáldi 1951 und 1952, Neubearbeitungen 1959 und 1964) zu übernehmen und die bei späteren Auflagen notwendigen Neubearbeitungen zu betreuen.

6. Literatur (in Auswahl)

6.1. Wörterbücher

Alvarus 1703 = Syllabus Vocabulorum Grammaticae Emmanuelis Alvari [...] Tyrnaviae 1703 [96 S.; zuletzt 1837].

Babos 1865 = Babos Kálmán: Közhasznu magyarázó szótár a leggyakrabban előforduló idegen szavak megértésére. Pest 1865 [328 S.; 4. Aufl. 1899].

Bakos 1957 = Bakos Ferenc: Idegen szavak szótára. Budapest 1957 [848 S.; 5. Aufl. 1978].

Bakos 1973 = Bakos Ferenc: Idegen szavak és kifejezések szótára. Budapest 1973 [927 S.; 9. Aufl. 1989].

Balassa 1940 = Balassa József: A magyar nyelv szótára. Budapest 1940 [857 S. 2 Bde].

Ballagi 1854 = Ballagi Mór: Új teljes német és magyar szótár [...] Pest 1854, 1857 [1485 S. 2 Bde; 6. Aufl. 1890].

Ballagi 1868 = Ballagi Mór: A magyar nyelv teljes szótára. Pest 1868—73 [1447 S. 2 Bde].

Baranyai Decsi 1598 = Baranyai Decsi János: Adagiorum Graecolatino-ungaricorum Chiliades quinque. Bartphae 1598 [111 fol.].

Bernolák 1825 = Anton Bernolák: Lexicon Slavicum-Bohemico-Latino-Germanico-Ungaricum. Budae 1825—27 [5299 S. 6 Bde].

Bobb 1822 = Ioan Bobb: Dicţionariul rumanesc, lateinesc şi unguresc. Cluj 1822—23 [1234 S. 2 Bde].

Cal. 1585 = Ambrosius Calepinus: Dictionarivm Decem Lingvarum [...] Lvgdvni 1585 [1153 S.].

Cellarius 1719 = Christophorus Cellarius: Latinitatis probatae et exercitae Liber memorialis. Nori[n]bergae 1719 [zuletzt 1768].

Cellarius 1798 = ut supra. [...] cum interpretatione Hungarica aucta [...] ab Esaia Budai. Debrecen 1798 [663 S.].

CzF. 1862 = Czuczor Gergely/Fogarasi János: A magyar nyelv szótára. Budapest 1862—74 [9339 S. 6 Bde].

CsángSz. 1936 = Yrjö Wichmanns Wörterbuch des ungarischen Moldauer Nordcsángó- und des Hétfaluer Csángódialektes [...]. Hrsg. von Bálint Csűry und Artturi Kannisto. Helsinki 1936 [219 S.].

Dankovszky 1833 = Gregor Dankovszky: Kritisch-etymologisches Wörterbuch der ungarischen Sprache. Pozsony 1833 [1000 S.].

Erdélyi 1851 = Magyar közmondások könyve [...] Szerk. és kiadja Erdélyi János. Pest 1851 [461 S.].

ÉKsz. 1972 = Magyar értelmező kéziszótár. Szerkesztette Juhász József et alii. Budapest 1972 [1550 S.; 8. Aufl. 1990].

ÉrtSz. 1959 = A magyar nyelv értelmező szótára. Budapest 1959—62 [7378 S. 7 Bde; 4. Aufl. 1984—88].

EtSz. 1914 = Gombocz Zoltán/Melich János: Magyar etymologiai szótár. *A — geburnus.* Budapest 1914—44 [2860 S. 2 Bde].

Fábchich 1794 = Fábchich József: Magyar Kálepinus (Manuskript).

FNESz. 1978 = Kiss Lajos: Földrajzi nevek etimológiai szótára. Budapest 1978 [726 S.; Neubearbeitung: 1988 1643 S. 2 Bde].

Forstinger 1854 = Forstinger János: Irás és mindennapi társalkodásban előrduló idegen-szavakat magyarázó kézikönyv. Pest 1854 [1088 Spalten].

Hadrovics-Gáldi 1951 = Hadrovics László/ Gáldi László: Orosz-magyar szótár. Budapest 1951 [996 S.] Neubearbeitung: 1959 [1968 S.].

Hadrovics-Gáldi 1952 = Hadrovics László/Gáldi László: Magyar-orosz szótár. Budapest 1952 [1364 S.] Neubearbeitung: 1964 [2720 S.].

HKsz. 1988 = Helyesirási kéziszótár. Szerkesztők Deme László és Fábián Pál. Budapest 1988 [687 S.].

Horovitz 1908 = Horovitz Jenő: Idegen szavak magyarázata. Budapest 1908 [181 S.; 6. Aufl. 1947].

Imre 1973 = Imre Samu: Felsőőri tájszótár. Budapest 1973 [174 S.].

JuhászGySz. 1972 = Juhász Gyula költői nyelvének szótára. Szerkesztette Benkö László. Budapest 1972 [930 S.].

Kassai 1833 = Kassai József: Származtató 's gyökerésző magyar-diák szókönyv. Pest 1833—36 [1947 S. 5 Bde; der letzte Teil hrsg. von Gáldi László. Budapest 1962. 328 S.].

Kelemen B. 1929 = Kelemen Béla: Német-magyar, magyar-német nagy kézi szótár. Budapest 1929 [1924 S. 2 Bde; neue Aufl. bearb. von Tivadar Thienemann 1942].

Királyföldy 1846 = Királyföldy Endre: Újdon-új magyar szavak tára. Pest 1846 [408 S.].

Kiss J. 1979 = Kiss Jenő: Mihályi tájszótár. [Rábaköz] Budapest 1979 [76 S.].

Kis-Viczay 1713 = Selectiora adagia Latino-Hungarica [...]. Studio et vigilentia Petri Kis Viczay. Bartphae 1713 [552 S.].

Kresznerics 1831 = Kresznerics Ferenc: Magyar szótár gyökérrenddel és deákozattal. Buda 1831—32 [693 S. 2 Bde].

Kunoss 1834 = Kunoss Endre: Szófüzér [...]. Pest 1834 [78 S.; 4. Aufl. 1843].

Kunoss 1835 = Kunoss Endre: Gyalulat [...]. Pest 1835 [116 S.].

Leschka 1825 = Stephanus Leschka: Elenchus vocabulorum Europaeorum, cumprimis Slavicorum Magyarici usus. Budae 1825 [271 S.].

LexBud. 1825 = Lexicon Valachico-Latino-Hungarico-Germanicum [...]. Buda 1825.

LexMars. = Il „Lexicon Marsilianum", dizionario latino-rumeno-ungherese del sec. XVII [Hrsg. von Carlo Tagliavini]. Bucureşti 1930 [282 S.].

Lexicon Ianuale 1652 = Comenius Johannes Amos: Eruditionis Scholasticae Pars II. Ianua [...] Sylva Latinae Lingvae [...] Sive Lexicon Januale. Sárospatak 1652 [362 fol.].

MA. 1604 = Albertus Molnár Szenciensis: Dictionarivm Latinovngaricvm. II. Dictionarivm Vngarico-Latinvm. Nürnberg 1604 [491 S.].

MA. 1611 = Albertus Molnár Szenciensis: Lexicon Latino Graeco Hungaricum. Hanau 1611 [1241 S.].

Magay 1974 = Magay Tamás: Idegen nevek kiejtési szótára. Budapest 1974 [501 S.; 3. Aufl. 1986].

Margalits 1896 = Margalits Ede: Magyar közmondások és közmondásszerű szólások. Budapest 1896 [770 S.].

Márton 1803 = Márton József: Német-magyar és magyar-német lexicon, vagyis szókönyv. Bécs 1803, 1807 [3442 S. 4 Bde].

Márton 1823 = Márton József: Német-magyardeák lexicon [...]. Bécs 1823 [1990 S. 2 Bde].

MathMűsz. 1834 = Mathematikai műszótár. Közre bocsátja a Magyar Tudós Társaság. Buda 1834 [110 S.].

MSzFgrE. 1967 = A magyar szókészlet finnugor elemei. Etimológiai szótár. Főszerkesztő Lakó György. Budapest 1967—78 [857 S. 4 Bde].

MSzK. 1966 = O. Nagy Gábor: Magyar szólások és közmondások. Budapest 1966 [860 S.; 4. Aufl. 1985].

MTsz. 1893 = Szinnyei József: Magyar tájszótár. Budapest 1893—1901 [2664 Spalten 2 Bde].

MUSz. 1873 = Budenz József: Magyar-ugor öszszehasonlító szótár. Budapest 1873—81 [983 S.].

Műszaki Értelmező Szótár. Lexikográfiai szaktanácsadó Skripecz Sándor. 1—69. Budapest 1958—1989 [Die Serie wird fortgesetzt].

Noszkó 1791 = Virág Szó-tár, mellyet öszve-szedett [. . .] Noszkó Aloiszius. Pest 1791 [358 S.].

NySz. 1890 = Szarvas Gábor/Simonyi Zsigmond: Magyar nyelvtörténeti szótár [. . .]. Budapest 1890—93 [4600 Spalten 3 Bde].

NyUSz. 1902 = Szily Kálmán: A magyar nyelvújítás szótára a legkedveltebb képzők és képzésmódok jegyzékével. Budapest 1902, 1908 [662 S. 2 Bde].

OklSz. 1902 = Szamota István/Zolnai Gyula: Magyar oklevél-szótár. Pótlék a Magyar nyelvtörténeti szótárhoz. Budapest 1902—06 [1210 Spalten].

OrmSz. 1952 = Ormánysági szótár. Kiss Géza hagyatékából szerk. Keresztes Kálmán. Budapest 1952 [611 S.].

Országh 1953 = Országh László: Magyar-angol szótár. Budapest 1953 [1444 S.] Neubearbeitung: 1963 [2144 S.].

Országh 1960 = Országh László: Angol-magyar szótár. Budapest 1960 [2336 S.] Neubearbeitung: 1976 [2318 S.].

PetőfiSz. 1973 = Petőfi Sándor életművének szókészlete. Szerkesztette J. Soltész Katalin et alii. Budapest 1973—1987 [3921 S. 4 Bde].

PhilMűsz. 1834 = Philosophiai műszótár. Közre bocsátja a Magyar Tudós Társaság. Buda 1838 [212 S.].

Póra 1907 = Póra Ferenc: A magyar rokonértelmű szók és szólások kézikönyve. Budapest 1907 [523 S.].

PP. 1708 = Franciscus Pápai Páriz: Dictionarium manuale Latino-Ungaricum et Ungarico-Latinum. Leutschoviae 1708 [922 S.; weitere neu bearb. Auflagen 1767, 1801].

Radó 1904 = Radó Antal: Idegen szavak szótára [. . .] Budapest 1904 [182 S.; 10. Aufl. 1942].

Rédei 1986 f. = Károly Rédei: Uralisches Etymologisches Wörterbuch. Budapest 1986 f. [Bd. I, Lfg. 1—5, Bd. II, Lfg. 6—7; bisher 906 S.].

RMG. 1984 = Régi magyar glosszárium. Szótárak, szójegyzékek és glosszák egyesített szótára. Szerk. Berrár Jolán és Károly Sándor. Budapest 1984 [805 S.].

Rubinyi 1910 = Rubinyi Mózes: Mikszáth Kálmán stílusa és nyelve. Budapest 1910 [246 S.; Wörterverzeichnis 108—246].

Sauvageot 1932 = Aurélien Sauvageot: Franciamagyar és magyar-francia nagy kéziszótár. Budapest 1932, 1937 [2537 S. 2 Bde; 2. Aufl. 1942].

Schlandt 1913 = Heinrich Schlandt: Deutsch-magyarisches Sprichwörter-Lexikon. Budapest 1913 [383 S.].

Simai 1809 = Simai Kristóf: Vég tagokra szedetett Szó-tár [. . .]. Buda 1809—10 [386 S.].

Simai 1833 = Simai Kristóf: Gazdag szótár 1814—33 [Manuskript 5354 Blät.].

Sirisaka 1890 = Sirisaka Andor: Magyar közmondások könyve. Pécs 1890 [279 S.].

Szaitz 1788 = [Szaitz Leo Mária] Kis magyar frázeológyia. Közre bocsátá Máriafi István. Pozsony 1788 [159 S.].

SzamSz. 1935 = Csűry Bálint: Szamosháti szótár. Budapest 1935—36 [1052 S. 2 Bde].

SzD. 1784 = Baróti Szabó Dávid: Kis-ded Szó-tár [. . .] Kassa 1784 [104 S.; 2. Aufl. 1792. 292 S.].

SzegSz. 1957 = Bálint Sándor: Szegedi Szótár. Budapest 1957 [1567 S. 2 Bde].

SzikszF. 1590 = Szikszai Fabricius Balázs: Nomenclatvra sev Dictionarivm Latino-vngaricvm. Debrecen 1590 [235 S.; zuletzt 1641].

SzinSz. 1978 = O. Nagy Gábor/Ruzsiczky Éva: Magyar Szinonimaszótár. Budapest 1978 [593 S.; 4. Aufl. 1989].

Szirmay 1804 = Szirmay Antal: Hvngaria in parabolis [. . .]. Buda 1804 [150 S.].

SzlavSz. 1967 = Penavin Olga: Szlavóniai [kórogyi] szótár. Újvidék 1967—78 [1084 S. 3 Bde].

SzófSz. 1941 = Bárczi Géza: Magyar szófejtő szótár. Budapest 1941 [348 S.].

SzT. 1975 = Szabó T. Attila: Erdélyi magyar szótörténeti tár. I—IV. *A-házsongárdi.* Bukarest 1975 [4908 S. 4 Bde].

TESz. 1967 = A magyar nyelv történeti-etimológiai szótára. Főszerk. Benkő Loránd. Budapest 1967—84 [3977 S. 4 Bde].

Tsaholci-Bihari 1647 = Index Vocabvlorvm J. A. Comenii [per Johannem Tsaholci et Franciscum Bihari]. Albae Iuliae 1647 [508 S.].

Tsz. 1838 = Magyar Tájszótár. Kiadta a' Magyar Tudós Társaság. Buda 1838 [400 S.].

Tzs. 1835 = Magyar és német zsebszótár. Közrebocsátá a' Magyar Tudós Társaság. Buda 1835, 1838 [1636 S. 2 Bde].

ÚMTsz. 1979 = Új magyar tájszótár. Főszerk. B. Lőrinczy Éva. Bd. 1.: A—D. 1053 S.; Bd. 2.: E—J. 1175 S. Budapest 1979, 1988 [Die Redaktion setzt sich fort].

VégSz. 1969 = A magyar nyelv szóvégmutató szótára. Szerk. Papp Ferenc. Budapest 1969 [594 S.].

Verantius 1595 = Faustus Verantius: Dictionarivm qvinqve nobilissimarvm Evropae Lingvarum [. . .]. Venetiis 1595 [135 S.].

Verborum 1648 = Verborum in institutione grammaticâ [. . .] translatio. Tyrnaviae 1648 [50 S.].

Wagner 1750 = Franciscus Wagner: Universae phraseologiae Latinae corpus [. . .]. Tyrnaviae 1750 [1328 S.].

Wagner 1822 = ut supra. Editio 3 novissimis curis emendata et aucta [per Franciscus Versegi]. Budae 1822 [1607 S.].

6.2. Sonstige Literatur

Bakos 1966 = Ferenc Bakos: La lexicographie hongroise d'aujourd'hui. In: Cahiers de Lexicologie 9. 1966/II, 89—101.

Gáldi 1957 = Gáldi László: A magyar szótárirodalom a felvilágosodás korában és a reformkorban. Budapest 1957.

Kelemen J. 1970 = Kelemen József: A magyar szótárírás főbb kérdései a múlt század közepétől 1920-ig. In: Tanulmányok a magyar és a finnugor nyelvtudomány történetéből [1850—1970]. Budapest 1970, 77—97.

Melich 1907 = Melich János: A magyar szótárirodalom a legrégibb szójegyzékektől P. Páriz szótáráig. Budapest 1907.

Országh 1960 = László Országh: Problems and principles of the new dictionary of the Hungarian language. In: ALH. 10. 1960, 211—73.

Ferenc Bakos, Budapest (Ungarn)

228. Die Lexikographie der uralischen Sprachen II: Finnisch

1. Einleitendes
2. Lexikographie des Finnischen vom 17. bis 19. Jh.
3. Lexikographie des Finnischen im 20. Jh.
4. Karelisch
5. Literatur (in Auswahl)

1. Einleitendes

Finnisch ist der Hauptvertreter der sog. ostseefinn. Sprachen, zu denen noch Karelisch, Estnisch, Livisch, Wotisch, Ingrisch und Wepsisch gehören. Finn. und Karel. bilden gemeinsam das Nord-Ost-

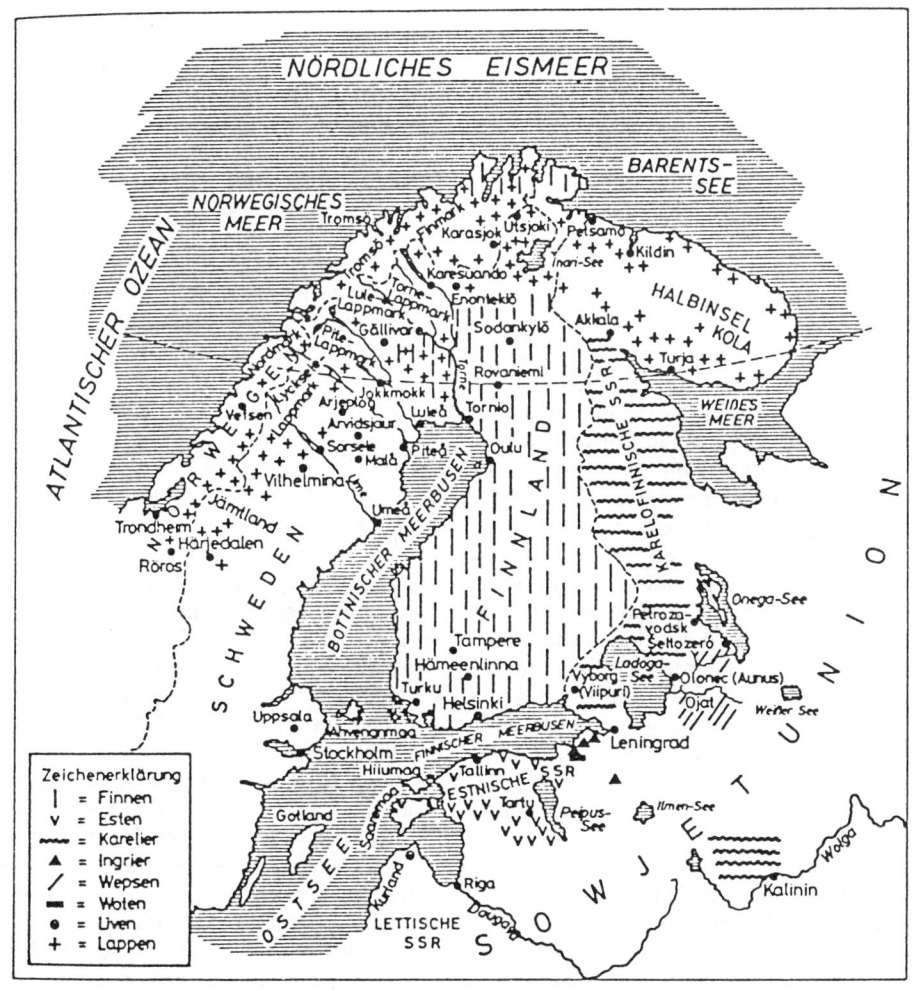

Karte 228.1: Siedlungsgebiete der ostsee-finnischen Völker und der Lappen (aus: Hajdú/Domokos 1987, 139)

see-finn. — Finnland war seit dem Mittelalter zweisprachig: Zunächst diente das Lat., später das Schwed. in unterschiedlicher Gewichtung als Kirchen-, Bildungs- und Amtssprache. Die Verfassung von 1919 garantiert die offizielle Gleichstellung von Finn. und Schwed. als Nationalsprachen der Republik Finnland. — Auf die finn. Lexikographie hatte Finnlands staatliche Zugehörigkeit zu Schweden oder sein Status als russisches Großfürstentum keinen negativen Einfluß. Charakteristisch ist vielmehr das Bemühen, das Finn. durch bewußte Sprachentwicklung und Sprachpflege, durch Aktivierung der eigenen Voraussetzungen der Sprache von einer reinen Volks- zu einer Bildungssprache zu machen. Auch als Kultursprache ist das Finn. wohl am stärksten uralisch geblieben. Sein eigenständig wirkender Wortschatz enthält jedoch zahlreiche alte Entlehnungen aus dem Baltischen und Germanischen sowie Lehnübersetzungen aus idg. Sprachen. — Der agglutinierende Charakter des Finnischen wird in der Lexikographie erstaunlich wenig berücksichtigt: Aufgenommen sind in der Regel die Nominative (mitunter auch Gen.) von Nomina und die Inf. I-Formen der Verben (mitunter auch 1. P. Sg.). — Übersichten über finnische Lexikographie sind selten. An neueren Darstellungen sei auf Kuusi 1968 und bes. Hakulinen 1974 hingewiesen.

2. Lexikographie des Finnischen vom 17. bis 19. Jh.

Die ersten Anfänge bestehen in mehrsprachigen Wörterlisten. Schroderus 1637 enthält ca. 2400 Wörter, in 36 Sachgruppen lat.-schwed.-dt.-finn. geordnet, nicht alphabetisch; Flexionsangaben fehlen. Kurze Beispielsätze enthält bereits die Neuauflage eines kleinen, ursprünglich lat.-schwed. Wörterbuches, *Variarum rerum* 1644. Florinus 1678 bringt eine lat.-schwed.-finn. Wörterliste, die verbesserten Auflagen enthalten ca. 3000 Wörter. Neu bei Florinus war, daß die lat. und schwed. Wörter häufig durch zwei und mehr finn. Synonyme erklärt wurden. — Erst Juslenius 1745 verdient den Namen eines Wörterbuches des Finn. Die finn. Lemmata sind lat. und schwed. übersetzt, Beispielsätze fehlen. Ein Register der schwed. Entsprechungen ermöglicht das Auffinden der finn. Synonyme. Juslenius 1745 bildet eine wertvolle Quelle für die historische Forschung, besonders für die Semantik, wenn auch einige etymologische Zusammenstellungen nicht den heutigen Erkenntnissen entsprechen. Die Lexik spiegelt die SW-Dialekte wider, auf denen ja auch die alte finn. Schriftsprache basierte. 1968 wurde das interfoliierte Wörterbuch von Juslenius mit zahlreichen wertvollen Eintragungen von H. G. Porthan als Faksimiledruck veröffentlicht. — Ganander 1787 erschien erstmalig 1937—1940 mit ca. 30 000 Lemmata, schwed. und lat. erklärt. Die zahlreichen Redewendungen und Beispielsätze sowie Synonyme sind meist genau belegt. — Renvall 1826 baute auf Porthans interfoliiertem Juslenius-Exemplar, Gananders Manuskript, eigenen Sammlungen und Wörterlisten von Zeitgenossen auf. Die ca. 22 000 Lemmata, alphabetisch nach etymologischen Gruppen geordnet, zeichnen sich aus durch präzise Bedeutungserklärungen, Beispielsätze und Verbreitungsangaben. — Finnisch wurde erst im Laufe des 19. Jhs. zu einer eigentlichen Kultursprache. Lönnrot 1847 ('Schwed.-finn.-dt. Sprachführer'), Europaeus 1852 f. ('Schwed.-finn. Wörterbuch') und Eurén 1860 ('Finn.-schwed. Wörterbuch') sind als lexikographische Errungenschaften zu erwähnen. Lönnrot 1880 ('Finn.-schwed. Wörterbuch') enthält an die 200 000 Lemmata und erstmals auch die reichen ostfinn. Dialekte. Das Wörterbuch war für finn. Muttersprachler bestimmt, erklärt aber die Lexik schwedisch. Ableitungen sind z. T. mechanisch gebildet oder erfunden; Neologismen sind sporadisch aufgenommen. Die 1930 und 1958 erschienene Faksimile-Ausgabe enthält auch das Supplement mit Neuaufnahmen und Ergänzungen von Lönnrots Mitarbeiter A. H. Kallio. Als Materialsammlung und Forschungsquelle ist Lönnrot 1880 nach wie vor unverzichtbar.

3. Lexikographie des Finnischen im 20. Jh.

3.1. Allgemeine einsprachige Wörterbücher

Das einzige abgeschlossene Werk, das hier genannt werden kann, ist *Nykysuomen sanakirja* 1978 (= NS; 'Wörterbuch der finn. Gegenwartssprache'). Diese Gemeinschaftsarbeit umfaßt ca. 201 000 Lemmata und fußt im großen und ganzen auf Exzerpten aus der Literatur des Zeitraums 1880 — 50er Jahre des 20. Jhs.; aus früheren Zeiten wurden nur das Kalevala und das literarische Schaffen von Aleksis Kivi sprachlich berücksichtigt. Außer standardsprachlichem registriert das NS in gewissem Umfang auch weiteres sprachvarietätenbezogenes Wortgut, so u. a. bei Schriftstellern auftretende Dialektwörter sowie bestimmte Ausdrücke von Fach- und Gruppensprachen. Im NS wurden zwei Aufgabenbereiche, ein deskriptiver und ein normativer, vereint, wenn auch die Unterscheidung dieser beiden Seiten für den Leser nicht immer einfach ist. Es gibt zwei Arten von Lemmata, und zwar sog. Hauptlemmata, die in alphabetischer Reihenfolge aufgeführt sind, und sog. Unterlemmata, die im etymologischen Zusammenhang erscheinen, z. B. **ahker/a** *a.* -asti *adv.* -uus *omin.*, wobei *a.* = 'Adjektiv', *adv.* = 'Adverb' und *omin.* = 'substantivische Eigenschaftsbezeichnung'. Die Bedeutung von Lemmata wird durch Definitionen oder sinnverwandte Ausdrücke erläutert, allerdings kann eine Bedeutungserläuterung bei Ableitungen und Zusammensetzungen oft fehlen. Zum syntaktischen Verhalten des Wortes werden in der Regel keine expliziten Angaben gemacht, vielmehr sind die Verwendungsweisen den jeweiligen Beispielkonstruktionen zu entnehmen. Nominale und verbale Lemmata sind mit hochgestellten Nummern versehen, die sich auf Flexionstypen beziehen. Die Flexionstabelle der Nomina enthält 85, die der Verben 45 Typen. Für die Flexionstypen werden folgende Formen angegeben: Nom., Gen., Partit., Ess. und Illat. Sg. sowie Gen., Partit. und Illat. Pl. (Nomina); Inf. I, Präs. Ind. Akt. 1. P. Sg., Imperf. Ind. Akt. 3. P. Sg., Präs. Konditional Akt. 3. P. Sg., Imperat. Akt. 3. P. Sg., Part. II Akt. und Imperf. Ind. Pass. (Verben). — Das systematische Sammeln von Material für NS wurde bereits 1938 beendet, weshalb sich dieses Wörterbuch heute in gewissen Fragen als veraltet erweist. Derzeit wird im Forschungszentrum für die Landessprachen Finnlands an einem neuen Wörterbuch gearbeitet, in das ca. 80 000 Lemmata aufgenommen werden sollen. Materialquellen des neuen Wörterbuchs sind das NS und Sammlungen, die sich aus Belegen aus der Belletristik und der Fachliteratur sowie aus Zeitungen und Zeitschriften zusammensetzen. Der normative Standpunkt soll stärker herausgearbeitet werden als im NS, ebenso soll der Rektion der Wörter größere Beachtung geschenkt werden. Die Kennzeichnung der Flexion der Lemmata erfolgt wie im NS, die Flexionstabellen aber sollen erneuert werden.

3.2. Weitere Wörterbuchtypen

In die Kategorie syntagmatische Spezialwörterbücher lassen sich u. a. Virkkunen 1983 ('Finn. Phrasenwörterbuch'), Sinnemäki 1983 ('Geflügelte Worte') und Laine 1983 ('Großes Zitatenwörterbuch') einordnen, wenngleich einige davon, vor allem Virkkunen 1983, auch eine Reihe von Einzelwörtern verzeichnen, was insbes. im Hinblick auf phraseologische Wörterbücher theoretisch problematisch ist. — Paradigmatische Spezialwörterbücher sind Jäppinen 1989 ('Synonymwörterbuch') und Tuomi 1980 ('Rückläufiges Wörterbuch des Finn.'). In Jäppinen 1989 wird zu einem Lemma, dem eine Wortartangabe folgt, ein Synonym oder eine Synonymreihe angeführt. Die verschiedenen Bedeutungen unter einem Lemma werden mit Hilfe arabischer Ziffern gegliedert, und vor einer Synonymreihe erscheint ein zentraler Begriff in Klammern. Tuomi 1980 beruht auf dem NS: Es enthält alle Lemmata des NS mit Ausnahme der Abkürzungen und eines überwiegenden Teils der Zusammensetzungen. Dem Lemma ist ein Kodeteil zugeordnet, wo eventuelle Homonymie, Wortart, Flexionstyp, Unvollständigkeit oder Unpersönlichkeit im Paradigma sowie eventueller Stufenwechsel und eventuelle Pluralität zum Ausdruck gebracht werden. — An Spezialwörterbüchern zu markierten Lemmata der Standardsprache existieren erstens *Uudissanasto 80* ('Neue Lexik 80'; eine Ergänzung zum NS), in dem anhand von ca. 6000 Lemmata Neuwörter und Neubedeutungen festgehalten werden, und *Nykysuomen sivistyssanakirja* 1979 ('Fremdwörterbuch der finn. Gegenwartssprache'; ca. 30 000 Lemmata); etymologische Angaben sind hier nicht vorhanden, dafür wird aber besonderer Wert gelegt auf Fragen der Rechtschreibung, Silbentrennung, Aussprache und Bedeutung. Außerdem gehören in diese Kategorie Karttunen 1979 ('Wörterbuch des heutigen Jargons'), eine Zusammenstellung von ca. 6000 Lemmata aus dem Gemeinjargon und einigen Sonderjargons vorrangig der 60er und 70er Jahre, und Vesikansa 1976 ('Präzisierungswörterbuch'), das leicht verwechselbare Wörter in Gruppen präsentiert. — Im Zusammenhang mit Wörterbüchern zu bestimmten weiteren Lemmatypen ist nur Vesikansa 1980 ('Abkürzungen') zu nennen. Das Material besteht aus finn. und internationalen Abkürzungen. — Das wichtigste Namenwörterbuch ist Vilkuna/Huitu/Mikkonen u. a. 1988, in dem Personennamen (Vor- und Nachnamen voneinander getrennt) in bezug auf ihre Geschichte und Verbreitung dargestellt werden. — Unter die Rubrik Spezialwörterbücher mit bestimmten Informationstypen fallen Saukkonen/Haipus/Niemikorpi u. a. 1979 ('Finn. Frequenzwörterbuch') und Toivonen/Itkonen/Joki u. a. 1955 ff. ('Etymologisches Wörterbuch des Finn.'). In Saukkonen/Haipus/ Niemikorpi u. a. 1979 wurden 12 663 von den insges. 43 670 verschiedenen Wörtern aufgenommen, die in einem Korpus aus dem Sprachgebrauch der Belletristik, des Rundfunks, der Presse und der Fachliteratur der 60er Jahre vorkommen. In Toivonen/Itkonen/Joki u. a. 1955 ff. folgt auf die genaue Bedeutungserklärung eine detaillierte Aufzählung der etymologischen Entsprechungen in den verwandten Dialekten und Sprachen, die z. T. noch keine Kultursprachen sind und keine feste Schriftsprache besitzen. Hinweise auf mögliche Entlehnungen werden gegeben. Dialektwörter und Elemente der Volkssprache als Lemmata sind hier zahlreicher als üblich, Fremdwörter sind nicht behandelt. Das Wörterbuch ist eine riesige lexikalische und semantische Materialsammlung; erklärende Ausführungen und wertende Stellungnahmen im Falle unterschiedlicher etymologischer Theorien sind selten. Der 1981 erschienene Band 7 bringt ein nach Sprachgruppen geordnetes Verzeichnis der in Band 1—6 etymologisch behandelten Wörter. — Den Typus sprachvarietätenbezogene Wörterbücher vertreten *Vanhan kirjasuomen sanakirja* 1985 (= VKS; 'Wörterbuch der alten finn. Schriftsprache', Bd. 1), *Suomen murteiden sanakirja* 1985 ff. (= SMS; 'Wörterbuch der finn. Dialekte', Bd. 1—2), Hämäläinen 1963 ('Finn. Militärjargon') und Penttinen 1984 ('Wörterbuch des Militärjargons'). Als Quellenmaterial des VKS dient finnischsprachige Literatur von der Zeit Mikael Agricolas bis 1810. Ein Wortartikel setzt sich aus folgenden Daten zusammen: Lemma (Form wie im heutigen Finn.), eventuelle Formvarianten, Wortartabkürzung, Bedeutungserläuterung durch Denotatsbeschreibung oder Synonyme bzw. bedeutungsverwandte Wörter, Informationen älterer Wörterbücher, Belege mit Quellenangaben in chronologischer Reihenfolge, Aufzählung von Zusammensetzungen mit dem Lemma als Determinat. Das Material des SMS basiert auf 8,5 Mio. Wortbelegen, 1900—1974 aus der mündlichen Rede aufgezeichnet. Als finn. Dialekte gelten alle vor 1940 in den Grenzen Finnlands gesprochenen Mundarten mit Ausnahme der schwed. Dialekte Finnlands und der in Ladogakarelien gesprochenen olonetzischen Dialekte. Ingermanland, Nordschweden (Västerbotten) und Norwegen (Finnmarken) sowie Mittelschweden (Värmland-Finnen) lieferten ebenfalls finn. Dialektmaterial. Die Wortartikel berücksichtigen mit ihrem Beispielmaterial Dialektgeographie, Semantik, Morphologie und Syntax gleichermaßen. Auffälligerweise haben die beiden gruppenbezogenen Wörterbücher Hämäläinen 1963 und Penttinen 1984 das gleiche Beschreibungsobjekt, den Militärjargon. Hämäläinen 1963 basiert weitgehend auf einem Material aus der Zeit von 1926 bis 1946, Penttinen 1984 wiederum erfaßt etwa den Zeitraum Mitte der 50er Jahre bis Anfang der 80er Jahre. — Textbezogene Wörterbücher sind schließlich Turunen 1979 ('Die Wörter des Kalevala') und *Index Agricolaensis* 1980. In Turunen 1979 wird der Wortschatz des Kalevala in seiner Gesamtheit (7830 verschiedene Wörter) semantisch und etymologisch erklärt, während der *Index Agricolaensis* 1980 die Belegstellen der konkreten Wortformen in den gesammelten Werken Mikael Agricolas festhält.

4. Karelisch

Die genuine Bevölkerung der Karelischen ASSR (gegr. 1923) — Karelier, Finnen, Wepsen — bildet heute ein Fünftel der Gesamteinwohnerschaft der Republik. Knapp die Hälfte aller Karelier lebt jedoch außerhalb der Republik, wie z. B. die Tver-Karelier am Oberlauf der Wolga im Gebiet Kalinin. Die karelische Sprache umfaßt folgende Dialekte: Nord- oder Weißmeerkarelisch und Südkarelisch mit Olonetzisch oder Livisch; das ebenfalls ostseefinn. Lüdische mit stark wepsischem Substrat bildet den Übergang zwischen Wepsisch und Olonetzisch. In der heute zu Finnland gehörenden Provinz Karelien wird, solange Dialekt gesammelt wurde, kein Karel. mehr gesprochen, sondern der ostfinn. Dialekt. — Trotz entsprechender Versuche konnte keine gesamtkarel. Schriftsprache eingeführt werden. Das Karel. ist eine schriftlose Volkssprache; in der Karelischen ASSR wird heute Finn. als eine Art regionale Amtssprache neben dem Russischen benutzt. Karel. wird heute nur zu wissenschaftlichen Zwecken publiziert (Sprachproben und Mundarttexte folkloristischen und ethnographischen Inhalts). — Kujola 1944 vereinigt das bislang gesammelte lüdische Dialektmaterial; die Lemmata und die reichen Belege sind ins Finn. übersetzt. Jede Eintragung ist durch Abkürzungen belegt; Name und Alter des Informanten, Zeit und Ort der Aufzeichnung sind genannt. Für ein nominales Lemma sind Gen. und Partit. Sg. sowie Nom. und Partit. Pl. angegeben, bei Verben folgt auf den Inf. I in der Regel die

1. P. Sg. und Imperf. — Virtaranta 1968 ff. baut auf bisher unveröffentlichten lexikalischen Aufzeichnungen des Karel. seit 1894 auf, aus Texten, Volksdichtung, mündlicher Rede bis in unsere Tage. Die Transkription der verschiedenen Quellen ist vereinheitlicht und vereinfacht. Als Lemma ist die nord- oder weißmeerkarel. Form gewählt, die ins Finn. übersetzt ist. Es folgen Wort- und Satzbelege aus den einzelnen karel. Dialekten, als solche durch Abkürzungen belegt. Die Wortarten sind gekennzeichnet; Querverweise auf lautliche Entsprechungen bzw. dialektale Synonyme werden gegeben. Nur im Falle eines unvollständigen Paradigmas sind bei Nomina auch andere Kasusformen angegeben als der Nom.

5. Literatur (in Auswahl)

5.1. Wörterbücher

Eurén 1860 = G. E. Eurén: Suomalais-Ruotsalainen Sanakirja. Hämeenlinna 1860 [506 S.].

Europaeus 1852 f. = D. E. D. Europaeus: Ruotsalais-Suomalainen Sanakirja. Helsingfors 1852—1853 [727 S.; 2 Bde.].

Florinus 1678 = Henrik Florinus: Nomenclatura Rerum brevissima Latino-Sveco-Finnonica. Turku 1678 [148 S.; 2. verb. Aufl. 1683; 3. Aufl. Stockholm 1695: Vocabularium Latino-Sveco-Germanico-Finnicum; zwei weitere Aufl. in Stockholm 1708 bzw. 1733, finn. Name: Yxi Lyhykäinen Sana-Kirja; Faksimile Pieksämäki 1976].

Ganander 1787 = Christfrid Ganander: Nytt Finskt Lexicon. Manuskript. [Faksimile Porvoo. Helsinki 1937—1940: Christfrid Ganander in Uusi suomen sanakirja; XIV, 1463 S.; 3 Bde.].

Hämäläinen 1963 = Simo Hämäläinen: Suomalainen sotilasslangi. Helsinki 1963 [331 S.].

Index Agricolaensis 1980 = Index Agricolaensis. Hrsg. v. Kotimaisten kielten tutkimuskeskus. Helsinki 1980 [VI, 879 S.; 2 Bde.].

Jäppinen 1989 = Harri Jäppinen: Synonyymisanakirja. 2. Aufl. Porvoo. Helsinki. Juva 1989 [485 S.; als Bd. 7 der Neuaufl. von NS; 1. Aufl. 1989].

Juslenius 1745 = Daniel Juslenius: Suomalaisen Sana-Lugun Coetus. Stockholm 1745 [XVI, 567 S.; Faksimile Helsinki 1968].

Karttunen 1979 = Kaarina Karttunen: Nykyslangin sanakirja. Porvoo. Helsinki. Juva 1979 [333 S.; Nachdr. in Bd. 5 der Neuaufl. von NS; 1980, 113—292].

Kujola 1944 = Juho Kujola: Lyydiläismurteiden sanakirja. Helsinki 1944 [X, 543 S.].

Laine 1983 = Jarkko Laine: Suuri sitaattisanakirja. 2. Aufl. Helsinki 1983 [556 S.; 1. Aufl. 1982].

Lönnrot 1847 = Elias Lönnrot: Ruotsin, Suomen ja Saksan tulkki. Helsingfors 1847 [VIII, 232 S.].

Lönnrot 1880 = Elias Lönnrot: Suomalais-Ruotsalainen Sanakirja. Helsinki 1880 [VIII, 2203 S.; 2 Bde.; Supplement 1886, 212 S.; Faksimile Porvoo 1930 und 1958].

Nykysuomen sanakirja 1978 = Nykysuomen sanakirja. Hrsg. v. Suomalaisen Kirjallisuuden Seura. 6. Aufl. Porvoo. Helsinki. Juva 1978 [XVIII, 4588 S.; 3 Bde.; 1. Aufl. 1951—1961, 6 Bde.].

Nykysuomen sivistyssanakirja 1979 = Nykysuomen sivistyssanakirja. Hrsg. v. Nykysuomen laitos. 5. Aufl. Porvoo. Helsinki. Juva 1979 [XVI, 448 S.; als Bd. 4 der Neuaufl. von NS; 1. Aufl. 1973; XVI, 462 S.].

Penttinen 1984 = Antti Penttinen: Sotilasslangin sanakirja. Porvoo. Helsinki. Juva 1984 [299 S.].

Renvall 1826 = Kustaa Renvall: Suomalainen Sana-Kirja. Turku 1826 [XVI, 695 S.; 2 Bde.].

Saukkonen/Haipus/Niemikorpi u. a. 1979 = Pauli Saukkonen/Marjatta Haipus/Antero Niemikorpi/Helena Sulkala: Suomen kielen taajuussanasto. Porvoo. Helsinki. Juva 1979 [536 S.].

Schroderus 1637 = Ericus Schroderus: Lexicon Latino-Scondicum. Stockholm 1637 [XXV, 106 S.; Faksimile Uppsala 1941].

Sinnemäki 1983 = Maunu Sinnemäki: Lentävien lauseiden sanakirja. 2. Aufl. Helsinki 1983 [564 S.; 1. Aufl. 1982].

Suomen murteiden sanakirja 1985 ff. = Suomen murteiden sanakirja. Hrsg. v. Kotimaisten kielten tutkimuskeskus. Helsinki 1985—1988 [XXXIX, 1833 S.; bisher Bd. 1: *a-elää*, 1985; Bd. 2: *emaali-havuvasta*, 1988].

Toivonen/Itkonen/Joki u. a. 1955 ff. = Y. H. Toivonen/Erkki Itkonen/Aulis J. Joki/Reino Peltola: Suomen kielen etymologinen sanakirja. Helsinki 1955—1981 [XXVI, 2293 S.; 7 Bde.].

Tuomi 1980 = Tuomo Tuomi: Suomen kielen käänteissanakirja. 2. Aufl. Hämeenlinna 1980 [XXXII, 546 S.; 1. Aufl. 1972; XXXII, 545 S.].

Turunen 1979 = Aimo Turunen: Kalevalan sanat ja niiden taustat. Lappeenranta 1979 [415 S.].

Uudissanasto 80 = Uudissanasto 80. Hrsg. v. Kotimaisten kielten tutkimuskeskuksen kielitoimisto. Porvoo. Helsinki. Juva 1979 [X, 195 S.; Nachdr. in Bd. 5 der Neuaufl. von NS; 1980, 5—111].

Vanhan kirjasuomen sanakirja 1985 = Vanhan kirjasuomen sanakirja. Hrsg. v. Kotimaisten kielten tutkimuskeskus. Helsinki 1985 [XLIV, 918 S.; bisher Bd. 1: *A—I*].

Variarum rerum 1644 = Variarum rerum vocabula Latina, cum Svetica et Finnonica Interpretatione. Stockholm 1644 [121 S.; spätere Aufl. u. a. 1658 und 1668; Faksimile Stockholm 1925].

Vesikansa 1976 = Jouko Vesikansa: Täsmennyssanasto. Porvoo. Helsinki 1976 [128 S.].

Vesikansa 1980 = Jouko Vesikansa: Lyhenteet. 2. Aufl. Porvoo. Helsinki. Juva 1980 [In Bd. 5 der Neuaufl. von NS, 293—379; 1. Aufl. 1979, 174 S.].

Vilkuna/Huitu/Mikkonen u. a. 1988 = Uusi suomalainen nimikirja. Bearb. v. Kustaa Vilkuna unter Mitwirkung v. Marketta Huitu und Pirjo Mikkonen (Vornamen) sowie v. Pirjo Mikkonen und Sirkka Paikkala (Nachnamen). Helsinki 1988 [1031 S.; 1. Aufl. 1984: Suomalainen nimikirja, 925 S.].

Virkkunen 1983 = Sakari Virkkunen: Suomalainen fraasisanakirja. 5. Aufl. Helsinki 1983 [420 S.; 1. Aufl. 1974; X, 656 Sp.].

Virtaranta 1968 ff. = Pertti Virtaranta: Karjalan kielen sanakirja. Helsinki 1968—1983 [CXI, 1751 S.; bisher Bd. 1: *A—J*, 1968; Bd. 2: *K*, 1974; Bd. 3: *L—N*, 1983].

5.2. Sonstige Literatur

Hajdú/Domokos 1987 = P. Hajdú/P. Domokos: Die uralischen Sprachen und Literaturen. Budapest 1987.

Hakulinen 1974 = Lauri Hakulinen: Die finnische lexikographische Literatur. In: Ural-Altaische Jahrbücher 46. 1974, 84—98.

Kuusi 1968 = Matti Kuusi: Sanakirjat. In: Suomen kirjallisuus. Bd. 7. Hrsg. v. Matti Kuusi. Helsinki 1968, 588—592.

Jarmo Korhonen, Turku (Finnland)
Ingrid Schellbach-Kopra, München
(Bundesrepublik Deutschland)

228 a. Die Lexikographie der uralischen Sprachen III: Lappisch

1. Allgemeines
2. Süddialekte
3. Mitteldialekte
4. Ostdialekte
5. Literatur (in Auswahl)

1. Allgemeines

Das Sprachgebiet des Lappischen *(sápmi)* verteilt sich auf vier Staaten: Norwegen, Schweden, Finnland und die Sowjetunion (vgl. Karte 228 a. 1). In einer Breite von einigen hundert Kilometern reicht es von Mittelskandinavien entlang der Küste des Nördlichen Eismeers bis an die Ostküste der Halbinsel Kola. Die Schätzungen über die Anzahl der Lappen schwanken je nach den verwendeten Kriterien zwischen 30 000 und 70 000. Die Anzahl der lappischen Muttersprachler dürfte höchstens ²⁄₃ der Gesamtzahl ausmachen. Fast in ihrem gesamten Wohngebiet leben die Lappen heute als Minderheit; in keinem Staat hat das Lappische den Rang einer offiziellen Sprache. In einigen Schulen des

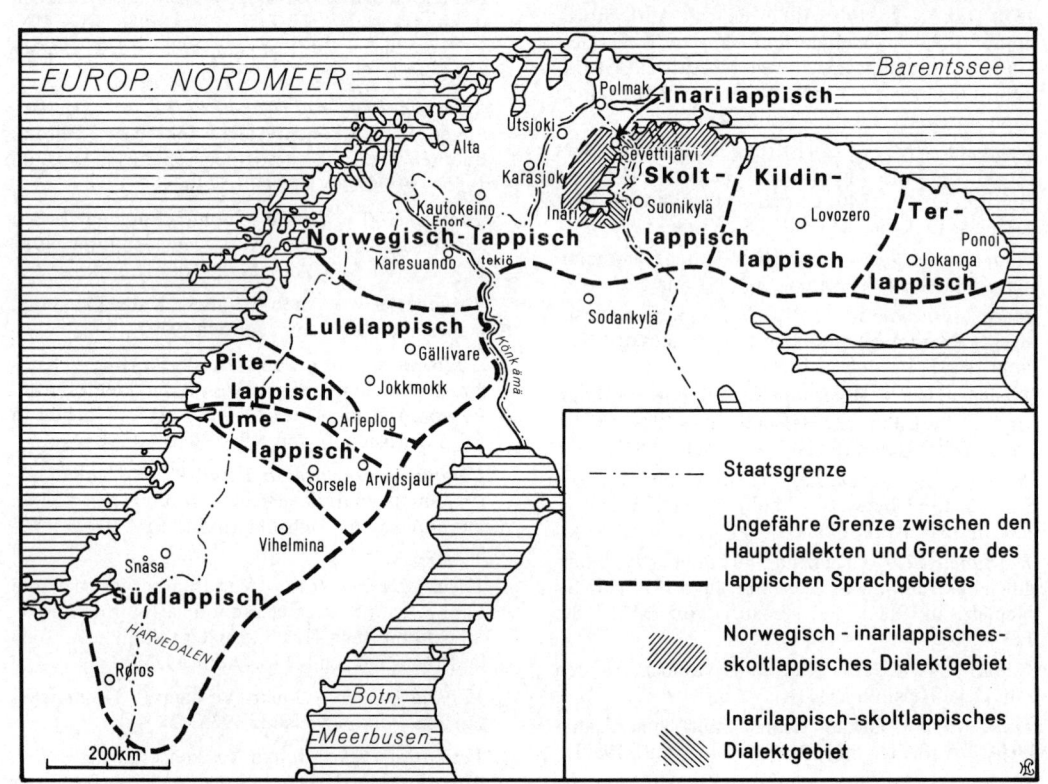

Karte 228 a. 1: Das lappische Sprachgebiet

Lappengebietes wird das Lappische und in lappischer Sprache unterrichtet. Regionale Rundfunkstationen in Norwegen, Schweden und Finnland strahlen auch Programme in lapp. Sprache aus, und es erscheinen einige Zeitungen auf lappisch. Die lappischsprachige Literatur entstand im 17. Jh. und war zu Beginn vorwiegend religiös. Heute liegt das Hauptgewicht auf Belletristik und Sachbüchern sowie u. a. auf Schulbüchern. — Das Lappische gliedert sich in sieben Hauptdialekte, die sich so stark voneinander unterscheiden, daß sie als eigene lapp. Sprachen bezeichnet werden können. Im folgenden sind diese Dialekte in drei größere Gesamtheiten gruppiert: a. Süddialekte: eigentliches Südlapp. und Umelapp., b. Mitteldialekte: Pite-, Lule- und Norwegisch- bzw. Nordlapp., c. Ostlapp.: Inari-, Skolt-, Kildin- und Terlapp. — Die frühesten lapp. Wörterbücher sollten in erster Linie der Christianisierung und der sonstigen religiösen Tätigkeit dienen. Die Ende des 19. Jhs. aufkommende wissenschaftliche Lappologie hat bislang zur Entstehung mehrerer umfangreicher Dialektwörterbücher geführt, die dank ihres reichen und detaillierten Inhalts nicht nur für die Sprachwissenschaft, sondern auch für die Volkskunde wertvolle Sammlungen darstellen. Die meisten sind auf ein größeres oder kleineres Dialektgebiet beschränkt. Eine Ausnahme bildet Lagercrantz 1939, wo das vom Verf. gesammelte Material zahlreiche Süd- und Mitteldialekte umfaßt, angefangen von Härjedalen in Mittelschweden bis zum Varangerfjord im östlichen Finnmarken. Aufgenommen sind auch Eigennamen. Die etymologisch zusammengehörenden Wörter sind in einem Wortartikel behandelt. Jeder Wortartikel besteht aus einem oder mehreren Punkten. Im ersten (oft einzigen) Punkt steht das Grundwort der betr. Sippe oder die einfachste Ableitung, gleichzeitig als Lemma alphabetisch geordnet. Es folgen — jeweils als eigener Punkt — eventuelle (sonstige) Ableitungen sowie Komposita, deren Anfangskomponente als Wort im betr. Artikel erscheint. Jede Dialektform ist in sehr genauer phonetischer Transkription angegeben. Als Quelle wird das Dorf der Aufzeichnung und oft auch der Informant mitgeteilt. Flexionsformen und Phraseologie sind ebenfalls vertreten. Die Erklärungen sind in dt. Sprache abgefaßt. Das Wb. enthält 8859 Wortartikel mit über 20 000 Punkten. Am Schluß findet sich ein ausführliches Sachregister. — In unserem Jh. sind ferner einige kleinere, praktischen Zwecken dienende Wb. und Verzeichnisse erschienen, mit Norw., Schwed., Finn. oder Russ. als zweiter Sprache.

2. Süddialekte

Das älteste bekannte lapp. Wb. ist Fiellström 1738, ein kurzgefaßtes Wörterverzeichnis, das vor allem vom Umelapp. ausging und die Grundlage schuf für die sog. südlapp. Schriftsprache. Im lapp.-schwed.-lat. Wb. von Lindahl/Öhrling 1780 sind auch die nördlicheren Dialekte in gewissem Umfang mitberücksichtigt; dieses Wb. war schon bedeutend umfangreicher und enthielt auch einen Index sowie die Hauptzüge der Grammatik. Die Reihe der wissenschaftlichen Wb. eröffnet Halász 1891, ein kurzgefaßter südlapp.-ung.-dt. Wortschatz, dessen Material der Verf. selbst gesammelt hatte. Im 20. Jh. folgen dann einige ebenfalls kleinere, auf Sammlungen des jeweiligen Herausgebers basierende Dialektwörterbücher, wie Lagercrantz 1926 mit der Lexik der nördl. Gruppe des Südlapp., Collinder 1943 mit einem bescheidenen Wörterverzeichnis aus dem südlichsten Lappendialekt sowie Schlachter 1958, ein verdienstvolles Wb. über das Waldlapp. von Umeå, das auch die Grundzüge der Morphologie sowie Texte enthält. Danach erschien dann in drei gewichtigen Bänden Hasselbrink 1981—85, mit einer umfassenden grammatischen Einführung. Das Wb. baut auf dem Material auf, das zahlreiche Forscher aus den vielen südlapp. Dialekten zu unterschiedlichen Zeiten gesammelt haben. Die Belege sind in grober Transkription angegeben, wo nötig, auch phonetisch. Genaue Angaben zu Quellen und Verbreitung sind vorhanden; die Bedeutungen werden auf dt. gegeben. Die Zahl der Lemmata beträgt über 35 000.

3. Mitteldialekte

Die zahlenmäßig größte und auch schriftlich am meisten benutzte lapp. Sprache ist das Nordlapp. bzw. Norwegischlapp., das zusammen mit dem Pite- und dem Lulelapp. zur Gruppe der Mitteldialekte gehört. Die ältesten nordlapp. Wb., Leem 1756, 1768—81 und Stockfleth 1852, waren ebenfalls hauptsächlich für die Bedürfnisse der Missionstätigkeit und der Kirche zusammengestellt worden. Sie, wie auch die zur gleichen Zeit erschienenen Grammatiken, schufen die Grundlage für die nordlapp. Schriftsprache. Noch wichtiger wurden in dieser Hinsicht die Arbeiten von J. A. Friis, vor allem sein großes lapp.-lat.-norw. Wb. (Friis 1887), das über 40 000 Lemmata enthält. Friis nahm auch Material aus dem Schwedischlapp. (vor allem nach Lindahl/Öhrling 1780) sowie aus dem Ostlapp. in sein Wb. auf. Den Anfang des Wb. bildet ein recht umfassender Überblick über die Laut- und Formenlehre. Nielsen 1932—62 ist vielleicht das inhaltlich reichste aller lapp. Wb. Von den fünf Bänden bringen die drei ersten das eigentliche Lexikon, Band 4 enthält ein Sachregister und Band 5 Ergänzungen und Korrekturen. Das Wb. stellt den Wortschatz der drei Finnmarken-Dialekte vor, wobei Polmak den östlichen Dialekttyp des Finnmarken-Lapp. vertritt, Karasjok den mittleren und Kautokeino den westlichen. Die Lemmata sind in der von Nielsen selbst entwickelten Orthographie geschrieben, die phonologisch und morphophonologisch wesentlich genauer ist als die Orthographie von Friis. Nielsens Orthographie wird vor allem in der wissenschaftlichen Literatur bis in unsere Tage für die Wiedergabe lappischsprachigen Materials verwendet. Sonst hat sie sich jedoch nicht eingebürgert, offenbar wegen ihrer gewissen morphophonologischen Abstraktheit und ihrer zahlreichen, auch typographisch schwierigen Sonderzeichen. Nach dem Lemma folgen die Angaben zur Verbreitung und die phonetische Gestalt des Wortes in einem jeden Dialekt. Die Bedeutung der Wörter ist auf engl. und norw. angegeben. Die Wortartikel enthalten auch Phraseologie, Beispielsätze, Komposita und — falls es sich um eine Ableitung handelt — einen Hinweis auf das Grundwort. Die Zahl der Lemmata beträgt ca. 25 000. In dieser Zahl sind nicht die Komposita enthalten, da sie nicht als Lemma erscheinen, sondern unter einem Stichwort, das einer ihrer Komponenten entspricht. Das Sachregister ist illustriert und enthält auch viele ethnographisch wertvolle Angaben. — Für das Nordlapp. sind einige Spezialwörterbücher erschienen, wie Qvigstad 1935, 1938 und 1944 über die norwegischlapp. Ortsnamen sowie Egel/Utsi 1984 über Gesundheitspflege und Sozialwesen. In der letzten Zeit sind auch mehrere kurzgefaßte zweisprachige Wb. für schulische und andere praktische Zwecke erschienen.

Seit der ersten Hälfte des 19. Jhs. ist in geringem Umfang das Lulelapp. als Schriftsprache verwendet worden. K. B. Wiklund publizierte 1890 anhand eigener Sammlungen ein kurzgefaßtes Wörterbuch. Diesbezügliches sprachliches Material ist vor allem von schwed. Forschern gesammelt worden, hauptsächlich von Wiklund, Björn Collinder und Harald Grundström. Von diesem Material geht Grundström 1946—54 aus. Das Wb. umfaßt an die 18 000 Lemmata. Die Lemmaformen sind in genormter grober Transkription wiedergegeben; darauf folgen die Vertretungen der einzelnen Dialekte in phonetischer Transkription. Die Bedeutungen sind schwed. und dt. angegeben. Vor allem mit der lapp. Kultur zusammenhängende Begriffe sind recht ausführlich erklärt worden. Unter der sonstigen Lexik findet sich auch eine Anzahl Ortsnamen; die Personennamen bilden dagegen eine eigene Abteilung. Der letzte Band des Wb. enthält ein Register jener nordlapp. Wörter in Nielsen 1932 ff., die in Grundström 1946—54 eine etymologische Entsprechung haben, ferner Angaben über das Material, die Dialekte sowie die Transkription; schließlich folgt auf ca. 200 Seiten ein Verzeichnis der Flexionstypen der verschiedenen Nominal- und Verbaltypen in sechs lulelapp. Dialekten. — Die einzige veröffentlichte lexikalische Quelle für das Pitelapp. ist ein kurzgefaßter Wortschatz in Halász 1896, wo die Bedeutung der Wörter auf ungar. und dt. angegeben ist.

4. Ostdialekte

Die Ostdialekte bilden eine wesentlich heterogenere Gruppe als die beiden vorangehenden. Die dazugehörenden vier Dialekte unterscheiden sich stark voneinander; alle vier werden jeweils von einer Gemeinschaft mit weniger als 1000 Sprechern unterhalten. Die schriftliche Verwendung dieser Dialekte war sehr gering, andererseits waren sie aber Gegenstand intensiven wissenschaftlichen Interesses. Die Lexikographie des Ostlapp. begann in der zweiten Hälfte des 19. Jhs. im Zuge des starken Aufschwungs der finnisch-ugrischen Sprachwissenschaft und der damit verbundenen Feldforschung. Genetz 1891 beruht auf dem Material, das der Autor selbst aus den skolt-, kildin- und terlapp. Dialekten gesammelt hat.

Wissenschaftsgeschichtlich interessant ist die für die Lemmata verwendete Transkription. Da die Lautgestalt ein und desselben Wortes große interdialektale Differenzen aufweisen kann, steht man bei der Stichwortfindung und der Reihenfolge der Darstellung vor schwierigen Problemen. Genetz gab in Stichwörtern eine abstrakte morphophonologische Form, von der man die phonetische Form des betr. Wortes in einem jeden Dialekt sowie auch die im Wortstamm auftretenden paradigmatischen Wechsel ableiten kann. Es ist zu betonen, daß die Stichwortformen, die zum Unterschied von den in phonetischer Transkription geschriebenen „Oberflächenformen" in den Dialekten in Klammern mit großen Buchstaben geschrieben sind, keine sprachgeschichtlichen Rekonstruktionen darstellen, sondern zunächst an die Art der Darstellung der Morphemebene erinnern, wie sie in der Sprachwissenschaft unserer Tage üblich ist. (Näher dazu Korhonen 1986, 119—20.)

Auch das Material von T. Itkonen 1958 wurde größtenteils vom Verf. selbst gesammelt; zusätzlich dazu wurde auch älteres skolt- und kolalapp. Material aufgenommen, z. B. von Genetz und aus in der Sowjetunion veröffentlichten Texten. Das Material ist etymologisch geordnet (vgl. 5.1., Lagercrantz 1939), Itkonens eigenes Material ist in genauer phonetischer Transkription wiedergegeben, das übrige Material normalerweise der Quelle entsprechend, Kyrillika jedoch latinisiert. Die Erklärungen stehen in Finn. und Dt. Am Ende der Wortartikel finden sich etymologische Hinweise auf Entsprechungen in anderen Dialekten des Lapp. sowie auf eine eventuelle Lehnherkunft. Der eigentliche Wörterbuchanteil umfaßt ca. 7000 Wortartikel, einschließlich der Komposita und Ableitungen über 30 000 Wörter. Band 2 enthält Ergänzungen zu Band 1, umfangreiche Orts- und Personennamenverzeichnisse sowie Register in Norwegischlapp., Finn. und Dt. — Für das Inarilapp. standen lange nur einige kleinere Wörterverzeichnisse zur Verfügung (Lönnrot 1855, Andelin 1861 und Sammallahti/Morottaja 1983). Ein umfassendes Großwörterbuch wissenschaftlichen Formats (E. Itkonen 1986—91) ist neulich erschienen. Das Material geht auf mehrere Sammler zurück, zum größten Teil jedoch auf E. Itkonen selbst. — Kurutsch 1985 ist ein Wb. mit 8000 Lemmata, das auf den in der Sowjetunion gesprochenen lapp. Dialekten aufbaut.

5. Literatur (in Auswahl)

5.1. Wörterbücher

Andelin 1861 = A. Andelin: Enare-lapska språkprof med ordregister. In: Acta Societatis Scientiarum Fennicae VI. Helsingfors 1861, 385—495.

Collinder 1943 = Björn Collinder: Lappisches Wörterverzeichnis aus Härjedalen. Uppsala 1943 [X, 110 S.].

Egel/Utsi 1984 = Mákke Jovsset Egel/Egil Utsi: Dearvvasvuođa- ja sosialsuorggi sánit ja dadjanvuogit. Narvik 1984 [221 S.].

Fiellström 1738 = Dictionarium sueco-lapponicum. Af Petro Fiellström. Holmiae 1738 [190 S.].

Friis 1887 = Jens Andreas Friis: Lexicon lapponicum cum interpretatione latina et norvegica adiuncta brevi grammaticae lapponicae adumbratione. Christianiae 1887 [LIX, 868, 6 S.].

Genetz 1891 = Arvid Genetz: Kuollan Lapin murteiden sanakirja ynnä kielennäytteitä. — Wörterbuch der Kola-lappischen Dialekte nebst Sprachproben. Helsinki 1891 [XLVI, 292 S.].

Grundström 1946—54 = Harald Grundström: Lulelappisches Wörterbuch — Lulelapsk ordbok. Uppsala 1946—54 [VI, 1920 S., 4 Bde.].

Halász 1891 = Ignácz Halász: Déli-lapp szótár. (Svéd-lapp nyelv 4) Budapest 1891 [V, 264 S.].

Halász 1896 = Ignácz Halász: Pite lappmarki szótár és nyelvtan. (Svéd-lapp nyelv 6) Budapest 1896 [XLI, 201 S.].

Hasselbrink 1981—85 = Gustav Hasselbrink: Südlappisches Wörterbuch. Uppsala 1981—85 [1488 S., 3 Bde.].

E. Itkonen 1986—91 = Erkki Itkonen: Inarilappisches Wörterbuch (Lexica Societatis Fenno-Ugricae XX.) [1331, 217 S., 4 Bde.].

T. Itkonen 1958 = Toivo I. Itkonen: Wörterbuch des Kolta- und Kolalappischen. — Koltan- ja kuolanlapin snakirja. (Lexica Societatis Fenno-Ugricae XV) Helsinki 1958 [XLIV, 1236 S., 2 Bde.].

Kurutsch 1985 = Rimma D. Kurutsch: Saamsko-russkij slovar'. Moskva 1985 [568 S.].

Lagercrantz 1926 = Eliel Lagercrantz: Wörterbuch des Südlappischen nach der Mundart von Wefsen. Oslo 1926 [XI, 214 S.].

Lagercrantz 1939 = Eliel Lagercrantz: Lappischer Wortschatz. (Lexica Societatis Fenno-Ugricae VI) Helsinki 1939 [IV, 1250 S., 2 Bde.].

Leem 1756 = Knud Leem: En lappesk Nomenclator efter den Dialect, som bruges af Fjeld-Lapperne i Porsanger-Fjorden. Tronhiem 1756 [666 S. 8°].

Leem 1768—81 = Knud Leem: Lexicon Lapponicum bipartitum. Pars prima lapponico-danico-latina. Nidarosiae 1768 [1610 S. 4:o] — Pars secunda danico-latina-lapponica. Havniae 1781 [512 S. 4°].

Lindahl/Öhrling 1780 = Ericus Lindahl/Johannes Öhrling: Lexicon lapponicum, cum interpretatione vocabulorum sveco-latina et indice svecano-lapponico, auctum grammatica lapponica. Holmiae 1780 [LXXX, 716 S.].

Lönnrot 1855 = Elias Lönnrot: Ueber den Enarelappischen Dialekt. In: Acta Societatis Scientiarum Fennicae IV. Helsingfors 1855, 133—279.

Nielsen 1932—62 = Konrad Nielsen: Lapp dictionary — Lappisk ordbok. Oslo 1932—62 [1. Bd. 1932: LXVII, 666 S.; 2. Bd. 1934: 718 S.; 3. Bd. 1938: 876 S.; 4. Bd. 1956: 560 S.; 5. Bd. 1962: 283 S., 2. Aufl. 1979].

Qvigstad 1935 = Just Knud Qvigstad: De lappiske stedsnavn i Troms fylke. Oslo 1935 [162 S.].

Qvigstad 1938 = Just Knud Qvigstad: De lappiske stedsnavn i Finnmark og Nordland fylker. Oslo 1938 [275 S.].

Qvigstad 1944 = Just Knud Qvigstad: De lappiske appellative stedsnavn. Oslo 1944 [82 S.].

Sammallahti/Morottaja 1983 = Pekka Sammallahti/Matti Morottaja: Säämi — suoma — säämi škovlasänikirja. Inarinsaame — suomi — inarinsaame koulusanakirja. Helsinki 1983 [IV, 214 S.].

Schlachter 1958 = Wolfgang Schlachter: Wörterbuch des Waldlappendialekts von Malå und Texte zur Ethnographie. (Lexica Societatis Fenno-Ugricae XIV) Helsinki 1958 [XI, 294 S.].

Stockfleth 1852 = Nils Vibe Stockfleth: Norsklappisk Ordbog. Christiania 1852 [IV, 892 S.].

Wiklund 1890 = Karl Bernhard Wiklund: Lulelappisches Wörterbuch. (Mémoires de la Société Finno-Ougrienne 1) Helsinki 1890 [187 S.].

5.2. Sonstige Literatur

Korhonen 1981 = Mikko Korhonen: Johdatus lapin kielen historiaan, 53—75. Helsinki 1981.

Korhonen 1986 = Mikko Korhonen: Finno-Ugrian language studies in Finland 1828—1918. Helsinki 1986.

Qvigstad 1899 = Just Knud Qvigstad: Uebersicht der Geschichte der lappischen Sprachforschung. In: Journal de la Société Finno-Ougrienne XVI, 3, 11—29. Helsinki 1899.

Mikko Korhonen, Helsinki (Finnland)

229. Lexicography of the Uralic Languages IV: Estonian and Livonian

1. 1637—1918
2. 1919—1940
3. After 1944
4. Livonian
5. Selected Bibliography

1. 1637—1918

Earlier there were two Estonian literary languages: North Estonian and South Estonian. However, the latter gradually lost its literary status. The first printed book in Estonian appeared in 1535 but the first vocabulary of Estonian is found in Stahl 1637 where on circa 100 pages 3200 North Estonian correspondences are offered to over 2000 German words. Gutslaff 1648 was a similar work for South Estonian, giving on 39 pages Estonian correspondences of c. 1100 German words. Much more comprehensive is the next German-Estonian vocabulary: Göseken 1660. Here on 412 pages c. 10000 Estonian correspondences of c. 9000 German words are offered. In the introductory etymological section c. 400 alleged German borrowings in Estonian are listed for the first time. Also Estonian phrases and sentences are served. All three quoted authors were German pastors whose handling of the Estonian lexicon evidently was better than their understanding of the Estonian grammar. Beside the German-Estonian printed word lists also handwritten Estonian-German dictionaries circulated, in the first half of the 18th century especially J. Chr. Clare's *Cellarius* with c. 7500 South Estonian words and S. H. Vestring's *Lexicon* with 8000—9000 North Estonian words, both provided with sentence examples. The first printed Estonian-German vocabulary in Thor Helle 1732 actually is a reduced version of Vestring's dictionary. For the first time Thor Helle also lists technical terms and Russian borrowings in Estonian. The dictionary part of Hupel 1780 combines the data of its predecessors and consists of two sections: Estonian-German (192 pages) and German-Estonian (216 pages). Altogether Hupel 1780

56

VOcabula Germanica, id eſt, á Germanicis mutuata Oeſthonicis meritó præmittuntur, ut á Tyronibus arrepta faciliorem ad reliqua viam ijs ſtruant. Quæ etſi non ſint absq; neceſſitate intermiſcenda, quia Germanismum ſapiunt, nec á ruſticis, præſertim ijs, qui vel procul á Germanis vivunt, vel cum illis non converſantur, intelligi queunt, utpote, quæ nunquam apud eos in uſu fuerunt: (quare, qui cum illis loqvi & eos rectè informare cupit, ejusmodi germanismos vitet, neceſſe eſt, & purè Oeſthonicè cum illis loquatur; ut, quæ jubeat doceátve, percipere & intelligere queant:) Nihilominus, quia Oeſthones plurima vocabula á Germanis acceperunt, quæ ante apud eos in uſu non fuerunt, ideoq; nec Oeſthonico idiomate nominare ea potuerunt, in uſum ſuum translata adhuc retinent, & uſurpant;
ut ſunt ſequentia:

26/

Dictionary excerpt 229.1: Göseken 1660, 86

offers c. 14000 and its second ed. c. 21000 Estonian words.

In the early 19th century a limited secularization of the Estonian literature started and some native Estonian authors appeared. The best expert of Estonian of that period was O. W. Masing who also was active in coining new words. For more than thirty years he worked on his large Estonian-German and German-Estonian dictionary whose manuscript, however, was lost.

The need for a real comprehensive Estonian-German dictionary was finally satisfied by Wiedemann 1869. The author was a linguist, botanist, and jurist in one person who was eager to cover all varieties of Estonian. The first edition of his dictionary offered c. 50000 headwords, the second, edited by J. Hurt, c. 60000 (among them 18000 compounds). Actually, up to the present time this work has not been superseded.

The last quarter of the 19th century was characterized both by increased Estonian national activities and by Russian administrative efforts at Russification. In any case, a number of Estonian-Russian and Russian-Estonian dictionaries appeared on the market and this process continued in the early 20th century. Probably the best such dictionary was J. Jurkatam's (1904, 1913) which offered 45000 Russian words with adequate but at times clumsy Estonian comments. The first German-Estonian dictionary (with about 35000 German words) by J. Ploompuu appeared in 1902. The first Finnish-Estonian dictionary (30000 words) was published by M. Neumann in 1911 and the first Estonian-Finnish one (over 20000 words) by L. Kettunen in 1917.

Two energetic persons, Dr. K. A. Hermann and J. Muide, tried their luck at assembling an encyclopedic dictionary in Estonian. Since neither time nor the authors themselves were ripe for such an undertaking, Hermann (1900, 1906) only could reach from **A** to **Bras** and Muide (1908/1909) with his shorter work from **A** to **Def.** But Hermann was a prolific puristic neologist of whose c. 1200 proposals c. 140 have survived (mainly grammatical terms). Since there was a burning need for Estonian terminological dictionaries, five of such were published still under the last czar's rule, mostly by the Language Commission of the Estonian Literary Society. The first of them was a glossary of mathematics (1909/1917/1922) which offered 1300 terms, followed by a glossary of geography (1910/1911) with 750 terms. In 1914 a relatively large (149 pages) medical glossary, offering 3000 medical and related terms, appeared. But in 1914 also two competing chemistry dictionaries were published, one in Tartu and the other in Petrograd (later Leningrad), the former offering 647 and the latter 1136 terms. Understandably enough, this created considerable confusion. On the contrary, a harmonious achievement was the normative dictionary Tammemägi 1918, with 20000 entries, much needed not only in view of the dialect diversity of Estonian.

2. 1919—1940

This was the period of the Estonian independence during which, first of all, the work on terminological dictionaries continued, mainly under the leadership of J. V. Veski (1873—1968) who participated in the compiling of more than thirty such glossaries. He claimed having coined more than 180000 words during his lifetime. Veski was a conservative neologist, preferably operating with stems and suffixes already existing in the lan-

Dictionary excerpt 229.2: Göseken 1660, 87

guage. In 1925 he began publishing a normative dictionary of Estonian in three volumes, the third volume being completed by E. Muuk. This work offers c. 120000 entries, among them numerous derivatives. For everyday use the small normative dictionary Muuk 1947 (1933) served the purpose. Veski's counterpart in coining neologisms was Johannes Aavik (1880—1973) who mostly strove for the beauty of sound and therefore could not care much for the actual origin of the proposed neologisms. During the independence larger bilingual dictionaries with these source languages were published: Finnish (J. Mägiste 1931), English (J. Silvet 1939), German (G. Tuksam, E. Muuk 1939), and Swedish (P. Wieselgren, P. Ariste, G. Suits 1940). Much smaller were the dictionaries with Estonian first, like M. Wrangell's Estonian-French and two Estonian-German dictionaries (by A. Graf and E. Sell). May it be added that an Estonian encyclopedic dictionary in eight volumes was published in 1932—1937.

3. After 1944

During the Second World War nothing new could be produced. After the war lexicographic activities were resumed both abroad, where several Estonian linguists had emigrated, and in the old homeland under the Soviet rule.

In the emigration three large dictionaries have been published: an Estonian thesaurus, Saareste 1958/1968, an Estonian etymological dictionary (first draft), Mägiste 1982, and an Estonian-English dictionary, Saagpakk 1982. The rest are reprinted and/or reedited Swedish and English dictionaries and a small Estonian etymological vocabulary, Raun 1982. Under the Soviet rule a very important task was to revise the Veski 1925/1937 normative dictionary. This was achieved by Nurm 1960 which contains c. 105000 words. The second edition of the same dictionary — Kull/Raiet 1976 — offers 115000 words, the additions consisting of special terms, colloquialisms, and derivative neologisms. Silvet 1965 is a handy Estonian-English dictionary of 30000 words. The first large Russian-Estonian dictionary was started in 1940 by P. Arumaa and B. Pravdin, and completely published by the latter and J. V. Veski in 1947. A comparable large German-Estonian by E. Kibbermann, S. Kirotar, and P. Koppel appeared in 1975. Smaller dictionaries of various languages and numerous terminological glossaries complete the list. Brochures explaining neologisms are continuously published. Pall 1982/1989 is the first preliminary Estonian dialect dictionary. A Soviet Estonian encyclopedia in eight volumes and a supplement was published in 1968—1978.

The theory of lexicography has only been touched upon in some reviews of larger bilingual dictionaries and in Saareste 1958/1963.

4. Livonian

Livonian, a close relative of Estonian, is still spoken by 17 persons in present-day (May 1990) Latvia. There are two scholarly dictionaries of Livonian: Sjögren/Wiedemann 1861 and Kettunen 1938, the latter also offering etymologies.

5. Selected Bibliography

5.1. Dictionaries

Göseken 1660 = Henricus Göseken: Manuductio ad Linguam Oesthonicam. Reval 1660 [547 p.].

Gutslaff 1648 = Johannes Gutslaff: Observationes Grammaticae circa linguam Esthonicam. Dorpat 1648 [XIV, 127 p.].

Hupel 1780 = A. W. Hupel: Ehstnische Sprachlehre für beide Hauptdialekte, den revalschen und den dörptschen; nebst einem vollständigen Wörterbuch. Riga.Leipzig 1780 [XIV, 539 p., 2nd ed. 1818].

Kettunen 1938 = Lauri Kettunen: Livisches Wörterbuch mit grammatischer Einleitung. Helsinki 1938 [LXXII, 648 p.].

Kull/Raiet 1976 = R. Kull/E. Raiet: Õigekeelsussõnaraamat. Tallinn 1976 [928 p.; 2nd ed. 1978, 3rd ed. 1980, 4th ed. 1984].

Mägiste 1982 = Julius Mägiste: Estnisches etymologisches Wörterbuch I—XII. Helsinki 1982 [LXXVI, 4106 p.].

Muuk 1947 (1933) = Elmar Muuk: Väike õigekeelsus-sõnaraamat. 9th ed. Stockholm 1947 [458 p.; 1st ed. 1933].

Nurm 1960 = E. Nurm/E. Raiet/M. Kindlam: Õigekeelsuse sõnaraamat. Tallinn 1960 [872 p.].

Pall 1982/1989 = Valdek Pall, editor: Väike murdesõnastik I/II. Tallinn 1982/1989 [503, 783 p.].

Raun 1982 = Alo Raun: Eesti keele etümoloogiline teatmik. Rooma.Toronto 1982 [XV, 222 p.].

Saagpakk 1982 = Paul Saagpakk: Estonian-English Dictionary. New Haven.London 1982 [CXI, 1180 p.].

Saareste 1958/1963 = Andrus Saareste: Eesti keele mõisteline sõnaraamat I/IV. Stockholm 1958/1959/1962/1963 [XV p., 1320, 1330, 1316, 964 columns].

Silvet 1965 = J. Silvet: Eesti-inglise sõnaraamat. Tallinn 1965 [509 p.; 2nd ed. 1980].

Sjögren/Wiedemann 1861 = Joh. Andreas Sjögren's Livisch-deutsches und deutsch-livisches Wörterbuch. Im Auftrage der Kaiserlichen Akademie bearbeitet von Ferdinand Johann Wiedemann. St. Petersburg 1861 [398 p.].

Stahl 1637 = Henricus Stahl: Anführung zu der Esthnischen Sprach. Revall 1637 [XIV, 136 p.].

Tammemägi 1918 = J. Tammemägi et al.: Eesti keele õigekirjutuse-sõnaraamat. Tartu 1918 [149 p.].

Thor Helle 1732 = Anton Thor Helle: Kurzgefaßte Anweisung zur Ehstnischen Sprache. Halle 1732 [XLII, 419 p.].

Veski 1925/1937 = Johannes Voldemar Veski: Eesti õigekeelsuse-sõnaraamat I/III. Tartu 1925/1930/1937 [1720 p.].

Wiedemann 1869 = Ferdinand Johann Wiedemann: Ehstnisch-deutsches Wörterbuch. St. Petersburg 1869 [VIII p., 1672 columns, CLVIII p.; 2nd. ed. 1893].

Note. In modern Estonian dictionaries the diacritic vowels õ, ä, ö, and ü are placed between w and x.

5.2. Other Publications

A. Kask: Ülevaade eesti leksikograafiast 1917. aastani. Keele ja Kirjanduse Instituudi uurimused I 140—169. Tallinn 1956.

J. Tuldava: Razvitie leksiki estonskogo jazyka po dannym slovarej XVII—XX vv. Tartu Riikliku Ülikooli Toimetised 684 115—129. Tartu 1984.

Alo Raun, Indiana University, Bloomington, Indiana (USA)

230. Lexicography of the Uralic Languages V: Other Uralic Languages

1. Introductory
2. Word Lists
3. Fieldwork and Corpus-Based Dictionaries
4. (Semi-)Normative Dictionaries
5. Selected Bibliography

1. Introductory

Apart from Hungarian, Finnic, and Lapp, the Uralic language family today comprises ten languages, all spoken in the Soviet Union. Listed roughly from west to east, these are (older designations, and approximate number of native speakers in thousands, are given in brackets): Mordva (Mordvinian, both Erźa and Mokša, 980), southwest and southeast of Kazan, but also widely scattered to the south and east of the Mordvinian ASSR; Mari (Cheremis, 550), centered between the Vetluga and Vyatka rivers; Udmurt (Votyak, 580), chiefly in the Votyak ASSR (between the Vyatka and Kama); Komi (Zyrian, 400), most of whose speakers live in the vast (415,000 km^2) Zyrian ASSR (a southern group of dialects is classified separately as *permjackiĭ* by Soviet scholars, and a literary norm is evolving: cf. Batalova/Krivoščekova-Gantman 1985); Mansi (Vogul, 4) and Khanty (Ostyak, 14), spoken along the lower Obj and its tributaries; Nenets (Yurak, 24), most of whose speakers live north of the Arctic Circle from the Kanin peninsula to the Yenisei; Enets (Yenisei-Samoyed, .4), mouth of the Yenisei; Nganasan (Tavgi, .9), Taimyr peninsula; and Selkup (Ostyak-Samoyed, 2), chiefly along the Taz and Turukhan rivers. Other Samoyedic groups (e. g. Karagass, Taigi, Mator) had already been assimilated to non-Uralic groups by the first half of the 19th century, with one exception: Kamassian. Fieldwork in this now extinct language conducted just before World War I has secured a vital lexicographic source (Donner/Joki 1944).

Lexicographic sources for these languages may be classified into three broad categories: word lists; corpus and/or fieldwork dictionaries; normative and seminormative dictionaries intended to reflect or nurture nascent literary standard languages. These three types are exemplified at 2., 3., and 4. below; here we offer a general characterization. — Semantically, most of these dictionaries are weak. Most are bi- or multilingual; many present little more than glosses, e. g. Savvaitov 1850, Koljadenkov/Cyganov 1949. In compensation, some are extensive, e. g. Wiedemann 1880 (20,000 entries according to Fokos-Fuchs 1959,15 note), Batalova/Krivoščekova-Gantman 1985 (ca. 27,000 entries). Sebeok/Zips 1961 compensates with a high level of organization and perspicuity. Note also Janhunen 1977 and Honti 1982, which aim at exhaustiveness (the target lexica in these latter two cases are common Samoyedic and Obugrian [Mansi + Khanty], respectively). — Many suffer from phonetic overdifferentiation or phonological underdifferentiation. Perhaps the most egregious examples of the former are Karjalainen/Toivonen 1948 and Lehtisalo 1956; work with these sources would be much more difficult were it not for their German indexes. Phonological underdifferentiation is usually the result of inadequate Roman (in the 1930's) or Cyrillic orthographies, in the dictionaries themselves or in their sources, e. g. Potapkin/Imjarekov 1949, Erdélyi 1970, but also occasionally stems from incorrect analysis, e. g. Juhász/Erdélyi 1961 (marking of hissing vs. hushing, palatalization, cf. Keresztes 1986,22). — Probably the most pervasive and characteristic challenge facing lexicographers of Uralic languages is that these languages, although widely thought of as "agglutinating", in fact show a considerable amount of phonologically unpredictable allomorphy. This challenge is often shirked, e. g. Vakhrušev 1983, which does not indicate whether a given noun takes -*e*- or -*y*- in its singular possessive forms, or Munkácsi/Kálmán 1986, which does not give a uniform indication of the infinitival suffix variant selected by verbs (-*aŋkwe* vs. -*uŋkwe*).

2. Word Lists

The earliest lexicographic sources are word lists compiled in the early 18th century by English merchants (Richard James and Peter Mundy), a Dutch diplomat (Nicolaes Witsen) and a Swedish officer taken prisoner after the Battle of Poltava (Philip Johann von Strahlenberg); see Mikola 1975 and Hajdú/Domokos 1987, 410—411. Further material, e. g. Pallas 1786—9, was furnished by participants in the Orenburg expedition (1768—72). Exceptionally plenteous is the material assembled by the Göttingen-trained Bishop of Nižegorod, Demetrius Semenov-Rudnev Damaskin (1785), which according to Keresztes 1986,18 contains some 11,000 items; cf. also Feoktistov 1971.

3. Fieldwork and Corpus-Based Dictionaries

The first linguistically sophisticated compiler of Uralic lexicographic matter was Mathias Alexander Castrén (Castrén/Schiefner 1855, Castrén/Lehtisalo 1960). After Castrén, the pace of fieldwork gradually quickened, to peak around the turn of the century. Few dictionaries presenting this material appeared during their collector's lifetime, however, and the lag between closing year of fieldwork and publication-date is frequently stunning, e. g. 40 (Wichmann/Uotila 1942), 42 (Lehtisalo 1956), 47 (Karjalainen/Toivonen 1948), even 93 (Wichmann/Uotila/Korhonen 1987) and 97 years (Munkácsi/Kálmán 1986). These are all large dictionaries, but the delay in their publication does not reflect a linguistic coming of age. — Yet two dictionaries of this magnitude manage to present complex data in a uniform and accessible way. The first to appear was Fokos-Fuchs 1959, which was published in the compiler's 75th year (fieldwork took place just before and during World War I). On page 959 of this work, we read that in the Udora dialect *śir* means 'grösserer, grosser Hecht', and a footnote adds that, also in Udora, a small pike is *kaneĭ*, while a medium-sized pike ('bis zu 1 Pfund Gewicht') is *žuń*. — But the most massive dictionary is the as yet only half-published Steinitz 1966 —. This work is a model of thoroughness (internal and external references; etymologies; folkloristic variants and parallel-words) and clarity, both of transcription and typography. Based on fieldwork conducted between the wars but also incorporating data from previous Khanty dictionaries, its publication has been overseen by Steinitz' students since his death in 1967. — Among other dictionaries of this type which merit special notice are Munkácsi 1896, for its detailed definitions (in Hungarian and German), and Wichmann/Uotila 1942, which is cross-referenced for synonyms and collocations, and can be quite circumstantial in its treatment of cultural data (e. g., s. v. *pyž* there is the gloss 'Boot', followed by an 80-word description of the Komi boat). Finally, mention should be made of Tereškin 1982, compiled by a native speaker from his (1950's) fieldwork.

4. (Semi-)Normative Dictionaries

The dictionaries discussed above at 3. are addressed to a highly specialized public. In the young Soviet Union, however, particularly in the 1930's, there was a fresh surge in the writing of grammars and dictionaries intended for native speakers. For example, Vakhrušev 1983,6;12 reports eight Udmurt lexicographic publications between the years 1924—1939, all with practical applications, including orthographic, elementary school, and synonym dictionaries, and even an aid

(1926) to the reading of Udmurt newspaper articles (the first Udmurt newspaper dates from 1913 [Haarmann 1974,189]). — Asylbaev/Basil'ev/Rybakova 1956, despite its title, is more than a Mari-Russian dictionary. It is tri-dialectal (with normative weighting: peripheral [Hill, Eastern] dialect forms refer to core [Meadow] entries, but not vice versa). Furthermore, grammatical apparatus, semantic subdivisions within articles, and definitions of cultifacts unique to Mari subgroups (e. g. *šarpàn* 695) are in Russian, but new words acquired from or via Russian (e. g. *putëvka* 473, *kalorimetr* 173) are defined in (Meadow) Mari. — Normative in a similarly liberated way is Sakharova/Kosnyreva/Sel'kov 1985. This orthographic dictionary is twice the size of its predecessor (Sakharova 1959 [1976]) because it includes archaisms and 'dialect words which have entered the literary language' (p. 3); unfortunately, such new items are not identified in the body of the dictionary.

5. Selected Bibliography

5.1. Dictionaries

Asylbaev/Basil'ev/Rybakova 1956 = A. A. Asylbaev/V. M. Basil'ev/P. G. Rybakova et al.: Marijsko-russkij slovar'. Moskva 1956 [863 p., including 68-page grammatical sketch by A. Savatkova and Z. Učaev].

Batalova/Krivoščekova-Gantman 1985 = R. M. Batalova/A. S. Krivoščekova-Gantman: Komipermjackij-russkij slovar'. Moskva 1985 [621 p., including grammatical sketch by A. S. Krivoščekova-Gantman pp. 596—621; ca. 27,000 entries].

Castrén/Lehtisalo 1960 = Mathias Alexander Castrén: Samojedische Sprachmaterialien. Hg. von Toivo Vilho Lehtisalo. Helsinki 1960 [462 p.; vol. 122 of Mémoires de la Société Finno-Ougrienne].

Castrén/Schiefner 1855 = Mathias Alexander Castrén: Wörterverzeichnisse aus den samojedischen Sprachen. Bearb. von Anton Schiefner. St. Petersburg 1855 [XXXIV, 404 p.].

Donner/Joki 1944 = Kai Donner: Kamassisches Wörterbuch nebst Sprachproben und Hauptzügen der Grammatik. Bearb. und hg. von Aulis J. Joki. Helsinki 1944 [LI, 216 p.; dictionary section p. 3—82; German index p. 200—215].

Erdélyi 1970 = István Erdélyi: Selkupisches Wörterverzeichnis. Tas-Dialekt. Bloomington. The Hague 1970 [316 p.; based on elementary school readers; articles arranged by grammatical forms; indexed].

Fokos-Fuchs 1959 = D. R. Fokos-Fuchs: Syrjänisches Wörterbuch. Budapest 1959 [1,564 p.; numerous dialectological, ethnographic, and methodological footnotes; indexed].

Hajdú/Pápai 1953 = Péter Hajdú: Pápai Károly szelkup szójegyzéke (Károly Pápais selkupisches Wörterverzeichnis). In: Nyelvtudományi közlemények 54. 1953, 141—184.

Janhunen 1977 = Juha Janhunen: Samojedischer Wortschatz. Gemeinsamojedische Etymologien. Helsinki 1977 [186 p.; landmark integration of common Samoyedic vocabulary; 650 reconstructed lemmata. Vol. 17 in the series Castrenianumin toimitteita].

Juhász/Erdélyi 1961 = Jenő Juhász: Moksamordvin szójegyzék. Ed. István Erdélyi. Budapest 1961 [262 p.; Hungarian index; ca. 15,000 entries].

Karjalainen/Toivonen 1948 = Kustaa Fredrik Karjalainen: Ostjakisches Wörterbuch. I—II. Hg. von Yrjö Heikki Toivonen. Helsinki 1948 (Lexica Societatis Fenno-Ugricae 10).

Katzschmann/Pusztay 1978 = Michael Katzschmann/János Pusztay: Jenissej-samojedisches (enzisches) Wörterverzeichnis. Hamburg 1978 (Lexica Societatis Fenno-Ugricae 5) [283 p.; entries numbered; indexed].

Koljadenkov/Cyganov 1948 = M. N. Koljadenkov/N. F. Cyganov: Russko-èrzjanskij slovar'. Moskva 1948 [413 p.; 25,000 entries].

Koljadenkov/Cyganov 1949 = M. N. Koljadenkov/N. F. Cyganov: Èrzjansko-russkij slovar'. Moskva 1949 [292 p.; 20-page grammatical sketch by M. N. Koljadenkov; 15,000 entries].

Kortt/Simčenko 1985 = I. R. Kortt/Ju. B. Simčenko: Wörterverzeichnis der nganasanischen Sprache. Berlin 1985.

Lehtisalo 1956 = Toivo Vilho Lehtisalo: Juraksamojedisches Wörterbuch. Helsinki 1956 (Lexica Societatis Fenno-Ugricae 13) [CIX, 601 p.; narrow phonetic transcription throughout; indexed].

Lytkin/Guljaev 1970 = V. I. Lytkin/E. S. Guljaev: Kratkij ètimologičeskij slovar' komi jazyka. Moskva 1970 [386 p.; introduction lists numbered Lautgesetze, to which articles refer; indexes. See Lytkin/Guljaev 1975].

Lytkin/Guljaev 1975 = V. I. Lytkin/E. S. Guljaev: Dopolnenija k kratkomu slovarju komi jazyka. Syktyvkar 1975 [Appeared as *priloženija* in Komi Filologija, trudy instituta jazyka, literatury i istorii, number 18; paginated separately, 1—45].

Munkácsi 1896 = Bernát Munkácsi: A voták nyelv szótára. Budapest 1896 [XVI, 836 p.; indicates -y- alternant of nominal stems; order of entries on articulatory basis; definitions in Hungarian and German].

Munkácsi/Kálmán 1986 = Bernát Munkácsi: Wogulisches Wörterbuch. Geordnet, bearb. und hg. von Béla Kálmán. Budapest 1986 [950 p.; separate German and Hungarian indexes (747—950)].

Paasonen/Donner 1926 = Heikki Paasonen: Ostjakisches Wörterbuch nach den Dialekten an der Konda und am Jugan. Zusammengestellt, neu transkribiert und hg. von Kai Donner. Helsinki 1926 (Lexica Societatis Fenno-Ugricae 2).

Paasonen/Siro 1948 = Heikki Paasonen: Osttscheremissisches Wörterbuch. Bearb. u. hg. von Paavo Siro (Lexica Societatis Fenno-Ugricae 11).

Pallas 1786—9 = Peter Simon Pallas: Linguarum totius orbis vocabularia comparativa ... I—II. St. Petersburg 1786—9 [Reissued Hamburg 1977].

Potapkin/Imjarekov 1949 = S. G. Potapkin/A. K. Imjarekov: Mokšansko-russkij slovar'. Moskva 1949.

Ravila 1959 = Paavo Ravila: Ersjamordwinisches Wörterverzeichnis aus Malyj Tolkaj. Helsinki 1959 [= Journal de la Société Finno-Ougrienne 61/3].

Rédei 1986—8 = Károly Rédei: Uralisches etymologisches Wörterbuch. Unter Mitarbeit von Marianne Bakró-Nagy, Sándor Csúcs, István Erdélyi et al. Budapest 1986—8 [State of the art. For a conservative control cf. Janhunen 1982 below at 5.2.].

Rogov 1869 = N. Rogov: Permjacko-russkij i russko-permjackij slovar'. St. Petersburg 1869.

Sakharova 1976 = M. A. Sakharova: Komi orfografičeskój slovar'. Syktyvkar 1976 [2nd ed.; 215 p. including orthoëpic supplement by N. N. Sel'kov (206—215); ca. 10,500 words and collocations. First ed. 1959].

Sakharova/Kosnyreva/Sel'kov 1985 = M. A. Sakharova/R. I. Kosnyreva/N. N. Sel'kov: Komi orfografičeskój slovar'. Syktyvkar 1985 [414 p.; ca. 23,000 words and collocations].

Savvaitov 1850 = P. I. Savvaitov: Zyrjansko-russkij i russko-zyrjanskój slovar'. St. Petersburg 1850.

Sebeok/Zips 1961 = Th. A. Sebeok/V. J. Zips: Concordance and Thesaurus of Cheremis Poetic Language. 's-Gravenhage 1961.

Steinitz 1966 = Wolfgang Steinitz: Dialektologisches und etymologisches Wörterbuch der ostjakischen Sprache. Unter Mitarbeit von Lieselotte Hartung, Gert Sauer und Brigitte Schulze. Berlin 1966 — [1,504 p. as of 12th fascicle (1988)].

Tereškin 1982 = N. I. Tereškin: Slovar' vostočnokhantyjskikh dialektov. Leningrad 1982 [540 p.; quasiphonemic Roman transcription; indicates stem-vowel ablaut].

Tereščenko 1965 = N. M. Tereščenko: Neneckorusskij slovar'. Moskva 1965 [942 p.; 80-page grammatical sketch].

Timušev/Kolegova 1961 = D. A. Timušev/M. A. Kolegova: Komi-russkij slovar'. Moskva 1961 [923 p.; with grammatical sketch by V. I. Lytkin and D. A. Timušev 837—923; based on Syktyvkar (literary) norm, but includes many dialect forms (identified solely as "dial.")].

Vakhrušev 1983 = V. M. Vakhrušev: Udmurtskorusskij slovar'. Moskva 1983 [591 p.; ca. 35,000 entries. Grammatical sketch by V. I. Alatyrev, 540—559].

Wichmann/Uotila 1942 = Yrjö Wichmann: Syrjänischer Wortschatz. Bearb. u. hg. von T. E. Uotila. Helsinki 1942 [XVI, 487 p.; gives Udmurt pendants; indexed].

Wichmann/Uotila/Korhonen 1987 = Yrjö Wichmann: Wotjakischer Wortschatz. Bearb. von T. E. Uotila u. Mikko Korhonen; hg. von Mikko Korhonen. Helsinki 1987 (Lexica Societatis Fenno-Ugricae 21) [XXIII, 421 p.; gives Komi pendants].

Wiedemann 1880 = F. J. Wiedemann: Syrjänischdeutsches Wörterbuch nebst einem wotjakischdeutschen und einem deutschen Register. St. Petersburg 1880.

5.2. Other Publications

Comrie 1981 = Bernard Comrie: The languages of the Soviet Union. Cambridge 1981.

Décsy 1965 = Gyula Décsy: Einführung in die finnisch-ugrische Sprachwissenschaft. Wiesbaden 1965.

Feoktistov 1971 = A. P. Feoktistov: Russko-mordovskij slovar'. Moskva 1971 [Russian-Mordva section of Damaskin Ms.; cf. 2.].

Haarmann 1974 = Harald Haarmann: Die finnisch-ugrischen Sprachen. Soziologische und politische Aspekte ihrer Entwicklung. Unter Mitarbeit von Anna-Liisa Värri Haarmann. Hamburg 1974 [vol. 1 in the series Fenno-Ugrica].

Hajdú/Domokos 1987 = Péter Hajdú/Péter Domokos: Die uralischen Sprachen und Literaturen. Budapest 1987.

Honti 1982 = László Honti: Geschichte des obugrischen Vokalismus der ersten Silbe. Budapest 1982 [vol. 6 in the series Bibliotheca uralica. Pages 123—206 give a synoptic view of 829 Khanty/Mansi etymologies with abundant documentation].

Honti/Zaicz 1970 = László Honti/Gábor Zaicz: Jurák a tergo toldalékár. Rückläufiges jurakisches Suffixverzeichnis. In: Nyelvtudományi közlemények 72. 1970, 363—398 [cf. section 1. above].

Janhunen 1982 = Juha Janhunen: Uralilaisen kantakielen sanastosta. In: Journal de la Société Finno-Ougrienne 77:9. 1982, 272—274 [Proto-Uralic lexical core; German glosses].

Keresztes 1986 = László Keresztes: Geschichte des mordwinischen Konsonantismus II. Etymologisches Belegmaterial. Szeged 1986 [557 entries with extensive utilization of early compilations; indexes of cognates and of German glosses].

Mikola 1975 = Tibor Mikola: N. Witsens Berichte über die uralischen Völker. Szeged 1975 (Studia Uralo-altaica 7).

Schlachter/Ganschow 1983 = Wolfgang Schlachter/Gerhard Ganschow: Bibliographie der uralischen Sprachwissenschaft 1830—1970. Band II. Finnisch-Permisch/Obugrisch/Samojedisch. München 1983.

Sinor 1988 = Denis Sinor (ed.): The Uralic Languages: Description, History and Foreign Influences. Leiden. New York. København. Köln 1988 (Handbuch der Orientalistik, achte Abteilung, 1).

Daniel Abondolo, London (Great Britain)

231. Die Lexikographie der Turksprachen I: Osmanisch-Türkisch

1. Definition
2. Entwicklung
3. Gegenwärtiger Stand
4. Literatur (in Auswahl)

1. Definition

Unter „Türkisch" kann man die heute vor allem in der Türkei gesprochene Sprache oder die Gesamtheit der Sprachen aller Türkvölker verstehen. Zur Unterscheidung dieser beiden Begriffe verwendet die Sprachwissenschaft für die erstere Sprache zumeist den Terminus „Osmanisch-Türkisch", obwohl darunter auch die vor der Gründung des osmanischen Staates vom 11.—13. Jh. von den kleinasiatischen Türken gesprochene Sprache verstanden wird ebenso wie die der heutigen Türkischen Republik. Für die seit 1928 in Lateinschrift geschriebene moderne Form wird auch der Terminus „Türkeitürkisch" gebraucht. In der Türkei und neuerdings auch vielfach im westlichen Hochschulbetrieb wird das Osmanisch-Türkische in arabischer Schrift kurzweg als „Osmanisch" bezeichnet.

Eine bibliographische Übersicht über die osmanisch-türkische Lexikographie findet sich bei Deny (1959, 222—238). Zu älteren Wörterbüchern in Handschriftensammlungen siehe Babinger (1919), Majda (1976), Akyüz (1959, Bibliothèque Nationale), Çağatay (1961, Bodleian, British Library), Pamukciyan (1986, armenische Hss.). Es gibt auch Übersichtsartikel über die neugriechische (Chidiroglou 1975—77, 278—281) und über die sowjetische (Aganin 1978) Lexikographie des Osmanisch-Türkischen. Betrachtungen zur Problematik der türkischen Lexikographie bei Tietze (1962).

2. Entwicklung

2.1. Die Anfänge der osmanischen Lexikographie

Die osmanische Bildungstradition fußte auf der Kenntnis der klassischen islamischen Sprachen, d. h. neben dem Türkischen auf dem Arabischen und Persischen. Dem Schreibenden stand es frei, sich sämtlicher nominaler Lexeme (inklusive der Verbalnomina) dieser Sprachen auch im Osmanischen zu bedienen. Demgemäß gab es schon früh einen Bedarf an lexikalischen Hilfsmitteln.

Diese „Bildungswörterbücher", wie wir sie nennen können, zerfallen in zwei Gruppen.

2.1.1. Pädagogisch-mnemotechnische Wörterbücher (Reimwörterbücher)

Schulwörterbücher in Gedichtform, die arabische bzw. persische Vokabeln ihren türkischen Äquivalenten gegenüberstellten (wie etwa unser „Le bœuf der Ochs, la vache die Kuh, fermez la porte die Tür macht zu"), waren sehr beliebt. Sie konnten leicht auswendig gelernt werden. Außerdem dienten sie als Wörterbücher in beiden Richtungen gleichzeitig. Am bekanntesten waren Ferişteoğlu (15. Jh.) für den arabischen Wortschatz des Korans und für das Persische Şâhidî (1514—15). Auch ein bosnisch-türkisches Wörterbuch dieser Art gibt es (Üsküfî 17. Jh.; vergl. Smailović 1983). Noch im 18. und 19. Jh. wurden solche Reimwörterbücher für das Arabische (Vehbî 1805) und Persische (Vehbî 1798) und sogar für das Französische (Yûsuf Hâlis 1849—50) geschaffen.

2.1.2. Alphabetische Wörterbücher

Dem Gebildeten standen die großen, von arabischen oder persischen Gelehrten verfaßten Wörterbücher der klassischen islamischen Sprachen zur Verfügung. Manche wurden auch von osmanischen Gelehrten verfaßt (z. B. Muḥammad 1450). Obwohl kein Türkisch enthaltend, waren sie für den Gebildeten verwendbar. Außerdem entstanden türkische Übersetzungen. Z. B. das ca. 140 000 Lemmata enthaltende einsprachige arabische Wörterbuch des Ǧauharî (10. Jh.) wurde im 16. Jh. übersetzt und im 18. als erstes osmanisches Buch gedruckt (Vankuli 1728—29); ein anderes, noch umfangreicheres (Fîrûzâbâdî +1415) wurde in türkischer Übersetzung im 19. Jh. mehrmals aufgelegt (Âsım 1814—18). Beliebt war auch ein kürzeres, einfach alphabetisch (d. h. nicht wie die anderen unter Zusammenfassung der Wortwurzeln) angeordnetes arabisches Wörterbuch (Ahterî 1545). Unter den persisch-türkischen Wörterbüchern waren die wichtigsten Şuᶜûrî (1742) und Âsım (1799). Ein verdienstvolles modernes Werk derselben Tradition (Şükûn 1944) belegt jedes Lemma mit Zitaten aus der persischen Poesie. Das Bedürfnis nach Wörterbüchern in der umgekehrten Richtung war weniger entwickelt. Ein größeres solches stammt erst aus der ersten Hälfte des 18. Jhs.

(Mehmed Es'ad 1801—02). Es ist zwar nach den türkischen Lemmata angeordnet, aber sein Anliegen ist nicht die Kodifizierung des türkischen Wortschatzes, sondern der Zugang zu den klassischen Bildungssprachen. Bis in die Mitte des 19. Jhs. beschäftigte sich die osmanische Lexikographie fast ausschließlich mit den beiden Bildungssprachen und zeigte keinerlei Interesse an der Erfassung des eigenen Wortschatzes oder (wenn wir von dem unter 2.1.1. erwähnten Kuriosum des Bosnischen absehen) des Wortschatzes irgendeiner anderen Sprache mit Ausnahme des Tschagataischen (Vámbéry 1862), das während einer begrenzten Periode (16. Jh.) dank dem Auftreten sehr bedeutender tschagataischer Dichter den Status einer dritten osmanischen Bildungssprache angenommen hatte.

2.1.3. Fremdwörterlexika

Die Nachfolger der Bildungswörterbücher sind im 19. Jh. einerseits die zahlreichen sog. Galatât-Wörterbücher (z. B. Mehmed Hafîd 1806), orthoepisch-orthographische Lexika, die arabische oder persische, dem Türkischen angepaßte Lehnwörter mit ihrer ursprünglichen („korrekten") Form (oder Bedeutung) vergleichen; andererseits sind es die Fremdwörterlexika (wie Salâhî 1897—1906, Naci 1901), die ebenfalls auf das arabische und persische Wortmaterial eingestellt sind — im Gegensatz zu denen der neuesten Zeit, die ganz der internationalen Terminologie in ihrer französischen Ausprägung gewidmet sind (Özön 1962). In republikanischer Zeit hat das Französische die Rolle der Bildungssprache übernommen.

2.2. Die Anfänge der europäischen Lexikographie des Osmanisch-Türkischen

Die ersten abendländischen Wörterbücher waren für die mündliche Verständigung der Reisenden (Diplomaten, Kaufleute, Missionäre) gedacht, daher bringen sie das Türkische nur in lateinischer Transkription und überwiegend sind sie nur in der Richtung ins Türkische angelegt. Oft sind sie von einem Abriß der türkischen Grammatik begleitet. Solche oft recht primitive Verständigungswörterbücher hat es wahrscheinlich schon früher gegeben, wenngleich sie uns erst seit dem 17. Jh. bekannt sind (handschriftlich das älteste Ferraguto 1611), und dank dem Bedarf hat es sie auch später immer wieder gegeben (von türkischer Seite ist ihr Bedarf erst in unserer Zeit durch den Strom der Arbeitsemigranten fühlbar geworden, der die Entstehung solcher Behelfe besonders für das Deutsche, Holländische und Schwedische veranlaßt hat). Das älteste gedruckte türkische Wörterbuch, Megiser 1612, geht vom Lateinischen aus, enthält aber auch einen Index der türkischen Wörter (insgesamt etwa 1100). Verfaßt ist es von einem Gelehrten, der sein Interesse für Sprachen durch zahlreiche Publikationen bewiesen hat (Megiser 1592a, 1592b, 1593, 1603), in denen er manchmal auch türkisches Material verwendete. Selbst beherrschte er die Sprache kaum, muß also mit einem Informanten gearbeitet haben. Anders Molino (1641), der Dolmetscher der venezianischen Gesandtschaft in Konstantinopel war, oder der Neapolitaner Mascis (1677), der sich Dolmetscher des Großfürsten Cosimo III. von Toscana nennt. Ein nicht alphabetisches, sondern nach Sachgruppen geordnetes Wörterverzeichnis dieser Art ist das Dictionarium turco-latinum von 1668, veröffentlicht von Németh (1970).

Neben den reinen Verständigungswörterbüchern gab es bald auch schon von Orientalisten, oft von Lehrern oder Schülern an Lehranstalten für orientalische Sprachen (vor allem zur Ausbildung von Missionären, etwa in Rom) verfaßte Werke. In diesen wird auch die arabische Schrift gebraucht. So etwa verfaßte der französische Konsul in Ägypten, Übersetzer des Korans und anderer orientalischer Werke, Du Ryer, eine türkische Grammatik (Du Ryer 1630) und später ein (nur handschriftlich erhaltenes) türkisches Wörterbuch (Du Ryer 17. Jh.) mit den türkischen Wörtern in arabischer und Lateinschrift. Ebenso verfuhr ein Franziskanermissionär (Carradori 1635?) in Oberägypten, dessen türkisches Vocabularium (vielleicht deswegen?) ungedruckt blieb (die erste Seite siehe Zetterstéen 1907). Nur in arabischer Schrift werden die türkischen Wörter in dem italienisch-osmanischen Lexikon des Bernardo da Parigi (1665) vorgestellt, das offensichtlich für die Studenten der orientalischen Sprachen bestimmt war. Mehrere andere, teilweise schon recht umfangreiche Werke der Zeit wie William Seaman 1665—73 [569 S.], Antoine Galland 1672—73 [551 S.], Joseph Delacroix 1679 [470 S.], Jean Baptiste de Fiennes 1689 [1233 S.], Arcère 17. Jh. [2020 S.] sind ebenfalls nie im Druck erschienen. In manchen Fällen mag daran das Erscheinen des Thesaurus (Meninski 1680) schuld gewesen sein, des „orientalistischen Wörterbuchs" par excellence, das wir unter 2.3. behandeln wollen.

2.3. Das orientalistische Wörterbuch

Unter 2.2. wurden schon mehrere von Orientalisten verfaßte Wörterbücher des 17. Jhs. erwähnt, aber das eigentlich orientalistische beginnt erst mit der Vereinigung des unter 2.1.2. beschriebenen osmanischen Bildungswörterbuchs mit den unter 2.2. dargestellten abendländischen Unternehmungen. Durch die Aufnahme des Wortschatzes, den die Bildungstradition dem gebildeten Osmanen auferlegte, in das der Registrierung des türkischen Wortschatzes dienende zweisprachige Lexikon entstand ein Zwitterding, das die Realität der Umgangssprache mit dem Trugbild einer Idealkonzeption auf *einer* Ebene vorlegte (etwa wie ein mittelhochdeutsches Wörterbuch mit einem ganzen lateinischen Lexikon durchsetzt, oder ein frühneuhochdeutsches mit einem französischen). Das primum exemplum dieser Novität ist der monumentale Thesaurus Meninskis (1680).

Der Lothringer Franciscus à Mesgnien, später Meninski (Abrahamowicz 1975), in Rom bei den Jesuiten ausgebildet (wahrscheinlich auch schon in den orientalischen Sprachen), wirkte als Sprachlehrer des Französischen und Italienischen in Polen (wo er drei Grammatiken veröffentlicht: Meninski 1649a, 1649b, 1649c). 1653—56 weilt er als Dolmetscher des polnischen Gesandten in Konstantinopel, gleichzeitig bei guten Lehrern die türkische Sprache studierend (Sajkowski 1966). 1658—59 und 1659—60 als Gesandter des polnischen Königs wieder in der osmanischen Hauptstadt, tritt er 1662 in kaiserliche Dienste. Seitdem arbeitet er in Wien, wo er seinen erlernten und erlesenen osmanischen Wortschatz, ergänzt durch den arabischen nach Golius (1653) und den persischen nach Golius (1669), in seinem Hauptwerk (Meninski 1680 u. 1687) niederlegt.

Der Thesaurus (Meninski 1680), 4 starke Großquartbände, entspricht allen Anforderungen wissenschaftlicher Akribie. Auf eine knappe, aber alles Wichtige (z. B. Erklärung der Transkriptionszeichen, Abkürzungen, Quellenangaben) enthaltende Einleitung folgt das Lexicon (6508 Sp.) mit einem Appendix von weiteren 430 Spalten. Die einzelnen Eintragungen beginnen mit dem Stichwort in arabischer Schreibung und in lateinischer Transkription (mit Aussprachehilfen), Herkunftsangabe (z. B. a = arabisch), Wortklasse, etwaige grammatische Besonderheiten (z. B. unregelmäßige Pluralbildung), dann folgt die Bedeutung in — je nach Häufigkeit des Wortes — zwei bis fünf Sprachen: lateinisch, deutsch, italienisch, französisch, polnisch. Sodann Anwendungsbeispiele aus literarischen Texten (mit Angabe der Quelle), gebräuchliche Wortzusammensetzungen und Redensarten (alles in Originalschreibung, lateinischer Umschrift und Übersetzung), und zum Abschluß bei seltenen Vokabeln ein Hinweis auf das Lexikon, dem es entnommen ist. Bei wichtigen Lexemen kann so eine Eintragung 200 bis 300 Zeilen umfassen. Im ganzen dürfte der Thesaurus etwa 62 000 Lemmata enthalten. Verglichen etwa mit Megisers (1612) ca. 1 100 ist der Umfang des Thesaurus gigantisch. Von diesen 62 000 gehören nach einer groben Berechnung 28 % der Umgangssprache (Türkisch und eingebürgerte Lehnwörter) und 72 % dem gelehrten Bildungswortschatz an. Dieses Verhältnis illustriert den Charakter des „orientalistischen" Wörterbuches.

Meninski selbst veröffentlichte später noch einen Ergänzungsband (Meninski 1687), der unter anderem auch ein lateinisch-osmanisches Wörterbuch enthielt. Im 18. Jh. wurde der Thesaurus von Bernhard von Jenisch überarbeitet und noch einmal herausgegeben (Meninski 1780). Dies ist auch heute noch die in der Wissenschaft verwendete Standardausgabe. Für praktische Zwecke entstanden im 18. Jh. einige Handwörterbücher — der Thesaurus war teuer und wog 17,7 kg! — wie Clodius (1730), Preindl (1787), Viguier (1790), oft in Verbindung mit Grammatiken, größtenteils Kompilationen, die nichts Neues brachten. Auch die großen orientalistischen Wörterbücher des 19. und 20. Jhs. fußen auf dem Thesaurus (siehe unter 2.5., 2.6.).

اغارمق *agharmak* Albefcere, canefcere, *ut* صاچ صغال اغرمق *fač fakal agharmak*. Crines, barbam albefcere, canefcere. Weiß vnd graw werden/ grawen/ faſt alten. *Imbianchire, imbianchirſi, biancheggiare, incanutire.* Blanchir, devenir blanc, & gris, ou chenu, grifonner. Białym y śiwym ſtać śie/ bieleie / śiwieie. Item صباح اغارمق *ſæbāh agharmak*. Diefcere, diem albefcere. Tag anbrechen. *Spuntar il giorno, l' alba.* Se faire iour, poindre. Świtać / zorza pokazać śie/ dnieie. Sic صباح اغاردوغى كبى *ſæbāh aghardughy gibi*. Statim atque diefcere cœpit, ipſo diluculo. So bald der Tag anbricht/ vmb die Morgen-Röthe. *Nello ſpuntar del giorno, all' alba.* A l'aube duiour. Na świtániu/ iak śie zorza pokaza/albo pokázały.

Textbeispiel 231.1: Artikel aus Meninski 1680

2.4. Minderheiten und Staatssprache

Das wirtschaftliche und politische Erstarken der Minderheiten seit dem 18. Jh. hatte Auswirkungen auf die osmanische Lexikographie, ausgelöst durch eine wesentliche Verbesserung des nationalen Schulwesens (besonders der Griechen und Armenier) und durch die Entstehung einer neuen (nicht klerikalen) Intelligenz im öffentlichen Leben, die einer guten Beherrschung der Staatssprache bedurfte. Die vorhandenen Wörterbücher eigneten sich nicht für die Schulen, ein neuer Typ mußte geschaffen werden. Typisch ist etwa Agioreitês (1804), ein äußerst primitives Vokabular zur mündlichen (die türkischen Wörter werden nur in griechischer Schrift vorgestellt) Einführung in die Staatssprache oder ins Griechische für turkophone (sog. Karamanli-)Griechen. Dem letzteren Zweck dient auch Alexandridês (1812), wo schon das Titelblatt vermerkt, das Buch sei „zum Nutzen der in Anatolien lebenden Christen" geschrieben. Eine Liste von 22 griech.-türk. oder türk.-griech. gedruckten Wb. findet sich bei Chidiroglu (1978, 278—280). Das vollständigste und beste ist Chlôros (1899). Auch die Armenier haben auf dem Gebiet der osmanischen Lexikographie Wichtiges geleistet. Der in Wien tätige Dolmetscher und Lehrer des Türkischen Artin Hindoglu veröffentlichte Wörterbücher (Hindoglu 1831 u. 1838) für Studenten der orientalischen Sprachen. Sie vermitteln eine modernere Sprachstufe als die alten Behelfe. Das 19. Jahrhundert war eine Zeit, in der viel westliches Kulturgut in die osmanische Welt und Sprache eindrang. Die beiden Armenier Tinghir und Sinapian (1891—92) bemühten sich, die ausländische Fachterminologie in eine osmanische umzuprägen (zumeist auf Grund der alten Bildungssprachen). Auch noch im 20. Jahrhundert haben Armenier wichtige Beiträge zur osmanischen Lexikographie geliefert (Kelekian 1911, Kerestedjian 1912, Devedjian 1926, Bedevian 1936). Der Albaner Şemseddin Sami Fraschery hat durch seine zweisprachigen Wörterbücher (Fraschery 1883a und b), besonders aber durch das einsprachige (1899—1900), das als das Standardlexikon des modernen Osmanischen angesehen werden kann, dem einheimischen Kulturleben den größten Dienst geleistet. So waren es gerade die Minderheiten, die durch ihre profunde Vertrautheit mit der Staatssprache in der Lexikographie eine moderne, lebensnahe, sachliche Richtung durchsetzten.

2.5. Diplomatie und Handel

Die fortschreitende Integration des Osmanischen Reiches in das politische und ökonomische System der europäischen Staaten erweiterte den Bereich der Kommunikationskanäle besonders auf den Gebieten der Diplomatie und des Handels, woraus sich auch für die Lexikographie neue Bedürfnisse und neue Ausrichtungen ergeben mußten. Die vorhandenen älteren Wörterbücher, sowohl die ganz allgemein der Verständigung dienenden als auch die „orientalistischen" genügten für diese Zwecke nicht. Zwar gab es jetzt eine Neufassung des Thesaurus in stark verkürzter, handlicher Form (Kieffer/Bianchi 1835—37), aber darin gab es kaum Fortschritte in Richtung auf das, was jetzt gebraucht wurde, obgleich schon das Titelblatt eine solche Zielsetzung ankündigt. Auch das bald danach erschienene französisch-osmanische Wörterbuch des Dolmetschers der kaiserlich russischen Botschaft in Konstantinopel (Handjéri 1840—41), das ankündigt, es sei „fait pour guider les traducteurs dans leurs travaux", ist noch ganz im Geiste des orientalistischen Wörterbuchs verfaßt (der Autor liebt den traditionellen barocken Stil der diplomatischen Korrespondenz); kein Wunder, daß sein Werk bei Orientalisten bis heute beliebt ist. Die Praktiker der Diplomatie hingegen griffen längst nach kompakteren Fachwörterbüchern wie dem von Schlechta-Wssehrd (1870) oder nach den moderneren französischen Wörterbüchern (Barbier de Meynard 1881—86, Fraschery 1883a u. b). Französisch war die Weltsprache des 19. Jahrhunderts, die Sprache der Diplomatie und des Handels, und gleichzeitig der Weg, über den modernes europäisches Gedankengut die osmanischen Länder erreichte. Englisch und Deutsch hatten dagegen weniger praktische als akademische Bedeutung: ihre lexikographischen Bemühungen konnten daher leichter die orientalistische Tradition fortsetzen.

2.6. Das moderne orientalistische Wörterbuch

Wer die osmanische Literatur verstehen will, muß ein orientalistisches Wörterbuch benützen. Wenn ihm der Thesaurus (Meninski 1680 oder 1780) nicht zur Verfügung steht, greift er im deutschen oder französischen Sprachbereich nach Zenker (1866), im englischen nach Redhouse (1890). James W. Redhouse, der schon als 14jähriger nach Istanbul gekommen war und jahrzehntelang in türkischen Diensten stand (vgl. Findley 1980), schuf, nach bescheideneren Anfängen (Redhouse 1856), ein großangelegtes Lexikon (Redhouse 1890), das den Wortschatz des Thesaurus mit dem Wortschatz seiner eigenen Zeit zu vereinigen suchte. Ganz in seinem Geiste wurde es ein Dreivierteljahrhundert später von einem Team auf den jüngsten Stand gebracht (Redhouse 1968). Während aber die älteren Ausgaben von der arabischen Schreibung ausgingen, geht in der neuen die Lateinschreibung voran und die arabischen Schreibungen werden nur zusätzlich angeführt.

2.7. Das nationale türkische Wörterbuch

In der 2. Hälfte des 19. und im 1. Viertel des 20. Jahrhunderts erringen viele Nationalitäten des Osmanischen Reiches ihre Unabhängigkeit. Parallel mit dieser Entwicklung wird auch ein türkisches Nationalbewußtsein geboren. Man beginnt sich für das türkische Element in der osmanischen Sprache, also für die eigene Kulturtradition stärker zu interessieren. Ein Aufstand gegen das alte osmanische Bildungsideal hat begonnen. In der Lexikographie meldet sich die neue Richtung mit einem einsprachigen Wörterbuch (Ahmed Vefik 1876) an, das in einem Band nur die türkischen Elemente mit großer Ausführlichkeit behandelt, die arabischen und persischen aber stark reduziert in einen zweiten Band verbannt. Die mit diesem Werk einsetzende neue Richtung setzte sich alsbald durch. Ihre Wirkung läßt sich in den bald darauf erschienenen zweisprachigen (Barbier de Meynard 1881—86, Fraschery 1883 a u. b) und einsprachigen (Fraschery 1899—1900) Wb. erkennen. Im Ergebnis hat sich das osmanische Wörterbuch der letzten osmanischen Zeit dem in Europa geläufigen Wörterbuchkonzept angepaßt. Die türkische Republik übernahm diese Richtung und führte sie weiter. Durch den Übergang zur Lateinschrift 1928 war der Bruch mit der osmanischen Kultur- und Bildungstradition ein vollständiger geworden. Eine radikale puristische Bewegung, zeitweise von der Regierung unterstützt, trat für die Ersetzung der Fremdelemente durch vergessenes türkisches Sprachgut oder von türkischen Stämmen gebildete Neologismen ein. Ein Wörterbuch, das den arabischen und persischen Lehnwörtern Entsprechungen gegenüberstellte, die aus den anatolischen Dialekten und aus anderen (nicht-osmanischen) Turksprachen geschöpft waren (Tarama dergisi 1934), sollte diesem Zweck dienen. Ihm folgten zwei Taschenwörterbücher (Osmanlıcadan Türkçeye cep kılavuzu 1935, Türkçeden Osmanlıcaya cep kılavuzu 1935), die das Schreiben und Verstehen der purifizierten Sprache ermöglichen sollten. Für den Wortschatz der anatolischen Dialekte gab es damals nur wenig Behelfe (Koşay/Işıtman 1932, Hüsnü 1934), aber die für die Sprachreinigung eintretende Türkische Sprachgesellschaft entwickelte eine rege Sammeltätigkeit, die sich in einem groß angelegten Dialektwörterbuch (Türkiyede halk ağzından söz derleme dergisi 1939—57; verbesserte 2. Ausg.: Türkiye'de halk ağzından söz derleme sözlüğü 1963—82) niederschlug. Ein paralleles Unternehmen derselben Gesellschaft war ein Belegwörterbuch, das die außer Gebrauch gekommenen türkischen Lexeme zur etwaigen Wiedererweckung sammelte (XIII. asırdan günümüze kadar kitaplardan toplanmış tanıklariyle tarama sözlüğü 1943—54; verbesserte 2. Ausg.: XIII. yüzyıldan beri Türkiye Türkçesiyle yazılmış kitaplardan toplanan tanıklariyle tarama sözlüğü 1963—77).

Während diese beiden Unternehmen das Material für etwaige sprachliche Neuschöpfungen liefern sollten, war das von der Sprachgesellschaft herausgegebene Türkçe sözlük (1943) als ein normatives Standardwörterbuch für Verwaltung, Schule und Presse gedacht. Erst seine 7. Ausgabe (1983) hat dergleichen ideologische Ziele in starkem Maße abgelegt und will in erster Linie den bestehenden Wortschatz möglichst vollständig erfassen. Darin äußert sich der konservativere Trend der jüngsten Vergangenheit. Immer wieder zeigt sich die enge Verknüpfung der Lexikographie mit der Zeitgeschichte.

3. Gegenwärtiger Stand

3.1. Allgemeine Wb.

3.1.1. Einsprachige

3.1.1.1. Für das Osmanische: Fraschery 1899—1900.

3.1.1.2. Modernes Türkeitürkisch: Türkçe sözlük 1943.

3.1.2. Zweisprachige

3.1.2.1. Für das Osmanische: Meninski 1680 oder 1780; Zenker 1866; Redhouse 1890 oder 1968.

3.1.2.2. Für das moderne Türkeitürkisch: Bonelli 1939; Redhouse 1968; Steuerwald 1972 u. 1974; vorhanden sind auch: bulgarische, finnische, georgische, neugriechische, niederländische, polnische, rumänische, russische, schwedische, serbokroatische zweisprachige Wb.

3.2. Spezialwörterbücher

3.2.1. Alt- u. Mittelosmanisch: XIII. yüzyıldan beri Türkiye Türkçesiyle yazılmış kitaplardan toplanan tanıklariyle tarama sözlüğü 1963—77.

3.2.2. Argot: Mikhailov 1930; Mehmet Halit 1934; Devellioğlu 1941.

3.2.3. Belegwörterbücher: XIII. yüzyıldan beri Türkiye Türkçesiyle yazılmış kitaplardan toplanan tanıklariyle tarama sözlüğü 1963—77; Eyüboğlu 1973—75.

3.2.4. Dialektwörterbücher: Koşay/Işıtman 1932; Aksoy 1945—46; Türkiye'de halk ağzından söz derleme sözlüğü 1963—82; und viele andere (Bibliographie: Gülensoy 1981).

3.2.5. Etymologische Wb.: Kerestedjian 1912; Räsänen 1969; Sevortjan 1974—80.

3.2.6. Fachwörterbücher: Nutki 1917 (Seewesen), Devedjian 1926 (Fischerei); Bedevian 1936 (Pflanzennamen); Büngül 1939 (Antiquitätenmarkt); Türk hukuk lugati 1944 (Jus); Pakalın 1946—51 (historische Terminologie); Zanaat terimleri sözlüğü 1976 (Handwerk); und viele andere.

3.2.7. Fremdwörterlexikon: Özön 1962.

3.2.8. Neologismen: Püsküllüoğlu 1966; Antelava 1985.

3.2.9. Phraseologische Wb.: Özön 1943; Eyüboğlu 1973—75; Aksoy 1976.

3.2.10. Rechtschreibewörterbuch: Imlâ lûgati 1928.

3.2.11. Rückläufiges Wb.: Vietze/Zenker/Warnke 1975.

3.2.12. Synonymenwörterbuch: Ağakay 1956.

3.2.13. Volkskunde: Türkiyede halk ağzından söz derleme dergisi 1939—57, Bd. 6 (1952).

3.3. Osmanisch/Türkeitürkisch im Rahmen der Turksprachen: Budagov 1868—71, Radloff 1893—1911, Kadri 1927—45; Räsänen 1969; Sevortjan 1974—80.

3.4. Bibliographie: Deny 1959; Akyüz 1959; Çağatay 1961; Redhouse 1968, XIV—XVIII; Chidiroglou 1975—77; Aganin 1978.

4. Literatur (in Auswahl)

4.1. Wörterbücher

Ağakay 1956 = Mehmet Ali Ağakay: Türkçede yakın anlamlı kelimeler lugati. Bir deneme. Ankara 1956 [115 S.].

Agioreitês 1804 = Zacharias Agioreitês: Lexikòn tourkikòn kai graikikón. Venedig 1804 [Aufl. 1819 56 S.].

Ahmed Vefik 1876 = Ahmed Vefik [Pascha]: Lehçe-i osmânî. Istanbul 1876 [2 Bde., 1293 S.; 2. Aufl. 1900, 1455 S.].

Ahterî 1545 = Karahisarî Mustafâ b. Şemseddîn Ahterî: Ahterî-i kebîr. Abgefaßt 1545, viele Drucke ab 1826 [700 + 875 S.].

Aksoy 1945—46 = Ömer Asım Aksoy: Gaziantep ağzı. Istanbul 1945—46 [3 Bde., Wb. im 3. Bd., 826 S.].

Aksoy 1976 = Ömer Asım Aksoy: Deyimler sözlüğü. Ankara 1976 [S. 399—968; Bd. 2 seines Atasözleri ve deyimler sözlüğü, Ankara 1971. Stark erweiterte Fassung der Ausgabe von 1965.].

Alexandridês 1812 = Dêmêtrios Alexandridês: Lexikòn tourkikó-graikikòn. Wien 1812 [445 + 159 S.].

Antelava 1985 = G. I. Antelava: Turecko-russkij slovar' (neologizmy). Tbilisi 1985 [167 S.].

Arcère +1699 = Antoine Arcère de l'Oratoire: Dictionnaire français-turc. 17. Jh. [2 Bde., 1034 u. 986 S.; Hs., Bibliothèque Nationale, Paris].

Asım 1799 = Ahmed Asım: Tibyân-i nâfi' der tercüme-i Burhân-i kâti'. Istanbul 1799 [863 S.; viele spätere Aufl.].

Asım 1814—18 = Ahmed Asım: El-okyânûs el-basît fî tercümeti l-Kâmûsi l-muhît. Istanbul 1814—18 [3 Bde., ca. 3000 S.; mehrere spätere Aufl.].

Barbier de Meynard 1881—86 = A. C. Barbier de Meynard: Dictionnaire turc-français. Paris 1881—86 [2 Bde., 786 u. 898 S.; Reprint 1971].

Bedevian 1936 = Armenag K. Bedevian: Illustrated polyglottic dictionary of plant names in Latin, Arabic, Armenian, English, French, German, Italian and Turkish languages. Cairo 1936 [456 S.].

Bernardo da Parigi 1665 = M. R. P. F. Bernardo da Parigi: Dittionario della lingua italiana turchesca sive Lexicon italo-turcicum. Rom 1665 [3 Bde., 2458 S.; aus dem Franz. übersetzt von P. F. Pietro d'Abbavilla].

Bonelli 1939 = Luigi Bonelli: Lessico italiano-turco. Rom 1939 [2. Aufl. 1952, 359 S.].

Budagov 1868—71 = Lazar Budagov: Sravnitel'nyj slovar' turkotatarskich narečij. St. Petersburg 1868—71 [2 Bde., 810 u. 416 S.; Reprint 1961.].

Büngül 1939 = Nureddin Rüşdü Büngül: Eski eserler ansiklopedisi. Istanbul 1939 [270 S.].

Carradori 1635? = Frate Arcangelo de Carradori: Dizionario turco-italiano. Girge 1635? [269 S.; Hs., Biblioteca Fortiguerriana, Pistoia].

Chlôros 1899 = Iôannês Chlôros: Lexikòn tourko-hellênikón. Konstantinopel 1899 [2 Bde., 2102 S.].

Clodius 1730 = Johannes Christianus Clodius: Compendiosum lexicon latino-turcico-germanicum. Leipzig 1730 [928 + ca. 400 unpaginierte S.].

Delacroix 1679 = Joseph Delacroix: Dictionnaire turc-français. Konstantinopel 1679 [470 S.; Hs., Bibliothèque Nationale, Paris].

Devedjian 1926 = Karekin Devedjian: Pêche et pêcheries en Turquie. Konstantinopel 1926 [169 S.].

Devellioğlu 1941 = Ferit Devellio*ğlu: Türk argosu*. Ankara 1941 *[Verb. u. erw. Ausg. 1945, 1955, 1959; 206 S.].*

Du Ryer 17. Jh. = André Du Ryer: Dictionarium turcico-latinum. 17. Jh. [285 Bl.; Hs., Bibliothèque Nationale, Paris].

Eyüboğlu 1973—75 = E. Kemal Eyüboğlu: Şiirde ve halk dilinde atasözleri ve deyimler. Istanbul 1973—1975 [2 Bde., 329 u. 528 S.].

Ferişteoğlu 15. Jh. = ᶜAbdullatîf Ferişteo*ğlu:* Lugat-i Ferişteoğlu. 15. Jh. [viele Hss.].

Ferraguto 1611 = Pietro Ferraguto: Dittionario della lingua turchesca. 1611. [Teil 2 seiner Grammatica turchesca. Hs., Biblioteca Nazionale, Neapel. Nach A. Bombaci: Padre Pietro Ferraguto e la sua Grammatica turca (1611). In: Annali del R. Istituto Superiore Orientale di Napoli, N.S. 1 (1940) 205—236.

Fiennes 1689 = Jean Baptiste de Fiennes: Dictionnaire turc-français. Konstantinopel 1689 [1233 S.; Hs.- Bibliothèque Nationale, Paris].

Fîrûzâbâdî +1415 = Muḥammad b. Yaᶜqûb Fîrûzâbâdî: Qâmûs. [viele Hss.; Drucke seit 1815].

Fraschery 1883a = Ch. Samy-Bey Fraschery: Dictionnaire français-turc. Istanbul 1883 [1630 S.].

Fraschery 1883b = Ch. Samy-Bey Fraschery: Dictionnaire turc-français. Istanbul 1883 [1208 S.; mehrere spätere Ausg.].

Fraschery 1899—1900 = S. Sami [Fraschery]: Kamus-u türkî. Istanbul 1899—1900 [2 Bde., 1575 S.].

Galland 1672—73 = Antoine Galland: Fransız tercümesi ile Türkî lugat. Konstantinopel 1672—73 [551 S.; Hs., Bibliothèque Nationale, Paris].

Golius 1653 = Jacobus Golius: Lexicon arabico-latinum. Leiden 1653 [2922 S.].

Golius 1669 = Jacobus Golius: Dictionarium persico-latinum. Teil 2 von Edmundus Castellus: Lexikon heptaglotton. London 1669.

Handjéri 1840—41 = Prince Alexandre Handjéri: Dictionnaire français-arabe-persan et turc. Moskau 1840—41 [3 Bde., 992, 658, 805 S.].

Hindoglu 1831 = Artin Hindoglu: Dictionnaire abrégé français-turc. Wien 1831 [562 S.].

Hindoglu 1838 = Artin Hindoglu: Dictionnaire abrégé turc-français. Wien 1838 [516 S.].

Hüsnü 1934 = Hüsnü: Kayseri sözlüğü. Kayseri 1934 [96 S.].

İmlâ lugati 1928 = [Rechtschreibewörterbuch]. Istanbul 1928 [371 S.; viele spätere Ausg.].

Kadri 1927—42 = Hüseyin Kâzim Kadri: [Büyük] Türk lûgati. Istanbul 1927—42 [4 Bde., XCIX+855, 981, 928, 894 S.].

Kelekian 1911 = Diran Kelekian: Dictionnaire turc, français. Istanbul 1911 [1373 S.].

Kerestedjian 1912 = Bedros Efendi Kerestedjian: Quelques matériaux pour un dictionnaire étymologique de la langue turque. London 1912 [364 + 40 S.].

Kieffer/Bianchi 1835—37 = J. D. Kieffer/T. X. Bianchi: Dictionnaire turc-français. Paris 1835—37 [2 Bde., 784 u. 1304 S.].

Koşay/Işıtman 1932 = Hamit Zübeyr [Koşay]/İshak Refet [Işıtman]: Anadilden derlemeler. Ankara 1932 [448 S.].

Mascis 1677 = Antonio Mascis: Vocabolario toscano e tvrchesco. Arricchito di molti voci arabe, persiane, tartare e greche, necessarie alla perfetta cognizione della stessa lingua turchesca. Firenze 1677 [290 S.].

Magiser 1592a = Hieronymus Megiser: Paroemiologia polyglotta. Graz 1592 [250 S.].

Megiser 1592b = Hieronymus Megiser: Dictionarium quatuor linguarum. Graz 1592 [188 S.].

Megiser 1593 = Hieronymus Megiser: Specimen 40 linguarum. Frankfurt 1593 [47 S.].

Megiser 1603 = Hieronymus Megiser: Thesaurus polyglottus. Frankfurt 1603 [750 S.].

Megiser 1612 = Hieronymus Megiser: Dictionarium latino-turcicum. Leipzig 1612 [Bd. 4 von: Institutionum linguæ turcicæ libri quatuor. Bd. 4 hat 57+54 S.].

Mehmed Es'ad 1801—02 = Mehmed Es'ad: Lehcet el-lugât. Istanbul 1801—02 [851 S.].

Mehmed Hafîd 1806 = Mehmed Hafîd: Galatât-i meşhûre. Istanbul 1806 [534 S.].

Mehmet Halit 1934 = Mehmet Halit: Istanbul argosu ve halk tabirleri. Istanbul 1934 [210 S.].

Meninski 1680 = Franciscus à Mesgnien Meninski: Thesaurus linguarum orientalium turcicæ, arabicæ, persicæ... lexicon turcico-arabico-persicum. Wien 1680 [4 Bde., 6079 Sp., +276 S.].

Meninski 1687 = Franciscus à Mesgnien Meninski: Complementum thesauri linguarum orientalium seu Onomasticum latino-turcico-arabico-persicum... Wien 1687 [1998 Sp.].

Meninski 1780 = Franciscus à Mesgnien Meninski: Lexicon arabico-persico-turcicum... Wien 1780 [2. Ausg., 4 Bde., 660, 822, 1086, 1207 S.].

Mikhailov 1930 = M. S. Mikhailov: Matériaux sur l'argot et les locutions populaires turc-ottomans. Leipzig 1930 [41 S.].

Molino 1641 = Giovanni Molino: Dittionario della lingua italiana turchesca. Rom 1641 [494 Sp.].

Muhammad 1450 = as-Sayyid Muḥammad b. as-Sayyid Ḥasan: Ǧâmiᶜ al-luġa. Edirne 1450 [Hss.].

Naci 1901 = Muallim Naci: Lugat-i Naci. Istanbul 1901 [1426 S.; mehrere spätere Aufl.].

Nutki 1917 = Süleyman Nutki: Kamus-u bahrî. Istanbul 1917 [425 S.].

XIII. asırdan günümüze kadar kitaplardan toplanmış tanıklariyle tarama sözlüğü 1943—54 = [osmanisches Belegwörterbuch]. Istanbul 1943—54 [3 Bde., jeweils mit vollständigem Alphabet; 862, 1090, 840 S.].

XIII. yüzyıldan beri Türkiye Türkçesiyle yazılmış kitaplardan toplanmış tanıklariyle tarama sözlüğü 1963—77 = [osmanisches Belegwörterbuch]. Ankara 1963—77 [8 Bde.; 4814 + 295 + 419 S.].

Osmanlıcadan Türkçeye cep kılavuzu 1935 = Istanbul 1935 [369 S.].

Özön 1943 = Mustafa Nihat Özön: Türkçe tabirler sözlüğü. Istanbul 1943 [Bd. 1, 400 S.; nicht mehr erschienen].

Özön 1962 = Mustafa Nihat Özön: Türkçe — yabancı kelimeler sözlüğü. Istanbul 1962 [244 S.].

Pakalın 1946—51 = Mehmet Zeki Pakalın: Osmanlı tarih deyimleri ve terimleri sözlüğü. Istanbul 1946—51 [3 Bde., 840, 784, 870 S.].

Preindl 1787 = [Preindl]: Vocabulaire de la langue turque. Schleswig 1787 [S. 175—591; Teil von: Essai d'une grammaire turque].

Püsküllüoğlu 1966 = Ali Püsküllüoğlu: Öz Türkçe sözcükler ve terimler sözlüğü. Ankara 1966 [192 S.].

Radloff 1897—1911 = Wilhelm Radloff: Versuch eines Wörterbuches der Türk-Dialecte. St. Petersburg 1897—1911 [4 Bde., 1914 Sp. + 66 S., 1814 Sp. + 64 S., 2204 Sp. + 98 S., 2230 Sp. + 107 S.; Reprint Haag 1960].

Räsänen 1969 = Martti Räsänen: Versuch eines etymologischen Wörterbuchs der Türksprachen. Helsinki 1969 [533 S.].

Redhouse 1856 = Sir James William Redhouse: An English and Turkish dictionary. London 1856 [1149 S.; 2. Aufl. 1861; 3. Aufl. 1880].

Redhouse 1890 = Sir James William Redhouse: A Turkish and English lexicon. London. Konstantinopel 1890 [2224 S.; Reprint 1921].

Redhouse 1950 = Yeni Redhouse lugati. İngilizce-Türkçe/Revised Redhouse dictionary, English-Turkish. Istanbul 1950 [1193 S.; 2. Aufl. 1953, 1214 S.; später weitere Auflagen].

Redhouse 1968 = Redhouse yeni Türkçe-İngilizce sözlük. Istanbul 1968 [1292 S.; 2. Aufl. 1974, mit 45 S. Supplement].

Resden 1822 = Dr. Mikayel Resden: Pararan [Medizinisch-pharmakologisches Wb.]. Venedig 1822 [2. Aufl., Venedig 1832, 502 S. Zitiert nach Kevork Pamukciyan: Dr. Mikayel Resden (1774—1844) ve dokuz dildeki tıp sözlüğü. In: Tarih ve toplum (Istanbul), Jahrg. 2, Heft 17 (1985), 334—336].

Şâhidî 1514—15 = İbrahim Şâhidî: Tuhfe-i Şâhidî. Verfaßt 1514—15. Druck Istanbul 1858 [63 S.].

Salâhî 1897—1906 = Mehmed Salaheddin Salâhî: Kamus-u osmanî. Istanbul 1897—1906 [4 Bde., 501, 371, 485, 668 S.].

Schlechta-Wssehrd 1870 = O. de Schlechta-Wssehrd: Manuel terminologique français-turc contenant les principales expressions et locutions techniques usitées dans les pièces diplomatiques, administratives et judiciaires... Wien 1870 [400 S.].

Seaman 1665—73 = William Seaman: [türkisch-lateinisches Wb.], 1665—73 [569 S.; Hs., British Library].

Sevortjan 1974—80 = È. V. Sevortjan: Etimologičeskij slovar' tjurkskich jazykov. Moskau 1974—80 [3 Bde., 766, 348, 394 S.; noch nicht abgeschlossen].

Steuerwald 1972 = Karl Steuerwald: Türkisch-deutsches Wörterbuch. Wiesbaden 1972 [1057 S.; Reprint Istanbul 1982].

Steuerwald 1974 = Karl Steuerwald: Deutsch-türkisches Wörterbuch. Wiesbaden 1974 [669 S.].

Şükûn 1944 = Ziya Şükûn: Farsça-Türkçe lugat; Gencinei güftar; Ferhengi Ziya. Istanbul 1944 [2040 S.].

Şu'ûrî 1742 = Hasan Şu'ûrî: Ferheng-i Şu'ûrî. Istanbul 1742 [2 Bde.; 454 u. 451 S.].

Tarama dergisi 1934 = Tarama dergisi. Istanbul 1934 [2 Bde., 1309 S.].

Tinghir/Sinapian 1891 = Ant. B. Tinghir/K. Sinapian: Dictionnaire français-turc des termes techniques des sciences, des lettres et des arts. Konstantinopel 1891 [2 Bde., 423 u. 565 S.].

Türk hukuk lugati 1944 = [türkisches juridisches Wb.]. Ankara 1944 [582 S.].

Türkçe sözlük 1943 = [einsprachiges türk. Wb.]. Istanbul 1944 [669 S.; 2. Aufl. 1955, 823 S.; 3. Aufl. 1959, 856 S.; 4. Aufl. 1966, 808 S.; 5. Aufl. 1969, 832 S.; 6. Aufl. 1974, 893 S.; 7. Aufl. 1983, 2 Bde., 1353 S.].

Türkçeden Osmanlıcaya cep kılavuzu 1935 = [Taschenwörterbuch Türkisch-Osmanisch]. Istanbul 1935 [340 S.].

Türkiyede halk ağzından söz derleme dergisi 1939—57 = [türkisches Dialektwörterbuch]. Istanbul 1939—1957 [6 Bde., 1709, 427, 152 S.].

Türkiye'de halk ağzından söz derleme sözlüğü 1963—82 = [türkisches Dialektwörterbuch]. Ankara 1963—82 (12 Bde., 4842 S.].

Üsküfî 17. Jh. = Muhamed Hevai Üsküfî: Makbûl-i 'ârif. Bosnien, 17. Jh. [Hss.].

Vámbéry 1862 = Ármin Vámbéry: Abuska: csagatajtörök szógyüjtemény. Budapest 1862 [117 S.].

Vankuli 1728—29 = Mehmed b. Mustafâ Vankuli: Lugat-i Vankuli. Istanbul 1728—29 [2 Bde., 666 u. 756 S.; 2. Aufl. 1755—56; 3. Aufl. 1802—03].

Vehbî 1798 = Sünbülzâde Mehmed Vehbî: Tuhfe-i Vehbî. Istanbul 1798 [55 S.; viele weitere Drucke].

Vehbî 1805 = Sünbülzâde Mehmed Vehbî: Nuhbe-i Vehbî. Istanbul 1805 [123 S.].

Vietze/Zenker/Warnke 1975 = Hans-Peter Vietze/Ludwig Zenker/Ingrid Warnke: Rückläufiges Wörterbuch der türkischen Sprache. Leipzig 1975 [197 S.].

Viguier 1790 = Viguier: Élémens de la langue turque. Konstantinopel 1790 [462 S.; enthält ein franz.-türk. Wörterverzeichnis].

Yûsuf Hâlis 1849—50 = Yûsuf Hâlis: Miftâh-i lisân. Istanbul 1849—50 [52 S.].

Zanaat terimleri sözlüğü 1976 = [Wb. gewerblicher Fachausdrücke]. Ankara 1976 [215 S.].

Zenker 1866 = Julius Theodor Zenker: Dictionnaire turc-arabe-persan/Türkisch-arabisch-persisches Handwörterbuch. Leipzig 1866—76 [2 Bde., 980 S.; Reprint Hildesheim 1976].

4.2. Sonstige Literatur

Abrahamowicz 1975 = Zygmunt Abrahamowicz: Mesgnien Meninski Franciszek. In: Polski słownik biograficzny XX. (1975, 464—466).

Aganin 1978 = R. A. Aganin: Tureckaja leksikografija v SSSR (1917—1977). In: Sovetskaja Tjurkologija 1978, Heft 3, 80—94.

Akyüz 1959 = Kenan Akyüz: Paris Millî Kütüphanesinde ilk Türkçe-Fransızca ve Fransızca-Türkçe yazma eserler. In: Türk dili araştırmaları yıllığı belleten (Ankara) 1959, 249—292.

Babinger 1919 = Franz Babinger: Die türkischen Studien in Europa bis zum Auftreten Josef von Hammer-Purgstalls. In: Die Welt des Islams (Berlin) VII. 1919, 103—129.

Çağatay 1961 = Saadet Çağatay: Yazma sözlük ve gramerler. In: Ankara Üniversitesi Dil ve Tarih-Coğrafya Fakültesi Dergisi (Ankara) 19 (1961), 129—135.

Chidiroglou 1975—77 = Pavlos Chidiroglou: Bibliographikè symbolè eis tèn hellênikèn tourkologian (1788—1975). In: Epetêrís (Nikosia) 8. 1975—77, 253—405.

Deny 1959 = Jean Deny: L'osmanli moderne et le türk de Turquie. In: Philologiae turcicae fundamenta. Bd. 1, Wiesbaden 1959, 182—239.

Du Ryer 1630 = André Du Ryer: Rudimenta grammaticæ linguæ turcicæ. Paris 1630 [96 S.; 2. Aufl. 1633].

Findley 1980 = Carter V. Findley: Sir James W. Redhouse (1811—92): the making of a perfect Orientalist? In: Journal of the American Oriental Society 99. 1980, 573—600.

Gülensoy 1981 = Tuncer Gülensoy: Anadolu ve Rumeli ağızları bibliyografyası. Ankara 1981.

Majda 1976 = Tadeusz Majda: Present state and perspectives of the studies of Ottoman Turkish linguistic monuments in phonetic transcription (non-Arabic scripts). In: Studi preottomani e ottomani. Atti del Convegno di Napoli (24—26 settembre 1974). Napoli 1976, 179—189.

Meninski 1649a = Franciscus à Mesgnien [Meninski]: Grammatica gallica in usum iuventutis maxime polonae. Danzig 1649.

Meninski 1649b = Franciscus à Mesgnien [Meninski]: Compendiosa italicæ linguæ institutio in Polonorum gratiam collecta. Danzig 1649.

Meninski 1649c = Franciscus à Mesgnien [Meninski]: Grammatica seu institutio polonicae linguae ... in usum exterorum edita. Danzig 1649.

Meninski 1746 = Franciscus à Mesgnien Meninski: Institutiones linguae turcicae. 2. Ausg., Wien 1756. [Die 1. Ausg. war in Meninski 1680, Bd. 4, letzter Abschnitt, 1—276].

Németh 1970 = J. Németh: Die türkische Sprache in Ungarn im siebzehnten Jahrhundert. Budapest 1970.

Pamukciyan 1986 = Kevork Pamukciyan: Ermeni harfli Türkçe yazma sözlükler. In: Tarih ve toplum (Istanbul), III/25. 1986, 52—54.

Sajkowski 1966 = Alojzy Sajkowski: Franciszek Mesgnien-Meninski w Konstantynopolu. In: Odrodzenie i Reformacja u Polsce (Warschau) 11. 1966, 181—192.

Smailović 1983 = Ismet Smailović: O jednom vrlo zanimljivom rječniku iz 17. stoljeća. In: Studia Linguistica Polono-Jugoslavica (Sarajevo) 3. 1983, 151—161.

Tietze 1962 = Andreas Tietze: Problems of Turkish lexicography. In: Problems of lexicography (ed. F. Householder/S. Saporta), Bloomington, Indiana, 1962, 263—273.

Zetterstéen 1907 = K. V. Zetterstéen: A specimen of the Turkish dictionary. In: Le Monde Oriental (Uppsala) 1. 1907, 234—236.

Andreas Tietze, Wien (Österreich)

232. Die Lexikographie der Turksprachen II: Sonstige Turksprachen

1. Die zu behandelnden Sprachen
2. Turklexikographie der UdSSR
3. Turklexikographie Chinas
4. Turklexikographie Irans
5. Turklexikographie anderer Länder
6. Lexikographie des Alt- und Mitteltürkischen
7. Vergleichende Turklexikographie
8. Literatur (in Auswahl)

1. Die zu behandelnden Sprachen

Nach sowjetischer (streng *politischer*) Definition gibt es 40 Türk„sprachen", d. h. Idiome, die z. T. als Literatursprache anerkannt sind (auch wenn ihre Differenzen linguistisch minimal sind). *Linguistisch* sollte man eher 9 Türk-Sprachen unterscheiden, nämlich

(1) *Oghusisch* (Texte seit 13. Jh.),
(2) *Kiptschakisch,*
(3) *Zentraltürkisch* (Texte (2/3) seit 14. Jh.),
(4) *Uigurisch* (Texte seit 8. Jh.),
(5) *Südsibirisch* (erst seit 18. Jh. erforscht),
(6) *Jakutisch* (erst seit 18. Jh. erforscht),
(7) *Chaladsch* (erst seit 1968 näher erforscht),
(8) *Čuvašisch* (Texte seit 13. Jh.),
(9) *Gelbuigurisch* (erst seit 19. Jh. erforscht).

Diese Türkvölker leben v. a. in der UdSSR, s. Abschn. 2. Ausnahmen: in China: (teilweise) Kasachisch, Kirgisisch (zu 3), Neuuigurisch (zu 4), (ganz) Salarisch (zu 4), Gelbuigurisch; im Iran: (teilw.) Azeri, Südoghusisch, Chorasantürkisch, Türkmenisch (alle zu 1), (ganz) Sonqori (zu (1)), Qašqa'i-Aynallu (zu (1)), Chaladsch; im Irak: Kerkük (zu 1); in Afghanistan: (teilw.) Südoghusisch Chorasantürkisch, Türkmenisch, Kasachisch, Karakalpakisch (zu 3), Kirgisisch, Özbekisch (zu 4), Neuuigurisch; in Rumänien: Dobrudschatatarisch (zu 2), -nogaiisch (zu 3).

2. Turklexikographie der UdSSR

Die Erforschung der Türksprachen Rußlands setzt Ende des 17. Jh. (Witsen) ein; auch Fischer, Pallas und andere haben kleinere Wörterlisten im 18. Jh. zusammengestellt. Erst im 19. Jh. jedoch erscheinen ansehnlichere Glossare, etwa 2300—17 000 Wörter umfassend, der Sprachen Kasachisch, Westsibirisch, Kasantatarisch, Baschkirisch, Frühözbekisch, Altaitürkisch, Krimtatarisch (vgl. Kononov 1982). Diese Werke waren jedoch den heute in der UdSSR publizierten nicht ebenbürtig (oft Verwendung unzulänglicher arab. Schrift, ungenaue Transkription). Freilich, auch kein modernes sowjet. Werk weist den Rang eines Webster, Grimm oder des Slovar' sovremennogo russkogo literaturnogo jazyka auf. Am nächsten kommt dem: N. I. *Ašmarin: Thesaurus linguae tschuvaschorum,* 17 Bde., Kazan' 1928—50. — Als die Bolschewiki die Macht übernehmend an die Gleichstellung der Völker der UdSSR, auch Schaffung von Literatursprachen, gingen, standen sie einer Fülle politischer Tendenzen gegenüber: a) Großrussische Tendenzen. Diese zeigen sich (abgesehen von Termini wie *pivo* 'Bier', *avtomobil'*) in Vernachlässigung ethnologisch/ideologisch wichtiger Termini einheimischer Völker, auch darin, daß in der Stalinzeit weit mehr größere russisch-türkische (RT) als türkisch-russische (TR) Wörterbücher erstellt worden sind (s. Tabelle). Hier war „der größere Nutzeffekt ... bei der Vermittlung des Russischen als der offiziell angestrebten Zweitsprache aller Nationen maßgebend" (Brands 1973, 9). — b) Bedürfnisse der Internationalisierung. So sind zwischen 1929 und 1941 Wörterbücher im lateinischen Alphabet verfaßt worden. Dann setzte sich Tendenz a) durch: Verwendung des russischen Alphabets. — c) Bedürfnisse der Sowjetmacht: Politik des divide et impera. So hätte sich leicht eine einheitliche Idel-Uralsprache schaffen lassen, statt dessen sind die zwei „Sprachen" Kasantarisch und Baschkirisch konstruiert worden. Die ältere, auf dem Norddialekt beruhende, vielen Türksprechern verständliche özbekische Schriftsprache ist durch ein extremes, iranisiertes Muster ersetzt worden usf. Selbst die Transkription teilt die Türksprachen, das Phonem /ö/ z. B. erscheint als *ob, ö, ө* und *o*. — d) Pantürkische Tendenzen Einheimischer (wie der von Türkmenen vorgebrachte Vorschlag, das Türkeitürkische als Schriftsprache zu übernehmen) sind nicht durchgedrungen. — e) Ebenso scheiterten panislamische Tendenzen, die auf Beibehaltung der arabischen Schrift drangen. (Diese war gerade durch ihre Ungenauigkeit ein hervorragendes Instrument der Einheit der Türkvölker: „kwl" 'See' konnte, ganz verschieden gesprochen, überall verstanden werden.) — f) Es gab ferner lokale Tendenzen, oft einander widerstrebend. Das Krimtatarische z. B. stellt ein buntes Gemisch von Dialektformen dar. Die türkischen Literatursprachen der UdSSR sind nützliche, aber *künstliche* Schöpfungen.

Eine ideale lexikographische Situation sollte u. a. folgenden Anforderungen genügen: (a) die Wörterbücher sollten genügenden Umfang aufweisen. — (b) Dies sollte für beide Richtungen gelten: TR + RT. Hierzu folgende Tabelle, die je umfangreichsten Wörterbücher in der UdSSR markierend. Jahreszahlen i. a. nur bei den beiden ersten Kategorien, zuweilen kleinere Wörterbücher in [ ] gegeben, vor-sowjetische in ( ); ! = an der unteren Grenze. Angaben in 10^3.

Wir konstatieren: Bei den größeren Sprachen (kursiv) überwiegen bis 1956 größere RT Wörterbücher gegen TR (8:4), nach 1956 gilt dagegen RT:TR = 0:4. Bei den kleineren Sprachen herrscht Ausgewogenheit (RT:TR bis 1956 7:5, danach 7:4). Erstaunlich ist die Unterrepräsentation des Azeri, auch daß das kleine Karakalpakisch weit besser dasteht als das Kasachische. Meist aber sind die kleineren Sprachen schlechter erschlossen als die größeren: praktisch-politisches Denken. (Linguistisch wären die kleinen Sprachen Sibiriens interessanter.) Dem Umfange nach ist ein befriedigender Stand erreicht. — (c) Das Idealwörterbuch sollte exhaustiv sein — in sowjetischen Werken werden aber obszöne Termini grundsätzlich, religiöse oft ausgelassen, auch Argot selten behandelt. Andererseits ist eine Fülle terminologischer Werke auf technisch-naturwissenschaftlichem Gebiet zu konstatieren. — (d) Die Erfassung aller Sprachen sollte gleichmäßig sein, s. dazu

	TR				RT			
	45—30	25—10	10—3	<3	45—30	25—10	10—3	<3
Gagaus.			+					
Krimosman.								
Azeri		1941			1940			
Chorasantürk.			+					
Özbek-oghus.			+					
Türkmen.	1968				1956			
Krimtatar.			1980!				(1906)	
Karaim.		1974						
Kar-Balkar.				(1909)	1967			
Kumük.		1969		(1911)	1960!			
Kasantatar.	1966	(1950)			1955			
Westsibir.			+					(1804!)
Baraba		(+!)	+					
Baschkir.		1958			1948	[1954]		
Kasach.		1954		1946	1954			
Karakalpak.	1958!				1967			
Özbekkipčak.			+					
Kirgis.	1940				1944			
Nogai.		1969			1956			
Özbek.	1959				1954			
Neuuigur.		1939			1956!			(1955)
Altai/Nord			+					
Altai/Süd		1947!			1964			
Schor.			(+)					
Chakass.		1953			1961			
Čulymtürk.				(+)				
Tuvin.		1955			1980	[1953]		
Tofalar.			(+!)	+				
Jakut.		1907			1949?	1968		
Čuvaš.	1928				1951			

Abb. 232.1: Die Lexikographie der Turksprachen in der UdSSR

oben. — (e) „Wörter und Sachen", ethnologische Beschreibungen sind spärlich (Ausnahme:Ašmarin). — (f) Viele Zitate aus der Literatur sind erwünscht — unerreicht, oft werden zwar Sprichwörter zitiert, vielfach aber erfundene Sätze (linguistische Todsünde). — (g) Diachronisches und Etymologisches liegt nur von wenigen Sprachen (wie Čuvaš., Kasachisch, in recht dürftiger Form) vor. Talât Tekins Wort über Sevortjans vergleichendes Wörterbuch „Die etymologischen Erklärungen sind höchst schwach und unzulänglich" wird dem riesigen Werk nicht gerecht, trifft aber im Kerne zu. — (h) Es gibt jedoch eine Fülle teilweise recht guter Dialektwörterbücher. Seit einiger Zeit wird an einem Sprachatlas gearbeitet, vgl. dazu Sovetskaja Tjurkologija 1976: 3.3—9; 1979: 2.3—8; 1981:3.71—5; 1982:3.3—9. — (i) Die Transkription sollte die Phoneme, aber auch wichtige Allophone, exakt widerspiegeln. Da die Türksprachen der UdSSR meist neugeschaffen sind, wäre dies realisierbar gewesen, sie ist auch meist geleistet worden. Es gibt aber manche Inkonsequenzen, so erwies sich die Schaffung von Rechtschreibwörterbüchern für mehrere Türksprachen (z. B. Türkmenisch) als notwendig. — (j) Im Laufe der Wörterbucharbeit sollte eine systematische, kohärente Aufarbeitung des Materials erfolgen. Dies ist nicht durchweg der Fall. Hier nur *ein* Beispiel: Ein Vergleich der mit *ab-* beginnenden Wörter in den azeri Werken von Hüsejnov („1941", 17 000 Wörter) und Azizbekov („1965", 23 000 Wörter) zeigt: „1965" enthält 25 Termini, die in „1941" fehlen — aber auch „1941" enthält 9 in „1965" fehlende Lemmata; auch erscheint abweichende Lautung [„1941" *abïr-haya* = „1965" *abïr-häya* usw.); die Transkription hat sich verändert: 1958 ist der (lateinische!) Buchstabe *j* eingeführt worden; dadurch entfielen gewisse russische Zeichen, ist aber auch die alphabetische Folge verändert worden (ferner steht Ы direkt nach И). Im Zeitraum von nur 29 Jahren ist das Azeri auf vier Weisen geschrieben worden: bis 1929 in arabischer Schrift, bis 1940 in Lateinschrift, 1940—58 in puristisch-russischer Schrift, danach in leicht latinisierter Form. Ein ähnlicher Übergang ist auch bei vielen anderen Türksprachen festzustellen. — (k) Es sind vorzügliche erklärende Wörterbücher für die einheimische Bevölkerung geschaffen worden (z. B. für Azeri, Türkmenisch, Kasachisch). — Abschließend sei bemerkt: Es gibt eine Fülle von Artikeln zu bestimmten Lebensbereichen, teilweise vorzügliche (so Šćerbaks Studie über die Bezeichnungen der Haustiere in Ubrjatova 1961). Seltener sind Monographien (wie Laude-Cirtautas: Der Gebrauch der Farbbezeichnungen in den Türkdialekten, Wiesbaden 1961 oder Doerfer 1963—75). Bisher scheint es aber nur *eine* Arbeit zu geben, die abstrakt-wissenschaftlich Probleme der türkischen Lexikographie im Zusammenhang behandelt: Brands 1973, s. § 12. — Die Zahl solcher Wörterbücher unseres Gebiets, die in anderen Sprachen als der russischen erschienen, ist recht gering. Zwar gibt es schon seit alters kleine Wörterlisten, z. B. Fischer ca. 1730, Castrén 1857, Paasonen 1908, Pröhle 1909, Németh 1911—12; s. Sinor 1963 (vgl. § 12). Auch in sowjetischer Zeit sind noch einige kleine Wörterbücher erschienen (z. B. Kowalski 1929, Buronov 1969, Waterson 1980, Indjoudjian 1983, Kydyrbaeva 1983, s. Sinor 1963, *Turkologischer Anzeiger*). Umfangreich sind aber allein: Shitnikov 1966 und Jäfärov 1971.

3. Turklexikographie Chinas

Aus dem 11. Jh. stammt ein hervorragendes Wörterbuch des Kaschgharer Philologen Maḥmūd, das folgende (in Abschn. 1. aufgeführte) Sprachen erfaßt: 1, 2/3, 4, 7, 8; es ist in der Art arabischer Reimlexika (nach al-Fārābī) zusammengestellt, als Hauptsprache dient das Karachanidische (ein Vorläufer des Neuuigurischen). — Schon früh hat es in China Dolmetscherämter zum Ziele des Verkehrs mit den Fremdvölkern gegeben. Schon in der Yüan-Zeit sind mongolisch-chinesische Wörtersammlungen veranstaltet worden (Gründung des Dolmetscheramts Hui-t'ung kuan 1276). Besonders in der Ming-Zeit waren Dolmetscher auf vielen Gebieten tätig (Abfassung des Hüa-yi yi-yü von 1389 durch Ho Yüan-chieh, Gründung des Übersetzungsamtes Sse-yi kuan im Jahre 1407 in Ablösung des Hui-t'ung kuan); hierbei sind 10 Sprachen behandelt worden, darunter auch das Uigurische (ca. 1500 fertiggestelltes Ming-Vokabular). Während in älterer Zeit die Fremdsprachen gewöhnlich in chinesische Schrift transkribiert und mit chinesischer Interlinearübersetzung versehen wurden, ist der uigurische Text des Sse-yi kuan in uigurischer Schrift verfaßt. Seine Sprache ist noch altuigurisch. Sicher Neuuigurisches bietet dagegen das *Wu-t'i ch'ing wên chien* (zwischen 1771 und 1800). Das Werk enthält in der japanischen Ausgabe Tamura et alii 1966, 1968 18 671 Termini. Es ist, wie alle chinesischen Ausgaben älterer Zeit, nach Sachkategorien geordnet (Himmel, Zeit, Geographie, Herrscher usw.). Das Neuuigurische ist in arabischer und zusätzlich in mandschu Schrift exakt geschrieben. — Kirgisen und Kasachen haben in größerer Masse erst im 20. Jh. (teilweise schon in der Zarenzeit) in China gesiedelt. Auch in der VR China spiegeln sich die politischen Wandlungen deutlich in den Wörterbüchern wider. Burhan *Šähidi: Uyġurča-xanča-rusča luγat* (1953) enthält etwa 13 000 Wörter, ist im reformierten arabischen Alphabet (das lediglich *o* und *ö*, *u* und *ü* nicht scheidet, sonst aber exakt ist) gehalten (Angaben über Sachkunde: Chemie, Botanik, Mythologie, veraltete und vulgäre Termini, über chinesische Etymologie usw. finden sich); auffällig: Auch eine russische Übersetzung ist beigegeben. Ganz anders das *Hänzuqä-uyǧurqä luǧät* 1974: Es enthält 41 000 Eintragungen in Lateinschrift (die 1959/60 eingeführt worden war), auch die chinesischen Charaktere sind in diese umschrieben (Pinyin-Fang-System). Wegen der Entzweiung zwischen der UdSSR und der VR China ist also das Russische in den Hintergrund getreten und ist die Transkription internationalisiert worden. Charakteristischerweise ist das etwa gleichzeitig in der UdSSR erschienene *Uyγurča-rusča luγät* (s. unten) im arabischen Alphabet gehalten. Bezeichnend für beide modernen Werke ist immerhin die Abkehr von der alten sachkundlichen Ordnung, wie sie noch im *Wu-t'i ch'ing wên chien* üblich war. Zu nennen ist noch das *Uyǧurqä-Hanzuqä luǧät* 1982, in Lateinschrift. Es gibt auch ein Rechtschreibwörterbuch für das Neuuigurische (ca. 9500 Wörter). Wörterbücher des Kasachischen sind (für beide Richtungen) verfaßt worden: Bingji 1979 und *Hanzuxa-Qazaqxa sözdik* 1979; ferner ein kleines Rechtschreibwörterbuch (4000 Wörter). Gute Spezialwörterbücher der Flora Sinkiangs in Uigurisch (1974) und Kasachisch (1973) liegen vor. — Freilich, ohne die Mitarbeit vieler europäischer

Gelehrter wäre der Wortschatz der Türksprachen Chinas unvollständig erfaßt. Am besten ist das Neuuigurische untersucht: R. Shaw 1878, M. Hartmann 1904/5, Raquette 1914/1927, Menges 1933, 1936, 1955, Malov 1954, 1956, 1961, Nadžip 1954, Baskakov 1970. Ein besonders wichtiges Wörterbuch stammt aus der Feder G. Jarrings (Jarring 1964); es basiert auf der Auswertung von wichtigen folkloristischen Texten. Noch umfangreicher ist jedoch Nadžip 1968 (33 000 Wörter im reformierten arabischen Alphabet), ein Werk, das hohen Ansprüchen gerecht wird, auch Dialekt- und sachkundliche Angaben enthält. Grundsätzlich befriedigt die Erforschung des Neuuigurischen Sinkiangs, wenngleich einzelne Dialekte noch wenig erforscht sind.

Weniger günstig steht es um die Lexikographie des Kirgisischen und der beiden kleinen Türksprachen Chinas. Es gibt geringe Wörterlisten aus älterer Zeit (Gelbuigurisch, Salarisch bei Potanin 1893, Gelbuigurisch bei Mannerheim 1911). Aber auch die Vokabulare des Gelbuigurischen bei Malov 1957 und Tenišev 1976 b umfassen nur 6000 bzw. 2500 Termini, das salarische Vokabular bei Tenišev 1976 a ist zwar 6500 Lemmata stark, darunter befinden sich aber viele Varianten bzw. Eigennamen. Von chinesischer Seite sind mir keine größeren Vokabulare bekannt. Nach einer Mitteilung von Geng Shimin (Peking) ist kürzlich in Ürümči eine kirgisische Abteilung eingerichtet worden, und Arbeiten über das Gelbuigurische und Salarische sind im Druck.

4. Turklexikographie Irans

Eines der wichtigsten Länder für die Turkologie ist Iran. Dieses Land hat 900 Jahre unter türkischen oder mongolischen Dynastien gelebt. Etwa ein Fünftel der Bevölkerung dürfte türkisch sein (wobei das Türkische teilweise noch expandiert). In der Bearbeitung von Turcica durch einheimische Autoren mag man vier Perioden unterscheiden: (a) In ältester Zeit (Seldschuken usw.) Behauptung des iranischen Elements, Desinteresse am Türkischen; (b) seit dem 14. Jh. (Mongolenzeit) Bewußtwerdung der türkischen Suprematie. Es wird eine Reihe von türkischen Wörterbüchern geschaffen, wobei das Čaghataische (Vorläufer des Özbekischen) im Vordergrund steht. Die Wörterbücher sind teilweise recht akzeptabel, sowohl qualitativ (z. B. Zitate von Dialektformen), wie auch quantitativ (Muḥammad Mahdī Xān z. B., etwa von 1759, hat 7000 Lemmata gesammelt). Daß das Osttürkische so stark berücksichtigt wurde, trotz des überwiegend oghusischen Charakters der Türkbevölkerung Irans, erklärt sich daraus, daß es als die „edelste der Türksprachen" galt (so Ibn Muhannā, etwa um 1300). — (c) Während der Pahlevi-Dynastie, die sich puristisch-iranisch gebärdete, war das Türkische verpönt. Nur schüchtern (z. B. als „iranischer Dialekt" getarnt) konnte es behandelt werden. Während es in der UdSSR und in Iran etwa gleichviel Azeris gibt, waren bis 1960 1442 sowjetische Werke über sie erschienen, dagegen nur 11 einheimisch-iranische (dazu 7 europäische). Darunter befanden sich nur zwei Wörterbücher, beide minimal, eines (von 1343 h. š.; = 1945) 593 Wörter des Westazeri (etwa Tebriz) enthaltend, das andere genau 700 azeri Wörter aus Zentraliran. Immerhin enthielt letzteres auch rund 300 Wörter des chaladsch Dialekts und hat damit einen Anstoß zu einer hoffnungsvollen Entwicklung gegeben. — (d) In der Chomeini-Zeit ist durch die Rückbesinnung auf die Gleichheit aller Nationen vor dem Islam eine für turkologische Sprachuntersuchungen günstigere Situation eingetreten. Der kräftezehrende Krieg mit Irak hat jedoch bisher wissenschaftliche Forschungen erschwert. Immerhin ist z. B. in der Zeitschrift Qäläm uju das Chorasantürkische behandelt worden, dessen Existenz früher peinlich verschwiegen wurde — obwohl es sich um etwa 1 000 000 Bewohner Irans handelt. Ferner ist erschienen Payfūn 1983: 16 000 Wörter, charakteristischerweise mit einem in russischer (!) Schrift beigegebenen Index. — Wichtiger als die einheimischen Arbeiten zur Turkologie Irans waren jene ausländischer Forscher: (a) Das Azeri Irans, gesprochen von mehreren Millionen Menschen, war gleichwohl bisher nur dürftig erfaßt. In grammatischen Darstellungen finden sich zuweilen Listen von einigen hundert Wörtern (Szapszal 1935, Monteil 1956, Householder 1965). Auch die Wörterliste des Azeri von Galūgāh (am Kaspischen Meer), ca. 700 Wörter, ist erst kürzlich ediert worden (Doerfer et al. 1990). Das relativ umfangreichste Wörterbuch (gleichwohl nur 197 Seiten stark) stammt von Koichi Haneda: Tabrizi Vocabulary, Tokyo 1979. — (b) Vom Qašqa'i existiert bisher keine Wörterliste, vom Aynallu nur eine ganz dürftige (400 Wörter). — (c) Vom Türkmenischen und Südoghusischen sowie Sonqori Irans ist erschienen: Doerfer/

Hesche 1989. — (d) Zum Chorasantürkischen sind bisher drei Dissertationen (Bozkurt 1975 und Fázsy 1977, Tulu 1989) mit Wörterlisten von 700 bzw. 1500 bzw. 1200 Lemmata erschienen. Die Auswertung einer Liste von 714 Wörtern von 22 weiteren Mundarten ist in Göttingen in Angriff genommen. Da Chorasantürken in Iran wie auch in der UdSSR siedeln, wäre eine Zusammenarbeit mit sowjetischen Stellen wünschenswert. — (e) Die einzige Türksprache Irans, von der ausreichendes Material erarbeitet worden ist, ist gleichzeitig die kleinste (aber linguistisch wegen ihrer Archaismen wichtigste): das Chaladsch. Ein 1980 in Budapest publiziertes „Wörterbuch des Chaladsch" (Doerfer/ Tezcan 1980) enthält 4000 Wörter (mit Varianten 5000). Eine Gesamtbehandlung der 48 chaladsch Orte, mit Sprachatlas, ist erschienen: Doerfer 1987. — Alles in allem muß die lexikalische Erfassung der Turksprachen Irans als unbefriedigend bezeichnet werden. Eine kurze Periode relativer Liberalisierung erlaubte es Göttinger Forschern 1968—1973 in drei Expeditionen vier neue Sprachen zu entdecken. Es gibt Anzeichen dafür, daß noch viele weitere Entdeckungen möglich wären.

5. Turklexikographie anderer Länder

Als der gagausische Sprachraum noch zu *Rumänien* gehörte, ist von dieser Seite ein kleines Wörterbuch publiziert worden (Ceachir 1938). Heute leben vor allem in der Dobrudscha Tataren und Nogaier. W. Zajączkowski hat das Dobrudschatatarische 1975 bearbeitet und dabei eine Liste von 2500 Wörtern gegeben. Ebenso ist in *Polen* seinerzeit das Karaimische bearbeitet worden. (Das erste größere Wörterbuch stammt jedoch aus sowjetischer Zeit.) — In *Irak* scheinen größere einheimische Arbeiten über den Wortschatz des dortigen Türkischen zu fehlen. Jedoch sind in der Türkei einige anspruchslose Dissertationen über den Dialekt von Kerkük erschienen (Haydar 1979, Hassan 1979, je 3—4000 Wörter im Anhang einer Textsammlung). — Über die sprachlichen Verhältnisse *Afghanistans* haben Jarring 1939, Ligeti 1955 und Schurmann 1962 ausgezeichnete Berichte hinterlassen. Gleichwohl sind auch die Türksprachen dieses Landes kaum erfaßt. Nur kleinere Wörterlisten sind bisher verfaßt worden: Jarring 1938 (1600 Wörter), Hesche et al. 1978 (700 Wörter), Boeschoten 1983 (500 Wörter) — alles zum Özbekischen (in Vorbereitung sind auch Listen von Hesche und Baldauf); Hesche untersucht ferner das Türkmenische von Andxoy; Bozkurt hat 1977 520 kabul-afscharische Wörter ediert. Redard und Kieffer (Bern) bereiten einen Sprachatlas Afghanistans vor, der auch 11 türkische Punkte umfaßt. Zu Iran und Afghanistan vgl. allgemein Doerfer 1970. — In der *Mongolei* siedeln u. a. Kasachen, Tuviner, auch einige Özbeken und Uiguren. Es scheint bisher keine einigermaßen umfangreichen Wörterbücher über deren Sprachen von mongolischer Seite zu geben. — Fassen wir Kapitel 2—5 zusammen, so ist zu sagen, daß bisher allein in der UdSSR befriedigende Resultate in puncto Lexikographie erbracht worden sind. Die VR China dürfte bald denselben Stand erreicht haben.

6. Lexikographie des Alt- und Mitteltürkischen

Während die Bearbeitung der modernen Türksprachen riesige Lücken aufweist, sind die bisher edierten Texte älterer Sprachstadien weitaus besser lexikalisch erfaßt. Neben zwei größeren Wörterbüchern des Alttürkischen (etwa 16 000 Lemmata: Nadeljaev, Clauson) erscheint auch ein umfangreiches Wörterbuch des Uigurischen (Röhrborn) in freilich zögernder Edition (4 Lieferungen, 298 Seiten). In den beiden zuerst genannten Werken ist auch der Wortschatz des Karachanidischen erfaßt, das sich als Westdialekt des älteren Türkischen darstellt. Besser sind jedoch die Spezialarbeiten dazu (Konkordanzen), so Arat 1979 und vor allem die treffliche Arbeit Dankoffs (die als einzige bisher philologischen Ansprüchen genügt). — Auch die mitteltürkischen Sprachstadien sind teilweise recht gut erforscht, sowohl (a) das ältere Azeri (das oft sub „Altosmanisch" figuriert) als auch (b) die beiden Türksprachen Mamluk-Osmanisch und Mamluk-Kiptschakisch mit Quellen aus dem 14.—17. Jh., ebenso das Kiptschakische „Komanische" der Krim (14. Jh.), Zentralasiens (14. Jh.) und schließlich das Armeno-Kiptschakische (16./17. Jh.); all die sub (b) genannten Sprachen sind heute ausgestorben, stellen jedoch eine sprachhistorisch wichtige Übergangsstufe dar. Die Turkologie hat sich bisher vornehmlich der Erfassung des älteren Materials zugewandt; jüngeres Material ist (teilweise wegen politischer Verhältnisse) weniger erforscht.

7. Vergleichende Turklexikographie

Es gibt (neben weniger bedeutsamen und heute überholten Werken wie Budagov und Hüseyin Kâzim Kadri) drei größere, den Wortschatz der Türksprachen zusammenfassende Arbeiten. Das älteste ist Radloff 1893—1911, bis heute ein Standardwerk; es registriert freilich nur die Termini und gibt selten Etymologien: v. Gabain und Veenker haben dazu einen Index der deutschen Bedeutungen herausgegeben. Es folgt Räsänens meist zuverlässige (aber noch recht unvollständige) Arbeit. Schließlich sind bisher vier Bände des Wörterbuchs von Sevortjan erschienen (vgl. 2.); das Werk hat wegen der Sammlung umfangreichen sowjetischen Materials hohe Verdienste, behandelt aber fast nur Wörter türkischen Ursprungs. Eine allen Ansprüchen etymologischer und sprachgeographischer Forschungen genügende Arbeit steht für die Turkologie noch aus.

8. Literatur (in Auswahl)

8.1. Wörterbücher

Arat 1979 = Reşid Rahmeti Arat: Kutadgu Bilig, III, Indeks (ed. Kemal Eraslan et alii). Istanbul 1979 [65 S.].

Bingji 1979 = Jin Bingji: Qazaqxa Hanzuxa sözdik. Urümči 1979 [897 S.].

Bozkurt 1975 = Mehmet Fuat Bozkurt: Untersuchungen zum Bojnurd-Dialekt des Chorasantürkischen. Göttingen 1975.

Bozkurt 1977 = Mehmet Fuat Bozkurt: Kabil Avşar ağzı. Türk Dili Araştırmaları Yıllığı Belleten 1977 [keine Seriennummer!], 205—261.

Buronov et al. 1969 = J. B. Buronov et alii: Uzbek-English school dictionary. Toshkent 1969.

Ceachir 1938 = M. Ceachir: Dicţionar găgăuz-român. Chişinău 1938.

Clauson 1972 = Sir Gerard Clauson: An Etymological Dictionary of Pre-Thirteenth Century Turkish. Oxford 1972 [XLVIII, 989 S.].

Dankoff 1982—85 = Robert Dankoff: Maḥmūd al-Kāšγarī: Compendium of the Turkic Dialects. 3 Bde. Harvard 1982—1985 [416, 381, 337 S.].

Doerfer 1963—75 = Gerhard Doerfer: Türkische und mongolische Elemente im Neupersischen. 4 Bde. Wiesbaden 1963—75.

Doerfer 1987 = Gerhard Doerfer: Lexik und Sprachgeographie des Chaladsch. Wiesbaden Charrab). Budapest 1980 [5000 Wörter].

Gabain/Veenker 1969—72 = A. v. Gabain/W. Veenker: „Radloff", Index der deutschen Bedeutungen. Wiesbaden 1969—72 [913 S.].

Hänzuqä-uyğurqä luğat 1974 = Hänzuqä-uyğurqä luğat. Urümči 1974 [1190 S.].

Hanzuxa-Qazaqxa sözdik 1979 = Hanzuxa-Qazaqxa sözdik. Urümči 1979 [1150 S., ca. 68 000 Eintragungen].

Hesche 1989 = Wolfram Hesche: Südoghusische Materialien aus Afghanistan und Iran. Wiesbaden 1989.

Hesche et al. 1978 = Wolfram Hesche et alii: Das Moyolî in Badachschan (Afghanistan). Göttingen 1978.

Indjoudjian 1983 = D. Indjoudjian: Dictionnaire kazakh-français. Paris 1983.

Jäfärov 1971 = J. M. Jäfärov: Deutsch-aserbaidschanisches Wörterbuch. Baku 1971 [35 000 Wörter].

Jarring 1964 = G. Jarring: An Eastern Turki-English Dictionary. Lund 1964 [9000 Wörter].

Kydyrbaeva 1983 = L. Kydyrbaeva: Dictionnaire français-kazakh. Paris 1983.

Menges 1936, 1955 = Karl Heinrich Menges: Volkskundliche Texte aus Ost-Türkistan I/II. Sitzungsberichte der Preußischen Akademie der Wissenschaften. Berlin 1933, 1936. Glossar zu den volkskundlichen Texten aus Ost-Türkistan II. Wiesbaden 1955.

Nadeljaev 1969 = Nadeljaev et alii (red.): Drevnetjurkskij slovar'. Leningrad 1969 [XXXVIII, 676 S.].

Nadžip 1968 = Nadžip: Uyyurča-rusča luyät. Moskva 1968 [33 000 Wörter].

Németh 1911—1912 = Julius Németh: Kumükisches und balkarisches Wörterverzeichnis. In: Keleti Szemle 12. 1911—1912, 91—153.

Paasonen 1908 = Heikki Paasonen: Csuvas szójegyzék. Budapest 1908.

Payfün 1983 = Muḥammad Payfün: Farhang-i āzarbāyjānī-fārsī. Teheran 1381 h.š. (= 1983) [535 S., 16 000 Wörter].

Pröhle 1909 = Wilhelm Pröhle: Karatschaisches Wörterbuch. In: Keleti Szemle 10. 1909, 83—150.

Radloff 1893—1911 = Wilhelm Radloff: Versuch eines Wörterbuches der Türk-Dialecte. 4 Bde. Sanktpetersburg 1893—1911 [XVIII, 1914, 66; 1814, 64; 2203, 48; 2230, 107 S.].

Raquette 1914 = G. Raquette: Eastern Turki grammar, practical and theoretical, with vocabulary. In: Mitteilungen des Seminars für orientalische Sprachen (W) 17. 1914, 170—232.

Raquette 1927 = G. Raquette: English-Turki dictionary based on the dialects of Kashgar and Yarkend. Lund 1927.

Räsänen 1969—71 = Martti Räsänen: Versuch eines etymologischen Wörterbuchs der Türksprachen. 2 Bde. Helsinki 1969—71 [XV, 533; 136 S.].

Röhrborn 1977—88 = Klaus Röhrborn: Uigurisches Wörterbuch. 4 Lieferungen. Wiesbaden 1977—88 [298 S.].

Šähidi 1953 = Burhan Šähidi: Uyğurča-xančarusča luğat. Peking 1953 [827 S.].

Sevortjan 1974—80 = È. V. Sevortjan: Ètimologičeskij slovar' tjurkskich jazykov. Bisher 4 Bde. Moskva 1974—89 [767, 349, 395, 292 S.].

Shaw 1878 = R. B. Shaw: A vocabulary of the language of Eastern Turkestan. In: Journal of the Asiatic Society of Bengal, 1878 (extra number).

Shitnikov 1966 = B. N. Shitnikov: Kazakh-English Dictionary. London 1966 [22 000 Wörter].

Tamura et al. 1966, 1968 = Jitsuzo Tamura et alii: Wu-t'i ch'ing wên chien. Tokyo 1966, 1968.

Uyğurqä-Hanzuqä luğät 1982 = Uyğurqä-Handzuqä luğat. Urümči 1982 [798 S., in Lateinschrift].

Waterson 1980 = Natalie Waterson: Uzbek-English dictionary. Oxford 1980.

8.2. Sonstige Literatur

Baskakov 1972 = N. A. Baskakov (red.): Voprosy soveršenstvovanija alfavitov tjurkskich jazykov SSSR. Moskva 1972.

Boeschoten 1983 = H. E. Boeschoten: Özbekisches aus Aibak. Utrecht 1983.

Brands 1973 = Horst Wilfrid Brands: Studien zum Wortbestand der Türksprachen. Leiden 1973.

Castrén 1857 = Alexander Castrén: Versuch einer koibalischen und karagassischen Sprachlehre..., ed. A. Schiefner. St. Petersburg 1857.

Central Asiatic Journal. Wiesbaden 1955—1990.

Dmitriev/Baskakov 1962 = N. K. Dmitriev/N. A. Baskakov: Issledovanija po sravnitel'noj grammatike tjurkskich jazykov. Moskva 1962.

Doerfer 1970 = Gerhard Doerfer: Irano-Altaistica. In: Current Trends in Linguistics VI. The Hague 1970. 217—34.

Doerfer et al. 1990 = Gerhard Doerfer/Wolfram Hesche/Jamshid Ravanyar: Oghusica aus Iran. Wiesbaden 1990.

Fázsy 1977 = Szabolcs Fázsy: Das Bodschnurdi, ein türkischer Dialekt in Chorasan, Ostpersien. Zürich 1977.

Fischer ca. 1730 = Gerhard Doerfer: Ältere westeuropäische Quellen zur kalmückischen Sprachgeschichte. Wiesbaden 1965 (darin S. 40—182 Faksimile von Johann Eberhard Fischer: Vocabularium continens trecenta vocabula triginta quatuor gentium, maxima ex parte Sibiricarum).

Hartmann 1904, 1905 = Martin Hartmann: Ein türkischer Text aus Kašgar. In: Keleti Szemle 5. 1904, 21—35, 161—184, 330—343; Keleti Szemle 6. 1905, 26—65.

Hassan 1979 = Hussin Shahbaz Hassan: Kerkük ağzı. Istanbul 1979.

Haydar 1979 = Choban Khıdır Haydar: Irak türkmen ağızları. Istanbul 1979.

Hazai 1960 = Georg Hazai et alii: Sovietico-Turcica. Budapest 1960.

Householder 1965 = Fred W. Householder: Basic courses in Azerbaijani. Bloomington. The Hague 1965. Indiana University Publications 45.

Jarring 1938 = Gunnar Jarring: Uzbek texts from Afghan Turkestan with glossary. Lund. Leipzig ohne Jahrgang (laut Vorwort 1938).

Jarring 1939 = Gunnar Jarring: On the distribution of Turk tribes in Afghanistan. Lund. Leipzig 1939.

Keleti Szemle, 1—21. Budapest 1900—32.

Kononov 1982 = A. N. Kononov: Istorija izučenija tjurksskich jazykov v Rossii. Leningrad 1982.

Kowalski 1929 = Tadeusz Kowalski: Karaimische Texte im Dialekt von Troki. Kraków 1929.

Ligeti 1955 = L. Ligeti: O mongol'skich i tjurkskich jazykach i dialektach Afganistana. In: Acta Orientalia Hungarica 4. 1955, 93—117 (mit französischem Resümee).

Loewenthal 1957 = Rudolf Loewenthal: The Turkic Languages and Literatures of Central Asia. 's-Gravenhage 1957.

Malov 1954 = S. E. Malov: Ujgurskij jazyk, teksty, perevody i slovar'. Moskva. Leningrad 1954.

Malov 1956 = S. E. Malov: Lobnorskij jazyk. Frunze 1956.

Malov 1957 = S. E. Malov: Jazyk želtych ujgurov. Alma-Ata 1957.

Malov 1961 = S. E. Malov: Ujgurskie teksty Sin'czjana, teksty, perevody i slovar'. Moskva 1961.

Mannerheim 1911 = C. G. E. Mannerheim: A visit to the Sarö and Shera Yögurs. In: Journal de la Société Finno-ougrienne 1911,2.

Menges 1968 = Karl Heinrich Menges: The Turkic Peoples and Languages. Wiesbaden 1968.

Monteil 1956 = Vincent Monteil: Sur le dialecte turc de l'Azerbâydjân iranien. In: Journal Asiatique 1956, 1—77.

Musaev 1984 = K. M. Musaev: Leksikologija tjurkskikh jazykov. Moskva 1984.

Poppe 1965 = Nicholas Poppe: Introduction to Altaic Linguistics. Wiesbaden 1965.

Potanin 1893 = G. N. Potanin: Tangutsko-tibetskaja okraina Kitaja i Central'naja Mongolija. 2 Bände. Sankt-Petersburg 1893.

PTF 1959 = Philologiae Turcicae Fundamenta. I. Aquis Mattiacis 1959.

Schurmann 1962 = H. F. Schurmann: The Mongols of Afghanistan. 's-Gravenhage 1962.

Sinor 1963 = Denis Sinor: Introduction à l'étude de l'Eurasie Centrale. Wiesbaden 1963.

Sovetskaja Tjurkologija, Baku 1970—1988.

Szapszal 1935 = H. Seraja Szapszal: Proben der Volksliteratur der Türken aus dem persischen Azerbaidschan. Kraków 1935.

Tenišev 1976a = È. R. Tenišev: Stroj salarskogo jazyka. Moskva 1976.

Tenišev 1976b = È. R. Tenišev: Stroj saryg-jugurskogo jazyka. Moskva 1976.

Turkologischer Anzeiger 1977—1989 (Türksprachen Zentralasiens usw., aufgenommen ab Band 6).

Tulu 1989 = Sultan Tulu: Chorasantürkische Materialien aus Kalāt bei Esfarāyen. Berlin 1989.

Ubrjatova 1961 = E. I. Ubrjatova (red.): Istoričeskie razvitie leksiki tjurskich jazykov. Moskva 1961.

Ungarische Jahrbücher 1—23, Berlin. Leipzig 1921—43; fortgeführt als Ural-altaische Jahrbücher 24—46, Wiesbaden 1952—74; weiter fortgeführt als Ural-Altaische Jahrbücher, Neue Folge 1—8, Wiesbaden 1981—1988.

Zajączkowski 1975 = Włodzimierz Język i folklor tatarów z Dobrudży rumuńskiej. Kraków 1975.

*Gerhard Doerfer, Göttingen
(Bundesrepublik Deutschland)*

233. Lexicography of the Caucasian Languages I: Georgian and Kartvelian

1. Introduction
2. Survey
3. Selected Bibliography

1. Introduction

Georgian, Svan, Laz and Mingrelian (the last two sometimes jointly termed Zan) are structurally sufficiently alike to allow the salient features of the family to be illustrated by data from any one of them; below Georgian examples will be used as this is (a) the best known, (b) the most widely spoken, (c) the only member for which comprehensive dictionaries exist, and (d) the only one to have a literary tradition, which dates back to the 5th century and which employs its very own script, which is phonemic. All four languages are most conveniently written in this script with minor modifications, and all lexicons (with one exception) referred to in 2 do use it. Presentation of the non-verbal part of the vocabulary causes no difficulty — nouns (and adjectives) will be cited in the nominative, though any peculiar oblique and/or plural formation (e. g. presence of syncopating vowel in the stem) should be indicated (as should declension-class in Svan). Problems arise with the verb, for the verbal system, though not as polysynthetic as in North West Caucasian, is complicated by much greater irregularity and unpredictability. To take the root *c'er*, the following formations exist: (i) Neutral Version (NV) *c'er-s* 'X writes (Y)' — some verbs mark their NV by a pre-radical *a-* (*a-k'et-eb-s* 'X makes Y'); (ii) Subjective Version (SV) *i-c'er-s* 'X writes Y for himself/his own Y'; (iii) Objective Version (OV) *u-c'er-s* 'X writes Y for Z//Z's Y'; (iv) Locative Version (LV) *a-c'er-s* 'X writes (Y) on Z'; (v) Indirect Object Relation *s-c'er-s* 'X writes (Y) to Z'; (vi) Absolute Passive (AP) *i-c'er-eb-a* 'X is being written'; (vii) Relative Passive (RP) *e-c'er-eb-a* 'X is being written for/on/to Y'; (viii) Stative Passive *c'er-i-a* 'X is written'; (ix) Indirect Stative Passive *s-c'er-i-a* 'X is written for Y'; (x) Objective Stative Passive *u-c'er-i-a* 'X has it written'; (xi) Locative Stative Passive *a-c'er-i-a* 'X is written on Y'; (xii) Causative *a-c'er-in-eb-s* 'X makes Y write (Z)'; (xiii) Active Participle *da-m-c'er-i* 'who writes/has written'; (xiv) Future Participle *da-sa-c'er-i* 'for writing/to be written'; (xv) Passive Participle *da-c'er-i-l-i/da-na-c'er-i* 'written'; (xvi) Negative Participle *da-u-c'er-el-i* 'unwritten', and the single masdar (the normal term for the only existing verbal noun) of all the non causative forms is (xvii) *c'-er-a*, whose perfective form will usually be (xviii) *da-c'er-a* but (xix) *mi/mo-c'er-a* in the case of (v) and its equivalent passives — the causative masdar is (xx) *(da/mi/mo-) c'er-in-eb-a*. If the masdar alone were entered in a lexicon, the wealth of formations associated with *c'er* would remain opaque, and one could not even be sure how to form the Present tense as the masdar of a verb with Present Stem Format (PSF)

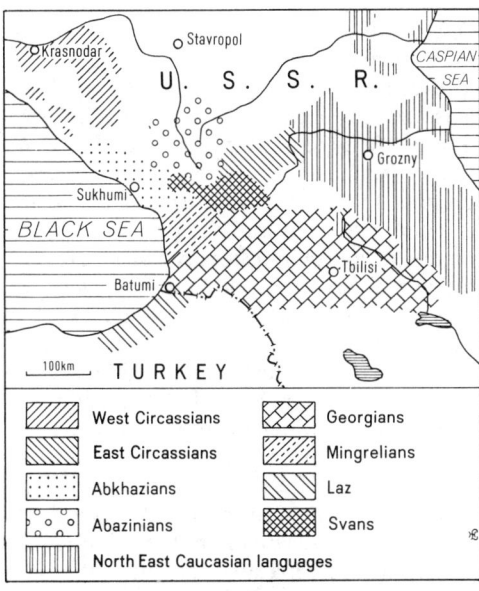

Map 233.1: Current distribution of the indigenous languages of the Caucasus (with detailed reference to the North West and South Caucasian families)

-i- (gzavn-i-s 'X sends Y') would end like (xvii) *(gzavn-a).* Given the Present tense, one could only be sure of forming the Imperfect and the Present Subjunctive, as for most verbs the remaining Series I forms (Future, Conditional and Future Subjunctive) differ from these respectively by the addition of a preverb, which in most cases is lexically determined and thus unpredictable — preverbs generally serve to mark perfective aspect, and, as most occurrences of Series II (Aorist and Aorist Subjunctive) and Series III (Perfect, Pluperfect and IIIrd Subjunctive) forms are of perfective aspect, one needs to know the relevant preverb before any of these too may be produced. As there are 'strong' and 'weak' Aorist conjugations, one must know which pattern a root will follow; concerning the Aorist it is also necessary to know (a) if a non-syllabic root is expanded by a vowel and whether this occurs in all three persons or only in the first two; (b) whether the extra vowel is *-a-* or *-e-*; (c) whether the end of the root will show an extra *-v-* in the first two persons; (d) precisely how the passive of verbs in *-ev-* behaves. The Aorist alone will not suffice as lexical entry, as it will not then be clear which PSF is taken by the root. Nor will the Future (+ Aorist) suffice, as at least one group of verbs, the Medials, do not differentiate Future from Present by addition of a preverb (*i-t'ir-eb-s* 'X will cry' vs *t'ir-i-s* 'X cries', where the Future *i-* is the SV vowel). For active verbs knowledge of the Future allows one to form the Perfect, and (for Georgian) knowledge of the Aorist allows one to form the Pluperfect and IIIrd Subjunctive; for APs knowledge of the passive participle allows one to form the IIIrd Series as a whole, and for RPs knowledge of the masdar allows the same. If the AP is not formed as in (vi) by *i-* but by either *-d-* (*k'et-d-eb-a* 'X is being made') or absence of affix (*kr-eb-a* 'X goes out, disappears'), the RP will be formed by the use of the OV-vowel and not by *e-*. This already complex picture is further complicated in a number of ways: some verbs obligatorily take SV or OV where a formal NV might be expected (*mo-i-q'van-s* 'X will bring Y (animate)'; *ga-u-šv-eb-s* 'X will release Y'); a whole class of 'inverted' verbs exists where the logical subject stands in the dative and is marked in the verb by an indirect object prefix (a) alone (*h-q'av-s* 'X *h-* has Y(animate) *-s*'), (b) followed by the OV vowel ((*Ø-*)*u-q'var-s* 'X Ø-loves Y *-s*'), (c) followed by the LV vowel (*Ø-*)*a-kv-s* 'X Ø- has Y(inanimate) *-s-*), (d) followed by the RP vowel *e-* ((*Ø*)*e-mɣer-eb-a* 'X Ø- has a desire to sing'), though the Futures of (a)-(c) pattern alike; the 'relative' (i. e. with indirect object) forms and active participles of Medials are notoriously varied; and some roots may combine with a variety of preverbs to produce a range of lexical items, so that the Present *šl-i-s* may, according to context, correspond to any of the Futures: *a-šl-i-s* 'X will upset/disturb Y', *ga-šl-i-s* 'X will unfold Y', *da-šl-i-s* 'X will split Y', *še-šl-i-s* 'X will derange Y', *c'a-šl-i-s* 'X will erase Y', *ča-šl-i-s* 'X will ruin Y', *mo-šl-i-s* 'X will destroy Y'.

2. Survey

2.1. Both masdars and finite verb-forms appear as independent entries in the very earliest monolingual Georgian dictionary, compiled by Sulxan Saba Orbeliani (finished 1716; first published 1884 and most recently 1965—6 in two volumes). This work incorporates both contemporary vocabulary and many words from Old and Mediaeval Georgian texts with frequent referencing of sources (especially the Bible). Where finite verb-forms are entered, they may take the form of Aorist (1st, 2nd or 3rd person singular subject), Present or Imperfect (3rd person singular subject), and some Presents even contain the 2nd person object prefix, which locates them under the letter *g*. This confusion is perhaps understandable in a pioneering lexicographical work. Under an entry are often included words in the same semantic field, so that under 'horse' are also quoted the words for 'stallion', 'mare', 'foal', 'colt', 'pack-horse' etc ..., though these extra nouns are also entered separately at their appropriate alphabetical place. Unlike many of his successors Saba does not shrink from including such taboo-items as words for the sexual organs and bodily functions. Based on Saba (and also on the manuscript of his uncle Nik'o's parallel dictionary, published only in 1961) was Čubinov's (Čubinašvili's) Georgian-Russian dictionary (1887; reprinted 1984) but with expansion to 70,000 entries for Old, Mediaeval and contemporary materials with source-referencing. Both perfective (preverbal) and imperfective (preverbless) masdars are entered, followed by information on the type of active and passive formations associated with them. The 1st person singular Present and, where necessary, Aorist is cited either in full (e. g. *vxdi, vxade* 'I remove(d) (clothing) from X'; *vixdi, vixade* 'I remove(d) my own (clothing)'; *vixdebi, vixade* 'I am being/was stripped', all of which are given under *gaxda,* the first two pairs being repeated under *xda,* where the OV *vuxdi, vuxade* 'I remove(d) it (hat) for X' is added and for which the preverb is *mo-*) or, if the ending is predictable, by showing only the first two letters (e. g. under *(ga)k'eteba* 'make' the formation of the NV is shown by *va-* alone). Causatives and participles are either entered separately or under the base-form. Georgian synonyms are also usually given. A shorthand method of indicating a masdar's range of versional active and passive formations was devised by Šanidze (1946), slightly modified at his suggestion by Imnaišvili (1948—9), and used principally by them alone in their various Old Georgian word-lists. It combines reference to morphological properties and a form's valence, so that *dabadeba* 'give birth' is styled 0-(3)2, meaning that the NV is marked by zero and that (in *Old* Georgian) this *bi*valent verb nevertheless had formally a *tri*valent structure. Different from all approaches examined so far is Tschenkéli's three-volume Georgian-German dictionary (1965/1970/1974): verbs are entered not by masdar but by root. Under the root are then given all finite active and passive types, all preverb-root combinations, masdars and causative according to a rigid pattern of presentation explained in the Introduction. 1st person singular subject-forms are used in the order: Present, Future, Aorist, Perfect; the 3rd person singular subject Aorist is added either if the ending is *-o* or if the root is in any person expanded by a vowel. 3rd person forms are used if the verb's meaning precludes the presence of a 1st person argument. At the end of each letter of the alphabet an index of all incorporated verb-roots is given with meanings. Because of the nature of the verbal system some entries in such a lexicon are very long, that for *svla* 'go' here extending to 22 pages. Whilst recognising the advantage to the philologist of a lexicon where all forms associated with a given root are drawn together, Čikobava (1965,62), under whose general editorship the eight-volume Georgian Academy Dictionary (KEGL) (Čikobava 1950—1964) was prepared, felt such a lexicon to be difficult for the non-specialist user. The result is that virtually all forms (i)-(xx) listed in 1 are entered separately in KEGL — the exceptions are (v) and (ix), which are listed under (i) and (viii) respectively, as personal affixes on verbs (and also the nominative case-ending *-i* in consonant-stem nouns) were judged to be irrelevant to a word's placement in the dictionary. 3rd person singular subject verb-forms were chosen by the editorial board without explanation (1950,011). In brackets the lexical entry is followed by the 3rd person Aorist and Perfect (imperfective alongside a Present entry, perfective alongside a Future). If a Present (such as *šl-i-s*) can correlate with more than one preverb + root combination in perfective forms, the reader is referred to the relevant Futures for the meanings. KEGL includes 113,000 entries, is rich in illustrative materials with referencing to sources, and represents the Modern Georgian literary language to the exclusion of Old Georgian, taboo and dialectal words — dialectal forms are included only if they occur in some literary work; their regional provenance is indicated. For nouns the genitive is bracketed after the nominative citation-form and this shows whether a syncopating vowel is present. However, it is normal for parallel dictionaries of Georgian to enter only the masdar (with possibly separate entries for perfective and imperfective forms) and one or more of the participles (Gvarjaladze/Gvarjaladze 1979); Cherkesi (1950) sometimes presents past participles and derivatives like abstract nouns under the entry for the base-form. Xucišvili/Xat'iašvili (1977) add in brackets after the masdar a single finite form (usually the 3rd person singular Aorist, though for some verbs the Future, for others the Imperfect is given) to indicate the type of finite formation(s) taken by the root.

2.2. The idea of using the root as lexical entry in Kartvelian lexicography goes back to at least the 115-page vocabulary appended by Marr to his grammar of Laz (1910). A verbal root is followed by the masdar and a variety of finite and non-finite forms, including the Present, Future and Aorist, regularly (though not always only) with 1st person singular subject — clearly there is no attempt to present all potentially occurring forms of a root. This principle is followed by Kipšidze (1911).

2.3. Kipšidze followed the same principle in the 232-page lexicon appended to his Mingrelian grammar (1914). The treatment of verbs is, however, much more exhaustive — 1st, 2nd and 3rd person subjectforms of the various tenses often being quoted, possibly in recognition of the complexity introduced both by the large number of preverbs existing here and by the phonetic changes occasioned by preverb-personal prefix-version vowel collocations. The Perfect is regularly quoted along with other finite and non-finite forms, Georgian equivalents are sometimes placed beside the Russian glosses.

2.4. Marr's extract of a Svan-Russian lexicon (1922) follows this same pattern, with masdar and a selection of finite and non-finite formations accompanying verbal roots. The order of the Georgian alphabet is not entirely followed, vowel- and semi-vowel-initial words precede all consonant-initial ones. Gudjedjiani/Palmaitis' (Upper) Svan-English lexicon (1985) uses a Roman-based transcription but adheres to the ordering of the Georgian alphabet; long and/or umlauted vowels (marked by macron and/or diaeresis) are not kept separate from their plain counterparts. Declension-class and presence of syncopating vowel is indicated for nouns and adjectives. Verbal meanings (along with valence, (in)transitivity and stative/dynamic status) are given alongside masdars. As there is no published grammar of Svan and as phonetic changes within verbs are just as complicated as in Mingrelian, the bulk of the dictionary consists of finite verb-forms that a non-native speaker might find difficult to analyse. Each such citation is then parsed according to a shorthand method described in the Introduction, and cross-reference is given to the masdar for the meaning.

3. Selected Bibliography

3.1. Dictionaries

Cherkesi 1950 = Ekaterine Cherkesi: Georgian-English Dictionary. Oxford 1950 [275 p.].

Čikobava 1950—1964 = Arnold Čikobava (editor): kartuli enis ganmart'ebiti leksik'oni 1—8. Tbilisi 1950—1964 [096, 12302 p.].

Čubinov (Čubinašvili) 1887; 1984 = Davit Čubinov (Čubinašvili): kartul-rusuli leksik'oni. St. Petersburg.Tbilisi 1887; 1984 [xvi, 1780 p.].

Gudjedjiani/Palmaitis 1985 = Chato Gudjedjiani/ Letas Palmaitis: Svan-English Dictionary. Edited by B. George Hewitt. New York 1985 [vii, 369 p.].

Gvarjaladze/Gvarjaladze 1979 = Thamar and Isidor Gvarjaladze: kartul-inglisuri leksik'oni. Tbilisi 1979 [527 p.].

Imnaišvili 1948—9 = Ivane Imnaišvili: kartuli otxtavis simponia-leksik'oni. Tbilisi 1948—1949 [032, 839 p.].

Kipšidze 1911 = Ioseb Kipšidze: Dopolnitel'nyja svedenija o čanskom jazyke. St. Petersburg 1911 [vi, 33 p.].

Kipšidze 1914 = Ioseb Kipšidze: Grammatika mingrel'skago (iverskago) jazyka s khrestomatieju i slovarem. St. Petersburg 1914 [xl, 0150, 424 p.].

Marr 1910 = Nikolai Jakovlevič Marr: Grammatika čanskago (lazskago) jazyka s khrestomatieju i slovarem. St. Petersburg 1910 [xxx, 240 p.].

Marr 1922 = Nikolai Jakovlevič Marr: Izvlečenie iz svansko-russkago slovarja. Petrograd 1922 [viii, 39 p.].

Saba 1965—6 = Sulxan Saba Orbeliani: txzulebani IV$_1$, IV$_2$; sit'q'vis k'ona kartuli, romel ars leksik'oni. Edited by Ilia Abuladze. Tbilisi 1965 [638 p.], 1966 [655 p.].

Tschenkéli 1965/1970/1974 = Kita Tschenkéli: Georgisch-Deutsches Wörterbuch. Zürich 1965/ 1970/1974 [xxxviii, 2470 p.].

Xucišvili/Xat'iašvili 1977 = Otar Xucišvili/Tamar Xat'iašvili: kartul-germanuli leksik'oni. Tbilisi 1977 [534 p.].

3.2. Other Publications

Čikobava 1965 = Arnold Čikobava: iberiul-k'avk'asiur enata šesc'avlis ist'oria. Tbilisi 1965 [xv, 412 p.].

Šanidze 1946 = Ak'ak'i Šanidze (editor): cxovreba iovanesi da eptwimesi. Tbilisi 1946 [xii, 171 p.].

Brian George Hewitt, London (Great Britain)

234. Lexicography of the Caucasian Languages II: Northwest Caucasian Languages

1. Introduction
2. Survey
3. Selected Bibliography

1. Introduction

Abkhaz-Abaza, Circassian and Ubykh [=Ubyx] are characterised by large consonantal inventories (coupled with minimal vowel-systems), by mainly monosyllabic root-morphemes, and by an extreme polypersonalism within the verbal system, whereby virtually the entire syntactic structure of the clause is recapitulated in the verbal complex. This makes it impossible for any dictionary of manageable proportions to list all potentially occurring verb-forms (even if restricted uniquely to 3rd person illustrations, as in some Soviet lexicons). But, since morphological irregularity is not typical of these languages, one can question whether there is any need to include such entirely predictable formations as reflexive, reciprocal, benefactive, potential, causative, 'participial' and tense-modal forms for the verbs, and (in)definite and/or plural forms for the nouns. For nouns one certainly needs to indicate irregular plural formations, after the manner of Džanašia (1954); for verbs it is essential to identify the root (sc. where the lexical meaning is not determined solely by the root but is a function of some preverb + root combination), as certain exponents must stand immediately before it — this can be achieved typographically in a number of ways; it is really immaterial whether entry is by root/stem or masdar (the regular term for the only existing verbal noun), but, as masdars are not always available, perhaps the former is to be preferred. In addition it is necessary to state (a) whether a verb is stative, dynamic (processual) or freely capable of either classification (e.g. the Abkhaz root $t^{o'}a$ is stative for the meaning 'X is seated' = $də-t^{o'}a-w+p'$, but dynamic for 'X is sitting down' = $də-t^{o'}a-wa-yt'$), (b) whether a form is transitive or intransitive, and what changes, if any, are involved if a given root/stem may be either (e.g. Circassian $tχə$ 'write(trans)' vs $tχe$ 'write(intrans)'), and (c) any unpredictable feature of morphology or semantics (e.g. in Abkhaz the causative marker r usually stands between preverb and root but for some verbs it irregularly precedes the preverb, as in the stem $q'a-c'a$ 'do' ⇒ $r-q'a(-)c'a$ 'cause to do'; equally where the preverb a: is used normally to mark orientation 'hither', as in $(a:-)št$ 'send (hither)', this need not be listed [sc. as long as this and similar intraverbal items have their own entries in the lexicon], but, where it has modal force, as in 'X sat down *slowly*' = $d-a:-t^{o'}a-yt'$, this must be mentioned). In languages so rich in compositionality cross-referencing for elements in compounds that have entries of their own is to be recommended. All the family has a rich oral tradition (e.g. the Nart epic), was first represented by individual texts in such late 19th century publications as *Sbornik materialov dlja opisanija mestnostei i plemen kavkaza,* and gained four orthographies thus: Abaza 1932 (Latin); Abkhaz c. 1900 (Uslar's script; 1928 Latin); East Circassian 1924 (Latin); West Circassian 1918 (Arabic; 1927 Latin).

2. Survey

2.1. Closest to the approach outlined above stand the Ubykh-French lexicon of Vogt (1963) (Ubykh is almost extinct and since the 1864 migration has been spoken only in Turkey), the Abkhaz-English lexicon of Lucassen/Starreveld (forthcoming), and Paris' rendition into French of two West Circassian dialects: (a) the 69-page lexicon attached to her collection of Šapsugh texts (1974), and (b) her comprehensive treatment (forthcoming) of Abzakh. In all four cases the script used is Roman-based, but, whereas Vogt and Paris basically follow the alphabetic order (with additional/adapted signs accommodated appropriately), Lucassen/Starreveld first group together the sonants and then order the consonants according to point of articulation from front to back of the mouth (plosives precede affricates, which precede fricatives; plain sounds precede palatalised ones, which precede labialised ones, and ejectives precede non-ejectives). Whilst entry is by root/stem in Vogt and Paris, Lucassen/Starreveld use citation-forms, so that all nouns, including masdars, and adjectives begin with the definite-generic article a-, which has no bearing on a word's alphabetic placement. Whilst certain of the predictable formations are quoted under the root/stem by Vogt, Paris (1974) assigns such forms separate articles with cross-references under the root/stem, though in the later work she seems to avoid their wholesale incorporation. In all cases compounds are entered under their initial component, and entries have cross-references to places where the relevant form appears as non-first element in a compound. Illustrative examples are freely provided. Kuipers' specialised proto-Circassian root-dictionary (1975), based on Bžedugh (West Circassian) and Kabardian (East Circassian) cognates for open mono- and bisyllabic items, also uses a Roman-based script with the contruct-phonemes ordered for point of articulation from front to back of the mouth. But, as the non-finite members of consonant-clusters have no independent laryngal articulation, they are written with capitals in the reconstructed forms (e.g. Pz = [bz]) and placed according to the final element of the cluster (except for segments with $*-q'$, $*-q'^{o}$).

2.2. Within the USSR the West Circassian and East Circassian literary languages (based on the Temirgoi and Kabardian dialects respectively) have, together with Abaza, been written with a Cyrillic-based script since 1938 (1936 for Kabardian), though there is often no uniform representation of identical sounds. In each case the one additional letter is the old Cyrillic capital I, which marks all ejectives in Temirgoi, some ejectives in Kabardian and either ejectivity or pharyngal articulation in Abaza: Cyrillic ordering is followed. The rich consonantism of these languages can only be handled in this way by the use of di- and trigraphs, and Kabardian even has one tetragraph КХБУ = /q^{o}/. In the Abaza-Russian lexicon (Tugov 1967) words are entered in their citation-forms (i.e. without the definite article a-), though stative verbs, having no natural masdar, are cited in the Present tense (3rd person singular subject). A number of verbs merit separate entries not only for the basic lexical meaning but also for the predictable categories listed in 1. Temirgoi's monolingual dictionary (Khatanov/Keraševa 1960), where however a single Russian equivalent is given as well as the native definition, quotes verbs in the Simple Past (3rd person singular subject), adding the Present in brackets. Where the subject-prefix is ы = /ə/, this has no influence on the word's alphabetic placement (similarly for 'participles' starting with ы). The usual list of predictable forms (plus masdars) are also entered separately. Citation-form for nouns is the indefinite absolutive singular, the predictable definite and plural forms then standing in brackets. Šaov's Temirgoi-Russian lexicon (1975) differs by excluding 'participles' and by quoting finite verbs in their Present tense only, nouns appearing only in the indefinite absolutive singular. The Kabardian-Russian lexicon (Kardanov 1957) then differs again only insofar as it cites verbs exclusively in the masdar, be this for the basic lexeme or for the usual list of predictable categories. Jakovlev's compilation (1927) was limited to the 400 open monosyllabic roots that reflect the core-vocabulary of the language.

2.3. Although the Abkhaz literary language (based on the Abžui dialect) has used a Cyrillic-based script since 1954, no monolingual or parallel dictionary has been produced in the USSR since then. From 1938 to 1954 a Georgian-based script was used, and this is how the language is presented in Džanašia's Abkhaz-Georgian dictionary (1954, though compiled in 1938). The ordering is basically that of Georgian. Labialisation of velars and uvulars is shown by use of the Georgian character for *u,* and words beginning with such phonemes are placed under the relevant plain consonantal sign (e.g. *a-k°'a* 'breast-pocket' appears under *k'*), whilst other labialised and all palatalised segments have separate headings. Though the modern script uses the Russian sign for *u* to mark labialised velars and uvulars, it can be seen from such specialised lexicons as Aršba (1980) that each phoneme is assigned its own heading in the alphabet. Words are cited as in Lucassen/Starreveld's work, the artificial masdars of stative verbs being bracketed. For all verbs the finite Past (and sometimes the Present) with 3rd person singular subject is quoted in brackets. The two previous Abkhaz(-Russian) dictionaries were both based on the phonetically richer Bzyp dialect. Marr (1928) used his idiosyncratic Japhetic alphabet, first listing the vowels, semi-vowels and schwa, and then arranging the consonants according to the Georgian pattern, fitting in non-Georgian sounds at the phonetically most appropriate place. All 67 consonantal phonemes are recognised, though an extra one is also proposed. Citations are as in the other Abkhaz lexicons. Illustrated are the indefinite singular and definite plurals for nouns, and a variety of (predictable) finite and non-finite forms for verbs (plus variants from non-Bzyp-speaking areas). Uslar appended a 64-page lexicon to his grammar (1862 lithograph; 1887 in print). His script was Cyrillic-based with additional characters, a number of which were borrowed when the present orthography was devised — his inconsistent marking by diacritic of non-ejectivity for voiceless plosives but of ejectivity for affricates is today retained. Entry was by roots, with a typical verbal article showing the Present (1st person singular subject), Imperative (singular) and masdar; adjectives were shown in the normal citation-form, in the abstract-noun and in the phrase 'I became ADJ'; nouns were treated as by Marr. Not quite all the phonemes were identified, but for a pioneering study the work is impressive.

3. Selected Bibliography

3.1. Dictionaries

Aršba 1980 = Nelli Vladimirovna Aršba: Slovar' životnovodčeskikh terminov. Sukhumi 1980 [183 p.].

Džanašia 1954 = Bagrat Džanašia: apkhazur-kartuli leksik'oni. Tbilisi 1954 [VIII, 468 p.].

Jakovlev 1927 = Nikolai Feofanovič Jakovlev: Materialy dlja kabardinskogo slovarja I: Slovar' odnosložnykh korennykh slov i kornei tipa otkrytogo sloga. Moscow 1927. Komitet po izučeniju jazykov i ètničeskikh kul'tur vostočnykh narodov SSSR, VI.

Kardanov 1957 = Buba Matsikovič Kardanov (editor): Kabardinsko-russkij slovar'. Moscow 1957 [576 p.].

Khatanov/Keraševa 1960 = Abdul Akhmedovič Khatanov/Zajnab Ibragimovna Keraševa: Tolkovyj slovar' adygejskogo jazyka. Majkop 1960 [XIV, 696 p.].

Kuipers 1975 = Aert H. Kuipers: A Dictionary of Proto-Circassian Roots. Lisse/Netherlands 1975 [93 p.].

Lucassen/Starreveld Forthcoming = Wim Lucassen/Albert Starreveld: Abkhaz-English Dictionary. Delmar. New York Forthcoming.

Marr 1928 = Nikolaj Jakovlevič Marr: Abkhazsko-russkij slovar'. Leningrad 1928 [LV, 159 p.].

Paris 1974 = Catherine Paris: La princesse Kahraman, Contes d'Anatolie en dialecte chapsough (tcherkesse occidental). Paris 1974 [301 p.].

Paris Forthcoming = Catherine Paris: Dictionnaire du dialecte Abzakh. Paris Forthcoming.

Šaov 1975 = Žorž A. Šaov (editor): Adygejsko-russkij slovar'. Majkop 1975 [440 p.].

Tugov 1967 = Vladimir V. Tugov (editor): Abazinsko-russkij slovar'. Moscow 1967 [536 p.].

Uslar 1887 = Baron Pëtr Karlovič Uslar: Étnografija Kavkaza, jazykoznanie, abkhazskij jazyk. Tiflis 1887 [XV, 194 p.].

Vogt 1963 = Hans Vogt: Dictionnaire de la langue oubykh. Oslo 1963 [265 p.].

Brian George Hewitt, London (Great Britain)

235. Lexicography of the Caucasian Languages III: Northeast Caucasian Languages

1. Introduction
2. Grammatical Structure
3. The Dictionaries
4. Selected Bibliography

1. Introduction

The Northeast Caucasian (NEC), or Nakh-Daghestanian, family comprises some 30 languages divided among four or five branches. Some languages are spoken in a single village; others have several hundred thousand speakers. Serious description began in the 19th century, when Uslar (1888—96; 1979) provided extensive grammars with texts and glossaries. There was limited and local early writing in the Arabic alphabet for a few languages (Avar, Lak, Dargi), but official literary status — orthography, publishing, some schooling — dates from the 1920's. There are now seven written languages: Chechen, Ingush, Avar, Lak, Dargi, Tabassaran, Lezghi. The first orthographies used the Latin alphabet, but all were converted to the Russian alphabet (supplemented, typically by "I" for pharyngeals and/or laryngeals) in 1938. The descriptive, grammatical, and lexicological traditions are not indigenous in origin, although native contributions have been essential to them.

2. Grammatical Structure

NEC languages have structural features which challenge lexicography. Most have gender classes, with which (some but usually not all) verbs agree by mutating their initial consonants; this complicates alphabetization. They are ergative or stative-active, i.e. have more than one case for subject; so the received Soviet practice of giving illustrative examples in the infinitive, hence without the subject, removes essential information about case government. The consonant inventories are complex. Multilingualism, functional restriction of indigenous languages, and recourse to Russian (and, earlier, Arabic and Turkic languages) as the language of intergroup communication, higher education, and technology complicates the treatment of technical vocabulary. On the other hand, the following simplify lexicography: the languages are agglutinating, there are few or no prefixes, an infinitive is regularly derived and retrievable for every verb, and there is generally a clear default gender — so citation forms are natural, transparent, and informative.

The gender problem was solved intelligently by Uslar: with each noun, cite the gender markers it requires (rather than naming or numbering the genders); cite the verb without the mutating consonant and with an initial hyphen, or in the default gender with an asterisk (to distinguish it from verbs which begin with the same consonant but do not take gender agreement; the asterisk goes back at least to Žirkov 1936).

3. The Dictionaries

Uslar's glossaries (1888 ff.) set high standards: they contain upwards of a thousand words, with useful citation forms, principal parts shown, gender indicated, irregularities listed, and phonemic writing. 20th-century dictionaries are mostly bilingual defining dictionaries. Caucasian-Russian ones give morphological information (gender, principal parts), salient idioms and fixed phrases, usually an illustrative example phrase (with verbs in the infinitive), and often a gazetteer and grammatical sketch (the latter generally excellent on morphological paradigms). Russian-Caucasian dictionaries give little information about either language. There are

детта²* [летта, диттнра, дит-
тина] дойть; етт бетта дойть
корову.

Dictionary excerpt 235.1: Maciev 1961, 142

დ-ეთარ² d-etaar² ქართ. ფრ.

წველა (მიწველის) დოითь,
сдоить. სუ ესხუნეგ კი
ეთრა ბეთად — წელი ჶოოოო
ხამ ფურს წველის.

Dictionary excerpt 235.3: Kadagidze/Kadagidze 1984, 224

доить несов., кого 1) детта, оза 2) перен.
дакха

Dictionary excerpt 235.2: Karasaev/Maciev 1978, 137

119. ДОИТЬ <кто:эрг; кого:ном>

АВЧД √=ec'; AOR 3 běc'rɨ; IMP 3 běc'ɨ; PRH 3 běc'ugɨ; INF 3 běc'Žɨ ∗ АНД
√=erč'ɨ; AOR 3·berč'ɨ/HF, 3pl jerč'ɨ; IMP 3 berč'o/HR, 3pl jerč'o; INF 3 berč'ɨ-
du/HHL ∗ ЧАМ √can; AOR can/L; IMP cana/LR; PRF ca:n/L ɨda; IMP caɨna/L ∗ ЧАМГ
√canɨ; AOR canɨ/L; IMP cană/L; INF canɨnă/L ∗ ТИНД √čal; AOR čalo; IMP čala; INF
čalɨɨa ∗ БЕЖТ √t'äLe; AOR t'äLerö; pl t'ä:Lerö; PRS t'äLeč; IMP t'äLä; INF t'ä-
Läɨ ∗ БЕЖХ √t'äLe; PRS t'äLec; INF t'äLäɨ ∗ ЛАК √čiz; AOR čɨ:zundɨ; IMP čɨza;
INF čɨzin; INFD čɨzlan ∗ ДАРЧ √=ircǁɨc; AOR 3 bɨrcɨb, 3,1p bɨrcɨbda; PRS ɨcle,
1p ɨcanda; IMP 3 bɨrca; PRH mějce; INF 3 bɨrcɨ: ∗ АРЧ =сеять, сажать (√=aca) ∗
ТАБД √gv-ɨ=t; PRS 1p gɨltunda:za/F; PRF 1p,2 gɨʔɨwtunuza; INF 2 gɨwtus, pl gɨtus ∗
ТАБК √kud-u=3; INF 2 kudub3ŭz, pl kudur3ŭz ∗ АГБШ =пахать, сеять {√uz-a} ∗ АГРИ
=сеять {√uz} ∗ РУТ =сеять {√=ez} ∗ ЦАХ √gya=z/L; AOR 3 gya:zɨ, 3pl gyazɨ; PRS 3
gya:za, 3pl gyaza; FUT 3 gya:zas, 3pl gyazas ∗ КРЫЗ √=äz(ä); AOR 3 väzäžu; PRS

Dictonary excerpt 235.4: Kibrik/Kadzasov 1988, 131

school dictionaries, primarily Russian-Caucasian. There are no monolingual dictionaries of any kind, no bilingual dictionaries involving any language other than Russian, no technical or terminological dictionaries (although there were a few attempts in the 1920's and 1930's: see Crisp 1985). All of this is consistent with the official and quasi-official functional restriction of these languages: there is little schooling *in* the languages, although some are taught as subjects; Russian is the language of research and technical communication; Russian is the only language for inter-group and international communication; translation is done only from and into Russian.

The major dictionaries for the literary languages are as follows. For each language the number of speakers is given (1979 census figures); "C—R" = Caucasian-Russian dictionaries; "R—C" = Russian-Caucasian; for each dictionary, the number of words is given (where known). School dictionaries are not shown. Languages are listed in approximate west-east order.

Ingush (186,000)
  R—C Ozdoeva/Kurkiev 1980 (40,000)
Chechen (756,000)
  C—R Maciev 1961 (13,250)
  R—C Karasaev/Maciev 1978 (40,000)
Avar (483,000)
  C—R Žirkov 1936 (9,000)
      Saidov 1967 (18,000)
  R—C Saidov/Mikailov 1951
Lak (100,000)
  C—R Khajdakov 1962 (13,000)
  R—C Murkelinskij 1963
Dargi (287,000)
  R—C Abdullaev 1950
Tabassaran (75,000) [no dictionaries]
Lezghi (383,000)
  C—R Talibov/Gadžiev 1966 (28,000)
  R—C Gadžiev 1951

For non-literary languages we have e.g. Mejlanova 1984 (8000 words) for Budukh, a useful description along standard lines, with a Russian-Budukh key as well; for Batsbi, Kadagidze/Kadagidze 1984 — handwritten; forms cited in Georgian alphabet, then in

Latin-based transliteration; glosses in Georgian and Russian; examples only in the Georgian alphabet and only with Georgian translation. Kibrik et al. 1977 give 3000 Archi words with government and morphological information, and a Russian-Archi index. There are a few 'comparative' dictionaries, with disparate materials from the various languages assembled by gloss. Kibrik/Kodzasov 1988 is a highly systematized landmark in this genre: 220 selected basic verbal meanings typical of the whole Daghestanian subfamily, plus valence; each entry gives the roots, principal parts, valence, and other grammatical information for the relevant verb in each of 19 languages. A second volume on the noun is in press.

Samples: Maciev 1961, 142, glossing the Chechen verb 'milk (e.g. a cow)': "*" marks the initial *d-* as a gender marker; the superscript numeral distinguishes homonyms; the example is cited with infinitive (only knowledge of grammatical structure tells the reader that the subject would be ergative). Karasaev/Maciev 1978, 37, Russian translation of same verb (note the lack of grammatical information); Kadagidze/Kadagidze 1984, 224, cognate verb in Batsbi; Kibrik/Kodzasov 1988, 131 entry for this meaning (Cyrillic capital abbreviations for languages; roots, underlined; principal parts; glosses and comments).

4. Selected Bibliography

4.1. Dictionaries

Abdullaev 1950 = S. N. Abdullaev: Russko-darginskij slovar'. Makhačkala 1950.

Gadžiev 1951 = M. M. Gadžiev: Russko-lezginskij slovar'. Makhačkala 1951 [964 p.].

Kadagidze/Kadagidze 1984 = David and Nik'o Kadagidze: Cova-tušur-kartul-rusuli leksik'oni. Tbilisi 1984 [935 p.].

Karasaev/Maciev 1978 = A. T. Karasaev/A. G. Maciev: Russko-čečenskij slovar'. Moscow 1978 [728 p.].

Khajdakov 1962 = S. M. Khajdakov: Laksko-russkij slovar'. Moscow 1962 [422 p.].

Kibrik/Kodzasov 1988 = A. E. Kibrik/S. V. Kodzasov: Sopostavitel'noe izučenie dagestanskikh jazykov: glagol. Moscow 1988 [226 p.].

Kibrik et al. 1977 = A. E. Kibrik/S. V. Kodzasov/I. P. Olovjannikova/D. S. Samedov: Arčinskij jazyk, 4: Teksty i slovari. Moscow 1977 [392 p.].

Maciev 1961 = A. G. Maciev: Čečensko-russkij slovar'. Moscow 1961 [631 p.].

Mejlanova 1984 = U. A. Mejlanova: Budukhsko-russkij slovar'. Moscow 1984 [253 p.].

Murkelinskij 1963 = G. B. Murkelinskij: Russko-lakskij slovar'. Makhačkala 1963 [826 p.].

Ozdoeva/Kurkiev 1980 = F. G. Ozdoeva/A. S. Kurkiev: Russko-ingušskij slovar'. Moscow 1980 [831 p.].

Saidov 1967 = Magomedsajid Saidov: Avarsko-russkij slovar'. Moscow 1967 [806 p.].

Saidov/Mikailov 1951 = Magomedsajid Saidov/Š. Mikailov: Russko-avarskij slovar'. Makhačkala 1951.

Talibov/Gadžiev 1966 = V. Talibov/M. Gadžiev: Lezginsko-russkij slovar'. Moscow 1966 [603 p.].

Uslar 1888—96 = P. K. Uslar: Ètnografija Kavkaza, Jazykoznanie: 2, Čečenskij jazyk (1888); 3, Avarskij jazyk (1889); 4, Lakskij jazyk (1890); 5, Khjurkilinskij jazyk [Dargi] (1892); 6, Kjurinskij jazyk [Lezghi] (1896). Tbilisi [52, 276, 71, 117; 242, 275, 20; 422, 14; 497 p.].

Uslar 1979 = P. K. Uslar: Ètnografija Kavkaza, Jazykoznanie: 7, Tabasaranskij jazyk. (Edited and with an introduction by A. A. Magometov.) Tbilisi 1979 [1070 p.].

Žirkov 1936 = L. I. Žirkov: Avarsko-russkij slovar'. Moscow 1936 [187 p.].

4.2. Other Publications

Crisp 1985 = Simon Crisp: The formation and development of literary Avar. In: I. T. Krindler, ed., Sociolinguistic Perspective on Soviet National Languages. Berlin 1985.

Johanna Nichols, University of California, Berkeley, California (USA)

XXII. Lexikographie der Einzelsprachen VI:
Die semitohamitischen Sprachen
Lexicography of Individual Languages VI:
The Hamito-Semitic Languages
Lexicographie des langues particulières VI:
Langues chamito-sémitiques

236. Hebrew and Aramaic Lexicography

1. Hebrew and Aramaic Languages
2. Hebrew, Aramaic and Other Semitic Languages in Comparative Dictionaries
3. Development of Hebrew and Aramaic Lexicography
4. Biblical Hebrew

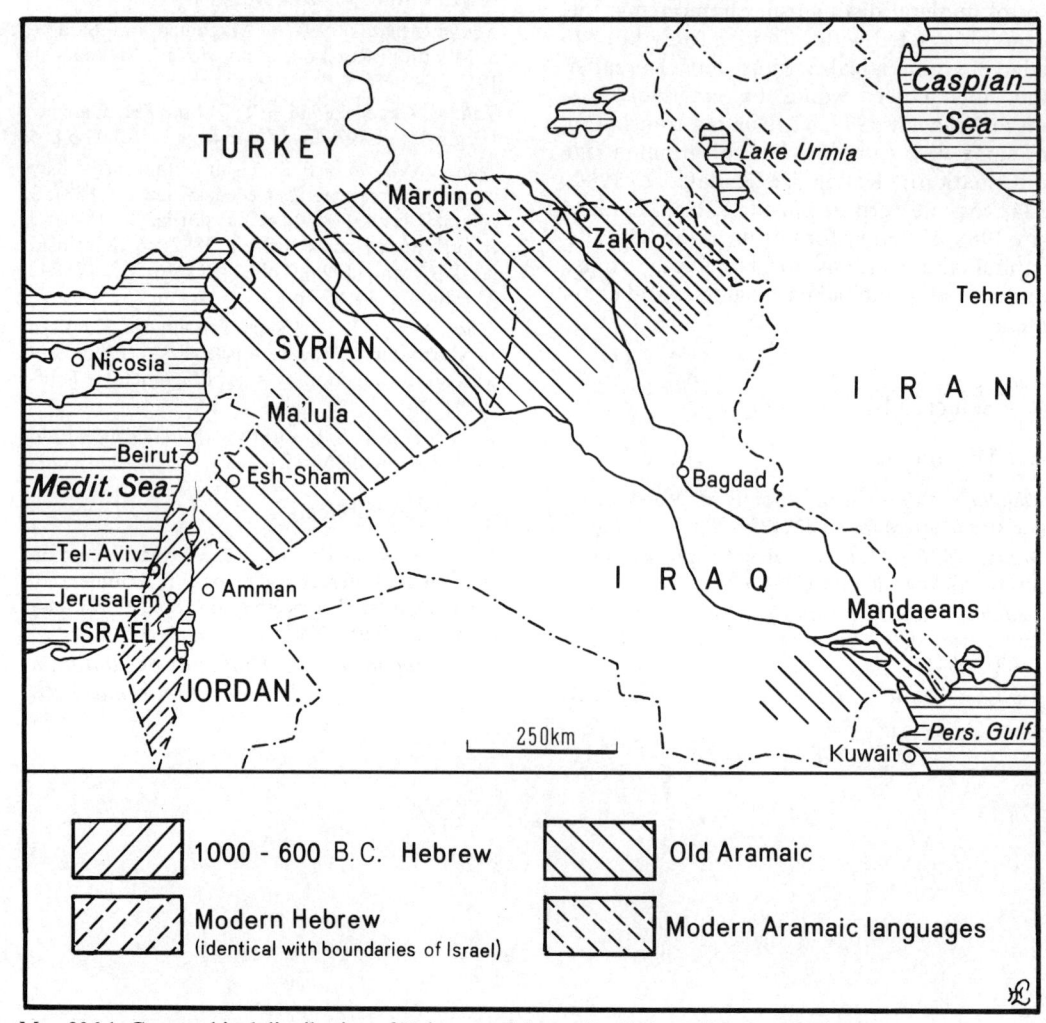

Map 236.1: Geographical distribution of Hebrew and Aramaic: 1000—600 B.C. and in modern times

236. Hebrew and Aramaic Lexicography

5. Hebrew and Aramaic of Jewish Traditional Literature
6. Modern Hebrew
7. Lexicography of Ancient and Medieval Aramaic Languages
8. Lexicography of Modern Aramaic Languages
9. Selected Bibliography

1. Hebrew and Aramaic Languages

1.1. Linguistic Affinities

Northwest Semitic languages, attested since the 3rd millennium B.C. until the present time, can be divided into two branches, Canaanite and Aramaic. The Ancient Canaanite, Ugaritic and Phoenician, are dealt with in Article 177. Hebrew and all Aramaic languages are presented here below. The phonological systems of Hebrew and the Aramaic languages are similar. The main differences are in the development of the interdental protophonemes, to sibilants in Hebrew, and to dentals in Aramaic; and in the retaining of long /ā/ in Aramaic, while in Hebrew it was subjected to the Canaanite shift to /ō/. Hebrew has prepositive article /ha-/, Aramaic has postpositive stressed /-ā/. Since the 6th cent. B.C. Hebrew was exposed to a strong influence from the commonly spoken and written Aramaic.

1.2. Historical and Cultural Connections

In the 1st millennium B.C. Aramaic was the common language of the area between Persia and Egypt — Mesopotamia, Syria, Palestine — and the official language of the Persian Empire (538—332 B.C.) (cf. Map 236.1). Hebrew in Palestine was gradually replaced by Aramaic since the 6th cent. B.C. Jewish communities in the Babylonian exile adopted Aramaic. Aramaic was used beside Hebrew in the Jewish liturgy and religious literature: prayers and blessings, 1 % of the Bible canon (in Ezra and Daniel), targums — Aramaic versions of the Bible, talmuds — Aramaic discussions of the Hebrew legal texts of the Mishna. Also, Samaritans used Aramaic in their targum and in their religious poetry and prose.

1.3. Sources and Approaches

The main source for ancient Hebrew is the Hebrew Bible (Old Testament). Epigraphic material from the Biblical (12th — 2nd cent. B.C.) period is scarce. From the later period (2nd cent. B.C. — 2nd cent. A.D./C.E.), great parts of the apocryphal book of Yeshu ben Sira (Ecclesiasticus), Essene writings found in the Qumran area, documents from the Bar

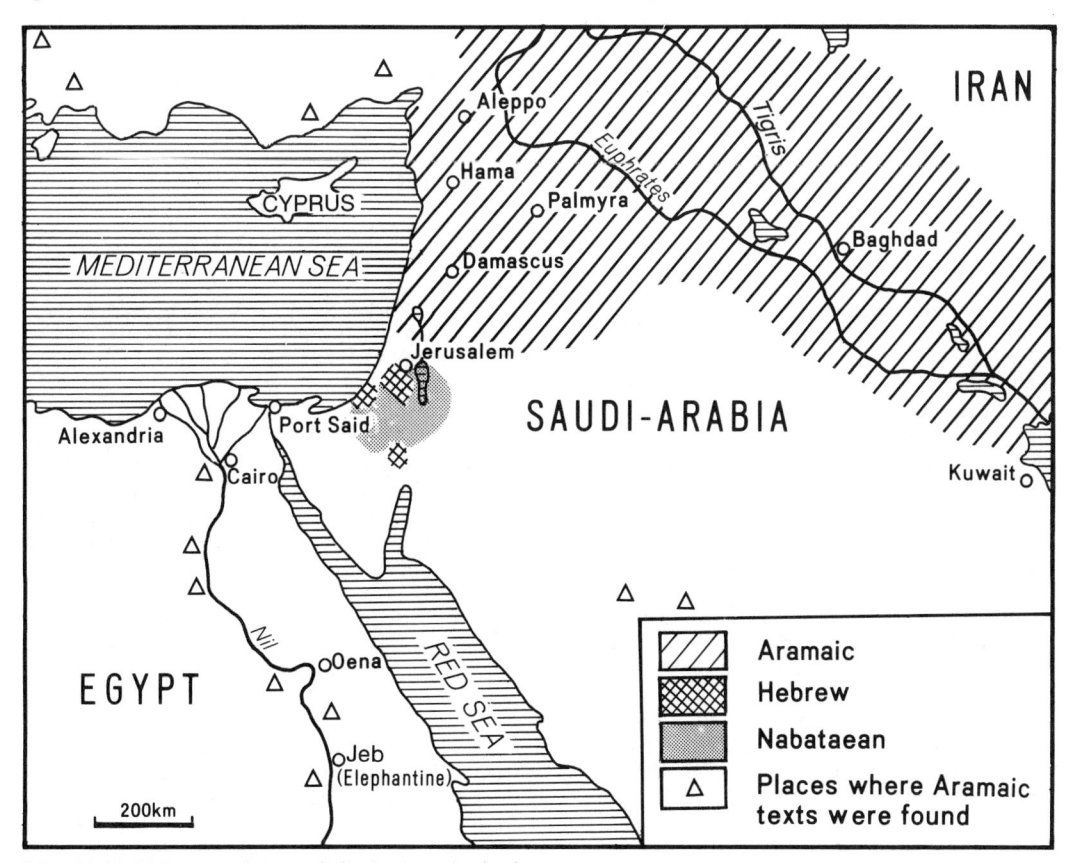

Map 236.2: Hebrew and Aramaic in the Late Antiquity

Kokhba time, and inscriptions are preserved. While until the end of the 19th cent. the Aramaic material known from the Pre-Christian period was limited to the Aramaic portions of the Old Testament, this material has been and still is being enriched by finds of inscriptions in many countries of the Near East, from Indus to Hellespont, from Caucasus to Southern Egypt. Texts on papyrus have been excavated on the island Jeb/Elephantine in the Nile across from Seven (now Assuan), at Saqqara and in other localities in Egypt. Many Aramaic texts have been found in the Qumran area and in the valleys south of it, on the western shore of the Dead Sea. The proportion of epigraphic sources for the later periods of Hebrew and Aramaic is small, in comparison to the Jewish traditional literature in both these languages, to the very rich Christian literature in Syriac, and to the Mandaic religious texts. For Modern Hebrew many printed texts serve as sources, while a great part of the lexical evidence for Modern Aramaic dialects is based on recordings of the spoken language.

Lexicographic approaches vary accordingly. Besides dictionaries, concordances are convenient tools for the study of the vocabulary of canonical collections. Standard dictionaries have to be supplemented by the words from the glossaries accompanying the editions of newly published texts.

1.4. Writing Systems

With few exceptions, the lexicographical material for Hebrew and Aramaic languages is available in texts using the West Semitic alphabet. Some ancient words, mostly proper names, are attested in Egyptian scripts and in cuneiform syllabic writing. In Greek and Latin translations of Biblical and other texts the names are rendered in the alphabetic writing with vowels. From the Hexaplaric rendering of the Hebrew Old Testament in Greek letters only some Psalms have survived. Aramaic texts, mostly poetic ones from a 2nd cent. B.C. papyrus in Egyptian Demotic writing are now being published. All of these texts are useful for a reconstruction of Hebrew and Aramaic vowels, which were only rarely and inconsistently indicated in the in principle consonantal West Semitic alphabetic script.

In modern scholarly publications Semitic alphabets are often transliterated by Roman letters with the help of various diacritic signs. One such system was used around 1930 for the Eastern Neo-Aramaic readers in the Soviet Union.

The principle of a West Semitic alphabetic writing is to indicate one consonant sound by one letter. This initial limitation to consonants corresponds to their function in Semitic languages: they express basic concepts, while the vowels are used to modify them. To indicate vowels, letters for phonetically related consonants and special signs were used if for some reason this help for readers was considered necessary — to ascertain correct pronunciation of sacred texts and to assist those who were not well acquainted with the language system.

The tradition locates the origin of the Semitic alphabet to the city of Byblos, a Canaanite commercial center on the Mediterranean coast under the Lebanon mountains. From the 2nd millennium B.C. several alphabetic inscriptions from Lebanon, Palestine and the Sinai Peninsula are known. The oldest from the 17th cent. B.C. were excavated at Lahav (north of Beersheva in Southern Palestine). Phoenicians and Israelites used an alphabet of 22 consonantal letters, Aramaeans the same number of letters, with slightly different shapes. Since Early Aramaic (first half of the 1st millennium B.C.) possessed more consonantal phonemes, some letters indicated more than one phoneme, e.g. the letter z also indicated the voiced interdental /ḏ/. Some long vowels were indicated by letters for phonetically related consonants, long /ī/ by y, /ū/ by w. This device was used, both for morphologically significant end vowels and for middle vowels, already in the Aramaic inscription from Gozan (Tell Fekheriye in Northern Syria) from the 9th cent. B.C. This device was used also in Hebrew texts of the Biblical period and even later. It helped to distinguish traditional Hebrew forms from those used in commonly spoken Aramaic; e.g. the negative particle "not", written in Hebrew texts l', was then written lw', to ascertain the pronunciation /lō/, in contrast to Aramaic /lā/. The "vowel letters" were not and are not now consistently used in Hebrew and Aramaic; only in Mandaic writing was the consistency achieved. This is well reflected in Macuch's (v. infra 7.5.) transliteration system using the letters $a, i,$ and u.

Other signs than originally consonantal letters were introduced for indicating vowels first by the Nestorians in the Eastern tradition of Syriac in the 7th cent. A.D. They developed from the devices distinguishing full or less full vocalism of words. These signs were different also in their graphical shapes, points being used in various combinations and positions. The Western (monophysite, Jacobite) Syriac writing uses for indicating vowels signs imitating Greek vowel letters. Hebrew vocalization systems, Babylonian and Palestinian, followed the Eastern Syriac model. The prevailing Hebrew vocalization system, developed in Tiberias in Palestine, is very exact. Besides vowels it indicates also the doubling of consonants. In both Syriac and Hebrew, the vocalization is used for Biblical texts, for poetry and for language textbooks, while other written and printed texts, to be read by people acquainted with the word structures, are presented in consonant letters only.

2. Hebrew, Aramaic and Other Semitic Languages in Comparative Dictionaries

2.1. Middle Ages

The use of both Hebrew and Aramaic in Jewish religious literature (v. supra 1.2) led to the relating of these languages in the area of lexicography. The beginning of Arabic lexicography stimulated similar efforts by Jewish scholars using Arabic in the Near East and in Spain. The affinity of Arabic to the traditional languages of Jewish literature, Hebrew and Aramaic, led to their comparison. A trilingual dictionary, Hebrew-Arabic-Aramaic, *ha-mēlīṣ*, ("Translator"), was completed by Samaritans about 1200; ed. Ben-Ḥayyim 1957.

2.2. 17th Century

Renaissance and Reformation efforts for a better understanding of the Bible and especially of the editions of polyglot Bibles fostered a development of the lexicography of mutually related Semitic languages. *Lexicon pentaglotton* by Valentin Schindler (1612) contained Hebrew, Biblical and Talmudic Aramaic and Syriac, together with Arabic. Seven languages were presented in *Etymologicum Orientale* by Heinrich Hottinger (1661), and in *Lexicon heptaglotton* by Edmund Castell (1669), an addition to the London Polyglot Bible.

2.3. Recent Attempts

Many of the achievements of the comparative Semitic lexical studies are referred to in the recent dictionaries of Biblical Hebrew and Aramaic, Syriac, Akkadian and Ge'ez, but no comparative dictionary is available now (1991). The dictionary of Semitic roots by David Cohen (1970, 1976), in which also the material collected by Jean Cantineau is used, ceased to be published after the first two installments. A comparative dictionary was started with the help of computer in Prague (cf. Segert 1960, 1969) and is now being continued in Los Angeles. I. M. D'jakonov works on a dictionary which will contain also material from the African languages of the Hamito-Semitic (Afroasiatic) family.

3. Development of Hebrew and Aramaic Lexicography

3.1. Middle Ages

As Aramaic was being replaced as an everyday language of Jewish and Christian communities by Arabic, since the 7th cent., lexical tools were developed to preserve the correct reading and understanding of Biblical and other religious literature.

In the second half of the 7th cent. 'Enānīšō' compiled a lexicon of Syriac words written with the same letters but pronounced differently, with different meanings. Later Syriac lexicography concentrated on explaining Greek technical terms used in Syriac texts. A detailed Syriac lexicon with references to sources was compiled in the 10th cent. by Abū-l-Ḥasan bar Bahlūl (ed. Duval 1886—1903). In the following century Elīyā bar Šīnayā put together a Syriac-Arabic dictionary (ed. de Lagarde 1879). Jewish academies in Mesopotamia began to cultivate Hebrew and Aramaic lexicography. The Aramaic material from the Babylonian Talmud was treated in the 9th cent. in the lexical work called *'Aruk* ("The Set (Table))". In the beginning of the 10th cent. Sa'adya, head of the academy in Sura, compiled *Egron* ("Vocabulary"), a collection of Hebrew words arranged — as in the Arabic models — according to their first root consonants and then according to their last root consonants, with Arabic equivalents added. Biblical Hebrew was completely covered in *Maḥberet* ("Connection") by Menaḥem ben Saruq (10th cent.). Yona ibn Ǧanāḥ (Abū-l-Walīd) wrote his lexicon, "Book of Roots", in Spain in the 11th cent. in Arabic *(Kitāb al-uṣūl);* it was then translated into Hebrew *(Sep̄er ha-šorašim)*. The same title was given by David Qimḥi (1160—1235) to the second part of his *Miklol* ("Compendium") in which derivatives from the roots are presented. Even more influential became *'Aruk,* an encyclopedic Aramaic lexicon to Talmud by Nathan ben Yeḥiel (1020—1106). For the Samaritan trilingual dictionary, cf. supra 2.1.

3.2. Renaissance and Enlightenment

Christian interest in Biblical Hebrew and Aramaic (called "Chaldaean", cf. Daniel 2, 4) is reflected in dictionaries of these languages, i.a. those by Johannes Reuchlin (1506), Alfonso de Zamora (1515/1522), and Johann Buxtorf (1607). Elias Levita (1467—1549), a Jewish scholar active in Germany and Italy, contributed to these efforts by his *Meturgeman* ("Translator") covering Biblical and targumic Aramaic. For dictionaries containing more Semitic languages, cf. supra 2.2.

The first concordance to the Hebrew Bible by Isaac Nathan ben Kalonymus, composed in the middle of the 15th cent., was published in 1523. It served as the basis for a concordance by Johann Buxtorf (1632). Equally basic became *Lexicon Chaldaicum, Talmudicum et Rabbinicum* by Johann Buxtorf (1639—1640).

The Hebrew and Aramaic dictionary and Manual Lexicon with Latin equivalents by Johannes Simonis (1752, 1793) were widely used.

3.3. 19th Century

Biblical Hebrew and Aramaic lexical material was critically summarized by Wilhelm Gesenius (1786—1842), in *Thesaurus philologicus criticus* (1829—1842), and in *Hebräisch-deutsches Handwörterbuch* (1810), a basis for reeditions and reworkings even now. The concordance by Buxtorf (v. supra 3.2.) served as a basis for the work by Julius Fürst (1840). Further revision by Solomon Mandelkern (1896) brought further improvements.

Lexicography of Jewish traditional literature was intensively cultivated. M. J. Landau published *Rabbinisch-aramäisch-deutsches Wörterbuch* (1819—1824). Alexander Kohut edited and expanded the collected material under the title *Seper 'aruk ha-šalem* (1878—1892); cf. supra 3.1. Jakob Levy composed dictionaries to the targumic and related writings (1867—1868) and to talmudic and midrashic literature (1876—1889). Some other important, still widely used contributions to Aramaic lexicography were begun at the end of the 19th cent. and completed later; cf. infra 5.; 7.4.

4. Biblical Hebrew

4.1. Hebrew Bible

Gesenius' dictionary, reedited and revised during the whole 19th cent., has remained the basic tool for Biblical Hebrew (and Aramaic), as edited by Frants Buhl (1915) and in the English version by Francis Brown, S. R. Driver and Charles A. Briggs (1907). A new revision begun by Rudolf Meyer is being continued by Herbert Donner (1987). A new *Lexicon in Veteris Testamenti libros,* with German and English equivalents, was published in 1953 by Ludwig Koehler. The Aramaic section was provided by Walter Baumgartner, who also then began to prepare the revised edition, with German equivalents only (1967, 1990—); this lexicon is now being edited by Johann Jakob Stamm. All of these dictionaries give detailed references to texts, comparative material and secondary literature.

Another new dictionary for Biblical Hebrew only, with Latin equivalents, was produced by F. Zorell (1940—1954); for its Aramaic complement by Vogt, cf. infra 7.1. A great amount of material about the function of words in the Old Testament is collected in theological dictionaries: a more detailed one, edited by G. Johannes Botterweck and Helmer Ringgren, began to be published in the original German in 1970, and in English translation in 1974. Shorter works of this kind are a German dictionary, edited by Ernst Jenni and Claus Westermann (1971), and an English one, edited by R. Laird Harris (1980). For the benefit of students, many shorter dictionaries for the Hebrew Bible were published, e.g. by W. L. Holladay (1965); and by Georg Fohrer (1971), whose dictionary was translated into English by W. Johnstone (1973). Lexical material is in some of them presented also according to the meanings (cf. Weinheimer 1918), according to biblical books or even according to the verses. For dictionaries containing Biblical Hebrew together with the later stages, cf. infra 6.2. Mandelkern's Old Testament Concordance has been published in revised editions by Chayim Mordecai Brecher (1955) and by Moshe Goshen-Gottstein (1959). From the concordance with dictionary by Samuel E. Loewenstamm and Joshua Blau, 2 volumes have appeared (1957, 1959), the third was edited by M. Z. Kaddari (1968). A new concordance by Abraham Even-Shoshan was published in 1980. Gerhard Lisowsky wrote his concordance, provided with German, English and Latin equivalents, by hand (1958).

A concordance of the Samaritan Pentateuch, according to its traditional pronunciation, rendered in Roman letters, was produced by Zeev Ben-Ḥayyim (1977).

Hebrew words referring to the original text are listed in some Bible concordances for the Greek Septuagint and for some other versions, i.a. English and Czech.

A useful tool is the retrograde Hebrew lexicon, containing also words from epigraphic and Qumran texts, edited by Karl Georg Kuhn (1958).

A classification of Hebrew Bible vocabulary according to semantic fields is being prepared by Eugene A. Nida and Johannes P. Louw.

4.2. Epigraphic Texts

Hebrew inscriptions from Biblical and early Post-Biblical periods are covered by DISO/ Hoftijzer (1965) and by glossaries to their editions, such as Donner/Röllig (1969).

4.3. Yeshu ben Sira

Of the Hebrew original of the Wisdom of Yeshu ben Sira, which was not accepted into the Hebrew Bible canon, great parts were discovered; in medieval copies in the Cairo Geniza beginning in 1896, and in ancient fragments of leather scrolls from the ruins of Masada, the last Jewish fortress conquered by the Romans in 74 A.D. (according to new evidence), in 1964, during the excavations conducted by Yigael Yadin. The Hebrew text was published, together with a concordance and lexical lists, within the Dictionary Project of the Academy of the Hebrew Language (Z. Ben-Ḥayyim, ed., 1973).

4.4. Texts From the Qumran Region/Dead Sea Area

Hebrew texts from the 3rd cent. B.C. — 1st cent. A.D./C.E., from 11 caves near the ruins of the Essene center (Ḥirbet Qumran) destroyed by the Romans in 68 A.D. discovered beginning in 1947/8, are not yet (1991) completely published. The lexical material as was then available, was collected in the concordance edited by Karl Georg Kuhn (1960) and in that by Bilhah Habermann, accompanying the edition by A. M. Habermann (1959). These collections have to be complemented by the material from the glossaries to the later editions of the texts. The same approach is necessary for the words contained in the documents found in Masada and in the caves with the relics from the Bar Kokhba War (132—135 A.D.), situated in the valleys west of the Dead Sea.

5. Hebrew and Aramaic of Jewish Traditional Literature

5.1. Mishnaic Hebrew

The Hebrew language as used in the beginning of the Christian era is preserved in the collection of 63 legal treatises, called Mishna ("Repetition", of oral laws), in additional texts to them, called Tosephta, in expositions of some books of the Tora ("Law", Books of Moses), and in the sayings of Jewish scholars preserved in the talmudic literature.

This Hebrew lexical material is — together with the Aramaic words — treated in the dictionary by Marcus Jastrow (1886—1903), with many context quotations, and in the shorter dictionary by Gustaf Dalman (1897—1901). The material is presented according to books in concordances composed by members of the Kasowski (also written Kosovsky, Q'sswsqy) family; namely, father Chayim Yehoshua and sons Moshe and Binjamin. The father composed the concordances to Mishna (1928/1956) and to Tosephta (1932—1961).

5.2. Palestinian Jewish Aramaic

Recently original texts in this dialect from the period around the beginning of the Christian era have been uncovered in caves of Qumran (the so-called Genesis Apocryphon and other texts) and of Wadi Murabba'āt (relics from the Bar Kokhba War). Their lexical material is presented, together with later synagogal and other inscriptions, by K. Beyer (1984). The traditional literature in this Western Aramaic dialect is contained in the lexical works by Levy (cf. supra 3.3.) and Jastrow (cf. supra 5.1.). In this dialect, close to the older Imperial Aramaic, the targums, versions of the Biblical text, are written. Some are straight translations, some rather paraphrastic. The concordance to the Targum Onqelos to the Tora was compiled by Ch. Y. Kasowsky (1940). For the recently published Targum Neofiti no lexical tool is available. The talmudic literature in this dialect is mostly concentrated on the Jerusalem/Palestinian Talmud, for which the concordance is being compiled by M. Kosovsky (1979). A Dictionary of Palestinian Jewish Aramaic was prepared by M. Sokoloff (1990).

5.3. Babylonian Jewish Aramaic

The main corpus of this Eastern dialect is the Babylonian Talmud. Its lexical material is listed in the general dictionaries by Levy and Jastrow (cf. the references to 5.2.). The concordance for this collection was prepared by Ch. Y. Kasowsky (1954—1982).

5.4. Samaritan Hebrew and Aramaic

The Hebrew and Aramaic liturgical texts, which are to a great extent poetical, Aramaic exegetical literature — including *Mēmar Marqē* —, and related texts are not yet (1991) covered by a detailed dictionary; as a provisional tool the Samaritan-Aramaic index by Ben-Ḥayyim (1957) can serve well. Abraham Tal is preparing a dictionary to his edition (1980—1983) of the Samaritan targum (Aramaic version) of the Pentateuch.

6. Modern Hebrew

6.1. Enrichment of the Vocabulary

In the 18th cent. in Europe, Haskala, the Jewish Enlightenment, brought a revival of literary activity in the Hebrew language. The traditional vocabulary did not suffice to express contemporary concerns, and new words had to be introduced. The immigration of Jews from Czarist Russia at the end of the 19th cent. and the Zionism attracting Jews from the diaspora to their ancient homeland required a common Hebrew language which could serve all needs of a modern society. The most active worker for this revival was Eliezer Ben Yehudah (1858—1922). He was also instrumental in founding a Language Committee *(Waʿad ha-lašon)* in 1890. It cared for the orderly development of the vocabulary, and published normative word lists for various scholarly and professional fields. The establishment of the State of Israel in 1948 meant new requirement for the Hebrew language. In 1954 the responsible institution was reorganized as the Academy of the Hebrew Language in Jerusalem. While Modern Hebrew morphology and to a great extent syntax follow the Biblical Hebrew model, for the vocabulary later stages of Hebrew were also utilized: mishnaic and rabbinic — which were continued in the traditional scholarship —, the medieval Hebrew of poetry and philosophy, and innovations of the Haskala period. Words of Aramaic and Arabic origin, which were accepted earlier, were revived, and new words were drawn from these source languages. Modern meanings were assigned to some ancient words; e.g. ḥašmal "electricity" meant a shiny metal in Ezechiel 1:4, rendered as "electrum" in the Latin Bible. New words were coined from old roots. Modern European languages served as a model, e.g. for *šiddur* "broadcast", from Post-Biblical Hebrew and Aramaic root *š-d-r* "cast". The adoption of words from non-Semitic languages had to be avoided, as they did not fit well into Semitic word structures. But some widely used terms had to be accepted. E.g. "telephone" as a noun, *telefon,* was not changed, but in the verbal forms the Hebrew patterns are applied: *tilpen* "he telephoned", *yetalpen* "he will telephone" (but instead of /p/, corresponding to the Hebrew phonological system, the original foreign /f/ is pronounced by some speakers). In colloquial Hebrew many words from the immigrant languages, Yiddish and Arabic especially, and from English are used.

6.2. Hebrew Dictionaries

The pioneer of the Hebrew language revival Eliezer Ben Yehudah collected all lexical material from all periods of Hebrew and compiled the *Millon ha-lašon ha-ʿivri ha-yešana we-ha-ḥadaša* (Thesaurus totius Hebraitatis et veteris et recentioris). Publication began in 1910, and the last volume appeared in 1959. A larger project of a Historical Dictionary of the Hebrew Language was inaugurated by the Academy of the Hebrew Language in 1954, under the editorship of Z. Ben-Ḥayyim. A sample was published in 1982.

Besides these monumental, amply documented undertakings several lexicons for practical use were published; some presenting complete lexical material beginning with the Bible, some concentrating on Modern (Standard Israeli) Hebrew. The "New Dictionary" by Avraham Even-Shoshan appeared in several editions, the last of which was published in 1980. The *Modern Hebrew Dictionary* by Moshe Goshen-Gottstein is introduced by a volume entitled *Introduction to the Lexicography of Modern Hebrew* (1969). The material in the lexicons by Ṣevi Scharfstein (1939), by Nahum Stutchkoff (1968), and by Chaim Rabin and Zevi Raday (1970—1973), is organized according to semantic fields.

The Language Council and the Academy of the Hebrew Language (v. supra 6.1.) published many normative vocabularies for various scientific disciplines, professions and trades, e.g. for ceramics (1950).

6.3. Bilingual Dictionaries

The official languages of the State of Israel are Hebrew, English, and Arabic. Many immigrants arrived from Arab countries, including those where French was used, in North Africa. This situation influenced the lexical activities.

M. H. Segal composed *A Concise Hebrew—English Dictionary* (1958) and edited the *Compendious Hebrew—English Dictionary* by R. Grossmann (1955), both comprising all periods of Hebrew, and worked with H. Danby on *A Concise English—Hebrew Dictionary* (1958). Other Hebrew—English dictionaries include the one by R. Alcalay (1962), and *The Megiddo Modern Dictionary* by R. Sivan (1972) and E. Levenston (1966), who also provided a shortened version (1975), similar in size to the Pocket Dictionary by Ehud Ben-Yehuda (1961). Dictionaries connecting Hebrew with French and Arabic were provided by Elmaleh and Goshen-Gottstein (cf. Banitt). A Hebrew—Russian dictionary prepared by F. Šapiro in cooperation with B. M. Grande was published in Moscow in 1963.

7. Lexicography of Ancient and Medieval Aramaic Languages

Glossaries to selected texts in 13 Aramaic languages are published in *An Aramaic Handbook,* edited by Franz Rosenthal (1967). *Comprehensive Aramaic Lexicon* is being prepared under the editorship of S. Kaufman and others.

7.1. Ancient Aramaic: Early, Imperial, Biblical

The texts from the early period of the Aramaic language (9th—7th cent. B.C.) are epigraphic, most of them from Syria. Three inscriptions written in the archaic dialect of Ya'udi (Šam'āl) were found at Zincirli, north of Antioch. The problem of the affiliation of the language to which the inscription of Deir 'Alla (East of the river Jordan) belongs is under discussion; it seems that it is basically an Aramaic language, affected by the common Canaanite-Aramaic poetic dialect. The lexical material from this period is listed in Vinnikov 1958—1965, DISO/Hoftijzer 1965, Donner/Röllig 1969, Segert 1975.

The term for the language used in the 6th—4th cent. is "Imperial" (or "Official"), as it served as the official language for the Persian Empire. This language found a wide area of usage, as the inscriptions found in countries between Hellespont and Indus, between Caucasus and Southern Egypt attest. In Egypt many texts, legal, epistolar and literary, written on papyrus or leather have been uncovered, most of them on the island Jeb/Elephantine in the Nile at Seven (Assuan), where a colony of Aramaic speaking Jewish soldiers in Persian service protected the southern boundary of Egypt. The type of Aramaic language cultivated in Persian ofices survived the collapse of the Persian Empire in 332 B.C. The major monument of this late period is a papyrus presenting Aramaic religious and epic poetry in the Egyptian Demotic script. For the lexical tools, cf. DISO/Hoftijzer, Vinnikov, Segert (v. supra), and Beyer 1984 (v. 5.2.).

The Biblical Aramaic used in the documents and historical narratives in the Book of Ezra (cc. 4—7) and in the stories and visions of the Book of Daniel (cc. 2—7) is of the Imperial Aramaic type. Its lexical material is presented mostly in the dictionaries and concordances of Biblical Hebrew (cf. supra 4.1.). Cf. also the glossaries by F. Rosenthal (1961) and H. L. Ginsberg (1967) and the lexicon with Latin equivalents and many quotations from Aramaic texts by E. Vogt (1971).

7.2. Nabataean, Palmyrenian, Hatraean

Aramaic was used by Arabic speaking Nabataeans for their inscriptions in the 2nd cent. B.C. — 1st cent. A.D. They were preserved in the area southeast of the Dead Sea. From the first three centuries of the Christian era many inscriptions have been preserved in the ruins of the commercial center Palmyra in the Syrian Desert. Inscriptions in the local dialect from the 1st—2nd cent. A.D. have been excavated from the ruins of Hatra (el-Ḥadr), west of the Middle Tigris in Iraq. For lexical material cf. DISO/Hoftijzer (1965); for Hatra texts, Donner/Röllig (1969); and for Nabataean texts, Cantineau (1932).

7.3. Christian Western Aramaic

For this dialect, similar to contemporary Jewish Western Aramaic (cf. 5.2.), preserved mostly in Bible translations from the 4th—7th cent. A.D., the *Lexicon Syropalaestinum* was provided by Schulthess (1903).

7.4. Syriac

The local dialect of Edessa (*'Ūrhōy;* now Urfa in Eastern Turkey) was used in the 1st—3rd cent. A.D., in inscriptions (cf. the glossary in the edition by Drijvers 1972), and then it became the liturgical and literary language of

Syriac churches. Two traditions of pronunciation and script were formed according to denominational lines: Eastern, dyophysitic, Nestorian; and Western, monophysitic, Jacobite. Bible translation and commentaries, religious poetry, history and sciences were cultivated in Syriac, from the 2nd to 13th cent.

The modern lexicography continued indigenous works (cf. supra 3.1.). Two detailed dictionaries with Latin equivalents were finished around 1900: *Thesaurus Syriacus* by R. Payne Smith (1879—1901), containing also material from other Christian dialects, and *Lexicon Syriacum* by C. Brockelmann (1895), to the 2nd edition (1928) of which were added comparative data. The daughter of the author of the *Thesaurus,* J. Payne Smith, abridged it and edited it with English equivalents in 1903. Less detailed are *Vocabularium Syriacum* by R. Köbert (1956) and the dictionary with French, English and Arabic equivalents by L. Costaz (1963).

7.5. Mandaic

Mandaeans, a gnostic religious community which originated probably in Palestine around the beginning of the Christian era, survived until now in Lower Iraq. The access to their old and rich religious literature, written in an Eastern Aramaic dialect, was provided by *A Mandaic Dictionary,* by E. R. Drower and R. Macuch (1963). The latter's transliteration system (cf. supra 1.4.) was used. In similar Eastern Aramaic dialects, magical bowls with spiralic inscriptions and other magical texts were written in Mesopotamia. Ch. D. Isbell added a glossary to the edition of these texts (1975). The words from the magic gnostic text from the 2nd cent. on the letter "wāw", edited by A. Dupont-Sommer (1946), are included in DISO/Hoftijzer (1965).

8. Lexicography of Modern Aramaic Languages

8.1. Western

The western type of Aramaic survived only in Anti-Lebanon, north of Damascus, in the Christian town of Ma'lūla and in two Moslem towns. The always growing impact of Arabic did not affect the Semitic character of this Western Aramaic dialect. Folk narratives and everyday conversations provided a basis for the glossary by G. Bergsträsser (1921).

8.2. Eastern: Ṭūrōyō

This eastern dialect, spoken by the Christian Jacobites in the Ṭūr ʿAbdīn area (near Mardin in Eastern Turkey) exhibits some features similar to the Western (Jacobite) tradition of Syriac, such as the shift of long /ā/ toward /ō/. As for Western Aramaic (cf. 8.1.), this central dialect was made accessible to lexicography on the basis of non-literary records by H. Ritter (1979).

8.3. Eastern: Christian and Jewish Dialects

Several Eastern Aramaic dialects are spoken in Northern Iraq, in adjacent areas of Iran, Turkey, and Syria, and in secondary settlements in the Caucasus area, in some European countries, and in the United States (Detroit, California). A translation of the Bible into the Christian dialect of Lake Urmia (in northwest Iran) was made in the 19th cent.; it served as a basis for other religious and literary activity. The languages of all these areas were comprised in the dictionary by A. J. Maclean (1901), containing also material from the western and central dialects (cf. 8.1—2). G. Krotkoff composed a vocabulary of Kurdistan Aramaic (1982). The languages of those who emigrated during World War I to Russia were studied by K. Cereteli (1958). While the Eastern Aramaic Christians — who are also called "Assyrians" — use the Syriac script in its eastern (Nestorian) variant, for some time around 1930 the Roman transliteration was introduced for those living in the Soviet Union. The Jewish dialect of Zakho (near Mosul, in Northern Iraqi Kurdistan), the speakers of which mostly moved to Jerusalem, was presented in publications of Biblical traditions and of folklore texts by Y. Sabar, with glossaries and indexes (1976—1990).

These dialects (cf. also 8.2. and 8.4.) were exposed to the strong influence of languages spoken in the environment: Semitic Arabic, non-Semitic Kurdish, Persian and Turkish. Many loanwords from these languages were adopted.

8.4. Modern Mandaic

Members of the Mandaen gnostic religious community in Lower Iraq and in the adjacent area of Iran (Ahwāz) use a modern version of their Eastern Aramaic language. From the information provided by native speakers, R. Macuch compiled a vocabulary arranged according to the English equivalents (1965), cf. 9.7.2., and a glossary (1989).

9. Selected Bibliography

9.1. Bibliography to Section 1

Barr 1973 = James Barr: Hebrew Lexicography. In: Fronzaroli 1973, 103—126.

Chomsky 1957 = William Chomsky: Hebrew: The Eternal Language. Philadelphia 1957.

Donner 1973 = Herbert Donner: Aramäische Lexikographie. In: Fronzaroli 1973, 127—143.

Drijvers 1973 = H. J. W. Drijvers: Syriac and Aramaic. In: Hospers 1973, 283—335.

Driver 1970 = G. R. Driver: Semitic Writing from Pictograph to Alphabet. London 1970.

Encyclopaedia Judaica 1971 = Encyclopaedia Judaica (Jerusalem): Aramaic, 3.260—287; Hebrew Language, 16.1561—1662; Linguistic Literature, Hebrew, 16.1352—1401.

Even-Shoshan 1980 = Abraham Even-Shoshan: ha-qonqordancyot ha-'ivriyot la-miqra': sqyrh byblywgr'pyty. [Hebr.]. In: Even-Shoshan 1980 (v. infra 9.4.1.), 15—35.

Fronzaroli 1973 = Pelio Fronzaroli (ed.): Studies on Semitic Lexicography. Firenze 1973.

Gelb 1963 = I. J. Gelb: A Study of Writing. Chicago. London 1963.

Goshen-Gottstein = (v. infra 9.6.1.).

Habermann 1957 = A. M. Habermann: Bible and Concordance. In: Loewenstamm/Blau 1957 (v. infr. 9.4.1.), XIX—XXXVIII; h-mqr' w-h-qwnqwrdncyh, ib. 1—44 [Hebr.].

Hospers 1973 = J. H. Hospers (ed.): A Basic Bibliography for the Study of the Semitic Languages. Vol. I. Leiden 1973 [Semitic Writing, 375—383].

Hospers/de Geus 1973 = J. H. Hospers/C. H. J. de Geus (et al.): Hebrew. In: Hospers 1973, 176—282.

Jones 1963 = D. R. Jones: Aids to the Study of the Bible (Appendix I). In: S. L. Greenslade (ed.): The Cambridge History of the Bible 3, 520—530.

Kutscher 1970 = Eduard Yechezkel Kutscher: Aramaic. In: Sebeok 1970, 347—412.

Kutscher 1984 = Eduard Yechezkel Kutscher: A History of the Hebrew Language. Jerusalem 1984.

Malachi 1955 = A. R. Malachi: Otzar Halexicografia Haivrit. In: Mandelkern/Brecher 1955 (v. infra 9.4.1.), 1—63.

Rabin 1970 = Chaim Rabin: Hebrew. In: Sebeok 1970, 304—46.

Rosenthal 1964 = Franz Rosenthal: Die aramaistische Forschung seit Th. Nöldeke's Veröffentlichungen. Leiden 1939 (1964).

Sebeok 1970 = Thomas A. Sebeok (ed.): Current Trends in Linguistics. Vol. 6. The Hague. Paris 1970.

Waxman 1960 = Meyer Waxman: A History of Jewish Literature. Vols. I—V. New York. London 1960.

9.2. Bibliography to Section 2
9.2.1. Dictionaries

Ben-Hayyim 1957 = Ben-Hayyim (ed.): h-mlyṣ, A Hebrew-Arabic-Aramaic Samaritan glossary. In: Z. Ben-Hayyim: The Literary and Oral Tradition of Hebrew and Aramaic amongst the Samaritans [Hebr.], I. Jerusalem 1957, 435—616.

Castellus 1686 = Edmund Castellus: Lexicon heptaglotton Hebraicum, Chaldaicum, Syriacum, Samaritanum, Aethiopicum, Arabicum conjunctim et Persicum separatim. London (1669) 1686.

Cohen 1970—1976 = David Cohen: Dictionnaire des racines sémitiques ou attestées dans les langues sémitiques. 1—2: —GLGL, 1970, 1976. Paris. La Haye 1970—1976 [XXXIV, 119 pp.].

Hottinger 1661 = Johann Heinrich Hottinger: Etymologicum orientale sive Lexicon harmonicum heptaglōtton (...). Frankfurt 1661.

Schindler 1612 = Valentin Schindler: Lexicon pentaglotton Hebraicum, Chaldaicum, Syriacum, Talmudico-Rabbinicum et Arabicum (...). Hanau 1612.

9.2.2. Other Publications

Cohen 1973 = David Cohen: La lexicographie comparée. In: Fronzaroli 1973 (v. supra 9.1), 183—208.

Fronzaroli 1973 = Pelio Fronzaroli: Problems of a Semitic Etymological Dictionary. In: Fronzaroli 1973 (v. supra 9.1.), 1—24.

Hospers 1973 = J. H. Hospers: Comparative Semitics. In: Hospers 1973 (v. supra 9.1.), 365—86.

Segert 1960 = Stanislav Segert: Considerations on Semitic Comparative Lexicography. In: Archiv Orientální 28. 1960, 470—487.

Segert 1969 = Stanislav Segert: Die Arbeit am vergleichenden Wörterbuch der semitischen Sprachen mit Hilfe des Computer IBM 1410. In: Zeitschrift der Deutschen Morgenländischen Gesellschaft, Supplementa I, XVII. Deutscher Orientalistentag, Vorträge, Teil 2. Wiesbaden 1969, 714—717.

Ullendorff 1970 = Edward Ullendorff: Comparative Semitics. In: Sebeok 1970 (v. supra 9.1.), 261—73.

9.3. Bibliography to Section 3
9.3.1. Dictionaries

Abu-l-Ḥasan Bar Bahlul 1888—1901 = Rubens Duval (ed.): Lexicon syriacum auctore Hassano Bar Bahlule, I—III. Paris 1888—1901 (Amsterdam 1970) [XXXIX, 246 pp., 2098 cols.].

Buxtorf 1607 = Johann Buxtorf [father]: Epitome radicum Hebraicarum et Chaldaicarum. Basileae 1607 [14, 983, 71 pp.].

Buxtorf 1632 = Johann Buxtorf [father]: Concordantiae Bibliorum Hebraicae (...). Basileae 1632 [462 pp].

Buxtorf 1639 = Johann Buxtorf [father], [son] (ed.): Lexicon chaldaicum, talmudicum et rabbinicum. Basileae 1639 [8 pp., 2680 cols., 63 pp.].

David ben Abraham = The Hebrew-Arabic Dictionary as Kitab Jami al-alfaz (Agran) of David Ben Abraham al-Fasi the Karaite, Solomon Solomon L. Skoss (ed.). I—II. Philadelphia 1945 [CLI, 600, 6; CLX, 756, 6 pp.].

Elīyā bar Šīnāyā = Eliae Nisibeni interpres, P. de Lagarde (ed.): Praetermissorum libri duo. Göttingen 1879, 1—96.

Fürst 1840 = Julius Fürst: Librorum sacrorum Veteris Testamenti Concordantiae Hebraicae atque Chaldaicae (...). Lipsiae 1840 [XII, 770 pp.].

Fürst 1868 = Julius Fürst: Hebräisches und chaldäisches Handwörterbuch über das Alte Testament. Leipzig 1868 [654 pp.].

Gesenius 1810 = Wilhelm Gesenius: Hebräisch-deutsches Handwörterbuch über die Schriften des Alten Testaments. Halle 1810.

Gesenius 1829 = Wilhelm Gesenius: Thesaurus philologicus criticus linguae Hebraicae et Chaldaicae Veteris Testamenti. Leipzig 1829—1842—1858 [1522, 116 pp.].

Gesenius 1833 = Wilhelm Gesenius: Lexicon manuale Hebraicum et Chaldaicum in Veteris Testamenti libros. Leipzig 1833 [X, 1123 pp].

Isaac Nathan ben Kalonymus = spr m'yr ntyb hnqr' qwnqwrdnśyyš šḥybr ... mrdky ntn ... Venezia 1524.

Isaac Nathan ben Kalonymus = Concordantiarum Hebraicarum capita, (...) a (...) Mordechai Nathan (...) conscripta, nunc (...) translata per Ant. Reuchlinum. Basel 1556 [10 fol., 980 pp.].

Levita 1541 = mtwrgmn (...) mlwt (...) blšwn 'rmy (...) 'lyh [h-lwy] (...) Lexicon Chaldaicum (...) Authore Elia Leuita (...) Isnae 1541 [7 pp., 70 + 164 fol., 3 pp.].

Levy 1867 = Jacob Levy: Chaldäisches Wörterbuch über die Targumim und einen großen Teil des rabbinischen Schrifttums, I—IV. Leipzig 1867—1868.

Levy 1876 = Jacob Levy: Neuhebräisches und chaldäisches Wörterbuch über die Talmudim und Midraschim, I—IV. Leipzig 1876—1884 [VIII, 567; 542; 736; 741 pp.]. Nachträge, ed. L. Goldschmidt, Berlin. Wien 1924.

Mandelkern 1896 = (v. infra 9.4.1.).

Munster 1525 = Sebastian Munster: Dictionarium Hebraicum ex Rabbinorum commentariis collectum (...). Basileae 1525 [10, 718 pp.].

Nathan ben Yehiel = h-'rwk 'šr 'rk mlyn ... Moses Landau (ed.) m- ... Ntn ... br ... Yḥ'l ... Mšh Lnd' [Landau]. Pr'g [Praha] 1818—1824. I—IV [46, 1676, XL pp.].

Nathan ben Yeḥi'el = Alexander Kohut (ed.): 'rwk h-šlm ... spr h-'rwk ... m't Yḥy'l ... Aruch completum. Viennae 1878—1892. I—VIII [Additamenta, ed. S. Krauss. New York 1955].

Qimḥi = T. J. H. R. Bienenthal/F. Lebrecht (eds.): spr h-šršym l- (...) Dwd bn Ywsp Qmḥy (...). Rabbi Davidis Kimchi Radicum liber (...). Berlini 1847 [906, XLII, 10 cols.].

Reuchlin 1506 = Johannes Reuchlin: Rudimenta linguae hebraicae una cum Lexico. Pforzheim 1506.

Saʿadya = Sa'adya: spr h-'grwn; cf. A. E. Harkavy: zkrwn l-r'šwnym, 5: zkrwn ... S'dyh ... St. Petersburg 1892.

Simonis 1793 = Johannes Simonis: Lexicon manuale Hebraicum et Chaldaicum. Halae 1793 [3rd ed. 1st ed. 1752].

Yona ibn Ǧanāḥ = spr h-šršym ... ḥbrw b-lšwn 'rb ... Ywnh bn Ǧn'ḥ ... [Hebr.] Yhwdh bn Tbwn. B. Z. Bacher (ed.). Berlin 1896 [XLII, 3, 596, 1 pp.].

Zamorensis 1515 = Alfonsus Zamorensis: Vocabularium Hebraicum et Chaldaicum Veteris Testamenti. Complutum 1515.

9.4. Bibliography to Section 4
9.4.1. Dictionaries

Baumgartner 1967 = Walter Baumgartner: Hebräisches und aramäisches Lexikon zum Alten Testament. Leiden. I'-ṭebaḥ; I—III. '-r'h. 1967: 1974, 1983 [LIV, 1—1080].

Botterweck/Ringgren 1970 = G. Johannes Botterweck/Helmer Ringgren (eds.): Theologisches Wörterbuch zum Alten Testament. I. Stuttgart 1970—.

Botterweck/Ringgren 1974 = G. Johannes Botterweck/Helmer Ringgren (eds.): Theological Dictionary of the Old Testament. Grand Rapids, Michigan 1974. I, 1977 [XXI, 479 pp.]; II, 1977 [XX, 488 pp.]; III, 1978 [XIX, 463 pp.]; IV, 1980 [XIX, 493 pp.]; V, 1986 [XXI, 521 pp.]; VI, 1990 [XXII, 491 pp.].

Brown/Driver/Briggs 1907 = Francis Brown/S. R. Driver/Charles A. Briggs (eds.): A Hebrew and English Lexicon of the Old Testament. Oxford 1907 [xix, 1127 pp.].

Buhl 1915 = Frants Buhl (ed.): Wilhelm Gesenius' hebräisches und aramäisches Handwörterbuch über das Alte Testament. 17. Auflage. Leipzig 1915 [XIX, 1013 pp.].

DISO 1965 = (v. Hoftijzer 1965).

Donner/Röllig 1969 = H. Donner/W. Röllig: Kanaanäische und aramäische Inschriften, III: Glossare und Indizes (...). 2. Aufl. Wiesbaden 1969 [vii, 84 pp.].

Donner 1987 = (v. Meyer 1987).

Even-Shoshan 1980 = Abraham Even-Shoshan (ed.): qonqordancya ḥadaša l-tora nevi'im u-ktuvim. A New Concordance of the Bible. 4 vols. Jerusalem 1980. I—IV [37, 2307 pp.].

Fohrer 1971 = Georg Fohrer (ed.): Hebräisches und aramäisches Wörterbuch zum Alten Testament. Berlin. New York 1971.

Fohrer 1973 = Georg Fohrer (ed.) (English version W. Johnstone): Hebrew and Aramaic Dictionary of the Old Testament. Berlin. New York 1973 [XV, 332 pp.].

Habermann 1959 = A.M. Habermann (ed.): mgylwt mdbr Yhwdh. The Scrolls from the Judean Desert. Jerusalem 1959. — Bilha Habermann: Concordance [213, 175, XVI pp.].

Harris 1980 = R. Laird Harris (ed.): Theological Wordbook of the Old Testament. I—II. Chicago 1980 [xvii, 1124 pp.].

Hoftijzer 1965 = *DISO 1965* = Charles-F. Jean/ Jacob Hoftijzer: Dictionnaire des inscriptions sémitiques de l'Ouest. Leiden 1965 [XXXI, 342 pp.].

Holladay 1971 = W. L. Holladay: A Concise Hebrew and Aramaic Lexicon of the Old Testament. Leiden 1971 [XIX, 425 pp.].

Jenni/Westermann 1971—1976 = Ernst Jenni/ Claus Westermann (eds.): Theologisches Handwörterbuch zum Alten Testament. I—II. München 1971, 1976.

Koehler 1953 = Ludwig Koehler: Lexicon in Veteris Testamenti libros. Leiden 1953, 1—1044. (Aramaic Part, 1045—1138, v. Baumgartner 1953, infra 9.7.1.).

Koehler/Baumgartner 1958 = Ludwig Koehler/ W. Baumgartner (eds.): Supplementum ad Lexicon in Veteris Testamenti libros. Leiden 1958 [XXXIV, 227 pp.].

Kuhn 1958 = Karl Georg Kuhn (ed.): Rückläufiges hebräisches Wörterbuch. Göttingen 1958 [15, 144 pp.].

Kuhn 1960 = Karl Georg Kuhn (ed.): Konkordanz zu den Qumrantexten. Göttingen 1960 [XII, 237 pp.].

Lisowsky 1958 = Gerhard Lisowsky: Konkordanz zum hebräischen Alten Testament. Stuttgart 1958 [XVI, 1672 pp.].

Loewenstamm/Blau 1957 = Samuel E. Loewenstamm/Joshua Blau (eds.):'wcr lšwn h-mqr'. Thesaurus of the Language of the Bible. Jerusalem I, 1957 [XVI, 42. 413 ('), XXXVIII]; II, 1959 [8, 441 (b—w), 4 pp.]; III, 1968 M. Z. Kaddari (ed.) z—y [323 pp.].

Mandelkern 1896 = Solomon Mandelkern: hekal ha-qodeš... qonqordanciya 'ivrit wa-'aramit... Veteris Testamenti Concordantiae Hebraicae atque Chaldaicae... Lipsiae 1896 [XX, 1532 pp.].

Mandelkern/Brecher 1955 = Šlmh Mndlqrn: qwnqwrdncyh l-twrh, nby'ym w-ktwbym. Concordance on the Bible by... Solomon Mandelkern; Chaim Mordecai Brecher (ed.). New York 1955 [XVII, 63, 1550 pp.].

Mandelkern/Goshen-Gottstein 1959 = Šlmh Mndlqrn (Moshe Henry Goshen-Gottstein, ed.): Qonqordancya la-Tenak. Jerusalem 1959 [XVIII, 1565 pp.].

Meyer/Donner 1987 = Rudolf Meyer/Herbert Donner (eds.): Wilhelm Gesenius Hebräisches und aramäisches Handwörterbuch über das Alte Testament. 18. Auflage. 1. Lieferung '-g. Berlin. 1987 [XXX, 233 pp.].

Mitchel 1984 = Larry A. Mitchel: A Student's Vocabulary for Biblical Hebrew and Aramaic. Grand Rapids, Michigan 1984 [xxiv, 88 pp.].

Murtonen 1960 = A. Murtonen: An etymological vocabulary to the Samaritan Pentatech. Helsinki 1960.

Raday/Rabin 1989 = Zvi Raday/Ḥayim Rabin: ha-million he-ḥadaš la-tenak. Jerusalem. Tel Aviv (1989) [16, 749 pp].

Weinheimer 1918 = H. Weinheimer: Hebräisches Wörterbuch in sachlicher Ordnung. Tübingen 1918 [VIII, 96 pp.].

Zorell 1940—1954 = F. Zorell (ed.): Lexicon Hebraicum et Aramaicum Veteris Testamenti. Romae 1940—1954 [912 pp.].

9.4.2. Other Publications

Ben-Hayyim 1973 = Z. Ben-Ḥayyim (ed.): spr bn Syr'. The Book of Ben Sira. Text, Concordance and an Analysis of the Vocabulary. [Hebr.] Jerusalem 1973 [16, 517, XIX pp.].

Palache 1959 = J[ehuda] L[ion] Palache (tr., ed. R. J. Zwi Werblowsky): Semantic Notes on Hebrew Lexicon. Leiden 1959

9.5. Bibliography to Section 5
9.5.1. Dictionaries

Dalman 1938 = Gustaf Dalman: Aramäisch-neuhebräisches Handwörterbuch zu Targum, Talmud und Midrasch. 3. Aufl. Göttingen 1938.

Jastrow 1886—1903 = Marcus Jastrow: A Dictionary of the Targumim, the Talmud Babli and Yerushalmi, and the Midrashic Literature. London. New York 1903 (1926). I—II [XVIII, 1736 pp.].

Kasovsky 1940 = Chaim Yehoshua Kasovsky: 'wcr htrgwm. qwnqwrdncyh ltrgwm 'wnqlws. Jerusalem 1940. I—II [564, 58, 10, 22, 130 pp.].

Kasovsky 1956 = Chaim Yehoshua Kasovsky (Q's'wwsqy): 'wcr lšwn h-mšnh. Thesaurus Mishnae. 4 vols. Jerusalem 1956 I—IV [8, 1889 pp.].

Kasowski 1932—1961 = Chaim Josua Kasowski: 'wcr lšwn h-twspt'. Thesaurus Tosephthae. Jerusalem 1932—1961. 6 vols. I—VI [XII, 674; VI, 513; IV, 634; IV, 498; IV, 624; 6, 677 pp.].

Kasowski 1954—1982 = Chaim Josua Kasowski: 'wcr lšwn h-Tlmwd. Thesaurus Talmudis. Concordantiae verborum quae in Talmude Babilonico reperiuntur. Vol. I. Jerusalem I 1954 [VIII, 537 pp.; XLI, 1982].

Kosovsky 1965—1966 = Biniamin Kosovsky: 'wcr lšwn h-tn'ym, mkylt' d-rby Yšm"l. Concordantiae verborum quae in Mechilta d'Rabbi Ismael reperiuntur. 4 vols. Jerusalem 1965—1966. I—IV.

Kosovsky 1967—1969 = Biniamin Kosovsky: 'wcr lšwn h-tn'ym, spr'... Concordantiae verborum... in Sifra... 4 vols. Jerusalem 1967—1969 I—IV [VIII, 1816, 42 pp.].

Kosovsky 1970—1974 = Biniamin Kosovsky: spr h-t'ymwt l-spry. Thesaurus Sifrei. 3 vols. Jerusalem 1970—1974 I—III [VIII, 1922, 56 pp.].

Kosovsky 1979—1984 = Moshe Kosovsky: 'wcr lšwn Tlmwd Yrwšlmy ... Concordance to the Talmud Yerushalmi. Jerusalem 1979—I, 1979 [12, 960, 4]; II, 1982 [938]; III, 1984 [790 pp.].

Krupnik/Silbermann 1927 = Baruch Krupnik/ A. M. Silbermann: millon šimmuši la-talmud la-midraš w-la-targum. A Dictionary of the Talmud, the Midrash and the Targum. 2 vols. London 1927 I—II [461; 439 pp.].

Sokoloff 1990 = Michael Sokoloff: A Dictionary of Jewish Palestinian Aramaic of the Byzantine Period. Ramat-Gan 1990 [823 pp.].

9.5.2. Other Publications

Ben-Hayyim 1947—1977 = Z. Ben-Hayyim: 'bryt w-'rmyt nwsh Šwmrwn 'l py t'wdwt š-b-ktb w-'dwt š-b-'l ph. The Literary and Oral Tradition of Hebrew and Aramaic amongst the Samaritans. Jerusalem 1957—1977. I—V. II, 1967, 642—666: Index to the Aramaic part of hamlys; IV, 1977, 1—349: [Samaritan Pentateuch] Words, Names.

Beyer 1984 = Klaus Beyer: Die aramäischen Texte vom Toten Meer samt den Inschriften aus Palästina, dem Testament Levis ..., der Fastenrolle und den alten talmudischen Zitaten ... Wörterbuch. Deutsch-aramäische Wortliste. Göttingen 1984 [779 pp.].

9.6. Bibliography to Section 6

Academy of the Hebrew Language 1982 = Hrsg. The Historical Dictionary of the Hebrew Language. Specimen Pamphlet: The Root 'rb. Lěšonenu 46. 1982, 165—267.

Alcalay 1962 = Reuben Alcalay: The complete English-Hebrew Dictionary. 4 vols. Hartford 1962 I—IV [4270 cols.].

Alcalay 1969 = Reuben Alcalay: Millon 'ivri šalem. The Complete Hebrew Dictionary. 3 vols. Ramat Gan 1969 I—III [12, 1828 pp.].

Banitt 1983 = Menahem Banitt: Dictionnaire français-hébreux. I—IV. Tel Aviv 1983 [XXXI pp., 4736 cols.].

Ben-Hayyim 1982 = (v. supra Academy 1982).

Ben-Yehuda 1961 = Ehud Ben-Yehuda (ed.): Ben-Yehuda's Pocket English—Hebrew, Hebrew—English Dictionary. New York 1961 [IV, xxviii, 306, 320, xxiv pp.].

Ben-Yehuda 1910—1959 = Eliezer Ben-Yehuda: millon ha-lašon ha-'ivrit hyšnh w-h-hdšh. Thesaurus totius Hebraitatis et veteris et recentioris. Jerusalem. Berlin 1910—1929. 16 vols. Jerusalem 1939—1959 I—XVI [15, 7944 pp.].

Danby/Segal 1958 = H. Danby/M. H. Segal: A Concise Hebrew—English Dictionary comprising the Hebrew of all ages. Tel Aviv 1958 [X, 462, 260, 8 pp.].

Eichenbaum 1981 = M. D. Eichenbaum: Autor 'Aruk hamašma 'im. A Thesaurus of the Hebrew language arranged according to meaning. A compilation [!] of synonyms. Vol. I. Giveon 1981 [23, 502 pp.].

Elmaleh = Abraham Elmaleh: Nouveau dictionnaire complet hébreux-français. I—V. Tel Aviv 1950—1957 [4675 cols.] Millon hadaš w-šalem 'ivri-carfati. Tel Aviv 1961. I—V. Millon hadaš carfati-'ivri. Tel Aviv 1966 [726 cols.] Millon 'arvi-'ivri. Jerusalem 1968 [XV, 1590 pp.].

Even-Shoshan 1966 = Avraham Even-Šošan: ha-millon he-hadaš. I—VII. Jerusalem 1966—1970 [26, 3109 pp.] — Kerek millu'im. 1983 [XII, 324 pp.]

Even-Shoshan 1980 = Abraham Even-Shoshan 'Avraham 'Even-Šošan (ed.): ha-millon he-hadaš. 3 vols. Jerusalem 1980 I—III [11th ed.; 26; 15; 16; 1603 pp.].

Goshen-Gottstein 1969— = Moshe Henry Goshen-Gottstein: Mylwn h-lšwn h-'bryt h-hdšh. The Modern Hebrew Dictionary. Jerusalem. Tel Aviv. Introductory Volume: Introduction to the Lexicography of Modern Hebrew. mbw' l-mlwn'wt š-l h-'bryt h-hdšh. I, 1969 [15, 354, XIV, 4 pp.].

Kena'ani 1960—1987 = Y'qb Kn'ny: 'ocar ha-lašon ha-'ivrit li tqufoteha ha-šonot. Jerusalem. Tel Aviv 1960—1987 I—XVIII [28, 6164 pp.].

Klatzkin 1928—1933 = Jacob Klatzkin: 'wcr h-mwnhym h-pylswpyym. Thesaurus philosophicus linguae Hebraicae. 4 vols. Berlin 1928—1933 I—IV [338; 329; 360; 222 pp.].

Levenston/Sivan 1966 = Edward A. Levenston/ Reuven Sivan: The Megiddo Modern Dictionary. English-Hebrew. Tel Aviv 1966 [XVI, 1267 pp.].

Rabin/Raday 1970 = Chaim Rabin/Zevi Raday: Thesaurus of the Hebrew Language in Dictionary Form. 2 vols. Jerusalem 1970 I—II [11, 1272, XX pp.].

Sappan 1965 = Raphael Sappan: Millon ha-sleng ha-yisra'eli. Jerusalem 1965.

Šapiro/Grande 1963 = F. L. Šapiro/B. M. Grande: Ivrit-russkij slovar'. Moskva 1963 [766 pp.].

Scharfstein 1939 = Ṣevi Šarfšteyn: 'ocar ha-millim we-ha-nivim. Tel Aviv 1939 [XV, 422 pp. 2nd ed.] 1964, 531 pp.].

Segal 1958 = (v. supra Danby/Segal 1958).

Segal 1986 = M. Segal/M. B. Dagut: English-Hebrew Dictionary. — Menachem Dagut: Hebrew-English Dictionary of Contemporary Hebrew. Jerusalem 1986 [XVI, 840; XVI, 539 pp.].

Sivan 1972 = Reuven Sivan: Millon Megiddo he-hadaš 'ivri-angli. Tel Aviv 1972 [xiv, 715 pp.].

Sivan/Levenston 1975 = Reuven Sivan/Edward A. Levenston: The New Bantam-Megiddo Hebrew & English Dictionary. New York 1975 [xxii, 399, 294, xviii pp.].

Stutchkoff 1968 = Nahum Stutchkoff: 'ocar ha-śapa ha-'ivrit. Thesaurus of the Hebrew Language. New York 1968 [34, 584 pp.].

9.7. Bibliography to Section 7
9.7.1. Dictionaries

Aufrecht/Hurd 1975 = Walter E. Aufrecht/John

C. Hurd: A Synoptic Concordance of Aramaic Inscriptions. Missoula, Montana 1975 [7, 158 pp.]

Baumgartner 1953 = (v. supra 9.4.1.: Koehler 1953, 1045—1138).

Beyer 1984 = (v. supra 9.5.2.).

Brockelmann 1928 = Carolus Brockelmann: Lexicon Syriacum. Halis Saxonum 1928 [2nd ed.; VII, 930 pp.].

Costaz 1963 = Louis Costaz: Dictionnaire Syriac-Français. Syriac—English Dictionary. qāmūs sūryānī c_arabī. Beyrouth 1963 [XIII, 421 pp.].

DISO 1965 = (v. supra 9.4.1.: Hoftijzer 1965).

Donner/Röllig 1969 = (v. supra 9.4.1.).

Drower/Macuch 1963 = E. S. Drower/R. Macuch: A Mandaic Dictionary. Oxford 1963 [XII, 491 pp.].

Hoftijzer 1965 = (v. supra 9.4.1.).

Köbert 1956 = R. Köbert: Vocabularium Syriacum. Roma 1956 [VIII, 216 pp.].

Schulthess 1903 = Friedrich Schulthess: Lexicon Syropalaestinum. Berlin 1903 [XVI, 226 pp.].

Smith 1879—1901 = R. Payne Smith: Thesaurus Syriacus. 2 vols. Oxford 1879—1901 I—II [4516 cols. P. Margoliouth: Supplement to the Thesaurus Syriacus. Oxford 1927, XIX, 345 pp.].

Smith 1903 = J. Payne Smith (Margoliouth) (ed.): A Compendious Syriac Dictionary. Oxford 1903 [viii, 626 pp.].

Vinnikov 1958—1965 = I. N. Vinnikov: Slovar' aramejskich nadpisej (Dictionary of the Aramaic Inscriptions). In: Palestinskij sbornik 3. 1958, 171—216; 4. 1959, 196—240; 7. 1962, 192—237; 9. 1962, 141—158; 11. 1964, 189—232; 13. 1965, 217—262.

Vogt 1971 = Ernestus Vogt: Lexicon linguae Aramaicae Veteris Testamenti documentis antiquis illustratum. Roma 1971 [13, 192 pp.].

9.7.2. Other Publications

Altheim/Stiehl 1963 = Franz Altheim/Ruth Stiehl: Die aramäische Sprache unter den Achaimeniden. Frankfurt am Main. I, 1963 (262—277, Wortschatz aramäischer Inschriften (...) aus parthischer Zeit).

Cantineau 1932 = Jean Cantineau: Le Nabatéen. Paris 1932.

Drijvers 1972 = H. J. W. Drijvers (ed.): Old-Syriac (Edessean) Inscriptions. Leiden 1972.

Dupont-Sommer 1946 = A. Dupont-Sommer: La doctrine gnostique de la lettre "Wâw"... Paris 1946.

Fitzmyer/Harrington 1978 = Joseph A. Fitzmyer/Daniel J. Harrington (eds.): A Manual of Palestinian Aramaic Texts. Rome 1978.

Isbell 1975 = Charles D. Isbell (ed.): Corpus of the Aramaic Incantation Bowls. Missoula, Montana 1975.

Macuch 1965 = Rudolf Macuch: Handbook of Classical and Modern Mandaic. Berlin 1965.

Rosenthal 1961 = Franz Rosenthal: A Grammar of Biblical Aramaic. Wiesbaden 1961.

Rosenthal 1967 = Franz Rosenthal (ed.): An Aramaic Handbook. Wiesbaden 1967. Glossary. I/2 [6, 76 pp.]; II/2 [6, 120 pp.].

Segert 1975 = Stanislav Segert: Altaramäische Grammatik mit (...) Glossar. Leipzig 1975.

9.8. Bibliography to Section 8

9.8.1. Dictionaries

Bergsträsser 1921 = Gotthelf Bergsträsser: Glossar des neuaramäischen Dialekts von Ma'lūla. Leipzig 1921 [123 pp.].

Krupnik 1967 = Baruch Krupnik: Millon ha-'Aramit ha-ḥayyah ba-'ivrit she-bi-khetav u-ve-dibbur. Tel Aviv 1967.

Maclean 1901 = Arthur John Maclean: A Dictionary of the Dialects of Vernacular Syriac, as Spoken by the Eastern Syrians of Kurdistan, North-West Persia, and the Plain of Mosul, with Illustrations from the Dialects of the Jews of Zakhu, and Azerbaijan, and of the Western Syrians of Tur 'Abdin and Ma'lula. Oxford 1901 [Reprint Amsterdam 1972].

Oraham 1943 = Alexander Joseph Oraham: Dictionary of the Stabilized and Enriched Assyrian Language and English. Chicago 1943 [576 pp.].

Yohanan 1900 = Abraham Yohanan: A Modern Syriac—English Dictionary. Part 1. New York 1900 [65 pp.].

9.8.2. Other Publications

Cereteli 1958 = K. G. Cereteli: Chrestomafija sovremennogo assirijskogo jazyka. Tbilisi 1958.

Cerulli/Pennachietti 1971 = E. Cerulli/F. A. Pennachietti: Testi neo-aramaici dell'Iran settentrionale. Napoli 1971.

Friedrich 1960 = J. Friedrich: Zwei russische Novellen in neusyrischer Übersetzung und Lateinschrift. Wiesbaden 1960.

Garbell 1965 = Irene Garbell: The Jewish Neo-Aramaic Dialect of Persian Azerbaijan. Linguistic Analysis and Folkloric Texts. The Hague 1965.

Ishaq 1983 = Yusuf Ishaq et al.: Toxu Qorena. Stockholm 1983.

Kalašev 1894 = A. I. Kalašev: Ajsorskie teksty. Sbornik materialov dl'a opisanija mestnostej i plemen Kavkaza. Tiflis 1894.

Krotkoff 1982 = G. Krotkoff: A Neo-Aramaic Dialect of Kurdistan. Texts, Grammar and Vocabulary. New Haven 1982.

Lidzbarski 1896 = Mark Lidzbarski: Die neuaramäischen Handschriften der kgl. Bibliothek zu Berlin. Weimar 1896.

Macuch 1989 = Rudolf Macuch/(Klaus Boekels): Neumandäische Chrestomathie. Wiesbaden 1989 (Glossar: 197—263).

Macuch/Panoussi 1974 = R. Macuch/E. Panoussi: Neusyrische Chrestomathie. Wiesbaden 1974.

Rosenthal 1967 = (9.7.2).
Sabar 1976 = Yona Sabar: Pěšaṭ Wayěhî Běšallaḥ. A Neo-Aramaic Midrash on Beshallaḥ (Exodus). Wiesbaden 1976.
Sabar 1983 = Yona Sabar: The Book of Genesis in Neo-Aramaic in the Dialect of the Jewish Community of Zakho, including selected texts in other Neo-Aramaic dialects. Jerusalem 1983 [Exodus, 1988. Leviticus, 1990].

Sabar 1984 = Yona Sabar: Homilies in the Neo-Aramaic of the Kurdistani Jews on the Parashot Wayḥi, Beshallaḥ and Yitro. Jerusalem 1984.

Stanislav Segert (sections 8. and 9.8.:
Yona Sabar), University of California,
Los Angeles, California (USA)

237. Arabic Lexicography

1. Origins: The Language and Lexicography
2. *Kitāb al 'Ain* and the Phonetical-Anagrammatical Arrangement
3. The 'Rhyme Arrangement'
4. The Modern Dictionary Arrangement
5. Miscellaneous Matters: Vocabularies, Definitions, Arrangement Within Entries
6. The Influence of Arabic Lexicography
7. Selected Bibliography

1. Origins: The Language and Lexicography

When Islam arose at the beginning of the 7th C., Arabic was spoken in various dialects by tribes inhabiting the Arabian Peninsula and the deserts between Syria and Iraq (ct. Map 237.1). There was a highly developed poetical literature going back at least a hundred years; but it was transmitted orally, the writing of Arabic being then extremely rare. However, from 610 onwards, the Qur'ān was recited piecemeal in Mecca and Medina, by the Prophet Muhammad, as God's final Revelation to mankind. The preservation and preparation of an authoritative text made the writing of Arabic essential after his death in 632, while those who had heard it, including some who had written down parts of it, were still alive. This in its turn encouraged linguistic studies, including grammar and lexicography.

1.1. The Language and Its Script

The Qur'ān was 'revealed' in a dialect resembling that of the early poetry, and having much in common with the speech of the Quraish tribe of the Hedjaz, whose chief town, Mecca, was an important cultural, religious and mercantile centre. This dialect became the standard written Arabic. Being a Semitic language, Arabic is based on consonantal roots, largely triliteral, though it includes also many biliterals, quadriliterals and quinquiliterals. Consequently, early forms of the script tended to omit vowels, particularly the short ones. In addition there were groups of letters which were nearly identical in shape, especially when initial or medial, e.g. *r-z, j-ḥ-kh, b-t-th-n-y*. The introduction, over and under letters, of small vowel-signs, and also dots to distinguish letters otherwise identical, was sponsored by al-Ḥajjāj (d. 714), a schoolmaster appointed Governor of Iraq by the Umaiyad Caliph 'Abd al-Malik (Nicholson 1907, 200 ff.). This Caliph also substituted coins with Arabic inscriptions for the Byzantine and Persian currency previously used, and made Arabic the language of financial transactions. Thenceforward the cumbersome square Kufic script, in which the early copies of the Qur'ān were written, was gradually superseded by the cursive naskhī. Without these developments, the writing of serviceable dictionaries would have been difficult. Even so, there was reluctance to use the vowel-signs, because they were time-consuming, and because careless copyists or readers might confuse them. Lack of confidence in them persisted so long as dictionaries were handwritten, and this was one of the lexicographers' problems.

1.2. Factors Favouring Lexicography

By the end of the 8th C., the Arabic script was capable of coping with lexicography, and the time was ripe for it. Under the first three caliphs (532—44) an authoritative manuscript of the Qur'ān had been prepared. But there were grammatical and lexical difficulties which required elucidation and this led to variant readings, and disputes exacerbated by sectarian divisions. Moreover, as the Arabs built up their empire stretching from Iberia to India, a vast number of non-Arabs embraced Islam, whilst those who did not still needed a knowledge of the language for official business and trade. A further stimulus for lexicography was the Arabs' interest in their poetry, the older the better, and their enthusiasm rubbed off on non-Arab users of the language. The dictionaries and vocabularies are full of poetical quotations, to explain rare words and usages. The over-riding aim of the Arabic lexicographers during much of the Medieval period was to establish the 'pure Arabic' of the Qur'ān and the early poets, and to preserve it from corruption because it was the language of Divine Revelation. The speech of desert Arab tribes, their

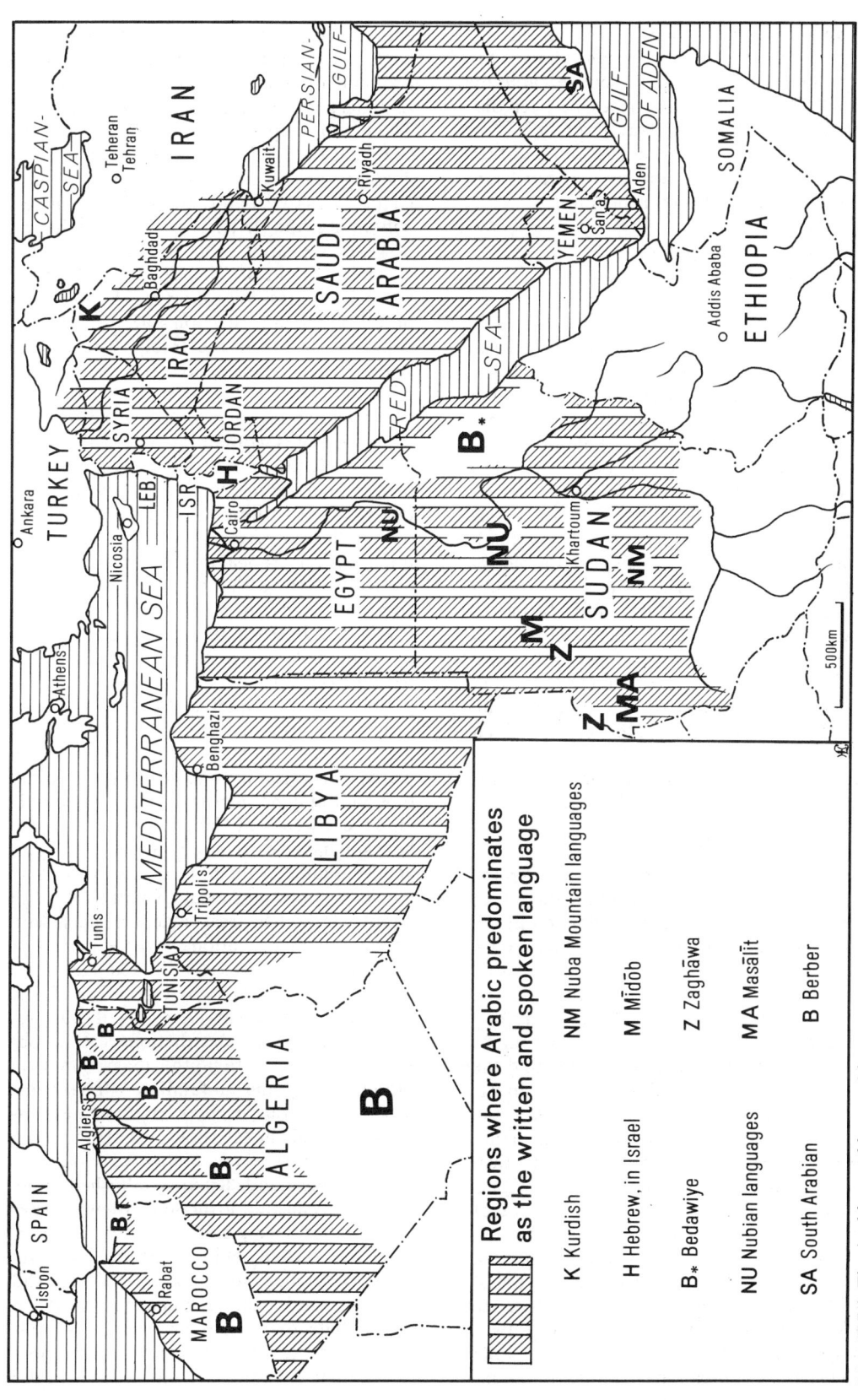

Map 237.1: The Arabic-speaking world

proverbs and their poetry, were considered important evidence: though how far dictionary-compilers carried out research by actually staying with such tribes has been disputed, e.g. by L. Kopf (Haywood 1959, 17). Nevertheless, in linguistics, as well as other studies, there was a sort of mystique surrounding the desert and the bedouin.

2. Kitāb al 'Ain and the Phonetical-Anagrammatical Arrangement

The earliest Arabic lexicographical works were short monographs, each devoted to the vocabulary of some specific topic, arranged not alphabetically, but according to meaning, word form, or haphazardly. Favourite subjects included the camel, the horse, man and his qualities, rare words in the Qur'ān or Ḥadīth (Traditions of the Prophet) and various topics of philological interest such as aḍdād' (words having two meanings, each an antonym of the other). The 'Fihrist', a bibliography of Arabic literature dating from 988 (Ibn al-Nadīm, 1871−2) lists many such works, some of them by younger contemporaries of Khalīl: but it is difficult to prove that he definitely used them in compiling the 'Ain. He does mention some authorities — albeit infrequently, without naming their works: but these were in the main probably Bedouins expert in language. (Sezgin 1982, 41).

2.1. Kitāb al'Ain (Khalīl 1980−85)

The two famous centres or 'schools' of Arabic linguistic studies were Basra and Kufa in Iraq (Haywood 1965, 92). Khalīl belonged to the former, but he started writing his dictionary while on a visit to Khurāsān, and was assisted by al-Laith, a native of that province, the extent of whose involvement was hotly disputed by later scholars and lexicographers. However, it is reasonable to assume that the unusual plan was Khalīl's as set out in his long introduction. It may be described as the 'Phonetical anagrammatical arrangement'. Rejecting the accepted Arabic alphabetical order, on the grounds that it begins with a 'weak' letter, the alif ('/a), he devised one of his own, based on the place of pronunciation of consonants. He began with the gutturals, as being the lowest, the first and lowest of which, the 'ain, gave the book its title. He ended with the labials *f/b/m* followed by a group of four weak letters, *w(u)/y(i)*/long *a/hamza* (a soft breathing). (Some Indian inspiration may have played a role in this, because the Indian sequence also is based on pronunciation and the consonants also start with the gutturals and proceed to the labials.) There is a chapter for each of these letters, save that the four weak letters form a single chapter, making 26 in all. The aim in each chapter was to list all roots (with derivatives) containing the letter concerned, without, however, repeating roots already included in previous chapters. The chapters therefore become progressively shorter. The first, that of the letter 'ain, occupies 180 of the 590 pages of the MS in the Iraqi National Museum. Each chapter is divided into six types of root: the biliteral (e. g. *m-rr /m-r-m-r*), the sound triliteral (e. g. *q-t-l*), the weak *(mu'tall)* triliteral, that is, containing one weak radical (e. g. *w-s-l*), the doubly weak *(lafīf)* triliteral, that is, containing two weak radicals (e. g. *q-w-y*), the quadriliterals (e. g. *d-h-r-j*) and the quinquiliterals (e. g. *'-n-k-b-t*). In each of these sections, roots are dealt with anagrammatically. Thus with the root *q-t-l* would also come *q-l-t, t-q-l, t-l-q, l-t-q* and *l-q-t*. Wherever a certain permutation does not actually occur in the language, whether by chance, or because certain letters are mutually incompatible, Khalīl explains this. Indeed he is rather pre-occupied with phonetics as a means of distinguishing Arabic from foreign words. He certainly had an original mind, though it may be suspected that his phonetic alphabet owed something to Sanscrit, which he could have heard of in Khurāsān. The 'Ain achieved fame as the first Arabic dictionary; but its complicated arrangement — though adopted by other great lexicographers, with or without modifications, over a period of 300 years — must have militated against its use, and may explain why only a handful of manuscripts have survived. Yet it was frequently quoted in later dictionaries. Its obvious weaknesses are (a) the anagrammatical principle, (b) the unfamiliar alphabetical order, (c) separate sections based on the number of radicals in the root, and (d) the separate listing of roots containing weak radicals. On the other hand, Khalīl established many features of the Arabic dictionary entry: types of definition (see 5.2.), supporting citations from the Qur'ān, Ḥadīth, poetry and orations, reference to spoken dialects and proverbs, and naming language experts to substantiate definitions and usages — this last, however, understandably much more rarely than later became the vogue. He did not, however, devise any regular sequence for mentioning the various derivatives under a given root. Indeed, he obviously makes no attempt to include all the derivatives. Nor is it possible to determine what his criteria are for including some and omitting others. Thus the 'Ain is fairly exhaustive as to roots, but selective as to vocabulary.

2.2. Later Dictionaries Using Khalīl's Arrangement

The second attempt to compile an exhaustive Arabic dictionary was the [al-] *Jamhara* [fi l-lugha] of [Muḥammad ibn al-Ḥasan] Ibn Duraid (?837—934), the title of which probably means 'the all-embracing in language' (Ibn Duraid 1925—38). Ibn Duraid rejects Khalīl's phonetic alphabet, and uses the normal alphabetical order, as being more in keeping with most men's knowledge and capacity. But he retains the anagrammatical principle, and the separation of roots according to the number of their radicals, though slightly differently from Khalīl. But confusion is caused by a number of supplementary chapters on various classes of words, which appear to have been added rather haphazardly to the body of the dictionary. These are at times interesting: one listing Persian loanwords and their origins breaks fresh ground, for in the 'Ain there are words clearly Persian in origin, but Khalīl does not mention the fact, though he must surely have known! But apart from the untidiness and inconvenience, there is also the result that some words occur two or three times in various parts of the dictionary. The fat 4th vol. in the Hyderabad edition listing all words entered is thus doubly necessary. — Ibn Duraid's use of the normal alphabetical order was an important, if modest landmark in Arabic lexicography, which was to be followed in due course. Meanwhile several major dictionaries were compiled following Khalīl's system more or less slavishly, while correcting some of his errors, adding new words, supplementing, and in some cases identifying, his citations. Of these dictionaries, *Tahdhīb* [al-lugha] by [Abū Manṣūr al-] Azharī (895—981) is very copious, and particularly rich in religious references (Azharī 1964—7). Azharī was born in Herat, Khurāsān, and studied in Baghdad. His knowledge of Arabic was further enhanced by travels in Arabia, part of the time as a captive of nomads, on whose knowledge of correct Arabic he placed great reliance. Even more copious is the [al-] *Muḥkam* [wa l-Muḥīṭ al-a'ẓam] written by a blind scholar of Arab Spain, Ibn Sīdā (1006—1066) (Ibn Sīdā, Muḥkam 1958—72). Among other dictionaries in the Khalīl arrangement, mention must be made of [al-Ṣāḥib] Ibn 'Abbād's [al-] Muḥīṭ [fi l-lugha], archetype of the exhaustive Arabic dictionary of modest proportions. Ibn 'Abbād (938—995) — a statesman as well as a man of letters — achieved brevity without sacrificing fulness, by omitting most citations: but even so, he managed to include hundreds of proverbs (Ibn 'Abbād 1976/8).

3. The 'Rhyme Arrangement'

It was a contemporary of Ibn 'Abbād who initiated the arrangement which replaced that of Khalīl for major dictionaries, and lasted to the 19th century, despite some efforts to establish the modern dictionary arrangement, as we shall see. [Ismā'īl ibn Ḥammād al-] Jauharī (d. c. 1007) was born in Transoxiana, studied in Baghdad, and spent some time among tribes of Arabia, then settled in Khurāsān where he died. It was there that he compiled his dictionary [Tāj al-lugha wa] *Ṣaḥāḥ* [al- 'Arabiyya] (the crown of language and the authentic of Arabic) (Jauharī 1956—8). Like Ibn Duraid he used the normal alphabetical order. But he arranged roots first according to their final radicals — hence the term 'rhyme arrangement', then according to their first and intermediate radicals. He abolished Khalīl's separation of roots according to the number of radicals, irrespective of whether radicals were sound or weak, and rejected the anagrammatical principle. As the title suggests, the Ṣaḥāḥ was designed to establish 'correct' Arabic: with this proviso, it was meant to be exhaustive. Scholars have been puzzled as to why he chose to base his arrangement on final radicals. Certainly, a pioneer of Hebrew lexicography, Saadia Gaon (892—942) had done this in one part of his *Agron*. But it is probable that Jauharī took it from his maternal uncle, [Isḥāq ibn Ibrāhīm al-] Fārābī (d.961), who had used it in the various sections of his *Dīwān al-adab,* a general vocabulary. This is a very substantial work, in which each of the many Arabic word forms has a section. The words in each section are listed in rhyme order, and defined briefly. There are many citations from scholars and texts (Fārābī 1978—9). However, Jauharī was the first to make this arrangement the basis of a major dictionary. Another innovation was Jauharī's use of a regular system for indicating the vowels of words, and other orthographical signs such as the tashdīd, a sign placed over a consonant to show that it is doubled without any intervening vowel, as the two b's in ṭabbākh (= cook). The system may be summarised thus. Vowels are indicated in full wording where words differ from certain norms, and familiar words are used as models. (For further details, see Haywood 1965, 74). This system was adopted by subsequent lexicographers. The Ṣaḥāḥ was immediately successful, and remained the standard dictionary for 300 years. It generated a large literature, and gave rise to a number of enlargements on the one hand and abridgements on the other. A good example of the former is that of [Ḥasan Muḥammad ibn al-Ḥasan al-] Ṣaghānī (1177—1262) entitled [al-] *Takmila* [wa l-dhail wa l-ṣila li-Kitāb Tāj al-lugha wa Ṣaḥāḥ al 'Arabiyya] (Ṣaghānī, Takmila 1970—77). The key-word of this title is 'Takmila' (= completion), its aim being to include roots and words omitted by Jauharī, whether deliberately, in his passion for 'pure Arabic', or from carelessness or ignorance. The many abridgements include *Tahdhīb al-Ṣaḥāḥ* by [Muḥmūd ibn Aḥmad al-] Zinjānī (1177—1258) (Zinjānī 1952). This reduced the original by 90% by omitting almost all quadri- and quinqui-literals, dispensing with citations, and giving few derivatives. The best-known abridgement is *Mukhtār al-Ṣaḥāḥ* by [Muḥammad ibn Abī Bakr al-] Rāzī, completed in 1262 (Rāzī 1865 and 1918). Rāzī had students of the Qur'ān and Ḥadīth in mind, and incorporated material from the Tahdhīb. So important was this book considered that in 1904 the Egyptian Ministery of Education financed the preparation and publication of a new edition by Maḥmūd Khāṭir Bey, and prescribed its use in state schools. Rāzī's entries were re-arranged in the modern alphabetical order, to facilitate its use by students.

3.1. Subsequent Dictionaries in the Rhyme Arrangement

Ṣaghānī, already mentioned for his Takmila, was an outstanding lexicographer. Suyūṭī, the famous 15th-century Egyptian polymath, described him as 'the bearer of the banner of philology in his time'. Apart from the Takmila, he wrote two other rhyme-order dictionaries: *Majma' al-Baḥrain* and [al-] *'Ubāb* [al-zākhir wa l-lubāb al-fākhir], a large-scale work much admired by later scholars. It was said that he completed only two-thirds of it. An extract containing the roots ending in the letter ghain has been published (Ṣaghānī, 'Ubāb 1980). It is to be hoped that more of Ṣaghānī's work will be published, to permit a more accurate assessment of his stature. While Jauharī's rhyme arrangement appeared to find favour, his purism in rejecting some words, the expansion of Arabic vocabulary to meet different needs, and a general tendency towards verbosity and rich vocabulary — as, for example, in the *Maqāmāt* (séances) of al-Hamadhānī (d. 1008) and al-Ḥarīrī (1054—1122) — made the compilation of a gigantic dictionary, incorporating, as far as possible, the contents of all previous dictionaries, only a matter of time. [Muḥammad ibn Mukarram] Ibn Manẓūr (1232—1311) performed this task with his *Lisān al- 'Arab* (Ibn Manẓūr 1955/6). Born in Tunis, Ibn Manẓūr worked for the Mameluke rulers of Egypt, and died in Cairo. His dictionary is still widely regarded by Arabs as the best exhaustive dictionary in Classical Arabic. In his Introduction (v,1, 7 ff.) Ibn Manẓūr praises the Tahdhīb and the Muḥkam, but laments their non-availability, which he ascribes to their unsatisfactory arrangement. He commends the Ṣaḥāḥ for its arrangement, but describes it as 'a mere drop in the ocean of the language' because of its omissions. He frankly disclaims any originality stating that he has merely quoted from previous dictionaries. It is interesting to note that he likens his Lisān to Noah's Ark, because Arabic is threatened (and, by implication, the Lisān is designed to save it). People, he says, are vying with each other to translate Arabic books into other languages. We must remember that by this time, the Caliphate had split up into a number of independent states, mostly ruled by non-Arab dynasties — Iranian, Turkish and so on, and the position of Arabic, except in the Arab heart-lands, had become not unlike that of Latin in the later Middle Ages. With its supposed 80,000 words, and numerous citations from the Qur'ān, Ḥadīth, proverbs and poetry, the Lisān is a rich store of Arabic, comparable in size and scope to the Oxford English Dictionary. Ibn Manẓūr is at pains to give full and accurate definitions of words. Unfortunately, the usual lack of any regular sequence of entering derivatives under their roots is made even more frustrating by its fulness. Nor can the charge of unneccessary verbosity be refuted. For example, too often, in citing poetry to support a definition, two verses are given when one might suffice. And Ibn Manẓūr feels obliged to explain several other words in the quotation, in addition to the one he is seeking to define.

3.1.1. A century later, the Lisān was paralleled by another dictionary, perhaps more copious, yet of modest size, the *Qāmūs* of [al-] Fīrūzābādī. It may be compared with Ibn 'Abbād's *Muḥīṭ*, in that he achieved its modest proportions by the omission of citations. Fīrūzābādī (1326—1414) was born near Shiraz in Persia, and spent his life as a wandering scholar and qāḍi (judge), settling temporarily in a succession of countries of the Islamic world, including Syria, Egypt, Iraq, the Yemen, Turkey and India, carrying loads of books wherever he went. He began compiling a gigantic dictionary, based primarily on the *Muḥkam* and the *'Ubāb*, but realising that its anticipated 60 volumes would render it inaccessible to students, he compiled a short one with the same lexical content, by removing the citations (v. 1, 2—7) (Fīrūzābādī, various Cairo editions). The Qāmūs obviously filled a pressing need, for manuscripts proliferated: indeed, it became, in modern terms, a 'best-seller'. And even to this day few selfrespecting Arab teachers of the language or religious studies would be without a copy, as it is cheap, as well as full and reliable. Fīrūzābādī was a pioneer in using abbreviations: *m* (= ma'rūf) for common words requiring no definition; *j* (= jam') for plurals, and other signs for geographical names. Among the many virtues of the Qamus is that Fīrūzābādī does not hesitate to admit that certain words are foreign loan-words. The full title of the dictionary is *al-Qāmūs al-muḥīṭ* (= the surrounding ocean). We have already seen the word *muḥīṭ* in other dictionary titles. As an active participle it means 'surrounding'; but as a noun it may mean 'sea'. But such was the popularity of Fīrūzābādī's dictionary, the 'qāmūs' — which may be derived from Greek 'okeanos' became, and has remained, the commonest Arabic word for 'dictionary'. In the 'silver age' of Classical Arabic, it became the custom to give ornate metaphorical titles to books. Words associated with the ocean were regarded as apt for the Arabic language, because it was considered so vast and complex that no one man could 'plumb its depths'. The word *'Ubāb* used by Ṣaghānī for one of his dictionaries means 'billows'; the title of another, *Majma' al-baḥrain*, means 'the meeting of the two seas'.

3.1.2. From the early 16th c. the Arabic-speaking peoples of the Near East and N.Africa fell under Ottoman Turkish rule, while in Spain, the last Moorish principality, Granada, had submitted to the armies of Ferdinand and Isabella in 1492. In the East, the Persian language had revived in Iran, and it ousted Arabic in N.India as the language of government and culture. In the Arab lands of the Fertile Crescent, the conquering Turks adhered to their own language. Lexicography, like Arabic literature in general, stagnated. Yet in 18th-century Egypt, a final rhyme-order dictionary — and the most copious of all Arabic dictionaries — appeared, entitled *Tāj al-'Arūs* [min jawāhir al-Qāmūs] (= the bride's crown from the pearls of the Qamus/ocean. The word *Qāmūs* is a pun here). The author was [Murtaḍā al-] Zabīdī (1732/3—1791). It is a commentary on, or more accurately an enlargement of, the Qāmūs. Material from the latter is given in brackets, and Zabīdī adds fresh material of several kinds: correction of errors, amplification of definitions, the inclusion of additional words under existing roots or new roots altogether, and the insertion of citations, though not so fully as in the earlier large-scale dictionaries, especially the Lisān. E. W. Lane drew attention to Tāj al-'Arūs by basing his Lexicon on it (Lane 1863—93). In his Introduction (v 1, xx) he mentions his discovery that over three-quarters of Zabīdī's additional material is quoted almost verbatim from the Lisān, but without acknowledgement. Despite its additions and its greater length (said to total 120,000 defined words), it has not supplanted the Lisān. It remains to be seen whether the new Kuwait edition, to replace the Bulaq, Cairo edition, will change this (Zabīdī 1889 and 1965—).

4. The Modern Dictionary Arrangement

By this expression, we mean a system whereby words or roots are listed according to the normal alphabetical order letter by letter. Groping efforts in this direction began early — possibly while Khalīl was still alive. And throughout the medieval period a spasmodic succession of dictionaries was compiled based on this system to a greater or lesser extent. But they were largely specialised rather than general, and apparently included no exhaustive dictionaries. The first was the [Kitāb al-] *Jīm* by [Abu 'Amr al-] Shaibānī (d.828 aged over 100; Shaibānī 1974/5). Why it was called 'The book of the letter Jīm' is difficult to say, since it begins with the letter alif, and lists words beginning with it in seemingly haphazard order; then it does the same for the letters bā', tā', and so on. No attempt is made to deal with roots, only words, rarely more than one or two for a given root, often without mentioning any verb. Shaibānī was of the Kufan school, and was a noted collector of poetry. The Jīm includes many dialect words of various tribes as exemplified in their poetry (Diem 1968, 60—69). The arrangement makes it difficult to look up words: yet this arrangement continued to be used from time to time, the most notable example being [Kitāb al-] *Mu'arrab* by al-Jawālīqī (1073—1134) (Jawaliki 1867). This is a dictionary of foreign loan-words which were frequently used in Arabic. Lexicographers had often been reluctant to admit that a word acceptable in Arabic could really be of foreign origin. This was probably due more to inhibition than ignorance, as we have seen that many of them lived in Iran and adjoining countries. The Mu'arrab (= Arabicised) was at once a sign of and a stimulus to recognition by the experts that the notion of 'pure Arabic' had to give way in the face of common usage.

4.1. In the meantime, some lexicographers moved from Shaibānī's method — which has been called the 'Kufan method' (Haywood 1965, 96) — nearer towards the modern dictionary arrangement. Ibn Fāris (d.1000), an outstanding philologist who enjoyed the patronage of Ibn 'Abbānd, compiled two dictionaries: [al-] *Mujmal* [fi l-lugha] and *Maqāyīs* [al-lugha] (Ibn Fāris 1985 and 1366—71 AH). Both are arranged on the same plan. The normal alphabetical order is used for each initial letter, but bi-, tri-, quadri- and quinqui-literal roots are dealt with separately. The latter two types are listed haphazardly, but for the former two, roots are then given in the order of their subsequent radicals. But Ibn Fāris imagined that the letters of the alphabet were written round the circumference of a circle, around which one could move only in one direction. Thus under r, the first root listed would be $r+z$ (the next letter in the alphabet). Roots in which the second radical came earlier in the alphabet had to be deferred. Thus $r+$', $r+b$, $r+t$ etc. would come after $r+y$, y being the last letter in the alphabet. Ibn Fāris does not attempt to include many derivatives, or even numerous roots, and he is sparing with citations. Indeed his avowed aim is to concentrate on the usage of his time — a novel attitude for those days. In the Maqāyis, a further aim is to give the basic meaning(s) of roots. For example, he gives those of $w+d+$' (= to put) as to lower/ place something on the ground, or for a woman to give birth to a child. Presumably the main practical use of these basic root-meanings is that knowledge of them can help one to deduce the meaning of an unfamiliar derivative encountered in reading, without having to consult a large dictionary. Yet one could well be wrong, such is the waywardness of languages!

4.1.1. Further progress was made towards the modern dictionary arrangement by compilers of specialised dictionaries of religious terminology. The first to adopt this method in toto was probably [al-] Rāghib [al-Isfahānī] (d.1108) in his *Kitāb mufradāt alfāẓ al-Qur'ān* (= the Book of individual words of the Qur'ān) (Rāghib 1324 AH). The greatest lexicographer to use this arrangement was undoubtedly [Abū l-Qāsim al-] Zamakhsharī (1075—1144), born in Transoxiana. He won fame for a Qur'anic commentary, a grammar, and a geographical dictionary, in addition to three language dictionaries. The first, his Arabic-Persian Dictionary, is mentioned elsewhere (article 325). The second [al-] *Fā'iq* [fī gharīb al-Ḥadīth] (The outstanding in rare words of the Ḥadīth) (Zamakhsharī, Fā'iq, 1324 AH) follows the alphabetical order for the first two radicals only. The third, *Asās* [al-balāgha] (the foundation of rhetoric) (Zamakhsharī, Asās, 1953) is fully in the modern arrangement. It was designed to distinguish between the literal and metaphorical use of words. In those days, balāgha (rhetoric) was an important subject, and it had been codified to meet the requirements of the ornate rhymed prose and rich poetic diction then in fashion. Each entry in this dictionary is divided into two parts, the first giving literal meanings, and the second — usually longer — the metaphorical (majāz). There are many citations from literature and the spoken language, and many compound expressions and idiomatic phrases and sentences are given under each root. Yet another ḥadīth dictionary was composed by al-Muṭṭarizī (d.1213) entitled [al-] *Mughrib* [fī tartīb al-muʻrab] (the extraordinary in the arrangement is expressed) (Muṭṭarizī 1328 AH). This is arranged alphabetically insofar as 1st, 2nd and final radicals are concerned, the 3rd (and 4th) radicals of quadri- (and quinqui-) literals are treated haphazardly.

4.2. As has been shown, the modern arrangement in Arabic dictionaries, despite its early origins in the 'Kufan method' of Shaibānī, was slow to develop to its logical conclusion, and it found favour in restricted or specialised rather than general dictionaries. It seems to have been considered suitable for religious dictionaries in particular. Meanwhile the general dictionaries used the Khalīl method at first, then switched over to Jauharī's rhyme order. It was probably European influence which led Arabs to adopt the modern dictionary arrangement from the second half of the 19th c. (see article 325). Buṭrus al-Bustānī's *Muḥīṭ al-Muḥīṭ* (Bustānī 1867/70) was based on the Qāmūs, but rearranged — like G. W. Freytag's Lexicon (Freytag 1830/37). But it did not fully solve the problem of how to arrange derivatives under roots (see 5.3). Various small-scale monolingual dictionaries have appeared in the Arab world during the last 100 years, few, it would seem, of great moment with the exception of Louis Maaloufs's *Munjid*, which has gone through numerous editions (Maalouf n. d.). In 1932, an Egyptian royal decree called for the compiling of a comprehensive historical dictionary. The great German scholar August Fischer was in Cairo, and had collected information on 360,000 pieces of paper. But his death in 1939 put paid to the project. Language academies have been flourishing in Cairo, Damascus and Baghdad, but we still await the hoped-for dictionary. By contrast, in Persian, Dekhoda's monumental *Loghet-nameh* was completed a few years ago. The Arabs have done some superb work, following the 19th century Bulaq tradition, especially in the last 25 years, in searching out manuscripts of the old dictionaries, many of them long considered lost, then editing and publishing them. As for the compiling of new dictionaries, they appear to prefer the bi-lingual, particularly with English or French. The mantle of the great medieval Arab lexicographers dealt with in this study has, for the time being, fallen on the shoulders of Western Orientalists. The true modern successors of Ibn Manẓūr, Fīrū-zābādī and their likes are the editors of *Wörterbuch der klassischen arabischen Sprache* and Hans Wehr. (See article 235.)

5. Miscellaneous Matters: Vocabularies, Definitions, Arrangement Within Entries

5.1. Vocabularies

In the foregoing account, we have dealt almost entirely with dictionaries in the narrow sense, but mention has been made of vocabularies, many short and specialised, and some extensive and general. For examples of the former category, the reader can only be referred to Haywood (1965, 110—114, 133) and Sezgin (1982, passim). The general vocabularies were usually arranged according to subject matter, with perhaps a few short sections on word-forms. The various sections coincided with the subjects of the different specialised vocabularies. Some, however, were based wholly on word-form. Fārābī's *Dīwān al-adab* has already been mentioned. Another, devoted to certain verb forms, is *Kitāb al-afʻāl* (= the book of verbs) by Ibn Qūṭiyya (d.Cordoba 977) (Haywood 1965, 135 f.). Of the general vocabulary arranged by subject-matter, two outstanding examples will be mentioned. The first is *Gharīb al-muṣannaf* (= roughly 'rare words found in books') by Abu 'Ubaid (773—837) (Abu 'Ubaid MS). This is a book frequently quoted in the major dictionaries. The second is Ibn Sīdā's *Mukhaṣṣaṣ*, which leans heavily on the aforementioned work. It is as full, in its way, as Ibn Sīdā's *Muḥkam*, being characterised by exact definitions with ample citations. (Ibn Sīdā, Mukhaṣṣaṣ, 1316—21 [anno hidžrae], see Haywood 1965, 64 ff., 134 f.).

5.2. Definitions in Dictionaries and Vocabularies

Ways of defining words changed very little from the *ʻAin* to the 19th c. The following are the chief methods: — (a) the simple antonym e. g. *ʻilm naqīd al-jahl* (= knowledge — the opposite of ignorance); (b) the simple synonym, e. g. *ʻalima — ʻarafa* (both words meaning 'to know', though with different shades of meaning); (c) more exact definition by sentence or phrase; (d) sometimes definition was by implication, such as by an example of the word's use in prose, poetry, or speech, the reader being expected to deduce the meaning from meanings already given for the root verb or some derivative; (e) for common words, no definition might be given, or (f) the word *ma'rūf* (= well-known) might be added; (g) in the Ṣaḥāḥ there are examples of 'non-definitions' on the following pattern: *dawā', wāḥid al-adwiya* (= medicine, the singular of medicines). Fortunately, this type is rather rare.

5.3. Word Order Within the Root Entries

Arabic lexicographers, though concerned with the order in which they listed roots, did not devote the same attention to the order in which derivatives should be listed in a root entry. Indeed, it is difficult to find any consistency at all even within any one dictionary. As we have seen, Arabic roots are based on consonants. A root is most conveniently indicated by the 3rd person perfect masc. sing. of the simple verb. This is formed for bi-literals simply by vowelling both radicals with a short *a*, e. g. *marra* (= 'to pass', lit. 'he passed'). For the reduplicative bi-literal, the vowelling is like that for the quadriliteral, e. g. *gharghara* (= 'he gargled') and *dahraja* (= 'he rolled', transitive). In the triliteral, the first and third radicals have short *a*, and the second *i, a* or *u* (e. g. *raja'a* = 'he returned', *ḥasiba* = 'he estimated', and *kabura* = 'he grew'). The above are merely brief specimen translations, and the masculine singular subject of a verb may be animate or inanimate, there being no neuter in Arabic. Nouns are masculine or feminine, either because of their meaning, or by grammatical convention. Quinquiliteral roots cannot be verbs, but in determining their position in a dictionary, only consonants are taken into account. The practice of beginning a root-entry with the simple verb on a regular basis was probably established by European orientalists. The root verb is then logically followed by a regular sequence of derived-form verbs, formed by adding certain letters to it initially, medially or finally. These give various shades of meaning, such as *qattala* (= 'he massacred') from *qatal* (= 'he killed'). Ten or more are possible with triliterals, and with biliterals like *marra* (= 'he passed'), which double the second radical, and behave almost like triliterals. In practice, the number of these derived verbs differs from root to root. Quadriliterals and reduplicative bi-literals rarely form more than one derived verb, e. g. *tadahraja* (= 'he/it rolled', intrans.), though three are possible. After the verbs, the modern convention is to list nouns and adjectives according to their length, which of course depends on the number of 'letters of increase' they contain over and above the root, the shorter ones being given first. Certain derivations have a prefixed *m,* as *makhzan* (= 'store'), from *khazana* (= 'to store up'), and these usually come at the end of the entry. This makes consulting an Arabic dictionary much easier and speedier. The first Arabic monolingual dictionary to be arranged thus was probably Sa'īd al-Shurṭūnī's *Aqrab al-mawārid* (late 19th c.) (Darwish 1956, 134—5). When one considers that a common root like *'alima* (= 'to know') has around 100 derivatives, one can appreciate the need for a regular order.

6. The Influence of Arabic Lexicography

The medieval Arabic dictionaries are a treasure-house of information not only on the language, but on every aspect of Arabic and Islamic culture. They also represent an important stage in the world history of lexicography. The influence of Arabic lexicography can be seen, to varying degrees, in the languages of other Muslim peoples, and other peoples which came under Arab rule or influence. This is apparent in the early dictionaries in Persian, Ottoman Turkish, Pashto, various languages of India and Pakistan such as Urdu, Panjabi and Sindhi, in Malay/Indonesian, and African languages such as Swahili and Hausa. To these might be added Hebrew. This influence took several forms. (a) Many Arabic words were taken into the languages of non-Arab Muslims, and for the definitions of these words lexicographers turned to the old Arabic dictionaries. In non-Semitic languages, Arabic loan-words brought special problems, for example, the broken plurals which are so important a feature of Arabic. (b) In some cases, famous Arabic dictionaries were reproduced with definitions translated into the native language. Thus the Ṣaḥāḥ and Qāmūs were translated into Turkish; the former by Vanquli (d.1591/2), the latter by 'Aintābī (c.1759—1819) (see Haywood 1965, 120). (c) Another, and less helpful, influence was in dictionary arrangement. For example, the earliest Persian dictionary is the short *Lughat al-Furs* of Asadī yi-Ṭūsī, compiled c. 1050. It is in the rhyme order, but words are listed haphazardly so far as their initial and medial letters are concerned. This is rather like the

'Kufan method' in reverse (Asadī yi-Ṭūsī 1897 and 1957). In a 13th-century dictionary by Nakhjavānī, pointedly called *Ṣaḥāḥ al-Furs* (the Ṣaḥāḥ of the Persians) (Nakhjavānī 1963), the rhyme order is followed, but only the initial in addition to the final letters are followed alphabetically. Turning to Hebrew lexicography, we have seen that Saadia Gaon may have influenced Jauharī. But the influence must surely have been mutual, since Saadia must have seen some Arabic dictionaries. Arabic lexicography possibly taught the Jews to distinguish between radicals and letters of increase. Jewish scholarship flourished in Muslim Spain, and it was there that a contemporary of Azharī, Menahim ben Saruk (910—970) compiled his Mehbaret, the first exhaustive dictionary of biblical Hebrew.

7. Selected Bibliography

7.1. Dictionaries

Abū 'Ubaid = Abu 'Ubaid, Gharīb al-musannaf, MS 1628, Iraqi National Museum. Baghdad.

Asadī yi-Ṭusī = Asadī yi-Ṭusī, Lughat al-Furs, (1) ed. Paul Horn. Göttingen 1897 [133, 37 p.]. (2)ed. M. D. Syaqi. Teheran 1957 [70, 210 p.].

Azharī 1964—7 = Abū Manṣūr Muḥammad ibn Aḥmad al-Azharī, Tahdhīb al-lugha, ed. Ibrāhīm al-Abyārī, 15 vv. Cairo 1964—7 [7601 p.].

Bustānī 1867—70 = Buṭrus al Bustānī, Muḥīṭ al-muḥīṭ, 2 vv. Beirut 1867—70 [2452 p.].

Fārābī 1867—9 = Isḥāq ibn Ibrāhīm al-Fārābī, Dīwān al-adab, 5 vv. Cairo 1974—9 [2443 p.].

Fīrūzābādī = Majd al-Dīn Muḥammad al-Fīrūzābādī, al-Qāmūs al Muḥīṭ, 4 vv. Cairo, amny editions [c.1600 p.].

Freytag 1830—37 = G. W. Freytag, Lexicon Arabico-Latinum, 4 vv. Halle 1830—37 [694 p.].

Ǧawaliki 1867 = Ǧawaliki's Muarrab, ed. E. Sachau. Leipzig 1867 [267 p.].

Ibn 'Abbād 1976 = al-Ṣāḥib ibn 'Abbād, al-Muḥīṭ fi l-lugha, ed. Muhammad Ḥasan Āl-Yāsīn, vv. 1 and 2, Baghdad 1976—8 [515, 381 p.].

Ibn Duraid 1925—38 = Muḥammad ibn al-Ḥasan ibn Duraid, al-Jamhara fi l-lugha, 4 vv. Hyderabad, India 1925—38 [2115 p.].

Ibn Fāris Maqāyīs 1366—71 AH = Ibn Fāris, Maqāyīs al-lugha, 6 vv. Cairo 1366—71 AH [3014 p.].

Ibn Fāris, Mujmal 1985 = Ibn Fāris, al-Mujmal fi l-lugha, 5 vv. Kuwait 1985 [2307 p.].

Ibn Manẓūr 1955—6 = Muḥammad ibn Mukarram ibn Manẓūr, Lisān al-'Arab, 15 vv. Beirut 1955—6 [c.8000 p.].

Ibn Sīdā, Muhkam 1958—72 = Ibn Sīdā, al-Muḥkam wa l-muḥīṭ al-a'ẓam, vv. 1—3. Cairo 1958—72.

Ibn Sdā, Mukhaṣṣaṣ 1316—21 AH = Ibn Sīdā, al-Mukhaṣṣaṣ, 17 parts. Bulaq. Cairo, 1316—21 AH.

Jauharī 1956—8 = Ismā'il ibn al-Ḥammād al-Jauharī, Tāj al-lugha wa-Ṣaḥāḥ al-'arabiyya, 7 vv. Cairo 1956—8 [2563 p.].

Khalīl 1980—85 = al Khalīl ibn Aḥmad, Kitāb al-'Ain, ed. Makhzūmī and Sāmurrā'ī. 8 vv. Baghdad 1980—85 [3476 p.].

Lane 1863—93 = Edward W. Lane, Arabic-English Lexicon. The last 4 volumes ed. Stanley Lane-Poole. 8 vv. London 1863—93 [xxi, 3064 p.].

Maalouf n. d. = Louis Maalouf, al-Munjid, Beirut n.d. (?1923), ill. [1094 p.]; also 23rd ed., 2 vv. 1982 [1014, 800 p.].

Muṭṭarizī 1328 AH = al-Muṭṭarizī, al-Mughrib fī tartīb al-mu'rab. Hyderabad, India, 1328 AH.

Nakhjavānī 1963 = Muḥammad ibn Hendushqh-e Nakhjavani, Sahah'ol Fors, ed. Abd'ol Ali Ta'ati. Teheran 1963 [vi, 343 p.].

Rāghib 1324 AH = al-Rāghib al-Isfahānī, Kitāb mufradāt alfāẓ al-Qur'ān, Cairo 1324 AH.

Rāzī 1865 = Muḥammad ibn Abī Bakr al-*Rāzī*, Mukhtār al-Ṣaḥāḥ, Bulaq, Cairo 1865.

Rāzī 1918 = ibn ed. Maḥmūd Khāṭir Bey. Cairo 1918 [745 p.].

Ṣaghānī, Takmila 1970—77 = Ḥasan Maḥmūd al-Ṣaghānī, al-Takmila wa-l-dhail wa-l-ṣila li-kitāb Tāj al-lugha wa-Ṣaḥāḥ al-arabiyya, ed Tajāwī and Ḥasan, vv. 1—5. Cairo 1970—77 [2795 p.].

Ṣaghānī, 'Ubāb 1980 = ibid. al-'Ubāb al-zakhir wa-l-lubāb al-fakhir, 1 v. (letter ghain only). Baghdad 1980 [128 p.].

Shaibānī 1974—5 = Abū 'Amr al-Shaibānī, Kitāb al-Jīm, ed. Ibrāhīm-al-Abyārī, 3 vv. Cairo 1974—5.

Zabīdī 1889 = Martaḍa al -Zabīdī, Tāj al-'Arūs min jawāhir al-Qāmūs, 10 vv. Bulaq. Cairo 1889 [5020 p.].

Zabīdī 1965— = ibid, vv. 1—10, Kuwait 1965—83 [5000 p.] (Not yet completed).

Zamakhsharī Asās 1953 = Abū l-Qāsim al-Zamakhsharī, Asās al-balāgha, Cairo 1953 [514 p.]. (Also photometric reprint, Beirut 1982).

Zamakhsharī Fā'iq 1324 AH = ibid., al-Fā'iq fī gharīb al-Hadīth. Hyderabad, India, 1324 AH.

Zinjānī 1952 = Maḥmūd ibn Aḥmad al-Zinjānī, Tahdhīb al-Ṣaḥāḥ, ed. 'Aṭṭār and Hārūn, 3 vv. Cairo 1952 [1384 p.].

7.2. Other Publications

Darwīsh 1956 = A. Darwīsh: al Ma'ājim al-'Arabiyya. Cairo 1956.

Diem 1968 = Werner Diem: Das Kitab al Ǧim des Abu 'Amr as-Ṣaibani — ein Beitrag zur arabischen Lexikographie. Munich 1968.

Haywood 1959, [2]1965 = John A. Haywood: Arabic lexicography — its History and its place in the general History of Lexicography. Leiden 1959, ²1965.

Ibn al-Nadīm 1871—2 = Fihrist Ibn Nadīm, 2 vv. ed. G. *Fluegel.* Leipzig 1871—2.

Nicholson 1907 = R. A. Nicholson: Literary History of the Arabs. London 1907, several reprints.

Sezgin 1982 = Fuat Sezgin: Geschichte des arabischen Schrifttums, Band VIII, Lexikographie bis ca. 430 H. Leiden 1982.

* For the system of transliteration of Arabic used in this article, see that given in Haywood, p. viii (Notes).

John A. Haywood, Lewes (Great Britain)

238. Lexicography of the Semitic Languages of Ethiopia

1. Introduction
2. Geʻez
3. Tigré
4. Tigrinya
5. Amharic
6. Argobba
7. Gafat
8. Gurage
9. Harari
10. Selected Bibliography

1. Introduction

From the descriptive and geographical point of view the Ethiopian-Semitic languages (cf. Map

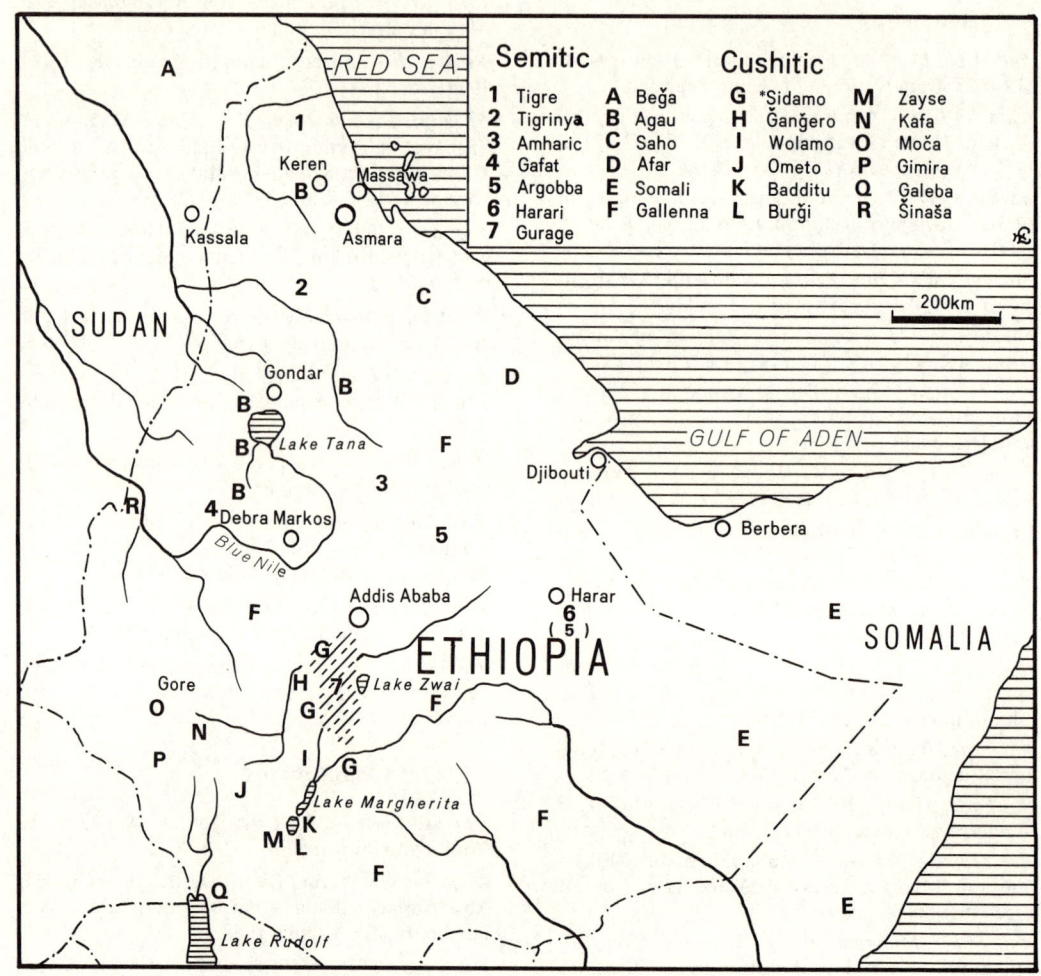

Map 238.1: Languages of Ethiopia

238.1) are divided into North Ethiopic including Ge'ez, Tigré and Tigrinya; and South Ethiopic including Amharic, Argobba, Gafat, Gurage and Harari.

The Ethiopian languages have preserved some features inherited from Proto-Semitic, and developed a few new ones. Some of the innovations are due to Cushitic influence.

(a) Phonology. The interdentals disappeared: $\underline{d} > z$, $\underline{t} > s$, $\underline{z} > \underline{s}$; the velar $\dot{g} > g$ — Innovations in Ethiopic are: the labiovelar series g^w, k^w, q^w, h^w (in the West Gurage dialects the labials have likewise the rounded phonemes: b^w, f^w, m^w, and p^w), and the labials p, $\underline{p}$ beside the labio-dental f. — The "emphatic" consonants of Semitic are glottalized or ejectives in Ethiopic. — In all the modern languages $\underline{d}$ became $\underline{s}$, or even $\underline{t}$; $\underline{h}$ became h in Tigré and Tigrinya, zero in most southern languages (except in Harari where $\underline{h}$, h and h are also preserved as $\underline{h}$; in Argobba h and $\underline{h}$ are likewise preserved); ' and ' became zero except in Harari where ' and ' became ' in special situations. — A new prepalatal series has developed in the modern languages: $\check{s}$, $\check{z}$, $\check{c}$, $\check{c}$, $\check{g}$, $\check{n}$; in West Gurage also g^y, k^y, x^y, q^y.

(b) Morphology. Noun. The plural is external and internal in North Ethiopic as in Arabic. The southern languages have an internal plural only; some Gurage dialects preserved the internal plural. — The marker -t of the feminine is preserved in the northern languages, but only occasionally in South Ethiopic. In the substantive of all the languages -t has lost its original value as feminine. — Of case endings only the accusative -a (ä) remained in Ge'ez and in the Gurage dialects of Selṭi and Zway. The same ending serves in the expression of the construct state.

Verb. Nearly all the derived stems are formed not only from the basic stem, but also from the so-called types B and C, which correspond formally to the intensive and conative stem of Semitic, but semantically became a basic stem in Ethiopic. — A special stem (so-called "Reduplicative") formed by the repetition of the second radical (*qātatälä) is used in all the modern languages. It expresses an intensive, repeated or augmentative action. — The prefixed morpheme n does not serve for the expression of the passive. — Ge'ez preserved two verbal patterns: nagara (nägärä), and labsa (läbsä) in the type A, but the modern languages have only one pattern in the perfect. — The imperfect has a vowel after the first radical yəqät(t)əl, as in Akkadian (but the origin may be different). — Ge'ez has two patterns for the jussive: yəngər, and yəlbäs; these patterns are preserved in some West Gurage dialects. — Ge'ez, Tigrinya, Amharic and Argobba have developed a gerund; some West Gurage dialects have a 'pseudo-gerund'. — The suffix of the 1st and 2nd person, perfect, is k as opposed to t of most other Semitic languages.

(c) Syntax. The word order is influenced by Cushitic, especially in the spoken languages. The order of a main clause is: Subject + direct or indirect complement + verb. — The qualifier is placed before the qualified. — The subordinate clause can precede or follow the main clause in the northern languages, but it always precedes the main clause in the southern languages.

(d) Alphabet. The Ethiopic script is a syllabic system of writing in which each character consists of a consonant to which a vocalic symbol is attached. There are seven "orders" or vocalic symbols. They are: ä (a), u, i, a (ā), e, ə (or zero), o. The alphabet derived from the South Arabic alphabet. The first inscriptions that date from the 3rd or 4th century have only the consonant symbol with the vowel ä (a). In the fourth century A.D. one comes across an inscription with the vocalic symbols added to the consonant. The question about the origin of these vocalic symbols is not yet answered. The Ethiopic alphabet has two drawbacks: 1) there is no special symbol for the gemination of the consonant, an important phonetic and phonemic feature; 2) the sixth "order" is ambiguous since the consonant of the 6th order can be pronounced either with a shva or with a vowel zero.

2. Ge'ez

The first inscription dates from the 3rd or 4th century. The Bible translation was accomplished between the 5th and the 7th century. The bulk of the Ge'ez literature dates from the 13th to the 17th century. It is mainly religious in content. Some of the writings were translated from Greek, Syriac, or Arabic. For the Ge'ez literature, see Guidi 1933, Cerulli 1956. It is difficult to determine when Ge'ez ceased to be spoken. This possibly occurred between the 12th and the 14th century, but the language still continues as the language of the liturgy. For the pronunciation of Ge'ez we rely on what is called "traditional pronunciation" preserved in the religious schools.

The dictionaries for Ge'ez are: Wemmers 1638: Ge'ez-Latin dictionary, pp. 1—319. Second part, 56 unnumbered pages: Latin-Ge'ez index. — Ludolf 1661: Ge'ez-Latin dictionary: 1st ed., cols. 1—474; 2nd ed., cols. 1—632. Latin-Ge'ez index: 1st ed., 40 unnumbered pages; 2nd ed., 42 unnumbered pages. It gives references for the majority of the lexemes. There are also comparisons with Hebrew, Aramaic, and Arabic. — Dillmann 1865: Cols. 1—1292: Ge'ez-Latin dictionary; cols. 1303—1434: various indices; cols. 1435—1522: Latin index, the numbers referring the reader to the page where the Ge'ez lexeme is treated. The dictionary gives references to the Ge'ez writings (books and manuscripts) known to Dillmann. In his comparisons he makes use of Arabic, Hebrew, Aramaic, and Syriac. — Grébaut 1952:

Geʿez-French supplement to Dillmann's Lexicon containing either new meanings or new forms. Only occasionally are references given. It also contains the Geʿez-Latin-French-Amharic dictionary collected by Juste d'Urbin. — Maggiora 1953: Geʿez-Italian-Latin dictionary. It is arranged in the alphabetical order of the forms, and not in the order of the roots. Thus, the derived stems are listed in different places. The dictionary is a translation of Dillmann augmented by the dictionaries of a few Ethiopian lexicographers. — Leslau 1987: Geʿez-English, pp. 1—649; English-Geʿez, pp. 653—761; Index of Semitic roots, pp. 765—813. It contains the dictionaries of all the Western and Ethiopian lexicographers. It is arranged in the order of the Roman alphabet, in phonetic transcription, except for the main entry that is also rendered in the Ethiopic alphabet. Comparisons are made with all the Semitic languages, the Ethiopian-Semitic languages, and the Cushitic languages. — Leslau 1989: Geʿez-English dictionary. The arrangement of the lexemes is in the traditional order of the Geʿez dictionaries. All the lexemes and their derivations are in the Ethiopic alphabet and in phonetic transcription.

Dictionaries compiled by Ethiopian lexicographers include: Tayyä 1889: Geʿez-Amharic dictionary, pp. 89—190. The derived stems are not listed with the root. No references are given. — Kidanä Wäld 1948: Introduction, pp. 1—191; vocabulary, pp. 193—908. It is a Geʿez-Amharic dictionary, arranged in the order of the Hebrew alphabet. The references used to illustrate the lexemes are nearly all taken from Dillmann 1865.

For smaller dictionaries by (Abba) Ya'qob Gäbrä Iyyäsus (1920 = 1927/8), Täsfa Səllase (1938 = 1945/6) and others, and for the glossaries known as Säwasəw 'ladder', see Leslau 1987.

3. Tigré

Tigré is spoken in the eastern, western and northern lowlands of Eritrea, including the Massawa region and the Dahlak islands in the east. The New Testament, the Psalter, religious books and some customary law codes have been published by Swedish missionaries. There is a considerable amount of texts in prose and poetry collected by E. Littmann. Littmann 1910—14 contains Tigré texts in the Ethiopic alphabet, with a translation into English and German.

Only a selection of dictionaries for Tigré is given. The most important ones are: Munzinger 1863: Cols. 7—52: Tigré-French vocabulary, in the Ethiopic alphabet and in transcription. Cols. 53—64: Tigré-French vocabulary of d'Abbadie, Extrait du vocabulaire de langue tigré à Muçawwʿa, in the Ethiopic alphabet, published in Dillmann 1865. — Camperio 1894: Pp. 127—177: Tigré-Italian vocabulary, in transcription. — Missione Cattolica dell'Eritrea 1919 (Grammatica della lingua tigré): Pp. 91—186: Tigré-Italian vocabulary, in the Ethiopic alphabet. — Piccirilli 1938: Pp. 53—421: Vocabulary in Italian-Amharic-Tigrinya-Galla-Tigré, arranged according to subjects. Pp. 425—808: Vocabulary in Amharic-Tigrinya-Galla-Tigré-Italian, arranged according to subjects. — Littmann/Höfner 1962: The dictionary is in the Ethiopic alphabet. The homonyms are placed together. Comparisons are made with Geʿez, Tigrinya, and Amharic. — Leslau 1982: Comparisons with Geʿez, Tigrinya, and Amharic, dealing with the entries mentioned in Littmann/Höfner 1962. — Nakano 1982: Pp. 1—143: English-Tigré, in phonetic transcription and Ethiopic script, according to subjects; pp. 144—159: English index.

4. Tigrinya (Təgrəñña)

Tigrinya is spoken in the Tigrai province and in Eritrea in the regions of Hamasen, Serae, Akkele Guzay. There are dialectal variants in Tigrinya. Mission societies have published the Bible, and some religious books. Since the 1940s there is a beginning of a Tigrinya literature.

Since Eritrea was an Italian colony there is a number of Tigrinya-Italian dictionaries compiled for practical purposes. Only some of these dictionaries will be mentioned here. The most important dictionaries for Tigrinya are: Vito 1896: Pp. 7—133: Tigrinya-Italian dictionary, in the Ethiopic alphabet and in transcription; pp. 135—166: Italian-Tigrinya index. — Cimino 1904: Pp. 1—203: Italian-Tigrinya dictionary; pp. 205—325: Tigrinya-Italian dictionary, in the Ethiopic alphabet. — Ronciglione 1912: Pp. 1—164: Vocabulary in Italian-French-Tigrinya; in the Ethiopic alphabet and in phonetic transcription, arranged according to subjects. — Coulbeaux/Schreiber 1915: Tigrinya-French dictionary in the Ethiopic alphabet only, with special signs for the vowel of the 6th order, and for the gemination. It contains only the letters H—N (in the alphabetical order of Ethiopic). No more published. — Bassano 1918: Cols. 1—1020: Tigrinya-Italian dictionary; cols. 1053—1304: Italian-Tigrinya index. It is the most copious dictionary available. — Piccirilli 1938 (see section 3) treats also Tigrinya. — Milano 1936: Pp. 13—163: Italian-Tigrinya-Amharic vocabulary, in transcription; pp. 167—239: Tigrinya-Italian vocabulary, in transcription. — Information Center 1985: English-Tigrinya-Arabic; 1986: Tigrinya-English, in Ethiopic alphabet only — Ullendorff 1985: Pp. 155—236: Tigrinya-English: in the Ethiopic alphabet only.

Dictionaries by Ethiopian lexicographers include: Ḥagos 1903: Pp. 27—195: Tigrinya-Italian-Arabic vocabulary. — Yoḥannəs 1949: Tigrinya-Amharic dictionary. The derived nominal and verbal forms are in the alphabetical order and not under the root. — Gərma Ṣəyon 1976: A Tigrinya-Tigrinya dictionary.

5. Amharic (Amarəñña)

Amharic is the national language of Ethiopia. It is spoken in the central part of the country and also in other parts of Ethiopia with enclaves of other languages. There are slight regional variants in the phonology and morphology. The oldest known writings in Amharic are songs written in the 14th or 15th century in praise of various emperors. Modern Amharic literature started appearing at the beginning of the 20th century. On the Amharic literature, see Kane 1975.

During the Italian occupation of Ethiopia a number of Amharic dictionaries in Italian appeared for practical purposes. Only a small number of them is given here. Important dictionaries of Amharic are: Ludolf 1668: Pp. 1—163, in two columns: Amharic-Latin; pp. 1—15: Latin index in three columns, with numerals referring the reader to the page where the Amharic word is treated. Occasionally comparisons with Ge'ez are made. — Isenberg 1841: Amharic-English, English-Amharic; in the Ethiopic alphabet only. — d'Abbadie 1881: Cols. 1—1106: Amharic-French; cols. 1107—1336: French index with numerals referring the reader to the page where the Amharic word is treated. The dictionary is printed in the Ethiopic alphabet with partial transcription. — Guidi 1901: Amharic-Italian dictionary, in the Ethiopic alphabet and in phonetic transcription. — Armbruster 1910: English-Amharic; in the Ethiopic alphabet and in phonetic transcription. — Armbruster 1920: incomplete Amharic-English dictionary; in the Ethiopic alphabet and in phonetic transcription. The dictionary is partially comparative. — Walker 1928: English-Amharic; in phonetic transcription only. The lexemes are illustrated with sentences that are often a free translation of the English text. — Baeteman 1929: First part, 1262 cols.: Amharic-French dictionary. Second part, 426 cols.: French-Amharic index. The words are arranged in the order of the vowels following the consonants. The transcription is only partially indicated. There are 1000 proverbs throughout the dictionary, translated into French. — Bevilacqua 1937: Italian-Amharic vocabulary, in two columns, in the Ethiopic alphabet and in transcription. — Fusella/Girace 1937: Italian Amharic dictionary, in phonetic transcription. — Piccirilli 1938 (see section 3) also treats Amharic. — Guidi 1940 (con il concorso di Francesco Gallina ed Enrico Cerulli). A supplement to Guidi 1901. There is no transcription. — Gankin/Käbbädä 1965: Russian-Amharic, in the Ethiopic script and in phonetic transcription. — Klingenheben 1966: German-Amharic, in phonetic transcription only. — Gankin 1969: Amharic-Russian; in the Ethiopic alphabet and in phonetic transcription. — Amsalu/Mosback 1973: English-Amharic, in Ethiopic script only. — Leslau 1973: English-Amharic; in the Ethiopic alphabet only. Each entry is illustrated with an English sentence translated into Amharic. — Leslau 1976: Pp. 1—253, in two columns: Amharic-English; pp. 257—535: English-Amharic, in Ethiopic alphabet and in phonetic transcription. — Amsalu 1987: Amharic-English, in the Ethiopic alphabet only. The dictionary is arranged in the order of the vowels following the consonant. — Kane 1990: Amharic-English; in the Ethiopic script and in phonetic transcription.

Dictionaries by Ethiopian lexicographers include: Täsämma 1951: Amharic-Amharic, pp. 193—1398. It is arranged in the order of the vowel after the consonant. The derived nominal and verbal forms are listed separately, and not under the basic root. The dictionary occasionally lists Ge'ez nouns and verbs. — Dästa 1962: Amharic-Amharic, pp. 60—1284, arranged in the order of the

Hebrew alphabet. The derived nominal and verbal forms are listed under the root.

6. Argobba

Argobba was spoken in the region of Harar. At present the speakers of that region speak Oromo (Galləñña). In the region of Ankober to the north of Addis Ababa, Argobba was spoken in the 1950s by the older people and the women only. The young people speak Amharic at present. F. M. C. Mondon-Vidailhet published a collection of poems, in Ethiopic script, that he considers to be Argobba, but they seem to be written in corrupt Amharic (see Mondon-Vidailhet 1913, pp. 95—119). Of all the South Ethiopian languages Argobba comes the closest to Amharic.

A vocabulary of Argobba was published by Leslau 1973—77. Leslau 1966 analyzes the Argobba vocabulary.

7. Gafat

Gafat was spoken in the province of Gojam (Gog̈am) in the region of the Blue Nile. At present the Gafat speak Amharic. In 1946 the author found only four speakers still speaking the language. The only written document is the Song of Songs translated from Amharic into Gafat at the initiative of James Bruce in the 18th century. The manuscript was published by Leslau in 1945. Gafat is related to Soddo of the Gurage group.

Dictionaries and vocabularies for Gafat include: Bruce 1804 which contains pp. 494—497 a vocabulary of "(English,) Amharic, Falashan, Gafat, Agaw, Tcheretch Agow". Bruce's vocabulary is reproduced in Murray 1808, and in Beke 1846. — Leslau 1945: Gafat-English, pp. 139—181; English-Gafat, pp. 183—188. The dictionary is based on the Song of Songs mentioned above. The dictionary is also comparative. — Leslau 1956: Gafat-French, pp. 169—252; French-Gafat, pp. 253—260. The dictionary was collected through fieldwork in Ethiopia. It is also a comparative dictionary.

8. Gurage (Guragué)

The region of Gurage is situated southwest of Addis Ababa. It is bordered on the north by the river Awash, on the east by Lake Zway, and on the south and west by the river Omo. Gurage has twelve dialects. There are three distinct groups in the cluster: East Gurage which includes Selṭi, Wolane, and Zway. West Gurage which includes Čaha, Eža, Ennemor, Endegeň, and Gyeto; North Gurage, with Soddo as the only representative; and Muher, Masqan, and Gogot the position of which still remains to be investigated. East Gurage is linguistically related to Harari; Soddo is related to Gafat. As for West Gurage, even though it has for the most part south Ethiopian features, it has no particularly close connection with any specific south Ethiopian language. The only indigenous text of Gurage is a Čaha catechism in Ethiopic script entitled Aččər təmhərta krəstiyan bägurage bäčäha qʷanqʷa [. . .]., Dire-Daoua 1926 (= 1933/4), 95 pp. Texts in the various Gurage dialects were generated at the initiative of Wolf Leslau in the series "Ethiopians Speak: Studies in Cultural Background" (see Leslau 1966—83).

Dictionaries and glossaries of Gurage include: Mayer 1878: Pp. 8—18: vocabulary in English-German-Amharic-Gurage, in the Ethiopic alphabet and partially in transcription. — Mondon-Vidailhet 1913: Pp. 9—92: French-Gurage (Čaha, Ulbarag, Gogot-Amharic) vocabulary, partially in the Ethiopic alphabet and in phonetic transcription. — Cohen 1931: Pp. 216—230: vocabulary in French-Gurage (Muher, Čaha, Soddo [called Aymellel by Cohen], Wolane, in phonetic transcription, arranged according to subjects. — Leslau 1950: Pp. 145—168: Čaha-English vocabulary, in two columns, in phonetic transcription. — Leslau 1979: Vol. I: Individual dictionaries (twelve dialects), vol. II: English-Gurage Index, vol. III: Etymological section with comparisons with Semitic, Ethiopian-Semitic, and Cushitic. The dictionary includes an index of the Semitic roots, of the Arabic loanwords, and of the Ethiopic roots.

9. Harari

Harari (called ge sinān 'the language of the city' by the inhabitants, and Adare by the Oromo) is spoken only in the city of Harar in eastern Ethiopia. The Harari are Muslims and their religious writings in "Ancient Harari" are written in the Arabic script. These writings became known mostly through Cohen 1931 (pp. 325—354), Cerulli 1936 (pp. 282—343), and Wagner 1983. Modern Harari texts were generated at the author's initiative in: Ethiopians Speak: Studies in

Cultural Background (Vol. 1, Univ. of Calif. Publ., Near Eastern Studies, vol. 7, 1965, 262 pp. [See also Leslau 1966—83]). Harari is related to East Gurage (see above).

Dictionaries and glossaries of Harari include: Salt 1814: Appendix I, pages vi—x: "Vocabularies of the Hurrur and the Southern Galla dialects" (Hurrur referring to Harar). — Burton 1856: Pp. 536—582: English-Harari vocabulary in transcription. — Bricchetti-Robecchi 1890: Vocabulary in Italian-Harari-Galla (Oromo), in transliteration. — Cerulli 1936: Pp. 229—281: Harari-Italian vocabulary with comparisons; pp. 406—437: vocabulary of "Ancient Harari" on the basis of the Kitāb al-farā'iḍ, with comparisons; pp. 443—462: Italian-Harari index, in two columns. — Leslau 1937: Pp. 460—479, 529—591: Harari-French vocabulary with comparisons; pp. 592—606: Harari-French index, in two columns. The material is taken from the various authors. — Leslau 1963: Pp. 15—168: Harari-English dictionary; pp. 171—175: index of the Semitic roots; pp. 176—186: index of the Arabic loanwords; pp. 187—240: English-Harari index. The dictionary is comparative and etymological. The lexemes were collected through fieldwork added to the previous sources. — Wagner 1983: Pp. 267—318. A glossary of the lexemes taken from the text published by the author.

10. Selected Bibliography

10.1. Dictionaries

d'Abbadie 1881 = Antoine d'Abbadie: Dictionnaire de la langue amariñña. Paris 1881 [xlviii, 1336 cols.].

Amsalu 1987 = Amsalu Aklilu: Amharic-English Dictionary. Addis Ababa 1987 [344 pp. in two cols.].

Amsalu/Mosback 1973 = Amsalu Aklilu/G. P. Mosback: English-Amharic Dictionary. Addis Ababa 1973 [299 pp. in two cols.].

Armbruster 1910 = Charles Hubert Armbruster: Initia Amharica. An introduction to spoken Amharic. Part II. English-Amharic vocabulary with phrases. Cambridge 1910 [xxviii, 504 pp.].

Armbruster 1920 = Charles Hubert Armbruster: Part III. Amharic-English Vocabulary, with phrases. Vol I. H—S (in the Ethiopic order). Cambridge 1920 [xxx, 966 pp.].

Baeteman 1929 = Joseph Baeteman: Dictionnaire amarigna-français. Dire-Daoua (Ethiopie) 1929 [xxi, 1262, 426 cols.].

Bassano 1918 = Francesco da Bassano: Vocabolario tigray-italiano e repertorio italiano-tigray. Roma 1918 [xvi, 1308 cols.].

Beke 1846 = C. T. Beke: On the languages and dialects of Abyssinia and the countries to the south. In: Proceedings of the Philological Society 2. 1846, 97—107.

Bevilacqua 1937 = Amleto Bevilacqua: Nuovo vocabolario italiano-amarico. Roma 1937 [vii, 306 pp.].

Bricchetti-Robecchi 1890 = Luigi Bricchetti-Robecchi: Lingue parlate, somali, galla e harari. Note e studi raccolti ed ordinati nell'Harar. In: Bolletino della società geografica italiana, ser. 3, vol. 3. 1890, 257—271, 380—391, 689—708.

Burton 1856 = Sir Richard Francis Burton: First footsteps in East Africa; or An exploration of Harar. London 1856.

Camperio 1894 = Manfredo Camperio: Manuale tigrè-italiano. Milano 1894.

Cerulli 1936 = Enrico Cerulli: Studi etiopici. Vol. I. La lingua e la storia di Harar. Roma 1936.

Cimino 1904 = Alfonso Cimino: Vocabolario italiano-tigrai e tigrai-italiano. Asmara 1904 [xiv, 338 pp.].

Cohen 1931 = Marcel Cohen: Etudes d'éthiopien méridional. Paris 1931.

Coulbeaux/Schreiber 1915 = P. S. Coulbeaux/J. Schreiber: Dictionnaire de la langue tigraï. Wien 1915 [504 pp.].

Dästa 1962 = Dästa Täklä Wäld: Addis yamarəñña mäzgäbä qalat. Addis Ababa 1962 (= 1969/70) [1284 pp. in two cols.].

Dillmann 1865 = August Dillmann: Lexicon linguae aethiopicae, cum indice latino. Lipsiae 1865 [xxxii, 1522 cols.].

Fusella/Girace 1937 = Luigi Fusella/Alfonso Girace: Dizionario pratico e frasario per conversazione italiano-amarica (con elementi di grammatica). Napoli 1937 [xxxviii, 234 pp.].

Gankin 1969 = Emanuel Gankin: Amkharsko-Russkiy slovar'. Moskva: Sovetskaya Entsiklopediia, 1969 [967 pp].

Gankin/Käbbädä 1965 = Emanuel Gankin/Käbbädä Dästa: Russko-Amkharskii slovar'. Moskva 1965 [1013 pp.].

Gərma Ṣəyon 1976 = Gərma Ṣəyon Mäbrahtu: Ləsanä'ag'azi. Asmara 1976 (= 1983/4) [650 pp.].

Grébaut 1952 = Sylvain Grébaut: Supplément au Lexicon linguae aethiopicae de August Dillmann (1865) et édition du Lexique de Juste d'Urbin (1850—55). Paris 1952 [v, 520 pp.].

Guidi 1901 = Ignazio Guidi: Vocabolario amarico-italiano. Roma 1901 [xv, 918 cols. Photostatic reproduction. Roma: Istituto per l'Oriente, 1953.].

Guidi 1940 = Ignazio Guidi: Supplemento al Vocabolario amarico-italiano, compilato con il concorso di Francesco Gallina ed Enrico Cerulli. Roma 1940 [vii, 268 cols.].

Ḥagos 1903 = Ḥagos Täkästa: Nə'əštoy tərgʷam 'erətra. Asmara 1903.

Information Center 1985 = English-Tigrigna-Arabic. Ed. by the Information Center on Eritrea. Roma 1985 [718 pp.].

Information Center 1986 = Dictionary Tigrigna-English. Ed. by the Information Center on Eritrea. Roma 1986 [632 pp.].

Isenberg 1841 = Charles William Isenberg: Dictionary of the Amharic language. Amharic and English, and English and Amharic. London 1841 [vii, 215, 218 pp. in two cols.].

Kane 1990 = Thomas Leiper Kane: Amharic Dictionary. Wiesbaden 1990 [XXIII 2351 pp.].

Kidanä Wäld 1948 = Kidanä Wäld Kəfle: Mäṣhafä säwasəw wägəss wämäzgäbä qalat ḥaddis, published by Dästa Täklä Wäld. Addis Ababa 1948 (= 1955/6) [908 pp.].

Klingenheben 1966 = August Klingenheben: Deutsch-amharischer Sprachführer. Wiesbaden 1966 [169 pp.].

Leslau 1937 = Wolf Leslau: Contributions à l'étude du harari (Abyssinie méridionale). In: Journal Asiatique 229. 1937.

Leslau 1945 = Wolf Leslau: Gafat Documents. Records of a South Ethiopic Language. New Haven 1945 [188 pp.].

Leslau 1950 = Wolf Leslau: Ethiopic Documents: Gurage. New York 1950 (Viking Fund Publications in Anthropology, no. 14).

Leslau 1956 = Wolf Leslau: Etude descriptive et comparative du gafat (Ethiopien méridional). Paris 1956 [260 pp.].

Leslau 1963 = Wolf Leslau: Etymological Dictionary of Harari. Berkely. Los Angeles 1963 (Univ. of Calif. Publ., Near Eastern Studies, vol. 1) [xv, 240 pp. in two cols.].

Leslau 1966 = Wolf Leslau: Analysis of the Argobba vocabulary. In: Journal of African Languages 5. 1966, 102—112.

Leslau 1973 = Wolf Leslau: English-Amharic Context Dictionary. Wiesbaden 1973 [xviii, 1503 pp.].

Leslau 1973—77 = Wolf Leslau: Argobba Vocabulary. In: Rassegna di studi etiopici 26. 1973—77, 21—43.

Leslau 1976 = Wolf Leslau: Concise Amharic Dictionary. Amharic-English, English-Amharic. Wiesbaden 1976 [xiv, 538 pp.].

Leslau 1979 = Wolf Leslau: Etymological dictionary of Gurage (Ethiopic). Wiesbaden 1979 [3 volumes: Vol. I. Individual dictionaries. xix, 1244 pp. in two cols., in phonetic transcription. Čaha, 1—137; Endegeň, 139—256; Ennemor, 257—390; Eža, 391—529; Gogot, 531—618; Gyeto, 619—750; Masqan, 751—830; Muher, 831—960; Selṭi, 961—1031; Soddo, 1033—1120; Wolane, 1121—1193; Zway, 1195—1231; additions, 1233—1239. Vol. II. English-Gurage Index. x, 702 pp. in 12 cols. Vol. III. Etymological section. cvi, 856 pp.].

Leslau 1982 = Wolf Leslau: North Ethiopic and Amharic cognates in Tigre. Supplemento n. 31 agli Annali. Istituto Orientale di Napoli, vol. 42. 1982 [fasc. 2, 86 pp.].

Leslau 1987 = Wolf Leslau: Comparative Dictionary of Ge'ez (Classical Ethiopic). Wiesbaden 1987 [xlix, 813 pp.].

Leslau 1989 = Wolf Leslau: Concise Dictionary of Ge'ez (Classical Ethiopic). Wiesbaden 1989 [x. 247 pp.].

Littmann/Höfner 1962 = Enno Littmann/Maria Höfner: Wörterbuch der Tigrē-Sprache. Tigrē-Deutsch-Englisch. Wiesbaden 1962 [774 pp.].

Ludolf 1661 = Hiob Ludolf: Lexicon aethiopico-latinum [...]. Edited by J. M. Wansleben. Londini: Apud Thomam Roycroft, 1661 [560 cols.; 2nd edition, 1669, 664 cols.].

Ludolf 1668 = Hiob Ludolf: Lexicon Amharicum-Latinum. Francofurti ad Moenum: Prostat apud Johannem David Zunnerum, 1668.

Maggiora 1953 = Gabriele de Maggiora: Vocabolario etiopico-italiano-Latino. Asmara 1953 [(12+) 579 pp.].

Mayer 1878 = Johannes Mayer: Kurze Wörtersammlung in Englisch, Deutsch, Amharisch, Gallanisch, Guraguesch, herausgegeben von Dr. L. Krapf. Basel 1878 [32 pp.].

Milano 1936 = Prospero Maria da Milano: Vocabolario pratico italiano-tigrai-amarico. Milano 1936 [345 pp.].

Missione Cattolica dell'Eritrea 1919 = Grammatica della lingua tigré. Published by the Missione Cattolica dell'Eritrea. Asmara 1919.

Mondon-Vidailhet 1913 = François Marie Casimir Mondon-Vidailhet: Etudes sur le guragiē. Ed. by Erich Weinzinger. Wien 1913 (Kaiserliche Akademie der Wissenschaften. Sprachen-Kommission. [Schriften] Bd. 5).

Munzinger 1865 = Werner Munzinger: Vocabulaire de la langue tigré. Leipzig 1865 [x, 93 pp.].

Nakano 1982 = Aki'o Nakano: A Vocabulary of Beni Amer dialect of Tigré. Institute for the study of languages and cultures of Asia and Africa (Tokyo University), 1982 [159 pp.].

Piccirilli 1938 = Tito Piccirilli: Dizionario di alcune lingue parlate nell' A.O. I. (amarico-tigrai-galla-tigre). Empoli 1938.

Ronciglione 1912 = P. Angelo da Ronciglione: Manuale tigray-italiano-francese. Roma 1912 [xvi, 428 pp.].

Salt 1814 = Henry Salt: A voyage to Abyssinia and travels into the interior of that country. London 1814.

Täsämma 1951 = Täsämma Habtä Mika'el: Käsate bərhan täsämma wägəss wämäzgäbä qalat ḥaddis. Addis Ababa 1951 (= 1958/9) [1398 pp., in two cols.].

Tayyä 1889 = Gäbrä Maryam Tayyä (known as Aläqa Tayyä): Mäṣḥafa Säwasəw. Monkullo 1889 (= 1896/7).

Ullendorf 1985 = Edward Ullendorff: A Tigrinya (Təgrəñña) Chrestomathy. Stuttgart 1985, 155—236.

Vito 1896 = Ludovico de Vito: Vocabolario della lingua tigrigna. Roma 1896 [xii, 166 pp.].

Wagner 1983 = Ewald Wagner: Harari-Texte in arabischer Schrift (Äthiopistische Forschungen, vol. 13). Wiesbaden 1983 [xii, 318 pp.].

Walker 1928 = C. H. Walker: English-Amharic dictionary. London 1928 [xi, 236 pp.].

Wemmers 1638 = Jacob Wemmers: Lexicon aethiopicum. Romae [...]: Typis Sac. Congreg. de Propaganda Fide, 1683 [319 pp. 56 pages.].

Yoḥannəs 1949 = Yoḥannəs Gäbrä Egzi'abəher, Abba: Mäzgäbä qalat təgrəñña amharəñña. Ethiopian Dictionary. Tigrigna-Amharic. Asmara 1949 (= 1956/7) [855 pp.].

10.2. Other Publications

Bruce 1804 = James Bruce: Travels to discover the source of the Nile in the years 1768, 1769, 1770, 1771, 1772, 1773. 2nd ed. Edinburgh 1804.

Cerulli 1956 = E. Cerulli: Storia della letteratura etiopica. Milano 1956.

Guidi 1933 = I. Guidi: Storia della letteratura etiopica. Roma 1933.

Kane 1975 = T. L. Kane: Ethiopian Literature in Amharic. Wiesbaden 1975.

Leslau 1966—83 = Wolf Leslau: Ethiopians Speak: Studies in Cultural Background. Vol. 2: Čaha (Univ. of Calif. Publ., Near Eastern Studies, vol. 9, 1966), vol. 3: Soddo (Univ. of Calif. Publ., Near Eastern Studies, vol. 11, 1968), vol. 4: Muher (Äthiopistische Forschungen, vol. 11. Wiesbaden 1981), vol. 5: Čaha and Ennemor (Äthiopistische Forschungen, vol. 16. Wiesbaden 1983).

Littmann 1910—14 = E. Littmann: Publications of the Princeton Expedition to Abyssinia. 4 vols. Leiden 1910—14.

Murray 1808 = Alexander Murray: Account of the Life and Writings of James Bruce. Edinburgh 1808.

Wolf Leslau, University of California, Los Angeles, California (USA)

239. La lexicographie berbère

1. Le statut du berbère
2. La lexicographie utilitaire
3. La lexicographie dialectale
4. La lexicographie scientifique
5. Problèmes actuels
6. Bibliographie choisie

1. Le statut du berbère

Le berbère est une langue chamito-sémitique. Elle est encore parlée dans plusieurs pays d'Afrique (Egypte, Lybie, Tunisie, Algérie, Maroc, Mauritanie, Mali et Niger). Elle est aussi vieille que les grandes langues méditerranéennes. Sans écriture depuis la plus haute antiquité, elle fut et reste orale, vivant successivement sous la domination du phénicien, du grec, du latin et, enfin, de l'arabe. Ce statut (oralité et domination) a eu deux conséquences: (a) une forte dialectalisation; (b) le grand retard de la recherche linguistique et, par conséquent, lexicographique. Nous ne disposons d'aucune étude, dans ce domaine, même chez les Arabes malgré leur tradition philologique. Il fallut attendre les Français pour qu'apparût un intérêt pour la description du berbère. La lexicographie berbère est donc essentiellement européenne. On peut la classer en trois tendances qui reflètent trois types de préoccupations: une lexicographie utilitaire, une autre dialectale et, enfin, une lexicographie scientifique.

2. La lexicographie utilitaire

Elle est née dans la période précoloniale et de ‹pacification› (1820—1918). Elle s'adresse, quand elle n'est pas leur œuvre, aux commerçants, aux voyageurs, à l'armée et à l'administration installée après 1830 en Algérie. Ses traits essentiels sont: (a) le parler de base est le dialecte kabyle (Algérie) parlé dans une région reconnue par sa résistance traditionnelle à tout envahisseur. Il faut donc connaître cette population à travers sa langue. Il en sera de même pour le Rif et l'Atlas marocains. Néanmoins, les lexicographes ne tiendront pas compte de la dialectalisation du berbère. Certains (Paradis 1844) amalgament deux dialectes très éloignés (le kabyle et le chleuh). Ajoutons que la variation lexicale interne à un dialecte n'est pas abordée non plus. (b) Les dictionnaires sont souvent bilingues et parfois trilingues. Ceci pose le problème de la transcription qui est plus que fautive et oublie de se pencher sur la structure morphophonologique de la langue. On suppose, parfois, qu'elle est équivalente à celle de l'arabe. (c) Ce qui implique que la théorie et la méthodologie sont sommaires. En fait, c'est un travail d'amateurs. Les articles sont réduits à la traduction de lexèmes français. Seuls les dictionnaires de la génération du XIXe siècle et quelques rares lexiques du XXe siècle adoptent la transcription arabe. C'est donc la transcription latine qui domine d'autant plus que les études berbères sont autonomes par rapport aux études arabes, en France du moins.

3. La lexicographie dialectale

Elle correspond à la période coloniale proprement dite (1918—1950) et reste marquée par un dictionnaire (Foucauld 1951) et des recherches lexicographiques systématiques (Laoust 1920 et Destaing 1944). Les caractères de cette période peuvent être résumés ainsi: (a) On s'intéresse de manière systématique au lexique d'un dialecte (Tahaggart, Chleuh, etc.). (b) La structure morphophonologique de la langue est mieux étudiée; la transcription phonétique est d'une grande précision et le classement par racine prend de l'importance (Foucauld 1951). (c) L'article est mieux structuré: il comporte une définition de chaque lexème et des dérivés. Souvent, on cite des exemples. (d) Des enquêtes ethnographiques (Laoust 1920) et des recueils de textes (Foucauld 1930, Destaing 1938, Boulifa 1904) rendent les définitions et les comparaisons plus précises. Néanmoins des problèmes théoriques et méthodologiques restent et seront repris par les lexicographes suivants.

4. La lexicographie scientifique

Même si les travaux préparatoires ont commencé avant les indépendances, on peut dire que cette lexicographie est post-coloniale. Elle profite des acquis de la période précédente et, surtout, des progrès de la linguistique elle-même. En plus donc des qualités citées en 3. on peut ajouter: (a) le respect des normes scientifiques actuelles (traitement des racines et leur classement, une meilleure structuration de l'article avec des indications grammaticales, etc.) (b) Un appareil de sigles et de signes important précise le sens péjoratif ou familier, son utilisation dans un jargon. (c) Une information ethnographique d'une grande précision. Avec cette période, on peut dire que la lexicographie berbère scientifique est bien partie.

Les dictionnaires de Dallet (1982) et de Delheure (1984), le premier consacré au parler kabyle des Aït Meuguellet et le second au dialecte mozabite, peuvent être considérés comme les premiers dictionnaires de la génération scientifique. Voici les raisons que l'on peut invoquer:

— une transcription phonétique fine basée sur les derniers travaux de linguistique descriptive.
— une documentation riche et critiquée de manière scientifique.
— une présentation formelle et typographique des articles d'une rigueur et d'une clarté dignes des grands dictionnaires des langues comme le français.
— une introduction sociolinguistique et linguistique qui situe bien le dictionnaire dans la recherche actuelle (pp. XV—XXIX).
— le contenu des articles fournit, en plus des sens des items, des renseignements grammaticaux de tout genre: a) pour le verbe nous disposons de toutes ses variations morphologiques; b) il en est de même du nom; certains comportements syntaxiques sont signalés (l'état d'annexion, par exemple) car ils ont des conséquences sur la forme phonétique de l'item.

On trouve une liste des abréviations de ces renseignements dans l'ouvrage.

Ceci nous amène à dire que ces dictionnaires développent les acquis du dictionnaire de Ch. de Foucauld.

Les articles sont introduits par une racine de base consonantique. Ils sont ensuite subdivisés selon les grandes catégories grammaticales: la particule, le verbe puis le nom.

Chacune de ces catégories est présentée avec des variations morphophonologiques.

Prenons l'exemple du verbe. On le présente d'abord sous sa forme simple puis dérivée. A l'intérieur de chaque forme, on présente l'impératif de l'aoriste, puis l'intensif et enfin le prétérit.

Le nom est présenté aussi avec le souci de rendre compte des variations morphophonologiques. Certains renseignements syntaxiques — ceux qui ont des effets de variation phonétique comme l'état d'annexion — sont présents. Néanmoins, ils sont insuffisants.

C'est, sans doute, dans ce secteur et celui du classement par racine (voir Dallet, p. XXIII) que des progrès restent à faire. Mais ceci relève des lacunes de la recherche en syntaxe et non du travail lexicographique.

5. Problèmes actuels

Sans aborder les questions théoriques et méthodologiques très discutées en milieu berbérisant, on fera l'inventaire des grands problèmes purement liés à la lexicographie berbère: (a) tous les dialectes ne sont pas aussi bien décrits que le touareg et le kabyle. Certains ne le sont pas du tout. (b) Cette remarque conditionne l'élaboration d'une recherche sur le lexique panberbère qui doit déboucher sur le problème de l'histoire de la langue et donc sur des questions comme l'étymologie, la synonymie, etc. (c) La lexicographie berbère reste tributaire des langues européennes et une recherche en langue berbère semble à l'ordre du jour. Ces problèmes retiennent l'attention des linguistes berbérophones. Mais le statut socio-politique du berbère pèsera encore lourdement sur la recherche.

6. Bibliographie choisie

6.1. Dictionnaires

Dallet 1982 = Jean-Marie Dallet: Dictionnaire kabyle-français. Paris 1982 (XI + 1056 p.; 2ème vol. français-kabyle).

Delheure 1984 = Jean Delheure: Dictionnaire mozabite-français. Paris 1984 (XXVI + 319 p.).

Destaing 1938 = Edmond Destaing: Vocabulaire français-berbère. Paris 1938 (XIV + 300 p.; 2e vol. Textes + berbère-français).

Foucauld 1951 = Charles de Foucauld: Dictionnaire touareg-français, dialecte de l'Ahaggar. Alger 1951 (XVI + 2030 p.; 4 vol.).

Huygue 1906 = Georges Huygue: Dictionnaire français-chaouia. Alger 1906 (VIII + 752 p.).

Paradis 1844 = Jean-Michel de Venture de Paradis: Grammaire et dictionnaire abrégés de la langue berbère revus par P. Amédée Jaubert et publiés par la société de géographie. Paris 1844.

6.2. Textes et glossaires

Basset 1963 = André Basset: Textes berbères du Maroc (parler des Aït Sadden). Paris 1963.

Boulifa 1904 = Ammar Boulifa: Recueil de poésies kabyles. Alger 1904.

Foucauld 1930 = Charles de Foucauld: Poésies touarègues, dialecte de l'Ahaggar. 2 vol. Paris 1925—1930.

Galand 1979 = Lionel Galand: Langue et littérature berbères. Vingt cinq ans d'études. Paris 1979.

Laoust 1920 = Emile Laoust: Mots et choses berbères, notes de linguistique et d'ethnographie, dialectes du Maroc. Paris 1920.

Abdallah Bounfour, Montrouge (France)

240. Lexicography of the Chadic Languages

1. Hausa and Chadic
1.1. Smaller Chadic Languages
1.2. Hausa
2. Selected Bibliography

1. Hausa and Chadic

The Chadic family (cf. Map 240.1) includes approximately 140 different languages spoken in Nigeria, Niger, Cameroon, and Chad (Newman 1977). One of these, Hausa, is a large, widely-spoken language with a long tradition of literacy. The others are small languages, still unwritten or only recently reduced to writing. Because the status of Hausa is so different from that of its sister languages, it will be discussed separately.

1.1. Smaller Chadic Languages

Lexicographic work on the smaller Chadic languages dates from the beginning of the 19th century, e.g. Seetzen's 1816 word list of Affade (Sölken 1967). Studies of these languages since then, whether by explorers, colonial officers, missionaries, or academic linguists, have been primarily for scholarly interest. Thus there is no correlation between the importance of individual languages and the extent of grammatical and lexical materials on them. There are four general types of lexicographic works available. For most Chadic languages there are only "wordlists" (from English, French, or German into the local language) in the 500—1,000 word range, often appended to grammatical sketches or included in comparative lexical compendia (e.g. Koelle 1854, Barth 1862—66, Lukas 1937, Kraft 1981). These lists generally lack basic morphological information (e.g. noun plurals or verb inflections) and are in many cases phonologically inaccurate, especially with respect to vowel length and tone. Somewhat larger "vocabularies" (generally from the Chadic language to English/French/German, often with a reverse index) exist for a few languages, e.g. Kanakuru (Newman 1974), Pa'a (Skinner 1979), Pero (Frajzyngier 1985), Ron (Jungraithmayr 1970), and Tumak (Caprile 1975). "Small dictionaries" (essentially expanded "vocabularies"), which provide essential morphological information, exist for Glavda (Rapp et al. 1968—69), Gude (Hoskison 1983), Kera (Ebert 1976), and Masa (Caïtucoli 1983). "Full dictionaries", which are still restricted in size by comparison with those of major world languages, exist only for Dangaléat (Fédry 1971, de Montgolfier 1973), Lamé (Sachnine 1982), and Ngizim (Schuh 1981). These dictionaries, all of which are fully tone marked, are high quality scholarly works. Fédry's is particularly noteworthy in its inclusion of plates illustrating items distinctive to the local culture.

1.2. Hausa

Vocabularies of Hausa collected by travellers and explorers began to appear at the end of the 18th century and continued for the next 50 years. All of these works were inexact and superficial. The vocabularies of Schön 1843 and Barth 1862—66 were greatly superior to anything published earlier, but were still limited in scope. The missionary J. F. Schön (1876) produced the first real Hausa dictionary. It contains a Hausa-English section of some 3,800 head entries and a somewhat smaller English-Hausa section. Phonologically the work is poor by modern standards, but the definitions are quite good and the words are amply illustrated by lively examples taken from natural Hausa narratives.

At the turn of the century, three dictionaries appeared, totally independent of each other, that mark a significant advance in Hausa lexicography: Robinson 1899/1900 (Hausa—English/English—Hausa); Mischlich 1906 (Hausa—German only); and Landeroin/Tilho 1909 (Hausa—French/French—Hausa). All three works are still phonologically inadequate, e.g. the contrast between the glottalized and non-glottalized consonants is not recognized, and tone, which is phonemically distinctive in Hausa, is not noted. However, in the presentation of definitions, idiomatic expressions, and grammatical information (e.g. gender, plurals, nominal/verbal derivations), these dictionaries, especially Mischlich, seem quite modern. In Mischlich and Robinson, the Hausa head entries are given in Arabic script (with vocalization marked) as well as in Roman script, a feature that was discontinued in all later works (including subsequent editions of Robinson). The use of Arabic script was of minor value to the Europeans for whom the

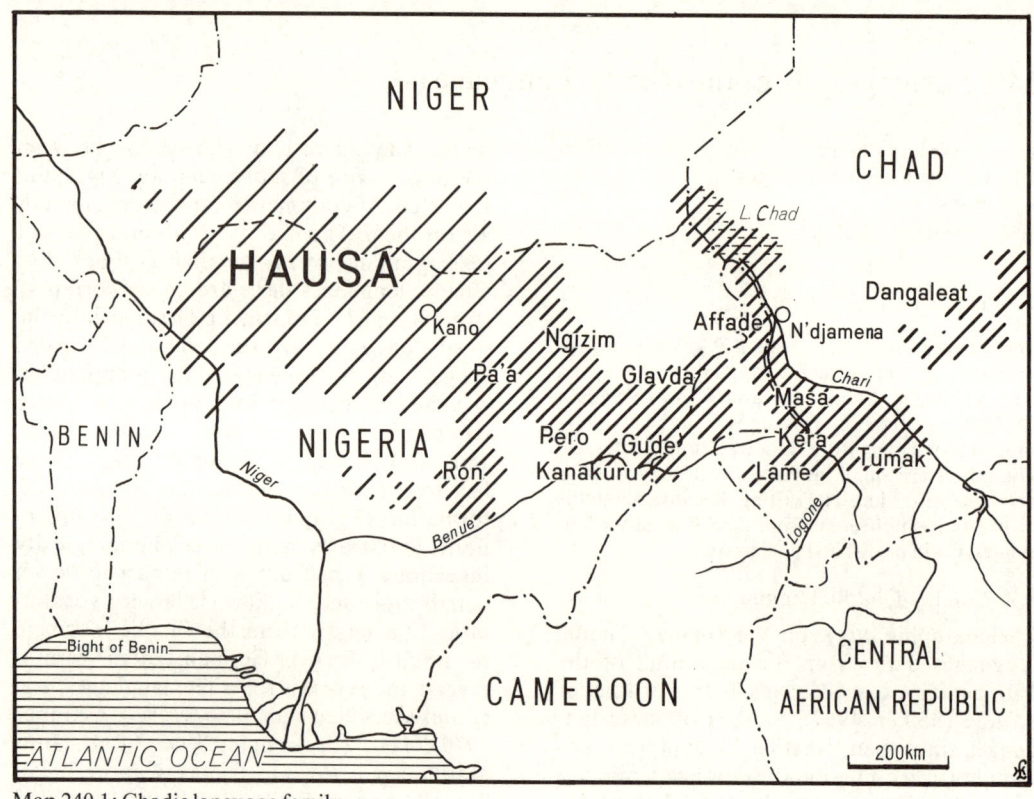

Map 240.1: Chadic language family

dictionaries were intended, but it signalled a new role for the traditionally educated Hausa class in lexicographic endeavors.

The pinnacle of Hausa lexicography was reached with the dictionary of Bargery 1934. This monumental work consists of a Hausa— English section of some 1,150 tightly packed pages (over 39,000 head entries) plus a concise 70-page English-Hausa index. For the first time, all head entries are given in a phonologically accurate transcription: the glottalized consonants are indicated, the flap and tap R's are distinguished, vowel length is noted, and tone is carefully marked. The definitions are remarkable in their fullness and in the appropriateness of the accompanying phrases, proverbs, and epithets. Bargery's deep knowledge of Hausa language and culture—he spent over 20 years preparing the work—is clearly evident in those entries where he groups related semantic items. For example, under the word *k'ato* 'huge', he lists over 300 words (nouns, adjectives, and ideophones) that connote hugeness in some way. Under *goro* 'kolanut', he devotes two full columns to describing terms for varieties, sizes, and provenience of different kinds. (For botanical terms, Bargery depended upon the specialized lexicon of Dalziel 1916.)

In addition to Bargery, there is one other first-class comprehensive Hausa-English dictionary, that of Abraham 1949. In most respects, Abraham has to be viewed not as an entirely new work but as a revised edition of Bargery, with the tone marking system simplified and more semantic collocations included. In two areas, however, Abraham's dictionary marks a significant step forward. First, Abraham marks tone and vowel length for each and every Hausa word in the dictionary. (By contrast, Bargery only transcribes the headwords phonologically, but elsewhere uses standard Hausa orthography, in which tone and vowel length are not noted.) Second, Abraham provides more extensive entries for "grammatical" words. For example, while Bargery treats the word *sai* 'until, except, then...' in 15 lines, Abraham devotes some 4 pages (double columns) to the description and elucidation of this multifaceted little word.

The Hausa/Russian dictionaries (Olderogge 1963, Laptukhin 1967) are the last of the large bilingual dictionaries to appear. Although relatively recent, these works are inexplicably anachronistic in their failure to transcribe Hausa with tone or vowel length.

The final scholarly work that needs mentioning is the specialized dictionary of Hausa music and musical instruments of Ames/ King 1971, an interesting and culturally informative work that suffers from the lack of adequate photographs, diagrams, and drawings.

From the late 1950s to the present, a period marked by the emergence of Nigeria and Niger as independent states, the trend in Hausa lexicography has been towards practical applications. For example, Hanyar 1957 and Skinner 1965 were designed for Hausas learning English, while Skinner 1959 was aimed at English speakers wishing to use Hausa. The Hausa dictionaries of Newman/ Newman 1977 and Newman 1990 are linguistically up-to-date works which incorporate recent loanwords and semantic extensions. While they are primarily intended for practical use by native Hausa speakers and Hausa language learners, they also serve as a modern reference work for scholars, since both Bargery and Abraham have long been out of print.

The most recent focus in Hausa lexicography has been the efforts by Hausas themselves to create needed technical vocabulary. Lists of proposed technical terms have been published covering, among others, language and literature (Tsarin 1983, Mijinguini 1983), history and geography (Petit 1983), and general science and technology (Mahamane 1982). Interestingly, while items and concepts introduced into Hausa culture over the past half century were usually expressed as loanwords, the conscious creation of new technical vocabulary has been done primarily through semantic extension and lexical derivation based on native Hausa words.

The next big step in Hausa lexicography, the creation of a monolingual dictionary, has been undertaken by a team of Hausa scholars in Nigeria. Their dictionary is now awaiting publication.

2. Selected Bibliography

2.1. Dictionaries and Wordlists

Abraham 1949 = R. C. Abraham: Dictionary of the Hausa Language. 2nd ed. London 1962 [992 p.; 1st ed. with Mai Kano listed as co-author, 1949].

Ames/King 1971 = David W. Ames/Anthony V. King: Glossary of Hausa Music and its Social Contexts. Evanston 1971 [184 p., 10 plates].

Bargery 1934 = G. P. Bargery: A Hausa-English Dictionary and English-Hausa Vocabulary. London 1934 [1226 p.].

Barth 1862—66 = Heinrich Barth: Sammlung und Bearbeitung Zentral-Afrikanischer Vokabularien. Gotha 1862—66.

Caïtucoli 1983 = Claude Caïtucoli: Lexique masa. Paris 1983 [205 p.].

Caprile 1975 = Jean-Pierre Caprile: Lexique tumak-français. Berlin 1975 [137 p.].

Dalziel 1916 = J. M. Dalziel: A Hausa Botanical Vocabulary. London 1916 [107 p.].

de Montgolfier 1973 = Paul de Montgolfier: Dictionnaire dangaléat. Lyon 1973 [353 p.].

Ebert 1976 = Karen H. Ebert: Sprache und Tradition der Kera (Tschad). II. Lexikon/Lexique. Berlin 1976 [213 p.].

Fédry 1971 = Jacques Fédry: Dictionnaire dangaléat. Lyon 1971 [434 p., 16 plates].

Frajzyngier 1985 = Zygmunt Frajzyngier: A Pero-English and English-Pero Vocabulary. Berlin 1985 [93 p.].

Hanyar 1957 = Hanyar Tadi da Turanci. Zaria 1957 [337 p.].

Herms 1987 = Irmtraud Herms: Wörterbuch Hausa-Deutsch. Leipzig 1987 [186 p.].

Hoskison 1983 = James T. Hoskison: A Grammar and Dictionary of the Gude Language. Ann Arbor 1983 [University Microfilms dissertation].

Jungraithmayr 1970 = Herrmann Jungraithmayr: Die Ron-Sprachen. Glückstadt 1970.

Koelle 1854 = S. W. Koelle: Polyglotta Africana. London 1854 [Reprinted with an historical introduction by P. E. H. Hair, 1963].

Kraft 1981 = Charles H. Kraft: Chadic Wordlists. 3 vols. Berlin 1981.

Landeroin/Tilho 1909 = M. Landeroin/J. Tilho: Dictionnaire haoussa. Paris 1909 [332 p.].

Laptukhin 1967 = V. Laptukhin: Russko-khausa slovar. Moscow 1967 [411 p.].

Lukas 1937 = Johannes Lukas: Zentralsudanische Studien. Hamburg 1937.

Mahamane 1982 = Issoufou Mahamane: Lexique scientifique français-hausa. Niamey 1982 [86 p.].

Mijinguini 1983 = Abdou Mijinguini: Vocabulaire technique des sciences du langage (français-hausa). Niamey 1983 [71 p.].

Mischlich 1906 = Adam Mischlich: Wörterbuch der Hausasprache. Berlin 1906 [692 p.].

Newman 1974 = Paul Newman: The Kanakuru Language. Leeds 1974.

Newman/Newman 1977 = Paul Newman/Roxana Ma Newman: Modern Hausa-English Dictionary. Ibadan 1977 [153 p.].

Newman 1990 = Roxana Ma Newman: An English-Hausa Dictionary. New Haven 1990 [327 p.].

Olderogge 1963 = D. A. Olderogge: Khausarusskii slovar. Moscow 1963 [459 p.].

Petit 1983 = Petit lexique français-hausa d'histoire et de géographie. Niamey 1983 [69 p.].

Rapp et al. 1968—69 = Eugen L. Rapp/Brigitta Benzing/Christraud Mühle: Dictionary of the Glavda Language. 2 vols. Frankfurt 1968—69 [220 p.].

Robinson 1899/1900 = Charles H. Robinson: Dictionary of the Hausa Language. 2 vols. Cambridge 1899/1900 [487 p.; 4th ed. 1925].

Sachnine 1982 = Michka Sachnine: Dictionnaire lamé-français. Lexique français-lamé. Paris 1982 [306 p.].

Schön 1843 = J. F. Schön: Vocabulary of the Hausa Language. London 1843 [190 p.].

Schön 1876 = J. F. Schön: Dictionary of the Hausa Language. London 1876 [457 p.].

Schuh 1981 = Russell G. Schuh: A Dictionary of Ngizim. Berkeley 1981 [231 p.].

Skinner 1959 = A. Neil Skinner: Hausa-English Pocket Dictionary. Zaria 1959 [107 p.; 2nd revised ed. 1968].

Skinner 1965 = A. Neil Skinner: Kamus na Turanci da Hausa. Zaria 1965 [191 p.; 2nd revised ed. 1970].

Skinner 1985 = A. Neil Skinner: Hausa Lexical Expansion since 1930: A Supplement to Bargery's Dictionary. Madison 1985 [54 p.].

Skinner 1979 = Margaret G. Skinner: Aspects of Pa'anci Grammar. Ann Arbor 1979 [University Microfilms dissertation].

Tsarin 1983 = Tsarin Kamus na Keɓaɓɓun Kalmomi na Ilmin Harsuna da Adabi. Zaria [1983] [177 p.].

2.2. Other Publications

Hair 1967 = P. E. H. Hair: The Early Study of Nigerian Languages. Cambridge 1967.

Newman 1974a = Roxana Ma Newman: Dictionaries of the Hausa language. In Harsunan Nijeriya 4, 1974, 1—25.

Newman 1977 = Paul Newman: Chadic Classification and Reconstructions. Malibu 1977. [= Vol. 5, no. 1 of Afroasiatic Linguistics]

Sölken 1965 = Heinz Sölken: Seetzens Affadéh. Berlin 1967.

Paul Newman/Roxana Ma Newman, Indiana University, Bloomington, Indiana (USA)

241. Lexicography of the Cushitic Languages

1. The Cushitic(-Omotic) Languages
2. Earliest Vocabularies and Dictionaries
3. Systematic Lexicography
4. Selected Bibliography

1. The Cushitic(-Omotic) Languages

The term "Cushitic(-Omotic)" is used to designate a highly differentiated group of some seventy Afroasiatic (Hamito-Semitic) languages spoken: 1) along the Red Sea coastal plains and hills of Sudan — Bedja, or Northern Cushitic (ca. 100,000 speakers); 2) in scattered speech-communities in highland Ethiopia — Agaw, or Central Cushitic (ca. 100,000 speakers); 3) in central Ethiopia, and from the Rift Valley to the Indian Ocean in Eastern Ethiopia, Djibouti, Somalia, and Northern Kenya — Eastern Cushitic (more than 15,000,000, including at least 4,000,000 Somalis and 8,000,000 Oromos); 4) in isolated pockets among Bantu and Nilotic speakers in Southern Kenya and Northern Tanzania — Southern Cushitic (perhaps 240,000); 5) in Southwest Ethiopia, roughly in the Omo River watershed — a large group of languages formerly regarded as Western Cushitic, now commonly referred to as the independent Afroasiatic family "Omotic" (perhaps 1,300,000 speakers) (cf. Map 241.1). Although these language families are clearly related to one another, and to Afroasiatic, the exact genetic structure of the group "Cushitic" is still the subject of considerable debate and research (as witness Hetzron 1980, Zaborski 1986; for statistics and bibliographic and other background see contributions by Bender, Elderkin, Fleming, Pankhurst, Zaborski, and others in Bender 1976, and also Sasse 1981).

Up until relatively recently our lexical knowledge for most Cushitic languages depended on more-or-less incidental word lists brought back by travelers, missionaries, and explorers — and for many languages this is still the case. Lexical coverage of Cushitic thus follows a pattern largely determined by the political, intellectual, and religious currents that directed outside attention to one or another area of the Horn and adjacent regions in East Africa.

2. Earliest Vocabularies and Dictionaries

From the earliest reliable and widespread accounts of Ethiopia (Ludolph 1681) (a translation into English appeared in 1682, and into French in 1684, while the accounts of the early Seventeenth Century Portuguese Jesuits were already accessible in English in, for example, Tellez 1710) the outside world had long been aware that there existed, alongside the Semitic-speaking Christian highlanders, other groups like the Agaw, Galla (now, Oromo), Danakil (now Afar), Somalis, Bedja (known already from classical and early Christian sources as Blemmyes), and the mysterious sacral kingdoms of the Southwest. However, apart from a handful of isolated words, the sources yielded nothing by way of lexical or grammatical description. The most informative eighteenth century traveler, James Bruce (1790), brought back vocabularies of Oromo and three Agaw languages (along with a translation into these languages of the "Song of Salomon"!). Samples of these were incorporated into later editions of his travel narrative, but the bulk remained in manuscript (Bruce MS), accessible only to a few scholars who went to consult them at Oxford.

The first published vocabularies are owing to Henry Salt (1814), with about one hundred words each in Somali, Oromo, Afar, Saho, Bedja, and Agaw, culled during two diplomatic missions to Ethiopia, and to Ulrich Seetzen, who worked with native speakers of a number of African languages during a long residence in Cairo. Seetzen (1809) is a vocabulary of a Somali dialect, while Seetzen (1816), published posthumously in a volume

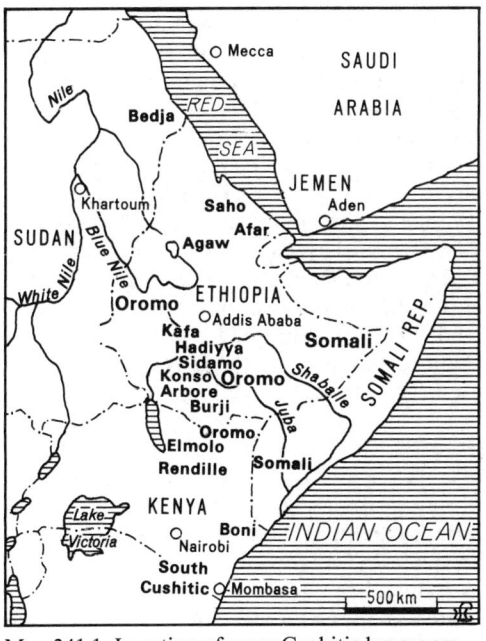

Map 241.1: Location of some Cushitic languages

of Johann Vater, is a short Oromo word-list, and a rather extensive (750 words) vocabulary of Bedja. As travelers began to frequent coastal locations on the Red Sea and Indian Ocean, lexical information on Cushitic languages spoken there began to trickle in. An early polyglot vocabulary in Swahili, Somali, and Oromo comes to us from Captain Smee (1844), who in 1811 sailed down the East African coast under orders from the Bombay government, and in the same genre from the German soldier of fortune Kielmeyer (1840). From similar sources, Koenig (1839) reproduced Afar and Somali word-lists, while the explorer Rochet d'Héricourt (1841) included Oromo material, Lefebvre (1845) Afar and Oromo, and Guillain (1856—57) Somali. Rigby, later to be English consul at Zanzibar, furnished material on Afar in 1844 and Somali in 1850. Antoine d'Abbadie's many contributions to Ethiopian linguistics and philology start with a Somali vocabulary (d'Abbadie 1839) and the first publication on Saho (d'Abbadie 1843). Separately printed dictionaries appear as missionaries first attempt a serious penetration of the Horn of Africa. Isenberg (1840) is a short dictionary and phrase book of Afar, while the Oromo dictionary of his associate, Krapf (1842), is the fruit of an intensive but unsuccessful attempt to establish a mission among the "Gallas". Krapf, who went on to do linguistic work among Swahili-speaking East Africans, also included Oromo in a polyglot dictionary (Krapf 1850). The Catholic missionary Sapeto includes an Agaw (Bilin) vocabulary in a travel book (1857), while the Chrishona missionary Waldmeier published a short contribution to Agaw lexicography in 1868. The latter's colleague, Mayer, was active in Ethiopia at this period and later (1878) included Oromo in a polyglot dictionary. An influential and rather unusual lexical effort from this period is Tutschek 1845. Karl Tutschek was engaged by Count Maximilian of Bavaria as tutor for four African boys purchased from households or the slave market in Alexandria and Cairo. One of them was an Oromo and became in informant for an Oromo dictionary. Note that lexical information from a freed Oromo slave had already been published in Jomard 1839.

To the Southwest Antoine d'Abbadie in 1843 became the first European to penetrate deeply into Omotic territory beyond the Gibe River, and was gathering material there shortly after Charles Beke crossed the Northern fringe of the Omotic area. However, except for a short notice in d'Abbadie 1845, in which he argues for the relatedness of these new languages to the already known "Hamitic" languages of Ethiopia, d'Abbadie's material was not published until 1859, and then only partially. The first published Omotic materials appeared in Beke 1845, a polyglot vocabulary including wordlists from three Agaw languages, Oromo, and the Omotic languages Gonga, Kaffa, Dauro, Welamo, and Janjero. Beke is more skeptical about the genetic relation of the Omotic languages to the rest. But by this time enough evidence was in place to clearly highlight the unity of the more "central" Cushitic languages and their relatedness to Semitic, Egyptian, and Berber (i. e., Afroasiatic or Hamito-Semitic language family). This conclusion seems to have been explicitly drawn for the first time by Lottner 1861, who relied on Oromo material from Tutschek, and Saho from d'Abbadie, and referred in fact to what we now call Cushitic languages as "Saho-Galla." The term "Cushitic" in approximately its contemporary linguistic sense seems to have been first used by Lepsius 1880, who earlier (1863) refers to the language family as "Ethiopic"; note however that Renan (1863, 339) talks about how the "Hamitic" languages of Ethiopia conserve "remnants of the ancient language of the Cushites."

The arrival of a major Italian scientific expedition under the leadership of Antonio Cecchi in 1877 signaled a newly awakened European interest in things Ethiopian from scholars and statesmen alike. Volume III of the report (Cecchi 1887) has vocabularies collected by Cecchi, Giovanni Chiarini (note also Chiarini 1897 for Somali), and Léon des Avanchers for Hadiyya, Kaffa, Jenjero, and Afar (for the latter see also Cecchi 1885—87). The Oromo material from the expedition was entrusted for publication to Ettore Viterbo, who had no first-hand experience with Oromo, and appeared also as a separate volume; with all its defects, this remained for a long time one of the principal sources for lexical information on this important representative of the Cushitic family. Italian explorers and travelers continued to collect material, as witness Serra-Caraccioli 1883, Colizza 1887, Candeo 1893, Derchi 1895, and Capomazza 1907 for Afar, Capomazza 1910—11 for Saho, da Palermo 1915 for Somali, Robecchi-Bricchetti 1891—92 for

Oromo, as well as the polyglot Scholart 1888, which includes Oromo. Oehlschlager 1891 and Henry 1897, both from the Imprimerie Administrative, show awakened French interest in the practical aspects of Afar and Somali respectively; while the English geographer Foot (1913) furnished a small lexical compilation of Oromo "in the hope that it may prove of service to those of my countrymen whose duties, official or other, may call them to have dealings with the Gallas." The Austrian Paulitschke (1886) gives lexical information about Oromo and Somali in an ethnographic context. Interestingly enough the dictionary of the French Franciscan Evangeliste de Larajasse (1897) is Somali-English; another missionary compilation with French, Oromo, and Amharic is Anonymous 1928. Finally, at the end of the pre-WWII period, there is a spate of, for the most part, polyglot vocabularies drawn up in conjunction with Italy's push into Ethiopia and the Horn of Africa. To this genre belong: Storaci 1935, Ducati 1935/1937, Anonymous 1936, Caressa 1938, d'Arpino 1938, and Piccirill: 1938.

Meanwhile, information on unknown, or less well-known languages was being put in the public domain by explorers like the Dutch traveler Schuver 1883, who brought back 100 words in a Shinasha-like language, and the Frenchman Borelli 1890, who contributed lists of several hundred words from the as yet scantily attested Rift-Valley languages, Hadiyya, Timbaro, Kembata, Alaba. Other lexical material from the South and Southwest was brought back by the American Smith 1897 (Konso, Arbore, and the Southern Omotic Hamer and Dume), the British Wellby 1901 (also some Hamer, as well as Welamo, Arbore, Dasenech, and Oromo) and Crosby 1901 (Shinasha, Northern Omotic), and the Swiss explorer Montandon 1913 (Gimirra). The Austrian Bieber published in 1920 a detailed description of the Kaffa, with much lexical information, based on fieldwork done in 1905, complementing previous studies done in Bieber (1908 and 1903). Finally word-lists began to filter in from languages of an apparently "Hamitic" character spoken by small, (largely) hunter-gatherer tribes living among the Bantu and Nilotic pastoralists and cultivators in Southern Kenya, and in Northern Tanzania in the Rift Valley in the vicinity of Kilimanjaro (Shaw 1885; Baumann 1894; Seidel 1900; Kannenberg 1900; Meinhof 1906; Dempwolff 1917). The linguistic affinity of these peoples remained for a long time obscure or disputed, until Greenberg 1963 mustered the lexical evidence justifying their incorporation into Afroasiatic as "Southern Cushitic" — an initially controversial position which had gained general acceptance by the mid-1970's.

3. Systematic Lexicography

Systematic scholarly investigation of the Cushitic languages has to be dated to the Austrian Leo Reinisch. Between 1873 and 1911 he wrote articles and monographs on a wide range of Cushitic and other non-Semitic languages of the Horn of Africa, most of which contain important lexical information. In particular one has to point out his dictionaries of Bilin (1887), Saho (1890), Bedja (1895), and Somali (1902). In spite of deficiencies and inconsistencies in transcription, and a tendency toward sometimes fanciful etymologies, Reinisch's dictionaries and grammars constitute one of the foundations of modern Ethiopic studies. Reinisch's successor as dean and founder of scientific Ethiopian studies was the Italian Carlo Conti Rossini. Although most of his activity was in the domains of history, culture, and Ethiopic Semitic, he did do a substantial amount of original field work in the Agaw languages. However, his most important monograph in this domain (1912), which contains a French-Kemant and Kemant-French vocabulary, is based entirely on material gathered more than a half-century earlier by d'Abbadie. Among other major scholarly *éthiopisants* of the pre-World War II era, Enrico Cerulli produced a stream of articles and monographs on the languages and cultures of Southern Ethiopia; in particular his books of Janjero (1938) and Kaffa (published in 1951 on the basis of work done in the 30's) remain our best lexical sources for these Omotic languages. Mario Moreno included important vocabulary supplements in his grammars of Ometo (1938) and Sidamo (1940). In this context belongs mention of the compilation of the Italian Capuchin da Thiene (1939), one of the most complete Oromo dictionaries to date, based on collections made during more than fifty years among the Eastern Oromo by Andrea Jarosseau. This dictionary, based as it is on long experiences with the Oromo, is a rich source of lexical information, even if the phonological information is incomplete (consonant representation is fairly reliable, but representation of vowel-length is frequently inaccurate). Finally, although Marcel Cohen's field work in Ethiopia was largely limited to Semitic, his Essai (1947), essentially compiled before 1940, using the Cushitic materials of Reinisch, Conti Rossini, Cerulli, and Moreno, integrated Cushitic into the first authoritative attempt at a synthesis of the lexicon of Afroasiatic.

After World War II, in spite of an unprecedented amount of publication of new information on things Cushitic, especially from 1970 on, lexical coverage in Cushitic has been quite uneven. (Note that for this period I mention only dictionaries or works with an explicit vocabulary section, although of course incidental lexical information is inevitably included in any linguistic and cultural investigation.) Thus there is nothing new to report for Bedja, while for Agaw there is only an index of verbs appended to Hetzron 1969. For the vast and little explored domain of Omotic, the only new dictionary is Mocha (Leslau 1959); Bender (1989) and Fleming (1989) however make available lexical material, some of it previously accessible only in widely scattered publications and a considerable amount of it new. In South Cushitic Ehret 1980 is a comparative dictionary which utilizes all previous sources, and adds a great deal of new material. For the Cushitic family as a whole, Dolgopol'skij (1973) has fairly exhaustively scoured the pre-World War II literature for possible cognate sets, although his reconstructions suffer from failure to take into account the genetic subgroupings (e. g., one should not directly compare an Oromo and a Kaffa word, but a proto-East-Cushitic reconstructed form with a proto-North-Omotione), as well as from the mistakes in and the inconsistent and heterogeneous nature of his sources' transcription systems; additional material is contained in Dolgopol'skij 1983, while Ehret 1987 is an important corrective and supplement. Gragg (1988) announces a project for a collectively maintained Cushitic cognate data-base in electronic form.

The one area where substantial progress can be noted is in East Cushitic. Here Black 1974 and Sasse 1979 have provided a solid lexical cognate base for the family as a whole. Konso and Giddole dictionaries exist at least in draft form (Black 1973 a, b); there are published dictionaries of Borana (Southern Oromo) (Venturino 1973; 1976), (Western) Oromo (Gragg 1982), Sidamo (Gasparini 1983), and Afar (Parker/Hayward 1985), and a comparative dictionary of Highland East Cushitic (Hudson 1989). Explicit vocabulary lists now exist for Rendille (Schlee 1978), Dullay (Amborn et al. 1980), Bayso (Hayward 1978/1979), Boni (Heine 1982), Arbore (Hayward 1984), for the Southern Oromo Borana-Orma-Wata dialects (Heine 1981) and (Stroomer 1987), and for the highland East Cushitic language/dialect chain, Kembata-Timbaro-Alaba-Hadiyya-Libido-Quabena (Korhonen et al. 1986). Finally, there is a comparative dictionary of Burji (Sasse 1983), which serves practically as an etymological dictionary of East Cushitic. Of course, the most substantial progress has been made, as could be expected, in Somali, the only Cushitic language which is the national language of a practically monolingual country, and in which moreover there has been a substantial effort, since independence in 1960, to create an orthography, spread literacy, and encourage the use of Somali written materials in education, administration, and mass media (Andrzejewski 1978; 1979; 1980a; 1983; Caney 1984). A practical vocabulary for Italian speaking medical workers appeared in Maino/Yasin 1953, an English counterpart was created in Peate 1982. For a full Somali-English and English-Somali dictionary there is Abraham 1962; 1967; note also the shorter glossary Nakano 1976, and Spitler/Spitler 1966 (mentioned in Lamberti 1986), while Saciid/Cabduraxmaan n.d. is an English-Somali dictionary for Somali speakers. The most recent English-Somali dictionary is Luling 1987, and another (Caney forthcoming) is on the way. Stepanchenko/ Mohamed 1969 is a Russian-Somali dictionary; Italian, in addition to earlier works, has had Minozzi/Poletti-Turbini 1962 a, b, and more recently a major lexicon in Agostini et al. 1985. A short French-Somali dictionary appeared in Philibert 1976, but a more substantial effort is represented by the two-volume work of Maxamed 1985; 1988. However, the most important recent development in Somali lexicography, marking the onset of full lexicographic maturity, has been the appearance of a substantial monolingual dictionary (Yaasiin 1976); note also the shorter Cabdulqaadir 1976 and the bilingual dictionaries mentioned above by Maxamed and Saciid.

It remains to be seen how many other Cushitic languages will be able to follow suit, but at least in Oromo the necessary preliminaries are already taking place (Andrzejewski 1980b) and a major monolingual dictionary project seems completely feasible.

4. Selected Bibliography

4.1. Dictionaries

Abraham 1962 = Roy Clive Abraham: Somali-English Dictionary. London 1962 [332 p.].

Abraham 1967 = Roy Clive Abraham: English-Somali Dictionary. London 1967 [208 p.].

Agostini et al. 1985 = Francesco Agostini et al: Dizionario somalo-italiano. Roma 1985 [xxiii, 656 p.].

Anonymous 1928 = Anonymous: Vocabulaire Français, Oromo, Abyssin. Diré-Daoua 1928 [127 p.].

Black 1973a = Paul Black: First Draft of a Konso Dictionary. MS 1973.

Black 1973b = Paul Black: Preliminary Draft of a Gidole Dictionary. MS 1973.

Cabdulqaadir 1976 = Cabdulqaadir F. Bootan: Qaamuus Kooban ee Af Soomali Ah: Qaamuuska Af Soomaaliga. Mogadiscio 1976 [374 p.].

Caney forthcoming = John Charles Caney: Modern Somali-English, English-Somali Dictionary. London in press.

Capomazza 1907 = Ilario Capomazza: La Lingua degli Afar: Vocabolario Italiano-Dankalo e Dankalo-Italiano. Macerata 1907.

da Palermo 1915 = Padre Giovanni Maria da Palermo: Dizionario somalo-italiano e italiano-somalo. Asmara 1915.

da Thiene 1939 = Gaetano da Thiene: Dizionario della lingua galla con brevi nozioni grammaticali: Opera compilate sugli scritti editi ed inediti di Mons. Andrea Jarosseau (Vic. Apos. dei galla (1881—1938). Harar 1939 [1x, 340 163 p.].

de Larajasse 1897 = Evangeliste de Larajasse: Somali-English and English-Somali Dictionary. London 1897.

Dolgopol'skij 1973 = Aron B. Dolgopol'skij: Sravnitel'no-istoricheskaja Fonetika Kushitskikh Jazykov. Moscow 1973 [398 p.].

Ehret 1980 = Christopher Ehret: The Historical Reconstruction of Southern Cushitic Phonology and Vocabulary. (Kölner Beiträge zur Afrikanistik 5) Berlin 1980 [407 p.].

Foot 1913 = Edwin C. Foot: Galla-English, English-Galla Dictionary. Cambridge 1913 [118 p.].

Gasparini 1983 = Armido Gasparini: Sidamo-English Dictionary. Bologna 1983 [362 p.].

Gragg 1982 = Gene B. Gragg: Oromo Dictionary. East Lansing MI 1982 [462 p.].

Henry 1897 = Léon Henry: Essai de vocabulaire pratique Français-Issa (Somalis), avec prononciation figurée. Melun 1897 [100 p.].

Hudson 1989 = Grover Hudson: Highland East Cushitic Dictionary. Hamburg 1989. (Kuschitische Sprachstudien/Cushitic Language Studies) [424 p.].

Isenberg 1840 = Charles W. Isenberg: A Small Vocabulary of the Dankali Language, in Three Parts: Dankali and English, English and Dankali, and a Selection of Dankali Sentences with English Translations. London 1840 [xiv, 22 p.].

Keenadiid 1976 = Keenadiid Yaasiin Cismaan: Qaamuuska af-Soomaaliga. Mogadishu. Florence 1976 [xxx, 498 p.].

Krapf 1842 = Johann L. Krapf: Vocabulary of the Galla Language. London 1842 [ii, 42 p.].

Leslau 1959 = Wolf Leslau: A Dictionary of Moca (Southwestern Ethiopia). Berkeley. Los Angeles 1959 [83 p.].

Luling 1987 = Virginia Luling: Somali-English Dictionary. Wheaton Md. 1987 [vii, 605 p.].

Maino/Yasin 1953 = Mario Maino/Yasin 'Isman Kenadid: Terminologia medica e suevoci nella lingua somala. Alessandria (Italy) 1953 [358 p.].

Maxamed 1985 = Maxamed Cabdi Maxamed: Dictionnaire Français-Somali/Qaamuus Fransiis-Soomaali. Paris 1985 [598 p.].

Maxamed 1988 = Maxamed Cabdi Maxamed: Eraybixin soomaali-faransiis (=Lexique somali-francais). Besancon 1988 [ix, 128 p.].

Minozzi/Poletti-Turbini 1962a = M. T. Minozzi/C. Poletti-Turbini: Dizionario italiano-somalo. Milan 1962.

Minozzi/Poletti-Turbini 1962b = M. T. Minozzi/C. Poletti-Turbini: Dizionario somalo-italiano e migiurtino-italiano. Milan 1962.

Nakano 1976 = Aki'o Nakano: Basic Vocabulary in Standard Somali. Tokyo 1976 (Stud. Culturae Islamicae 1) [139 p.].

Oehlschager 1891 = A. L. Oehlschager: Vocabulaire français-dankali. Melun 1891 [109 p.].

Parker/Hayward 1985 = Enid Parker/Dick Hayward: An Afar-English-French Dictionary (with Grammatical Notes in English). London 1985 [306 p.].

Peate 1982 = Wayne F. Peate: English-Somali Phrase Book of Common and Medical Terms (for travelers, health field workers, etc.). Tuscon 1982 [84 p.].

Philibert 1976 = Christophe Philibert: Petit Lexique Somali-Français. Paris 1976 [57 p.].

Plazikowsky-Brauner 1964 = Herma Plazikowsky-Brauner: Wörterbuch der Hadiya-Sprache. In: Rassegna di Studi Etiopichi 20. 1964, 133—182.

Reinisch 1887 = Leo Reinisch: Wörterbuch der Bilin-Sprache (= Bilin-Sprache 2). Vienna 1887 [vi, 426 p.].

Reinisch 1890 = Leo Reinisch: Wörterbuch der Saho-Sprache (= Die Saho-Sprache 2). Vienna 1890 [ix, 492 p.].

Reinisch 1895 = Leo Reinisch: Wörterbuch der Bedauye-Sprache. Vienna 1895 [vi, 365 p.].

Reinisch 1902 = Leo Reinisch: Wörterbuch der Somali-Sprache (= Die Somali-Sprache 2). Vienna 1902 (Südarab. Exped.) [vii, 540 p.].

Saciid/Cabduraxmaan n.d. = Saciid Warsame Xirsi/Cabduraxmaan Ciise Oomaar: Qaamuus Ingiriisi-Soomaali/English-Somali Dictionary. Mogadiscio n.d.

Sasse 1982 = Hans-Jürgen Sasse: An Etymological Dictionary of Burji. Hamburg 1982 (Kuschitische Sprachstudien/Cushitic Language Studies 1) [256 p.].

Spitler/Spitler 1966 = Keene A. Spitler/Helen Spitler: English-Somali Dictionary. Pasadena (California) 1966.

Stepanchenko/Mohamed 1969 = D. I. Stepanchenko/Mohamed Haaji Cosman: Kratkij Somali-Russkij i Russko-Somali Slovar': Abwan Urursan Af Soomalli iyo Rusha Rush iyo af Soomaaliya. Moscow 1969 [319 p.].

Tutschek 1845 = Karl Tutschek: Dictionary of the Galla language. Composed by Charles Tutschek, published by Lawrence Tutschek (Subtitle: Lexikon der Galla-Sprache) (Galla-English-German). Munich 1844—1845 [126 p.].

Venturino 1973 = Bartolomeo Venturino: Dizionario Borana-Italiano. Bologna 1973.

Venturino 1976 = Bartolomeo Venturino: Dizionario Italiano-Borana. Marsabit, Kenya 1976 [164 p.].

Viterbo 1887 = Ettore Viterbo: Vocabulario della lingua oromonica. In: Antonio Cecchi: Da Zeila alle frontiere del Caffa. Rome 1887, 101—398 [Also appeared as separate book: Grammatica e dizionario della lingua oromonica (galla). 2 vols. Milan 1892].

Waldmeier 1868 = Theophilus Waldmeier: Wörtersammlung aus der Agau-Sprache. Von einem Freund der orientalischen Sprachen zum Druck befördert. St. Chrischona 1868 [29 p.].

4.2. Vocabularies, Polyglot Collections, and Cognate Lists

Amborn et al. 1980 = Herrmann Amborn et al.: Das Dullay: Materialien zu einer ostkuschitischen Sprache. Berlin 1980 (Beiträge zur Afrikanistik 6).

Anonymous 1936 = Anonymous: Nomenclatura elementare ed espressioni nelle lingue amarica, galla, arabo (dialetto tripolino). Rome 1936.

Baumann 1894 = Oscar Baumann: Durch Masailand zur Nilquelle. Berlin 1894.

Beke 1845 = Charles T. Beke: On the Languages and Dialects of Abyssinia and the Countries to the South. In: Proceedings of the Philological Society 2. 1845, 89—107.

Bender 1988 = M. Lionel Bender: Proto-Omotic Phonology and Lexicon. In: Proceedings of the First Symposium on Cushitic and Omotic Languages. Edited by Marianne Bechhaus-Gerst/Franz Serzisko. Hamburg 1988, 121—162.

Bieber 1903 = Friedrich Julius Bieber: Beiträge zu einem erotischen Lexicon der Abessinien (Amhara), Galla und Kaffitscho. In: Antropophyteia 5. 1903, 22—24; 82—95 [also vol. 8. 1911, 193].

Bieber 1908 = Frederico Friedrich Bieber: Dizionario della Lingua Cafficio. In: Bolletino della Reale Societa Geogr. Italiana 45. 1908, 368—80, 452—56.

Bieber 1920 = Friedrich Bieber: Kaffa: Ein altkuschitisches Volkstum in Inner-Afrika. Münster 1920.

Black 1974 = Paul Black: Lowland East Cushitic: Subgrouping and Reconstruction. Ann Arbor Microfilms 1974.

Borelli 1890 = Jules Borelli: Ethiopic Méridionale. Paris 1890.

Bruce MS = James Bruce: Manuscript 33. Ethiopian Collection, Bodleian Library, Oxford.

Bruce 1790 = James Bruce: Travels to Discover the Source of the Nile in the Years 1768—73. London 1790.

Candeo 1893 = G. Candeo: Vocabolario dancalo. In: Bolletino della Società Africana Italiana 1893.

Capomazza 1910/1911 = Ilario Capomazza: L'Assaorta-saho. Vocabolario italiano-assaorta-saho ed assaorta-saho-italiano. In: Bolletino della Società Africana Italiana 1910; 1911, 161—181, 213—224; 131—139, 173—181.

Caressa 1938 = Feruccio Caressa: Dizionario africana: Italiano-amarico-tigrino-galla-migiurtino-benadirese. Milan 1938.

Cecchi 1885/1887 = Antonio Cecchi: Vocaboli e modi di dire della lingua Afar. In: Società geografica Italiana 3 19. 1885—1887, 485—490.

Cecchi 1887 = Antonio Cecchi: Da Zeila alle frontiere del Caffa. Rome 1887.

Cerulli 1938 = Enrico Cerulli: Il Linguaggio dei Giangerò ed alcune lingue Sidama dell'Omo (Basketo, Ciaro, Zaissè). Rome 1938 (Studi Etiopici 3).

Cerulli 1951 = Enrico Cerulli: La Lingua Caffina. Rome 1951 (Studi Etiopici 2).

Chiarini 1897 = Giovanni Chiarini: Raccolta dei vocaboli dei Somali-Isa. In: Memoria della Società Geografica Italiana 1. 1897, 209—15.

Chiomo 1938 = Giovanni Chiomo: Brevi Appunti di lingua Uollamo (A.O.I.): Grammatica e dizionario. Turin 1938.

Cohen 1947 = Marcel Cohen: Essai comparatif sur le vocabulaire et la phonétique du chamito-sémitique. Paris 1947 (Bibliothèque de l'École des Hautes Études 291).

Colizza 1887 = Giovanni Colizza: Lingua 'Afar nel Nord-Est dell'Africa: Grammatica, Testi e Vocabolario. Vienna 1887.

Conti Rossini 1912 = Carlo Conti Rossini: La langue des Kemant en Abyssinie. Vienna 1912 (Kaiserliche Akademie der Wissenschaften, Schriften der Sprachkommission 4).

Crosby 1901 = Oscar Terry Crosby: Notes on a Journey from Zeila to Khartoum. In: Geographical Journal 18. 1901, 46—61.

d'Abbadie 1839 = Antoine d'Abbadie: Liste des noms de lieux situés sur la partie de la côte africaine, habitée principalement par les tribus des Somalis. In: Bulletin de la Société de Géographie de Paris sér. 2 12. 1839.

d'Abbadie 1843 = Antoine d'Abbadie: Lettres à M. Jules Mohl sur la langue saho. In: Journal Asiatique Série II, Vol. XVII; XVIII. 1843, 170—180; 355.

d'Abbadie 1859 = Antoine d'Abbadie: Note sur le Kafa. In: Bulletin de la Société de Géographie de Paris ser. 4 17/18. 1859, 170—180, 355.

d'Arpino 1938 = Ludovico d'Arpino: Vocabolario dall'italiano nelle versioni galla (oromo), amara, dancala, somala. Milano 1938.

da Trento 1941 = Gabriele da Trento: Vocaboli in lingue dell'Etiopia meridionale. In: Rassegna di Studi Etiopici 1. 1941, 203—207.

Dempwolff 1917 = O. Dempwolff: Beiträge zur Kenntnis der Sprachen in Deutsch-Ostafrika. In: Zeitschrift für Kolonialsprachen 7. 1916—1917.

Derchi 1895 = F. Derchi: Dizionario e frasario italo-dancala (afar). In: Memorie della Società Geografica Italiana 5. 1895.

Dolgopol'skij 1983 = Aron B. Dolgopol'sky: Semitic and East Cushitic: Sound Correspondences and Cognate Sets. In: Ethiopian Studies Dedicated to Wolf Leslau on the Occasion of his Seventy-Fifth Birthday, November 14th 1981 by Friends and Colleagues. Edited by Stanislaw Segert/Andreas J. E. Bodrogligeti. Wiesbaden 1983, 123—142.

Ducati 1935 = Bruno Ducati: L'amharico, il suaheli, il galla: Dizionarietto delle tre principali lingue parlate in Abissinia. Rome 1935.

Ducati 1937 = Bruno Ducati: Dizionario galla-italiano e italiano-galla. Rome 1937.

Ehret 1987 = Christopher Ehret: Proto-Cushitic Reconstruction. In: Sprache und Geschichte in Afrika 8. 1987, 7—180.

Ewald 1844 = Heinrich von Ewald: Über die Saho-Sprache in Aethiopien. In: Zeitschrift für die Kunde des Morgenlands 5. 1844, 410—424.

Fleming 1988 = Harold C. Fleming: Reconstruction of Proto-South Omotic. In: Proceedings of the First Symposium on Cushitic and Omotic Languages. Edited by Marianne Bechhaus-Gerst/Franz Serzisko. Hamburg 1988, 163—178.

Guillain 1856—1857 = Charles Guillain: Documents sur l'histoire, la géographie et le commerce de l'Afrique Orientale. Paris 1856—1857.

Hayward 1978/1979 = Richad J. Hayward: Bayso Revisited: Some Preliminary Linguistic Observations. In: Bulletin of the School of African and Oriental Studies 41—42. 1978—1979, 539—570; 101—132.

Hayward 1984 = Richard J. Hayward: The Arbore Language: A First Investigation, Including a Vocabulary. Hamburg 1984 (Kuschitische Sprachstudien 2).

Heine 1973 = Bernd Heine: Vokabulare ostafrikanischer Restsprachen I: Elmolo. In: Afrika und Übersee 56. 1973, 276—83.

Heine 1981 = Bernd Heine: The Waata Dialect of Oromo: Grammatical sketch and vocabulary. Berlin 1981 (Language and Dialect Atlas of Kenya 4).

Heine 1982 = Bernd Heine: Boni Dialects. Berlin 1982 (Language and Dialect Atlas of Kenya 10).

Hetzron 1969 = Robert Hetzron: The Verbal System of Southern Agaw. Berkeley. Los Angeles 1969 (University of California Publications: Near Eastern Series 12).

Kannenberg 1900 = Kannenberg: Reise durch die Hamitischen Sprachgebiete um Kondoa. In: Mitteilungen aus den Deutschen Schutzgebieten 13. 1900.

Kielmayer 1840 = C. Kielmayer: Sammlung von Wörtern aus den Sprachen der Küstenbewohner des östl. Afrika zwischen dem neunten bis sechzehnten Grad nördl. Breite. In: Ausland 13. 1840, 303.

Koenig 1839 = E. Koenig: Vocabolari somali e dankali. In: Vocabulaires appartenant à diverses contrées ou tribus de l'Afrique, recueillis dans la Nubie supérienne. Paris 1839.

Korhonen et al. 1986 = Elsa Korhonen et al.: A Dialect Study of Kambaata-Hadiyya (Ethiopia) Part 2: Appendices. In: Afrikanistische Arbeitspapiere 6. 1986, 71—121.

Krapf 1850 = Johann L. Krapf: Vocabulary of Six East-African Languages (Kisuaheli, Kinika, Kikamba, Kipokomo, Kihiau, Kigalla). Tübingen 1850.

Lefebvre 1845 = Th. Lefebvre: Voyage en Abyssinie exécuté pendant les années 1839, 1840, 1841, 1842, 1843. Paris 1845—48.

Mayer 1878 = Johannes Mayer: Kurze Wörter-Sammlung in Englisch, Deutsch, Amharisch, Gallanisch, Guraguesch. Basel 1878.

Meinhof 1906 = Karl Meinhof: Linguistische Studien in Ost Afrika 10, 11. In: Mitteilungen des Seminars für Orientalische Sprachen 9. 1906, 293—333.

Montandon 1913 = George Montandon: Au pays Ghimirra: Récit de mon voyage à travers le Massif ethiopien 1909—1911. Neuchâtel 1913.

Moreno 1938 = Mario Martino Moreno: Introduzione alla lingua Ometo [Gofa]. Milan 1938.

Moreno 1940 = Mario Martino Moreno: Manuale di Sidamo. Milano 1940.

Paulitschke 1886 = Philipp Paulitschke: Beiträge zur Ethnographie und Anthropologie der Somal, Galla und Harari. Leipzig 1886.

Piccirilli 1938 = Tito Piccirilli: Dizionario di alcune lingue parlate nell'A.O.I. (Amarica-Tigray-Galla-Tigré). Naples 1938.

Rigby 1844 = Christopher P. Rigby: Specimen of the languages spoken on the Western Shore of the Red Sea and the Gulf of Aden. In: Transactions of the Bombay Geographical Society 6. 1844, 93—94.

Rigby 1850 = Christopher P. Rigby: An Outline of the Somali Language, with Vocabulary. In: Transactions of the Bombay Geographical Society 9. 1850, 129—184.

Robecchi-Bricchetti 1890 = Luigi Robecchi-Bricchetti: Vocabolario Harari, Somali, Galla. 1890.

Robecchi-Bricchetti 1891/1892 = Luigi Robecchi-Bricchetti: Vocaboli della lingua oromonica raccolti nei paesi Galla. In: Bolletino della Società Africana d'Italia 10; 11. 1891—92, 98—104, 168—73, 191—93, 214—222; 7—17, 60—68, 92—93, 162—169.

Rochet d'Héricourt 1841 = Charles E. Xavier Rochet d'Héricourt: Voyage sur la côte orientale de la Mer Rouge, dans le pays d'Adel et le royaume de Choa. Paris 1841.

Salt 1814 = Henry Salt: A Voyage to Abyssinia, and Travels into the Interior of that Country, Executed under the Order of the British Government, in the Years 1809 and 1810 ... and Some Particulars Respecting the Aboriginal African Tribes, Extending from Mosambique to the Borders of Egypt; together with Vocabularies of their Respective Languages. London 1814.

Sapeto 1857 = G. Sapeto: Viaggio e missione cattolica fra i Mensa, i Bogos e gli Habab, con un cenno geografico e storico dell'Abissinia. Rome 1857.

Sasse 1979 = Hans-Jürgen Sasse: The Consonant Phonemes of Proto-East-Cushitic (PEC): A First Approximation. In: Afroasiatic Linguistics 7. 1979, 1—67.

Schlee 1978 = G. Schlee: Sprachliche Studien zum Rendille. Grammatik, Texte, Glossar. With English summary of Rendille Grammar. Hamburg 1978 (Heidelberg. Phil. Stud. 46).

Scholart 1888 = Lucio Scholart: Frasario e vocaboli in lingua amarica-oromona-araba-inglese, con le preghiere in etiopico, ad uso dei viaggiatori in Abissinia. Naples 1888.

Schuver 1883 = Juan Maria Schuver: Kleene wordenlijst der Sienetjo-Taal. De Reisen van Juan Maria Schuver. 1883.

Seetzen 1809 = Ulrich Jaspers Seetzen: Wörterverzeichnis aus der Sprache der Gibberty in dem Lande Jedschu in Habbesch. In: Monatl. Correspondenz 20. 1809, 552—563.

Seetzen 1816 = Ulrich Jaspers Seetzen: [Wörter-Sammlungen aus Nordost-Afrikanischen Sprachen]. In: Proben Deutscher Volks-Mundarten, Dr. Seetzen's linguistischer Nachlass, und andere Sprach-Forschungen und Sammlungen, besonders über Ostindien. Edited by Johann S. Vater. Leipzig 1816 [Ch. XII].

Seidel 1900 = August Seidel: Die Sprache von Ufiomi in Deutsch-Ostafrika. In: Zeitschrift für Afrikanische und Ozeanische Sprachen 5. 1900, 165—175.

Serra-Caraccioli 1883 = P. Serra-Caraccioli: Saggio di vocabolario della lingua danakil. In: l'Esplorazione 1883.

Shaw 1885 = A. Downes Shaw: A Pocket Vocabulary of the Ki-Swahili, Ki-Nyika, Ki-Taita and Ki-Kamba Languages; also a Brief Vocabulary of the Kibwyo Dialect. Collected by Archbishop Farler. London 1885.

Smee 1844 = T. Smee: Specimens of different languages used on the East Coast of Africa (Suaheli, Somali, Galla). In: Transactions of the Bombay Geographical Society 6. 1844, 50—55.

Smith 1897 = A. Donaldson Smith: Through Unknown African Countries. London 1897.

Storaci 1935 = E. Storaci: Il poliglotta africano. Vademecum per l'Africa Orientale Italiana, arabo, swahili, somalo, galla, tigrino, tigre. Raccolta dei vocaboli piu usati. Milan 1935.

Stroomer 1987 = Harry Stroomer: A Comparative Study of Three Southern Oromo Dialects in Kenya (Phonology, Morphology and Vocabulary). Leiden 1987.

Toselli 1939 = Giovanni Toselli: Elementi di Lingua Magi. Turin 1939.

Wellby 1901 = Montagu S. Wellby: A Limited Vocabulary of Different Tribes. In: Twixt Sirdar and Menelik. Edited by Montagu S. Wellby. London 1901.

4.3. Other Publications

Agostini 1981 = Francesco Agostini: Ragguáglio sui lavori del vocabulario somalo-italiano. In: Studi Somali. Vol. 1: Fonologia e lessico. Edited by Comitato Tecnico Linguistico per l'Università Nazionale Somala (a cura di Giorgio R. Cardona e Francesco Agostini). Rome 1981, 143—187.

Andrżejewski 1978 = B. W. Andrzejewski: The Development of National Orthography in Somalia and the Modernization of the Somali Language. In: Horn of Africa 1. 1978, 39—45.

Andrzejewski 1979 = B. W. Andrzejewski: The Development of Somali as National Medium of Education and Literature. In: African Languages/Langues Africaines 5. 1979, 1—9.

Andrzejewski 1980a = B. W. Andrzejewski: Some Observations on the Present Orthography for Oromo. In: L'Ethiopie moderne: De l'avènement de Menelik II à nos jours/Modern Ethiopia: From the Accession of Menilek II to the Present. Edited by Joseph Tubiana. Rotterdam 1980, 125—132.

Andrzejewski 1980b = B. W. Andrzejewski: The Use of Somali in Mathematics and Science. In: Afrika und Übersee 63. 1980, 103—117.

Andrzejewski 1983 = B. W. Andrzejewski: Language Reform in Somalia and the Modernization of the Somali Vocabulary. In: Language Reforms — History and Future. Edited by Istvan Fodor/Claude Hagège. Hamburg 1983, 69—84.

Banti 1980 = G. Banti: Problemi di lessicografia somala. In: Atti del Sodalizio Glottologico Milanese. 1979—1980, 34—57.

Bender 1976 = M. Lionel Bender: The Non-Semitic Languages of Ethiopia. East Lansing 1976.

Bliese 1970 = Loren Bliese: The Lexicon — a Key to Culture: with Illustrations from 'Afar Word Lists'. In: Journal of Ethiopian Studies 8. 1970, 1—19.

Caney 1984 = John Charles Caney: The Modernization of Somali Vocabulary, with Particular Reference to the Period from 1972 to the Present. Hamburg 1984.

d'Abbadie 1845 = Antoine d'Abbadie: Letter of April 12, 1845 to Athenaeum (London) [cited in Beke 1845].

Gragg 1988 = Gene B. Gragg: An Etymological Cushitic Database. In: Proceedings of the First Symposium on Cushitic and Omotic Languages. Edited by Marianne Bechhaus-Gerst/Franz Serzisko. Hamburg 1988, 187—204.

Greenberg 1963 = Joseph Greenberg: The Languages of Africa. In: International Journal of American Linguistics 29/1 Part II. 1963.

Hair 1969 = P. E. H. Hair: The Brothers Tutschek and their Sudanese Informants. In: Sudan Notes and Records 50. 1969, 53—62.

Hetzron 1980 = Robert Hetzron: The Limits of Cushitic. In: Sprache und Geschichte in Afrika 2. 1980, 7—126.

Jomard 1839 = François Jomard: Notice sur les Gallas de Limou. In: Bulletin de la Société de Géographie ser. 2 11/12. 1839.

Lamberti 1986 = Marcello Lamberti: Somali Language and Literature. Hamburg 1986 (African Linguistic Bibliographies 2).

Lepsius 1863 = Richard Lepsius: Standard Alphabet for Reducing Unwritten Languages and Foreign Graphic Systems to a Uniform Orthography in European Letters. 2nd Edition. London 1863.

Lepsius 1880 = Richard Lepsius: Nubische Grammatik, mit einer Einleitung über die Völker und Sprachen Afrikas. Berlin 1880.

Lottner 1861 = C. Lottner: On Sister Families of Languages, Specially Those Connected with the Semitic Family. In: Transactions of the Philological Society 1860—61, 20—27; 112—132.

Ludolf 1681 = Hiob Ludolf: Historia aethiopica. Frankfurt 1681.

Parker 1979 = Enid M. Parker: Prerequisites for an Adequate Lexicography of 'Afar. London 1979 [Ph. D. Dissertation, London University].

Renan 1863 = Ernest Renan: Histoire générale et système comparé des langues sémitiques. 3rd edition. Paris 1863.

Sasse 1981 = Hans-Jürgen Sasse: Die kuschitischen Sprachen. In: Die Sprachen Afrikas. Edited by Bernd Heine et al. Hamburg 1981, 187—216.

Tellez 1710 = Balthazar Tellez: The Travels of the Jesuits in Ethiopia. London 1710.

Wolff 1981 = Ekkehard Wolff: Die omotischen Sprachen. In: Die Sprachen Afrikas. Edited by Bernd Heine et al. Hamburg 1981, 217—224.

Zaborski 1986 = Andrzej Zaborski: Can Omotic Be Reclassified as West Cushitic? In: Ethiopian Studies: Proceedings of the Sixth International Conference. Edited by Gideon Goldenberg. Rotterdam. Boston 1986, 525—530.

Zholkovskij 1967 = A. K. Zholkovskij: K leksikograficheskomu opisaniju somalijiskikh sushchestvitelnikh. In: Narodi Azii i Afriki 1967, 93—102.

Zholkovskij 1970 = A. K. Zholkovskij: Materiali k russko-somalijsskomu slovarju. In: Mashinnij Perevod i Prikladnaja Lingvistika 13. 1970, 35—63.

Gene Balford Gragg,
The University of Chicago,
Chicago, Illinois (USA)

XXIII. Lexikographie der Einzelsprachen VII: Die iranischen Sprachen
Lexicography of Individual Languages VII: The Iranian Languages
Lexicographie des langues particulières VII: Langues iraniennes

242. Altiranische Lexikographie

1. Der altiranische Sprachbestand
2. Lexikographie des Avestischen
3. Lexikographie des Altpersischen
4. Literatur (in Auswahl)

1. Der altiranische Sprachbestand

Von der größeren Menge iranischer Sprachen im Altertum, die aus der Vielzahl mittel- und neuiranischer Sprachen zu folgern ist, sind nur zwei altiranische Corpus-Sprachen, Avestisch und Altpersisch, erhalten geblieben (vgl. Karte 242.1). Zwar wird die Existenz der altiranischen Sprache der Meder schon durch antike Nachrichten bestätigt, so durch Herodot (Historien I 110), nach welchem z. B. *spaka- das medische Wort für „Hund" sei (τὴν γὰρ κύνα καλέουσι σπάκα Μῆδοι); aus lautgesetzlich nicht-persischen Wörtern im Lexikon des Altpersischen (vgl. 3) hat man Teile des medischen Wortschatzes zu rekonstruieren versucht (s. darüber die Literatur bei Mayrhofer 1971, 46ff., Schmitt 1980, 28; sehr skeptisch zuletzt Skjærvø 1983, 244ff.). Noch andere altiranische Sprachen im Achaimenidenreich scheinen sich in der „Nebenüberlieferung" niedergeschlagen zu haben (s.

Karte 242.1: Verbreitung altiranischer Corpussprachen

Hinz 1975, 7 ff.; Mayrhofer 1979 a, 111 ff., mit Lit.; Schmitt 1984, 183 ff.). — Ein Sonderfall sind die vornehmlich bei Herodot überlieferten Wörter und Namen aus dem südrussischen Bereich, die, soweit deutbar, einer weiteren altiranischen Sprache anzugehören scheinen; man nennt diese üblicherweise, mit einem in den antiken Quellen nicht eindeutig gebrauchten Namen, Skythisch (s. Vasmer 1923, 7 ff.; Zgusta 1955, 20 ff.; Humbach 1960, 322 ff.; Schmitt 1984, 206 f.). — Während es für diese Nebenüberlieferungssprachen nur Listen des möglichen (zumeist rekonstruierten) Wortgutes geben kann (s. Hinz 1975, 17—279; vgl. Vasmer 1923, 11 ff.), bleiben eigentliche Wörterbücher den beiden Sprachen mit Text-Corpora, Avestisch und Altpersisch, vorbehalten.

2. Lexikographie des Avestischen

2.1. Als Folge der Pflege des Avesta im Bereich mittelpersischer Sprache (s. Hoffmann 1979, 89 ff.) war, vielleicht schon im 9./10. Jahrhundert, ein Avestisch-Pahlavi-Glossar nötig geworden, *Farhang-i ōīm* (s. die Lit. bei Schlerath 1968 a, 240 a; Klingenschmitt 1968, 1 f.; Art. 243); dieses Glossar ist auch für die westliche Wissenschaft von Belang, da es „nicht allein viele Awestaworte, sondern ganze Phrasen und Citate aus verlorenen Awestabüchern bewahrt hat" (Geldner 1896—1904, 9).

2.2. Auf den für die einzelnen Teile des Avesta sehr verschieden zu bewertenden Traditionen der Parsen beruhend, und undenkbar ohne die indogermanistische und indoiranistische Sprachvergleichung, vollzog sich in den rund hundert Jahren zwischen dem späten 18. und dem späten 19. Jahrhundert die wesentliche Erschließung des Avesta und seiner Sprache (s. Geldner 1896—1904, 40 ff.). Das erste größere Wörterbuch dieser Sprache, die dort noch „Altbaktrisch" genannt wird, steht im Banne der Überbewertung jener Tradition (Justi 1864). Stärker zur sprachvergleichenden Methode hingewandt sind die Glossare in später erschienenen Handbüchern (Geiger 1879, 175 ff.; de Harlez 1882, 281 ff.; besonders Jackson 1893, 51 ff.). Diese lexikographischen Arbeiten sind durch Christian Bartholomaes *Altiranisches Wörterbuch* überholt, das, wie sein Titel aussagt, beiden altiranischen Sprachen gewidmet ist (Bartholomae 1904); während es für das Altpersische kaum noch verwendet wird (u. 3.1.2), ist es für das Avestische ein unentbehrliches Lexikon geblieben. Durch das *Awesta-Wörterbuch* Bernfried Schleraths wird es erst ersetzt werden, wenn dessen lexikalischer Teil vollständig vorliegt; zur Stunde sind zwei sehr nützliche Bände mit *Vorarbeiten* erschienen (Schlerath 1968 a, 1968 b), aber noch kein Wörterbuch-Lemma.

2.2.1. Glossare des Avestischen der Gāthās bieten Insler 1975, 339 ff. und Monna 1978, 117 ff.

2.3. Ein Teilgebiet des avestischen Lexikons, die Personennamen, bisher nur im Rahmen des gesamtiranischen Namenbuches (Justi 1895) und sorgfältiger in Bartholomae 1904 behandelt, liegt jetzt in einem kleinen Onomastikon vor (Mayrhofer 1977); ein älteres avestisches Namenbuch war aus sprachlichen Gründen auf einen schmalen Benützerkreis beschränkt (Modi 1892).

3. Lexikographie des Altpersischen

3.1. In den Jahren 1802—1846 vollzog sich die Entzifferung der altpersischen Schriftzeichen (s. Kent 1953, 11 a—11 b). Lassens Versuch (1836, 176), „ein Verzeichnis der [in den Inschriften] vorkommenden Wörter auf[zu]stellen", und auch noch sein neun Jahre späteres „Wortverzeichnis" (Lassen 1845, 186 ff.) fallen somit in die Zeit einer noch nicht voll erreichten richtigen Umschrift der Texte; Benfeys Glossar (1847, 70 ff.) ist eine bewundernswerte Leistung, die ebenfalls nur noch der Wissenschaftsgeschichte angehört. Unvollständig (bis *darsh* reichend) blieb das Vokabular, das H. C. Rawlinson vorlegte (1849).

3.1.1. Vollständig erschienen und nach dem Abschluß der Entzifferung verfaßt ist das Glossar von F. Spiegels in erster Auflage 1862 erschienenem, vielbenutztem Buch (Spiegel 1881, 201 ff.). Von diesem Werk, das sich selbst zu oft auf Sekundärquellen verlassen hatte, ist Kossowicz 1872 (darin ein „Glossarium Palaeo-Persicum") weitgehend abhängig; von geringem Wert sind Tolman 1908 und Johnson 1910.

3.1.2. Durch den starken Zufluß neuen inschriftlichen Materials in diesem Jahrhundert ist aber auch eine eigenständige Meisterleistung, Bartholomae 1904 (s. o. 2.2), im Bezug auf das Altpersische veraltet. Wer heute auf diesem Gebiet arbeitet, ist in erster Linie auf Kent 1953 (darin „Lexicon" 164—215) angewiesen. Zur Ergänzung sind heranzuziehen: der anders (nach Einzelbelegen, und dadurch für Nicht-Linguisten zugänglicher) aufgebaute *Altpersische Wortschatz* von W. Hinz (Hinz 1942), drei Jahrzehnte später in neuer (und zum Teil problematischer) Umschrift nochmals dargeboten (Hinz 1973, 119 ff.); ferner das lexikalische Material aus den seit Kent 1953 gefundenen (bzw. bei Kent übersehenen) Inschriften (Mayrhofer 1978, 49 ff.). — S. u. 3.3.

3.2. Dem lexikalischen Sonderbereich der Personennamen ist Mayrhofer 1979b gewidmet.

3.3. Ein gutes altpersisches Lexikon bleibt trotz der oben 3.1.2. genannten Literatur ein Desiderat. Es sollte den Wortschatz nicht in den üblichen interpretierenden Transkriptionen, sondern in einer Transliteration der tatsächlich auf den Inschriften stehenden Zeichenfolgen darbieten; stärker als bisher sollte es, was zum Teil heute noch nicht leistbar ist, die nichtpersischen Entsprechungen in den mehrsprachigen Inschriften heranziehen. Es hätte schließlich die seit Kent 1953 erreichten sicheren Erkenntnisse auf den Gebieten von Sprachvergleichung, grammatischer Analyse und Etymologie zu vermerken, was mit Hilfe der nach dem Lexikon in Brandenstein/Mayrhofer 1964, 99 ff. erschienenen Forschungsberichte (Mayrhofer 1970, 283 ff.; 1971, 53 ff.; Schmitt 1980, 28 ff.) leicht zu erstellen wäre. — Fraglich bleibt, ob aus der Nebenüberlieferung jenes lexikalische und morphologische Material in das Lexikon übernommen werden müßte, das altpersisches Gepräge trägt und offenbar nur wegen der Eingeschränktheit des altpersischen inschriftlichen Corpus nicht in diesem erscheint (wie z. B. */astu/ „er sei!", Hinz 1975, 47).

4. Literatur (in Auswahl)

4.1. Wörterbücher

Bartholomae 1904 = Christian Bartholomae: Altiranisches Wörterbuch. Straßburg 1904 [XXXII, 2000 S.; letzter Nachdruck Berlin. New York 1979].

Hinz 1942 = Walther Hinz: Altpersischer Wortschatz. Leipzig 1942 [VIII, 160 S.; Nachdruck Nendeln 1966].

Johnson 1910 = Edwin Lee Johnson: Index Verborum to the Old Persian Inscriptions. Anhang (IV, 51 S.) zu Herbert Cushing Tolman: Cuneiform Supplement to the Author's Ancient Persian Lexicon and Texts.... [s. Tolman 1908]. New York. Cincinnati. Chicago 1910.

Justi 1864 = Ferdinand Justi: Handbuch der Zendsprache. Altbactrisches Woerterbuch. Grammatik. Chrestomathie. Leipzig 1864 [XXII, 424 S.; Nachdruck Wiesbaden 1969].

Schlerath 1968 a = Bernfried Schlerath: Awesta-Wörterbuch. Vorarbeiten I: Index locorum zur Sekundärliteratur des Awesta. Wiesbaden 1968 [XXXII, 264 S.].

Schlerath 1968 b = Bernfried Schlerath: Awesta-Wörterbuch. Vorarbeiten II: Konkordanz. Wiesbaden 1968 [XVI, 199 S.].

Tolman 1908 = Herbert Cushing Tolman: Ancient Persian Lexicon. New York. Cincinnati. Chicago 1908 [XII, 134 S.].

4.2. Sonstige Literatur

Benfey 1847 = Theodor Benfey: Die persischen Keilinschriften mit Uebersetzung und Glossar. Leipzig 1847.

Brandenstein/Mayrhofer 1964 = Wilhelm Brandenstein/Manfred Mayrhofer: Handbuch des Altpersischen. Wiesbaden 1964.

Geiger 1879 = Wilhelm Geiger: Handbuch der Awestasprache. Grammatik, Chrestomathie und Glossar. Erlangen 1879.

Geldner 1896—1904 = K[arl] F[riedrich] Geldner: Awestalitteratur. In: Grundriß der Iranischen Philologie 2. Band (Straßburg 1896—1904), 1—53.

de Harlez 1882 = C[harles] de Harlez: Manuel de l'Avesta. Grammaire, Anthologie, Lexique. Paris 1882.

Hinz 1973 = Walther Hinz: Neue Wege im Altpersischen. Wiesbaden 1973.

Hinz 1975 = Walther Hinz: Altiranisches Sprachgut der Nebenüberlieferungen. Wiesbaden 1975.

Hoffmann 1979 = Karl Hoffmann: Das Avesta in der Persis. In: J[ános] Harmatta [ed.]: Prolegomena to the Sources on the History of Pre-Islamic Central Asia (Budapest 1979), 89—93.

Humbach 1960 = Helmut Humbach: Scytho-Sarmatica. In: Die Welt der Slaven, Vierteljahrsschrift für Slavistik 5. 1960, 322—328.

Insler 1975 = S[tanley] Insler: The Gāthās of Zarathustra. Teheran. Lüttich. Leiden 1975.

Jackson 1893 = A[braham] V[alentine] Williams Jackson: Avesta Reader. First Series. Easier Texts, Notes, and Vocabulary. Stuttgart 1893 [Nachdruck New York 1975].

Justi 1895 = Ferdinand Justi: Iranisches Namenbuch. Marburg 1895 [Nachdruck Hildesheim 1963].

Kent 1953 = Roland G[rubb] Kent: Old Persian. Grammar. Texts. Lexicon. Second Edition, Revised. New Haven/Connecticut 1953 [1. Aufl. 1950].

Klingenschmitt 1968 = Gert Klingenschmitt: Farhang-i ōīm. Edition und Kommentar. Erlangen-Nürnberg [phil. Diss., maschinenschr.] 1968.

Kossowicz 1872 = Cajetanus Kossowicz: Inscriptiones Palaeo-Persicae Achaemenidarum quot hucusque repertae sunt. St. Petersburg 1872.

Lassen 1836 = Christian Lassen: Die Altpersischen Keil-Inschriften von Persepolis. Entzifferung des Alphabets und Erklärung des Inhalts. Bonn 1836.

Lassen 1845 = Christian Lassen: Die Altpersischen Inschriften nach Hrn. N. L. Westergaard's Mittheilungen. In: Zeitschrift für die Kunde des Morgenlandes 6. 1845, 1—188.

Mayrhofer 1970 = Manfred Mayrhofer: Das Altpersische seit 1964. In: W. B. Henning Memorial Volume (London 1970), 276—298.

Mayrhofer 1971 = Manfred Mayrhofer: Neuere Forschungen zum Altpersischen. In: Donum Indogermanicum, Festschrift für Anton Scherer (Heidelberg 1971), 41—66.

Mayrhofer 1977 = Manfred Mayrhofer: Die avestischen Namen. Faszikel 1 von M. M.: Die altiranischen Namen [s. Mayrhofer 1979b]. Wien 1977.

Mayrhofer 1978 = Manfred Mayrhofer: Supplement zur Sammlung der altpersischen Inschriften. Wien 1978.

Mayrhofer 1979a = Manfred Mayrhofer: Zur Frage nicht medisch-persischer Personennamen in Persepolis. In: J[ános] Harmatta [ed.]: Prolegomena to the Sources on the History of Pre-Islamic Central Asia (Budapest 1979), 111—118.

Mayrhofer 1979b = Manfred Mayrhofer: Die altpersischen Namen. Faszikel 2 (II/1—II/32), zusammen mit Indices (III/1—III/33) und Mayrhofer 1977 (s. d.) = Mayrhofer, Die altiranischen Namen [Iranisches Personennamenbuch I], Wien 1979.

Modi 1892 = Jivanji Jamshedji Modi: A Dictionary of Avestic Proper Names. Bombay 1892 [in Gujarati, Titelblatt englisch].

Monna 1978 = Maria Cornelia Monna: The Gathas of Zarathustra. Amsterdam 1978.

Rawlinson 1849 = H[enry] C[reswicke] Rawlinson: Memoir on Cuneiform Inscriptions. Chapter VI: Vocabulary of the Ancient Persian Language.... In: Journal of the Royal Asiatic Society 11, Part 1. 1849, 1—192.

Schmitt 1980 = Rüdiger Schmitt: Altpersisch-Forschung in den Siebzigerjahren. In: Kratylos 25. 1980, 1—66.

Schmitt 1984 = Rüdiger Schmitt: Zur Ermittlung von Dialekten in altiranischer Zeit. In: Sprachwissenschaft 9. 1984, 183—207.

Skjærvø 1983 = Prods O. Skjærvø: *Farnah-:* mot mède en vieux-perse? In: Bulletin de la Société de Linguistique de Paris 78, 1. 1983, 241—259.

Spiegel 1881 = Fr[iedrich] Spiegel: Die altpersischen Keilinschriften. Im Grundtexte mit Uebersetzung, Grammatik und Glossar. Zweite vermehrte Auflage. Leipzig 1881 [Nachdruck Amsterdam 1971].

Vasmer 1923 = Max Vasmer: Untersuchungen über die ältesten Wohnsitze der Slaven I: Die Iranier in Südrußland. Leipzig 1923 [IV, 79 S.; Wiederabdruck in M. Vasmer, Schriften zur slavischen Altertumskunde und Namenkunde (Berlin 1971) 108—170].

Zgusta 1955 = Ladislav Zgusta: Die Personennamen griechischer Städte der nördlichen Schwarzmeerküste. Die ethnischen Verhältnisse, namentlich das Verhältnis der Skythen und Sarmaten, im Lichte der Namenforschung. Prag 1955.

Manfred Mayrhofer, Wien (Österreich)

243. Middle Iranian Lexicography

1. Western Middle Iranian
2. Sogdian
3. Khwarezmian
4. Saka
5. Bactrian
6. Selected Bibliography

1. Western Middle Iranian

The languages classed as Middle Iranian of which any substantial records survive fall conveniently into two groups. To the Western group belong the relatively similar Parthian and Middle Persian. The Eastern group comprises four languages of more disparate character: Sogdian, Khwarezmian, Saka and Bactrian (cf. Map 243.1). The earliest, but sparsely, attested is Parthian, in the form of documents on ostraca from the Arsacid royal city of Nisa (1st cent. B. C.) and on parchment from Avroman in Kurdistan (A. D. 53). It is only as second language of the Sasanians that Parthian appears in literary form. Middle Persian, the dialect of Persis proper between the invasions of Alexander the Great (4th cent. B. C.) and of the Arabs (7th cent. A. D.), and official language of the Sasanian Empire, first appears in royal and priestly inscriptions of the 3rd century A. D. A complete glossary of these has been published by Gignoux (1972). Like Parthian before it,

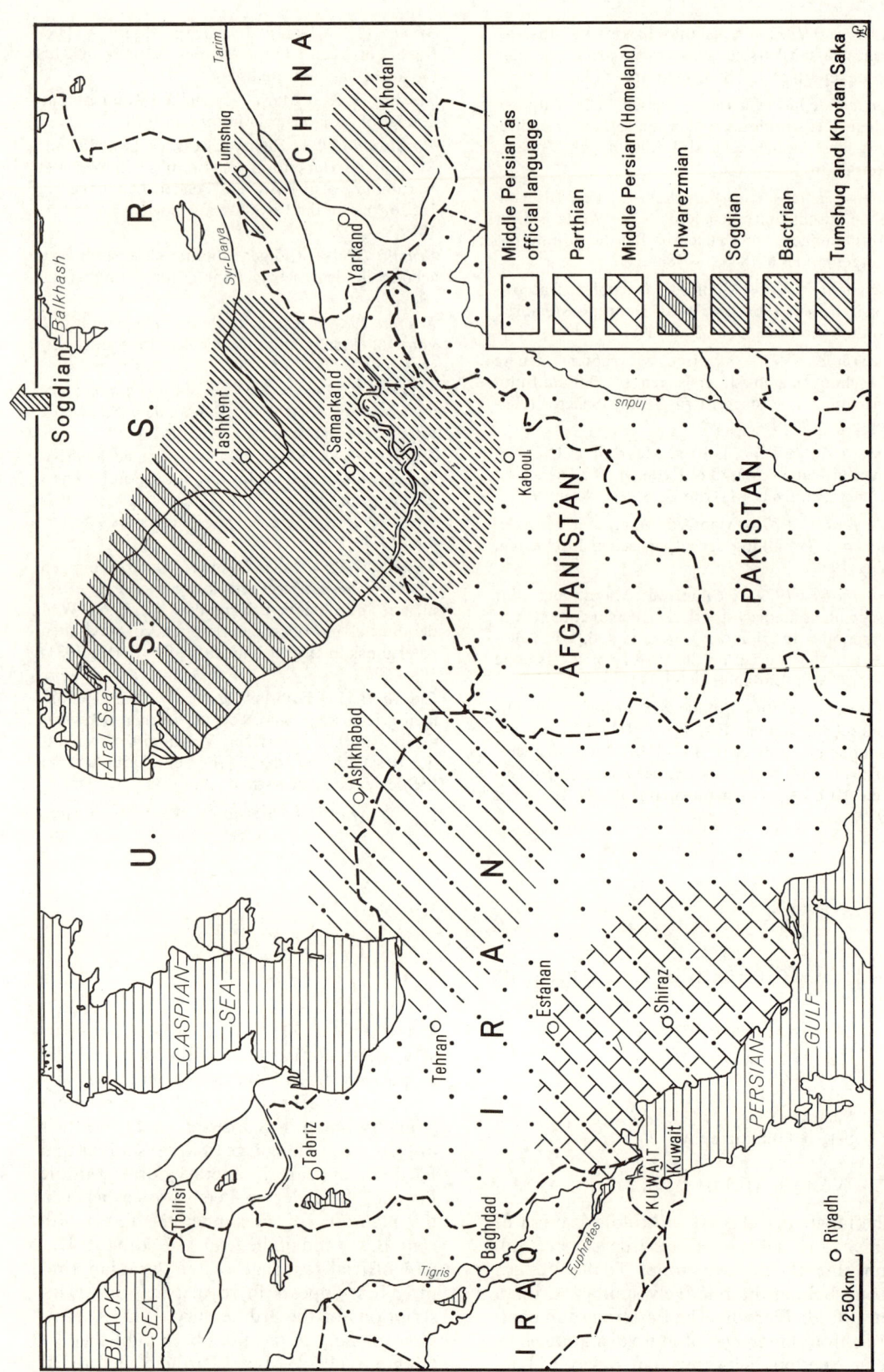

Map 243.1: Middle Iranian languages

Middle Persian was written in its own development of the consonantic Imperial Aramaic script of Achaemenian times. In an increasingly cursive form this was also the vehicle of Zoroastrian writings of the Sasanian period, though the earliest extant works written with it, in so-called Pahlavi, actually date from after the Islamic conquest, by which time it was a dead language. A feature of this writing system, besides historical spellings such as *štr* for *šaϑr*, later *šahr*, 'town', was the frequent use of heterograms (generally misnamed ideograms), i. e. more or less well preserved Aramaic forms for the corresponding Persian words, e. g. MP *šāh* 'king' written *MLK'*, or *ōzad* 'killed' written *YKTLWNt* (Aram. *yqtlwn* 'they kill'). The first dictionary (MP *frahang*) in Iran, a list of Avestan words (from the Zoroastrian scriptures) explained in Pahlavi, is called *Frahang ī oīm* after its first entry, Av. *oīm* = Pahl. *ēk* 'one' (editions Jamaspji 1867, Reichelt 1900; Art. 242). In the course of time dictionary-like lists of the heterograms and their Persian equivalents, following a tradition dating from Akkadian times, became necessary. The most important is the *Frahang ī pahlawīg*, of unknown date. Such lists naturally served only mnemonic purposes and made no attempt to explain the foreign forms. This task modern scholarship has set itself, with so far only partial success. A first critical edition of the Frahang, which contains a large proportion of heterograms not actually occurring in surviving texts, was published by Junker (1912). This, with all its faults, served Ebeling (1941) as source for his study of the origins of the heterograms, in which credibility is sometimes stretched beyond breaking point. His results were nevertheless incorporated uncritically in Junker 1955. A new edition of the Frahang has been published from the Nachlass of Nyberg (Nyberg/Utas 1988), from whose pen came the first book to ease the study of the language (Nyberg 1928), containing an etymological glossary of selected texts. In the new edition of this work (Nyberg 1964) a too fertile imagination has been given rein, with deleterious effects: an unacceptably high percentage of the glossary consists either of misrepresented or of totally "ghost" words. Several problems have bedevilled Pahlavi studies. One is the order in which the Pahlavi letters are presented in different works. In some (e. g. Junker 1912; 1955) the alphabet is arranged quite arbitrarily, in others in the order of the corresponding letters of the Arabo-Persian alphabet. Later, more comprehensive works (Abrahamjan 1965, MacKenzie 1971) follow the order of the basic Aramaic alphabet. While scholars are by and large agreed on its transliteration, despite the ambiguity of several letters, the transcriptions employed range from representations of the presumed pronunciation of the earliest Middle Persian (of some five centuries before the earliest actual text), through attempts (doomed to failure) to combine transcription and transliteration, to those giving the pronunciation of the early or late Sasanian periods. Thus the same word, e. g. later Persian *pay(γ)ām* 'message', < Old Persian **patigāma-*, can be found represented as *patigām*, *pītām* (Abrahamjan 1965, 212) and *paitām* (Nyberg 1964, 149, both misrepresentations of the corrupt spelling *pgt'm*), and *paygām* (MacKenzie 1971, 67), to the confusion of the layman.

From the 3rd century onwards the prophet Mani and his disciples used both Middle Persian and Parthian for their missionary writings, employing a beautiful variety of the Syriac script which gave a much clearer picture of the actual pronunciation of the languages, e. g. *šhr, š'h, 'wzd, pyg'm* for the exx. above. The lexicon of this material has been most comprehensively dealt with by Boyce (1977).

2. Sogdian

West Iranian Manichaean missionaries also brought these languages, with their faith, to the Sogdians of Central Asia (cf. Map 243.2), who carried them further to the confines of China. The Sogdian Manichaeans, besides using the Persian and Parthian scriptures, also made translations into their own lan-

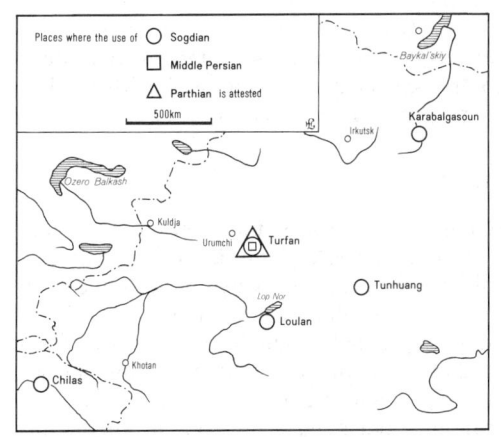

Map 243.2: Languages of the Sogdian diaspora

guage. A number of word-lists have survived from this period (6th—8th centuries) containing Middle Persian words, arranged alphabetically by the first one or two letters only, with Sogdian equivalents (Henning 1940, 12—58). These are, however, the only lexicographical works known in the whole considerable corpus of Buddhist, Christian, Manichaean or lay Sogdian texts. Although most editions of these texts hitherto have contained glossaries, the steady progress of Sogdian studies has overtaken the earlier of these. No comprehensive dictionary of any dialect of Sogdian has yet been compiled.

3. Khwarezmian

Khwarezmian is only attested in pre-Islamic times on coins and ossuary inscriptions. The language survived, however, at least until the catastrophic Mongol conquest of the 13th century. By good chance knowledge of it, apart from a few hundred short sentences quoted in Arabic law books, comes mainly from the numerous Khwarezmian interlinear glosses in a manuscript of the famous Arabic dictionary *Muqaddimat al-adab* (ca. 1135 A. D.) by al-Zamakhsharī, which has been published in facsimile (Togan 1951). By mischance not all these glosses, in an augmented Arabic script, are fully pointed. Although some of the resulting uncertainty can be removed by the comparison of several entries much remains obscure, owing to the ambiguity of unpointed Arabic letters. So far only a fragment of this material has been published in dictionary form (Henning/MacKenzie 1971). A full edition (Benzing 1968), but with serious faults (not all of which have been noted in the copious reviews), has led to the publication of a more than copious word index (Benzing 1983). This, however, by no means fills the need for a complete dictionary of the Khwarezmian material. Such a work is in preparation by MacKenzie.

4. Saka

Of the languages of the once mighty Saka (Scythian) tribes of Central Asia the only mediaeval records surviving are those of the 7th—10th century from Khotan and Tumshuq, two small kingdoms of probably mixed Indian, Iranian and Chinese Buddhist population, which at some time came under the rule of Saka kings. However, in all the copious literary relics from Khotan and the sparser remains from Tumshuq, both written in forms of the Indian Brāhmī script, there are no lexical works, and only two bilingual texts at all (a school exercise Sanskrit-Saka, and part of a book of Chinese-Khotanese phrases). As the culmination of his nearly 50 years occupation with the material Bailey (1979) has published his etymological dictionary of the Iranian element of the language. Not only for its omission of the considerable number of Sanskritic loan-words, this has drawn much criticism, leading to the founding of a new series of Khotanese lexical studies (Emmerick/Skjaervø 1982).

5. Bactrian

The language of the Kushan kingdom of Bactria at the beginning of the first millennium is known from one complete inscription and several fragments in Greek uncials, and from the few later so-called Hephthalite documents. The only comprehensive dictionary of this material, the interpretation of which is still much debated, is by Davary (1982).

6. Selected Bibliography

6.1. Dictionaries

Abrahamjan 1965 = R. Abrahamjan: Pexlevijsko-persidsko-armjano-russko-anglijskij slovar'. Erevan 1965 [VIII, 338 p.].

Bailey 1979 = Harold Walter Bailey: Dictionary of Khotan Saka. Cambridge 1979 [xviii, 559 p.].

Boyce 1977 = Mary Boyce: A word-list of Manichaean Middle Persian and Parthian. Teheran.Liège 1977 [iv, 172 p.].

Davary 1982 = Gholam Djelani Davary: Baktrisch. Ein Wörterbuch auf Grund der Inschriften, Handschriften, Münzen und Siegelsteine. Heidelberg 1982 [306 p.].

Gignoux 1972 = Philippe Gignoux: Glossaire des inscriptions pehlevies et parthes. London 1972 [68 p.].

Henning/MacKenzie 1971 = Walter Bruno Henning (†), ed. David Neil MacKenzie: A fragment of a Khwarezmian dictionary. London. Teheran 1971 [iv, 56 p.].

MacKenzie 1971 = David Neil MacKenzie: A concise Pahlavi dictionary. London 1971 [xx, 236 p.].

6.2. Other Publications

Benzing 1968 = Johannes Benzing: Das chwaresmische Sprachmaterial einer Handschrift der "Muqaddimat al-Adab" von Zamaxšarī. Wiesbaden 1968.

Benzing 1983 = Johannes Benzing: Chwaresmischer Wortindex. Wiesbaden 1983.

Ebeling 1941 = Erich Ebeling: Das aramäisch-mittelpersische Glossar Frahang-i-pahlavīk im Lichte der assyriologischen Forschung. In: Mitteilungen der Altorientalischen Gesellschaft XIV/1. Leipzig 1941.

Emmerick/Skjaervø 1982 = Ronald Eric Emmerick and Prods Oktor Skjaervø: Studies in the vocabulary of Khotanese. I. Vienna 1982.

Henning 1940 = Walter Bruno Henning: Sogdica. London 1940.

Jamaspji 1867 = Hoshangji Jamaspji: An old Zend-Pahlavi glossary. Bombay. London 1867.

Junker 1912 = Heinrich F. J. Junker: The Frahang i Pahlavik. Heidelberg 1912.

Junker 1955 = Heinrich F. J. Junker: Das Frahang i Pahlavīk in zeichengemäßer Anordnung. Leipzig 1955.

Nyberg 1928 = Henrik Samuel Nyberg: Hilfsbuch des Pehlewi. I. Texte und Index der Pehlewi-Wörter. II. Glossar. Uppsala 1928—31.

Nyberg 1964 = Henrik Samuel Nyberg: A manual of Pahlavi. I. Texts. II, Ideograms, Glossary, ... Wiesbaden 1964—74.

Nyberg/Utas 1988 = Henrik Samuel Nyberg (†), ed. Bo Utas: Frahang i Pahlavīk. Wiesbaden 1988.

Reichelt 1900 = Hans Reichelt: Der Frahang i oīm. In: Wiener Zeitschrift für die Kunde des Morgenlandes XIV. 1900, 177—213; XV. 1901, 117—186.

Togan 1951 = Zeki Velidi Togan: Documents on Khorezmian culture, Part 1, Muqaddimat al-Adab. Istanbul 1951.

David Neil MacKenzie, Göttingen
(Federal Republic of Germany)

244. Modern Iranian Lexicography: Persian/Tajik

1. Evolution of New Persian Lexicography
2. Traditional Monolingual Dictionaries
3. The European Contribution
4. Modern Persian Lexicography
4. Afghan Darī and Tajik
6. Selected Bibliography

1. Evolution of New Persian Lexicography

New Persian *(fārsī)*, the literary language of Iran and much of Central Asia from the 10th century, is characterized by the use of Arabic script and the massive incorporation of Arabic loanwords. In phonology, morphology and orthography, however, it has changed comparatively little in the past 1,000 years, during which it became the chief vehicle of eastern Islamic literature and a catalyst in the rise of Turkish and Urdu to literary status. Today it is the official and majority language of Iran, the lingua franca of Afghanistan (there called *darī* or *kābulī*) and the national language of the Tajik SSR *(tojikī;* Russ. *tadžikskij)* (cf. Map 244.1). Dictionaries *(farhang,* also meaning 'learning, culture'; *lughat, lughāt* 'vocabulary' and *lughatnāma* 'lexicon') number approximately 150 monolingual and 150 multilingual. For the first three centuries after the Arab conquest (ca. 650—950) the literary language of Muslim Iranian intellectuals was Arabic, which throughout the Islamic world enjoyed a status analogous to that of Latin in the Christian west. Lexicography was accordingly in and of Arabic; several of the earliest monolingual Arabic dictionaries were the work of Iranians. Arabic-Persian glossaries modeled on these appeared from at least the 11th century (Elwell-Sutton 1983, 245; McKenzie 1975, 525). By the 10th century, a Persian court literature based on the educated vernacular of northeast Iran and Central Asia *(darī, pārsī)* began to spread westward, and monolingual dictionaries were first compiled for poets speaking western dialects who could not understand some of the vocabulary of their models (Lazard 1975, 595—606; Nafīsī 1959, 178—80). The earliest such work extant is the *Lughat-i Furs* of Asadī Ṭūsī, compiled ca. 1060: this glosses some 1,200 rare or archaic words of the eastern poets, arranged alphabetically by rhyme, and each supported by a verse citation (Horn 1897). In 1328, Shams-i Munshī of Nakhjivān compiled the *Ṣiḥāḥu'l-Furs,* modeled on a 10th-century Arabic dictionary; this, as also a dictionary of 1344 forming part of a treatise on poetics, the *Mi'yār-i Jamālī* by Shams-i Fakhrī of Isfahan, employed the arrangement by rhyme initiated by Asadī. The last and most important medieval dictionary pro-

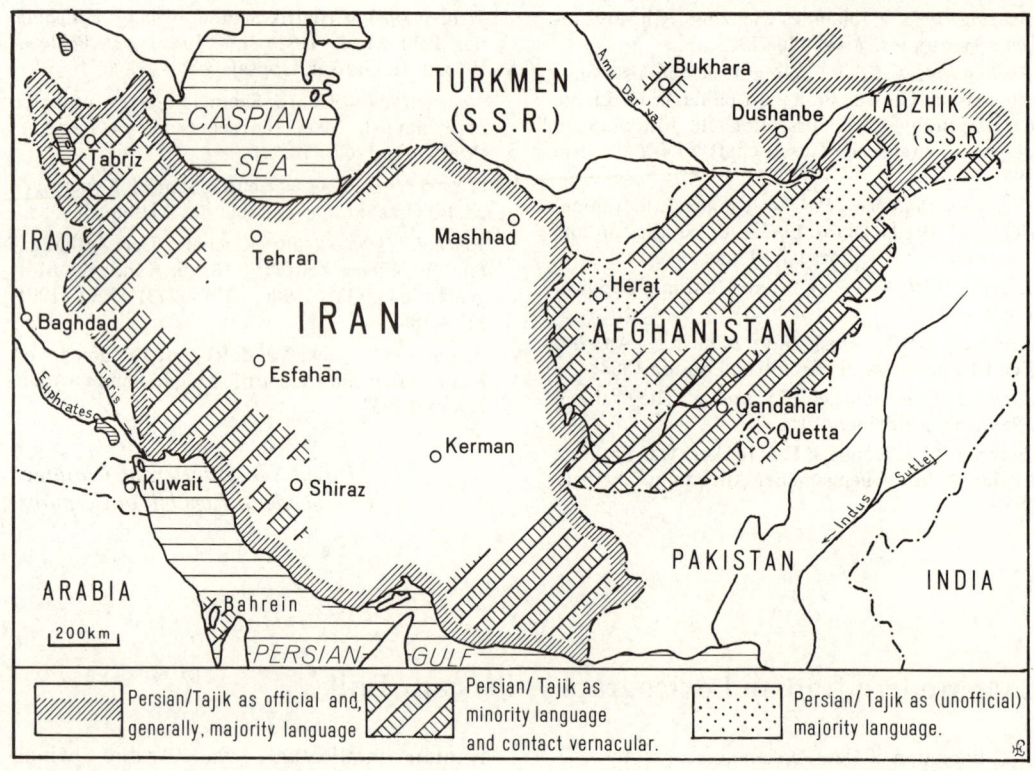

Map 244.1: Area of Persian/Tajik

duced in Iran was the *Majma'u'l-Furs* (1600) by Muḥammad Qāsim Surūrī of Kāshān, dedicated to Shah 'Abbās: its nearly 6,000 entries, with citations from 60 literary classics, rely on 38 earlier dictionaries, many since lost. In a revised edition of 1629 Surūrī profited from the *Farhang-i Jahāngīrī* (1609) by Jamālu'l-dīn Ḥusayn Īnjū, an emigrant from Shiraz to India: commissioned by Akbar, this monumental citation lexicon acknowledges 44 earlier dictionaries.

2. Traditional Monolingual Dictionaries

From the 14th century, as the political and cultural empire of Iranized Islam rolled eastward, until the 19th, when the British Indian civil service was still staffed on the basis of examinations in the Persian classics, scores of Persian dictionaries appeared in India. Earlier ones include the *Sharafnāma-yi Ibrāhīm* (1474; based on the works of poets from Firdawsī to Ḥāfiẓ, with citations), the *Tuḥfatu'l-sa'āda* (1510; without citations, but including compounds and idioms) and the *Mu'ayyidu'l-afāḍil* (1519; listing separately words of Persian, Arabic, and Turkish origins). During the 16th century Ottoman Turkish lexicographers also paid homage to their classics: Luṭfullāh Ḥalīmī compiled three different Persian dictionaries, and Ibrāhīm ibn Khudāydede composed one, the *Tuḥfa-yi Shahīdī*, in verse. In India, the *Farhang-i Jahāngīrī* inspired the much-used *Burhān-i qāti'* by Muḥammad Ḥusayn Tabrīzī (Hyderabad, 1652): conceived as a practical condensation of Īnjū's work, it dispensed with attestations and citations, but — setting a fortunate precedent — arranged the 20,000 entries in strict alphabetical order by initials. The *Burhān* inspired further efforts criticizing and supplementing it, notably the *Sirāju'l-lughāt* by the poet Ārzū (1735); this also utilized the influential *F. Rashīdī* (1654) by 'Abdu'l-rashīd Tattavī, whose introduction constitutes the first critical essay on Persian philology. Henceforth Persian dictionaries increased greatly in number and volume, and began to include post-classical and contemporary vocabulary: of note is the *F. Nāṣirī* (1870), compiled in Iran by Riḍā qulī Khan Hidāyat (McKenzie 1975, 526; Nafīsī 1959, 179ff.; Storey 1984, 3—61; Tauer 1968, 429—32). The principal defects of traditional

Persian dictionaries — in part carried over into modern ones — are: inadequacy of the Arabic script to represent the sounds (particularly the vowels) of Persian; errors perpetuated from poorly-written manuscript sources and from original misreadings of Middle Persian logograms; inclusion of spurious vocabulary — notably from the *dasātīr,* a fake Zoroastrian text — and of spurious citation verses (McKenzie 1975, 526; Yar-shater 1970, 677). Distribution was severely restricted: printing was not established in Iran until the 1820s, nor lithography before the 1840s, and literacy was never widespread.

3. The European Contribution

European dictionaries of Persian — by nature multilingual — begin with the valuable *Codex Cumanicus,* a Turkic-Persian-Latin glossary of ca. 1350 compiled in the field; most works until the present century, however, relied largely uncritically on Persian scholarly tradition (McKenzie 1975, 526; Windfuhr 1979, 158—60). Steingass' *Comprehensive Persian-English Dictionary* (1892), at the confluence of the European and Indian traditions — its basis is the *F. Rashīdī* — exhibits the defects mentioned, but makes use of contemporary vernacular material culled from L. Schlimmer's *Terminologie médico-pharmaceutique et anthropologique française-persane* (Tehran lithograph 1874) and Nāṣiru'l-dīn Shah's travel diaries. A score of modern bilingual dictionaries — compiled by Europeans, by Iranians, and in collaboration — now exist for all six major European languages (Elwell-Sutton 1983, 243—4; Moayyad 1962, 32—81).

4. Modern Persian Lexicography

During the present century a number of Iranian scholars trained in Indo-European philology at French and German universities began to produce critical editions of the literary and lexicographical classics. The foundation in 1935 of the University of Tehran and of the Persian Language Academy *(farhangistān)* gave impetus to such endeavors, though the Academy's projected dictionary never materialized. The *F. Nafīsī* (ca. 100,000 Arabic and 60,000 Persian entries; no citations) marks the transition: compiled before 1919 by Nāẓimu'l-aṭibbā, a Qajar court physician, it was later published in 5 volumes (Tehran, 1939—56) with pronunciation indi-

يار . (ا َ اِ) (۲) اعانت كننده . (برهان) .
(شرفنامه) . معين . (دهار) . مدد . مددكار .
(غياث ا للغات) . عون . معاون . ناصر .
نصير . عضد . معاضد . ظهير . پشت . ياور .
مدد . ساعد . دستگير . طرفدار . دستيار .
مساعد . ولى . رده :
واين سه گروه بايكديگر بحربند وچون دشمنى
پديد آيد با يكديگر يار باشند .
(حدود العالم) .
خرد باد هموارہ سالار تو
مباد ازجهان جز خرد يار تو .
ابوشكور .
ترا يار كردارها باد و بس
كه باشد بهرجات فرياد رس .
فردوسى .

Dictionary excerpt 244.1 (from: *Lughatnāma*)

cated by Roman transcription. The outstanding result so far is the encyclopedic *Lughatnāma* begun by 'Ali Akbar Dihkhudā in 1946, continued after his death in 1956 by Muḥammad Mu'īn and others, and completed in 1981: it comprises over 26,000 folio pages. Etymology and usage are faithfully recorded, though page references of sources cited are often lacking, meanings are not listed in order of frequency or chronology, and much undisciplined geographical and biographical material is included. Mu'īn's 6-volume *F. fārsī* (1963—73), less ambitious and better organized, is modeled on Larousse, with topical subsections. A systematic historical dictionary, the *F. tārīkhī-yi zabān-i fārsī,* was initiated by the Iranian Cultural Foundation in 1978 (Vol. 1, A—B, has 735 pages). Continuing problems of Persian lexicography include: selection of headwords for the many composite verbal idioms (cf. English phrasal verbs); selection by register *(Fremdwort* vs. *Lehnwort)* of the Arabic vocabulary; and incorporation of vernacular usage (Moayyad 1962, 13—26; Yar-shater 1970, 678). This last defect is being remedied by the appearance of separate dictionaries of colloquial Persian: by Yūsuf Raḥmatī (1951), M. 'A. Jamālzāda (1962), Amīrqulī Amīnī (1960s—70s) and Aḥmad Shāmlū (*Kitāb-i Kūcha,* from 1978).

5. Afghan Darī and Tajik

Afghan Darī lexicography is not distinct from that of standard Persian before the present century. The only modern monolingual dictionary is the *F. 'āmiyāna-yi fārsī-yi Afghānistān* (1961; ca. 12,000 entries) by 'Abdullāh *Afghānī-navīs,* who has also compiled a Persian-Pashto dictionary (1956). The trilingual *Russko-pushtu-dari slovar'* by K. A. Lebedev et al. (Moscow, 1983; 20,000 entries) is a practical response to political realities. Tajik attained separate literary status during the Soviet period, using a modified Russian alphabet from 1940. Two contrasting goals inform Tajik lexicography: the promotion of a practical, national, vernacular-based literary language, enriched by native neologisms and Russian loanwords; and the preservation of the literary heritage of (eastern) Classical Persian. Both trends are exemplified in the pioneering *Lughati nimtafsilī* 'semi-explicatory dictionary' compiled by Sadriddin Aynī in 1938 (published 1976): its 11,400 entries — in Cyrillic, with Arabic transliteration and checklist, and selected citations — preserve local craft terms and idioms as well as literary words. The first goal is uppermost in M. Fozilov's 2-volume *F. iborahoi rekhta* 'phraseological dictionary' of 1963—4 (ca. 6,500 entries; Cyrillic only), with extensive citations from modern Tajik writers, and the second in the 2-volume *F. zaboni tojikī* by M. Shukurov et al. (1969; Cyrillic with Arabic transliteration and checklist): its 45,000 entries, based on Persian literature from the 10th to the early 20th centuries, are supported by citations from classical writers, chiefly poets of eastern Iran. The *Tadžiksko-russkij slovar'* of 1954 (40,000 entries; no citations; Arabic checklist) is the definitive dictionary of the modern literary language, though already out of date (Oranskij 1975, 39—45).

6. Selected Bibliography

6.1. Dictionaries (mentioned in the text)

For editions of these (and others), see Elwell-Sutton 1983; for manuscripts, Storey 1984.

6.2. Other Publications

Blochmann 1868 = H. Blochmann: Contributions to Persian Lexicography. In: Journal of the Asiatic Society of Bengal, N. S. Vol. XXXVII, Part I No. 1, Calcutta 1868, 1—72.

Elwell-Sutton 1983 = L. P. Elwell-Sutton: Bibliographical Guide to Iran. Brighton. New Jersey 1983.

Horn 1897 = Paul Horn: Asadî's neupersisches Wörterbuch Lughat-i Furs. In: Abhandlungen der Königlichen Gesellschaft der Wissenschaften zu Göttingen, Philologisch-historische Klasse, N. F. Bd. 1. Nr. 8. Göttingen 1897 [Introduction, 1—37; Persian text, 1—133].

Lazard 1975 = Gilbert Lazard: The Rise of the New Persian Language. In: Cambridge History of Iran IV, Cambridge 1975, 595—632.

McKenzie 1975 = D. N. McKenzie: Ķāmūs, 2. In: Encyclopaedia of Islam, New Edition IV, Leiden 1975, 525—7.

Moayyad 1962 = Heshmat Moayyad: Zum Problemkreis und Stand der persischen Lexikographie. In: Annali dell'Istituto Universitario Orientale di Napoli, N. S. Vol. XII, Rome 1962, 1—81.

Nafīsī 1959 = Sa'īd Nafīsī: Farhanghā-yi fārsī (Persian [monolingual] dictionaries). In: Lughat-nāma-yi Dihkhudā Fasc. 40 (Introduction), Tehran 1959/1338, 178—379.

Oranskij 1975 = I. M. Oranskij: Die Neuiranischen Sprachen der Sowjetunion. Trans. Werner Winter. Paris. The Hague 1975.

Storey 1984 = C. A. Storey: Persian Literature, A Bio-Bibliographical Survey. Vol. III, Part 1. Ed. V. M. Shepherd. Leiden 1984.

Tauer 1968 = Felix Tauer: Persian Learned Literature to the End of the 18th Century, III: Philology. In: Jan Rypka, History of Iranian Literature. Dordrecht 1968, 429—37.

Windfuhr 1979 = Gernot L. Windfuhr: Persian Grammar — History and State of its Study. (Trends in Linguistics, State-of-the-Art Reports 12). The Hague 1979.

Yar-shater 1970 = Iran and Afghanistan. In: Current Trends in Linguistics 6, Paris. The Hague 1970, 669—89.

ЕР يار 1. дӯст, рафиқ.

Даст дар сӯроххо дорӣ, зи мор андеша кун,
Ёрро ҳам ёр ҳаст, аз ёри ёр андеша кун.*
Ёрон чу ҷавоб гӯш карданд,
Аз гуфтаи худ хамӯш карданд. *Хилолӣ*

ёри кухан ёри дерина, дӯсти қадим.
Аз ёри кухан намекунӣ ёд,
Ин пешаи нав муборакат бод. *Ҷомӣ*

2. ҳамкор, шарик; мувофиқ.
Маъшуқа ба ранги рӯзгор аст,
Бо гардиши рӯзгор ёр аст. *Анварӣ*
Ёре дар паҳлӯи ӯ истода буд, ки номи ӯ Холид бинни Асад буд. «*Таърихи Табарӣ*»

Dictionary excerpt 244.2 (from: M. Shukurov et al., *F. zaboni tojikī*. 1969)

*John R. Perry, University of Chicago,
Chicago, Illinois (USA)*

245. Die Lexikographie der übrigen neuiranischen Sprachen

1. Einteilung der neuiranischen Sprachen
2. Kurdisch
3. Pašto
4. Ossetisch
5. Balōčī
6. Schriftlose Sprachen
7. Literatur (in Auswahl)

1. Einteilung der neuiranischen Sprachen

1.1. Nach einer von den altiran. Verhältnissen ausgehenden Klassifizierung, die allerdings nicht völlig unumstritten ist, zerfallen die iran. Sprachen in zwei große Gruppen, eine westliche und eine östliche. Diese Bezeichnungen sind in bezug auf die neuiran. Sprachen jedoch nur mehr bedingt geographisch zu verstehen, da sich die Besiedlungsverhältnisse durch Migrationen und politische Gegebenheiten im Laufe der Zeit beträchtlich verändert haben (vgl. Karte 245.1). Dies gilt auch für die aufgrund lautlicher Kriterien erfolgte weitere Unterteilung in eine nordwestl. und eine südwestl. sowie in eine nordöstl. und eine südöstl. Untergruppe. Für die neuiran. Sprachen ergibt sich folgendes Schema:

Südwestiran.: N(eu)pers(isch, gesprochen im Iran); Tādž(īkisch; UdSSR: Tadž. SSR); Darī (Afghanistan; für diese Sprachen vgl. Art. 244); Xazara-Dialekte (Afghanistan; Westiran; UdSSR: Turkmen. SSR); Tātī (UdSSR: Azerbajdžan. SSR).

Nordwestiran.: Kurd(isch; Türkei, Irak, Iran, Syrien; UdSSR: Kaukasusrepubliken, Turkmen. SSR); Gūrānī (Nordwestiran); Zāzā (Osttürkei, Irak); Lur-Dialekte (Südwestiran); Balōčī (Iran, Pakistan, Afghanistan, Nordindien, UdSSR: Turkmen. SSR); „Kasp. Dialekte": Semnānī, Gīlānī (oder Gīlakī), Māzandarānī, Tālišī (Nordwestiran; das letztere auch in UdSSR: Azerbajdžan. SSR).

Südostiran.: Pašto; Ōrmuṛī, Parāčī (Afghanistan, Pakistan); „Pamirdialekte": Xūfī, Bartangī, Orošōrī, Šughnī-Rošānī, Sarikōlī, Waxī, Yazgulāmī, Iškāšmī-Sanglēčī, Munǯī-Yidgha (alle im Gebiet Afghanistan, UdSSR, China, Pakistan).

Nordostiran.: Oss(etisch; UdSSR: am Nord- und Südhang des zentralen Kaukasus); Yaghnōbī (UdSSR: Tadž. SSR).

1.2. Die hier zu behandelnden Sprachen sind in lexikographischer Hinsicht höchst unterschiedlich erschlossen. Dies hängt mit dem Status zusammen, der ihnen in ihrem jeweiligen Verbreitungsgebiet zukommt. So hat sich z. B. das Pašto in den letzten Jahrhunderten zu einer rel. einheitlichen Literatursprache entwickelt, wodurch auch das in den Wörterbüchern erfaßte Material vergleichsweise homogen ist. Anders steht es z. B. mit dem Kurd., das durch die extreme politische und geographische Zersplitterung seines Verbreitungsgebiets starke dialektale Divergenzen zeigt, durch die auch die Lexikographie der Sprache geprägt ist. Wieder anders ist z. B. die Situation der sog. „Pamirdialekte" oder der „kasp. Dialekte", die z. T. von nur wenigen hundert Sprechern gesprochen werden, wobei diese sämtlich noch eine andere Sprache als „Verkehrssprache" benutzen (v. a. das Tādž. bzw. das Npers.); hier dient die Lexikographie fast ausschließlich linguistischen Zwecken, Wörterbücher für den täglichen Gebrauch gibt es kaum. Während diese „schriftlosen" Sprachen en bloc behandelt werden können, bedürfen das Kurd., Pašto, das Oss. und das Balōčī aufgrund ihrer jeweiligen Sonderstellung einer ausführlicheren Diskussion.

2. Kurdisch

Um der besonderen Situation des Kurd. gerecht zu werden, ist es nötig, eine Übersicht über das Dialektgefüge dieser Sprache vorauszuschicken.

2.1. Bezüglich der Benennung und Klassifizierung der kurd. Dialekte herrscht in der Fachliteratur keine Einheitlichkeit. Am verbreitetsten ist eine Einteilung in zwei Hauptdialektgruppen; dabei umfaßt die eine Gruppe das Kurd. im türk. Kurdistan (Ostanatolien), im nördl. Teil des Irak, im Nordwesten des Iran, im Nordosten Syriens und in der UdSSR; die zweite Gruppe bilden die Dialekte des südl. Teils von iran. und irak. Kurdistan. Als Bezeichnung der beiden Gruppen haben sich weitgehend die Termini „Nord-" und „Südkurd." durchgesetzt, die die geographischen Verhältnisse aber nur grob wiedergeben, wie die daneben existierenden Begriffspaare „West-" und „Ostkurd." (Socin 1898-1901, 250) oder „Nordwest-" und „Südostkurd." (Oranskij 1963, 135) zeigen, die im großen und ganzen dieselbe Dialektspaltung meinen. Im gleichen Sinn werden einander bisweilen auch die Namen „Kurmandžī" und „Soranī" gegenübergestellt (so v. a. in der sowjet. Kurdologie, cf. z. B. Kurdoev 1978, 20); dieses Begriffspaar ist terminologisch jedoch nicht einwandfrei, da *kurmandž* eine von den Kurden überregional gebrauchte Eigenbezeichnung ist (als Synonym zu *kurd*) und *soranī* sich ursprünglich nur auf die Mundarten der Ortschaften Arbil und Rewandīz in irak. Kurdistan bezieht. Die tiefergehende linguistische Erforschung des Kurd. in jüngerer Zeit hat

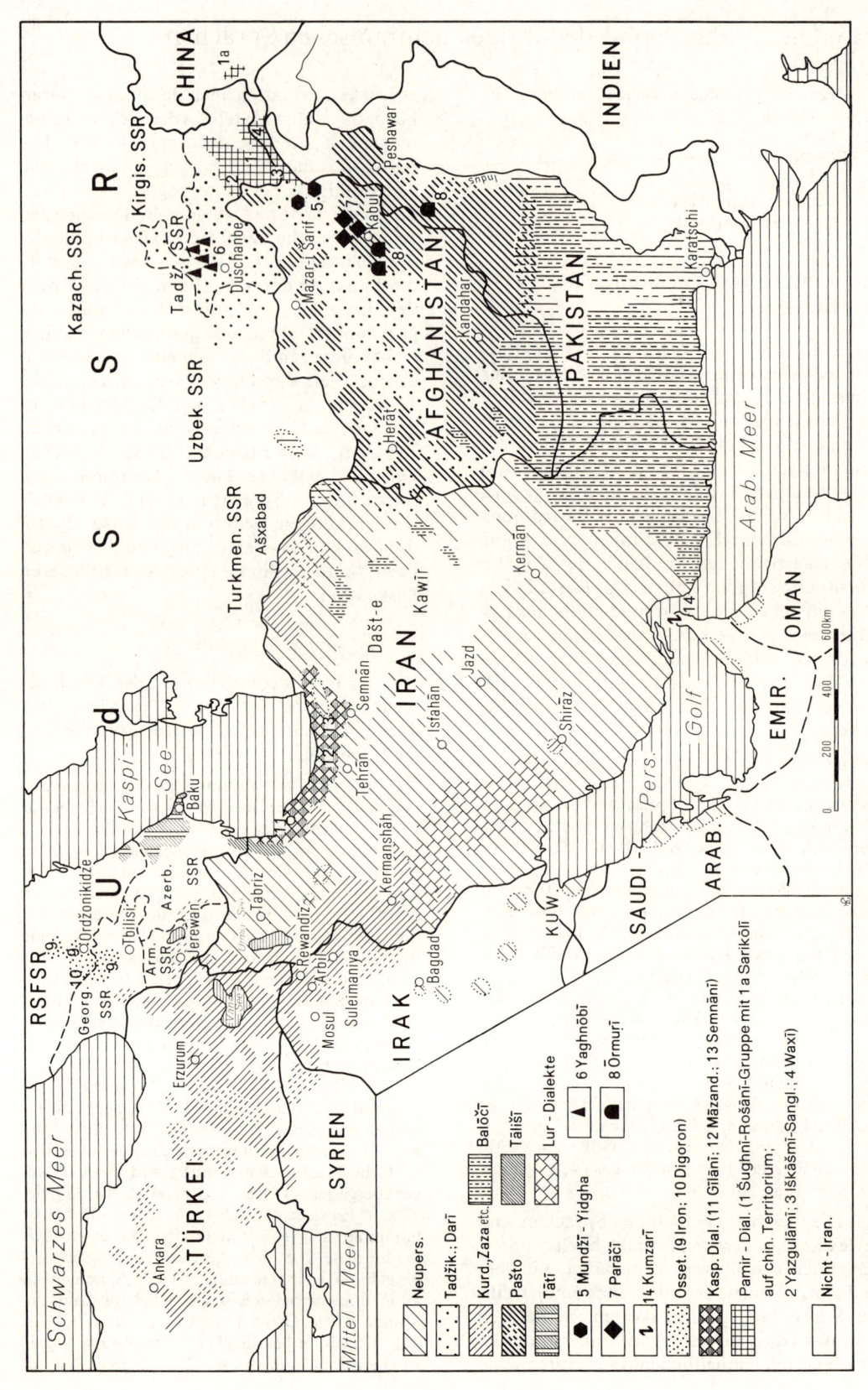

2482 XXIII. Lexikographie der Einzelsprachen VII: Die iranischen Sprachen

Karte 245.1: Skizze des Verbreitungsgebietes sonstiger neuiranischer Sprachen

245. Die Lexikographie der übrigen neuiranischen Sprachen

es nötig gemacht, von einer Dreiteilung der Dialekte auszugehen, wobei dem „Nordkurd." ein „Zentral-" und ein „Südkurd." gegenüberstehen (MacKenzie 1963, 162 ff.). Strittig ist das Verhältnis des Kurd. zu den benachbarten Gūrānī, Lurī und Zāzā, die bisweilen ebenfalls als kurd. Dialekte aufgefaßt werden (Wahby 1951, 31 ff.).

2.2. Eine zusätzliche Diskrepanz ergibt sich daraus, daß die Kurden zu verschiedenen Zeiten und in verschiedenen Gebieten unterschiedliche Schriftsysteme adaptiert haben. Während die seit den Anfängen kurd. Schrifttums im Mittelalter verwendete arab. Schrift bei den irak. und iran. Kurden noch heute in Gebrauch ist, benutzen die syr. Kurden seit 1931 ein Lateinalphabet, das nach dem Muster der modernen türk. Graphie ausgerichtet ist. Die Kurden der UdSSR schrieben 1921—29 in einer Abart der armen. Schrift; 1929 führte man ebenfalls das lat. Alphabet ein, das aber 1946 wieder durch die kyrill. Schrift abgelöst wurde. Sprachwissenschaftliche Werke bedienen sich zumeist eines in der Iranistik üblichen Umschriftsystems.

2.3. Für die kurd. Lexikographie ist festzuhalten, daß die bisher erschienenen Werke zum größten Teil an bestimmte Einzelmundarten oder Dialekte gebunden sind. Dies gilt vor allem für die mehr wissenschaftlich orientierten Wörtersammlungen, die mit Garzoni 1787 beginnen (erste kurd. Grammatik mit ital.-kurd. Wörterverzeichnis in „ital." Graphie; behandelt ist die nordkurd. Mundart von 'Amādiya, Irak, auch Bahdīnānī genannt); ebenfalls auf nordkurd. Mundarten basiert Jaba 1879 (erstes eigentliches „Wörterbuch", kurd.-franz. in arab. Schrift mit lat. Transkription; Erzurum, Osttürkei; Nordwestiran), unter den neueren Sammlungen dann z. B. Blau 1975 ('Amādiya und Djabal Sindjār, Irak). Die Liste bei Fossum 1919 (262 ff.) und das Wörterbuch von Mukriānī (1961) sind dem zentralkurd. Dialekt Mukrī (Nordiran) gewidmet (ein kleines etymologisches Glossar zum selben Dialekt bieten Smirnova/Ėjjubi 1985, 303 ff.). Bérésine 1853 stellt eine ost- und eine westkurd. Wörterliste gegenüber. — Auch unter den „Gebrauchswörterbüchern" gibt es solche, die einen bestimmten Dialekt repräsentieren, wie z. B. die beiden am Zentralkurd. von Suleimanīya (Irak) orientierten Arbeiten von Wahby/Edmonds (1966; kurd.-engl., Lateinschr.) und McCarus (1967; kurd.-engl., arab. Schr. mit lat. Transkription), oder auch Bakaev (1957; kurd.-russ., kyrill. Schr.), der das Nordkurd. der UdSSR darstellt (ebenso die orthographischen Wörterbücher von Avdal 1958 und Bakaev 1983). In immer größerem Maße ist hier aber ein Streben nach überdialektaler Verwendbarkeit zu beobachten; so erhebt z. B. Farizov 1957 (russ.-kurd., lat. Schr.) den Anspruch, allen „Kurmandžī"-Dialekten gerecht zu werden, während Kurdoev/Jusupova 1983 (kurd.-russ.; arab. Schr.) den gesamten „südkurd." Wortschatz („Soranī") repräsentieren wollen. Kurdoev 1960 (kurd.-russ.; lat. Graphie) basiert auf dem „Kurmandžī", enthält aber auch einige Einträge aus dem „Soranī". Das kurd.-franz.-engl. Wörterbuch von Blau (1965; lat. Graphie) versucht erstmalig, Bestandteile des nord- und südkurd. Wortschatzes gleichermaßen zu erschließen. Ein umfassendes kurd. Lexikon, das sowohl die vorhandenen Literaturwerke als auch die heutigen Dialekte berücksichtigen würde, bleibt ebenso ein Desiderat wie ein etymologisches Wörterbuch.

3. Pašto

3.1. Auch das Pašto oder Afghanische zerfällt in zahlreiche Mundarten, die sich in zwei Hauptgruppen zusammenfassen lassen: eine West- oder Südwestgruppe mit dem Zentrum in Kandahar (Afghanistan) und eine Ost- oder Nordostgruppe um Peshawar (Pakistan). In diesen beiden Zentren waren zunächst seit dem Mittelalter unabhängige literarische Traditionen entstanden, die eine Hochblüte im 17./18. Jh. erlebten. Nachdem das Pašto 1936 zur zweiten Staatssprache Afghanistans erhoben worden war (neben dem Darī, vgl. Art. 244), entwickelte es sich mehr und mehr zu einer einheitlichen Hochsprache, für die beide Dialekte gleichermaßen die Grundlage bilden.

3.2. Zur Niederschrift des Pašto wird seit jeher die arab. Schrift verwendet, die, dem Phoneminventar der Sprache entsprechend, um einige Buchstaben und Zusatzzeichen erweitert werden mußte. Auch die Graphie, für die es früher wegen der dialektalen Scheidung keine festen Normen gab, wurde erst in diesem Jh. fixiert.

3.3. Nach der Veröffentlichung der ersten Wortlisten (Güldenstädt 1791; Elphinstone 1815, 66 ff.; Klaproth 1823, 56 ff.) erschienen bereits in der Mitte des vorigen Jhs. recht umfangreiche Wörterbücher, die sich anders als im Falle des Kurd. nicht auf einzelne Mundarten bezogen, sondern von Anfang an an den literarischen Werken orientiert waren und so bis heute nicht an Aktualität verloren haben. Dabei ist vor allem das *Dictionary* von Raverty (1860; pašto-engl.) zu nennen, das immer wieder nachgedruckt wurde, obwohl die Graphie nicht mehr der heutigen Norm entspricht; von bleibender Bedeutung sind auch Bellew 1901 (pašto-engl./engl.-pašto) und Gilbertson (1932; engl.-pašto). Mit dem *Paxto qāmūs* (1951—54; pašto-npers.) und dem *Afğān qāmūs* (o. J.; npers.-pašto) publizierte die Afghanische Akademie in Kabul zwei philologisch besonders ergiebige Lexika; den Stand der heutigen Staatssprache verkörpern Aslanov 1966 (pašto-russ.), Zudin 1955 (russ.-pašto) und Lebedev/Jacevič/ Konarovskij 1983 (russ.-pašto-darī). Wie beim Kurd. fehlt auch für das Pašto noch ein eigentliches etymologisches Wörterbuch; erste Einzelstudien legten Geiger (1893) und Morgenstierne (1927) vor.

4. Ossetisch

4.1. Das Oss(etische) ist die Schrift- und Verwaltungssprache der Nordoss. ASSR (Zentrum Ordžonikidze, 1990 wieder in Vladikavkaz rückumbenannt; alter osset. Name: Dzæwdžyqæw) innerhalb der RSFSR und der Südoss. AO (Zentrum Cxinvali) innerhalb der Georgischen SSR in der Sowjetunion; die Grundlage bildet der Iron-Dialekt, dem der morphologisch und phonologisch archaischere digor. Dialekt im westl. Nordossetien gegenübersteht.

4.2. Anders als bei den beiden zuvor besprochenen Sprachen, die über eine rel. reiche literarische Tradition verfügen, entwickelte sich das Schrifttum des Oss. erst im Laufe der letzten hundert Jahre; dabei gingen gerade von lexikographischen Arbeiten entscheidende Impulse aus. Nachdem auch hier zunächst einige kleinere Wortlisten veröffentlicht worden waren (Pallas 1786—89; Reineggs 1796, 216f.; Klaproth 1814, 197ff.), erschien mit der „Ossetischen Sprachlehre" von A. Sjögren (1844) die erste eigentliche Grammatik mit ausführlichem Wörterverzeichnis; das hierin verwendete Alphabet auf der Basis der Kyrillica, das auch der in Vladikavkaz residierende Bischof Joseph für sein umfangreiches russ.-oss. Wörterbuch übernahm (Iosif 1884), bildete die Grundlage für das oss. Schrifttum, als dessen Initiator der Dichter Kosta Khetagurov (1859—1906) gilt. Mit dem dreibändigen oss.-russ.-dt. Lexikon von Vs. Miller (1927—34) wurde schon bald darauf ein deskriptives Wörterbuch vorgelegt, das den Anspruch erheben konnte, den oss. Wortschatz vollständig zu erfassen, und dabei neben dem schriftsprachlichen Iron als erstes und einziges auch den digor. Dialekt berücksichtigte; das Werk ist auch heute noch unentbehrlich, obwohl das Oss. seither zwei Schriftreformen durchgemacht hat (nach einer kurzen lateinschriftl. Episode in den 20er Jahren dieses Jhs. wurde wieder eine kyrill. Graphie eingeführt) und sich der heutige Zustand in zahlreichen Gebrauchswörterbüchern niedergeschlagen hat (Abaev 1970, Isaeva/Cagaeva 1978: russ.-oss.; *Osetinsko-russkij slovar'* 1962: oss.-russ.; Bagaev 1963: Orthographiewörterbuch; Gabaraev 1964: Erklärendes Wörterbuch). Einen besonderen Stellenwert innerhalb der neuiran. Lexikographie nimmt das etymologische Wörterbuch des Oss. von V. I. Abaev (1958—89) ein: Hier wird für jedes Lemma sowohl die iron. als auch die digor. Dialektform angegeben (in Umschrift); die Bedeutung wird durch Belege aus der oss. Literatur illustriert, wobei zahlreiche Zusatzinformationen zu Mythologie, Folklore und Geschichte anfallen. Nicht zuletzt durch dieses Werk gehört das Oss. in lexikographischer Hinsicht zu den besterschlossenen neuiran. Sprachen.

5. Balōčī

Mehr noch als die des Kurd. ist die Situation des Bal(ōčī) dadurch geprägt, daß seine Sprecher auf verschiedene Länder verstreut leben und keinerlei gemeinsame Kommunikationsbasis haben; so konnte sich nie eine eigentliche Literatursprache herausbilden. Lediglich in Pakistan gibt es bescheidene Ansätze zu einem eigenen Schrifttum (in arab. Schrift; Volksdichtung, Zeitungen); nicht durchsetzen konnten sich Bestrebungen in den 30er Jahren, für die Balōčen in der UdSSR ein lateinschriftliches Alphabet einzuführen.

Dementsprechend ist auch die lexikographische Erfassung des Bal. bisher noch nicht weit gediehen. Obwohl bereits im vorigen Jh. erste Glossare veröffentlicht wurden (z. B. bei Marston 1877), existieren mit Gilbertson 1925 (engl.-bal.) und Elfenbein 1963 (bal.-engl.) bis heute nur zwei umfangreichere Wörterbücher. Auch die etymologische Arbeit blieb bisher auf die Studien von Geiger (1890) beschränkt.

6. Schriftlose Sprachen

Es gab zwar Bestrebungen, auch andere neuiran. Sprachen zu Schriftsprachen zu machen wie z. B. bei den „kasp. Dialekten" Tālišī (mit einem lateinschriftlichen, später einem kyrill. Alphabet), Gīlānī und Māzandarānī (arab. Schrift); diese Versuche blieben jedoch ohne Erfolg. Für die meisten dieser Sprachen existieren deshalb nur wissenschaftliche Wortsammlungen oder Glossare (im Anschluß an Textproben und Grammatiken), die mit der vergleichenden Wortliste (u. a. Gīlānī, Māzandarānī) bei Bérésine 1853 und dem Tālišī-Vokabular bei Riss 1855 (38 ff.) beginnen. Besonders zahlreich sind die Arbeiten zu den „Pamirdialekten", die teils übergreifend gehalten (Morgenstierne 1929—38, Smith 1936, Badakhshi 1960), teils auf einzelne Sprachen bezogen sind (z. B. Capus 1889, Pachalina 1975: Waxī; Zarubin 1930: Orošorī; Sokolova 1960: Bartangī; Ivanov 1895, Tumanovič 1908, Zarubin 1960: Šughnī; dazu auch das kurze etymologische Wörterbuch von Morgenstierne 1974). Recht gut erforscht sind auch das Yaghnōbī (Benveniste 1955, Andreev/Livšic/Pisarčik 1957) und das Tātī (Miller 1905). Eigentliche Wörterbücher (von kleinerem Umfang) gibt es lediglich für das Yazgulāmī (Ėdel'man 1971), das Sarikōlī (Pachalina 1971), das Tālišī (Pirejko 1976) und das Gīlānī (Kerimova/Mamedzade/Rastorgueva 1980).

7. Literatur (in Auswahl)

7.1. Wörterbücher

Abaev 1958—89 = Vasilij Ivanovič Abaev: Istoriko-ėtimologičeskij slovar' osetinskogo jazyka. Leningrad 1958ff. [Bd. 1: A—K, 1958, 655 S.; Bd. 2: L—R, 1973, 448 S.; Bd. 3: S—T', 1979, 358 S.; Bd. 4: U—Z. 1989].

Abaev 1970 = Vasilij Ivanovič Abaev: Russko-osetinskij slovar'. 2. Auflage. Moskva 1970 [583 S.].

Afġān qāmūs o. J. = Afġān qāmūs, 'Abdullāh Afġānī nawīs. Kābūl 1957—58 [Bd. 1: ā—č, 552 S.; Bd. 2: h—ġ, 490 S.; Bd. 3: f—ī, 619 S.].

Andreev/Livšic/Pisarčik 1957 = Jagnobsko-russkij slovar', sost. M. S. Andreevym, V. A. Livšicem i A. K. Pisarčik. In: M. S. Andreev/E. M. Peščereva: Jagnobskie teksty. Moskva. Leningrad 1957, 223—391.

Aslanov 1966 = Martiros Grigor'evič Aslanov: Avgansko-russkij slovar'. Moskva 1966 [994 S.; 2. Auflage: Puštu-russkij slovar', 1985: 1007 S.].

Avdal 1958 = A. Avdal: Orfografičeskij slovar' kurdskogo jazyka. Erevan 1958.

Badakhshi 1960 = Shah Abdullah Badakhshi: A dictionary of some languages and dialects of Afghanistan. Kabul 1960.

Bagaev 1963 = Nikolaj Konstantinovič Bagaev (Bagaty N.): Iron ævzadžy orfografion dzyrduat. Ordžonikidze 1963 [400 S.].

Bakaev 1957 = Čerkes Chudoevič Bakaev: Kurdsko-russkij slovar'. Moskva 1957 [618 S.].

Bakaev 1983 = Čerkes Chudoevič Bakaev: Osnovy kurdskoj orfografii. Moskva 1983 [272 S.].

Bellew 1901 = Henry Walter Bellew: A dictionary of the Pukkhto or Pukshto language. Lahore 1901 [355 S.; Reprint Peshawar 1982].

Benveniste 1955 = Emile Benveniste: Une lexique du Yaghnobi. In: Journal Asiatique 243. 1955, 139—162.

Bérésine 1853 = E. Bérésine: Recherches sur les dialectes persans. 3. Teil. Casan 1853 [149 S.].

Blau 1965 = Joyce Blau: Dictionnaire kurde-français-anglais. Bruxelles 1965 [263 S.].

Capus 1889 = G. Capus: Vocabulaires de langues prépamiriennes. In: Bulletin de la Société d'Anthropologie de Paris 12. 1889, 203—216.

Elfenbein 1963 = Joseph Elfenbein: A Vocabulary of Marw Baluchi. Naples 1963 [106 S.].

Ėdel'man 1971 = Džoj Iosifovna Ėdel'man: Jazguljamsko-russkij slovar'. Moskva 1971 [354 S.].

Farizov 1957 = Ivan Omarovič Farizov: Russko-kurdskij slovar'. Moskva 1957 [781 S.].

Gabaraev 1964 = N. Ja. Gabaraev: Tolkovyj slovar' osetinskogo jazyka. Cxinval 1964.

Gilbertson 1925 = George Waters Gilbertson: English-Baluchi Colloquial Dictionary. Hertford 1925 [2 Bände].

Gilbertson 1932 = George Waters Gilbertson: The Pakkhto Idiom: A Dictionary. Hertford 1932 [Bd. 1: a—l, 496 S.; Bd. 2: m—z, 468 S.].

Iosif 1884 = Iosif Ėpiskop Vladikavkazskij: Russko-osetinskij slovar' s kratkoju grammatikoju. Vladikavkaz 1884 [579 S.].

Isaeva/Cagaeva 1978 = Zoja Georgievna Isaeva/Anastasija Dzaboelaevna Cagaeva: Kratkij russko-osetinskij slovar'. Moskva 1978 [616 S.].

Ivanov 1895 = K. G. Zaleman [Carl Salemann]: Šugnanskij slovar' D. L. Ivanova. In: Vostočnyja zamětki. Sanktpeterburg 1895, 269—320.

Jaba 1879 = Auguste Jaba: Dictionnaire kurde-français, publié par Ferdinand Justi. St.-Pétersbourg 1879 [463 S.; Reprint Osnabrück 1975].

Kerimova/Mamedzade/Rastorgueva 1980 = Aza Alimovna Kerimova/Achmed Kerimovič Mamedzade/Vera Sergeevna Rastorgueva: Giljansko-russkij slovar'. Moskva 1980 [465 S.].

Kurdoev 1960 = Kanat Kalaševič Kurdoev: Kurdsko-russkij slovar'. Moskva 1960 [890 S.].

Kurdoev/Jusupova 1983 = Kanat Kalaševič Kurdoev/Zara Alievna Jusupova: Kurdsko-russkij slovar' (Sorani). Moskva 1983 [752 S.].

Lebedev/Jacevič/Konarovskij 1983 = Konstantin Aleksandrovič Lebedev/Ljudmila Stanislavovna Jacevič/Michail Alekseevič Konarovskij: Russko-puštu-dari slovar'. Moskva 1983 [768 S.].

McCarus 1967 = Ernest N. McCarus: A Kurdish-English Dictionary. Dialect of Sulaimania, Iraq. Ann Arbor 1967 [194 S.].

Miller 1927—34 = Vsevolod Fedorovič Miller: Osetinsko-russko-nemeckij slovar'. Leningrad 1927ff. [Bd. 1: A—Z, 1827 [618 S.]; Bd. 2: I—S, 1929 [S. 619—1176]; Bd. 3: T—H, 1934 [S. 1177—1729. Repr. The Hague. Paris 1972].

Morgenstierne 1927 = Georg Morgenstierne: An Etymological Vocabulary of Pashto. Oslo 1927 [120 S.].

Morgenstierne 1974 = Georg Morgenstierne: Etymological Vocabulary of the Shughni Group. Wiesbaden 1974 [119 S.].

Mukriāni 1961 = Gīvī Mukriāni: Fərhəngi Məhā-bād. Həwlēr 1961.

Osetinsko-russkij slovar' 1962 = Osetinsko-russkij slovar'. S priloženiem grammatičeskogo očerka .. V. I. Abaeva. 2. izdanie. Ordžonikidze 1962 [662 S.].

Pallas 1786—9 = Peter Simon Pallas: Linguarum totius orbis vocabularia comparativa. Bd. 1 [411 S.]; Bd. 2 [491 S.] St. Peterburg 1786f. [Reprint Hamburg 1977f.].

Pachalina 1971 = Tat'jana Nikolaevna Pachalina: Sarykol'sko-russkij slovar'. Moskva 1971 [312 S.].

Paxto qāmūs 1951—54 = Paxto qāmūs. Kābūl 1330ff. [Bd. 1: '—s, 1951; 668 S. Bd. 2: š—ī, 1954; 322 S.].

Pirejko 1976 = Lija Aleksandrovna Pirejko: Talyšsko-russkij slovar'. Moskva 1976 [352 S.].

Raverty 1860 = H. G. Raverty: A Dictionary of the Pukkhto, Pushto or Language of the Afghans. London 1860 [diverse Reprints].

Smith 1936 = Helmer Smith: Wörterverzeichnisse. In: Hannes Sköld: Materialien zu den iranischen Pamirsprachen. Lund 1936, 131—317.

Wahby/Edmonds 1966 = T. Wahby/C. J. Edmonds: A Kurdish-English Dictionary. Oxford 1966 [179 S.].

Zudin 1955 = Petr Borisovič Zudin: Russko-afganskij slovar'. Moskva 1955 [1176 S.].

7.2. Sonstige Literatur

Blau 1975 = Joyce Blau: Le Kurde de 'Amādiya et de Djabal Sindjār. Paris 1975.

Elphinstone 1815 = Mount Stuart Elphinstone: Account of the Kingdom of Caubul. London 1815 [Reprint: Karachi u. a. 1972].

Fossum 1919 = Ludvig O. Fossum: A Practical Kurdish Grammar. Minneapolis 1919.

Garzoni 1787 = Maurizio Garzoni: Grammatica e vocabolario della lingua kurda. Roma 1787 [288 S.; Vocabulario: S. 79—282].

Geiger 1890 = Wilhelm Geiger: Etymologie des Balūčī. München 1890.

Geiger 1893 = Wilhelm Geiger: Etymologie und Lautlehre des Afghanischen. München 1893 [Abh. d. I. Cl. d. K. Ad. d. Wiss.; Bd. 20, 1. Abtl. S. 169—222].

Güldenstädt 1791 = Johann Anton Güldenstädt: Reisen durch Rußland und im Caucasischen Gebürge. [Hrsg. v.] Peter Simon Pallas. 2. Band. St. Petersburg 1791 [S. 535—544].

Klaproth 1814 = Julius von Klaproth: Kaukasische Sprachen. Anhang zur Reise in den Kaukasus und nach Georgien. Halle. Berlin 1814 [Reprint Leipzig 1970].

Klaproth 1823 = Julius von Klaproth: Asia polyglotta. (Awganish, Dugorisch, Ossetisch.) Paris 1823.

Kurdoev 1978 = Kanat Kalaševič Kurdoev: Grammatika kurdskogo jazyka. Moskva 1978.

MacKenzie 1963 = David Neil MacKenzie: Kurmandži, kurdi i gurani. In: Narody Azii i Afriki 1963, 162—170.

Marston 1877 = E. W. Marston: Grammar and Vocabulary of the Mecranee Balochee Dialect. Bombay 1877.

Miller 1905 = Vsevolod Fedorovič Miller: Tatskie ètjudy. Čast' 1. Moskva 1905.

Morgenstierne 1929—38 = Georg Morgenstierne: Indo-Iranian Frontier Languages. Oslo 1929ff. [Bd. 1: Parachi and Ormuri: 414 S. Bd. 2: Iranian Pamir Languages: 564 S.; Engl.-franz. Index: 66 S.].

Oranskij 1963 = Iosif Machailovič Oranskij: Iranskie jazyki. Moskva 1963.

Pachalina 1975 = Tat'jana Nikolaevna Pachalina: Vachanskij jazyk. Moskva 1975.

Reineggs 1796 = Jakob Reineggs: Allgemeine historisch-topographische Beschreibung des Kaukasus. Hrsg. v. Friedrich Enoch Schröder. 1. Theil. Gotha. St. Petersburg 1796.

Riss 1855 = P. F. Riss: O Talyšincach, ich obraze žisni i jazykě. In: Zapiski Kavkazskago Otděla Imperatorskago Russkago Geografičeskago Obščestva 3. 1855, 1—72.

Sjögren 1844 = Andr. Joh. Sjögren: Iron Ävzagaxur, d. i. Ossetische Sprachlehre [...] St. Petersburg 1844 [russ. Ausgabe: A. Šegren: Osetinskaja grammatika ... St. Peterburg 1844].

Socin 1898—1901 = Albert Socin: Die Sprache der Kurden. In: Grundriß der iranischen Philologie, I/2. Straßburg 1898—1901, 249—286.

Smirnova/Èjjubi 1985 = Iraida Anatol'evna Smirnova/Kerim Rachmanovič Èjjubi: Fonetika kurdskogo jazyka. Dialekt Mukri. Leningrad 1985.

Sokolova 1960 = Valentina Stepanovna Sokolova: Bartangskie teksty i slovar'. Moskva. Leningrad 1960.

Tumanovič 1908 = O. B. Tumanovič: Kratkaja grammatika i slovar' šugnanskogo narečija. Taškent 1908.

Wahby 1951 = Taufiq Wahby: Rock Sculptures in Gunduk Cave. Baghdad 1951.

Zarubin 1930 = Ivan Ivanovič Zarubin: Orošorskie teksty i slovar'. Leningrad 1930.

Zarubin 1960 = Ivan Ivanovič Zarubin: Šugnanskie teksty i slovar'. Moskva. Leningrad 1960.

Sonja Fritz, Berlin
(Bundesrepublik Deutschland)

XXIV. Lexikographie der Einzelsprachen VIII:
Die Sprachen des indischen Subkontinents
Lexicography of Individual Languages VIII:
The Languages of the Indian Subcontinent
Lexicographie des langues particulières VIII:
Les langues du sous-continent Indien

246. Lexicography of Old Indo-Aryan: Vedic and Sanskrit

1. Linguistic Background
2. Ancient Vedic Lexicography
3. The Classical *kośas* (Lexicons)
4. Later Indigenous Vedic Lexicography
5. Early Modern Lexicons in Europe
6. Peak of European Sanskrit Lexicography
7. Recent Lexicographical Works
8. Special Dictionaries
9. Comparative Etymological Lexicons
10. Work on a Comprehensive Historical Sanskrit Dictionary
11. Selected Bibliography

1. Linguistic Background

The origin of Indo-Aryan lexicography goes back to the last century of the 2nd millennium B.C. The Vedic Aryans carried their sacred hymns with them when they entered India at the beginning of that millennium. The transmission of these hymns was through continuous oral tradition; during the long period of the Aryan settlement, this tradition split itself into several schools. By 1500 B.C. these hymns were organized into four separate collections, meant for specific purposes: the Ṛg Veda for singing the praises of divinities, the Yajur Veda for the performance of sacrifices, the Sāma Veda for musical chanting and the Atharva Veda for magical incantations. In the course of oral transmission these collections were subject to slight alterations, leading to several recensions and versions. Pantañjali (c. 2nd cent. B.C.) has already recorded their number as 21 for the Ṛg Veda, 101 for the Yajur Veda, 1000 for the Sāma Veda and 9 for the Atharva Veda. As early as 1000 B.C. the continuous text of the Ṛg Veda was split up into its constituent word forms, each with its own accents. Thus from the continuous text (Saṁhitā-pāṭha) was derived its first modification known as the Padapāṭha; further modifications were also derived by taking two, three and four contiguous word-forms and arranging them in all their combinations and permutations in order to preserve the purity of the original received text. Due to this elaborate mode of oral transmission the Vedic texts have come down to us with very few variants. The analysis of the continuous text into its constituent word forms was one of the major steps which led to the development of Indo-Aryan lexicography.

2. Ancient Vedic Lexicography

The need for a collection of vocables is the first step in building up a lexicon. That such collections were attempted from the earliest times is recorded by Patañjali for Vedic and post-Vedic Sanskrit in his reference to a lost compilation called Śabdapārāyaṇa (recitation of words) attributed to Bṛhaspati, the divine preceptor. The only such collection which has come down to us is the *Nighaṇṭu*, consisting of three *kāṇḍas* (major sections). The first, divided into three chapters, deals with synonyms, listing groups of nouns indicating a specific object; the second deals with homonyms and the last with the names of divinities. The need for such lists arose from the fact that the language of the hymns differed in many respects from the current speech of the settlers whose contact with the local inhabitants in the region brought about changes in the phonology and morphology of Indo-Aryan. The obsolete forms required glosses, and the continuing effort to provide glosses gave rise to several ancillary branches of Vedic scholarship *(Vedāṅgas)* of which the following four have a bearing on lexicography: (1) *Śikṣā* (articulatory phonetics) since the transmission of the texts was through oral tradition; (2) *Vyākaraṇa* (grammatical analysis), (3) *Nirukta* (etymology) and (4) *Chandas* (prosody) which defined the exact nature of the Vedic verse. For the practical application of Vedic hymns in the observation of rituals and sacrifices in the daily life of the Vedic Aryans two more branches (5) *Kalpasūtras* and (6) *Jyotiṣa* (astronomy) constitute a supplement of Vedic studies. For the correct recitation of Vedic hymns a class of special treatises bearing the general title of *Prātiśākhya* (text dealing with each recension or version of a Veda) came into existence, dealing with articulatory phonetics and related matters. All of these branches were intended to preserve the purity of the sacred texts and their utilization in daily observances. The prose appendages to the Vedic texts, known as *Brāhmaṇas*, attempt to indicate the meanings of some of the expressions found in the hymns, and a large number of folk etymologies are given to explain some of them. This is the forerunner of the Nirukta literature which comments upon the Nighaṇṭu. It is clearly stated by Patañjali that the object of grammatical analysis is to validate the structure of speech and to describe the relationship between word and meaning as current in the usage of the community speaking that language. To elicit the meaning of expressions which have become obsolete recourse must necessarily be had to their derivation and to the study of their substitute expressions which have come into vogue in their place. Since usage is the primary indicator for determining the import of a word, Yāska (c. 7th cent. B.C.) cites Vedic passages in his Nirukta to illustrate the meaning of words listed in the Nighaṇṭu using an etymological approach. Yāska's is the sole representative of Nirukta literature which has come down to us, and it constitutes a running commentary on the Nighaṇṭu and deals with the words included in it. There is no alphabetical arrangement of the words as they are presented in groups indicating specific objects. Besides nouns the Nirukta illustrates the use of prepositions and particles with ample citations from Vedic passages and indicates how they bring about the subordinate meaning of nouns and verbs. So far as Vedic lexicography is concerned, it is the oldest extant work and represents the latest contribution to a continuous effort toward Vedic interpretation. The Nirukta tradition necessarily precedes that of Vyākaraṇa (grammatical analysis) which culminated in the work of Pāṇini (c. 6th cent B.C.) whose building blocks are (1) *prātipadika* (nominal stem), (2) *dhātu* (verbal stem) and (3) *praty-aya* (affix), versus the fourfold classification of Nirukta: (1) *nāman* (nomen), (2) *ākhyāta* (verbum), (3) *upasarga* (preverb/preposition) and (4) *nipāta* (particle). Among grammarians Pāṇini alone deals with accent as phonemic and while describing the current speech he has also noted peculiarities of Vedic expressions which differ from current usage. The Kalpasūtras also comment on Vedic hymns used in their ritual setting and provide a sort of commentary which is helpful in determining the meaning of words.

2.1. Since one of the founders of the Nirukta tradition, Śākaṭāyana (c. 8th cent. B.C.?), laid down the principle that every noun is derived from a verbal stem, this ancillary branch of Vedic grammar must have attempted such an analysis and tried to derive nominal stems from verbal stems. The *Aṣṭādhyāyī* of Pāṇini consists of 8 chapters and contains approximately 4000 *sūtras* (aphoristic or algebraic statements) and is accompanied by two lexicons, for verbal stems *(dhātupāṭha)* and for nominal stems undergoing specific grammatical operations *(gaṇa-pāṭha)*, respectively. The verb-list is divided into ten classes, each with its own class marker, and contains nearly 2000 stems. Their arrangement is in groups according to the alphabetical order of the final consonants, but within each group there is no further alphabetization according to initial letters. It may be noted that in both lists the lemmata are given as stems, except in a few cases in the nominal list. Meanings are not assigned to either list; however, meanings came to be assigned to the verbal list by about 300 A.D., following the pattern indicated in some of Pāṇini's rules. Pāṇini uses the locative case for illustrating meanings and this has provided the model for subsequent works. The meanings attached to the verb list range from one to many. The Nirukta tradition of denoting meaning was to use the word *karman* as a second member of a compound, the first of which denoted the meaning of the stem in the form of a nominal stem. The nominative case is used to denote the lexeme since, according to Pāṇini, it is the only case which indicates both gender and number. The meanings are usually supplied by means of synonyms, while occasionally the synonyms may be qualified by other qualifying words. An important contribution has been made by Patañjali in this respect. He criticizes this system of meaning explication by synonyms and suggests simple definitions while commenting on the meaning of the word *dhātu* (verbal stem, 1.3.1.). Occasionally Pāṇini indicates the gender of nominal stems. The verblist also utilizes special markers to indicate voice (active or middle) or some grammatical operation peculiar to a specific verb. In generating primary or secondary derivations of nominal stems from verbal stems he indicates the general scope of the meanings. Pāṇini's work was commented upon by a large number of succeeding grammarians, chief among them being Kātyāyana (c. 4th cent. B.C.) and Patañjali (2nd cent. B.C.); they provide definitions of many words used by Pāṇini. In turn these grammarians were commented upon by others in the succeeding centuries, providing further explanation of both Pāṇini's as well as Kātyāyana's and Patañjali's words.

3. The Classical *kośas* (Lexicons)

It is only in the later centuries of the Christian Era that lexicons of Sanskrit came to be compiled. The earliest available is the fragment found in the bundle of Weber Manuscripts purchased by the Missionary F. Weber in Leh in Ladakh; they are from Kashgar. The 8 leaves give fragments of a synonymical lexicon. The lexicons *(kośas)* produced in this period, when classical

Sanskrit literature was flourishing, belong under the caption of Kośa Literature. A search among catalogues of Sanskrit manuscripts deposited in various libraries has uncovered over 370 distinct lexicons, varying in extent as well as in scope, over a period of almost 1800 years. A number of citations in various works of commentarial literature refer to some lexicons which are not extant. Just as Pāṇini's work overshadowed all previous grammars, so also in the field of Kośa literature Amara's work under the title *Nāma-liṅgānuśāsana* occupies the premier position and enjoys a host of commentaries. Earlier lexicographers like Kātya and Vyāḍi are known only through quotations in commentaries and their works have not survived in later days. Amara's work is divided into three major sections called *kāṇḍas*. Unlike works produced before the Christian Era all lexicons produced in this era are in verse form. The first kāṇḍa deals with words relating to objects to be found in heaven; in the second words relating to objects found on the earth are listed; the third contains adjectives, compound words and a section on homonyms, indeclinables and genders. The arrangement is not alphabetical and is clumsy from the point of view of the user. But for the time of its production, when oral tradition was the most popular way of transmitting texts, it was adequate, since these texts were learned by rote and one could draw on them with the aid of one's highly developed memory. Such lexicons were intended mainly for the use of poets or literary artists. Following the pattern of the Nighaṇṭu, the kośas collected synonymous words in groups. Some, like Amara, have included a section of homonyms, while special homonymous lexicons came to be written in the following centuries. Puruṣottamadeva compiled a supplement to Amara under the title *Tri-kāṇḍa-śeṣa* on the same pattern. It is noteworthy that he has included words which are attested only in inscriptions, and the number of words added is quite large. This is indicative of the continuous search for new words or meanings to be found in the literature or current usage, not previously recorded by earlier lexicographers.

3.1. Among purely homonymous lexicons, mention should be made of the *Anekārtha-samuccaya* of Śāsvata. The arrangement here is peculiar. First are recorded words which require a whole verse to indicate their meanings; next follow words requiring half a verse, and finally those requiring only a quarter verse. Other works in this category are the *Abhidhāna-ratna-mālā* of Halāyudha (c. 10th cent. A.D.) and the *Vaijayantī* of Yādava-prakāśa; in this last lexicon words are arranged according to the number of syllables, then according to gender, and in each section again according to the order of the initial letter. As a lexicon it represents an improvement over previous works. It also contains a large number of words that are missing in other lexicons. The *Anekārtha-kośa* of Maṅkha (c. 12th cent. A.D.) is important in that he has suggested a large number of meanings not included in other lexicons. In all of these lexicons no literary references are given to illustrate the usage of the words. Of great significance are the lexicons compiled by the polymath Hemacandra (c. 12th cent. A.D.). The *Abhidhāna-cintāmaṇi* is a synonymical lexicon; the *Nighaṇṭu-śeṣa* is a glossary of botanical terms while the *Anekārtha-saṁ-graha* is a homonymical lexicon and is characterized by its arrangement of headwords according to the number of syllables and, within each group, according to the initial as well as final letters. The *Nānārtha-ratna-mālā* of Irugappa Daṇḍādinātha (c. 14th cent. A.D.) consists of six chapters, beginning with monosyllabic words, followed serially in succeeding chapters by words of 2, 3 and 4 syllables, the fifth chapter being of miscellaneous words and the sixth dealing with indeclinables.

3.2. Specialized glossaries were also compiled for specific technical subjects. The *Dhanvanti-nighaṇṭu* (c. 5th cent. A.D.) is a glossary of *materia medica* and lists names of medicinal plants and herbs with their synonyms. In addition to the vocables it also lists the properties of the herbs and plants. The *Paryāya-ratna-mālā* of Mādhavakara is a similar lexicon, but in addition it contains general vocabulary also. One of the largest collections of vocables pertaining to *materia medica* is the *Madana-vinoda-nighaṇṭu* of Madana-pāla (c. 14th cent. A.D.); it also deals with the properties of drugs. A noteworthy contribution to lexicography is the *Mahā-vyutpatti* which is a voluminous lexicon, containing not only the names of the Buddha and Buddhist technical terms, but also in addition pronouns, names of animals, plants and diseases, etc. A special feature of this lexicon is that it not only gives synonyms, but also phrases, verbal forms and complete sentences.

4. Later Indigenous Vedic Lexicography

While most Kośa works deal with general classical Sanskrit vocables, interest in Vedic studies was still maintained in the post-Christian Era. The great commentaries of Sāyaṇa, Veṅkatamādhava, and others provide a rich source for explanation of Vedic words. Some of the important commentaries on the Nirukta provide a fresh source of lexical importance. Durga's commentary (c. 14th cent. A.D.) is an important aid in fixing the text of the Nirukta as he cites every word of that text. An earlier commentary of Skandasvāmin and Maheśvara also provides important data on the meanings of Vedic words. The latest in the area of Vedic lexicography is the short Vaidikakośa of Bhaskararaya (c. 1880 A.D.), a compilation in seven sections.

5. Early Modern Lexicons in Europe

Except for the Pada-pāṭha and the small collection of words listed in the Nighaṇṭu and commented upon by the Nirukta, we have no remnants of the basic tools employed by the early lexicographers in the compiling of their lexicons; the same situation also obtains in the case of the classical kośas. How words were selected and from what sources is not made explicit in these works. It is to be inferred from general references in later kośas that work on extracting material from literary compositions helped the collection of texts to grow. It is only in the beginning of the 19th century that evidence for the manner in which the newer lexicons came to be compiled becomes evident.

5.1. With the inauguration of the Asiatic Society of Bengal in 1786 and the significant pronouncement of Sir William Jones about the probable relationship between the classical languages of Europe and Iran and India, and their descent from a common parent speech which was no longer extant, began a new era which led to the establishment of two major disciplines: Comparative Philology and Linguistics. Interest in the study of Sanskrit in the West assumed gigantic proportions, both in relation to Comparative Philology and the Vedic literature. Collections of Sanskrit manuscripts began to be made and deposited in various Western libraries. These became the source of much editorial work and the texts of the Vedas were published. Max Müller's edition of the Ṛg Veda provided a complete index verborum arranged alphabetically as the single words occurred in their full forms in that text. Roth and Whitney provided a similar one for the Atharva Veda. Böhtlingk provided a similar index of words in Pāṇini's grammar in his edition of it. Such collections of words and glossaries were frequent in the two centuries following the foundation of the Asiatic Society of Bengal. Chief examples are Stenzler's for the Gṛhlya-sūtras and Renou's (1954) for the sacrificial terms in Vedic literature and his special glossary (1942) of technical terms in grammar. Sorensen's index of personal names in the Mahābhārata is also a pioneer work in this direction.

5.2. The first bilingual dictionary of Sanskrit to be published is that of H. H. Wilson with assistance from the Pandits of the College of Fort William in 1818, with a revised edition in 1832. It is a digest of indigenous lexicography, principally based on six kośas. The second edition used one more kośa as well as the published parts of Śabdakalpadruma. The meanings are illustrated by suitable examples but are not traced to any literary sources. In the revised edition of 1832, use is made of the matter extracted from important literary works such as the *Śiśupāla-vadha, Hitopadeśa,* etc. and the total number of words listed is between fifty and sixty thousand. All of this work was done in India. But the interest in Sanskrit studies in Europe also provided the impetus for the teaching of the Sanskrit language, and a number of important aids in the form of Chrestomathies and Readers by Bhandarkar, Benfey, Bopp, Böhtlingk, Lanman, Lassen, Liebich and others provided miniature lexicons at the end as student aids. Bopp's Glossarium (1847) contains material drawn from both Vedic and classical Sanskrit texts on a small scale, extending to about 400 pages. Indo-European cognates are indicated, confirming in some cases the genuineness of some Sanskrit verbal stems which are not attested in Sanskrit literature. Citations are given from the selected texts for the usages recorded. Bopp sets the model for including preverbs under the verbal stem and not according to the normal alphabetical order of the compounded stem.

A gradual evolution from the glossaries attached to various readers for instruction in Sanskrit was in a way a serious preparation for more elaborate lexicons. Benfey's Glossary designed for his Handbook, was developed into a regular dictionary (1866) by combining the information and words contained in different chrestomathies and selections. One peculiar feature of this work is that compound expressions are listed under the second member with the result that second members are listed as head-words as in the case of *rāja-* for *rājan-* ending in a special affix at the end of a compound. Under each verbal stem are given not only the preverbs but also the class of particles defined by Pāṇini with the technical term *Gati*. The head-words are given in Devanāgarī script followed by Roman transliteration. Accents are not marked. References to citations are given, but none quoted. Indo-European cognates are listed at the end of each article. Meanings are indicated by Roman numerals and minor sections by Arabic numerals. Another dictionary in French was provided the same year by E. Burnouf on a similar basis for the use of students. Both Devanāgarī and Roman transliteration are used to indicate the head-words. Compounds beginning with a given word are listed under each in transliteration. Verbal stems are given in the first person singular; conjugated forms of the same are given separately under each stem. Within the limitations of the time and availability of Sanskrit literature Burnouf's aim was to present the meanings in the order of their historical occurrence and the primary meaning of each word was assumed from its etymological derivation. A revised version of Wilson's dictionary was undertaken by Th. Goldstücker and only the first volume appeared in 1856. It has taken on the aspect of an encyclopedia, containing a lot of information not strictly relevant to a lexicon. Citations are given in full, with the names of authors as well as works indicated, but with no references with which to check them. Manuscript sources appear to have been used in many places, but with no indications of their sources.

6. Peak of European Sanskrit Lexicography

The most important event in the 19th century was the appearance of the Sanskrit Wörterbuch (1855—75) of Böhtlingk and Roth which was published in 7 volumes in St. Petersburg. This dictionary is a monument of scholarship and has remained the principal source for scholarly research in the history of Sanskrit from Vedic times to the early classical period. It covers a total of 9478 large sized half-pages. Cooperation of various scholars enabled the editors to cover a number of valuable texts for extraction of material. At the time this monumental work appeared, the amount of Sanskrit literature available in print was limited in extent and consequently the editors could concentrate on a more detailed analysis of what was available. The long period involved in producing the printed volumes enabled the editors to add to and correct material in the earlier volumes as appendices to later volumes. The head-words are given in Devanāgarī characters, with the accent shown by a superscript over the accented syllable; so are the exhaustive citations, particularly from the Vedas and the two great Epics Mahābhārata and Rāmāyaṇa. Grammatical information is fully supplied as well as references to traditional lexicons. What is very significant is that in the absence of critical editions of texts, the editors have suggested emendations in some of the cited passages. Proper names as well as the names of authors and titles of works available in the language are listed. Inscriptional material is meagerly used, and similar is the case pertaining to specialized treaties in the arts, science and technology. Compound expressions are given as head-words in so far as nominal stems are concerned, but in the case of verbal stems the preverbs and particles associated with them are listed under the main entry of the stems themselves. The importance of this dictionary can be realized from the fact that it has made possible the production of such major contributions to the historical study of Sanskrit as Wackernagel-Debrunner's *Altindische Grammatik*. Indeed the editors of the critical edition of the Mahābhārata in Poona have often found the citations of this text in the dictionary helpful, revealing the wonderful coverage of material accomplished by the two lexicographers. Though a century has elapsed since the completion of that dictionary, it is still the standard by which all other lexicographical work in the field of Indo-Aryan is to be judged. A reprint of this lexicon has been much appreciated by discerning scholars. The different addenda and corrigenda which the editors had to append to later volumes, involving new words or meanings, necessitated the production of a shorter lexicon which incorporated all of the material of the larger work in one place in proper alphabetical sequence. This was done by Böhtlingk in 7 volumes (1879—89) covering a total of 2107 large pages with three columns on each page. The reduction was accomplished by eschewing all citations except when new words were added. Thus both versions, the larger edition and the shorter edition of the Petersburg Lexicons, provided the maximum number of entries. A later supplement to these is a volume of additions brought out by J. Schmitt (1924) as an addition to the shorter lexicon of Böhtlingk. Together, these lexicons have used about 500 texts for extracting their material and contain a little over 300,000 entries if we count the compound expressions as separate words. Since these three lexicons are in German, an English version is now being prepared in Delhi; this version should incorporate words found in the supplements of the main lexicon in their proper alphabetical order, with a revised transliteration of Avestan forms according to Bartholomae (see Art. 242) and of Greek words in Roman transliteration.

6.1. Following the tradition of H. H. Wilson, Monier-Williams brought out a *Sanskrit-English Dictionary* while holding the Boden Professorship in Oxford (1872) with a much enlarged revised edition in 1899. This work, while relying largely on the great Petersburg Lexicon, is organized on an entirely different plan. Moreover, in the revised edition new matter has been added from texts not utilized in the two lexicons. The main entries are indicated in Devanāgarī script, followed by transliteration in italic roman; and within this paragraph, a branch line similarly printed groups second members of compounds, with a further branch line in italic roman listing compounds of compounds. This arrangement is at once etymological and philological, and saves a lot of space. Thus within 1333 pages, each with three columns, the Editor has compressed all of the material to be found in the Petersburg Lexicons by excluding the citations except for new words or new meanings. Accent marks are indicated in the transliterated forms of words wherever they are available from Vedic texts. For those who have little access to the great Petersburg Lexicons in German, this dictionary has become the general standard of reference in the field of Sanskrit studies. This merit is not diminished by Böhtlingk's allegations that Monier-Williams' dictionary was plagiarized from the St. Petersburg thesaurus; the contention was studied by Zgusta (1988; Dvaikośyam) with the conclusion that Monier-Williams should be exonerated, at least to a large extent. Monier-Williams also brought out a kind of reverse lexicon, giving Sanskrit equivalents for English words (1851, 1861).

6.2. More recently, during the present century a number of important lexicons have appeared in Europe. Mention should be made here of A. A. Macdonel's *Practical Sanskrit Dictionary with transliteration, accentuation and etymological analysis* (1924). The Vedic language is illustrated from 120 hymns of the Ṛg Veda, Aitareya Brāhmaṇa and some Gṛhya- and Dharma-sūtras; classical Sanskrit is represented by about 40 works in all. A good number of words from grammatical and rhetorical works are included as an aid to reading commentaries on the poetical and dramatic works. The Vedic words are given with their accent marks in Roman transliteration, but no citations are included except to mark words as occurring in specific Vedic texts. Economy is aimed at by the inclusion of compounds under the initial member, while preverbs are given under the verbal stems. According to the Editor, he has tried to give the meanings in an orderly manner (i.e. "not in an arbitrary manner") and he has been able to cover about 50,000 entries within 382 pages. Macdonel also provided a full glossary to his *Vedic Reader,* drawing his vocabulary from the selections given therein, with complete references. In 1932 Stchoupak, Nitti and Renou published their *Dictionnaire Sanscrit-Français,* containing 897 pages, mainly addressed to students, excluding Vedic texts and Buddhist literature. Thirteen Upaniṣads and some 30 authors from the classical period were drawn upon for the selection of the vocabulary. Words are given in transliteration; compound words are given under the first member. Accent marks are not included. Verbal stems with preverbs are given as separate main entries. Under each verbal stem the basic forms are listed and they are not repeated under their prefixed forms. No citations or references are given. Mention should also be made of Capeller's *Sanskrit-Wörterbuch* (1887) and its English version (1891) containing about 50,000 entries in Devanāgarī script, with accent marks shown. Words from Vedic are restricted to a few while those occurring in the Brahmanas are excluded as being of no use to beginners.

7. Recent Lexicographical Works

With the interest shown by British administrators, beginning with Sir William Jones and the establishment of the Asiatic Society of Bengal, two significant monolingual Sanskrit dictionaries came to be compiled in Bengal: the *Śabda-kalpa-druma* of Rādhākānta Deva (1818 ff.) and *Vācaspatya* of *Tārānāth Tarkavācaspati* (in 7 volumes). The former was partially utilized in the second edition of Wilson's dictionary. Here, for the first time, Sanskrit vocabulary is presented in its proper alphabetical order, breaking the earlier tradition of the kośas. A similar lexicon was brought out by Sukhānandanātha from Agra entitled *Śabdārtha-cintā-maṇi* in four volumes (1865). In the lexicons produced in Bengal the principal source used was the kośa literature, most of which was still in manuscript form, with a few references from classical literature. Though citations were given, they could not be easily traced as many of these sources were still un-published.

7.1. With the establishment of Universities in India in the middle of the 19th century and the introduction of English as the medium of instruction, the need for providing for the study of Sanskrit according to the western system of education on the model of London University was the impetus for the production of Sanskrit-English lexicons towards the last decades of that century. Classical Sanskrit was the main subject studied at the high school and university undergraduate levels; yet existing lexicons produced in Europe lacked full citations and their price was beyond the ability of students to buy them. Moreover, new literature was being edited and published, providing fresh material. One of the earliest dictionaries to be issued was that of Principal V. S. Apte of Fergusson College in Poona under the title *A Practical Sanskrit-English Dictionary* (1890) concentrating on these aspects. Its emphasis is primarily on classical Sanskrit, and copious citations with exact references are provided from texts which students were generally expected to read for their courses. The success of this lexicon is seen in the number of its reprints in succeeding years and the production of a shorter version as a *Student's Sanskrit-English Dictionary*. A new revised edition in three volumes (1957—59) has appeared under the editorship of P. K. Gode and C. G. Karve, incorporating some new material. Advantage was taken of the major lexicons published earlier in Europe, but this material was copiously supplemented with full citations from the standard literary works usually read by candidates at university examinations. Accent marks are not indicated since the main appeal of the dictionary is to students of classical Sanskrit. Compounds are indicated serially under the first member. The dictionary includes almost all words occurring in post-Vedic literature, the six systems of philosophy, the Tantras, medicine, grammar, poetics, astronomy, music and similar branches of scientific and technical literature. Verbal stems occurring with preverbs are shown as major head-words in their regular alphabetical order. This lexicon helps in supplying the gaps to be found in earlier dictionaries by including new material extracted from texts not available to previous editors. School and college bilingual lexicons have appeared in almost all of the major languages of India, but they depend largely upon the more scholarly lexicons produced in India as well as in Europe.

8. Special Dictionaries

Already in the 19th century Grassman published his *Wörterbuch zum Rig-Veda* (1873). It purports to be not only a lexicon, but also a complete index verborum. The declensional or conjugational forms of nominal and verbal stems respectively, are indicated with exact references to all occurrences in the text. Meanings are indicated without citation or reference, but the grammatical forms occurring are listed in an orderly manner. Similarly the words occurring syntactically with such forms are also indicated with exact references to such occurrences. For the time of its publication, it is a monumental contribution as a lexicon of a single text. The Sanskrit used in Buddhist text differs considerably from classical Sanskrit since it is greatly influenced by Middle Indo-Aryan dialects. Edgerton's *Buddhist Hybrid Sanskrit Grammar and Dictionary* (1953) is a significant contribution. Special encyclopedias on *Śrauta* (tradition), *Dharma* (Law), *Mīmāṁsā* (one of the six systems of philosophy), and *Nyāya* (Logic) have appeared. A lexicon with full citations from the Upaniṣads by G. S. Jacob was published in 1891. In the field of science and technology, an *Āyurveda-mahā-kośa* with Sanskrit-Marathi meanings was published in 1968 (Joshi et al. 1968). Similarly, a *Bharata-kośa* on dramaturgy appeared in 1951 (Kavi 1951).

8.1. Of special significance for Vedic lexicography is the *Vaidika-padānu-krama-kośa*, an index verborum of every word-form occurring in the whole range of Vedic literature (Visva Bandhu Shastri 1942—65). This index provides the basis for a comprehensive lexicon of Vedic. Two lexicons dealing with grammatical literature have been compiled by Renou and Abhyankar. Sanskrit manuscripts deposited in various libraries all over the world have had descriptive catalogues or lists published. These were consolidated by Th. Aufrecht in his Catalogus Catalogorum, giving the names of authors as well as their works. This catalogue was revised by the University of Madras with note being taken of additional matter which came to light after Aufrecht's work. Specialized lexicons have also been published listing geographical names and names occurring in the Purāṇas.

9. Comparative Etymological Lexicons

A number of important contributions in the field of comparative etymology have been published. The most important are Sir Ralph Turner's *Comparative Etymological Dictionary of Indo-Aryan* which deals with the post-Sanskrit evolution of Indo-Aryan, and Mayrhofer's *Concise Etymological Sanskrit Dictionary* which takes Sanskrit back to its Indo-European setting.

10. Work on a Comprehensive Historical Sanskrit Dictionary

10.1. With a lapse of a century since the publication of the great Petersburg Lexicons and their offshoots, in which the corpus of basic texts extended to no more than 600 Vedic and post-Vedic works, a need was felt for compiling a new dictionary of Sanskrit on historical principles, drawing its material from a very much extended body of texts published since the beginning of this century. The plan, as originally proposed, of doing this work in Europe with Renou as the likely Editor, did not materialize. When the Deccan College in Poona was reestablished as a foundation for post-graduate study and research in the fields of Sanskrit, Linguistics, History and Social Sciences, the department of Linguistics embarked on this project with the active participation of Renou, drew up a minimum program and began work on this major lexicon in 1948. With the active support of the Government of India, a special department was set up to extract material from about 2000 texts, covering the whole range of Sanskrit literature, including inscriptions and coin legends as well as scientific and technical works. The project (directed at that time by the author of this article) received active support from the University Grants Commission, the Maharashtra State Government, UNESCO and its agency CIPSH. A scriptorium has been built up of all the material extracted housing more than 12 million excerpts from about 1500 texts. This lexicon under the new title *An Encyclopaedic Dictionary of Sanskrit on Historical Principles* began appearing in fascicules in 1976, covering volumes 1 and 2 and part 1 of volume 3, extending over 1638 large pages, the last entry being **adhi-maśa-hata-,** and corresponding to 21 pages of Monier-Williams' dictionary (Ghatage 1976). In its scope and treatment it far exceeds any of the great lexicons on the classical languages of Europe such as Greek and Latin, since Old Indo-Aryan has a continuous history of almost four millennia. The general principles on which this lexicon is being constructed is discussed in full in the introductory essay of the *Dictionary of Sanskrit on Historical Principles* (pp. I—XXVIII) with ample illustrations. When completed it will include material selected from the whole range of Sanskrit literature from the Vedic period up to 1800 A.D. and it will provide a source of inestimable value to scholars in their study of the history of words in their space-time context. Aside from the citations included in the lexicon, a full scriptorium is being maintained of all the material extracted. A good illustration is Kiparski (1980): *Pāṇini as a Variationist*.

10.2. One particular feature has to be noted with regard to accentuation. While the Petersburg Lexicons indicate accents wherever available, either from accented Vedic texts or from grammatical operations indicated by Pāṇini, later lexicons restrict them, if they include them at all, to accented words in Vedic. Since accent was phonemic in Pāṇini's time, as seen in such examples as aṣṭa-má- 'eighth' versus áṣṭam-a- 'one eighth', the two have to be indicated as separate head-words. Full use of the accent rules of Pāṇini have to be utilized for separating homophonous words where a different placement of the accent also changes the meaning, i.e. when accent is phonemic. The definitions of meaning should be clearly stated in order to be precise. Old Indo-Aryan tradition treats the role of meaning as a central point in philosophical, rhetorical and grammatical treatises; and the large number of commentaries on poetical, dramatical as well as technical and scientific literature provide ample material in this direction and they have been fully utilized in the Poona lexicon. When completed, it will mark a new achievement in the field of Indo-Aryan as well as Indo-European lexicography.

11. Selected Bibliography

11.1. Dictionaries

Abhyankar 1969 = K. V. Abhyankar: A Dictionary of Sanskrit Grammar. Baroda: Oriental Institute, 1969 [15 + 415 p.].

Apte 1890 = Vaman Shivram Apte: A Practical Sanskrit-English Dictionary. Poona 1890 [13 + 1196 p.; Revised edition by P. K. Gode/C. G. Karve, Poona: Prasad Prakashan, 3 vols.: I 1957, 631 p.; II 1958, 663—1296 p.; III 1959, 1297—1768 + appendix 112 p.].

Benfey 1866 = Theodor B. Benfey: Sanskrit-English Dictionary. London 1866 [xi + 1145 p.].

Böhtlingk 1879 = Otto Böhtlingk: Sanskrit Wörterbuch in kurzer Fassung. St. Petersburg 1879 [vols. 1—2: 299, 301 p.; 3—4: 265; iv + 302 p.; 5—7: 264, 306; 2,390 p.].

Böhtlingk/Roth 1855—75 = Otto Böhtlingk/Rudolph Roth: Sanskrit Wörterbuch. St. Petersburg 1855—75 [7 vols.: I 1855, xiii, 1142 p.; II 1858, 1100 p.; III 1861, 1016 p.; IV 1865, 1214 p.; V 1868, 1600 p.; VI 1871, 1506 p.; VII 1875, 1822 p.; Anastatic reprint, Wiesbaden 1966.]

Bopp 1813 = Franz B. Bopp: Glossarium Sanscriticum. Berlin 1830 [412 p.].

Burnouf/Leupol 1866 = Emile Burnouf/L. Leupol: Dictionnaire classique Sanscrit-Français. Paris 1866 [viii + 782 p.].

Capeller 1891 = Carl Capeller: Sanskrit-English Dictionary. Strassburg 1891 [viii + 672 p.].

Edgerton 1953 = Franklin Edgerton: Buddhist Hybrid Sanskrit: Grammar and Dictionary. New Haven 1953 [vol. 1 Grammar, xxx + 239 p.; II Dictionary, 627 p.].

Ghatage et al. 1976 = A. M. Ghatage et al.: An Encyclopaedic Dictionary of Sanskrit on Historical Principles. Poona 1976 [vol. I: 1 1976, lxxxviii + 216 p.; I: 2 1977, 217—504 p.; I: 3 1978, 505—719 p.; II: 1 1979, 721—976 p.; II: 2 1980, 977—1224 p.; II: 3 1981, 1225—1477 p.; III: 1 1982, 1479—1638 p.].

Goldstücker 1856 = Th. Goldstücker: A Dictionary of Sanskrit and English, with Supplement as English-Sanskrit Vocabulary. Berlin 1856 [ii + 480 p.].

Grassman 1873 = H. Grassman: Wörterbuch zum Rig-Veda. Leipzig 1873 [viii + 1776 p.].

Macdonnel 1924 = Arthur Anthony Macdonnel: A Practical Sanskrit Dictionary, with Transliteration, Accentuation and Etymological Analysis Throughout. London 1924 [xii + 382 p.].

Mayrhofer 1953—56 = Manfred Mayrhofer: A Concise Etymological Sanskrit Dictionary. Heidelberg 1953—56 [vol. I, xxxv + 570 p.; II, 700 p.; III, x + xii + 808 p.; IV, viii + 384 p.].

Monier-Williams 1851 = Monier Monier-Williams: A Dictionary: English-Sanskrit. London 1851 [xiv + 859 p.].

Monier-Williams 1872 = Monier Monier-Williams: A Sanscrit-English Dictionary. Oxford 1872 [XXV + iii + 1186 p.; Revised edition 1899, 2 + 1333 + 2 p.].

Radhakanta Deva 1886—92 = Radhakanta Deva: Śabda-kalpa-druma. Reprint edition ed by Varadaprasada Vasu, Calcutta 1886—92 [vol. I 1886, xiv + 8 + 315 p.; II 1886, 4 + 937 p.; III 1891, 792 p.; IV 1892, 565 p.; V, 555 p.].

Renou et al. 1932 = Louis Renou et al.: Dictionnaire Sanskrit-Français. Paris 1932 [iv + 897 p.].

Renou et al. 1942 = Louis Renou et al.: Terminologie grammaticale du sanscrit. Paris 1942 [vol. I, xi + 185 p.; II, iv + 163 p.; III, viii + 185 p.; Reprint in one volume, Paris 1957].

Renou et al. 1954 = Louis Renou et al.: Vocabulaire du rituel védique. Paris 1954 [iv + 176 p.].

Schmitt 1924 = Richard Schmitt: Nachträge zum Sanskrit Wörterbuch in kurzer Fassung v. Böhtlingk. Hannover 1924 [Reprint, Leipzig 1928, viii + 398 p.].

Sukhānanda-nātha 1864—85 = Sukhānanda-nātha: Śabdārtha-cintāmaṇi. Sanskrit Printing Press (vols. I—II); Udaipur (vols. III—IV). [vol. I 1864, 7 + 876 p.; II, 877—1469 p.; 1883, 684 + 52 p.; IV 1885, 1060 + 42 p.].

Vācaspati 1873 = Tārānātha Tarka Vācaspati: Vācaspatyam. Calcutta 1873 [vol. 1, 586 p.; II, 587—11292 p.; III, 1293—2412 p.; IV, 2413 bis 3002 p.; V, 3003—3834 p.; VI, 3835—4616 p.; VII, 4617—5442 p.].

Visva Bandhu Shastri 1942—65 = Visva Bandhu Shastri: Vedic Word Concordance (Vaidika-padānukrama-kośa). Lahore (vols. I—III); Hoshiarpur (vols. IV—V). [vol. I: 1 1942, cliv + 592 p. (reprint Hoshiarpur 1956); I: 2 1955, 595—1282 p.; I: 3, 1955, 1285—1872 p.; I: 4 1959, 1875—2702 p.; I: 6 1963, 3545—4016 p.; II: 1 1935, liv + 441 p. (revised Hoshiarpur 1973); II: 2, 1135 p.; III: 1 1945, 11 + 468 p.; III: 2 1945, 471—1185 p.; IV: 1 1958, 18—760 p.; IV: 2 1958, 763—1456 p.; IV: 3 1959, 1459—2115 p.; IV: 4 1961, 2119—2992 p.; V: 1 1964, 3 + 878 p.; V: 2 1965, 3 + 628 p.].

Wilson 1818 = Horace Hayman Wilson: Dictionary of Sanskrit and English. Calcutta 1818 [Revised edition 1832, x + 982 p.].

Wüst 1935 = Walter Wüst: Vergleichendes und Etymologisches Wörterbuch des Alt-Indo-arischen (Altindischen). Heidelberg 1935 [208 p.].

11.2. Other Publications

Acharya 1927a = Prasanna Kumar Acharya: Dictionary of Hindu Architecture. London 1927 [xx + 861 p.].

Acharya 1927b = Prasanna Kumar Acharya: Encyclopaedia of Hindu Architecture. Bombay 1927 [xxiv + 984 + 18 + 18 p.].

Aufrecht 1891—1903 = Theodor Aufrecht: Catalogus Catalogorum. Leipzig 1891—1903 [vol. I 1891, viii + 795 p.; II 1896, iv + 239 p.; III 1903, iv + 161 p.].

Aufrecht, ed. 1861 = Abhidhāna-ratna-mālā of Halayudha. London 1861 [viii + 400 p.].

Benfey 1853—4 = Theodor Benfey: Chrestomathie aus Sanskritwerken. Leipzig 1853—54 [vol. I Text, 1853, vi + 330 p.; II Glossar, 1854, 374 p.].

Bhandarkar 1868 = Ramkrishna Gopal Bhandarkar: Second Book of Sanskrit. Bombay 1868 [13 + 201 p.].

Böhtlingk 1839—40 = Otto Böhtlingk: Pāṇini's acht Bücher grammatischer Regeln. Bonn 1839—40 [2 vols., CXXV + 556 p.; Revised edition titled Pāṇini's Grammatik, Leipzig: 1887, xx + 480 + *357 p.].

Böhtlingk 1845 = Otto Böhtlingk: Sanskrit Chrestomathie. St. Petersburg 1845 [x + 452 + 2 p.].

Böhtlingk 1847 = Otto Böhtlingk with Charles Rieu: Abhindhāna-citāmaṇi of Hemacandra. St. Petersburg 1847 [12 + 443 p.].

Bopp 1832 = Franciscus Bopp: Nalus Mahabharti episodium. Berolini 1832 [15 + 235 p.].

Chaudhuri, ed. 1946 = Tarapad Chaudhuri, ed.: Paryāya-ratnamālā of Mādhavakara. Patna 1946 [x + 142 p.].

Deslongschamps, ed. 1839 = A. Loiseleur Deslongschamps, ed.: Aamara-kośa. Paris 1839 [xvi + 380 p.].

Durgāprasāda et al., eds. = Durgāprasāda et al., eds.: Abhidhāna-saṃgraha (A Collection of Ancient Sanskrit Lexicons) 1. Nāmaliṅgānuśāsana, 2. Trikāṇḍaśeasa, 3. Hārāvali, 4. Ekākṣarakośa, 5. Dvirūpakośa, 6. Abhidhānacintāmaṇi, 7. Abhindhānacintāmaṇi-pariśuṣita, 8. Anekārthasaṃgraha, 9. Nighaṇṭu-śeṣam, 10. Liṅgānuśāsanam, 11. Abhidhāna-cintāmaṇi-śiloñcha [6 + 38 p.].

Godabole, ed. 1888 = N. B. Godabole, ed.: Vaidika-kośa of Bhāskararāya. Bombay 1888 [8 + 3 + 32 + 25 p.].

Jacob 1891 = Jacob: Upaniṣad-vākya-kośa. Bombay 1891 [8 + 1083 p.].

Jhalkikar 1874—75 = Bhimacharya Jhalkikar: Nyāya-kośa. Bombay 1874—75 [267 p.; Revised ed. 1893 and 1912, 1001 + 36 + 13 p.].

Joshi 1937—74 = Laxmanashastri Joshi: Dharmakośa. 1937—74 [vol. I: 1 1937, xxiv + 598 + 19 + 84 + 82 + 4 p.; I: 2 1938, xxxi + 599—1589 p.; I: 3 1941, xxxiv + 1590—1988 + 139 + 162 + 10 p.; II: 1 1950, 2 + 155 + 20 + 524 p.; II: 2 1949, 14 + 15 + 8 + 525—986 + 31 p.; II: 3 1949, 3 + 18 + 987—1683 p.; II: 4 1953, 10 + 460 p.; III: 1 1959, 380 + 814 p.; IV: 1 1973, 18 + 529 p.; IV: 2 1973, 44 + 532—1164 p.; IV: 3 1974, 53 + 1166—1883 p.].

Joshi et al. 1968 = Venimadhava-sastri Joshi et al.: Āyurveda-mahā-kośa (Sanskrit-Sanskrit/Marathi). Bombay 1968 [vol. I, 19 + 804 p.; II 805—1729 + 47 p.].

Kavi 1951 = M. R. Kavi: Bharata-kośa. Tirupati 1951 [xxvi + 984 p.].

Kielhorn, ed. 1880—85 = Lorenz Franz Kielhorn, ed.: The Vyākaraṇa-mahābhāṣya of Patañjali. Bombay 1880—85 [vol. I 1880, 546 p.; II 1883, 493 p.; III 1885, 539 p.; 3rd ed. ed. by K. V. Abhyankar, Poona, vol. I 1962, 572 p.; II 1965, 504 p.; III 1972].

Kuvalayanada 1952—62 = Sarasvati Kuvalayanada: Mīmāṃsā-kośa. Wai 1952—62 [vol. I 1952, 84 + 603 p.; II 1953, 10 + 605—1200 p.; III 1954, 136 + 1201—1800 p.; IV 1956, 5 + 1801 — 2407 p.; V 1960, 14 + 2409 — 2995 p.; VI 1962, 11 + 2997—3631 p.].

Lanman 1884 = Charles Lanman: Rockwell Sanskrit Reader with Vocabulary and Notes. Boston 1884 [20 + 2 + 292 + 2 p.].

Lassen 1838 = Christianus Lassen: Anthologia Sanscritica. Bonnae 1838 [iv + 358 p.].

Liebich 1905 = Bruno Liebich: Sanskrit Lesebuch. Leipzig 1905 [10 + 6520 p.].

Patkar 1981 = Madhukar M. Patkar: History of Sanskrit Lexicography. Delhi 1981.

Raghavan, ed. 1949—77 = V. Raghavan, ed.: New Catalogus Catalogorum: An Alphabetical Register of Sanskrit and Allied Works and Authors. Madras 1949—77 [vol. I 1949, 36 + 380 p.; II 1946, 40 + 415 p.; III 1967, iv + 398 p.; IV 1968, 374 p.; V 1969, 359 p.; VI 1971, 4 + 2 + 412 p.; VII 1973, 10 + 389 p.; VIII 1974, 371 p.; IX 1977, 419 p.].

Sharma, ed. 1954 = B. Ramachandra Sharma, ed.: Nānārtha-ratna-mālā of Iruguppa Daṇḍādinātha. Poona 1954 [vi + 279 p.].

Sorensen 1904 = Sorensen: Index to Names in the Mahābhārata with Short Explanations and Concordance to Bombay and Calcutta Editions. London 1904 [vol. I: 1—4, XLI + 352 p.; II: 5—6, 353—809 p.].

Stenzler 1886 = Adolph Friedrich Stenzler: Wortverzeichniss zu den hausregeln von Āśvalāyana, Pāraskara Śāṅkhāyana und Gobhila. Leipzig 1886 [120 p.].

Umeshacandra 1914 = S. Gupta Umeshacandra: Vaidyaka-śabda-sindhu. Ed. by Nagendranath Sen. Calcutta 1914 [vol. I, 20 + 346 p.; II, 347 — 722 p.; III, 732 — 1212 + 4 p.; original ed. by Umeshacandra 1894, xviii + 1122 p.].

Whitney 1881 = William Dwight Whitney: Index Verborum to Published Texts of Atharvaveda. New Haven 1881 [= JAOS 12; 383 p.].

Zachariae 1897 = Theodor Zachariae: Die indischen Wörterbücher. Strassburg 1897 [45 p.].

Zachariae, ed. 1893 = Theodor Zachariae, ed.: Anekārthasaṃgraha of Hemachandra with Extracts from the Commentary of Mahendra. Vienna 1893 [xviii + 132 + 206 p.].

Zachariae, ed. 1897 = Theodor Zachariae, ed.: Maṅka-kosha. Vienna 1897 [7 + 73 + 160 p.].

Zgusta 1988 = Ladislav Zgusta: Copying in Lexicography: Monier-Williams' Sanskrit Dictionary and Other Cases (Dvaikośyam). In: Lexicographica 4. 1988, 145—164.

Sumitra M. Katre, San José, California (USA)

247. Lexicography of Middle Indo-Aryan

1. Middle Indo-Aryan (Sociolinguistic Conditions, Sources, Language Development)
2. Classical Indian Lexicography
3. Modern Lexicography
4. Current Projects and Desiderata
5. Selected Bibliography

1. Middle Indo-Aryan (Sociolinguistic Conditions, Sources, Language Development)

1.1. Middle Indo-Aryan is a term used by scholars in the 20th century; it characterizes the language(s) as being mid-way between Old and New Indo-Aryan, which is to a large extent correct when seen from the formal point of view of linguistic development; by implication this could be taken to mean that chronologically it was used after the former and before the latter, which is, however, not the case. The names given by the native grammarians are more adequate: *Prakrit* and *Apabhraṃśa*. As is frequently the case with names, these were also nicknames, interpreted according to persuasion as meaning respectively *"(prākṛta a.) 1. Original, natural, unaltered, unmodified. 2. Usual, common, ordinary. 3. Uncultivated, vulgar, unrefined, illiterate. 4. Insignificant, unimportant; trifling. 5. Derived from Prakṛti, q.v. 6. Provincial, vernacular (as a dialect); (prākṛtam) A vernacular or provincial dialect derived from and akin to Sanskrit. (Many of these dialects are spoken by the female characters and inferior personages of Sanskrit plays).* — *(apabhraṃśaḥ) 1. Falling down or away, a fall. 2. A corrupted word, corruption; (hence) an incorrect word whether formed against the rules of grammar or used in a sense not strictly Sanskrit. 3. A corrupt language, one of the lowest forms of the Prākrita dialect used by the cow-herds etc. (in kāvyas); (in śāstras) any language other than Sanskrit."* (cf. Apte 1970). It is thus clear from the above — and it has been established by later linguistic research — that Middle Indo-Aryan was used side by side with what was for most grammarians the norm, the refined language of *Sanskrit*, but for quite different purposes. Whereas Old Indo-Aryan was the language of the gods, the revealed word to be preserved by the priestly inner-circle, Middle Indo-Aryan was the language of the world, the man-made natural means of daily communication; there are, however, also Jainas who take the dialect of their teacher to be the language of the gods. In terms of lexicography this sociolinguistic situation implied that every effort was made by the pandits to memorize, define and describe *Sanskrit*, both Vedic and Classical; it is, therefore, possible to maintain that a scientific treatment of these languages was a matter of vital importance for the Brahmanic scholars; the common language, being everybody's idiom, could not expect similar attention from learned circles. It was only later when *Prakrit* and *Apabhraṃśa* in their turn became means of literary composition, that they were treated by the learned lexicographers. It was then realized that these languages contained not only elements relatable to, if not directly derived from, Old Indo-Aryan but also non-related vocabulary and structural features representative of local language substrata which modern research has shown to be of partly Dravidian and partly Munda types. Middle Indo-Aryan thus holds a key position for the understanding of linguistic development on the South Asian continent as it contains elements as old as, or even older than, Vedic as well as the germs of the New Indo-Aryan languages (cf. Turner 1968). Culturally Middle Indo-Aryan also stands out as the medium of two of the old un-orthodox religions of India, viz. Jainism and Buddhism. The study of Middle Indo-Aryan can therefore also throw light on the dark ages, the events surrounding the waning and waxing of classical orthodox Hindu culture in India — or the waxing and waning of the un-orthodox religions which may reflect the popular beliefs current even before the advent of Vedic culture.

1.2. The *Prakrit* and *Apabhraṃśa* sources which have been preserved cover a time span of about 1500 years, from approximately 450 B.C. to 1100 A.D. They comprise the canon and other literature of Theravāda Buddhism written in *Pāli*, a composite, perhaps partly artificial, language believed to represent more than one regional idiom. The rest of the Prakrits (Prakrit in the narrow sense of the word) have been given regional names. To this Buddhist literature also belongs the Dhammapada of the Northwest, written in *Gāndhārī*. This is also the language of the official documents found in Niya. Inscriptional Prakrits are found in all corners of the subcontinent with the exception of the far South, but including Ceylon. The edicts of Emperor Aśoka, whose administrative language was *Māgadhī*, constitute an important corpus of inscriptions; these underwent regional and other modifications when employed in the various parts of his empire. Prakrit for administrative (inscriptional) purposes predates inscriptional Sanskrit by several centuries. The Jaina canon accepted by the Śvetāmbaras is written in *Ardhamāgadhī* "half M." whereas *Jaina Māhārāṣṭrī* is used for a huge non-canonical literature. *Jaina Śaurasenī* is the name given by most modern scholars to the language of the Digambara canon, although some regard it as old *Ardhamāgadhī*. As the Prakrits became literary languages, their original regional application was extended to a more or less theoretically established, partly socially stratified all-Indian use. *Māhārāṣṭrī* was the language of the epics and lyrics which were also included in Sanskrit dramas, whereas *Śaurasenī* and *Māgadhī* were used for conversation among "female characters and inferior personages". *Paiśācī* is said to be the language of the original collection of tales, the *Bṛhatkathā*, which is now preserved to us only in its famous Sanskrit version, the *Kathāsaritsāgara* "the ocean of streams of story". *Apabhraṃśa* regional dialects have been preserved very sporadically and fragmentarily whereas literary Apabhraṃśa was used in numerous compositions written mostly by Digambara Jainas. To this sketch of Prakrit and Apabhraṃśa literature it must be added that much has been lost and much is still to be discovered and published, such as inscriptions or literature including scientific works such as dictionaries.

1.3. The characteristics of Middle Indo-Aryan as compared with Old Indo-Aryan include a gradual reduction in the number of vowels, and assimilation or even complete elision of consonants in certain positions resulting in a considerable simplification in the declension and conjugation systems. Non-Indo-Aryan vocabulary and syntax further enlarged the gap between Vedic-Sanskrit on the one hand and Prakrit-Apabhraṃśa on the other. In view of the many various dialectal differences which developed in the course of 1500 years, it is not surprising that a detailed analysis resulting in a critical dictionary is a desideratum which remains a somewhat distant goal.

2. Classical Indian Lexicography

2.1. The native lexicography of Middle Indo-Aryan is the lexicography of the literary language only. It depends wholly on Sanskrit models; one might say that native Middle Indo-Aryan lexicography and grammar are for the most part treated as sort of ancillary subdisciplines of their Old Indo-Aryan counterparts. The method adopted is somewhat inadequate. The method applied in Indian lexicography (cf. Vogel 1979 and Franke 1902) usually consists of a miscellany of approaches: with organization by subject, by form (length or order in the Indian alphabet) and by both in a hierarchy often explained by the lexicographer himself at the outset, but more often than not deviated from, for a number of reasons which modern linguists would call unscientific. The product, i.e. the dictionary, is not intended for reference but for learning by heart in the traditional oriental way of learning and remembering. The majority of Old Indo-Aryan lexica are in verses and so are the three extant dictionaries of Middle Indo-Aryan; they are metrical though not in rhyme. Lexicography means, as a rule, an inventory of nouns, which are invariably given in the nominative.

2.2. The oldest extant native dictionary of Middle Indo-Aryan is the *Pāiyalacchī* "beauty of the Prakrit language" (cf. Dhanapāla 1879). According to its concluding stanzas it was composed in A.D. 972/973. The author is a certain Dhanapāla who has expressed himself both in Sanskrit and Prakrit in a range of literary genres. It is a synonymic dictionary of 279 stanzas and consists of four parts of unequal length containing sets of synonyms requiring a verse, a hemistich, or a line respectively, ending with single words explained by one synonym and sporadically by a sentence extending over a hemistich. In the first three parts the names of gods, saints and sacred things are treated. This work is of historical interest only.

One of the great masters of Sanskrit lexicography, Hemacandra, is the author of the only other extant dictionary of literary Prakrit, namely the *Rayaṇāvali* "string of pearls", more commonly known as the *Deśī-nāmamālā (Deś.)* "garland of *deśī* nouns or provincialisms" (cf. Hemacandra 1880). The date of composition is not known, but it is supposed to be around A.D. 1158. It is both synonymic and homonymic. The 783 stanzas are divided into eight chapters; these are subdivided on formal principles into paragraphs which in their turn are split into two: words with only one meaning and homonyms. These, for their part, are arranged according to alphabetical order and length. Both Dhanapāla and Hemacandra profess to deal only with *deśī* words or "provincialisms" as defined by them. For a survey of discussions of the term, cf. Bhayani 1966 and Shriyan 1969; Kuiper 1968 deals with recent Western research. In actual practice they include also pure Sanskrit or only slightly prakritized Sanskrit. They also profess to include only nouns, but Dhanapāla also treats adverbs, particles, and affixes as well as verbal forms. As for the verbs, they are by tradition dealt with in the native grammars and thus fall outside of the present subject. Only the phenomenon of *dhātvādeśas* "root-substitutes" deserves mention. These are Prakrit *(deśī)* root substitutes for Sanskrit roots. The native grammarians classed them according to the equivalence of meaning and not according to their derivation. A study and alphabetical arrangement of the *dhātvādeśas* collected from five grammars has been made by Grierson 1924. Hemacandra also touches upon this phenomenon in his *ṭīkā* or commentary in Sanskrit to his *Deś.* In order to illustrate the meaning of the *deśī* word in question, Hemacandra adds examples in verses, probably composed by himself. Manuscripts of a work by Vimala Sūri, a combined Prakrit index and Sanskrit glossary to the *Deś.*, have been preserved but have not yet been printed (cf. Vogel 1979, 344). The *Deś.*, composed by a major grammarian of the classical school and built on the (now lost) work of a number of his predecessors, has acquired the status of being a standard reference book; there have, therefore, been attempts both by Western and by modern Indian scholars to translate it into English, but so far nobody has succeeded. As already mentioned, native lexicographers were not consistent in their distinction between Sanskrit and Prakrit *(deśī)* vocabulary. Consequently, native Sanskrit dictionaries have been shown by modern scholars to contain quite a number of Prakrit words. These have, however, not been collected into a supplement to Prakrit lexicography. In Sanskrit itself, what were considered irregularities, e.g. in the epics, have been proven to be Middle Indo-Aryan in Sanskrit garb. Finally, so-called Sanskrit may in some cases denote rather a form of *Sanskritized Prakrit* like that termed *Buddhist Hybrid Sanskrit* (Edgerton 1953) or *Jaina Sanskrit* (Sandesara/Thaker 1962).

2.3. *Pāli* stands apart from the other Prakrits as not representing one definite regional language; whatever its relation was to the language(s) spoken by the Buddha, it became *the* language of Theravāda Buddhism par excellence. Its history is thus closely connected with that of this particular school of Buddhism. Its only extant native lexicon was composed in the late 12th century in one of the countries of S. and S. E. Asia which was to preserve Theravāda Buddhism when it became extinct in India, namely Ceylon. Nevertheless, the author Moggallāna, traditionally to be distinguished from the grammarian of the same name, shares the same method with Dhanapāla and Hemacandra, namely that developed by lexicographers of Old Indo-Aryan, particularly Amarasiṃha in his Sanskrit dictionary. Inadequate though this may seem, whole portions of this Sanskrit dictionary were thus copied by converting the Sanskrit words into Pāli according to the normal rules of phonological development. This meant that Pāli words which did not exist in actual Pāli literature were codified because this Pāli dictionary (cf. Moggalāna 1865) came to represent the norm. *Abhidhānappadīpikā (Abh.)* is therefore somewhat misleading as a title, since the name implies that it proposes to throw light on the meanings of (Pāli) nouns only, not to form new ones. The *Abh.* is predominantly synonymic, and as for the lists of genuine Pāli synonyms, their beginnings can be traced back to certain commentarial-style portions of the canon (cf. Dhadphale 1971 & 1980, Norman 1983, 166). *Abh.* is also composed in verses. 1—179 deal with nouns belonging to the sphere of the celestial, 180—690 the terrestrial and 691—776 the miscellaneous, which ends the synonymic part. Verses 777—1135 deal with homonyms, whereas 1136—1203 treat indeclinables. The terms for the Buddha, Nirvāṇa and wise men are illustrated by 32, 46 and 24 synonyms respectively; the majority are given only one to five synonyms. The number of synonyms is, however, not used as a means of structuring the subsections of the dictionary. A commentary entitled *Abhidhānappadīpikatthasaṃvaṇṇanā,* but popularly called *Abh.-ṭīkā* (cf. Caturaṅgabalāmacca 1903) was composed by a Burmese officer of state, named after his title Caturaṅgabalāmacca, who lived in the middle of the 14th century. Another Burmese, a monk named Saddhammakitti, composed a short list of monosyllabic words, hence the title *Ekakkharakosa,* in the year 1465, again on the model of Sanskrit works (cf. Saddhammakitti 1865). There exists a *ṭīkā* (commentary) on it, written by a Burmese (cf. under Saddhammakitti 1865). As in the case of verbs of literary Prakrit, Pāli verbs are also listed in grammars. A separate study of the lists of Pāli roots in old native grammars has been made by Katre 1940.

2.4. The classical lexicography of Old Indo-Aryan and Middle Indo-Aryan has met with strong criticism from Western scholars. Some of the harshest reactions (cf. Hemacandra 1880, 8) were provoked by seemingly nonsensical elements which, as the standard of critical editing improved, were discovered to be misreadings and misunderstandings on the part of modern scholars and editors. Other features which to us seem unreasonable may have their background in factors no longer known to us, especially in Middle Indo-Aryan where so few lexica are extant. The fact is that the works established a norm for later users and are also historically important as the primary objects of the pioneering studies of Middle Indo-Aryan by modern Western Indologists.

3. Modern Lexicography

3.1. The new phase of Middle Indo-Aryan lexicography started in the 1820's and by then the political, cultural and linguistic scene had changed considerably from the period of classical lexicography. Whereas the speakers of one Middle Indo-Aryan dialect are presumed to have easily understood the other dialects, and a schooling in the classical culture as a rule included the literary Prakrits, a speaker of a New Indo-Aryan language will understand considerably less of other such languages and nothing of Middle Indo-Aryan. Of Old Indo-Aryan, Sanskrit has been the best preserved due to its sacred character in Brahmanism and Hinduism; in modern India 82% of the population are Hindus. Jainism is no longer a politically and culturally important religion, but is reduced to a sort of sect of Hinduism, only 0.5% of the modern Indian population being Jainas. The Jaina religious circles had to turn to Sanskrit for their later literature, and knowledge of the old canonical and other texts in Middle Indo-Aryan dwindled to become the privilege of the few. Theravāda Buddhism had migrated from India, and thanks to its missionary zeal had taken root elsewhere where it again enjoyed a politically and culturally domineering status in Ceylon and S.E. Asia. This required in the course of time not only monolingual dictionaries but also bilingual ones to and from totally unrelated languages such as Burmese and Thai (cf. the list of modern bi- and multilingual Pāli dictionaries of S., S.E. and E. Asia). Much of the modern lexicographical work on Middle Indo-Aryan is thus done outside of India, to the West or to the East of the country of origin.

3.2. Clough 1824 was the first to publish in print for the Western audience the old Pāli dictionary. At the same time Burnouf had collected a Pāli-French dictionary of 6.087 entries and some thirty years later Trenckner was preparing his edition of the *Abh.,* whereas Spiegel had worked out a lexicon Palicum of 10.000 entries. All of these works remained unprinted (cf. Bechert 1970). The actual publication of the *Abh.* dates from 1865. The Western version of it (Childers 1875) followed a decade later, and as might be expected, this pioneering work met with severe criticism of both its contents and its form; like so many other pioneers in Indology, the author was trained as a civil servant and had taken up Pāli studies on his own with some help from a Buddhist monk. Later on he was helped by some European philologists. Childers chose to arrange the Indian words according to the Western alphabet. His successors all preferred to arrange them according to the Indian sequence, on phonological lines. In all it contains some 12.000 words and nearly 40.000 references and quotations. Soon preparations were under way for a dictionary based on Western lexicographical principles (cf. also Kern 1916). Pāli texts had been published since the middle of the century. As an impetus to serious philological work on the sources, the Pāli Text Society was founded in London in 1881 by T. W. Rhys Davids "to foster and promote the study of Pāli texts". The text editions were, at the express request of the founder, furnished with full indices, forming the foundation for lexicographical work. Eventually the society was to sponsor the first modern Pāli dictionary; plans for a more comprehensive dictionary which had been worked out by an international group of scholars were shattered by the First World War. Some material had in the meantime appeared as articles in the journal of the society. The editors were both professional philologists, namely the first president of the society, Professor T. W. Rhys Davids, and a German assistant, Stede, and their work was supported by a grant from the München Academy (cf. Rhys Davids/Stede 1925). In view of the results achieved in Middle Indo-Aryan studies at the time the work was meant by the authors to be essentially preliminary; nevertheless, it remains the standard one-volume Pāli-English dictionary, containing many etymologies and Indo-European comparisons not acceptable today. The authors can rightly claim in the foreword that the days were over when one English word, i.e. 'desire' was used for a translation of sixteen distinct Pāli words — on the other hand they omitted those 900 Pāli words included in Childers 1875 which were taken over from Sanskrit by the *Abh.* in spite of the fact that their inclusion in the *Abh.* had given them a legitimacy of their own since it led to their being used by later Pāli poets (cf. Warder 1981, 204). In size this dictionary marks an increase over Childers' work by 50 % in head-words to some 18.000, and in references by 300 % to some 146.000.

The scale of the international critical dictionary of Pāli (Trenckner 1924) is planned to be ten times that of this preliminary dictionary. The first fascicle of the former was published at the time when the latter was being finished and it started out as a Danish undertaking, mainly because of the lexicographical material prepared in the 19th century by Trenckner on the basis of the rich Pāli manuscript collection in Copenhagen. The professed aim of this critical dictionary is the testing of the readings of the Pāli canon and the younger books appertaining to it. Thereby material should be provided for that higher criticism which checks the canon of Theravāda with the documents left by other Buddhist schools as well as with deeper strata of Jaina lore. The carrying out of this aim was naturally most consistent while the work was in very few hands, those of the initiators of vol. I, Dines Andersen/Helmer Smith (cf. Hinüber 1980 & 1986). However, as the project progressed extremely slowly, international collaboration with other scholars became essential; this resulted in occasional deviations from the original plan; at the end of vol. II the dictionary includes among its authors the leading specialists in Middle Indo-Aryan from England, France and Germany, while work for vol. III is being done in India. The present editor-in-chief is the Presi-

ULLOCO, and -CAṀ, A canopy, awning [उल्लोच]. Ab. 299.

Dictionary excerpt 247.1: *ulluco* (in: Childers 1875, 523)

Ulloka [ud + lok°] doubtful in its meaning; occurs at Vin 1.48 = II.209 as ullokā paṭhamaṇ ohāreti, trsl. *Vin Texts* by "a cloth to remove cobwebs", but better by Andersen, *Pāli Reader* as "as soon as it is seen"; at Vin II.151 the translators give "a cloth placed under the bedstead to keep the stuffing from coming out". See on term Morris *J P T S.* 1885, 31. — In cpd. ulloka-paduma at J VI.432 it may mean "bright lotus" (lit. to be looked at). See ulloketi.

Dictionary excerpt 247.2: *ulloka* (in: Rhys Davids/ Stede 1925, 156)

ulloka, *m.* [*sa.* *ulloka; *Amg.* ulloga, ulloya, ullova; *cf.* ulloca; *see* Morris, JPTS 1885 p. 31 and O. von Hinüber, "Pāli ulloka-", KZ LXXXI 1967, pp. 247 foll.; *cf. also* S. Kramrisch. "Einige Typen indischer Deckenmalerei", Artibus Asiae VIII 1940], **1.** *canopy, covering;* **2.** *protective covering (between bedstead and bolster*); — **1.** sace vihāre santānakaṃ hoti, ~ā paṭhamaṃ ohāretabbaṃ, Vin I 48,7 (~ato paṭhamaṃ ~aṃ ādiṃ katvā avaharitabban ti attho, Sp 980,22; uddhaṃ oloketabba-ṭṭhānaṃ, upari-bhāgan ti attho, Vmv; gehassa upari-bhāgato paṭṭhāya, paṭhamaṃ upari-bhāgo sammajjitabbo ti vuttaṃ hoti, Sp-ṭ) = Vin II 209,6 = 218,26 *quoted* Vism-mhṭ Be 1960 I 68,1; — **2.** ~aṃ akaritvā saṃharanti heṭṭhato nipphaṭanti (bhisiyo); anujānāmi ~aṃ karitvā santharitvā bhisiṃ onandhituṃ, Vin II 150,38 *foll.* (~aṃ akaritvā ti heṭṭhā cimilikaṃ adatvā, Sp 1218,31); — °-**pada**, *n., the word* "ulloka"; Bv-a 45,13; — °-**paduma,** *n., lotus-flower decoration on a canopy;* upari ~āni dassesuṃ, Ja VI 432,24; ākāsesu ~āni paṭhavi-talaṃ bhinditvā daṇḍaka-padumāni pupphiṃsu, Sv 575,27 (= heṭṭhā olokentāni viya tiṭṭhana-padumāni, Sv-pṭ II 227,7-8) = Thūp 22,34; — °-**mattikā,** *f., ceiling stucco, a kind of white siliceous earth or pipeclay;* matthake padara-cchannaṃ kāretvā ~āya lepetvā seta-kammaṃ kāresi, Ja VI 432,7; — °**āharaṇa,** *n., putting up a canopy* (?); sammajjana-paribhaṇḍādi-karaṇe olokitassa, ~ādisu ullokitassa . . . sambhavo, Spk-pṭ *Be* 1961 II 464,3.

ulloca, *mn.* [= *sa.* since Amarakośa; *prob. hyper-Sanskritization fr. prakr.* ulloya; *cf.* ulloka], **1.** *awning, canopy;* Abh 299 (uddhaṃ locyate bandhīyate ti ~aṃ, u-pubbo luca dassane, ettha bandhanatthe, Abh-sūci; *cf.* Sadd 337,32); **2.** *covering, coverlet;* Abh 974 (~e ti seyyādīnaṃ uparibhāge rajopātanivāraṇatthaṃ ṭhapite dussa-mayādike, ṭ).

Dictionary excerpt 247.3: *ulloka, ulloca* (in: Trenckner 1924, II, 554—555)

dent of the Pāli Text Society, K. R. Norman. The project is sponsored by the Royal Danish Academy of Sciences and Letters in collaboration with the Mayence (Mainz) Academy in West Germany. The costs of the first two volumes have been borne almost entirely by Danish foundations, but the funding of the production of vol. III is, as yet, an open question. At the present rate of progress the project will continue well into the 21st century. A sample article from the latest fascicle will demonstrate the advances made in method and scope during the first century of modern Pāli lexicography. As has so often been the case, Sanskrit figures only with a confusing backformation *ulloca* from *ulloya* whereas the Prakrit parallels show to what extent Pāli lexicography depends on the lexicography of all the (other) Prakrits. This latter is, unfortunately, still in its initial stages (cf. Dict. excerpts 247.1—3). While the critical dictionary is in progress, the Pāli Text Society is preparing a revised edition of its dictionary; the society is likewise publishing a concordance to the canonical texts, which is now two-thirds complete (cf. Woodward/Hare 1952). A much shorter index to the same literature has been published in recent years in India (*Pālitipiṭakasaddānukkamanikā* 1979); also a small German-Pāli dictionary has seen the day (Klar 1982).

3.3. The modern lexicography of the rest of the Prakrits started at the same time as Pāli lexicography. If the former has until now reached less spectacular results than the latter, it is not only due to the factors mentioned earlier, but also to the considerably more complex character of the sources of these Prakrits. If the impetus in modern Pāli studies came predominantly from English scholars, the greater part of Jaina and other literary Prakrit studies was initiated and followed up by German Indologists in collaboration with Indian specialists. The foundation was laid by Lassen 1837, to which was added, as the first Prakrit word list printed in the West, Delius 1839. Later in the century the old native dictionaries were published, along with a number of texts, by leading Indologists such as Pischel and Jacobi. Jacobi was directly and indirectly instrumental in the preparation of the first modern Prakrit dictionary. His pioneering translations of Jaina texts into a Western language met with appreciation in India, but some of his misinterpretations aroused dissatisfaction in Jaina circles; the practical outcome was the collection by a Jaina scholar of material for an Ardha-Māgadhī-English dictionary in 1910. Soon after, Jacobi publicly supported the plans by the Italian scholar, Luigi Suali, to work out the first practical Prakrit-English dictionary (cf. Suali 1912). The Indian material was sent to him as a major contribution, but these plans were shattered by the outbreak of the war in 1914. The Indian material was returned and this formed the nucleus of Ratnachandra 1923, which contains some 50.000 words drawn from nearly the whole of the Śvetāmbara canon and important supplementary works. Only that meaning which a word bears in the *sūtras* is given — others are excluded. A major practical difficulty in the production of the work was the obligation upon its author and collaborators to move incessantly from place to place in accordance with the prescriptions for Jaina monks as recorded in the canon. (The original rule allowed the monk to stay in a village one day, in a town five days only.) A much smaller work by the same author is Ratnachandra 1929. Simultaneously an encyclopedia of Śvetāmbara Jainism was published, a monumental undertaking having all of the characteristics of native Indian learning (Vijayarājendra 1913). Its particular relevance for lexicography is that it constitutes at the same time a concordance to the Jaina texts, including some 60.000 Prakrit words with Sanskrit synonyms, commentaries, etc. Another dictionary of Jaina Prakrit is Ānandasāgarasūri 1954. Contemporary with the big Jaina lexicographical works, the one-volume dictionary of Jaina and secular literary Prakrit which remains the standard handbook, Sheth 1928, was published. *Pāia-sadda-mahaṇṇavo* "the ocean of Prakrit words" contains some 70.000 Prakrit entries translated into Hindi with Sanskrit equivalents and references to texts and to the *Deś*. As was the case with the one-volume Pāli dictionary, so this author too saw his work as preliminary only, leaving it to later generations to produce *the* critical dictionary of Prakrit. Modern native dictionaries of minor importance are Jaini 1918, Kāpaḍiā 1941 and Pathak 1951.

4. Current Projects and Desiderata

A precondition for a critical dictionary is the availability of critical editions with indices. In order to further this work, the Prakrit Text Society was founded in 1953, on the lines of the old Pāli Text Society. The chief patron and one of the six founding members was the then President of the Republic of India, Dr. Rajendra Prasad. Included in their series of text editions was a slightly revised edition of the dictionary by Sheth. As a consequence of religious rules which made banking, money-lending, trade in precious stones and metals proper occupations for Jainas while forbidding all of these (and some more) to Hindus in general and Brahmans in particular, quite a number of Jaina families have acquired considerable wealth which is often channelled into supporting scholarly work on Jaina religious texts. The Prakrit Text Society enjoys their liberality, and so do other Jaina publication series with the Lalbhai Dalpatbhai Series, Ahmedabad, being the foremost. The basis for preparing a critical dictionary meeting modern standards of lexicography has thus been consolidated in recent years and a bibliographical survey of the Jaina part of it can be gained from Schubring 1935, supplemented with Tripāṭhī 1975 & 1981. Whereas the few secular Prakrit literary compositions such as Hāla's Sattasaī have been studied so well that lexicographical work can be based on them, the same is far from being true about the Prakrit passages of (Sanskrit) dramas. At a stage in the linguistic and cultural history when Prakrits were no longer universally understood, the tradition and manuscripts were provided with a *chāyā* "shadow" in Sanskrit, an arrangement which in its turn discouraged the study of the original Prakrit text. Etymologically and phonetically, such a replacement was entirely unjustified since it crippled the melodious play on ambiguity suggestive of two or even more meanings which is the characteristic of the Prakrit. Editors of dramas thus printed the Prakrit text along with "its" traditional *chāyā;* even if the dramatic Prakrits were the object of a study in their own right, the result was not necessarily an acceptable edition. In what has become a classic in the study of dramatic Prakrits, Rājaśekhara's *Kārpūramañjarī* or "Camphor-cluster", so called after the name of the heroine, the editor tries to justify his introduction of Prakrit forms against all of the eleven manuscripts at his disposal and he corrects the readings on the basis of native Prakrit grammar, although Prakrit grammars are not meant to be normative in the way that Sanskrit grammars are (cf. Konow 1901).

Inscriptional Prakrits have been the object of detailed study ever since the start of the Archaeological Survey of India by the British. The material from inscriptions is published for the most part in *Epigraphia Indica* and *Corpus Inscriptionum Indicarum* and, for the Sinhalese Prakrits, in *Epigraphia Zeylanica,* for which cf. De Silva 1979. In spite of the wealth of detailed philological analyses, in particular of the Aśokan inscriptions, no dictionary of this type of Prakrit material has seen the light of day; a lexical work based on a number of glossaries of the above-mentioned series centres of the Sanskrit inscriptions, and Prakrit words have been given in their Sanskrit forms (Sircar 1966).

A large scale project currently (1971—) under preparation at the Freie Universität in Berlin with the support of the Deutsche Forschungsgemeinschaft well illustrates the problems of Prakrit lexicography. A Jaina concordance (cf. Bruhn/ Tripāṭhī 1977) is being prepared based on two types of metrical commentaries of the Śvetāmbara canon, the Niryuktis and the Bhāṣyas, numbering at this stage 49.805 verses. Its purpose is primarily to trace the occurrence of verse parallels and their variants, but when completed it will serve also as an important contribution to linguistic studies. The Prakrit employed is often "above the niceties of grammar: to say nothing of syntax" (cf. Bruhn/ Tripāṭhī 1977, 76); the vocabulary is to a large extent not found — or not found with the required meaning — in the standard Prakrit dictionary. The reason is that the authors not only coined new words, but also strove to develop a vocabulary which was *only* understood in the community. As for the form, the question of some sort of standardization imposes itself when a word such as Sanskrit *yathā* has in this material no less than six different Prakrit correspondences, i.e. *jahā, jaha, jah', jadhā, jadha* and *aha*. Even if a system of rigid standardization is applied, the original forms will remain on record. The collected material will be published in partial concordances, starting with a bhāṣya concordance of 23.336 verses. The nature of the corpus of the Jaina concordance has led the compilers to give up the use of computers, because only the editors themselves could cope with the textual criticism of the uncommonly numerous variant readings. The availability of this technical aid has, on the other hand, led to the first project of a dictionary of *Apabhraṃśa* (cf. Mayrhofer 1983a & b). Owing to its strongly different phonological and morphological structure, this language is only to a very limited extent and indirectly included in general Prakrit lexicography. The Australian National University in Canberra possesses a considerable amount of technical equipment and is now processing a critically edited text in order to produce an index verborum and an *index formantium* (Colin Mayrhofer). The initiator invites other scholars to contribute to the project by listing other well-edited texts. While it may take some time before any tangible outcome is produced in this modern scheme, Indian scholarship has succeeded in bringing out by way of traditional methods a glossary of the *deśī* words contained in the works of the leading *Apabhraṃśa* author known to us, namely Puṣpadanta (cf. Shriyan 1969). He lived in the ninth century A.D., some 300 years before Hemacandra (12th century). One of the purposes of this recent study is to investigate the basis and authenticity of Hemacandra's *Deś*. Hemacandra was prepared for criticism, for he expressly states in the commentary to his dictionary that "to collect all the words known in different regions is not possible not even for the intellect of Vācaspati, the

Lord of Speech, even if he works for thousands of divyayugas ("heavenly eras")" (*Deś.* I, 4. commentary). While lexicographers may at times feel inclined to sympathize with the pessimistic outlook of the old Master, it remains a challenge to modern scholars of Middle Indo-Aryan to prove him wrong.

5. Selected Bibliography

5.1. Dictionaries

Note: No attempt was made at unifying the transcriptions and transliterations as used in available materials.

Ānandasāgarasūri 1954 = Ānandasāgarasūri: Alpaparicitasaiddhāntikaśabdakosah, Śresthidevacandalālabhāījainapustakoddhārakośa, 101; 115; 116; 125. Surat 1954—1974.

Apte 1970 = Vaman Shivram Apte: The Student's Sanskrit — English Dictionary. Delhi 1890 [8, 664 p. Reprint 1970].

Caturaṅgabalāmacca (14. cent.) 1903 = Caturaṅgabalāmacca: Abhidhānappadīpikaṭṭhasamvannanā or Abhidhānaṭīkā. Rangoon 1903 [I, 329 p.]; 1909 [452, 682 p.]; 1910—1911 [567, 598 p.]; 1956 [508 p.]; 1964 [XVI, 744 p.].

Childers 1875 = Robert Caesar Childers: A Dictionary of the Pali Language. London 1875 [XVII, XII, 624 p.; reprints Rangoon 1974; Kyoto 1976; Delhi 1979.].

Clough 1824 = Benjamin Clough: A Compendious Pali grammar with a copious vocabulary in the same language. Colombo 1824 [IV, 147, 20, 157 p.].

Delius 1839 = Nicolaus Delius: Radices Pracriticae. Bonn 1839 [XIII, 93 p.].

Dhanapāla (10. cent.) *1879* = Dhanapāla: Pāiyalacchī Nāmamālā, ed. G. Bühler. Göttingen 1879 [101 p.]; Bhavnagar 1916—1917; ed. Vikramavijaya Muni, Patan 1946—1947 [VIII, 43 p.] ed. B. J. Dośī, Bombay 1960 [VIII, 38, 112 p.].

Edgerton 1953 = Franklin Edgerton: Buddhist Hybrid Sanskrit Grammar and Dictionary. New Haven 1953 [XXX, 239; 627 p.; reprints Delhi 1970, 1973, 1977.].

Grierson 1924 = George Abraham Grierson: The Prakrit Dhātv-ādeśas [...]. In: Memoirs of the Asiatic Society of Bengal, vol. VIII, no. 2, 77—170. Calcutta 1924.

Hemacandra (12. cent.) *1880* = Hemacandra: Deśīnāmamālā, ed. R. Pischel. Bombay 1880 [XI, 300 p.]; ed. M. Banerjee. Calcutta 1931 [LXI, 248, 72 p.]; ed. P. V. Ramanujaswami. Poona 1938 [XXXI, 345, 121 p.] ed. B. J. Dośī. Bombay 1947 [VI, 448 p.]; ed. S. M. Sharma. Jaipur 1980 [II, 88; VIII, 311 p.].

Jaini 1918 = Jagmandar Lāla Jaini: Jaina Gem Dictionary. Arrah 1918 [156 p.].

Kāpadiā 1941 = Hīralāla Rasikadāsa Kāpadiā: The Student's English — Paiyā Dictionary. Surat 1941 [IX, 190 p.].

Klar 1982 = Helmut Klar: Deutsch—Pāli Wörterbuch. Wien 1982 [364 p.].

Moggallāna (12. cent.) *1865* = Moggallāna: Abhidhānappadīpikā, ed. W. Subhūti. Colombo 1865 [XV, 204, XI p.]; 1883 [XV, 340, XX p.]; 1893 [XXXIV, 528 p. (with index)]; 1900 [XVI, 272 p.; reprint 1938]; ed. T. Pannamolitissa. Colombo 1895 [II, 161, III p.]; ed. V. Siddhattha. Velitota 1900 [VI, 113 p.]; ed. Nanobhasatissa. Colombo 1929 [284 p.]; 1960 [307 p.]; rearranged in the order of the Indian alphabet: Akārādikosha, ed. Pāntiyesīlavamsa/Bellana Saranaṅkara, Colombo 1891 [II, 75 p.]. *Indian editions:* ed. Jñānānanda Svāmī. Calcutta 1913 [IX, 337 p.; reprint Allahabad 1918]; ed. Jinavijaya. Ahmedabad 1923 [162 p.]; ed. Bh. J. Bhāskara, 1974; ed. Dwarikadas Shastri. Benaras 1981. *Burmese editions:* ed. Paññālaṅkāra, in Abhidhānakkharāvalī, Mandalay 1896 [VI, 449 p.]; with Alaṅkā and Chan. Rangoon 1898 [IV, 165 p.; reprint 1899, 1906.] ed. with Nissaya by Kyaw-aung-san-tā Hsaya. Rangoon 1900 [446 p.]; Mandalay 1914 [XLVI, 456 p.]; Rangoon 1922 [I, 850 p.]; Mandalay 1959 [659 p.]; in Saddatthabhedacintā [...], Mandalay 1903 [118, VIII p.]; ed. with comm. Ganthipadavinicchaya [...]. Rangoon 1925 [X, 402 p.]; ed. Visuddhābhivamsa, in: Laksvai abhidhān. Mandalay 1937 [316 p.]; with Alaṅkā and Chan. Rangoon 1957, 1966, 1968, 1973 (ed. Icchāsaya) [264 p.]. *Mon edition:* Akkharavidhāna Abhidhānappadīpikā. Pak Lat 1910. *Thai editions:* ed. Jinavarasirivadhana. Bangkok 1913; index by N. Sarpraserith, 1921; 2nd revised ed. Bangkok 1965 [517 p.; reprint 1980.].

Pālitipiṭakasaddānukkamanikā 1979 = Pālitipiṭakasaddānukkamanikā ed. by the Sampurnanand Sanskrit Vishvavidyalaya, I—II. Varanasi 1979—1983 [954, 317 p.].

Pathak 1951 = P. B. Pathak: Dictionary for students, Ardhamāgadhī-English, English-Ardhamāgadhī. Poona 1951 [135 p.].

Ratnachandra 1923 = Ratnachandra: An illustrated Ardha-Magadhi Dictionary [...] with Sanskrit, Gujarati, Hindi and English Equivalents I—V. Ajmer 1923—1938 [LIV, 19, 511; VII, 1002; VI, 701; VII, 912, 17, 103; XIV, 857, 12, 21 p.; reprint Tokyo 1977].

Ratnachandra 1929 = Ratnachandra: Jainagam sabda sangraha. Kathiawad 1929 [818, 12 p.].

Rhys Davids/Stede 1925 = Thomas William Rhys Davids/William Stede: The Pāli Text Society's Pāli-English Dictionary. London 1925 [XV, 738 p.; reprints London 1972, 1979; Delhi 1975].

Saddhammakitti (15. cent.) *1865* = Saddhammakitti: Ekakkharakosa as an appendix to Moggallāna 1865 and later editions, both Sinhalese, Indian, Burmese and Thai, [approx. 10 p.]. ed. separately by Nanatilaka. Colombo 1886 [55 p.]; another (anonymous) ed., same year and place [113 p.]; included in Saddā-ngay. Rangoon 1898, reprint 1899; Saddā ṅay 15 coṅ pāṭh. Rangoon 1954; ed. with Burmese Nissaya. In: Saddā-ngay V, Rangoon 1898—1900 [1—139]; Ekakkharakosa-ṭīkā ed. in Saddā Ngay Ṭīkā, Rangoon 1918; Saddā-ṅaya-ṭīkā. Rangoon 1968?

Sandesara/Thaker 1962 = Bhogilal Jayachandbai Sandesara/Jayant P. Thaker: Lexicographical Studies in 'Jaina Sanskrit'. Baroda 1962 [241 p.].

Sheth 1928 = Hargovind Das Trikamchand Sheth: Pāia-sadda-mahaṇṇavo. A comprehensive Prakrit Hindi dictionary [...]. Calcutta 1928 [LVIII, 1229 p.]; 2nd slightly rev. ed., Varanasi 1963 [LXXII, 952 p.].

Shriyan 1969 = Ratna Nagesh Shriyan: Critical study of Mahāpurāṇa of Puṣpadanta [...]. Ahmedabad 1969 [VIII, 348 p.].

Sircar 1966 = Dines Chandra Sircar: Indian Epigraphical Glossary. Delhi 1966 [560 p.].

Trenckner 1924 = Vilhelm Trenckner: A Critical Pāli Dictionary [...], vol. I (a), Copenhagen 1924—1948 [XXXIX, 561, 99 p.]; vol. II, fasc. 1—16 (ā — odissaka), 1960—1989 [XXVI, 728 p.].

Turner 1968 = Ralph Lilley Turner: A Comparative Dictionary of the Indo-Aryan Languages I—III + addenda. London 1968—1985 [XX, VIII, 841; IX, 357; VIII, 235; XI, 168 p.].

Vijayarājendra 1913 = Manmohan Vijayarājendra: Abhidhānarājendraḥ Kośaḥ I—VII. Ratlam 1913—1934 [in all approx. 10.000 p.; reprint Delhi 1985].

Woodward/Hare 1952 = Frank Lee Woodward/ E. M. Hare: Pāli Tipiṭaka Concordance [...], vol. I (a—o). London 1956; II (k—n), 1973; III, fasc. 1—6 (p—bahujana), 1973—1984 [VI, 454; I, 542; VI, 358 p.].

Yuvācārya Mahāprajña 1980 = Yuvācārya Mahāprajña: Āgama Śabdakośa: Aṅgasuttāni śabdasūcī I. Ladnun 1980 [X, 823 p.].

5.2. Modern Bi- and Multilingual Pāli Dictionaries of S., S.E. and E. Asia

5.2.1. Ceylon

Buddhadatta, Ambalangoda Polvatte: Concise Pali-English Dictionary, Colombo 1949 [XII, 281 p.]; 1957 [249 p.]; 1968 [VIII, 294 p.] Pali-Siṃhala Akārādiya, Colombo 1950 [VII, 568 p.; reprint 1960.] English-Pali Dictionary, Pāli Text Society, Colombo 1955 [XIII, 588 p.; reprint London 1970.] Pāligadyapadyaracanā, Colombo 1962 [147 p.].

De Silva, J. W. Paulus: Pāli padamālāva 1. Ambalangoda 1970 [218 p.].

De Silva, W. A.: A vocabulary to aid to speak Hindu and Pali languages. Colombo 1903 [53 p.].

Jinavacanakośaya: Pāli-Sinhalese Dictionary of religious technical terms 1, a—o, 1956 [803 p.].

Karuṇāratna, T.: The Tribhashadarpana or Mirror of Sanskrit, Pali and Sinhalese. Colombo 1862 [III, 60 p.].

Nyanatiloka = Anton Gueth: Buddhist Dictionary [...]. Colombo 1950 [VI, 189 p.; reprints 1956, 1972; German ed. Konstanz 1953; French ed. Paris 1961; American ed. New York 1983].

Paññāsīha, Madihē: Siṃhala-Pāli śabdakoṣaya, vol. I, fasc. 1— (a—akkhabhañjana). Maharagama 1975 [XLIV, 4, 80 p.]. Tripiṭakadharmakoṣaya, vol. I, fasc. 1 — (Aṃsavaṭṭaka—akamma), Maharagama 1978.

Perera, Johanis: Bhaiṣajyadarpaṇaya; A glossary of medical plants in Sanskrit, Tamil, Elu and Pali, with their equivalents in Sinhalese. Colombo 1873 [II, 92 p.].

Piyatissa, Vidurupola: English-Pali dictionary. Colombo 1949 [XVII, 747 p.].

Sasanaratana, Moratuve: Vinaya Koshaya I (a). Panadura 1955 [XLIV, 198 p.]; II (ā—o), 1958 [199—374]

Sirisumedha, Kosgoḍa: Aṭṭhakathāsūci I (a). Kālaniya 1960 [318 p.] II (ā—o), 1962 [p. 319—630].

Sumangala, Maditiyavela: Pāli-Siṃhala Śabdakoṣaya. Colombo 1965 [XVIII, 528 p.].

Vimalabuddhitissa, Timbirigaskatuve: Śabda muktāvaliya. Borella 1959 [III, 225 p.].

5.2.2. India

Kausalyāyana, Ānanda Bhadanta: Pāli-Hindī kośa. Delhi 1975 [367 p.].

Tick Twon: A short dictionary of Buddhist Hybrid Pāli. Kalimpong 1969.

Upasak, Chandrika Singh: Dictionary of Early Buddhist Monastic Terms based on Pāli literature. Varanasi 1975 [III, 245 p.].

5.2.3. Burma

Agarwal, R. C. S.: Pali-Burmese Dictionary. Mandalay [339 p.].

Anekaitha, a Pali-Burmese glossary. Rangoon 1883 [140 p.].

Ba, Maung/Maung *Tha Din:* Pāḷi abhidhān, [...]. Rangoon 1914 [III, 326 p.].

Dhammapāla: Pāli-bhāṣā-saṅgahat-sā ôk: A Pali-Burmese Glossary. Rangoon 1895 [72 p.].

Hut Cin: Pāli-Mranmā abhidhān I—IV. Rangoon 1956—1959 [1380 p.].

Kyaw Aung Sanda Sadaw: Abidan neikthaya. Rangoon 1900 [446 p.].

Kyaw Yan: Mula hse abhidhān kyan: list of Pali and other Indian terms for drugs, with their Burmese equivalents. Mandalay 1912 [54 p.].

Lū To Kyin Sin Kyan, a dictionary of Buddhist doctrinal terms, chiefly Pali [...]. Mandalay 1912 [II, 17, 144 p.].

Moṅ Krī, Lay tī paṇḍita: Pāḷi-Abhidhān-Khyup. Rangoon 1914 [VIII, 595 p.]; 1954 [755 p.]; 1965 [VII, 524 p.] without year [622 p.].

Maung Tin, Pe: Student's Pali-English dictionary. Rangoon 1920 [VI, 257 p.; reprint 1961].

Myataung, Sayadaw: Paṇyat net kyān. Mandalay 1927 [394 p.].

Ñāṇuttara, Sayadaw: Tipiṭaka-Pāḷi-Mranmā abhidhān, Buddha Sāsanā Council, I—IV, 1 (a bis utrāsseyyaṃ); V—X (ka—da); XV (pha—bhovādī). Rangoon 1963—1982 [4.183; 5.236 p.; 824 p.].

Pāḷipada piṭaka-kyam ññvhan, I—IV (ya—sā-ḷakāra, Buddha Sāsanā Council. Rangoon 1972—1985 [904; 880; 928].

Pye, U: Porāṇa-mūla-kathā-abhidhān, 1926.

Somābhisiri, Sayadaw: Saddattharatanāvali, I—IV, 1927—1937.

Sudassana, U.: Pāṭhānusāra myanmā bhāsā kyan. Rangoon 1918 [117 p.].

Tejavantābhivamsa, Paṭhama kyo: Mranmā pāḷi abhidhān. Rangoon 1939 [327 p.].

Thvan Mran, U.: Pāḷi sak vohāra abhidhān, Pāli loanwords in Burmese and Sanskrit. Rangoon 1968 [627 p.].

Vaṇṇakkama-dīpaṇī. Rangoon 1882 [266 p.].

5.2.4. Thailand

Bunlǭi, Chalāt, Sathīan Phantharangsi & Prayut Payuttō: Photchanānukrom Bālī-Sansakrit-Thai-Angkrit, I—III (a—u). Bangkok [5100 p.].

Chandaburinarünath, Kitiyakara Krommaphra: Pali-Thai-English-Sanskrit Dictionary. Bangkok 1970 [117, 906 p.; reprint 1977].

Chettuphon, Samākhom Samnak: Khamphī phra aphithān sap chabap. Bangkok 1974 [IX, 321 p.].

Nakhprathip, Sarpraserith: Pāli-Thai Dictionary. Bangkok 1922.

Rātwǭramuni, Prayut: Photcanānukrom Phutthasāt. A Dictionary of Buddhism, Pali, English and Thai. Bangkok 1977 [374 p.].

Sonthirak, Plaek: Photcanānukrom Pāli Thai. Bangkok 1963 [IX, 358 p.].

Thailand, Ministry of Education: Photchanānukrom Bālī-Thai-Angkrit, fasc. 1—8 (a—niggacchati). Bangkok 1962— [1.280 p.].

Thailand, Ministry of Education: Sapthānukrom rākkham. Dictionary of Pali and Sanskrit words used in Thai. Bangkok 1971 [161 p.].

Yen-Nguan, Liang Sathirasut & Songvit Kaesri: A dictionary of Buddhism Thai-Pali-Chinese. Bangkok 1978 [866 p.].

5.2.5. Malaysia

Aik, Lim Teong: A glossary of Buddhist terms in four languages. Penang 1960.

5.2.6. Cambodia

Menetrier, E.: Le vocabulaire cambodgien dans ses rapports avec le sanscrit et le pali. Phnom-Penh 1933 [V, 17, 168 p.].

5.2.7. Vietnam

Ho Giac, Thich: Pāli Việt tuđiên. Saigon 1965 [100 p.].

5.2.8. Japan

Kumoi, Shōzen: Pawa Shōjiten. Kyoto 1955—1960 [IV, 353, 2 p.].

Midzuno, Kōgen: Pārigo Jiten. Tokyo 1968 [VIII, 384, 4 p.; revised ed. 1984].

5.3. Other Publications

Bechert 1970 = Heinz Bechert: Some side-lights on the early history of Pāli lexicography. In: Añjali. Felicitation volume presented to O. H. de Alwis Wijesekera. Peradeniya 1970, 1—3.

Bhayani 1966 = Harivallabh C. Bhayani: Studies in Hemacandra's Deśīnāmamālā. Varanasi 1966.

Bruhn/Tripāṭhī 1977 = Klaus Bruhn/Chandra Bhāḷ Tripāṭhī: Jaina concordance and Bhāṣya concordance. In: Beiträge zur Indienforschung, Ernst Waldschmidt [...] gewidmet. Berlin 1977, 67—80.

De Silva 1979 = Manikku W. Sugathapala De Silva: Sinhalese and other island languages in South Asia. Tübingen 1979.

Dhadphale 1971 = M. G. Dhadphale: The development of Pali lexicography. In: Proceedings of the Seminar in Prakrit Studies. University of Bombay 1971, 237—248.

Dhadphale 1980 = M. G. Dhadphale: Synonymic collocations in the Tipiṭaka: A Study. Poona 1980.

Franke 1902 = Rudolf Otto Franke: Geschichte und Kritik der einheimischen Pāli-Grammatik und Lexicographie. Strassburg 1902 [V, 99 p.; reprinted in R. O. Franke: Kleine Schriften, I. Wiesbaden 1978, 9—111].

Hinüber 1980 = Oskar von Hinüber: Bemerkungen zum CPD II. In: (Kuhns) Zeitschrift für Vergleichende Sprachforschung 94. 1980, 10—31.

Hinüber 1986 = Oskar von Hinüber: Das ältere Mittelindisch im Überblick, Österreichische Akademie der Wissenschaften, Phil.-Hist. Klasse, Sitzungsberichte, 467. Band. Wien 1986.

Katre 1940 = Sumitra Mangesh Katre: The roots of the Pāli dhātupāṭhas. Poona 1940.

Kern 1916 = Heinrich Kern: Toevoegselen op't Woordenboek van Childers. Amsterdam 1916 [179; 140 p. (two parts in one)].

Konow 1901 = Rāja-Śekhara's Karpūra-Mañjarī critically edited [...] by Sten Konow [...]. Cambridge, Mass. 1901.

Kuiper 1968 = Franciscus Bernardus Jacobus Kuiper: Review of H. C. Bhayani 1966. In: Indo-Iranian Journal X 1967—1968, 305—307.

Lassen 1837 = Christian Lassen: Institutiones linguae pracriticae. Bonn 1837.

Mayrhofer 1983a = Colin Mayrhofer: Proposal for an Apabhraṃśa dictionary. In: Indologica Taurinensia XI. 1983, 339.

Mayrhofer 1983b = Colin Mayrhofer: L'utilisation de l'ordinateur dans la réalisation d'un lexique apabhraṃśa. In: Bulletin d'Études Indiennes I. 1983, 87—88.

Norman 1983 = Kenneth Roy Norman: Pāli literature [. . .]. A History of Indian Literature, VII, 2. Wiesbaden 1983.

Schubring 1935 = Walther Schubring: Die Lehre der Jainas [. . .]. Grundriß der indo-arischen Philologie und Altertumskunde, III, 7. Berlin. Leipzig 1935.

Suali 1912 = Luigi Suali: On an intended Prākṛt Dictionary. In: Zeitschrift der Deutschen Morgenländischen Gesellschaft LXVI. 1912, 544—548.

Tripāṭhī 1975 = Chandra Bhāl Tripāṭhī: Catalogue of the Jaina Manuscripts at Strasbourg, Indologia Berolinensis, Band IV. Leiden 1975.

Tripāṭhī 1981 = Chandra Bhāl Tripāṭhī: The Jaina concordance in Berlin: a bibliographical report. In: Studien zum Jainismus und Buddhismus. Gedenkschrift für L. Alsdorf, Alt- und Neu-Indische Studien XXIII. Wiesbaden 1981, 301—329.

Vogel 1979 = Claus Vogel: Indian lexicography. A History of Indian Literature, V, 4. Wiesbaden 1979.

Warder 1981 = Anthony Kennedy Warder: Some problems of the later Pāli literature. In: Journal of the Pāli Text Society IX. 1981, 198—207.

Elisabeth Strandberg,
Copenhagen (Denmark)

248. Lexicography of New Indo-Aryan

1. Introduction: the Sanskrit Tradition
2. Modern Lexicography
2.1. Assamese
2.2. Bengali
2.3. Gujarati
2.4. Hindi
2.5. Kashmiri
2.6. Marathi
2.7. Oriya
2.8. Panjabi
2.9. Sindhi
2.10. Urdu
2.11 Other Languages
3. Selected Bibliography

1. Introduction: the Sanskrit Tradition

The tradition of Sanskrit (Skt.) lexicography continued for a long time, even after the period of Middle Indo Aryan (MIA), and the earlier dictionaries of Modern or New Indo Aryan (NIA) languages follow the trend. *Amarakośa* was translated into different languages, and it also provided a model for dictionaries of various languages. Dictionaries of synonyms *(ekārtha* or *samānārtha),* wherein words were grouped by subjects and which had the character of encyclopaedias and dictionaries of homonyms or polysemous words *(nānārtha* or *anekārtha)* were compiled in different languages. These dictionaries, in verse form, compiled generally by poets, contain selective word lists useful for composing poems. These dictionaries include only nouns — *nāmamālā* is the earlier word for dictionaries. There is no alphabetical arrangement as in the European style but some dictionaries present the arrangement of words on the basis of the last letters rather than of the initial letters.

The legacy of Skt. lexicography has been so strong that many dictionaries, even today, contain a large number of Skt. words or meanings not current in the language.

Another type of earlier dictionary consists of the bilingual vocabularies of Persian and NIA languages or vice versa compiled for administrative purposes.

2. Modern Lexicography

Real lexicographical work, in the modern sense, started with the beginning of contact with the west and obtained firm footing with the subsequent establishment of British rule. The practical needs of communicating with the local people for trade or administration motivated the British rulers and others to learn the local languages. The Christian missionaries, who came to propagate their religion, felt it necessary to learn the language of the people in order to be able to converse with them in their mother tongue. This led to the compilation of many word lists for unwritten languages and the writing of dictionaries and grammars for written languages. These dictionaries introduced a new feature, the inclusion of words from spoken languages collected from actual speakers along with words from literary languages. Bilingual dictionaries of NIA and English and vice versa, and similarly of Portuguese (only a very few), of different sizes and extent of coverage were compiled by Fort William College and Serampur Missionaries. Most of these dictionaries were general purpose reference dictionaries, meant to help the foreign speaker learn NIA languages or NIA speaker learn English. These dictionaries introduced most of the present lexicographical techniques viz. giving pronunci-

Map 248.1: New Indo-Aryan languages

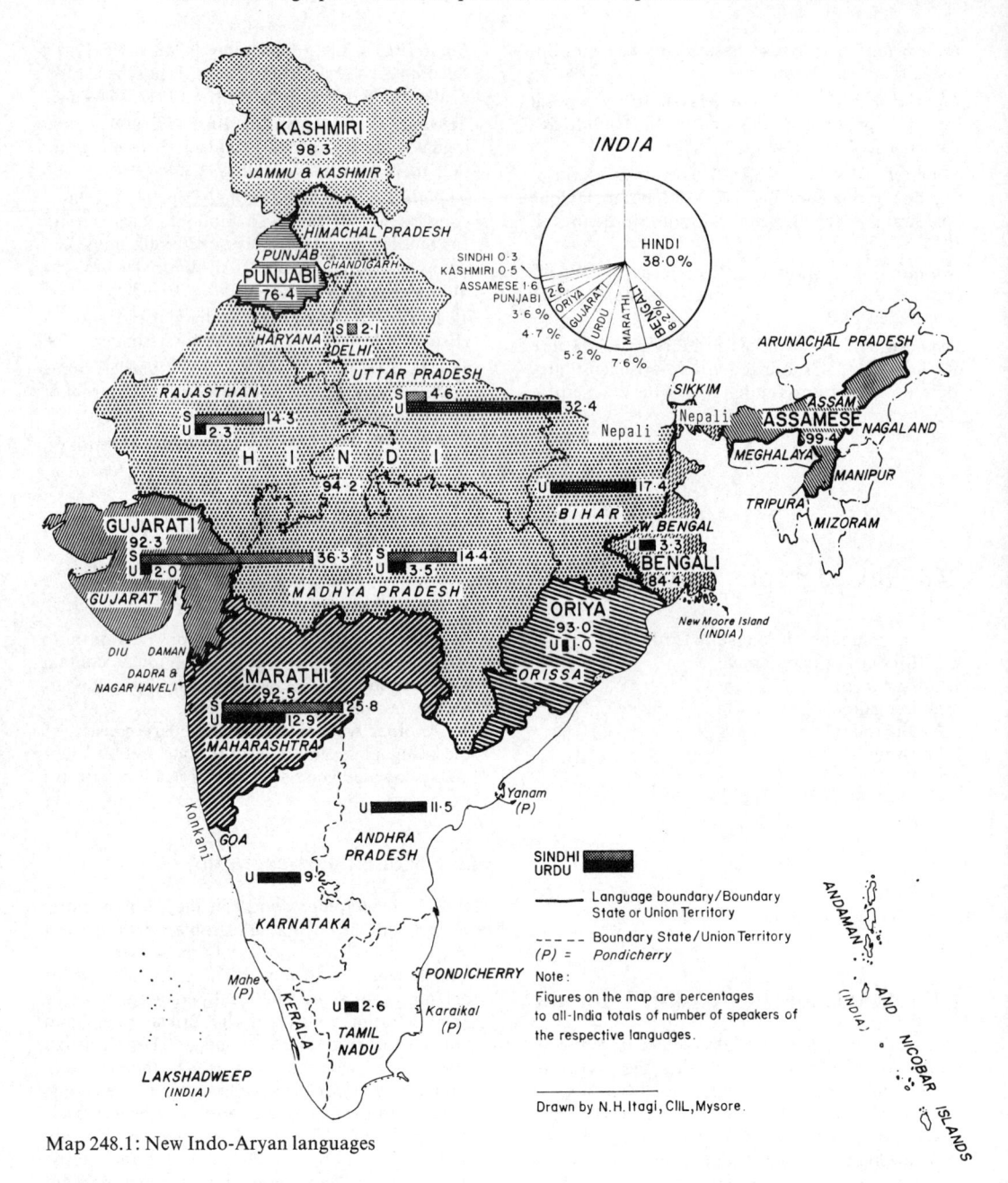

ation, parts of speech, arrangement of different meanings, labels and cross reference and the alphabetical arrangement of entries — though the last was not totally unknown. With the spread of the English education the need was felt for more and more bilingual dictionaries as a help to the students for learning languages. Some dictionaries in some languages have mono-bi-lingual character e.g. Gujarati-Gujarati English and vice versa.

Monolingual dictionaries, except in few cases, appeared late on the scene. Projects, individual or institutional, on larger dictionaries were taken up around the turn of the last century. These dictionaries provided a lot of encyclopaedic information. Some of them were inspired by the nationalistic zeal for the development of regional languages during freedom struggle days.

After independence, the NIA languages were required to play a greater role in the field of education, administration and mass communication. In order to meet the diverse needs different types of dictionaries have been compiled. The Central and State Governments have set up commissions or bodies for coining technical terms although earlier attempts are not negligible. The result has been not only the compilation of dictionaries of technical terms but also the enrichment and expansion of the word lists of general dictionaries. The need for interlingual communication among different language speakers has led to the compilation of bilingual dictionaries between NIA languages. And also, bilingual dictionaries of NIA and foreign languages have appeared. A brief account of the major lexicographical works in the major NIA languages follows.

2.1. Assamese

The first dictionary, *A Dictionary in Assamese and English* (Bronson 1867), contains 14 000 entries, covering the general vocabulary of the spoken language, *tatsama* words (i. e., borrowings from Sanskrit) used in texts, common idioms and figurative expressions. The words are given 'in the way as they dropped from the lips of the people' and written according to the system of orthography framed by the Baptist monthly Orunodoi (1846) so that the written form corresponds to actual pronunciation. Each entry contains the head-word, grammatical information and meanings in Assamese and English. The orthography and the meanings were questioned by Hemachandra Barua as 'absolutely wrong and not come to be desirable'.

Barua, in order to remove the shortcomings, compiled a new dictionary *Hemakośa* or an Etymological Dictionary of the Assamese language with Capt. P. R. T. Gordon (1900, several reprints) on the model of Webster and taking help from Wilson's *Sanskrit Dictionary* and Hindi and Bengali dictionaries. The orthography retains all of the consonants. The vowel length distinction is represented in the script. It gives the prevalent alternate Assamese spellings of *tatsama* words. The dictionary, with its abridged monolingual version *Asamiyā Bhāṣāra pārhāsalīyā abhidhāna* (The School Dictionary of Assamese, 1906), stabilized the spelling and grammar of Assamese. But the etymologies in this dictionary are not scientific as material from old Assamese literature is not exploited fully.

Chandrakānta Abhidhāna, A Comparative Dictionary (Assam Sahitya Sabha 1933, 36 000 words), gives the meanings of Assamese words in Assamese and English with adequate etymologies and illustrative examples from literature, especially from Buranjis or old Assamese chronicles. A second edition of the dictionary (1962), revised in the light of the linguistic studies of the language by B. K. Kakati, aims at being an all purpose dictionary, embracing old and mediaeval Assamese and giving revised etymologies and meanings.

Other Assamese-English dictionaries are meant for the use of students and there is very little special about them.

Of the English-Assamese dictionaries, *A Brief Vocabulary in English and Assamese* (S. R. Ward 1864) is the earliest. Among the many others, the *Anglo Assamese Dictionary* (1950), comprising a full range of words and phrases with their adequate and elaborate meanings in Assamese, is widely used. The *Pronouncing Anglo Assamese Dictionary* (B. N. Bhattacharya 1931) is remarkable in that it gives pronunciations and includes several appendices containing hints on Assamese grammar for non-Assamese, scientific terms etc.

A comprehensive monolingual dictionary of Assamese is still a desideratum. However, *Ādhunik Asamiyā Abhidhāna,* Modern Assamese Dictionary by the Publication Board, Assam (1971), a small and handy volume, may be useful for students and general readers.

2.2. Bengali

Modern Bengali lexicography begins in the 18th century. *Vocabularies Em Idioma Bengalia Portuguez* (Manoel da Assumpcan 1743) using Roman script, and *Ingarājī O Vangāli Vokebilari* (Up John 1793), using Bengali characters, are the two pioneer works in this field. The latter, designed to help natives to learn English and beginners to learn Bengali gives consonants before vowels in the arrangement of words.

William Carey's *A Dictionary of the Bengali Language* (1818—25, 2 vols., 80 000 words), an early comprehensive dictionary, includes words from both the literary and spoken languages. The entries give words in Bengali script and in Roman transcription, parts of speech and various meanings. Among the other Bengali-English dictionaries, and most of those compiled afterwards were meant for students, V. Gangopadhyaya's *Students' dictionary of Bengali words and phrases done into English* (1903) and the *Samsad Bengali English Dictionary* by Sailendra Biswas (1968) are popular, both giving detailed entries with phrases and set expressions.

In *The English Bengali Dictionary* by M. P. Thakur (1810), words are arranged in semantic groups. Thakur's *Bengali English Vocabulary* (1805) in Bengali and Romanised Bengali characters gives terms for theology, physiology, medicine, etc. Raj Kamal Sen's *Dictionary in English and Bengali* (1834, 2 vols.), a translation of Johnson's English Dictionary, gives a short list of French and Latin words and phrases commonly used by English authors. T. N. Barat's *Barat's pronouncing, etymological and pictorial dictionary of the English and of the Bengali language* (English to English and Bengali, Bengali to Bengali and English; 1887) is notable for its extensive coverage. *The Modern Anglo Bengali Dictionary* by Charu Chandra Guha (1916—19, 3 vols.) is by far the best and biggest comprehensive dictionary, including literary, scientific and technological words and terms.

Various other bilingual dictionaries with Bengali as both source and target language were compiled before and after Independence. Of these, *Bāṅglā Hindi Śabdakośa* (Gopalachandra Chakrabarti 1958), *Bāṅgāli Marāthī Kośa* (V. K. Apte 1925) in Nagari script, and *Bengalsko Ruskii Slovar* (Bāṅglā Rus abhidhāna, Bikova et al. 1957) are notable.

The first monolingual dictionary is *Baṅga Bhāṣābhidhāna*, Vocabulary of the Bengali language, (R. Vidyāvāgīśa 1817—18), containing a large number of Sanskrit *(tatsama)* words, a characteristic shared by many Bengali and other NIA language dictionaries, a notable exception being *Bāṅglā Śabdakośa* by Y. C. Ray Vidyānidhi (1913) dealing mostly with *tadbhava* (i. e., not immediately borrowed from Sanskrit) words of common usage. A notable feature of Bengali dictionaries, shared by some Marathi dictionaries, is the inclusion of either a skeleton grammar or some notes on grammatical features or pronunciation.

Bāṅglā Bhāṣār Abhidhāna (Jnanendra Mohan Das 1916, 2 vols. 75 000 words), a landmark in Bengali lexicography, is a pronouncing, etymological and explanatory dictionary, considered the most reliable dictionary for meaning and usage. Its etymologies are substantiated by comparative forms from different cognate languages. Borrowings are marked for the source language and form. The definitions are simple, precise and clear. The meanings are supported by examples of usage. It has an appendix on the rules of orthography and pronunciation.

Baṅgīya Śabdakośa (Haricharan Bandyopadhyaya 1933—44), another major achievement, includes all of the necessary and notable words from the works of old literature up to present day literature. It gives the etymologies of tadbhava words from Sanskrit to NIA, through Pali and Prakrit, as well as cognates in other NIA languages and the original word for borrowings. The entries contain copious examples from texts for clarification of meanings.

In the alphabetical arrangement of Bengali dictionaries, nasalized vowels come in sequence after oral vowels and before consonants. *Calantikā*, The Dictionary of Modern Bengali Language (Basu 1951; many eds., 30 000 words), a handy and commonly used dictionary, contains words collected mostly from the spoken language as opposed to other dictionaries which include words mostly collected from *Sādhu bhāṣā* (the higher variety). The entries give variant spellings, different meanings, grammatical category, etymology and synonyms. Its ten appendices give rules of orthography, pronunciation, some grammatical forms, technical terms etc.

Subalchandra Mitra's *Ādarśa Bāṅglā Abhidhāna* (1909, 1936) is a comprehensive dictionary containing current words, their etymologies and quite a few pieces of encyclopaedic information relating to history, geography, science, etc.

Among more than 400 other dictionaries the following are worth noting:

Laukika Śabda Kośa (Kamini Kumar Roy 1971, 2 vols.) is a dialect dictionary which gives a glossary of colloquial terms arranged in 14 broad semantic groups.

Bāṅglā Deśer Āñchalik Bhāṣār Abhidhāna, A Lexicon of Bāṅglā Deś Dialects, (Mohammed Shahidullah, Bangla Academy Dacca 1965) — prepared after extensive linguistic fieldwork — is the first exhaustive dictionary of regional and dialectal words in Bengali and it gives all of the district variations with their meanings. Homonyms are given separate entries. The front matter contains a detailed treatment of the orthography and pronunciation.

An Etymological Dictionary of Bengali (c. 1000—1800 A. D., Sukumar Sen 1971, 2 vols., 20 000 words) attempts to give accurate meanings and correct etymologies of words with a citation for each word.

A Dictionary of Foreign Words in Bengali (Govindalal Banerjee 1960) gives pronunciation, language of origin and sometimes illustrative sentences.

2.3. Gujarati

Mugdhavodha Auktika (Kulamandana Gani 1394), the only dictionary in Gujarati available prior to the 19th century, contains peculiar and uncommon words which were used in those days with their Sanskrit equivalents.

Father Drummond's *Glossary* (*Gujarati English* 1808, with a short grammar) is the first bilingual dictionary of Gujarati and it contains 463 Gujarati words with full explanations in English. *Dictionary of Goojaratee and English* (Mirza Mahomed Cauzim 1846, 15 000 words), the first major Gujarati dictionary, gives in several places Marathi, Hindustani, Zend, Turkish, Portuguese, French, Greek, Hebrew, Arabic and Persian equivalents. The spelling of Persian and Arabic words is given in Perso-Arabic script. It presents also the etymologies of words.

Among the number of Gujarati-English dictionaries, the majority of them designed for students, the *Pocket Gujarati English Dictionary* (Karsandas Mulji 1862, 10 000 words), *The Dictionary of Gujarati and English* (Shapur Edalji 1863, 27 000 words), and *Gujarātīno Gujarātī ane Ingrejikośa*, A Dictionary English-Gujarati and Gujarati-English (Cassidass & Balkrishnadass Brijbhukhandas 1885, 1147 pp.), are prominent.

Of the English Gujarati dictionaries, Nanabhai Rustomji Remina's *The Dictionary of English and Gujarati* (1857, 8 pts, 50 000 words) is one of the biggest. Robert Montgomery's *Dictionary of English and Gujarati* (1877), notable for the preciseness of its Gujarati equivalents, is a well conceived effort.

Among bidirectional bilingual (combined) dictionaries of Gujarati the following are more notable: *Students' modern combined dictionary*: English into English and Gujarati and Gujarati into Gujarati and English (D. M. Desai and K. M. Mehta 1969, 1122 pp.) and the *Standard English Gujarati Dictionary* by V. Vyas, and S. G. Patel, based on Webster's International dictionary, 1891 (1894).

In *Narmakośa* (poet Narmada Shankar Dave 1873, 25 000 words), the first major monolingual dictionary, words are divided into the categories of tatsama, tadbhava and foreign. The introduction gives a detailed history of the language. The definitions and explanations are clear and precise. The dictionary subsequently became the basis of many lexicographical works. *Gujarati Śabda Sangrah*, Gujarati Dictionary, (J. T. and T. G. Patel 1876) contains 1200 words not found in *Narmakośa*.

The Gujarat Vernacular Society (est. 1848, presently known as the Gujarat Vidyapith) launched a scheme of compiling an authentic Gujarati Dictionary with proper orthography. *Śuddha Śabda Pradarśana* (J. K. Bhakta), an etymological dictionary showing the correct form of words used in Gujarati with vocalic changes from Sanskrit, Persian, Arabic, English, Portuguese, etc. was an earnest effort in this direction. In order to standardize the spelling of Gujarati, the Vidyapith, inspired by Mahatma Gandhi, framed rules for consistent spellings which were incorporated in *Gujarati Jodnī Kośa* (1929). The most outstanding feature of this dictionary is the enunciation of spelling rules in which preference was given to current practice and certain optional spellings were permitted for certain words. The dictionary was instrumental in getting the spelling system fully established. But subsequently, because its scope was enlarged to include etymology, dialect, etc., its original orthographical character deteriorated and the originally useful dictionary developed into a disorganised jumble of words with fanciful etymologies.

The biggest monolingual encyclopaedic dictionary is *Bhagawad Gomandal* Bhagavatsimhaji (1944—1955, 9 vols., 2,81,377 words, 5,40,455 meanings and 28,156 idioms). Its major distinguishing features are the inclusion of occupational terms, especially from rural life, exemplification of meaning by quotation, the presentation of different types of detailed meanings, etc. The Gujarat Vidyapith has brought out different bilingual dictionaries with Gujarati as the source and target language. The following dictionaries of other types are remarkable: *Dhātumañjarī* (Haridas Hirachand 1865) and *Dhātukośa* (S. Taylor), the latter giving Sanskrit verbal roots with their Gujarati derivations and equivalents; etymological dictionaries include. *Vyutpatti Prakāśa* (M. R. Nilkanth

1881) and the *Etymological Gujarati English Dictionary* (M. B. Belsare 1895): the latter tracing etymologies back to Sanskrit. The intermediate forms in Pali and Prakrit and cognate words from other NIA languages are given.

2.4. Hindi

The earliest dictionary *Khaliqbārī* (in verse, ascribed to Amir Khusro 14th cent., 475 words with Persian, Arabic and Turkish synonyms) was compiled with the purpose of helping the Persian speaker learn Hindi. *Lughāte Hindi* (Mirza Khan 1675, 3500 words explained in Persian or with synonyms in Arabic and Persian) contains hints about pronunciation. J. Ferguson's *Dictionary of Hindustani Language* (1773, 2 Pts. English-Hindustani and Hindustani-English) is the earliest Hindi English dictionary with a brief grammar. W. Kirkpatrick's *Vocabulary Persian, Arabic and English* (1785) contains words adopted from Persian and Arabic in Hindi. John Gilchrist's *Anti-Jargonist* (1800, with an extensive vocabulary) and *Oriental Linguist* (1789, 10 000 words) are the best among the earlier dictionaries. These dictionaries had very limited coverage and audience and they employed few lexicographic techniques. Bigger dictionaries of larger scope and purpose appeared in the 19th century. John Shakespear's *Dictionary: Hindustani English* (1817, 70 000 words) which made use of all available dictionaries and other materials is the first organised lexicographic work giving words in Devanagari and marking the origin of words by language name. The *New Hindustani English Dictionary* (S. W. Fallon 1879), aimed at the collection of local words (the methodology of collection is given), is valuable on account of the numerous proverbs and quotations from poets it contains. John Platt's *Dictionary of Urdu, Classical Hindi and English* (1884), the best so far, gives words of Sanskrit origin in both Arabic and Devanagari scripts but Arabic-Persian words in Arabic script only, with Roman spelling for all, Roman only for subentries. The main features of this dictionary are its copious etymologies (with names of source languages given), the indication of which post-positions words take with transitive and intransitive verbs, the large number of precise equivalents, the inclusion of many colloquial words and the detailed treatment of entries. Later dictionaries were mostly based on Platt's. Prominent among them is the *Dictionary of the Hindee Language* (J. D. Bate 1918, 25 000 words), giving possible derivations of words and including dialect words with proper labels.

A number of dictionaries of Hindi and Indian languages or Hindi and foreign languages have appeared after this, especially after Independence, most of them intended for students. Among these, the *Practical Hindi English Dictionary* (M. Chaturvedi and B. N. Tiwari 1970, 20 000 words) with each entry containing pronunciation and semantically precise equivalents, and the *Minakshi Hindi English Dictionary* (Brajmohan and B. N. Kapur) with pronunciation and syllable-cuts indicated, are more widely used dictionaries. Of the Hindi-foreign language dictionaries, K. Doi's *Hindi Japanese Dictionary*, a bidirectional dictionary dealing with common words, and the *Hindi Russian Dictionary* (B. M. Breskovny et al. 1972, 75 000 words) with profuse examples of usage are prominent.

Among English-Hindi dictionaries, J. Ferguson's, noted previously, is the earliest. The *New English Hindustani Dictionary* (Fallon 1883) with illustrations from English literature is remarkable for its popular Hindustani rendering. One dictionary of this type (and there are many of them) is Raghuvira's *Comprehensive English Hindi Dictionary* (1955, 150 000 specific words and terms) which is highly scholastic because of the emasculated coinages exclusively from Sanskrit it contains. H. Bahri's *Bṛhat Angreji Hindi kośa* (1960, 100 000 words, 5000 idioms and phrases) includes examples of usage and indicates slang items and examples of colloquial usage. The *English Hindi Dictionary* (Camille Bulcke 1968, 54 000 words) is notable for the preciseness of its equivalents in common Hindi and its inclusion of technical terms.

The early monolingual dictionaries of Hindi are metrical and contain selected words which were not current at the time, and were meant to help poets. They were of 1) synonyms — words grouped under various subjects with some encyclopaedic information given, (2) polysemous words — mostly religious words selected without any basis and (3) letters (*ekākṣarī*) explaining individual letters — all types based on Skt. models. Most of them are unpublished. Nandadāsa's *Anekārthamañjarī* (1568, verse, 120 couplets containing polysemous words) and Bhikhari

Das's *Nāma prakāśa* (1738, 23 sections), a dictionary of nouns selected from different works, are the earliest monolingual Hindi dictionaries.

Hindi Kośa Sangraha, Hindvi Dictionary (Father M. T. Adam 1829, 2000 words) was the first dictionary compiled using modern techniques, and in the entries it gives grammatical category, labels, excerpts from the colloquial language, compounds, phrases and idioms, and meanings in simple Hindi. The words are arranged in alphabetical order. *Sridhara Bhāṣākośa* (Sridhara Tripathi, 1894), containing words collected from text books, and *Hindi Śabdārtha Pārijāt* (Dwarika Prasad Chaturvedi 1914), containing words used by eminent poets are the notable dictionaries which appeared before the publication of *Hindi Śabda Sāgar* (HSS, eds. Syamsudardas et al. 1916—1928, 4 vols., revised 1965—75, 11 vols.) the most exhaustive encyclopaedic dictionary of Hindi. It contains 100 000 words taken from all possible genres of literature and the local dialects. Its main features are: the large number of meanings given, the use of quoted or constructed examples to clarify meanings, and the treatment of set expressions. But this dictionary contains an abundance of Skt. words and meanings which are not used currently. The dialectal and stylistic variations have not been specifically marked as such. The later dictionaries follow HSS without adding anything significant. *Saṅkṣipta Hindi Śabda Sāgar* (R. C. Varma 1933), an abridgement of HSS, is quite popular. *Prāmāṇik Hindi Kośa* (R. C. Varma 1949) shows a definite improvement over earlier dictionaries in the selection of common words, scientific etymologies, accurate meanings and appropriate definitions and explanations. Among the several dictionaries compiled after Independence, three are important. HSS has already been noted. *Bṛhat Hindi Kośa* (K. P. Srivastav et al. 1952) is a useful one volume dictionary which includes compounds within the entry. *Mānak Hindi Kośa* (R. C. Varma 1962—65, 5 vols.) is a dictionary of standard (*mānak*) Hindi and has the following significant features: inclusion of modern vocables from newspapers and other types of mass media, presentation of meanings arranged in order of frequency, and an attempt to distinguish synonyms.

Hindi has a number of dialect dictionaries, the most exhaustive being *Rajasthani Sabad Kosa* (Sitaram Lalas 1962—1978, 4 vols., 125 000 words), an encyclopaedic dictionary containing words from literature, from different subjects and professions, and from colloquial speech. The definitions are free of complex words so that they are easily understandable.

There has been considerable lexicographic work done on technical terminology for Hindi. The work of the Commission for Scientific and Technical Terminology and the Central Hindi Directorate is notable. An etymological dictionary and a historical dictionary are still desiderata in Hindi.

2.5. Kashmiri

Except for a few vocabularies and glossaries of Kashmiri by M. P. Edgeworth (1841), H. S. Godwin Austin (1866), L. B. Bowring (1866) and William J. Elmslie (1872), there is no earlier proper dictionary of Kashmiri barring a small *Kashmiri Persian Dictionary* (Sonti Pandit 1893) and an incomplete Kashmiri-Sanskrit Dictionary by Ishwara Kaula.

Using the material left by Ishwara Kaula and supplements of his own, G. A. Grierson compiled the only exhaustive dictionary of the language, *A Dictionary of the Kashmiri Language* (1916—1932, 4 parts). The entries are arranged in the Roman alphabetical order and contain Kashmiri words in Roman script with transliteration in Devanagari, grammatical category, meanings in Sanskrit and English, variant spelling forms, and idioms and phrases explained with illustrations from well known Kashmiri texts. The 'Preliminary Note' gives a detailed sketch of the orthography and pronunciation with a full phonetic description of each sound and also tables of declensions and conjugations.

There is no monolingual dictionary of Kashmiri designed on modern lines except for *Kashir Dikshanari* (ed. S. K. Toshkhani 1972—79, 7 vols.) by the Jammu and Kashmir Academy of Arts, Culture and Languages. It includes the words of Grierson's dictionary and also new words and expressions currently used in literary and spoken Kashmiri, the latter collected by an extensive linguistic survey. The script is a broad adaptation of that used for Urdu with diacritic marks added to suit Kashmiri phonology.

Another dictionary prepared under the direction of the Academy is *Urdu Kashmiri Farhang* (1969—80, 9 vols.), a very exhaustive and comprehensive dictionary.

2.6. Marathi

Rājavyavahāra Kośa (Raghunatha Narayana Adhwani, minister in the court of Shivaji, 384 verses) is the only earlier dictionary of Marathi. It is written in Sanskrit verse in *Amarakośa* style and it gives Marathi alternatives for current Persian words, especially for the field of administration.

The *Dictionary of Mahratta language* (William Carey 1810) is the first modern bilingual dictionary of Marathi. The words of the spoken language are given in Modi Script with Roman transliteration, with grammar and different meanings indicated. *Mahārāṣṭra Bhāṣeca Kośa* (G. Molesworth and T. Candey 1829), based on the language of Pune, also includes words from other territories but very few old Marathi words. Persian and Arabic words are omitted. Etymologies are not given.

The *Marathi English Dictionary* (Molesworth assisted by G. and T. Candey 1831, 40 000 words) is the most systematic dictionary of Marathi so far. The words it contains have been meticulously selected. Persian and Arabic words have not been rejected, nor are Sanskrit words unduly preferred. It includes slang items, phrases, and the derivatives of a few words. The meanings of typical polysemous words are exemplified by illustrations from literature and common language. The source language of every borrowed word is given. The Preface of the dictionary, especially the section 'General Intimation', elucidates the constituent elements of the language, morphological peculiarities, etc. This dictionary uses cross references and labels judiciously.

Later dictionaries have been inspired by Molesworth: M. K. Deshpande's *Marathi English Dictionary* (1908, 26 000 words) which is one of the more popular among the recent dictionaries. N. B. Ranade's *20th Century English Marathi Dictionary* (1903), a pronouncing, etymological, literary, scientific dictionary, and V. V. Bhide's *English Marathi Dictionary* (1910, 30 000 words) with syllables, accents, roots, etc. indicated are the two earlier English-Marathi dictionaries. Many dictionaries which do justice to different Indian and foreign languages have appeared subsequently.

Hemakośa (R. B. Godbole 1863) with 7000 difficult words used by renowned poets of the last 6 centuries is the earliest monolingual dictionary of Marathi. Etymologies are not given but the source language of borrowed words is noted. Godbole's *Marāṭhī Bhāṣeca navīnakośa* (1870) for students does not include either difficult Sanskrit words or very simple commonly known words, but it does include Persian and Arabic words. It neither gives etymological details nor quotations from authors. *Śuddha Marāṭhī Kośa* (V. R. Bapat and B. V. Pandit 1891) does not include words from old Marathi literature or common English words but it contains some scientific and technical terms as well as names of birds and animals. *Marathi Śabda Ratñakara* (V. G. Apte 1922, 39 000 words) includes many English words used in Marathi, but leaves out difficult words from old literature and scientific terms. *Saraswati Śabda Kośa* (V. V. Bhide 1930, 2 vols.) gives the etymologies and derivations of words and also the development of meanings. It does not include slang items, technical terms or quotations.

Mahārāṣṭra Śabdakośa (Y. R. Date et al. 1932—38, 7 vols., a supplementary volume 1950), by far the largest encyclopaedic monolingual dictionary of Marathi, contains a lengthy preface dealing elaborately with topics connected with the history and study of the language, and gives an account of the Marathi people, language, and history and a skeleton grammar. It includes words from all dialects and various trades, as well as slang words, obsolete words, technical terms, etc. The entries give parts of speech, different derivations, all possible meanings arranged according to frequency, copious illustrations, either constructed or quotations taken from standard writers, and also etymologies (sparingly). Homonyms are given separately. For borrowings the original form in the source language is given. The dialect forms are suitably marked.

Ādarśa Marāṭhī Śabdakośa (P. N. Joshi 1970) gives new words not found in *Mahārāṣṭra Śabda kośa*. *Marāṭhī Śabdakośa* (started 1970, Maharastra State Board for Literature and Culture) proposes to contain all of the features of an ideal lexicon. In addition to the words of Date's dictionary the compilers intend to include as far as possible all words from all books from the last 750 years (about 140 000 words). Rare and obsolete words would be omitted. It would have the following special features: etymological details, grammatical information (in different morphological patterns), elaborate information on pronunciation, citations and illustrations, and explanations of technical terms.

Also to Marathi lexicography belong an etymological dictionary, *Marathi Vyutpatti kośa* (K. P. Kulkarni 1947), and several other dictionaries of technical terminology, etc.

2.7. Oriya

Gītābhidhāna (Upendra Bhanja 17th cent.), in verse, was compiled on the model of *Amarakośa,* giving synonyms for each word, and is the earliest Oriya dictionary. The words are arranged in the sequence of their last letters.

In *A Vocabulary : Oriya English for use of students* (M. P. Thakur 1811), the first Oriya English dictionary, Oriya words, classified into 32 sections, e. g. gods, parts of the body, trade and commerce etc., are written in Roman script, giving the actual pronunciation.

The Oriya Dictionary (A. Sutton and B. Nyāyālankāra 1841—43, 3 vols., I: English and Oriya, II: A Oriya English Dictionary with Oriya synonyms, III: Oriya and English Dictionary) is the first dictionary compiled using lexicographic techniques. It gives grammar and meanings in Oriya and English.

Pūrnachandra Oḍia Bhashakosha (G. C. Praharaj 1931—40, 7 vols. 185 000 words and phrases with their Oriya, English, Bengali and Hindi meanings) is the largest Oriya dictionary. It includes slang words, words from dialectal and colloquial speech, and words from mediaeval and old and modern literature. It gives copious encyclopaedic notes and the English transliteration for every word. The author has used 'chaste, idiomatic and homely language in preference to polished, laboured and Sanskritised style' for defining words. Labels are used to indicate regional and stylistic variations. The origins of head-words are indicated.

The *Comprehensive English Oriya Dictionary* (J. G. Pike and Gordon S. Williams 1916, 30 000 entries) is an earlier dictionary of note. Binayaka Padhi's *Jyotirmaya Iṅgrājī-Oḍia Iṅgrājī abhidhāna* (1947) and the *Ramakrishna English Oriya Dictionary* (1951) have been widely used. The latter gives parts of speech, idioms, phrases and proverbs, etc. But the most popular dictionary is the *Students Diamond Dictionary* of words, phrases and idioms (J. Pattanayak 1962—64, 2 vols., 30,000 words).

Śabdanidhi (Chaturbhuj Pattanayak and Shivanarayan Nayak, 1983) and *Utkal abhidhāna* (Jagannath Rao 1891, 22 000 words; arranged alphabetically) mark the beginning of Oriya monolingual lexicography. *Śabdatattva Abhidhāna* (Gopinath Nanda Sharma 1916, 35 000 words) is a major dictionary in this tradition. The words are culled from literary as well as colloquial Oriya and they are classified in terms of tatsama, tadbhava and desaja types. For borrowed words, the name of their source language is given. The entries contain copious examples of use for the clarification of meanings. There has been no improvement in later monolingual lexicography, with the exception of *Pramoda abhidhana* (P. C. Deb and Damodara Misra 1942, 150 000 words) which contains many words not found in Praharaj.

A small etymological dictionary, *Moola Śabda Bodhikā* (Mrityunjay Rath 1914), is a notable earlier attempt in the field.

2.8. Panjabi

The *Dictionary of the Punjabi language,* (Rev. E. P. Newton 1841, 2 pts.: Panjabi-English and English-Panjabi) and *the Punjabi Dictionary* (Rev. L. Jarivier 1854) mark the beginning of Panjabi lexicography. The latter gives words transcribed carefully from every dialect. It marks grammatical categories and gives examples of idiomatic usage.

Bhai Maya Singh's *The Panjabi Dictionary* (1895) uses Gurumukhi script for Panjabi words, as well as Roman script. The word list has been drawn from different available materials, e. g. dictionaries, glossaries, gazetteers, etc.

Of English-Panjabi Dictionaries, Captain Starkey's *A Dictionary English and Panjabee* (1949) is one of the earliest, followed by T. Graham Bailey's *English Panjabi Vocabulary* (1919, 5800 words) issued to meet the needs of Europeans. *An English Panjabi Dictionary* (Rev. W. P. Hares 1929, 15 000 entries) gives several meanings for polysemous words in Panjabi in Roman script. The *English Punjabi Dictionary* (Panjab University 1981), based on the pattern of the concise Oxford Dictionary, gives the pronunciation of English words in Gurumukhi with modifications suitable for English. The equivalents are very meticulously arranged; first Panjabi *tadbhava* words, followed by Sanskrit *tatsama* words and other words, arranged in order of frequency.

Teja Singh's various English-Panjabi dictionaries have been widely used. The Language Department of Punjab has brought out several bilingual dictionaries of Panjabi and other Indian languages.

Bishandas Puri's *Punjabi Sabad Bhandar* (1922), the first major Panjabi monolingual dictionary, contains common words, phrases, idioms and proverbs, and limited grammatical information. *Panjabi kośa* (Language Dept. 1955 onwards) uses modern lexicographical techniques and contains words from different dictionaries and local dialects. The entries give a detailed description of the lexical units, viz. etymology, various shades of meaning, examples of use, and idioms and proverbs. Among the encyclopaedic exegetic dictionaries of Guru Granth Saheb, the holy scripture of Sikhism, the largest, *Mahān Kośa* (Bhai Kahan Singh 1930, 1960), comes from the Ṭīkā (commentary) tradition of helping the understanding of the message of Sikh teachers and saints. S. Obrien's *Glossary of the Multani language* (1880), with entries in Roman script, and the *Dictionary of the Jatki or Western Panjabi Language* (Jukes 1900), with entries in Perso-Arabic script, are earlier dialect dictionaries of Panjabi.

2.9. Sindhi

The earliest lexicographical works in Sindhi (unpublished) are brief Sindhi-Persian and Persian-Sindhi vocabularies (1783—1843) compiled for court use. Capt. George Stack's *A Dictionary English-Sindhi* (1849, 15 000 words) and *A Dictionary Sindhi-English* (1855, 17 000 words, including and marking loans from Sanskrit, Persian and Arabic sources) are the first modern lexicographical works of Sindhi. Both give Sindhi words in Sindhi Devanagari script. Father G. Shirt's *Sindhi English Dictionary* (1879) uses Sindhi Arabic characters for Sindhi words. Each entry contains part of speech, the various meanings of polysemous words, and the source of the Sindhi word. This widely used dictionary has served as the basis for many other dictionaries, *A Sindhi English Dictionary* (Parmanand Mewaram 1910) being most popular. The word list of Mewaram's dictionary is 'largely drawn from Shirt's compilation' and it has been supplemented by a fairly large number of words from different sources, viz. the words of Shahjo Rasalo, scientific and technical terms, dialectal, homely and colloquial words and a good number of Sanskrit, Persian, Arabic and Urdu words. Parmanand Mewaram's *A New English Sindhi Dictionary* (1933) enjoys similar popularity. These dictionaries have greatly influenced almost all of the later bilingual dictionaries of Sindhi, most of which are meant for students; these do not even show much improvement in the word list or meanings. The dictionaries of A. T. Sahani, the *Sindhi English Dictionary* (1956) and the *English Sindhi Dictionary,* the latter giving the pronunciation of English words in Sindhi Arabic script, are commonly used. *The Sindhi English Dictionary* presently being prepared by Deccan College, Poona, is based on contemporary Standard usage, and it carefully employs most lexicographic techniques such as labels, cross references, nesting, etc. The entry words are given both in Devanagari Sindhi and Arabic Sindhi scripts. The entries provide a meticulous treatment of phrases and compounds. A single entry of *ākhi* (eye) runs several pages. Sindhi-Urdu and Urdu-Sindhi are the most numerous types of bilingual dictionaries. Notable among these are the *Urdu Sindhi Dictionary* (Ibn Ilyas 1950, 14 000 words) and the *Sindhi Urdu Lughāt-*Sindhi Urdu Dictionary (Nabi Baksh Khan Baloch and Ghulam Mustafa Khan 1959, 24 000 words).

There has been no serious attempt in the field of Sindhi monolingual lexicography. The only comprehensive dictionary of classical and current Sindhi is the *Sindhi Sindhi Dictionary* (ed. Nabi Baksh Khan Baloch, Sindhi Adabi Board Karachi 1960, 5 vols.). It contains words collected from 35 works and all walks of life and dialects (except Kacchi) and a number of compound words, noun and verb phrases. Among exegetic dictionaries based on the *Shahjo Rasalo* of Shah Abdul Latif from 17th century, notable are E. Trumpp's (1862), *Gharibul Lughāt* (B. M. Advani 1907), *Lughat-e latifi* (Mirza Qaleech Beg 1913), and H. M. Gumbuxani's edition of *Shahjo Rasalo* in 3 volumes. Among other types of dictionaries, an etymological dictionary *Sindhi Vaipati Kośa* (J. N. Vasnani 1866) giving Sanskrit roots and words with their Sindhi derivatives is notable.

2.10. Urdu

The account of earlier bilingual dictionaries of Hindi covers Urdu dictionaries also, because most of them deal with Hindi, Hindustani and Urdu, many using the Perso Arabic script also. The *Twentieth Century Urdu English Dictionary* (Y. Sen 1912) is an earlier dictionary. Abdul Haq's *Standard English Urdu Dictionary* (1937, 200 000 words and phrases with illustrative examples) is the most popular of the several Urdu and Indian language dictionaries. *Devanagari Urdu Hindi Kośa* (R. C. Varma 1948, 11 335 words in Nagari script) and *Urdu Hindi Śabda Kośa* (M. Mustafa Khan 1959) giving various pronunciations, are notable.

The first great monolingual dictionary of Urdu is *Farhang-e Āsifiā* (Syed Ahmed, 1908, 4 vols.), followed by two others, *Nurul Lughāt* (Nurul Hasan Naiyyar 1924—31, 4 vols.), and *Jāmeul lughāt* (Abdul Majid 1933—35, 4 vols). These dictionaries are rich in their vocabulary and their treatment of entries with illustrative examples. Other notable dictionaries are: *Farhang-e asar* (Jafar Ali Khan Ásar' 1961), a commentary on *Nurul Lughāt* giving prominence to the Urdu of Lucknow, *Muhazzab-ul-lughāt* (Mohmmad Meerza Mohazzab 1958, 7 vols.), for which the point of reference of standard usage is the author himself, and *Lughāt-i-Urdu* (Taraqqie Urdu Board Karachi, 1961) which is based on the pattern of the Oxford English Dictionary and is notable for its wide coverage.

Dakhini Urdu Kī lughāt (M. H. Khan and G. U. Khan 1969), a classical Dakhani Urdu dictionary, is a dictionary of a variety of Urdu.

2.11. Other Languages

Other notable lexicographical works in New Indo Aryan include *The Nepali Dictionary* (R. L. Turner 1931, 26 000 entries), a comparative, etymological and philological dictionary. This dictionary is the supreme landmark in Nepali lexicography and it has been the most authentic etymological dictionary of any NIA language. In it, Nepali words, printed in Devanagari and Roman scripts are accompanied by English equivalents and illustrated by citations and examples of idiomatic usage. Each entry includes a list of cognate words in other NIA languages. Its index contains a series of lists of words from over 50 languages. The introduction gives a profile of the language and notes on orthography discussing spelling problems. *Nepālī Śabda Kośa* (ed. B. C. Sharma 1962) is another notable recent dictionary for Nepali.

Turner's *A Compative Dictionary of Indo-Aryan Languages* (1966) is the most reliable source of etymology, and it contains 15 000 Skt. head words, extant or reconstructed, followed by their developed forms in over 50 languages and dialects of the family. It has two index volumes, one giving lists of words in each language and the other giving the phonetic analysis of 1500 sounds and sound groups showing their history in NIA.

3. Selected Bibliography

3.1. Dictionaries

3.1.1. Assamese

Barua 1900 = Hemachandra Barua: Hemakośa. Gauhati 1900 [XXII, 1972 pp.].

Barua 1906 = Hemachandra Barua: Asamiyā Bhāṣāra Pārhāsaliyā Abhidhāna (The School Dictionary of Assamese). Ed. by Tulasiram Barua. Gauhati 1906 [XIII, 482 pp.].

Barua, ed. 1933 = M. K. Barua: Chandrakānta Abhidhāna. Gauhati 1933 [2nd ed. 1962, XXX, 1044 pp., 36,819 words].

Bhattacharya 1931 = B. N. Bhattacharya: Pronouncing Anglo Assamese Dictionary. Gauhati 1931 [XXVI, 876 pp.].

Bronson 1867 = Rev. M. Bronson: A Dictionary in Assamese and English. Sibsagar 1867 [VIII + 609 pp.].

Neog et al. 1971 = Maheshawar Neog et al.: Ādhunik Asamiyā Abhidhāna. Gauhati 1971 [10 + 581 pp.].

Ward 1864 = S. R. Ward: A Brief Vocabulary in English and Assamese. Sibsagar 1864 [XII, 104 pp.].

Ward 1950 = S. R. Ward: Anglo Assamese Dictionary. Gauhati 1950 [XXIII, 859 pp.].

3.1.2. Bengali

Apte 1925 = V. G. Apte: Bangalī Marāthī Kośa. Poona 1925 [VIII, 248 pp.].

Bandyopadhyaya 1933—44 = Haricharan Bandyopadhyaya: Bangiya Śabdakośa. 1933—44 [105 pts.; 2nd ed., New Delhi 1969, XXX, 2435 pp.].

Banerjee 1960 = Govindalal Banerjee: A Dictionary of Foreign Words in Bengali. Calcutta 1960 [VI, 337 pp.].

Barat 1887 = T. N. Barat: Barat's Pronouncing Etymological and Pictorial Dictionary of the English and of the Bengali Language. Calcutta 1887 [6 vols.].

Basu 1951 = Rajshekhar Basu: Calantikā. Calcutta 1951 [XII, 698 pp.; many eds.].

Bikova et al. 1957 = E. M. Bikova et al.: Bengalsko Ruskii Slovar (Bāṅglā Rūs Abhidhāna). Moscow 1957 [908 + 46 pp.].

Biswas = Birendranath Biswas: Rabindra Śabdakośa.

Carey 1818—25 = William Carey: A Dictionary of the Bengali Language. Serampur 1818—25 [8, 1544 pp.].

Carey 1903 = William Carey: A Dictionary of the Bengali Language. Edition 12. 1903 [revised and edited by Rasamaya Mitra Vrajendranath Ghoshal].

Chakrabarti 1958 = Gopalachandra Chakrabarti: Bāṅglā Hindī Śabdakośa. Calcutta 1958 [VIII, 383 pp.].

da Assumpcan 1743 = Manoel da Assumpcan: Vocabularies Em Idioma Bengalia Portuguez. Lisbon 1743.

Das 1916 = Jnanendra Mohan Das: Bāṅglā Bhāṣār Abhidhāna. Calcutta 1916 [2 vols., XXVII, 1577 pp.].

Gangopadhyaya 1903 = V. Gangopadhyaya: Students' Dictionary of Bengali Words and Phrases Done into English. Calcutta 1903 [VIII, 829, XII pp.].

Guha 1916—19 = Charu Chandra Guha: Modern Anglo Bengali Dictionary. Dacca 1916—19 [3 vols.].

Kundu Asoka = Asoka Kundu: Bankim Abhidhāna.

Mitra 1909 = Subalachandra Mitra: Saral Bāṅglā Abhidhāna. Calcutta 1909 [1595 pp.].

Ray Vidyanidhi 1913 = Yogesh Chandra Ray Vidyanidhi: Bāṅglā Bhāsā Śabdakośa. Calcutta 1913 [IV, 479 pp.].

Roy 1971 = Kamini Kumar Roy: Laukika Śabda Kośa. Calcutta 1971 (vol. I); Calcutta 1971 (vol. II) [vol. I, 320 pp.; II, 258 pp.].

Sen 1834 = Ram Kamal Sen: Dictionary in English and Bengali. Serampore 1834 [2 vols.].

Sen 1971 = Sukumar Sen: An Etymological Dictionary of Bengali (c. 1000—1800 A. D.). Calcutta 1971, [2 vols., XVI, 968 pp.].

Shahidullah, ed. 1965 = Mohammed Shahidullah, ed.: Bāṅglā Deśer Āncalik Bhāṣār Abhidhāna. Dacca 1965 [3 vols.: I, 22 + 468 pp.; III, 590 pp.].

Thakur 1810 = M. P. Thakur: The English Bengali Dictionary. Calcutta 1810.

Thakur 1805 = M. P. Thakur: Bengali English Vocabulary. Calcutta 1805 [166 pp.].

Thakur 1875 = Saurindra Mohan Thakur: Yantra-Kośa. Calcutta 1875 [XII, 296 pp.].

Up John 1793 = Up John: Ingaraji O Vangali Vokebilari. Calcutta 1793 [455 pp.].

Vidyavagisa 1817—18 = Ram Chandra Vidyavagisa: Baṅga Bhāṣābhidhāna. Calcutta 1817—18 [IV, 516 pp.].

Viswas Sailendra 1968 = Viswas Sailendra: Samsad Bengali English Dictionary. Calcutta 1968 [1278 pp.].

3.1.3. Gujarati

Belsare 1895 = M. B. Belsare: Etymological Gujarati English Dictionary. Ahmedabad 1895 [1209 pp.].

Bhagavat Simhaji 1944—55 = Bhagavat Simhaji: Bhagawad Gomadal. Gondal 1944—55 [9270 pp.].

Bhakta = T. K. Bhakta: Śuddha Śabda Pradarśana. Ahmedabad [170 pp.].

Brijbhukhandas/Brijbhukhandas 1885 = Cassidass Brijbhukhandas/Balkicanadass Brijbhukhandas: Gujaratino Gujarati ane Ingrejikośa (A Dictionary Gujarati and Gujarati English). Rajkot 1885 [XIV, 1147, 15 pp.].

Dave Narmada Shankar 1871 = Narmadashankar Lal Shankar Dave: Narmakosa. Surat 1871 [XXVI, 619 pp., 25 000 words].

Desai/Mehta 1969 = D. M. Desai/K. M. Mehta: Students' Modern Combined Dictionary. Bombay 1969 [510 pp.].

Drummond 1808 = Father Drummond: Glossary, Gujarati English. 1808.

Gujarat Vidyapith 1929 = Gujarat Vidyapith: Gujarati Jodni Kośa. Ahmedabad 1929 [XVI, 376 pp.; 5th ed., Sārtha Gujarati Jodnikośa, 42- 904 pp.].

Hirachand 1865 = Haridas Hirachand: Dhātumanjari. 1865.

Karsandas Mulji 1862 = Karsandas Mulji: Pocket Gujarati English Dictionary. Bombay 1862 [XII, 632 pp.].

Kulamandana Gani 1394 = Kulamandana Gani: Mugdhāvabodha Auktika.

Mahomed Cauzim Mirza 1846 = Mahomed Cauzim Mirza: Dictionary of Goojaratee and English. Bombay 1846 [XIII, 420 pp.].

Montgomery 1877 = Robert Montgomery: Dictionary of English and Gujarati. Surat 1877 [ii, 976 pp.].

Nanabhai Rustomji Remina 1857 = Nanabhai Rustomji Remina: The Dictionary of English and Gujarati. 1857 [8 parts].

Nilkanth 1881 = M. R. Nilkanth: Vyutpatti Prakasa. 1881 [75 pp.].

Patel/Patel 1878 = J. T. Patel/T. G. Patel: Gujarati Sabda Sangraha. 1878.

Shapur Edalji 1863 = Shapur Edalji: The Dictionary of Gujarati and English. Bombay 1863 [XXIV, 862 pp.].

Taylor 1870 = D. S. Taylor: Dhātusangraho. Bombay 1870 [204 pp.].

Vyas/Patel 1894 = V. Vyas/S. G. Patel: Standard English Gujarati Dictionary. 1894 [1st ed., 1244 pp.; 5th ed., Ahmedabad 1688 pp.].

3.1.4. Hindi

Adam 1829 = Father M. T. Adam: Hindi Kośa Sangrah (Hindvi Dictionary). Calcutta 1829 [374 pp.].

Bahri 1960 = H. Bahri: Bṛhat Angrejī Hindī Kośa. Varanasi 1960 [VI, 1797 pp.; 2nd. ed. 1969, 2 vols., XI, 2196 pp.].

Bate 1918 = J. D. Bate: Dictionary of the Hindee Language. Allahabad 1918 [810 pp.].

Brajmohan/Kapur 1980 = Brajmohan/B. N. Kapur: Minakshi Hindi English Dictionary. Meerut 1980 [XV, 798 pp.].

Breskovny et al. 1972 = B. M. Breskovny et al.: Hindu Russian Dictionary. Moscow 1972 [2 vols., 8 + 1819 pp.].

Bulcke 1968 = Camille Bulcke: English Hindi Dictionary. Ranchi 1968 [XII, 891 pp.; 3rd. ed., New Delhi 1981].

Chaturvedi 1914 = Dwarika Prasad Chaturvedi: Hindī Śabdārtha Pārijāt. Allahabad 1914 [676 pp.].

Chaturvedi/Tiwari 1970 = M. Chaturvedi/B. N. Tiwari: Practical Hindi English Dictionary. Delhi 1970 [16 + 730 pp.].

Das et al., eds. 1916—28 = Syamsundar Das et al.: Hindī Śabda Sāgar. Kashi 1916—28 [2nd ed. 1965—75, 11 vols., 32 + 16 + 5570 pp.].

Doi = K. Doi: Hindi Japanese Dictionary. Tokyo [466 pp.].

Fallon 1879 = S. W. Fallon: New Hindustani English Dictionary. Banaras 1879 [XXVII, 1216 pp.].

Fallon 1883 = S. W. Fallon: New English Hindustani Dictionary. Banaras 1883 [277 pp.].

Ferguson 1773 = J. Ferguson: Dictionary of Hindustani Language. London 1773 [VIII, 58 (112) pp.].

Gilchrist 1800 = John Gilchrist: Anti — Jargonist. Calcutta 1800 [LXVIII, 290 pp.].

Khusro 14th cent. = Amir Khusro: Khaliq bārī.

Kirkpatrick 1785 = W. Kirkpatrick: Vocabulary Persian, Arabic and English. London 1785 [32, VIII, 190 pp.].

Lalas 1962—78 = Sitaram Lalas: Rajasthani Sabadkosa. Jodhpur 1962—78 [238 + 5902 + 234 pp.].

Mirza Khan 1675 = Mirza Khan: Tuhapatula-Hind 1675 [286 pp].

Platts 1884 = John Platts: Dictionary of Urdu, Classical Hindi and English. London 1884 [VIII, 1259 pp.].

Raghuvira 1955 = Raghuvira: Comprehensive English Hindi Dictionary of Governmental & Educational Words & Phrases. New Delhi 1955 [1572 pp.].

Shakespear 1817 = John Shakespear: Dictionary, Hindustani English. 1817 [VIII, 837 pp.; 4th ed., London 1949, 2241 pp.].

Srivastav et al. 1952 = Kalka Prasad Srivastav et al.: Bṛhat Hindi Kośa. Varanasi 1952 [IV, 1608 pp.; another ed. 1965, 2020 pp.].

Tripathi 1894 = Sridhar Tripathi: Śrīdhara Bhāṣākośa. Lucknow 1894 [764 pp.].

Varma 1933 = Ramchandra Varma: Sankshipta Hindī Śabda Sāgar. Banaras 1933 [2 + 2 + 1097 pp.].

Varma 1949 = Ramchandra Varma: Prāmāṇik Hindī Kośa. Banaras 1949 [XII, 1256 pp.; 2nd ed. 1951, XVI, 1586 pp.].

Varma, ed. 1962—65 = Ramchandra Varma, ed.: Mānak Hindī Kośa. Allahabad 1962—65 [5 vols., 3177 pp.].

3.1.5. Kashmiri

Bowring 1866 = L. B. Bowring: Kashmiri Vocabulary and Grammatical Forms. In: Journal of the Asiatic Society 35.1866, 225—250.

Edgeworth 1841 = M. P. Edgeworth: Grammar and Vocabulary of the Cashmiri Language. In: Journal of the Asiatic Society 10.1841, 1038—1064.

Elmslie 1872 = William Elmslie: A Vocabulary of the Kashmirī Language. London 1872 [264 pp.].

Godwin Austin 1866 = H. S. Godwin Austin: A Vocabulary of Balti and Kashmiri. In: Journal of the Asiatic Society 35.1866, 233 ff, 267 ff.

Grierson 1916—32 = G. A. Grierson: A Dictionary of the Kashmiri Language. Calcutta 1916—32 [4 parts, 1254 pp.].

Pandit 1893 = Sonti Pandit: Kashmiri Persian Dictionary 1893.

Toshkhani, ed. 1972—79 = S. K. Toshkhani, ed.: Kashir Dikshanari. Srinagar, Jammu and Kashmir: Academy of Arts, Culture and Language, 1972—79 [7 vols.].

3.1.6. Marathi

Adhwani 1860 = Raghunath Narayana Adhwani (alias Pandit Rao): Rajavyavahāra Kośa. 1860.

Apte 1922 = V. G. Apte: Marāṭhī Śabda Ratnākara. Poona 1922 [4th ed., Poona 1956, LXX, 775 pp.].

Bapat/Pandit 1891 = V. R. Bapat/B. V. Pandit: Śuddha Marāṭhī Kośa. Poona 1891 [XIV, 257 pp.].

Bhide 1910 = V. V. Bhide: English Marathi Dictionary. Bombay 1910 [3rd ed. 1933, X, II, 652 pp.].

Bhide 1930 = V. V. Bhide: Saraswatī Śabda Kośa. Poona 1930 [2 vols., 2 + 2050 pp.].

Carey 1810 = William Carey, assisted by Pt. Vidyanidhi: Dictionary of Mahratta Language. Serampore 1810 [652 pp.].

Date et al. 1932—38 = T. R. Date et al.: Maharāṣtra Śabdakośa. 1932—38 [7 vols.; a supplementary vol. 1950, Poona 332 + 3233 pp.; supplement, 8 + 254 pp.].

Deshpande 1908 = M. K. Deshpande: Marathi English Dictionary. Nagpur 1908 [604 pp.].

Godbole 1863 = Raghunath Bhaskar Godbole: Hemakośa. Poona 1863 [288 pp.].

Godbole 1870 = Raghunath Bhaskar Godbole: Marāṭhī Bhāṣecā Navīna Kośa. Bombay 1870 [632 pp.].

Joshi 1970 = P. N. Joshi: Ādarśa Marāṭhī Śabdakośa. Poona 1970 [43 + 1369 pp.].

Kulkarni 1947 = K. P. Kulkarni: Marāṭhī Vyutpatti Kośa: aitihasika va taulanik. Bombay 1947 [2nd ed., Poona 1964, 8 + 829 pp.].

Molesworth 1831 = G. Molesworth, assisted by George and Thomas Candey: Marathi English Dictionary [4 + 20 + 1164 pp.; 2nd ed., Bombay: Gov't. of Bombay, XXX, 921 pp.].

Molesworth/Candey 1829 = G. Molesworth/ T. Candey: Mahārāṣṭra Bhāṣeca Kosa. Bombay 1829.

Ranade 1903 = N. B. Ranade: 20th Century English Marathi Dictionary. Bombay 1903 [2nd ed. 1916, XX, 2012 pp.].

3.1.7. Oriya

Bhanja 17th cent. = Upendra Bhanja: Gitalamkara. Cuttack 1933 [38 pp.].

Nanda Sharma 1916 = Gopinath Nanda Sharma: Śabdatattva bodha abhidhāna. Cuttack 1916 [XX, 1072 + 48 pp.].

Padhi 1947 = Binayaka Padhi: Jyotirmaya Ingraji Odiā Ingraji Abhidhāna. Parlakimedi 1947 [525 pp.].

Padhi 1951 = Binayaka Padhi: Ramakrishna English Oriya Dictionary. Berhampur 1951 [323 pp.].

Pattanayak/Nayak 1883 = Chaturbhuj Pattanayak/Shivanarayan Nayak: Sabda Nidhi. Balasore 1883 [164 pp.].

Pattanayaka 1962—64 = Jaganmohan Pattanayaka: Student's Diamond Dictionary. Cuttack 1962—64 [2 vols., VIII, 2488 pp.].

Pike/Gordon 1910 = J. G. Pike/S. W. Gordon: The Comprehensive English Oriya Dictionary. Cuttack 1910 [418 pp.].

Prahraj 1931—40 = Govinda Chandra Prahraj: Pūrnachandra Odia Bhashakosha. Cuttack 1931—40 [61 + 9248 pp.].

Rao 1891 = Jagannatha Rao: Utkala Abhidhana. Cuttack 1891 [2nd ed., 1915, IV, 768 + 54 pp.].

Rath 1914 = Mṛtyunjay Rath: Moola Śabda Bodhikā. Cuttack 1914 [VI, 48 pp.].

Sutton/Nyayalankara 1841—43 = A. Sutton/ B. Nyayalankara: The Oriya Dictionary. Cuttack 1841—43.

Thakur 1811 = M. P. Thakur: A Vocabulary; Oriya English for Use of Students. Serampur 1811 [VIII, 209 pp.]

3.1.8. Panjabi

Graham Bailey 1919 = T. H. Graham Bailey: English Panjabi Vocabulary. Calcutta (the author) 1919 [XVI, 159 pp.].

Hares 1929 = Rev. W. P. Hares: An English Panjabi Dictionary. Gojra (Lyallpur) 1929 [III, 478 pp.].

Jarivier 1854 = Rev. L. Jarivier: The Panjabi Dictionary. 1854.

Jukes 1900 = A. Jukes: A Dictionary of the Jatki or Western Punjabi Language. Lahore 1900 [X, 344 pp.].

Language Department 1955 = Language Department: Panjabi Kosh. Patiala 1955 [4 vols.].

Newton 1841 = Rev. E. P. Newton: Dictionary of the Panjabi Language. Ludhiana 1841 [438 pp.].

Obrien 1880 = S. Obrien: Glossary of the Multani Language. Lahore 1880.

Puri 1922 = Bishandas Puri: Panjabi Sabad Bhandar. Lahore 1922 [1058 pp.].

Sandhu, ed. 1981 = B. S. Sandhu, chief ed.: The English Punjabi Dictionary. Chandigarh 1981 [16 + 1407 pp.].

Singh 1895 = Bhai Maya Singh: The Panjabi Dictionary. Lahore 1895 [IV, 1221 pp.].

Singh 1930 = Bhai Kahan Singh: Mahan Kosa. Patiala 1930 [3338 pp.].

Starkey 1849 = Capt. Samuel Cross Starkey: Dictionary English and Punjabee. Calcutta 1849 [IV, 286, XXXV, 116 pp.].

3.1.9. Sindhi

Advani 1907 = B. M. Advani: Gharib-ul-Lughat. 1907.

Baloch 1960 = Nabi Baksh Khan Baloch: Jami Sindhi Lughat (Sindhi Sindhi Dictionary). Karachi Sindhi Adabi Board, 1960 [5 vols.].

Baloch/Khan 1959 = Nabi Baksh Khan Baloch/ Ghulam Mustafa Khan: Sindhi Urdu Dictionary. Hyderabad 1959 [866 pp.].

Beg 1913 = Mirza Qaleech Beg: Lughat-e-Latifi (Glossary of Words Occurring in Shah Latif's Works). 1913.

Deccan College = Deccan College: The Sindhi English Dictionary [under preparation, vol. 1 released].

Ibn Ilyas 1950 = Ibn Ilyas: Urdu Sindhi Lughat (New Urdu Sindhi Dictionary). Hyderabad (Sind) 1950 [14 000 words).

Mewaram 1910 = Parmanand Mewaram: A Sindhi English Dictionary. Hyderabad (Sind) 1910 [XXVI, 664 pp.].

Mewaram 1933 = Paramanand Mewaram: A New English Sindhi Dictionary. Hyderabad (Sind) 1933 [Reprint, New Delhi Sahitya Akademy, 1981, 465 pp.].

Sahani = A. T. Sahani: English Sindhi Dictionary. Bombay [936 pp.].

Sahani 1956 = A. T. Sahani: Sindhi English Dictionary. Bombay 1956.

Shirt 1879 = Father G. Shirt: Sindhi English Dictionary. Karachi 1879 [IV, 919, XIV pp.].

Stack 1849 = Capt. George Stack: A Dictionary English Sindhi. Bombay 1849 [VI, 130 pp.].

Stack 1855 = Capt. George Stack: A Dictionary Sindhi English. Bombay 1855 [VI, 437 pp.].

Vasnani 1886 = J. N. Vasnani: Sindhi Vaipatikośa — A Glossary of Sanskrit Roots and Words with Sindhi Derivative. 1886 [Reprint, Karachi 1904, 43 pp.].

3.1.10. Urdu

Abdul Haq 1937 = Abdul Haq: Standard English Urdu Dictionary. Delhi 1937 [VI, 1513 + 13 + 8 pp.].

Abdul Majid 1933—35 = Abdul Majid: Jamiul-Lughat. Lucknow 1933-35 [4 vols.].

Jafar Ali Khan Asar 1961 = Jafar Ali Khan Asar: Farhang-e-asar. Lucknow 1961.

Khan 1959 = M. Mustafa Khan: Urdu Hindi Sabda Kosa. Lucknow 1959 [XXII, 755 pp.].

Khan/Khan 1969 = Masood Husain Khan/Ghulam Khan: Dakhini Urdu Ki Lughat. Hyderabad 1969 [12 + 381 pp.].

Mohammed Meerza Mohazzab 1958 = Mohammed Meerza Mohazzab: Mahazzab-el-Lughat. Lucknow 1958 [7 vols.].

Nurul Hasan 1924—1931 = Naiyyar Nurul Hasan: Nurul-Lughat. Lucknow 1924—1931 [4 vols.].

Sen 1912 = Y. Sen: Twentieth Century Urdu English Dictionary. Allahabad 1912 [568 pp.].

Syed Ahmed 1908 = Syed Ahmed: Farhang-i-Āsifiyah. Lahore 1908 [4 vols.].

Taraqqi-e-Urdu Board 1961 = Taraqqi-e-Urdu Board: Lughat-i-Urdu. Karachi 1961 [40 pp.].

Varma 1948 = Ramchandra Varma: Devanagari Urdu Hindi Kośa. Bombay 1948 [494 pp.].

3.1.11. Others

Turner 1931 = R. L. Turner: The Nepali Dictionary. London 1931 [XXIV, 932 pp.].

Turner 1966 = R. L. Turner: A Comparative Dictionary of Indo Aryan Languages. London 1966 [vol. 1, XX, 841 pp.; 2, IX, 375 pp.].

3.2. Other Publications

National Library (Calcutta) 1964 = National Library, Calcutta: A Bibliography of Dictionaries and Encyclopaedias in Indian Languages. Calcutta 1964.

Navalani/Gidwani 1972 = K. Navalani/N. N. Gidwani: Dictionaries in Indian Languages. Jaipur 1972.

Singh 1982 = Ram Adhar Singh: An Introduction to Lexicography. Mysore 1982 (Central Institute of Indian Languages. Occasional Monographs Series 26).

Ram Adhar Singh, Mysore (India)

249. Dravidian Lexicography

1. Introduction
2. Literary Languages
2.1. Tamil
2.2. Kannaḍa
2.3. Telugu
2.4. Malayāḷam
3. Non-Literary Languages
4. Comparative and Etymological Dictionaries
5. Dialect Dictionaries/Special Dictionaries
6. Selected Bibliography

1. Introduction

The Dravidian family of languages consists of over twenty-five members spanning the entire South Asia (cf Map 249.1). With the exception of Brāhūī (spoken in Pakistan), the rest of the languages are spoken in India. The population figures (Census 1981) are as follows (in millions): Southern group — Tamil 44.7, Malayāḷam 26, Kannaḍa 27, Tuḷu 1.4, Koḍagu .09, Toda (.0009), Kōta (.0013), Iruḷa (.0052); South-Central group — Telugu 54.2, Gondi (incl. Kōya) 2.2, Koṇḍa .011, Kui .5, Kuvi .2, Pengo (.0013), Manḍa (?); Central group — Kolami .08, Naiki (.054), Parji .03, Ollari (.009), Gadba (.011); Northern group — Kuṟukh 1.3, Malto .9, Brāhūī (.3). [The figures in parentheses are taken from the 1971 or an earlier Census. See Krishnamurti 1969, 1985 a]. Four of these languages, viz. Tamil, Malayāḷam, Telugu and Kannaḍa, have literatures dating from the early Christian era for Tamil, the 8th century for Kannaḍa, the 11th century for Telugu and the 12th for Malayāḷam. Lexicography for Dravidian falls into four stages/phases: (a) Versified lexicons of synonyms and homonyms modelled after Sanskrit dictionaries traditionally found in the literary languages only; (b) Monolingual and bilingual dictionaries which came into existence after the exposure of these languages to Western scholarship and influence. These are prepared by foreign missionaries, merchants and administrators as well as regional scholars under the influence of the former; (c) Comparative and etymological dictionaries; (d) Specialized dictionaries/vocabularies. Phases (a) and (b) are treated under each of the literary languages; (c) and (d) are treated in sections 4 and 5 respectively.

2. Literary Languages

2.1. Tamil

The earliest literary work of Tamil, Tolkāppiyam (early pre-Christian era), classifies

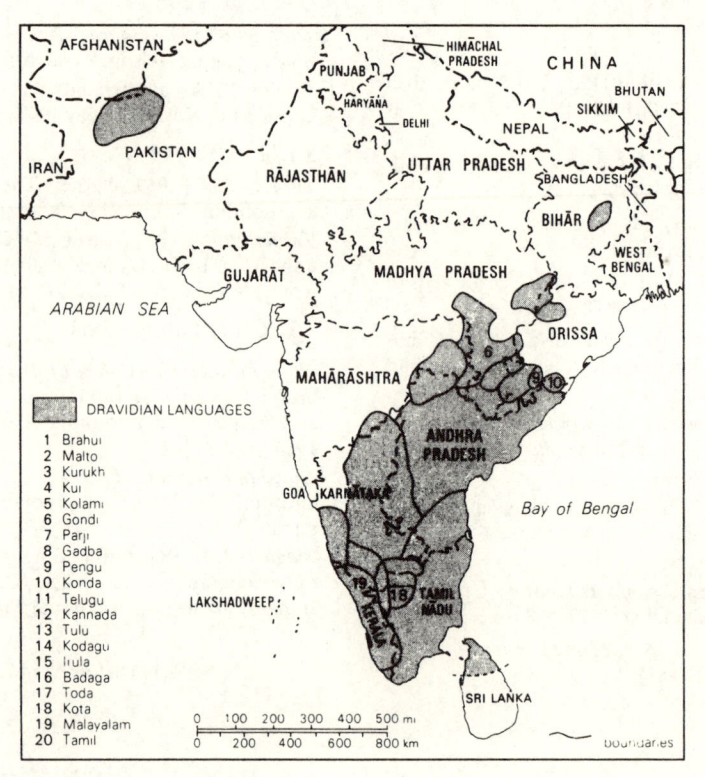

Map 249.1: Dravidian languages in South Asia

words as common, standard, dialectal, and Sanskrit/Prakrit (*Tamil Lexicon,* Introduction). From the 8th century onwards there have been numerous lexicons with the following properties: (a) They are composed in verse; (b) These works classify words into semantic fields, viz. names of gods, heavenly bodies, ranks among men, body parts, birds, beasts, plants and trees, tools and weapons, names of places, natural products, actions, etc.; entries are given under each without following any alphabetical order; (c) There are separate sections dealing with synonyms and homonyms, following the Sanskrit model of *samānārtha* (several words having the same meaning) vs. *nānārtha* (each word having several meanings). The second type includes historically related meaning-shifts as well as homonyms. For instance, **tāram** is given as many as 27 meanings in traditional dictionaries; the *Tamil Lexicon* sets up 9 different homonymous entries, some native and some borrowed from Sanskrit. The important ones among the traditional dictionaries are: (1) *Tivākaram;* c. 8th cent. It has 12 semantically differentiated sections; the 11th section deals with homonyms and the 12th with synonyms. (2) *Piṅkaḷantai;* c. 11—12th cent. It has 10 sections; there are 14,700 words in 9 sections. This work is often cited as an authority. (3) *Nikaṇṭucūṭāmaṇi;* c. 1520. It has 12 sections; in the first ten sections 11,000 words are dealt with. This work is considered the most popular of the nikaṇṭus (dictionaries). Eight other such dictionaries follow in the same style of writing. Some dictionaries are exclusively devoted to words with different meanings (nānārthanighaṇṭu), e.g. *Nānārthatīpikai* has 5430 words with nānārthas. In 1594 a breakthrough came with the composition of *Akarāti-nikaṇṭu* (dictionary beginning with *a-* etc.), the first alphabetical dictionary in South Indian languages. This work has 3368 words. The alphabetical order must have been suggested by a genre of writing where the stanzas are arranged on the first-letter order, called *varukka-kkōvai*. This work was followed by *Potikainikaṇṭu* (1750) which employed the alphabetical order based on the first two letters; all sectional classification is abandoned in favour of alphabetical arrangement. The focus shifted to referencing in preference to memorizing as the goal of lexicography. The next phase is alphabetically arranged monolingual and bilingual dictionaries produced by Western missionaries. The

கூடு. Coula baldada, அபப
பொழுடெ ாநிஇகு-
Gaſtar o tempo baldadamente.
அபநா உ. Infamia.
அபபதநீபம - Quebra do regi-
mento, no comer.

Dictionary excerpt 249.1: The first two entries from page 1 of Proença (1679)

introduction of the printing press aided the preparation of many dictionaries. In 1679 a Tamil-Portuguese Dictionary by Father Antaõ de Proença was published in Cochin. There are 16,546 main entries in the dictionary with meanings given in Portuguese or Latin.

Father Beschi (1710) published his Thesaurus called *Catur-akarāti* 'Alphabetized Four-part Dictionary'. This is an alphabetized index of traditional dictionaries arranged in four parts: (a) words with multiple meanings (incl. homonyms), (b) words with the same meaning (synonyms), (c) technical and general terms of science and literature, and (d) a rhyming lexicon. In 1779, two German Lutheran missionaries prepared Fabricius's *Tamil-English Dictionary* with 9000 entries. The most significant bilingual dictionaries of this period are: *A Dictionary of the Tamil and English Languages* by Rev. J.P. Rottler (1830—1837) in four parts running into 1425 pages (extensively revised by others) with 37 000 words. This is followed by Rev. Winslow's *Comprehensive Tamil and English Dictionary* (1862) with over 67,000 entries. This work has introduced many innovations: (a) The verb root is cited as the entry and not its nominal form, e. g. **cey** 'to do' rather than **ceytal** 'to do, doing', followed by tense and person inflection in 1st person and the infinitive marker; (b) Sanskrit-derived entries are marked with an asterisk before them; (c) Tamil meanings are provided beside English glosses.

A shorter and a handy bilingual dictionary of the 19th century is the Tranquebar Dictionary, based on Fabricius's Malabar-English Dictionary but refined after Winslow's. A number denoting the conjugational class of the verb is given to obviate citing inflected forms. There are 11,590 words and 21,305 derivatives and phrases arranged alphabetically. Obsolete and rare words are dropped. A monolingual Tamil-Tamil dictionary of some significance was the *Sangam Dictionary* (1910—23) in three volumes with 63,900 words. Finally came the monumental *Tamil Lexicon* (1924—39) of Madras University in 6 volumes with 107,715 words. It is now being revised and expanded into 10 volumes. The first volume was published in 1988. The *Tamil Lexicon* is the most comprehensive and modern dictionary in many respects. The entry is given both in Tamil script and in Roman transliteration. The grammatical classification of the word is given, followed by cognates from the other literary languages. Loanwords are identified by source language; homonyms are separated as headwords with raised numbers; meanings are given in English and Tamil, arranged, by and

வரி, இடெறன், ர்டென், வேன், ய, v. a. To write, to draw lines, எழுத. 2. To paint, சித்திரமெழுத. 3. To bind sticks in regular order for covering a hut, வளைகட்ட. 4. To tie together the openings of two bags to be laid on a bullock, சாக்குகட்ட. (c.)
அவன்சம்மாவரிகிறான். He is going on writing.
சேலைவரிந்துகட்டிக்கொண்டான். He gathered up and tied the folds of his garment round his waist.
வீவரிக்தாய்ற்று. The roof-sticks are regularly tied.
வரிக்யிறு, s. A rope to tie the loading of a cart.
வரிகோணியல், s. A bag joined with another.
வரிவடிவெழுத்து, s. Written, in distinction from spoken, letters.

Dictionary excerpt 249.2: An entry from Winslow's Dictionary (1862)

பாடு¹-தல் pāṭu-, 5 v. tr. [K. hāḍu.] 1. To sing; to chant; பண்ணிசைத்தல். மறம்பாடிய பாடினியும்மே (புறநா. 11). 2. To warble, as birds; to hum, as bees or beetles; வண்டு முதலியன இசைத்தல். வண்பல விசைபாட (திவ். பெரியதி. 3, 9, 3). 3. To make verses, compose poems; கவிபாடுதல். பாடினூர் பல்புகழைப் பல்புலவர் (பு. வெ. 8, 1). 4. To recite verses from a book; பாட்டு ஒப்பித்தல். (w.) 5. To speak endearingly; பாராட்டுதல். தகைகள் காதலினுள் நகைபாடினூர் (சீவக. 1337). 6. To praise; துதித்தல். பாடகம் வம்மிேே பரிசின் மக்கள் (புறநா. 32). 7. To declare, proclaim; கூறுதல். அறம் பாடிற்றே (புறநா. 34). 8. To abuse; வைதல். (w.) 9. To sing in the

Dictionary excerpt 249.3: An entry from the *Tamil Lexicon* (1934—39)

large, chronologically and numbered; one or two citations from literature are given. The conjugational class of the verb is indicated by a number keyed to an explanation in the preface. The *Tamil Lexicon* has drawn heavily on Rev. M. Winslow's Dictionary.

The *Tamil Lexicon* is perhaps the only dictionary of the Dravidian literary languages which has been extensively used both by native and foreign scholars in literary and linguistic studies. Burrow and Emeneau have used it as the major source for *DED(R)* (1961, 1984). During the recent decades a number of school dictionaries and dictionaries of technical terms have come into existence. The following total count of dictionaries available in Tamil is based on Jayadevan 1985: Tamil-Tamil 58; Tamil-English 27; Tamil-French 7; Tamil-Portuguese 6; Tamil-Russian 1; Tamil-Sinhalese 3; Tamil-Burmese 1; Tamil-Hindi 1; Tamil-Telugu 1; Tamil-Sanskrit 1. Recent dictionaries for specialized clientele 50.

2.2. Kannaḍa

Ranna (c. 993) gave the meanings of difficult Kannaḍa words in the *kanda* verse, of which only 12 verses are available. A standard grammarian of Classical Kannaḍa, Kēśirāja (1260) in his *Śabdamaṇidarpaṇa* gives a list of 2140 words of rare literary worth with meanings, some in Kannaḍa and some in Sanskrit. Proto-Dravidian *ẓ (retroflex fricative) was maintained in Kannaḍa until about the 9th century and then merged with *ḷ* and *r* in complementary environments. After the completion of this change, the poets had a problem of distinguishing the original *ẓ (> ḷ, r) from underlying *ḷ* and *r* (< *ḷ, *r). So Śabdamaṇidarpaṇa gives a list of words with original ẓ with meanings as an aid to poets to help them discriminate older words in their writings. The meanings are in prose and no alphabetical order is followed. *Karṇāṭaka Śabdasāram* (c. 1400) is a prose work which gives the meanings of 1416 words without classification. *Caturāsyanighaṇṭu* (c. 1450) is a lexicon laid out in 130 *kanda* verses; this work too does not follow either semantic or alphabetical classification. It classifies words into native, *tadbhava* (assimilated loans) and *tatsama* (unassimilated loans). The other Kannaḍa-Kannaḍa verse-based dictionaries are: *Kabbigārakaipiḍi* (c. 1530), *Karṇāṭaka-śabdamanjari* (c. 1560) with 120 verses, *Karṇāṭakasanjīwana* (c. 1600) with 35 verses, *Śabdāgama* (?) with 202 verses and *Bhārata-*

nighaṇṭu with 67 verses. Therefore, it appears that no traditional Kannaḍa dictionary in verse has followed the Amarakōśa tradition of Sanskrit, unlike Tamil and Telugu. Between the 12th and 17th centuries many Sanskrit-Kannaḍa bilingual dictionaries were prepared to aid Kannaḍa writers in their knowledge of Sanskrit, viz. *Abhidhāna-vastukōśa* by Nāgavarma II (c. 1145), and *Nācirājīya* (c. 1300), a Kannaḍa commentary of Sanskrit Amarakōśa. The first Kannaḍa-English Dictionary (as well as English-Kannaḍa) was prepared by Rev. William Reeve (1824—32) called *Carnāṭaka-English Dictionary*. The most standard of the bilingual dictionaries was prepared by Rev. F. Kittel, a German missionary. His *Kannaḍa-English Dictionary* consisting of 70,000 entries was published by Basel Mission Press, Mangalore in 1894. It has both literary and colloquial words with regional and social variants; the headwords are written in Kannaḍa as well as in Roman; the meanings are given in both Kannaḍa and English with literary or colloquial usage; derived or extended forms are given under the same entry. Native headwords are set in large bold type-face and non-native ones in small regular type. Cognates from Tamil, Telugu, Malayāḷam and Tuḷu are provided in many cases. The printing of this work was excellent for the 19th century. The Madras University has published a revised and enlarged edition of it (Kittel 1968—71) but the major part of Kittel's work remains

ಪಾಡು pâṛu. 2. = (ಪಟು, etc.), ಹಾಡು 2. Running, flying, etc. 2, a kind of boat or ship (ವಹಿತ್ರ ಭೇದ Śmd. Dh., o. r. ಬಹಿತ್ರ-; ಬಹಿತ್ರಭೇದ Śmd. II, Śm. 35; ಬಹಿತ್ರ Śm. 117; ಬಹಿತ್ರದ ಭೇದ Kk. 93; ಹಡಗುಗಳ ಭೇದ Ct. I, 77; T., M.; Tu. ಪಾಡಿ; M. ಪಾಡಿಲ್, a float, raft). 3, a flying vehicle: a self-moving chariot of the gods (ನಡೆವೂಡು, ವಿಮಾನ Kś.; ನಡೆವಾಡ, ವ್ಯೋಮಯಾನ Śm. 10, o. r. ನಡೆವಾಡು; 800 ಗಟ-). — ಪಾಡಿಟ್. -ಅಟ್. = ಪಾಡುಗೆಡು. (Rêv. 14, after 106). — ಪಾಡುಗೆಡು. -ಕೆಡು. Leaping, running, etc. to cease (Śêv. 3, after 35). — ಪಾಡುವಿನಿ. -o-ವನಿ. Flying drops, drizzling rain (ತುಷಾರ Mr. 44; M. ಪಾಡಿಲ್). — ಪಾಡುವಪ್ಪಳಿ. -o-ಬಳಿ. (Śmd. 204). A discus (ಚಕ್ರ Ct. I, 77; II, 75; Abh. P. 13,89; 14, 188; Rêv. 6, after 11; J. 20, 50). — ಪಾಡುವಪ್ಪಳಿಗೆಯುಳ್ಳ. -ಕೆಯ್ಯ. (ಎನ್ನು Kś.). — ಪಾಡುವಪ್ಪಳಿಯ ಕೆಯ್ಯ. Vishṇu (ಉಪೇನ್ದ್ರ Kk. 7). — ಪಾಡೀ ಬಿಲ್. -ಏಟ್. To commence to run, to run away (ನಿಧಾವನ Śmd. Dh.). 2, to become contemptuous (ಅವಮಾನ Śmd. Dh.).

Dictionary excerpt 249.4: An article from Kittel (1894)

unchanged. The revised edition has 7800 new items (Kedilaya 1980).

In the preface to this monumental dictionary, Kittel gives a list of 420 Dravidian words 'probably borrowed by Sanskrit' (Kittel 1894, Preface xvii-xliii) which opened up a new area of research on Dravidian loanwords in Sanskrit. A major endeavour is now being made by Kannaḍa Sāhitya Pariṣat, Bangalore, to bring out a comprehensive Kannaḍa-Kannaḍa dictionary called *Kannaḍa-nighaṇṭu,* on historical principles under the chief editorship of G. Venkatasubbiah. So far five volumes of this work have been published (1966—1988) (Basavardhya 1980). The estimated number of entries is over 150,000 in seven volumes. The chronological coverage of the usage of words dates from the earliest, i.e. 450 A. D. to 1800 A. D. Dialectal forms, regional and social, are included. All published inscriptions and classics have been surveyed for usage in framing definitions. All pre-existing dictionary entries have been taken into account. The headword is given grammatical classification as [n.], [v.], [adj.] and so on in Kannaḍa. Meanings follow, arranged chronologically, from the earliest to recent times. Compounds are analysed into component elements. The source language of non-native words is indicated wherever it is known. Among the school dictionaries, the most widely used is the IBH Kannaḍa-Kannaḍa-English Dictionary (G. Venkatasubbiah et al. 1981) with 90,000 entries. The parts of speech and meanings are given both in Kannaḍa and English.

2.3. Telugu

An early Telugu grammar (c. 11th century), *Āndhrabhāṣānuśāsanam,* composed in Sanskrit sūtras, classifies words into *tadbhava* 'derived from that' (Sanskrit or Prakrit), *tatsama* 'same as that' (Sanskrit or Prakrit), *deśya* 'native', and *grāmya* 'rustic, vulgar'. Perso-Arabic words had not entered Telugu by that time. Early Telugu dictionaries were composed in verse and followed the Sanskrit Amarakośa, i.e. meaning-based categories of words were arranged into synonyms and homonyms including polysemous items. The important among them are as follows: (i) *Cawḍappa Sīsamulu* (c. 1619—37); *sīsamu* is a certain metrical form of verse in which dictionaries were composed. There are 30 verses covering 600 lexical items. The author gave meanings of words which rhymed in the last syllable, e.g. **wiri** 'flower', **newiri** 'today', **kāwiri** 'excess', **pari** 'sword', **rūpari** 'a beautiful woman', etc. He also listed synonyms without subjecting these to any major classification. Many of his meanings are not attested by later dictionaries or literature. He cited quite a few loanwords (nearly 52) from Perso-Arabic sources but treated them as native; for 'pen' he cites **kalam** (Arabic) and **pēnā** (perhaps French). (ii) Ganapawarapuweṅkaṭakawi's *Āndrhra nighaṇṭuwu* (1674—89) has 128 verses in *sīsa* metre. He classifies words, following Amarakośa, into 'gods, humans, non-human non-mobile, and non-human mobile'. There is also a part dealing with words having *nānārthas* (different meanings). For instance, he gives 25 names for **Viṣṇu,** one of the Hindu Trinity. He cites synonymous verbs which rhyme in the last syllable, e.g. **bēpaḍe, agapaḍe, paṭṭuwaḍe** 'surrendered'. He also gives meanings of certain words that begin with *a-,* followed by *ā-, e-, k-, c-,* etc. Words beginning with a given letter are covered in one verse. These indicate the author's awareness of the alphabetical order. He then gives a list of homonyms, e.g. **kari** 'border' (native), 'elephant' (**karin-** Sanskrit), etc. His synonyms include regional, stylistic or social variants, e.g. **palu, pallu** 'tooth', **kayi, kay** 'hand', **trāgu, trāwu** 'to drink' etc. He has also coined many native translation equivalents of Sanskrit words taking the originals from Amarakośa. (iii) The same author also wrote *Āndhradwirūpakośam* following Sriharṣa's *Dvirūpakośa* in Sanskrit. This is a dictionary of variants, viz. dialectal, grammatical and phonological, e.g. **wēḍuka/wēḍka** 'wish', **bayalu/baylu** 'open space', **kalimi/kalmi** 'wealth'. It has classified items with two variants, three variants, four variants, etc., e.g. **īwala/iwwala/iwala** 'this side'. One clitic is cited with as many as seven variants. Therefore, this is a unique lexicon in Telugu. (iv) Paydipāṭi Lakṣmaṇakawi's *Āndhranāmasangrahamu* (c. late 17th century). This is the most popular of the versified dictionaries in Telugu. There are 209 verses covering 1788 words. The words, as usual, are classified according to meaning; gods, human, inanimate, animate (non-human). There are 29 verses involving 79 words with multiple meanings. The lexical items covered in versified dictionaries are all either native words or assimilated loans from Sanskrit or Prakrit. However, glosses are given in Sanskrit. Phonological variants are also treated as synonyms. (v) Kastūri Ranga Kawi's *Sāmba-*

nighaṇṭuwu (c. 18th century A.D.) is composed in the *sīsa* metre and has four semantic groups plus a chapter on *nānārthas*. There are in all 108 verses covering 2906 words. The synonyms of common verbs in the 3rd person sg. are given under the 'human' group. (vi) *Āndhrabhāṣārṇawamu* by Nudurupāṭi Wenkanna (18th century), like the others, also follows the model of Sanskrit Amarakōśa. There are three *kāṇḍas* (chapters), each with several semantic sub-groups. There are 624 verses covering over 3000 words. The author has used different metres unlike his predecessors. C. P. Brown reported of having seen a Telugu-French dictionary in England, said to have been written around 1720 by a French Missionary (Usharani 1974, 491-3). A manuscript of this is in the India Office Library, London. The first published Telugu-English Dictionary is *A Vocabulary of Gentoo and English* (1818) by 'A Senior Merchant' of the Madras Establishment. At the end of the preface the author's name is given as William Brown. Apparently the Telugu language was called 'Gentoo' by some people of the East India Company at that time. There are 3434 entries in Telugu script alphabetically arranged. The alphabetization was based purely on phonetic criteria; front vowels (*i ī e ē*) are cited with the onglide *y-* (*yi, yī, ye, yē*) and those with back vowels are cited with the onglide *w-* (*wu, wū, wo, wō*). Consequently, under vowels only items with *a* and *ā* occur. The onglides *y* and *w* are predictable and therefore non-phonemic. William Brown replaced Sanskritic vocalic *ṛ* by *ru, r̄* by *r* and *ai, au* by *ayi* and *awu*. In the Telugu alphabet, the anuswāra is included among the vowels. It is a cover symbol for homorganic nasals which fall into three phonemes; *m* (before *p b s ś ṣ h*), *n* (before *t d c j k g*), and *ṇ* (before retroflex *ṭ ḍ*). Brown correctly locates the anuswāra with non-labial articulation in the alphabetical order after V*n*] and anuswāra with labial articulation after V*m*]. Only popular words are included, not the literary ones. The verbs are cited in their nominalized form, e.g. **aḍagaḍam** v.a. 'to ask, to require' (V + **aḍam** = V + *ing*); the entry in Telugu script is followed by a grammatical label, e.g. v.a. = verb-adverb; sub. = substantive; v.n. = verb-noun, etc. For verbs, following the grammatical label, the durative and perfective participles are cited, e.g. **aḍugutū/aḍigi** 'asking, having asked'. For substantives, the singular and plural forms are cited. If the oblique in the singular is different from the stem, it is cited; e.g. "**ceyyi** sub. **cēti, cētulu**". Here **cēti-** is oblique sg. and **cētulu** is nominative plural. The oblique of the plural is formed by adding *a* to the plural stem, whereas there are no strict rules to predict the singular oblique. In a sense, the author has shown his sensitivity to the complex morphophonemics of Telugu in his dictionary, which none of his successors have either understood or followed. He said he wrote a grammar of Telugu, but it was not finalized. He therefore indicated the morphophonemic variations of lexical items in the dictionary. He included native items as well as borrowings from Sanskrit, Prakrit, Perso-Arabic and English found in current usage. There were 15 English words like *nambaru* = number, *ḍikrī* = decree, etc. (judiciary and revenue terms).

Campbell's *A Dictionary of the Teloogoo Language* (1821) is superior to William Brown's in coverage and methodology. The dictionary has 14,862 entries. He prefixed labels for native Telugu words, Sanskrit derivatives, colloquial words and borrowings from Arabic, Persian and Hindustani. One 'Mamidi Venkayya, a learned native at Masulipatnam, has been of material assistance to the Author' (Campbell 1821, advertisement page, paras 3,4,5). Māmiḍi Venkayya had written a monolingual dictionary called *Āndhradīpika* by then. He distinguished *r̄* and *r* in the alphabetical order, whose difference was valid only in classical literature; the phonemes /c j/ were listed as [ts, tś, dz, dź] although the difference was predictable in terms of the following vowel. It appears that he did not know of William Brown's dictionary. After each vowel, the first consonant listed is anuswāra, ahead of the other consonants, i.e. *aṃk/g/c/j/t/d*, etc. and then *ak, ag*, etc. This order of anuswāra was followed

√ అదరడం *v. a.* అదురుతూ। అదిరి. To start; to shake. ఫిరంగి ధ్వనిచేతను గోడ అదిరినది The report of the gun made the wall *shake*. నేను పిడుగుధ్వనిచేతను అదిరిపడ్డాను The noise of the thunderbolt made me *start* and tumble down. Some write it అదురడం.

Dictionary excerpt 249.5: An entry from William Brown (1818)

by the later lexicographers. For the first time, Campbell includes as lexical entries certain nominal derivative suffixes e.g. **-kāḍu** 'he' (agentive suffix) and clitics like **kadā** (tag question). The causative forms are given under non-causative stems, *neṭṭince* 'one caused somebody to be pushed' under **neṭṭu** 'to push'. He separated, by and large, homonyms as separate entries, e.g. **ālu** 'wife', **ālu**, plural of **āwu** 'cow'. He entered verbal roots as headwords rather than their nominal forms, unlike William Brown. He tried to keep the distinction of *ṛ* and *r* but was not correct throughout, e.g. **ceruwu, ceruku** should have been **ceruwu, ceṛuku**. He introduced nasalization by a diacritic following grammatical description, but not current usage. He numbered glosses; sometimes usages are given. The next major bilingual dictionary was *A Dictionary of English and Teloogoo* (1835—39) by John Cormac Morris, who served as a 'Deputy Telugu Translator to the Government'. It has two volumes, vol. 1: 584 pages, vol. 2: 532 pages. He was assisted by a former Telugu pundit Rāwipāṭi Gurumūrtiśāstri. This was mainly meant for English speakers learning Telugu words. C. P. Brown's *Telugu-English Dictionary* (1852) is a monumental contribution to Telugu bilingual lexicography. No foreign scholar has done as much for Telugu literature and lexicography as C. P. Brown. He had all Telugu palm-leaf manuscripts copied on paper and edited them. He studied Telugu language and literature in depth. He also prepared an English-Telugu Dictionary (1853) as well as a Dictionary of 'mixed dialects' (1854). He has not only drawn on Campbell but also on earlier grammars and classical literature, besides current usage. He has included almost all the words occurring in earlier dictionaries — both the versified ones and European ones. (1) In the alphabetical order he treated each series of homorganic consonants as a single letter, e.g. *k, kh, g, gh; c, ch, j, jh;* etc. He also treated the sibilants as a single letter, viz. *s, ś, ṣ*. He dropped the obsolete nasalized vowel, indicated by a semi-circle (ardhānuswāra), occurring in words after vowels in Telugu. He has also not maintained the distinction between the two trill consonants, viz., *ṛ* and *r*. (2) Brown used an asterisk before loanwords from Sanskrit and Prakrit. No marking was used for other loanwords. However, he prepared a separate dictionary for loanwords from Perso-Arabic, English, Portuguese etc., called *Miśramabhāṣānighaṇṭuwu* (Mixed Language Dictionary). He has also included a number of colloquial expressions which had not found a place in the earlier dictionaries. He did not follow Campbell in giving derivative suffixes as separate entries. Derived items like **koṇṭetanamu** 'indecency', **tiyyadanamu** 'sweetness' are given as separate entries and not under the stems **koṇṭe** and **tiyya**, respectively. Sometimes even the verbs which can be used as intransitives and transitives are given as separate headwords. The verbs are cited in their infinitive form ending in *ṭa,* e.g. **caduvuṭa, pampuṭa** instead of **caduvu, pampu**, etc. Homonyms are meticulously separated but not numbered. The part of speech of each entry is indicated after the headword in almost all cases. Certain conjunctive suffixes and clitics are given the status of separate entries. Sanskrit vocalic *ṛ* is given in two spellings, e.g. *ṛṣi, ruṣi* 'a prophet'. The meanings are given in explanatory Telugu as well as in English.

Galletti (1935) is the next important bilingual dictionary. The author calls it a manual rather than a dictionary. It was meant for administrators, missionaries, business people and Telugu students learning English. The English alphabetical order is followed. The Telugu items are given in Roman script. It draws vocabulary from popular and official usage, but was not based on the material of the earlier dictionaries. It can be called a dictionary of current usage in every respect. There has been no standard Telugu-English dictionary after Galletti's. G. V. Ramamurty published a Telugu-Savara dictionary in 1904. (Savara is a Munda language which was extensively studied by G. V. Ramamurty.) The most standard of Telugu dictionaries is *Śabdaratnākaramu* (1885) by Bahujanapalli Sītārāmācāryulu. It has since been reprinted 6 times. There are nearly 34,000 entries in the dictionary. The headwords are followed by a

వాచుట *v. n.* To swell. To pine, long, be eager. (The Hindus like the Musulmans imagine the face and the legs to swell with desire or want.) వాడు కూటికి వాచియున్నాడు he is perishing for want of food. మేము దానికి వాచిన వాండ్ల ముకాము I am not pining for it. I do not care for it. Vish. 6. 100. మేము సై తమ్మీ వాచిన వారియట్ల గరువంబున గన్గొనుచుంటి మవ్వి భర, నొప్పిచేత లావోట, కెప్పుటెంచుట. D.

Dictionary excerpt 249.6: An entry from C. P. Brown (1852)

symbol indicating the source language as well as the part of speech. This includes both literary and colloquial words, with usages wherever possible. It follows the Devanagari order in the alphabet. Words with anuswāra occur before other consonants. This work includes 123 English loanwords, 16 Tamil loanwords, and 4 Kannaḍa loanwords. The grammatical classification is given after the entry. The verbs are given in their basic form, e.g. **winu** 'to hear' and not **winuṭa**. Meanings are numbered and homonyms are separated. The 6th edition of Śabdaratnākaramu was revised by Sri N. Venkata Rao who added an Appendix of 116 pages involving 3,115 new loanwords. The most comprehensive Telugu-Telugu dictionary is *Sūryarāyāndhranighaṇṭuwu (SAN)* in 7 volumes (1936—1972). Jayanti Rāmayya edited the first and second volumes (1936/39); the third and fourth volumes were edited by Kāśībhaṭṭa Subbayyaśāstri (1942/44). The publication of volumes 5, 6 and 7 was entrusted to Dr. G. Sitapati under the editorship of Sri K. Subbayyaśāstri. Volume 7 was completed and published by the Andhra Pradesh Sahitya Akademi in 1972. *SAN* is still considered the most comprehensive dictionary. Though usages are cited from the earliest to more recent literary sources, it cannot claim to be a dictionary prepared on historical principles. Native words, loanwords and grammatical categories are suitably identified. The most widely prevalent meaning is first given followed by meanings with restricted usage. In the earlier volumes, cognates from Tamil and Kannaḍa have been identified. Burrow and Emeneau used the Sankaranārāyaṇa's Telugu-English dictionary (1907) based on *Śabdaratnākaramu* as the main source for Telugu entries in *DED(R)*.

2.4. Malayāḷam

Bilingual dictionaries precede monolingual ones in Malayāḷam. Rev. H. Gundert (1872) refers to "two very valuable dictionaries compiled by the Portuguese and Italian missionaries of Verapoli, works which, although completed in 1746, rest upon materials accumulated in the 17th, perhaps even 16th century, and rank as the oldest monuments extant of the study of Indian languages by Europeans" (Preface, p. iv). These were published by the "Cottayam Press" but are not available. The next known bilingual dictionary was Rev. Benjamin Bailey's *A Dictionary of High and Colloquial Malayalam and English* (1846). Since Malayāḷam is more heavily influenced by Sanskrit than any other literary Dravidian language, Rev. Bailey included many Sanskrit words in the dictionary, even if they were not supported by literary or popular usage. Sanskrit-derived and native Malayāḷam words were also not distinguished (Gundert 1872, Preface, p. vi). Bailey drew his Sanskrit vocabulary from H. H. Wilson's Sanskrit-English Dictionary. The glosses were given only in English. This work was followed by the first monumental bilingual dictionary in Malayāḷam by Rev. Herman Gundert, *A Malayalam and English Dictionary* (1872), printed by the Basel Mission Press, Mangalore. This was prepared on sound lines: (1) It took vocabulary from literature as well as from regional and social dialects; (2) Sanskrit expressions not used in literature were excluded (unlike Bailey); (3) loanwords were identified and source languages indicated; (4) for native words, the other literary languages which have cognates have been pointed out, though the cognates are not always cited; (5) the entries are given both in Malayāḷam and in Roman script; (6) the part of speech of the entry is indicated; (7) glosses are given in English; followed by usage and source; (8) homonyms are separated by prefixed Roman numbers, e.g. I **tikku** *Tbh*. (Skt. *dik-*) 'direction'; II **tikku** 'straining, pressure'; (9) verbs are cited in their infinitive form by adding *-ka* or *-kka* (see Pref. pp. iv to xviii). This dictionary is used widely by scholars for comparative purposes.

തൂങ്ങുക tūṅṅuya (v. n. of തൂക്കുക) 1. To hang. ത്രാസു ശരിയായി തൂങ്ങി Arb. hung even. പിടിച്ചു തൂങ്ങുന്ന രഥത്തിനെ ചിലർ KR. so as to detain the chariot. — to be suspended, dangle, എല്ലു തൂങ്ങി Bhr. (of an old man). അടുത്തു തൂങ്ങിയും, തൂങ്ങി.അടുക്കു Bhr. to lean forward in fencing. വാങ്ങിയും നീങ്ങിയും തൂങ്ങിയെടുക്കയും PatR. തൂങ്ങിമരിച്ചു = തൂങ്ങന്നു So. 2. to be weighed. അന്നു ഏറ്റത്തൂങ്ങിയ സത്യം Bhr. when Brahma weighed truth & untruth, the former weighed more. ആ മാംസം പ്രാചീന ശരിയായി തൂങ്ങാതെ Arb. 3. T. Te. to be drowsy, to sleep.

VN. തൂങ്ങൽ hanging, inclination, reliance, drowsiness.

Dictionary excerpt 249.7: An entry from Gundert (1872)

Based on Bailey's dictionary, a Malayāḷam-Malayāḷam dictionary was prepared by Richard Collins (1865). *Śabdaratnāvaḷi* (1923) by Sreekandeswaram Padmanabha Pillai is considered a standard dictionary for language scholars. *Navayugubhāṣānighaṇṭu* by Narayana Paṇikkar (1954) is the next one which included a large number of words borrowed from English also. A major effort is *Malayāḷam Lexicon* (1965) planned in 1953 on the same lines as the *Tamil Lexicon* of Madras University. It is edited by Suranad Kunjan Pillai and is being published by the University of Kerala. Three volumes have so far come out (1965, 1970, 1976). The first volume has a long introduction (pp. i—xxx) which sets out the goals of the undertaking, the scope and methodology. It is a comprehensive bilingual dictionary prepared on historical principles like the great Oxford English Dictionary: (a) It has drawn data from all written documents from the earliest times and also from popular usage; (b) meanings are given in Malayāḷam as well as English with usages and authorities; (c) cognates are given but the dictionary has not drawn on *DED* (1961) although the 1st volume was printed in 1965; (d) meanings are arranged chronologically; (e) homonyms are separated; (f) entries are in Malayāḷam and Roman script; (g) loanwords are identified by source. It is, therefore, a modern dictionary in all respects. It is proposed to publish the lexicon in seven volumes of 1000 pages each.

3. Non-Literary Languages

Only Tuḷu and Kurukh have anything that can be called good dictionaries among the non-literary languages. Rev. A. Männer's *Tuḷu-English Dictionary* (1886) runs 687 pages with nearly 20,000 entries. The Tuḷu entries are given both in the Kannaḍa script and in Roman. Glosses in English are numbered; extended words and phrases are given under the same headword. The verbs are cited with infinitive suffixes, viz. *-uni, -pini, -puni* which help in identifying the conjugational class of the verb. Forms from both regional and social dialects are given without identification. This dictionary has been the major source of Tuḷu vocabulary for all Dravidian comparativists for nearly a century. Recently a major 'Tulu Lexicon Project' was undertaken by K. S. Haridas Bhat and U. P. Upadhayaya at the P. G. Research Centre of the M. G. M. College, Udupi, Karnataka. It is proposed to bring out the Lexicon in six volumes. The first volume of the *Tuḷu nighaṇṭu* (1988) covers four vowels *a* to *ī*. It is very comprehensive in its coverage. Regional and social dialects, as well as modern Tuḷu literature, written and oral, have been thoroughly studied and covered. The entries are in Kannaḍa and Roman and the meanings in Kannaḍa and English. This is a definite improvement on Männer (1886). The vocabularies of the Nilagiri languages — Toda, Kota and Badaga — collected by Emeneau in the 1930s, are included in *DED(R)* (1961, 1984). Kurukh (Oraon) has a standard dictionary by Rev. A. Grignard, S. J. (1924) entitled *An Oraon-English Dictionary,* published by the Administration of "Anthropos" in Austria. The entries follow the English alphabet. Broadly phonemicized Roman transcription is employed for the headwords. The grammatical category is given next to the entry followed by indication of source language in parentheses in case of loanwords. Meanings are accompanied by usages of words in sentences with English translation. Different meanings under the same entry are numbered. For verbs, the past tense 3rd sg. forms are given after the entry in parentheses before the grammatical label. Homonyms are separated by bold numbers following the headwords. There has been no attempt to revise or reprint it. This work is now out of print.

The Brāhūī language, Part III *Etymological Vocabulary* by Sir Denys Bray (1934) running 265 pages has a comprehensive vocabulary. Brāhūī has about 5 % of Dravidian vocabulary; the rest of the vocabulary is mostly borrowed from the neighbouring Indic and Iranian languages, viz. Jatki, Sindhi, Urdu, Persian, Balochi, Pashto, etc. There are over 7000 entries in this work. Meanings are followed by usage. All entries are in Roman

---

pocgō S. Any small worm, caterpillar or fleshy larve, esp. of beetle. The earth worm and the worm which develops in the human stomach are better called *leṇḍā*. The latter is sometimes also called *kūltā pocgō*, stomach worm.

poc-ha Adj. Lousy. *Poc-has*, a low fellow, a scoundrel.

Dictionary excerpt 249.8: An entry from Grignard (1924)

with adequate diacritics; meanings are only in English. At the end of the entry, in the case of loanwords, the source language and the source form are cited in square brackets. Grammatical labels are not given after the entries. However, there are frequent cross-references to the sections in the grammar (Part I) published in 1909. For the rest of the non-literary languages, there are vocabularies published and prepared by missionaries and administrators during the British period and recently also by linguists. These languages are Toda, Iruḷa, Koraga of Southern Dravidian, Kui, Kuvi, Gondi, Koṇḍa, Pengo and Manḍa of South-Central Dravidian, Parji, Kolami, Naiki, Ollari and Gadba of Central Dravidian (Emeneau 1969). These are not treated here since they do not contribute much either to the theory or practice of lexicography.

4. Comparative and Etymological Dictionaries

As early as 1816, Francis Whyte Ellis of the Indian Civil Service discovered the fact that Tamil, Malayāḷam, Telugu, Kannaḍa, and Tuḷu belong to the same family of languages (DEDR, 1; Krishnamurti 1969, 311—2). It was Caldwell's comparative grammar published in 1856 that established the extended membership of the Dravidian family. However, no attempt at the preparation of a comparative and/or etymological dictionary was made until the middle of this century. R. P. Sethupillai et al. (1959) edited the first volume of Dravidian Comparative Vocabulary, published by the Madras University. It covers the major South Indian languages. Burrow and Emeneau collaborated for over two decades and published *A Dravidian Etymological Dictionary* (*DED* 1961) which opened a new era in comparative Dravidian studies. This work has 4,572 numbered entries (pp. 1—385) followed by word indexes for individual languages (pp. 387—574), an index of English meanings (pp. 585—604), and an index of flora and fauna (pp. 605—609). Taking entries from the *Tamil Lexicon* as base words, the authors have cited cognates from all available Dravidian languages. The unpublished field-notes of the authors on many of the non-literary languages have been included. No attempt was made to reconstruct the proto-Dravidian forms. The second edition of the dictionary was published in 1984 incorporating the material of two supplements issued since 1961 and with many revisions. The revised edition *DEDR* (1984) follows the same format as the first edition. There are 5557 entries (pp. 1—507), followed by a supplement of Dravidian borrowings from Indo-Aryan and other sources with 61 entries (pp. 509—14), word-indexes of languages and an index of English meanings (pp. 515—816), and an index of flora (Latin) (pp. 817—821). Finally an index of entries in *DEDR* corresponding to *DED* are given (pp. 825—53), followed by a list of the numbers of new items. *DEDR* is more thorough and comprehensive than *DED*. It is a monumental work which has positively contributed to research in comparative Dravidian. Cognates are cited from 26 languages, each with several dialects in the following order: Tamil, Malayāḷam, Iruḷa, Kurumba, Kōta, Toda, Kannaḍa, Koḍagu, Tuḷu, Belari, Koraga; Telugu, Kolami, Naikṛi, Naiki of Chanda, Parji, Gadba; Gondi, Koṇḍa, Pengo, Manḍa, Kui, Kuwi; Kuṛux, Malto and Brahui. Here Telugu could have been followed by Gondi — Kuwi, with which it is closer rather than by the Parji sub-group. Even suspected IA borrowings into Dravidian have been included. In the case of certain items an Indo-Aryan source is suggested with a question mark at the end. At the end of each *DEDR* entry, the corresponding number of the *DED (S, N)* entry is given.

An etymological dictionary of Telugu has been brought out in 5 volumes by the Andhra University. It draws cognates from *DED* (1961). It does not add new etymologies not covered by *DED(R)* 1961, 1984. T. Burrow and S. Bhattacharya (1960) have compiled 'A Comparative Vocabulary of Gondi dialects' published as a supplement to the Journal of the Asiatic Society, Calcutta (Vol. 2, 73—251). They have drawn their material from about twenty sources scattered in various publications with different degrees of phonetic or phonological reliability. This is a

---

1252 *Ta.* kayal, cēl carp. *Ma.* kayal a fish, *Cyprinus*; kayyan a river fish. *Te.* kakka fish; cēpa id. *Kol.* kaye id. *Nk.* kayye id. *Nk. (Ch.)* kayye (*pl.* -l) id. *Pa.* key sp. fish. *Go.* kīke (Mu. Ma.) a small fish, (M. Ko.) fish (*Voc.* 706). / ? Cf. kai-, ke- in Skt. kaivarta-, kevarta- fisherman, Pali Pkt. kevaṭṭa- id. (Turner, *CDIAL*, no. 3469). DED(S) 1050.

Dictionary excerpt 249.9: An entry from *DEDR* (1984)

very useful compendium and has been fully utilized by the authors of *DEDR* (1984).

5. Dialect Dictionaries/Special Dictionaries

The Andhra Pradesh Sahitya Akademi (the State Academy of Letters), established in 1957, has brought out a series of dialect dictionaries of occupational vocabularies in Telugu since 1962 (Telugu Dialect Dictionary). The first volume covering the words used in agriculture was edited by Bh. Krishnamurti (1962, repr. 1974); the second volume covering the handloom vocabulary was published in 1971. The project was proposed and implemented by Bh. Krishnamurti. This is the first work of its kind in Indian languages. The vocabulary was collected by trained fieldworkers from about 120 villages covering the whole state. All synonyms and phonological variants are grouped together. A widely used item with phonetic stability has been taken as the master entry. Under this all dialectal synonyms, whether phonologically related or not, are cross-referred. This is followed by a descriptive meaning; a reference to a line diagram is given wherever necessary; at the end of the entry a list of numbers where the entry is recorded is given, keyed to the names of the villages selected. The methodology used in this volume is described in detail in Krishnamurti 1985 b. So far four volumes have been published; Vol. I.: Agriculture, Vol. II: Handloom (Krishnamurti 1962, 71), Vol. IV: House-building and Architecture (Radhakrishna 1968), Vol. V: Pottery (Reddy 1976). Volume III dealing with Fisheries and Boat Construction has not gone to press yet. In 1983, the Andhra Pradesh State Government dissolved all Academies. The newly established Telugu University has taken over the functions of the A. P. Sahitya Akademi. All literary languages have had a large number of dictionaries of a specialized nature published during the last two decades. These deal with terminologies in science and technology, proverbs, idioms and phrases, quotations, concordances of classical works etc. Since these have been prepared mostly in the respective languages, they are not easily accessible to students of lexicography outside the language area. None of these is highly original in attaining national and international visibility. Therefore, no effort has been made to treat them here.

6. Selected Bibiliography

6.1. Dictionaries

Abhidhānavastukośa c. 1145 = Nāgavarma II: Abhidhānavastukośa. Ed. by A. Venkata Rao/H. Sesha Iyengar. Madras 1933.

Akarāti-nikaṇṭu 1594 = Citampara Rēwaṇacittar: Akarāti-nikaṇṭu (A dictionary beginning with letter a). Ed. by D. Narayana Aiyangar. Tamil Sangam. Madurai 1921 (3368 words).

Āndhra nighaṇṭuwu 1674—89 = Gaṇapawarupuwēnkaṭakawi 1674—89.: Also called wēnkaṭēsāndhramu. Kākināda 1898; Madras 1933. Āndhra nighaṇṭuwu [128 verses].

Āndhrabhāṣānuśāsanamu c. 11 cent. = Nannayabhaṭṭu (First Telugu grammar written in Sanskrit ascribed to the first known Telugu poet) (11 cent.): Āndhrabhānuśāsamu or Āndhraśabdacintāmaṇi. Kakinada 1932.

Āndhrabhāṣārṇawamu c. 18 cent. = Nudurupāṭi Wenkanna: Āndhrabhāṣārṇawamu. 18 cent. Visakhapatnam, 1891, 1900; Madras 1910, 1912, 1931 (A dictionary of native Telugu words in 108 verses of the sīsa metre; 3000 words).

Āndhradīpika = Māmiḍi Venkayya: Āndhradīpika (First alphabetical Telugu dictionary in Devanāgari script). Masulpatnam 1848.

Āndhradwirūpakōśam = Gaṇapawarupuwēnkaṭakawi: Āndhradwirūpakōśam. Unpublished. Oriental Mss. Literary, Tirupalī (120 verses).

Āndhranāmasangrahamu c. 17 cent. = Payḍipāṭi Lakshmaṇakawi: Āndhranāmasangrahamu. c. late 17 cent. First published in 1840. Revised ed. by Vavilla Press. Madras 1913, 1923, 1953 [209 verses, 1788 words].

Bailey 1846 = Benjamin Bailey: A Dictionary of High and Colloquial Malayalam and English. 1846.

Beschi C. 1732 = (Father Beschi: Caturakarāti (Alphabetized Four-part Dictionary). Tirukkavalur 1732.

Bhāratanighaṇṭu [67 verses].

Bray 1934 = Sir Denys Bray: The Brahūī Language, Part III — Etymological Vocabulary. Delhi 1934 [49—313 p.].

Brown 1818 = William Brown: A Vocabulary of Gentoo and English. Madras 1818. Revised edn. Madras 1953 [6+378 p.].

Brown 1852 = Charles Philip Brown: A Dictionary, Telugu-English. Madras 1852. 2nd edn. Revised and enlarged by M. Venkata Ratnam, W. H. Campbell and K. Veeresalingam. Madras 1905. Reprinted by Asian Educational Services. New Delhi 1979 [viii+1416 p.].

Brown 1853 = Charles Philip Brown: English-Telugu Dictionary. 1853.

Brown = Charles Philip Brown: Miśramabhāṣānighaṇṭuwu (Mixed Language Dictionary).

Burrow/Bhattacharya 1960 = Thomas Burrow/ Sudhibhushan Bhattacharya: A Comparative Vocabulary of the Gondi Dialects. In: Journal of the Asiatic Society. Calcutta 1960 [73—251 p.].

Campbell 1821 = Campbell: A Dictionary of the Teloogoo Language 1821 [14, 862 entries].

Caturāsyanighaṇṭu c. 1450 [130 verses]

Cauḍappa sīsamulu c. 1619—37 = Cauḍappa: sīsamulu. Printed in: Bulletin of the Government Oriental Mss. Library 3. No. 1, 53—70 Madras?).

Collins 1865 = Richard Collins: (Malayāḷam-Malayāḷam)

DED(R) 1961/1984 = T. Burrow/M. B. Emeneau: A Dravidian Etymological Dictionary. Oxford 1961. [1st edn. xxix + 609 p.]; Oxford 1984 [2nd revised edn. xli + 853].

Dvirūpakōśa = Śrīharṣa: Dvirūpakōśa.

Fabricius c. 1779 = John Philip Fabricius: A Dictionary, English and Tamil. Madras 1779 (9000 entries). Revised by L. P. Haubroe/Sperschneider/T. Brotherton and published by Christian Knowledge Society's Press in two parts. Madras 1852.

Fabricius c. 1786 = John Philip Fabricius/John Breithaupt: A Dictionary of the English and Malabar Languages (2 vols.) Madras 1786.

Galletti 1935 = A. Galletti Di Cadilhac: Galletti's Telugu Dictionary: A Dictionary of Current Telugu. London 1935 (xvii + 434 p.].

Grignard 1924 = A. Grignard: An Oraon-English Dictionary. Calcutta. Vienna 1924 (vii + 697 p.].

Gundert 1872 = H. Gundert: A Malayalam and English Dictionary. Mangalore 1872 (xviii + 1116 p].

Kabbigārakaipidi c. 1530

Karṇāṭakaśabdamanjari c. 1560 [120 verses]

Karṇāṭaka Śabdasāram c. 1400 [1416 words]

Karṇāṭakasanjīwana c. 1600 [35 verses]

Kittel 1894 = F. Kittel: A Kannaḍa-English Dictionary. Mangalore 1894 [l + 1752 p.]. Reprinted by Asian Educational Services. New Delhi 1983. Revised and enlarged by M. Mariappa Bhat. Madras 1968—71 [XVIII, 1781 p.].

Malayalam Lexicon 1965—76 = A Comprehensive Malayalam-Malayalam-English Dictionary: Vols. I/II, ed. by Suranad Kunjan Pillai. Trivandrum 1965/1970; vol. III, ed. by K. V. Namboodiripad. Trivandrum 1976.

Männer 1886 = A. Männer: Tuḷu-English Dictionary. Mangalore 1886. Repr. by Asian Educational Services. New Delhi 1983 [688 p.].

Morris 1835—39 = John Cormac Morris: A Dictionary of English and Teloogoo. (Assisted by Rāwipāṭi Gurumūrtiśāstri). 2 vols. 1835—1839 [584, 532 pp.].

Nācirājiya c. 1300

Nānārthatipikai = Mutucāmi Piḷḷai: Nanārthatipikai. Ed. with commentary by S. Anavaratha Vinayakam Piḷḷai. Madras 1936 (5430 words).

Navayugabhāṣānighaṇṭu 1954 = Narayana Paṇikkar: Navayugabhāṣānighaṇṭu. 1954.

Nikaṇṭucūṭāmmaṇi c. 1520

Piṅkaḷantai c. 11—12 cent. = Pinkaḷar: Piṅkaḷantai ennum Piṅkaḷanikaṇṭu. Ed. by V. T. Sivanpillai/T. K. Subramania Chettiar. Hindu Theological Press. Madras 1890 (14 700 words).

Potikainikaṇṭu c. 1750 = Cāminātakkaviyar: Potikainikaṇṭu, 1750. Ed. by S. Vaiyapuri Pillai. Madras 1934.

Proença 1679 = Antaō De Proença: Tamil-Portuguese Dictionary A. D. 1679. Prepared for publication by Xavier S. Thani Nayagam. Kuala Lumpur 1966.

Ramamurty 1904 = G. V. Ramamurty: (Telugu-Savara).

Ranna c. 993 =

Reeve 1858 = William Reeve: A Dictionary, Canarese and English, revised by Daniel Sanderson. Bangalore 1858 [1468 p.]. Reprinted by Asian Educational Services. New Delhi 1979/1980.

Rottler 1830—37 = J. P. Rottler: A Dictionary of the Tamil and English Languages. 1830—37. [4 pts.]

Śabdāgama (?) [202 verses]

Śabdamaṇidarpaṇa 1260 = Kēsirāja: Śabdamaṇidarpaṇa, 1260 with commentary by Linganaradhya. Ed by A. Venkata Rao/H. Sesha Iyengar. Madras 1939.

Śabdaratnākaramu 1885 = Bahujanapalli Sītārāmācāryulu: Śabdaratnākaramu. Madras 1885. Repr. 1912, 1922, 1929, 1937; with Appendix 1958 [xxviii + 868 + App. 122 p.].

Śabdaratnāvali 1923 = Sreekandeswaram Padmanabha Pillai: Śabdaratnāvali 1923

Sāmbanighaṇṭuwu c. 18th c. = Kastūri Ranga Kawi: Sāmbanighaṇṭuwu. c. 18th cent. Visakhapalnam 1891, Madras 1913, 1951 [108 verses 2906 words].

SAN = Sūryarāyāndhranighaṇṭuwu. By a committee of scholars headed by K. Brahmayya Sastri. Kakinada. 1936—72 (7 vols.): vol. 1 *a-au*, 1936 [9 + 14 + 994 p.], vol. 2 *ka-ja*, 1939 [14 + 1000 p.], vol. 3 *ca-tr*, 1942 [930 + 20 p.], vol. 4 *te-nr*, 1944, 1972 [935 p.], vol. 5 *pa-bhrē*, 1958 [1236 p.], vol. 6 *ma-lau*, 1958 [994 p.], vol. 7 *wa-hṛ* 1958, 1972 in two parts [1248 p.].

Sangam Dictionary 1910—23 = Sangam Dictionary. (Tamil-Tamil) 1910—23 [3 vols., 63,900 words].

Sankaranarayana 1907 = P. Sankaranārāyana. A Telugu-English Dictionary. Madras 1907; 2nd ed. 1927, repr. 1953, 1964.

Sethupillai et al. 1959 = Dravidian Comparative Vocabulary. R. P. Sethupillai (ed.): Vol. I. Madras University 1959 [V, 178 p.].

Tamil Lexicon 1924—39 = Tamil Lexicon, published under the authority of the University of Madras. Madras 1924—39. Vol. 1 [632 p.]; vol. 2

[633+1208 p.]; vol. 3 [1209+1700 p.]; vol. 4 [1701—1932 p.]; vol. 5 [1933—2974 p.]; vol. 6 [2975—3928 p.]. Introduction by Vaiyapuripillai in vol. 6, 1936 [cv p.] deals with Tamil lexicography. Repr. with a supplement [423 p.] Madras 1982.

Telugu Dialect Dictionary 1962, 1974/ 1971/1968/1976 = Māṇḍalikavr̥ttipadakōsam (A Telugu Dialect Dictionary of Occupational Vocabularies). Hyderabad. Vol. I: Agriculture, ed. by Bh. Krishnamurti. 1962, (repr. 1974) [122+405 p.]; vol. II: Handloom. ed. by Bh. Krishnamurti. 1974 [56+464 p.]; vol. III: Fisheries and Boat Construction (in press); vol. IV: House Construction and Architecture. ed. by Budaraju Radhakrishna. 1968 [x+100+574 p.]; vol. V: Pottery. ed. by G. N. Reddy. 1976 [vi+36+195].

Tivākaram = Tivakarar: Cēntan̲tivākaram, c. 8 cent. Madras 1958.

Tolkāppiyam = Tolkāppiyar: Tolkāppiyam (The earliest extant Tamil grammar of early Christian era). Ed. with English commentary by P. S. Subrahmanya Sastri. Vol. I. Madras 1930; Vol. II. Annamalainagar 1945.

Tranquebar Dictionary 19th c.

Tulu Lexicon 1988 = U. P. Upadhayaya (ed.): Tuḷu nighaṇṭu (Tuḷu-Kannaḍa-English Dictionary): vol. 1. Mangalore 1988 [90+338 p.].

Venkatasubbiah 1966—88 = G. Venkatasubbiah: Kannaḍa-Kannaḍa Dictionary. Bangalore vol. 1 [XIX+1322 p.], vol. 2 [1323—2474 p.], vol. 3 [2475—3482 p.], vol. 4 [3483—4490 p.], vol. 5 [4491—5471 p.]. Vol. 1 ed. by D. L. Narasimhachar.

Venkatasubbiah et al. 1981 = G. Venkatasubbiah et al.: IBH Kannaḍa-Kannaḍa-English Dictionary. Bangalore 1981 (viii+677 p.].

Winslow 1862 = Miron Winslow: A Comprehensive Tamil and English Dictionary of High and Low Tamil. Madras 1862 (x+1976 p.] Repr. by Asian Educational Services. New Delhi 1987.

6.2 Other Publications

Basavaradhya 1980 = N. Basavaradhya: Preparation of Kannaḍa-Kannaḍa Dictionary on Historical Principles. In: B. G. Misra (ed.): Lexicography in India. Mysore 1980, 79—88.

Census 1981 = Census of India 1981. Paper I of 1987: Households and Household Population by Language Mainly Spoken in the Household. New Delhi 1987.

Emeneau 1969 = Murray B. Emeneau: The Non-Literary Dravidian Languages. In: Thomas A. Sebeok (ed.): Current Trends in Linguistics, Vol. 5. The Hague 1969, 334—342.

Jayadevan 1985 = V. Jayadevan: tamiz̲ akarāti iyal val̲arci varalāru [History and development of the Tamil Lexicography]. Anbunulagam, Madras 1985.

Kedilaya 1980 = A. S. Kedilaya: History of Dictionaries in Kannaḍa with Special Reference to Bilingual Dictionaries. In: B. G. Misra (ed.): Lexicography in India. Mysore 1980, 70—78.

Krishnamurti 1969 = Bh. Krishnamurti: Comparative Dravidian Studies. In: T. A. Sebeok (ed.), Current Trends in Linguistics Vol. 5. The Hague 1969, 309—33.

Krishnamurti 1985 a = Bh. Krishnamurti: An Overview of Comparative Dravidian Studies since Current Trends 5 (1969). In: Veneeta Z. Acson/Richard L. Leed (eds.), For Gordon Fairbanks. Honolulu 1985, 212—231.

Krishnamurti 1985 b = Bh. Krishnamurti: A Survey of Telugu Dialect Vocabulary Used in Native Occupations. In: International Journal of the Sociology of Language 55. 1985, 7—21.

Usharani 1974 = T. Usharani: telugu nighaṇṭuwula pariśīlana (A Study of Telugu Dictionaries). Tirupati 1974. Unpublished Ph. D. Dissertation submitted to S. V. University.

Bhadriraju Krishnamurti,
Hyderabad (India)

250. Lexicography of Other Languages of the Indian Subcontinent: The Munda Languages

1. Introduction
2. North Munda
3. South Munda
4. Selected Bibliography

1. Introduction

There are (depending on what counts as 'a language') a dozen Munda languages, all of them spoken in largely hilly tracts of eastern and central India: in Bengal, Bihar, Orissa, Madhya Pradesh, northern Andhra, and the easternmost parts of Maharashtra.

Munda is the western branch of the Austroasiatic family of languages, Mon-Khmer (with many more languages, perhaps c 150) being the eastern branch. The Munda languages are not particularly close to each other (clearly less so than, for instance, the Indo-Aryan languages of peninsular

India). The main cleavage is between North Munda (four or five comparatively closely related languages) and South Munda (seven or eight not very closely related languages). Some of the Munda languages (Gutob, Gorum, Kharia) have borrowed very heavily from their Indo-Aryan (and, to a lesser extent, Dravidian) neighbors, and all of the Munda languages participate to a fair degree in the Indian linguistic area.

Dictionaries were and are for the literate minority of speakers of Munda languages — and for some Munda languages it is a very small minority — used sometimes in learning the important regional language(s), but not often for any purpose involving their own native languages. The four major dictionaries (for four of the Munda languages), Bodding's *A Santal Dictionary* (Bodding 1929—35, sect. 2.6.), Hoffmann's and his associates' *Encyclopaedia Mundarica* (Hoffmann 1930—79, sect. 2.4.), Ramamurti's English-Sora and Sora-English dictionaries (Ramamurti 1933, 1938, sect. 3.6.), and Deeney's Ho-English dictionary (Deeney s. a., sect. 2.5.) were all compiled by non-native speakers (three of them foreign missionaries) for non-native users. The fourth dictionary maker, G. V. Ramamurti was an unusual man, a man of Telugu letters very active in literary, linguistic and cultural matters in the Telugu-speaking regions. In his own — Parlakimedi (Parlakhemundi) — region there was a large Sora population.

(When Andhra, the Telugu state, was finally established, Parlakimedi went not to Andhra but to Orissa, to Ramamurti's great displeasure.) Ramamurti interested himself in the Sora 'hill tribesmen', and spent more than twenty years working in their areas, using and studying the language with the collaboration of native-speaking tutors and consultants. All four prepared grammars and other materials for the languages. Despite the fact that English was neither the first nor second language of three of these men (all but Deeney) the dictionaries were written in English, and the phonetic/phonemic transcriptions of the languages were in a roman-based quasiphonemic transcription. (See Bodding's remarks in his Introduction on the earlier use of Indian scripts, Devanagari and the Bengali script, and his reasons for not using them.) Deeney gives Devanagari as well as roman-based transcriptions, but his definitions are given in English only, in this differing from earlier trilingual formats, e.g. the Korku-Hindi-English dictionaries. Deeney does use Devanagari in other materials of his in Ho. The dictionaries were made for the use of missionaries, civil servants, and educators, but also with an eye to the scholarly interests of (largely European) philologists and linguists, some of whom encouraged Bodding and the others. Ramamurti's and Deeney's books were published fairly cheaply in India and were locally available whereas Bodding's five volumes were published in Norway and were not available or affordable in Bihar and Bengal. Hoffmann's volumes were published cheaply by the Bihar government, and some of the volumes reprinted in 1950. In the sixties it was difficult to find a full set of the thirteen volumes, worm-eaten or not.

The Tea Districts Labour Association prepared 'handbooks' in English for several Munda and Dravidian languages (among the Munda languages: Sora, Kharia, Mundari and Santali) to help their tea-garden overseers in Assam and north Bengal communicate with the laborers brought in from Bihar and Orissa. The Kharia dictionary (Floor et al. 1934, sect. 3.1.) was a by-product of the lexical overflow from the vocabulary in the Kharia Handbook.

The old canard that 'primitive languages' such as the Munda languages have only a few hundred words, and communication is 'eked out' with gestures is still alive and taken seriously in some higher administrative circles in India. Some of these lexicographers explicitly discuss and reject such notions. (They do this implicitly with their dictionaries.) Thus Deeney quotes an English ICS (Indian Civil Service) officer who published a small book on Ho in 1915 and should have known better; Lionel Burrows (Burrows 1915, sect. 2.5.) wrote that 'the number of words used by an average Ho is not more than four hundred at the outside', and Deeney comments that his own dictionary has twelve thousand entries and he has not exhausted the Ho lexicon.

More recently (see Soy s. a., sect. 2.4. and Kisku/Soren 1951, sect. 2.6.), small dictionaries have been published compiled by native speakers (of Mundari and of Santali in these cases). I don't know whether they were made for local non Mundas, e.g. IAS (Indian Administrative Service) officers who must pass examinations in the languages of the regions they are assigned to, or for people in the Munda communities. For Kharia, the big dictionary now being compiled by several native Kharia scholars may be intended not only to preserve the older lexicon which is in the Ranchi area being replaced by Indo-Aryan borrowings, but to maintain and promote the language where it is being lost. Several books on the Kharia language have been published by native scholars recently, and folklore material as well as lexical material has been collected. But, with regard to the dictionary project, there have been disagreements on format and transcription which may hold up the completion and publication of the dictionary since those holding opposing positions — on, e.g., whether the nasal release of final preglottalized stops should be written or not (it is completely predictable), i.e. should one write *uḍṇ* or *uḍ* for 'mushroom' — may be intransigent enough to refuse to compromise, the need for a large Kharia dictionary in hand being less than the need to transcribe Kharia in one's own correct transcription and no other way.

The publication history of the last two volumes of the *Encyclopaedia Mundarica* (published by the Bihar state government press) is indicative of the low esteem and low priority such works have had in post-independence Bihar. The two volumes appeared in 1979 after several persons then influential on the state government, persons interested in Mundari, Chota Nagpur and 'tribals', had applied sufficient pressure (the manuscript had been ready for thirty years and more), but the two volumes were never officially released for sale. The official excuse is that the officials in charge have not been able to decide on a price for the books. The galleys were semi-surreptitiously photocopied, and it is copies of volumes 14 and 15 made from these photocopies that have been made available to a small number of libraries and individuals. I am told that a commercial publisher has now reprinted all the volumes very expensively. Presumably Indian library budgets and academics and libraries outside India are expected to underwrite publication costs.

For several of the Munda languages there are no proper dictionaries, and for these I mention the best (or only) wordlists we have for them. The Linguistic Survey of India — the Munda material is in the fourth volume (Konow 1906) is still useful, particularly for such North Munda dialects as Asuri, which have received no linguistic attention since the LSI. A new linguistic survey of India under the direction of Dr. B. P. Mahapatra is now under way. This should provide more and better data and analyses on the Munda languages (and the others), Dr. Mahapatra having studied Juang and Sora and being thoroughly familiar with the field of Munda linguistics. The new LSI project has also collected a lot of the older published lexicons, including 'bazaar booklets' elsewhere ignored. When and how the lexical material will be presented I don't know. Probably publication is in the fairly distant future since data-gathering has only just begun.

The Orissa government Academy of Tribal Cultures and Dialects under the directorship of Professor Khageshwar Mahapatra (another Orissan linguist and literary scholar who has done research on the Munda languages) is interested in preparing short grammars and lexicons of several of the tribal languages of Orissa, and the first batch to be published will include volumes on Gtaʔ (Ḍiḍayi, Ḍidei) and Sora. I am told these will be trilingual, either Munda-Oṛia-Hindi or Munda-Oṛia-English.

Several new scripts have been devised for various Munda languages by their speakers, the most notable and durable of these being Raghunath Murmu's Ol (Ol Ciki, formerly called 'Ol Cemet') script for Santali, Lako Bodra's 'Varang Kshiti' script for Ho, and the Sora script of Mangay Gomang(o). I know of only one dictionary using any of these scripts, the unpublished trilingual Ho-Hindi-English dictionary of Lako Bodra, but this is an esoteric work (see sect. 2.5.) which is not mainly concerned with the everyday meanings of everyday Ho (*ho kaji*). The Santal proponents of the Ol script are now assiduously promoting the script not only for Santali but for the other tribal languages of Chota Nagpur, without much success. The distinguished Bengali novelist Mahashveta Devi who is very familiar with the Chota Nagpur area characterized the Santals as the brahmins of Chota Nagpur.

2. North Munda

2.1. Korku

There is an early (English-Korku only) glossary made by Miss E. W. Ramsay (Ramsay 1914) which is still useful to linguists in that it describes a Melghat dialect different from those described elsewhere, i.e. in the Nagpur dictionary (1940), Girard's dictionary (s. a.), and N. Zide's dissertation (1960) (see below). I am told that Ramsay's data came from the Ghatang area where there are now no Korku settlements. In Ramsay's glossary verbstems with initial *s*-, elsewhere reduplicated with *s*- (*sod-*, *so-sod*), reduplicate with *c*- (*co-sod*) in Ramsay.

I was told that Father Thevenet — /ṭionet/ in Korku — worked in the Dharni area, and had compiled extensive lexicographic materials, but that these were destroyed by fire. He published nothing, and so far as I can learn, left no archival materials. Some of his data were made available to the compiler of the Nagpur dictionary (see below).

The Korkū-Hindī-Aṃgrezī Sabdkoṣ, published by the Government Press of the Central Provinces and Berar, in the introduction by G. G. R. Hunter is credited to Mr Nilkanth Prasad of the Central Provinces Educational Service (Thevenet is duly acknowledged).

I was told by Korku friends that Prasad appropriated the materials of a man called Shiv Pujan, who was connected with local cooperatives. This work — I will refer to it as the Nagpur dictionary — has a fairly extensive representative vocabulary of Korku. The transcription of Korku words (in Devanagari) is defective in a number of ways: glottal stop is not indicated, ḍ and ṛ are transcribed identically, and vowel length (which is a real problem) is transcribed erratically. Little morphological information is given: verbs are sometimes listed in stem form, sometimes as reduplicated stems, sometimes with various affixes, e.g. -e, and the cislocative -lī. The definitions are brief, but seem to be as accurate as brevity will permit. In a few cases someone's confusing English pronunciation derailed the correct translation: the word transcribed uaa (my romanization of their Devanagari) means not 'odour' (Hindi bās) as they have it, but 'udder'.

Miss Beryl Girard's Korku-Hindi-English Dictionary is the best Korku dictionary we have. Miss Girard has additional Korku lexical materials and, it is hoped, she will enlarge the dictionary, and perhaps make it more widely available in a more pukka form. She describes a Melghat dialect that she worked with for more than twenty years before retiring from the Baptist mission back to the United States.

The same mission has had missionaries working on Hoshangabad (Village Lahi) District Korku, a very different dialect, but no linguistic materials have been published on that dialect.

Girard's dictionary has a brief introduction on phonetics, phonemics and the transcription used. Girard does write the glottal stop (with a raised apostrophe), but does not transcribe tone. There are two phonemic tones: high-unmarked and low, the low tone being relatively uncommon, and bearing a low functional load. The book is roughly mimeographed and not always easily legible. There are five columns on each page: the Korku form in a Devanagari phonemic transcription (the vowel length as written is not phonemic but can be converted easily enough to a phonemic transcription); Hindi translation; Part of Speech; phonemic transcription in roman; English meaning. She gives some dialect variants found in the Melghat region, e.g., alam, alom 'we two (dual inclusive)'. The material is carefully presented and analyzed. The six page supplement gives the verbal (tense and mood) suffixes, the declension of nouns and pronouns, and Korku kinship terms, also a list of irregular verbs. The introduction has a few words on borrowing, and on the formation of verbstems from borrowed verbs. The borrowings are not identified in the body of the dictionary, but where the Korku and Hindi are obviously very similar the Korku has borrowed from Hindi. Where the borrowing has been from a language other than Hindi (usually Marathi), or where the Hindi translation uses an unrelated word the borrowing is less apparent. Thus Korku sutar 'carpenter', where the word comes from Marathi, but is not unknown in Hindi. The Hindi definition in Girard is baṛhai (sic). Girard uses dental and retroflex non-nasal stops for reasons she discusses in her introduction, although she says dental stops are not phonemic — i. e. phonemically distinct from retroflex post-alveolar stops — in Korku. This was certainly true of older speakers, but apparently is changing, the earlier single phonemes [t, ṭ], [d, ḍ] having split into two.

2.2. Korwa

The Korwa Lexicon of Kali Charan Bahl (Bahl 1962) is the only dictionary we have for Korwa. There are a few early, scrappy, brief vocabularies. Bahl's dictionary is based on a summer's fieldwork with the Korwa. It is carefully done, but further research would clarify and modify some of the entries and the interpretation of Korwa vocalism (Bahl has long and short vowels for Korwa within morphemes). The earlier vocabulary of Crooke (Crooke 1892) seems to represent either a different dialect or an earlier stage, and has unexpected vowels (i.e. e where Bahl finds i), which need to be taken into consideration for the reconstruction of Proto-Kherwarian.

2.3. Birhor

The Chicago Munda Languages Project wordlists (Birhor-English; Sinha s. a.) are all that there is for Birhor.

2.4. Mundari

The major dictionary, an encyclopaedic dictionary, for Mundari is Father Hoffmann's *Encyclopaedia Mundarica* in fifteen volumes (Hoffmann 1930—79). Other more and less useful dictionaries are: Bhaduri's Mundari-English dictionary (Bhaduri 1931) which does not transcribe the glottal stop, indicates some borrowings but not most of them, gives fairly adequate definitions, and has the usual problems with North Munda vowel length; Soy's Mundari-English-Hindi Mundari Vocabulary (Soy s. a.) of which apparently only the first part (a to na was published. Soy's transcriptions and definitions are better than Bhaduri's. He does not indicate borrowings, but remarks that in Horọ Jagar (Mundari) 'there is no word with aspirates' . . . 'but now some have crept in', i.e. in borrowed forms; there are two dictionaries (in Hindi) put out by the Bihar Tribal Welfare and Research Institute, compiled by Mrs Svarnlata Prasad, a Mundari-Hindi dictionary (Prasad 1973), and a Hindi-Mundari dictionary (Prasad 1976). Mrs Prasad, who has worked on Ho and Mundari, worked with informants and made use of the *Encyclopaedia Mundarica*. Her dictionaries are useful, particularly the Hindi-Mundari dictionary, but would have been more so had the definitions been better and fuller.

The *Encyclopaedia* is a major contribution to the study of the Mundari language, and to Munda linguistics, and a knowledgeable study of Munda (i.e. Mundari) life. Hoffmann wrote a grammar of Mundari much earlier (Hoffmann 1903), and his revisions and elaborations of topics treated in the grammar, e.g. negation, are to be found in the *Encyclopaedia* (e.g., see the entry under *alo*, the prohibitive particle). There are long articles on history, ethnography, music, folklore (see for instance the entry under *bhuiñāri* on land-holding and settlement). Hoffmann gives a fair amount of information on dialect variation of the three main Mundari dialects, Hasada, Naguri and Kera. Hoffmann does give some cognate forms in other Munda languages, but along with this, somewhat confusingly, words in other, often European, languages that look something like the Mundari.

Hoffmann's entries are rich in exemplifications (see Dict. excerpt 250.1) of Mundari sentences, and provide a great deal of subtle syntactic and semantic ethnographic analysis. These volumes *are* a mine of information. The volume published in commemoration of Hoffman and his work (Ponette 1978) on the fiftieth anniversary of his death tells something about his collaborators on the *Encyclopaedia*, Menas Orea, a native speaker of Mundari, and Arthur Van Emmelen, a Belgian Jesuit. The editor of that volume, Father P. Ponette, restored — i.e. wrote — the entries for a few pages which were missing after thirty years, when the Bihar government finally got around to printing the last two volumes of the Encyclopaedia.

2.5. Ho

The only 'conventional' dictionary of Ho is that of Father Deeney (Deeney s. a.), which is a fuller lexical compilation than the one at the back of his Ho Grammar and Vocabulary (Deeney 1975), the Ho-English vocabulary occupying pages 120—184, and an English-Ho vocabulary pages 185—216 of that volume. Deeney, like Bodding, Hoffmann and Ramamurti, first wrote a grammar of the language, and later completed a dictionary. Deeney, who has been working with the Ho for more than thirty years, also published several selections of ethnographic texts in Ho with the collaboration of D. S. Purty.

In his dictionary Deeney gives first the Ho form in a (roman) phonemic transcription, then a Devanagari equivalent, and then the definition in English. His introduction gives background on the language, discusses 'categories of word presenting special problems', lays out the conventions used in the dictionary, etc. The dictionary is admirably full and clear, the definitions careful and not overly brief. He gives sentences usefully exemplifying his definitions. The only cavil I have is that the transcription *ā* ('long a'), e.g. in *hām* 'old man, husband', probably should be geminate *a*, i.e. *haam*, to best represent Ho phonology. Perhaps here, as elsewhere (i.e. in Korku), the 'Schriftgefühl' when using the Devanagari script (which is the usual one for Ho) comes more from what looks 'right' (well-formed) for writing Hindi, rather than what best describes Ho (e.g. vowel sequences in Ho). See Dictionary excerpt 250.2.

The unconventional dictionary of Ho is the as yet unpublished trilingual dictionary (Ho-Hindi-English) of Lako Bodra, the Ho being written in Bodra's 'Varang Kshiti' script (Bodra s. a.). Pinnow, in his (Pinnow 1972) long article on Lako Bodra's script, writes that Bodra, a Ho shaman, claimed to have rediscovered the script in a shamanistic vision.

Pinnow mentions several esoteric works of Lako Bodra, but he was not aware of a dictionary. Pinnow writes that 'the language employed by Bodra is not standard Ho (Ho Kaji), but a distinct dialect closely related to Ho Kaji which is called Ho Hayam. The position of Ho Hayam within the Kherwari group of Munda languages is still unclear; it may be an old secret language of the Ho shamans which Bodra wished to raise to the level of an Adivasi literary language — an aim he was unable to achieve.' He has been more successful recently.

The dictionary is an esoteric work of considerable interest, but since I could only examine it briefly, and am no Ho Kaji scholar, to say nothing of Ho Hayam, I can offer only some preliminary observations. I know nothing of shamanic languages in Munda-speaking communities. Perhaps Carrin-Bouez (for Santali) or Vitebsky (for Sora) know of parallels. Some of Bodra's ideas on language owe something to Hindu notions about language. Bodra seems to have read (in Hindi) and heard all sorts of things, and B. Pat Pingua, the disciple of Bodra's who promoted the script to me, has read widely in English, and incorporated into Bodra's system everything promising that turned up in his reading: e.g., genes and DNA, the Harap-

hon (Kh. *ćhūn*, son or daughter; Sk. *sūnu*, son) I. sbst., (1) a child. When it is desired to distinguish between the sexes, the words *koṛa*, *kuṛi*, are prefixed, or sometimes affixed, to *hon*: *koṛahon*, a boy, a son; *kuṛihon*, a girl, a daughter. In the meaning of son, daughter, *honkoṛa* and *honkuṛi* must be used when specified by the prsl. prns. *iṇ*, *me*, *te*, inserted between the two words: *honiṇkoṛa*, my son, *honmekuṛi*, thy daughter; but when the pos. adjectives *aiñq*, *amq*, *aěq*, *akiṇq*, *akoq*, etc. are used, *koṛahon* and *kuṛihon* are preferred. In the meaning of boy, girl, *honkoṛa* and *honkuṛi* are never used of infants and children up to about ten years of age; and the same terms are preferred when there is question of an intended or actual bride or bridegroom. (2) the young of any animals: maěno *honkoe* apirkeḍkoa, the myna has induced its young to leave the nest.

II. adj., with *hoṛoko*, syn. of *haturen honko*, the children of one's village, in cntrd. to *eṇga hoṛoko*, the mothers of one's village: ape *hon* hoṛoko apu hoṛokolo enka eperaṇ ciulaǒ alope heǒana, you, children, take never such a habit of quarrelling with elder people in the village. (2) of any animal, a young one: *hon* merom *hon* miṇḍi, *hon* sim. *Hon* is never used with *keṛa*, *uṛi* or *karkom* because there are special terms to designate a buffalo-calf, a calf, and a young crab. (3) with *cẹṛê*, bird, *bani*, *raṇga*, coloured stripes along the border of a cloth, *daṛo*, *ganḍa*, *kaṭu*, finger or toe: smaller or narrower in comparison to another or others, described by the adj. *eṇga*. In these connections, *hon* may be used as adj. noun when the context or circumstances make the meaning sufficiently clear. (4) of a plant or tree, young: *hon* tamrasdaru. (5) of a fruit or any other object, small-sized: *hon* tamras, a small guava; *hon* ari, a small saw.

III. trs., to give birth to (impolite when used of a woman): aleạ seta turuiae *honkeḍkoa*, our bitch has brought forth six pups.

IV. intrs., (1) to call smb. a child: samagem *honaiṇtana*, moḍnoɡejālaṇ umarakana, thou hast no reason to call me a child, we must be of about the same age. (2) to address smb. with the vocative *hon*: Nagurikodo babuako oṛo mâiakoko *honakoa*, in Naguri they use *hon* as vocative of address even for grown boys and girls, for whom in Hasada they use *babu* and *mǎi*. Note the idiom: ne kuṛido jilu naman ca hai naman urlusurluge namaia, hon kae *honakoa*, koṛao kae koṛaaia, this woman when she gets hold of some meat or fish, has a fit of ungovernable greediness and gives no part of it either to her children or to her husband.

hon-en rflx. v., to do smth. which only children do, v.g., to ask for a meal in the morning: ne haṛam *honentana*.

hon-ọ p. v., (1) to be born: aleạ oṛaṛe turuia setako *honjana*. (2) in the past tenses, of a child, animal, tree, fruit or other object, to be small: inią honko *honakangea*; nekan kamimente puṛạe *honjana*, he is far too young for this kind of work; ne kuḍlamdo *honiana* maraṇnoạ auipe, this hoe is too small, bring a larger one.

V. afx. (1) to *hoṛo*: *hoṛohon*, a child of man, a human being. (2) to proper nouns of races or castes, a member of the said race or caste: *Munḍahon*, *Hoṛohon*, a Munda; *Dikuhon*, a Hindu; *Uraṇhon*, an Oraon. (3) to names of animals, trees, plants, fruits, or other objects. The cpds. thus formed are syns. of the phrases in which *hon* stands as adj.

Dictionary excerpt 250.1: Dictionary article (from: Hoffmann 1930—79, 1789—90)

baṭi (बटि) – a small measuring cup (about ⅛ seer)

baṭi (बटि) – to overturn, to knock over something standing upright; refl. to turn over; to turn from side to side

*baṭi-ādu – to overturn causing to go down; refl. – to turn over and descend

*baṭi-atom – to remove out of the way by knocking over

*baṭi bandi – a paddy bundle, the outer ropes (*bandi bayer*) of which are fixed by rolling the bundle along the ground

*baṭi-chakaḍen – to pretend to fall over (refl. form)

*baṭi gunu-gunu – to overturn and repeatedly roll over

*baṭin-baṭin – (refl. form repeated) roll over (said playfully at the end of a verse by one playing the *banam* or playing a flute)

*baṭi uru – another name for the *guri: uru* (dung beetle), so called because making a ball of dung, it rolls it over (*baṭi*) into a hole which it has made

baṭiḍ (बतिड़) – same as *batil*, q.v.

batil, batī:l (बतिल) (बती:ल) – a word (not translatable in a uniform way) put after a word or phrase to which the main subject is compared, usually unfavourably, indicating that the subject would rather do or could more easily do the action to which *batil* is attached than that to which it is compared, e.g. *achādo ka rāsakowa, kako herdaiyanredo rowa batilko rowaya*, 'They do not like to sow in water; if they have not been able to sow, they would rather transplant (they prefer to transplant)'. Sometimes used after a noun or pronoun e.g. *Ae: alom emaiya, am batil jomeme*, 'Do not give it to him, rather you eat it'

batilo – used in a story-song in the term *bēṭ batilo* apparently meaning the same as *bēṭ danḍa:*, 'a rattan cane' (*batilo* is not a Ho word. Some story songs are a mixture of Ho and Oriya).

batiṅ (बतिञ) – same as *batil*, q.v.

bātiṅ (बातिञ) – a poetic parallel to *hiyatiṅ*, 'to feel pity' (more often *chakatiṅ* is used for this)

Dictionary excerpt 250.2: Dictionary articles (from: Deeney s. a., 31)

pan civilization and its (as yet undecipherable) script, Partha Mitter's book *Much Maligned Monsters* about the English reception of Indian art in the nineteenth century. All of this — how much of this is Pat Pingua and how much Bodra, I can't say — goes to promote Ho as the Ursprache and Urkultur, the one language that survived an ancient South Asian deluge, the language through which one can truly etymologize words in other Asian and European languages using archaic, true Ho meanings for e.g. (Pat Pingua's example) English 'Birmingham'.

The letter shapes, drawn and colored perhaps by Lako Bodra himself, represent organs of the body, and the meanings of the letter/sound and its name derive (partly?) from the body part and its connotations. Each word — and this includes letter names — has a range of meanings, arranged by Bodra in 'registers', e.g. linguistic, biological-zoological, biological-botanical, technical, philosophical-religious, etc. I don't know whether the registers somehow determine these meanings, but Ho words in Bodra's Ho Hayam have a great variety — diversity — of meanings. Thus N (the roman equivalent of) 'the twentieth varang kshiti script (letter, character), tenth consonant, and fourth nasal consonant ... It is to be pronounced by pressing the breath amidst the disk (sic) to throw out (the sound) through the mouth with buzzing echo (release) through the nose. Being a divine wind the phonetic effects from the testicle to the prostate all over the masculine gender, i.e. the special organ of the male. (The glosses are) in biological science: youth, spirit, ape, gender or sexual part of male, semen, valour, vigour. (Biological science, botanical:) the pollen or farina of a flower. Physical science: earth, brick, mortar, kneaded clay. Philosophy: creation, the universe, the world, history (description). Technology: hammer, G.n.p.m. (??) Vishwakarma, artist of the gods, God, mason, carpenter. n. com. (common noun?): egg, semen or vigour, metal, mineral, ore, the root of a verb, wealth.' One more example: 'G The first non-nasal consonant, and the twelfth character of 'Varangkshiti' script of Ho language. It is pronounced by the normal opening of the mouth pressing up the breath from the stomach grinding the backbones to come out through the mouth. The sound of this form is 'ga?'. Its meaning is air, back part of body, shoulder joint, neck, and refers to shoulder blade or scapula in biology and zoology. It is an echo in philological science, and inflation of joint in physics, and a balance or weighing scale in technology.'

I don't know how these meanings are selected and put into effect. It does not appear that ex-

hoṇ, n. A son, child; offspring (also of animals). The word is now only used in compounds. *Apa h.*, father and child (son or daughter); *eṅga h.*, mother and child, dam and young; *sim mǫ̃ṛẹ̃ eṅga h. menakkoa*, the fowls are five, hen and four chickens; *h. hopoṇ*, children; *h. hopoṇ cele hõ baṇukkotaea*, he has no children at all; *nitok do apnar hat tulạteṅ jometa, h.kimin tite do ceṭ leka coṅ hoeoktiṅ hapẹn*, now I eat as much as I myself may take, who knows how it will be in the future when I shall get my food at the hands of my son and daughter-in-law; *h. jāwāe*, daughter and son-in-law; *h. jāwāe koṭaṅ sahan, tatāoge koṭ koṭoka*, a daughter and a son-in-law and crooked firewood when heated get still more crooked (i. e., the more fuss you make of a son-in-law, the more offence he will take). (Muṇḍari *hon*; Kurku *kon*.)

hoṇ, dem. element. There yonder (showing), mostly used followed by other demonstratives commencing with *hon*. *H.hona*, dem. pr. That there shown at a little distance (inanim.).

   h.honka, dem. pr. and adv. Such as that there; thus, in that way; v. a. m. Do, be, become do.;

   h.honka leka, dem. adv.; v. a. m. In that way there; do, be, become do.;

   h.honka lekan, dem. adj. Like that there (-*ič*, -*kin*, -*ko*; -*ak̇*, -*ak̇kin*, -*ak̇ko*);

   h.honkan, dem. adj. Such as that there (-*ič*, -*ak̇*, etc.);

   h.hontẹ, dem. adv. Thither, over in that direction; v. a. m. Do, settle, send do. (with suffixes -*khon*, -*re*, -*reak̇*, -*ren*, -*seč*, -*te*, etc.);

   h.hontẹn, dem. adj. Such as that there (-*ič*, -*kin*, -*ko*; -*ak̇*, *ak̇kin*, -*ak̇ko*);

   h.hoṇḍẹ, dem. adv. Over there at a distance.

   h.hoṇḍẹn, dem. adj. That one over there (-*ič*, -*kin*, -*ko*; -*ak̇*, -*ak̇kin*, -*ak̇ko*).

hoṇ barduṛŭč, n. A species of bat (v. *barduṛŭč*).

hoṇ baṭaṛič (or *h. baṭaṛič*), adj. Equal to, like that (v. *hoṇ* and *baṭaṛ*).

hoṇḍroṅ, the same as *haṇḍruṅ*, q. v.

hoṇẹ, dem. pr. That, that there, there (a little distance off; inanim.; -*kin*, -*ko*). *H. do ceṭ kana*, what is that over there; *h. ṅẹlme*, look at that there; *h.laṅ ṅapamlen ṭhẹč*, the place over there where we two met; *h.koa dare do*, those over there are the trees. *H.ak̇, -an, -aṅ, -reak̇, -reaṅ, -ren*, of that there; *h. anaṅ, -anẹč, -ena, enaṅ, -ẹnẹč*. That there now only;

   h.coṅ, why, there you see; *h. do*, that there;

   h.hona, dem. pr. That there, that over there at a distance;

   h.honka, dem. pr. and adv.; v. a. m. Such as that there (shown); in such a way as that there; do, be, become do.

Dictionary excerpt 250.3: Dictionary articles (from: Bodding 1929—35, III, 139—140)

pressives — as Diffloth has described them for other Austroasiatic languages, and which are probably found in Santali — occur in Ho, and that there is a systematic semantic value given to particular phonemes in one portion of the lexicon. What and whom Bodra's dictionary is for remains a mystery.

2.6. Santali

Santali has more speakers (in Bengal, Bihar, Orissa and Assam) than any of the other Munda languages, about three and a half million, and there have been more books published in and on Santali. There were a number of wordlists published before Campbell's dictionary, but only two dictionaries (neither of which I have seen): Puxley's *Vocabulary* (Puxley 1868), and Martin's English-Santali dictionary (Martin 1898). Campbell's Santali-English dictionary was first published in 1899—1902 (Campbell 1899—1905). I know only the third edition of the Santali-English dictionary (Campbell/Macphail 1953 b), and the third of the English-Santali dictionary (Campbell/Macphail 1954), and my comments are based on those editions. I contrast Campbell's Santali-English dictionary (see below) with Bodding's (Bodding 1929—35). The Campbell/Macphail English-Santali dictionary is the best such dictionary we have. It is less than half the size of the Santali-English lexicon, and lacks the detail and the sentences exemplifying Santali usage, and presumably finds that sort of exemplification unnecessary for English. A sizable stock of English words is defined in Santali. One complaint could be that the English word often is defined in Santali by, say, ten words (see below on 'languid') where the Santali words can and should be semantically distinguished, and a fuller gloss given for the English word. Presumably, one can go to the Santali-English dictionaries, Campbell's or Bodding's, for more specificity on the Santali.

P. O. Bodding, a Norwegian missionary working in Santal Parganas District, first built on the lexical materials left him by his predecessor, L. O. Skrefsrud, and continued his lexicographic work (along with work on Santali grammar) for more than thirty years.

I am told by Dr Marine Carrin-Bouez, an anthropologist who has worked on Santali religion and society, and used the Oslo archives, that Bodding's original dictionary sheets (which are in the Oslo archives) are in Santali, i.e. the definitions as well as the words to be defined are Santali. The published volumes give the definitions in English. Bodding provides a full, authoritative, masterly treatment of the Santali lexicon. A fuller treatment of the verb conjugations, the demonstratives, etc. can be found in his grammar (Bodding 1929). His entries are clear, detailed, semantically discriminating, and generous with sentences exemplifying relevant usage. (See Dict. excerpt 250.3)

In his introduction Bodding discusses the earlier dictionaries, Campbell in particular, and lays out and justifies his own procedures. He gives grammatical — part-of-speech — labels to his lexical items, something Campbell finds it difficult and perhaps inappropriate to do. For example Bodding's entry *ā ā* ('groan, grunt') is labelled 'noun, adjective, active and medium (mediopassive) verb'. Campbell gives no label, and glosses the word 'Grunt of buffalo'. Bodding gives cognates — or possible cognates — in other Munda languages, and possible sources of words identified as loans. There is a problem with Santali dialects. Bodding takes Santal Parganas Santali as standard, and marks with C forms that he finds in Campbell, but has not 'heard among the Santals with whom (he) has come into contact.' He writes that 'in many cases such words are in a form written by persons who have had little proper training. In other cases they are words used only by persons who have been accustomed to speak or write especially Hindi.' It is not clear to me to what extent Campbell's Santali represents a different regional dialect, characterized by something more (lexicon, phonology) than a sizable number of loans not found in good Santal Parganas Santali, and a degree of what is to Bodding contamination or sloppiness. The southern Santali spoken in the Mayurbhanj District of Orissa (which has, for instance, six vowels, not the eight of Santal Parganas Santali) is not discussed. That is, Bodding's dictionary is a dictionary of the standard, Santal Parganas, language. He comments elsewhere on the language as spoken in a region where Ko̱lhe̱s (Mundari speakers) are found, and how funny his Santal companions found the Santali spoken by some Santals in that area. Campbell and Bodding seem to have influenced each other, so that parallel entries (Bodding and Campbell/Macphail's third edition) are quite similar. Thus, Bodding defining *bal* v. a. m. (active and medium verb) 'Burn a hole (with a redhot iron, mostly a spindle); puncture. *Tirio are sakwa do̱ ṭakudhipa̱ukateko bal bhuga̱ga* 'they burn holes in flutes and horns having made a spindle red-hot'; *ojoko b. kedea* 'they punctured his boil' (in order not to get the redhot iron too far in a potsherd with a small hole is put on the boil; the iron is pushed through this hole).' Campbell on *bal*: 'To bore a hole, or to puncture with a red hot iron, *ojo baltiṅme*. 'Puncture the boil for me with a red hot needle.' *Tirioṅ balkeda*, 'I bored the finger holes in my flute with a red hot iron.' Bodding's Santali sentences tend to be longer, and he provides more ethnographic background detail. His English is less idiomatic than Campbell's.

For the linguist interested in comparative Austroasiatic, browsing through Campbell/Macphail's English-Santali dictionary one comes across entries suggesting that Santali does (or did) have 'expressives' (see Diffloth 1976), something widespread in Mon-Khmer, but not described elsewhere for a Munda language. Thus, under 'languid' we find *bijr bojo̱r, do̱gdo̱g, ha̱rur, pico̱ć poco̱ć, ropropo* and *rubrubu* in Campbell. See too the Santali words (more than fifty) for 'fat' in Campbell/Macphail, and the glosses of these — and related others not given in Campbell/Macphail — in Bodding. Many of these words have to do with movement, describing and presenting how these 'fatnesses' are perceived — in motion, and at rest. In Bodding words glossed as 'wriggle' (among other things) include *biḍić, biḍić biḍić, beḍeć beḍeć* (?), *buḍuć buḍuć, biḍir biḍir, bikir bikir, bikiṭ bikiṭ, biryo̱ṅ boryo̱ṅ, biryo̱ṅ biryo̱ṅ,* etc.

3. South Munda

3.1. Kharia

There is no Kharia dictionary comparable to those of the other developed (literary) Munda languages of the Chota Nagpur region (Santali, Mundari, Ho), but several members of the Kharia community in and around Ranchi have been preparing one over a number of years. About this lexicon Veena Malhotra (Malhotra 1982) writes:

'attempts have also been made to compile an elaborate prescriptive lexicon of Kharia, which minimizes on loanwords, the work initiated by J. B. Soreng, and continued by Ilias Kerketta, Julius

Baʔ and Herman Kiṛo. Kiṛo particularly has devised and recommended use of prescriptive Kharia day/month names, technical vocabulary relating to farming implements and household goods borrowed from the Aryan culture but these terms have not entered into popular, current usage, and Kiṛo's may be regarded as theoretical.'

A great deal of Kharia vocabulary has been collected from all over the Kharia-speaking area, and I believe that collection still continues. The lexical entry slips I have seen (in 1988) were Kharia-Hindi only — the intention is to publish a Kharia-Hindi-English dictionary, and the definitions (in Hindi) were overly brief, with no exemplifications and little grammatical information. Even if the dictionary is published with no further expansions and elaborations, however, it will be a great improvement over the earlier lexical materials.

The earlier materials consist of a short Kharia-English and English-Kharia dictionary prepared by Catholic missionaries in the thirties, and sizable vocabularies in recent books prepared by native Kharia scholars: Kullū 1981 and Ḍungḍung 1986. Books by non-Kharia linguists that include some lexical material are Biligiri's *Kharia Phonology, Grammar and Vocabulary* (Biligiri 1965), Pinnow's *Versuch einer Historischen Lautlehre der Kharia-Sprache* (Pinnow 1959) and *Kharia Texte* (Pinnow 1965). The missionary dictionary (Floor et al. 1934) has an English-Kharia section of fifty pages done by Floor, Gheysens and others, and a Kharia-English section of seventy-one pages by Father Druart. This dictionary gives some grammatical information, careful definitions and a reliable transcription. There are brief sentences exemplifying Kharia usage, and there is a short 'foreword' on the various ways Kharia handles a sizable stock of loanwords. Biligiri includes an eighty-four page Kharia-English vocabulary, carefully transcribed and grammatically analysed, but with no information on borrowed items. Pinnow must have extensive lexical files for Kharia, but he has no glossary in the book of texts (he does translate the texts) and the Kharia vocabulary in the *Versuch* is chosen for comparative — reconstructive — purposes. There is more of a Kharia lexicon in his Juang monograph (Pinnow 1960; sect. 3.2.), where he gives Kharia cognates for an extensive Juang vocabulary.

There is a short vocabulary (*saṃkṣipt śabdkoś*) after the grammar in P. Kullū's book, which is quite useful.

It is arranged by syntactic/semantic categories, i.e. transitive verbs, intransitive verbs, humans, animals, etc. Kullu transcribes Kharia in Devanagari in a standard (with the nasal released written in) fashion. The definitions are brief, but careful. Not much explicit information on loanwords is provided. Dr (Father) Mathiyas Ḍungḍung's book — originally a dissertation — on Hindi and Kharia has a twenty-four page Hindi-Kharia glossary, and a twenty-seven page Kharia-English vocabulary. He provides the briefest of glosses and no further information on the words.

3.2. Juang

There are no dictionaries of Juang, but there are three wordlists: the long vocabulary (Kharia-German with some quoted English glosses) with Kharia and other cognates in Pinnow's unpublished Beiträge (Pinnow 1960), the Mahapatra/Matson wordlists (Juang-English and English-Juang) in Matson's unpublished dissertation (Matson 1964), and the Juang-English vocabulary in Das Gupta's study of Juang (Das Gupta 1978). Das Gupta's Dhenkanal Juang has a large number of loanwords which he doesn't identify as such. The Dhenkanal dialect has borrowed a great deal of vocabulary and, apparently, morphology and syntax as well, but it is conservative in some of its phonology, e.g., in preserving aspiration (or preserving something which comes out as aspiration in Dhenkanal Juang). Matson has some interesting grammatical information on the verb-stems in his lexicon, marking stems that are (roughly) intransitive, transitive, and stems which can take both transitive and intransitive verb suffixes, apparently without difference in meaning. This last presumption seems unlikely. B. P. Mahapatra has a paper in which he compares these verbs — and transitivity — in Juang with cognate verbs in Kharia (Mahapatra 1976). Pinnow's unpublished monograph (based on his field study of the language) is an extensive, carefully analysed Juang vocabulary with phonological, morphological and syntactic analysis, information on borrowing, cognates in other Munda languages, and references to relevant ethnographic literature.

3.3. Gutob (Gad(a)ba)

There is no Gutob dictionary. There are wordlists, Gutob-English and English-Gutob, done by N. Zide, B. P. Das and R. De Armond (Zide et al. 1963) for the Munda Languages Project of the University of Chicago. These vocabularies and most of the other Munda lexical material have been put on computer tape (after reorganization and analysis by David Stampe and Patricia Donegan). (I have no index of the contents of the Stampe/Donegan Munda archive in Honolulu.) The Gutob Verb Lexicon of N. Zide and B. P. Das (Zide/Das 1963) lists and describes the morphology and (some) syntax of c. four hundred verbs, half of the original list. The slips with the data on the second half were sent back to Chicago from India and lost in transit.

The lexicon gives information on transitivity, causativity, derived nominals, noun incorporation in verbstems, and borrowed verbstems — of which Gutob has many (c. forty percent of the total). A later paper by Zide (Zide 1985) on forming derived transitives and causatives from native and borrowed verbstems in Gutob has some notes on the preparation of the lexicon and the problems of working with informants of slightly differing dialects; the judgments of the two informants on the use of certain transitive/intransitive suffixes were influenced by the dictionary-making procedures, and the judgments of each informant were affected by those of the other. The difficult judgments in some cases were resolved by generalizing different derivational rules (for the two informants), and by normalizing what looked like interpersonal dissimilation behavior, i.e. the feeling that they spoke differently and should speak differently and then, somewhat arbitrarily — for their purposes, not mine — fixing how this should be actualized and formalized.

3.4. Remo (Boṇḍa)

For Remo (Boṇḍa) we have Bhattacharya's A Bonda Dictionary (Bhattacharya 1968) with an English index, and the Remo-English and English-Remo vocabularies in Fernandez' dissertation (Fernandez 1968).

There is a long review by N. Zide of Bhattacharya's dictionary (Zide 1972). Bhattacharya has recorded a large sample of the Remo lexicon, and with his glosses given some grammatical information. His introduction describes the Remo verb, discusses 'the Munda problem', gives cognate sets of words for Remo and most of the other Munda languages. If one uses both Bhattacharya and Fernandez together (they describe slightly differing dialects, Fernandez having worked with Hill Remo (Boṇḍa)) and Bhattacharya with Plains Boṇḍa (Remo), one can get a fairly good idea of the Remo language. Bhattacharya includes some texts at the back of the dictionary; Fernandez has none in his dissertation. I would stand by my earlier criticisms of Bhattacharya's dictionary (in Zide 1972): that the verb system is confusingly and inefficiently presented, the nominal combining forms (although Bhattacharya clearly knows where they are and what they do) are not apparent to the casual reader, that morphological analysis of the interesting demonstrative system (and a better semantic analysis) is not provided, etc., but I have continued to consult Bhattacharya's dictionary and find it invaluable in reconstructing Proto-Gutob-Remo Gtaʔ and Proto-South Munda.

Fernandez' lexicon, Remo-English, smaller than Bhattacharya's, is carefully put together, but there are some questionable morphological analyses in it. The few differences noted between the Hill and Plains dialects have to do with morphology (no reciprocal in the Plains dialect), and phonology: in Andrahal village, not the home of most of Fernandez' informants but the source of a little of his data, Remo *u* elsewhere corresponds to *i* (like the cognate forms in Gutob).

3.5. Gtaʔ (Ḍiḍayi, Ḍiḍei)

There are two Gtaʔ dialects — or closely related languages (with some intermediate dialects): Plains Gtaʔ and Hill/Riverside Gtaʔ. On Hill/Riverside (H/R) Gtaʔ K. Mahapatra and N. Zide collected a small vocabulary in a very short period of fieldwork in 1988, eliciting cognate forms (and some others) from the plains Gtaʔ lexicon. For Plains Gtaʔ there is an unpublished lexicon by K. Mahapatra and N. Zide (Mahapatra/Zide 1980 revised), the long glossary to Gtaʔ Texts (Mahapatra/Zide 1979), and the first part — about a fifth — of a larger Gtaʔ dictionary (Zide/Mahapatra 1988). The first of these is somewhat larger than Bhattacharya's Remo dictionary, and gives along with somewhat extended definitions some morphological and grammatical analysis. The larger dictionary gives examples, greater syntactic detail, considerable morphological analysis of complex verbstems, nouns and demonstratives, along with information on borrowings from standard Oria and from the local Desia dialect (of Oria).

3.6. Sora (Saora)

For Sora we have G. V. Ramamurti's English-Sora dictionary (Ramamurti 1933), and his Sora-English dictionary (Ramamurti 1938). He published his grammar of Sora in 1931 (Ramamurti 1931), and teaching materials in Telugu had been published earlier. Ramamurti's dictionaries are large and detailed, giving precise definitions and sample sentences (see Dict. excerpt 250.4). There is a good deal of morphological information: e.g. on reduplication, tagwords, nominal combining forms. There are appendices on personal names, village names, names of plants, etc. Familiarity with Ramamurti's grammar makes the dictionaries more useful, but is not

soi-'me-, *n.*, yellow colour of the bile, vomitted, or of purgings.

soi-soi-'aŋel, *n.*, fuel, *see* soi-.

soi-soi-'mar-ən, *n.*, a hunter.

soi-suŋ-'mar-ən, *n.*, *lit.* burn-house-man ; incendiary.

soi-'tar-, *v.t.*, to roast, to scorch (cashewnuts so as to remove the bitter sap, so that they may be easily shelled).
Ex. oloj-ja:ŋ-ən soi-tarren-ende:n-pa:lte:n. pu-pu:-n obseŋ-a: ; soi-tar-do:ŋ.

soj-'soj-, *v.t.*, to jeer; to mock, to mimic.

'so:kər-, (*dial.*), *v.i.* (*impl.*) to feel disappointed.

'soked-, *v.i.*, to be bent, to become curved, to sag.
adj., bent, curved.
soked-ji:-mar-ən, *lit.* irregular teeth man.
soked-tam-mar-ən, *lit.* curved mouth man.

'so:l-ən-, ? contr. of so:lda:-n as in kuppu:-so:l-ən, a clod of earth; lakij-so:l-ən, sandy soil. jobba:-so:l-ən.
[*See* lo:-n, *cf.* Mundari, loso:d, ' earth ', ' mud '.]

'so:la:-, *v.i.* (*impl.*) to be affected by an ' evil eye '.

'so:la:-'mad-, *v.t.*, to look at with an ' evil eye '.
so:la:-mad-ən, *n.*, evil eye.
so:la:-mad:-bo:j-ən, *n.*, a woman that has an evil eye.
so:la-mad-mar-ən, *n.*, a man who has an evil eye.

'so:la:-n-'mo:la:-n, evil spirits ; as in (so:la:n-mo:la:n) pum-pum-gare:b-ən-ə-so:la:, an evil spirit.

'so:lda:-n, *n.*, mud prepared for building a wall.

so:'lo:-, *v.i.*, to be overgrown with under wood, etc., as roads, fields and village-sites that are deserted.

so:'lo:-n, *n.*, coppice, brushwood.

so:lo:-'bur-ən, (an-sənɪd-da:-bur-ən) a clearing on the hill which has been left uncultivated for two or three years.

'somba:-'ne:b-ən, *var.* sumba:-ne:b-, somma:-ne:b-, so:mi-ne:b-, *n.*, a tree called so:mida in Telugu. (The bark is used as medicine.)

-so:-n, a particle, used with taŋ-, as in ə-taŋ-so:-n = alone (*3rd pers. sing.*) ; taŋ-so:n-ɲen-n = alone (*1st pers. sing.*), taŋ-so:-n-am = *2nd pers. sing*). *Ex.* ə-taŋ-so:-n dimman-ne:te:n = he slept alone. taŋ-soi-n-am bərun ille po:ŋ? didst thou go to the hill alone ?

Dictionary excerpt 250.4: Dictionary articles (from: Ramamurti 1938)

presupposed. The dictionaries provide a variety of relevant information: on dialect variation, sources of loanwords, cognates in other Munda languages, and notes on phonetics. Ramamurti's phonetic transcriptions have been criticised, and (see below) corrected by B. P. Mahapatra and R. Mahapatra. Ramamurti does not clearly and consistently distinguish the (presumably) nine phonemic vowels of the dialect he worked on. Sora vowels have not been easy (for non-Soras) to hear, produce and analyse. (A survey of the Sora dialects is very much worth doing.) The distinctions between the high and higher mid vowels, and between some back and central vowels are not wholly accurate in Ramamurti. A corrected transcripton of Ramamurti's Sora is to be found in Mahapatra and Mahapatra's revision of Ramamurti (Mahapatra/Mahapatra 1968). Mahapatra and Mahapatra retranscribe Ramamurti's Sora (they worked with several informants in the Serango area) and give a more authoritative transcription (the changes are almost entirely in the vocalism) of the Sora forms. The revised transcription of the full and combining forms of nouns is particularly useful for historical reconstruction. Mahapatra and Mahapatra rely on Ramamurti for semantic detail — not that they don't make corrections when necessary, their glosses are brief and they don't include sentences exemplifying usage. Stampe and Donegan have incorporated their own Sora material and Stanley Starosta's materials as well as those of Ramamurti and the Mahapatras into their computer archive of Munda materials.

3.7. Juray

There is no published dictionary or wordlist of Juray. Arlene Zide's lexical materials on Juray are made use of in her reconstruction of Proto-Sora-Juray-Gorum. Juray has been considered to be a Sora dialect. If so, it must be considered a very divergent dialect, or a closely related language.

3.8. Gorum (Parenga, Parengi)

For Gorum in print there are the Parengi wordlists of F. Richard Aze in an SIL (Summer Institute of Linguistics) compilation of wordlists for a number of Indian languages. Texts and grammatical descriptions of these same languages are provided in other volumes of the series. Aze's wordlists (Aze 1973) — the Parengi words are given along with (in parallel columns) Kolami and Dhangar-Kudux (both Dravidian) glosses for the same English words on the same page — are standard SIL lists, and arranged in semantic sets, e.g. 'human body parts', 'tools, instruments, metals', 'Verbs: Activities and States of the Human Body', 'Activities concerning Clothing', etc. The Gorum word or phrase is carefully transcribed, but, if a phrase, not further glossed. Thus, for 'rude', we get the Gorum *niman inkoʔnuʔ lok*, without the literal translation of this phrase, roughly 'not good people'. There is a large unpublished Gorum-English lexicon (A. Zide 1968) with full morphological analyses, and a fair amount of syntactic information, particularly in the verb entries. A. Zide has also prepared a shorter English-Gorum lexicon (A. Zide 1971). Her material is incorporated in the Stampe/Donegan archive.

4. Selected Bibliography

4.1. General

Diffloth 1976 = G. Diffloth: Expressives in Semai. AS I. 1976, 249—64.

Huffman 1986 = Franklin Huffman: Bibliography and Index of Mainland Southeast Asian Languages and Linguistics. New Haven 1986.

Konow 1906 = S. Konow: Munda and Dravidian languages. Vol. IV of the Linguistic Survey of India. Ed. by G. Grierson. Calcutta 1906.

4.2. North Munda

4.2.1. Korku

4.2.1.1. Dictionaries

Girard s. a. = Beryl Girard: Korku-Hindi-English Dictionary. Nimar District, M. P., India s. a. [99 p. + Supplement].

Nagpur Dictionary 1940 = Government Press, Central Provinces and Berar: Korku-Hindi-English Dictionary (Korkū-Hindī-Aṃgrezī Śabdkoṣ). Nagpur 1940 [118 p.].

Ramsay 1914 = E. W. Ramsay: Vocabulary of Words in the Kūrkū Language, English-Kūrkū. Ellichpur, Berar 1914 [26 p.].

4.2.1.2. Other Publications

Zide 1960 = N. Zide: Korku phonology and morphophonemics. Ph.D. dissertation, University of Pennsylvania 1960.

4.2.2. Korwa

4.2.2.1. Dictionaries

Bahl 1962 = Kali Charan Bahl: Korwa Lexicon. Chicago 1962 [150 p. mimeographed].

4.2.2.2. Other Publications

Crooke 1892 = W. Crooke: Vocabulary of the Korwa language. In: JRAS, 1st ser., 61.1. 1892, 125—8.

4.2.3. Birhor

Sinha s. a. = N. K. Sinha: Birhor Wordlists, Birhor-English. Chicago s. a. [mimeographed].

4.2.4. Mundari

4.2.4.1. Dictionaries

Bhaduri 1931 = Manindra Bhushan Bhaduri: A Mundari-English Dictionary. Calcutta 1931 [229 p.].

Hoffmann 1930—79 = Father Johann Hoffmann with A. Van Emmelen and others: Encyclopaedia Mundarica. Patna, Bihar 1930—79 [15 vols; 4889 p.].

Prasad 1973 = Svarnlata Prasad: Muṇḍarī-Hindī Śabdkoṣ (Mundari-Hindi Dictionary). Ranchi 1973 [464 p.].

Prasad 1976 = Svarnlata Prasad: Hindī-Muṇḍarī Śabdkoṣ (Hindi-Mundari Dictionary). Ranchi 1976 [238 p.].

Soy s. a. = N. Soy: Mundari Vocabulary (Horo Kajī Puthī). Part 1, *a* to *na*, P. D. Kandulna, Jamshedpur s. a. [172 p.].

4.2.4.2. Other Publications

Hoffmann 1903 = Father Johann Hoffmann: Mundari grammar. Calcutta 1903.

Ponette 1978 = Father P. Ponette: Hoffmann's two important collaborators ... van Emmelen and Menas Orea. In: The Munda world. Hoffman commemoration volume. Ed. by P. Ponette. Ranchi 1978, 42—46.

4.2.5. Ho

4.2.5.1. Dictionaries

Bodra s. a. = Lako Bodra: Ho Halang Galang. Jhinkpani s. a. [manuscript].

Burrows 1915 = Lionel Burrows: Ho Grammar (With Vocabulary). Calcutta 1915 [194 p.].

Deeney 1975 = John Deeney: Ho Grammar and Vocabulary. Chaibasa 1975 [216 p.].

Deeney s. a. = John Deeney: Ho-English Dictionary. Chaibasa s. a. [375 p.].

4.2.5.2. Other Publications

Pinnow 1972 = Heinz-Jürgen Pinnow: Schrift und Sprache in den Werken Lako Bodras im Gebiet der Ho von Singbhum (Bihar). In: Anthropos 67. 1972, 822—57.

4.2.6. Santali

[I am told that the Bihar government has published Hindi-Santali and Santali-Hindi dictionaries. I have not seen them, or references to their publication.]

4.2.6.1. Dictionaries

Bodding 1929—35 = P. O. Bodding: A Santal Dictionary. Oslo 1929—1935 [5 vols.; I, 652 p., II 548 p., III 752 p., IV 750 p., V 704 p.].

Campbell 1899—1905 = Andrew Campbell: A Santali-English Dictionary. Part I 1899, Part II 1900, Part III, 1902. Pokhuria 1899—1902 [707 p.; Index published as Supplement, Pokhuria 1905, 708—888].

Campbell/Macphail 1953 a = Andrew Campbell/R. M. Macphail: A Santali-English and English-Santali Dictionary. Second edition of Campbell 1899—1905. Pokhuria 1933.

Campbell/Macphail 1953 b = Andrew Campbell/R. M. Macphail: Third edition of Campbell's Santali-English Dictionary. Benegaria 1953 [816 p.].

Campbell/Macphail 1954 = Andrew Campbell/R. M. Macphail: Third edition of Campbell's English-Santali Dictionary. Benegaria 1954 [234 p.; reprinted, Calcutta 1984].

Kiskū/Soren 1951 = P. C. Kiskū/K. R. Soren: Sātālī Śabd-Koṣ. Deoghar 1951 [Not seen by me; the reference is from Huffman, who suggests that this may be a Santali-Santali dictionary. This seems unlikely; it is probably Santali-Hindi].

Kumār/Murmū 1980 a = Braj Bihārī Kumār/Bhagavat Murmū: Sātālī-Hindī Koś. Kohima 1980 [164 p.; Not seen].

Kumār/Murmū 1980 b = Braj Bihārī Kumār/Bhagavat Murmū: Hindī-Sātālī Koś. Kohima 1980 [264 p.; The copy of this book that I have seen has a title page of the Santali-Hindi Dictionary and an introduction by Kumar, who says that Bh. Murmu has been a co-compiler of the volume. Whether his name is on the correct title page or not I don't know].

Martin 1898 = W. Martin: English-Santali Vocabulary. Benares 1898 [192 p.].

Murmū 1967 = Bhagavat Murmū: Hindī-Sātālī Śabdkoṣ (Hindi-Santali Dictionary). Deoghar 1967 [208 p.; Not seen by me].

Puxley 1868 = E. L. Puxley: A Vocabulary of the Santali Language. London 1868 [139 p.].

Soren 1976 = Dilīpa Soren: Sāotāla Śabda Paricaya (in Bengali). Howrah 1976 [119 p.].

4.2.6.2. Other Publications

Bodding 1929 = P. O. Bodding: Materials for a Santali grammar. Part II (mostly morphological). Benegaria 1929.

4.2.7. Nihali

Kuiper 1962 = F. B. J. Kuiper: Nahali: A Comparative Study. In: Mededelingen der Koninklijke Nederlandsche Akademie van Wetenschappen, Afd. Letterkunde, N.R., deel 25.5. 1962, 229—352.

Mundlay 1972 = Asha Mundlay: Nihali Lexicon. Pune 1972 (?). Unpublished typescript [54 p. 1660 items].

4.3. South Munda

4.3.1. Kharia

4.3.1.1. Dictionaries

Biligiri 1965 = H. S. Biligiri: Kharia Phonology, Grammar and Vocabulary. Poona 1965 [206 p.].

Dungdung 1986 = Mathiyas Ḍungdung: Hindī aur Kharịyā (Hindi and Kharia). Ranchi 1986 [426 p.].

Floor et al. 1934 = H. Floor et al.: Dictionary of the Kharia Language. English-Kharia by H. Floor and V. Gheysens. Kharia-English by G. Druart. Calcutta 1934 [125 p.].

Kullū 1981 = Paulus Kullū: Kharịyā Vyākaraṇ evaṃ Saṃskipt Śabdkoś (Kharia Grammar and Short Vocabulary). Ranchi 1981 [160 p.].

4.3.1.2. Other Publications

Malhotra 1982 = Veena Malhotra: The structure of Kharia: A study of linguistic typology and language change. New Delhi 1982.

Pinnow 1959 = Heinz-Jürgen Pinnow: Versuch einer Historischen Lautlehre der Kharia-Sprache. Wiesbaden 1959.

Pinnow 1965 = Heinz-Jürgen Pinnow: Kharia-Texte. Wiesbaden 1965.

4.3.2. Juang

Das Gupta 1978 = Dipankar Das Gupta: Linguistic studies in Juang, Kharia Thar, Lodha, Malpahariya, Ghatoali, Pahariya. Calcutta 1978.

Mahapatra 1976 = B. P. Mahapatra: Comparative notes on Juang and Kharia finite verbs. In: AS II. 1976, 801—14.

Matson 1964 = Dan Matson: A grammatical sketch of Juang, a Munda language. PhD dissertation, University of Wisconsin 1964.

Pinnow 1960 = Heinz-Jürgen Pinnow: Beiträge zur Kenntnis der Juang-Sprache. Berlin 1960 [unpublished manuscript].

4.3.3. Gutob

4.3.3.1. Dictionaries

Zide/Das 1963 = Norman Zide/B. P. Das: Gutob Verb Lexicon. 1963.

Zide et al. 1963 = Norman Zide/B. P. Das/R. DeArmond: Gutob-English Wordlist, English-Gutob Wordlist. Chicago 1963.

4.3.3.2. Other Publications

Zide 1985 = Norman Zide: Notes mostly historical on some participant roles in some Munda languages. In: Proceedings of the conference on participant roles: South Asia and adjacent areas. Eds. Arlene Zide, D. Magier and E. Schiller. Bloomington 1985, 92—103

4.3.4. Remo

4.3.4.1. Dictionaries

Bhattacharya 1968 = S. Bhattacharya: A Bonda Dictionary. Poona 1968 [212 p.].

4.3.4.2. Other Publications

Fernandez 1968 = Frank Fernandez: A grammatical sketch of Remo, a Munda language. Ph.D. dissertation, University of North Carolina 1968

Zide 1972 = N. Zide: Review of S. Bhattacharya. A Bonda Dictionary. In: JAOS 92.4. 1972, 506—513.

4.3.5. Gtaʔ

4.3.5.1. Dictionaries

Mahapatra/Zide 1980 = Khageshwar Mahapatra/N. Zide: A Gtaʔ Lexicon, revised. Bhubaneshwar. Shantiniketan 1980.

Zide/Mahapatra 1988 = Norman Zide/Khageshwar Mahapatra: A Gtaʔ Dictionary (incomplete). Bhubaneshwar. Chicago 1988.

4.3.5.2. Other Publications

Mahapatra/Zide 1979 = Khageshwar Mahapatra/N. Zide: Gtaʔ texts. Bhubaneshwar. Shantiniketan 1979.

4.3.6. Sora

4.3.6.1 Dictionaries

Mahapatra/Mahapatra 1968 = B. P. Mahapatra/Ranganayaki Mahapatra: Revision of Ramamurti's Sora-English Dictionary. 1968 [printout].

Ramamurti 1933 = G. V. Ramamurti: English-Sora Dictionary. Madras 1933 [257 p.].

Ramamurti 1938 = G. V. Ramamurti: Sora-English Dictionary. Madras 1938 [254 p.].

4.3.6.2. Other Publications

Ramamurti 1912—14 = G. V. Ramamurti: Sora readers (in Telugu script). 1912—14.

Ramamurti 1931 = G. V. Ramamurti: A manual of So:ra: (or Savara) language. Madras 1931.

4.3.7. Juray

A. Zide 1982 = Arlene R. K. Zide: A reconstruction of Proto-Sora-Juray-Gorum phonology. Ph.D. dissertation, University of Chicago 1982.

4.3.8. Gorum

4.3.8.1. Dictionaries

A. Zide 1968 = Arlene R. K. Zide: A Gorum Lexicon. Chicago 1968 [503 p.; plus addenda].

A. Zide 1971 = Arlene R. K. Zide: An English-Gorum Lexicon. Chicago 1971 [202 p.; manuscript].

4.3.8.2. Other Publications

Aze 1973 = F. Richard Aze: Part IV, 1700 word vocabulary. In: Patterns in clause, sentence and discourse in selected Indian languages of India and Nepal. Kathmandu 1973, 12—208.

Norman Zide, University of Chicago, Chicago, Illinois (USA)

XXV. Lexikographie der Einzelsprachen IX: Die tibetobirmanischen Sprachen
Lexicography of Individual Languages IX: The Tibeto-Burman Languages
Lexicographie des langues particulières IX: Les langues tibéto-birmanes

251. Tibetan Lexicography

1. Introduction
2. Early Dictionaries
3. Modern Dictionaries
4. Selected Bibliography

1. Introduction

The Tibetan alphabet was created during the 7th century based on a northern form of the Indian Gupta alphabet. It consists of 30 consonants and 4 vowels, the vowel "a" being unwritten—implicit if none of the other written vowels appear. The language is read from left to right and includes a number of different scripts (e.g. cursive, block printed, headless).

2. Early Dictionaries

The earliest Tibetan dictionary is contained in the *Bstan 'gyur* (Tengyur), the great Buddhist commentary on the Kangyur which was written about the time of *Khri ral pa can* (Tri Repajen), i.e. the early 9th century. This has two chapters known as *sgro sbyong bam po gnyis pa* (Drojong bambo nyiba). The first is concerned with translating Sanskrit into Tibetan. The second, known as *chos kyi rnam grangs* (chöki namdrang) is a Sanskrit to Tibetan dictionary of religious terms.

Since that work, scores of indigenous Tibetan dictionaries have been compiled. These can be categorized into six broad classes:

(a) Those that are specialized by topic, e.g., for religious or medical terms.

(b) Those limited to the vocabulary used in a single text. These were compiled to facilitate comprehension of that particular text, and are usually called *brda bkrol (dadrö)* or *brda 'grol (dadrö)*. Some examples of the texts for which such *brda bkrol* exist are: (a) *sa skya legs bshad* (Sakya legshe), (b) *lam rim chen mo* (Lamrim chemmo), (c) *chu shing bstan bcos* (chushing denjö), (d) *be bum rngon po* (bebum ngönbo), (e) *'dul ba'i gling 'bum* (dülwe lingbum), (f) *'jam dbyangs bzhad pa'i phar phyin dang dbu ma'i brda bkrol* (Jamyang Shepe parchin dang ume dadrö).

(c) General dictionaries that contain explanations and definitions. The most famous classical examples of these are: (a) *dag yig ngag sgron* (Tayi ngagdrön) compiled by Dpal sgang lo tsa ba (Began lotsawa) at the time of the 3rd Dalai Lama (1543—88). (b) *dag yig sgron gsal* (Tayi drönsel) compiled by Bra sti dge bshes rin chen don grub (Drati geshe rinchen döndrup) at the time of the 7th Dalai Lama (1708—57). (c) *dag yig za ma tog* (Tayi samatog) compiled by Zhwa lu chos skyong bzang po (Shalu chögyong sangbo) at the time of the 2nd Dalai Lama (1475—1542).

(d) Dictionaries specialized to aid in spelling, i.e., they do not include any definition of terms. They are usually called *dag yig* (tayi), but this term is also used for a real dictionary containing definitions.

(e) Dictionaries for reading or translating from other languages, i.e., Mongolian, Chinese, Sanskrit, and Manchu. One of the most famous of these is the Chinese-Manchu-Tibetan dictionary *dag yig mkhas pa'i byung gnas* (Tayi kebe chungne) compiled by Lcang skya rol pa'i rdo rje (Janggya röbe dorje) during the reign of the Ch'ien lung Emperor (1736—96). Another is the 4 volume Chinese-Manchu-Mongolian-Tibetan dictionary known as *gsung rab kyi tshig mdzod* (Sungrab gi tsingdzö). A third famous one is the Tibetan to Sanskrit dictionary called *kaa li'i phreng bsgrigs*. It was compiled by Zhwa lu mchod dpon yon tan 'byung gnas during the reign of the 7th Dalai Lama (1708—57).

These bilingual dictionaries were often restricted to a particular lexical genre, for example, medicine, as in the Chinese-Tibetan dictionary of medical terms known as *sman ming rgya bod shan sbyar*. It was compiled by Sog po lo tsaa ba mgon po skyobs during the reign of the 8th Dalai Lama (1758—1804).

(f) Dictionaries of ancient terms. One of the most famous of these is the *brda gsar rnying gi rnam gzhag le shi'i gur khang* written by Phyongs ston rin chen bkra shis in 1476.

The early Tibetan dictionaries and spelling aids had no organized system of internal alphabetization and were written with the intent that the user would memorize the entire volume rather than use it as a reference book. In other words, lexical entries were not listed in alphabetical order. This is not surprising given the emphasis on memorization in the monastic education system, but it is also in part due to the complex nature of syllables in the Tibetan language.

The structure of Tibetan syllables makes alphabetization complicated because the initial letter (the first one written) is often not the root letter. For example, the root letter of the three syllables *gi, rgyal* and *bsgrubs* is "g" and all three would be alphabetized under "g" in the contemporary system of lexical alphabetization. This complexity results from prefixed, affixed, subjoined and final letters being attached in various combinations to a root letter. These various combinations affect pronunciation making it widely divergent from spelling. For example, whereas *gi* is pronounced (gi), *rgyal* is pronounced (gye), and *bsgrubs* is pronounced (drup). This, in turn, explains the need for specialized spelling texts.

Bsgrubs illustrates all of the possible letter slots in syllables (Fig. 251.1 and 251.2).

Traditional Tibetan lexical alphabetization is illustrated by one of the most famous indigenous dictionaries, the 16th century *Dag yig ngag sgron gyi rtsa ba* (Tayi ngagdrön gi dzawa) compiled by Dpal khang lo tsaa ba (Began lotsawa). It contained separate sections for each of the thirty letters in the Tibetan alphabet, but did not contain any form of internal alphabetization based on prefixed, affixed, subjoined and final letters beyond that. In other words, *gi, rgyal* and *bsgrubs* were grouped under "g", but all the words beginning in "rg" were not listed together nor were those starting with "bsg".

By the 18th century, alphabetization had become more sophisticated and lexical items were grouped within each of the thirty "root" letters based on the system of prefixes and affixes, e.g. all the "kh" words before all the "khy" words before all the "khr" words. However, there was still no ordering within these subsections, i.e., within all the words starting with "khy".

3. Modern Dictionaries

The Western tradition of Tibetan dictionaries began in 1834 with the publication of a Tibetan-English dictionary compiled by the Hungarian Alexander Csoma de Körös. This appears to be the first time the modern system of alphabetization was utilized. This pioneering work was followed by H. A. Jaschke's excellent Tibetan-English dictionary in 1881, and soon after that in 1902, by S.C. Das' Tibetan-English Dictionary, and in 1905 by Bell's English-Tibetan colloquial dictionary.

The first modern dictionary compiled in Tibet was Geshe Chödrak's *brda dag ming tshig gsal ba bzhugs so*. It was completed in 1946 and carved into wood blocks in 1949. It is the first indigenous dictionary to use a modern system of alphabetization. It was printed in Western book format with Chinese glosses in 1957.

Over the past 25 years, a number of substantial new dictionaries have appeared in Tibet, China and the West. All of these follow the modern format of dictionaries and include both detailed alphabetization and definitions. Some of the most important of these

1. block printed ("big head"): བསྒྲུབས་

2. cursive: [Tibetan cursive script]

3. headless: [Tibetan headless script]

Fig. 251.1: The word *bsgrubs* in different scripts

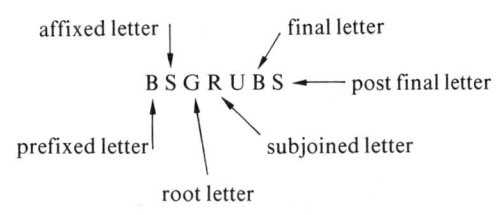

affixed letter — final letter
B S G R U B S ← post final letter
prefixed letter — subjoined letter
root letter

Fig. 251.2: Letter slots analysis of *bsgrups*

are: Melvyn C. Goldstein's *Tibetan-English Dictionary of Modern Tibetan* and *English-Tibetan Dictionary of Modern Tibetan*, Eberhardt Richter's *Tibetan-German Dictionary*, N. Roerich's *Tibetan-Russian-English Dictionary*, B. V. Semichov's (et al.) *Tibetan-Russian Dictionary*, Yu Dao-chu's *Tibetan Chinese Dictionary of Colloquial Lhasa Tibetan*, and the new three volume Tibetan-Tibetan-Chinese dictionary recently published in 1985 in China (Zhang, 1985).

China's post-Cultural Revolution reform policies have led to a resurgence of interest in Tibetan language in Tibet (now the Tibet Autonomous Region) and surrounding areas with large ethnic Tibetan populations such as the Qinghai and Sichuan Provinces. Many traditional dictionaries and other Tibetan language books have been republished, and a variety of Tibetan language magazines have appeared.

Some variance in terms has developed between the Tibetan refugees living outside of China and Tibetans in Tibet with the former adopting a number of English and Hindi terms where the latter have adopted Chinese terms. For example, whereas the Tibetans in exile use "rediyo" for radio, the Tibetans in Tibet generally use the Chinese term "hruyinji". By and large, though, these are relatively minor and neither of these Tibetan language communities has any difficulty communicating with the other in speech or writing, nor is it likely that this will become a problem in the future.

4. Selected Bibliography

Bell 1965 = Charles A. Bell: English-Tibetan Colloquial Dictionary. Calcutta 1965 (first published as part two of the Manual of Colloquial Tibetan, Calcutta 1905; published as separate book with above title in Calcutta 1920) [562 p.].

Das 1983 = Sarat Chandra Das: A Tibetan-English Dictionary with Sanskrit Synonyms. Delhi 1983 (first published in 1902) [1351 p.].

De Körös 1973 = Alexander Csoma De Körös: Essay Towards a Dictionary Tibetan and English. New Delhi 1973 (first published in 1834) [391 p.].

Geshe 1957 = Geshe Chödrak: brda dag ming tshig gsal ba bzhugs so. Peking 1957.

Goldstein 1978 = Melvyn C. Goldstein: Tibetan-English Dictionary of Modern Tibetan. Kathmandu 1978 [1234 p.].

Goldstein 1984 = Melvyn C. Goldstein: English-Tibetan Dictionary of Modern Tibetan. Berkeley 1984 [485 p.].

Jaschke 1980 = Heinrich August Jaschke: A Tibetan-English Dictionary. Delhi 1980 (first published in 1881) [671 p.].

Richter 1966 = Eberhardt Richter: Tibetisch-Deutsches Wörterbuch. Leipzig 1966 [444 p.].

Roerich 1983—87 = N. H. Roerich: Tibetan-Russian-English Dictionary. Vol. 1—9. Moscow 1983—87.

Semichov et al. 1983—87 = B. V. Semichov/J. M. Parfionovich/B. D. Dandaron: Tibetsko-russkij slovar'. Moscow 1963.

Yu 1983 = Yu, Dao-chu (ed.): Tibetan-Chinese Dictionary of Colloquial Tibetan. Beijing 1983 [1077 p.].

Zhang 1985 = Yi-sen Zhang (ed.): The Great Tibetan-Chinese Dictionary. 3 Volumes. Beijing 1985.

Melvyn C. Goldstein, Case Western Reserve University, Cleveland, Ohio (USA)

252. Burmese Lexicography

1. Pali-Burmese Dictionaries
2. Burmese-Burmese Dictionaries
3. Dictionaries of Burmese and Modern Foreign Languages
4. Features of Burmese that Affect Lexicography
5. Selected Bibliography

1. Pali-Burmese Dictionaries

The Burmese embraced Theravāda Buddhism in the 11th century, and have a strong tradition of scholarship in Pali, the classical language in which the sacred texts are written. The Burmese word for dictionary, *abhidhān*, is itself derived from the name of a Pali dictionary of synonyms, the *Abhidhānappadīpikā* (Moggallāna 12th cent.). (S. art. 247.) Despite — or perhaps because of — the abundance of editions, commentaries and translations of Pali texts that Burmese scholars produced over the centuries, alphabetically ordered Pali-Burmese dictionaries were late to appear. One of the earliest was written in the mid 19th century (Mra-toṅ 1927), and the most recent is a comprehensive work in 9 large volumes (Mran-mā Sāsanā 1975).

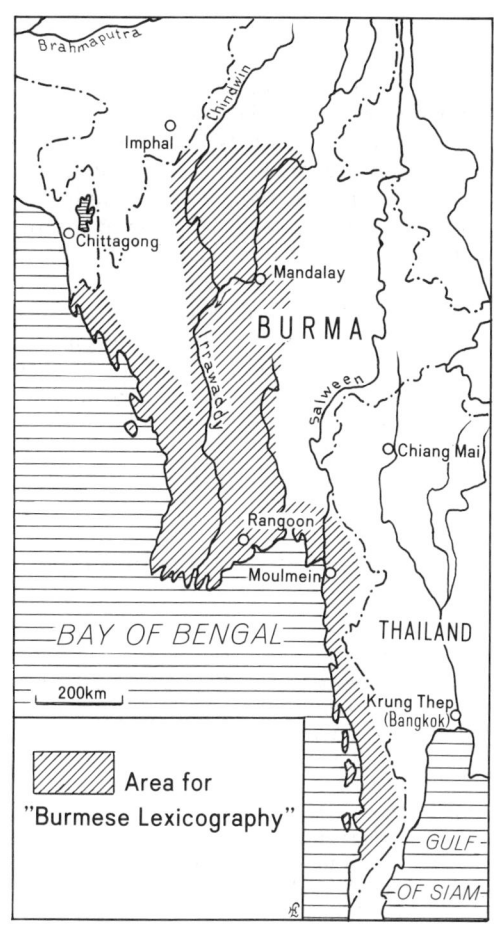

Map 252.1: Area for Burmese lexicography

2. Burmese-Burmese Dictionaries

By the mid 18th century Burmese language and literature came to be accepted as worthy of scholarly study alongside Pali. One outcome of this was the appearance of *porāṇa* dictionaries: dictionaries of words found in 16th and 17th century literature which had subsequently become obsolete. The earliest porāṇa dictionary was written in 1794 (Tvaṅ:-saṅ: 1794) and others are still appearing.

Part of the Kingdom of Burma was annexed by the British in 1826, and by 1886 the whole country was under British rule. The English language came to acquire high prestige as a requirement for entering the civil service and as the medium of instruction in the university. In the 1940s, when nationalist sentiment was strong, a comprehensive monolingual dictionary was seen as a powerful aid in preserving Burmese culture (see e.g.

Obhāsa 1948 pt 2, *ka* ff.): The aims of the association which supported this work include: 1. collecting and publishing works of older Burmese literature; 2. establishing the meaning of Burmese words and compiling a dictionary; ... 5. preventing Burmese culture from being lost. A dictionary was needed to help standardize usage as well as to aid the understanding of the older literature. Some early attempts (see Wun 1956, 176 ff.) had to be abandoned before completion, but the impetus gained strength after Burma regained independence in 1948, and in 1963 the government set up a body now named the Burma Language Commission, which was charged with the compilation of a grammar, a spelling book, and various dictionaries. Their first dictionary is in 5 volumes (Mran-mā-cā 1980). This excellent work contains about 28,000 entries, gives the pronunciation for every entry, and has illustrations where appropriate. It is aimed primarily at the needs of office workers and students, but has also proved very useful to foreign scholars of Burmese (cf. Dictionary excerpt 252.2).

The Burma Language Commission is currently (1986) engaged in compiling further dictionaries, one of which is a more comprehensive Burmese-Burmese dictionary of about 100,000 entries, including many more words from the older literature and words of restricted regional currency.

3. Dictionaries of Burmese and Modern Foreign Languages

The arrival in the early 19th century of Christian missionaries from North America, and of the civil servants and others who came with the British administration, created a need for dictionaries of Burmese and English, both for English speakers who wanted to learn Burmese, and for Burmese who wanted to be proficient in English. Of the many dictionaries published it is those of the American Baptist missionaries which stand preeminent. The earliest was an English-Burmese dictionary (Hough 1825) explicitly intended for foreigners — presumably members of the American mission; but this was superseded by the dictionaries of the Rev. Adoniram Judson, both English-Burmese and Burmese-English, which have survived through many editions, and are still in use at the present day (Judson 1849, 1852, 1887, 1902).

Several attempts at more comprehensive

and up-to-date Burmese-English dictionaries have been made and abandoned, notably the monumental work of J. A. Stewart and his successors (Stewart 1980), of which six fascicles were published out of a projected 30 or more. Of the Burmese-English dictionaries that have been completed the most useful is that of U Hoke Sein (1981), which gives a Pali and a Sanskrit equivalent, as well as an English one, for each Burmese entry (see further Okell 1983). Another Burmese-English dictionary is currently (1986) being prepared by the Burma Language Commission (see 2 above), and is expected to contain about 30,000 entries.

For users of English-Burmese dictionaries, publishers in Burma have produced a rich crop of new ones in the years since the Second World War and Burma's independence. The largest is the dictionary by Dr. Ba Han (1966), with some 60,000 entries.

In the same period, scholars from Russia, Germany, France and Japan have taken an active interest in Burmese language studies, and several dictionaries have appeared as a result of their work. Others were compiled as aids to foreign language teaching at the Institute of Foreign Languages in Rangoon. Noteworthy dictionaries in this group are those of Minina (1976), Esche (1976), Bernot (1978), and Ono (1984). There is also an excellent Burmese-Chinese dictionary (Chen 1970) containing about 30,000 entries, that was compiled in Burma. For further information on modern bilingual dictionaries see Wun 1956, Allott 1979, Okell 1982.

4. Features of Burmese that Affect Lexicography

4.1. Spelling

"There is no writer in Burmese who has uniformly followed any mode of orthography ... for every copyist writes after his own fashion, or without any fashion, spelling each word that occurs, as the whim of the moment dictates" (Judson 1852, v.). Judson clearly suffered acutely from the affliction that all Burmese lexicographers have to bear. The vagaries of Burmese spelling also account for the appearance of guides to spelling (*sat-puṁ* and other genres) from the 16th century onwards.

The problems arise from the way that the pronunciation of Burmese has changed since it was first written down in the 12th century. The sound written *r*, for example, has merged with the sound written *y*; and at the end of the syllable *t* merged with *p*, and *n* with *m*. In time people lost sight of the original spelling for many words, and the variants that so distressed Dr. Judson came into being.

The situation improved dramatically in 1978 when the Burma Language Commission published its authoritative standardized spelling book (Mranmā-cā 1978). The approved spellings were enforced and are now in widespread use by writers and editors all over the country. A new edition with minor revisions was published in 1986.

4.2. Alphabetical Order

Burmese has an established and widely known order of consonants and an order of vowels. However, neither set is entirely complete or systematic (e.g. the consonant set includes *ññ* but not *ñ*, *-ṁ* is listed with the vowels instead of with the consonants, *ī:* and *ū:* are omitted from the vowels, and *ā:* comes in the wrong place, etc.). As a result, different dictionaries insert the missing elements at different points in the set, causing confusion and irritation for readers familiar with other orders.

ခြောက် [chauɔ] trocken | ထင်း~ trockenes Feuerholz *n*

~ခန်း [~'khaŋ] vertrocknet, ausgetrocknet

~ခန်းလာ [~'khaŋla] vertrocknen, austrocknen

အခြောက်လှန်း [achauɔ'hlaŋ] trocknen *tr*

~အခန်း [~a'khaŋ] Trockenkammer *f*

~စက် [~seɔ] Trockenapparat *m*, Dörranlage *f*

ခြောက်လာ [chauɔla] trocknen *intr*, trocken werden

ခြောက်လုံးပြူးသေနတ် [chauɔ'louŋ-'byuθanaɔ] (Trommel-) Revolver *m*

အခြောက်အလေးချိန် [achauɔa'leijeiŋ] Trockengewicht *n*

ခြောက်သွေ့ [chauɔɢwei'] trocken; einsam, verlassen

~မှု [~hmu'] Trockenheit *f*; Einsamkeit *f*, Verlassenheit *f*

~အောင်ပြုလုပ် [~auŋpyu'iauɔ] trocknen, trocken machen

~အောင်ပြုလုပ်ခြင်း [~auŋpyu'louɔ-'chiŋ] Trocknen *n*, Trocknung *f*

Dictionary excerpt 252.1: Alphabetical order (from: Esche 1976)

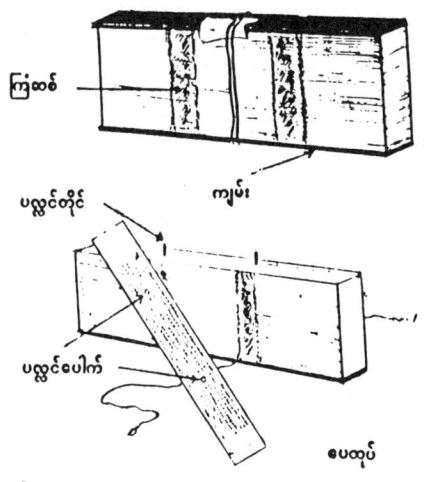

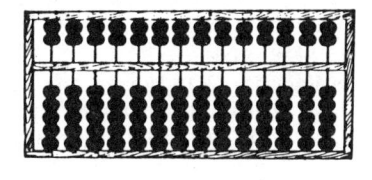

Dictionary excerpt 252.2: Illustrative sketches (from: Mran-ma-ca 1978)

A more fundamental difference of approach splits lexicographers into two camps. Those more familiar with Pali and Western dictionaries favour an order which takes the elements of a word one by one from the beginning (e.g. Hoke Sein, Judson). The other camp takes its direction from the traditional schoolroom method of teaching Burmese script (saṅ-pun:-krī:) which is the order adopted by the spelling books (sat-puṁ). This order takes first, under each consonant, all the syllables with a vowel ending, and then all the syllables with a consonant ending, and the latter are ordered, not by vowel but by final consonant; e.g.

not: *mak, maṅ, mac, mañ, mat, man*, . . .
but: *mak, mok, muik; maṅ, moṅ, muiṅ; mac; mañ; mat, mit, mut; man*, . . .

The latter approach is that adopted by the Burma Language Commission, and most modern dictionaries, whether produced in Burma or abroad, follow its lead. For fuller details see Okell (1968).

4.3. Prefixes

Burmese has only three common prefixes (*a-, ma-,* and *ta-*), but they are very frequently used, and lexicographers have so far evolved no standard procedure for handling forms that occur both with and without a prefix.

Prefix *a-* is found (1) with all nouns derived from verbs (e.g. *me:-* "to ask" and *ame:* "question", and (2) on many nouns not derived from verbs (e.g. *asā:* "flesh"). In the case of the nouns in group (1), many lexicographers make an entry for the derived noun, even though there is one for the verb anyway, which leads to a wasteful duplication of information. And in all cases of words with prefix *a-*, problems arise because the prefix is sometimes omitted (e.g. *akhwaṅ.* "permission", but *khwaṅ.pru-* "to give permission"; *asaṁ* "sound", but *raysaṁ* "sound of laughing"). One solution is to ignore prefix *a-* when ordering entries alphabetically, so that *akhwaṅ.* and *khwaṅ.pru-* would be listed alongside each other instead of in widely separated sections of the dictionary (see further Okell 1968). This expedient has been adopted in one dictionary (Esche 1976), which as a result is much more convenient to use, but so far other lexicographers have been reluctant to take this unorthodox step (cf. Dictionary excerpt 252.1).

Similar problems occur with the prefix *ta-* (sometimes "one" and sometimes an adverb formative, e.g. *rwe.-* "to crawl", *tarwe.rwe.* "creeping"), and with prefix *ma-* (negative). There are many entries which make it hard to decide whether the word should appear under the prefix or under the root. Currently lexicographers make arbitrary decisions, and users have to learn to look in both places.

5. Selected Bibliography

5.1. Dictionaries

Ba Han 1966 = Ba Han: The University English Burmese dictionary. Rangoon 1951—1966 [10 vols] [2293 p.].

Bernot 1978 = Denise Bernot: Dictionnaire birman-français. Paris 1978- [in progress]. [vol 1: 227 p., 2: 209, 3: 195, 4: 206, 5: 199, 6: 206, 7: 201, 8: 204].

Chen 1970 = Chen Yi Sein: A model Burmese-Chinese dictionary. Tokyo 1970 [1st ed. Rangoon 1962] [xviii + 682 p.].

Esche 1976 = Annemarie Esche: Wörterbuch Burmesisch-Deutsch. Leipzig 1976 [546 p.].

Hoke Sein 1981 = U Hoke Sein: The Universal Burmese-English-Pali dictionary. Rangoon 1981 [10+1064+2 p.].

Hough 1825 = G. H. Hough: An English and Burman vocabulary. Serampore 1825 [ii + 424 p.].

Judson 1849 = Rev Adoniram Judson: A dictionary, English and Burmese. 1st ed. Maulmain 1849 [10th ed. Rangoon 1966] [589 p.].

Judson 1852 = Rev Adoniram Judson: A dictionary, Burmese and English. 1st ed. Maulmain 1852 [An earlier unauthorized ed. was published in Calcutta in 1826. 10th ed. Rangoon 1966] [viii + 786 p.].

Judson 1887 = Rev Adoniram Judson: Burmese pocket dictionary, compiled from Dr. Judson's dictionaries: English-Burmese by F. D. Phinney, Burmese-English by F. H. Eveleth. 1st ed. Rangoon 1887 [5th ed. Rangoon n.d. ("post-war")] [iv + 382 p.].

Judson 1902 = Rev Adoniram Judson: Judson's English and Burmese dictionary abridged. 1st ed. Rangoon 1902 [repr. Rangoon 1919; V, 544 p.].

Minina 1976 = G. F. Minina/Kyaw Zaw: Birmansko-Russkiy slovar'. Moscow 1976 [783 p.].

Moggallāna 12th cent. = Moggallāna Thera: Abhidhānappadīpikā [written in 12th cent.]. in: Subhūti: Abhidhānappadīpikāsūci. Rangoon 1905, 673—765.

Mran-mā-cā 1980 = Mran-mā-cā Aphvai: Mran-mā abhidhañ akyañ:-khyup. Rangoon 1978-80 [5 vols] [vol 1: 59 + 242 p., 2: 17 + 228, 3: 17 + 252, 4: 17 + 251, 5: 17 + 275].

Mran-mā-cā 1978 = Mran-mā-cā Aphvai.: Mran-mā cā-luṁ:-poṅ: sat-puṁ kyam:. Rangoon 1978 [rev. ed. 1986; 16 + 292 p.].

Mran-mā Sāsanā 1975 = Mran-mā Sāsanā Aphvai.: Tipiṭaka Mran-mā abhidhān. Rangoon 1964-1975 [9 vols]. [vol 1: not seen, vol 2: not seen, vol 3: ka to ga + 1167 pp, vol 4: not seen, vol 5: ka to ghō + 840, vol 6: ka to na + 1016, vol 7: ka to ñi + 800, vol 8: ka to la + 808, vol 9: ka to ghō + 840].

Mra-toṅ c. 1870 = Mra-toṅ Charā-tō: Paññat-nak kyam: [written ca. 1870]. Mandalay 1927 [394 p.].

Obhāsa 1948 = Arhaṅ Ū: Obhāsa: Caṁ-pra Mran-mā abhidhān kyam:. Rangoon 1947-48 [vol 1 pts 1 &2]. [part 1: not seen, part 2: 216 p.].

Ono 1984 = Ono Toru: Biruma-go joyo 6,000-go. Tokyo 1984 [viii + 525 p.].

Stewart 1980 = J. A. Stewart et al: A Burmese-English dictionary. Rangoon.London 1941-80 [6 vols]. [part 1: xxxvi + p.1 to 40, part 2: viii + 41 to 120, part 3: vi + 121 to 200, part 4: iv + 201 to 280, part 5: viii + 281 to 360, part 6: iv + 361 to 373].

Tvaṅ:-saṅ: 1794 = Tvaṅ:-saṅ:-tuik-van: Porāna-kathā [written 1794]. In: Sudhammavati Press: Poranākathāṭīkā. Rangoon 1904 [and in other collections] [p. 1 to 41].

5.2. Other Publications

Allott 1978 = Anna Allott: Review of Minina 1976 and Esche 1976]. In: Bulletin of the School of Oriental and African Studies 42, 1. 1979, 168f.

Okell 1968 = John Okell: Alphabetical order in Burmese. In: Journal of the Burma Research Society 51. 1968, 145-171.

Okell 1982 = John Okell: [Review of Bernot 1978]. In: Linguistics of the Tibeto-Burman Area 6.2. 1982, 89-103.

Okell 1983 = John Okell: [Review of Hoke Sein 1981]. In: Linguistics of the Tibeto-Burman Area 7.2. 1983, 115-120.

Wun 1956 = Maung Wun: Some problems of a lexicographer in Burmese. In: Journal of the Burma Research Society 39.2. 1956, 176-181.

John Okell, University of London,
London (Great Britain)

253. Lexicography of Other Tibeto-Burman Languages

1. Introduction
2. Special Problems Posed by the Typological Characteristics of TB Languages
3. Further Desiderata
4. Selected Bibliography

1. Introduction

There are at least 250 languages in Tibeto-Burman (TB), which along with Chinese (over 1 billion speakers) comprises the great Sino-Tibetan (ST) family. The total number of speakers of TB languages is about 56 million, with about 9 languages having over a million speakers (including 22M Burmese, 5M Tibetan), but with over 200 having less than 100,000. TB languages are spoken over a wide area, including W and SW China, the Himalayan region, NE India, Burma, and northern peninsular SE Asia. It is useful to distinguish between "Indospheric" and "Sinospheric" branches of TB — those languages which have been under Indian or Chinese cultural influence, respectively.

There are only a handful of "literary" TB languages. Tibetan (attested since A.D. 600), Burmese (since around A.D. 1100), Newari and Meithei (=Manipuri) from the 17th/18th c., and Karen (since the 19th c.) have Indic-derived "devanāgarī" systems. On the Sinospheric side, Xixia (=Tangut), an extinct language spoken in the 11th—13th centuries A.D. in a once powerful empire on the western fringes of China, developed a complex homegrown logographic script; the Lolo (=Yi) devised a syllabary with more than 500 symbols perhaps as early as the 16th c.; the Naxi/Moso long ago created an intricate pictographic writing system reminiscent of Egyptian hieroglyphics. For most TB languages, however, if a tradition of writing exists at all, it goes back no further than a romanization introduced by Western missionaries within the past 150 years. Very recently, it has been official Chinese policy to create romanized orthographies for the 55 officially recognized minority languages of China, including 17 TB languages.

The history of TB lexicography begins in the 19th century, with the dictionaries of missionaries and colonial administrators, some of which are remarkable feats of scholarship (see sect. 4, Selected Bibliography). Though parts of the TB world (Burma, Laos, Vietnam, most of China and NE India) are still closed to outsiders, there has been a recent spate of linguistic fieldwork, including the collection of abundant lexical material, both through government- and institution-sponsored research projects (especially in China and India), and fieldwork by individual scholars and students (especially in Thailand and Nepal).

The *Bibliography* included with this survey is organized both by "*genre*" and by *subgroup* of the TB family:

We may roughly taxonomize the available TB lexicographical material into several "genres": *dictionaries* (D), *glossaries* (G), and *wordlists* (W). *Dictionaries* are large-scale lexica with nuanced glosses, abundant examples, and perhaps etymological and grammatical information. *Glossaries* are fairly extensive compilations that typically appear appended to a grammatical study of their language. By *wordlist* I mean a bare list of words, often arranged according to semantic category, with little or no analysis or exemplification, and minimal glosses. In addition I cite some important multilingual lexicographical works: *etymological dictionaries* (ED) and *etymological/comparative wordlists* (EW), as well as a few *bibliographies* (B) and a theoretically oriented *dictionary review* (RD).

The seven major subgroups of TB currently recognized have received unequal shares of lexicographical attention. These subgroups are as follows:

Kamarupan (NE India, W Burma): large and heterogeneous, including the Kuki-Chin-Naga, Abor-Miri-Dafla, and Bodo-Garo groups; Indospheric.

Himalayish (Tibet, Nepal, Bhutan, Sikkim): phonologically conservative, often morphologically complex; Indospheric.

Qiangic (Sichuan): a recently discovered group of about 12 languages; may include the closest living relatives of extinct Xixia; Sinospheric.

Kachin-Nung (N. Burma, Yunnan): geographically and genetically central; relatively free from both Chinese and Indic influence.

Lolo-Burmese (Sichuan, Yunnan, Burma, Thailand, Laos, Vietnam): Sinospheric; depleted consonants, rich tonal systems; most southerly and easterly of TB groups; best-studied group so far.

Baic (NW Yunnan): dialects of a single language, very heavily influenced by

Chinese; only Baic and Karenic have SVO order.

Karenic (Burma, Thailand): phonologically similar to Lolo-Burmese, but syntactically divergent from most of the rest of TB, with SVO order.

2. Special Problems Posed by the Typological Characteristics of TB Languages

2.1. Alphabetical Order of Consonants

Indic-derived devanāgarī writing systems, where the consonants appear in a sequence determined by their position and manner of articulation, were adopted for all the great literary languages of Southeast Asia except Vietnamese (Mon, Khmer, Cham, Old Javanese, Burmese, Tibetan, Thai, Lao), as well as by several minority languages with writing systems devised much more recently (e.g. Karen, Shan, Newari, Manipuri). There has also been a tradition going back to the 19th c. of arranging bilingual dictionaries of SE Asian languages in a devanāgarī-style order even when the words are in a romanized orthography (e.g. Mainwaring/Grünwedel 1898, sect. 4.3.; Srinuan 1976, sect. 4.7.; Grüssner 1978, sect. 4.5.; Matisoff 1988, sect. 4.7.), through most TB lexicographers now adopt the ABC order of romanization.

The five "cardinal" vowels also appear in a conventional order (*a i u e o*) in Indic-influenced alphabets, with additional or modified symbols intercalated or added to these basic five according to the needs of the particular language.

Dictionaries of monosyllabic multitonal languages must be alphabetized on another dimension as well, by *tone*. The many syllables which are homophonous with respect to consonants and vowels, but which differ in tone, must be presented in a consistent order. Symbologically, tonal contrasts may be indicated in several ways, e.g. by diacritics (acutes, graves, circumflexes, etc.), by superscribed numerals, or by arbitrary syllable-final consonants (this last option works particularly well in languages with no "real" final consonants). Lately some Chinese-English dictionaries have abandoned the traditional arrangement in terms of graphic elements ("radicals" and number of strokes) in favor of a listing according to the alphabetical order of their transcription in the excellent "pinyin" romanization of Mandarin used in the People's Republic of China.

2.2. Morphology

The relatively complex morphophonemics of some Indospheric TB languages sometimes requires the listing of several variants in an entry, e.g. the 4 "principal parts" of Tibetan verbs, the independent vs. subjunctive forms of Kuki-Chin verbs, or the pairs of Newari verb-forms both with and without a thematic stem-final consonant.

Sometimes prefixes pose lexicographical problems. The nominalizing or bulk-providing Lahu prefix ɔ̂- occurs as the first syllable in 6 % (86 pages) of the entries in Matisoff 1988 (1414 pages; see sect. 4.7.). Similarly 11.8 % of Judson's 1061-page Burmese-English Dictionary begins with the functionally identical prefix ʔə-. Even at the cost of the extra space, it is a good idea to list each of these prefixed morphemes twice, both in prefixed and unprefixed form, since there is often semantic differentiation and their syntactic properties are different.

2.3. Homophony and Compounding

The monosyllabic ST/TB languages (especially the phonologically reduced TB languages of the Sinospheric type) have compensated for their endemic homophony problem by creating countless disyllabic compounds, where each syllable by and large has a relatively clear meaning of its own. (I have applied the term *morphan* (i.e. orphan morph) to semantically obscure syllables which only occur in one or two collocations.)

In principle all recurrent morphs should be listed as separate head entries even if they do not occur initially in compounds — and it is often a good idea to list morphans separately as well (especially for comparative purposes — a bound morpheme in one language may well be cognate to a free morpheme in another).

Particularly distressing is the widespread practice of "pernicious interalphabetization" (see Matisoff 1987, sect. 4.7.), where homophonous monosyllables are listed *en bloc*, after which all the collocations that begin with the same phonological syllable appear in strict alphabetical order according to the initial of their second syllables, regardless of what the morphemic identity of their first syllables may be. Unless the meanings of the first syllables are quite disparate, it is often unclear which collocations relate to which homophone. Folk etymologies and conflations can go unrecognized.

This problem does not exist for Chinese, thanks to the logographic writing system, in which each character represents a single syllable (and usually a separate morpheme), so that nothing is more natural than to group together all collocations containing a certain character.

3. Further Desiderata

The humble unwritten languages which form the vast majority of the TB family are worthy of the most careful lexicographical attention. They are all rich and subtle instruments of expression, priceless repositories of human experience. Many of them are endangered, and will not survive the current generation of speakers. For some languages, the best that can be hoped for is a quick "salvage job", recording as much as possible, *tant bien que mal,* in a race against the clock. Ideally, however, the TB lexicographer should strive for excellence along several dimensions:

3.1. Lexico-Semantic Precision and Exhaustiveness

No area of the lexicon should go unrecorded, with special attention paid to such areas as cultural vocabulary, flora and fauna. Entries should be labelled for their stylistic level, affective value, or sociolinguistic flavor (e.g. *animist, archaic, babytalk, dialectal, euphemistic, insulting, jocular, neologistic, onomatopoetic, poetic*). Subsenses of polysemous morphemes should be carefully distinguished, and cases where it is difficult to decide between polysemy and homophony should be pointed out. Synonyms and antonyms should be provided, along with cross-references to other morphemes which cooccur with the head-entry in collocations. Culturally specific or arcane items should be explained at length (with pictures if possible!).

3.2. Grammatical Precision and Exemplification

There is certainly a limit to the amount of grammatical information that can be crammed into a dictionary, yet much more can be done than is usual in this regard. At a minimum, the form-class of each head-entry should be indicated (e.g. *N, V, Prt, Adv*), with the criteria for assignment to a grammatical category explained in the dictionary's preface. It is desirable to capture the internal structure of "higher-order" compounds (i.e. those with more than 2 constituents) by a system of several different kinds of hyphens between their syllables. For real understanding of a morpheme's grammatical properties, it is essential to provide examples of its use in context, both in simple collocations and in complex clauses or whole sentences. These examples shoud also be labelled according to their construction-type (e.g. Obj + V, Instr + V, N + Adj, Num + Clf, etc.). This is especially necessary in the case of Sinospheric TB languages with minimal morphology, where grammatical relationships (e.g. the relation of NP's to the VP of their clause) are often covert.

Because of the vastly different "information packaging strategies" of TB and European languages, the inclusion of complex clausal or sentential examples can present severe problems. While it is usually impractical to give morpheme-by-morpheme interlinear glosses (tremendously space-consuming!), it is often necessary to include "literal" paraphrases of a TB expression in order to give the dictionary user a reasonable chance of figuring out how the example sentence is put together.

3.3. Etymological Information

If possible, intralingual etymological connections among morphemes should be suggested (as, e.g. a good English dictionary would point out that *whole, heal,* and *hale* descend from the same etymon). When different morphemes are phonosemantically similar, the lexicographer should give his best judgment as to whether this is accidental or the result of a true etymological relationship. Loanwords should be traced and identified. In the case of native etyma, cognates from other TB languages should be suggested.

Very few dictionaries of minority TB languages actually meet the above desiderata, but it is good to keep the ideal in mind. Many major TB dictionaries are now in preparation (see the items marked *D in the *Bibliography*), and the lexicographical future of TB seems bright.

4. Selected Bibliography

4.1. General Sino-Tibetan/Tibeto-Burman

4.4.1. Dictionaries

Benedict 1972 = Paul K. Benedict: Sino-Tibetan: A Conspectus. Contributing Editor J. A. Matisoff.

(Princeton-Cambridge Series in Chinese Linguistics 2). New York 1972 [232 p.]. (ED)

Coblin 1986 = W.S. Coblin: A Sinologist's Handlist of Sino-Tibetan Lexical Comparisons. (Monumenta Serica Monograph Series 18). Nettetal 1986. (ED)

Grierson/Konow, eds. 1903—28 = Sir G.A. Grierson/S. Konow, eds.: Linguistic Survey of India. Vol. III, Parts 1—3, Tibeto-Burman Family. 1903—28 [Reprinted Delhi. Varanasi. Patna 1967]. (W)

Luce 1981 = G.H. Luce: A Comparative Wordlist of Old Burmese, Chinese, and Tibetan. London 1981 [88 p.]. (EW)

Shafer 1966/67 = R. Shafer: Introduction to Sino-Tibetan. Wiesbaden 1966 (Part I), 1967 (Part II). (ED)

Shafer/Benedict 1939—41 = R. Shafer/P.K. Benedict: Sino-Tibetan Linguistics. Berkeley 1939—41 [Bound typescript, 14 vols]. (ED)

4.4.2. Other Publications

Hale 1982 = B. Hale: Research on Tibeto-Burman Languages. (Trends in Linguistics, State of the Art Report 14). New York 1982. (B)

Huffman 1985 = F.E. Huffman: Bibliography and Index of Mainland Southeast Asian Languages and Linguistics. New Haven. London 1985. (B)

La Polla/Lowe 1989 = R.J. La Polla/J.B. Lowe: Bibliography of the International Conferences on Sino-Tibetan Languages and Linguistics, I—XXI. (STEDT Monograph Series 1, Institute of International Studies). Berkeley 1989. (B)

4.2. Baic
4.2.1. Dictionaries

Dell 1981 = F. Dell: La langue Bai, Phonologie et Lexique. Paris 1981 [174 p.]. (G)

Xu/Zhao 1984 = Xu Lin/Zhao Yansun: Outline Grammar of the Bai Language. Beijing 1984 [in Chinese]. (G)

Zhao (in prep.) = Zhao Yansun: A Bai-Chinese Dictionary. Ed. and trans. by G. Wiersma. In prep. (*D)

4.3. Himalayish
4.3.1. Dictionaries

Allen 1975 = N.J. Allen: Sketch of Thulung Grammar, with Three Texts and a Glossary. (Cornell University East Asia Papers 6). Ithaca, N.Y. 1975. (G)

Driem 1987 = G.L. van Driem: A Grammar of Limbu. Berlin 1987. (G)

Driem 1991 = G.L. van Driem: Dumi Bai Grammar. Berlin (to appear). (G)

Hale, ed. 1973 = A. Hale, ed.: Clause, Sentence, and Discourse Patterns in Selected Languages of Nepal, Vol. IV. [Contains wordlists of Chepang, Gurung, Jirel, Kham, Kaike, Khaling, Magari, Newari, Tamang, Thakali, Sherpa, Sunwari]. (W)

Mainwaring/Grünwedel 1898 = G.B. Mainwaring/A. Grünwedel: Dictionary of the Lepcha Language. Berlin 1898. (D)

Mazaudon (in prep.) = M. Mazaudon: Dictionnaire tamang-français. In prep. (*D)

Watters (in prep.) = D. Watters: Kham-English Dictionary. In prep. (*D)

Winter 1985 = W. Winter: Materials Towards a Dictionary of Chamling. Kiel 1985 [MS 78 p.].

4.4. Jingpho-Nung
4.4.1. Dictionaries

Dai, et al. 1981/83 = Dai Qingxia, et al.: Chinese-Jingpho Dictionary. Kunming 1981 [in Chinese]. Jingpho-Chinese Dictionary. Kunming 1983 [in Chinese]. (D)

Hanson 1906 = O. Hanson: A Dictionary of the Kachin Language. 1906 [Reprinted Rangoon 1954]. (D)

Maran (in prep.) = L. Maran: A Dictionary of Modern Jinghpaw. In prep. [Revised and enlarged version of Hanson 1906, with tones indicated; MS, 1441 p.]. (*D)

Sun 1982 = Sun Hongkai: A Brief Description of the Dulong Language. (in Chinese). Beijing 1982. (G)

Sun/Liu 1986 = Sun Hongkai/Lu Liu: A Brief Description of the Nu Language: Nusu Dialect. Beijing 1986 [in Chinese]. (G)

4.5. Kamarupan
(Including Kuki-Chin-Naga, Bodo-Garo, Abor-Miri-Dafla.)

4.5.1. Dictionaries

Anonymous = Wordlists of Angami, Ao, Chakhesang, Chang, Garo, Kheza, Konyak, Kuki, Liangmai, Lotha, Mao, Phom, Pochury, Rengma, Sangtam, Sema, Yimchungru, Zeliang. Published by the Nagaland Bhasha Parishad (Linguistic Circle of Nagaland), Kohima. (W)

Bhat 1969 = D.N.S. Bhat: Tankhur Naga Vocabulary. Poona 1969. (D)

Bor 1938 = N.L. Bor: Yano Dafla Grammar and Vocabulary. Journal of the Royal Asiatic Society of Bengal 4:2. 1938, 17—81 [64 p.]. (W)

Burling 1969 = R. Burling: Proto-Bodo. Language 35. 1969, 435—53 [18 p.]. (EW)

Clark 1911 = E.W. Clark: Ao Naga Dictionary. Calcutta 1911. (D)

Das Gupta 1963 = K. Das Gupta: An Introduction to the Gallong Language. Shillong 1963. (W)

Das Gupta 1968 = K. Das Gupta: An Introduction to Central Monpa. Shillong 1968. (W)

Das Gupta 1971 = K. Das Gupta: An Introduction to the Nocte Language. Shillong 1971. (W)

French 1983 = W.T. French: Northern Naga: a Tibeto-Burman Mesolanguage: New York 1983 [City Univ. of New York Ph.D. thesis, 737 p.].

Grüssner 1978 = K.-H. Grüssner: Arleng Alam, die Sprache der Mikir. Wiesbaden 1978. (G)

Grüssner (in prep.) = K.-H. Grüssner: Mikir-English Dictionary. In prep. [unpaginated MS]. (*D)

Henderson 1965 = E.J.A. Henderson: Tiddim Chin: a Descriptive Analysis of Two Texts. London 1965. (G)

Lorrain, J.H. 1907 = J.H. Lorrain: A Dictionary of the Abor-Miri Language. Shillong 1907. (D)

Lorrain, J.H. 1940 = J.H. Lorrain: Dictionary of the Lushai Language. (Bibliotheca Indica 261). Calcutta 1940. (D)

Lorrain, R.A. 1951 = R.A. Lorrain: Grammar and Dictionary of the Lakher or Mara Language. Gauhati, Assam 1951. (D)

Marrison 1967 = G.E. Marrison: The Classification of the Naga Languages of North East India. London 1967 [Univ. of London D.Phil. thesis; Vol. I, 292 p., Vol. II, 460 p.]. (EW)

Pettigrew 1918 = W. Pettigrew: Tangkhul Naga Grammar and Dictionary (Ukhrul Dialect). Shillong 1918. (D)

Simon 1972 = I.M. Simon: An Introduction to Apatani. Gangtok, Sikkim 1972. (G)

Sun, et al. 1980 = Sun Hongkai/Lu Shaozun/Zhang Jichuan/Ouyang Jueya: The Languages of the Menba, Loba, and Deng Peoples. Beijing 1980 [in Chinese]. (G)

Thoudam 1980 = P.C. Thoudam: A Grammatical Sketch of Meiteiron. Delhi 1980 [Jawaharlal Nehru Univ. Ph.D. thesis, 252 p.]. (G)

Walker 1925 = G.D. Walker: A Dictionary of the Mikir Language. Shillong 1925. (D)

4.6. Karenic

4.6.1. Dictionaries

Henderson (to appear) = E.J.A. Henderson: Bwe Karen-English Dictionary. To appear. (*D)

Jones 1961 = R.B. Jones: Karen Linguistic Studies: Description, Comparison, and Texts. (University of California Publications in Linguistics 25). Berkeley. Los Angeles 1961. (ED)

Solnit (in prep.) = D. Solnit: Dictionary of Kayah (Red Karen). In prep. (*D)

4.7. Lolo-Burmese

4.7.1. Dictionaries

Bradley 1978 = D. Bradley: Proto-Loloish. (Scandinavian Institute of Asian Studies Monograph Series 39). Copenhagen. London 1978. (ED)

Bradley 1979 = D. Bradley: Lahu Dialects. (Oriental Monograph Series 23). Canberra 1979. (W)

Burling 1968 = R. Burling: Proto-Lolo-Burmese. Special Publication of International Journal of American Linguistics 33.2, Part II. (Issued simultaneously as Indiana Publications in Anthropology and Linguistics 43). The Hague 1968. (ED)

Dai/Cui 1985 = Dai Qingxia/Cui Zhichao: A Brief Description of the Achang Language. Beijing 1985 [in Chinese]. (G)

Fraser 1922 = J.O. Fraser: Handbook of the Lisu (Yawyin) Language. Rangoon 1922. (G)

Fu 1950 = Fu Maoji: A Descriptive Grammar of Lolo. Cambridge 1950 [Cambridge Univ. D.Phil. thesis]. (W)

Gai 1981 = Gai Xingzhi: A Brief Description of the Jinuo Language. Beijing 1981 [in Chinese]. (G)

Gao 1958 = Gao Huanian: A Study of the Grammar of the Yi Language. Beijing 1958 [in Chinese]. (G)

Hansson (in prep.) = I.-L. Hansson: Akha-English Dictionary. In prep. (*D)

He/Jiang 1985 = He Jiren/Jiang Zhuyi: A Brief Description of the Naxi Language. Beijing 1985 [in Chinese]. (G)

Hope (in prep.) = E. Hope: Lisu-English Dictionary. In prep. (*D)

Lewis 1968 = P. Lewis: Akha-English Dictionary. (Southeast Asia Program Data Paper 70). Ithaca, N.Y. 1968. (D)

Lewis 1986 = P. Lewis: Lahu-English-Thai Dictionary. Bangkok 1986 [Thailand Lahu Baptist Convention]. (D)

Lewis 1989 = P. Lewis: Akha-English-Thai Dictionary. Bangkok 1989 [Development and Agricultural Project for Akha]. (D)

Liétard 1911 = A. Liétard: Essai de dictionnaire lolo-français, dialecte A-hi. T'oung Pao 12. 1911, 1—37, 123—56, 316—46, 544—58 [113 p.]. (D)

Ma 1949 = Ma Xueliang: Annotated Translation of the Lolo Classic of Rites, Cures, and Sacrifices. Academia Sinica Bulletin of the Inst. of History and Philology 20. 1949, 577—666 [89 p.]. (G)

Ma 1951 = Ma Xueliang: A Study of Sani, a Yi Dialect. (Chinese Academy of Sciences Monograph 2). Shanghai 1951 [in Chinese]. (G)

Matisoff 1988 = J.A. Matisoff: The Dictionary of Lahu. (Univ. of California Publications in Linguistics, Vol. 111). Berkeley. Los Angeles. London 1988 [80 plates, xxv + 1436 p.]. (D)

Rock 1963 = J.F. Rock: A Na-khi (Moso) — English Encyclopedic Dictionary, Part I. (Serie Orientale Roma 28.1). Rome 1963. (D)

Srinuan 1976 = D. Srinuan: An Mpi Dictionary. Ed. by W. Pantupong. (Working Papers in Phonetics and Phonology, vol. I. Indigenous Languages of Thailand Research Project). Bangkok 1976. (D)

Telford 1938 = J.H. Telford: Handbook of the Lahu (Muhso) Language and English-Lahu Dictionary. Rangoon 1938. (G)

Vial 1909 = P. Vial: Dictionnaire français-lolo, dialecte Gni. Hong Kong 1909. (D)

Yabu 1982 = S. Yabu: A Classified Dictionary of the Atsi or Zaiwa Language (Sadon Dialect), with Atsi, Japanese and English Indexes. Tokyo 1982 [in Japanese]. (W)

Yuan 1953 = Yuan Jiahua: The Folksongs and the Language of the Ahi People. Beijing 1953 [in Chinese]. (G)

4.7.2. Other Publications

Matisoff 1987 = J.A. Matisoff: Review of D. Bernot, Dictionnaire birman-français. Bulletin of the School of Oriental and African Studies 50.1. 1987, 191—5. (R)

4.8. Qiangic
4.8.1. Dictionaries

Lu 1980 = Lu Shaozun: A Brief Description of the Pumi Language. Minzu Yuwen 4. 1980, 58—72 [in Chinese; 14 p.]. (G)

Nishida 1964/66 = T. Nishida: A Study of the Hsi-hsia Language: Reconstruction of the Language and Decipherment of the Script. Tokyo 1964 (Vol. I), 1966 (Vol. II) [in Japanese]. (D)

Sun 1981 = Sun Hongkai: A Brief Description of the Qiang Language. Beijing 1981 [in Chinese]. (G)

James A. Matisoff,
University of California, Berkeley, California
(USA)

XXVI. Lexikographie der Einzelsprachen X: Die austronesischen Sprachen
Lexicography of Individual Languages X: The Austronesian Languages
Lexicographie des langues particulières X: Les langues austronésiennes

254. Javanese Lexicography

1. Background
2. The Old Language
3. New Javanese
4. Linguistic Problems
5. Selected Bibliography

1. Background

Javanese documents date back to the eighth century A. D. Javanese dictionaries are of two kinds: those which deal with Old and Middle Javanese (signal forms from texts which antedate the sixteenth century) and those which deal with New Javanese. Since Javanese has an unbroken literary tradition, many archaic forms and formulae survive to the present day, especially in the language of the Wayang-theater, so that much of the Old and Middle Javanese lexicon needs also to be treated in a complete dictionary of New Javanese.

2. The Old Language

Native Javanese lexicographical work dates to the earliest times in dictionaries and wordlists which were made to explain difficult words in texts (mostly of Sanskrit origin). Also Sanskrit lexicographic works were partially adapted with Javanese glosses. The eighteenth and nineteenth centuries saw a flowering of interest in Javanese literature, both older materials and contemporary productions, and numerous lexicons were compiled to explain poetic forms, including both Sanskrit forms from the more traditional literature and Malay and Arabic forms which were borrowed into Javanese with the composition or adaptation of Islamic texts. The poetic language or register is called *Kawi*, and many of these word lists are called Kawi dictionaries.

An all-Javanese compilation of poetic language glosses by Winter was published in 1880 and 1928. This book was a transition to work carried on by scholars with European philological training and outlook. The ground work in the European tradition was H. N. van der Tuuk's *Kawi-Balineesch-Nederlandsch woordenboek*, which was prepared over a period of 20 years and published 1897—1912. This work was in its organization totally unaccessible and unusable for scholars, so that people who read Old Javanese had to rely on a glossary of the Javanese Ramayana by Juynboll (1902) until 1982, when P. J. Zoetmulder's magnum opus, an Old-Javanese-English dictionary appeared. This dictionary covers Javanese from the earliest inscriptions up to modern times, and is based entirely on citations of forms which occur in 89 published and 39 unpublished works plus the corpus of published inscriptions. The contents of these works are treated exhaustively in this dictionary.

3. New Javanese

The lexicography of New Javanese begins with a short dictionary by Roorda van Eysinga in 1835, which in 1847 was eclipsed by a substantial dictionary by Gericke and Roorda. This dictionary went through four editions, to which Roorda, as well as a number of other scholars, devoted many years of work. The fourth edition of 1901 is still the standard reference work for Javanese. Th. Pigeaud spent much of his career to making a New Javanese dictionary, but World War II intervened to make this impossible. His files are said to have survived and remain unedited in Jakarta. A condensation of these materials which Pigeaud published in 1938 remains a basic research tool for Javanese. There is also a short monolingual Javanese dictionary by Peorwadarminta which contains original material. A somewhat unreliable Javanese-English dictionary was published by E. Horne in 1972. Other Javanese dictionaries contain nothing that is original.

The great Javanese dictionary by Gericke-Roorda is published with Javanese orthography and with the alphabetical order of the Javanese script. To use this work necessitates a detailed familiarity with the Javanese script which few people possess, as the Javanese script has practically been out of use for a half a century. Later dictionaries have used Roman transcriptions.

4. Linguistic Problems

Romanization presents a problem in that the contrast between dental and alveolar stops is not indicated in a consistent way. I.e., no decision was reached on how to present the contrast between (d) and (ḍ) and between (t) and (ṭ) (it was ignored, indicated with a dot or indicated with an *h*); and this gives rise to problems of alphabetization.

As Javanese is a language with a fairly limited number of affixes and uncomplicated morphophonemics, the practice of most of the cited dictionaries is to list strictly by root and list all affixed forms under them. Pigeaud's work of 1938 lists the roots and in addition, for roots which begin with a vowel, lists these same roots under *ng*- (if they occur with the prefix *ng*- — which is the case for an overwhelming majority of Javanese roots). Thus, forms which should be looked at together are treated in separate places and there is much duplication.

Another problem which is especially serious for Javanese is the stylistic variation. In the first place there is the language which harks back to the literary tradition. This comes up in proverbs and set phrases, and also these forms are very much alive in the Wayang theater literature which is widely known and widely quoted. Further, there is the matter of speech levels — that is, honorifics and sets of vocabularies which indicate the relative status of the interlocutors and the degree of intimacy. This vocabulary is extensive; some of it is considered correct and some incorrect; and it covers well over a thousand items. The status of the word as honorific or of high, low, or mid level, correct or incorrect, all must be signaled in a dictionary. Also Javanese suffers from or enjoys a very large amount of dialectal variation, in which significantly large numbers of variants occur according to the area and also according to the ethnic make-up of the speaker of Chinese, Javanese or Arab descent. Gericke/Roorda made notations of areas in which cited forms occur, but the information is by no means full or up-to-date. Pigeaud gives stylistic notations, but they seem not to hold water. A third problem is the extensive amount of contraction which Javanese allows, shortenings which derive from rapid-speech forms. These are rarely listed in any dictionaries, although almost all of the high-frequency vocabulary has shortened alternates in spoken Javanese (though not all of these are written).

Another problem which is posed for Javanese dictionaries is the current status of Javanese as second to the national language, Indonesian, and the strong influence which Indonesian exerts in the current language. Pigeaud and Horne list a fairly large number of Indonesian items, but this listing is far below the actual number of Indonesian forms which are currently widely used, even by monolingual speakers.

Javanese, with its long literary tradition and as the language of important empires in the past and currently one of the major world languages is probably better provided with dictionaries than any other Austronesian language except Indonesian (Malay). Yet much basic information about the vocabulary, from a simple signaling of the existence of a form to detailed information on the stylistic range, era, area of usage, or domain, remains unrecorded. There is no historical or etymological work. Now that Javanese has sunk to the status of a regional language which should always give way to the national language, Indonesian, the chances appear dim for serious lexicographical research on Javanese in this generation or next.

5. Selected Bibliography

5.1. Dictionaries

Gericke 1847 = J. F. C. Gericke: Javaansch-Nederduitsch woordenboek, vermeerderd en verbeterd door T. Roorda. 4th Edition: Javaansch-Nederlandsch Handwoordenboek vermeerderd en verbeterd door Dr. A. C. Vreede met medewerking van Dr. J. G. H. Gunning. Leiden 1901 [viii, 1051 pp.].

Horne 1972 = E. Horne: A Javanese-English Dictionary. New Haven 1972 [xl, 728 pp.].

Juynboll 1902 = H. H. Juynboll: Kawi-Balineesch-Nederlandsch glossarium op het Oudjavaansche Ramayana. The Hague 1902 [vi, 644 pp.].

Pigeaud 1938 = The. Pigeaud: Javaans-Nederlands handwoordenboek. Groningen. Batavia 1938 [xxi, 624 pp.].

Poerwadarminta 1939 = W. J. S. Poerwadarminta: Baoesastra Djawa. Groningen. Batavia 1939 [670 pp.].

Roorda van Eysinga 1835 = Roorda van Eysinga: Javaansch en Nederduitsch woordenboek in de kromo-, ngoko-, modjo- en kawische taal. Kampen 1835.

Tuuk 1897—1912 = H. N. van der Tuuk: Kawi-Balineesch-Nederlandsch woordenboek vol. 1 1897, vol. 2 1899, vol. 3 1901, vol. 4 1912. Batavia 1897—1912.

Winter 1880 = C. F. Winter: Kawi-Javaansch woordenboek. Batavia 1880 [576 pp.].

Zoetmulder 1982 = P. J. Zoetmulder: Old Javanese-English Dictionary. s-Gravenhague 1982 [xxxi, 2368 pp.].

*John U. Wolff, Cornell University,
Ithaca, New York (USA)*

255. Lexicography of Indonesian

1. Background
2. The Dictionaries
3. Problems of Linguistic Structure
4. Selected Bibliography

1. Background

Indonesian (Bahasa Indonesia) is the official language of Indonesia. The same language is the official language of Malaysia, where it is called Malay (Bahasa Malaysia) (ct. Map 255.1). During the period of Dutch colonization, the language was called Malay.

2. The Dictionaries

Indonesian lexicography starts with word lists gathered by early travelers. The first of these is a Chinese-Malay word list published by Blagden/Edwards in 1930, which dates from some time in the fifteenth century. Pigafetta gathered a Malay word list probably for the Moluccas in 1522. The first dictionary of substance or value was a Malay-English dictionary published by Marsden in 1812. In 1875 Abbé P. Favre published an extensive Malay-French dictionary. The first comprehensive Malay-Dutch dictionary was published by Klinkert in 1885, the latest and best edition of which is a revision by C. Spat in 1947.

The finest Indonesian or Malay dictionary is the Malay-English dictionary by J. Wilkinson. This dictionary first appeared in 1901—2 and was based on citations from classical Malay texts which the author had gathered over the course of approximately ten years. The author produced an expanded and revised edition published in 1932 in Mytilene, Greece. This dictionary is still the standard lexicographic source for classical Malay.

A large number of practical dictionaries of modern Indonesian and Malay have appeared. Most are plagiarisms or uncritical copies of previously printed materials, but a few rest on original research. An all-Indonesian dictionary was the *Kamus Umum* by W. J. Poerwadarminta, first published in 1953. This book has gone through several revisions but has not been much changed. In 1978 it was published as *Kamus Umum Bahasa Indonesia,* under the editorship of H. Kridalaksana. In 1968 the Dewan Bahasa dan Pustaka of Malaysia published a monolingual *Kamus Umum* under the editorship of Teuku Iskandar. This dictionary incorporates Poerwadarminta's entries almost wholesale with some alteration of examples, expanded citation of affixed forms, and listing of some additional forms used only in Malaysia. Important bilingual dictionaries based on citations have been published for English, French, Russian, and Dutch in the past thirty-five years. For English there is the dictionary of Echols and Shadily 1960, revised in 1963, a completely revamped edition of which was prepared by John Wolff and James Collins and published in 1989. For French a very thoroughgoing and well-documented dictionary by P. Labrousse was published in 1984. For Dutch two dictionaries were published in 1950, one by van Pernis and the second by Teeuw and Poerwadarminta. Taken together, these two dictionaries show good coverage.

Numerous technical word lists, lists of abbreviations and dialect dictionaries have appeared in the past twenty years. However, neither Indonesia nor Malaysia has produced a thoroughgoing lexicographical work based on citations from Malay and Indonesian from classical or modern writings.

3. Problems of Linguistic Structure

Indonesian lexicography faces numerous problems which are occasioned by the historical political

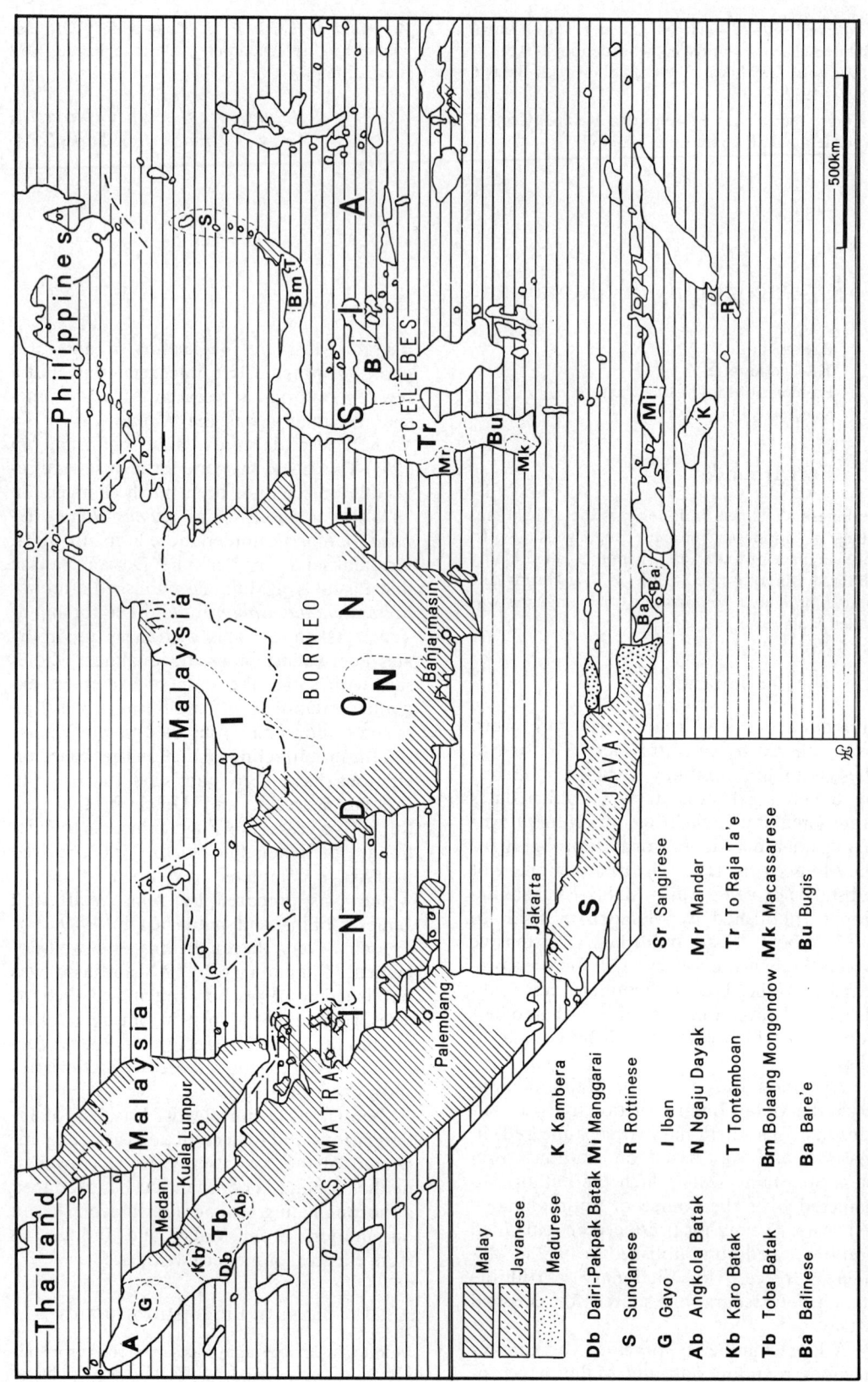

Map 255.1: Location of selected languages in Malaysia, Indonesia, and Brunei

background of Indonesia and Malaysia. First, there is the matter of orthographical tradition and lack of standardization. Originally Malay was written in Arabic script, but early grammars established modes of transcription which were taken up as conventions in the orthography of books printed in Roman script beginning at the end of the last century. In the Dutch Indies Indonesian spellings were based on Dutch orthographic conventions, and in the areas under British control the spelling conventions reflected English spelling. These conventions were maintained until 1972, when reforms aimed at standardizing all Indonesian and Malaysian orthography were introduced. The new orthography which resulted, however, is not totally phonemic in that non-contrastive elements are written (or optionally may not be written), the same sound may be represented by more than one letter, and one letter or sequence may represent several sounds. Further, words of foreign origin often are spelled as in the donor language.

Edicts have been issued by the language academies of both Indonesia and Malaysia as to which spellings are the accepted ones, but these are not followed with total conformity by editors and publishers, and alternative spellings exist for a large portion of the lexicon. These alternative spellings need to be signaled in a comprehensive dictionary. A more intractable problem is that posed by the strong regional and dialectal differences. The dialects of Malay vary in their vowel inventory from three to ten. This also leads to spelling variations and further renders it practically impossible to indicate pronunciation in a consistent way. The regional variations in vocabulary raise problems of what items to include in the dictionary. There is a tendency for regional terms which are widely known to be used for special effects in the nationwide press. Differences in usage in Malaysia and Indonesia also present problems. This is especially true for some of the most common entries, where meaning and patterns of affixation are different in Malaysia and Indonesia.

Typologically, Indonesian like most of the Austronesian languages lends itself to lexicographical listing by root under which affixed forms are subsumed. There is little by way of morphophonemic complexity to render identification of morphemes difficult. In Indonesian there is little by way of predictability in the affixational system — that is, the existence of an affix in a given meaning does not presuppose the existence of any other affix or affixes. No patterns or paradigms of affixation are ascertainable. Therefore, a complete dictionary must list out all the affixes with which a given root occurs. In Indonesian the total number of affixes is small, so that few listings need be extraordinarily long. Otherwise, however, there is little of irregularity or capriciousness in the morphology or syntax which needs be registered in a dictionary.

The lexicography of Indonesian is still in its infancy. Basic research on Indonesian etymology remains to be undertaken. The dictionary of Wilkinson incorporated all etymological information that had been known before 1932 and adds some original discoveries as well. Labrousse also gives a fair amount of etymological information for loanwords. Otherwise, etymological information is rarely given in modern lexicographical work. Further, much of the Indonesian lexicon remains unrecorded. There are large and broad semantic fields which have not been worked through with precision, and for much of the Indonesian lexicon accurate definitions and information on the usage is not recorded. This is true of high-frequency as well as for low-frequency items. A project is needed to gather large numbers of citations on which to base revised definitions and include common items which are nowhere listed.

4. Selected Bibliography

Blagden/Edwards 1930 = Charles O. Blagden/ E. D. Edwards: A Chinese Vocabulary of Malacca Malay Words and Phrases Collected Between AD 1403 and 1511(?). London 1930.

Echols/Shadily 1960 = John Echols/Hassan Shadily: An Indonesian-English Dictionary. Ithaca, New York 1960 [3rd ed., edited by John Wolff and James Collins, 1989, xix, 618 p.].

Favre 1875 = Pierre Etienne Favre: Dictionnaire Malais-Français. Paris 1875.

Iskandar 1970 = Teuku Iskandar: Kamus Dewan. Kuala Lampur 1970 [1,352 p.].

Klinkert 1885 = Hildebrandus C. Klinkert: Nieuw Maleisch-Nederlandsch woordenboek. 1885 [5th ed. ed. by C. Spat, Leiden 1947, viii, 1,047 p.].

Labrousse 1984 = Pierre Labrousse: Dictionnaire Général Indonésien-Français. Paris 1984 [xxi, 934 p.].

Marsden 1812 = William Marsden: A Dictionary of the Malayan Language. London 1812 [xv, 589 p.].

Pernis 1950 = H. D. van Pernis: Woordenboek bahasa Indonesia-Nederlands. Groningen 1950 [317 p.].

Pigafetta 1903 = Antonio Pigafetta: Magellan's Voyage Around the World. In: E. H. Blair/J. A. Robertson, eds., The Phillipine Islands 1493—1803. Cleveland 1903 [2 vols.].

Poerwadarminta 1953 = W. J. S. Poerwadarminta: Kamus Umum Bahasa Indonesia. 6th ed. H. Kridalaksana. Jakarta 1978 [903 p. 1st ed. 1953].

Poerwadarminta/Teeuw 1950 = W. J. S. Poerwadarminta/A. Teeuw: Indonesisch-Nederlands woordenboek. Groningen 1950 [369 p.].

Wilkinson 1932 = Richard J. Wilkinson: A Malay-English Dictionary (romanized). Mytilene, Greece 1932 [iv, 1,288 p.].

John U. Wolff, Cornell University, Ithaca, New York (USA)

256. Lexicography of the Languages of Indonesia Aside From Indonesian and Javanese

1. Background
2. The Dictionaries
3. Linguistic and Cultural Problems
4. Selected Bibliography

1. Background

There are literally hundreds of languages spoken in Indonesia aside from Indonesian and Javanese. A few of these have large numbers of speakers and are spoken over wide areas, but most are small and isolated. Except for some of the languages of the Northern Moluccas and West Irian and one on Timor, they are all members of the Austronesian family.

2. The Dictionaries

Most of these languages have only short and sketchy dictionaries for them. However, in the case of some of these languages, unusually good and complete lexicographical materials have been prepared. They are the works of missionaries and other Dutch colonial officials, many of whom spent a lifetime in given areas and devoted years to the preparation of a dictionary of the local language.

In some cases the dictionaries were the work of two generations of lexicographers, and a few of these could be considered to be monumental in scope and content. The earliest of these dictionaries is the Nadju-Dayak (Kalimantan) dictionary by Hardelandt of 1859 and van der Tuuk's Toba-Batak dictionary of 1861. These were followed by several other monumental works: For Celebes: a Makassarese dictionary by Matthes in 1859, revised by Cense in 1979, Bugis by Matthes in 1874, Bolaan Mongondow by Dunnebier, 1951, Bare'e by Adriani, 1928, Sangirese by Steller and Aebersold, 1959, Tontemboan by Schwartz, 1908; for the lesser Sundas: Rottinese by Jonker, 1908, and Kanbera of Sumba by Onvlee, 1984; other areas: Madurese by Kiliaan, 1904—5, Sundanese by Coolsma, 1884, 2nd ed. 1930, Achinese by Hoesein Djajadiningrat, 1934. Another excellent Sundanese dictionary by Eringa appeared in 1984. An extensive Iban-English dictionary (western Kalimantan and Sarawak) was published by Richards in 1981. Fairly extensive dictionaries but not monumental works as those cited above also exist for Gayo, Karo Batak and Angkola Batak in Sumatra, Balinese, for Mandar and Toradja (Ta'e) in Celebes, Manggarai in Flores, for Graged in Irian and for a few other local languages (see items 6, 10, 12, 20, and 21 in the bibliography). For Toba Batak, Sundanese, and Iban other extensive dictionaries exist aside from the monumental works cited above.

For most of the local languages, however, word lists or glossaries to texts offer the only lexicographical information. In the past decade the Institute of National Language in Jakarta *(Pusat Pembinaan dan Pengembangan Bahasa)* has sponsored the preparation of dictionaries for regional languages or regional varieties of Malay and Javanese. Most of these have the character of extensive word lists, but a few of them, among these the dictionary of Dairi-Pakpak Batak (Sumatra) by Radja Manik Tindi, 1977, are of considerable scope.

These regional language dictionaries are all bilingual and have the aim of explaining the meaning and usage of vocabulary in the foreign language. They are all Dutch except that the Ngaju-Dyak dictionary is in German and the Iban dictionary is in English, and some of the shorter dictionaries are in Indonesian. For the very extensive dictionaries there are full citations often from oral or published literature and thorough treatment of affixed forms as well as of the roots. The Bare'e dictionary gives equivalents in other languages of Central Celebes, but otherwise there is little by way of etymology.

3. Linguistic and Cultural Problems

These languages for the most part have a rich morphology which necessitates a listing by root and an extremely long entry if completeness is to be aimed at, or a working out of the paradigm — that is, stating which affixes occur and which fail to occur together with a given root, such that not all affixed forms need be listed for a complete description. None of the above-mentioned dictionaries come to grips with this problem in a satisfactory way. For languages which do not possess a rich morphology, this problem is not as severe as for languages with a complex and extensive morphology.

Cultural matters also present difficult problems. Not only are there artifacts, ceremonies and other activities, beliefs, supernatural or natural phenomena, flora and fauna, and the like, the terms for which require a complete explanation of the entire culture if they are to be understandibly defined, but also there are attitudes, ways of behaving, Weltanschauungen, and states of mind, which can be understood only in terms of the ethics of the community. This means that much of the vocabulary and many of the citations defy explanation. In addition there is the problem of the total semantic structure of the language, which makes it impossible to find accurate equivalents. This is solved in these works for the most part by giving a plethora of meanings, which allow the reader to obtain an impression of the range of the root. In some of the big works, there are given episodically very detailed and involved explanations for selected difficult vocabulary.

Most of these works are based primarily on written texts or transcriptions of oral literature and confine themselves to formal styles. Since all of the regional languages are spoken as a local language in conjunction with Indonesian as the national language, the current spoken language is far more heavily influenced by Indonesian than would be apparent from these dictionaries. There is nothing in any of these dictionaries which looks as though it comes from the daily colloquial language. The exception is the very early Ngadju-Dayak dictionary of Hardelandt, which lists not only large numbers of colloquialisms and contractions, but also is replete with loanwords from the Banjarese dialect of Malay, a dialect which even at that time (nearly 150 years ago) already played an important role in the Ngadju speech community.

In some areas the local language is regarded as not much more than peasant talk or at best something to be used around the house, and Indonesian (or an Indonesian dialect) is used for many social as well as formal purposes. This is especially true in Eastern Indonesia and in Sumatra except for Aceh and the Batak regions. In other cases — especially in the Batak, Sundanese, Achinese, Balinese and some other ethnic regions — the local languages have an important role in literature, religion, ceremonial functions and to some extent in schools and intellectual life. The status of the languages has repercussions on how well or accurately the language is spoken by its speakers. The question arises if inaccurate usage by poor speakers should be signaled as well as the usage of good speakers of the language (especially when the good speakers of the language tend to be the population with the least prestige and the prestigeful members of the community are the ones who are likely to have the poorest command of the local language).

The chances are very slender that this generation or the next will produce more great monuments for any of these regional languages. National policy emphasizes the development and spread of Indonesian as the national language, and there is not the type of policy and financial support which existed in the colonial era which allowed generations of scholars to devote years of effort to producing a dictionary of one unimportant language.

4. Selected Bibliography

Adriani 1928 = N. Adriani: Bare'e-Nederlandsch woordenboek. Leiden 1928 [xv, 1,074 p.].

Cense 1979 = A. A. Cense: Makassaars-Nederlands woordenboek (A Reworking of the Dictionary of B. F. Matthes, 1859). The Hague 1979 [xxxi, 989 p.].

Coolsma 1884 = S. Coolsma: Soendaneesch-Hollandsch woordenboek. Leiden 1884 [2nd ed. 1930, xxxiv, 729 p.].

Djajadiningrat 1934 = Hoesein Djajadiningrat: Atjehsch-Nederlandsch woordenboek. Batavia 1934 [xxi, 2,360 p.].

Dunnebier 1951 = W. Dunnebier: Bolaang Mongondowsch-Nederlandsch woordenboek. The Hague 1951 [xxi, 635 p.].

Enggink 1936 = H. Enggink: Angkola en Mandailing Bataksch-Nederlandsch woordenboek. Batavia 1936 [260 p.].

Eringa 1984 = F. S. Eringa: Soendaas-Nederlands woordenboek. Dordrecht 1984 [xc, 846 p.].

Hardelandt 1859 = August Hardelandt: Dajacksch-Deutsches Woerterbuch. Amsterdam 1859 [xiii, 638 p.].

Jonker 1908 = J. C. G. Jonker: Rottineesch-Hollandsch woordenboek. Leiden 1908 [xii, 806 p.].

Joustra 1922 = M. Joustra: Nederlandsch-Karosche woordenlijst. 2. vermeerde druk. Leiden 1922 [xi, 244 p.].

Kiliaan 1904—1905 = H. N. Kiliaan: Madoereesch-Nederlandsch woordenboek. Leiden 1904—05 [846 p.].

Mager 1952 = John F. Mager: Gedaged-English Dictionary. Columbus, Ohio 1952 [xiv, 353 p.].

Matthes 1874 = B. F. Matthes: Boegineesch-Hollandsch woordenboek. The Hague 1874 [viii, 1,180 p.; Supplement 1889, 150 p.].

Onvlee 1984 = L. Onvlee: Kamberaas (Oostsoembaas)-Nederlands woordenboek. Dordrecht 1984 [xxii, 628 p.].

Richards 1981 = Anthony Richards: An Iban-English Dictionary. Oxford 1981 [xxx, 417 p.].

Schwartz 1908 = J. Alb. T. Schwartz: Tontembonsch-Nederlandsch woordenboek. Leiden 1908 [x, 690 p.].

Steller/Aebersold 1959 = K. G. F. Steller/W. E. Aebersold: Sangerees-Nederlands woordenboek. The Hague 1959 [xi, 622 p.].

Tindi 1977 = Manik Tindi: Kamus Bahasa Dairi-Pakpak-Indonesia. Jakarta 1977 [333 p.].

Tuuk 1861 = H. N. van der Tuuk: Bataksch-Nederduitsch woordenboek. Amsterdam 1861 [viii, 549 p.].

Veen/Tammu 1972 = H. van der Veen/J. Tammu: Kamus Toradja-Indonesia. Rantepao 1972 [692 p.].

Verheijen 1967—70 = Jiri A. J. Verheijen: Kamus Manggarai-Indonesia. The Hague 1967—70 [xxiii, 772 p.].

John U. Wolff, Cornell University, Ithaca, New York (USA)

257. Tagalog Lexicography

1. Background
2. Orthography and Accent
3. Headword, Derivations, and Entries
4. Promulgation of a National Language
5. Some Practical Problems
6. Future Directions
7. Selected Bibliography

1. Background

Dictionaries of Tagalog (= Tag) have had a relatively long and illustrious history. The first known publication (San Buenaventura 1613) is housed in the British Museum.

Until 1986, all have been bilingual, the target language being Spanish (up to 1914) or English (after 1900). Some comparative wordlists are in German, French, and other Philippine languages.

2. Orthography and Accent

It is fortunate that the first contacts with the Philippines were by the Spanish who could phonetically record the forms they heard. Even the earliest documents are decipherable, which might not have been the case of an "English invasion". By the time of US intervention, consistent orthographic principles had been established.

In the following table, spellings which have differed from the official orthography are given in parentheses.

```
p            t            k (c, cq,qu)   ʔ(see
b (v)        d (r)        g (gu)          below)
f            ch (ts)      j (di, dy)
m            n            ng(ñg)
             s (z, x)                    h (j, g, x)
w (v, o, u)  y (j, i)
   l         r (rr)
VOWELS
i (y, e)                  u (o)
e            a            o
```

Fig. 257.1: Modern Tagalog consonants and vowels

Glottal stop [ʔ] is ignored initially and between vowels; in clusters it is written as a hyphen. Otherwise it and accent are treated by the Institute of National Language (= INL) and early Spanish sources (= ES) under accent conventions with reference to the penult (= pn.). An unmarked form is accented on the penult (ES *producta*) with corresponding vowel length if the syllable is open; a marked form is accented on the ultima (ES *correpta*) as in the following illustrations:

PHONETIC	EARLY SPANISH	
bá:ga	baga (pp)	= pn. producta grave
bá:gaʔ	baga (ppa)	= pn. producta pausal
bagá	bagá (pc)	= pn. correpta grave
bagáʔ	baga(pca)	= pn. correpta guttural
gabʔï	gabï	diaeresis

PHONETIC	INL/MODERN	GLOSS
bá:ga	baga	ember
bá:gaʔ	bagà	lungs
bagá	bagá	is it?
bagáʔ	bagâ	tumor
gabʔï	gab-í	night

Thus ES *palay* (pp) = INL *palay* [pá:lay] 'rice (plant, unhusked)', ES *bigas* (pc) = INL *bigás* 'husked rice', ES *busa* (pca) = INL *busâ* [busáʔ] 'popped rice', ES *digäs* = INL *dig-ás* [digʔás] 'third pounding of rice', ES = INL *sinaing* [siná:ʔiŋ] 'boiled rice'.

3. Headword, Derivations, and Entries

Even the earliest dictionaries showed sparks of ingenuity in isolating roots. Differences in treatment reflect the linguistic acumen of the author rather than his first-language background. The format of most includes the headword followed by translational gloss(es); occasionally sentence examples or derivations were given. Basic grammatical information, although rarely stated explicitly, can be deduced from either the Spanish equivalents or Tagalog examples, e. g., *bayo* 'arroz o algo en mortero' [= noun], *nagbabayo* 'molerlo asi' [= active verb], *binabayo* 'ser molido' [= passive verb].

Nevertheless, Tagalog has a rich and complicated inflectional system, e. g., the subtle intricacies between *mag-* and *-um-* verbs (Pittman 1966) or their active and passive counterparts (McFarland 1976). Although lexicographic practice still lags behind linguistic discoveries, it was only in this century that scholars have attempted to deal *systematically* with such phenomena: by formulae and/or example. The provision of examples or derivations has proven more comprehensible to a non-technical audience. Such information is given under the root within the main entry. Panganiban 1972, 220 is an example of such an entry:

kain[1] n. consumption of food. Cf. *lamon.* — Bk. kakan; Kpm. Ilk. Ind. Mal. Png. mangán; Hlg. Sb. SL. kaon (cf. Tg. *kaón*); Ibg. Mar. kan; Ivt. kanen (cf. Tg. *kanin*); Mgd. kaan; Tau kimun.
— *Kakákain-kain ko pa lamang.* I have just finished eating.
— *Kakanín,* q.v.
— *Kainan,* var. *kanan,* v. to eat off (x, as a dish) or in (x), as a place). Vide *kanan.*
— *Káinan,* n. (a) simultaneous eating of several (persons or animals) — (b) place or utensil from which or in which feeding or eating is done, as *silíd-káinan:* dining room, Syn. *komedór; mesang káinan:* dining table; *pinggáng káinan:* dish or china used in eating.
— *Kainin,* var. *kanin,* v. to eat (x). Syn. *kumain,* vtr. Vide *kanin.*
— *Kanin*—(a) v. var. of *kainin,* q.v.—(b) n. boiled or steamed rice (out of pot and ready to eat). **Note: *palay,* rice grains still in shell, and also the whole rice plant; *bigás,* hulled rice; *sinaing,* hulled rice being boiled or steamed; *kaninglamíg,* cold boiled or steamed rice, usually leftover *kanin* kept for another meal; *sinangág,* fried *kanin; murisketa tustada* Sp.: fried *kanin* mixed with meats and condiments; *ampáw,* puffed rice, sweetened puffed rice; *mumo:* grains of *kanin* fallen off dish on table; *lugaw, nilugaw* Ch.: rice porridge; *aruskalùs.:* rice porridge with chicken or meat; *arusbalensyana* Sp.: spiced soft-fried *kanin* styled after the manner done in Valencia (Spain).
— *Ikain,* v. to use (x) as tool or means of eating.
— *Kapakanán,* q.v. n. interests, affairs, welfare.
— *Maáaring makain, makákain* adj. edible, can be eaten.
— *Makain,* v. to be able to eat (x) — *Waláng makain:* none of the supply can be eaten; nothing is edible. — *Di-makakain:* cannot eat, having no appetite, unable to eat.
— *Mákain* v. to have something to eat; to happen to eat (x). — *Waláng mákain:* to have nothing to eat.
— *Makakain,* v. to be able to eat. — *Nang makakain na kamí...* After we have eaten...
— *Makikain,* v. to join others at meal; to ask others to be allowed to eat or be given food.
— *Magkaín, magkakaín,* v. to eat continuously or repeatedly.
— *Magpakain,* v. to feed; to allow others to eat.
— *Pakainin,* var. *pakanin,* v. to feed (x).
— *Pákainín,* var. *pákakanin,* n. person or animal one has to feed. Cf. *sustentuhin, alagà.*
— *Pagkain,* n. food. — Bk. Sb. kakanon; Kpm. pámangán; Hlg. Sb. pagkaon; Ibg. kanan; Ibg. kanan; Ilk. Ivt. Png. kanon; Ind. Mal. makanan; Mar. pangunungkan; Mgd. kan; Tau. kakaon.

Dictionary excerpt 257.1: *kain* (from: Panganiban 1972, 220)

4. Promulgation of a National Language

As early as 1897 Tagalog was proposed as the National Language, which was officially named *Pilipino* in 1939 and rechristened *Filipino* in 1973. Regardless of recurring opposition, some form of Tagalog is now spoken or understood by almost 70 % of the population, the cumulative result of bilingual education, movies, comics, and news media (see Gonzalez 1980).

As the medium of communication around busy Manila Bay for centuries, Tagalog had been borrowing from nearby Pampango, Sambal, or Pangasinan, and contact languages (Brunei-Malay, Spanish) resulting in an enriched vocabulary and a rapidly developing literary genre.

The 1940's saw a period of purism in the contruction of Pilipino. Coinages such as *salumpuwít* 'seat' or *banyuhay* 'metamorphosis' were introduced to replace already assimilated loans *silya* 'chair' (Sp.), *metamórposis* (Sp./Eng.). Some such scientific terms introduced in textbooks have now been accepted and are in use. Recent trends have again been recognising Tag as the Koine it is: freely incorporating Spanish and English loans, forms from other Philippine languages which have no Tag counterpart, or widely used words as acceptable synonyms [*baláy* 'house' = Tag *bahay, danóm* 'water' = Tag *tubig*]. Panganiban (1972) already represented a step in this direction.

Some native authors feel that more information on derivatives is necessary for non-Tagalog users, e. g., *kakainín* 'tidbit, snack' should have its own entry rather than be under *kain* 'eat'. This trend has resulted in dictionaries with thick sections where prefixes like *ka-* [noun], *ma-* [adjective], *mag-* [verb] were involved (Santos 1978). Since a fully-inflected verb may have up to 144 forms, strict adherence to this procedure could result in a *basic* lexicon with over half a million entries! Clearly some grammatical mastery must be supplied to or be assumed on the part of the user.

5. Some Practical Problems

While it is hoped that a dictionary would foster national language development, the majority of the population simply cannot afford one of the more comprehensive volumes — costing 20% of a teacher's already low monthly salary.

Furthermore, most publications in Tagalog do not use the accent symbols required in the official orthography. Although context can enlighten the curious as to meaning, information about the glottal stop or accent is more often obtained from a friend or teacher than by a painstaking search through a tome.

Given this situation, a dictionary is unlikely to replace media and word-of-mouth as *the* vehicle of National Language formation in the Philippines.

6. Future Directions

Several inexpensive lexicons are available (de Guzman 1968 and Sagalongos 1968 costing about 20 pesos each) and the educational system has come to rely heavily on them. Such works could be upgraded and expanded along with their lexicographic scholarship.

Bilingual dictionaries (especially into English) have served an important role, since English formerly was understood by more educated people than any indigenous language. However, a new age in Tagalog lexicography dawned in the late 1980's when a group of Manila teachers published a monolingual dictionary (1986). Shortly thereafter (1989) the INL released a larger monolingual dictionary, which certainly is an important next step in National Language development as it has proven in the development of any standard language.

There is a need to make a comprehensive dictionary drawing on all previous studies and as many Tagalog/Filipino publications as possible. Authors thus far appear to have set out alone leaving the valuable work of others aside; codes could be devised to credit sources thereby insuring the widest possible coverage of both archaic and current forms.

Filipinos are lovers of etymology; such data have long been included within most studies. Nevertheless, fact and fancy have been mixed, e. g., relating *supsóp* 'suck' to Sp. *chupar* rather than Austronesian *supsup. The *Core Etymological Dictionary of Filipino* offers future lexicographers a more reliable and comprehensive source, although it is suggested that these data come at the end of each entry (Zorc 1979—).

7. Selected Bibliography

7.1. Dictionaries

de Guzman 1968 = Maria Odulio de Guzman: Bagong Diksionaryo Pilipino-English, English-Pilipino. Manila 1968.

INL 1989 = Linangan ng mga sa Pilipinas. Diksyunaryo ng Wikang Filipino. Manila 1989.

Manila Teachers 1986 = Anonymous. Diksyunaryo Filipino-Filipino. Manila 1986.

Panganiban 1972 = José Villa Panganiban: Diksyunaryo-Tesauro Pilipino-Ingles. Quezon City 1972.

Sagalongos 1968 = Felicidad T. E. Sagalongos: Diksiyunaryong Engles-Pilipino, Pilipino-Engles. Manila 1968.

San Buenaventura 1613 = Pedro de San Buenaventura: Vocabulario de Lengua Tagala. Manila 1613.

Santos 1978 = Vito C. Santos: Pilipino-English Dictionary. Manila 1978.

Zorc 1979— = R. David Zorc: Core Etymological Dictionary of Filipino. Linguistic Society of the Philippines Publications 12—14. Manila 1979.

7.2. Other Publications

Gonzalez 1980 = Andrew B. Gonzales, FSC: Language and Nationalism. Ateneo de Manila University Press 1980.

McFarland 1976 = Curtis D. McFarland: A Provisional Classification of Tagalog Verbs. Study of Languages & Cultures of Asia & Africa Monograph 8. Tokyo 1976.

Pittman 1966 = Richard Pittman: Tagalog -um- and mag-, an interim report. In: Papers in Philippine Linguistics No. 1. Pacific Linguistics A.8. 1966, 9—20.

R. David Paul Zorc,
School of Australian Linguistics,
Batchelor, N. T. (Australia)

258. Lexicography of Other Philippine Languages

1. Overview
2. Phonologies and Orthographies
3. The Head Word and Morphophonemics
4. Verb Stem Classification
5. Future Directions
6. Selected Bibliography

1. Overview

There are 20 major linguistic groups within the Philippines (cf. Map 258.1). These can be further split into at least 50 subgroups representing over 500 known dialects. Of the latter, at least 30 have had reasonably thorough coverage (e. g., Fernandez Cosgaya 1865 for Pangasinan, Vanoverbergh 1956 for Ilokano, Wolff 1972 for Cebuano), while short word lists can be found for about 300 more. All such studies have been bilingual. [For comprehensive references consult Ward 1971.]

Spanish missionaries produced some of the first lexicons for Bikol, Ilokano, Kapampangan, Pangasinan, Maguindanao, and Cebuano-Bisayan, of roughly the same calibre as for Tagalog (see art. 257).

This was followed by American interest in languages spoken by ethnographically smallish societies (e. g., the Subanon or Palawan Batak), and more recently by the missionary activities of the Summer Institute of Linguistics (e. g., Western Bukidnon Manobo).

The era of modern dictionaries has seen some excellent studies on Cebuano, Tausug, and Casiguran Dumagat. Many have been produced by staff of the University of Hawaii, e. g., Bontok, Maranao. The needs of the U. S. Peace Corps led to several volumes within the PALI language series (University of Hawaii Press) and also a set of lexicons produced by Dr. Ernesto Constantino.

2. Phonologies and Orthographies

The offical orthography for Tagalog (Pilipino) has been applied with certain language-specific solutions, e. g., [γ] = *x* in Itbayaten, **g** in West.Bukidnon Manobo, *e* in Aklanon. Glottal stop cannot be assumed intervocalically in some dialects, e. g., Kuyonon *kaen* 'eat' = [kaən] not *[kaʔən]. Vowels vary the most: *e* often = [ə]; accent symbols may designate different vowels rather than stress or length, e. g., in Tboli *ó* = [o], *o* = [ɔ]; in Dumagat *é* = [ə], *ë* = [ɛ].

3. The Head Word and Morphophonemics

Most Philippine languages have complex morphophonemics that must be represented in the dictionary so that forms can be properly used or identified.

For example, Ilokano has geminate consonants after short penult vowels (mainly shwa). After prefixation, these geminates reduce to single consonants and the short vowel is lost, e. g., *gellóoŋ* 'resound' — *gumlóoŋ* 'to resound', *sunnóp* 'prefer' — *masnóp* 'be preferred'; however, neither is lost when suffixation occurs, *sunnopén* 'will be preferred'. Vanoverbergh (1956) handles this quite adequately by sample derivations within the main entry.

Aklanon and other Bisayan dialects have a complex system of syncope and metathesis, e. g., *inúm* 'drink', *imna* 'Drink it!', *bíhod* 'roe', *bidhánan* 'having roe; meaningful (maxim)'. Whether the lexicographer chooses to list the head word and its variant shapes as a formula (*inum, imn-*) or include sample derivations is a matter of preference.

More complex still is the situation in some Sambal dialects where the postulation of some roots would be total abstractions (they are never uttered independent of affixation), e. g., *bumdeŋ* 'to fear', *bedŋen* 'be feared';

Map 258.1: Location of other Philippine languages

*bedeŋ 'fear' does not occur, although it would appear to be the logical form for a head entry. Any solution requires much thought and consultations with prospective users.

Even a relatively simple matter such as suffixation has sometimes failed to receive explicit attention. When -*an* 'locative', -*un* or -*ən* 'direct passive' are added to stems ending in a vowel, some languages (like Tausug or Tboli) require that an *h* be inserted, e. g., Tausug *asawa-hun* 'will be married'. Others may unpredictably insert *h*, ʔ, or a homorganic semivowel. One cannot tell from the treatment in Elkins (1968) that forms should be *depa-han* 'to fathom', *duma-ha* 'Accompany him!' as opposed to *kuwa-ʔa* 'Get it!' or *huna-ʔan* 'be preceded' (data from Elkins, personal communication May 1980). Similar information is sometimes not available for Cebuano in Wolff (1972) when suffixed examples are not cited.

4. Verb Stem Classification

Philippine languages have a complex system of agreement between the semantic role of the *topic* and the verb (focus [= *rheme*]) involving a choice of active as opposed to three or more kinds of passive. Approaches to the problem of grammatical representation may be described as *morphological* (Reid) vs *formulaic* (Wolff), exemplified respectively by the dictionary excerpts 258.1 and 258.2.

ekan ek-ekan + N. Feast. (1)
   Nalpas nan kena, ek-ekan si baballo. *After the* kena *ceremony, the young men feast.*
  kak-akan To have just eaten.
  kan +V, A O._A:mang-/-om- (komman) (+part), O: -en. To eat. (1) Kommankas akit. *Eat a little of it.*
  makan + N. Cooked rice. Cf. teda; bináyo.
  makmakan Edible.
  manganan +N, _GEN. Any pot or jar in which rice is usually cooked. (1) into kay nan manganantakos na? *Where is our pot for cooking rice?*
  pakan +V, _A B O. B: -en, O:i-. To feed; to raise, as an animal. (1) Esámi pakanen nan esay ókenyo. *We will raise one of your puppies.* (2) Ipakanmo nan lokmog. *Feed it cooked sweet potato.*
  pan-ekan +T₂. Meal time; time for eating.
  pangan +V, A B O. B: -en, O:i-. To feed; to feed on.

Dictionary excerpt 258.1: *ekan* (from: Reid 1976, 103)

káun *v* 1 [A2S3S; a] eat. *Nagkaun ka na?* Have you eaten? *Nakakaun na kug amù,* I have eaten monkey meat. *Unsa may kan-un sa masakitun?* What should the patient eat now? **1a** [a 3] be eaten to get one to act in an unusual way. *Unsay nakáun sa táwu? Mangúhit man,* What got into you that you touched me? **2** [A; a 2] destroy by fire, erosion, corrosion. *Ang asidu mukáun ug tayà,* Acid eats away rust. *Ang balay gikaun sa kaláyu,* The house was destroyed by the fire. *Nahánaw siya kay gikaun man sa kangitngit,* He suddenly vanished because he was engulfed in darkness. **3** [A 12] consume, use up. *Ang ímung plansa mukáun ug dakung kurinti,* Your iron consumes a lot of electricity. **4** [A; ab 7] take a man in games of chess, checkers, and the like. *Wà pa kan-i ang ákung mga piyun,* None of my pawns has been captured yet. **4a** [b 48] when one returns the shuttlecock in *takyan* (by kicking it), for the return kick to be caught and kicked by the opponent. *Hikan-an ang ákung pátid kay ang ákung patid napatiran níya. Sa átù pa, hikan-an ku,* My kick was returned (lit. eaten) because he returned the shuttlecock when I kicked it. In other words, I had my kick returned. **5** [A] for a man to have sexual relations with a blood relative. *Háyup ka mukáun kag kaugalingung anak,* You're a beast. You have intercourse with your own child. **5a** [a 3] for a girl to be old enough to be had for sexual intercourse. **6** [b 4] for a fish to bite on one's line. *Wà ku kan-i gabíi,* I didn't get a bite last night. *n* **1** food served. *Sa míting adúna usáhay puy káun,* In the meeting they sometimes serve food. *Sa pagpabulan lábut na ang káun,* If you work as a maid, food is included. **1a** action of eating. *Tris díyas kung way káun,* I went three days without food. **2** consumption, amount of s.t. that is used up. *Dakug káun sa gasulína ning kutsíha,* This car consumes a lot of gas. ... **kan-anan, kalan-an** *n* place to eat (eating table, dining room, restaurant). **hiN-***a* fond of eating. *Hingáun kug mga prútas,* I'm fond of fruits. **-in-** *n* s.t. eaten, consumed. *Kináun sa gabas,* Sawdust (what was eaten by the saw). **kinan-an** *n* way of eating. **kakan-unun, ka-un(→)** *a* feel very much like eating. *Kakan-unun kug bága,* I'm so angry I could eat coals. **ma-** *n* food ready to eat. *Inig-ulì ni Máma, daghan siyag dáng makáun,* When Mom comes home, she will bring lots of food. **pag-** *n* 1 meal.

Dictionary excerpt 258.2: *kaun* (from: Wolff 1971, 457)

5. Future Directions

Many Philippine languages await such work. Scholars need to consider the points raised here as well as principles of *use, users,* and *predictability* (i. e., if form or meaning is sufficiently deviant, the word or collocation needs to be represented). In furthering National Language Development, should Tagalog or Pilipino be included in the definitions?

If one is working on a language that has had a dictionary or wordlist, should that data be included (even words no longer verifiable, e. g., found in an old Spanish study)? To what extent should written or oral literature be covered? How much cross-referencing is worthwhile (e. g., including the phases of the moon under the entry for 'moon', all monetary units under 'money', etc.)?

Much has been done, but there is yet much to do towards the production of comprehensive studies on the dozens of dialects not yet represented in the literature. Hopefully Filipino scholars themselves will work on the rich legacy of their own languages. This would finally off-set a long period of domination (albeit benign) by foreign scholars.

6. Selected Bibliography
6.1. Dictionaries

Elkins 1968 = Richard E. Elkins: Manobo-English Dictionary. Oceanic Linguistics Special Publication No. 3. Honolulu 1968.

Fernandez Cosgaya 1865 = Lorenzo Fernandez Cosgaya: Diccionario Pangasinan-Español. Manila 1865.

Reid 1976 = Lawrence A. Reid: Bontok-English Dictionary. Canberra 1976 (Pacific Linguistics C. 36).

Vanoverbergh 1956 = Morice Vanoverbergh: Ilokano-English Dictionary. Baguio 1956.

Wolff 1972 = John U. Wolff: A Dictionary of Cebuano Visayan. Manila 1972 (Special Monograph 4).

6.2. Other Publications

Ward 1971 = Jack H. Ward: A Bibliography of Philippine Linguistics and Minor Languages. Ithaca 1971 (Data Paper 83, SE Asia Program).

R. David Paul Zorc,
School of Australian Linguistics,
Batchelor, N. T. (Australia)

259. Polynesian and Melanesian Lexicography

1. Background
2. Fiji and Polynesia
3. Maori
4. Samoan and Other Languages
5. Probable Future Developments
6. Problems of Linguistic Structure
7. Selected Bibliography

1. Background

There are literally hundreds of languages in Oceania, most of which belong to the Austronesian group. Only a few of these languages have status as a language of importance outside their immediate local area, and most remain poorly described and poorly recorded. There is no great dictionary with full citations, full affixational listings and complete coverage for any of the Oceanic languages. Even the best dictionaries, with a couple of exceptions, have no more than ten or twelve thousand entries. All of these dictionaries aim at a user who wishes to know what the items mean and how they are used.

2. Fiji and Polynesia

The earliest dictionary from languages in this area come from Fiji and Polynesia, where missionary activity began in the early nineteenth century. In Fiji Hazlewood came out with a compendious dictionary of Bauan in 1850, revised in 1872. This dictionary was updated but not much revised by Capell in 1941. This is the best published work, although a thorough-going monolingual dictionary of Bauan is in preparation. There is also an unpublished dictionary of the Fijian language of Wayan by Andrew Pawley. In Polynesia extensive lexicographic work was done on Hawaiian, Maori, Samoan, and Tongan beginning early in the last century, and fairly full dictionaries are in existence. For Hawaiian there is a word list printed in Vol. III of Captain James Cook's *A Voyage to the Pacific Ocean,* compiled in 1778, the year of Cook's discovery of the Hawaiian Islands. The first word list of any extent was a five thousand-word dictionary published in 1836 by Lorrin Andrews which was expanded to a 15,000-entry work in 1865 and completely revamped in 1922. A more extensive Hawaiian dictionary containing 25,000 entries was prepared by Pukui and Elbert in

1957 with an extensively corrected edition appearing in 1965. There is no dictionary of another Oceanic language of comparable fullness.

3. Maori

For Maori a word list was collected as early as 1828, and a dictionary was published by Williams in 1844. This was revised many times and reworked into the best existing Maori dictionary by Herbert W. Williams in 1917, a sixth edition of which appeared in 1957. A full dictionary with comparisons to other Oceanic languages was published by Tregear in 1891. Numerous other dictionaries exist for Maori, including an extensive treatment of Rarotongan Maori by Steven Savage, 1962.

4. Samoan and Other Languages

The earliest Samoan dictionary is George Pratt's Samoan-English dictionary of 1862. This went through four editions, the fourth being a considerably enlarged version in 1911. Louis Violette published a fairly full Samoan-French-English dictionary in 1879. Probably the best dictionary for any Oceanic language apart from Elbert and Pukui's *Hawaiian dictionary* is George Milner's *Samoan-English dictionary* of 1966. This has more than 12,000 entries and complete listings of inflections and derivations for each root with thorough illustrations.

Tongan is also represented with an ample dictionary. For Tongan the earliest word list is Stephen Rabone's vocabulary from 1845. In 1890 A. Colomb published a full Tongan-French dictionary, and in 1959 C. Maxwell Churchward published an extensive Tongan-English dictionary.

There are dictionaries also in existence for the following languages: Melanesia: Aneityum, Rotuman, Lau, Nggela, Sa'a and Ulawa, Raluana; Micronesia: Nukuoro, Marshallese, Gilbertese, Trukese, Ponapean, Ulathian, Palauan and Chamorro (the last two genetically classified with the Philippine languages); Polynesia: Futunan, Tahitian, Easter Island, Tuamotuan, Marquisan, Uvean, Mangarevan.

5. Probable Future Developments

Most of the Oceanic languages have minority status, and for most of them it is unlikely that any sort of extensive lexicographic treatment will ever appear. Many of them are dying. In Western Oceania the local languages are rapidly losing ground in their functions and domains in which they are employed to the English Creoles (Neo-Melanesian, Tok-Pisin, and Beslamar), so that although the languages may still be very much alive in the sense that they are spoken, good speakers with a deep knowledge of them are rapidly passing away. Hawaiian has given way to English or to the English creole of Hawaii except for a few isolated groups.

6. Problems of Linguistic Structure

Aside from problems related to linguistic status the Oceanic languages offer their own special problems for lexicography. In structure most of these languages consist of roots plus a small set of derivative affixes. The morphophonemics may be complex and for many of the dictionaries referred to above, the compilers failed to come to grips with procedures for establishing the root as a head word. Accordingly, affixed forms as well as roots are listed as entries, which gives rise to organizational problems such that forms which should be looked at in context of each other are listed at scattered places and there is much duplication and repetition. There are in some languages capricious grammatical facts which should be signaled by a dictionary. For example, for many of the Oceanic languages there is a series of possessives, the choice of which is determined arbitrarily by the root. The choice of which possessive a root takes thus is something like gender in European languages, except that for some roots several "genders" are possible depending on the meaning. Insofar as this "gender" is arbitrary, it should be signaled, something which none of the referred dictionaries do.

Phonemicization offers a problem mainly in that the early dictionaries for the most part failed to indicate important contrasts, and in some cases still fail to indicate the long-short vowel contrasts which most of these languages show. In the case of Fijian and some of the other early-treated Oceanic languages, unusual spelling conventions arose in the course of early attempts to reflect the phonology of the language. This has led to letter assignments of sounds which are far afield from the practice of Western languages.

7. Selected Bibliography

Andrews 1865 = Lorrin Andrews: A Dictionary of the Hawaiian Language. Honolulu 1865 [Revised by H. H. Parker, 1922, Special Publications of the Bishop Museum, No. 8, xx, 674 p.].

Capell 1941 = A. Capell: A New Fijian Dictionary. Glasgow 1941 [x, 464 p.].

Churchward 1959 = C. Maxwell Churchward: Tongan Dictionary. London 1959 [xiv, 863 p.].

Colomb 1890 = A. Colomb: Dictionnaire tonga-français et français-tonga-anglais. Paris 1890 [xxii, 422 p.].

Hazlewood 1850 = D. Hazlewood: A Feejeean and English Dictionary. Vewra 1850 [349 p.].

Milner 1966 = Georg B. Milner: A Samoan Dictionary. London 1966 [li, 464 p.].

Pawley 1967—70 = A. Pawley: Wayan Dictionary 1967—70 [Typescript].

Pratt 1862 = G. Pratt: Grammar and Dictionary of the Samoan Language. 4th ed. revised by J. E. Newell. Malua 1911 [643 p.].

Pukui/Elbert 1957 = Mary K. Pukui/Samuel H. Elbert: Hawaiian-English Dictionary. 1957 [3rd ed. Honolulu 1965, xxxiii, 365 p.].

Rabone 1845 = Stephen Rabone: A Vocabulary of the Tonga Language. Vavau Neiafu 1845 [217 p.].

Savage 1962 = Stephen Savage: A Dictionary of the Maori Language of Rarotonga. Wellington 1962 [460 p.].

Tregear 1891 = Edward Tregear: The Maori-Polynesian Comparative Dictionary. Wellington 1891 [lxxiv, 675 p.].

Violette 1879 = Louis Violette: Dictionnaire Samoa-Français-Anglais. Paris 1879 [xcii, 468 p.].

Williams, H. 1957 = Herbert W. Williams: A Dictionary of the Maori Language. 6th ed. Wellington 1957 [xxv, 499 p.].

Williams, W. 1844 = William Williams: A Dictionary of the New-Zealand Language. Paihia 1844 [xli, 195 p.].

John U. Wolff, Cornell University, Ithaca, New York (USA)

XXVII. Lexikographie der Einzelsprachen XI: Südostasiatische Sprachen
Lexicography of Individual Languages XI: The Languages of South-East Asia
Lexicographie des langues particulières XI: Langues du Sud-Est asiatique

260. Lexicography of the Thai Language

1. Introduction
2. Thai Phonology and Orthography
3. The First Monolingual Thai Dictionary
4. The History of the Official Thai Dictionary 1884—1989
5. Summary and Discussion
6. Selected Bibliography

1. Introduction

Thai, a term which has been used by some linguists to refer to the family of languages spoken over a wide area embracing southern China, northern Vietnam, Laos, Thailand, northern and northeastern Burma, and the state of Assam in India, is used by many people more specifically to designate the language of this family spoken by the majority of the people in Thailand, and it is this latter use which is followed here. It is true that there is a large number of local varieties spoken by the people in Thailand. Vocabulary of not a few of these has been collected in compilations varying in both size and purpose; some, for example, compare local forms with those of Bangkok while others include only forms not found in Bangkok. However, space limitations preclude consideration of any of these works and the authors will treat only dictionaries of Bangkok Thai, also known as Standard Thai and, prior to about 1950, as Siamese. — There are monolingual, bilingual, and polyglot dictionaries of Bangkok Thai, all of which can be described as synchronic dictionaries. Here, only monolingual dictionaries are considered. Such works may be divided into overall linguistic dictionaries, which attempt to cover all of the words in the language, and specialized dictionaries, which include only words used in a certain field. Again, monolingual dictionaries may be divided into those compiled by government agencies and those compiled by private individuals or organizations. In this article, the authors limit themselves to describing only overall linguistic dictionaries and exclude dictionaries compiled by private individuals or organizations in the twentieth century. Thus, four dictionaries come within the scope of this article and the authors believe these will provide a picture of lexicography as it has been practiced in Thailand. — To permit the reader unfamiliar with Thai to follow the remainder of the article, a few words need to be said about the phonology and orthography of the language, for the order of words in the dictionary is related to the letters and the writing system.

2. Thai Phonology and Orthography

2.1. Phonology

Thai is a tonal language and the majority of words in use in everyday life are monosyllabic. Nevertheless, the number of multisyllabic words is by no means small; these tend to be borrowings from other languages, such as Pali, Sanskrit, and Khmer, or words recently coined in response to technological advances. — The stressed or full syllable has these significant components:
Ci (Ci) V Cf T or Ci (Ci) VV (Cf) T, where Ci = initial consonant, V = short vowel, VV = long vowel or diphthong, Cf = final consonant, and T = tone.
Initial consonants: p t c k ʔ ph th ch kh b d f s h m n ŋ l r w j pl pr tr kl kr kw phl phr thr khl khr khw
Vowels: i ii e ee ɛ ɛɛ ɨ ɨɨ ə əə a aa u uu o oo ɔ ɔɔ iə iiə iə ɨɨə uə uuə
Final consonants: p t k ʔ m n ŋ w j
Tones: Mid (no mark) Low (`) Falling (ˆ) High (´) Rising (ˇ)

2.2. Orthography

The Thai writing system, devised 700 years ago, is an alphabetic system. At present, one symbol may represent two or more sounds and one sound may be represented by more than one letter.
Consonant symbols: A total of 44 consonant symbols represent the 21 phonemes. The traditional order of the letters is, from left to right beginning with the top row:

⟨ก⟩ = /k/, ⟨ข⟩ = /kh/, ⟨ฃ⟩ = /kh/,
⟨ค⟩ = /kh/, ⟨ฅ⟩ = /kh/, ⟨ฆ⟩ = /kh/,
⟨ง⟩ = /ŋ/, ⟨จ⟩ = /c/, ⟨ฉ⟩ = /ch/,
⟨ช⟩ = /ch/, ⟨ซ⟩ = /s/, ⟨ฌ⟩ = /ch/,
⟨ญ⟩ = /j/, ⟨ฎ⟩ = /d/, ⟨ฏ⟩ = /t/,
⟨ฐ⟩ = /th/, ⟨ฑ⟩ = /th/, ⟨ฒ⟩ = /th/,
⟨ณ⟩ = /n/, ⟨ด⟩ = /d/, ⟨ต⟩ = /t/,
⟨ถ⟩ = /th/, ⟨ท⟩ = /th/, ⟨ธ⟩ = /th/,
⟨น⟩ = /n/, ⟨บ⟩ = /b/, ⟨ป⟩ = /p/,
⟨ผ⟩ = /ph/, ⟨ฝ⟩ = /f/, ⟨พ⟩ = /ph/,
⟨ฟ⟩ = /f/, ⟨ภ⟩ = /ph/, ⟨ม⟩ = /m/,
⟨ย⟩ = /j/, ⟨ร⟩ = /r/, ⟨ล⟩ = /l/,
⟨ว⟩ = /w/, ⟨ศ⟩ = /s/, ⟨ษ⟩ = /s/,
⟨ส⟩ = /s/, ⟨ห⟩ = /h/, ⟨ฬ⟩ = /l/,
⟨อ⟩ = /ʔ/, ⟨ฮ⟩ = /h/.

Vowel symbols: Vowels are represented with both simple and complex symbols. In writing, these must be positioned properly with respect to consonant and tone symbols in order to form a meaningful syllable. The position may be to the left, to the right, above, and/or below the initial consonant symbol. Currently, the order of the 32 vowel symbols is, from left to right beginning with the top row:

⟨-ะ⟩ = /a/, ⟨-า⟩ = /aa/, ⟨-ิ⟩ = /i/,
⟨-ี⟩ = /ii/, ⟨-ึ⟩ = /ɨ/, ⟨-ื⟩ = /ɨɨ/,
⟨-ุ⟩ = /u/, ⟨-ู⟩ = /uu/, ⟨เ-ะ⟩ = /e/,
⟨เ-⟩ = /ee/, ⟨แ-ะ⟩ = /ɛ/, ⟨แ-⟩ = /ɛɛ/,
⟨โ-ะ⟩ = /o/, ⟨โ-⟩ = /oo/, ⟨เ-าะ⟩ = /ɔ/,
⟨-อ⟩ = /ɔɔ/, ⟨เ-ือ⟩ = /ua/, ⟨-ัว⟩ = /uua/,
⟨เ-ียะ⟩ = /ia/, ⟨เ-ีย⟩ = /iia/, ⟨เ-ือะ⟩ = /ɨa/,
⟨เ-ือ⟩ = /ɨɨa/, ⟨เ-อะ⟩ = /ə/, ⟨เ-อ⟩ = /əə/,
⟨ฤ⟩ = /rɨʔ/, ⟨ฤๅ⟩ = /rɨɨ/, ⟨ฦ⟩ = /lɨʔ/,
⟨ฦๅ⟩ = /lɨɨ/, ⟨-ำ⟩ = /am/, ⟨ไ-⟩ = /aj/,
⟨ใ-⟩ = /aj/, ⟨เ-า⟩ = /aw/.

In some cases, the presence of a final consonant alters the representation of a vowel sound; in some cases, consonant letters may represent vowel sounds; and in some cases, consonant letters with no vowel symbol may be read with a vowel sound.

Tone symbols: ⟨◌่⟩ = /máaj ʔèek/, ⟨◌้⟩ = /máaj thoo/, ⟨◌๊⟩ = /máaj trii/, ⟨◌๋⟩ = /máaj càttawaa/.

In continuous text, words are not separated; a space thus serves as one punctuation symbol. Normally, punctuation marks such as the comma, semi-colon, colon, and period, are little used; they are, however, employed in dictionary definitions in the interests of conciseness and clarity, as well as of economical use of page space. — While the writing system has been important in the ordering of words in the dictionary, the arrangement of main entries has varied in dictionaries compiled at different times because of the interpretations, the notions of appropriateness, and the conventions guiding those carrying out the work. In some dictionaries, the order of the letters has been the sole determinant, while in other works, both alphabetical order and pronunciation have been criteria.

3. The First Monolingual Thai Dictionary

In a survey of dictionaries in such large libraries in Bangkok as the National Library, the Siam Society Library, and the Chulalongkorn University Library, it was found that books which list Thai words and explain their meanings have been called by a wide variety of names. Some of these names, here written, as are all proper names in Thai appearing in this article, in phonemic transcription (see Sec. 2.) are: ʔàkkharaaphíʔthaansàp (Bradley 1873), pàthaanúʔkrom (Textbook Department 1927), phótcànaanúʔkrom (Education Department 1891), khamrítsàdii (paramaanúchít chíʔnoorót et al. 1905), khamphiisàpphá ʔphótcanaanúʔjôok (Smith 1899—1908), sàpphá ʔphácanáʔ (Pallegoix 1854), líʔpìʔkaráʔmaajon (Michell 1891), sàri'ʔphót (Pallegoix/Vey 1896), wácànaanúkrom (maalaj 1923), wáʔcànaaphíʔthaan (wíʔsìt 1961), and sàpthaannúʔkrom (plɛɛk 1976). All of these names were coined from Pali or Sanskrit words and only three, namely phótcànaanúʔkrom, pàthaanúʔkrom, and sàpthaanúʔkrom, are still used as names for dictionaries; the others have passed from use. — Among the compilations of Bangkok Thai vocabulary of whatever name, the oldest known monolingual dictionary is ʔàkkharaaphíʔthaansàp: Dictionary of the Siamese Language by Dr. Dan Beach Bradley. This was published in 1873 by the American Missionary Association Press, which Bradley had established and for which he had brought a press and Thai type from Singapore (nuǝncan et al. 1981). The number of copies issued in the first printing is not known. The dictionary, a quarto volume of 428 pages, contains about 40,000 words used in everyday life, in literature, in religion, in other areas such as law, government, traditional medicine, the arts, crafts, and also the names of plants and animals. The year of publication, 1873, was the year of Bradley's death, and the dictionary has no prefatory sections explaining the background of the undertaking, the principles governing the arrangement of the entries, the meanings of the abbreviations used in it and other such matters. All there is a five-line advertisement which, in addition to specifying in detail the time and place of publication, says that the work is a compendium of Thai words with their meanings explained and that the person who defined the words and transcribed the work was ʔaacaan thát. — About 98 years after publication, the Teachers' Institute Press reprinted the dictionary. The reprint is provided with an introduction but this gives no further information on the compilation of the work. For insight into the background of the work, the authors are thus indebted to ʔaacaan chalɔ̌ɔŋ sǔntharaawaanít, who advised them of the *Abstract of the Journal of Rev. Dan Beach Bradley, M D., Medical Missionary in Siam, 1837—1873* (Fetus 1936), many passages in which refer to the dictionary project. Bradley began collecting words in 1838 and the manuscript was completed in 1855 and sent to the printery. At the time of Bradley's death in 1873, the work was still in press and it was his son, Dan F. Bradley, who saw it through publication. — In a journal entry dated February 21, 1838, Bradley states his goals in undertaking the work: "Made some preparations to commence writing on my Dictionary of Siamese words with Siamese definitions only. My object in preparing such a work is first for the benefits of missionaries in acquiring the language, and second for a standard work for the Siamese themselves. It appears to me that after a person has been studying a language or two a dictionary with purely Siamese definitions will be found far better than one with English definitions, for in the former he will have the great advantage of learning synonyms whereas in the latter he would not. And it strikes me that we ought to improve and settle the Siamese language which is now entirely destitute of anything like a dictionary and although there is a small book which bears the name of a grammar, yet it is almost useless because there are no two copies of it that do not contradict each other. Consequently there is much confusion among Siamese teachers touching the questions what is right and what is wrong" (Fetus 1936, 49 f.). — In gathering information for his dictionary, Bradley was assisted by a wordlist prepared by Mr. Gutstuff (Fetus 1936, 49). It is also possible that he consulted works that either had been or were being prepared at that time. These include a monolingual dictionary of literary words, paramaanúchítchíʔnoorót et al. (MS, n.d., published later in 1905), which had been in manuscript several decades before publication, two Thai-English dictionaries, Jones (1846) and McFarland (1865), a Thai-Latin-French-English dictionary, Pallegoix (1854), and also a handwritten manuscript prepared by a Catholic bishop that is mentioned in Fetus (1936, 173).

In the compiling of the dictionary, Bradley was assisted by his Thai teachers, ʔaacaan thát (Kru That) and naaj mɨɨəŋ (Nai Muang). To Kru That fell the task of defining the words and in this he was helped by Nai Muang. The authors are convinced that Kru That was a Buddhist monk, for in many journal entries Bradley writes of conversing with Kru That in the company of monks at a monastery, as in this extract dated August 12, 1851: "Visited Wat Kru That again and had a good time talking to a company of priests. They came around me at my request and heard me preach Christ Jesus, with much apparent interest" (Fetus 1936, 141). It may thus be said that the dictionary was the fruit of the cooperative effort of an American missionary and a Thai monk; the American, Bradley, served as producer and director and laid out the structure and the form of the work while the writing of the definitions was the responsibility of the Thais, Kru That and Nai Muang.

As in other Thai dictionaries, entries in Bradley 1873 are arranged by word initial consonant according to the traditional alphabetical order from ⟨ก⟩ = /k to ⟨ฮ⟩ = /h/. It is interesting, however, that entries with initial ⟨ข⟩ = /kh are not separated from those with initial ⟨ค⟩ = /kh/; rather, words with these two initials are integrated in one section ordered by vowel. In like manner, words with initial ⟨ศ⟩ = /s/ and ⟨ส⟩ = /s/ are presented together in one section. This differs from other dictionaries, in which entries with these initial letters are separated. Also unlike other dictionaries, words with initial ⟨ฤ,ฤๅ,ฦ,ฦๅ⟩ = /rɨʔ, rɨɨ, lɨʔ, lɨɨ/, which in Thai orthography are regarded as vowels, are in Bradley 1873 placed after ⟨ฮ⟩ = /h/, the 44th and final consonant. Furthermore, entries written with two contiguous initial consonant letters are ordered on the basis of their pronunciation. Entries under each initial are arranged by their vowels according to the order of vowels in a Thai primer of Bradley's time, *prathǒmakɔɔkaa* (MS, n.n., n.d.), which was: ⟨-า⟩ = /aa/, ⟨-ิ⟩ = /i/, ⟨-ี⟩ = /ii/, ⟨-ึ⟩ = /ɨ/, ⟨-ื⟩ = /ɨɨ/, ⟨-ุ⟩ = /u/, ⟨-ู⟩ = /uu/, ⟨เ-⟩ = /ee/, ⟨แ-⟩ = /ɛɛ/, ⟨ไ-⟩ = /aj/, ⟨ใ-⟩ = /aj/, ⟨โ-⟩ = /oo/, ⟨เ-า⟩ = /aw/, ⟨-ำ⟩ = /am/, ⟨-ะ⟩ = /a/. Beyond this, the arrangement of entries depended upon the vowel in combination with the final consonants, which were ordered ⟨-ก⟩ = /-k/, ⟨-ง⟩ = /-ŋ/, ⟨-ด⟩ = /-t/, ⟨-น⟩ = /-n/, ⟨-บ⟩ = /-p/, ⟨-ม⟩ = /-m/. The order of vowels with the final consonant ⟨-บ⟩ = /-p/ is an example: ⟨-บ⟩ = /op/, ⟨-ับ⟩ = /ap/, ⟨-าบ⟩ = /aap/, ⟨-ิบ⟩ = /ip/, ⟨-ีบ⟩ = /iip/, ⟨-ึบ⟩ = /ɨp/, ⟨-ืบ⟩ =

/ɨɨp/, ⟨ㅜบ⟩ = /up/, ⟨ㅡบ⟩ = /uup/, ⟨เ–ึบ⟩ = /ep/, ⟨เ–บ⟩ = /eep/, ⟨แ–บ⟩ = /ɛɛp/, ⟨โ–บ⟩ = /oop/, ⟨–อบ⟩ = /ɔɔp/, ⟨–ับ⟩ = /uuəp/, ⟨เ–ีบบ⟩ = /iiəp/, ⟨เ–ือบ⟩ = /ɨɨəp/, ⟨เ–อ⟩ = /əəp/. The order of the tone markers in Bradley 1873 is the same as that in other Thai dictionaries; words with no tone marker are first, followed by those with ⟨–่⟩ = /máaj ʔèek/, ⟨–้⟩ = /máaj thoo/, ⟨–๊⟩ = /máaj trii/, and ⟨–๋⟩ = /máaj càttawaa/ in succession. — In the grouping of entries it can be seen that sometimes sub-entries are not related to the main entry in terms of meaning; the only similarity is in pronunciation. — The punctuation marks used in Bradley 1873 are the comma, which immediately follows each entry word and which separates senses in the definition, and the period, which marks the end of a definition and which thus separates the definitions of homographs grouped under one entry word. Bradley 1873 does not indicate the pronunciation, the syntactic function, or the etymology of entries. — It is nevertheless a useful dictionary of value in research on the meanings of Thai words and expressions of an earlier time. It was the first Thai dictionary to bring together a large number of words from many fields. Most importantly, it stimulated the interest of Thais in the lexicography of their language. The compilers of the official dictionaries which followed used the entries in Bradley 1873 as a foundation; they did not have to break new ground.

4. The History of the Official Thai Dictionary 1884—1989

Between 1884 and 1891, the Department of Education produced a Thai dictionary with phráyaa paríyátthamthadaa (phɛɛ taalalák) as head of the project, and 500 copies of an octavo edition of 587 pages were issued in 1892 under the title *phótcànaanúʔkrom: lamdàp lɛɛ plɛɛ sàp thîi cháj naj năŋ sɨɨ thaj* [Dictionary: Thai Vocabulary Ordered and Explicated] Education Department 1891). In 1901 an additional 1,000 copies, these 447 pages in length, were issued with the new title *phótcànaanúʔkrom: pen kham plɛɛ sàp phaasăa thaj săm̀rap khĭiən kham cháj hâj thùuk tôŋ tua sakòt* [Dictionary: Explication of Thai Words for Correctness in Spelling] (Education Department 1901). Following this, a lexicography unit was set up in the Royal Pundits Department, a part of the Ministry of Public Instruction responsible for producing textbooks, and assigned the task of improving Education Department 1901. A reorganization gave rise to the Textbook Department and this agency published the revision under the title *pàthaanúʔkrom săm̀rap rooŋriiən* [Dictionary for Schools] (Textbook Department 1920), issuing 1,000 copies in 1920 and another 5,000 in 1924. The work of revising and enlarging the dictionary continued under the Textbook Department, Ministry of Public Instruction, and in 1927, the department issued 10,000 copies of a new edition, entitled *pàthaanúʔkrom ...* [Dictionary ...] (Textbook Department 1927). In 1933, the Royal Institute was established, and from that time, it has carried forward the task of compiling and editing the official dictionary. A revision of Textbook Department 1927 was published in duodecimo in 1950 with the title *phótcànaanúʔkrom* [Dictionary] (Royal Institute 1950), the same as the title of the first official dictionary, Education Department 1891. The reason for this change in title was that after considering the meanings of the Pali and Sanskrit roots from which the two words were formed, the dictionary committee decided that *phótcànaanúʔkrom* was a more accurate name for this type of work than *pàthaanúʔkrom*. At present, Thais generally refer to the official dictionary as *phótcànaanúʔkrom chabàp râatchabandìttajáʔsathăan phɔ̌ɔ sɔ̌ɔ sɔ̌ɔŋ phan sìi rɔ́ɔj kâaw sìp săam* [The B.E. (= Buddhist Era) 2493 (= A.D. 1950) Royal Institute Edition Dictionary]. This work has gone through a total of 20 printings with alteration limited for the most part to the correction of typographical errors. In 1977, twenty-seven years after its publication, the government ordered that Royal Institute 1950 be brought up to date by incorporating words that had recently entered the language, including coined terms. The revision, Royal Institute 1982, took five years in preparation and was completed in time to be published during the Bangkok bicentennial celebration in 1982. Royal Institute 1982 has gone through three printings, the latest in 1988, and work toward improving the dictionary continues. — Organizationally, the dictionary committee functions within the Office of Arts of the Royal Institute, which in turn has the status of a department under the Ministry of Education (carəən 1975). The fifteen members of the committee are appointed by the Cabinet. Each member has fine credentials and a high standing in Thai studies. For the most part they are experts in the fields of Thai literature, Thai dialectology, Pali and Sanskrit, Khmer, or folk art and culture, and many are retirees from government service. The committee meets weekly for a few hours. There are also many subcommittees charged with coining terminology and defining words in specific fields, e.g., the sub-committees on botanical and on zoological terminology. — The lexicographical work of the Royal Institute proceeds at a gradual pace, for most of those involved are regularly engaged in other pursuits. The methodology, administration, and organization of the project still adhere to a classical model. Though widely employed in Thailand, the computer has yet to be introduced into the lexicographical project of the Royal Institute. This slow response to the needs of dictionary users has provided a market for the many overall and specialized dictionaries produced by the private sector. Nevertheless, when disputes arise, particularly those concerning the fine points of spelling, the final arbiter is the Royal Institute dictionary, even though in some cases the majority of Thais may not agree.

4.1. The Textbook Department Dictionary 1927

Textbook Department 1927 was the first official dictionary in the compilation of which a rigorous system was applied, and it has provided the foundation used by the compilers of later Thai dictionaries both official and private. This dictionary has 19 pages of introductory matter: a title page, a preface, directions for finding words, and a key to the symbols indicating pronunciation. The title page specifies the printery, the year of printing, the printing history, the number of entries (26,230), the price (6.50 baht) and also bears a copyright notice. — Of primary interest is the direction for finding words. This is divided into nine sections, the first giving the order of initial consonant letters according to which entries are arranged. The order, as in Bradley 1873, is from ⟨ ก ⟩ = /k/ through ⟨ ฮ ⟩ = /h/ but there are some differences. First, a word spelled with two contiguous initial consonant letters such as ⟨ หน ⟩ = /năa/, which in Bradley 1873 was entered under ⟨ น ⟩ = /n/ on the basis of its pronunciation, is placed under ⟨ ห ⟩ = /h/, thus showing that the written form is the criterion in *Textbook Department 1927*, not the sound value. Second, words with initial ⟨ ฤ,ฤๅ ⟩ = /rɨʔ, rɨɨ/ follow those with initial ⟨ ร ⟩ = /r/ and words with initial ⟨ ฦ,ฦๅ ⟩ = /lɨʔ, lɨɨ/ follow those with initial ⟨ ล ⟩ = /l/. This differs from Bradley 1873, in which entries with these initials were placed after those with initial ⟨ ฮ ⟩ = /h/. Third, the order of entries under each initial consonant letter is very different from that in Bradley 1873, and again, this is because the written form of the word is the criterion. The rule is ⟨C1⟩, ⟨C1, C2⟩, ⟨C1 C2 C3⟩, ⟨C1 C2 C3 C4⟩, ⟨C1 C2 V⟩, ⟨C1 V⟩, ⟨C1 V F⟩; thus, words whose written form consists of consonant letters only are alphabetized on the basis of the second letter according to the same order as the initials: from ⟨ ก ⟩ = /k/ to ⟨ ฮ ⟩ = /h/, and then on the basis of a third letter and a fourth in succession. Only after such entries are exhausted are words with written vowel symbols entered, beginning with those written with two initial consonant letters. Final consonants (F) are ordered by point of articulation from velars to labials thus: ⟨ -ก, -ง, -ด, -น, -บ, -ม ⟩ = /-k, -ŋ, -t, -n, -p, -m/, as in Bradley 1873, however, the order of vowels is different. From left to right beginning with the top row, the order is: ⟨ -ะ ⟩ = /a/, ⟨ -ั ⟩ = /a/, ⟨ -ัว ⟩ = /uuə/, ⟨ -า ⟩ = /aa/, ⟨ -ํา ⟩ = /am/, ⟨ -ิ ⟩ = /i/, ⟨ -ี ⟩ = /ii/, ⟨ -ึ ⟩ = /ɨ/, ⟨ -ื ⟩ = /ɨɨ/, ⟨ -ุ ⟩ = /u/, ⟨ -ู ⟩ = /uu/, ⟨ เ- ⟩ = /ee/, ⟨ เ-ะ ⟩ = /e/, ⟨ เ-า ⟩ = /aw/, ⟨ เ-าะ ⟩ = /ɔ/, ⟨ เ-ิ ⟩ = /əə/, ⟨ เ-ี ⟩ = /iiə/, ⟨ เ-ีะ ⟩ = /iə/, ⟨ เ-ื ⟩ = /ɨə/, ⟨ เ-ื ⟩ = /ɨɨə/, ⟨ เ-ืะ ⟩ = /ɨə/, ⟨ แ- ⟩ = /ɛɛ/, ⟨ แ-ะ ⟩ = /ɛ/, ⟨ โ- ⟩ = /oo/, ⟨ โ-ะ ⟩ = /o/, ⟨ ไ- ⟩ = /aj/, ⟨ ใ- ⟩ = /aj/. — On the page, the text is printed in two columns with index words above and the page number centered above a rule separating the columns. Main entries and sub-entries are in boldface type, followed by pronunciation data enclosed in square brackets, next by an abbreviation in boldface indicating the language from which a borrowed word came, then by an abbreviation indicating the part of speech, and finally by the definition. The inclusion of information on the pronunciation, origin, and word class of the entries makes Textbook Department 1927 more complete a dictionary than Bradley 1873; the definitions, too, are clearer and more concise. — Three punctuation marks are used in Textbook Department 1927: the comma separates senses of a word, the semicolon separates the definitions of homographs grouped under one entry word, and the period marks the end of the matter presented under an entry word. — Textbook Department 1927 does not include colloquialisms, slang, or expressions of the spoken language, nor does it offer examples of usage or pictures to illustrate the meanings of words. Work on revision of Textbook Department 1927 continued and when completed, a revised edition was published in 1950 with the new title *phótcànaanú?krom chabàp râatchabandìttajá?sathăan phɔɔ sɔ̌ɔ 2493* (Royal Institute 1950) in duodecimo.

4.2. The Royal Institute Dictionary 1950

Royal Institute 1950 has won popularity and confidence both in official circles and among the general public. Between 1951 and 1981 there were 20 printings and a grand total of 187,000 copies were issued (Preface, Royal Institute 1982). Few emendations or additions distinguish one printing from the next. — Preceding the dictionary is a preface (and the prefaces of any earlier printings as well) and then an introduction with five sections explaining the order of the entries, their spelling, the way in which their pronunciation and language of origin are indicated, and the way in which they are defined. Following this are lists of abbreviations for parts of speech (e.g., ⟨น.⟩ = /n/ for ⟨คำนาม⟩ = /khamnaam/, meaning noun), usage (e.g., ⟨คณิต⟩ = /khanít/ for ⟨คณิตศาสตร์⟩ = /khaníttasàat/, meaning 'mathematics' and indicating that the word is used in this field), source languages of borrowed words (e.g., ⟨บ.⟩ = /b/ for ⟨บาลี⟩ = /baalii/, meaning Pali), and the reference works cited in the dictionary. — The dictionary begins with words with the initial consonant ⟨ก⟩ = /k/. Each main entry word is followed by pronunciation, usage and part of speech symbols; after this, the definition is given, and then source language and reference works, and for plants and animals, taxonomic names are cited. — The definitions of Royal Institute 1950 are clearer than those of *Textbook Department 1927*. Homographs appear as separate, numbered entries, thus showing clearly that although written and pronounced alike, they are different words. For example, *Royal Institute 1950* (p. 1) sets apart ⟨กก ๑⟩ = /kòk 1/, ⟨กก ๒⟩ = /kòk 2/, ⟨กก ๓⟩ = /kòk 3/, ⟨กก ๔⟩ = /kòk 4/, and ⟨กก ๕⟩ = /kòk 5/, each of which is a distinct word, differing from the others in meaning. — The punctuation marks in Royal Institute 1950 are the comma, semicolon, colon, and period; these are used in much the same way as they are in English. — The dictionary contains about 25,000 main entries. Other than common Thai words in general use, there are many literary and religious words, these constituting about 30 percent of the total. Of borrowed words, those of Pali and Sanskrit origin are the majority; only 590 borrowings from other languages, such as Khmer, Malay, Chinese, and English, appear. Few words from dialects or from specialized fields and no slang words are given (pràsìt 1974, 38). — Examples of usage, synonyms, and antonyms are rare. Thirty line drawings illustrate definitions, for the most part, of various types of basketry, of motifs in Thai art, and of artifacts of former times (pràsìt 1974, 42).

4.3. The Royal Institute Dictionary 1982

Royal Institute 1950 was used and reprinted for 27 years without being brought up to date. In 1976, as a step toward achieving the government policy goal of enabling all citizens of Thailand to use the national tongue with equal correctness, the then prime minister, a lawyer with experience in legal lexicography, decided to modernize *Royal Institute 1950* and appointed a committee to carry out the project on February 7, 1977. The committee, chaired by the president of the Royal Institute, met 280 times in all and followed the principles and procedures used in revising *Textbook Department 1927* to produce *Royal Institute 1950,* though adding certain features to enhance ease of use. Most of the matter of Royal Institute 1950 was retained intact; effort was directed primarily toward increasing the number of entries. Of words recently entering the language, only those which had gained wide currency were included. The 16 members of the committee established guidelines, divided the work among themselves, collected and defined words, and then considered the entries together. They also solicited criticism of the definitions of words in specialized fields from government agencies and other institutions and received many comments and suggestions from interested private individuals. The revision was completed in June 1982, in time for the 200th anniversary of the establishment of Bangkok as the royal capital (Preface, *Royal Institute 1982*). — A total of 160,000 copies of *Royal Institute 1982* have been issued in four printings, the latest in 1988. The dictionary is an octavo volume and is 947 pages long, exclusive of introductory matter and appendices containing pictures. — Overall, the structure and design of *Royal Institute 1982* are quite similar to those of *Royal Institute 1950;* the differences are mostly minor details. The most striking differences are: 1) *Royal Institute 1982* is issued in a volume of larger size, 2) index words have been moved to the upper right and left corners of the page while the page numbers occupy the lower left corner (verso) or right corner (recto), 3) main entry words are printed in bluish-green ink and other text in black to make word search easier and piracy by photo-offset more difficult, 4) a sloped typeface is used for cross reference between main entries, and 5) *Royal Institute 1982* contains more pictures: there are 74 line drawings in the dictionary and, in appendices, 48 color plates and 109 line drawings, showing flora and fauna, motifs in Thai art, watercraft, Thai musical instruments, equipment for capturing aquatic animals, and various types of machetes used in Thailand. — Compared with earlier editions of the official dictionary, *Royal Institute 1982* is much improved; in particular, the definitions and the grouping of words as main entries and sub-entries show that the revision committee paid greater attention to semantics than did their predecessors.

5. Summary and Discussion

The compilation of the first monolingual Thai dictionary was undertaken upon the initiative of an American missionary primarily to help Westerners gain a command of the vocabulary of Thai but also to serve in standardizing the written language. The fact that the leader of this pioneer effort was non-Thai and was not familiar with traditional orthographic conventions explains the importance of pronunciation as a criterion in the ordering of entries in Bradley 1873, as is seen in the merger of entries written with initials ⟨ข, ช⟩ and with initials ⟨ค, ฆ, ต⟩ and in the grouping of homographs as a single entry despite differences in their meanings. There are also inadequacies in the definition of words. On the other hand, the fact that pronunciation was an important criterion in this dictionary does provide information on the sound system of the language at the time of its compilation, indicating that the merger of initial /kh/ = ⟨ข⟩ and /x/ = ⟨ช⟩ had already taken place, and probably the same is true in the case of the initials ⟨ค, ฆ, ต⟩. — The official dictionaries, *Textbook Department 1927*, *Royal Institute 1950*, and *Royal Institute 1982*, show the leading significant role of the government in the standardizing of the language. The Royal Institute dictionaries have become important guides to language use despite their shortcomings, such as 1) the small number of entries, 2) the over-emphasis on literary and archaic words, 3) the exclusion of colloquialisms and slang, and 4) inadequacies in the definitions, some of which are unclear or do not cover actual current usage. Because of these deficiencies, a large number of dictionaries have been published by private concerns in the twentieth century, but even so, for the principles employed in compilation as well as for the definitions of most of the words they include, they follow the standards of the Royal Institute dictionaries. — The Royal Institute continues the revision of their dictionary and attempts to bring into it new words that have gained currency in the language. It also contends with the problem of coining new words constantly demanded by advances in technology. The slow pace at which this work proceeds is attributable to the fact that those so engaged have other duties and also to the fact that the Royal Institute has yet to employ modern data processing technology in its lexicographical project. Nevertheless, the Royal Institute dictionary is reasonably complete and contains accurate information so that it is useful as a reference in studies concerned with the Thai language.

6. Selected Bibliography

6.1. Dictionaries

Bradley 1873 = Dan Beach Bradley: ʔàkkharaaphíʔthaansàp: Dictionary of the Siamese Language. Bangkok 1971 [828 p.].

Education Department 1891 = krom sìksǎathíʔkaan: phótcànaanúʔkrom: lamdàp lɛɛ plɛɛ sàp thîi cháj naj nǎŋ sɯ̌ thaj. Bangkok 1892 [587 p.].

Education Department 1901 = krom sìksǎathíʔkaan: phótcànaanúʔkrom: pen kham plɛɛ sàp phaasǎa thaj sǎmràp khǐiən kham cháj hâj thùuk tɔ̂ŋ tua sakòt. Bangkok 1901 [447 p].

Jones 1846 = Taylor Jones: Siamese-English Dictionary. MS.

maalaj 1923 = maalaj cansǎncaj: wáʔcànaanúʔkrom rɯ̌ɯ tamraa plɛɛ lɛɛ pramuuən sàp. Bangkok 1923 [762 p.].

McFarland 1865 = Samuel Gamble McFarland: English and Siamese Dictionary. Bangkok 1865.

Michell 1891 = E. B. Michell: líʔpìʔkaráʔmaajon phaasǎa thaj plɛɛ pen phaasǎa ʔaŋkrìt: A Siamese-English Dictionary for the Students in Both Languages. Bangkok 1891 [323 p].

Pallegoix 1854 = Jean Baptiste Pallegoix: sàppháʔphacànáʔ phaasǎa thaj: Dictionarium linguae thai sive siamensis ... Paris 1854 [880 p.].

Pallegoix/Vey 1896 = Jean Baptiste Pallegoix/ J. L. Vey: sàrí?phót phaasǎa thaj: Siamese-French-English Dictionary. Bangkok 1896 [2,265 p].

paramaanúchítchí?noorót et al. 1905 = sǒmdètkrommaphrá? paramaanúchítchí?noorót lɛ́? sǒmdètkrommaphrá? deechaa?àdì?sɔ̌ɔn, krommalǔuaŋ phuunêet: khamrítsàdii. MS.

plɛɛk 1976 = plɛɛk sǒnthí?rák: sàpthaannú?krom. Bangkok 1976 [115 p.].

Royal Institute 1950 = râatchabandìttajá?sathǎan phɔɔ sɔ̌ɔ 2493. Bangkok 1950 [1,053 p.].

Royal Institute 1982 = râatchabandìttajá?sathǎan: phótcànaanú?krom chabàp râatchabandìttajá?sathǎan phɔɔ sɔ̌ɔ 2525. Bangkok 1987 [947 p.].

Smith 1899—1908 = Samuel J. Smith: khamphiisàpphá?phótcanaanú?jôok: A Comprehensive Anglo-Siamese Dictionary. Bangkok 1899—1908 [4512 p.].

Textbook Department 1920 = krom tamraa, kràsuuaŋ thammakaan: pàthaanú?krom sǎmràp rooŋriian. Bangkok 1920 [536 p.].

Textbook Department 1927 = krom tamraa, kràsuuaŋ thammakaan: pàthaanú?krom krom tamraa kràsuuaŋ thammakaan. Bangkok 1927 [906 p.].

wí?sít 1961 = wí?sít phútthí?bandìt: wannakhadii wá?cànaaphí?thaan. Thonburi 1961 [688 p.].

6.2. Other Publications

carəən 1975 = carəən ?inthará?kasèet: maa rúucàk kàp râatchabandìttajá?sathǎan [Get Acquainted with the Royal Institute]. In: waarasǎan râatchabandìttajá?sathǎan [Journal of the Royal Institute]. July—September 1975, 12—16.

Fetus 1936 = George Haws Fetus (ed.): Abstract of the Journal of Rev. Dan Beach Bradley, M. D., Medical Missionary in Siam 1837—1873. Cleveland 1936.

nuuəncan et al. 1981 = nuuəncan ráttanaakɔɔn lɛ? khaná?: pàkinnákà? rɨ̂aŋ nǎŋ sɨ̌ naj samǎj ráttaná?koosǐn [A Miscellany on Books in the Bangkok Period]. Bangkok 1981, 52—65.

prathǒmmakɔɔkaa = [A First Primer]. (n.n., n.d., n.p.) MS in possession of the Fine Arts Department published with permission. Bangkok 1970.

pràsìt 1974 = pràsìt kàapklɔɔn: wíkhrɔ́? phótcànaanú?krom thaj [An Analysis of the Thai Dictionaries]. In: waarasǎan raamkhamhɛ̌ɛŋ [The Ramkhamhaeng Journal]. July 1974, 30—61.

Theraphan L. Thongkum/ Pranee Kullavanijaya, Bangkok (Thailand)

261. Vietnamese Lexicography

1. The Missionary Period
2. The Colonial Period
3. The Independence and Partition Period
4. The Post-1975 Situation
5. Selected Bibliography

1. The Missionary Period

In traditional Vietnam, when the learning of Chinese classics dominated the intellectual scene, schoolchildren were taught basic written Chinese by means of locally authored texts entitled *The Book of 1,000 Characters, 3,000 Characters, 5,000 Characters,* etc., all of which are glossaries from Chinese to Vietnamese. These volumes use verse as mnemonic devices to provide native equivalents of Chinese lexemes in the so-called Sino-Vietnamese pronunciation with the headwords listed notionally in the manner of thesauri and the native terms transcribed in the demotic script called *nôm,* i. e. the southern script — as opposed to Chinese, referred to as the scholars' writing system (Nguyen D-H 1981).

As the product of Vietnamese romanization called quốc-ngữ — an international and collective undertaking — made its shy début in the 17th century, Western missionaries began to compile bilingual dictionaries going from Vietnamese to Latin and from Latin to Vietnamese and used to facilitate their religious purpose of converting the native population to Christianity. The period 1651—1884 was marked by the epoch-making pioneer efforts of Alexandre de Rhodes (1591—1660), who in addition to writing a Latin-Vietnamese Catechism, authored a trilingual volume, *Dictionarium Annamiticum Lusitanum et Latinum* (Rhodes 1651). This first dictionary printed in the Roman script gives some 8,000 Vietnamese entries with glosses in Portuguese and Latin. Inspired by two earlier works, since extinct, a Vietnamese-Por-

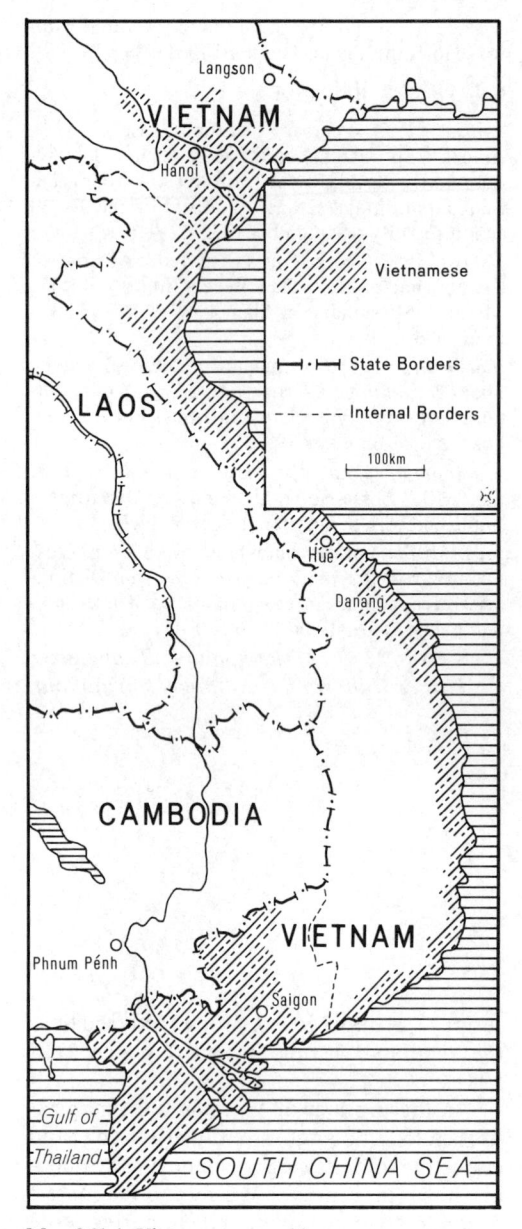

Map 261.1: Vietnamese speaking areas

tuguese dictionary and a Portuguese-Vietnamese dictionary authored by Gasparal de Amoral and by Antoine Barbosa, respectively, DALL is important for two reasons: it includes a *Brevis Declaratio* on Vietnamese grammar, and it records among other things some consonant clusters /bl- ml- mnh- tl-/ that reflect the pronunciation of the time, thus constituting a valuable document in historical linguistics (Nguyen D-H 1986a, b; K. Gregerson 1969). Alexandre de Rhodes' role as codifier of the novel script was later capably emulated by several generations of Catholic priests, all eager to perfect quốc-ngữ into a convenient tool in the evangelization of the country. Among those there was even the Bishop of Adran, Msgr Pigneau de Béhaine 1772, upon whose manuscript Bishop Taberd 1838 later built his excellent bidirectional Vietnamese-Latin and Latin-Vietnamese dictionary, which mirrored changes in the language in the second half of the 17th century and the 18th century, and which served as the foundation of a later work by Theurel 1877.

2. The Colonial Period

Following the French conquest, completed in 1884 with the capture of Hanoi, as the colonial administration encouraged both the teaching of French in local schools and the learning of Vietnamese by its civilian and military officers, there occurred an accelerated production of dictionaries going in both directions, with those going from Vietnamese (then called annamite) to French outnumbering those going the other way. Petrus Trương Vĩnh Ký 1887 wrote one of the earliest Vietnamese-French volumes, to be followed by several excellent works authored by Génibrel 1898, Bonet 1899, Vallot 1901, Barbier 1922, etc.

Works produced since 1931 have been mostly authored by native scholars. The policy of cultural assimilation by the French not only did not succeed, but unexpectedly led to reactions that were conducive to the development of the Vietnamese language: as a new press in the vernacular heralded by the two reviews *Nam-phong* and *Đông-dương Tạp-chí* contributed to the dissemination of knowledge and as political pamphlets, translations and textbooks also appeared in increasing numbers, previously published dictionaries failed to fulfill the needs of Western-oriented intellectuals. Thus Cordier 1930 *(Dictionnaire annamite-français)* required a supplement two years later, after a *Petit Passe-Partout de la Presse Indigène* was contributed by G. Huế 1931.

In order to keep up with the newly enriched and cultivated language and also to assist in the learning of Western languages, modern bilingual volumes had to be compiled. Three native scholars with the same family name brought forth their contributions: Đào Duy Anh 1936, author of an excel-

450

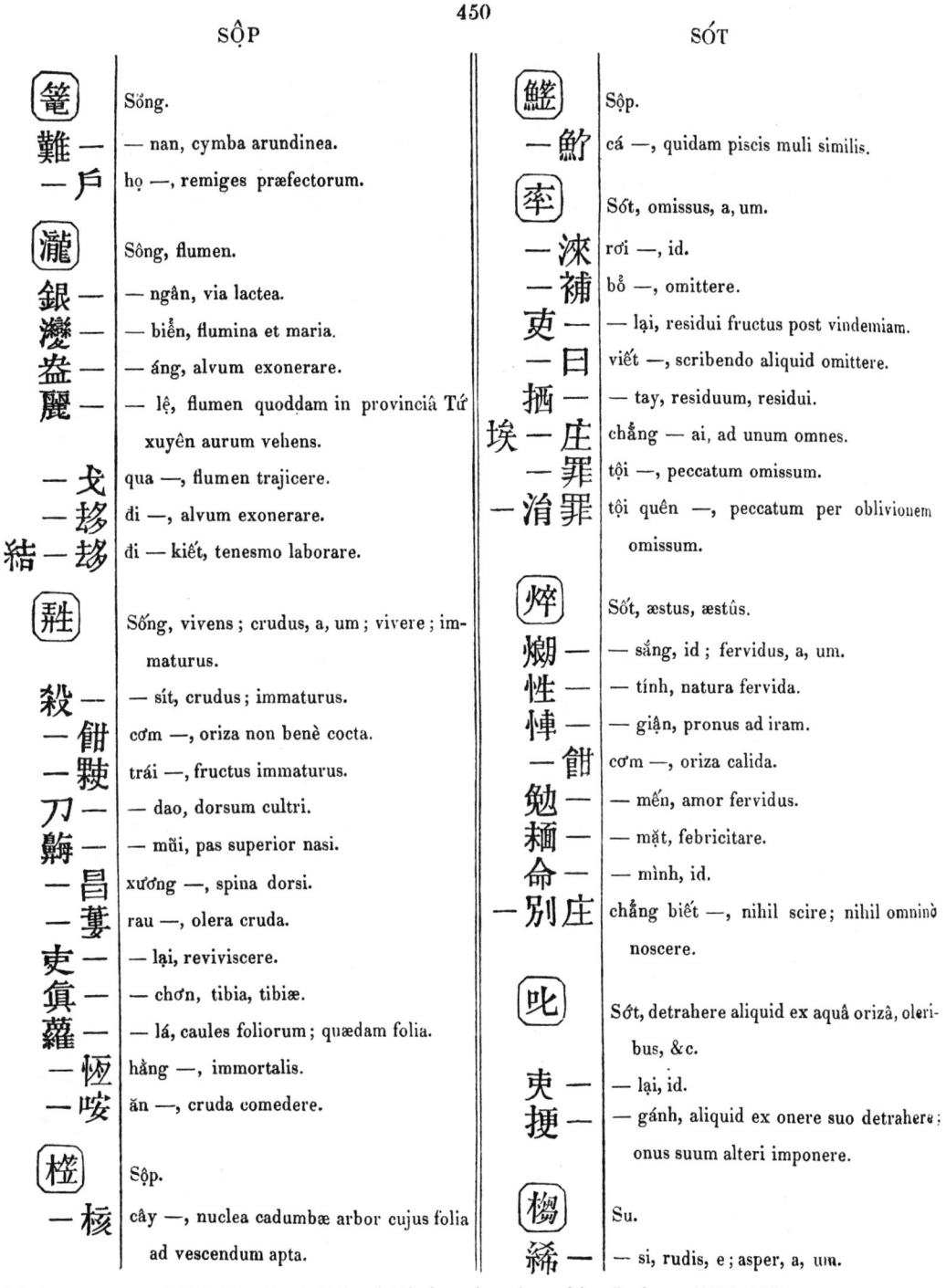

SỘP

箯 Sŏng.
難— — nan, cymba arundinea.
—戶 họ —, remiges præfectorum.

瀧 Sông, flumen.
銀— — ngân, via lactea.
瀁— — biển, flumina et maria.
益— — áng, alvum exonerare.
麗— — lệ, flumen quoddam in provinciâ Tứ xuyên aurum vehens.
—戈 qua —, flumen trajicere.
—珍 di —, alvum exonerare.
結—珍 di — kiết, tenesmo laborare.

胜 Sŏng, vivens; crudus, a, um; vivere; immaturus.
殺— — sít, crudus; immaturus.
—𩛄 cơm —, oriza non benè cocta.
—鞭 trái —, fructus immaturus.
刀— — dao, dorsum cultri.
齂— — mũi, pas superior nasi.
—昌 xương —, spina dorsi.
—薯 rau —, olera cruda.
吏— — lại, reviviscere.
真— — chơn, tibia, tibiæ.
蘿— — lá, caules foliorum; quædam folia.
—恆 hằng —, immortalis.
—唵 ăn —, cruda comedere.

橙 Sộp.
—核 cây —, nuclea cadumbæ arbor cujus folia ad vescendum apta.

SÓT

鰺 Sộp.
—魣 cá —, quidam piscis muli similis.

率 Sót, omissus, a, um.
—淶 rơi —, id.
—補 bỏ —, omittere.
吏—日 — lại, residui fructus post vindemiam.
拰— — viết —, scribendo aliquid omittere.
埃—庄 — tay, residuum, residui.
—罪 chẳng — ai, ad unum omnes.
—消罪 tội —, peccatum omissum.
tội quên —, peccatum per oblivionem omissum.

烊 Sót, æstus, æstûs.
爛— — sắng, id; fervidus, a, um.
性— — tính, natura fervida.
悻— — giận, pronus ad iram.
—䭊 cơm —, oriza calida.
勉— — mến, amor fervidus.
緬— — mặt, febricitare.
命— — mình, id.
—別庄 chẳng biết —, nihil scire; nihil omninò noscere.

叱 Sót, detrahere aliquid ex aquâ orizâ, oleribus, &c.
吏— — lại, id.
捷— — gánh, aliquid ex onere suo detraherᴇ; onus suum alteri imponere.

樞 Su.
絺— — si, rudis, e; asper, a, um.

Dictionary excerpt 261.1: Jean Louis Taberd, Dictionarium Anamitico-Latinum (1838, 450)

lent French-Vietnamese dictionary, in which Chinese characters are provided for those Vietnamese equivalents that are loan compounds, Đào Văn Tập, 1950, who produced the well-known French-Vietnamese and Vietnamese-French pair, and Đào Đăng Vỹ 1952, whose French-Vietnamese volume distinguished itself in thoroughness and accuracy. D-A Đào meant his French-Vietnamese volume to be a supplement to his Hán-Việt Từ-

Dictionary excerpt 261.2: Đào Duy Anh, Giản-yếu Hán-Việt tù-điê'n, Dictionnaire sino-vietnamien (1932, 382 f.)

điển 1932, a list of Chinese-borrowed words and expressions. V-T Đào's more selective corpus included only those Sino-Vietnamese terms that had been thoroughly integrated into the recipient language, and Đ-V Đào later even tried to publish an encyclopedic dictionary, of which only three volumes had appeared in print 1960—61.

A second category included those monolingual dictionaries which aim at standardizing Vietnamese through meaning discriminations as well as clarifications of synonyms and antonyms, and even explanations of literary allusions used in works of poetry and prose. A third category, that of spelling dictionaries, numbers a dozen or so volumes, the most scholarly of which is certainly Lê Ngọc Trụ 1959, which won a literary prize and was reissued in a revised edition in 1973. The fourth group consists of what can be termed "cultural dictionaries" since they all include lexemes and graphemes borrowed from Chinese, a language often considered the Latin of Vietnam, having served for centuries as the language of education and government at least in its written form.

3. The Independence and Partition Period

The most popular of those dictionaries of Sino-Vietnamese (Hán-Việt), i. e. Chinese loanwords pronounced in Vietnamese, is D-A Đào 1932, whose two parts record 40,000 compounds printed in the quốc-ngữ script and derived from 5,000 individual Chinese characters. Some definitions are also accompanied by French equivalents. All four-syllable compounds follow Chinese syntax: e.g. the entry kinh-tế 'economy' is followed by kinh-tế-chiến-tranh 'guerre économique', kinh-tế chính-sách 'politique économique', etc. Cf. the reverse word order in Vietnamese: chiến-tranh kinh-tế, chính-sách kinh-tế, etc. Its good feature remains the inclusion of Chinese graphs next to quốc-ngữ spellings, which helps the discrimination of homonyms in both of its parts. Several authors quickly emulated the pioneer lexicographer: T-M Nguyễn 1940, T-T Hoàng 1939, Bửu-Cân 1937, V-K Nguy-ễn 1960. But the most valuable real dictionary of Sino-Vietnamese was authored by a Buddhist monk, Thiều Chửu 1942: it lists Chinese characters by radicals and the number of strokes. In his Preface, the scholarly monk deplored that Han, i.e. Chinese studies, were losing ground, and that "only through Buddhist studies perhaps some parts could be preserved." His objective was to help people already able to read Buddhist scriptures understand individual characters, which would be "a foundation on which to rebuild the resplendent monument of Confucianism" (Thiều-Chửu 1942, iii-v).

The primers mentioned in Section 1 present both the Chinese graphs and the *nôm* characters that represent vernacular glosses, and have thus served as practical schooltexts for generations. Analytic articles existed that discuss this novel script, based on Chinese. However, real repertoires of those "southern" or demotic characters made their appearance relatively late as classroom materials before two valuable works were successively published in South and North Vietnam. Nguyễn/Vũ 1971 lists about 10,000 characters with cross references from romanized spellings; its 100-page body was later reproduced in the back matter of the Vietnamese-German dictionary by Karow 1972. The contribution of the Viện Ngôn-ngữ-học 1976 in Hanoi, modestly called a finder list, gives 8,187 nôm characters representing 12,000 syllables and culled from fifteen literary works.

The earliest monolingual dictionary of modern times is Việt-nam tự-điển by the Khaiœtrí Tiến-đức Society 1931. But actually some decades before a French-educated scholar had already produced a monumental work: Huình-Tịnh 1895—96 meant at first to be a Vietnamese-French volume turned out as an excellent monolingual dictionary which reflected the southern dialect with many Cambodian and Fukien or Chiuchow loanwords. The cooperative efforts of the scholars in the KTTĐ, on the other hand, resulted in clear and succinct definitions of both native and Sino-Vietnamese lexemes, the latter accompanied by written graphs, with citations in popular collocations. Later works by Đào 1951 and Thanh Nghị 1952 were more recently surpassed by Lê Văn Đức 1970 and Văn Tân 1977 in both coverage and methodology, and of a larger work sponsored by the Hanoi Linguistics Institute there has appeared only the first volume, A—C.

Bilingual dictionaries using another language than French as SL or TL are latecomers. A Beijing-published Vietnamese-Chinese volume by Hà Thành 1966 was found good enough for a U. S. government agency to translate the Chinese glosses into

English, resulting in a two-volume *Vietnamese-English Dictionary* (JPRS 1966).

4. The Post-1975 Situation

Although English has been taught at the secondary level as a second foreign language (next to Vietnamese in French-medium schools of the colonial period, and next to French since 1945), dictionaries involving English did not appear until the 1950's: Lê 1955, Lê Bá 1955, V. K. Nguyễn 1955, D. H. Nguyễn 1959, 1967, Bùi 1978, for Vietnamese-English, and for English-Vietnamese Viện Ngôn-ngữ-học 1975, Đặng and Bùi 1976 are the most rigorously compiled ones produced inside the country recently while abroad D. H. Nguyễn 1980 displays more consistency and accurary. Other languages involved are German, Russian, Norwegian, Esperanto, Japanese, Pali, Khmer, Thai, Tày-Nùng, with the Summer Institute of Linguistics 1975 contributing a "tentative" edition giving glosses of Mường, the archaic sister language of Vietnamese (SIL 1975).

Technical glossaries started appearing early in the 1940's (e.g. Hoàng 1948, Đào 1945) as Vietnamese began its status as medium of instruction at all three levels. Teachers in both halves of the country during partition (1954–75) competed in the compilation of technical dictionaries in the natural and social sciences, using native words as well as translations and transliterations.

Since 1984, a new institute within the Social Sciences Commission has been publishing Tri-thức Bách-khoa, a finely edited journal which contains technical discussions as well as draft entries for a "small-size" encyclopedic dictionary of Vietnamese and an encyclopedia of Vietnam. As linguists, scientists and scholars and writers are working together to enhance the purity and clarity of the mother tongue lexicographic work in Vietnamese promises to be both rigorous and comprehensive.

5. Selected Bibliography

5.1. Dictionaries

Barbier 1922 = Victor Barbier: Dictionaire annamite-français. Hanoi 1922 [951 p.].

Bonet 1899 = Jean Bonet: Dictionnaire annamite-français. Paris 1899–1900 [xxv, 440, 532 p.].

Bùi 1978 = Bùi Phụng: Từ-điển Việt-Anh. Hanoi 1978 [1322 p.].

Bửu Cân 1937 = Bửu Cân: Hán-Việt Thành-ngữ. Lexique des expressions sino-vietnamiennes. Huế 1937 [2nd ed. Saigon 1971] [625 p.].

Cordier 1930 = Georges Cordier: Dictionnaire annamite-français à l'usage des écoles et des annamitisants. Hanoi 1930 [1433 p.].

Đặng and Bùi 1976 = Đặng Chấn Liêu and Bùi Ý: Từ-điển Anh-Việt. Hanoi 1976 [1022 p.].

Đào D. A. 1932 = Đào Duy Anh: Giản-yếu Hán-Việt từ-điền. Dictionnaire sino-vietnamien. Huế 1932 [2nd ed. Paris 1950] [592 p. + 605 p.].

Đào D. A. 1936 = Đào Duy Anh: Pháp-Việt tự-điển. Dictionnaire français-vietnamien avec transcription en caractères chinois de termes sino-vietnamiens [Second edition Paris 1952] [1958 p.].

Đào D. V. 1952 = Đào Đăng Vỹ: Pháp-Việt tự-điển. Dictionnaire français-vietnamien. Saigon 1952 [1280 p.].

Đào D. V. 1960–61 = Đào Đăng Vỹ: Việt-nam bách-khoa tự-điển. Vietnamese encyclopedic dictionary with annotations in Chinese, French and English. Saigon 1960–61, vols 1–3, each 240 p.

Đào V. T. 1950 = Đào Văn Tập: Tự-điển Pháp-Việt phổ-thông. Dictionnaire général français-vietnamien. Saigon 1950 [1242 p.].

Đào V. T. 1951 = Đào Văn Tập: Tự-điển Việt-nam phổ-thông. Saigon 1951 [839 p.].

Đào 1945 = Đào Văn Tiến: Danh-từ khoa-học, Vocabulaire Scientifique. 2nd ed. Paris 1950 [106 p.].

Génibrel 1898 = J. F. M. Génibrel: Dictionnaire annamite-français. Saigon 1898 [987 p.].

Gouin 1957 = Eugène Gouin: Dictionnaire vietnamien-chinois-français. Saigon 1957 [1606 p.].

Hà Thành 1966 = Hà Thành: Từ-điển Việt-Hán. Beijing 1966 [1372 p.].

Hội Khai-trí Tiến-đức 1931 = Hội Khai-trí Tiến-đức: Việt-Nam tự-điển. Hanoi 1931 [663 p.].

Hoàng T-T 1939 = Hoàng Thúc Trâm: Hán-Việt Tân tự-điển. Hanoi 1939 [1505 p.] [Saigon reprint 1972].

Hoàng 1948 = Hoàng Xuân-Hãn: Danh-từ khoa-học. Vocabulaire scientifique. Saigon 1948 [197 p.].

Huế 1931 = Gustave Huế: Petit Passe-Partout de la Presse Indigène. Hanoi 1931 [698 p.].

Huế 1937 = Gustave Huế: Dictionnaire annamite-chinois-français. Hanoi 1937 [1199 p.] [Saigon reprint 1971].

Huình-Tịnh 1895–96 = Huình-Tịnh Paulus Của: Dictionnaire annamite. Đại-Nam Quấc-âm Tự-vị. Saigon 1895 vol. I [608 p.], 1896 vol. II. [596 p.].

JPRS 1966 = Joint Publications Research Service: Vietnamese-English Dictionary. Washington, DC 1966 [A–L 751 p.; M–Y 735 p.].

Karow 1972 = Otto Karow: Vietnamesisch-Deutsches Wörterbuch. Từ-điển Việt-Đức. Wiesbaden 1972 [1086 p.].

Lê 1955 = Lê Văn Hùng: Vietnamese-English Dictionary. Paris 1955 [820 p.].
Lê Bá 1955 = Lê Bá Kông: English-Vietnamese Dictionary. Saigon 1955 [491 p.].
Lê Ngọc Trụ 1959 = Lê Ngọc Trụ: Việt-ngữ chánh-tả tự-vị. Saigon 1959 [512 p. Rev. ed. Saigon 1973, 706 p.].
Lê Văn Đức 1970 = Lê Văn Đức: Việt-Nam Tự-điển. A-L, M-X. Saigon 1970 [1865 p. + 376 p. of Proverbs and Sayings + 273 p. of Proper names].
Nguyễn Đ-H 1959 = Nguyễn Đình-Hoà: Vietnamese-English Dictionary. Saigon 1959 [568 p.] [Repr. Tokyo 1966].
Nguyễn Đ-H 1967 = Nguyễn Đình-Hoà: Vietnamese-English Student Dictionary. Saigon 1967 [675 p.] [Reprint Carbondale, Illinois 1971].
Nguyễn Đ-H 1980 = Nguyễn Đình-Hoà: Essential English-Vietnamese Dictionary. Carbondale 1980 [316 p., Tokyo reprint 1983].
Nguyễn / Vũ 1971 = Nguyễn Quang Xỹ / Vũ Văn Kính: Tự-điển chữ Nôm. Saigon 1971 [863 p.].
Nguyễn T-M = Nguyễn Trần Mô: Nam-Hoa tự-điển. Hanoi 1940.
Nguyễn V-K 1955 = Nguyễn Văn Khôn: English-Vietnamese Dictionary. Saigon 1955 [1741 p.].
Nguyễn V-K 1960 = Nguyễn Văn Khôn: Hán-Việt từ-điển. Saigon 1960 [1161 p.].
Pigneau 1772 = Pigneau de Béhaine: Dictionarium annamitico-latinum. Ms.
Rhodes 1651 = Alexandre de Rhodes: Dictionarium Annamiticium Lusitanum et Latinum. Rome 1651 [900 columns].
SIL 1975 = Summer Institute of Linguistics: Mường-Vietnamese-English Dictionary. Dallas, Texas 1975 [532 p.].
Taberd 1838 = Jean Louis Taberd: Dictionarium Anamitico-Latinum. Serampore 1838 [722 p.].
Thanh-Nghị 1952 = Thanh Nghị: Việt-Nam tân-từ-điển. Saigon 1952 [1669 p.].

Theurel 1877 = J. S. Theurel: Dictionarium annamitico-latinum. Ninh-phú 1877 [566 p.].
Thiều Chửu 1942 = Thiều Chửu: Hán-Việt tự-điển. Hanoi 1942 [817 p.] [Saigon repr. 1966].
Trương 1887 = Petrus Trương Vĩnh Ký: Petit dictionnaire français-annamite. Saigon 1887 [1192 p.].
Uỷ-ban Khoa-học xã-hội 1975 = Uỷ-ban Khoa-học xã-hội Việt-Nam: Từ-điển tiếng Việt phổ-thông. Volume 1 (A–C). Hanoi 1975 [308 p.].
Vallot 1901 = Pierre Gabriel Vallot: Dictionnaire annamite-français [291 p., second ed. 1904].
Văn Tân 1977 = Văn Tân: Từ-điển tiếng Việt. Second ed. Hanoi 1977 [894 p.; 1967 edition has 1172 p.].
Viện Ngôn-ngữ-học 1975 = Viện Ngôn-ngữ-học: Từ-điển Anh-Việt. Hanoi 1975 [1959 p.].
Viện Ngôn-ngữ-học 1976 = Viện Ngôn-ngữ-học: Bảng tra chữ Nôm. Hanoi 1976 [426 p.].

5.2. Other Publications

Gregerson 1969 = Kenneth Gregerson: A study of Middle Vietnamese phonology, In: Bulletin de la Société des Etudes Indochinoises 44.2.135–193.
Nguyen D-H 1981 = Nguyễn Đình-Hoà: Bilingual Lexicography in Vietnam: The state of the art, In: Papers of the Dictionary Society of North America 1979, 149–171.
Nguyen D-H 1986a = Nguyễn Đình-Hoà: The Vietnamese-Portuguese-Latin dictionary by De Rhodes 1651, In: Papers in Linguistics 19.1, 1–18.
Nguyen D-H 1986b = Nguyễn Đình-Hoà: Middle (17th-century) Vietnamese Lexicon, Paper presented before the 19th International Conference on Sino-Tibetan Languages and Linguistics, Columbus, Ohio, September 1986.

Dinh-Hoa Nguyen, San Jose State University, San Jose, California (USA)

262. Lexicography of Other Southeast Asian Languages

1. Background
2. Types of Main Entry Ordering
3. Content
4. Format
5. Publication Form
6. Languages
7. Specialized Lexicography
8. Selected Bibliography

1. Background

Lexicography in the smaller languages of Southeast Asia (cf. Map 262.1) is still in its preliminary stages, with very little having been done before 1900, and most of the lexicography having been done only in the last 20—30 years, almost all of it being done by outsiders, not by native speakers of the lan-

Map 262.1: Smaller languages of Southeast Asia

guages. These languages range from a few hundred speakers to about five million (Khmer), and are predominantly members of the Mon-Khmer family. Khmer, being a national language, has had considerably more lexicographic attention paid to it than have the smaller languages.

For a full bibliography of the lexicographical work done in Southeast Asia see Huffman 1986.

2. Types of Main Entry Ordering

2.1. Roman Alphabetical Order

Bilingual dictionaries organized from French or English, or using a romanization based on French or English, follow the standard order for those two languages. Vietnamese adds the modified letters ă, â, đ, ê, ô, ơ, ư, which follow their respective unmodified forms. The alphabetization normally proceeds from left to right. Tone marks are generally written above or below the vowel, and tones are alphabetized last in a word. The digraphs and trigraph *ch, gh, gi, kh, ng, ngh, nh, ph, qu, th, tr* are frequently alphabetized as single complex units, not as sequences of letters. Languages such as Yao (Lombard 1960) and Meo (Heimbach 1966) which indicate tones by a word-final consonant also alphabetize the tone last in the word.

2.2. Reverse Roman Alphabetizing

In most Mon-Khmer languages the stressed syllable at the end of a word is more stable cross-dialectally than an unstressed syllable at the beginning of the word, and many of these languages have prefixes but virtually none have suffixes. So it is more advantageous to alphabetize them in reverse order, proceeding from right to left. This tends to keep dialectally different forms close together in the dictionary, and tends to keep affixed words close to their root. The published Pacoh dictionary (Watson 1979), for example, is arranged in this order, as is also the Ngeq rhyme dictionary (Smith 1968?) and the manuscript rhyme books of many linguists. In some of these the alphabetization is strictly right to left, in some the vowel is taken before the final consonant, and in some the alphabetizing is not carried beyond the final consonant and vowel but is left unordered. Some linguists have recommended starting with the first consonant of the last syllable, proceeding to the right, then taking the first syllable (if any), thus building from the most stable part of the word.

2.3. Phonetic Ordering

The dictionaries in the Indigenous Languages of Thailand Research Project (ILTRP) series, e.g. the Surin Khmer dictionary (Dhanan 1978), are arranged phonetically, with consonants arranged from the front of the mouth (bilabials) to the back (laryngeals), and from closed (stops) to open (semivowels) degrees of openness: *p ph b m w t th d n l r s tç tçhɲ j k kh ŋ ʔ h.* The vowels are arranged from front to back and high to low: *i ii ɩ ɩɩ e ee ɛ ɛɛ a aa m mm ɤ ɤɤ ə əə ʌ ʌʌ u uu ʊ ʊʊ o oo ɔ ɔɔ ɑ ɑɑ.* Then the diphthongs are arranged by their second element: *ei ɛi ai aai ɤɤi əəi ʌi ʌʌi ui ʊi i oi ɔɔi ɑɑi iu ɩɩu eu eeu ɛɛu au aau ɤu əu ʌu ia iia ma mma ua uua.* Then the triphthongs *iai uai iau.*

2.4. Indic Alphabetical Order

Languages using the Indian-derived Thai, Cambodian, or Cham alphabets generally follow the Sanskrit phonetic order, i.e. first the velar stops and nasals, then the palatal stops and nasals, the alveolars, the bilabials, then followed by the liquids, the sibilants, and finally the laryngeals. The vowels are ordered by their written position relative to the consonant, first those written following the consonant, then those above, those below, and those preceding. When there is an initial consonant cluster the second consonant is alphabetized before the vowel, even though the vowel may have been written before the first consonant. And in Cambodian, even though the second consonant is sometimes written before the first consonant it is alphabetized second. Indic scripts are organized by syllables rather than by phonemes, so syllables are written in strict left to right order but the component phonemes aren't.

2.5. Semantic Ordering

A number of vocabularies in the Summer Institute of Linguistics series have followed the Chrau (Thomas 1966) and Sedang (Smith 1967) thesaurus organization, grouping entries by semantic fields. Theraphan 1984 (Nyahkur) is also organized semantically. Most of these have an alphabetical index in the back, in one, two, or three languages. In simpler fashion, most of the word lists available in little known languages and dialects are also arranged by semantic fields.

3. Content

3.1. Full dictionaries with illustrative sentences have been appearing recently, especially in the ILTRP series, for Mpi (Srinuan 1976), Surin Khmer (Dhanan 1978), Kui (Prasert 1978), and Bruu (Theraphan 1980), and in the Lawa (Suriya 1986) and forthcoming Karen dictionaries from Mahidol University, and in Nhim/Donaldson (1970). This last also has some illustrative drawings.

Full dictionaries including semantic field crossreferencing may be seen in the (microfiche only) dictionaries of Chrau (Thomas 1975) and Sedang (Smith 1975). Thus a typical full Chrau entry might give the form(s) of the word, the dialects where it has been recorded, a Vietnamese gloss, the definition, etymological information, the generic term to which it is subordinate (sub.), the terms for which it is itself the generic (gen.), the terms with which it is contrastive (contr.), the parts for which it is the whole (pt.), words with which it is commonly associated (ass.), synonyms (=), antonyms (opp.), and parallel terms used in doublets (//).

A full dictionary with context-sensitive sense discriminations is seen in Huffman/Proum 1978, each sense shown by an illustrative phrase.

3.2. There are quite a few good-sized dictionaries with just simple definitions, as for Mon (Halliday 1922, Shorto 1962), Cham (Aymonier/Cabaton 1906, Moussay 1971), Radê (Davias-Baudrit 1966, Shintani 1981, Tharp 1980), Bahnar (Banker 1979), Khmer (Headley 1977, Sakamoto 1976, and others), Wa (Zhou 1981), White Hmong (Heimbach 1979), Khmu' (Delcros 1966), Ngeq (Smith 1968?), Pacóh (Watson 1979) and a number of others. For a full listing see Huffman 1986.

3.3. For a number of languages only glossaries are available, i.e. simple one-word equivalents, as in the SIL vocabularies series, or Phạm Xuân Tín's vocabularies (Tín 1955, 1962).

3.4. For many languages and dialects the only lexicographic data available is that found in brief word lists. This is especially true of the small languages of southern Laos and of northern Vietnam. Some of these word lists have been published, as in Cabaton 1905 or Tuyên 1963, but most remain as manuscripts. Much lexicographic work needs to be done.

4. Format

4.1. Layout

The White Meo dictionary of Heimbach (1966) has the main entry flush with the right margin, the definitions start on the next line flush with the left margin, and the illustrative sentences are indented from the left margin.

1. Late bearing; slow in bearing (Contr. 'cauj') taj
   pobkws taj — late corn
   hniav taj — teeth that come in late
   hais lus taj tsawv — slow of speech (Cf. 'nrho')

Dictionary excerpt 262.1: Heimbach 1966, p. 311

ตลาด   ka:t กาด (น)   ʔoʔyɔh ta *ka:t*   ฉันไปตลาด

market   โอ๊ะ ย็อฮ ตะ กาด

Dictionary excerpt 262.2: Suwilai 1979, p. 105

The Khmu dictionary of Suwilai (1979) has the Thai and English glosses in the left column, the Khmu word in the middle column, and illustrative sentences in the right column with Thai translations. Other dictionaries tend to follow more standard formats.

4.2. Scripts

The Cham dictionary of Moussay (1971) has the old Cham (Phanrang) script form as its first column, then the roman script form as a second column. Keller 1976, which gives definitions and explanations in Khmer, has Khmer standard script and phonetic script on alternating pages.

MU'TUY mu·tuĕi	mồ côi (cha hay mẹ)	orphelin de père ou de mère
— mu·tuy ți ame'	mồ côi mẹ	orphelin de mère
— mu·tuy ți amur	mồ côi cha	orphelin de père

Dictionary excerpt 262.3: Moussay 1971, 226

More common is to have the script form as the main entry, followed immediately by a phonetic transcription, as in Headley 1977, or followed by a romanized form, as in Aymonier/Cabaton (1906).

The ILTRP dictionaries have the main entry in IPA phonetic script as the left column, with a Thai-based phonetic script directly under it.

phlù?
ผลุ

จ๋ม (ต้นไม้, หลัก)   to topple over (as of a tree, pole, etc.)

khàl lùuaŋ phlù? khrùum
ต้นไม้ล้มดังโครม   The tree toppled over with a crash

Dictionary excerpt 262.4: Prasert 1978, 30

Some use the Thai numerals for numbering Thai prefatory pages and indexes and roman numerals for the English prefatory pages and indexes.

5. Publication Form

Because lexicography in the smaller languages of Southeast Asia is still in such a preliminary state, only a small percentage of the works are published dictionaries. Many of the dictionaries are just small mimeographed editions, even the ILTRP series, many of them being run off by hand in remote mission stations. Some of the manuscript materials are available in microfiche, especially those from SIL. And with the advent of economical photocopying, some, e.g. Gray 1985, are available as photocopies upon demand.

6. Languages

6.1. Monolingual

The only monolingual dictionaries that I am aware of in this group of languages are those in Cambodian, a language with more than a millenium of recorded literary work and the only language in this group that is currently a national language. The Khmer dictionary of the Institut Bouddhique in its several editions has been the standard work.

6.2. Bilingual

Most dictionaries in the smaller languages are bilingual, usually with English or French, but occasionally with Thai, Vietnamese, Chinese, or Japanese. The large majority of these works have the local language as the main entry, but often with an index or finder list in the back of the book for English or French.

6.3. Multilingual

A number of the dictionaries are trilingual, consisting of the local language, the national language, and an international language, English or French. Shintani 1981 has Japanese as the third language with Rađê and Vietnamese. The ILTRP dictionaries and the SIL vocabularies are all trilingual. I have seen only two quadrilingual vocabularies: Tín 1955 (Jơrai, Chru, Vietnamese, English) and Woykos/vanderHaak 1986 (Kui, Northern Khmer, Thai, English).

7. Specialized Lexicography

Keller 1976 is an English-Khmer dictionary of medical terms. Suwilai 1985 is an analysis of diarrhea terms in several languages.

Shorto 1971 is a dictionary of Mon inscriptions. This is essentially a dictionary of Old and Middle Mon.

The manuscript rhyme books of many linguists are designed to facilitate phonological analysis and phonological reconstructions (see Sec. 2.2). The glosses are solely for the purpose of identifying morphemes, not for defining meanings.

8. Selected Bibliography

8.1. Dictionaries

Aymonier/Cabaton 1906 = Etienne Aymonier/Antoine Cabaton: Dictionnaire Cam-Français. Paris 1906 [xlvi, 587 p.].

Banker 1979 = John and Elizabeth Banker/Mơ: Bahnar Dictionary. Huntington Beach 1979 [xvi, 204 p.].

Davias-Baudrit 1966 = J. Davias-Baudrit: Dictionnaire Rhade-Français. Dalat 1966 [5, 514 p.].

Delcros 1966 = Henri Delcros/Jean Subra: Petit dictionnaire du language des Khmu' de la region de Xieng Khouang. Vientiane 1966 [138 p.].

Dhanan 1978 = Dhanan Chantrupanth/Chartchai Phromjakgarin: พจนานุกรมเขมร (สุรินทร์) — ไทย — อังกฤษ /Khmer (Surin)-Thai-English Dictionary. Bangkok 1978 [๒๖, xxv, 593, 4, ๒๐, 17, 3 p.].

Gray 1985 = Ian Gray: Khmu-English English-Khmu Dictionary. Belfast 1985 [iv, 93, 135 p.].

Halliday 1922 = Robert Halliday: A Mon-English Dictionary. Bangkok 1922 [xxx, 512 p.].

Headley 1977 = Robert Headley et al.: Cambodian-English Dictionary. Washington 1977 [xxvii, 1—708, 709—1495 p.].

Heimbach 1966 = Ernest E. Heimbach: White Meo to English Dictionary. Chiangmai 1966 [223 p.].

Heimbach 1979 = Ernest E. Heimbach: White Hmong Dictionary. Ithaca 1979 [xxv, 497 p.].

Huffman/Proum 1978 = Franklin Huffman/Im Proum: English-Khmer Dictionary/.

វចនានុក្រម អង់គ្លេស - ខ្មែរ
New Haven 1978 [xix, 690 p.].

Institut Bouddhique = Institut Bouddhique: Vacananukrama Khmera. Phnom Penh 1967—68 [5th ed., 2 vols.].

Keller 1976 = Sally Keller:
វចនានុក្រម ពេទ្យ អង់គ្លេស-ខ្មែរ
English-Khmer Medical Dictionary. Grand Forks 1976 [viii, 190 p.].

Lombard 1960 = Sylvia J. Lombard: Yao-English Dictionary. Ithaca 1960 [xvi, 363 p. Ed. by H. Purnell].

Moussay 1971 = Gerard Moussay et al.:
ꩀꩌꨯꨂ ꨚꨀꨳꨯꨩꩀ
Dictionnaire Căm-Vietnamien-Français/Tự-điển Chàm-Việt-Pháp. Phanrang 1971 [xli, 498, 95 p.].

Nhim/Donaldson 1970 = Điêu Chinh Nhim/Jean Donaldson: Tai-Vietnamese-English Vocabulary. Saigon 1970 [xvii, 476 p.].

Prasert 1978 = Prasert Sriwises: พจนานุกรมกูยส่วย-ไทย—อังกฤษ Kui (Suai)-Thai-English Dictionary. Bangkok 1978 [ฬ, xxvii, 434, 18, 13, 23 p. Ed. by Theraphan L. Thongkum/Jerry W. Gainey].

Sakamoto 1976 = Yasuyuki Sakamoto: アフリカ.アフリカ語の計海研究 (Khmer-Japanese Dictionary]. Tokyo 1976 [444 p.].

Shintani 1981 = Tadahiko L. A. Shintani (Y. Mrâo Ênao-Mrô): Boh Blŭ Êđê — Yuan — Za Pô Nê/Từ Vựng Êđê — Việt — Nhật/ ラテン語―ベトナム語―日本語 Tokyo 1981 [448 p.].

Shorto 1962 = Harry L. Shorto: A Dictionary of Modern Spoken Mon. London 1962 [xvi, 614 p.].

Shorto 1971 = Harry L. Shorto: A Dictionary of the Mon Inscriptions from the Sixth to the Sixteenth Centuries. Oxford 1971 [xli, 406 p.].

Smith 1967 = Kenneth D. Smith: Sedang Vocabulary. Saigon 1967 [xi, 128 p.].

Smith 1975 = Kenneth D. Smith: Sedang Dictionary. Dallas 1975 microfiche [2265 p.].

Smith 1968? = Ronald Smith: Ngeq Rhyme Dictionary: Ngeq-English. Dallas 1975 microfiche [c. 300 p.].

Srinuan 1976 = Srinuan Duanghom: An Mpi Dictionary. Bangkok 1976 [xvi, 477 p.].

Suriya 1986 = Suriya Ratanakul/Lakhana Daoratanahong: พจนานุกรมภาษาละว้า - ไทย /Lawa — Thai Dictionary. Bangkok 1986 (BE.2529) [20, 421 , ก].

Suwilai 1979 = Suwilai Premsrirat/Phikulthong Ruchirapha/Sukhumawadee Khamhiran/Phayao Memanas: พจนานุกรมไทย — ขมุ [Thai-Khmu Dictionary]. Bangkok 1979 (BE.2522) [xxx, 315, ๒๒, 27].

Tharp 1980 = J. A. Tharp/Y-Bham Buon-Ya: A Rhadé-English Dictionary, with English-Rhadé finderlist. Canberra 1980 [xi, 271 p.].

Theraphan 1980 = Theraphan L. Thongkum/See Puengpa: พจนานุกรมบรู — ไทย — อังกฤษ Bruu-Thai-English Dictionary. Bangkok 1980 [ฎ, xiii, 614 p.].

Theraphan 1984 = Theraphan L. Thongkum: Nyah Kur (Chaobon)-Thai-English Dictionary. Bangkok 1984 [xii, 522].

Thomas 1966 = David Thomas/Thổ Sang Luc: Chrau Vocabulary. Saigon 1966 [xv, 128 p.].

Thomas 1975 = David Thomas/Dorothy Thomas: Chrau Dictionary. Dallas 1975 microfiche (c 1300 p.].

Tín 1955 = Phạm Xuân Tín: Lexique Polyglotte. Dalat 1955 [154 p.].

Tín 1962 = Phạm Xuân Tín: Bahnar Golar Vocabulary. Đờnduờng 1962 [77 p.].

Tuyên 1963 = Vương Hoàng Tuyên: Các dân tộc nguồn gốc Nam Á miền bác Việt Nam. Hànội 1963.

Watson 1979 = Richard Watson/Saundra Watson/Cubuat: Pacóh Dictionary. Huntington Beach 1979 [xv, 447 p.].

Woykos/vanderHaak 1986 = (anon.): พจนานุกรมภาพสี่ภาษา [Four-language picture dictionary]. Bangkok 1986 [95 p.].

Zhou 1981 = Zhou Zhi Zhi/Yan Xi Xiang et al.: Pug Lai Cix Ding Yiie Si Ndong Lai Vax Mai Lai Hox/佤汉简明词典 Beijing 1981 [16, 332 p.].

8.2. Other Publications

Cabaton 1905 = Antoine Cabaton: Dix dialectes indochinois recueillis par Prosper Odend'hal; étude linguistique. In: Journal Asiatique 10th ser., 5. 1905, 265—344.

Huffman 1986 = Franklin Huffman: Bibliography and Index of Mainland Southeast Asian Languages and Linguistics. New Haven 1986.

Suwilai 1985 = Suwilai Premsrirat: Language and Diarrheal Diseases. Paper presented at 19th Sino-Tibetan Conference, Bangkok, 1985.

David Thomas, Summer Institute of Linguistics, Bangkok (Thailand)

XXVIII: Lexikographie der Einzelsprachen XII: Ostasiatische Sprachen
Lexicography of Individual Languages XII: The Languages of East Asia
Lexicographie des langues particulières XII: Langues est-asiatiques

263. Chinese Lexicography

1. Introduction
2. Lexicography and the Chinese Language
3. Types of Chinese Dictionaries
4. Arrangement of Chinese Dictionaries
5. Summary
6. Selected Bibliography

1. Introduction

The Chinese language is a member of the Sino-Tibetan language family. It is the language of the Han (汉) people, the major Chinese racial group, and is the national language of the People's Republic of China ("Mainland China") and of the Republic of China (on the island of Taiwan or Formosa), as well as various Overseas Chinese communities such as Hong Kong (cf. Map 263.1). It has been estimated that there are more than one billion speakers of Chinese, making it the world's most commonly spoken language. Lexicography in China has enjoyed a long and interesting history. At times lexicography and lexicographers have been at the forefront of nation-wide language reform movements, and at other times both have been ignored or dismissed as irrelevant. Some dictionaries have been included among the great books of China and others have been suppressed or destroyed. While some lexicographers have enjoyed privilege and fame at court or in the scholarly community, others, in the not too distant past, have been ignominiously dispatched to the countryside to "learn from the peasants." To a certain extent, Chinese lexicography reflects the history of China, of the Chinese language, and of the Chinese people. — The existence of dictionaries in China was mentioned as early as the Yin (殷) Dynasty (14th—11th century B.C.) (Chen 1985). One of the first known dictionaries was Shizhoupian (史籀篇, 'Chanted Histories Chapters'), a fifteen chapter work by the court historian during the reign of King Xuan (宣王, 827 B.C. — 781 B.C.) of the Zhou (周) Dynasty (11th century B.C. — 256 B.C.). Unfortunately, Shizhoupian, like many other early Chinese dictionaries, did not survive the centuries. The dictionaries that have survived attest to the diversity and vitality of lexicography in China.

2. Lexicography and the Chinese Language

The Chinese language is more than 6,000 years old. Throughout its long history, the language has undergone evolutionary and, at the same time, revolutionary changes. Lexicography has played an important role in this process. Initially, dictionaries served as tools to stabilize Chinese script styles and standardize the written language. In former times, dictionaries were also closely identified with the scholar-official class and not a few were compiled under imperial auspices. In recent years, dictionaries have been instrumental in popularizing language reform efforts. Overall, dictionaries have been important resources in the study of the Chinese language and linguistics.

2.1. The Chinese written language is made up of symbols commonly called characters. A character is made up of a series of strokes written in the general pattern of top to bottom and left to right. Characters are formed according to set principles known as the Six Categories (六书, liùshū). The Six Categories are:

(1) Self-explanatory characters (e.g., "上" (shàng, 'above') and "下" (xià, 'below')), characters whose shape indicate their meaning;

(2) Pictographic characters (e.g., "月" (yuè, 'moon') and "日" (rì, 'sun')), charac-

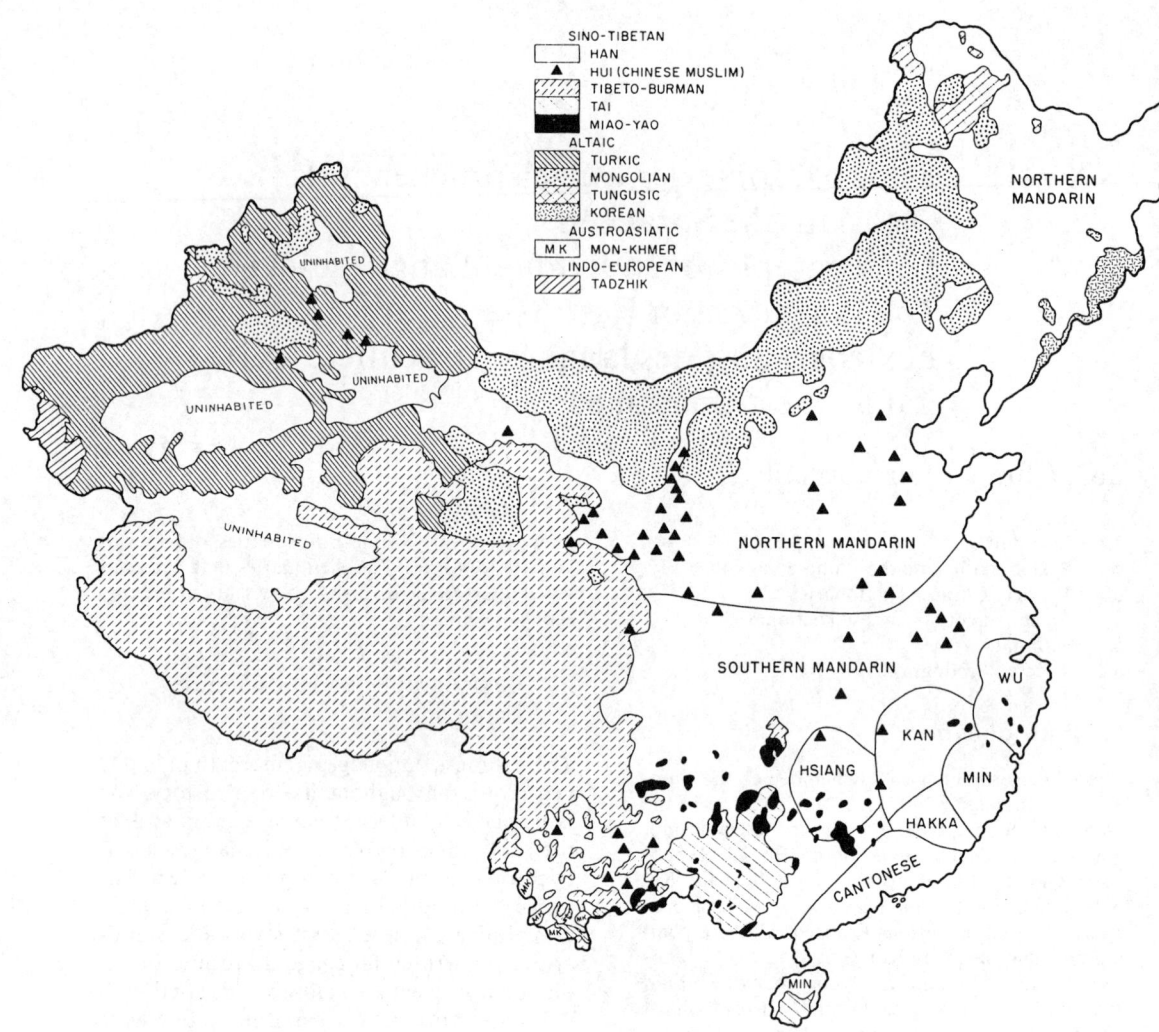

Map 263.1: People's Republic of China: Ethnolinguistic distribution (in: Area Handbook for the People's Republic of China 1972, 89)

ters whose ancient shapes were simple pictographs;

(3) Picto-phonetic characters (e.g., the character "河" which combines the element indicating water (氵) with the phonetic (可, pronounced kě) to mean "river" which is pronounced hé);

(4) Associative compounds (e.g., the components "止" (zhǐ, stop) and "戈" (gē, 'spear') are combined to form the character "武" meaning "military");

(5) Synonymous characters (e.g., "老" (lǎo, 'old') which is synonymous with "考" (kǎo, 'long life')); and

(6) Phonetic loan characters (e.g., the ancient character for wheat "来" which was pronounced lái was borrowed to represent the sound lái meaning "to come, to arrive").

The earliest known characters date from the Shang (商) Dynasty (c. 16th—11th century B.C.). At that time characters were simple pictographs carved first on oracle bones and tortoise shells (甲骨文, jiǎgǔwén) and later on bronze objects (金文, jīnwén). By the time of the Qin (秦) Dynasty (221 B.C.—207 B.C.) there were eight major forms of characters in use. Although short-lived, the Qin was a significant dynasty in many respects. In addition to bringing together the various Chinese states into a unified empire, the leaders of the Qin also instituted a number of significant reforms. One of the more important reforms was the stabilization of the Chinese script. The script stabilization movement was spearheaded by Li Si (李斯, d. 208 B.C.), Prime Minister of the Qin. Li adopted the small seal (小篆, xiǎozhuàn) script, a simplification and refinement of the great seal (大篆, dàzhuàn) script as the official script of the Qin Dynasty and used it in his dictionary Cangjiepian (苍颉篇, 'The Cang Jie Chapters'). The small seal script, was also used by Zhao Gao (赵高), Grand Councillor of the Qin, in Yuanlipian (爰历篇, 'The Yuan Li Chapters'), and by Hu Wujing (胡毋敬), Qin Chariot Master, in Boxuepian (博学篇, 'The Erudite Chapters'). These dictionaries, collectively known as the 'Three Cangs' (三苍), were used throughout the Qin empire as textbooks to teach writing and were instrumental in establishing the primacy of the small seal script. It was also during the Qin Dynasty that the official script (隶书, lìshū) became current, especially in legal circles. Official script is a further simplification of the small seal script and is the basis of modern Chinese script styles. The following chart shows the development of characters from earliest times up to the Qin:

Oracle bone				
Bronze				
Great Seal				
Small Seal				
Official	車	馬	魚	塵
	cart	horse	fish	dust

Fig. 263.1: Qin Dynasty Scripts (in: Zhang 1980, 52)

By the time the Qin fell to the Han (汉) Dynasty (206 B.C.—220 A.D.), China was not only unified politically, but also linguistically by a common written language. — The Han was the first great Chinese dynasty. The more than four hundred years of relative stability that it enjoyed was highlighted by the flowering of the arts, the establishment of Confucianism as the dominant philosophy at court, and the continued expansion and consolidation of the empire. The first true Chinese dictionary, Shuowen Jiezi (说文解字, 'Explaining Pictographic Characters and Analyzing Composite Characters') (Xu 100 A.D.), appeared during the Han Dynasty. Shuowen was compiled by Xu Shen (许慎, 58—147), a local government official, and contained 9,000 entries ranging from the oracle bone characters of ancient times to the common characters of the day. The dictionary was a watershed in both history of the Chinese language and Chinese lexicography. In Shuowen, Xu introduced a number of innovations including the concept of radicals (cf. 4.1.1.) and the Six Categories, both of which are still used in Chinese lexicography. Shuowen Jiezi also had a significant impact on the Chinese language. Up to the Han, the language had developed almost unchecked as scribes, either ignorant or unconcerned about correct usage, introduced numerous character variants into the language. This trend was temporarily halted after the dissemination of Shuowen and other Han Dynasty reference works that served as authoritative guides to correct language usage.

2.2. To help govern their far-flung empire, the Han rulers instituted an examination system to recruit "men of talent" which, over the centuries, developed into the Chinese civil service system. Success in the civil service examination system became one of the highest ideals in Chinese society and led to the rise of the scholar-official class. Almost from the beginning examination success depended more on literary erudition and mastery and memorization of the classical literature than on the practical matters of governance. It is safe to assume that the examination candidates at least were familiar with the major lexicographic works such as Shuowen Jiezi and Erya (cf. 3.2.2.). Certain specialized dictionaries such as rhyme books (cf. 3.4.) were especially useful to examination candidates because the tests were composed of a series of highly stylized essays that had to be written in intricate rhyme patterns. One dictionary in particular, Li Bu Yunlue (礼部韵略, 'The Board of Rites Outline of Rhymes'), was widely used during the Song (宋) Dynasty (960—1279) if for no other reason than it was the official guide to correct rhymes used by the Board of Rites, the overseers of the civil service examination system (Waters 1889, Chen 1985). In a sense, dictionary-making and preparation for the civil service were inter-related in that most of the dictionaries before the fall of Imperial China in 1911 were compiled by scholars who were in some way involved in the examination system. Only this elite class could afford the time-consuming effort to achieve literacy, much less to prepare for the civil service examinations, which for many was a life-long endeavor.

2.3. As the written Chinese language slowly evolved, the vocabulary dramatically expanded. With the natural increase in the language inventory due to advances in all segments of society over the centuries and particularly because of China's rich and illustrious literary heritage, the number of characters multiplied. During the Qing (清) Dynasty (1644—1911), Emperor Kangxi (r. 1662—1722), commissioned a dictionary to catalog the language. The dictionary, Kangxi Zidian (康熙字典, 'The Kangxi Character Dictionary') (Kangxi 1716), named in honor of the emperor, contained almost 47,000 individual characters. Like Shuowen Jiezi, the Kangxi Zidian was a milestone in the history of Chinese lexicography. It was the most comprehensive Chinese dictionary until the twentieth century and chronicled the almost five-fold increase in the number of characters in the language since the time of Shuowen Jiezi. Kangxi Zidian was the first dictionary to be given the title 'zidian'. The emperor declared that the dictionary was so complete and authoritative that it was indeed a "diǎn" or "canon" of characters (Xue 1982). — It was also during the Qing Dynasty that textual criticism flourished as scholars, for philosophical as well as philological reasons, engaged in rigorous analyses of ancient texts, including dictionaries. Important works on ancient dictionaries such as Wang Niansun's (王念孙, 1744—1832) study on Guangya (cf. 3.2.2.) entitled Guangya Shuzheng (广雅疏证, 'Exegetical Evidence for Guangya') (Wang 1778?) and Hao Yixing's (郝懿行, 1757—1825) investigation of Erya (cf. 3.2.2.) called Erya Yishu (尔雅义疏, 'Exegesis of Erya') (Hao 1865) helped scholars recreate ancient pronunciations, furthered the study of etymologies, and led to a general awakening of language studies. Undoubtedly, the most impressive philological study during the Qing Dynasty was Duan Yucai's (段玉裁, 1735—1815) Shuowen Jiezi Zhu (说文解字主, 'Commentary on Shuowen Jiezi') (Duan 1807), a masterful recreation and commentary on Shuowen Jiezi. Duan's work is considered to be a landmark in the study of the ancient Chinese language and itself has been the object of numerous studies and commentaries.

2.4. In recent decades, the Chinese language has undergone radical changes. Since 1949 and the victory of the Chinese Communist Party over the Kuomintang Party and the establishment of two Chinas, i.e., the People's Republic of China (PRC) on the Asian mainland and the Republic of China (ROC) on the island of Taiwan, two varieties of standard Chinese have emerged. In the PRC, the government promotes a standard spoken language based on the Beijing (Peking) dialect and a written language that employs simplified characters (简体字, jiǎntǐzì) and is written in lines, Western-style, from left to right. In the ROC, the government advocates a standard language generally based on the Beijing dialect and a written language that features complex characters (繁体字, fántǐzì) that, in most cases, is written in lines in the traditional Chinese style of top to bottom and right to left. A marked difference in the vocabulary of the two brands of standard Chinese has developed over the years that is somewhat comparable to the difference between American and British English. It has even been suggested that the two brands of Chinese will eventually develop into two separate languages (Li 1985). — The Chinese Communists began experimenting with simplified characters in the 1930s in an attempt to increase literacy. After 1949, character simplification became official policy in the PRC. In 1956 a list of 554 approved simplified characters was issued, followed by another list of 2,238 characters and character components in 1964. A third list of characters to be simplified was issued in 1977, but was later recalled after it was roundly criticized as being too drastic in that it made certain characters virtually indistinguishable. The general principles of simplification are to reduce the number of strokes needed to write a character and to reduce the number of characters in everyday use. In reducing the number of strokes, a character is abbreviated, usually based on the way in which it is written cursively. For example, the characters listed in Fig. 263.1 are written in their simplified forms as follows: "车", "马", "鱼" and "尘". The number of characters in everyday use is reduced by subsuming variants under one common form. For example, the characters "城", "硷", "礆", "鹼" and "鼸" are now represented by the single character "碱" in the PRC. — The educational systems and the mass media have been the driving forces in the language reform and standardization movements in the PRC and the ROC, but several dictionaries have also played an important role. In the PRC, the character dictionary Xinhua Zidian (新华字典, 'The New China Character Dictionary') (Xinhua 1953), first published by the Ministry of Education and later by the Commercial Press, has been revised periodically to reflect changes in language policy. Because it is considered an authoritative source on pronunciation and simplified characters and because of its relatively inexpensive price, Xinhua is one of the most popular dictionaries in the PRC. Another important PRC dictionary supporting language efforts is Xiandai Hanyu Cidian (现代汉语词典, 'A Dictionary of Contemporary Chinese') (Xianhan 1979). Xiandai Hanyu Cidian was the first major dictionary of character-combinations published in the PRC. It was compiled by the Chinese Academy of Social Sciences at the direction of the State Council of the PRC for the express purpose of unifying the Chinese language by standardizing the vocabulary and popularizing the common spoken language (普通话, pǔtōnghuà). The counterpart to Xiandai Hanyu Cidian in the ROC is Guoyu Ribao Cidian (国语日报辞典, 'The Mandarin Daily News Dictionary') (He 1974) edited by He Rong (何容) and published by the Mandarin Daily News of Taibei. Both He and the newspaper are closely identified with the language standardization movement in Taiwan. The dictionary is especially useful for reading newspapers and other literature from Taiwan and Overseas Chinese communities.

3. Types of Chinese Dictionaries

Of the literally thousands of Chinese dictionaries that have been compiled over the centuries, all can be divided into four general categories. The four categories are character dictionaries, character-combination dictionaries, dialect dictionaries, and rhyme dictionaries. The first two categories concern the composition of the entry word, while the second two categories pertain to the content of the dictionary.

3.1. Character Dictionaries

The purpose of a character dictionary or 字典, 'zìdiǎn' is to define individual characters. An individual character is often a complex lexical unit. It is not uncommon for a character to have a dozen or more separate meanings. The character "一" (yī), for example, has more than thirty definitions, in addition to its basic meaning of "one, the number one". Many characters have multiple pronunciations as well. For instance, the character "番" has six pronunciations (fān, fán, bō, pó, pān and pán), with each pronunciation value having a distinct meaning. In general, 'zìdiǎn' are intended for language scholars working with the classical or literary language where an individual character often assumes the dimension of a phrase or an entire sentence. Because 'zìdiǎn' usually contain many difficult or rare characters, they are often arranged according to the shape of the characters (cf. 4.1.). The more noteworthy 'zìdiǎn' such as Zhonghua Da Zidian and Hanyu Da Zidian, tend to be encyclopedic and contain between 40,000 and 50,000 entries. Even in the more modern 'zìdiǎn' definitions are often written in a classical or semi-classical style, perhaps as much to save space as to lend a literary elegance to the dictionary. Although somewhat difficult to use because of their size and style of definitions, 'zìdiǎn' represent the essence of Chinese lexicography.

3.1.1. One of the first 'zìdiǎn' and one of the most respected of all Chinese dictionaries is Xu Shen's Shuowen Jiezi (cf. 2.1.). Despite the fact that Kangxi Zidian (cf. 2.3.) was the first dictionary to be given the title 'zìdiǎn', it is often criticized for its inadequate definitions, inaccurate citations and difficult arrangement. A sometimes overlooked 'zìdiǎn' is Mei Yingzuo's (梅膺祚) Zihui (字汇, 'A Collection of Individual Characters') (Mei 1615). Mei, like Xu Shen, was an innovator in Chinese lexicography. He revised Xu's radical system, arranged entries within each section by the number of strokes in a character (cf. 4.1.2.), and popularized a straightforward defining style (Xue 1982). Other major 'zìdiǎn' include the Zhonghua Da Zidian and Hanyu Da Zidian. Zhonghua Da Zidian (中华大字典, 'An Encyclopedic Dictionary of Chinese Characters') (Zhonghua 1915), is a 48,000 entry dictionary compiled under the editorship of Lu Feikui, (陆费逵). Until recently it was the most complete and was considered by many to be the finest 'zidian'. Zhonghua Da Zidian most likely will be supplanted by Hanyu Da Zidian (汉语大字典, 'An Encyclopedic Character Dictionary of the Chinese Language') (Han Da Zi 1986) currently being compiled in the PRC. Hanyu Da Zidian is to contain more than 56,000 individual characters, making it the largest 'zidian' ever produced. It will be published in eight large volumes between late 1986 and 1991.

3.1.2. 'Zidian' not only serve the needs of the language scholar by their encyclopedic treatment of tens of thousands of characters, but are also useful tools for those learning the basic meaning of a character. 'Zidian' aimed at the learner usually contain between one and six thousand characters. The definitions in these smaller dictionaries often include everyday character combinations to help the student learn the use of the individual character in relation to other characters.

3.2. Character-combination dictionaries

Character-combination dictionaries or 词典'cídiǎn' are general language dictionaries for the everyday dictionary user. They contain both individual characters and characters used in combination with other characters. Although 'cidian' existed in ancient times, they are essentially a product of the twentieth century. It was not until the language reforms brought about during the May Fourth (1919) Movement that the primarily monosyllabic-based classical written language was replaced by the modern written language based on the decidedly polysyllabic-based vernacular language. The need for 'cidian' increased as the new literature of this movement began to proliferate and as the reading public gradually expanded.

3.2.1. The distinction between a 'zidian' and a 'cidian' is sometimes confused when the latter is referred to as a "word" dictionary. This tends to leave the mistaken impression that the individual characters in a 'zidian' are not "words", suggesting that they derive their meaning only as elements used in combination with other characters to form "words". Although some characters such as "琵" (pí) and "琶" (pá) can be used only in combination (琵琶, meaning a plucked stringed musical instrument), most individual characters have a lexical meaning as a single character unit and therefore must also be considered "words". Titles can further contribute to the confusion between the two types of dictionaries. Strictly speaking, 'zidian' should be used only with character dictionaries and 'cidian' only with character-combination dictionaries. However, 'zidian' is sometimes used in the title of character-combination dictionaries in an attempt to borrow on the prestige of Kangxi Zidian. — Although confusion may arise between a 'zidian' and 'cidian', there can be no confusion between the two when the contents are examined. The treatment of the individual character "另" (lìng) in the 'zidian' Zhonghua Da Zidian and in the 'cidian' Xiandai Hanyu Cidian illustrates the difference between the two types of dictionaries.

Zhonghua

Xiandai Hanyu

Dictionary excerpt 263.1: 'Zidian' vs. 'Cidian' (in: Zhonghua 1980, 204 and Xianhan 1979, 715)

As can be seen from the entry in Zhonghua Da Zidian, the character "另" is defined only as an individual character with two separate definitions. In the example from Xiandai Hanyu Cidian, the character "另" is not only defined as an individual character, but also as a character bound with others to form the lexical units "另起炉灶", "另外" and

"另眼相看" and in free combination with other characters such as "选", "议", etc. — The problem of determining lexical units for 'cidian' is a difficult one. The Chinese language lexicographer cannot even fall back on the notion that whatever is separated by a space in written text may be considered a lexical unit because in written Chinese there are spaces between every character. There are, nevertheless, definite bound or semi-bound forms of character combinations such as "另外" (lìngwài, 'besides, in addition to') in the example above that make up the lexical inventory for 'cidian' dictionaries. Much work remains to be done on the problem of word units.

3.2.2. Perhaps the first Chinese reference work to collect and define character combinations was Erya (尔雅, literally "approaching refined"), which, unfortunately, is no longer extant. Erya is believed to have been compiled by Confucian scholars sometime before the second century B.C. It has a revered place in Chinese literature and is one of the books included in the Thirteen Confucian Classics. Following Erya a number of dictionaries such as Guangya (广雅, 'Extension of (Er)Ya') by Zhang Yi (张揖) of the Wei (魏) Dynasty (220—265) were either named in honor of it or like Shiming (释名, 'Explanation of Names') (Liu 200?) by the Han Dynasty scholar Liu Xi (刘熙) were modelled after it. — In addition to the medium-sized Xiandai Hanyu Cidian and Guoyu Ribao Cidian (cf. 2.4.), three important large-size 'cidian' are Ciyuan, Cihai and Guoyu Cidian. Ciyuan (辞源, 'Origin of Words') (Ciyuan 1915) was compiled by a team of scholars headed by Lu Erkui (陆尔奎) and published in 1915, making it one of the first dictionaries compiled after the fall of Imperial China. Coming at the beginning of the vernacular movement of the 1910s and 1920s, Ciyuan retains the flavor of the classical language in both entry selection and its defining language. Cihai (辞海, 'Sea of Words') (Cihai 1938) was compiled under the direction of Shu Xincheng (舒新城). Although Cihai is somewhat smaller than Ciyuan (85,830 entries as compared to 98,994), Cihai tends to have more complete and encyclopedic-type definitions (Chen 1985). Both dictionaries are more in the European tradition of dictionaries of "hard words" than of the everyday vocabulary. In 1958 the PRC government, at the suggestion of Mao Zedong (毛泽东, 1893—1976), decided to revise both Ciyuan and Cihai. After years of work, the revised Ciyuan (volume one of four volumes) and Cihai (in three volumes) were published in 1979 to commemorate the thirtieth anniversary of the founding of the PRC. According to a pre-arranged division of labor, coverage of the language in Ciyuan stops at about the Opium War (1840), while Cihai remains a general reference work including ancient and modern terms, scientific and technical terms, and personal and place names. Guoyu Cidian (国语辞典, 'A Dictionary of the National Language') (Guoyu 1937) was published in 1937 under the sponsorship of the Chinese Ministry of Education as part of an effort to help standardize the language. The dictionary has been reprinted a number of times in various forms. In 1979 the ROC Ministry of Education issued a revised and enlarged edition of the dictionary. The original dictionary, although professing to be of the "national language", tended to emphasize the Beijing colloquial language. Nonetheless, Guoyu Cidian was one of the first general language Chinese dictionaries and was used as a basis for several bilingual dictionaries with Chinese.

3.2.3. Despite the long and active history of lexicography in China, only two encyclopedic 'cidian' have been compiled. In fact, the first such dictionary, Morohashi Tetsuji's Dai Kan Wa Jiten (大汉和辞典, 'A Chinese-Japanese Encyclopedic Dictionary') (Morohashi 1957), was compiled in Japan. The first encyclopedic 'cidian' published by the Chinese was Zhongwen Da Cidian (中文大辞典, 'An Encyclopedic Dictionary of the Chinese Language') (Zhongwen 1962). Zhongwen Da Cidian was produced by a team of more than 125 scholars at the Institute of Advanced Studies in Taibei, Taiwan under the direction of Zhang Qiyun (张其昀) and was based on Dai Kan Wa Jiten. Zhongwen is a massive dictionary of almost 50,000 individual characters and more than 370,000 character combinations. The first comprehensive 'cidian' to be published in the PRC will be Hanyu Da Cidian (汉语大词典, 'An Encyclopedic Dictionary of the Chinese Language') (Han Da Ci 1986). In a division of labor similar to that between Cihai and Ciyuan, Hanyu Da Cidian and Hanyu Da Zidian were conceived as complementary dictionaries. Therefore, Hanyu Da Cidian will not emphasize individual characters to the extent of Hanyu Da Zidian. According to pre-publication information, Hanyu Da Cidian will contain approximately 20,000 individual characters and more than 350,000 character combinations. It is to be published in ten volumes between late 1986 and 1990 at a projected rate of about two volumes per year.

3.3. Dialect Dictionaries

It is no exaggeration to say that China is a nation of dialects. There are seven major dialect groups, namely,

(1) the Northern dialect (e.g., Beijing),
(2) the Wu (吳) dialect (of the central-coastal provinces of Jiangsu and Zhejiang),
(3) the Xiang (湘) dialect (of Hunan province in central China),
(4) the Gan (贛) dialect (of Jiangxi province in southeastern China),
(5) the Hakka (客家) dialect (of a people living primarily in southern China and Taiwan),
(6) the Yue (粵) or Cantonese dialect (spoken in the southern provinces of Guangdong and Guangxi Zhuang Autonomous Region), and
(7) the Min (閩) dialect (spoken in the southern coastal province of Fujian and in Taiwan).

Within each dialect group there are numerous subgroups. For example, there are more than twenty varieties of the Wu dialect. Across the dialects there is enough variation or "mutual unintelligibility" that the dialects can be considered separate spoken languages (Kratochvil 1968, DeFrancis 1984). Although a person speaking only the Shanghai dialect cannot intelligently converse with a person speaking only the Cantonese dialect, they can communicate in writing. It is the common written language, more than the common spoken language, that bridges the gap between the dialects.

3.3.1.
One of the first and still most impressive dialect dictionaries is Yang Xiong's (揚雄, 53 B.C.—18 A.D.) Fangyan (方言, 'Dialects') (Fangyan 18 A.D.). Yang spent twenty-seven years gathering regionalisms from central China and as far north as Korea. The original Fangyan was a fifteen chapter work of between 9,000—11,000 entries and, following in the style of Erya, defined entries in synonym clusters. A typical entry in Fangyan is Dictionary excerpt 263.2.

黨, 曉 and 哲 all mean knowledge. In the state of Chu [present-day Hubei and Hunan Provinces in central China] 黨 [...] was used with 曉 as a variant. In the area between the States of Qi [present-day Shandong in northeast China] and Song [present-day Henan Province also in northeast China] 哲 was used.

Dictionary excerpt 263.2: Fangyan (in: Fangyan 1936, 1)

Like the other great dictionaries, Fangyan spawned an entire genre in Chinese lexicography that has continued to the present. The government of the PRC has been sensitive to the need to develop dialect dictionaries and similar language material even though it is actively trying to promote a common spoken language. Two noteworthy PRC works are Hanyu Fangyin Zihui (汉语方音字汇, 'A Glossary of Regional Pronunciations of Chinese Characters') (Han Fang Zi 1962) and Hanyu Fangyan Cihui (汉语方言词汇, 'A Glossary of Chinese Dialects') (Han Fang Ci 1964). Hanyu Fangyin Zihui contains 2,700 individual characters with their ancient and modern pronunciations for seventeen major dialect regions, while Hanyu Fangyan Cihui lists 905 vocabulary items with their equivalents in eighteen regions. Pronunciation in both dictionaries is given in the International Phonetic Alphabet.

3.4. Rhyme Dictionaries

Poetry may be the highest form of Chinese literature. From as early as the 'Book of Poetry' (诗经, Shi Jing), a collection of poems from before the seventh century B.C., to the great poets of the Tang and Song dynasties, and up to the present, poetry has captured the imagination of the Chinese people. Chinese poetry is as stylized as it is spontaneous. Poems are usually written in lines of four, five or seven syllables, and follow strict rhyme and tonal patterns. For example, in a poem of seven syllables per line, the seventh character in lines one, two, four, six and eight should rhyme (Liu 1962). Rhymes were equally important in the dramatic verse of the Yuan Dynasty (1271—1368) and in opera. Rhyme dictionaries (韵书, yùnshū) came into being to help writers make the correct rhymes.

3.4.1. The first Chinese rhyme dictionary was Sheng Lei (声类, 'Sound Categories'), a ten chapter work by Li Deng (李登) of the Wei Dynasty. Sheng Lei contained more than 11,000 entries and was arranged according to the ancient five-tone musical scale. The prototype for rhyme dictionaries is Lu Fayan's (陆法言) Qie Yun (切韵, 'Spelling Rhymes'), which was completed in 601. Qie Yun was a five volume dictionary arranged under 193 rhyme classifications. Although no longer extant, much of Qie Yun was incorporated in the rhyme dictionary Guangyun (广韵, 'Extension of Rhymes') (Guangyun 1011). Guangyun was compiled under imperial auspices by a team of scholars headed by Chen Pengnian (陈彭年). It is arranged under 206 rhymes and contains 26,194 head characters. A typical entry includes a definition, notes on pronunciation, homonyms, variant pronunciations, and variant character forms. The character "冬" (dōng, 'winter') is entered as in Dictionary excerpt 263.3.

In addition to its rhyme information, Guangyun is an important source of information on early Chinese pronunciation. Another important rhyme dictionary is Ji Yun. Ji Yun (集韵, 'Collection of Rhymes') (Ji

冬又姓前燕慕容皝左司馬冬壽都宗切七

冬四時之末尸子曰冬爲信北方爲冬冬終也

Winter. The last of the four seasons. According to Shi Zi [a disciple of Confucius] 冬 is a marker, the north is 冬. 冬 means the end. It is also a surname. [There was a] Dong Shou [who] held the office of Zuo Sima under the early emperor Morong Huang. It is pronounced d[u][z]ong. [There are] Seven [more characters under the same sound].

Dictionary excerpt 263.3: dōng (in: Guangyun 1704, 21)

Yun 1037) was compiled under the direction of Ding Du (丁度, 990—1053) and also benefited from imperial patronage. Ji Yun, with its 52,525 entries, is the largest rhyme dictionary.

4. Arrangement of Chinese Dictionaries

The graphic nature of the Chinese language has challenged the lexicographer to devise inventive look-up schemes that enable the user to quickly find the character(s) in question. Some lexicographers have been very inventive indeed by creating arrangement systems with intriguing names such as "the head and tail method", "the root-shape-number index method", and "the video codes". In general, all of the arrangement schemes used in Chinese dictionaries are based on either the shape or sound of a character or by subject categories.

4.1. Shape

Perhaps the most common arrangement scheme is by the shape of a character. The major shape-based arrangement schemes include radicals, the configuration of the character, and the Four-Corner System.

4.1.1. Radicals

A radical (部首, bùshǒu), also called signific, key, classifier or determinative, is the element that generally indicates the basic meaning of a Chinese character. For example, characters having to do with water (e.g., "河" (hé, 'river') and "湖" (hú, 'lake')) contain the "water" radical (氵), while those concerning metal (e.g., "锡" (xī, 'tin') and "铜" (tóng, 'copper')) include the "metal" radical (钅). Usually, the radical is found at the left, top or bottom of a character. — Looking up characters in a radical-sorted dictionary is a three-

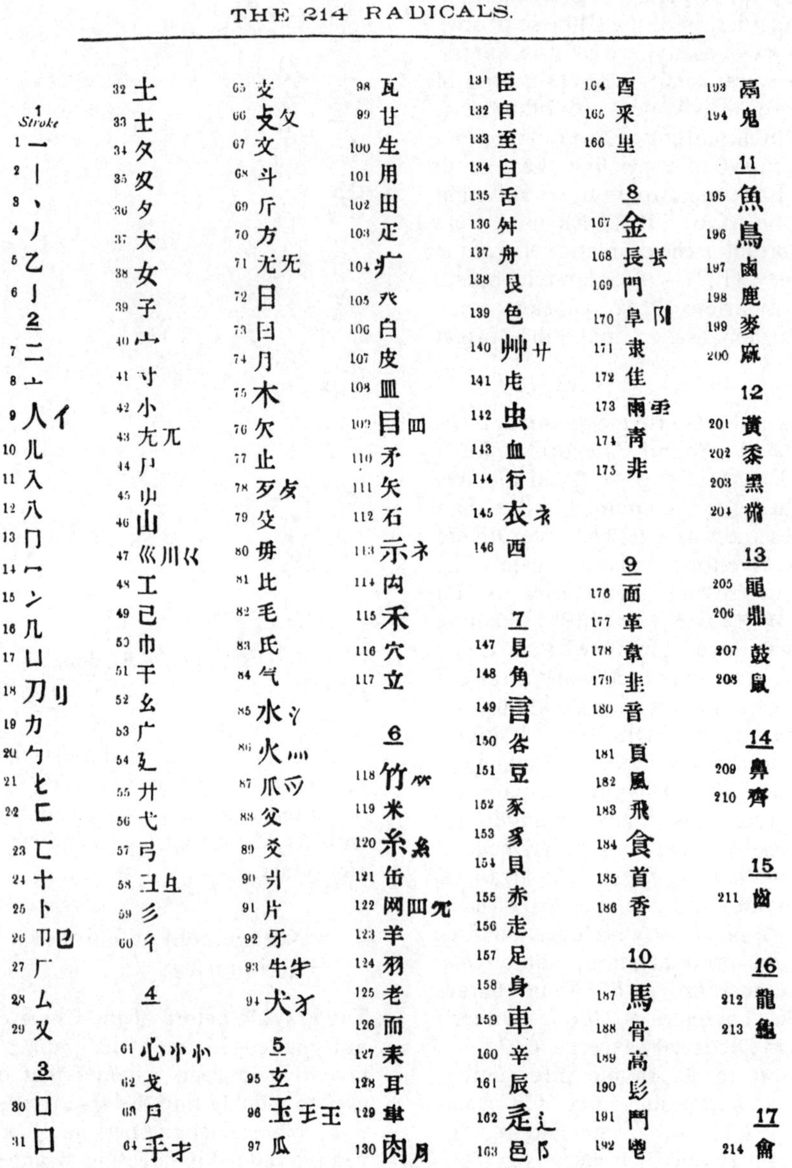

Fig. 263.2: The Kangxi Radicals (in: Devloo 1969, n.p.).

step process. Taking the character "河" as an example, the first step is to determine that it contains the "water" radical and then locate that section in the dictionary. The second step is to count the number of strokes minus the radical, in this case five, and then find that subsection under the "water" radical. The third, and often the most confusing, step is to search the subsection for the character. The tertiary arrangement scheme is usually based on the first stroke in that part of the character minus the radical, in this case the horizontal stroke "一". — The concept of radicals was introduced by Xu Shen in Shuowen Jiezi. Xu devised a system of 540 radicals and arranged the dictionary accordingly. Xu's system, based on the structure of a character, was revolutionary in that it broke with the tradition of topically arranged wordbooks, but was cumbersome to use because of the number of radicals that had to be distinguished to find a character. Later, Mei Yingzuo created a system of 214 radicals for his dictionary Zi Hui (cf. 3.1.1.). Mei's system, now commonly called the Kangxi radical system (see Fig. 263.2) because it was popularized in the dictionary Kangxi Zidian, was the standard radical system for Chinese dictionaries until character simplification in the early 1950s.

Character simplification altered the shape as well as the number of strokes in a radical. For example, the "grass" radical was changed from four strokes (⺿) to three strokes (艹), the "silk" radical from six strokes (糸) to three strokes (纟), and the "dragon" radical from sixteen strokes (龍) to five strokes (龙). Because radicals are arranged in sequence by the total number of strokes in a radical (from one (一) to seventeen (龠) in the Kangxi system), character simplification also necessitated a fundamental change in the ordering of radicals. Presently, there is no standard radical system for simplified characters. Each major dictionary

〔一〕

轘(huàn 换) 即"车裂"(49页)。
鞫狱 鞫通鞠。我国古代指审理刑事案件。秦时亦称"治狱",即讯问犯人。《汉书·刑法志》"今遣廷史与郡鞫狱"颜师古注引李奇曰:"鞫,穷也,狱事穷竟也。"鞫狱官指审讯犯人的官吏,《唐律疏议》称为"推鞫主司"。
擦拭状血痕 痕迹检验中指人体出血部位或血滴、血流柱、血泊受到摩擦拖带而出现的形状。其特征为:起端色深,痕宽,线条多;末端色浅,痕细,线条少。常见于命案现场。擦拭状血痕部位高低,对确定死亡性质有一定价值。
藐视法院罪 亦称"藐视法庭罪"。干扰或妨碍法庭审理、执行的行为。是英美等国所谓妨害公共正义与法权罪之一种。藐视行为分直接、间接两种:直接藐视法院行为,是指行为人在法院审理案件时,以语言或举动扰乱法庭秩序或干涉法院活动的行为;间接藐视法院行为,是指妨碍、阻挠法院裁决的执行的行为。
戴西(Albert Venn Dicey,1835—1922) 英国宪法学家。长期任牛津大学英国法教授。主要著作有《英宪精义》(1885年)、《十九世纪英国法与舆论关系讲义》(1905年)等。认为英国政府制度具有三个主要原则:(1)正式的法律规则与非正式的宪法传统之间的密切联系;(2)国会在立法方面的主权;(3)法治,即任何人都不应因从事法律所未禁止的行为而受罚,任何人的法律权利和责任都应由普通法院审理。在政治上倾向自由党,在经济观点上支持自由贸易论。
戴修瓒(1887—1957) 字君亮,湖南常德人。早年留学日本中央大学法律系。解放前,曾任京师地方检察厅检察长、河南省司法厅长、最高法院首席检察官等。先后在京师政法大学、北京大学、清华大学、中国公学等校担任教授。中华人民共和国成立后,历任中央人民政府法制委员会委员、国务院参事、中国国际贸易促进委员会对外贸易仲裁委员会副主席、九三学社中央委员。主要著作有《民法债编总论》、《民法债编各论》、《票据法》、《刑事诉讼法释义》等。

〔丨〕

羁押 把依法逮捕或拘留的现行

Dictionary excerpt 263.4: Total Stroke Arrangement System (in: Faxue 1980, 736)

now devises its own scheme ranging anywhere from 188 to 250 radicals.

4.1.2. Strokes

Most Chinese dictionaries employ the concept of how a character is written or stroked in their arrangement systems. Some dictionaries use the total number of strokes in a character as their primary look-up system, while others use the sequence and shape of the strokes in a character as a secondary sorting scheme. — In dictionaries arranged by total strokes, entries are listed by the number of strokes in a character regardless of the pronunciation or other sort method. For instance, in Dictionary excerpt 263.4, all characters with seventeen strokes are entered as a group.

A supplementary sort is frequently used to facilitate look-up because there are often many characters under each total stroke section. One supplementary sorting method is to arrange entries by the shape of the first stroke of a character. Although the sequence varies, the strokes are usually arranged according to the traditional Chinese calligraphy strokes, namely, horizontal stroke (一), vertical stroke (丨), dot (丶), stroke slanting to the left (丿), stroke shaped like the character 乙, and strokes with a "hook" (e.g., [亅, 乚]). In Dictionary excerpt 263.4 the sequence of the strokes is indicated in brackets in the middle of the columns, i.e., 一 and 丨. — Another supplementary sorting method is to arrange characters according to the shape of a shared component. In Dictionary excerpt 263.5, entries are first arranged by the Chinese Phonetic Alphabet (cf. 4.2.1.) and then by shared components. The common components are 兼, 青 and 斩.

4.1.3. Four-Corner System

The Four-Corner System was created by Wang Yunwu (王云五, Westernized as Y. W. Wong) in 1925. Wang's system was an attempt to speed the dictionary look-up process by assigning a four-digit code based on the strokes at the four corners (upper left, upper right, lower left and lower right) of a character. To look up a character the user must first determine the four corners of a character and then assign a number from 0 to 9 according to the shape of stroke in each corner. For example, a level or upward-slanting stroke (the stroke 一 in 元) is assigned the number 1, a vertical stroke (the stroke 丨 in 山) is assigned the number 2, and so on. If a character does not have a stroke in one of its corners (e.g., 今 which does not have a stroke in its lower

Dictionary excerpt 263.5: Shared Components (in: Xianhan 1979, 906)

Fig. 263.3: The Revised Four-Corner System (in: Xianhan 1979, 75)

left corner) it is assigned the number zero. In the event several characters are grouped under the same four digit numbers a fifth digit is added after a decimal point to further distinguish its location in the dictionary. — Wang's four-corner look-up system has been somewhat revised in recent years. The concept of a numbering system keyed to the four corners of a character remains the same, but the designation of the numbers has changed. In addition, following character simplification, the structure of many characters have changed, resulting in a change in the configuration of the strokes in the corners. Although the four-corner look-up system is not widely used today as the primary arrangement scheme, it is often included in dictionaries as a supplemental look-up index. Fig 263.3 is the primary scheme for the revised four-corner system.

4.2. Sound

Arranging dictionaries by the sound of a character is as ancient as it is modern. First used in rhyme dictionaries many centuries ago, sound arrangement is becoming the most popular ordering scheme, especially in the PRC with the widespread use and acceptance of pinyin (cf. 4.2.1.). Chinese is a tone language and the tones are incorporated in the various sound-based look-up systems. Modern standard spoken Chinese, variously called Mandarin, Guoyu (国语, the 'National Language'), or Putonghua (普通话,

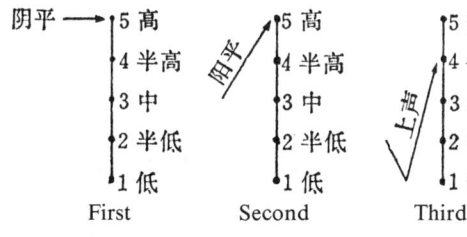

Fig. 263.4: The Four Tones (in: Huang 1981, 79)

Fig. 263.5: The Scheme for the Chinese Phonetic Alphabet (in: Xinhua 1980, 610, 611)

'Common Spoken Language'), is based on the Beijing dialect and has four major tones. The four major tones are: first tone, a high and level tone; second tone, a rising tone; third tone, a rising then falling tone, and fourth tone, a falling tone. The pitch of the four tones can be graphically represented as in Fig. 263.4 (with 5 indicating the highest pitch and 1 the lowest).

The symbols ¯, ´, ˇ and ` are used over the vowel of a romanized Chinese syllable to indicate the tone. When Chinese is spoken in phrases and sentences the tones may vary in accordance with a tone sandhi pattern.

4.2.1. Chinese Phonetic Alphabet

In February 1958, the Chinese government adopted the Chinese Phonetic Alphabet (汉语拼音, Hanyu Pinyin) as the official romanization system for Chinese. The Chinese Phonetic Alphabet, usually abbreviated to pinyin (拼音, "sound spelling"), uses the Latin alphabet to represent Chinese sounds. It is now the most common method of arranging Chinese dictionaries in the PRC. The scheme for the Chinese Phonetic Alphabet is as in Fig. 263.5.

Although the Chinese Phonetic Alphabet is firmly established, the major difficulty in its use, in dictionaries and elsewhere, is the grouping of syllables to represent multi-character words and phrases. For example, the "People's Republic of China" can be written "Zhong Hua Ren Min Gong He Guo" or "Zhonghua Renmin Gongheguo" or even "Zhonghuarenmingongheguo". The determination of syllabication (or of 'word' boundaries) directly affects how words are entered alphabetically in a dictionary. As yet no consensus of opinion on syllabication of the phonetic alphabet has been reached.

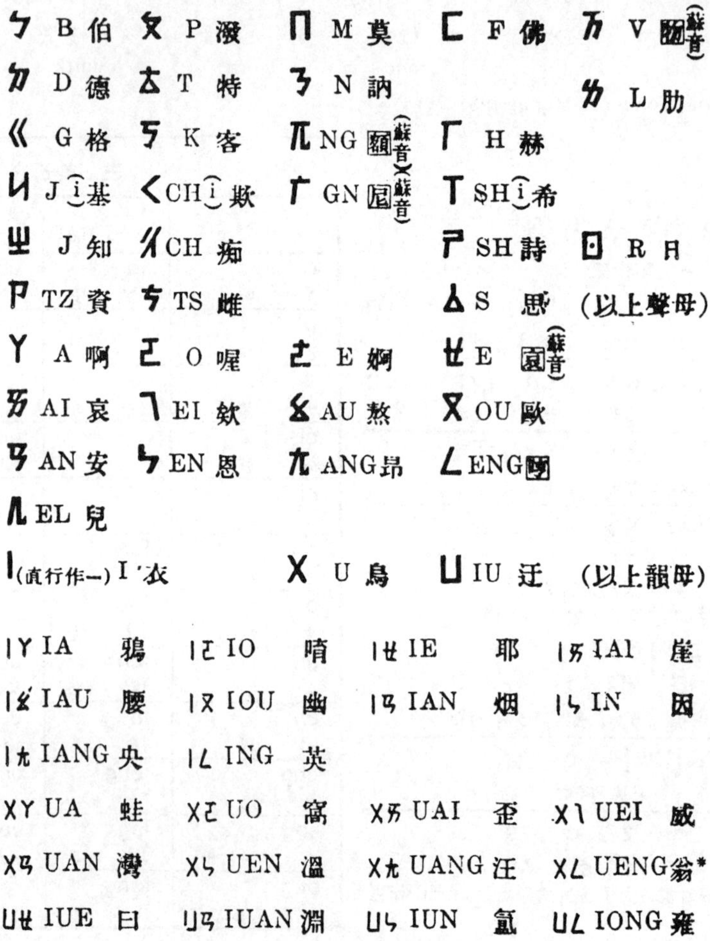

Fig. 263.6: The Scheme for the National Phonetic Alphabet (in: Guoyu 1959, 1)

4.2.2. The National Phonetic System

After the downfall of the monarchy in 1911, the new Chinese government became concerned with language reform and language unification, along with raising the literacy of the people. In 1913, the Ministry of Education sponsored the Conference on Unification of Pronunciation as a first step in the creation of a national language. The conference decided to use the Beijing dialect as the basis for the national language. In addition, the conference developed a list of thirty-nine phonetic symbols to represent standard pronunciation. The phonetic symbols (注音符号, zhùyīn fúhào), also known as 'phonetic alphabet' (注音字母, zhùyīn zìmǔ), are a group of symbols representing twenty-four initial consonants and sixteen simple and compound vowels used alongside a character to indicate its pronunciation. Pronunciation is indicated by a combination of symbols representing the initial and final sounds and the tone. The phonetic notation for the character "八" (bā, 'eight'), for instance, is "ㄅㄚ", the initial "b" being the symbol "ㄅ" and the final "a" being the symbol "ㄚ". The National Phonetic System has been used both as a primary and secondary sorting scheme in dictionaries and is a common method of indicating the pronunciation of a character in dictionaries and in language learning materials. The scheme for the National Phonetic Alphabet is as in Fig. 263.6.

平聲: 東、冬、江、支、微、魚、虞、齊、
佳、灰、真、文、元、寒、刪、先、蕭、肴、豪、
歌、麻、陽、庚、青、蒸、尤、侵、覃、鹽、咸。

上聲: 董、腫、講、紙、尾、語、麌、薺、
蟹、賄、軫、吻、阮、旱、潸、銑、篠、巧、皓、
哿、馬、養、梗、迥、有、寢、感、儉、豏。

去聲: 送、宋、絳、寘、未、御、遇、霽、
泰、卦、隊、震、問、願、翰、諫、霰、嘯、效、
號、箇、禡、漾、敬、徑、宥、沁、勘、豔、陷。

入聲: 屋、沃、覺、質、物、月、曷、黠、
屑、藥、陌、錫、職、緝、合、葉、洽。

Fig. 263.7: The Pingshui Rhyme Scheme (in: Ciyuan 1979, 0995)

4.2.3. Rhymes

The first attempts to arrange Chinese dictionaries by the sound of a character instead of its shape or meaning was in rhyme dictionaries. Moreover, it is thought that early Chinese dictionaries such as Shizhoupian were arranged by rhymes. The primary arrangement scheme in rhyme-sorted dictionaries is an index of characters arranged according to the finals of a Chinese syllable. The indexes have varied from as many as 206 finals to as few as 105. One common rhyme index was the Pingshui (平水) rhymes keyed to 106 finals. The Pingshui scheme is as in Fig. 263.7.

The secondary arrangement scheme is according to the four tones of ancient Chinese, namely, level tone (平, píng), rising tone (上, shǎng), falling tone (去, qù) and entering tone (入, rù). To find a character "中" (zhōng, 'middle, center') in a rhyme dictionary the user must know that it is pronounced in the level tone and that its final is "ong", putting it under the "东" (dōng) rhyme. Because of the number of rhymes that must be distinguished, rhyme books are among the most difficult of Chinese dictionaries to use.

4.3.3. Subject Categories

Dictionaries arranged by subject categories are known as 'classified dictionaries' (类书, lèishū). The arrangement of dictionaries by subject categories is less common than the shape or sound based arrangement systems, but it is a useful look-up option and one often preferred by subject specialists. The first classified Chinese dictionary was Erya (cf. 3.2.). Erya was arranged under nineteen categories or chapter headings. The first three categories concerned the general language (e.g., verbs, adjectives, particles and adverbs) and were followed by chapters on kinship terms, architectural terms, utensils, music, Heaven, earth, hills, mountains, watercourses, plants, trees, insects, fishes, birds, wild animals and domestic animals. Liu Xi's Shi Ming (cf. 3.2.2.) was also arranged by categories. Liu expanded the Erya classification scheme to twenty-seven categories by adding chapters on clothing, food and drink, boats, sickness and disease, and so on. One classified dictionary in the modern era is Hanyu Fangyan Cihui (cf. 3.3.1.). Entries in it are first divided into parts of speech and then into specific categories. The order of the parts of speech are nouns (with seventeen subcategories), verbs (with ten subcategories), adjectives (with six subcategories), pronouns (with four subcategories), classifiers or measure words (with two subcategories), adverbs, and prepositions and conjunctions. Occasionally, a large dictionary such as Cihai will be divided into subject categories and published in fascicles.

4.3.4. Each dictionary arrangement system has advantages and disadvantages. Dictionaries arranged by the shape of a character enable the user to find a character without knowing its pronunciation or meaning. However, it is no mean task to learn to efficiently use the various shape-based systems with their inherent idiosyncrasies. In dictionaries arranged by the sound of a character, the user can go directly to the character being looked up without having to determine the radical, count strokes or assign numbers to the various strokes. The obvious disadvantage in using such dictionaries is that the user often may not know the pronunciation and especially the tone of the character being looked up. Classified dictionaries allow the user to quickly find a character by only having to know its general meaning, but even knowing the general meaning of a character is, at times, difficult. Because no one look-up system is clearly superior to the other, Chinese dictionaries almost always include indexes to head character entries keyed to several different look-up schemes. For example, Xiandai Hanyu Cidian (cf. 2.4.) is arranged by the Chinese Phonetic Alphabet and it includes a radical and four-corner index, while the revised Cihai (cf. 3.2.2.) is arranged by its own radical system and includes total stroke and pinyin indexes. It is also a common practice to use several different arrangement schemes in the same dictionary. For example, the head characters in the revised Ciyuan (cf. 3.2.2) are arranged by Kangxi radicals, while the character combinations are arranged first by total strokes and then by word units.

5. Summary

From its beginning more than two millenniums ago, lexicography in China has been a fascinating endeavor. Lexicographers of Chinese have had to contend with the graphic nature of the language, the allure of the dialects and the great body of Chinese literature to pursue their art. Many have produced dictionaries that rival the great lexicographic works of the world. There can be little doubt that the grand tradition of Chinese lexicography will continue into the future.

6. Selected Bibliography

6.1. Dictionaries

Cihai 1938 = Shu Xincheng (舒新城) et al.: Cihai (辞海, 'Sea of Words'). Shanghai 1938 [Other editions include: Taibei 1956; revised edition Shanghai 1979].

Ciyuan 1915 = Lu Erkui (陆尔奎) et al.: Ciyuan (辞源, 'Origin of Words'). Shanghai 1915 [Other editions include: Shanghai 1931, 1939; Changsha 1949; Taibei 1968; Beijing 1979].

Devloo 1969 = Edmond Devloo: An Etymological Chinese-English Dictionary. Taibei 1969.

Duan 1807 = Duan Yucai (段玉裁): Shuowen Jiezi Zhu (说文解字注, 'Commentary on Shuowen Jiezi'). n.p. 1807 [Reprints include Taibei 1970].

Fangyan 18 A. D. = Yang Xiong (扬雄): Fangyan (方言, 'Dialects'). n.p. 18 A.D. [Reprints include: Shanghai 1936, 1937, 1939].

Faxue 1980 = Faxue Cidian (法学词典, 'Law Dictionary'). Shanghai 1980.

Guangyun 1011 = Chen Pengnian (陈彭年) et al.: Guangyun (广韵, 'Extension of Rhymes'). n.p. 1011 [Reprints include Beijing? 1704; Taibei 1956, 1961].

Guoyu 1937 = Guoyu Cidian (国语辞典, 'A Dictionary of the National Language'). Shanghai 1937 [Other editions include Taibei 1953; Hong Kong, 1961; Shanghai 1957 and Taibei 1979].

Han Da Ci 1986 = Hanyu Da Cidian (汉语大词典, 'An Encyclopedic Dictionary of the Chinese Language'). Shanghai 1986.

Han Da Zi 1986 = Hanyu Da Zidian (汉语大字典, 'An Encyclopedic Character Dictionary of the Chinese Language'). Wuhan 1986.

Han Fang Ci 1964 = Hanyu Fangyan Cihui (汉语方言词汇, 'A Glossary of Chinese Dialects'). Beijing 1964.

Han Fang Zi 1962 = Hanyu Fangyin Zihui (汉语方言字汇, 'A Glossary of Regional Pronunciations of Chinese Characters'). Beijing 1962.

Hao 1865 = Hao Yixing (郝懿行): Erya Yishu (尔雅义疏, 'Exegesis of Erya'). n.p. 1865 [Reprints include: Taibei 1974; Shanghai 1982].

He 1974 = He Rong (何容): Guoyu Ribao Cidian (国语日报辞典, 'The Mandarin Daily News Dictionary'). Taibei 1974.

Ji Yun 1037 = Ding Du (丁度): Ji Yun (集韵). n.p. 1037 [Reprints include: Taibei 1966].

Kangxi 1716 = Kangxi Zidian (康熙字典, 'The Kangxi Character Dictionary'). Beijing 1716 [Reprints include: Beijing 1887, 1958, 1980; Taibei 1965].

Liu 200? = Liu Xi (刘熙): Shi Ming (释名, 'Explanation of Names'). n.p. 200? [Reprints include: Shanghai 1919, 1936].

Mei 1615 = Mei Yingzuo (梅膺祚): Zihui (字汇, 'A Collection of Individual Characters'). n.p. 1615 [Reprints include: Suzhou 1685].

Morohashi 1957 = Morohashi Tetsuji (诸桥辙次): Dai Kan Wa Jiten (大汉和辞典, 'A Chinese-Japanese Encyclopedic Dictionary'). Tokyo 1957—1960.
Wang 1778? = Wang Niansun (王念孙): Guangya Shucheng (广雅疏证, 'Exegetical Evidence for Guangya'). n.p. 1778? [Reprints include: Taibei 1972; Shanghai 1983].
Xian Han 1979 = Zhongguo Shehuiyuan Yuyan Yanjiusuo Cidian Bianjishi:(中国社会科学院语言研究所词典编辑室, 'The Dictionary Compilation Office of the Linguistics Research Institute of the Chinese Academy of Social Sciences'). Xiandai Hanyu Cidian (现代汉语词典, 'A Dictionary of Contemporary Chinese'). Beijing 1979.
Xinhua 1953 = Xinhua Zidian (新华字典, 'The New China Character Dictionary'). Beijing 1953 [Revisions include: Beijing 1957, 1971, 1979].
Xu 100 A.D. = Xu Shen (许慎): Shuowen Jiezi (说文解字, 'Explaining Pictographic Characters and Analyzing Composite Characters). n.p. 100 A.D. [Reprints include: Shanghai 1914; Taibei 1956, 1959; Beijing 1963, 1979].
Zhonghua 1915 = Lu Feikui (陆费逵): et al.: Zhonghua Da Zidian (中华大字典, 'An Encyclopedic Dictionary of Chinese Characters'). Shanghai 1915 [Reprints include: Shanghai 1927; Beijing 1958, 1981; Taibei 1960].
Zhongwen 1962 = Zhang Qiyun (张其昀) et al.: Zhongwen Da Cidian (中文大辞典, 'An Encyclopedic Dictionary of the Chinese Language'). Taibei 1962—1968 [Original edition in 40 volumes, reprinted in 1973 in 10 volumes].

6.2. Other Publications

Chen 1985 = Chen Bingzhao (陈炳迢): Cishu Gaiyao (辞书概要, 'An Outline of Chinese Lexicography'). Fuzhou 1985.
DeFrancis 1984 = John DeFrancis: The Chinese Language. Fact and Fantasy. Honolulu 1984.
Huang 1981 = Huang Borong (黄伯荣) et al.: Xiandai Hanyu (汉代汉语, 'Modern Chinese'). Gansu 1981.
Kratochvil 1968 = Paul Kratochvil: The Chinese Language Today. London 1968.
Li 1985 = David Chen-ching Li: Problems and Trends of Standardization of Mandarin Chinese in Taiwan. In: Anthropological Linguistics 27. 1985, 122—140.
Liu 1962 = James J. L. Liu: The Art of Chinese Poetry. Chicago. London 1962.
Waters 1889 = Thomas Waters: Essays on the Chinese Language. Shanghai 1889.
Xue 1982 = Xue Shiqi: Chinese Lexicography Past and Present. In: Dictionaries 4. 1982, 151—169.
Zhang 1980 = Zhang Jing (张静): Xiandai Hanyu (现代汉语, 'Contemporary Chinese'). Shanghai 1980.

Thomas B. I. Creamer,
Takoma Park, Maryland (USA)

264. Korean Lexicography

1. Introduction
2. Korean Spelling and Dictionaries
3. Monolingual Dictionaries
4. Dictionaries of Ancient Korean
5. Dictionaries of Dialects
6. Bilingual Dictionaries
7. Dictionaries of Specialized Subjects
8. Conclusion; Desiderata
9. Selected Bibliography

1. Introduction

The origin of the Korean people and of their language has long been an enigma. They are a people of antiquity arising ca. 3,000 B.C. on the prairies of Manchuria, now North China. Pre-historic Koreans left behind no written records, no heroic poems, no histories, no literature, but only artifacts and short fragments of official or religious inscriptions. Some of these survived because they were buried in tombs underground. These remains provide a glimpse of the early Koreans' geographical habitat, manners and customs, and especially their language, which was distinctly alien compared to that of their neighbours, the Chinese and Tartars, including Mongols and Manchus.

The Korean language is believed to trace its ancestry to the language spoken in the Korean kingdom of Ko Chosŏn and other kingdom of Korea (ca. B.C. 108). Puyŏ (B.C. 1), Koguryŏ (B.C. 37—668); Paekche (B.C. 188—660), Silla (B.C. 57—935), Parhae (699—926), Koryŏ (918—1392) and Chosŏn (1392—1910).

In the monumental publication of McCune/Reischauer, (1939, 4), it is aptly stated that "Korean is a polysyllabic agglutinative language, bearing close resemblance in structure and grammar to the Altaic languages and to Japanese, but not to Chinese. The vocabulary is composed primarily of words of two types, native words and Sino-Korean words. The latter are either borrowed words from the Chinese, but pronounced in the Korean manner, or are new words coined in Korea from Chinese characters. Recently many words of Japanese and Western origin have been added."

It was in 1447 that King Sejong in the fourth reign of the Yi Dynasty of the Chosŏn Kingdom proclaimed "Hunmin chŏngŭm," literally meaning "to instruct people in correct sound" and now called "Han'gŭl" (unified spelling system), a phonetic alphabet of 28 letters with 14 consonants and 10 vowels.

In spite of the fact that both the Korean native language and "Han'gŭl" were phonetic in nature and syllabic in structure, "Chŏngŭm" was written in the fashion of Chinese characters to denote the combination of the three elements of consonant, vowel, consonant as syllables.

Because of this arbitrary spelling device contradicting Korean morphology, coupled with the irregularities and diversity of both Korean grammar and dialects, standardization of Korean orthography and grammar was an inevitable prerequisite for a meaningful dictionary. To solve this, the Chosŏnŏ Hakhoe (Korean Language Research Society) was formed in 1923 by noted Korean linguists and philologists of the time to tackle the herculean task of unifying spelling, grammar, pronunciation and word-division.

In 1933, after 10 years of painstaking endeavor, the Korean orthography named "Han'gŭl match'umpŏp t'ongiran" (Rules for the Unification of Spelling to conform to the Unified System for the Korean Language) was adopted; subsequently it became the foundation of the Korean orthography in Korea. As of March 1, 1989, the revised version of the orthography was announced by the Ministry of Education of the Republic of Korea.

2. Korean Spelling and Dictionaries

"Sajŏn" is the term for "dictionary" in modern Korean. Korean lexicography in this paper refers specifically to dictionaries whose entries are arranged according to the Korean alphabet with definitions in Korean of Korean words and vocabulary items. The words and vocabulary items are of both native and Sino-Korean origin. The Korean native language is the colloquial language while Sino-Korean is the language of books and the language used for technical terms. Also included in this paper are several bilingual dictionaries, for they may be seen as the prototypes of modern monolingual dictionaries.

Korean dictionaries are invariably called "Urimal sajŏn" (Our Language Dictionary), "Kugŏ sajŏn" (National Language Dictionary), "Chosŏnmal sajŏn" (Korean Language Dictionary) or "Han'gŭl sajŏn" (Unified Spelling System Dictionary).

Omitted from this study are Chinese character dictionaries, which are arranged according to the character radicals and the number of strokes, and provide mere renderings of Chinese characters into Korean without definitions; and encyclopedic works called "paekkwa sajŏn". During the Korean traditional period, lexicons appeared generally in encyclopedic works.

Excluded from consideration here are also foreign words used in science, technology, and specialized subjects, and acronyms, the majority of which are English. Inevitable for Korea today in its quest for Western knowledge is an awareness of Western languages. To illustrate the magnitude of Korea's need to incorporate and assimilate terms for new Western concepts, techniques, and products, there are over 450,000 entries in the *Webster's Collegiate English Dictionary,* whereas the largest unabridged Korean dictionary contains 200,000 words at most.

Dictionaries of the Korean language abound. Selected for this paper are those dictionaries representing the Korean vernacular lexicon which contain Korean words in "Han'gŭl". In order to facilitate the organization of this paper, the titles are introduced according to the following five categories of dictionaries: 1. Korean-Korean dictionaries; 2. Archaic Korean language dictionaries; 3. Dictionaries of dialects; 4. Bilingual dictionaries; 5. Specialized dictionaries.

3. Monolingual Dictionaries

Chosŏnmal k'ŭn sajŏn (Unabridged Korean Language Dictionary) in six volumes compiled by the Han'gŭl Hakhoe (Unified System Research Society — formerly the Korean Language Research Society) and published by Ŭryu Munhwasa in Seoul, 1947, is the unofficial standard dictionary of the Korean language in South Korea. The 1950 edition was published under the shortened title of *K'ŭn sajŏn.*

Analogous to this dictionary is *Chosŏnmal sajŏn* (Korean Language Dictionary), also in six volumes, compiled by the Chosŏn Minjujuŭi Inmin Konghwaguk Kwahagwŏn Ŏnŏ Munhak Yŏnguso Sajŏn Yŏngusil (Democratic People's Republic of Korea, Academy of Sciences, Language and Literature Research Institute, Dictionary Compilation Unit) and published by the Kwahagwŏn Ch'ulp'ansa in Pyongyang, 1960. This is an official standard dictionary of North Korea. This North Korean dictionary was published in 1962 in a single volume comprising 5054 pages.

The standard dictionaries of both South and North Korea contain more than 170,000 Korean words, and the vocabulary items in common usage are arranged according to the order of the Korean alphabet; both share practically the same definitions, except that the North Korean dictionary, *Chosŏnmal sajŏn,* draws its illustrations from North Korean literary sources.

The comparatively late advent of these standard dictionaries of the Korean language is partly attributed to the fact that in the case of *K'ŭn sajŏn,* the leading linguists, such as Ch'oe Hyŏn-bae (1894—1970), Kim Yun-gyŏng (1894—1969) and Yi Yun-jae (1888—1943), engaged in the Han'gŭl Hakhoe's dictionary project, were imprisoned in 1936 by the Japanese authorities and were only released on August 15, 1945 after the liberation of Korea from Japan; and in the case of *Chosŏnmal sajŏn,* the project for its compilation was interrupted from 1950—1953, during the Korean War. As an interim measure, however, the Language and Literature Institute of the North Korea Academy of Sciences published *Chosŏnŏ so sajŏn* (Concise Dictionary of the Korean Language) in 1955 (709 pages).

The guiding principles of the North Korean government with regard to language is worth noting. According to a 1949 Cabinet decision, vernacular Korean script (Han'gŭl in South Korea) was authorized as the sole national and official written language; the use of Chinese characters in writing was abolished; all publications printed in Han'gŭl were to be read from left to right as in English; the Pyongyang dialect was designated the standard language (Note: the Seoul dialect is standard for South Korea); a nationwide campaign was started to revitalize the native Korean language by exploring and rediscovering it, and the official Korean orthography called "Chosŏnŏ ch'ŏlchapŏp" (Rules of the Korean System of Spelling) was finally adopted.

The rules for the Korean spelling system were published in 1956 in a dictionary by the Academy of Sciences in Pyongyang under the title of *Chosŏnŏ ch'ŏlchapŏp sajŏn* (Korean Language Orthographic Dictionary) comprising 537 pages. The Korean orthography both in South and North Korea followed the principles set by Chu Si-gyŏng (1876—1914), who is known as the father of Korean grammar.

A dictionary purposely compiled to reflect the North Korean language policy of 1949 is *Hyŏndae Chosŏnmal sajŏn* (Modern Korean Language Dictionary), compiled by the Ŏnŏhak Yŏnguso (The Language Research Institute) and published by the Sahoe Kwahagwŏn Ch'ulp'ansa in Pyongyang in 1968 (1350 pages). It contains 50,000 entries of native Korean words in common usage. Subsequently another edition in 1060 pages, *Chosŏn munhwaŏ sajŏn* (Polished Korean Language Dictionary), was compiled and published in 1973 by the same publisher of *Hyŏndae Chosŏnmal sajŏn.* A significant feature of this latter editions is that out of a total of 130,000 entries, 50,000 are not found in the South Korean *K'ŭn sajŏn.*

The forerunner of Korean monolingual dictionaries is a dictionary entitled *Malmoi* (Collection of Words), compiled by Kim Tu-bong (1889—), one of the pioneers among Korean grammarians who later became the Speaker of the Parliament in North Korea. This dictionary is believed to have been published in 1910 by Chosŏn Kwangmunhoe in Seoul.

Korean-Korean dictionaries prepared and compiled by professional lexicographers are *Urimal sajŏn* (Our Language Dictionary), by Mun Se-yŏng; and *Kugŏ tae sajŏn* (Unabridged National Language Dictionary), by Yi Hŭi-sŭng. The former was published in Seoul by Sammunsa, 1938 (1634, 21 pages), and the latter, was published by Minjung Sŏrim in Seoul, 1981 (4482 pages).

Dictionaries to reflect a new revised orthography of the Korean language (effective March 1, 1989) published in Seoul in 1989, are *Tonga sae kugŏ sajŏn* (Tonga New National Language Dictionary) by Tonga Ch'ulp'ansa; *Nyu eisu kugo sajon* (New A's National Language Dictionary) by Kŭmsŏng Kyokwasŏ and *Essensŭ kugŏ sajŏn* (Essence National Language Dictionary) by Minjung Sŏrim.

4. Dictionaries of Ancient Korean

The archaic Korean language is preserved in the form of "Idu", a transliteration system of the Korean language using Chinese characters phonetically as in the case of the use of Man'yōgana in Japan. "Idu" was generally in use up to the 15th century.

The complexity and diversity of the "Idu" form require special philological training to decipher. Pioneering in these efforts were two Japanese scholars, Ayugai Fusanoshin, the eminent philologist specializing in Korean archaic languages who published his commentary on "Idu" in *Zakkō* (Miscellaneous Studies) in twelve volumes; and Maema Kyōsaku, the renowned philologist and bibliographer, who was the author of the language of Koryŏ, *Kyerim yusa Yŏŏngo.*

Zakkō, published by the Tōyō Bunko in Tokyo in 1931, comprises the philological commentaries on "Idu" of the Silla period (B.C. 37—935 A.D.), while the *Kyerim yusa Yŏŏngo,* also published by the Tōyo Bunko in 1915, is an annotation of the Koryŏ language as it was recorded in the *Chi-lin lei shih,* a work of the 12th century compiled by Sun Mu (ca. 1100), a Chinese envoy to the Koryŏ court. This work is the sole extant reminder of the Koryŏ language, specifically the dialect of Kaesŏng, the capital of Koryŏ, situated north of Seoul.

Among the major dictionaries concerned with Idu, the Archaic Korean language, are: *Chosŏn yenmal sajŏn* (Old Korean Language Dictionary), compiled by Yi Sang-ch'un and published by Ŭryu Munhwasa in Seoul, 1949 (275, 30 pages); *Idu charyo sŏnjip* (Selected Collection of Idu), published as the *Han'gukhak ko sajŏn ch'ongsŏ* (Studies on Korean Dictionary Series), by Asea Munhwasa in Seoul, 1975 (534 pages); and *Idu sajŏn* (Idu Dictionary) published by Chŏngŭmsa in Seoul, 1976, compiled by Chang Chi-yŏng, one of the founding members of the Korean Language Research Society, *Han'gŭl Hakhoe.* Contained in Chang's dictionary are early Idu dictionaries such as *Nayŏ Idu* (Silla and Koryŏ Idu of 1789), *Idu pyŏllam* (Directory of Idu of 1829), and *Idu chipsŏng* (Comprehensive Collection of Idu of 1937).

For Middle Korean, of the 15th century, *Yijoŏ sajŏn* (Dictionary of the Yi Dynasty Language) in one volume was authored by a Korean lexicographer, Yu Ch'ang-don and published by the Yonsei University Press in Seoul, 1964 (830 pages). Yu also compiled a dictionary of Idu in 1953 (686 pages), under the title, *Koŏ sajŏn* (Old Language Dictionary), published by Tongguk Munhwasa in Seoul.

5. Dictionaries of Dialects

In general, Korean dialects are regionally distinguished along provincial lines (cf. Map 264.1); for example, Central, Ch'ungch'ŏng; Chŏlla, Kyŏngsang, P'yŏngan, Hamgyŏng and Cheju Island. Other than the dialect of Cheju Island, located at the southwestern tip of the Korean peninsula, which has some distinct differences in its roots, Korean dialects are differentiated largely by accent and intonation.

Available are dictionaries representing each of these provincial dialects. Representing all these dialects are two dictionaries. One

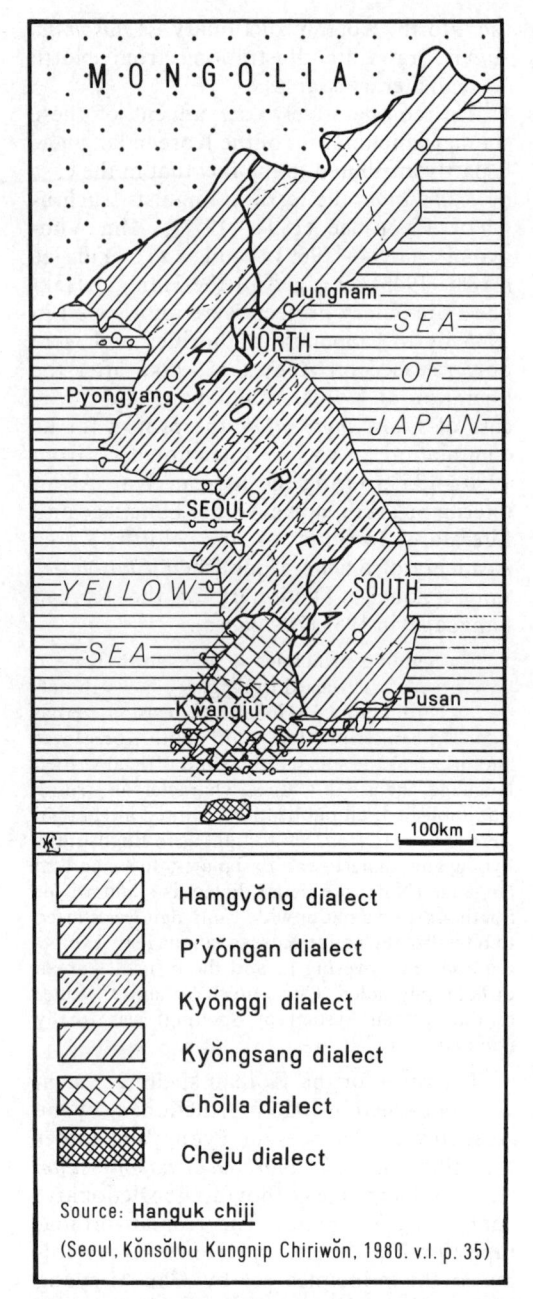

Map 264.1: Korean dialects

is *Pangŏn sajŏn* (Dialect Dictionary) prepared by Kim Pyŏng-je, one of the noted specialists on dialects and folklore in North Korea. It was published in Pyongyang by the Kwahak Paekkwa Sajŏn Ch'ulp'ansa, 1980 (499 pages); the other is *Han'guk pangŏn sajŏn* (Korean Dialect Dictionary), prepared by Ch'oe Hak-kŭn and published by Hyŏnmunsa in Seoul, 1978 (1695 pages). The former is arranged according to the order of the

Korean alphabet with designations of the province(s) where the dialects are spoken, while the latter, also arranged alphabetically, is classified by subjects such as nature, geography, plants, animals, utensils and parts of speech, with a general index.

6. Bilingual Dictionaries

Korean and major foreign language dictionaries are available due to Korea's growing intercourse with foreign countries. Nevertheless, titles introduced here are limited to those bilingual dictionaries which have directly contributed to Korean lexicography, especially the *K'ŭn sajŏn*. In reverse order of the titles listed below, each has attributed indebtedness to preceding dictionaries.

First to be introduced is the *Translation of a Comparative Vocabulary of the Chinese, Korean and Japanese Languages (Chosŏn Oeguk chahŭi)* by Philo Sinesis, a French Jesuit priest, published in Batavia, 1835, and printed at the Parapattan Press. Arranged according to English words and phrases followed by Korean, Japanese and Chinese characters and words, it was prepared for the Jesuit mission in the Far East.

Next are the *Dictionnaire Coréen Français... par les Missionnaires de Corée de la Société des Missions Étrangères de Paris (Hanbul chajŏn)*, published by C. Levy in Yokohama, Japan, 1880 (714 pages); and *A Korean-English Dictionary* by James S. Gale, published in Yokohama, 1897 (1781 pages); and finally, *Chōsengo jiten* (Korean Language Dictionary), published by Chōsen Sōtokufu in Seoul, 1920 (983 pages).

Encouraged by the publication of these dictionaries, the Japanese colonial government, the Chōsen Sōtokufu, commissioned Korean scholars to compile a Korean dictionary. But when it was ready for publication, it was published as a Korean-Japanese dictionary with the Korean version of the definitions translated into Japanese. Although lacking in uniformity in its Korean spelling, this dictionary of the *Chōsengo jiten* is considered unique in that it covers traditional terms and phrases, and includes drawings of Korean things as illustrations.

The French-Korean dictionary is considered the first comprehensive dictionary compiled according to the norm and styles of western lexicography. Arranged according to the Korean alphabetical order followed by the French romanization and definitions, it contains brief descriptions of Korean grammar and geographical names.

Gale's dictionary is significant in that attempts were made to emphasize Korean native words, an area into which even today Korean lexicography has yet to venture. Gale was a Canadian missionary in Korea, who is one of the most illustrious western Koreanologists in history down to the present day. In his preface, Gale stated that "In the work of preparing the dictionary, the list of words compiled by the French Fathers has been used as a basis."

Gale's second edition was published in Seoul in 1911 by the Christian Literature Society, and the Third edition, entitled *Unabridged Korean-English Dictionary (Hanyŏng tae chajŏn)*, edited by Alexander A. Pieters, was published by the Christian Literature Society of Korea in Seoul, 1931 (1781 pages), because the plates for the second edition, which were stored in the Yokohama Press, were destroyed by the Great Tokyo fire of 1923. The first edition contained 35,000 Korean words, the second edition 50,000 and the third edition 75,000 words.

7. Dictionaries of Specialized Subjects

There are dictionaries for Korean loanwords, acronyms, newly coined words and so forth. The works introduced here, however, are limited to dictionaries which primarily deal with Korean onomatopoeic words.

Chosŏnmal ŭisŏng ŭit'aeŏ sajŏn (Korean Dictionary of Onomatopoeic Words), compiled by Chosŏnŏ Yŏnguhoe and published by Hagu Sŏbang in Tokyo in 1971, contains over 4,000 Korean reduplicating words. It is arranged according to the Korean alphabet.

Using this Tokyo publication as a basis, the Yŏnbyŏn Ŏnŏ Yŏnguso (Language Research Institute), a Korean ethnic language institute in Yanbien (Yŏnbyŏn in Korean) in Manchuria, compiled and published *Chosŏnmal ŭisŏng ŭit'aeŏ pullyu sajŏn* (Classified Dictionary of Korean Onomatopoeic Words) in 1981. Unlike the Tokyo edition, this dictionary is arranged according to subjects such as people, animals and objects. It contains 8,000 reduplicating Korean words, doubling the size of the Tokyo edition.

Urimal yŏksun sajŏn (A Dictionary of Our Language in Reverse Order) was compiled by Yi Chae-wŏn and published by Chŏngŭmsa in Seoul, 1985. This dictionary is a listing of Korean words which have the same ending and are arranged in reverse order of the Korean alphabet.

Finally, *Urimal pullyu sajŏn* (Classified Dictionary of Our Language) was compiled by Nam Yong-sin and published by Hangang Munhwasa in Seoul, 1987. Korean words are arranged according to 18 classified subjects. Included also are the latest Korean orthography and standardized spelling systems adopted by the Ministry of Education on June 30, 1987.

8. Conclusion; Desiderata

Contemporary Korea, both South and North, has produced dictionaries in large numbers on a variety of subjects and for a number of purposes. Nevertheless, still unavailable is a genuine Korean lexicography for the Korean colloquial and the archaic languages of the three kingdom period of Koguryŏ, Paekche and Silla.

This deficiency can be remedied by arousing interest in scholarship on philology, bibliography and encyclopedic works, as well as by emphasizing the qualities of accuracy and exactness, which in defining words are the two most salient elements of lexicography.

Obviously outside of the main domain of Korean lexicography, but nevertheless desirable, is a Korean-English/English-Korean dictionary with standardized romanization. The McCune-Reischauer romanization system is a widely-adopted transliteration system for Korean in the United States, whereas the MOC (Ministry of Education) system is the official romanization system in South Korea.

The absence of a standardized romanized Korean dictionary is one of the factors impeding Korean studies among non-Koreans.

9. Selected Bibliography

9.1. Dictionaries

Chōsengo jiten 1920 = Chōsengo jiten (Korean Language Dictionary). Seoul 1920 [983 p.].

Chosŏn munhwaŏ sajŏn 1973 = Ŏnŏhak Yŏnguso (The Language Research Institute): Chosŏn munhwaŏ sajŏn (Polished Korean Language Dictionary). Pyongyang 1973 [1060 p.].

Chosŏn yenmal sajŏn 1949 = Yi Sang-ch'un: Chosŏn yenmal sajŏn (Old Korean Language Dictionary). Seoul 1949 [275, 30 p.].

Chosŏnmal k'ŭn sajŏn 1947 = Han'gŭl Hakhoe (Unified System Research Society): Chosŏnmal k'ŭn sajŏn (Unabridged Korean Language Dictionary). Seoul 1947 [6 vols.].

Chosŏnmal sajŏn 1960 = Chosŏn Minjujuŭi Inmin Konghwaguk Kwahagwŏn Ŏnŏ Munhak Yŏnguso Sajŏn Yŏngusil (Democratic People's Republic of Korea, Academy of Sciences, Language and Literature Research Institute, Dictionary Compilation Unit): Chosŏnmal sajŏn. Pyongyang 1960 [6 vols.].

Chosŏnmal ŭisŏng ŭit'aeŏ pullyu sajŏn 1981 = Yŏnbyŏn Ŏnŏ Yŏnguso (Language Research Institute): Chosŏnmal ŭisŏng ŭit'aeŏ pullyu sajŏn (Classified Dictionary of Korean Onomatopoeic Words). Yanbien, Manchuria 1981.

Chosŏnmal ŭisŏng ŭit'aeŏ sajŏn 1971 = Chosŏnŏ Yŏnguhoe: Chosŏnmal ŭisŏng ŭit'aeŏ sajŏn (Korean Dictionary of Onomatopoeic Words). Tokyo 1971.

Chosŏnŏ ch'ŏlchapŏp sajŏn 1956 = Academy of Sciences: Chosŏnŏ ch'ŏlchapŏp sajŏn (Korean Language Orthographic Dictionary). Pyongyang 1956 [537 p.].

Dictionnaire Coréen Français 1880 = Dictionnaire Coréen Français... par les Missionnaires de Corée de la Société des Missions Étrangères de Paris (Hanbul chajŏn). Yokohama 1880 [714 p.].

Essensŭ kugŏ sajŏn 1989 = Minjung Sŏrim: Essensŭ kugŏ sajŏn (Essence National Language Dictionary). Seoul 1989.

Gale 1897 = James S. Gale: A Korean-English Dictionary. Yokohama 1897 [1781 p.; 2nd ed. Seoul 1911].

Gale 1931 = James S. Gale: Unabridged Korean-English Dictionary (Hanyŏng tae chajŏn). Alexander A. Pieters (ed.). Seoul 1931 [1781 p.].

Han'guk pangŏn sajŏn 1978 = Ch'oe Hak-kŭn: Han'guk pangŏn sajŏn (Korean Dialect Dictionary). Seoul 1978 [1695 p.].

Han'gukhak ko sajŏn ch'ongsŏ = (see *Idu charyo sŏnjip 1975*).

Hyŏndae Chosŏnmal sajŏn 1968 = Ŏnŏhak Yŏnguso (The Language Research Institute): Hyŏndae Chosŏnmal sajŏn (Modern Korean Language Dictionary). Pyongyang 1968 [1350 p.].

Idu charyo sŏnjip 1975 = Idu charyo sŏnjip (Selected Collection of Idu). Published as the Han'gukhak ko sajŏn ch'ongsŏ (Studies on Korean Dictionary Series). Seoul 1975 [534 p.].

Idu sajŏn 1976 = Chang Chi-yŏng: Idu sajŏn (Idu Dictionary). Seoul 1976.

Koŏ sajŏn 1953 = Yu Ch'ang-don: Koŏ sajŏn (Old Language Dictionary). Seoul 1953 [686 p.].

Kugŏ tae sajŏn 1981 = Yi Hŭi-sŭng: Kugŏ tae sajŏn (Unabridged National Language Dictionary). Seoul 1981 [4482 p.].

K'ŭn sajŏn 1950 = 1950 edition of *Chosŏnmal k'ŭn sajŏn 1947*.

Malmoi 1910(?) = Kim Tu-bong: Malmoi (Collection of Words). Seoul 1910 (?).

Nyu eisŭ kugŏ sajŏn 1989 = Kŭmsŏng Kyokwasŏ: Nyu eisŭ kugŏ sajŏn (New A's National Language Dictionary). Seoul 1989.

Pangŏn sajŏn 1980 = Kim Pyŏng-je: Pangŏn sajŏn (Dialect Dictionary). Pyongyang 1980 [499 p.].
Sinesis 1835 = Philo Sinesis: Translation of a Comparative Vocabulary of the Chinese, Korean and Japanese Languages (Chosŏn Oeguk chahŭi). Batavia 1835 [176, 1].
Tonga sae kugŏ sajŏn 1989 = Tonga Ch'ulp'ansa: Tonga sae kugŏ sajŏn (Tonga New National Language Dictionary). Seoul 1989.
Urimal pullyu sajŏn 1987 = Nam Yong-sin: Urimal pullyu sajŏn (Classified Dictionary of Our Language). Seoul 1987.
Urimal sajŏn 1938 = Mun Se-yŏng: Urimal sajŏn (Our Language Dictionary). Seoul 1938 [1634, 21 p.].
Urimal yŏksun sajŏn 1985 = Yi Chae-wŏn: Urimal yŏksun sajŏn (A Dictionary of Our Language in Reverse Order). Seoul 1985.
Yijoŏ sajŏn 1964 = Yu Ch'ang-don: Yijoŏ sajŏn (Dictionary of the Yi Dynasty Language). Seoul 1964 [1 vol.; 830 p.].

9.2. Other Publications

McCune/Reischauer 1939 = McCune/Reischauer: Romanization of the Korean Language. In: Transactions of the Korea Branch of the Royal Asiatic Society 29. 1939.

Key P. Yang, The Library of Congress, Washington, D.C. (USA)

265. Japanische Lexikographie

1. Schrift und Lexikon
2. Geschichtliche Entwicklung
3. Lexikographie der Randsprachen
4. Ainu
5. Literatur (in Auswahl)

1. Schrift und Lexikon

Die Verschriftung des Japanischen auf der Basis der chinesischen Schriftsprache hat eine traditionsreiche Lexikographie hervorgebracht. In ihr spiegelt sich die Adaption der Wortschrift einer monosyllabisch-isolierenden Sprache für die Erfassung des Wortschatzes einer polysyllabisch-agglutinierenden Sprache (s. Müller-Yokota 1987). Das Resultat, eine sinojap. Mischschrift aus chin. Wortschriftzeichen *(kanji)* und von ihnen abgeleiteten Silbenschriftzeichen *(kana)*, ist für die jap. Lexikographie ein bestimmender Faktor, wobei das chin. Element früh als inkorporierter Bestandteil des Japanischen angesehen wurde, so daß echte mehrsprachige Wörterbücher erst nach der Berührung mit dem Westen erscheinen und mit ihnen die einzellautliche Erfassung mittels der lateinischen Buchstabenschrift *(rōmaji* „römische Schrift").

Der Leitschrift entsprechend lassen sich in der jap. Lexikographie die drei Gruppen der (1) Kanji-Lexika, (2) Kana-Lexika, (3) Rōmaji-Lexika unterscheiden. In dieser Reihenfolge treten sie auch historisch in Erscheinung. Die Kanji-Lexika (1) sind nach dem Zeichenbau (1 a: *jikeibiki*-Typ), der Zeichenaussprache (1 b: *ombiki*-Typ) oder der Zeichenbedeutung (1 c: *bunruitai*-Typ) angeordnet (früher häufig mit Typenkombinationen). Ordnungsprinzip des *jikeibiki*-Typs sind strukturelle Konstituenten der Kanji (meist sog. Klassenhäupter/Radikale zur Klassifizierung) mit zusätzlicher Gliederung nach der Zeichenstrichzahl. Ordnungsprinzip des *ombiki*-Typs ist die anlautende Silbe des Lexems in der Abfolge des Kana-Syllabars nach dem Merkvers *Iroha-uta (iroha-jun:* 1 b/a) oder der Systematik der 50-Laute-Tafel *(gojūon-jun:* 1 b/b). Ordnungsprinzip des *bunruitai*-Typs sind kategoriale Klassifizierungen *(bunrui)* nach chin. Vorbild, wobei das lexikalische Inventar in der Ordnung des Kana-Syllabars je Anlautsilbe nach Sachgruppen (1 c/a) oder in der Gliederung der Sachgruppen syllabarisch geordnet (1 c/b) auftritt. Die Kana-Lexika (2) haben Einträge in Hiragana oder/und Katakana und sind nach dem Iroha (2 a), in moderner Zeit fast nur noch nach dem Gojūon (2 b) geordnet. In der Regel werden den Kana-Stichwörtern die bedeutungswertigen Kanji nachgestellt. Rōmaji-Lexika (3) sind für mehrsprachige Wörterbücher charakteristisch und, soweit japanischer Provenienz, früher statt alphabetisch auch nach dem Iroha oder Gojūon angeordnet worden. Sie setzen in der Regel Kanji und/oder Kana zu dem latinisierten Eintrag. Die jap. Lexika erfassen die Schreibung, Lautung und Bedeutung der Wörter. Betrachtet man ihre Geschichte, so stehen die graphische Erfassung der Kanji, ihre (japanisierte) Aussprache *(jion/on:* „Zeichenlautung") und die Klärung ihrer Bedeutung, gegeben zumindest durch den Zusatz des jap. Wortäquivalentes *(wakun/kun:* „jap. Lesung"), voran. Sie dienen alsdann zur Feststellung der chinesischen Schreibung japanischer Wörter. All diese Aufgaben erfüllen die Kanji-Lexika, inhaltsgemäß auch „chin.-jap. Wörterbücher" *(kanwa-jiten)* genannt. Die Erfassung des jap. Wortschatzes und dessen Erläuterung in jap. Sprache folgte erst im Mittelalter, beginnend mit syllabisch geordneten Wörtersammlungen *(ombiki*-Typ) und der Anlage einsprachiger

Kana-Lexika, auch „Wörterbücher der Landessprache" *(kokugo-jiten)*, genannt. In ihrem Bereich haben sich in der Neuzeit Lexika für sprachl. Teilbereiche und für Fachsprachen entwickelt (sog. *semmon-jiten)*, die das hohe Niveau der modernen jap. Lexikographie mitprägen.

2. Geschichtliche Entwicklung

Die Geschichte der jap. Lexikographie setzt im ausgehenden 7. Jh. ein und läßt sich in eine frühe (ab 683), späte (ab 1598) und moderne (ab 1868) Phase gliedern. „Vorgeschichtlich" ist der Zeitraum seit Einführung der chin. Schrift mit dem 5. Jh., in dessen Verlauf alte chin. Lexika in Japan bekannt geworden sein dürften. Die frühe Phase der jap. Lexikographie (s. Bailey 1960) nimmt ihren Ausgang 683 mit der Order des Temmutennō, ein „neues Zeichenlexikon" (sinojap. *Shinji,* jap. *Niina)* zu schaffen (nicht überliefert), dessen Titel auf die Kenntnis älterer chin. Lexika hinweist. Lexika der Nara-Zeit (710—784), wie das *Yōshi-kangoshō* aus späteren Zitaten bekannt, sind nicht überliefert; allenfalls buddhistische chinesische Texte mit lexikalischen Lese- und Verständnishilfen (sog. *ongi),* die als Vorstufe echter Lexika gelten können.

Diese entstanden erst in der Heian-Zeit (794—1185), beginnend mit dem *Tenreibanshō-meigi* (ca. 830) des Mönches Kūkai, einem Kanji-Lexikon mit 16 200 Zeichen, ähnlich dem chin. *Yü-p'ien*. 898—901 wurde von dem Mönch Shōjū der „Neu zusammengestellte Zeichenspiegel" *(Shinsen-jikyō,* 21 300 Zeichen, 160 Klassen: Typ 1 a+1 c) abgeschlossen, mit Angabe der chin. Aussprache (nach dem *fan-ch'ieh* Verfahren; vgl. Art. 234), der Bedeutung (durch Setzung von Synonym-Kanji) und in ca. 3700 Fällen der äquivalenten jap. Wörter (mittels lautwertig gebrauchter Kanji, sog. *man'yōgana).* Aufgrund vergleichbarer chin. Lexika kompiliert, kann es doch wegen der zahlreichen Zusätze jap. Wortäquivalente *(wakun)* als erstes Kanwa-jiten angesprochen werden. Die „Klassifizierte Aufzeichnung jap. Namen" *(Wamyō-ruijushō)* des Minamoto Shitagō von 934 (abgek. *Wamyōshō,* Typ 1 c), überliefert in zwei Versionen von 10 u. 20 Büchern (s. Karow 1951), gliedert das Wortmaterial in 24 bzw. 32 Sachgruppen, verzeichnet Quelle, Aussprache, Bedeutung der Kanji und gibt die entspr. jap. Namen in Man'yōgana. Wegen der Einbeziehung der jap. Bezeichnungen gilt es als ältestes Lexikon des Japanischen *(kokugo-jiten);* wegen der Sachgliederung und des umfangreichen Quellenmaterials (insges. 290 chin. u. jap. Quellen zitiert) auch als ältestes enzyklopädisches Wörterbuch *(hyakka-jiten)* Japans. Seit dem 10. Jh. zeigen die Kanji-Lexika eine Japonisierung durch Aufnahme jap. Lesungen *(wakun),* mithin jap. Wortmaterials. Dieser Trend verstärkte sich in der späteren Heian-Zeit, ablesbar an den jap. Bearbeitungen chin. Lexika vom Typ *Chi'ieh-yün* (jap. *setsuin)* oder *Yü-p'ien* (jap. *gyokuhen).* Sie sind großenteils verloren oder nur in Zitaten späterer Werke überkommen. Einen Höhepunkt dieser Entwicklung markiert die erhaltene „Klassizierte Aufzeichnung von Aussprache u. Bedeutung" *(Ruijū-myōgishō,* anonym, frühes 12. Jh.). Mit ca. 32 000 Kanji und deren Komposita, nach dem *Yü-p'ien* in 120 Radikale gegliedert und mit Intonationszeichen *(shōten)* versehen, enthält es an die 10 000 jap. Lesungen in Man'yōgana und Katakana mit Akzentangaben. Es zitiert aus ca. 130 chin. u. jap. Quellen, darunter zahlreichen *ongi-* und *setsuin*-Werken (die einen wichtigen Teil des Rohmaterials späterer Lexika bildeten), und ist von hohem sprachhistorischen Wert.

Während all diese Wörterbücher noch von chin. Zeichen ausgehen, entwickeln sich seit der 2. Hälfte der Heian-Zeit Lexika, die vom jap. Wort ausgehen. Sie entstammen der Hochblüte jap. Waka-Dichtung und verzeichnen den poetischen Wortschatz in sachlicher Ordnung. Die erste allgemeine jap. Wörtersammlung ist die „Klassifizierte Kanji-Aufzeichnung in syllabarischer Ordnung" *(Iroha-jiruishō,* Typ 1 b) des Tachibana Tadakane (Erstfassung um 1145 in 2 Bd. nicht überliefert, spätere Neufassungen in 3 u. 10 Bd.). Sie ordnet das jap. Wortmaterial nach den 47 Silben des *Iroha-uta,* unterteilt aber jede Silbengruppe *(bu)* in 21 gleiche Sachgruppen *(mon).* Titelgemäß bezweckte dies Lexikon die Feststellung der Kanji-Schreibung des jap. Wortschatzes, der syllabarisch geordnet, in Kanji gegeben und durch Man'yōgana oder Katakana lautlich fixiert wurde. Das spätere Mittelalter der Kamakura- u. Muromachi-Zeit (1192—1573) hat viele weitere Lexika hervorgebracht. Es entstanden Kanwa-jiten in der Nachfolge des *Ruijū-myōgishō* wie das *Jikyō* (12. Jh.?), das auf ihm aufbauende *Jikyōshū* (1. Hälfte 13. Jh.). und das *Wagokuhen* (15. Jh.); letzteres blieb mit vielen Überarbeitungen bis in die Neuzeit als Prototyp eines sinojap. Zeichenlexikons populär. Relativ groß ist die Zahl der enzyklopädischen Sachgruppenlexika des Mittelalters, die einen klassifizierten Wort- und Zeichenschatz geben, stellenweise auch mit etymologischen Hinweisen, u. a. das *Chiribukuro* (2. Hälfte 13. Jh.), *Shūgaishō* (um 1300) und das *Kagakushū* (1444), das wohl verbreitetste dieser Art. In diese Epoche fällt das Erscheinen der „Aufzeichnungen über Nomina u. andere Wörter" *(Myōgoki,* 1268) des Mönchs Kyōson, des ersten etymologischen Wörterbuches der jap. Sprache.

Deutlich zugenommen hat im Mittelalter der Anteil der jap. Wortlexika gegenüber den sinojap. Zeichenlexika. Ordnungselemente sind hier Sachgruppen und Kana-Syllabar (meist *iroha*-Folge); der Wortschatz erscheint in Kanji mit Katakana-Lesungen. Das populärste Lexikon Japans vom Mittelalter bis in die Neuzeit, die „Leicht faßliche (Wörter)Sammlung für den Alltagsgebrauch" *(Setsuyōshū,* anonym, 2. Hälfte 15. Jh.), basierend auf dem *Kagakushū* und der Struktur des *Iroha-jiruishō,* repräsentiert diese Tradition und hat viele Überarbeitungen erfahren. Etwa gleichzeitig (1484) ist das erste solcher Lexika in *Gojūon-* statt *Iroha-*Folge erschienen: das *Onko-chishinsho* des Ōtomo Hirokimi.

Einen wesentlichen Fortschritt erreichte die traditionelle jap. Lexikographie in ihrer späten, der Tokugawa-Zeit (1600—1868) entsprechenden Phase, gefördert auch durch die Verbreitung des Buchdrucks. Damals wurden die ersten großen jap. Lexika geschaffen, die den Wortschatz in Kana und syllabarischer Ordnung (Typ 2 a, 2 b) darbieten und jap. kommentieren (Kanji-Schreibung der Stichwörter nur als Zusatzinformation). Prototyp ist der „Leitfaden der jap. Aussprache" *(Wakun no shiori)* des Tanigawa Kotosuga (1777 in Druck, abgeschlossen 1887). Er enthält in 82 Fasz. und Gojūon-Folge die bis dahin größte Sammlung des klass. und zeitgen. jap. Wortschatzes mit Erläuterungen und Quellenbelegen. Speziell den Wortschatz der Heian-Literatur sammelte mit Quellenbelegen der „Konspekt der klass. Sprache" *(Gagen-shūran)* des Ishikawa Masamochi (21 Fasz. in *iroha*-Folge, 1826—1849, unvoll., erw. Ausg. 1887 von Nakajima Hirotari), während der „Konspekt der Umgangssprache" *(Rigen-shūran)* des Ōta Zensai (26 Fasz. in *gojūon*-Folge, Entstehungszeit ungewiß, erw. Ausg. 1900) den Wortschatz der zeitgen. Sprache einschließlich Dialektismen zusammentrug. Weiterhin ist diese Periode durch das Erscheinen zahlreicher Speziallexika gekennzeichnet, eine Entwicklung, die sich in der modernen jap. Lexikographie fortgesetzt hat. Zu nennen sind erste Dialektwörterbücher, etymologische Wörterbücher oder Dichterlexika, sodann auch enzyklopädische Lexika, von denen das *Wakan-sanzai-zue* (1715) des Terajima Ryōan die weiteste Verbreitung fand.

Um 1600 erschienen dank der portugiesischen Christenmission die ersten mehrsprachigen Wörterbücher des Japanischen, und damit begann ein neuer Abschnitt der jap. Lexikographie (vgl. Laures 1957). Erstmals wurde das Jap. in Lateinschrift transkribiert u. in seinem damaligen Lautstand nach port. System erfaßt. Neben einer Sammlung von 282 „goldenen Worten" (Quincuxŭ = Kinkushū, 1593), Sprichwörtern zumeist chin. Provenienz, und einem ebenfalls für Lernzwecke verfaßten Kanji-Lexikon *(Racuyoxu* = *Rakuyōshū,* 1598, vgl. Bailey 1962, 214) gaben die port. Jesuiten in ihrer Druckerei auf Amakusa (W. Kyūshū) 1595 das *Dictionarium Latino-Lusitanicum, ac. Iaponicum* heraus. Mit seinen annähernd 30 000 Einträgen erfaßt es wesentliche Teile des damaligen jap. Wortschatzes. Es folgte das 1603 in Nagasaki gedruckte *Vocabulario da lingoa de Iapam com adeclaração em Portugues* mit 32 800 Wörtern der jap. Umgangssprache, einschl. Dialektismen, mit gram. Hinweisen und exakten port. Bedeutungsangaben — ein großer Wurf der vormodernen Lexikographie (s. Cooper 1976). 1632 wurde in Rom das kleinere *Dictionarium sive Thesauri Linguae Iaponicae Compendium* herausgegeben, ein lat.-span.-jap. Wörterbuch des spanischen Dominikaners Diego Collado. Zusammen mit Grammatiken und transkribierten Texten besitzen diese Werke höchsten sprachhist. Wert. Der anschließende Kontakt mit den holländischen Händlern in Nagasaki/Dejima führte zu jap. Initiativen der sog. Hollandkunde *(rangaku)* mit wesentlichem Anteil des Sprachstudiums und der Schaffung holl.-jap. Lexika wie dem *Haruma-wage* (1796) von Inamura Sampaku nach F. Halma's „*Nederduits Woordenboek"*, dem *Dōfu-Haruma* (1833), nach Halma's „*Woordenboek der Nederduitsche en Fransche taalen"* von H. Doeff zusammen mit japan. Dolmetschern für das Jap. bearb., und dessen überarbeitete Druckausgabe *Oranda-jii* (1858). In diese Periode fällt auch das Erscheinen des ersten jap.-russ. Wörterbuches *Novyj leksikon slaveno-japonskij* (St. Petersburg 1738) von Gonza, einem schiffbrüchigen Japaner, und A. I. Bogdanov (s. Murayama 1985). Der erste englische Versuch einer jap. Wörtersammlung, *An English and Japanese and Japanese and English Vocabulary,* stammt von W. H. Medhurst (Batavia 1830, ca. 7 000 jap. Wörter). Nach der Landesöffnung folgen seit der Mitte des 19. Jh. zahlreiche zwei- und mehrsprachige Lexika (s. Art. 328).

Die moderne jap. Lexikographie konnte an eine reiche Tradition anknüpfen. Sie hat hervorragende Werke auf den Gebieten der Kanwa-jiten, Kokugo-jiten und Semmon-jiten hervorgebracht und seit den 50er Jahren dieses Jhs. eine besondere Produktivität entwickelt. Dabei haben allg. Schulpflicht und Ausbau eines modernen Bildungswesens die massenhafte Herstellung und Verbreitung der Wörterbücher und Nachschlagewerke entscheidend vorangetrieben. Die Szene der jap. Zeichenlexika (*kanwa-jiten,* Typ 1 a, seit den 50er Jahren manche mit Veränderungen der Radikal-Anordnung) wird von denjenigen beherrscht, die den sinojap. Wortschatz jap. Druckerzeugnisse nach Lesung und Bedeutung erklären. Unter den älteren ragt heraus das *Daijiten* („Großes Zeichenlexikon", 1917) von Ueda Kazutoshi, unter den jüngeren das *Gakken Kanwa-daijiten* (1978) von Tōdō Akiyasu. Moderne Zeichenlexika sind durch Lesungs- und Strichzahl-Indizes über die Radikal-Anordnung hinaus zugänglich. Zur Erschließung des klass. chin. Wortschatzes inkl. wesentlicher Teile des sinojap. dient das umfassende Zeichenlexikon *Dai-Kanwa-jiten* (13 Bde., 1955—60; erw. Aufl. 1984—86) von Morohashi Tetsuji mit 48 902 bzw. 50 294 Zeichen (*Daijiten:* 14 924) und deren Komposita (insg. 526 000), eine der großen Leistungen der mod. jap. Lexikographie. Die Herstellung enzyklopädischer Wörterbücher des Japanischen wurde seit der frühen Meiji-Zeit im Zuge sprachreformerischer Maßnahmen von Regierungsseite gefördert. 1889—91 erschien ein Lexikon der damaligen Hochsprache *(futsūgo)* unter dem Titel „Wortmeer" (*Genkai,* 4 Bde.), im Regierungsauftrag kompiliert von Ōtsuki Fumihiko, einem führenden Mitglied der amtl. Sprachkommission (in erw. Form als *Daigenkai,* 5 Bde. 1932—37, noch heute verwendet). Mit seinen annähernd 40 000 Stichwörtern, etymolog. u. Quellenangaben erfaßt es große Teile des damaligen jap. Wortschatzes, inkl. der westl. Fremdwörter. Das *Nihon-daijisho* (12 Bde., 1892—93) des Yamada Bimyō zeichnet sich durch Akzentangaben u. umgangssprachliche Erklärungen aus. In den gleichen Zeitraum gehört noch das *Kotoba no izumi* (5 Bde., 1898—99) von Ochiai Naobumi, eine Sammlung von ca. 120 000 Wörtern. Das *Dainihon kokugo-jiten* (4 Bde., 1915—1919) von Ueda Kazutoshi u. Matsui Kanji enthält mehr als 200 000 Wörter, wird aber noch weit übertroffen vom „Großen Wörterbuch" (*Daijiten,* 26 Bde., 1934—36) des Verlages Heibonsha: es enthält ca. 700 000 Wörter in einer großen Synthese des erreichbaren lexikogr. Materials aus Vergangenheit und Gegenwart mit Quellenangaben. Selektiver doch detaillierter und präziser in den Worterläuterungen ist das „Große Wörterbuch der jap. Sprache" (*Nihon-kokugo-daijiten,* 20 Bde., 1972—76, verkl. Ausg. 1979—81 in 10 Bdn.) des Verlages Shōgakkan. Es repräsentiert den bisherigen Höhepunkt der jap. Lexikographie. Doch auch einbändige Standardlexika wie das *Kōjien* (1955, ^{3}1983), aus dem *Jien* (1935) von Shimmura Izuru hervorgegangen, besitzen enzyklopädische Aussagekraft auf hohem Niveau, aufgefächert von der klass. Schriftsprache bis zu mod. Sondersprachen, Wörter und Sachen gleichermaßen erklärend. Weit zahlreicher sind die Lexika für die getrennte Behandlung der vormodernen Sprache (meist bis 1868: *kogo-jiten*) und der modernen Sprache *(kokugo-jiten, gendai-kokugo-jiten);* großformatig u. höchst instruktiv wie z. B. das *Jidaibetsu kokugodaijiten* (ab 1967) oder das *Kadokawa-kogo-daijiten* (ab 1982), doch auch im Taschenbuchformat noch äußerst nützlich wie z. B. das *Meikai Kokugo-jiten* (1952) und das *Meikai Kogo-jiten* (1953) des Verlages Sanseidō (viele Aufl.). Außerordentlich umfangreich ist schließlich das Gebiet der jap. Speziallexika *(semmon-jiten),* das sich nach 1945 vehement entwickelte und Tausende von Titeln hervorgebracht hat, die nahtlos in das Gebiet der Sachlexika und Enzyklopädien übergehen (vgl. Yamagiwa 1968: 1 092 Titel; Sōgō u. Asakura 1977: über 5 000 Titel für 1868—1972; „List of dictionaries & encyclopedia", 1982, 6 092 lieferbare jap. Nachschlagewerke), kann hier nur summarisch berührt werden. Zum modernen Japanischen gibt es Speziallexika der Dialekte und Soziolekte, der Fachsprachen und Geheimsprachen, der Neologismen, Fremdwörter und Modewörter, der Synonyme und Antonyme, der Intonation und Orthographie, der Orts- u. Eigennamen, Sprichwörter u. Redensarten. Hinzu kommt die große Gruppe der zwei- und mehrsprachigen Wörterbücher. Weit entwickelt sind auch die Speziallexika zur Erfassung des Wortschatzes traditioneller literarischer Genres, lit. Werke und Autoren, sowie die Wortindizes *(sakuin)* zu klass. Werken. Demgegenüber spielen einschlägige Werke nicht-jap. Provenienz in moderner Zeit eine äußerst geringe Rolle und dienen in der Regel eher didaktischen als lexikographischen Zwecken.

3. Lexikographie der Randsprachen

Das einzige dem Japanischen nachweislich verwandte Sprachgebiet ist das der Ryūkyū-Inseln. Dialektal stark differenziert des Inselcharakters wegen, gilt es insb. unter jap. Linguisten als jap. Dialektgruppe. Über mittelalterliche Wörtersammlungen ist wenig bekannt. 1711 erschien unter der einheimischen Sho-Dynastie am Hofe von Shuri das erste Lexikon der alten Sprache von Okinawa: *Konkōken-shū.* Die modernen lexikographischen Arbeiten begannen mit B. H. Chamberlains „*Luchuan*-English Vocabulary" (Chamberlain 1895) und dem Wörterbuch *Okinawa-goten* (1896) von Nakamoto Seisei (mit gram. Notizen). Der Wortschatzerschließung der alten Liedersammlung *Omoro-sōshi* (1532, Aufzeichnung in Hiragana) ist das *Omorosōshi-jiten sōsakuin* (1967) von Nakahara Zenchū u. Hokama Shuzen gewidmet. Auch das *Ryūka-kogo-jiten* (Naha 1983) von Awagon Chōshō erläutert den Wortschatz der alten Lieder. Es gibt eine Reihe von Wörtersammlungen der Inseldialekte (s. Brower 1950); das erste große Wörterbuch des zentralen Shuri-Dialekts von Okinawa wurde 1963 vom National Language Research Institute in Tōkyō herausgegeben (*Okinawago-jiten,* Wortmaterial in Lateinschrift mit jap. Erklärungen). Eine dialektgeographische Übersicht der Bezeichnung von 206 Begriffen in 13 Sachgruppen gibt das *Zusetsu Ryūkyūgo-jiten* (1981) von Nakamoto Masachie.

4. Ainu

Das genetisch noch umstrittene, fast ausgestorbene Ainu hat als nördliche Nachbarsprache des Japanischen relativ starkes lexikographisches Interesse gefunden. Die ersten Wörtersammlungen stammen aus dem frühen 17. Jh., so eine portugiesische des Jesuiten Jeronymo de Angelis von 1621 mit 54 Wörtern und eine japanische (*Ezo-kotoba no koto,* vor 1626), die 117 Wörter u. Wendungen mit jap. Äquivalenten, wohl für den Handelsverkehr bestimmt, enthält. Insg. gibt es weit über 100 bekannt gewordene ältere Glossare als Wortlisten in Beschreibungen der Ainu-Sprache oder als selbständige Wörterbücher (vgl. Dettmer 1967 u. 1969). Das erste umfangreiche Lexikon ist das Werk „Miszellen zum Ainu-Dialekt" (*Ezo-hōgen moshiogusa,* 1792) von Uehara Kumajirō u. Abe Chōzaburō, das ca. 3 000 Wörter mit regionaler Differenzierung enthält, sich um exakte Lautwiedergabe bemüht und die Grundlage für die moderne jap. Ainu-Lexikographie bildet. Es diente u. a. als eine wichtige Quelle für das *Ainsko-russkij slovar* (Kazan 1875) von M. M. Dobrotvorskij. Ein weiterer Ausgangspunkt der mod. Ainu-Lexikographie ist das Werk des engl. Missionars John Batchelor, insb. *An Ainu-English-Japanese Dictionary and Grammar* (Tōkyō 1889). Große mod. jap. Ainu-Wörterbücher sind erst nach 1945 erschienen, so das nach Sachgruppen geordnete *Bunrui Ainugo-jiten* (1953—1962) von Chiri Mashiho und das Dialektwörterbuch *Ainugo-hōgen-jiten* (1964) von Hattori Shirō.

5. Literatur (in Auswahl)

5.1 Wörterbücher

Angelis 1621 = Jeronymo de Angelis. In: Hubert Cieslik: Hoppō tanken-ki. Tōkyō 1962 [S. 29 f.].

Awagon 1983 = Chōshō Awagon: Ryūka-kogo-jiten. Naha 1983 [463 S.].

Batchelor 1889 = John Batchelor: An Ainu-English-Japanese Dictionary and Grammar. Tōkyō 1889, ⁴1938. Reprint 1981 [insg. 876 S.].

Chamberlain 1895 = Basil Hall Chamberlain: Luchuan-English Vocabulary. In: Essay in Aid of a Grammar and Dictionary of the Luchuan Language. Transactions of the Asiatic Society of Japan 23. 1895, 188—267.

Chiri 1953—1962 = Mashiho Chiri: Bunrui Ainugo-jiten. 3 Bde. Tōkyō 1953—1962 [insg. 1493 S.].

Chiribukuro 13. Jh. = Yoshitane Toki(?): Chiribukuro. Ausg. Nihon-koten-zenshū. Tōkyō 1934—1935. 2 Bde. [ca. 400 S.].

Collado 1632 = Diego Collado: Dictionarium sive Thesauri Linguae Iaponicae Compendium. Rom 1632 [355 S.].

Daijiten 1934—1936 = Yasaburō Shimonaka (Hrsg.): Daijiten. 26 Bde. Tōkyō 1934—1936. Verkl. Ausg. 13 Bde. Tōkyō 1953—1954 [insg. 16 337 S.]. Verkl. Nachdruck 2 Bde. 1974 (4 209 S.].

Dictionarium 1595 = Dictionarium Latino-Lusitanicum, ac Iaponicum. Amakusa 1595 [908 S.].

Dobrotvorskij 1875 = Michail Michailovič Dobrotvorskij: Ainsko-russkij slovar'. Kazan 1875 [654 S.].

Doeff 1833 = Hendrik Doeff u. a.: Dōfu-Haruma. Nagasaki 1833 [insg. ca. 3 000 S.].

Doeff 1858 = Hendrik Doeff u. a.: Oranda-jii. Edo 1858. [insg. 1876 S.] Hrsg. v. Tsutomu Sugimoto, Tōkyō 1974.

Ezo-kotoba no koto ca. 1626 = Anonym: Ezo-kotoba no koto. In: Kindaichi-hakase kijukinen henshū-iinkai (Hrsg.): Kindaichi-Kyōsuke-senshū. Bd. 1. Tōkyō 1960, 486—491.

Gonza/Bogdanov 1738 = s. Murayama 1985.

Hattori 1964 = Shirō Hattori: Ainugo-hōgen-jiten. Tōkyō 1964 [556 S.].

Inamura 1796 = Sampaku Inamura: Harumawage. Edo 1796 [2181 S.].

Ishikawa 1826—1849 = Masamochi Ishikawa: Gagen-shūran 1826—1849 (unvollendet). Ergänzt v. Hirotari Nakajima: Zōho Gagen-shūran. Tōkyō 1887. Nachdrucke 3 Bde. Tōkyō 1903—1904, 1965 [2536 S.].

Jidaibetsu Kokugo-daijiten 1967 f. = Jidaibetsu kokugo-daijiten. Jōdai-hen. Tōkyō 1967 [58, 904, 190 S.]. Muromachi-jidai-hen I. Tōkyō 1985 [13, 1256 S.].

Jikyō 12. Jh.(?) = Anonym: Jikyō. Ausg. Kojisho-ongi-shūsei. Tōkyō 1980 [370 S.]. Indexbd. 1983 [240 S.].

Jikyōshū (1. Hälfte 13. Jh.) = Tamenaga Sugawara: Jikyōshū. Ausg. Kojisho-sōkan-kankōkai. Tōkyō 1977 [ca. 2000 S.].

Kadokawa-kogo-daijiten 1982 f. = Yukihiko Nakamura/Masao Okami/Atsuyoshi Sakakura: Kadokawa-kogo-daijiten. Tōkyō 1982 f. Bd. 1, a—ka [938 S.], Bd. 2, ki-sa [789 S.].

Kagakushū 1444 = Anonym: Kagakushū. Vorw. 1444. Druck 1617 (Genna-sannen-bon). Ausg. Kojisho-sōkan-kankōkai. Tōkyō 1968 [171, 248 S.].

Kindaichi 1952, 1953 = s. Meikai Kokugo/Kogojiten.

Konkōken-shū 1711 = Konkōken-shū. Shuri 1711. In: Iha Fuyū: Ko-Ryūkyū. 4. verb. Aufl. Suppl. Naha 1942, 391—454.

Kūkai ca. 830 = Sunao Saeki (Kōbō-daishi): Tenrei-banshō-meigi. Ausg. Kōzanji-shiryō-sōsho Bd. 6. Tōkyō 1977 [502 S. inkl. Index].

Kyōson 1268 = Kyōson: Myōgoki. Ausg. Benseisha. Tōkyō 1983 [1409 S.].

List of dictionaries & encyclopedia = Shuppan-nyūsusha (Hrsg.): Jiten-jiten-sō(go)-mokuroku. Tōkyō 1961, 1974, 1982.

Medhurst 1830 = Walter Henry Medhurst: An English and Japanese and Japanese and English Vocabulary. Batavia 1830 [9, 344 S.].

Meikai Kogo-jiten 1953 = Kyōsuke Kindaichi (Red.), bearb. v. Haruhiko Kindaichi u. a. Meikai Kogojiten. Tōkyō 1953 [1136 S.].

Meikai Kokugo-jiten 1952 = Kyōsuke Kindaichi u. a.: Meikai Kokugo-jiten kaiteiban. Tōkyō 1952 [978 S.].

Minamoto 934 = Shitagō Minamoto: Wamyō-ruijushō. 934. Hrsg. v. Atsuo Masamune. 2 Bde. u. 1 Indexbd. [insg. 954, 402 S.].

Morohashi 1955 = Tetsuji Morohashi: Daikanwa-jiten. 12 Bde. 1 Indexbd. Tōkyō 1955—1960. 2. verb. Aufl. 1984—1986 [13757, 1174 S.].

Murayama 1985 = Shichirō Murayama/Sadayoshi Igeta /Noriko Koshimizu (Hrsg.): Gonza's New Slavonic-Japanese Lexicon. Japanese Edition. Tōkyō 1985 [572 S.].

Nakahara/Hokama 1967 = Zenchū Nakahara/ Shuzen Hokama: Omorosōshi-jiten, sōsakuin. Tōkyō 1967 [566 S.].

Nakamoto 1896 = Seisei Nakamoto: Okinawa-goten. Naha 1896 [279 S.].

Nakamoto 1981 = Masachie Nakamoto: Zusetsu Ryūkyūgo-jiten. Tōkyō 1981 [463 S.].

Nakamura/Okami/Sakakura 1982, s. Kadokawa-kogo-daijiten.

Nihon-kokugo-daijiten 1972—1976 = Nihon-daijiten-kankōkai (Hrsg.): Nihon-kokugo-daijiten. 20 Bde. Tōkyō 1972—1976. Verkl. Ausg. 10 Bde. Tōkyō 1979—1981 [insg. 14 073 S.].

Ochiai 1898—1899 = Naobumi Ochiai: Kotoba no izumi. 5 Bde. Tōkyō 1898—1899. Verb. Aufl. bearb. v. Yaichi Haga. 5 Bde. u. 1 Indexbd. 1921—1928 [5154, 873 S.].

Okinawago-jiten 1963 = Okinawago-jiten. Hrsg. v. The National Language Research Institute. Tōkyō 1963 [854 S.].

Ōta o. J. = Zensai Ōta: Rigen-shūran. O. J. Erw. v. Yorikuni Inoue/Heijō Kondō: Zōho Rigen-shūran. Tōkyō 1900. Nachdruck 3 Bde. Tōkyō 1965—1966 [insg. 2536 S.].

Ōtomo 1484 = Hirokimi Ōtomo: Onko-chi-shinsho. Ausg. Hakuteisha. Tōkyō 1962 [182 S.].

Ōtsuki 1889—1891 = Fumihiko Ōtsuki: Genkai. 4 Bde. Tōkyō 1889—1891. Verkl. Ausg. 1904 [1110 S.].

Ōtsuki 1932—1937 = Fumihiko Ōtsuki: Daigenkai. 4 Bde. 1 Indexbd. Tōkyō 1932—1937 [insg. 3842, 695 S.]. Verb. Aufl. 1 Bd. 1956 [16, 15, 2213, 25, 2, 3 S.].

Quincuxú 1593 = Kinkushū. Amakusa 1592—1593. Hrsg. v. Sumio Yoshida: Amakusaban Kinkushū no kenkyū. Tōyō-bunko-ronsō 24. Tōkyō 1938 [21, 340, 12, 48 S.].

Racuyoxu 1598 = Rakuyōshū. Nagasaki 1598. s. Bailey 1962.

Ruijū-myōgishō o. J. = Anonym: Ruijū-myōgishō (frühes 12. Jh.). Nachdruck des Ms. Kanchiinbon 3 Bde. Tenri 1976 [insg. 1360 S.].

Setsuyōshū (15. Jh.) = Anonym: Setsuyōshū. 2. Hälfte 15. Jh. Ausg. Nihon-koten-zenshū. Tōkyō 1926 [3, 3, 280 S.].

Shimmura 1935 = Izuru Shimmura: Jien. Tōkyō 1935 [2285 S.].

Shimmura 1955 = Izuru Shimmura: Kōjien. Tōkyō 1955 [2359 S.], ³1983 [2667 S.].

Shōjū 898—901 = Shōjū: Shinsen-jikyō. Nachdruck der Hs. Tenjibon. Kyōto 1967 [889 S.].
Shūgaishō (um 1300) = Kinkata Tōin (?): Shūgaishō. Ausg. Zōtei Kojitsu-sōsho 11. Tōkyō 1928 [287 S.].
Tachibana ca. 1145 = Tadakane Tachibana: Iroha-jiruishō. ca. 1145. Hrsg. v. Atsuo Masamune. Tōkyō 1965 [insg. 1823 S.].
Tanigawa 1777 = Kotosuga Tanigawa: Wakun no shiori. Erw. v. Yorikuni Inoue/ Onson Kosugi: Zōho Gorin Wakun no shiori. 3 Bde. Tōkyō 1898 [insg. 2595 S.].
Terajima 1712 = Ryōan Terajima: Wakan-sansaizue. Tōkyō. Erstdruck 1824. Nachdrucke 1884, 1902, 1906, 1929, 1970 [1469, 100 S.].
Tōdō 1978 = Akiyasu Tōdō: Gakken Kanwa-daijiten. Tōkyō 1978 [1740, 90 S.].
Ueda 1917 = Kazutoshi (Mannen) Ueda: Daijiten. Tōkyō 1917. Amerik. Ausg. Harvard 1942, 1963 [73, 26, 2596, 10, 110 S.].
Ueda/Matsui 1915—1918 = Kazutoshi (Mannen) Ueda/Kanji Matsui: Dainihon-kokugo-jiten. 4 Bde. Tōkyō 1915—1919. Indexbd. 1928. Verb. Aufl. 1940—1941 [insg. 5377 S.].
Uehara/Abe 1792 = Kumajirō Uehara/Chōzaburō Abe: Ezo-hōgen moshiogusa. O. O. 1792, ²1804, unveränd. Nachdruck 1972 [insg. 110 S.].
Vocabulario 1603 = Vocabulario da lingoa de Iapam com adeclaração em Portugues. Nagasaki 1603. Hrsg. v. Tadao Doi: Nippo-jisho. Tōkyō 1960 [822 S.].
Wagokuhen 15. Jh. = Anonym: Wagokuhen (Wagyokuhen). Ausg. Nihon-koten-zenshū. Tōkyō 1936 [486 S.].
Yamada 1893 = Bimyō Yamada: Nihon-daijisho. Tōkyō 1892—1893. 12 Liefr. [1431 S.].

5.2 Sonstige Literatur

Aoki 1961 = Takashi Aoki: Jisho sakuin no rekishi. In: Kokugo-kokubungaku-kenkyūshi-taisei. Bd. 15: Kokugogaku. Tōkyō 1961, 226—279.
Bailey 1960 = Don Clifford Bailey: Early Japanese lexicography. In: Monumenta Nipponica 16. 1960, 1—52.
Bailey 1962 = Don Clifford Bailey: The Rakuyōshū. In: Monumenta Nipponica 17. 1962, 214—264.
Brower 1950 = Robert H. Brower: A bibliography of Japanese dialects. In: Univ. of Michigan, Center for Jap. Studies, Bibliogr. Ser. No. 2, Ann Arbor 1950.
Cooper 1976 = Michael Cooper: The Nippo Jisho. In: Monumenta Nipponica 31. 1976, 417—430.
Dettmer 1967/1969 = Hans A. Dettmer: Beiträge zur Geschichte der Ainu-Lexikographie. In: Oriens Extremus 14,2. 1967, 235—256, u. 16,1. 1969, 15—40.
Doi 1977 = Toshio Doi: The study of language in Japan. Tōkyō 1977.
Karow 1951 = Otto Karow: Die Wörterbücher der Heianzeit und ihre Bedeutung für die japanische Sprachgeschichte. In: Monumenta Nipponica 7. 1951, 156—197.
Kawase 1955 = Kazuma Kawase: Kojisho no kenkyū. Tōkyō 1955.
Laures 1940 = Johannes Laures: Kirishitan Bunko. A manual of books and documents on the early christian mission in Japan. Tōkyō 1940.
Müller-Yokota 1987 = Wolfram Müller-Yokota: Abriß der geschichtlichen Entwicklung der Schrift in Japan. In: Bochumer Jahrbuch zur Ostasienforschung 1987, 1—75.
Satō 1977 = Kiyoji Satō (Hrsg.): Kokugogaku-kenkyū-jiten, shiryōhen, Abschn. jisho. Tōkyō 1977, 292—293.
Sōgō 1977 = Masaaki Sōgō u. Haruhiko Asakura: Jisho-kaidai-jiten. Tōkyō 1977.
Yamagiwa 1968 = Joseph K. Yamagiwa: Bibliography of Japanese encyclopedias and dictionaries. Ann Arbor 1968.
Yoshida 1971 = Kanehiko Yoshida: Jisho no rekishi. In: Kōza kokugoshi. Bd. 3: Goishi. Tōkyō 1971, 413—537.

Bruno Lewin, Bochum
(Bundesrepublik Deutschland)

266. Mongolische Lexikographie

1. Vorbemerkung
2. Die mongolischen Sprachen
3. Mittelmongolische Periode
4. Das 18./19. Jahrhundert
5. Die Moderne
6. Literatur (in Auswahl)

1. Vorbemerkung

Es wird das System der einheimischen Lexikographie dargestellt, das europäische Lexika bzw. Bearbeitungen originaler Wörterbücher (Wb.) oft u. a. durch eine lateinisch-alphabetische Gliederung verdecken (Poppe 1938, 1972; Lessing 1960).

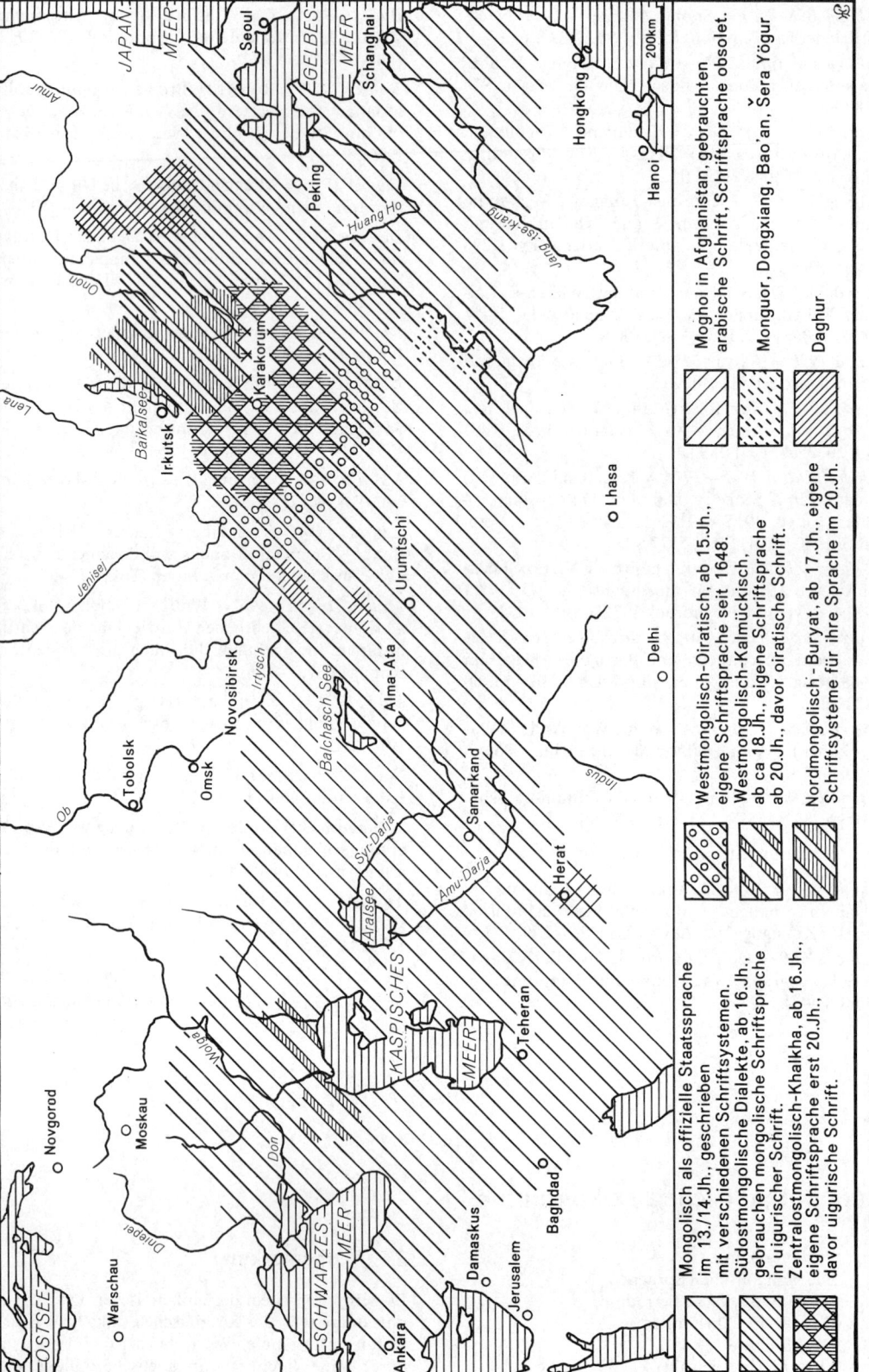

2624　XXVIII. Lexikographie der Einzelsprachen XII: Ost-asiatische Sprachen

Karte 266.1: Verbreitungsgebiet des Mongolischen

2. Die mongolischen Sprachen

Eine mongolische (mo.) Sprache existiert heute als lebende Einzelsprache ebensowenig wie eine Einzelsprache Semitisch. Allerdings haben sich die elf modernen mo. Sprachen (vgl. Karte 266.1) aus einer in der Norm im 13./14. Jh. noch einheitlichen Sprache herausentwickelt. Für die Beschreibung dieser Entwicklung und der u. a. damit verbundenen Lexikographie eignet sich deswegen eine diachronisch ausgerichtete Gliederung.

3. Mittelmongolische Periode

Aus dieser Periode (13.—16. Jh.) sind die frühesten Dokumente mo. Sprachen überliefert — abgefaßt in verschiedenen Schriftsystemen:

3.1. In chinesischer (chin.) Schrift

Das chin. *Yung-loh ta-tien* enthält ein mo.-chin. *ih-yü* „Übersetzungsvokabular" (um 1270), begrifflich gegliedert, mo. in phonetischen chin. Silbenzeichen, ein Gebrauchshandbuch für das mo. Dolmetschamt in China. Ebenso gegliedert erschien 1389 das mo.-chin. *Hua-I ih-yü* mit 17 Abschnitten nur nominaler Begriffe und mit chin. Angaben zur Aussprache des Mo. Eine spätere Kopie bringt das Mo. zusätzlich in uigurischer (uig.) Schrift. Diese mo.-chin. *ih-yü* sind die Vorläufer der chin.-fremdsprachlichen *ih-yü* mit bis zu 10 Sprachen (Haenisch 1957).

3.2. In arabischer (ar.) Schrift

Anfang 14. Jh. wurde von Ibn al-Muhannā in drei Teilen ein ar. Sprachenführer für die Sprachen Persisch (Per.), Türkisch (Tü.) und Mo. verfaßt. Der dritte, ar.-mo. Teil enthält 25 Kapitel, davon Kap. 2 und 3 Grammatik; die übrigen haben nach Sachgruppen gegliederte nominale Lexeme, diese jeweils nach dem ar. Alphabet geordnet (Weiers 1972). Vom Jahr 1343 stammt ein „Handbuch für tü., ar., mo. und per. Dolmetscher", wohl in Ägypten von Kiptschaq-Mongolen verfaßt, das Mo. betreffend ein mo.-per. und ein mo.-ar. Vokabular mit mo. Sätzen und ar. Übersetzung. Die Lexeme sind begrifflich gegliedert, Wortbildungsmorpheme gehören zum Lemma. Als kanonische Formen des verbalen Paradigmas finden sich *-ba* (finite Vergangenheit) und *-ji* (Konverb), als solche des nominalen Paradigmas Singular, Plural und auch Kasus (Poppe 1972). Aus dem 15. Jh. stammt die sog. Mukaddimat al-Adab, ein ar.-per.-tü.-mo. Einzel- und Satz-Wb. Die Lexeme und danach verbundene lexikalische Einheiten richten sich nach dem onomasiologisch gegliederten ar. Eintrag. Die verbundenen lexikalischen Einheiten bieten zahlreiche Konnotationen. Konzipiert war das Werk als polyglottes Gesprächsbuch für Händler und Reisende in Zentralasien (Poppe 1938). Endlich existiert ohne Jahr ein ar.-per.-tü.-mo. Vokabular eines Anonymus, gegliedert nach Sachgruppen, darunter grammatische Teile mit Pronomina und Verbformen (Ligeti 1962). Die Vokabulare enthalten von einigen 100 bis ca. 6 000 Lexeme.

4. Das 18./19. Jahrhundert

Nach einem an Schrifttum armen 15./16. Jh. wurde das 18./19. Jh. zur Blütezeit der mo. Lexikographie im Osten. Sie kann allerdings nur eingebunden in diejenige der mandschuchin. Ch'ing-Dynastie behandelt werden. Damals entstanden Hunderte von Wb. und Vokabularen, meist polyglotte, das Mo. stets in uig. Schrift. Im 18. Jh. mehr begrifflich gegliedert, hatten sie neben der Zusammenstellung von Lexemen für die Hauptsprachen des Reichs — Mandschu (Ma.), Chin., Mo., Tibetisch (Tib.), Tü. — auch als Wb. für Ortsnamen, religiöse Termini (tib.-mo.), Verwaltung, Ränge und Titel die Erfassung eines technolektischen Wortschatzes zum Ziel. Bild-Wb. kamen hinzu. Berühmt ist der „Fünf-Sprachen Wörterspiegel", 36 Bände, und von 1708 das ma.-mo. Wb., 21 Bände mit mo. Glossen. Ende 18. und Anfang 19. Jh. werden die Wb. auch alphabetisch gegliedert, das mo. Alphabet silbisch aufgefaßt, so daß z. B. die Lexeme mit *b*-Anlaut sich unter den Silben *ba, be, bi, bo, bu, bö, bü* ordnen. Danach entstanden als Anleitung für die Benutzung von Wb. die Syllabare. Als kanonische Form für die 22 finit-verbalen, 9 verbalnominalen und 16 konverbalen Paradigmaformen wurde das Verbalnomen *-qu* festgelegt. Die Ableitungssuffixe blieben Bestandteil des Lemmas. Alles das gilt bis heute für Wb. in uig. Schrift. Von den vielen alphabetischen Wb. sei das 17bändige mo.-chin.-ma. Wb. von 1891 erwähnt. Bei den Westmongolen entstanden nur wenige Wb., die als kalmükkisch (in oiratischer Schrift) — russische Wb. wohl von Europäern erstellt wurden.

5. Die Moderne

Die Wb.-Struktur des 18./19. Jh. und die uig. Schrift haben sich bis heute nur bei den Ostmongolen Chinas, Autonomes Gebiet Innere Mongolei, erhalten.

5.1. Innere Mongolei

Den Alphabetsilben (*ba, be..*) fügt man heute die Aussprache im IPA bei. Nach westlichen Vorbildern entstanden einsprachige enzyklopädische Wb. (A) und neue ein- und zweisprachige Wb.-Typen: Orthographie- und Aussprache-Wb. mit Artikulation im IPA (B), Wb. wissenschaftlicher Termini (C), Wb. des modernen Wortschatzes (D) und Wb. der gebräuchlichsten Wörter (E), ferner Wb. für andere mo. Sp., z. B. für Oiratisch (F).

5.2. Khalkha (K.)

Mit Einführung der Lateinschrift 1927 und seit 1941 der kyrillischen Schrift wurde das bis dahin schriftlose K.-Mo. zur Staatssprache der Mongolischen Volksrepublik. Alle Typen der in der UdSSR erstellten Wb. entstanden mit der Zeit auch hier (G). Von der alten Wb.-Struktur blieben die im K. entsprechende kanonische Form -*h* und die Ableitungssuffixe als Bestandteile des Lemmas erhalten. Neu sind Wb. mit dem Stamm als Lemma + Sigla, die auf die je möglichen Ableitungs- und Paradigmaformen verweisen (H). Wenn vorhanden, geben die Wb. die Entsprechungen der uig. geschriebenen Schriftsprache an.

5.3. Buryat

Über die noch laufenden lexikographischen Bemühungen der Buryaten unterrichtet Budaev (1978). Bisher gibt es nur ein einheimisches Standard-Wb. (Čeremisov 1973).

5.4. Kalmückisch (Ka.)

Ka. Wb. in oiratischer Schrift und Wb. des gesprochenen Ka. sind von Europäern verfaßt. Mit Einführung der kyrillischen Schrift erhielt das vom Oiratischen abweichende Ka. eine eigene Schriftsprache und eine an russischen Wb. orientierte einheimische Lexikographie (Mumin 1977).

5.5. Moghol

Die Moghol von Afghanistan schrieben ihre Sprache in ar. Schrift. Erhalten sind Vokabulare, begrifflich und nach dem ar. Alphabet gegliedert, zwei- und dreisprachig, auch mnemotechnisch in Gedichtform (Weiers 1975, 9—21).

5.6. Dongxiang

Seit 1980 ist Dongxiang versuchsweise Schriftsprache in mit IPA-Zeichen modifizierter Lateinschrift, bisher existiert ein etymologisches Wb. (Böke 1983).

5.7. Übrige moderne Sprachen und Dialekte

Einheimische Wb. für die schriftlosen mo. Sprachen Monguor, Daghur, Bao'an, Šera Yögur und Dialekte wie Ordos, Tsakhar usw. sind nicht vorhanden; hier gibt es nur europäische Werke.

6. Literatur (in Auswahl)

A = Mongγol üsüg-ün dürim-ün toli bičig. Kalgan 1951.

B = Mongγol kelen-ü jöb daγudalγ-a jöb bičilge-yin toli. Sining 1977.

Böke 1983 = Böke: Düngsiyang kelen-ü üges. o. O. 1983.

Budaev 1978 = C. B. Budaev: Leksika burjatskih dialektov v sravnitel'no-istoričeskom osveščenii. Novosibirsk 1978.

C = Mongγol udqa-yin jüil qubiyaγsan toli bičig. Peking 1956.

Čeremisov 1973 = K. M Čeremisov: Burjad-oros slovar'. Moskva 1973.

D = Mongγol kitad toli bičig. o. O. 1975.

E = Kebsigsen üge-yin toli. Kuehua 1984.

F = Xudum-todo keleni toli. o. O. 1979.

G = Standard-Wb. Luvsandendev: Mongol oros tol'. Moskva 1957. Einsprachig: Ja. Cevel: Mongol helnij tovč tajlbar tol'. Ulaanbaatar 1966.

H = Mongol üsgijn dürmijn tol'. Ulaanbaatar 1983.

Haenisch 1957 = Erich Haenisch: Sinomongolische Glossare. Berlin 1957.

Lessing 1960 = Ferdinand Lessing: Mongolian-English Dictionary. Berkeley 1960.

Ligeti 1962 = Louis Ligeti: Un vocabulaire Mongol d'Istanboul. In: Acta Orientalia Hungarica 14. 1962, 3—99.

Mumin 1977 = Mumin Bembe: Hal'mg-oros tol'. Moskva 1977.

Poppe 1938 = Nikolaj Poppe: Mongol'skij slovar' Mukaddimat Al-Adab. Moskva 1938.

Poppe 1972 = Nikolaus Poppe: Das mongolische Sprachmaterial einer Leidener Handschrift. Reprint: Westmead 1972.

Weiers 1972 = Michael Weiers: Ein arabisch-mongolischer Wörterspiegel aus der Biblioteca Corsini in Rom. In: Zentralasiatische Studien 6. 1972, 7—61.

Weiers 1975 = Michael Weiers: Schriftliche Quellen in Moġolī 2. Opladen 1975.

Michael Weiers, Bonn
(Bundesrepublik Deutschland)

XXIX. Lexikographie der Einzelsprachen XIII: Arktische und pazifische Sprachen
Lexicography of Individual Languages XIII: The Languages of the Arctic and of the Pacific
Lexicographie des langues particulières XIII: Les langues de l'Arctique et de l'Océanie

267. Lexicography of the Paleosiberian Languages

1. Introduction
2. Older Lexicography
3. Soviet Lexicography
4. Selected Bibliography

1. Introduction

1.1. The Paleosiberian languages (cf. Map 267.1) are Ket (also called Yenisei-Ostyak), Yukagir (Odul), Gilyak (Nivkh), and the small Chukotian

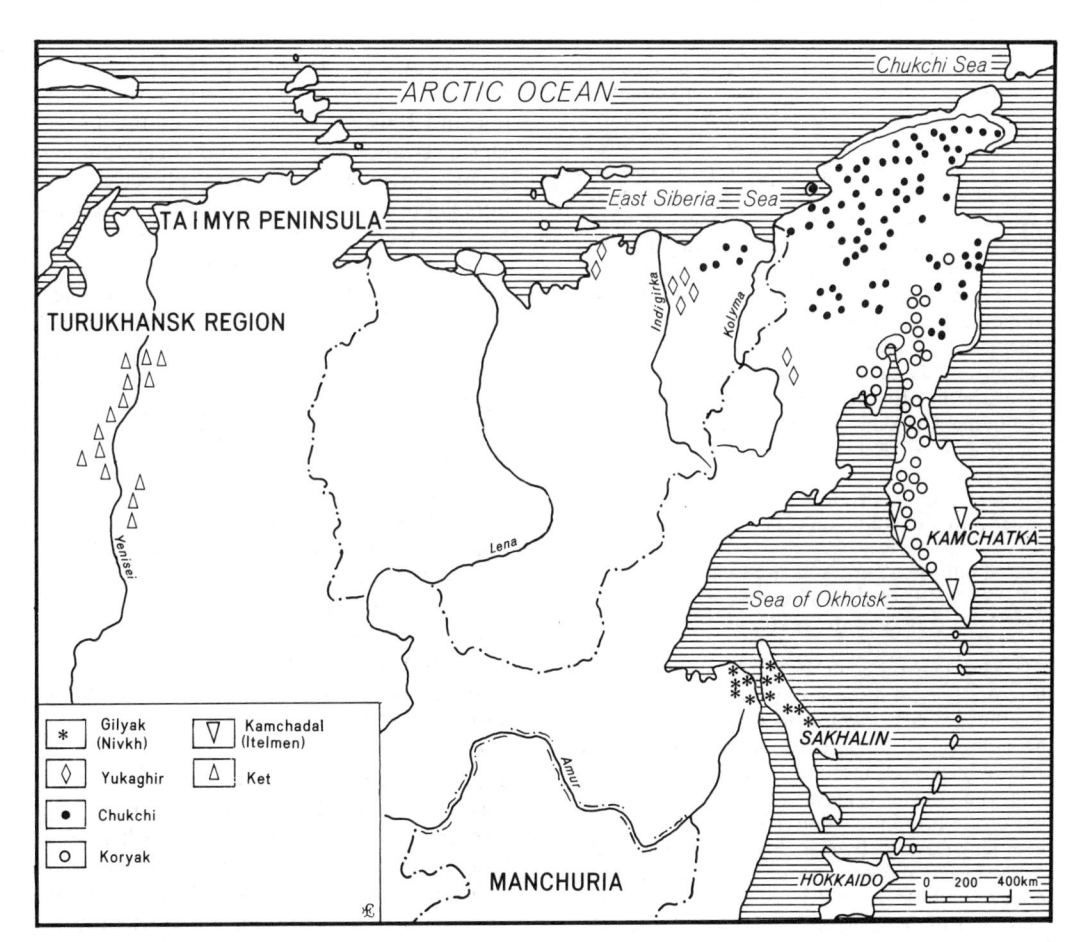

Map 267.1: Paleosibirian languages

family which consists of Chukchi, Koryak (also Nymylan) and Kamchadal (also Itelmen). (Two languages, Kerek and Alyutor, are also assigned to Chukotian, although they are considered to be Koryak dialects by some.) All of these languages are spoken in the northern half of Siberia, from the Yenisei to the Amur and from the Arctic Ocean to the South as far as the 50th parallel. See the map on page 2627. According to the latest census (USSR 1979), there were 1,100 Ket, 800 Yukagir, 4,400 Gilyak, 14,000 Chukchi, 7,900 Koryak, and 1,400 Kamchadal speakers. Precisely how many of these are competent native speakers of these languages is not known. It is unlikely that there are any completely monolingual speakers left. While there is therefore an obvious trend toward Russification (or of melting into other populations — mainly Tungus and, in the case of Yukagir, Yakut), the fact remains that in relative terms some of the Paleosiberian groups have recently increased while the largest group in the U.S.S.R., Russian, with more than 137 million speakers in 1979, has grown much less. This does not mean that the number of Paleosiberian speakers will rise but does mean that these languages are not doomed to immediate extinction, as some prophets predicted in the 1960s and 1970s.

1.2. The four Paleosiberian groups enumerated above (Ket, Yukagir, Gilyak and Chukotian) do *not* form a family. Rather, each group is probably a vestige of linguistic groups which covered larger areas in the North of Asia in the past. The first three have not been conclusively shown to be related to any other language or language families, although Yukagir has been assigned to the Uralic family (Finno-Ugric and Samoyed). Yukagir does in fact resemble Uralic. Ket is thoroughly aberrant (infixes, gender, a complicated verbal system), the structure of Gilyak is reminiscent of those of Korean and Japanese, and Chukchi and Koryak are of the incorporating type. Kamchadal, while resembling Chukchi and Koryak, is even more complicated. — Ket also has extinct congeners: Arin, Assan, and Kott. Yukagir, likewise, is related to Omok and Chuvan, which are extinct and known only from older sources.

1.3. Eskimo-Aleut and Ainu are sometimes classed as Paleo-Asiatic or Paleosiberian but are excluded from this survey. See articles 265 and 268.

1.4. The Paleosiberian peoples and languages therefore present a set of enigmas to the linguist, the ethnographer, and the historian: How old are the cultures? Do they reflect earlier stages in the cultural history of northern Asia? Were these languages and linguistic types more widespread in the past or are they innovations? What loanwords do these languages harbour and what do these loanwords suggest about the earlier ethnic and cultural history of Northern Asia? Can contacts or connections with the languages of the New World (Eskimo-Aleut, Athapascan) be traced or surmised? Can the trajectories of the migrations of the peoples who spoke these and related (and now extinct) languages in the past be traced through the minute study of languages (e.g., topographical terms, metallurgy, plant life)?

1.5. The most useful bibliographical tool for these languages is still Jakobson et al. 1957. Jazyki 1934, 1968, and 1979 (the three volumes do *not* form a series) contain the basic grammatical and bibliographical information. Comrie 1981 can be consulted for basic details. Matthews 1951 and Austerlitz 1974 are cursory introductions.

2. Older Lexicography

2.1. Paleosiberian lexicography (if such a designation may be used) is dictated primarily by three factors: the point in time when a particular language was first recorded, the degree of linguistic sophistication of the first field-workers, and the ultimate purpose of the compilation (word-list, lexicon for philology, linguistics, practical use).

2.2.1. Castrén 1858 is a posthumous publication. M. A. Castrén himself (1813—1852) was primarily interested in materials for launching and bolstering the study of the Finno-Ugric (Uralic) and Altaic language families, as he conceived them. This objective took him as far as Ket (and its extinct congeners). His Ket word-list (1858, 156—192) contains information from four dialects and is followed by Kott-German and German-Ket/ Kott lists (193—227, 229—261). Castrén 1858 can be called the first Paleosiberian dictionary and is still usable and used today. Grube 1892 is the work of an expert editor; Grube himself (1855—1908) was a Sinologist. This work is a tidy presentation of materials, collected during the Imperial expedition to Siberia of 1854—1856 primarily by two non-professionals, Leopold von Schrenck and P. von Glehn. The dictionary proper (43—113) is ordered on the principles of the Sanskrit alphabet. It is an amazingly durable and usable work, considering the inexpertise of the collectors, and contains remarks on grammar and loanwords.

2.2.2. Castrén 1858 and Grube 1892 form a class by themselves. Another class, represented by Angere 1957 and Worth 1969, is that of 20th-century compilations based on older texts and word-lists. Thus, Angere's dictionary is basically an alphabetically ordered list of words from the publications of

Wörterbuch

der

üblichen Sprache der Koriäcken,

von

Tumana bis Aklan.

Gott	Kamakaelin auch Aenigo.
Teufel	Manachteik.
Götzenbild	Ningivit.
Himmel	Cherwol.
Hölle	Wiálal.
Luft	Giwniuw.
Erde	Nutölut.
Wasser	Mimal.
Feuer	Milgan.
Wolke	Giniaeing.
Wind	Aénaeg.
Sturmwind	Ujalg.
Regen	Machumuch.
Schnee	Aá - al.
Hagel	Aéngaeriwii.
Eiß	Gilgil.
Thau	Pangopan.
Reif	Allapango.
Nebel	Wulch.
	Donner

Dictionary excerpt 267.1: Sample (from: Steller 1774)

Waldemar Jochelson (V. Jokhel'son) on Yukagir. Similarly, Worth 1969 is based primarily on Jochelson's (printed, manuscript, published and unpublished) Kamchadal collections and secondarily on some other sources (Erman 1848, Kraśeninnikov 1755, Radliński 1892—1895). Neither publication claims to contribute or contributes to the study of the grammar or history of the respective language. See Volodin 1971 and Volodin 1975.

2.3. Donner 1955/1958 contains word-lists based mostly on Donner's own work with informants. Since this material was not processed by the collector himself, it is published faithfully, but with a minimum of editorial interpretation.

2.4. Tailleur 1959 is a work of pure philology which salvages materials from Omok, an extinct language, and correlates them with Yukagir.

3. Soviet Lexicography

3.1. Soviet lexicography has had the advantage of direct access to prime materials, the enthusiasm of Soviet linguists of the 1920's and 1930's, and the stimulus of practical necessity.

3.2. Bogoraz 1937 gives the Chukchi forms in Roman letters. This practice was later abandoned in favour of Cyrillic alphabets with modifications designed to accommodate the phonology of each language, e.g. K_o for the post-velar (uvular) voiceless stop. Bogoraz 1937 and Korsakov 1939 are good examples of guardedly ambitious projects: they are serviceable dictionaries, with grammatical apparatus, designed by scholars for both scholars and practical use.

3.3. Skorik 1946 appeared at a point in history when its distribution was impeded. It is almost impossible to find.

3.4. Moll/Inènlikèj 1957 is a more modest attempt than Bogoraz 1937; presumably it was produced so as to provide a Chukchi-Russian dictionary with Cyrillic entries.

3.5. Žukova 1967 seems to be the most recent product of Soviet Chukotian lexicography. It is more ambitious than Bogoraz 1937, Korsakov 1939, and Moll/Inènlikèj 1957 (its title page indicates 18,500 entries). Pages 643—749 contain a very useful Koryak grammar "as contrasted with Russian" and two essential Koryak root lists.

3.6. Savel'eva/Taksami 1965 and 1970 (Russian Gilyak and Gilyak-Russian) constitute a felicitous set on a number of counts. (1) This is the only *set* of two dictionaries, compiled by one and the same team. (2) Savel'eva is a trained linguist-fieldworker and Taksami an ethnographer. (3) Taksami is a part-native-speaker and has first-hand knowledge of Gilyak culture. (4) The two works appeared within five years of each other and are therefore organically related. (5) The Gilyak-Russian volume (1970) contains very valuable bits of ethnographical information (on death rites, tabu, fishing equipment) which will serve the ethnographers of future generations. (6) These works (like others of the post-war period, but perhaps more so) make an attempt to explain and interpret Russian or Western-European cultural and every-day terms to the Gilyak user not only by simply introducing a foreign term into Gilyak by fiat (e.g., *America*) but also by interpreting it (e.g., *atomic ice-breaker,* 1965, 59).

3.7. Taksami 1983 is an innovation: It is intended explicitly for use in elementary schools, it is recommended by the Ministry of Education of the R.S.F.S.R., it introduces a number of judiciously chosen new symbols and a considerable number of words from the Sakhalin dialect, so as to permit its use in two dialect areas.

3.8. The treasures of the lexicon of the surviving Paleosiberian languages still remain to be mined, both in the field, with living informants, and in the old sources, by means of good philological work. One such source is Steller 1774.

4. Selected Bibliography

4.1. Dictionaries and Word-Lists

Angere 1957 = Johannes Angere: Jukagirisch-deutsches Wörterbuch. Zusammengestellt auf Grund der Texte von W. Jochelson. Stockholm 1957 [xviii + 272 p.].

Bogoraz 1937 = Vladimir Germanovič Bogoraz: Luoravetlansko-russkij (Čukotsko-russkij) slovar'. Leningrad 1937 [xlvi + 164 p.].

Castrén 1858 = Matthias Alexander Castrén: Versuch einer jenissei-ostjakischen und kottischen Sprachlehre nebst Wörterverzeichnissen aus den genannten Sprachen. Ed. by Anton Schiefner. St. Petersburg 1858 [xxii + 264 p.].

Donner 1955/1958 = Kai Donner: Ketica — Materialien aus dem Ketischen oder Jenisseiostjakischen. Aufgezeichnet von Kai Donner, bearbeitet und herausgegeben von Aulis J. Joki. Helsinki 1955, 1958 (Mémoires de la Société Finno-ougrienne 108, 108: 2) [136, 36 p.].

Grube 1892 = Wilhelm Grube: Giljakisches Wörterverzeichnis nebst grammatischen Bemerkungen. St. Petersburg 1892 (Reisen und Forschungen in Amur-Lande i. d. J. 1854—1856 ... herausgeg. v. Leopold von Schrenck. Anhang zum 3. Bd., 1. Lieferung.) [v + ii + 150 p.].

Korsakov 1939 = G. M. Korsakov: Nymylansko (koriaksko)-russkij slovar'. Ed. by Sergej Nikolaevič Stebnickij. Moskva 1939 [350 p.].

Moll/Inènlikèj 1957 = Tat'jana Aleksandrovna Moll/Petr Ivanovič Inènlikèj: Čukotsko-russkij slovar'. Ed. by P. Ja. Skorik. Leningrad 1957 [196 p.].

Radliński 1892—1895 = Ignacy Radliński: Słowniki narzeczy ludów kamczackich. Ze zbiorów Prof. B. Dybowskiego. Polska Akademia Umietjętności, Wydział Filologiczny. Rozprawy II. Kraków 1892, 1895 [I: 130—217, II: 103—124, III: 81—164, VII: 149—229.].

Savel'eva/Taksami 1965 = Valentina Nikolaevna Savel'eva/Čuner Mikhajlovič Taksami: Russko-nivkhskij slovar'. Moskva 1965 [480 p.].

Savel'eva/Taksami 1970 = Valentina Nikolaevna Savel'eva/Čuner Mikhajlovič Taksami: Nivkhsko-russkij slovar'. Moskva 1970 [536 p.].

Skorik 1946 = Petr Jakovlevič Skorik: Russko-čukotskij slovar' (s kratkim grammatičeskim očerkom čukotskogo jazyka). Leningrad 1946.

Tailleur 1959 = Oliver Guy Tailleur: Les uniques données sur l'omok, langue éteinte de la famille youkaghire. In: Orbis 8. 1959, 78—108.

Taksami 1983 = Čuner Mikhajlovič Taksami: Slovar' nivkhsko-russkij i russko-nivkhskij. Leningrad 1983 [288 p.].

Worth 1969 = Dean S. Worth: Dictionary of Western Kamchadal. Berkeley. Los Angeles 1969 [vii+320 p.].

Žukova 1967 = Alevtina Nikodimovna Žukova: Russko-korjakskij slovar'. Moskva 1967 [750 p.]

4.2. Other Publications

Austerlitz 1974 = Robert Austerlitz: Paleosiberian languages. In: Encyclopaedia Britannica, 15th ed. Chicago 1974, 914—916.

Comrie 1981 = Bernard Comrie: The Languages of the Soviet Union. Cambridge 1981.

Erman 1848 = [Georg] Adolph Erman: Reise um die Erde durch Nord-Asien und die beiden Oceane in den Jahren 1828, 1829 and 1830. 1. Abtl.: Historischer Bericht. 3. Band.: Die Ochozker Küste, das Ochozker Meer und die Reisen auf Kamtschatka im Jahre 1829. Berlin 1848.

Jakobson et al. 1957 = Roman Jakobson/Gerta Hüttl-Worth/John Fred Beebe: Paleosiberian Peoples and Languages: A Bibliographical Guide. New Haven 1957.

Jazyki 1934 = Jazyki i pis'mennost' narodov severa, 3: Jazyki i pis'mennost' paleoaziatskikh narodov. Ed. by E. A. Krejnovič. Moskva-Leningrad 1934.

Jazyki 1968 = Jazyki narodov S.S.S.R., 5: Mongol'skie, tunguso-man'čžurskie i paleoaziatskie jazyki. Ed. by P. Ja. Skorik et al. Leningrad 1968.

Jazyki 1979 = Jazyki Azii i Afriki, 3: Jazyki drevnej perednej Azii—nesemitskie; Iberijsko-kavkazskie jazyki, Paleoaziatskie jazyki. Moskva 1979.

Krašeninnikov 1755 = Stepan Petrovič Krašeninnikov: Opisanie zemli Kamčatki. Sanktpeterburg 1755.

Matthews 1951 = William Kleesman Matthews: Languages of the U.S.S.R. Cambridge 1951.

Steller 1774 = Georg Wilhelm Steller: Beschreibung von dem Lande Kamtschatka, dessen Einwohnern, deren Sitten, Nahmen, Lebensart und verschiedenen Gewohnheiten. Frankfurt. Leipzig 1774. Reprinted Stuttgart 1974 (facsimile).

Volodin 1971 = Aleksandr Pavlovič Volodin: Rev. of Worth 1969. In: Voprosy Jazykoznanija 1971, 134—136.

Volodin 1975 = Aleksandr Pavlovič Volodin: Itelmenskij jazyk. Leningrad 1975.

Robert Austerlitz, Columbia University, New York, N. Y. (USA)

268. Lexicography of the Eskimo-Aleut Languages

1. Background
2. Types of Dictionaries
3. Format
4. Coverage
5. Lexical Work in Progress
6. Selected Bibliography

1. Background

The Eskimo-Aleut language family extends from Southcentral Alaska and the Aleutian Islands north to Bering Strait, including the coast of the Chukchi Peninsula in the U.S.S.R., and east across the Alaskan and Canadian Arctic to Greenland. Besides Aleut are found five Eskimo languages: Alutiiq or Pacific Yupik, Central Alaskan Yupik, Siberian Yupik, Old Sirenik, and Inuit, which includes considerable dialect diversity. That Aleut was related to Greenlandic Eskimo was first noticed by Rasmus Rask in 1819. The first known written recordings of these languages stem from early Arctic explorers, who sometimes made maps with Native place names and compiled word lists with translations. The oldest such list is Frobisher 1578 collected in Inuit on Baffin Island.

All Eskimo-Aleut languages now have practical phonemic orthographies, although these vary considerably from one language to another. Most are Latin-based with adaptations such as diacritics and conventions applying to predictable morphophonemic processes, especially in the Yupik languages.

Inuit writing varies considerably from one area to another. West Greenlandic adopted a new, more phonemic orthography in the early 1970's, but earlier dictionaries are in the old writing system developed by Samuel Kleinschmidt. A cyrillic orthography is used for Siberian Yupik in the U.S.S.R., and historical Russian sources for Alaskan Yupik and Aleut also employ cyrillic. A syllabary based on one designed for Cree is in wide use throughout Eastern Canada and figures in several dictionaries.

2. Types of Dictionaries

2.1. Early Dictionaries

Most early dictionaries of Eskimo-Aleut languages were compiled by missionaries in conjunction with work on translation of religious materials. Of these languages especially West Greenlandic and Aleut have an important tradition of early lexical and linguistic work by missionaries. The first Eskimo dictionary is Egede 1750 for West Greenlandic; other important early dictionaries for this language are Fabricius 1804 and Kleinschmidt 1871. An extensive dictionary of Aleut was prepared by Iakov Netsvetov circa 1840, and Veniaminov 1846 includes an Aleut dictionary along with a grammar. For Western Canada Petitot 1876 is a valuable French-Eskimo dictionary of the Siglit dialect.

2.2. Current Dictionaries

The twentieth century has seen the publication of many Eskimo-Aleut dictionaries. Most have continued to list Eskimo-Aleut entries with translation in a European language (English, French, Russian, or Danish). Most are alphabetical, but some are topical, e.g. the Lowe 1983—1984 series on Western Canadian Inuit dialects. Some dictionaries include an index which allows the user to look up words in the European language and find a brief Eskimo entry. Missionaries continued making dictionaries, especially in Canada, e.g. Schneider 1970 (French-Eskimo, Eskimo-French) remains the most complete source for Eastern Canadian Inuit, along with the English version published in 1985. Métayer 1953, although rare, is the most extensive source for Western Canadian Inuit. For West Greenlandic Schultz-Lorentzen 1926 (Eskimo-Danish) and 1927 (Eskimo-English) continue as important resources, alongside Petersen 1951, which is the only major Eskimo-Eskimo dictionary to date, and Berthelsen et al. 1990 (Eskimo-Danish). Noteworthy among Alaskan Eskimo dictionaries are those published by the Alaska Native Language Center, Jacobson 1984 for Central Alaskan Yupik and Badten et al. 1987 for Siberian Yupik. A number of school dictionaries have been produced which, although limited in coverage, are often the best published sources for some languages, e.g. Leer 1978 a and 1978 b (Alutiiq), Bergsland/ Dirks 1978 and Bergsland 1980 (Aleut), and MacLean 1980 (North Slope Alaskan Inuit). The major Soviet work for Siberian Yupik (Chaplino) is Rubtsova 1971; Menovshchikov 1964 gives a vocabulary of the nearly extinct Old Sirenik language, along with a comparative table, and Menovshchikov 1975 gives a vocabulary of Naukan Yupik.

3. Format

Eskimo-Aleut languages are polysynthetic, with a word stem followed by derivational suffixes, called postbases, and finally an inflection. Prefixes are virtually non-existent, and morphophonemic processes do not radically alter word structure, making the languages ideally suited for alphabetical representation in a dictionary. Nouns are always listed in the absolutive singular form, and verbs are listed either in an abstract stem form (Jacobson 1984, Badten 1987) or in third person indicative forms (Schneider 1985, Schultz-Lorentzen 1926, Rubtsova 1971). In the tradition of Kleinschmidt, a main section containing stems is followed by an alphabetical listing of derivational suffixes.

4. Coverage

4.1. Derived Words

All the dictionaries strive to include fully lexicalized derived words. To varying extents dictionaries list derivations which have predictable meanings, especially when the meaning corresponds to a single European-language term, or when there is a frequently-occurring combination of base and suffix(es). The treatment of derivationally related lexemes varies widely. Schneider 1985 and Rubtsova 1971 do not have sub-entries or other indication of morphological relationship among entries, while Egede 1750, Schultz-Lorentzen 1926, Jacobson 1984 and others group derived forms under a basic entry.

4.2. Borrowings and Neologisms

All dictionaries include borrowings which have unquestionably become part of the language, especially in cases where the Eskimo-Aleut language is no longer in contact with the source language (e.g. English borrowings in Soviet Siberian Eskimo from the 19th century whaling era, and Russian borrowings in Alaskan languages). Also included are borrowings from other native languages such as the many Chukchi words in Siberian Yupik and the very few Indian words in various Eskimo languages. The dictionaries differ considerably in the degree to which they list phonologically unassimilated borrowings from the local European language of power, because this category is large and open-ended. Rubtsova 1971 lists many Russian words even retaining their exact Russian spelling up to the word ending, and Berthelsen et al. 1990 does the same for Danish borrowings, but other dictionaries omit commonly-used European words, listing only those whose phonology and/or meaning has changed significantly in the borrowing process.

Dictionary compilers have generally avoided coining new terms, though most dictionaries include recently established terminology. Prescriptive coinage of neologisms is left to specialized terminology lists (e.g. Utatnaq et al. 1989), while Dorais 1983 lists recent coinages and borrowings for Eastern Canada.

4.3. Dialect Differences

Most dictionaries cover more than one dialect, with entries indicating dialect restrictions or variation (Jacobson 1984, Schneider 1985). Lowe 1983, 1984a and 1984b and Dorais 1976 a, b, 1977, and 1978 represent series of dictionaries for related dialects. West Greenlandic dictionaries do not emphasize dialects. The divergent dialect of East Greenland is treated in Robbe 1986.

5. Lexical Work in Progress

The Alaska Native Language Center is preparing dictionaries for Aleut, Alutiiq, and North Slope Alaskan Inuit. The Sukaq Institute of Quebec is reportedly producing a monolingual dictionary, which will be the first of its kind outside Greenland. A comprehensive new monolingual dictionary is also projected for Greenland. The Alaska Native Language Center and the Institute of Eskimology (University of Copenhagen) are compiling a comparative Eskimo dictionary, which also incorporates Aleut information and groups Eskimo words in cognate sets under a reconstructed protoform.

6. Selected Bibliography

Badten et al. 1987 = Linda Womkon Badten/Vera Oovi Kaneshiro/Marie Oovi: A Dictionary of the St. Lawrence Island/Siberian Yupik Eskimo Language Ed. by Steven A. Jacobson. Fairbanks 1987 [410 p.].

Bergsland/Dirks 1978 = Knut Bergsland/Moses Dirks: Qawalangim Tunugan Kaduuĝingin: Eastern Aleut Grammar and Lexicon. Anchorage 1978 [iii, 190 p.].

Bergsland 1980 = Knut Bergsland: Atkan Aleut — English Dictionary. Anchorage 1980 [161 p.].

Berthelsen et al. 1990 = Chr. Berthelsen/Birgitte Jacobsen/Frederik Nielsen/Inge Kleivan/Robert Petersen/Jørgen Rischel: Oqaatsit Kalaallisuumit — Qallunaatuumut; Grønlandsk-Dansk Ordbog. Nuuk, Greenland 1990. [472 p.].

Birket-Smith 1928 = Kaj Birket-Smith: Five Hundred Eskimo Words: A Comparative Vocabulary from Greenland and Central Eskimo Dialects. Report of the Fifth Thule Expedition 1921—24. Copenhagen 1928 [64 p.].

Dorais 1976 a = Louis-Jacques Dorais: Aivilingmiut Uqausingit: The Aivilik Inuit Language: Le Parler Inuit Aivilik. Quebec 1976 [iii, 87 p.].

Dorais 1976 b = Louis-Jacques Dorais: Iglulingmiut Uqausingit: The Inuit Language in Igloolik N. W. T.: Le Parler Inuit d'Igloolik T. N. O. Quebec 1976 [iii, 90 p].

Dorais 1977 = Louis-Jacques Dorais: Inuit Kupaimmiut Uqausingit: The Language of the Northern Quebec Inuit. Quebec 1977 [81 p.].

Dorais 1978 = Louis-Jacques Dorais: Iglulingmiut Uqausingit: The Inuit Language of Igloolik NWT: Le Parler Inuit d'Igloolik TNO. Quebec 1978 [117 p.].

Dorais 1983 = Louis-Jacques Dorais: Uqausigusiqtaat: An Analytical Lexicon of Modern Inuktitut in Quebec-Labrador. Quebec 1983 [x, 168 p.].

Egede 1750 = Poul Egede: Dictionarium Grönlandico-Danico-Latinum. Havniae 1750 [312 p.].

Fabricius 1804 = Otho Fabricius: Den grønlandske Ordbog, forbedret og forøget. 1804 [795 p.].

Frobisher 1578 = Sir Martin Frobisher: A true Discourse of the Late Voyages of Discovery for Finding of a Passage to Cathaya and India by the North West. (Reprinted in the Principall Navigations, Voiages and Discoveries of the English Nation [1589]. Cambridge 1965).

Jacobson 1984 = Steven A. Jacobson: Yup'ik Eskimo Dictionary. Fairbanks 1984 [755 p.].
Jeddore 1976 = Rose Jeddore: Labrador Inuit Uqausingit. St. John's Newfoundland 1976 [vi, 217 p.].
Jenness 1928 = Diamond Jenness: Comparative Vocabulary of the Western Eskimo Dialects. Report of the Canadian Arctic Expedition 1913—1918. Ottawa 1928 [134 p.].
Kleinschmidt 1871 = Samuel Petrus Kleinschmidt: Den Grønlandske Ordbog Omarbejdet. Copenhagen 1871 [460 p.].
Leer 1978a = Jeff Leer: A Conversational Dictionary of Kodiak Alutiiq. Fairbanks 1978 [119 p.].
Leer 1978b = Jeff Leer: Nanwalegmiut Paluwigmiut-llu Nupugnerit: Conversational Alutiiq Dictionary Kenai Peninsula Alutiiq. Anchorage 1978 [306 p.].
Lowe 1983 = Ronald Lowe: Kangiryuarmiut Uqauhingita Numiktittitdjutingit: Basic Kangiryuarmiut Eskimo Dictionary. Inuvik, NWT 1983 [xxiv, 241 p.].
Lowe 1984a = Ronald Lowe: Uummarmiut Uqalungiha Mumikhitchiŕutingit: Basic Uummarmiut Eskimo Dictionary. Inuvik, NWT 1984 [xxvii, 262 p.].
Lowe 1984b = Ronald Lowe: Siglit Inuvialuit Uqausiita Kipuktirutait: Basic Siglit Inuvialuit Eskimo Dictionary. Inuvik, NWT 1984 [xxviii, 305 p.].
MacLean 1980 = Edna Ahgeak MacLean: Abridged Iñupiaq and English Dictionary. Fairbanks 1980 [xx, 168 p.].
Menovshchikov 1964 = Georgii Alekseevich Menovshchikov: Iazyk sirenikskikh ėskimosov: Fonetika, ocherk morfologii, teksty i slovarí. Moscow and Leningrad 1964 [219 p.].
Menovshchikov 1975 = Georgii Alekseevich Menovshchikov: Iazyk naukanskikh ėskimosov: foneticheskoe vvedenie, ocherk morfologii, teksty, slovarí. Leningrad 1975 [512 p.].
Métayer 1953 = R. P. Maurice Métayer: Dictionnaire Esquimau-Français. Aklavik 1953 [158, 118 p.].
Netsvetov ca. 1840 = Jakov Netsvetov: Russian Aleut Dictionary. ms. Library of Congress.

Peacock 1974a = F. W. Peacock: English-Eskimo Dictionary. St. John's Newfoundland 1974 [605 p.].
Peacock 1974b = F. W. Peacock: English-Eskimo Dictionary. St. John's Newfoundland 1974 [432 p.].
Petersen 1967 = Jonathan Petersen: Ordbogêrak. Nuuk, Greenland 1951. København 1967 [235 p.].
Petitot 1876 = Emile Petitot: Vocabulaire Français-Eskimo, dialecte des Tchiglit des Bouches du Mackenzie. Paris 1876 [78 p.].
Rasmussen 1941 = Knud Rasmussen: Alaskan Eskimo Words. Report of the Fifth Thule Expedition 1921—1924. Copenhagen 1941 [83 p.].
Robbe 1986 = Pierre Robbe/Louis-Jacques Dorais: Tunumiit Oraasiat. Quebec 1986 [xxvii, 265 p.].
Rubtsova 1971 = Ekaterina Semenovna Rubtsova: Ėskimossko-russkii slovar': Eskimo-Russian Dictionary. Moscow 1971 [644 p.].
Schneider 1970 = Lucien Schneider: Dictionnaire Français-Esquimau du Langage esquimau de L'Ungava et Contrées Limitrophes. Quebec 1970 [421 p.].
Schneider 1985 = Lucien Schneider: Ulirnaisigutiit: An Inuktitut-English Dictionary of Northern Quebec, Labrador and Eastern Arctic Dialects. Quebec 1985 [x, 507 p.].
Schultz-Lorentzen 1926 = C. W. Schultz-Lorentzen: Den Grønlandske Ordbog. Kjøbenhavn 1926, 1964 [360 p.].
Schultz-Lorentzen 1927 = C. W. Schultz-Lorentzen: Dictionary of the West Greenlandic Eskimo Language. Copenhagen 1927, 1967 [303 p.].
Utatnaq et al. 1989 = Alexis Utatnaq: Interpreter Translator Word List Book. Iqaluit, NWT 1989 [99 p.].
Veniaminov 1846 = Ivan Evfeevich Popov: Opyt grammatiki aleutskoliśevskago fazyka. St. Petersburg 1846 [126 p.]
Webster 1970 = D. H. Webster/Wilfried Zibell: Iñupiat Eskimo Dictonary. Fairbanks 1970 [xii, 211 p.].

Steven A. Jacobson/Lawrence D. Kaplan, Alaska Native Language Center, Fairbanks, Alaska (USA)

269. Lexicography of the Languages of New Guinea

1. Background Information
2. Missionaries' Dictionaries
3. Summer Institute of Linguistics
4. Linguists and Anthropologists
5. New Guinea Pidgin (Tok Pisin)
6. Selected Bibliography

1. Background Information

The New Guinea region is the linguistically most complex area in the world, with close to 1 000 languages. Many of these are early immigrant Austronesian languages, but 740 are non-Austronesian

269. Lexicography of the Languages of New Guinea

Location Map of the Languages mentioned in 269, S.A. Wurm, Lexicography of the Languages of New Guinea

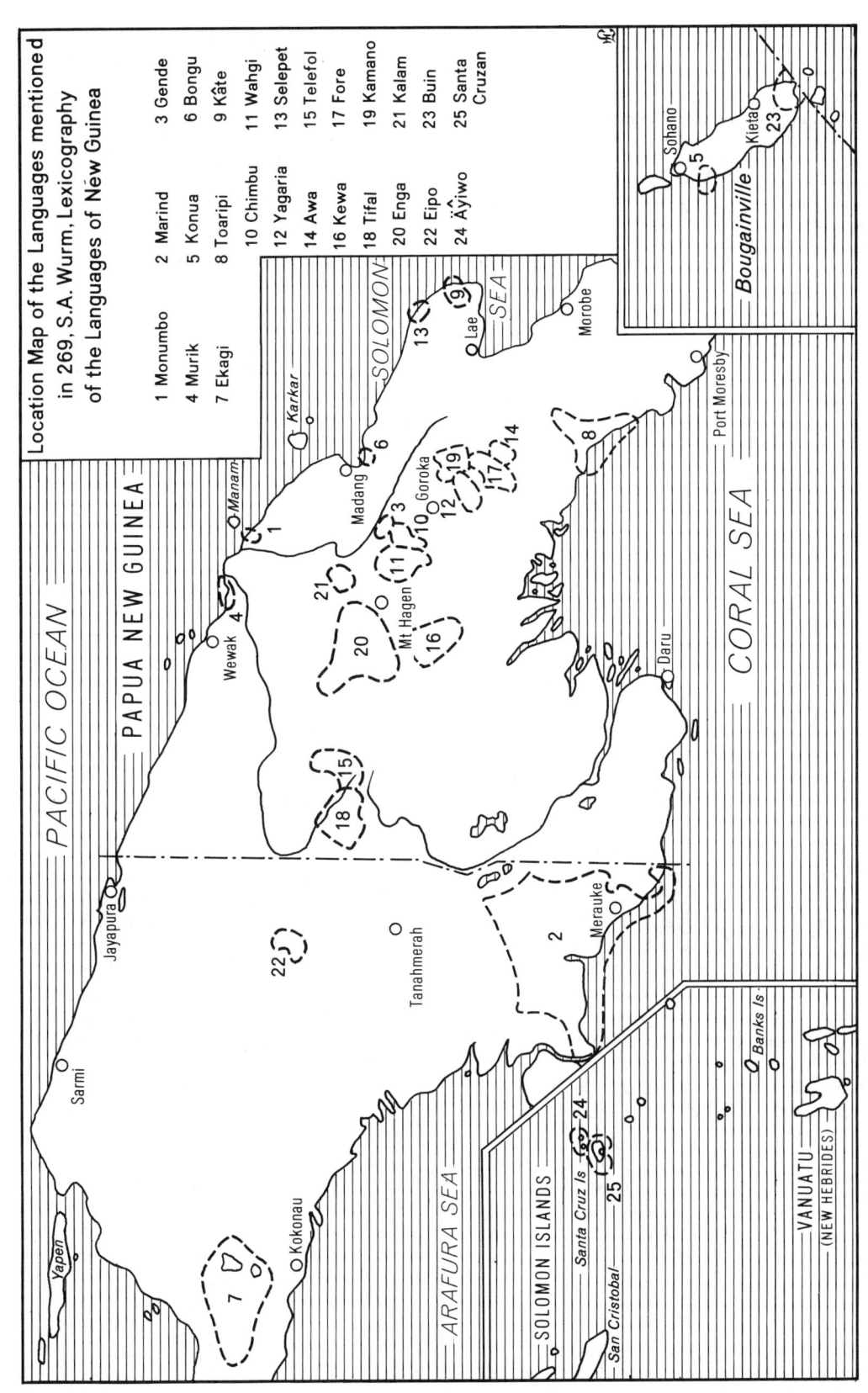

1 Monumbo	2 Marind	3 Gende
4 Murik	5 Konua	6 Bongu
7 Ekagi	8 Toaripi	9 Kâte
10 Chimbu	11 Wahgi	
12 Yagaria	13 Seleppet	
14 Awa	15 Telefol	
16 Kewa	17 Fore	
18 Tifal	19 Kamano	
20 Enga	21 Kalam	
22 Eipo	23 Buin	
24 Äyiwo	25 Santa Cruzan	

Map 269.1: Location of the languages referred to in article 269

or Papuan languages (Wurm 1982, 13, Wurm/Hattori 1981—83: maps and texts 1—14, 40, 45). The existence of Papuan languages, as distinct from Austronesian, was recognized only towards the end of the 19th century. Only in the 1950s, large-scale systematic linguistic surveying and research work had begun mainly through the Research School of Pacific Studies of the Australian National University, and the Summer Institute of Linguistics. This work produced the present-day, still somewhat tentative and changing picture and a large amount of information on individual languages and language groups. Still, the number of dictionaries in published form or in preparation for publication, or in generally inaccessible MS form, is very small indeed when considering the vast number of languages involved.

2. Missionaries' Dictionaries

Of the 70-odd dictionaries and vocabularies of Papuan languages published or otherwise made available (e.g. mimeographed), or in advanced preparation, about 50 have been prepared by missionaries. They vary greatly in quality, scope and size from simple listings of items with glosses to larger-size dictionaries meeting more advanced lexicographic requirements, e.g. supplying grammatical information and illustration of usage, cross-referencing, and ethnographic information. Of the simpler type (language names added) Vormann/Scharfenberger 1914 (Monumbo), Kolk/Vertenten 1922 (Marind), Aufenanger 1952 (Gende), Schmidt 1953 (Murik) and Müller 1954 (Konua) are examples. More sophisticated are for instance Hanke 1909 (Bongu), Geurtjens 1933 (Marind), Doble 1960 (Ekagi or Kapauku), Brown 1968 (Toaripi), and Steltenpool 1969 (Ekagi). Missionaries' dictionaries showing the most advanced level of compliance with lexicographic requirements are Keysser 1925 (Kâte), Nilles 1969 (Chimbu), Ramsey 1975 (Wahgi), Renck 1977 (Yagaria) and Flierl/Strauss 1976 (Kâte). All except Keysser 1925 have English-other language sections.

A number of missionaries' dictionaries are known to have existed, in manuscript form, e.g. of New Britain languages, but their whereabouts are not known, and several appear to have been destroyed during World War II.

3. Summer Institute of Linguistics

The Summer Institute of Linguistics, a religious organisation with linguistically trained members, has been in the New Guinea area since the mid-fifties and worked in over 150 local languages, many of them Papuan. Some sizeable Papuan dictionaries based on their work have been published, notably McElhanon and McElhanon 1970 (Selepet), Loving and Loving 1975 (Awa), Healey/Healey (Telefol), Franklin and Franklin 1978 (Kewa) and Scott 1980 (Fore). All of these are lexicographically sophisticated, with Franklin and Franklin 1978 in particular containing extensive ethnographic data. The Summer Institute also holds a number of Papuan manuscript dictionaries ranging from simple listings to quite sizeable dictionaries of some sophistication. Some have been mimeographed or put on microfiche, for instance Healey and Steinkrauss 1972 (Tifal) and Drew and Payne 1973 (Kamano).

4. Linguists and Anthropologists

Papuan dictionaries by secular authors are few, but almost all are lexicographically sophisticated. Lang 1973 (Enga), Bulmer/Pawley/Biggs 1974 (Kalam), Heeschen/Schiefenhövel 1983 (Eipo), Laycock forthcoming (Buin), Wurm/Bwakolo/Moŷiya forthcoming) (Äŷiwo) and Wurm/Mealue/Lapli/Yöpusë forthcoming (Lödäi = Santa Cruzan) may be mentioned. Lang 1973 lacks illustrative examples, while Bulmer/Pawley/Biggs and the last four have a heavy ethnographic and natural science content. Heeschen/Schiefenhövel 1983 has no German (or English)-Eipo index.

The morphology of Papuan languages is amongst the richest and most complex in the world, but much of it is regular and predictable. However, there are unpredictable phenomena such as irregular stem suppletions in verb forms, the unpredictable appearance of subject markers as prefixes or as suffixes, the unpredictable use of certain aspect markers with certain verbs as opposed to different ones with other verbs etc. Such unpredictable features should be indicated in dictionaries and in fact are in the more sophisticated ones. With verbs, some dictionaries give verbal roots as head words, others give citation forms, others forms which are the bases for derived forms. In some dictionaries, derived forms appear under the basic form as head words, but other dictionaries give them as entries of their own, because derivations are often quite irregular and unpredictable in Papuan languages. A few examples of the grammatical treatment taken from a sophisticated dictionary (Äŷiwo Language, Wurm/Bwakolo/Moŷiya forthcoming) are given below:

bobwa̱ (verbal noun) hole or hollow inside a (usually wooden or plant) thing; deformed Tahitian chestnut; hollow log drum (cavities in wood and hard vegetables noun class, no noun class concordance; hole or hollow: general possession possessive class with marker *nou¹*, deformed Tahitian chestnut: food possessive class with marker *nugo²*, hollow log drum: utensils possessive class with marker *nugû¹*; intrusive presence construct class with marker *-ngä³*, with the noun base changing to **bobo-* in constructs). From **bwa¹-*. Example: *bobongä nyenaa* a hole in a tree. Cf. *bo³-*, *nûmobwa̱*, *nwobwa̱*.

vä̱va (verbal noun) baby chicken; small chicken (chicken noun class, noun class concordance with adjectives, numerals and possessives; as food: food possessive class with marker *nugo²*, otherwise general possession possessive class with marker *-nou¹*; background or material construct class with marker *-ä̂³*). From *va¹*. Example: *väva väwopwa välakî väŷeve vänûgo* my three small white chickens (for food). Cf. *vä̱-*, *giva*, *sîva*, *meva*, *bova*, *uva*.

vägäte (active verb) to slit or tear something (by hand) (subject indicated by prefixes; common aspect prefix *ki¹-*; imperative sg form *vägäsî*). From **-gä-*. Example: *dyikivägäte nupwää* we two tear calico (by hand). Cf. *vägäsî*, *vä̱³-*, *-te³*, *lägäte*, *ägäte*.

5. New Guinea Pidgin (Tok Pisin)

Several dictionaries of Tok Pisin, the major lingua franca of Papua New Guinea, have been published. The most important are Mihalic 1971 and Steinbauer 1969, of which especially the former played an important role in providing reference tools for standardized forms of the language. A major etymological dictionary is in the early stages of preparation by Peter Mühlhäusler (Oxford) in collaboration with others.

6. Selected Bibliography

6.1. Dictionaries

Aufenanger 1952 = Heinrich Aufenanger: Vokabular und Grammatik der Gende-Sprache in Zentral-Neuguinea. Fribourg 1952 (Microbibliotheka Anthropos 5) [301 pp.].

Brown 1968 = Herbert Brown: A dictionary of Toaripi. 2 vols. Sydney 1968 (Oceania Linguistic Monographs 11) [VIII, 389 pp.].

Bulmer/Pawley/Biggs 1974 = Ralph Bulmer/Andrew Pawley/Bruce Biggs: A First Dictionary of Kalam. Mimeo. Auckland 1974 [300 pp.].

Doble 1960 = Marion Doble: Kapauku-Malayan-Dutch-English dictionary. The Hague 1960 [VIII, 156 pp.].

Drew/Payne 1973 = Dorothy Drew/Audrey Payne: A small Kamano dictionary. Mimeo. Ukarumpa 1973 [219 pp.].

Flierl/Strauss 1976 = Wilhelm Flierl/Hermann Strauss, eds: Kâte dictionary. Canberra 1976 (Pacific Linguistics C-41) [XXXIII, 499 pp.].

Franklin/Franklin 1978 = Karl Franklin/Joice Franklin: A Kewa dictionary. Canberra 1978 (Pacific Linguistics C-53) [XI, 514 pp.].

Geurtjens 1933 = Henrikus Geurtjens: Marindineesch-Nederlandsch woordenboek. (Verhandelingen van het Koninklijk Bataviaasch Genootschap van Kunsten en Wetenschappen 71, 5e stuk). Bandoeng 1933 [433 pp.].

Hanke 1909 = August Hanke: Grammatik und Vokabularium der Bongu-Sprache (Astrolabe-Bai, Kaiser-Wilhelmsland). (Archiv für das Studium deutscher Kolonialsprachen 8). Berlin 1909 [XII, 252 pp.; Vokabularium 118–252 pp.].

Healey/Healey 1977 = Phyllis Healey/Alan Healey: Telefol dictionary. Canberra 1977 (Pacific Linguistics C-46) [XVII, 358 pp.].

Healey/Steinkrauss 1972 = Phyllis Healey/Walter Steinkrauss: Preliminary Vocabulary of Tifal with grammar notes. (Language Data Microfiche AP5). Huntington Beach 1972 [VII, 143 pp.].

Heeschen/Schiefenhövel 1983 = Volker Heeschen/Wulf Schiefenhövel: Wörterbuch der Eipo-Sprache, Eipo-Deutsch-Englisch. (Mensch, Kultur und Umwelt im zentralen Bergland von West-Neuguinea 6). Berlin 1983 [249 pp.].

Keysser 1925 = Christian Keysser: Wörterbuch der Kâte-Sprache gesprochen in Neuguinea. Zeitschrift für Eingeborenensprachen. Berlin 1925 [XII, 612 pp.].

Kolk/Vertenten 1922 = Jos van de Kolk/Piet Vertenten: Marindineesch woordenboek. Deel I: Nederlandsch-Marindineesch. Weltevreden 1922 [160 pp.].

Lang 1973 = Adrianne Lang: Enga dictionary with English index. Canberra 1973 (Pacific Linguistics C-20) [LXII, 219 pp.].

Laycock forthcoming = Donald Clarence Laycock: Basic materials in Buin: grammar, texts, and dictionary. Canberra (Pacific Linguistics).

Loving/Loving 1975 = Richard Loving/Aretta Loving: Awa dictionary. Canberra 1975 (Pacific Linguistics C-30) [XLIV, 203 pp.].

McElhanon/McElhanon 1970 = Kenneth McElhanon/Noreen McElhanon: Selepet-English dictionary. Canberra 1970 (Pacific Linguistics C-15) [XXI, 144 pp.].

Mihalic 1971 = Francis Mihalic: The Jacaranda dictionary and grammar of Melanesian Pidgin. Milton 1971 [XVI, 375 pp.; earlier version Techny 1957, XXIV, 318 pp.].

Müller 1954 = Adam Müller: Grammar and Vocabulary of the Konua Language. Fribourg 1954 (Microbibliotheca Anthropos 12) [140 pp.].

Nilles 1969 = Johann Nilles: Kuman-English dictionary. Kundiawa 1969 [V, 291 pp.].

Ramsey 1975 = Evelyn Ramsey: Middle Wahgi dictionary. Mount Hagen 1975 [XVI, 457 pp.].

Renck 1977 = Günther Renck: Yagaria dictionary. Canberra 1977 (Pacific Linguistics C-37) [XXVII, 327 pp.].

Schmidt 1953 = Josef Schmidt: Vokabular und Grammatik der Murik-Sprache in Nordost-Neuguinea. Fribourg 1953 (Microbibliotheca Anthropos 3) [300 pp.].

Scott 1980 = Graham Scott: Fore Dictionary. Canberra 1980 (Pacific Linguistics C-62) [XIII, 243 pp.].

Steinbauer 1969 = Friedrich Steinbauer: Concise Dictionary of New Guinea Pidgin (Neo-Melanesian). Madang 1969 [223 pp.].

Steltenpool 1969 = Jan Steltenpool: Ekagi-Dutch-English-Indonesian Dictionary. (Verhandelingen van het Koninklijk Instituut voor Taal- Land- en Volkenkunde 56). The Hague 1969 [VIII, 269 pp.].

Vormann/Scharfenberger 1914 = Franz Vormann/Wilhelm Scharfenberger: Die Monumbo-Sprache: Grammatik und Wörterverzeichnis. Vienna 1914 [252 pp.; Wörterverzeichnis 141—252].

Wurm/Bwakolo/Moŷiya forthcoming = Stephen Adolphe Wurm/Patrick Bwakolo/Martin Moŷiya: Äŷiwo dictionary. Canberra (Pacific Linguistics).

Wurm/Mealue/Lapli/Yöpusë forthcoming = Stephen Adolphe Wurm/John Mealue/John Ini Lapli/Frank Bollen Yöpusë = Santa Cruzan (Lödäi) dictionary. Canberra (Pacific Linguistics).

6.2. Other Publications

Wurm 1982 = Stephen Adolphe Wurm: Papuan Languages of Oceania. Tübingen 1982.

Wurm/Hattori 1981—83 = Stephen Adolphe Wurm/Shirô Hattori, eds: Language Atlas of the Pacific Area, parts I and II. Canberra 1981—83.

Stephen A. Wurm, Australian National University, Canberra (Australia)

270. Australian Lexicography

1. Australian Aboriginal Languages — Nature and Classification
2. Tasmanian Languages
3. Historical Sketch of Lexicographic Research
4. Issues in Australian Lexicography
5. Selected Bibliography

1. Australian Aboriginal Languages — Nature and Classification

At first European settlement of Australia (1788), it is estimated there were 600 'tribes' on the continent, each with its own form of speech. These comprise some 250 languages (Dixon 1980); a quarter are now extinct and a further 100 are moribund. The languages are morphologically complex and typically agglutinative. Typologically, there are those having both suffixes and prefixes (northern third of continent; see map) and those with just suffixes (southern two-thirds). The genetic picture is unclear but the southern languages (plus eastern Arnhemland) show grammatical and lexical homogeneity and are generally referred to as Pama-Nyungan. Non-Pama-Nyungan languages are quite diverse.

2. Tasmanian Languages

The linguistic situation in Tasmania is very poorly known — existing records are fragmentary and of low quality, mostly collected by amateurs last century. Schmidt 1952 collated the materials and attempted to analyse them. Plomley 1976 is a full compilation of all the Tasmanian vocabularies — Crowley/Dixon 1981 discuss possible phonological and grammatical interpretations of Plomley.

3. Historical Sketch of Lexicographic Research

O'Grady 1971 discusses in detail the development of Australian lexicography until 1968. Two periods of research are distinguished: early (1770—1920) collections of vocabulary by amateurs and missionaries, and later (1930—68) dictionary compilation by trained linguists. All lexicography in Australia has been bilingual, mostly Aboriginal-English and/or English-Aboriginal, and primarily dictionaries of 1000 or fewer headwords. Early dictionaries are generally phonologically underdifferentiated and lack morphosyntactic information, although some provide semantic and ethnographic detail (O'Grady 1971, 795). Later dictionaries are linguistically more sophisticated and larger (several thousand entries), but most were and remain unpublished. Since 1968 the situation has improved, yet, as Heath (1982, ix) notes:

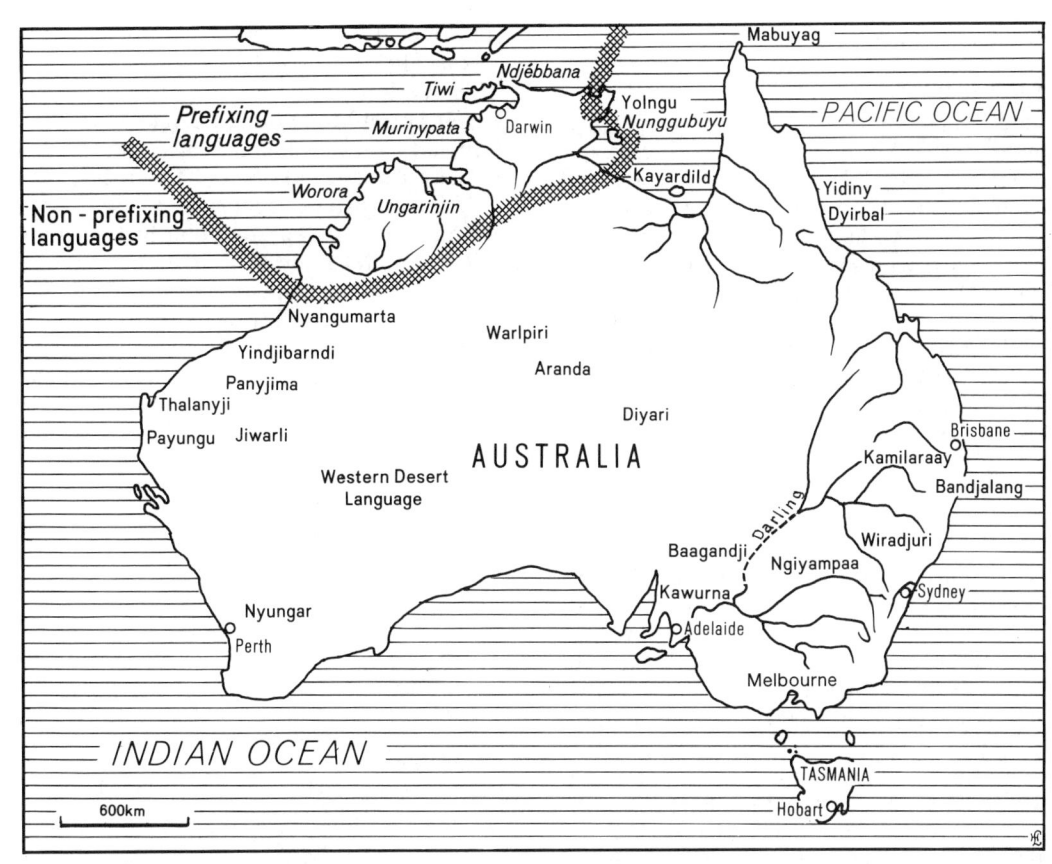

Map 270.1: Location of the Australian Aboriginal languages referred to in article 270

'although many fieldworkers ... have extensive lexical files, the number of published dictionaries is scandalously low ... linguists have essentially contented themselves with long grammatical studies, ... and have as yet published few or no texts and no adequate dictionaries'. Quite a number of grammars have been published, usually with accompanying vocabulary lists (see Dixon/Blake 1981 for examples). Just four large dictionaries (4000 entries or more) have appeared: Coate/Elkin 1975, Hansen/Hansen 1977, Heath 1982 and Reuther 1981 (English translation of a four-volume Diari-German dictionary collected in the 1880's). Only Heath 1982 is fully comprehensive (others lack sufficient specification of morphology and syntax), incorporating ethnographic, sociolinguistic and grammatical details, plus reference to published text examples. A sample is Dictionary excerpt 270.1:

=nᵍala:ga- VIntrN to wade, to walk in water. 108.6.1.
  Cf. =lu:lha-, =lalalha-.

nᵍalaji NcAnaWu freshwater long-tom fish, Strongylura kreffti. Syn: mada (more common, even though this also means 'grass').
nᵍa:lal NCWara frog, toad (all species).
  Syn: dhabararag, nᵍa:nᵍu.
nᵍala:ligi NcNa green turtle, Chelonia midas (by far the most salient marine turtle). 14. 6. 3, 14. 10. 2, 64. 8. 1, 18.6.1/2, Texts 19 and 42, 166.10.1.
  Stages: nᵍulguru, rujuru, ramba:ri. Cf. wugalij, =nᵍurga-. Other turtles: nᵍalhuwa, gariwa, jadaga:miri, nibunᵍa:yu(nᵍ), and synonyms. Tortoises: dalma:ranᵍ, etc.

Dictionary excerpt 270.1: Articles (from: Heath 1982, 131)

Several current projects will result in dictionaries of this level of detail, including Yolngu (Schebeck 1983, Zorc 1983), Warlpiri (Hale 1983, Laughren/Nash 1983, Hale/Laughren/Nash 1986), Dyirbal (Dixon 1982), Kayardild (Evans 1985), Aranda (Breen p. c.), Ndjébbana (McKay 1983), and southern Pilbara languages (Austin 1983 — see map for locations). There are important issues of organization and presentation raised by recent publications and research.

4. Issues in Australian Lexicography

4.1. Language and Dialect

Traditional Aboriginal society was highly multilingual, with great dialectal and sociolectal variation. Zorc 1983 will code his Yolngu dictionary for all variation; Schebeck 1983 questions whether variation is linguistic or political. Hansen/Hansen list numerous synonyms without extra-linguistic details, Heath 1982 mentions currency of words while Austin (1983, 10) includes informant codes. Dixon 1982 will give both ordinary and taboo (mother-in-law) vocabulary (see also Dixon 1971).

4.2. The Lemma

Pama-Nyungan languages have generally transparent roots to serve as headwords. Non-Pama-Nyungan prefixing languages pose difficulties as verb roots without bound cross-referencing prefixes (and nominals without gender prefixes) are meaningless to native speakers (McKay 1983). Additionally, complex morphophonemics obscure underlying roots (McKay 1983, Heath 1982, xiv ff); in Heath 1982, for example, roots beginning with a, w, w_1, w_2 all appear under W. Suppletion is a problem for some languages; McKay 1983 lists the 'principal parts' of Ndjébbana verbs to handle it. Morphology is highly productive, questions arise concerning the number of derived forms to be listed — linguists differ widely on this issue.

4.3. Glosses

All recent and current Australian dictionaries are bilingual; English is the glossing language. There is debate about the style of glosses: 'ordinary English', or Latinate terms or technical linguistic vocabulary (see Hale 1983, Wierzbicka 1983, Evans 1985). For Warlpiri both ordinary and technical glosses are included, for example (Laughren/Nash (1983, 131)): "PAKA-RNI (V): 1. Contact/effect: xERG produces concussion on the surface of yABS, by some entity coming into contact with y: hit, strike, bump, crash into, beat, thrash, thresh." Few lexicographers follow the Warlpiri model. Some (Evans 1985, Austin 1983) include Aboriginal English glosses.

4.4. Semantic Domains and Ethnographica

Lexicographers have tried to capture Aboriginal language semantics: Dixon 1982 organizes his Dyirbal dictionary as a thesaurus (informed by taboo language semantics — Dixon 1971), Hale/Laughren/Nash 1986 give Warlpiri ethno-semantic classes (also Schebeck 1983 for Yolngu), Evans 1985 mentions a thesaurus/domains dictionary based on Kayardild semantics and Heath 1982 has a thesaurus-style supplement (see also Dixon/Blake 1981). All published dictionaries are alphabetical in the main body. Many dictionaries include ethnographic information (especially as traditional lifestyles rapidly change), either in the gloss (Hansen/Hansen 1977, Heath 1982), as a separate field (Hale/Laughren/Nash 1986, Austin 1983) or in example sentences.

YAKANGKU (N): 1. *Flora: watiya:* small tree with edible larva: **salt bush**
Yakangkuju watiya muluwurrungawurrpa. Laju ka palka nguna yarturarla. Kalalu pajurnu ngalkirdipiyajuku. Kalalu purranjarla ngarnu. Watiya ka karri yulyurdupiya. Parrka ka kaninjarrakari waraly-wanti. Rdangkarlpa ka karri watiya yakangkuju. Karrinyarrarla karlarra ka palka karrimi yakangkuju. The *yakangku* is a tree which grows near claypans. There is an edible grub in its roots. People get grubs from it as from the *ngarlkirdi* tree. They cook them and eat them. The tree is grey coloured. The leaves hang downwards. The *yakangku* tree is short and compact. They grow west of Karrinyarra (Mt. Wedge).
2. *Flora related: pama: laju:* edible grub found in 1. **witchetty grub sp.**
YAKANKU (N): 1. See JANMARDA
Karntalpalu yakankurla-jarrija. The women were engaged in gathering bush onions.
YAKIRLIPURRUNY (N): 1. *Flora: watiya:* Psoralea leucantha **plant sp.**
Yakirlipurrunyu, ngulaji watiya wita-wita, parla pilirripilirrikirli kunjuru-kunjurukurlu. Karrungkapirntipirnti ka pardimi. Ngulajika parntimi janyungupiyayijala. Ngulanya kalalu ngarnu janyungupiyayijala nyurruwiyi. Yakirlipurrunyu is a smallish bush with flat grey leaves. It grows near sandy creeks. It smells like tobacco. In the old days they used to chew it like tobacco. Cf. WIRNINYWIRNINYPA

Dictionary excerpt 270.2: Warlpiri examples (from: Hale/Laughren/Nash 1986, 77)

4.5. Etymology

Concern for historical linguistic issues (including the Pama Nyungan/non-Pama Nyungan distinction) has lead several lexicographers to incorporate etymons in their dictionaries (Austin 1983, Hale 1983, Evans 1985). Koch 1983 discusses Australian etymological issues.

4.6. Computer Applications

Most Australian lexicographers now make use of computers, usually for text editing and sorting. Laughren/Nash 1983 report development of LISP programs for concordances and finder lists, and describe use of laser printers to typeset the Warlpiri dictionary (see Hale/Laughren/Nash 1986). Austin/Nathan 1986 describe a large complex relational database (using the entity-relationship model) and associated input/output and manipulation software for single language and multilingual dictionary compilation. The lexical database interfaces with text manipulation software for attestations and concordance listing (Webb/Austin 1986).

5. Selected Bibliography

5.1. Dictionaries

Coate/Elkin 1975 = H. H. J. Coate/A. P. Elkin: Narinjin-English dictionary. 2 volumes. Sydney 1975 [534 pages].

Hale/Laughren/Nash 1986 = Ken Hale/Mary Laughren/David Nash. Warlpiri-English dictionary: flora section. Cambridge MA 1986 [95 pages].

Hansen/Hansen 1977 = K. C. Hansen/L. E. Hansen: Pintupi/Luritja dictionary. 2nd ed. Alice Springs 1977 [277 pages].

Heath 1982 = Jeffrey Heath: Nunggubuyu dictionary. Canberra 1982 [399 pages].

Plomley 1976 = N. J. B. Plomley: A word-list of the Tasmanian Aboriginal languages. Tasmania 1976 [486 pages].

Reuther 1981 = J. G. Reuther: The Diari. Canberra 1981.

Schmidt 1952 = W. Schmidt: Die tasmanischen Sprachen. Utrecht. Anvers 1952.

5.2. Other Publications

Austin 1983 = Peter Austin (ed.): Papers in Australian linguistics No. 15: Australian Aboriginal lexicography. Canberra 1983.

Austin/Nathan 1986 = Peter Austin/David Nathan: The Gascoyne-Ashburton languages project — dictionary database description. Melbourne 1986.

Crowley/Dixon 1981 = Terry Crowley/R. M. W. Dixon: Tasmanian. In: Dixon/Blake 1981, 395—421.

Dixon 1971 = R. M. W. Dixon: A method of semantic description. In: Danny D. Steinberg/Leon A. Jakobovits, Semantics. Cambridge 1971, 436—71.

Dixon 1980 = R. M. W. Dixon: The languages of Australia. Cambridge 1980.

Dixon 1982 = R. M. W. Dixon: Dyirbal thesaurus and dictionary. Canberra 1982.

Dixon/Blake 1981 = R. M. W. Dixon/Barry J. Blake: Handbook of Australian languages vol. 2. Canberra 1981.

Evans 1985 = Nicholas Evans: The Kayardild dictionary project. Canberra 1985.

Hale 1983 = Kenneth Hale: A lexicographic study of some Australian languages: project description. In: Austin 1983, 71—107.

Koch 1983 = Harold Koch: Etymology and dictionary making for Australian languages (with examples from Kaytej). In: Austin 1983, 149—173.

Laughren/Nash 1983 = Mary Laughren/David Nash: Warlpiri dictionary project: aims, method, organization and problems of definition. In: Austin 1983, 109—133.

McKay 1983 = G. R. McKay: Lexicography and Ndjébbana (Kunibidji) bilingual education program. In: Austin 1983, 57—70.

O'Grady 1971 = Geoffrey N. O'Grady: Lexicographic research in Aboriginal Australia. In: Thomas A. Sebeok: Current trends in linguistics 8. The Hague 1971, 779—803.

Schebeck 1983 = Bernhard Schebeck: Dictionaries for Australian languages: some general remarks. In: Austin 1983, 41—55.

Webb/Austin 1986 = Geoffrey I. Webb/Peter Austin: The Gascoyne-Ashburton languages project — text and concordance system description. Melbourne 1986.

Wierzbicka 1983 = Anna Wierzbicka: Semantics and lexicography: some comments on the Warlpiri dictionary project. In: Austin 1983, 135—144.

Zorc 1983 = R. David Zorc: A Yolngumatha dictionary — plans and proposals. In: Austin 1983, 31—40.

Peter Austin, La Trobe, Victoria (Australia)

XXX. Lexikographie der Einzelsprachen XIV: Die Sprachen Schwarzafrikas
Lexicography of Individual Languages XIV: The Languages of Black Africa
Lexicographie des langues particulières XIV: Les langues d'Afrique noire

271. Lexicography of Nilo-Saharan

1. The Nilo-Saharan Languages
2. Families Other Than Sudanic
3. East and Central Sudanic
4. Selected Bibliography

1. The Nilo-Saharan Languages

Nilo-Saharan (N-S) is one of four generally accepted African language phyla along with Afrasian (AA), Niger-Kordofanian (N-K), and Khoisan. N-S has about 120 languages, about 10% of the African total of 1200, and perhaps 20,000,000 speakers, about 3% of Africa's total of 600,000,000 in 1989. Ranging roughly west to east, N-S families are A Songay, B Saharan, C Maban, D For, E East Sudanic, F Central Sudanic, G Berta, H Kunama, I Koman, J Gumuz, K Kuliak, L Kado. This follows my modification of Greenberg's genetic classification (1963). For the history of N-S classification, see Greenberg 1971, Ruhlen 1987, who point out that the pioneering work was that of Westermann 1911 and later. My ongoing work (e.g. Bender 1991) indicates that N-S has five branches: four independent "outliers" (A, B, H, K) plus a core group (E, I, J, L) and a periphery to the core (G, F, C, D). Henceforth I will refer to E and F as "Sudanic" with no implication of special relationship. Suggestions that epigraphic Meroitic is East Sudanic cannot be settled because of paucity of evidence.

The demographically leading N-S languages are (in millions of estimated speakers): Kanuri 4, Kenya Luo 2, Kalenjin 1.65, Jieng (Dinka) 1.1, Songay 1.

Since N-S languages have been little written, most sources are bilingual in English, French, German, Italian, or Arabic (I will not deal with Arabic). All dictionaries etc. named below are assumed to be with English as target language unless otherwise specified; "index" will mean the reverse (e.g. English to L as against L to English). A thorough bibliography up to the time is found in Tucker/Bryan 1956 (for Songay, Westermann/Bryan 1952). I will thus concentrate on recent and forthcoming items.

N-S languages are tonal, but most older sources lack tone-marking.

For all of N-S, see lexicon in the main sources above: e.g. Greenberg 1963 has 161 widespread items of rather limited distribution and reliability while Gregersen 1972 goes further to suggest possible items linking N-S and N-K into a giant Kongo-Kordofanian. Ehret forth. and Bender forth. a will provide supporting items for their classifications.

Two well-known 19th-century sources contain N-S material: Koelle 1854 has about 282 items each of "Timbuktu" (A Songay), Kanuri-Kanembu (of B), and Bagirmi of Central Sudanic, while Barth 1862 (2nd ed., 1961 in parallel German/English) has about 1500 items in A Songay, B Kanuri, Teda, C Maba, and Bagirmi.

For brevity, I will have to omit older sources, newer ones without lexica, and unpublished archives.

2. Families Other Than Sudanic

Families A, D, G, H, J are single languages (better: dialect clusters). For A, for historical reasons, most material is in French. I know of no more recent dictionary than the extensive but not very reliable lexicon in Prost 1956.

Nicolai 1990 lists 412 items in support of his argument that Songay is a post-creole, not Nilo-Saharan at all. Tersis 1968, titled Dendi, is on a Zerma variety.

Family B is dominated by Kanuri, for which there is a new dictionary (Hutchison/Cyffer et al. 1990, with about 11000 items. Teda and Tubu have only older sources, Berti and Zagawa only fragments.

C Maba also has a forthcoming dictionary (Edgar forth. a) of all varieties (Maba, Mesalit, Runga-Kibet, "Mimi") reviewing all older sources in 450 pages. Nougayrol 1991 has ca. 2000 Aiki-French items with index.

Family D For (= Fur): an older inadequate grammar with word lists (Beaton 1968) and Jakobi et al. forth. For Biltine (= Amdang or "Mimi of Jungraithmayr") and other "Mimis" there is a survey in Doornbos/Bender 1983. G, Berta has nearly 1000 items I collected from several varieties and notes on some of the older sources (Bender 1989). See also E4 Jebel Group under Sudanic.

Kunama (H) has both Italian and German older dictionaries; Bender forth. b will have several thousand items tentatively tone-marked.

Greenberg included "Mao" with I Koman, but it is now known that most "Mao" varieties are Omotic languages of the AA phylum (Bender 1990). About 224 Proto-Koman words are reconstructed in Bender 1983. The only dictionary of a Koman language is Beam/Cridland 1970, with about 3600 tone-marked Uduk (Twampa) entries, but no English index. Sisto Verri 1982 is a privately circulated list of all that is known of Gule, probably now extinct. Fleming 1991 lists about 220 items of the recently discovered Shabo, which may be Koman. Komo, Kwama, and Opo have only older published fragments of up to 200 items.

Gumuz (J) is close to Koman as a "sister" family (dialect cluster). The best lexical source is probably Unseth 1985, a dialect survey. We can hope that much unpublished material for both I and J soon becomes available.

For K Kuliak, considered by Greenberg to be East Sudanic, Heine's work is definitive: 1975/6 for Ik (ca. 1050 German-Ik items), 1974/5 for Nyangi and So (= Tepes, ca. 550 items each), and 1976 for Proto-Kuliak (about 200 words).

Finally, Kado (= Kadugli-Krongo) is now seen by most cognoscenti as belonging to N-S rather than N-K. It has three branches: Kadugli, Krongo, and Tulishi. Reh 1985 has about 1300 German-Krongo items, while Matsushita 1984, 1986 lists Kadugli-English and reverse with much duplication. An earlier source, Stevenson 1956—7 covers some other varieties.

3. East and Central Sudanic

According to current classifying work, East Sudanic divides into sub-groups Ek (1 sg. pronoun with old N-S k) and En (1 sg. innovated n). Ek consists of E1, 3, 5?, 7. Nubian (E1) has one of the older dictionaries of an African language: the Kenzi one of Carradori 1635, conveniently reissued as Spaulding 1975 with about 600 Italian-Nubian words and phrases. Armbruster 1965 treats the same dialect with about 11,000 entries plus index (work done in early 20th century). Other recent work on Nile Nubian are Hofmann 1986 (about 2580 items based on an earlier source), Hohenwart-Gerlachstein 1979 with about 1870 German-Nubian items of Fadijja, Werner 1987 with ca. 900 words and 400 phrases of Nobiin-German. There is no recent work on Hill Nubian. For reconstructions of all Nubian, see Bechhaus-Gerst 1984.

For E3 Nera (= Barea, a pejorative), only Bender 1968 can be added to Reinisch 1874 (!). E5 Nyima has only Stevenson 1956—7. E7 Tama has about 226 reconstructions in Edgar 1991 and Edgar forth. b will provide 250 pages of lexicon from all main sources on the group (main languages: Tama, Erenga, Sungor, Merarit, Misiiri).

En includes E2, 4, 6?, 8, 9. Surmic (E2) has Lyth 1971 (ca. 1500 Murle items, not tone-marked, plus index). Ricci 1974 is based on a 1940's source, with ca. 2400 Me'en-Italian items with etymological notes to many Sudan-Ethiopia border languages plus Italian index. Unseth 1988 is perhaps best for Majang, the most divergent E2 language, but much data on all languages (Mursi, Didinga, Kwegu, etc.) awaits publication, e.g. Will forth. has ca. 2000 items Me'en-English-Me'en with Amharic glosses. Jebel (E4) has one modest dictionary (Bender/Malik 1980) of the main variety, Gaam (= Tabi = Ingessana), with ca. 1500 tone-marked items plus index; the three other varieties, discovered by Evans-Pritchard ca. 1926 and considered to be Berta, are now known to belong with Gaam (I have unpublished lexicon). E6 Temein has varieties: Ronge (= Temein), Doni

(= Jirru), Dese (= Teis-umm-Danab; only fragments exist, e.g. Stevenson 1956—7). For E8 Daju, Thelwall 1981 gives five varieties and proto-forms based on these; otherwise only fragments exist (main vars. Shatt-Liguri, Nyala, Lagowa, Sila, Mongo, † Beygo, Nyalgulgule).

E9 Nilotic, the largest group in N-S, must be treated even more briefly here. Dimmendaal 1988 reconstructs 204 proto-Nilotic items and many sub-group items, while Rottland 1982 treats E9c (South) and Vossen 1982 does E9b (East). There is no such published work for the larger E9a (West) yet. There is a 1974 reprint of the Heasty 1937 dictionary of E9a Colo (Shilluk, not tone-marked). Kokwaro 1972 is an example of special lexicon (Kenya Luo botany). For E9b, Spagnolo 1960 is Bari-Italian-English, no index, while Tucker/Mpaayei 1955 has Masai lexicon and Vossen 1988 is an exhaustive study of Masai dialects. For Teso there is Hilders/Lawrance 1958. For E9c, important forthcoming dictionaries are Creider/Creider (Nandi) and Larsen (Sabaot-English-Sabaot, 3000 entries).

Central Sudanic. Fp ("peripheral", perhaps not a genetic group, consists of F1—3, 7—9). For F1, Tucker 1940 is definitive: ca. 900 items in 15 varieties plus "Lendu" (Baledha, F8); otherwise, only Crazzolara 1960 for Logbara and Goyvaerts/Tauli forth. for Logo. F2 ("Mangbutu") has grammars but no lexica that I know of. F3 (Mangbetu) has Larochette 1958 (1800 items plus French index). Kresh (F7) and Aja (F9) have Santandrea 1970b with ca. 560 items plus notes on dialects and several N-K languages of the area.

Fc: Core Central Sudanic (F4—6). For F4, Sara languages: Keegan forth. will be definitive for Mbay with thousands of entries. Ngambay: Boukar et al. 1983 has ca. 2500 items in economics and socio-politics with contextual examples; Thayer/Thayer 1971 has ca. 400 items, Vandame 1963 over 800. Kaba (Kyabe village, Chad): Danay et al. 1986 with ca. 3000 items. Nougayrol 1991 is a grammar/lexicon of the little-known Gula. Nothing new on F4 Bagirmi. F5 (Shemya = Sinyar) has only a published fragment (Doornbos/Bender 1983), while for F4 Kara, Baka, Yulu and F6 Bongo there is Santandrea 1970 a (about 400 items each with comparative notes to other area languages). Andersen 1981 has ca. 600 items of F6 Modo plus index.

4. Selected Bibliography

4.1. Dictionaries

Armbruster 1965 = Charles Hubert Armbruster: Dongolese Nubian: A Lexicon. Cambridge 1965 [269 p.].

Beam/Cridland 1970 = Mary S. Beam/A. Elizabeth Cridland: UDUK-English Dictionary. Khartoum 1970 [183 p.].

Bender forth. b = M. Lionel Bender: Kunama-English-Kunama.

Bender/Malik 1980 = M. Lionel Bender/Malik Agaar Ayre: Preliminary Gaam-English-Gaam Dictionary. Carbondale 1980 [267 p.].

Boukar et al. 1983 = B. L. G. Boukar et al.: 1. Activités Economiques et sociales Sara-ngambay. Paris 1983 [481 p.].

Creider/Creider forth. = Chet A./Jane Tapsubei Creider: Nandi Dictionary.

Danay et al. 1968 = Kamis Danay et al.: Dictionnaire Sara-Kab-Na-Français. Sarh 1968 [217 p.].

Edgar forth. a = John Edgar: Maba Group Dictionary. Hamburg [ca. 450 p.].

Edgar forth. b = John Edgar: Tama Group Dictionary. Hamburg [ca. 250 p.].

Heasty 1937 (1974) = J. A. Heasty: English-Shilluk-English Dictionary. Doleib Hill, Sudan 1937 [109 p.].

Hilders/Lawrance 1958 = J. H. Hilders/J. C. P. Lawrance: An English-Ateso and Ateso-English Vocabulary. Nairobi 1958 [58 p.].

Hofmann 1986 = Inge Hofmann: Nubisches Wortverzeichnis. Berlin 1986 [238 p.].

Hutchison/Cyffer et al. 1990 = John Hutchison/Norbert Cyffer et al.: Dictionary of the Kanuri Language. Dordrecht 1990.

Jakobi et al. forth. = Angelika Jakobi et al.: Dictionary of Fur.

Keegan forth. = John Keegan: Mbay Dictionary. Hamburg.

Kokwaro 1972 = J. O. Kokwaro: Luo-English Botanical Dictionary. Nairobi 1972 [200 p.].

Larsen forth. = Iver Larsen: Sabaot-English-Sabaot Dictionary.

Nougayrol 1991 = Pierre Nougayrol: Les parlers gula [...] grammaire comparée et lexique. Paris 1991.

Spagnolo 1960 = Fr. Lorenzo Spagnolo: Bari-English-Italian Dictionary. Verona 1960 [377 p.].

Spaulding 1975 = Jay Spaulding: Carradori's Dictionary of Kenzi Nubian. Bergen 1975 [298 p.].

Will forth. = Hans-Georg Will: Me'en-English-Me'en (+Amharic) Dictionary.

4.2. Other Publications

Andersen 1981 = Torben Arensen: A Grammar of Modo. Aalborg 1981.

Barth 1862 = Henry Barth: Central African Languages (2nd ed. by A. H. M. Kirk-Greene 1971). London 1862.

Beaton 1968 = A. C. Beaton: A Grammar of the Fur Language. Khartoum 1968.

Becchaus-Gerst 1984 = Marianne Becchaus-Gerst: Sprachliche und historische Rekonstruktion [...] Nubischen [...]. In: Sprache und Geschichte in Afrika 6. 1984, 7—134.

Bender 1968 = M. Lionel Bender: Analysis of a Barya Word List. In: Anthropological Linguistics 10. 9. 1968, 1—24.

Bender 1981 = M. Lionel Bender: Some Nilo-Saharan Isoglosses. In: Thilo Schadeberg/M. Lionel Bender: Nilo-Saharan. Dordrecht 1981, 253—68.

Bender 1983 = M. Lionel Bender: Proto-Koman Phonology and Lexicon. In: Afrika und Übersee 66.2. 1983, 259—97.

Bender 1989 = M. Lionel Bender: Berta Lexicon. In: M. Lionel Bender, ed.: Topics in Nilo-Saharan Linguistics. Hamburg 1989, 271—304.

Bender 1990 = M. Lionel Bender: The Limits of Omotic. In: Richard Hayward, ed.: Omotic Language Studies. London 1990, 584—616.

Bender 1991 = M. Lionel Bender: Subclassification of Nilo-Saharan. In: M. Lionel Bender, ed.: Proceedings of the 4th Nilo-Saharan Linguistics Colloquium. Hamburg 1991, 1—34.

Bender forth. a = M. Lionel Bender: Nilo-Saharan Reconstructions.

Crazzolara 1960 = J. P. Crazzolara: A Study of the Logbara (Ma'di) Language. Oxford 1960.

Dimmendaal 1988 = Gerrit J. Dimmendaal: The Lexical Reconstruction of Proto-Nilotic. In: Afrikanistische Arbeitspapiere 16. 1988, 5—67.

Doornbos/Bender 1983 = P. Doornbos/M. L. Bender: Languages of Wadai-Darfur. In: M. Lionel Bender, ed.: Nilo-Saharan Language Studies. East Lansing 1983, 42—79.

Edgar 1991 = John Edgar: First Steps toward Proto-Tama. In: M. Lionel Bender, ed.: Proceedings of the 4th Nilo-Saharan Linguistics Colloquium. Hamburg 1991.

Ehret forth. = Christopher Ehret: Monograph on Nilo-Saharan Reconstruction.

Fleming 1991 = Harold C. Fleming: Shabo. In: M. Lionel Bender, ed.: Procs. of the 4th Nilo-Saharan Linguistics Colloquium. Hamburg 1991.

Goyvaerts/Tauli forth. = Didier Goyvaerts/Agasuru Tauli: English-Logoti Lexicon. Tervuren.

Greenberg 1963 = Joseph H. Greenberg: The Languages of Africa. Indiana. Berlin 1963.

Greenberg 1971 = Joseph H. Greenberg: Nilo-Saharan and Meroitic. In: Jack Berry/Joseph H. Greenberg, eds.: Current Trends in Linguistics Vol. 7: Sub-Saharan Africa. Berlin 1971, 426—442.

Gregersen 1972 = Edward A. Gregersen: Kongo-Saharan. In: Journal of African Languages 11. 1972, 69—89.

Heine 1974/5 = Bernd Heine: Tepes and Nyang'i. In: Afrika und Übersee 58.3—4. 1974/75, 263—300.

Heine 1975/6 = Bernd Heine: Ik. In: Afrika und Übersee 59.1. 1975/6, 31—56.

Heine 1976 = Bernd Heine: The Kuliak Languages of Eastern Uganda. Nairobi 1976.

Hohenwart-Gerlachstein 1979 = Anna Hohenwart-Gerlachstein: Nubienforschungen. Vienna 1979.

Koelle 1854 = Sigismund W. Koelle: Polyglotta Africana. Graz 1963.

Larochette 1958 = J. Larochette: Grammaire des Dialectes Mangbetu et Medje. Tervuren 1958.

Lyth 1971 = R. E. Lyth: The Murle Language. Khartoum 1971.

Matsushita 1984, 1986 = Shuji Matsushita: A Preliminary Sketch of Kadugli Vocabulary. In: Morimichi Tomikawa, ed.: Sudan Sahel Studies I. Tokyo, 15—73, 111—138.

Nicolai 1990 = Robert Nicolai: Parentés linguistiques (á propos du songhay). Paris 1990.

Prost 1956 = R. P. A. Prost: La langue songay et ses dialectes. Dakar 1956.

Reh 1985 = Mechtild Reh: Die Krongo-Sprache. Berlin 1985.

Ricci 1974 = Lanfranco Ricci: Materiali per la lingua Mekan. In: Rassegna di studi Etiopici 25. 1974, 90—455.

Rottland 1982 = Franz Rottland: Die südnilotischen Sprachen. Berlin 1982.

Ruhlen 1987 = Merritt Ruhlen: A Guide to the World's languages Vol. 1: Classification. Stanford 1987.

Santandrea 1970a = Stefano Santandrea: Brief Grammar Outlines of the Yulu and Kara Languages. Rome 1970.

Santandrea 1970b = Stefano Santandrea: The Kresh Group [...]. Rome 1970.

Stevenson 1956/7 = Roland C. Stevenson: [...] Nuba Mountain Languages [...]. In: Afrika und Übersee 40. 1956, 27—65, 73—84. 41. 1957, 117—152, 171—196.

Tersis 1968 = Nicole Tersis: Le parler dendi [...]. Paris 1968.

Thayer/Thayer 1971 = Linda J./James E. Thayer: 50 Leçons en Sara-Ngambay (3 vols.). Indiana 1971.

Thelwall 1981 = Robin Thelwall: ... Lexical Reconstruction of the Daju Group. In: Thilo Schadeberg/M. Lionel Bender eds.: Nilo-Saharan. Dordrecht 1981, 161—184.

Tucker 1940 = Archibald N. Tucker: The Eastern Sudanic Languages. London 1940.

Tucker/Bryan 1956 = Archibald N. Tucker/Margaret A. Bryan: The Non-Bantu Languages of North-Eastern Africa. Oxford 1956.

Tucker/Mpaayei 1955 = Archibald N. Tucker/J. Tompo Ole Mpaayei: A Maasai Grammar. London 1955.

Unseth 1985 = Peter Unseth: Gumuz Dialect Survey. In: Journal of Ethiopian Studies 18. 1985, 91—114.

Unseth 1988 = Peter Unseth: Majang Noun Plurals. In: Studies in African Linguistics 19. 1988, 75—91.

Vandame 1963 = R. P. Charles Vandame: Le Ngambay-Moundou. Dakar 1963.

Verri 1982 = Sisto Verri: English-Gule Vocabulary. Padova 1982.

Vossen 1982 = Rainer Vossen: The Eastern Nilotes. Berlin 1982.

Vossen 1988 = Rainer Vossen: [...] Maa Dialects [...]. Hamburg 1988.

Werner 1987 = Roland Werner: Grammatik des Nobiin. Hamburg 1987.

Westermann 1911 = Diedrich Westermann: Die Sudansprachen. Hamburg 1911.

Westermann/Bryan 1952 = Diedrich Westermann/Margaret A. Bryan: The Languages of West Africa. Oxford 1952.

Zyhlarz 1928 = E. Zyhlarz: Grundzüge der Nubischen Grammatik. Leipzig 1928.

M. Lionel Bender,
Southern Illinois University,
Carbondale, Illinois (USA)

272. Lexicography of the Niger-Kordofanian Languages

1. Introduction
2. Historical Sketch
3. Methodology and Sampling
4. Selected Bibliography

1. Introduction

The Niger-Kordofanian languages — more commonly known as Congo-Kordofanian (a term coined by J. Greenberg 1963) — include two major

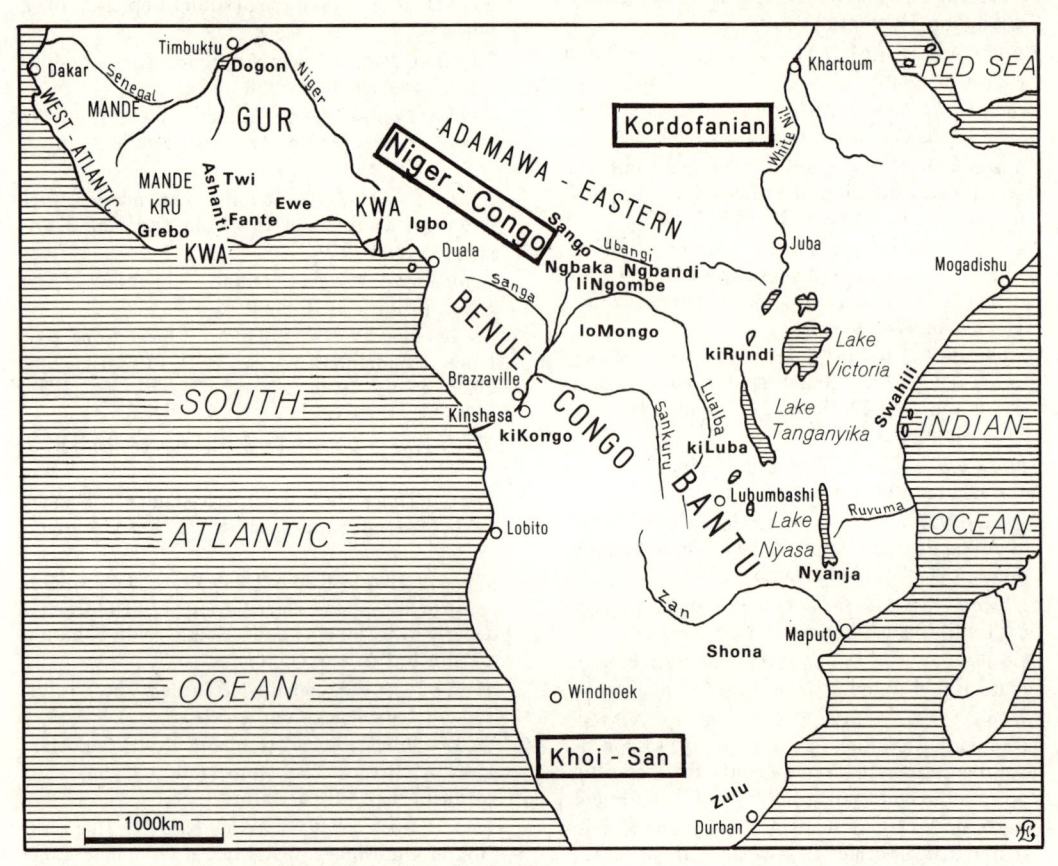

Map 272.1: Languages of Africa referred to in article 272

groups: (a) Niger-Congo, and (b) Kordofanian (cf. Map 272.1). Whereas the latter constitutes a set of small languages spoken in the Nuba mountain area of southern Kordofan in the Sudan, the former covers a vast territory which stretches from Senegal to Kenya and down to the southern tip of Africa, with the exception of the southwestern areas occupied by Khoi-San peoples. Niger-Congo is usually subdivided into six subgroups: (a) West-Atlantic (mainly in Senegal and Guinea-Bissau), (b) Mande (mainly in Mali, Guinea, Sierra Leone, Liberia and the Ivory Coast), (c) Gur (in the Upper Volta area), (d) Kwa — including Kru (in the coastal regions, from Liberia to western Nigeria), (e) Adamawa-Eastern (from northern Nigeria to Chad, the Central African Republik and northern Zaire), and (f) Benue-Congo — a large subgroup that encompasses the whole Bantu territory and the related language areas in eastern Nigeria and Cameroon (De Wolf 1981, Möhlig 1981, Schadeberg 1981, Manessy 1981/1981a, Lacroix 1981, Houis 1981, Innes 1981, Hérault 1981, Hagège 1981, Thomas 1981, Alexandre 1981).

2. Historical Sketch

The compilation of vocabularies of the Niger-Kordofanian languages goes back to the earliest days of evangelization: It was essentially the work of missionaries who put together, for strictly practical purposes, rather unsystematic glossaries of the languages they were in contact with. The oldest example of such an original lexical work is the *Vocabularium Latinum, Hispanicum, et Congense,* preserved in Rome in a manuscript dating back to 1651—52. It was compiled in the old Congo kingdom by a San Salvador mulatto priest called Emmanuel Roborero, and written down by a Flemish capuchin, Friar Joris van Geel (van Wing/Pengers 1928). Another important milestone in Niger-Kordofanian lexicography is the publication in 1854 of S. W. Koelle's *Polyglotta Africana. Comparative Vocabularies of More than 100 Distinct African Languages.* Whatever its merits and the value of the information it provides, it is, however, no substitute for a regular dictionary: breaking new ground in this regard is the first Swahili dictionary, compiled by the Rev. L. Krapf around 1850 while working in East Africa for the Church Missionary Society. Though completed in 1860, it unfortunately appeared only in 1882 in London. What distinguishes this work from its predecessors is the deliberate effort of its author to provide detailed information on the usage of the terms, their background and their sociocultural context.

The second half of the XIXth century witnessed the great expansion of missionary work in Subsaharan Africa: as a result, many vocabularies, glossaries and dictionaries of various degrees of sophistication and extent of coverage were compiled by missionaries — some printed locally, some published in their homeland, some merely written down in notebooks which sometimes were saved from destruction by enlightened local librarians or museum curators (cf. for the Bantu area, Doke 1967; for West Africa Westermann/Bryan 1952). In the XXth century, better linguistic training led to the production of some lexical works of higher quality, but for many of the languages, all that is available as yet are still the word lists patiently compiled by local missionaries (cf. for East Africa, Whiteley/Guthrie 1958; for Tanzania, Polomé 1980).

3. Methodology and Sampling

Word lists were compiled in recent years by linguists with various aims: some merely followed the example of their XIXth century predecessors like J. Last in his *Polyglotta Africana Orientalis* (1885) to provide samples of various languages and dialects (e.g., Nurse 1979); others wanted to gather a comprehensive set of materials covering a large number of languages within a definite family or group to examine the lexical correspondences between them (e.g., Johnston 1919—1922). Such lists could serve several purposes: using Johnston's data, L. B. de Boeck (1942) tried to derive historical conclusions from the geographical distribution of the relevant terms, and since then, modified Swadesh lists have been used repeatedly for the purpose of glottochronology. Ultimately, Guthrie's reconstruction of Proto-Bantu (1967—1971) rests essentially on extended vocabulary lists that he and his collaborators collected over the years in Africa. But the major dictionaries published in recent years are based on the patient gathering of material from all sources: daily conversation, proverbs, tales, fables, songs, epic poetry and other types of oral literature, bargaining, palavers, ritual formulas and other magico-religious forms of speech, etc. Mostly, they merely supply a literal translation without much further comment (e.g., Höftmann 1979) or with a periphrastic rendering of the term in the original language, as in the *Kamusi ya KiSwahili Sanifu* (1981) or in the Swahili "explanations" of Kajiga 1975. Some, however, are works of high scientific standing in which the phonological and grammatical information is precise and accurate, the analysis of the semantic connotations of the terms, thorough and adequately illustrated by concrete examples, and the coverage of the vocabulary extensive and properly documented. Particularly worth mentioning are, in this respect, the dictionaries produced by the Royal Museum for Central Africa in Tervuren, Belgium, e.g., van Avermaet 1954 (kiLuba), Lekens 1955 (Ngbandi), Hulstaert 1957 (loMongo), Rood 1958 (liNgombe), Maes 1959 (Ngbaka), Rodegem 1970 (kiRundi), etc.

In the former British territories, the regional Literature Bureaus sponsored the publication of translating dictionaries of the main vernaculars, mainly for educational purposes, but some of them are excellent tools for the study of the vocabulary and its meaning in context, though the linguist will miss the tones in such languages as Shona (Hannan 1974) or Nyanja (Scott/Hetherwick 1957). The latter is actually a slightly updated reprint of a 1929 work which contains a lot of ethnographic information which one misses in the more recent Portuguese Nyanja dictionary (1963) where new loanwords from English and Portuguese are also listed. Lexicographical work had an early start in southern Africa, where Colenso's Zulu dictionary (1861) opened a tradition which culminated in the excellent Zulu dictionary of Doke and Vilikazi (1948), after being illustrated in 1905 by the remarkable work of A. T. Bryant. This dictionary arranged about 22,000 Zulu lexical entries according to (verbal) stems and derivations, gave hints about pronunciation and intonation (albeit not always very accurately), and listed idiomatic expressions, proverbs and *hlonipha* forms of respect. Although older dictionaries are available for a number of West African languages, the work done under the sponsorship of the *Institut Français d'Afrique Noire* in colonial times and by the institutions that have replaced it after the French territories gained their independence, is more limited than in the Bantu area (Barreteau 1978). For some major languages there are, however, dictionaries produced by experienced linguists, e.g. Westermann 1954 (Ewe), Berry 1960 (Twi-Fante-Ashanti), Innes 1967 (Grebo), Calame-Griaule 1968 (Dogon), Williamson 1972 (Igbo), Bouquiaux 1978 (Sango), etc. See also Murphy/Goff 1969.

4. Selected Bibliography

4.1. Dictionaries

Berry 1960 = J. Berry: English, Twi, Asante, Fante Dictionary. London. Accra 1960 [146 p.].

Bouquiaux 1978 = Luc Bouquiaux: Dictionnaire sango-français. Paris 1978. (Langues et civilisations à tradition orale 29) [663 p.].

Bryant 1905 = A. T. Bryant: Zulu-English Dictionary. Pinetown (Natal) 1905 [cxi + 778 p.].

Calame-Griaule 1968 = G. Calame-Griaule: Dictionnaire dogon (dialecte tóro). Paris 1968.

Doke/Vilikazi 1948 = C. M. Doke/B. W. Vilikazi: Zulu-English Dictionary. Johannesburg 1948 [903 p.; 1972, 918 p.].

Hannan 1974 = M. Hannan: Standard Shona Dictionary. 2nd ed. Salisbury 1974 [996 p.].

Höftmann 1979 = Hildegard Höftmann: Wörterbuch Swahili-Deutsch. Leipzig 1979 [402 p.].

Hulstaert 1957 = G. Hulstaert: Dictionnaire loMóngo-français. 2 volumes. Tervuren 1957. (Annales du Musée Royal du Congo Belge. Linguistique. Vol. 16). [1948 p.].

Innes 1967 = Gordon Innes: A Grebo-English dictionary. Cambridge 1967. (Journal of West African Languages Monograph 6). [v, 131 p.].

Kajiga 1975 = Balihuta Kajiga: Dictionnaire de la langue Swahili. Goma (Zaire) 1975 [680 p.].

Kamusi = The Institute of Swahili Research (Dar es Salaam): Kamusi ya KiSwahili Sanifu (Dictionary of Standard Swahili). Nairobi 1981 [325 p.].

Lekens 1955 = B. Lekens: Ngbandi Idioticon. Part I: A—K. Tervuren 1955. (Annales du Musée Royal du Congo Belge. Linguistique. Vol. 3). [1091 p. A shorter complete Dictionnaire Ngbandi, 348 p., was published in 1952 at Tervuren in the Annales du Musée Royal du Congo Belge. Linguistique. Vol. 1].

Maes 1959 = V. Maes: Dictionnaire ngbaka-français-néerlandais, précédé d'un aperçu grammatical. Tervuren 1959. (Annales du Musée Royal du Congo Belge. Linguistique. Vol. 25). [200 p.].

Nyanja = Junta de Investigações do Ultramar: Dicionário cinyanja-português. Lisbon 1963 [291 p.].

Rodegem 1970 = F. M. Rodegem: Dictionnaire rundi-français. Tervuren 1970. (Annales du Musée Royal d'Afrique Centrale. Sciences Humaines. Vol. 69). [644 p.].

Rood 1958 = N. Rood: Dictionnaire ngombe-néerlandais-français. Tervuren 1958. (Annales du Musée Royal du Congo Belge. Linguistique. Vol. 21). [414 p.].

Scott/Hetherwick 1957 = David Clement Scott/Alexander Hetherwick: Dictionary of the Nyanja Language. Revised ed. London 1957 (reprint of 1929 ed.) [614 p.].

van Avermaet 1954 = E. van Avermaet: Dictionnaire kiLuba-français. Tervuren 1954. (Annales du

Musée Royal du Congo Belge. Linguistique. Vol. 7). Tervuren 1954. [838 p.].
van Wing/Penders 1928 = V. van Wing/G. Penders (eds.): Le plus ancien dictionnaire bantu. Vocabularium P. Georgii Gelensis. Bibliothèque Congo. Louvain 1928 [365 p.].
Westermann 1954 = Dietrich Westermann: Wörterbuch der Ewe-Sprache. Berlin 1954 [795 p.].
Williamson 1972 = Kay Williamson (ed.): Igbo-English dictionary. Benin City 1972 [lxx, 568 p.].

4.2. Other Publications

Alexandre 1981 = Pierre Alexandre: Les langues bantu. In: Manessy 1981, 351—397.

Barreteau 1978 = Daniel Barreteau (ed.): Inventaire des études linguistiques sur les pays d'Afrique noire d'expression française. Paris 1978.

Bouquiaux 1981 = Luc Bouquiaux: Les langues Bénoué-Congo et leur classification. In: Manessy 1981, 159—180.

de Boeck 1942 = L. B. de Boeck: Premières applications de la géographie linguistique aux langues bantoues. (Institut Royal Colonial Belge. Mémoire X, 5). Brussels 1942.

De Wolf 1981 = P. P. De Wolf: Das Niger-Kongo (ohne Bantu). In: Heine 1981, 45—76.

Doke 1967 = Clement M. Doke: Bantu. Modern Grammatical, Phonetical and Lexicographical Studies since 1860. London 1967.

Greenberg 1963 = J. H. Greenberg: The Languages of Africa. International Journal of American Linguistics 29.1, Part II. Bloomington 1963 (reprint The Hague 1966; first published as: Studies in African Linguistic Classification. In: Southwestern Journal of Anthropology 5. 1949, 79—100, 190—198, 309—317; 6. 1950, 47—63, 143—160, 223—237, 388—398).

Guthrie 1967—1971 = Malcolm Guthrie: Comparative Bantu. An Introduction to the comparative linguistics and prehistory of the Bantu languages. 4 volumes. Farnborough 1967—71 [the last 2 volumes being a "catalogue of Common Bantu with commentary"].

Hagège 1981 = Claude Hagège: Les langues de l'Adamawa et leur classification. In: Manessy 1981.

Heine 1981 = Bernd Heine/Thilo C. Schadeberg/Ekkehard Wolff: Die Sprachen Afrikas. Hamburg 1981.

Hérault 1981 = Georges Hérault: Les langues kwa. In: Manessy 1981, 137—157.

Houis 1981 = Maurice Houis: Les langues du groupe mandé. In: Manessy 1981, 65—82.

Innes 1981 = Gordon Innes: Les langues kru. In: Manessy 1981, 123—135.

Johnston 1919—1922 = H. H. Johnston: A Comparative Study of the Bantu and Semi-Bantu Languages. 2 volumes. Oxford 1919—1922.

Lacroix 1981 = Pierre François Lacroix: Les langues "ouest-atlantiques". In: Manessy 1981, 9—63.

Manessy 1981 = Gabriel Manessy (ed.): Les langues dans le monde ancien et moderne. 1. Les langues de l'Afrique subsaharienne. Paris 1981.

Manessy 1981a = Gabriel Manessy: Les langues voltaïques. In: Manessy 1981, 101—115.

Möhlig 1981 = Wilhelm J. G. Möhlig: Die Bantusprachen im engeren Sinn. In: Heine 1981, 77—116.

Murphy/Goff 1969 = John D. Murphy/Harry Goff: A Bibliography of African Languages and Linguistics. Washington 1969.

Nurse 1979 = Derek Nurse: Description of 14 Bantu Languages of Tanzania. In: African Languages 5.1, 1—150. London 1979.

Polomé 1980 = Edgar C. Polomé: The Languages of Tanzania. In: Edgar C. Polomé/P. C. Hill (eds.): Language in Tanzania. London 1980, 3—25.

Schadeberg 1981 = Thilo C. Schadeberg: Das Kordofanische. In: Heine 1981, 117—128.

Thomas 1981 = Jacqueline M. C. Thomas: Les langues du sous-groupe oriental ou oubangien et leur classification. In: Manessy 1981, 197—233.

Westermann/Bryan 1952 = Dietrich Westermann/M. A. Bryan: Languages of West Africa. Handbook of African Languages. Part II. London 1952.

Whiteley/Guthrie 1958 = W. H. Whiteley/A. M. Guthrie: A Linguistic Bibliography of East Africa. Revised ed. Kampala 1958.

Edgar C. Polomé, University of Texas, Austin, Texas (USA)

273. Lexicography of the Khoisan Languages

1. Preliminaries
2. Classification of Languages
3. Development of Study of Khoisan Languages
4. Exploration of Their Grammar; Nama
5. Lexical Studies
6. Selected Bibliography

1. Preliminaries

1.1. This unusual family of languages presents a lexicography with almost none of the features that occupy the modern technical field. Rather, it affords a special focus on difficulties and experience in bringing a challenging area of study into the range of formal linguistic analysis and accomplishment. Khoisan lexicography is as yet poorly distinguished from demography, genetic classification, dialectology, phonology, morphosyntax, cultural semantics, ethnography, folklore, text collection and recording, field philology, manuscript paleography, bibliography, and librarian's data processing. Our study is still in its infancy while the data retreat perilously from view; for an impassioned and reasoned statement of this urgency see Traill 1974.

1.2. This impoverished lexicography can be credited to a number of factors: in particular, the late start of Khoisan studies, forbidding phonology whose mastery is essential to the identification of lexemes, and the long and informed study needed to disengage Khoisan from Bantu. Satisfactory coverage of varieties had to await the discernment of genetic classification, in the early period especially by Tindall and W. H. I. Bleek, later in the recognition during the 1920s of the placement of Bushman, and in the modern period by the attachment of Sandawe and Hadza. Thus the disclosure of Khoisan has been unlike that of e.g. many indigenous North American families.

The work of missionaries has been a great asset, but their primary aim at practical results leads to much traditional and simplifying analysis: Technically trained analysis has been slow and understaffed; this aspect of inadequacy has been particularly noticeable with these difficult and unfamiliar phonologies.

Such conditions have shaped the whole lexicography of Khoisan; with few real dictionaries, it is largely an account of the collection of improved word lists, heavily a story of the philology and search to identify the proper objects of study, the progress of salvage, the refining of inventories of social units. Much of the early 20th century literature was occupied with sorting out tribes, names and their spellings, and speech differences.

1.3. Two important confusions have impeded, though not defeated, the correct and principled genetic identification of Khoisan: the reliance on a single phonetic and phonological characteristic and the intrusion of a typological trait of morphological category as a guiding criterion. So, while click consonants turn out to be highly characteristic of the family, they are not intrinsically diagnostic any more than is retroflexion of Dravidian. Likewise, German, Icelandic, and Gothic show rich gender systems which agree also in detail, while English, Afrikaans, and Danish show varying degrees of absence of this category.

2. Classification of Languages

The taxonomy of the members of this linguistic family is important in assessing the number of objects of lexicographic study to be reckoned with and the degree of success in attaining relevant goals.

2.1. The Khoisan (< Europeanized Nama *khoi*+-*sa-n*, credited to L. Schultze) languages, numbering between a dozen and two dozen languages and varieties centering on the Kalahari (less than 50 000 Bushmen, or San) and Namibia (nearly 100 000 Hottentots, Bergdama, and Bushmen speaking Nama), are found in discontinuous groups, enclaves and relics (on the ethnography and identification see basically Schapera 1930) in South Africa, Namibia with southern Angola, Botswana and Zambia, with outliers in Tanzania (Sandawe [Dempwolff 1916] and Hadza, or Hatsa [D. F. Bleek 1931a, 1931b]). For a full listing see D. F. Bleek 1929, 1956, Westphal 1971, Köhler 1971, 1974, Snyman 1974, Traill 1973.

2.2. The internal subgrouping of the southern African languages is agreed to comprise a compact and populous Central group, a Northern group of three dialects, and a divergent Southern group with three major clusters; these groups are superficially dissimilar, as is Sandawe, which has been dubiously claimed as a Central language, and more notably so the distant Hadza. Bushman has also been divided into A, B, C, and D groups, of which A matches D. F. Bleek's Northern (including !K(h)ung), thus validating D. F. Bleek's 1929 trichotomy into Northern, Central, and Southern. The Tshu-Khwe (Khoe) San, of which the largest language is Nharo, or Naro(n), belong with Hottentot to the Central group. On these relations see for detailed discussion which space here will not permit D. F. Bleek 1929, Maingard 1963, Köhler 1961, 1971, Stanley 1968, Baucom 1970, Tanaka 1978, Barnard 1985, Traill 1985 (p. 5—7). From among the Southern group, sadly, Traill 1974 (p. 41—43) documents the presence of the last /ʔauni speaker, and Traill 1985 reports that for three or four Southern languages only a couple of speakers survived; therefore the solitary remnant Southern language was !Xóõ, with ca. 2000 speakers in southwest Botswana and eastern Namibia.

A relation between Hottentot and Sandawe was recognized in 1910 by Trombetti, but obviously on unsatisfactory data (s. Fleming 1986, Elderkin 1982).

3. Development of Study of Khoisan Languages

Through a review of classificatory results we have tried to discern how many and which languages are representative of the familiy, but we cannot avoid a glance at the history of the field. Leibnitz 1717 was aware of these languages and includes Cape Hottentot data from before 1679, published in 1691 and reprinted by W. H. I. Bleek in 1858 (1869). But serious documentation for Hottentot begins only with Wallmann 1854 and especially Tindall 1857.

The first modern scholar to enter this field was W. H. I. Bleek, with a German doctorate (W. H. I. Bleek 1851), whose *Comparative Grammar* (1862—9) was a landmark, inspired by the advances of the day and by such figures as Max Müller and the new Comparative Philology; thus he wrote (p. vii) that Comparative Philology and Ethnology were superior in certainty to that of the historical record, and that up to twelve years previously the field had been groping. Bleek's goal was to classify the African languages south of the Equator; as his basis he chose "Kafir" and Hottentot (cf. W. H. I. Bleek 1857), since (p. 1) Bushman was still too little known, while Hottentot was known in 3 to 4 dialects, and Nama best through missionary literature. Bleek goes on to mention (p. 3) a manuscript grammar of Bushman by the Rev. C. F. Wuras (cf. W. H. I. Bleek 1869) in Sir George Grey's Library (see Mendelssohn 1910) and (p. 4) a manuscript dictionary of !Kora (cf. Wuras 1920); he observes that for Eastern Hottentot scanty vocabularies were all that one had. Bleek's enlightened scholarship praised the literary

dance, the supposed difficulty in mastering the language, and on early manuscripts and learners; opposite p. 168 are shown 10 numerals from 1626 to 1725 in Old Cape dialects, from 1773 to 1797 in Eastern dialects, from 1801 to 1812 in Kora, from 1812 to 1814 in Nama, from 1835 in Griqua, and then the modern Nama, Kora, and Griqua forms; the higher numerals then follow.

4.1. The most noticeable and unavoidable fact of Khoisan is the set of click consonants in every language. Often cited on this subject but long out of date is Stopa 1935; the classic work however remains Beach 1938. Simply to consult the literature and lexicography, to master the alphabetization of these characteristically frequent stop sounds with double articulation, rarefaction, and egressive velar release, one must learn to recognize 3 to 5 elements and their notation (ct. Fig. 273.1). The

Customary	Ingressive	IPA	Nguni romanization
⊙	bilabial (affricate)	no symbol	
/	dental affricate	ǀ	c
≠	alveolar non-affricate	ǂ	
//	lateral affricate	ǁ	x
!	(alveo-)palatal non-affricate	ǃ	q

Fig. 273.1: Frequent stop sounds

capacity and refinement of Hottentot, sought (W. H. I. Bleek 1875) to preserve aboriginal literature, expressed (W. H. I. Bleek 1873b) humane aims in using convicts in 1870 as sources to expand the traveller Dr. H. Lichtenstein's short vocabularies and sparse sentences that then constituted the total corpus of Bushman data, and observed (W. H. I. Bleek 1873a) that philology could have refuted the error alleging that the Bushmen were Hottentots robbed of their cattle by Boers.

As a measure of the sparseness of accumulated study we may note that Mendelssohn 1910 furnishes us mostly with Nama, and that Doke's 1933 Bushman listing came to 2 pages. A more updated picture is given by Westphal 1971.

4. Exploration of Their Grammar; Nama

Although our proper subject is lexicography, to understand the field we must take brief account of grammatical study. It is striking how this field has been dominated by work on Nama. A rich and varied collection of information is found in Nienaber 1963 on early contacts, the word Hottentot, the history of theories on its origin, the Hotten-

customary notation goes back to W. H. I. Bleek. Clicks in Khoisan are notable in occurring only initially almost only in major form-class roots. The bilabial is found only in the Southern group.

4.2. These phonologies display distinctive word tones, and until very recently the tones have been inadequately recognized, analyzed, and notated. The role of nasality (also in syllabics) is important and can be intricate. Features of glottalization, pharyngealization, aspiration, and velar spirant release are important and result in conflicting faulty orthographies. The best phonological studies are Beach 1938 (for Nama and Korana/Griqua), von Essen (but defective in part) 1957, 1962, 1966, Doke 1925, Snyman 1975 (for the Northern group), Traill 1985 (from the Southern group) on !Xóõ, and Ladefoged/Traill 1984.

4.3. The only language whose grammar has been repeatedly and diligently studied is Nama. Hagman 1977 observes that between

1855 and 1905 six Nama grammars had appeared, although all are now surpassed; there is no need to name all of them, just as we pass over some vocabulary and meritorious text collections. The earliest grammar of real merit was Tindall 1857; after that we have a serious analysis by a first-class linguist in Dempwolff 1934—5. Then we must wait until Rust 1965, which, expanding on J. Olpp and H. Vedder, is the culmination of German missionary South West African didactic traditional Latin-based grammar; this practical work, with exercises, based on deep firsthand knowledge immediately became the best and fullest handbook, but unfortunately ignores Beach, who must always be consulted. Hagman 1977 followed, with a brief but interesting modern grammar with new syntactic perspectives. More recently we have the handbook of Köhler 1981 and the introduction by Böhm 1985. Recent studies on separate grammatical topics can be traced in the standard bibliographies.

Although C. Meinhof's Lehrbuch (Berlin: Reimer 1909) is superseded, the 3rd part on Wortbildungslehre is still useful and, because of the resources in word formation which characterize the Central group, is relevant to lexicography.

4.4. Outside of Nama, serviceable grammatical literature is sparse. The Northern group is represented by Snyman 1970. From the Southern group we have D. F. Bleek 1928—30 and Meriggi 1928/9 for /xam and Maingard 1937 for ≠Khomani. For Sandawe there is only the sketch in Dempwolff 1916.

5. Lexical Studies

We now comment chronologically on the work devoted separately to lexical documentation, without segregating the genetic groupings; for references see sect. 6.1. All works are overtly or implicitly bilingual. Wallmann 1854 is now a brief pioneering collection of historical interest only.

Tindall 1857 was an important landmark in the documentation of Khoisan (cf. sect. 4.3.). Declaring that the Hottentot language had been neglected, Tindall distinguished 4 dialects: Hottentot Proper, Coranna, Namaqua, and Bushman; the last was said to have numerous brogues, mutually intelligible and not, but similar in grammatical structure. This intelligent work demonstrates that in Khoisan studies lexicography was not yet a discernable field. W. H. I. Bleek 1858 is a philological document directed at the earliest documentation of Khoisan linguistic history. W. H. I. Bleek 1875 documents for us the true beginnings of Bushman lexicography.

Olpp (1888) was a serious scholar, but still a precursor of sustained lexicography; cf. his other work. Kroenlein 1889 brings us suddenly to the heart of Khoisan lexicography. Though the size of this dictionary is modest, Hagman 1977 is still able to declare it the best. Note also that this corresponds to the leading position in Khoisan scholarship that Nama (or German-trained scholars?) has taken. That Kroenlein was not new to such high-quality work is shown by the fact that W. H. I. Bleek refers in 'Reynard the Fox in South Africa: or, Hottentot Fables and Tales' (London: Trübner 1864, xxxi+94 p.) to Rev. G. Kronlein and a 65-page manuscript including 24 fables and songs, proverbs, riddles, etc, from Namaqua and Bushman.

Schils 1894 took its place beside a grammar of 1891, but these seem to have had little impact on the field.

Dempwolff 1916 contains a very brief glossary, yet it is our only solid source for Sandawe; it illustrates Dempwolff's imperturbable enterprise. One must recall that Dempwolff was a founder of exact modern comparativism in the huge Austronesian family.

Wandres 1918—19 and 1925—26 deserve our gratitude but contribute nothing essentially new to the scholarship which we have seen unfolding.

Wuras 1920 is really a modest contribution; considering the close relationship of Korana to Nama we should like to know much more about Korana. Indeed, Maingard 1962 has given us welcome material on this language lying just west of Kimberley, and Beach 1938 is invaluable on the phonetics of Korana. Yet it seems ironical that Wuras' Korana Catechism has been presented and discussed at least by Vedder in 1927, by Maingard (Bantu Studies 5, 1931, 111—65) and by F. Hestermann in 1954—55 without our yet having an updated lexical register. Here the passage of time has not been well exploited.

D. F. Bleek 1929 is a very valuable piece of work, but is aimed at the problem of comparison and not at that of descriptive or analytic lexicography.

D. F. Bleek 1937 belongs to the ethnographic genre that we have already seen in Dempwolff 1916, D. F. Bleek 1928—30, and Maingard 1937. It also belongs now to the category of salvage documentation in view of what we have reported above in sect. 2.2. from Traill 1974. We must therefore be grateful for what we have of this precious Southern relic. — D. F. Bleek 1956 is a major foundation stone for the basic lexicography of this family of moribund remnant languages and rapidly absorbed cultures. — Rust 1969: While we must accord Kroenlein his proper place in the scholarship of this field (see above), we must also recognize Rust 1969 as one of the central lexicographic accomplishments and tools of this field, and Rust himself as one of the immortals of Khoisan studies (cf. sect. 4.3. above). Rust 1960 completes the work at this stage by providing a matching bilingual dictionary in the other direction. It is significant that these tasks have been accomplished for the important Nama language. — Snyman 1975 provides the first major lexicographic work for a variety of !K(h)ung. The dictionary portion of this book contains 166 pages, each with two columns of typewriter size type and ca. ten entries per column, i.e. a total of ca. 3300 headwords each carrying a gloss a few words in length. This work should be considered alongside that author's grammar of 1970 (cf. sect. 4.4.).

Tanaka 1978 results from 24 months of anthropological fieldwork. The work comprises a simple listing of lexemes broken into sub-lists as shown; the two dialects are mutually intelligible. It is very valuable to have this ample documentation of etyma from another variety of the Central group, to be placed alongside Nama. Barnard 1985 supplies representation from one more variety of the Central group with 6000 speakers in Ghanzi, Botswana. This volume is a careful piece of work. — W. G. H. Haacke is in charge of a group at work on a new Nama dictionary.

5.2. We now comment on the listings in sect. 6.2. D. F. Bleek 1924, Marshall 1957, 1962, Fabian 1965, and Gruber 1973 may be placed alongside Tanaka 1978, as may also Wandres 1927. D. F. Bleek 1936 should be associated with D. F. Bleek 1928—30 (cf. sect. 4.4.). Seven items have taken us into the sphere of toponyms and geography. Nama no longer dominates these recent special studies.

5.3. Up to the present it seems that the main aims of Khoisan lexicography have concentrated on practical and especially missionary needs, ethnography, and basic vocabulary for linguistic comparison. The most damaging gaps at present are in the Southern and Tanzanian groups.

6. Selected Bibliography

6.1. Dictionaries and Lexical Collections

Barnard 1985 = Alan Barnard: A Nharo Wordlist: with notes on grammar (Occasional Publications No. 2, Dept. of African Studies, Univ. of Natal). Durban 1985 [x + 238 p.; 31 p. preamble and grammar; wordlist with simple glosses to p. 170; 171—177 bibliography; 178—236 reverse index].

Bleek, D. F. 1929 = Dorothea Frances Bleek: Comparative Vocabularies of Bushman Languages (University of Cape Town Publications of the School of African Life and Language). Cambridge 1929 [assembles eleven languages].

Bleek, D. F. 1937 = Dorothea Frances Bleek: Grammatical Notes and Texts in the /ʔauni Language; /ʔauni Vocabulary. In: Bushmen of the Southern Kalahari. Ed. by John David Rheinallt Jones and C. M. Doke. Johannesburg 1937 [p. 195—200; 201—220; = Bantu Studies 11,3, 253—258; 259—278; cf. Traill 1974].

Bleek, D. F. 1956 = Dorothea Frances Bleek: A Bushman Dictionary (American Oriental Series 41). New Haven 1956 [10 + 773 p.; reproduction of the typescript; a compilation of all extant material except Hottentot].

Bleek, W. H. I. 1858 = Wilhelm Heinrich Immanuel Bleek: The Hottentot Language. In: The Cape Monthly Magazine 3. 1858, 34—41, 116—119 [containing a translation from Juncker's Life of Ludolf, and the Collectanea Etymologica of Leibnitz 1717, with Hottentot vocabulary in four languages from Cape Hottentot of before 1679, published in 1691, as well as examples of prayers rendered in Hottentot; cf. O. M. Spohr 1963, First Hottentot Vocabulary, Quarterly Bulletin of the South African Library 18, 27—33].

Bleek, W. H. I. 1875 = Wilhelm Heinrich Immanuel Bleek: A Brief Account of Bushman Folklore and other Texts... by W. H. I. Bleek, Ph. D. Curator of the Grey Library, Foreign Member of the R. Bavarian Academy of Sciences & c. Second Report... both Houses of Parliament of the Cape of Good Hope... London 1875 [21 p.; This account argues for the preservation of aboriginal literature, referring to the work of Kro[e]nlein and Rath for Hottentot and Damara; up to then 7200 half-pages in 84 volumes of Bushman literature had been collected. Mendelssohn (1910) summarizes: "In the course of the translation of the Bushman texts a Bushman-English dictionary had been compiled, which at the time of writing contained 11,000 entries, from which, as well as the author's older dictionary, an index, or Bushman-English dictionary, comprising 10,000 entries, had been formed." Cf. D. F. Bleek 1956].

Dempwolff 1916 = Otto Dempwolff: Die Sandawe. s. l. 1916 [the grammatical section includes a glossary].

Kroenlein 1889 = Johann Georg Kroenlein (Krönlein in Rust 1969, SAB 3, 1979; Kronlein in Mendelssohn): Wortschatz der Khoi-khoin (Namaqua-Hottentotten). Berlin 1889 (dated 1899 in Mendelssohn 1910 and Hagman 1977) [vi+350 p; Additional information about this in Rust 1969].

Olpp 1888 = Johannes Olpp: Nama-deutsches Wörterbuch. Elberfeld (1888) [iii+3—118 p.; not in Mendelssohn, but in SAB 1979; Olpp also wrote a grammar 1917, which was translated into Afrikaans 1964].

Rust 1960 = F. Rust: Deutsch-Nama Wörterbuch. Windhoek 1960.

Rust 1969 = F. Rust: Nama Wörterbuch (Krönlein Redivivus). Pietermaritzburg 1969 [x+390 p.; expansion of Kroenlein 1889; cf. Rust 1965, Namagrammatik].

Schils 1894 = G. H. Schils: Dictionnaire étymologique de la langue des Namas. Louvain 1894 (cover and preface 1895) [106 p.].

Snyman 1975 = J. W. Snyman: žu/'hõasi Fonologie & Woordeboek (Communication 37 of University of Cape Town School of African Studies). Kaapstad. Rotterdam 1975 [vii+xi+196+xvii+166 p.; PhD dissertation 1972; foreword by E. O. J. Westphal. See also Some phonetic and lexical aspects of žu/'hõasi. In: A. Traill (ed.): Bushman and Hottentot Studies, University of Witwatersrand African Studies Institute Communication No. 2. 1975, 61—76.].

Tanaka 1978 = Jiro Tanaka: A San Vocabulary of the Central Kalahari: G//ana and G/wi Dialects (African Languages and Ethnography VII). Tokyo 1978 [xxvii+158 p.; 110 p. English — //Ganakhoe — /Gui-khoe, ca. 15 lexemes per page = ca. 1650 entries, +20 p. grouped by semantic class+131 p. personal pronouns+132—3 kin term charts+134—158 G//ana index].

Tindall 1857 = Henry Tindall: A Grammar and Vocabulary of the Namaqua-Hottentot Languages. (Capetown 1857) [124 p.; The review of this by W. H. I. Bleek 1858, South African Philology, The Cape Monthly Magazine 3, 21—27 gives additional information].

Wallmann 1854 = Johann C. Wallmann: Vocabular der Namaqua-Sprache nebst einem Abrisse der Formenlehre derselben. Barmen 1854 [32 p.; Wallmann published a 95-p. *Formenlehre* in Berlin 1857, in which some lexical material can be found].

Wandres 1918—19 = Carl Wandres: Alte Wortlisten der Hottentottensprache. In: Zeitschrift für Kolonialsprachen 9, 26—42; Wandres 1925—26 = Carl Wandres: Namawörter. In: Zeitschrift für Eingeborenen-Sprachen 16, 275—297.

Wuras 1920 = C. F. Wuras: Vocabular der Korana-Sprache. Berlin 1920 [cf. the mention W. H. I. Bleek 1862, p. 4, of a manuscript dictionary of !Kora].

6.2. Special Vocabularies

Bleek, D. F. 1924 = Dorothea Frances Bleek: Bushman terms of relationship. In: Bantu Studies 2. 1924, 57—70.

Bleek, D. F. 1936 = Dorothea Frances Bleek: Special speech of animals and moon used by the /Xam Bushmen. Edition based on W. H. I. Bleek and L. C. Lloyd. In: Bantu Studies 10, 2. 1936, 163—199.

Bourquin 1951 = W. Bourquin: Click-words which Xhosa, Zulu and Sotho have in common. In: African Studies 10. 1951, 59—81.

Dove 1900 = K. Dove: Geographische Bezeichnungen in der Namasprache. In: Mitteilungen des Seminars für Orientalische Sprachen zu Berlin 3. 1900, 57—65 [Dove was a German University-lecturer in geography].

Fabian 1965 = Johannes Fabian: !Kung Bushman kinship componential analysis and alternative interpretations. In: Anthropos 60. 1965, 663—718.

Gruber 1973 = Jeffrey S. Gruber: ≠Hõã kinship terms. In: Linguistic Inquiry 4. 1973, 427—449.

Kingon 1918 = J. R. L. Kingon: A Survey of aboriginal place-names. In: South African Journal of Science 15. 1918, 712—779.

Lanham/Hallowes 1956 = L. W. Lanham/D. P. Hallowes: Linguistic relationships and contacts expressed in the vocabulary of Eastern Bushman. In: African Studies 15. 1956, 45—48; Outline of the structure of Eastern Bushman, 97—118 [grammar and borrowing from Zulu-Swazi, English, Afrikaans, and earlier Sotho and Tsonga by a variety close to ≠khomani].

Marshall 1957 = L. Marshall: The kin terminology system of the !Kung Bushmen. In: Africa 27. 1957, 1—24.

Marshall 1962 = Lorna Marshall: !Kung Bushman religous beliefs. In: Africa 32. 1962, 221—252 [names of gods].

Nienaber 1966 = P. J. Nienaber: South African place-names, with special reference to Bushmen, Hottentot and Bantu place names. In: PICOS 8. 1966, 334—345.

Nienaber/Raper 1977—80 = G. S. Nienaber/P. E. Raper: Toponymica Hottentotica A I: A—G, II: H—Z. Pretoria 1977 [xviii + 503 + 505—1126 pp.]; B: A—Z, 1980 [xviii + 822 pp.] [also P. E. Raper: Onoma 22. 1978, 225—233; PICOS 13 (Kraków) 1982, 291—297].

Ten Raa 1966 = Eric Ten Raa: Geographical names in south-eastern Sandawe. In: Journal of African Linguistics 5. 1966, 175—207.

van Vreeden 1965 = B. F. van Vreeden: Die Khoisan naamgewing in Griekwaland-Wes. In: Tydskrif vir Volkskunde en Volkstaal (Johannesburg) 21. 1965. 4, 12—32 [toponyms].

Vedder 1928—29 = Heinrich Vedder: Bedeutung der Stammes- und Ortsnamen in Südwestafrika. In: Journal of the South West African Scientific Society 4. 1928—29, 11—28.

Wandres 1927 = Carl Wandres: Tiernamen in der Nama- und Bergdama-Sprache. In: Festschrift Meinhof. Hamburg 1927.

6.3. Other Publications

Baucom 1970 = Kenneth Baucom: More on the indigenous languages of South West Africa. In: Anthropological Linguistics 12. 1970, 343—348.

Beach 1938 = D. M. Beach: The phonetics of the Hottentot Language. Cambridge 1938 [good map].

Bleek, D. F. 1928—30 = Dorothea Frances Bleek: Bushman grammar: A Grammatical sketch of the language of the /xam-ka-!k'e'. In: Zeitschrift für Eingeborenen-Sprachen, 1928—30, 19—20.

Bleek, D. F. 1931 a = Dorothea Frances Bleek: The Hadzapi or Watindega of Tanganyika Territory. In: Africa 4. 1931, 273—286.

Bleek, D. F. 1931 b = Dorothea Frances Bleek: Traces of former Bushman occupation in Tanganyika Territory. In: South African Journal of Science 28. 1931, 423—429.

Bleek, W. H. I. 1851 = Wilhelm Heinrich Immanuel Bleek: De Nominum Generibus Linguarum Africæ Australis, Copticæ, Semiticarum Aliarumque Sexualium, Scripsit Gulielmus Bleek. Bonnæ 1851.

Bleek, W. H. I. 1857 = Wilhelm Heinrich Immanuel Bleek: Researches into the relations between the Hottentots and the Kaffirs. In: The Cape Monthly Magazine 1. 1857, 199—212, 289—296.

Bleek, W. H. I. 1862—69 = Wilhelm Heinrich Immanuel Bleek: A Comparative grammar of South African languages. London 1862—69 [322 p.; vol. I 1862; II 1869, Concord — the Noun. According to Mendelssohn 1910, this work was never completed. For a fragment in continuation: Bantu Studies 10, 1, 1—7].

Bleek, W. H. I. 1869 = Wilhelm Heinrich Immanuel Bleek: The Bushman Language. In: The Cape and its people and other essays. Ed. by Prof. Roderick Noble. Cape Town 1869, 269—284 p. 270, footnote, states that a manuscript of 8 p. quarto "Outline of the Bushman Language" by Wuras was presented by the author to Sir George Grey, Nov. 11, 1858].

Bleek, W. H. I. 1873 a = Wilhelm Heinrich Immanuel Bleek: Scientific reasons for the study of the Bushman Language. In: The Cape Monthly Magazine (new series) 7. 1873, 149—153.

Bleek, W. H. I. 1873 b = Wilhelm Heinrich Immanuel Bleek: Report ... concerning his researches into the Bushman Language, presented to the Hon. the House of Assembly by command of His Exc. the Governor, Cape of Good Hope [8 p.].

Böhm 1985 = Gerhard Böhm: Khoe-Kowap. Wien 1985 [Einführung in Nama].

Dempwolff 1934—35 = Otto Dempwolff: Einführung in die Sprache der Nama-Hottentotten. In: Zeitschrift für Eingeborenen-Sprachen 25. 1934—35, 30—66, 89—134, 188—229.

Doke 1925 = Clement M. Doke: An outline of the phonetics of the language of the Chū: Bushmen of the North-West Kalahari. In: Bantu Studies 2. 1925, 129—166.

Doke 1933 = Clement M. Doke: An Alphabetic bibliography of the Bushman Language and literature. In: Bantu Studies 7. 1933, 34—35.

Elderkin 1982 = E. D. Elderkin: On the classification of Hadza. In: Sprache und Geschichte in Afrika 4. 1982, 67—82.

Essen 1957 = Otto von Essen: Das Phonemsystem des Nama-Hottentottischen. In: Zeitschrift für Phonetik 10. 1957, 127—143.

Essen 1962 = Otto von Essen: Sprachliche Ermittlungen im Nama-Hottentottischen, nach einer Tonbandaufnahme. In: Zeitschrift für Phonetik 15. 1962, 65—92.

Essen 1966 = Otto von Essen: Über die Anschlußarten Schnalz-Vokal im Nama-Hottentottischen. In: Afrika und Übersee 49. 1966, 53—58.

Fleming 1986 = Harold C. Fleming: Hadza and Sandawe genetic relations. In: Sprache und Geschichte in Afrika 7/2. 1986, 157—187.

Hagman 1977 = Roy S. Hagman: Nama Hottentot grammar (Language Science Monographs 15). Bloomington 1977 [This grammar uses a mixed structural and mildly transformational approach].

Köhler 1961 = Oswin R. A. Köhler: Die Sprachforschung in Südwestafrika. In: Festschrift Dr. h. c. Heinrich Vedder. Windhoek 1961, 61—71.

Köhler 1971 = Oswin R. A. Köhler: Die Khoesprachigen Buschmänner der Kalahari: Ihre Verbreitung und Gliederung. In: Kölner Geograph. Arbeiten. Festschrift Kurt Kayser, 1971, 373—411.

Köhler 1974 = Oswin R. A. Köhler: Khoisan languages. In: African Languages, Encyclopædia Britannica, 1974.

Köhler 1981 = Oswin R. A. Köhler: Présentation d'ensemble; bibliographie. In: J. Perrot (ed.), Les langues du monde. Paris 1981, 459—482.

Ladefoged/Traill 1984 = P. Ladefoged/A. Traill: Linguistic phonetic description of clicks. In: Language 60. 1984, 1—20.

Leibnitz 1717 = G. W. von Leibnitz: Collectanea Etymologica. Hanover 1717, 375—384 [includes Cape Hottentot specimens; cf. W. H. I. Bleek 1858].

Maingard 1937 = L. F. Maingard: The ≠Khomani Dialect of Bushman. In: Bushmen of the Southern Kalahari. Ed by J. D. Rh. Jones and C. M. Doke. Johannesburg 1937.

Maingard 1957—8 = L. F. Maingard: Three Bushman languages. In: African Studies 16. 1957, 37—71; 17, 1958, 100—115.

Maingard 1961 = L. F. Maingard: The Central group of the click languages of the Kalahari. In: African Studies 20. 1961, 114—122.

Maingard 1962 = L. F. Maingard: Korana Folktales, Grammar and Texts. Johannesburg 1962.

Maingard 1963 = L. F. Maingard: Comparative study of Naron, Hietshware, and Korana. In: African Studies 22. 1963, 97—108.

Mendelssohn 1910 = Sidney Mendelssohn: Mendelssohn's South African Bibliography. London 1910 [2 vols.; Vol. II contains indexes p. 925 ff.: see under *Philology* Cape Colony 963—964 (mostly Kaffir); German South-West Africa 977 (Nama); South Africa in General 1046—47. Vol. I, xiii lists allonyms; NB esp. Bushman: Boscheman, Bosjesman, Boshies-man, Boschmane; Coranna: Korrana(h), Koran(n)a, Korunna, Corans; Griqua: Grikwa, Grigriquaas, Giriquas; Kaffir: -f-, -er, -re, C-, Caffra, Saphre; Kalahari: -a, Callighari, -garee; Namaqua: -cq-, Amaqua, Nemiqua. Valuable listing of W. H. I. Bleek's work and literature on Sir George Grey; of which note esp. W. H. I. Bleek, South African Languages and Books, The Cape Monthly Magazine (CMM) 3. 1858, 321—337, on Sir George Grey's collection in the South African Public Library, Cape Town; Sir George Grey's Library, CMM 11. 1862, 163—171, 235—239, 315—319, 385—389; W. H. I. Bleek et alii, The Library of His Excellency Sir George Grey, 1858 (or 1862)—67, a catalogue in 4 vols., to which Theophilus Hahn, Index, Cape Town 1884; cf. further Spohr 1962].

Meriggi 1928—9 = P. Meriggi: Versuch einer Grammatik des /xam-Buschmännischen. In: Zeitschrift für Eingeborenen-Sprachen 19. 1928—9, 117—153, 188—205.

Nienaber 1963 = G. S. Nienaber: Hottentots. Pretoria 1963 [dedicated to Rust; 192—200a detailed retrospective bibliography, and 201—539 an annotated comparative word list].

Rust 1965 = F. Rust: Praktische Namagrammatik. Cape Town 1965 (Communication 31 from the School of African Studies).

SAB 1979 = A South African Bibliography to the year 1925. London 1979 [4 vols.; continues Mendelssohn 1910; only alphabetic by author or issuer].

Schapera 1930 = I. Schapera: The Khoisan peoples of South Africa: Bushmen and Hottentots. London 1930.

Snyman 1970 = J. W. Snyman: An Introduction to the !Xũ (!Kung) Language. Cape Town 1970.

Snyman 1974 = J. W. Snyman: The Bushman and Hottentot languages of Southern Africa. In: LIMI (Departement Bantoetale, Universiteit van Suid-Afrika) 2/2. 1974, 28—44.

Spohr 1962 = Otto M. Spohr: W. H. I. Bleek: A bio-bibliographical sketch. Cape Town 1962 (Varia series no. 6).

Stanley 1968 = George Edward Stanley: The indigenous languages of South West Africa. In: Anthropological Linguistics 10, 3. 1968, 5—18.

Stopa 1935 = Roman Stopa: Die Schnalze, ihre Natur, Entwicklung und Ursprung. Kraków 1935.

Traill 1973 = Anthony Traill: "N4 or S7": another Bushman language. In: African Studies 32. 1973, 25—32 [see also 33. 1974, 243—247; 249—255].

Traill 1974 = Anthony Traill: The Complete guide to the Koon. Johannesburg 1974 (A. S. I. Communication No. 1, 1974) [50 p. photo-offset + 4 maps; on salvage and study plans for what Traill wrote then !xõ, and p. 41—43 on the last /ʔauni speaker].

Traill 1985 = Anthony Traill: Phonetic and phonological studies of !xóõ Bushman. Hamburg 1985.

Westphal 1971 = E. O. J. Westphal: The click languages of southern and eastern Africa. In: Linguistics in Subsaharan Africa (Current Trends in Linguistics 7). Ed. by T. A. Sebeok. The Hague 1971, 367—420.

Eric P. Hamp, The University of Chicago, Chicago, Illinois (USA)

XXXI. Lexikographie der Einzelsprachen XV: Die Indianersprachen Amerikas während der Kolonialzeit
Lexicography of Individual Languages XV: The Languages of the American Indians in the Colonial Period
Lexicographie des langues particulières XV: Les langues amérindiennes pendant la période coloniale

274. Nahuatl Lexicography

1. Background
2. Molina's Dictionaries
3. Works Derived From Molina
4. The Practical Phrase Book of Pedro de Arenas
5. Works Recognizing Vowel Length and Glottal Stop
6. New Collections
7. Selected Bibliography

1. Background

Nahuatl is the major indigenous language of central Mexico. In addition to a rich oral tradition, it has a vast written literature of poems, theatricals, history, ethnography, and notarial documentation written down during the Spanish colonial period. Today it is spoken by a million people in communities in the Huasteca, the Sierra de Puebla, on the Veracruz coast, in the Federal District, and in the states of Puebla, Tlaxcala, Morelos, Guerrero, Michoacan, and Mexico. There are also a few speakers in the western states of Nayarit, Jalisco, and Colima. There are two major dialect groups, the central and the peripheral. The central dialects are characterized by a laterally released consonant written *tl*, while in the peripheral group the lateral release has been lost, yielding simple *t* except in a western area where it is the stop articulation that has been lost, yielding *l* (see map). Pipil, a related language, is spoken further to the south and east as far as Central America. Prior to European intrusion into the area, Aztec economic and political expansion spread Nahuatl throughout Mesoamerica. Upon arrival, Catholic missionary friars began compiling dictionaries of the indigenous languages of the area, using Antonio de Nebrija's Spanish/Latin dictionary, probably the 1516 edition, as an elicitation list. In the Edward E. Ayer Collection of the Newberry Library in Chicago there is a notebook containing Nebrija's dictionary copied out by hand with blank lines left after each entry. Nahuatl glosses have been written in red using some of the conventions used by Alonso de Molina but also employing a diacritic to mark stressed syllables, a convention not seen again until Macazaga Ordoño 1979, since Nahuatl stress is predictable.

2. Molina's Dictionaries

Alonso de Molina was brought to Mexico as a child in the years immediately following the European conquest and grew up bilingual in

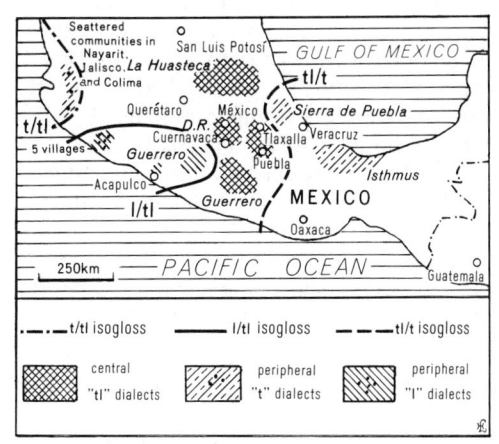

Map 274.1: Location of Nahuatl-speaking communities in the 20th century

Spanish and Nahuatl. While still very young he became a Franciscan friar and devoted his long and productive life to translating devotional literature into Nahuatl and creating grammatical and lexical reference works in the language. The first of the great Mesoamerican dictionaries of the sixteenth century to be published was Molina's Spanish/Nahuatl dictionary of 1555. This follows Nebrija closely, but the entries have been edited somewhat to exclude those without significance in the New World and to include additional material peculiar to Nahuatl. As in the Newberry ms. Nahuatl verbs are given in first-person present form and those that are transitive with the third-person singular object prefix, but here the prefixes are separated from the rest of the verb by punctuation. Whereas there are very few Spanish loanwords in the Newberry ms., Molina 1555 contains about two hundred nouns borrowed from Spanish, some in unassimilated form indicated by the gloss *lo mismo* and some altered to the morphology of Nahuatl and fully spelled out. An example of both conventions in a single entry is *sayo de varon. lo mismo. vel, oquich xaiotli* (f. 219 v), where *xaiotli* is the assimilated Nahuatl form of Spanish *sayo* 'jacket'. Molina's second dictionary was published in 1571. It is a bilingual dictionary in which the Spanish/Nahuatl side is an edited version of the 1555 dictionary, while the Nahuatl/Spanish side is a new compilation rather than a reversal of the Spanish/Nahuatl section. The dictionary as a whole contains more entries about things indigenous to Mesoamerica. It also contains additional Spanish loanwords into Nahuatl. Here Molina experiments with variant spellings and sporadically represents Nahuatl's segmental glottal stop with *h*, but neither of the dictionaries consistently indicates glottal stops or contrastive vowel length, which leads to ambiguity in the dictionary. For instance, Molina's *Auatl* represents three different Nahuatl nouns: *āhuatl* 'oak', *āhuātl* 'woolly caterpillar', and *ahhuatl* 'thorn' (where the first of the *h*'s represents a glottal stop). These have been merged into a single entry with three glosses as though the words were homophonous, which they are not.

Auatl. enzina, roble, guſano lanudo. o eſpina.

Dictionary excerpt 274.1: Dictionary entry for *Auatl* (in facsimile edition of Molina 1571, folio 9 recto).

For the most part noun entries are in absolutive form, as with those just cited, but some entries are in possessed form with a possessive prefix, and those few plural forms given appear as separate entries. For verbs Molina provides information about transitivity and reflexivity by listing after the verb a sample set of the prefixes it may take. He also provides the form of the preterit, which is not predictable from the citation form. The preterit follows the Spanish gloss and has, in addition to the antecessive prefix $\bar{o}$-, all the same sample prefixes that appear at the head of the entry. For instance, the transitive verb *ihtoā* 'to say something' appears in three contiguous entries, all with the first person singular subject prefix *ni-*. The first of these entries has the reflexive object prefix *n(o)-*; the second has the third person singular specific object prefix *qu(i)-*; and the third has the nonspecific human object *tē-*. The preterit form is prefixed with $\bar{o}$-, drops the final $\bar{a}$, and ends in a final glottal stop, but the length of the vowels is not indicated, nor are the two glottal stops, one within the stem and the other at the end of the preterit form.

Itoa. nin. comedirſe, o ofrecerſe a hazer alguna coſa. Pret. oninito.
Itoa niqu. dezir alguna coſa. Pret. oniquito.
Itoa. nite. dezir bien, o mal de otro. Pr. oniteito.

Dictionary excerpt 274.2: Dictionary entries (in facsimile edition of Molina 1571, folio 43 recto).

3. Works Derived From Molina

In addition to laying the foundation for the 1571 bilingual dictionary, Molina 1555 also served as an elicitation list for Alonso Urbano's 1605 trilingual Spanish/Nahuatl/Otomí dictionary. All other publications derived wholly or in part from Molina have used Molina 1571 as their source. These include two major works, Siméon 1885 and Campbell 1985. Siméon's work is a compilation drawing on Molina, the lexical material in the grammars of Andrés de Olmos, Horacio Carochi, Francisco Xavier Clavijero, Ignacio Paredes, and several other sources, but since Molina's dictionary is by far the largest of these sources, Siméon's entries mainly replicate Molina's, though in somewhat different format. Siméon compresses many of Molina's multiple entries for verbs and lists possessed and plural forms within entries for nouns. His entries also contain etymological or derivational material, which serves as a cross-referencing device within the dictionary. Unfortunately this material is unreliable, partly due to Siméon's not having comprehensive information about distinctive vowel length and glottal stop in Nahuatl. Originally published in French, this dictionary appeared in excellent Spanish translation in 1977.

The most recent treatment of Molina is R. Joe Campbell's morpheme index to the Nahuatl/Spanish section of the 1571 dictionary. It consists of three sections. The first is an alphabetical list of 1,339 morphemes that Campbell has identified in the dictionary. The second section repeats this list, giving under each morpheme in alphabetical order all the entries in Molina that contain that morpheme together with Campbell's morphological analysis of each entry and an English translation of Molina's gloss. Hence, a complete English translation of the Nahuatl/Spanish section of Molina 1571 is subsumed in this section. The final section is an alphabetical listing of the entries in Molina as they actually appear there with prefixes and variant spellings, each together with the first entry under which it appears in the second section. All works derived from Molina share the characteristics of not indicating vowel length and only rarely indicating the location of segmental glottal stops.

4. The Practical Phrase Book of Pedro de Arenas

Arenas 1611 is a collection of basic vocabulary and phrases mainly concerned with practical information, commerce, and domestic management. Of enduring usefulness to householders in central Mexico, it went through at least eleven editions, including a French one in 1862.

5. Works Recognizing Vowel Length and Glottal Stop

At the end of the sixteenth century the grammarian Antonio de Rincón published a list of Nahuatl words that contrast in vowel length and/or the presence of glottal stops. In his 1645 grammar Horacio Carochi expanded on this list and employed a set of diacritics to indicate these two features of Nahuatl phonology which the traditional Spanish-based orthography does not recognize. When Carochi's grammar was reprinted in 1892, errors in the diacritics were introduced. Errors and omissions of diacritics also are characteristic of the eighteenth-century works of Clavijero and Paredes, both derivative of Carochi. For this reason the word list appended to Clavijero's grammar is not wholly reliable. Adrian et al. 1976 is a morpheme index to Carochi based on the 1892 reprinting. (Macazago Ordoño 1979 is also derived from Carochi but omits vowel length and glottal stops while sporadically marking stress). Swadesh and Sancho 1966 is a list of a thousand morphemes felt by the authors to have been fundamental to older Nahuatl. It also contains errors and inconsistencies in its diacritics. The glossary of J. Richard Andrews' grammar of Nahuatl exhaustively marks vowel length and glottal stops. The lexical material is drawn principally from Carochi but also from other Nahuatl sources that sporadically or systematically indicate them. Entries in this glossary are grouped in derivational families. Karttunen 1983 is an alphabetically organized dictionary based on all sources that provide information about vowel-length contrasts and glottal stops: Carochi, one manuscript written with diacritics like those of Carochi, Clavijero, Paredes, and three dictionaries compiled by linguists in the twentieth century. Bierhorst 1985 contains a glossary of all the lexical material in the collection of sixteenth-century poems known as the *Cantares mexicanos*, marking all the long vowels and indicating all the glottal stops that Bierhorst can deduce from older Nahuatl sources but not drawing from any sources later than the mid-seventeeth century. The glosses reflect Bierhorst's interpretation of the *Cantares*.

6. New Collections

The date on a manuscript dictionary (Araoz 1778) preserved at Tulane University has been incorrectly read as 1598 but it is actually a late eighteenth-century production. This is a new collection in the sense that it is not derived from Nebrija or Molina, but it adds nothing of substance to earlier works and is not up to their standards. Modern dictionaries and word lists based on original elicitation in Nahuatl-speaking communities include Key/Ritchie de Key 1953 (Zacapoaxtla, Puebla), Brewer/Brewer 1971 (Tetelcingo, Morelos), García de León 1976 (Pajapan, Veracruz), Beller/Cowan de Beller 1976 and 1979 (Huautla, Hidalgo), Ramírez/

Dakin 1979 (Xalitla, Guerrero), Guzmán Betancourt 1979 (Santa Catarina, Morelos), Lastra de Suárez 1980 (Tetzcoco), Stiles 1980 (Huasteca, Hidalgo), Kimball 1980 (Huatzalinguillo), and Wolgemuth (Mecayapan, Veracruz) 1981. These works do not all share the same notational conventions. In some of these communities, notably Tetelcingo, vowel length and glottal stops are clearly maintained and are indicated in the dictionary notation. Some of the dictionaries do not indicate these things, either because the community does not give phonetic realization to them or because the person doing the elicitation has not recorded them. Moreover, these dictionaries vary among themselves in format, especially with respect to whether or not inflectional prefixes are included in Nahuatl citation forms and how much grammatical information is provided in an entry.

7. Selected Bibliography

7.1. Dictionaries

Adrian et al. 1976 = Karen Adrian/Una Canger/Kjeld K. Lings/Jette Nilsson/Anne Schlanbusch: Diccionario de vocablos aztecas contenidos en *El arte de la lengua mexicana* de Horacio Carochi. Copenhagen 1976 [iii, 231 p.].

Araoz 1778 = Francisco Xavier Araoz: Vocabulario mexicano. Manuscript in Tulane University Latin American Library. New Orleans 1778.

Arenas 1611 = Pedro de Arenas: Vocabulario manual de las lenguas castellana y mexicana. (second edition) Mexico City 1611 [5 +7 p. unnumbered, 160] (Facsimile edition 1982 by Universidad Nacional Autónoma de México).

Arenas 1862 = Pedro de Arenas: Guide de la conversation en trois langues: Français, Espagnol et Mexicain. M. Charles Romey, transl. Paris 1862 [72 p.].

Bierhorst 1985 = John Bierhorst: A Nahuatl-English dictionary and concordance to the Cantares Mexicanos with an analytical transcription and grammatical notes. Stanford, California 1985 [75 p.].

Brewer/Brewer 1971 = Forrest Brewer/Jean G. Brewer: Vocabulario mexicano de Tetelcingo, Morelos (second printing). Mexico City 1971 [vii, 274 p.].

Campbell 1985 = R. Joe Campbell: A morphological dictionary of Classical Nahuatl: a morphological index to the *Vocabulario en lengua mexicana y castellana*. Madison, Wisconsin 1985 [xi, 485 p.].

Clavijero 1974 = Francisco Xavier Clavijero: Reglas de la lengua mexicana con un vocabulario. Arthur J. O. Anderson, ed. and transl. Mexico City 1974 (Composed in the second half of the eighteenth century. Anderson's 1973 English translation omits the word list).

Karttunen 1983 = Frances Karttunen: An analytical dictionary of Nahuatl. Austin, Texas 1983 [xxxiv, 349 p.].

Key/Ritchie de Key 1953 = Harold Key/Mary Ritchie de Key: Vocabulario Mejicano de la Sierra de Zacapoaxtla, Puebla. Mexico City 1953 [xii, 232 p.].

Kimball 1980 = Geoffrey Kimball: A dictionary of the Huatzalinguillo dialect of Nahuatl. With grammatical sketch and readings. New Orleans 1980 [131 p.].

Macazaga Ordoño 1979 = César Macazaga Ordoño: Diccionario de la lengua náhuatl. Mexico City 1979 [122 p.].

Molina 1555 = Alonso de Molina: Aqui comiença un vocabulario en la lengua castellana y mexicana. Mexico City 1555 [261 f.].

Molina 1571 = Alonso de Molina: Vocabulario en lengua castellana y mexicana y mexicana y castellana. Mexico City 1571 [283 f.] (Most recent facsimile edition 1970 by Biblioteca-Porrua, Mexico City).

Ramírez/Dakin 1979 = Cleofas Ramírez/Karen Dakin: Vocabulario náhuatl de Xalitla, Guerrero. Mexico City 1979 [227 p.].

Siméon 1885 = Rémi Siméon: Dictionnaire de la langue nahuatl ou mexicain. Paris 1885 [lxxv, 710 p].

Siméon 1977 = Rémi Siméon: Diccionario de la lengua náhuatl o mexicana. (Josefina Oliva de Col, transl.) Mexico City 1977 [xcvi, 783 p.].

Stiles 1980 = Neville Stiles: A Huasteca Nahuatl (Hidalgo) fieldworker's vocabulary. St. Andrews, Scotland 1980 [v, 121 p.].

Swadesh/Sancho 1966 = Mauricio Swadesh/Madalena Sancho: Los mil elementos del mexicano clásico, base analítica de la lengua nahua. Mexico City 1966 [ix, 92 p.].

Urbano 1605 = Alonso Urbano: Vocabulario trilingüe español mexicano otomí. Mexico City 1605.

(author unknown) nd. = Vocabulario trilingüe. Cast.Lat.Mex. Aztec ms. 1478. Edward E. Ayer Collection, Newberry Library. Chicago.

7.2. Other Publications

Andrews 1975 = J. Richard Andrews: Introduction to Classical Nahuatl. Austin 1975

Beller/Cowan de Beller 1976, 1979 = Ricardo Beller N./Patricia Cowan de Beller: Curso del náhuatl moderno. Náhuatl de la Huasteca. Vols. 1,2. Mexico City 1976, 1979.

Carochi 1645 = Horacio Carochi: Arte de la lengua mexicana con la declaracion de los adverbios della. Mexico City 1645. (Facsimile edition 1983 by Universidad Nacional Autónoma de México).

Carochi 1892 = Horacio Carochi: Arte de la lengua mexicana con la declaracion de los adverbios

della. Reimpreso por el Museo Nacional de Mexico. In Colección de gramáticas de la lengua mexicana. Mexico City 1892.
García de León 1976 = Antonio García de León: Pajapan, un dialecto mexicano del golfo. Mexico City 1976.
Guzmán Betancourt 1979 = Ignacio Guzmán Betancourt: Gramática del náhuatl de Santa Catarina, Morelos. Mexico City 1979.
Karttunen 1981 = Frances Karttunen: Nahuatl lexicography. In: Texas Linguistic Forum 18. Nahuatl Studies in Memory of Fernando Horcasitas. Frances Karttunen, ed. Austin, Texas 1981. 105—118.
Karttunen 1988 = Frances Karttunen: The roots of sixteenth-century Mesoamerican lexicography. In: Studies in Memory of Thelma D. Sullivan. J. Kathryn Josserand Karen Dakin, eds. Oxford 1988.
Karttunen/Amsler 1983 = Frances Karttunen/ Robert Amsler: Computer-assisted compilation of a Nahuatl dictionary. In: Computers and the Humanities 17. 1983, 175—184.

Lastra de Suárez 1980 = Yolanda Lastra de Suárez: El náhuatl de Tetzcoco en la actualidad. Mexico City 1980.
Nebrija 1516 = Antonio de Nebrija: Vocabulario de romance en latín. Seville 1516 (Recent transcription and critical edition by Gerald J. MacDonald. Philadelphia 1973).
Olmos 1985 = Andrés de Olmos: Arte de la lengua Mexicana y vocabulario. (Thelma Sullivan and René Acuña, eds.) Mexico City 1985 (composed 1547).
Paredes 1759 = Ignacio Paredes: Compendio del arte de la lengua mexicana del P. Horacio de Carochi... Mexico City 1759.
Rincón 1595 = Antonio del Rincón: Arte mexicana. Mexico City 1595.
Wolgemuth 1981 = Carl Wolgemuth: Gramática náhuatl del municipio de Mecayapan, Veracruz. Mexico City 1981.

Frances Karttunen, The University of Texas, Austin, Texas (USA)

275. Lexikographie der Mayasprachen

1. Einführung
2. Enzyklopädische Wörterbücher
3. Praktisch orientierte zweisprachige Wörterbücher
4. Wörterbücher anderen Typs
5. Vokabulare
6. Zusammenfassende Bemerkungen
7. Literatur (in Auswahl)

1. Einführung

Gegenwärtig rechnet man die folgenden 23 Sprachen zu den Mayasprachen, wobei zehn in jüngerer Zeit als eigenständige Sprachen anerkannte Mundarten und vier früher gültige Bezeichnungen in Klammern mit angeführt, aber nicht gesondert gezählt werden: Aguakatek, Cakchikel, Chikomuseltek (= Cotoque), Chol, Chontal (incl. Yocotan), Chorti (= Cholti), Chuh, Huastek, Ixil, Hakaltek, Kanhobal (incl. Akatek, Solomek), Kekchi, Kiche (incl. Achi, Sakapultek, Sipakapa), Mam (incl. Teko), Mocho (= Motozintlek), Pokomam, Pokomchi, Toholabal (= Chaneabal), Tzeltal (incl. Subinha), Tzotzil, Tzutuhil, Uspantek, Yukatek (incl. Itza, Lakandon, Mopan). Von diesen 23 Sprachen ist lediglich eine bereits ausgestorben.

2. Enzyklopädische Wörterbücher

Unter den 22 noch lebenden Mayasprachen existieren nur zu vier Sprachen Wörterbücher, die sich als enzyklopädisch charakterisieren lassen: zu Cakchikel (Acuña 1983), Kiche (Edmonson 1965), Tzotzil (Laughlin 1975) und Yukatek (Barrera V. 1980).

Das von R. Acuña herausgegebene Wörterbuch (Spanisch-Cakchikel) stellt eine Neuedition des 1656 von Tomás de Coto auf der Basis der älteren Vokabulare Alonsos (XVI), Vareas (1699) und Vicos (XVII) erarbeiteten Werks dar. Dieses wurde seinerseits von Alonso nach dem Vorbild des spanisch-lateinischen Wörterbuchs von Nebrija (1492) begründet und von Coto mit autochthonen und aus dem Ausland stammenden theolo-

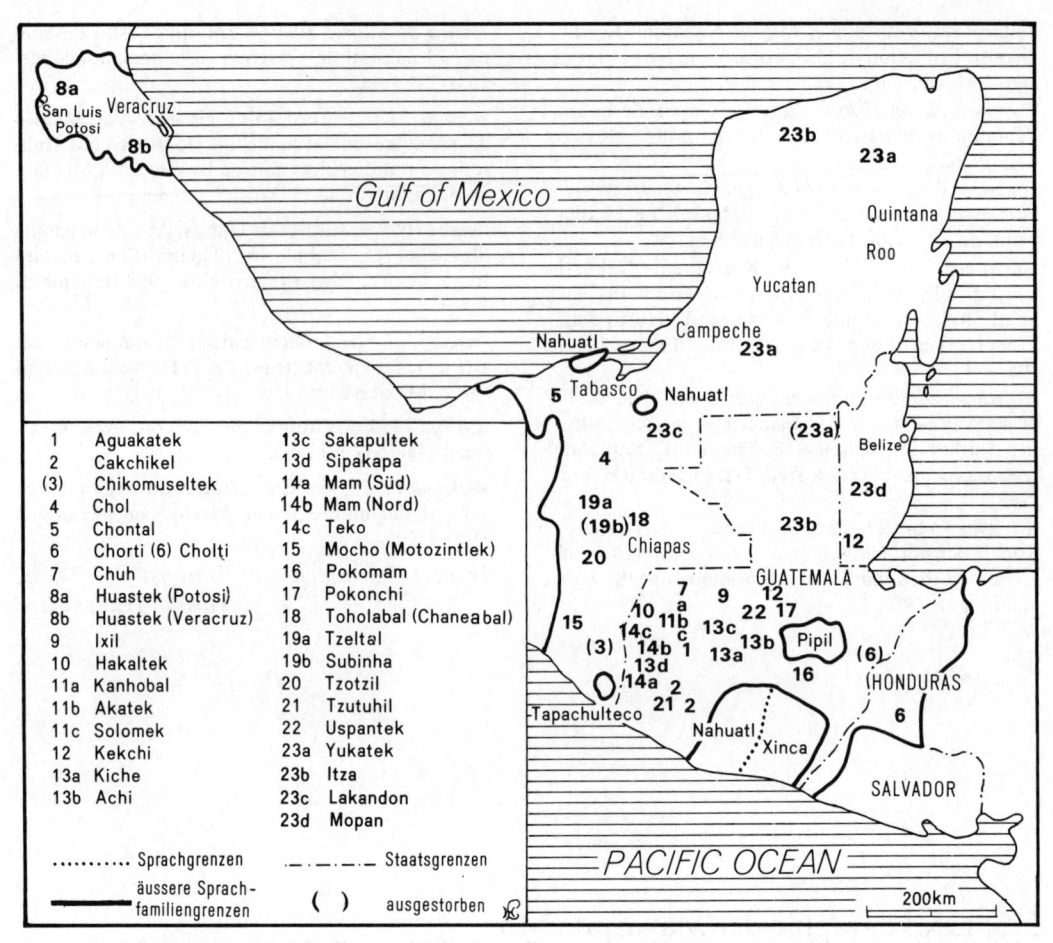

Karte 275.1: Maya-Sprachen Mexikos und Mittelamerikas

1	Aguakatek	13c	Sakapultek
2	Cakchikel	13d	Sipakapa
(3)	Chikomuseltek	14a	Mam (Süd)
4	Chol	14b	Mam (Nord)
5	Chontal	14c	Teko
6	Chorti (6) Cholţi	15	Mocho (Motozintlek)
7	Chuh	16	Pokomam
8a	Huastek (Potosi)	17	Pokonchi
8b	Huastek (Veracruz)	18	Toholabal (Chaneabal)
9	Ixil	19a	Tzeltal
10	Hakaltek	19b	Subinha
11a	Kanhobal	20	Tzotzil
11b	Akatek	21	Tzutuhil
11c	Solomek	22	Uspantek
12	Kekchi	23a	Yukatek
13a	Kiche	23b	Itza
13b	Achi	23c	Lakandon
		23d	Mopan

gisch-exegetischen Materialien ergänzt. Coto benutzte die von Francisco de la Parra (o. D.) erdachten Alphabetzusätze *(tt 4, 4h 4ε) (= t' ꞓ' č' k' q')* und versuchte, alle Mundarten zu erfassen. Acuña fügte seiner Ausgabe, die wegen drucktechnischer Schwierigkeiten auf Parras neue Zusätze verzichten mußte, einen Index Cakchikel-Spanisch hinzu. Bedauerlicherweise war ihm eine Faksimile-Edition des Originals nicht möglich.

Munro Edmonson (1965) stellte in seinem Wörterbuch Materialien aus 41 früheren Quellen zusammen (z. B. Basseta 1698, Barrera 1745, Schultze-Jena 1933, Xec/Maynard 1954) und versuchte, zwischen östlicher, zentraler und westlicher Mundart zu differenzieren und aus etymologischen Vergleichen mit den anderen Mayasprachen historisch-chronologische Informationen zu gewinnen. Er hat alle Wurzeln mit modernen Kichesprechern (Xecul, Cantel, San Francisco el Alto) und Cakchikelsprechern (Solola, Panajachel) ausprobiert und das bei Xec und Maynard (Totonicapan) gefundene Material berücksichtigt. Edmonsons einzigartiges Alphabet ist halb praktisch *(ch = č, ch' = č', tz' = ꞓ', x = š)* und halb wissenschaftlich *(k = k, k' = k', q = q, q' = q')* ausgerichtet, wobei bisweilen Unklarheiten in der Unterscheidung zwischen *k* und *q* bzw. *C* und *C'* auftreten. Im einzelnen ermöglichen jedoch die Quellen eine Erklärung der zweifelhaften Fälle (z. B. *q'ooh = k'oh, q'uluh = k'uluh).* Edmonson hat ferner viele ethnographische Daten eingearbeitet.

Das Wörterbuch von Robert Laughlin (1975) basiert gänzlich auf modernem Material, das aus der gegenwärtigen Umgangssprache stammt. Es beinhaltet ein vollständiges Wurzelinventar, eine spezielle ethnobotanische Sammlung sowie toponymische Angaben und behandelt alle Formen in ihrem ethnographischen Kontext. Bei gänzlich wissenschaftlichem Alphabet steht die Mundart von Zinacantan im Zentrum. Dieses Werk, das durch eine kurze Grammatik ergänzt wird, ist das erste vollständige Wörterbuch einer modernen Mayasprache.

Alfredo Barrera V. (1980) kompiliert in seinem enzyklopädischen Werk Materialien aus 10 älteren (Anón. Y XVIa, Anón. Y XVIb, Anón. Y XVII, Anón. Y 1976, Anón. Y 1898, Beltrán 1859, Pérez 1898, Swadesh 1970, Roys 1931—1957, Edmonson o. D.) und 18 modernen Quellen (Barrera M. 1976, Barrera V. 1980, Bastarrachea 1975, Blair 1974, Brito 1980, Dzul 1977, Echeverría 1980, Edmonson o. D., Gann 1918, Pacheco 1939, Palomo 1935, Pearse 1945, Romero C. 1976, Romero F. 1910, Standley 1945, Thompson 1930, Thompson 1962, Vermont 1980). In seinem Alphabet findet sich nur ein spezielles Zeichen ('). Da viele der von ihm benutzten Quellen keine Unterscheidungen zwischen langen (= doppelten) und kurzen Vokalen, zwischen Hoch-, Mittel- und Niederton zulassen und das Vorkommen des Kehlkopfverschlußlauts (') nicht anzeigen, mußte sich Barrera meist mit einfachen Transkriptionen der Originale begnügen. Sein Wörterbuch, das Maya-Spanisch angelegt ist, stellt gleichwohl das erste der Sprachfamilie dar, das einen direkten Zugang zu allen früheren Quellen bietet.

3. Praktisch orientierte zweisprachige Wörterbücher

Einen praktisch orientierten zweisprachigen Wörterbuchtyp, dessen Modell von den Normen der Lexikographen des Instituto Lingüístico de Verano abgeleitet ist, findet man zu folgenden sechs Mayasprachen: Chol, Huastek, Kiche, Mopan, Tzeltal und Tzotzil.

Das Wörterbuch von W. und E. Aulie (1978) zur Mayasprache Chol, das von J. Eric S. Thompson eingeleitet wird, beinhaltet einen Anhang, in dem grammatikalische Fragen am Beispiel von Verbkonjugationen und der Flexion von Pflanzen- und Tierbezeichnungen behandelt werden. Das Huastek-Wörterbuch Larsens (1955) ist mit einer grammatikalischen Beschreibung und einer von Guy Stresser-Péan skizzierten Landkarte von San Luis Potosí versehen. Das Wörterbuch von M. und R. Ulrich (1976b), das sich aus einem Mopan- und einem Spanisch-Teil zusammensetzt, bietet zu jedem der Teile eine für Spanisch- und Mopan-Sprecher gleichermaßen nützliche grammatikalische Einleitung. Das Kiche-Wörterbuch Hennes (1980), das aus dem älteren Wörterbuch Xecs und Maynards (1954) hervorgegangen ist und dessen aus Totonicapan stammende Quellen mit Wortmaterial moderner Sprecher aus Cantel, Nahuala und Chichicastenango ergänzte, umfaßt viele Satzbeispiele und einführende grammatikalische Bemerkungen. Das auf Bachajón konzentrierte Tzeltal-Wörterbuch von Slocum und Gerdel (1965) enthält für das Spanische spezielle Listen mit Wochentagen, Gewichts- und Maßeinheiten und für Tzeltal partielle Listen mit Numeralsuffixen, Familien-, Tauf- und Ortsnamen. Das von Delgaty und Ruiz (1978) erstellte Wörterbuch zur Mayasprache Tzotzil beinhaltet sprachliches Material aus Larráinzar, Chamula, Chenalhó, Iztapa und Zinacantan. Hinzugefügt sind ein vollständiger grammatikalischer Anhang, Tabellen mit Bezeichnungen der Tage, der Monate, der Zahlen und der nominalischen Klassifikatoren sowie Zusammenstellungen der Verwandtschaftsterminologie, der Bezeichnungen der Körperteile und der Ausdrücke mit o'onil ('Herz, Magen, Wille'). Ferner sind Pflanzen- und Tierbezeichnungen auch graphische Erläuterungen beigegeben.

4. Wörterbücher anderen Typs

Von den 14 Mayasprachen, zu denen Wörterbücher anderen Typs vorliegen, existiert zu folgenden 13 Sprachen je eines: Cakchikel, Chol, Chuh, Huastek, Hakaltek, Kekchi, Kiche, Mam, Pokomam, Pokomchi, Toholabal, Tzeltal und Tzotzil. Unter den 16 derartigen Werken zu Yukatek sind drei glyphisch, zehn aus der Kolonialzeit und drei neueren Datums. Zu diesen insgesamt 29 Wörterbüchern zählen Vokabulare sprachlicher Einführungskurse (Wick 1975 a, b, Blair 1974) und Konkordanzen (Andrade 1975a, Day 1977, Owen 1970 a, b), zahlreiche gedruckte Bände (Saenz 1940, Beekman 1953, Sedat 1955, Maldonado 1987, Mayers 1956, Lenkersdorf 1979, Slocum 1953, Sarles 1962, Weathers 1949, Pacheco 1969, Pérez 1877, 1898, Schumann 1973, Solís 1949, Andrews 1978, Beltrán 1859, Swadesh 1970, Gates 1939, Thompson 1962, Zimmermann 1956) und einige Manuskripte (Ara 1571, Hopkins 1976, Anón. C XVII a, Anón K o. D. a, b).

5. Vokabulare

Zu 31 Mayasprachen (einschließlich der in 1. nicht gezählten Mundarten) gibt es schließlich die folgenden, den in alphabetischer Folge aufgeführten Sprachen zuzuordnenden 124 Vokabulare größeren oder kleineren Umfangs, die aus kolonialer oder moderner Zeit stammen und gedruckt oder handschriftlich vorliegen:

zu *Achi* existieren 2 Vokabulare: Shaw 1962 (Cubulco), Brawand 1962 (Rabinal);

zu *Aguakatek* 1: Andrade 1945 a;

zu *Cakchikel* 12, davon kolonial: Alonso XVI, Angel XVII, XVIII, Anón. C XVII a, b, 1813, Guzmán 1704, Santo Domingo 1693, Varea 1699, Vico XVII; davon modern: Andrade 1945 c (Panajachel), Otzoy 1976;

zu *Chikomuseltek* 2: Termer 1930, Zimmermann 1955;

zu *Chol* 2: Schumann 1973 (Tila), Aulie 1948 (Tumbalá);

zu *Cholti* 1: Morán 1695;

zu *Chontal* 3, davon kolonial: Smailus 1975; davon modern: Becerra 1934, La Farge 1927;

zu *Chorti* 3: Andrade 1976, McQuown 1976 e, Wisdom 1950;

zu *Chuh* 4: McQuown 1976 f (Coatán), Andrade 1945 b (Ixtatán), Hopkins 1967, 1969;

zu *Huastek* 8: a) San Luis Potosí, davon kolonial: Tapia Zenteno 1767; davon modern: Alcorn 1983, McQuown 1976 a; b) Veracruz, davon kolonial: Cruz 1571; davon modern: Alejandre 1890, Salvador 1945, Silva 1987, Staub 1924;

zu *Ixil* 2, davon kolonial: Anón I 1935; davon modern: Elliott 1962;

zu *Hakaltek* 2: Church 1955, Stoll 1887;

zu *Kanhobal* 4: Andrade 1945 d, e, f (Ixcoy), McQuown 1976 g (Santa Eulalia);

zu *Kekchi* 4, davon kolonial: Estrada 1979; davon modern: Andrade 1945 g, McQuown 1976 b (Chamelco), Wirsing 1930;

zu *Kiche* 17, davon kolonial: Anón. K. o. D. a, b, c, XVII, XVIII, XIX a, XIX b, XIX c, 1787, Barrera 1745, Basseta 1698, Calvo 1726; davon modern: Alvarado 1975, Andrade 1946 a, b, León 1954, McQuown 1976 m, Schultze-Jena 1933;

zu *Lakandon* 2: Andrade 1945 h, Bruce 1968;

zu *Mam* 6, davon kolonial: Elgueta o. D., Reynoso 1916; davon modern: McQuown 1976 h (Ixtahuacán), McQuown 1976 i (Ostuncalco), Sywulka 1975;

zu *Mayaner* 6: Campbell 1977, Fox 1978, Grimes 1972, Kaufman 1964, Jacks 1972 a, Stoll 1958;

zu *Mochó* 1: Kaufman 1967;

zu *Mopan* 1: Ulrich 1976 a;

zu *Pokomam* 4, davon kolonial: Morán 1720; davon modern: McQuown 1976 k (Jilotepeque), Ruano 1892, Sapper 1906;

zu *Pokomchi* 3, davon kolonial: Zúñiga 1608; davon modern: Fernández 1937, McQuown 1976 l (Purulhá);

zu *Sakapulas* u. Sipakapa 1: Kaufman 1976;

zu *Subinha* 1: Ortiz 1892 (kolonial);

zu *Teko* 1: Kaufman 1969;

zu *Tzeltal* 9, davon kolonial: Ara 1571 (Copanaguastla), Guzmán XVII; davon modern: Berlin 1962, 1968, McQuown 1976 n (Bachajón), 1977 a (Oxchuc), Pineda 1888, Robles 1962 (Bachajón), Sarles 1961 (Oxchuc);

zu *Tzotzil* 6, davon kolonial: García 1971; davon modern: Cowan 1961 (Huixtán), Delgaty 1964 (Larráinzar), Hopkins 1977 (Chalchihuitán), McQuown 1976 o (Iztapa);

zu *Tzutuhil* 1: Andrade 1946 c, d;

zu *Uspantek* 3: Jacks 1972 b, McQuown 1976 c, Stoll 1896;

zu *Yukatek* 13, davon kolonial: Alvarez 1980, Brasseur 1872, Charencey 1884, McQuown 1967; davon modern: Andrade 1987, McClaran 1972, McQuown 1976 j, Miram 1983, Owen 1968, Pacheco 1939, Pérez o. D., Roys 1931—1957, Zavala 1898.

6. Zusammenfassende Bemerkungen

Die in den Abschnitten 3. bis 5. behandelten Wörterbuchtypen bieten insbesondere für die Mayasprachen Chol, Chontal, Chorti, Chuh, Huastek, Kekchi, Mam, Pokomam und Tzeltal reiche Materialgrundlagen, die die baldige Ausarbeitung enzyklopädischer Wörterbücher in Aussicht stellen. Hingegen ist für die Sprachen Aguakatek, Ixil, Hakaltek, Kanhobal, Mocho, Mopan, Pokomchi, Sakapultek, Sipakapa, Tzutuhil und Uspantek noch ein weit größeres Pensum lexikographischer Arbeit zu leisten. Die seit 450 Jahren betriebene Lexikographie der Mayasprachen hat bislang 4 enzyklopädische und 6 praktisch orientierte zweisprachige Wörterbücher sowie 29 Wörterbücher anderen Typs hervorgebracht. Für die 11 Sprachen, die bislang in keinem dieser in den Abschnitten 2. bis 4. behandelten Wörterbuchtypen erfaßt sind, besteht indessen die Hoffnung, daß bis zum

Jahrhundertende einige Lücken geschlossen werden können.

7. Literatur (in Auswahl)

Abkürzungen:

ADV = Akademische Druck- u. Verlagsanstalt. — AHG = Antropología e Historia de Guatemala. — AISC = American Indian Studies Center. — AMNAHE = Anales del Museo de Arqueología, Historia y Etnografía, Mexiko. — APSL = American Philosophical Society. — ASGH = Anales de la Sociedad de Geografía e Historia, Guatemala. — ASP = Actes de la Société Philologique, Alençon. — BAE = Bureau of American Ethnology. — BLA = Biblioteca Linguistica Americana. — BMC = Bancroft Manuscript Collections, Berkeley. — BNP = Bibliothèque Nationale, Paris; FA = Fonds américain; FM = Fonds mexicain; FN = Fonds Angrand; FS = Fonds Smith-Lesouëf. — BYUL = Brigham Young University Library. — CEMC = Centro de Estudios Mayas: Cuadernos, Universidad Nacional Autónoma, Mexiko. — CPO = Computer Printout. — EL = Editorial Landívar. — EY = Enciclopedia Yucatanense. — FMNH; AS = Field Museum of Natural History: Anthropological Series, Chicago. — fs = folios. — HMAI = Handbook of Middle American Indians. — HU; PM = Harvard University, Peabody Museum. — ICA = International Congress of Americanists. — IIN = Instituto Indigenista Nacional, Guatemala. — IL = Investigaciones Lingüísticas, Universidad Nacional Autónoma, Mexiko. — ILV = Instituto Lingüístico de Verano. — INAH; CRS; CC = Instituto Nacional de Antropología e Historia; Centro Regional del Sureste; Colección Científica, Mérida. — INAH; DIP = Instituto Nacional de Antropología e Historia; Departamento de Investigaciones; Publicaciones, Mexiko. — JCBL = John Carter Brown Library, Providence. — JLSP = Janua Linguarum: Series Practica, Mouton. — JML = Journal of Mayan Linguistics. — MA = El México Antiguo. — MARI = Middle American Research Institute, New Orleans. — MCMCA = Microfilm Collection of Manuscripts on Cultural Anthropology, University of Chicago Library. — McQL = McQuown, Personal Library. — mf = Microfilm. — mgr = Mimeograph. — ms = Manuskript. — MSP = Maya Society Publications, Baltimore. — NL = Newberry Library, Chicago. — Pht = Photokopie. — PUL = Princeton University Library. — SCA = Smithsonian Contributions to Anthropology. — SM = Secretaría de Fomento, Mexiko. — SI; SCA = Smithsonian Institution; Smithsonian Contributions to Anthropology. — SIU; UM; RR = Southern Illinois University; University Museum; Research Records, Carbondale. — SMA; MR = Sociedad Mexicana de Antropología; Mesa Redonda, Mexico. — typscr = typescript. — UCB; LBRL; WP = University of California, Berkeley; Language Behavior Research Laboratory; Working Papers. — UCDA = University of Chicago, Department of Anthropology. — UCL = University of Chicago Library. — UCLA = University of California, Los Angeles. — UH; ABAK; B(VkKgSpr) = Universität Hamburg; Abhandlungen aus dem Gebiet der Auslandskunde; B (Völkerkunde, Kulturgeschichte und Sprachen). — UNAM = Universidad Nacional Autónoma de México. — UPL = University of Pennsylvania Library. — USC = Universidad de San Carlos, Guatemala. — VIMSA = Vocabularios Indígenas Mariano Silva y Aceves, ILV, Mexiko. — YU = Yale University. — ZdGfE = Zeitschrift der Gesellschaft für Erdkunde. — ZfE = Zeitschrift für Ethnologie.

Acuña 1983 = René Acuña (ed.): Fray Tomás de Coto [Thesaurus verborum] Vocabulario [español-cakchiquel]. México [883 S.].

Alcorn 1983 = Janis Alcorn and Cándido Hernández: Plants of the Huastec region of Mexico. JML 4.1.11—118 [111 S.].

Alejandre 1890 = Marcelo Alejandre: Cartilla huasteca. México [179 S.].

Alonso XVI = Fray Juan Alonso: Vocabulario castellano-cakchiquel. ms. [= PUL ms. Garrett 266] [610 S.].

Alvarado 1975 = Miguel Alvarado L.: Léxico médico quiché-español. IIN Guatemala [115 S.].

Alvarez 1980 = María Cristina Alvarez: Diccionario etnolingüístico del yucateco colonial I: mundo físico. UNAM México [385 S.].

Andrade 1945 a = Manuel Andrade and Abraham Halpern: Aguacatec-Spanish vocabulary. ms. 1937 [= MCMCA 10 (II)] [101 S.].

Andrade 1945 b = Manuel Andrade: Apuntes chujes. ms. 1934 [= MCMCA 10 (II)] [33 S.].

Andrade 1945 c = Manuel Andrade: Cakchiquel (Panajachel) vocabulary. ms. 1936 [= MCMA 10 (II)].

Andrade 1945 d = Manuel Andrade: Kanhobal vocabulary. ms. 1935 [= MCMCA 10 (II)] [42 S.].

Andrade 1945 e = Manuel Andrade: Kanjobal vocabulary. ms. 1937 [= MCMCA 10 (II)] [51 S.].

Andrade 1945 f = Manuel Andrade: Kanjobal [Ixcoy] vocabulary. ms. 1937 [= MCMA 10 (II)] [33 S.].

Andrade 1945 g = Manuel Andrade: Kekchi vocabulary. ms. 1939 [= MCMCA 12 (II)] [217 S.].

Andrade 1945 h = Manuel Andrade: Lacandone notes (vocabulary, texts, grammar). ms. 1939 [= MCMCA 10 (II)] [31 S.].

Andrade 1945 i = Manuel Andrade: Mam-Kanjobal miscellany; Kanjobal vocabulary. ms. 1937 [= MCMCA 10 (II)].

Andrade 1945 j = Manuel Andrade: Mam vocabulary [Ostuncalco, Necta, Tacaná]. ms. 1935 [= MCMCA 10 (II)].

Andrade 1946 a = Manuel Andrade: Quiché-Mam-Kanjobal comparative vocabulary. ms. 1935 [= MCMCA 11 (II)].

Andrade 1946 b = Manuel Andrade: Quiché vocabularies. ms. 1936 [= MCMCA 11 (II)].

Andrade 1946 c = Manuel Andrade: Tzutuhil vocabulary. ms. 1936 [= MCMCA 11 (II)] [99 S.].

Andrade 1946 d = Manuel Andrade: Cakchiquel-Tzutuhil comparative vocabularies [11 dialects]. typscr 1936 [= MCMCA 11 (II)].

Andrade 1975 a = Manuel Andrade/Norman McQuown/James Redd: Huastec text word-concordance, UCL [= MCMCA 165—166 (XXXI)] [1558 S.].

Andrade 1975 b = Manuel Andrade: Mam miscellany (vocabulary, verb conjugation). ms. 1935 [= MCMCA 302 (LVII)].

Andrade 1976 = Manuel Andrade: Notes on Chorti. ms. 1932—1934 [= MCMCA 158 (XXIX)].

Andrade 1987 = Manuel Andrade: Yucatec vocabularies. ms. 1931 [= MCMCA 162 (XXX)] [8 S.].

Andrews 1978 = Dorothy Andrews: Vocabulario de mayathan [Viena] [índice maya-español]. Mérida, Yucatán [607 S.].

Angel XVII = Fray Angel: Vocabulario cakchiquel. ms. [= BNP; FA 41] [= NL (4) Pht] [= BYUL Gates b-75 # 1] [452 S.].

Angel XVIII = Fray Angel: Vocabulario cakchiquel. ms. [= NL 9150 Pht] [718 S.].

Anón. C XVII a = Anónimo: Vocabulario cakchiquel. ms. [= NL (15) Pht] [718 S.].

Anón. C XVII b = Anónimo: Noticia cakchiquel. ms. [= BNP: FA 47] [= NL (21) Pht] [706 S.].

Anón. C 1813 = Anónimo: Vocabulario cakchiquel-español. ms. [= BNP: FA 47] [244 S.].

Anón. I 1935 = Anónimo: Arte y vocabulario ixil. Baltimore [= MSP 14] [24 S.].

Anón. K o. D. a = Anónimo: Borrador de vocabulario kiché. ms. [= NL (9) Pht] [56 S.].

Anón. K o. D. b = Anónimo: Vocabulario kiché. ms. [= NL (72) Pht] [78 S.].

Anón. K o. D. c = Anónimo: Vocabulario quiché-[-español]. [= NL (72) Pht] [372 S.].

Anón. K XVII = Anónimo: Vocabulario quiché[-español]. ms. [= BNP:FN 9] [278 S.].

Anón. K XVIII = Anónimo: Vocabulario [español-] quiché. ms. [= BNP: FA 64] [= NL (69) Pht] [200 S.].

Anón. K XIX a = Anónimo: Vocabulario español-kiché. ms. [= BNP: FA 12] [32 S.].

Anón. K XIX b = Anónimo: Vocabulario kiché y cakchiquel. ms. [= BNP: FA 65] [= NL (70) Pht] [151 S.].

Anón. K XIX c = Anónimo: Vocabulario español-quiché. ms. [= BNP: FA 12] [= NL (73) Pht] [32 S.].

Anón. K 1787 = Anónimo: Vocabularios quichés [copiados por Fermín Joseph Tirado en Sacapulas] [= BYUL Gates] [432 S.].

Anón. Y XVI a = Anónimo: Diccionario de Motul 1 [maya-español] [= JCBL T 9 b case] ms. [= Martínez 1929] [465 fs].

Anón. Y XVI b = Anónimo: Diccionario de Motul 2 [español-maya] [= JCBL T 9 b case] [236 fs].

Anón. Y XVII = Anónimo: E. Mengin (ed.): Bocabulario de Mayathan [español-maya] [Facsimile-Ausgabe] ms. [= Codex Vindobonensis S. N. 3833] ADV Graz 1972 [444 S.].

Anón. Y 1898 = Anónimo: Diccionario de Ticul. ms. 1690 [Original jetzt verloren] [aber in Pérez 1898 eingearbeitet: S. 123—296].

Anón. Y 1976 = Anónimo: Diccionario de San Francisco (Oscar Michelon, ed.) [Facsimile-Ausgabe] ADV Graz [786 S.].

Ara 1571 = Domingo de Ara: Bocabulario [español-tzeltal] (Copanaguastla) ms. [= UPL] [= NL (2) Pht] [328 S.].

Aulie 1948 = Evelyn Aulie: Chol dictionary. ms. 1948 [= MCMCA 26 (IV)] [18 S.].

Aulie 1978 = Wilbur y Evelyn Aulie: Diccionario ch'ol-español y español-ch'ol. ILV México [215 S.].

Barrera 1745 = Francisco Barrera: Vocabulario castellano-quiché, ... doctrina, ... confessionario ms. [= NL (6) Pht] [201 S.].

Barrera M. 1976 = Alfredo Barrera M.: Nomenclatura etnobotánica maya [= INAH; CRS; CC 36] México.

Barrera V. 1980 = Alfredo Barrera V.: Diccionario maya Cordemex: maya-español; español-maya. Mérida, Yucatán [1415 S.].

Basseta 1698 = Domingo de Basseta: Vocabulario español-[quiché y quiché-español]. ms. [= BNP: FA 59] [fs 1—160 = NL (7) Pht (320 S.) [fsa 240—248 = NL (7) Pht (172 S.)] [492 S.].

Bastarrachea 1975 = Juan Bastarrachea: Vocabulario de Cobá, Quintana Roo. ms.

Becerra 1934 = Marcos Becerra: Los chontales de Tabasco. IL 2.29—36 UNAM México.

Beekman 1953 = John Beekman/Elaine Beekman: Vocabulario chol. ILV México [70 S.].

Beltrán 1859 = Pedro Beltrán: Arte y semilexicon yucateco [México 1746]. Mérida de Yucatán [= NL (9)] [260 S.].

Berlin 1962 = Brent Berlin/Terrence Kaufman: Diccionario tzeltal de Tenejapa. [= MCMCA 281 (LIII)] [141 S.].

Berlin 1968 = Brent Berlin: Tzeltal numeral classifiers. 's Gravenhage [243 S.].

Blair 1974 = Robert Blair/Refugio Vermont: Yucatec Maya-English vocabulary [= MCMCA 160 (XXX)]; English-Yucatec Maya vocabulary [= MCMCA 161 (XXX)] [350 S.].

Brasseur 1872 = Étienne Brasseur de Bourbourg: Dictionnaire, grammaire et chrestomathie de la langue maya. Paris [= NL (17).

Brawand 1962 = John Brawand/Alice Brawand: Achi vocabulary. Guatemala [50 S.].

Breedlove 1970 = Dennis Breedlove/Nicholas Hopkins: A study of Chuj (Mayan) plants. The Wasmann Journal of Biology 28. (1970) 275—298; 23. (1971) 107—205.

Brito 1980 = William Brito Sansores (Secretario de la Academica de la Lengua Maya) ms.

Bruce 1968 = Robert Bruce: Gramática del lacandón [con listas de vocablos]. México [= INAH: DIP 21] [152 S.].

Calvo 1726 = Tomás Calvo: Bocabulario español-quiché. ms. [= NL (15) Pht] [144 S.].

Campbell 1977 = Lyle Campbell: Historical linguistics and Quichean linguistic prehistory [lists]. Los Angeles [144 S.].

Charencey 1884 = Hyacinthe de Charencey: Vocabulaire français-maya. Alençon [= ASP 13] [89 S.].

Church 1955 = Clarence Church/Katherine Church: Vocabulario castellano-jacalteco [y] jacalteco-castellano. ILV Guatemala [68 S.].

Coto 1656 = Tomás de Coto: Voacabulario [español-]cakchiquel. ms. [= APSL] [= NL (10) Pht] [955 S.].

Cowan 1961 = Marion Cowan: Huixteco (Maya Tzotzil) place names. SMA:MR 8. 1961, 195—200.

Cruz 1571 = Juan de la Cruz: Doctrina christiana en la lengua guasteca [Veracruz] con la lengua castellana [listas de vocablos]. México [= JCBL S 13 a V 17 b R (51 fs)] [102 S.].

Day 1977 = Christopher Day: Diccionario jacalteco-español [y] español-jacalteco. Rochester CPO [241 S.].

Delgaty 1964 = Colin Delgaty: Vocabulario tzotzil de San Andrés [tzotzil-españól y español-tzotzil]. [= ILV: VIMSA 10] México [90 S.].

Delgaty 1978 = Alfa Delgaty/Agustín Ruiz: Diccionario tzotzil de San Andrés [Larráinzar, Chamula, Chenalhó, Iztapa, Zinacantan] [tzotzil-español y español-tzotzil]. [= ILV: VIMSA 22] México [498 S.].

Dzul 1977 = Domingo Dzul Poot: [vocabulario de voces del dialecto maya de Bécal, Campeche]. ms.

Echeverría 1980 = Víctor Echeverría: [lengua maya moderna]. ms.

Edmonson o. D. = Munro Edmonson: U xe oher tzih (U chun uchben t'an) [preliminary lexicon of roots of historical Yucatec] ms.

Edmonson 1965 = Munro Edmonson: Quiché-English dictionary. New Orleans [= MARI 30] [168 S.].

Elgueta o. D. = Manuel Elgueta: Vocabulario mam i español. ms. [= NL (4) Pht] [17 S.].

Elliott 1962 = Ray Elliott/Helen Elliott: Ixil [Nebaj] Mayan vocabulary. Guatemala [50 S.].

Estrada 1979 = Agustín Estrada: El vocabulario k'ekchí-español de Fray Eugenio de Góngora (1739). AHG (II) 1. 1979, 149—193.

Fernández 1937 = Jesús Fernández: Diccionario poconchí. ASGH 14. 1937, 47—70, 184—200.

Fox 1978 = James Fox: Proto-Mayan accent, morpheme-structure conditions, and velar innovations (283 cognate sets). Chicago [324 S.].

Gann 1918 = Thomas Gann: The Maya Indians of Southern Yucatan and Northern British Honduras. [= BAE Bulletin 64] Washington [146 S.].

García 1971 = Antonio García: Los elementos del tzotzil colonial y moderno [San Andrés Chamula]. México [= UNAM;CEMC 7] [111 S.].

Gates 1931 = William Gates: An outline dictionary of Maya glyphs. Baltimore [= MSP 1] [186 S.].

Grimes 1972 = James Grimes: The phonological history of the Quichean languages. Carbondale, Illinois [= STU:UM:RR 1] [106 S.].

Guzmán XVII = Alonso de Guzmán: Bocabulario de lengua tzeldal [Copanaguastla]. ms. [= NL (11) Pht] [294 S.].

Guzmán 1704 = Pantaleón de Guzmán: Libro de nombres en lengua cakchiquel. ms. [= NL (14) Pht] [346 S.].

Henne 1980 = David Henne/Abraham García/Santiago Yac Sam: Diccionario quiché-español [y español-quiché]. ILV Guatemala [294 S.].

Hopkins 1967 = Nicholas Hopkins: The Chuj language [San Mateo Ixtatán] [word lists]. Austin [University of Texas] [278 S.].

Hopkins 1969 = Nicholas Hopkins: Compound placenames in Chuj and other Mayan languages. Austin [University of Texas] [38 S. mgr].

Hopkins 1976 = Nicholas Hopkins: Chuj-English dictionary. ms.

Hopkins 1977 = Nicholas Hopkins: Some loan words in Chalchihuitan Tzotzil [= MCMCA 271 (LI)] [3 S. typscr].

Jacks 1972 a = Lewis Jacks: Macro-Mayan cognate sets [SIU:UM:RR].

Jacks 1972 b = Lewis Jacks: The phonological history of Uspantec. Carbondale, Illinois.

Jackson 1952 = Frances Jackson/Julia Supple: Vocabulario tojolabal[-español y español-tojolabal]. ILV México [60 S.].

Kaufman 1964 = Terrence Kaufman: Materiales lingüísticos de la familia de idiomas mayanos [listas de cognadas]. In: Evon Vogt/Alberto Ruz (eds.): Desarrollo cultural de los mayas] México 1964, 81—136.

Kaufman 1967 = Terrence Kaufman: Preliminary Mochó vocabulary. [= UCB:LBRL:WP 5] Berkeley [321 S. mgr].

Kaufman 1969 = Terrence Kaufman: Teco — a new Mayan language. IJAL 35.154—174.

Kaufman 1972 = Terrence Kaufman: El prototzeltal-tzotzil: fonología comparada y diccionario reconstruido. [= UNAM:CEMC 5] México [161 S.].

Kaufman 1976 = Terrence Kaufman: New Mayan languages in Guatemala [Sacapulas, Sipacapa]. [= UCLA:AISC:Mayan Linguistics 1 (Marlys McClaran ed.) S. 67—89].

La Farge 1927 = Oliver La Farge: Comparative word-lists: Yocotan, Chontal, Tzeltal, Chaneabal, Jacalteca. In: MARI 2.465—485. New Orleans.

Larsen 1955 = Raymond Larsen: Vocabulario huasteco[-español y español-huasteco] de San Luis Potosí. ILV México [218 S.].

Laughlin 1975 = Robert Laughlin: The great Tzotzil dictionary of San Lorenzo Zinacantan. Washington [= SI:SCA 19] [612 S. + 5 Landkarten].

Lenkersdorf 1979 = Carlos Lenkersdorf: Diccionario tojolabal-español [Vol. 1] [425 S.] español-tojolabal [Vol. 2] [812 S.] México [1237 S.].

León 1954 = Juan de León: Diccionario quiché-español. Guatemala.

McClaran 1972 = Marlys McClaran: Lexical and syntactic structures in Yucatec Maya. Cambridge, Massachusetts [289 S.].

McQuown 1967 = Norman McQuown: Classical Yucatec Maya [monosyllable index to Motul 1; particle inventory from Coronel]. Austin In: HMAI 5.201—247].

McQuown 1976 a = Norman McQuown: Huastec morpheme list [huasteco-español]. CPO [= MCMCA 67 (XXXI)] [889 S.].

McQuown 1976 b = Norman McQuown: Kekchi (San Juan Chamelco) vocabulary. ms. 1948 [= MCMCA 171 (XXXII)] [106 S.].

McQuown 1976 c = Norman McQuown: Notes on comparative Mayan: Uspantec. McQL [5 S.].

McQuown 1976 d = Norman McQuown: Vocabulario chol de La Cueva. ms. 1949 [= MCMCA 156 (XXIX)] [25 S.].

McQuown 1976 e = Norman McQuown: Vocabulario chortí. ms. 1949 [= MCMCA 157 (XXIX)] [47 S.].

McQuown 1976 f = Norman McQuown: Vocabulario chuj de San Sebastián Coatán. ms. 1949 [= MCMCA 226 (XLII)] [33 S.].

McQuown 1976 g = Norman McQuown: Vocabulario kanjobal de Santa Eulalia. ms. 1949 [= MCMCA 195 (XXXVII)] [108 S.].

McQuown 1976 h = Norman McQuown: Vocabulario mame de Ixtahuacán. ms. 1949 [= MCMCA 243 (XLV)] [48 S.].

McQuown 1976 i = Norman McQuown: Vocabulario mame de San Juan Ostuncalco. ms. 1948 [= MCMCA 129 (XXIII)] [65 S.].

McQuown 1976 j = Norman McQuown: Vocabularios maya-yucatecos [Valladolid, Dzilam González, Ich Ek, Bécal (2), Bacu, Xocempich, Tzucacab, Maxcanu]. ms. 1949 [= MCMCA 261 (XLTX)] [193 S.].

McQuown 1976 k = Norman McQuown: Vocabulario pocomame de San Luis Jilotepeque. ms. 1949 [= MCMCA 251 (XLVII)] [33 S.].

McQuown 1976 l = Norman McQuown: Vocabulario pocomchí de Purulhá. ms. 1949 [= MCMCA 256 (XLVIII)] [34 S.].

McQuown 1976 m = Norman McQuown: Vocabularios quichés de Totonicapán y Chichicastenango. ms. 1948 [= MCMCA 113 (XX)] [66 S.].

McQuown 1976 n = Norman McQuown: Vocabulario tzeltal de Bachajón y Yajalón. ms. 1949 [= MCMCA 181 (XXXIV)] [30 S.].

McQuown 1976 o = Norman McQuown: Vocabulario tzotzil de Iztapa. ms. 1949 [= MCMCA 233 (XLIII)] [32 S.].

McQuown 1977 a = Norman McQuown: Léxico tzeltal-español y español-tzeltal [Oxchuc]. ms. 1958 [= MCMCA 320 (LX)] [69 S.].

McQuown 1977 b = Norman McQuown: Tojolabal vocabulary. ms. 1949 [= MCMCA 266 (L)] [36 S.].

Maldonado 1987 = Juan Maldonado et al.: Diccionario mam de Ixtahuacán. EL Guatemala [513 S.].

Martínez 1929 = Juan Martínez (ed.): Diccionario de Motul [1] maya-español. Mérida, Yucatan [= Anónimo Y XVI a] [= NL (32) Pht] [954 S.].

Mayers 1956 = Marvin Mayers: Vocabulario pocomchí-español y español-pocomchí. ILV Guatemala [106 S.].

Mengin 1972 = Ernst Mengin (ed.): Bocabulario de Mayathan [1625]. ADV Graz [= Anón. Y XVII] [444 S.].

Michelon 1976 = Oscar Michelon: Diccionario [maya] de San Francisco. ADV Graz [= Anón. Y 1976] [786 S.].

Miram 1983 = Helga Miram: Numeral classifiers im yukatekischen Maya. Hannover [317 S.].

Morán 1695 = Francisco Morán: Arte en lengua choltí ... libro ... confessionario ... vocabulario. ms. [= NL (4) Pht] [182 S.].

Morán 1720 = Pedro Morán: Bocabulario ... pokoman de Amatitán [español-pocomam]. ms. (fs 91) [= BNP:FA 50] [= BYUL Pht (180 S.)] [182 S.].

Nebrija 1492 = Antonio de Nebrija: Vocabulario romance en latín.

Ortiz 1892 = José Ortiz: Vocabulario subinha. ms. 1789 [In: León Fernández (ed.); Lenguas indígenas de Centro América en el siglo XVIII].

Otzoy 1976 = Flora Otzoy Cutzal: Vocabulario cakchiquel-español médico. USC Guatemala [130 S.].

Owen 1968 = Michael Owen: The semantic structure of Yucatec verb roots. Ann Arbor, Michigan [113 S.].

Owen 1970 a = Michael Owen: Concordance of the Chilam Balam de Chumayel. Seattle [359 S.].

Owen 1970 b = Michael Owen: Concordance of the Ritual of the Bacabs. Seattle [297 S.].

Owen 1971 = Michael Owen: A morphosyntactic root dictionary of Yucatec Maya. Seattle [235 S.].

Pacheco 1939 = Santiago Pacheco: Léxico de la fauna yucateca. Mérida, Yucatán [= NL (70)] [171 S.].

Pacheco 1969 = Santiago Pacheco: Hahil tzolbichunil t'an Mayab (Verdadero diccionario de la lengua maya) [el primer intento de explicar la lengua maya en el mismo idioma]. Mérida, Yucatán [472 S.].

Palomo 1935 = Florencio Palomo: [vocabularios inéditos del maya hablado actual] ms.

Parra o. D. = Francisco de la Parra [con Pedro de Betanzos]: Arte, pronunciación y orthographia de ... cakchequel. ms.

Pearse 1945 = A. S. Pearse: La fauna. In: EY 1.109—271. Mérida, Yucatán.

Pérez o. D. = Juan Pío Pérez: [recetarios de indios] Indices de plantas medicinales y de enfermedades combinados. ms. [= NL (75) Pht] [58 S.].

Pérez 1877 = Juan Pío Pérez: Diccionario maya. Mérida, Yucatán [= NL (74)] [467 S.].

Pérez 1898 = Juan Pío Pérez: Coordinación alfabética del maya. Mérida, Yucatán [= NL (73)] [307 S.].

Pineda 1888 = Vicente Pineda: Gramática tzeltal y diccionario [Oxchuc?]. Chiapas, México [= NL (15)] [498 S.].

Reynoso 1916 = Diego de Reynoso: Vocabulario de la lengua mame [1644]. México [144 S.].

Robles 1962 = Carlos Robles: Manual del tzeltal de Bachajón [con vocabularios]. México [115 S.].

Romero C. 1976 = Moisés Romero C.: [notas sobre elementos de la lengua maya yucateca].

Romero F. 1910 = Luis Romero F.: La lengua maya. Mérida, Yucatán [100 S.].

Roys 1931—1957 = Ralph Roys: The ethnobotany of the Maya [1931], Place names of Yucatan [1935], Personal names of Yucatan [1940], Indian background of colonial Yucatan [1940], The political geography of the Yucatan Maya [1957].

Ruano 1892 = Alberto Ruano: Estudios y vocabularios, pokoman y chortí. ms. [= NL (3) Pht] [121 S.].

Saenz 1940 = Carmelo Saenz: Diccionario cakchiquel-español. Guatemala [434 S.].

Salvador 1945 = Juan Salvador: Huastec (Veracruz) vocabularies. ms. 1930 [= MCMCA 9 (II)].

Santo Domingo 1693 = Tomás de Santo Domingo: Vocabulario en lengua cakchiquel y castellana. ms. [= BNP:FA 44] [= NL (23) Pht (286 S.)] [139 fs].

Sapper 1906 = Karl Sapper: Vocabular in Chorti, Chol und Pocoman von Jilotepeque. In: ICA 15. 1906, 440—465 [= NL (40)].

Sarles 1961 = Harvey Sarles: Monosyllable dictionary of the Tzeltal language [Oxchuc]. UCDA Chicago [82 S. mgr].

Sarles 1962 = Harvey Sarles: San Bartolomé Tzotzil dictionary. UCDA Chicago [99 S. mgr].

Schultze-Jena 1933 = Leonhard Schultze-Jena: Indiana I — Leben, Glaube und Sprache der Quiché von Guatemala. Jena [= NL (53)] [334 S.].

Schumann 1971 = Otto Schumann: Descripción estructural del maya-itzá ... con un diccionario itzá-español, español-itzá [San José Soccotz]. México [= UNAM:CEMC 6] [134 S.].

Schumann 1973 = Otto Schumann: La lengua chol de Tila (Chiapas) [con vocabularios chol-español, español-chol]. México [= UNAM:CEMC 8] [115 S.].

Sedat 1955 = Guillermo Sedat: Nuevo diccionario k'ekchi'-español, español-k'ekchi' [San Juan Chamelco]. Guatemala [273 S.].

Shaw 1962 = Mary Shaw/Helen Neuenswander: Achi [Cubulco] vocabulary. Guatemala [45 S.].

Silva 1987 = Ismael Silva Fuenzalida: Veracruz Huastec grammar and vocabulary. UCDA Chicago 1953 ms. [= MCMCA 105 (XVII)].

Slocum 1953 = Marianna Slocum: Vocabulario tzeltal-español [y] español-tzeltal [Oxchuc]. ILV México [169 S.].

Slocum 1965 = Marianna Slocum/Florencia Gerdel: Vocabulario tzeltal de Bachajón. ILV México [= VIMSA 13] [216 S.].

Smailus 1975 = Ortwin Smailus: El maya-chontal de Acalan [vocabularios]. México [= UNAM:CEMC 9] [234 S.].

Solís 1949 = Ermilo Solís: Diccionario español-maya. Mérida, Yucatán [503 S.].

Standley 1945 = Paul Standley: La flora. In: EY 1. 273—527. Mérida, Yucatán.

Staub 1924 = Walther Staub: Zur Kenntnis der indianischen Ortsnamen in der Huasteka (Ost-Mexiko). In: ZdGfE 1924. 215—234.

Stoll 1887 = Otto Stoll: Die Sprache der Ixil Indianer [Jacalteca S. 131—146]. Leipzig [= NL (3)].

Stoll 1896 = Otto Stoll: Die Maya-Sprachen der Pokomgruppe. Zweiter Theil. Die Sprache der K'ekchi Indianer. Nebst einem Anhang: die Uspanteca. Leipzig [229 S.].

Stoll 1958 = Otto Stoll: Etnografía de Guatemala [vocabulario comparativo]. Guatemala [255 S.].

Swadesh 1970 = Mauricio Swadesh et al.: Diccionario de elementos del maya yucateco colonial. México [= UNAM:CEMC 3] [137 S.].

Sywulka 1975 = Edward Sywulka: Mam vocabulary [Ixtahuacán]. ms. 1938 [= MCMCA 241 (XLV)] [52 S. typscr].

Tapia Z. 1767 = Carlos de Tapia Z.: Noticia de la lengua huasteca [con vocabularios]. México [137 S.].

Termer 1930 = Franz Termer: Über die Mayasprache von Chicomucelo. In: ICA 23. 1928, 926—936.

Thompson 1930 = Eric Thompson: Ethnology of Southern and Central British Honduras. [= FMNH:AS 17.2] Chicago [194 S.].

Thompson 1962 = Eric Thompson: A catalogue of Maya hieroglyphs. Norman, Oklahoma [472 S.].

Ulrich 1976 a = Matthew Ulrich/Rosemary Ulrich: Mopan Maya vocabulary [San Luis]. Guatemala 1962 [= MCMCA 247 (XLVI)] [47 S.].

Ulrich 1976 b = Mateo Ulrich/Rosemary Ulrich: Diccionario mopán-español y español-mopán. SIL Guatemala [393 S.].

Varea 1699 = Francisco de Varea: Calepino español-cakchiquel [Comalapa]. ms. [= APSL 497.43; No. V 42] [400 fs].

Vermont 1980 = Refugio Vermont [co-author with Robert Blair of "Spoken Yucatec Maya"] UCDA Chicago 1965—1967.

Vico XVII = Domingo de Vico: Vocabulario cakchiquel-español. ms. [= BNP:FA 46] [286 fs].

Weathers 1949 = Kenneth Weathers/Nadine Weathers: Diccionario español-tzotzil y tzotzil-español [Nabenchauc]. SIL México [57 S.].

Wick 1975 a = Stanley Wick/Remigio Cochojil: Quiché-English vocabulary. [= MCMCA 78 (XII)] [238 S.] English-Quiché vocabulary. [= MCMCA 79 (XII)] [238 S.].

Wick 1975 b = Stanley Wick et al.: Quiché-English vocabulary [end-sort]. CPO UCDA Chicago 1974 [= MCMCA 112 (XX)] [237 S.].

Wirsing 1930 = Paul Wirsing: German-Kekchi dictionary. ms. [HU:PM].

Wisdom 1950 = Charles Wisdom: Materials on the Chorti language: texts, vocabulary, grammatical notes, and classified lists of terms. [= MCMCA 28 (V)] [1138 S.].

Xec 1954 = Patricio Xec/Gail Maynard: Diccionario preliminar quiché-español [y] español-quiché. Quezaltenango [207 S. mgr].

Zavala 1898 = M. Zavala/Alejandro Medina: Vocabulario español-maya. Mérida, Yucatán [= NL (116)] [72 S.].

Zimmermann 1955 = Günter Zimmermann: Das Cotoque — die Maya-Sprache von Chicomucelo. In: ZfE 80. 1955, 59—87.

Zimmermann 1956 = Günter Zimmermann: Die Hieroglyphen der Maya-Handschriften. Hamburg [= UH:AGAK:B (VkKGSpr) 34] [183 S. + 8 Tafeln].

Zinn o. D. = Raymond Zinn: Diccionario de pocomam oriental. ILV Guatemala [80 S.].

Zúñiga 1608 = Dionysio de Zúñiga: Diccionario pocomchí [= BYUL Gates Collection (typscr)].

Norman A. McQuown, The University of Chicago, Chicago, Illinois (USA)

276. Die Lexikographie des Tupí-Guaraní

1. Einleitung
2. Die frühe Lexikographie des Tupí
3. Die frühe Lexikographie des Guaraní
4. Die neuere Lexikographie des Tupí-Guaraní
5. Literatur (in Auswahl)

1. Einleitung

Von den zahlreichen heute bekannten Tupí-Guaraní-Sprachen sind in der Kolonialzeit nur zwei Vertreter Gegenstand grammatischer und lexikographischer Beschreibung geworden, nämlich Tupí an der brasilianischen Küste und Guaraní vornehmlich in Paraguay, (vgl. Karte 276.1), von denen die o. g. Sprachfamilie dann ihren Namen bekommen hat. Beide nah verwandten Sprachformen dienten der Jesuitenmission in Brasilien und Paraguay seit der 2. Hälfte des 16. Jhs. als Verkehrs- und Unterrichtssprache (*língua geral* oder auch *língua brasílica* in Brasilien) zwischen Missionaren und verschiedenen Tupívölkern, die damals gerade die Küste entlang nach Norden wanderten und so bei der Missionierung immer wieder in Erscheinung traten. Nach der Vertreibung der Jesuiten übernahmen die Franziskaner die Pflege der „língua geral" (vgl. zur Geschichte der Tupí-Lexikographie auch Edelweiss 1969, 112—158 und passim, wenn auch z. T. polemisch). Als Grundlage für die schon früh erfolgten Beschreibungen und Lehrbücher der beiden Sprachen dienten das Tupinambá der Gegend um Rio de Janeiro (vgl. z. B. Anchieta 1595, Anonymus 1621) und das Guaraní des südlichen Paraguay (Ruiz de Montoya 1639, Restivo 1724). Das von den Jesuiten kodifizierte Tupinambá (Alttupí) ist nach dem Aussterben der Tupí sprechenden Küstenvölker vor allem im Amazonasraum in lautlich und grammatisch vereinfachter Form als Verkehrssprache verbreitet geblieben und dort bis heute in reduzierter Funktion als solche unter dem Namen Nheengatú ('gute Sprache') bekannt, während das von Restivo (1724) und Späteren normierte und durch europäisches Gedankengut beeinflußte Guaraní (zur Sprachplanung und Sprachpolitik der Jesuiten vgl. Tovar 1964 und Meliá 1969) heute als Umgangssprache in Paraguay (neben Spanisch) Avañe'ẽ ('Menschensprache') genannt wird.

2. Die frühe Lexikographie des Tupí

Die Lexikographie des Tupí besteht in der Kolonialzeit Brasiliens vor allem aus handschriftlichen Verzeichnissen anonymer oder kaum bekannter Jesuitenmissionare bzw. Franziskanermönche, die mit einer Ausnahme alle erst in den dreißiger Jahren unseres Jahrhunderts gedruckt wurden, jedoch

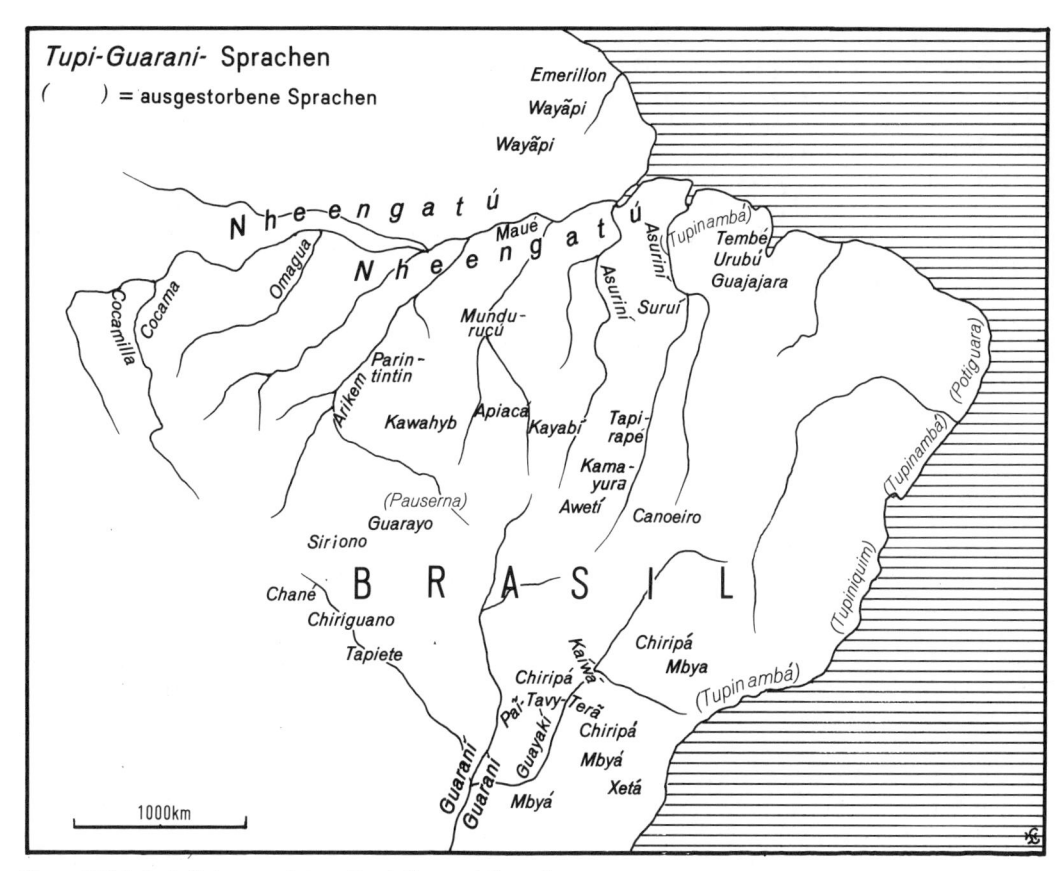

Karte 276.1: Lokalisierung einiger Tupí-Guaraní-Sprachen

vorwiegend nicht als selbständige Wörterbücher für ein größeres Publikum, sondern als kommentierte Ausgaben in wissenschaftlichen Zeitschriften. Nicht behandelt werden hier die neueren recht zahlreichen populären Wörterbuchkompilationen des Alttupí (d. h. Tupí der frühen Kolonialzeit) geringen Umfangs sowie unsicherer Herkunft und Qualität. — Das älteste und daher wichtigste Vokabular des alten Tupí der brasilianischen Küste ist der in einer Handschrift von 1621 überlieferte „Vocabulario na lingoa Brasilica", dessen Autorschaft trotz vieler Versuche bis heute ungeklärt ist (Anonymus 1621). Nach Meinung des ersten Herausgebers, Plínio Ayrosa, war eventuell schon Padre Anchieta, der Vater der brasilianischen Jesuitenmission und Verfasser der ersten Grammatik des Tupí (Anchieta 1595), ein Mitautor dieses möglicherweise kollektiven Werkes. Ob die beiden existierenden Handschriften Kopien einer gemeinsamen Vorlage oder die Lissaboner eine leicht abweichende, aber besser lesbare Abschrift des in Rio de Janeiro befindlichen Manuskripts ist, ist ebenfalls nicht sicher. Es handelt sich um ein Wörterverzeichnis Portugiesisch-Tupí, das deutlich den Charakter eines alphabetisch geordneten Glossars für die praktischen Zwecke der Verständigung der Missionare hat. Eine tiefere Erschließung der Sprache, wie sie wenig später Montoya für das Guaraní zeigt (vgl. § 3), indem er die Zusammensetzung der Wörter aus einzelnen Elementen und deren Bedeutung angibt, sie mit den Ableitungen in Wortfamilien aufführt, Konstruktionen erklärt und vor allem ein reiches Beispielmaterial für den Gebrauch bringt, fehlt hier und in der ganzen weiteren Tradition der Tupí-Lexikographie der Kolonialzeit. Es mangelt für die ganze Zeit an einem größeren Werk, das vom Tupí ausgeht und dessen lexikalische Strukturen repräsentiert. Der „Vocabulário na língua brasílica" von 1621 (entstanden sicher früher) bietet ausführliche lexikalische Information über die Fauna, Flora und andere für die Portugiesen neue Dinge des Brasilien der frühen Kolonialzeit, allerdings nicht unter Lemmata, die diese Erscheinungen mit dem Tupí entlehnten Wörtern im Portugiesischen benennen, sondern unter allgemeinen Begriffen, wie z. B. „palma ou palmeira" (Palme) oder „peixe" (Fisch), mit zahlreichen Hyponymen. Eine so typische Sache wie das schon längst belegte *tabaco* fehlt als Lemma, das Wort für 'Tabak' ist aber unter *Fumaça que se bebe* 'Rauch, den man trinkt' zu finden, nämlich *petigma* (d. h. [petĩma]). In der Darstellung der dem Tupí eigenen Laute (insbesondere [ɨ, ĩ]; [mb, nd, ŋg] im Anlaut) ist der „Vocabulário" ebenso inkonsequent wie Anchieta in seiner Grammatik. Wegen der frühen Dokumentation ist das Werk dennoch von großem sprachhistorischem Wert. Eine erste Druckfassung des „Vocabulário" wurde 1938 von Plínio Ayrosa (mit ausführlicher Diskussion der Autorfrage im Vorwort) in São Paulo besorgt. Eine zweite, verbesserte Ausgabe unter Berücksichtigung einer Parallelhandschrift in Lissabon (die den Titel „Vocabulario da lingoa Brasilica" trägt) erschien 1952 und 1953 in 2 Bänden ebenfalls in São Paulo. — Erst Ende des 18. Jhs. erschien im Druck ein schmales, ebenfalls anonymes Wörterbuch Portugiesisch-Tupí („Diccionario Portuguez-Brasiliano", Frei Onofre 1795). Die Publikation des im Manuskript in der Nationalbibliothek in Lissabon vorliegenden zweiten und wertvolleren Teils Tupí-Portugiesisch erfolgte erst 1934 (Frei Onofre 1934). Die durch den Tupinologen Plínio Ayrosa besorgte Ausgabe von 1934 enthält im Vorwort (S. 19—34) auch die verwickelte Verfasserfrage und die Geschichte der Plagiatausgaben des ersten Teils in der ersten Hälfte des 19. Jhs. Danach ist sicher, daß beide Teile des Tupí-Wörterbuches von einem Franziskanerbruder namens Onofre (Frei Onofre), wohl einem Missionar aus dem Maranhão (NO-Brasilien), einige Zeit vor 1751 verfaßt wurden. Es handelt sich dabei nicht mehr um das ursprüngliche Tupí, sondern um die schon morphologisch und syntaktisch europäisierte „língua geral" (vgl. Edelweiss 1969, 109 f.). Ein besonders botanisch interessierter Franziskaner, Frei Velloso, ebenfalls aus dem Maranhão, vervollständigte das nur skizzierte Manuskript des 2. Teils und publizierte 1795 den 1. Teil, der im Zeichen des erwachenden brasilianischen Nationalismus in der 1. H. des 19. Jh. mehrfach unter verschiedenen Titeln nachgedruckt wurde und u. a. von Martius — der jedoch auch das Manuskript des 2. Teils kannte — in seiner „Wörtersammlung brasilianischer Sprachen", Erlangen 1863, 31—97, verarbeitet wurde. Platzmann wiederum druckte 1896 nicht nur den 1. Teil nach, als einziger vollständig und getreu, sondern auch den Teil Tupí-Portugiesisch, allerdings nicht nach dem Manuskript des Frei Velloso, sondern nach eigener Umkehrung („reverso") des 1. Teils. Platzmann kannte wohl auch nicht das unter dem Titel „Poranduba Maranhense" (etwa 'Bericht über den/Geschichte des Maranhão') 1826 von Frei Prazeres Maranhão verfaßte und 1891 unter dem Titel „Diccionario da língua geral do Brasil" (Frei Prazeres 1891) publizierte Wörterbuch, das ebenfalls nur eine Umkehrung des Werkes des Frei Onofre ist, also vom Tupí ausgeht. Es ist nicht genau bekannt, wann und wo das Material zu dem Wörterbuch des Frei Onofre gesammelt wurde. Wahrscheinlich wurde es in den zwanziger Jahren des 18. Jhs. in einem Kloster im Maranhão aus der dortigen „língua geral" zusammengestellt. Die Sprache zeigt die gegenüber dem Alttupí typischen Formen des „dialeto brasiliano" (Edelweiss 1969, 109), indem von den auslautenden Konsonanten *-b* nicht mehr, *-m* selten erscheint, sondern durch das mechanisch angefügte nominalisierende Morphem *-a* verdeckt wird (z. B. *pytyma* 'Tabak' statt *petym*). Auch sind gegenüber dem Alttupí und dem Guaraní Vokal- und Konsonantenveränderungen zu beobachten, wie man sie aus dem Nheengatú und heutigen amazonischen Tupí-Sprachen kennt. Z. T. erscheinen auch Varianten, wie z. B. *abaxí* neben *abatí* 'Mais', vgl. Guaraní *avatí*. Nachteilig ist nicht nur die spärliche Berücksichtigung und unzureichende Beschreibung grammatischer Morpheme (z. B. Lokalsuffixe), sondern auch die alphabetische Anordnung, bei der z. B. Verben, die wegen des inexistenten Infinitivs immer mit dem Personenpräfix der 1. Person Sg. gebraucht werden, alle unter diesem Präfix anstatt unter dem Buchstaben des Wortstammes aufgeführt werden. Beispielsätze, die den Gebrauch eines Wortes erläutern, sind auch im 2. Teil selten. Sehr ausführlich sind dagegen Pflanzen- und Tierbeschreibungen. — Kleinere handschriftlich überlieferte Wörterverzeichnisse sind der anonyme, wohl um 1700 entstandene „Vocabulário português-brasílico" (Voc.port.-bras. 1951) und der damit nicht identische „Vocabulário português-tupi" des João de Arronches. Beide Verfasser waren wohl Franziskaner. — Die amazonische *língua geral (nheengatú)*, die gegenüber dem alten Tupí starke Vereinfachungen aufweist, ist 1910 von Constant Tatevin grammatisch skizziert worden, samt einem

„Dictionnaire Tupï-Français" genannten Wörterbuchteil (Tatevin 1910, 99—237). Wesentlich umfangreicher, aber durch die Aufnahme aller möglichen Ableitungen stark aufgebläht (nahezu 7000 Wortformen) ist der Teil „Língua geral-Portugiesisch" in Stradellis „Vocabulário" (1929). Es war Grundlage mehrerer kleiner „Tupí"-Wörterbücher.

3. Die frühe Lexikographie des Guaraní

Das herausragende Werk unter den Wörterbüchern des Tupí-Guaraní insgesamt ist bis heute das zweiteilige (*Vocabulario,* d. h. Spanisch-Guaraní, und *Tesoro,* d. h. Guaraní-Spanisch) Wörterbuch von Antonio Ruiz de Montoya (1639—1640), einem der Väter der Jesuitenmission in Paraguay (vgl. Dietrich 1984, 89—91). Es ist von allen das umfassendste und die grundlegenden Sprachstrukturen am besten darstellende Wörterbuch und geht somit weit über die sonst häufig anzutreffende einfache Sammlung von Wörtergleichungen hinaus. Montoyas Wörterbuch ist bis gegen 1950 das einzige eigenständige lexikographische Werk des paraguayischen Guaraní gewesen. Restivo (1722) stellt lediglich eine Bearbeitung des „Vocabulario" dar, während der bedeutendere, weil vom Guaraní ausgehende und auch umfangreichere „Tesoro" keine Neuausgabe während der Kolonialzeit erfuhr. — Der sprachwissenschaftliche Wert beider Teile des Wörterbuchs von Montoya ist durch folgende Faktoren begründet: (a) Die Authentizität des Materials ist durch die selbständige Sammlertätigkeit des Autors gesichert, der in jahrzehntelangem Umgang (seit 1612) mit den Indios die lebendige Sprache mit allen Varianten kennengelernt hat. (b) Der von Montoya notierte Dialekt entspricht nicht völlig dem sog. Paraguay-Guaraní, sondern der Sprachform der Provinz Guairá im heutigen brasilianischen Staat Paraná, wo Montoya zunächst als Missionar arbeitete. Damit stellt die von ihm beschriebene Sprache z. T. eine Übergangsmundart zwischen Guaraní und Tupí dar, was auch der Herausgeber der Werke Montoyas, Franz Adolph von Varnhagen, 1876 bemerkte, indem er dem im Titel erscheinenden „Guaraní" jeweils „ò más bien Tupí" hinzufügte. Montoya selbst sagt nichts zu dialektalen Unterschieden. Immerhin ist aber sein Werk so eher auch als eine Art etymologisches Wörterbuch der heutigen Tupí-Guaraní-Sprachen zu gebrauchen, als wenn es ganz auf die paraguayische Sprachform beschränkt wäre. Das als Unterscheidungskriterium zwischen Tupí und Guaraní geltende Merkmal -s- im Tupí, dem im Guaraní -h- entspricht (*osó* vs. *ohó* 'er/sie ging/geht'; *kwarasy* vs. *kwarahy* 'Sonne'), erscheint bei Montoya z. T. auch in der für das Tupí typischen Lautung. Daher können bei ihm sowohl heutige Formen des Guaraní als auch des Tupí wiedergefunden werden (vgl. Dietrich 1984). (c) Montoya hat nicht nur über 6000 Guaraníwörter in ca. 5500 Lemmata gesammelt, ihre Bedeutung und ihren Gebrauch beschrieben, meist auch die Wurzeln zusammengesetzter Lexeme angegeben, wenngleich vielfach spekulativ, sondern enthält auch reichliche idiomatische und dadurch ebenfalls grammatische und syntaktische Informationen. Etwa 580 nicht durch ein eigenes Lemma vertretene und daher nicht in alphabetischer Ordnung auffindbare

LENGVA GVARANI. 151

uembé rembópiyâ, no fe fuella bien el baftago del embe. Hembopirĩ, defue fe bien el baftago. Ïbagïbó, cuerda, ò baftago fube hafta el cielo, vfanlo ra la dificultad de efconrfe, ò fubirfe al cielo. agembórâmõpae erehópe che hegũine, no te efparàs de mis manos. uembópĭpé chemõãngai-, con fu miembro pecò nmigo dize la muger. *Hemõrẽ.* Vna efpecie de bora. *Hendĭ.* Refplandor, refandecer, luzir, encender. guendĭpĭpéñânde reça-, alumbronos con fu refãndor. Yaçïendĭ, refplan-r de Luna. Tatáendĭ, veencendida, o apagada, z del fuego. Quaraçĭ en-, Sol refplandeciente, o plandor del Sol. Teçá dĭ, ojos claros, y garços. ñõendĭ tatá, encender ẽgo. Amõendĭyá tatá, fa-r fuego con pedernal. ñõendĭpú, hazer luzir. ñõendĭpúberá, hazer refĩndecer mucho. Hendĭ- çó ndiçóg, llamaradas. Hẽ dĭpõng, eftallido del fuego. Hendĭyâyâ, llamaradas grandes. Hendĭpû, reluziente. Hendĭpúberá, muy reluziente. Hendĭ vnĩ vnĩ, falir algunas llamaradas entre el humo, y de los relampagos entre nubes. c. d. hendĭ. yhû, negro. y. (ĩ) diminutiuo. Amõendĭpuyeog .l. Amõendĭpupỹtû, apagar llamas, y borrar lo refplandeciente. Ahendĭpûmonã, desluzir. Amõendĭpúmõnã cherapichára reco márãngatú, des luftrar la fama del proximo.

Hendú. b. Oyr, cherendú, me oye. h. gu. Ahendú, yo oygo, pa pára. bo. hara. Ahendubaí, entreoyr. Ahẽ dú catú .l. caracatú, oyr atentamente. Ahendú aũ, oyr de mala gana, no guftar de lo que fe dize. Ahendú vmbĭgĩ, oyr el eco, o fonido folo. Ahenduñẽmĩ, efcuchar a efcondidas. ñeẽñẽmỹngûera ahendú, oyr el fecreto. Ahenduorĭcatú yñãngaohába, oyr murmurar con gufto. Ndacherorĭ-

Textbeispiel 276.1: Wörterbuchausschnitt (aus: Montoya 1876a)

weitere Wörter sind bei Cadogan (1963) gesammelt. (d) Montoya ist sich bewußt, daß das Guaraní eine Sprache mit einsilbiger, höchstens zweisilbiger Wurzelstruktur ist, und versucht daher, längere Wortstämme durch semantisch sinnvolle Zusammensetzung einfacher Wurzeln zu erklären. Diese Erklärungen sind aus heutiger Sicht häufig richtig, teils jedoch auch willkürlich und unbegründet. (e) Homonyme werden in eigenen Lemmata getrennt und durchnumeriert aufgeführt. Dabei werden z. T. auch polyseme Wörter auseinandergerissen. Die Differenzierung beruht in Wirklichkeit auf der Homographie, wobei diakritische Zeichen nicht berücksichtigt werden, so daß z. B. *tatá* 'Feuer' als *1 tatá* und *tatā* 'hart' als *2 tatá* erscheint, obwohl beide Wörter durch Oralität und Nasalität phonologisch deutlich geschieden, also nicht homophon sind. (f) Außer den Lexemen werden auch alle Morpheme samt Allomorphen alphabetisch geordnet aufgeführt und durch Beispiele hinsichtlich ihres Gebrauchs illustriert. — Beide Teile des Wörterbuchs von Montoya wurden erst im 19. Jh. wieder aufgelegt, und zwar in einem von Julius Platzmann besorgten Faksimilenachdruck (Montoya 1876 a) und gleichzeitig durch Francisco Adolfo de Varnhagen, der jedoch den Satzspiegel änderte, indem er die Guaraní-Elemente kursiv setzen ließ und einige offensichtliche Versehen Montoyas emendierte (Montoya 1876 b). Der durch Restivo bearbeitete „Vocabulario" Montoyas (SpanischGuaraní) wurde 1893 durch Christian Friedrich Seybold wieder nachgedruckt (Restivo 1893).

4. Die neuere Lexikographie des Tupí-Guaraní

4.1. Die erste Hälfte des 20. Jahrhunderts

Dieser Zeitraum ist wiederum durch einige von Missionaren verfaßte ausführliche und zuverlässige Wörterbücher gekennzeichnet, nun aber auch zu den kleineren, nicht von den Jesuiten beeinflußten Sprachen, nämlich dem Chiriguano, genauer zum Chané-Dialekt dieser südostbolivianisch-nordargentinischen Sprache (Romano-Cattunar 1916), zum Guarayo oder Guarayu in Ostbolivien (Hoeller 1932) und zum benachbarten Siriono (häufig auch Sirionó; Schermair 1958, 1962). Die Arbeiten von Romano-Cattunar und Hoeller beruhen auf Vorarbeiten anderer Franziskaner, die jedoch kritisch gesichtet und dem jeweils aktuellen Sprachgebrauch angepaßt wurden. Dem nur im Manuskript bestehenden „Diccionario chiriguano-español etimológico, filológico, etnográfico, histórico" des P. Doroteo Giannecchini (1899) fügten Romano und Cattunar neu den Teil Spanisch-Chiriguano hinzu. Sie sagen jedoch nirgendwo, daß beide Teile des Wörterbuchs die typischen Lautungen, Formen und Lexeme des Chané-Dialekts, nicht des Chiriguano schlechthin abbilden. Das Wörterbuch enthält eine kurzgefaßte Grammatik (44 S.) und bei allen Lemmata allgemeineren Charakters zahlreiche Satzbeispiele. Noch systematischer sind bei Hoeller neben Beispielen auch Ableitungen angegeben, die die Wortfamilie deutlich machen, sowie bei prädikativen Ausdrücken (verbal und nominal) deren syntaktische Valenzen. Die beiden Teile des Siriono-Wörterbuchs von Schermair (Schermair 1958, 1962) scheinen dagegen ganz auf eigener Beobachtung zu beruhen. Sie enthalten den bisher einzigen systematischen Versuch, in dieser von den klassischen Tupí-Guaraní-Sprachen lautlich, grammatisch und lexikalisch sehr stark abweichenden Sprache die lexikalischen und grammatischen Morpheme zu identifizieren und zueinander in Beziehung zu setzen. Das Wörterbuch ist ebenfalls reich an Beispielen und bis heute eine der wichtigsten Quellen unserer Kenntnis des Siriono. — Das moderne Paraguay-Guaraní wird neben vielen kleineren vor allem in zwei Wörterbüchern dargestellt: Jover Peralta/Osuna (1950) enthält zwar keine Beispiele und kaum grammatische Hinweise, ist aber sehr zuverlässig und reichhaltig (1. Teil 183 S., 2. Teil 240 S., abschließend eine kurze Grammatik (S. 429—488), sowie Orts- und Personennamen). Beispiele und genauere syntaktische Informationen finden sich bei Guasch (1961), auch im umfangreicheren spanischen Teil (487 S. gegenüber 275 S. im 2. Teil).

4.2. Neueste Lexikographie

Die Mehrzahl der neuesten Wörterbücher ist im Gegensatz zu früher von Linguisten bzw. linguistisch geschulten Missionaren, hier vor allem Mitarbeitern des in den USA beheimateten sehr aktiven Summer Institute of Linguistics, verfaßt (Betts 1981, Dooley 1982). Sie zeichnen sich vor allem durch genaue morphologische Analysen und Verweise zu Ableitungen oder Synonymen aus. Außerordentlich reichhaltig ist Boudin (1978), der die Lexeme und Morpheme des bis dahin kaum dokumentierten, südlich der Amazonasmündung gesprochenen Tembé systematisch in Bezug zum älteren und modernen Guaraní bringt (Bd. 1: „Tembé-ténêtéhar — português", 344 S.; Bd. 2: „Português — tembé-ténêtéhar e sinopse gramatical", 393 S.). Betts (1981) beschreibt eine kleine, sehr konservative Tupí-Guaraní-Sprache des südlichen zentralen Amazonasraums, mit vielen synonymischen Verweisen und einer grammatischen Skizze im Teil „Parintintín-Português" (219 S.; „Português-Parintintín", 108 S.), aber ohne Beispiele. Reiche Phraseologie enthält dagegen Dooley (1982) im Teil „Guarani (Mbyá) — Português" (S. 23—207), eine deutliche Kennzeichnung von grammatischen gegenüber lexikalischen Elementen im Teil „Português — Guaraní" (S. 208—322). Hier wird zum ersten Mal das in Südostbrasilien gesprochene Mbyá lexikographisch erfaßt. — Das umfangreichste Wörterbuch (6000 Stichwörter) zum Wayãpi in Französisch Guayana, das besonders reich an Fachwortschatz zu Fauna und Flora ist und in Zusammenarbeit mit Botanikern und Zoologen erstellt wurde, ist der „Dictionnaire wayãpi" von Françoise Grenand (1989). Er zeichnet sich zudem durch genaue sprachstrukturelle und ethnologisch relevante Bedeutungsangaben (mit Zeichnungen), Angaben der möglichen Etymologie und durch Beispiele aus. Dies ist sicherlich die größte lexikographische Leistung dieses Jahrhunderts im Bereich der Tupí-Guaraní-Sprachen. Der Teil Französisch-Wayãpi umfaßt die Seiten 47—87, ein Verzeichnis Lateinisch-Wayãpi der wissenschaftlichen Tier- und Pflanzennamen die Seiten 79—112, der Teil Wayãpi-Französisch die Seiten 113—538.

5. Literatur (in Auswahl)

5.1. Wörterbücher der Kolonialzeit

Arronches 1935/37 = João de Arronches: O caderno da língua ou Vocabulário portuguez-tupi de João de Arronches, 1739. Notas e commentarios á margem de um manuscripto do século XVIII. Hrsg. von Plínio Ayrosa. In: Revista do Museu Paulista 81, 1937, 49—322. Als Separatum: São Paulo 1935.

Anonymus 1621 = Vocabulário na língua brasílica. Manuscrito português-tupi do séc. XVII, 1621, transcrito e prefaciado por Plínio Ayrosa. São Paulo 1938; 2.ª ed. revista e confrontada com o Ms. fg., 3144 da Biblioteca Nacional de Lisboa por Carlos Drumond. Universidade de São Paulo, Faculdade de Filosofia, Ciências e Letras, Bd. I (A—H), Boletim n.º 137 (Série Etnografia e Tupi-Guarani, n.º 23), 1952 [154 S.]; Bd. II (I—Z), Boletim n.º 164, (Série Etnografia e Tupi-Guarani, n.º 26), 1953 [149 S].

Montoya 1639 = Pe. Antonio Ruiz de Montoya, S. J.: Tesoro de la lengua guaraní Compuesto por el Padre Antonio Ruiz, de la Compañía de Iesús, Dedicado a la Soberana Virgen María. Madrid 1639 [407 S. zu 4 Spalten (2 Sp. r., 2 Sp. v.)].

Montoya 1640 = Pe. Antonio Ruiz de Montoya, S. J.: Arte, y Bocabulario de la lengua guaraní, Compuesto por el Padre Antonio Ruiz, de la Compañía de Iesús, Dedicado a la Soberana Virgen María. Madrid 1640 [508 S. zu 2 Spalten].

Montoya 1876 a = Pe. Antonio Ruiz de Montoya: Arte Bocabulario Tesoro y Catecismo de la lengua guaraní por Antonio Ruiz de Montoya, publicado nuevamente sin alteración alguna por Julio Platzmann. 4 Bde. Leipzig 1876.

Montoya 1876 b = Antonio Ruiz de Montoya: Arte, Vocabulario y Tesoro de la lengua Guaraní, ò más bien Tupí. Viena. Paris 1876 [XII S. + 510 Sp. Auf dem Titelblatt ohne Angabe des Herausgebers Francisco Adolfo de (Franz Adolph von) Varnhagen, Visconde de Porto Seguro].

Frei Onofre 1795 = [Frei Onofre]: Diccionario Portuguez e Brasiliano. Obra necessaria aos ministros do altar ... por ... Primeira parte. Lisboa 1795.

Frei Onofre 1896 = [Frei Onofre]: O Diccionario anonymo da lingua Geral do Brasil publicado de novo com o seu reverso por Julius Platzmann. Leipzig 1896 [164 S.].

Frei Onofre 1934 = [Frei Onofre]: Diccionario Portuguez-Brasiliano e Brasiliano-Portuguez. Reimpressão integral de edição de 1795, seguida da 2ª parte, até hoje inédita, ordenada e prefaciada por Plínio M[arqués] da Silva Ayrosa. In: Revista do Museu Paulista, São Paulo, 18. 1934, 17—322.

Frei Prazeres 1891 = [Frei Prazeres Maranhão]: Diccionario da língua geral do Brasil. In: Revista do Instituto Histórico do Brasil, Rio de Janeiro, 54. 1891, 1—281 [Verkürzte Ausgabe des „Poranduba Maranhense", 1826, von Frei Prazeres].

Restivo 1722 = P. Paulo Restivo: Vocabulario de la lengua guaraní, compuesto por el P. A. Ruiz de la Compañía de Jesús. Revisto y augmentado por otro religioso de la misma Compañía. En el Pueblo de Santa María la Mayor, 1722.

Restivo 1893 = P. Paulo Restivo: Vocabulario de la lengua guaraní. Lexicon Hispano-Guaranicum inscriptum a Rev. P. Iesuita Paulo Restivo secundum uocabularium Antonii Ruiz de Montoya..., denuo editum et adauctum. Stuttgart 1893 [545 S.; Angabe des Herausgebers Christian Friedrich Seybold nur im Vorwort].

Vocabulário Português-Brasílico 1951 = Vocabulario Português-Brasílico, hrsg. von Plínio Ayrosa, Universidade de São Paulo, Faculdade de Filosofia, Ciências e Letras, Boletim n.º 135 (Série Etnografia e Tupi-Guarani, n.º 21), 1951.

5.2. Wörterbücher des 20. Jahrhunderts

Betts 1981 = LaVera Betts: Dicionário Parintintín-Português, Portugués-Parintintín. Brasília 1981 [326 S.].

Boudin 1978 = Max H. Boudin: Dicionário de tupi moderno (Dialeto tembé-ténêtéhara do alto do rio Gurupi). 2 Bde. São Paulo 1978 [344, 393 S.].

Cadogan 1968 = León Cadogan: Diccionario guayakí-español y español-guayakí. Paris 1968 [VIII, 196 und VII, 30 S.].

Dooley 1982 = Robert A. Dooley: Vocabulário do Guarani. Vocabulário Básico do Guarani Contemporâneo (Dialeto Mbüá do Brasil). Brasília 1982 [322 S.].

Grenand 1989 = Françoise Grenand: Dictionnaire wayãpi-français, Lexique français-wayãpi. Paris 1989 [538 p].

Guasch 1961 = P. Antonio Guasch, S. J.: Diccionario castellano-guaraní y guaraní-castellano. Sintáctico, fraseológico, ideológico. Sevilla ⁴1961 [789 S.].

Hoeller 1932 = P. Fray Alfredo Hoeller (Höller): Guarayo-Deutsches Wörterbuch. Guarayos (Bolivia) 1932.

Jover Peralta/Osuna 1950 = Anselmo Jover Peralta/Tomás Osuna: Diccionario guaraní-español y español-guaraní. Buenos Aires 1950, ³1952. Nachdruck Asunción 1984.

Romano/Cattunar 1916 = P. Santiago Romano/ P. Hermán Cattunar: Diccionario Chiriguano-Español y Español (...). 2 Bände. Tarija (Bolivia) 1916.

Schermair 1958 = P. Fray Anselmo Schermair E.: Vocabulario sirionó-castellano, Innsbruck 1958 [Umschlag 1957] [Innsbrucker Beiträge zur Kulturwissenschaft, Sonderheft 5].

Schermair 1962 = P. Fray Anselmo Schermair E.: Vocabulario castellano-sirionó. Innsbruck 1962 [Innsbrucker Beiträge zur Kulturwissenschaft, Sonderheft 11].

Stradelli 1929 = Ermano Stradelli: Vocabulários da língua geral portuguez-nheêngatú e nheêngatú-portuguez (...). In: Revista do Instituto Histórico e Geográfico Brasileiro (Rio de Janeiro) 104, 158, 9—768.

5.3. Sonstige Literatur

Anchieta 1595 = Pe. José de Anchieta, S. J.: Arte de grammatica da lingoa mais usada na costa do Brasil. Coimbra 1595.

Cadogan 1963 = León Cadogan: Registro de algunas voces internas del 'Tesoro de la lengua guaraní' del P. Antonio Ruiz de Montoya, S. J. In: Bulletin de la Faculté des Lettres. Strasbourg, 3,8. 1963, 517—532.

Dietrich 1984 = Wolf Dietrich: Ruiz de Montoyas Bedeutung für die Erforschung des Guaraní. In: Navicula Tubingensis. Festschrift für Antonio Tovar zum 70. Geburtstag. Tübingen 1984, 89—101.

Edelweiss 1969 = Frederico G. Edelweiss: Estudos tupis e tupi-guaranis. Confrontos e revisões. Rio de Janeiro 1969.

Meliá 1969 = Bartomeu Meliá: La création d'un langage chrétien dans les réductions des guarani au Paraguay. 2 hektogr. Bde. Thèse. Strasbourg, Faculté de Théologie, 1969.

Restivo 1724 = P. Paulo Restivo: Arte de la lengua guaraní. Pueblo de Santa María la Mayor 1724.

Tatevin 1910 = P. Constant Tatevin: La langue tapïhïya dite tupï ou ńeêngatu (belle langue). Grammaire, dictionnaire et textes. Vienne 1910 [Kaiserl. Akademie der Wissenschaften, Schriften der Sprachenkommission, Band II. „Dictionnaire Tupï-Français", S. 99—237].

Tovar 1964 = Antonio Tovar: Español y lenguas indígenas: algunos ejemplos. In: Presente y futuro de la lengua española, II. Madrid 1964, 245—257.

Wolf Dietrich, Münster
(Bundesrepublik Deutschland)

277. Lexicography of Colonial Quechua

1. The Socio-Cultural Context of Colonial Quechua Lexicography
2. Types of Lexicographic Sources
3. Lexicographic Interpretation
4. Major Sources
5. Selected Bibliography

1. The Socio-Cultural Context of Colonial Quechua Lexicography

The lexicography of Quechua languages under Spanish colonial rule (1532—1821) was shaped to meet the needs of colonial priests and administrators. It was a practical, rather than theoretical, activity shaped to meet the requirements of explaining Catholic dogma in a foreign context, and of providing the minimal translations which would serve as a necessary guide to a person who did not speak Quechua as a first language. The imperial

Map 277.1: Departments in which Southern Peruvian Quechua is spoken today

administrative and religious concerns of the earliest lexicographers also explain why the greater part of their work was on Southern Peruvian Quechua, especially as spoken in the Inka capital, Cuzco, to the exclusion of other Quechua languages. For the colonial era, Southern Peruvian Quechua, a member of the Peripheral branch of the Quechua language family (Mannheim 1985, 489—91), is far better documented than other Peripheral Quechua languages, or than the Central Quechua languages. (For a discussion of subgrouping within the Quechua family, see Parker 1963, Torero 1964, and Mannheim 1985.)

The first lexicographers of Quechua might be compared to modern-day ethnographers. They often provided important and subtle insights into the nature of Quechua language and culture; their grammatical and cultural insights have sometimes remained unsurpassed up to the present. On the other hand, they also distorted Quechua terms and cultural patterns by forcing them into Western frameworks. After all, Westerners were the lexicographers' audience. The strongest evidence for both aspects of colonial lexicography is to be found in translations of religious terminology, for it is in the missionizing field that Spain legitimized its presence in America, and it was on the religious front that the Spanish empire encountered the most robust threats to its military, political, and cultural hegemony.

The first impetus for lexicographic work in colonial Peru was standardization of the catechism (Mannheim 1984, 294—95). The wordlist of religious vocabulary appended to the *Doctrina del Tercer Concilio* (1584) and the religious vocabulary scattered through the *Vocabulario* of Gonçález Holguín have proven to be essential sources in understanding colonial and pre-conquest cultural and religious life; they still constitute underutilized sources.

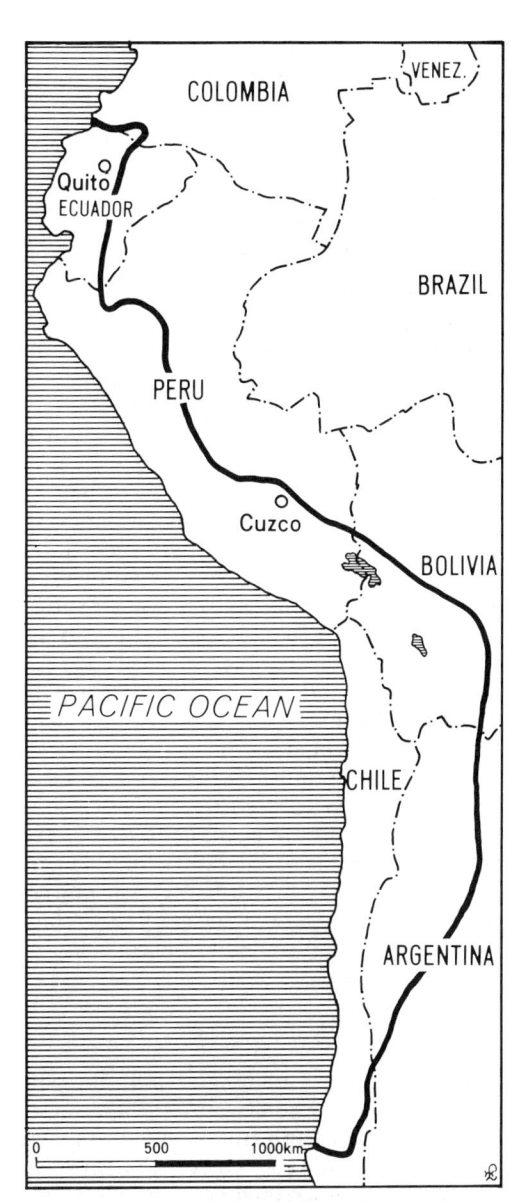

Map 277.2: The Inca Empire at the time of conquest

All of these materials were filtered through the perceptions and scribal practices of Spanish speakers. No colonial Quechua texts were produced by monolingual Quechua speakers, and only a handful (none were lexicographic works) were written by native speakers of Quechua. Because colonial linguistic work was carried out in a foreign language in an *ad hoc* manner, there is no evidence of a scribal tradition, even a Spanish-based one. Every source has its own history and particular orthographic and lexical characteristics. This means that each source requires careful interpretation in its own right. But if there was no direct tradition of lexicographers building on one another's work, their works both reflected and contributed to the development of a vernacular translation tradition between the Quechua languages and Spanish.

2. Types of Lexicographic Sources

2.1. Translation Manuals

Translation manuals were explicitly lexicographic in intent, and frequently appeared as separate volumes, often accompanying a volume of grammar and rhetoric (*gramática* or *arte*). They frequently consisted of stem listings in Quechua with single-word Spanish translations, and Spanish stem-listings with one-word Quechua translations. The best of these was the *Vocabulario* (1608) of the Jesuit Diego de Gonçález Holguín, who understood the complexities of Quechua agglutination, and provided multiple entries for derivative forms from single stems. Gonçález Holguín's lexicon frequently includes a derived and inflected word or phrase in Quechua defined by a phrase in Spanish. Gonçález showed a clear concern for the nuanced differences between Quechua and Spanish lexical and cultural worlds. But even as careful a scholar as Gonçález appears to have been, he based his entries on unsystematic elicitations in both languages, essentially a "card file." The entries sometimes make sense in terms of a Quechua cultural logic, and sometimes make sense in Spanish.

2.2. Specialized Vocabularies

Priests' manuals, grammars, and bureaucratic documents sometimes include short bilingual lexicons appended to the main text. The Doctrina of the Tercer Concilio Limense, for example, includes a religious lexicon in the "annotations" of its *Doctrina Christiana y cathecismo* (1584), along with discussions of dialect variation in the Quechua linguistic family, and of translation difficulties involving grammatical morphology. The *Arte* by Diego de Torres Rubio (1619) includes an appendix discussing kinship terminology, which has proven useful to modern scholars interested in contact-era Quechua social structure (Lounsbury 1978; Zuidema 1977).

2.3. *Ad hoc* Vocabularies

Bureaucratic documents, such as a set of unpublished, early seventeenth century wills from Calca, Cuzco (cf. Mannheim 1988), sometimes included short word lists of Quechua administrative neologisms based on their Spanish equivalents. These neologisms were loan translations, or semantic calques, from the Spanish.

Dictionary excerpt 277.1: Translation manuals: Domingo de Santo Tomás, *Lexicon* (1560)

2.4. Implicit Lexicography

By 'implicit lexicography', I mean the common practice of including native terms and translations in the texts of colonial chronicles of indigenous cultural and religious life. The linguistic quality of these materials is uneven. Those reports which were written by mestizos and others who were in close contact with Quechua speakers, such as the manuscripts by Molina *"el Cuzqueño"*, Santacruz Pachacuti Yamqui Salcamaygua, Guamán Poma, and the anonymous manuscript of Huarochirí are of particular interest.

De los nombres del parentesco.

¶ Curac churi, o vsusi. El hijo o hija mayor del padre.

¶ Sullcachuri, o vsusi. El hijo o hija menor del padre.

¶ Çapay churi, o vsusi. Dize el padre a su hijo, o hija vnicos, y piui churi, o vsusi al hijo, o hija primogenito del.

¶ Assi los llamã el padre y sus hermanos varones no mas q̃ son tios porq̃ los hermanos de su madre llamã a sus sobrinos cõcha, a varones y hẽbras, y los hermanos de padre churi.

¶ Y assi Concha es el sobrino, o sobrina de solos tios varones ora sea hermanos o primos de su madre, q̃ los hermanos de padre les dizen Churi.

¶ Y tambien aqui se distinguẽ assi yumasca churiy, o quiquinchuriy, mi proprio hijo, o engendrado de mi.

¶ Huaoque. Hermano varon de varon, huaoquepura, o huaoquentin dos hermanos, o mas ambos varones.

¶ Curac huauque. Hermano mayor, Sullca hermano menor.

¶ Pana. La hermana del hermano varon. Panantin. El hermano y la hermana.

¶ Huaoquepura, o huaoquentin, Los hermanos varones.

¶ Huaoquentin ñanantin. Los hermanos y las hermanas.

¶ Huaoquentin ñañantinpura. Los hermanos con las hermanas.

¶ Curac huahua. El hijo, o hija mayor de ella.

¶ Sullca huahua. El hijo, o hija menor de ella.

¶ Çapay huahua. Dize la madre a su hijo, o hija vnicos, Piuihuahua El hijo, o hija primogenito della.

¶ Assi los llaman la madre, y sus hermanas, mas tambien estas hermanas de madre con las hermanas y primas de padre y madre llaman a los sobrinos y sobrinas mulla.

¶ Mulla. Son sobrinos y sobrinas de solas las tias mugeres, ora sea hermanas o primas de sus padres, mas las hermanas y primas de madre les dizẽ huahua

¶ Quiquin huahuay, o huachac cahuahuay. Mi proprio hijo o hija nacido de mi.

¶ ñaña. La hermana hembra de otra hembra, ñañapura, o ñañantin Dos o mas hermanas hembras.

¶ Curac ñaña. Hermana mayor. Sullcañaña Hermana menor.

¶ Tora. El hermano de la hermana muger solamente, Toratin la hermana y su hermano.

¶ ñaña pura, o ñañantin. Las hermanas hembras.

¶ Ñañantin huaoquentin. Las hermanas y los hermanos.

¶ ñañantin huaoquentinpura, las hermanas con los hermanos.

¶ Papa

Dictionary excerpt 277.2: Specialized vocabularies: Kinship terms, Gonçález Holguín, *Gramática* (1607) (Nineteenth century reedition)

Dictionary excerpt 277.3: Ad hoc vocabularies: Legal terminology, Anonymous notary, Calca, Cuzco, late sixteenth century

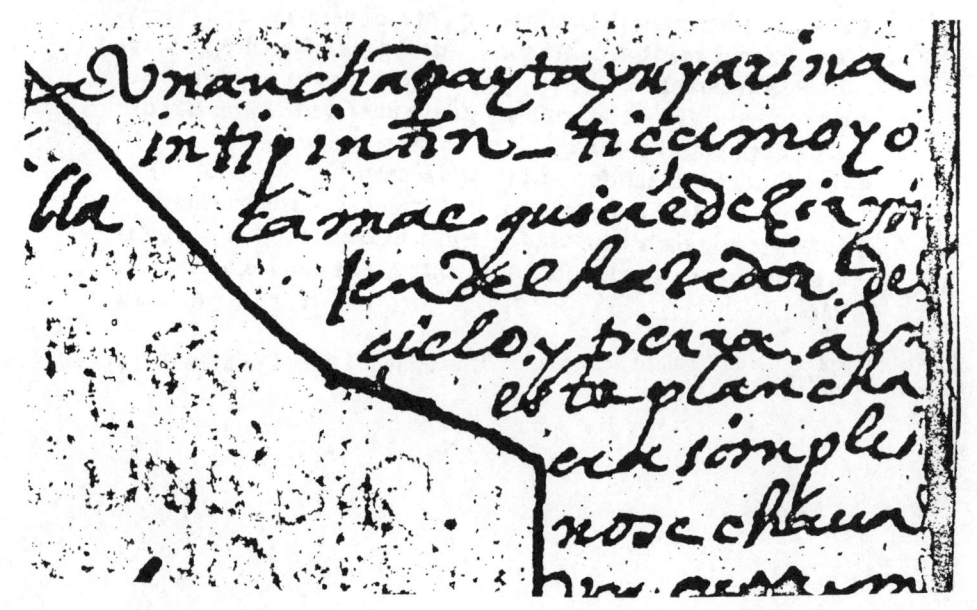

Dictionary excerpt 277.4: Implicit lexicography: Cosmology, Santacruz Pachacuti Yamqui (early seventeenth century)

3. Lexicographic Interpretation

From a lexicographic standpoint, no single source can be used alone or "as is". Apart from the biases introduced by the purposes for which they were written (as translation manuals for Spanish speakers and toward specific politico-religious ends), colonial Quechua lexicographers unconsciously imported the morpho-syntactic typological biases of Spanish such that they assume Quechua word stems are functionally equivalent to those in Spanish. The most frequent entries and translations are single word stems. But the Quechua languages are exceptionally rich in derivational processes, and these give derived forms a precision and breadth not found in Spanish, and conversely, do not allow a one-word translation into Spanish to approximate either the abstractness of the Quechua stem, nor its range of uses. Apart from González Holguín's *Vocabulario*, colonial Quechua lexicography is extremely impoverished as a representation of the lexical richness of Quechua. The same, incidentally, may be said for most contemporary Quechua lexicography. Thus any lexicographic source must be cross-checked against other lexical and cultural sources, especially colonial texts. Also, there are problems of orthographic interpretation. All sources use a Spanish-based orthography, which underdifferentiates Quechua segmental distinctions at critical points. These include the distinction between ejective, aspirate, and plain stops, which are phonemic in some varieties of Southern Peruvian Quechua (including the Inka *koiné*), and the distinction between velar and uvular places of articulation, which are distinctive in most Quechua languages. In addition, during the early colonial period, Spanish was losing a distinction which was also lost in Southern Peruvian Quechua, between apical and dorsal sibilants ($s/\underline{s}$, or orthographic s-ss/z-ç-c, respectively). The sibilant distinction is attested in some colonial sources and not in others (Landerman 1983, Mannheim 1988). I refer to some of the orthographic problems in the short sketches in section 4.

4. Major Sources

This section is restricted to some of the most important and most cited sources. For additional sources, consult the first volume of the four-volume *Bibliographie des langues aymará et kičua* by Rivet and Créqui-Montfort, and Dedenbach-Salazar's excellent study of the vocabulary of agriculture in the earliest lexicographic sources (Dedenbach-Salazar 1985).

4.1. Domingo de Santo Tomás, O. P., *Lexicon* (1560)

Santo Tomás (1499—1570) arrived in Peru in 1540 and spent much of his first five years in America on the coast and in the Central highlands (Porras 1951; Rivet/Créqui-Montfort 1951, 1, 3; Barnadas 1973; Dedenbach-Salazar 1985, 10—15). He quickly rose through the Church hierarchy and emerged as a major spokesman for indigenous autonomy (Murra 1980, xviii, cf. Guamán Poma c. 1615). Santo Tomás's *Grammatica,* and by implication, his Lexicon as well, are reported to have been written by 1550. Santo Tomás spent the five-year period from 1556—1561 in Italy and Spain where he arranged the publication of his *Grammatica* and *Lexicon*. He was named Bishop of Charcas (modern-day Bolivia, northern Argentina, and northern Chile) by Felipe II in 1561.

Santo Tomás worked with informants from both the Central and Peripheral branches of the Quechua language family (Santo Tomás 1951 [1560 b], 15). The *Grammatica* shows Southern inflectional morphology, and both the Central and Peripheral words for 'four', *chuzco* and *tagua,* respectively (Santo Tomás 1560a, 19 r). Entries in the *Lexicon* with sibilants often appear in two forms, an [ʃ]-form, representing Central Quechua pronunciation, and an [s]-form, representing Southern pronunciation. Likewise, Santo Tomás cites both variants of the Peripheral/Central *hamuy ~ xamuy* ([ʃamuy]) lexical shibboleth. Another possible dialectal shibboleth is that Santo Tomás reported a single palatal stop, although it is not clear whether this reflects Spanish orthography or the merger of č̣ > č in most Peripheral languages. Palatal stops spirantize syllable-finally. Dentals appear to be sporadically lenited in the same environment. There is no evidence of the ejectives and aspirates that — exluding Ayacucho Quechua — are characteristic of Southern Quechua. Santo Tomás systematically distinguished dorsal and apical sibilants, {ç} (= [s]) and {s} (= [s̱]), just as other formally educated lexicographers of the sixteenth century did. In less formal lexicography, especially of the third and fourth type enumerated in 3, the sibilants were confused with one another. By the end of the seventeenth century, the distinction was on its way out of Southern Quechua (see Aguilar 1690).

Santo Tomás' *Lexicon* is essentially a listing of stems, with verbs cited in first and second person. By his own admission, the *Grammatica* is an approximation designed for the practical use of Spanish speakers who required rudimentary knowledge of the language for evangelical purposes (Santo Tomás 1951 [1560 b], 14). There is evidence that Santo Tomás over-regularized the inflectional paradigm (Mannheim 1982, 148 ff.).

4.2. Tercer Concilio Limense, *Anotaciones* to the *Doctrina Christiana y cathecismo* (1584)

The linguistic materials designed by the Tercer Concilio Limense were written by committee. The council was concerned with standardization of the catechism and other religious instruction in the vernacular languages, and so charged a committee headed by José de Acosta (c. 1539—1600) with writing an official catechism, cartilla, and sermon collection which were translated into Quechua and Aymara (Rivet/Créqui-Montfort 1951, 1, 10 f.; Vargas Ugarte 1951—1954, 1, 266, 1, 317, 3, 94 ff.; Bartra 1967, 359—72; Mannheim 1984). The *Doctrina* itself consists of a twenty-page *doctrina*, a simple catechism, an extended catechism, and *plática*, all in Quechua, Aymara, and Spanish. A set of annotations explaining points of the orthography and culturally-sensitive translation problems is appended. The Quechua annotations briefly discuss dialect variation and make a point of explaining the inclusive/exclusive distinction in the person system. A short lexicon of religious figures and untranslatable terms follows. Three of the four translators, Alonso de Martínez and Francisco Carrasco, both from Cuzco, and Bartolomé de Santiago, from Arequipa, were speakers of a Cuzco variety of Southern Peruvian Quechua. But the committee complained about the ostentatiousness of Cuzco Quechua and settled on a simplified version by which they hoped the work would be of wider use. Ejectives and aspirates are therefore not marked as such in the orthography though the translators stated that they were writing in the Quechua of Cuzco. The Tercer Concilio clearly distinguished the two sibilants, as did Santo Tomás and Gonçález Holguín.

4.3. Anonymous, *Arte y vocabulario en la lengua general del Peru* (1586)

The anonymous *Vocabulario* is a stem lexicon of Quechua with occasional derived forms and phrases, and phrase translations. Verb stems are cited in the first person. There is a short appendix describing the kinship terminology. The sibilants are distinguished. The *Vocabulario* and the *Arte* which accompanied it in the first edition were published by the printer Antonio Ricardo, who established his printshop in Lima in order to produce the *Doctrina* and *Sermones* of the Tercer Concilio Limense; for this and other reasons, both works are associated with the Tercer Concilio. They appear to be separate works, joined together by the printer. The authorship of the Anonymous *Vocabulario* has been a subject of considerable conjecture, most of which has attempted to associate it with one of the other major lexicographic works in this list, including Santo Tomás' *Lexicon,* Gonçález Holguín's *Vocabulario,* and Torres Rubio's *Arte* (Escobar 1951; Rivet/Créqui-Montfort 1951—1956, 1, 16—18; Dedenbach-Salazar 1985, 18—20). While Gonçález Holguín would probably have been familiar with the work, no attribution of the work apart from a participant in the Tercer Concilio committee appears likely.

4.4. Diego de Gonçález Holguín, S. J., *Vocabulario de la lengua general* (1608)

Gonçalez Holguín (1552—1618) was the best colonial grammarian of Quechua. He was sent to Cuzco shortly after his arrival in Peru in 1581 where he was ordained and where he began his study of Quechua (Porras 1952; Dedenbach-Salazar 1985, 20—23). Gonçález Holguín's linguistic training includes serving as Superior at the Jesuit Aymara language training parish in Juli. The *Vocabulario* has entries for fully inflected and derived Quechua words and phrases along with the usual stem listings and so is a particularly rich cultural source (cf. Golte 1973). Gonçález Holguín's lexicographic methodology appears to have been some form of a "card file" system (see 2.1.). The phrase entries are sometimes loan translations, in both directions, from Spanish to Quechua and from Quechua to Spanish. Therefore, the phrase entries should be used with caution. Gonçález Holguín was an exceptional scholar and observer. His *Gramática y arte nueva* (1607) included a Latinate treatment of the inflectional system, and a detailed, semantically sensitive analysis of the complex verbal derivational system. It ranks with the best linguistic descriptions of a Quechua language for any period.

Gonçález Holguín stated that he was describing the court language of Cuzco. Ejectivity and aspiration are both attested in his orthography, but they are not always distinguished. The sibilants are distinguished clearly. Gonçález Holguín carefully indicated lexical variation in stems, particularly for the sibilants, as in the following entry (325):

Ssecssehuanmi. Tengo comezón. Vease cec cec, y cec cihuan con (ç) pocos lo dizen con (ss).

Along with the stems which Gonçález pointed out were variable, he also lists multiple entries for variable stems, such as *sapsi ~ çapçi, çocco ~ soqos* and *çucçu ~ sucsu.*

4.5. Diego de Torres Rubio, S. J., *Arte de lengua quichua* (1619)

Torres Rubio wrote an important early work on Aymara, as well as the *Arte* of 1619 on Quechua. He was most intimately acquainted with the Quechua of Bolivia, especially the area around Chuquisaca (Dedenbach-Salazar 1985, 23—25). The *Arte* includes a stem vocabulary, and an important discussion of kinship terminology. It can be inferred from the array of kin terms that Torres Rubio's informants were all male.

Note

I am grateful to Dr. Joyce Marcus and Dr. Deborah A. Poole for their comments on an earlier version of this article.

5. Selected Bibliography

5.1. Dictionaries

Anonymous 1586 = Anonymous: Arte y vocabulario en la lengua general del Peru llamada Quichua y en la lengua Española. Lima 1586. Additional editions: Grammatica y vocabulario en la lengua general del Peru llamada Quichua, y en la lengua Española. Seville 1603. Juan Martínez (editor): Vocabulario en la lengua general del Peru llamada Quichua, y en la lengua española. Lima 1604. Arte, y vocabulario en la lengua general del Peru llamada Quichua, y en la lengua española. Lima 1614. G. Escobar R. (editor): Vocabulario y phrasis en la lengua general de los Indios del Perú, llamada Quichua (Dictionary only). Lima 1951. R. Aguilar P. (editor): Gramática quechua y vocabularios. Lima 1970 [Escobar's reedition includes a word-by-word comparison of the four colonial texts. Aguilar's edition revised the orthography].

Gonçález Holguín 1608 = Diego de Gonçález Holguín: Vocabulario de la lengua general de todo el Perú llamada lengua Qquichua o del Inca. Los Reyes 1608 [Modern edition, Lima 1989]

Santo Tomás 1560 a = Domingo de Santo Tomás: Lexicon o vocabulario de la lengua general. Valladolid: Fernández de Cordova 1560 [Facsimile edition, Lima 1951].

Tercer Concilio Provincial 1584 = Tercer Concilio Provincial: Doctrina Christiana y cathecismo para instrucción de los Indios, y de las demás personas que han de ser enseñados en nuestra sancta Fé. Lima 1584 [Modern edition Madrid 1985].

Torres Rubio 1619 = Diego de Torres Rubio: Arte de lengua quichua. Lima 1619 [This may be based on an earlier work, Gramatica y vocabulario en lengua Quichua, Aymara y Española, published in Rome in 1603].

5.2. Other Publications

Aguilar 1690 = Juan de Aguilar M.: Arte de la lengua quichua general de Indios del Perú. Facsimile of holographic manuscript. Tucumán (1939).

Anonymous — Huarochirí = Anonymous: Runa yn.° niscap Machoncuna ñaupa pacha [...] manuscript 3169, ff. 64R—114R, Biblioteca Nacional, Madrid, late 16th—early 17th century. Editions: H. Galante, (1942) De priscorum huaruchiriensium origene et institutis, (transcription, Latin translation, photocopy of most of the manuscript). Madrid. H. Trimborn/A. Kelm, (1967) Francisco de Ávila (transcription, German translation). Berlin. José María Arguedas/Pierre Duviols/Karen Spalding, (1966) Dioses y hombres de Huarochirí (transcription, Spanish translation), Lima. Gerald Taylor, (1980) Rites et traditions de Huarochiri: Manuscrit quechua du début du 17e siècle (transcription, French translation) Paris.

Barnadas 1973 = Josep M. Barnadas: Charcas, orígenes históricos de una sociedad colonial. La Paz 1973.

Bartra 1967 = Enrique Bartra: Los autores del catecismo del Tercer Concilio Limense. In: Mercurio Peruano 52. 1967, 259—372.

Dedenbach-Salazar 1985 = Sabine Dedenbach-Salazar Sáenz: Un aporte a la reconstrucción del vocabulario agrícola de la época incaica. Bonn 1985 (Bonner Amerikanistische Studien 14).

Escobar 1951 = Guillermo Escobar Risco: Introducción [to] Vocabulario y phrasis en la lengua general de los Indios del Perú, llamada Quichua. Lima 1951.

Golte 1973 = Jürgen Golte: El concepto de *sonqo* en el *runa simi* del siglo XVI. In: Indiana 1. 1973, 213—18.

Gonçález Holguín 1607 = Diego de Gonçález Holguín: Gramática y arte nueva de la lengua general de todo el Perú llamada lengua Qquichua o del Inca. Los Reyes 1607.

Guamán Poma c. 1615 = Felipe Guamán Poma de Ayala: El primer nveva coronica i bvẽ gobierno manuscript, c. 1615. Facsimile edition. Paris 1936. Edition by Rolena Adorno/John V. Murra/ Jorge Urioste: Nueva corónica y buen gobierno. México (D. F.) 1980.

Landerman 1983 = Peter Landerman: Las sibilantes castellanas, quechua y aimaras en el siglo xvi: Un enigma tridimensional. In: Rodolfo Cerrón-Palomino (ed.), Aula quechua. Lima 1983, 203—34.

Lounsbury 1978 = Floyd Lounsbury: Aspects du système de parenté inca. In: Annales, e. s. c. 33. 1978, 991—1005.

Mannheim 1982 = Bruce Mannheim: Person, number and inclusivity in two Andean languages. In: Acta Linguistica Hafniensia 17. 1982, 138—154.

Mannheim 1984 = Bruce Mannheim: "Una nación acorralada": Southern Peruvian Quechua language planning and politics in historical perspective. In: Language in Society 13. 1984, 291—309.

Mannheim 1985 = Bruce Mannheim: Southern Peruvian Quechua. In: Harriet E. Manelis Klein/ Louisa A. Stark (eds.), South American Indian languages, retrospect and prospect. Austin 1985, 481—515.

Mannheim 1988 = Bruce Mannheim: On the sibilants of colonial Southern Peruvian Quechua. In: International Journal of American Linguistics 54. 1988, 168—208

Molina (el Cuzqueño) c. 1575 = Cristóbal de Molina (el Cuzqueño): Relación de las fabulas y ritos de los Yngas [...]. Biblioteca Nacional de Madrid, Manuscript 3169, ff. 2—36, c. 1575. Reprinted in: Carlos A. Romero/Horacio Urteaga, Colección de libros y documentos referentes a la historia del Perú (series 1, volume 1). Lima 1916.

Parker 1963 = Gary J. Parker: La clasificación genética de los dialectos quechuas. In: Revista del Museo Nacional 32. 1963, 241—252.

Porras 1951 = Raúl Porras Barrenechea: Prólogo. In: Santo Tomás 1951 [1560 a] reedition.

Porras 1952 = Raúl Porras Barrenechea: Prólogo. In: Gonçález Holguín 1952 [1608].

Rivet/Créqui-Montfort 1951—1956 = Paul Rivet/ Georges de Créqui-Montfort: Bibliographie des langues aymará et kičua. 4 vols. Paris 1951—1956.

Santacruz Pachacuti Yamqui c. 1615 = Juan de Santacruz Pachacuti Yamqui: Relación de antigüedades deste reyno del Piru, manuscript 3169, ff. 132—169. Biblioteca Nacional, Madrid c. 1615.

Santo Tomás 1560 b = Domingo de Santo Tomás: Grammatica o arte de la lengua general de los indios de los reynos del Peru. Valladolid: Fernández de Cordova 1560. Facsimile edition. Lima 1951.

Tercer Concilio Limense 1585 = Tercer Concilio Provincial: Tercero cathecismo y exposición de la doctrina Christiana, por sermones. Lima 1585 (1773 reprint).

Torero 1964 = Alfredo Torero: Los dialectos quechuas. In: Anales Científicos de la Universidad Agraria 2. 1964, 446—478.

Vargas 1951—1954 = Ruben Vargas Ugarte: Concilios Limenses. Lima 1951—1954.

Zuidema 1977 = R. Tom Zuidema: The Inca kinship system. In: Ralph Bolton and Enrique Mayer (eds.), Andean kinship and marriage. Washington 1977, 240—281.

Bruce Mannheim, The University of Michigan, Ann Arbor, Michigan (USA)

278. Aymara Lexicography

1. Jaqi Family of Languages
2. Overview
3. Pre-Linguistic Dictionaries
4. Linguistic Dictionaries
5. Work in Progress
6. Conclusion
7. Selected Bibliography

1. Jaqi Family of Languages

Aymara is a member of the Jaqi family of languages, and is currently spoken by some three and a half million people in the Andes mountains of South America. Aymara is the native language of one third of the population of Bolivia, the major language of Southern Perú, and the native language of northern Chile. The other two extant languages that are members of the Jaqi family, Jaqaru and Kawki, are spoken by a few people in the Yauyos valley of Lima Province, Perú (Hardman 1978) (cf. Map 278.1).

Jaqi was once the dominant language of the Andean region, being the imperial language of the so-called Tiwanaku horizon (400—800 A. D.), extending north through what is today northern Perú and Ecuador and south into what is today Argentina and Chile. Early Aymara was the first language of Inca expansion. Aymara was the second language in importance at the time of the arrival of the Spaniards (Hardman 1985). It was during the colonial period that the languages became contracted to their current distribution in the Yauyos Province of Lima, Perú, and, in the case of Aymara, pushed further south and eliminated in the more northern area around Cuzco.

An excellent review of the linguistic studies of Aymara, focusing primarily on grammars, can be found in Briggs 1985. The primary bibliography of Andean languages is Rivet 1951—6, complete up to date of publication.

2. Overview

After the conquest, Aymara quickly fell from interest, while the Cuzco variety of Quechua grew to

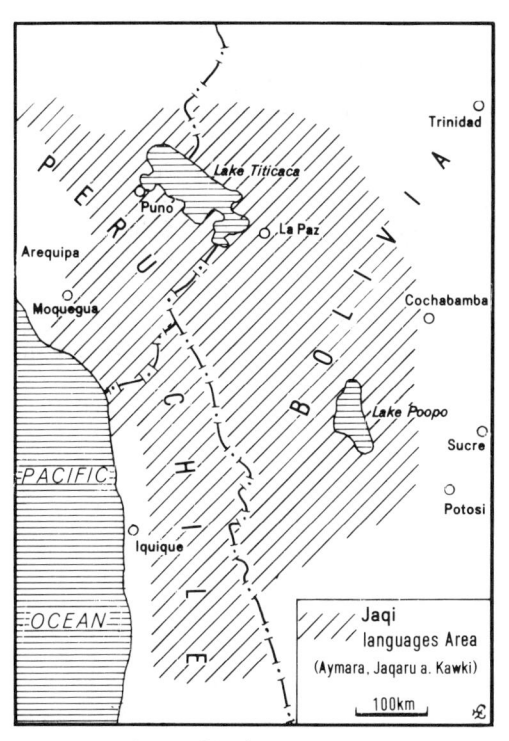

Map 278.1: Areas of Jaqi Language (Aymara, Jaqaru, and Kawki) in Peru, Bolivia, and Chile

monumental proportions. In the early seventeenth century the works that came to be considered the fundamental works, a grammar and a dictionary, were written by a Jesuit priest working in Chucuito on what is now the Peruvian side of Lake Titicaca, Ludovico Bertonio (Bertonio 1603, 1612). These works are only now being superseded, primarily by the work of the Aymara people themselves.

In this overview of Aymara lexicography, given space constraints, we will deal briefly with Bertonio and his followers, and then more extensively with current dictionary efforts, especially those by the Aymara people themselves.

The separation of the dictionaries into the periods of pre-linguistic, linguistic, and Aymara-centered follows the organization suggested in Briggs 1985.

After the initial flurry of activity in the 17th century, there was a dearth of activity until recent times; during 200 years almost nothing was published. In many respects, this loss of interest in the indigenous languages paralleled political interests which were focused on Europe.

3. Pre-Linguistic Dictionaries

Pre-linguistic dictionaries are those traditional works written without the benefit of the techniques of modern linguistic scholarship. These seventeenth-century word lists are useful but need careful reinterpretation in the light of contemporary linguistic scholarship and recent discoveries concerning Aymara language and culture. Many, if not most, of the Aymara terms and sentences given as examples are more or less awkward translations of Spanish rather than native words and expressions. This is not surprising, as Bertonio himself, whose work became the model for all others, indicated in the introduction to his dictionary (Bertonio 1612) that he took his entries from translations of religious texts into Aymara. This work, in addition to being the primary model for all later work also laid the basis for Aymara usages that persist today among native speakers and other persons associated with missionaries; such usages are referred to by certain other native speakers as Missionary Aymara (Briggs 1981).

3.1. Bertonio

Ludovico Bertonio's dictionary, *Vocabulario de la lengua Aymara,* has been the measure of all dictionaries of Aymara, and has itself been reedited and republished a number of times, the most recent being in 1984 (see Bertonio 1612), with two new introductions, one by a Jesuit priest and one by an Aymara speaker. It is still considered the "best" dictionary of Aymara, and is even popularly believed by non-Aymara speakers to be absolutely accurate. Aymara speakers, however, have quite a different view, as seen in a review of this new edition (Yapita 1985 a).

The dictionary itself, for its time and place, is indeed remarkable. It has two sections, Spanish > Aymara and Aymara > Spanish, nearly 400 pages, for approximately 5000 words. Bertonio includes phrases as well as words, and gives example sentences and *observaciones* he believes will be of use to the readers. However, as he himself states, and as is also true for his grammar, he takes his examples from liturgical sources, which means that, at least by the judgement of the Aymara speakers of today, there are serious distortions and ecclesiastical impositions of meaning ignoring Aymara categories (cf. Briggs 1981). For example, he gives *wawachatha* as the word meaning 'to give birth', a term used only for animals, never for humans, thus violating one of the fundamental linguistic postulates of the language (Hardman 1979). In church contexts such a usage would (and did) reinforce the treatment and mutual perceptions imposed by the conquest. The actual form of the word, as cited by Bertonio, is grammatically impossible, as he himself said in his grammar. He writes the words with all underlying vowels added so as not to annoy the reader with what he calls syncope, or vowel dropping. Therefore, very little in the dictionary is immediately usable other than forms that are primarily simple noun roots. Nevertheless, the dictionary is valuable as an historical document, if used carefully, understanding the ethnohistory of the Conquest period and of the Spanish Jesuits of the time.

3.2. Torres Rubio

The other major dictionary of the 17th century is Torres Rubio 1616. It is much smaller than Bertonio, and looks to be very much influenced by Bertonio. The dictionary portion of the small text is basically a word list.

3.3. The *Vocabularios*

Other than the two mentioned above, all other dictionaries up to the twentieth century, of which there were very few, were either copies of Bertonio or very small specialty lists, such as of toponyms, or medicine. These are all listed in Rivet 1951—6 and will not be relisted here.

However, activity in the native languages fell off markedly in the 18th and 19th centuries, more so for Aymara than for Quechua, so that the little that was done tends to be of little interest, either because it is so very little, or because even that mostly consists of copying earlier sources.

The one curiosity is a paperback appearing apparently for the first time in the middle of the 19th century, of about 24 pages, called *Vocabulario de las voces usuales de aymará al castellano y quéchua* (Vocabularios). No authors are ever listed, only the various presses. It has gone through endless versions, some straight copies of each other, some slightly different, each press doing it as they wished. It has varied in size up to 44 pages and has varied slightly in title, mostly to *Catálogo* instead of *Vocabulario*. It is available almost always, in one version or another, at newsstands, and is still being reprinted. This little *Vocabulario* is clearly the most widely disseminated dictionary of the Aymara language. It is a very simple word list with only the most commonly accepted translation tradition glosses. Rivet lists 49 republications. It continues to be published, the most recent republication of which I am personally aware being that of 1971.

3.4. 19th—20th Century

From the late 19th century into the 20th century there has been renewed interest in the Aymara language, primarily by academic foreigners. One of the earliest of this type is Forbes 1880, where dictionary type information is included in an ethnographic report. A more significant early effort which merits comment is Sebeok 1951, which includes Villamor 1940 as well as the material from the early anthropologists in the field, from La Barre, Tschopik, and Pike, as well as his own materials.

Sebeok uses an orthography that is approximately phonetic, but not phonemic. He has included whatever material was available to him. The stated purpose is primarily historical, for comparative use with other languages of the Americas.

Related words are listed as part of the main entry, e.g., there are 12 related words listed under **aka** 'this'; however, the listing of the related words clearly shows no knowledge of the grammar of the language; roots bearing suffixes with highly predictable meanings, like relationals, are treated as entirely different — which is how there come to be, e.g., 12 words based on **aka**. While valuable historically, actual use demands careful reading and interpretation. The main headings are presented in alphabetical order by Aymara only, and are approximately 2000 in number.

Some word lists were included in other studies, some anthropological (La Barre 1959), others in an attempt to prove some historical point or other (Farfán 1955). The anthropological materials are the most useful today to scholars, but are not generally available. The La Barre study, for example, gives some 410 terms related to medicine, illness and medicinal plants, grouped by Linnean terms, with descriptive statements, pictures, and including some excellent comments on borrowing from Aymara into Quechua. The definitions and descriptions are clear and informative. Works intended to be more available are almost entirely missionary efforts, both Protestant (Ross 1958) and Catholic (Ebbing 1965). These works, even when done by people with linguistic training, reflect many of the same design properties as Bertonio, and in many cases owe a great deal to Bertonio.

Other works were produced by people who spoke the language but primarily as members of the (former) landowning class; these works were frequently inspired by those of the 17th century, e.g. Mario Franco Inojosa 1965, citing forms used in Puno, and Miranda 1970, for forms used in La Paz. Both of these are Catholic, and use the Catholic alphabet with 5 vowels and difficult consonantal representation.

4. Linguistic Dictionaries

Linguistic studies are those reflecting contemporary linguistic theory and practice. The first one in this vein is the Protestant one cited above (Ross 1958) which has been reprinted. It uses the CALA alphabet, which is designed to make Aymara look as much like Spanish as possible, even if such an effort makes Aymara difficult to read. For example, the alphabet writes five vowels, even though there are only three phonemic vowels in Aymara. That alphabet also imports all of the European-type inconsistencies in the use of *c, k,* and *qu*. Other similar efforts have been made by, e.g., the Peace Corps, but have not resulted in any lexicographical materials.

4.1. European-Centered

European-centered linguistic studies have given rise to at least two dictionaries, one in Bolivia and one in Perú.

The Bolivian one (de Lucca 1983) is mostly a rewrite of Bertonio.

The cover shows a llama, which, according to the Aymara, shows exactly the intent of the dictionary — to deny the language, and the people, human status. The entire effort is considered higly insulting by all Aymara people, regardless of the author's protestations in the Introduction concerning the importance of valuing the culture. The definitions are universally believed to be poorly done, and quite useless. Because the Aymara are hungry for a good contemporary dictionary, and because there are so many non-Aymara needing a good dictionary (as shown by the active international participation), this dictionary attracted a lot of attention. In fact, the edition of 5000 sold out almost immediately, clearly validating the claim that such a dictionary is needed as never before. The book is nearly 900 pages, with a listing of both Aymara > Spanish and Spanish > Aymara, with a total of approximately 4,500 Aymara words. A large section is given over to Aymara surnames, gleaned from documents of the colonial period. Some regional information is given, but accuracy is a problem. Also, some words are listed separately by gloss, e.g., he gives 36 words for **llevar** 'to carry' and 35 for **andar** 'walk'. The alphabet used is CALA, with all its problems. The entire work is Spanish-focused, and all explanations are in terms of Spanish. He clearly has no notion of Aymara grammar, and gives all root plus suffix combinations as though all were derived, as different vocabulary items, e.g. he gives **aca** 'this, here' with all possible nominal suffixes in a very long entry. All examples are straight Spanish word-for-word translations. The real authorities on Aymara are considered to be the colonial, mainly priestly, documents. In spite of its pretensions, this work is not a dictionary of modern Aymara; it continues all of the errors of early works, incorporates the church view, and ignores all Aymara-centered explanations, e.g. **acchuña** is glossed only as 'producir', but it is, in fact, a non-human verb and cannot take a human subject without derivation, again ignoring one of the most fundamental linguistic postulates of the Aymara language. In fact, more space is given to explaining the Spanish gloss in Spanish of an Aymara item than in giving the Aymara. In some ways the work would be more useful for a study of Andean Spanish.

Aymara people in Bolivia who have serious need of a dictionary, I am told, import the Peruvian one (Büttner 1984), which, while not the best, at least avoids the more egregious errors of this one.

Büttner 1984 was done under the aegis of the German bilingual education project in Puno, Perú.

While done with Büttner as the major decision maker, there was a great deal more input from Aymara people, including some with some knowledge of linguistics. Büttner himself does not know the Aymara grammar particularly well, and in fact misunderstands some very fundamental concepts, as shown not only here but in other publications, but the input not only from his co-author, but from the revision team, has led to the production of a dictionary that is actually useful if limited. The cover, a real inspiration, is of an Aymara weaving. Given the value system of the Aymara, it is hard to think of a better one, unless involving people; it gives no offense and is seen as dignified. The dictionary consists of alphabetical Aymara > Spanish only, 258 pages, for a total of approximately 7,500 words. The alphabet used is a modified Aymara one (see Layme 1980 and below); the difference being the use of **h** instead of " for aspiration; the result is phonemic, but the statement is that they will not be dependent on an Aymara speaker for the alphabet. There is some cross referencing; derived forms are referred to the root; there are occasional example sentences. Synonym listing is remarkably frequent, e.g. *liju* is said to have the synonyms *qaña* and *taqi*. They are all glossed as 'all'; the actual usage is vastly different, however: *liju* is used for grains and other food substances only, and then usually when transference from one container to another is indicated; *taqi,* alone of the three, may be used for people, and implies participation, although it may also be used for things thought of as discrete entities; *q"aña* is unknown to us, and is not otherwise listed in their dictionary, but may be a variant of *q'alpacha* (or *q'ala*), which is also glossed as 'all'; this may be used in almost all of the cases in which *liju* is appropriate, but it may also be used in the non-human contexts where *taqi* could be used, and again, the human/non-human linguistic postulate is ignored, leaving the synonymity as a translation phenomenon rather than being internal to Aymara. The grammatical weakness is seen in grammatical errors in the examples as well. Glosses for the entries are almost always minimal, without significant cultural information. The offset production of the dictionary is quite good; the typescript is well done and quite readable, making the dictionary the most attractive one currently available.

Most interesting, however, is the beginning of real work by Aymara speakers themselves. Inspired by the development of the Aymara alphabet by an Aymara linguist (Yapita 1981), a number of Aymara people have begun the real work of compilation of a dictionary reflecting the actual Aymara language. This is not as simple as it might appear; literate Aymara must frequently overcome Spanish-style thinking learned in school in order to discover their own, but Aymara institutions, such as ILCA and COPLA, have been established to make Aymara studies Aymara-centered. Two fascinating works which came out of this type of scholarly endeavor are Kispi 1974 and P"axsi 1980, 1983 on medicinal herbs in Aymara. It would be interesting to compare these two works with the earlier work by La Barre. Both authors have been working consistently, so that subsequent publications are each time much improved over the preceding. P"axsi 1983 has a paragraph on each herb in Aymara followed by an explanation in Spanish. The paragraphs include such material as how to use the herb, dosage, and for what diseases and/or parts of the body each is good. At the end there is an index to all herbs listed. It is an excellent work, with much detail.

The major efforts today are coming out of ILCA, founded and directed by Juan de Dios Yapita Moya. The literary production of the several thousand associated with ILCA, or working in harmony, is impressive in and of itself. All materials are printed in the Aymara alphabet, also called the phonemic alphabet. Many Aymara intellectuals have associated themselves with ILCA, even though they had begun some work earlier, and continue to work both with and independently of ILCA. One such person is Felix Layme, cited above for his alphabet work, but who has also prepared a dictionary (Layme 1982) as yet unpublished. The work on the alphabet, Layme 1980, contains many short lists of words illustrating Aymara phonemes coming to a total of some 20 pages of word lists by phoneme. Layme 1982 is an Aymara > Spanish Spanish > Aymara dictionary aimed at the Aymara community, with a direct goal of literary use. In a 70 page introduction Layme gives an historical survey of all other dictionary efforts, discussing specifically the purposes of the authors and the alphabets used. Layme also discusses the current revitalization of the Aymara language. The glosses are short definitions with some descriptive material and some dialectal material.

At one time there was a promise of publication; Layme has told me that he made the definitions shorter than he would have preferred under the instructions of the presumptive publisher. This has led to a number of errors of the type made in earlier dictionaries; a fact that Layme himself recognizes. This dictionary, however, contains more words than any previous effort, some 11,000 entries, without the redundancies of considering grammatical formations as separate words.

Yapita himself began dictionary work before founding ILCA, which culminated in the publication of Yapita 1974, a number of years later.

This work is trilingual, Spanish, Aymara, English, listed alphabetically by Spanish. By the three-column page make-up, entries are necessarily limited in size to a word or a short phrase. Importantly, this quite popular work is a statement of Aymara involvement and interest in international affairs and in languages other than the one of conquest. This statement fits very well with Aymara cultural values, including great estimation of the language and the multilingualism of the Aymara businesswomen who act as brokers across language barriers, both Andean and European, in the Andes.

Since the founding of ILCA, there have been three additional works in lexicography, each adding to the other. Yapita 1977 is a brief study and listing of names in Aymara. Yapita et al. 1980 is a more ambitious, if more circumscribed effort, listing words of two syllables only. The list includes nearly 1100 words with excellent and long example phrases, listed in Aymara phonemic order, with an alphabetic index. The work is carefully done, and is a step towards a more complete Aymara dictionary. The work is as yet unpublished, although mimeographed copies are limitedly available to those associated with ILCA. Yapita et al. 1981 is a redoing of his earlier trilingual glossary. This one is phonemically ordered by Aymara, with the number of words starting with each phoneme indicated; entries have been improved, corrected, and, to some extent, expanded. Yapita 1985 b lists 296 verbs, first simple and then derived; only the simple are given Spanish glosses.

A separate effort, partially inspired by ILCA, is that of the Aymara community in Chile. Mamani 1985 is a listing of Aymara toponyms found in northern Chile, presented trilingually, listed alphabetically by the Aymara term, for which is given the current rendering, the etymology or ordinary language form, and glosses in Spanish and English. Included is a very short Aymara > Spanish vocabulary. This publication is part of a larger northern Chile geographical names project, currently mostly in the hands of the author.

5. Work in Progress

A number of projects are currently in progress which promise much more in Aymara lexicography than has previously been available. One such is the Aymara dictionary being prepared in Chile (Mamani in preparation). The emphasis is on the Aymara of Chile; so far nearly four thousand words have been collected. The material is in the Aymara alphabet. A second is the current project at ILCA to produce an Aymara > Aymara dictionary. The young students are gradually accumulating a pool of words that they have defined in their own language. The third major project currently in progress is that of the Aymara Language Materials Program of the University of Florida. In this case, the dictionary is trilingual, but the definitions are aiming at including all relevant cultural material necessary to know how to use the word in Aymara, following, in part at least, the theoretical constructs of Wierzbicka 1985.

6. Conclusion

Up until modern times, the dictionaries have been ad hoc lists, occasionally focused for specific purposes such as medicine. Behind them was the unspoken assumption that languages simply had different terms for identical items. I do not think that Bertonio actually thought that; his dictionary gives much evidence of attempting to cope with differing frames of reference; but his basic orientation was that of changing that frame of reference to the "correct" one, even if he, personally, could appreciate these differences. In the end, his dictionary actually fomented the belief in the one-to-one correlation, by forcing the language into the ecclesiastical mold. Subsequent authors were even more naive in terms of appreciation of alternate lexical structures. Also, all dictionaries have been conceived of in terms of usefulness to outsiders, who either wished to convert and/or exploit the Aymara. At no point was any consideration given to the use an Aymara speaker might have for a dictionary of any kind. In modern times all of the previous statements continue to apply, with very few exceptions. The Layme 1982 dictionary does have the Aymara community as its goal; Yapita 1974 and the word lists published by ILCA are for the Aymara people; the projects currently underway at ILCA and at UF are also taking into account the Aymara audience. Furthermore, except for the toponymics done in Chile and the UF project, all are ad hoc word collections, collected as the authors could, without direct theoretical considerations. This does not detract from their usefulness, particularly given the need for dictionaries, and the dearth of even reasonably useful ones. Particularly in the area of what definitions should look like and what should be included have the works been ad hoc, and it is in this area that the dictionaries are weakest. It is to be hoped that the project currently at UF can move forward the art of multilingual defining, in the framing of definitions such that they take into account what a native speaker must know about the word in order to use it accurately. The activity of Aymara speakers in this and the other projects currently in progress also promises a clearer view of the lexicon of the Aymara language.

7. Selected Bibliography

7.1. Dictionaries

Bertonio 1612 = Ludovico Bertonio: Vocabulario de la lenga Aymara. Juli: Francisco del Canto 1612. Republication noted: La Paz: CERES, IFEA, and MUSEF 1984.

Büttner 1984 = Thomas Büttner/Dionisio Condori Cruz: Diccionario Aymara-Castellano/Arunakan liwru Aymara-Kastillanu. Puno, Perú, INIDE, GTZ 1984 [258 p.].

de Lucca 1983 = Manuel de Lucca D.: Diccionario Aymara. La Paz: CALA (with SIL, Brazil and Norway) 1983 [897 p.].

Ebbing 1965 = Juan Enrique Ebbing: Grammática y diccionario aymara. La Paz 1965.

Farfán 1955 = J. M. B. Farfán: Estudio de un vocabulario de las lenguas quechua, aymara y jaqeuaru. In: Revista del Museo Nacional 24. Lima 1955.

Franco Inojosa 1965 = Mario Franco Inojosa: Breve vocabulario castellano aymara. Puno: Departamento de Integración Cultural de la CORPUNO 1965.

Layme 1982 = Félix Layme Pairumani: Diccionario bilingüe aymara (written 1982; unpublished) [70+417 p.].

Mamani 1985 = Manuel Mamani M.: Ensayo de topónimos más comunes de la primera región de Tarapacá. Arica, Chile: Univ. de Tarapca 1985.

Mamani in prep. = Manuel Mamani M.: Aymara dictionary. In preparation.

Miranda 1970 = Pedro Miranda: Diccionario breve castellano-aymara, aymara-castellano. La Paz 1970.

P"axsi 1980 = Rufino P"axsi Limachi: Vocabulario aymara castellano de enfermedades. Mimeographed 1980 [24 p.].

Ross 1958 = Ellen M. Ross: Diccionario aymaracastellano, castellano-aymara. La Paz: Misión Cristiana Pro-Alfabetización, mimeographed 1958. Reissued La Paz: CALA 1973.

Sebeok 1951 = Thomas A. Sebeok: Materials for an Aymara dictionary. Journal de la Société des Américanistes, n. s. 40. 1951, 89—151.

Torres Rubio 1616 = Diego de Torres Rubio: Arte de la lengua Aymara. Lima 1616. Edition cited: Mario Franco Inojosa, ed. Lima.: LYRSA, 1967.

Villamor 1940 = German G. Villamor: Moderno Vocabulario de Kechua y del Aymara. La Paz 1940.

Vocabularios = Vocabulario de las voces usuales de aymará al castellano y quéchua *or* Catálogo de las voces usuales del aymara con la correspondencia en castellano y quechua. See Rivet 745, etc. Under the second name published La Paz: Gisbert 1953, 1963, 1971.

Yapita 1974 = Juan de Dios Yapita Moya: Vocabulario castellano-inglés-aymara. Oruro, Bolivia: Indicep 1974 [6+76 p.].

Yapita 1977 = Juan de Dios Yapita Moya: Los rios, 24 April 1977.

Yapita et al. 1980 = Juan de Dios Yapita Moya with the committee of Berta Villanueva/Basilia Copana/Teresa Elizabeth Argani Villanueva: Lexicografía Aymara. Unpublished 1980 [132 p.].

Yapita 1981 = Juan de Dios Yapita Moya with the committee of Berta Villanueva/Basilia Copana: Vocabulario aymara inglés castellano. La Paz: ILCA 1981 [27 p.].

7.2. Other Publications

Bertonio 1603 = Ludovico Bertonio: Arte y grammatica muy copiosa de la lengua Aymara. Rome 1603.

Briggs 1981 = Lucy Therina Briggs: Missionary, Patrón, and Radio Aymara. In: Aymara Language in its Cultural and Social Context, ed. M. J. Hardman. Gainesville 1981.

Briggs 1985 = Lucy Therina Briggs: A Critical Survey of the Literature on the Aymara Language. In: South American Indian languages, retrospect and prospect, ed. Harriet E. Manelis Klein/Louisa R. Stark. Austin, Texas 1985.

Forbes 1880 = David Forbes: On Aymara Indians of Bolivia and Peru. Journal of the Ethnological Society of London n. s. 2/13. 1880. 193—305.

Hardman 1978 = Martha J. Hardman: Jaqi: The Linguistic Family. IJAL 44:2: 1978. 146—50.

Hardman 1979 = Martha J. Hardman: Linguistic Postulates and Applied Anthropological Linguistics. In: Papers on Linguistics and Child Language. Ruth Hirsch Weir Memorial Volume, ed. M. J. Hardman/Vladimir Honsa. The Hague 1979.

Hardman 1985 = Martha J. Hardman: The Imperial Languages of the Andes. In: Language of Inequality, eds. Nessa Wolfson/Joan Manes. University of Pennsylvania 1985, 183—193.

Kispi 1974 = Gabino Kispi H.: Aymaranakan q"ichwanakan qullapa. Plantas, yerbas medicinales en nuestros campos. Tiahuanaco: Comisión para la Promoción de la Lengua Aymara (COPLA) y Centro de Servicio Cultural de Tiwanaku 1974.

La Barre 1959 = Weston La Barre: Materia Medica of the Aymara. In: Webla, Vol. XV/1. 1959, 47—99.

Layme 1980 = Félix Layme Pairumani: Desarrollo del alfabeto aymara. La Paz, Bolivia: ILCA 1980.

P"axsi 1983 = Rufino P"axsi Limachi and Mallku Askjani: Medicina andina y popular: medicina natural: Cultura Aymara y Kechua: Mundo Aymar Qullasuyu, Bolivia. La Paz: Industria Graficas 1983.

Rivet 1951—6 = Paul Rivet/Georges de Créqui-Montfort: Bibliographie des langues Aymará et Kiçua. Institut d'ethnologie. 4 vols. Paris 1951—6.

Wierzbicka 1985 = Anna Wierzbicka: Lexicography and Conceptual Analysis. Ann Arbor 1985.

Yapita 1981 = Juan de Dios Yapita Moya: The Aymara Alphabet: Linguistics for Indigenous Communities. In: Aymara Language in its Cultural and Social Context, ed. M. J. Hardman. Gainesville 1981.

Yapita 1985 a = Juan de Dios Yapita Moya: Review of 1984 reprint of Bertonio Dictionary. In: Historia Boliviana 5. 1985, 1—2.

Yapita 1985 b = Juan de Dios Yapita Moya: Estructura morfológica verbal aymara. La Paz: ILCA 1985.

Martha J. Hardman-de-Bautista, University of Florida, Gainesville, Florida (USA)

XXXII. Lexikographie der Einzelsprachen XVI: Die Indianersprachen Amerikas seit ca. 1800
Lexicography of Individual Languages XVI: The Languages of the American Indians From About 1800 On
Lexicographie des langues particulières XVI: Les langues indiennes d'Amérique depuis env. 1800

279. Lexicography of the Languages of the North American Indians

1. The Native Languages of North America
2. Survey of Lexicographic Materials
3. Problems of Lexicography in North American Languages
4. Selected Bibliography

1. The Native Languages of North America

The number and variety of languages indigenous to the North American continent north of Mexico is unparalleled. At the time of white contact there were in excess of 700 languages in 12 major families and about 20 further small families and language isolates. But these languages have always had very small numbers of speakers by comparison with the languages of the rest of the world. Discounting moribund languages, they range in size from a few hundred speakers in the smallest groups up to the largest groups with speakers numbering into the tens of thousands.

The twelve major language families of North America with their general locations are: Eskimo-Aleut, in the Arctic; Athabaskan, in north central Canada and the American southwest; Algic, comprising the Algonquians of the Canadian subarctic, the Great Lakes area, and the American northeast and the Ritwan branch in northern California; Iroquoian in the eastern Great Lakes area and in the southeast; Siouan and Caddoan, on the American plains; Muskogean, in the southeast; Uto-Aztecan, in the Great Basin and southwest extending into California and Mexico; Tanoan, in the southwest; Penutian and Hokan, in California and Oregon; Wakashan and Salishan, in the Pacific northwest. A great amount of controversy surrounds the macro-classification of these languages, but for the purposes of discussing lexicography, the more conservative, if somewhat uneven, classification given here is the most useful.

2. Survey of Lexicographic Materials

Some of the numerous languages of North America are known only through short word lists taken by early missionaries and explorers. Others are documented more fully. The extent of documentation varies greatly from language to language, but for almost every documented language the record includes some sort of wordlist, glossary, lexicon, or dictionary. These vocabularies vary greatly in size — from short wordlists through extensive dictionaries — and in quality — from the ad hoc spellings of the linguistically naïve explorer to the thoroughly accurate transcriptions of talented linguists. Unfortunately, not only is much of the lexicography of North American languages too brief and linguistically uninformed, but a sizeable portion of it exists solely in manuscript or semipublished forms accessible only to the serious scholar. Typical of this condition is Fox, an important Algonquian language aboriginally in Michigan but currently spoken in Iowa and Oklahoma. There are two significant Fox lexicons. One is a semi-published paperbound photocopy of Leonard Bloomfield's notebook, a collation of Fox words from his lexical file, written in his own nearly illegible hand (Bloomfield 1984).

This work is linguistically accurate, but quite short by the standards of general lexicographic practice, ca. 3000 words. A more extensive Fox lexicon is James Geary's lexical file comprising some 10,000 cards in the National Anthropological Archives. This work is completely unpublished (Geary n. d.).

Dictionary excerpt 279.1: Six articles (from: Bloomfield 1984, 80)

There are, however, important published dictionaries for languages from most of the major North American families. Eskimo: *Den Grønlandske Ordbog* (Schultz-Lorentzen 1958), Algonquian: *Dictionary of the Otchipwe Language* (Baraga 1878) and *A Dictionary of the Cree Language* (Faeries 1938), Iroquoian: *Cherokee-English Dictionary* (Feeling 1975) and *Seneca Morphology and Dictionary* (Chafe 1967), Siouan: *Dakota-English Dictionary* (Riggs 1890) and *Crow Word Lists* (Lowie 1960), Athapaskan: *The Navajo Language* (Young/Morgan 1980), and Penutian: *Klamath Dictionary* (Barker 1963), among others. Particularly worthy of mention is the University of California Publications in Linguistics series. It contains many good dictionaries of North American languages.

3. Problems of Lexicography in North American Languages

There are two general sorts of problems found in the practice of lexicography of North American languages — those stemming from limited resources and those stemming from linguistic complexity. The problems of limited resources have to do with the specialized nature of the work and the problems of complexity have to do with the fact that the typological characteristics of many North American languages make it difficult to apply traditional lexicographic approaches. We will deal with these problems in order.

3.1. Problems of Manpower

The field of American Indian linguistics is highly specialized. The number of linguists seriously engaged in their study is small and, at any given time, most languages in this area are not being actively studied. Therefore the resources for producing primary data materials are severely limited.

Because the resources are so limited, much of the lexicographical work on North American languages is produced incidentally to other language work by fieldworkers with little or no formal training in lexicography. Few man-years are spent in producing a lexicon. Thus the dictionaries tend to be small — frequently 3000 entries or less — and tend to display a general quality that is far below that of the lexicography of major world languages. Consider the *Menominee Lexicon* (Bloomfield 1975), an excellent dictionary by the standards of work in North American languages. The articles have few examples, even where they are needed, and almost no fixed expressions. Only about 8000 articles comprise the entire work and there is no English-Menominee section. To the reader's eye the work lacks polish. It is an 8½" × 11" offset reproduction of a typescript, poorly bound in paperback.

The major exceptions to this are some of the dictionaries of the 19th century produced by missionaries, e. g. *Dictionary of the Otchipwe Language* [...] (Baraga 1878) and *Dictionnaire Français-Algonquin* (Lemoine 1909).

With the advent of cheap personal computers it has become possible for a single fieldworker with limited time to produce longer lexicons with a higher quality of production, e. g. *Chippewa-Ottawa-Eastern Ojibwa Dictionary* (Rhodes 1985).

napa·kekew AI, napa·kekɛn II 'he, it is flat in natural shape'; nɛ·pakeket,
  nɛ·pakekɛh; N napa·kekew AN 'flat timber or board'
napa·ko·s (napa·ko·nan) 'raft' 14.363
napo·p (napu·pyan) 'soup, broth'; nena·popem; AN (pl napu·pyak) 'loose woman'
  14.304
napo·pe·hkanɛw TA, napo·pe·hkatam TI 'he makes soup over him, it';
  nena·pope·hkanaw, nena·pope·hkatan 16.86
napu·pi·qsiw TA, napu·pi·qsam TI 'he cooks him, it in soup'; nena·popi·qswaw,
  nena·popi·qsan 16.169

Dictionary excerpt 279.2: Five articles (from: Bloomfield 1975, 143)

Ishpimissagong, adv. Up-stairs, on the upper floor.
Ishpina, (*nind*) (*nan*). I raise or lift him up; p. *esh..nad*.
Ishpinibin. The summer is high, is far advanced; p. *esh. ing*.
Ishpishinog. There is a high heap of objects; p. *eshpishingig*. — *Ishpishinog nobagissagog;* there is a high heap or pile of boards. — Also in the sing.; as: *Ishpishin joniia*, there is a high heap of money.
Ishpissin. There is a high heap, (something heaped up;) p. *eshpissing*. — *Ishpissinon missan;* there is a high heap of wood, (for fuel.)

Dictionary excerpt 279.3: Five articles (from: Baraga 1878, 161)

3.2. Problems of Morphology and Morphophonemics

The languages of North America also present significant problems to the lexicographer due to their typology. They tend to be either polysynthetic or agglutinative. The boundaries between morphemes are frequently obscured by complex morphophonemics, even in inflection. This complexity presents a number of significant problems to the lexicographer, mostly because the potential audience for these works is split between a few highly-trained professional linguists on the one hand and larger numbers of native speakers on the other, many in language revival and language maintenance programs, most of whom have little or no linguistic training. These two groups make very different de-

S 657. -ǰèèh, -ǰééʔ, -ǰàh (12331) (mom.); -ǰèèh, -ǰèʔ, -ǰàh (12331)
  (trans.) 'several move'. Active of S 652.

  657.1 ∅-pr. (n-ipf., n-pf. AI)-∅- (mom.) 'several move along to a
    given point'.
    Base 657.1 preceded by P 9 0-í- 'overtake 0': 'several overtake 0'.
    Base 657.1 preceded by tààh- (1) 'into the water': 'several take a bath, move into the water'.
    Base 657.1 preceded by N 104 táčééh 'sweathouse': 'several take a sweat bath'.
  657.2 0-àà- (P 1) dì- (6) ('away from 0') (y-ipf., y-pf. AI)-∅- (mom.)
    'several run away from 0'.
  657.3 0-àà- (P 1) tį̀į̀h- (1) ('go after 0') (y-ipf., y-pf. AI)-∅- (mom.)
    'several come to attack 0'.

Dictionary excerpt 279.4: Four articles (from: Hoijer 1974, 205)

(315) didishjááh(I), dińdíshjih (déédíshjih)(R), didííjaa'(P), didideeshjih(F), didóshjááh(O)(∅), to put them into or close to the fire (plural objects). Hooghan góne' honiik'aaz. Chizh dilk'is ła' didíjááh, it's chilly in the hogan. Put some juniper sticks on the fire! (*∅jááh: to handle --- plural objects.) (didi-³)

(315) didishjeeh(I), déédíshjah(R), didííłjéé'(P), didideeshjah(F), didóshjeeh(O)(ł), to make a fire, to build a fire, to kindle a fire, to start a fire. Didishjeeh ńt'éé' tsitł'éłí 'ádin lá, I was going to build a fire but I found that I had no matches. (*łjeeh: to cause them to lie --- firewood.) (didi-³)

(315) didishjooł(I), dińdíshjoł (déédíshjoł)(R), didííłjool(P), didideeshjoł(F), didóshjooł(O)(ł), to put it into the fire (or close to the fire) (wool, loose hay, a wig). 'Éechx̨ǫ́'í doo chonáánáot'į́į́' 'át'éhígíí didííłjool, I put the old useless shirt into the fire. (*łjool: to handle --- non-compact matter.) (didi-³)

Dictionary excerpt 279.5: Three articles (from: Young/Morgan 1980, 314)

mands on dictionaries. Two general approaches have been used to cope with them. One approach caters to the linguistically sophisticated audience. Such works contain highly analyzed and often very abstract forms which need to be combined with other morphological material and worked through morphophonemics to produce fully grammatical words. *A Navajo Lexicon* (Hoijer 1974) is an example of this strategy.

The other solution is aimed at a wider audience. The lexicographer chooses a citation form from among the inflected forms — because there is often no natively recognized citation form — and develops an apparatus for indicating how each stem is inflected. *The Navajo Language* (Young/Morgan 1980) is an example. Whole words are listed as citation forms, as excerpt 279.5 shows.

The parenthesized form at the end of each article and the page number in the margin at the lower left cross-index the word with an example paradigm. The paradigm for the articles in excerpt 279.5 is given as excerpt 279.6.

There are drawbacks to each of these general approaches. In practice the analytic approach is often woefully inadequate in that the lexicographer never goes far enough in supplying the constraints on the combinations of morphemes and only rarely addresses the specialized semantics that accrue to certain morphological combinations. Furthermore, even trained linguists who are not specialists in the language or language family in question often have a hard time assembling words correctly, even when an adequate description is provided, because of the amount of morphological and morphophonemic complexity typical of these languages.

The whole word approach has weaknesses in practice, too. It is difficult, particularly for field-workers with little or no lexicographic training and limited resources, to make principled decisions on which forms to include. Most North American languages present the lexicographer with a continuum of types of words from semantically opaque com-

didi-³			YI-		
PERSON	IMPERFECTIVE ∅	ITERATIVE	PERFECTIVE ∅ - Ł	FUTURE	OPTATIVE
1	didish-	dińdísh- / déédísh-	didíí-	didideesh-	didósh-
2	didí-	dińdí- / déédí-	didííní-	dididíí-	didóó-
3o	diidi-	dinéidi- / déédidi-	diidíí-	diididoo-	diidó-
3a	dizhdi-	dinį́zhdí- / déézhdí-	dizhdíí-	dizhdidoo-	dizhdó-
1	didii-	dińdii- / déédii-	didii-	dididii-	didoo-
2	didoh-	dińdóh- / déédóh-	didoo-	dididooh-	didooh-
1	didadii-	dińdadii- / déédadii-	didadii-	didadidii-	didadoo-
2	didadoh-	dińdadoh- / déédadoh-	didadoo-	didadidooh-	didadooh-
3o	dideidi-	dińdeidi- / déédeidi-	dideideez-(s)	dideididoo-	dideidó-
3a	didazhdi-	dińdazhdi- / déédazhdi-	didazhdeez-(s)	didazhdidoo-	didazhdó-
PASS. A	didi-	dińdí- / déédí-	didoo-	dididoo-	didó-
PASS. B REV.	dibidi'di- dińdísh- / déédísh-	dinábidi'di-	dibidi'doo- dińdíí- / déédíí-	dibidi'doo- dińdideesh- / déédideesh-	dibidi'dó- dińdósh- / déédósh-
SEMELIT.	dináádísh-		dináádíí-	dináádideesh-	dináádósh-

Dictionary excerpt 279.6: One paradigm article (from: Young/Morgan 1980, 315) dendewid *vai* be a bullfrog, become a bullfrog, turn into a bullfrog, *Ot*; *pres* ndendew; *cc* e-dendewid, dyendewid.

nden'gom *na* my snot, *CL*; *obv* wden'goman; *loc* nden'goming.

ndengway *ni* my face; *loc* nde=ngyaang, ndengwaang.

ndenig *na* my nostril, *M*, *CL*; *pl* nden'goog; *loc* nden'gong.

ndenniw *ni* my tongue; *loc* ndenni=waang, ndenniwing.

de-pii *ni* sufficient room, *M*, *CL*; *loc* de-pii.

Dictionary excerpt 279.7: Six articles (from: Rhodes 1985, 108)

binations of derivational morphemes to transparently derived forms. On the transparent end of this scale the number of possible words is enormous, being more akin to a catalogue of possible phrases or clauses in Indo-European languages than to a simple list of words. Most lexicographers employing the whole word approach implicitly acknowledge this problem by adding productive morphemes among the citations, e. g. Baraga 1878, or by providing an appendix of morphemes, e. g. Young/Morgan 1980.

Another problem for lexicographers using a whole word approach is found in those languages which have a class of words that require prefixes. For example, in Algonquian languages there are nouns which can only appear with a possessive prefix. Occasionally lexicographers will devote a special section of their work to that word class, thereby avoiding problems in alphabetization that arise from the presence of the obligatory prefixes. In the *Menominee Lexicon* (Bloomfield 1975), for example, the first section is comprised of all nouns that are obligatorily possessed. Another technique to accomodate obligatorily prefixed forms to alphabetization is to alphabetize by the stem and indicate the prefix typographically. Such a technique is used in the *Chippewa-Ottawa-Eastern Ojibwa Dictionary* (Rhodes 1985).

Not all dictionaries of North American languages fall neatly into these two categories. For example there is an approach which supplements an analytic organization of the whole lexicon with hierarchically structured subentries of increasingly complex words containing the citation morpheme. A good example of this is the *Klamath Dictionary* (Barker 1963) in which the layout on the page reflects the structure of the article.

The *Fox-English Lexicon* (Bloomfield 1984) is similarly organized but all the citation forms are full words and the hierarchical structure is indicated by the use of underlining rather than placement on the page.

Some native speakers prefer semantically organized word lists to alphabetically organized dictionaries. The orthographically troubled *Ojibway Language Lexicon* (Johnston 1978) is an example.

One other organizational matter is worth noting. Some dictionaries of Indian languages have been created by using an English or French dictionary as a keyword list and translating each word, regardless of whether there is a corresponding regular native word. Examples of this approach can be found in the *Dictionnaire Français-Algonquin* (Lemoine 1909) and in *The Michif Dictionary* (Laverdure/Allard 1983).

```
ačw    10sv    on the head, hair.  Also  čw.  See Sec. 352.
    ʔičwa  :  /ʔičwa/   puts pl. objs. on the hair, puts oil or grease on
        the hair
            seʔičwa  :  /siʔačwa/   puts on one's own head, hair
        ʔičw!  :  /ʔičo·!/   put on someone's hair!
            seʔičwdk  :  /siʔačo·tk/   having (oil, grease, etc.) on one's own
                head
    nᵉačwa  :  /načwa/   puts a flat obj. on someone's head.  (N.B. Hats
        are treated as flat objects in Klamath.)
            nᵉačwo·la  :  /načwo·la/   takes off someone's hat
        sʼaq̓čwo·la  :  /sʼaq̓čwo·la/   is getting bald
```

Dictionary excerpt 279.8: Article (from: Barker 1963, 42)

Dictionary excerpt 279.9: Article (from: Bloomfield 1984, 65)

4. Selected Bibliography

Baraga 1878 = Frederic J. Baraga: A Dictionary of the Otchipwe Language, explained in English. Parts I and II. 2nd ed. Montréal 1878 [New ed. Minneapolis 1966, repr. 1973. 1st ed. 1858. Part I: 302 p. Part II: vii + 422 p.].

Barker 1963 = M. A. R. Barker: Klamath Dictionary. Berkeley 1963 (University of California Publications in Linguistics, 31) [550 p.].

Bloomfield 1975 = Leonard Bloomfield: Menominee Lexicon. Ed. Charles F. Hockett. Milwaukee 1975 (Milwaukee Public Museum Publications in Anthropology & History, No. 3) [289 p.].

Bloomfield 1984 = Leonard Bloomfield: Fox-English Lexicon. Ed. Charles F. Hockett. New Haven 1984 (Language and Literature Series: Native American Linguistics, I) [119 p.].

Chafe 1967 = Wallace L. Chafe: Seneca Morphology and Dictionary. Washington 1967 (Smithsonian Contributions to Anthropology Volume 4) [126 p.].

Faeries 1938 = R. Faeries: A Dictionary of the Cree Language [...]. Toronto 1938 [based on E. A. Watkins 1865 dictionary. x + 530 p.].

Feeling 1975 = Durbin Feeling: Cherokee-English Dictionary. Ed. William Pulte. Tahlequah, Oklahoma 1975 [xix + 355 p.].

Geary n.d. = James A. Geary: File 4860. National Anthropological Archives. Eighteen total boxes. Five boxes of word slips [ca. 10,000 cards].

Hoijer 1974 = Henry Hoijer: A Navajo Lexicon. Berkeley 1974 (University of California Publications in Linguistics, Vol. 78) [314 p.].

Johnston 1978 = Basil Johnston: Ojibway Language Lexicon. Ottawa 1978 [143 p.].

Laverdure/Allard 1983 = Patline Laverdure/Ida Rose Allard: The Michif Dictionary. Ed. John C. Crawford. Winnipeg 1983 [387 p.].

Lemoine 1909 = Georges Lemoine: Dictionnaire Français-Algonquin. Chicoutimi 1909 [512 p., no pages are numbered past page 258].

Lowie 1960 = Robert H. Lowie: Crow Word Lists. Berkeley 1960 [x + 411 p.].

Rhodes 1985 = Richard A. Rhodes: Chippewa-Ottawa-Eastern Ojibwa Dictionary. Berlin 1985 [liii + 530 p.].

Riggs 1890 = Stephen R. Riggs: A Dakota-English Dictionary. Ed. J. Owen Dorsey. Washington 1890 (Contributions to North American Ethnology, Vol. 7) [x + 665 p.].

Schultz-Lorentzen 1958 = Christian W. Schultz-Lorentzen: Den Grønlandske Ordbog: Grønlandsk-Dansk. Ny Udgave. Danish Packing 1958 [360 p.].

Young/Morgan 1980 = Robert W. Young/William Morgan: The Navajo Language: A Grammar and Colloquial Dictionary. Albuquerque 1980 [1st edition, xxvii + 472 + 1069 p.].

Richard A. Rhodes, University of California, Berkeley, California (USA)

280. Lexicography of the Languages of the Mesoamerican Indians

1. The Nebrija Latin-Spanish Model
2. Early Vocabularies of the S.I.L.
3. Root Dictionaries
4. Recent Dictionaries of the S.I.L.
5. Ethnological Dictionaries
6. The Great Tzotzil Dictionary
7. New Domains Dictionary
8. A Guide to Orthography
9. Lexical-Semantic Relations
10. Selected Bibliography

1. The Nebrija Latin-Spanish Model

The first dictionaries of Mesoamerican Indian languages, done in the 16th and 17th centuries, were heavily influenced by the Latin-Spanish dictionary compiled by Antonio de Nebrija and published in 1492 and the Spanish-Latin dictionary published in 1495 (Nebrija 1981).

Dictionaries done on this model gave special attention to word formation. They grouped together a word and its derivatives and close-knit phrases, e.g.: *Meter, Metido, Metido estar, Metedor, Meter muchas vezes, Meter debaxo de tierra, Metido assi, Metido en el alfora, Metida cosa assi, Metedor tal, Meter debajo del agua, Metido assi.*

The Spanish-Latin dictionary served as a model for the Indian languages. It, or a dictionary patterned after it, served as a word list for other languages. Fray Alonso de Molina acknowledged his debt to Nebrija in his Spanish-Aztec dictionary in 1555, one of the first books published in the New World. In turn, his dictionary served as a word list for Matlatzinca; the copy of the first edition of this dictionary in the library of the Museum of the American Indian in New York City has Matlatzinca equivalents written in throughout by Fray Andrés de Castro during the first two years after its publication. The Gilberti Tarascan dictionary at the New York Public Library has Otomi glosses supplied throughout, representing the speech of a colony of Otomi miners at Tzintzuntzan.

The Mesoamerican Indian dictionaries were far from mere calques on the Nebrija Spanish-Latin dictionary, however, as Miguel León Portilla points out in his introduction to the 1970 reprinting of the Molina Aztec dictionary. Molina explained his choice of possessed noun entry forms for body parts because "the natives never use these nouns without a possessive prefix".

Molina always noted the preterite form in the entry for a verb because of its importance in predicting the rest of the paradigm. Although obviously influenced by Nebrija's Spanish bilingual lexicography, Molina and the compilers of other early dictionaries were sensitive to the unique characteristics of those languages.

Early dictionaries in the Nebrija model include: Aztec (Molina 1555, 1571), Tarascan (Gilberti 1559), Zapotec (Córdoba 1578) and Mixtec (Alvarado 1593).

There have been two recent dictionaries which echo the practice of the 16th century. A Tarascan dictionary was produced by a native speaker who had some training in linguistics from Swadesh and Pike (Velázquez Gallardo 1978). It includes words from all major Tarascan towns, but without identifying the sources. Thus, on the Spanish side there is often a string of Tarascan equivalents with no indication of whether they represent sense discriminations or if they represent geographical variants. It has a wealth of flora and fauna terms, many of them glossed with technical names in Latin. The other modern dictionary in the Nebrija model is the Rarámuri (Tarahumara) dictionary (Brambila 1976). This dictionary also has words collected from all over the Tarahumara area, but again without documenting the source of the words. They are treated as synonyms. It is rich in illustrative phrases and sentences.

2. Early Vocabularies of the S.I.L.

The Summer Institute of Linguistics published a series of vocabularies of Mexican Indian languages in the late 1950's and the 1960's. Some of the vocabularies were fairly extensive, e.g., the Tetelcingo Aztec (Brewer 1962) and the Totontepec Mixe (Schoenhals 1965). Many included sense discriminations and subentries for compounds and derivatives. Some included stem alternants and a few gave part of speech designations.

3. Root Dictionaries

Morris Swadesh promoted the production of dictionaries which would identify the basic morphological elements of a language. The first were done for languages well covered by previous dictionaries and grammars: Classical Aztec (Swadesh/Sancho 1966), Classical Yucatec Mayan (Swadesh/Álvarez/ Bastarrachea 1970), Colonial and Modern Tzotzil (García de León 1971), Tarascan (Swadesh 1969), Ancient Mixtec (Arana and Swadesh 1965), Yaqui-Mayo (Lionnet 1977).

4. Recent Dictionaries of the S.I.L.

Since 1970 the S.I.L. dictionaries have attempted to include the best features of the early vocabularies and add to these the perspective of the Indian users, who are newly literate (Bartholomew/Schoenhals 1983). Entry forms are restricted to full words which can be used by themselves, as opposed to abstract roots or stems which never occur by themselves. For instance, an obligatorily possessed noun would be cited with a possessive prefix and a transitive verb with an obligatory object prefix would be cited with an object prefix. A root dictionary would cite only the root form; some other "linguistic dictionaries" would also favor roots as entry forms. The translation equivalents given as glosses are further defined by the use of illustrative sentences, constructed by native speakers, which place the word in a natural context, both grammatically and culturally. Some of the dictionaries which are in this model are: Chatino (Pride 1970), Papantla Totonac (Aschmann 1973), Xicotepec de Juarez Totonac (Reid/Bishop 1974) Chayuco Mixtec (Pensinger 1974), Chicahuaxtla Triqui (Good 1978), Ch'ol (Aulie 1978), Tzotzil (Delgaty/Ruiz 1978), Copainalá Zoque (Harrison 1981), Huave (Stairs 1981), Oluta Popoluca (Clark 1981), Cuicatec (Anderson 1983), Juárez Zapotec (Nellis 1983), Rayón Zoque [without sentences] (Harrison 1985), San Juan Colorado Mixtec (Stark/Johnson 1986).

All of the dictionaries just listed have some grammatical notes; many have rather complete grammatical sketches.

5. Ethnological Dictionaries

A great deal of interest has been evidenced in the investigation of the folk classification systems in flora and fauna, in numeral shape classifiers, etc. Tzeltal plant classification was studied in detail by Berlin/Breedlove/Raven (1974); Tzeltal fauna was explored by Hunn (1977). Dictionaries produced in Guatemala by the Proyecto Francisco Marroquín include information about folk taxonomies, with cross-referencing between hyperonym and hyponym (Day 1976).

6. The Great Tzotzil Dictionary

This dictionary explored in great depth the lexical resources of the Zinancantan dialect of Tzotzil. Laughlin (1975) used a computer to put together all the possible combinations of consonants and vowels in the canonical patterns for roots and derivational affixes. Next he used the computer to put these elements together in all possible words. He then worked with teams of native speakers to check out which of these possible words were actual Tzotzil words and to determine what they meant. (Cf. al-Khalil, Art. 237.) The dictionary also has a detailed listing of flora and fauna terms.

7. New Domains Dictionary

The Tojolobal dictionary (Lenkersdorf 1979) consciously explores the capacity of the language to talk about the domain of land reform in Mexico. Many of the entries include sense discriminations that developed as the need arose to talk about social justice and land reform.

8. A Guide to Orthography

A Zapotec dictionary (Jiménez Girón 1980) was planned as a guide in the correct writing of the language. The author is a poet who has expressed himself in writing in his mother tongue on many occasions. He includes separate verb entries for each of the three major verb aspects. He also lists many homophones and partial homophones (minimal pairs) even when one of the members of the pair is not the ordinary citation form. This practice is helpful for a user who wants to learn to write his language and needs to learn the symbols for the contrastive phonemes of his language.

9. Lexical-Semantic Relations

The Huichol lexical study (Grimes 1981) makes reference to some 50 lexical-semantic relations (after Mel'chuk and Zholkovskij 1970). It reflects lexical investigation in the field directed toward an internally consistent network of semantic relationships which would permit definitions in the Indian language. For the approximately 5,000 words in his semantic inventory of Huichol, Grimes lists the semantic relations uncovered and includes a detailed cross-reference to related words. A computer was utilized to track down the multitude of cross-references to assure completeness of the circuits. One of the monolingual definitions cited is that for *hablar* (speak, talk): "Mi hermano (= 1) hace un sonido para que otro llegue a saber una cosa por haber oído a mi hermano" (My brother [actant 1] makes a sound so that another comes to know something for having heard my brother).

10. Selected Bibliography

10.1. Dictionaries

Alvarado 1593 = Fray Francisco de Alvarado: Vocabulario en lengua misteca. México 1593 [Facsimile edition 1962, 153 p. + 204 leaves].

Anderson/Concepción 1983 = Richard Anderson/Hilario Concepción R: Diccionario cuicateco. (Serie de Vocabularios y Diccionarios "Mariano Silva y Aceves" 26) México 1983 [802 p.].

Arana/Swadesh 1965 = Evangelina Arana/Mauricio Swadesh: Los elementos del mixteco antiguo. México 1965 [138 p.].

Aschmann 1973 = Herman Pedro Aschmann/Elizabeth D. Aschmann: Diccionario totonaco de Papantla. (Serie de Vocabularios y Diccionarios "Mariano Silva y Aceves" 16) México 1973 [xiii + 268 p.].

Aulie 1978 = Wilbur Aulie/Evelyn W. Aulie con la colaboracion de Cesar Meneses Díaz/Cristobal López Vázquez: Diccionario ch'ol. (Serie de Vocabularios y Diccionarios "Mariano Silva y Aceves" 21) México 1978 [215 p.].

Brambila 1976 = David Brambila: Diccionario rarámuri-castellano (tarahumar). Mexico 1976 [xxii + 614 p.].

Brewer 1962 = Forrest Brewer/Jean G. Brewer: Vocabulario mexicano de Tetelcingo, Morelos. (Serie de Vocabularios y Diccionarios "Mariano Silva y Aceves" 8) México 1962 [vii + 274 p.].

Clark 1981 = Lawrence E. Clark: Diccionario popoluca de Oluta. (Serie de Vocabularios y Diccionarios "Mariano Silva y Aceves" 25) México 1981 [xvii + 162 p.].

Córdoba 1578 = Fray Juan de Córdoba: Vocabulario en lengua zapoteca. México 1578 [Facsimile edition 1942, 432 p.].

Delgaty/Ruiz 1978 = Alfa Hurley viuda de Delgaty y Agustín Ruíz Sánchez: Diccionario tzotzil de San Andrés, con variaciones dialectales. (Serie de Vocabularios y Diccionarios "Mariano Silva y Aceves" 22) México 1978 [xvii + 481 p.].

García de León 1971 = Antonio García de León: Los elementos del tzotzil colonial y moderno. México 1971 [107 p.].

Gilberti 1559 = Fray Maturino Gilberti: Diccionario de la lengua tarasca o de Michoacan. México 1559 [Facsimile edition 1962, 516 p.].

Good 1978 = Claude Good: Diccionario triqui de Chicahuaxtla. (Serie de Vocabularios y Diccionarios "Mariano Silva y Aceves" 20) México 1978 [122 p.].

Grimes 1981 = Joseph E. Grimes et al.: El Huichol: apuntes sobre el léxico. Ithaca, New York 1981 [295 p.].

Harrison/García 1981 = Roy Harrison/Margaret Harrison/Cástulo García H.: Diccionario zoque de Copainalá. (Serie de Vocabularios y Diccionarios "Mariano Silva y Aceves" 23) México 1981 [ix + 489 p.].

Harrison 1985 = Roy Harrison/Margaret Harrison: Vocabulario zoque de Rayón. (Serie de Vocabularios y Diccionarios "Mariano Silva y Aceves" 28) México 1985 [200 p.].

Jiménez Girón 1980 = Eustaquio Jiménez Girón: Guía gráfico fonémica para la escritura y lectura del zapoteco: cómo se escribe el zapoteco de Juchitán. Juchitán, Oaxaca 1980 [155 p.].

Laughlin 1975 = Robert M. Laughlin: The Great Tzotzil Dictionary. Washington 1975 [xii + 598 p.].

Lenkersdorf 1979 = Carlos Lenkersdorf: Diccionario tojolabal-español: idioma mayance de los altos de Chiapas. Mexico 1979 [425 p.].

Lenkersdorf 1981 = Carlos Lenkersdorf: Diccionario español-tojolabal. México 1981 [812 p.].

Lionnet 1977 = Andres Lionnet: Los elementos de la lengua tarahumara. México 1977 [104 p.].

Molina 1555, 1571 = Fray Alonso de Molina: Vocabulario de la lengua castellana y mexicana. Mexico 1555, 1571 [Facsimile edition 1977. Con un estudio preliminar de Miguel León Portilla, xiv + viii + 124 + iv + 164 pp.].

Nebrija 1981 = Antonio de Nebrija: Vocabulario de romance en latín. Transcripción crítica de la edición revisada por el autor (Sevilla 1516) con una introducción de Gerald J. MacDonald. Madrid 1981 [xiv + 200 p.].

Nellis 1983 = Neil Nellis/Jane Goodner Nellis: Diccionario zapoteco de Juárez. (Serie de Vocabularios y Diccionarios "Mariano Silva y Aceves" 27) México 1983 [xxiii + 484 p.].

Pensinger 1974 = Brenda J. Pensinger: Diccionario mixteco de Chayuco. (Serie de Vocabularios y Diccionarios "Mariano Silva y Aceves" 18) México 1974 [xii + 159 p.].

Pride 1970 = Leslie Pride/Kitty Pride: Vocabulario chatino de Tataltepec. (Serie de Vocabularios y Diccionarios "Mariano Silva y Aceves" 15) México 1970 [103 p.].

Reid/Bishop 1974 = Aileen A. Reid/Ruth Bishop: Diccionario totonaco de Xicotepec de Juárez, Puebla. (Serie de Vocabularios y Diccionarios "Mariano Silva y Aceves" 17) México 1974 [xiii + 418 p.].

Schoenhals 1965 = Alvin Schoenhals/Louise Schoenhals: Vocabulario mixe de Totontepec. (Serie de Vocabularios y Diccionarios "Mariano Silva y Aceves" 14) México 1965 [ix + 353 p.].

Stairs 1981 = Glen Stairs/Emily Stairs; Proceso Olivares Oviedo/Tereso Ponce Villanueva, colaboradores principales: Diccionario huave de San Mateo del Mar. (Serie de Vocabularios y Diccionarios "Mariano Silva y Aceves" 24) México 1981 [xxiii + 423 p.].

Stark/Johnson 1986 = Sharon Stark/Audrey Johnson: Diccionario mixteco de San Juan Colorado. (Serie de Vocabularios y Diccionarios "Mariano Silva y Aceves" 29) México 1986 [300 p.].

Swadesh/Alvarez/Bastarrachea 1970 = Mauricio Swadesh/Cristina Alvarez/Juan R. Bastarrachea: Diccionario de elementos del maya yucateco colonial. México 1970 [137 p.].

Swadesh/Sancho 1966 = Mauricio Swadesh/ Magdalena Sancho: Los mil elementos del mexicano clásico. México 1966 [89 p.].

Velázquez Gallardo 1978 = Pablo Velázquez Gallardo: Diccionario de la lengua phorhépecha: español-phorhépecha, phorhépecha-español. México 1978 [226 p.].

10.2. Other Publications

Bartholomew/Schoenhals 1983 = Doris A. Bartholomew/Louise C. Schoenhals: Bilingual Dictionaries for Indigenous Languages. México 1983.

Berlin/Breedlove/Raven 1974 = Brent Berlin/ Dennis E. Breedlove/Peter H. Raven: Principles of Tzeltal Plant Classification. New York 1974.

Day 1976 = Christopher Day: Structural semantics and the Jacaltec dictionary. In: Mayan Linguistics 1. 1976, 19—26.

Hunn 1977 = Eugene S. Hunn: Tzeltal Folk Zoology: The Classification of Discontinuities in Nature. New York 1977.

Mel'chuk/Zholkovskij 1970 = I. A. Mel'chuk/A. K. Zholkovskij: Towards a functioning "meaning-text" model of language. In: Linguistics 56. 1970, 10—47.

*Doris Bartholomew,
Summer Institute of Linguistics,
Ixmiquilpan, Hidalgo (Mexico)*

281. Lexicography of the Languages of the Indians of the Orinoco and Amazon Area

1. Discussion
2. Selected Bibliography

1. Discussion

The vast land area of the second longest river in the world encompasses nine countries and hundreds of languages in the northern part of South America. The Amazon River drains the tropical rain forest, and its dozens of branches are the means of travel and source of food for the nomadic Indians and the forest hunters and gatherers, as well as for the farming Indians. All of the major language families of South America had representatives in the Orinoco and Amazon areas (cf. Map 281.1): Chibchan, Cariban, Tucanoan, Arawakan, Pano-Tacanan, Tupian, and Gê. The Chibchan people are mostly located in the Andean regions; and those languages will be dealt with in the following article. The Gê languages are dealt with in Art. 283. The bibliography of South American languages is now enormous, with an exponential growth in this latter half of the century. The linguistic data have improved significantly during this time, along with the growth of the discipline of linguistics and with entrance into the scholarly community of native speakers who give a more accurate account of their own languages. Thus, the prospects of better theoretical explanations of language structures and change are enhanced for the next century of scholarship. The following listing is a selective representation of available lexicons. Special attention has been given to publications since the widely-known handbooks, which are listed in detail in Key 1979 and Tovar/Larrucea 1984. Except for generally accepted close family units, genetic relationships are not used in this presentation. The languages are presented, roughly, along geographical lines, starting from the north and moving south, where following articles 283 and 284 will pick up and cover the southern part of South America. Major works will be listed here, but the reader should remember that there are many word lists and vocabularies of obscure languages which are available in local research centers of the various countries where the languages are or were spoken. These may be found in series publi-

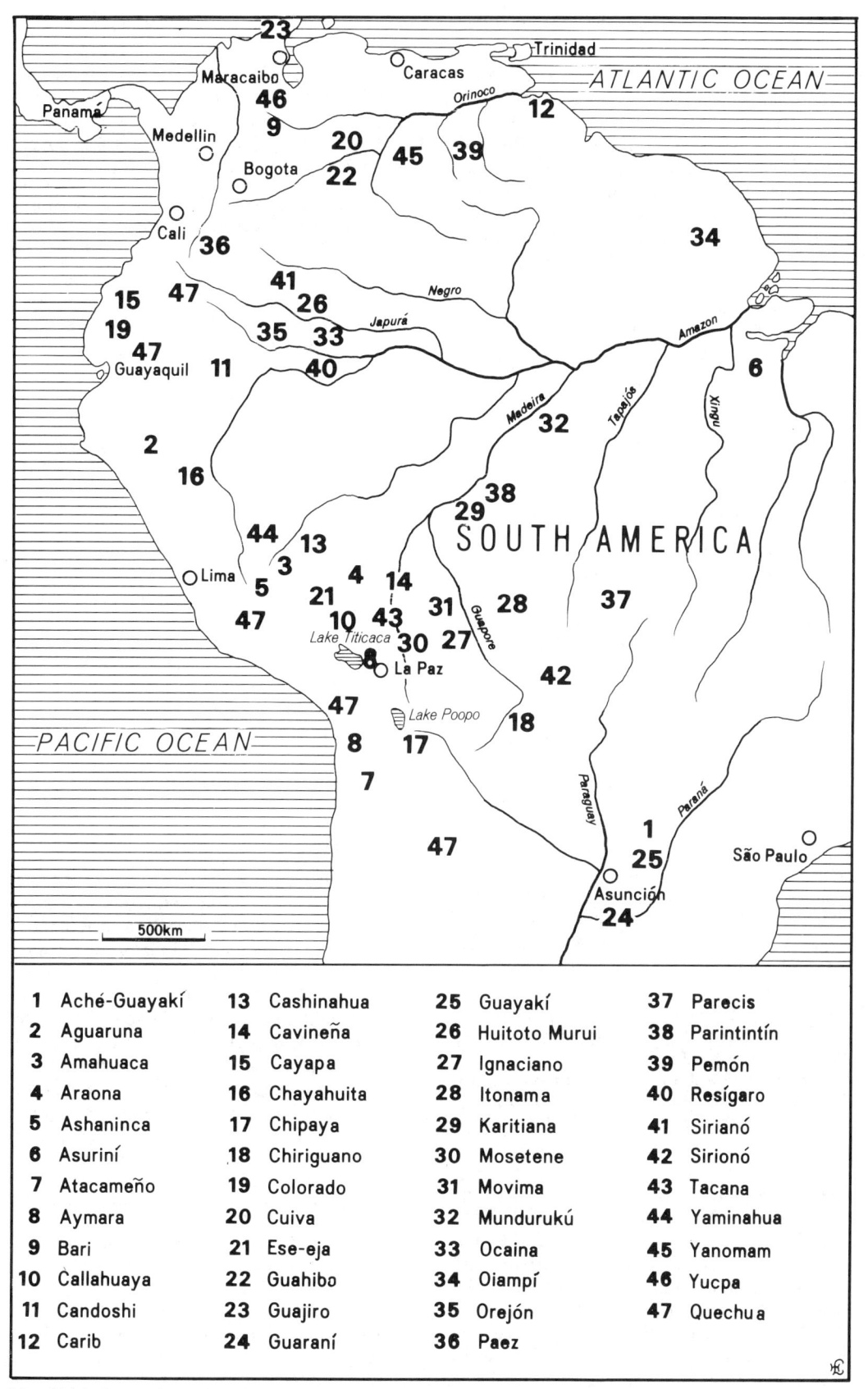

1 Aché-Guayakí	13 Cashinahua	25 Guayakí	37 Parecis
2 Aguaruna	14 Cavineña	26 Huitoto Murui	38 Parintintín
3 Amahuaca	15 Cayapa	27 Ignaciano	39 Pemón
4 Araona	16 Chayahuita	28 Itonama	40 Resígaro
5 Ashaninca	17 Chipaya	29 Karitiana	41 Sirianó
6 Asuriní	18 Chiriguano	30 Mosetene	42 Sirionó
7 Atacameño	19 Colorado	31 Movima	43 Tacana
8 Aymara	20 Cuiva	32 Mundurukú	44 Yaminahua
9 Bari	21 Ese-eja	33 Ocaina	45 Yanomam
10 Callahuaya	22 Guahibo	34 Oiampí	46 Yucpa
11 Candoshi	23 Guajiro	35 Orejón	47 Quechua
12 Carib	24 Guaraní	36 Paez	

Map 281.1: Approximate locations of some South American Indian groups

cations, in local journals of museums, and in private collections. A complete coverage would require a visit to each center. Bibliographies by countries are also useful, as Angel Rivas et al. 1983 and Ortega Ricaurte 1978. Special vocabularies are useful beyond linguistic analyses, in that they indicate something of the culture or the history of a people. Migrations and history are reflected in the toponymy and flora and fauna of the Indian areas, as seen in Drumond/Rocha 1982 and Moncayo Rosales 1983. A medical vocabulary focuses on anatomy and physiology, as in Wise 1978.

2. Selected Bibliography

2.1. General

Angel Rivas/Obregón et al. 1983 = Rafael Angel Rivas/Hugo Obregón/Gladys García Riera/Ramón *Vivas*: Bibliografía sobre las lenguas indígenas de Venezuela. Caracas 1983.

Drumond/Rocha 1982 = Carlos Drumond/Arlinda Rocha Nogueira: Estudo toponímico do Rio Tietê. Anais do Museu Paulista 31. 1982, 59—182.

Key 1979 = Mary Ritchie Key: The grouping of South American Indian languages. Tübingen 1979.

Klein/Stark 1985 = Harriet E. Manelis Klein/Louisa R. Stark, eds.: South American Indian languages. Austin 1985.

Matteson 1972 = Esther Matteson et al.: Comparative studies in Amerindian languages. The Hague 1972.

Moncayo Rosales 1983 = Leonardo Moncayo Rosales: Influencias lingüísticas del Guane en la toponimia, fitonimia y ornitonimia en el español de Santander. Bucaramanga, Colombia 1983.

Ortega Ricaurte 1978 = Carmen Ortega Ricaurte: Los estudios sobre lenguas indígenas de Colombia. Bogotá 1978.

Tovar/Larrucea 1984 = Antonio Tovar/Consuelo Larrucea de Tovar: Catálogo de las lenguas de América del Sur. Madrid 1984.

Wise 1978 = Mary Ruth Wise: Vocablos y expresiones médicos más usuales en veinte idiomas vernáculos peruanos. Yarinacocha, Peru 1978.

2.2. Cariban

The Cariban languages are mostly located in the Guianas and Venezuela along the Caribbean Sea, which took its name from the linguistic family. Small clusters of Cariban languages are found south and west of the main areas, some as far south as the Mato Grosso. The Cariban lexicon included differences in male and female language in the areas where Arawakan people were invaded by the more aggressive Carib groups. These maritime people were known in ancient times for extensive travel and trade, and it is easy to understand why Creole languages are spoken in the areas of the Cariban peoples.

Armalleda/Gutiérrez S. 1981 = Cesáreo de Armalleda/Mariano Gutiérrez S.: Diccionario Pemón. Caracas 1981.

Hoff 1968 = B. J. Hoff: The Carib language. The Hague 1968.

Vegamián 1978 = Félix María de Vegamián: Diccionario ilustrado Yupa-Español. Caracas 1978.

2.3. Tucanoan

The Tucanoan people are known for their multilingualism, and thus this language area lends itself to studies of languages in contact. Tucano is used as a lingua franca.

Anon. 1973 = Anon.: Pequeño diccionario. Museo Etnográfico Miguel Angel Builes, Medellín 1973.

Mountain 1978 = Kathy Mountain: Lista de palabras Swadesh y Rowe. Inst. Lingüístico de Verano, Colombia 1978.

Trujillo/Delgaty et. al. 1980 = Olga Trujillo/Joan Delgaty de Osorio et al.: Vocabulario Siriano y Español. Lomalinda, Colombia 1980.

Velie/Velie 1981 = Daniel Velie/Virginia Velie: Vocabulario Orejón. Yarinacocha, Peru 1981.

Waltz/Wheeler 1972 = Nathan E. Waltz/Alva Wheeler: Proto Tucanoan. In: Matteson 1972, 119—149.

2.4. Arawak

The territory of this group is said to be the most widespread of South American families. The area extends across the northern and western regions of the Amazon basin, and even up into the foothills of the Andes, where the Campa live. The southern groups extend into Bolivia and the Gran Chaco, and to the sources of the Xingu River in Brazil and the Mato Grosso. Because of the affixial nature of these languages, with long strings of short morphemes, they lend themselves to studies of word formation. Also significant are shape morphemes. The largest comparative word list has been gathered by Matteson, with over 1500 entries among the various subgroups.

Allin 1979 = Trevor R. Allin: Vocabulario Resígaro. Ministerio de Educación and Inst. Lingüístico de Verano, Peru 1979.

Kindberg 1980 = Lee Kindberg: Diccionario Ashaninca. Inst. Lingüístico de Verano, Pucallpa, Peru 1980.

Matteson 1972 = In: 2.1.

Ott/Burke de Ott 1983 = Willis Ott/Rebecca Burke de Ott: Diccionario Ignaciano y Castellano. Cochabamba 1983.

Rowan/Rowan 1978 = Orland Rowan/Phyllis Rowan: Dicionário Parecis-Português. Summer Inst. of Linguistics, Brasília 1978.

2.5 Guajiro (Arawak).

Goulet 1981 = Jean-Guy Goulet: The Guajiro kinship system. In: Anthropological Linguistics 23. 1981, 298—325.

Hildebrandt 1963 = Martha Hildebrandt: Diccionario Guajiro-Español. Lenguas Indigenas de Venezuela 2. 1963, 1—273.

Jusayú/Olza 1981 = Miguel Angel Jusayú/Jesús Olza Zubiri: Diccionario de la lengua Guajira. Universidad Católica Andrés Bello, Caracas 1981.

2.6. Bora-Huitotoan

The Bora language is a tone language, which carries tone on each syllable. This is the basis for the signaling system with drums carrying varying pitches.

Burtch 1983 = Shirley Burtch: Diccionario Huitoto Murui. Inst. Lingüístico de Verano, Yarinacocha, Peru 1983.

Leach 1969 = Ilo M. Leach: Vocabulario Ocaina. Inst. Lingüístico de Verano, Yarinacocha, Peru 1969.

2.7. Jivaroan/Shuar

Larson 1966 = Mildred L. Larson: Vocabulario Aguaruna de Amazonas. Inst. Lingüístico de Verano, Peru 1966.

Tuggy 1966 = John Tuggy: Vocabulario Candoshi de Loreto. Inst. Lingüístico de Verano, Peru 1966.

2.8. Pano-Tacanan

The Panoan languages are spoken along the Ucayali River in Peru and across the border into Brazil and Bolivia. The Tacanan languages also overlap borders, but are spoken mainly in Bolivia, in the northern area along the Madidi and Beni Rivers, up into the foothills of the Andes bordering the Andean languages. Lexicons are available for both these families, starting with excellent materials for the Tacanan languages done in the previous century by missionaries, in particular Bishop Armentia. Two large comparative studies bring together a substantial array of cognate sets, with over 500 sets in Panoan (Shell 1965) and about 700 sets that include both Panoan and Tacanan (Key 1968 [1963]).

D'Ans 1972 = André-Marcel D'Ans: Léxico Yaminahua. Universidad Nacional Mayor de San Marcos, Peru 1972.

Armentia 1902 = Nicolás Armentia: Arte y vocabulario de la lengua Takana. In: Revista del Museo de La Plata 10. 1902, 63—172, 283—312.

Armentia 1906 = Nicolás Armentia: Arte y vocabulario de la lengua Cavineña. In: Revista del Museo de La Plata 13. 1906, 1—120.

Chavarría M. 1980 = María C. Chavarría Mendoza: Léxico Ese-eja-Español. Universidad Nacional Mayor de San Marcos, Peru 1980.

Hyde/Russell et. al. 1980 = Sylvia Hyde/Robert Russell/Delores Russell/María Consuelo de Rivera: Diccionario Amahuaca. Inst. Lingüístico de Verano, Yarinacocha 1980.

Key 1968 = Mary Ritchie Key: Comparative Tacanan phonology: with Cavineña phonology and notes on Pano-Tacanan relationship. The Hague 1968.

Montag 1981 = Susan Montag: Diccionario Cashinahua. Inst. Lingüístico de Verano, Yarinacocha 1981.

Pitman 1981 = Mary de Pitman: Diccionario Araona y Castellano. Riberalta, Bolivia 1981.

Shell 1965 = Olive Shell: Pano reconstruction. University of Pennsylvania Dissertation. 1965.

2.9. Mosetene

Armentia 1901—1902 = Nicolás Armentia: Los indios Mosetenes y su lengua. In: Anales de la Sociedad Científica Argentina 52—54. Buenos Aires 1901—1902.

Bibolotti 1917 = Benigno Bibolotti: Moseteno vocabulary and treatises. Evanston, Illinois 1917.

2.10. Itonama

Camp/Liccardi 1967 = Elizabeth Camp/Millicent Liccardi: Itonama: Castellano e Inglés. Riberalta, Bolivia 1967.

2.11. Movima

Judy/Judy 1962 = Roberto Judy/Judit Emerich de Judy: Movima y Castellano. Cochabamba, Bolivia 1962.

2.12. Tupian/Guaranian

Most of the Tupian languages are spoken south of the Amazon River down into Paraguay, with a couple of exceptions in French Guiana: Emerillon and Oyampi. Cocama, in Peru, is the farthermost western representative of the family. Guaraní is noted for being a dominant language in Paraguay, where the country is significantly bilingual with Spanish. Tupinambá is known for being the lingua franca along the Atlantic coast.

Betts 1981 = La Vera Betts: Dicionário Parintintín-Português. Summer Institute of Linguistics, Brasília 1981.

Caldas 1984 = Luis Caldas Tibiriçá: Dicionário Tupi-Português. Liberdade, S. P. 1984.
Crofts 1981 = Marjorie Crofts: Dicionário bilíngüe em Português e Munduruku. Summer Institute of Linguistics. Brasília 1981.
Dietrich 1986 = Wolf Dietrich: El idioma Chiriguano. Madrid 1986.
Gómez Perasso 1975 = J. A. Gómez Perasso: Vocabulario Aché-Guayakí. In: Antropológico 10 (Supplement). 1975, 93—134.
Guasch 1981 = Antonio Guasch: Diccionario Castellano-Guaraní (revised). Asunción 1981.
Landin 1983 = David Landin: Dicionário e léxico: Karitiana/Português. Summer Institute of Linguistics, Brasília 1983.
Lemle 1971 = Miriam Lemle: Internal classification of the Tupi-Guarani linguistic family. In: Tupi Studies I, Summer Institute of Linguistics. 1971, 107—129.
Nicholson 1982 = Velda Nicholson: Breve estudo da língua Asuriní do Xingu. Summer Institute of Linguistics, Brasília 1982.
Olson 1978 = Roberta Olson: Dicionário por tópicos nas línguas Oiampi (Wajapï)-Português. Summer Institute of Linguistics, Brasília 1978.
Rodrigues 1985 = Aryon D. Rodrigues: Evidence for Tupi-Carib relationships. In: Klein/Stark 1985, 371—404.
Schermair 1962 = Anselmo Schermair: Vocabulario Castellano-Sirionó. Innsbruck 1962.
Silveira Bueno 1983 = Francisco da Silveira Bueno: Vocabulário Tupi-Guaraní: Português. São Paulo 1983.

Susnik 1974 = Branislava Susnik: Estudios Guayakí: vocabulario Ače. Asunción 1974.

2.13. Guahiban

Christian/Matteson 1972 = Diana R. Christian/ Esther Matteson: Proto Guahiban. In: Matteson 1972, 150—159.
Ortiz/Queixalos 1981 = Francisco Ortiz/Francisco Queixalos: Ornitología Cuiva-Guahibo. In: Amerindia 6. 1981, 125—147.

2.14. Bari

Lizarralde 1976 = Roberto Lizarralde: Vocabulario Bari. In: Boletín Bibliográfico de Antropología Americana 38. Mexico 1976, 207—215.
Villamañán 1978 = Adolfo de Villamañán: Vocabulario Barí comparado. Universidad Católica Andrés Bello, 1978.

2.15. Cahuapanan

Hart 1988 = Helen Long Hart: Diccionario Chayahuita-Castellano. Yarinacocha, Pucallpa 1988.

2.16. Yanomamɨ

Lizot 1975 = Jacques Lizot: Diccionario Yanomamɨ-Español. Caracas 1975.

Mary Ritchie Key, University of California, Irvine, California (USA)

282. Lexicography of the Languages of the Andean Indians

1. Discussion
2. Selected Bibliography

1. Introduction

The South American languages which follow the coast line along the great range of the Andes are, of course, among the earliest recorded. The lexical material of the early centuries, however, was sparse. Today, after almost four centuries of documenting these non-Western languages, there is an abundance to give linguistic studies a better perspective for theory and to correct the distortions that scholars in previous centuries held about the languages and cultures of non-European peoples. The resources for historical and comparative studies are plentiful. Documentation is not complete by any means, and dictionary-making must be encouraged as much as possible before the languages are lost forever. The Inca culture dominated the discussions of South American peoples because of its greatness, which can be described only in superlatives. This discussion begins with the Quechuan languages along the Andes of the central part of South America; other Andean languages will be taken up on a geographical route both south and north of the Quechua territory. Some word lists which were presented for comparative purposes are included here along with descriptive-type dictionaries. The relationships which were proposed in the comparative studies may or may not be proved eventually, but the word lists are valuable in that they contain raw data which might not be available in other form. The comparative word lists are of value because the linguists who made the studies are experts in the languages and have sorted and sifted the vocabulary to find basic, core items. The loanwords have been sifted out, or identified; further, the word lists may have been retrieved from publications which are difficult to locate, or they may be taken from unpublished materials. Because of the limitations which are necessarily imposed here, bibliographical material from Rivet/Créqui-Montfort 1952—56 and the handbooks of South American languages is not repeated. Rather, the emphasis is on recent publications. Other recent bibliographical material is available in Key 1979, Klein/Stark 1985, and Tovar/Larrucea 1984. The rich display of dialect material has opened up discussions of differences of dialect or different Quechuan languages and other important matters of language change. Special mention should be made of the series of Quechua dictionaries edited by Alberto Escobar Zambrano at the Instituto de Estudios Peruanos. Topical vocabularies such as Valda 1972, give information on the culture and industries (e. g. wool, pottery) of the people. A particular study done at the University of St. Andrews, Scotland, is a model for future work, with the availability of good dictionaries. This study focuses on the word 'heart' *sonqo* in Quechua, with word formation and meaning relationships examined (Dedenbach 1979). Difficult-to-locate vocabulary of the Callahuaya, Chipaya, Haquearu, Quechua and Aymara languages has been assembled in word lists in Büttner 1983.

2. Selected Bibliography

2.1. General

Büttner 1983 = Thomas Th. Büttner: Las lenguas de los Andes Centrales. Madrid 1983.

Dedenbach [1979] = Sabine Dedenbach: "The lexical unit *sonqo* 'heart', its derivatives and compounds: use and treatment in the Quechua dictionaries". University of St. Andrews [1979].

Key 1979 = Mary Ritchie Key: The grouping of South American Indian languages. Tübingen 1979.

Klein/Stark 1985 = Harriet E. Manelis Klein/Louisa R. Stark, eds.: South American Indian languages. Austin 1985.

Rivet/Créqui-Montfort 1952—1956 = Paul Rivet/Georges de Créqui-Montfort: Bibliographie des langues Aymará et Kičua. Paris 1952—1956.

Tovar/Larrucea 1984 = Antonio Tovar/Consuelo Larrucea de Tovar: Catálogo de las lenguas de América del Sur. Madrid 1984.

Valda 1972 = Luisa Valda de Jaimes Freyre: Cultura Aymara en La Paz. La Paz, Bolivia 1972.

2.2. Quechuan

Adelaar 1977 = Willem F. H. Adelaar: Tarma Quechua. Lisse 1977.

Bravo 1977 = Domingo Bravo: Diccionario Castellano-Quichua Santiagueño. Buenos Aires 1977.

Cerrón-Palomino 1976 = Rodolfo Cerrón-Palomino: Diccionario Quechua: Junín-Huanca. Inst. de Estudios Peruanos 1976.

Cusihuamán 1976 = Antonio Cusihuamán Gutiérrez: Diccionario Quechua: Cuzco-Collao. Inst. de Estudios Peruanos 1976.

Landerman 1973 = Peter Landerman: Vocabulario Quechua del Pastaza. Yarinacocha, Peru 1973.

Lara 1978 = Jesús Lara: Diccionario Qheshwa-Castellano. La Paz, Bolivia 1978.

Levinsohn/Galeano 1981 = Stephen H. Levinsohn/Luis G. Galeano L.: Inga Yachaycusunchi. Universidad de Nariño, Pasto, Colombia 1981.

Orr 1978 = Carolyn Orr: Dialectos Quichuas del Ecuador. Quito 1978.

Orr/Longacre 1968 = Carolyn Orr/Robert E. Longacre: Proto-Quechumaran. In: Language 44. 1968, 528—555.

Orr/Wrisley 1965 = Carolyn Orr/Betsy Wrisley: Vocabulario Quichua del Oriente del Ecuador. Inst. Lingüístico de Verano, Quito 1965 [1981].

Park/Weber/Cenepo 1976 = Marinell Park/Nancy Weber/Victor Cenepo Sangamá: Diccionario Quechua: San Martín. Inst. de Estudios Peruanos 1976.

Parker/Chávez 1976 = Gary J. Parker/Amancio Chávez: Diccionario Quechua: Ancash-Huailas. Inst. de Estudios Peruanos 1976.

Perroud/Chouvenc 1970 = Pedro Clemente Perroud/Juan María Chouvenc: Diccionario Castellano Kechwa: dialecto de Ayacucho. Lima 1970.

Plaza/Quiroz 1979 = Pedro Plaza Martínez/Alfredo Quiroz V.: Diccionario Quechua-Castellano. Inst. Nacional de Estudios Lingüísticos, La Paz 1979.

Quesada 1976 = Félix Quesada C.: Diccionario Quechua: Cajamarca-Cañaris. Inst. de Estudios Peruanos 1976.

Quiroga 1979 = Miguel Angel Quiroga: Diccionario Kollasuyano Español-Quechua. Cochabamba, Bolivia 1979.

Soto 1976 = Clodoaldo Soto Ruiz: Diccionario Quechua: Ayacucho-Chanca. Inst. de Estudios Peruanos 1976.

Tandioy/Levinsohn/Maffla 1978 = Domingo Tandioy Chasoy/Stephen H. Levinsohn/Alonso Maffla Bilbao: Diccionario Inga del Valle de Sibundoy. Lomalinda, Colombia 1978.

Taylor 1979 = Gerald Taylor: Diccionario normalizado y comparativo Quechua: Chachapoyas-Lamas. Paris 1979.

2.3. Aymaran/Jaqaru

Büttner/Condori/et. al. 1984 = Thomas Büttner/ Dionisio Condori Cruz/et. al.: Diccionario Aymara-Castellano. Puno, Peru 1984.

Clair-Vasiliadis 1976 = Christos Clair-Vasiliadis [Clairis]: Esquisse phonologique de l'Aymara parlé au Chili. In: La Linguistique 12. 1976, 143—152.

Cotari/Mejía/Carrasco 1978 = Daniel Cotari/ Jaime Mejía/Victor Carrasco: Diccionario Aymara-Castellano. Inst. de Idiomas, Padres de Maryknoll, Cochabamba, Bolivia 1978.

Ebbing 1965 = Juan Enrique Ebbing: Gramática y diccionario Aimará. La Paz 1965.

Hardman 1978 = Martha J. Hardman-de-Bautista: Jaqui: the linguistic family. In: International Journal of American Linguistics 44. 1978, 146—153.

Miranda 1970 = Pedro Miranda S.: Diccionario breve Castellano-Aymara. La Paz 1970.

Ross 1957 = Elena M. Ross: Diccionario Castellano-Aymara. La Paz 1957.

Sebeok 1951 = Thomas A. Sebeok: Materials for an Aymara dictionary. In: Journal de la Société des Américanistes 40. 1951, 89—151.

Yapita 1981 = Juan de Dios Yapita: Vocabulario Aymara-Inglés-Castellano. La Paz 1981.

2.4. Chipaya

The Chipaya people live in the barren altiplano of Bolivia, at extreme altitudes. The lexical items display an unusually high percentage of loan words, about a third of the Chipaya lexicon.

Olson 1965 = Ronald D. Olson: Mayan affinities with Chipaya of Bolivia II: cognates. In: International Journal of American Linguistics 31. 1965, 29—38.

2.5. Callahuaya

Oblitas 1955 = Enrique Oblitas Poblete: El Machchaj-juyai o idioma Callawaya. In: Khana 5. La Paz 1955, 122—129.

Stark 1972 = Louisa R. Stark: Machaj-juyai: secret language of the Callahuayas. In: Papers in Andean Linguistics 1. 1972, 199—227.

2.6. Atacameño/Cunza

The Cunza language was spoken in the barren desert in northern Chile. It is now extinct. Scholars at the Universidad Católica de Valparaiso have brought together the vocabularies in a computer data-base.

Saez 1974 = Leopoldo Saez Godoy: Diccionario Español-Kunsa: Kunsa-Español. Universidad Católica de Valparaiso, Computer printout. 1974.

2.7. Chibchan

The Chibchan languages connect North and South America. In Colombia the Muisca people had a highly developed culture and the goldwork of their artifacts is a marvel to behold. Extensive trade undoubtedly spread linguistic examples throughout their market areas.

González 1980 = María Stella González de Pérez: Trayectoria de los estudios sobre la lengua Chibcha o Muisca. Bogotá 1980.

Slocum/Gerdel 1983 = Marianna C. Slocum/ Florence L. Gerdel: Diccionario Páez-Español. Lomalinda, Colombia 1983.

Wheeler 1972 = Alva Wheeler: Proto Chibchan. In: Esther Matteson et. al.: Comparative studies in Amerindian languages. The Hague 1972, 93—108.

2.8. Barbacoan

The Barbacoan languages are located along the Ecuadorian coastal jungle. The Cayapa people live in high houses on stilts and travel mainly by river.

Lindskoog/Lindskoog 1964 = John N. Lindskoog/Carrie A. Lindskoog: Vocabulario Cayapa. Inst. Lingüístico de Verano, Quito 1964.

Moore 1966 = Bruce R. Moore: Diccionario Castellano-Colorado. Inst. Lingüístico de Verano, Quito 1966.

Mary Ritchie Key, *University of California, Irvine California (USA)*

283. Lexicography of the Indian Languages of Southern Brazil and the Rio de la Plata Region

1. Discussion
2. Selected Bibliography

1. Discussion

The geographic scope of this article is the area between the southernmost branches of the Amazon River in Brazil and the Rio de la Plata in Argentina. It includes therefore the indigenous languages (except for Tupian and Arawakan, see art. 281) spoken in the states of São Paulo, Parana, Santa Catarina, Rio Grande do Sul, Minas Gerais, Mato Grosso and Mato Grosso du Sul in Brazil, as well as those spoken in the Gran Chaco region of Paraguay, Bolivia and Argentina. These languages have been mentioned in the literature as far back as the 16th century and vocabularies and dictionaries have been produced from that time to the present.

For the area where the Jesuits built their missions, lexicographical materials are readily available (e.g. Bárcena 1893 in sect. 2.7., Machoni de Cerdeña 1732 in 2.9.). The earliest word lists we have are based on voyages of missionaries in the 16th century. By the end of the 17th century there were quite a few vocabularies; by the end of the 18th there were attempts to group languages along lines of lexical similarity. From the end of the 18th to the end of the 19th centuries many language catalogues, vocabularies and partial grammars had been produced (e.g. *Martius 1867* in 2.2.). By the end of the 19th century, classification of South American Indian languages began in earnest; however, it was based for most languages on short word lists and for comparative purposes is insufficient. The result of subsequent classificatory works, in which relationship and grouping have been postulated only on lexical comparisons of resemblant forms and presumed cognates, has been large scale tentative classifications of doubtful validity. Today the situation is quite different. Vocabularies and dictionaries can be found for most languages, although all are not of equal quality. Probably the most important comment to make on contemporary lexicography for this area is that there is less of it: scholars are more intent on describing and analyzing the languages than they are on compiling word lists. Thus for many languages in this region, contemporary lexicographical citations are lacking. The recent works cited in the general section (2.1.) cover such issues as language distribution, classification, and contain significant bibliographies. For the language families or stocks, the citations tend to be recent; however, there are some earlier ones that are representative of dictionaries of different epochs which deserve special mention. The presentation of the bibliography begins with general works (2.1.) and anthologies (2.2.) and then the languages geographically from north to south as follows: Macro-ge (2.3.), Nambiquara (2.4.), Zamuco (2.5.), Mascoi (2.6.), Guaykuru (2.7.), Mataco/Mataguayo (2.8.), and Lule-Vilela (2.9.). Languages of the southern cone not included here will be found in art. 284.

2. Selected Bibliography

Note: Lexicographic material, vocabularies, and similar sources are interspersed in publications of different character; real dictionaries are rare: therefore, a division of this bibliography into Dictionaries and Other Publications is not possible.

2.1. General

Key 1979 = Mary Ritchie Key: The grouping of South American Indian languages. Tübingen 1979.

Klein/Stark 1985 = Harriet E. Manelis Klein/Louisa R. Stark, eds.: South American Indian languages. Austin 1985.

Payne 1990 = Doris Payne, ed.: Amazonian Linguistics: Studies in Lowland South American Languages. Austin 1990.

Rodrigues 1986 = Aryon Rodrigues: Línguas Brasileiras. São Paulo 1986.

Tovar/Larrucea 1984 = Antonio Tovar/Consuelo Larrucea de Tovar: Catálogo de las lenguas des América del Sur. Madrid 1984.

2.2. Anthologies

These works contain lexicographic materials for more than one language family and are therefore grouped separately.

Abregú Virreira 1942 = Carlos Abregú Virreira: Idiomas aborígenes de la República Argentina. Buenos Aires 1942.

Martius 1867 = Karl Friederich Philipp von Martius: Beiträge zur Ethnographie und Sprachenkunde Americas zumal Brasiliens. Leipzig 1867.

2.3. Macro-ge

These languages are found in the south-eastern part of the Amazon region, south of the lower Amazon river and extending as far as the southern part of Brazil.

Albisetti/Venturelli 1962 = César Albisetti/Angelo Jayme Venturelli: Enciclopedia Bororo, vol. I: Vocabulários e etnografia. Campo Grande 1962.

Guérios 1940 = R. F. Mansur Guérios: Estudos sobre a língua camacã. Curitiba 1940.

Wiesemann 1981 = Ursula Wiesemann, comp.: Dicionario Kaingang-Portugues, Portugues-Kaingang. Brasilia 1981.

2.4. Nambiquara

These languages are located in the northwestern part of Mato Grosso and nearby Rondonia. The works cited demonstrate major problems, contain many erroneous entries and are examples of how not to compile a dictionary.

Albuquerque 1910 = Severiano Godofredo de Albuquerque: Relatório do serviços executados em Campos-Novos da serra do Norte. Rio de Janeiro 1910.

Roquette-Pinto 1935 = E. Roquette-Pinto: Rondônia. 3rd Ed. São Paulo 1935.

2.5. Zamuco

These languages are found in western Bolivia and northern Paraguay.

Sušnik 1970 = Branislava Sušnik: Chamacocos II: Diccionario etnográfico. Asunción 1970.

2.6. Mascoi

Boggiani 1896 = Guido Boggiani: Vocabulario dell'idioma Guana, Parte I. In: Atti della R. Academia de Licel Memorie 3. 1896, 57—80.

Coryn 1922 = Alfredo Coryn: Los Indios Lenguas, sus Costumbres y su Idioma, con Compendio de Gramática y Vocabulario. In: Annuario Sociedad Científica Argentina 93. 1922, 221—82.

Lowes 1954 = R. H. G. Lowes: Alphabetical List of Lengua Indian Words with English Equivalents. In: Journal de la Société des Américanistes (Paris) 43. 1954, 85—109.

2.7. Guaykuru

Bárcena 1893 = Alonso de Bárcena: Arte de la lengua toba... con vocabularios facilitados por los Sres. Ángel J. Carranza, Pelleschi y otros, editados y comentados por Samuel A. Lafone Quevedo. Bibl. Ling. del Mus. de la Plata, vol. 2, parte 1 (In: Revista del Museo de La Plata 5. 1893, 129—84; 305—87).

Brigniel 1896 = Joseph Brigniel: Vocabulario castellano-abipón con frases y verbos... edited by Samuel Lafone Quevedo. In: Boletín de la Academia Nacional de Ciencias XV. 1896, 185—253.

Bruno/Najlis 1965 = Lidia Bruno/Elena Najlis: Estudio comparativo de vocabulario Tobas y Pilagás. Buenos Aires 1965.

Bucca 1981 = Salvador Bucca: Palabras y frases mocovíes de Colonia Dolores. In: Cuadernos del Sur 14, 231—238. Bahía Blanca 1981.

Buckwalter 1980 = Alberto S. Buckwalter: Vocabulario toba. President Roque Sáenz Peña 1980.

Rocha 1938 = Alberto Rocha: Vocabulario comentado pilagá-castellano y castellano-pilagá. (Ministerio del Interior. Comisión honoraria de Reducciones de Indios. Publicación no. 7). Buenos Aires 1938.

Sánchez-Labrador 1972 = José Sánchez-Labrador: Familia Guaycuru: vocabulario eyiguayegi, según ms. del siglo XVIII, parte 1. a, letras M—Z. Resumen Etnográfico del vocabulario eyiguayegimbayá. Asunción 1972 (Lenguas chaqueñas 3).

2.8. Mataco/Mataguayo

These works are examples of how lexicography can be useful in comparative linguistics.

Sušnik 1962 = Branislava Sušnik: Vocabularios inéditos de los idiomas Emok-Toba y Choroti recogidos por el doctor Max Schmidt. In: Boletín de la Sociedad Científica del Paraguay y del Museo Andrés Barbero VI, 3. 1962.

Tovar 1964 = Antonio Tovar: Relación entre las lenguas del grupo mataco. Madrid 1964.

2.9. Lule-Vilela

The work below was written originally just one hundred years after Bárcena "civilized these Indians". It reappeared in an 1877 version in which the editor altered the orthography, punctuation, made some stylistic changes, and presented his philosophy on the "poverty" of the language as compared to "Guarani, Quechua and even Araucanian".

Machoni de Cerdeña 1732 = P. Antonio Machoni de Cerdeña: Arte y vocabulario de la lengua Lule y Tonocoté compuestos con facultad de sus superiores. Madrid 1732.

Harriet E. Manelis Klein, Montclair State College, Upper Montclair, New Jersey (USA)

284. Lexicography of the Indian Languages of Southern South America

1. Discussion
2. Selected Bibliography

1. Discussion

Although the Andes mountain range continues southward into this part of South America, the languages discussed in this section will not include the Quechua and Aymara spoken in western Argentina and northern Chile (discussed in art. 282). Rather, the focus will be on the indigenous languages of Argentina and Chile not covered in art. 283.

Included in this grouping is the rich lexicography of the Araucanian or Mapuche language which started as early as 1607, with Valdivia's dictionary on Mapuche and continues with the most recent dictionary written by Erize 1987 (in sect. 2.2), a grandson of the lexicographer of the same name. Araucanian therefore is one of the few languages of South America for which there is both good time depth and adequate data available. For this reason the presentation of languages in the bibliography begins with the Araucanian language (2.2.). The other languages are presented from west (Qawasqar 2.3.) to south (Yagan, 2.4.) to east (Chon, 2.5. and Gununa Kune, 2.6.). The lexicography of languages that are now extinct are not included; however, references to them can be found in Key 1979 and Tovar/Larrucea 1984 (in 2.1).

2. Selected Bibliography

Note: Lexicographic material, vocabularies, and similar sources are interspersed in publications of different character; real dictionaries are rare: therefore, a division of this bibliography into Dictionaries and Other Publications is not possible

2.1. General

Key 1979 = Mary Ritchie Key: The grouping of South American Indian languages. Tübingen 1979.

Klein/Stark 1985 = Harriet E. Manelis Klein/ Louisa R. Stark, eds.: South American Indian languages. Austin 1985.

Tovar/Larrucea 1984 = Antonio Tovar/Consuelo Larrucea de Tovar: Catálogo de las lenguas de América del Sur. Madrid 1984.

2.2. Araucanian

Some older works are cited here because they demonstrate the rationale for writing dictionaries. For example, Febrés 1765 is included because its brief dictionary serves a didactic purpose. Consisting of only a few frequently used words, the author noted that those studying the language would not be intimidated by too many new forms and would therefore be more likely to use these precise and common words to conjugate verbs and to converse, an activity Febrés called most important. The work of Mitre 1894 is interesting because explanations are provided for the inclusion of items. This work also includes a discussion of the works of Valdivia. The 17th century work of Valdivia 1606 is more a manual than a dictionary. It was supposed to be useful for priests to minister to the people. The foreword also contains a statement of the phonetic value of the indigenous words listed in the dictionary in Araucanian alphabetic order.

Abregú Virreira 1942 = Carlos Abregú Virreira: Idiomas aborígenes de la República Argentina. Buenos Aires 1942.

Augusta Félix 1916 = Fr. José de Augusta Félix: Diccionario araucano-español y español-araucano, dos tomos. Santiago de Chile 1916.

Erize 1960 = Esteban Erize: Diccionario comentado mapuche-español. Bahía Blanca 1960.

Erize 1987 = Esteban Erize: Mapuche 1. Buenos Aires 1987.

Febrés 1765 = Andrés Febrés: Arte de la lengua general del reyno de Chile, con un diálogo chileno-hispano y un vocabulario hispano-chileno y Calepino chileno-hispano. Lima 1765 [reprinted Santiago de Chile 1846].

La Grasserie 1902 = Raoul de La Grasserie: Contribution à l'étude des langues de la Patagonie. Vocabulaire Pehuelche. Paris 1902.

Mitre 1894 = Bartolomé Mitre: Lenguas Americanas: Estudio Bibliográfico-Lingüístico Huarpe de los obras del P. Luis de Valdivia sobre el Araucano y el Allentiak, con un vocabulario razonado del Allentiak. La Plata 1894.

Moesbach 1963 = P. Ernesto Wilhelm de Moesbach: Idioma Mapuche. Padre las Casas 1963.

Outes 1914 = Félix F. Outes: Un texto y un vocabulario en dialecto pehuenche de fines del siglo XVIII con introducción y notas. Buenos Aires 1914.

Ramírez 1979 = Carlos Ramírez Sánchez: Diccionario de topónimos de procedencia indígena de la provincia de Cautín (Chile). Valdivia 1979.

Ramírez 1986 = Carlos Ramírez Sánchez: Voces Mapuche. Valdivia 1986.

Sáez-Godoy 1976 = Leopoldo Sáez-Godoy: El indoamericanismo mare [Madia sativa Molina, nombre araucano]. In: Archiv für das Studium der neueren Sprachen und Literaturen 213. 1976, 345—347.

Valdivia 1606 = Luis de Valdivia: Arte y gramática general de la lengua que corre en todo el Reyno de Chile con un vocabulario y confessionario, juntamente con la Doctrina Christiana y Cathecismo del Concilio de Lima en español y dos traducciones dél en lengua de Chile. Lima 1606.

2.3. Qawasqar

The work by Marcel 1892 is included here because it contains a brief vocabulary which serves as an example of an early dictionary of the language. Clairis 1987, on the other hand, provides an excellent analysis of the language as well as a sizable dictionary, useful as a contemporary source.

Aguilera 1978 = Óscar Aguilera: Léxico kawesqar-español, español-kawesqar [alacalufe septentrional]. In: Boletín de Filología, Universidad de Chile 29. 1978, 7—149.

Clairis 1987 = Christos Clairis: El qawasqar: lingüística fueguina teoria y descripción. Valdivia 1987.

Marcel 1892 = Gabriel Marcel: Vocabulaire des Fuégiens à la fin du XVIIe siècle. Paris 1892.

2.4. Yagan

Considering the amount of excellent scholarship now being done on Yagan, lexicography is one area not yet covered. Both Platzmann 1882 and Vignati 1940 are examples of lexicography gone wrong. The former work is just a listing of terms and gives no background or explanation of format of the entries provided. The latter author criticizes Bridges 1933 because that work is only Yamana-

English and not English-Yamana. However, his own dictionary consists of limited word lists with minimum details and only a few examples are given for each letter.

Bridges 1933 = Thomas Bridges: Yamana-English: A Dictionary of the Speech of Tierra del Fuego. Mödling, Austria 1933.

Platzmann 1882 = Julius Platzmann: Glossar der feuerländischen Sprache. Leipzig 1882.

Vignati 1940 = Milcíades Alejo Vignati: Glosario yámana de fines del siglo XVIII. In: Boletín de la Academia Argentina de Letras 8, 30. 1940, 637—663.

2.5. Chon

Beauvoir 1915, a dictionary by a Salesian missionary, also contains some ethnographical material. The author notes that there are three "nations" inhabiting Tierra del Fuego which are different from other in customs and language. Unfortunately, the utility of this work for lexicographers is limited since no phonetics or grammatical information is provided. Vignati 1940 is interesting because of its discussion of the problems of re-editing a critical edition of Patagonian dictionaries. He notes that Elizalde's vocabulary has — like others of the same period — some socio-linguistic value because it demonstrates the degree to which the Indians adopt certain Spanish words as loan words. The organization of the dictionary also deserves mention because it is both a bilingual dictionary and divided by semantic domains.

Beauvoir 1915 = José Maria Beauvoir: Pequeño diccionario del idioma fuegino-ona, con su correspondiente castellano. Buenos Aires 1915.

Vignati 1940 = Milcíades Alejo Vignati: Materiales para la lingüística patagona. El vocabulario de Elizalde. In: Boletín de la Academia Argentina de Letras 8, 30. 1940, 159—202.

2.6. Gununa Kune

Rosas 1947 is a reedition of a work done by General Rosas in 1825. Given the non-missionary and non-scholarly background of the author, it is well-done and worth looking at as an example of early 19th century dictionaries.

Rosas 1947 = Juan Manuel de Rosas: Gramática y diccionario de la lengua pampa. Buenos Aires 1947.

Harriet E. Manelis Klein, Montclair State College, Upper Montclair, New Jersey (USA)

XXXIII. Theorie der zwei- und mehrsprachigen Lexikographie I: Prinzipien und Bauteile
Theory of Bilingual and Multilingual Lexicography I: Principles and Components
Théorie de la lexicographie bilingue et plurilingue I: Principes et éléments

285. Principles of Bilingual Lexicography

1. History of the Dictionaries
2. Essentials of Modern Bilingual Lexicography
3. State of Research
4. Main Principles of Bilingual Lexicography
5. Consequences for Dictionary Entries and Vocabulary
6. Perspectives
7. Concluding Remarks
8. Selected Bibliography

1. History of the Dictionaries

When asked about the historical age of bilingual dictionaries compared with that of monolingual dictionaries one is often at a loss for an answer. If one looks, for example, at the history of dictionaries in the English language, one can find support in Stein (1985 a) for the view that bilingual glossaries, vocabularies and dictionaries came first. The earliest known, *The Leiden Glossary*, is from the 8th century: here Latin words are explained for English speakers. Later other glossaries and vocabularies followed, usually with Latin as one of the languages. In the 15th century genuine Latin-English and English-Latin dictionaries began to appear. But it was not until the 16th century that the first bilingual dictionaries of English and other modern languages like French, Italian or Spanish were produced (Stein 1985 a, 122), while the first English-German dictionary appeared as late as 1706, and a German-English dictionary in 1716, both compiled by Christian Ludwig (Stein 1985 b).

Besides proper bilingual dictionaries, vocabularies and glossaries, after the invention of printing in the 15th century a large number of dictionaries appeared for six, seven or eight languages, meant to meet the needs of travellers and traders between countries. According to Stein's chronological list (1985 a) these polyglot dictionaries enjoyed great popularity and went through innumerable editions and reprints in the course of the next two centuries. After this, bilingual dictionaries proper seem to have gained ground gradually as they were compiled (see Hausmann/Cop 1985). In contrast to almost a thousand years' dominance of bilingual or multilingual glossaries in English, the beginnings of English monolingual lexicography, as late as 1604 with Cawdrey's *Table Alphabeticall*, seem almost inconspicuous. Thus, viewed in the English perspective, it seems reasonable to say that bilingual or multilingual lexicography was the natural predecessor of monolingual lexicography, and that there was a natural evolution from a primitive lexicography of translation to a highly-developed and sophisticated monolingual lexicography. But the truth is less simple if one considers the rather older cultural languages like Arabic and Hebrew.

While the Germanic languages were beginning to get their first, primitive bilingual glossaries of Latin from the 7th and 8th centuries on, several major methodically sophisticated monolingual, semasiological dictionaries of Arabic were being compiled (see Haywood 1965 and Art. 237). According to Haywood a proper bilingual dictionary with Arabic as one language does not seem to have been compiled until the middle of the 11th century, i.e. Al-Zamakhshari's *Arabic-Persian Dictionary*, intended for speakers of Persian who wished to understand Arabic — presumably especially the Koran.

The lexicographical pioneer work in Arabic had its effect on Hebrew lexicography in Spain, which also flourished in the Middle Ages. The difficulty of making a clear distinction between a monolingual semasiological dictionary and a bilingual dictionary with explanations is illustrated by one of the major works of Hebrew lexicography, *The Book of Hebrew Roots* by Abu'l-Walîd Marwan Ibn Janâh, otherwise called Rabbi Yônâh, from 1050 (see Fürst 1876). The dictionary was intended for Arabic-speaking Jews in Spain, so the Hebrew headwords are transcribed into the Arabic alphabet, their meaning is explained in Arabic, and parallels are drawn to Arabic. There is a rich body of Hebrew example material from the Scriptures illustrating the meanings of words, including explanations of hapax legomena. As was the case with Arabic, genuine bilingual dictionaries of Hebrew and another language in this period were the exception rather than the rule (see Fürst 1876).

Given the lack of research on the history of dictionaries of both ancient and modern languages — for example Germanic and Romance — it is difficult to say anything about the purposes mono-, bi-, tri- or multilingual dictionaries originally served. The development of lexicography in the individual languages was, as we have seen, extraordinarily diverse, and what is true of the ancient religion-bearing languages like Hebrew, Arabic, Greek and Latin is not necessarily true of more modern languages like the Germanic and Romance ones. It does however seem reasonable to assume with Haywood (1965) that the manuscript dictionaries of the old languages first and foremost served religion, and were thus an aid to the exegesis of religious (and thereby legal) texts for administrative purposes in the society of the day. Whether this is also true of the first glossaries for Latin texts in the Germanic languages deserves closer investigation. It was not until the 15th century — with the spread of printing — that the needs of trade and travel led to mass production of multilingual dictionaries in particular.

As we have said, the bilingual and multilingual glossaries and dictionaries in English seem rather primitive compared with the high standard of Arabic and Hebrew lexicography from the 8th to the 15th century. In addition, the Arabic and Hebrew lexicographers were excellent linguists who wrote major grammatical works. This was the case with Al-Khalil, Al-Zamakhshari and Ibn Janâh, for example. Such an integral view of lexicographical and grammatical linguistic description is only exceptionally found in descriptions of English, for example in Palsgrave (see Stein 1985 a, 122 ff.).

In more recent times bilingual lexicography can be said to have served a variety of purposes determined by the development of society. Now as ever, bilingual dictionaries are important tools in language-learning all the way from primaryschool to university level. They are useful aids to travel abroad and communication in foreign languages, necessary tools in the commercial world and public administration, and indispensable for secretaries dealing with foreign-language correspondence, translators and interpreters. Specialized translation dictionaries are an essential factor in international specialized communication between companies, public authorities and international organizations. To this we may add translation dictionaries of the scholarly historical-philological type, which serve research in the humanities and the interpretation of older texts and cultures — for example translation dictionaries with Biblical Hebrew, Classical Greek and Latin as the source languages.

Normally the term bilingual dictionary is applied to dictionaries of two national languages, where the source language lemmata of the dictionary are supplied with equivalents in the target language. Such a dictionary may be general, specialized, or a mixture of the two. But one could also justifiably consider dictionaries of older stages of national languages or of their dialects not only as monolingual historical-philological dictionaries, but as bilingual historical-philological and dialect dictionaries respectively, since they are to a great extent subject to the same principles as monofunctional bilingual dictionaries (see 2.1.). But in practice they differ from normal bilingual dictionaries in being corpus-based, and thus usually have a sound empirical foundation.

Regardless of the diversity of translation purposes they can serve (see also Zgusta 1971, 304 ff.) bilingual dictionaries have the common function that they are involved as tools in a pattern of action where the user makes a translation from a foreign language to his mother tongue (or from an older to a modern language-stage, or from a dialect to the standard language), or from his native language to a foreign one. It is true that certain types of monolingual dictionaries (and of course tri- or multilingual dictionaries) also serve these two purposes, but they do not satisfy all the demands a user can justifiably make on a translation dictionary (see Kromann/Riiber/Rosbach 1984 a, 207—208; 1984 b, 178—182). In the following, therefore, we discuss only recent bilingual lexicography, concentrating on the essential aspects (Section 2), the progress of research so far (Section 3), the main principles of the lexicography of translation (Section 4), the consequences entailed by the main principles (Section 5), demonstrating by means of a specific dictionary entry significant shortcomings in widespread lexicographical practice in the light of these principles (Section 6).

2. Essentials of Modern Bilingual Lexicography

In evaluating existing translation dictionaries and compiling new ones it is important to see them from three points of view which — different as they are — are inextricably connected in dictionaries: the *user aspect,* which involves consideration on the part of the lexicographer for the dictionary's target group, its needs and competence, and the types of user situations that occur; the *linguistic aspect,* which demands that the lexicographer deals with equivalence relations between fields of lexical units in the language pair as well as the other paradigmatic and syntagmatic relations of these fields; the *empirical aspect,* which on the basis of the overall user aspect includes the establishment of relevant text corpora and the excerpting of lexical units. Of these, the user aspect and the empirical aspect in particular seem to have remained unclarified in recent lexicographical practice. We will come to the linguistic aspect in 3.2.

2.1. The User Aspect

One often finds that no addressee group is specified for a bilingual dictionary; if the matter is mentioned, it is often couched in such general, non-committal terms that a member of any of the user groups of the language might well believe that the dictionary is useful to him. Even though school dictionaries, for example, might as a type seem to have a clearly formulated addressee group, it is far from guaranteed that the dictionary will fully satisfy the needs of pupils learning foreign languages. Nor can the size of a dictionary be taken as an implicit statement of who it is meant for. Often small dictionaries, which in reality assume an extraordinarily high degree of competence in the foreign language, are meant for users with little competence; while the largest dictionaries, containing an overwhelming amount of information about the foreign language, are aimed at those who already master it. The vague conceptions of lexicographers and publishers as regards users and their needs can similarly be seen from the fact that some of them supplement the main alphabetical section with things like lists of names, lists of abbreviations, fragments of the morphology of the language and (in very rare cases) of its syntax — sometimes even a section where idioms and proverbs can be found translated. This kind of presentation completely loses sight of the user aspect.

Even though many dictionaries give no details of their user group, most of them can still be classified in one of the following two groups: monofunctional or bifunctional dictionaries. A *monofunctional* translation dictionary for a language pair A + B is in the following a dictionary meant for *either* A-speakers *or* B-speakers: for example, in the language direction A → B either for A-speakers in $L_1 \to L_2$ translation or for B-speakers in $L_2 \to L_1$ translation. A *bifunctional* translation dictionary for a language pair A + B is a dictionary aimed at *both* the A-speakers *and* the B-speakers: for example, in the A → B direction both for A-speakers in $L_1 \to L_2$ translation and for B-speakers in $L_2 \to L_1$ translation.

These two main categories can each again be subdivided according to whether the bilingual dictionary consists of an independent reference work for each of the two possible directions, or an integrated work for both directions, so that the dictionary for each direction complements the other in one or more respects, and common editorial principles have been laid down on the basis of a coordinated view of the whole dictionary work. There can thus be extremely varied bilingual dictionary concepts and consequently widely differing editorial principles for the actual dictionaries. We will exemplify this subdivision with some existing dictionaries, classifying the dictionaries according to their declared intended functions.

(1) The monofunctional bilingual dictionary for A-speakers:

(1 a) The dictionary is conceived as an independent dictionary for only one of the two possible language directions A → B or B → A: Lötzsch: Dt.-russ. Wörterbuch ($L_1 \rightarrow L_2$);
Bielfeldt: Russ.-dt. Wörterbuch ($L_2 \rightarrow L_1$).
(1 b) The dictionary is conceived as an integrated work for both language directions, constituting a whole in which the two dictionaries are complementary in one or more respects:
van Dale: Nederlands-Duits ($L_1 \rightarrow L_2$)
Duits-Nederlands ($L_2 \rightarrow L_1$)
(2) The bifunctional bilingual dictionary for both A- and B-speakers:
(2 a) The dictionary is conceived as an independent dictionary for one of the two possible language directions:
Vinterberg/Bodelsen: Dansk-Engelsk Ordbog ($L_1 \rightarrow L_2 + L_2 \rightarrow L_1$)
Kjærulff Nielsen: Engelsk-dansk Ordbog ($L_2 \rightarrow L_1 + L_1 \rightarrow L_2$)
(2 b) The dictionary is conceived as an integrated work for both language directions, constituting a whole in which the two dictionaries in one or more respects complement each other:
Pons Collins: Deutsch-Englisch ($L_1 \rightarrow L_2 + L_2 \rightarrow L_1$), Englisch-Deutsch ($L_2 \rightarrow L_1 + L_1 \rightarrow L_2$)

The user aspect must be said to be one of the areas that really need to be examined in more detail — we need to know more about the way people use bilingual dictionaries, and especially about their linguistic competence in the areas of pronunciation, grammar, semantics, style and their general or specialized knowledge of the foreign language and its culture (see for example Hartmann 1982 or Wiegand 1985).

2.2. The Empirical Aspect

The second of the three aspects is the empirical basis of bilingual dictionaries. It is easy to demonstrate the empirical dependence of the large bilingual dictionaries on the major national monolingual dictionaries, and the dependence of the smaller bilingual dictionaries on the larger ones, as in a system of Chinese boxes. This dependence is not only a matter of directly taking over an inventory of words from a dictionary (often historical-philological) of the vocabulary of the national language; it also involves taking over the explanations and descriptions of the lexical units in these dictionaries and the order in which they are presented. Another area where translation dictionaries are not based on representative corpora is the more specialized component in these dictionaries. Not only is the selection of words arbitrary; it is to a great extent based on the obsolete lemma inventories of older dictionaries or on inadequate definitions of the specialized concepts.

Empirical dependence on national monolingual dictionaries is very much in evidence in the presentation of lexicographical information in the dictionary entries themselves. Labelling conventions, the semantic structure of the entry, collocations etc. are often taken over uncritically and without reflection from the big monolingual dictionaries. For example large translation dictionaries — like the corresponding monolingual dictionaries — classify animals as zoological entities [*Känguruh* — Zoologie *kangaroo* (Fam. Macropodidae)]; plants as botanical entities [*Tulipan* — Botanik (Tulipa) *tulip*] or list the place name *London* as a geographical entity [*London* (geogr.) *Londres*]. One finds just as often in the examples in translation dictionaries that it is the usual collocations from monolingual dictionaries that are translated, despite the fact that they may be trivial or uninteresting in the bilingual context: for example, under *dog* or *Hund* one finds the extremely obvious collocation *bark* or *bellen*, simply designating the usual action associated with this animal.

2.3. Overall View of Aspects

Clearly, the bilingual lexicographer has considerable problems incorporating the user aspect when compiling a dictionary, and there is a conspicuous absence of any original empirical foundation for dealing with the special problems of bilingual lexicography. Such a foundation could improve the quality of bilingual lexicographical work instead of competing in terms of quantity as in the publisher's prospectuses. We lack the guidelines that could provide us with a sound definition of the user group at which a given dictionary project is aimed. In other words, we need sociological user surveys that describe potential user groups, their linguistic competence and their needs. We also need to acknowledge that a bilingual lexicography with any claim to scientific rigour must establish and maintain its own representative corpora in accordance with the nature of the target groups the projects are aiming at. There are of course many other problems in bilingual lexicography, but the two mentioned here are quite fundamental and essential and therefore merit special treatment. We will indicate other metalexicographical problems in bilingual lexicography in the following sections.

3. State of Research

3.1. Research on the User Aspect

Research on bilingual lexicography has an unusually short history considering the long history of these socially important dictionaries themselves. It is true that the front matter of bilingual dictionaries often contains reflections on questions of principle: for example material on how the dictionary in question has been compiled; in older dictionaries, one may also find major excursions on the history of lexicography — for example in Fürst (1876); but no actual unified theory of bilingual lexicography has ever been published, although certain essential partial aspects have been discussed. Of general interest, however, is Reichmann (1986), who reviews in a 164-page "lexikographische Einleitung" the theoretical and methodological principles underlying the conception of the dictionary, including principles for the empirical foundation and other essential principles of bilingual lexicography.

The first attempt in recent times to clarify the user aspect of bilingual dictionaries must be credited to the Russian linguist L. V. Ščerba, who in the preface to the first edition of his Russian-French dictionary (1936) and in his famous treatise on dictionary types (1940) established important principles for dictionaries meant for translation from a native to a foreign language, while for pedagogical reasons he specified requirements of a quite different nature for the so-called explanatory dictionary meant for translation from the foreign to the native language. Ščerba, unlike previous lexicographers, thus placed crucial emphasis on the fact that a dictionary user has native-language competence, and that translation is done in two different directions in terms of this competence. Out of these ideas have grown more elaborated proposals for a typology of translation dictionaries, operating with four dictionaries per language-pair. Along with Smolik (1969) we will call the dictionary meant to serve the user for translation from the native to the foreign language an *active* dictionary, and the one meant for translation from a foreign to a native language a *passive* dictionary. Incidentally, the Ščerba literature, which is not easily accessible for the non-Russian speaker, is briefly but expertly summarized in Duda/Frenzel/Wöller et al. (1986, 11—22), although they extend the typology and argue for six dictionaries per language-pair (1986, 5 f.). In Eastern Europe, Ščerba's proposals and criticisms of the translation dictionaries of his contemporaries have inspired lexicographical practice (Bielfeldt, Kopeckij, Lötzsch among others) and led to metalexicographical debate on translation dictionaries, as is evident from Bielfeldt (1956), Gak (1964), Golovaščuk (1970), Kopeckij (1971), Duda/Müller (1974), Berkov (1977), Lötzsch (1978), Mel'čuk (1984) and others. In Western Europe and the USA there has been little awareness of Eastern European metalexicography and lexicology; other linguistic issues have dominated the debate, and as "publishers' lexicography" bilingual lexicography has had no very high scientific status. Yet there was an important, now almost forgotten discussion of the lexicography of translation at the end of the 50s between Iannucci, Williams and others. Another important event was the symposium held at Indiana University in 1960, published with some delay in Householder/Saporta (1962 and 1967). What had given rise to the scholarly debate was Iannucci's pioneering work on meaning discrimination (1957) in dictionary entries, where he stated that lexicographical practice is inadequate and inconsistent, and remarks that "it also reveals very little evidence that any serious thought has been given to the purposes which meaning discrimination should serve in a bilingual dictionary" (Iannucci 1957, 272). Williams, in his discussion of the problems of bilingual lexicography, establishes very clearly (more systematically in fact than Ščerba, but without reference to Eastern European metalexicography) the four functions bilingual dictionaries must have. He points out that "a Spanish and English dictionary should be designed to fulfill four purposes, two to serve the Spanish-speaking user (the reader-listener and the writer-speaker), two [to serve] the English-speaking user, and that therefore each of the two parts has to fulfill two purposes" (Williams 1959, 251). Williams proposes that the problem should be solved by introducing meaning discrimination for both languages in one and the same dictionary entry, but does admit at the same time that this solution is not realistic because of the space requirements.

While Zgusta (1971, 299 f.) expresses no views on William's clear distinction among the four functions, he does add another important dimension to the classification of dictionaries — the dimension he calls "purpose", which has to do with whether the dictionary is addressed to "the public (learned, educated, general)" or is to be used for "literary translation, business contracts, general use". Al-Kasimi (1977, 20 ff.) lists a number of the criteria for a dictionary typology, partly those specified by Zgusta, partly criteria applying to monolingual dictionaries, while Al-Kasimi (1983) supports Williams word for word. Hausmann (1977) suggests a more differentiated typology of bilingual dictionaries: besides the four dictionaries per language-pair, the active and passive dictionaries which he very aptly calls "Hinübersetzungswörterbücher" and "Herübersetzungswörterbücher" he proposes a "Lesewörterbuch" meant for understanding a foreign language text without necessarily translating it into the native language, and a "Schreibwörterbuch" meant for the free production of texts in the foreign language. Taken to its logical conclusion, this proposal would mean eight dictionaries per language-pair. The Dutch publishers van Dale have initiated a major project where the active-passive typology is represented by the concepts "dictionnaire de thème" and "dictionnaire de version", and has already to some extent been observed in practice for the language-pairs Dutch/French, Dutch/German and Dutch/English (van Sterkenburg/Martin/Al, 1982; Al 1983). In Kromann/Riiber/Rosbach (1984 a and 1984 b) the point of departure is also the active-passive principle, and the consequences of using the principle for meaning discrimination, collocations, grammar etc. are demonstrated systematically. In Kromann/Riiber/Rosbach (1984 b) there is a more detailed review of the progress of research up to 1982/1983.

There are hardly any surveys of user sociology in connection with bilingual dictionaries (see Hartmann 1987); but the contributions that have been made to the typology of bilingual dictionaries may help to create a conceptual framework for such surveys. The theoretical and practical consequences of Ščerba's initial idea of incorporating the user aspect in bilingual lexicographical work have first and foremost been drawn by the Eastern European lexicographers mentioned above. Willams has supplied a very precise formulation of the problem, and the van Dale dictionaries can be counted as a large-scale practical dictionary project with a theoretical foundation which is also innovative in other ways.

3.2. Research on the Linguistic Aspect

While it is true that there are a number of interesting works comparing the vocabularies of two languages — one of the pioneer works is Leisi (1952) — there are only a few Western works that are directly concerned with bilingual lexicography and a related semantic methodology. One of these works is Baldinger (1971), which calls for a full semantic analysis of both languages in order to establish relations of equivalence between the individual meanings of the two languages' lexical units. Detailed consideration of equivalence relations between sememes in languages as different as German and Chinese can be found in Karl (1982). Rettig (1985) argues against the equivalence types proposed by Hausmann ("Kongruenz", "Divergenz", "Konvergenz"). But what one misses in attempts to classify equivalence relations between lexicographical units in a language pair is a clear view of whether the equivalence relation is posited between a lemma and its equivalents or between the individual meanings of the lemmatized word and the particular meaning of the equivalent word: for this distinction leads to very different results, depending on the approach used. Let us look at the following example:

news [nju:z] *n, no pl* **(a)** (*report, information*) Nachricht *f*; (*recent development*) Neuigkeit(en *pl*) *f.* **a piece of** ~ eine Neuigkeit; **I have** ~/**no** ~ **of him** ich habe von ihm gehört/nicht von ihm gehört, ich weiß Neues/nichts Neues von ihm; **there is no** ~ es gibt nichts Neues zu berichten; **have you heard the** ~? haben Sie schon (das Neueste) gehört?; **have you heard the** ~ **about Fred?** haben Sie schon das Neueste über Fred gehört?; **tell us your** ~ erzähl uns die Neuigkeiten *or* das Neueste; **let us have** *or* **send us some** ~ **of yourself** lassen Sie mal von sich hören, schreiben Sie mal, was es Neues gibt; **what's your** ~? was gibt's Neues?; **is there any** ~? gibt es etwas Neues?; **I have** ~ **for you** (*iro*) ich habe eine Überraschung für dich; **bad/sad/good** ~ schlimme *or* schlechte/traurige/gute Nachricht(en); **that is good** ~ das ist erfreulich zu hören, das sind ja gute Nachrichten; **when the** ~/**the** ~ **of his death broke** als es/sein Tod bekannt wurde; **who will break the** ~ **to him?** wer wird es ihm sagen *or* beibringen?; **that is** ~/**no** ~ (**to me)**! das ist (mir) ganz/nicht neu!; **that isn't exactly** ~ das ist nichts Neues; **it will be** ~ **to him that** ... er wird staunen, daß ...; ~ **travels fast** wie sich doch alles herumspricht; **bad** ~ **travels fast** schlechte Nachrichten verbreiten sich schnell; **no** ~ **is good** ~ keine Nachricht ist gute Nachricht.
(b) (*Press, Film, Rad, TV*) Nachrichten *pl.* ~ **in brief** Kurznachrichten *pl*; **financial** ~ Wirtschaftsbericht *m*; **sports** ~ Sportnachrichten *pl*; **it was on the** ~ das kam in den Nachrichten; **to be in the** ~ von sich reden machen; **to make** ~ Schlagzeilen machen; **that's not** ~ damit kann man keine Schlagzeilen machen.

Dictionary excerpt 285.1: article **news** (from *Pons, Collins Deutsch-Englisch, Englisch-Deutsch*, 428)

When the equivalence relation is established between the lemma word *news* and the equivalents *Nachricht, Neuigkeit(en)* and *Nachrichten* (pl.), the result is partial equivalence between the units ("divergence" from English to German, "convergence" from German to English). But when the equivalence relation is established between the sub-meanings of the lemma — or, as here, rather between nuances of meaning — and the corresponding sub-meanings of the equivalents, there is full equivalence. In the following we assume that the latter approach is the most appropriate.

The analysis of equivalence relations and paradigmatic semantic relations has been the object of several Eastern European metalexicographical and lexicological treatises which also deal with the subject in detail as it applies to bilingual dictionaries. See for example Gak (1964), Kopeckij (1971), Sukalenko (1976), Berkov (1977), Karl (1982). Rigorous scientific research on collocations and idioms in the bilingual dictionary must also be sought in Eastern Europe.

3.3. Overall View of Research

As we have seen, research on bilingual lexicography has been of very modest proportions. As regards the user aspect there is disagreement about typology, and analytical procedures for clarifying user needs and competence are practically non-existent. The arrangement of the dictionaries, too, understood as the selection and presentation of lexicographical information — including the structure of the entry —, must be regarded as a problem that is far from solved.

As for the linguistic aspect, it is especially the concept of equivalence at the lexical level (both paradigmatic and syntagmatic) that has aroused particular interest. Related to this are first and foremost all the problems implicit in the concept of connotative meaning, and those of so-called pragmatic information (Wiegand 1981). The need for a more thorough definition of the concepts of collocation and idiom increases with the ever more intensive discussion of the syntagmatic level in translation dictionaries. Similarly we must expect a radical revision of the concept of grammar in translation dictionaries, especially as new theoretical advances in linguistics gradually penetrate into lexicographical practice.

As for the empirical aspect, several issues arise — for example the selection and classification of texts for building up corpora, the principles of excerpting and storing lexical units, as well as the inevitable use of computers and development of the necessary software. Last of all, but closely related to the other aspects, there is the need for a specifically bilingual metalexicographical terminology. Research on the lexicography of translation is thus still in its infancy.

4. Main Principles of Bilingual Lexicography

4.1. The Concept of Translation

By translation we understand here a language-pair-related unidirectional activity where the translator uses his or her native language as one of the two languages, translating to or from the native language. The function of the translation dictionary is, then, to be an aid to the translator *either* in decoding a foreign-language text to an equivalent text in the native language *or* encoding a native-language text as an equivalent text in the foreign language. The words "translator" and "translation" are not to be understood as applying literally to professional translators and translations, and "text" is not to be understood exclusively as written text, but also as oral text — so the definition also includes oral translation and oral texts.

4.2. Equivalence

Equivalence is the axis about which the activity of translation turns. As mentioned in 3.2., we propose that equivalence is understood as a relation between the individual meanings of the lemmatized word and the equivalents. We are thus disregarding syntactic equivalence in this context. If one begins with the three logically possible equivalence relations — full, partial and zero equivalence — an initial categorization of the conceivable equivalence relations between the individual meanings of lexical units in a language-pair can operate with three main types of equivalents:

(i) Full equivalents

Eng. *square root*	— Ger.	*Quadratwurzel*
Ger. *Achse*	— Da.	(mek.) *aksel*
		(geom.) *akse*
Da. *aksel*	— Ger.	*Achse* (mek.)
Da. *akse*	— Ger.	*Achse* (geom.)
Eng. *bride*	— Ger.	*Braut* (am Hochzeitstag)
Ger. *Braut*	— Eng.	*bride* (am Hochzeitstag)
	— Eng.	*fiancée (Verlobte)*

Here we have full equivalence, even in the examples like *Achse: aksel/akse* and *Braut: bride,* where, depending on the sub-meanings, there are different equivalents. *Bride* is fully equivalent to one of the meanings of *Braut.* No denotative or connotative elements are lost that could justify classifying the examples in the category for partial equivalence. In the cases used here one is justified in speaking of interlingual synonymy between particular meanings of the lexical units.

(ii) Partial equivalents

This group includes a great variety of types of equivalence, only two of which will be mentioned:

Eng. *girlhood*	— Fr.	*adolescence, periode de jeunesse (d'une femme)*
Fr. *adolescence*	— Eng.	(d'une femme) *girlhood* (d'un garçon) *boyhood*
Eng. *aunt*	— Da.	(maternal) *moster* (paternal) *faster*

In these cases — depending on the direction of translation — some more specific information must be given (as here in brackets) to avoid loss of information. In such cases of anisomorphism we may be justified in speaking of divergence and convergence: there is divergence when a lemma, contrasted with the lexical units of the target language, must be divided into several "sub-meanings", as in the examples with *adolescence* and *aunt.* There is convergence when two or more "sub-meanings" with their lexical units correspond to one and the same lexical unit in the target language, as would be the case, for example, with *moster* and *faster* as lemmata and *aunt* as equivalent. If the translator in a specific instance considers it desirable to avoid a loss of information, he can add the specifying elements shown in brackets, or similar compensatory elements, to his text. The type of partial equivalence shown here could reasonably be called interlingual hyperonymy or hyponymy respectively. In contrast to this there is another type:

Eng. *streetcar*	— Ger.	[US] *Straßenbahn*
Ger. *Samstag*	— Eng.	[Western & South German] *Saturday*

In these cases there will always be a loss of information in translation. In contrast to the first type, the labelling in the square brackets cannot be directly inserted as compensatory material in the target text. The comment in brackets is uninsertable and in practice untranslatable: if there is no compensatory information in the general context, information is lost.

(iii) Non-equivalents (surrogate equivalents)

In the vocabulary of every language there are considerable numbers of lexical units that are language and culture-specific — for example the vocabulary of religious observance, art, science, handicrafts and politics. In these cases the lexicographer must seek solutions that meet the needs of the user as far as possible by providing brief, precise encyclopaedic explanations and suggestions for translation. In Schnorr (1986) there is an illustrative review of examples from various areas, e.g.:

Eng. *muffin*	Ger.	[Brit.] (weiches, flaches) *Milchbrötchen* (meist warm gegessen).
	Ger.	[US] (kleiner pfannkuchenartiger) *Fladen*

The lexicographer cannot predict all the conceivable types of text where words like these could occur, and how they could be translated there; but by giving some form of brief encyclopaedic explanation in the foreign language he at least provides the translator with some basic elements that can form a point of departure for the insertion of a suitable surrogate equivalent in the given text (see also Articles 301 and 295).

Zgusta has an excellently formulated statement on the fundamental anisomorphism between the lexical units of languages: "The fundamental difficulty of such co-ordination of lexical units is caused by the differences in the organisation of the designate in the individual languages and by the differences between languages" (Zgusta 1971, 294). The three types of equivalents outlined here can of course only be considered as three stages on a scale of lexical units going from isomorphism through increasing to extreme anisomorphism. It goes without saying that the more distantly related and culturally foreign to one another two languages are, the more anisomorphism one must expect to have to describe in the relevant bilingual dictionaries.

4.3. The Language-Pair

That one meaning of a lexical unit can be related to a meaning of a lexical unit in another language, and that the equivalence relation for a sub-meaning can change from language to language is due to the familiar fact of semantics that the number of lexical units in the same lexical field can change from language to language, as can be seen from the examples cited as partial equivalents in 4.2.; this could be illustrated with many other examples even by remaining within the group of lexical units designating family relations.

Certain culture-specific aspects of the phenomenal world and certain specialized concepts are of course structured differently from language to language and from country to country, which means that there are words which only apply to the particular circumstances of each country. Such words should only be included in bilingual dictionaries as lemmata when the language in question is the source language of the dictionary, while in the opposite case their surrogate equivalents should not be given lemma status.

For example, there are a number of feast-days connected with the Rhineland Shrovetide season — *Rosenmontag, Fastnacht, Aschermittwoch,* etc. The Danish *fastelavn* is a much more modest one-day affair in comparison with these, and in a German-Danish translation dictionary it would be very relevant to have these lexical units as headwords with their explanations. The same is true of the special German holidays in November — *Allerheiligen, Volkstrauertag, Buß- und Bettag, Totensonntag;* but it seems pointless to list the surrogate equivalent for *Volkstrauertag* as a headword in a Danish-German dictionary for Danes who are not familiar with the concept. In such cases the so-called mirror-imaging of surrogate equivalents is confusing to the user, as it may give a false impression that the phenomena are identical in the two societies.

There have been proposals to use the same semantic structuring for a given lemma in both a monolingual and a bilingual dictionary (Iannucci 1957, Steiner 1982), but this approach is rejected with strong arguments by Hietsch (1958) among others, and indirectly by Lötzsch (1978). The latter cites the example of German *intensiv,* which is given four meanings in *Wörterbuch der deutschen Gegenwartssprache* and has the same semantic structure in Russian, so it would be a waste of space to list the same Russian equivalent four times in the dictionary entry. On the other hand it would be relevant to reduce the polysemic structure when specifying equivalence relations with English:

intensiv *adj Arbeit, Forschung, Landwirtschaft* intensive; *Farbe, Gefuhl* intense; *Geruch* powerful, strong; *Blick* intent, intense. **jdn ~ beobachten** to watch sb intently.

Dictionary excerpt 285.2: article **intensiv** (from *Pons, Collins Deutsch-Englisch, Englisch-Deutsch,* 370)

Thus it is best when contrasting the lexical units of the respective languages to determine how the meanings of a lemma are to be structured, and thereby how the equivalence relations are to be presented for the user. This is one of the points where bilingual lexicography must break free of monolingual lexicography.

4.4. The Active-Passive Dichotomy

There is a stubborn tradition in scholarly literature on bilingual lexicography (and for that matter on translation theory) of only operating with the concepts of source language and target language. Yet these concepts are inadequate when it comes to the principles for the selection and presentation of lexicographical information in bilingual dictionaries and dictionary entries with due consideration for the competence and needs of the user. Here it is of crucial importance to make use of the further distinction between native and foreign language. On the basis of these two criteria one can establish a typology for bilingual dictionaries with far-reaching consequences. The first criterion involves the fact that the user of translation dictionaries has native-language competence, as mentioned in 3.1., i.e. he knows the meaning and usage of words in his own language. The other criterion takes into account the fact that translation can be done in two directions — from the native to the foreign language or from the foreign to the native language. This is the basis on which the now familiar typological distinction between active and passive dictionaries is built — in principle entailing that four dictionaries must be compiled per language-pair. By an active dictionary, then, we understand a monofunctional $L_1 \rightarrow L_2$ dictionary; by a passive dictionary, a monofunctional $L_2 \rightarrow L_1$ dictionary. If we take the language-pair English and German and make each language L_1 in turn, the four dictionaries can be shown schematically like this:

active dictionary (monofunctional $L_1 \rightarrow L_2$)
    English-German for English users
    German-English for German users
passive dictionary (monofunctional $L_2 \rightarrow L_1$)
    German-English for English users
    English-German for German users

This basic typology determines the lexicographical information to be selected and how it is to be presented in the most useful way for the user. In the active dictionary the information is primarily concerned with the equivalents, i.e. the lexical units of the foreign language which are to be used by the user to produce foreign-language texts. In the passive dictionary the information is primarily about the lemmata, i.e. the lexical units of the foreign language which occur in foreign-language texts the user wants to understand and translate into his native language. If we use the word "comment" as the inclusive concept for information that can be supplied for a lemma and its individual meanings or for an equivalent and its individual meanings — whether this is implicit material in the illustrative examples or explicit phonetic, grammatical, semantic or stylistic information — the principles for comments in monofunctional dictionaries can be summarized in the following form:

	LEMMA	EQUIVALENT
ACTIVE DICTIONARIES	— comm.	+ comm.
PASSIVE DICTIONARIES	+ comm.	— comm.

Great advantages are to be gained from the conception of dictionaries for a language-pair as monofunctional dictionaries (see 2.1.), so that two sets of active-passive dictionaries are compiled for each language-pair. Some of the advantages are that there will be considerable savings on transparent words in the word inventory; that a user-orientated grammatical description can be established for each of the languages in each of the two sets of dictionaries; and that the comments needed by the user can be written in the user's own language.

The active-passive principle thus enables us to eliminate superfluous detail systematically and maximize necessary information, and is thus in accordance with lexicographical principles of economy.

5. Consequences for Dictionary Entries and Vocabulary

5.1. Comments and Meaning Discrimination

In the following we will show some of the most obvious consequences of the active-passive dichotomy. These apply in particular to the selection and presentation of commentatory information in the dictionary entries, and to a more limited extent to the selection and presentation of lexical units. In the dictionary entries the active-passive dichotomy in particular determines comments of a linguistic nature on equivalence, semantics, style, grammar and phonetic features, and comments of a non-linguistic nature like the classification of the lexical units in subject fields, encyclopaedic explanations, culture-specific and subject-specific facts. Apart from the fact that such comments can constitute useful information in themselves, they can serve as aids to meaning discrimination, for example when meanings of the lemma are to be distinguished in order to provide different potential equivalents, or when the correct meaning among the possible meanings of the equivalents is to be identified for the user of the dictionary.

Meaning discrimination is done by many different means: semantic paraphrases in the form of hyperonyms, hyponyms, synonyms, antonyms; subject or stylistic labels; but also grammatical categories or phonetic symbols. In addition, examples can be important for meaning discrimination. There are reviews of these devices in Iannucci (1957) and Hausmann (1977). Meaning discrimination is essential throughout in active dictionaries, while it can be omitted in passive dictionaries with a few special exceptions (see Kromann/Riiber/Rosbach 1984 b, 200 f.).

5.2. Meaning Discrimination and Meaning Identification

In any pair of languages one can find lexical units which are monosemous and completely isomorphic with one another in both denotative and connotative terms. In such cases there is no need for comments on the lemma or equivalent in either the active or passive bilingual dictionary:

Eng.	Ger.
dictator	*Diktator*
diode	*Diode*

At first glance the same might appear to be the case with the following examples:

Eng.	Ger.
neigh	*wiehern*

But if we turn the latter example round it emerges that English has two lexical units to designate the sound horses make. In such a case of anisomorphism it is necessary to discriminate between the meanings of the two equivalents for the German user. Here the active-passive dichotomy comes into the picture, with its clear distinction between the two functions that the translation dictionary for one and the same direction can have:

Active	Ger.	— Eng.
	wiehern	— *neigh,*
		(leise) *whinny*
Passive	Ger.	— Eng.
	wiehern	— *neigh, whinny*

Thus the English units here are what we have called partial equivalents (see 4.2.), like *aunt* and its Danish equivalents. It emerges that anisomorphic structures like these in a given language-pair require special treatment when we observe the active-passive dichotomy:

Passive	Eng.	— Da.
	aunt	*moster, faster*
Active	Eng.	— Da.
	aunt	(mother's sister)
		moster
		(father's sister) *faster*

In these cases the comments quite unequivocally have a meaning-discriminating function for the English user. But when the English speaker reads a Danish text where words like *faster* and *moster* occur it is reasonable for the lexicographer not only to give *aunt* as equivalent, but to add the comments "(father's sister)" and "(mother's sister)" respectively, to identify the meaning of the lemma with complete precision and no information loss:

Passive	Da.	— Eng.
	faster	— *aunt* (father's sister)
	moster	— *aunt* (mother's sister)

This comment does not discriminate between meanings of the equivalent, as was the case with the preceding example; the comments identify the meaning of the lemma for the user, and can at the same time be used to compensate for a possible loss of information in a translation.

However, it may also be necessary to identify an equivalent only, i.e. where the equivalent has several meanings, but only one of them is relevant for a given lemma. We will use the example from the full equivalents in 4.2.:

Passive	Eng.	— Ger.
	bride	— *Braut* (am Hochzeitstag)

In contrast, the same comment has a meaning-discriminating function in the following model:

Active	Ger.	— Eng.
	Braut	— (am Hochzeitstag)
		bride
		(Verlobte) *fiancée*

In the same way, stylistic, regional, technical and other labels can serve two purposes: meaning discrimination or meaning identification. Let us take one of the simple examples again to illustrate how the active-passive dichotomy brings out two different functions for one and the same comment:

Active	Ger.	— Eng.
	Straßenbahn	— [Brit.] *tram(car)*
		[US.] *streetcar*
Passive	Ger.	— Eng.
	Bub	— [South German,
		Austr., Swiss] *boy*

In the active dictionary the comments here are meaning-discriminating for the equivalents; in the passive dictionary the comment is meaning-identifying for the lemma.

Meaning discrimination and meaning identification are thus language-pair-related. For example there is no anisomorphism between German and English *aunt — Tante;* nor is there any need for comment in a Danish-English dictionary on *brud — bride*. In these cases the need for meaning discrimination and identification disappears.

5.3. Collocations and Idiosyncratic Constructions

Since bilingual dictionaries are an aid to translation, the user of the dictionary should be able to find the relevant information for the given language-pair about so-called collocations and idioms containing the lexical units in question. We will not discuss here the widely differing views on the collocation concept or idiomaticity; but we will point out some of the types of phrases that are of interest to bilingual lexicography. By "phrase" we understand here first and foremost possible semantic combinations of lexical units in accordance with the norms of the given language.

Monolingual lexicography as a rule describes the phrases that are possible in connection with a given lexical unit. Thus in a monolingual, semasiological dictionary a reasonable approach to the description of collocations is to classify and illustrate the possible objects of, for example, the verb *to have*. The same classification and illustration in a bilingual dictionary — English-German, for example — would lead to a huge entry on *to have* full of superfluous information, because most of the possible constructions would be directly translatable into German. It is however an indispensable requirement that the English-German dictionary presents exactly those constructions that cannot be translated directly into German. Consequently not all the possible phrases should be selected and presented in the bilingual dictionary — only those that are unpredictable for the translator (cf. dictionary excerpt 285.3).

3 *vt* **(a)** (*possess*) haben. **she has (got** *esp Brit*) **blue eyes** sie hat blaue Augen; **~ you (got** *esp Brit*) *or* **do you ~ a suitcase?** hast du einen Koffer?; **I ~n't (got** *esp Brit*) *or* **I don't ~ a pen** ich habe keinen Kugelschreiber; **I must ~ more time** ich brauche mehr Zeit; **~ you (got** *esp Brit*) *or* **do you have a cigarette?** hast du (mal) eine Zigarette?; **I ~ (got** *esp Brit*) **no German** ich kann kein (Wort) Deutsch; **he had her on the sofa** er nahm sie auf dem Sofa; **I ~ it!** ich hab's!; **what time do you ~?** (*US*) wieviel Uhr hast du?; (*inf*), wie spät hast du es?; **judge Smith has it ...** Kampfrichter Smith bewertet es mit ...
(b) to ~ breakfast/lunch/dinner frühstücken/zu Mittag essen/zu Abend essen; **to ~ tea with sb** mit jdm (zusammen) Tee trinken; **will you ~ tea or coffee/a drink/a cigarette?** möchten Sie lieber Tee oder Kaffee/möchten Sie etwas zu trinken/eine Zigarette?, hätten Sie lieber Tee oder Kaffee/gern etwas zu trinken/gern eine Zigarette?; **what will you ~?** — **I'll ~ the steak** was möchten *or* hätten Sie gern(e)? — ich hätte *or* möchte gern das Steak; **he had a cigarette/a drink/a steak** er rauchte eine Zigarette/trank etwas/aß ein Steak; **how do you ~ your eggs?** wie hätten *or* möchten Sie die Eier gern(e)?; **he had eggs for breakfast** er aß Eier zum Frühstück; **will you ~ some more?** möchten Sie *or* hätten Sie gern(e) (noch etwas) mehr?; **do you ~ coffee at breakfast?** trinken Sie zum Frühstück Kaffee?; **~ another one** nimm noch eine/einen/eines; trink noch einen; rauch noch eine; **he likes to ~ his steak medium** er hat sein Steak gern(e) halb durch(gebraten).
(c) (*receive, obtain, get*) haben. **to ~ news from sb** von jdm hören; **I ~ it from my sister that ...** ich habe von meiner Schwester gehört *or* erfahren, daß ...; **to let sb ~ sth** jdm etw geben; **I must ~ the money by this afternoon** ich muß das Geld bis heute nachmittag haben; **I must ~ something to eat at once** ich brauche dringend etwas zu essen, ich muß dringend etwas zu essen haben; **we had a lot of visitors** wir hatten viel Besuch; **there are no newspapers to be had** es sind keine Zeitungen zu haben; **it's nowhere to be had** es ist nirgends zu haben *or* kriegen (*inf*); **it's to be had at the chemist's** es ist in der Apotheke erhältlich, man bekommt es in der Apotheke.
(d) (*maintain, insist*) **he will ~ it that Paul is guilty** er besteht darauf, daß Paul schuldig ist; **he won't ~ it that Paul is guilty** er will nichts davon hören, daß Paul schuldig ist; **as gossip has it** dem Hörensagen nach, wie man so munkelt; **as the Bible/Shakespeare has it** wie es in der Bibel steht/wie Shakespeare sagt; **as Professor James would ~ it** (*according to*) laut Professor James; (*as he would put it*) um mit Professor James zu sprechen.
(e) (*neg: refuse to allow*) **I won't ~ this nonsense** dieser Unsinn kommt (mir) nicht in Frage!; **I won't ~ this sort of behaviour!** diese Art (von) Benehmen lasse ich mir ganz einfach nicht bieten; **I won't ~ it!** das lasse ich mir nicht bieten!; **I won't ~ him insulted** ich lasse es nicht zu *or* dulde es nicht, daß man ihn beleidigt; **I won't ~ him insult his mother** ich lasse es nicht zu, daß er seine Mutter beleidigt; **we won't ~ women in our club** in unserem Klub sind Frauen nicht zugelassen; **I'm not having any of that!** (*inf*) mit mir nicht! (*inf*); **but she wasn't having any** (*sl*) aber sie wollte nichts davon wissen.

Dictionary excerpt 285.3: extract of article **to have** (from: *Pons, Collins Deutsch-Englisch, Englisch-Deutsch*, 294)

One could say that there are two extremes on the scale between free and restricted phrases. At the free end, as with *to have*, there are a multitude of options for semantic complementation. When the free phrases are convergent in the language pair (as they are to all intents and purposes for the main meaning of *to have, to see, to buy, to sell* and the corresponding words in German) the convergent semantics of the complements mean that one is justified in not selecting and presenting such phrases in the dictionary entries. But, as demonstrated above, this is not permissible when the semantics of the phrases are divergent. At the restricted end of the scale we find at least two very different types. On the one hand we have the bound, lexicalized phrases — the true idioms — whose individual elements cannot be replaced, and whose meaning is metaphorical: for example, *to kick the bucket/ins Gras beißen* (for these, see Article 290). On the other we have cases with relatively narrow (from the denotative point of view) semantic restrictions as regards complementation etc. — for example words like *bark/bellen* which as subject can only have *dog/Hund* and similar animals making the same noise. The true idioms must be given in both active and passive dictionaries, because they have the same status as lexical units. With the *bark/bellen* type we can say that the restriction, if convergent in both languages, does not need to be presented in the dictionary.

At the middle of the scale there is a large group of phrases, difficult to define, which we will call idiosyncratic phrases here. It is typical of these that one phrase out of several possible (from the denotative point of view) is either the only usual or preferred one. For example, English has two expressions, *to get on a bicycle* or *to mount a bicycle*. German, correspondingly, has (at least) two expressions, *auf ein Fahrrad (auf)steigen* or *ein Fahrrad besteigen*. Danish also has two expressions, *at stå på en cykel* or *at stige (op) på en cykel*. In all three languages the first of the two phrases is the most frequent and preferred, while the second can be said to belong to a more formal style in all three languages. The translation dictionary now has the job of giving as precise an account as possible of which of the two expressions is preferred. This requirement is absolute in the active dictionary, but can be dispensed with in the passive dictionary, where one could omit it in cases of transparence; but non-transparent idiosyncratic phrases must be included not only in the active, but also in the passive dictionary.

5.4. Grammar

Much grammatical knowledge is necessary for translation. In recent years it has also been shown that the need for grammatical information in dictionaries, including bilingual dictionaries, is greater than one might immediately assume (see for example Hartmann 1982, and especially Wiegand 1985, as well as several of the papers in Bergenholtz/ Mugdan 1985). In active bilingual dictionaries it is first and foremost the equivalents that need to be supplied with grammatical information; in passive dictionaries, it is the lemmata.

The grammatical information could conceivably be given in several different places in the dictionary: it could be provided along with the lexical units it concerns; one also finds it in separate sections on grammar in appendices to the dictionary; and sometimes there is a combination of these two (in principle very different) modes of presenting grammatical information (see Article 287).

Strictly speaking — if one accepts the theory of four functions distributed over four dictionaries per language-pair — it should be sufficient to list grammatical information as follows:

(active English-German dictionary)
goose   *Gans*, die, pl. *Gänse*
old   *alt (älter, am ältesten)*
roast   *braten (brät, briet, gebraten)*
(passive English German dictionary)
elder   siehe *old*
eldest   siehe *old*
geese   siehe *goose*
goose, pl. *geese* *Gans*
old (older, oldest)
oder *elder, eldest)* *alt*
roast schw. Vb   *braten*

The extent of grammatical information will depend on the grammatical system of the individual language and the function of the dictionary. For example, German has a far more complex morphology than English, and bilingual dictionaries for non-Germans with German as one language will therefore need detailed information on the morphology of German, whether the dictionary is intended for active or passive use. Dictionaries intended for Germans with German as one of the languages, on the other hand, can do without the morphological information on German. Article 287, on constructions, deals with syntactic constructions in bilingual dictionaries.

5.5. Vocabulary: Selection and Presentation

As stated in Section 1, bilingual dictionaries today are compiled for such fundamentally different purposes as use in schools, intercultural communication, specialist use, etc. These overall purposes will of course give the main criteria for the inventory of words that will form the basis of the dictionary. The selection of lexical units on the basis of such criteria may in turn be restricted by the size of the dictionary and the economic resources of the project. Here we will point out some further consequences of the theory of active and passive dictionaries for the selection and presentation of lexical units.

In the section above on grammar it was already evident that the lemmatization of the lexical units is approached differently depending on whether the dictionary is active or passive. Similar considerations apply to orthographic variants like German *Telefon* and *Telephon,* both of which must be listed in a passive German-English dictionary; but in an active German-English dictionary the normal form *Telefon* is sufficient. Conversely, it is quite sufficient to list *Telefon* alone in both the active and passive English-German dictionary.

The dichotomy between active and passive dictionaries emerges clearly in the case of regionalisms, which should first and foremost be included in the passive dictionary. For example, in German there are many dialect and regionalese words for *butcher: Fleischhauer, Fleischhacker, Metzger, Schlächter;* and these should be in a passive German-English dictionary with comments identifying them as regionalisms. But an active German-English dictionary can content itself with the standard-language lemmata *Fleischer* and *Metzger* and their equivalent *butcher*. In the English-German dictionary (both active and passive) it will be sufficient to give the standard-language equivalent *Fleischer.*

The active-passive principle can also be of interest in small dictionaries, where the vocabulary has to be greatly reduced. In this context, for example, internationalisms that are convergent and transparent in the language-pair in question can be omitted in a passive dictionary. If one takes the German sentence *Religion ist das Opium des Volks,* the words *Religion* and *Opium* are unlikely to pose any problems for an English speaker. Internationalisms like these can therefore be omitted in a small passive German-English dictionary, but not of course in an active English-German dictionary, where English-speaking users may need to make sure that they exist and perhaps look up grammatical information on the two words.

An area of the vocabulary with particularly subtle problems is that of compounds and derivatives. For this we can refer to Article 288 and Kromann/Riiber/Rosbach 1984 b, 219—221.

6. Perspectives

The considerations of principle in Sections 4 and 5 concerning the presentation and selection of lexicographical information have their most far-reaching consequences for the practical lexicographical editing of bilingual dictionaries. But it may be added that theoretical and methodical guidelines like these can also be applied to the critical analysis and evaluation of existing bilingual dictionaries and the creation of programs for the electronic storage and presentation of lexicographical information. In the following we will briefly touch on these two areas.

In the critical analysis and evaluation of existing dictionaries one will often find two opposing tendencies in one and the same dictionary, especially in the intentionally bi-functional dictionaries. We cannot go into all the details here, but will restrict ourselves to giving an example of a recurring and typical failing in a single dictionary entry which may stand as an archetypal instance of a widespread lexicographical practice.

If a German speaker wishes to translate the sentence *Wir haben einen bedauerlichen Fall von Interessenlosigkeit* into English and is doubtful about the correct equivalent of *Fall*, the lexicographer responsible for the following dictionary entry does not afford him the necessary assistance in finding the proper equivalent with any certainty:

> **Fall**, *m.* (-es, ⸚e) fall, tumble, accident; decay, ruin, decline, downfall, failure; waterfall, cataract; case, instance, event; condition, situation; *auf jeden* -, *auf alle Fälle*, in any case, by all means, at all events; *auf keinen* -, on no account, by no means; *im* -*e*, *daß*, in case; *in dem* -*e*, in that case; *im* – *der Not*, in case of necessity; (*coll.*) *Knall und* -, like a bolt from the blue; *ich setze den* -, I make the supposition, suppose; *einen* – *tun*, have a fall; *von* – *zu* -, as the case may be; (*Prov.*) *Hochmut kommt vor dem* -, pride goes before a fall; *der vorliegende* -, the case in point; *der Wen*-, the accusative case; *der Wer*-, the nominative case; *zu* -*e bringen*, ruin, seduce; *zu* -*e kommen*, be ruined.

Dictionary excerpt 285.4: article **Fall** (from: *Cassells Wörterbuch Deutsch-Englisch, Englisch-Deutsch*, 147)

In this entry the German speaker not only lacks meaning-discriminating comments — a semicolon between different meanings is not enough — but for each of the equivalents to the meanings of the lemma a couple of extra "synonyms" are provided: for example, for *case* also *incident* and *event,* neither of which can be inserted with the same meaning as *case*. It is claimed that the dictionary is of use to both English and German speakers. This entry is in reality only useful to English speakers — i.e. in the passive function of the dictionary — while it fails in its active function.

It is one of the ancient and deadly sins of translation lexicography in bi-directional dictionaries to provide lists of equivalents and accompanying quasi-synonyms without meaning-discriminating comments. The user of the dictionary is then obliged to guess at the correct answer or to investigate further in other sources of information — a time-consuming activity and in practice impossible for most users, as they will not usually in the here-and-now situation in question have such extra sources at hand.

As for the development of software, an extra dimension can be added to the preparation, editing and printing of lexical entries if one incorporates potential theoretical guidelines for translation dictionaries. Much interest has centred in recent years on the work of developing a prototype for a so-called multifunctional, multidimensional lexical database with structured and formalized information suitable for interactive use by many categories of potential users, and intended for on-line processing and retrieval. In the future realization of such LDBs it will be necessary to develop a variety of search profiles for on-line retrieval; and in compiling dictionaries with a view to future storage on magnetic and electronic media it will be necessary to select from the total mass of information precisely those items that are relevant for a given user (group) with particular needs and a particular level of competence.

If the user is not simply to be presented with a computerized version of traditional dictionary entries, it is precisely the theoretical considerations underlying the active-passive principle that will prove of crucial importance in developing the user-oriented search profiles. Computer technology, which has already made its entry into the production of dictionaries, thus opens up possibilities that can also benefit the user in that he will only be presented with the exact information he needs (see also Steiner 1975).

Apart from the two perspectives mentioned here, the basic theoretical considerations on which the active-passive principle rests can also be applied in the area of foreign-language teaching, partly in vocabulary acquisition for translation purposes, partly in error analysis and the teaching of dictionary skills.

7. Concluding Remarks

There is a clear area of common ground for the authors of dictionaries and theoreticians (most of whom are also, or have also been, involved in the making of dictionaries): the wish to meet the needs of the user in the translation situation. Yet the discrepancies between the conclusions drawn by radical theoreticians and hardened practitioners are striking. On the one hand the radicals demand that the active and passive functions should be observed in the dictionaries, and that the consequences of the active-passive typology should penetrate far into the entry structure — consequences that would seem to favour monofunctional dictionaries. On the other hand the lexicographers (and publishers) claim in their prefaces that their dictionaries do in fact cater for the needs of users of both languages.

The objection may be made against the theoretically-based demand for active and passive dictionaries that it would be too expensive to make four dictionaries for each language-pair. This may be countered by pointing out that in the first place theory formation must not be determined by economic considerations; that in the second place the active-passive function can be observed in one and the same dictionary; and that in the third place research on the lexicography of translation has just begun and there is a vast amount of development work ahead, in which electronic facilities will also have a decisive influence on the functions to be performed and their mode of realization.

That theory formation in bilingual lexicography is gathering impetus is evident from the very fact that within the last ten years a number of theories based on the active-passive principle have emerged. If we look at Hausmann (1977 and 1988) we find a proposal for eight dictionaries per language-pair; Kromann/Riiber/Rosbach (1984 b) propose four per language-pair, and Duda/Frenzel/Wöller et al. (1986) suggest six; while Zaiping/Wiegand (1987) propose a solution with just one dictionary which is to perform all four functions — admittedly with an order of priorities: translation from German to Chinese and Chinese to German in one and the same dictionary for both Chinese and German speakers, with first priority for the Chinese users. Perhaps there are realistic solutions to be gained by following the suggestion that Williams (1960) once made of catering for all four functions in two dictionaries. At any rate, so much new knowledge must by now have been amassed concerning the principles of the lexicography of translation that no scientifically sound translation dictionary will in future be able to neglect consideration of the active-passive principle.

The primary function of the bilingual dictionary — regardless of its theoretical background or lack of the same — is to serve as an aid to translation. In this it clearly differs from tri- or multilingual dictionaries, which in practice can only be used in the passive function (cf. Kromann/Riiber/Rosbach 1984 b, 177—181). Compared with the monolingual dictionary, including so-called learners' dictionaries, the ideal bilingual dictionary has the following clear (and acknowledged) advantages from the point of view of the tranlator:
— direct access to equivalents;
— orientation towards a specific language pair;
— immediately insertable equivalents;
— scope for an adequate metalanguage;
— no superfluous material in the form of etymology, lexical definitions and encyclopaedic information etc.

In practice the bilingual dictionaries are perhaps subject to a number of weaknesses; but this is because we have not fully acknowledged their "true nature" or proper purpose: to serve the user in translation from his native language to a foreign language, or from a foreign language to his native language.

Note: The first version of this article was written by Hans-Peder Kromann, while he was supported by a fellowship of the Alexander von Humboldt-Stiftung during a stay at the University of Heidelberg.

8. Selected Bibliography

8.1. Dictionaries

Bielfeldt: Russ.-dt. Wörterbuch = Russisch-Deutsches Wörterbuch, unter Leitung und Redaktion von Hans Holm Bielfeldt. 14., durchgesehene Auflage. Berlin 1982 [1119 p.; 1. ed. 1958].
Cassells Wörterbuch Deutsch-Englisch, Englisch-Deutsch = Cassells Wörterbuch Deutsch-Eng-

lisch, Englisch-Deutsch. Teil I, Deutsch-Englisch, auf der Grundlage der Ausgaben von Karl Breul vollständig neu bearbeitet und herausgegeben von Harold T. Betteridge. Sonderausgabe. München 1984 [646, 632 p.; 1. ed. 1957].

van Dale: Duits-Nederlands = Groot woordenboek Duits-Nederlands door prof. dr. H. L. Cox (...). Utrecht. Antwerpen 1983 [1576 p.].

van Dale: Nederlands-Duits = Groot woordenboek Nederlands-Duits door prof. dr. H. L. Cox (...). Utrecht. Antwerpen 1986 [1560 p.].

Kjærulff Nielsen: Engelsk-dansk Ordbog = B. Kjærulff Nielsen: Engelsk-dansk Ordbog. Medredaktør: Jens Axelsen. Konsulent: C. A. Bodelsen. Anden udgave. 2. oplag. København 1984 [1273 p.].

Lötzsch: Dt.-russ. Wörterbuch = Deutsch-Russisches Wörterbuch. Begründet von Hans Holm Bielfeldt. In der Endfassung erarbeitet von einem Autorenkollektiv unter der Leitung von Ronald Lötzsch. 1. Band. Berlin 1983. 2. und 3. Band. Berlin 1984 [XXXI, 761, 706, 786 p.].

Pons, Collins Deutsch-Englisch, Englisch-Deutsch = Pons Collins Großwörterbuch Deutsch-Englisch, Englisch-Deutsch von Peter Terrell, Veronika Calderwood-Schnorr, Wendy V. A. Morris, Roland Breitsprecher. Nachdruck. Stuttgart 1986 [792, 790 p.; 1. ed. 1980].

Vinterberg/Bodelsen: Dansk-Engelsk Ordbog = Hermann Vinterberg og C. A. Bodelsen: Dansk-Engelsk Ordbog. Anden reviderede og udvidede udgave ved C. A. Bodelsen. Medredaktør: Jens Axelsen, B. Kjærulff Nielsen og Edith Frey. Ottende oplag med tillæg. Bd. I og II. København 1986 [918, 928 p.].

8.2. Other Publications

Al 1983 = B. P. F. Al: Dictionnaire de thème et dictionnaire de version. In: Revue de Phonétique Appliquée 66—67—68. 1983, 203—211.

Al-Kasimi 1977 = Ali M. Al-Kasimi: Linguistics and Bilingual Dictionaries. Leiden 1977.

Al-Kasimi 1983 = Ali M. Al-Kasimi: The interlingual/translation dictionary. Dictionaries for translation. In: Lexicography: Principles and Practice. Ed. R. R. K. Hartmann. London 1983, 153—162.

Baldinger 1971 = Kurt Baldinger: Semasiologie und Onomasiologie im zweisprachigen Wörterbuch. In: Interlinguistica — Sprachvergleich und Übersetzung. Festschrift zum 60. Geburtstag von Mario Wandruszka. Tübingen 1971, 384—396.

Baunebjerg Hansen 1988 = Gitte Baunebjerg Hansen: Stand und Aufgaben der zweisprachigen Lexikographie. Nachlese zum Kopenhagener Werkstattgespräch 12.—13. Mai 1986. In: Lexicographica. International Annual for Lexicography 4. 1988, 186—202.

Bergenholtz/Mugdan 1985 = Lexikographie und Grammatik. Akten des Essener Kolloquiums zur Grammatik im Wörterbuch 28.—30. 6. 1984. Ed. by Henning Bergenholtz and Joachim Mugdan. Tübingen 1985. (Lexicographica. Serie, Maior 3).

Berkov 1977 = V. P. Berkov: Slovo v dvujazyčnom slovare. Akademija Nauk ESSR. Tallin 1977.

Bielfeldt 1956 = Hans Holm Bielfeldt: Fragen des russisch-deutschen Wörterbuches. In: Zeitschrift für Slawistik 1. 1956, 19—34.

Duda/Frenzel/Wöller et al. 1986 = Walter Duda/Maria Frenzel/Egon Wöller/Tatjana Zimmermann: Zu einer Theorie der zweisprachigen Lexikographie. Überlegungen zu einem neuen russisch-deutschen Wörterbuch. Linguistische Studien, Reihe A, Arbeitsberichte 142. Berlin 1986.

Duda/Müller 1974 = Walter Duda/Bärbel Müller: Zur Problematik eines aktiven deutsch-russischen Wörterbuchs. In: Fremdsprachen 1974, H. 3, 175—180.

Duda/Müller/Müller 1978 = Walter Duda/Bärbel Müller/Klaus Müller: Zu spezifischen Aspekten der Darstellung des russischen Wortschatzes für Deutschmuttersprachler. In: Wissenschaftliche Zeitschrift der Humboldt-Universität zu Berlin, Ges.-Sprachw. R. XXVII, 4. 1978, 455—457.

Duda/Müller/Müller 1981 = Walter Duda/Bärbel Müller/Klaus Müller: Fragen der Darstellung des deutschen Wortschatzes in einem zweisprachigen Wörterbuch. In: Fremdsprachen 25. H. 1. 1981, 42—44.

Fürst 1876 = Julius Fürst: Zur Geschichte der hebräischen Lexikographie. Fortsetzung und Nachträge von Victor Ryssel. In: Julius Fürst: Hebräisches und chaldäisches Handwörterbuch über das Alte Testament. Dritte verbesserte und vermehrte Auflage, bearbeitet von V. Ryssel. Erster Band. Leipzig 1876, XV—XLIII.

Gak 1964 = V. G. Gak: O raznych tipach dvujazyčnych slovarej. In: Tetradi perevodčika 2. 1964, 71—78.

Gedney 1967 = William Gedney: Comments. In: Householder/Saporta 1967, 229—234.

Gold 1978 = David L. Gold: Problems in Interlingual Lexicography. In: Babel 24. 1978, 161—178.

Golovaščuk 1970 = S. I. Golovaščuk: Rozmežuvannja značen sliv u dvomovnomu slovniku. Movoznavstvo nr. 4, juli-august 1970. Kiew, vidavnictvo "Naukova Dumka".

Good Dictionaries 1978 = ATA Forum: Good Dictionaries — A Call for Action — How Translators Would Like Dictionaries Prepared 1978. (Summary. Workshop on specialized bilingual dictionaries held at the 1977 Annual Meeting of the American Translators Association). In: Babel 24. 1978, 52—53.

Harrell 1967 = Richard S. Harrell: Some Notes on Bilingual Lexicography. In: Householder/Saporta 1967, 51—61.

Hartmann 1982 = R. R. K. Hartmann: Das zweisprachige Wörterbuch im Fremdsprachenerwerb. In: Studien zur neuhochdeutschen Lexikographie II. Ed. by H. E. Wiegand. Germanistische Linguistik 3—6/80. Hildesheim. New York 1982, 73—86.

Hartmann 1987 = Reinhard R. K. Hartmann: Wozu Wörterbücher? Die Benutzungsforschung in der zweisprachigen Lexikographie. In: Lebende Sprachen. 32. 1987, 154—156.

Hausmann 1977 = Franz Josef Hausmann: Einführung in die Benutzung der neufranzösischen Wörterbücher. Tübingen 1977 (Romanistische Arbeitshefte 19).

Hausmann 1988 = Franz Josef Hausmann: Grundprobleme des zweisprachigen Wörterbuchs. In: K. Hyldgaard-Jensen/A. Zettersten (eds.): Symposium on Lexicography III. Proceedings of the Third International Symposium on Lexicography May 14—16, 1986 at the University of Copenhagen. Tübingen 1988 (Lexicographica. Series Maior 19), 137—154.

Hausmann/Cop 1985 = Franz Josef Hausmann/ Margaret Cop: Short History of English-German Lexicography. In: Karl Hyldgaard-Jensen/Arne Zettersten (eds.): Symposium on Lexicography II. Proceedings of the Second International Symposium on Lexicography May 16—17, 1984 at the University of Copenhagen. Tübingen 1985 (Lexicographica. Series Maior 5), 183—197.

Haywood 1965 = John A. Haywood: Arabic Lexicography. Its History and its Place in the General History of Lexicography. 2. Aufl. Leiden 1965 (1. Aufl. 1959).

Hietsch 1958 = Otto Hietsch: Meaning Discrimination in Modern Lexicography. In: Modern Language Journal 42. 1958, 232—234.

Householder/Saporta 1967 = Fred W. Householder/Sol Saporta: Problems in Lexicography. Bloomington, Indiana University 1967.

Iannucci 1957 = James E. Iannucci: Meaning Discrimination in Bilingual Lexicography: A New Lexicographical Technique. In: Modern Language Journal 41. 1957, 272—281.

Iannucci 1959 = James E. Iannucci: Explanatory Matter in Bilingual Dictionaries. In: Babel 5. 1959, 195—199.

Karl 1982 = Ilse Karl: Linguistische Probleme der zweisprachigen Lexikographie. Eine Nachlese praktischer Wörterbucharbeit. Linguistische Studien, Reihe A, Arbeitsberichte 96. Berlin 1982.

Kelemen 1957 = Bela Kelemen: Contributions à la méthode de rédaction des dictionnaires bilingues. In: Mélanges linguistiques. Bucarest 1957, 235—248.

Kopeckij 1971 = L. V. Kopeckij: Raboty po semantičeskomu sintezu i dvujazyčnyj slovar. In: Československá Rusistika XVI, nr. 5. 1971.

Kromann 1983 = Hans-Peder Kromann: Paradigmatische und syntagmatische Relationen im zweisprachigen Wörterbuch: In: Die Lexikographie von heute und das Wörterbuch von morgen. Analysen — Probleme — Vorschläge. Ed. by J. Schildt/D. Viehweger. Linguistische Studien 109. Berlin 1983, 330—348.

Kromann 1987 = Hans-Peder Kromann: Zur Typologie und Darbietung der Phraseologismen in Übersetzungswörterbüchern. In: J. Korhonen (ed.): Beiträge zur allgemeinen und germanistischen Phraseologieforschung. Oulu 1987, 183—192.

Kromann/Riiber/Rosbach 1979 = H.-P. Kromann/Th. Riiber/P. Rosbach: Betydningsbeskrivelse og ordbogstyper inden for tosprogs-leksikografien med særligt henblik på en dansk-tysk ordbog. ARK, Sproginstitutternes Arbejdspapirer, Handelshøjskolen i København, 1. 1979.

Kromann/Riiber/Rosbach 1984a = H.-P. Kromann/Th. Riiber/P. Rosbach: "Active" and "Passive" Bilingual Dictionaries: The Ščerba Concept Reconsidered. In: R. R. K. Hartmann (ed.): LEXeter '83 Proceedings. Tübingen 1984 (Lexicographica. Series Maior 1), 207—215.

Kromann/Riiber/Rosbach 1984b = H.-P. Kromann/Th. Riiber/P. Rosbach: Überlegungen zu Grundfragen der zweisprachigen Lexikographie. In: Studien zur neuhochdeutschen Lexikographie V. Ed. by H. E. Wiegand. Germanistische Linguistik 3—6/84. Hildesheim. Zürich. New York 1984, 159—238.

Leisi 1952 = Ernst Leisi: Der Wortinhalt. Seine Struktur im Deutschen und Englischen. 5. Aufl. Heidelberg 1975.

Levitzky 1957 = Leon D. Levitzky: Bilingual Dictionaries: Suggestions. In: Mélanges linguistiques. Bucarest 1957, 249—256.

Lötzsch 1978 = Ronald Lötzsch: Ein aktives Deutsch-Russisches Wörterbuch. Interview mit Dr. phil. Ronald Lötzsch. In: Spektrum — Monatszeitschrift für den Wissenschaftler Nr. 1. 1978, 28—30.

Lötzsch 1979 = Ronald Lötzsch: Einige Fragen der Entwicklung der zweisprachigen russischen Lexikographie an der AdW der DDR. In: Zeitschrift für Slawistik 24. 1979, 402—408.

Malige-Klappenbach/Bielfeldt 1966 = Helene Malige-Klappenbach/Hans Holm Bielfeldt: Deutsch-Tschechisches Wörterbuch; unter Leitung und Red. von Prof. Dr. H. Siebenschein; 2 Bde., Prag. In: Zeitschrift für Slawistik 11, H. 1. 1966, 98—103.

Mel'čuk 1984 = Igor Mel'čuk: Dictionnaire explicatif et combinatoire du français contemporain. Recherches lexico-sémantiques 1. Montréal 1984.

Meyersteen 1960 = R. S. Meyersteen: Bilingual Dictionaries and Applied Linguistics. In: Modern Language Journal 44. 1960, 163—167.

Nguyen 1980 = Dinh-Hoa Nguyen: Bicultural Information in a Bilingual Dictionary. In: Theory and Method in Lexicography. Western and Non-Western Perspectives. Ed. L. Zgusta. Courtwood Drive, Columbia 1980, 163—175.

Ponten 1975 = Jan-Peter Ponten: Kontrastive Semantik und bilinguale Lexikographie. In: Grundfragen der Methodik des Deutschunterrichts und ihrer praktischen Verfahren. Ed. H. G. Funke. München 1975, 210—217.

Ponten 1976 = Jan-Peter Ponten: Das Übersetzungswörterbuch und seine linguistischen Implikationen. In: Probleme der Lexikologie und Lexikographie. Ed. H. Moser. Düsseldorf 1976, 200—210.

Reichmann 1986 = Oskar Reichmann: Frühneuhochdeutsches Wörterbuch. Einleitung. Quellenverzeichnis. Literaturverzeichnis. In: Frühneuhochdeutsches Wörterbuch. Herausgegeben von Robert R. Anderson, Ulrich Goebel, Oskar Reichmann. Band 1. Lieferung 1. Berlin. New York 1986, 10—164.

Rettig 1985 = Wolfgang Rettig: Die zweisprachige Lexikographie Französisch-Deutsch, Deutsch-Französisch. Stand, Probleme, Aufgaben. In: Lexicographica. International Annual for Lexicography 1. 1985, 83—124.

Ščerba 1936 = L. V. Ščerba: Vorwort in: Russko-Frančuzski slovar'. Pod. red. D. V. Sezemana. Moskau 1959 (1. ed. 1936).

Ščerba 1940 = L. V. Ščerba: Versuch einer allgemeinen Theorie der Lexikographie (= Opyt obščej teorii leksikografii). In: W. Wolski (ed.): Aspekte der sowjetrussischen Lexikographie. Übersetzungen, Abstracts, bibliographische Angaben. Tübingen 1982 17—62. (1. ed. 1940).

Schnorr 1986 = Veronika Schnorr: Translational Equivalent and/or Explanation? The Perennial Problem of Equivalence. In: Lexicographica. International Annual for Lexicography 2. 1986, 53—60.

Smolik 1969 = W. Smolik: „Aktives" Wörterbuch Deutsch-Russisch. In: Nachrichten für Sprachmittler H. 3. 1969, 11—13.

Snell-Hornby 1984 = Mary Snell-Hornby: The Bilingual Dictionary — Help or Hindrance? In: R. R. K. Hartmann (ed.): LEXeter '83 Proceedings. Tübingen 1984 (Lexicographica. Series Maior 1), 274—281.

Snell-Hornby 1987 = Mary Snell-Hornby: Towards a Learner's Bilingual Dictionary. In: The Dictionary and the Language Learner. Ed. Anthony Cowie. Tübingen 1987 (Lexicographica. Series Maior 17), 159—170.

Stein 1985a = Gabriele Stein: The English Dictionary before Cawdrey. Tübingen 1985 (Lexicographica. Series Maior 9).

Stein 1985b = Gabriele Stein: English-German/German-English Lexicography: Its early beginnings. In: Lexicographica. International Annual for Lexicography 1. 1985, 134—164.

Steiner 1975 = Roger J. Steiner: Monodirectional Bilingual Dictionaries (A Lexicographical Innovation). In: Babel 21. 1975, 123—124.

Steiner 1982 = Roger J. Steiner: How a Bilingual Dictionary best Serves the Writer. In: Papers of the Dictionary Society of North America 1977. Ed. Donald Hobar. Terre Haute, IN 1982, 24—31.

Sterkenburg/Martin/Al 1982 = P. van Sterkenburg/ W. Martin/B. Al: A new Van Dale project: bilingual dictionaries on one and the same monolingual basis. In: J. Goetschalckx/L. Rolling (eds.): Lexicography in the electronic age. Amsterdam 1982, 221—237.

Sukalenko 1976 = N. J. Sukalenko: Dvujazyčnyje slovari i voprosa perevoda. Charkow 1976.

Svensén 1987 = Bo Svensén: Handbok i lexikografi. Principer och metoder i ordboksarbetet. Tekniska Nomenklaturcentralen, Stockholm 1987 (TNC 85).

Tomasczyk 1983 = Jerzy Tomasczyk: On bilingual dictionaries. The Case for Bilingual Dictionaries for Foreign Language Learners. In: (Ed.) R. R. K. Hartmann: Lexicography: Principles and Practice. London 1983, 41—51.

Werner 1979 = Reinhold Werner: Formaler Vergleich einiger spanisch-deutscher und deutsch-spanischer Wörterbücher. In: Lebende Sprachen 24. 1979, 75—81.

Werner 1980 = Reinhold Werner: Ein technisches Detail der Stilebenenkennzeichnung im zweisprachigen Wörterbuch. In: Lebende Sprachen 25. 1980, 154—158.

Werner 1982 = Reinhold Werner: Zur Reihenfolge der Definitionen bzw. Übersetzungsäquivalente im Wörterbuchartikel (mit besonderer Berücksichtigung spanischer Beispiele). In: Lebende Sprachen 27. 1982, 150—156.

Wiegand 1981 = Herbert Ernst Wiegand: Pragmatische Informationen in neuhochdeutschen Wörterbüchern. Ein Beitrag zur praktischen Lexikologie. In: H. E. Wiegand (ed.): Studien zur neuhochdeutschen Lexikographie I. Hildesheim. New York 1981 (Germanistische Linguistik 3—4/79), 139—271.

Wiegand 1985 = Herbert Ernst Wiegand: Fragen zur Grammatik in Wörterbuchbenutzungsprotokollen. Ein Beitrag zur empirischen Erforschung der Benutzer einsprachiger Wörterbücher. In: Lexikographie und Grammatik. Akten des Essener Kolloquiums zur Grammatik im Wörterbuch, 28.—30. 6. 1984. H. Bergenholtz/J. Mugdan (eds.). Tübingen 1985 (Lexicographica. Series Maior 3), 20—98.

Williams 1959 = Edwin B. Williams: The Problem of Bilingual Lexicography Particularly as Applied to Spanish and English. In: Hispanic Review 27. 1959, 246—253.

Williams 1960 = Edwin B. Williams: Analysis of the Problem of Meaning Discrimination in Spanish and English Bilingual Lexicography. In: Babel 6. 1960, 121—125.

Zaiping/Wiegand 1987 = Pan Zaiping/Herbert Ernst Wiegand: Konzeption für das Große Deutsch-Chinesische Wörterbuch. In: Lexicographica. International Annual for Lexicography 3. 1987, 228—241.

Zgusta 1971 = Ladislav Zgusta et al.: Manual of Lexicography. The Hague. Paris 1971.

Zgusta 1984 = Ladislav Zgusta: Translational equivalence in the bilingual dictionary. In: R. R. K. Hartmann (ed.): LEXeter '83 Proceedings. Tübingen 1984, 145—154. (Lexicographica. Series Maior 1).

Zgusta 1987 = Ladislav Zgusta et al.: Lexicography Today. An annotated bibliography of the theory of lexicography. Tübingen 1987 (Lexicographica. Series Maior 18).

Hans-Peder Kromann/Theis Riiber/Poul Rosbach (†), Copenhagen (Denmark)

286. Spezifische Bauteile und Strukturen zweisprachiger Wörterbücher: eine Übersicht

1. Grundbegriffe
2. Hierarchische Adressierung und Mehr-Wort-Adressen
3. Einsprachige und zweisprachige Bearbeitungseinheiten
4. Bedeutungs- und äquivalenzdifferenzierende Angaben
5. Beispiel- und Kotextangaben
6. Glossen
7. Zusammenwirken von Glossen, Kotextangaben und Markierungsangaben
8. Inhaltliche Beziehungsgeflechte zwischen Artikelbauteilen
9. Sprachrichtungen und Funktionen des zweisprachigen Wörterbuchs
10. Zum Status der sog. Äquivalente im zweisprachigen Wörterbuch
11. Makrostrukturen zweisprachiger Wörterbücher
12. Mikrostrukturelle Profile zweisprachiger Wörterbücher
13. Literatur (in Auswahl)

1. Grundbegriffe

Entsprechend Art. 36, 1. besteht eine 'lexikographische Bearbeitungseinheit' aus zwei Zeichenkomplexen (Zeichen, in sich strukturierten Zeichengebilden, Mengen von Zeichen oder Mengen von strukturierten Zeichengebilden), die einander nach dem Prinzip Thema/Rhema zugeordnet sind. Für den thematischen Zeichenkomplex wird der Terminus *Adresse,* für den rhematischen der Terminus *Angabe* verwendet. Die Adresse bildet ein Element einer lexikographischen Zugriffsstruktur, auf das mindestens eine Angabe 'adressiert' wird. Im Extremfall können Adresse und Angabe in ein und demselben Zeichenkomplex zusammenfallen. Die Form der Adresse oder ein Bestandteil ihrer Form liefert in diesem Fall Information über das Zeichen oder die Zeichen, das/die mittels der Adresse erwähnt wird/werden.

Lexikographische Bearbeitungseinheit

Adresse	→ Zugriff auf	Angabe
(Thema)	Information über ←	(Rhema)

Abb. 286.1: Schema der lexikographischen Adressierung

Wichtigster Typ von Adresse im Wörterbuch ist als Teil der wichtigsten Zugriffsstruktur (Art. 36), d. h. in der Regel der Makrostruktur (Art. 38), das Lemma (Art. 37). In der lexikographischen Praxis lassen sich sowohl nach formalen wie nach inhaltlichen Kriterien Hunderte von Angabentypen unterscheiden. Im Gegensatz zum einsprachigen Wörterbuch, in dem Adresse und Angaben immer derselben Sprache angehören, kann das zweisprachige Wörterbuch sowohl Bearbeitungseinheiten mit Adresse und Angabe(n) in derselben Sprache als auch Bearbeitungseinheiten mit je verschiedener Sprache für Adresse und Angabe(n) enthalten. Ersterer Typ von Bearbeitungseinheit soll im folgenden einfach als 'einsprachig', letzterer als 'zweisprachig' bezeichnet werden (vgl. unten 3.).

Zentrale Bedeutung im allgemeinen zweisprachigen Wörterbuch kommt einem Typ zweisprachiger Bearbeitungseinheit zu, welcher sich aus einer Wortschatzeinheit der Ausgangssprache (als Adresse) und einer darauf adressierten, als äquivalent angenommenen Wortschatzeinheit der Zielsprache (als Angabe) zusammensetzt. Diese zentrale Bearbeitungseinheit wird im angelsächsischen Sprachraum als *bilingual item* bezeichnet.

bilingual item

(Ausgangssprache A)	(Zielsprache B)
Wortschatzeinheit aus A	Wortschatzeinheit aus B
(Adresse)	(Angabe)

Abb. 286.2: Schema des 'bilingual item'

Die Probleme der Äquivalentsetzung und ihrer Grenzen werden in Art. 285, 4. und 5., sowie in Art. 295 abgehandelt (vgl. auch Marello 1989, 51—55). Ein erster besonderer Problemkreis ist mit den Mehr-Wort-Adressen verbunden, die aufgrund der Äquivalenzverhältnisse zwischen Sprachen zahlreich sind (vgl. Art. 303, 1.), in der Regel aber nicht der Makrostruktur angehören, sondern in die Mikrostruktur abgeschoben werden. Mehr-Wort-Adressen haben also meist keinen lemmatischen Status (auch keinen sublemmatischen, vgl. unten 11.), sondern einen infralemmatischen (vgl. Art. 36, Fig. 36.14; dort wird für *infralemmatisch* der Terminus *non-*

lemmatic verwendet). Infralemmatische Adressen können in Übereinstimmung mit Art. 36, 8. auch *Subadressen* genannt werden. In der Übersicht:

Lemma = lemmatische Adresse (Makrostruktur)
Sublemma = sublemmatische Adresse (Makrostruktur)
Subadresse = infralemmatische Adresse (Mikrostruktur)

Der mit den Mehr-Wort-Adressen verbundene Problemkreis sowie allgemein die Probleme von Makro- und Mikrostruktur im zweisprachigen Wörterbuch werden in den Abschnitten 2., 11. und 12. behandelt (vgl. ferner Art. 287—290).

Ein zweiter Problemkreis ergibt sich aus der Polyäquivalenz. Einer Wortschatzeinheit der Ausgangssprache stehen nämlich in der Regel mehrere äquivalente Einheiten der Zielsprache gegenüber. Die Polyäquivalenz erfordert mannigfache Techniken der Äquivalenzdifferenzierung (E. *meaning discrimination,* vgl. Art. 285, 5., doch ist dieser Terminus unpassend und sollte durch *equivalence discrimination* ersetzt werden) (vgl. unten 4.—8. und Marello 1989, 55—61).

Schließlich sind die Bauteile und Strukturen vielfachen Funktionen zuzuordnen, die wiederum zu differenzieren sind, je nachdem ob Ausgangs- oder Zielsprache Mutter- oder Fremdsprache des Benutzers ist (vgl. unten 9.). Daraus ergibt sich, daß die sogenannten Äquivalente (E. *equivalents,* F. *traduisants* oder *équivalents*) einen vielgestaltigen Status haben können, der unten in Abschnitt 10. erläutert wird.

Es brauchen in diesem Artikel nicht alle Bauteile des zweisprachigen Wörterbuchs besprochen zu werden, da viele sich im Vergleich zum allgemeinen einsprachigen Wörterbuch (s. Art. 36, Fig. 36.9) als unspezifisch erweisen, z. B. Orthographie- und Ausspracheangaben. Der (sporadisch auftretenden) paradigmatischen Information ist Art. 291 gewidmet. Selten sind auch etymologische Angaben (z. B. Essence 1983).

2. Hierarchische Adressierung und Mehr-Wort-Adressen

2.1. Hierarchische Adressierung

Wie im einsprachigen Wörterbuch kann auch im zweisprachigen die Adressierung in hierarchischen Strukturen erfolgen. Mehrere Artikel zusammen können auf ein Nest- oder Nischeneingangslemma adressiert sein (vgl. Art. 37, 3., s. auch unten 11.). Das Nest- bzw. das Nischeneingangslemma stellt eine übergeordnete Adresse dar, der die Lemmata der einzelnen Artikel als Adressen untergeordnet sind. Innerhalb eines Artikels kann das Lemma wieder übergeordnete Adresse sein. Im zweisprachigen Wörterbuch ist es dies in folgenden Fällen:

(a) Bei einsprachigen Bearbeitungseinheiten (3.). Beispiel: Eine Genusangabe ist auf ein zielsprachliches Äquivalent des ausgangssprachlichen Lemmazeichens adressiert. Das Äquivalent ist in diesem Fall nicht nur Angabe zur Adresse Lemma, sondern ist dieser auch als eigene Adresse untergeordnet.

(b) Bei mehrfacher Präsentation des Lemmazeichens unter einem gemeinsamen Lemma zum Zweck der Artikelgliederung entsprechend verschiedenen Kriterien der Unterscheidung von Einzelbedeutungen oder der Anordnung von Äquivalenten, wobei jede der einzelnen Präsentationen von irgendeiner Charakterisierung begleitet wird, aus der die Anordnungskriterien ersichtlich sind (zur Präsentation des Lemmazeichens können wie beim Lemma des gesamten Artikels Platzhaltersymbole herangezogen werden). Beispiel: In einem Artikel zu einer Präposition, die in je verschiedenen Einzelbedeutungen je verschiedene Kasus regieren kann, etwa altgriechisch ἐπί, kann die Präsentation der Präposition jeweils zusammen mit der Kasusangabe — „ἐπί (Genitiv)", „ἐπί (Dativ)" und „ἐπί (Akkusativ)" — als Adresse dem Lemma untergeordnet werden.

(c) Dem Lemma untergeordnete Adressen können für Verwendungen des Lemmazeichens stehen, bei denen die Präsentation des Lemmazeichens in der für die Lemmatisierung gewählten Nennform (etwa Nominativ Singular oder Infinitiv) nicht ausreicht. Dies ist z. B. der Fall, wenn Einzelbedeutungen oder Äquivalente auf bestimmte grammatikalische Formen, auf Vorkommen in durch bestimmte Interpunktionszeichen gekennzeichneten Verwendungen oder auf bestimmte syntagmatische Umgebungen des Lemmazeichens (einschließlich des Vorkommens in Komposita) beschränkt sind, wie etwa in folgenden Fällen (Spanisch-Deutsch):

(aa) **padre**... Vater...
padres... Eltern...
(bb) **miércoles**... Mittwoch...
¡miércoles!... Scheibenkleister!
(cc) **carnet**... Ausweis
carné de conducir (Spanien)... Führerschein

Statt „**padres**", „**¡miércoles!**" und „**carné de conducir**" könnte die untergeordnete Adressierung in den Beispielen aa — cc mittels „~ s", „¡ ~ !" bzw. „~ de conducir" erfolgen. Es liegt auf der Hand, daß sich zahlreiche weitere Hierarchisierungsmöglichkeiten ergeben. Eine bestimmte grammatikalische Form (Plural, reflexives Verb, finite Verbform etc.) kann als Adresse der üblichen Nennform untergeordnet sein und ihrerseits übergeordnete Adresse für das Wort in derselben grammatikalischen Form, aber z. B. mit Ausrufezeichen zur Kennzeichnung der exklamativen Funktion, sein; eine Mehr-Wort-Einheit kann einer Ein-Wort-Einheit in einer bestimmten grammatikalischen Form untergeordnet sein und diese wiederum der Nennform, die als Lemma gewählt wurde; etc.

Weitere Hierarchisierungen ergeben sich durch die Verbindung aller bisher genannten Möglichkeiten der untergeordneten Adressierung. Man könnte sich also z. B. folgende Adressierungshierarchie vorstellen: Nischeneingangslemma → Nischenlemma (Substantiv im Singular) → Adresse für die Pluralform des Lemmazeichens → Adresse für Mehr-Wort-Einheit, welche die Pluralform des Lemmazeichens mitumfaßt (Nominalsyntagma) → Adresse für die Mehr-Wort-Einheit mit Ausrufezeichen (exklamative Funktion) → zielsprachliches Äquivalent der Mehr-Wort-Einheit in exklamativer Funktion → [Stilebenenangabe zum Äquivalent].

Zur terminologischen Vereinfachung sei folgende Sprachregelung getroffen. Eine Adresse wird im Hinblick auf eine ihr untergeordnete Adresse als 'Oberadresse' und im Hinblick auf eine ihr übergeordnete Adresse als 'Unteradresse' bezeichnet. Soll eine Adresse als solche unterhalb der Adressierungsebene des Lemmas (bzw. des Sublemmas, vgl. Abschnitt 11.) charakterisiert werden, so kann sie als 'infralemmatische Adresse' bezeichnet werden.

2.2. Mehr-Wort-Einheiten in der Adressierungshierarchie

In den meisten, nicht allen, zweisprachigen Wörterbüchern läßt sich folgender Bezug zwischen Adressierungshierarchie und Behandlung von Mehr-Wort-Einheiten der Wörterbuchausgangssprache feststellen. Mehr-Wort-Einheiten der Ausgangssprache wird in der Regel kein eigener Artikel gewidmet. Sie fungieren meist als infralemmatische Adressen zweisprachiger Bearbeitungseinheiten. Umgekehrt stehen die meisten infralemmatischen Adressen zweisprachiger Bearbeitungseinheiten für aus mehreren Wörtern bestehende Wortschatzeinheiten der Ausgangssprache.

Als Mehr-Wort-Einheiten werden hier nicht nur Wortschatzeinheiten mit einem bestimmten lexikologischen Status (Lexikalisierung, phraseologische Fixierung etc.) bezeichnet, sondern beliebige aus mehreren Einheiten in derselben Verwendungsinstanz (zum Begriff 'Verwendungsinstanz' s. Art. 37, 2.) bestehende Wortkombinationen. In Frage kommen neben phraseologischen Einheiten der verschiedensten Art sowie Kollokationen z. B. auch Wortverbindungen ohne jegliche syntagmatische Fixierung, für die als zielsprachliche Äquivalente Wörter oder Wortkombinationen stehen, die vom Wörterbuchbenutzer nicht ohne weiteres über die Äquivalente der einzelnen Wörter der ausgangssprachlichen Wortkombination erschlossen werden können.

Zweisprachige Wörterbücher machen in der Regel auch keine oder nur geringe Versuche, den lexikologischen Status von Mehr-Wort-Einheiten zu bestimmen. Gewöhnlich findet man weder Angaben zum lexikologischen Status noch typographische Unterscheidung verschiedener Arten von Mehr-Wort-Einheiten (allenfalls läßt sich der idiomatische Charakter aus einer Glosse oder einem Transferindikator wie „fig." erschließen). Das wichtigste Kriterium für die Ansetzung von Mehr-Wort-Einheiten als Adressen ist die Tatsache, daß für die betreffende ausgangssprachliche Wortkombination Äquivalente als Angaben für nötig erachtet werden, die sich nicht einfach aus den Äquivalenten erschließen lassen, die das Wörterbuch für die Einzelwörter angibt, aus denen die Wortkombination besteht.

Die Bearbeitungseinheiten, derentwegen aus Mehr-Wort-Einheiten bestehende Adressen erforderlich sind, bringen also in der Regel Information, die dem Wörterbuchartikel nicht anderweitig zu entnehmen ist. Ihre Funktion ist meist nicht die, im Artikel bereits anderweitig vermittelte Aussagen zu exemplifizieren oder zu illustrieren. Sie enthalten nicht redundante, sondern grundsätzlich neue, zentrale und unersetzbare Information. Deshalb empfiehlt sich keineswegs ihre übliche Benennung mit den Termini *Beispiel* und *Anwendungsbeispiel*.

Übrigens bleibt bei aus Mehr-Wort-Einheiten, insbesondere Sätzen, bestehenden

Adressen oft implizit, welcher Information wegen (z. B. kollokationeller, konstruktioneller oder gleichzeitig kollokationeller und konstruktioneller Information wegen) sie als notwendig erachtet wurden. Der Benutzer ist oft auf Hypothesen angewiesen. Der Mangel an grundsätzlich wünschenswerter Explizitheit ist jedoch aus Gründen ökonomischer Zwänge und der ratsamen Vermeidung zu komplexer lexikographischer Mikrostrukturen entschuldbar.

3. Einsprachige und zweisprachige Bearbeitungseinheiten

In der einsprachigen Bearbeitungseinheit stehen Adresse und Angabe(n) in derselben Sprache. Einsprachige Bearbeitungseinheiten können sowohl auf der ausgangs- wie auf der zielsprachlichen Seite vorkommen. So können z. B. Ausspracheangaben sowohl für ein ausgangssprachliches Lemmazeichen wie für dessen zielsprachliche Äquivalente vorgenommen werden (letzteres ist in der Praxis seltener anzutreffen). Ähnliches gilt für weitere Angabentypen, wie Wortarten-, Flexions- und Konstruktionsangaben sowie für alle Arten glossierender und markierender Angaben.

In der zweisprachigen Bearbeitungseinheit wird auf eine sprachliche Einheit der Ausgangssprache eine zielsprachliche Einheit adressiert. Wichtigster Typ zweisprachiger Bearbeitungseinheit ist der, welcher aus der Präsentation einer ausgangssprachlichen Wortschatzeinheit und der Angabe eines zielsprachlichen Äquivalents besteht. Während in den meisten Wörterbüchern die einsprachigen Bearbeitungseinheiten an Zahl gegenüber den zweisprachigen überwiegen, enthalten die zweisprachigen die zentrale Information.

bestatten [bə'ʃtatn̩] *tr. V. (geh.)* inter *(formal);* bury; **bestattet werden** be laid to rest

Textbeispiel 286.1: Wörterbuchartikel *bestatten* (aus: Duden Oxford, 957)

Der in Textbeispiel 286.1 wiedergegebene Wörterbuchartikel enthält folgende Bearbeitungseinheiten:

(a) Zweisprachige Bearbeitungseinheiten:
bestatten inter
bestatten bury
bestattet werden be laid to rest

(b) Einsprachige Bearbeitungseinheiten:

(ba) Ausgangssprachliche Bearbeitungseinheiten
bestatten [bə'ʃtatn̩] (Ausspracheangabe)
bestatten *tr.V.* (Konstruktionsangabe)
bestatten *(geh.)* (Markierungsangabe)
(bb) Zielsprachliche Bearbeitungseinheit
inter *(formal)* (Markierungsangabe)

4. Bedeutungs- und äquivalenzdifferenzierende Angaben

4.1. Der ambivalente informative Status äquivalenzdifferenzierender Angaben

Einigen Typen von Angaben (meist in einsprachigen Bearbeitungseinheiten) können prinzipiell zwei verschiedene Funktionen (je nach Fall die eine oder die andere oder auch beide zusammen) zukommen. Sie können einerseits einfach eine Angabe zu der Wortschatzeinheit bilden, welche die Adresse (in der Wörterbuchausgangs- oder in der Wörterbuchzielsprache) präsentiert, sie können aber auch die Beziehung zwischen ausgangssprachlicher Wortschatzeinheit und zielsprachlichem Äquivalent betreffen. Siehe das folgende Beispiel (Deutsch-Englisch):

erschöpfen *v/t* to exhaust.
erschrecken *v/t* to frighten; *v/i* to be frightened.

Das Artikelsegment „*v/t*" im Artikel zu *erschöpfen* beinhaltet nur die Aussage, daß *erschöpfen* transitives Verb ist. Die Artikelsegmente „*v/t*" und "to frighten" im Artikel zu *erschrecken* können in doppelter Weise interpretiert werden. Erstens: *erschrecken* kann als transitives Verb gebraucht werden, und als Äquivalent zu *erschrecken* kommt *to frighten* in Frage. In diesem Fall bildet „**erschrecken**" die Adresse einer einsprachigen Bearbeitungseinheit (Angabe „*v/t*") und gleichzeitig einer zweisprachigen (Angabe "to frighten"). Zweitens (und so wird der Wörterbuchbenutzer das Textsegment „**erschrecken** *v/t* to frighten" eben eher interpretieren): Dem deutschen *erschrecken* als transitivem Verb entspricht im Englischen *to frighten*. Fragt man nach Adressen und Angaben im Artikel zu *erschrecken*, so hat man theoretisch die Wahl zwischen vier verschiedenen Lesarten:

(a) Der Adresse „**erschrecken**" stehen vier Angaben gegenüber: „*v/t*", "to frighten", „*v/i*" und "to be frightened".

(b) Der Adresse „**erschrecken**" stehen die Angaben "to frighten" und "to be frightened" gegenüber. Zwischen Adresse und Angabe stehen jeweils „v/t" und „v/i", die weder als Adresse noch als Angabe gewertet werden, sondern als eine Art 'Angabenmodifikator'. Damit könnten zweisprachige Bearbeitungseinheiten aus drei Arten von Elementen bestehen. Da „v/t" im Artikel zu *erschöpfen* nicht 'Angabenmodifikator', sondern nur Angabe sein kann, müßte parallel dazu „v/t" im Artikel zu *erschrecken* als Angabe und 'Angabenmodifikator' interpretiert werden.

(c) Man betrachtet im Sinne des oben (s. 3.) Gesagten „v/t" und „v/i" gleichzeitig als Angaben und als Unteradressen zur lemmatischen Adresse „**erschrecken**". Der Artikel bestünde dann aus Elementen nur mit Adressenstatus („**erschrecken**"), Elementen nur mit Angabenstatus ("to frighten" und "to be frightened") und Elementen mit Adressen- und Angabenstatus („v/t" und „v/i").

(d) Man geht von mehrgliedrigen Adressen aus, einer, die aus den Elementen „**erschrecken**" und „v/t", sowie einer, die aus den Elementen „**erschrecken**" und „v/i" besteht. Erstere würde mit der Angabe "to frighten", letztere mit der Angabe "to be frightened" eine Bearbeitungseinheit bilden. Lesart d bringt keine Vorteile gegenüber Lesart c. Sie ist komplizierter, insbesondere, wenn man den Artikel, wie dies naheliegt, als hierarchisch gegliedert ansieht. In letzterem Fall müßte man das Lemma „**erschrecken**" als Oberadresse und dazu zwei Unteradressen „**erschrecken** v/t" sowie „**erschrecken** v/i" annehmen. Mit Lesart d ist Lesart c folgender Nachteil gemeinsam. Sie ergeben wenig Sinn, wenn nicht allen jeweiligen parallelen Artikelsegmenten parallele Angaben vorausgehen, etwa in Fällen wie diesem:

Ursprung *m* origine *f,* principe *m; (Anfang)* commencement *m; (Entstehung)* naissance *f; (Quelle)* source *f; (Herkunft)* provenance *f.*

Man könnte Lesart d z. B. in diesem Fall nur beibehalten, wenn man annimmt, daß „origine" und „principe" direkt, „commencement", „naissance", „source" und „provenance" dagegen über „*(Anfang)*", „*(Entstehung)*", „*(Quelle)*" bzw. „*(Herkunft)*" auf das Lemma „**Ursprung**" adressiert sind. Lesart d könnte jedoch in bestimmten Fällen wie in folgendem Sinn ergeben. In einem Wörterbuch Tagalog-Englisch nur für Benutzer mit Muttersprache Tagalog, in dem für das Lemmazeichen (Tagalog) in der Regel keine Ausspracheangaben erfolgen, werden fallweise Ausspracheangaben zur Bedeutungs- oder Äquivalenzdifferenzierung eingesetzt, etwa so:

kainan [ka·ˈi·nan] party; [kaɪna·n] place for eating
tubo [tu·bo] tube, pipe; [tʊbo·] sugar cane

Auch in diesem Fall ist Lesart d jedoch nicht unbedingt erforderlich. Lesart b würde grundsätzlich eine kompliziertere Lösung als das binäre Prinzip nach dem Muster Adresse/Angabe erfordern.

Bei Lesart a scheint sich der Nachteil zu ergeben, daß die eigentliche Funktion mancher Angaben gar nicht berücksichtigt wird. „*(Anfang)*" im Artikel *Ursprung* in einem deutsch-französischen Wörterbuch soll nichts in bezug auf das deutsche Lemmazeichen erklären, sondern es soll besagen, wann für deutsch *Ursprung* französisch *commencement* in Frage kommt. Der entsprechende Einwand greift jedoch nicht, wenn prinzipiell zwischen adressenhierarchischen Strukturen einerseits und Angabenfunktionen andererseits unterschieden wird. Die Tatsache, daß eine Angabe auf einen bestimmten anderen Bauteil eines Artikels adressiert ist, muß nicht bedeuten, daß die der Angabe zu entnehmende Information nur für die durch die Adresse vertretene Wortschatzeinheit gilt.

Die strenge Unterscheidung zwischen Zuordnung einer Angabe per Adressierung und Zuordnung hinsichtlich informativem Wert erweist sich gerade deshalb als vorteilhaft, weil bei der metalexikographischen Analyse offengelassen werden kann, ob ein Angabentyp deswegen eingesetzt wird, um Information über ein bestimmtes Wortschatzelement oder Information über Beziehungen zwischen einem ausgangssprachlichen und einem zielsprachlichen Element zu liefern. In vielen Wörterbüchern ist nämlich nicht offensichtlich, zu welchem Zweck bestimmte Angabentypen genau eingesetzt werden sollen. Häufig liegt der Verdacht nahe, daß vor der Redaktion des Wörterbuches keine entsprechende grundsätzliche Festlegung getroffen wurde.

Einer Angabe können auch verschiedene informative Funktionen je nach aktiver oder passiver Wörterbuchbenutzung (s. 9.2.) zugeordnet sein. Beispiel (Spanisch-Deutsch):

polla *f* junge Henne *f,* Junghenne *f; fam* (junges) Mädchen *n; vulg* Schwanz *m* (= Penis)

Die Stilebenenangaben „*fam*" und „*vulg*" könnten hier dem Benutzer mit Muttersprache Spanisch zur Äquivalenzdifferenzierung dienen. Mit ihrer Hilfe kann er die Entscheidung fällen, ob er als Äquivalent für *polla* im Deutschen *Junghenne, Mädchen,* oder *Schwanz* wählen soll. Die Stilebenenangaben bringen ihm keine Information, die er suchen würde, sie stellen für ihn nur Leitelemente bei der Suche nach dem einschlägigen Äquivalent dar. Anders liegt der Fall für den deutschsprachigen Benutzer. Er entnimmt den Stilebenenangaben tatsächlich Information zur Markierung von *polla*. Er erfährt, daß *polla* in der Einzelbedeutung 'junges Mädchen' im Gegensatz zum gebotenen deutschen Äquivalent als familiär und in der Einzelbedeutung 'Penis' in Übereinstimmung mit dem deutschen *Schwanz* als vulgär markiert ist.

Angaben, die nicht nur die sprachliche Einheit betreffen, auf die sie adressiert sind, sondern auch die Beziehung zwischen einer ausgangssprachlichen Wortschatzeinheit und einem zielsprachlichen Äquivalent, müssen nicht grundsätzlich auf eine ausgangssprachliche, sondern können auch auf eine zielsprachliche Einheit adressiert sein. Im folgenden Beispiel (Deutsch-Spanisch) geht es wieder um grammatikalische Angaben:

Radio *m* radio *f*.
Radius *m* radio *m*.

Die Genusangabe „*f*" im Artikel zu *Radio* kann so interpretiert werden, daß sie besagt, daß *radio* nur in femininer Verwendung als Äquivalent zu *Radio* in Frage kommt. Analoges gilt für *radio* in maskuliner Verwendung und *Radius*.

4.2. Äquivalenzdifferenzierung mittels verschiedener Typen von Angaben

Als bedeutungs- und äquivalenzdifferenzierende Angaben kommen oft Angaben verschiedener Typen in Frage. Im Artikel zu spanisch *polla* könnte die Bedeutungs- und Äquivalenzdifferenzierung in einem spanisch-deutschen Wörterbuch für Spanier statt durch die Stilebenenangaben „*fam*" und „*vulg*" auch durch denotative Identifizierung, z. B. durch „*(jovencita)*" bzw. „*(pene)*" geleistet werden:

polla *f (gallina)* junge Henne *f*, Junghenne *f*; *(jovencita)* (junges) Mädchen *n*; *(pene)* Schwanz *m*.

Häufig wechseln in ein und demselben Wörterbuch in bedeutungs- und äquivalenzdifferenzierender Funktion Angaben verschiedener Typen in bunter Reihenfolge. Oft werden sie kumuliert. Und sehr häufig werden verschiedene Angabentypen auch typographisch nicht unterschieden. Insbesondere folgende Angabentypen werden in vielen zweisprachigen Wörterbüchern formal und funktional nicht hinreichend differenziert

(s. 7.): Kotextangaben, Glossen und Markierungsangaben. Diese drei Typen von Angaben werfen für das zweisprachige Wörterbuch auch besondere Probleme auf. Probleme im Zusammenhang mit Markierungsangaben werden in Art. 292 behandelt, im übrigen gilt das in Art. 36, 6.3. über Markierung Gesagte (vgl. ferner die Art. 53—61). Im folgenden soll auf spezielle Probleme im Zusammenhang mit Kotextangaben (5.) und Glossen (6.) im zweisprachigen Wörterbuch eingegangen werden.

5. Beispiel- und Kotextangaben

5.1. Wider den üblichen Beispielbegriff

Im Unterschied zum Sprachgebrauch vieler Wörterbucheinleitungen, die als Beispiele zweisprachige Bearbeitungseinheiten bezeichnen, die aus einer Mehr-Wort-Einheit der Ausgangssprache und einem zielsprachlichen Äquivalent oder Äquivalentsurrogat bestehen, definiert Art. 289 den Bauteil 'Beispiel' als Angabe zur Syntagmatik in einsprachigen Bearbeitungseinheiten. Für 'Beispiele' im Sinne von Art. 289 soll im folgenden der Terminus *Kotextangabe* verwendet werden. Der Terminus *Beispiel* suggeriert von seiner vorwissenschaftlichen Bedeutung her primär exemplifizierende oder illustrierende Funktion. Den hier als Kotextangaben bezeichneten Angaben kommt diese Funktion jedoch häufig nicht oder nur sekundär zu. Im übrigen können zu diesen Angaben noch formal deutlich unterschiedene Bauteile treten, denen tatsächlich eine Beispielfunktion im vorwissenschaftlichen Sinne zugedacht ist.

5.2. Kotext- und Beispielangaben, am Beispiel eines altsprachlichen Wörterbuchs

Zur Veranschaulichung eignen sich gut Artikel aus einem modernen Wörterbuch mit einer toten Sprache als einer der beiden Sprachen des zweisprachigen Wörterbuchs, weil sie eindeutig nicht sowohl für Benutzer mit der Ausgangs- wie solche mit der Zielsprache als Muttersprache bestimmt sind und deshalb nicht je verschiedene Angabenfunktionen für je nach ihrer Muttersprache definierte Zielgruppen angenommen werden müssen. Ein lateinisch-englisches Wörterbuch ist sicher nicht für Muttersprachler des Latein definiert, die Information für die sprachliche Produktion des Englischen suchen. In den

marīnus ~a ~um, *a.* [MARE+-INVS]
1 Of or belonging to the sea, marine, sea-. **b** (of deities). **c** (of animals or plants, esp. those named after land varieties). **d** (of the products of the sea); *aqua* ~*a* (and sim.), seawater. **e** (as dist. from river-); (esp. of ships or sailors) seagoing.
~as. plagas ENN.*Sat.*65; ~is aestibus CIC.*Div.*2.34; ~is fluctibus LUCR.5.1079; casus pariter timuisse ~os Ov.*Pont.*2.10.39; me.. ~o lauacro trado APVL.*Met.*11.1. **b** ~as.. Nymphas CATVL.64.16; ~ae..Veneris HOR.*Carm.*3.26.5; uirginis.. ~ae (*i.e.* Thetidis) Ov.*Met.*11.228; dis.. ~is 13.964; iuuenes.. ~os JVV.14.283. **c** (*animals*) mustela ~a ENN.*var.*34; ~am urticam PL.*Rud.*298; canibus.. ~is VERG.*Ecl.*6.77; ostreas ~as AFRAN.*com.*142; uolucres.. ~ae PROP.3.7.11; ~is beluis SEN.*Apoc.*5.3; testudini ~ae PLIN.*Nat.*11.180; leporis ~i uenenum 20.223; muris ~i cinis 32.67;—(*plants*) ~a lactuca COL.6.15.2; ~a brassica PLIN.*Nat.*20.96. **d** harena fossicia, fluuiatica aut ~a lota VITR.1.2.8; limum ~um PLIN.*Nat.*19.178; salis ~i LARG.217;—aquae ~ae ueteris Q. II CATO *Agr.*24; colorem..habet ~ae aquae CELS.7.7.14; SUET.*Aug.*82.2;—concipiunt..multum ..~um umorem LUCR.6.503; laticis.. ~i Ov.*Pont.*3.1.17. **e** siue..Boreae uis saeua ~as, siue redundatas flumine cogit aquas Ov.*Tr.*3.10.51; cum cancris ~is uel fluuiatilibus PLIN.*Nat.*20.120;—qui naues ~as fabricauerunt SCAEV.*dig.*50.5.3; nauem accipere debemus siue ~am siue fluuiatilem ULP.*dig.*1.1.1.6; NAVICLARIO ~O *CIL* 13.1942.
2 Relating to ships or seamanship, nautical.
de ~is machinationibus VITR.10.13.8.
3 *ros* ~*us*, The plant rosemary.
Culex 403; coronantem ~o rore deos HOR.*Carm.*3.23.15; PLIN.*Nat.*11.38; PLIN.*Ep.*2.17.14.

marītō ~āre ~āuī ~ātum, *tr.* [MARITVS²+ -O³]
1 To provide with a husband or wife, marry; (pass.) to get married, marry. **b** to contract (a marriage).
Vitelli..filiam splendidissime ~auit SUET.*Ves.*14.1; (*poet.*) dum Pelea dulce ~at Pelion STAT.*Ach.*2.56;—QVI NONDVM SVNT ~ATI *CIL* 6.32323.55; quando ~andum principem cuncti suaderent TAC.*Ann.*12.6; quouis alio felicius ~are APVL.*Met.*8.8; (*in the title of a law of Augustus*) LEGE DE ~A⟨NDIS ORDINIBVS⟩ *CIL* 6.32323.55; SUET.*Aug.*34.1; GAIUS *Inst.*1.178. **b** matrimonia..non priuatim ~anda esse APVL.*Pl.*2.25.
2 To mate or pair (animals, birds).
(canes) dicuntur catulire, id est ostendere uelle se ~ari VAR.*R.*2.9.11; ternae (gallinae) singulis ~antur COL.8.2.12; 8.8.7.
3 To fertilize (plants).
illum (*sc.* palmam marem)..adflatu uisuque ipso et puluere etiam reliquas ~are PLIN.*Nat.*13.35; hoc (*sc.* uento fauonio) ~antur uiuescentia e terra 16.93.
4 To join or 'wed' (vines and trees grown to support them); (also w. vines as subj.).
adulta uitium propagine altas ~at populos HOR.*Epod.*2.10; si teneram ulmum ~aueris COL.5.6.18; ulmi..uitibus recte ~antur 11.2.79; PLIN.*Nat.*17.200;—caules..qui possint..sua ~are statumina COL.4.22.6; ut uiduum ramum ~et (uitis) 5.6.31.

Textbeispiel 286.2: Wörterbuchartikel *marinus, -a, -um* und *marito* (aus: OLD 1982, 1079—1080)

Artikeln *marinus, -a, -um* und *marito* (Textbeispiel 286.2) kann man deutlich folgende Bauteile voneinander unterscheiden:

(a) Zweisprachige Bearbeitungseinheiten für Mehr-Wort-Einheiten der Ausgangssprache. Sie finden sich nur im Artikel *marinus, -a, -um*. Adressen sind „*aqua* ~*a*" und „*ros* ~*us*".

(b) Kotextangaben zu ausgangssprachlichen und zielsprachlichen Wortschatzeinheiten. Der Artikel zu *marinus, -a, -um* ist reich an Kotextangaben zum ausgangssprachlichen Lemma: "(of deities)", "(of animals or plants, esp. those named after land varieties)", "(of the products of the sea)", "(esp. of ships or sailors)". Es handelt sich hier um den in Wörterbüchern, deren Ausgangs- und deren Zielsprache je eine moderne Sprache ist, selten vorkommenden Fall, daß die Kotextangabe zu einer Wortschatzeinheit einer Sprache in der anderen Sprache des Wörterbuchs formuliert ist. Dieses Verfahren läßt sich jedoch nur bei Kotextkategorisatoren anwenden, nicht bei Nennung spezifischer Wortschatzeinheiten, die ja autonym präsentiert werden müssen. Auf den Kotext wird hier über die Nennung von Referentenklassen in Englisch hingewiesen, nicht über lateinische Kotextpartner. Im vorliegenden Wörterbuch werden durch Nennung von Kotextkategorisatoren erfolgende Kotextangaben zu den ausgangssprachlichen Wortschatzeinheiten gern mit "of" eingeleitet. Ihre Funktion besteht primär eindeutig darin, mehrere Verwendungsweisen einer lateinischen Wortschatzeinheit zu unterscheiden, wobei übrigens nicht jeder nach Kotext unterschiedenen Verwendungsweise eigene Äquivalente zugeordnet werden. Diese Kotextangaben dienen dem Wörterbuchbenutzer als Leitelemente bei der Suche nach der einschlägigen Einzelbedeutung bzw. dem einschlägigen Äquivalent.

Auch der Artikel *marito* ist reich an Kotextangaben: "(a marriage)", "(animals, birds)", "(plants)", "(vines and trees grown to support them)". Beim Segment "(also w. [with] vines as subj. [subject])" handelt es sich eindeutig um eine Kotextangabe zur ausgangssprachlichen Wortschatzeinheit. Bei den anderen Kotextangaben in diesem Artikel liegt der Fall schwieriger. Von ihrer Stellung her liegt es nahe, anzunehmen, daß sie auf die englischen Äquivalente und nicht auf das lateinische Lemma adressiert sind. Allerdings ist diese Zuordnung nicht zwingend. Man kann den Angaben auch zweierlei Information zuordnen. Sie monosemieren einerseits die englischen Äquivalente. Das Äquivalent *to fertilize* etwa gilt als Äquivalent zu *maritare* nur in einer einzigen Einzelbedeutung, in der das Verbum Objekte regieren kann, die auf Pflanzen referieren ('befruchten'). Man könnte sie aber auch in dem Sinne interpretieren, daß mehrere Verwendungsweisen von *marito* je nach Kotext zu unterscheiden und diesen je eigene Äquivalente (jeweils die den Kotextangaben vorausgehenden) zuzuordnen sind. Von der Intention des Wörterbuchs her ist folgende Deutung am vernünftigsten. In der Wörterbuchzielsprache Englisch werden nicht in erster Linie Äquivalentvorschläge dafür gemacht, wie Wörter eines lateinischen Ausgangstextes in einem englischen Zieltext wiedergegeben werden können, vielmehr sollen Bedeutungsangaben formuliert werden. Deshalb bieten viele Artikel des Wörterbuchs statt Äquivalenten oder neben diesen auch (englische) Bedeutungsparaphrasen (wie "of or belonging to the sea, marine" im Artikel zu *marinus, -a, -um*). Häufig reicht ein Äquivalent als Bedeutungsangabe nicht aus. Deshalb wird ihm die Angabe in Klammern beigefügt. Diese bildet zusammen mit dem Äquivalent die zielsprachliche Bedeutungserklärung.

(c) Beispielangaben, welche die Verwendung der ausgangssprachlichen Wortschatzeinheiten exemplifizieren (Schlicht Petit), z. B. „~ as. . plagas" im Artikel *marinus, -a, -um* oder „Vitelli. . filiam splendidissime ~ auit" im Artikel *marito*. Auf diese sind die Beispielquellenangaben adressiert, die ihrerseits wieder folgende obligatorische Teilangaben umfassen: Autorenangabe (Kapitälchen Petit: „ENN." etc. bzw. „SUET." etc.), Werkangabe (Kursiv Petit: „*Sat.*" etc. bzw. „*Ves.*" etc.) und Stellenangabe (Ziffern in Schlicht Petit: „65" bzw. „14.1."). In der "Publisher's Note" ist ohne weitere terminologische Präzision (die dort auch nicht nötig ist) von Beispielen bzw. Zitaten die Rede (OLD, v): "quotations are arranged in chronological order, the first example showing, where practical, the earliest known instance of that particular sense or usage". Die Tatsache, daß als erstes "example" in der Regel der früheste zugängliche Beleg gewählt wurde, legt nahe, anzunehmen, daß den Beispielen nicht nur im Sinne von 'illustrieren' exemplifizierende, sondern auch belegende (nachweisende) Funktion zukommt. Für Korpussprachen werden in der Regel Belege als Beispiele verwendet. Für moderne Sprachen kommen jedoch auch vom Lexikographen formulierte Beispiele in Betracht. Die Beispiele müssen auch nicht grundsätzlich der Wörterbuchausgangssprache gelten, sondern können ebensogut, wenn das Wörterbuch für Benutzer mit der Wörterbuchausgangssprache als Muttersprache bestimmt ist, die Wörterbuchzielsprache betreffen. Beispielangaben im hier gemeinten Sinne treten in Wörterbüchern für aus zwei modernen Sprachen bestehende Sprachenpaare selten auf.

5.3. Kotextangaben

In Textbeispiel 286.3 finden sich folgende Kotextangaben, die allesamt auf Äquivalente adressiert sind: "⟨bachelor⟩" (adressiert auf "confirmed"), "⟨smoker⟩" (adressiert auf "inveterate") und "⟨habit, prejudice⟩" (adressiert auf "deep-rooted" und "ingrained").

eingefleischt [ˈaɪngəflaɪʃt] *Adj., nicht präd.* confirmed ⟨*bachelor*⟩; inveterate ⟨*smoker*⟩; deep-rooted, ingrained ⟨*habit, prejudice*⟩

Textbeispiel 286.3: Wörterbuchartikel *eingefleischt* (aus: Duden Oxford, 1040, vergrößert)

anbrechen *sep irreg* **I** *vt* **1.** *Packung, Flasche etc* to open; *Vorrat* to broach; *Ersparnisse, Geldsumme, Geldschein* to break into; *siehe* **angebrochen.**
2. (*teilweise brechen*) *Brett, Gefäß, Knochen etc* to crack. **angebrochen sein** to be cracked.
II *vi aux sein* (*Epoche etc*) to dawn; (*Tag auch*) to break; (*Nacht*) to fall; (*Jahreszeit*) to begin; (*Winter*) to close in.

Textbeispiel 286.4: Wörterbuchartikel *anbrechen* (aus: Pons Global, 50, vergrößert)

Während die Kotextangaben in Textbeispiel 286.3 auf die Äquivalente adressiert sind, ziehen es die Autoren des in Textbeispiel 286.4 zitierten Wörterbuchs vor, Kotextangaben auf das Lemma zu adressieren. Im Artikel *anbrechen* sind es die Angaben „*Packung, Flasche etc*", „*Vorrat*", „*Ersparnisse, Geldsumme, Geldschein*", „*Brett, Gefäß, Knochen etc*", „(*Epoche etc*)", „(*Tag auch*)", „(*Nacht*)", „(*Jahreszeit*)" und „(*Winter*)". Dabei unterscheidet das Wörterbuch Subjekte (in Klammern) und Objekte (ohne Klammer) für das Verbum *anbrechen*. Der Unterschied zwischen der Adressierung der Kotextangaben aufs Lemma und der auf die Äquivalente kann einer methodischen Entscheidung folgen, deren Vor- und Nachteile im Zusammenhang mit der Wörterbuchfunktion (siehe 9.) diskutiert werden müssen.

Kotextangaben benennen entweder Kollokationspartner (*Packung* ist z. B. Partner von *anbrechen* in der Kollokation *Packung anbrechen*) oder Kotextkategorisatoren (*Jahreszeit* vertritt klassematisch die Kollokationspartner *Jahreszeit, Frühling, Frühjahr, Lenz, Sommer, Herbst, Winter* und eventuell einige mehr; „*Eßwaren*" als Angabe zur Adresse „einen ~ haben" im Artikel *Stich*

an|brechen 1. *unr. tr. V.* **a)** crack; **sich (Dat.) einen Knochen ~:** crack a bone; **b)** *(öffnen)* open; start; **eine angebrochene Flasche** an opened bottle; **c)** *(zu verbrauchen beginnen)* break into ‹*supplies, reserves*›; **einen Hundertmarkschein ~:** break into *or (Amer.)* break a hundred mark note; **was machen wir mit dem angebrochenen Abend?** *(fig. ugs.)* what shall we do for the rest of the evening? 2. *unr. itr. V.; mit sein (geh.: beginnen)*‹*dawn*› break; ‹*day*› dawn, break; ‹*darkness, night*› come down, fall; ‹*age, epoch*› dawn; ‹*autumn, winter*› set in; ‹*spring, summer*› begin

Textbeispiel 286.5: Wörterbuchartikel *anbrechen* (aus: Duden Oxford, 872, vergrößert)

eingefleischt *adj* 1. *attr* (*überzeugt*) confirmed; (*unverbesserlich*) dyed-in-the-wool. **~er Junggeselle** (*hum*) confirmed bachelor. 2. (*zur zweiten Natur geworden*) ingrained, deep-rooted.

Textbeispiel 286.6: Wörterbuchartikel *eingefleischt* (aus: Pons Global, 328, vergrößert)

steht für *die Butter hat einen Stich, die Milch hatte einen Stich* etc.). Oft wird nicht klar, ob die genannten Kollokationspartner als offenes oder als geschlossenes Inventar zu verstehen sind. Noch unklarer ist oft, welche der unter einem als Kotextkategorisator genannten Oberbegriff subsumierbaren Kollokationspartner tatsächlich in Texten vorkommen oder in solche einsetzbar sind.

Die Textbeispiele 286.5 und 286.6 zeigen, daß Information zu Kollokationen statt über Kotextangaben auch über zweisprachige Bearbeitungseinheiten, bestehend aus Mehr-

připevniti attacher (les feuilles sont attachées sur la tige; la malle était attachée derrière l'auto; pour faire un cerf-volant, j'attache en croix la latte et la baguette d'osier); fixer (les bretelles sont fixées aux boutons de la ceinture du pantalon par des pattes; le manche est fixé dans le trou de la tête de la hache; le rail est fixé au ballast de la voie par des traverses; la montre est fixée par un anneau à une chaîne); mettre des patins à des souliers; adapter la roue à l'extrémité d'un essieu; assujettir (une table qui vacille, un chapeau sur sa tête (, *aby se nehnul*); p. passé: le tableau est assujetti, la chaîne est assujettie).

Textbeispiel 286.7: Wörterbuchartikel *připevniti* (aus: Stehlík 1936, 707)

Wort-Einheit der Ausgangssprache (Adresse) und zielsprachlichen Äquivalenten dazu (Angaben), erfolgen kann. Die jeweiligen Adressen sind „sich [...] einen Knochen ~", „eine angebrochene Flasche", „einen Hundertmarkschein ~", „was machen wir mit dem angebrochenen Abend?" (Artikel zu *anbrechen*) und „ ~ er Junggeselle" (Artikel zu *eingefleischt*).

Manche Wörterbücher legen großes Gewicht auf zielsprachliche Kotextangaben (vgl. auch Art. 289). Ein extremer Fall ist Stehlík 1936 (Textbeispiel 286.7), dessen Methode nur im Rahmen einer Funktionstypologie begründet werden kann (in diesem Fall handelt es sich um das Extrembeispiel eines aktiven Wörterbuchs, siehe 9.). Allerdings darf die Tatsache, daß nahezu alle Angaben auf der mikrostrukturellen Ebene einsprachig sind, nicht zu der Annahme verleiten, man könne diese Art zweisprachigen Wörterbuchs gleich durch ein einsprachiges mit ausführlichen syntagmatischen Angaben ersetzen. Das allgemeine einsprachige Wörterbuch für muttersprachliche Benutzer hätte keine Veranlassung, dieselben Kotexte zu spezifizieren wie das zweisprachige Wörterbuch mit einer der beiden Sprachen als Fremdsprache des Wörterbuchbenutzers.

6. Glossen

Da im zweisprachigen Wörterbuch Wortschatzeinheiten zweier verschiedener Sprachen aufeinander bezogen und nach dem Gesichtspunkt der Äquivalenz verglichen werden, ergibt sich das Problem des Tertium comparationis. Dieses muß identifiziert und offengelegt werden, vor allem bei Polyäquivalenzbeziehungen zwischen einer ausgangssprachlichen Wortschatzeinheit (repräsentiert durch eine Adresse) und mehreren zielsprachlichen Äquivalenten. Die Identifikation des gemeinten Ausschnitts aus der Gesamtbedeutung einer Wortschatzeinheit erfolgt vornehmlich mit Hilfe der sog. Glosse (E. *gloss*, F. *glose*). Die Glosse steht zu der glossierten Einheit in einem paradigmatischen Verhältnis. In Frage kommen synonymische Paraphrasen, Synonyme und Hyperonyme. Die auf das Lemma adressierte Angabe „(*teilweise brechen*)" in Abschnitt I 2. des Artikels *anbrechen* des Pons Global (Textbeispiel 286.4) ist eine Glosse.

Das aufwendigste Identifikationsverfahren sind voll ausformulierte Bedeutungsparaphrasen sowohl auf der ausgangssprachlichen wie auf der zielsprachlichen Seite. Dieses Verfahren wird z. B. im deutsch-französischen Wörterbuch von Schwan 1782 angewandt, das auf zwei einsprachigen Wörterbüchern aufbaut und deren Bedeutungserklärungen (Definitionen) übernimmt. Wie in Art. 316, 2.6. dargestellt, schlägt sich eine vergleichbare italienische Tradition noch heute in Robert-Signorelli 1981 nieder (vgl. Marello 1989, 58 u. 151). Aus Platzgründen begnügen sich die meisten Wörterbücher mit Synonymen oder kurzen synonymischen Paraphrasen. So findet man z. B. in Pons Global folgende acht Bedeutungsausschnittsidentifikationen für das deutsche Lemmazeichen *hart*:

1. *(nicht weich, nicht sanft)*
2. *(scharf)*
3. *(rauh)*
4. *(widerstandsfähig, robust)*
5. *(stabil, sicher)*
6. *(streng, gnadenlos, kompromißlos)*
7. *(schwer zu ertragen)*
8. *(mühevoll, anstrengend)*

Bei der Lektüre wird sofort klar, daß mit derlei Synonymen der gemeinte Bedeutungsausschnitt nicht präzise identifiziert werden kann, da die glossierenden Synonyme ihrerseits polysem und an den semantischen Grenzen unscharf sind. Deshalb bedarf es in einem guten Wörterbuch der Kotextangaben und der infralemmatischen Adressen für Mehr-Wort-Einheiten zur Ergänzung der Glossen. Man mag sogar Kotextangaben als die besseren Identifikatoren ansehen. Mehrere Bauteile, darunter Markierungsangaben, können auch kumulativ zur Identifikation beitragen.

Glossen treten vornehmlich auf der ausgangssprachlichen Seite auf, weil sie dort für die Bedeutungs- oder die Äquivalenzdifferenzierung für unumgänglich erachtet werden können. Auf der zielsprachlichen Seite dienen sie meist zur kompensierenden Vervollständigung partieller Äquivalente (vgl. Art. 285, 4.2. das Beispiel "*girlhood = adolescence (d'une femme)*") und als Erläuterung zu Äquivalenten, deren Kenntnis seitens des Wörterbuchbenutzers nicht als selbstverständlich vorausgesetzt werden kann. Umschreibungen, die anstelle von Äquivalenten stehen oder von Lexikographen eigens in der Zielsprache eingeführte Äquivalente ergänzen, sogenannte 'Äquivalentsurrogate' (E. *non-equivalents*, vgl. Art. 285, 4.2.), werden hier nicht unter dem Begriff der Glosse mitverstanden.

7. Zusammenwirken von Glossen, Kotextangaben und Markierungsangaben

Die Grenzlinien zwischen Glossen, Kotextangaben und Markierungsangaben sind fließend, und zwar sowohl formal als auch inhaltlich. Formal gilt, daß viele Wörterbücher die Bauteile aller drei Typen gleich präsentieren, z. B. kursiv in Klammern. Ein solches Verfahren hat seine Berechtigung, insofern Bauteile aller drei Typen an der Äquivalenzdifferenzierung mitwirken. Inhaltlich gehen Kotextkategorisatoren und der Markierungsangabentyp 'Fachbereichsmarkierungsangaben' ineinander über.

In dem in Textbeispiel 286.8 zitierten Artikelausschnitt gehen den Äquivalenten zu *hart* und zu Mehr-Wort-Einheiten, die *hart* mitumfassen, kursiv gedruckt teils Glossen — z. B. „*(streng, scharf)*" —, teils Markierungsangaben — z. B. „*jur.*", „*econ.*", „*med.*", „*tech.*", „*phys.*" und „*phot.*" — und Kotextangaben — z. B. „*Leib:*", „*Haut:*" und „*Stuhl:*" — voraus. Teils wirken Markierungs- und Kotextangaben zusammen, um die nötige Äquivalenzdifferenzierung herzustellen: „*med.*" mit „*Leib:*", „*Haut:*" sowie „*Stuhl:*", „*tech.*" mit „*Schaumstoff:*", „*phys.*" mit „*Strahlen etc:*" und „*phot.*" mit „*Negativ etc.*". So monosemiert die Markierungsangabe „*med.*" die Kotextangabe „*Stuhl:*", und

firm. **5.** *fig.* (*streng, scharf*) hard, harsh, severe (*face, punishment, voice, winter, etc*); ~er **Kampf** stiff (*od.* hard) fight; ein ~es **Los** a hard lot, a cruel fate; e-e ~e **Politik** a tough (*od.* hard-line, get-tough, no-nonsense) policy; e-n ~en **Kurs** verfolgen take a hard line; ein ~er **Krimi** a hard-boiled (*od.* tough) crime story; ~e **Tatsachen** hard facts; ~es **Urteil** a) *jur.* heavy sentence, b) *weitS.* harsh judg(e)ment (*od.* verdict); ~e **Zeiten** hard times; ~e **Farben** (**Gegensätze**) harsh colo(u)rs (contrasts); mit (*od.* zu) j-m ~ sein be hard on s. o., be severe with s. o.; das war ~! that was tough!; das war ~ für ihn that was hard on him, that hit him hard. **6.** *Spirituosen etc*: hard, strong (*drink, liquor*); ~e **Drogen** hard drugs. **7.** *econ.* ~es **Geld** coin(s *pl*), hard cash; ~e **Währung** hard currency. **8.** *med.* a) *Leib*: constipated, costive, b) *Haut*: hard, sclerotic, c) *Stuhl*: hard. **9.** *tech. Schaumstoff*: rigid. **10.** *phys. Strahlen etc*: hard (*X-rays, etc*). **11.** *phot. Negativ etc*: contrasty. **II** *adv* **12.** *allg.* hard, a.

Textbeispiel 286.8: Ausschnitt aus Wörterbuchartikel *hart* (aus: LGWB, 555, vergrößert)

nur auf diese Weise wird der einschlägige Bedeutungsausschnitt von *hart* hinreichend präzisiert. Umgekehrt reicht etwa die Gebrauchsbereichsmarkierungsangabe „*tech.*" allein nicht aus, um die Verwendungsweise von *hart* zu identifizieren, in der zu diesem *rigid* äquivalent ist. Es bedarf zusätzlich des Kotextkategorisators „*Schaumstoff:*". In gewisser Weise kann die Angabe „*Schaumstoff:*" also auch als präzisierender Teil einer zusammengesetzten Angabe „*tech. Schaumstoff:*" angesehen werden, der zu entnehmen ist, innerhalb welches thematischen Bereichs als Äquivalent zum Deutschen *hart* das englische *rigid* in Frage kommt.

An weiteren Bauteilen zwischen präsentierten ausgangssprachlichen Wortschatzeinheiten und zielsprachlichen Äquivalenten fallen die semantischen Transferindikatoren „*fig.*" und „*weitS.*" auf, die ebenfalls zur Äquivalenzdifferenzierung beitragen. Im zitierten Artikelausschnitt findet man neben auf die präsentierte ausgangssprachliche Wortschatzeinheit adressierten auch auf das Äquivalent adressierte Kotextangaben, einmal — "(*face, punishment, voice, winter, etc*)" — zusammen mit den lemmaadressierten Angaben „*fig.*" (Transferindikator) und „(*streng, scharf*)" (Glosse), einmal — "(*drink, liquor*)" — zusammen mit der lemmaadressierten Kotextangabe „*Spirituosen etc:*" (Kotextkategorisator) und einmal — "(*X-rays, etc*)" — zusammen mit den lemmaadressierten Angaben „*phys.*" (Gebrauchsbereichsmarkierungsangabe) und „*Strahlen etc:*" (Kotextkategorisator). In letzterem Fall treffen also eine lemma- und eine äquivalenzadressierte Kotextangabe (jeweils Kotextkategorisator) zusammen.

8. Inhaltliche Beziehungsgeflechte zwischen Artikelbauteilen

Im Artikel *anbringen* (Abschnitt 3.) aus Pons Global (Textbeispiel 286.9) findet man das englische "to" als Äquivalent auf das deutsche „*bei*" adressiert. Nach demselben Muster bilden eine zweisprachige Bearbeitungseinheit „*an + dat*" und "(on)to" im zitierten Artikel (Abschnitt 2.).

Im Artikel *anbringen* aus Duden Oxford (Textbeispiel 286.10) wird die Parallelität zwischen der Bearbeitungseinheit „**an** + *Dat.* on" und der Bearbeitungseinheit (infralemmatische Adresse für Mehr-Wort-Einheit) „**an etw.** (*Dat.*) **angebracht sein** be fixed [on] to

anbringen *vt sep irreg* **1.** (*hierherbringen*) to bring (with one); (*nach Hause*) to bring home (with one).
2. (*befestigen*) to fix, to fasten (*an* +*dat* (on)to); (*aufstellen, aufhängen*) to put up; *Telefon, Feuermelder etc* to put in, to install; *Stiel an Besen* to put on; *Beschläge, Hufeisen* to mount. **sich** (*dat*) **Tätowierungen ~ lassen** to have oneself tattooed.
3. (*äußern*) *Bemerkung, Bitte, Gesuch, Beschwerde* to make (*bei* to); *Kenntnisse, Wissen* to display; *Argument* to use. **er konnte seine Kritik/seinen Antrag nicht mehr ~** he couldn't get his criticism/motion in; *siehe* **angebracht.**
4. (*inf: loswerden*) *Ware* to get rid of (*inf*).
5. (*dial*) *siehe* **anbekommen.**

Textbeispiel 286.9: Wörterbuchartikel *anbringen* (aus: Pons Global, 50, vergrößert)

an|bringen *unr. tr. V.* **a)** (*befestigen*) put up ⟨*sign, aerial, curtain, plaque*⟩ (**an** + *Dat.* on); fix ⟨*lamp, camera*⟩ (**an** + *Dat.* [on] to); **an etw.** (*Dat.*) **angebracht sein** be fixed [on] to sth.-; **b)** (*äußern*) make ⟨*request, complaint, comment, reference*⟩; **c)** (*zeigen*) display, demonstrate ⟨*knowledge, experience*⟩; **d)** (*ugs.: herbeibringen*) bring; (*nach Hause*) bring home; **e)** (*ugs.: verkaufen*) sell; move

Textbeispiel 286.10: Wörterbuchartikel *anbringen* (aus: Duden Oxford, 872, vergrößert)

sth.-" noch durch die typographische Gleichbehandlung unterstrichen.

Andererseits unterscheiden sich die beiden Artikelsegmente (s. Textbeispiel 286.5)

(a) **an** + *Dat.* [on] to
(b) **was machen wir mit dem angebrochenen Abend?** (*fig. ugs.*) what shall we do for the rest of the evening?

erheblich, was die Einbettung in die lexikographische Textstruktur betrifft. Während b ohne Berücksichtigung anderer Bauteile des Artikels brauchbare Information vermittelt (die aus präsentierter Mehr-Wort-Einheit der Ausgangssprache und zielsprachlichem Äquivalent bestehende Bearbeitungseinheit ist von ihrem Informationsgehalt her relativ autonom), muß der Wörterbuchbenutzer bei a unbedingt folgende Bauteile mitrezipieren, um zu angemessener Information zu gelangen:

— das Lemma „**an|bringen**"
— das Äquivalent "fix"
— die Kotextangaben "⟨*lamp, camera*⟩"

Nicht nur ist also "[on] to" (zu lesen als "*onto* oder *to*") als Äquivalent auf „**an**" adressiert, sondern es ist darüber hinaus auch als Konstruktionsangabe auf das voraufgehende "fix" (seinerseits als Äquivalent auf das Lemma adressiert) und auf die Kotextangaben zu "fix", nämlich "⟨lamp, camera⟩", zu beziehen, was besagt, daß das angegebene Konstruktionsmuster einer syntagmatischen Restriktion unterworfen ist, wobei unklar bleibt, welche Substantive nicht von der Präposition abhängen können (alle außer *lamp* und *camera*?). Das Artikelsegment „**an**" im zitierten Artikel *anbringen* stellt einerseits die Adresse zur Äquivalentangabe "[on] to" und andererseits eine auf das Lemma adressierte Konstruktionsangabe dar.

Es besteht jedoch auch ein inhaltlicher Bezug zwischen den Artikelsegmenten „**an**" und "⟨lamp, camera⟩". Zum Ausdruck gebracht wird nämlich auch eine syntagmatische Beschränkung für *an*, die so formuliert werden kann: *an*, wenn davon ein Substantiv abhängt, dem ein Äquivalent wie *lamp* oder *camera* entspricht. Hier besteht also eine inhaltliche Beziehung zwischen auf das Lemma adressierter Konstruktionsangabe und auf ein Äquivalent adressierten Kotextangaben.

Ähnlich ist auch Glossen Rechnung zu tragen. So ist „**an**" nicht nur einfach Konstruktionsangabe zum Lemma, sondern die Konstruktionsangabe bezieht sich auf das Lemmazeichen im Bereich des mittels der Glosse „(*befestigen*)" identifizierten Bedeutungsausschnittes.

Inhaltliche Beziehungsgeflechte, die weiter reichen als die den Adressierungsstrukturen entsprechenden Relationen, sind typisch für Artikel zweisprachiger Wörterbücher. Auf ihr Vorkommen wurde hier nur anhand von Beispielen hingewiesen. Eine umfassende Typologie solcher Beziehungsgeflechte kann hier nicht geleistet werden.

9. Sprachrichtungen und Funktionen des zweisprachigen Wörterbuchs

9.1. Der Skopus des Wörterbuchs

Ein Wörterbuch für ein bestimmtes Sprachenpaar kann 'monoskopal' oder 'biskopal' angelegt sein. Bietet ein Wörterbuch Äquivalente nur einer bestimmten Sprache für Wortschatzeinheiten nur einer bestimmten anderen Sprache, so handelt es sich um ein monoskopales Wörterbuch. Pro Sprachenpaar sind nach dem Kriterium der Sprachrichtung zwei verschiedene Wörterbuchtypen möglich, für das Sprachenpaar Deutsch/Englisch etwa ein deutsch-englisches und ein englisch-deutsches. Bietet ein Wörterbuch sowohl Äquivalente in einer Sprache für Wortschatzeinheiten einer zweiten als auch Äquivalente in letzterer Sprache für Wortschatzeinheiten ersterer, dann liegt der Fall eines biskopalen Wörterbuchs vor.

Die meisten biskopalen Wörterbücher sind 'getrennt biskopal', d. h. sie bestehen aus getrennten Teilen für verschiedene Sprachrichtungen. Biskopale Wörterbücher für das Sprachenpaar Deutsch/Englisch bestehen in der Regel aus einem Teil Deutsch-Englisch und einem Teil Englisch-Deutsch. Möglich ist jedoch auch ein 'integriert biskopales' Wörterbuch. Dieses enthält im Rahmen einer einzigen Makrostruktur Einträge für beide Sprachrichtungen.

Integriert biskopale Wörterbücher sind heute selten. Ansatzweise tritt dieser Wörterbuchtyp unter Reisewörterbüchern (vgl. Art. 305 a) noch auf, mit Artikeln für beide Sprachrichtungen im Rahmen einer einzigen Makrostruktur und teils sogar mit Einträgen

Telefon el teléfono
   kann ich hier telefonieren? ¿puedo llamar por teléfono? [pu-*e*do ljamar ...]
   kann ich ... sprechen? ¿se puede poner ...? [sse pu-*e*de ...]
   könnten Sie die Nummer für mich wählen? ¿podría marcarme el n*ú*mero?
   MAN HÖRT EVTL.
   diga *hallo*
   ¿quién llama? *wer ist am Apparat?*
   espere un momento *Augenblick bitte*
   está comunicando *es ist besetzt*
  » *REISE-TIP: Auskunft: wählen Sie 009 fürs Inland und 008 für Auslandauskunft; Vorwahl für Deutschland ist 07, Ton abwarten 49, für Österreich 07-43 & für die Schweiz 07-41; erste Null der Ortsvorwahl weglassen*

Vanille la vainilla [bain*i*lja]
Vater: mein Vater mi p*a*dre
Vd., Vds.=usted, ustedes *Sie*
Vegetarier vegetariano [bech*e*tariano]
velocidad limitada
   Geschwindigkeitsbegrenzung
venta de sellos Briefmarken
Ventilator un ventilador [bentil*a*dor]
Verabredung: ich habe eine Verabredung
   tengo una cita [teng-go una ss*i*ta]
verärgert: ich bin sehr verärgert estoy muy enfadado [eßt*e*u mui ...]
Verband (*Wunde*) un vendaje [bend*a*che]
Verbandskasten un botiquín [botik*i*n]
verbessern mejorar [mech*o*rar]
Verbindung (*Reisen*) el enlace [enl*a*sse]

Textbeispiel 286.11: Wörterbuchartikel *Telefon* und *Vanille* bis *Verbindung* (aus: Lexus D−S 1983, 106 u. 111)

für beide Sprachrichtungen innerhalb eines einzigen Artikels.

Der aus den Artikeln *Vanille* bis *Verbindung* bestehende Wörterbuchausschnitt aus Lexus D—S 1983 (Textbeispiel 286.11) z. B. setzt sich aus Artikeln für die Sprachrichtung Deutsch-Spanisch (Lemmata „**Vanille**", „**Vater**", „**Vegetarier**", „**Ventilator**", „**Verabredung**", „**verärgert**", „**Verband**", „**Verbandskasten**", „**verbessern**" und „**Verbindung**") und solchen für die Sprachrichtung Spanisch-Deutsch (Lemmata „**Vd., Vds.**", „**velocidad limitada**" und „**venta de sellos**") zusammen. Im Artikel Telefon aus demselben Wörterbuch (Textbeispiel 286.11) werden spanische Äquivalente zu deutschen Wortschatzeinheiten (*Telefon, kann ich hier telefonieren?, kann ich ... sprechen?* und *könnten Sie die Nummer für mich wählen?*) und deutsche Äquivalente zu spanischen Wortschatzeinheiten (*diga, ¿quién llama?, espere un momento* und *está comunicando*) geboten. Aus den beiden Ausschnitten wird jedoch ersichtlich, daß das zitierte Wörterbuch primär eines für die Sprachrichtung Deutsch-Spanisch und nur sekundär eines für die Sprachrichtung Spanisch-Deutsch sein will.

Getrennt biskopale Wörterbücher bestehen aus mindestens zwei 'monoskopalen Wörterbuchteilen'. Zweisprachige Wörterbücher können auch aus mehreren Wörterbuchteilen für dieselbe Sprachrichtung bestehen. Wörterbücher oder Wörterbuchteile für ein und dieselbe Sprachrichtung können nämlich für verschiedene 'Funktionen' bestimmt sein.

9.2. Die Funktion des Wörterbuchs

Ein Wörterbuch(teil) für eine bestimmte Sprachrichtung kann für eine oder beide der folgenden Benutzungszwecke vorgesehen sein: Erwerb oder Erweiterung von Fremdsprachenkompetenz und Konsultation bei aktuellen Problemen im Umgang mit Texten. Bei den weiteren Unterscheidungen wird vom Sprachenpaartyp Muttersprache/Fremdsprache (= MS/FS) ausgegangen, bei anderen Sprachenpaartypen (Erstsprache/Zweitsprache, Zweitsprache/Fremdsprache, Fremdsprache/Fremdsprache) kann jedoch teilweise das im Hinblick auf die Muttersprache des Wörterbuchbenutzers Gesagte auf eine der beiden Sprachen des Wörterbuchs bezogen werden.

Wörterbücher können entweder dem Erwerb und der Erweiterung von Kompetenz in der Wörterbuchausgangssprache (Sprache der Äquivalente ist Muttersprache) oder dem Erwerb und der Erweiterung von Kompetenz in der Wörterbuchzielsprache (Sprache der Äquivalente ist Fremdsprache) dienen. Ein Wörterbuch Englisch-Deutsch kann eine 'Lernfunktion' hinsichtlich des Englischen (für Benutzer mit Muttersprache Deutsch) und hinsichtlich des Deutschen (für Benutzer mit Muttersprache Englisch) erfüllen. Oder anders gesehen: Sowohl ein deutsch-englisches als auch ein englisch-deutsches Wörterbuch können für einen Benutzer mit Deutsch als Muttersprache einer Lernfunktion im Hinblick auf Englisch als Fremdsprache gerecht werden. Die Lernfunktion soll im folgenden außer acht bleiben. Für die Benutzung bei aktuellen Problemen im Umgang mit Texten bestimmte Wörterbücher erfüllen jedoch fast immer sekundär auch eine Lernfunktion.

Für die Unterscheidung von Funktionen im Hinblick auf Benutzungssituationen im Zusammenhang mit der Bewältigung aktueller Probleme beim Umgang mit Texten sind zwei Kriterien maßgeblich. Zu fragen ist einerseits, ob das Wörterbuch bei der Rezeption oder der Produktion fremdsprachlicher Texte zu verwenden ist, und andererseits, ob es als Hilfsmittel bei Translationsvorgängen oder beim translationsunabhängigen Umgang mit Texten nur der Fremdsprache dient. Translationsvorgänge umfassen jeweils eine Komponente Rezeption in der Fremdsprache (Herübersetzung) oder Produktion in der Fremdsprache (Hinübersetzung). An die Rezeption fremdsprachlicher Texte gebundene Wörterbuchfunktionen werden als 'passive', an die Produktion fremdsprachlicher Texte gebundene Funktionen werden als 'aktive' Funktionen bezeichnet.

Die Begriffe 'aktiv' und 'passiv' dürfen nicht in dem Sinne verstanden werden, daß sie Aktivität oder Passivität des Wörterbuchbenutzers im Umgang mit einem Text bedeuten. Der Begriff 'aktiv' bezieht sich einfach auf die Produktion, der Begriff 'passiv' auf die Rezeption eines fremdsprachlichen Textes.

Ein passiver Wörterbuchteil kann zwei passiven Funktionen dienen, der Instruktion für die translationsunabhängige Rezeption fremdsprachlicher Texte (fremdsprachliche Dekodierung) und der Instruktion für die Herübersetzung (fremdsprachliche Dekodierung + muttersprachliche Enkodierung). Auch ein aktiver Wörterbuchteil kann zwei Funktionen dienen, der Instruktion für die translationsunabhängige Produktion (fremdsprachliche Enkodierung) und der Instruktion für die Hinübersetzung (muttersprachliche Dekodierung + fremdsprachliche Enkodierung). Ein 'monoskopaler Wörterbuchteil' Englisch-Deutsch kann einem Benutzer mit Muttersprache Deutsch für folgende Funktionen dienen:

(a) Instruktion für Rezeption des Englischen (FS →)
(b) Instruktion für Herübersetzung aus dem Englischen (FS → MS)
(c) Instruktion für Produktion des Englischen (→ FS)
(d) Instruktion für Hinübersetzung ins Englische (MS → FS)

Die Funktionen a und b sind passiv, die Funktionen c und d aktiv. Die Reihenfolge in der Anführung der Funktionen spiegelt die funktionale De-facto-Gewichtung der meisten existierenden zweisprachigen Wörterbücher wider. Der Wörterbuchteil Englisch-Deutsch (bzw. das nur aus diesem Teil bestehende Wörterbuch) hat in der Hand des Benutzers mit Deutsch als Muttersprache vorwiegend passive Funktionen zu erfüllen. Es kommen ihm aber auch aktive Funktionen zu. Man denke z. B. an die Ausspracheangaben oder an die eventuelle Nutzung der Information über Kollokationen des Englischen (wenn der Wörterbuchteil derartige Information in Form von Adressen für Mehr-Wort-Einheiten oder in Form von Kotextangaben zu wörterbuchausgangssprachlichen Adressen in reichlichem Umfang bietet), nicht zuletzt auch an die Möglichkeit der Gegenprobe zu Information, die dem Wörterbuchteil Deutsch-Englisch entnommen wurde.

In der Hand des Benutzers mit Muttersprache Englisch kann ein Wörterbuchteil Englisch-Deutsch folgenden aktiven Funktionen dienen:

(e) Instruktion für Produktion des Deutschen (→ FS)
(f) Instruktion für Hinübersetzung ins Deutsche (MS → FS)

Passive Funktionen für den Wörterbuchbenutzer mit Muttersprache Englisch spielen im Wörterbuchteil Englisch-Deutsch praktisch keine Rolle. Bei der Dekodierung eines muttersprachlichen Textes entstehen entweder keine mit dem Wörterbuch zu lösenden Probleme, oder, soweit solche entstehen, werden diese in der Regel nicht mit Hilfe eines zweisprachigen Wörterbuchs gelöst. Auch eine Gegenprobe beim Einsatz des Wörterbuchs für die fremdsprachliche Textrezeption bzw. das Herübersetzen wird wegen der Kompetenz des Wörterbuchbenutzers in der Wörterbuchzielsprache kaum nötig. Der anglophone Benutzer eines deutsch-englischen Wörterbuchs macht keine Gegenprobe im englisch-deutschen Wörterbuch.

Genauso wie es denkbar ist, daß ein Wörterbuchteil Englisch-Deutsch vom Benutzer mit Muttersprache Deutsch in allen vier und vom Benutzer mit Muttersprache Englisch in zwei Funktionen herangezogen wird, ist es vorstellbar, daß ein Wörterbuchteil (bzw. ein nur aus einem monoskopalen Teil bestehendes Wörterbuch) auf eine einzige Funktion nur für Adressaten mit einer bestimmten der beiden Wörterbuchsprachen als Muttersprache zugeschnitten ist. Die Regel unter den existierenden Wörterbüchern sind für mehrere Funktionen bestimmte 'plurifunktionale' (auf zwei Funktionen ausgerichtete 'bifunktionale' und vor allem auf mehr als zwei Funktionen ausgerichtete 'polyfunktionale') Wörterbuchteile.

9.3. Die Direktion des Wörterbuchs

Mögen 'monofunktionale' Wörterbuchteile als Luxus erscheinen, so gilt dies auf keinen Fall für nur auf Adressaten mit einer bestimmten Wörterbuchsprache als Muttersprache ausgerichtete bifunktionale, entweder nur aktive oder nur passive, Wörterbuchteile. Auf Adressaten nur einer der beiden Wörterbuchsprachen als Muttersprache ausgerichtete Wörterbuchteile seien hier als 'monodirektional', auf Muttersprachler beider Muttersprachen ausgerichtete Wörterbuchteile als 'bidirektional' bezeichnet.

Die mit -*direktional* und -*funktional* gebildeten Termini werden von verschiedenen Autoren in je verschiedenem Sinne verwendet. So bezieht sich der Begriff der 'Direktionalität' in der metalexikographischen Literatur teils auf die Sprachrichtung eines Wörterbuchs oder Wörterbuchteils und teils auf die Ausrichtung auf nach Muttersprachen definierte Adressatengruppen. Auf letzteres Kriterium wird teils auch mittels der Termini auf -*funktional* Bezug genommen. Die hier getroffene Sprachregelung gilt nur ad hoc und erhebt nicht den Anspruch, die einzig brauchbare zu sein:

-*skopal*   Sprachrichtung
-*funktional*   Instruktionszweck
-*direktional*   Ausrichtung auf nach Muttersprachen definierte Adressatengruppen

Bidirektionale Wörterbuchteile können entweder ihren Zielen nicht voll gerecht werden oder müssen wesentlich umfangreicher und komplexer strukturiert (besonders auf der mikrostrukturellen Ebene) ausfallen als monodirektionale. Monodirektionale Wörterbuchteile würden gegenüber bidirektionalen also Platzersparnis bzw. größere Benutzerfreundlichkeit bedeuten.

Dies sei exemplifizierend im Hinblick auf Information über transparente Kollokationen verdeutlicht. Im Wörterbuchteil Englisch-Deutsch ist im Hinblick auf die rezeptionsbezogene Funktion für Benutzer mit Deutsch als Muttersprache diesbezügliche Information überflüssig. Im Hinblick auf die produktions- und die hinübersetzungsbezogene Funktion für Benutzer mit Muttersprache Deutsch ist Information zu Kollokationen des Englischen wertvoll. Es bedarf jedoch dabei keiner Information über Äquivalenzen zwischen ausgangs- und zielsprachlichen Kollokationen. Letzterer bedarf es auch im Hinblick auf die herübersetzungsbezogene Funktion für Benutzer mit Muttersprache Deutsch nicht unbedingt. Die umfassende Registrierung von Kollokationen der Zielsprache Deutsch ist jedoch im Hinblick auf die produktions- und die hinübersetzungsbezogene Funktion für Benutzer mit Muttersprache Englisch unabdingbar. Zumindest was die hinübersetzungsbezogene Funktion betrifft, ist dabei auch unbedingt die Herstellung von Äquivalenzen zwischen Kollokationen des Englischen und ihnen entsprechenden deutschen Wortschatzeinheiten (Kollokationen und anderen Wortschatzeinheiten) sowie zwischen Kollokationen des Deutschen und englischen Wortschatzeinheiten (Kollokationen und anderen Wortschatzeinheiten), denen diese als Äquivalente entsprechen, erforderlich.

Ein bidirektionaler Wörterbuchteil Englisch-Deutsch, der auch als aktiver Wörterbuchteil für Benutzer mit Muttersprache Englisch dienen soll, muß also Information bieten, die der Benutzer mit Muttersprache Deutsch nicht sucht. Umgekehrt gilt, daß ein bidirektionaler Wörterbuchteil Englisch-Deutsch auch viel Information vorsehen muß, die den Benutzer mit Muttersprache Englisch nicht oder selten interessiert, so z. B. die in Bearbeitungseinheiten mit peripheren Wortschatzeinheiten als Adressen gebotene. Man denke nur an den ganz unterschiedlichen Nutzen von Adressen für wörterbuchausgangssprachliche Archaismen im Hinblick auf passive und auf aktive Funktionen.

Im übrigen gilt, daß ein guter als aktiv intendierter Wörterbuchteil für Adressaten mit einer der beiden Wörterbuchsprachen als Muttersprache auch mit Gewinn als passiver Wörterbuchteil für Adressaten mit der anderen der beiden Sprachen als Muttersprache benutzt werden kann, dagegen umgekehrt ein als passiv intendierter Wörterbuchteil für Adressaten mit einer der beiden Sprachen als Muttersprache als aktiver Wörterbuchteil für Adressaten mit der anderen Sprache als Muttersprache nur sehr begrenzt taugt. Gleichzeitig gilt, daß ein als passiv intendierter Wörterbuchteil für Benutzer mit einer Sprache als Muttersprache auch aktive Funktionen für dieselben Benutzer abdeckt (die Wörterbuchausgangssprache ist in diesem Fall die Sprache der fremdsprachlichen Produktion, im Falle der Translation Zielsprache), nicht so gut jedoch ein als aktiv intendierter Wörterbuchteil für Adressaten einer Sprache als Muttersprache passive Funktionen für dieselben Adressaten.

9.4. Kombinationsmöglichkeiten von Skopus, Funktion und Direktion

Aus den Kriterien Skopus, Funktion und Direktion ergeben sich folgende Möglichkeiten der Zusammensetzung eines getrennt biskopalen Wörterbuchs aus zwei monoskopalen Wörterbuchteilen:

(a) bidirektional + bidirektional (z. B. Englisch-Deutsch für Deutschmuttersprachler und Englischmuttersprachler sowie Deutsch-Englisch für Englischmuttersprachler und Deutschmuttersprachler),

(b) aktiv + passiv (z. B. Englisch-Deutsch für Englischmuttersprachler sowie Deutsch-Englisch für Englischmuttersprachler),

(c) aktiv + aktiv (z. B. Englisch-Deutsch für Englischmuttersprachler sowie Deutsch-Englisch für Deutschmuttersprachler),

(d) passiv + passiv (z. B. Englisch-Deutsch für Deutschmuttersprachler sowie Deutsch-Englisch für Englischmuttersprachler),

(e) bidirektional + aktiv (z. B. Englisch-Deutsch für Deutschmuttersprachler und Englischmuttersprachler sowie Deutsch-Englisch für Deutschmuttersprachler),

(f) bidirektional + passiv (z. B. Englisch-Deutsch für Deutschmuttersprachler und Englischmuttersprachler sowie Deutsch-Englisch für Englischmuttersprachler).

Historisch sind alle diese Typen nachweisbar. Zu Typ d zählt z. B. ein Wörterbuch für das Sprachenpaar Deutsch/Spanisch mit einem deutsch-spanischen und einem spanisch-deutschen Teil, das in Spanien herausgegeben wurde, nur in Spanien vertrieben wird und dessen spanisch-deutscher Teil, d. h. der Teil, von dem man annehmen möchte, daß er als aktiver Wörterbuchteil für Spanier gedacht sei, dem spanischen Benutzer für die Äquivalentauswahl nicht mehr Hilfestellung leistet als der passive Teil Deutsch-Spanisch und deswegen allenfalls vom Benutzer mit Muttersprache Deutsch gewinnbringend zu benutzen ist (Textbeispiel 286.12).

Nebenbei zeigt dieses Beispiel auch, wie wenig sich die Feststellung von Funktionen und Direktionalität eines Wörterbuchs oder Wörterbuchteils auf die Erklärungen von Autoren oder Verlagen verlassen sollte oder auf die Tatsache, daß Wörterbucheinleitungsteile in einer bestimmten Sprache redigiert sind. Die Funktions- und Direktionsbestimmung sollte sich unbedingt auf die Analyse des lexikographischen Textes stützen.

Ein Wörterbuch kann im übrigen auch aus zwei monoskopalen Teilen jeweils mit

> **bre'chen.** *v. tr.* **(h.) (brichst, bricht; brach; gebrochen)** romper; quebrar; partir; despedazar, cascar; (p. us.) frangir; dividir, separar; refrenar, contener, reprimir; (mar.) desguazar; demoler; sacar, arrancar, quitar; hender; infringir; conculcar; reflejar (rayos); refringir; violar, quebrantar, machacar; espadar; espadillar; agramar (lino, etc.); vomitar; desgarrar (el alma); coger (fruta); doblar (papel); (fis.) refractar (rayos); paralizar, neutralizar, vencer (resistencia); superar (una marca); desmontar (terreno); degradar (colores): *Flachs brechen*, tascar; *die Kanten brechen*, descornar, achaflanar; *sein Wort brechen*, faltar a la palabra; *aus einer Mauer brechen*, desempotrar. — *v. intr.* **(s.)** mudar (la voz); romperse; quebrarse; romper (las olas); cortarse (seda); hundirse, desplomarse; venirse abajo: *aus dem Gefängnis ausbrechen*, fugarse, evadirse; *mit j-m brechen*, romper con uno; *es bricht mir das Herz*, se me parte el alma; *wer bricht, der zahlt*, el que rompe paga. — *v. r.* vomitar; disiparse (nubes); ceder (la fiebre); trabarse (la lengua). — **brechend.** *p. a.* rompedor. — **gebrochen.** *p. p.* fracturado, cascado; (mat.) fraccionario (número); refracto (rayo); chapurrado (idioma); destrozado; quebrantado.
>
> **pensión.** *f.* Pensión, Kost, *f.*; Reisestipendium, Jahrgeld, Kostgeld, *n.*; Gnadengehalt, Ruhegehalt, Ehrensold, *m.*; Freistelle, *f.*; Kosthaus; Fremdenheim, Pensionat, *n.*; Gnadengeld, amtliches Stipendium, *n.*: *pensión completa*, volle Pension, Kost mit Wohnung, *f.*; *pensión de vejez*, Altersrente, *f.*; *poner a pensión*, in Pension geben; *con derecho a pensión*, pensionsberechtigt; *pensión vitalicia*, Leibrente, *f.*; *media pensión*, Halbpension, *f.*

Textbeispiel 286.12: Wörterbuchartikel *brechen* und *pensión* (aus: Martínez Amador 1969, 155, 1412)

derselben Wörterbuchausgangs- und derselben Wörterbuchzielsprache bestehen (z. B. aktiver Wörterbuchteil Englisch-Deutsch für Englischmuttersprachler sowie passiver Wörterbuchteil Englisch-Deutsch für Deutschmuttersprachler). Denkbar sind ohne weiteres auch aus drei oder vier monoskopalen Teilen bestehende getrennt biskopale Wörterbücher. So könnte man sich ein Wörterbuch vorstellen, das sich aus folgenden Teilen zusammensetzt:

(a) aktiver Wörterbuchteil Englisch-Deutsch für Englischmuttersprachler,
(b) passiver Wörterbuchteil Deutsch-Englisch für Englischmuttersprachler,
(c) aktiver Wörterbuchteil Deutsch-Englisch für Deutschmuttersprachler,
(d) passiver Wörterbuchteil Englisch-Deutsch für Deutschmuttersprachler.

Sinnvoll im Hinblick auf die Benutzung ist eigentlich nur die Zusammenfassung von Wörterbuchteilen, die jeweils für Adressaten mit derselben Sprache als Muttersprache konzipiert sind. Alle anderen Kombinationen ergeben allenfalls unter verlegerischen Gesichtspunkten Sinn.

10. Zum Status der sog. Äquivalente im zweisprachigen Wörterbuch

10.1. Äquivalente als Angabentypen

Was besagt eigentlich die Ausdrucksweise „im Wörterbuch verzeichnete Äquivalente"? Das zweisprachige Wörterbuch präsentiert zielsprachliche Wortschatzeinheiten in ihrer Eigenschaft als Äquivalente ebenfalls präsentierter ausgangssprachlicher Wortschatzeinheiten. Mittels der Präsentation zielsprachlicher Wortschatzeinheiten in der Eigenschaft von Äquivalenten ausgangssprachlicher Wortschatzeinheiten werden Angaben vorgenommen. Angaben worüber? Von Wörterbuchfunktionen ausgehend (siehe Abschnitt 9.) sind drei Antworten möglich:

(a) Mittels der zielsprachlichen Äquivalente werden Angaben zum semantischen und pragmatischen Potential ausgangssprachlicher Wortschatzeinheiten vorgenommen, auf die sie als Angaben adressiert sind. Die Aufgabe der Äquivalente ist in diesem Fall die einer lexikographischen Kommentarsprache; sie ist der Aufgabe der Bedeutungsparaphrasen im allgemeinen einsprachigen Wörterbuch vergleichbar. Der Status der ausgangssprachlichen Wortschatzeinheiten, auf welche die Äquivalente adressiert sind, entspricht dann dem der Wortschatzeinheiten, auf die im einsprachigen Wörterbuch Bedeutungserklärungen adressiert sind. Die beiden Wörterbuchartikel (Slowenisch-Deutsch, schematisch).

svinčnik Bleistift
hvala danke

sind dann wie folgt zu lesen: Das Wort *svinčnik* bedeutet 'Bleistift', das Wort *hvala* bedeutet 'danke'. Mit anderen Worten: Mittels *svinčnik* wird üblicherweise auf Bleistifte referiert, *hvala* dient üblicherweise dazu, die verbale Handlung des Dankens durchzuführen.

(b) Mittels der Äquivalente werden Angaben darüber vorgenommen, mittels welcher Wortschatzeinheiten in der Zielsprache des Wörterbuches bestimmte außersprachliche Einheiten (Ideen, Begriffe, Intentionen etc.) versprachlicht werden. In diesem Fall werden die wörterbuchausgangssprachlichen Einheiten nicht dazu präsentiert, um über sie selbst Angaben zu machen. Sie stehen vielmehr für Außersprachliches (Referentenklassen etc.). Im Gegensatz zu a stehen jedoch in diesem Fall die zielsprachlichen Einheiten für sich selbst. Es ergibt sich also eine Analogie zum onomasiologischen Wörterbuch. Die beiden Artikel (Deutsch-Rumänisch, schematisch)

Bleistift craion
danke mulţumesc

sind dann folgendermaßen zu lesen: Ein Bleistift wird üblicherweise mit *craion* bezeichnet, Dank kann durch *mulţumesc* ausgedrückt werden. Mit anderen Worten: Auf die Referentenklasse der Bleistifte wird üblicherweise mittels des Wortes *craion* referiert, die verbale Handlung des Dankens kann mittels des Aussprechens von *mulţumesc* vollzogen werden.

(c) Mittels der Äquivalente werden Angaben darüber gemacht, welche Wortschatzeinheiten der Wörterbuchzielsprache bestimmten Wortschatzeinheiten der Wörterbuchausgangssprache als Äquivalente (in einem linguistischen Sinne, den das Wort außerhalb der Lexikographie hat) entsprechen. Die Artikel (Spanisch-Französisch, schematisch)

lápiz crayon
¡gracias! merci

sind dann so zu lesen: Französisches Äquivalent zu spanisch *lápiz* ist *crayon*, französisches Äquivalent zu spanisch *¡gracias!* ist *merci*. Oder: Dem spanischen *lápiz* entspricht im Französischen *crayon*, dem spanischen *¡gracias!* entspricht im Französischen *merci*.

Die sogenannten Äquivalente des zweisprachigen Wörterbuchs sind also auf jeden Fall Angaben mittels wörterbuchzielsprachlicher Wortschatzeinheiten in der Eigenschaft von Äquivalenten in einem vorlexikographischen Sinn.

10.2. Systemäquivalente und Übersetzungsäquivalente

Der Begriff 'Äquivalent' wird außerhalb der Lexikographie in verschiedenen weiteren sprachwissenschaftlichen Teildisziplinen verwendet. Von Bedeutung für die zweisprachige Lexikographie ist einerseits die Verwendung des Begriffs im Sinne des Vergleichs von Sprachsystemen und andererseits im Sinne der Übersetzungswissenschaft. Zur Vereinfachung der Ausdrucksweise sei im folgenden einfach von 'Systemäquivalenten' (Sprachsystemvergleich) und 'Übersetzungsäquivalenten' (Übersetzungswissenschaft) die Rede.

'Systemäquivalente' sind diejenigen Einheiten, die im System einer bestimmten Sprache in einer bestimmten Einzelbedeutung dem funktionalen (semantischen, pragmatischen, eventuell syntagmatischen) Stellenwert am nächsten kommen, den eine bestimmte Einheit im System einer bestimmten anderen Sprache einnimmt. 'Übersetzungsäquivalente' sind diejenigen Einheiten einer bestimmten Zielsprache (im Sinne der Translation), die bei Translationsvorgängen als zu bestimmten Bauteilen eines bestimmten Textes in einer bestimmten Quellsprache parallele Bauteile eines zum Quelltext kommunikativ äquivalenten Textes in Frage kommen. Ein zu einem Quelltext kommunikativ äquivalenter Zieltext setzt sich nicht einfach aus den zielsprachlichen Systemäquivalenten der den Quelltext konstituierenden quellsprachlichen Einheiten zusammen. Dies ist aus verschiedenen Gründen nicht so ohne weiteres möglich, z. B. wegen Restriktionen der Zielsprache, was die Kombination sprachlicher Zeichen betrifft, oder aus kompensatorischen Notwendigkeiten (ein semantisches oder stilistisches Element, das an einer bestimmten Stelle des Zieltextes nicht parallel zum Quelltext zum Ausdruck gebracht werden kann, muß an anderer Stelle zum Ausdruck gebracht werden, wo im Quelltext kein entsprechendes Element vorkommt).

10.3. Äquivalenttypen

Aus der Kombination der Unterscheidung von 'Systemäquivalenten' und 'Übersetzungsäquivalenten' mit der Unterscheidung drei verschiedener Typen von Angaben, die im zweisprachigen Wörterbuch mittels der sog. Äquivalente vorgenommen werden, ergeben sich acht theoretische Möglichkeiten dessen, was die sogenannten Äquivalente des Wörterbuches sein könnten:

(a) Systemäquivalente als Bedeutungsangaben
(b) Systemäquivalente als onomasiologische Angaben
(c) Systemäquivalente als Angaben von Systemäquivalenten
(d) Systemäquivalente als Angaben von Übersetzungsäquivalenten
(e) Übersetzungsäquivalente als Bedeutungsangaben
(f) Übersetzungsäquivalente als onomasiologische Angaben
(g) Übersetzungsäquivalente als Angaben von Systemäquivalenten
(h) Übersetzungsäquivalente als Angaben von Übersetzungsäquivalenten

Sicher ist die Präsentation von Äquivalenten in einem Sinne nicht das geeignete Mittel der Angabe von Äquivalenten in einem anderen Sinne. Damit scheiden die Möglichkeiten d und g als sinnvolle Deutungen des Status der sogenannten Äquivalente in einem zweisprachigen Wörterbuch von vornherein grundsätzlich aus.

Die restlichen Deutungen sind zur Funktionstypologie des zweisprachigen Wörterbuchs (siehe Abschnitt 9.) in Beziehung zu bringen. Für die Rezeption in der Fremdsprache eignen sich am besten Systemäquivalente, die dann als Bedeutungsangaben zu lesen sind (a). Für die fremdsprachliche Produktion werden Äquivalente als onomasiologische Angaben benötigt. Der Translationsaspekt spielt dabei keine Rolle. Jedoch ist für den Wörterbuchbenutzer ein breites Angebot an zielsprachlichen Ausdrucksmöglichkeiten von Interesse. Deshalb zieht er aus einer breiten Auswahl von Übersetzungsäquivalenten (f) in der Regel mehr Gewinn als aus wenigen Systemäquivalenten (b), allerdings nur, wenn erstere nicht einfach kumulativ angeführt sind, sondern weitere Angaben die Unterschiede in ihrem Gebrauchswert verdeutlichen. Im Hinblick auf die Herübersetzung bedeuten Angaben von Übersetzungsäquivalenten mittels der Präsentation dieser Übersetzungsäquivalente (h) eine optimale Hilfe. Angesichts der muttersprachlichen Kompetenz des Wörterbuchbenutzers kann sich das Wörterbuch aber gegebenenfalls auch auf Bedeutungsangaben oder Angaben von Systemäquivalenten mittels der Präsentation von Systemäquivalenten (a bzw. c) beschränken. Dagegen benötigt der Wörterbuchbenutzer für die Hinübersetzung unbedingt die Angabe von Übersetzungsäquivalenten, was nur mittels der Präsentation dieser Übersetzungsäquivalente zu bewerkstelligen ist (h). Bedeutungsangaben mittels der Präsentation von Übersetzungsäquivalenten (e) sind im Hinblick auf keine Funktion die optimale Möglichkeit, da sie weniger präzise Aussagen implizieren als solche mittels der Präsentation von Systemäquivalenten.

11. Makrostrukturen zweisprachiger Wörterbücher

11.1. Einführung

In Artikel 38 (Abb. 38.2) werden drei Typen initialalphabetischer Makrostrukturen unterschieden:

(1) glattalphabetisch (= striktalphabetisch, ohne Gruppierung)
(2) nischenalphabetisch (= striktalphabetisch, mit Gruppierung)
(3) nestalphabetisch (= nicht striktalphabetisch, mit Gruppierung)

Diese Typologie ist aus der Sicht des zweisprachigen Wörterbuchs zu kommentieren und zu ergänzen.

11.2. Das nestalphabetische Wörterbuch

Das nestalphabetische Wörterbuch gruppiert unter morphosemantischen Gesichtspunkten (meist) mit den Vorteilen Platzersparnis und Begünstigung der Lernfunktion. Textbeispiel 286.13, in dem das Wort *Buchzeichen* vor *Buchecker* und das Wort *Buchweizen* vor *Buche* behandelt wird, so daß die entsprechenden Artikel zwischen denen zu *Buchungsunterlage* und *Buckel* fehlen, zeigt aber auch den Nachteil des Verfahrens für den Benutzer in passiver Funktion. Zur Auffindung der Wörter wird eine semantische Analysefähigkeit vorausgesetzt, deren Fehlen die Nachschlagehandlung ja gerade bedingt. Dennoch ist das Verfahren keineswegs selten (vgl. z. B. Robert-Collins), offenbar, weil man auf den Suchwillen des Benutzers vertraut.

11.3. Das nischenalphabetische Wörterbuch

Auch wenn das Wörterbuch auf Nester verzichtet und striktalphabetisch angeordnet ist,

Buch|abschluß [″buːxˈapʃlus] m. (es, ″e). Comm. arrêté m. (du livre) de comptes. | *auf Grund eines Buchabschlusses,* en vertu d'un arrêté de compte. ‖″**-ausstellung** f. (-, en). Comm. exposition (f.) de livres. ‖″**-auszug** m. (es, ″e). Comm. extrait (m.) d'un compte courant. ‖ Littér. extrait (m.) d'un livre. ‖″**-besprechung** f. (-, en). Littér. compte rendu m. ‖″**-binder** m. (s, -) relieur m. ‖°**-decke** f. (-, n) couverture (f.) de livre ; reliure f. ‖°**-druck** m. (s, e) imprimerie f. ; typographie f. ‖ Par ext. imprimé m. ‖°**-druckerm.** (s, -) imprimeur m. ; typographe m. ‖°**-druckerei** f. (-, en) imprimerie f. ; typographie f. ‖°**-drucker|kunst** [″-/--/″-] f. (-) art (m.) typographique ; typographie f. ; imprimerie f. ‖°**-drucker|schwärze** f. (-, n) encre (f.) d'imprimerie. ‖°**-forderung** f. (-, en). Comm. créance (f.) comptable ; dette active. ‖″**-führung** f. (-, en) comptabilité f. ; tenue (f.) des livres. | *einfache, doppelte Buchführung,* comptabilité en partie simple, en partie double. ‖″**-geld** n. (s, er). Comm. monnaie (f.) de compte ; monnaie-virement f. ; monnaie scripturale. ‖″**-gelehrsamkeit** f. (-) érudition f. ; science (f.) livresque. ‖″**-halter** m. (-). Comm. comptable m. ; teneur (m.) de livres. ‖°**-haltung** f. (-, en) comptabilité f. ‖″**-handel** m. (s). Comm. librairie f. | *im Buchhandel sein,* être en vente. ‖″**-händler** m. (s, e) libraire m. ‖″**-handlung** f. (-, en) librairie f. ‖″**-hülle** f. (-, n) liseuse f. ‖″**-hypothek** f. (-, en). Comm. hypothèque sans cédule, inscrite au livre foncier. ‖°**-macher** m. (s,-). Sport. bookmaker m. ‖″**-mäßig** adj. Comm. suivant le système comptable. | *buchmäßige Berechnung, Forderung,* calcul actuariel ; créance comptable. ‖″**-prüfer** m. (s, -). Comm. expert-comptable. ‖°**-prüfung** f. (-, en) vérification (f.) des livres. | *Buch- und Betriebsprüfung,* contrôle (m.) des livres et de l'entreprise. ‖″**-schuld** f. (-, en) dette (f.) comptable ; dette (f.) en compte. ‖″**-verleih** m. (s, e) [Leihbuchhandlung] prêt (m.) de livres. ‖″**-wert** m. (s, e). Comm. valeur (f.) en compte. ‖″**-zeichen** n. (s, -) ex-libris m.
Buch|ecker [″buːxˈɛkər] f. °**-eichel** [-aiçəl] f. Bot. faîne f. ‖″°**-fink** m. (s, e). Zool. pinson m. ‖″**-weizen** m. (s, -). Bot. sarrasin m. ; blé noir.
Buche [ˈbuːxə] f. (-, n). Bot. hêtre m.
Büchelchen [ˈbyːçəlçən] n. (s, -) petit livre ; livret m. ; opuscule m.
buchen [ˈbuːxən] v. tr. Comm. passer écriture ; passer en compte ; comptabiliser. | *ins Haben*

Textbeispiel 286.13: Wörterbuchausschnitt (aus: Grappin, 148)

ist der Lexikograph oft versucht, aus Gründen der Platzersparnis typographische Blöcke zu bilden, in denen die Lemmata ohne Absatz eingetragen werden können. Zieht sich solchermaßen die alphabetische Makrostruktur des Wörterbuchs durch die Blöcke hindurch, so spricht man statt von Nestern von Nischen. Die Makrostruktur eines solchen Wörterbuchs ist 'nischenalphabetisch'. Die Einträge in der Nische sind (ebenso wie im Nest) Teil der alphabetischen Makrostruktur.

Bei der Nischenbildung sind wiederum zwei Typen zu unterscheiden. Bei der 'semantischen Nische' wird der Lexikograph darauf achten, daß nur solche Ableitungen und Zusammensetzungen als Nischenlemmata in eine Nische gruppiert werden, die auch nach den Gesetzen der (vorwiegend synchronischen) Wortbildung zusammengehören. Er wird also etwa die Nische mit dem Nischeneingangslemma **Bau** nur vom Artikel **Bauabschnitt** bis zum Artikel **Baubüro** führen, weil anschließend dem Alphabet nach das Lemma **Bauch** kommt, das mit **Baubüro** nichts zu tun hat. Der Zufall der alphabetischen Verteilung wird ihm dann erlauben, die Nische mit **Bauch** als Nischeneingangslemma vom Artikel **Bauchatmung** bis zum Artikel **Bauchweh** zu Ende zu führen, um dann neue Lemmazeichen aus der Serie der Zusammensetzungen mit *Bau* aufzunehmen, nämlich **Baudenkmal** usw.

Das Prinzip der semantischen Begrenzung der Nische reicht jedoch als Garantie für sinnvolle Nischenbildung nicht aus. Denn bei strikter Einhaltung des Alphabets spiegelt die Abfolge der Lexeme in vielen Fällen nicht die intuitiv erkannten Wortbildungsabhängigkeiten wider. Das bedeutet z. B., daß das Verbum *brummeln* des Alphabets wegen vor dem ihm als Wortbildungsbasis zugrundeliegenden Verbum *brummen* behandelt wird und daß ebenfalls aus Gründen des Alphabets beide möglicherweise unter dem Nischeneingangslemma **Brummbär** stehen, womit selbstverständlich die sprachlichen Verhältnisse sehr unbefriedigend abgebildet sind.

Ein besonders krasser Gegensatz der Nischenbildung zu der intuitiv erkannten Realität der sprachlichen Wortbildungsabhängigkeiten ergibt sich bei der 'graphischen Nische', die gerade in zweisprachigen Wörterbüchern außerordentlich beliebt ist. Rettig 1985, 110 hat in diesem Zusammenhang vom „relativ rücksichtslosen Umgang mit den Lexemen als offenbar bloß graphischem Material" gesprochen. Das gilt z. B. für die französische Nische **néo**, in der zwischen **néologisme** und **néophyte** auch **néon** eingetragen ist.

Die in Nischen und Nestern gruppierten Lemmata heißen *Sublemmata*. Die auf sie adressierten Angaben sind sublemmatisch adressiert. Sublemmata gehören zur Makrostruktur. Das erste Lemma einer Gruppe von Sublemmata heißt *Eingangslemma* (*Nischeneingangslemma/Nesteingangslemma;* es kommen auch Leitadressen des Typs „**Bau-**" vor, vgl. oben). Es ist also streng zwischen Sublemma und infralemmatischer Adresse (Subadresse) zu unterscheiden. Während Sublemmata der Makrostruktur angehören — sie können über einen alphabetischen Suchpfad gefunden werden (der freilich im Falle der Nester recht kurvenreich verlaufen kann) —, kommt infralemmatischen Adressen nur mikrostruktureller Rang zu.

11.4. Das glattalphabetische Wörterbuch

Verzichtet das alphabetische Wörterbuch auf Nester und Nischen, so kann man es mit Rettig 1985 *glattalphabetisch* nennen. Aber auch dann gibt es immer noch zwei Möglichkeiten, das Material glattalphabetisch einzutragen. Die erste und üblichere Möglichkeit ist die 'artikelalphabetische' Anordnung, d. h.: Zwar sind alle Wörter glattalphabetisch lemmatisiert, z. B. französisch *bouton, boutonner, boutonneux, boutonnière* usw., viele der Artikel enthalten jedoch zahlreiche infralemmatische Adressen.

Die artikelalphabetische Anordnung ist nicht selbstverständlich. Sowohl in der Geschichte der Lexikographie als auch in aktuellen fachsprachlichen Wörterbüchern ist das Prinzip zu beobachten, auf infralemmatische Adressen völlig zu verzichten. Da in diesem Falle jede zweisprachige Bearbeitungseinheit

> **Notar** *m*
> (Re) notary public
> – (GB) Commissioner for Oaths
> *(ie, lawyer, free professional, qualified as a judge, officially appointed; no equivalent in British and American law)*
> **Notar-Anderkonto** *n* (Fin) banking account kept by a notary public in his own name for a third party on a trust basis
> **Notariatsgebühr** *f* (Re) notarial fee
> **Notariatskosten** *pl* (Re) notarial charges
> **notariell beglaubigen**
> (Re) to notarize
> – to record in notarial form
> **notariell beglaubigt** (Re) notarially authenticated
> **notariell beurkundetes Rechtsgeschäft** *n* (Re) notarized legal transaction
> **notarielle Beglaubigung** *f* (Re) notarial authentication
> **notarielle Bescheinigung** *f* (Re) notarial certificate (*or* attestation)
> **notarielle Beurkundung** *f*
> (Re) notarial record
> – recording by a notary
> – authentication by public act
> **notarieller Vertrag** *m* (Re) notarized agreement (*or* contract)
> **notarielle Urkunde** *f* (Re) notarial act (*or* instrument)
> **Notbestellung** *f* (Re) emergency appointment. § 29 BGB
> **Notbetrieb** *m*
> (IndE) emergency operation
> – plant operation on a care and maintenance basis
> **Notenausgabe** *f* (Vw) issue of bank notes

Textbeispiel 286.14: Wörterbuchausschnitt (aus: Schäfer 1983, 446)

(E. *bilingual item*) lemmatisiert wird, kann man dieses Prinzip das *itemalphabetische Prinzip* nennen (vgl. Textbeispiel 286.14).

12. Mikrostrukturelle Profile zweisprachiger Wörterbücher

Wie im einsprachigen Wörterbuch lassen sich auch im allgemeinen zweisprachigen Wörterbuch drei typische Profile von Mikrostrukturen unterscheiden (vgl. Art. 39 und Marello 1989, 77—85):

(a) die integrierte Mikrostruktur
(b) die nichtintegrierte Mikrostruktur
(c) die partiell integrierte Mikrostruktur

12.1. Die integrierte Mikrostruktur

Die integrierte Mikrostruktur ordnet alle Adressen für Mehr-Wort-Einheiten in eine Polysemiestruktur ein, die gelegentlich auch *Mediostruktur* genannt wird. Der Terminus *Polysemiestruktur* wird in vereinfachender Redeweise gebraucht. Genaugenommen handelt es sich um eine Polyäquivalenzstruktur, da die Polysemie des Lemmazeichens im Lichte der Äquivalenzverhältnisse reinterpretiert werden muß. Besteht die Polysemiestruktur z. B. aus sechs 'Integraten' (vgl. zu diesem Begriff Art. 39, 5.1.), so muß für jede der Adressen für Mehr-Wort-Einheiten entschieden werden, in welches Integrat sie gehört. Der Standardbausatz des Integrats besteht aus:

Glosse + Markierungsangabe(n) + Äquivalent(e) + Kotextangaben + Subintegrate für Bearbeitungseinheiten zu Mehr-Wort-Einheiten

Jedes einzelne Bauteil ist fakultativ. Nicht selten bestehen Integrate ausschließlich aus Subintegraten für Mehr-Wort-Einheiten. Die integrierte Mikrostruktur entspricht dem Profil B nach Marello 1989, 82. Man findet sie z. B. in Duden Oxford und in Pons Global.

Integrate bilden Teilstrukturen innerhalb der Mikrostruktur auf einer ersten Unterordnungsstufe. Bedient sich ein Wörterbuch hierarchischer Strukturen mit sekundären und tertiären Stufen, so spricht Art. 39 (S. 487) von 'Subintegraten'. Diese kommen selbstredend auch in zweisprachigen Wörterbüchern vor (vgl. Textbeispiel 286.8). Des weiteren versteht es sich, daß Adressen für Mehr-Wort-Einheiten (seien sie integriert oder nicht) eigene Polysemiestrukturen haben können (vgl. Textbeispiel 286.8, s. v.

„~es Urteil"). Schließlich ist auch denkbar, daß Subintegrate durch Leitelemente eingeführt werden, die als Subintegratseingänge ('Leitadressen') fungieren. Die Leitadresse muß nicht selbst Teil einer zweisprachigen Bearbeitungseinheit sein. Ist sie es, so haben wir es mit einer infralemmatischen Adresse (Subadresse) zu tun, die gleichzeitig als Leitadresse fungiert, auf die andere Subadressen adressiert sind. Z. B. (vgl. Textbeispiel 286.17)

s. v. cœur
(1) *par cœur* by heart
(2) *je la connais par cœur...*
(3) *dîner/déjeuner par cœur...*

Legende: 1 enthält eine Subadresse, welche als Leitadresse für 2 und 3 fungiert. Da die Leitadresse nicht formal kenntlich gemacht ist, können wir von einer versteckten Leitadresse sprechen.

s. v. **cœur**
(1) PAR CŒUR
(2) *réciter/apprendre par cœur* by heart
(3) *je la connais par cœur...*
(4) *dîner/déjeuner par cœur...*

Legende: 1 ist formal als solche kenntlich gemachte Leitadresse für die Subadressen 2—4. Die Leitadresse ist selbst nicht Subadresse, sie ist reines Leitelement.

12.2. Die nichtintegrierte Mikrostruktur

Die nichtintegrierte Mikrostruktur, die sich in zweisprachigen Wörterbüchern entschieden häufiger findet als in einsprachigen, trennt Polysemiestruktur und Mehr-Wort-Teil. Dem kompakten polysemen 'Artikelkopf' (bestehend z. B. aus sechs Positionen, die jeweils den Standardbausatz „Glosse + Marker + Äquivalent(e)" aufweisen) folgt ein erheblich längerer 'Artikelkörper' mit dem Gesamt der Mehr-Wort-Adressen (vgl. Art. 297, wo auch die Organisation dieses Mehr-Wort-Annexes diskutiert wird: rein alphabetisch nach dem Kotextpartner, kategoriell-alphabetisch, d. h. mit Wortartensortierung der Kotextpartner, oder schließlich kategoriell-semantisch-alphabetisch, d. h. mit einer semantischen Sortierung innerhalb der Wortartensortierung). Die nichtintegrierte Mikrostruktur entspricht dem Profil C bei Marello 1989. Die rein alphabetische Sortierung des Mehr-Wort-Annexes findet sich in Sansoni 1984 (Textbeispiel in Marello 1989, 83), die kategoriell-alphabetische Sortierung in Pan Zaiping (vgl. Textbeispiel 286.15), die kategoriell-semantisch-alphabe-

Grundsatz m. ① 原则, 准则, 原理 ② 【数】公理 ‖ ❶ 〈与形容词连用〉 *pädagogische* Grundsätze 教育原理, 教学法原理 / die *richtigen* Grundsätze 正确的原则 / *strenge* [moralische] Grundsätze 严格的[道德的]准则 ❷ 〈与动词连用〉 von seinen Grundsätzen nicht *abgehen* (或 abweichen) 不背离自己的原则 / von einem bestimmten ~ *ausgehen* 从一定的原则出发 / Grundsätze *befolgen* [vertreten] 遵循 [维护]原则/ an den richtigen Grundsätzen *festhalten* 坚持正确的原则 / (keine) Grundsätze *haben* (没)有原则 / seine Grundsätze *preisgeben* 放弃原则 ❸ 〈与连词、介词连用〉 **Das** habe ich mir *als* ~ aufgestellt. 我把这当作原则. / ein Mensch *mit* (或 von) Grundsätzen 有原则(性)的人

Textbeispiel 286.15: Wörterbuchartikel *Grundsatz* (aus: Pan Zaiping, 537)

tische in Van Dale 1983—1986 (vgl. Art. 297 und Marello 1989, 89—98, ferner Hausmann 1985 und Baunebjerg Hansen 1990).

Der Mehr-Wort-Annex kann aus mehreren Blöcken bestehen. So teilt das von Marello 1989, 84 als Beispiel für Profil D vorgestellte Wörterbuch den Mehr-Wort-Körper in einen terminologischen Block und einen idiomatischen Block auf.

Als semiintegriert darf eine Mikrostruktur bezeichnet werden, in der der syntagmatikbezogene Körper zwar vom Artikelkopf getrennt ist, beide Teile aber gleichwohl deckungsgleich organisiert sind, so daß sich durch rein mechanische Umsortierung eine vollständig integrierte Mikrostruktur herstellen ließe. Ein solches Profil weist z. B. Stowasser 1980 auf. Stowasser hat einen vollpa-

disciplīna, altl. discipulīna, ae, *f.*

I. 1. Unterweisung, Lehre, Unterricht; 2. *meton.* Bildung, Kenntnis, Wissen, Kunst; *occ. a.* Methode, Lehrgang; *b.* System, Schule.
II. 1. *met.* Erziehung, Zucht; *occ.* Kriegszucht, Disziplin; 2. *meton.* Ordnung, Einrichtung, Gewohnheit; *occ.* Staatsverfassung, -ordnung.

I. 1. adhibere disciplinam puero angedeihen lassen *L.* 2. disciplinis erudiri in Fächern (Gegenständen) unterrichtet werden *N,* iusti Ethik, memoriae Mnemotechnik. **a.** Hermagorae. **b.** Stoicorum; *pl.* konkr. Schulen. II. 1. familiae der Sklaven, veterum Sabinorum *L.* occ. vetus *T.* 2. tenax disciplinae bei seiner Lebensweise beharrend *Cu,* sacrificandi Ritus *L.* occ. Lycurgi, rei p. Von

Textbeispiel 286.16: Wörterbuchartikel *disciplina* (aus: Stowasser 1980, 141)

rallelisierten syntagmatischen Annex (vgl. Textbeispiel 286.16).

Teilparallelisiert ist z. B. das genannte Van Dale-Profil, insofern dort die Mehr-Wort-Adressen in zweiter Ordnung (die erste ist die nach Wortarten) nach dem Schema des Artikelkopfes deckungsgleich organisiert sind. Eine Beziehung zwischen Mehr-Wort-Körper und Artikelkopf läßt sich, wie Wiegand 1988 b, 594—596 gezeigt hat, (auch ohne jede Parallelisierung) mittels Indizes durchführen, welche alle Mehr-Wort-Adressen, bei denen das möglich ist, einer Lesart der Polysemiestruktur zuordnen.

Die für nichtintegrierte Mikrostrukturen typische formale Organisation der Mehr-Wort-Adressen (kategoriell und/oder alphabetisch) kann auch in integrierten Mikrostrukturen verwirklicht werden (was freilich selten geschieht). So zeichnet sich etwa im Artikel **cœur** von Weis 1979 das Integrat 2. (als eines von acht Integraten) nicht nur durch seine Länge (mehr als zwei Drittel des Artikels), sondern auch durch seine relativ straffe Organisation in drei durch Rhomben getrennte kategoriell bestimmte Gruppen aus, in denen die jeweiligen Kotextpartner (Substantive, Präpositionen, Verben) alphabetisch geordnet sind. Die Präpositionen sind sogar als Leitelemente durch Fettdruck herausgehoben.

12.3. Die partiell integrierte Mikrostruktur

Die partiell integrierte Mikrostruktur ordnet einen Teil der Mehr-Wort-Adressen in die Polysemiestruktur ein und verweist den Rest (wegen der Unmöglichkeit der zweifelsfreien Zuordnung) in den Artikelkörper, oft unter der Überschrift „Phraseologie". Die partiell integrierte Mikrostruktur entspricht dem Profil A in Marello 1989, 81. Man findet sie z. B. in Robert-Collins s. v. «**cœur**», wo die Mehr-Wort-Adresse «**avoir mal au** ∼ » integriert (adressiert auf **cœur (b)** (*fig: estomac*)), «**par** ∼ » hingegen dem Phraseologie-Annex **(k)** (*loc*) zugewiesen ist (vgl. Textbeispiel 286.17).

Die partiell integrierte Mikrostruktur ist doppelt interpretationsgebunden. Nicht nur muß der Lexikograph entscheiden, wohin er die Mehr-Wort-Adresse integriert, er muß zuvor entscheiden, ob er sie überhaupt integriert. Der Gewinn für die Lernfunktion wird mit Zeitverlust beim Suchvorgang bezahlt.

cœur [kœR] *nm* **(a)** (*Anat*) heart. (*lit, hum*) c'est une chance que j'ai le ∼ solide it's a good thing I haven't got a weak heart; il faut avoir le ∼ bien accroché pour risquer ainsi sa vie you need guts* ou a strong stomach to risk your life like that; serrer ou presser qn contre ou sur son ∼ to hold ou clasp ou press sb to one's heart ou breast; opération à ∼ ouvert open-heart operation; on l'a opéré à ∼ ouvert he had an open-heart operation; maladie de ∼ heart complaint ou trouble; avoir le ∼ malade to have a weak heart ou a heart condition; V **battement, greffe¹**.
(b) (*fig: estomac*) avoir mal au ∼ to feel sick; cela me soulève le ∼ it nauseates me, it makes me (feel) sick; ça vous fait mal au ∼ de penser que it is sickening to think that; une odeur/un spectacle qui soulève le ∼ a nauseating ou sickening smell/sight; V **haut**.
(c) (*siège des sentiments, de l'amour*) heart. (*forme d'adresse*) mon ∼† dear heart!; (*à un enfant*) sweetheart; avoir un ou le ∼ sensible to be sensitive ou tender-hearted; un dur au ∼ tendre someone whose bark is worse than his bite; elle lui a donné son ∼ she has lost her heart to him ou given him her heart; mon ∼ se serre/se brise ou se fend à cette pensée my heart sinks/breaks at the thought; chagrin qui brise le ∼ heartbreaking grief ou sorrow; un spectacle à vous fendre le ∼ a heartrending ou heartbreaking sight; avoir le ∼ gros ou serré to have a heavy heart; il avait la rage au ∼ he was inwardly seething with anger; cela m'a réchauffé le ∼ de les voir it did my heart good ou it was heartwarming to see them; ce geste lui est allé (droit) au ∼ he was (deeply) moved ou touched by this gesture, this gesture went straight to his heart; V **affaire, courrier** *etc*.
(d) (*bonté, générosité*) avoir bon ∼ to be kind-hearted; avoir le ∼ sur la main to be open-handed; manquer de ∼ to be unfeeling ou heartless; il a du ∼ he is a good-hearted man, his heart is in the right place; c'est un (homme) sans ∼, il n'a pas de ∼ he is a heartless man; il a ou c'est un ∼ de pierre/d'or he has a heart of stone/gold; un homme/une femme de ∼ a noble-hearted man/woman.
(e) (*humeur*) avoir le ∼ gai ou joyeux/léger/triste to feel happy/light-hearted/sad ou sad at heart; je n'ai pas le ∼ à rire/à sortir I do not feel like laughing/going out, I am not in the mood for laughing/going out; il n'a plus le ∼ à rien his heart isn't in anything any more; si le ∼ vous en dit if you feel like it, if you are in the mood.
(f) (*âme, pensées intimes*) c'est un ∼ pur ou candide he is a candid soul; la noirceur de son ∼ his blackness of heart; la noblesse de son ∼ his noble-heartedness; connaître le fond du ∼ de qn to know sb's innermost feelings; des paroles venues (du fond) du ∼ words (coming) from the heart, heartfelt words; dévoiler son ∼ à qn to open one's heart to sb; elle a vidé son ∼ she poured out her heart; au fond de son ∼ in his heart of hearts; il m'a parlé à ∼ ouvert he had a heart-to-heart talk with me; V **cri**.
(g) (*courage, ardeur*) heart, courage. le ∼ lui manqua (pour faire) his heart ou courage failed him (when it came to doing); mettre tout son ∼ dans qch/à faire qch to put all one's heart into sth/into doing sth; comment peut-on avoir le ∼ de refuser?; how can one have ou find the heart to refuse?; donner du ∼ au ventre à qn* to buck sb up*; avoir du ∼ au ventre* to have guts*; avoir du ∼ à l'ouvrage to put one's heart into one's work; il travaille mais le ∼ n'y est pas he does the work but his heart isn't in it; cela m'a redonné du ∼ that gave me new heart.
(h) (*partie centrale*) *[chou]* heart; *[arbre, bois]* heart, core; *[fruit, pile atomique]* core; *[problème, ville]* heart. au ∼ de région, ville, forêt in the heart of; aller au ∼ du sujet to get to the heart of the matter; au ∼ de l'été in the height of summer; au ∼ de l'hiver in the depth ou heart of winter; fromage fait à ∼ fully ripe cheese; ∼ de palmier heart of palm; (*lit*) ∼ d'artichaut artichoke heart; (*fig*) il a un ∼ d'artichaut he falls in love with every girl he meets.
(i) (*objet*) heart. en (forme de) ∼ heart-shaped; volets percés de ∼s shutters with heart-shaped holes; V **bouche**.
(j) (*Cartes*) heart. valet/as de ∼ knave/ace of hearts; avez-vous du ∼? have you any hearts?; V **atout, joli**.
(k) (*loc*) par ∼ réciter, apprendre by heart; je la connais par ∼ I know her inside out, I know her like the back of my hand; dîner/déjeuner par ∼† to have to do without dinner/lunch; sur le ∼: ce qu'il m'a dit, je l'ai sur le ∼ ou ça m'est resté sur le ∼ what he told me still rankles with me, I still feel sore about what he told me; je vais lui dire ce que j'ai sur le ∼ I'm going to tell him what's on my mind; à ∼ joie to one's heart's content; de tout mon ∼ with all my heart; je vous souhaite de tout mon ∼ de réussir I wish you success with all my heart ou from the bottom of my heart; être de tout ∼ avec qn dans la joie/une épreuve to share (in) sb's happiness/sorrow; je suis de tout ∼ avec vous I DO sympathize with you; ne pas porter qn dans son ∼ to have no great liking for sb; je veux en avoir le ∼ net I want to be clear in my own mind (about it); avoir à ∼ de faire to want ou be keen to do; prendre les choses à ∼ to take things to heart; prendre à ∼ de faire to set one's heart on doing; ce voyage me tient à ∼ I have set my heart on this journey; ce sujet me tient à ∼ this subject is close to my heart; trouver un ami selon son ∼ to find a friend after one's own heart; V **donner**.

Textbeispiel 286.17: Wörterbuchartikel *cœur* (aus: Robert-Collins, 130)

13. Literatur (in Auswahl)

13.1. Wörterbücher

Duden Oxford = Duden Oxford Großwörterbuch Englisch. Englisch-Deutsch/Deutsch-Englisch. Hrsg. v. d. Dudenredaktion und Oxford University Press. Red. Leitung: Werner Scholze-Stubenrecht/ John Sykes. Mannheim. Wien. Zürich 1990 [1696 S.].

Essence 1982/83 = Hyungkun Heo/Koreanische Gesellschaft für Germanistik: Minjungseorims Essence Deutsch-Koreanisches/Koreanisch-Deutsches Wörterbuch. 2 Bde. Seoul 1982/83 [2051, 2103 S.].

Grappin = Pierre Grappin: Dictionnaire allemand-français. Paris 1963 (Collection Saturne) [XIV, 898 S. Neuaufl. 1989: Großwörterbuch Deutsch-Französisch, XVIII, S. 707—1463].

Lexus D—S 1983 = Huebers Kleines Reise-ABC Spanisch. Hrsg. v. LEXUS mit R. Krause Morales/ Hugh O'Donnell. München 1983 [127 S.].

LGWB = Langenscheidts Großwörterbuch der englischen und deutschen Sprache. „Der Kleine Muret-Sanders". Deutsch-Englisch. Von Heinz Messinger und der Langenscheidt-Redaktion. Berlin. München. Wien. Zürich 1982 [1296 S.].

Martínez Amador = Emilio M. Martínez Amador: Diccionario alemán-español, español-alemán. Ed. rev. y ampl. Barcelona 1969 [1616 S.].

OLD = P. G. W. Glare (Hrsg.): Oxford Latin Dictionary. 8 Fasz. Oxford 1968—1982 [XXIV, 2126 S.].

Pan Zaiping = Autorenkollektiv unter der Leitung von Pan Zaiping: Deutsch-Chinesisches Wörterbuch. Shanghai 1984 [1527 S.].

Pons Global = Roland Breitsprecher/Peter Terrell/Veronika Calderwood-Schnorr/Wendy V. A. Morris: Pons Globalwörterbuch Deutsch-Englisch. Stuttgart 1983 [XXIII, 1380 S.].

Robert-Collins = Beryl T. Atkins/Alain Duval/ Rosemary C. Milne/Pierre Henri Cousin/Hélène M. A. Lewis/Lorna A. Sinclair/Renée O. Birks/ Marie-Noëlle Lamy: Robert-Collins Dictionnaire français-anglais, anglais-français. Nouvelle éd. Paris 1987 [XXIX, 768, 830 S.].

Robert-Signorelli 1981 = Robert Signorelli. Dictionnaire italien-français, français-italien. Paris 1981 [3002 S.].

Sansoni 1984 = Vladimiro Macchi (Hrsg.): Dizionario delle lingue italiana e tedesca. 2 Bde. Florenz 1984 [3228 S.].

Schäfer 1983 = Wilhelm Schäfer: Wirtschaftswörterbuch. Band II: Deutsch-Englisch. München 1983 [XXX, 721 S.].

Schwan 1782 = Christian Friedrich Schwan: Nouveau Dictionnaire de la langue allemande et françoise. 2 Bde. Mannheim 1782—1784 [2115 S.].

Stehlík 1936 = Oldrich Stehlík: Dictionnaire tchèque-français. 2 Bde. Prag 1936.

Stowasser 1980 = Der Kleine Stowasser. Lateinisch-deutsches Schulwörterbuch. Von J. M. Stowasser/M. Petschenig/F. Skutsch. Bearb. u. erw. v. Robert Pichl u. a. Gesamtredaktion Herbert Reitterer/Wilfried Winkler. München 1980 [XXXII, 507 S.; geht zurück auf: Joseph Maria Stowasser, Lateinisch-Deutsches Schulwörterbuch. Wien 1894, XX, 1092 S. 2. Aufl. 1900, 1104 S. Nachdruck 1969].

Van Dale 1983/85 = B. P. F. Al et al.: Van Dale Groot woordenboek Frans-Nederlands. Van Dale Groot woordenboek Nederlands-Frans. 2 Bde. Utrecht 1983, 1985 [1579, 1565 S.].

Van Dale 1983/86 = H. L. Cox et al.: Van Dale Groot woordenboek Duits-Nederlands. Van Dale Groot woordenboek Nederlands-Duits. 2 Bde. Utrecht 1983, 1986 [1576, 1560 S.].

Van Dale 1984/86 = W. Martin/G. A. J. Tops et al.: Van Dale Groot woordenboek Engels-Nederlands. Van Dale Groot woordenboek Nederlands-Engels. 2 Bde. Utrecht 1984, 1986 [1594, 1560 S.].

Weis 1979 = Erich Weis (Hrsg.): Langenscheidts Großwörterbuch Französisch. Teil 1: Französisch-Deutsch. Begründet von Prof. Dr. Karl Sachs und Prof. Dr. Césaire Villatte. Völlige Neubearb. 1979. Berlin. München. Wien. Zürich 1979 [XXIX, 1048 S.].

13.2. Sonstige Literatur

Abend 1988 = Heike Abend: Das Reisewörterbuch verdient die Aufmerksamkeit der Wörterbuchforschung. In: Lebende Sprachen 33. 1988, 98—101 u. 156—159.

Abraham/Wuite 1984 = Werner Abraham/Eva Wuite: Kontrastive Partikelforschung unter lexikographischem Gesichtspunkt. Exempel am Deutsch-Finnischen. In: Folia Linguistica 18. 1984, 155—192.

Académie 1957 = Académie de la République Populaire Roumaine: Mélanges linguistiques publiés à l'occasion du VIIIe Congrès International des Linguistes à Oslo, du 5 au 9 août 1957. Comité de rédaction: Iorgu Iordan/Émile Petrovici/A. [Alexandru] Rosetti. Bucarest 1957.

Adrados 1979 = Francisco R. Adrados: La Lexicografia griega: su estado actual y el Diccionario Griego-Español. In: Revista Española de Lingüística 9. 1979, 413—439.

Adrados 1986 = Francisco R. Adrados: The Greek-Spanish Dictionary and Lexicographic Science. In: Lexicographica 2. 1986, 8—32.

Akademija 1976 = Akademija Nauk SSSR. Naučnyj Sovet po Leksikologii i Leksikografii: Problematika opredelenij terminov v slovarjach raznych tipov. Redakcionnaja kollegija: S. G. Barchudarov (predsedatel')/V. P. Petruškov/V. P. Sorokoletov. Leningrad 1976.

Akademija 1984 = Akademija Nauk SSSR, Otdelenie Literatury i Jazyka, Naučnyj Sovet po Teorii

Sovetskogo Jazykoznanija, Naučnyj Sovet po Leksikologii i Leksikografii: Slovo v grammatike i slovare. Redakcionnaja kollegija V. N. Jarceva (otvetstvennyj redaktor) et al. Moskva 1984.

Al 1983a = Bernard Al: Dictionnaire de thème et dictionnaire de version. In: Revue de Phonétique Appliquée 66—67—68. 1983, 203—211.

Al 1983b = Bernard Al: Principes d'organisation d'un dictionnaire bilingue. In: Lexique 2. 1983, 159—165.

Al 1987 = Bernard Al: Ordinateur et lexicographie. In: Studies in Honour of Roberto Busa S.J. = Linguistica Computazionale 4—5. 1987, 1—21.

Al 1988 = Bernard Al: Langue source, langue cible et métalangue. In: Aspects de linguistique française. Hommage à Q. I. M. Mok. Ed. Ronald Landheer. Amsterdam 1988, 15—29.

Al-Kasimi 1977 = Ali M. Al-Kasimi: Linguistics and Bilingual Dictionaries. Leiden 1977 (photomechanical reprint, 1983).

Al-Kasimi 1983 = A. [Ali] Al-Kasimi: The interlingual/translation dictionary. Dictionaries for translation. In: Hartmann 1983a, 153—162.

Alvar 1981 = Manuel Alvar Ezquerra: Los diccionarios bilingües: su contenido. In: Lingüística Española Actual 3. 1981, 175—196.

Anderson 1978 = James David Anderson: The Development of the English-French, French-English Bilingual Dictionary: A Study in Comparative Lexicography. New York 1978 (Supplement to Word. Volume 28, No. 3, Monograph No. 6).

Andrianov 1964 = S. N. Andrianov: Nekotorye voprosy postroenija slovarej special'noj terminologii. In: Tetradi perevodčika. Pod redakciej L. S. Barchudarova. Moskva 1964 (Učenye zapiski No. 2), 78—91.

Antor 1988 = Heinz Antor: Einsprachige Wörterbücher für Muttersprachler — eine Alternative für den deutschen Schüler? In: Neusprachliche Mitteilungen aus Wissenschaft und Praxis 40. 1988, 223—228.

Ard 1982 = Josh Ard: The Use of Bilingual Dictionaries by ESL Students While Writing. In: ITL 58. 1982, 1—27.

Armogathe 1983 = Jean-Robert Armogathe: Les Dictionnaires allemand-français et la langue philosophique au début du XIXème siècle. In: Beiträge zur Romanischen Philologie 22. 1983, 267—270.

Atkins 1985 = Beryl T. Atkins: Monolingual and Bilingual Learner's Dictionaries: a comparison. In: Robert Ilson (ed.): Dictionaries, Lexicography and Language Learning. Oxford 1985 (ELT Documents 120), 15—24.

Babić 1970 = Stjepan Babić: Varijante u dvojezičnim rječnicima. In: Jezik 1/2. 1970, 46—54.

Baganz 1987 = Lutz Baganz: Scientific and Practical Problems of a Hindi-German Dictionary. In: Ilson 1987, 101—114.

Baldinger 1971 = Kurt Baldinger: Semasiologie und Onomasiologie im zweisprachigen Wörterbuch. In: Bausch/Gauger 1971, 384—396.

Baldinger 1985 = Kurt Baldinger: Semasiologie und Onomasiologie im zweisprachigen Wörterbuch. In: Zgusta 1985, 136—149 (Erstveröffentlichung Baldinger 1971).

Bantaş 1982 = Andrei Bantaş: Aspects of Applied Semantics: for Modernizing Bilingual Dictionaries. In: Revue Roumaine de Linguistique 27. 1982, 219—226.

Bartholomew/Schoenhals 1983 = Doris A. Bartholomew/Louise C. Schoenhals: Bilingual Dictionaries for Indigenous Languages. México 1983.

Baskakov 1976 = N. A. Baskakov: Ètnografičeskaja leksika: terminologija v nacional'no-russkich slovarjach (na materiale tjurkskich jazykov). In: Akademija 1976, 236—243.

Baudouin de Courtenay 1963 = I. A. Boduèn de Kurtenè [Baudouin de Courtenay]: Zamečanija o russko-pol'skom slovare. In: Leksikografičeskij sbornik 6. 1963, 139—147.

Baunebjerg Hansen 1988a = Gitte Baunebjerg Hansen: En undersøgelse af dansk-tyske/tyskdanske ordbøgers brug og brugbarhed i en oversættelsessituation. In: ARK 41. 1988.

Baunebjerg Hansen 1988b = Gitte Baunebjerg Hansen: Stand und Aufgaben der zweisprachigen Lexikographie. Nachlese zum Kopenhagener Werkstattgespräch 12.—13. Mai 1986. In: Lexicographica 4. 1988, 186—202.

Baunebjerg Hansen 1990 = Gitte Baunebjerg Hansen: Artikelstruktur im zweisprachigen Wörterbuch. Überlegungen zur Darbietung von Übersetzungsäquivalenten im Wörterbuchartikel. Tübingen 1990 (Lexicographica Series Maior 35).

Baunebjerg/Wesemann 1983 = Gitte Baunebjerg/Monika Wesemann: Partikelwörterbuch Deutsch-Dänisch, Dänisch-Deutsch. Ein Arbeitsbericht. In: Harald Weydt (Hrsg.), Partikeln und Interaktion. Tübingen 1983, 119—129.

Bausch/Gauger 1971 = Karl-Richard Bausch/Hans-Martin Gauger (Hrsg.): Interlinguistica. Sprachvergleich und Übersetzung. Festschrift zum 60. Geburtstag von Mario Wandruszka. Tübingen 1971.

Baxter 1980 = J. Baxter: The Dictionary and Vocabulary Behaviour: A Single Word or a Handful? In: TESOL Quarterly 14. 1980, 325—336.

Beattie 1973 = Nicholas Beattie: Teaching Dictionary Use. In: Modern Language 54. 1973, 161—168.

Bergenholtz 1990 = Henning Bergenholtz: Lexikographische Instruktionen für ein zweisprachiges Wörterbuch. In: Zeitschrift für Phonetik, Sprachwissenschaft und Kommunikationsforschung 43. 1990, 19—37.

Bergenholtz/Mugdan 1985 = Henning Bergenholtz/Joachim Mugdan (Hrsg.): Lexikographie und Grammatik. Akten des Essener Kolloquiums zur Grammatik im Wörterbuch 28.—30. 6. 1984. Tübingen 1985 (Lexicographica Series Maior 3).

Berkov 1970 = V. [Valerij Pavlovič] Berkov: Izučenie russkogo jazyka i dvujazyčnyj slovar'. In: Russkij jazyk v nacional'noj škole Jg. 1970, 4—10.

Berkov 1973 = V. P. [Valerij Pavlovič] Berkov: Voprosy dvujazyčnoj leksikografii (slovnik). Leningrad 1973.

Berkov 1977 = V. P. [Valerij Pavlovič] Berkov: Slovo v dvujazyčnom slovare. Tallin 1977.

Berkov 1990 = Valerij P. [Pavlovič] Berkov: A Modern Bilingual Dictionary — Results and Prospects. In: BudaLEX 1990, 97—106.

Berni-Canani/Fumel/Pristipino 1985 = M. Berni-Canani/Y. Fumel/P. Pristipino: Analyse linguistique des dictionnaires bilingues. Premières réflexions. In: Repères 1. 1985, 75—102.

Berni-Canani/Pristipino 1987 = M. Berni-Canani/P. Pristipino: La transcription phonétique dans les dictionnaires bilingues français-italien/italien-français: problèmes. In: Repères 2. 1987, 86—109.

Bertaux 1983 = Pierre Bertaux: Contrastivité et lexicographie. In: Contrastes. Hors Série A 3. 1983, 17—21.

Bielfeldt 1956 = H. H. [Hans Holm] Bielfeldt: Fragen des russisch-deutschen Wörterbuches. In: Zeitschrift für Slawistik 1/2. 1956, 19—34.

Birkenhauer/Birkenhauer 1989 = Klaus Birkenhauer/Renate Birkenhauer: Shaping Tools for the Literary Translator's Trade. In: Snell-Hornby/Pöhl 1989, 89—98.

Blumenthal 1987 = Peter Blumenthal: Sprachvergleich Deutsch-Französisch. Tübingen 1987 (Romanistische Arbeitshefte 29).

Boas 1978 = Hans-Ulrich Boas: Lexical Entries for Verbs in a Contrastive Lexicon English-German. In: Werner Abraham (Hrsg.), Valence, Semantic Case, and Grammatical Relations. Amsterdam 1978 (Studies in Language Comparison Series 1), 191—216.

Boch 1989 = Raoul Boch: Faire un bilingue français/italien. In: Le Français dans le Monde Numéro Spécial: Lexiques, ed. Amr Helmy Ibrahim. Août-Septembre 1989, 78—83.

Boelcke/Thiele 1983 = J. B. Boelcke/P. Thiele: Wie entsteht ein Wirtschaftswörterbuch? Einige lexikographische Anmerkungen. In: Nouveaux cahiers d'allemand 1. 1983, 256—266.

Bogaards 1987 = Paul Bogaards: Tweetalige handwoordenboeken voor enigszins gevorderde taalverwervers. In: Toegepaste Taalwetenschap in Artikelen 27. 1987, 42—49.

Bogaards 1988 = P. [Paul] Bogaards: A propos de l'usage du dictionnaire de langue étrangère. In: Cahiers de lexicologie 52. 1988, 131—152.

Bogaards 1990 = Paul Bogaards: Où cherche-t-on dans le dictionnaire? In: International Journal of Lexicography 3. 1990, 79—102.

Bogin 1967 = G. I. Bogin: Nekotorye voprosy racionolizacii postroenija slovarnoj stat'i v nacional'no-inostrannom slovare. In: Tezisy dokladov i soobščenij 1-j naučno-metodičeskoj konferencii Kokčetavskogo pegadogičeskogo instituta. Kokčetav 1967, 54—57.

Bogusławski 1979 = Andrzej Bogusławski: Zum Problem der Phraseologie in zweisprachigen Wörterbüchern. In: Kwartalnik neofilologiczny 26. 1979, 29—36.

Bordier/Szende 1988 = Evelyne Bordier/Tamás Szende: Termes d'adresse et de salutation dans un dictionnaire hongrois-français. In: Contrastes 17. 1988, 93—104.

Bork 1983 = Egon Bork: Prinzipien und Entwicklung der Gyldendalschen Wörterbücher Deutsch-Dänisch und Dänisch-Deutsch in den Zeiträumen 1902/1912/1932/1982. In: Hyldgaard-Jensen/Zettersten 1983, 163—167.

Bornemann 1989 = Eva Bornemann: Translation and Lexicography: A Practical View. In: Snell-Hornby/Pöhl 1989, 99—104.

Borovkov 1957 = A. K. Borovkov: Iz opyta sostavlenija russko-nacional'nych slovarej. In: Leksikografičeskij sbornik 1. 1957, 135—159.

Borsdorf/Gross 1981 = Wolfgang Borsdorf/Helmut Gross: Zur Zeitökonomie bei der Erarbeitung zweisprachiger Fachwörterbücher. In: Gunter Neubert (Hrsg.), Rechnerunterstützung bei der Bearbeitung fachlexikalischer Probleme. Ein Sammelband. Leipzig 1981, 94—114.

Braasch 1988 = Anna Braasch: Zur lexikographischen Kodifizierung von Phrasemen in einsprachigen deutschen Wörterbüchern aus der Sicht eines ausländischen Buchbenutzers. In: Hyldgaard-Jensen/Zettersten 1988 b, 83—100.

Bray 1988 = Laurent Bray: La Lexicographie Bilingue Italien-Allemand, Allemand-Italien du Dix-Septième Siècle. In: International Journal of Lexicography 1. 1988, 313—342.

Bucksch 1973 = Herbert Bucksch: Das technische Übersetzungswörterbuch. In: Mitteilungsblatt für Dolmetscher und Übersetzer 19/5. 1973, 6—8.

BudaLEX 1990 = T. Magay/J. Zigány (eds.): BudaLEX '88 Proceedings. Papers from the 3rd International EURALEX Congress, Budapest, 4—9 September 1988. Budapest 1990.

Bühler 1990 = Hildegund Bühler: Das Arnold-Lissance-Archiv an der Universität Wien. Gedanken zum Konzept eines Translator's Dictionary. In: BudaLEX 1990, 411—419.

Bujas 1974 = Željko Bujas: A Manual Conversion Procedure in Bilingual (Croatian—English) Lexicography. In: Studia romanica et anglica zagrabiensia 37. 1974, 187—203.

Bujas 1975 = Željko Bujas: Testing the Performance of a Bilingual Dictionary on Topical Current Texts. In: Studia romanica et anglica zagrabiensia 39. 1975, 193—204.

Calzolari 1988 = Nicoletta Calzolari/Antonio Zampolli: From Monolingual to Bilingual Automated Lexicons: Is There a Continuum? In: Lexicographica 4. 1988, 130—144.

Čanturišvili 1975 = D. S. Čanturišvili: Iz istorii dvujazyčnoj leksikografii. In: Voprosy jazykoznanija Jg. 1975/Nr. 1. 1975, 104—110.

Carstensen 1970 = Broder Carstensen: Englische Wortschatzarbeit unter dem Gesichtspunkt der Kollokation. In: Neusprachliche Mitteilungen 23. 1970, 193—202.

Chivescu 1984 = Romeo Chivescu: Elemente de tipologie a dicţionarelor bilingve — Din experienţa alcătuirii unor lucrări lexicografice cu profil didactic. In: Romanoslavica 22. 1984, 307—327.

Chivescu 1986 = Romeo Chivescu: Unele aspecte ale oglindirii informaţiei generale în dicţionarele bilingve (cu privire specială la dicţionarele ruso-române. In: Romanoslavica 24. 1986, 137—153.

Chorochorin 1964 = L.G. Chorochorin: Nekotorye zamečanija o mnogoznačnosti slov v dvujazyčnych slovarjach. In: Tetradi perevodčika. Pod redakciej L. S. Barchudarova. Moskva 1964 (Učenye zapiski No. 2), 91—99.

Choul 1987 = Jean-Claude Choul: Contrôle de l'équivalence dans les dictionnaires bilingues. In: Ilson 1987, 75—90.

Christmann/Troebes/Witt 1981 = Kurt Christmann/Otto Troebes/Rudolf Witt: Probleme bei der Erarbeitung eines Fügungswörterbuches deutsch-russisch für Wissenschaftler und Studenten. In: Wissenschaftliche Zeitschrift. Martin-Luther-Universität Halle-Wittenberg. GSR 30. 1981, 43—48.

Collinson 1939 = W.E. Collinson: Comparative Synonymics. Some Principles and Illustrations. In: Transactions of the Philological Society. London 1939, 54—77.

Cop 1984 = Margaret Cop: Zur Qualität der englisch-deutsch, deutsch-englischen Lexikographie unter besonderer Berücksichtigung der Großwörterbücher von Klett-Collins und Langenscheidt. Erlangen 1984 (unveröffentlichte Magisterarbeit).

Cousin 1982 = Pierre-Henri Cousin: La mise en équation des entités lexicales françaises et anglaises dans un dictionnaire bilingue. In: D. Calleri/C. Marello (Hrsg.), Linguistica contrastiva. Roma 1982, 255—277.

Cowie 1981 = Anthony P. Cowie (ed.): Lexicography and its Pedagogical Applications. In: Applied Linguistics 2 (Thematic Issue). 1981.

Cowie 1987 = Anthony Cowie (ed.): The Dictionary and the Language Learner. Papers from the EURALEX Seminar at the University of Leeds, 1—3 April 1985. Tübingen 1987 (Lexicographica Series Maior 17).

Creamer 1987 = Thomas Creamer: Beyond the definition: some problems with examples in recent Chinese-English and English-Chinese bilingual dictionaries. In: Cowie 1987, 238—245.

Cydendambaev 1969 = C.B. Cydendambaev: Nekotorye voprosy sostavlenija burjatsko-russkogo slovarja. In: Akademija Nauk, Sibirskoe Otdelenije, Burjatskij Filial, K izučeniju burjatskogo jazyka. Ulan-Udė 1969 (Trudy Burjatskogo instituta obščestvennych nauk 6), 117—128.

Czochralski 1977 = Jan A. Czochralski: Deutschpolnische Wörterbücher in Volkspolen. In: Ulrich Engel (Hrsg.), Deutsche Sprache im Kontrast. Tübingen 1977 (Forschungsberichte des Instituts für deutsche Sprache Mannheim. Band 36), 198—205.

Dalitz 1975 = Günter Dalitz: Zur Darstellung von Präpositionen in einem Übersetzungswörterbuch. In: Linguistische Arbeitsberichte 11. 1975, 85—90.

Dalitz 1978 = Günter Dalitz: Zur lexikographischen Bearbeitung von Präpositionen in einem deutsch-russischen Übersetzungswörterbuch. In: Fremdsprachen 22. 1978, 102—108.

DANLEX-Group 1987 = The DANLEX-Group: Ebba Hjorth/Bodil Nistrup Madsen/Ole Norling-Christensen/Jane Rosenkilde Jacobsen/Hanne Ruus: Descriptive Tools for Electronic Processing of Dictionary Data. Studies in Computational Lexicography. Mit einer deutschen Zusammenfassung/Avec un résumé français. Tübingen 1987 (Lexicographica Series Maior 20).

Darbelnet 1970 = Jean Darbelnet: Dictionnaires bilingues et lexicologie différentielle. In: Langages 19. 1970, 92—102.

Debyser 1971 = Francis Debyser: Comparaison et interférence lexicales (français-italien). In: Le français dans le monde 81. 1971, 51—57.

De Martino 1981 = G. De Martino: Il dizionario bilingue come componente dell' insegnamento glottodidattico. In: F. Albano Leoni/N. De Blasi (Hrsg.), Lessico e semantica. Roma 1981, 161—181.

Ditten 1959 = Hans Ditten: Über die Arbeit an einem neugriechisch-deutschen Lexikon. In: Johannes Irmscher in Zusammenarbeit mit Hans Ditten und Marika Mineemi (Hrsg.), Probleme der neugriechischen Literatur. I. Berlin 1959 (Berliner byzantinistische Arbeiten. Band 14), 43—49.

Dittmer 1981 = Arne Dittmer: Feste Syntagmen im Dänisch-Deutschen Wörterbuch. In: Kopenhagener Beiträge zur Germanistischen Linguistik 17. 1981, 110—125.

Dittmer 1983 = Arne Dittmer: Partizipien im Dänisch-Deutschen Wörterbuch. In: Hyldgaard-Jensen/Zettersten 1983, 189—197.

Duda 1986 = Walter Duda: Ein „aktives" russisch-deutsches Wörterbuch für deutschsprachige Benutzer? In: Günther 1986, 9—15.

Duda/Frenzel/Wöller/Zimmermann 1986 = Walter Duda/Maria Frenzel/Egon Wöller/Tatjana Zimmermann: Zu einer Theorie der zweisprachigen Lexikographie. Überlegungen zu einem neuen russisch-deutschen Wörterbuch. Berlin 1986 (Linguistische Studien. Reihe A. Arbeitsberichte 142).

Duda/Müller 1974 = Walter Duda/Bärbel Müller: Zur Problematik eines aktiven deutsch-russischen Wörterbuchs. In: Fremdsprachen 18. 1974, 175—180.

Duda/Müller 1976 = Walter Duda/Klaus Müller: Die Bedeutung der Phraseologie für ein Übersetzungswörterbuch. In: Fremdsprachen 20. 1976, 168—171.

Duda/Müller/Müller 1977 = V. Duda/B. Mjuller/K. Mjuller [Walter Duda/Bärbel Müller/Klaus Müller]: K nekotorym voprosam nemecko-russkogo slovarja dlja govorjaščich na nemeckom jazyke. In: Aktual'nye problemy metodiki i obučenija russkomu jazyku graždan GDR. Konferencija prepodavatelej vysšej i srednej školy GDR i SSSR. Berlin 16—18 marta 1977 g. Doklady i tezisy vystuplenij. Redakcionnaja kollegija B. Brandt et al. Berlin 1977, 169—171.

Duda/Müller/Müller 1978 = Walter Duda/Bärbel Müller/Klaus Müller: Zu spezifischen Aspekten der Darstellung des russischen Wortschatzes für Deutschmuttersprachler. In: Wissenschaftliche Zeitschrift der Humboldt-Universität zu Berlin. Ges.-Sprachw. R. 27. 1978, 455—457.

Duda/Müller/Müller 1981 = Walter Duda/Bärbel Müller/Klaus Müller: Fragen der Darstellung des deutschen Wortschatzes in einem zweisprachigen Wörterbuch. In: Fremdsprachen 25. 1981, 42—45.

Duval 1986 = Alain Duval: La métalangue dans les dictionnaires bilingues. In: Lexicographica 2. 1986, 93—100.

Ehegötz 1973 = Erika Ehegötz: Zur Konzeption eines polnisch-deutschen phraseologischen Wörterbuchs. In: Zeitschrift für Slawistik 18. 1973, 227—234.

Ehegötz 1986 = Erika Ehegötz: Zur Darstellung des phraseologischen Materials im allgemeinsprachlichen Übersetzungswörterbuch. In: Günther 1986, 132—140.

Eismann 1989 = Wolfgang Eismann: Zum Problem der Äquivalenz von Phraseologismen. In: Gréciano 1989, 83—93.

Elia 1984 = A. Elia: Etude formelle des différents emplois sémantiques d'un mot. Un exemple d'application du Lexique-Grammaire de l'italien et du français. In: Cahiers de lexicologie 44. 1984, 51—62.

Engelmann/Rackebrandt 1970 = Gudrun Engelmann/Renate Rackebrandt: Zu einigen Problemen bei der Arbeit an einem Deutsch-Suaheli-Wörterbuch. In: Kaspar Riemschneider (Hrsg.), Probleme der Lexikographie. Berlin 1970 (Deutsche Akademie der Wissenschaften zu Berlin, Institut für Orientforschung. Veröffentlichung Nr. 73), 101—110.

Ettinger 1987 = Stefan Ettinger: Einige «apontamentos» zur modernen zweisprachigen Lexikographie Deutsch-Portugiesisch und Portugiesisch-Deutsch. In: Vox Romanica 46. 1987, 180—247.

Ettinger 1988 = Stefan Ettinger: Vom möglichen Nutzen der Übersetzung für die zweisprachige Lexikographie. Einige Anmerkungen zur Bedeutung und Bezeichnung anhand französischer Beispiele. In: Energeia und Ergon. Bd. III: Das sprachtheoretische Denken Eugenio Coserius in der Diskussion (2). Hrsg. v. Jens Lüdtke. Tübingen 1988, 421—434.

Ettinger 1989 = Stefan Ettinger: Einige Probleme der lexikographischen Darstellung idiomatischer Einheiten (Französisch-Deutsch). In: Gréciano 1989, 95—115.

Ezawa 1988 = Kennosuke Ezawa/Seiichi Okoma: Computergestützte Herstellung eines japanisch-deutschen Satzlexikons. In: Snell-Hornby 1988, 427—436.

Fábián 1990 = Zsuzsanna Fábián: Historische Untersuchung der italienisch-ungarischen und ungarisch-italienischen Wörterbücher. In: BudaLEX 1990, 177—187.

Faluba/Morvay 1986 = Kálmán Faluba/Károly Morvay: Noticia del diccionario manual catalán-húngaro. In: Acta Universitatis Szegedensis. Acta Romanica. Tomus XI: Studia Lexicographica Neolatina. Szeged 1986, 52—81.

Fedorov/Chazanović 1976 = A. V. Fedorov/A. P. Chazanović: Überlegungen zum deutsch-russischen Anna-Seghers-Wörterbuch (anhand des Romans „Die Toten bleiben jung"). In: Deutsch als Fremdsprache 13. 1976, 262—268.

Fedorov/Krylova/Lilič/Trofimkina 1975 = A. V. Fedorov/G. V. Krylova/G. A. Lilič/O. I. Trofimkina: Perevodnoj ob-jasnitel'nyj slovar' jazyka pisatelja (mesto v leksikografii i v metodike prepodavanija perevoda). In: Moskovskij gosudarstvennyj pedagogičeskij institut inostrannych jazykov imeni Morisa Toreza 1975, Čast' I, 58—60.

Fel'dman 1952 = N. I. Fel'dman: O specifike nebol'šich dvujazyčnych slovarej. In: Voprosy jazykoznanija 1952/2, 62—84.

Fel'dman 1957a = N. I. Fel'dman: Ob analize smyslovoj struktury slova v dvujazyčnych slovarjach. In: Leksikografičeskij sbornik 1. 1957, 9—35.

Fel'dman 1957b = N. I. Fel'dman: O granicach perevoda v inojazyčno-russkich slovarjach. In: Leksikografičeskij sbornik 2. 1957, 81—109.

Figge 1989 = Udo L. Figge: Internationale Fachkonferenz über zweisprachige Lexikographie: Deutsch und Portugiesisch. Ruhr-Universität Bochum, Oktober 1987. In: Lexicographica 5. 1989, 221—225.

Filipec 1973 = Josef Filipec: Ekvivalenty a synonyma v slovní zásobě. In: Jozef Ružička/Ivan Poldauf (ed.), Slovo a slovník: Zborník referátov z lexikologicko-lexikografickej konferencie v Smoleniciach, 4.—7. mája 1970. Bratislava 1973, 131—144.

Filipova-Bajrova 1959 = Marija Filipova-Bajrova: Izrabotane na dvuezični rečnici. In: Izvestija na Instituta za bălgarski ezik 6. 1959, 222—262.

François 1979 = Jacques François: *Ersticken* vs. *étouffer:* analyse contrastive et traitement lexicographique des polysémies. In: Documentation et recherche en linguistique allemande contemporaine — Vincennes 21. 1979, 88—100.

François 1980 = Jacques François: Kontrastive Analyse des Verblexikons und zweisprachige Lexikographie am Beispiel der deutschen Entsprechungen von frz. *quérir.* In: Edda Weigand/Gerhard Tschauder (Hrsg.), Perspektive: textintern. Akten des 14. Linguistischen Kolloquiums Bochum 1979. Band 1. Tübingen 1980 (Linguistische Arbeiten 88), 35—49.

François 1982 = Jacques François: Explizite bilinguale Lexikoneinträge als Darstellungsmethode vergleichender Wortschatzanalysen (erörtert am Beispiel der deutschen Entsprechungen von frz. *apprendre).* In: Klaus Detering/Jürgen Schmidt-Radefeldt/Wolfgang Sucharowski (Hrsg.), Sprache beschreiben und erklären. Akten des 16. Linguistischen Kolloquiums Kiel 1981. Band 1. Tübingen 1982 (Linguistische Arbeiten 118), 91—103.

Franke 1966 = Wolfgang Franke: Zur Neuauflage von Werner Rüdenberg, Chinesisch-Deutsches Wörterbuch. In: Oriens Extremus 13. 1966, 243—256.

Fuchs 1988 = Volker Fuchs: Grammatische Angaben im zweisprachigen Wörterbuch. In: Wissenschaftliche Zeitschrift der Ernst-Moritz-Arndt-Universität Greifswald. Gesellschaftswissenschaftliche Reihe 37/2. 1988, 26—29.

Gak 1964 = V. G. Gak: O raznych tipach dvujazyčnych slovarej. In: Tetradi perevodčika. Pod redakciej L.S. Barchudarova. Moskva 1964 (Učenye zapiski 2), 71—78.

Gak 1970 = V. G. Gak: La langue et le discours dans un dictionnaire bilingue. In: Langages 19. 1970, 103—115.

Gallina 1959 = Annamaria Gallina: Contributi alla storia della lessicografia italo-spagnola dei secoli XVI e XVII. Firenze 1959 (Biblioteca dell' »Archivum Romanicum«. Serie I: Storia — Letteratura — Paleografia. Vol. 58).

Gatzlaff 1975 = M. Gatzlaff: Das erste Wörterbuch 'Deutsch-Hindi', an der Karl-Marx-Universität Leipzig entwickelt. In: Wissenschaftliche Zeitschrift der Universität Leipzig 24. 1975, 181—185.

Geeraerts 1987 = Dirk Geeraerts: Types of Semantic Information in Dictionaries. In: Ilson 1987, 1—10.

Gerbert 1980 = Manfred Gerbert: Kollokationen im fremdsprachlichen Wörterbuch. In: Fremdsprachen 24. 1980, 133—135.

Glanze 1978 = W. D. Glanze (ed.): Methodological Problems in Monolingual and Bilingual Lexicography. New York 1978 (Studies in Lexicography as a Science and an Art 2, 1).

Göller 1983 = Alfred Göller: Lücken im französisch-deutschen Wörterbuch. Dargestellt an Langenscheidts Großwörterbuch Französisch-Deutsch. In: Französisch heute 14. 1983, 93—99.

Goetz/Herbst 1984 = Dieter Goetz/Thomas Herbst (Hrsg.): Theoretische und praktische Probleme der Lexikographie. 1. Augsburger Kolloquium. München 1984.

Gold 1973 = David L. Gold: Raising the Standards of Portuguese-English Bilingual Lexicography — A Plea. In: Babel 19. 1973, 25—30.

Gold 1978a = David L. Gold: New Perspectives in Spanish Bilingual Lexicography. In: Babel 24. 1978, 57—64.

Gold 1978b = David L. Gold: Problems in Interlingual Lexicography. In: Babel 24. 1978, 161—168.

Gossing 1968 = G. Gossing: Zum Problem der Übersetzungswörterbücher. In: Albrecht Neubert (Hrsg.), Grundfragen der Übersetzungswissenschaft (Beiheft 2 zur Zeitschrift „Fremdsprachen"). Leipzig 1968, 133 ff.

Gréciano 1989 = Gertrud Gréciano (éd.): Europhras 88. Phraséologie contrastive. Actes du Colloque International Klingenthal-Strasbourg 12—16 mai 1988. Strasbourg 1989 (Collection Recherches Germaniques 2).

Greidanus 1985 = Tine Greidanus: Tweetalig woordenboek en taalonderwijs op tertiair niveau. In: Toegepaste Taalwetenschap in Artikelen 21. 1985, 72—83.

Grindsted 1988a = Annette Grindsted: Geographical Varieties (and Regionalisms) in Bilingual Lexicography. In: Hyldgaard-Jensen/Zettersten 1988b, 181—192.

Grindsted 1988b = Annette Grindsted: Principper for præsentation af aekvivalenter i oversættelsordbøger. Odense 1988 (Odense University Studies in Linguistics Vol. 8).

Guckler 1975 = Gudrun Guckler: Zweisprachiges Wörterbuch für angewandte operationelle Analyse semantischer Entsprechungen mittels EDV. Tübingen 1975 (Tübinger Beiträge zur Linguistik 53).

Günther 1986 = Erika Günther (Hrsg.): Beiträge zur Lexikographie slawischer Sprachen. Berlin 1986 (Linguistische Studien. Reihe A: Arbeitsberichte 147).

Gutschmidt 1986 = Karl Gutschmidt: Lexikalische Äquivalenz grammatikalischer Bedeutungen im bulgarisch-deutschen Wörterbuch. In: Günther 1986, 44—50.

Haas 1962 = Mary R. Haas: What Belongs in a Bilingual Dictionary? In: Householder/Saporta 1962, 45—50.

Haensch/Wolf/Ettinger/Werner 1982 = Günther Haensch/Lothar Wolf/Stefan Ettinger/Reinhold Werner: La lexicografía. De la lingüística teórica a la lexicografía práctica. Madrid 1982 (Biblioteca Románica Hispánica III. Manuales 56).

Hardaway 1950 = R. Travis Hardaway: The Making of German-English, English-German Dictionaries of the Spoken Word. In: The German Quarterly 23. 1950, 84—92.

Harrell 1962 = Richard S. Harrell: Some Notes on Bilingual Lexicography. In: Householder/Saporta 1962, 51—61.

Hartmann 1975 = Reinhard R. K. Hartmann: Semantics Applied to English-German Lexical Structures. In: Folia Linguistica 7. 1975, 357—369.

Hartmann 1979 = Reinhard R. K. Hartmann (ed.): Dictionaries and their Users. Papers from the 1978 B. A. A. L. Seminar on Lexicography. Exeter 1979 (Exeter Linguistic Studies 4).

Hartmann 1980 = Reinhard R. K. Hartmann: Contrastive Textology. Comparative Discourse Analysis in Applied Linguistics [Kapitel 8: Bilingual Lexicography]. Heidelberg 1980, 82—90.

Hartmann 1982 = Reinhard R. K. Hartmann: Das zweisprachige Wörterbuch im Fremdsprachenerwerb. In: Wiegand 1982, 73—86.

Hartmann 1983a = Reinhard R. K. Hartmann (ed.): Lexicography: Principles and Practice. London. New York 1983.

Hartmann 1983b = Reinhard R. K. Hartmann: The bilingual learner's dictionary and its uses. In: Multilingua 2. 1983, 195—201.

Hartmann 1984 = Reinhard R. K. Hartmann (ed.): LEXeter '83 Proceedings. Papers from the International Conference on Lexicography at Exeter, 9—12 September, 1983. Tübingen 1984 (Lexicographica Series Maior 1).

Hartmann 1985 = Reinhard R. K. Hartmann: Contrastive Text Analysis and the Bilingual Dictionary. In: Hyldgaard-Jensen/Zettersten 1985, 121—132.

Hartmann 1987 = Reinhard R. K. Hartmann: Wozu Wörterbücher? Die Benutzungsforschung in der zweisprachigen Lexikographie. In: Lebende Sprachen 32. 1987, 154—156.

Hartmann 1988 = Reinhard R. K. Hartmann: Equivalence in Bilingual Lexicography. From Correspondence Relation to Communicative Strategy. In: Papers and Studies in Contrastive Linguistics 22. 1988, 21—28.

Hartmann 1989 = Reinhard R. K. Hartmann: Lexicography, Translation and the So-called Language Barrier. In: Snell-Hornby/Pöhl 1989, 9—20.

Hausmann 1977 = Franz Josef Hausmann: Einführung in die Benutzung der neufranzösischen Wörterbücher. Tübingen 1977 (Romanistische Arbeitshefte 19).

Hausmann 1985 = Franz Josef Hausmann: Lexikographie. In: Christoph Schwarze/Dieter Wunderlich (Hrsg.), Handbuch der Lexikologie. Königstein/Ts. 1985, 367—411.

Hausmann 1988a = Franz Josef Hausmann: Grundprobleme des zweisprachigen Wörterbuchs. In: Hyldgaard-Jensen/Zettersten 1988a, 137—154.

Hausmann 1988b = Franz Josef Hausmann: Les dictionnaires bilingues (et multilingues) en Europe au XVIIIe siècle. Acquis et suggestions de recherche. In: La lexicographie française du XVIIIe au XXe siècle. Colloque International de Lexicographie tenu à l'Institut de Langues et Littératures Romanes, Université de Düsseldorf, du 23 au 26 septembre 1986. Actes publiés par Barbara von Gemmingen et Manfred Höfler. Paris 1988 (Actes et Colloques 27), 11—32 (= in: Travaux de Linguistique et de Littérature 26/1 = Travaux de Linguistique et de Philologie 1).

Hausmann 1989a = Franz Josef Hausmann: Points noirs dans la lexicographie bilingue. In: Dieter Kremer (Hrsg.), Actes du XVIIIe Congrès International de Linguistique et de Philologie Romanes. Université de Trèves (Trier) 1986. Tome IV. Section VI: Lexicologie et lexicographie. Tübingen 1989, 39—40.

Hausmann 1989b = Franz Josef Hausmann: „im Tunnel ist es immer dunkel". Fremdsprachenunterricht und Wörterbuch. In: Fremdsprachenunterricht zwischen Sprachenpolitik und Praxis. Festschrift für Herbert Christ zum 60. Geburtstag. Hrsg. v. Eberhard Kleinschmidt. Tübingen 1989, 152—160.

Hausmann/Cop 1985 = Franz Josef Hausmann/ Margaret Cop: Short History of English-German Lexicography. In: Hyldgaard-Jensen/Zettersten 1985, 183—197.

Hausmann/Honig 1982 = Franz Josef Hausmann/Winfried Honig: A propos alpha 8. Steht das Wörterbuch am Scheideweg zwischen Buch und Computer? In: Linguistik und Didaktik 49/50. 1982, 108—112.

Havas 1957 = L. Havas: Words with Emotional Connotations in Bilingual Dictionaries. In: Acta Linguistica Academiae Scientiarum Hungaricae 6. Budapest 1957, 449—468.

Hawkes 1976 = Harry Hawkes: Some Criteria for Evaluating a Dictionary. In: Lenguaje y Ciencias 16. 1976, 195—202.

Heid 1988 = Ulrich Heid: Zweisprachige Wörterbücher für maschinelle Übersetzung. In: Hyldgaard-Jensen/Zettersten 1988b, 193—217.

Heid 1990 = Ulrich Heid: Bilingual Lexicography and Transfer Dictionaries for Machine Translation — Treating Structural Differences Between French and German. In: BudaLEX 1990, 107—119.

Heltai 1988 = Pál Heltai: Contrastive Analysis of Terminological Systems and Bilingual Technical Dictionaries. In: International Journal of Lexicography 1. 1988, 32—40.

Henke/Pätzold 1985 = Käthe Henke/Kurt Michael Pätzold: Englische Wörterbücher und Nachschlagewerke. In: Bielefelder Beiträge zur Sprachlehrforschung 14. 1985, 98—180.

Herbst 1985 = Thomas Herbst: Das zweisprachige Wörterbuch als Schreibwörterbuch: Informationen zur Syntax in zweisprachigen Wörterbüchern Englisch-Deutsch/Deutsch-Englisch. In: Bergenholtz/Mugdan 1985, 308—331.

Herbst/Stein 1987 = Thomas Herbst/Gabriele Stein: Dictionary Using Skills: A Plea for a New

Orientation in Language Teaching. In: Cowie 1987, 115—127.

Hermes 1987 = Liesel Hermes: Einführung in den Umgang mit einem zweisprachigen Wörterbuch in einer 6. Hauptschulklasse. In: Englisch 22. 1987, 68—71.

Herzog 1912 = E. Herzog: Französische Lexikographie. In: Karl Vollmöller (Hrsg.), Kritischer Jahresbericht über die Fortschritte der romanischen Philologie 1909/1910. 1912. I, 184—189.

Hessky 1980 = Regina Hessky: Überlegungen zum Idiom als Problem der zweisprachigen Lexikographie. In: Acta Linguistica Academiae Scientiarum Hungaricae 30. 1980, 163—171.

Hiddemann 1980 = Herbert Hiddemann: Des Lehrers und Schülers „ständiger Begleiter" — das Wörterbuch: ein Wegweiser für Englisch. In: Praxis des neusprachlichen Unterrichts 27. 1980, 243—249.

Hietsch 1958 = Otto Hietsch: Meaning Discrimination in Modern Lexicography. In: Modern Language Journal 42. 1958, 232—234.

Hietsch 1980 = Otto Hietsch: The Mirthless World of the Bilingual Dictionary: A Critical Look at Two German-English Examples, and a Glossary. In: Linguistica (Ljubljana) 20. 1980, 183—218.

Hobar 1982 = Donald Hobar (ed.): Papers of the Dictionary Society of North America 1977. Indiana 1982.

Hochmuth 1975 = Horst Hochmuth: Ermittlung von Äquivalenzkriterien durch semantischen Valenzvergleich (am Beispiel des militärischen Terminus **befördern** und seiner russischen Entsprechungen). In: Linguistische Arbeitsberichte 11. 1975, 106—112.

Hohulin 1986 = E. Lou Hohulin: The Absence of Lexical Equivalence and Cases of its Asymmetry. In: Lexicographica 2. 1986, 43—52.

Holm 1983 = Gösta Holm: Some Innovations in a New Swedish-Icelandic Dictionary. In: Hyldgaard-Jensen/Zettersten 1983, 87—91.

Holovaščuk 1970a = S. I. Holovaščuk: Do specyfiky perekladnoï leksykohrafiï blyz'koporidnemych sliv. In: Movoznavstvo 4/1. 1970, 3—10.

Holovaščuk 1970b = S. I. Holovaščuk: Rozmežuvannja značen' sliv u dvomovnomu slovnyku. In: Movoznavstvo 4/4. 1970, 15—24.

Householder/Saporta 1962 = Fred Householder/Sol Saporta (eds.): Problems in Lexicography. Report of the Conference Held at Indiana University, November 11—12, 1960. Bloomington 1962 (Part IV International Journal of American Linguistics Volume 28 Number 2. Publication Twenty-one of the Indiana University Research Center in Anthropology, Folklore, and Linguistics).

Householder/Saporta 1975 = Fred W. Householder/Sol Saporta (eds.): Problems in Lexicography. Report of the Conference on Lexicography Held at Indiana University November 11—12, 1960. 3. Aufl. Bloomington 1975 (Indiana University Publications. General Publications. Volume 21).

Hyldgaard-Jensen 1983 = Karl Hyldgaard-Jensen: Zum Einsatz des Computers in einigen dänischen Wörterbüchern. In: Hyldgaard-Jensen/Zettersten 1983, 207—209.

Hyldgaard-Jensen/Larsen 1988 = Karl Hyldgaard-Jensen/H. Verner Larsen: Die zweisprachige Lexikographie Deutsch-Dänisch, Dänisch-Deutsch. Stand, Probleme, Aufgaben. In: Lexicographica 4. 1988, 165—173.

Hyldgaard-Jensen/Zettersten 1983 = Karl Hyldgaard-Jensen/Arne Zettersten (eds.): Symposium zur Lexikographie. Proceedings of the Symposium on Lexicography, September 1—2, 1982 at the University of Copenhagen. Hildesheim. Zürich. New York 1983 (Germanistische Linguistik 5—6/82).

Hyldgaard-Jensen/Zettersten 1985 = Karl Hyldgaard-Jensen/Arne Zettersten (eds.): Symposium on Lexicography II. Proceedings of the Second International Symposium on Lexicography May 16—17, 1984 at the University of Copenhagen. Tübingen 1985 (Lexicographica Series Maior 5).

Hyldgaard-Jensen/Zettersten 1988a = Karl Hyldgaard-Jensen/Arne Zettersten (eds.): Symposium on Lexicography III. Proceedings of the Third International Symposium on Lexicography May 14—16, 1986 at the University of Copenhagen. Tübingen 1988 (Lexicographica Series Maior 19).

Hyldgaard-Jensen/Zettersten 1988b = Karl Hyldgaard-Jensen/Arne Zettersten (eds.): Symposium on Lexicography IV. Proceedings of the Fourth International Symposium on Lexicography April 20—22, 1988 at the University of Copenhagen. Tübingen 1988 (Lexicographica Series Maior 26).

Iannucci 1957 = James E. Iannucci: Meaning Discrimination in Bilingual Dictionaries: A New Lexicographical Technique. In: Modern Language Journal 41. 1957, 272—281.

Iannucci 1959 = James E. Iannucci: Explanatory Matter in Bilingual Dictionaries. In: Babel 5. 1959, 195—199.

Iannucci 1962 = James E. Iannucci: Meaning Discrimination in Bilingual Dictionaries. In: Householder/Saporta 1962, 201—216.

Iannucci 1974 = James E. Iannucci: Sense discrimination in English and Spanish bilingual dictionaries. In: Babel 20. 1974, 142—148.

Iannucci 1976 = James E. Iannucci: Subcategories in bilingual dictionaries. In: J. D. [James David] Anderson/R. [Roger] J. Steiner (eds.), Lexicography as a Science and as an Art. Louisville, Ky 1976.

Iannucci 1985 = James E. Iannucci: Sense Discrimination and Translation Complements in Bilingual Dictionaries. In: Dictionaries 7. 1985, 57—65.

Iliescu 1957 = Maria Iliescu: Grundfragen der zweisprachigen Wörterbücher. In: Académie 1957, 207—221.

Ilson 1987 = Robert Ilson (ed.): A Spectrum of Lexicography. Papers from AILA Brussels 1984. Amsterdam. Philadelphia 1987.

Institut 1977 = Institut russkogo jazyka im. A. S. Puškina, Sektor učebnoj leksikografii: Problemy učebnoj leksikografii. Pod redakciej P. N. Denisova i V. V. Morkovkina. Moskva 1977.

Isbăşescu 1988 = Mihai Isbăşescu: Der Beitrag des Deutschunterrichts und der rumänisch-deutschen Lexikographie zur Entwicklung der rumänisch-deutschen Kulturbeziehungen im 19. Jahrhundert. In: Kurier der Bochumer Gesellschaft für rumänische Sprache und Literatur 14. 1988, 122—141.

Ivir 1988 = Vladimir Ivir: Collocations in Dictionaries: Monolingual and Bilingual. In: T. L. Burton/Jill Burton (eds.), Lexicographical and Linguistic Studies. Essays in Honour of G. W. Turner. Cambridge 1988, 43—50.

Jackson 1975 = Howard Jackson: What's in a Bilingual Dictionary? In: Modern Languages 56. 1975, 85—89.

Jackson 1979 = Howard Jackson: German-English Dictionaries and How to Use Them. Exeter 1979 (Exeter Tapes, G771).

Jones 1969 = Trevor Jones: Some Problems of Bilingual Lexicography. In: Siegbert S. Prawer/R. Hinton Thomas/Leonard Forster (eds.), Essays in German Language, Culture and Society. London 1969, 24—35.

Jørgensen 1982 = Mogens Wied Jørgensen: Die grammatischen Angaben zu den Lemmata in zweisprachigen Wörterbüchern, besonders im Hinblick auf das DTO (Dänisch-Deutsches Wörterbuch). In: Kopenhagener Beiträge zur Germanistischen Linguistik 20. 1982, 67—85.

Jørgensen 1983 = Mogens Wied Jørgensen: Die grammatischen Informationen in bezug auf die dänischen Lemmata im DTO (Dänisch-deutsches Wörterbuch). In: Hyldgaard-Jensen/Zettersten 1983, 199—206.

Kade 1973 = Otto Kade: Interferenzprobleme bei der Arbeit mit dem zweisprachigen Wörterbuch. In: Linguistische Arbeitsberichte 8. 1973, 210—222.

Karl 1982 = Ilse Karl: Linguistische Probleme der zweisprachigen Lexikographie. Eine Nachlese praktischer Wörterbucharbeit. Berlin 1982 (Linguistische Studien, Reihe A: 96).

Karl 1986 = Ilse Karl: Einige Probleme zur semantiktheoretischen Fundierung von Wörterbuchartikeln. In: Linguistische Studien, Reihe A: Arbeitsberichte 148. 1986, 107—118.

Kelemen 1957 = Béla Kelemen: Contributions à la méthode de rédaction des dictionnaires bilingues. In: Académie 1957, 235—248.

Keppler 1951 = Kurt Keppler: Some Inaccuracies in German-English Dictionaries. In: The German Quarterly 24. 1951, 137—150.

Keppler 1954 = Kurt Keppler: Misleading German Words of Foreign Origin. In: The German Quarterly 27. 1954, 31—40.

Keppler 1957 = Kurt Keppler: Problems of German-English Dictionary Making. In: Modern Language Journal 41. 1957, 26—29.

Kharma 1984 = Nayef N. Kharma: Contextualization and the bilingual learner's dictionary. In: Hartmann 1984, 199—206.

Kibbee 1985 = Douglas A. Kibbee: Progress in Bilingual Lexicography During the Renaissance. In: Dictionaries 7. 1985, 21—31.

Kim 1981 = S. S.-D. Kim: Voprosy, kompleksnoj razrabotki tipovoj russkoj časti dlja russko-nacional'nych slovarej (Zametki praktika). In: Voprosy jazykoznanija 1981/5. 1981, 39—53.

Kim 1984 = S. S. Kim: Grammatičeskij apparat v akademičeskich russko-nacional'nych slovarjach. In: Akademija 1984, 205—211.

Klaudi 1975 = K. Klaudi: Sostavlenie special'nogo slovarja dlja perevodčikov. In: Moskovskij gosudarstvennyj pedagogičeskij institut inostrannych jazykov imeni Morisa Toreza 1975, Časť I, 164—167.

Klein 1952 = Hans W. [Wilhelm] Klein: Über die Qualität unserer führenden deutsch-französischen Wörterbücher. In: Die Neueren Sprachen N.F. 1. 1952, 215—218.

Klein 1972 = Hans-Wilhelm Klein: Scheinentsprechungen bei französischen und deutschen Idiomatismen. Ein Beitrag zur Lexikographie. In: Der fremdsprachliche Unterricht 6/3 (Heft 23). 1972, 44—51.

König 1981 = Ekkehard König: Kontrastive Analyse und zweisprachige Wörterbücher: Die Gradpartikel *even* und ihre Entsprechungen im Deutschen. In: Harald Weydt (Hrsg.), Partikeln und Deutschunterricht. Abtönungspartikeln für Lerner des Deutschen. Heidelberg 1981, 277—304.

König/Stark 1987 = Ekkehard König/Detlef Stark: Function Words in a Bilingual German-English Dictionary: A New Approach. In: Lexicographica 3. 1987, 158—177.

Kopeckij 1962 = L. Kopeckij: Iz zametok teorii dvujazyčnoj leksikografii. In: Slavica pragensia 4. 1962, 515—524.

Korlètjanu 1964 = M. G. Korlètjanu: Voprosy frazeologii v dvujazyčnych i tolkovych slovarjach. In: Materialy V Vsesojuznogo leksikografičeskogo soveščanija. Frunze 1964, 8—27.

Koval'ov 1965 = V. P. Koval'ov: Obsjah rejestru zahal'nomovnoho perekladnoho slovnyka. In: Doslihžennja z leksykolohiï ta leksykohrafiï. Mižvidomčyj zbornyk. Redakcijna kolehija: S. I. Holovaščuk et al., L. S. Palamarčuk (holovnyj redaktor), N. I. Švydka (vidpovidal'nyj sekretar'). Kyïv 1965, 41—51.

Kratochvíl/Novotná/Stovičková/Zgusta 1962 = P. Kratochvíl/Z. Novotná/D. Stovičková/L. Zgusta: Some Problems of a Czech-Chinese Dictionary. In: Archiv orientální 30. 1962, 258—313.

Kretov/Laomonen/Nikkila 1988 = A. Kretov/A. Laomonen/E. Nikkila: O novom tipe dvujazyčnogo slovarja. In: Russkij Jazyk za Rubežom Jg. 1988/5. 1988, 49—56.

Kromann 1977 = Hans-Peder Kromann: Grammatischer Problemkatalog bei der Erarbeitung des Dansk-Tysk Ordbog (DTO). Ein Arbeitsbericht. In: Kopenhagener Beiträge zur germ. Ling. 12. 1977, 162—169.

Kromann 1983 = Hans-Peder Kromann: Paradigmatische und syntagmatische Relationen im zweisprachigen Wörterbuch. In: Schildt/Viehweger 1983, 330—348.

Kromann 1985 = Hans-Peder Kromann: Zur Selektion und Darbietung syntaktischer Informationen in einsprachigen Wörterbüchern des Deutschen aus der Sicht ausländischer Benutzer. In: Bergenholtz/Mugdan 1985, 346—357.

Kromann 1986 = Hans-Peder Kromann: Die zweisprachige Lexikographie: ein Stiefkind der Germanisten. In: A. Schöne (Hrsg.), Akten des VII. Kongresses der Internationalen Vereinigung für germanische Sprach- und Literaturwissenschaft. Band 3: Textlinguistik contra Stilistik? Wortschatz und Wörterbuch. Hrsg. v. W. E. Weiss/H. E. Wiegand/M. Reis. Tübingen 1986, 177—181.

Kromann 1987a = Hans-Peder Kromann: Zur Syntax im Übersetzungswörterbuch. In: Mogens Dyhr/Jørgen Olsen (Hrsg.), Festschrift für Karl Hyldgaard-Jensen. Zum 70. Geburtstag am 3. Februar 1987. Kopenhagen 1987 (Kopenhagener Beiträge zur Germanistischen Linguistik. Sonderband 3), 143—150.

Kromann 1987b = Hans-Peder Kromann: Zur Typologie und Darbietung von Phraseologismen in Übersetzungswörterbüchern. In: Jarmo Korhonen (Hrsg.), Beiträge zur allgemeinen und germanistischen Phraseologieforschung. Internationales Symposium in Oulu 13.—15. Juni 1986. Oulu 1987 (Universität Oulu, Finnland. Veröffentlichungen des Germanistischen Instituts 7), 183—192.

Kromann 1989a = Hans-Peder Kromann: Neue Orientierung der zweisprachigen Wörterbücher. Zur funktionellen zweisprachigen Lexikographie. In: Snell-Hornby/Pöhl 1989, 55—65.

Kromann 1989b = Hans-Peder Kromann: Zur funktionalen Beschreibung von Kollokationen und Phraseologismen in Übersetzungswörterbüchern. In: Gréciano 1989, 265—271.

Kromann/Riiber/Rosbach 1979 = Hans-Peder Kromann/Theis Riiber/Poul Rosbach: Betydningsbeskrivelse og ordbogstyper inden for tosprogs-leksikografien med særligt henblik på en dansk-tysk ordbog. In: ARK 1. 1979.

Kromann/Riiber/Rosbach 1984a = Hans-Peder Kromann/Theis Riiber/Poul Rosbach: 'Active' and 'passive' bilingual dictionaries: the Ščerba concept reconsidered. In: Hartmann 1984, 207—215.

Kromann/Riiber/Rosbach 1984b = Hans-Peder Kromann/Theis Riiber/Poul Rosbach: Überlegungen zu Grundfragen der zweisprachigen Lexikographie. In: Herbert Ernst Wiegand (Hrsg.), Studien zur neuhochdeutschen Lexikographie V. Hildesheim. Wien. Zürich 1984 (Germanistische Linguistik 3—6/84), 159—238.

Kromann/Riiber/Rosbach 1986 = Hans-Peder Kromann/Theis Riiber/Poul Rosbach: Om principper for oversættelses leksikografi. In: Festskrift til Jens Rasmussen i anledning af hans 70 års fødselsdag. Redigeret af Niels Davidsen-Nielsen og Finn Sørensen. Copenhagen 1986 (CEBAL Publikation 8), 264—287.

Krytenko 1963 = A. P. Krytenko: Absoljutna i vidnosna omonimija ta ïï podača v ukraïns'ko-rosijskomu slovnyku. In: Leksykohrafičnyj bjuleten' 9. 1963, 13—30.

Kunin 1964 = O perevode anglijskich frazeologizmov v anglo-russkom frazeologičeskom slovare. In: Tetradi perevodčika. Pod redakciej L. S. Barchudarova. Moskva 1964 (Učenye zapiski No. 2), 3—20.

Landheer 1983 = Ronald Landheer: Ambiguïté et dictionnaire bilingue. In: Lexique 2. 1983, 147—158.

Larsen 1983 = H. Verner Larsen: Überlegungen zur Erstellung eines dänisch-deutschen Wörterbuchs. In: Hyldgaard-Jensen/Zettersten 1983, 153—162.

Leëmets 1977 = Ch. D. Leëmets: Ob ėstonsko-russkom škol'nom slovare. In: Red'kin 1977, 192—194.

Leëmets 1984 = Ch. D. Leëmets: Otraženie semantiki slova v dvujazyčnom slovare (Na materiale «Russko-ėstonskogo slovarja». AN ESSR). In: Akademija 1984, 200—205.

Leisi 1962 = Ernst Leisi: Deutsche und englische Wortinhalte. Zonen der Deckung, Zonen der Verschiedenheit. In: Wirkendes Wort 12. 1962.

Lejeune 1971 = Josef Lejeune: Zum deutsch-französischen Großwörterbuch „SACHS-VILLATTE". In: Revue des langues vivantes 37. 1971, 264—281 u. 414—432.

Leningradskij universitet 1981 = Leningradskij ordena Lenina i ordena trudovogo krasnogo znameni gosudarstvenyj universitet imeni A. A. Ždanova, Mežkafedral'nyj slovarnyj kabinet imeni Prof. B. A. Larina: Očerki leksikografii pisatelja (dvujazyčnye slovari). Leningrad 1981.

Lépinette 1989 = B. Lépinette: Vers un dictionnaire explicatif et combinatoire bilingue: bases théoriques et élaboration de quelques articles. In: Cahiers de lexicologie 54. 1989, 105—162.

Levčenko 1951 = S. P. Levčenko: Terminolohična leksyka v rosijsko-ukraïnskych slovnykach. In: Leksykohrafičnyj bjuleten' 1. 1951, 45—57.

Levitzky 1957 = Leon D. Levitzky: Bilingual Dictionaries. Suggestions. In: Académie 1957, 249—256.

Liebold 1975 = Harald Liebold: Probleme des Verhältnisses von Lexikologie und Lexikographie. In: Beiträge zur Romanischen Philologie 14. 1975, 299—304.

Lindquist 1983 = Hans Lindquist: Dictionaries and the Translator. In: Hyldgaard-Jensen/Zettersten 1983, 93—98.

Lindstrom 1980 = Naomi Lindstrom: Making the Bilingual Dictionary Safer for Students. In: Hispania 63. 1980, 718—722.

Lippert 1983—86 = Wolfgang Lippert: [Rezension] Das Große Chinesisch-Russische Wörterbuch in vier Bänden, hrsg. v. I. M. Osanin. Moskva 1983/1984. In: Oriens Extremus 30. 1983—86, 263—277.

Lissance 1949 = Arnold Lissance: The translator's dictionary. A Twentieth Century German-English Dictionary. In: The German Quarterly 22. 1949, 134—144.

Lloshi 1990 = Xhevanat Lloshi: Compiling and Editing Bilingual Dictionaries in Albania. In: BudaLEX 1990, 379—387.

Lötzsch 1978 = Ronald Lötzsch: Ein aktives deutsch-russisches Wörterbuch. Interview mit R. Lötzsch. In: Spektrum — Monatszeitschrift für den Wissenschaftler 1978/1, 28—30.

Lötzsch 1979a = Ronald Lötzsch: Einige Fragen der Entwicklung der zweisprachigen russistischen Lexikographie an der AdW der DDR. In: Zeitschrift für Slawistik 24. 1979, 402—408.

Lötzsch 1979b = Ronald Lötzsch: Einige Probleme der zweisprachigen Lexikographie (Russisch-Deutsch, Deutsch-Russisch). In: Sprachpflege 28. 1979, 243—245.

Lötzsch 1985 = Ronald Lötzsch: Zur Konzeption und zu den Probearbeiten des „Deutsch-Obersorbischen Wörterbuchs". In: Letopis 32/2. 1985, 121—126.

Lötzsch/Heinze/Hinze 1979 = R. Ljëč/S. Chaince/F. Chince [Ronald Lötzsch/S. Heinze/F. Hinze]: Principy sostavlenija aktivnogo dvujazyčnogo slovarja i ich realizacija v trechtomnon nemecko-russkom slovare. In: Četvertyj meždunarodnyj kongress prepodavatelej russkogo jazyka i literatury. Berlin 1979. Doklady i soobščenija delegacii Germanskoj Demokratičeskoj Respubliki. Berlin 1979, 75—79.

Lovatt 1984 = Edwin A. Lovatt: Illustrative Examples in a Bilingual Colloquial Dictionary. In: Hartmann 1984, 216—220.

Lowe 1970 = Pardee Lowe Jr.: Postulates for Making Bilingual Dictionaries. In: Hreinn Benediktsson (ed.), The Nordic Languages and Modern Linguistics. Reykjavík 1970, 404—416.

Magay 1979 = T. [Tamás] Magay: Problems of indicating pronunciation in bilingual dictionaries with English as the source language. In: Hartmann 1979, 98—103.

Magay 1984 = Tamás Magay: Technical or general: problems of vocabulary selection in a medium-size bilingual dictionary. In: Hartmann 1984, 221—225.

Magay 1988 = Tamás Magay: On some problems of the bilingual learner's dictionary. In: Snell-Hornby 1988, 171—180.

Magometov 1976 = A. A. Magometov: Terminologičeskaja leksika v kubačinsko-russkom slovare. In: Akademija 1976, 258—261.

Mai/Mai 1969 = Elisabeth Mai/Joachim Mai: Die deutsch-russischen und russisch-deutschen Fachwörterbücher aus der Zeit von 1850—1917 in ihrer ökonomisch-politischen Bedingtheit. In: W. Krauss/Z. Stieber/J. Belik/V. J. Borkovskij (Hrsg.): Slawisch-deutsche Wechselbeziehungen in Sprache, Literatur und Kultur. Berlin 1969 (Deutsche Akademie der Wissenschaften zu Berlin. Veröffentlichungen des Instituts für Slawistik 44), 110—119.

Majtinskaja 1957 = K. E. Majtinskaja: Otraženie različij grammatičeskogo stroja v dvujazyčnych slovarjach (na materiale finno-ugorskich jazykov s privlečeniem tjurkskich). In: Leksikografičeskij sbornik 1. 1957, 160—171.

Malige-Klappenbach/Bielfeldt 1966 = H. [Helene] Malige-Klappenbach/H.H. [Hans Holm] Bielfeldt: [Rezension] Deutsch-Tschechisches Wörterbuch; unter Leitung und Redaktion von Prof. Dr. H. Siebenschein; 2 Bde., Praha. In: Zeitschrift für Slawistik 11. 1966, 98—103.

Malíková 1953 = O. Malíková: Problem ekvivalentu v dvojjazyčnom slovníku. In: Lexikografický sborník. Bratislava 1953, 119—125.

Malina 1979 = Anneliese Malina: Bemerkungen zur Problematik der Einbeziehung des gesellschaftlichen Wortschatzes in ein neugriechisch-deutsches Wörterbuch. In: Zur Herausbildung des modernen gesellschaftlichen Wortschatzes in Südosteuropa. Beiträge zur Balkanlinguistik IV. Berlin 1979 (Linguistische Studien. Reihe A: Arbeitsberichte 58), 179—186.

Malone 1962 = Kemp Malone: Structural Linguistics and Bilingual Dictionaries. In: Householder/Saporta 1962, 111—118.

Man 1967 = O. Man: Některé problémy odborného dvojjazyčného (rusko-českého) slovníku. In: Československá rusistika Jg. 1967/3, 162—167.

Manley 1983 = James Manley: The Bilingual Dictionary: Problems of Normativity, Selection and Semantic Classification. In: Hyldgaard-Jensen/Zettersten 1983, 119—125.

Manley 1985 = James Manley: Processing of Excerpts for the Bilingual Dictionary. In: Hyldgaard-Jensen/Zettersten 1985, 245—254.

Manley/Jacobsen/Pedersen 1988 = James Manley/Jane Jacobsen/Viggo Hjørnager Pedersen: Telling Lies Efficiently: Terminology and the Microstructure in the Bilingual Dictionary. In: Hyldgaard-Jensen/Zettersten 1988a, 281—302.

Manthey 1985 = Fred Manthey: Mehr Aufmerksamkeit der systematischen Steigerung des Schwierigkeitsgrades in der Arbeit mit dem Wörterbuch. In: Fremdsprachenunterricht 29. 1985, 25—29.

Marello 1987 = Carla Marello: Examples in contemporary Italian bilingual dictionaries. In: Cowie 1987, 224—237.

Marello 1989 = Carla Marello: Dizionari bilingui con schede sui dizionari italiani per francese, inglese, spagnolo, tedesco. Bologna 1989 (Fenomeni Linguistici 6).

Marín 1987 = Rafael Marín: Los diccionarios bilingües Español/Alemán y Alemán/Español. Dos lenguas distintas y un mismo diccionario. Propósitos y resultados. In: Hispanorama 46. 1987, 160—166.

Marín 1989 = Rafael Marín: De la necesidad imperiosa del uso de diccionarios monolingües para la traducción inversa. In: Hispanorama 52. 1989, 166—168.

Martem'janov/Rozencvejg 1975 = Ju. S. Martem'janov/V. Ju. Rozenc'vejg: Slovar' i sintaksis v processe perevoda. In: Moskovskij gosudarstvennyj pedagogičeskij institut inostrannych jazykov imeni Morisa Toreza 1975, Část' I, 48—49.

Martin 1962 = Samuel E. Martin: Selection and Presentation of Ready Equivalents in a Translation Dictionary. In: Householder/Saporta 1962, 153—159.

Martin 1985 = Willy Martin: Reflections on Learner's Dictionaries. In: Hyldgaard-Jensen/Zettersten 1985, 169—181.

Martin/Al/Sterkenburg 1981 = W. [Willy] Martin/B. [Bernard] Al/P. [Piet] van Sterkenburg: Text-Processing and Lexicographical Information — a State of the Art. In: ALLC Journal 2. 1981, 61—68.

Martin/Al/Sterkenburg 1983 = W. Martin/B. Al/P. van Sterkenburg: On the processing of a text corpus. From textual data to lexicographical information. In: Hartmann 1983, 77—87.

Maslova-Lašanskaja 1961 = S. S. Maslova-Lasanskaja: Zametki o russko-švedskich slovarjach. In: Scandinavica 1. 1961, 84—107.

Mbogho 1985 = Kalumbo Mbogho: Observations on Bilingual Lexicography Involving Bantu and Indo-European Languages. In: Babel 31. 1985, 152—162.

McCawley 1989 = James D. McCawley: Making Life Easier for Users of Chinese-English Dictionaries. In: Journal of the Chinese Language Teachers Association 24. 1989, 105—109.

Megen 1983 = Jan van Megen: Valenzanalyse und kontrastive Lexikographie. Die Beschreibung deutscher Verben in einem niederländisch-deutschen Wörterbuch. In: Hans Estler/Guillaume von Gemert/Jan van Megen (Hrsg.), Ars et ingenium. Studien zum Übersetzen. Festgabe für Frans Stoks zum 70. Geburtstag. Amsterdam. Maarssen 1983, 27—43.

Messelaar 1983 = P. A. Messelaar: Le contexte et la structure du dictionnaire général bilingue; quelques réflexions d'ordre lexicographique. In: Langue, dialecte, littérature. Etudes romanes à la mémoire de Hugo Plomteux. Leuven 1983, 379—395.

Messelaar 1987 = P. A. Messelaar: Réflexions sur le contenu de l'article lexicographique et le passage d'une langue à l'autre. In: ITL 72. 1987, 53—82.

Messelaar 1988 = P. A. Messelaar: Tentative de systématisation en lexicographie bilingue malgré les limites de la sémantique. In: ITL 79—80. 1988, 113—133.

Metrich 1985 = René Metrich: Proposition pour le traitement des 'mots du discours' en lexicographie bilingue français-allemand: l'exemple de *d'accord, donc* et *enfin*. In: Nouveaux cahiers d'allemand 3. 1985, 33—52, 159—172 u. 237—247.

Metrich 1988 = René Metrich: *Tiens* und *tenez* im französisch-deutschen Wörterbuch. Ein Beitrag zur bilingualen lexikographischen Erfassung von „Gesprächswörtern". In: Zeitschrift für französische Sprache und Literatur 98. 1988, 23—40.

Meyer 1985 = Ingrid Meyer: Translation and the General Bilingual Dictionary. In: P. Newman (ed.), Proceedings of the American Translators Association Conference 1985, Medford, N.J. 1985, 181—186.

Meyer 1988 = Ingrid Meyer: The General Bilingual Dictionary as a Working Tool in *Thème*. In: Meta 33. 1988, 368—376.

Meyersteen 1960 = R. S. Meyersteen: Bilingual Dictionaries and Applied Linguistics. In: Modern Language Journal 44. 1960, 163—167.

Miller 1982 = Elisabeth Miller: Bilingual Dictionaries: Spanish-English, English-Spanish. In: Translation Review 9. 1982, 34—39.

Møller 1977 = Elisabeth Møller: Das DTO-Projekt. In: Kopenhagener Beitr. z. germ. Ling. 12. 1977, 150—161.

Møller 1978 = Elisabeth Møller: Korpusprobleme und Systematisierungsaspekte am Beispiel des dänisch-deutschen Wörterbuchprojekts. In: Zeitschrift für Germanistische Linguistik 6. 1978, 313—325.

Møller 1983 = Elisabeth Møller: Homonymie bzw. Polysemie. Kriterien für die Ansetzung des Lemmas im dänisch-deutschen Wörterbuch (DTO). In: Hyldgaard-Jensen/Zettersten 1983, 169—188.

Møller 1984 = Elisabeth Møller: Gedanken und Vorschläge zu einer operationalen Basis für die Übersetzung lexikalischer Signeme aus Sprachsystem 1 (AS) in Sprachsystem 2 (ZS). Am Beispiel des DTO-Projektes (Dänisch-Deutsches Wörterbuch). In: Kopenhagener Beiträge zur Germanistischen Linguistik 22. 1984, 69—91.

Møller 1985 = Elisabeth Møller: Die 'optimale' autonom-semasiologische Operation eines lexikalischen Signems der Zielsprache. In: Hyldgaard-Jensen/Zettersten 1985, 303—317.

Møller 1988 = Elisabeth Møller: Komposita — ihre Behandlung in ein- bzw. zweisprachigen Wörterbüchern. In: Hyldgaard-Jensen/Zettersten 1988a, 503—515.

Morkovkin 1977 = V. V. Morkovkin: Russko-inojazyčnyj slovar' sočetaemosti, ego lingvističeskie osnovy i struktura. In: Institut 1977, 84—110.

Moser 1976 = Hugo Moser (Hrsg.): Probleme der Lexikologie und Lexikographie. Jahrbuch 1975 des IdS. Düsseldorf 1976 (Sprache der Gegenwart 39).

Moskovskij gosudarstvennyj pedagogičeskij institut inostrannych jazykov imeni Morisa Toreza 1975 = Ministerstvo vysšego i srednego special'nogo obrazovanija SSSR, Moskovskij gosudarstvennyj pedagogičeskij institut inostrannych jazykov imeni Morisa Toreza: Teorija perevoda i naučnye osnovy podgotovki perevodčikov. Materialy vsesojuznoj konferencii. Moskva 1975.

Müller 1982 = Oskar Müller: Bedeutungs- und Kompatibilitätsmarkierung in einem deutsch-russischen Wörterbuch. In: Karl Gutschmidt/Ronald Lötzsch (Hrsg.), Beiträge zum synchronen Sprachvergleich (am Material der slawischen Sprachen, des Deutschen und des Ungarischen). Berlin 1982 (Linguistische Studien. Reihe A: Arbeitsberichte 94/I), 120—130.

Müller 1984 = Bärbel Müller: Zu einigen spezifischen Besonderheiten unterschiedlicher Wörterbuchtypen. In: Fremdsprachen 28. 1984, 236—239.

Müller 1986 = Bärbel Müller: Probleme der Darstellung von Funktionswörtern im zweisprachigen Wörterbuch. In: Günther 1986, 93—102.

Mylius 1973 = K. Mylius: Ein neues Handwörterbuch Sanskrit-Deutsch, an der Karl-Marx-Universität entwickelt. In: Wissenschaftliche Zeitschrift der Universität Leipzig 22. 1973, 91—97.

Nakao 1989 = Keisuke Nakao: English-Japanese Learners' Dictionaries. In: International Journal of Lexicography 2. 1989, 295—314.

Nakashima 1989 = Hisashi Nakashima: Klassifikation von Wörtern aufgrund von Übersetzungswörtern in einem japanisch-deutschen Wörterbuch. In: Quantitative Linguistics 39. 1989, 77—89.

Nelson 1979 = R. J. Nelson: Translation and Translating Dictionaries. In: Lebende Sprachen 24. 1979, 53—54.

Nelson 1981 = R. J. Nelson: The Problem of Meaning Across the Boundary Between Spanish and English: An Expanding Role for the Bilingual Dictionary. In: Dictionaries 2—3. 1981, 52—56.

Nelson 1987 = R. J. Nelson: El diccionario bilingüe y el roce de los idiomas. In: The Linguist 26/3. 1987, 118.

Nelson 1988 = R. J. Nelson: Alice's *Quel long nez* and the Wonderland of the Translating Dictionary. In: Dictionaries 10. 1988, 59—68.

Neubert 1986 = Albrecht Neubert: Dichtung und Wahrheit des zweisprachigen Wörterbuchs. Berlin 1986 (Sitzungsberichte der Sächsischen Akademie der Wissenschaften zu Leipzig, Phil.-hist. Klasse. Bd. 126. Heft 4).

Nguyen 1979 = Dinh-Hoa Nguyen: Bilingual Lexicography in Vietnam: The State of the Art. In: Papers of the Dictionary Society of North America Jg. 1979. 1979, 149—171.

Nguyen 1980 = Dinh-Hoa Nguyen: Bicultural Information in a Bilingual Dictionary. In: Zgusta 1980, 163—175.

Nguyen 1981 = Dinh-Hoa Nguyen: Teaching Culture Through Bilingual Dictionaries. In: Dictionaries 2—3. 1981, 57—68.

Nguyen 1986 = Dinh-Hoa Nguyen: How to Present Grammatical Information in a Learner's Dictionary of English. In: Lexicographica 2. 1986, 61—77.

Nikitevič 1977 = V. M. Nikitevič: Principy sostavlenija dvujazyčnych slovarej s vključeniem derivacionnych sočetanij. In: Red'kin 1977, 195—197.

Oehler 1984 = Jürgen Oehler: Zweisprachige englische Wörterbücher im Vergleichstest. In: Die Neueren Sprachen 83. 1984, 209—218.

Ol'šanskij 1975 a = I. [Igor] G. Ol'šanskij: Perevod i problemy dvujazyčnoj leksikografii. In: Moskovskij gosudarstvennyj pedagogičeskij institut inostrannych jazykov imeni Morisa Toreza 1975, Čast' II, 24—27.

Ol'šanskij 1975 b = I. [Igor] G. Ol'šanskij: Zu einigen Problemen der Erarbeitung eines russisch-deutschen Kombinationswörterbuches (Vorläufige Überlegungen). In: Linguistische Arbeitsberichte 11. 1975, 126—138.

Ol'šanskij 1977 = I. [Igor] G. Ol'šanskij: O russko-nemeckom slovare sočetaemosti slov. In: Institut 1977, 134—142.

Ol'šanskij 1978 = I. [Igor] G. Ol'šanskij: Landeskundliche Informationen und ihre lexikographische Erfassung. In: Deutsch als Fremdsprache 15. 1978, 277—279.

Országh 1968 = Ladislas Országh: Wanted: Better English Dictionaries. In: English Language Teaching 23. 1968, 216—222.

Orudžev 1963 = A. A. Orudžev: K voprosu ob otraženii v russko-tjurkskich slovarjach leksiko-grammatičeskich osobennosti russkogo jazyka (na materiale russko-azerbajdžanskich slovarej). In: Leksikografičeskij sbornik 6. 1963, 53—61.

Osselton 1979 = N. [Noel] E. Osselton: Some Problems of Obsolescence in Bilingual Dictionaries. In: Hartmann 1979, 120—126.

Paepcke 1982 = Fritz Paepcke: Brauchbarkeit und Grenzen eines zweisprachigen Wörterbuchs. Bemerkungen zu Langenscheidts Großwörterbuch Französisch-Deutsch (1979). In: Mitteilungsblatt für Übersetzer und Dolmetscher 1982, 6—9 (= In: Fritz Paepcke, Im Übersetzen leben. Hrsg. V. K. Berger/H.-M. Speier. Tübingen 1986 (TBL 281)).

Palamarčuk 1961 = L. S. Palamarčuk: Pro odnu poznačku v perekladnych slovnykach. In: Leksykohrafičnyj bjuleten' 8. 1961, 48—52.

Pálfy/Burján/Réti 1986 = Miklós Pálfy/Mónika Burján/Attila Réti: Quelques critères supplémentaires pour un dictionnaire scolaire français-hongrois. In: Acta Universitatis Szegedensis. Acta Romanica. Tomos XI: Studia Lexicographica Neolatina. Szeged 1986, 1—9.

Pan/Wiegand 1987 = Pan Zaiping/Herbert Ernst Wiegand: Konzeption für das Große Deutsch-Chinesische Wörterbuch (Zweiter Entwurf). In: Lexicographica 3. 1987, 228—241.

Papachristos 1990 = Evthymios Chr. Papachristos: Die deutsch-neugriechische Lexikographie von 1796 bis 1909. Tübingen 1990 (Lexicographica Series Maior 32).

Pasch 1987 = Renate Pasch: Ja, Lexikographie kann angewandte Sprachwissenschaft sein und muß es auch. In: Zeitschrift für Germanistik 8. 1987, 577—582.

Patyal 1980 = Hukam Chand Patyal: The Problem of Homonymy in a Bilingual Dictionary. In: Indian Linguistics 41. 1980, 67—72.

Peck 1989 = Charles Peck: Some Notes on Making Bilingual Dictionaries. In: Notes on Linguistics 46. 1989, 49—61.

Pedersen 1983 = Viggo Hjørnager Pedersen: The Danish-English Dictionary Project at Copenhagen. In: Hyldgaard-Jensen/Zettersten 1983, 113—117.

Pedersen 1984 = Viggo H. [Hjørnager] Pedersen: Reflections on the treatment of prepositions in bilingual dictionaries, and suggestions for a statistical approach. In: Hartmann 1984, 258—267.

Perl 1976 = Matthias Perl: Wörterbucheintragungen für Verben. In: Fremdsprachen 20. 1976, 274—279.

Petermann 1983 = J. Petermann: Zur Erstellung ein- und zweisprachiger phraseologischer Wörterbücher: Prinzipien der formalen Gestaltung und der Einordnung von Phrasemen. In: J. Matešić (Hrsg.), Phraseologie und ihre Aufgaben. Beitrag zum 1. Internationalen Phraseologie-Symposium vom 12. bis 14. Oktober 1981 in Mannheim. Heidelberg 1983 (Mannheimer Beiträge zur slawischen Philologie 3), 172—193.

Petkov 1985 = Pawel Petkov: Zur Typologisierung der zweisprachigen Wörterbücher. In: G. Stötzel (Hrsg.): Germanistik — Forschungsstand und Perspektiven. Vorträge des Deutschen Germanistentages 1984. 1. Teil Germanistische Sprachwissenschaft. Berlin. New York 1985, 74—79.

Petti 1989 = Vincent Petti: Notes on Dictionary Making. In: Moderna Språk 83. 1989, 201—207.

Pfeffer 1956 = Allan J. Pfeffer: Bilingual Lexicography. In: Modern Language Journal 40. 1956, 127—128.

Piitulainen 1987 = Marja-Leena Piitulainen: Zum Problem der Äquivalenz in der kontrastiven Lexikographie. In: Welke/Neurath 1987, 117—123.

Piotrowski 1987 = Tadeusz Piotrowski: Indication of English Pronunciation in Bilingual Dictionaries. In: Applied Linguistics 8. 1987, 37—45.

Piotrowski 1988 = Tadeusz Piotrowski: English and Russian: Two Bilingual Dictionaries. In: Dictionaries 10. 1988, 127—141.

Piotrowski 1989a = Tadeusz Piotrowski: [Rezension] English-Czech Dictionary Prag 1984—85. In: Dictionaries 11. 1989, 231—242.

Piotrowski 1989b = Tadeusz Piotrowski: Monolingual and Bilingual Dictionaries: Fundamental Differences. In: M. L. Tickoo (ed.), Learner's Dictionaries: State of the Art. Singapore 1989 (Anthology Series 23), 72—83.

Piotrowski 1990 = Tadeusz Piotrowski: Towards a Theory of Bilingual Lexicography: Basic Issues. Diss. Universität Wrocław [Breslau] 1990 (Manuskript).

Pöhl 1987 = Esther Pöhl: Dictionaries as Tools for the Translator: A Critical Analysis of German-Italian Dictionaries. In: Snell-Hornby/Pöhl 1987, 129—137.

Pöhl 1990 = Esther Pöhl: Vorschläge zu einem neuen zweisprachigen Übersetzungswörterbuch (Deutsch-Italienisch). In: BudaLEX 1990, 429—437.

Ponten 1975 = Jan-Peter Ponten: Kontrastive Semantik und bilinguale Lexikographie. In: H. G. Funke (Hrsg.), Grundfragen der Methodik des Deutschunterrichts und ihrer praktischen Verfahren. München 1975.

Ponten 1976 = Jan-Peter Ponten: Das Übersetzungswörterbuch und seine linguistischen Implikationen. In: Moser 1976, 200—210.

Ponten 1985 = Jan-Peter Ponten: Zum Programm eines bilingualen Wörterbuchs. Ein Beitrag zur niederländisch-deutschen Lexikographie. In: Zgusta 1985, 199—221 (zuerst in: Deutsche Sprache 3. 1975, 131—146).

Powers 1982 = Michael D. Powers: El sentido de las palabras en los diccionarios bilingües. In: Yelmo 52 y 53. 1982, 28.

Quemada 1960 = B. [Bernard] Quemada: L'inventaire des dictionnaires bilingues. In: Cahiers de lexicologie 2. 1960, 67—78.

Rasmussen 1985 = Jens Rasmussen: Enquête sur l'emploi du dictionnaire danois-français de Blinkenberg et Høybye. In: Copenhagen School of Economics and Business Administration Language Department (CEBAL). Publication no. 7. Copenhagen 1985, 130—154.

Rathmayr 1989 = Renate Rathmayr: Übersetzung gesprochener Sprache. Probleme der Lexikoneintragung von Partikeln und gestischen und mimischen Zeichen. In: Snell-Hornby/Pöhl 1989, 149—161.

Recker 1975 = Ja. I. Recker: Leksikografičeskie pomoščniki perevodčika (O frazeologii v slovarja). In: Moskovskij gosudarstvennyj pedagogičeskij institut inostrannych jazykov imeni Morisa Toreza 1975, Čast' II, 48—51.

Red'kin 1977 = V. A. Red'kin (ed.): Aktual'nye problemy učebnoj leksikografii. Moskva 1977.

Reed 1971 = Carroll E. Reed (ed.): The Learning of Language. New York 1971.

Rettig 1982 = Wolfgang Rettig: Les dictionnaires bilingues des langues française et allemande au 18e siècle: Questions de méthode. In: La lexicographie française du XVIe au XVIIIe siècle. Actes du Colloque International de Lexicographie dans la Herzog August Bibliothek Wolfenbüttel (9—11 octobre 1979) publiés par Manfred Höfler. Wolfenbüttel 1982 (Wolfenbütteler Forschungen 18), 103—113.

Rettig 1985 = Wolfgang Rettig: Die zweisprachige Lexikographie Französisch-Deutsch, Deutsch-Französisch. Stand, Probleme, Aufgaben. In: Lexicographica 1. 1985, 83—124.

Reuther 1986 = Tilmann Reuther: Zur Lexikographie des Imperativs: Deutsch und Russisch. In: Neue Entwicklungen der Angewandten Linguistik. Hrsg. v. Wolfgang Kühlwein. Tübingen 1986 (Forum Angewandte Linguistik 9), 77—79.

Rey 1986 = Alain Rey: Les écarts culturels dans les dictionnaires bilingues. In: Lexicographica 2. 1986, 33—42.

Ripfel 1989 = Martha Ripfel: Ergebnisse einer Befragung zur Benutzung ein- und zweisprachiger Wörterbücher. In: Lexicographica 5. 1989, 178—201.

Rivers 1969 = Wilga M. Rivers: Teaching Foreign Language Skills. Chicago. London 1969.

Robinson 1969 = Dow F. Robinson: Manual for Bilingual Dictionaries. 3 Bde. Santa Ana, Calif. 1969.

Rode 1982 = Matej Rode: Frazeologija u dvojezičkom rečnicima. In: Srpska akademija nauka i umetnosti — Odeljenje jezika i književnosti et al., Leksikografija i leksikologija. Zbornik referata. Uređivački odbor Darinka, Gortan-Premk et al., odgovorni urednik Drago Ćupić. Beograd. Novi Sad 1982, 275—278.

Rohwedder 1988 = Eberhard Rohwedder: Algunas consideraciones en relación con la elaboración de un nuevo diccionario español-alemán. In: Fremdsprachen 32. 1988, 110—114.

Roos 1975 = Eckhard Roos: Kollokationsmöglichkeiten der Verben des Sehvermögens im Deutschen und Englischen. Bern. Frankfurt a. M. 1975.

Rossenbeck 1975a = Klaus Rossenbeck: „En rak vänster" — ein gerader Linker? Bemerkungen zu einem neuen schwedisch-deutschen Wörterbuch. In: Moderna Språk 69. 1975, 21—34.

Rossenbeck 1975b = Klaus Rossenbeck: „Zwei durch acht macht vier". Weiteres zum schwedisch-deutschen Wörterbuch des Prisma-Verlages. In: Moderna Språk 69. 1975, 316—333.

Rossenbeck 1977 = Klaus Rossenbeck: 'Beratt mod' — berauschter Sinn? Bemerkungen zum Fachwörterbuch für Recht und Wirtschaft Schwedisch-Deutsch — Deutsch-Schwedisch von G. Parsenow, Köln 1975. In: Moderna Språk 71. 1977, 77—86.

Rossenbeck 1978 = Klaus Rossenbeck: Fachsprachlicher Wortschatz des Schwedischen und Deutschen als Problem der bilingualen Lexikographie. In: Skandinavistik 8/1. 1978, 1—5.

Rossenbeck 1979 = Klaus Rossenbeck: Einige Typen fachsprachlicher Wortbildung im Schwedischen und im Deutschen: methodische Probleme ihrer Beschreibung unter dem Gesichtspunkt der einsprachigen und zweisprachigen Lexikographie. In: Fachsprache 1. 1979, 197—209.

Rossenbeck 1981 = Klaus Rossenbeck: „Der 'Unfall-tüchtige' und 'die Einundfünfzige' — oder: *Goddag, yxskraft!*" Zur zweiten Auflage von Modern svensk-tysk ordbok (Stockholm: Bokförlaget Prisma, 1980). In: Germanistisches Bulletin 5. 1981, 75—103.

Rossenbeck 1986 = Klaus Rossenbeck: Zur gegenwärtigen Lage der deutsch-schwedischen Lexikographie. In: Die Brüder Grimm. Erbe und Rezeption. Stockholmer Symposium 1984. Hrsg. v. Astrid Stedje. Stockholm 1986 (Acta Universitatis Stockholmiensis. Stockholmer Germanistische Forschungen 32), 142—154.

Rossenbeck 1987 = Klaus Rossenbeck: Zur Gestaltung zweisprachiger Fachwörterbücher. In: A.-M. Cornu/J. Vanparijs/M. Delahaye/L. Baten (eds.), Beads or Bracelet? How do we approach LSP? Selected Papers from the Fifth European Symposium on LSP. Oxford 1987, 274—283.

Rossenbeck 1988 = Klaus Rossenbeck: Passabel — doch auf das deutsch-schwedische 'Traumlexikon' warten wir noch! Bemerkungen zu Prismas *Modern tysk-svensk ordbok*. In: Moderna Språk 82. 1988, 211—225.

Rossenbeck 1989 = Klaus Rossenbeck: Lexikologische und lexikographische Probleme fachsprachlicher Phraseologie aus kontrastiver Sicht. In: Snell-Hornby/Pöhl 1989, 197—210.

Sakari 1977 = A. Sakari: Les sens «fantômes» des dictionnaires bilingues. In: Actes du XIVᵉ Congrès international de linguistique et philologie romanes, Napoli 1974. Vol. IV. Naples 1977, 71—77.

Šarčević 1988 = Susan Šarčević: The challenge of legal lexicography. Implications for bilingual and multilingual dictionaries. In: Snell-Hornby 1988, 307—314.

Šarčević 1989a = Susan Šarčević: Conceptual Dictionaries for Translation in the Field of Law. In: International Journal of Lexicography 2. 1989, 277—293.

Šarčević 1989b = Susan Šarčević: Lexicography and Translation Across Culture. In: Snell-Hornby/Pöhl 1989, 211—221.

Šarčević 1990 = Susan Šarčević: Terminological Incongruency in Legal Dictionaries for Translation. In: BudaLEX 1990, 439—446.

Ščerba 1940 = L.V. Ščerba: Opyt obščej teorii leksikografii. In: Izvestija Akademii Nauk SSSR. Otdelenie Literatury i Jazyka 3. 1940, 89—117 [neu in L. V. Ščerba, Jazykovaja sistema i rečevaja dejatel'nost. Redaktory: L. R. Zinder, M. I. Matusevič. Leningrad 1974].

Schade 1973 = Walter Schade: Zur Verwendung des Kontextes bei der Auswahl von Wörterbuchäquivalenten. In: Fremdsprachen 17. 1973, 239—245.

Schade 1975 = Walter Schade: Valenztheorie und Übersetzungswörterbücher. In: Linguistische Arbeitsberichte 11. 1975, 91—94.

Schelbert 1972 = Tarcisius Werner Schelbert: Wörterbuch und konstruierte Mehrdeutigkeit mit besonderer Berücksichtigung des Englischen. Diss. Zürich 1972.

Schildt/Viehweger 1983 = J. Schildt/D. Viehweger (Hrsg.): Die Lexikographie von heute und das Wörterbuch von morgen. Analysen — Probleme — Vorschläge. Berlin 1983 (Linguistische Studien, Reihe A: Arbeitsberichte 109).

Schlipf 1956—1959 = Wolfgang Schlipf: Einige Bemerkungen zur Entwicklungsgeschichte des spanischen Woerterbuchs in Deutschland. In: Boletín de Filología (Santiago de Chile) 9. 1956/1957, 189—234. 10. 1958, 303—401. 11. 1959, 87—132.

Schmid 1989 = Annemarie Schmid: Wörterbücher als Hilfe zur Übersetzung von Phraseologismen. In: Snell-Hornby/Pöhl 1989, 121—127.

Schmitz 1960 = Siegfried Schmitz: Englische Wörterbücher. In: Die Neueren Sprachen 59. 1960, 226—242.

Schmuck/Voigt 1986 = Anton Schmuck/Walter Voigt: Zweisprachige elektronische Wörterbücher: am Beispiel des Langenscheidt-Wörterbuchs „alpha 8". In: Lexicographica 2. 1986, 284—290.

Schnorr 1986 = Veronika Schnorr: Translational Equivalent and/or Explanation? The Perennial Problem of Equivalence. In: Lexicographica 2. 1986, 53—60.

Schoenhals 1982 = Louise Schoenhals: Towards a valid linguistic check of bilingual dictionaries. In: (SIL) Notes on Linguistics 24. 1982, 15—20.

Schorr 1987 = Gabrielle Schorr: Deux types de dictionnaires bilingues de poche. In: Ilson 1987, 91—100.

Schregle 1969 = Götz Schregle: Probleme eines deutsch-arabischen Wörterbuches. In: Wolf-Dietrich Fischer (Hrsg.), Festgabe für Hans Wehr. Wiesbaden 1969, 130—135.

Schröer 1894 = Arnold Schröer: Über neuere englische Lexikographie. Vortrag, gehalten auf dem 6. allgemeinen Neuphilologentag zu Karlsruhe am 15. Mai 1894. In: Die Neueren Sprachen 2. 1894, 193—210.

Schröer 1903 = Arnold Schröer: [Rezensionen] Muret-Sanders Encyclopädisches Wörterbuch der englischen und deutschen Sprache, Große Ausgabe, Teil II: Deutsch-Englisch (1897—1901) und Kleine Ausgabe. In: Beiblatt zur Anglia 14. 1903, 193—211.

Schulz 1982 = Werner Schulz: Zur Grundkonzeption für ein großes Wörterbuch vom Typ Muttersprache/Fremdsprache (am Beispiel Deutsch-Russisch). In: Fremdsprachen 26. 1982, 258—263.

Sciarone 1983 = Bondi Sciarone: Analyse sémantique: l'homme et la machine. In: Lexique 2. 1983, 133—146.

Sciarone 1984 = Abondio Sciarone: The Organization of the Bilingual Dictionary. In: Hartmann 1984, 413—419.

Segoviano 1984 = Carlos Segoviano: Criterios para la valoración de diccionarios bilingües. In: Carlos Segoviano/José M. [María] Navarro (Hrsg.), Spanien und Lateinamerika. Beiträge zu Sprache, Literatur, Kultur. Homenaje a Anton [e] Inge Bemmerlein. Nürnberg 1984, 474—495.

Serre 1984 = R. Serre: The Contextual Dictionary: A Bilingual Dictionary Designed Specifically for Translators. In: P. Newman (ed.), Proceedings of the American Translators Association Conference 1984. Medford, N.J. 1984, 83—88.

Shaikevich/Oubine 1988 = A. Shaikevich/I. Oubine: Translators and researchers look at bilingual terminological dictionaries. In: Babel 34. 1988, 10—16.

Sharpe 1988 = Peter A. Sharpe: Japanese Speech Levels and How to Indicate Them in an English-Japanese Dictionary. In: Dictionaries 10. 1988, 69—80.

Sharpe 1989 = Peter A. Sharpe: Pragmatic Considerations for an English-Japanese Dictionary. In: International Journal of Lexicography 2. 1989, 315—323.

Sherwood 1990 = Peter Sherwood: Grammar in the Bilingual Dictionary, with Special Reference to English and Hungarian. In: BudaLEX 1990, 129—140.

Smith 1978 = R. N. Smith: Computational Bilingual Lexicography: A la recherche du mot juste. In: Computer Support for Translation: Proceedings of the Foreign Broadcast Information Seminar. Washington 1978, 84—112.

Snell-Hornby 1984 = Mary Snell-Hornby: The bilingual dictionary — help or hindrance? In: Hartmann 1984, 274—281.

Snell-Hornby 1986 = Mary Snell-Hornby: The Bilingual Dictionary — Victim of its own tradition? In: R.R.K. [Reinhard Rudolf Karl] Hartmann (ed.), The History of Lexicography. Papers from the Dictionary Research Centre Seminar at Exeter, March 1986. Amsterdam. Philadelphia 1986 (Amsterdam Studies in the Theory and History of Linguistic Sciences, Volume 40), 207—218.

Snell-Hornby 1987 = Mary Snell-Hornby: Towards a learner's bilingual dictionary. In: Cowie 1987, 159—170.

Snell-Hornby 1988 = Mary Snell-Hornby (ed.): ZüriLEX '86 Proceedings. Papers read at the EURALEX International Congress, University of Zürich, 9—14 September 1986. Tübingen 1988.

Snell-Hornby 1990 = Mary Snell-Hornby: Bilingual Dictionaries — Visions and Revisions. In: BudaLEX 1990, 227—236.

Snell-Hornby/Pöhl 1989 = Mary Snell-Hornby/Esther Pöhl (eds.): Translation and Lexicography. Papers read at the EURALEX Colloquium held at Innsbruck 2—5 July 1987. Kirksville, Missouri 1989.

Sommerfeldt 1977 = Karl Ernst Sommerfeldt: Bedeutungsanalyse und Valenztheorie im Dienste der Konfrontation (Gedanken zur Erarbeitung eines konfrontativen Wörterbuches deutscher und russischer Verben und Adjektive für den Fremdsprachenunterricht). In: Zeitschrift für Phonetik, Sprachwissenschaft und Kommunikationsforschung 30. 1977, 251—260.

Sora 1984 = F. Sora: Study of the Use of Bilingual and Monolingual Dictionaries by Italian Students of English. In: Papers on Work in Progress 12. 1984, 40—46.

Standop 1985 = Ewald Standop: Englische Wörterbücher unter der Lupe. Tübingen 1985 (Lexicographica Series Maior 2).

Stein 1985 = Gabriele Stein: English-German/German-English Lexicography: Its early beginnings. In: Lexicographica 1. 1985, 134—164.

Stein 1990 = Gabriele Stein: From the Bilingual to the Monolingual Dictionary. In: BudaLEX 1990, 401—407.

Steiner 1971 = Roger J. Steiner: A Cardinal Principle of Lexicography: Equivalence. In: ITL 14. 1971, 23—28.

Steiner 1975 = Roger Steiner: Monodirectional Bilingual Dictionaries (a Lexicographical Innovation). In: Babel 21. 1975, 123—124.

Steiner 1976 = Roger J. Steiner: Neologisms and Scientific Words in Bilingual Lexicography: Ten Problems. In: Lebende Sprachen 21. 1976, 145—150.

Steiner 1982 = Roger J. Steiner: How a Bilingual Dictionary Best Serves the Writer. In: Hobar 1982, 24—31.

Steiner 1984 = Roger J. Steiner: Guidelines for Reviewers of Bilingual Dictionaries. In: Dictionaries 6. 1984, 166—181.

Steiner 1986 = Roger J. Steiner: How Many Languages Should a 'Bilingual' Dictionary Offer? In: Lexicographica 2. 1986, 85—92.

Steiner 1989 = Roger J. Steiner: The Absence of Text: The Bilingual Dictionary as an Index. In: International Journal of Lexicography 2. 1989, 249—257.

Sterkenburg 1983 = P. G. J. van Sterkenburg: Johann Hendrik Van Dale en zijn Opvolgers. Utrecht 1983.

Sterkenburg 1985 = P. G. J. van Sterkenburg: Groot woordenboek van hedendags Nederlands en Grote Van Dale: een eerste vergelijking. In: Spektator 14—2. 1984/1985, 135—152.

Sterkenburg/Martin/Al 1982 = P. G. J. van Sterkenburg/Willi Martin/Bernard Al: A New Van Dale Project: Bilingual Dictionaries on One and the Same Monolingual Basis. In: J. Goetschalckx/L. Rolling (eds.), Lexicography in the Electronic Age. Amsterdam 1982, 221—237.

Stolze 1988 = Radegundis Stolze: Das begriffliche Bedeutungspotential als Problem der Lexikographie. In: Snell-Hornby 1988, 27—36.

Strand-Juchansen 1977 = E. Strand-Juchansen: Russko-norvežskie jazykovye kontakty i nekotorye problemy sovremennoj russko-norvežskoj učebnoj leksikografii. In: Institut 1977, 123—134.

Strevens 1978 = Peter Strevens (ed.): In Honour of A. S. Hornby. Oxford 1978.

Stupin 1967 = L. P. Stupin: Neobchodimy dvujazyčnye slovari imen sobstvennych. In: Tetradi perevodčika. Pod redakciej L. S. Barchudarova. Moskva 1967 (Učenye zapiski No. 4), 55—62.

Sukalenko 1976 = Nonna Ivanovna Sukalenko: Dvujazyčnye slovari i voprosy perevoda. Charkov 1976.

Sunaga 1986 = Koichi Sunaga: Zweisprachige Wörterbücher und die Interferenz. Am Beispiel deutsch-japanischer sprachlicher Interferenzen. In: A. Schöne (Hrsg.), Akten des VII. Kongresses der Internationalen Vereinigung für germanische Sprach- und Literaturwissenschaft. Band 3: Textlinguistik contra Stilistik? Wortschatz und Wörterbuch. Hrsg. v. W. E. Weiss, H. E. Wiegand u. M. Reis. Tübingen 1986, 182—186.

Swanson 1962 = Donald C. Swanson: The Selection of Entries for a Bilingual Dictionary. In: Householder/Saporta 1962, 63—77.

Takebayashi 1988 = S. Takebayashi: [Probleme der zweisprachigen Lexikographie (in japanischer Sprache)]. In: Philologica Anglica (Tokio) 1988, 467—475.

Tatišvili 1961 = Ju. G. Tatišvili: Perevodnye slovari i problema slovasočetanija v lingvistike (Po materialam russko-nemeckich slovarej). In: Učenye zapiski Pjatigorskogo GPIIJa 24. 1961, 407—473.

Teichmann-Nadiraschwili 1988 = Christine Teichmann-Nadiraschwili: Makrostrukturelle Beziehungen im Übersetzungswörterbuch — ein Beitrag zur zweisprachigen Lexikographie unter Berücksichtigung des Sprachenpaares Deutsch-Französisch. In: Zeitschrift für Phonetik, Sprachwissenschaft und Kommunikationsforschung 41. 1988, 801—806.

Thiele 1988 = Johannes Thiele: Les phraséologismes dans les dictionnaires bilingues. In: Wissenschaftliche Zeitschrift der Ernst-Moritz-Arndt-Universität Greifswald. Gesellschaftswissenschaftliche Reihe 37/2. 1988, 49—51.

Thompson 1984 = Sandra A. Thompson: Bilingual dictionaries and the notion of 'lexical categories' in Chinese. In: Hartmann 1984, 282—288.

Thompson 1987 = Geoff Thompson: Using bilingual dictionaries. In: ELT Journal 41. 1987, 282—286.

Tiitula 1987 = Liisa Tiitula: Pragmatischer Aspekt in einem zweisprachigen aktiven Wörterbuch. In: Welke/Neurath 1987, 124—128.

Titova 1977 = L. N. Titova: Sopostavitel'no-perevodnoj associativnyj slovar' i vozmožnosti ego lingvodidaktičeskogo ispol'zovanija. In: Red'kin 1977, 183.

Tomaszczyk 1976 = Jerzy Tomaszczyk: On establishing equivalence between lexical items between two languages. In: Papers and Studies in Contrastive Linguistics 5. 1976, 77—81.

Tomaszczyk 1979 = Jerzy Tomaszczyk: Dictionaries: Users and Uses. In: Glottodidactica 12. 1979, 103—119.

Tomaszczyk 1981 = Jerzy Tomaszczyk: Issues and Developments in Bilingual Pedagogical Lexicography. In: Cowie 1981, 287—296.

Tomaszczyk 1983 = J. [Jerzy] Tomaszczyk: On bilingual dictionaries. The case of bilingual dictionaries for foreign language learners. In: Hartmann 1983 a, 41—51.

Tomaszczyk 1984 = Jerzy Tomaszczyk: The culture-bound element in bilingual dictionaries. In: Hartmann 1984, 289—297.

Tomaszczyk 1988 = Jerzy Tomaszczyk: The bilingual dictionary under review. In: Snell-Hornby 1988, 289—298.

Tomaszczyk 1989 = Jerzy Tomaszczyk: L1—L2 Technical Translation and Dictionaries. In: Snell-Hornby/Pöhl 1989, 177—186.

Toury 1989 = Gideon Toury: The Meaning of Translation Specific Lexical Items and Its Representation in the Dictionary. In: Snell-Hornby/Pöhl 1989, 45—53.

Traupmann 1985 = John C. Traupmann: Modern Trends in German-English Lexicography. In: Lexicographica 1. 1985, 165—171.

Turabaev 1968 = A. Turabaev: O principach peredači i osnovnoj formy glagola v tjurksko-russkich slovarjach. In: Vestnik Karapalkakskogo filiala AN Uzbekskogo SSR 4. Nukus 1968, 70—76.

Umarchodžaev 1974 = M. I. Umarchodžaev: K voprosu o vybore ėkvivalentov frazeologičeskich edinic pri sostavlenija slovarja. In: Fremdsprachen 18. 1974, 191—197.

Umarchodžaev 1975 = M. I. Umarchodžaev: Principy ustanovlenija mežjazykovych sootvetstvii pri sostavlenii frazeologičeskogo slovarja v uslovijach otsutstvija neposredstvennogo o prjamogo kontakta jazykov. In: Moskovskij gosudarstvennyj pedagogičeskij institut inostrannych jazykov imeni Morisa Toreza 1975, Čast' II, 104—107.

Van Roey 1990 = J. Van Roey: French-English Contrastive Lexicology. An Introduction. Louvain 1990 (Série pédagogique de l'Institut de linguistique de Louvain 14).

Veselytskyj 1963 = V. V. Veselytskyj: Dsjaky pryjomy podavannja pryjmennykiv u velykomu Rosijs'ko-čes'komu slovnyku. In: Leksykohrafičnyj bjuleten' 9. 1963, 103—106.

Vietze 1981 = Hans-Peter Vietze: Äquivalenzprobleme bei der Arbeit am deutsch-mongolischen Wörterbuch. In: Zeitschrift für Phonetik, Sprachwissenschaft und Kommunikationsforschung 34. 1981, 78—83.

Vietze 1983 = Hans-Peter Vietze: Theoretische und praktische Probleme bei der Erarbeitung der Wörterbücher Deutsch-Mongolisch und Mongolisch-Deutsch. In: Zeitschrift für Phonetik, Sprachwissenschaft und Kommunikationsforschung 36. 1983, 228—234.

Vinay/Dariault 1958 = Jean-Paul Vinay/P. Dariault: Dictionnaires Canadiens I: Les dictionnaires bilingues. In: Journal des Traducteurs 3. 1958, 109—113.

Vlachov 1990 = Sergej I. Vlachov: Učastie illjustrativnogo materiala v semantizacii ischodnoj slovarnoj edinicy. In: BudaLEX 1990, 75—82.

Vlček/Denisov 1977 = J. Vlček/P. Denisov: O russko-českom slovare sočetaemosti slov. In: Institut 1977, 111—122.

Voigt 1981 = Walter Voigt: Wörterbuch, Wörterbuchmacher, Wörterbuchprobleme. Ein Werkstattgespräch. In: Wort und Sprache 1981, 24—33.

Voigt 1984 = Walter Voigt: Der Wörterbuchverlag und das „optimale" Wörterbuch. In: Goetz/Herbst 1984, 334—349.

Wagner 1989 = Horst Wagner: Les dictionnaires du français langue de spécialité/langue économique. In: Dieter Kremer (Hrsg.), Actes du XVIIIe Congrès International de Linguistique et de Philologie Romanes. Université de Trèves (Trier) 1986. Tome IV. Section VI: Lexicologie et lexicographie. Tübingen 1989, 209—219.

Welke/Neurath 1987 = Klaus Welke/Renate Neurath (Hrsg.): Lexikologie und Lexikographie. Vorträge der IV. sprachwissenschaftlichen Konferenz DDR-Finnland. Humboldt-Universität zu Berlin, 3.—5. September 1986. Berlin 1987 (Linguistische Studien. Reihe A: Arbeitsberichte 160).

Werner 1979 = Reinhold Werner: Formaler Vergleich einiger spanisch-deutscher und deutsch-spanischer Wörterbücher. In: Lebende Sprachen 24. 1979, 75—81.

Werner 1980 = Reinhold Werner: Ein technisches Detail der Stilebenenkennzeichnung im zweisprachigen Wörterbuch. In: Lebende Sprachen 25. 1980, 154—158.

Werner 1981 = Reinhold Werner: Umgangssprache im zweisprachigen Wörterbuch: lexikographische Probleme, aufgezeigt an zwei spanisch-deutschen Wörterbüchern. In: Zielsprache Spanisch 1/2. 1981, 69—75.

Werner 1982a = Reinhold Werner: Das Bild im Wörterbuch. Funktionen der Illustration in spanischen Wörterbüchern. In: Linguistik und Didaktik 49/50. 1982, 62—94.

Werner 1982b = Reinhold Werner: La definición lexicográfica. In: Haensch/Wolf/Ettinger/Werner 1982, 259—328.

Werner 1982c = Reinhold Werner: Zur Reihenfolge der Definitionen bzw. Übersetzungsäquivalente im Wörterbuchartikel. In: Lebende Sprachen 27. 1982, 150—156.

Werner 1984 = Reinhold Werner: Ein nicht genügend ernstgenommener Wörterbuchtyp: das Reisewörterbuch. Mit Bemerkungen zu Reisewörterbüchern des Spanischen für Deutschsprachige. In: Hispanorama 38. 1984, 153—162.

Werner 1986 = Reinhold Werner: Zum Stand der zweisprachigen Lexikographie Deutsch-Spanisch, Spanisch-Deutsch. In: Lexicographica 2. 1986, 127—155.

Wexler 1987 = P. J. Wexler: Affix-entries in bilingual dictionaries. In: Cahiers de lexicologie 50. 1987, 237—243.

Wheeler 1957 = Marcus Wheeler: Meaning in Bilingual Dictionaries. In: Studia Linguistica 11. 1957, 65—69.

White 1989 = Linda White: Feminism and Lexicography: Dealing with Sexist Language in a Bilingual Dictionary. In: Frontiers 10/3. 1989, 61—64.

Wiegand 1982 = Herbert Ernst Wiegand (Hrsg.): Studien zur neuhochdeutschen Lexikographie II. Hildesheim. New York 1982 (Germanistische Linguistik 3—6/80).

Wiegand 1988a = Herbert Ernst Wiegand (Hrsg.): Studien zur neuhochdeutschen Lexikographie VI. 2. Teilband. Hildesheim. Zürich. New York 1988 (Germanistische Linguistik 87—90/1986).

Wiegand 1988b = Herbert Ernst Wiegand: „Shanghai bei Nacht". Auszüge aus einem metalexikographischen Tagebuch zur Arbeit beim Großen Deutsch-Chinesischen Wörterbuch. In: Wiegand 1988a, 521—626.

Wiegand 1988c = Herbert Ernst Wiegand: Bibliographie zur Wörterbuchforschung von 1945 bis auf die Gegenwart. 2200 Titel. Ausgewählt aus germanistischer Perspektive. In: Wiegand 1988a, 627—821.

Williams 1959 = Edwin B. Williams: The Problem of Bilingual Lexicography Particularly as Applied to Spanish and English. In: Hispanic Review 27. 1959, 246—253.

Williams 1960 = Edwin B. Williams: Analysis of the Problem of Meaning Discrimination in Spanish and English Lexicography. In: Babel 6. 1960, 121—125.

Willnat 1986 = Heinz Willnat: Zur Problematik der Darstellung sog. tentativ-transformativer Verben in zweisprachigen Wörterbüchern. In: Günther 1986, 68—72.

Wöller 1985 = Egon Wöller: Valenzangaben im zweisprachigen Wörterbuch. In: Linguistische Arbeitsberichte 48. Leipzig 1985, 74—80.

Wöller 1986 = Egon Wöller: Zur systematischen Darstellung von Lexemgruppierungen in zweisprachigen Wörterbüchern. In: Günther 1986, 35—43.

Wolski 1982 = Werner Wolski (Hrsg.): Aspekte der sowjetrussischen Lexikographie. Übersetzungen, Abstracts, bibliographische Angaben. Tübingen 1982 (Reihe Germanistische Linguistik 43).

Wort und Sprache = Wort und Sprache. Beiträge zu Problemen der Lexikographie und Sprachpraxis veröffentlicht zum 125jährigen Bestehen des Langenscheidt-Verlages. Berlin. München. Wien. Zürich 1981.

Wörterbuch als Fehlerquelle = Wörterbuch als Fehlerquelle. Eine Untersuchung der bekanntesten englischen Wörterbücher und Dictionaries nach linguistischen Gesichtspunkten (von einem studentischen Kollektiv). Hamburg 1970.

Wu 1982 = Wu Ying: Shuangyu cidiande shouci. In: Cishu Yanjiu 198 2/1. 1982, 27—33.

Zgusta 1971 = Ladislav Zgusta: Manual of Lexicography. Den Haag 1971 [Kapitel 7: The Bilingual Dictionary, 294—344].

Zgusta 1980 = Ladislav Zgusta (ed.): Theory and Method in Lexicography: Western and Non-Western Perspectives. Columbia, S.C. 1980.

Zgusta 1984 = Ladislav Zgusta: Translational Equivalence in the Bilingual Dictionary. In: Hartmann 1984, 147—154.

Zgusta 1985 = Ladislav Zgusta (Hrsg.): Probleme des Wörterbuchs. Darmstadt 1985 (Wege der Forschung 612).

Zgusta 1986 = Ladislav Zgusta (ed.): Problems of the Bilingual Dictionary. In: Lexicographica 2. 1986, 1—161.

Zgusta 1987 = Ladislav Zgusta: Translational Equivalence in a Bilingual Dictionary: Báhukośyam. In: Dictionaries 9. 1987, 1—47.

Zimmer 1990 = Rudolf Zimmer: Theoretische Überlegungen. In: Rudolf Zimmer, Äquivalenzen zwischen FRANZÖSISCH und DEUTSCH. Theorie — Korpus — Indizes. Ein Kontextwörterbuch. Tübingen 1990, 5—176.

Zorc 1979 = R. David Zorc: An Etymological Bilingual Dictionary — Esoteric or Essential? In: Philippine Journal of Linguistics 10. 1979, 63—73.

Franz Josef Hausmann, Erlangen/
Reinhold Otto Werner, Augsburg
(Bundesrepublik Deutschland)

287. Grammatical Constructions in the Bilingual Dictionary

1. Types of Construction With Reference to Bilingual Dictionaries
2. The Specification of Constructions in Lexicographical Practice
3. Arguments for Specifying Constructions
4. Conclusion: Guidelines for Specifying Constructions
5. Selected Bibliography

1. Types of Construction With Reference to Bilingual Dictionaries

Lexicography deals not only with the denotative and connotative meaning of the individual lemma, but also with its combinatory properties — that is, its ability to combine with other lexical units. Such combinations, which we will call constructions here, present a number of problems, especially for anyone translating into a foreign language, and are thus of particularly great significance for the bilingual lexicographer.

Constructions in bilingual dictionaries can be classified into two main groups: grammatical and idiosyncratic. Grammatical constructions are formed according to the rules of grammar or as deviations (exceptions) from these, while the idiosyncratic phrases are typified by the fact that one phrase out of several possible (from the denotative point of view) is either the only usual or the preferred one, entailing that the idiosyncratic constructions, in encoding a native-language text as an equivalent text in the foreign language, are in principle unpredictable, while in decoding a foreign-language text as an equivalent text in the native language they may be transparent (cf. Article 285).

In the (not particularly intensive) research on constructions in dictionaries (Zgusta 1971, Al-Kasimi 1978, 48—57, Hausmann 1977, 70—88, Svensén 1987, 79—105, Brauße 1987) the grammatical constructions have been given most attention, especially valency, verb patterns and the like, which have been described and discussed in published valency lexica — for example Helbig/Schenkel 1973, Sommerfeldt/Schreiber 1977 a, b, Engel/Savin 1983, Schumacher 1986, to some extent in the so-called learners' dictionaries and publications concerned with these — see for example contributions to the collections Bergenholtz/Mugdan 1985, Cowie 1987, Hyldgaard-Jensen/Zettersten 1988 and Lemmens/Wekker 1986.

2. The Specification of Constructions in Lexicographical Practice

Like monolingual dictionaries, bilingual dictionaries list — with varying degrees of thoroughness depending on the size of the dictionaries — construction specifications for verbs, adjectives and substantives. Within the verb class, however, auxiliaries like *to be, to have,* modal verbs, and verbs like *to take* and *to let* constitute particularly construction-rich lexical units. In the same category are pronouns, prepositions, conjunctions and adverbs, but given the lack of metalexicographical research on these lexical/grammatical units (see however Bergenholtz 1984) it is not possible to deal with them here.

Morphosyntactic indications like part of speech and inflexion are as a rule among the standard information on the lexical units of at least one of the two languages in the dictionary (see Bergenholtz/Mugdan 1982, Jørgensen 1982, Bergenholtz 1983), but in bilingual lexicographical practice there is no consensus on what syntactic information should be selected for the individual parts of speech — cf. Bergenholtz/Mugdan 1982, Bergenholtz 1983.

For verbs, the grammatical categories transitive, intransitive, reflexive etc. are usually given. Auxiliaries also appear as constructional specifications. No systematic selection of constructional specifications is made for adjectives: apart from indications of their comparison, some dictionaries specify restrictions in their attributive, predicative or adverbial use, while others show whether they can be used substantivally. As for substantives, in large and medium-sized dictionaries there may be important information on their constructional potential hidden away in the often not particularly well-arranged examples in the individual entries.

Constructional features are presented in bilingual dictionaries by means of three main types of specification: grammatical category, examples in sentence form and elliptic constructions (cf. also Svensén 1987, 80 ff.).

Grammatical category is given for the lexical unit by means of an abbreviation — for example in Collins Pocket 1983 we find **schließen** vtir (= transitive, intransitive, reflexive) = *close, shut.* ... These catch-all grammatical categories may also serve as means of structuring the dictionary entry, as in Muret/Sanders: "*schließen* I tr. . . . II intr. . . . III refl. . . ."

Sentence examples (see also Article 288) take the form of independent indicative, interrogative, optative or exclamatory sentences: *schließ das Fenster, bitte!* = *shut the window, please!; er schloß seine Rede mit den Worten* = *he concluded (or wound up) his speech by saying* (Muret/Sanders). The examples serve not only to illustrate the grammatical category transitive, but also to show other syntactic constructions with the verb *schließen* as well as its semantic context and idiosyncratic constructions.

schlie·ßen [ˈʃliːsṇ] ⟨f⟩ ⟨→t 120⟩
 I ⟨onov. ww.⟩ **0.1** *sluiten* ⇒*dichtgaan* **0.2** *sluiten* ⇒*eindigen, besluiten* **0.3** *concluderen* ⇒*opmaken, een gevolgtrekking maken, afleiden* ♦ **1.2** die Autoaktien schlossen DM 3,- höher *de autoaandelen sloten DM 3,- hoger* **3.2** ⟨in brieven⟩ laß mich für heute ~ *voor vandaag wil ik er een eind(e) aan maken, er een punt achter zetten* **3.3** so darf man nicht ~ *zo mag men niet redeneren* **5.1** der Schlüssel schließt schlecht *de sleutel past niet goed (in het slot);* ich schloß zweimal *ik draai de sleutel twee keer om* **6.1** ⟨reg.⟩ der Schlüssel schließt zu dieser Tür *de sleutel past op deze deur* **6.2** mit diesem Satz schließt das Drama *met deze zin eindigt het drama* **6.3** die Polizei konnte **auf** den Täter ~ *de politie kon afleiden, opmaken wie de dader was;* er schloß auf Mord *hij kwam tot de conclusie dat er van moord sprake was;* ich schloß **aus** seinen Worten, daß . . . *ik maakte uit zijn woorden op dat . . . ;* **vom** Besonderen auf das Allgemeine ~ *het algemene uit het bijzondere afleiden;* ⟨inf.⟩ du sollst nicht von dir auf andere ~ *je moet anderen niet naar jezelf beoordelen;*
II ⟨ov. ww.⟩ **0.1** *sluiten* ⇒*dichtmaken* **0.2** *(be)sluiten* ⇒*beëindigen, eindigen* **0.3** *(in)sluiten* ⇒*opsluiten, opbergen* **0.4** *sluiten* ⇒*aangaan* **0.5** *aansluiten* ♦ **1.1** ⟨fig.⟩ darüber sind die Akten noch nicht geschlossen *deze zaak is nog niet afgedaan;* eine geschlossene Anstalt *een gesloten inrichting;* die Augen ~ *zijn ogen sluiten, toedoen,* ⟨ook⟩ *sterven;* einen Hahn ~ *een kraan dichtdraaien;* ein geschlossener Jahrgang *een volledige jaargang;* eine Lücke ~ *een lacune opvullen;* geschlossene Vokale *gesloten klinkers;* den Zugang ~ *de toegang afsluiten* **1.2** eine Rede ~ *een rede besluiten;* eine Versammlung ~ *een vergadering sluiten;* Sympathisanten schlossen den Zug *sympathisanten besloten de optocht, stoet* **1.4** eine Bekanntschaft ~*kennismaken, (elkaar, iem.) leren kennen;* einen Bund ~ *een verbond, sluiten, aangaan;* (mit jmdm.) die Ehe ~ *(met iem.) een huwelijk sluiten, trouwen* **6.1** die Hand **um** einen Gegenstand ~ *de hand om een voorwerp klemmen, sluiten;* die Hand **zur** Faust ~ *de hand tot een vuist maken, sluiten* **6.2** einen Brief mit den Worten ~ *. . . een brief met de woorden besluiten . . .* **6.3** jmdn. **an** die Brust ~ *iem. aan zijn borst drukken, sluiten;* jmdn. in die Arme ~ *iem. in zijn armen sluiten, omarmen;* jmdn. (mit) in das Gebet ~ *iem. in zijn gebed(en) opnemen;* etwas in die Hand ~ *iets in zijn hand klemmen, sluiten;* jmdn. in sein Herz geschlossen haben *iem. in zijn hart gesloten hebben* Geld in den Schrank ~ *geld in de kast opbergen;* etwas in sich ~ *iets bevatten, inhouden, insluiten, met zich meebrengen* **6.4** mit jmdm. den Lebensbund ~ *met iem. in de echt treden* **6.5** er schloß daran die Worte *. . . aansluitend zei hij . . . ;*
III sich ~ ⟨wk. ww.⟩ **0.1** *zich sluiten* ⇒*dichtgaan, sluiten* **0.2** *volgen* ⇒*zich aansluiten* ♦ **1.1** der Kreis schließt sich *de kring, cirkel wordt gesloten;* die Reihen ~ *de rijen sluiten aaneen;* die Wunde schließt sich *de wond gaat dicht, sluit zich* **6.2** an die Diskussion schloß sich noch ein gemütliches Beisammensein *op de discussie volgde nog een gezellig samenzijn;*→**geschlossen.**

Dictionary excerpt 287.1: Dictionary article **schließen** (from: van Dale 1983, 1106 f.).

Elliptic constructions appear when the lexicographer omits certain constructional elements, e. g. for reasons of space or because he assumes that the user can interpolate them. This is a well-known, economical way of indicating constructions with verbs — like *aus etwas auf etwas schließen* = *to judge (infer, conclude, deduce) something from something*. This way of using ellipses can be further abbreviated, as in *schließen* = *infer (aus* = *from)*. In a language like German, though, it is not sufficient for users with German as the foreign language to specify *auf etwas* without at the same time giving the case the preposition governs.

As an interesting innovation in the otherwise rather hidebound bilingual lexicographical tradition we should mention the Dutch van Dale series which has made the grammatical constructions a basic structuring principle in all their large dictionaries with Dutch and English, German or French as the foreign language — see Sterkenburg/Martin/Al 1982. In the dictionary entries the way each lemma combines with lexical units of other parts of speech is systematically reflected. If we choose the German **schließen** in the German-Dutch dictionary, the structure of the entry looks fairly traditional at first glance: I stands for intransitive, II for transitive and III for reflexive, but the structure within each of these categories is determined by a strictly grammatical principle according to which the figure 1.0 indicates the ability to combine with substantives, 2.0 with adjectives, 3.0 with verbs, 4.0 with pronouns, 5.0 with adverbs, 6.0 with prepositions, etc. The digit after the point in the code refers to the meaning number (cf. Hausmann 1988 on this entry structure).

3. Arguments for Specifying Constructions

The special problems of constructions in bilingual dictionaries are primarily due to the lack of guidelines for the selection and indication of constructions. We will present three important arguments that can form a basis for establishing guidelines for the selection and presentation of constructions.

In the first place it is the function of the dictionary that determines how many constructional specifications should be selected and presented in a bilingual translation dictionary, as the need for information on constructions depends on whether the dictionary is active, i. e. designed for encoding a native-language text as an equivalent text in the foreign language, or passive, i. e. designed for decoding a foreign language text into an equivalent text in the native language; or whether the dictionary is to fulfil both functions at once (cf. Article 285).

Irrespective of which language is the source language of the dictionary, it is necessary in the entries in an active dictionary with German as the foreign language to specify a number of grammatical and idiosyncratic constructions with their respective German equivalents, for example:
— relevant valency specifications for verbs, adjectives and substantives;
— cases governed by prepositions that govern two cases (accusative and dative) in fixed-valency combinations with verbs *(Geld* **in** *einem Safe deponieren),* adjectives *(müde* + genitive), substantives *(Hoffnung* **auf** + accusative);
— obligatory or facultative use of correlatives for subordinate clauses or infinitives (*Er hofft* (**darauf**), *ihn bald wiederzusehen/daß er ihn bald wiedersieht; es gehört eine Frechheit* **dazu**, *so zu tun*);
— the use of articles in phrases in certain constructions (*jemanden* **zum** *Direktor ernennen*).

The idiosyncratic constructions should be made clear by the examples given with the German equivalents — for example, under **bike, bicycle** or **wheel** the idiosyncratic phrase *das Fahrrad schieben.* With the equivalent *Frage* one must cite the functional verb *an jemanden eine Frage stellen.*

What is common to such grammatical or idiosyncratic constructions is that they cannot be described as the result of regular grammatical or lexical combination rules, and that they must therefore be included in an active dictionary.

In a passive dictionary, on the other hand, such grammatical or idiosyncratic constructions can be omitted insofar as they are transparent to the target-language users. In a bifunctional (active *and* passive) dictionary the demands on the active dictionary's construction descriptions must be given priority over those of the passive dictionary.

Yet in lexicographical practice this is not the case. The smaller and smallest dictionaries largely neglect information on the grammatical and idiosyncratic constructions a given lexical unit may enter into. The equivalent of a lemma is often simply given as substantives and adjectives, as if these parts of speech did not establish constructions: **Frage** = *question;* **groß** = *big, large, tall, great.* But regardless of the size of the dictionary, such information is needed if it has the active function.

The specialist bilingual dictionaries, too, and the tri- or multilingual (terminological) dictionaries leave much to be desired in this vital area for active translation dictionaries (Rossenbeck 1989). For example, in an English-German dictionary it will be important that the English-speaking user is presented with the prepositions that are associated with German substantives like *Anbringung, Befestigung, Änderung,* etc. Conversely, it is important for the German user to be told the prepositions that go with the corresponding English substantives in the technical dictionary's German-English part. The same is true of the verbs in technical language whose association with particular prepositions and cases governed may indicate differing states, processes or actions — for example *anbringen (an, auf)* or *schalten (auf, in, zu).*

In the second place, the selection and presentation of construction specifications must be based on the fact that the need for construction specification may vary from language pair to language pair. It follows from this language-pair relatedness that the divergent constructions in the respective languages must be given priority in the bilingual dictionary for the language pair in question. Grammatical and idiosyncratic constructions which are not predictable in translation between the language pair in question must be included in the bilingual dictionary concerned.

As an example, the lexicographer must reflect on the extent to which he will describe language-pair-related grammatical, systematic differences in the dictionary entries — like the fact that certain groups of intransitive perfective verbs in English take the auxiliary *have,* while the same groups in German take *sein:* e. g. *to fall asleep/einschlafen, to blush/erröten, to arrive/ankommen.* In these cases the Danish auxiliary *være* corresponds to the German, and in that respect does not have to be given in a Danish-German or German-Danish dictionary, but it does of course in a Danish-English or English-Danish active dictionary.

In Danish we have some clear transitive verbs that take the auxiliary *have,* while German verbs in the same constructions take the auxiliary *sein*, as in the following sentences: *han har indgået ægteskab = er ist eine Ehe eingegangen; han har efterkommet sine forpligtelser = er ist seinen Verpflichtungen nachgekommen*. In these cases English and Danish have the corresponding auxiliary *have*. Language-pair-related idiosyncratic constructions, as shown by examples, may feature a lexical unit in a divergent idiosyncratic construction, which thus cannot be translated word for word — for example, *groß* in *unsere Firma war groß vertreten (auf einer Messe) = our firm was well represented; ich möchte nicht groß essen = I don't want to eat very much* (Muret/Sanders). While in the construction *the fuse has blown*, German *die Sicherung ist durchgebrannt* and Danish *sikringen er gået (sprunget)* we have three mutually divergent idiosyncratic constructions, the German and Danish constructions *Auskunft, Rat, Gutachten... einholen/indhente oplysninger, råd, responsum...* are convergent, unlike the corresponding divergent constructions in English: *to ask for information, to make enquiries, to obtain advice from somebody*.

Consideration of the dictionary user's needs and competence in the foreign language is a strong argument for including such constructions in active dictionaries, which are meant precisely for the production of foreign-language texts.

In the third place, in the selection and presentation of constructions one must take into account the user's grammatical competence in the foreign language, and anticipate a reasonably well-balanced division of work between the dictionary and grammar.

Empirical studies of dictionary use for translation into foreign languages (Wiegand 1985, 73) show that grammatical problems may account for up to 55 % of consultations. Of these, questions about syntactic problems, the use of prepositions and word formation make up at least half. Similarly, Hartmann 1982 documents that grammatical constructions should be assigned more importance than they have in lexicographical practice; but the problem we are left with then is how much competence in constructions the dictionary user can be expected to have, and where in the dictionary the information should be placed.

Let us reflect on a couple of points of principle. First and foremost, there is the natural division of work between the grammar and the dictionary. It is normally regarded as the job of the grammar to state general rules, including the general rules for particular parts of speech, while the dictionary deals with "the word" — that is, the combinatory properties of the individual members of word classes; for example, the grammar describes transitivity, but does not give a list of all the transitive verbs. Thus, while it is true in principle that there is a clear division of work between the grammar and the dictionary, in practice one gets fluid boundaries and considerable overlapping, which the lexicographer can justify on the grounds of the user's anticipated lack of grammatical competence in the foreign language.

Secondly, the grammatical constructions pose special problems of selection and presentation to do with demarcation between the grammar and the dictionary. However, it is obvious that constructions whose translation follows unproblematically from elementary grammatical (and semantic) rules should not be included in the dictionary — for example an active bilingual dictionary with German as the target language should not provide the information, in entries on verbs, that the verb takes a subject, that this is in the nominative in German, and that the subject of, for example, *denken* must have the semantic feature [+ HUMAN].

Finally, the lexicographer — in consideration of the grammatical competence of the potential users of the dictionary — must make a fundamental decision as to which construction specifications should be selected and presented in the dictionary entries, which should be selected and presented in a separate grammatical component in the dictionary, and which can be taken as known to the users — cf. the examples mentioned above, where the verb's ability to take a subject in the nominative in German is regarded as redundant information in the dictionary entry and can therefore be assigned to expected grammatical knowledge or, alternatively, can be put in a separate grammatical component in the dictionary. At all events, it is necessary in the initial stage of compiling a dictionary to establish the grammatical descriptive apparatus which is to form the basis of the grammatical information in it. In this connection it should be considered whether the dictionary is to be provided with an independent grammatical component, which not only includes morphological tables, but also vital elements of syntax, as practiced, for example, in the van Dale series (see also Kromann 1987).

4. Conclusion: Guidelines for Specifying Constructions

Against the background of the above arguments we can summarize by formulating the following overall guidelines, which can be used in compiling new dictionaries as well as revising existing ones:

(a) *The needs and competence of the users*

The typical needs of the potential dictionary users, and their competence in the foreign language, which, it is true, will be difficult to define in practice, should determine the selection and presentation of construction specifications. The less foreign-language competence the user has, the greater the need for the specification of constructions in the bilingual dictionary.

(b) *The language pair*

The language pair is a determinant of which grammatical or idiosyncratic constructions, as a minimum, should be selected and presented and should thus take priority.

(c) *The function of the dictionary*

The function of the dictionary — monofunctional active or passive, or bifunctional active and passive — should determine the selection and presentation of construction specifications so that, while in the passive dictionary a minimum of syntactic constructions plus nontransparent idiosyncratic constructions will suffice, the active dictionary must exhaustively select and present whatever relevant syntactic and idiosyncratic constructions serve the production of texts in the foreign language.

(d) *Independent grammatical component in the dictionary*

The grammatical description that forms the basis of the description of the vocabulary in the dictionary can be presented (in selected relevant sections) in an independent component in the dictionary and will thus help on the one hand to supplement or reduce information on syntactic constructions in the dictionary entries themselves, and on the other to meet the user's possible need for supplementary (or complementary) syntactic information concerning the constructions, which means that any information that is necessary for the production of texts in the foreign language, and which is implicitly contrastive, should be given priority. The grammatical component will thus reflect the competence in the grammar of the foreign language anticipated by the lexicographer: the less the grammatical competence in the foreign language, the more exhaustive the grammatical component needed in the dictionary itself.

5. Selected Bibliography

5.1. Dictionaries

Collins Pocket 1983 = Collins Pocket German Dictionary. German-English/English-German. London. Glasgow. First Reprint 1983 [1st Ed. 1982. 441 p.].

van Dale 1983 = Groot woordenboek Duits-Nederlands door prof. dr. H. L. Cox (...). Utrecht. Antwerpen 1983 [1576 p.].

Engel/Savin 1983 = Ulrich Engel/Emilia Savin: Valenzlexikon deutsch-rumänisch. Dictionar de valenta german-roman. Heidelberg 1983 (Deutsch im Kontrast 3) [456 p.].

Helbig/Schenkel 1973 = Gerhard Helbig/Wolfgang Schenkel: Wörterbuch zur Valenz und Distribution deutscher Verben. 2. überarbeitete und erweiterte Auflage. Leipzig 1973 [1. Aufl. 1969. 458 p.].

Muret/Sanders = Ernst Muret/Daniel Sanders: Langenscheidts enzyklopädisches Wörterbuch der englischen und deutschen Sprache. Englisch-Deutsch. Teil I, 1—2. Berlin. München. Wien. Zürich 1962—63. Deutsch-Englisch. Teil II, 1—2. Ibid. 1974—75.

Schumacher 1986 = Verben in Feldern. Valenzwörterbuch zur Syntax und Semantik deutscher Verben. Hrsg. Helmut Schumacher. Berlin. New York 1986 [882 p.].

Sommerfeldt/Schreiber 1977a = Karl-Ernst Sommerfeldt/Herbert Schreiber: Wörterbuch zur Valenz und Distribution deutscher Adjektive. 2. überarbeitete Aufl. Leipzig 1977 [1. Aufl. 1974. 435 p.].

Sommerfeldt/Schreiber 1977b = Karl-Ernst Sommerfeldt/Herbert Schreiber: Wörterbuch zur Valenz und Distribution der Substantive. Leipzig 1977 [1. Aufl. 432 p.].

5.2. Other Publications

Al-Kasimi 1978 = Ali M. Al-Kasimi: Linguistics and Bilingual Dictionaries. Leiden 1977.

Bergenholtz 1983 = Henning Bergenholtz: Grammatik im Wörterbuch: Zur Terminologie und zur empirischen Basis. In: Kopenhagener Beiträge zur Germanistischen Linguistik 21. 1983, 70—92.

Bergenholtz 1984 = Henning Bergenholtz: Grammatik im Wörterbuch: Syntax. In: Studien zur neuhochdeutschen Lexikographie V. Hrsg. v. H. E. Wiegand. Hildesheim. Zürich. New York 1984 (Germanistische Linguistik 3—6/84), 1—46.

Bergenholtz/Mugdan 1982 = Henning Bergenholtz/Joachim Mugdan: Grammatik im Wörterbuch: Probleme und Aufgaben. In: Studien zur neuhochdeutschen Lexikographie II. Hrsg. v. H. E. Wiegand. Hildesheim. Zürich. New York 1982, 17—36.

Bergenholtz/Mugdan 1985 = Lexikographie und Grammatik. Akten des Essener Kolloquiums zur Grammatik im Wörterbuch 28.—30. 6. 1984. Hrsg. v. Henning Bergenholtz und Joachim Mugdan. Tübingen 1985 (Lexicographica. Series Maior 3).

Brauße 1987 = Ursula Brauße: Kollokations- und Valenzrelationen. In: Studien zu einem Komplexwörterbuch der lexikalischen Mikro-, Medio- und Makrostrukturen ("Komplexikon"). Linguistische Studien 169/I. 1987, 269—322.

Cowie 1987 = Anthony Cowie (ed.): The Dictionary and the Language Learner. Papers from the EURALEX Seminar at the University of Leeds, 1—3 April 1985. Tübingen 1987 (Lexicographica. Series Maior 17).

Hartmann 1982 = Reinhard R. K. Hartmann: Das zweisprachige Wörterbuch im Fremdsprachenerwerb. In: Studien zur neuhochdeutschen Lexikographie II. Hrsg. v. H. E. Wiegand. Hildesheim. New York 1982, 73—86.

Hartmann 1984 = LEXeter '83 PROCEEDINGS. Papers from the International Conference on Lexicography at Exeter, 9—12 September 1983. Ed. by R. R. K. Hartmann (Lexicographica. Series Maior 1).

Hausmann 1977 = Franz Josef Hausmann: Einführung in die Benutzung der neufranzösischen Wörterbücher. Tübingen 1977 (Romanistische Arbeitshefte 19).

Hausmann 1988 = Franz Josef Hausmann: Grundprobleme des zweisprachigen Wörterbuchs. In: Hyldgaard-Jensen/Zettersten 1988, 137—154.

Hyldgaard-Jensen/Zettersten 1988 = Symposium on Lexicography III. Proceedings of the Third International Symposium on Lexicography, May 14—16 1986 at the University of Copenhagen, by Karl Hyldgaard-Jensen and Arne Zettersten. Tübingen 1988 (Lexicographica. Series Maior 19).

Jørgensen 1982 = Mogens Wied Jørgensen: Die grammatischen Angaben zu den Lemmata in zweisprachigen Wörterbüchern, besonders im Hinblick auf das DTO (Dänisch-Deutsches Wörterbuch). In: Kopenhagener Beiträge zur germanistischen Linguistik 20. 1982, 67—85.

Kromann 1977 = Hans-Peder Kromann: Grammatischer problemkatalog bei der erarbeitung des Dansk-Tysk ordbog (DTO). In: Kopenhagener Beiträge zur germanistischen Linguistik 12. 1977, 162—169.

Kromann 1987 = Hans-Peder Kromann: Zur Syntax im Übersetzungswörterbuch. In: Kopenhagener Beiträge zur germanistischen Linguistik. Sonderband 3. Festschrift für Karl Hyldgaard-Jensen. Kopenhagen 1987, 143—150.

Lemmens/Wekker 1986 = Marcel Lemmens/Herman Wekker: Grammar in English Learner's Dictionaries. Tübingen 1986 (Lexicographica. Series Maior 16).

Rossenbeck 1989 = Klaus Rossenbeck: Lexikologische und lexikographische Probleme fachsprachlicher Phraseologie aus kontrastiver Sicht. In: M. Snell-Hornby/E. Pöhl: Translation and Lexicography. Papers read at the EURALEX-Colloquium held at Innsbruck 2—5 July 1987. Paintbrush. A Journal of Poetry, Translation and Letters. Vol. XVI. August 1989, 197—210.

Sterkenburg/Martin/Al 1982 = P. van Sterkenburg/W. Martin/B. Al: A New van Dale Project: Bilingual dictionaries on one and the same monolingual basis. In: J. Goetschalckx/L. Rolling (eds.): Lexicography in the Electronic Age. Amsterdam 1982, 221—237.

Svensén 1987 = Bo Svensén: Handbok i lexikografi. Principer och metoder i ordboksarbetet. Stockholm 1987 (TNC 85).

Wiegand 1985 = Herbert Ernst Wiegand: Fragen zur Grammatik in Wörterbuchbenutzungsprotokollen. Ein Beitrag zur empirischen Erforschung der Benutzer einsprachiger Wörterbücher. In: Bergenholtz/Mugdan 1985, 20—98.

Zgusta 1971 = Ladislav Zgusta et al.: Manual of Lexicography. The Hague. Paris 1971 (Janua Linguarum. Series Maior 39).

Hans-Peder Kromann/Theis Riiber/Poul Rosbach (†), Copenhagen (Denmark)

287a. Collocations in the Bilingual Dictionary

1. Collocations
2. General Bilingual Dictionaries vs. Specialized Dictionaries of Collocations
3. Explanatory Bilingual Dictionaries
4. Translatory Bilingual Dictionaries
5. Selected Bibliography

1. Collocations

Collocations are affinitive, bipartite lexical combinations which, in terms of the attractive force between their two component parts, can be situated between free combinations and idioms (see Art. 95 and Cop 1990). Incorrect collocations have a comical effect on the NL (native language) receiver while correct ones are accepted as "passwords" to NL fluency in a foreign language (Korosadowicz-Strużyńska 1980, 115). This is why collocations are important units for the language learner. Collocations consist of a base and a collocator which are not on the same hierarchical level, and so they fulfil differing functions in dictionaries (Art. 95, 1010 and Cop 1990). However, the principles that apply to monolingual dictionaries do not apply to bilingual ones, and the bilingual dictionary type determines the role that collocations will play in it. Both Ivir 1988 and Kromann 1989 do not sufficiently distinguish between the role of collocations in mono- and bilingual dictionaries and in general the necessary distinction between the criteria for selection and presentation of collocations in general and specialized collocational dictionaries is not made.

2. General Bilingual Dictionaries vs. Specialized Dictionaries of Collocations

General bilingual dictionaries have a much larger job than just presenting collocations. They aspire to provide information on all linguistic aspects of the languages involved and thus have a complex macro-, medio- and microstructure. Bilingual dictionaries of collocations complement the general bilingual dictionary and thus have a simpler structure. Here, collocations are listed in their role as collocations and need not double in their roles as meaning discriminators (see Jain 1981 on the preference of collocators over synonyms as meaning discriminators in learner's dictionaries), meaning illustrators and examples. The microstructure is not as complicated as that of a general bilingual dictionary, so it can limit itself to supplying a maximum of collocations. Also, the macrostructure can be limited to nouns, verbs, adjectives and adverbs or to one or more of these (Bratus 1979, Bratus 1987 and Ilgenfritz/Stephan-Gabinel/Schneider 1989 have only noun entries, Günther/Förster 1987 have only verb entries supplemented by an index of nouns occurring with the verbs, and Troebes/Christmann 1985 have noun and verb entries). Beinhauer 1978 and Reum 1931 see themselves as writers' dictionaries and therefore add a paradigmatic dimension (synonyms and antonyms) to the syntagmatic one.

3. Explanatory Bilingual Dictionaries

Explanatory (from Russian *tol'kovyj*; German *Erklärungswörterbuch*) bilingual dictionaries are FL-NL dictionaries primarily intended to aid in decoding FL texts when subsequent encoding of the FL text in the NL is not intended (Duda/Frenzel/Wöller/Zimmermann 1986, 5). They are thus primarily concerned with meaning or semasiology. The most convenient means of showing meaning in a FL—NL dictionary is to give a small selection of NL equivalents chosen in their function as "prototypes" rather than insertable equivalents. These "prototypical equivalents" (Neubert 1986, 12—13) replace a clumsier definition. The equivalents in this dictionary thus have the predominantly metalinguistic function of conveying meaning. The chances of a collocation being predictable are smaller than the chances of it being transparent (Hausmann 1988). Therefore only such collocations as are not transparent need be included in this type of dictionary.

4. Translatory Bilingual Dictionaries

There are two types of translatory dictionary: active and passive. Active translatory dictionaries (NL—FL) help produce FL texts based on free or bounded encoding, i.e. writing a FL text or translating a NL text into a FL, while passive dictionaries are FL-NL and aid in translating texts from the foreign into the native language.

Translatory dictionaries (Russian *perevodnye slovarie,* German *Übersetzungswörterbücher*) are explicitly made for producing texts. It thus follows that even transparent collocations must be present because they are not predictable. This is especially true of the active dictionary but also applies to the passive one because it is used to produce texts, albeit NL ones. In translatory dictionaries the equivalents have a double function: not only must they convey meaning, but they must be actually usable in a given text. Here semasiology and onomasiology are combined and the equivalents have both a linguistic and metalinguistic function. When linguistic data belongs to the metalanguage it is logical to give it in the user's NL. When it is part of language it should appear in the target language of the dictionary. In the active dictionary this is the FL while in the passive dictionary it is the NL. This is of fundamental importance when considering the language in which collocations are presented in the bilingual dictionary (see 4.2. below).

4.1. Secondary Dictionary Function

Beyond the dictionary functions described above, looking up a word in the bilingual dictionary, even when it remains a more or less punctual action, almost always has a secondary learning function. Thus, by scanning the meaning structure (German *Mediostruktur*) of a FL—NL or NL—FL collocator entry, the user can gain an impression of its collocational range (for example s.v. **einhalten**; passive dictionary: *einhalten* collocates with *Termin, Spielregeln, Diät, Vertrag* and *Ärmel;* active dictionary: *einhalten* is "meet" when used with *deadline,* but "keep to" when used with *diet* and "gather" when used with *sleeve).* This is of help in anchoring the looked-up element in the user's memory (*einhalten* means "meet" when it occurs with *Termin* but "gather" when it occurs with *Ärmel;* one says *meet (einhalten) a deadline* but *keep to (einhalten) a diet).* This is also beneficial because a collocator realizes its full semantic identity in collocation, i.e. together with the base (Hausmann 1979, 192). This is of interest here because bases are frequently used as glosses for meaning discrimination:

EINHALTEN	(Termin)	meet
	(Spielregeln)	obey
	(Diät, Vertrag)	keep to
	(Ärmel)	gather

The secondary function of the passive dictionary is an active one, i.e. it provides the user with information for later active use of the word he or she has looked up.

4.2. Active Dictionaries

Here, access to FL collocations is only possible via the system of the NL. A German-speaking user wishing to express "finish a task in advance of a set due date" in English could conceivably have no idea at all how to verbalize what he or she wishes to say. This is a case for the thesaurus-type dictionary. Or, the user may think of a collocation such as *den Termin einhalten;* or he or she may only think "there's something with *Termin,* what is it?" Or he or she may know that "Termin" is *deadline* in English and wonder "how do anglophones say "einhalten". Or he or she may think "what do you do to a *deadline?"* The latter is a case for a monolingual L2 dictionary or an L2—L1 general bilingual dictionary (the Dutch Van Dale dictionaries, French-Dutch, English-Dutch and German-Dutch, are very rich in this respect; see e.g. Al 1983), or better yet a specialized collocational bilingual dictionary. If the German user is translating a German text, he or she will know the collocation in German and thus would have the choice of looking under *Termin* or *einhalten.* We thus see that the collocations should ideally be accessible under both base and collocator entries.

Giving the base *(Termin)* in the collocator entry **(einhalten)** serves meaning discrimination in the active dictionary. Because this information is aimed at the native speaker of the dictionary's source language, *Termin* is given in German and not translated. This is a common practice used, for example, in Collins 1981. Yet at the same time a collocation is being given and it should therefore appear entirely in the FL:

EINHALTEN	Termin	to meet a deadline
	Spielregeln	to obey rules
	Diät, Vertrag	to keep to a diet, a contract

Collocators, when given in a base entry, do not contribute so much to the meaning of the base. In the case of **Termin,** collocators show how the equivalent to *Termin* is characteristically contextualized. This too, is important to learning the meaning and range of *deadline:*

TERMIN
~ einhalten meet a deadline
einen ~ setzen set, establish a deadline
einen ~ überschreiten miss a deadline

It thus follows that collocations have important functions in both base and collocator entries as well as active and passive dictionaries. They should thus be accessible in all four. Space-saving devices such as the cross-referencing system suggested by Hausmann 1988 are better avoided.

DEADLINE meet ~ : Termin einhalten
   Termin: see deadline
   Frist: see deadline
   einhalten: see deadline

This procedure would only interfere with clear presentation of the meaning structure of the collocator and inhibit coherence in the general bilingual dictionary articles of both bases and collocators. If redundancy is tolerated in natural language, then it should, at least to some extent, be tolerated in a dictionary of natural language made for human users. Cross-referrencing is better applied to dictionaries of collocations because their structure is less complex and their aim not as multiple as that of a general bilingual dictionary.

5. Selected Bibliography

5.1. Dictionaries

Al 1983 = Bernard P. F. Al (ed.): Van Dale Groot Woordenboek Frans-Nederlands. Utrecht. Antwerpen 1983 [1579 pp.].

Bratus 1979 = Boris Vasil'evič Bratus et al.: Russian word-collocations. Learner's dictionary. Moskva 1979 [367 pp.].

Bratus 1987 = Boris Vasil'evič Bratus et al.: Slovné spojenia ruského jazyka. Ruskoslovensky slovník — príručka pre štúdium ruštiny. Moskva. Bratislava 1987 [373 pp.].

Beinhauer 1978 = Werner Beinhauer: Stilistisch-phraseologisches Wörterbuch spanisch—deutsch. München 1978 [1043 pp.].

Collins 1981 = Peter Terrell/Veronika Calderwood-Schnorr/Wendy V. A. Morris/Roland Breitsprecher: Collins German—English, English—German Dictionary. London. Glasgow. Stuttgart 1981 [XVII, 790 pp.].

Günther/Förster 1987 = Erika Günther/Waldtraut Förster: Wörterbuch verbaler Wendungen Deutsch—Russisch. Eine Sammlung verbal-nominaler Fügungen. Leipzig 1987 [223 pp.].

Ilgenfritz/Stephan-Gabinel/Schneider 1989 = Peter Ilgenfritz/Nicole Stephan-Gabinel/Gertraud Schneider: Langenscheidts Kontextwörterbuch Französisch—Deutsch. Berlin. München. Wien. Zürich. New York 1989 [320 pp.].

Lötzsch 1983 = Ronald Lötzsch et al.: Deutsch-russisches Wörterbuch, begründet von Hans Holm Bielfeldt. Berlin 1983—1984 [Vol. 1: A—G, XXXI, 761 pp. Vol. 2: H—R, 706 pp. Vol. 3: S—Z, 787 pp.].

Reum 1931 = Albrecht Reum: A dictionary of English style. Leipzig 1931 [VIII, 771 pp.].

Troebes/Christmann 1985 = Otto Troebes/Kurt Christmann: Fügungswörterbuch Deutsch—Russisch. Eine Sammlung häufig gebrauchter Wendungen für Wissenschaftler und Studenten. Leipzig 1985 [200 pp.].

5.2 Other Publications

Cop 1990 = Margaret Cop: The function of collocations in dictionaries. In: Tamás Magay/Judit Zigány (eds): BudaLEX '88. Papers from the EURALEX third International Congress in Budapest, September 1988. Budapest 1990.

Duda/Frenzel/Wöller/Zimmermann 1986 = Walter Duda/Marie Frenzel/Egon Wöller/Tatjana Zimmermann: Zu einer Theorie der zweisprachigen Lexikographie. Überlegungen zu einem neuen russisch—deutschen Wörterbuch. Berlin 1986 (Linguistische Studien, Reihe A, Arbeitsberichte 142).

Hausmann 1979 = Franz Josef Hausmann: Un dictionnaire des collocations est-il possible? In: Travaux de linguistique et de littérature 17/1. 1979, 187—195.

Hausmann 1988 = Franz Josef Hausmann: Grundprobleme des zweisprachigen Wörterbuchs. In: Karl Hyldgaard-Jensen/Arne Zettersten (eds): Symposium on Lexicography III. Proceedings of the third International Symposium on Lexicography, May 14—16, 1986 at the University of Copenhagen. Tübingen 1988 (Lexicographica Series Maior 22), 137—154.

Hausmann 1989 = Franz Josef Hausmann: Le dictionnaire de collocations. In: Franz Josef Hausmann/Oskar Reichmann/Herbert Ernst Wiegand/Ladislav Zgusta (eds): Dictionaries. International Encyclopedia of Lexicography. First Volume. Berlin. New York 1989, 1010—1019.

Hausmann 1991 = Franz Josef Hausmann: Collocations in monolingual and bilingual English dictionaries. In: V. Ivir et al. (eds): Languages in contact and contrast. Berlin. New York. 1991, 225—236.

Ivir 1988 = Vladimir Ivir: Collocations in dictionaries, monolingual and bilingual. In: T. L. Burton/Jill Burton (eds): Lexicographical and linguistic studies. Essays in honour of G. W. Turner. Cambridge. Wolfeboro, New Hampshire 1988, 43—50.

Jain 1981 = Mahavir P. Jain: On meaning in the foreign learner's dictionary. In: Applied Linguistics 2. 1981, 109—120.

Korosadowicz-Strużyńska 1980 = Maria Korosadowicz-Strużyńska: Word collocations in FL vocabulary instruction. In: Studia Anglica Posnaniensia 12. 1980, 109—120.

Kromann 1989 = Hans-Peder Kromann: Zur funktionalen Beschreibung von Kollokationen und Phraseologismen in Übersetzungswörterbüchern. In: Gertrud Gréciano (ed.): EUROPHRAS 88. Phraséologie contrastive. Actes du Colloque International Klingenthal-Strasbourg. 12—16 mai 1988. Strasbourg 1989, 65—271.

Neubert 1986 = Albrecht Neubert: Dichtung und Wahrheit des zweisprachigen Wörterbuchs. Berlin 1986 (Sitzungsberichte der sächsischen Akademie der Wissenschaften zu Leipzig, Philologisch-historische Klasse Band 126, Heft 4).

Margaret Cop, Erlangen
(Federal Republic of Germany)

288. Die Komposita im zweisprachigen Wörterbuch

1. Theoretische Voraussetzungen
2. Postulat der optimalen Platzverwendung
3. Frequenz und Transparenz der Komposita als Kriterien für die Aufnahme
4. Typologische Spezifik von Ausgangssprache und Zielsprache eines aktiven Wörterbuchs und Möglichkeiten der Nichtaufnahme von Komposita
5. Adjektivische Äquivalenz des ersten Kompositionsgliedes
6. Übersetzung syntaktischer Auflösungen
7. Einordnung der Komposita
8. Literatur (in Auswahl)

1. Theoretische Voraussetzungen

Ausgangspunkt für die Behandlung der Komposita im zweisprachigen Wörterbuch ist ihre Stellung im grammatischen und lexikalischen System der beiden Sprachen, die im Wörterbuch Ausgangs- und Zielsprache bilden. Dabei ist davon auszugehen, daß die These, die traditionell als „Wort" bezeichnete Phonem- oder Morphemfolge sei die Grundeinheit des Lexikons, in doppelter Hinsicht anfechtbar ist. Einerseits verfügen auch die sog. flektierenden Sprachen, in denen grammatische Beziehungen durch Veränderungen am Wortkörper ausgedrückt werden können, über sog. analytische Formen, die aus mehreren Wörtern bestehen. So setzen sich z. B. die Formen des deutschen Futurs, Perfekts oder Passivs aus finiten Formen eines Hilfsverbs und infiniten Formen eines sog. Vollverbs zusammen. — Andererseits haben in manchen Sprachen — dazu gehören die germanischen und insbesondere das Deutsche (Pavlov 1972) — die Wortzusammensetzungen nicht automatisch den Charakter von Grundeinheiten des Lexikons, obwohl sie unbestreitbar die formalen Merkmale von Wörtern aufweisen. Wörter, Phonem- und Morphemverbindungen mit spezifischen formalen Merkmalen sind demnach grundsätzlich zu unterscheiden von Lexemen, in denen Begriffe sprachlich fixiert sind. Semantisch kann es sich bei Wörtern um Teile von Lexemen (um Bestandteile analytischer Lexemformen oder sog. Mehrwortlexeme), Lexeme oder Lexemverbindungen (Syntagmen) handeln. Den Status von Lexemverbindungen, also von Wortsyntagmen, hätten die in manchen Sprachen ad hoc bildbaren Komposita, deren Bedeutungen genau der Summe der Bedeutungen ihrer Komponenten entspricht und die mit den entsprechenden Mehrwortsyntagmen synonym sind (vgl. z. B. im Deutschen *Holzhaus* mit *hölzernes Haus* bzw. *Haus aus Holz*). — Die Unterscheidung von *Wort* und *Lexem* hat eminent praktische Bedeutung für die Lexikographie. Obwohl deren in Buchform verbreitete Ergebnisse in vielen Sprachen „Wörterbücher" genannt werden, stellen sie entsprechend den Intentionen und/oder Möglichkeiten ihrer Verfasser und/oder der Verlage mehr oder weniger vollständige Verzeichnisse der Lexeme der jeweiligen Sprachen dar. Den Grundstock bilden dabei jene Lexeme, die in formaler Hinsicht auch Wörter sind. Die Mehrwortlexeme erscheinen als „Beispiele" unter den von der einen oder anderen ihrer Komponenten gebildeten Stichwörtern. Viele real existierende Mehrwortlexeme bleiben beim derzeitigen Stand ihrer Erforschung und Erfassung dabei sicher unberücksichtigt. — Die Aufnahme nicht nur aller potentiell bildbaren, sondern auch der in realen Texten verwendeten Komposita in Wörterbücher von Sprachen, für die Wortsyntagmen charakteristisch sind, ist praktisch nicht möglich (vgl. Art. 89). Dies ist auch nicht nötig, denn die Wörterbucheintragungen sollen Lexeme sein. In Sprachen des genannten Typs aber bedürfen Komposita, ebenso wie Mehrwortsyntagmen, der besonderen Lexikalisierung, um den Status von Grundeinheiten des Lexikons zu erlangen.

2. Postulat der optimalen Platzverwendung

In der zweisprachigen Lexikographie ist grundsätzlich zu unterscheiden zwischen passiven und aktiven Wörterbüchern. Dennoch besteht in einer Hinsicht zwischen den beiden Wörterbuchtypen kein wesentlicher Unterschied. Für beide gilt das Primat der optimalen Platzverwendung. Passive Wörterbücher brauchen viel Platz, um möglichst viele Lexeme der Ausgangssprache erfassen zu können. Aktive Wörterbücher können zwar die weniger gebräuchlichen Synonyme, insbesondere Regionalismen und Archaismen, entbehren, benötigen aber um so mehr Platz für die Explizierung der Bedingungen für unterschiedliche Äquivalenz (Lötzsch 1979, 1985). Eine sinnvolle Beschränkung der Aufnahme von Komposita könnte dazu beitragen, den Umfang zweisprachiger Wörterbücher ohne Beeinträchtigung ihrer Informativität zu reduzieren und so ihre Handhabbarkeit zu verbessern.

3. Frequenz und Transparenz der Komposita als Kriterien für die Aufnahme

In bisher angestellten Überlegungen über die Aufnahme von Komposita in zweisprachige Wörterbücher (Møller 1981, 100 ff.; Kromann 1985, 408) spielten sowohl ihre Frequenz als auch ihre Transparenz eine Rolle. Møller hat darauf hingewiesen, daß die Aufnahme von Komposita nach ihrer Frequenz „ein unsicherer Faktor" sei, zumal gezielte Frequenzuntersuchungen fehlten. Kromann plädiert für die Anwendung folgender „Transparenzregel": „die Elemente der Zusammensetzung behalten bei der syntaktischen Auflösung ihre Bedeutung bei, d. h. die Bedeutung der Zusammensetzung kann aus den Bestandteilen erschlossen werden". Solche Komposita, also Wortsyntagmen nach der hier verwendeten Terminologie, könnten im „passiven Taschenwörterbuch" weggelassen werden. Diese Auffassung erscheint plausibel. Hinzuzufügen ist, daß zweisprachige Wörterbücher im Interesse ihrer Handhabbarkeit generell nur einbändig sein sollten, auch solche, deren Verfasser den allgemeinen Wortschatz des bearbeiteten Sprachenpaares möglichst vollständig aufzunehmen bestrebt sind. (Daß dies machbar ist, beweist insbesondere die Serie „Woordenboeken voor hedendaags taalgebruik" des Verlags van Dale, z. B. Cox 1983 und 1986).

4. Typologische Spezifik von Ausgangssprache und Zielsprache eines aktiven Wörterbuchs und Möglichkeiten der Nichtaufnahme von Komposita

Bei der Erarbeitung aktiver zweisprachiger Wörterbücher kann es nicht nur um die Abgrenzung von Syntaktischem und Lexikalischem gehen. Über die Aufnahme oder Nichtaufnahme eines Kompositums, das in der Ausgangssprache den Charakter eines Wortsyntagmas hat, muß letztlich die Äquivalenz in der Zielsprache entscheiden. Selbst wenn zwei Sprachen hinsichtlich der Möglichkeiten der Wortkomposition annähernd den gleichen Typ vertreten, können sich die Verfasser eines Wörterbuchs, in dem Sprachen dieses Typs sowohl als Ausgangs- als auch als Zielsprache figurieren, nicht einfach damit begnügen, lediglich die unter Umständen spezifischen Formen der Erstglieder von Komposita (vgl. z. B. deutsche Ableitungen von Feminina mit Fugen-*s* des Typs *Arbeits-, Gesellschafts-* usw.) anzugeben.

Welche Schwierigkeiten sich beispielsweise bei der Arbeit an einem dänisch-deutschen Wörterbuch ergeben, machen die diesbezüglichen Überlegungen von Møller (1981, 100 ff.) deutlich. Immerhin ist ein Artikeltyp *skole/- Schul/-* vorgesehen, in dem das dänische erste Kompositionsglied als Stichwort und das deutsche als Äquivalent figurieren und der als „Generierungsmuster" dienen soll. Es liegt auf der Hand, daß die Einführung eines solchen „Generierungsmusters" die Aufnahme der meisten Wortsyntagmen mit dem Erstglied *skole-* überflüssig machen dürfte. In van Dales „Groot woordenboek Nederlands-Duits" (Cox 1986), das für Sprecher des Niederländischen bestimmt ist und somit als aktives Wörterbuch konzipiert sein sollte, wird dagegen zwischen lexikalisierten Komposita und Wortsyntagmen keinerlei Unterschied gemacht. Es enthält sogar zahlreiche Artikel, in denen sich das deutsche Äquivalent vom niederländischen Stichwort lediglich auf der phonologischen Ebene, nicht aber semantisch oder morphologisch unterscheidet.

Unvergleichlich größer sind die Schwierigkeiten, wenn die Möglichkeiten der Wortkomposition in der Zielsprache stark eingeschränkt sind. So verwenden beispielsweise die slawischen Standardsprachen die Wortkomposition praktisch nur zur Bildung von Fachtermini. Den syntaktischen Substantivkomposita germanischer Sprachen stehen hier entweder freie Lexemverbindungen gegenüber, in denen dem Erstglied der Ausgangssprache eine Kasusform des substantivischen Äquivalents mit oder ohne Präposition bzw. ein von dem substantivischen Äquivalent abgeleitetes Beziehungsadjektiv entspricht. Äquivalent des Kompositums kann auch eine Ableitung sein, in der gleichsam dem Zweitglied des Stichworts ein Derivationssuffix entspricht. Diese spezifischen Äquivalenzen müssen explizit signalisiert werden, gerade auch im Falle der Nichtaufnahme eines Kompositums. Nicht vertreten werden kann m. E. auch bei solchen Sprachenpaaren die Aufnahme möglichst vieler Wortsyntagmen als Stichwörter. Dies ist aber die bisher geübte Praxis, wie die vorliegenden Wörterbücher mit einer germanischen Ausgangs- und einer slawischen Zielsprache beweisen. Auch in das dreibändige „Deutsch-Russische Wörterbuch" des Akademie-Verlags Berlin (Lötzsch 1983/84), das als konsequent aktives Wörterbuch konzipiert ist, wurden entschieden zu viele Wortsyntagmen aufgenommen, deren russische Äquivalente genau ihrer syntaktischen Struktur entsprechen. Dabei bestehen m. E. auch dann gewisse Möglichkeiten, die Anzahl der als Stichwörter aufzunehmenden Komposita zu reduzieren, wenn eine Sprache slawischen Typs als Zielsprache figuriert.

5. Adjektivische Äquivalenz des ersten Kompositionsgliedes

Wenn einem syntaktischen Kompositum der Ausgangssprache in der Zielsprache eine attributive Verbindung mit Beziehungsadjektiv entspricht und mehrere Komposita mit dem gleichen Erstglied ein Äquivalent mit dem gleichen Adjektiv aufweisen, erscheint es sinnvoll, das Erstglied als Stichwort aufzunehmen und ihm das Adjektiv als Äquivalent beizugeben. Soweit das Stichwort in dem Sinne monosem ist, daß es nur ein Äquivalent besitzt (eine im Stichwort und Äquivalent gleichermaßen vorhandene Polysemie könnte vernachlässigt werden) und keinerlei Lexikalisierungen vorliegen, wäre dies der ganze Artikel. Dieser Fall ist jedoch äußerst selten. Dennoch kommt er gelegentlich vor.

So könnte z. B. ein aktives deutsch-russisches Wörterbuch einen Artikel enthalten, in dem das Stichwort *Backstein-* als Äquivalent lediglich das von кирпи́ч 'Backstein' abgeleitete Adjektiv кирпи́чный hätte. Daß die Struktur eines Artikels mit dem Erstglied eines Kompositums als Stichwort in der Regel komplizierter ist, zeigt ein Vergleich mit den Komposita, die als Erstglied das mit *Backstein-* teilsynonyme *Ziegel-* aufweisen. Es geht dabei nicht nur um die Polysemie 'Backstein' : 'Dachziegel', die sich entsprechend der denkbaren asymmetrischen Struktur eines Artikels *Ziegel* кирпи́ч ... *Dachziegel* черепи́ца unter Verwendung einer auf diese Sememgliederung verweisenden Klammerung etwa folgendermaßen darstellen ließe: *Ziegel-* кирпи́чный [черепи́чный]. Diese Beziehungsadjektive kämen also normalerweise als Äquivalente von *Ziegel-* mit der Bedeutung 'aus Ziegeln gebaut', 'mit Ziegeln gedeckt' in Frage. Komposita wie *Ziegeldach, Ziegelhaus, Ziegelmauer* usw. brauchten also nicht ins Wörterbuch aufgenommen zu werden. (Es ist bezeichnend, daß sich Cox 1986 mit der Aufnahme des Adjektivs *bakstenen* begnügt, wobei als Äquivalente neben den syntaktischen Auflösungen *aus Back-, Ziegelstein* die Kompositionsglieder *Backstein-, Ziegelstein-, Ziegel-* angegeben werden. Anderseits geht aus Cox 1983 hervor, daß Wortsyntagmen mit *baksteen-* als Erstglied kaum seltener sein dürften als deutsche mit *Backstein-, Ziegel-*.) — In manchen Fällen wirken sich die semantischen Unterschiede zwischen den syntaktischen Auflösungen eines Erstgliedes auf die im Prinzip auch hier mögliche adjektivische Äquivalenz aus. *Gold-* z. B. kann bedeuten 'aus Gold bestehend', 'aus Gold gemacht', 'vergoldet', 'goldig schimmernd'. In den ersten beiden Bedeutungen entspräche ihm im Russischen das Adjektiv золото́й, in der dritten золочёный, in der vierten золоти́стый. All dies müßte in einem Artikel *Gold-* berücksichtigt werden. Ähnliche Probleme entstünden bei der Aufnahme eines Artikels *Glas-* mit adjektivischer Äquivalenz. Der allgemeinen Bedeutung 'eine Beziehung zu Glas besitzend' entspräche im Russischen стеко́льный, dann kämen стекля́нный 'aus Glas hergestellt' und застеклённый 'verglast'. — Bei extrem polysemen Erstgliedern könnte sich eine pragmatische Lösung als zweckmäßig erweisen, bei der eine einzige, besonders produktive und hinsichtlich ihrer Äquivalenz einheitliche Bedeutungsvariante ausgeworfen wird. Als Beispiel sei nur *Holz-* genannt, das, auch wenn man von den Bedeutungen 'Wald', 'Holzblasinstrumente', 'Kegel' absieht, im Russischen fünf verschiedene Äquivalente besitzt. Sie alle kommen in den Äquivalenten der Wortsyntagmen mit *Holz-* vor, namentlich als Grundwörter adjektivischer Ableitungen, in Fachtermini auch als Erstglieder von Komposita. *Holz-* in der Bedeutung 'aus Holz hergestellt' kann dagegen stets mit den Adjektiv деревя́нный wiedergegeben werden (in Lötzsch 1983/84, 56 Beispiele). Auch die Auswerfung eines einzigen Semems *Holz-* 'aus Holz hergestellt' wäre also sinnvoll. — Auch ein auf maximale Platzersparnis orientiertes aktives Wörterbuch müßte die syntaktischen Komposita enthalten, deren Äquivalenz vom Normaltyp abweicht. In einem Artikel *Ziegel-* eines deutsch-russischen Wörterbuchs beträfe dies z. B. *Ziegelbrenner,* dessen Äquivalente suffixale Ableitungen (кирпи́чник, черепи́чник) sind.

6. Übersetzung syntaktischer Auflösungen

Komposita, deren Äquivalente die genaue Übersetzung ihrer syntaktischen Auflösungen darstellen, brauchen grundsätzlich nicht aufgenommen zu werden. Bei der Wiedergabe im Russischen z. B. gilt dies nicht nur für mehrere Typen zusammengesetzter Substantive, sondern auch für Komposita anderer Lexemklassenzugehörigkeit. Zu nennen sind hier insbesondere Komposita, deren Grundwort ein Nomen agentis oder Nomen actionis ist und deren Erstglied mit einem „Genitivus obiektivus" korrespondiert. Das Äquivalent von *Ziegelformer* bzw. *Feuerbekämpfung* wäre dementsprechend 'Former von Ziegeln' und 'Kampf mit dem Feuer'. Gleiches hätte für mit einer Quantifikation synonyme Komposita zu gelten. Äquivalent von *Goldklumpen* wäre also die Übersetzung von 'Klumpen Gold'. Weiter gehören hierher zusammengesetzte Adjektive, deren Erstglieder die Gegenstände benennen, mit deren Eigenschaften die vom Grundwort bezeichnete verglichen wird. Die Äquivalente von *bärenstark, bienenfleißig, bleischwer, eselgrau, glashart* wären also Syntagmen des Typs 'stark wie ein Bär', 'fleißig wie eine Biene', 'schwer wie Blei', 'grau wie ein Esel', 'hart wie Glas'. — Für alle jene Fälle, in denen dem Wörterbuchbenutzer zugemutet wird, die syntaktischen Äquivalente für Komposita selbst bilden zu müssen, ist eine entsprechende Anleitung in den Benutzerhinweisen erforderlich. Außerdem müßten die Artikel, in denen die als Kompositionsglieder in Frage kommenden Lexeme dargestellt werden, die Voraussetzungen dafür bieten, daß die Äquivalente für nicht aufgenommene Komposita wirklich gebildet werden können.

7. Einordnung der Komposita

Da nicht nur die echte Lexeme darstellenden Komposita, sondern auch die syntaktischen mit vom Normaltyp abweichender Äquivalenz ins Wörterbuch aufgenommen werden müssen, ergibt sich die Frage, ob sie Bestandteil des Artikels sein sollten, in dem das Erstglied abgehandelt wird. Dafür spräche, daß auch die Mehrwortlexeme nicht als gesonderte Lemmata ausgeworfen werden und daß manche Komposita kontextbedingt sowohl Wortsyntagmen als auch Lexeme sein können. Dagegen spräche die Tatsache, daß viele Kompositaartikel einen zu großen Umfang annehmen würden. Denkbar wäre eine pragmatische Lösung, bei der Komposita mit komplexerer Semantik und/oder Äquivalenz besondere Lemmata bilden.

8. Literatur (in Auswahl)

8.1. Wörterbücher

Cox u. a. 1983 = Groot woordenboek Duits-Nederlands door prof. dr. H. L. Cox in samenwerking met prof. drs. F. C. M. Stoks, lic. F. Beersmans, dr. D. Otten, dr. W. de Cubber. Utrecht. Antwerpen 1983 [1576 S.].

Cox u. a. 1986 = Groot woordenboek Nederlands-Duits door prof. dr. H. L. Cox in samenwerking met prof. drs. F. C. M. Stoks, lic. F. Beersmans, drs. G. A. van de Garde, dr. J. van Megen, dr. D. Otten. Utrecht. Antwerpen 1986 [1560 S.].

Lötzsch u. a. 1983/1984 = Deutsch-Russisches Wörterbuch. Begründet von Hans Holm Bielfeldt. In der Endfassung erarbeitet von einem Autorenkollektiv unter der Leitung von Ronald Lötzsch. 3 Bde. Berlin 1983—1984 [XXXI, 761, 706, 787 S.].

8.2. Sonstige Literatur

Kromann 1985 = Hans-Peder Kromann: Die zweisprachige Lexikographie: ein Stiefkind der Germanisten. In: Kontroversen, alte und neue. Akten des VII. Kongresses der Internationalen Vereinigung für germanische Sprach- und Literaturwissenschaft. Hrsg. v. A. Schöne. Band 3. Tübingen 1985, 407—409.

Lötzsch 1979 = Ronald Lötzsch: Einige Fragen der Entwicklung der zweisprachigen Lexikographie an der AdW der DDR. In: Zeitschrift für Slawistik 24. 1979, 402—408.

Lötzsch 1985 = Ronald Lötzsch: Zur Konzeption und zu den Probeartikeln des „Deutsch-obersorbischen Wörterbuches". In: Lětopis (Jahresschrift des Instituts für sorbische Volksforschung) A, 32/2. 1985, 121—126.

Møller 1981 = Elisabeth Møller: Die Arbeit am DTO (Dansk-Tysk Ordbog). In: Kopenhagener Beiträge zur Germanistischen Linguistik 17. 1981, 94—109.

Pavlov 1972 = Vladimir M. Pavlov: Die substantivische Zusammensetzung im Deutschen als syntaktisches Problem. München 1972.

Ronald Lötzsch, Berlin
(Bundesrepublik Deutschland)

289. Examples in the Bilingual Dictionary

1. Synopsis
2. Preliminaries
3. The Definition, Make-Up, and Proper Use of Examples
4. Exemplification by Other Means Than Formal Examples
5. Selected Bibliography

1. Synopsis

This article falls into three main sections:
    (1) A review of critical utterances on examples, and of the way they function in a number of bilingual dictionaries, leading up to the formal definition of *example* used below.

(2) A definition of *example* as we intend to use the term, comments on the differences between examples, glosses, and sub-entries, suggestions for the proper use and functions of examples in bilingual dictionaries, and proposals on the language in which examples should be given.

(3) A discussion of other types of verbal illustrative material not covered by our formal definition.

2. Preliminaries

2.1. Earlier Points of View

Under this head two questions may be raised: what is an example? and how should examples be used? But however pertinent these questions may seem, we have not really come across any systematic answers. — Zgusta 1971, 263 ff. states — about monolingual dictionaries — that "The purpose of the example is to show how the entry-word functions in combination with other lexical units"; — and about the bilingual dictionary entry he says (Zgusta 1971, 337) that "there is a considerable amount of overlapping between glosses and examples." — Al-Kasimi 1983 is silent on the exact nature of the example in contrast to other forms of explanatory matter in the dictionary, while Bergenholtz 1984 draws a useful distinction between explicit, half-explicit and implicit information, true examples obviously belonging in the last category. — Zöfgen 1986, discussing monolingual learners' dictionaries, draws a distinction between made-up examples and authentic quotations — a distinction which as we shall see is not very relevant for modern bilingual dictionaries. Further he observes that using examples is the best way of throwing light on syntax. He suggests 4 different ways in which this may be done: (a) by giving indications of grammatical properties, (b) through the use of collocations and (c) lemmatized collocations of high frequency, plus (d) by introducing clauses and phrases containing (a) + (b) or (c) as implicit information. He himself recognizes only (b) and (d) as true examples; for reasons that will appear we intend to be even more restrictive, recognizing only members of category (d) as examples.

The dictionaries themselves are not very helpful. We agree with Zöfgen 1986 that most comments on "examples" in the prefaces to bilingual dictionaries are mere casual remarks ("Randbemerkungen"). A few instances: Svensk-engelsk Fackordbok 1977 does not distinguish between examples and what it calls *phrases*. Gyldendal's small German-Danish dictionary (= Gyldendals blå ordbøger T-D 1980) proposes using examples to indicate TL word-classes. VB 1976 uses the word *eksempel* both about SL-phrases to be illustrated and about asterisked TL-phrases without any SL equivalent, and uses the terms *example* and *combination* (of words) interchangeably. Several other bilingual dictionaries that we have examined do not comment on the category *example* at all and do not appear to have any clear conception of what examples are or ought to be. — These are just some instances of the more general problem of terminology in bilingual lexicography. For a critical discussion of this, see Manley/Jacobsen/Pedersen 1988.

2.2. Towards a Definition of the Term *Example*

There are two main reasons why the term *example* should be considered as a strictly formal category in the microstructure of the bilingual dictionary: (1) As we have seen, the term has been used very loosely in the literature. This is primarily due to its wide range of reference in normal language. For instance, it is true in a sense to say that everything in a bilingual dictionary that is not the headword or explicit metalinguistic information exemplifies the use of the headword or its translation equivalents. Therefore lexicographers tend to use *example* vaguely when referring to sub-entries (idioms, collocations and other syntagms with their translation equivalents). This situation is largely due to the historical dependence of bilingual dictionaries on the content and categories of monolingual dictionaries, in which there is considerably more justification for seeing sub-entries as exemplifications of the headword. In bilingual dictionaries, however, the majority of sub-entries provide one-to-one translation equivalents. They *exemplify* nothing. A related problem is the fact that there is no distinction between *examples* which truly exemplify (in the sense that one can generalize from them) and those that present instances of contexts in which the word in question can be used, but from which one cannot generalize.

(2) Examples proper, as defined below, are multifunctional. Functionally, they overlap with many of the *explicit* categories of information provided in the entry (glosses, meaning discrimination, syntactic/stylistic/cultural/encyclopaedic information). Furthermore, examples can provide several of

these types of information at once. Inasmuch as one of the chief functions of examples is to provide information about the collocational force of a headword or translation equivalent, they also overlap functionally with sub-entries (i.e. formal units consisting of an SL-phrase and its translation equivalent). Clearly, one of the main considerations must therefore be: when does one use a formal sub-entry? when a gloss? when a formal example? when does one give two, or all three of these categories? Since examples cannot be defined in terms of *function*, they must be defined *formally* before we can even begin to make such a decision.

Our use of the term *example*, then, is not based on the ordinary language *meaning* of the word *example*; nor can it be functionally defined in terms of the type of information it provides; it follows from this that it is not (meta)linguistically defined in terms of the linguistic categories (syntax, semantics, morphology) involved. One cannot, for instance, distinguish between an *example* and an *idiom*, as *idiom* is a lexicological category, whereas an example is a formal category in the dictionary entry. Our use of *example* is based on the internal requirements of the entry: it is a lexicographical category. (We use *lexicographical* of the formal categories — the slots on the dictionary page for the insertion of information — in contrast to *lexicological* categories used to distinguish between e.g. idioms, collocations, and free syntagms).

3. The Definition, Make-Up, and Proper Use of Examples

We therefore define *example* as a supplement to a translation equivalent, providing implicit information about the equivalent or headword. To be even more precise, the example provides information about the equivalent insofar as it enters into the same range of contexts as the headword, while in some cases it provides information about the headword insofar as it can be translated by a given equivalent. In other words, in a dictionary entry on the Danish word *fast*, we have among the simple equivalents in the head of the entry "[...] firm (fx it is my firm conviction) [...]". This consists, clearly, of an *equivalent* and a *supplementary example*. Later in the entry we have a *sub-entry*: "[...] *en fast abonnent* a regular subscriber (fx to a paper) [...]". This consists, in our terminology, of a *sub-lemma* (*en fast abonnent*), an *equivalent* (*a regular subscriber*), and an *example* (fx to a paper). — *En fast abonnent* is not present in the entry to exemplify the use of the word *fast*, as it might be in a monolingual dictionary, but to show how the phrase *en fast abonnent* is translated. The *example* is the part (to a paper) from which we can generalize.

3.1. Distinctions Between Examples and Other Categories

As an illustration of the above, consider the following extract from VB 1976:

> **samfund** *et pl d. s.* 1 *(det borgerlige ~ som begreb)* society (fx he is an enemy of s.); *(enkelt konkret ~)* community (fx the c. in which he lived); 2 *(tros-)* (religious) society (fx the S. of Friends; Methodist societies); (religious) community (fx the Jewish c.); communion (fx belong to the same c.); denomination (fx Christians of many denominations); 3 *(forening)* association, society, league; 4 *(rel: i Gud)* communion; *(rel: med Gud)* fellowship; 5 *(biol)* society (fx of beavers, of bees); *-et* (1) society, the community, the social system;
> *som danner ~ (biol)* social (fx animals, trees); *-ets dyb se I. dyb; de helliges ~* the Communion of Saints; *individet og -et* the individual and the community; *det menneskelige ~* human society; *»det rige ~«* the Affluent Society; *-ets stedbørn* the underprivileged, those not favoured by fortune; *-ets støtter* the pillars of society; *de troendes ~* the congregation; *-ets udskud* the dregs of society; *-ets vel* the public welfare (el. weal), the common good;
> [*forb med præp*] *de små i -et* the humbler members of the community; *være (, komme) på kant med -et* have offended against the laws of society; have got on the wrong side of the law; be a (social) misfit; *pligt* **over for** *-et* (1) social duty; duty towards the community; ☆ *(bibl)* the communion of the Holy Ghost be with you all.

Dictionary excerpt 288.1: Dictionary entry (from VB 1976 II., 270)

This section can be analysed as follows:

———— (1) ————
samfund *et pl d.s.* 1 *(det borgerlige — som begreb)*
—·(2) – ———— (3) ————
society (fx he is an enemy of s.); *(enkelt konkret -)*
community (fx the c. in which he lived); 2 *(tros-)*
—— (4) ——
(religious) society (fx the S. of Friends; Methodist
societies); (religious) community (fx the Jewish c.);
communion (fx belong to the same c.); denomination (fx Christians of many denominations); 3
—— (5) ————   ———— (6) ———— —— (7) ——
(forening) association, society, league; 4 *(rel: i Gud)*
————————————————————— – (8) -
communion; *(rel: med Gud)* fellowship; 5 *(biol)* society (fx of beavers, of bees); *-et* (1) society, the community, the social system;

——————— (9) ———————
som danner — *(biol)* social (fx animals, trees); *-ets dyb se I. dyb; de helliges* — the Communion of Saints; *individet og -et* the individual and the community; *det menneskelige* — human society; *"det rige* —*"* the Affluent Society; *-ets stedbørn* the underprivileged, those not favoured by fortune;
——— (10) ———
-ets støtter the pillars of society; *de troendes* — the congregation; *-ets udskud* the dregs of society; *-ets vel* the public welfare (*el.* weal), the common good; */forb med præp/ de små i -et* the humbler members of the community; *være (,komme) på kant med -et* have offended against the laws of society; have got on the wrong side of the law; be a (social)
——— (11) ———
misfit; *pligt over for -et* (1) social duty; duty to-
——————— (12) ———
wards the community; * *(bibl)* the communion of the Holy Ghost be with you all.

Item (1) has been called a *gloss*, a *definition*, *meaning discrimination*, an *indicator*, a *label*, an *explanation*, etc. Item (2) has been called a *translation*, an *equivalent*, and even a *definition*. Item (3) has been called an *illustration*, a *collocator* or an *example*. It is what we call an example. Item (4) we consider to be part of an *equivalent*, but it has also been called a type of *gloss*. Item (5) has been called a *gloss* and all the other terms for Item (1) above, but it has also been called a *synonym* (as the word it contains can be regarded as a synonym of the headword). The words in Item (6) have also been called *synonyms* of the first equivalent. Item (7), a whole "sense" of the headword according to this dictionary, has been called a *semantic subdivision*, a *sub-entry*, a *meaning*, etc. Item (8) (*biol*, for "biological") has been called a *gloss* or a *label*. — Moving to the next section of the entry, dealing with phrases of various kinds, Item (9) has been called an *example*, a *set phrase*, an *idiom*, a *collocation*, a *multi-word lexical unit*, a *sub-entry*. This unit also contains an *equivalent*. Items (10), (11) and (12) have all been called by the same names as Item (9).

The reader who is not familiar with Danish may object that he or she is in no position to judge how many, if any, of these terms can reasonably be applied. It is precisely one of the points we are making that this should be irrelevant. We should have terms for the components of the entry that do not make any assumptions about their contents or the lexicological status of the words concerned in the source language. Obviously, there are many different names for the same thing. As far as different categories with the same name are concerned, we have *gloss* used of Items (1), (4), (5) and (8); *definition* of Items (1) and (2); *synonym* of (5) and (6); *example* of (3), (9), (10), (11) and (12); and *sub-entry* of Items (7) and (9). — *Synonym* in the sense of Item (5) belongs to a different broad type from *synonym* in the sense of Item (6); *gloss* in Items (1), (5) and (8) to a different category from *gloss* in Item (4); *example* in the sense of Item (9) contains an example in the sense of Item (3), and so on. — The moral that we draw from this terminological confusion is that we need precise, formal lexicographical (rather than lexicological, functional or semantic) definitions of terms like example, gloss, and sub-entry.

To round off these observations on the ambiguity of terms, we would like to enlarge on our definition of *example,* and to discuss the use of examples in different types of bilingual dictionaries. We have suggested that the use of the term *example* for what we have defined as *sub-lemmas* is based on techniques taken over from the monolingual dictionary. Phrases containing the headword are included in the monolingual dictionary to illustrate the use of the headword in special contexts. Whether *idioms* containing the headword illustrate anything about the headword is a moot point, even in the monolingual dictionary, except when it is a historical dictionary, which illustrates the diachronic *development* of idioms. The purpose of sub-lemmas in the bilingual dictionary, however, is to index phrases in the source language conveniently and allow for the provision of equivalents in the target language. It is the equivalents that may need exemplifying, not the headword. Therefore a sub-lemma and its equivalent should as far as possible be given in a "canonical" form. But sometimes one may also wish to *exemplify* the use of the equivalent, and this is what *examples* should be used for. The extent to which this should be done depends on the type and size of the dictionary in question. Obviously large dictionaries have room for more examples than small ones. But equally important is the type of dictionary involved. So-called *active* dictionaries, which we prefer to call *encoding* dictionaries (cf. Manley/Jacobsen/Pedersen 1988) as they go from the language of the user to the foreign language, do not need exemplification of SL lemmas and sub-lemmas, since the competent dictionary user may be supposed to be able to furnish such examples himself. *Passive* or *decoding* dictionaries, since they go from the foreign language to the language of the user, either do not need examples at all in our sense, or in some cases need a rather more subtle kind of example — a type whose function is more difficult to describe.

As an illustration, consider the following from KN 1981: "**cross** [. . .] gå over (fx *the street, a bridge, the frontier*); [. . .]". Superficially, the examples here seem to be illustrating the headword. Does this invalidate our definition of *example* as a supplement to the equivalent? In terms of sheer physical position in the entry, obviously not; since this placing could be an arbitrary decision. The essential point is that the examples do not primarily illustrate the "use" of the headword. They are there to show *in what circumstances* the headword may be translated by the equivalent *gå over*. They are thus still essentially supplementary to the equivalent.

As for the large group of combined encoding and decoding dictionaries that exist in the real rather than the ideal world, they must be treated as encoding dictionaries, and be furnished with examples. — We can best illustrate what we mean by citing a dictionary which does not use the technique of exemplifying the equivalent described above. Collins E-G/G-E 1981 deals with the sub-lemma *lock, stock and barrel* as follows (s.v. *lock*):

> *he offered me the house —, stock and barrel* er bot mir das Haus mit allem Drum und Dran an (*inf*); *they destroyed it —, stock and barrel* sie haben es total zerstört; *to condemn sth —, stock and barrel* etw in Grund und Boden verdammen; *they rejected the idea —, stock and barrel* sie lehnten die Idee in Bausch und Bogen ab; *he swallowed my story —, stock and barrel* er hat mir die Geschichte voll und ganz abgenommen; *it is finished —, stock and barrel* es ist ganz und gar fertig."

This gives an excellent selection of the contexts in which *lock, stock and barrel* and its equivalents can be used. Compared with Harrap F and E 1982, for example, it is obviously more useful to the user. The latter dictionary has: "[. . .] 1. *lock, stock and barrel,* tout sans exception; tout le fourbi [. . .]" — i.e. it provides a couple of general "canonical" equivalents without illustrating either the usage of the sub-lemma or the equivalents. What it gains in economy of space, it loses in usefulness. — The Collins E-G/G-E 1981 entry, however, involves a lot of repetition. It establishes the "canonicity" of *lock, stock and barrel* by a commutative process. Only the idiom itself is common to all the "examples". For in the case of the Collins entry, the "sub-lemmas" combine the functions of what we call sub-lemmas and examples.

The logic of our approach would be as follows: in an encoding dictionary, only the equivalents need exemplification. We would thus give the canonical form *lock, stock and barrel,* followed by as many equivalents as possible, *with examples where necessary of the use of the equivalents*. The examples of the use of the equivalents would be untranslated, as there would be nothing particularly idiosyncratic about anything except the equivalents themselves. In a decoding dictionary, of course, the situation is more complex (cf. this section above). — Our version of the Collins E-G/G-E 1981 entry (assuming that we used all the same exemplifying material) would thus look something like this:

> [. . .] *lock, stock and barrel* mit allem Drum und Dran (*e.g.* er bot mir das Haus mit a. D. u. D. an); total (*e.g.* sie haben es t. zerstört); in Grund und Boden (*e.g.* etw in G. u. B. verdammen); in Bausch und Bogen (*e.g.* sie lehnten die Idee in B. u. B. ab); voll und ganz (*e.g.* er hat mir die Geschichte v. u. g. abgenommen); ganz und gar (*e.g.* es ist g. u. g. fertig) [. . .].

This gives the English-speaking user the canonical form of the equivalents; it takes up less space; and it provides the user with almost as much information as the other version. What it lacks is the English version of the non-canonical parts of the examples. But the examples should be chosen so as to pose no problems for anyone with a basic knowledge of the target language. In any case, the user *has* a sentence he wants to translate. What interests him is how to translate *lock, stock and barrel*. The other parts of his sentence he either knows how to translate already, or will have to look up anyway. The chances that the *examples* will include precisely the sentence he wants are minimal. Their function should therefore be to demonstrate, using the simplest possible forms of the target language, the syntactic and contextual behaviour of the equivalent. Nothing in the examples apart from the equivalent itself should be idiosyncratic.

It should now be clear why we advocate a formal distinction between *sub-lemmas* and *examples*. Rather simplistically stated, sub-lemmas should be items of *langue,* and examples should be items of *parole.*

3.2. When to Use Examples

When considering whether to use an example or one of the other formal lexicographical categories (sub-entry or gloss), there are three interrelated factors to take into account:

(1) degree of idiosyncrasy
(2) amount of information
(3) "true" or "false" exemplification (basis for generalization).

The *degree of idiosyncrasy* of a syntagm can be seen as its position on a scale going from idioms where none of the elements are replaceable (*once in a blue moon,* which exhibits complete idiosyncrasy) through more flexible idioms (where, for example, syntactic features can be altered) via relatively frequent collocations to completely free syntagms (cf. Pedersen 1986). The fact that there are all sorts of gradations on this scale, and that it may be difficult to place a syntagm exactly, does not preclude its intuitive usefulness. Obviously, a completely idiosyncratic syntagm is more suitable for presentation as a sub-entry (sub-lemma + a translation equivalent which is as far as possible a corresponding fixed syntagm in the TL) than as an *example.*

The *amount of information* is a matter of how many features of the word or syntagm concerned can be conveyed by a well-chosen example compared with the space that would be taken up by an explicit formulation of these features. Examples, if judiciously selected, can demonstrate collocational, stylistic, syntactic, morphological, and cultural features of words and phrases.

The Danish word *dask* is, among other things, a slang term for one Danish krone. If the relevant part of the entry on *dask* in a Danish-English dictionary reads: "**dask** [. . .] bob (fx it cost me ten bob) [. . .]" — the example tells the user that *bob* is used with numerals, that it has no -*s* in the plural, and that it is used in a conversational context. This is of course reinforced by the fact that the Danish user knows how *dask* is used. A great deal of information is conveyed which would take up a lot of space if stated explicitly.

The distinction between "true" and "false" examples is based on how far one can generalize from a given example. If we were to give s.v. *ivrig* in a Danish-English dictionary the equivalent: "[. . .] avid (fx reader) [. . .]" we would be giving a "false" example. *Reader* is one of the few words (if not the only one) that can be used with an attributive *avid.* By giving an example of this form one is also giving the implicit information that the user is free to generalize. Even if the word can be extended to other contexts, how is one to generalize? You cannot be *an * avid diner-out, philanderer,* etc. In VB 1976 we find s.v. *dækning*: "[. . .] coverage (fx insurance coverage, news coverage) [. . .]". If we added *press* and *media* coverage, that would more or less have exhausted the collocational possibilities of *coverage* in this sense. This would have been better dealt with by means of a gloss (whereas the *avid* example approaches an idiom and should have been a sub-entry). The greater the extent to which one can generalize, then, the more justification there is for an example rather than a sub-entry. As mentioned earlier in this section, the three criteria are interrelated. A non-idiosyncratic example enabling the user to generate free syntagms provides more information than a sub-entry giving an idiom + equivalent, and more of a basis for generalization.

3.3. Should Examples Be Translated?

Given these criteria, we can now say that if an example has to be translated, it is probably because the information in it should not be given in a formal example at all, but in a sub-entry or a gloss. In particular, it is probably because it is not a free syntagm. The transparency of the translation is thus an added factor to consider when choosing between an example and a sub-entry. When we consider that most dictionaries with examples would grow to twice the size if all examples in them were translated, these considerations become important.

3.4. Practical Considerations

There are some further considerations, which incidentally apply equally to glosses. For reasons of space, examples should be as few, as brief and as illustrative as possible. There is no need to give several more or less parallel examples of near-synonyms. One must take a global view of the entry. Examples, like meaning discrimination devices, should bring out the major *differences* between possible translations of a word or phrase. Sometimes both a gloss and one or more examples will be necessary, in which case the example will also be illustrating the sense specified in the gloss. There is no need to give a whole sentence where a brief phrase (or a single collocable word) will do. But often more than a micro-context is needed if an example is meant to illustrate a feature at sentence-level or above, as with the following example from KN 1981 (an English-Danish dictionary for Danes, or at least published in Denmark): "**hope** *v.* [...] *I hope* gid (fx *I ~ he will never regret what he has done*) [...]", i.e. SL headword, SL sub-lemma, TL equivalent, SL example. *Gid* is an old verbal form which now more or less has the force of an optative particle. The Danish user knows how to use *gid*; so there is no reason for the example to be in Danish. What is interesting in the context is how a sentence with *I hope [...]* can be translated using *gid*. Other types of example seem superfluous in the strictly passive dictionary. For instance, we also find in KN 1981: "**bold** *adj* dristig (fx *plan; speech; art design*) [...]". The question here is: who is the example for? The Danish user has a context he wants to understand. Strictly speaking, a list of equivalents would allow him to choose the right one. The only function of the English examples here (for the Dane) seems to be to instruct him in the finer points of his own language. In fact the problem is that the author is trying to serve the double purpose of providing a passive dictionary for Danes and an active one for English-speakers. Yet to be really useful in the latter case, the examples should be in Danish! The result is a compromise typical of the small linguistic community, where it is a hard fact of life that no one is going to produce four bilingual dictionaries for one language pair. It is also unlikely that an English publisher, for example, would be interested in producing an active English-Danish dictionary for English-speakers.

Any comments on or explanations of the example should be in the language of the user, i.e. in SL in an encoding and in TL in a decoding dictionary.

It is a good thing to take one's examples from authentic SL and TL texts if possible, or from monolingual dictionaries using such examples, or at least it is good to derive them from such examples: often an authentic example can be abbreviated or paraphrased without losing any of its illustrative value. Besides, for a competent bilingual dictionary maker (ambiguities intended) it should be quite possible to coin examples illustrating well-established usage. — If large dictionaries have more space for examples than small ones, space is still important, and the users of large dictionaries may be assumed to have more knowledge of the foreign language than the users of small ones. This means that in a dictionary that is large enough to have extensive exemplification, the user can be assumed to be capable of understanding transparent syntagms without translation.

Cultural distance between the languages involved also plays a role. A bilingual dictionary of two languages from very different cultures will need many examples illustrating cultural/encyclopædic factors, whereas if the non-linguistic background of the two languages is largely the same, fewer examples are needed (cf. art. 301).

4. Exemplification by Other Means Than Formal Examples

There are good arguments for including in the larger dictionaries material that is not based on a *direct* translation of the headword. For instance, in VB 1976 there is at the end of many entries a component known as "asterisk examples". Thus we find at the end of the entry on the Danish word *fest:*

"∗ The Salzburg *Festival*/the inauguration *ceremony* took place in the Town Hall/a *celebration* to commemorate the foundation of the university."

— where the Danish equivalents of the words we have underlined might be *festspil* (or *festival*), *indvielsesfest* and *jubilæumsfest* respectively. — At the end of the entry on *ambassadør* (or any other official title) one could provide the correct form of address for an ambassador, etc. Such a category is particularly useful for certain types of speech acts related to the meaning of the headword but not directly translated by a phrase using it. E.g. at the end of an entry on *overraskelse* (surprise), phrases like *Well, I'll be blowed!/wonders will never cease!/Blimey!.* These may not be formal examples, but one should always keep in mind that the user is looking for inspiration in a given linguistic context.

5. Selected Bibliography

5.1. Dictionaries

Collins E-G/G-E 1981 = Peter Terrell/Veronika Calderwood-Schnorr/Wendy W. A. Morris/Roland Breitsprecher: Collins English-German German-English Dictionary. London. Glasgow 1981 [XVII, 792, 790 pp.].

Gyldendals blå ordbøger T-D 1980 = Gyldendals blå ordbøger. Hovedredaktør: Svend Brüel. Tyskdansk ordbog. Udarbejdet af Egon Bork. Tredje, omarbejdede udgave. Tønder 1980.

Harrap F and E = Harrap's Shorter French and English Dictionary. Edited by Peter Collin/Helen Knox/Margaret Ledésert/René Ledésert. London 1982 [XXII, 983, 32, 798 pp.].

KN 1981 = Bernhard Kjærulff Nielsen: Engelskdansk Ordbog. Anden udgave. Haslev 1981 [1273 pp.].

Svensk-engelsk Fackordbok 1977 = Ingvar E. Gullberg: Svensk-engelsk Fackordbok för näringsliv, förvaltning, undervisning och forskning. Andra reviderade upplagan med supplement. Stockholm 1977.

VB 1976 = Hermann Vinterberg/Carl Adolf Bodelsen: Dansk-engelsk ordbog. Anden reviderede og udvidede udgave ved C. A. Bodelsen. Tredje oplag med tillæg. I. A-Måttevæver, II. N—Åsyn og tillæg. Haslev 1976 [I. 918 pp., II. 928 pp., Første udgave 1954—1956. Anden udgave 1966].

5.2. Other Publications

Al-Kasimi 1983 = Ali M. Al-Kasimi: Linguistics and Bilingual Dictionaries. Leiden 1983.

Bergenholtz 1984 = Henning Bergenholtz: Grammatik im Wörterbuch: Syntax. In: Studien zur neuhochdeutschen Lexikographie V. Herausgegeben von Herbert Ernst Wiegand (Germanistische Linguistik 3—6/84). Hildesheim. Zürich. New York 1984, 1—46.

Manley/Jacobsen/Pedersen 1988 = James Manley/Jane Jacobsen/Viggo Hjørnager Pedersen: Telling Lies Efficiently: Terminology and the Microstructure in the Bilingual Dictionary. In: Symposium on Lexicography III. Ed. by K. Hyldgaard-Jensen/A. Zettersten. Tübingen 1988 (Lexicographica Series Maior 19), 281—302.

Pedersen 1986 = Viggo Hjørnager Pedersen: The Translation of Collocations and Idioms. In: Proceedings from the Second Scandinavian Symposium on Translation Theory. Lund 1986.

Zgusta 1971 = Ladislav Zgusta: Manual of Lexicography. The Hague. Paris 1971.

Zöfgen 1986 = Ekkehard Zöfgen: Kollokation — Kontextualisierung — Belegsatz. Anmerkungen zur Theorie und Praxis des lexikographischen Beispiels. In: Französische Sprachlehre und *bon usage*. Festschrift für H.-W. Klein. Ed. A. Barrera-Vidal et al. München 1986, 219—238.

Jane Rosenkilde Jacobsen/James Manley/
Viggo Hjørnager Pedersen,
University of Copenhagen
(Denmark)

290. Die Phraseologie im zweisprachigen Wörterbuch

1. Die Erwartungshaltung des Wörterbuchbenutzers
2. Tendenzen zur Berücksichtigung der Phraseologie im zweisprachigen Wörterbuch
3. Die formalen Probleme der lexikographischen Darstellung phraseologischer Ausdrücke
4. Die Probleme einer exakten Bedeutungsangabe der phraseologischen Ausdrücke
5. Literatur (in Auswahl)

1. Die Erwartungshaltung des Wörterbuchbenutzers

Jemand, der in einem zweisprachigen Wörterbuch einen phraseologischen Ausdruck nachschlägt, möchte diesen Ausdruck überhaupt (2), rasch (3.1., 3.2.) und zuverlässig finden. Dabei heißt „zuverlässig" der Sache nach: der Ausdruck ist in seiner Form — oder seinen Formen — (bes. 3.3.) und in seiner Bedeutung — oder seinen Bedeutungen — (4) dem aktuellen Sprachgebrauch der entsprechenden Sprache nach korrekt angegeben; der Methode nach: er ist so angegeben, daß Mißverständnisse so weit wie möglich ausgeschlossen sind, zumindest also ein adäquates passives Verständnis (4), im Optimalfall indessen auch eine einwandfreie aktive Verwendung (5) durch den Wörterbuchbenutzer gesichert ist.

2. Tendenzen zur Berücksichtigung der Phraseologie im zweisprachigen Wörterbuch

Da eine vergleichende Untersuchung über die Berücksichtigung phraseologischer oder idiomatischer Ausdrücke — diese Bezeichnungen sollen hier unterschiedslos gebraucht werden — in den zweisprachigen Wörterbüchern fehlt, lassen sich hierüber nur ungefähre Angaben machen. — Die großen oder mittelgroßen Wörterbücher gaben den Phraseologismen schon zu einer Zeit einen relativ breiten Raum, als die Idiomatik in der Linguistik noch keine oder kaum eine Rolle spielte. In den letzten Jahrzehnten hat die Idiomatik dann vor allem auch in den Wörterbüchern mittleren bis kleineren Umfangs zunehmend Berücksichtigung gefunden. Unterrepräsentiert ist sie nur noch in den Taschenwörterbüchern. Trotzdem aber — und das ist für den einzelnen Wörterbuchbenutzer wie für den Zustand bzw. spezifische Mängel der (Fremd-)Sprachenausbildung und -vermittlung insgesamt von größter Bedeutung — bieten bis heute die großen einsprachigen Wörterbücher zugleich eine meist weitaus größere Anzahl phraseologischer Einheiten und ebenfalls meist weitaus zuverlässigere Angaben als die zweisprachigen, d. h. stellen selbst die großen unter diesen in der Phraseologie immer noch Auswahlwörterbücher dar (und dies wiederum gilt nicht nur für die Aufnahme der Einheiten, sondern auch für die Angabe von Äquivalenten in der Zielsprache).

3. Die formalen Probleme der lexikographischen Darstellung phraseologischer Ausdrücke

3.1. Wenn man eine Einheit rasch finden will, muß man wissen, wo sie steht bzw. wo man sie zu suchen hat. Leider herrscht wohl in keinem Bereich der Lexikographie (und Lexikologie) eine solche Verwirrung wie in der Frage der alphabetischen Anordnung phraseologischer Einheiten. Das gilt zunächst für die Makrostruktur. Wo finde ich *an js. Händen klebt Blut* (und seine engl., frz., span., port., ... Äquivalente)? Unter **Hand, Blut** oder **kleben**? — Ebenso verwirrend ist die Anlage der Mikrostruktur. Warum steht die Einheit im Langenscheidt D-E bei den „Verbindungen mit Verben?" Wer vermutet *jen. an Händen und Füßen fesseln* in der Untergruppe „Verbindungen mit Präpositionen" (eba.)? Warum steht *Blut klebt an seinen Händen* im Langenscheidt D-Sp hinter *am Buchstaben kleben*?

Unser Vorschlag zur alphabetischen Anordnung ist folgender: Hat ein idiomatischer Ausdruck ein Substantiv, entscheidet dies, sonst das Verb. Gibt es weder Subst. noch Verb, zählt, falls vorhanden, das Adj., sonst das Adv. Fehlen alle genannten Kategorien, zählen Pronomen, Partikel usw. — Hat ein Idiom zwei oder mehrere Konstituenten gleicher Kategorie, zählt die, die an erster Stelle steht. — Haben mehrere Ausdrücke dasselbe alphabetische Leitwort (oder dieselben alphabetischen Leitwörter), entscheiden über ihre Anordnung die übrigen Kategorien, und zwar wiederum in der Abfolge Subst. — Verb — Adj. — Adv. (Pron. — Partikel — ...); d. h., gibt es ein zweites Subst., entscheidet dies, andernfalls das Verb, usw. Hierbei kommen zunächst die Idioms, die neben dem Leitwort alphabetisch relevante Konstituenten vor diesem Leitwort haben, danach die mit alphabetisch relevanten Konstituenten nach dem Leitwort. Gibt es vor und nach dem Leitwort solche Konstituenten, zählen nur die nachfolgenden. — Phraseologismen, die nur in bestimmten Formen vorkommen, werden nach diesen Formen angeordnet, und nicht nach einer (idiomatisch nicht vorliegenden) „Grundform". Das heißt, bei Idioms mit Substantivkonstituenten im Plural zählen auch diese Formen als Konstituenten — in unserem Beisp. *(an js. Händen klebt Blut):* **Händen**; bei Idioms, die nur in bestimmten Tempora, Modi (bzw. Sprechakten) u. ä. vorkommen, ist, falls möglich, leitend die 3. Pers. Sing. der entsprechenden Tempora, Modi usw. bzw. der Imp. Sing.; dabei wird das Paradigma bzw. die Variablen durch eine zweite Form nach einem Schrägstrich angedeutet: *er kann mir/die können uns/... den Buckel herunterrutschen,* und nicht: *jem. den Buckel herunterrutschen,* so, als könnte man (ohne Ironie oder andere rhetorische Absicht) sagen: *Karl rutschte Barbara gestern den Buckel herunter.* — Nicht zählen für die alphabetische Anordnung die (durch Schrägstriche angedeuteten) Variablen, Ergänzungen *(an js. Händen klebt Blut),* Artikel (falls sie nicht idiomatisch fixiert sind), die Verben *sein, haben, tun,* (die übrigen) Hilfsverben, Zahlwörter u. ä. (ebenfalls: wenn nicht idiomatisch fixiert und falls sie nicht aufgrund des Fehlens aller übrigen übergeordneten Kategorien alphabetisch relevant werden). — Die Bestimmung der Kategorien einer Idiomkonstituente erfolgt nach ihrer Funktion im Idiom und nicht aufgrund einer angenommenen Grundform, Grundbedeutung o. ä.

Ohne eine bis ins Detail geregelte und einheitliche Alphabetisierung idiomatischer Einheiten ist ein „reeller" lexikographischer (und lexikologischer) Fortschritt in der Phraseologie aus folgenden Gründen nur schwer denkbar: (1) Der Wörterbuchbenutzer hat immer weniger Zeit, und ist auch immer weniger geneigt, seine Zeit mit langwierigem Aufsuchen von Einheiten zu „vertun"; (2) Ein Vergleich der Angaben in verschiedenen Wörterbüchern ist nur dann ohne Schwierigkeiten durchzuführen, wenn die Artikel (wenigstens in etwa) nach dem gleichen Schema angelegt sind; (3) Folgen Makro- und Mikrostruktur (wie hier vorgeschlagen) denselben Prinzipien, wird das Nachschlagen zu einem gleichsam automatischen Prozeß; d. h., die

Aufmerksamkeit des Wörterbuchbenutzers kann sich ganz auf das konzentrieren, was sie sucht; sie wird nicht durch die mangelhafte Artikelstruktur von ihrer Zielrichtung abgelenkt; (4) Ist (3) gegeben, sind allgemeine einsprachige wie zweisprachige Wörterbücher einerseits und einsprachige wie zweisprachige idiomatische Wörterbücher andererseits mühelos aufeinander zu projizieren bzw. miteinander zu vergleichen: die Mikrostruktur des idiomatischen Teils eines Artikels eines allgemeinen Wörterbuchs ist dann dieselbe wie die Makrostruktur eines idiomatischen Wörterbuchs; (5) Zahlreiche Fehler und Ungenauigkeiten bei den Angaben zu Form und Inhalt der Phraseologismen werden fast zwangsläufig vermieden, wenn der Lexikograph die formale Gestaltung eines Artikels so konsequent wie möglich handhabt.

3.2. Auch in der Frage, wo der idiomatische Block innerhalb eines Artikels zu stehen hat, d. h. wie die gesamte Mikrostruktur aussehen sollte, sind die Wörterbücher verwirrend uneinheitlich, wenn die Tendenz auch generell dahin geht, drei oder vier Blöcke zu unterscheiden: (a) die Einzelbedeutungen des infragestehenden (Ausgangs-) Lexems; (b) Präpositionalphrasen u. ä., die e i n e Gesamtbedeutung haben *(anhand von, unterderhand* usw.); Gefüge mit Adj., Adv. u. ä., deren Gesamtbedeutung der einer ihrer Konstituenten gleich oder ähnlich ist *(mit milder Hand* „milde"); (d) die Idioms im engeren Sinn. — Dabei werden die Einzelbedeutungen in der Regel an den Anfang gesetzt, in manchen Wörterbüchern jedoch ans Ende; (b) und (c) bilden häufig eine einzige Gruppe; in wieder anderen Fällen wird nach den Einzelbedeutungen expressis verbis unterteilt in: (Ausgangslexem) + Präp., + Adj., + Verb usw. — wobei die Detailanordnung indessen schon deswegen inkohärent ist, weil bei den Kategorien nicht nach der Gesamtfunktion der (gesamten) Einheit (im Satz) und der Funktion der Konstituenten im Phraseologismus streng unterschieden wird. — Ist der Artikelaufbau schon in den allgemeinen Leitlinien nicht einheitlich, so gehen die Kriterien im Detail völlig durcheinander.

Unser Vorschlag für den Aufbau eines Artikels ist: (1) Einzelbedeutung(en); (2) phraseologische Ausdrücke im engeren Sinn (Weinreich), deren Kontext frei ist *(blau machen:* genau wie bei der die Bedeutung umschreibenden freien Paraphrase „nicht zur Arbeit gehen" kann als Subj. jedes beliebige Lexem für „Mensch" eintreten); (3) Gefüge aus zwei oder mehreren Konstituenten, von denen nur eine Lexemstatus im strengen Sinn hat. (Zusammengeschriebene Einheiten sind dabei genauso zu behandeln wie funktionell identische, aber auseinandergeschriebene Einheiten: *unterderhand* — *unter der Hand*. — *Unter* und *der* haben Morphemstatus (Relationsglieder)); (4) Idioms aus zwei oder mehreren Konstituenten mit Lexemstatus, deren Kontext im strengen Sinn zwar nicht gebunden, aber auch nicht frei ist *(mit milder Hand regieren/leiten/verwalten/...)*. — Diese Gruppe bildet einen Zwischenbereich, insofern als die Kontextgebundenheit zwar nicht lexematisch eindeutig angebbar, aber trotzdem nicht aus der (Gesamt-)Bedeutung folgend, d. h. frei ist. Man kann sagen: *Er verhält sich ihr gegenüber sehr milde,* nicht aber: [...] *mit milder Hand*); (5) die Idioms mit freiem Kontext nach 3.1. — Hier pflegen die Wörterbücher, wenn auch unsystematisch, (wenigstens) zu unterscheiden zwischen: (aa) kollokationsähnlichen Gefügen, in denen die Konstituenten zwar gebunden, doch nicht übertragen sind, und die, als ganze, (lediglich) eine Geste, ein Bild o. ä. gleichsam nachzeichnen *(in die Hände klatschen)*; (bb) Einheiten, insbesondere Verbalphrasen, bei denen eine Konstituente, insbes. das Verb, in normaler Bedeutung fungiert *(die Hand von etw. lassen)*: (cc) die gesamt-übertragenen Einheiten *(jen. auf Händen tragen)*; (dd) pragmatische Einheiten *(Hand drauf!)*. Hier würde unser Vorschlag sein, n i c h t zu differenzieren, und zwar aus zwei Gründen. Einmal gibt es zahllose Fälle, die nicht eindeutig zu entscheiden sind. Zum andern gehen die Differenzierungen, fängt man damit an, in diesem Punkt leicht ins Uferlose.

Alle fünf Blöcke sind intern wiederum zu untergliedern nach der Satzfunktion der (Gesamt-) Einheiten, in der Reihenfolge Subst. — Verb — Adj. — Verb (Pron. — Partikel — ...).

3.3. In bezug auf die Form sind insbesondere folgende Anforderungen zu stellen: (1) die Einheiten müssen, als ganze, in jeder ihrer Konstituenten und in ihrer Konstruktion zutreffend angegeben sein. — Selbstverständlich gibt es in diesem Bereich mannigfache Zweifelsfälle. — (2) Die Restriktionen in Tempus, Modus usw. sind möglichst exakt zu verzeichnen (vgl. 3.1. *jem. den Buckel herunterrutschen*). — Hier sind die Zweifelsfälle vielleicht noch zahlreicher, und ein besonderes (technisches) Problem stellt die sehr häufig auftretende Schwierigkeit dar, solche Restriktionen auf knappem Raum exakt anzugeben. — (3) Die relative Kontextgebundenheit ist so präzis wie möglich anzugeben (vgl. 3.2. *mit milder Hand*). — (4) Die verzeichneten Einheiten müssen korrekt ab- bzw. ausgegrenzt sein. (Also nicht: *mit vollen Händen* — wie im Bertaux/Lepointe 1968 —, sondern: [...] *ausgeben*). — Der Usus zahlreicher Wörterbücher, Idiomkonstituenten und Idiomblöcke wie freie Einzellexeme zu verzeichnen und Konstituenten sowie Blöcke inkorrekt zu verbinden, stellt einen der schwerwiegendsten Mängel in der lexikographischen Praxis der Phraseologie dar; jeder Benutzer, der nicht aufgrund eigener Sprachkompetenz die Idioms korrekt „wiederherstellen" kann, wird dadurch völlig irregeleitet.

Ähnlich wie in der Frage der alphabetischen Anordnung der idiomatischen Einheiten und des Artikelaufbaus im ganzen liegt auch hier eine Chance der Lexikographie zur Verbesserung der Wörterbücher, die der Benutzer sofort vermerkt.

4. Die Probleme einer exakten Bedeutungsangabe der phraseologischen Ausdrücke

4.1. Vor besondere Probleme stellt die Lexikographie bekanntlich auch die Bedeutungsangabe der phraseologischen Einheiten. Zunächst aufgrund der spezifischen Motiviertheit des idiomatischen Sprachzeichens, bei dem die Sprachbedeutung durch eine mehr oder weniger komplexe Bildbedeutung sehr häufig mitkonstituiert wird. Die grundlegende Aufgabe besteht demnach darin, die Relation Sprach-/Bildbedeutung zutreffend mitzuberücksichtigen.

Eine Einheit wie *immer/... Ausreden/Argumente/... bei der Hand haben* etwa hat als Basis zunächst die Bildbedeutung „'bei der Hand haben'", d. h. (vereinfachend) „'in der Nähe/im Umkreis/... der Hand — der Person (der die Hand gehört)/... haben'" (wobei wir die prinzipielle Möglichkeit außer acht lassen, daß der Block — hier *bei der Hand* — schon in einer ganz spezifischen (Teilgesamt-)Bedeutung vorliegen kann, so daß das Idiom als ganzes nicht oder nur teilweise auf den „normalen" Konstituentenbedeutungen, sondern (zusätzlich) auf dieser Teilbedeutung aufbaut). Die erste Sprachbedeutung ist mit dieser Bildbedeutung nahezu identisch. *(Mein Wörterbuch muß ich immer bei der Hand haben; wenn ich immer erst aufstehen müßte, um ein Wort nachzuschlagen, könnte ich nicht arbeiten).* Die zweite Sprachbedeutung ergibt sich durch eine Teilübertragung (Übertragung eines Idiomblocks): Nähe, direkt bei der Hand → räumliche Nähe, als Verfügungsgewalt (mit der Hand) *(Hast du den Larousse gerade bei der Hand? Ich brauche da eine Angabe... — Warte, er steht in einem der Regale da drüben).* Die dritte Sprachbedeutung schließlich wird gebildet durch Übertragung der zweiten auf den Bereich: „Ausreden/Entschuldigung/..." *(Unsere älteste Tochter läßt sich nie zu Spaziergängen mit uns bewegen. Wenn man sie darum bittet, hat sie immer eine Ausrede bei der Hand.)*

In der zweiten und dritten Bedeutung dieses Idioms wird deutlich, daß die lexikographisch üblichen Vermerke *konkr., abstr., fig.* u. ä. viel zu grob sind, um dem Benutzer eine genaue Bedeutungserfassung zu ermöglichen. Die zweite Bedeutung liegt gleichsam zwischen dem Konkreten und dem Abstrakten: „Nähe als Verfügungsraum", und die dritte schränkt die Verwendung auf der abstrakten Ebene auf einen ganz spezifischen Bereich ein (Wortfeldproblematik). Angaben, die dem Benutzer Bedeutungen wie die zweite erschließen, vermißt man in allen (ein- wie zweisprachigen) Wörterbüchern; ein sehr großer Teil der idiomatischen Ausdrücke kann schon aus diesem Grund von einem Nicht-native-speaker nicht korrekt verwandt werden, wenn er seine Kenntnisse (nur) aus Wörterbüchern bezieht. Und Angaben zu Bedeutungen wie der dritten — etwa Zusatz in Klammern (Argumente/...) oder ein in diesem Sinn kontextuell zu verstehender Beispielsatz (u. U. in Kurzform) — sind in der zweisprachigen Lexikographie seltener als in der einsprachigen und finden sich — wenn überhaupt — fast nur für freie Lexeme, nicht aber für phraseologische Ausdrücke.

4.2. Eine äußerst „tückische" Problematik stellt für ein zweisprachiges Wörterbuch die Tatsache dar, daß gleiche, fast gleiche, ähnliche Bilder und Bildbedeutungen (von Idioms als ganzen wie von Idiomblöcken) in zwei oder mehreren Sprachen sehr oft zu unterschiedlichen Sprachbedeutungen führen, und zwar entweder so, daß diese Bedeutungen wenig, im Grenzfall nichts miteinander zu tun haben, oder aber, häufiger, so, daß sich (Teil-)Überschneidungen ergeben: die idiomatischen *faux amis* (vgl. Art. 304) sind ganz besondere „falsche Freunde", die in ihrer Besonderheit bisher kaum untersucht wurden. Ein Verständnis für diese Problematik läßt sich etwa an span. Ausdrücken mit *echar/meter/poner* ± Artikel + *mano(s)* ± Präp. (*a/de/en/...*) und ihren dt. Äquivalenten gewinnen. Das die span. Einheiten fundierende Bild ist: „'die Hand/Hände an/auf/zu/... etw./jen. tun'"; die Bildbedeutungen: „'die Hand versus die Hände an versus auf versus gegen... etw. versus jen. heften versus legen versus halten...'". In den unterschiedlichen Sprachbedeutungen aber liegen dann, vom Bild und von den Bildbedeutungen her gesehen, die vielfachsten impliziten, d. h. von Bild und Bildbedeutung nicht erschließbaren Restriktionen vor, d. h.

spezifische Relationen, in welchem raumzeitlichem Zusammenhang, warum und mit welchem Zweck man „die Hand/Hände an/auf/ gegen ... etw/jen. tut"; „(um/...:) etw./jen. festhalten/festnehmen/stützen/beistehen/ fördern/...". Die klassische Stilistik faßte diese Relationen unter der Bezeichnung Metonymie zusammen; die moderne Linguistik ist einem Teilbereich davon insbesondere in der Erforschung der Illokutionen von Sätzen nachgegangen. Die Lexikalisierung von idiomatischen Ausdrücken nun, verstanden als fixierte Illokutionen eines im Bild bzw. in der Bildbedeutung abgesteckten Meinungspotentials, ist ein überaus breites und vielversprechendes Forschungsgebiet, das die Idiomatik mit dem non-verbalen Sprechen in Beziehung bringt und letztlich ins Anthropologische führt, das indessen bisher kaum in Angriff genommen wurde. In den Fällen, in denen aus den zur Auswahl stehenden Äquivalenten der Zielsprache keines die durch die illokutionären Relationen bedingten Restriktionen der Einheiten der Ausgangssprache zureichend trifft, geht unser Vorschlag dahin, in zweisprachigen Wörterbüchern hinter das Äquivalent (bzw. die Äquivalente), in Klammern, mit anderthalb Anführungsstrichen, die metonymische Relation zuzufügen (*echar mano de u.c.* — „sich einer S. bedienen" (,'die Hände an etw. tun — um es zu gebrauchen/...'"). In einem Satz wie „Er bedient sich der und der Argumente..." läßt sich, so wird aus dem Zusatz sofort klar, das Idiom nicht verwenden).

Mit den Angaben der Übertragungs**form** (Metapher, 4.1.; Metonymie, 4.2.), der Übertragungs**basis** (Idiomkonstituente, Idiomblock, Idiom als Ganzes), des Übertragungs**bereichs** (d. h. des spezifischen Kontexts, der für den idiomatischen Ausdruck nach und aufgrund der Übertragung gilt; vgl. unser Beispiel in 4.1.: „Argumente/Ausreden/...") und der — mit der Relation Bild-/Sprachbedeutung häufig implizierten — Kontextrestriktionen (bes. 4.2.) sind keineswegs alle Probleme gelöst, vor die sich der Lexikograph besonders dann gestellt sieht, wenn er die Bedeutung von idiomatischen Einheiten präzis angeben will, bei denen die Bildbedeutung (noch) nicht (ganz) verblaßt ist. Doch scheint uns damit ein methodologisch durchsichtiger und kohärenter Weg gezeigt, auf dem sie sich schrittweise lösen lassen. — Der Teil der idiomatischen Ausdrücke, der lediglich durch syntaktische Anomalien konstituiert wird, pflegt der Bedeutungserfassung auch durch Nicht-nativespeaker, die ihnen zum ersten Mal begegnen, keine größeren Schwierigkeiten zu machen: die Anomalien sind durchweg durchschaubar. (Vgl. dt. *alle Hände voll zu tun haben*: auch ein Nicht-Deutscher, der die Gesamtbedeutung aufgrund des weiteren Kontexts auch nur einigermaßen erfaßt, durchschaut die syntaktische Anomalie des Blocks *alle Hände voll* sofort, so daß er (re-)konstruieren kann: „'so viel Arbeit/zu tun/... haben, daß — fig. — die Hände (gleichsam immer) voll sind'" — „mit Arbeit/... (mehr als) eingedeckt sein"). Die Kontextrestriktionen und Bedeutungsspezifizierungen, die auf Übertragungen zurückgehen, sind dagegen ungleich schwerer zu durchschauen. Von den übertragenen idiomatischen Einheiten machen nun die metaphorisch oder metonymisch übertragenen den bei weitem größten Anteil aus. Auch aus diesem Grund scheint uns der angegebene lexikographische Weg der vielversprechendste. — Zwischen der lebendigen Metapher und Metonymie, die in der Kommunikation „spontan" gebildet wird, und der völlig verblaßten, bei der so wenig Kontextrestriktionen auftreten wie bei einem nichtübertragenen Lexem, bildet die gleichsam auf halbem Weg steckengebliebene Übertragung, bei der das Bild die Bedeutung (noch) mitkonstituiert, sowohl unter theoretischem als auch unter praktischem Gesichtspunkt den schwierigsten — und den interessantesten — Bereich der phraseologischen Ausdrücke.

5. Literatur (in Auswahl)

5.1. Wörterbücher

Bertaux/Lepointe 1968 = F. Bertaux/E. Lepointe: Dictionnaire Allemand-Français. Ed. Pierre Bertaux. Paris 1968 [1392 p.].

Langenscheidt D-E = Heinz Messinger: Langenscheidts Großwörterbuch der englischen und deutschen Sprache. Deutsch-Englisch. Berlin 1982 (Der kleine Muret-Sanders) [1296 p.].

Langenscheidt D-Sp. = Enrique Alvarez-Prada: Langenscheidts Handwörterbuch Spanisch. Deutsch-Spanisch. Ed. Gisela Haberkamp de Antón. Berlin 1985 [640 p.].

5.2. Sonstige Literatur

Boguslawski 1979 = A. Boguslawski: Zum Problem der Phraseologie in zweisprachigen Wörterbüchern. In: Kwartalnik Neofilologiczny 26. 1979, 29—36.

Dittmer 1981 = A. Dittmer: Feste Syntagmen im Dänisch-Deutschen Wörterbuch. In: Kopenhagener Beiträge zur Germanistischen Linguistik 17. 1981, 110—125.

Ettinger 1989 = Stefan Ettinger: Einige Probleme der lexikographischen Darstellung idiomatischer Einheiten (Französisch-Deutsch). In: Europhras 88, 95—116.

Europhras 88 = Europhras 88. Phraséologie Contrastive. Actes du Colloque International Klingenthal — Strasbourg, 12—16 mai 1988. Ed. Gertrud Gréciano. Strasbourg 1989 (Collection Recherches Germaniques Nr. 2).

Hessky 1980 = Regina Hessky: Überlegungen zum Idiom als Problem der zweisprachigen Lexikographie. In: Acta Linguistica Academiae Scientiarum Hungaricae 30. 1980, 163—171.

Kromann 1987 = Hans-Peder Kromann: Zur Typologie und Darbietung der Phraseologismen in Übersetzungswörterbüchern. In: Beiträge zur allgemeinen und germanistischen Phraseologieforschung. Internationales Symposium in Oulu 13.—15. Juni 1986. Hrsg. v. Jarmo Korhonen. Oulu 1987 (Universität Oulu, Finnland. Veröffentlichungen des Germanistischen Instituts 7), 183—192.

Kromann 1989 = Hans-Peder Kromann: Zur funktionalen Beschreibung von Kollokationen und Phraseologismen in Übersetzungswörterbüchern. In: Europhras 88, 265—272.

Weinreich 1969 = Uriel Weinreich: Problems in the Analysis of Idioms. In: Substance and Structure of Language. Ed. J. Puhvel. Berkeley 1969, 23—81.

Hans Schemann, München
(Bundesrepublik Deutschland)

291. Die Paradigmatik im zweisprachigen Wörterbuch

1. Einführung
2. Synonymie und Antonymie
3. Analogie und Wortbildung
4. Literatur (in Auswahl)

1. Einführung

Im allgemeinen zweisprachigen Wörterbuch schaut der Benutzer durch das Lemma der Ausgangssprache wie durch ein Fernrohr auf einen lexikalischen Ausschnitt der Zielsprache, der in den meisten Fällen nicht aus einem Wort, sondern aus mehreren synonymen Wörtern besteht. Wer z. B. in Weis 1979, 374 s. v. *étourdi* nachschlägt, findet unter I. 1. *Person* folgende Liste: „gedankenlos; unbesonnen; leichtsinnig; leichtfertig; kopflos; vergeßlich; zerstreut". Zweisprachige Wörterbücher sind immer auch Synonymwörterbücher und werden oft ausdrücklich in dieser Funktion genutzt, z. B. die lateinisch-französischen Wörterbücher des 16. Jh. als Synonymwörterbücher des Französischen oder ein heutiges englisch-isländisches Wörterbuch als Synonymwörterbuch des Isländischen, in beiden Fällen in Ermangelung spezieller Synonymwörterbücher. Daneben dienen Synonyme (und Antonyme) in guten zweisprachigen Wörterbüchern zur Glossierung (*meaning discrimination*) (cf. Marello 1989, 58).

Im vorliegenden Artikel soll jedoch nicht von der *automatischen* Paradigmatik, sondern von der *intentionellen* Paradigmatik die Rede sein. Eine solche ist bislang ausgesprochen selten. Es wäre deshalb wünschenswert, daß von der Sichtung intentioneller paradigmatischer Beschreibung im allgemeinen zweisprachigen Wörterbuch Anregungen für künftige Lexikographie ausgehen.

2. Synonymie und Antonymie

Die allgemeine Begeisterung des 18. Jh. für die distinktive Synonymik schlug sich im

> ABYSS (a-biss'), s. [a bottomless gulf] abîme, m. gouffre, m. profondeur énorme, f. Infinite —, abîme immense, infini. Time's —, the common grave of all, l'abîme des temps où tout s'engloutit. (DRYDEN.) In the — of light, of darkness, au sein de la lumière, des ténèbres. (Poet.) An — of misery, of woe, abîme de malheurs, de misère. | Abyss [hell, in the language of Scripture], abîme, m. enfer, m. The rebellious angels have been cast headlong into the —, les anges rebelles ont été précipités dans l'enfer ou l'abîme. [Gr. a, sans, bussos, fond.]
>
> [Abyss, abîme; gulf, gouffre (synon.): These words are more frequently used in a figurative than a literal sense; the first conveys an idea of unmeasurable depth, whose bottom we can never reach; the second, of insatiable voracity, which drags in and consumes all that approaches; thus we say: plunged in an abyss of darkness, in an abyss of sorrow; swallowed up by a gulf of woe, by the gulf of dissipation. A gulf is supposed to have many turns and windings, of which when we have once set a step in, we can not possibly get out, but are carried on, in spite of all our endeavours to the contrary. An abyss is supposed to have many uncertain and obscure roads, without end, in which though we may sometimes stop, in hopes of finding a way out, yet, being deceived, we become disheartened, bewildered with doubts, and overwhelmed with despair.]

Textbeispiel 291.1: Artikel *abyss* (aus: Fleming/Tibbins 1839, 10)

19. Jh. in dem Versuch nieder, sie in allgemeine Wörterbücher, einsprachige wie zweisprachige, zu integrieren. Da distinktive Synonymik Platz kostet, leisten sich diesen Luxus nur die ganz großen Wörterbücher. Textbeispiel 291.1 zeigt einen Ausschnitt aus Fleming/Tibbins 1839. Als Übernahme aus Littré 1863—73 erklärt sich daneben die distinktive Synonymik in Sachs 1869 (Textbeispiel 291.2). Ein später und stark reduzierter Nachklang findet sich bei Grappin 1963 (vgl. Textbeispiel 291.3). Im Prinzip dient diese Synonymik der Rezeptions-, Produktions- und Lernfunktion. Allerdings wird man dem Grappinschen Verfahren der Beschränkung auf Wortäquivalenzen reserviert gegenüberstehen, weil damit keine angemessene Distinktion erzielt werden kann.

Textbeispiel 291.2: Artikel *atelier* (aus: Sachs 1869, 101)

Textbeispiel 291.3: Artikel *Dieb* (aus: Grappin 1963, 172)

Für Textproduktions- und Lernfunktion wird man das Anführen von Antonymen unter strukturalistischen Gesichtspunkten für genauso wichtig halten wie das Verzeichnen von Synonymen. Tolhausen 1888/89 integriert als einziger Antonymik ins Wörterbuch, wenn er z. B. s. v. *consumidor* anführt: „ant. producidor" (ohne Äquivalent).

3. Analogie und Wortbildung

Unter Analogie wollen wir hier die lexikalischen Beziehungen in Wort-, Sach- und Situationsfeldern zusammenfassen. Zwei- und mehrsprachige Sachgruppenwörterbücher gehören bekanntlich zu den ältesten europäischen Sprachmitteln. Die Integration solcher Sachgruppen in ein alphabetisches zweisprachiges Wörterbuch ist hingegen ausgesprochen selten. Man findet sie in dem dreisprachigen Wörterbuch Pomay 1740, z. B. die Sachgruppe *corps* unter dem Lemma **corps** mit mehr als 150 Körperteilen, ferner den Exkrementen und den Adjektiven für Körperfehler von *borgne* bis *eunuque*. An anderer Stelle stehen Listen von Farbnamen, Pflanzennamen oder den Teilen einer Uhr. Solche Zusammenstellungen machen sich vor allem Wörterbücher zunutze, die einen starken didaktischen Akzent tragen, z. B. Dubois-Charlier 1980, 29 mit einer zweisprachigen Liste der *arts and sciences* (vgl. auch die Tabellen in Grappin 1963, z. B. die Tabelle *Eisenbahn*).

In diesen Zusammenhang fällt auch die Nutzung von Abbildungen zur Präsentation sachgebundener Terminologie (z. B. Grappin 1963, 71 zu den Einzelteilen des Automobils). In größerem Umfang bedienten sich dieses Präsentationsmittels die Brockhaus Bildwörterbücher Französisch-Deutsch, Englisch-Deutsch und Italienisch-Deutsch (z. B. Brockhaus 1978). Man muß sich wundern, daß in unserer so terminologisierten Welt dieses Verfahren nicht häufiger genutzt wird (vgl. auch Marello 1989, 218 f.). Nach Sprechakten und Situationsanlässen zusammengestellten Wortschatz Französisch-Englisch und Englisch-Französisch enthält (annexiert und nicht integriert) Robert-Collins 1987, 859—930.

Die Kompositanester, welche manche zweisprachige Wörterbücher aus Gründen der Platzersparnis einrichten (Grappin 1963 Deutsch-Französisch, Robert-Collins 1987 Anglais-Français), sind nicht als explizite Paradigmatik zu verstehen. Systematische Gruppierung zur Abbildung der Wortbildungsbeziehungen im Wortschatz scheitert im allgemeinen zweisprachigen Wörterbuch (noch mehr als im einsprachigen Wörterbuch) an dem Gebot der Benutzerfreundlichkeit, das keine Durchbrechung des Alphabets und kein Übermaß an Verweisung zuläßt.

4. Literatur (in Auswahl)

4.1. Wörterbücher

Brockhaus 1978 = Brockhaus Bildwörterbuch Englisch-Deutsch, Deutsch-Englisch. 8. Aufl. München 1978 [680, 773 S.].

Dubois-Charlier 1980 = Françoise Dubois-Charlier: Dictionnaire de l'anglais contemporain. Paris 1980 [863 S.].

Fleming/Tibbins 1839 = Charles Fleming/J. Tibbins: The Royal Dictionary English and French. Vol. I. English and French. Paris 1839 [1234 S.].

Grappin 1963 = Pierre Grappin: Dictionnaire moderne français-allemand, allemand-français. Paris 1963 [848, 898 S.; später unverändert ohne „moderne"].

Littré 1863—73 = Emile Littré: Dictionnaire de la langue française. 4 Bde. Paris 1863—1873 [2040, 2628 S.].

Pomay 1700 = François Pomay: Dictionnaire royal français-latin-allemand. Frankfurt 1700 [1. Aufl. 1681, 7. Aufl. 1740: 984, 244, 355, 64 S.].

Robert-Collins 1987 = Beryl T. Atkins/Alain Duval/Rosemary C. Milne et al.: Robert Collins Dictionnaire français-anglais, anglais-français. Paris 1987 [768, 930 S.].

Sachs 1869 = Karl Sachs: Enzyklopädisches französisch-deutsches Wörterbuch. A-Bl. Berlin 1869.

Tolhausen 1888/9 = Louis Tolhausen: Neues spanisch-deutsches und deutsch-spanisches Wörterbuch. 2 Bde. Leipzig 1888, 1889 [764, 828 S.].

Weis 1979 = Langenscheidts Großwörterbuch Französisch. Teil I: Französisch-Deutsch. Hrsg. v. Erich Weis. Berlin 1979 [1047 S.].

4.2. Sonstige Literatur

Marello = Carla Marello: Dizionari bilingui. Bologna 1989.

Franz Josef Hausmann, Erlangen
(Bundesrepublik Deutschland)

292. Die Markierungen im zweisprachigen Wörterbuch

1. Markierungen im ein- und im zweisprachigen Wörterbuch: gemeinsame und spezifische Aspekte
2. Funktionen der Markierungsangaben im zweisprachigen Wörterbuch
3. Markierungen, Äquivalenz und Typen zweisprachiger Wörterbücher
4. Formale Regeln für die Zuordnung von Markierungskennzeichnungen
5. Literatur (in Auswahl)

1. Markierungen im ein- und im zweisprachigen Wörterbuch: gemeinsame und spezifische Aspekte

Die Thematik der Markierungen im zweisprachigen Wörterbuch umfaßt eine Reihe von Aspekten, die auch einsprachige Wörterbücher betreffen (vgl. Art. 53). Spezifische Aspekte für das zweisprachige Wörterbuch ergeben sich vor allem in zwei Punkten: (1) Zentrales Element der Mikrostruktur im allgemeinen einsprachigen Wörterbuch ist meist die sog. Definition (vgl. Art. 39), im allgemeinen zweisprachigen Wörterbuch spielt eine zentrale Rolle die Angabe sog. Äquivalente (vgl. Art. 295). Definitionen und Äquivalente beeinflussen in je verschiedener Weise die Notwendigkeit und die Form zusätzlicher (von Definition bzw. Äquivalenten nicht schon geleisteter) Hinweise auf die Markierung sprachlicher Elemente. (2) Während im allgemeinen einsprachigen Wörterbuch sich die Angaben zur Markierung immer auf die eine Sprache beziehen, der das Wörterbuch gewidmet ist, können sie im allgemeinen zweisprachigen Wörterbuch Elemente der Ausgangs- und der Zielsprache betreffen. Daraus ergeben sich zusätzliche Komplikationen für die Festlegung der lexikographischen Mikrostruktur. Fragen, die im Rahmen der Festlegung der Mikrostrukturen gestellt werden müssen, sind vor allem, inwieweit sich die Inventare standardisierter Markierungskennzeichnungen für Ausgangs- und Zielsprache decken können bzw. sollen, und, wie die eindeutige Zuordnung von Markierungskennzeichnungen zu ausgangs- bzw. zielsprachlichen Elementen gewährleistet werden kann.

2. Funktionen der Markierungsangaben im zweisprachigen Wörterbuch

Markierungskennzeichnungen in zweisprachigen Wörterbüchern sind oft nicht eindeutig zu interpretieren und verfehlen je nach

Fall ihre Funktion völlig oder teilweise insofern, als nicht klar wird, worauf sie sich genau beziehen (Werner 1980, Werner 1981). Dies trifft selbst für solche Wörterbücher zu, die (wie Langenscheidts Großwb. F-D/D-F 1980, Teil I, XVII für die „Bezeichnung der Sprachgebrauchsebene") explizit Regeln für die Zuordnung von Markierungskennzeichnungen angeben (Werner 1980, 156—157). Ein besonders häufiger Grund dafür ist, daß nicht genügend zwischen allen Möglichkeiten der Zuordnung der Markierungsangaben zu Elementen der Ausgangs- und der Zielsprache des Wörterbuches unterschieden wird.

Hinsichtlich der Zuordnung von Markierungsangaben im zweisprachigen Wörterbuch zu Elementen der jeweiligen Sprachen können u. a. folgende Fragen gestellt werden. (1) Für welche sprachlichen Größen wird eine Markierung angegeben? (2) Für wie viele Elemente einer Größe gilt eine Markierungsangabe? (3) Was bezweckt die Markierungsangabe?

Die Markierungsangabe kann auf folgende Größen bezogen werden. (1 a) Auf die Verwendung einer lexikalischen Einheit der Ausgangssprache allgemein.

Beispiel: In einem Wörterbuch mit Ausgangssprache Deutsch und Zielsprache Spanisch, in dem deutsch *Arschloch* zwei Einzelbedeutungen (eine auf einen Körperteil und eine auf eine Person zu beziehende) und pro Einzelbedeutung mehrere Äquivalente (Körperteil: *ojete, ojo del culo, ojo moreno*; Person: *mierda, hijo de puta* usw.) zugeordnet werden, kann der Verwendung der lexikalischen Einheit *Arschloch* allgemein eine Angabe zur pragmatischen Markierung (etwa *vulgär*) gewidmet sein.

(1 b) Auf die Verwendung einer lexikalischen Einheit der Ausgangssprache in bestimmten Einzelbedeutungen.

Beispiel: In einem Wörterbuch mit Ausgangssprache Spanisch und Zielsprache Deutsch können spanisch *pico* mehrere Einzelbedeutungen und jeder Einzelbedeutung ein oder mehrere Äquivalente zugeordnet werden, u. a.: *Schnabel* (von Tieren); *Schnabel, Maul* usw. (von Menschen); *Spitze, Gipfel* (von Bergen); *Schwanz* usw. (für den Penis). Dem Gebrauch des Wortes *pico* in den Einzelbedeutungen, die auf Körperteile bezogen sind, können Angaben zur pragmatischen Markierung (etwa *populär* oder *vulgär*) gewidmet werden. Dem Gebrauch des Wortes in der Einzelbedeutung, die auf den Penis bezogen ist, kann ferner eine Angabe zur diatopischen Markierung gewidmet sein (chilenisches Spanisch).

(1 c) Auf zielsprachliche Äquivalente in der Verwendung, in der sie jeweils einer berücksichtigten Verwendung einer erfaßten lexikalischen Einheit der Ausgangssprache entsprechen.

Beispiel: Für die ausgangssprachliche lexikalische Einheit *stamp* kann in einem Wörterbuch mit Ausgangssprache Englisch und Zielsprache Deutsch eine Vielzahl von Einzelbedeutungen unterschieden werden. Als Äquivalente für *stamp* in einer bestimmten Einzelbedeutung können *Briefmarke* und *Postwertzeichen* angeführt werden. Dem Äquivalent *Postwertzeichen* kann dabei eine Markierungsangabe beigefügt werden, die darüber Auskunft gibt, daß *Postwertzeichen* im Deutschen für offiziösen Sprachgebrauch typisch ist.

(1 d) Auf lautliche, orthographische, morphologische und syntaktische Varianten des Gebrauchs einer lexikalischen Einheit der Ausgangs- oder der Zielsprache. Solche Fälle kommen im Wörterbuch vergleichsweise selten vor. Die Markierungsangabe wird dabei in der Regel auch in einer Weise vorgenommen, die eine eindeutige Interpretation ermöglicht, z. B., wenn der Gebrauch von *un espèce de* für *une espèce de* im Französischen folgendermaßen als *familier* und *abusif* gekennzeichnet wird: „une ~ de < F *abus oft mit dem Genus des nachfolgenden Substantivs* un ~ de...>" (Langenscheidts Großwb. F-D/D-F 1980, Teil I, 366).

In vielen zweisprachigen Wörterbüchern ist im Einzelfall — sei es mangels systematischer Regelung, sei es mangels konsequenter Einhaltung der Regelung — nicht zu erkennen, ob sich eine Markierungskennzeichnung auf (2 a) eine Einzelbedeutung oder (2 b) mehrere einer ausgangssprachlichen lexikalischen Einheit bzw. auf (2 a) ein Äquivalent oder (2 b) mehrere bezieht.

So muß in einem großen französisch-deutschen Wörterbuch die Markierungsangabe *populaire* wohl für die vier aufeinander folgenden Äquivalente des französischen *fumier* — „Schimpfwort P Mistvieh *n*; Miststück *n*; *für einen Mann auch* Drecksack *m*; Saukerl *m*; (Langenscheidts Großwb. F-D/D-F 1980, Teil I, 435) — gelten, während im selben Wörterbuch die Äquivalente von *esquinter* gruppenweise als *familier* gekennzeichnet werden: „F ka'puttmachen; rampo'nieren; *Person* F übel, bös zurichten;" (Langenscheidts Großwb. F-D/D-F 1980, Teil I, 367).

Was schließlich den Zweck von Markierungsangaben betrifft, so müssen wieder zwei Funktionen unterschieden werden. Oft erfüllt eine Markierungsangabe im zweisprachigen Wörterbuch nicht (3 a) die Funktion, die Verwendung eines sprachlichen Elementes näher zu charakterisieren, sondern nur (3 b) eine reine Diskriminierungsfunktion. Was damit gemeint ist, läßt sich an folgendem Beispiel erklären. In einem spanisch-deutschen Wörterbuch könnten für das Substantiv *bocadillo* der Ausgangssprache Spanisch mehrere deutsche Äquivalente angegeben werden, die dem je verschiedenen Gebrauch des spanischen Wortes im peninsularen und kolumbianischen Spanisch entsprechen. Im peninsularen Spanisch bezeichnet *bocadillo* eine Art belegtes Brötchen, im kolumbianischen eine Süßigkeit, meist aus Guavengelee. Werden nun die zwei verschiedenen Einzelbedeutungen von *bocadillo* mit Markierungsangaben versehen, die auf die Verwendung des Wortes im peninsularen bzw. im kolumbianischen Spanisch hinweisen, so erfüllen diese Markierungsangaben verschiedene Funktionen, je nachdem, ob das Wörterbuch von einem Benutzer mit Muttersprache Spanisch konsultiert wird, der zumindest eine der beiden Einzelbedeutungen von *bocadillo* kennt, nicht aber deren deutsche Entsprechung, oder aber von einem Benutzer mit Muttersprache Deutsch, der das Wort *bocadillo* nicht kennt. Für letzteren werden die beiden Einzelbedeutungen des Wortes *bocadillo* hinsichtlich ihrer Gebrauchsbedingungen näher charakterisiert. Für den Benutzer mit Muttersprache Spanisch hingegen spielen die Markierungsangaben nicht die Rolle einer Instruktion für das richtige Verständnis des Wortes *bocadillo,* sondern die Rolle einer Instruktion zur Identifizierung der Einzelbedeutung, für die er ein deutsches Äquivalent sucht. Die Instruktion zum Gebrauch der lexikalischen Einheit in Form einer standardisierten oder nicht standardisierten Markierungsangabe ist für den Benutzer mit Muttersprache Deutsch nicht zu ersetzen. Dagegen können die Funktion der Diskriminierung von Einzelbedeutungen auch spanische Glossen in Definitionsform (*panecillo abierto y relleno con algo como jamón, queso, etc.* und *dulce, generalmente de guayaba*) oder in Form eines verkürzten Hinweises zur Bedeutung (etwa *panecillo relleno* und *dulce*) übernehmen.

In vielen Fällen sind andere Formen der Diskriminierung von Einzelbedeutungen sogar viel zweckmäßiger als eine Markierungsangabe. So dürfte in einem zweisprachigen Wörterbuch mit Ausgangssprache Deutsch für den Benutzer mit Muttersprache Deutsch für die Diskriminierung einer bestimmten Einzelbedeutung des Wortes *Karren* eine

¹**pico** *m* Schnabel m ‖ fig *Spitze* f ‖ fig *Bergspitze* f ‖ *hoher Berg* m ‖ ⟨Agr⟩ *Karst* m, *Pickel-, Spitz|haue* f ‖ ⟨Mar⟩ *Gaffel* f ‖ *Eispickel* m ‖ *Mundstück* n, *Schnabel* m, *Tülle* f *e-s Gefäßes* ‖ *Ausguß* m ‖ ⟨An⟩ *Zacke* f ‖ *Zipfel* m ‖ *Überschuß* m *e-r runden Summe* ‖ pop *Mund* m, *Schnabel* m, vulg *Maul* n ‖ *Beredsamkeit* f, *Mundwerk* n ‖ ~ de flauta ⟨Zim⟩ *schräger Blattstoß* m ‖ ~ de frasco → **tucán** ‖ ~ de gas *Gasflamme* f ‖ ~ de oro fig *ausgezeichneter Redner* m ‖ el ~ de una uña figf *ein klein bißchen* ‖ de ~ iron *nicht mit dem Mund (aber nicht mit der Tat)* ‖ mil pesetas y ~ fam *et über tausend Pesetas* ‖ tiene 40 y ~ *er ist in den Vierzigern* ‖ es un ~ fam *es ist ein hübsches Sümmchen* ‖ cortado a ~ fig *steil (Felsen)* ‖ ◊ hacer el ~ pop *den Rest bezahlen* ‖ hincar el ~ pop *sterben,* vulg *krepieren* ‖ se lo quita del ~ pop *er spart es sich am Munde ab* ‖ tener buen ~, tener un ~ de oro fam *ein tolles Mundwerk haben* ‖ ¡calla el ~! ¡cierra el ~! fam *halt den Mund (od den Schnabel),* vulg *halt's Maul!* ‖ andar (od irse) de (od a, con) ~s pardos figf *die Zeit unnütz vertrödeln* ‖ figf *flirten, jdm den Hof machen* ‖ → **sombrero**

Textbeispiel 292.1: Wörterbuchartikel (aus: Slabý/Grossmann 1975/1989, I., 833)

Glossierung durch das Wort *Auto* geeigneter sein als eine sog. Stilschichtenkennzeichnung. Zur Illustration aller Schwierigkeiten, die Markierungsangaben aufgrund mangelnder Unterscheidung ihrer Funktionen dem Benutzer zweisprachiger Wörterbücher häufig bereiten, müßte man (wie Werner 1980) mehrere Artikel je eines und desselben Wörterbuchs miteinander vergleichen, um typische Inkonsequenzen aufzuzeigen. Aber auch ein einziger Artikel kann bereits ein Bild von der Problematik vermitteln (Textbeispiel 292.1).

Der abgebildete Artikel ist reich an standardisierten Angaben, die auf technolektale Markierungen — „⟨Agr⟩": „Agrikultur, Landwirtschaft", „⟨Mar⟩": „Marine, Seewesen", „⟨An⟩": „Anatomie", „⟨Zim⟩": „Zimmermannshandwerk, Schreinerei, Tischlerei" — und sog. Stilebenen — „fam": „familiär, vertraulich", „pop": „populär, volkstümlich", „vulg": „vulgär, derb, gemein" — hinweisen (Auflösung der Kennzeichnungen nach Slabý/Grossmann 1975/1989, I., unpaginierte Liste der Abkürzungen). Dabei sind die Stilebenenkennzeichnungen in einer Weise verwendet, daß sie nur derjenige richtig interpretieren kann, der das Wörterbuch gar nicht dazu braucht, um die Bedeutung von spanisch *pico* nachzuschlagen oder dafür deutsche Äquivalente zu suchen. Die Kennzeichnung „pop" vor „*Mund*" in Zeile 6 des Artikels gilt für die Einzelbedeutung von *pico,* der die folgenden drei Äquivalente entsprechen. Sie ist für den Benutzer deutscher Muttersprache deshalb von Nutzen, weil als erstes Äquivalent „*Mund*" angegeben wird, dem keineswegs die Markierung von *pico* zuzuordnen ist. Den Benutzer mit Muttersprache Spanisch kann die Kennzeichnung verwirren. Er könnte aufgrund der im Wörterbuch geltenden Äquivalenzbeziehungen ohnedies schon glauben, *Mund* sei dieselbe Markierung wie *pico* zuzuordnen. Die Kennzeichnung „pop" könnte ihn in dieser Ansicht bestärken, ebenso die Kennzeichnung „vulg", die tatsächlich dem deutschen Äquivalent „*Maul*" zuzuordnen ist, obwohl die Kennzeichnung in derselben Weise vor dem Äquivalent steht wie „pop" vor „*Mund*". Der Benutzer mit Muttersprache Spanisch könnte auch annehmen, das Wort *Schnabel* sei in der einschlägigen Einzelbedeutung nicht markiert, weil im Gegensatz zu „*Mund*" und „*Maul*" dem deutschen Äquivalent keine Kennzeichnung vorausgeht. Die Kennzeichnung „fam" nach „mil pesetas y ~ " bezieht sich auf die spanische Wendung und ist für den Benutzer mit Muttersprache Deutsch von Nutzen, weil dem deutschen *etwas über tausend Pesetas* die Markierung nicht zukommt (die etwa durch *tausend Peseten und ein paar zerquetschte* mitwiedergegeben werden könnte). Den Benutzer mit Muttersprache Spanisch kann die Kennzeichnung irreführen. Er könnte am ehesten zu der Auffassung gelangen, die Markierung sei auch dem deutschen Äquivalent zuzuordnen. Ähnliches kann bei der Angabe „pop" nach „hacer el ~ ", „hincar el ~ " und „se lo quita del ~ " passieren. Sie bezieht sich vor „den Rest bezahlen" und vor „sterben" auf die spanische Wendung, während „vulg" vor „*krepieren*" auf das deutsche Äquivalent bezieht. Das „fam" nach „¡calle el ~ ! ¡cierra el ~ !" kann sowohl auf die spanischen Wendungen wie auf die deutschen Äquivalente „*halt den Mund (od den Schnabel)*" bezogen werden, nicht dagegen „vulg" vor „*halt's Maul*". Letzteres gilt nur für das deutsche Äquivalent. Weil es nur für das deutsche Äquivalent gilt, könnte der Benutzer mit Muttersprache Deutsch das „fam" vor „*halt den Mund*" analog interpretieren und meinen, ¡calla el pico! sei keine Markierung zuzuordnen.

3. Markierungen, Äquivalenz und Typen zweisprachiger Wörterbücher

Schlägt man in einem spanisch-deutschen Wörterbuch die spanischen Wörter *joder* oder *jodienda*

jo|der vi/t (sehr vulg) *den Beischlaf ausüben,* vulg *vögeln, ficken* ‖ fig vulg *plagen, ärgern, belästigen* ‖ *jdm et vermasseln* ‖ *jdn abkanzeln,* pop *jdn zur Sau machen* ‖ *et völlig kaputt machen* ‖ ◊ ¡ ~! vulg *verflucht! verdammt noch mal!* ‖ ¡jódete! sehr vulg *scher' Dich zum Teufel! ätsch!* ‖ ¡que se joda! sehr vulg *zum Teufel mit ihm!* ‖ *er soll nur sehen, wie er (damit) fertig wird* ‖ ¡no jodas! sehr vulg *so was (gibt's ja gar nicht)!* ‖ ¡no me jodas! sehr vulg *laß mich in Frieden!* ‖ a mí ya no me jode V. más sehr vulg *von Ihnen lasse ich mir jetzt nichts mehr bieten* ‖ ~le a uno el empleo (*od* la plaza) sehr vulg *jdn um s-e Stellung bringen* ‖ estoy –dido vulg *ich bin schön angeschmiert!* ‖ estoy –dido de las muelas sehr vulg *ich habe e–n verdammten Zahnschmerz* ‖ ~se vr sehr vulg fig *sich belästigen lassen (müssen)* ‖ *sich abrackern* ‖ → a **jeringarse, fastidiarse** u **joder** ‖ **–dienda** *f* sehr vulg *Vögeln, Ficken* n ‖ *Koitus,* vulg *Fick* m ‖ fig *Plackerei, Schinderei* f ‖ fig *Scheiße* f

Textbeispiel 292.2: Wörterbuchartikel (aus Slabý/ Grossmann 1975/1989, I., 669)

nach, so kennt man wahrscheinlich als Benutzer mit Muttersprache Deutsch ihre Bedeutung nicht oder unvollständig, oder man kennt als Benutzer mit Muttersprache Spanisch die deutschen Äquivalente nicht und somit auch nicht ihre Markierungen. Der Benutzer mit beschränkter Kenntnis des Deutschen oder des Spanischen, der im Wörterbuch zu *joder* die Angaben „(sehr vulg) *den Beischlaf ausüben,* vulg *vögeln, ficken*" und zu *jodienda* „sehr vulg *Vögeln, Ficken* n ‖ *Koitus,* vulg *Fick* m" (Slabý/Grossmann 1975/1989, I., 669) findet, könnte aufgrund der Anordnung der Markierungskennzeichnungen u. a. zu folgenden Interpretationen kommen: *vögeln* und *ficken* vulgär, *den Beischlaf ausüben* dagegen sehr vulgär; *vögeln, ficken* dagegen nicht; *Vögeln* sehr vulgär, *Fick* vulgär, *Ficken* und *Koitus* unmarkiert; *jodienda* sehr vulgär, *Vögeln, Ficken* und *Koitus* dagegen nicht; *Vögeln* sehr vulgäres Äquivalent zu nicht markiertem *jodienda*; *Vögeln, Ficken* und *Koitus* gleich markiert wie sehr vulgäres *jodienda*, *Fick* dagegen nur vulgär, d. h. weniger vulgär als sehr vulgär. Wären zu *joder* einfach nur die Äquivalente *vögeln* und *ficken* oder zu *jodienda* die Äquivalente *Vögeln* und *Ficken,* jeweils ohne Markierungskennzeichnungen, angegeben, könnte, vorausgesetzt in vergleichbaren Fällen würde auch so zu verfahren, nicht so leicht ein Mißverständnis auftreten. Der Wörterbuchbenutzer mit Muttersprache Spanisch weiß um die Markierung von *joder* und dürfte bei Fehlen von Markierungsangaben annehmen, daß *vögeln* und *ficken* dazu nicht nur denotativ, sondern auch pragmatisch äquivalent sind; und der Wörterbuchbenutzer mit Muttersprache Deutsch könnte den Äquivalenten *vögeln* und *ficken* Information nicht nur über den denotativen Wert, sondern auch über die Markierung von *joder* entnehmen.

Um den Benutzer eines zweisprachigen Wörterbuches über die Markierung einer registrierten lexikalischen Einheit zu informieren, bedarf es nicht grundsätzlich und immer einer eigenständigen Markierungskennzeichnung. Hier unterscheidet sich die Instruktionstechnik des allgemeinen zweisprachigen Wörterbuches von der des einsprachigen Bedeutungswörterbuches. Um die Bedeutung von deutsch *scheißen* oder spanisch *cagar* zu erklären, könnte das einsprachige Wörterbuch eine Definition liefern. Dieser wäre jedoch nicht die Markierung der registrierten lexikalischen Einheit zu entnehmen. Die Ergänzung der Information durch eine Markierungsangabe ist deshalb unbedingt erforderlich. Die Frage, auf Elemente welcher Sprache sich die Markierungsangabe bezieht, stellt sich im einsprachigen Wörterbuch nicht. Im Gegensatz dazu muß im zweisprachigen Wörterbuch die Information über die Markierung lexikalischer Einheiten nicht grundsätzlich verselbständigt erfolgen. Im

Idealfall sollen sich nämlich lexikalische Einheiten der Ausgangs- und der Zielsprache im Rahmen der lexikographischen Äquivalenz (vgl. Art. 285) nicht nur denotativ, sondern auch in ihrer Markierung so weit wie möglich entsprechen.

Wenn jemand in einem spanisch-deutschen Wörterbuch zu spanisch (1) *cagar* transitiv, (2) *cagar* intransitiv, (3) *cagarse* oder (4) *cagada* nachschlägt, so wird er, ganz gleich, ob seine Muttersprache Deutsch oder Spanisch ist, mittels der Äquivalente (1, 2, 3) *scheißen* und *kacken* bzw. *Schiß* (Maskulinum) und *Haufen Scheiße* ohne Markierungsangaben besser informiert als mittels (1) „*durch den After ausleeren,* vulg *bescheißen*" (Slabý/Grossmann 1975/1989, I., 200), (2) „*seine Notdurft verrichten,* vulg *kacken, scheißen*" (Slabý/Grossmann 1975/1989, I., 200), (3) „*seine Notdurft verrichten*" (Slabý/Grossmann 1975/1989, I., 200) und (4) „V Kot, *m.*; Stuhlentleeren, *f.*" (Martínez Amador 1980, spanisch-deutscher Teil, 80).

Werden Markierungskennzeichnungen im zweisprachigen Wörterbuch nicht mehr grundsätzlich gebraucht, um über die Markierungen lexikalischer Einheiten der Ausgangs- und der Zielsprache zu unterrichten, so kann ihre Funktion anders festgelegt werden. Eine Funktion könnte auch sein, Markierungsunterschiede zwischen Ausgangs- und Zielsprache in solchen Fällen anzuzeigen, in denen die Information durch Äquivalente nicht möglich oder nicht ausreichend ist. Über das genaue Verhältnis von Angaben zu ausgangs- und zielsprachlichen Einheiten unter einem Lemma des zweisprachigen Wörterbuchs entscheidet nicht nur die jeweilige Äquivalenzbeziehung, sondern auch die Zweckbestimmung des Wörterbuches. Je nachdem, ob es als aktives oder passives Wörterbuch (vgl. Art. 285 u. 297), für translatorische Zwecke bestimmt oder unabhängig von solchen als zweisprachiges Rezeptions- bzw. Produktionswörterbuch (eine doppelte Unterscheidung zwischen aktivem und passivem sowie übersetzungsbezogenem und nicht übersetzungsbezogenem zweisprachigen Wörterbuch treffen z. B. Werner 1982, 285—294, speziell 286, u. Cop 1984, 18—26) konzipiert ist, müssen seine Strukturen verschieden ausfallen. Nur eine der beiden in einem zweisprachigen Wörterbuch behandelten Sprachen betreffende Markierungen können bei Berücksichtigung der genannten Faktoren vor allem in folgenden Fällen auftreten.

(1) Manche Markierungskategorien gelten grundsätzlich nur für eine Sprache. Der gängigste Fall solcher Markierungen ist die gesamte Klasse der diatopischen Markierungen. Dem deutschen *Glühbirne* entsprechen im Spanischen mehrere Wörter mit jeweils diatopischer Markierung, z. B. *bombilla* (Spanien), *bombillo* (Kolumbien, Panama, Mittelamerika, Dominikanische Republik), *bombito* (Argentinien), *ampolleta* (Chile) und *foco* (Argentinien, Peru). Zumindest in einem passiven Wörterbuch Spanisch-Deutsch und in einem aktiven Wörterbuch Deutsch-Spanisch muß die Markierung der genannten spanischen Wörter eigens angegeben werden, weil bei den deutschen Wörtern *Birne* und *Glühbirne* die Markierung nicht vorliegt. An nur eine der beiden in einem zweisprachigen Wörterbuch gegenübergestellten Sprachen können jedoch auch andere als diatopische Markierungskategorien gebunden sein. In einem aktiven Wörterbuch Niederländisch-Javanisch oder einem passiven Wörterbuch Javanisch-Bahasa Indonesia müßten etwa für das Javanische die klar abgegrenzten, das soziale Verhältnis zwischen Sprecher/Schreiber und Hörer/Leser betreffenden Markierungen Ngoko, Kromo und Kromo Inggil (vgl. Art. 235) unterschieden werden, für die es im Niederländischen bzw. Bahasa Indonesia keine Entsprechung gibt. Markierungen, die qua Definition nur eine der beiden Sprachen des Wörterbuches betreffen können, sind allerdings in dem Punkt Eindeutigkeit der Zuordnung zu Ausgangs- oder Zielsprache unproblematisch.

(2) Manchmal steht im Einzelfall in der Zielsprache des Wörterbuches für eine lexikalische Einheit der Ausgangssprache kein Äquivalent mit gleicher Markierung zur Verfügung, obwohl die betreffende Markierungskategorie in beiden Sprachen besteht. In solchen Fällen muß für eine markierte lexikalische Einheit der Ausgangssprache oft eine nicht oder anders markierte zielsprachliche Einheit als Entsprechung angegeben werden. Umgekehrt stehen manchmal als Entsprechungen für eine nicht markierte Einheit der Ausgangssprache in der Zielsprache nur markierte Einheiten zur Verfügung. In einem Wörterbuch mit Ausgangssprache Deutsch und Zielsprache Russisch muß für das im Deutschen stilistisch markierte Verb *kriegen* im Russischen als erste Entsprechung das denotativ ungefähr äquivalente, aber stilistisch nicht markierte получать/получить angesetzt werden. Ganz gleich, ob es sich um ein passives oder ein aktives Wörterbuch handelt, muß der Benutzer auf den Markierungsunterschied hingewiesen werden. Der Benutzer mit Muttersprache Russisch benötigt ei-

nen Hinweis auf die aus der russischen Entsprechung nicht ersichtliche Markierung von *kriegen*, der Benutzer mit Muttersprache Deutsch einen Hinweis auf die eingeschränkte Äquivalenz des russischen Verbs gegenüber dem Deutschen (er muß unter Umständen bei einer Übersetzung ins Russische die Markierung von *kriegen* auf der Textebene anderweitig in der Zielsprache zum Ausdruck bringen).

(3) Manchmal fehlt in der Zielsprache eine denotativ hinreichend äquivalente Entsprechung für eine lexikalische Einheit der Ausgangssprache. In solchen Fällen muß im passiven Wörterbuch die Einzelbedeutung der ausgangssprachlichen Einheit oft umschrieben werden. Die Umschreibung kann die Form einer sog. Definition (vgl. Art. 39 u. 264) nach Art des einsprachigen Wörterbuches annehmen (die als solche erkennbar gemacht werden sollte). Ist die ausgangssprachliche Einheit markiert, so muß zusätzlich zur Definition eine Markierungsangabe erfolgen.

Beispiel: Viele Wörterbücher mit Ausgangssprache Spanisch geben für das spanische *jamona* in der Zielsprache definitionsartige Entsprechungen an, von denen manche, wie deutsch „wohlerhaltene Frau" (z. B. Martínez Amador 1980, spanisch-deutscher Teil, 290), einem Benutzer nicht spanischer Muttersprache eine denotativ unzureichende Vorstellung von der Verwendung des Wortes vermitteln und andere den denotativen Wert des Wortes einigermaßen ahnen lassen, wie deutsch „rundliche Frau mittleren Alters" (Espasa-Calpe D-S/S-D 1978, 769), „*wohlerhaltene, mollige Frau f mittleren Alters*" und „*Fettpolster anlegende, rüstige Frau*" (beide Slabý/Grossmann 1975/1989, I., 665), oder estnisch „täidlane v. mabakas keskealine naime" (Kaasik u. a. 1983, 336). Die zitierten Angaben werden teilweise von Angaben zu einer familiären oder umgangssprachlichen Markierung begleitet (Martínez Amador 1980, Slabý/Grossmann 1975/1989, Kaasik u. a. 1983), teilweise nicht (Espasa-Calpe D-S/S-D 1978). In keinem der zitierten Wörterbücher wird dem Benutzer ein echtes Übersetzungsäquivalent angeboten. Benutzt man die betreffenden Wörterbücher als passives Wörterbuch, so verschmerzt man das Fehlen von echten Äquivalenten, benötigt jedoch als Deutscher, Engländer, Este usw. unbedingt eine Angabe zur Markierung. Konsultiert man dagegen die betreffenden Wörterbücher als aktives Wörterbuch, so benötigt man den Hinweis auf die Markierung von *jamona* nicht, und man könnte sogar auf den gesamten Eintrag zu *jamona* verzichten, solange einem nicht zusätzlich zur Bedeutungserklärung ein paar lexikalische Einheiten der Zielsprache angeboten werden, die gegebenenfalls trotz unzureichender denotativer Äquivalenz als Übersetzung in konkreten Fällen in Frage kommen könnten (z. B. deutsch *molliges Weibsbild, üppige Matrone, gut gebaute Dreißigerin/ Vierzigerin/ Mitdreißigerin* usw.). Von Nutzen sind solche zielsprachlichen Formulierungshilfen auch im passiven Übersetzungswörterbuch (Herübersetzungswörterbuch).

(4) Als Benutzer eines zweisprachigen Wörterbuches kann man in die Lage kommen, daß man auf eine unbekannte fremdsprachliche Einheit stößt, für die es in der eigenen Muttersprache mindestens ein denotativ wie hinsichtlich der Markierung treffendes Äquivalent gibt, daß man dieses Äquivalent jedoch genausowenig wie die fremdsprachliche Einheit kennt. Die alleinige Angabe eines genauen Äquivalents für eine ausgangssprachliche Einheit würde den Wörterbuchbenutzer in manchen Fällen zur anschließenden Benutzung eines Spezialwörterbuches seiner Muttersprache zwingen. Dergleichen kann z. B. passieren bei lexikalischen Einheiten aus den Sondersprachen des Drogen- oder Kriminellenmilieus und bei stilistisch markierten Ausdrücken aus dem Sexualbereich. So manchem deutschen Benutzer eines passiven Wörterbuches Spanisch-Deutsch wäre wohl mit den genauen deutschen Äquivalenten für spanisch *cacorro* oder *lengüetazo* wenig geholfen. Sollte er sich über eines der beiden spanischen Wörter informieren wollen, so könnte es für ihn hilfreich sein, wenn ihm per Umschreibung erklärt würde, daß mit *cacorro* im amerikanischen Spanisch auf eine männliche Person referiert werden kann, die beim homosexuellen Geschlechtsverkehr die männliche Rolle spielt, oder wenn ihn für *lengüetazo* die hinsichtlich der vulgärsprachlichen Markierung nicht äquivalente Entsprechung *Cunnilingus* zumindest über die denotative Seite einer seiner Einzelbedeutungen aufklärt. Nur ist für ihn in solchen Fällen zusätzlich zur Umschreibung bzw. zusätzlich zur bezüglich der Markierung nicht äquivalenten Entsprechung eine Angabe zur Markierung der ausgangssprachlichen Einheit nötig. Im aktiven Wörterbuch und im passiven Übersetzungswörterbuch (Herübersetzungswörterbuch) müssen in solchen Fällen unbedingt hinsichtlich der Markierung äquivalente zielsprachliche Einheiten (gegebenenfalls zusammen mit einer Umschreibung oder einem nur denotativ äquivalenten Ausdruck) angegeben werden.

(5) Im aktiven Wörterbuch ist es oft zweckmäßig, zusätzlich zu den exakteren zielsprachlichen Äquivalenten für nicht markierte lexikalische Einheiten der Ausgangssprache markierte, also nur denotativ äqui-

valente, Einheiten der Zielsprache anzugeben.

Wenn ein italienisch-deutsches Wörterbuch für die Einzelbedeutung ‚Nahrung zu sich nehmen' von italienisch *mangiare* die deutschen Äquivalente auf Italienisch glossiert — „**1** (*rif. a persone*) essen. **2** (*rif. ad animali*) fressen" (Langenscheidts Großwb. I-D/D-I 1984, Teil I, 391) —, so erweckt es den Anschein, als aktives Wörterbuch, also für den Benutzer mit Muttersprache Italienisch, konzipiert zu sein. Es ist jedoch nicht unwahrscheinlich, daß ein Italiener, der ein italienisch-deutsches Wörterbuch dieses Umfangs benutzt, die im Wörterbuch verzeichneten, pragmatisch nicht markierten deutschen Äquivalente *essen* und *fressen* von *mangiare* kennt und das Wörterbuch nur aufschlägt, um für *mangiare* in einem bestimmten Kontext oder Kotext weitere Übersetzungsmöglichkeiten zu finden. Die markierten Entsprechungen *fressen* (von Menschen), *speisen, verspeisen, verzehren* könnten für ihn von Interesse sein. Im nicht übersetzungsbezogenen aktiven Produktionswörterbuch, in dem der Benutzer zielsprachliche Formulierungsmöglichkeiten ohne Zwang zur Äquivalenz gegenüber einem ausgangssprachlichen Text sucht, könnte die Auswahl markierter zielsprachlicher Entsprechungen für nicht markierte lexikalische Einheiten der Ausgangssprache oft noch reichhaltiger ausfallen als im aktiven Übersetzungswörterbuch (Hinübersetzungswörterbuch). Im passiven Übersetzungswörterbuch (Herübersetzungswörterbuch) können markierte zielsprachliche Entsprechungen für nicht markierte lexikalische Einheiten der Ausgangssprache im Hinblick auf zielsprachliche Kotexte ebenfalls von Nutzen sein, im Gegensatz zum nicht übersetzungsbezogenen passiven Rezeptionswörterbuch, in dem als Entsprechungen zu *mangiare* die beiden Äquivalente *essen* und *fressen* (von Tieren) ohne Markierungsangabe ausreichen würden. Werden nun im aktiven Wörterbuch Italienisch-Deutsch für *mangiare* die Entsprechungen *speisen* und *fressen* angegeben, so muß für *speisen* ein Hinweis darauf erfolgen, daß es als einer gehobenen Stilschicht zugehörig markiert ist, während für auf Menschen bezogenes *fressen* vermerkt werden muß, daß es in die umgekehrte Richtung hin auf der Skala der Stilschichten markiert ist.

4. Formale Regeln für die Zuordnung von Markierungskennzeichnungen

Für die eindeutige Zuordnung von Markierungskennzeichnungen im zweisprachigen Wörterbuch ist eine strikte Orientierung an klar durchdachten Konzepten hinsichtlich verschiedener Typen von Äquivalenzbeziehungen zwischen ausgangssprachlichen Stichwörtern und zielsprachlichen Entsprechungen sowie hinsichtlich Adressaten und Zweckbestimmung des jeweiligen Wörterbuches äußerst wichtig. Das konsequente Beachten solcher Konzepte reicht jedoch noch nicht aus. Es müssen zusätzlich formale Regeln dafür aufgestellt werden, die u. a. folgende Fragen beantworten. (1) Für welche Art von Elementen gilt eine Markierungskennzeichnung jeweils? Beispiel: Gilt eine Kennzeichnung *poetisch* im Einzelfall für den Gebrauch der lexikalischen Einheit der Ausgangssprache allgemein, für ihren Gebrauch in bestimmten Einzelbedeutungen oder für den Gebrauch der zielsprachlichen Entsprechung(en)? (2) Für wie viele Elemente einer Art gilt eine Markierungskennzeichnung jeweils? Beispiel: Gilt eine Kennzeichnung *umgangssprachlich* im Einzelfall für nur ein Äquivalent oder für soundsoviele? (3) Wann gelten bei einem Nebeneinander von Markierungskennzeichnungen diese konjunktiv und wann disjunktiv? Beispiel: Besagt das Nebeneinander der Markierungskennzeichnungen *brasilianisch* und *veraltend* in einem portugiesisch-deutschen Wörterbuch, daß das so gekennzeichnete lexikalische Element nur im brasilianischen Portugiesisch vorkommt und auch dort immer seltener, oder daß es einerseits im brasilianischen Portugiesisch vorkommt, ohne dort veraltend zu sein, und andererseits auch im europäischen Portugiesisch, aber in diesem nur in veraltendem Sprachgebrauch? Die formalen Regeln, die der Lexikograph zu dem Zwecke festlegt, dem Wörterbuchbenutzer eine eindeutige Zuordnung von Markierungskennzeichnungen zu ermöglichen, können den verschiedensten Elementen der lexikographischen Mikrostruktur eine auf Markierungskennzeichnung bezogene Funktion zuweisen, beispielsweise der Position der Markierungskennzeichnungen, mikrostrukturellen Gliederungsmitteln oder Formen der typographischen Gestaltung. Selbstverständlich müssen diese Regeln in den jeweiligen Anleitungen zur Benutzung des Wörterbuches (vgl. Art. 66) erläutert werden.

5. Literatur (in Auswahl)

5.1. Wörterbücher

Espasa-Calpe D-S/S-D 1978 = Diccionario alemán-español español-alemán. Preparado por Félix Díez Mateo y Frida Hochleitner. Madrid 1978 [952 S.].

Kaasik u. a. 1983 = Imbi-Reet Kaasik u. a.: Hispaania-eesti sõnaraamat. Tallinn 1983 [705 S.].

Langenscheidts Großwb. F-D/D-F 1980 = Langenscheidts Großwörterbuch Französisch. Große Ausgabe in 4 Bden, begründet von Karl Sachs u. Césaire Villatte. Hand- und Schulausgabe in 2 Bden. Teil I: Französisch-Deutsch. Völlige Neubearb. 1979, hrsg. von Erich Weis. 2. Aufl. Berlin. München. Wien. Zürich 1980. Teil II: Deutsch-Französisch. Völlige Neubearb. 1968, hrsg. von Walter Gottschalk u. Gaston Bentot. 6. Aufl., mit Nachtrag 1979, Berlin. München. Wien. Zürich 1980 [XXVII, 1047, XXLX, 1080 S.; 1. Bearb. Teil I 1874, Teil II 1880].

Langenscheidts Großwb. I-D/D-I 1984 = Langenscheidts Großwörterbuch Italienisch. Hrsg. vom Lexikographischen Institut Sansoni unter der Leitung von Vladimiro Macchi. 2 Bde. Teil I: Italienisch-Deutsch. 2. Aufl. Berlin. München. Wien. Zürich 1984. Teil II: Deutsch-Italienisch. 2. Aufl. Berlin. München. Wien. Zürich 1984 [XIX, 784, XVII, 938 S.; 1. Aufl. beider Bde. 1978].

Martínez Amador 1980 = Emilio María Martínez Amador: Diccionario manual alemán-español. 18. Aufl. Barcelona 1980 (Diccionarios Cuyás) [XII, 444, XII, 467 S.; 1. Aufl. 1935].

Slabý/Grossmann 1975/1989 = Rudolf J. Slabý/Rudolf Grossmann: Wörterbuch der spanischen und deutschen Sprache. 2 Bde. I.: Spanisch-Deutsch. 3. Aufl., völlig neu bearb. u. erw. von José Manuel Banzo y Sáenz de Miera, Wiesbaden 1975. II.: Deutsch-Spanisch. 4. Aufl., neu bearb. von Carlos Illig, Wiesbaden 1989 [1139, XXVIII, 1319 S.; Vorspann von I. unpaginiert; 1. Aufl. beider Bde 1953; Nachtrag zu I., zusammengestellt von José Manuel Banzo, Antonín Kučera u. H. Elsebach 1978, 18 S.].

5.2. Sonstige Literatur

Cop 1984 = Margaret Cop: Zur Qualität der englisch-deutschen, deutsch-englischen Lexikographie unter besonderer Berücksichtigung der Großwörterbücher von Klett-Collins und Langenscheidt. Erlangen 1984 [Unveröffentlichte Magisterarbeit, vorgelegt an den Philosophischen Fakultäten der Universität Erlangen-Nürnberg].

Werner 1980 = Reinhold Werner: Ein technisches Detail der Stilebenenkennzeichnung im zweisprachigen Wörterbuch. In: Lebende Sprachen 25. 1980, 154—158.

Werner 1981 = Reinhold Werner: Umgangssprache im zweisprachigen Wörterbuch: lexikographische Probleme, aufgezeigt an zwei spanisch-deutschen Wörterbüchern. In: Zielsprache Spanisch 1/2 — 1981. 1981, 69—75.

Werner 1982 = Reinhold Werner: La definición lexicográfica. In: Günther Haensch u. a.: La lexicografía. De la lingüística teórica a la lexicografía práctica. Madrid 1982 (Biblioteca Románica Hispánica III. Manuales, 56), 259—328.

Reinhold Werner, Erlangen
(Bundesrepublik Deutschland)

XXXIV. Theorie der zwei- und mehrsprachigen Lexikographie II: Ausgewählte Beschreibungsprobleme
Theory of Bilingual and Multilingual Lexicography II: Selected Problems in Description
Théorie de la lexicographie bilingue et plurilingue II: Problèmes choisis de description

293. Dictionnaire bilingue et ordinateur

1. L'ordinateur au service du lexicographe
1.1. Introduction
1.2. Analyse (semi-)automatique d'un corpus de référence
1.3. De la saisie à la photocomposition
1.4. Gestion d'une base de données dictionnairiques bilingue
2. L'avènement du dictionnaire bilingue électronique
2.1 Dictionnaires de poche
2.2. Dictionnaires bilingues pour micro-ordinateurs
2.3. Formatage des données lexicales
3. Perspectives
4. Bibliographie choisie

1. L'ordinateur au service du lexicographe

1.1. Introduction

Le lexicographe moderne, quel que soit son objectif (dictionnaire monolingue ou bilingue), ne pourrait plus se passer de l'ordinateur. En effet, les possibilités qu'offre aujourd'hui l'informatique facilitent grandement le travail du lexicographe, aussi bien au niveau de l'analyse préliminaire du matériel de référence (paragraphe 1.2.) qu'à celui de la constitution du texte dictionnairique proprement dit (paragraphe 1.3.). Il est évident, par ailleurs, que l'ordinateur peut rendre de grands services lorsqu'il s'agit de mettre à jour un ouvrage existant ou de générer, à partir de l'information sous-jacente à de tels ouvrages, un produit nouveau (paragraphe 1.4.).

1.2. Analyse (semi-)automatique d'un corpus de référence

Dans le domaine de la lexicographie monolingue le corpus de référence a toujours joué un rôle prépondérant. Mais les limitations inhérentes au dispositif documentaire qu'est le fichier traditionnel obligeaient le lexicographe à ne noter que des extraits de la documentation textuelle qui, au fond, sous-tend depuis toujours le dictionnaire. On imagine sans peine que la seule constitution manuelle d'un fichier d'une certaine importance prenait facilement plusieurs dizaines d'années. Il est clair aussi que la gestion par le lexicographe d'un tel fichier, avec toutes les opérations de classement, de triage, de comparaison, de sélection et de regroupement que cela implique, l'empêchait de se consacrer entièrement à sa spécialité véritable: la rédaction d'une définition ou le choix du ‹bon exemple›. Aussi n'est-il pas étonnant, comme le souligne à juste titre Quemada (1983, 102) que «de toutes les disciplines linguistiques, c'est la lexicographie textuelle, celle qui se fonde sur l'analyse de corpus étendus, qui a su tirer de l'ordinateur le parti le plus évident (...). Les enquêtes extensives sur les mots et leurs emplois dans des ensembles de textes très vastes ont trouvé dans l'ordinateur un collaborateur, certes sans imagination, mais d'une force à la mesure de la tâche».

De nos jours ce ne sont plus des citations, mais des textes complets qui sont enregistrés, puis analysés par voie (semi-)automatique. Les dactylos des années soixante ont depuis longtemps cédé leur place à des machines à lire. Quant à l'analyse qui, durant les premières années de l'ère informatique, était exclusivement séquentielle et se faisait par lots (c'est-à-dire en *batch*), elle est complétée aujourd'hui par des opérations de type relationnel, tandis que la procédure d'interrogation s'est enrichie d'une composante conversationnelle. Traduit en termes pratiques cela revient à dire que le lexicographe peut non seulement obtenir de la machine la documentation traditionnelle, qui est essentiellement constituée d'index et de concordances (cf. Martin/Al/van Sterkenburg 1983), mais qu'il peut également retrouver tous les éléments d'un (sous-)ensemble de textes qui correspondent à tel ou tel critère (catégorie grammaticale, niveau de langue, type de contexte, etc.). En outre, il n'a plus besoin d'attendre les résultats parfois surprenants d'une requête définie la veille, mais il peut, si besoin est, réajuster son tir en cours de route, par exemple si la quantité des données sélectionnées en première instance s'avère trop importante ou si, au contraire, telle ou telle intersection de deux ensembles contient trop peu d'éléments. Il va sans dire que ces progrès sont dus en grande partie au développement des moyens techniques. Mais il ne faut pas sous-estimer non plus les efforts qui ont été faits en matière de programmation. En effet, tout traitement relationnel présuppose un classement correct des mots-occurrences qui composent le texte. Or ce classement ne peut être obtenu que si l'ordinateur est doté d'un dictionnaire de machine accompagné d'un programme de lemmatisation adéquat. C'est donc seulement lorsqu'on dispose d'un logiciel d'analyse linguistique perfectionné qu'il est possible de convertir *automatiquement* une base de données textuelles en base de données lexicographiques véritable. A vrai dire, de tels programmes commencent seulement à faire leur apparition sur le marché (cf. pour l'anglais, par exemple, Garside/Leech/Sampson 1987 ou encore Martin/Heymans/Platteau 1988). En attendant les lexicographes devront se contenter de procédures semi-automatiques. Signalons pour terminer que la technique des ‹fenêtres›, à laquelle peut accéder désormais tout utilisateur de micro-ordinateurs, va mettre fin à une pratique commune mais périmée, à savoir celle qui consiste à ‹aider› le lexicographe en mettant à sa disposition des quantités incroyables de pages-paravents d'ordinateur. C'est une erreur, car «ainsi sortis du circuit informatique, ces documents deviennent des données statiques, c'est-à-dire qu'ils retrouvent les caractères, et les inconvénients, des fonds documentaires traditionnels» (Quemada 1983, 112).

Le moment est venu de se demander si les corpus et les moyens techniques dont se sert la lexicographie bilingue diffèrent de ceux dont il vient d'être question. A priori on ne voit pas pourquoi ce serait le cas, car la lexicographie bilingue pourrait très bien s'appuyer sur les résultats fournis par l'analyse des deux corpus monolingues concernés. Et pourtant la réalité est différente. Plutôt que de recourir à des corpus textuels, la lexicographie bilingue préfère utiliser des bases de données dictionnairiques. La raison en est simple: comme le contenu de la plupart des dictionnaires monolingues récents a été stocké dans une base de données de type relationnel — c'est par exemple le cas du COBUILD de 1987 (cf. Sinclair 1987) et du monolingue néerlandais de Van Dale de 1984 — un éditeur peut réaliser des économies considérables s'il réussit à construire ses dictionnaires de thème sur le fondement informatisé constitué par le dictionnaire monolingue (cf. Van Sterkenburg/Martin/Al 1982). Pour ce qui est du dictionnaire de version, l'éditeur cherchera à conclure un accord avec un collègue étranger. Nous reviendrons sur ce type d'opérations informatiques dans la section 1.4. Du point de vue lexicologique la méthode qui vient d'être esquissée nous semble parfaitement acceptable, à condition toutefois que l'éditeur reste conscient des deux risques qu'elle comporte. Le premier risque consiste en ceci que dans ces conditions la qualité du dictionnaire bilingue dépend de manière essentielle de la qualité de la source monolingue. Si celle-ci, par exemple, présente une microstructure relativement pauvre, les dictionnaires de thème correspondants ont toutes les chances de ne pas convenir à leurs usagers. Le deuxième risque réside dans le fait qu'un dictionnaire monolingue, par définition, ne tient pas compte des différences structurelles qui peuvent exister entre deux langues, aussi bien sur le plan de la grammaire que sur celui du vocabulaire. Il faut donc nécessairement compléter l'opération décrite plus haut par une analyse contrastive dont les résultats doivent être incorporés dans le dictionnaire bilingue en question.

Il nous reste à faire remarquer que jusqu'à présent, pour autant que nous sachions, aucun dictionnaire bilingue n'a été directement fondé sur une base de données textuelles bilingues. Pourtant de tels corpus informatisés existent. Nous pensons en premier lieu à la collection des *Canadian Hansard Data,* qui contient les Actes du parlement canadien. Ce corpus compte aujourd'hui plus de 2,8 millions de phrases anglaises avec leur traduction française. Les quelque 100 millions d'occurrences pour chaque langue sont réparties sur 60 000 mots anglais et 82 000 mots français. Mais les Nations Unies et la Communauté européenne possèdent aussi des corpus multilingues. Ces données sont utilisées dans plusieurs projets de traduction automatique et les terminologues s'en servent aussi. Il serait donc intéressant d'examiner dans quelle mesure les rédacteurs de dictionnaires bilingues pourraient tirer profit d'une analyse automatique de ce type de données.

1.3. De la saisie à la photocomposition

Saisir un texte en machine est une chose, le traitement automatique qui y fait suite en est une autre. Pour ce qui est de la saisie, nous avons décrit de façon détaillée dans Al (1986, 6—12) un processus qui permettait, au début des annéees 80, d'obtenir automatiquement l'article de dictionnaire *pension*

pension [pãsjõ]⟨f.⟩⟨v.⟩ **0.1** *uitkering* ⇒*jaargeld, toelage, pensioen* **0.2** **pension** ⇒*kosthuis, kostgeld, kost en inwoning* **0.3** **kostschool** ⇒*pensionaat, internaat* ♦ **1.1** ~ de retraite, ~ de vieillesse *(ouderdoms)pensioen;* ~ de réversion *weduwenpensioen* **1.2** ~ de famille *familiepension* **2.1** ~ alimentaire *alimentatie;* ~ réversible *weduwenpensioen;* ~ viagère *lijfrente* **3.2** prendre ~ chez qn. *bij iem. in pension gaan, zijn* **6.2 avec, en** ~ complète *met vol pension;* être en ~ chez qn. *bij iem. in de kost zijn;* prendre qn. chez soi en ~ *iem. in de kost nemen* **6.3** mettre ses enfants **en** ~ *zijn kinderen op kostschool doen.*

Extrait textuel 293.1: Article de dictionnaire (tiré de: Van Dale 1983, 1007).

à partir de la séquence suivante :

+V+pension [p@7sjc7]<f> <12> 0.1 uitkering = jaargeld, toelage, pensioen; 0.2 pension = kosthuis, kostgeld, kost en inwoning; 0.3 kostschool = pensionaat, internaat; ++ 1.1 -- +R+de retraite, -- de vieillesse +C+(ouderdoms)pensioen; -- +R+de re2version +C+weduwenpensioen; 1.2 -- +R+de famille +C+familiepension; 2.1 -- +R+alimentaire +C+alimentatie; -- +R+re2versible +C+weduwenpensioen; -- +R+viage3re +C+lijfrente; 3.2 +R+prendre -- chez qn. +C+bij iem. in pension gaan, zijn; 6.2 +V+avec, en -- +R+comple3te +C+met vol pension +R+e4tre +V+en -- +R+chez qn. +C+bij iem. in de kost zijn; +R+prendre qn. chez soi +V+en -- +C+iem. in de kost nemen; 6.3 +R+mettre ses enfants +V+en -- +C+zijn kinderen op kostschool doen;;

Ill. 293.1: Extrait de la base de données Van Dale (première version)

Depuis, les choses ont beaucoup changé. Au lieu de saisir un texte continu où des éléments de codage alternent avec des mots, le claviste — souvent d'ailleurs il s'agit du lexicographe lui-même — a pour tâche de compléter un canevas préétabli. A titre d'illustration nous reproduisons ci-dessous le fragment de la base de données actuelle de Van Dale qui correspond à l'entrée *pension*.

<TREFW>	pension
<FONET>	p˜@sj˜c
<FREQU>	f
<GRAMT>	12
<NULCO>	0.1
<HVERT>	uitkering
<SYNON>	jaargeld, toelage, pensioen
<NULCO>	0.2
<HVERT>	pension
<SYNON>	kosthuis, kostgeld, kost en inwoning
<NULCO>	0.3
<HVERT>	kostschool
<SYNON>	pensionaat, internaat
<CIJCO>	1.1
<VOORB>	__ de retraite, de vieillesse
<VVERT>	(ouderdoms)pensioen
<VOORB>	__ de réversion
<VVERT>	weduwenpensioen
<CIJCO>	1.2
<VOORB>	__ de famille
<VVERT>	familiepension
<CIJCO>	2.1
<VOORB>	__ alimentaire
<VVERT>	alimentatie
<VOORB>	__ réversible
<VVERT>	weduwenpensioen
<VOORB>	__ viagère
<VVERT>	lijfrente
<CIJCO>	3.2
<VOORB>	prendre __ chez qn.
<VVERT>	bij iem. in pension gaan, zijn
<CIJCO>	6.2
<VOORB>	@avec, @en __ complète
<VVERT>	met vol pension
<VOORB>	être @en __ chez qn.
<VVERT>	bij iem. in de kost zijn
<VOORB>	prendre qn. chez soi @en __
<VVERT>	iem. in de kost nemen
<CIJCO>	6.3
<VOORB>	mettre ses enfants @en__
<VVERT>	zijn kinderen op kostschool doen

Ill. 293.2: Extrait de la base de données Van Dale (deuxième version)

La différence est claire : la séparation entre forme et contenu est désormais totale. Le lexicographe est concerné seulement par la colonne de droite, les responsables de la production, dont le typographe, s'appuient sur l'information que contient la première colonne. Mais il est clair aussi qu'une telle organisation des données présuppose que le format d'une entrée lexicale, dans le sens informatique du terme, soit très bien défini. Etant donné ce format, cette grammaire formelle qui permet de distinguer les articles de dictionnaire bien formés de ceux qui ne le sont pas, l'ordinateur se charge de la normalisation et de la vérification des diverses données et références (y compris la correction orthographique), de l'arrangement par ordre alphabétique des entrées, du contrôle de la typographie et de la fabrication de la bande magnétique destinée à la photocomposition.

Des systèmes analogues à celui dont nous venons de décrire partiellement les fonctions et qui a été mis au point par la maison d'édition Van Dale, ont été développés entre autres par la société danoise DataSats Informatik (système Compulexis, cf. Danlex 1987, 175—230) et par Siemens (système Team, cf. Vollnhals 1984).

Un dernier développement récent dans ce domaine de la technique qui mérite d'être signalé est l'établissement en 1986 d'une norme ISO pour le marquage d'un texte (cf. ISO 8879, 1986). Ce langage standard et généralisé de marquage porte le nom de SGML (Standard Generalized Mark-up Language). Tout texte qui respecte cette norme peut être traité automatiquement par tous les éditeurs qui disposent d'un programme d'analyse SGML. Pour ce qui est de l'application de SGML à la lexicographie bilingue nous empruntons à Danlex (1987, 144) la séquence suivante, rédigée conformément à la norme SGML (version abrégée), qui correspond à une partie de l'entrée *navle* du dictionnaire danois-anglais de Vinterberg/Bodelsen (1976).

```
<ENTRY PRGPH = «YES»>
  <HOMGR>I
    <LEMMA>navle
    <LGRAM>en -r
      <DISCR>anat
        <EQUIV>navel
      <DISCR>fagl
        <EQUIV>umbilicus
    <SEGMl>
      <DISCR>&FLOWER;
        <EQUIV>hilum
    ...
    <SEGMl>
      <DISCR>glasnavle
        <EQUIV>punty (el. pontil) mark
    ...
```

```
      <SBLEM>stirre på sin egen &-;
        <DISCR>fig
          <EQUIV>be self-centred
          <EQUIV>be a narcissist
          <EQUIV>be narcistic
</ENTRY>
```

Ill. 293.3: Exemple de séquence SGML

1.4. Gestion d'une base de données dictionnairiques bilingue

L'avantage de pouvoir accéder directement à la base de données qui sous-tend un dictionnaire peut difficilement être surestimé. Ainsi, le lexicographe qui douterait de la consistance de son dictionnaire dans tel ou tel domaine grammatical, technique ou stylistique peut obtenir sans peine les sorties correspondantes sur son écran ou sur papier. Sa requête pourrait porter sur un seul paramètre (exemple: toutes les expressions familières ou tous les verbes exclusivement intransitifs). Mais elle pourrait également avoir pour objet une sélection plus complexe qui fait intervenir les opérateurs logiques ‹ou›, ‹et›, ‹sans› (exemple: toutes les expressions familières de nature verbale, sauf celles qui contiennent un verbe exclusivement intransitif). L'éditeur, de son côté, profite du fait que l'investissement requis pour la préparation d'une nouvelle édition d'un dictionnaire ou d'un dérivé est nettement moins important que dans le passé, sans compter la durée de la production qui ne représente plus qu'une fraction de ce qu'elle était.

Mais l'intérêt principal d'une base de données dictionnairique réside ailleurs. Deux cas précis, représentatifs des problèmes pratiques de la lexicographie bilingue, serviront à montrer que l'accès direct à des données lexicales déjà enregistrées facilite considérablement la création de nouveaux produits.

Le premier cas concerne l'utilisation d'un dictionnaire monolingue et d'un dictionnaire de version lors de la préparation du dictionnaire de thème correspondant. Comme cette méthode a déjà été décrite dans Al (1986, 12—20), nous nous contentons d'en résumer les traits caractéristiques essentiels. Contrairement à ce que semblent croire un certain nombre d'éditeurs, un dictionnaire de thème convenable diffère profondément du produit qu'on obtient en inversant simplement le dictionnaire de version complémentaire (cf. les art. 285 et 297 pour une argumentation détaillée). Mais cela n'implique nullement qu'une telle opération est inutile par principe, bien au contraire. Il faut faire remarquer en premier lieu que l'opération d'inversion est parfaitement justifiable lorsqu'il s'agit de termes techniques à caractère monosémique. Et tout dictionnaire d'une certaine importance contient au moins 25 % d'entrées de ce type. Mais il y a plus. Prenons comme exemple la création d'un dictionnaire de thème néerlandais-français de Van Dale, étant donnés le dictionnaire monolingue néerlandais de Van Dale (1984) d'une part et le dictionnaire de version français-néerlandais de 1983 d'autre part. Un listage des mots néerlandais qui avaient été utilisés comme traductions des entrées françaises du tome français-néerlandais était facile à produire à partir de la base de données. Quelques opérations de triage et de classement ont suffi. Or, de la confrontation de cette liste avec la macrostructure du dictionnaire monolingue néerlandais qui a servi de base à tous les dictionnaires de thème de Van Dale, il a résulté automatiquement un sous-ensemble de mots qui étaient propres au seul dictionnaire français-néerlandais inversé. Ces mots ont très utilement complété la liste monolingue, parce qu'il s'agissait dans la plupart des cas de mots composés qui, pour être parfaitement transparents en néerlandais, étaient pourvus d'un équivalent français qui ne l'était pas du tout. Les exemples suivants en constituent l'illustration:

— *appel = pomme*
— *appelbrandewijn* = *cidre* et non pas **alcool de pommes*
— *appelboom* = *pommier*
— *appelboomgaard* = *pommeraie* et non pas **verger de pommiers*

Un dictionnaire inversé constitue donc une véritable mine d'or. Le lexicographe y trouve non seulement la traduction de nombre de termes techniques, mais aussi la plupart des entrées à valeur contrastive qu'il convient d'ajouter lorsqu'un dictionnaire de thème est basé essentiellement sur un dictionnaire monolingue. En soi, ce qui vient d'être dit n'est pas vraiment nouveau. Depuis toujours les lexicographes ont essayé de se servir du premier tome d'un dictionnaire bilingue lors de la rédaction du tome complémentaire. Mais l'ordinateur permet de combiner des données qui n'étaient pas facilement accessibles à l'époque des fichiers traditionnels.

Le deuxième cas que nous aimerions décrire brièvement est plus original. Souvent on nous a demandé si, étant donnés nos dictionnaires français-néerlandais et néerlandais-allemand, il nous était possible de constituer automatiquement un dictionnaire français-allemand. La réponse à cette question est nécessairement négative. En effet, même en supposant que le mot néerlandais *navel* soit la seule traduction possible du mot *nombril* (en réalité deux autres traductions devraient entrer en ligne de compte), il est impossible de savoir si la traduction allemande est *Navel (orange)* ou *Nabel*. Ce choix peut seulement être fait à base du sens du mot néerlandais *navel*, information qui n'est pas disponible lorsqu'on applique la formule FN + ND = FD (D de Deutsch) pour créer un dictionnaire français-allemand. Faisons remarquer entre parenthèses que Byrd e. a. 1987 se sont heurté au même type d'obstacles lorsqu'ils ont essayé de constituer automatiquement un dictionnaire de synonymes italien à partir d'un dictionnaire de synonymes anglais en utilisant un bilingue anglais-italien comme véhicule de transfert. Pour revenir au dictionnaire français-allemand, ce résultat pourrait être obtenu par voie semi-automatique à condition de disposer de deux dictionnaires de thème XF et XD, qui possèdent une base monolingue X strictement commune. Cela est vrai, par exemple, dans le cas des dictionnaires de thème Van Dale, comme le prouve l'extrait textuel 297.3 qui figure dans l'article 297 de cette encyclopédie. Dans ces conditions une première opération consiste à réunir automatiquement ces données dans un tableau synoptique. Pour l'exemple qui nous intéresse ici, le mot néerlandais *navel*, le résultat de cette opération se présente comme suit:

navel

0.1 [mbt. een mens, zoogdier]	nombril, ombilic	Nabel
0.2 [sinaasappel]	navel	Navel(orange)
0.3 [mbt. planten]	hile, cicatricule, ombilic	Nabel

Ill. 293.4: Tableau synoptique des traductions de *navel*

De la sorte il est possible d'établir une relation directe entre les éléments de la colonne française et ceux de la colonne allemande, relation qui est décrite de manière précise au moyen du ‹commentaire› néerlandais entre crochets. Le néerlandais, dans ce contexte, ne fonctionne donc plus comme langue source, mais il sert véritablement de métalangue. Afin de rendre accessible l'information autrement que par le biais du néerlandais, il convient de trier et de classer par ordre alphabétique les éléments de la colonne française (ou allemande) tout en sauvegardant les correspondances avec les autres colonnes du tableau. Cela ne signifie pas, bien entendu, qu'il suffit désormais d'appuyer sur un bouton pour obtenir un nouveau dictionnaire bilingue. Un traitement rédactionnel postopératoire s'impose pour plusieurs raisons, qui sont exposées de façon détaillée dans Al 1988. Le but de ce paragraphe a simplement été de montrer que l'ordinateur joue désormais un rôle utile, voire indispensable à chaque stade de la réalisation d'un dictionnaire bilingue.

2. L'avènement du dictionnaire bilingue électronique

2.1. Dictionnaires de poche

L'accueil qui a été réservé en 1982 aux premiers dictionnaires de poche électroniques n'a guère été chaleureux. En fait, ces produits que Langenscheidt a introduits sur le marché allemand sous le nom de *alpha 8* ne contiennent que 4.000 mots avec leurs traduction(s), c'est-à-dire le tiers du contenu des dictionnaires Lilliput qui coûtent dix fois moins (cf. Hausmann/Honig 1982). En outre, l'usager doit acheter une nouvelle calculatrice chaque fois qu'il s'intéresse à une autre langue étrangère (anglais, français, espagnol, italien ou latin). Et pourtant, d'un point de vue purement technique, ces machines sont des merveilles si on les compare aux ‹engins› qui se vendaient surtout au Japon et aux Etats-Unis entre 1975 et 1980 (cf. Schmuck/Voigt 1986, 285).

Cependant, dans ce domaine la technique progresse à pas de géant. Les sociétés américaines Franklin et SelecTronics, qui se partagent le marché du dictionnaire électronique aux Etats-Unis, se contentaient jusqu'à présent de sortir des produits monolingues. Mais les deux sociétés préparent actuellement des versions bilingues, dont l'introduction est prévue pour 1991. Ces machines ont une capacité qui, avec 20 Mo, dépasse très largement celle qui serait requise pour contenir l'information d'un gros dictionnaire d'un volume. En outre, elles sont dotées d'une carte à mémoire amovible. Et comme leur écran permet de représenter jusqu'à 160 lettres ou symboles à la fois (répartis sur 4 lignes), on peut prévoir qu'une nouvelle génération de dictionnaires de poche électroniques va bientôt prendre la relève des *alpha 8,* qui auront tout de même eu le mérite d'avoir fait fonction de premier jalon (cf. aussi l'art. 35).

2.2. Dictionnaires bilingues pour micro-ordinateurs

Les éditeurs ne se sont pas pressés pour publier des dictionnaires bilingues sur support magnétique. En 1988, une tentative de commercialisation de la série des dictionnaires de poche de Collins sur disquette, sous le nom évocateur de ‹Collins On-line›, s'est soldée par un échec. Il est encore trop tôt pour se prononcer sur les chances du produit bilingue sur disquette que vient de lancer la société danoise Textware en coopération avec l'éditeur Gyldendal, mais là non plus on ne s'attend pas à un miracle. Et il faut bien avouer que les problèmes qui se posent sont réels. En effet, quelle que soit la technique de compression utilisée, la capacité d'une disquette reste très limitée. Il faut ajouter que le support est relativement fragile et qu'il est difficile sinon impossible de prévenir la reproduction illégale de ce type de produits. Du point de vue de l'usager, un des inconvénients majeurs consiste en ceci que même après avoir été copiés sur disque dur, ces dictionnaires, malgré leur contenu limité, bloquent en permanence une partie trop importante de la mémoire disponible. Il n'est donc pas étonnant que dans la pratique c'est seulement dans le secteur du vocabulaire spécialisé que les dictionnaires sur disquette se sont imposés. Citons à titre d'exemple le cas du produit *TermTracer,* développé par la société INK International, qui est un logiciel d'aide à la traduction et dans le cadre duquel des dictionnaires bilingues spécialisés — donc de volume modeste — sont vendus comme produits annexes.

Mais ici encore la technique, en l'occurrence celle du CD-ROM, a récemment permis de surmonter la plupart des obstacles. Et on constate aujourd'hui qu'un nombre grandissant de dictionnaires souvent volumineux est désormais disponible sur disque compact. En combinaison avec un logiciel de traitement de texte, un dictionnaire sur CD-ROM constitue un outil extrêmement souple et puissant. La capacité utile d'un CD-ROM est gigantesque avec près de 600 mégaoctets (norme ISO 9660) et les possibilités de protection du copyright sont, pour le moment, réelles. Le seul inconvénient est que l'usager a besoin d'un lecteur de disque compact spécifique qu'il doit brancher sur son micro-ordinateur. Les deux premiers disques compacts bilingues qui aient été mis en vente sont les suivants. Le premier s'intitule *CD-Word*. Il comprend 18 dictionnaires avec un volume total de 7 millions de mots-occurrences, répartis sur 12 langues différentes. Certes, du point de vue lexicographique on peut formuler de nombreuses critiques, la plus importante étant le manque total de cohérence. Cela n'est guère étonnant si l'on se rend compte du fait que les dictionnaires en question proviennent de 11 éditeurs différents et qu'aucun effort d'harmonisation n'a été entrepris. Cependant, on ne saurait nier qu'il s'agit là d'un développement technique important. L'autre disque, publié par Walters Lexikon, porte le nom de *Termdok*. La version de 1989 de ce dictionnaire technique multilingue contient 7 bases de données avec un total de plus de 400 000 entrées, suivies de leur définition et de leurs équivalents en d'autres langues.

Nombre d'autres disques sont en préparation et on peut tenir pour certain que ce type de dictionnaire bilingue électronique, dans l'environnement spécifique du micro-ordinateur muni d'un logiciel de traitement de texte, remplacera au moins partiellement son équivalent imprimé dans un avenir pas trop lointain.

2.3. Formatage des données lexicales

Si le lecteur a cru pouvoir déduire de ce qui précède qu'il est relativement facile de produire un dictionnaire électronique à condition de disposer d'un support magnétique adéquat, le moment est venu de le détromper. La grande majorité des dictionnaires bilingues existants n'a pas été conçue pour être consultée autrement que sur papier. Et dans ces cas-là seule la typographie donne prise au traitement automatique. C'est ainsi que l'alternance de caractères gras, italiques et romains a permis à l'équipe lexicographique d'IBM de transformer les articles de certains dictionnaires bilingues de Collins en structures automatiquement manipulables. L'exemple suivant, emprunté au texte d'une conférence faite par Mary Neff lors d'un séminaire IBM en 1989, illustre la procédure suivie. L'entrée originale se présente comme suit :

consist [...] *vi* **(a)** *(be composed)* **to** ~ **of** bestehen aus. **(b)** *(have as its essence)* **to** ~ **in sth** in etw *(dat)* bestehen; **his happiness** ~**s in helping others** sein Glück besteht darin, anderen zu helfen.

L'entrée correspondante du dictionnaire électronique WordSmith (utilisé par les traducteurs d'IBM) est dérivée de la structure suivante, que l'ordinateur a construite à base des alternances typographiques :

```
entry
+-hdw: consist
  +-pronunc:...
   +-pos: v
   +-feat: intrans
   +-sens
   |+-sensnum: a
   |+-collocat
   |  +-usage_note: be composed
   |  +-source: to ~ of
   |  +-targ
   |   +-target
   |    +-word: bestehen aus
   |
  +-sens
   +-sensnum: b
   +-collocat
   |+-usage_note: have as its essence
   |+-source: to ~ in sth
   |+-targ
   |  +-target
   |   +-phrase: in etw. (dat). bestehen
   |
   +-collocat
    +-source:   his happiness ~s in helping
                others
    +-targ
     +-target
      +-word:   sein Glück besteht
                darin, anderen zu helfen
```

Il n'est pas difficile d'imaginer que toute erreur typographique — et on en rencontre inévitablement dans un dictionnaire traditionnel — est fatale. Par conséquent, le contrôle manuel d'une telle opération de conversion demeure indispensable.

Lorsqu'au contraire un texte de dictionnaire a été saisi conformément aux principes exposés plus haut (section 1.3.), la situation est bien sûr totalement différente. On peut, par exemple, adapter automatiquement les données lexicales au format spécifique d'une base de données relationnelle et interroger cette base au moyen de commandes très simples. La démonstration en a été faite par Huber (1989, 67—75, 94—102), à qui nous empruntons les schémas relationnels suivants (légèrement modifiés), qui s'appliquent à quelques entrées du dictionnaire Van Dale néerlandais-français de 1985.

Voici, pour terminer, comment se présente le protocole d'une session de consultation de la base de données relationnelle dont nous venons de préciser le contenu.

293. Dictionnaire bilingue et ordinateur

relation	attributes
keywords	kw_id, kword, art_id
gramcat	art_id, cat
tr_profile	art_id, meaningno, label_id, transltxt, comment_id
labels	label_id, nature, text
comments	comment_id, comment
combi	art_id, combi_cat, meaningno, src_txt, transl_txt, transl_text

relation **keywords**

kw_id	kword	art_id
1	druif	1
2	druiven	1
3	correct	2
4	correcte	2
5	correctheid	3

relation **gramcat**

art_id	cat
1	de
2	bn/bw
3	de(v)

relation **tr_profile**

art_id	meaningno	label_id	transltxt	comment_id
1	1	1	raisin	
1	1	1	grain de raisin	
1	2	2	(un drôle d')oiseau	
1	2	2	farceur, -euse	
1	2	2	loustic	
2	1	3	correct	1
2	1	3	correctement	2
2	2	4	correct	3
2	2	4	impeccable	3
2	2	4	irréprochable	3
2	2	4	correctement	4
2	2	4	impeccablement	4
3	1	5	correction	
3	2	6	correction	

relation **labels**

label_id	nature	text
1	def	vrucht
2	def	mal mens
3	def	zonder fouten
4	def	onberispelijk
5	def	juistheid, zuiverheid
6	def	onberispelijkheid

relation **comments**

comment_id	comment
1	bn
2	bw
3	bn
4	bw

relation **combi**

art_id	combi_cat	meaningno	src_text	trans_text
1	1	1	een tros druiven	une grappe de raisins
1	2	1	witte, blauwe druiven	du raisin blanc, noir
1	2	2	een rare druif	un drôle de pistolet, zèbre
1	$	2	wat ben jij toch een druif!	sacré farceur, va!
2	1	1	correct werk	du bon travail
2	3	1	correct schrijven	écrire correctement
3	1	1	correctheid van taal, stijl	pureté de langue, de style

Ill. 293.5: Schémas d'une base de données relationnelle pour les dictionnaires Van Dale

```
DEMONSTRATION DATABASE for DIC-
TIONARY Van Dale N-F. Type '.h' for help, '.q'
for quit
< > .h
Summary of commands:
INPUT          EFFECT
.h             help, prints the information
.q             quit, terminates the session
any keyword    prints the translation profile sec-
               tion for the entered keyword
line number    prints the part of context section
               related with the indicated line
               from the translation profile that
               was printed last.
< > druif
1   0001   0.1    [vrucht] raisin
2                    grain de raisin
3   0001   0.2    [mal mens] (un drôle d')oiseau
4                    farceur, -euse
5                    loustic
< > 1
1   0001   1.1    een tros druiven :: une grappe de
                     raisins
2   0001   2.1    witte, blauwe druiven :: du raisin
                     blanc, noir
< > 4
1   0001   2.2    een rare druif :: un drôle de pis-
                     tolet, zèbre
2   0001   $.2    wat ben je toch een druif! :: sacré
                     farceur, va!
< > cor*
correct
1   0002   0.1    [zonder fouten] correct <bn>
2                    correctement <bw>
3   0002   0.2    [onberispelijk] correct <bn>
4                    correctement <bw>
5                    impeccable <bn>
6                    impeccablement <bw>
7                    irréprochable <bn>
correctheid
8   0003   0.1    [juistheid, zuiverheid] correction
9   0003   0.2    [onberispelijkheid] correction
< > 8
1   0003   1.1    correctheid van taal, stijl :: pu-
                     reté de langue, de style
< > .q
```

Ill. 293.6: Protocole d'une session de consultation d'un dictionnaire électronique

Pour conclure cette section, nous aimerions insister sur le fait que tout dictionnaire électronique est nécessairement dérivé d'une base de données. Mais seuls les dictionnaires électroniques dont l'information est stockée dans une base de données relationnelle répondent pleinement aux besoins de leurs usagers.

3. Perspectives

Jusqu'à présent il a seulement été question de dictionnaires conçus pour être consultés par l'homme. Et nous avons pu constater qu'à condition d'être muni d'une base de données convenable, l'ordinateur peut effectivement faciliter cette consultation.

Mais nous aurions tort de ne pas faire mention ici des efforts qui ont été déployés ces dernières années pour dériver à partir des dictionnaires (bilingues) existants de véritables dictionnaires-machine, c'est-à-dire des dictionnaires qui faciliteraient les opérations d'analyse, de traduction et de synthèse automatiques. On ne peut que se réjouir de cette redécouverte du lexique par les linguistes et les informaticiens, qui pendant de trop longues années n'avaient eu d'yeux que pour la syntaxe. Il est encore trop tôt pour faire le bilan définitif de ces travaux (cf. par exemple les contributions à la partie thématique du numéro 4 (1988) de la revue Lexicographica), mais il est déjà clair néanmoins que même dans les dictionnaires les plus récents et les plus complets de nombreuses informations indispensables à la traduction automatique font défaut ou n'y figurent pas de manière suffisamment explicite, notamment dans le domaine de la structure thématique des entrées lexicales. On peut prévoir que ces lacunes seront comblées dans la prochaine décennie. On peut prévoir également qu'étant données les techniques décrites dans la première partie de cet article, les dictionnaires bilingues pour êtres humains profiteront au même titre de ces résultats que les dictionnaires pour machines.

4. Bibliographie choisie

4.1. Dictionnaires

CD-Word = CD-ROM Multilingual Dictionary Database. Tokyo 1989.
COBUILD 1987 = Collins Cobuild English Language Dictionary. London. Glasgow 1987 [XXIV, 1703 p.].
Collins On-line 1988 = Collins On-line Electronic Dictionary. Neuchâtel 1988.
Termdok 1989 = TERMDOK på CD-ROM. New ed. Bromma 1989 [1e éd. 1987].
Van Dale 1983 = B. P. F. Al e. a. : Van Dale Groot woordenboek Frans-Nederlands. Utrecht 1983 [1579 p.].
Van Dale 1984 = P. G. J. van Sterkenburg e. a. : Van Dale Groot woordenboek van Hedendaags Nederlands. Utrecht 1984 [1569 p.].

Van Dale 1985 = B. P. F. Al e. a. : Van Dale Groot woordenboek Nederlands-Frans. Utrecht 1985 [1565 p.].

Van Dale 1986 = H. L. Cox e. a.: Van Dale Groot woordenboek Nederlands-Duits. Utrecht 1986 [1560 p.].

Vinterberg/Bodelsen 1976 = H. Vinterberg/C. A. Bodelsen: Dansk-Engelsk Ordbog. Tredje oplag København 1976 [1e éd. 1954—56].

4.2. Travaux

Al 1986 = Bernard Al: Ordinateur et lexicographie. In: A. Zampolli (ed.): Scritti in onore di Roberto Busa. Pisa 1986, 1—21.

Al 1988 = Bernard Al: Langue source, langue cible et métalangue. In: Ronald Landheer (éd.): Aspects de linguistique française. Amsterdam 1988, 15—29.

Byrd e. a. 1987 = R. J. Byrd/N. Calzolari/M. S. Chodorow/J. L. Klavans/M. S. Neff/O. A. Rizk: Tools and Methods for Computational Lexicology. In: Computational Linguistics 13. 1987, 219—240.

Danlex 1987 = The DANLEX-GROUP: Descriptive Tools for Electronic Processing of Dictionary Data. Studies in Computational Lexicography. Tübingen 1987 (Lexicographica. Series Maior 20).

Garside/Leech/Sampson 1987 = R. Garside/G. Leech/G. Sampson (eds.): The Computational Analysis of English: a corpus-based approach. London 1987.

Hausmann/Honig 1982 = F. J. Hausmann/W. Honig: A propos alpha 8. Steht das Wörterbuch am Scheideweg zwischen Buch und Computer? In: Linguistik und Didaktik 49/50, 13. 1982, 108—112.

Huber 1989 = Omno Huber: The Construction of Lexically Analysed Text Corpora on the Computer. Amsterdam 1989.

ISO 8879, 1986 = International Standard: Information Processing — Text and office systems — Standard Generalized Mark-up Language (SGML). Geneva 1986.

Martin/Al/van Sterkenburg 1983 = W. J. R. Martin/B. P. F. Al/P. G. J. van Sterkenburg: On the processing of a text corpus. In: R. R. K. Hartmann (ed.): Lexicography: Principles and Practice. London. New York etc. 1983, 77—87.

Martin/Heymans/Platteau 1988 = W. Martin/R. Heymans/F. Platteau: DILEMMA, An Automatic Lemmatizer. In: Antwerp Papers in Linguistics 56. 1988, 5—62.

Quemada 1983 = Bernard Quemada: Bases de données informatisées et dictionnaires. In: Lexique 2 (Le dictionnaire). 1983, 101—120.

Schmuck/Voigt 1986 = A. Schmuck/W. Voigt: Zweisprachige elektronische Wörterbücher: Am Beispiel des Langenscheidt-Wörterbuchs 'alpha 8'. In: Lexicographica 2. 1986, 284—290.

Sinclair 1987 = John M. Sinclair (ed.): Looking Up. An account of the COBUILD Project in lexical computing. London. Glasgow 1987.

Van Sterkenburg/Martin/Al 1982 = P. van Sterkenburg/W. Martin/B. Al: A new Van Dale project: bilingual dictionaries on one and the same monolingual basis. In: J. Goetschalckx/L. Rolling (eds.): Lexicography in the electronic age. Amsterdam 1982, 221—237.

Vollnhals 1984 = Otto Vollnhals: Utilization of a commercial linguistic database-system for electronic storage and automated production of dictionaries. In: R. R. K. Hartmann (ed.): LEXeter '83 Proceedings. Tübingen 1984 (Lexicographica. Series Maior 1), 430—434.

Bernard P. F. Al, Amsterdam
(Pays-Bas)

294. Problems of Lemmatization in the Bilingual Dictionary

1. The Base Form
2. One or Several Lemmas Versus Base Form
3. Lemma or No Lemma
4. Inclusion of Non-Base Forms
5. Selected Bibliography

Lemmatization is — a word not to be found in most dictionaries. The German Normenausschuß Terminologie (NAT) im DIN Deutsches Institut für Normung e. V. defines lemmatization this way: „Lemmatisierung ist die Zuordnung einer Wortform eines Textes zu der zugehörigen Grundform" (DIN 2342). In the English translation it is the „creation of the base form corresponding to a given word form, usually achieved by transforming the word form" (DIN 2342).

1. The Base Form

Most dictionaries for European languages state in their notes to the user that headwords or entry words are given in their base form. There seems to be a lexicographical convention on what is generally accepted to be a base form. For most European languages this means that adjectives are listed in their undeclined singular positive form, verbs in the infinitive and nouns in the singular. To arrive at the base form writers and users of a dictionary have to transform a given word form by a process of deinflection and disambiguation, i. e., inflectional elements have to be stripped, inserted or replaced, homonyms have to be assigned to their meaning or word class. Thus, in the sentence *The country arms for war,* the word form „arms" has to be deinflected, i. e., reduced to the base form „arm" and disambiguated according to its word class as a verb, as opposed to the noun *arm* as a part of the body and the noun *arms* meaning „weapons". While these aspects of lemmatization are difficult in the computer-assisted compilation of corpora, they pose fewer problems in the compilation of bilingual dictionaries for most European languages. In writing bilingual dictionaries, lexicographers start out with the base form rather than an inflected form. Even for languages which do not have base forms, there usually is a lexicographical convention that defines the form of the entry word. The languages German, English, French and Italian, which are taken into consideration in this article, all have base forms. Yet lexicographers dealing with them still encounter the following problem areas, for which there are insufficient conventions, and lack of theoretical support resulting in quite a lot of bad practice.

1.1. Spelling Variants

The German word ['fo:to] has two spelling forms, i. e. *Photo* or *Foto*. A non-normative dictionary will list both forms, treat the word in one place and cross-refer the other form. The main problem in a bilingual dictionary is to achieve consistency as to the preferred spelling in both parts of the dictionary.

1.2. No Undeclined Base Form

There are cases where there is no undeclined base form. This is true for certain German adjectives like "besondere ..." and superlatives like "höchste ..." and German nouns of the type „der Angestellte, ein Angestellter". So far no lexicographical convention seems to have been agreed upon for cases like these. In the superlative, in any case, it seems misleading to list the adjectival use under the adverb, i. e. suggesting that "höchst" is the base form of "höchste".

1.3. Singular Base Form Not Usual or Possible

There are clear cases where there is no singular base form of nouns. German words like *Kosten, Genitalien* and *Leute* cannot be reduced to a singular form or be assigned a gender and would therefore be listed in their plural form. This, however, poses a problem for the non-German user who might look for the base forms *Kost, *Genitalie* or *Leut;* the non-French user who might look for *gen* instead of "gens"; or the non-English user who tries to find information on "arms" in the entry **arm**.

There is a second problem area where a lexicographer might opt to give the base form in the singular but immediately add the information that the singular is rarely used as with words like *Eßgewohnheiten, Investitionsgüter* and *Möbel*.

Thirdly, there are cases where the syntax and semantics of a lexeme clash with the assumptions that non-native and native speakers make about its base form. Is it really justifiable to give information on "Daten" in the informational sense under the base form **Datum**, or to treat "Medien" in the entry **Medium**, to pretend that "arms" in the meaning of weapons exists in the singular form "arm"? The meaning of these plural forms is not reflected in their singular form, and it is, therefore, debatable whether the singular is their base form. I think there is a strong case to treat them as separate lemmas.

1.4. Several Base Forms

Although the question of homonyms cannot be dealt with here in any detail, I want to consider briefly how many base forms should be assigned to words with the same spelling. It seems to me that a bilingual dictionary with a strictly synchronic approach reduces the number of entries for homonyms to a minimum. The decision on entries for homonyms also largely depends on whether the dictionary is a decoding or an encoding dictionary. The encoding user, more aware of etymological roots in their own language, might appreciate more homonyms; the decoding user might find them disconcerting.

1.5. Feminine Forms

In most dictionaries feminine forms, if mentioned at all, are treated under the masculine form, which is generally assumed to be the base form. However, strange inconsistencies can arise when feminine forms are treated as base forms in their own right. Why do, for example, so many dictionaries mention "Lehrerin" under the base form of **Lehrer**, but not mention "Professorin" at all, ignore the masculine form "Kindergärtner" or "Schwesternhelfer", and have separate entries for **Friseur** and **Friseuse**, **König** and

Königin, Löwe and **Löwin** or **Putzmann** and **Putzfrau**? It might be argued that in a bilingual dictionary the decision could be influenced by the target language. If there are the equivalents "king" and "queen", "lion" and "lioness", there could be two separate entries. Many articles have been written about sexism in language. To avoid laying oneself wide open to this criticism a consistent handling of feminine forms should be aimed at. It seems reasonable to use the masculine form as base form where the feminine form consists of masculine form + feminine ending. With the comfort of the user in mind, I think it appropriate to have two entries in those cases where the feminine form is not masculine form + feminine ending, i. e., "Putzmann" and "Putzfrau". Yet it is highly debatable whether what happens in the target language should influence the decision on how many entries to list. It is not easy to decide where to draw the line. For example, it is not very user-friendly to treat words like "la belle" = dans un jeu, partie qui doit départager deux adversaires (Le Petit Robert) in the entry for **beau** and "la bonne" = domestique in the entry for **bon**. Interestingly enough, in "Le Petit Robert" "la belle" is lemmatized under **beau** whereas "la bonne" is a separate headword. In a bilingual dictionary, where native and non-native speakers of the target language have to be considered, it is certainly more user-friendly to have separate entries in such cases and cross-references where the information might be looked up in different places.

1.6. Participle or Adjective

According to the principle of base forms, present and past participles should be dealt with in the entry of the infinitive. However, problems develop where there is no infinitive form in use, e. g., *ausgebufft, ausgefuchst, abgefeimt*. And problems occur where the participle in its adjectival use has lost most of its connection with the verb, e. g., *sich zerschlagen fühlen, geplättet sein, brennende Frage, ätzende Bemerkung*. Finally problems arise where the form is syntactically more like an adjective than a participle, e. g., *gestiefelt und gespornt, gebrannte Mandeln, ein gemachter Mann*. It is to be hoped that lexicographers will get more theoretical support in this area, which might lead to a practicable solution obvious to both lexicographers and users.

2. One or Several Lemmas Versus Base Form

Words written together or hyphenated, no matter how many distinguishable lemmas they consist of, will be lemmatized in most dictionaries as one entry word.

2.1. Words Beginning With a Single Detached Letter

Exceptions are frequently found where a word starts with a single letter before the hyphen, as in **T-bone steak, V-neck** etc. To me, there is no reason why they should not be considered as base words and thus alphabetized in their entire length.

2.2. Compound Forms

A blank is usually a delimiter between words. Therefore, the biggest problem in lemmatization is to ascertain the base form for words or expressions consisting of several detached items. It is hoped that research into dictionary use will give the lexicographer an indication of how to solve this problem. With the user in mind, I think that the solution to this problem should be based on practical considerations rather than sophisticated theory.

The first step is to reduce a compound form to its minimum. Thus, for example, the German expressions *in flagranti, in petto, instand halten, hau ruck* cannot be reduced further. Likewise the expression *niet- und nagelfest* cannot be reduced further, because there is no word **nietfest*. However, *in- und auswendig* can be further reduced to "inwendig" and "auswendig". So the base words would be **in flagranti, in petto, instand halten, hau ruck, niet- und nagelfest,** and **inwendig**. However, it can be argued that the native and non-native speaker of German cannot identify these as the base forms. Therefore it is justifiable to list these expressions where the user is likely to look for them, i. e., **flagranti:** in ~, **petto:** in ~, **instand:** ~ halten, **hau:** ~ ruck.

Compound nouns consisting of two nouns like *data processing, cottage cheese, space shuttle* will not pose too many problems to a German or English user of an English-German dictionary because compounds are formed similarly in both languages. Despite the blank, these compounds will be identified as one concept and therefore one base form, so they can be listed as one entry word in their alphabetical place. The German user of a dictionary of a Romance source language might have more difficulties identifying a compound as one concept and thus one base word. One can assume that the decoding German user who looks up *femme de chambre, pomme de terre, chambre de commerce, elaborazione dati,* or *pigiama palazzo,* not knowing what they mean, will identify them as separate words. At first glance, there might be little or no difference for the user between "la femme du maire" and "la femme de chambre". Therefore, it is justifiable to list these compounds under the first identifiable element. However, to demonstrate the fact that they are one unit, they can be grouped together in one block as was done in Collins-Robert (1987).

Compounds consisting of an adjective and a noun, like *brown study, hot jazz, dark room; fromage blanc, nuit blanche,* are the most difficult for the lexicographer. Here the transition from fixed collocation of several base forms to one concept, and thus one base form, is fluid. A first evaluation of the Euralex research into dictionary use (Euralex/AILA Research Project) leads to the following conclusion. First, rather than identify these compounds as compounds, the user is much more likely to consider them as noun + adjective. Secondly, since nouns are looked up more often than other parts of speech, it is in the noun entry that they should be dealt with.

Set phrases and idioms such as *sich grün und blau ärgern, das Pferd beim Schwanz aufzäumen; jamais deux sans trois; to kick the bucket, few and far between* pose the problem of where a user would look them up. Some dictionaries lemmatize them "under the first meaningful element" (PONS-Collins), some do not give the user any indication on where to look. Schemann (Dicionário Idiomático) and Cox (van Dale) lemmatize according to a certain hierarchy of parts of speech. Both list the noun in first place, followed by the adjective in the van Dale dictionaries and the verb in the Schemann dictionary. This means that a phrase or idiom containing a noun is listed in the entry of this noun, and so on. Since the knowledge of parts of speech is expected of a bilingual dictionary user, using this hierarchy based on parts of speech as a criterion for lemmatization is the clearest solution which can be applied consistently.

3. Lemma or No Lemma

In mono- and bilingual dictionaries it is common practice to list names and abbreviations in separate lists. Perhaps this is because they cannot always be treated like a lemma, i. e., attributed to a part of speech, gender, or inflected forms.

3.1. Proper Names and Geographical Names

For whatever reasons, proper names and geographical names are often banned from the alphabetical wordlist, to me this is not a very user-friendly practice. Why should the user have to look up **Elizabeth** in a separate list, which usually has no indication of its pronunciation, but find "Elizabethan" as an entry word in the dictionary section? It is even less understandable why the dictionary section should only mention **French letter** and **French window,** but not the adjective "French" as pertaining to France.

3.2. Abbreviations and Acronyms

More and more abbreviations and acronyms are being used in present-day language and should, therefore, be given due recognition, i. e. be listed in the dictionary section in their alphabetical place. Was there ever a logical reason to put **FKK, TÜV, Nato** in a separate list, yet treat **FKK-Anhänger, TÜV-Plakette, Natogegner** as headwords in the dictionary?

4. Inclusion of Non-Base Forms

Bilingual dictionaries are used for two quite different purposes, i. e. decoding and encoding. Because of this dual purpose, more than just base forms are listed. While the encoding user is expected to know the base form, the decoding user will often have difficulties knowing which is the base form for the given word form they find in the respective contexts. Therefore, a bilingual dictionary aimed at the decoding user will list as many non-base forms as possible and refer the user to the appropriate base form.

5. Selected Bibliography

5.1. Dictionaries

Collins-Robert = Beryl T. Atkins/Alain Duval/Rosemary C. Milne: Robert & Collins Dictionnaire français-anglais anglais-français. Nouvelle édition. Paris. Glasgow 1987 [XXIX, 768, 930 p.].

Le Petit Robert = Paul Robert: Le Petit Robert, dictionnaire alphabétique et analogique de la langue française. Paris 1986 [XXXI, 2173 p.].

PONS-Collins = Peter Terrell/Veronika Calderwood-Schnorr/Wendy V. A. Morris/Roland Breitsprecher: PONS Großwörterbuch Englisch. Stuttgart 1981 [792, 790 p.].

Van Dale = H. L. Cox et al.: Groot woordenboek Duits-Nederlands. Utrecht. Antwerpen 1983 [1576 p.].

Dicionário Idiomático = Hans Schemann/Luiza Schemann-Dias: Dicionário Idiomático português-alemao. München 1979 [XLVII, 859 p.].

5.2. Other Publications

DIN 2342 = DIN 2342. Grundbegriffe der Terminologie; maschinelle Hilfen für die Terminologiearbeit und Lexikographie. Normenausschuß Terminologie (NAT) im DIN Deutsches Institut für Normung e. V. September 1986.

Euralex/AILA Research Project = Beryl T. Atkins/Frank E. Knowles: Interim Report on the Euralex/AILA Research Project into dictionary use (Forthcoming publication).

Veronika Schnorr, Stuttgart
(Federal Republic of Germany)

295. L'équivalence dans le dictionnaire bilingue

1. Introduction
2. Les équivalences, le réel et la langue
3. Les équivalences, la dénotation et la connotation
4. Les équivalences, l'extension et la compréhension
5. Les équivalences, les faits de langue et les faits de parole
6. Conclusion
7. Bibliographie choisie

1. Introduction

1.1. Tous les ouvrages lexicographiques de référence, qu'il s'agisse de dictionnaires monolingues, de dictionnaires bilingues, de glossaires plurilingues ou d'encyclopédies, ont pour propos d'établir des passerelles entre ce que l'usager connaît et ce qu'il ne connaît pas. Leur rôle consiste à montrer qu'il existe une équivalence entre l'adresse, c'est à dire le mot de la nomenclature à partir duquel la recherche commence, et le corps de l'article.

1.2. Dans le dictionnaire monolingue, l'article est presque toujours composé de la même façon: un hyperonyme indique le champ sémantique et un spécificateur affine le sens en apportant les attributs spécifiques de l'adresse permettant de distinguer celle-ci de tous les autres hyponymes.

Ainsi le mot *fauteuil*
i) désigne un meuble,
ii) désigne un meuble sur lequel on s'asseoit,
iii) désigne un meuble avec un dossier sur lequel on s'asseoit,
iv) désigne un meuble avec un dossier et des bras, sur lequel on s'asseoit,
v) désigne un meuble avec un dossier et des bras, prévu pour une personne, sur lequel on s'asseoit.

Il y a donc plusieurs degrés de précision dans l'équivalence. A partir de l'hyperonyme *meuble* le spécificateur apportera le *nombre d'éléments suffisants* permettant de distinguer entre tous les hyponymes possibles, qui sont par exemple:
— tabouret/chaise/canapé/fauteuil ... en ii)
— chaise/canapé/fauteuil en iii)
— canapé/fauteuil en iv).

1.3. Dans l'encyclopédie, le corps de l'article donne des éléments de connaissance sur la portion du réel désignée par l'adresse. La somme de ces éléments a pour but d'apporter un certain niveau de culture.

Ainsi à l'article **Europe** on trouvera des indications sur la position géographique de ce continent, sur la répartition politique des pays qui la composent, sur l'histoire, l'économie, la démographie, etc ... Il y a là aussi plusieurs degrés de précision dans l'équivalence. Toutefois, puisqu'il ne s'agit plus de permettre de faire la distinction entre plusieurs hyponymes possibles (Afrique/Amérique/Asie/Europe/Océanie), la notion de *nombre d'éléments suffisants* fait place à la notion de *nombre d'éléments nécessaires* selon l'importance de l'ouvrage et le niveau de culture que l'on désire apporter.

1.4. Dans le dictionnaire bilingue, c'est la traduction qui a pour fonction de donner des équivalents dans la langue cible de l'adresse de la langue source.

La traduction est considérée par l'usager comme un synonyme de l'adresse en langue étrangère. Dans son esprit, la traduction est toujours possible et ne doit pas poser de problèmes. Les langues ont en effet pour rôle de décrire le réel, dont on pense intuitivement qu'il est le même pour tous. L'équivalence devrait donc exister nécessairement.

En fait le mot étant un signe formé d'un signifié, qui renvoie à la réalité extérieure, et d'un signifiant, qui renvoie à sa représentation dans la langue, les problèmes d'équivalence vont se poser sur deux plans: le plan du réel et le plan de la langue: Le réel existe-t-il ou non dans la culture des locuteurs? Le mot qui le désigne existe-t-il ou non dans la langue des locuteurs?

1.5. Les exemples servant à illustrer ces points seront pris à partir d'une comparaison entre le français et l'anglais, qui forment peut-être le couple de langues ayant donné lieu à la plus forte production d'ouvrages de référence bilingues. Il est évident que les cas présentés se rencontrent à des degrés divers dans la confrontation de toutes autres langues étrangères.

2. Les équivalences, le réel et la langue

2.1. Le cas le plus simple se rencontre lorsque le signifié renvoie à une même réalité culturelle, et que le signifiant est représenté par un élément du lexique dans les deux langues. Par exemple:

F: *ordinateur*   A: *computer*

L'item lexical est ici monosémique et inambigu dans les deux langues, immédiatement compréhensible et utilisable par les locuteurs de l'une et l'autre.

L'usager considère a priori que c'est le cas le plus courant, voire le seul qui puisse exister. Cette vision des choses est généralisée dans les dictionnaires de petit format. Les deux langues sont assimilées à deux codes parallèles avec une correspondance exacte terme à terme.

2.2. Un cas différent se rencontre lorsque le mot existe bien en tant qu'élément du lexique dans les deux langues, alors que le réel ne fait pas partie de l'univers culturel des locuteurs de la langue cible, ou n'est pas reconnu en tant que tel par la majorité d'entre eux. Par exemple:

F: *le 14 juillet*   A: *Bastille Day*

L'item lexical est ici également monosémique et inambigu dans les deux langues, mais il n'est en général pas immédiatement compréhensible par le locuteur de la langue cible. Il y a bien équivalence au niveau de la langue, mais au niveau du réel, du réseau d'associations d'idées liées aux termes, l'équivalence sera plus ou moins réalisée suivant le degré de culture des locuteurs.

2.3. Plus fréquemment qu'on ne le pense, il se peut que le réel n'existe que dans l'univers culturel et le lexique du locuteur de la langue source. Par exemple:

F: *ballotage*   A: *situation in a political election when no candidate has an absolute majority in the first ballot and people have to vote again*

L'item lexical est là encore monosémique et inambigu, mais il n'a de réalité que dans la langue de départ. L'équivalence se réalise au niveau d'une glose contextuelle qui prend la forme d'une définition, analogue à celles que l'on rencontre dans les monolingues.

Il est intéressant de constater la position inconfortable de cette définition, qui est un compromis entre la forme de l'article de dictionnaire monolingue et celle de l'article d'encyclopédie.

Du dictionnaire monolingue, on retrouve un hyperonyme et un spécificateur. Toutefois, le rôle de ce dernier n'est pas de faire le départ entre plusieurs hyponymes possibles puisque le référent est en langue étrangère.

De l'encyclopédie, on retrouve les éléments de connaissance apportant un certain niveau de culture. Toutefois, il y a une impossibilité logique évidente à la présence même de l'article puisqu'il décrit une absence de réel et une non-existence de l'adresse à partir de laquelle on pourrait effectuer la recherche dans l'ouvrage.

La glose contextuelle du bilingue est donc une équivalence qui a la structure de l'article de dictionnaire monolingue et le contenu de l'article d'encyclopédie.

3. Les équivalences, la dénotation et la connotation

3.1. Toute traduction d'un texte suivi (article de revue, roman, poème) offre ou impose au traducteur, selon la nature du contenu, différents degrés d'équivalences: traduction fidèle, adaptation, transposition, recréation. Ces mêmes degrés se retrouvent au niveau du dictionnaire bilingue, à ceci près que l'environnement contextuel doit se faire le plus elliptique possible pour des raisons évidentes de place.

L'équivalence parfaite implique un même niveau de dénotation, c'est à dire la référence à un même élément de la réalité extérieure, et un même niveau de connotation, c'est à dire le même réseau d'associations culturelles liées au terme dans les deux langues. Le lecteur pense là encore intuitivement que les traductions de dictionnaire donnent toujours ces équivalences parfaites. En réalité, suivant le type de problèmes, le dictionnaire rendra plus ou moins compte de l'un ou de l'autre niveau de traduction.

Les exemples qui suivent sont tirés du bilingue Larousse Saturne. Seuls les traits pertinents pour l'illustration du présent propos ont été pris en compte.

3.2. La traduction a la même valeur dénotative et connotative que l'adresse. Par exemple:

F: *synovie*   A: *synovia*

L'emploi du terme, sa fréquence, son caractère technique sont ressentis de manière identique par les locuteurs des deux langues.

3.3. L'adresse reçoit plusieurs traductions, identiques du point de vue de la dénotation, mais différentes du point de vue de la connotation. Par exemple:

F: *tibia*   A: *tibia, shinbone*

Un grand nombre de termes à coloration scientifique se traduisent en anglais par un terme d'origine latine en langue de spécialiste, et par un terme d'origine saxonne en langue de tous les jours. Ainsi la seconde traduction sera employée par les locuteurs dans des conditions normales de conversation, alors que la première sera utilisée par un médecin ou un professeur d'anatomie. Les deux équivalents proposés sont interchangeables du point de vue du sens, mais non du point de vue de la fréquence et de l'emploi.

3.4. La traduction rend compte de l'adresse sur le plan de la dénotation, mais n'est absolument pas connotée dans la langue cible. Par exemple:

F: *étrille*   A: *swimming crab*

Alors que le terme français est plus ou moins bien connu du locuteur, que le mot figure à l'étal des poissonniers et sur les menus de restaurants, le terme anglais ne se rencontre jamais dans la vie courante. Il est absent de la nomenclature des dictionnaires monolingues courants et ne se trouve que dans des manuels spécialisés de zoologie. Le dictionnaire bilingue fournit dans ce cas une équivalence à la fois rigoureuse et partielle.

3.5. La traduction n'a qu'une valeur dénotative relative, mais une valeur connotative satisfaisante. Par exemple:

F: *ministère de l'Intérieur*
A: *Home Office*

Le signifié français n'a aucun rapport avec le signifié anglais. L'un fait référence à une réalité spécifiquement française, l'autre à une réalité spécifiquement britannique. Cependant la fonction décrite est sensiblement la même dans les deux pays, et sur le plan de la connotation, il y a équivalence au niveau de reconnaissance du terme, de fréquence et d'associations d'idées. L'opération a ses limites et n'est pas sans dangers dans le cadre du dictionnaire bilingue. Elle suppose le passage par un hyperonyme théorique, non exprimé dans l'article, dont adresse et traduction seraient les réalisations hyponymiques dans chacune des deux langues. En poursuivant le raisonnement jusqu'à l'absurde, on pourrait aboutir à une équivalence de ce type:

F: *président de la République*
A: *queen of England*

par le truchement d'un hyperonyme non exprimé ayant la valeur de:

chef d'État.

3.6. La traduction n'a aucune valeur dénotative, mais tente de donner une équivalence partielle au niveau de la connotation. Par exemple:

F: *jeu de l'oie*   A: *snakes and ladders*

ou encore:

F: *pain d'épices*   A: *gingerbread*

Le signifié français n'ayant pas de correspondance exacte en anglais, l'équivalence de traduction va se réaliser au niveau du champ sémantique, par la recherche d'un item présentant les caractéristiques suivantes:
— le signifié anglais n'a pas non plus de correspondance exacte en français,
— il a un niveau de fréquence sensiblement identique,
— il renvoie à une réalité extérieure ressentie comme très proche, dont on a regroupé un maximum de caractéristiques:

Dans le premier cas, on retrouve parmi les traits pertinents le domaine des jeux de société pour enfants, utilisant un carton imprimé, des dés et des pions;

Dans le second cas, il s'agit d'un même type de gâteau très sucré, de consistance molle et de couleur marron au goût caractéristique et familier (anis pour le premier, gingembre pour le second).

L'équivalence prend en quelque sorte une valeur de remplacement, se présente comme un succédané linguistique.

3.7. Le rédacteur, conscient du caractère imparfait des équivalences qu'il fournit, va souvent tenter de réduire l'écart entre le plan de la dénotation et le plan de la connotation par l'adjonction d'éléments supplémentaires de traduction. Examinons par exemple, pour reprendre le domaine culinaire, trois séries présentant chacune des caractéristiques différentes:

F: *camembert* A: *camembert*

Dans ce premier exemple, une seule traduction. On considère que l'équivalence, évidente au niveau de la dénotation, l'est également au niveau de la connotation, le mot comme l'aliment étant supposés suffisamment connus. C'est de toute évidence au locuteur de la langue source, utilisant l'ouvrage dans un but d'encodage, que l'article est destiné.

F: *munster* A: *Munster, Munster cheese*

Dans ce second exemple, deux traductions. La première apporte une équivalence dénotative, la seconde apporte une précision connotative à l'aide d'un hyperonyme de champ sémantique, le signifié risquant d'être peu connu. C'est surtout pour le locuteur de la langue cible, utilisant l'ouvrage dans un but de décodage, que le deuxième équivalent est indiqué.

F: *girolle* A: *mushroom, chanterelle*

Dans ce troisième exemple, deux traductions également. C'est la première, cette fois, qui apporte l'équivalence connotative à l'aide d'un hyperonyme de champ sémantique. La seconde donne l'équivalence dénotative. L'ordre d'apparition n'est pas neutre et a une valeur discriminante en mettant implicitement en garde le locuteur de la langue source contre une utilisation abusive de A: *chanterelle,* le mot comme la plante étant pratiquement inconnus en anglais.

Il est à noter que la précision apportée dans les deux derniers exemples est faible, et se situe à un degré trop élevé d'hyperonymie pour constituer une explication sémantiquement signifiante. Elle a cependant été ressentie comme nécessaire par le rédacteur, qui n'a pas voulu (ou pas osé?) offrir à l'usager anglophone utilisant le dictionnaire dans un but de décodage, des articles elliptiques et déconcertants se présentant sous la forme:

F: *munster* A: *Munster*
F: girolle A: chanterelle

Il est à noter aussi que toute glose plus étoffée aurait nécessité un développement encyclopédique conséquent, hors de proportion avec l'importance relative des mots dans la langue.

4. Les équivalences, l'extension et la compréhension

4.1. Les termes d'extension et de compréhension sont pris ici au sens que leur donne la logique. L'extension d'un concept regroupe l'ensemble des objets auxquels il s'applique. La compréhension d'un concept regroupe l'ensemble des caractères qui lui sont spécifiques. Ainsi *meuble* aura une extension beaucoup plus grande et une compréhension beaucoup plus faible que *fauteuil* et inversement.

4.2. Examinons les termes anglais suivants et leurs équivalents français, tirés du bilingue Robert-Collins:

i) A: *traffic warden*
F: *contractuel/-elle*
ii) A: *lollipop man/lady*
F: *contractuel/-elle*
iii) A: meter maid
F: *contractuelle*

4.2.1. Si l'on ne tient pas compte des problèmes de niveau de langue, ni des différences entre usage britannique et usage américain, qui ne sont pas pertinents ici, et si l'on fait abstraction des indications métalinguistiques qui dans l'ouvrage guident l'usager et lèvent les ambiguïtés, les termes anglais reçoivent une même traduction en langue cible, ce qui tendrait à prouver qu'ils sont synonymes. Or ce n'est pas le cas.

traffic warden et *contractuel/-elle* ont sensiblement la même extension et la même compréhension. Ils désignent des auxiliaires de police, généralement des femmes ou des retraités, chargés de s'occuper des problèmes de circulation dans les villes.

lollipop man/lady ne désigne qu'une espèce spécifique de *contractuel/-elle,* assurant la protection des enfants à la sortie de l'école.

meter maid pour sa part désigne uniquement une personne de sexe féminin, spécialisée dans la surveillance du stationnement excessif des véhicules.

4.2.2. Il y a donc dans les deux derniers cas une «extensionnisation» artificielle de la langue source, et une «compréhensionnisation» artificielle de la langue cible.

4.2.3. Si l'information est présentée telle quelle dans le bilingue, elle ne nuit pas ponctuellement à la qualité de la traduction. L'anglophone utilisant le bilingue comme dictionnaire actif pourra sans problème encoder *lollipop man* en *contractuel* dans le sens thème. Le francophone utilisant le bilingue en tant que dictionnaire passif pourra décoder *meter maid* en *contractuelle* dans le sens version. Ils ne feront aucune faute d'interprétation, aucune erreur de traduction.

4.2.4. La faute risque d'apparaître plus tard après mémorisation lorsque l'anglophone réutilisera *lollipop man* pour traduire *contractuel* dans le sens version en compréhensionnisant abusivement le français, et lorsque le francophone utilisera *meter maid* pour traduire *contractuelle* dans le sens thème, en extensionnisant abusivement l'anglais.

4.2.5. On peut noter également que *traffic warden* fait figure d'hyperonyme, dont *lollipop man/lady* et *meter maid* seraient les hyponymes. En conséquence, l'ambiguïté n'apparaîtra que dans la partie anglais/français, car dans la partie français/anglais, l'adresse *contractuel/-elle* peut se contenter de la traduction *traffic warden,* qui a la même extension et la même compréhension.

4.3. Examinons maintenant les termes suivants:

A: *stoat*   F: *hermine*
A: *ermine* F: *hermine*

4.3.1. Il y a là encore une extensionnisation abusive de la langue source par la langue cible.

A: *stoat* désigne un animal à fourrure brune habitant le sud d'un territoire et A: *ermine* désigne la même espèce d'animal dans la partie nord de ce territoire, arborant une fourrure blanche pendant l'hiver.

F: *hermine* désigne indifféremment l'un ou l'autre.

4.3.2. Contrairement au cas précédent, il n'y a pas d'hyperonyme immédiat en anglais dont *stoat* et *ermine* seraient les hyponymes directs.

4.3.3. L'équivalence est à la fois exacte et mensongère. Mensongère parce que la traduction a une extension plus grande. Exacte parce que toute tentative de compréhensionnisation de la traduction, par l'adjonction d'un spécificateur du type:

A: *stoat*   F: *hermine (dans le sud)*
A: *ermine* F: *hermine (à pelage blanc l'hiver)*

n'aurait aucune pertinence au niveau de la langue cible, aveugle à la distinction.

4.3.4. L'anglais présente dans ce cas une puissance supérieure d'analyse du réel, et met en évidence la carence du français à fournir un outil précis de différenciation.

4.4. Examinons maintenant l'information à partir du français langue source:

F: *hermine*   A: *ermine; stoat*

4.4.1. Le phénomène inverse se produit au niveau de l'équivalence: c'est la langue cible qui compréhensionnise abusivement la langue source. Les traductions ne sont pas interchangeables. C'est la somme des deux qui rend pleinement le sens de l'adresse. L'adresse joue en quelque sorte le rôle d'hyperonyme en langue étrangère.

4.4.2. Le français présente dans ce cas une puissance supérieure de synthèse et met en évidence la carence de l'anglais à fournir un outil pratique de classification.

4.5. Examinons un dernier cas à partir d'un mot ayant une orthographe identique dans les deux langues:

F: *pneumothorax*   A: *pneumothorax*

4.5.1. La lecture des monolingues en langue française et en langue anglaise montre que les deux signifiants se réfèrent à un même signifié polysémique, désignant soit une affection accidentelle, soit une intervention chirurgicale. L'équivalent anglais a donc une extension et une compréhension théoriques égales à celles du français.

4.5.2. Dans la pratique courante, les deux langues ont effectué une compréhensionnisation du sens, en ne retenant qu'une seule acception:

— L'anglais a privilégié le sens «affection accidentelle».
— Le français a privilégié le sens «intervention chirurgicale».

4.5.3. Cela conduit à deux résultats:
— chaque terme se trouve pratiquement être un faux-ami pour l'autre car il ne donne pas un équivalent valable de la langue source.

— l'affection accidentelle étant rarissime, le terme anglais a un degré extrêmement faible de fréquence. Il est par exemple intéressant de noter que l'adresse *pneumothorax* figure à la nomenclature de la partie français/ anglais du Larousse Saturne, du Harrap's New Shorter et du Robert-Collins, alors qu'aucun de ces trois dictionnaires ne la mentionne à la nomenclature de la partie anglais/ français.

4.5.4. Il y a donc bien ici une véritable équivalence sur le plan technique et sur le plan diachronique. Il y a en revanche absence d'équivalence sur le plan synchronique de l'acception courante.

5. Les équivalences, les faits de langue et les faits de parole

5.1. Le traducteur d'un article scientifique doit s'effacer au maximum derrière les mots qu'il traduit, respecter scrupuleusement la propriété des termes, se faire discret et impersonnel. Aucune fantaisie n'est autorisée, son rôle est de donner à chaque terme une équivalence, qui est un *fait de langue* généralement bien balisé, répertorié dans les glossaires techniques.

5.2. Le traducteur littéraire doit rendre à la fois la matière et l'esprit du texte. Il doit souvent faire preuve d'originalité et montrer des qualités d'écrivain, créer des trouvailles qui sont autant de *faits de parole* nécessaires à la transposition authentique du texte dans la langue cible.

5.3. L'auteur de dictionnaire se trouve pris entre deux feux. En tant que rédacteur d'un ouvrage de référence, il doit décrire la langue telle qu'elle est, enregistrer une norme indépendante de lui qui pourra être reprise de manière neutre par l'usager. Il doit recenser des *faits de langue*. Pourtant, surtout au niveau des expressions figées, métaphoriques, l'équivalence n'existe pas toujours, et il doit alors créer des *faits de parole,* qui lui sont personnels, et les imposer à l'usager.

5.4. Une illustration des problèmes qui se posent alors peut être faite à partir des équivalences possibles à donner à une catégorie d'expressions figurées solidement établies dans la langue: les proverbes.

Les exemples seront tirés des quatre pages intérieures de la couverture du Harrap's New Shorter qui recensent: «50 famous English proverbs» et «50 famous French proverbs».

5.5. Quelques proverbes sont des faits de langue dûment répertoriés, et figurent à la fois dans la liste des proverbes anglais et dans celle des proverbes français. Par exemple:

A: *once bitten twice shy*
F: *chat échaudé craint l'eau froide*
F: *tout ce qui brille n'est pas or*
A: *all that glitters is not gold*

Ce sont des items lexicaux présentant tous les critères d'équivalence requis.

5.6. D'autres proverbes sont des faits de langue répertoriés, mais ils ne figurent que dans une seule liste. Par exemple:

A: *all's well that ends well*
F: *tout est bien qui finit bien*
F: *tel père, tel fils*
A: *like father like son*

La raison de leur absence dans l'autre liste est arbitraire, due uniquement au choix personnel des auteurs ayant établi chaque liste séparément. Tous les critères d'équivalence requis sont là aussi réunis.

5.7. D'autres proverbes, répertoriés dans la langue source, n'ont pas d'équivalent figé dans la langue cible. Ils sont traduits par des faits de parole impersonnels. Par exemple:

A: *people who live in glass houses shouldn't throw stones*
F: *il faut être sans défauts pour critiquer autrui*
F: *de deux maux il faut choisir le moindre*
A: *one must choose the lesser of two evils*

L'équivalent proposé ne rend compte, dans ce cas, que du sens du point de vue de la dénotation. Il rend *la lettre* et non *l'esprit* du proverbe. Il permet à l'utilisateur-version de comprendre la langue source, mais prive l'utilisateur-thème de la force d'évocation qu'il voulait donner à sa pensée. Le rédacteur, n'ayant pas à sa disposition les moyens de fournir une équivalence parfaite, préfère ne pas prendre de risque et fournit une glose peu compromettante.

5.8. Certains autres proverbes, n'ayant pas non plus d'équivalent figé dans la langue cible, sont traduits par des calques. Par exemple:

A: *too many cooks spoil the broth*
F: *trop de cuisinières gâtent la sauce*
F: *l'habit ne fait pas le moine*
A: *it is not the cowl that makes the monk*

Le calque a le mérite de proposer une traduction plus évocatrice, mais il présente un danger en cela qu'il donne une équivalence au niveau de la langue, du signe, et non au niveau conceptuel. Ce qui apporte deux types d'inconvénients:

— L'utilisateur-version ne sera que peu éclairé par la traduction, dont il pourra plus ou moins deviner le sens métaphorique sans certitude absolue, puisque l'item n'existe pas dans la langue cible.

— L'utilisateur-thème sera faussement incité à croire qu'il est en présence d'un équivalent authentique. S'il possède suffisamment d'intuition, il aura le sentiment inconfortable que la mariée est trop belle (it's too good to be true) et que le message qu'il veut faire passer risque d'être faussé par un parallélisme formel trop parfait.

5.9. D'autres proverbes encore, n'ayant pas d'équivalent figé dans la langue cible, sont traduits par des faits de parole originaux. Par exemple:

A: *you can't have your cake and eat it*
F: *on ne peut pas avoir le drap et l'argent*

Le rédacteur, frustré d'être le témoin passif des carences de la langue cible, ou n'ayant pas présent à l'esprit une équivalence reconnue, va faire œuvre de création personnelle. Il peut aussi penser à une équivalence sortie de l'usage et d'un niveau de fréquence pratiquement nul.

Ce souci est louable chez le traducteur littéraire, mais il n'est pas sans inconvénient dans le cadre du bilingue. Il laisse en effet l'utilisateur-version tout aussi peu éclairé que dans le cas précédent, mais il enlève à l'utilisateur-thème la possibilité intuitive de sentir le danger d'un fait de parole usurpatoire déguisé en fait de langue (a wolf in sheep's clothing).

5.10. D'autres proverbes enfin présentent les caractéristiques de la rétrotraduction: un fait de parole est mentionné en tant qu'item de la langue source en apparaissant avec toutes les caractéristiques d'un fait de langue, dans le seul but de recevoir un équivalent idéal sous la forme d'un proverbe répertorié de la langue cible. Par exemple:

F: *c'est dans le malheur qu'on connaît ses vrais amis*
A: *a friend in need is a friend indeed*

5.10.1. L'utilisateur-thème ne sera pas gêné par la présence de l'expression. Il ne cherchera jamais à l'encoder. Tout au plus pourra-t-il être surpris de sa présence.

5.10.2. L'utilisateur-version ne sera pas surpris par la présence de l'expression. Il s'agit d'un fait de parole parfaitement plausible. Il ne sera bien sûr pas induit en erreur par la traduction qui lui offre une sorte de «suréquivalence».

5.10.3. C'est au niveau de la mémorisation que l'utilisateur-version risque de pâtir de l'information. Ayant consciencieusement enregistré le message, il peut être amené par la suite à réutiliser spontanément la pseudo-équivalence en s'exprimant dans la langue étrangère. Il aura alors faussement l'impression de produire un énoncé authentique et figé par l'usage.

6. Conclusion

L'équivalence absolue entre langue source et langue cible, qui est la demande légitime de l'utilisateur de dictionnaire, est réalisée beaucoup plus rarement qu'on ne le pense. Elle exige une adéquation parfaite entre le réel, tel qu'il est perçu dans les deux cultures, et les mots de la langue qui le décrivent.

A défaut d'équivalence absolue, le rédacteur de dictionnaire a à sa disposition un ensemble de moyens lui permettant de fournir une équivalence relative en jouant sur les éléments dénotatifs et connotatifs, sur les possibilités d'extension et de compréhension des termes, sur les faits de langue présents dans l'un et l'autre code.

C'est par un étiquetage métalinguistique minutieux, désambiguïsant chaque traduction et mettant en garde l'usager contre tout risque de généralisation abusive, que le degré d'équivalence lui sera indiqué et que les erreurs habituellement liées à l'utilisation en aveugle des dictionnaires bilingues seront en partie évitées.

7. Bibliographie choisie

7.1. Dictionnaires

Harrap's New Shorter 1982 = Peter Collin/Helen Knox/Margaret Ledésert/René Ledésert (éd.): Harrap's New Shorter French and English Dictionary. London. Paris 1982 [XXII, 983, 32, 798 p.].

Larousse Saturne 1981 = Marguerite-Marie Dubois avec la collaboration de Charles Cestre/Barbara Shuey/Denis J. Keen/W. Ian James: Dictionnaire français-anglais Saturne. Nouv. éd. augm. de 10 000 termes par Michèle Beaucourt/Jacqueline Blériot/David Jones. Paris 1981 [XVI, 796, XVI, XVI, 782 p.].

Robert-Collins 1987 = Beryl T. Atkins/Alain Duval/Rosemary C. Milne (éd.): Robert-Collins dictionnaire français-anglais, anglais-français. Collins-Robert French-English, English-French Dictionary. Nouv. éd. Paris. London. Glasgow. Toronto 1987 [XXIX, 768, 930 p.].

7. 2. Travaux

Baunebjerg Hansen 1988 = Gitte Baunebjerg Hansen: Stand und Aufgaben der zweisprachigen Lexikographie. Nachlese zum Kopenhagener Werkstattgespräch 12.—13. Mai 1986. In: Lexicographica 4. 1988, 186—202.

Choul 1987 = Jean-Claude Choul: Contrôle de l'équivalence dans les dictionnaires bilingues. In: Ilson 1987, 75—90.

Duval 1986 = Alain Duval: La métalangue dans les dictionnaires bilingues. In: Lexicographica 2. 1986, 93—100.

Ettinger 1988 = Stefan Ettinger: Vom möglichen Nutzen der Übersetzung für die zweisprachige Lexikographie. Einige Anmerkungen zur Bedeutung und Bezeichnung anhand französischer Beispiele. In: Energeia und Ergon. Bd. III: Das sprachtheoretische Denken Eugenio Coserius in der Diskussion (2), éd. Jens Lüdtke. Tübingen 1988, 421—434.

Hohulin 1986 = E. Lou Hohulin: The Absence of Lexical Equivalence and Cases of its Asymmetry. In: Lexicographica 2. 1986, 43—52.

Ilson 1987 = Robert Ilson (éd.): Spectrum of Lexicography. Amsterdam 1987.

Schade 1973 = Walter Schade: Zur Verwendung des Kontextes bei der Auswahl von Wörterbuchäquivalenten. In: Fremdsprachen 17. 1973, 239—245.

Schnorr 1986 = Veronika Schnorr: Translational Equivalent and/or Explanation? The Perennial Problem of Equivalence. In: Lexicographica 2. 1986, 53—60.

Zgusta 1984 = Ladislav Zgusta: Translation Equivalence in the Bilingual Dictionary. In: LEXeter '83 Proceedings. Hrsg. R. Hartmann. Tübingen 1984, 147—154.

Zgusta 1987 = Ladislav Zgusta: Translational Equivalence in a Bilingual Dictionary: Bahukoṣyam. In: Dictionaries 9. 1987, 1—47.

Alain Duval, Paris (France)

296. Grammatische und lexikalische Kategorisierung im zweisprachigen Wörterbuch

1. Zum Begriff der Kategorie in der Linguistik. Grammatische und lexikalische Kategorien
2. Kategorien im bilingualen Wörterbuch
2.1. Kategorien flektierender Sprachen
2.2. Kategorien im Chinesischen und Probleme ihrer Behandlung im Wörterbuch
3. Prinzipien der grammatischen und lexikalischen Kategorisierung
4. Literatur (in Auswahl)

1. Zum Begriff der Kategorie in der Linguistik. Grammatische und lexikalische Kategorien

Der Begriff der Kategorie in der Sprachwissenschaft ist im Verlauf seiner Entwicklung von Aristoteles bis heute in bezug auf verschiedene Erscheinungen verwendet worden. Er ist auch in der neueren linguistischen Literatur nicht einheitlich und eindeutig bestimmt. Wenn von Kategorien der Sprachwissenschaft die Rede ist, sind in der Regel grammatische Kategorien gemeint. Der Begriff der lexikalischen Kategorie wird in der Linguistik kaum detailliert behandelt. Lyons 1972, 286 erwähnt ausdrücklich 'Zählbarkeit', 'Kollektivum', 'Menge'; Allgem. Sprachwiss. 2, 1975, 349, 365—366 bezeichnet mit dem Terminus Wortkategorien Subklassen von Wortarten auf verschiedenen Stufen, die aufgrund bestimmter Merkmale gebildet werden, wie z. B. 'Beseeltheit/Nichtbeseeltheit', 'Teilbarkeit/Nichtteilbarkeit'. Abweichend von diesen Auffassungen wird der Begriff der lexikalischen Kategorie in Chomskys Konzept einer generativen Grammatik für nicht weiter durch Verzweigungsregeln ersetzbare Endkategorien, wie Nomen, Verb usw., verwendet. Im folgenden wird versucht, ausgehend von den in der linguistischen Literatur verbreiteten Auffassungen, den Begriff der Kategorie für die lexikographische Beschreibung von Wortschatzelementen einheitlich und präziser zu fassen.

Eine Kategorie zeichnet sich durch eine innere Systematik aus, sie bildet eine Einheit von Inhalt und Form. Sie wird aus zwei oder mehr Gliedern gebildet, die zueinander in Opposition stehen. Die Bedeutung der Glieder einer Kategorie beruht auf der ihnen gemeinsamen kategorialen Basis, d. h. einer allgemeinen Bedeutung oder Grundeigenschaft der Sprache.

Je nach Anzahl und Art ihrer Glieder werden binäre vs. mehrgliedrige sowie asymmetrisch privative vs. äquipollente Oppositionen unterschieden (vgl. Grundzüge 1981, 276—277). In den asymmetrisch privativen Oppositionen ist in der Regel ein Glied gegenüber dem (den) anderen bezüglich des distinktiven Merkmals unmarkert. Seine Kennzeichnung geschieht allein durch die kategoriale Basis. In den äquipollenten Oppositionen ist jedes Glied sowohl durch die kategoriale Basis als auch durch ein oder mehrere distinktive Merkmale erklärt. Die Kategorie wird in einer gegebenen Sprache durch Systeme der morphologischen Formen/Paradigmen und/oder Systeme (zusätzlicher) syntaktischer Mittel/Funktionen und/oder Systeme zusätzlicher lexikalischer Mittel, die Wortbildungsmittel einschließen, ausgedrückt. Die Kategorien sind sprachspezifisch. Für ihre Charakterisierung und Klassifizierung ist ein einheitliches Kriterium anzusetzen: ihr Inhalt, der im wesentlichen auch ihre Funktion bestimmt, oder ihre Form. Die Ausdrucksmittel einer Kategorie sind immer nur der Indikator für ihren Inhalt; ein und dieselbe Kategorie kann verschiedene Formen haben. Nicht die Form ist die wesentliche Bedingung für die Bildung einer Kategorie, sondern die Existenz von gegensätzlichen „Bedeutungen" mit einem gemeinsamen Nenner. Der Unterscheidung zwischen grammatischen und lexikalischen Kategorien liegt die traditionelle Zweiteilung in 'Wortschatz' und 'Grammatik' (Sprachlehre) in der Sprachbeschreibung zugrunde. Lexikalische Kategorien sind dadurch von grammatischen Kategorien abgegrenzt, daß sie auf einem kategorialen semantischen Merkmal beruhen, das Bestandteil der semantischen Struktur des betreffenden Wortschatzelements und folglich allen seinen Wortformen eigen ist. Kategorien, die die Wortbildung betreffen, können ebenfalls zu den lexikalischen Kategorien gerechnet werden. Die Allgemeinbedeutung grammatischer Kategorien existiert unabhängig von den konkreten lexikalischen Bedeutungen.

2. Kategorien im bilingualen Wörterbuch

Die grammatische und lexikalische Kategorisierung der Wörter im zweisprachigen Wörterbuch ist ein wesentliches Element seiner Gestaltung mit einer langen Tradition.

2.1. Kategorien flektierender Sprachen

In der folgenden Übersicht wird versucht, Kategorien, die in der zweisprachigen Lexikographie eine Rolle spielen, systematisch zusammenzufassen (vgl. Abb. 296.1).

Außer diesen Kategorien kommen in Wörterbüchern Kennzeichnungen vor wie 'Abkürzung', 'Interjektion', 'Attribut' u. a. m., deren Status als Kategorie(nglied) nicht geklärt ist. Schon ein oberflächlicher Vergleich verschiedener bilingualer Wörterbücher zeigt, daß die Kategorien in recht unterschiedlichem Umfang für die Gestaltung der Wörterbuchartikel genutzt werden. Keine oder nahezu keine Kategorisierung enthalten z. B. Chin.-dt. Wb. 1924, Chin.-dt. Wb. 1985, Chin.-engl. Wb. 1956, Chin.-russ. Wb. 1977, Gr. Chin.-russ. Wb. 1984. Demgegenüber sind Wörterbücher mit einem indoeuropäischen Sprachenpaar sowie einige der zweisprachigen indoeuropäisch-chinesischen Wörterbücher relativ umfangreich mit Angaben zu grammatischen und zu einem geringen Teil zu lexikalischen Kategorien versehen (u. a. z. B. Dt.-chin. Wb. 1983, Neues Engl.-chin. Wb. 1975, Russ.-dt. Wb. 1956). Diese Angaben betreffen insbesondere die Kategorien, die ihren Ausdruck in Flexionsformen finden, wie Kasus, Numerus, Person, Tempus, Modus, Aspekt, Komparation, Determination. Eine mehr oder weniger durchgängige Wortartenmarkierung ist in der Regel ebenfalls nur in Wörterbüchern mit indoeuropäischen Sprachen zu finden. Die chinesischen Wortarten sind fast nie ausgezeichnet. Nur „besondere" oder „schwierige" Wortklassen, wie Zähleinheitswörter (z. B. Chin.-engl. Wb. 1956), dazu Interjektionen und Onomatopoetika (z. B. Chin.-russ. Wb. 1977) sowie darüber hinaus Präpositionen, Personalpronomen, Partikeln u. a. (z. B. Chin.-dt. Wb. 1985) sind gekennzeichnet. Die Kategorisierung der Verben entsprechend ihrer Subjekt-/Objektgebundenheit erfolgt in der Mehrzahl der Wörterbücher durch die Subklassifizierung derselben als intransitive und transitive bzw. auch reflexive, reziproke und impersonelle (z. B. Dt.-chin. Wb. 1983, Russ.-dt. Wb. 1956). Außerdem liefern einzelne Wörterbücher Informationen zu häufig passivischem Gebrauch von Verben (z. B. Neues Engl.-chin. Wb. 1975). Für die Einordnung von Lexemen in lexikalische Kategorien werden die Begriffe 'Kollektivum' (z. B. Chin.-russ. Wb. 1977, Russ.-dt. Wb. 1956) und, je nach Stichwortauswahl, auch 'Eigenname', 'Abkürzung', 'Maßangabe' (z. B. Chin.-dt. Wb. 1985, Chin.-russ. Wb. 1977, Gr. Chin.-russ. Wb. 1984, Neues Engl.-chin. Wb. 1975) verwendet. Die Kategorisierungen in den Wörterbüchern haben in der Regel keine Basis in einer Grammatik, die Teil des Wör-

Kategorie/kategoriale Basis	distinktives Merkmal	Kategorienglieder/Bezeichnung
Genus	männlich	Maskulinum
	weiblich	Femininum
	sächlich	Neutrum
Kasus		Nominativ
		Genitiv
		.
		.
		.
Numerus	ein	Singular
	zwei	Dual (Sorbisch, Slowenisch)
	mehr	Plural
Person	Sprecher	1. Person
	Angesprochener	2. Person
	Dritter	3. Person
Tempus	Verlauf allgemein	Präsens
	Verlauf vollzogen	Präteritum
	Vollzug allgemein	Perfekt
	.	
	.	
	.	
Modus	1. Wirklichkeit	Indikativ
	Möglichkeit	Konjunktiv
	2. Aufforderung	Imperativ
	Feststellung	
	Frage	
Genus verbi	±agensbezogen	Aktiv
	−agensbezogen	Passiv
		Medium (Griechisch)
Aspekt	Gesamtheit der Handlung	vollendeter Aspekt
	Verlauf der Handlung	unvollendeter Aspekt (slawische Sprachen)
Komparation		Positiv
	relativ zu ...	Komparativ
	Höchstform	Superlativ
Wortart		Substantiv
		Verb
		.
		.
		.
Subjekt-/Objektgebundenheit		intransitiv
		transitiv
		reflexiv
		reziprok
		impersonell
Generalisierung	+generell und ±individuell	Gattungsname
	−generell und +individuell	Eigenname
Teilbarkeit	+teilbar	Gattungsname
	−teilbar	Kollektivum (Russisch)
Art des Dinges	+beseelt	
	−beseelt	
Maß des Dinges	Vergrößerung	Augmentativum
	Verkleinerung	Diminutivum
Bestimmtheit		
1. Verb	unbestimmt	
	bestimmt	Infinitiv
2. Nomen	unbestimmt	
	bestimmt	

Abb. 296.1: Lexikographisch relevante Kategorien einiger flektierender Sprachen

terbuchs ist bzw. auf die sich das Wörterbuch explizit bezieht. Einige Langenscheidts Taschenwörterbücher Deutsch-Fremdsprache enthalten Teil- bzw. Kurzgrammatiken für die Zielsprache. Im Hinblick auf das Sprachen p a a r ist zu konstatieren, daß Wortarten generell nur bei den Stichwörtern der Ausgangssprache (AS) verzeichnet sind, wohingegen Informationen zu syntaktischen Eigenschaften der Wörter meist nur bei der Zielsprache (ZS) gegeben werden. Nur wenige Wörterbücher machen syntaktische Angaben auch zum Wortschatz der AS. Kategorien, die die Flexion betreffen, sind zumeist nur für die AS oder für die ZS verzeichnet, wobei es sich in der Regel um die Fremdsprache für den (vermutlichen) Benutzer handelt.

2.2. Kategorien im Chinesischen und Probleme ihrer Behandlung im Wörterbuch

Die mangelhaft erscheinende Kategorisierung chinesischer Lexeme liegt offenbar in den Eigenschaften des Chinesischen begründet. Es verfügt, als eine seiner größten Besonderheiten, nicht über Merkmale der Morphologie im engen Sinne. Im Chinesischen sind Kategorien mit lexikalischen bzw. Wortbildungsmitteln oder durch die Ordnung der Wörter im Syntagma, durch syntaktische Beziehungen oder Funktionen ausgedrückt. Im folgenden sind einige Kategorien aufgeführt (vgl. Abb. 296.2).

Die Kategorien des Chinesischen sind m. W. noch nirgends umfassend beschrieben. Deshalb kann diese Aufstellung nur vorläufig sein (vgl. u. a. Peng Chunan 1957, Lü Shuxiang 1980, 10, Jachontov 1975). Einige der hier angeführten Kategorien sind in ihrer Allgemeingültigkeit eingeschränkt, d. h. die kategorialen Ausdrucksmittel, wie z. B. *men* (Plural) oder *le* (Vollendung), dürfen nicht, müssen oder können im Satz erscheinen. Darüber hinaus lassen usuelle oder semantische Bedingungen die Verbindung bestimmter Verben mit *zhe, le* und *guò* oder deren Reduplikation nicht zu. Daraus ergibt sich

Kategorie	distinktives Merkmal	Ausdrucksform
Numerus	ein/mehr	
	mehr	Pronomen/Nomen (Person) + *men*
Art des Dinges		Zähleinheitswort + Nomen
z. B.:	lang u. dünn *(Strick)*	*tiáo* + Nomen
	flach u. eben *(Tisch)*	*zhāng* + Nomen
Aspekt	1. Verlaufsform Nichtverlaufsform	Verb + *zhe*
	2. Vollendung Nichtvollendung	Verb + *le*
	3. Erfahrung Nichterfahrung	Verb + *guò*
	4. Kurzzeitigkeit/geringe Frequenz normale Dauer	Reduplikation des Verbs
	5. Möglichkeit Wirklichkeit	Verb + *de/bu* + Komplement
Aktionsart	Resultat ohne Resultat	Verb + Komplement
Orientierung (Richtung)	Zum Sprecher hin	Verb + (...) *lai*
	vom Sprecher weg	Verb + (...) *qu*
Maß der Eigenschaft	Verstärkung/ Abschwächung normal	Reduplikation + Satzstellung des Adj.
Komparation	Positiv	
	Komparativ	*gèng* + Adj.
	Superlativ	*zuì* + Adj.

Abb. 296.2: Ausgewählte chinesische Kategorien

die Frage, ob und wie die betreffenden Lexeme im Wörterbuch kategorisiert werden können. Andere Kategorien berühren das Problem der Bestimmung der Lemmata. Es gibt Auffassungen, daß Verben zusammen mit ihrem Komplement der 'Orientierung' oder des 'Resultats' als lexikalische Einheiten behandelt werden sollten. Probleme wirft auch die Kategorie 'Wortart' auf. Der Mangel an wortartentypischen flexionsmorphologischen Merkmalen bedingt die Bestimmung der Wortarten nach ihrer (allgemeinen) lexikalischen Bedeutung und nach ihren grammatischen Funktionen. Dabei ist jedoch eine mögliche Asymmetrie im Verhältnis Wortart — Satzglied zu konstatieren, die sich in einer relativen Beweglichkeit der Stellung einer Wortart im Satz, besonders in der mündlichen Rede, oder auch in der zeitweiligen Annahme von Merkmalen anderer Wortarten (Adjektive haben verbale Merkmale, Verben treten als Substantive auf) zeigt. Aus diesem Grunde erscheint die Wortartenkennzeichnung besonders bei den Substantiven, Verben und Adjektiven in Wörterbüchern problematisch.

3. Prinzipien der grammatischen und lexikalischen Kategorisierung

Grammatische und lexikalische Kategorisierungen sind ein wichtiger Bestandteil der Wörterbucheinträge. Sie ergänzen die anderen Informationen, die ein Benutzer für den richtigen Gebrauch eines gesuchten Lexems der Zielsprache als der zentralen Größe in einem bilingualen Wörterbuch benötigt. In einem solchen kann die Kategorisierung nicht gleichmäßig auf beide Sprachen verteilt sein. Sie sollte in Abhängigkeit von der Funktion eines Lexems im Wörterbuch erfolgen, nämlich, ob es Stichwort oder Übersetzungsäquivalent, eine muttersprachliche oder fremdsprachliche Einheit für den Benutzer ist. Kategorisierungen hängen ferner von der Größe eines Wörterbuchs, einschließlich der Stichwortauswahl (Einbeziehung von Namen, Abkürzungen usw.), vom Typ der Sprachen, von ökonomischen Aspekten und von der Handhabbarkeit ab. Nicht zuletzt spielt die Verteilung derartiger Informationen auf Wörterbuch und Grammatik (Sprachlehre) eine Rolle. Bestimmte Strukturen und Beziehungen in zweisprachigen Wörterbüchern haben für die Kategorisierung Bedeutung, wie die Monosemierung des Stichworts oder die Äquivalenzbeziehungen. Das gilt insbesondere bei Nichtübereinstimmung von Kategorien der beiden Sprachen. Lexikalische Kategorien des Lemmas können oft durch das Äquivalent der Zielsprache ausgedrückt werden. Ihre Angabe ist hingegen unentbehrlich, wenn sie zur Monosemierung beiträgt, z. B. *foot* — *Fuß* als Körperteil und als Maßangabe. Diminutive könnten als reguläre Bildungen im Wörterbuch entfallen. Treten sie im Zusammenhang mit asymmetrischen Äquivalenzbeziehungen auf, sind sie zu kategorisieren, z. B. hat das Chinesische für *Gärtchen* und *Kleingarten* nur einen Ausdruck. Zu überlegen ist auch, ob auf traditionell lexikographisch relevante Kategorien aufgrund neuer sprachtheoretischer Erkenntnisse verzichtet werden sollte. Das betrifft z. B. die Unterteilung der Verben in intransitive vs. transitive. Diese sagt für die Syntagmenbildung nicht viel aus, da sowohl syntaktische Anschlüsse (Präpositionen, Rektion) als auch semantische Kontextpartner(klassen) nicht darin enthalten sind. An Stelle der Kategorie 'Subjektiv-/Objektgebundenheit' könnte die Kategorie 'Valenz' treten.

Die Kategorisierung von Lexemen kann explizit durch Nennung des Kategorienglieds bzw. des distinktiven Merkmals oder durch die Angabe der Formenmittel vorgenommen werden. Eine implizite Kategorisierung kann ebenfalls informativ sein. Als solche können z. B. Satzmodelle gelten, wie sie systematisch u. a. im Dt.-chin. Wb. 1983 gegeben werden. Aus ihnen können ggf. die Wortklassenzugehörigkeit, der attributive bzw. prädikative Gebrauch von Adjektiven u. ä. m. abgelesen werden. Die Wahl dieser oder jener Kategorienmarkierung sollte prinzipiell von der damit zu erreichenden Informationsintensität und Ökonomie bei der Wörterbuchgestaltung abhängen.

4. Literatur (in Auswahl)

4.1. Wörterbücher

Chin.-dt. Wb. 1924 = Werner Rüdenberg: Chinesisch-deutsches Wörterbuch. Hamburg 1924 [IX, 687 S.].

Chin.-dt. Wb. 1985 = Chinesisch-deutsches Wörterbuch. 2 Bde. Berlin (DDR) 1985 [XVI, 044, 1381 S.].

Chin.-engl. Wb. 1956 = Mathew's Chinese-English Dictionary. 7. Druck. Cambridge, Massachusetts 1956 [XXIV, 1226 S., 1. Auflage 1931].

Chin.-russ. Wb. 1977 = Han E Cidian. Beijing 1977 [29, 1235 S.].

Dt.-chin. Wb. 1983 = De Han Cidian. Shanghai 1983 [9, 1227 S.].

Gr. Chin.-russ. Wb. 1984 = Bol'šoj kitajsko-russkij slovar'. 4 Bde. Moskva 1983—1984 [insges. 3917 S.].

Neues Engl.-chin. Wb. 1975 = Xin Ying Han Cidian. Shanghai 1975 [12, 1688 S.].

Russ.-dt. Wb. 1956 = Russko-nemeckij slovar'. 3. überarbeitete und ergänzte Aufl. Moskva 1956 [919 S.].

4.2. Sonstige Literatur

Allgem. Sprachwiss. 2. 1975 = Allgemeine Sprachwissenschaft. Bd. 2. V. einem Autorenkollektiv u. d. Ltg. v. B. A. Serébrennikow, ins Deutsche übertr. und hrsg. v. Hans Zikmund u. Günter Feudel. Berlin 1975.

Grundzüge 1981 = Grundzüge einer deutschen Grammatik. V. einem Autorenkollektiv u. d. Ltg. v. Karl-Erich Heidolph, Walter Flämig u. Wolfgang Motsch. Berlin 1981.

Lyons 1972 = John Lyons: Einführung in die moderne Linguistik. 2. durchgesehene Aufl. München 1972.

Jachontov 1975 = Sergej Evgenevič Jachontov: Grammatičeskie kategorii amorfnogo jazyka [Grammatische Kategorien der amorphen Sprache]. In: Tipologija grammatičeskich kategorii: Meščaninovskie štenija [Eine Typologie grammatischer Kategorien: Lesung zum Gedenken an I. I. Meščaninov]. Moskva 1975, 105—119.

Lü Shuxiang 1980 = Lü Shuxiang: Xiandai Hanyu ba bai ci [800 Wörter des modernen Chinesisch]. Beijing 1981.

Peng Chunan 1957 = Peng Chunan: Yufa fanchou [Grammatische Kategorien]. In: Zhongguo Yuwen 59. 1957, H. 5, 26—32. 61. 1957, H. 7, 1—6.

Ilse Karl, Berlin
(Bundesrepublik Deutschland)

297. L'organisation microstructurelle dans le dictionnaire bilingue

1. Introduction
2. Typologie du dictionnaire bilingue
3. Moyens techniques pour structurer le contenu d'un dictionnaire
4. Principes d'organisation de la microstructure
5. Bibliographie choisie

1. Introduction

Lorsqu'on dresse l'inventaire des défauts que présentent les dictionnaires au dire de leurs usagers, trois ‹défectuosités› viennent en tête de liste: la non-attestation de tel ou tel sens, l'absence de tel ou tel mot et la présentation confuse, en tout cas peu systématique des articles d'une certaine complexité (Dodd 1988, 13, Marello 1989, 99—129). En ce qui concerne le troisième point, ces usagers n'ont malheureusement pas tort. La cause profonde en est que très souvent les décisions touchant la présentation des données sont prises indépendamment des choix stratégiques concernant la fonction et le contenu du dictionnaire au lieu d'y être subordonnées. Fort heureusement, sous l'influence de la lexicographie computationnelle (cf. aussi l'art. 293), on se rend compte aujourd'hui qu'il est essentiel de séparer totalement les questions de formatage de celles qui concernent le contenu d'un dictionnaire (cf. Danlex 1987). C'est en effet dans ces conditions seulement qu'on peut envisager d'utiliser à plusieurs fins l'information lexicale enregistrée dans une base de données non-orientée. A chaque emploi correspondrait alors une orientation spécifique et un format conséquent (Martin/Al 1990).

Dans la perspective de ce qui précède il est logique que cette contribution est structurée comme suit. Nous commencerons par rappeler les principes qui devraient sous-tendre toute typologie du dictionnaire bilingue. Puis nous examinerons de quels moyens techniques peut disposer un lexicographe pour structurer ses données. Finalement, pour ce qui est des principes d'organisation de la microstructure, nous ferons la distinction entre la partie paradigmatique (les équivalents) et la partie syntagmatique (les ‹exemples›) du dictionnaire bilingue.

2. Typologie du dictionnaire bilingue

2.1. Deux distinctions fondamentales

L'article 285 traite des principes de la lexicographie bilingue. Le lecteur y trouvera un aperçu bien documenté. C'est pourquoi nous nous contentons ici de rappeler que c'est à Ščerba (1940) que nous devons la distinction fondamentale entre le dictionnaire actif (ou dictionnaire de production) et le dictionnaire passif (ou dictionnaire de compréhension). C'est lui aussi qui a souligné que l'opposition langue cible/langue source n'est pas très intéressante. Ce qui importe en réalité c'est le contraste langue maternelle/langue étrangère. Ces deux distinctions nous autorisent à constater, comme le font aujourd'hui la plupart des lexicographes (cf. e. a. Zgusta 1971, Lötzsch 1978, Hausmann 1977 et 1988, Al-Kasimi 1983, Kromann e. a. 1984), que pour toute paire de langues il nous faudrait en principe les quatre dictionnaires suivants:

— deux dictionnaires actifs
 A → B (pour A-phones)
 B → A (pour B-phones)
— deux dictionnaires passifs
 B → A (pour A-phones)
 A → B (pour B-phones)

Faire la distinction entre un dictionnaire actif (ou dictionnaire de thème) et un dictionnaire passif (ou dictionnaire de version) revient à dire qu'il est possible et souhaitable, pour ne pas dire indispensable, de tenir compte dans l'organisation du dictionnaire bilingue de la compétence linguistique de l'usager, compétence qui, bien entendu, ne concerne que sa langue maternelle. Imaginons, en effet, la situation d'un locuteur germanophone qui se sert de son dictionnaire français-allemand afin de comprendre un texte français qu'il est en train de lire. Cet usager du dictionnaire ne peut s'appuyer que sur la forme du mot français dont il cherche à saisir le sens et sur le contexte où ce mot figure. Par conséquent, si l'on veut faciliter la tâche de l'utilisateur, le dictionnaire doit refléter cette démarche qui va de la forme au sens. Pour le francophone qui se servirait d'un dictionnaire français-allemand il s'agit, au contraire, de trouver une forme allemande correspondant à un mot français dont le sens lui est parfaitement clair. Pour lui le problème se situe, par conséquent, au niveau des propriétés combinatoires de la langue cible, au sujet de laquelle il possède une compétence linguistique pour le moins insuffisante (voir e. a. Al 1983).

2.2. Distinctions secondaires

Hausmann (1977, 144—156, 1988, 138) et Werner (1982a, 286) font remarquer à juste titre qu'il convient de mieux préciser encore ce qu'il faut entendre par un dictionnaire actif. Ils distinguent deux emplois actifs: pour la production d'un texte en langue étrangère à partir de zéro (0 → texte) l'usager fait appel à d'autres propriétés de son dictionnaire que lorsqu'il s'en sert pour produire une véritable traduction (texte → texte). De manière analogue on peut définir deux emplois passifs: la compréhension pure et simple d'une part (texte → 0) et la traduction au sens propre d'autre part (texte → texte).

A la suite de Tomaszczyk (1983) on pourrait par ailleurs se demander s'il n'y a pas lieu de faire la différence entre un dictionnaire bilingue d'apprentissage (par opposition au dictionnaire d'apprentissage monolingue) et un dictionnaire bilingue ordinaire.

De manière plus générale on peut poser qu'un dictionnaire ‹scolaire› qui ne se distinguerait d'un exemplaire plus volumineux que sur le plan quantitatif, comme c'est souvent le cas des dictionnaires dits dérivés, ne saurait convenir parfaitement au public auquel il est destiné (Martin/Al 1990).

Bien que ces distinctions nous semblent parfaitement justifiées et qu'elles devraient donc se répercuter sur l'organisation microstructurelle de ces dictionnaires, nous nous contenterons dans cette contribution d'examiner les effets des deux distinctions fondamentales traitées dans le paragraphe 2.1. Mais considérons tout d'abord de quels moyens techniques nous disposons.

3. Moyens techniques pour structurer le contenu d'un dictionnaire

Le lexicographe, ou son éditeur, dispose de quatre types de ressources pour formaliser la structure de ses données lexicographiques (cf. Duval 1986, 93 s.). Il y a d'abord la *typographie* avec ses différentes polices de caractères (romain, italique, etc.), plusieurs graisses (gras, demi-gras), plusieurs corps ainsi qu'un certain nombre de possibilités pour la mise en page (nombre de colonnes, alinéas). Puis il y a la *ponctuation* (point, virgule, point-virgule), les signes apparentés (parenthèses, crochets, barres verticales, tirets) et des symboles de toutes sortes (losanges, flèches, éléments idéographiques, etc.). En troisième lieu il faut citer les *systèmes de numérotation* (chiffres romains et arabes, lettres majuscules et minuscules) qui permettent de découper l'article en plusieurs parties. Il y a finalement l'*étiquetage*, qui peut être standardisé (abréviations pour indiquer les catégories grammaticales, les champs sémantiques, les niveaux de langue ou les emplois spécifiques), mais ne l'est pas nécessairement (il suffit de penser aux gloses contextuelles et autres commentaires métalinguistiques). Indispensables pour accentuer un profil délibérément choisi par le lexicographe, ces procédés induisent souvent en erreur. En effet, on peut aussi s'en servir pour masquer un manque de structure véritable. L'usager s'en rendra compte bien après avoir acheté son dictionnaire.

4. Principes d'organisation de la microstructure

4.1. Généralités

L'ordre dans lequel sont présentées les différentes composantes d'un dictionnaire bilingue varie grandement d'un ouvrage à l'autre. Dans beaucoup de cas d'ailleurs le format des articles varie également à l'intérieur d'un seul dictionnaire. Cela s'explique par le fait que les directives rédactionnelles, souvent très sommaires, n'ont pas été interprétées de la même manière par les rédacteurs, ou que les responsables ont modifié ces instructions en cours de projet sans avoir eu le courage de retourner à leurs marques. L'ordinateur peut rendre de grands services dans ce domaine (cf. art. 293), mais la grande majorité des dictionnaires bilingues disponibles aujourd'hui n'a pas encore pu profiter de ces facilités.

On peut néanmoins constater que tout article de dictionnaire bilingue comprend les trois composantes suivantes: (a) la *tête* de l'article qui, dans un dictionnaire de thème, se limite le plus souvent à l'entrée lexicale (l'adresse) et sa catégorie grammaticale, mais qui, dans un dictionnaire de version, comprend une sélection délibérée des éléments suivants, généralement dans l'ordre que nous indiquons: variante(s) graphique(s), prononciation(s), informations grammaticales (flexion, schéma dérivationnel, valence, renvois aux annexes éventuels) et informations sémantico-stylistiques (niveau de langue, champ sémantique, etc.), (b) les *traductions* (ou équivalents) de l'entrée lexicale (cf. aussi art. 295) et (c) les *contextes* dans lesquels l'entrée lexicale peut figurer, c'est-à-dire la partie syntagmatique de l'article, où se trouvent réunis les exemples (cf. art. 289), les collocations (cf. art. 287 a) et les combinaisons phraséologiques (cf. art. 290).

morceau, pl ∼x [mɔRSO] nm (a) (*comestible*) [*pain*] piece, bit; [*sucre*] lump; [*viande*] (*à table*) piece, bit; (*chez le boucher*) piece, cut. ∼ **de choix** choice cut *ou* piece; c'était un ∼ de roi it was fit for a king; **manger** *ou* **prendre un** ∼ to have a bite (to eat) *ou* a snack; (*fig*) **manger** *ou* **lâcher le** ∼⁑ to spill the beans*, come clean*, talk*; (*fig: gagner*) il a emporté le ∼* he carried it off; V **bas¹**, **sucre**.
  (b) (*gén*) piece; [*bois*] piece, lump; [*fer*] block; [*ficelle*] bit, piece; [*terre*] piece, patch, plot; [*tissu*] piece, length. **en** ∼**x** in pieces; **couper en** ∼**x** to cut into pieces; **mettre qch en** ∼**x** to pull sth to bits *ou* pieces; **essayant d'assembler les** ∼**x du vase** trying to piece together the bits of the vase *ou* the broken vase.
  (c) (*Littérat*) passage, extract, excerpt; (*Art, Mus*) piece, item, passage; (*poème*) piece. (recueil de) ∼**x choisis** (collection of) selected extracts *ou* passages; **un beau** ∼ **d'éloquence** a fine piece of eloquence; ∼ **de bravoure** purple passage; ∼ **de concours** competition piece; ∼ **pour piano/violon** piece for piano/violin.
  (d) (**loc*) **beau** ∼ (*femme*) nice bit of stuff⁑ (*Brit*), nice chick⁑ (*US*); c'est un sacré ∼ he (*ou* it *etc*) is a hell of a size*.

Extrait textuel 297.1: Article de dictionnaire (tiré de: Robert/Collins 1987, 456)

Certains dictionnaires, comme le Robert/ Collins (1987, fr.-angl./angl.-fr.) ou Il nuovo Boch (1985, ital.-fr./fr.-ital.), font suivre chaque traduction des syntagmes qui s'y rapportent, à l'exception de la phraséologie qui est donnée en fin d'article. Cette manière de présenter le matériel est très proche de celle qui se retrouve dans la plupart des dictionnaires monolingues (cf. Extrait textuel 297.1). L'inconvénient majeur de cette présentation réside en ceci que l'usager ne peut détecter le syntagme recherché avec suffisamment de rapidité que si sa compétence linguistique conduit au même découpage sémantique de l'entrée lexicale en question que celle du lexicographe qui a rédigé l'article. C'est donc un mode d'organisation qui peut à la rigueur convenir au dictionnaire de thème, mais qui est carrément inadéquat dans le cas du dictionnaire de version.

Dans d'autres dictionnaires, comme le Sansoni/Larousse (1981, fr.-ital./ital.-fr.), les dictionnaires bilingues Van Dale ou le Blinkenberg/Høybye (1975—77, dan.-fr.), on sépare nettement les traductions, qui constituent le *corps* de l'article, de la partie syntagmatique (ou *queue*). L'exemple suivant montre que cette présentation n'est pas seulement utilisée pour les dictionnaires de version, mais tout aussi bien pour des dictionnaires de thème.

besøg n (-) A) (1) visite* (2) passage (3) [court] séjour. B) (= besøgende) (4) visite* (5) visiteur (6) invité. ‖ aflægge én et ~, aflægge et ~ hos én faire (el. rendre) [une] visite à q., visiter q.; besvare et ~ (personligt) rendre une visite (en personne); ~ på et biblioteks læsesal séance*; gengælde éns ~ rendre la (el. sa) visite à q.; godt ~ beaucoup de monde, un grand nombre de visiteurs (de spectateurs, etc.); gøre ~, v. aflægge ~; gøre ~ i et musæum visiter un m.; have ~ avoir de la visite; han har ~ il a du monde, il y a du monde chez lui, il y a q. chez lui; efter et ~ hos grevinden après une visite à la comtesse; hyppigt ~ (på et sted, hvor mange samles) fréquentation*; officielt ~ (1); på ~ en visite; her har været ~ il est venu du monde; udstillingen er vel et ~ værd ... mérite d'être vue.

Extrait textuel 297.2: Article de dictionnaire (tiré de: Blinkenberg/Høybye 1975—7, 135)

Dans ce qui suit il sera d'abord question de l'organisation du corps de l'article, puis de celle de la queue.

4.2. Les traductions

La première question à laquelle il faut apporter une réponse est celle de savoir si l'analyse de l'entrée lexicale que nous fournit le dictionnaire monolingue pourrait convenir au dictionnaire bilingue. Tous les métalexicographes s'accordent pour dire qu'on ne peut pas reprendre telle quelle une analyse monolingue du signifié. Seules sont utilisables les analyses qui tiennent compte de la langue d'arrivée. Mais à partir de là deux options sont envisageables: soit rejeter carrément tout recours à l'analyse monolingue — telle semble être la position de Duval (1986), Hausmann (1977, 1988), Kromann (1984; cf. aussi art. 285) et Lötzsch (1978) — soit prendre le profil sémantique fourni par le dictionnaire monolingue comme point de départ, en l'adaptant, bien sûr, en fonction des résultats de l'étude différentielle de la paire de langues concernée. Pour ce faire le lexicographe dispose des moyens techniques dont il a été question dans le paragraphe 3. Le deuxième point de vue est partagé e. a. par Marello (1989), Martin/Al (1990) et Zgusta (1971). Leurs arguments sont les suivants. L'un des buts du dictionnaire de *version* est d'informer l'usager sur la structure et les particularités de la langue étrangère. Dans ces conditions on ne lui rend pas service en lui présentant cette langue à travers le prisme déformant de sa langue maternelle. Prenons un cas classique de divergence, à savoir la traduction du verbe anglais *to land* en français. Il serait tout de même bizarre de vouloir distinguer deux mots *land* dans un dictionnaire de version anglais-français pour la seule raison que le français distingue *atterrir* de *débarquer,* alors qu'en anglais on désigne les deux notions par le même terme (pour plus de détails et plus d'exemples, voir Darbelnet 1970; cf. aussi art. 295). Pour des raisons analogues nous sommes d'avis que, si la microstructure d'une entrée lexicale polysème peut parfois paraître redondante dans le contexte d'un dictionnaire de version, à savoir dans les cas où l'entrée est traduite dans plusieurs de ses significations par le même mot de la langue cible, il faut tout de même, dans la présentation, respecter le caractère polysémique du mot de la langue source. En théorie, ce qui vient d'être dit va à l'encontre du principe d'économie tel qu'il est défini par Lötzsch (1979). Mais dans la pratique le sacrifice consenti n'est pas aussi grand qu'il n'y paraît. En effet, dans la plupart des cas un dictionnaire de version offre plus d'un équivalent par signification. Et c'est au niveau de ces ‹synonymes› que la polysémie du mot de la langue source réapparaît dans la langue cible, comme le montre l'exemple suivant:

travail: (1) Arbeit, Arbeiten
(2) Arbeit, Tätigkeit, Beschäftigung
(3) Arbeit, Aufgabe
(4) Arbeit, Werk
(5) ...

Si le dictionnaire de version permet donc à celui qui s'en sert de mieux comprendre une culture étrangère, parce qu'elle est traduite en termes qui lui sont familiers, le but du dictionnaire de *thème* est différent. Dans ce cas il s'agit, pour ainsi dire, de traduire en termes étrangers la réalité quotidienne de l'usager. Rien de plus logique, dans ces conditions, que de prendre un dictionnaire monolingue comme point de départ, tout en ajoutant, bien entendu, les accents contrastifs qui s'imposent. C'est ce que fait de manière systématique le Robert/Signorelli (1981). C'est aussi ce que font les dictionnaires de thème de Van Dale (1985, néerl.-fr.; 1986a, néerl.-all.; 1986b, néerl.-angl.), qui sont fondés tous les trois sur le même Van Dale monolingue (1984), comme le montrent les extraits suivants:

navel ⟨de (m.)⟩ **0.1** [mbt. een mens, zoogdier] **nombril** ⟨m.⟩ ⇒*ombilic* ⟨m.⟩ **0.2** [sinaasappel] *navel* ⟨v.⟩ **0.3** [mbt. planten] *hile* ⟨m.⟩ ⇒*cicatricule* ⟨v.⟩, *ombilic* **0.4** [mbt. schelpen] *ombilic*

navel ⟨de (m.)⟩ **0.1** [mbt. een mens/zoogdier] *navel* ⇒*umbilicus*, ⟨inf.⟩ *belly button* **0.2** [sinaasappel] *navel orange* **0.3** [mbt. planten] *hilum* **0.4** [mbt. schelpen] *umbo*.

navel ⟨de (m.)⟩ **0.1** [mbt. een mens, zoogdier] *Nabel* ⟨m.5⟩ **0.2** [sinaasappel] *Navel* ⟨v.10⟩, *Navelorange* ⟨v.19⟩ **0.3** [mbt. planten] *Nabel*.

Extrait textuel 297.3: Articles de dictionnaire (tirés de: Van Dale 1985, 808; 1986a, 807; 1986b, 824)

Mais même en admettant qu'un dictionnaire monolingue pourrait constituer le fondement d'un ou de plusieurs dictionnaires bilingues, il reste à déterminer quel type d'ouvrage peut être considéré comme un point de départ adéquat. Faisons remarquer tout d'abord que les dictionnaires fortement homonymiques, comme le Lexis (1975), ne conviennent d'aucune manière comme base d'un dictionnaire de version, puisque pour l'usager étranger, qui ne peut que procéder de la forme au sens, un tel découpage constitue un obstacle insurmontable. Hausmann (1977, 1988) et Werner (1982b) distinguent quatre critères pour ordonner les significations d'une entrée lexicale: (a) le critère historique (avec comme variantes: une approche chronologique stricte ou un agencement qui tient davantage compte de l'étymologie), (b) le critère logique (raisonnements du type: du général au particulier, du cas non-marqué aux cas marqués, du propre au figuré, etc.), (c) le critère de la fréquence (du plus fréquent au moins fréquent) et (d) le critère distributionnel. Les dictionnaires dont le profil sémantique suit la chronologie ne convient guère, tous les lexicographes bilingues sont d'accord là-dessus. Le problème du critère de la fréquence est qu'à notre connaissance il n'existe pas de données concernant la fréquence d'emploi des *significations* d'un mot. Par conséquent, les lexicographes qui disent se servir de ce critère utilisent en réalité l'idée qu'ils se font de la fréquence des différents sens d'un mot. Ce n'est pas tout à fait la même chose. D'ailleurs l'application du seul critère de la fréquence dans un dictionnaire monolingue conduirait à des résultats très peu satisfaisants. En effet, le profil qui en résulterait serait dépourvu de toute logique (dans le sens susmentionné). Du point de vue du lexicographe bilingue le critère formel de la distribution d'un mot présente des avantages certains, mais s'il est vrai que pratiquement tous les dictionnaires monolingues se servent de quelques propriétés distributionnelles pour structurer leurs données (le trait de la transitivité pour les verbes, le régime pour les prépositions, le trait ‹comptable› pour les noms), il n'existe que très peu de dictionnaires monolingues à profil exclusivement distributionnel. Dans la pratique le lexicographe est donc forcé de recourir à une combinaison de critères pour arranger son matériel. On ne peut que lui demander, comme le fait Werner (1982b, 156), d'établir au préalable un ordre prioritaire parmi les critères choisis et de respecter strictement ces priorités pendant la rédaction de son dictionnaire.

En résumé, pour ce qui est de l'organisation du corps d'un dictionnaire bilingue, il est à conseiller de choisir comme point de départ un dictionnaire monolingue dont l'ordre des significations est déterminé par une combinaison régie des critères suivants: logique, distribution et fréquence intuitive. Ce canevas, après une adaptation qui est fonction des résultats de l'analyse contrastive de la paire de langues concernée, doit être respecté même si cela peut entraîner une certaine redondance.

4.3. La partie syntagmatique

Nous considérons comme acquis le fait qu'il convient dans tout dictionnaire, mais surtout dans un dictionnaire bilingue de faire la différence entre faits de langue et faits de parole (Gak 1970; Baunebjerg Hansen 1988, 195; cf. aussi art. 295), par exemple, comme le fait le Robert/Collins (1987), en utilisant l'infinitif pour marquer les collocations verbales et la forme finie pour les exemples purement illustratifs.

Nous nous contenterons par ailleurs de la simple bipartition qui oppose les syntagmes dont au moins un des éléments peut être mis en rapport avec le profil sémantique, énoncé dans le corps de l'article (c'est le cas des collocations) aux syntagmes de nature phraséologique où une telle relation est exclue par définition. En effet, du point de vue de l'organisation de la microstructure il n'y a pas de différence de principe entre les collocations d'une part et les exemples illustratifs d'autre part. Aussi laisserons-nous de côté la question de savoir s'il faut incorporer ceux-ci dans le dictionnaire bilingue. Pour ce qui est des collocations, la question ne se pose pas. Elles doivent être incluses impérativement dans le dictionnaire de thème et elles ne sont pas nécessairement superflues dans un dictionnaire de version (cf. Hausmann 1988, 148—151).

Quant aux principes d'organisation dont nous disposons pour ordonner les contextes sélectionnés, ils sont au nombre de trois.

On pourrait tout d'abord essayer de classer les exemples selon le sens de l'entrée lexicale qu'ils illustrent. Mais dans ce cas-là il n'y aurait pas intérêt à les séparer de la signification à laquelle ils se rapportent. Or nous venons de voir (paragraphe 4.1.) qu'il est souhaitable, au moins dans un dictionnaire de version, de faire une distinction entre le corps et la queue d'un article, car c'est alors seulement que l'usager peut procéder de la forme au sens, conformément au principe que nous avons défini plus haut (paragraphe 2.1.).

La deuxième possibilité consiste à classer les exemples par ordre alphabétique. Cette solution à première vue facile à mettre en œuvre exige quand-même de la part du lexicographe un effort non négligeable. Il doit en effet indiquer pour chaque contexte sélectionné le mot à partir duquel l'exemple pourra être classé alphabétiquement. Bien que le principe de l'arrangement alphabétique soit considéré par tous les lexicographes comme indispensable, il présente un inconvénient majeur. Prenons comme exemple le cas du verbe *promettre*. Dans tout dictionnaire de version il faut au moins incorporer les constructions suivantes: *promettre (qqch.) (à qqn.), promettre (à qqn.) de + inf.* et *promettre que + proposition*. Cela étant, on a le choix: soit sélectionner des contextes qui illustrent ces constructions (*le baromètre nous promet la tempête, elle m'a promis de venir,* etc.), ce qui entraînerait un classement sous le *n* de *nous* ou le *t* de *tempête* dans le premier cas, soit insérer la construction telle quelle sous la lettre *q* (de *qqch.*). La première solution relève de l'arbitraire, car le choix des mots *nous* et *tempête* dans le premier exemple n'est nullement significatif. La deuxième solution n'est pas très révélatrice non plus, puisqu'en réalité *qqch.* représente la catégorie des substantifs.

Le troisième principe de classement, qui est de nature distributionnelle, a justement pour but de remédier au défaut que nous venons de signaler. Dans cette perspective les exemples sont classés en fonction de la catégorie grammaticale du mot avec lequel l'entrée lexicale se combine. L'idée est intéressante parce qu'elle permet d'incorporer dans le dictionnaire bilingue les résultats des nombreux travaux sur la valence des entrées lexicales. L'élaboration la plus révolutionnaire

1. *X promet Y à Z* = X communique à Z que X est certain qu'il y aura un événement (lié à) Y qui concerne Z (et X communique que X s'engage à causer cet événement).

Régime

1 = X	2 = Y	3 = Z
1. N	1. N 2. *de* V_{inf} 3. *que* $PROP_{fut}$ obligatoire	1. *à* N

1) C_2 : si $C_2 = \Lambda$, alors Y = 'X fait cela'

C_1 : *Pierre a promis*

$C_1 + C_2$: *Le vieillard a promis la tempête ; Pierre a promis ce livre ⟨une récompense, une fessée, son aide⟩; Pierre a promis de venir ; Le vieillard a promis que la tempête aurait lieu demain*

$C_1 + C_3$: *Mais tu m'as promis!*

$C_1 + C_2 + C_3$: *Tu ne riras pas toujours, je te le promets ; Le vieillard a promis la tempête aux paysans ; Pierre a promis à Paul de venir ; Pierre a promis à Paul que son fils s'en repentirait*

Extrait textuel 297.4: Article de dictionnaire (tiré de: Mel'čuk 1984, 143)

de cette idée est illustrée par Mel'čuk e. a. (1984), à qui nous empruntons la représentation partielle suivante du verbe *promettre*.

Dans le domaine bilingue une initiative un peu moins radicale a été prise par les responsables de la série de dictionnaires Van Dale. Ils distinguent les 9 catégories suivantes: (1.) substantif, (2.) adjectif, (3.) verbe, (4.) pronom, (5.) adverbe, (6.) préposition, (7.) article/déterminant, (8.) conjonction et (9.) interjection. Dans tous les contextes sélectionnés le mot clef est marqué et pourvu d'une des catégories susmentionnées. Ensuite les exemples sont rangés dans l'ordre indiqué, donc d'abord les syntagmes dans lesquels l'entrée lexicale se combine avec un substantif, puis ceux où est illustrée la combinaison avec un adjectif, puis les combinaisons avec un verbe, et ainsi de suite. A l'intérieur de chaque catégorie les exemples sont classés par ordre alphabétique.

Selon Hausmann des principes analogues ont été appliqués de manière particulièrement systématique dans le dictionnaire allemand-chinois de Pan (1984). Mais Hausmann fait également remarquer que le système préconisé par Van Dale soulève aussi des questions. Dans quelle mesure l'usager domine-t-il la taxinomie catégorielle? N'est-il pas préférable de la réduire aux cinq catégories suivantes, jugées indispensables par Hausmann: substantif, adjectif, verbe, préposition, ainsi qu'une catégorie résiduelle qui regrouperait les autres classes grammaticales? Et, par ailleurs, comment l'usager peut-il savoir quel est le mot clef d'un contexte (c'est-à-dire le mot qui a servi à classer l'exemple)? En d'autres termes, la procédure suivie par le lexicographe est-elle vraiment transparente pour l'usager?

A la première question on peut répliquer, après sept ans d'expérience pratique, que les usagers se sont vite habitués à ce nouveau mode de présentation. Les clients interrogés à ce sujet n'avaient souvent aucune connaissance explicite de la grammaire, mais ils étaient capables d'indiquer après très peu de consultations du dictionnaire concerné que toutes les constructions que les lexicographes appellent prépositionnelles sont précédées du chiffre (6.). Cela n'empêche qu'il faudra certainement déterminer par voie expérimentale quel est le nombre idéal de distinctions catégorielles du point de vue de l'usager.

La réponse à l'autre question, celle concernant la transparence de la procédure suivie par le lexicographe, est plus délicate. En effet, seule une procédure strictement formelle peut être retenue dans le cas du dictionnaire de version. L'équipe responsable des dictionnaires Van Dale a opté pour une solution qui a également été adoptée par Schemann (cf. art. 290). Elle peut être résumée comme suit: si une expression contient un ou plusieurs substantifs, c'est le premier substantif qui servira à classer cet exemple; si l'expression ne comporte pas de substantif, c'est le premier adjectif qui est considéré comme le mot clef; si l'expression ne contient pas d'adjectif non plus, c'est le premier verbe qui est choisi. Cette ligne de conduite est décrite avec plus de détails par Marello (1989, 94 s.).

Il reste pourtant deux problèmes à résoudre. Nous avons dit à plusieurs reprises qu'un dictionnaire de version doit tenir compte du fait que les usagers d'un tel dictionnaire procèdent de la forme au sens. Le principe d'organisation que nous venons de décrire est en effet strictement formel, mais conduit-il l'usager au sens d'une expression? Certes, l'exemple est suivi d'une traduction appropriée. Mais aucun rapport n'est établi dans ces conditions avec les significations énumérées dans le corps de l'article. Pour compenser ce défaut inhérent au mode de présentation distributionnel, les responsables des dictionnaires Van Dale ont élaboré le système suivant, qui est appliqué dans tous les dictionnaires bilingues de cette maison d'édition. Dans le corps de l'article les significations sont numérotées de 0.1, 0.2 à 0.n. Dans la partie syntagmatique tous les exemples sont précédés d'un code de deux chiffres, dont le premier élément indique la catégorie grammaticale du mot clef de l'exemple (1. = substantif, 2. = adjectif, 3. = verbe, 4. = pronom, 5. = adverbe, 6. = préposition, etc.); le deuxième chiffre renvoie à celle des significations énumérées dans le corps de l'article qui s'applique dans le cas concret. Si le sens d'une expression ne peut pas être mis en rapport avec une des significations autonomes de l'entrée lexicale — et cela est nécessairement le cas lorsqu'il s'agit d'une expression idiomatique — on se sert du signe ¶. L'extrait textuel 297.5, que nous empruntons à Marello (1989, 92) illustre l'effet de ce mode d'organisation si on l'applique à un dictionnaire existent, en l'occurrence le Ragazzini (1984).

Même en admettant avec Marello (1989, 89—97) que l'organisation de la microstructure telle que nous venons de la décrire soit adéquate dans le cas d'un dictionnaire de

to **answer** ['ɑːnsə*], v. t. e i. **1** rispondere (in quasi tutti i sensi): **to a. a letter (the phone, the door, the bell)**, rispondere a una lettera (al telefono, alla porta, al campanello); **This instrument does not a. my purpose**, questo strumento non risponde al mio scopo; **The ship wouldn't a. her rudder**, la nave non rispondeva al timone **2** pagare lo scotto; pagare di persona: **The guilt was mine and I answered for it**, la colpa fu mia e pagai lo scotto **3** (anche **to a. a purpose**) rispondere a uno scopo; esser utile; servire: **That won't a. at all**, ciò non servirà affatto. ● (fam.) **to a. back**, rispondere (in modo impertinente e sgarbato); ribattere; rimbeccare ☐ **to a. blow with blow**, ribattere colpo su colpo ☐ **to a. for**, rispondere di; essere responsabile di; farsi garante di ☐ (naut.) **to a. (to) the helm**, ubbidire al timone; sentire il timone ☐ **to a. to**, rispondere a; reagire a (una sollecitazione) ☐ **to a. to the name of**, rispondere al nome di; chiamarsi ☐ **to a. (to) one's hopes (a description, etc.)**, rispondere (o corrispondere) alle proprie speranze (a una descrizione, ecc.) ☐ (tel.) **answering machine**, segreteria telefonica.

(to) **answer** ['ɑːnsə*] <v.> **0.1** *rispondere* ⇒ *ribattere* **0.2** *pagare lo scotto* ⇒ *pagare di persona* **0.3** *rispondere a uno scopo* ⇒ *esser utile, servire* ♦ **1.1** to ~ the bell, the door, a letter, the phone *rispondere al campanello, alla porta, a una lettera, al telefono*; to ~ a blow with a blow *ribattere colpo su colpo*; to ~ (to) the helm *ubbidire al timone, sentire il timone*; this ship wouldn't ~ her rudder *la nave non rispondeva al timone*; answering machine *segreteria telefonica* **1.3** to ~ a purpose *rispondere a uno scopo*; this instrument does not ~ my purpose *questo strumento non risponde al mio scopo* **1.¶** to ~ (to) one's hopes, a description *rispondere, corrispondere alle proprie speranze, a una descrizione* **5.1** to ~ back *rispondere (in modo impertinente e sgarbato), ribattere, rimbeccare* **5.3** that won't ~ at all *ciò non servirà affatto* **6.1** to ~ **to** *rispondere a, reagire a* ; to ~ **to** the name of *rispondere al nome di, chiamarsi* **6.2** to ~ **for** *rispondere di, essere responsabile di, farsi garante di*; the guilt was mine and I answered **for** it *la colpa fu mia e pagai lo scotto*.

Extrait textuel 297.5: Articles de dictionnaire (tirés de: Marello 1989, 92)

version — mais tout le monde n'est pas totalement d'accord à ce sujet (cf. Hausmann 1988, 146—8) — qu'en est-il du dictionnaire de thème? Ne faudrait-il pas être logique et organiser la partie syntagmatique d'un tel dictionnaire à base de critères sémantiques, conformément au principe que l'usager cherche à associer une forme étrangère à un sens connu? Le système développé par Van Dale pourrait être adapté sans trop de difficultés à ce principe. En effet, comme l'illustre l'extrait textuel 297.5, les exemples du dictionnaire de version sont rangés dans un ordre numérique strict: d'abord les codes qui commencent par 1., puis les codes commençant par 5., et finalement les codes qui commencent par 6.; à l'intérieur de chacune de ces sections formelles (rappelons encore une fois que le premier chiffre de chaque code a trait à la catégorie grammaticale du mot clef) l'ordre dépend du deuxième chiffre, qui représente le côté sémantique du code (les différentes significations de l'entrée lexicale): d'abord 1.1, puis 1.2, etc. Rien de plus simple en principe que d'inverser la procédure automatique de classement et de subordonner, par conséquent, la division formelle à la division sémantique. Si l'éditeur des dictionnaires Van Dale n'a pas voulu entrer dans cette logique, c'est essentiellement pour deux raisons.

La première est d'ordre théorique: pour un locuteur natif il est généralement possible de reconstruire après coup le raisonnement du lexicographe qui a rédigé le profil sémantique d'une entrée lexicale, mais il lui serait pratiquement impossible, malgré sa compétence linguistique, d'aboutir au même résultat (cf. Werner 1982b et Hausmann 1988, 141 s.). Pourquoi, dans ces conditions, fatiguer inutilement l'usager du dictionnaire de thème, puisqu'une organisation formelle des données primaires est disponible? La deuxième raison est d'ordre strictement pratique: l'éditeur n'a pas voulu prendre le risque de désorienter complètement ses clients qu'il venait justement d'habituer à un code dont le premier chiffre représentait une caractéristique formelle.

Si nous terminons sur cette décision éditoriale qui témoigne avant tout de bon sens, c'est parce que nous croyons qu'il s'agit là d'un critère qu'il ne faut jamais perdre de vue lorsqu'on cherche à organiser la microstructure d'un dictionnaire bilingue.

5. Bibliographie choisie

5.1. Dictionnaires

Blinkenberg/Høybye 1975—7 = Andreas Blinkenberg/Poul Høybye: Dansk-Fransk Ordbog. 3ème éd. København 1975—1977 [2077 p.; 1ère éd. 1930—7].

Il nuovo Boch 1985 = Raoul Boch: Dizionario francese italiano italiano francese. II ed. Bologna 1985 [2178 p.; I ed. 1978].

Lexis 1975 = Jean Dubois e. a.: Lexis. Dictionnaire de la langue française. Paris 1975 [1950 p.].

Mel'čuk 1984 = Igor Mel'čuk e. a.: Dictionnaire explicatif et combinatoire du français contemporain. Recherches lexico-sémantiques I. Montréal 1984 [172 p.].

Pan 1984 = Pan Zaiping: Deutsch-Chinesisches Wörterbuch. Shanghai 1984 [1527 S.].

Ragazzini 1984 = Giuseppe Ragazzini: Il nuovo Ragazzini Dizionario inglese italiano italiano inglese. II ed. Bologna 1984 [2112 p.; I ed. 1967].

Robert/Collins 1987 = Beryl T. Atkins/Alain Duval e. a.: Robert/Collins Dictionnaire français-anglais anglais-français. 2ème éd. Paris 1987 [XL, 768 + 930 p.; 1ère éd. 1978].

Robert/Signorelli 1981 = Paul Robert/Augusto Arizzi e. a.: Robert & Signorelli Dictionnaire français-italien italien-français. Paris 1981 [3008 p.].

Sansoni/Larousse 1981 = Claude Margueron/Gianfranco Folena: Dizionario Sansoni Larousse francese-italiano italiano-francese. Firenze 1981 [XXXVII, 714; L, 797 p.].

Van Dale 1984 = P. G. J. van Sterkenburg e. a.: Van Dale Groot woordenboek van Hedendaags Nederlands. Utrecht 1984 [1569 p.].

Van Dale 1985 = B. P. F. Al e. a.: Van Dale Groot woordenboek Nederlands-Frans. Utrecht 1985 [1565 p.].

Van Dale 1986a = H. L. Cox e. a: Van Dale Groot woordenboek Nederlands-Duits. Utrecht 1986 [1560 p.].

Van Dale 1986b = W. Martin/G. A. J. Tops e. a.: Van Dale Groot woordenboek Nederlands-Engels. Utrecht 1986 [1560 p.].

5.2. Travaux

Al 1983 = Bernard P. F. Al: Dictionnaire de thème et dictionnaire de version. In: Revue de Phonétique Appliquée 66—68. 1983, 203—211.

Al-Kasimi 1983 = Ali M. Al-Kasimi: The interlingual/translation dictionary. In: R. R. K. Hartmann (ed.): Lexicography: Principles and Practice. London. New York e. a. 1983, 153—162.

Baunebjerg Hansen 1988 = Gitte Baunebjerg Hansen: Stand und Aufgaben der zweisprachigen Lexikographie. Nachlese zum Kopenhagener Werkstattgespräch 12.—13. Mai 1986. In: Lexicographica 4. 1988, 186—202.

Danlex 1987 = The DANLEX-GROUP: Descriptive Tools for Electronic Processing of Dictionary Data. Studies in Computational Lexicography. Tübingen 1987 (Lexicographica. Series Maior 20).

Darbelnet 1970 = Jean Darbelnet: Dictionnaires bilingues et lexicologie différentielle. In: Langages 19. 1970, 92—102.

Dodd 1988 = W. Steven Dodd: The Exeter Coditext Project. In: Lexicographica 4. 1988, 11—18.

Duval 1986 = Alain Duval: La métalangue dans les dictionnaires bilingues. In: Lexicographica 2. 1986, 93—100.

Gak 1970 = V. G. Gak: La langue et le discours dans un dictionnaire bilingue. In: Langages 19. 1970, 103—115.

Hausmann 1977 = Franz Josef Hausmann: Einführung in die Benutzung der neufranzösischen Wörterbücher. Tübingen 1977 (Romanistische Arbeitshefte 19).

Hausmann 1988 = Franz Josef Hausmann: Grundprobleme des zweisprachigen Wörterbuchs. In: K. Hyldgaard-Jensen/Arne Zettersten (eds.): Symposium on Lexicography III. Tübingen 1988 (Lexicographica. Series Maior 19), 137—158.

Kromann e. a. 1984 = Hans-Peder Kromann/Theis Riiber/Poul Rosbach: Überlegungen zu Grundfragen der zweisprachigen Lexikographie. In: Herbert Ernst Wiegand (Hrsg.): Studien zur Neuhochdeutschen Lexikographie V. Germanistische Linguistik 3—6. 1984, 159—238.

Lötzsch 1978 = Ronald Lötzsch: Ein aktives Deutsch-Russisches Wörterbuch. Interview mit Dr. phil. Ronald Lötzsch. In: Spektrum — Monatszeitschrift für den Wissenschaftler 1. 1978, 28—30.

Lötzsch 1979 = Ronald Lötzsch: Einige Fragen der Entwicklung der zweisprachigen russischen Lexikographie an der Akademie der Wissenschaften der DDR. In: Zeitschrift für Slawistik 24. 1979, 402—408.

Marello 1989 = Carla Marello: Dizionari bilingui con schede sui dizionari italiani per francese, inglese, spagnolo, tedesco. Bologna 1989.

Martin/Al 1990 = Willy Martin/Bernard P. F. Al: User-orientation in dictionaries: 9 propositions. In: Tamás Magay/Judit Zigáni (eds.): BudaLEX '88. Papers from the EURALEX 3rd International Congress (Budapest, September 1988). Budapest 1990.

Ščerba 1940 = L. V. Ščerba: Opyt obščej teorii leksikografii I. In: Izvestija Akademii Nauk SSSR 3. 1940, 89—117. [Traduction allemande: Versuch einer allgemeinen Theorie der Lexikographie. In: W. Wolski (Hrsg.): Aspekte der sowjetrussischen Lexikographie. Übersetzungen, Abstracts, bibliographische Angaben. Tübingen 1982, 17—62 (Reihe Germanistische Linguistik 43).

Tomaszczyk 1983 = J. Tomaszczyk: On bilingual dictionaries. The case for bilingual dictionaries for foreign language learners. In: R. R. K. Hartmann (ed.): Lexicography: Principles and Practice. London. New York e. a. 1983, 41—51.

Werner 1982a = Reinhold Werner: La definición lexicográfica. In: G. Haensch e. a.: La lexicografía. Madrid 1982, 259—328.

Werner 1982b = Reinhold Werner: Zur Reihenfolge der Definitionen bzw. Übersetzungsäquivalente im Wörterbuchartikel (mit besonderer Berücksichtigung spanischer Beispiele). In: Lebende Sprachen 4. 1982, 150—156.

Zgusta 1971 = Ladislav Zgusta e. a.: Manual of Lexicography. The Hague/Paris 1971 (Janua linguarum. Series maior 39).

Bernard P. F. Al, Amsterdam (Pays-Bas)

298. Formen der Textverdichtung im zweisprachigen Wörterbuch

1. Vorbemerkungen
2. Wörterbuchfunktionen zweisprachiger Wörterbücher und Verfahren der Textverdichtung
3. Literatur (in Auswahl)

1. Vorbemerkungen

In Art. 90a sind die wichtigsten texttheoretischen und metalexikographischen Annahmen, die dem Verständnis von Textverdichtung zugrunde liegen, am Beispiel allgemeiner einsprachiger Wörterbücher des Deutschen im Zusammenhang erläutert. Die Verfahren der Textverdichtung (bzw. Textverdichtungsoperationen, Kondensierungsverfahren bzw. -operationen) sind in zweisprachigen Wörterbüchern keine anderen als die in den einsprachigen Wörterbüchern angewandten.

Zur Vorbereitung auf Probleme des Einsatzes solcher Verfahren in zweisprachigen Wörterbüchern, welche unter 2.1. nach Wörterbuchfunktionen differenziert werden, sei nachfolgend der Argumentationsgang nochmals kurz erläutert; in Ergänzung der Ausführungen in Art. 90a werden dabei mehrere Anregungen aus Art. 38a, Art. 44 und vor allem aus Wiegand (1990) berücksichtigt.

1.1. Der Textverdichtungsprozeß wird als Prozeß der Überführung eines hypothetischen bzw. rekonstruierbaren Volltextes (oder Volltextteils) in ein Kondensat (oder Teilkondensat) aufgefaßt. Insbesondere für stark standardisierte und verdichtete Wörterbücher lassen sich entsprechende Artikeltexte in der Weise interpretieren, daß Textverdichtungsoperationen nach vorgesehenen Standards wenigstens einmal auf sie angewandt wurden, so daß alle Angaben mehr oder weniger elliptisch ausfallen.

Die verschiedenen Textverdichtungsoperationen können als Handlungsmuster aufgefaßt werden, nach denen entsprechende Handlungen unter Anwendung bestimmter Vorschriften vollzogen werden (vgl. Wiegand 1990, 89). Sie bilden eine Unterklasse allgemeiner textverarbeitender Operationen. Zu den Textverdichtungsverfahren zählen mindestens (vgl. Art. 90a unter 3, 961 ff.) folgende Grundverfahren:

Das Auslassen von Formulierungsbestandteilen, die Bildung von Abkürzungen, die Ersetzung von Teilen eines Volltextes durch Angabesymbole, die Ersetzung bzw. Substitution (von Teilen) des Lemmazeichens durch Platzhaltersymbole, die Ineinanderschachtelung, das Belegschnittverfahren.

Auf diese Grundverfahren bauen auf: die Nischen- und Nestbildung und das Verfahren der Auslagerung von Textsegmenten.

Alle Typen textverdichtender Operationen, die wenigstens einmal ausgeführt werden müssen, um von einem bestimmten Volltext zu einem Wörterbuchartikel zu gelangen, lassen sich mit Wiegand zu einer Menge zusammenfassen:

„Die n-malige Ausführung der Operationen aus dieser Menge, welche erforderlich ist, um als Kondensat einen Artikel zu erhalten, heißt erste Stufe der lexikographischen Textverdichtung" (Wiegand 1990, 99 f.).

Zu dieser ersten Stufe zählen die in Art. 90a so bezeichneten Grundverfahren. Sie gelten für Artikel sämtlicher Art und sie gehen der Anwendung weiterreichender Operationen logisch voraus. Abgeschlossen ist die Textverdichtung für Artikel monosemer Lemmazeichen, wenn diese erste Stufe durchlaufen ist.

Was Artikel zu polysemen Lemmazeichen angeht, muß zusätzlich die Operation des Auslagerns berücksichtigt werden, die die zweite Stufe der lexikographischen Textverdichtung bildet. Auf die mit der Linksauslagerung verbundenen Skopusprobleme kann hier nicht eingegangen werden; vgl. Wiegand (1990, 100 ff.). Erforderlich werden in solchen Artikeln gegebenenfalls zusätzlich Skopusregulierungen, und die hierarchischen

Artikelstrukturen werden wesentlich komplexer, was Auswirkungen auf die Lesbarkeit entsprechender Artikeltexte hat.

Schließlich sei auf die druckraumersparende Operation der Zusammenrückung hingewiesen; es handelt sich dabei um ein Sonderverfahren, das angewandt wird, um aus mehreren Verweisartikeln einen verdichteten Verweisartikel zu erhalten, der ein „Lemmacluster" aufweist; vgl. dazu aus Wiegand (1990,112): „**äherkorn, äherlesung, äherspitze,** s. *äher* 1". — Dieses Verfahren ist dem der Nest- und Nischenbildung verwandt und wurde in Art. 90a nicht eigens angeführt. Als Sonderform des Verfahrens der Auslassung von Formulierungsbestandteilen (vgl. Art. 90a, 961) kann das in Wiegand (1990, 89) so bezeichnete Verfahren des „Kürzens" erfaßt werden.

1.2. Im Ergebnis der Anwendung textverdichtender Verfahren auf einen Volltext (bzw. auf einen historisch vorausgehenden Leittext) zeichnet sich das Kondensat, i.e. der Artikeltext eines standardisierten Wörterbuchs, durch eine vergleichsweise größere propositionale Dichte aus. Ein Ausgangstext A (Volltext, Leittext) steht zu seinem Kondensat B in mehreren Beziehungen:
— A wurde verdichtet zu B
— B ist propositional dichter als A
— A ist propositional weniger dicht als B.

Der Term *propositionale Dichte* dient in Anschluß an Wiegand (1990, 95) dazu, eine der auffallendsten Eigenschaften von Artikeltexten standardisierter Wörterbücher, welche als mehr oder weniger erhebliche Komplexität erfaßt wird, zu präzisieren:

Aus jeder Angabe eines Wörterbuchartikels kann eine propositionale Information zum Wörterbuchgegenstand entnommen werden, die sich durch mindestens einen Aussagesatz mitteilen läßt (vgl. Art. 38a, 4.3.2.). Bildet man den Quotienten aus der Anzahl elementarer propositionaler Gehalte und der Anzahl der Textoberflächeneinheiten (i.e. Wortformen, einschließlich Ziffern und Abkürzungen) eines Textes A und vergleicht den Quotienten mit dem eines Textes B, dann läßt sich die propositionale Dichte als Vergleichseinheit angeben (vgl. Wiegand 1990, 95). Dies sei an einem Beispiel erläutert:

Als Beispiel dient der Ausschnitt aus dem Wörterbuchartikel (WA$_1$) des Dicţionar Romîn-German (vgl. den ganzen Artikel: Abb. 298.10 unter 2.2.2.):

WA$_1$ „**joc**, ~ uri, s.n. [. . .]"

Ein möglicher Volltext (VT$_1$) zu WA$_1$ kann lauten (die Buchstaben in Klammern sind zur weiteren Bezugnahme eingefügt):

VT$_1$: (a) Wörterbuchartikel zu *joc*; (b) *joc* lautet im Plural *jocuri*; (c) es handelt sich um ein Substantiv, (d) dessen Genus das Neutrum ist.

Der Übergang von dem Volltext VT$_1$ zu dem propositional dichteren Kondensat WA$_1$ läßt sich für (a)—(d) folgendermaßen skizzieren, wobei elementare propositionale Gehalte (p) jeweils in der *daß*-Formulierung angegeben werden:

Auf den texttheoretisch als Zwischentitel auffaßbaren Textteil (a) wird beim Übergang von VT$_1$ zu WA$_1$ die Operation des Kürzens angewandt; (a) kann der propositionale Gehalt p$_1$: „daß ein Wörterbuchartikel zu *joc* folgt" zugeordnet werden. Die Pluralbildungsangabe in WA$_1$ wird durch das Verfahren der Ersetzung eines Teils des Lemmazeichens gemacht; hier kann der propositionale Gehalt gefaßt werden als p$_2$: „daß der Plural *jocuri* lautet". Auf (c) und (d) wird das textverdichtende Verfahren der Bildung von Abkürzungen angewandt. Die entsprechenden propositionalen Gehalte lauten: p$_3$: „daß *joc* ein Substantiv ist" und p$_4$: „daß das Genus von *joc* das Neutrum ist".

Ein Vergleich der Textteile (a)—(d) aus VT$_1$, die zu dem Formkommentar von WA$_1$ verdichtet wurden, mit WA$_1$ zeigt für dieses Beispiel: Die entsprechenden propositionalen Gehalte gehen beim Übergang von VT$_1$ zu WA$_1$ nicht verloren; allerdings sind aus dem Kondensat die propositionalen Gehalte p$_1$—p$_4$ aus weniger formkommentarinternen Textoberflächeneinheiten (Ausdruck aus Wiegand 1990, 95) erschließbar. Nunmehr läßt sich der Quotient für die propositionale Dichte folgendermaßen angeben:

Im Falle von WA$_1$ mit 4 Textoberflächeneinheiten und 4 propositionalen Gehalten ist dieser Quotient 4:4 = 1. — VT$_1$ hingegen enthält 19 Textoberflächeneinheiten. Der Quotient für die propositionale Dichte ist in diesem Fall 4:19 = 0,21 . . .; er ist also wesentlich geringer als derjenige für WA$_1$.

Bei anderer sprachlicher Abfassung, d. h. für mögliche Volltexte VT$_2$, VT$_3$ usw., wäre dieser Wert zwar jeweils ein anderer, würde aber ebenfalls stets den von WA$_1$ übertreffen; dies auch dann, wenn Textoberflächeneinheiten und propositionale Gehalte nicht im Verhältnis 1:1 stünden wie in dem Beispiel für WA$_1$ der Fall. Wird, wie hier, bei der Berechnung die Zahl der Textoberflächeneinheiten in den jeweiligen Divisor gestellt, fällt der Ziffernwert parallel zur Formulierung „geringerer" propositionaler Dichte (für VT$_1$) bzw. „größerer" propositionaler Dichte (für WA$_1$) aus.

Der Sinn entsprechender Berechnungen kann darin gesehen werden, die Verdichtungsgrade von Wörterbuchartikeln und auch ganzer Wörterbücher einer vergleichenden Analyse zugänglich zu machen.

1.3. In den modernen und hier untersuchten Wörterbüchern ist die Textverdichtung und damit das Ergebnis, nämlich das propositional dichtere Kondensat, standardisiert. Bei unterschiedlichen Graden der Textverdichtung gibt es nämlich weitgehende Festlegungen dazu, auf welche Teile welche Textverdichtungsverfahren anzuwenden sind. Standardisierung und Textverdichtung stehen — mit Blick auf die Benutzer — im Dienst der Orientierung und damit des raschen Zugriffs auf benötigte Daten; was die (Text-)Produzenten angeht, dienen Standardisierung und Textverdichtung der Druckraumersparnis.

Von einer gewissen Stufe des Einsatzes entsprechender Textverdichtungsverfahren an (die auf der Basis der metalexikographischen Untersuchung solcher Verfahren erstestet werden könnte) stellt sich allerdings für den Benutzer der Nachteil der Desorientierung und Textunverständlichkeit ein.

Die nichtbeabsichtigten Folgen der Anwendung von Verfahren der Textverdichtung sind für zweisprachige und einsprachige Wörterbücher gleich: Wenn die Verfahren gehäuft angewandt werden, insbesondere wenn (nicht bereits aus anderen Texten bekannte) Abkürzungen und Angabesymbole zahlreich vorkommen, ist gegebenenfalls selbst ein kundiger Benutzer zu ständigem Nachschlagen in den Außentexten (Benutzerhinweisen, Tabellen zur Grammatik, u. a. m.) des eigentlichen Wörterverzeichnisses gezwungen.

Sind Wörterbuchartikel eines Wörterbuchs nurmehr verständlich aufgrund wiederholt notwendig werdender Konsultation entsprechender Außentexte, dann besteht zwischen diesen und den Artikeltexten ein Verhältnis ausgeprägter Intertextualität, weswegen eben die Benutzung erschwert sein kann.

Werden hingegen Artikeltexte nicht oder nur geringfügig durch den Einsatz spezieller Verfahren verdichtet, kann den Außentexten eines Wörterbuchs eine bloß marginale Rolle zukommen (jedenfalls was Benutzeraspekte angeht). — Dies ist gewöhnlich der Fall in sehr umfangsarmen kleinen Wörterbüchern. Aber auch in Wörterbüchern mittleren Umfangs kann in Abhängigkeit von Zielsetzungen wie Durchsichtigkeit der Artikeltexte und — was zweisprachige Wörterbücher angeht — bloße Befähigung zum Verstehen einfachster fremdsprachlicher Texte darauf verzichtet werden, sämtliche oder einen Großteil verfügbarer Textverdichtungsverfahren auszuschöpfen.

1.4. Was die jeweils eingeführten Textverdichtungsverfahren und ihre Erläuterung in den Außentexten eines Wörterbuchs angeht, sei schließlich auf folgendes hingewiesen:

Manche der Textverdichtungsverfahren sind insofern „natürlich", als auf Vertextungsregeln zurückgegriffen wird, wie sie z. B. als elliptische Formen aus anderen Texten bekannt sind; über sie verfügt der kompetente Sprecher auch sonst bei der Produktion von Äußerungen (vgl. dazu auch Art. 44). Solche eingespielten Traditionen der Textverdichtung, die den Lesegewohnheiten von Benutzern im Rahmen allgemeiner Benutzungspraxis entsprechen, werden insofern bei der Artikeltextgestaltung einkalkuliert, als diese nicht mehr in den Metatexten (i.e. Außentexten) der Wörterbücher erläutert werden (müssen).

Das gilt z. B. für das Auslassen von Relationsprädikaten wie *bezeichnet, bedeutet* bei Bedeutungsparaphrasenangaben zu Lemmazeichen aus dem Bereich der Nennlexik (vgl. Art. 90a unter 3., 962 und Wolski 1986, 117). Und das gilt sogar in Fällen, in denen bei Adressierungsbeziehungen die lexikographische Syntax mit der normalen Syntax kollidiert, so bei der Nachstellung von Artikelangaben: *Lexikon, das* versus *das Lexikon*.

Demgegenüber werden nur noch die für speziell erachteten Verfahren der Textverdichtung in der Wörterbucheinleitung eigens erklärt, so der Gebrauch von Angabesymbolen, Abkürzungen u. a. m.

Grundsätzlich entstehen dem Textproduzenten bei jeder Abweichung von der natürlichen Textkonstruktion Erklärungsverpflichtungen. Abgesehen von den soeben erläuterten Fällen, in denen eine Verläßlichkeit auf vorhandene Leserfertigkeiten garantiert zu sein scheint, ist es auch sonst nicht immer sinnvoll, jede Kommentierungshandlung zu standardisieren, d. h. hier, für jedes Formulierungsresultat ein vorgeschriebenes Textverdichtungsmuster zu entwerfen; vgl. dazu Wiegand (1990, 248).

So kann u. a. im Falle selten zu berücksichtigender Glossate oder anderer Textsegmente darauf verzichtet werden, für diese z. B. Abkürzungen zu verwenden; vgl. ein Beispiel unter 2.2.1.2.

1.5. Im Vergleich zu den allgemeinen einsprachigen Wörterbüchern ist die Zahl möglicher Angaben in den zweisprachigen Wörterbüchern von vornherein größer, weil es zwei Adressierungsrichtungen gibt: Es werden — unabhängig von den zu unterscheidenden Wörterbuchfunktionen (vgl. unter 2.1.) — jeweils Angaben zu der lexikographischen Ausgangssprache, i.e. der lemmagebenden Sprache, gemacht, und zu der lexikographischen Zielsprache.

Einige der in Art. 90a und in diesem Beitrag erläuterten Textverdichtungsverfahren spielen dabei für die berücksichtigten zweisprachigen Wörterbücher nur eine untergeordnete oder gar keine Rolle, so das Belegschnittverfahren, aber auch die Nestbildung.

Bei dem Übergang von einem Volltext oder einem Leittext (wenn dieser einem zweisprachigen Wörterbuch zugrunde liegt) können für das vorliegende zweisprachige Wörterbuch durch die im Textbearbeitungsprozeß angewandten Operationen des Auswählens bzw. Selektierens propositionale Gehalte verlorengehen. Dies ist der Fall, wenn in Abhängigkeit von Wörterbuchfunktionen oder aufgrund von Einfachheitserwägungen für die lexikographische Ausgangssprache Betonungsangaben, grammatische Angaben, Bedeutungsangaben, Stilschichtenangaben oder andere Angaben entfallen. Von entsprechenden textbearbeitenden Operationen des Auslassens/Selektierens können betroffen sein: Die Lemmareihe im Vergleich zu einem Leitwörterbuch (äußere Selektion), oder auch die einzelnen Angaben eines Wörterbuchartikels (innere Selektion).

2. Wörterbuchfunktionen zweisprachiger Wörterbücher und Verfahren der Textverdichtung

2.1. Wörterbuchfunktionen

Seit der grundlegenden Arbeit von L. V. Ščerba (1940; vgl. auch Art. 324) werden in der sprachenpaarbezogenen Lexikographie nach den Kriterien von Textproduktion/Textrezeption und der Übersetzungsrichtung Muttersprache—Fremdsprache/Fremdsprache—Muttersprache je Sprachenpaar vier zweisprachige Wörterbuchtypen unterschieden; für das Sprachenpaar Russisch und Deutsch z. B. sind dies:

(a) deutsch-russisches Wörterbuch für deutschsprachige Benutzer: Übersetzung aus der deutschen Muttersprache in die russische Fremdsprache;

(b) russisch-deutsches Wörterbuch für russischsprachige Benutzer: Übersetzung aus der russischen Muttersprache in die deutsche Fremdsprache;

(c) deutsch-russisches Wörterbuch für russischsprachige Benutzer: Übersetzung aus der deutschen Fremdsprache in die russische Muttersprache;

(d) russisch-deutsches Wörterbuch für deutschsprachige Benutzer: Übersetzung aus der russischen Fremdsprache in die deutsche Muttersprache.

Die Wörterbücher unter (a) und (b) werden nach Hausmann (1977) als „Hinübersetzungswörterbücher" bezeichnet (vgl. auch Hausmann 1988), als „Hinproduktionswörterbücher" nach Wiegand (1988), weil sie Zwecken der Textproduktion dienen.

In Hausmann (1988, 150) wird zwischen dem Produzieren von Texten ohne Ausgangstext in einer Fremdsprache (i.e. „hinproduzieren") und der aktiven „Hinübersetzung" unterschieden.

In Anschluß an Lötzsch (1979) (vgl. auch die Wörterbucheinleitung zu dem deutsch-russischen Wörterbuch, erarbeitet unter der Leitung von R. Lötzsch und die dort angegebene Literatur; s. zu dem Wörterbuch 2.2.1.1., dort unter a, und Art. 324) werden diese Wörterbücher meist als „aktive" Wörterbücher bezeichnet, so in Kromann/Riiber/Rosbach (1984, 185), Kromann 1983 und Art. 285.

Die Wörterbücher unter (c) und (d) mit der Übersetzungsrichtung von der Fremdsprache in die Muttersprache werden parallel als „Herübersetzungswörterbücher" bzw. als „passive" Wörterbücher bezeichnet, die der Textrezeption dienen.

Für diesen Beitrag wird für die Wörterbücher unter (a) und (b) die Bezeichnung *Hinproduktionswörterbuch* gewählt, für diejenigen unter (c) und (d) die Bezeichnung *Herübersetzungswörterbuch*.

Mit der Wahl dieser Ausdrücke kann den immer wieder gegebenen Verwechslungsmöglichkeiten zwischen „Hin-" und „Her-" („Übersetzungswörterbuch"), und vor allem „aktiv" und „passiv" bis zu einem gewissen Grad begegnet werden. So wird beispielsweise der Ausdruck *passiv* auf das Wörterbuch bezogen („passives Wörterbuch"), damit aber dem Benutzer dieses Wörterbuchtyps eine passive Rolle bei der Textrezeption zugeschrieben; „passiv" kann dabei allerdings insofern in „aktiv" uminterpretiert werden, als der Benutzer bei der

Textrezeption stets Wissensbestände, d. h. eigene Kenntnisse (Sprach- und Sachkenntnisse) aktivieren muß, mithin auf der Basis solcher Kenntnisse Texte durchaus aktiv rezipiert. Zu ähnlichen Einwänden gegen die Terminologie vgl. Manley/Jacobson/Pedersen (1988, 283).

Andere Bezeichnungen als die genannten sind „encoding dictionary" und „decoding dictionary" z. B. nach Manley/Jacobson/Pedersen (1988, 284); vgl. dort zu einer zusätzlichen „re-encoding function of the decoding dictionary"; vgl. auch Schnorr (1986, 54) und Standop (1983) zur „Enkodierung" und „Dekodierung".

An diese Ausdrücke wird in dem vorliegenden Beitrag nicht angeschlossen, weil sie eine zu große Nähe zu den Dekodierungs- und Enkodierungsvorstellungen der älteren Kommunikations- und Texttheorie aufweisen.

Daneben werden auch noch die Ausdrücke „dictionnaire de thème" und „dictionnaire de version" verwendet (vgl. dazu Steiner 1986, 87 und Baunebjerg Hansen 1988, 187), oder auch dem „aktiven" Wörterbuch das „rezeptive" gegenübergestellt, so z. B. in Tomaszczyk (1981).

In Werner (1982, 286) werden für das aktive Wörterbuch „Hin-Übersetzen" und „Hin-Produzieren" unterschieden, für das passive „Her-Verstehen" und „Her-Übersetzen" (vgl. dazu Hausmann 1988). Zu weiteren Problemen um „Verstehen" und „Übersetzen" sei auf Steiner (1986, 86) verwiesen und auf Standop (1983).

Nur wenige Wörterbücher scheinen den Zuschnitt auf jeweilige Benutzergruppen konsequent entlang dieser Typologie durchzuführen, was die Auswahl und das Arrangement von Textsegmenten, aber auch die gewählte Sprache für kommentierende Textsegmente (Kommentarsprache) angeht. Meist wollen die zweisprachigen Wörterbücher gleichzeitig Hinproduktionswörterbücher und Herübersetzungswörterbücher sein. Vgl. dazu auch Hausmann 1988, 151 und Baunebjerg Hansen (1988, 187). F. J. Hausmann schreibt dazu:

„Wenn das Wörterbuch für den aktiven Benutzer gemacht ist, hilft es auch dem passiven, nicht aber umgekehrt. Im Falle eines bidirektionalen Wörterbuchs gelten also die Gesetze des aktiven Wörterbuchs." (Hausmann 1988, 151)

Wenn ein solches Wörterbuch, das in diesem Beitrag als *bifunktionales*, nicht als „bidirektionales" bezeichnet werden soll, weder muttersprachlichen noch fremdsprachlichen Benutzern in ausreichendem Maße dienlich ist, wird es relativ zu den in der Theorie unterschiedenen — monofunktionalen — Wörterbuchtypen zu einem Mischwörterbuch.

In Rettig (1985, 101) wird darauf hingewiesen, daß der heutige Wörterbuchmarkt weit davon entfernt ist, „daß jeweils nur die Benutzer der einen Sprache in einem bestimmten Wörterbuch Auskunft suchen". Gerade in Gebieten mit „unmittelbarer Sprachnachbarschaft" oder gemischtsprachiger Bevölkerung" kann man nach W. Rettig „kaum ein Wörterbuchprogramm der einen oder der anderen Ausrichtung empfehlen".

Es gibt allerdings auch Wege, unter Beachtung der grundlegenden vier Wörterbuchfunktionen ein „polyfunktionales Mehrwegwörterbuch" zu erstellen. Hingewiesen sei auf die Vorschläge zum Großen Deutsch-Chinesischen Wörterbuch aus Wiegand (1988); dort werden die zentralen Wörterbuchfunktionen gewichtet und durch Hinzufügen von Registern Zugriffsmöglichkeiten für unterschiedliche Benutzergruppen zu schaffen versucht.

Auf der Basis der Unterscheidung von Hinproduktionswörterbüchern, Herübersetzungswörterbüchern und bifunktionalen Wörterbüchern werden nachfolgend die Ergebnisse der Anwendung von Textverdichtungsverfahren am Beispiel zweisprachiger Wörterbücher aufgezeigt. Dabei wird auf mögliche weitergehende Differenzierungen von Wörterbuchtypen verzichtet (vgl. z. B. solche aus Steiner 1986, 87 ff.).

Die ausgewählten Sprachenpaare sind Deutsch und Russisch, Deutsch und Englisch sowie Deutsch und Rumänisch. Obwohl es um die zu diesen Sprachenpaaren jeweils berücksichtigten Wörterbücher per se nicht geht und deren Auswahl in Hinblick auf interessante Fälle für das Artikelthema erfolgt, ist es in einigen Fällen notwendig, entsprechende Wörterbücher kurz vorzustellen.

Dies gilt insbesondere für die Wörterbücher zu dem Sprachenpaar Deutsch und Rumänisch, die in Rumänien erschienen sind, bei uns nicht als bekannt gelten können, auf dem freien Buchmarkt nicht erhältlich sind (jedenfalls noch nicht zur Zeit der Abfassung dieses Beitrags kurz nach der Revolution), und denen kein Handbuchartikel gewidmet ist, weshalb durch deren Berücksichtigung eine Lücke geschlossen werden kann. Denn im Unterschied zu anderen räumlich recht begrenzten Sprachen (z. B. Dänisch) haben die Wörterbücher mit Rumänisch keine theoretischen Fürsprecher. Lediglich in Art. 189 wird auf die — ältere — rumänische Lexikographie eingegangen. Von den zweisprachigen Wörterbüchern mit Deutsch wird dort nur das neubearbeitete Wörterbuch von H. Tiktin berücksichtigt, das nicht als Wörterbuch der rumänischen Gegenwartssprache gelten kann; vgl. auch unter 2.2.3.2.

2.2. Abstufung und Gewichtung der Textverdichtung in Abhängigkeit von Wörterbuchfunktionen

Die in der Theorie voneinander unterschiedenen Wörterbuchfunktionen sind einzelnen zweisprachigen Wörterbüchern meist erst nach der Untersuchung von Wörterbuchartikeln und Sichtung der Wörterbucheinleitungen (auch mit Blick auf die dort verwendete Sprache) entsprechender Wörterbücher klar zuzuordnen. Auf die Wörterbucheinleitungen ist — von Ausnahmen abgesehen — wenig Verlaß, was Ausführungen zur angestrebten Wörterbuchfunktion angeht.

Die theoretischen Differenzierungen zur Typologie zweisprachiger Wörterbücher, nach der zu einem Sprachenpaar vier monofunktionale Wörterbücher erwartet werden können, wird in der lexikographischen Praxis nicht nur durch das Vorhandensein bifunktionaler Wörterbücher unterlaufen. Vor allem in Wörterbüchern mit ganz spärlichen Angaben zur lexikographischen Zielsprache werden Zuordnungskriterien zu dem einen oder anderen Typ von Wörterbuch verwischt.

In Herübersetzungswörterbüchern ist z. B. die Kommentarsprache diejenige der lexikographischen Zielsprache, so im deutsch-englischen Wörterbuch für Engländer die englische Sprache. Die Wahl der Kommentarsprache ist ein wichtiges Kriterium für die Einordnung in diesem Falle als Herübersetzungswörterbuch. Werden in einem Kleinwörterbuch keine oder nur ganz spärliche Angaben gemacht, und ist somit die propositionale Dichte in den Wörterbuchartikeln ganz und gar gering, muß für solche Wörterbücher die Differenzierung nach Wörterbuchfunktionen als unnötig aufwendig angesehen werden: Wörterbücher dieser Art werden in diesem Beitrag nicht berücksichtigt. Es sind aber gerade diejenigen Wörterbücher, zu denen R. J. Steiner festgestellt hat:

„This is the type of ‚dictionary‘, which gives some people the erroneous impression that lexicography is only one step removed from stenography." (Steiner 1986, 87).

Grundsätzlich läßt sich eine Abstufung der Textverdichtung von Wörterbuchartikeln in folgender Reihenfolge, wie nachfolgend ausgeführt wird, ansetzen: Hinproduktionswörterbuch — bifunktionales Wörterbuch — Herübersetzungswörterbuch. Diese Abfolge nach dem Grad der Textverdichtung, den Wörterbuchartikel entsprechender Wörterbücher insgesamt stets dann aufweisen, wenn die Kommentierung möglichst exhaustiv ist (in sozusagen prototypischen Wörterbuch-Kandidaten), wird bedingt durch die unterschiedliche Gewichtung von Angaben in Wörterbüchern unterschiedlicher Funktionstypzugehörigkeit.

2.2.1. Hinproduktionswörterbücher

In Hinproduktionswörterbüchern besteht die Kommentierungsaufgabe darin, die lexikographische Zielsprache (die zielsprachlichen Äquivalente) zu kommentieren. Entsprechend ist die propositionale Dichte auf seiten der Zielsprache erheblich größer als für die lemmagebende Sprache. Für die lemmagebende Sprache kann die Kenntnis des Benutzers vorausgesetzt werden; außer der obligatorischen Lemmazeichengestaltangabe müssen nur in besonderen Fällen weitere Angaben gemacht werden.

Wenn man die Lemmazeichengestaltangabe und die im Artikelkopf (Terminus nach Wiegand 1988) an diese adressierten Formangaben als den „linken Teil des Wörterbuchartikels" (in Anlehnung an Denisov 1977; dort ist der „linke Teil des Wörterbuchs" der Lemmabestand) bezeichnet, die an die lexikographische Zielsprache adressierten Angaben als den „rechten Teil" des Wörterbuchartikels, dann ist das Hinproduktionswörterbuch eines mit Rechtsgewichtung der Angaben. Es kommt somit auf der rechten Seite eine (in den einzelnen Wörterbüchern unterschiedlich ausgeprägte) propositionale Dichte zustande; die Verfahren der Textverdichtung greifen auf dieser rechten Seite.

Kromann/Riiber/Rosbach (1984, 222) fassen dies für das dort so bezeichnete „aktive" Wörterbuch so:

„Zu den fremdsprachlichen lexikalischen Einheiten bedarf der Benutzer eines Maximums an grammatischen Informationen, zu den muttersprachlichen genügt ein Minimum."

In den nachfolgenden Abschnitten ist für die lexikographische Zielsprache jeweils diejenige eingesetzt, für die entsprechende Wörterbuchfunktionen in der Menge der berücksichtigten Wörterbücher belegbar sind.

2.2.1.1. Ausgangssprache: Deutsch — Zielsprache: Russisch; für deutschsprachige Benutzer

Diese Wörterbuchfunktionen haben (von den berücksichtigten) nur die Wörterbücher unter a) und b); das prototypische Wörterbuch mit dieser Funktion ist

a) Das „Deutsch-Russische Wörterbuch", begründet von H. H. Bielfeldt und erarbeitet unter der Leitung von Ronald Lötzsch. In dem Abschnitt der Wörterbucheinleitung „Passive und aktive deutsch-russische Wörterbücher" wird erläutert, was sich in der Artikelgestaltung konsequent niederschlägt: Es handelt sich um ein „aktives" Wörterbuch, um ein Hinproduktionswörterbuch, das „für die Anwendung der Fremdsprache bzw. für das Übersetzen in die Fremdprache" (vgl. die Einleitung) für deutschsprachige Benutzer gedacht ist, die das Russische nur unvollkommen beherrschen.

Die Angaben in diesem Wörterbuch sind an den Interessen des deutschsprachigen Benutzers orientiert. Deshalb kommt es hier auf die russ. Äquivalente an und auf ihre Kommentierung in der Muttersprache des Benutzers, i.e. in deutscher Sprache.

Die deutschen Lemmazeichen erhalten entsprechend der Wörterbuchfunktion (mit Rechtsgewichtung der Angaben) keine Akzentangaben, Ausspracheangaben oder grammatische Angaben, weil die ausgebildete Sprachkompetenz des deutschsprachigen Benutzers vorausgesetzt werden kann.

In einem Herübersetzungswörterbuch wären solche Angaben aber notwendig enthalten und bei polysemen Lemmazeichen das Verfahren der Linksauslagerung angewandt.

Das Wörterbuch weist eine große propositionale Dichte auf Zielsprachenseite auf. Es werden zahlreiche Abkürzungen für morphologische und akzentologische Besonderheiten der russischen Äquivalente verwendet, sowohl natürlichsprachliche also auch erst über die Wörterbucheinleitung erschließbare.

Bei homonymen Lemmazeichen werden diese nicht mit Homonymenindex versehen (vgl. Textbeispiel 298.1); Polysemieangaben entfallen dann, wenn im Russischen keine verschiedenen Äquivalente zu berücksichtigen sind (vgl. Textbeispiel 298.2). Deutschsprachige Synonymenangaben wie *hochheben* und Glossate zum Bezugsbereich wie *Sitzung, Versammlung* dienen lediglich dazu, die Gliederungspunkte des Artikeltextes mit Blick auf die zu unterscheidenden Äquivalenzangaben zu etikettieren — nicht dazu, die lemmagebende Sprache zu kommentieren (vgl. Textbeispiel 298.3).

In geschweifte Klammern gesetzt, wird mit kyrillischen Buchstaben (und Zerozeichen) auf morphologische Besonderheiten verwiesen, durch Vokalbuchstaben und Ziffern auf das Deklinationsparadigma, u. a. m. Mittels arabischer Ziffern wird auf Betonungstypen verwiesen, durch das hochgestellte Sternchen unter anderem auf zusätzliche (irreguläre) morphologische und/oder akzentologische Besonderheiten. Phrasemangaben ist ein Strukturanzeiger in Form der Raute vorangestellt.

Tau I der ~ pocá. ~ fällt pocá выпадáет ◆ vor ~ und Tag чуть свет / ни свет, ни заря
II das ~ канáт. *Naut auch* трос. am ~ klettern лáзить {ж} по канáту. das ~ lösen ⟨kappen⟩ отвязывать/-вязáть {7ж/е} канáт ⟨трос⟩. ein ~ um etw. schlingen обмáтывать/-мотáть канáт вокрýг чего́-н., обвя́зывать/-вязáть {7ж/е} что-н. канáтом

Textbeispiel 298.1: Wörterbuchartikel (aus: Deutsch-Russisches Wörterbuch)

Ente *Vogel*; *Med*; *Falschmeldung* ýтка {o} ◆ wie eine bleierne ~ schwimmen плáвать как топóр. jd. läuft wie eine ~ у когó-н. утиная похóдка. das ist eine lahme ~ это тюфя́к {1}. kalte ~ *Bowle* (холóдный) ⟨лимóнный⟩ крюшóн

Textbeispiel 298.2: Wörterbuchartikel (aus: Deutsch-Russisches Wörterbuch)

aufheben I *trans* 1 *hochheben*; *emporstrecken* поднимáть/поднять* 2 *beenden* a) *Sitzung, Versammlung* закрывáть/-крыть*. die Tafel ~ давáть*/дать* знак к окончáнию трáпезы b) *Blockade, Belagerungszustand* снимáть*/снять* 3 *abschaffen* отменять/-менить {7} 4 *aufbewahren* сохраня́ть/-хранить. sich etw. (zu etw.) ~ оставля́ть/-стáвить {л} (себé) чегó-н. ⟨что-н.⟩ (на что-н.) ◆ den Handschuh ~ принимáть/принять* вы́зов. aufgeschoben ist nicht aufgehoben отложить — не значит отменить
II sich ~ v. *Widersprüchen* исчезáть/исчéзнуть 2 *Math* взаимно уничтожáться/уничтóжиться

Textbeispiel 298.3: Wörterbuchartikel (aus: Deutsch-Russisches Wörterbuch)

b) Das „Nemecko-Russkij Učebnyj Slovar'"/„Deutsch-Russisches Lehrwörterbuch" (von N. Liperovskaja und E. Ivanova: Moskau 1966) ist ebenfalls ein Hinproduktionswörterbuch. Es ist vom Lemmabestand her wesentlich beschränkter als das zuvor genannte Wörterbuch; und es werden auch weniger grammatische Angaben unter Anwendung von Verfahren der Textverdichtung gemacht.

„Die Aufgabe des Wörterbuches soll es sein, Anfängern und Fortgeschrittenen das russische Wortgut zu vermitteln, das für ein Gespräch bzw. für eine Übersetzung mittleren Schwierigkeitsgrades aus dem Deutschen ins Russische notwendig ist" (vgl. das „Vorwort").

Der Benutzer soll sich einen „Grundwortschatz" aneignen; der Wörterbuchnachspann enthält Leseregeln der russischen Sprache sowie grammatische Tabellen; die Ziffern zu russischsprachigen Äquivalenten verweisen auf diese Tabellen:

Ente *f* 1. ýтка ^{16c} *f*; 2. *übtr* (газéтная ^{23}) ýтка ^{16c} *f*; die Nachricht hat sich als ~ erwiesen извéстие оказáлось (газéтной) ýткой.

Textbeispiel 298.4: Wörterbuchartikel (aus: Nemecko-Russkij Učebnyi Slovar')

Tau *m* pocá ¹³ᵉ *f*; diese Nacht fiel ~ этой ночью выпала роса.

Textbeispiel 298.5: Wörterbuchartikel (aus: Nemecko-Russkij Učebny Slovar')

> **aufheben 1.** поднимать ³⁵, *perf* поднять ⁷⁰ᵃ; ein Stück Papier vom Fußboden ~ поднять с пола клочок бумаги; einen Gefallenen von der Erde ~ поднять упавшего человека с земли; beide Arme ~ поднять обе руки; **2.** *aufbewahren* сохранять ³⁵, *perf* сохранить ³⁹ᶠ; sie hebt alle Nummern dieser Zeitschrift [alte Briefe] auf она сохраняет все номера этого журнала [старые письма]; etw. gut [sorgfältig] ~ хорошо [тщательно] сохранять что-л.; etw. zum Andenken | zur Erinnerung ~ сохранять что-л. на память; der Junge ist dort gut aufgehoben мальчик там хорошо устроен; **3.** *ungültig machen* отменять ³⁵, *perf* отменить ³⁹ʰ; ein Gesetz [eine Verfügung] ~ отменить закон [распоряжение].

Textbeispiel 298.6: Wörterbuchartikel (aus: Nemecko-Russkij Učebny Slovar')

Ausgelassen sind für das „Lehrwörterbuch" gewisse Bedeutungen der deutschsprachigen Lemmazeichen (vgl. zu **Tau** Textbeispiel 298.1 und 298.5) ebenso wie Phrasemangaben (vgl. Textbeispiele 298.2 und 298.4). Bei Verben wird der zweiten russischen Verbvariante, dem Verb mit perfektivem Aspekt, jeweils die Abkürzung *perf.* hinzugestellt, was für diejenigen, die die russische Sprache als Anfänger erlernen, eine wichtige Angabe ist. Die Synonymenangaben zu Verben (vgl. Textbeispiel 298.6) dienen wie in dem zuvor genannten Wörterbuch nur dazu, über die angenommene Grundbedeutung hinausgehende Bedeutungen für die lexikographische Zielsprache zu differenzieren. Durch das Verfahren der parallelen Ineinanderschachtelung von Formulierungsbestandteilen werden Entsprechungen in den deutschsprachigen und russischsprachigen Beispielangaben (vgl. Textbeispiel 298.6) aufgezeigt.

2.2.1.2. Ausgangssprache: Rumänisch/Russisch — Zielsprache: Deutsch; für rumänischsprachige/russischsprachige Benutzer

a) Das „Dicţionar Român-German/German-Român" (Bucureşti 1986) ist in dem rumänisch-deutschen Teil ein Hinproduktionswörterbuch für rumänischsprachige Benutzer, die aus ihrer Muttersprache ins Deutsche übersetzen wollen.

In dem rumänischsprachigen Vorwort („Prefaţa") wird erläutert, daß das Wörterbuch — auch — für Benutzer gedacht ist, die nur über Elementarkenntnisse im Deutschen verfügen.

Deutschsprachigen Wortäquivalenten und Beispieläquivalenzangaben sind grammatische Angaben hinzugestellt; Ziffern verweisen auf grammatische Tabellen. Von der Wörterbuchfunktion her sind nur die den rumänischsprachigen Lemmazeichen nachgestellten Genusangaben überflüssig.

> **joc** *n. s* Spiel, -(e)s/-e; *a cîştiga/a pierde un* ~ ein Spiel gewinnen (50)/verlieren (170); *Jocurile Olimpice* die Olympischen Spiele *(pl.);* ~ *ul s-a terminat* das Spiel ist aus; ~ *ul de-a v-aţi ascunselea s* Versteckenspiel*, -s/, *s* Versteckspiel, -(e)s/-e; *a face* ~ *dublu* ein doppeltes Spiel spielen (-te, -t); *a ieşi din* ~ das Spiel a u f - geben (42), sich aus dem Spiel z u r ü c k ziehen (187); *(fig.) a pune in* ~ aufs Spiel setzen (-te, -t); *a-şi bate* ~ *de* Spott treiben (161) +*mit*+*D*), sich lustig machen (-te, -t) +*über*+*A; a-şi pune capul/onoarea in* ~ seinen Kopf/seine Ehre aufs Spiel setzen (-te, -t)

Textbeispiel 298.7: Wörterbuchartikel (aus: Dicţionar Român-German)

Die Artikelbildungsangaben zu deutschen Ausdrücken werden dadurch gemacht, daß der letzte Buchstabe deutscher bestimmter Artikel als Abkürzung verwendet wird (*r, e, s*). Auf den Einsatz von Verfahren der Textverdichtung, die gegebenenfalls zu wiederholtem Nachschlagen in der Wörterbucheinleitung Anlaß geben könnten, wird in dem Wörterbuch verzichtet.

Während sich in den anderen hier berücksichtigten Wörterbüchern Trennungsangaben zu deutschsprachigen Äquivalenten nicht finden, werden diese für jeden (oder fast jeden) in Frage kommenden Fall dadurch ad hoc gemacht, daß durch ein Sternchen (vgl. Textbeispiel 298.7 zu *Versteckenspiel*) auf eine Fußnote verwiesen wird: „*despărţirea în silabe: k/k" (Silbentrennung: k/k). Diese Fußnoten finden sich auf fast jeder Druckseite, auch mehrfach. Es werden somit Trennungsangaben zu deutschsprachigen Ausdrücken nicht durch ein generell angewandtes Textverdichtungsverfahren der Art gemacht, welches den Außentexten des Wörterbuchs größeres Gewicht zukommen ließe.

Das Wörterbuch, in dem so viel Wert darauf gelegt wird, dem Benutzer die Schwierigkeiten der deutschen Sprache für die mündliche und schriftliche Textproduktion (aus der Sicht dessen, was für rumänischsprachige Benutzer die Schwierigkeiten ausmacht) unter Einsatz nur weniger textverdichtender Verfahren zu vermitteln, trägt den Charakter eines „Lernerwörterbuchs". Wie in diesen so bezeichneten Wörterbüchern gibt es eine Beschränkung auf gewisse Grundbedeutungen der lexikographischen Ausgangssprache.

Der Benutzer findet für *joc* nur den deutschen Ausdruck *Spiel* als Äquivalent vor; die anderen Bedeutungen, die *joc* im Deutschen haben kann (vgl. ein anderes Wörterbuch unter 2.2.2.), sind ausgelassen.

b) Das „Russko-Nemeckij Slovar'"/„Russisch-Deutsches Wörterbuch" (von E. I. Leping, N. P. Strachova u. a., Moskva 1983) kann unter Berücksichtigung des Gros der Artikeltexte ebenfalls als Hinproduktionswörterbuch gelten. Dies nicht nur, weil die Kommentarsprache Russisch ist, sondern auch wegen der propositionalen Dichte auf Seiten der lexikographischen Zielsprache: Pragmatische Angaben, Genitivangaben u. a. m. sind an diese adressiert.

Bei starken und unregelmäßigen Verben (vgl. 298.9) wird durch den Stern auf Konjugationstabellen in den Außentexten des Wörterbuchs verwiesen, bei Substantiva durch Ziffern (vgl. Textbeispiel 298.8) auf Deklinationstabellen.

Das Angabesymbol „ ‖ " in der Lemmazeichengestaltangabe zeigt den „unveränderlichen" ersten Teil (vgl. die Wörterbucheinleitung S. 18) an, der in lexikographischen Beispielen durch die Tilde ersetzt wird. Die Ausspracheangabe zur Getrenntaussprache (bei *i* vor *e*) ist durch einen gepunkteten Strich angegeben (vgl. 298.8 zu *Baufluchtlinie*).

Das Wörterbuch soll „sowohl von russisch Sprechenden als auch von deutschsprachigen Benutzern gebraucht werden" (vgl. die Wörterbucheinleitung S. 18). Es weist durchaus eine Tendenz zu einem bifunktionalen Wörterbuch auf (wie jedes Hinproduktionswörterbuch auch der anderen Funktion mehr oder weniger dienen kann; vgl. Hausmann 1988, 151), unterscheidet sich aber deutlich von einem Herübersetzungswörterbuch (vgl. ein solches russisch-deutsches Wörterbuch unter 2.2.3.2.). Begünstigt wird die Tendenz zu einem bifunktionalen Wörterbuch in vorliegendem dadurch, daß Synonymenangaben, Glossate und vor allem die pragmatischen Angaben relativ ausführlich gemacht werden; vgl. Textbeispiel 298.8 unter „3" (übersetzt ins Deutsche:) „*in subst.[antivischer] Bed.[eutung] masculinum* (Revolutionär) Röte *m*(19)[...]."

2.2.2. Bifunktionale Wörterbücher

Als *bifunktionale Wörterbücher* werden hier solche Wörterbücher bezeichnet, in denen die — unter Einsatz verschiedener Verfahren der Textverdichtung — gemachten Angaben an die lexikographische Ausgangssprache und auch an die Zielsprache adressiert sind. Dabei gibt es meist eine Gewichtung auf eine primäre Wörterbuchfunktion. Ein mittlerer Grad der Textverdichtung von Artikeltexten im Vergleich zu Hinproduktions- und Herübersetzungswörterbüchern kommt dadurch zustande, daß die propositionale Dichte für beide Wörterbuchfunktionen sozusagen reduziert wird (vgl. zu diesbezüglicher „Ökonomie" auch Art. 324). Denn bei exhaustiver Kommentierung an zwei Adressen (Ausgangssprache und Zielsprache) würden entsprechende Wörterbuchartikel schnell unübersichtlich.

Das deutsch-russische Wörterbuch von R. Lötzsch (vgl. 2.2.1.1. unter a) weist eine große propositionale Dichte auf Zielsprachenseite auf; würden die deutschsprachigen Ausdrücke (Lemmazeichen und Äquivalente) ebenso ausführlich

---

красн‖ый *прил.* 1. rot; ~ый цвет Rot *n* -(e)s, róte Fárbe; ~ый карандáш Rótstift *m* (1); ~ый свет (*у светофора*) Stópplicht *n* (5), rótes Líchtsignal; ~ое винó Rótwein *m* (1); 2. (*революционный*) rot; 3. *в знач. сущ. м* (*революционер*) Röte *m* (14); ◇ Крáсная Áрмия die Röte Armée; Крáсное знáмя das Röte Bánner; óрден Крáсного Знáмени Rótbannerorden *m* (7); Крáсный флот die Röte Flótte; Крáсная плóщадь der Röte Platz; ~ый уголóк Röte Écke; ~ая доскá róte Táfel, Éhrentafel *f* (11); ~ая строкá Alínea *n* -s, -s; néue Zéile mit Ábsatz; ~ая рыба Knórpelfische *pl*, Störe *pl*; ~ый зверь *уст.* Rótwild *n* -(e)s, Édelwild *n*; ~ое дéрево Rótholz *n* -s, Mahagóni *n* -s; ~ые дни *фольк.* schöne Táge, glückliche [glückselige] Zeit; ~ая дéвица 1) *фольк.* schöne [hólde] Júngfrau [Maid]; 2) *ирон.* schüchterner Mensch; ~ое сóлнышко *фольк.* die liebe Sónne, die stráhlende Sónne; Крáсная Шáпочка *фольк.* Rótkäppchen *n* -s; ~ое крыльцó Parádetreppe *f* (11), Parádeaufgang *m* (1*) (*in altrussischen Häusern*); ~ая лúния *стр.* Báufluchtliniḙ *f* (11); ~ради слóвцá der schönen Wórte wégen; ~ая ценá *разг.* gúter Preis, höchstmöglicher Preis; проходи́ть ~ой ни́тью sich wie ein róter Fáden hindúrchziehen*

Textbeispiel 298.8: Wörterbuchartikel (aus: Russko-Nemeckij Slovar')

пробр‖áть *разг.* 1. (*выбранить*) j-m den Kopf wáschen* [zuréchtsetzen]; 2. (*прохватить*) (dúrch)dríngen* *vt*, durch und durch géhen*; хóлод меня ~áл ich bin ganz durchfróren, mir friert das Herz im Léibe, die Kälte geht mir durch Mark und Bein; меня дрожь ~алá ein Zittern überlíef mich; 3. (*прополоть*) áusjäten *vt*; ~áть свёклу Rüben verzíehen*; ◇ егó не проберёшь er hat ein díckes Fell

Textbeispiel 298.9: Wörterbuchartikel (aus: Russko-Nemeckij Slovar')

kommentiert, wäre der Artikeltext mit Angaben allzu überfrachtet.

Wörterbücher, die mehreren Wörterbuchfunktionen gleichzeitig gerecht werden sollen, weisen aus der Perspektive der einen Funktion jeweils einen gravierenden Überschuß an Textsegmenten auf. Diese Textsegmente sind sozusagen redundant relativ zu einer Theorie der Wörterbuchfunktionen, nach der die Auswahl der (meist durch den Einsatz von Textverdichtungsverfahren kondensierten) Textsegmente bestimmt wird. Wenn aber aus wörterbucheigener Perspektive eben verschiedene Wörterbuchfunktionen abgedeckt werden sollen, sind die an unterschiedliche Benutzergruppen gerichteten Textsegmente im Rahmen des Gesamtartikels durchaus nicht redundant.

a) Das „Dicţionar Romîn-German" (Bucureşti 1963) ist z. B. ein bifunktionales Wörterbuch; zum Vergleich mit dem Hinproduktionswörterbuch von 1986 (siehe unter 2.2.1.2. Textbeispiel 298.7) sei der Wörterbuchartikel zu dem Lemmazeichen *joc* angeführt.

> **joc,** ~*uri, s.n.* **1.** Spiel *n.*; ~ *de societate* Gesellschaftsspiel *n.*; ~ *de cuvinte* Wortspiel *n.*; ~ *de scenă* Bühnenspiel *n.*; ~*uri olimpice* olympische Spiele; ~ *de cărţi* Kartenspiel *n.*; ~ *de culori* Farbenspiel *n.*; *a pune în* ~ aufs Spiel setzen; einsetzen; *a fi în* ~ auf dem Spiele stehen; *piesele maşinii au un* ~ *prea mare* die Maschinenteile haben ein zu großes Spiel. **2.** Tanz *m.*; Volkstanz *m.*; *a ieşi la* ~ a) am Tanze teilnehmen; b) erwachsen sein, zu den Erwachsenen gehören. **3.** *a-şi bate* ~ (*de cineva*) spotten, (jn.) verspotten, (mit jm.) Spott treiben.

Textbeispiel 298.10: Wörterbuchartikel (aus: Dicţionar Romîn-German)

Das Wörterbuch soll ein Hinproduktionswörterbuch für den rumänischsprachigen Benutzer sein, daneben aber auch ein Herübersetzungswörterbuch für den deutschsprachigen Benutzer. Diese dem Wörterbuch zugedachte Doppelfunktion wird im Vorwort so erläutert:

„În felul acesta, deşi dicţionarul este destinat în primul rînd cititorului romîn — întrucît explicaţiile însoţitoare sînt date în limba romînă — el poate fi deopotrivă folosit şi de străinii care învaţă limba romînă ori studiază literatura noastră." [Somit kann das Wörterbuch, obwohl es in erster Linie für den rumänischen Leser bestimmt ist — weil die Begleitkommentare in rumänischer Sprache angegeben sind —, gleichzeitig auch von Ausländern benutzt werden, die die rumän. Sprache erlernen oder unsere Literatur studieren].

Dem rumänischsprachigen Benutzer gelingt es (bei guten Deutschkenntnissen), mit Hilfe dieses Wörterbuchs z. B. *joc* aus *dumenica după masa în sat se iese la joc* richtig zu übertragen als *Volkstanz* (das angegebene Äquivalent *Tanz* ist nicht korrekt; dafür rumän. *dans*), oder auch *joc* in *Maria nu se mai joacă cu păpuşile cîci a ieşit deja la joc* als „erwachsen"; vgl. das Wörterbuch unter 2.2.1.2., in dem lediglich auf das deutschsprachige Äquivalent verwiesen wird.

Das Wörterbuch ist ein gewichtetes bifunktionales Wörterbuch. Es setzt für beide Benutzergruppen bereits eine gute Kompetenz in den Sprachen voraus. Der rumänischsprachige Benutzer erhält nur wenige grammatische Angaben zu den deutschsprachigen Äquivalenten, meist nicht einmal bedeutungsdifferenzierende Angaben dazu, welche Übersetzungswahl er wann zu treffen hat (vgl. „erwachsen sein" und „zu den Erwachsenen gehören"). Die Formkommentare zu den Lemmazeichen sind für diesen Benutzer überflüssig. Der deutschsprachige Benutzer aber wird bei Äquivalentreihungen aufgrund seiner Muttersprachenkompetenz z. B. zwischen „aufs Spiel setzen" und „einsetzen" differenzieren können. Die wenigen grammatischen Angaben zur Valenz sind für die rumänischsprachigen Beispielangaben in rumänischer, für die deutschsprachigen in deutscher Sprache gefaßt. Die Artikeltexte sind nur unter Einsatz einiger Verfahren verdichtet; sie können ohne Rückgriff auf die Wörterbucheinleitung rezipiert werden.

b) „Langenscheidt's Encyclopaedic Dictionary of the English and German Languages" (LED) und „Langenscheidts Großwör-

> **dis·pute** [dis'pju:t] **I** *v/i* **1.** dispu'tieren, debat'tieren, streiten (on, about über *acc*): there is no disputing about tastes über den Geschmack läßt sich nicht streiten. – **2.** (sich) streiten, zanken. – **II** *v/t* **3.** disku'tieren, erörtern, debat'tieren. – **4.** bestreiten, in Zweifel ziehen: it cannot be ~d es kann nicht bestritten werden, es läßt sich nicht bestreiten. – **5.** streiten um, kämpfen um, sich bemühen um, sich (*etwas*) streitig machen: to ~ the **victory** to s.o. j-m den Sieg streitig machen; to ~ the **victory** sich den Sieg streitig machen, um den Sieg kämpfen. – **6.** (an)kämpfen gegen, (*dat*) wider'streben, -'stehen, (*dat*) 'Widerstand leisten. – *SYN.* cf. **dis**·**cuss**. – **III** *s* **7.** Dis'put *m*, Diskussi'on *f*, Wortstreit *m*, Kontro'verse *f*, De'batte *f*: in ~ zur Diskussion *od.* Debatte stehend, umstritten, strittig; beyond (*od.* past, without) ~ außerhalb jeder Diskussion stehend, unzweifelhaft, fraglos, zweifellos, unstreitig; a matter of ~ eine strittige Sache. – **8.** (mündliche) Ausein'andersetzung, (heftiger) Streit, Zank *m*. – **9.** *obs.* Kampf *m*.

Textbeispiel 298.11: Wörterbuchartikel (aus: LED)

> **dis·pute** [dɪˈspjuːt] **I** v/i **1.** streiten, (*Wissenschaftler a.*) dispuˈtieren (**on, about** über *acc*): **there is no disputing about tastes** über den Geschmack läßt sich nicht streiten. **2.** (sich) streiten, zanken. **II** v/t **3.** streiten über (*acc*), (*Wissenschaftler a.*) dispuˈtieren über (*acc*). **4.** in Zweifel ziehen, bezweifeln: **a ~d decision** *sport* e-e umstrittene Entscheidung. **5.** kämpfen um, sich bemühen um: **to ~ the victory to s.o.** j-m den Sieg streitig machen; **to ~ the victory** um den Sieg kämpfen. **6.** (an)kämpfen gegen. **III** s [a. ˈdɪspjuːt] **7.** Disˈput m, Kontroˈverse f: **in** (*od.* **under**) **~** umstritten; **beyond** (*od.* **past, without**) **~** unzweifelhaft, fraglos, unbestritten; **a matter of ~** e-e strittige Sache. **8.** (heftiger) Streit.

Textbeispiel 298.12: Wörterbuchartikel (aus: Muret-Sanders kl. E-D)

terbuch der englischen und deutschen Sprache. Englisch—Deutsch" (Muret-Sanders, kl. E-D): Mit Blick auf die Wahl der Kommentarsprache, der ausführlichen Formkommentare zu englischsprachigen Lemmazeichen u. a. m. können die beiden Wörterbücher als Herübersetzungswörterbücher für deutschsprachige Benutzer angesehen werden.

Für diese Funktion allerdings sind Betonungsangaben, Genusangaben, grammatische Angaben wie *dat* und *acc* zu den deutschsprachigen Äquivalenten entbehrlich; für englischsprachige Benutzer sind hingegen Aussprachangaben, Silbentrennungsangaben u. a. m. zur lemmagebenden Sprache entbehrlich. Insgesamt herrscht ein Gleichgewicht der propositionalen Dichte auf Ausgangs- und Zielsprachenseite:

Formulierungsalternativen werden zu Ausdrücken aus beiden Sprachen angegeben, so „*od.* past, without", „Diskussion *od.* Debatte"; Zusätze zum Gebrauch für Präpositionen, vgl. „on, about über *acc*", enthalten grammatische Angaben (hier *acc*), die für beide Sprachen gelten; auch das Glossat *Wissenschaftler* (vgl. Textbeispiel 298.12) gilt für das Lemmazeichen und für das zielsprachige Äquivalent.

In manchen Partien stehen die Wörterbuchartikel aus LED und dem „kleinen Muret-Sanders" im Verhältnis der Textverdichtung zueinander. Im „kleinen Muret-Sanders" sind z. B. unter „7." einige Äquivalente ausgelassen; vgl. auch unter „8." in Textbeispiel 298.11 und 298.12.

Der „kleine Muret-Sanders" Deutsch—Englisch richtet sich an englischsprachige Benutzer (vgl. das „Vorwort"). Es handelt sich von hierher um ein Herübersetzungswörterbuch für Benutzer, die aus deutschsprachigen Texten in ihre eigene Muttersprache übersetzen möchten. Allerdings widerspricht dem, daß als Kommentarsprache die deutsche

> ˈaufˌhe·ben v/t ⟨*irr, sep, -ge-, h*⟩ **1.** (*Äpfel, Zettel etc*) lift (up), take up; **j-n ~** lift (*od.* help) s. o. up. **2.** (*Arm, Augen*) raise, lift; *fig.* **die Hand gegen j-n ~** lift (*od.* raise) one's hand against s. o. **3.** (*aufbewahren*) keep, save *s. th.* up, preserve, (*lagern*) store; **et. für später ~** keep s. th. for later; → **aufgehoben. 4.** (*Versammlung etc*) close, terminate, (*vertagen*) adjourn, (*Boykott, Streik*) call off; → **Belagerung 2, Tafel 7. 5.** (*abschaffen*) abolish (*capital punishment, etc*); **ein Verbot** (**Embargo**) **~** lift a ban (an embargo). **6.** *jur.* (*Vertrag etc*) cancel, rescind, (*a. Ehe etc*) annul, (*Gesetz*) abrogate, repeal, *zeitweilig*: suspend, (*Beschlagnahme etc*) lift, raise; **ein Testament ~** revoke (*od.* set aside) a will; **ein Verlöbnis ~** break off an engagement; **ein Urteil ~** quash (*od.* set aside) a judg(e)ment. **7.** *fig.* (*ausgleichen*) compensate, neutralize, (*counter*)balance, offset, (*Wirkung*) a. negative; **die Schwerkraft ~** neutralize gravity; **sich** (*od.* **einander**) **~** cancel each other out, neutralize one another, *math.* cancel out.
> ˈAufˌhe·ben n ⟨-s; *no pl*⟩ fuss, to-do, ado; **viel ~(s)** (*od.* **großes ~**) **von et.** (**um j-n**) **machen** make a great fuss (*colloq.* noise) about s. th. (s. o.), fuss about s. th. (s. o.); **davon braucht man kein ~(s) zu machen** that's nothing to make a song and dance about; **viel ~(s) um nichts** much ado about nothing.
> ˈaufˌhe·bend *adj Bestimmung, Urteil*: rescissory.

Textbeispiel 298.13: Wörterbuchartikel (aus: Muret-Sanders kl. D-E)

Sprache gewählt ist; vgl. aus Textbeispiel 298.13 zu den Lemmazeichen *aufheben* und *Aufheben* das Glossat „(*Äpfel, Zettel* etc.)", „*od.*" für *oder* u. a. m. Die dem Formkommentar zugehörigen Angaben wie „*sep*" (für *separable*), „*no pl*" (zu *Aufheben*), aber auch pragmatische Angaben wie „*colloq.*" werden hingegen in englischer Sprache gemacht.

> ˈaufˌhän|gen **I** v/t ⟨*sep, -ge-, h*⟩ **1.** (*Mantel etc, teleph. den Hörer, a. v/i*) hang up. **2.** (**an** *dat*) (*Lampe etc, a. tech. Räder*) suspend (from *the ceiling, etc*), (*Bild etc*) hang (on *the wall*). **3.** (*Wäsche*) hang *s. th.* out (to dry). **4.** **j-n ~** hang s. o. (by the neck), *colloq.* string s. o. up. **5.** *fig. colloq.* **j-m et. ~** → **aufhalsen**; **j-m ein Märchen ~** tell s. o. a (whopping) lie; **er hat ihr ein Kind aufgehängt** he's got her with child; **e-n Zeitungsartikel an e-m bestimmten Fall ~** hang an article on a specific case. **II** v/reflex **sich ~ 6.** hang o. s.; *colloq.* (**ach,**) **häng dich** (**doch**) **auf!** go and be hanged!; *humor.* **wo kann ich mich ~?** where can I hang up my things? ⁀**ger** m ⟨-s; -⟩ **1.** (*Mantel⁀ etc*) loop, hanger, tab. **2.** *colloq.* **für e-n Zeitungsartikel etc**: peg (on which to hang a story), *colloq.* gimmick. ⁀**gung** f ⟨-; *no pl*⟩ **1.** hanging up (*etc*). **2.** *tech.* a) (*Rad⁀ etc*) suspension, b) *Batterie*: mounting.

Textbeispiel 298.14: Wörterbuchartikel (aus: Muret-Sanders kl. D-E)

Die deutschsprachigen Lemmazeichen sind reichhaltig unter Einsatz von Angabesymbolen und Abkürzungen kommentiert. Bei polysemen Lemmazeichen (vgl. *aufheben*) sind die Angaben durch Linksauslagerung in den Artikelkopf den jeweiligen ersten Polysemieangaben vorangestellt.

Wo aber artikelintern ein transitives Verb („*v/t*") und z. B. ein reflexives Verb („*v/reflex*") unterschieden wird, nimmt die Linksauslagerung eine besondere Form an; vgl. Textbeispiel 298.14.

Der Formkommentar unter „I" wird unter „II" nur teilweise dadurch getilgt, daß nun „*v/t*" durch „*v/reflex*" ersetzt wird; die Angaben in spitzen Klammern, nämlich „*sep*" (für „separable"/„trennbar") und die Angaben zur Bildung des Partizip Perfekt (mit *ge* oder ohne, mit *haben* oder *sein*), behalten ihre Gültigkeit, wenn sich die Verbkategorie ändert. Es handelt sich bei diesem Verfahren der Textverdichtung um eines der restbildenden Linksauslagerung unter die erste Polysemieangabe (welche zur Unterscheidung der Wortarten dient), als Sonderfall der Linksauslagerung; vgl. auch Art. 38 a.

2.2.3. Herübersetzungswörterbücher

In den Herübersetzungswörterbüchern liegt das Gewicht der Kommentierung (damit die propositionale Dichte) auf seiten der lemmagebenden Sprache. An diese sind grammatische und andere Angaben adressiert, die gegebenenfalls linksausgelagert werden. Die Kommentarsprache ist jeweils die der Zielsprache.

2.2.3.1. Ausgangssprache: Deutsch —
Zielsprache:
Russisch/Englisch/Rumänisch; für Benutzer mit der Zielsprache als Muttersprache

a) Im Vergleich z. B. zu dem Hinproduktionswörterbuch von R. Lötzsch (siehe unter 2.2.1.1.) sind in dem „Nemecko-Russkij Slovar'"/„Deutsch-Russisches Wörterbuch" (von A. A. Leping und N. P. Strachova) die Textverdichtungsmittel wesentlich sparsamer eingesetzt. Denn für dieses Herübersetzungswörterbuch für russischsprachige Benutzer, die zum Lesen und Übersetzen deutscher Literatur befähigt werden sollen (vgl. das Vorwort des Verlages), kann auf die vielfältigen grammatischen und anderen Angaben zu russischen Äquivalenten verzichtet werden, für welche in dem Hinproduktionswörterbuch der Großteil druckraumersparender Textverdichtungsverfahren eingesetzt wird; vgl.:

Tau I *m* -(e)s, *редко pl* -е роса́; vor ~ und Tag чуть свет, ни свет ни заря́.
Tau II *n* -(e)s, -е кана́т, трос; das ~ um etw. *(A)* schlíngen* обмота́ть кана́т вокру́г чего́-л.; das ~ um etw. *(A)* wérfen* набро́сить кана́т на что-л.

Textbeispiel 298.15: Wörterbuchartikel (aus: Nemecko-Russkij Slovar')

Énte *f* =, -n 1. у́тка *(Anas L.)*; er schwimmt wie éine bléierne ~ он совсе́м не уме́ет пла́вать; ≅ он пла́вает как топо́р; 2. (газе́тная) у́тка; 3. *мед.* у́тка *(сосуд)*; ◇ die kálte ~ (холо́дный) крюшо́н.

Textbeispiel 298.16: Wörterbuchartikel (aus: Nemecko-Russkij Slovar')

áufheben* *vt* 1. поднима́ть; 2. прекраща́ть, ока́нчивать; die Táfel [den Tisch] ~ конча́ть обе́д [у́жин], встава́ть из-за стола́; die Sitzung ~ закрыва́ть заседа́ние; die Belágerung ~ снима́ть оса́ду; die Schúle ~ закрыва́ть шко́лу; 3. отменя́ть, упраздня́ть; ликвиди́ровать; ein Gesétz ~ отменя́ть зако́н; ein Verbót ~ снять запре́т; aufgeschoben heißt nicht áufgehoben *посл.* отложи́ть не значит отмени́ть; 4. выла́вливать; ликвиди́ровать *(банду)*; éinen Dieb ~ излови́ть во́ра; die Fálschmünzerei ~ вы́ловить фальшивомоне́тчиков; 5. раскрыва́ть *(заговор)*; 6. сохраня́ть, обеспе́чивать; устра́ивать; séine Sáchen ~ убира́ть ве́щи для сохра́нности; das Kind ist (dort) gut áufgehoben ребёнок (там) хорошо́ устро́ен; 7. *мат.* сокраща́ть; éinen Bruch ~ сокраща́ть дробь; sich ~ *мат.* взаи́мно уничтожа́ться; +10 und —10 hében sich gégenseitig auf +10 и —10 взаи́мно уничтожа́ются.

Textbeispiel 298.17: Wörterbuchartikel (aus: Nemecko-Russkij Slovar')

Pragmatische Angaben („*med*", „*mat.*", „*posl.*"/letztere Angabe für „Sprichwort"), Glossate und Häufigkeitsangaben (vgl. „*redko*"/„selten" aus Textbeispiel 298.15) sind in russischer Sprache formuliert. Durch den Stern nach deutschen Verben wird auf deren Veränderung bei Konjugation und auf Tabellen im Wörterbuchnachspann verwiesen; „ ≅ " zeigt ungefähre Entsprechung an, das Gleichheitszeichen „ = " (siehe Textbeispiel 298.16), daß der Genitiv mit dem Nominativ übereinstimmt.

Ergänzend sei darauf hingewiesen, daß das „Bol'šoj Nemecko-Russkij Slovar'" (erstellt von E. I. Leping, N. P. Strachova u. a., unter der Leitung von O. I. Moskal'skaja) ein ganz ähnlich angelegtes Herübersetzungswörterbuch ist.

b) „Harrap's Standard German and English Dictionary" zeichnet sich als Herüberset-

Ente, *f.* -/-n. 1. *Orn:* duck; Türkische E., Muscovy duck, Barbary duck, musk-duck; *Cu:* gebratene E., roast duck; *F:* gehen, watscheln, wie eine E., to waddle like a duck; schwimmen wie eine bleierne E., to swim badly, *F:* to swim like a stone; tanzen wie eine bleierne E., to dance like a sack of potatoes; aussehen wie eine E. wenn's donnert, to look like a dying duck in a thunderstorm; *Navy: F: (of submarine)* eine E. machen, to crash-dive. 2. *F: (pers., ship, etc.)* eine lahme E., a lame duck. 3. *(drink)* kalte E., (a kind of) white wine cup. 4. *F:* false report, hoax, *F: canard.* 5. *Med: F:* (bed) urinal. 6. *Av:* = Entenflugzeug.

Textbeispiel 298.18: Wörterbuchartikel (aus: Harrap's Standard)

zungswörterbuch für englischsprachige Benutzer dadurch aus, daß deutschsprachige lexikographische Beispiele halbfett hervorgehoben sind; entsprechend der Funktion sind pragmatische Angaben und Glossate zu den deutschsprachigen Ausdrücken in englischer Sprache abgefaßt. Verfahren der Textverdichtung sind Linksauslagerung von Formkommentaren und Abkürzungen (z. B. „F" für „familiar"/„umgangssprachlich").

Aus Äquivalentreihungen kann der kompetente englischsprachige Benutzer die jeweils in einer Benutzungssituation zutreffenden Ausdrücke auswählen. Grammatische Angaben zur lemmagebenden Sprache sind in dem Wörterbuch relativ knapp; es scheint an fortgeschrittene englischsprachige Benutzer gedacht zu sein, denn Ausspracheangaben, Silbentrennungsangaben und Betonungsangaben werden nicht gemacht.

c) Die zweisprachigen Wörterbücher mit Deutsch als lemmagebender Sprache und Rumänisch als lexikographischer Zielsprache sind durchweg, soweit in Rumänien erschienen, Herübersetzungswörterbücher.

Das bereits unter 2.2.1.2. (Textbeispiel 298.7) genannte „Dicţionar Român-German/German-Român (Bucureşti 1986) ist in dem Deutsch-Rumänischen Teil ein konsequentes Herübersetzungswörterbuch für Rumänen als Muttersprachler. Die Angaben zu den deutschsprachigen Lemmazeichen sind reichhaltig und in Abhängigkeit von den jeweils hervorzuhebenden Schwierigkeiten des Deutschen dem Bestand nach variabel gehalten.

Bei den Verben werden abtrennbare Präfixe gesperrt gedruckt; Imperfektiv- und Partizipialformen sind ausgeschrieben; die Ziffern verweisen auf Verbtabellen. Der Strich unter den Vokalen *a* und *u* (vgl. Textbeispiel 298.19) im Lemmazeichen ist sowohl Wortakzentangabe bei Länge, als auch eine Angabe zur Aussprache von *a* und *u* als Diphthong.

a u f heben, hob auf, aufgehoben (62) *vt.* 1. a ridica; *heb den Bleistift auf!* ridică creionul! 2. a păstra, a pune bine; *heben Sie bitte mein Buch auf, bis ich zurückkomme* păstrați-mi, vă rog, cartea pînă mă întorc. 3. a anula, a desființa; *man hob das Urteil auf* sentinţa s-a anulat. 4. a suspenda, a ridica *(o şedinţă etc.)*

Textbeispiel 298.19: Wörterbuchartikel (aus: Dicţionar Român-German/German-Român 1986)

Die Kommentarsprache ist Rumänisch; vgl. neben Textbeispiel 298.19, dort „*o şedinţă*", auch „*e* Ente,-/-n 1. raţă 2. ştire falsă (*apărută în presă*)" — deutsch: „Falschmeldung (*die in der Presse erscheint*)".

Die Artikelbildungsangabe ist in diesem Wörterbuch vor die Lemmazeichengestaltangabe linksausgelagert und abgekürzt (vgl. aus Textbeispiel 298.20: „*e* Bahn"); innerhalb der Wörterbuchartikel wird für nur im Plural gebrauchte Ausdrücke der bestimmte Artikel ausgeschrieben und den Ausdrücken vorangestellt (vgl. Textbeispiel 298.20 zu „*die* Bahamas"). Die Lemmazeichengestaltangabe ist in Textbeispiel 298.20 dadurch verdichtet, daß Varianten hintereinander gestellt werden:

bahamanisch; bahamisch[...ha...] *adj.* bahaman *die* Bahamas; die Bahama|inseln [...ha...] *(pl.)* Bahamas, insulele Bahamas; *die Union ~* Uniunea Bahamas

e Bahn, -/-en 1. cale, drum ◊ *ihn auf die rechte ~ bringen (18)* a-l aduce pe drumul cel bun 2. *mit der ~ fahren (29)* a merge cu trenul/ tramvaiul 3. traiectorie

Textbeispiel 298.20: Wörterbuchartikel (aus: Dicţionar Român-German/German-Român 1986)

Die lemmagebende Sprache ist in diesem konsequenten Herübersetzungswörterbuch insofern reichhaltig kommentiert, als auch partizipiale Formen von Verben zum Lemmabestand gehören.

Entweder handelt es sich um Verweisartikel („**geschrieben**, *v.* schreiben") oder um Artikel mit Phrasemangaben und anderen Verwendungen der Partizipialformen (so zu „**aufgehoben**").

Dem rumänischsprachigen Benutzer gelingt es mit Hilfe des Wörterbuchs, einfache deutsche Texte zu übersetzen; für verschiedene Bedeutungen deutschsprachiger Ausdrücke vermißt man Äquivalenzangaben.

So finden sich unter *Bahn* (vgl. 298.20) als Äquivalente nur *cale* und *drum* (dt. 'Weg', 'Fahrt'), *tren* ('Zug') und *traiectorie* ('(Flug-)Bahn'). *Bahn* im Sinne von 'eine Bahn Stoff' (rumän. *fîşie*), *Bahn* 'im Sport' (rumän. *pistă*), *Bahn* im Sinne von 'Straße' (rumän. *pistă*), 'Straßenbahn' (rumän. *linie*) oder auch 'Verwaltung der Bahn als Institution' (rumän. *calea ferată*) sind nicht verzeichnet.

Wie das genannte Wörterbuch sind zwei weitere deutsch-rumänische Wörterbücher

Herübersetzungswörterbücher: Das „Dicționar German-Român" (București 1966) und das „Dicționar German—Romîn" (von 1958). Sie zeichnen sich durch eine ähnliche Artikeltextgestaltung aus wie das Wörterbuch von 1986; auch in diesen Wörterbüchern sind nur wenige Verfahren der Textverdichtung eingesetzt, so daß die Außentexte bei der Benutzung eine ganz untergeordnete Rolle spielen.

2.2.3.2. Ausgangssprache: Russisch/Rumänisch/Englisch — Zielsprache: Deutsch; für Benutzer mit Deutsch als Muttersprache

Für diese Herübersetzungsrichtung seien drei Wörterbücher angeführt:

a) In dem Wörterbuch von H. H. Bielfeldt (Leitung und Redaktion; Berlin, 14. Aufl. 1982), „Russisch-Deutsches Wörterbuch", ist die Funktion des Herübersetzungswörterbuchs prototypisch verwirklicht. Kommentiert werden Bedeutungen und grammatische Eigenschaften von Ausdrücken der lemmagebenden Sprache in deutscher Sprache. Um das Wörterbuch „durch die grammatischen Angaben nicht zu überlasten, sind die russischen Wörter durch Chiffren auf ein System von Typen bezogen" (H. H. Bielfeldt im Vorwort); vgl. dazu den Metatext zur „Grammatik".

Die Ziffern 1—15 bezeichnen den Flexionstyp und die Wortart. Das Verfahren der

> кра́сный 10 I. -сен, -сна́, -сно rot *Farbe*: -ое зна́мя. II. rot *auf die revolutionäre Tätigkeit, auf das sowjetische Staatssystem bezogen*: -ые войска́; -ые обо́зы Massentransport des Getreides an die Ablieferungsstellen für den Staat. III. -сен, -сна́, -сно schön *in der Volkssprache und folkl.*: ~ денёк; ~ у́гол Ehrenplatz; -ая де́вица schönes Mädchen; долг платежо́м кра́сен *Sprichw.* IV. sehr wertvoll *bezeichnet in Verb. mit best. Subst. eine sehr wertvolle Gattung*: -ая ры́ба grätenloser Fisch, *z. B. Stör*; ~ зверь das wertvollste Wild für den Jäger, *z. B. Bär, Fuchs, Wolf*. — кра́сная строка́ neue Zeile mit Absatz. кра́сная цена́ äußerster annehmbarer Preis: кра́сная цена́ э́тому костю́му 50 рубле́й, а с меня́ про́сят 100. | кра́сный гриб Rotkappe *Pilz*. кра́сное словцо́ geistreiche Bemerkung. кра́сного петуха́ пусти́ть den roten Hahn aufsetzen, in Brand stecken. кра́сной ни́тью *oder* ли́нией проходи́ть sich wie ein roter Faden hindurchziehen. кра́сное де́рево Rotholz. кра́сный това́р Schnitt-, Ellenware *Stoffe, alt.* кра́сный уголо́к Rote Ecke *Raum für kulturelle Aufklärungsarbeit*. Кра́сное мо́ре Rotes Meer

Textbeispiel 298.21: Wörterbuchartikel (aus: Russisch-Deutsches Wörterbuch)

> пробра́ть *v., wie* брать; про́бранный. кого́/что I. *1., 2. Pers. ungebr.* durchdringen, jem. durch und durch gehen *von Kälte, Angst*: моро́з пробра́л меня́ ich bin ganz durchfroren; дрожь пробрала́ меня́ ein Schauer überlief mich; страх пробра́л его́. II. *übertr.* jem. gehörig rügen, ausschimpfen, jem. den Kopf waschen: ~ шалуна́. III. von Unkraut und unbrauchbaren Pflanzen säubern; (aus)jäten; Rüben verziehen; ~ расса́ду; ~ свёклу. ‖ *uv.* пробира́ть 1

Textbeispiel 298.22: Wörterbuchartikel (aus: Russisch-Deutsches Wörterbuch)

> кра́йний 11 äußerster I. am Ende befindlich: ~ дом на у́лице; на кра́йнем се́вере im hohen Norden. II. letzter: ~ срок; -яя цена́ niedrigster Preis. III. *übertr.* heftig, sehr (stark), extrem: -яя нужда́; -ие ме́ры; -е ва́жно; ~ реакционе́р Erzreaktionär. — в кра́йнем слу́чае im Notfalle. по кра́йней ме́ре wenigstens

Textbeispiel 298.23: Wörterbuchartikel (aus: Russisch-Deutsches Wörterbuch)

Textverdichtung kann bezeichnet werden als das der Ersetzung eines möglichen Volltextes zur Grammatik durch Ziffern. Bei polysemen Lemmazeichen sind diese Ziffern linksausgelagert; linksausgelagert sind auch gegebenenfalls allgemeine deutschsprachige Äquivalente (vgl. Textbeispiel 298.23), aber auch z. B. Angaben zum Aspekt bei Verben und andere grammatische Angaben (vgl. vor allem Textbeispiel 298.22). Es werden (außer den Ziffern) keine Angabesymbole verwendet, die in den Außentexten des Wörterbuchs nachzuschlagen wären. Der Gedankenstrich (nicht eine Raute o. a.) steht als Strukturanzeiger vor Phrasemangaben (vgl. Textbeispiel 298.21). Durchweg wird offenbar angestrebt, die Artikel für den Benutzer lesbar zu halten.

So wird bei Bedeutungsparaphrasenangaben auf Abkürzungen oft verzichtet; auch das Verfahren der Auslassung von Formulierungsbestandteilen wird oftmals nicht angewandt.

Vgl. dazu Textbeispiel 298.21 unter „IV": „*bezeichnet in Verb. mit best. Subst. eine sehr wertvolle Gattung*". Vgl. auch z. B. zu *jamskoj*: „*sich auf die Beförderung von Post, Lasten und Passagieren mit der Postkutsche beziehend*". Die Relationsprädikate wie *bezeichnet, sich ... beziehend* sind im Unterschied zu der Praxis in anderen Wörterbüchern mit standardisierten Artikeltexten hier auch für die Nennlexik nicht ausgelassen; vgl. dazu Art. 90 a unter 3.

b) Unter den ohnehin an Zahl geringen rumänisch-deutschen Wörterbüchern hat eines die Funktion der Herübersetzung, nimmt aber eine Sonderstellung ein: H. Tiktin, „Rumänisch-Deutsches Wörterbuch" (Neubearbeitung von Paul Miron).

Das Wörterbuch ist ein bedeutungsgeschichtliches Belegtextwörterbuch, in dem Belegtexte und Belegstellenangaben obligatorisch sind; genauer könnte man es als historisches Stellenhinweiswörterbuch bezeichnen, weil nur auf Verwendungsinstanzen der Lemmazeichen in Belegtexten der Wörterbuchbasis hingewiesen wird, ohne diese ausführlich zu kommentieren.

Das Wörterbuch ist dem Lemmabestand und den angegebenen Bedeutungen nach kein Wörterbuch der rumänischen Gegenwartssprache. Daß das „Gewicht" ausschließlich „auf der Ebene der Sprachgeschichte" liegt, wird aus der allzu knappen Wörterbucheinleitung nicht deutlich. Für die Neubearbeitung hat man sich die Ergebnisse der neueren metalexikographischen Literatur in keiner Weise zu eigen gemacht; auch gibt es keinerlei Orientierung an ähnlichen Wörterbuchunternehmungen. — Die erste Lieferung der Urfassung des Wörterbuchs von Heyman Tiktin (1850—1936) erschien 1895. Für die Neubearbeitung wurden Zitate aus Quellen überprüft und ergänzt.

Das Wörterbuch kommt mit wenigen Verfahren der Textverdichtung aus. Im wesentlichen sind es (a) Abkürzungen für die ausgewerteten Quellen (die im „Literaturverzeichnis" aufgeführt werden), z. B. „PO" für „Palia de la Orastie 1581/82 (Ed. Viorica Pamfil). Bucureşti 1968", (b) nicht einmal im Abkürzungsverzeichnis enthaltene Abkürzungen (vgl. Textbeispiel 298.24: „Z", „Ex" u. a. m.),

(c) Abkürzungen wie „ET", das am Schluß der Artikel für „Etymologie, Angaben zur Wortgeschichte" steht.

Die wenigen Angabesymbole, von denen in dem Wörterbuch Gebrauch gemacht wird, findet man — abgesehen von der Wortakzentangabe — nur selten verwendet, z. B. den Stern für „erschlossene, nicht belegte Form", „(+)" für „untergegangene Lexie". Ohne weitreichende Kenntnisse in der rumänischen Sprache ist nicht erschließbar, ob ein Lemmazeichenformativ noch der rumän. Gegenwartssprache entspricht, denn Angaben wie „(+)" oder auch „veralt." (für „veraltet") werden nicht nur ganz gelegentlich, sondern auch offenbar völlig unkontrolliert gemacht. Die zugeordneten deutschsprachigen Äquivalente geben meist veraltete Bedeutungen wieder (abgesehen davon, daß oft auch veraltete deutschsprachige Ausdrücke vorkommen); veraltete Bedeutungen stehen neben noch heute gebräuchlichen ohne differenzierende Angaben; und wo Angaben wie „ugs." (für „umgangssprachlich") gemacht werden, sind diese in den untersuchten Fällen meist nicht zutreffend.

So gibt es heute das Verb *răzbuna'* noch (vgl. Textbeispiel 298.24). Allerdings ist die auf den heutigen Sprachgebrauch zugeschnittene (bzw. einen solchen Zuschnitt zumindest suggerierende) Angabe „ugs." unzutreffend; die angegebene Bedeutung existiert nicht mehr. Unter „II.V.intr." findet sich „2. veralt. *a-şi răzbuna* R a c h e ü b e n". Aber

---

răzbuna´ Präs. -bu´n (1581/2 PO)
I. V.tr. 1. ugs. a u f h e i t e r n, e r f r e u e n.
Calul bun şi mîndra bună la inimă mă răzbună (I.-B.15). -
2. jdn. od. etw. r ä c h e n. *Apolon şi Diana răzbunară
pe mama lor ucizînd copiii Niobeei* (OLL.HOR.301). - II.
V.intr. 1. LV. a u s r u h e n; a u f h ö r e n. *În şase
dzile lucrează în a şaptea dzi tu răzbună de-a ararea
şi de-a secerarea* (PO² 295b;Ex 34,21;VULGATA: *cessabis
arare et metere*). - 2. veralt. *a-şi răzbuna* R a c h e
ü b e n. *Capra face stricăciuni scumpiei şi scumpia îşi
răzbună cu pielea ei* (PANN,Z.I,395). - III. *a se răzbuna*
1. (*pc.,asupra cuiva*) s i c h (a n j d m.) r ä c h e n.
*De cîte ori se ciudea pe bărbatul său, trebuia să se răz-
bune pe copil* (MELH.CH.373). *Noi înfulicăm cu lăcomie; ne
răzbunăm pe cele şease săptămîni de post* (VLAH.IC.97). -
2. (vom Wetter) s i c h a u f k l ä r e n, s i c h a u f-
h e i t e r n. *De se răzbună cîte-o leacă vremea înspre
amiază* (NĂD.NUV.I,30). - ET. *răz* + *bun*.

Textbeispiel 298.24: Wörterbuchartikel (aus: Tiktin)

auch diese Angabe ist falsch; denn es handelt sich dabei gerade um die einzige heute noch gültige Bedeutung von *răzbuna*. Unter „III." ist die Angabe *asupra cuiva* veraltet, ohne daß dies verzeichnet wird; unter „2. (vom Wetter)" etc. kann heute nur noch in veralteten Kotexten wie *vremja se răzbune* verstanden werden: 'das Wetter ändert sich' (diese Angabe fehlt); aber die angegebenen deutschen Entsprechungen gibt es heute nicht mehr; etc. etc.

c) Für die Wörterbücher mit Englisch sei als Beispiel ein Lernwörterbuch angeführt: „Harrap's Lernwörterbuch Grundwortschatz Englisch—Deutsch".

In dem Lernwörterbuch wird durch den Nichteinsatz möglicher Textverdichtungsverfahren (und bei Beschränkung auf einen „Grundwortschatz") dafür gesorgt, dem Buch einen gewissen Umfang zu geben. Um aus den Angaben Informationen zu entnehmen, brauchen die Benutzer so gut wie keine Verfahren der Textverdichtung beim Lesen rückgängig zu machen. Aber die Benutzer benötigen zur Vertiefung die „Übungen und Spiele" im Anhang des Buches, in denen auch auf die Wörterbuchartikel eingegangen wird.

> **machine** [mə'ʃiːn] *Substantiv*
> Maschine; **washing machine** = Waschmaschine; **sewing machine** = Nähmaschine; **the factory has put in a new machine for making electric light bulbs.**
> **machinery,** *Substantiv*
> Maschinen; **the factory has put in a lot of new machinery.**
> *NB:* kein Plural: **some machinery** = einige Maschinen; **a piece of machinery** = eine Maschine, ein Gerät

Textbeispiel 298.25: Wörterbuchartikel (aus: Harrap's Lernwörterbuch)

> **pretty** ['prɪtɪ] *Adjektiv*
> hübsch; **he has two pretty daughters; she is prettier than her sister; what a pretty little village!**
> **pretty—prettier—prettiest**
> *NB:* wird gesagt von Mädchen und Gegenständen, aber nie von Männern

Textbeispiel 298.26: Wörterbuchartikel (aus: Harrap's Lernwörterbuch)

In einem grauen Feld am Ende vieler Artikel werden Zusatzangaben zur Grammatik und zum sonstigen Gebrauch meist in vollständigen Sätzen gemacht; abgekürzt sind selbst Wortartenangaben wie „*Substantiv*" nicht, so daß zusammenhängende Benutzerhinweise mit Erklärungen zu verwendeten Abkürzungen etc. entfallen (können).

2.3. Nachbemerkungen

Wie in den vorangehenden Abschnitten gezeigt wird, sind die Textsegmente von Wörterbuchartikeln zweisprachiger Wörterbücher je nach Wörterbuchfunktion unterschiedlich gewichtet: Rechtsgewichtung mit propositionaler Dichte auf Zielsprachenseite, Linksgewichtung mit propositionaler Dichte auf Ausgangssprachenseite und relative Gleichgewichtung im Rahmen bifunktionaler Wörterbücher. Daß die überwiegende Zahl zweisprachiger Wörterbücher nicht den Nachschlagebedürfnissen nur einer Benutzergruppe gerecht werden will, kommt insofern in der Darstellung nicht zum Ausdruck, als zu Illustrationszwecken jeweils nur wenige Wörterbücher herangezogen werden (zu jedem Sprachenpaar etwa gleich viele und in der Rolle als Belege für die Wörterbuchfunktionen nur jeweils einige Wörterbücher). Und bei diesen Wörterbüchern handelt es sich um solche, in denen die für die jeweilige Wörterbuchfunktion konstitutiven Eigenschaften in hohem Maße (oder zumindest der Tendenz nach gut) hervortreten. Im einzelnen kann sogar innerhalb ein und desselben Wörterbuchs — auf der Folie einer Theorie von Wörterbuchfunktionen und dementsprechend auszuwählender Textsegmente — inkonsequent verfahren werden.

Wie über die in diesem Artikel berücksichtigten Sprachenpaare hinaus angenommen werden kann, sind die Verfahren der Textverdichtung in zweisprachigen Wörterbüchern keine anderen als diejenigen, die in Art. 90a anhand einsprachiger Wörterbücher unterschieden werden. (Selbstverständlich ließen sich für die Verfahren selbst jeweils weitere interne theoretische Differenzierungen anbringen; um die durchsichtigen und oft bescheidenen Wege der lexikographischen Praxis vom möglichen Volltext zum Kondensat zu verfolgen, genügt der gemachte theoretische Aufwand). Die Untersuchungen zur Anwendung entsprechender Verfahren der Textverdichtung in zweisprachigen Wörterbüchern (in der Gewichtung von Textsegmenten nach Wörterbuchfunktionen) ist nicht darauf ausgerichtet, Forderungen für die Artikeltextgestaltung zweisprachiger Wörterbücher abzuleiten — sei es in Richtung einer Gestaltung als Serie monofunktionaler Wörterbücher zu einem Sprachenpaar, sei es als Wörterbuch, das gleichzeitig mehrere Funktionen wahrnehmen will.

3. Literatur (in Auswahl)

3.1. Wörterbücher

Bol'šoj = Bol'šoj Nemecko-Russkij Slovar'. Das große Deutsch-Russische Wörterbuch. Erstellt von E. I. Leping, N. P. Strachova u. a., unter der Leitung von O. I. Moskal'skaja. 2., unveränd. Aufl. Moskva 1980 [Bd. 1: A—K: 760 S.].

Deutsch-Russisches Wörterbuch = Deutsch-Russisches Wörterbuch. Begründet von Hans Holm Bielfeldt. In der Endfassung erarbeitet von einem Autorenkollektiv unter der Leitung von Ronald Lötzsch. 3 Bde. Berlin 1983 [Bd. 1: 761 S.; Bd. 3: 787 S.].

Dicţionar German-Român = Dicţionar German-Român. [Bucureşti]: Academia Republicii Socialiste România, Institutul de Lingvistică 1966 [1172 S.].

Dicţionar German-Romîn = Dicţionar German-Romîn. Redactor responsabil: Mihai Isbăşescu. Bucureşti 1958 [1183 S.].

Dicţionar Român-German = Dicţionar Român-German/German-Român. Von Emilia Savin (Coordinator), Ioan Lăzărescu und Katharina Tăntu. Bucureşti 1986 [400 + 494 S.].

Dicţionar Romîn-German = Dicţionar Romîn-German. Redactor responsabil: Mihai Isbăşescu. Bucureşti 1963 [733 S.].

Harrap's Lernwörterbuch = Harrap's Lernwörterbuch Grundwortschatz Englisch-Deutsch. Hrsg. von P. H. Collin, in Zusammenarbeit mit Eva-Maria Sawers und Robin Sawers. London 1985 [304 S.].

Harrap's Standard = Harrap's Standard German and English Dictionary. Ed. by Trevor Jones. Part One: German-English, A-E. London [usw.] 1963 [117 S.].

LED = Langenscheidt's Encyclopaedic Dictionary of the English and German Languages. Part I: English-German. 1. Bd.: A-M. Völlige Neubearbeitung. Hrsg. von Otto Springer. Berlin 1962 [XXXVII, 883 S.].

Muret-Sanders kl. D-E = Langenscheidts Großwörterbuch der englischen und deutschen Sprache. „Der kleine Muret-Sanders". Deutsch-Englisch. Von Heinz Messinger und der Langenscheidt-Redaktion. 1. Aufl. Berlin. München [usw.] 1982 [1296 S.].

Muret-Sanders kl. E-D = Langenscheidts Großwörterbuch der englischen und deutschen Sprache. „Der kleine Muret-Sanders". Englisch-Deutsch. Von Helmut Willmann, Heinz Messinger und der Langenscheidt-Redaktion. 1. Aufl. Berlin. München [usw.] 1985 [1200 S.].

Nemecko-Russkij Slovar' = Deutsch-Russisches Wörterbuch. Red.: A. A. Leping und N. P. Strachova. 5., unveränd. Aufl. Moskva 1968 [987 + 5 S.].

Nemecko-Russkij Učebnyi Slovar' = Deutsch-Russisches Wörterbuch. Deutsch-Russisches Lehrwörterbuch. Von N. Liperovskaja und E. Ivanova. Moskva 1966 [749 S.].

Russisch-Deutsches Wörterbuch. = Russisch-Deutsches Wörterbuch. Unter Leitung und Redaktion von Hans Holm Bielfeldt. 14., durchgesehene Aufl. Berlin 1982 [1119 S.].

Russko-Nemeckij Slovar' = Russisch-Deutsches Wörterbuch. Hrsg. von E. I. Leping/N. P. Strachova/K. Leyn/R. Eckert. 9., unveränd. Aufl. Moskva 1983 [848 S.].

Tiktin = Heyman Tiktin: Rumänisch-Deutsches Wörterbuch. 2., Tiktin, H.: Rumänisch-Deutsches Wörterbuch. 2., überarbeitete und ergänzte Aufl. von Paul Miron. Lfg. 1 ff. Wiesbaden 1985 ff.

3.2. Sonstige Literatur

Baunebjerg Hansen 1988 = Gitte Baunebjerg Hansen: Stand und Aufgaben der zweisprachigen Lexikographie. Nachlese zum Kopenhagener Werkstattgespräch 12.—13. Mai 1986. In: Lexicographica 4. 1988, 186—202.

Denisov 1977 = P. N. Denisov: Ob universal'noj strukture slovarnoj stat'i [Zur universellen Struktur des Wörterbuchartikels]. In: Aktual'nye problemy učebnoj leksikografii. Hrsg. von V. A. Red'kin. Moskva 1977, 205—225 [Deutschsprachige Übersetzung in: Aspekte der sowjetrussischen Lexikographie. Übersetzungen, Abstracts, bibliographische Angaben. Übersetzt, herausgegeben und eingeleitet von Werner Wolski. Tübingen 1982, 89—111 (Reihe Germanistische Linguistik 43)].

Hausmann 1977 = Franz Josef Hausmann: Einführung in die Benutzung der neufranzösischen Wörterbücher. Tübingen 1977 (Romanistische Arbeitshefte 19).

Hausmann 1988 = Franz Josef Hausmann: Grundprobleme des zweisprachigen Wörterbuchs. In: Symposium on Lexicography III. Proceedings of the Third International Symposium on Lexicography, May 14—16, 1986, at the University of Copenhagen. Ed. by Karl Hyldgaard-Jensen and Arne Zettersten. Tübingen 1988 (Lexicographica Series Maior 19), 137—154.

Kromann 1983 = Hans-Peter Kromann: Paradigmatische und syntagmatische Relationen im zweisprachigen Wörterbuch. In: Die Lexikographie von heute und das Wörterbuch von morgen. Hrsg. von J. Schildt und D. Viehweger. Berlin (Linguistische Studien, Reihe A: Arbeitsberichte 109), 330—345.

Kromann/Riiber/Rosbach 1984 = Hans-Peder Kromann, Theis Riiber, Poul Rosbach: Überlegungen zu Grundfragen der zweisprachigen Lexikographie. In: Studien zur neuhochdeutschen Lexikographie V. Hrsg. von Herbert Ernst Wiegand. Hildesheim. Zürich. New York 1984 (Germanistische Linguistik 3—6/84), 159—238.

Lötzsch 1979 = Ronald Lötzsch: Einige Fragen der Entwicklung der zweisprachigen Lexikographie an der AdW der DDR. In: Zeitschrift für Slawistik 24. 1979, 402—408.

Manley/Jacobson/Pedersen 1988 = James Manley/Jane Jacobson/Viggo Hjørnager Pedersen: Telling Lies Efficiently: Terminology and the Microstructure in the Bilingual Dictionary. In: Symposium on Lexicography III. Proceedings of the Third International Symposium on Lexicography, Mai 14—16, 1986, at the University of Copenhagen. Ed. by Karl Hyldgaard-Jensen and Arne Zettersten. Tübingen 1988 (Lexicographica Series Maior 19), 281—302.

Rettig 1985 = Wolfgang Rettig: Die zweisprachige Lexikographie Französisch—Deutsch, Deutsch—Französisch. Stand, Probleme, Aufgaben. In: Lexicographica 1. 1985, 83—124.

Ščerba 1940 = L. V. Ščerba: Opyt obščej teorii leksikografii [Versuch einer allgemeinen Theorie der Lexikographie]. In: Leksikografičeskij Sbornik III. 1940, 89—117 [Übersetzung ins Deutsche in: Aspekte der sowjetrussischen Lexikographie. Übersetzungen, Abstracts, bibliographische Angaben. Übersetzt, eingeleitet und herausgegeben von Werner Wolski. Tübingen 1982 (Reihe Germanistische Linguistik 43), 17—62].

Schnorr 1986 = Veronika Schnorr: Translational Equivalent and/or Explanation? The Perennial Problem of Equivalence. In: Lexicographica 2. 1986, 53—60.

Standop 1983 = Ewald Standop: Englische Wörterbücher unter der Lupe. In: Würzburger Anglistische Mitteilungen. Sondernummer 1. 1983, 1—71.

Steiner 1986 = Roger J. Steiner: How Many Languages Should a 'Bilingual' Dictionary Offer? In: Lexicographica 2. 1986, 85—92.

Tomaszczyk 1981 = Jerzy Tomaszczyk: Issues and Developments in Bilingual Pedagogical Lexicography. In: Applied Linguistics 2. 1981, 287—296.

Werner 1982 = Reinhold Werner: La definición lexicográfica. In: G. Haensch u. a., La lexicografía. Madrid 1982, 259—328.

Wiegand 1988 = Herbert Ernst Wiegand: Shanghai bei Nacht. Auszüge aus einem metalexikographischen Tagebuch zur Arbeit am Großen Deutsch-Chinesischen Wörterbuch. In: Studien zur neuhochdeutschen Lexikographie VI. 2. Teilband. Hrsg. von Herbert Ernst Wiegand. Hildesheim. Zürich. New York (Germanistische Linguistik 87—90/86), 521—626.

Wiegand 1989 = Herbert Ernst Wiegand: Wörterbuchforschung. Studien zur Theorie der Lexikographie. Typoskript Heidelberg 1989.

Wiegand 1990 = Herbert Ernst Wiegand: Über die Strukturen der Artikeltexte im Frühneuhochdeutschen Wörterbuch. Zugleich ein Versuch zur Weiterentwicklung einer Theorie lexikographischer Texte. Typoskript. Heidelberg 1990.

Wolski 1986 = Werner Wolski: Partikellexikographie. Ein Beitrag zur praktischen Lexikologie. With an English Summary. Tübingen 1986 (Lexicographica Series Maior 14).

Wolski 1989 = Werner Wolski: Art. 90 a. Formen der Textverdichtung im allgemeinen einsprachigen Wörterbuch. In: Wörterbücher. Dictionaries. Dictionnaires. Ein internationales Handbuch zur Lexikographie. Hrsg. von Franz Josef Hausmann/Oskar Reichmann/Herbert Ernst Wiegand/Ladislav Zgusta. Erster Teilband. Berlin. New York 1989, 956—967.

Werner Wolski, Heidelberg,
(Bundesrepublik Deutschland)

299. Contrastive Linguistics and Bilingual Lexicography

1. Introduction
2. Contrastive Linguistics and Its Divisions
3. Contrastive Linguistics Applied to Bilingual Lexicography
4. Open Questions
5. Selected Bibliography

1. Introduction

In spite of the long tradition of comparative studies in linguistics, 'contrastive analysis' is a relatively young discipline. Its relevance to bilingual lexicography (here taken to include all types of interlingual or polyglot dictionaries) has not been explored in a systematic fashion before, except perhaps in connection with the notion of translation 'equivalence' (cf. Art. 295). — This article is intended to give an outline of contrastive linguistics and its most important divisions in relation to the main issues of bilingual lexicography; examples will be drawn largely from English, German and French.

2. Contrastive Linguistics and Its Divisions

2.1. General Contrastive Analysis

Most statements about language in general may be called contrastive in the sense that they deal with similarities and differences (and thus need a common denominator, the so-called *tertium comparationis,* cf. Hartmann 1980, 22 ff.). Any language or any of its varieties or subsystems is thus capable of being contrasted with any other language or corresponding variety or sub-system. — Contrastive analysis can be carried out on these for a number of different purposes. The object may be to elucidate the production of errors in the acquisition of a foreign language, to explain the complexities of bilingualism, to analyse the processes of translation and interpreting, to aid the compilation of teaching grammars and bilingual dictionaries, or to isolate a set of common linguistic universals. — The antecedents of contrastive linguistics in the widest sense go back to diachronic, genetic and other variants of historical-comparative linguistics (referred to as 'philology' in some quarters); in the narrower sense, however, contrastive analysis is barely 100 years old. — Contrastive studies can take many forms, according to the period or place when or where they are carried out, and no single or unified paradigm has emerged yet. Indeed, there are striking differences in approach even between the various treatments of relatively closely related language areas (compare, e. g., such diverse traditions as [for English and German] Leisi 1953 and Kufner 1971, [for English and French] Vinay/Darbelnet 1958 and Delattre 1966, and [for French and German] Malblanc 1961 and Ternes 1976). Some language pairs are still inadequately covered: the selective bibliography by Siegrist (1977) lists 977 studies for European languages and only 56 for African, Asian and American languages. — Two sets of distinctions are sometimes made to characterise the main types of contrastive linguistics (also called 'differential' or 'confrontative' linguistics, in the Romance and Slavonic domains, respectively). One is the dichotomy, already hinted at, between historical-comparative (or diachronic) studies and descriptive-contemporary (or synchronic) studies, the other is between typological-theoretical (or discipline-based) studies and practical-applied (or problem-based) studies.

2.2. Special Divisions of Contrastive Linguistics

Several constituent branches or divisions of contrastive linguistics may be distinguished, using two time-honoured classifications in linguistics, structural 'levels' and semiotic 'dimensions'. The first starts from the assumption of a layered ranking of basic units from simple (and short) to complex (and large), e. g. in phonology from phoneme to syllable, in graphology from grapheme to logogram, in lexicology from lexeme to idiom, in grammar from morpheme to sentence, in textology from speech act to discourse. The second classification posits linguistic relationships in terms of the three aspects: paradigmatic (choice of items from an

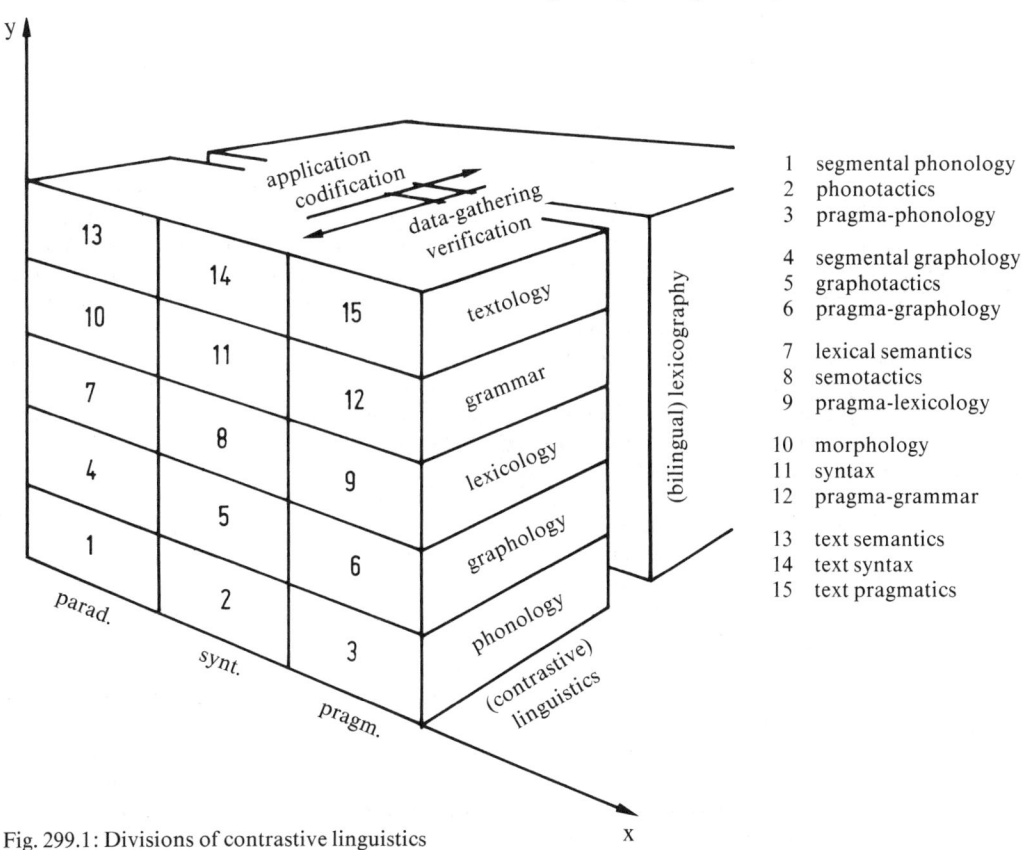

1   segmental phonology
2   phonotactics
3   pragma-phonology

4   segmental graphology
5   graphotactics
6   pragma-graphology

7   lexical semantics
8   semotactics
9   pragma-lexicology

10 morphology
11 syntax
12 pragma-grammar

13 text semantics
14 text syntax
15 text pragmatics

Fig. 299.1: Divisions of contrastive linguistics

inventory), syntagmatic (sequence of items in chains), and pragmatic (communicative effect in context). — Combining these two classifications, we can establish a grid like the one in Fig. 299.1. The main divisions are formed by arranging linguistic levels, along the y-axis, from patterns of substance (phonology and graphology) at the bottom, via patterns of form (lexicology and grammar) in the middle, to patterns of interaction (textology) at the top, and by correlating them, along the x-axis, with the three semiotic dimensions (paradigmatic or semantic, syntagmatic or syntactic, and pragmatic or contextual).

It may be that not all these 15 divisions of contrastive linguistics turn out to be relevant to the concerns of bilingual lexicography. But at least some forms of (especially 'synchronic' and 'applied') contrastive analysis are suitable for solving some of the problems of bilingual dictionary-making. Some specific examples follow in Section 3.

3. Contrastive Linguistics Applied to Bilingual Lexicography

The relation between (various forms of) contrastive analysis and (various forms of) bilingual lexicography is never even, direct, or mutual. It is sometimes claimed that a descriptive comparison of a set of phenomena from a particular pair of languages can lead to an improved codification of items representing these phenomena in the interlingual dictionary. However, it is doubtful whether such contrastive work has always materially affected lexicographical practice; what is more, it may well have been the bilingual dictionary that provided the contrastive linguist with appropriate data, or their verification, in the first place (cf. Di Pietro 1971). — The comparability criterion that both contrastive linguistics and interlingual lexicography share is the translating competence of their respective practitioners. Because of the 'anisomorphism' (or non-correspondence of surface forms) between any two languages, it is only the bilingual analyst who, via his/her mental lexical stores, can approximate any formal or functional equivalence: "Da es keine echte sprachliche Kongruenz gibt, ist der Lexikograph gezwungen, sich bei der Festlegung zweisprachiger Entsprechungen stets nur mit Annäherungswerten zu begnügen." (Schmitz 1960, 234) — To illustrate some of the methods and results of contras-

contrast [kən'trɑːst] **1** *vt* mettre en contraste, contraster (*one thing with another* une chose avec une autre).
2 *vi* contraster, faire contraste (*with* avec). *[colour]* to ~ **strongly** contraster (*with* avec), trancher (*with* sur).
3 ['kɒntrɑːst] *n* (*gen, TV*) contraste *m* (*between* entre). **in** ~ **par** contraste; **in** ~ **to par** opposition à, par contraste avec; **to stand out in** ~ (*in landscapes, photographs*) se détacher (*to* de, sur); ressortir (*to* sur, contre); *[colours]* contraster (*to* avec), trancher (*to* sur).
contrasting [kən'trɑːstɪŋ] *adj colours, opinions* opposé, contrasté.

Dictionary excerpt 299.1: Entry *contrast* (from: Atkins 1978, 119)

contrast ['kɒntrɑːst] **1** *n* (a) (*contrasting*) Gegenüberstellung *f*. a ~ **of the two reveals that ...** bei einer Gegenüberstellung der beiden zeigt sich, daß ...
(b) Gegensatz *m* (*with, to* zu); (*visual, striking difference of opposites*) Kontrast *m* (*with, to* zu). **by** *or* **in** ~ im Gegensatz dazu; **to be in** ~ **with** *or* **to sth** im Gegensatz/in Kontrast zu etw stehen; **the red makes a good** ~ das Rot stellt einen guten Kontrast dar; **she's quite a** ~ **to her sister** es besteht ein ziemlicher Gegensatz *or* Unterschied zwischen ihr und ihrer Schwester; **the** ~ **between the state of the £ now and last year** der Unterschied zwischen dem jetzigen Stand des Pfundes und seinem Wert im letzten Jahr; **and now, by way of** ~ und nun etwas ganz anderes; **what a** ~! welch ein Gegensatz!
(c) (*Art, Phot, TV*) Kontrast *m*.
2 [kən'trɑːst] *vt* einen Vergleich anstellen (*with* zwischen +*dat*), gegenüberstellen (*with dat*).
3 [kən'trɑːst] *vi* im Gegensatz *or* in Kontrast stehen (*with* zu), kontrastieren (*with* mit); (*colours also*) sich abheben (*with* von), abstechen (*with* von). **to** ~ **unfavourably with sth** bei einem Vergleich mit *or* im Vergleich zu etw schlecht abschneiden; **his promises and his actions** ~ **sharply** seine Versprechungen und seine Handlungsweise stehen in scharfem Kontrast *or* Gegensatz zueinander; **blue and yellow** ~ **nicely** Blau und Gelb ergeben einen hübschen Kontrast.
contrasting [kən'trɑːstɪŋ] *adj opinions, lifestyle etc* gegensätzlich, kontrastierend (*form*); *colours* kontrastierend, Kontrast-.
contrastive [kən'trɑːstɪv] *adj* gegenüberstellend; (*Ling*) kontrastiv.

Dictionary excerpt 299.2: Entry *contrast* (from: Terrell 1980, 132—133)

tive linguistics, an arbitrarily chosen pair of specimen entries from two bilingual dictionaries (see dictionary excerpts 299.1 and 299.2) will be referred to.

What is interesting about these entries is not the fact that they differ superficially in terms of the ordering of the information or by the fact that only one of them lists the technical term *contrastive linguistics,* but rather the apparently greater weight given to the English-German entry. Rather than exploring the possible reasons for this, we turn to the problem of converting contrastive knowledge into dictionary text.

3.1. Contrastive Phonology

At the level of phonology, contrastive analysis can help to specify differences between the sound systems of the languages in question. To isolate the segmental units, various systems of phonetic/phonological description and classification compete, depending on the state of the art of linguistic scholarship for each particular language pair. The transcription symbols devised by the IPA are employed in many (but by no means all) monolingual and interlingual dictionaries. Thus, both Collins dictionaries adopt [ɒ] as in ['kɒntrɑːst] and [ə] as in [kən'trɑːst] to distinguish the stressed and unstressed variants of English *o*; German and French share with English the pronunciation [ə], but not [ɒ]. However, both phonemes are transcribed by symbols whose significance may not be obvious to the dictionary user (cf. Art. 15, 300). — Recent contrastive 'suprasegmental' or phonotactic analysis has produced interesting new evidence (Ternes 1976, 4 explains the apparent 'singing' quality of Welsh speakers of English and Swiss speakers of German in terms of inversely correlated stress and intonation patterns), but most interlingual dictionaries are still notoriously deficient in reflecting the prosodic facts of connected speech. — Much less is known about the pragmatics of sound systems, e. g. how such features as strong emphasis, ridicule, emotion and attitude are conveyed in different languages. — Progress in contrastive linguistics may lead to new advances in bilingual lexicography here, perhaps even to the development of new genres of interlingual dictionaries of pronunciation (cf. Art. 141).

3.2. Contrastive Graphology

Some languages contrast sharply in their use of (especially non-alphabetic) writing systems (cf. Art. 32). An example of how this affects the lack-of-fit between sound and spelling may be gleaned from the specimen entries: in word-initial position we note (disregarding loan orthographies) that French uses the letter *c* to represent the sound [k] as in *contraste,* German uses *k* as in *Kontrast,* while English uses either *c* as in *contrast* or *k* as in *kindred.* Dictionary users may or may not be familiar with such conventions. Whether special bilingual forms of the spelling dictionary (cf. Art. 140) are likely to become available, to reflect the paradigmatic, syntagmatic and pragmatic facts of written language, cannot be predicted here.

3.3. Contrastive Lexicology

At the level of lexicology, anisomorphic relationships are even more awkward. 'Meaning discrimination' is the lexicographical technique which is supposed to clarify the various multiple relationships between words (lexemes) and their meanings (senses). In the monolingual dictionary, semantic similarity is shown by paraphrase or definition or the use of synonyms, in the bilingual dictionary equivalence is achieved by metaphrase or translation or the use of glosses. For the contrastive analysis of these complex lexico-semantic relations, a 'componential approach' is often suggested as a solution: just as phonological units may be broken down into distinct phonetic features, lexemes are held to be capable of analysis into senses as 'complexes of semantic features' (James 1980, 91). Thus, a contrastive analysis of the different senses of a word like *contrast* ('comparison', 'opposition', 'distinction' etc.) would not only be regarded as revealing their equivalent(s) in other languages (French *contraste, opposition,* etc. and German *Gegenüberstellung, Gegensatz, Unterschied* etc.), but also seen as improving the arrangement of the information within the dictionary entry itself. However, in view of the known indeterminacy of interlingual interference in the language acquisition progress (cf. Nemser/Vincenz 1972) and the apparent inability of existing dictionaries to capture the complexities of 'directionality' and 'multivergence' (cf. Kromann/Riiber/ Rosbach 1984, Rettig 1985), such a straightforwardly direct application of contrastive linguistics to bilingual lexicography will be very difficult to execute. Could it explain, e. g., the fact that *contrast(e)* in English (and French) has a greater semantic range than German *Kontrast* and therefore requires more glosses and a larger entry in the English-German dictionary? — It is possible that further advances in contrastive lexical semantics, semotactics and pragma-lexicology may bring limited benefits to bilingual lexicography. Suggestions have been put forward, e. g., for a 'contrastive dictionary of synonyms' (Snell-Hornby 1984, 278 f.) or for better codifications of 'false friends' (cf. Art. 304) and technical terminology (cf. Art. 307).

3.4. Contrastive Grammar

The contrastive analysis of the word, its formation from smaller building blocks (morphology) and its functioning in sentences (syntax) is fairly well developed for many pairs of languages, using a variety of theoretical models (cf. Art. 296). Thus, in the extracts 299.1 and 299.2, word classes are marked by the labels *n* and *v,* as are subclasses of verbs (note that English *contrast,* but not all its equivalents, can function either as *vi* or *vt*). Systemic differences in degrees of collocability are sometimes indicated by means of examples, e. g. *in contrast with/to // par opposition à, par contraste avec // im Gegensatz/in Kontrast zu.* — But many problems remain unsolved; does a phrase like *and now, by way of contrast* have literal or idiomatic equivalents, and could they be found by the means of an as yet inadequately constituted contrastive pragma-grammar? — Some specialised dictionary genres are open to interlingual adaptation in this area, e. g. the dictionary of 'constructions' (cf. Art. 287) and 'idioms' (cf. Art. 290).

3.5. Contrastive Textology

If the objective of bilingual lexicography is to find "lexical units of the target language which, when inserted into the context, produce a smooth translation" (Zgusta 1984, 147), we need to know how discourse is structured into text and how this works in different languages. There have been several attempts, since Vinay/Darbelnet 1958, to develop a contrastive linguistics at the level of the text, but none have resulted in models that can be easily applied to the design of the interlingual dictionary. The problem seems to lie, once more, in our inability so far to model the bilingual text competence of the translator-lexicographer. Can a systematic analysis of 'parallel texts' (Hartmann 1980, 37 f.) help us explain the various communicative strategies that are at work when functional equivalence is produced? How does such a model incorporate semantic, syntactic and pragmatic dimensions? — At its most advanced and ambitious, contrastive discourse analysis also needs to address itself to problems of culture-specificity (cf. Art. 301), which might in turn lead to a new generation of dictionaries of cross-cultural information.

4. Open Questions

Contrastive linguistics has much more to do than it has already done, particularly in its 'pragmatic' divisions. The ever-dominant question is what *tertium comparationis* to choose: is it a linguistic notion akin to formal 'congruence', does it reside in the situational context as functional similarity, or is it part of the approximative act performed by the bilingual analyst? — If more systematic contrastive treatments of increasing numbers of languages were forthcoming, would they transcend the mere catalogues of similarities and differences that have been offered by conventional studies? (Hawkins 1986 presents interesting evidence, from German and English grammar, that interlingual contrasts in one sub-system of the language can be compensated by those in another and thus accounted for in a unified framework of contrastive typological analysis.) — Given a further boost to contrastive linguistics, will bilingual lexicography manage to process this additional information in ways that can benefit the user of dictionaries? More has to be done to assess real user needs (cf. Art. 12) and to improve textual transparency (e. g. by means of usage labelling, cf. Art. 292) in general and specialised bilingual dictionaries. — Another question is the interdisciplinary nature of research in this field. Many problems are multidimensional, requiring collaboration with fields like psycholinguistics (errors in interference) and sociolinguistics (language contact and variation). One interesting side-issue is whether a contrastive analysis of bilingual dictionaries for different language pairs would uncover new principles that might be valid for the whole of bilingual lexicography.

5. Selected Bibliography

5.1. Dictionaries

Atkins 1978 = Beryl T. Atkins et. al.: Collins/Robert [French-English &] English-French Dictionary. Glasgow. London. Paris 1978 [XXVII, 717 & 781 p.].

Terrell 1980 = Peter Terrell et al.: Collins/Pons [German-English &] English-German Dictionary. Glasgow. London. Stuttgart 1980 [XVII, 792 & 790 p.].

5.2. Other Publications

Delattre 1966 = Pierre Delattre: Studies in French and Comparative Phonetics: Selected Papers in French and English. The Hague 1966.

Di Pietro 1971 = Robert J. Di Pietro: Language Structures in Contrast. Rowley, Mass. 1971.

Hartmann 1980 = Reinhard Rudolf Karl Hartmann: Contrastive Textology. Comparative Discourse Analysis in Applied Linguistics. Heidelberg 1980 (Descriptive Linguistics 5).

Hawkins 1986 = John A. Hawkins: A Comparative Typology of English and German. Unifying the Contrasts. London 1986.

James 1980 = Carl James: Contrastive Analysis. Harlow 1980.

Kromann/Riiber/Rosbach 1984 = Hans-Peder Kromann/Theis Riiber/Poul Rosbach: Überlegungen zu Grundfragen der zweisprachigen Lexikographie. In: Germanistische Linguistik 3—6/84, 159—238.

Kufner 1971 = Herbert L. Kufner: Kontrastive Phonologie Deutsch-Englisch. Stuttgart 1971.

Leisi 1953 = Ernst Leisi: Der Wortinhalt. Seine Struktur im Deutschen und Englischen. Heidelberg 1953 [4th ed. 1971].

Malblanc 1961 = Alfred Malblanc: Stylistique comparée du français et de l'allemand. Essai de représentation linguistique comparée et étude de traduction. Paris 1961.

Nemser/Vincenz 1972 = William Nemser/Ileana Vincenz: The indeterminacy of semantic interference. In: Revue Roumaine de Linguistique 17. 1972, 99—120.

Rettig 1985 = Wolfgang Rettig: Die zweisprachige Lexikographie Französisch-Deutsch/Deutsch-Französisch. Stand, Probleme, Aufgaben. In: Lexicographica 1. 1985, 83—124.

Schmitz 1960 = Siegfried Schmitz: Englische Wörterbücher. In: Die Neueren Sprachen 9. 1960, 226—242.

Siegrist 1977 = Leslie Siegrist: Bibliographie zur kontrastiven Linguistik. Trier 1977.

Snell-Hornby 1984 = Mary Snell-Hornby: The bilingual dictionary — help or hindrance? In: R. R. K. Hartmann (ed.): LEXeter '83 Proceedings. Tübingen 1984 (Lexicographica. Series Maior 1), 274—281.

Ternes 1976 = Elmar Ternes: Probleme der kontrastiven Phonetik. Hamburg 1976 (Forum Phoneticum 13).

Vinay/Darbelnet 1958 = Jean-Paul Vinay/Jean Louis Darbelnet: Stylistique comparée du français et de l'anglais. Méthode de traduction. Paris 1958.

Zgusta 1984 = Ladislav Zgusta: Translation equivalence in the bilingual dictionary. In: R. R. K. Hartmann (ed.): LEXeter '83 Proceedings. Tübingen 1984 (Lexicographica. Series Maior 1), 147—154.

Reinhard Rudolf Karl Hartmann, Exeter (Great Britain)

300. La métalangue dans les dictionnaires bilingues

1. Le dictionnaire de langues
2. Les échanges de contenus
3. Langues-objets et langues de description
4. Construction d'un modèle et réalisations effectives
5. Les informations de microstructure
6. Bibliographie choisie

1. Le dictionnaire de langues

1.1. L'article en deux langues

Le dictionnaire bilingue est un excellent représentant du dictionnaire de langue, tel qu'on l'oppose au dictionnaire encyclopédique. Aucune ambiguïté ne se manifeste dans la lecture des articles, entre les signes et les choses (art. 33), et il s'agit constamment des signes. La seule exception s'applique aux noms propres souvent intégrés à la nomenclature, à la fois pour le signe (aménagement graphique, calque, prononciation) et pour son référent. Mais dans un article quelconque, le caractère métalinguistique du texte est notamment vérifié parce que la longue phrase qui a pour sujet le mot-entrée est un mélange de deux langues; elle n'est donc interprétable qu'au niveau métalinguistique, autrement elle serait inacceptable (*«un lit est un bed», *«un bed est un lit» ou, en anglais, *«a lit is a bed», *«a bed is a lit»). Il s'agit, au contraire, d'une mise en relation de deux signes, l'entrée qui est autonyme (= le mot *lit*) et l'équivalent qui l'est également (= le mot *bed*).

1.2. Le connu et l'inconnu

Le dictionnaire bilingue est donc obligatoirement un dictionnaire de langue. Les dictionnaires de langue monolingues sont traditionnellement faits pour aller de l'inconnu au connu (décodage) ou plus récemment dans l'histoire de ces ouvrages, du connu à l'inconnu (encodage: utilisation du mot dans la phrase, autres sens, recherche onomasiologique/analogique, etc.). Les dictionnaires bilingues suivent le même modèle, d'abord et historiquement, de l'inconnu au connu (version), puis du connu à l'inconnu (thème). La différence fondamentale, de ce point de vue, est celle qui existe entre l'inconnu dans sa propre langue, qui est toujours plus ou moins accessible (graphie, prononciation, morphologie) et l'inconnu dans une langue étrangère qui peut être total (langue non alphabétique pour un francophone, par exemple). En admettant que l'on apprenne ponctuellement un mot chinois, l'exemple en chinois ne peut ni aider à comprendre le mot, ni illustrer un emploi particulier, et il perd son utilité. C'est un lexique bilingue extrêmement fruste qui conviendrait. Il faut donc considérer que le dictionnaire bilingue est un ouvrage où la langue «inconnue» est partiellement connue du lecteur, ce qui le rapproche du monolingue pour le lecteur dont c'est la langue. On voit que, pour un locuteur de langue L_1 qui veut comprendre L_2, existent plusieurs ouvrages selon une compétence croissante pour L_2: le simple lexique L_2/L_1, le dictionnaire $L_2/L_1 - L_1/L_2$, enfin le dictionnaire monolingue L_2, le plus difficile (Atkins 1982).

Par ailleurs, on rappellera l'existence de deux types de dictionnaires bilingues différents du modèle étudié ici. Ce sont les faux bilingues ou dictionnaires monolingues donnant une information de microstructure sur (ou dans) une langue étrangère (cf. Wooldridge 1982, Zgusta 1986); ce sont aussi les dictionnaires terminologiques bilingues (non généraux) qui empruntent au monolingue sa fonction définitoire et/ou encyclopédique, les mots des deux langues étant également mal connus (Rey-Debove 1983).

2. Les échanges de contenus

2.1. Équivalences de signes

Le dictionnaire bilingue ne fait pas d'analyse de contenu comme le fait le monolingue avec les définitions. Il ne donne que des équivalences lexicales non analytiques (mot, syntagme codé, locution) par un transcodage d'unité d'une langue à unité de l'autre. C'est seulement quand il n'existe pas d'équivalent codé du mot-entrée que le lexicographe recourt à une glose définitionnelle dans la langue cible, celle de l'équivalent.

Le monolingue établit une relation entre le signe et le référentiel (signifié dénotatif lié à la connaissance du monde), et son lexique offre un découpage du monde idiosyncrasique, c'est-à-dire différent pour chaque langue. Le bilingue établit une relation entre les signes de langues différentes sans s'occuper du référentiel; il confronte deux lexiques et deux découpages du monde, mais ne s'intéresse qu'au découpage en signes. Passant d'un signe à l'autre, il conserve à peu près le contenu (car il n'y a pas de «synonymie» possible entre langues différentes) mais il ne fait pas d'analyse sémantique, même s'il donne des indications dans ce domaine (cf. 5.2.).

En l'absence de copules entre le mot-entrée et ses prédicats, la lecture d'un bilingue doit être explicitée par un verbe exprimant la relation entre signes. Soit par exemple, pour l'anglais et le français, à l'usage d'un francophone:

(1) L'anglais **bed** a pour traduction *lit*
(2) **Lit** se dit *bed* en anglais

Dans les deux cas on peut lire aussi «se traduit par, a pour équivalent, correspond à, etc.»

2.2. Signification et dénomination

On s'avise que pour (1), il existe un autre type de prédication beaucoup plus fréquent en français (aussi en allemand):

(1 *bis*) L'anglais *bed* signifie «lit»,

ce qui est sémiotiquement différent puisque «lit» est un nom de signifié et non pas un nom de signe. Dans cette mesure, la prédication bilingue de contenu est très proche de la définition synonymique du monolingue (*plumard* signifie «lit»). Or, il est important de savoir que, dans un monolingue, ce type de prédicat ne peut fonctionner que de l'inconnu au connu, du moins courant au plus courant, du spécial au général, du marqué au non marqué, puisqu'il n'y a pas d'analyse sémantique. La phrase *«*lit* signifie *plumard*» est improbable, alors que «*lit* se dit *plumard* dans le langage familier» est normal. La même contrainte se manifeste dans les bilingues: «*bed* signifie ‹lit› » est normal, mais non pas *«*lit* signifie ‹bed› ». Il semble qu'il en soit ainsi dans toutes les langues pour les verbes de signification, car le nom de signifié n'est pas un véritable autonyme puisqu'il a le statut d'une définition à signifié déterminé dont les signes sont aléatoires. Dans «*bed* signifie ‹lit› », *lit* pourrait être remplacé par une définition; son signifiant n'est pas obligatoire comme celui du mot-entrée, et son signifié ne peut jamais être inconnu (Rey-Debove 1978, 189).

On a toujours, dans la version, l'illusion d'une signification (qu'est-ce que ça veut dire?) qui prend la place du transcodage. Inversement, pour le thème, on a l'illusion d'une dénomination, d'une opération onomasiologique, bien qu'on ne parte pas du tout d'un signifié ou d'une notion, mais d'un signe. Il faut éviter de tomber dans une erreur d'interprétation (s'appliquant aussi aux monolingues) qui consisterait à croire que le dictionnaire bilingue attribue tantôt un signifié à un signifiant (version), tantôt un signifiant à un signifié (thème). Signifiant et signifié étant solidaires, il ne peut s'agir que de signifié inconnu ou de signifiant inconnu d'un signe. La prédication de version est en fait: «*bed* a le même sens que *lit*» (*lit* désignant un signe à signifiant déterminé), alors que la prédication d'encodage du monolingue implique le verbe *signifier* dont le complément est libre (le synonyme a le statut de la définition).

D'ailleurs chaque langue exprime la relation métalinguistique de transcodage à sa façon; en anglais, la phrase la plus naturelle met clairement en jeu deux autonymes, et on préférera aussi un modèle qui évite *signifier* pour le français :

(anglais)   version   The English for *lit* is *bed*
            thème   The French for *bed* is *lit*
(français) version   L'anglais *bed* se traduit par *lit*
            thème   *Lit* se dit *bed* en anglais

Le modèle des relations d'échange de signes est pour la version :

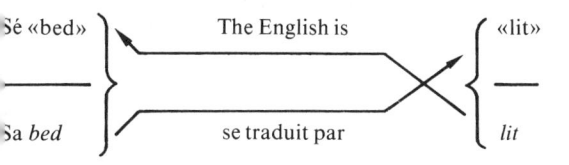

Sé «bed»   The English is   «lit»
Sa *bed*   se traduit par   *lit*

et pour le thème :

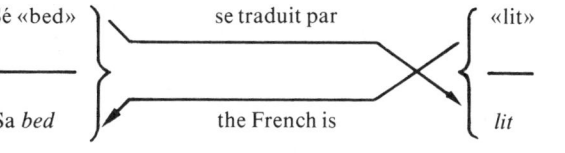

Sé «bed»   se traduit par   «lit»
Sa *bed*   the French is   *lit*

Dans ce schéma apparaissent les mouvements croisés Sa × Sé (signifiants × signifiés) dus à la méconnaissance de l'un ou de l'autre selon la situation.

3. Langues-objets et langues de description

Le dictionnaire bilingue a pour objet deux langues L_1 et L_2 qu'il met en relation. Par ailleurs, pour parler de ces langues, il lui faut choisir une langue de description qui soit comprise de l'utilisateur. Le bilingue est un ouvrage dont le modèle maximal possède deux fonctions (thème et version) pour deux communautés linguistiques : il possède quatre lectures, alors que le monolingue n'en possède que deux (décodage/encodage) et souvent une seule (décodage). Le bilingue $L_1/L_2 - L_2/L_1$ offre quatre situations de consultation (Duval 1986) :
Le lecteur de langue L_1 traduit L_2 en L_1 (version), L_1 en L_2 (thème) ;
Le lecteur de langue L_2 traduit L_1 en L_2 (version), L_2 en L_1 (thème).

Chaque lecteur d'un bilingue fait les mêmes opérations, quelle que soit la langue qu'il parle, ce qui est version pour l'un étant thème pour l'autre, et vice versa. À étudier le métalangage des articles de dictionnaires bilingues, on observe des constantes.

(1) Répartition des autonymes et des mots métalinguistiques : *a*) le mot-entrée, son équivalent dans l'autre langue et les expressions ou phrases contenant le mot-entrée sont autonymes ; lorsqu'il n'existe pas d'équivalent du mot-entrée, la périphrase qui le remplace est autonyme pour le lecteur dont ce n'est pas la langue *b*) le reste du discours (information sur la catégorie grammaticale, niveaux de langue, domaines, contraintes de contenu, etc.) n'est pas autonyme ; il utilise des mots neutres et métalinguistiques pour commenter le passage d'un autonyme de L_1 à un autonyme de L_2 et vice versa.

(2) Répartition des langues : *a*) l'article contient des mots appartenant aux deux langues, et parfois des signes non langagiers *b*) le mot-entrée et les expressions ou phrases le contenant (ou son symbole) sont dans la même langue, L_1 ou L_2 *c*) les équivalents du mot-entrée sont dans l'autre langue, L_2 ou L_1.

(3) La langue de description qui constitue le tissu où sont pris les autonymes est beaucoup plus difficile à caractériser d'emblée, d'autant qu'il s'agit surtout d'abréviations. La langue de description est généralement unique, L_1 ou L_2, dans la plupart des dictionnaires. Or, on a vu qu'un bilingue complet mettait en jeu deux langues-objets et deux communautés linguistiques, et l'on s'attendrait donc à deux langues de description, deux métalangages L_1 et L_2, pour que l'utilisation par les deux communautés soit parfaitement symétrique.

3.1. Incertitudes sur la langue de description

3.1.1. Titres, préfaces, annexes grammaticales

On prendra comme exemple de métalangage le titre des dictionnaires bilingues, pour bien distinguer les langues-objets des langues de description. Soit le Harrap's Shorter 2 vol. publié chez Bordas (= HSB). Le premier volume porte en titre de jaquette *Dictionnaire français-anglais,* et le second, *Dictionnaire anglais-français.* Pour ces titres, les langues-objets (L_o) sont bien le français et l'anglais : L_{o1}, L_{o2}. La langue de description (L_d) est le français : L_{d1}. La formule complète du dictionnaire est alors : L_{o1}/L_{o2} en L_{d1} et L_{o2}/L_{o1} en L_{d1}. Ce dictionnaire serait donc destiné aux francophones. Mais on est surpris de voir en lettres d'or, sur les couvertures cartonnées : *1. French/English, 2. English/French,* titre qui correspond à la formule L_{o1}/L_{o2} en L_{d2} et L_{o2}/L_{o1} en L_{d2}. Ce même dictionnaire est donc destiné aux anglophones. Cette dernière interprétation semble corroborée par le fait que, dans les bilingues, la première partie est généralement pour la version, opération plus facile et plus courante que le thème. Ici, le lecteur anglophone du HSB *French/English* fait de la version. Pour plus d'information, on se reporte à la préface de ce premier volume: elle est écrite en anglais à propos de l'anglais et du français, et aussitôt suivie d'une traduction en français. Cette fois la double expression en L_{d2}, L_{d1} est respectée, mais le contenu de l'information sur les langues-objets est complètement inadapté, puisque les informations dont ont besoin un anglophone et un francophone sont spécifiques; dans les deux langues, on parle des verbes français, mais pas des verbes anglais. Si l'on consulte le volume 2, *English/French,* on constate que la même préface est répétée; autrement dit, le HSB présente quatre textes de même contenu sans rapport avec les quatre fonctions du bilingue précédemment envisagées et destinés aux anglophones.

3.1.2. Abréviations et indications de microstructure

Un autre repère est constitué par la liste des abréviations. Dans un bilingue, le métalangage de description est presque uniquement fait d'abréviations, et pour que le dictionnaire soit lisible par les deux communautés linguistiques, ces abréviations devraient figurer dans les deux langues. À consulter le HSB, on trouve au début de chaque volume la même liste présentée en anglais *(abbreviations used in the dictionary).* Cette liste comporte trois colonnes en regard: les abréviations, le mot complet en anglais, et le mot correspondant en français, par exemple:

Needlew.	*Needlework*	Couture
Jew.	*Jewish*	Juif; juive
phr.	*Phrase*	Locution

L'abréviation est celle du mot anglais et, en ce qui concerne le français, elle devient un code arbitraire à mémoriser pour le lecteur francophone. Si ce dernier cherche le mot anglais pour *point* (de couture) il trouvera «*Needlew*: Stitch»; et s'il cherche la traduction de *stitch,* il lira «*Needle*: Point». Or, le mot désambiguïsateur pour *point* et *stitch* (polysémiques) n'est pas *Needlework* pour le francophone, mais *Couture.*

La communauté des racines latines et grecques peut produire des abréviations communes pour des mots savants:

acc.	Accusative	Accusatif
Adm.	Administration	Administration
adv.	Adverb, adverbial	Adverbe, adverbial

Il n'en reste pas moins que cette rencontre est de pur hasard, selon les mots et les langues comparées (pour évacuer toute ambiguïté, on vérifiera ce qui se passe dans des bilingues dont L_1 et L_2 ont un alphabet différent). La liste des abréviations du HSB est donc en anglais, les auteurs ont fait une seule exception pour *qch., qn, sth., s.o.* (*quelque chose* et *quelqu'un* dans les deux langues). Si l'on observe, à l'intérieur des articles, l'indication des contraintes de contenu contextuel (sujet obligé, objet obligé, etc.), on remarque qu'elles sont également en anglais dans les deux volumes, par exemple la mention «of wind»:

(anglais) **howl,** *v.i. & tr. 1.* Hurler, pousser des hurlements; *(of wind)* mugir, rugir.
(français) **hurler** [yʀle]. *1. v.i.* (of dog, wolf) To howl; (of wind, storm) to roar;

On peut donc déduire de toutes ces observations que la langue de description du bilingue HSB est l'anglais, et qu'en dépit du titre français de la jaquette, ce dictionnaire est destiné aux anglophones pour la version et pour le thème. Et si, effectivement, des francophones l'utilisent, ils doivent bien maîtriser l'anglais pour en tirer profit. Dans les niveaux de difficulté liés à la compétence (cf. 1.2.), il s'agit, pour le locuteur de langue L_1, d'un dictionnaire $L_{o2}/L_{o1}-L_{o1}/L_{o2}$ qui est écrit en L_{d2}, et qui se rapproche du monolingue L_{o2} en L_{d2}.

4. Construction d'un modèle et réalisations effectives

Le métalangage de tout dictionnaire bilingue contient les autonymes de deux langues, et c'est l'étude du discours métalinguistique de liaison sur ces autonymes qui caractérise la communauté à laquelle il est destiné. L'étude des articles, des abréviations, des préfaces, des titres de divers bilingues montre une grande variété d'utilisation du métalangage, variété qui atteint parfois l'incohérence et qui n'est jamais explicitée, pour des raisons d'édition, de co-édition, de diffusion et de commercialisation. Le modèle complet d'un dictionnaire bilingue pour deux communautés serait:

L_1/L_2 métalangage en L_2 sur L_1
 métalangage en L_1 sur L_2
L_2/L_1 métalangage en L_2 sur L_1
 métalangage en L_1 sur L_2

Ces doubles commentaires en deux langues seraient extrêmement lourds dans l'article, aussi adopte-t-on souvent une solution moyenne, comme dans le Robert & Collins en un volume, 1978 (= RC):

L_1/L_2 métalangage en L_1 sur L_2
L_2/L_1 métalangage en L_2 sur L_1

où le métalangage est dans la langue de celui qui fait un thème (qu'il parle L_1 ou L_2), c'est-à-dire l'opération la plus difficile de l'encodage, non soutenue par un contexte:

(anglais) **howl**(...) *2 vi [person, animal]* hurler; *(*:cry)* pleurer: *[baby]* brailler; *[wind]* mugir.
(français) **hurler** ['yʀle] (l) *1 vi* (a) *[personne]* (de douleur) to roar, yell (out), bellow; *(de peur)* to scream, yell; (...) (b) *[chien]* to howl; *[vent]* to howl, roar ... etc.

Pour des langues lexicalement apparentées (langues romanes ou romanisées, par exemple anglais et français) on peut aussi éviter les abréviations en deux langues par une sorte de neutralisation des abréviations. Le RC en fournit une liste intéressante où la recherche de mots voisins, avec l'aide de la coupe, permet de restreindre les abréviations spécifiques de chacune des langues à une quinzaine sur 175 (compte non tenu des accents, de l'ordre adjectif/nom). Ainsi, il n'est pas gênant pour un francophone de trouver l'abréviation *Rail (railways)* pour *chemin de fer*, ni pour l'anglophone l'abréviation *Constr (construction)* pour *building trade*. L'abréviation *Culin* est commode pour *cookery* et *cuisine (culinary, culinaire)*. D'autre part, les symboles non langagiers (astérisques, vignettes diverses) sont statutairement neutres par rapport à L_1 et L_2. C'est dans les bilingues que ces symboles sont pleinement justifiés (comme le code iconique international des aéroports), alors que dans le monolingue ils ne servent qu'à réaliser une économie de place. Malheureusement, les possibilités iconiques des symboles métalinguistiques sont très restreintes, et les symboles arbitrairement forgés nécessitent un apprentissage du lecteur.

Le métalangage d'un bilingue est donc, comme dans le monolingue, un espace d'ambiguïté: ambiguïté langue/monde pour le monolingue, ambiguïté lecteur L_1/lecteur L_2 pour le dictionnaire traitant de L_1 et L_2 (Rettig 1982). C'est l'étude du métalangage d'un bilingue relativement à L_1, L_2 qui permet de le caractériser. Ainsi, HSB est un dictionnaire version/thème pour anglophones, le RC un dictionnaire version/thème pour anglophones et francophones (néanmoins, la jaquette du RC réservé à la vente en Grande-Bretagne est entièrement rédigée en anglais: French/English-English/French, alors que celle du même livre vendu en France est bilingue: français/anglais-English/French). Le Collins anglais-espagnol (= CSD) est, comme le HSB, fait pour les anglophones; comme lui, son titre est en anglais, avec deux sous-titres dans chacune des langues.

Il existe aussi, évidemment, des bilingues simples à deux fonctions, par exemple le dictionnaire Shogakukan-Random House 1980 (= SR), dont la nomenclature est en anglais, les équivalents en japonais. Là aussi, c'est la métalangue qui indique si le SR est un dictionnaire de version anglaise pour les Japonais ou de thème japonais pour les anglophones, ce qui semble être le cas, l'essentiel du métalangage étant en anglais.

Mais on peut penser que, dans la mise en relation de deux langues inégalement connues (le Japonais pratique plus l'anglais que l'Anglais ne pratique le japonais), le lexicographe réserve le plus gros effort au lecteur qui parle la langue la moins connue. La nature L_{d1} ou L_{d2} du métalangage constitue une présomption sur la langue du lecteur; mais le lecteur n'ignorant pas tout de la langue L_2 sur laquelle il s'informe, on peut penser que le métalangage L_{d2} admet aussi le lecteur parlant L_1.

5. Les informations de microstructure

5.1. Les informations sur le signe

Ce sont à peu près les mêmes que dans un dictionnaire monolingue, et elles sont données pour les deux langues: notation de la prononciation (seulement pour le mot-entrée dans les dictionnaires L_1/L_2–L_2/L_1, ce qui oblige, pour le thème, à consulter l'équivalent en situation de mot-entrée), catégorie grammaticale et morphologie, niveau de langue pour L_1 et L_2.

Le découpage d'un article polysémique a_1 en L_1 est spécifique du dictionnaire bilingue. En effet, les structures lexicales de L_1 et L_2 ne sont jamais isomorphes (l'isomorphisme n'existe que pour les langages subrogés et/ou artificiels). Les cas où un mot polysémique en L_1 aurait un équivalent en L_2 présentant la même polysémie ne sont pas très fréquents, et il suffirait alors de mettre les deux mots en équivalence sans évoquer du tout leur polysémie (une des deux langues étant connue du lecteur). La polysémie est une articulation faible, plus ou moins arbitraire (elle varie selon les dictionnaires); or cette articulation peut être mise en équivalence avec une polylexie (b_2, c_2, x_2 de L_2). Plusieurs mots correspondent alors à plusieurs sens d'un seul mot; par exemple, le français *mouton* → *sheep* et *mutton* (entre autres) et l'anglais *scientist* → *scientifique* et *savant*. Cette position forte de la langue cible, qui oppose des unités formelles (signes) à des unités non formelles (sens), est de nature à imposer l'organisation polysémique de la langue source. Les exemples-contextes écrits dans la langue source n'ont d'autre but que d'amener les mots différents de la langue cible, comme les exemples des monolingues destinés à amener des synonymes. C'est donc la polylexie dans la langue cible qui articule la polysémie de la langue source, et, ce faisant, qui articule le discours métalinguistique.

Aussi bien, seule la mise en relation de deux langues est-elle possible, et le «dictionnaire général plurilingue» n'est qu'un dictionnaire monolingue ou bilingue indiquant des équivalents en L_3, L_4, etc. parmi d'autres informations (cf. 1.2.). Le plurilinguisme n'est possible que dans les dictionnaires spéciaux des terminologies (un signe, un sens, une notion, donc une relation biunivoque entre les langues).

5.2. La poussée du métalangage de contenu

La description des équivalences qui permettent de passer de L_1 à L_2 et vice versa s'est récemment améliorée au profit de la fonction thème. L'encodage d'une phrase contenant le mot-entrée ne peut se faire acceptablement que grâce à des informations métalinguistiques concernant le contenu (pratiquement, des indications exprimées par des mots non métalinguistiques). Ces informations sont de quatre sortes; elles ont une fonction de désambiguïsation qui permet parfois de faire l'économie de certaines d'entre elles. Ce sont *a*) le domaine sémantique (en anglais *field*) dans lequel le mot-entrée se manifeste *b*) les contraintes de contenu exercées par les co-occurrents du mot-entrée dans la phrase (sujet, complément, etc.), leur contenu étant résumé par un hyperonyme *c*) le classificateur *d*) la définition synonymique ou analytique.

En fait, le simple programme d'«équivalences de signes» est mis en défaut pour toutes les indications non définitionnelles qui permettent effectivement l'emploi des mots. On observe un contournement de l'analyse sémantique des monolingues qui parfois la rejoint, ou parfois laisse simplement dans l'ombre «la différence spécifique». Ces quatre sortes d'information de contenu, qui figurent dans les dictionnaires les plus complets, ont parfois des présentations typographiques permettant de les distinguer. Par exemple, dans le RC le contexte notionnel (*a*) est entre parenthèses, et le contexte phrastique (*b*) est entre crochets, afin que le lecteur ne confonde pas ces deux indications de contenu. Récemment le Dictionnaire italien/français-français/italien de Robert & Signorelli (= RS) a introduit des définitions analytiques dans la langue de l'entrée. Cette intéressante tentative de réunir l'acquisition d'une compétence pour deux langues à la fois (Werner 1982, 6.4.) entraîne une certaine dés-

organisation du modèle bilingue, la polysémie de la langue source se trouvant imposée à la langue cible sans raison valable (sans polylexie correspondante).

Parti d'un modèle très simple de juxtaposition d'autonymes (de L_1 et de L_2), le dictionnaire bilingue enrichit constamment la description et pose des problèmes de compréhension du métalangage en relation avec la langue du lecteur. Un soin particulier doit être apporté à l'explicitation du statut du dictionnaire (à qui il est destiné et pour quelles opérations) et à la traduction en clair de tous les signes et abréviations métalinguistiques.

6. Bibliographie choisie

6.1. Dictionnaires

CSD = Collins Spanish Dictionary. Spanish-English/English-Spanish. Glasgow 1971.

HSB = Harrap's Shorter Bordas. Dictionnaire Français-Anglais (vol. 1), Dictionnaire Anglais-Français (vol. 2). Paris 1967.

RC = Robert/Collins. Dictionnaire français-anglais/English-French Dictionary. Paris 1978.

RS = Robert/Signorelli. Dictionnaire français-italien/italien-français. Paris 1981.

SR = Shogakukan Random House English-Japanese Dictionary for personal use. New York 1980.

6.2. Travaux

Atkins 1985 = Beryl T. Atkins: Monolingual and bilingual learners' dictionaries: comparison. In: Dictionaries, lexicography and language learning. Ed. R. Ilson. Oxford 1985, 15—24.

Carpenter/Latiri 1986 = Edwin Carpenter/Dora Latiri: Mystères et démystification du dictionnaire bilingue. In: Euralex Bulletin 3, 1. June 1986.

Duval 1986 = Alain Duval: La métalangue dans les dictionnaires bilingues. In: Lexicographica 2. 1986, 93—100.

Rettig 1982 = Wolfgang Rettig: Les dictionnaires bilingues des langues française et allemande au 18e siècle: Questions de méthode. In: La Lexicographie française du XVIe au XVIIIe siècle. Ed. M. Höfler (Wolfenbütteler Forschungen 18). Wolfenbüttel 1982, 103—114.

Rey-Debove 1978 = Josette Rey-Debove: Le métalangage. Paris 1978.

Rey-Debove 1983 = Josette Rey-Debove: La lexicographie terminologique bilingue. In: Actes du colloque GISTERM-UQAM. Montréal 1983.

Werner 1982 = Reinhold Werner: La definición lexicográfica. In: La Lexicografía. De la lingüística teórica a la lexicografía práctica. Madrid 1982, 259—328.

Wooldridge 1982 = Terence R. Wooldridge: Projet de traitement informatique des dictionnaires de Robert Estienne et Jean Nicot. In: La lexicographie française du XVIᵉ au XVIIIᵉ siècle. Ed. M. Höfler. Wolfenbüttel 1982 (Wolfenbütteler Forschungen 18), 21—32.

Zgusta 1986 = Ladislav Zgusta: Introduction. In: Lexicographica 2. 1986, 1—7.

Josette Rey-Debove, Paris (France)

301. Divergences culturelles et dictionnaire bilingue

1. L'explicitation des contenus culturels dans le dictionnaire bilingue
2. Nature et contrastes des contenus culturels
3. Ecart chronologique et écart culturel : les dictionnaires bilingues langue morte — langue vivante
4. Du dictionnaire plurilingue de la Renaissance au monolingue et au bilingue moderne
5. Divergences culturelles et normes : nature des écarts
6. Le traitement des divergences culturelles
7. Ecarts et linguistique contrastive
8. Bibliographie choisie

1. L'explicitation des contenus culturels dans le dictionnaire bilingue

Dans les dictionnaires bilingues modernes, l'explicitation des contenus culturels est fonction des écarts, soit internes à une langue, soit, plus visiblement, liés à la dualité des langues mises en rapport (Rey 1986). La nomenclature, avec ses «entrées» et ses exclusions, la microstructure, avec ses contenus lexicaux (sous-entrées), idiomatiques et discursifs, ces derniers souvent choisis pour des raisons pédagogiques concernant le fonctionnement de la langue, peuvent être culturellement pertinents : mais cette pertinence est en général sous-entendue, et elle est subordonnée à un objectif didactique : faire accéder à un code B, assimilé à une langue, les usagers maîtrisant un code A, et vice versa. Cet objectif entraîne un point de vue différentiel qui élimine de nombreuses informations pertinentes dans l'analyse interne d'une langue et a fortiori dans ses implications culturelles.

2. Nature et contrastes des contenus culturels

Cependant, cette notion du dictionnaire bilingue ne s'applique correctement qu'à ceux qui mettent en relation des langues *vivantes de statut culturel comparable :* allemand, anglais, espagnol, français, italien, russe, ou chinois, vietnamien, japonais, etc. Déjà, les mises en rapport entre de telles langues correspondant à des traditions de description lexicale éloignées (anglais-arabe, français-chinois, allemand-japonais) peuvent revêtir d'autres caractères.

L'importance des écarts culturels nécessite alors, sans même prendre en considération les aspects théoriques du problème, une explicitation des différences, chaque fois qu'une simple équivalence lexicale ou idiomatique ne suffit pas. Parfois apparaissent alors des éléments définitionnels, ou au moins des gloses descriptives. Enfin, l'inclusion de noms propres dans la macrostructure, avec un contenu «encyclopédique», c'est-à-dire extralinguistique, peut d'ailleurs perturber le modèle linguistique pur.

Il en va de même pour les contenus terminologiques, appliqués majoritairement à des syntagmes, et donc intégrés à la microstructure. Ces contenus correspondent à la totalité du système désignatif de la langue, envisagée dans une perspective originale («terminologique»), à la fois onomasiologique et systématique. Ils peuvent fort bien s'appliquer à des systèmes de dénomination propres à une seule culture — mais pas à une seule langue, car il s'agit d'onomasiologie. Ils ne s'appliquent pas seulement, comme on le pense trop souvent, aux sciences et aux techniques modernes, lesquelles tendent à l'universalité transculturelle. Les contenus terminologiques des dictionnaires bilingues généraux sont plus ou moins importants ; leurs éléments non scientifiques et non «techniques» au sens moderne, et par exemple les «taxinomies populaires» *(folk taxonomies)* dénommant les animaux, les plantes, les réalités quotidiennes, — comme les mots de la nourriture ou de la vie rurale, comme la description des croyances et des rites, etc. —, relèvent tous de l'anthropologie culturelle, et sont fréquemment très différentiels, non seulement d'une culture à l'autre, mais éventuellement aussi à l'intérieur d'une même langue. Il n'en va pas autrement pour les terminologies institutionnelles — terminologie administrative, juridique, politique, etc. — et pour les techniques traditionnelles, qui sont loin d'être universelles.

Ces remarques, qui concernent aussi les dictionnaires unilingues extensifs, s'appliquent surtout aux dictionnaires bilingues, lorsque ces derniers ne sont pas élémentaires. D'ailleurs, la perspective terminologique, onomasiologique, s'accommode particulièrement bien d'une présentation bilingue ou multilingue, qui garantit son caractère translinguistique.

3. Ecart chronologique et écart culturel: les dictionnaires bilingues langue morte — langue vivante

L'écart chronologique peut jouer, dans l'économie des ouvrages, un rôle analogue à celui de l'écart culturel. La combinaison des deux écarts est représentée dans les dictionnaires bilingues langue morte — langue vivante, dont la nature sémiotique, en termes de communication, est profondément différente de celle des autres descriptions bilingues. En effet, un dictionnaire latin-anglais et anglais-latin, ou grec-allemand et allemand-grec, contient apparemment la même information qu'un dictionnaire allemand-anglais et anglais-allemand. Mais, alors que ce dernier modèle inclut quatre contenus fonctionnels, les premiers, n'étant pas destinés, et pour cause, à des locuteurs spontanés du latin et du grec antiques, ne renferment que deux contenus fonctionnels (la version et le thème latins pour un locuteur anglophone, grecs pour un locuteur germanophone, dans les exemples proposés) et ne contiennent aucun élément culturel, sinon induit par effet différentiel de traduction, quant aux civilisations correspondant à la langue vivante (anglais ou allemand, dans nos exemples). Tout au contraire, l'absence d'utilisateurs pour qui le latin ou le grec ancien correspondent à une langue maternelle ou maîtrisée activement, l'écart à la fois chronologique et social entre les civilisations exprimées par les deux langues mises en rapport, enfin la nature philologique de ces dictionnaires, tous ces facteurs ont pour effet que l'information culturelle sur les civilisations ayant parlé et écrit la langue morte y est assez abondante, au moins en ce qui concerne les unités pour lesquelles une équivalence lexicale ne suffit pas — ce qui est très fréquent — et dès que les exemples mentionnés, qui sont souvent signés d'auteurs-témoins et extraits du corpus clos que constitue, par exemple, «le latin classique», manifestent un contenu culturel transmissible, et non seulement une illustration fonctionnelle pour l'unité lexicale concernée.

4. Du dictionnaire plurilingue de la Renaissance au monolingue et au bilingue moderne

L'histoire de la lexicographie occidentale, on le sait, témoigne d'une évolution qui va du dictionnaire bilingue ou plurilingue impliquant presque toujours le latin, cette langue possédant un statut très particulier, vers: (a) le dictionnaire quasi unilingue, conservant un repérage latin (exemple français: le Trésor de Nicot, 1606, cf. art. 185), puis le dictionnaire absolument unilingue; et (b) le dictionnaire bilingue moderne, mettant en rapport, pour deux types linguistiques d'utilisateurs, deux langues simultanément en usage. Ce dernier type est largement antérieur au premier (ex.: Vocabulary of French and English, imprimé par William Caxton vers 1480).

Bien que cette évolution ne semble pas universelle, puisque les traditions arabe et chinoise manifestent très antérieurement l'élaboration de recueils unilingues, elle représente assez clairement le rapport entre informations fonctionnelles sur la langue — prépondérant dans le modèle bilingue et dans le dictionnaire pour apprenants *(learner's dictionary)* qui apparaît plus tard — et informations non fonctionnelles, de nature philologique et culturelle, avec une insistance obligatoire pour les divergences.

Les bilingues originels, qu'ils confrontent une langue morte et une langue moderne ou deux langues mortes (hébreu-latin, etc.), ainsi que les plurilingues articulés sur le latin, nombreux du XVIe au XVIIIe siècle, développent forcément des contenus culturels. Ces contenus sont liés à la langue ancienne, décrite plus ou moins philologiquement et, dans les dictionnaires polyglottes, aux langues modernes par la description différentielle des langues.

Moins faible que dans les dictionnaires bilingues confrontant deux langues vivantes, l'information culturelle contrastive de ces dictionnaires est néanmoins souvent implicite. Dans les descriptions d'une langue jamais encore décrite lexicographiquement, au moyen d'une métalangue différente, on a affaire à un «faux bilingue». En effet, les dictionnaires d'ethnologues, s'ils décrivent préférentiellement, à l'intérieur de la culture visée, les éléments divergents par rapport à une notion, d'ailleurs implicite et vague, de la culture du descripteur, n'opèrent pas la mise en rapport explicite des contenus sémantiques (représentés par exemple par les définitions avec leurs stéréotypes) ni la comparaison des produits discursifs (représentée par des traductions). La langue de description (anglais, français, allemand, espagnol, italien, russe, japonais, etc.) reçoit par définition un statut métalinguistique qui la «décroche» de la langue décrite et de ses contenus, et qui interdit de parler, sur le plan de la sémiotique de la langue, de «divergences» comme de «convergences» ou de «similitudes».

5. Divergences culturelles et normes: nature des écarts

L'objet principal d'une étude des divergences culturelles concernera donc le dictionnaire bilingue courant, mettant en relation deux langues vivantes A et B et comportant en principe deux parties, A vers B et B vers A, chacune ayant deux utilisations, commodément désignées par les termes «thème» (locuteurs de A pour la partie A → B; de B pour la partie B → A) et de «version» (les autres). Ce dictionnaire est donc quadruple: La formule n.2 (n-1) donne 12 parties pour trois langues, 24 pour trois langues, etc., ce qui explique l'impossibilité pratique de maîtriser de tels programmes. Il existe cependant des exceptions: dictionnaires doubles conçus pour un seul type d'utilisateurs; dictionnaires simples A → B.

Il existe, il est vrai, d'assez nombreux dictionnaires trilingues, notamment dans les pays multilingues (U.R.S.S., Inde) ou bien lorsqu'une langue peu décrite est mise en rapport avec deux langues de description elles-mêmes associées. Dans de tels cas, le statut de diglossie établi entre la langue-objet et les deux langues servant à la décrire correspond à un affaiblissement du modèle général; il en allait de même pour les plurilingues de la Renaissance. Un dictionnaire comme le *Hindi-Aptani-English* de Braj Bihari Kumar (1974) traite l'anglais un peu comme certains dictionnaires du XVIe ou du XVIIe siècle européens traitaient le latin, c'est-à-dire comme un repère commun. Il s'agit plutôt d'un bilingue enrichi que d'un trilingue. L'importance de l'expérience indienne du trilingue et le caractère particulier de ce genre lexicographique a été relevé avec pertinence, à propos d'un article de Sumitra M. Katre (1980), auquel j'emprunte la référence ci-dessus, par L. Zgusta (1980).

Dans ces descriptions bilingues usuelles, les divergences culturelles jouent entre deux normes, unifiant chacune des deux langues. On y néglige le plus souvent les divergences internes à une langue, très importante dans les cas où celle-ci est employée simultanément dans plusieurs contextes culturels.

Les unités concernées, mots ou syntagmes, correspondent fréquemment à des domaines proprement culturels (coutumes, croyances, activités artisanales ou agricoles, nourriture, habillement, logement...) ou à l'appréhension culturelle spécifique de réalités naturelles elles-mêmes variables (faunes, flores, milieux géographiques). Parmi les premières, les désignations de réalités institutionnelles (droit, politique) forment une classe à part, où le critère n'est plus une civilisation mais une entité politique, et souvent un État. Cette dernière catégorie manifeste de nombreuses divergences internes à une langue (institutions d'Espagne et des différents États d'Amérique latine pour l'espagnol, de l'Allemagne, de l'Autriche et d'une partie de la Suisse pour l'allemand) et peut concerner des usages seconds, officiels et non pas spontanés ou maternels, de la langue (institutions de l'Inde et d'Afrique en anglais, du Maghreb et d'Afrique noire en français).

Aux écarts linguistiques proprement dits, qui font l'objet du dictionnaire bilingue dans son ensemble et concernent (a) le plan formel, graphique et phonique; (b) le plan sémantique-dénotatif, se superposent donc des écarts culturels plus ou moins importants, qui concernent parfois le plan sémantique dénotatif, mais surtout le plan connotatif. Dans le premier cas, il s'agit de la désignation, lorsque le désigné est spécifique d'une culture. La nature «translinguistique» — plutôt qu'extralinguistique — des terminologies, notamment lorsqu'il s'agit de la désignation de concepts «universels» (ceux de la science et de la technique modernes, pourtant liées à un groupe de cultures-sources spécifiques) correspond à une neutralisation importante, sinon totale, de ces écarts. Ainsi, les termes qui correspondent à *atom — atome...* ou à *computer — ordinateur...* donnent lieu à des équivalences lexicales qui suffisent pour l'effet requis du dictionnaire. Il est vrai que les emprunts culturels, pourtant liés à une source spécifique et variables dans leurs connotations, sont traités (à tort et insuffisamment) comme les termes scientifiques interlinguistiques: on trouvera *hamburger* = *hamburger, sheriff* = *shérif,* comme *spin* = *spin,* dans un dictionnaire anglais-français, alors que les trois cas sont différents, le troisième seul ne nécessitant aucune glose.

6. Le traitement des divergences culturelles

Plusieurs facteurs commandent l'existence de ces divergences culturelles. On l'a vu, certaines langues manifestent une variation importante selon les lieux et éventuellement les cultures différentes où elles fonctionnent. Ainsi, le français correspond non seulement au monde urbanisé d'Europe occidentale — avec ses spécificités par rapport à l'allemand, à l'anglais de Grande-Bretagne, etc. — mais aussi, par exemple, au monde rural méditerranéen de la vigne et de l'élevage extensif, comme l'italien ou le grec, et encore au monde urbain nord-américain — celui de Montréal, proche de celui de Toronto, anglophone, ou même de celui de New York. On ne mentionnera pas ici les divergences culturelles manifestées dans les grands dictionnaires unilingues plurinormes et dans les dictionnaires consacrés à une sous-norme culturelle d'une langue, dont l'étude serait fort nécessaire.

Ainsi, un dictionnaire anglais-espagnol ou français-arabe, décrivant très imparfaitement les véhicules de plusieurs univers culturels, manifestera encore plus imparfaitement leurs divergences multipliées: anglais des États-Unis-espagnol d'Espagne; anglais de Grande-Bretagne-espagnol du Mexique, etc. La neutralisation de ces divergences est encore plus forte que la neutralisation des divergences internes à une langue dans un dictionnaire unilingue.

Plusieurs taux d'écart culturel, d'ailleurs difficiles à établir sociologiquement et anthropologiquement, caractériseront donc un même dictionnaire bilingue. Faible entre le français et l'allemand en Suisse, le taux est plus fort entre le français du Québec et ce même allemand. On imagine la variété des taux d'écart culturel impliqués par un seul dictionnaire espagnol-anglais ou arabe-russe, par exemple; alors, de nombreuses combinatoires de mises en rapport sont impliquées (par ex. Argentine-Australie ou Espagne-Singapour, dans le premier cas.)

Enfin, certaines langues étant majoritairement employées dans des types de culture fortement divergents, le dictionnaire bilingue manifestera alors un important taux moyen d'écart, et ceci quelles que soient les neutralisations pratiquées (ex.: anglais-chinois; espagnol-japonais).

La définition des entrées manifestant plus ou moins un tel écart, leur typologie par domaines culturels et enfin les implications lexicographiques de ces écarts nécessiteraient une description détaillée. On en trouvera une esquisse, à propos du *Dictionnaire indonésien-français* de Pierre Labrousse (1984), dans Rey 1986. Dans ce dictionnaire, cas exceptionnel et exemplaire, les «écarts culturels» sont marqués, «traduits» par un emprunt à la langue source ou définis par une glose en français typographiquement distincte des équivalences habituelles, et souvent explicités par une illustration. Ce sous-ensemble, qui correspond à 6,5 % de la nomenclature, concerne ce qu'on pourrait appeler l'«inexprimable lexical dénotatif» d'une langue par rapport à une autre; il concerne essentiellement des noms et quelques verbes, mais on pourrait l'enrichir quant aux entrées non substantives. Ce traitement constitue un excellent point de départ pour une prise en charge plus sérieuse du problème en lexicographie bilingue, et un préalable avant d'aborder la sémantique connotative et, sur le plan syntagmatique, la phraséologie, lesquelles distinguent, à la fois linguistiquement et culturellement, la quasi-totalité d'un usage lexical de tout autre.

7. Ecarts et linguistique contrastive

La mise en perspective des écarts culturels dans les dictionnaires bilingues dépend essentiellement des données fournies par la linguistique comparée, lorsque ces données concernent, non pas et trop vaguement une langue, mais un usage chronologiquement, géographiquement et socialement bien défini. Elle est voisine des considérations développées par certains spécialistes de la traduction — tels Nida ou Yuen-Ren Chao — et reçoit ses bases théoriques de l'anthropologie linguistique dont les hypothèses balayent le continuum qui va de l'homogénéité universaliste — et de la traduisibilité quasi parfaite — à la différenciation des visions du monde et des modes de raisonnements, considérée comme plus ou moins inscrite dans les langues, de par leurs différences à différents niveaux, syntactiques aussi bien que sémantique, — on parle moins des pragmatiques —, grammaticaux aussi bien que lexicaux. Malgré ses excès, l'hypothèse de Sapir et Whorf sous-tend de manière indispensable un examen des écarts sémioculturels inscrits dans les lexiques, et donc celui de leur traitement, très imparfait, dans les dictionnaires.

Ainsi, la mise en rapport de champs lexicaux, de champs désignatifs ou sémantiques — selon des perspectives différentes — entre deux usages correspondant à des univers culturels éloignés, ou même entre deux langues dont la majorité des usages se trouvent dans cette situation d'éloignement, révèle les difficultés du traitement lexicographique. Des champs désignatifs (après les exemples classiques de celui du «chameau» en arabe, de la «neige» dans les langues de la famille inuit, du «cheval» dans l'ancien français, on signalera celui du «riz» en vietnamien [Nguyen 1980b, 60]), posent, entre chacune des langues considérées et un autre usage culturellement éloigné (par exemple, arabe-anglais en ce qui concerne le «chameau»; vietnamien-français pour le «riz»), le problème du découpage référentiel d'univers culturellement différents. Les différences de découpage proviennent (a) de la nature des référents, (b) des constructions conceptuelles effectuées par la culture à leur égard, (c) de la prise en charge de ces conceptualisations par un usage d'une langue, lui-même conditionné par les moyens — morphologiques, syntagmatiques, sémantiques... — qu'une langue met à la disposition d'une culture. Les domaines représentés par la langue le sont de manière différente selon l'action de ces trois types de facteurs. Cette question a été bien étudiée par les spécialistes de la traduction, par exemple lorsque l'univers référentiel de la Bible (celui de la Méditerranée orientale antique) doit «passer» en anglais, en quechua ou en inuktituk.

Très provisoirement, on peut distinguer trois types de difficultés à gérer lexicographiquement: (a) différences structurales, dans des systèmes où des traits pertinents sont réalisés dans une langue (un usage) et non dans une autre: le lexique des relations de parenté en fournit un excellent exemple; (b) différences structurales et quantitatives, dans les deux sens: (b1) richesse lexicale et phraséologique correspondant à une pauvreté relative dans l'autre langue; (b2) pauvreté relative par rapport aux ressources lexico-phraséologiques de l'autre langue. Un cas important en (a) est l'existence dans un seul des systèmes d'une unité lexicale générique (hyperonyme), qui a souvent fait conclure hâtivement à une incapacité abstractive dans la culture où la langue présente une lacune lexicale de ce type. On a trop parlé de vocabulaires «concrets», sans lexicalisation des «abstractions», en particulier par négligence des moyens phraséologiques, métaphoriques, pragmatiques, des langues jugées plus «concrètes».

Ira-t-on dire que le français est incapable d'abstraction puisqu'il ne fournit pas à une série comme *chien, chat, hamster, souris blanche, poisson rouge...* l'hyperonyme très usuel que l'anglais suscite à ses équivalents: *pet?* Cependant, une difficulté lexicographique évidente en résulte: l'équivalence classique des dictionnaires: *pet = animal familier,* ne convient pas en discours; celle qui se contente de *animal (no pets allowed = les animaux sont interdits)* n'est qu'une équivalence pragmatique, non pertinente sémantiquement. Dans un tel cas — extrêmement fréquent entre langues culturellement distantes et, on vient de le voir, facile à évoquer entre langues proches — le dictionnaire se devrait, au moins, de signaler la difficulté par un symbole signifiant «pas d'équivalence sémantique acceptable dans l'usage-cible» et de la résoudre (a) en donnant, comme on l'a vu plus haut, le statut de «glose», et non d'équivalence lexicale, à la représentation suggérée du sens visé; (b) en fournissant des équivalences en discours (exemples traduits) assortis d'un signe de non-équivalence analytique. Un tel procédé serait en fait indispensable pour la plupart des équivalences phraséologiques contenues dans les dictionnaires bilingues. Or, dans tous les cas, le dictionnaire bilingue est soumis à une règle constante: cette équivalence doit s'intégrer au système de l'utilisateur pour lequel la langue décrite est la cible (Zgusta 1984, qui cite cet aphorisme essentiel: «[Dictionary] Translations must be in the idiom of the reader» (Lissance 1949). Cette homogénéité pragmatique requise s'oppose aux éventuelles hétérogénéités interculturelles et pose au lexicographe comparatiste un redoutable problème. Par ailleurs, certaines langues (par ex. le japonais, le vietnamien) peuvent recourir dans leur fonctionnement discursif et pragmatique à des procédés morpho-lexicaux inconnus d'autres langues. Il en est ainsi des termes d'adresse et même de la morphologie exprimant des différences de statut entre interlocuteurs, comparativement lacunaires dans d'autres langues (par ex. indo-européennes) où pourtant distinctions hiérarchiques et politesse ne sont pas absentes. Les difficultés lexicographiques suscitées par de telles situations sont vastes, comme celles qui surgissent lorsque le dictionnaire — et c'est heureux — prétend noter les «niveaux d'usage» des unités traitées (voir par exemple Nguyen 1980).

Qu'il s'agisse des différences structurelles lexicales (ex.: termes de parenté) ou des différences pragmatiques, il semble que les taux d'écart soient de plus en plus importants. Pour le dernier point, tous les usages correspondant à des situations culturelles tant soit peu différentes, que ce soit entre deux langues ou entre deux usages d'une même langue, sont concernés. Donc, tous les dictionnaires le sont aussi.

La métalexicographie a consacré peu d'études à cette question; mais les sociolinguistes, les spécialistes de linguistique comparée et les théoriciens de la traduction montrent la voie pour l'étude de ce problème, essentiel dans l'économie de tout dictionnaire bilingue de qualité.

8. Bibliographie choisie

8.1. Dictionnaires

Kumar 1974 = Brai Bihari Kumar: Hindi-Aptani-English Vocabulary. Kohima 1974.

Labrousse 1984 = Pierre Labrousse et al: Dictionnaire général indonésien-français. Paris 1984 [XXI, 934 p.].

8.2. Travaux

Chao 1976 = Yuen-Ren Chao: Problems in Chinese-English Lexicography. In: Aspects of Chinese Sociolinguistics. Ed. Anwar S. Dil. Standford 1976, 170—179.

Echols 1978 = John M. Echols: Dictionaries and dictionary making: Malay and Indonesian. In: Journal of Asian Studies 38. 1978, 11—24.

Hohulin 1986 = Lou Hohulin: The Absence of Lexical Equivalences and Cases of Asymmetry. In: Lexicographica 2. 1986, 43—52.

Katre 1980 = Sumitra M. Katre: Current Trends in Indian Lexicography. In: Theory and Method in Lexicography. Ed. L. Zgusta. Columbia, South Carolina 1980, 177—189.

Lissance 1949 = A. Lissance: The Translator's Dictionary. In: The German Quarterly 22. 1949, 134—144.

Nguyen 1980 (a) = Dinh-Hoa Nguyen: Bicultural Information in a Bilingual Dictionary. In: Theory and Method in Lexicography. Ed. L. Zgusta. Columbia, South Carolina 1980, 163—175.

Nguyen 1980 (b) = Dinh-Hoa Nguyen: Teaching culture through bilingual dictionaries: In: Dictionaries 2—3. 1980—81, 57—68.

Rey 1986 = Alain Rey: Les écarts culturels dans les dictionnaires bilingues. In: Lexicographica 2. 1986, 33—42.

Schnorr 1986 = Veronika Schnorr: Translational equivalence and/or explanation? The perennial problem of equivalence. In: Lexicographica 2. 1986, 53—60.

Tomaszczyk 1984 = Jerzy Tomaszczyk: The culture-bound element in bilingual dictionaries. In: LEXeter' 83 Proceedings. Ed. R. Hartmann. Tübingen 1984, 289—297.

Zgusta 1971 = Ladislav Zgusta: Manual of Lexicography. Paris. La Haye 1971.

Zgusta 1980 = L. Zgusta: Introduction. In: Theory and Method in Lexicography. Columbia, South Carolina 1980, 3—29.

Zgusta 1984 = L. Zgusta: Translation Equivalence in the Bilingual Dictionary. In: LEXeter '83 Proceedings. Ed. R. Hartmann. Tübingen 1984, 147—154.

Zorc 1986 = David R. Zorc: Linguistic 'Purism' and Subcategorizational Labels in Yongu-Matha. In: Lexicographica 2. 1986, 78—84.

Alain Rey, Paris (France)

302. Problèmes de description lexicographique des langues pidgins et créoles

1. Pidgins et créoles
2. Historique
3. La nomenclature
4. L'orthographe
5. La microstructure
6. Travaux en cours
7. Bibliographie choisie

1. Pidgins et créoles

Les pidgins et les créoles sont des langues nées des contacts entre plusieurs groupes linguistiques qui se trouvent devant la nécessité de créer un moyen d'intercompréhension. Si les contacts sociaux entre les locuteurs hétéroglosses restent limités à des situations de commerce ou de travail, une langue de relation à grammaire et vocabulaire réduits peut suffire. Tant que cette langue de relation ne devient pas la première langue d'une nouvelle génération, elle est appelée *pidgin*, ou aussi *sabir* dans le monde francophone — terme qui, au XIXᵉ siècle, ne désignait que la langue franque de la Méditerranée (Pérégo 1968). Du moment qu'un pidgin devient la langue maternelle d'un groupe de locuteurs, on l'appelle *créole:* «A creole language arises when a pidgin becomes the native language of a speech-community» (Hall 1966, xii). Le présent article ne prend en considération que les créoles issus de langues européennes (français, espagnol, portugais, néerlandais) à l'époque coloniale, c'est-à-dire aux XVIIᵉ et XVIIIᵉ siècles, à l'exception des pidgins et créoles à base lexicale anglaise, traités dans l'article 158. En ce qui concerne les pidgins non anglais, ils ne sont pas nombreux et beaucoup d'entre eux ont disparu après l'époque de l'expansion européenne; le seul ouvrage lexicographique qu'on pourrait nommer ici est le vocabulaire du «petit-nègre» compilé par Delafosse 1904. Cependant, les problèmes de la description lexicographique seraient fondamentalement les mêmes pour les pidgins comme pour les créoles.

2. Historique

Les premiers auteurs de glossaires et lexiques créoles avaient pour objectif d'élaborer des outils pratiques: c'étaient soit des missionnaires soit des amateurs qui voulaient donner une orientation linguistique aux nouveaux venus dans les colonies. Les «premiers créolistes» furent les Frères Moraves, qui, en 1736, commencèrent à propager l'Evangile à St. Thomas (la plus importante des Îles Vierges). Pour ce faire, ils se servirent de la langue des esclaves, un créole néerlandais appelé *negerhollands* (aujourd'hui disparu), dont Oldendorp donna plus tard une description détaillée. Celui-ci a également composé un dictionnaire allemand-créole (probablement en 1767/68), un manuscrit de presque 200 pages avec environ 3.500 entrées. P. Stein prépare actuellement une édition de ce premier dictionnaire d'une langue créole (Stein 1986). Dix ans plus tard, en 1778, Ch. L. Schumann, un autre missionnaire morave, rédigea un petit lexique bilingue du saramaccan, créole portugais de Suriname (manuscrit inédit de 80 pages, v. Perl 1986). Le premier glossaire d'un créole français, du créole haïtien en l'oc-

currence, se trouve dans le *Manuel des habitans de Saint-Domingue* de Ducœurjoly 1802, «premier vocabulaire français-créole, et [...] conversations françaises-créoles, pour donner une idée de ce langage, et se faire entendre des nègres [...]». La quatrième tentative lexicographique dans le domaine créole a comme objet le papiamentu, un créole à base espagnole et portugaise: le *Nederlandsch-Papiamentsch-Spaansch woordenboekje* de Van Ewijk 1875, cité dans Reinecke 1975, mais introuvable dans les bibliothèques européennes.

Les dictionnaires du papiamentu compilés au XXᵉ siècle (Hoyer 1918; Jansen 1945, 1947; Hassell 1953; Dijkhoff 1985) ont également été publiés dans une optique pratique — le statut sociolinguistique de cette langue, qui joue le rôle de langue nationale acceptée par toutes les couches de la population des îles ABC (Curaçao, Aruba, Bonaire) et employée par les médias, les écrivains, les églises, ainsi que dans le système éducatif (à côté du néerlandais, langue officielle), rend un dictionnaire d'usage indispensable.

Les créoles français (et portugais dans une moindre mesure), en revanche, ont bénéficié d'un intérêt scientifique croissant depuis les années trente, début de la deuxième période importante de la créolistique (la première, marquée surtout par les travaux de Schuchardt entre 1881 et 1909, n'ayant pas engendré d'ouvrages lexicographiques). L'étude linguistique des créoles a toujours débuté par des grammaires, mais celles-ci étaient souvent accompagnées, ou suivies, de glossaires ou descriptions lexicologiques importantes (Faine 1936, Jourdain 1946/56, Funk 1953, Hall 1953, Lopes da Silva 1957, Morgan 1960, Günther 1973, Bollée 1977, Neumann 1985). Le «glossaire étymologique» du linguiste amateur Faine (133 pages, 1.566 entrées) s'insère dans le débat séculaire sur la genèse du créole: Faine s'est proposé de démontrer — par des étymologies parfois aberrantes — que le créole d'Haïti est «une langue néo-romane issue de la langue oïl, en passant par les anciens dialectes normand, picard, angevin, poitevin, et composée en outre de mots empruntés à l'anglais et à l'espagnol et, dans une faible mesure, à l'indien caraïbe et à des idiomes africains» (XI).

Voir extrait textuel 302.1.

Un dictionnaire français-créole, d'environ 17.000 mots, laissé en notes manuscrites, fut publié après sa mort par G. Lefebvre (Faine 1974).

CAMPER v. cr. angev. et pic. Appliquer un coup: «Camper eine baffe».— M'«camper» l'ioun paire soufflett.—À l'acception de: lancer une saillie, un trait mordant etc.: «Li *camper* l' 400 sottises».
CAMOMINE s. cr. et norm. pour: camomille. «Dans les comptes de 1374 de l'Hôtel-Dieu d'Evreux figurent des achats d'huile de *camomine*». (L'Agric. en Norm. au moyen-âge de M. Delisle).
CANARI s cr. Vase de terre, caraïbe.

Extrait textuel 302.1: Articles de dictionnaire (tiré de: Faine 1936, 219)

Jourdain 1956 (rédigé en 1946) partage avec Faine la perspective diachronique, mais vise à un inventaire beaucoup plus complet du vocabulaire créole de la Martinique, présenté sous forme de classement par champs conceptuels.

A partir des années cinquante, les descriptions des langues créoles suivent en partie les orientations méthodologiques du structuralisme nord-américain; les glossaires de Hall 1953, Morgan 1960, Bazerque 1969, Germain 1980, ainsi que les dictionnaires de Bentolila 1976, Valdman 1981 et Poullet/Telchid/Montbrand 1984 donnent des descriptions purement ou essentiellement (Bazerque) synchroniques du vocabulaire créole. Toutefois, les recherches étymologiques reprennent, pour ce qui est des créoles de l'Océan Indien (réunionnais, mauricien, seychellois) avec Chaudenson 1974, D'Offay/Lionnet 1982 et Baker/Hookoomsing (1987).

3. La nomenclature

Les langues créoles, beaucoup plus riches que les pidgins (le dictionnaire du Tok Pisin de Mihalic, p. ex., enregistre environ 1.500 mots [cf. Art. 158], celui du créole haïtien de Valdman environ 10.000), doivent néanmoins être considérées comme langues «en voie de développement». Leur situation actuelle est comparable à celle des langues romanes au moyen âge et à l'époque de la Renaissance: leur vocabulaire scientifique et technique est déficient et doit être enrichi si le créole est destiné à s'émanciper de ses domaines traditionnels afin de servir à tous les besoins d'expression de la vie moderne. Tous les pidgins et créoles existent dans des situations de diglossie (p. ex. dans les D.O.M. français) ou de multilinguisme (p. ex. aux îles ABC et à l'île Maurice). Il est donc tout à fait naturel qu'ils aient recours à la langue officielle ou dominante pour l'enrichissement, voire la modernisation de leur lexique: le papiamentu se tourne vers le néerlandais pour l'extension de son vocabulaire scientifique et administratif (Lenz 1928, 210 a compté 30 % de mots d'origine hollandaise dans Hoyer 1918), le créole mauricien fourmille d'anglicismes, et pour la plupart des créoles français, c'est le français qui comble les lacunes dans le vocabulaire abstrait et technique. Le fait que tout mot français est, virtuellement, un mot créole, pose le problème de la démarcation entre créole et français. Dans son rapport sur la composition du premier dictionnaire bilingue créole réunionnais-français (1987), Baggioni constate que «pour l'élaboration de la nomenclature [...] la question de la frontière avec la langue dominante (envahissante dans le cas du réunionnais) est difficile à résoudre» (1985, 73; une remarque semblable se lit dans Valdman 1981, i). On peut, en effet, mettre en cause le caractère «créole» de mots comme *demisyone, determinasyon, devosyon, entansifye, envestisman,* empruntés *ad hoc* par un journaliste, seychellois en l'occurence, qui rédige un article d'après une source française ou anglaise; D'Offay/Lionnet 1982 ne les ont pas admis dans leur dictionnaire (ils sont également absents dans Valdman 1981). D'autre part, le dictionnaire seychellois a accueilli *adverb, alfabetizasyon, analfabet, apostrof:* le rôle accordé au créole dans l'enseignement aux Seychelles implique la nécessité de «créoliser» la terminologie de toutes les disciplines scolaires. Les tentatives de modernisation du créole, en cours aux Seychelles depuis 1982, et qui ne manqueront pas d'élargir considérablement la nomenclature de futurs dictionnaires, semblent être uniques dans le monde créolophone; pour l'haïtien, dont le statut sociolinguistique s'est beaucoup amélioré récemment, l'enrichissement systématique du vocabulaire reste à faire: «No major program has been launched to codify the grammar and to enunciate principles for lexical expansion» (Valdman 1981, Foreword). La plupart des lexicographes (exceptions notables: Baker/Hookoomsing) se montrent très réservés envers les néologismes et s'efforcent plutôt de mettre en relief la distance entre créole et français. La raison d'être d'un dictionnaire créole est pour Poullet/Telchid/Montbrand de sauvegarder le créole authentique face à l'influence funeste du français:

Peut-être allez-vous vous demander pourquoi nous avons voulu faire un dictionnaire créole? Tout simplement parce que nous constatons tous les jours, dans la rue comme à la radio, que nous parlons peu à peu un créole à tel point mêlé de français qu'en fin de compte la langue que nous employons n'est plus du créole sans être pour autant du français. Dans cette lutte inégale, le créole est perdant [...] (1984, 6).

3.1. La documentation

Le problème de savoir comment délimiter le «lexique créole authentique» (Baggioni 1985, 73) est lié à celui de la documentation dont dispose le lexicographe. Les créoles sont, jusqu'à nos jours, essentiellement des langues parlées, et les sources écrites — abondantes seulement dans le cas du papiamentu — constituent une base trop mince pour l'élaboration d'un dictionnaire de quelque envergure, même si le compilateur a le temps et les moyens de les dépouiller systématiquement. Aucun auteur de dictionnaire créole n'a pu travailler avec un corpus qui réponde aux exigences de la lexicographie moderne. Dijkhoff, qui annonce «un dikshonario mas amplio i revisà» (1985, 5), passe sous silence la question de la documentation. Bentolila et son équipe ont enregistré 60 heures de conversation à partir desquelles ils ont réalisé un *Dictionnaire élémentaire créole haïtien-français* de 3.400 entrées. Valdman, qui a dépouillé tous les glossaires et dictionnaires du créole haïtien, en y ajoutant beaucoup de mots tirés d'autres ouvrages et de ses propres enquêtes sur le terrain, a pu rassembler 10.000 mots, mais il déclare sans fausse modestie: «In a sense, this Dictionary should be viewed as preliminary» (Foreword). La même remarque pourrait être faite pour Baggioni (1987), dont la nomenclature de 13.000 mots dépasse celles de toutes les tentatives lexicographiques entreprises jusqu'à présent: il a utilisé Chaudenson 1974 (environ 5.000 mots), l'*Atlas Linguistique et Ethnographique de la Réunion* (Carayol/Chaudenson/Barat 1985) et «la littérature nouvelle d'expression créole», mais n'a pas pu effectuer des «enquêtes auprès des jeunes générations en milieu urbain» (Marimoutou/Baggioni 1986, 103), qui auraient complété avantageusement sa documentation.

Le seul dictionnaire à perspective historique est Baker/Hookoomsing (1987): Baker et ses collaborateurs ont dépouillé tous les textes imprimés en créole mauricien au XIXe siècle et admis bon nombre de mots tombés en désuétude entretemps.

3.2. La variation et la norme

Les créoles ne sont pas seulement des langues en voie de développement, mais aussi en voie de standardisation. Le problème de la norme est partout posé — sauf dans certaines situations de diglossie. Dijkhoff 1985, encore une fois, ne se prononce pas, mais tient compte des variétés du papiamentu de Curaçao, Aruba et Bonaire en marquant beaucoup de mots et de variantes avec les lettres (C), (A) ou (B). Valdman, face à un créole qui montre une variation géographique considérable, s'est vu obligé, pour des raisons pratiques, de décrire «the basic lexical stock of Haitian Creole as spoken in Port-au-Prince and vicinity» et d'ignorer, à quelques exceptions près, régionalismes et variantes régionales. Son choix serait d'ailleurs, théoriquement, parfaitement justifiable s'il avait eu pour objectif d'établir une norme, du fait qu'il décrit «the standard dialect [...] in which all existing materials have been written» (1981, i). Pour Poullet/Telchid/Montbrand, évidemment, le problème d'un «créole standard» ne se pose pas: la place, pour eux incontestée, du français dans la diglossie aux Antilles françaises, assigne au créole le rôle d'une «langue populaire, parlée, familière», dont ils se proposent d'enregistrer toutes les richesses, y compris les mots grossiers et les expressions très vulgaires. Baggioni, aux prises avec un créole qui existe sous forme d'un continuum, une variation entre deux pôles, l'un acrolectal ou «créole petit blanc», l'autre basilectal ou «créole cafre», se voit forcé, pour éviter «la guerre civile ou la défection *a priori* d'une partie de la population créolophone», d'intégrer dans son dictionnaire les variantes acrolectales, option sans doute discutable aux yeux de lexicographes qui définissent le «vrai créole» par son éloignement par rapport au français (p. ex. Poullet/Telchid/Montbrand ou le GEREC [Groupe d'Etudes et de Recherches en Espace Créolophone] à la Martinique, v. 6).

4. L'orthographe

Le problème de la graphie, «question délicate entre toutes en terre créolophone» (Baggioni 1985, 72), débattu depuis les années trente (p. ex. en Haïti), peut être considéré comme plus ou moins résolu. Tous les dictionnaires présentés dans cet article ont opté pour la solution d'une orthographe de type phonologique. Vu les difficultés pratiques que pose le système graphique de l'A.P.I., surtout pour les machines à écrire traditionnelles, on s'est orienté vers les conventions graphiques de langues en contact avec les créoles (français, espagnol, anglais).

Voici quelques graphies qui ont donné lieu à des discussions (parfois violentes, comme dans le cas du *w* refusé en Haïti comme symbole de l'impérialisme américain):

A.P.I.	Dijkhoff papia- mentu	Vald- man cr. haït.	Poullet cr. ant.	Baggioni cr. réun.	D'Offay/ Lionnet cr. seych.
/ʃ/	sh	ch	ch	(ch)*	--
/ʒ/	sj	j	j	(j)*	--
/ɲ/	ñ	ny	gn	gn	gn/ny
/ŋ/	--	ng	ng	ng	ng
/j/	y	y	y	y	y
/w/	w/u	w	w	w	w
/ɛ̃/	--	en	en	in	en
/ã/	--	an	an	an	an
/õ/	--	on	on	on	on

* existe seulement dans la variante acrolectale

Ill. 302.1: Tableau synoptique de quelques graphies créoles

On peut regretter que les lexicographes, dans le domaine des créoles français, n'aient pas pu se mettre d'accord sur une orthographe «pan-créole», mais on peut constater que, au cours des discussions et modifications, les divers systèmes se sont graduellement rapprochés.

5. La microstructure

Il n'est guère étonnant que la microstructure des dictionnaires discutés ici — tous des dictionnaires bilingues ou trilingues, œuvres de pionniers, élaborées par un ou deux auteurs ou de très petites équipes, et parfois sous la pression d'un public qui attendait la publication avec impatience — ne soit pas très riche et laisse à désirer. Dijkhoff 1985, D'Offay/Lionnet et Baker/Hookoomsing se contentent en général de simples traductions des entrées. Les exemples, très rares dans D'Offay/Lionnet, sont un peu plus nombreux dans Baggioni, tandis que Bentolila, Valdman et Poullet/Telchid/Montbrand donnent un ou deux exemples pour chaque mot, avec traduction dans Poullet/Telchid/Montbrand, sans traduction dans Valdman. Dans tous les cas, il s'agit d'exemples forgés par les lexicographes ou de proverbes.

Voici quelques specimens d'articles:

konbit [kɔ̃bit] *var.* **konbi, koumbit, koumbi**
- coumbite (travail collectif des champs)
Konpè Sovè ap fè on konbit demen, nou tout prale.
L'ami Sauveur fait une coumbite demain, on y va tous.

Extrait textuel 302.2: Article de dictionnaire (tiré de: Bentolila 1976, 254)

kichòy. n. F chose, quelque chose. E thing, something. 1) Ou ta ban m kichòy tou, li mèt yon moso pen. 2) Pòv-yo pa mande ou yon ti kichòy ankò, pase yo pap pran senk kòb nan men-ou. cf: bagay

Extrait textuel 302.3: Article de dictionnaire (tiré de: Valdman 1981)

KENBWA (vwè DAWA) : Quimbois, maléfice, sortilège
• **Yo touvé on kenbwa an katchimen-la** : On a trouvé un quimbois dans le carrefour. (Ensemble d'objets ensorcelés destinés à nuire à quelqu'un : boîte en forme de cercueil, petite poupée, cheveux, cadenas, etc.)
KENBWAZÈ (vwè GADÈZAFÈ) : Sorcier, « quimboiseur », voyant, féticheur

Extrait textuel 302.4: Article de dictionnaire (tiré de: Poullet/Telchid/Montbrand 1984, 145)

> **raska** (verbo, II), krassen, bekrassen
> **raská,** geprikkeld, kribbig; schram (A); kras (A)
> **raskamentu** (A ... o), (het) krassen, (het) bekrassen
> **rasku** (C), kras
> **raso,** woedend, razend
> **rason,** gelijk; *tin -,* gelijk hebben
> **rasonabel,** redelijk
> **raspa** (verbo, II), afkrabben, schrapen, raspen; raspinstrument (A)

Extrait textuel 302.5: Article de dictionnaire (tiré de: Dijkhoff 1985, 119)

6. Travaux en cours

Le Groupe d'Etudes et de Recherches en Espace Créolophone [GEREC] de l'Université Antilles-Guyane a mis en chantier un *Dictionnaire des Créoles caribéens à base lexicale française* (dictionnaire créole-français avec un index français-créole). Le coordonnateur du projet est Jean Bernabé; les territoires concernés sont pour l'essentiel Martinique, Guadeloupe, Guyane, Dominique, Ste Lucie, Haïti. L'objet de la recherche est le créole basilectal, que Bernabé définit par le critère de «déviance maximale» par rapport au français (1983, 16).

A l'Université de Bamberg, un *Dictionnaire étymologique des créoles* (DEC) est préparé sous la direction d'Annegret Bollée (v. Bollée 1984). Sous la vedette de l'étymon français (ou non-français), le DEC enregistre les attestations du mot dans tous les parlers créoles français de l'Amérique et de l'Océan Indien. Les données pour l'Océan Indien ont été mises sur ordinateur et sont disponibles sous formes de listings; pour les créoles de la zone caribéenne, la collecte des données ainsi que la recherche étymologique sont encore en cours.

7. Bibliographie choisie

7.1. Dictionnaires

Armand 1987 = Alain Armand: Dictionnaire Kréol Rénioné Français. Saint-André (Réunion) 1987 [399 p.].

Baggioni 1987 = Daniel Baggioni: Petit Dictionnaire Créole réunionnais/Français. Saint-André (Réunion) 1987 [359 p.].

Baker/Hookoomsing 1987 = Philip Baker/Vinesh Y. Hookoomsing: Morisyen-English-Français. Diksyoner kreol morisyen. Dictionary of Mauritian Creole. Dictionnaire du créole mauricien. Paris 1987 [365 p.].

Bentolila 1976 = Alain Bentolila: Ti diksyonnè kreyol-franse. Dictionnaire élémentaire créole haïtien-français. Paris. Port-au-Prince 1976 [511 p.].

Cifoletti 1980 = Guido Cifoletti: Il Vocabolario della Lingua Franca. Padova 1980 [154 p.].

Delafosse 1904 = Maurice Delafosse: Vocabulaires comparatifs de plus de 60 langues ou dialectes parlés à la Côte d'Ivoire et dans les régions limitrophes [. . .]. Paris 1904 [284 p.].

Dictionnaire 1830 = Dictionnaire de la langue franque ou petit mauresque. Marseille 1830 [107 p.].

Dijkhoff 1985 = Mario Dijkhoff: Dikshonario, Woordenboek. Papiamentu-Ulandes, Ulandes-Papiamentu. Zutphen 1985 [310 p.].

D'Offay/Lionnet 1982 = Danielle D'Offay/Guy Lionnet: Diksyonner kreol-franse. Dictionnaire créole seychellois-français. Hamburg 1982 (Kreolische Bibliothek 2) [422 p.].

Faine 1974 = Jules Faine: Dictionnaire français-créole. Ottawa 1974 [483 p.].

Hassel 1953 = E. A. L. Hassell: Dictionary English Papiamentu — Papiamentu English. Aruba 1953 [144 p.].

Hoyer 1918 = Willem Manuel Hoyer: Woordenlijst en samenspraak: Hollandsch-Papiamentsch-Spaansch. Curaçao 1918 [72 p.] 7ᵉ éd. geheel herzien [. . .] en omgezet in de fonologische spelling door Antoine J. Maduro. Curaçao 1980 [99 p.].

Jansen 1945 = Gerrit P. Jansen: Diccionario Papiamentu-Holandés. Curaçao 1945 [166 p.].

Jansen 1947 = Gerrit P. Jansen: Nederlands-Papiaments handwoordenboek. Curaçao 1947 [229 p.].

Jourdain 1956 = Elodie Jourdain: Le vocabulaire du parler créole de la Martinique. Paris 1956 [303 p.].

Ledikasyon 1985 = Ledikasyon pu travayer: Diksyoner Kreol-Angle. Port Louis (Mauritius) 1985 [250 p.].

Poullet/Telchid/Montbrand 1984 = Hector Poullet/Sylviane Telchid/Danièle Montbrand: Dictionnaire des expressions du créole guadeloupéen. Fort-de-France 1984 [349 p.].

Valdman 1981 = Albert Valdman: Haitian Creole-English-French Dictionary. 3 vol. Bloomington, Indiana 1981 [894 p.].

Van Ewijk 1875 = Petrus A. H. J. van Ewijk: Nederlandsch-Papiamentsch-Spaansch woordenboekje. Arnhem 1875.

7.2. Travaux

Baggioni 1985 = Daniel Baggioni: L'élaboration d'un dictionnaire bilingue créole/français. Réflexions sociolinguistiques, praxématiques et/ou pragmatiques d'un lexicographe désabusé. In: Cahiers de praxématique 5. Montpellier 1985, 67—84.

Bazerque 1969 = Auguste Bazerque: Le langage créole. Artra (Guadeloupe) 1969.

Bernabé 1983 = Jean Bernabé: Fondal-natal. Grammaire basilectale approchée des créoles guadeloupéen et martiniquais. 3 vol. Paris 1983.

Bollée 1977 = Annegret Bollée: Le Créole Français des Seychelles: Esquisse d'une grammaire, textes, vocabulaire. Tübingen 1977 (Beihefte zur Zeitschrift für romanische Philologie 159).

Bollée 1984 = Annegret Bollée: Dictionnaire étymologique des créoles. In: Wörterbücher der deutschen Romanistik. Hrsg. H. Stimm. Weinheim 1984, 49—59.

Carayol/Chaudenson/Barat 1985 = Michel Carayol/Robert Chaudenson/Christian Barat: Atlas linguistique et ethnographique de la Réunion. Paris 1985.

Chaudenson 1974 = Robert Chaudenson: Le lexique du parler créole de la Réunion. 2 vol. Paris 1974.

Ducœurjoly 1802 = S. J. Ducœurjoly: Manuel des habitans de Saint Domingue [. . .]. 2 vol. Paris 1802.

Faine 1936 = Jules Faine: Philologie Créole: Etudes historiques et étymologiques sur la langue créole d'Haïti. 2ᵉ éd. Port-au-Prince 1937.

Funk 1953 = Henry Elwell Funk: The French Creole Dialect of Martinique: Its Historical Background, Vocabulary, Syntax, Proverbs and Literature. With a Glossary. Dissertation. Univ. of Virginia 1953.

Germain 1980 = Robert Germain: Grammaire Créole. Paris 1980.

Günther 1973 = Wilfried Günther: Das portugiesische Kreolisch der Ilha do Principe. Dissertation. Marburg 1973.

Hall 1953 = Robert A. Hall, Jr.: Haitian Creole: Grammar, Texts, Vocabulary. Philadelphia 1953.

Hall 1966 = Robert A. Hall, Jr.: Pidgin and Creole Languages. Ithaca. London 1966.

Lenz 1928 = Rodolfo Lenz: El Papiamento, la lengua criolla de Curazao (la gramática más sencilla). Santiago de Chile 1928.

Lopes da Silva 1957 = Baltasar Lopes da Silva: O dialecto crioulo de Cabo Verde. Lisboa 1957.

Marimoutou/Baggioni 1986 = Carpanin Jean Claude Marimoutou/Daniel Baggioni: Le roman créole réunionnais et le projet de dictionnaire. In: Lengas 19. Montpellier 1986, 101—126.

Morgan 1960 = Raleigh Morgan, Jr.: The Lexicon of Saint Martin Creole. In: Anthropological Linguistics 2 (1). 1960, 7—29.

Neumann 1985 = Ingrid Neumann: Le créole de Breaux Bridge, Louisiane. Etude morphosyntaxique, textes, vocabulaire. Hamburg 1985 (Kreolische Bibliothek 7).

Pérégo 1968 = Pierre Pérégo: Les sabirs. In: Le Langage, éd. A. Martinet. Paris 1968, 597—607.

Perl 1986 = Matthias Perl: Gedanken zu den ersten lexikographischen Beschreibungen der romanischen Kreolsprachen [...]. Beitrag zum Kolloquium „Aktuelle Problemstellungen der romanischen Lexikographie und Lexikologie [...]", Greifswald 2—3. Oktober 1986.

Reinecke 1975 = John E. Reinecke: A Bibliography of Pidgin and Creole Languages. Honolulu 1975.

Stein 1986 = Peter Stein: Les Premiers créolistes: Les Frères Moraves à St. Thomas au XVIIIe siècle. In: Creole Studies 51. 1986, 3—42.

Annegret Bollée, Bamberg
(République Fédérale d'Allemagne)

XXXV. Typologie und ausgewählte Typen der zwei- und mehrsprachigen Lexikographie
Typology and Selected Types of Bilingual and Multilingual Lexicography
Typologie et types choisis de la lexicographie bilingue et plurilingue

303. Typologie der zweisprachigen Spezialwörterbücher

1. Die Notwendigkeit des Spezialwörterbuchs
2. Zur Typologie der Spezialwörterbücher
3. Syntagmatische Spezialwörterbücher
4. Paradigmatische Spezialwörterbücher
5. Weitere Typen von Spezialwörterbüchern
6. Literatur (in Auswahl)

1. Die Notwendigkeit des Spezialwörterbuchs

Menschliche Rede wird vom Sprecher zum überwiegenden Teil nicht kreiert, sondern wiederholt. Unsere Sprachen sind idiomatisch, d. h. verfestigt. Das meiste, was gesagt wird, ist schon so gesagt worden. Die Sprache (*langue*) ist nicht ein Schatz von Wörtern, sondern von Formulierungen, die durch Auslöser (z. B. Situationen) spontan hervorgerufen werden. Sprachen sagen bevorzugt so oder so, blockieren hingegen zahlreiche theoretisch mögliche Formulierungen. Dem Durchschnittssprecher wird die Idiomatizität seiner Sprache gar nicht bewußt, da er nicht im Traum daran denkt, anders zu formulieren als durch die Sprache vorgegeben.

Bewußt wird die Idiomatizität der Sprache dem Fremdsprachler. Denn der neigt dazu, die Formulierungen seiner Sprache strukturgleich in der Fremdsprache zu wiederholen, mit dem Ergebnis, daß, wenn schon nicht alles, so doch das meiste falsch formuliert ist. Die Fremdsprache formuliert überwiegend anders. Nur wer das begriffen hat, begreift auch die Probleme des zweisprachigen Wörterbuchs. Er begreift, daß das vollständige zweisprachige Wörterbuch das Gesamt der Formulierungen einer Sprache (d. h. alles, was in irgendeiner Weise vorformuliert ist) mit dem Gesamt der Formulierungen einer anderen Sprache zu vergleichen hat. Die Grundeinheit des zweisprachigen Wörterbuchs ist gar nicht das Wort, sondern die Formulierung, d. h. eine syntagmatische, kontextuelle, phraseologische Einheit.

Das Wort steht in den üblichen zweisprachigen Wörterbüchern nur deshalb im Vordergrund, weil es in Form des Lemmas den Zugriff auf die Formulierungen ermöglicht. Anders als über die Wörter sind die Formulierungen lexikographisch nämlich nicht ordnungsfähig. Daraus läßt sich aber keine Autonomie des Wortes ableiten. Auf der Skala kontextueller (semiotaktischer) Abhängigkeit der Wörter gibt es zwar Unterschiede (die hier nicht erörtert werden können), entscheidend aber ist dies: die meisten der zentralen Wörter einer Sprache sind in ihrer Verwendung hochgradig kontextuell gebunden, anders gesagt, sie sind Teil von Formulierungen (Hausmann 1989 u. 1990).

Damit ist aber die Komplikation des zweisprachigen Wörterbuchs noch nicht hinreichend beschrieben. Während nämlich das einsprachige Wörterbuch die Ebene der Formulierung als einer kodierten Kontexteinheit nicht unterschreitet (sie höchstens exemplifiziert), sieht sich das zweisprachige Wörterbuch mit der Tatsache konfrontiert, daß jedes „Beispiel" des einsprachigen Wörterbuchs eine neue Übersetzung verlangt. Eine Einheit, die vom einsprachigen Wörterbuch als monosem behandelt wird, ist oft im zweisprachigen Wörterbuch hochgradig, wenn nicht unendlich, polyäquivalent. Das zweisprachige Wörterbuch ist wie das Faß der Danaiden. Voll wird es nie.

Dieser Unbegrenztheit des Beschreibungswürdigen steht die Begrenzung des Wörterbuchs als Buch gegenüber. Mit guter

Begründung scheuen die Verlage davor zurück, für einen Wörterbuchteil des zweisprachigen Wörterbuchs (z. B. E—D) mehr als 1000 Seiten zur Verfügung zu stellen. Wortlisten, die sich über mehrere Bände erstrekken, und Artikel, die sich über mehrere Seiten erstrecken, sind nicht mehr handhabbar und nicht mehr zugreifbar zu organisieren. Schon aus praktischen Gründen paßt die im zweisprachigen Wörterbuch wünschenswerte Information gar nicht in ein Buch. Hier bietet sich Arbeitsteilung an. Das allgemeine zweisprachige Wörterbuch kann nur das Flaggschiff einer ganzen Flotte von Spezialwörterbüchern sein, welche je eigene Information in einer Menge transportieren, die ohne Spezialisierung unbefördert bliebe.

2. Zur Typologie der Spezialwörterbücher

Es kann im folgenden nicht darum gehen, eine eigene Typologie zu entwerfen. Die im Art. 91 (7.) vorgestellte und in den Art. 92—166 durchbeschriebene Typologie ist auch für die zweisprachige Speziallexikographie gültig. Zahlreiche zweisprachige Wörterbücher werden dort mitbehandelt. Allerdings ist die benutzte Typologie für die zweisprachigen Wörterbücher unterschiedlich relevant. Drei Gruppen ließen sich unterscheiden.

(a) Nur wenige Wörterbuchtypen sind *genuin zweisprachig*. Dazu gehören das Faux-Amis-Wörterbuch (Art. 304, sowie Prado 1989, Wilczynska 1989) und das Reisewörterbuch (Art. 305 a). Viele Typen enthalten allerdings ein Element der Zweisprachigkeit, insofern sie verschiedene Subsysteme einer Sprache in Beziehung setzen („homoglosse Wörterbücher" nach der Typologie von Alain Rey, vgl. Art. 91, Abb. 91.5).

(b) Bestimmte Wörterbuchtypen existieren *vorwiegend einsprachig*. Das gilt z. B. für Zitatenwörterbücher (Art. 98) oder Orthographiewörterbücher (Art. 140). Für die Beantwortung der Frage, ob es *genuin einsprachige* Wörterbücher gibt, muß man zuvor klären, welche Art Information in der Zielsprache formuliert ist. Beschränkt man die Frage auf Wörterbücher, welche die typkonstitutive Information in der Zielsprache formulieren (z. B. die zweisprachige distinktive Synonymik, welche den Synonymenunterschied in der Zielsprache formuliert), so gibt es sehr wohl genuin einsprachige Wörterbücher, z. B. das Orthographiewörterbuch, insofern die Information über die Orthographie eines Wortes schlechterdings nicht anders denn durch Vorzeigen dieses Wortes in seiner graphischen Form geschehen kann. Dem kann freilich mancherlei Art nicht-typkonstitutiver Information in der Zielsprache hinzugefügt werden, z. B. können alle der orthographischen Schwierigkeit wegen aufgenommenen Wörter mit Äquivalenten versehen werden. Bezieht man demnach die Zweisprachigkeit auf nicht-typkonstitutive Information, so muß man genuin einsprachige Wörterbücher für inexistent erklären. Zwar scheint es z. B. zweisprachige Zitatenwörterbücher nicht zu geben, doch sind sie ohne weiteres denkbar und darüber hinaus sogar wünschenswert.

(c) Die dritte und wichtigste Gruppe zweisprachiger Spezialwörterbücher betrifft jene, die, wenn schon nicht genuin zweisprachig, so doch *spezifisch zweisprachig* sind. Damit ist gemeint, daß die in der Zielsprache formulierte Information typkonstitutiv ist und daß darüber hinaus Information über zwei Sprachen geliefert wird. Das spezifische zweisprachige Spezialwörterbuch vergleicht zwei Sprachen im Sinne von 1.

3. Syntagmatische Spezialwörterbücher

Spezifische Spezialwörterbücher sind zuerst einmal im Bereich der *Syntagmatik* nötig (vgl. Kap. VII). — Das kontrastive *Konstruktionswörterbuch*, das die falschen Freunde der Valenz miteinander kontrastiert, ist bislang erstaunlich selten (vgl. Art. 94, 1002 f.). — Ähnlich ausbaufähig erscheint der didaktisch unersetzliche Typ des zweisprachigen *Kollokationswörterbuchs* (vgl. Art. 287 a,2. und Zöfgen 1990). — Während die Kollokationen sich meist relativ eindeutig übersetzen lassen, zeigen die Redewendungen einer Sprache je nach Kontext so vielfältige Schattierungen und pragmatische Abhängigkeiten, daß sie in der Zielsprache fast in jedem Kontext mit anderen Äquivalenten versehen werden müssen. Diesem Phänomen stehen vor allem hinübersetzende zweisprachige Wörterbücher aus Mangel an Platz nahezu machtlos gegenüber. Das zweisprachige *phraseologische Wörterbuch* (vgl. Art. 96 und 290) kann hier für jede Redewendung eine große Zahl authentischer und belegter Beispiele in die Fremdsprache übersetzen und Nuancen diskutieren und kommentieren. Ein so geartetes, im wahren Sinne des Wortes kontrastives phraseologisches Wörterbuch ist allerdings bislang ein Desiderat. Denn auch die Spezialwörterbücher begnügen sich meist mit der Reduktion der Redewendung auf wenige Kontexte und wenige Äquivalente. — Dem in 1. dargestellten Umfang der Idiomatizität der Sprachen versuchen die zweisprachigen *Satzwörterbücher* gerecht zu werden, die früher mit dem Titel *Phraseologie* erschienen (vgl. Art. 99). Sie enthalten neben Kollokationen und Redewendungen jede weitere Art von Formulierungen mit kontrastiver Idiomatizität. Das Genre, das in letzter Zeit rar zu werden schien (vgl. aber Paffen 1980, das 43 000 deutsche Sätze ins Russische übersetzt), ist jetzt noch einmal durch Zimmer 1990 für das Französische und Deutsche belebt worden. Zimmers *Kontextwörterbuch* hat allerdings nur durch den Index Wörterbuchcharakter und enthält wohl auch zu viel Material, über das die allgemeinen zweisprachigen Wörterbücher bereits hinreichend informieren. — Weitere syntagmatische Spezialwörterbücher kommen zweisprachig vor, z. B. solche der Gesprächsformeln (Art. 100, 1.3). Viele weitere wären denkbar. So muß überraschen, daß es zwar das (einsprachige) Wörterbuch der altfranzösischen Grußformeln gibt (Lebsanft 1988), aber offenbar kein kontrastives Grußwörterbuch der Gegenwart.

4. Paradigmatische Spezialwörterbücher

Unter den paradigmatischen Spezialwörterbüchern (vgl. Kap. VIII) ist zweisprachig die *kontrastive Synonymik* von größtem theoretischem Interesse (vgl. etwa Krüger 1922, Klein/Friederich 1967, Kleineidam/Gottschalk 1972, Meldau/Whitling 1981). In der Praxis stößt allerdings dieses Spezialwörterbuch an ähnliche Grenzen wie das allgemeine zweisprachige Wörterbuch, da es, um leistungsfähig zu sein, syntagmatisch begründet werden müßte und deshalb vor der Unbegrenztheit der Kontexte kapitulieren muß. Theoretisch wäre für ein kontrastives Synonymwörterbuch zu fordern, daß in typischen Kontexten erläutert wird, wo Synonyme in Bedeutungsopposition stehen, wo sie ohne Bedeutungsunterschied austauschbar sind und wo das eine im Gegensatz zum anderen überhaupt nicht stehen kann. Hartmut Kleineidam, selber Autor eines umfangreichen zweisprachigen Synonymenwörterbuchs, hat diese Aufgabe mit Recht als unerfüllbar von sich gewiesen (Kleineidam 1976). Die grenzenlose Kompliziertheit der Verhältnisse wurde schon bei Collinson 1939 deutlich und ist seither durch die Schule von Christoph Schwarze herausgearbeitet worden

leicht

facile *adj.* Qui se fait sans effort, qui s'obtient sans difficulté. Terme usuel.

Une opération, un travail, un problème ~. C'est ~ comme bonjour *(kinderleicht).* Ce passage est ~ à traduire. Chemin ~ à trouver. Objet ~ à se procurer. C'est plus ~ à dire qu'à faire. Il est ~ à contenter. Il est ~ de le contenter. En amour, notre vanité dédaigne une victoire trop ~ (Stendhal). Un homme d'un abord ~ *(leicht zugänglich).*

aisé,e *adj.* Qui se fait sans peine (terme plus relevé et moins fréquent que *facile*). *Einfach, mühelos.*

C'est un jeu très simple et qu'il est ~ aux enfants de comprendre (DFC). C'est la chose la plus ~e du monde. Tu comprends que ça n'était pas ~ pour nous, qui n'avions rien (Maupassant). On comprend d'ailleurs ~ment qu'il n'ait pas voulu courir de risques.

simple *adj.* Qui est facile à utiliser, aisé à comprendre, parce qu'il est formé de peu d'éléments, parce qu'il n'est pas compliqué. *Einfach, unkompliziert.*

Un mécanisme très ~. Le français, qui nous semble si ~, est une langue très difficile, pleine de menus traquenards (Gide). Ce serait vraiment trop beau, ce serait aussi trop ~ (Duhamel). Vous ne savez pas comment il faut s'y prendre? C'est pourtant bien ~, ~ comme bonjour *(kinderleicht).*

commode *adj.* Qui offre de la facilité parce qu'il est bien approprié à l'usage requis. *Bequem und leicht.*

Machine ~ à manier. Je connais un moyen ~ pour réussir (DFC). C'est fort ~ et fort doux de n'avoir qu'un mot à dire pour faire tout plier autour de soi (Sand). Ce que vous me demandez là n'est pas ~ (Rob.).

Textbeispiel 303.1: Artikel *leicht* (aus: Kleineidam/Gottschalk 1972, 341)

(Schwarze 1983, 1985, Jessen 1979, Schepping 1982, Hartmann 1984; ähnliche Einblicke gibt Van der Elst 1983). Die kontrastiven Wortfeldanalysen, die Snell-Hornby 1984 als Basis der kontrastiven Synonymik und letztlich eines besseren allgemeinen zweisprachigen Wörterbuchs fordert, gibt es nur in Ansätzen. Man darf sich deshalb nicht wundern, daß bisherige Synonymiken kaum mehr leisten als die synonymische Zusammenstellung einer Reihe von Artikeln unter dem zielsprachigen Stichwort (vgl. Textbeispiel 303.1, sowie Häusler 1988).

Jahrhundertelange Tradition haben die zweisprachigen *Sachgruppenwörterbücher (E. Thesaurus F. Dictionnaire par ordre de matières,* vgl. Art. 105, 6.; 148; 152, 5.1.; 305,6., sowie einzelne Artikel aus den Kap. XVII—XX, z. B. Art. 185). Unter didaktischen Aspekten werden sie in Art. 305 behandelt.

Folgende methodische Fehler sind häufig zu beobachten (vgl. auch Vaslet 1990 a, b):
— Die Sachgruppen sind zu umfangreich, so daß das systematische Lernen in der Masse des lexikalischen Materials erstickt.
— Es wird nach Wortarten unterteilt, was man nur als lernpsychologischen Unfug betrachten kann. Die Verschiebung einer Bedeutung durch mehrere Wortarten hindurch (vor allem bei morphologischer Durchsichtigkeit) sollte Grundprinzip solcher Zusammenstellungen sein.
— Besonders unsinnig ist die Trennung der Wortarten durch das Prinzip der Verteilung von Grundwort und Ableitung in zwei verschiedene Wichtigkeitsstufen. Anstatt also die durchsichtige Ableitung mit dem Grundwort zusammenzulernen, wird sie unnötigerweise auf ein späteres Lernstadium verschoben.
— Die Anordnung in den einzelnen Sachgruppen ist oft prinzipienlos, manchmal gar alphabetisch, was in einem Sachgruppenwörterbuch als schlimmste Sünde angesehen werden muß.
— Viele Sachgruppenwörterbücher verzichten auf unabdingbare Kontexte. Statt dessen neigen sie zur sinnlosen Anhäufung von Nomenklatur.

Das (meist zweisprachige) *Bildwörterbuch* wird in Art. 108 behandelt. Die Art. 109—114 berücksichtigen sporadisch zweisprachige Ausprägungen paradigmatischer Spezialwörterbücher.

5. Weitere Typen von Spezialwörterbüchern

Die Spezialwörterbücher zu markierten Lemmata der Standardsprache (Kap. IX) sind überwiegend einsprachig. Dabei könnten manche dieser Wörterbuchtypen zweisprachig durchaus eine eigene Funktion haben, z. B. das *zweisprachige Sprechsprachenwörterbuch* (vgl. Art. 120). Es könnte belegte Kontexte übersetzen und sich in besonderer Weise um adäquate, vor allem markierungsgleiche, Äquivalente bemühen. Nuancen und Unterschiede, die das Äquivalent nicht vermitteln kann, wären in einem eigenen Kommentar zu beschreiben. Ein solches kontrastives Sprechsprachenwörterbuch gibt es bislang jedoch nicht.

Unter den Spezialwörterbüchern zu bestimmten weiteren Lemmatypen (Kap. X) ist das zweisprachige *grammatische Wörterbuch* naturgemäß gut vertreten (Art. 126). Von besonderem Interesse wären *wortklassenbezogene Spezialwörterbücher,* denn für die zweisprachigen Wörterbücher gilt ja in gleichem Maße wie für die einsprachigen das Gesetz der differenzierten lexikographischen Bearbeitung statt einer Schema-F-Bearbeitung (vgl. Art. 70). Bahnbrechend ist nun das deutsch-englische Partikelnwörterbuch von König u. a. 1990. Musterartikel für zwei französische Sprechaktformeln liefert Schneider 1989, 285—295, 301—311, 314—319.

Von essentieller Zweisprachigkeit sind ansonsten nur noch die zweisprachigen *Schulwörterbücher* (vgl. Art. 305). Hier wird man beklagen, daß viele Verlage glauben, sie könnten sich für die Herstellung von Schulwörterbüchern mit der syntagmatischen Ausdünnung und der typographischen Veränderung ihrer Hand- und Taschenwörterbücher begnügen, mit dem Ergebnis, daß zwar Fachsprachliches und Terminologisches reichlich, die Idiomatizität der Sprachen hingegen mehr als ärmlich vertreten ist.

6. Literatur (in Auswahl)

6.1. Wörterbücher

Klein/Friederich 1967 = Hans-Wilhelm Klein/Wolf Friederich: Englische Synonymik für Studierende und Lehrer. 3. Aufl. München 1967 [921 S. 1. Aufl. durch Klein, 1951].

Kleineidam/Gottschalk 1972 = Hartmut Kleineidam/Walter Gottschalk: Französische Synonymik. 6., völlig neu bearb. Aufl. München 1972 [657 S. 1. Aufl. durch Gottschalk, Heidelberg 1925, 2. Aufl. 1950].

König u. a. 1990 = Ekkehard König/Detlef Stark/Susanne Requardt: Adverbien und Partikeln. Ein deutsch-englisches Wörterbuch. Heidelberg 1990.

Krüger 1922 = Gustav Krüger: Französische Synonymik nebst Beiträgen zum Wortgebrauch. Leipzig 1922 [1230 S.].

Lebsanft 1988 = Franz Lebsanft: Studien zu einer Linguistik des Grußes. Sprache und Funktion der altfranzösischen Grußformeln. Tübingen 1988 (Beihefte zur ZRPh 217) [Wörterbuch 305—491].

Meldau/Whitling 1981 = Rudolf Meldau unter Mitwirkung von Ralph B. Whitling: Sinnverwandte Wörter der englischen Sprache. Heidelberg 1981 (Anglistische Forschungen 154) [642 S.].

Paffen 1980 = K. A. Paffen: Deutsch-russisches Satzlexikon. Hrsg. v. Christa Fleckenstein. Leipzig. München 1980 [1686 S.].

Zimmer 1990 = Rudolf Zimmer: Äquivalenzen zwischen Französisch und Deutsch. Theorie — Korpus — Indizes. Ein Kontextwörterbuch. Tübingen 1990 [917 S.].

6.2. Sonstige Literatur

Collinson 1939 = W.E. Collinson: Comparative Synonymics: Some Principles and Illustrations. In: Transactions of the Philological Society. 1939, 54—77.

Hartmann 1984 = Lily Maria von Hartmann: Modalitäten des Nichttuns. Analyse und Vergleich der 'negativ implikativen Verben' im Französischen und Deutschen. Konstanz 1984.

Häusler 1988 = Frank Häusler: Der Stichwortartikel im zweisprachigen Synonymwörterbuch. Zur Spezifik einer lexikographischen Textsorte. In: Potsdamer Forschungen der Pädagogischen Hochschule Karl Liebknecht. Potsdam. Reihe A 90. 1988, 54—63.

Hausmann 1989 = Franz Josef Hausmann: Was ist und was soll ein Kontextwörterbuch? In: Langenscheidts Kontextwörterbuch Französisch-Deutsch. (...) Von Peter Ilgenfritz u. a. Berlin 1989, 5—9.

Hausmann 1990 = Franz Josef Hausmann: La définition est-elle utile? In: Centre d'études du lexique: La définition. Paris 1990 (Langue et langage), 225—235.

Jessen 1979 = H. Jessen: Pragmatische Aspekte lexikalischer Semantik. Verben des Aufforderns im Französischen. Tübingen 1979.

Kleineidam 1976 = Hartmut Kleineidam: Lexikalische Synonymie unter kontrastivem Aspekt. In: Lebendige Romania. Festschrift für Hans-Wilhelm Klein. Göppingen 1976, 177—195.

Prado 1989 = Marcial Prado: Falsos amigos en lexicografía bilingüe. In: Hispania 72. 1989, 721—727.

Schepping 1982 = Marie Theres Schepping: Kontrastive semantische Analyse von Verben des Visuellen im Französischen und Deutschen. Tübingen 1982.

Schneider 1989 = Franz Schneider: Comment décrire les actes de langage? De la linguistique pragmatique à la lexicographie: «La belle affaire!» et «Tu m'en diras tant!». Tübingen 1989 (Linguistische Arbeiten 227).

Schwarze 1983 = Christoph Schwarze: Une typologie des contrastes lexicaux. In: Allgemeine Sprachwissenschaft, Sprachtypologie und Textlinguistik. Festschrift für Peter Hartmann. Tübingen 1983, 199—210.

Schwarze 1985 = Christoph Schwarze: Prinzipien eines kontrastiven Verblexikons. In: Chr. Schwarze (Hrsg.), Beiträge zu einem kontrastiven Wortfeldlexikon Deutsch-Französisch. Tübingen 1985.

Snell-Hornby 1984 = Mary Snell-Hornby: The Bilingual Dictionary — Help or Hindrance? In: LEXeter '83 Proceedings. Ed. R.R.K. Hartmann. Tübingen 1984 (Lexicographica Series Maior 1), 274—281.

Van der Elst 1983 = Gaston Van der Elst: Versuch einer kontrastiven semantischen Analyse (am Beispiel Deutsch-Niederländisch). In: Mehrsprachigkeit und Gesellschaft. Akten des 17. Linguistischen Kolloquiums. Bd. 2. Tübingen 1983, 211—221.

Vaslet 1990a = Daniel Vaslet: Kritik und Vergleich von zwei zweisprachigen Lernwörterbüchern. Emploi des mots und Thematischer Grund- und Aufbauwortschatz Französisch. In: Französisch heute 21. 1990, 31—38.

Vaslet 1990b = Daniel Vaslet: Kritik eines zweisprachigen Lernwörterbuches in Sachgruppen. D. Lübkes *Emploi des mots*. In: T. Magay/J. Zigány (Hrsg.): BudaLEX '88. Budapest 1990, 243—250.

Wilczynska 1989 = Veronica Wilczynska: Un dictionnaire de faux-amis: pour quoi faire? In: Le Français dans le Monde. Numéro Spécial: Lexiques, ed. A. H. Ibrahim. Août-Septembre 1989, 179—186.

Zöfgen 1990 = Ekkehard Zöfgen: Bewährungsprobe für das *Kontextwörterbuch Französisch-Deutsch*. In: Fremdsprachen lehren und lernen 19. 1990, 213—227.

Franz Josef Hausmann, Erlangen
(Bundesrepublik Deutschland)

304. The Dictionary of False Friends

1. What Are False Friends?
2. Model Example of a Dictionary Entry
3. What Demands Should a False Friend Dictionary Meet?
4. Where False Friend Dictionaries Can Go Wrong
5. History of False Friend Dictionaries
6. Selected Bibliography

1. What Are False Friends?

False Friends (= FF) are words in two different languages which are graphically or phonetically very similar but have different meanings and can therefore be easily confused by foreign language learners. FF dictionaries aim at precluding confusion of this type. We can distinguish between total false

BRANCHE / BRANCH

I	1.	Le chat s'est réfugié sur la plus haute **branche** du cerisier	The cat fled to the highest **branch** of the cherry tree [a]
	2.	J'appartiens à la **branche** pauvre de la famille	I belong to the poor **branch** of the family
		Toutes les **branches** de la science [du savoir] sont représentées dans la bibliothèque	All **branches** of science [knowledge] are represented in the library [b] ⇨ 3
II	3.	Ma fille s'oriente vers une **branche** scientifique	My daughter is going towards the science **side**
		Il est de loin le meilleur dans sa **branche**	He is by far the best in his **field**
	4.	Les **branches** des lunettes [du compas, des ciseaux] sont tordues	The **arms** of the spectacles [the **legs** of the compasses, the **blades** of the scissors] are bent [c]
	5.	Alors, vieille **branche***, comment ça va ?	Well, (old) *(Brit)* **mate***/*(US)* **buddy***, how's it going ?
III	6.	One of the two **branches** of the river is extremely dangerous	Un des deux **bras** du fleuve est très dangereux [d] (*rarement :* **branche**)
	7.	Our shop has **branches** all over the country	Notre magasin a des **succursales/filiales** dans tout le pays [e]

a. *Petite branche :* twig
b. Branch désigne uniquement une subdivision d'un même domaine alors que branche peut avoir le sens plus général de 'domaine, orientation' (cf. 3).
c. Mais : *branche (d'un chandelier) :* branch
d. (Ch. de fer) *Branch line :* ligne secondaire
e. (Admin) *Branch (of government...) :* division, section

Dictionary excerpt 304.1: Dictionary article F *branche*/E *branch* (from: Van Roey 1988, 96)

friends, such as German *sensibel*/English *sensible,* and partial false friends, eg G *bringen*/E *bring,* with *bring* being reserved for movement towards the speaker. FF dictionaries may also include frequently confused word pairs such as G *selbstbewußt*/E *self-conscious,* where confusion arises less from formal similarity but from literal translation ('Germanisms', 'Anglicisms' etc). For further typology of FF, see Haschka 1989, Kudela 1980, Maillot 1981, Rasmussen 1978, Reiner 1983, Wandruszka 1977, Wotjak 1984.

FF dictionaries belong to the category of learning dictionaries. They can be subdivided into (a) *secondary learning dictionaries,* ie dictionaries that aim at being as comprehensive as possible and do not contain exercises (Van Roey 1988; Hill 1982) and (b) *primary learning dictionaries,* which should be worked through systematically, can contain exercises (Parkes/Cornell 1989) and occasionally try to amuse the readers, as well as inform them (Pascoe 1985; Parkes/Cornell 1989).

2. Model Example of a Dictionary Entry

Dictionary excerpt 304.1 shows the model of a FF dictionary entry which proceeds on the following principles:

— The false friend pair is printed on top.
— The entry is subdivided into three parts. Under I are listed all the senses in which the French and the English headwords are 'true friends', ie where their meaning(s) coincide(s):

$F_{a\,1,2} = E_{a\,1,2}$

Under II follow the instances in which the French headword corresponds to different English words:

$F_{a\,3,4,5} = E_{b,c,d}$

Under III the English headword is shown to correspond to different French words:

$E_{a\,3,4} = F_{b,c}$

Any of the three numbers can be missing, showing that there are no instances under the category concerned. This is a very clear, consistent and helpful arrangement.

— Priority is given to clear and idiomatic examples and their translations. Importance is attached to frequently used collocations. Users are supposed to derive their own rules.

— Where deemed necessary, explanatory notes are added in small print at the end of the entry; so are further less frequent or specialised meanings and idiomatic usages.

— Importance is attached to extensive and careful marking of style level, frequency, geographic varieties, areas of application.

— The arrangement of 'French headword left in I and II, English headword left in III' follows the learner's question: 'Well, what then does *branch* mean in French apart from *branche*'?

3. What Demands Should a False Friend Dictionary Meet?

(a) Careful *selection* of headwords: the selection should be based on frequency of error, supported by experience, not on fanciful conjecture. Accidental false friends or random homonyms without a common semantic origin or background should be excluded (cf Kipp 1986, 51: *electricity/elektrifizierte Stadt,* 24: *bluefish/Forelle blau;* Pascoe 1985, 44—45: *Fahrt/fart,* 128—9: *Ragwurz/ragwort;* Helliwell 1989, 40: *Igel/eagle,* 48: *Kittchen/kitchen;* Hill 1982, 32: *close/Kloß,* 33: *collier/Koller*).

(b) Idiomatic and clear *examples* reflecting present-day usage and their correct *translation* are essential. They illustrate explanations and can even replace them (exemplary: Van Roey 1988; Parkes/Cornell 1989; no examples are supplied by Hill 1982 and Kipp 1986; examples from 17th to 19th century literature are quoted in Klein 1968).

(c) *Explanations* of differences in meaning, if necessary, should be brief and to the point (Van Roey 1988 and Parkes/Cornell 1989 strike a happy compromise between Kipp 1986 and Hill 1982, who do not provide any explanations, and the unnecessarily wordy Pascoe 1985; cf Pascoe 1985, 35: *defective*).

(d) *Illustrations* are hardly ever essential; they may clarify explanations (Pascoe 1985, 26—27: *Pferdebox/horse-box;* Parkes/Cornell 1989, 21: *alarmieren/alert*) and motivate the reader, but they can be obscure and thereby confusing (Helliwell 1989, 174: *nagging a hole in the cupboard door;* 46: *Birthday cakes;* 10: *I never touch alcoholics*).

(e) The examples and their translation should be *arranged* in a user-friendly way, ie spaced out (Pascoe 1985 runs on; Van Roey 1988, Parkes/Cornell 1989 are exemplary).

(f) *Phonetic transcriptions* should be added where necessary (cf Van Roey 1988, Pascoe 1985).

(g) *Grammatical information* in easy-to-understand coding (countability of nouns, irregular plurals, attributive vs predicative usage etc) is important (and is contained in Van Roey 1988 and Pascoe 1985).

(h) *Labels* indicating style level, regional restrictions, specialised usage etc are essential, especially where taboo words are concerned. Most FF dictionaries contain labels of some sort; labelling is most consistently carried through in Van Roey 1988; Parkes/Cornell 1989; Pascoe 1985.

(i) Terms relating to *institutions* of one country that do not have an opposite number in the other language should be explained (as in Parkes/Cornell 1989, 71: *Pension;* Van Roey 1988, 508: *pension;* Pascoe 1985, 100—1: *Nougat,* 104—5: *Pantomime*).

(j) *Collocations, idiomatic expressions* in which the headwords occur typically should be included (as in Van Roey 1988; Parkes/Cornell 1989; Pascoe 1985; to a minor degree in Helliwell 1989; not at all in Kipp 1986 and Hill 1982).

(k) The inclusion of *exercises* in FF dictionaries of the primary learning dictionary type is most desirable (the only one to do this, and in exemplary fashion, is Parkes/Cornell 1989).

(l) The *difficulties that might arise from either of the two languages* should be taken into account. English *bring* presents no difficulty when translated into German (G *bringen*), German *bringen* does when translated into English (E *bring — take*). This problem is seen in all the FF dictionaries, but when carried out mechanically as in Kipp 1986, which simply turns the translations from the English-German first part into the headwords for the second German-English part, leads to absurd headwords such as 148: *baldiger Pate;* 199: *komischer Streifen;* 197: *Klosettwasser;* 231: *toter Ringer;* 241: *Schweinebacke.*

4. Where False Friend Dictionaries Can Go Wrong

(a) Examples should not reflect *outdated* usage (Klein 1968).

(b) A *subdivision by word-classes* (nouns, adjectives and adverbs, verbs) is as arbitrary as alphabetical ordering, but far less useful or user-friendly (Helliwell 1989).

(c) Primary learning dictionaries that print their examples and translations within *one running-on text* deprive users of useful translation practice (Pascoe 1985).

(d) *Rare, unrealistic and fanciful FF pairs* may amuse the author but will mislead the uninitiated user and will irritate the experienced one (Kipp 1986; occasionally Helliwell 1989 and Pascoe 1985, see under 3).

(e) FF dictionaries that compare *more than two languages* may be of some interest to teachers at language institutes catering for students from widely different languages, but are not at all helpful to the students themselves as they do not aid them in language production (Hill 1982: 15 languages).

(f) A bare minimum of information, *one-word by one-word equations,* can provoke errors (Helliwell 1989, 82—85: G *Salon* = E *salon* in *hairdressing salon,* but not when *Salon* refers to a private home (= *drawing-room*), a ship (= *saloon*), a fair (= *stand*) or an art exhibition (= *exhibition room*) — none of which are mentioned. The same applies to the following: 171—174: G *parieren* = E *parry* in *to parry questions,* but not when G *parieren* means 'to obey', which is the more frequently used meaning; Kipp 1986, 62: E *garn* is used as an interjection; equating it with G *Quatsch* without any labelling provokes sentences like: 'He's talking a load of garn.')

(g) *Printing, translation, grammar errors* and downright *wrong information* confuse and mislead the user (Kipp 1986, 256: un*e*sthetisch, 114: s*k*ythe, 188: hist*e*rical; 85: *filing cabinet* = *Mappenkasten* instead of *Aktenschrank, -regal,* 48: *dog days* = *Hundetage* instead of *Hundstage,* 99: *first aid kit* = *Pflasterkasten* instead of *Erste-Hilfe-Ausrüstung,* 134: *woman* = *Weib* instead of *Frau;* 117: *slim diet* instead of *slimming diet,* 70: *high-seasoned* instead of *highly seasoned;* 54: *faggot* = *Fagott* instead of *bassoon,* 126: *templet* — *Schläfe* instead of *temple,* 84: *magistrate* = *hoher richterlicher Beamter* instead of *Friedensrichter* etc, 74: *inflammable* (Am) = *nicht brennbar,* instead of *feuergefährlich*).

5. History of False Friend Dictionaries

The first contribution to a short history of false friend dictionaries is given in Reiner 1983, 66—70. According to Reiner a first systematic treatment of the subject is to be found in an extensive work by Mauvillon 1747. For the French-German language pair Reiner further mentions Portitor 1788, Bigot 1845 and several minor titles in the second half of the 19th century. Other authors mention Grangier 1864 and Dubray 1894 as further predecessors. The more recent tradition begins with Koessler/Derocquigny 1928, who apparently also created the term *faux amis.* Since then, especially since the Second World War, there have been numerous successors dealing with a variety of language pairs (cf. 6.1.).

6. Selected Bibliography
6.1. Dictionaries

Akulenko 1969 = V. V. Akulenko/C. Ju. Komisarčik/R. V. Pogorelova/V. A. Jucht: English-Russian and Russian-English Dictionary of Misleading Words. Moskva 1969.

Altrocchi 1935 = Rudolph Altrocchi: Deceptive Cognates. Italian-English and English-Italian. Chicago 1935 [72 p.].

Anderson 1938 = James Gauchez Anderson: Le mot juste. A Dictionary of English and French Homonyms. Ed. L. C. Harmer. New York 1938 [205 p.; first ed. 1932].

Bigot 1845 = Charles Bigot: Germanismes corrigés, ou Remarques sur les fautes ordinaires aux Allemands, qui parlent le français. Stuttgart 1845 [144 p.].

Birbrajer 1987 = Julian Birbrajer: Friends and False Friends. A Dictionary of "False Friends" Between Polish and Russian With an English Translation of All Entries. Stockholm 1987 [70 p.].

Boch 1988 = Raoul Boch/Carla Salvioni: Les faux amis aux aguets. Dizionario di false analogie e ambigue affinità tra francese e italiano. Bologna 1988 [316 p.].

Boillot 1930 = Félix Boillot: Le vrai ami du traducteur anglais-français et français-anglais. Paris 1930 [266 p.].

Boillot 1956 = Félix Boillot: Le second vrai ami du traducteur anglais-français et français-anglais. Paris 1956 [250 p.].

Bouscaren/Davoust 1977 = Christian Bouscaren/Eugène Davoust: Les mots anglais qu'on croit connaître. 2. Les mots-sosies. Paris 1977 [256 p.].

Broussous 1972 = Monique Broussous: Les mots-pièges dans la version italienne et leurs analogues français dans le thème. Paris 1972 [149 p.].

Buhl 1977 = Ingeborg Buhl: Lumske ord og vendinger: Engelsk. Copenhagen 1977 [110 p.; first ed. 1968].

Buhl 1977a = Ingeborg Buhl: Lumske ord og vendinger: Fransk. Copenhagen 1977 [112 p.; first ed. 1968].

Buhl 1977b = Ingeborg Buhl: Lumske ord og vendinger. Copenhagen 1977 [87 p.; first ed. 1968].

Causse 1978 = Jean-Pierre Causse: Dictionnaire des vrais amis. Dictionnaire français-anglais de locutions similaires placées dans un contexte. S. l. 1978 [156 p.].

Derocquigny 1931 = Jules Derocquigny: Autres mots anglais perfides. Paris 1931 [107 p.].

Downes 1977 = Leonard S. Downes: Palavras Amigas da Onça: A Vocabulary of False Friends in English and Portuguese. Portsmouth 1977 [77 p.].

Dubray 1894 = Gabriel Dubray: Fautes de français. Tableau des fautes les plus fréquentes que font les Allemands en parlant et en écrivant le français. 4e éd. Wien 1894 [111 p.; 13th ed. Max Seidner-Weiser 1935, 212 p.].

Dubray 1910 = Gabriel Dubray: L'Allemand a son français que le Français ne connaît pas. 2e éd. Wien 1910 [15 p.].

Dumont 1970 = Maurice-Alex Dumont: Espagnol-Français. Les fausses concordances lexicales. Louvain 1970 [178 p.].

Dupont 1961 = Louis Dupont: Les faux amis espagnols. Paris 1961 [167 p.].

Dupont 1965 = Louis Dupont: Les pièges du vocabulaire italien. Genève 1965 [199 p.].

Ernolv 1958 = Carl Ernolv: False friends — förrödiska ord. In: Moderna Språk 52. 1958, 347—368.

Gonzalez 1982 = Blanca Gonzalez Marimon: Diccionario de "falsos amigos" francés-español. Madrid 1982 [53 p.].

Gottlieb 1986 = Karl Heinrich Gottlieb: Sprachfallen im Russischen. Wörterbuch der "falschen Freunde" Russisch-Deutsch/Deutsch-Russisch. München 1986 [160 p.; russ. Orig. Moskau 1972].

Grangier 1864 = Louis Grangier: Tableau des germanismes les plus répandus en Allemagne et dans les pays limitrophes, suivi d'un aperçu des principaux gallicismes. Leipzig 1864 [91 p.].

Hammer 1976 = P. Hammer/M. J. Monod: English-French Cognate Dictionary. Edmonton 1976.

Helliwell 1983 = Margaret Helliwell: False Friends — Falsche Freunde. Eine Sammlung tückischer Wörter Deutsch-Englisch. Brühl 1983 [183 p.].

Helliwell 1989 = Margaret Helliwell: Can I become a beefsteak? Trügerische Wörter zum Nachschlagen und Üben Deutsch-Englisch. Berlin 1989 [191 p.].

Hill 1982 = Robert J. Hill: A Dictionary of False Friends. London 1982 [VIII, 319 p.].

Kanivé 1950 = Joseph Kanivé: Les Faux Amis — Recueil pratique de listes lexicologiques. Esch-s.-A. 1950 [86 p.].

Kipp 1986 = Harald Kipp: Non-Verwexlikon. Englische Vokabeln, die am häufigsten verwechselt werden. Bergisch-Gladbach 1986 [266 p.].

Kirk-Green 1968 = Christopher W. Edward Kirk-Green: Les mots-amis et les faux-amis. London 1968 [127 p.].

Kirk-Green 1981 = Christopher W. Edward Kirk-Green: French False Friends. London 1981 [197 p.].

Klein 1968 = Hans-Wilhelm Klein: Schwierigkeiten des deutsch-französischen Wortschatzes. Germanismen — Faux Amis. Stuttgart 1968 [305 p.; Sec. ed. 1975, 400 p.].

Koessler/Derocquigny 1928 = Maxime Koessler/Jules Derocquigny: Les Faux amis des vocabulaires anglais et américain. Paris 1975 [584 p.; first ed. Les faux amis ou les pièges du vocabulaire anglais. Conseils aux traducteurs. Paris 1928, 387 p.].

Konder 1982 = Rosa W. Konder: Longman English Dictionary for Portuguese Speakers. London 1982 [552 p.].

Kozielewski 1959 = Ignacy Kozielewski: Slownik wyrazów o podobnym brzmienie. Warszawa 1959 [100 p.].

Kühnel 1979 = Helmut Kühnel: Kleines Wörterbuch der "faux amis" Deutsch-Französisch, Französisch-Deutsch. Leipzig 1979 [127 p.].

Lyon 1961 = John E. Lyon: Pitfalls of Spanish Vocabulary. London 1961 [120 p.].

Mascherpe 1968 = Mario Mascherpe: A tradução do inglês para o português. Os falsos cognatos. São Paulo 1968 [100 p.].

Mauvillon 1747 = Eléazar de Mauvillon: Remarques sur les germanismes. 2 vols. Amsterdam 1753, 1754 [386, 485 p.; T. 1 also 1747].

Messner 1977 = Dieter Messner: Dictionnaire chronologique des langues ibéroromanes. IV: Répertoire chronologique des mots français. Heidelberg 1977.

Munch 1962 = Valfrid Palmgren Munch/Ellen Hartmann: Farlige ord og lumske ligheder i svensk og dansk. Copenhagen 1962 [260 p.; first ed. 1944].

Murav'ev 1969 = V. L. Murav'ev: Faux amis ili "ložnye druzja" perevodčika. Moskva 1969.

Nash 1980 = Rose Nash: Parallexicon: A Dictionary of Shared Vocabulary. In: Readings in Spanish-English Contrastive Linguistics. Vol. 2. Ed. by Rose Nash et al. San Juan 1980, 136—153.

Neck 1925 = M. G. van Neck/M. van Neck: Nederlandsch-Engelsche klank- en zinverwante woorden. Leiden 1925 [296 S.].

Onelli 1955 = Onelli: Gli scogli del francese moderno. Roma 1955.

Ossiannilsson 1947 = Sølve Ossiannilsson/Martin Tamsen: Farliga ord och fällör i tyskan: Jömförande svensk-tysk ordbok. Lund 1947 [178 p.].

Panis 1967 = Augustin Panis: Les mots perfides de l'espagnol. 10e éd. Paris 1967 [60 p.; 3e éd. 1953].

Parkes/Cornell 1989 = Geoff Parkes/Alan Cornell: German-English False Friends. Reference and Practice. Book 1. Southampton 1989 [104 p.].

Pascoe 1985 = Graham Pascoe/Henriette Pascoe: Sprachfallen im Englischen. Wörterbuch der falschen Freunde Deutsch-Englisch. München 1985 [181 p.].

Paulovsky 1949 = Louis H. Paulovsky: Errors in English. A Collection of common pitfalls in British and American usage as an aid to conversation and translation for German-speaking students. Wien 1949 [248 p.].

Péan 1971 = François Y. Péan: Les mots-pièges dans la version espagnole et leurs analogues français. Paris 1971 [320 p.].

Pollak 1956 = Wolfgang Pollak: Fallstricke des französischen und deutschen Wortschatzes. Wien 1956 [44 p.].

Portitor 1788 = Henri Portitor: Petit Traité des gallicismes et germanismes, dans lesquels ces deux langues sont le plus opposées l'une à l'autre. Salzburg 1788 [92 p.].

Prevost = Arthur Prevost: Dictionnaire Français-Anglais Dictionary. Ile Perrot (Kanada) s. d.

Rancoule 1974 = Ludovic Rancoule/Françoise Péan: Les mots-pièges dans la version anglaise et leurs analogues français. Paris 1974 [240 p.].

Reinheimer 1952 = Maurice Reinheimer: Les faux amis du vocabulaire allemand-français. Lausanne 1952 [58 p.].

Rossetti 1937 = Carlo Rossetti: Tranelli dell'inglese; ovvero il traduttore avvertito e consigliato. Third ed. Milano 1937 [232 p.; ed. M. V. Rossetti. Milano 1974, 425 p.].

Rossetti 1944 = Carlo Rossetti: Tranelli del francese ossia del ben tradurre. Roma 1944 [245 p.].

Sassu 1984 = Marina Sassu Frescura: Interferenze Lessicali: Italiano-Inglese/Lexical Interference: Italian-English. Toronto 1984 [172 p.].

Schwarz 1973 = Helge Schwarz: False Friends. Faldgruber i engelsk. Kopenhagen 1973 [120 p.].

Seward 1947 = Robert D. Seward: Dictionary of French [Deceptive] Cognates. New York 1947 [227 p.].

Storni 1975 = Bruno Storni: Schwierigkeiten des deutsch-italienischen Wortschatzes. Stuttgart 1975 [335 p.].

Thody 1985 = Philip Thody/Howard Evans: Mistakable French: A Dictionary of Words and Phrases Easily Confused. New York 1985 [224 p.].

Thorin 1984 = Agnès Thorin: Vrais et faux amis du vocabulaire anglais. Lycées et formation continue. Paris 1984 [143 p.].

Van Roey 1988 = Jacques Van Roey/Sylviane Granger/Helen Swallow: Dictionnaire des faux amis français-anglais. Gembloux 1988 (XXXIII, 792 p.].

Veslot 1923 = H. Veslot/J. Banchet: Les traquenards de la version anglaise. Paris 1928 [First 1923; see Les mots-sosies, 145—167].

Weeren 1977 = Jan van Weeren: Interferenz und Valenz. Zum Problem der "falschen Freunde" für niederländische Germanistikstudenten. Meppel 1977 [Dictionary p. 67—88].

Wotjak 1984 = Gerd Wotjak/Ulf Hermann: Wörterbuch der 'falschen Freunde'. Deutsch-Spanisch/Spanisch-Deutsch. Leipzig 1984 [168 p.].

6.2. Other Publications

Baldinger 1981 = Kurt Baldinger: *Stupide* bei Rabelais: *faux amis* in der Übersetzung. In: Europäische Mehrsprachigkeit. Festschrift für Mario Wandruszka. Tübingen 1981, 349—358.

Bolinger 1948 = Dwight L. Bolinger: 1464 Identical Cognates in English and Spanish. In: Hispania 31. 1948, 271—279.

Darbelnet 1981 = Jean Darbelnet: Réflexions sur les faux amis. In: Traduire 106. Mars 1981, 2—6.

Dolamore 1984 = C. E. J. Dolamore: Faux amis et agents doubles. In: Modern Languages 65. 1984, 75—81.

Gauger 1982 = Hans-Martin Gauger: Falsche Freunde. In: Romania historica et Romania hodierna. Festschrift für Olaf Deutschmann zum 70. Geburtstag. Ed. P. Wunderli/W. Müller. Frankfurt. Bern 1982, 77—92.

Gociman 1976 = A. Gociman/A. Bantas: Main Aspects of Deceptive Cognates in English, Romanian, French, Italian and Spanish. Bukarest 1976.

Gottlieb 1986 = Karl Heinrich Gottlieb: Grundprinzipien eines Wörterbuchs der "Falschen Freunde des Übersetzers". Ein Beitrag zur praktischen Lexikographie. In: Germanistische Linguistik 3—6/84. 1986, 103—134.

Granger/Swallow 1988 = Sylviane Granger/ Helen Swallow: False Friends: A Kaleidoscope of Translation Difficulties. In: Langage et l'Homme 23. 1988, 198—210.

Hammer 1976 = P. Hammer/M. J. Monod: English-French Cognates: A Re-Examination. In: Alberta Modern Language Journal 15. 1976, 23—41.

Hammer 1979 = P. Hammer: The Utility of Cognates in Second-Language Acquisition. In: Alberta Modern Language Journal 17. 1979, 28—31.

Haschka 1989 = Christine Haschka: Zur Entwicklungsgeschichte der "faux amis"-Forschung. In: Lebende Sprachen 34. 1989, 148—152.

Hayward/Moulin 1984 = Timothy Hayward/ André Moulin: False Friends Invigorated. In: LEXeter '83 Proceedings. Papers from the International Conference on Lexicography at Exeter, 9—12 September 1983. Ed. Reinhard Hartmann. Tübingen 1984 (Lexicographica Ser. Mai. 1), 190—198.

Johnston 1941 = Marjorie C. Johnston: Spanish-English Cognates of High Frequency. In: Modern Language Notes 25. 1941, 405—417.

Juilland 1978 = Alphonse Juilland: Les 'faux amis' dans le vocabulaire de Céline. In: Stanford French Review 2. 1978, 323—349.

Keppler 1954 = K. Keppler: Misleading German Words. In: The German Quarterly 17. 1954.

Keppler 1957 = K. Keppler: Irreführende Fremdwörter. In: Lebende Sprachen 2. 1957.

Klein 1972 = Hans-Wilhelm Klein: Scheinentsprechungen bei französischen und deutschen Idiomatismen. Ein Beitrag zur Lexikographie. In: Der fremdsprachliche Unterricht 23. 1972, 44—51.

Koppenburg 1976 = Rudolf Koppenburg: Konvergenzen in einigen europäischen Kultursprachen. Ein deutsch-englisch-französisch-italienisch-spanisch-russischer Übersetzungsvergleich. Tübingen 1976.

Kudela 1980 = Jean Kudela: Processus de déétymonisation et typologie des "faux-amis" français en serbo-croate. In: Cahiers de l'Institut de linguistique de Louvain 6. 1980, 153—180.

Kühnel 1974 = H. Kühnel: Die französischen "faux amis" im deutschen Wortschatz. In: Deutsch als Fremdsprache 11. 1974, 115—117.

Le Huche 1975 = Jean-Marie Le Huche: 235 faux amis. In: Moderna Språk 69. 1975, 152—168.

Maillot 1981 = Jean Maillot: La traduction scientifique et technique. Sec. ed. Paris 1981.

Malone 1982 = Joseph L. Malone: False Friendship. In: Babel 28. 1982, 21—24.

Mikó 1983 = Marianne Mikó: Remarques sur quelques vrais "faux-amis" voire faux "vrais-amis". In: Contrastes. Hors Série A 2. Actes du Colloque de linguistique contrastive Français-Hongrois, 1976. 1983, 43—51.

Moers 1884 = Joseph Moers: Die Form- und Begriffsänderung der französischen Fremdwörter im Deutschen. Bonn 1884.

Müller 1981 = Bernhard Müller: Faux amis und mots-pièges — Eine kritische Zusammenstellung. In: Französisch heute 12. 1981, 250—258.

Neuhaus 1982 = Hans Joachim Neuhaus: Englisch-deutsche Wortentsprechungen. Plan für ein systematisches Wörterbuch. In: Sprachen und Computer. Festschrift zum 75. Geburtstag von Hans Eggers. Ed. H. Fix et al. Dudweiler 1982, 37—48.

Polo 1976 = José Polo: El Español como lengua extranjera, enseñanza de idiomas y traducción. Tres Calas Bibliográficas. Madrid 1976.

Ranson 1955 = Helen M. Ranson: Cognates, Deceptive and Otherwise. In: Hispania 38. 1955, 56—61.

Rasmussen 1978 = Jens Rasmussen: Essais d'une typologie des "faux amis" danois-français. In: Copenhagen School of Economic and Business Administration. Language Department 4. 1978, 7—22.

Reiner 1983 = Erwin Reiner: Etudes de linguistique dualiste. Essai sur la stylistique envisagée comme complément de la grammaire. Essai sur les "pénidentèmes" (les "faux amis" et les "vrais amis") de deux vocabulaires. Wien 1983.

Scatori 1932 = S. Scatori: Deceptive Cognates in Spanish. In: The Modern Language Journal 16. 1932, 395—401.

Schwarze 1979 = Christoph Schwarze: Réparer-Reparieren. A Contrastive Study. In: Semantics From Different Points of View. Ed. R. Bäuerle et al. Berlin 1979, 304—323.

Svobodová 1982 = Jitka Svobodová-Chmelová: Problèmes de la traduction. I. Interférences lexicales: internationalismes, faux internationalismes et les problèmes liés à leur traduction. Praha 1982.

Taylor 1976 = I. Taylor: Similarity Between French and English Words. In: Journal of Psycholinguistic Research 5. 1976, 85—94.

Thiemer 1979 = E. Thiemer: Die "falschen Freunde" als Erscheinung zwischensprachlicher und innersprachlicher Interferenz. In: Fremdsprachen 1979, 263—271 [Spanish].

Van Roey 1984 = Jacques Van Roey: Le traitement lexicographique des "mots-sosies" anglais-français. In: Cahiers de l'Institut de linguistique de Louvain 10. 1984, 287—303.

Wandruszka 1977 = Mario Wandruszka: "Falsche Freunde": Ein linguistisches Problem und seine Lösung. In: Festgabe für Julius Wilhelm zum 80. Geburtstag. Hrsg. v. H. Laitenberger. Wiesbaden 1977 (Zeitschrift für französische Sprache und Literatur. Beiheft Neue Folge, 5), 53—77.

Wotjak 1984 = Gerd Wotjak: Kongruenzen und Divergenzen im spanischen und deutschen Wortschatz. In: Beiträge zur romanischen Philologie 23. 1984, 109—152.

Adeline Gorbahn-Orme/
Franz Josef Hausmann, Erlangen
(Federal Republic of Germany)

305. Bilingual Learner's Dictionaries

1. Progress in Pedagogical Lexicography
2. Types of Bilingual Learner's Dictionaries and Their Functions
3. Alphabetical Versus Topical Arrangement of the Macro-Structure
4. Problems of Vocabulary Selection
5. The "Intensity" of the Micro-Structure
6. Bilingual Learner's Dictionaries: Past and Present
7. A Bilingual Learner's Dictionary for Encoding Tasks: Some Proposals
8. Selected Bibliography

1. Progress in Pedagogical Lexicography

The remarkable progress which has been made in pedagogical dictionary design over the last two decades has led to the compilation of a whole series of monolingual learner's dictionaries. Pedagogical lexicography, which is evidently trying to meet the needs of the foreign user more and more, seems to be well established within the wide range of different types of monolingual dictionaries, despite its minor deficiencies (cf. Zöfgen 1985a) and the lack of empirically supported information about the user's reference needs and reference skills. On the other hand, research in various countries on the use of dictionaries has confirmed that a vast majority of foreign language learners tend to turn to the bilingual rather than to the monolingual dictionary (cf. Baxter 1980, 333; Hartmann 1982; 1983, 197; Tomaszczyk 1983, 45 f; 1988, 294). Neither innovative practices which aim at designing the monolingual learner's dictionary as a tool for learning (Lamy 1985), nor instructions about how to make full use of the wealth of information provided by these dictionaries have so far been able to change this attitude. It is therefore all the more surprising that in a market saturated with language learning material a bilingual dictionary developed along the lines of pedagogical lexicography and especially designed for the foreign learner is, with the exception of only a few language pairs (cf. section 6), still not available.

2. Types of Bilingual Learner's Dictionaries and Their Functions

In the literature concerned with metalexicographical problems there is a widespread tendency to focus on alphabetically arranged learner's dictionaries. This priority has led to a neglect of those types of 'dictionaries' which have always, traditionally, followed explicitly pedagogical goals. The bilingual subject-matter (i.e. topically arranged) dictionaries deserve first mention; they contain

"einen begrenzten, lernenswert erscheinenden Wortschatz [...], der so arrangiert und kombiniert wird, wie er für das Vokabellernen am geeignetsten ist [a limited vocabulary evidently worth the learning effort and arranged in combinations appropriate for the learning of vocabulary]" (Lübke 1982, 22).

Apparently the chief emphasis lies on the arrangement and limitation of the vocabulary. Not least because we have empirical evidence that the alphabetical arrangement of items is detrimental rather than helpful to systematic learning, words are organized in the macro-structure according to semantically relevant associational fields (**thinking, touching and moving,** etc.). In this way the macro-structure reflects an important principle of progression in learning: that of relating what is known to what is yet to be learned. With entries thematically selected to utilize the associational relationships of meanings and to promote situationally appropriate speech behaviour such bilingual subject-matter dictionaries are well qualified to serve as **primary learning dictionaries** ["primäre Lernwörterbücher"] (Hausmann 1976, 102), which are, even if severely limited in range of entries (see below section 4), clearly different from dictionaries of basic vocabulary (see Art. 148). — Primary learning dictionaries can be divided into two groups with regard to the number of entries: (a) Selective ones (with up to 5,000 headwords) are generally used in school training. They are not only suited for use independent of particular textbooks at practically every stage of learning for the effective revision of the basic vocabulary of a given field, but also lend themselves to brushing up vocabulary already dealt with at an earlier stage of learning. Beginners can draw on them to extend and/or differentiate their vocabulary. (b) This final aspect comes to the fore in connection with extensive learning dictionaries, which are intended first and foremost for advanced learners or academic students of the language. With as many as 25,000 entries (Barnier/Delage 1974), they open up a special field, not just its vocabulary; they sometimes claim to serve the learner both as learning dictionary and as reference book.

In contrast to subject-matter dictionaries, which may be used without necessarily having a concrete textual or communicative context in mind, the use of an alphabetically arranged (learner's) dictionary presupposes a communicative situation, and requires skill in acknowledging lexical deficits as well as the ability to find a reference form for them. Since the look-up situation is generally initiated by a single problem, it is largely restricted to the micro-structure of a particular entry. It has not been possible to determine significant conditions of or motivation for using bilingual learner's dictionaries which may be said to differ from those which apply to general bilingual dictionaries, whether for use in the direction of the target (L1 → L2) or of the mother tongue (L2 → L1). Although we do not yet possess a full profile of needs as conditioned by the various activities of the learner, what characterizes the alphabetically arranged bilingual learner's dictionary most stringently is its selective macro-structure, on the one hand, and its generous use of contextualization in the micro-structure, especially in the case of words of high frequency, on the other.

The so-called 'translated versions' of monolingual learner's dictionaries of English, as attempted by the Chinese (Hornby et al. 1966), the Israelis (Hornby/Reif 1986), the Japanese and the Italians (cf. Tomaszczyk 1983, 47) deserve only limited mention here. Apart from the fact that native language 'glosses' of the lexicographical definitions meet the demands which have been made for monolingual learning dictionaries (cf. Zöfgen 1985 a, 68 ff), these so-called 'semi-bilingual' learner's dictionaries are insufficient in regard to the standards which ought to be set for a true bilingual learner's dictionary (see section 7).

3. Alphabetical Versus Topical Arrangement of the Macro-Structure

The organization of vocabulary in alphabetical order, which is recognized as a distinct disadvantage from the point of view of foreign language teaching, has undisputed advantages from the point of view of the lexicographer: Since the sequence is, in principle, predetermined, the arrangement of the entries is no longer dependent on the editor of the dictionary. This gives the macro-structure of bilingual learner's dictionaries a relatively unified appearance. The alphabetical order is only broken in the case of the Dictionnaire de l'anglais contemporain (DAC), which, for example, regroups derivatives; that is, it treats them as run-on entries thus transferring parts of the macro-structure into the micro-structure (cf. dictionary excerpt 305.2). — The situation is quite different if we start from the content/meaning of the words and if we try to arrange the macro-structure according to topics. Since the lexicographer cannot rely on a generally accepted system of categorization, all attempts to 'develop' the vocabulary systematically with reference to onomasiological principles seem to have something arbitrary about them. Hence the inclusion of a particular entry within a given subject group remains, in many cases, at the discretion of the editor. Fig. 305.1 illustrates in exemplary fashion the deep-seated problems (including those of an ontological nature) which arise in the overall organization of a **primary learning dictionary** and the variety of solutions offered towards an approach to language and world.

	Dictionaries	Categories (major groupings)	Subject areas	Subject groups	Degrees of "importance"	Words (Entries)
Selective English	Langenscheidt/E 1984	20	56	70	2	2500 (4000)
	Weis 1977 (1963)	—	13	73	2	4500
	Häublein/Jenkins 1987	—	21	98	2	4263 (5437)
	Pollmann 1982	—	38	201	—	4200 (5400)
	Berold 1987	—	9	46	4	4980
Selective French	Langenscheidt/F 1984	22	56	76	2	2500 (4000)
	Lübke 1975	7	19	270	—	3500 (4500)
	Nickolaus 1977 (1963)	—	13	73	2	4500
	Herrmann/Rauch 1987	6	35	171	2	4943 (6000)
Extensive English	Haase 1959	3	35	—	7	7 000
	Blass/Friederich 1956	—	30	35	—	10 000
	Fischer 1964	10	18	135	—	17 000
Extensive French	Vian 1961	—	10	86	2	8 000
	Borel 1949	—	52	300	—	10 000
	Fischer 1962	10	18	135	—	16 000
	Barnier/Delage 1974	—	20	80	—	25 000

Fig. 305.1: Overall organization of French and English subject-matter dictionaries (for German-speaking learners)

As supplementary explanations the following may be added: (a) The principle of a strictly topical arrangement of the macro-structure has not always been adhered to consistently. For example, the tendency is noticeable to separate and treat as an independent category the so-called grammatical words (e.g. Langenscheidt/E/F 1984, Herrmann/Rauch 1987). (b) Not only are the categories (major groupings), subject areas, and subject groups structured hierarchically in relation to each other, but the hierarchic arrangement applies to the subject groups among themselves as well. As the number of groups expands, so does the difficulty of maintaining a unified and consistent overall structure. Note that the principles of progression are many-sided in Pollmann 1982 and Lübke 1975 (opposition, synonymy, from general to specific, progression of actions, increasing intensity, etc.). It is, above all, those dictionaries that guarantee a manageable field size by limiting the number of entries within the subject groups, from 17 (Lübke 1975) to a maximum of 28 items (Herrmann/Rauch 1987), which offer a stimulus to learning. Langenscheidt/E/F 1984 with an average of 39 or Berold 1987 with an astonishing 108 units per subject group attempt to overcome the lack of sufficient differentiation by fixing two and four levels of learning (degrees of 'importance') respectively. Subject groups with 285 (Blass/Friederich 1956) or even 315 items (Barnier/Delage 1974) disregard all pedagogical principles and can no longer be justified under the aspect of systematic learning and controlled acquisition of lexical competence. (d) Appropriate speech behaviour demands paradigmatic learning in accordance with the organization of the 'world' as it is in the target language. For this reason the translational direction from L2 to L1 is mandatory for primary learning dictionaries. Fischer 1962, Fischer 1964, and Blass/Friederich 1956, which favour the opposite direction, as well as Barnier/Delage 1974 (which is primarily aimed at the French-speaking learner of German) all fail to meet the needs of the German-speaking L2 learner. (e) If subject-matter dictionaries are to be of use in situations in which the learner looks up an individual word, an alphabetical index has to be provided to make the macro-structure accessible. The selective subject-matter dictionaries respect this in principle; the extensive ones generally make do without an index. Haase 1959 is an exception to this rule; this work is exceptional in any case since the main body of the dictionary contains an alphabetical English-German word list whose foreign language part is given in an appendix according to subject areas. In addition to the alphabetical arrangement of the macro-structure Weis 1977, Nickolaus 1977 and Berold 1987 offer a German mother-tongue index. The latter is impressive above all because of its varied information about the use of words (cf. dictionary excerpt 305.1); in this way it combines the advantages of a learning dictionary with those of a frequency dictionary which is more or less adequate for productive language purposes.

There are also considerable differences as to the internal structure of the subject groups. In the comprehensive subject-matter dictionaries purely formal aspects usually predominate. In contrast to these the decisively selective ones published after 1980 — with the exception of Langenscheidt/E/F 1984 and Herrmann/Rauch 1987 — dispense not only with listings according to part of speech, but also with any semblance of alphabetical order. They do this by making an effort to project the structure of the vocabulary right into the subject groups as a network of semantically relevant paradigms (such as synonymy, antonymy, hyponymy, word families, etc.). — Consistent orientation along the lines of the content of a word involves numerous dangers, however, and is not completely unproblematic from a pedagogical point of view. First of all, no clearly organized micro-structure is likely to appear because of the variety of possible meaning and associational relations and because of their often complicated internal relationships. In those cases where pragmatic categories overlap with the paradigms of meaning and where these then expand into situational paradigms, there are innumerable cases where the attribution chosen does not make immediate sense to the learner (cf. for example *deserve* in the subject group **sports** [Häublein/Jenkins 1987, 208]). As a result it becomes increasingly difficult to grasp the principles of progression or to explain the unity of a subject group plausibly. Incidentally, we do not know whether learners can adopt the associations in the dictionary, or, indeed, whether they recognize them as paradigms at all. The pedagogical usefulness of topical arrangement can, in other words, turn out to be the contrary. Rather than providing help, the principle of consistent organization of the vocabulary according to paradigms of meaning can become an obstacle (cf. Hausmann 1976, 107 f).

4. Problems of Vocabulary Selection

In answering the question of how a "vocabulary list which is worth learning" should look and of how to evaluate the relative frequency of a word for selection in the macro-structure, 'pedagogical lexicography' seems to have taken a moderate position, one which may be reduced to the following thesis: a frequency list should not be regarded as equivalent to a basic vocabulary list; but it does represent an important basis for one (cf. also Hoffmann 1969, 49).

The concept of frequency does, actually, continue to play a central role in the controversy about the production of addressee-appropriate/user-oriented language inventories (for a summary in regard to French cf. Stammerjohann 1983, 176 ff). The fact that the validity of frequency studies has increasingly been called into question has to do with the shift of emphasis to the speech acts. By the way, criticism has been aimed less at the criterion of frequency itself than at the (statistical) appropriateness of the corpus or at the methodological weaknesses in connection with the exploitation of the data. As a result, the realization is gradually being accepted that the radical rejection of frequency as a criterion leads to methodological loss.

It is in this sense that the selective subject-matter dictionaries agree, on the one hand, that in addition to frequency of occurrence in textbooks, both a variety of minimal levels (such as the "Threshold Level" or "Niveau Seuil") and 'academic' sources — above all West's 'service list' (West 1953) for English and the studies on Français Fondamental (cf. Gougenheim 1958) — need to be considered. On the other hand, they agree that frequency alone is not a sufficient criterion for vocabulary selection and therefore has to be counterbalanced by considerations concerning: degree of familiarity, usefulness and accessibility in everyday situations, importance for the learner-user.

Two reasons for this are given: (α) Almost every available basic vocabulary list is, despite varying conceptions, based on the outdated frequency studies launched in the fifties for French or on the classical but antiquated general service list of West 1953 (an exception seems to be the use by Berold 1987 of Hindmarsh 1980). (β) There is no such thing as a thematically structured corpus; furthermore, the so-called "Aufbauwortschätze" [intermediate vocabularies] cannot be defended statistically with reference to the available frequency studies.

Methodologically speaking, such an approach to vocabulary selection can hardly be satisfying. It is obvious that any intuitive deletions or additions in these frequency lists which are not justified by some systematic procedure will increase the subjectivity already present in them (only Lübke 1975 provides for a certain degree of transparency by at least marking the entries which were not contained in Français fondamental). This holds to an even greater degree for the less strongly selective learner's dictionaries and for the alphabetically arranged ones. Both types simply mention in passing that 'frequency' and 'utility' have been taken into consideration, but give no further hints as to the methodological and empirical criteria used in vocabulary selection. — However, the picture is uneven not only in a qualitative (criteria for selection), but also in a quantitative sense (size and grading of the vocabulary). Structural parallels do not become evident until an overall comparison is made between topically and alphabetically arranged dictionaries: the (alphabetically arranged) bilingual learner's dictionaries developed in the USSR for the foreign learner of Russian have from 3,000 to 8,500 entries for those in which Russian is the target language (L1 → Russian); in the direction from Russian to the mother tongue (Russian → L1) they cover a vocabulary of from 9,000 to 16,000 words (cf. survey in Denisov 1977, 14). As demonstrated in Fig. 305.1, this corresponds more or less to the quantitative variations in subject-matter dictionaries. The DAC, which is intended for French-speaking learners of English, conforms totally to this pattern with its stock of 14 200 alphabetically ordered headwords (5 200 main entries [= vocabulaire essentiel], 9 000 secondary entries [= vocabulaire complémentaire]) and a supplementary list of 800 specialized terms.

5. The "Intensity" of the Micro-Structure

Words such as *nutmeg* or *chives* are peripheral rather than central to vocabulary. They belong to the so-called nomenclature, that part of the lexis of a language which is largely determined by the nature of the world, by things themselves. For this reason word for word equivalents from the area of **food** such as German *Nelke* = English *clove* are unobjectionable. This probably explains why the extensive subject-matter dictionaries, above all, which contain a high proportion of specialized words and nomenclature (e.g. flora and fauna), are so often confined to only one L2 equivalent in their micro-structure. Selective subject-matter dictionaries, in contrast, have to do with nomenclatures only secondarily (cf. Pollmann 1982 with, for example, the subject groups **occupations** or **animals**); the focus is on that part of the vocabulary in which the world is primarily organized according to differences imposed by the language and in which English/German and German/English equivalents such as *cook* = kochen and *kochen* = *cook, boil* (or French/German and German/French *sain* = *gesund* and *gesund* = *sain, en bonne santé*) are likely to cause confusion for learners. At such points there must be clarification beyond mere equivalents. One possibility for limiting the scope of an equivalent may be accomplished by attributing the various senses of a headword to various topics (*accident* = German *Unfall* to the area **traffic**; *accident* = German *Zufall* to the area **existence**).

The arrangement of entries according to their conceptual affinities has, however, some drawbacks as well. Unfortunately, the semantic unity of a word is often lost in this way: see, for example, Berold 1987, where *belief* is linked with the topic **Thinking and Learning**, whereas *belief (in God)* is to be found under **Education and Religion.**

When there is polysemy within a single subject group, explicit limitations on the context of use have to take over the function of disambiguation (for example *to be killed* **in** *an accident, a road accident/to meet s.o.* **by** *accident*). All of the more recent selective subject-matter dictionaries endeavour to use contextualization to distinguish aspects of equivalence and to prevent erroneous use in the context of a complete sentence.

The most significant effort in this direction (besides Lübke 1975) has been undertaken by Pollmann 1982, who proposes up to five syntagmatic combinations (preferably collocations and syntactic patterns) for each pair of equivalents. In the variety of information about the correct use of words he is, however, outdistanced by Berold 1987, who — even though he provides explicit information on valency in the English index — does not attain the wealth of syntagmatic information which Lübke 1975 and Pollmann 1982 have; his strength lies in adding paradigmatic information (synonymy, antonymy) as well as treating intralingual and interlingual interference and supplying so-called "remember boxes", illustrations, and a user-friendly lay-out of the pages, which enhance the didactic value of the book.

When it is a question of understanding situations and expressing thoughts in the foreign language, the weaknesses and limitations of learner's dictionaries of this type soon become highly evident.

To prevent any misunderstanding it should, first of all, be pointed out that a lack of skill in communicating is not always a sign of a limited vocabulary. Meaningful improvement in the area of productive language competence is dependent both on a sure knowledge of the variety of uses of the words and on a confident mastery of the syntactic patterns of a language. Since foreign language teaching in the schools neglects precisely the words of high frequency as far as their full range of meanings is concerned, it is this aspect which the learner's dictionaries should be emphasizing. It is therefore all the more unfortunate that the syntagmatic information in the subject-matter dictionaries is frequently not sufficient to prevent erroneous constructions such as * *je suis sain* (Lübke 1975), * *The water is cooking* (Berold 1987). Nowhere will the learner-user find such common expressions as *to attach importance to, to tackle a problem, to overcome difficulties, to make objections, to assume responsibility, to pass (adopt) a law on*

CATCH	... a cold	sich erkälten	COME TO	... an agreement	zu einer Einigung kommen
	... a bus/train	den Bus/Zug erreichen		... a conclusion	zu einer Folgerung gelangen
				... a decision	eine Entscheidung erreichen
DO	... one's best	sein Bestes geben		... somebody a favour	jemandem einen Gefallen tun
	... one's duty	seine Pflicht tun		... one's homework	seine Hausaufgabe(n) machen
				... somebody a service	jemandem einen Dienst erweisen

☐	to hear *v* [hɪə] heard [hɜːd] heard [hɜːd]	I couldn't ~ a sound.	hören
☐	to listen *v* [lɪsn]	Are you ~ing (**to** the music)?	zuhören
	noise *n* [nɔɪz]	There was so much ~ in the pub that I couldn't hear him.	Lärm
☐	noisy *adj* ['nɔɪzɪ]	≽ full of noise; ►◄ quiet	lärmend, geräuschvoll
☐	sound *n* [saʊnd]	Light travels faster than ~.	Ton, Klang, Schall
	quiet *adj* ['kwaɪət]	≽ with little noise	ruhig, leise
	silent *adj* ['saɪlənt]	►► quiet, calm; ►◄ loud, noisy	still, leise
	loud *adj* [laʊd]	►◄ quiet	laut
	aloud *adv* [ə'laʊd]	Shall I read ~ or silently?	laut
☐	to ring *v* [rɪŋ] rang [ræŋ] rung [rʌŋ]	The telephone was ~ing.	läuten
☐	to notice *v* ['nəʊtɪs]	≽ to see, hear, recognize	bemerken
	notice *n* ['nəʊtɪs]	Don't take any ~ of what he says. (≽ pay any attention to) The ~ on the wall says "NO PARKING"	Notiz, Beachtung Hinweis(schild)
☐	smell *n* [smel]	Roses have a sweet ~.	Geruch
	to smell *v* [smel]	I could ~ that the meat wasn't fresh. That man ~s **of** tobacco.	riechen (nach)
☐	to taste *v* [teɪst]	The cook ~d the soup. This soup doesn't ~ **of** anything.	kosten, versuchen schmecken (nach)
☐	taste *n* [teɪst]	Sugar has a sweet ~.	Geschmack

guesthouse	**Pension**		pension ['penʃn]	Rente
corridor	**Flur**	*Keep apart!*	floor [flɔː]	Stockwerk; Fußboden
trade	**Handel**		handle ['hændl]	Griff
button, key	**Taste**		taste [teɪst]	Geschmack

Dictionary excerpt 305.1: The micro-structure of a selective subject-matter dictionary (from: Berold 1987, 64)

sthg. This may be because the headword is missing (in Pollmann 1982, the following, for example, are not to be found: *to* beg, *to* bet, danger, difficulty, door, importance, problem, victory). Or it may be because they have been sacrificed to the limitations dictated by the micro-structure. An additional factor is that, in general, differentiation of meaning has not been carried far enough (cf. the entries *to* give, *to* get, *to* tell). As a result idiomatic and fixed expressions as well as figurative meanings are badly underrepresented (cf., for example, *to set an example, to be at stake, to take sthg. for granted,* etc.).

What we glean from these few critical remarks is the conviction that primary learning dictionaries do not ensure communicative success and need to be supplemented by secondary learning (learner's) dictionaries [sekundäre Lernwörterbücher] (Hausmann 1976, 102). These are primarily arranged alphabetically, it is true, but they have a tremendous advantage in the way they exploit the micro-structure by going far beyond the subject-matter dictionaries in quantity and, qualitatively, by orientating the whole of their content according to the needs of foreign language learners. One such serious and promising attempt to turn the lexicographical article into a complete learning package is the English-French dictionary by Dubois-Charlier (DAC). This

tell [tel] v., **-s** [-z], **told** [təʊld] ~ *sb sthg,* ~ *that,* ~ *wh-* ou ~ *sthg to sb Has she told her mother the news?*(Elle a annoncé la nouvelle à sa mère?) • *You must always tell the truth to me.*(Tu dois toujours me dire la vérité.) • *Tell us a story/your name.*(Racontez-nous une histoire/Dites-nous votre nom.) • *The postman told me that he had been ill.*(Le facteur m'a dit qu'il avait été malade.) • *God, he's not really going to tell her what he thinks of her, is he?*(Malheur, il ne va quand même pas lui dire ce qu'il pense d'elle, si?) • ~ *sb about sthg Did she tell him about her dream/Mark?*(Elle lui a parlé de son rêve/de Mark?) // ~ *sb to do,* ~ *sb wh- to do Then the doctor told me to get undressed.*(Puis le médecin m'a dit de me déshabiller.) • *Please tell them where to go.*(S'il te plaît, dis-leur où ils doivent aller.) // ~ *wh-/wh- to do How can you tell when the oven's hot enough?*(Comment fais-tu pour savoir si le four est assez chaud?) • *I couldn't tell which road to take.*(Je ne savais pas quel chemin prendre.) ~ *sthg/sb from sthg/sb Surely anybody can tell fresh vegetables from tinned!*(Oh quand même, n'importe qui peut distinguer les légumes frais des légumes en conserve!) **tell sb off** *If he's late again, you'll have to tell him off.*(S'il est en retard encore une fois, il faudra que tu le grondes.) **tell on sb** *The effort is beginning to tell on them.*(La fatigue commence à se voir/se faire sentir/se marquer sur leurs visages.) // *Please don't tell on us.*(Je t'en prie, ne nous dénonce/cafarde pas!)
◆ *I'll tell you what*(j'ai une idée, voilà ce qu'on devrait faire), *I tell you*(je t'assure, je te le répète), *I told you so*(je t'avais prévenu, je te l'avais bien dit), *You're telling me!*(C'est à moi que tu dis ça?!), *you can never tell*(on ne sait jamais), etc. ◆
-teller, cf. *table, fortune,* etc.; **telling** adj.(révélateur ǀǀ efficace, bien asséné); **telltale** adj. et n.(révélateur, indiscret, qui dévoile des secrets).

Dictionary excerpt 305.2: Entry **tell** (from DAC 1982, 624)

model is based on the same principles as those which have been implemented in the Dictionnaire du français langue étrangère (DFLE), a monolingual dictionary for French as a foreign language.

The characteristic features of the micro-structure are as follows (cf. Dubois 1981, 247): (a) The entries are organized on syntactic (and only secondarily on semantic) principles, and the syntactic patterns and the semantic distinctions are clearly shown. Each construction and each semantic aspect corresponds to a different meaning in French. (b) Whereas most of the bilingual dictionaries are patently aimed at translators or users occasionally looking up a difficult or unfamiliar word, the DAC concentrates on the active use of English which can best be conveyed by means of commonly occurring expressions and reference to everyday situations. Accordingly, it emphasizes collocations and fixed expressions which are found in realistic speech and demonstrates their use in entire sentences (sometimes imitating real life situations with a "minidialogue"). All the examples are translated into French completely. (c) Usage labels and information on stylistic levels, fixed phrases, derivatives, synonyms, etc. are separated from the example sentences and form a distinct part of the entry. This 'commentary' contains what the author calls 'complementary vocabulary'. The explanations of meaning are generally limited to the listing of a French equivalent (there may be some additional information about pronunciation, grammar, etc., as necessary). (d) Moreover, the dictionary has a French-English reverse, i.e. an index of 10,000 French words with translations and cross-references back to the English-French section.

With this carefully thought-out comprehensive concept, which includes a useful treatment of the function words (cf. the entries for **any, by, if**), the DAC is way ahead of the competition. Not even the German-Russian dictionary by Ivanova/Liperovskaja 1966 can dispute its exceptional position, though the latter not only employs a transparent micro-structure, but also emphasizes the syntagmatic dimension in its subtitle and, indeed, keeps that promise in the examples it chooses.

6. Bilingual Learner's Dictionaries: Past and Present

The idea and conception of French-German subject-matter dictionaries can be traced back to 1847, the year in which Karl Ploetz's Vocabulaire systématique (Ploetz 1847) appeared. In the year 1913 this classic compilation of words and phrases went through its twenty-second printing; however, Gillot/ Krüger 1912 had, in the meantime, appeared as a serious competitor. The German-French dictionary by Du Cloux 1678, which already employed the principle of topical arrangement, also deserves to be mentioned; it designated itself explicitly as a "learning dictionary" for the young people of Strasbourg. The idea of learning vocabulary with a (bilingual) dictionary (cf. Art. 23) is a distinctively older tradition. In fact, throughout its development, from the very beginning on, the history of bilingual dictionaries reveals a strong didactic orientation, in which "the chief motive underlying lexicography up to 1600 was to assist students of foreign languages" (Mathews 1933, 14). The 'vocabularies' played an important role in this connection. These were a very popular type of 'dictionary', which flourished from the Anglo-Saxon period until the nineteenth century and in which the items are not arranged alphabetically, but in related groups, according to specific subjects such as the earth, parts of the body, etc. It is this kind of compilation of vocabulary which stands in the long tradition of medieval topical (or 'class') glossaries, the so-called "summae" (or "nominales"). Throughout the Middle Ages they served the purposes of practical teaching, i. e. the translation of Latin texts and the exegesis of theological writings. Numerous examples from the German language area (cf. Püschel 1986 with extensive bibliography), from the French area (cf. Quemada 1967, 361 ff), and from the Italian area (cf. Tancke 1984) confirm without any doubt that this medieval tradition also persisted on the continent and that the type of dictionary which Withals in England first presented in 1553, viz. placing the vernacular before the Latin, began to displace other types by the middle of the 16th century at the latest (for an overview of the medieval and Renaissance vocabularies with English cf. the pioneering work of Starnes 1954 and Stein 1985). The vocabularies are, however, not the only books which are designed with the intention of building up a stock of vocabulary and which gave vogue to the topical arrangement of entries. Throughout the 17th and the 18th century most of the bilingual teaching materials devoted a great part of their space to the acquisition of vocabulary according to subject groups (cf. Schröder 1984, 309 ff; Düwell 1986, 275 ff). Thus they contributed to the maintenance of the tradition of 'class' glossaries into the 19th century and to the establishment of this practice as a lexicographical as well as a pedagogical principle for the teaching and learning of foreign languages. — This brief historical review suggests that the remote ancestors of topically arranged vocabularies for learning purposes are to be found in the glossaries of the early Middle Ages and therefore go back to the very beginnings of English lexicography, and, indeed, the lexicography of other European languages (cf. Hüllen 1989 a; 1989 b). A long line runs from Aelfric, who compiled a Latin-Anglo-Saxon vocabulary as early as the 10th century, via the vocabularies of the Renaissance, which frequently supplemented their alphabetical parts with topically arranged glossaries, down to the learning dictionaries of the 20th century, such as, for example, Weis 1977 (1963) and Nickolaus 1977 (1963), which combine an alphabetically arranged basic vocabulary with a topically arranged intermediate one. The success of both of these word lists from the early sixties for English-German and for French-German respectively quickly led to a series of similarly conceived works for other language pairs, all of which are still popular despite clear methodological weaknesses. For native speakers of German the following additional works are available: Giovannelli 1977 (Italian), Amorim-Braun 1972 (Portuguese), Vogt 1967 (Russian), Heupel 1977 (Spanish). For German as a foreign language the following have appeared since 1980: Oehler 1980a (for speakers of English), Oehler 1980b (→ French), Oehler et al. 1982 (→ Italian), Navarro et al. 1982 (→ Spanish), Aktaş/Meyer-Ingwersen 1983 (→ Turkish).

As stressed in section 4, frequency has been a criterion in learner's dictionaries throughout the 20th century. If the vocabulary used in the topical glossaries and teaching manuals from the 16th to the 19th century is compared with that of the basic word lists which were compiled using West 1953 and Français fondamental, then the suspicion is not altogether ungrounded that the results of modern frequency analyses were slowly being arrived at on an intuitive didactic basis. In any case it has already been pointed out that the macro-structures of the primary learning dictionaries are, overall, only relatively general approximations to the standards provided by the frequency lists (cf. Schröder 1984, 307 f).

For some time now there have been increasing signs that this conception will, in the long run, be replaced by the thematically organized basic and intermediate word list. Herrmann/Rauch 1987 and Häublein/Jenkins 1987, the only representatives of this approach to date, attach more importance to the syntagmatic dimension of a word; nevertheless, they are facing growing competition (cf. section 5). The influence of the foreign language research of the seventies and eighties is being felt here.

This survey can be rounded off with two extreme examples which also claim to present vocabulary according to pedagogically meaningful fields of association. At the lowest level of associational power there is the etymological principle, which appears in the grouping of words according to the historical root (cf. Fischer 1958). The opposite pole is represented by Leyton 1960, which combines the principle of topical arrangement of words with the presentation of vocabulary in narrative form.

The noteworthy change in the microstructural treatment of words (information on the use of a word, illustrations, etc.) and the LSP component in the extensive subject-matter dictionaries are, however, by no means without historical models (for further details cf. Starnes/Noyes 1946, 200 ff). This means that the new generation of learning dictionaries, which at first glance seem to be extremely innovative, takes up, in reality, a tradition of long standing, which they can hardly be conscious of. —

Since glossaries and vocabularies cannot be reckoned among dictionaries in the proper sense, the picture is fundamentally different when this historical review is restricted to alphabetically arranged dictionaries. Although most of the early multilingual dictionaries were at least in part designed to relieve the school-master of some of his duties, it is not possible to talk of bilingual pedagogical lexicography before the sixties of this century. It is true that Ščerba advocated a user-oriented typology of bilingual dictionaries as far back as 1936 (cf. Kromann et al. 1984, 166 ff), and it is also true that he argued the case for pedagogical dictionaries a few years later (cf. Ščerba 1940); in his rudimentary sketch of a theory of lexicography there was, however, no mention of the possibilities and, above all, of the form of such dictionaries. This explains why it was still such a long way from these initial thoughts to the often overlooked efforts of Russian lexicography in compiling bilingual learner's dictionaries for Russian as a second or foreign language since about 1960. While sporadic attempts have been made in various countries at developing a bilingual learners's dictionary, the Soviet Union was not only the first but also the only country which has given "sustained attention" to such dictionaries (Tomaszczyk 1981, 288 f).

Between 1961 and 1970 no fewer than twenty-four bilingual learner's dictionaries were published treating eleven different languages (cf. detailed bibliography in Denisov 1977, 13 ff). With the exception of German, which, originally, had to make do with an 'active' (contextual) dictionary (Ivanova/Liperovskaja 1966) — the Russian-German counterpart of which has only recently been published (Ivanova/Schenk 1987) —, all the important European languages were, from the beginning, represented with one encoding (or 'active': L1→ Russian) and one decoding (or 'passive': Russian→ L1) dictionary each. For English there is Folomkina/Weiser 1962 and Lapidus/Ševcova 1962; for French, there is Kobrina et al. 1963 and Zaliznjak 1961; for Italian, we can rely on Čerdanceva 1967 and Rozental' 1966; and finally, the Spanish speaking learners have at their disposal Gisbert/Nižskij 1962 and Nogueira/Turover 1962. These dictionaries meet the mark didactically inasmuch as they take adequate account not only of the learners' native tongue but also of their productive and receptive skills, while making the difference between encoding and decoding dictionaries clear thanks to the varying number of entries which they provide (cf. section 4). Nevertheless, there is still much left to be desired, especially concerning information about the use of words.

One of the most radical attempts to integrate pedagogy and lexicography and to do justice to the needs of the learner in regard to a full treatment of essential vocabulary is the French DAC, the merits of which have already been enumerated sufficiently (cf. section 5). It is according to the standard set by this unique example of a genuine bilingual learner's dictionary, above all in the syntagmatic area, that the contextual examples of the Arab World Dictionary (English-Arab), already announced in 1984 (cf. Kharma 1984), will have to be measured. In conclusion we may observe that many of the dictionaries which designate themselves as 'learner's dictionary' (for example the Arab-English dictionary by Salmoné 1972 or its English-Arab counterpart by Steingass 1960) do not show a pedagogical orientation either in the macro-structure or in the micro-structure.

7. A Bilingual Learner's Dictionary for Encoding Tasks: Some Proposals

"Dictionaries should be designed with a special set of users in mind and for their specific needs" (Householder 1967, 279).

This well-known recommendation issued at the end of the classic Conference on Lexicography (1960) marked a turning point in the history of lexicography insofar as it laid the foundations for the user perspective. For the alphabetically arranged bilingual dictionary the user-orientation entails at least two consequences: it must necessarily give proper consideration to the language base of its users and to the directionality of the language pair concerned (i.e. L1 → L2 or L2 → L1). In addition, there is agreement that the dictionary has more narrowly defined purposes to fulfill than has been claimed by traditional bilingual ones. An appropriate limitation of purpose would primarily have to account for the type of activity (i.e. reading comprehension vs. writing/translating). As a result every language pair requires four bilingual dictionaries (two each for encoding and for decoding).

A fourth parameter, namely the type of information provided by the dictionary (grammar, collocations, etc.), has to do with the difference between specialized and non-specialized dictionaries.

Theoretically, all four parameters could be combined with one another in any fashion. Even though it is not economic grounds alone which speak against the resulting diversification and specialization in the lexicographic landscape, the type of specialized learner's dictionary as represented, for example, by the bilingual valency dictionary of French for German learners, and as outlined by Zöfgen 1982, is justified on its own merits.

From these explanatory comments it follows that the orientation of a dictionary according to the needs of specific user-groups is a necessary, but by no means a sufficient condition for pedagogical lexicography. The demands to be made of bilingual learner's dictionaries developed along the lines of pedagogical lexicography include (1) that they take account of the specific requirements of foreign language teaching/acquisition; (2) that they assess the skills of the user realistically and therefore select the language material as well as linguistic information according to the level of proficiency of the users; (3) that they organize (where possible on the grounds of learning psychology) the whole of the lexicographical text according to relevant criteria from the teaching of vocabulary and from error analysis.

However, since there are no definitive principles in regard to language input or output nor in respect to the way in which lexicographical information is processed or retained, the realization of this final demand seems to be facing some insuperable obstacles. This concern is based in part on the mistaken assumption about the place and role of the dictionary in an integrated learning concept. It is fundamentally correct that using a bilingual dictionary is a specific type of communicative situation characterized by a competency gap between L1 and L2. The lexicographer must, therefore, anticipate this carefully because the language problems of the user cannot be dealt with discursively. Although this is true, too much would be demanded of lexicography if it were expected to provide a model of the highly complex thought processes involved in establishing equivalencies or, even more, the structure of the mental lexicon. All the same, there is no need for a pedagogical dictionary to give up its function as a learning aid or, in certain situations, as a "silent language teacher" (Stein 1984, 126). The achievement of such goals has not, however, been made easier by the fact that our knowledge about the situations of dictionary use has not increased in recent years nor by the fact that a theory of the bilingual learner's dictionary is, at best, only beginning to appear in the barest of outlines.

Against this background the lexicographer is well advised to restrict himself for the time being to the structural features which are likely to qualify a dictionary as potentially pedagogical. The following remarks are only a modest attempt to assemble some of these relevant components and to develop a framework within which research could be encouraged: (1) Bilingual learner's dictionaries should not only be modelled and based on monolingual pedagogical ones; over and above this, they should constitute an integral part of a language teaching programme. As Snell-Hornby 1987 has convincingly argued, the learner should not be confronted too early with independent reference works in which the items do not apply to a teaching text (as glossaries in teaching manuals, however, do), but in which they remain remote and abstract. The stage at which a bilingual dictionary is most valuable is reached when learners have a basic command of the foreign language, one which allows them to make the necessary comparisons between the two language systems. It goes without saying that the ultimate goal of such a teaching programme continues to be that of acquiring the ability to use monolingual dictionaries, including unabridged academic ones. (2) Most of the bilingual (school) dictionaries focus on the headword, for which they provide a selection of undefined, syntagmatically insufficiently described equivalents. Dictionaries of this kind may be useful for purposes of analysis and reading comprehension. They will, of course, hardly be able to close the gap to the pedagogical decoding dictionary needed for the intermediate learner. A full-sized L2-L1 dictionary — especially if supplemented by a monolingual learner's dictionary — will, nevertheless, serve the more advanced learner well in his attempts to identify unfamiliar meanings. Where the need for a pedagogical bilingual dictionary is most pressing and most urgent, however, is in the field of productive, truly 'generative' L1-L2 dictionaries, which are the only reference aids available when culture-specific vocabulary is involved (Tomaszczyk 1983, 47).

L2-L1 learner's dictionaries which are supplied with an L1-L2 index and cross-references to the main body of the dictionary (like the DAC) occupy a peculiarly hybrid position inasmuch as they try to perform both decoding and encoding tasks. It is obvious that such "semi-bi-directional" learner's dictionaries are not only less convenient (requiring the learner to find the proper equivalent in different articles instead of relying on clearly differentiated meanings and contextualizations within one article); they are also insufficiently suited to act as reference books for active language use.

(3) We are accustomed to judging the quality of bilingual dictionaries exclusively according to the number of items included. Recent studies show that this is the basic attitude taken by the average dictionary user; pupils, more than others, are not only prepared to put blind trust in a handy pocket dictionary with a large macro-structure (and, as a logical consequence, a poorly developed micro-structure), they also prefer ones like this to all others (cf. most recently Hernández 1989, 122). There is obviously a great potential not only for deliberate instruction in dictionary use, but also for the development of "better" dictionary users. After all, it is one of the basic principles of pedagogical lexicography that instead of trying to give equal coverage to a maximum number of entries, a learner's dictionary should treat the essential vocabulary as intensively as possible (according to the level of proficiency of the user). Such selective treatment should devote particular attention to the function words and to "culture-bound elements" (cf. Tomaszczyk 1984). While current school dictionaries proudly proclaim that they contain 100,000 words, pedagogical L1-L2 dictionaries of the same length will best range between 5,000 and 6,000 entries at an intermediate level; for reading comprehension, in contrast, the number of entries may be limited to 15,000 headwords at this level (for discussion cf. Zöfgen 1985 a, 24 ff).

(4) In the metalexicographical literature there is broad consensus that the generally accepted principles (i. e. the active-passive-principle, alphabetization, frequency, etc.) have far-reaching consequences for the presentation and organization of the micro-structure of a bilingual dictionary. Although we are far from certain about what the microstructural features of a learner's dictionary should be, suggestions like those made about the internal structure of bilingual dictionaries at the Copenhagen Colloquium, 1986 (cf. report by Baunebjerg Hansen 1988), are of fundamental relevance and great significance for this type of dictionary. This applies, on the one hand, to problems of the labelling of words and of the ordering of the micro-structure. It holds, on the other hand, for questions concerning the elicitation and selection of data, too. Syntagmatic and paradigmatic phenomena as well as the error analytic part of a lexicographic article, in contrast, demand finer distinctions. —

In a bilingual learner's dictionary which is intended for language encoding the following **syntagmatically relevant features** are in need of further exploration and detailed consideration: (a) Grammar codes: When there is grammatical-syntactical incongruency between L1 and L2, explicit information about the characteristics of the constructions in L2 is an absolute must; this information should always be illustrated with an example. As far as the grammar code itself is concerned, the description may be so elaborate as to be unserviceable; the lexicographer must therefore adopt a "transparent" type of notation, one which the user can transfer to a general statement about sentence structure without really knowing or being obliged to acquaint himself with the concept of grammar that lies behind it (see suggestions in Zöfgen 1982, 1985 b; Nguyen 1986). (b) Collocations and example sentences: When it is a question of translating collocations such as German *eine vernichtende Niederlage erleiden* (English *to suffer a crushing defeat;* French *subir (essuyer) une défaite écrasante),* the same procedures are in principle valid which apply to monolingual dictionaries (Hausmann 1988, 148 ff). In order to save space in a rational way it is advisable, as a rule, to list the collocations under the "base" or node (in this case *Niederlage)* and not under the collocates (*erleiden; vernichtend*). Along with the grammar codes given this list of lexical combinations makes up the explicit part of the syntagmatic information. In an active learner's dictionary these "patterns", which guide in the generation of sentences, need to be rounded out by implicit information about the proper use of a word; this should be accomplished with example sentences (and their complete translation into the foreign language). Examples should be chosen so as to enable the learner both to recognize grammatical usage and to situate the item in a context which highlights particular problems of its contextualization and of its pragmatic effect. As this type of dictionary is concerned with what is common to all speakers of a language, the examples ought to present the information in contexts of activity which illustrate use in the commonest types of everyday situations. In this sense they are, above all, "prototypes of *current* language use" (Snell-Hornby 1987, 167). There is no need to stress that 'made-up examples' are clearly to be preferred to 'quoted examples', which are seldom prototypical and which are usually inappropriate as instances for generalization (cf. Nikula 1986; Zöfgen 1986). (c) Idioms and fixed phrases: In most cases, there is no stringent way to alphabetize idioms and fixed phrases nor are there clear criteria for categorizing them. This methodological lack means that only a small percentage of users can profit from the rich idiomatic material contained in dictionaries. In order to find expressions such as German *(bei etwas) seine Hand im Spiel haben* in the microstructure, the pedagogical dictionary (i.e. the learner's dictionary) will have to list it under different entries and to equip its macro-structure with a sufficient number of cross-references. For sub-entries under a particular headword it might be recommendable to add all the idioms separately at the end of the article (on the model of the DAC).

Paradigmatic treatment: Because of the common practice of providing several equivalents for each item, paradigmatic treatments have always had a secure place in bilingual dictionaries. In pedagogical dictionaries, synonyms have to be defined in terms of the context in which they can be substituted for the item or the meaning of a headword in question. They should, therefore, as a matter of principle, only be used as variants (with the appropriate label, if any) which are a part of a collocation or an example sentence (= phrasal synonymy). In a decoding dictionary such a system is, however, only useful if the synonym is integrated in the overall conception, that is, if all the synonyms employed also appear in the macro-structure (with cross-references).

L1-L2 interference: Foreign language teachers are well acquainted with the (now empirically established) fact that the production of a text in a foreign language is greatly influenced by the mother tongue, even among advanced learners. So far all attempts to reduce the dominance of L1 in foreign language teaching or, more yet, to eliminate the native language altogether have, to date, been failures. Even the hypothesis of error analysts that negative transfer is of secondary significance for language acquisition may be regarded as refuted. More recent investigations have shown that a high proportion of lexical and grammatical errors are due to negative transfer (cf. Tomaszczyk 1983, 44). For the pedagogical L1-L2 dictionary these findings entail the obligation to treat interference between native language and target language in an appropriately salient fashion by devoting a separate 'commentary' to these questions (as well as to that part of the vocabulary which is specific to the source language). The metalinguistic information should, needless to say, always be given in the language of the user.

In summary we may say that the organization of the content and the formal arrangement of the dictionary article must be governed by the principle that not only the linguistic information, but also the means of access provided to it must correspond to the limited reference skills of an intermediate learner. — In conclusion, only a few of the numerous unanswered questions and unsolved problems with which the pedagogical lexicographer will have to struggle in the future can be raised: (a) If we stick to the demand that the bilingual learner's dictionary is to be consciously included in the process of language acquisition, we necessarily have to make efforts "to adjust the lexical substance [...] to the social role of the learner-user" (Hartmann 1988, 227). To what extent can this postulate be coordinated with the criterion of frequency, which has been recognized as absolutely necessary for questions of vocabulary selection? (b) We cannot deny that the proposals made here are largely based on assumptions, which means that further studies will have to assess the validity of the design outlined above. For the time being it is hardly possible to decide to what extent empirical investigations into the reference needs and reference skills of dictionary users (as Hartmann 1989 has once again demanded) are going to lead to new insights. Neither is it possible to say whether these investigations are going to show the way to a fundamental change in regard to the nature and content of pedagogical dictionaries or whether they only result in partial corrections of the concept sketched out here. (c) There is good reason to believe that (bilingual) learner's dictionaries may take their rightful place in the process of language learning. Nevertheless, as long as so many foreign language learners continue to be so completely unaware of their language deficits and as long as their insufficient reference skills make them incapable of using bilingual dictionaries appropriately, this assumption turns out to be quite a daring hypothesis. Yet even if it proves to be well-founded, we must not close our eyes to the fact that a (L1-L2) pedagogical dictionary is subject to severe limitations: It is not intended for the (professional) translator and it is far from being able to answer all the questions its users have for it. Finally, there can be no doubt "that language learning involves much more than the extensive use of reference books" (Tomaszczyk 1987, 147).

8. Selected Bibliography

8.1. Dictionaries

Aktaş/Meyer-Ingwersen 1983 = Grund- und Aufbauwortschatz Deutsch-Türkisch. Bearb. des türkischen Teils von Ahmet Aktaş und Johannes Meyer-Ingwersen. München 1983 [XXI, 340 p.].

Amorim-Braun 1972 = Grund- und Aufbauwortschatz Portugiesisch, bearb. von Maria Luisa Amorim-Braun. Stuttgart 1972 (1987) [207 p.].

Barnier/Delage 1974 = J[oseph] Barnier/E[dmond] Delage/Raymond-Fred Niemann: Les mots allemands [Deutsch/Französisch nach Sachgruppen]. Paris 1974 [335 p.; first ed.: J. Barnier/ E. Delage: Les mots allemands et les locutions allemandes groupés d'après le sens, 1939, VI + 282 p.].

Berold 1987 = Klaus Berold: Words you can use. Lernwörterbuch in Sachgruppen. Berlin 1987 [VI, 206 p.].

Blass/Friederich 1956 = Armin Blass/Wolf Friederich: Englischer Wortschatz in Sachgruppen. 11. überarb. Aufl. München 1976 [144 p., 1st ed. by Armin Blass 1956].

Borel 1949 = Pierre Borel: Vocabulaire systématique français-allemand. 2e éd. Berne 1959 [171 p.; 1st ed. 1949].

Čerdanceva 1967 = T[amara] Z[acharovna] Čerdanceva: [Ital'jansko-russkij učebnyj slovar'] Dizionario pratico italiano-russo. Contiene 8 500 voci. Compilato da T. Čerdanceva, include come appendice un compendio di grammatica russa preparato da A. Zaliznjak. 3 ed. stereotipata. Mosca 1984 [544 p.; 1st ed. 1967].

DAC = Françoise Dubois-Charlier [et al.]: Dictionnaire de l'anglais contemporain. Paris 1980 [XVI, 863 p.].

DFLE = Jean Dubois [et al.] (ed.): Dictionnaire du français langue étrangère. Niveau 1, Paris 1979 [XV, 911 p.], Niveau 2, Paris 1980 [XVI, 1088 p.].

Du Cloux 1678 = Louys Charles Du Cloux: Frantzösisches Wörterbuch/Mit angehängter Form Art und Weiß von jedem Ding zu reden/Zu nutzlichem Gebrauch und Dienst der Jugend in Straßburg. Vocabulaire François avec une Phraseologie convenable à tous ses mots [...]. Strasbourg 1678 [446 p.].

Fischer 1958 = Walter Fischer: Englischer Wortschatz. Für die Oberstufe nach Wortsippen geordnet. 6. durchges. Aufl. Göttingen 1973 [143 p.; 1st ed. 1958].

Fischer 1962 = Walter Fischer: Französischer Wortschatz in Sachgruppen. 7. Aufl. München 1986 [203 p.; 1st ed. 1962].

Fischer 1964 = Walter Fischer: Englischer Wortschatz in Sachgruppen. 4., verbess. Aufl. Göttingen 1978 [238 p.; 1st ed. 1964].

Folomkina/Weiser 1962 = S[ofja Kirillovna] Folomkina/H. Weiser: [Anglo-russkij učebnyj slovar'] The Learner's English-Russian dictionary for English speaking students: approximately 3,500 words. Compiled by S. Folomkina and H. Weiser. 5th Stereotype ed. Moscow 1981 [471 p.; 1st ed. 1962, 655 p.].

Gillot/Krüger 1912 = Hubert Gillot/Gustav Krüger: Dictionnaire systématique français-allemand. Französisch-deutsches Wörterbuch nach Stoffen geordnet. Dresden 1912 [1335 p.].

Giovannelli 1977 = Grund- und Aufbauwortschatz Italienisch, bearb. von Paolo Giovannelli. Stuttgart 1977 (1989) [256 p.; first publ. 1966 without index].

Gisbert/Nižskij 1962 = M. Gisbert: [Ispansko-russkij učebnyj slovar'] Diccionario manual español-ruso. Compuesto por M. Gisbert, V. A. Nižskij. 6 000 palabras. Con nociones breves de la morfología y tablas morfológicas del ruso por A. Zaliznjak. 2 ed. esteriotipada. Moscú 1963 [548 p.; 1st ed. 1962].

Gougenheim 1958 = Georges Gougenheim: Dictionnaire fondamental de la langue française. Nouvelle édition revue et augmentée. Paris 1958 [last print. 1967; 283 p.].

Haase 1959 = Alfred Haase: Englisches Arbeitswörterbuch. The Learner's Standard Vocabulary. Der aktive englische Wortschatz in Wertigkeitsstufen und Sachgruppen [...]. 7. Aufl. Frankfurt. Berlin. München 1979 [273 p. 1st ed. 1959].

Häublein/Jenkins 1987 = Thematischer Grund- und Aufbauwortschatz Englisch. Von Gernot Häublein und Recs Jenkins. Stuttgart 1987 [VIII, 352 p.].

Hermann/Rauch 1987 = Thematischer Grund- und Aufbauwortschatz Französisch. Von Reinhild Herrmann und Rainer Rauch. Stuttgart 1987 [XVIII, 341 p.].

Heupel 1977 = Grund- und Aufbauwortschatz Spanisch, bearb. von Carl Heupel. Stuttgart 1977 (1989) [240 p.].

Hindmarsh 1980 = Roland Hindmarsh: Cambridge English Lexicon: A Graded Word List for Materials Writers and Course Designers. 3rd ed. Cambridge 1987 [xiv, 210 p. 1st ed. 1980].

Hornby et al. 1966 = A[lbert] S[idney] Hornby/ E[dward] V[ivian] Gatenby/H. Wakenfield (eds.): The Advanced Learner's Dictionary of Current English. 2nd ed. Wu Xi-Zhen, Editor-in-chief. Taipei 1972 [1354 p.; 1st ed. 1966].

Hornby/Reif 1986 = The Oxford Student's Dictionary for Hebrew Speakers. A[lbert] S[idney] Hornby with the assistance of Christina Ruse. Hebrew editor Joseph A. Reif with the assistance of Yaacov Levy. Tel Aviv 1986 [xii, 824 p.].

Ivanova/Liperovskaja 1966 = E[vgenija] A[leksandrovna] Ivanova/N[ina] A[leksandrovna] Liperovskaja: [Nemecko-russkij učebnyj slovar'] Deutsch-russisches Wörterbuch für Lehrzwecke; etwa 6 200 Stichwörter. 3. verb. u. erw. Aufl. Moskau 1981 [796 p.; 1st ed. N. A. Liperovskaja/E. Ivanova [...] 6 000 Stichwörter in Wendungen [...] 1966, 749 p.].

Ivanova/Schenk 1987 = E[vgenija] A[leksandrovna] Ivanova/W[erner] Schenk: [Russko-nemeckij učebnyj slovar'] Russisch-deutsches Wörterbuch für Lehr- und Lernzwecke; etwa 5 000 Stichwörter. Moskau. Leipzig 1987 [544 p.].

Kobrina et al. 1963 = N[atalija] B[orisovna] Kobrina [et al.]: [Kratkij francuzsko-russkij učebnyj slovar'] Petit dictionnaire pratique français-russe. 5 000 mots. Par N. Kobrina [et al.]. Suivi des «Tableaux morphologiques russes» par A. Zaliznjak et de l'étude «Quelques particularités du russe par rapport au français» par Vladimir Gak. 2e éd. revue et corrigée. Moscou 1978 [668 p.; 1st ed. 1963, 716 p.].

Langenscheidt/E 1984 = Langenscheidts Grundwortschatz Englisch. Ein nach Sachgebieten geordnetes Lernwörterbuch mit Satzbeispielen. Erarbeitet von der Langenscheidt-Redaktion. Berlin. München. Wien. Zürich 1984 [XII, 324 p.].

Langenscheidt/F 1984 = Langenscheidts Grundwortschatz Französisch. Ein nach Sachgebieten geordnetes Lernwörterbuch mit Satzbeispielen. Erarbeitet von der Langenscheidt-Redaktion. Berlin. München. Wien. Zürich 1984 [XIII, 320 p.].

Lapidus/Ševcova 1962 = B[oris] A[ronovič] Lapidus/S[vetlana] V[asilevna] Ševcova: [Russko-anglijskij učebnyj slovar'] The Learner's Russian-English dictionary for foreign students of Russian: 13 000 words approx. 3rd stereotype ed. Moscow 1980 [552 p.; 1st ed. 1962 (10,000 words)].

Leyton 1960 = John Leyton: Modern English Vocabulary in narrative form with 2000 translated idioms (English-German). 8. Aufl. München 1988 [244 p.; 1st ed. 1960].

Lübke 1975 = Emploi des mots. Lernwörterbuch in Sachgruppen. Zusammengestellt und bearb. von Diethard Lübke. 13. Aufl. Dortmund 1987 [mit Diskette für Commodore 64, 190 p.; 1st ed. 1975; Neubearbeitung 1990 (with illustrations), 200 p.].

Navarro et al. 1982 = Grund- und Aufbauwortschatz Deutsch-Spanisch, bearb. von José Navarro, Graciela Vázquez und Carl Heupel. München 1982 (1987) [XXII, 372 p.].

Nickolaus 1977 = Grund- und Aufbauwortschatz Französisch, bearb. von Günter Nickolaus. Stuttgart 1977 (1989) [237 p.; first publ. 1963 without index].

Nogueira/Turover 1962 = J. Nogueira/G[enrich Iakovlevič] Turover: [Russko-ispanskij učebnyj slovar'] Diccionario manual ruso-español: 12 000 palabras con nociones breves de la morfología y tablas morfológicas del ruso por A. Zaliznjak. 3 ed. corr. y aumentada. Moscú 1976 [471 p.; 1st ed. 1962, 548 p.].

Oehler 1980a = Grund- und Aufbauwortschatz Deutsch-Englisch, bearb. von Heinz Oehler. München 1980 (1988) [XXI, 368 p.].

Oehler 1980b = Grund- und Aufbauwortschatz Deutsch-Französisch, bearb. von Heinz Oehler. München 1980 (1987) [XXI, 368 p.].

Oehler et al. 1982 = Grund- und Aufbauwortschatz Deutsch-Italienisch, bearb. von Heinz Oehler, M. Luisa Heinz-Mazzoni und Ingeborg Sörensen. München 1982 (1989) [XXI, 370 p.].

Ploetz 1847 = Karl Ploetz: Vocabulaire systématique et guide de conversation française. Sammlung der zum Französischsprechen nötigsten Wörter und Redensarten, nach einer das Lernen und Behalten derselben erleichternden Anordnung [. . .]. 22. Aufl. Berlin 1913 [230 p. 1st ed. 1847].

Pollmann 1982 = How to use your words. Lernwörterbuch in Sachgruppen. Zusammengestellt und bearb. von Carin Pollmann-Laverentz und Friedrich Pollmann. 5. Aufl. Dortmund 1987 [288 p.; 1st ed. 1982].

Rozental' 1966 = D[imitar] È[ljaševič] Rozental': [Russko-ital'janskij učebnyj slovar'] Dizionario pratico russo-italiano: 13 500 vocaboli/D. Rozental', in appendice un compendio di grammatica russa preparato da A. Zaliznjak. 2 ed. riv. e aggiornata. Mosca 1977 [496 p.; 1st ed. 1966, 712 p.].

Salmoné 1972 = H. Anthony Salmoné: An Advanced Learner's Arabic-English Dictionary: including an English Index by H. Anthony Salmoné. New impr. Beirut 1972 [xxiii, 1252 + 179 p.].

Steingass 1960 = F[rancis] Steingass: A Learner's English-Arabic Dictionary. Beirut 1960 [466 p.].

Vian 1961 = R[obert] Vian/M[aria] Vian: Vocabulaire et phraséologie modernes. Nach Sachgebieten geordnet. Einführung in den aktuellen französischen Wortschatz. 3., erw. Aufl. Wien 1969 [200 p.; 1st ed. 1961].

Vogt 1967 = Grund- und Aufbauwortschatz Russisch, bearb. von Helger Oleg Vogt. 2. Aufl. Stuttgart 1968 (1989) [328 p.; 1st ed. 1967].

Weis 1977 = Grund- und Aufbauwortschatz Englisch, bearb. von Erich Weis. Stuttgart 1977 (1989) [274 p.; first publ. 1963 without index].

West 1953 = Michael West: A General Service List of English Words, with semantic frequencies and a supplementary list for the writing of popular science and technology. Rev. and enl. ed. London. New York 1953 [xiii, 588 p.; 13th ed. 1974; first publ. 1936].

Withals 1553 = John Withals: A shorte dictionarie for yonge begynners. London 1553.

Zaliznjak 1961 = A[ndrej] A[natol'evič] Zaliznjak: [Kratkij russko-francuzskij učebnyj slovar'] Petit dictionnaire pratique russe-français. Environ 13 500 mots. Par A. Zaliznjak. Suivi d'un «Précis de déclinaison et de conjugaison russes» et d'«Éléments de phonétique russe». 3e éd. revue et augmentée. Moscou 1969 [688 p.; 1st ed. 1961 (10 000 mots), 632 p.; 2nd ed. 1964, 676 p.].

8.2. Other Publications

Barrera-Vidal et al. 1986 = Albert Barrera-Vidal/Hartmut Kleineidam/Manfred Raupach (eds.): Französische Sprache und *bon usage*. Festschrift für Hans-Wilhelm Klein zum 75. Geburtstag. München 1986.

Baunebjerg Hansen 1988 = Gitte Baunebjerg Hansen: Stand und Aufgaben der zweisprachigen Lexikographie. Nachlese zum Kopenhagener Werkstattgespräch 12.—13. Mai 1986. In: Lexicographica 4. 1988, 186—202.

Baxter 1980 = James Baxter: The Dictionary and Vocabulary Behavior: a Single Word or a Handful? In: Tesol Quarterly 14. 1980, 325—336.

Cowie 1987 = Anthony Cowie (ed.): The Dictionary and the Language Learner. Papers from the EURALEX Seminar at the University of Leeds, 1—3 April 1985, ed. by Anthony Cowie. Tübingen 1987 (Lexicographica. Series Maior 17).

Denisov 1977 = P[etr] N[ikitič] Denisov: Učebnaja leksikografija: itogi i perspektivy. In: P[etr] N[ikitič] Denisov/V[alerij] V. Morkovkin (eds.): Problemy učebnoj leksikografii. Moskau 1977, 4—22.

Dubois 1981 = Jean Dubois: Models of the Dictionary: Evolution in Dictionary Design. In: Applied Linguistics 2. 1981, 236—249.

Düwell 1986 = Henning Düwell: Mittler der französischen Sprache im deutschsprachigen Raum im 18. Jahrhundert, oder: Des neuen Versuchs, die französische Sprache auf eine angenehme und gründliche Art in kurzer Zeit zu erlernen, ... In: Barrera-Vidal et al. 1986, 267—283.

Hartmann 1982 = Reinhard R. K. Hartmann: Das zweisprachige Wörterbuch im Fremdsprachenerwerb. In: Herbert Ernst Wiegand (ed.): Studien zur neuhochdeutschen Lexikographie II. Hildesheim. New York 1982 (Germanistische Linguistik 3—6/80), 73—86.

Hartmann 1983 = Reinhard R. K. Hartmann: The bilingual learner's dictionary and its uses. In: Multilingua 2. 1983, 195—201.

Hartmann 1984 = Reinhard R. K. Hartmann (ed.): LEXeter '83 Proceedings. Papers from the International Conference on Lexicography at Exeter, 9—12 September 1983. Tübingen 1984 (Lexicographica. Series Maior 1).

Hartmann 1988 = Reinhard R. K. Hartmann: The Learner's Dictionary. Traum oder Wirklichkeit. In: Hyldgaard-Jensen/Zettersten 1988, 215—235.

Hartmann 1989 = Reinhard R. K. Hartmann: Bilingual Dictionary Reference Skills — Some Research Priorities. In: Language & Literature — Theory & Practice. A Tribute to Walter Grauberg, ed. by Christopher S. Butler [et al.]. Nottingham 1989, 17—26.

Hausmann 1976 = Franz Josef Hausmann: Sprache und Welt im Wörterbuch. Wortschatzlernen mit den „Wörterbüchern in Sachgruppen". In: französisch heute 7. 1976, 94—104.

Hausmann 1988 = Franz Josef Hausmann: Grundprobleme des zweisprachigen Wörterbuchs. In: Hyldgaard-Jensen/Zettersten 1988, 137—154.

Hernández 1989 = Humberto Hernández: Los diccionarios de orientación escolar. Contribución de la lexicografía monolingüe española. With an English Summary. Tübingen 1989 (Lexicographica. Series Maior 28).

Hoffmann 1969 = Lothar Hoffmann: Die Bedeutung statistischer Untersuchungen für den Fremdsprachenunterricht. Glottodidactica 3/4. 1969, 47—81.

Householder 1967 = Fred W. Householder: Summary Report. In: Fred W. Householder/Sol Saporta (eds.): Problems in lexicography. 2nd ed. with add. and corr. Bloomington. The Hague 1967 [1st ed. 1962: International Journal of American Linguistics 28].

Hüllen 1989 a = Werner Hüllen: In the beginning was the gloss. Remarks on the historical emergence of lexicographical paradigms. In: Gregory James (ed.): Lexicographers and their Works. Exeter 1989 (Exeter Linguistic Studies 14), 100—116.

Hüllen 1989 b = Werner Hüllen: Von Glossaren und frühen Lehrbüchern für den fremdsprachlichen Unterricht. In: Eberhard Kleinschmidt (ed.): Fremdsprachenunterricht zwischen Sprachpolitik und Praxis. Festschrift für Herbert Christ zum 60. Geburtstag. Tübingen 1989, 112—122.

Hyldgaard-Jensen/Zettersten 1988 = Karl Hyldgaard-Jensen/Arne Zettersten (eds.): Symposium on Lexicography III. Proceedings of the Third International Symposium on Lexicography May 14—16, 1986 at the University of Copenhagen. Tübingen 1988 (Lexicographica. Series Maior 19).

Kharma 1984 = Nayef N. Kharma: Contextualization and the bilingual learner's dictionary. In: Hartmann 1984, 199—206.

Kromann et al. 1984 = Hans-Peder Kromann/Theis Riiber/Poul Rosbach: Überlegungen zu Grundfragen der zweisprachigen Lexikographie. In: Herbert Ernst Wiegand (ed.): Studien zur neuhochdeutschen Lexikographie V. Hildesheim. Zürich. New York 1984 (Germanistische Linguistik 3—6/84), 159—238.

Lamy 1985 = Marie-Noëlle Lamy: Innovative practices in French monolingual learner's dictionaries as compared with their English counterparts. In: Robert Ilson (ed.): Dictionaries, Lexicography and Language Learning. Oxford [etc.] 1985 (ELT Documents 120), 25—34.

Lübke 1982 = Diethard Lübke: Das Wörterbuch im Französischunterricht. Überlegungen zu den Schulwörterbüchern von morgen. München 1982 (Langenscheidts Arbeitshilfen für den Fremdsprachenlehrer 17).

Mathews 1933 = M[itford] M[cleod] Mathews: A Survey of English Dictionaries. Oxford 1933.

Nguyen 1986 = Dinh-Hoa Nguyen: How to Present Grammatical Information in a Learner's Dictionary of English. In: Lexicographica 2. 1986, 61—77.

Nikula 1986 = Henrik Nikula: Wörterbuch und Kontext. Ein Beitrag zur Theorie des lexikalischen Beispiels. In: Walter Weiss/Herbert Ernst Wiegand/Marga Reis (eds.): Textlinguistik contra Stilistik? Wortschatz und Wörterbuch. Grammatische oder pragmatische Organisation von Rede? Tübingen 1986 (Kontroversen alte und neue; Band 3), 187—192.

Püschel 1986 = Ulrich Püschel: Vom Nutzen synonymisch und sachlich gegliederter Wörterbücher des Deutschen. Überlegungen zu ausgewählten historischen Beispielen: In: Lexicographica 2. 1986, 223—243.

Quemada 1967 = Bernard Quemada: Les dictionnaires du français moderne 1539—1863. Étude sur leur historie, leurs types et leurs méthodes. Paris. Bruxelles. Montréal 1967.

Ščerba 1940 = L[ev] V[ladimirovič] Ščerba: Opyt obščej teorii leksikografii. In: Leksikografičeskij sbornik 3. 1940, 89—117 [German translation in: Werner Wolski (ed.): Aspekte der sowjetrussischen Lexikographie. Übersetzungen, Abstracts, bibliographische Angaben. Tübingen 1982 (Reihe Germanistische Linguistik 43), 17—62].

Schröder 1984 = Konrad Schröder: Die Vermittlung von englischem Wortschatz in Lehrwerken des 17. und 18. Jahrhunderts. In: Dieter Götz/Thomas Herbst (eds.): Theoretische und praktische Probleme der Lexikographie. 1. Augsburger Kolloquium. München 1984, 300—333.

Snell-Hornby 1987 = Mary Snell-Hornby: Towards a learner's bilingual dictionary. In: Cowie 1987, 159—170.

Stammerjohann 1983 = Harro Stammerjohann: Französisch für Lehrer. Linguistische Daten für Studium und Unterricht. München 1983.

Starnes 1954 = De Witt T[almage] Starnes: Renaissance Dictionaries. English-Latin and Latin-English. Austin 1954.

Starnes/Noyes 1946 = De Witt T[almage] Starnes/ Gertrude E[lizabeth] Noyes: The English Dictionary from Cawdrey to Johnson 1604—1755. Chapel Hill [N.C.] 1946.

Stein 1984 = Gabriele Stein: Towards a theory of lexicography: principles and/vs. practice in modern English dictionaries. In: Hartmann 1984, 124—130.

Stein 1985 = Gabriele Stein: The English Dictionary before Cawdrey. Tübingen 1985 (Lexicographica. Series maior 9).

Tancke 1984 = Gunnar Tancke: Die italienischen Wörterbücher von den Anfängen bis zum Erscheinen des «Vocabulario degli Accademici della Crusca» (1612). Bestandsaufnahme und Analyse. Tübingen 1984 (Beihefte zur Zeitschrift für Romanische Philologie 198).

Tomaszczyk 1981 = Jerzy Tomaszczyk: Issues and Developments in Bilingual Pedagogical Lexicography. In: Applied Linguistics 2. 1981, 287—296.

Tomaszczyk 1983 = Jerzy Tomaszczyk: The case for bilingual dictionaries for foreign language learners. In: Reinhard R. K. Hartmann (ed.): Lexicography: Principles and Practice. London. New York 1983 (Applied Language Studies), 41—51.

Tomaszczyk 1984 = Jerzy Tomaszczyk: The culture-bound element in bilingual dictionaries. In: Hartmann 1984, 289—298.

Tomaszczyk 1987 = Jerzy Tomaszczyk: FL learners' communication failure: implications for pedagogical lexicography. In: Cowie 1987, 136—145.

Tomaszczyk 1988 = Jerzy Tomaszczyk: The bilingual dictionary under review. In: Mary Snell-Hornby (ed.): ZüriLEX '86 Proceedings. Papers read at the EURALEX International Congress, University of Zürich, 9—14 September 1986. Tübingen 1988, 289—297.

Zöfgen 1982 = Ekkehard Zöfgen: Verbwörterbücher und Verbvalenz im Französischunterricht. In: Linguistik und Didaktik 49/50. 1982, 18—61.

Zöfgen 1985a = Ekkehard Zöfgen: Lernerwörterbücher auf dem Prüfstand oder: Was ist ein Lernwörterbuch? In: Ekkehard Zöfgen (ed.): Wörterbücher und ihre Didaktik. Bad Honnef. Zürich 1985 (Bielefelder Beiträge zur Sprachlehrforschung 14. 1985), 10—89.

Zöfgen 1985b = Ekkehard Zöfgen: Definitionswörterbuch kontra Valenzwörterbuch. Zur lexikographischen Darstellung der Verbsyntax aus pragmatischer Sicht. In: Henning Bergenholtz/Joachim Mugdan (eds.): Lexikographie und Grammatik. Akten des Essener Kolloquiums zur Grammatik im Wörterbuch 22.—30. 6. 1984. Tübingen 1985 (Lexicographica. Series Maior 3), 130—158.

Zöfgen 1986 = Ekkehard Zöfgen: Kollokation — Kontextualisierung — (Beleg-)Satz. Anmerkungen zur Theorie und Praxis des lexikographischen Beispiels. In: Barrera-Vidal et al. 1986, 219—238.

Ekkehard Zöfgen, Bielefeld
(Federal Republic of Germany)

305 a. Das Reisewörterbuch

1. Funktion des Reisewörterbuchs
2. Inhaltliche und strukturelle Bestandteile des Reisewörterbuchs
3. Typen von Reisewörterbüchern
4. Vergleich ausgewählter Reisewörterbücher des Spanischen für Deutschsprachige
5. Das Reisewörterbuch in der Wörterbuchforschung
6. Literatur (in Auswahl)

1. Funktion des Reisewörterbuchs

Das Reisewörterbuch [= RWB] ist als lexikographisches Hilfsmittel für Reisende gedacht, die nur geringe oder keine Kenntnisse der Sprache ihres Urlaubslandes besitzen. Zweisprachig angeordnete Wörter, Satzteile und ganze Sätze sollen dem Benutzer eine elementare mündliche Verständigung in der fremden Sprache ermöglichen bzw. erleichtern. Das RWB dient als Nachschlagewerk auf Reisen, um aktuelle Kommunikationsprobleme durch punktuelle Konsultation zu beheben. Alle RWB unterliegen dem monodirektionalen Prinzip, so daß sie nur in der Richtung Ausgangssprache-Zielsprache sinnvoll genutzt werden können. Ein kompetenter Sprecher der Ausgangssprache benötigt Informationen zu der fremden Sprache und Kultur. RWB werden auch für die Reisevorbereitung und, in seltenen Fällen, für die Reisenachbereitung verwendet.

Abzugrenzen ist das RWB von dem *kleinen allgemeinen zweisprachigen Wörterbuch,* das durch eine Speisekarte und ein paar Redewendungen erweitert wurde, bei dem jedoch der allgemeinsprachliche Aspekt überwiegt. Die touristische Komponente allein, oft ausgedrückt durch den Zusatz „für Urlaub und Reise", macht noch kein RWB. In einem solchen wird das lexikalische Material nach eigenen Prinzipien geordnet (vgl. 3.). Außerdem soll der Wortschatz in Auswahl und Darstellung auf den Aspekt der Reise abgestimmt sein. Des weiteren ist das RWB vom *Reiseführer* abzusetzen. Der Reiseführer bietet sachliche Informationen zu Land und Leuten an. Die sprachliche Information beschränkt sich auf ein zweisprachiges Glossar. In einem RWB kann zusätzlich enzyklopädisches Wissen vermittelt werden. — Publikationen wie *Russisch für Reisende* oder *Englisch unterwegs* sind eher *Lehrwerke* als Nachschlagewerke, da ein gradueller Aufbau fremdsprachlicher Kompetenz angestrebt wird. Durch das RWB soll der Benutzer dagegen für einen beschränkten Zeitraum eine nur sehr partielle kommunikative Kompetenz erwerben. Funktionale und notionale Kategorien sind dabei wichtiger als grammatische Strukturen. Bei der Frage *En jakın benzin istasyonu nerededir? „Wo ist die nächste Tankstelle?"* (BerlTürk, 75) spielt der Kontext und die Handlung, die sich aus ihm ergibt, die entscheidende Rolle. Die Funktion des RWB kann sich sogar darauf beschränken, dem Gesprächspartner im Ausland das RWB zu zeigen und auf den entsprechenden Satz zu deuten. Dieser Fall tritt für Sprachen mit einem fremden Schriftsystem, wie z. B. Arabisch, ein. Im RWB sollte neben dem ausgangssprachlichen Lemma und der Lautumschrift als Äquivalent das Lemma in der Originalschrift erscheinen.

2. Inhaltliche und strukturelle Bestandteile des Reisewörterbuchs

RWB basieren meist auf einem Grundkonzept, das für eine Sprache entwickelt und auf die anderen Sprachen übertragen wird. Die RWB erscheinen deshalb in Reihen für mehrere Sprachen.

Inhaltlich ähneln sich die meisten Wörterbücher. Das lexikalische Material besteht aus sprachlichen Einheiten, z. B. Wörtern, Wendungen und Sätzen, die auf das reale Umfeld eines Reisenden referieren. Sie werden nach Kommunikationssituationen geordnet. Dabei entspricht die Reihenfolge der Situationen dem möglichen Verlauf einer Reise. Die Situationstexte sind bestimmten Themenbereichen zugeordnet, die sich auf Sachverhalte oder Sprechakte des Reiselebens wie Grenze, Unterkunft, Geldwechsel, Begrüßung, Sympathie ausdrücken beziehen. Am Ende jeden Kapitels finden sich alphabetische Einzelwortlisten, deren Wörter sich in vorgegebene Teilsätze einfügen lassen. . . . *ist nicht in Ordnung,* . . . *no funciona.* Einsetzen könnte man

Vorwort/Benutzerhinweise	Inhaltsverzeichnis	Erläuterungen zur Aussprache	Erläuterungen zur Grammatik	Illustration	Sachregister	Anhang	alphabetisches Wörterverzeichnis
				für Touristen typische Kommunikationssituationen (situationsspezifischer Wortschatz in Wörtern, Wendungen und Sätzen)			
				touristische Zusatzinformation			

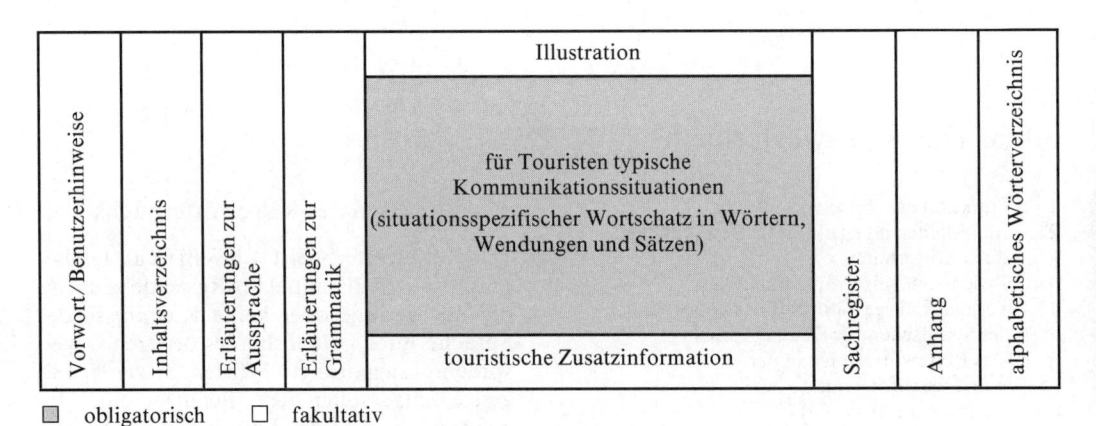

■ obligatorisch   □ fakultativ

Abb. 305 a. 1: Strukturelle Bestandteile des Reisewörterbuchs

Auspuff, escape (LAS, 52—53). Diesen Teil des RWB nenne ich Situationswörterbuch. Er bildet die konstitutive Komponente eines RWB. Das lexikalische Material wird in einer stilistisch möglichst neutralen Sprache angegeben. Die Mikrostruktur ist in einem RWB nur schwach ausgeprägt. Ab und zu werden grammatische und diatopische Kennzeichnungen vorgenommen. Im Vordergrund steht im RWB die textorientierte Makrostruktur. Zusätzlich kann ein RWB andere Textteile, z. B. zur non-verbalen Kommunikation, zu Aussprachebesonderheiten, zur Grammatik etc. beinhalten. Neben dem Situationswörterbuch enthalten einige RWB einen rein alphabetischen Wörterbuchteil in einer oder beiden Sprachrichtungen (vgl. Abb. 305 a. 1).

Viele kommunikative Handlungen sind so aufgebaut, daß eine Äußerung des einen Partners eine genau zugeordnete Reaktion des anderen Partners zur Folge hat. Im Situationswörterbuchteil des RWB wird diese Tatsache interkulturell verarbeitet, da dem situationsspezifischen Muster für die Sprechhandlung in der einen Sprache dasjenige der anderen entsprechend gegenübergestellt wird. Es handelt sich meist um Floskeln, stereotype Wendungen, feste Ausdrücke, die der Gebrauchsnorm unterliegen, weil sie ständig in denselben Situationen verwendet werden. Viele Redemittel haben dialogischen Charakter, z. B. Frage und Antwort im Kontext, Begrüßung und Erwiderung des Grußes u. ä. Eine wichtige Rolle spielt für die Verständigung mit Hilfe eines RWB die starke Kontextualisierung in der aktuellen Situation.

3. Typen von Reisewörterbüchern

Für RWB existieren bis jetzt weder einheitliche Bezeichnungen, noch besitzen sie Titel, aus denen genau hervorgeht, wofür das RWB nützlich ist, z. B. *Reisedolmetscher, Reise-ABC, Sprachführer, Reisewörterbuch, × für Globetrotter.* Allen ist der Situationswörterbuchteil im Kontext Reise gemeinsam. Wenn man in erster Linie die Struktur und in zweiter den Inhalt betrachtet, kristallisieren sich vier Gruppen von RWB heraus:

(a) Reisewörterbücher, die einen Situationswörterbuchteil und ein zweisprachiges, alphabetisches Wörterverzeichnis enthalten.
(b) Reisewörterbücher, die zum größten Teil aus einem Situationswörterbuch bestehen.
(c) Reisewörterbücher mit inhaltlichem Schwerpunkt.
(d) Sonderformen

Zu (a) gehören die *Kauderwelsch-Sprachführer.* Schon die Bezeichnung macht deutlich, welche Rolle der mündlichen Kommunikation zukommt. Dieser Reisewörterbuchtyp ist vor allem für Globetrotter und Individualreisende gedacht. Der relativ hohe Anteil an Erläuterungen zur Grammatik wird bereits mit landeskundlichen und lexikographischen Informationen in Form von zweisprachig angeführten Sätzen und deutschen Zusatzbemerkungen verknüpft. Zuerst wird der Text in der fremden Sprache abgedruckt, dazu mit Hilfe einer Interlinearversion der Satzbau verdeutlicht, und dann folgt der deutsche Text.

Kólim nem bilóng yu?
Nennen Name gehören du?
Wie heißt du (heißen Sie)?
Das ist zwar korrektes Tok Pisin, aber es ist ziemlich unhöflich, jemanden direkt nach dem Namen zu fragen.

Textbeispiel 305 a. 1: Interlinearversion und Zusatzhinweis (aus: KauPid 1986, 11)

Die sprachlichen Mittel sind in erster Linie nach Sprechakten wie *sich ärgern, schimpfen, Kontakt knüpfen* angeordnet. Sehr hoch ist der Anteil an Information zur non-verbalen Kommunikation und zum richtigen Verhalten im fremden Land, was besonders für Reisen in exotische Länder von Bedeutung ist.

Zu (b) gehören Publikationen, die weitläufig als Sprachführer bekannt sind, wie z. B. Polyglott.

RWB vom Typ (c) sind z. B. der *Auto- und der Menü-Sprachführer* von Polyglott. In dem Auto-Sprachführer findet der Benutzer den technischen Fachwortschatz für die Reise mit dem eigenen Wagen. Das RWB ist sehr anschaulich illustriert und bietet sehr viel zusätzliche Sachinformationen, wie Autobahngebühren, Unfallprotokolle in beiden Sprachen usw. In dem Menü-Sprachführer werden in einer fremdsprachlichen Speisekarte kulinarische Genüsse mit Übersetzung angeboten. Der Reisende bekommt Speisen, Getränke, Hinweise auf Eßgewohnheiten in alphabetischer Reihenfolge serviert, was ihm das Lesen einer Speisekarte erleichtern soll. RWB mit Titeln wie *Kiwi-Slang-das Englisch Neuseelands* legen den Schwerpunkt auf diatopische Varianten bestimmter Sprachen. Interessant ist auch die Zusammenfassung verschiedener RWB für eine größere Region. Für Südamerikareisende gibt es das *Sprachbuch Lateinamerika,* in dem RWB für Spanisch, Brasilianisch und Quechua zusammengefaßt sind.

Zu den Sonderformen (d) gehört *Huebers ReiseABC,* das eine strukturelle Besonderheit aufweist. In dem sehr kleinen Wörterbuch, nur 8 × 14 cm, wird ein altes Prinzip (vgl. Ruppert 1887) wieder aufgegriffen. In einer einzigen Wortliste wird das gesamte lexikalische Inventar in alphabetischer Reihenfolge aufgeführt: deutsche Lemmata und ihre fremdsprachlichen Äquivalente, fremdsprachliche Lemmata mit deutscher Entsprechung und touristische Zusatzinformationen sind in jeweils anderer Drucktype eingearbeitet.

> **Arzt** un médico
> **wo gibt es hier einen Arzt?** ¿dónde hay un médico? [donde ai ...]
> » *REISE-TIP: sehen Sie im Branchenfernsprechbuch unter 'Médicos' nach oder gehen Sie ins nächste 'Casa de Socorro'*
> MAN HÖRT EVTL.
> ¿ha tenido esto antes? *hatten Sie das schon einmal?*
> ¿dónde le duele? *wo tut es weh?*
> ¿está tomando algún medicamento? *nehmen Sie zur Zeit Medikamente?*
> tómese una/dos de éstas *nehmen Sie davon eine/zwei*
> cada tres horas/al día/dos veces al día *alle drei Stunden/täglich/zweimal täglich*
> **ascensor** *Aufzug*
> **Aschenbecher** un cenicero [ssenissero]
> *aseos* *Toiletten*
> **Assistent/-in** asistente [assißtente]
> **Asthma** el asma [aßma]
> **Atem** el aliento [ali-ento]
> **ich bin ganz außer Atem** estoy sin aliento [eßteu ssin ...]
> **atención al tren** *Achtung! unbeschrankter Bahnübergang*
> **atmen** respirar [reßpirar]

Textbeispiel 305 a.2: Zweisprachige Makrostruktur eines RWB (aus: Hueber, 11)

Eine interessante Sonderform stellt auch das zweisprachige RWB in Fächerform dar. Dieses RWB wird als Werbemittel an Kunden verteilt. Auf der einen Seite sind die einzelnen Fächerblätter z. B. mit einem deutsch-italienischen Wörterverzeichnis und einem Situationswörterbuchteil zu touristisch relevanten Themen bedruckt. Auf der Rückseite ist Entsprechendes in italienisch-deutscher Sprachrichtung verzeichnet.

4. Vergleich ausgewählter Reisewörterbücher des Spanischen für Deutschsprachige

Zehn RWB wurden anhand eines Kriterienkatalogs verglichen, der sich in der Hauptsache an den Bauteilen orientiert. Dieser Kriterienkatalog läßt sich auch auf RWB anderer Sprachenpaare anwenden (vgl. Abb. 305 a.2).

RWB sind im allgemeinen handlich und preisgünstig. In den meisten Fällen werden dem Benutzer Hinweise zum sinnvollen Nachschlagen gegeben. Allerdings sind sie oft unverständlich und zu wenig anwendungsbezogen. Inhaltsverzeichnis und Stichwortregister spielen eine wichtige Rolle für das schnelle Auffinden von Information. LAS und Berl verknüpfen das Stichwortregister geschickt mit dem alphabetischen Wörterbuchteil. Die Zahl der Einträge in diesem RWBteil schwankt zwischen 1000 und 4000 pro Sprachrichtung. Die Äquivalente stehen sich meistens im Verhältnis 1:1 gegenüber. Schwächen zeigen sich bei der Wortschatzauswahl hinsichtlich Adäquatheit, Aktualität und Konsequenz.

Erläuterungen zur Aussprache sind oft mißverständlich und zu theoretisch formuliert. Die Metasprache sollte besser auf den Benutzer abgestimmt werden. Die Lautumschrift ist in den meisten RWB an die deutsche Lautung und Orthographie angelehnt. Zu vielen RWB werden Begleitkassetten zum Einhören in die fremde Sprache und zum Nachsprechen angeboten. Die Grammatik ist nur bei Pons und Kauderwelsch didaktisch sinnvoll zusammengestellt.

Für die meisten Länder ist Spanien das Referenzland, nur KauLat bezieht sich auf hispanoamerikanische Länder und stellt damit das einzige RWB für den Sprachgebrauch des amerikanischen Spanisch dar. LAS bemüht sich darum, diesen Wortschatz differenziert in das lexikographische Inventar zu integrieren. Bei Pons erfolgt die Kennzeichnung von Amerikanismen willkürlich und inkonsequent.

Eine wichtige Rolle könnte im RWB die Illustration übernehmen, wenn sie lexikographisch und didaktisch sinnvoller eingesetzt würde. Illustrationen können dekorative, textgliedernde, landeskundliche und mnemotechnische Funktionen im RWB erfüllen (vgl. Textbeispiel 305 a.3).

Leider werden die Möglichkeiten nicht ausreichend ausgelotet und ausgeschöpft.

3 Reisen mit Bahn, Flugzeug oder Schiff Viajes en tren, en avión o en barco

Textbeispiel 305 a.3: Illustration im RWB (aus: Pons, 65)

305 a. Das Reisewörterbuch

Reisewörterbücher Kriterien	LAS 1990[9]	Lan 1989[13]	Pons Nachdruck 1987	Reisedol 1990	Berl 1988[2]	Poly 1986	Gold 1982[2]	Ull 1983	KauSpan 1988[2]	KauLat 1989[4]
Format (cm)	9,5 × 15	10,5 × 7,5	11 × 17,5	11 × 16	10,5 × 14,5	11,5 × 19,5	16,5 × 11,5	11,5 × 18	10,5 × 14,5	10,5 × 14,5
Umfang/Preis (DM, 1990)	256 S./10,80	256 S./7.80	232 S./13.80	144 S./12,80	192 S./9,80	48 S./4.80	64 S./5.80	126 S./6.80	144 S./12.80	112 S./12.80
Material/Einband	Plastik	Plastik	Plastik	Glanzkarton	Glanzkarton	Glanzkarton	Glanzkarton	Glanzkarton	fadengehefteter Karton	
Vorwort/Benutzerhinweise	−/+	+	+/−	+	−/+	+/−	+/−	−/+	+/+	+/+
Inhaltsverzeichnis	+	+	+	+	+	+	+	+	+	+
Sach-/Stichwortregister	+	+	−	−	−	+	+	−	−	−
alphabet. Wörterbuchteil										
deutsch-spanisch	+	−	+	+	+	−	−	−	+	+
spanisch-deutsch	−	−	+	−	+	+	+	−	+	+
Aussspracherläuterungen	+	+	−	−	+	−	+	+	+	−
durchgängig transkribiert	+	+	−	−	−	+	−	−	−	+
Cassette	−	−	−	+	+	−	−	−	+	+
Kurzgrammatik	+	+	+ +	+	+	+	−	+	+ +	+ +
tourist. Informationen										
Spanien	sehr wenig	sehr wenig	sehr wenig	−	+	−	−	+ +	+ +	−
Hispanoamerika	−	−	+	−	−	−	−	−	−	+ +
Kennzeichnung von amerikan. Wortschatz	differenziert	−	Am Arg Mex	−	−	−	−	−	−	Per Bol Arg Chi Ven
Kennzeichnung von zu hörendem Wortschatz	+	+	+	+	+	+	−	−	−	−
Illustration	einige Piktogramme	−	+ + Farbfotos, authent. Bildmaterial, Zeichnungen	+ Zeichnungen	+ Farben als Sortiermerkmal	einige Piktogramme	einige Piktogramme	−	+ + Fotos und Zeichnungen in schwarz-weiß	+ +
"Wichtiges auf einen Blick"	+	−	−	−	+	+	−	+	−	−

+ = vorhanden   − = nicht vorhanden   + + = in hohem Maß vorhanden

In allen Reisewörterbüchern werden die folgenden Bereiche je nach Umfang mehr oder weniger ausführlich thematisiert: Allgemeine Wendungen, Auto, andere Verkehrsmittel, Grenze, Polizei, Bank, Post, Einkauf/Geschäfte, Unterkunft, Essen/Trinken, Friseur, Gesundheit/Krankheit, In der Stadt, Zeitvertreib/Vergnügen

Abb. 305 a.2: Vergleich ausgewählter Reisewörterbücher des Spanischen für Deutschsprachige

5. Das Reisewörterbuch in der Wörterbuchforschung

Die Wörterbuchforschung hat dem RWB bisher nur wenig Aufmerksamkeit geschenkt. Es fehlt in den meisten Wörterbuchbibliographien (eine Ausnahme macht die Bibliografia Słowników 1981), und in Schriften zur zweisprachigen Lexikographie wird es nur am Rande erwähnt. Werner 1984 regte die wissenschaftliche Forschung mit Bemerkungen zu RWB und wörterbuchähnlichen Sprachführern des Spanischen für Deutschsprachige an. Abend 1988 entwirft eine Typologie der RWB und Kriterien für den Vergleich von RWB. Eine stärker an der Praxis und am Wörterbuchbenutzer orientierte Wörterbuchforschung wird das RWB in Zukunft stärker berücksichtigen müssen. Das RWB sollte in die Geschichte der Lexikographie integriert werden. Es stellt als Gesamttext einen Forschungsgegenstand für die Textlinguistik dar. Das RWB kann mit seinem Inhalt und dem Ordnungsprinzip nach Kommunikationssituationen Aufgaben eines Lehrwerkes übernehmen. Dem RWB können interessante Anregungen für die Lernlexikographie entnommen werden. Und nicht zuletzt kann die Wörterbuchkritik dazu beitragen, daß ein RWB-Benutzer beim Nachschlagen auf adäquate und korrekte Information stößt.

6. Literatur (in Auswahl)

6.1. Wörterbücher

Berl = Berlitz: Spanisch für die Reise. 4. Aufl. Lausanne 1990 [192 S.; 1. Aufl. 1971; in 13 weiteren Sprachen].

BerlTürk = Berlitz: Türkisch für die Reise. 2. Aufl. Lausanne 1990 [192 S.; 1. Aufl. 1974].

Gold = Goldstadt-Sprachführer Spanisch für Urlaub und Reise. 2. Aufl. Pforzheim 1982 [64 S.; 1. Aufl. 1979; in 8 weiteren Sprachen].

Hueber = Huebers kleines Reise-ABC Spanisch. München 1983 [128 S.; in 5 weiteren Sprachen].

KauLat = Kauderwelsch Spanisch für Latein-Amerika von Vicente Celi-Kresling. 4. Aufl. Bielefeld 1989 [112 S.; in 43 weiteren Sprachen].

KauPid = Kauderwelsch Pidgin-English für Papua-Neuguinea von Albrecht Schäfer. Bielefeld 1986 [144 S.].

KauSpan = Kauderwelsch Spanisch (nicht nur) für Globetrotter von O'Niel V. Som. 2. Aufl. Bielefeld 1988 [144 S.; 1. Aufl. 1987].

LAS = Langenscheidts Sprachführer Spanisch. 9. Aufl. Berlin. München 1990 [256 S.; 1. Aufl. 1963; in 26 Sprachen].

Lan = Universal-Sprachführer Spanisch. 13. Aufl. Berlin. München 1989 [256 S.; 1. Aufl. 1971; in 6 Sprachen].

Poly = Polyglott Sprachführer Spanisch. München 1986 [48 S.; in 30 Sprachen].

Pons = Pons Spanisch Reisewörterbuch. Nachdruck Stuttgart 1988 [232 S.; 1. Aufl. 1980; in 12 weiteren Sprachen].

Reisedol = Reisedolmetscher Spanisch. Ismaning 1990 [144 S.; in 12 Sprachen].

Ruppert 1887 = Heinrich Ruppert: Spanischer Sprachführer. Leipzig. Wien 1887 [300 S.].

Ull = Ullstein Sprach- und Reiseführer Spanisch in der Tasche von Maureen Herzfeld. Berlin 1983 [126 S.; in 2 weiteren Sprachen].

6.2. Sonstige Literatur

Abend 1988 = Heike Abend: Das Reisewörterbuch verdient die Aufmerksamkeit der Wörterbuchforschung. In: Lebende Sprachen 33. 1988, 98—101, 156—159.

Bibliografia Słowników = Bibliographie der Wörterbücher. Bd. IX. Berichtszeitraum 1977—78. Warschau 1981 [62—64, 72, 75, 86].

Werner 1984 = Reinhold Werner: Ein nicht genügend ernstgenommener Wörterbuchtyp: Das Reisewörterbuch. Mit Bemerkungen zu Reisewörterbüchern des Spanischen für Deutschsprachige. In: Hispanorama 38. 1984, 153—162.

Heike Abend, Augsburg
(Bundesrepublik Deutschland)

306. Die mehrsprachigen Wörterbücher und ihre Probleme

1. Einleitung
2. Geschichtlicher Überblick
2.1. Die mehrsprachige Lexikographie im 15., 16. und 17. Jahrhundert
2.2. Die mehrsprachige Lexikographie im 18. Jahrhundert
2.3. Die mehrsprachige Lexikographie im 19. Jahrhundert
2.4. Die mehrsprachige Lexikographie im 20. Jahrhundert
3. Typologie der mehrsprachigen Wörterbücher
3.1. nach dem dargestellten Wortschatz
3.2. nach der Makrostruktur
3.3. nach der Mikrostruktur
4. Äquivalenzprobleme der mehrsprachigen Wörterbücher
5. Ausblick
6. Literatur (in Auswahl)

1. Einleitung

Nach dem heutigen Stand der Forschung gibt es in Europa mehrsprachige Wörterbücher i. w. S. erst seit der 2. Hälfte des 15. Jh. Inhalt und Zweck dieser polyglotten Verständigungshilfen haben jedoch im Laufe der Jahrhunderte einen tiefen Wandel erfahren. So werden unter dem Oberbegriff „mehrsprachige Wörterbücher" so verschiedenartige Werke zusammengefaßt wie etwa ein relativ rudimentäres dreisprachiges „Vocabularietto" des 16. Jh. mit 200 Einträgen und ein umfangreiches, hochspezialisiertes Fachwörterbuch des 20. Jh. in 6 Sprachen mit 12 000 Einträgen, wobei beide Typen von Wörterbüchern nur das eine gemeinsam haben, daß sie eine bestimmte Wortschatzauswahl einer Sprache mit Äquivalenten in mehreren anderen Sprachen bringen.

In unserer Darstellung verstehen wir unter dem etwas vagen Terminus „mehrsprachige Wörterbücher" jede Art von lexikographischen Inventaren, in denen Wortschatz in mehr als zwei Sprachen erscheint, ganz gleich, ob es sich um Wörterbücher i. e. S., thematisch geordnete Vokabellisten, um polyglotte Gesprächsbücher *(phrase books)* oder um Glossare von Fachwörtern in wissenschaftlichen Werken handelt. Zur Terminologie ist noch anzumerken, daß wir im Dt., was die Zahl der Sprachen betrifft, nur die Termini *einsprachige, zweisprachige* und *mehrsprachige* Wörterbücher kennen. Im Engl., Frz. u. Span. ist die Terminologie nuancierter. Den einsprachigen Wörterbüchern *(dictionnaires monolingues, monolingual dictionaries, diccionarios monolingües)* stehen die *plurilingual dictionaries (dictionnaires plurilingues, diccionarios plurilingües)* gegenüber, die ihrerseits unterteilt werden in *bilingual dictionaries (dictionnaires bilingues, diccionarios bilingües)* und *multilingual dictionaries (dictionnaires multilingues, diccionarios multilingües)*, d. h. solche mit mehr als zwei Sprachen. Für die mehrsprachigen Wörterbücher ist seit der Renaissance auch die Bezeichnung *polyglott* gebräuchlich; manche Autoren, vor allem solche von Bibliographien, wenden sie jedoch nur auf Wörterbücher an, die mehr als vier oder sogar sechs Sprachen berücksichtigen (vgl. zur Terminologie auch Haensch et al. 1982 und Quemada 1967, 43). Die nachfolgende Darstellung möchte einen Überblick über das weite Feld der mehrsprachigen Lexikographie geben, und zwar zunächst einen geschichtlichen Überblick, wobei vom 15.—17. Jh. die Schwerpunkte deutlich bei den allgemeinsprachlichen Wörterbüchern liegen und nur wenige Fachwörterbücher bekannt sind, bis sich dann — nach einer Zeit des Wandels im 18. und 19. Jh. — der Schwerpunkt der mehrsprachigen Lexikographie auf die fachsprachlichen Wörterbücher verlagert. Hierbei werden wir auch die Frage aufwerfen müssen, ob und inwieweit allgemeinsprachliche Wörterbücher für mehr als zwei Sprachen heutzutage überhaupt noch einen Sinn haben. Der Verf. hat sich bemüht, in diesem Überblick Wörterbücher mit möglichst vielen, vor allem europäischen Sprachen zu berücksichtigen. Angesichts der Fülle des Materials kann hier aber nur, auch für das 16. und 17. Jh., eine Auswahl aus der umfangreichen mehrsprachigen lexikographischen Produktion vorgestellt werden, die Strömungen und Tendenzen erkennen läßt und den Versuch einer typologischen Klassifikation und die Erörterung methodischer Fragen ermöglicht. Eine vollständige Darstellung der mehrsprachigen Lexikographie in Europa, allein im 16. und 17. Jh., würde mehrere Bände füllen. Aus Gründen der Darstellungsökonomie verwenden wir für die einzelnen Sprachen (sowohl im Text als auch in der Bibliographie) Abkürzungen (die unmittelbar verständlich sind).

2. Geschichtlicher Überblick

2.1. Die mehrsprachige Lexikographie im 15., 16. und 17. Jahrhundert

Bei den mehrsprachigen Wörterbüchern (und anderen polyglotten Wortschatzinventaren), die vor dem 18. Jh. erschienen sind, stößt der Metalexikograph auf eine Reihe von Schwierigkeiten. Zunächst haben viele Wörterbücher lat. Titel, die irreführend sein können. So bedeutet bei vielen Werken *teutonicum* 'dtsch.', bei vielen anderen aber 'niederl.' (in Einzelfällen bedeutet sogar *duytsch* oder *duits* 'niederl.'). Das Niederl. (meist ist es hier das Flämische) wird z. T. auch noch als *belgicum*, z. T. als *flandricum* bezeichnet. Bei anderen Wörterbüchern ist mit *Illyrisch* 'Kroatisch', mit *Kymrisch* 'Walisisch' gemeint. Manche Wörterbücher oder einzelne Ausgaben davon sind noch gar nicht bibliographisch erfaßt, wie der Verf. z. B. in der Augsburger Universitätsbibliothek feststellen konnte, die eine Reihe von Originalausgaben des 16. und 17. Jh. besitzt, oder manche erscheinen nur in gewissen, aber nicht in allen Bibliographien und z. T. mit ungenügenden Daten. In vielen Fällen wird ein Wörterbuch zuerst unter dem Namen des Autors erwähnt, so z. B. die erste ital.-dt. Auflage des *„Introito e porta"*, eines thematisch aufgebauten Vokabulariums (Rottweil 1477). Dieses erschien später unter dem Namen des Druckers Franciscus Garonus (1526) und unter anderen Namen (vgl. weiter unten. Die Drucker waren ja oft auch gleichzeitig Bearbeiter bzw. Herausgeber und Verleger der Wörterbücher). Das ursprünglich von Noel de Berlaimont 1536 veröffentlichte *„Vocabulare"* (Frz.-Niederl.) z. B. erschien 1551 u. a. als *„Vocabulaer in vier spraken"* unter dem Namen des Druckers Bartholomy de Grave in Löwen. Die meisten Bibliographien zitieren aber diese Wörterbücher als völlig verschiedene Werke, mit verschiedenen Namen (oft dem des Druckers), oft auch anonym, ohne jedoch auf ihre Filiation hinzuweisen. Manche Bibliographien zitieren eine bestimmte Auflage eines Wörterbuchs mit deutschem oder französischem, oft übersetztem Titel, andere dieselbe Auflage mit lateinischem Titel. Auch sonst sind viele Angaben in den Bibliographien ungenau oder widersprüchlich. So zitiert Zaunmüller 1958 für die 1. Aufl. der *Sylva quinque linguarum* von Helfrig Emmelius das Jahr 1630, es gab aber schon eine Auflage mit den gleichen fünf Sprachen im Jahre 1592.

Bei der großen Zahl der polyglotten Wörterbücher des 16. und 17. Jh. konnten weder alle Werke noch alle Auflagen berücksichtigt werden. Der Verf. hat sich dennoch um eine möglichst breite und repräsentative Auswahl aus den Wörterbüchern zwischen 1480 und 1700 bemüht. Die vom Verf. vorsichtig formulierten Erkenntnisse zu einzelnen Aspekten der polyglotten Wörterbücher (erste Ausgaben bestimmter Wörterbücher, Sprachenkombinationen) haben deshalb provisorischen Charakter und können allenfalls als eine Art „Hochrechnung" aus einer repräsentativen Auswahl, nicht aber als endgültig angesehen werden. Hierzu fehlt noch die Übersicht über alle im 16. und 17. Jh. erschienenen oder gar nur als Manuskript vorhandenen mehrsprachigen Wörterbücher.

Die mehrsprachige Lexikographie im 16. und 17. Jh. muß als eine Einheit betrachtet werden, weil viele der im 16. Jh. erschienenen Wörterbücher im 17. Jh. neu aufgelegt oder neu bearbeitet wurden und weil die erste Blütezeit polyglotter Wortschatzinventare etwa von 1520—1680 reicht. Sicher sind am Anfang kürzere Vokabularien und Gesprächsbücher häufiger als umfangreiche Wörterbücher, die erst nach und nach in größerer Zahl auftreten, dennoch ist die Einheit dieses Wörterbuchtyps im 16. und 17. Jh. wegen des Zwecks, der Wahl der Sprachen und der Darstellung des Wortschatzes offensichtlich. Im 15. Jh., in das der Beginn der modernen Lexikographie in Europa fällt, beginnt die lexikographische Produktion zuerst in Italien, dann in Deutschland und Spanien, erst später in Frankreich mit zweisprachigen Wörterbüchern, zuerst meist des Lat. in Kombination mit einer modernen Sprache, bald auch von zwei neuen Sprachen. Schon früh beginnt man, bei den zweisprachigen Wörterbüchern eine, bald auch mehrere alte und moderne Sprachen hinzuzufügen, und so entsteht der für das 16. und 17. Jh. so charakteristische und allgemein beliebte Typ des mehrsprachigen Wörterbuchs, sogar meist noch (mit Ausnahme von Italien) bevor sich langsam auch das einsprachige Bedeutungswörterbuch durchsetzt. In nicht wenigen Fällen ist eine der modernen Sprachen schon in irgendeinem mehrsprachigen Wortschatzinventar vertreten, bevor sie als eine der beiden Sprachen in einem zweisprachigen Wörterbuch erscheint (z. B. Französisch im *Dictionarium sex linguarum* 1505, aber dann erst im frz.-lat. Wörterbuch von Robert Estienne von 1539). Häufig erscheint sogar ein bestimmtes Sprachenpaar zuerst in Kombination mit anderen Sprachen in einem polyglotten Wörterbuch, bevor es für dieses Sprachenpaar ein zweisprachiges Wörterbuch gibt (z. B. erscheinen Deutsch und Spanisch zuerst im *Dictionarium sex linguarum* 1505 und dann im zweisprachigen Wörterbuch des Mez de Braidenbach 1670).

Hier müssen jedoch gleich zwei Einschränkungen gemacht werden: Einerseits sind viele der frühen Wortschatzinventare z. T. bescheidene „Vocabolarietti" oder Nomenklaturen (meist thematisch geordnet), und die Zahl ihrer Wortstellen liegt weit unter der später erschienener mehrsprachiger alphabetisch geordneter Wörterbücher. Andererseits ist bei den eigtl. alphabetisch geordneten Wörterbüchern (wie z. B. bei Calepino) nur die Ausgangssprache, häufig das Lat., wirklich maßgebend, während die Äquivalente in den anderen Sprachen nur als Lernhilfe oder Erläuterung für das Lat. anzusehen sind und man die übrigen Sprachen nicht direkt nachschlagen kann.

In einer Zeit, in der sich ein ungeheurer Wissens- und Bildungsdrang ausbreitete und die alten Sprachen Griechisch und Latein, in gewissem Maße auch das Hebräische, wiederentdeckt wurden, brauchte man Wörterbücher zum Erlernen und Verstehen der alten Sprachen. Da ferner der Handel in Europa, aber bald auch mit der übrigen Welt (vor allem nach den überseeischen Entdeckungen und Eroberungen) einen großen Aufschwung nahm, brauchte man auch mehrsprachige Wörterbücher als praktische Verständigungshilfen. In der Tat wurde das polyglotte Wörterbuch in Europa Mode und erlebte seine Blütezeit zwischen 1520 und 1680. Erste Zeugnisse mehrsprachiger Lexikographie im 15. Jh. waren einige Wortschatzinventare, die man fast als Zufallsprodukte ansehen kann: (a) ein anonymer *Vocabularius gallico-belgico-latinus,* der in Löwen 1484—86 erschien (Vocabularius 1484 (Frz.-Niederl.-Lat.)), wohl eines der ersten mehrsprachigen Wortschatzinventare (erwähnt bei Claes 1980), (b) ein hebr.-arab.-ital. Glossar (Makre dardeke 1488; erwähnt bei Tancke 1984 und Zaunmüller 1958), (c) ein bretonisch-lat.-frz. Wörterbuch, das der bretonische Geistliche Jehan Lagadeuc 1499 unter dem Titel „*Catholicon*" für den bretonischen Klerus verfaßte, der sowohl Lat. als auch Frz. lernen mußte (Lagadeuc 1499).

Abgesehen von diesen sporadisch auftretenden Vorläufern erscheinen die ersten mehrsprachigen Wortschatzinventare, denen z. T. eine gewisse Kontinuität beschieden war, erst im 16. Jh.

Im 16. und 17. Jh. entstanden aus dem bereits erwähnten, ursprünglich dtsch.-ital., thematisch angeordneten Vocabularium des Adam von Rottweil (ital. auch Roduila) von 1477 nicht weniger als 3 Ausgaben dreisprachiger Vokabularien, 12 Ausgaben fünfsprachiger, 17 Ausgaben sechssprachiger Vokabularien, eine siebensprachige Fassung sowie 7 Ausgaben achtsprachiger Wörterbücher (Rottweil 1477 und Garon 1526). Die berücksichtigten Sprachen waren Ital., Dt., Lat., Altgr., Frz., Span., Engl., Niederl. und Tschechisch („Böhmisch").

Auch die meist als selbständige Werke zitierten *Quinque linguarum utilissimus vocabulista ... mit* Lat.-Ital.-Frz.-Span.-Dt. (Quinque linguarum 1513) bzw. mit Niederl. anstelle von Dt. (Quinque linguarum 1534), das *Dictionarium sex linguarum* 1505 und der *Dictionnaire des huit langages,* 1546, meist unter dem Namen des Druckers Pasquier Le Tellier zitiert, ferner der *Dictionnaire des sept langages* (Dictionnaire 1540) sind Weiterentwicklungen des ursprünglich nur ital.-dt. Vokabulariums von Adam von Rottweil, wobei diese Filiation bei den meisten Autoren nicht erwähnt wird (vgl. dagegen Gallina 1959, 38—40).

Das auf das lat.-span. Wörterbuch von Elio Antonio de Nebrija (vgl. Art. 182) zu-

rückgehende *Vocabularium Nebrissense ex siciliense sermone in Latinum* [...] des Andalusiers Cristóforo de Escobar wurde ein Jahr später vom Verf. auf Lat.-Sizilianisch-Span. erweitert (Escobar 1520), und so entstand auch hier ein mehrsprachiges Wörterbuch aus einem zweisprachigen. Aus einem zweisprachigen (Frz.-Niederl.) „*Vocabulare"* des Noel de Berlaimont (Berlaimont 1536), einem Gesprächsbuch, entstand eine Reihe von mehrsprachigen Ausgaben, die der Verf. selbst nicht mehr bearbeitet hatte und die teils unter dem Namen des jeweiligen Drukkers (Grave 1551 und 1558 sowie Trogney 1639), teils anonym (Colloquia 1560, 1610, 1630 und 1634) erschienen.

Insgesamt gehen auf das „*Vocabulare"* von 1536 zurück: 2 dreisprachige, 32 viersprachige, 25 sechssprachige, 13 siebensprachige und 20 achtsprachige Gesprächsbücher (nach Gallina 1959, 87—91). Die berücksichtigten Sprachen waren Niederl., Frz., Dt., Span., Ital., Lat., Engl., Port. und je in einer Ausgabe Tschechisch und Polnisch. Bei den Nachkommen des Berlaimont'schen „*Vocabulare"* wurden auch — wie bei vielen anderen mehrsprachigen Wörterbüchern der damaligen Zeit — einzelne Sprachen durch andere ersetzt.

Eines der erfolgreichsten mehrsprachigen Wörterbücher des 16. und 17. Jh., das immer wieder erweitert wurde, war das ursprünglich einsprachige lat. Wörterbuch des ital. Augustinermönchs Ambrogio Calepino, meist latinisiert zu Ambrosius Calepinus (1435—1511). Dieses nach Wortstämmen gegliederte Lateinwörterbuch, das nur gelegentlich altgr. Äquivalente angibt, erschien zuerst 1502 in Reggio und wurde in dieser Form häufig neu aufgelegt. In der Ausgabe von Venedig von 1550 kam das Ital. hinzu und die 2. Aufl. dieser Fassung von 1553 diente dann als Grundlage für zahlreiche Ausgaben mit 4 bis 11 Sprachen.

1545 kamen Span. und Frz. hinzu (Antwerpen), 1568 Dt., 1570 Hebr. und Niederl., 1581 Engl., 1585 Poln. und Ungar., 1595 erschien eine Ausgabe mit Lat.-Port.-Jap. Insgesamt erfuhr der „Calepinus" neben den zahlreichen Ausgaben in Lat. (teilweise mit Altgr. und Ital.) 1 viersprachige, 24 fünfsprachige, 5 sechssprachige, 42 siebensprachige, 21 achtsprachige, 7 neunsprachige, 5 zehnsprachige und 9 elfsprachige Ausgaben bzw. Auflagen (vgl. hierzu u. a. Gallina 1959 und vor allem Labarre 1975; s. auch die in 6.1. aufgeführten Ausgaben von 1502—1758, von denen die von 1572, 1574, 1581 und 1590 in der Augsburger Universitätsbibliothek eingesehen werden konnten).

Es muß aber bemerkt werden, daß der Calepino kein echtes mehrsprachiges Wörterbuch ist, sondern stets als Ausgangssprache Lat. hat. Auf das lat. Stichwort folgen lat. Definitionen und lat. Zitate; die anderen Sprachen erscheinen sozusagen als zusätzliche Information. Weitere Beispiele für Erweiterungen von Wörterbüchern bieten: der dreisprachige *Dictionarie newelye corrected* [...] von Huloet mit Lat.-Engl.-Frz. (Huloet 1572), der auf das *Abecedarium anglico-latinum* des gleichen Verf. von 1552 zurückgeht, und das sechssprachige Werk *Sylva [...] vocabulorum et phrasium* des protestantischen Theologen Heinrich Decimator mit Dt.-Hebr.-Chaldäisch-Lat.-Altgr.-Frz. (Decimator 1586), das auf das ursprünglich nur dt.-lat.-altgr. Vokabularium des gleichen Autors zurückgeht (Decimator 1580). Ausgangssprache ist bei beiden Werken Dt. (vgl. auch Decimator 1587). Insgesamt erfuhren die mehrsprachigen Fassungen des Werkes 13 Auflagen (vgl. Quemada 1967, 365 und Gallina 1959, 191—204).

Andere mehrsprachige Wörterbücher sind jedoch nicht aus ein- oder zweisprachigen Wörterbüchern hervorgegangen, sondern wurden von Anfang an mehrsprachig konzipiert, so z. B. der *Nomenclator omnium rerum* [...] von Adriaans de Jonghe, meist zu Hadrianus Junius latinisiert.

In dem thematisch aufgebauten, erstmalig 1567 erschienenen Werk folgt auf das lat. Stichwort die jeweilige Übersetzung ins Altgr., Dt., Niederl., Frz., Ital., Span. u. Engl. Diese Fassung erfuhr insgesamt 25 Auflagen. Im Gegensatz zu anderen Wörterbüchern, die um neue Sprachen erweitert wurden, wurde dieses Wörterbuch auf 4 Sprachen (1 Ausgabe), 3 Sprachen (8 Ausgaben) und 2 Sprachen (4 Ausgaben) reduziert, wobei aber das Lat. stets Ausgangssprache blieb (vgl. u. a. Gallina 1959, 133 ff. und Quemada 1967, 364 sowie in 6.1.: Junius 1567, 1588 und 1623 als Beispiele).

Ein weiteres selbständiges polyglottes Wörterbuch ist das in England erschienene Werk *Hegemon eistas glossas, id est Ductor in Linguas* von John Minshew (Minshew 1617a), das folgende Sprachen umfaßt: Engl., Walisisch., Dt., Niederl., Frz., Ital., Span., Port., Lat., Altgr. und Hebr.

Viele mehrsprachige Wortschatzinventare sind, wie wir gesehen haben, durch Erweiterung bzw. Kürzung oder durch Substitution einzelner Sprachen entstanden. In vielen Fällen ist der Name des ursprünglichen Autors weggefallen und wurde durch den des Drukkers bzw. Bearbeiters ersetzt bzw. das Werk wurde anonym veröffentlicht. In anderen Fällen wird die ursprüngliche Fassung ausdrücklich erwähnt (z. B. bei Escobar 1520) oder der Name des ursprünglichen Autors zusammen mit dem des Bearbeiters genannt; so werden z. B. Robert Estienne und John Vernon zusammen aufgeführt im Titel des *Dictionariolum puerorum,* das 1552 erschien und auf das frühere (Paris 1548) *Dictionarium puerorum* von Robert Estienne zurückgeht (Estienne/Vernon 1552). In anderen Fällen ist der Name des Urvaters einer Wörterbuchserie über die Jahrhunderte erhalten geblieben wie z. B. bei Calepino. Emmelius, der Autor eines dreisprachigen Wörterbuches (Emmelius 1586) erwähnt im Titel seines Werkes ausdrücklich seine Quellen: *Lexicon trilingue, ex Thesauro Roberti Stephani et Dictionario Joannis Frisii collectum...* Neben der Neubearbeitung oder Weiterführung bereits erschienener Wörterbücher waren auch Plagiate, z. T. auch noch zu Lebzeiten des ursprünglichen Autors sehr häufig. Einer der bekanntesten Fälle eines Plagiats ist der *Tesoro de las tres lenguas, española, francesa y italiana* von Hierosme Victor (auch: Girolamo Vittori) von 1606 oder 1609 (vgl. Victor 1609), der einfach eine Erweiterung um eine Sprache des *Tesoro de las lenguas francesa y española* von César Oudin (Paris 1607) darstellt, wobei Vittori nur jeweils die ital. Äquivalente hinzugefügt hat. Oudin beklagt sich übrigens ausdrücklich in der 2. Aufl. seines *Tesoro* (Paris 1616) über das Plagiat. Letzteres erfuhr immerhin 18 Auflagen (vgl. Gallina 1959, 229—246).

Die mehrsprachigen Wörterbücher erscheinen im 16. Jh. unter den verschiedensten Titeln, zuerst lat. wie *Porta, Vestibulum, Janua* (Idee des Zugangs zu den Sprachen), *Gazophylacium, Sylva, Thesaurus, Lexicon, Vocabulista, Vocabularium, Dictionarium* (und *Dictionariolum*). Nach 1550 werden die letzteren drei Bezeichnungen und ihre Entsprechungen in den einzelnen modernen Sprachen immer häufiger (*dictionnaire, Wörterbuch, Ordbok, Woordenboek* usw.), um im 18. Jh., bis auf wenige Ausnahmen, allgemein üblich zu werden.

Auf die oft kurzen Vokabularien („*Vocabolarietti", „nomenclaturae"* usw.) der 1. Hälfte des 16. Jh. folgen schon gegen Ende des Jh. und vor allem im 17. Jh. umfangreiche Wörterbücher. So umfaßt die Auflage des *Tesoro de las tres lenguas* des Hierosme Victor von 1613 bereits 3 Bde mit 570, 420 und 504 S. Zu den umfangreicheren Wörterbüchern gehören u. a. auch die verschiedenen großen Ausgaben von Calepino, der *Dictionnaire impérial* (Veneroni 1700), der *Dictionnaire François-Allemand-Italien et Latin* von

306. Die mehrsprachigen Wörterbücher und ihre Probleme

Levinus Hulsius (Hulsius 1631) und der *Grand Dictionnaire Royal* (Frz.-Lat.-Dt.) des François Pomai, von dem wir die 4. Auflage von 1709 (UB Augsburg) einsehen konnten (Pomai 1709).

Bei der Beurteilung der mehrsprachigen Lexikographie im 16. und 17. Jh. ist es auch aufschlußreich zu untersuchen, welche Sprachen zuerst in polyglotten Wortschatzinventaren vertreten sind. Wir beziehen uns hier auf das erste Auftreten der in 6.1. aufgeführten mehrsprachigen Wörterbücher und sind uns bewußt, daß hier sicher noch frühere Datierungen möglich sind (vgl. oben 1.). Dennoch lassen sich gewisse Tendenzen feststellen. Während in den drei mehrsprachigen Wortschatzinventaren des 15. Jh., die wir als Zufallsprodukte bezeichnet hatten, die Sprachen Lat., Hebr., Arab., Ital., Frz., Niederl. (Flämisch) und Bretonisch vertreten waren, ergibt sich für das 16. und 17. Jh. folgendes Bild.

Lat., Ital., Frz., Span., Dt. und Engl. sind bereits im *Dictionarium sex linguarum* 1505 vertreten, wobei das Engl. dann erst in der 2. Hälfte des 16. Jh. häufiger in mehrsprachigen Wörterbüchern erscheint. Tschech. erscheint erstaunlich früh (1513) im *Dictionarius trium linguarum, Latinae, Teutonicae et Boemicae potiora vocabula continens* (Dictionarius 1513) und dann noch bei Pesthi 1538 und Codicillus 1546. Niederl. (meist Flämisch und nicht Holländisch) ist bereits 1520 im anonymen *Vocabulario para aprender franches, espannol y flaminco* vertreten (Vocabulario 1520) und ist dann im 16. und 17. Jh. häufig eine der Sprachen in mehrsprachigen Wortschatzinventaren. Poln. ist auch relativ früh im *Dictionarium trium linguarum, Latinae, Teutonicae et Polonicae* [...] enthalten (Mymerus 1528). Als Ausgangssprache erscheint es dann bei Cnapius 1621. Ungar. ist bereits 1533 in einem mehrsprachigen Wörterbuch vertreten (Murmelius 1533). Altgr., das bereits als Erklärungssprache in der Urfassung des Calepino erscheint (Calepinus 1502), ist dann wiederum u. a. vertreten im viersprachigen Wörterbuch von Gelenius 1537, in dessen Neuauflage von 1544, bei Servilius 1545 und im anonymen *Dictionnaire des huit langages* 1546. Arab. kommt bereits in Form von arabischen Wortäquivalenten in den naturwissenschaftlichen Werken von Gesnerus 1551, Laguna 1555 und Dalechamps 1615 vor, aber noch in keinem allgemeinsprachlichen Wörterbuch. Persisch wird ebenfalls in den Wortlisten von Gesnerus 1551 berücksichtigt, tritt aber erst 1645 in einem allgemeinsprachlichen Wörterbuch auf und ist Ausgangssprache bei Saint-Joseph 1684. Port. erscheint als Äquivalentsprache im medizinischen Werk von Laguna 1555, dann in einem allgemeinen Wörterbuch erst bei Calepinus 1595. Katal. ist auch schon bei Laguna 1555 vertreten, erscheint aber dann erst wieder im allgemeinsprachlichen Wörterbuch von Lacavalleria 1641 (Span.-Kat.-Frz.). Baskisch ist erstaunlich früh im unveröffentlichten Werk des Landuchi 1562 vertreten, in einem veröffentlichten Wörterbuch dann 1642 (Thresor 1642). Türk. ist eine der Sprachen des *Vocabolario nuovo* 1567 und erscheint wiederum in einem „Dictionario" als Anhang zu einem Werk über die Türken (Crato 1596). Hebr. ist eine der im Calepinus 1581(?) vertretenen Sprachen, erscheint dann bei Decimator 1586 und als Ausgangssprache bei Pomis 1587. Schwed. erscheint erstmalig im schwed.-lat.-altgr. Wörterbuch von Helsingius 1587. Kroat. tritt zuerst bei Megiser 1592 auf und dann wiederum bei Verantius 1595. Jap. erscheint in einer dreisprachigen Ausgabe des Calepinus 1595. Slowenisch ist bei Megiser 1603 erstmalig vertreten. Malaiisch und Madagassisch sind erstmalig bei Houtman 1603 zu finden. Walisisch wird bei Minshew 1617a berücksichtigt. Chin. erscheint zuerst im Diccionario 1633. Finnisch tritt erstmalig bei Schroderus 1637 in Verbindung mit Schwed.-Lat.-Dt. auf, dann erscheinen beide Sprachen wiederum im Vocabularium Latinum 1664 (Lat.-Schwed.-Finnisch). Dän. erscheint erstmalig in dem frz.-dt.-ital.-dän. Wörterbuch von Mairas 1643 (bei Haugen 1984, 291). Was das Annamitische betrifft, so erschien beachtlich früh (1651) in Rom ein annamitisch (vietnamesisch)-port.-lat. Wörterbuch. Sprachenkombination, Erscheinungsjahr und Erscheinungsort deuten darauf hin, daß es für port. Missionare in Indochina verfaßt wurde (Rhodes 1651).

So sind bis Ende des 17. Jh. fast alle wichtigen europäischen Sprachen in mehrsprachigen Wörterbüchern vertreten, und zwar einschließlich der Sprachen des Altertums (Altgr., Lat., Hebr.). Russisch und Bulgarisch sind noch in keinem der mehrsprachigen Wörterbücher zu finden, dagegen die anderen slawischen Sprachen, deren Verbreitungsgebiete, u. a. auch durch ihre Zugehörigkeit zur römisch-katholischen Kirche eine stärkere Bindung an das übrige Europa hatten: Kroat. (als Illyricus oder Dalmatinus bezeichnet), Tschech. („Böhmisch"), Polnisch und Slowenisch. Lat. ist nicht nur als Ausgangssprache wie bei Calepinus, sondern häufig auch als Erklärungssprache vertreten, z. B. bei Stoer 1563. Den mannigfachen kriegerischen und friedlichen Kontakten zwischen Europa und dem Orient ist es wohl zuzuschreiben, daß Arabisch, Türkisch und Persisch relativ früh erscheinen. Wenn Jap., Annamitisch und Chin. früh auftreten, dann ist dies wohl durch die spanische und portugiesische Kolonisation im asiatisch-pazifischen Raum und die Tätigkeit spanischer und portugiesischer Missionare in Fernost zu erklären (Jap. erscheint erstmalig in der Kombination Lat.-Port.-Jap. bei Calepinus 1595 und Chin. im Diccionario 1633 in der Kombination Span.-Lat.-Chin.). Daß sogar Malaiisch und Madagassisch ziemlich früh auftreten, und zwar in der Kombination mit Niederl., ist sicher durch den Handel der Holländer im pazifischen Raum bedingt (Houtman 1603). Die Zahl der in einem Werk gegenübergestellten Sprachen wuchs seit 1505 ständig, und so finden wir bei Calepinus 1581 bereits 9 Sprachen, bei Calepinus 1605 11 Sprachen, ebenso bei Minshew 1617 a und bei Megiser 1603 sogar 16 Sprachen. Hierbei ist allerdings zu berücksichtigen, daß häufig mit wachsender Sprachenzahl die Zahl der Einträge sinkt, worauf schon Quemada 1967, 44 hingewiesen hat.

Im 16. und 17. Jh. kommen 6 Haupttypen von mehrsprachigen Wortschatzinventaren vor: (a) Wörterbücher i. e. S., d. h. meist alphabetisch geordnete Äquivalenzwörterbücher von einem gewissen Umfang. Beispiele: der „Calepinus" (vgl. 6. 1. u. weiter oben), das *Dictionarium triglotton* von Servilius 1545 und das Wörterbuch von Escobar 1520. Bei diesem Typ ist der Wortschatz meist alphabetisch nach der Ausgangssprache geordnet. Auch Kombinationen von alphabetischer und thematischer Anordnung finden sich, z. B. bei Howell 1659—60: 1. Teil alphabetisches Wörterbuch, 2. Teil thematisch gegliedertes Vokabularium. — Bei den Wörterbüchern i. e. S. sind wieder zwei Haupttypen zu unterscheiden. Bei (aa) unechten mehrsprachigen Wörterbüchern sind die Einträge der Ausgangssprache alphabetisch geordnet und dazu werden die Äquivalente in anderen Sprachen gegeben. Da letztere aber nicht in einer eigenen Wortliste als Ausgangssprache erscheinen, ist ein direkter Zugriff auf die übrigen Sprachen nicht möglich. Quemada 1967 spricht hier von „faux trilingues, quadrilingues" usw. und von „plurilingues à entrées simples". Es ist auch noch zu vermerken, daß in diesen Wörterbüchern oft die Äquivalente in einzelnen Sprachen nur teilweise angegeben werden und teilweise fehlen, so z. B. bei Toscanella 1568. Aus diesen beiden Gründen bedeutet im 16. und 17. Jh. Vielsprachigkeit keinesfalls Gleichwertigkeit der Darstellung für die einzelnen Sprachen. Diese finden wir in den (ab) echten mehrsprachigen Wörterbüchern (bei Quemada 1967: „plurilingues à entrées multiples"). Für diese möchten wir als Beispiele anführen: das dt.-frz.-ital. Wörterbuch von Hulsius 1616 und den *Dictionnaire impérial représentant les quatre Langues principales de l'Europe* (Ital.-Frz.-Dt.-Lat.) in 4 Teilen, wobei jede der vier Sprachen in einem besonderen Teil Ausgangssprache ist (Veneroni 1700). Dieser Typ, der maximal bis zu vier Sprachen umfaßt, meistens aber durch dreisprachige Wörterbücher vertreten ist, hat allmählich die Wörterbücher mit noch mehr Sprachen verdrängt. (b) Vokabularien, Wortschatzsammlungen, meist thematisch geordnet. Thematisch in 50 Kapiteln dargestellten Wortschatz in drei Sprachen (Ital., Frz., Span.) bieten z. B. die *Nomenclatura* [...] von Guillaume Alexandre de Noviliers (Noviliers 1629; vgl. a. Gallina 1959, 293 und Quemada 1967, 364) sowie die bereits in anderem Zusammenhang erwähnten Vokabularien von Adam von Rottweil, die später unter anderem Namen erschienen (Rottweil 1477), wie auch die von Adrianus Junius (Junius 1567) und von Decimator (Decimator 1580, 1586, 1587, 1595, 1600, 1606, 1633). Oft sind mehrsprachige thematisch aufgebaute Vokabularien Teil eines umfassenderen Werkes, z. B. einer Grammatik oder eines Gesprächsbuches. Der *Thesaurus fundamentalis quinque linguarum* von Johannes Angelus Sumarán umfaßt z. B. 3 Teile: 1. Teil: Grammatische Ausführungen Span., Frz. und Ital., 2. Teil: ein Gesprächsbuch, 3. Teil: ein in 29 Kapiteln dargestellter thematischer Wortschatz mit Lat. (Ausgangssprache), Ital., Frz., Span. und Dt. (vgl. Sumarán 1626). Unter den thematisch geordneten Wortschatzinventaren ist auch das *Vocabularium latino-svecogermanico-finnicum* von Henrik Florinus zu erwähnen (Florinus 1695, Probeseite bei Haugen 1984, 7). Ein thematisch aufgebautes Werk besonderer Art ist der *Orbis sensualium pictus* des Böhmen Jan Amos Komenský, dessen Name in den Titeln seiner Werke meist als Johann(es) Amos Comenius erscheint. Das Werk stellt, jeweils auf der linken Seite, Begriffe aus einzelnen Sachgebieten (z. B. Wetter, Landbau, Fischerei) in Form von Tafeln bildlich dar und gibt dazu auf der rechten Seite die entsprechenden Wörter, und zwar in der 1. Ausgabe lat. und dt. (Comenius, Orbis 1658), später auch in anderen Sprachen, meist in einem Kontext in kurzen Sätzen. Dieses Werk kann daher als der Vorläufer der modernen Bildwörterbücher gelten.

Bald wurde der *Orbis pictus* auch für andere Kombinationen von zwei oder mehr Sprachen bearbeitet, z. B. 1669 Engl.-Lat. und 1666

306. Die mehrsprachigen Wörterbücher und ihre Probleme

Lat.-Dt.-Ital.-Frz. Es gab vom *Orbis pictus* zwischen 1658 und 1966 z. T. erheblich umgestaltete zwei- und mehrsprachige Ausgaben, und zwar 125 zweisprachige, 56 dreisprachige, 50 viersprachige, 6 fünfsprachige und 2 sechssprachige, d. h. insgesamt 239 tatsächlich veröffentlichte Ausgaben in mehr als einer Sprache. Die berücksichtigten Sprachen (es werden nur Werke erwähnt, die mehr als 5 Ausgaben erfuhren) sind: Lat. 215, Dt. 180, Frz. 53, Ungar. 41, Tschech. 38, Poln. 37, Russ. 18, Engl. 15, Ital. 14, Schwedisch 10, Slowakisch 10, Slowenisch 6 (vgl. Hupka 1989 und Pilz 1967). Damit hat der *Orbis pictus* sogar noch die großen Erfolge des „Calepino" (vgl. oben) übertroffen.

(c) Gesprächsbücher (phrase books) enthalten Gespräche (ausgeformte Sätze) in der Ausgangssprache mit den Äquivalenten in verschiedenen anderen Sprachen. Diese Bücher waren für die Praxis gedacht. So bringt z. B. Berlaimont (Berlaimont 1536, vgl. weiter oben) sogar Muster von Handelsbriefen. Auch diese Wortschatzinventare treten z. T. in Kombination mit Sprachlehrwerken auf, z. B. thematisch aufgebauten Vokabularien, wie wir schon bei Sumarán 1626 gesehen haben. Ein berühmtes Gesprächsbuch, das viel Erfolg hatte, war das Werk *Janua Linguarum Reserata* des bereits erwähnten Johannes Amos Comenius, das zuerst 1631 als lat. Schulbuch erschien. Mit 8000 lat. Wörtern wurden ca. 1000 Sätze gebildet.

Bald erschienen dann auch mehrsprachige Ausgaben, z. B. 1638 Lat.-Frz.-Dt., im gleichen Jahr eine Fassung mit Lat.-Frz.-Ital., 1641 eine fünfsprachige Ausgabe mit Lat.-Dt.-Frz.-Ital.-Span., 1643 eine dreisprachige mit Lat.-Altgr.-Frz. und 1684 eine dreisprachige Ausgabe mit Lat.-Frz.-Niederl. (s. in 6.1.: Comenius 1638, 1638a, 1641, 1643, 1661 und 1684).

(d) Sprichwortsammlungen waren bereits im 16. Jh. beliebt, wie z. B. die *Proverbia Gallicana, una cum interpretatione tum Teutonica, tum Latina* von Zegers (1554: Frz.-Niederl.-Lat.). Megiser, der bereits als Autor des *Dictionarium quattuor linguarum* [...] (Megiser 1592) erwähnt wurde, hat auch eine Sammlung von Sprichwörtern in insgesamt 11 Sprachen verfaßt (Megiser 1605). Ein dreibändiges Werk über altgr., dt., niederl., ital., frz. und span. Sprichwörter verdanken wir Gruterus 1610. Floriato veröffentlichte 1636 sein Werk *Proverborum trilinguium collectanea latina, itala et hispanica* (Floriato 1636). Sprichwörter auf Frz., Dän., Ital. und Dt. finden wir bei Matras 1633.

(e) Wörterbücher mit besonderer Zielsetzung: Ein Wörterbuch zu einem Autor, nämlich zu Cicero, veröffentlichte Mario Nizzoli. Das Werk war zunächst einsprachig lat., mit Wörtern, Redensarten und Zitaten aus Cicero: *Marii Nizzolii Brixellensis Observationum in M. T. Ciceronem* (Nizzoli 1535); eine weitere Auflage erschien 1551 in Venedig unter dem Titel *Thesaurus Ciceronianus*. Ab 1606 wurde dieses Wörterbuch mit Übersetzungen ins Ital., Frz. und Span. veröffentlicht (ebenfalls in Venedig) und erfuhr insgesamt 68 Ausgaben (Gallina 1959, 215—218). Das Werk wurde geschrieben, um gutes, klassisches Lat. zu lehren. — Als Lehrwerk mit Ausgangssprache Hebräisch ist Hutterus 1597 zu erwähnen, mit Äquivalenten in Altgr., Lat. und Dt., vermutlich in erster Linie für Theologen verfaßt. Dasselbe gilt für das *Lexicon Novi Testamenti Graeco-Latino-Belgicum* (Pasor 1690). — In diesem Zusammenhang ist die berühmte *Biblia poliglota Complutense* (6 Bde., Alcalá 1514—17) mit dem Text in Hebr., Chaldäisch, Altgr. und Lat. zu erwähnen. Mit dem mehrsprachigen Glossar der Wörter, die im Text erscheinen, enthält diese Bibelausgabe schon zu Beginn des 16. Jh. eines der ersten polyglotten Wörterbücher.

(f) Wenn es auch im 16. und 17. Jh. noch keine Fachwörterbücher im heutigen Sinne gab, so erscheinen doch bereits die ersten mehrsprachigen Fachwortglossare — meist nicht als selbständige Publikationen, sondern in naturwissenschaftlichen Werken. Die vermutlich ersten Zeugnisse von Fachlexikographie finden wir in den Werken des Naturwissenschaftlers Konrad Gesner. In seinem Werk *Nomenclator Aquatilium Animantium* gibt der Verf., wenn auch nur teilweise, Äquivalente der lat. aufgeführten Tiernamen in anderen Sprachen (Gesnerus 1540), in seinem *Catalogus plantarum* (Gesnerus 1542) erscheinen die Pflanzennamen in Lat., Altgr., Dt. und Frz. In der *Historia animalium* (Gesnerus 1551) werden zu den lat. Namen Äquivalente in bis zu 12 Sprachen gegeben. Gesner schrieb natürlich diese Werke nicht als Lexikograph, sondern als Naturwissenschaftler, aber gewissermaßen als Nebenprodukt bietet er zoologischen und botanischen Wortschatz in mehreren Sprachen an. Auch die anderen ersten Zeugnisse mehrsprachiger Fachlexikographie erläutern meist Wortschatz der Botanik, Zoologie oder Medizin; so enthält z. B. das Werk *De aquatilibus* (Belon 1553) zoologischen Wortschatz in Altgr., Lat. und Frz. und ein anderes Werk desselben Verf., *Nature des poissons* (Belon 1555), Tafeln mit Altgr.-Lat.-Frz.-Ital. 1553 erschien in Straßburg bereits ein *Lexicon rei herbariae trilingue* mit Lat., Frz. und Dt. (Kyber 1553). In der *Materia medica,* der span. Übersetzung des Dioscorides (Laguna 1555) (auch mit Tier- und Pflanzennamen) gibt der Verf. meist die Namen auf Altgr., Lat. („Apothekerlatein"), Arab., Span., Katal., Port., Ital., Frz. und Dt. an (vgl. Colón/Soberanas 1985, 85—87). Der Botanik gewidmet sind das *Kruydtboeck* (Lobelius 1581) auf Niederl. mit Äquivalenten in Lat., Dt., Frz., Ital., Span. (z. T. Port.) und Engl. und ein weiteres *Cruydt-Boeck* (Dodoens 1608) mit Pflanzennamen auf Niederl., Dt., Lat. und Altgr. In seiner *Histoire générale des plantes* gibt Dalechamps sogar Äquivalente der Pflanzennamen in 10 Sprachen (Dalechamps 1615). Das auf Katal. verfaßte *Llibre dels secrets de agricultura, casa rústica y pastoril* von 1617 enthält Vokabellisten mit landwirtschaftlichen Termini auf Span., Katal., Lat., Port., Ital. und Frz. (Agustí 1617; vgl. Colón/Soberanas 1985, 100—102). Botanische Terminologie in mehreren Sprachen (Lat.-Niederl.-Frz.) enthält auch das *Lexicon novum herbarium tripartitum* von Vossius (1640). Ein regelrechtes Inventar der Pflanzennamen in 30 Sprachen bietet Mentzel 1682 (vgl. Claes 1980, 278). 1679 erschien noch das *Lexicon medicum, Graeco-Latinum in quo [. . .] Belgica nomina si quae fuerint adjunguntur* von Stephanus Blancardus mit Altgr.-Lat.-Niederl. (Blancardus 1679). So sind zwischen 1540 und 1680 bereits eine Reihe von Terminologiesammlungen der Botanik, Zoologie und Landwirtschaft entstanden, die man als Vorläufer und Wegbereiter der späteren Fachwörterbücher ansehen kann.

2.2. Die mehrsprachige Lexikographie im 18. Jahrhundert

Im 18. Jh. war die lexikographische Landschaft gegenüber den Anfängen im 15. Jh. stark verändert. Inzwischen war neben das zweisprachige Wörterbuch auch das einsprachige getreten, dessen Definitionen immer präziser wurden. Die großen Akademiewörterbücher waren entweder schon veröffentlicht (Italien, Frankreich) oder erschienen im 18. Jh. (Spanien). Auch einsprachige Fachwörterbücher wurden häufiger. Die Nationalsprachen setzten sich mehr und mehr gegen das Lat. durch, das sich zwar als Schulfach und z. T. noch als Wissenschaftssprache behauptete, aber doch Einbußen erlitt. Diese Entwicklung und ganz allgemein der Fortschritt der Wissenschaften, vor allem im Zeitalter der Enzyklopädie, konnten nicht ohne Auswirkungen auf die mehrsprachige Lexikographie bleiben. So ebbte die Welle der vielsprachigen Wörterbücher gegen Ende des 17. Jh. merklich ab. Wir finden noch einige viersprachige Wörterbücher, die meisten allgemeinsprachlichen Wörterbücher sind aber dreisprachig oder noch häufiger zweisprachig. Eine Ausnahme bilden hier nur wenige Werke:

— Das unter Förderung von Zarin Katharina II 1790—91 entstandene Wörterbuch „Pallas", meist als *Vocabularium Catherinae* zitiert, das Wortschatz aus 200 europäischen und asiatischen Sprachen bringt, dafür aber nur 130 Einträge hat (Pallas 1790). Hier geht es wie bei ähnlichen Werken von Sprachforschern, z. B. Hervás y Panduro, darum, eine Auswahl von Sprachproben für vergleichende Studien zu geben (Hervás 1784 und 1787). Im Zeichen der aufkommenden vergleichenden Sprachwissenschaft lebte dieser Typ von Wortschatzsammlung auch im 19. Jh. weiter.
— Das zweite Wörterbuch mit mehr als vier Sprachen ist das *Hexaglotton geminum, docens linguas* des Jesuitenpaters Weitenauer, in dem 10 Sprachen vertreten sind (Weitenauer 1762). —

Bezeichnenderweise sind die im 15. und 16. Jh. beliebten Wörterbücher von Berlaimont, Hadrianus Junius, Decimator, Hierosme Victor, Minshew, Sumarán, Noviliers Clavel und Howell nicht mehr aufgelegt oder neu bearbeitet worden. Nur die beiden beliebtesten mehrsprachigen Wörterbücher des 16. und 17. Jh. erschienen weiter in Neubearbeitungen: der Calepinus mit 17 siebensprachigen Ausgaben (vgl. Gallina 1959, 117—118 und als Beispiel in 6.1.: Calepinus 1758) und der *Orbis pictus* von Comenius (vgl. Pilz 1967). Die meisten Wörterbücher sind nunmehr echte mehrsprachige Nachschlagewerke, bei denen jede Sprache als Ausgangssprache eine eigene Wortliste oder zumindest ein Register besitzt und so ein Zugriff auf alle Sprachen möglich ist.

Neue Sprachen treten nun auch in mehrsprachigen Wörterbüchern auf, z. B. Neugriechisch (Vendoti 1790); Lappisch bei Lindahl/Öhrling 1780 (Lappisch-Schwed.-Lat.) und bei Leem/Sandberg 1768 in der Kombination Lappisch-Dän.-Lat. Grönländisch erscheint im grönl.-dän.-lat. Wörterbuch von Egede, dem „Apostel der Grönländer" (Egede 1750). Auch sonst erscheinen mehr Wortschatzinventare in Kombination mit einer skandinavischen Sprache: Dän.-Frz.-Lat. (Chamereau 1744); Schwed.-Engl.-Lat. (Serenius 1734 u. 1741); Schwed.-Engl.-Lat.-Frz. (Spegel 1712), Lat.-Schwed.-Dt. (Novum dictionarium 1700) und Finnisch-Lat.-Schwed. (Jusenius 1745). — Das Russ. tritt nunmehr in Kombination mit anderen nichtslawischen europäischen Sprachen auf, z. B. Frz.-Dt.-Lat.-Russ. im Dictionnaire 1762; Frz.-Ital.-Dt.-Russ. (Veneroni 1771), Russ.-Dt.-Frz. (Norstett

1780); Dt.-Lat.-Russ. (Volchkov 1755—64) sowie Russ.-Altgr.-Lat. (Polycarpius 1704). Poln. ist vertreten in der Kombination Frz.-Lat.-Poln. bei Danet 1743 und Frz.-Dt.-Poln. bei Troc 1742. — Baskisch erscheint in Kombination mit Span. und Lat. bei Larramendi 1745 und zusätzlich mit Frz. bei Etcheverri 1701. — Portugiesisch ist mit Frz. und Lat. kombiniert bei Costa e Sá 1794 und mit Niederl. und Malaiisch im *Nieuwe Woordenshat* 1780, eine Sprachkombination, die für die Holländer in den niederländischen Kolonien im pazifischen Raum (mit portugiesischen Nachbarkolonien) bestimmt war. — Bemerkenswert ist für das 18. Jh. die Sprachkombination Rumänisch-Albanisch-Griechisch-Mazedonisch im *Lexicon tetraglosson* von 1764 (Hadži P. Daniil 1764). Katal. erscheint kombiniert mit Span. und Lat. bei Anglés 1742. — Kombinationen, bei denen als eine Sprache Frz., Ital., Span., Dt., Engl. und Niederl. sowie Lat. oder Altgr. erscheint, sind, wie schon seit dem 16. Jh., weiterhin häufig vertreten. Um nur wenige Beispiele zu nennen: Ital.-Lat.-Frz. bei Antonini 1738; Dt.-Ital.-Frz. bei Rädlein 1711; Lat.-Dt.-Altgr.-Frz. bei Guertler 1731; Frz.-Span.-Lat. bei Sobrino 1769; Span.-Frz.-Lat. bei Séjournant 1749 und Span.-Frz.-Lat.-Ital. bei Terreros y Pando 1786; Frz.-Lat.-Dt. im *Dictionnaire orateur* 1709, bei Herbau 1716 und Pomai 1709.

In dreisprachigen Wörterbüchern ist Lat. als Ausgangssprache aus den oben erwähnten Gründen seltener geworden, erscheint jedoch häufig als zusätzliche Erklärungssprache, wie dies Antonini in seinem ital.-lat.-frz. Wörterbuch (Antonini 1738) klar zum Ausdruck bringt:

„Mon but a été uniquement de donner au Public un Dictionnaire Italien et François. Si j'y ai ajouté le Latin, ce n'a été que dans la seule vue d'amener mes Lecteurs à une plus juste intelligence de ces deux langues qui en dérivent. Permis à ceux qui ignorent cette troisième de ne me tenir aucun compte de ce surplus d'attention qui leur devient inutile. J'ai renfermé à dessein le Latin entre deux parenthèses, afin de leur épargner la peine de s'y arrêter". (Zitat nach Quemada 1967, 56).

Eine größere Anzahl von Sprachen hat sich — im Gegensatz zu den allgemeinsprachlichen Wörterbüchern — bei den Fachwörterbüchern behauptet und dies ist dann bis heute so geblieben. Die Themen bei den Fachwörterbüchern werden allmählich vielfältiger.

Botanik bei Munting 1702; Naturwissenschaften i. w. S. bei Nemnich 1793; Musik bei Brossard 1703; Mineralogie bei Reuss 1798; Handwerk und Technik i. w. S. im eindrucksvollen dreibändigen Werk von Terreros y Pando 1786; Holzkunde bei Houttuyn 1773; Marinewortschatz bei Röding 1794 und im Vocabulary 1799; Warenkunde bei Nemnich 1797. Hier begann eine Entwicklung, die bis heute andauern sollte.

Als Beispiel für eine **Sprichwortsammlung** sei der *Recueil de proverbes françois, latins, espagnols, italiens, allemands, hollandois, juifs, américains, russes* (Humières 1790) genannt. Ein viersprachiges **Gesprächsbuch** verfaßte Grandpre unter dem Titel *The traveller's interpreter in four languages* mit Engl.-Niederl.-Frz.-Ital. (Grandpre 1728). Als Beispiel für ein thematisch geordnetes dreisprachiges **Vokabularium** sei noch das *Promptuario* von Joseph Broch mit Katal.-Span.-Frz. zitiert (Broch 1771).

2.3. Die mehrsprachige Lexikographie im 19. Jahrhundert

Bei den mehrsprachigen Wörterbüchern dominieren im 19. Jh. einerseits die allgemeinsprachlichen Wörterbücher von Sprachen, die in Europa zunächst eher marginal oder „exotisch" und deshalb in den vorhergehenden Jh. seltener vertreten waren (z. B. Russisch, Schwedisch, Finnisch), andererseits die mehrsprachigen Fachwörterbücher, deren Themenbereiche immer differenzierter werden. So finden wir, was exotische Sprachen betrifft, allgemeinsprachliche Wörterbücher, in deren Sprachkombination folgende Sprachen vorkommen: Chinesisch bei Guignes 1813, Javanisch bei Bruckner 1842, Tamil (Tamulisch) im Dictionarium 1846, Georgisch bei Soulkhanov 1839, Armenisch bei Eminian 1853, Thai bei Pallegoix 1854, Isländisch bei Haldorson 1814, Arabisch und Türkisch bei Letellier 1838 und Neugr. bei Theocharopoulos 1834 und Schmidt 1837. Katal. ist infolge der sprachlich-kulturellen Erneurungsbewegung der „Renaixença" mit drei mehrsprachigen Wörterbüchern gut vertreten: Esteve 1803 (Katal.-Span.-Lat.), Labèrnia 1839 (Katal.-Span.-Lat.) und das von einer „Societat de catalans" verfaßte Diccionari català-castellà-llatí-francès-italià (Diccionari 1839). Baskisch enthält das viersprachige Wörterbuch von Chao 1836 (Baskisch-Frz.-Span.-Lat.). Von den bis zum 18. Jh. mehr „marginalen" Sprachen erscheinen die folgenden in Wörterbüchern: Port. bei Ionchère 1807; Russ. bei Heym 1802 und 1805 sowie bei Reiff 1879; Poln. im Nouveau dictionnaire 1807, Schwed. im Dictionnaire 1840, bei Lindberg 1835 und im Ordbok 1856; Dän. bei Valentin 1843.

Abgesehen von Polidori 1806 und Falletti 1822, beide mit der Kombination Ital.-

Engl.-Frz., sind die wichtigen europäischen Sprachen wie Dt., Frz., Engl., Span. u. Ital. in Kombination untereinander im 19. Jh. seltener in mehrsprachigen Wörterbüchern vertreten, vermutlich weil man mit den zweisprachigen Wörterbüchern bessere Erfahrungen gemacht hatte. Dagegen hat sich die Mehrsprachigkeit bei den Fachwörterbüchern behauptet. Mit der Entwicklung von Technik und Verkehr werden auch die behandelten Fachgebiete immer spezieller. Auffällig ist, daß unter den behandelten Fachgebieten der Marinewortschatz (besonders Schiffsbau und Seefahrt) an der Spitze steht, was wohl durch die starke Entwicklung des Seeverkehrs nach Einführung der Dampfschiffahrt zu erklären ist.

Diesem Gebiet sind gewidmet: Lantsheer 1811 (Frz.-Niederl.-Engl.); Twent 1813 (Niederl.-Engl.-Frz.); O'Scanlan 1829 (Frz.-Engl.-Ital.-Span.); Müller 1847 (Dän.-Dt.-Engl.-Span.-Frz.-Niederl.-Ital.-Port.-Russ.-Schwed.); Jal 1848 in 18 Sprachen; Lorenzo 1864 (Span.-Frz.-Engl.-Ital.); Bobrik 1878 in 9 Sprachen; Boom 1879 (Niederl.-Engl.-Frz.-, spätere Aufl. mit Dt.) und Badings 1880 (Niederl.-Malaiisch-Frz.-Engl.).

An zweiter Stelle stehen bereits im 19. Jh. die Wörterbücher der Technik, z. B. ein achtsprachiges technisches Wörterbuch von Reehorst 1842; ein dt.-frz.-engl. von Beil 1853; ein frz.-engl.-dt. von Tolhausen 1854; ein span.-frz.-engl.-ital. Wörterbuch der Architektur und des Ingenieurwesens von Clairac 1877 sowie ein dt.-engl.-span.-frz. Wörterbuch für Bergbau, Metallurgie und Chemie (Venator 1899). Ebenso gut vertreten ist die Wirtschaft mit einem *Comtoir-Lexikon in neun Sprachen für Geschäftsmänner* (Nemnich 1803), einem zwölfsprachigen Warenlexikon (Nemnich 1820), einem zehnsprachigen *Polyglot Commercial Dictionary* (Reehorst 1850), einem sechssprachigen Wörterbuch der Handels- und Geschäftssprache (Brutzer 1873), einem viersprachigen Handelswörterbuch (Oosting 1887) sowie einem neunsprachigen Wörterbuch der Handelskorrespondenz (Antonoff 1884). Militärwortschatz bringen ein niederl.-frz.-dt. Wörterbuch (Creutz Lechleitner 1839), ein dt.-engl.-frz. Wörterbuch (Duckett 1948), ein frz.-engl.-span. Werk (Enrile 1853) und ein frz.-dt.-engl.-niederl.-japan. Wörterbuch (Dictionnaire 1880). Den Wortschatz der Kavallerie behandelt Römer 1891 (Niederl.-Frz.; Niederl.-Dt.). Sonst gibt es u. a. Fachwörterbücher für Numismatik (Ambrosoli 1897); Botanik und Gartenbau (Jongkindt 1894) und Medizin, z. B. ein zwölfsprachiges Wörterbuch der Krankheitsnamen (Nemnich 1800).

Die Entwicklung der Philologie und vor allem der vergleichenden Sprachwissenschaft führte wie schon im 18. Jh. (vgl. Pallas 1790 sowie Hervás y Panduro 1784 und 1787) zur Entstehung weiterer Wörterbücher und anderer Werke, die eine Auswahl von Wortschatz in verschiedenen Sprachen zum Zwecke des Sprachvergleichs bringen, wie Adelung 1806 (der kein eigentliches Wörterbuch darstellt), Schischkoff 1838 mit einem vergleichenden Wörterbuch in 200 Sprachen, das *Specimen lexici comparativi omnium linguarum europearum* von Prinz Louis Lucien Bonaparte mit Wortschatzproben aus 52 Sprachen (Bonaparte 1846) und das *Comparative Vocabulary of forty-eight languages* [...] von Tomlin 1865.

Ist im 19. Jh. die Tendenz zu mehrsprachigen allgemeinsprachlichen Wörterbüchern mit wichtigen europäischen Sprachen eher rückläufig, so können wir gleichzeitig — wohl bedingt durch die Entwicklung von Handel, Verkehr und Tourismus — eine Zunahme bei mehrsprachigen Gesprächsbüchern feststellen.

Hier sind u. a. zu erwähnen: ein *Manuel interprète de correspondance* von Cambry 1805; ein Gesprächs- und Vokabelbuch Frz.-Russ.-Poln.-Dt. (Recueil 1832); ein sechssprachiges Gesprächsbuch von Núñez de Taboada 1833; ein Gesprächsbuch in 5 Sprachen von Smith 1843; ein dreisprachiges *Vocabulaire du voyageur* 1837; ein dreisprachiges und zwei viersprachige Gesprächsbücher von Smith (1840[1], 1840a, b); ein sechssprachiges Konversationsbuch (Smith 1843); ein dt.-engl.-frz.-ital. Gesprächsbuch von Mesnard 1841; ein sechssprachiger *Guide polyglotte* (Duarte 1859); ein viersprachiges Konversationsbuch von Ochoa 1860 sowie ein kurioser *Tornisterdolmetscher des deutschen Reichssoldaten im täglichen Verkehr mit den Grenzvölkern des deutschen Reiches* mit Dt.-Dän.-Niederl.-Frz.-Russ.-Poln.-Tschech. (Kasprowicz 1878). Ähnlichen Zwecken diente auch ein für die Teilnahme an den Napoleonischen Kriegen verfaßtes *Petit vocabulaire à l'usage des Français et des Alliés* [...] mit Frz. - Lat. - Hebr. - Niederl. - Dt. - Engl. - Schottisch - Span. - Ital. - Hannoveranisch - Badisch - Hessisch - Tirolerisch - Schweizerisch (Denys de Montfort 1815).

Wichtige Sprichwortsammlungen des 19. Jh. sind u. a. *A polyglot dictionary of foreign proverbs* mit Frz.-Ital.-Dt.-Niederl.-Span.-Port.-Dän.-Engl. (Bohn 1857), eine viersprachige Sprichwortsammlung (Frz.-Engl.-Dt.-Niederl.) von Calisch 1876 und eine weitere niederl.-frz.-dt.-engl. von Valette 1888.

Auch thematisch aufgebaute Vokabularien für Unterrichtszwecke gibt es weiterhin im 19. Jh., wie z. B. das *Manuel du Pensionnat en 3 langues* (Manuel 1875) mit Dt.-Frz.-Engl.

So sind gegen Ende des 19. Jh. die meisten im 20. Jh. anzutreffenden Typen mehrsprachiger Wortschatzinventare bereits vorhanden: das allgemeinsprachliche Wörterbuch, das Fachwörterbuch, die Sprichwortsammlung, das Gesprächsbuch, das thematisch geordnete Vokabularium und die Wortschatzinventare für vergleichende Sprachstudien.

2.4. Die mehrsprachige Lexikographie im 20. Jahrhundert

Wenn man die Tausende von Titeln mehrsprachiger Wörterbücher durchgeht, die in den verschiedenen Bibliographien für das 20. Jh. angezeigt sind, fällt auf, daß sich die Fachwörterbücher und anderen Fachwortschatzinventare gegenüber den allgemeinsprachlichen Wörterbüchern mit mehr als zwei Sprachen in einer erdrückenden Überzahl befinden. Sicher ist dies vor allem dem Umstand zuzuschreiben, daß der Wortschatz einer Ausgangssprache schon nur mit Mühe in e i n e r Zielsprache dargestellt werden kann und die Beschreibung von allgemeinem Wortschatz in mehr als zwei Sprachen fast unlösbare Probleme aufwirft, während dies bei dem schärfer definierten Fachwortschatz dagegen durchaus möglich ist (vgl. 4.).

Wenn wir dennoch eine Reihe von allgemeinen mehrsprachigen Wörterbüchern im 20. Jh. finden, dann hat dies z. T. sehr spezielle Gründe.

Solche Wörterbücher wurden zum Beispiel für Sprachen geschrieben, deren Sprachgebiet weit entfernt von Europa liegt. Wenn die Kongosprache Lingala in Kombination mit Frz. und Niederl. in einem dreisprachigen Wörterbuch erscheint, dann war dies der Sprachsituation des ehem. Belgisch-Kongo zuzuschreiben (Blavier 1953). Wenn Malaiisch in Kombination mit Engl. und Niederl. in einem Wörterbuch von 1946 auftritt, so ist das durch die damalige Kolonialsituation bedingt (Helsloot 1946). Dasselbe gilt für den *Dictionnaire annamite-chinois-français* (Hue 1937). Oder es geht darum, eine kleinere Sprache außerhalb ihres Verbreitungsgebietes bekannt zu machen, wie z. B. bei einem Wörterbuch Lappisch-Schwed.-Dt. von 1939 (Grundström 1939) und einem anderen Lappisch-Engl.-Norwegisch von 1932 (Nielsen 1932) oder bei einem Wörterbuch Rätoromanisch-Dt.-Frz.-Engl. (Velleman 1929). Erwähnenswert sind auch zwei dreisprachige Wörterbücher in der Kombination Arab.-Frz.-Engl. (Blachère 1967 und Sabek 1971).

Als in der neuen demokratischen Monarchie Spaniens die lange verfolgten oder z. T. nur geduldeten Regionalsprachen Katalanisch, Baskisch und Galicisch (gallego) im Jahre 1977 Amtssprachen neben Span. wurden, erschien, gewissermaßen als Symbol größerer Sprachfreiheit, ein viersprachiges Wörterbuch: Span.-Katal.-Galicisch-Bask. unter dem Titel *Diccionario de las lenguas de España* (Fontanillo 1985). Wenn das Wörterbuch von Azkúe Baskisch in Kombination mit Frz. und Span. behandelt, so ist dies durch die geographische Lage des Baskenlandes zu erklären (Azkúe 1905).

Sonst gibt es unter den eigentl. allgemeinsprachlichen Wörterbüchern relativ wenig vielsprachige; die Ausnahmen sind z. B. ein dreisprachiges Wörterbuch Dt.-Frz.-Niederl. von 1940 (Dreisprachiges Taschenwörterbuch 1940) und ein frz.-dt.-engl.-niederl. Wörterbuch von 1937 (van Goor's Woordenboek 1937). Allerdings gibt es daneben einige Wörterbücher, die eine größere Anzahl von Sprachen berücksichtigen. Ihr Zweck ist vielleicht u. a., Wortschatz für vergleichende Sprachstudien zu bieten, wie wir dies schon bei anderen Wörterbüchern im 18. und 19. Jh. gesehen hatten. Sicher ist auch beim Auflisten von Wörtern in mehreren Sprachen so etwas wie Spielerei dabei und wohl auch nicht wenig verlegerisches Gewinnkalkül, denn als echte Nachschlagewerke sind diese vielsprachigen Wörterbücher nicht zu gebrauchen. Als Beispiele wollen wir nur einige Werke zitieren: Kürschners *Lexikon der sechs Weltsprachen* (Engl.-Frz.-Ital.-Span.-Lat.-Dt.) ist, dem Druck nach zu urteilen, ein photomechanischer Nachdruck eines Vorkriegswerkes (Kürschner 1954).

Zu dieser Gruppe gehören noch ein fünfsprachiges Wörterbuch (Pisant 1958), ein siebensprachiges Wörterbuch (Capitol's concise dictionary), ein Wörterbuch für 21 europäische Sprachen und Türkisch (Ouseg 1962), der *Concise Dictionary of 26 languages,* der aber für die 26 Sprachen insgesamt nur über 400 Seiten verfügt (Concise dictionary 1967), ferner *The 5 Language European Dictionary* (Orefice 1977) und ein Bildwörterbuch für 23 Sprachen (Lux 1943). Auch die mehrsprachigen Wortlisten, die im großen Wörterbuch von Funk and Wagnall als Anhang erschienen sind, fallen unter diese Kategorie (Funk and Wagnalls 1954) und gehören mit Engl. als Ausgangssprache zu den „dictionnaires à entrées simples" wie die ersten mehrsprachigen Wörterbücher des 16. Jh.

Die wirklich professionelle mehrsprachige Lexikographie des 20. Jh. ist aber die der Fachwörterbücher und Fachglossare, auf die wir in 3.1. eingehen werden. Die übrigen, aus früheren Jahrhunderten übernommenen Typen mehrsprachiger Wortschatzinventare haben sich weiterhin behauptet: thematische Vokabularien (vor allem für Lernzwecke), Reiseführer und Gesprächsbücher sowie Sprichwortsammlungen. Die nach dem Zweiten Weltkrieg entstandenen Grundwortschatzsammlungen, die meist ein- oder zweisprachig sind, wurden in einigen Fällen auf 3 oder mehr Sprachen erweitert, wobei aber auch hier, wie schon bei den Wörterbüchern des 16. Jh., nur die Ausgangssprache, die erlernt werden soll, maßgebend ist, z. B. beim dreisprachigen Grundwortschatz Dt.-Engl.-Span. (Klett 1973) (vgl. auch 3.1.). Neu ist im 20. Jh. in der Art der Darstellung, wenn auch schon durch Comenius begründet, das mehrsprachige Bildwörterbuch.

3. Typologie der mehrsprachigen Wörterbücher

Um die Probleme der heutigen mehrsprachigen Wörterbücher in angemessener Form beurteilen zu können, ist es unerläßlich, ihre verschiedenen Typen nach der Auswahl ihres Wortschatzes, nach der Anordnung ihrer Materialien (Makrostruktur) und der Gestaltung der einzelnen Einträge (Mikrostruktur) vorzustellen.

3.1. Typen mehrsprachiger Wörterbücher nach dem dargestellten Wortschatz

Zunächst ist es wichtig festzustellen, welche Auswahl lexikalischer Einheiten ein mehrsprachiges Wörterbuch bringt. Hier haben wir an erster Stelle den Typ des allgemeinen Wörterbuches, das eine — dem Umfang nach variable — breite Auswahl von Standardwortschatz verzeichnet, eine noch relativ repräsentative Auswahl aus dem gehobenen bzw. literarischen Wortschatz, eine meist weniger repräsentative Auswahl aus dem Substandardwortschatz, den Soziolekten, den Regionalismen und dem Fachwortschatz. Bis heute ist der Anteil der einzelnen Teilbereiche am Inhalt allgemeinsprachlicher Wörterbücher, egal ob sie einsprachig, zwei- oder mehrsprachig sind, nie genauer bestimmt worden und die Auswahl aus einzelnen Teilwortschatzbereichen, die außerhalb des Standardwortschatzes liegen, ist immer nach subjektiven Maßstäben erfolgt. Wenn wir jedoch den in allgemeinen mehrsprachigen Wörterbüchern tatsächlich dargestellten Wortschatz untersuchen, so überwiegt hier eindeutig der Standardwortschatz; der Wortschatz der gehobenen bzw. literarischen Ebene wird zumindest z. T. berücksichtigt. Die verschiedenen Schichten des Substandards und die übrigen Teilbereiche kommen kaum zum Zuge, so z. B. bei Kürschner 1954 oder Orefice 1977.

In den mehrsprachigen Wörterbüchern, die nur eine Auswahl aus einem bestimmten Wortschatzbereich bringen, könnten theoretisch alle in ein- und zweisprachigen Wörterbüchern beschriebenen Bereiche vertreten sein, in der Praxis ist dies aber kaum der Fall. So haben wir nur sehr wenige Beispiele dafür, daß Wortschatz mit diastratischer Markierung in mehrsprachigen Wörterbüchern erscheint. Ein Fall ist das englische Slangwörterbuch von Farmer/Henley, das Äquivalente der engl. Slangwörter auf Dt., Frz., Ital. und Span. bringt. (Farmer/Henley 1890). Sonst sind die Wortschatzinventare der Slangs, Argots, Gerghi, Jergas usw. überwiegend einsprachig, wenn es auch einige zweisprachige Werke gibt (z. B. Deak 1959, Marks 1970 und Villatte 1888). — Es gibt dagegen einige Beispiele für mehrsprachige Wörterbücher, die diaphasisch markierten Wortschatz bringen, meist handelt es sich um Schimpfwörterbücher wie z. B. der, übrigens ziemlich mangelhafte, *Dizionario degli insulti* 1980 (Ital.-Engl.-Frz.-Span.-Dt.) (vgl. auch Schmutzige Wörter 1987).

Darüber hinaus wird Wortschatz aus folgenden Bereichen in mehrsprachigen Wörterbüchern beschrieben:

— Idiomatik: Die Auswahl des Wortschatzes beschränkt sich hier auf idiomatische Redensarten, wobei meist Äquivalente von Redensarten einer Ausgangssprache gegeben werden, so daß wir hier der Typ „dictionnaire multilingue à entrées simples" wiederfinden. Beispiele: Burvenich 1905, Pradez 1951, Dony 1956 und Schaufelbüel 1986.

— Wie schon seit dem 16. Jh. gibt es auch heute noch mehrsprachige Inventare von Sprichwörtern, z. B. Burvenich 1905, Gluski 1971, Heng 1933, Ilg 1960, Proverbia septentrionalia 1985, Schaufelbüel 1986 und Veer-Bertels 1971.

— Zu den mehrsprachigen Wortschatzinventaren gehören auch Reisewörterbücher, Reiseführer und für Reisende verfaßte Gesprächsbücher, wie z. B. Bruin 1900, *Zestalige Woordenlijst* 1928, Brinkley 1938, Kettridge 1945 und Gilanov 1966. Auch hier kann man feststellen, daß bei diesem Wörterbuchtyp die zweisprachigen Werke heute überwiegen.

— Nahe verwandt mit den Gesprächsbüchern sind auch die Satzlexika, die es vor allem für Handelskorrespondenz gibt, wie z. B. *The Multi-*

lingual Business Handbook 1983 (Dt.-Engl.-Span.-Frz.-Ital.) und Berset 1979 (parallele Texte von Handelsbriefen in Dt.-Engl.-Frz.-Span.).

— Eine besondere Auswahl von Wortschatz, die durch die Zwänge bildlicher Darstellung bestimmt wird, bringen die **mehrsprachigen Bildwörterbücher**, wie z. B. Medina 1960 (Span.-Engl.-Frz.-Dt.), Backhausen 1948 (Dän.-Engl.-Frz.-Dt.), Bildwörterbuch Meyer 1981 (Dt.-Engl.-Frz.), Kerler 1971 (Span.-Frz.-Engl.-Dt.-Ital.), ein für militärische Zwecke verfaßter Bilderduden für Soldaten 1941 (Dt.-Bulgarisch-Rumänisch) und Lux 1946 in 23 Sprachen. Hierher gehören auch die verschiedenen Ausgaben der Duden-Bildwörterbücher, vgl. Art. 108.

— Eine genau umrissene Teilmenge von Wortschatz bringen auch die Wortschatzinventare von **geographischen Eigennamen**, wie z. B. das *Viersprachen-Länderverzeichnis*, hrsg. vom Auswärtigen Amt, Bonn (Viersprachen-Länderverzeichnis), und *Names of Countries [. . .], FAO Terminology Bulletin,* 20, rev. 8, Bonn 1986. Wie schon an anderer Stelle erwähnt (vgl. 2.4.), gibt es neuerdings auch **Grundwortschatzsammlungen**, die den Grundwortschatz für eine bestimmte Sprache bringen und dazu die Äquivalente in mehreren anderen Sprachen angeben, die aber hier eher als Lernhilfen aufzufassen sind, z. B. Klett 1973.

Zu mehrsprachigen Wortschatzinventaren i. w. S. gehören auch **Sprachatlanten**, die neben dem Wortschatz, der Gegenstand der Darstellung ist, Äquivalente in mindestens zwei weiteren Sprachen bringen, wie dies z. B. beim *Atlas linguistico-etnográfico de Colombia* der Fall ist (ALEC 1980), der engl. und frz. Äquivalente bringt.

— Für alle bisher erwähnten Typen mehrsprachiger Wortschatzinventare gibt es Beispiele, wenn auch oft nur einige wenige. Die Mehrzahl der mehrsprachigen Wortschatzinventare (Wörterbücher, Vokabularien, Glossarien) unserer Zeit bringt jedoch, wie schon wiederholt hervorgehoben, **Fachwortschatz**, d. h. ausgewählten Wortschatz aus einzelnen Wissenschaftsbereichen (Chemie, Soziologie) oder aus den verschiedensten anderen Gebieten menschlicher Tätigkeit (z. B. Sport, Spiele, Diplomatie, Musik). Hierbei kann es sich um umfassendere Wortschatzbereiche handeln, wie z. B. Wirtschaft, Recht, Technik, Chemie usw., oder um einzelne Teilbereiche bzw. Unterfachgebiete, z. B. Investitionen, Jugendstrafrecht, Textilmaschinen, Petrochemie. Viele dieser Wortschatzinventare sind reine Nomenklaturen, die oft nur Substantive aufnehmen. Ein gutes Fachwörterbuch sollte jedoch auch Wortzusammensetzungen, Kollokationen, Phraseologie und formelhafte Ausdrücke bieten und sich nicht auf ein terminologisches Skelett beschränken, da der Übersetzer und jeder, der sonst eine sprachliche Äußerung produziert, ja das Wort meist nicht isoliert gebraucht, sondern in einem Kontext mit viel „wiederholter Rede" (im Sinne von Coseriu, vor allem Coseriu 1973), die fast immer in ihrer Formulierung in der Zielsprache ebenfalls vorgegeben ist, so z. B. dt. „*. . . mit der Bitte um weitere Veranlassung"*, im Frz. kürzer als „*. . . pour suite à donner"*. Fachwortschatzinventare sollten auch die im jeweiligen Fachgebiet üblichen Abkürzungen enthalten, z. B. in der Medizin Tbc, OP, o.B., EKG, EEG. Was die Auswahl lexikalischer Einheiten für ein fachsprachliches Wortschatzinventar betrifft, so sollte möglichst kein bekannter allgemeinsprachlicher Wortschatz aufgenommen werden, es sei denn, es gäbe im Einzelfall besondere Gründe dafür. Sonst wird das meist ohnehin kostspielige mehrsprachige Fachwörterbuch nur unnötig aufgebläht.

Umfangreichere Wortschatzinventare mit dem Anspruch breiter Repräsentativität (nicht „Vollständigkeit", die praktisch unerreichbar ist) werden als „Wörterbuch", „Lexikon" u. ä. bezeichnet, gelegentlich auch „Vokabularium" (auch bei alphabetischer Anordnung des Wortschatzes), kürzere Listen von Fachwortschatz als „Glossare". Solche Glossare, die immer wieder aktualisiert werden müssen, erscheinen häufig in Sprachzeitschriften wie „Lebende Sprachen" (Berlin-München) oder in periodischen Publikationen internationaler Organisationen wie z. B. in dem von der EG-Kommission in Luxemburg herausgegebenen Bulletin „Terminologie et Traduction". Hier sind sie dem interessierten Sprachmittler oder Lexikographen leicht zugänglich. Handelt es sich dagegen um Fachglossare, die in nichtsprachlichen Fachzeitschriften erscheinen und dem sprachlich Interessierten deshalb kaum zugänglich sind, spricht man von *hidden glossaries, vocabulaires cachés* oder *lexiques occultes*. Dieser Terminus erschien zuerst in „Lexicographical Information" (in: *Babel. Revue internationale de la traduction* 3/1959, 102). Informationen über solche „versteckte Glossare" geben u. a. *Infoterm Newsletter* (IN), und *Biblio Term* (BIT), beide hrsg. vom Österreichischen Normungsinstitut Wien. Was die fachsprachliche Lexikographie heute betrifft, ob sie nun ein- oder mehrsprachig ist, so ist anzumerken, daß sie sich meist unter dem Etikett „Terminologie" als Fachgebiet verselbständigt hat. Viele Fachglossare in mehreren Sprachen werden von internationalen Organisationen veröffentlicht, z. B. von der UNO, der Organisation Amerikanischer Staaten (OAS), der FAO (UN-Organisation für Ernährung und Landwirtschaft), verschiedenen Dienststellen der Europäischen Gemeinschaften, von Sprachendiensten von Ministerien oder großen Firmen. Dank der Pionierarbeit der beiden österreichischen Terminologen Eugen Wüster und Helmut Felber hat sich Wien zu einem der wichtigsten Zentren internationaler Zusammenarbeit auf dem Gebiet der Terminologie entwickelt. Dort befindet sich auch das 1988 errichtete *International Network for Terminology* (Term Net), wo u. a. die oben erwähnten bibliographischen Informationen über Fachterminologie sowie die Zeitschrift „*Fachsprache*. Internationale Zeitschrift für Fachsprachenforschung, -didaktik und Terminologie" (seit 1979) veröffentlicht werden. Aus Platzgründen müssen wir darauf verzichten, hier näher auf die mehr als 200 Zentren für terminologische Arbeit, die vielen Bibliographien über Fachwörterbücher, Fachglossare usw. und die Zeitschriften und Bulletins, die Fachglossare veröffentlichen, einzugehen. Sie alle leisten zusammen mit den Autoren von fachsprachlichen Wortschatzinventaren einen wesentlichen Beitrag zur internationalen Zusammenarbeit auf allen Gebieten.

3.2. Typologie der mehrsprachigen Wörterbücher nach ihrer Makrostruktur

Bei der Anordnung des Wortschatzes eines mehrsprachigen Wörterbuchs stellt sich zuerst die Frage: alphabetische Anordnung oder thematische oder eine andere nichtalphabetische Gliederung des darzustellenden Wortschatzes? Für die **alphabetische Ordnung** spricht der rasche Zugriff, für die **thematische** (oder eine ähnliche) die Darstellung des Wortschatzes in einem organischen Zusammenhang mit Wortfeldnachbarn, Synonymen, Antonymen, Hyponymen, Hyperonymen, Kollokationen, Phraseologie usw., die bei Einhaltung einer strikten alphabetischen Ordnung zum größten Teil auseinander gerissen werden. Die **alphabetische Anordnung** empfiehlt sich bei allgemeinsprachlichen Wörterbüchern (sofern diese überhaupt noch einen Sinn haben, vgl. 4.), Wörterbüchern von Gruppensprachen (Soziolekten), Inventaren von idiomatischen Redensarten, Sprichwörtern und geographischen Eigennamen sowie sehr umfassenden Fachwörterbüchern, z. B. einem allgemeinen Wörterbuch der Technik.

Die **thematische Anordnung**, die wir bereits bei den ersten „vocabolarietti" des 15. und 16. Jh. vorfinden und die wissenschaftlich von Hallig/Wartburg 1952 beschrieben wurde, wird man u. a. bei Wortschatzsammlungen für Lernzwecke wählen. Bei Sprachatlanten und Bildwörterbüchern ist die Anordnung des Wortschatzes ohnehin durch die einzelnen Karten bzw. Bildtafeln vorgegeben. Eine der thematischen Anordnung verwandte ist die Gliederung nach **Gesprächssituationen**, wie wir sie in Reiseführern (meist mit ausgeformten Sätzen und dem dazugehörigen wichtigen Wortschatz) und in Konversationsbüchern finden. Für Fachwortschatzinventare, die eigentlich in diesem Zusammenhang am wichtigsten sind, hat die thematische (oder systematische) Anordnung — wie schon oben erwähnt — sehr große Vorteile. Deshalb hat auch der Deutsche Industrie-Normenausschuß, der sich seit Jahrzehnten mit fachterminologischen Problemen befaßt, in seiner Schrift: *Deutsche Normen-Fachwörterbücher Stufen der Ausarbeitung* (DIN 2333) bereits im Jahre 1974 (S. 2) ausdrücklich empfohlen, bei Fachwörterbüchern der systematischen Anordnung des Wortschatzes den Vorzug zu geben. Da heute praktisch alle systematisch angeordneten mehrsprachigen Fachwörterbücher für jede der Sprachen ein eigenes alphabetisches Register haben, sollte diese Modalität der Anordnung (systematische Anordnung in einer Ausgangssprache und alphabetische Register für alle Sprachen) der Vorzug gegeben werden, da hier der Vorteil der Darstellung des Wortschatzes in seinem organischen Zusammenhang und der des raschen Zugriffs miteinander kombiniert werden können.

Es gibt hier auch Mischformen. So ist z. B. in einem sechssprachigen Wörterbuch der Landwirtschaft der Wortschatz in 17 Kapitel gegliedert, die meist mehrere Unterkapitel haben, also wird das Prinzip der thematischen Gliederung gewahrt. Innerhalb der einzelnen Unterkapitel ist der Wortschatz jedoch alphabetisch gegliedert (Haensch/Haberkamp 1987). Hier muß auch ein Typ von Fachwörterbüchern erwähnt werden, der in keiner Bibliographie erscheint, aber dem Benutzer unschätzbare Dienste erweist und den ich das „latente Fachwörterbuch" nennen möchte. Es handelt sich um Fachbücher (z. T. auch Sachbücher) über Botanik, Zoologie, Mineralogie, die sehr terminologieintensiv sind und — ähnlich wie die oben erwähnten Bildwörterbücher — in anderssprachigen, von hervorragenden Fachleuten bearbeiteten Fassungen vorliegen. Da hier nicht nur das gesuchte Stichwort (z. B. Tier- oder Pflanzennamen), sondern vieles andere, was dazu gehört (enzyklopädische Information und Abbildungen) in organischem Zusammenhang und in ausgeformten Sätzen erscheint, können solche Werke oft noch bessere Dienste leisten als ein reines Wörterbuch.

Beispiele: Muus/Dahlström 1966: *Guide des Poissons de Mer et Pêche;* Neuchâtel und Paris 1966; dt. Ausgabe 1968, span. Ausgabe 1977, ferner eine engl., niederl., norwegische, schwed. und finnische Ausgabe, die alle auf die Urfassung „Havfisk of Fiskeri i Nordvesteuropa", Kopenhagen 1964 zurückgehen oder Matz/Vanderhaege 1978 (Parallele Terrarienführer in Dt., Frz. und Span.).

Ähnliches gilt auch für Übersetzungen von Gesetzbüchern, Verfassungen, Gebrauchsanweisungen, Betriebsanleitungen, die zusammen mit dem Original durch parallelen Textvergleich sozusagen zum Fachwörterbuch mit Kontext werden, vorausgesetzt, daß die Übersetzungen absolut zuverlässig sind. In einem juristischen Wörterbuch findet man z. B. für dt. *Gewalt* = span. *poder*. In einer span. Übersetzung des Grundgesetzes findet man dagegen den ausgeformten Satz: *Alle Staatsgewalt geht vom Volke aus = Todo poder público emana del pueblo*. (Ley fundamental 1973). Solche wortschatzintensiven, in mehreren Sprachen vorliegenden Werke sollten daher, auch wenn sie keine eigentlichen Wörterbücher sind, unbedingt in die Bibliographien der mehrsprachigen Fachwörterbücher aufgenommen werden.

— Die Anordnung des Wortschatzes in mehrsprachigen alphabetischen Fachwörterbüchern kann auf die verschiedenste Weise erfolgen. Die häufigsten Typen der Anordnung sind bei Fachwörterbüchern, die uns hier in erster Linie interessieren, folgende:

(a) Das jeweilige Wörterbuch geht von einer Ausgangssprache aus, deren Wortschatz alphabetisch angeordnet ist, die Äquivalente in den übrigen Sprachen stehen daneben in mehreren Spalten. Der alphabetische Zugriff auf den Wortschatz der Ausgangssprache ist problemlos: dieser ist bereits alphabetisch geordnet, für die übrigen Sprachen gibt es hinter dem Hauptteil je ein alphabetisches Register mit Angabe einer Nummer, die jeweils vor dem Stichwort der Ausgangssprache steht, oder mit einer Seitenangabe. Dieses ist heute die häufigste und sicher auch die sinnvollste Anordnung eines alphabetischen Fachwörterbuches.

(b) Ist der Wortschatz in einem Wörterbuch thematisch (systematisch) geordnet, empfiehlt sich ebenfalls eine Anordnung in mehreren Spalten mit jeweils einer Nummer vor jedem Stichwort. In diesem Fall gibt es ein Alphabetregister für jede der Sprachen einschl. der Ausgangssprache. Dies ist in jeder Hinsicht die beste Anordnung des Wortschatzes, da sie, wie oben erwähnt, die Vorteile der systematischen Darstellung mit dem des raschen Zugriffs über die Alphabetregister ermöglicht.

(c) Eine weitere Möglichkeit ist die, das Stichwort der Ausgangssprache und dessen Äquivalente in den anderen Sprachen hintereinander zu setzen und dann — wie beim Typ 1 — Alphabetregister für die übrigen Sprachen vorzusehen (z. B. Weck 1966).

(d) Man findet auch häufig die Anordnung der Termini nach dem Alphabet in den einzelnen Sprachen untereinander, z. B.:

137 Vertrag *m*, Staatsvertrag *m*
    treaty
    traité *m*
    tratado *m*

Der Zugriff erfolgt wiederum über die jeweiligen Register. Manche Wörterbücher kennzeichnen die einzelnen Äquivalente zusätzlich durch Angabe der jeweiligen Sprache in Form von Abkürzungen oder Symbolen (z. B. E = Español, Dt = Deutsch usw.).

(e) Ein weiterer Anordnungstyp ist das Allsprachenkorpus, bei dem jedes Stichwort in jeder Sprache nach dem Alphabet eingeordnet wird und dann jeweils alle Äquivalente in den übrigen Sprachen gegeben werden. Diese Anordnung ist weder übersichtlich noch ökonomisch, z. B.:

bodega *(f) n* Es
De Laderaum *(m)*
En hold
Fr cale *(f)*
It stiva *(f)*
Pt porão *(m)*
Bodenfläche *(f) n* De
En floor space
Es superficie de piso *(f)*
Fr surface de plancher *(f)*
It superficie di pavimento *(f)*
Pt área de chão *(f)*

(f) Es gibt auch den Typ des Wörterbuches mit Mehrfachkorpus. Hier wird der Wortschatz in jeder Ausgangssprache alphabetisch geordnet und jeweils alle Äquivalente in den übrigen Sprachen angegeben.

(g) Eine weitere Möglichkeit ist, für jede Sprache ein getrenntes Corpus zu haben, in dem die Anordnung der Stichwörter identisch ist, und jedes Stichwort mit Nummern zu versehen, so daß in jedem Eintrag ein Äquivalent in jeder Sprache gesucht werden kann. Zusätzlich erscheint oft ein Register.

(h) Schließlich gibt es noch den Typ des mehrsprachigen Wörterbuches, bei dem jeder Sprache ein Band entspricht (auch „Vielsprachen-Wörterbuch nach der Einsprachen-Anordnung" genannt). Jeder der Bände hat einen ersten alphabetischen Teil mit Verweisnummern und einen zweiten (z. B. von 1—8500) numerierten Teil, in dem ausgehend von den Nummern jedes Wort in jedem der Bände gefunden werden kann. Dieser durchaus ökonomische Anordnungstypus ermöglicht es, nur die Bände zu benützen (und zu kaufen), die man wirklich braucht (Holtzmann 1937).

3.3. Typologie nach der Mikrostruktur

Bei der Darstellung der verschiedenen Typen der Anordnung des Wortschatzes in 3.2. haben wir bereits — bei der Beschreibung der Anordnung der Äquivalente innerhalb eines Eintrags — auf die Mikrostruktur der mehrsprachigen Wörterbücher Bezug genommen. Daneben ist bei mehrsprachigen Wörterbüchern (wobei uns wieder in erster Linie die Fachwörterbücher interessieren) hinsichtlich der Mikrostruktur noch zu erwähnen, daß man bei manchen guten mehrsprachigen Fachwörterbüchern neben den Termini auch Definitionen findet, was für den Benützer sehr nützlich ist, wenn man bedenkt, wie die Fachterminologien mancher Gebiete von Schule zu Schule verschieden sind, z. B. in der modernen Linguistik oder in der Soziologie. In den meisten Fällen steht die Definition hinter dem Stichwort, manchmal hinter den Äquivalenten (cf. Sánchez-Monge 1981 und *Terminologie forestière* 1975).

4. Äquivalenzprobleme der mehrsprachigen Wörterbücher

Ist es schon außerordentlich schwierig, die Äquivalente der lexikalischen Einheiten e i n e r Ausgangssprache in e i n e r Zielsprache zu geben, so vervielfachen sich die Schwierigkeiten, wenn es um mehr als zwei Sprachen geht. Vor allem kann hier wegen der Art der Darstellung meist nur eine Bedeutung einer lexikalischen Einheit der Ausgangssprache in den anderen Sprachen berücksichtigt werden, so daß die Polysemie der Wörter weder in der Ausgangssprache noch in den übrigen Sprachen berücksichtigt werden kann, von unentbehrlichen syntagmatischen Elementen wie Rektion, Kollokationen, Idiomatik usw. ganz zu schweigen. Wenn man bedenkt, daß z. B. ein englisch-deutscher Band eines Wörterbuches nicht einfach die „umgedrehte" Fassung des entsprechenden deutsch-englischen Bandes sein kann, wird einem klar, daß sich z. B. bei einem sechssprachigen Wörterbuch die Schwierigkeiten der Darstellung allgemeinsprachlichen Wortschatzes derart häufen, daß eine brauchbare Wortschatzbeschreibung nicht möglich ist, es sei denn, man wolle für anspruchslose Reisewörterbücher oder für sprachvergleichende Zwecke jeweils nur eine Bedeutung von Einzelwörtern in Form einer Nomenklatur auflisten, wie dies die ersten „vocabolarietti" des 16. Jh. getan haben. Es stellt sich daher die Frage, ob es überhaupt sinnvoll ist, umfangreiche allgemeinsprachliche mehrsprachige Wörterbücher herzustellen; wir möchten dies mit allem Nachdruck verneinen, eine Haltung, die auch Zgusta 1971 vertritt, wenn er lakonisch feststellt: „In any case, a general dictionary for the public, uninitiated or professional, requires a treatment of polysemy and is, therefore, bilingual par excellence, not multilingual" (297). Anders ist die Situation bei den Fachwörterbüchern, da die lexikalischen Einheiten der Fachsprache meist klar definiert und zumindest innerhalb eines bestimmten Bereiches monosem sind. Bezüglich der Äquivalenzprobleme in mehrsprachigen Fachwörterbüchern verweisen wir auf Art. 285, da die Äquivalenzprobleme der mehrsprachigen Fachlexikographie grundsätzlich die gleichen sind wie bei der zweisprachigen, wobei die größere Anzahl an Sprachen allenfalls noch als Erschwernis hinzukommt.

5. Ausblick

Beim Durchgehen der zahlreichen Bibliographien von Fachwörterbüchern der letzten Jahrzehnte fällt auf, daß die einzelnen Fachwörterbücher und -glossare immer speziellere Themen behandeln. Auch wird die Zahl der in der internationalen Kommunikation häufig verwendeten Sprachen immer größer. Man denke nur an den ungeheuren Ausstoß an Texten in den 9 Amtssprachen der Europäischen Gemeinschaft. Dazu kommt die Notwendigkeit der ständigen Aktualisierung des Fachwortschatzes. Man ist daher dazu übergegangen, bei den großen internationalen Organisationen, bei nationalen Behörden und in anderen Bereichen Hunderttausende von Fachausdrücken mit ihren Äquivalenten in anderen Sprachen im Computer zu speichern. Inzwischen sind eine Reihe von terminologischen Datenbanken entstanden, die immer stärker miteinander vernetzt werden. Aber auch wenn dem mehrsprachigen Fachwörterbuch im Computer ein gewichtiger Konkurrent entstanden ist, überflüssig wird es deshalb wohl trotzdem nicht werden.

6. Literatur (in Auswahl)

6.1. Wörterbücher

ABC 1958 = A.B.C. Magyar-Angol-Francis-Holland-Német-Olasz-Spanyol-Svéd. Den Haag 1958 [Ungar. - Engl. - Frz. - Niederl. - Dt. - Ital. - Span.- Schwed.].

Adelung 1806 = Johann Christoph Adelung/Johann Severin Vater: Mithridates oder allgemeine Sprachenkunde [. . .] 4 Bde. Berlin 1806—1817 [enthält Wörterverzeichnisse aus vielen Sprachen für sprachvergleichende Studien].

Agustí 1617 = Fra Miquel Agustí: El Llibre dels secrets d'agricultura, casa rústica y pastoril. Barcelona 1617 [enthält Vokabellisten auf Span.-Katal.-Lat.-Port.-Ital.-Frz.].

ALEC 1981 = Luis Flórez (Hrsg.): Atlas Lingüístico Etnográfico de Colombia. Instituto Caro y Cuervo. 6 Bde. Bogotá 1981—83.

Ambrosoli 1897 = Solone Ambrosoli: Vocabolarietto pei numismatici in sei lingue. Mailand 1897 [Frz.-Ital.-Dt.-Engl.-Span.-Lat.].

Anchorani 1631 = J. Anchorani: Porta linguarum. London 1631 [Lat.-Engl.-Frz.].

Anglés 1742 = Pedro Martir Anglés: Prontuario orthologigráphico trilingüe. En que se enseña a pronunciar, escribir y letrear correctamente en latín, castellano y catalano (sic), con una idiographía. Barcelona 1742.

Antonini 1738 = Annibale Antonini: Dictionnaire italien, latin et français. Paris 1738. Weitere Aufl. Lyon 1770.

Antonoff 1884 = A. Antonoff: Lexikon der Handelskorrespondenz in 9 Sprachen. Stuttgart 1884 [Dt. - Engl. - Frz. - Ital. - Port. - Poln. - Russ. - Span. - Schwed.].

Azkúe 1905 = Resurrección Ma. de Azkúe: Diccionario vasco-español-francés. 2 Bde. Bilbao. Paris 1905—1906.

Backhausen 1948 = Nelly Backhausen (Bearb.): Hvad hedder dat? Kopenhagen 1. Aufl. 1948, 3. Aufl. 1956 [Bildwörterbuch in Dän.-Engl.-Frz.-Dt.].

Bader 1614 = M. Bader: Nomenclator [. . .]. Straßburg 1614 [Lat.-Frz.-Dt.].

Badings 1880 = A.H.L. Badings: Woordenboek voor de Zeevaart. Schoonhoven 1880 [Niederl.-Malaiisch-Frz.-Engl.].

Barbier 1617 = Jean Barbier: Ianua linguarum quadrilinguis. London 1617 [Engl.-Frz.-Lat.-Span.].

Baret 1573 = John Baret: An Alvearie, or Triple Dictionarie, in English, Latin and French. London 1573 und öfter.

Bathe 1617 = William Bathe: Ianua linguarum, Quadrilinguis or a Messe of Tongues: Latine, English, French and Spanish. London 1617 [ursprünglich nur Span. und Lat. in der Ausgabe von 1611].

Bathe 1629 = William Bathe: Ianua linguarum silinguis, Latina, Germanica, Gallica, Italia, Hispanica, Anglica [. . .]. 1629.

Beil 1853 = J. Beil: Technologisches Wörterbuch. Wiesbaden 1853 [Dt.-Frz.-Engl.].

Belon 1553 = P. Belon: De aquatilibus. Paris 1553 [Zoolog. Wortschatz Altgr.-Lat.-Frz.].

Belon 1555 = P. Belon: Nature des poissons. Paris 1555 [Tafeln in Altgr.-Lat.-Frz.-Ital.].

Berlaimont 1536 = Noel de Berlaimont (auch: Berlemont): Vocabulare [. . .]. Antwerpen 1536 [Frz.-Niederl. Siehe auch Grave 1551].

Berset 1979 = Francis Berset: Correspondance commerciale en 4 langues [. . .]. Biel 1979 [Dt.-Engl.-Frz.-Span.].

Bilderduden für Soldaten 1941 = Bilderduden für Soldaten. Dt.-Bulgarisch-Rumänisch. Tornisterschrift des Oberkommandos der Wehrmacht. Heft 40. Leipzig 1941 [64 S.].

Bildwörterbuch Meyer = Meyers Enzyklopädisches Lexikon. Bd. 29. Bildwörterbuch Deutsch-Englisch-Französisch. Mannheim 1981.

Blachère 1967 = Régis Blachère et al.: Dictionnaire arabe-français-anglais (Langue classique et moderne). 3 Bde. Paris 1967—1975.

Blancardus 1679 = Stephanus Blancardus: Lexicon medicum, Graeco-Latinum in quo [. . .] Belgica nomina si quae fuerint adjunguntur. Amsterdam 1679 [Altgr.-Lat.-Niederl. In den Aufl. von 1690, 1717, 1739, 1748, 1777 u. 1832 zusätzlich Dt., Frz. u. Engl.].

Blavier 1953 = E. Blavier: Dictionnaire. Woordenboek, Français-Lingala-Néerlandais. Néerlandais-Lingala-Français. Lingala-Français-Néerlandais. Léopoldville 1953.

Bobrik 1878 = Eduard Bobrik: Allgemeines nautisches Wörterbuch [. . .]. Leipzig 1878 [Dt.-Engl.-Frz.-Span.-Port.-Ital.-Schwed.-Dän.-Niederl.].

Bohn 1857 = Henry G. Bohn: A polyglot dictionary of foreign proverbs. London 1857 [Frz.Ital.-Dt.-Niederl.-Span.-Port.-Dän.-Engl.].

Bonaparte 1846 = Louis Lucien Bonaparte: Specimen lexici comparativi omnium linguarum europearum. Florenz 1846 [Enthält Wortschatzproben aus 52 Sprachen].

Boom 1879 = Dignus J. Boom: Zeemans Woordenboek, in drie talen. Den Haag 1879 [Niederl.-Engl.-Frz.; 1888 um Dt. erweitert].

Bottarelli 1789 = F. Bottarelli: Dictionnaire de poche italien-anglois-françois. 3 Bde. London 1789.

Brinkley 1938 = J. Brinkley/S. Kasai/S. Asakune: Illustrated Handbook of Conservation in four languages. Tokio. London 1938 [Jap.-Engl.-Span.-Niederl.].

Broch 1771 = Joseph Broch: Promptuario trilingüe en el que se manifiestan con toda claridad todas las voces que generalmente sirven para el comercio político y sociable en los tres idiomas catalán, castellano y francés. Barcelona 1771 [216, II S.; thematisch angelegter Wortschatz].

Brossard 1703 = S. de Brossard: Dictionnaire de musique. Paris 1703 [Altgr.-Lat.-Ital.-Frz.; bei Quemada 1967, 578].

Bruckner 1842 = Gottlob Bruckner: Een klein Woordenboek der Hollandsche, Englesche en Javaansche Talen [...] Batavia 1842 [Niederl.-Engl.-Javanisch].

Bruin 1900 = Servaas de Bruin/J.G.B. Waanders: Beknopte woordenlijst voor de vier talen [...]. Amsterdam 1900 [Niederl.-Frz.-Dt.-Engl.].

Brutzer 1873 = H. Brutzer et alii: Wörterbuch der Handels- und Geschäftssprache [...] nebst ausführlichem Warenverzeichnis und 5 Sachregistern. Stuttgart 1873 [Dt.-Niederl.-Engl.-Frz.-Ital.-Span.].

Burvenich 1905 = Arthur Burvenich: English Idioms and Colloquialisms. Words and phrases of familiar or figurative use. Proverbs. With origins and equivalents. Zutphen 1905 [Engl.-Frz.-Niederl.].

Calagius 1595 = Andreas Calagius: Synonyma Latina, Polonica et Germanica. Preßburg 1595.

Calepinus 1502 = Ambrosius Calepinus: Dictionum latinarum e grecopariter derivantium: earundemque interpretationum collector studiosissimus [...]. Reggio 1502 [Lat., gelegentlich Altgr.].

Calepinus 1545 = Ambrosius Calepinus: Pentaglottos [...]. Antwerpen 1545 [Lat.-Altgr.-Dt.-Niederl.-Frz.].

Calepinus 1568 = Ambrosius Calepinus: Dictionarium [hexaglottum]. Basel 1568 [Lat.-Altgr.-Ital.-Frz.-Span.-Dt.].

Calepinus 1570 = Ambrosius Calepinus: Dictionarium septem linguarum [...]. Basel 1570 [Lat.-Altgr.-Ital.-Frz.-Span.-Dt.-Niederl.].

Calepinus 1572 = Ambrosius Calepinus: Dictionarium [...]. Antwerpen 1572 [Lat.-Altgr.-Frz.-Ital.-Span.].

Calepinus 1574 = Ambrosius Calepinus: Dictionarium linguarum septem. Basel 1574 [676 S., davon 355 S. Register. Lat.-Altgr.-Ital.-Frz.-Span.-Dt.-Niederl.].

Calepinus 1580 = Ambrosius Calepinus: Dictionarium [...]. Rom 1580 [1. Teil: Lat.-Altgr.; 2. Teil: Lat.-Ital.-Frz.-Span.-Altgr.; 444 + 447 S.].

Calepinus 1581 = Ambrosius Calepinus: [...] linguarum novem dictionarium. Lyon 1581 [628 S.; Lat.-Altgr.-Hebr.-Frz.-Ital.-Dt.-Span.-Engl.-Niederl.].

Calepinus 1584 = Ambrosius Calepinus: Dictionarium octo linguarum [...] Respondent autem vocabulis latinis, hebraica, graeca, gallica, italica, germanica, belgica, hispanica [...] Basel 1584 [315 S.].

Calepinus 1585 = Ambrosius Calepinus: Dictionarium decem linguarum [...]. Lyon 1585 [XIII, 484 S.; Engl.-Frz.-Dt.-Altgr.-Hebr.-Ungar.-Ital.-Lat.-Poln.-Span.].

Calepinus 1590 = Ambrosius Calepinus: Dictionarium undecim linguarum [...]. Basel 1590 [Lat.-Hebr. - Frz. - Ital. - Dt. - Niederl. - Span. - Poln. - Ungar.-Engl.-Port.].

Calepinus 1595 = Ambrosius Calepinus: Dictionarium Latino-Lusitanicum ac Japonicum. Amacusa 1595 [Weitere Aufl. Rom 1878].

Calepinus 1599 = Ambrosius Calepinus: Dictionarium octo linguarum. Paris 1599.

Calepinus 1647 = Ambrosius Calepinus: Dictionarium octo linguarum. 2 Bde. Lyon 1647.

Calepinus 1758 = Septem linguarum Calepinus, hoc est lexicon latinum variorum linguarum interpretatione adjecta. 2 Bde. Padua 1758 [Ital.-Hebr.-Dt.-Frz.-Span.-Altgr.].

Calisch 1876 = Isaac Marcus Calisch: Proverbes et locutions familières en quatre langues. Den Haag 1876 [Frz.-Engl.-Dt.-Niederl. Weitere Aufl. 1878 und 1901].

Cambry 1805 = Jaques Cambry: Manuel interprète de correspondance, ou vocabulaires polyglottes alphabétiques et numériques en tableaux. Paris 1805 [Frz.-Ital.-Engl.-Dt.-Span.-Niederl.-Bretonisch].

Capitol's concise dictionary 1972 = Capitol's concise dictionary [...]. Bologna 1972 [Engl.-Schwed.-Niederl.-Dt.-Frz.-Ital.-Span.].

Cawdrey 1604 = R. Cawdrey: Table alphabeticall. London 1604 [Engl.-Hebr.-Altgr.-Lat.-Frz.].

Chamereau 1744 = N. Chamereau: Nyt danskfransk of latinsk lexicon [...]. 2 Bde. Kopenhagen 1744 [Bei Haugen 1984 erwähnt; bei Quemada 1967 als Chambreau zitiert.].

Chao 1836 = Juan Agustín Chao: Dictionnaire basque-français-espagnol-latin. 2 Bde. Bayonne 1836—1858.

Clairac 1877 = Pelayo Clairac y Sáenz: Diccionario general de arquitectura e ingeniería. 5 Bde. Madrid 1877—91 [mit Äquivalenten der Fachtermini auf Frz., Engl. und Ital.].

Cnapius 1621 = Gregor Cnapius: Thesaurus polono-latino-graecus. 1. Bd. Krakau 1621, 2. Bd. 1625.

Cnapius 1698 = Gregor Cnapius: Thesaurus Latino-Germanico-Polonicus. Posen 1698 [Lat.-Dt.-Poln.; weitere Aufl. Krakau 1741].

Codicillus 1546 = Petrus Codicillus: Vocabulař latinský český a německý. W. Praze 1546 [Lat.-Tschech.-Dt.].

Colloquia 1560 = ... Colloquia Familiaria cum Dictionariolo Quatuor Linguarum Teutonicae, Gallicae, Latinae et Hispanicae [...]. Löwen 1560 [Niederl.-Frz.-Lat.-Span; Zahlreiche weitere Aufl. mit anderen Sprachen (vgl. Colloquia 1610)].

Colloquia 1610 = Colloquia et dictionariolum septem linguarum, belgicae, anglicae, teutonicae, latinae, italicae, hispanicae, gallicae. Lüttich 1610. Moderne Ausgabe: Colloquia et Dictionariolum septem Linguarum gedruckt door Fickaert te Antwerpen in 1616 opnieuw uitgeven door prof. Verdeyen. 2 Bde. Antwerpen 1926 [Weitere Auflage 1935].

Colloquia 1630 = ... Colloquia et dictionariolum octo linguarum [...]. Antwerpen 1630 [Fläm.-Engl.-Frz.-Dt.-Ital.-Lat.-Port.-Span.].

Colloquia 1634 = Colloquia et dictionariolum sex linguarum [...]. Genf 1634 [Lat.-Frz.-Dt.-Span.-Ital.-Engl.; Erweiterung von Berlaimont 1551].

Comenius 1638 = Johannes Amos Comenius: Janua linguarum. Genf 1638 [Lat.-Frz.-Dt.].

Comenius 1638a = Johannes Amos Comenius: Janua linguarum. Genf 1638 [Lat.-Dt.-Frz.-Ital.].

Comenius 1641 = Johannes Amos Comenius: Janua linguarum reserata, quinque linguis [...]. Amsterdam 1641 [Frz.-Dt.-Ital.-Lat.-Span.].

Comenius 1643 = Johannes Amos Comenius: Janua linguarum. 2 Bde. Amsterdam 1643 [Lat.-Altgr.-Frz.].

Comenius 1661 = Johannes Amos Comenius: Janua linguarum. Amsterdam 1661 [Lat.-Dt.-Frz.-Ital.-Span.].

Comenius 1684 = Johannes Amos Comenius: Novum vestibulum. Amsterdam 1684 [Lat.-Frz.-Niederl.].

Comenius, Orbis 1658 = Johannes Amos Comenius: Orbis sensualium pictus. Nürnberg 1658 [Lat.-dt. Ausg.].

Concise dictionary 1967 = The concise dictionary of 26 languages in simultaneous translations. New York 1967 [400 S.].

Costa e Sá 1794 = Joaquim José da Costa e Sá: Diccionario portuguez francez e latino. Lisboa 1794.

Crato 1596 = Adam Crato: Geheimnis der Türken von ihrer Religion, Kriegsmanier etc. samt einem Dictionario dreyer Sprachen, Lateinisch, Türkisch und Deutsch. Magdeburg 1596.

Crespin 1627 = Jean Crespin [Hrsg.]: Le Thresor des trois langues, espagnole, francoise et italienne. Genf 1627 [Weitere Aufl. Köln 1631].

Creutz Lechleitner 1839 = W. J. Creutz Lechleitner: Algemeen militair Zakwoordenboek. Den Haag 1839 [Niederl.-Frz.-Dt.].

Dalechamps 1615 = Jacques Dalechamps: Histoire générale des plantes. Ensemble des tables des noms en diverses langues. 2 Bde. Lyon 1615 [Frz.-Lat.-Altgr.-Arab.-Ital.-Span.-Dt.-Niederl.-Tschech.-Engl.].

Danet 1743 = Pierre Danet: Nouveau grand dictionnaire fr., lat., polonois. Warschau 1743.

Dasypodius 1567 = Petrus Dasypodius: Dictionarium Triglotton. Antwerpen 1567 [Lat.-Altgr.-Niederl.].

Deak 1959 = Etienne Deak/Simone Deak: A Dictionary of Colorful French Slanguage and Colloquialisms. Paris 1959.

Decimator 1580 — Henricus Decimator: Sylva vocabulorum et phrasium cum solutae, tum ligatae orationis [...]. Gifhorn 1580 [Dt.-Lat.-Altgr.].

Decimator 1586 = Henricus Decimator: Sylva vocabulorum [...]. Wittenberg 1586 [Dt.-Hebr.-Chald.-Lat.-Altgr.-Frz.].

Decimator 1587 = Henricus Decimator: Sylva vocabulorum [...]. Wittenberg 1587 [Dt.-Lat.-Altgr.-Chald.].

Decimator 1595 = Henricus Decimator: Sylva vocabulorum [...]. 2 Bde. Frankfurt 1595 [Dt.-Lat.-Hebr.-Altgr.-Frz.].

Decimator 1600 = Henricus Decimator: Thesaurus linguarum. Magdeburg gegen 1600 [Lat.-Altgr.-Hebr.-Frz.-Ital.-Dt.].

Decimator 1606 = Henricus Decimator: Tertia pars. Sylvae vocabulorum et phrasium sive nomenclator. Wittenberg 1606 [Lat.-Altgr.-Hebr.-Chald.-Frz.-Ital.-Dt.-Niederl.-Span.-Engl.].

Denys de Montfort 1815 = Pierre Denys de Montfort: Petit vocabulaire à l'usage des Français et des Alliés, renfermant les noms d'une partie des choses les plus essentielles à la vie. Paris 1815 [Frz.-Lat.-Hebr.-Niederl.-Dt.-Engl.-Schottisch-Span.-Ital.-Hannoveranisch-Badisch-Hessisch-Tirolerisch-Schweizerisch].

Diccionari 1839 = Diccionari català-castellà-llatí-francès-italià, per una Societat de Catalans. 2 Bde. Barcelona 1839 [Näheres bei Colon/Soberanas 1985, 161–164. Bei Fabbri 1979, 24 unter dem Namen Miguel Antón Martí zitiert].

Diccionario 1633 = ... Diccionario de la lengua de la China en castellano, latín y chino. Roma 1633.

Dictionariolum 1662 = Dictionariolum et colloquia octo linguarum [...]. Antwerpen 1662 [Lat.-Frz.-Fläm.-Dt.-Span.-Ital.-Engl.-Port.; nach Berlaimont].

Dictionarium 1507 = ... Dictionarium Latinis, Gallicis et Germanicis Vocabulis. Lyon 1507.

Dictionarium 1556 = Dictionarium quadrilingue. Löwen 1556 [Dt.-Frz.-Lat.-Span.].

Dictionarium 1562 = Dictionarium tetraglotton. Antwerpen 1562 [Lat.-Altgr.-Frz.-Dt.].

Dictionarium 1568 = Dictionarium quadrilingue cum instructione rationis. Antwerpen 1568.

Dictionarium 1578 = Dictionarium latinum, gallicum et germanicum. Lyon 1578.

Dictionarium 1591 = ... Dictionarium VII linguarum. Lüttich 1591 [Niederl.-Engl.-Dt.-Lat.-Ital.-Span.-Frz.].

Dictionarium 1846 = ... Dictionarium latino-gallico-tamulicum. Pondichéry 1846.

Dictionarium sex linguarum 1505 = Dictionarium sex linguarum Latinae, Gallicae, Hispanicae, Italicae, Anglicae et Teutonicae dilucidissimum. Zürich 1505 [Spätere Ausgaben mit 8 Sprachen (Vgl.

Claes 1974, 37—38). Eines der allerersten mehrsprachigen Wörterbücher in Europa. Niederehe 1987 gibt für die erste Aufl. dieses Wörterbuches 1518 und als Erscheinungsort Venedig, Claes 1974 dagegen 1505 und Zürich].

Dictionarium triglotton 1665 = ... Dictionarium triglotton. Lüttich 1665 [Lat.-Altgr.-Frz.].

Dictionarium trilingüe 1549 = Dictionarium trilingüe. Antwerpen 1549 [Frz.-Lat.-Dt.].

Dictionarius 1513 = Dictionarius trium linguarum, Latinae, Teutonicae, Boemicae, potiora vocabula continens: peregrinantibus apprime utilis. Wien 1513 [Lat.-Dt.-Tschech.].

Dictionnaire 1540 = Le Dictionnaire des Sept Langages (Ital., Dt., Lat., Frz., Span., Engl., Flämisch), Antwerpen 1540.

Dictionnaire 1762 = Dictionnaire françois-allemand-latin-russe. St. Petersburg 1762.

Dictionnaire 1840 = Dictionnaire français-anglais-allemand-suédois. 2 Bde. Stockholm 1840 [Beruht lt. Haugen 1984 auf Brockhaus: Dictionnaire français-allemand-anglais].

Dictionnaire 1880 = Dictionnaire polyglotte, militaire et naval. Tokio 1880 [Frz.-Dt.-Engl.-Niederl.-Jap.].

Dictionnaire des huict langaiges 1546 = Le Dictionnaire des huict langaiges: grec, latin, flamang, françois, espagnol, italien, anglois et aleman. Paris 1546 [z. T. unter dem Namen des Druckers Pasquier Letellier zitiert. Geht ebenfalls auf Rottweil 1477 zurück].

Dictionnaire orateur 1709 = ... Dictionnaire orateur françois-latin-allemand. Frankfurt 1709.

Dizionario degli insulti 1980 = ... Dizionario degli insulti. Come dire le parolacce in 5 lingue. Perugia 1980.

Dodoens 1608 = Rembert Dodoens: Cruydt-Boeck [...]. Leyden 1608 [Weitere Aufl. Leyden 1618 und Antwerpen 1644. Pflanzennamen auf Niederl., Dt., Lat. und Altgr.].

Dony 1951 = Yvonne P. de Dony: Léxico del lenguaje figurado. Buenos Aires 1951 [Span.-Engl.-Dt.-Frz.].

Dreisprachiges Taschenwörterbuch 1940 = ... Dreisprachiges Taschenwörterbuch Deutsch-Französisch-Niederländisch. Brüssel 1940.

Duarte 1859 = P. Duarte: Guide polyglotte français-anglais-allemand-italien-espagnol-portugais. Paris 1859.

Duckett 1848 = G. Duckett: Technological military dictionary. London 1848 [Dt.-Engl.-Frz.].

Duez 1642 = Nathaniel Duez: Dictionnaire français-allemand-latin et allemand-français-latin. 2 Bde. Leyden 1642 [3. Aufl. Dictionarium Gallico-Germanico-Latinum et dictionarium Germanico-Gallico-Latinum. Amsterdam 1664].

Egede 1750 = Paul Egede: Dictionarium grønlandico-danico-latinum [...]. Kopenhagen 1750 [Grönländisch-Dän.-Lat.].

Elert 1646 = Petrus Elert: Dictionarium hexaglossum [...]. Warschau 1646 [Frz.-Dt.-Ital.-Lat.-Poln.-Span.].

Eminian 1853 = S. Eminian: Dictionnaire français-arménien-turc. Wien 1853.

Emmelius 1586 = Helfricus Emmelius/David Schellingius: Lexicon Trilingue, ex Thesauro Roberti Stephani et Dictionario Joannis Frisii collectum. Straßburg 1586.

Emmelius 1592 = Helfricus Emmelius: Nomenclator quatrilinguis. Straßburg 1592 [Dt.-Lat.-Altgr.-Frz.].

Emmelius 1592a = Helfricus Emmelius: Sylva quinquelinguis. 5 Bde. Straßburg 1592 [Dt.-Lat.-Altgr.-Hebr.-Frz.].

Enrile 1853 = Joaquín María Enrile: Vocabulario militar francés, inglés, español. 1853.

Escobar 1520 = Cristoforo de Escobar: Vocabularium ex latino sermone in Siciliensem et hispaniensem denuo Traductum. Venedig 1520 [Lat.-Sizilianisch-Span.].

Esteve 1803 = Joaquim Esteve/Josep Bellvitges/Antoni Juglà i Font: Diccionario catalán-castellano-latino. Barcelona 1803—1805.

Estienne 1548 = Robert Estienne: Dictionarium puerorum. Zürich 1548 [Lat.-Frz.-Dt.].

Estienne/Vernon 1552 = Robert Estienne/John Vernon: Dictionariolum puerorum tribus linguis Latine, Anglica et Gallica conscriptum. London 1552 [Nach einem Werk von R. Estienne von Vernon bearbeitet.].

Etcheverri 1701 = Juan de Etcheverri: Diccionario vasco-francés, español y latín. San Sebastián 1701.

Falletti 1822 = F. Falletti: Vocabulaire encyclopédique de poche français, italien, anglais. Paris 1822.

Farmer/Henley 1890 = John Stephen Farmer/W. E. Henley: Slang and its analogues. Historical and comparative dictionary. 7 Bde. London 1890—94.

Fernández 1654 = Marcos Fernández: Nomenclator en castellano, francés y flamenco. Köln 1654.

Floriato 1636 = M. Floriato: Proverborum trilinguium collectanea latina, itala et hispanica. Neapel 1636 [322 S.].

Florinus 1695 = Henrik Florinus: Vocabularium latino-sveco-germanico-finnicum. Stockholm 1695.

Fontanillo 1985 = Enrique Fontanillo Merino (Hrsg.): Diccionario de las lenguas de España. Madrid 1985.

Frischlin 1586 = Nicodemus Frischlin: Nomenclator trilinguis graecolatino germanicus [...]. Frankfurt 1586 [Altgr.-Lat.-Dt. Weitere Aufl. Frankfurt 1612].

Frisius 1548 = Joannes Frisius: Dictionarium puerorum tribus linguis Latina, Gallica et Germanica conscriptum. Zürich 1548 [613 S.; beruht auf dem Wb. von Robert Estienne].

Frisius 1556 = Joannes Frisius: Novum dictionarium puerorum Latinogermanicum et e diverso Germanicolatinum. Zürich 1556.

Frisius 1587 = Joannes Frisius: Dictionarium puerorum. Straßburg 1587. [Lat.-Dt., teilweise Altgr.; mit Register].

Funk and Wagnalls 1954 = Funk and Wagnalls New Practical Standard Dictionary of the English Language. New York 1954 [im Anhang Wortlisten mit Engl.-Frz.-Dt.-Ital.-Span.-Schwed.-Jiddisch].

Garon 1526 = Franciscus Garon: Quinque linguarum utilissimus Vocabulista, Latine, Tusche, Gallice, Hyspane et Alemanice. Valde necessarius per mundum versari cupientibus. Venedig 1526 [Weitere Aufl. Nürnberg 1529; Venedig 1533, 1537 und 1542].

Gaudin 1666 = R. P. Gaudin: Novum Dictionarium. Limoges 1666 [Lat.-Altgr.-Frz.].

Gelenius 1537 = Sigismundus Gelenius [auch: Ghelen, Geneilus oder Jelený]: Lexicon symphonum quatuor linguarum Europae familiarum concordia consonantiaque indicatur. Basel 1537. 2. Aufl. 1544 [Altgr.-Lat.-Dt.-Tschech.].

Gesnerus 1540 = Conradus Gesnerus: Nomenclator Aquatilium Animantium [...]. Zürich 1540.

Gesnerus 1542 = Conradus Gesnerus: Catalogus plantarum. Zürich 1542 [Lat.-Altgr.-Dt.-Frz.].

Gesnerus 1551 = Conradus Gesnerus: Historia animalium. 5 Bde. Zürich 1551 [Lat.-Ital.-Span.-Lat.-Hebr.-Aram./Arab.-Berberisch-Pers.-Altgr.-Ital.-Span.-Frz.-Dt.-Engl.-Slawisch].

Gilanov 1966 = S. M. Gilanov: Kleiner Sprachführer in sechs Sprachen. Moskau 1966 [Frz.-Engl.-Dt.-Russ.-Ital.-Niederl.].

Gluski 1971 = Jerzy Gluski: Proverbs. Amsterdam 1971 [Engl.-Frz.-Dt.-Ital.-Span.-Russ.].

Gothus 1640 = Jonas Petri Gothus: Dictionarium: Latino-sveco-germanicum [...]. 2 Bde. Linköping 1640 [Schwed.-Lat.; Dt.-Lat.].

Grandpre 1728 = J. Grandpre: The traveller's interpreter in four languages. London 1728 [Engl.-Niederl.-Frz.-Ital.].

Grave 1551 = Bartholomy de Grave: Vocabulaer in vier spraken [...]. Löwen 1551 [Niederl.-Frz.-Lat.-Span. Erweiterung von Berlaimont 1536. Weitere Aufl. unter dem Titel „Colloquia ..." (siehe dort)].

Grave 1558 = Bartholomy de Grave: Vocabulario de quatro Lingue, Francese, Latina/Italiana e Spagnola [...]. Löwen 1558.

Grundström 1939 = Harald Grundström: Lapsksvensk-tysk ordbok. Uppsala 1939 [Lappisch-Schwed.-Dt.].

Gruterus 1610—12 = Janus Gruterus: Florilegium ethico-politicum. Accedunt gnomae paroemiaeque Graecorum, item proverbia Germanica, Belgica, Italica, Gallica, Hispanica. 3 Bde. Frankfurt 1610—12.

Guertler 1731 = N. Guertler: Novum lexicon universale quatuor linguarum. Basel 1731 [Lat.-Dt.-Altgr.-Frz.].

Guignes 1813 = Chrétien Louis Joseph de Guignes: Dictionnaire chinois-français et latin. Paris 1813.

Hadži P. Daniil 1764 = Hadži P. Daniil: Lexicon tetraglosson. Moschopolis 1764 [Rumänisch-Albanisch-Neugr.-Mazedonisch].

Haensch/Haberkamp 1981 = Günther Haensch/Gisela Haberkamp de Antón: Wörterbuch der Biologie 2. Aufl. München 1981 [Engl.-Dt.-Frz.-Span.].

Haensch/Haberkamp 1987 = Günther Haensch/Gisela Haberkamp: Wörterbuch der Landwirtschaft. München 1987 [Dt.-Engl.-Frz.-Span.-Ital.-Russ. Systematisch und alphabetisch.].

Haldorson 1814 = Biørn Haldorson/R. K. Raskii: Lexicon Islandico-Latino-Danicum. 2 Bde. Kopenhagen 1814.

Helsingius 1587 = Olaus Petri Helsingius: Synonymorum libellus. Stockholm 1587 [Schwed.-Lat.-Altgr.].

Helsloot 1946 = N. Helsloot: Malay, English, Dutch Pocket Vocabulary of 20 000 Words. Melbourne 1946.

Heng 1933 = E. Heng: Deutsche Sprichwörter im Spiegel fremder Sprachen [...]. Berlin. Leipzig 1933 [Dt.-Engl.-Frz.-Ital.-Lat.-Span.].

Henisch 1616 = Georg Henisch: Teutsche Sprache und Weissheit (sic). [...] Augsburg 1616 [Tschech.-Engl. - Frz. - Dt. - Altgr. - Hebr. - Span. - Ungar.-Ital.-Poln.].

Herbau 1716 = S. Herbau: Dictionnaire fr.-all.-lat. et all.-fr.-latin. Köln 1716 [bei Quemada 1967, 579].

Hervás 1784 = Lorenzo Hervás y Panduro: Catálogo de las lenguas de las naciones conocidas. Cesena 1784 [enthält vergleichende Wortlisten aus 300 europäischen, asiatischen und amerikanischen Sprachen].

Hervás 1787 = Lorenzo Hervás y Panduro: Vocabulario polyglotto con prolegomeni sopra più di CL lingue. Cesena 1787.

Hexaglosson 1646 = Hexaglosson dictionarium. Warschau 1646 [Lat.-Ital.-Poln.-Frz.-Span.-Dt.].

Heym 1802 = J. Heym: Nouveau dictionnaire russe-français-allemand. 2 Bde. Moskau 1802.

Heym 1805 = J. Heym: Dictionnaire portatif français-russe-allemand. 2 Bde. Riga 1805.

Holtzmann 1937 = Otto Holtzmann (Hrsg.): Vielsprachen-Wörterbuch nach der Einsprachen-Anordnung. Band Grundbegriffe der Technik (Dt.) — Band General Technical Terms (Engl.) — Band Technologie Générale (Frz.) — Band Technología general (Span.) — Band Termini fundamentali della tecnica (Ital.). Alle München. Berlin. Paris. London. Barcelona. Florenz 1937.

Hornkens 1599 = Henrico Hornkens: Recueil de Dictionnaires francoys, espagnolz et latins. Brüssel 1599.

Houtman 1603 = Frederick de Houtman: Spraeck- and Woord-boek inde Maleysche ende Madagaskaische talen. Amsterdam 1603 [2. Aufl. 1680. Malaiisch, Madagassisch, Niederl.].

Houttuyn 1773 = Martinus Houttuyn: Houtkunde [...]. Amsterdam 1773 [Niederl.-Dt.-Engl.-Frz.-Lat.; weitere Aufl. 1791—1795].

Howell 1659—1660 = James Howell: Lexicon tetraglotton, English-French-Italian-Spanish Dictionary. London 1659—1660 [gefolgt von einem thematisch aufgebauten Wortschatz im 2. Teil: A particular Vocabulary or Nomenclature in English, Italian, French and Spanish of The proper terms belonging to several arts and sciences. London 1659].

Hue 1937 = Gustave Hue: Dictionnaire annamite-chinois-français. Hanoi 1937.

Huloet 1572 = Richard Huloet: Dictionarie [...]. London 1572 [Lat.-Engl.-Frz.].

Hulsius 1616 = Levinus Hulsius: Dictionarium teutsch-frantzösisch-italiänisch; frantzösisch-teutsch-italiänisch; italiänisch-frantzösisch-teutsch. 5. Aufl. Frankfurt 1616.

Hulsius 1631 = Levinus Hulsius: Bd. I. Dictionnaire François-Allemand-Italien et Latin. 6. Aufl. Frankfurt 1631 [768 S.]. Bd. II. Dictionarium Teutsch - Frantzösisch - Italiänisch - Lateinisch. Frankfurt 1631 [531 S.]. Bd. III Dittionario Italiano-Francese-Tedesco. Frankfurt 1616 [595 S.].

Humières 1790 = L.J.P. d'Humières: Recueil de proverbes françois, latins, espagnols, italiens, allemands, hollandois, juifs, américains, russes à l'usage des écoles publiques et maisons d'éducation. Paris 1790 [Frz.-Lat.-Span.-Ital.-Dt.-Niederl.-Hebräisch-Engl.-Russ.-Türk.].

Hutterus 1597 = Elias Hutterus: Ein ABC-Büchlein darauß man die vier Hauptsprachen als Ebraisch, Griechisch, Lateinisch, Deutsch leicht buchstabieren und lesen lernen kann [...]. Nürnberg 1597 [890 S. + 393 S. Register].

Ilg 1960 = Gérard Ilg: Proverbes français, suivis des équivalents en allemand, anglais, espagnol, italien, néerlandais. Amsterdam. New York 1960 (Glossaria interpretum 4).

Ionchère 1807 = C. La Ionchère: Dictionnaire abrégé et portatif français, latin, italien, espagnol et portugais. 2. Aufl. Paris 1807.

Jal 1848 = Augustin Jal: Glossaire nautique. Répertoire polyglotte des termes de marine anciens et modernes. Paris 1848 [Frz.-Engl.-Dt.-Dän.-Schwed.-Niederl.-Ital.-Maltesisch-Span.-Port.-Altgr.-Neugr.-Russ.-Poln.-Bretonisch-Bask.-Malaiisch-Chin.].

Janua linguarum 1617 = Janua linguarum quadrilinguis. London 1659 [Lat.-Engl.-Frz.-Span. mit 1200 Sprichwörtern in diesen Sprachen].

Jongkindt 1894 = A.M.C. Jongkindt Coninck: Dictionnaire Latin-Grec-Français-Anglais-Allemand-Hollandais, des principaux termes employés en botanique et en horticulture. Haarlem 1894.

Junius 1567 = Hadrianus Junius: Nomenclator omnium rerum propia nomina variis linguis explicata indicans. Antwerpen 1567 [Weitere Aufl. London 1585. Frankfurt 1620. Lat.-Altgr.-Dt.-Niederl.-Frz.-Ital.-Span.-Engl.].

Junius 1588 = Hadrianus Junius [De Jonghe]: Nomenclator [...]. Köln 1588 [Lat.-Dt.-Frz.].

Junius 1623 = Hadrianus Junius: Nomenclator [...]. Antwerpen 1623 [Lat.-Niederl.-Frz.].

Jusenius 1745 = Daniel Jusenius: Finsk orda-boks försök [...]. Stockholm 1745 [Finnisch-Lat.-Schwed.].

Kasprowicz 1878 = Erazm Lucjan Kasprowicz: Tornisterdolmetscher des deutschen Reichssoldaten im täglichen Verkehr mit den Grenzvölkern des deutschen Reiches. Leipzig 1878 [Dt.-Dän.-Niederl.-Frz.-Russ.-Poln.-Tschech.].

Kerler 1971 = Richard Kerler: Conozca y hable 5 idiomas a la vez. Barcelona 1971 [Bildwörterbuch].

Kettridge 1945 = J. O. Kettridge: Traveller's Foreign Phrase Book. London 1945 [Engl.-Dt.-Span.-Frz.-Ital.-Niederl.].

Kilianus 1573 = Cornelius Kilianus: Etymologicum. Antwerpen 1573 [Niederl.-Lat.-Frz.].

Kilianus 1642 = Cornelius Kilianus: Dictionarium Teutonico-Latino-Gallicum. Amsterdam 1642.

Klett 1973 = Grundwortschatz Deutsch. Essential German — Alemán fundamental, bearb. von Heinz Oehler und Carl Heupel. Stuttgart 1973.

Kürschner 1954 = Joseph Kürschner: Lexikon der sechs Weltsprachen. Berchtesgaden 1954. 1. Aufl. als Welt-Sprachen-Lexikon Berlin. Eisenach. Leipzig. Chicago o. J. (aber sicher vor 1940) [Engl.-Frz.-Ital.-Span.-Lat.-Dt.; 1. Aufl. ohne Span.].

Kyber 1553 = D. Kyber: Lexicon rei herbariae trilingue. Straßburg 1553 [Lat.-Frz.-Dt.].

Labèrnia 1839 = Pere Labèrnia J. Esteller: Diccionari de la llengua catalana amb la correspondència castellana y latina. 2 Bde. Barcelona 1839—40.

Lacavalleria 1641 = Antoni Lacavalleria: Diccionario castellano. Dictionnaire français. Dictionari (sic) catala. Barcelona 1641.

Lagadeuc 1499 = Jehan Lagadeuc: Catholicon [Vorwort von 1464; gedruckt 1499 in Tréguier. Bretonisch-Lat.-Frz.].

Laguna 1555 = Andrés Laguna: Materia medica [Span. Übersetzung des Dioscorides 1555]. Moderne Ausgabe: César E. Dubler: La „Materia Médica de Dioscórides. Transmisión medical renacentista, vol. III: La „Materia Médica" de Dioscórides traducida y comentada por D. Andrés Laguna. Barcelona 1955 [Gibt meist die Namen auf Altgr.-Lat.-„Apothekerlatein"-Arab.-Span.-Katal.-Port.-Ital.-Frz.-Dt. an. Illustriert. Nach Colón/Soberanas 1985].

Landuchi 1562 = Nicolaus Landuchi (auch: Landuchius): Dictionarium linguae Toscanae [...] [Ms. 8341 der Biblioteca Nacional, Madrid. Span.-Ital.-Frz. u. Bask.].

Lantsheer 1811 = Hendrik Willem Lantsheer/ A. C. Twent: Dictionnaire des termes de marine français recueillis et traduits en termes techniques hollandais et en partie en anglais. 2 Bde. Amsterdam 1811 [Frz.-Niederl.-Engl.].

Larramendi 1745 = Manuel de Larramendi: Diccionario trilingüe del castellano, bascuence y latín. 2 Bde. San Sebastián. 1. Aufl. 1745. 2. Aufl. 1853.

Leem/Sandberg 1768 = Knut Leem/Gerhard Sandberg: Lexicon lapponicum bipartitum [...]. 2 Teile: Lappisch-Dän.-Lat. und Dän.-Lat.-Lappisch. Kopenhagen 1768 [bei Haugen 1984].

Letellier 1838 = L. Letellier: Vocabulaire oriental français-italien-arabe-turc-grec. Paris 1838.

Ley fundamental 1973 = Ley fundamental de la República federal alemana. Hrsg. vom Presse- und Informationsamt der Bundesregierung. Bonn 1973.

Lindahl/Öhrling 1780 = Erik Lindahl/Johann J. Öhrling: Lexicon Lapponicum, cum interpretatione sveco-latina et indice sveco-lapponico. Stockholm 1780 [Lappisch-Schwed.-Lat.].

Lindberg 1835 = Lorenz Lindberg: Ordbok på 6 språk: svenska, latin, italienska, fransyska, engelska och tyska. Wexiö 1835.

Lobelius 1581 = Matthias Lobelius: Kruydtboeck oft Beschrijvinghe van allerley Ghewasser, Kruyderen, Hesteren ende Gheboomten. Antwerpen 1581 [Niederl.-Lat.-Dt.-Frz.-Ital.-Span.-(Port.-)Engl.].

Lodereckerus 1605 = Petrus Lodereckerus: Dictionarium septem linguarum. Prag 1605 [Tschech.-Ital.-Dt.-Kroat.-Ungar.-Poln.-Lat.].

Lorenzo 1864 = José Lorenzo/Gonzalo de Murgo/Martín Ferreiro: Diccionario marítimo español. Madrid 1864—65 [mit Äquivalenten der Fachtermini auf Frz., Engl. und Ital.].

Lux 1943 = Sebastian Lux (Hrsg.): Europa in 23 Sprachen — 1000 Wörter bildhaft dargestellt. München 1943 [Neuaufl. unter dem Titel „Europa versteht sich". München 1946].

Mairas 1643 = D. Mairas: Nomenclature français-allemand-italien-danois. Kopenhagen 1643.

Makre dardeke 1488 = Makre dardeke, praeceptor puerorum, seu lexicon Hebraeo-Italico-Arabico-Rabbinicum. Neapel 1488 [Hebr.-Ital.-Arab.].

Manuel 1875 = ... Manuel du Pensionnat en 3 langues. 2. Aufl. München 1875.

Manutius 1672 = Aldus Manutius: Phrases instauratae et in meliorem ordinem digestae a P.P. Societatis Jesu. [...]. Leiden 1672 [Lat.-Frz.-Niederl.].

Marks 1970 = Joseph Marks: Harrap's French-English Dictionary of Slang and Colloquialisms. London 1970.

Martínez de Waucquier 1714 = Matthias Martínez de Waucquier/Nicoleides Joannes: Novum Dictionarium Tetraglotton Amsterdam 1714 [Lat.-Altgr.-Frz.-Niederl. Insgesamt 8 weitere Aufl. zwischen 1719 und 1796].

Matras 1633 = Daniel Matras: Proverbes, sentences, et mots durez [...] en François, Danois, Italien et Allemand. Copenhagen 1633.

Matz/Vanderhaege 1978 = Gilbert Matz/Maurice Vanderhaege: Guide du terrarium. Neuchâtel. Paris 1978 [Dazu dt. Ausgabe: BLV-Terrarienführer. München 1980. Span. Ausgabe: Guía del Terrario. Barcelona 1979].

Medina 1960 = G. Medina Zapater: Diccionario ideográfico políglota. Madrid 1960.

Megiser 1592 = Hieronymus Megiser: Dictionarium quattuor linguarum, videlicet Germanicae, Latinae, Illyricae [Serbokroatisch] et Italicae. Graz 1592 [Weitere Aufl. Graz 1744].

Megiser 1603 = Hieronymus Megiser: Thesaurus polyglottus. 2 Bde. Frankfurt 1603 [Lat.-Hebr.-Altgr.-Arab.-Syrisch-Ital.-Frz.-Span.-Dt.-Niederl.-Tschech.-Kroat.-Poln.-Ungar.-Slowenisch-Engl.].

Megiser 1605 = Hieronymus Megiser: Paroemiologia Polyglottes, hoc est: Proverbia et sententiae complurium linguarum. Leipzig 1605 [Hebr.-Altgr.-Lat.-Ital.-Span.-Frz.-Dt.-Niederl.-Slowenisch-Arab.-Türk.].

Meninski 1680 = Franz Meninski [Franz a Mesgnien]: Thesaurus linguarum orientalium praesertim Turcicae, Arabicae et Persicae cum interpretatione Latina, Germanica etc. 3 Bde. Wien 1680.

Mentzel 1682 = Christian Mentzel: Pinax Botanorymos Polyglottos. Index nominum plantarum universalis. Berlin 1682 [Nomenklatur der Pflanzen in 30 Sprachen].

Mesnard 1841 = A. Mesnard: Guide de la conversation allemand-anglais-français-italien. Leipzig 1841.

Mez de Braidenbach 1670 = Nicolas Mez de Braidenbach: Diccionario muy copioso de la lengua española y alemana [...]. Wien 1670.

Minshew 1617 = John Minshew (oder: Minscheu): Vocabularium hispanico-latinum et anglicum. A most copious Spanish dictionarie with Latin and English. London 1617 [erschien zus. mit Minshew 1617a].

Minshew 1617a = John Minshew (oder: Minscheu): Hegemon eistas glossas, id est Ductor in linguas. The guide into Tongues. London 1617 [Engl.-Kymrisch-(Walisisch)-Dt.-Niederl.-Frz.-Ital.-Span.-Port.-Lat.-Altgr.-Hebr. 1. Teil Ausgangssprache Engl. mit engl. Definitionen und Äquivalenten in 11 Sprachen, aber nur z. T. durchgeführt; 2. Teil ist Minshew 1617, alphabetisch geordnetes Vokabular Span. (Ausgangssprache)-Lat.-Engl. 2. Aufl. London 1617 (aber ohne das Vocabularium hispanico-latinum et anglium); nur noch 9 Sprachen statt 11].

Morel 1573 = G. Morel: Thesaurus vocum omnium [...]. Lyon 1573 [Lat.-Altgr.-Frz.].

Morel 1603 = F. Morel: Dictionariolum lat., graeco, gallicum. Paris 1603.

Mosimmanull 1574 = D. Mosimmanull: Dictionarium trium linguarum lat.-gallogerm. Straßburg 1574.

Müller 1847 = C. H. Müller: Polyglossarium nauticum. Hamburg 1847 [Dän.-Dt.-Engl.-Span.-Frz.-Niederl.-Ital.-Port.-Russ.-Schwed.].

Multilingual Business Handbook 1983 = The Multilingual Business Handbook. A Guide to International Correspondence. London. Sydney 1983 [Dt.-Engl.-Span.-Frz.-Ital.].

Multilingual Commercial Dictionary 1983 = A Multilingual Commercial Dictionary. London 1978 [Nachdruck 1983. Engl.-Dt.-Span.-Frz.-Ital.-Port.].

Munting 1702 = Abraham Munting: Phytographia curiosa, exhibens arborum fruticum, herbarum et florum icones [...]. Amsterdam 1702. [Lat.-Frz.-Ital.-Dt.-Niederl. Weitere Aufl. 1711, 1723 und 1727].

Murmelius 1533 = Johannes Murmelius: Lat.-ungar.-dt. Wörterbuch 1533. Kommentierte Ausgabe von István Szamota: A Murmelius-féle Latin-magyar-szójegyzék, bevezetéssel és magyaráza tokkal ellátra. Budapest 1896.

Muus/Dahlström 1966 = Guide des Poissons de Mer et Pêche. Neuchâtel. Paris 1966. Dänische Originalausgabe: Havfisk og Fiskeri i Nordvesteuropa. Kopenhagen 1964. Deutsche Fassung: BLV-Bestimmungsbuch Meeresfische. 2. Aufl. München 1968.

Mymerus 1528 = Franciscus Mymerus: Dictionarium trium linguarum, Latinae, Teutonicae et Polonicae, potiora vocabula continens. Krakau 1528 [Lat.-Dt.-Poln.].

Nemnich 1793 = Philipp Andreas Nemnich: Allgemeines Polyglottenlexicon der Naturgeschichte. Hamburg. Halle. Leipzig 1793—98 [Dt.-Niederl.-Dän.-Schwed.-Engl.-Frz.-Ital.-Span.-Port.].

Nemnich 1797 = Philipp Andreas Nemnich: Waaren-Lexicon in zwölf Sprachen [...]. 2 Bde. Hamburg 1797—1802 [Engl.-Dt.-Niederl.-Dän.-Schwed.-Frz.-Ital.-Span.-Port.-Russ.-Poln.-Lat.].

Nemnich 1800 = Philipp Andreas Nemnich: Lexicon nosologicum polyglotton omnium morborum. Hamburg 1800 [Engl.-Dt.-Niederl.-Dän.-Schwed.-Frz.-Ital.-Span.-Port.-Russ.-Poln.-Lat.].

Nemnich 1803 = Philipp Andreas Nemnich: Comtoir-Lexikon in neun Sprachen, für Geschäftsmänner. Hamburg 1803 [Dt.-Niederl.-Dän.-Schwed.-Engl.-Frz.-Ital.-Span.-Port.].

Nemnich 1820 = Philipp Andreas Nemnich: Neues Waaren-Lexicon in zwölf Sprachen. 3 Bde. Hamburg 1820 [Engl.-Dt.-Niederl.-Dän.-Schwed.-Frz.-Ital.-Span.-Port.-Russ.-Neugr.-Lat.].

Nielsen 1932 = Konrad Nielsen: Lappisk ordbok [...]. Oslo. London. Cambridge (Mass.) 1932—38 [Lappisch-Engl.-Norwegisch].

Nieuwe Woordenshat 1780 = Nieuwe Woordenshat uigt het Nedenduitsch in het gemeene Maleiisch en Portugeesch [...]. Batavia 1780 [Niederl.-Malaiisch-Port.].

Nirmutanus 1625 = Ch. Nirmutanus: Dictionarium harmonicum lat.-gall.-ital. Frankfurt 1625.

Nizzoli 1535 = Mario Nizzoli: Marii Nizolii Brixellensis Observatorium in M. T. Ciceronem. Prato Albino 1535 [Näheres über die folgenden Ausgaben bei Gallina 1959, 215—218].

Norstett 1780—82 = I. Norstett: Rossīĭskīĭ, s nêmetskim i frantzuskim perevodami, slovar'. 2 Bde. Katherinenburg 1780—82 [Russ.-Dt.-Frz.].

Nouveau dictionnaire 1807 = Nouveau dictionnaire portatif français, polonais et allemand. 2 Bde. Breslau 1807.

Noviliers 1629 = Guillermo A. de Noviliers Clavel: Nomenclatura Italiana, Francese e Spagnuola. Con i termini proprii di ciascun Capitolo. Venedig 1629 [411 S.].

Novum dictionarium 1700 = ... Novum dictionarium latino-sueco-germanicum [Lat.-Schwed.-Dt. und Schwed.-Lat.-Dt.]. 3 Bde. Hamburg 1700.

Núñez de Taboada 1833 = ... Núñez de Taboada: Guide de la conversation en VI langues. Paris 1833 [Engl.-Dt.-Frz.-Ital.-Span.-Russ.].

Ochoa 1860 = D. de Ochoa: Guide de la conversation français-espagnol-italien-anglais. Paris 1860.

Oosting 1887 = J. Oosting: Practisch Handelswoordenboek in vier talen. Gouda 1887—90 [Niederl.-Dt.-Frz.-Engl.].

Ordbok 1856 = Ordbok finsk, tysk, rysk och svensk. Viborg 1856.

Orefice 1977 = Guiseppe Alberto Orefice: The 5 Language European Dictionary. London 1977 [o. S.].

O'Scanlan 1829 = Timoteo O'Scanlan: Cartilla práctica de construcción naval, dispuesta en forma de vocabulario con algunos apéndices y las nomenclaturas francesa, inglesa e italiana, con su correspondencia castellana. Madrid 1829.

Oudin 1617 = César Oudin: Thrésor des III langues espagnole, françoise et italienne. Genf 1617 [ursprünglich nur Frz. und Span.].

Ouseg 1962 = H. L. Ouseg: 21 Language Dictionary. New York. London 1962 [20 europäische Sprachen und Türkisch].

Pajot 1645 = R. P. Pajot: Dictionarium novum. La Flèche 1645 [Lat.-Frz.-Altgr.].

Pallas 1790 = Petr Simon Pallas: Vocabularium linguarum totius orbis Augustissimae Catherinae II cura collectum. 2 Teile. Petersburg 1786—89. 2. Aufl. in 4 Bden., alphabetisch geordnet, hrsg. von Fedor Jankovic de Marjevo. Petersburg 1790—91 [Dieses Wb. wird meist „Vocabularium Catherinae" genannt. Es enthält 200 europäische und asiatische Sprachen].

Pallegoix 1854 = D. Pallegoix: Dictionarium linguae thai (et latinae-gallicae-anglicae). Paris 1854.

Paludanus 1544 = Joannes Paludanus: Dictionariolum rerum vulgarium linguae lat.-gall. et flam. Genf 1544 [Lat.-Frz.-Niederl.; geht auf das Dictionariolum puerorum von Robert Estienne von 1542 zurück].

Pasor 1690 = Georg Pasor/Everardus van der Hooght: Lexicon Novi Testamenti Graeco-Latino-Belgicum. Amsterdam 1690 [Altgr.-Lat.-Niederl.].

Pell 1735 = Guillaume Pell: The English, Dutch, French and Latin Vocabulary [...]. Utrecht 1735 [Engl.-Niederl./Frz.-Engl./Engl.-Lat.].

Percivall 1591 = Richard Percivall: Bibliotheca hispanica II. A Dictionaire in Spanish, English and Latine. London 1591.

Pesthi 1538 = Gabriel Pesthi: Nomenclatura sex linguarum Latinae, Italicae, Gallicae, Bohemicae, Hungaricae et Germanicae. Wien 1538.

Pisant 1958 = Emmanuel Pisant: International dictionary. Boulogne. Paris 1958 [Engl.-Frz.-Ital.-Span.-Dt.].

Plantin 1573 = Christophe Plantin: Thrésor du langage bas-allemand, français-latin. Antwerpen 1573.

Polidori 1806 = G. Polidori: Nuovo dizionario portatile italiano-inglese-francese. 3 Bde. London 1806.

Polycarpius 1704 = Theodor Polycarpius: Dictionarium trilingue hoc est dictionum Slavicarum, Graecarum et Latinarum thesaurus. Moskau 1704 [Russ.-Altgr.-Lat.].

Pomai 1709 = François Pomai (auch: Pomey): Le Grand Dictionnaire Royal. I. François-Latin-Allemand. II. Latin-Allemand-François. III. Allemand-François-Latin. Frankfurt 1709.

Pomis 1587 = David de Pomis: Dittionario (sic) novo hebraico. Venedig 1587 [Hebr.-Lat.-Ital.].

Pradez 1951 = Elisabeth Pradez: Dictionnaire des gallicismes les plus usités, expliqués brièvement, illustrés par des exemples et accompagnés de leurs équivalents anglais et allemands. Paris 1951. 2. Aufl. Paris 1965.

Proverbia Septentrionalia 1985 = Matti Kuüsi: Proverbia Septentrionalia. 900 Balto-Finnic Proverb types with Russian, Baltic, German and Scandinavian Parallels. Helsinki 1985 (FF Communications, Vol. CI, Nr. 236, Academia Scientiarum Fennica).

Quinque linguarum 1513 = Quinque linguarum utilissimus vocabulista Latine, Tusche, Gallice, Hyspane et Alemanice. Venedig 1513 [Lat.-Ital.-Frz.-Span.-Dt.].

Quinque linguarum 1543 = Quinque linguarum, Latinae, Theutonicae, Gallicae, Hispanicae, Italicae dilucidissimus dictionarius. Antwerpen 1543 [Lat.-Niederl.-Frz.-Span.-Ital.].

Rädlein 1711 = Johann Rädlein: Europäischer Sprachenschatz [...]. 3 Bde. Leipzig 1711 [Dt.-Ital.-Frz.].

Ravius 1645 = Chr. Ravius: Specimen lexici Arabico-Persico-Latini. Leyden 1645.

Recueil 1832 = Recueil de dialogues et mots usuels. Besançon 1832 [Frz.-Russ.-Poln.-Dt.].

Reehorst 1842 = Karel P. Fer Reehorst: New Dictionary of technical Terms. Amsterdam 1842 [8 Sprachen].

Reehorst 1850 = Karel P. Fer Reehorst: Polyglot commercial Dictionary in ten Languages. London 1850 [Engl.-Niederl.-Dt.-Dän.-Schwed.-Frz.-Ital.-Span.-Port.-Russ.].

Reiff 1879 = Carl Philipp Reiff: Parallel dictionaries of the Russian, French, German and English languages. 4 Bde. Karlsruhe 1879—81.

Reuss 1798 = F. Reuss: Lexicon mineralogicum (mit Index in Lat., Frz., Ital., Schwed., Dän., Engl., Russ., Ungar. und Dt.). Berlin 1798.

Rhodes 1651 = Alexandre de Rhodes: Dictionarium Annamiticum, Lusitanum et Latinum. Rom 1651.

Röding 1794 = Johann Heinrich Röding: Allgemeines Wörterbuch der Marine in allen europäischen Sprachen. Leipzig 1794—98 [Dt.-Niederl.-Dän.-Schwed.-Engl.-Frz.-Ital.-Span.-Port.].

Römer 1891 = G.P.A.G.H. Römer: De meest gebruikelijke Termen der Cavalerie vertaald in het Fransch en Duitsch. Den Haag 1891 [Niederl.-Frz. und Niederl.-Dt.].

Rottweil 1477 = Adam von Rottweil: Introito e porta de quele che volemo imparare e comprender todesco a latino, cioè italiano. Venedig 1477 [Ital.-dt. Sprachführer; Anordnung thematisch. Kommentierte Ausgabe von Vito R. Giustiniani: Adam von Rottweil. Dt.-ital. Sprachführer. (Lingua et traditio. Beiträge zur Geschichte der Sprachwissenschaft 8) Tübingen 1987. Das Werk wurde später unter dem Titel *Vocabulista* veröffentlicht, z. B. *Quinque linguarum utilissimus Vocabulista*, Nürnberg 1529. Für alle folgenden Ausgaben siehe Gallina 1959, 38—40].

Ruland 1586 = Martin Ruland: Dictionariolum et nomenclatura Germanico-Latino-Graecuon omnium rerum et locutionum usitatarum. Augsburg 1586.

Sabek 1971 = Jerwan Sabek: Trilingual dictionary Arabic-French-English. Beirut 1971.

Saint-Joseph 1684 = Angelus a S. Josepho [auch: Ange de Saint Joseph oder Joseph de la Brosse]: Gazophylacium linguae Persicae triplici linguarum clavi, Italicae, Latinae, Gallicae [...]. Amsterdam 1684 [Persisch-Frz.-Lat.-Ital.].

Sánchez-Monge 1981 = Enrique Sánchez-Monge y Parellada: Diccionario de Plantas Agrícolas. Madrid 1981 [Lat.-Span.-Katal.-Bask.-Galicisch-Dt.-Frz.-Engl.-Ital.-Port.].

Schaufelbüel 1986 = Adolf Schaufelbüel: Treffende Redensarten, viersprachig. 2000 Redewendungen und 500 Sprichwörter. Thun 1986 [Dt.-Frz.-Ital.-Engl.].

Schischkoff 1838 = Alex Schischkoff: Vergleichendes Wörterbuch in 200 Sprachen. 2 Bde. St. Petersburg 1838.

Schmidt 1837 = J. Schmidt: Nouveau dictionnaire complet français-grec moderne-allemand. Leipzig 1837.

Schmutzige Wörter 1987 = Schmutzige Wörter. Deutsch - Englisch - Französisch - Italienisch - Spanisch-Türkisch. Eichborns sechssprachiges Wörterbuch der Schimpfwörter, Beleidigungen und Flüche. Hrsg. von Hella Thall. Frankfurt 1987.

Schroderus 1637 = Ericus Schroderus: Dictionarium Latino Scondicum 1637 [nicht veröffentlicht]. Faksimileausgabe von Bengt Hesselmann. Uppsala 1941 [Finn.-Schwed.-Lat.-Dt.].

Séjournant 1749 = Nicolás de Séjournant: Nouveau dictionnaire espagnol, français et latin. Paris 1749 [Weitere Ausgaben 1759, 1775, 1785, 1786—1787, 1789—90, 1790—91].

Septem linguarum (...) dictionarius 1540 = Septem linguarum [...] dilucidissimus dictionarius [...]. Antwerpen 1540 [Lat.-Niederl.-Frz.-Span.-Ital.-Engl.-Dt.].

Serenius 1734 = Jacob Serenius: Dictionarium anglo-svethico-latinum [...]. Hamburg 1734 [Engl.-Schwed.-Lat.].

Serenius 1741 = Jacob Serenius: Dictionarium Svethico-anglo-latinum. Stockholm 1741 [Schwed.-Engl.-Lat.].

Serrey 1629 = Joannes Serrey: Nomenclator Latino-Gallico-Germanicus. Straßburg 1629.

Servilius 1545 = Joannes Servilius: Dictionarium triglotton [...]. Antwerpen 1545 [Zahlreiche weitere Aufl. von 1546—1620 (alphabetisch). Lat.-Altgr.-Niederl. Vgl. Claes 1980, 228].

Sewel 1793 = William Sewel/John Hiltrop/Thomas Berry: A new pocket-dictionary and vocabulary of the English, Flemish and French Languages [...]. Dünkirchen. Genf 1781—85 [Engl.-Niederl.-Frz.].

Sex Linguarum 1530 = ... Sex Linguarum Latinae, Gallicae, Hispanicae, Italicae, Anglicae et Teutonicae dilucidissimus Dictionarius. 1530.

Smith 1840 = L. Smith: Guide de la conversation français, anglais, italien. Paris 1840.

Smith 1840a = L. Smith: Guide de la conversation français-anglais-allemand-italien. Paris 1840.

Smith 1840b = L. Smith: Guide of English, French, German, Italian Conversation. London 1840.

Smith 1843 = L. Smith: Guide de la conversation français-anglais-allemand-italien-espagnol-portugais. Paris 1843.

Smith 1843a = L. Smith: Guide de la conversation français, anglais, italien, espagnol, portugais. Paris 1843.

Sobrino 1769 = F. Sobrino: Nouveau Dictionnaire françois, espagnol et latin. 3 Bde. Antwerpen 1769 [Erweiterung der ursprünglich zweisprachigen Fassung: Diccionario nuevo de las lenguas española y francesa. 2 Bde. Brüssel 1705. Z. T. auch unter dem Namen des Bearbeiters Cormón zitiert. Neuauflagen 1772, 1775—76, 1780, 1789, 1791].

Soulkhanov 1839 = A. Soulkhanov: Vocabulaire méthodique géorgien-francais-russe. St. Petersburg 1839.

Spegel 1712 = H. Spegel: Glossaire suédois-latin-anglois-françois. Lund 1712 [bei Quemada 1967, 579].

Stoer 1563 = Jacob Stoer: Dictionnaire français-allemand-latin et allemand-français-latin. 2 Bde. Genf 1563.

Storck 1983 = Fachausdrücke in vier Sprachen aus Handel und Verkehr. Hamburg o. J. [1983].

Sturmius 1590 = Joannes Sturmius: Lexicon trilingue, Latino-Graeco-Germanicum. Straßburg 1590.

Sumarán 1626 = Johannes Angelus Sumarán: Thesaurus fundamentalis quinque linguarum (Lat.-Span.-Frz.-Dt.-Ital.). 3 Bde. Ingolstadt 1626 [4, 339, 245, 156 S.].

Terminologie forestière 1975 = Terminologie forestière. Sciences forestières, technologie, pratiques et produits forestiers. Paris 1975.

Terreros y Pando 1786 = Esteban Terreros y Pando: Diccionario castellano con las voces de ciencias y artes. 4 Bde. Madrid 1786—1793 [Span.-Lat.-Frz.-Ital.].

Theocharopoulos 1834 = G. Theocharopoulos: Vocabulaire français, anglais, grec moderne et grec ancien. München 1834.

Thesaurus 1573 = Thesaurus teutonicae linguae [...]. Antwerpen 1573. [Niederl.-Frz.-Lat. Nachdruck mit einer Einführung von F. Claes, Den Haag 1972].

Thesaurus 1665 = ... Thesaurus Quinque Germanicae, Latinae, Hispanicae, Gallicae et Italicae Linguarum fundamentalis [...]. Wien 1665 [962 S.].

Thresor 1642 = ... Thresor des trois langues. Tresora hirour lenguaiectagra francesa, espagnola etu hasquara. Bayonne 1642 [Frz.-Span.-Bask.].

Tolhausen 1854 = A. und E. Tolhausen: Dictionnaire technologique français-anglais-allemand. 3 Bde. Paris 1854.

Tomlin 1865 = J. Tomlin: A Comparative Vocabulary of forty-eight languages, comprising one hundred and forty-six common English words. Liverpool 1865 [insges. 48 europäische, afrikanische und asiatische Sprachen einschl. Lat. und Altgr.].

Toscanella 1568 = Orazio Toscanella: Dittionario (sic) volgare et latino [...]. Venedig 1568 [248 Bl.; Ital.-Lat.-Niederl.-Span., nur z. T. auch Dt., Türk., Frz.; dann Niederl.-Ital. u. Span.-Ital.].

Tournes 1621 = Jean Antoine et Samuel de Tournes (Hrsg.): Tesoro de las tres lenguas española, francesa e italiana. Dictionnaire en trois langues divise en III. Parties. 1. Esp.-fr.-ital., 2. fr.-it.-esp., 3. ital.-fr.-esp. Genf 1621 [Andere Ausgabe: Köln 1671. 1. Teil: 570 S., 2. Teil: 420 S., 3. Teil: 504 S.; „le tout recueilli des plus célèbres auteurs"].

Troc 1742 = Michael Abraham Troc: Nouveau dictionnaire français-allemand-polonais et polonais-français. Leipzig 1742—64 [Neue Ausgabe Leipzig 1806—22, 4 Bde. Bei Quemada 1967 erscheint dieses Wörterbuch mit dem Namen Trotz und der Jahreszahl 1744].

Trogney 1639 = Joachim Trogney [od. Trognesius]: El grande diccionario y thesoro de las tres lenguas española, francesa y flamenca [...]. Antwerpen 1639 [Auch dieses Werk geht auf Berlaimont 1536 zurück].

Twent 1813 = A. C. Twent: Dictionnaire de Marine [...]. Den Haag. Amsterdam 1813 [Niederl.-Engl.-Frz.].

Udino 1634 = Antonio Udino: Nuevo et ampio Dittionario di tre lingue diviso en III Parti: I. Italiano-Francese-Tedesco, II. Francese-Italiano-Tedesco, III. Tedesco-Francese-Italiano. Frankfurt 1634.

Valentin 1843 = Ch. Valentin: Dansk italiensk-spansk-portugisik haandordbog. Kopenhagen 1843.

Valette 1888 = T.G.G. Valette: Verzameling van spreekwoorden een spreekwoordelijke uitdrukkingen in vier talen. Haarlem 1888 [Niederl.-Frz.-Dt.-Engl.].

Van Goor's Woordenboek 1937 = Van Goor's Woordenboek der moderne talen. Den Haag 1937 [Frz.-Dt.-Engl.-Niederl.].

Varini 1672 = Giulio Varini: Scielta de Proverbi, e sentenze Italiani tolti da varie lingue [...]. Venedig 1672 [Hebr.-Arab.-Aramäisch-Altgr.-Lat.-Dt.-Frz.-Span.-Niederl.-Ital.].

Veer-Bertels 1971 = E. T. van der Veer-Bertels: Spreekwoorden, Proverbs, Sprichwörter, Proverbes. Een verzameling Nederlandse spreekwoorden met Duitse, Engelse en Franse equivalenten. Amsterdam 1971 [Niederl.-Dt.-Engl.-Frz.].

Velleman 1929 = Antoine Velleman: Dicziunari scurznieu de la lingua ladina [...]. Samaden 1929 [Rätoromanisch-Dt.-Frz.-Engl.].

Venator 1899 = Max Venator: German-English-Spanish-French dictionary of terms employed in Mining, Metallurgy and Chemistry. 3 Bde. Leipzig 1899—1905.

Vendoti 1790 = G. Vendoti: Dictionnaire grec moderne, français, italien. 3 Bde. Venedig 1790.

Veneroni 1700 = Giovanni Veneroni: Le dictionnaire impérial représentant les quatre Langues principales de l'Europe. I. Ital.-fr.-allem.-latin, II. Fr.-ital.-allem.-latin, III. Allem.-fr.-latin-ital., IV. Latin-ital.-fr.-allem. Frankfurt 1700 [Spätere Aufl. Köln 1804].

Veneroni 1771 = Giovanni Veneroni: Dictionnaire manuel français-italien-allemand-russe. Moskau 1771.

Verantius 1595 = Faustus Verantius (= F. Verancsics): Dictionarium quinque nobilissimarum Europae linguarum, Latinae, Italicae, Germanicae, Dalmaticae [Kroatisch] et Ungaricae. Venedig 1595.

Victor 1609 = Hierosme Victor Bolonois (auch: Girolamo Vittori): Tesoro de las tres lenguas, Francesa, Italiana y Española. 2 Teile. Genf 1609 [oder 1606. Zum Streit über die Datierung vgl. Gallina 1959, 231 ff., dort auch eine Liste aller späteren Auflagen].

Viersprachen-Länderverzeichnis = Viersprachen-Länderverzeichnis. Hrsg. vom Auswärtigen Amt. Bonn o. J. [in Loseblattform, letzte Ergänzungslieferung von Januar 1989].

Villatte 1888 = Césaire Villatte: Parisismen: Alphabetisch geordnete Sammlung der eigenartigen Ausdrucksweisen des Pariser Argot. 2. Aufl. Berlin 1888.

Vlachus 1659 = P. Vlachus: Thesaurus enciclopaedicae basis quadrilinguis [...]. Venedig 1659 [Altgr.-Neugr.-Lat.-Ital.].

Vocabolario nuovo 1567 = Vocabolario nuovo. Con il quale da se stessi si può benissimo imparare diversi linguaggi, cioè Italiano e Greco, Italiano e Turco et todesco (gegen 1567 verf.). Venedig 1583 [Ital.-Altgr.-Türk.-Dt.].

Vocabulaer 1560 = Vocabulaer pour apprendre latin, romain et flamand. o. O. 1560 [Lat.-Ital.-Fläm.].

... Vocabulaire du voyageur 1837 = Vocabulaire du voyageur anglais-français, italien-français, espagnol-français. Paris 1837.

Vocabulario 1599 = Vocabulario nuovo italiano-greco, italiano-turcho et italiano-tedesco. Venedig 1599 [Ital.-Griech.-Türk.-Dt.].

Vocabulario 1520 = ... Vocabulario para aprender franches, espannol y flaminco [...]. Antwerpen 1520 [20 Bl. Frz.-Span.-Fläm.].

Vocabularium 1575 = Vocabularium Lat., Gall.-germanicum. 2 Bde. Basel 1575.

Vocabularium 1507 = Vocabularium Latinis, Gallicis et Theutonicis verbis scriptum. Lyon 1507 [Weitere Aufl. 1514 u. 1515. Neudruck Köln 1568].

Vocabularium 1669 = ... Vocabularium Latino-Gallico-Germanicum [...]. Genf 1669.

Vocabularium Latinum 1664 = Vocabularium Latinum cum Suecica et Finnonica interpretatione. Stockholm 1664.

Vocabularius 1484 = ... Vocabularius gallico-belgico-latinus. Löwen 1484—86 [80 Bl.; Frz.-Niederl.-Lat.].

Vocabulary 1799 = Vocabulary of sea phrases engl.-frz. frz.-engl. 2 Bde. London 1799 [zitiert bei Quemada 1967].

Volchkov 1755—64 = S. Volchkov: Novoi leksikon na nemetskom, latinkom, i na rossiiskom yahzykakh. 2 Bde. St. Petersburg 1755—64 [Dt.-Lat.-Russ. Bei Quemada 1967, 586 als Volechkoff zitiert].

Vossius 1640 = Lambert Vossius: Lexicon novum herbarium tripartitum. In: Anselmus Boetius de Boodt: Florum, herbarum et fructum selectiorum icones [...]. Brügge 1640 [Lat.-Niederl.-Frz.].

Warmer 1691 = Christophorus Warmer: Gazophylacium decem linguarum europearum apertum [...]. Kassel 1691 [Tschech.-Fläm.-Engl.-Frz.-Dt.-Ungar.-Ital.-Lat.-Poln.-Span.].

Weck 1966 = Johannes Weck: Wörterbuch der Forstwirtschaft. München 1966 [Dt.-Engl.-Frz.-Span.-Russ.].

Weitenauer 1762 = Ignatius Weitenauer, S. J.: Hexaglotton geminum, docens linguas [...]. 2 Bde. Augsburg. Freiburg 1762 [Frz.-Ital.-Span.-Altgr.-Hebr.-Aramäisch-Engl.-Dt.-Niederl.-Lat.-Port.-Syrisch].

Weleslawin 1586 = Daniel Adam de Weleslawin: Nomenclator omnium rerum propria nomina tribus linguis Latina, Bojemica et Germanica. Prag 1586 [Lat.-Tschech.-Dt.].

Zegers 1554 = Tacitus Nicolaes Zegers: Proverbia Gallicana, una cum interpretatione tum Teutonica, tum Latina. Antwerpen 1554 [28 Bl.; Frz.-Niederl.-Lat.].

Zestalige Woordenlijst 1928 = Zestalige Woordenlijst voor toeristen. Brüssel 1928 [Niederl.-Frz.-Dt.-Engl.-Ital.-Span.].

6.2. Sonstige Literatur

Alvar Ezquerra 1984 = Manuel Alvar Ezquerra: Apuntes para la historia de las nomenclaturas del español. In: Actas del VII Congreso, Asociación de Lingüística y Filología de América Latina. Bd. 1. Santo Domingo 1984, 457—470.

Claes 1974 = Frans Claes: Lijst van Nederlandse woordenlijsten en woordenboeken gedrukt tot 1600. Nieuwkoop 1974.

Claes 1980 = Frans M. Claes: A Bibliography of Netherlandic Dictionaries. Dutch-Flemish. München 1980.

Collison 1982 = Robert L. Collison: A History of Foreign-Language Dictionaries. London 1982.

Colón/Soberanas 1985 = Germà Colón i Domenech/Amadeu J. Soberanas i LLeó: Panorama de la lexicografia catalana. Biblioteca Universitària. Barcelona 1985.

Coseriu 1973 = Eugenio Coseriu: Einführung in die strukturelle Betrachtung des Wortschatzes. Tübingen 1973.

Fabbri 1979 = Maurizio Fabbri: A Bibliography of Hispanic Dictionaries. Catalan, Galician, Spanish [...]. Imola 1979.

Gallina 1959 = Annamaria Gallina: Contributi alla storia della lessicografia italo-spagnola dei secoli XVI e XVII. Florenz 1959.

Gili Gaya 1960 = Samuel Gili Gaya: Tesoro Lexicográfico (1492—1720). Madrid 1960.

Haensch et al. 1982 = Günther Haensch/Lothar Wolf/Stefan Ettinger/Reinhold Werner: La lexicografía. Madrid 1982. De la lingüística teórica a la lexicografía práctica. (Biblioteca Románica Hispánica III. Manuales, 56).

Hallig/Wartburg 1952 = Rudolf Hallig/Walther von der Wartburg: Begriffssystem als Grundlage für die Lexikographie. Versuch eines Ordnungsschemas. Berlin 1957 (Abhandlungen der Deutschen Akademie der Wissenschaften zu Berlin. Klasse für Sprachen, Literatur und Kunst. Jg. 1957, Nr. 4).

Haugen 1984 = Eva L. Haugen: A Bibliography of Scandinavian Dictionaries. New York 1984.

Hupka 1989 = Werner Hupka: Wort und Bild. Die Illustrationen in Wörterbüchern und Enzyklopädien. Tübingen 1989 (Lexicographica. Series Maior 22).

Krauß 1979 = Eberhard Krauß: Zu einigen Problemen bei der Ausarbeitung eines mehrsprachigen Fachwörterbuches. In: Theorie und Praxis der wissenschaftlich-technischen Information 1. 1979, 13—14.

Kühn 1978 = Peter Kühn: Deutsche Wörterbücher: Eine systematische Bibliographie. Tübingen 1978 (Reihe germanistische Linguistik 15).

Labarre 1975 = Albert Labarre: Bibliographie du Dictionnaire d'Ambrogio Calepino (1502—1779). Baden-Baden 1975.

Learmonth 1986 = Trevor Learmonth/Stuart Macwilliam: Historic English Dictionaries 1595—1899. Exeter 1986.

Niederehe 1986 = Hans Josef Niederehe: La lexicographie espagnole jusqu'à Covarrubias. In: Histoire. Epistémologie. Langage 8. 1986, 9—19.

Niederehe 1987 = Hans-Josef Niederehe: La lexicografía española desde los principios hasta el año 1599. In: Hans Aarsleff/Louis G. Kelly/Hans-Josef Niederehe: Papers on the History of Linguistics. Proceedings of the Third International Conference on the History of the Language Sciences, Princeton, 19—23 August 1984. Amsterdam. Philadelphia 1987 (Studies in the History of the Language Sciences, 38).

Pilz 1967 = Kurt Pilz: Johann Amos Comenius. Die Ausgaben des Orbis Sensualium Pictus. Eine Bibliographie. Nürnberg 1967.

Quemada 1967 = Bernard Quemada: Les dictionnaires du français moderne (1539—1863). Etude sur leur histoire, leurs types et leurs méthodes. Paris. Bruxelles. Montréal 1967.

Schwartze 1875 = Roderich Schwartze: Die Wörterbücher der französischen Sprache vor dem Erscheinen des „Dictionnaire de l'Academie française". 1350—1694. Ein Beitrag zur Geschichte der französischen Lexikographie. Diss. Jena 1875.

Serís 1964 = Homero Serís: Bibliografía de la lingüística española. Bogotá 1964 (Publicaciones del Instituto Caro y Cuervo 19).

Stein 1985 = Gabriele Stein: The English Dictionary before Cawdrey. Tübingen 1985 (Lexicographica Series Maior 9).

Tancke 1984 = Gunnar Tancke: Die italienischen Wörterbücher von den Anfängen bis zum Erscheinen des «Vocabolario degli Academici della Crusca» (1612). Tübingen 1984 (Beihefte zur Zeitschrift für romanische Philologie 198).

Viñaza 1893 = Cipriano Muñoz y Manzano, Conde de la Viñaza: Biblioteca histórica de la filología castellana. Madrid 1893.

Zaunmüller 1958 = Wolfram Zaunmüller: Bibliographisches Handbuch der Sprachwörterbücher.

Ein internationales Verzeichnis von 5600 Wörterbüchern der Jahre 1466—1958 für mehr als 500 Sprachen und Dialekte. Stuttgart 1958.

Zgusta 1971 = Ladislav Zgusta: Manual of Lexicography. Prag. Den Haag. Paris 1971.

Günther Haensch, Augsburg (Bundesrepublik Deutschland)

307. Die zweisprachige Fachlexikographie und ihre Probleme

1. Die zweisprachige Fachlexikographie vor dem 20. Jh.
2. Fachsprache und Lexikographie
3. Makrostruktur zweisprachiger Fachwortschatzinventare
4. Mikrostruktur zweisprachiger Fachwortschatzinventare
5. Äquivalenzprobleme
6. Ausblick
7. Literatur (in Auswahl)

1. Die zweisprachige Fachlexikographie vor dem 20. Jh.

Wie in anderen Beiträgen aufgezeigt wird, entstand die moderne Lexikographie im 15. Jh. in Europa, zuerst in Italien. Die ersten (allgemeinsprachlichen) Wörterbücher waren meist zweisprachig, und vor allem im 15. und 16. Jh. war ihre Ausgangssprache meist noch Latein. Bald wurden nicht wenige der zweisprachigen Wörterbücher zu vielsprachigen Wörterbüchern erweitert, oder solche entstanden auch als völlig eigenständige Neuschöpfungen (vgl. Art. 284). Wie steht es nun mit den Fachwörterbüchern? Hier finden wir einerseits schon relativ früh einsprachige Glossare und bald auch Definitionswörterbücher, oft mit viel enzyklopädischer Information, für bestimmte Sachgebiete, vor allem Seefahrt, Botanik, Zoologie, schon ab dem 16. Jh.; andererseits gibt es im 16. und 17. Jh. bereits **mehrsprachige Fachwörterbücher** wie in Art. 284 ausgeführt. Erstaunlich ist nun, daß das zweisprachige Fachwörterbuch noch bis in die Mitte des 19. Jh. relativ selten auftritt, obwohl die Zahl der einsprachigen Definitionswörterbücher und mehrsprachigen Äquivalenzwörterbücher für die einzelnen Fachgebiete bis dahin schon stark angewachsen war.

Der Zugang zur Information über zweisprachige Fachwörterbücher vor dem 19. Jh. ist schwierig. Zum Teil registrieren die vorhandenen Bibliographien nur andere Wörterbuchtypen, z. B. allgemeinsprachliche, oder sie sind sehr lückenhaft, meist aber ist die entsprechende Information sehr verstreut. Für die nachfolgenden Ausführungen haben wir jeweils folgende Bibliographien ausgewertet: Für das Deutsche: Zaunmüller 1958 (der kaum auf Fachwörterbücher eingeht), Zischka 1958 (der für die Zeit vor 1800 sehr wenig angibt) und Kühn 1978 (der ebenfalls für unser Thema wenig bietet); für das Englische: Stein 1985 und 1985 a, Collison 1971 und 1982; für das Französische: Quemada 1967; für das Spanische: Fabbri 1979, Seris 1964 und Viñaza 1893; für das Niederländische: Claes 1974 und Claes 1980; für das Italienische: Tancke 1984. Sicher gibt es vor dem 19. Jh. mehr zweisprachige Fachwortschatzinventare als in den Bibliographien verzeichnet, und es fehlen noch echte Fachwörterbuchbibliographien für die Zeit vor dem 20. Jh., dennoch dürften die verfügbaren Daten ein repräsentatives Bild vom Stand zweisprachiger Fachlexikographie zwischen dem 16. und 19. Jh. geben, der einfach zu charakterisieren ist: Vor dem 19. Jh. gibt es im Vergleich zur übrigen Wörterbuchproduktion erst spät Beispiele für zweisprachige Fachwortschatzinventare.

In England finden wir zwar schon im 12. Jh. Fachglossare von Pflanzennamen und Rechtsterminologie, meist lateinisch-altenglisch oder altenglisch-altfranzösisch (Stein 1985, 44 ff.), in denen wir mit Recht die Anfänge zweisprachiger Fachlexikographie sehen können. Um so erstaunlicher ist, daß dann später, im 16. und 17. Jh., keine weiteren zweisprachigen fachlexikographischen Inventare zu verzeichnen sind (so z. B. nicht laut Stein 1985 bis zum Jahr 1692 und laut Stein 1985 a bis 1716). Auch im 18. Jh. sind sie noch relativ selten. So registriert Quemada 1967 für das Sprachenpaar Englisch-Französisch nur zwei Seefahrtwörterbücher (Lescallier 1777 und Sea Phrases 1799) und Claes 1980 nur ein Kunstwörterbuch Englisch-Niederländisch (Buys 1768). Im 19. Jh. finden wir u. a. zweisprachige Fachwörterbücher für: Englisch und Deutsch: Post- und Telegrafenwesen (Hennicke 1889) und Landwirtschaft (Englisch-deutsches Landw. 1862); Englisch und Niederländisch: zwei Marinewörterbücher (Rees 1861 und Schokker 1841) und ein technisches Woordenboek 1888 (Engl.-Niederl./Niederl.-Engl.); Englisch und Französisch: Fachwortschatzinventare für Seefahrt (Bussy 1862); Technik (Colombier 1860); Archäologie (Berty 1853) und Chorgesang (Orphéonistes 1860). Wenn wir den französischen Sprachraum betrachten, so stellen wir fest, daß die Bibliographie von Quemada 1967 für das 16. Jh. acht mehrsprachige Fachwortschatzinventare verzeichnet, bei denen die Ausgangssprache Latein und eine der Zielsprachen Französisch ist (vgl. Art. 284), dagegen kein einziges zweisprachiges Fachwörterbuch. Die konsultierten Bibliographien verzeichnen wiederum für das 17. Jh. fünf mehrsprachige Fachwörterbücher, bei denen Französisch eine der Zielsprachen ist, von diesen ist aber nur eines in Frankreich erschienen (Dalechamps 1615), von den übrigen dagegen zwei in den Niederlanden (Vossius 1640; Lobelius 1681), eines in Katalonien (Agustí 1617, s. Art. 306) und eines in Berlin (Mentzel 1682). Wiederum finden wir auch hier für das 17. Jh. kein zweisprachiges Fachwortschatzinventar, bei dem Französisch Ausgangs- oder Zielsprache ist. Die Thematik all dieser Wörterbücher waren Tier- und Pflanzennamen, nur bei einem (Agustí 1617) Landwirtschaft und bei einem anderen Medizin (Laguna 1555). Es ist deshalb interessant festzustellen, welches die Thematik der im 18. Jh. nun allmählich in Frankreich und anderswo erscheinenden zweisprachigen Fachwörterbücher mit Ausgangs- oder Zielsprache Französisch war. Zunächst fällt auf, daß von 21 (bei Quemada 1967) für das 18. Jh. registrierten zweisprachigen Fachwortschatzinventaren nur drei in Frankreich erschienen sind, davon zwei frz.-lat. Medizinwörterbücher (Col des Villars 1740 und Péras 1753) und ein Seefahrtwörterbuch engl.-frz. (Lescallier 1777); ein weiteres engl.-frz./frz.-engl. Seefahrtwörterbuch (Sea Phrases 1799) erschien in London, wo auch zwei Wörterbücher der Pflanzennamen Lat.-Frz. (Buchoz 1786 und 1787) veröffentlicht wurden. Ein frz.-niederl. Wörterbuch der Pflanzennamen wurde in Brüssel herausgebracht (Roucel 1792), ein frz.-niederl. Marinewörterbuch in Holland (Aubin 1702). Ein technisch-militärisches Fachwörterbuch (Egger 1757) und ein Wörterbuch des Gartenbaus (Kroehndorf 1700) erschienen in Deutschland. Alle übrigen französisch-deutschen Fachglossare aus dem handwerklich-industriellen Bereich stammen aus Neuchâtel/ Schweiz, z. B. Glossare für Tuchkräuseln (Duhamel 1774); Köhlerei (Duhamel 1774 a); Wachszieherei (Duhamel 1776); Schlosserei (Duhamel 1776 a); Ziegelei (Duhamel 1776 b); Papierherstellung (La Lande 1776); Teppichherstellung (Duhamel 1777); Tuchherstellung (Duhamel 1777 a); Töpferei (Duhamel 1777 b); Böttcherei (Fougeroux 1777); Kupfertechnik (Galon 1777), Nadlerei (Réaumur 1777); Ankerherstellung (Réaumur 1781). Für die erste Hälfte des 19. Jh. registriert Quemada 1967 auch nur 12 zweisprachige Fachwörterbücher mit Französisch, von denen 7 in Frankreich und 5 in Deutschland erschienen sind. Die behandelten Fachgebiete waren: Militärwesen (Rouvroy 1829; Brandt 1841; Heinze 1846, Kazimirski 1846, Llave 1846, Parmentier 1849); Mineralogie (Pausner 1802; Kopp 1810); Seefahrt (Gérin Roze 1840); Handel (Spiers 1846) und Musik (Moreali 1839). In Spanien steht am Anfang der zweisprachigen Fachlexikographie ein bemerkenswertes Werk des berühmten Grammatikers und Lexikographen Elio Antonio de Nebrija (vgl. Art. 284), nämlich ein zweisprachiges *Juris Civilis Lexicon — Léxico de Derecho Civil,* das erstmals 1506 erschien (Nebrija 1506). Es ist zunächst ein enzyklopädisches Wörterbuch, in dem lateinische Wörter auf Latein mit viel enzyklopädischer Information erläutert werden, der gesamte lateinische Artikel erscheint dann daneben in spanischer Übersetzung, so daß man mit Recht von einem zweisprachigen Fachwörterbuch sprechen kann, das übrigens weit über die Rechtssprache hinausgeht und eine Reihe von Wörtern aus anderen Fachgebieten enthält (vgl. Textbeispiel 307.1).

Dann finden wir erstaunlicherweise bis ins 19. Jh. kein zweisprachiges Fachwörterbuch mit Spanisch mehr. Das erste wichtige Fachwörterbuch des Spanischen (Terreros y Pando 1786) ist viersprachig. Erst im 19. Jh. finden wir einzelne zweisprachige Fachwörterbücher, z. B. der Seefahrt (Martínez de Espinosa 1849), des Militärwesens (Moretti 1828, Llave 1846, Trepied 1889), der Technik (Cañada 1878 und Ponce de León 1893), des Handels (Lópes/Bensley 1864) und der Warenkunde (Hirche 1893).

Das Katalanische wurde zwar schon früh in zweisprachigen Fachwörterbüchern berücksichtigt (so z. B. bei Agustí 1617), der Beginn der zweisprachigen katalanischen Fachlexikographie fällt jedoch in das 20. Jh. (cf. Art. 184).

Was das Italienische betrifft, so sei nur erwähnt, daß sich in der Bibliothek der Academia della Crusca unter 77 Wörterbüchern des 19. Jh., darunter vielen zweisprachigen, nur zwei zweisprachige Fachwörterbücher befinden, ein Marinewörterbuch (Fincati 1870) und ein Musikwörterbuch (Vissian 1846). In der Bibliographie italienisch-kroatischer Wörterbücher 1649—1985 (Bruna 1987) mit insgesamt 110 Titeln erscheint kein zweisprachiges Fachwortschatzinventar für das 19. Jh., jedoch 9 für das 20. Jh. Hier wie praktisch fast in allen anderen Ländern ist die Geschichte der zweisprachigen Fachlexikographie vor dem 19. Jh. noch nicht geschrieben. Selbst für einen so wörterbuchfreudigen Sprachraum wie den niederländischen (Belgien und Niederlande) verzeichnet die außerordentlich zuverlässige und vollständige Bibliographie von Claes 1980 kein zweisprachiges Fachwörterbuch für das 16. und 17. Jh. und gibt nur 3 Titel für das 18. Jh.: ein frz.-niederl. Wörterbuch der Seefahrt (Aubin 1702), ein engl.-niederl.

393.—PARAPHERNA bona sunt quaecumque praeter dotem dantur sponsae. Unde paraphernica instrumenta dixit Sidonius Apollinaris puellae tradita, et dicuntur parapherna a para, quod est praeter, et pherne, dos; non ut vulgus loquitur, paraphrena. Ulpianus, libro XXIII Dig. titulo De Jure Dotium, 1. Si ergo: „Si res dentur, ea quae graeci parapherna vocant, quaeque galli peculium appelant"

393.—PARAFERNOS son toda clase de bienes que, aparte de la dote, se dan a la esposa. De ahí que Sidonio Apolinar diga que „fueron dados a la joven instrumentos paraférmicos", palabra formada de para — a excepción de — y pherne — Ulpiano en el libro 33 del Digesto, Del Derecho de la Dote, ley Si ego: „Si son dadas aquellas cosas que los griegos llaman parafernas y los galos peculio".

Textbeispiel 307.1: Wörterbuchartikel (aus: Nebrija 1506, 380 f.; neu gesetzt)

Kunstwörterbuch (Buys 1768) und ein frz.-niederl. Glossar in einem Botanikbuch (Roucel 1792). Im 19. Jh. gibt es einige zweisprachige Fachwörterbücher mehr: 4 für Niederl.-Englisch, davon zwei für die Seefahrt (Rees 1861 und Schokker 1841), ein Militärwörterbuch (Chantepie 1811) und eines für Technik (Technisch Woordenboek 1888); 9 für Niederl.-Frz., davon 3 für Militärwesen (Chantepie 1811, Hoefer 1881 und Serraris 1864), 3 für Gymnastik (Dockx 1878, 1878 a und 1879); 2 für Recht (Bellefroid 1897 und Géruzet 1830) und eins für Seefahrt (Flines 1806); 3 für Niederl.-Dtsch., davon zwei Fachwörterbücher für Handel (Nemnich 1821 und Halem 1811) sowie eines für Militärwesen (Hoefer 1881 a), ferner ein lat.-niederl. Fachwörterbuch der Medizin und Naturwissenschaften (Gabler 1858). Das bedeutet, daß zwischen dem Beginn der modernen Lexikographie im 16. Jh. und 1900 wahrscheinlich kaum mehr als insgesamt 17 zweisprachige Fachwörterbücher im niederländischen Sprachraum, einschl. des zweisprachigen Belgien, herauskamen.

Daß auch in den Ländern der vielsprachigen Donaumonarchie ein Bedarf an zweisprachigen Fachwörterbüchern bestand, davon zeugen u. a. fünf im 19. Jh. erschienene Werke: zwei deutschtschechische Rechtsterminologien (Nečas 1892 und Juridisch-politische Terminologie 1850), eine deutsch-slowenische Rechtsterminologie (Babnik 1894), ein deutsch-tschechisches Jagdwörterbuch (Spatny 1870) und ein ungarisch-deutsches Technikwörterbuch (Péch 1879). Für die im 19. Jh. sicher noch nicht zahlreichen zweisprachigen Fachwörterbücher mit Russisch seien als Beispiele erwähnt: ein Rechtswörterbuch Russisch und Deutsch (Deutsch-russisches Wörterbuch 1878); ein deutsch-russisches Forstwörterbuch (Krause 1889) und ein allgemeines Wissenschaftswörterbuch deutsch-russisch (Grachow 1872). Was schließlich den deutschen Sprachraum betrifft, so wissen wir wenig über zweisprachige Fachwortschatzinventare vor dem 19. Jh. Nach den sicher nicht vollständigen Bibliographien gab es vor dem 19. Jh. nur wenige zweisprachige Fachwortschatzinventare mit Deutsch als Ausgangs- oder Zielsprache. Auch hier sind die ersten Werke im 18. Jh. lateinisch-deutsche Wörterbücher, z. B. zwei für die Pharmazie (Hellwig 1711 und Sommerhoff 1713), ein Medizinwörterbuch (Hellwig 1711 a), ein lat.-dtsch. Rechtswörterbuch (Oberländer 1721) und zwei Botanikwörterbücher (Gmelin 1772 und Reuss 1781). Lediglich in der Kombination mit Französisch finden wir schon im 18. Jh. mehr zweisprachige Fachwörterbücher (vgl. oben). Im übrigen wächst auch im deutschen Sprachraum im 19. Jh., vor allem in dessen zweiter Hälfte, die Zahl der zweisprachigen Fachwortschatzinventare erheblich an (vgl. die Beispiele bei den einzelnen Fremdsprachen). Für das Sprachenpaar Deutsch und Französisch seien neben den bereits genannten Werken noch erwähnt: ein Wörterbuch für Bergbau und Hüttenwesen (Beurard 1809), eines für allgemeine Technik (Kaltschmidt 1860), eines für Dampfmaschinen (Witzel 1858) und eines für Festungsbauten (Duhamel 1801).

Hatte die Zahl der zweisprachigen Fachwortschatzinventare in der 2. Hälfte des 19. Jh. mit fortschreitender Technisierung und Industrialisierung und überhaupt Internationalisierung vieler Tätigkeiten bereits erheblich zugenommen, so erleben wir im 20. Jh. eine wahre Explosion von Fachwortschatzinventaren, die heute zahlenmäßig an der Spitze aller Wörterbuchtypen stehen.

2. Fachsprache und Lexikographie

Wie wir in 1. gesehen haben, konzentrierte sich die zweisprachige Fachlexikographie vor dem 19. Jh. lange Zeit auf bestimmte Gebiete wie Botanik, Zoologie, Medizin, Landwirtschaft, Seefahrt, Militärwesen und Bergbau. Erst allmählich erweiterte sich im 19. Jh. der Katalog der behandelten Fachgebiete mit den Fortschritten von Technik und Verkehr. Im 20. Jh. „ist mit der zunehmenden Auffächerung der traditionellen wissenschaftlichen Disziplinen und der Ausbreitung der Technik die Anzahl der theoretischen und praktischen Fachsprachen permanent und erheblich angewachsen" (Wiegand 1976, 39—40). Nicht nur die Zahl der Fachsprachen ist mit dem Aufkommen neuer Fachgebiete wie Luftfahrt, Psychoanalyse, Elektronik, Automation, EDV, Raumfahrt, Betriebswirtschaft usw. gestiegen, sondern auch in den schon bestehenden Fachgebieten (wie z. B. Biologie, Medizin, Wirtschaft) hat sich der Fachwortschatz erheblich vermehrt. All dies führte zu einer wahren Explosion der zwei- und mehrsprachigen Fachlexikographie im 20. Jh. Der Terminus „Fachwortschatz" sollte übrigens aus praktischen Gründen sehr weit ausgelegt werden, er gilt nicht nur für Wissenschaften und Technik, sondern überhaupt für jegliche Art menschlicher Aktivität, die eine gewisse Spezialisierung bedeutet, also auch für Sport, Jagd, Showbusiness, Amateurfunkwesen und Briefmarkensammeln.

Es ist hier nicht der Ort, die seit ca. 15 Jahren intensive Diskussion um den Begriff „Fachsprachen" darzustellen und zu erörtern. Es sei nur daran erinnert, daß zwar das wichtigste Element aller Fachsprachen die eigtl. Terminologie ist, daß aber Fachsprache auch durch gewisse Normen der Auswahl, des Gebrauchs und der Frequenz in der Gemeinsprache verfügbarer lexikalischer und morphosyntaktischer Ausdrucksmittel bestimmt wird, im Deutschen z. B. häufige Verwendung von Verbalsubstantiven (z. B. Ingangsetzung, Ausfiltern), oft mit rein funktionalen, sonst sinnentleerten Verben, häufiger Gebrauch des Passivs und unpersönlicher Verbkonstruktionen (z. B. *es liegt nichts vor; es heißt*...). Zum Teil gibt es auch fachspezifische Strukturwörter.

Z. B. wird die frz. Konjunktion *attendu que* ('da', 'in Anbetracht der Tatsache, daß') nur in Gerichtsurteilen, aber nicht in der allgemeinen Rechtssprache verwendet, bedeutet in der frz. Rechts- und Verwaltungssprache *dans cette hypothèse* nicht 'in dieser Hypothese', sondern 'in diesem Falle' und *dès lors* nicht 'seit damals', sondern 'infolgedessen'.

Hier stellt sich nun die Frage, was ein Fachwörterbuch enthalten soll, nur die reine Terminologie, also eine Art skelettartiger Nomenklatur, oder auch andere zur betr. Fachsprache gehörende lexikalische Einheiten wie Strukturwörter, im betr. Fachgebiet häufige Wörter von Nachbardisziplinen oder sogar allgemeinsprachliche lexikalische Einheiten, die in dem betr. Fachgebiet häufig vorkommen, wie z. B. beim Eherecht bzw. Scheidungsrecht: *getrennt leben, wilde Ehe, Ehe auf Probe, Hochzeitsgeschenke* (alles keine juristischen Fachtermini!). Wir sind mit den Autoren vieler Beiträge (z. B. Grin'ov 1989) darin einig, daß viele Fachwörterbücher allzusehr mit allgemeinsprachlichen Elementen überfrachtet sind, was vermieden werden sollte. Was wir jedoch für ausführlichere Fachwörterbücher vorschlagen, sind allgemeinsprachliche und „halbfachliche" Wörter, die in dem betr. Fachgebiet häufig, oft fast automatisch vorkommen, so daß ihre Aufnahme in ein Fachwörterbuch mit zuverlässigen Übersetzungsäquivalenten eine wirkliche Hilfe für den Übersetzer sein kann. Die meisten Autoren, die sich mit Fachsprache befassen, heben die Schwierigkeit hervor, Fachsprache und Allgemeinsprache, zwischen denen natürlich eine Übergangszone besteht, abzugrenzen. Eine solche Abgrenzung für Zwecke der Wörterbucharbeit ergibt sich meist von selbst. Wenn ich in einem frz. Rechtswörterbuch alle Arten von „Mieten" aufzählen will, muß ich, obwohl *Miete* kein spezieller Terminus technicus ist, z. B. zwangsläufig mit einem Stichwort *loyer* 'Miete' beginnen, auf das dann die verschiedenen Komposita und Kollokationen folgen. — Hier sei auch daran erinnert, daß zwischen den einzelnen Fachsprachen große Unterschiede bestehen, wie z. B. zwischen der Rechts- und Verwaltungssprache, einem der ältesten Technolekte, und der Fachsprache der Elektronik, einem der jüngsten. Bei letzterer wird im Normalfall ein Fachwörterbuch die reine Terminologie registrieren, bei ersterer jedoch im Sinne obiger Ausführungen weit mehr.

Man könnte nun meinen, hier ließen sich reine Terminologien von den Fachwörterbüchern unterscheiden, die neben der eigentl. Terminologie auch Terminologie von Nachbargebieten (z. B. Grundterminologie der elektronischen Datenverarbeitung in einem Wörterbuch der Betriebswirtschaft), Strukturwörter und im Zusammenhang mit dem betr. Fachgebiet häufige allgemeinsprachliche oder „halbfachliche" lexikalische Einheiten bringen. Leider wird dieser Unterschied zwischen „Terminologie" (i. e. S.) und „Fachwörterbuch" in der Praxis häufig nicht gemacht, und wie schon bei vielen allgemeinsprachlichen Wörterbüchern sagen auch bei den zweisprachigen Fachwörterbüchern die Titel oft wenig oder gar Irreführendes über deren Inhalt aus. Ebenso wenig präzis werden andere Bezeichnungen wie „Glossar" und „Vokabular" (und die entsprechenden fremdsprachlichen Bezeichnungen) gebraucht. Der Terminus „Glossar" besagt im allgemeinen, daß nur eine geringe oder zumindest nicht repräsentative, oft auch nicht systematische Auswahl lexikalischer Einheiten aus dem betr. Fachwortschatz getroffen wurde.

Wenn in Art. 159 und 160 das Fachwörterbuch für den Laien von dem des Spezialisten unterschieden wird, so ist das eine Idealvorstellung, die für einzelne Bereiche wie z. B. Technik mehr gelten mag als für andere. Bei der ungeheuren Fülle der heute vorhandenen zweisprachigen Fachwortschatzinventare gibt es aber meist das „Fachwörterbuch" für alle Zielgruppen. Ein solches kann zum Dekodieren der sprachlichen Aussagen dienen, aber auch zur Produktion von Aussagen. In vielen, vielleicht in den meisten Fällen, dient es jedoch zum Übersetzen. Dem sollten die Fachwörterbücher Rechnung tragen. Wie oben erwähnt, wird häufig gefordert, ein Fachwörterbuch solle sich auf die reine Fachterminologie beschränken. Dies mag bei einzelnen Typen von Fachwörterbüchern durchaus angebracht sein, z. B. bei technischen Normenwörterbüchern. Im übrigen sollte man für die Bedürfnisse des Übersetzens auch an das im obigen Sinne erweiterte Fachwörterbuch denken.

Das oft gepriesene Ideal der fachsprachlichen Terminologie „Ein Referent — ein Fachterminus" wird zwar oft, aber nicht immer erreicht. So gibt es für fachsprachliche Ausdrücke hochsprachliche diatopische Varianten, z. B. bedeuten in der Schweiz ein

Fürsprech 'ein Rechtsanwalt' und eine *Gant* 'Versteigerung', in Österreich *systemisieren* 'verbeamten'. Der Computer heißt in Spanien *ordenador* (< frz. ordinateur), in Lateinamerika *computadora* (< engl. computer). Die zweisprachige Fachlexikographie müßte solche Heteronyme unbedingt berücksichtigen. — Neben der eigtl. Fachsprache, die im wesentlichen durch den Gegenstand, aber nicht unbedingt durch eine menschliche Gruppe bestimmt wird, gibt es so etwas wie einen gleichzeitig diatechnisch und diatopisch markierten *Fachjargon* (Technosoziolekt), der sich auf Dinge des betr. Fachgebietes bezieht, aber meist nur von der Gruppe, die unmittelbar damit befaßt ist, gebraucht wird.

So kann ein deutscher Anwalt von einem Kollegen sagen, er habe einen Schriftsatz „im Keller machen lassen" (frz. „il a fait travailler ses nègres"); ein Elektriker, der feststellt, daß kein Strom da ist, sagt: „Kein Saft da" (frz. „y a pas d'jus"), und wenn im Wirtschaftsleben von Pleite, Flop, Ladenhüter (frz. rossignol) u. ä. die Rede ist, handelt es sich nicht um Terminologie, sondern um fachgebundenen Jargon, der aber unbedingt in Fachwörterbüchern — natürlich mit entsprechender Markierung — erfaßt werden sollte, weil er vor allem im mündlichen Sprachgebrauch des betr. Fachgebietes erscheint.

Auch die Fachsprachen haben so etwas wie „falsche Freunde". Diese können schon innerhalb eines Sprachsystems bei diatopischen Varianten auftreten. So bedeutet z. B. in der spanischen Rechtssprache in Spanien *allanamiento (de morada)* 'Hausfriedensbruch', also eine strafbare Handlung, während der Terminus in Lateinamerika „Hausdurchsuchung" (im allgemeinen auf richterliche Anordnung hin) bedeutet. Es gibt aber auch „falsche Freunde" in der Zweisprachigkeit. So heißen im Frz. z. B. 'Sachleistungen' *prestations en nature,* 'Barleistungen' dagegen *prestations en espèces.* Im Span. ist es umgekehrt: dort bedeutet *prestaciones en especie* 'Sachleistungen' (im Gegensatz zu den *prestaciones en metálico).* Auf diese Fehlerquellen kann und sollte ein Fachwörterbuch durchaus hinweisen. Schließlich sollte ein Fachwörterbuch auch die wichtigsten im betr. Fachgebiet benützten Abkürzungen erläutern. — Hinsichtlich seiner Zielsetzung kann ein zweisprachiges Fachwörterbuch rein deskriptiv sein. In diesem Falle kann und muß es auch Fremdwörter wie die z. B. im Französischen durch Gesetz verbannten Anglizismen aufnehmen, wenn sie entsprechend häufig auftreten, wie z. B. neben *oléoduc* 'Ölleitung' auch: *pipe-line* [piplín]. Es kann auch normativ sein und einen bestimmten Sprachgebrauch als ideal kodifizieren. Von den normativen Wörterbüchern (im linguistischen Sinne) sind die Normenwörterbücher zu unterscheiden, deren Ziel es ist, eine Sache mit einem Terminus zu bezeichnen und diesen klar zu definieren. Die ihnen zugrundeliegenden Normen werden von nationalen (in Deutschland DIN) und internationalen Organisationen (ISO = International Organization of Standardization) festgelegt. — Für die genaue Beschreibung lexikalischer Einheiten in der Ausgangs- und Zielsprache, ihre Konstruktion, häufige Kollokationen und andere syntagmatische Angaben, aber auch für zusätzliche Erläuterungen (Gebrauchseinschränkungen, Unterfachgebiete) hat das zweisprachige Fachwörterbuch den unschätzbaren Vorteil, daß es in der Ausgangs- wie auch in der Zielsprache viel mehr und genauere Angaben machen kann als ein mehrsprachiges Fachwörterbuch.

3. Makrostruktur zweisprachiger Fachwortschatzinventare

Die Makrostruktur eines Wörterbuches ist das Profil seines lexikographischen Inventars: Auswahl der Stichwörter und deren Anordnung im Wörterbuch, evtl. Anhänge und Tabellen. Was die Auswahl der Stichwörter betrifft, so wurden deren wesentliche Probleme in 2. erörtert. Auf jeden Fall sollten hier neben dem Stichwort etwa vorhandene Synonyme und Heteronyme (vor allem diatopische Varianten), alles mit entsprechender Markierung, berücksichtigt werden, ebenso die wichtigsten Komposita und Kollokationen. Hier sei auch daran erinnert, wie wichtig es ist, feste Formeln (Syntagmen, oft ganze Sätze) zu berücksichtigen, z. B. in der Rechts- und Verwaltungssprache *für die Richtigkeit der Abschrift, mit der Bitte um weitere Veranlassung,* im Sport *Auf die Plätze — Fertig — Los* oder in der Medizin *ohne Befund (o. B.).* Die zweisprachige Fachlexikographie kann, wenn sie sich nicht auf reine Terminologielisten beschränken will, hier noch einiges von den Fortschritten der allgemeinen ein- und zweisprachigen Lexikographie, vor allem im Hinblick auf paradigmatische und syntagmatische Erweiterung der einzelnen Artikel, übernehmen. Dies gilt besonders für die Rektion, z. B. *sich von jdm. scheiden lassen* ist frz. *divorcer d'avec qn.* Was die Anordnung des Wortschatzmaterials betrifft, so finden wir hier ähnlich wie bei den mehrsprachigen Fachwörterbüchern zwei Haupttypen: alphabetische und thematische (systematische) Anordnung, deren Vor- und Nachteile in Art. 306, 3.2. erörtert werden, auf das hier verwiesen sei (vgl. auch weiter unten 4.). Manche Fachwortschatzinventare bringen Anhänge wie Karten, Organisationsschemata, Abkürzungsglossare usw.

4. Mikrostruktur zweisprachiger Fachwortschatzinventare

Hier finden wir die verschiedensten Typen der Darstellung. Viele Glossare beschränken sich auf reine Wortlisten mit minimalen oder gar keinen grammatischen Angaben (vgl. Textbeispiel 307.2).

Glossar der Bienenzucht (D-S)

1. **Abfüllstelle** *f*	planta *f* de envase, envasadora *f*
2. **Absperrgitter** *n*	separador *m*
3. **Amöben** *plur*	amebasis *f*
4. **Backhonig** *m* → **Industriehonig** *m*	miel *f* industrial
5. **Bärenklauhonig** *m*	miel de acanto
6. **Beinschiene** *f*	segmento *m* (de las patas)
7. **Beute** *f*	alza *m*
8. **Bienenableger** *m*	núcleo *m*
9. **Biene,** *f* **deutsche** *adj*	abeja *f* alemana; abeja negra
10. **Biene,** *f* **junge** *adj*	ninfa *f*
11. **Bienenhaus** *n*	colmenar *m*
12. **Bienenstock** *m*	colmena *f*
13. **Blütenhonig** *m*	miel *f* de flores
14. **Brutwabe** *f*	panal *m* de cría
15. **Buchweizenhonig** *m*	miel *f* de alforfón
16. **Carnicabiene** *f*	abeja *f* carniola
17. **Diastase** *f*	diastasa *f*

Textbeispiel 307.2: Glossarausschnitt (aus: Falbi 1989, 134)

Andere dagegen machen die in der allgemeinen ein- und zweisprachigen Lexikographie üblichen grammatischen Angaben. Die phonetische Transkription von Wörtern sollte nur in Zweifelsfällen angegeben werden, z. B. bei frz. *détritus* 'Abfälle' [detritys]. Die übrigen Markierungen ergeben sich aus der Natur des betr. Fachwortschatzes, z. B. die sehr wichtige Angabe von Unterfachgebieten; Zugehörigkeit zum Fachjargon (vgl. 2.); geographische Verbreitung (oft mit Autokennzeichen, z. B. D, A, Ch); Angaben zu Gebrauchsrestriktionen (z. B. nur auf Personen bezogen, Adjektive nur attributiv oder prädikativ gebraucht). Außerordentlich nützlich sind Illustrationen, vor allem bei technischen Wörterbüchern.

Wie schon bei der Erörterung der mehrsprachigen Wörterbücher erwähnt (vgl. Art. 284, 3.3.), geben manche Fachwörterbücher, meist unmittelbar hinter dem Stichwort, Definitionen. Diese sind, auch für den Fachmann, außerordentlich nützlich und stellen eine wertvolle Bereicherung des betr. Wörterbuches dar. Dort wo keine Definitionen gegeben werden, kann mit Klammerzusätzen viel wichtige zusätzliche, meist sachbezogene (enzyklopädische) Information gegeben werden. So hatte z. B. Frankreich in den letzten Jahrzehnten drei verschiedene Systeme von Konkursrecht. In diesem Fall genügt eine Datumsangabe hinter dem jeweiligen Terminus, um die Zugehörigkeit des jeweiligen Terminus zu einem der drei Systeme zu klären. Oder man vergleiche die folgende Glossierung:

1. **crédit** *m* (1) *(prêt, avance)* (gewährtes) Darlehen *n*, Kredit *m*, (2) *(promesse d'un établissement financier)* Darlehenszusage *f* (einer Bank), Krediteröffnung *f*, (3) *(éc. pol.)* Kreditwesen *n*, Kreditverkehr *m*, (4) *(réputation de solvabilité)* (Vertrauen in die) Zahlungsfähigkeit *f*, Kreditwürdigkeit *f*, (5) *(dr. budgétaire)* Haushaltsmittel *npl*, Ausgabemittel *npl*, Staatsausgaben *fpl*, (6) *(partie du compte: avoir)* Haben *n*, Habenseite *f* (des Kontos), (7) *(fig.)* Ansehen *n*, Einfluß *m*, Gewicht *n*; **abattement de** – Krediteinschränkung; **accord de** – Kreditabkommen *n*, Kreditvereinbarung *f*; **accorder un** – einen Kredit gewähren *od* einräumen; **achat à** – Kauf auf Kredit, Kreditkauf; **allouer un** – einen Kredit bewilligen; **amputer un** – einen Kredit kürzen; **article de** – Einnahmeposten *m*; **assurance**– Kreditversicherung *f*; **atteinte au** – Kreditgefährdung *f*, Kreditverleumdung *f*, Kreditschädigung *f*; **atteinte au** – **de l'État** Staatsverleumdung; **autorisation d'ouverture de** – Kreditbewilligung; **avance sur** – in Anspruch genommener Kreditbetrag; **avis de** – Gutschriftzettel *m*, Gutschriftnote *f*, Gutschriftsanzeige *f*; **avis d'ouverture de** – Krediteinräumungsschreiben *n*; **avoir du** – Kredit genießen *od* haben; **avoir recours à un** – einen Kredit aufnehmen; **banque de** – Kreditbank *f*, Darlehensbank; **banque de** – **foncier** Hypothekenbank, Bodenkreditbank, Grundkreditbank; **banque de** – **mobilier** Mobiliarkreditbank; **bénéficiaire du** – Kreditempfänger *m*, Kreditnehmer;

Textbeispiel 307.3: Artikelausschnitt (aus: Doucet/Fleck 1980, 166 f.)

a) La vente	a) Der Kauf
On remarquera que la terminologie française parle de "contrat de vente", là où la terminologie juridique allemande parle de „Kaufvertrag", soit de "contrat d'achat".	Die deutsche Rechtsterminologie geht von der Seite des Käufers, die französische dagegen von der des Verkäufers aus. Wenn im Deutschen ganz allgemein vom „Kauf" oder der „Kaufsache" die Rede ist, sagt der Franzose deshalb "la vente", "la chose vendue" usw. Natürlich spricht der Käufer in seinem speziellen Fall "de l'achat" (= der Kauf), der günstig oder ungünstig war, und der Verkäufer "de la vente" (= der Verkauf), der etwa nach langen Verhandlungen zustandekam.
la vente; l'achat *(m)*, le marché	der Kauf
le vendeur	der Verkäufer
l'acheteur *(m)*	der Käufer
l'échange *(f)*, le troc	der Tausch
troquer	tauschen; Tauschhandel treiben
l'acquéreur *(m)*	der Erwerber
l'ordre *(m)* de vente	der Verkaufsauftrag
l'ordre *(m)* d'achat	der Kaufauftrag
le prix d'achat, le prix de vente	der Kaufpreis ("le prix de vente" kann auch der „Verkaufspreis" im Gegensatz zum „Einkaufspreis" heißen)
la chose vendue	die Kaufsache
acheter pour son propre compte, acheter pour son compte personnel	für eigene Rechnung kaufen
acheter pour le compte d'autrui, acheter pour le compte d'un tiers	für fremde Rechnung kaufen
le vice* de droit	der Rechtsmangel

* Les termes "défaut" et "vice" sont synonymes. Une différence dans l'emploi n'est qu'une question d'usage, donc relative à l'auteur, au pays, etc.

Textbeispiel 307.4: Textausschnitt (aus: Renner 1966, 38, gegenüber dem Original verkleinert)

mandat *m* d'amener = Vorführungsbefehl *m* (bei Nichterschienenen)
mandat *m* d'extraction = Vorführungsbefehl *m* (bei Gefangenen)

Der Vergleich der Textbeispiele 307.3 und 307.4 zeigt, warum ein systematisch aufgebautes zweisprachiges Fachwortschatzinventar, bei dem sich die Wörter in beiden Sprachen in zwei Spalten gegenüberstehen, für Lernzwecke wesentlich geeigneter ist als ein alphabetisches Fachwörterbuch. Man beachte die vielen Erläuterungen in Textbeispiel 307.4.

5. Äquivalenzprobleme

Der Idealfall von Äquivalenz ist auch hier nach der Terminologie von Karl 1982 die Volläquivalenz, z. B. *droit pénal* 'Strafrecht'. Im Gegensatz zur Meinung vieler Sprachwissenschaftler, die die Eindeutigkeit der Fachtermini gegenüber den lexikalischen Einheiten der Gemeinsprache betonen, gibt es auch in den Fachterminologien Fälle von Quasiäquivalenz und Nulläquivalenz.

Bei der Quasiäquivalenz handelt es sich um lexikalische Einheiten, die in der Zielsprache mit einem ähnlichen Terminus wiedergegeben werden können; z. B. haben *Ortszuschlag*, frz. *indemnité de résidence* im Beamtenbesoldungsrecht die gleiche Grundbedeutung (zusätzliche Vergütung für Beamte), aber verschiedene Inhalte: der Ortszuschlag ist in der ganzen BRD einheitlich, in Frankreich dagegen nach Zonen abgestuft. Demnach entsteht hier kein Schaden, wenn *Ortszuschlag* durch 'indemnité de résidence' wiedergegeben wird, entsprechende klärende Klammerzusätze sind aber eigentlich auch hier notwendig. — Die Nulläquivalenz ist problematischer. Zunächst ist die beste Methode, vor allem bei kulturspezifischem

Wortschatz, wie er z. B. auch in Recht, Politik, Verwaltung und Wirtschaft häufig auftritt, den Terminus der Ausgangssprache in der Zielsprache (in Kursivdruck oder in Anführungszeichen gesetzt) zu verwenden und dann in einem Klammerzusatz zu definieren, z. B.:

Landrat m frz. „Landrat *m*" (= Fonctionnaire qui est à la tête de l'administration d'un „Kreis").

Dies ist die sauberste Methode, um das Problem der Nulläquivalenz zu lösen. Wenn auch gelegentlich gegen ad hoc-Übersetzungen polemisiert wird, muß der Übersetzer doch in vielen Fällen zu solchen greifen, nur muß dem Leser klar sein, daß es sich hier um eine Behelfsübersetzung eines Terminus der Ausgangssprache in die Zielsprache und nicht um ein echtes Äquivalent in der Zielsprache handelt. Auch in diesem Fall empfiehlt sich ein erklärender Klammerzusatz, z. B.

Altenteil *n süddt.* Austrag *m*
  „part de vieillesse" (ensemble des biens ou droits qu'un paysan âgé conserve à son profit quand il abandonne l'exploitation de sa propriété à ses héritiers)
(Im folgenden Text würde dann „part de vieillesse" genügen).

Die einzelnen Bände des vom Internationalen Institut für Rechts- und Verwaltungssprache, Berlin, herausgegebenen Europa-Glossars der Rechts- und Verwaltungssprache verwenden hier folgende Symbole:

(a) Lexikalische Einheiten, die in beiden Sprachen inhaltsgleich sind, werden mit = gekennzeichnet (Volläquivalenz)

(b) Lexikalische Einheiten, die in der Zielsprache mit einem ähnlichen Terminus wiedergegeben werden können, werden mit ± gekennzeichnet (Quasiäquivalenz)

(c) Lexikalische Einheiten, für die es in der Zielsprache keine Entsprechung gibt (Nulläquivalenz), werden mit ≠ gekennzeichnet, Erklärungen mit ad hoc-Übersetzungen hierzu werden in Klammern gesetzt.

6. Ausblick

Auch im Zeitalter des Computers und der terminologischen Datenbanken werden die zweisprachigen Fachwörterbücher ihren Platz behaupten können. Wenn sie jedoch nicht gegen die leicht aktualisierbaren Datenbanken ins Hintertreffen geraten wollen, müssen sie wesentlich öfter als bisher überarbeitet und aktualisiert werden, was mit den neuen drucktechnischen Möglichkeiten auch leichter und wesentlich billiger geschehen kann als bei dem bisher üblichen, mit sehr hohen Kosten verbundenen Neusatz. Der Vorteil des Fachwörterbuches gegenüber der Datenbank kann hier vor allem in einer ausgefeilten Mikrostruktur liegen: Stichwort, Synonyme, Heteronyme, grammatische Angaben, Angaben von Unterfachgebieten, konnotative Markierungen, Angaben zu Gebrauchsrestriktionen, Rektion, Kollokationen, Illustrationen und evtl. Definitionen, alles Dinge, die eine auf Datenbank gespeicherte Terminologie nicht bietet. Auch für Lernzwecke wird die systematisch aufgebaute zweisprachige Fachterminologie (vgl. oben) mit vielen erklärenden Hinweisen weiterhin gute Dienste leisten. Eine mögliche Arbeitsteilung in der zweisprachigen Fachlexikographie könnte in Zukunft darin bestehen, daß es einerseits jeweils ein allgemeines Fachwörterbuch für einzelne Gebiete wie Recht, Technik, Wirtschaft, Medizin usw. mit einer stark entwickelten Mikrostruktur gibt, das als Einführungswerk und zum Nachschlagen der wichtigsten lexikalischen Einheiten des betr. Fachgebietes geeignet ist und hierfür viele Angaben für den Gebrauch im Kontext bietet, und andererseits für die zahlreichen Unterfachgebiete reine Terminologieglossare, z. B. über Patentrecht, Marketing, Nuklearmedizin, Mikroprozessoren.

7. Literatur (in Auswahl)

7.1. Wörterbücher

Aubin 1702 = Nikolaus Aubin: Dictionnaire de Marine contenant les termes de la navigation et de l'architecture navale. (Frz.-Niederl.). Amsterdam 1702 [Weitere Aufl. 1722, 1736, 1742, 1747, 1786].

Babnik 1894 = Janko Babnik: Deutsch-slovenische juridische Terminologie. Na Dunaju 1984 [833 S.].

Bellefroid 1897 = Paul Bellefroid: Dictionnaire Français-Néerlandais des Termes de Droit. Hasselt 1897 [Weitere Aufl. 1912, 1930].

Berty 1853 = A. Berty: Vocabulaire archéologique français-anglais et anglais-français. Oxford 1853.

Beurard 1809 = J. B. Beurard: Dictionnaire allemand-français des mines et métallurgie. Paris 1809.

Brandt 1841 = Brandt, dit Grierin: Vocabulaire militaire français-allemand. 2. Aufl. Berlin 1841.

Buchoz 1786 = P. Buchoz: Catalogue latin et français des plantes vivaces. London 1786.

Buchoz 1787 = P. Buchoz: Catalogue latin et français des arbustes et plantes. London 1787.

Bussy 1862 = Ch. de Bussy: Dictionnaire universel de marine (Frz.-Engl.). 2 Bde. Paris 1862.

Buys 1768 = E. Buys: New and complete Dictionary of terms of art. Datis, Nieuw en volkomen Konstwoordenboek. 2 Bde. (Engl.Niederl.) Amsterdam 1768—69.

Cañada 1878 = F. Cañada: Diccionario tecnológico inglés-español. Madrid 1878.

Chantepie 1811 = J. R. S. C. Chantepie de la Saussaye: Dictionnaire François et Hollandois. Hollandois et François à l'usage de l'Artilleur. [...]. Den Haag 1811.

Col de Villars 1740 = Elie Col de Villars: Dictionnaire français-latin des termes de chirurgie, avec leur définition, leur division et leur étymologie. Paris 1740.

Colombier 1860 = de Colombier: Vocabulaire technique usuel français-anglais. London gegen 1860.

Dalechamps 1615 = Jacques Dalechamps: Histoire générale des plantes. Ensemble des tables des noms en diverses langues. 2 Bde. Lyon 1615 [Frz.-Lat.-Altgr.-Arab.-Ital.-Span.-Dtsch.-Niederl.-Tschech.-Engl.].

Deutsch-russisches Wörterbuch 1878 = Deutschrussisches und russisch-deutsches Wörterbuch für juristische Ausdrücke aus dem Gebiete des Civil- und Handelsrechtes. St. Petersburg 1878.

Dockx 1878 = Willem Dockx: Tableau synoptique des commandements français-flamands pour la gymnastique des garçons. Namur 1878.

Dockx 1878a = Willem Dockx: Tableau synoptique des commandements français-flamands pour la gymnastique des filles. Namur 1878.

Dockx 1879 = Willem Dockx: Gymnastick voor meisjes. Synoptische tabel der bevelen. Namur 1879.

Doucet/Fleck 1980 = Michel Doucet/Klaus E. W. Fleck: Wörterbuch der Rechts- und Wirtschaftssprache. 3. erweiterte Auflage. München 1980.

Duhamel 1774 = Duhamel du Monceau: Art de friser les étoffes mit einem Vokabular frz.-dtsch. Neuchâtel 1774.

Duhamel 1774a = Duhamel du Monceau: Art du Charbonnier. mit einem Vokabular frz.-dtsch. Neuchâtel 1774.

Duhamel 1776 = Duhamel du Monceau: Art du Chandelier mit einem Vokabular frz.-dtsch. Neuchâtel 1776.

Duhamel 1776a = Duhamel du Monceau: Art du Serrurier mit einem Vokabular frz.-dtsch. Neuchâtel 1776.

Duhamel 1776b = Duhamel du Monceau: Art du Tuilier-Briquetier mit einem frz.-dtsch. Vokabular. Neuchâtel 1776.

Duhamel 1777 = Duhamel du Monceau: Art de faire les Tapis mit frz.-dtsch. Vokabular. Neuchâtel 1771.

Duhamel 1777a = Duhamel du Monceau: Art de la Draperie mit frz.-dtsch. Vokabular. Neuchâtel 1777.

Duhamel 1777 = Duhamel du Monceau: Art du Potier de terre mit frz.-dtsch. Vokabular. Neuchâtel 1777.

Duhamel 1801 = Duhamel: Dictionnaire portatif allemand et français des termes de mines. Paris 1801.

Egger 1757 = J. Egger: Nouveau dictionnaire allemand-français de l'ingénieur, de l'artilleur, du marin. 2 Bde. Dresden. Leipzig 1757.

Englisch-deutsches Landw. 1862 = Englisch-deutsches Wörterbuch für Landwirte. Stuttgart 1862.

Falbi 1989 = Lena Falbi: Glossar der Bienenzucht (D-S). In: Lebende Sprachen 1989, 134.

Fincati 1870 = Luigi Fincati: Dizionario di marina italiano francese e francese italiano. Genua. Torin 1870.

Flines 1806 = Q. de Flines: Scheeps-en Zeemanns-Woordenboek in het Nederduitsch en Fransch. Amsterdam 1806. Weitere Aufl. Rotterdam 1820.

Fougeroux 1777 = Fougeroux: Art du Tonnelier mit frz.-dtsch. Vokabular. Neuchâtel 1777.

Gabler 1858 = Ernst Gabler: Latijnsch-Hollandsch woordenboek over de geneeskunde en de natuurkundige wetenschappen. Utrecht 1858 [Weitere Aufl. Leiden 1881 und 1910].

Galon 1777 = Galon: Art de convertir le cuivre mit frz.-dtsch. Vokabular. Neuchâtel 1777.

Gérin Roze 1840 = M. de Gérin Roze: Manuel du navigateur français-anglais. Paris 1840.

Géruzet 1830 = J. B. Géruzet: Vocabulaire français-hollandais des termes propres à la science du notariat. Brüssel 1830.

Gmelin 1772 = Johann Friedrich Gmelin: Onomatologia botanica completa oder vollständiges botanisches Wörterbuch [...]. Frankfurt 1772—1777.

Grachow 1872 = J. Grachow: Deutsch-russisches wissenschaftlich-technisches Kunstwörterbuch. 2 Bde. St. Petersburg 1872.

Haensch 1965 = Günther Haensch: Französische Verwaltungssprache. München 1965.

Halem 1811 = F. W. von Halem: Kleines ächt Holländisches Handwörterbuch für Geschäftsmänner und Kaufleute. (Niederl.-Dtsch.) Bremen. Aurich 1811.

Heinze 1846 = A. Heinze: Dictionnaire portatif des armes. Frz.-dtsch. Leipzig 1846.

Hellwig 1711 = Christoph Hellwig: Thesaurus pharmaceuticus oder Apotheker-Schatz [...]. Leipzig 1711.

Hellwig 1711a = Christoph Hellwig: Neu eingerichtetes Lexicon medico-chymicum oder chymisches Lexikon. Frankfurt. Leipzig 1711.

Hennicke 1889 = F. Hennicke: Technisches Wörterbuch für Telegraphie und Post. Deutsch-englisch und englisch-deutsch. Berlin 1889.

Hirche 1893 = P. Hirche: Liste alphabétique des marchandises français et allemand. Berlin 1893.

Hoefer 1881 = F. A. Hoefer: Fransch-Nederlandsch Militair Technisch Woordenboek. Arnhem 1881 (Frz.-Niederl.).

Hoefer 1881a = F. A. Hoefer: Hoogduitsch-Nederlandsch militair woordenboek. Arnhem 1881.

Hoof 1989 = Henri van Hoof: Histoire des dictionnaires techniques. In: Terminologie diachronique. Actes du Colloque de Bruxelles 1988. Ed. C. de Schaetzen. Bruxelles 1989, 27—37.

Juridisch-politische Terminologie 1850 = Juridisch-politische Terminologie für die slawischen Sprachen Österreichs. Deutsch-böhmische Separatausgabe. Wien 1850.

Kaltschmidt 1860 = J. Kaltschmidt: Petit dictionnaire technoterminologique français-allemand. 2 Bde. Leipzig (gegen 1860).

Kazimirski 1846 = Kazimirski-Biberstein: Dictionnaire arabe-français (Marine und Militärwesen). 2 Bde. Paris 1846.

Kopp 1810 = J. Kopp: Mineralische Synonymik. Frz.-dtsch. Frankfurt 1810.

Kotzenberg 1875 = H. W. A. Kotzenberg: Deutsch-spanisches und spanisch-deutsches Wörterbuch des kaufmännischen Verkehrs und der Handelskorrespondenz. Bremen 1875.

Krause 1889 = A. Krause: Deutsch-russisches Forstwörterbuch. Riga 1889.

Kroehndorf 1700 = P. Kroehndorf: Instruction pour les jardins fruitiers (français-allemand) avec un petit dictionnaire des termes du jardinage plus utiles. Leipzig 1700.

Laguna 1555 = Andrés Laguna: Materia medica (Span. Übersetzung des Dioscorides 1555). Moderne Ausgabe: César E. Dubler: La „Materia Médica de Dioscórides: Transmisión medieval y renacentista, vol. III: La „Materia Médica" de Dioscórides traducida y comentada por D. Andrés Laguna. Barcelona 1955 [Gibt meist die Namen auf Altgr.-Lat.-„Apothekerlatein"-Arab.-Span.-Katal.-Port.-Ital.-Frz. u. Dtsch. an].

La Lande 1776 = J. de La Lande: Art du Papetier mit einem frz.-dtsch. Vokabular. Neuchâtel 1776.

Lescallier 1777 = D. Lescallier: Vocabulaire des termes de marine anglais-français. 2 Bde. Paris 1777.

Lhuillée 1810 = C. Lhuillée: Dictionnaires des termes de marine français-espagnol et espagnol-français. 2 Bde. Paris 1810.

Llave 1846 = P. de la Llave: Vocabulario francés-español de términos de artillería. Segovia 1846 [160 S.].

Lobelius 1681 = Matthias Lobelius: Kruydtboeck oft Beschrijvinghe van allerley Ghewassen, Kruyderen, Hesteren ende Gheboomten. Antwerpen 1681 [Niederl.-Lat.-Dtsch.-Frz.-Ital.-Span.-Port.-Engl.].

Lópes/Bensley 1864 = J. M. Lópes/E. R. Bensley: Nueva correspondencia comercial francesa-española con vocabulario francés-español. Paris 1864 [927 S.].

Martínez de Espinosa 1849 = Martínez de Espinosa y Tacón: Diccionario marino inglés-español y español-inglés. 1849.

Mentzel 1682 = Christian Mentzel: Pinax Botanorymos Polyglottos Index nominum plantarum universalis. Berlin 1682 [Nomenklatur der Pflanzen in 30 Sprachen].

Moreali 1839 = G. Moreali: Dictionnaire de musique italien-français. 2. Aufl. Paris 1839.

Moretti 1828 = Federico Moretti: Diccionario militar español-francés. Vocabulaire militaire français-espagnol. Madrid 1828 [XXXIX, 448, 184, 72 S.].

Nebrija 1506 = Elio Antonio de Nebrija: Léxico de Derecho Civil. Hrsg. von Carlos Humberto Núñez. Madrid 1944 [1.Aufl. unter dem Titel Aenigmata Juris Civilis ab Antonio Nebrissensi Edita, Salamanca 1506. Weitere Aufl. Lyon 1537 und Venedig 1606].

Nečas 1892 = Johan Nečas: Deutsch-böhmische juridische Terminologie. Brünn 1892—93.

Nemnich 1821 = Ph. A. Nemnich: Holländisches Waaren-Lexicon. Hamburg 1821.

Oberländer 1721 = Samuel Oberländer: Lexicon iuridicum Romano-Teutonicum das ist vollständiges lateinisch-teutsches juridisches Hand-Lexicon. Nürnberg 1721.

Orphéonistes 1860 = Vocabulaire et guide des orphéonistes. (Frz.-Engl.) Paris 1860.

Pausner 1802 = J. Pausner: Dictionnaire minéralogique français-allemand. Jena 1802.

Parmentier 1849 = Th. Parmentier: Vocabulaire allemand-français des termes de fortification. Paris 1849.

Péch 1879 = A. Péch: Magyar és német bányászati szótàr. Selmeczen 1879.

Péras 1753 = J. Péras: Dictionnaire anatomique latin-français. Paris 1753.

Ponce de León 1893 = Nestor Ponce de León: Diccionario technológico inglés-español y español-inglés de los términos y frases usadas en las ciencias aplicadas, artes industriales, bellas artes, mecánica, agricultura [...]. New York. Ponce de León 1893—1904 [1832 S.].

Réaumur 1777 = R. A. F. de Réaumur: Art de l'Epinglier mit frz.-dtsch. Vokabular. Neuchâtel 1777.

Réaumur 1781 = R. A. F. de Réaumur: Fabrication des ancres. Mit frz.-dtsch. Vokabular. Neuchâtel 1781.

Rees 1861 = P. A. van Rees: Engelsch-Nederduitsch technisch marinewoordenboek. Rotterdam 1861.

Renner 1966 = Rüdiger Renner/Günther Haensch/Michel Campart de Kostine: Französisch-deutsche Rechtssprache. München 1966.

Reuss 1781 = Christian Friedrich Reuss: Dictionarium botanicum oder botanisches lateinisches und teutsches Handwörterbuch. Leipzig 1781.

Roucel 1792 = F. Roucel: Traité des plantes avec nomenclature français-allemand. Brüssel 1792.

Rouvroy 1829 = F. von Rouvroy: Dictionnaire français-allemand contenant les termes techniques de l'artillerie. Dresden 1829.

Schokker 1841 = H. W. Schokker: Zakwoordenboek van Engelsche Zeetermen, in het Hollandsch overgebragt. Den Haag. Amsterdam 1841 [Engl.-Niederl.].

Sea Phrases 1799 = Vocabulary of Sea Phrases English-French/French-English. 2 Bde. London 1799.

Serraris 1864 = P. A. Serraris: Militair woordenboek betreffende de draagbare wapenen. (Frz.-Niederl.). Kampen 1864.

Sommerhoff 1701 = Johann C. Sommerhoff: Lexicon pharmaceutico-chymicum latino-germanicum et germanico-latinum. Nürnberg 1701 [Weitere Aufl. 1713].

Spatny 1870 = Franz Spatny: Deutsch-böhmisches Wörterbuch für Jäger und Jagdfreunde. Prag 1870.

Spiers 1846 = A. Spiers: Manuel des termes du commerce anglais et français. Paris 1846.

Technisch Woordenboek 1888 = Technisch Woordenboek. Engelsch-Hollandsch en Hollandsch-Engelsch Verzameling van technische woorden, ten dienste van den machinist. Helder 1888.

Terreros y Pando 1786 = Esteban Terreros y Pando: Diccionario castellano con las voces de ciencias y artes. 4 Bde. Madrid 1786—1793 [Span.-Lat.-Frz.-Ital.].

Trepied 1889 = Henry Trepied: Vocabulaire militaire espagnol-français. Paris 1889 [239 S.].

Vissian 1846 = Massimino Vissian: Dizionario della musica [...] (Frz.-Ital.). Mailand 1846.

Vossius 1640 = Lambert Vossius: „Lexicon novum herbarium tripartitum". In: Anselmus Boetius de Boodt: Florum, herbarum et fructum selectiorum icones [...]. Brügge 1640 [Lat.-Niederl.-Frz.].

Witzel 1858 = E. Witzel: Dictionnaire français-allemand des machines à vapeur. Paris 1858.

7.2. Sonstige Literatur

Barblan 1981 = Maria-Clotilde Barblan: Biblioteca dell'Academia della Crusca: Dizionari della lingua italiana, Sec. XIX—XX. In: Studi di lessicografia italiana a cura dell'Academia della Crusca 3. 1981, 191—281.

Boelcke 1983 = J. Boelcke/B. Straub/P. Thiele: Wie entsteht ein Wirtschaftswörterbuch? Einige lexikographische Anmerkungen. In: Nouveaux Cahiers d'Allemand. Revue de linguistique et didactique 4. 1983, 256—266.

Bruna 1987 = Maria Luisa Bruna: La lessicografia italo-(serbo)croata (1649—1985). In: Studi di lessicografia italiana a cura dell'Academia della Crusca 9. 1987, 21—45.

Claes 1974 = Frans Claes: Lijst van Nederlandse woordenlijsten en woordenboeken gedrukt tot 1600. Nieuwkoop 1974.

Claes 1980 = Frans M. Claes: A Bibliography of Netherlandic Dictionaries. Dutch-Flemish. München 1980.

Collison 1971 = Robert L. Collison: Dictionaries of English and Foreign Languages. A Bibliographical Guide to both General and Technical Dictionaries with Historical and Explanatory Notes and References. 2. Aufl. New York 1971.

Collison 1982 = Robert L. Collison: A History of Foreign-Language Dictionaries. London 1982.

Fabbri 1979 = Maurizio Fabbri: A Bibliography of Hispanic Dictionaries. Catalan, Galician, Spanish [...]. Imola 1979.

Grin'ov 1989 = S. V. Grin'ov: Some Problems of Terminological Dictionaries and their Classification. In: UNESCO. ALSED-LSP. Newsletter, Vol. 11, N. 2 (27) Januar 1989, 3—9.

Haugen 1984 = Eva L. Haugen: A Bibliography of Scandinavian Dictionaries. New York 1984.

Kalverkämper 1988 = Hartwig Kalverkämper: Die Fachwelt in der allgemeinen einsprachigen Lexikographie. In: Special Language. Fachsprache 10. 1988, 98—123.

Karl 1982 = Ilse Karl: Linguistische Probleme der zweisprachigen Lexikographie. Eine Nachlese praktischer Wörterbucharbeit. Berlin 1982 (Linguistische Studien, Reihe A, Arbeitsberichte 96).

Kromann 1984 = Hans-Peder Kromann/Theis Riiber/Poul Rosbach: Überlegungen zu Grundfragen der zweisprachigen Lexikographie. In: Germanistische Linguistik 3—6/84. 1984, (Studien zur neuhochdeutschen Lexikographie V. Hrsg. v. H. E. Wiegand). 159—238

Kühn 1978 = Peter Kühn: Deutsche Wörterbücher. Eine systematische Bibliographie. Tübingen 1978 (Reihe germanistische Linguistik 15).

Learmonth 1986 = Trevor Learmonth/Stuart Macwilliam: Historic English Dictionaries 1595—1899. Exeter 1986.

Quemada 1967 = Bernard Quemada: Les dictionnaires du français moderne (1539—1863). Etude sur leur histoire, leurs types et leurs méthodes. Paris. Bruxelles. Montréal 1967.

Serís 1964 = Homero Serís: Bibliografía de la lingüística española. Bogotá 1964 (Publicaciones del Instituto Caro y Cuervo XIX).

Stein 1985 = Gabriele Stein: The English Dictionary before Cawdrey. Tübingen 1985 (Lexicographica. Series Maior 9).

Stein 1985a = Gabriele Stein: English-German/German-English Lexicography: Its Early Beginnings. In: Lexicographica 1. 1985, 134—164.

Steiner 1976 = Roger J. Steiner: Neologisms and Scientific Words in Bilingual Lexicography: Ten Problems. In: Lebende Sprachen 4. 1976, 145—150.

Tancke 1984 = Gunnar Tancke: Die italienischen Wörterbücher von den Anfängen bis zum Erscheinen des Vocabolario degli Academici della Crusca

(1612). Tübingen 1984 (Beihefte zur Zeitschrift für romanische Philologie 198).

Viñaza 1893 = Cipriano Muñoz y Manzano, Conde de la Viñaza: Biblioteca histórica de la filología castellana. Madrid 1893.

Wiegand 1976 = Herbert Ernst Wiegand: Fachsprachen im einsprachigen Wörterbuch. Kritik, Provokationen und praktisch-pragmatische Vorschläge. In: Kongreßberichte der 7. Jahrestagung der Gesellschaft für Angewandte Linguistik GAL e. V. Trier 1976, 39—65.

Zaunmüller 1958 = Wolfram Zaunmüller: Bibliographisches Handbuch der Sprachwörterbücher. Ein internationales Verzeichnis von 5600 Wörterbüchern der Jahre 1400—1958 für mehr als 500 Sprachen und Dialekte. Stuttgart 1958.

Zischka 1958 = Gert A. Zischka: Index lexicorum. Bibliographie der lexikographischen Nachschlagewerke. Wien 1958.

Günther Haensch, Augsburg
(Bundesrepublik Deutschland)

XXXVI. Die zweisprachigen Wörterbücher in Geschichte und Gegenwart
Bilingual Dictionaries Past and Present
Les dictionnaires bilingues hier et aujourd'hui

308. Bilingual Lexicography: English-Spanish and Spanish-English

1. The Scope of the Study
2. The First Spanish–English Dictionary
3. Percyvall's Successor: Minsheu
4. The Eighteenth Century
5. A Turning Point: 1797–1802
6. The Neuman and Baretti
7. The Velázquez Dictionaries
8. Other Nineteenth-Century Dictionaries
9. The Cuyás Dictionaries
10. The Influence of World War II
11. The Williams Dictionaries
12. Three American Dictionaries
13. Dictionaries From England
14. Dictionaries From France
15. Dictionaries From Germany
16. Dictionaries From Spain
17. Conclusion
18. Selected Bibliography

1. The Scope of the Study

This survey includes the dictionaries necessary for an understanding of the history of Spanish and English bilingual lexicography. The importance of a dictionary is a reason for inclusion but the most important reason is the exemplary nature of the dictionary in showing the principles on which an author compiled it and the need it filled for the buying public. Dictionaries not listed in this survey may fall into one of three categories. (1) They are small or derivative. (2) They are published in Central or South America and are largely of regional use. (3) They are specialized dictionaries of: (a) commercial terms, (b) technical terms such as those used in engineering and medicine, (c) phrases and key words for conversation and the guidance of the traveler, or (d) types of speech (idioms, synonyms, proverbs, regionalisms, dialects, localisms, slang).

2. The First Spanish-English Dictionary

Sir Richard Percyvall, one of Queen Elizabeth's translators, compiled the first Spanish and English bilingual dictionary. Spanish had been included in Latin and Spanish bilingual works, in polyglot works, in a Spanish and Italian dictionary, and in brief equivalencies appended to grammars. Even though Percyvall's work also followed his grammar, it deserves the name of dictionary because of its scope and size. His publisher, Richard Watkins, had secured the copyright that had been given in 1590 for a dictionary by Dr. Thomas D'Oylie, who had practiced medicine in Belgium and Holland. Percyvall adopted the Latin tag that D'Oylie had used with each entry. For a short time, Percyvall received the help of native informants, two officers of the Spanish Armada, Don Pedro de Valdés and Don Vasco de Sylva, prisoners at the home of Sir Richard Drake. His main sources were Nebrija 1492 and Las Casas 1570. To words from these sources he added about two thousand entries, half of them derived forms or expressions from other entries in the dictionary. Percyvall's one-part Spanish-English dictionary had 184 pages and 12 500 entries. It was bilingual even though it used a third language, Latin, because the Latin tag served as meaning discrimination. It was monodirectional for the benefit of the speaker of English. It was inconsistent in its alphabetization and typography and in its treatment of articles, pronunciation, irregular forms, and words with multiple meanings. Percyvall often translated a transitive verb by an expression including the direct object even though the direct object was not part of the meaning of the verb.

> Matar, to kill, to murder, to destroy, to combate, to swing, to put out a candle, *Interficere, pugnare, mactare, urere, extinguere.*

Dictionary excerpt 308.1: Dictionary entry (in: Percyvall 1591, II, MA).

In the above entry, *matar* is a transitive word but *to put out a candle* is an intransitive expression.

3. Percyvall's Successor: Minsheu

In 1599, Edmund Bollifant was allowed a copyright but had to give top billing on the title page to "Ric. Perciuale *Gent*.", star each new entry, and reduce the emphasis on the title page for his own lexicographer, John Minsheu. It was not a new innovative dictionary even though its 391 pages were over twice the number of its predecessor, and each of those pages had twice as many entries as a page from Percyvall. Although he removed Percyvall's Latin glosses, Minsheu used Latin dictionaries and bookish sources. What expands his dictionary the most is his addition of the English-Spanish part, which often contains reversals from the other side of the dictionary. He goes beyond Percyvall in a more complete presentation of the inflection of irregular verbs and in indicating the stress and gender of the Spanish headword. The second edition in 1623 is virtually identical to the 1599. Minsheu 1617 is a new work containing, in its second part, a trilingual dictionary with Spanish headwords, and Latin and English glosses. The 50 000 brief entries use material from the polylingual Part I, are variants, or are cross-references.

4. The Eighteenth Century

4.1. Captain John Stevens

The Stevens 1705—6 makes the pretense of using a whole pageful of titles of Spanish works listed in the front matter of the dictionary, but actually, Stevens followed Minsheu 1599 slavishly. The two parts of the dictionary were unequal, the English-Spanish containing only 20 000 entries while the Spanish-English contained 50 000 entries. Stevens added a good many proverbs to Minsheu's work, an occasional etymology of a Spanish headword, and encyclopedic material. The grammar and dialogues borrowed from Minsheu were discontinued in the 1726 printing, with little else changed.

4.2. Peter Pineda

The first Spanish and English bilingual dictionary compiled by a Spaniard was that of the émigré Pedro Pineda. He added about 18 000 entries to the 60 000 entries taken from Stevens. He used Nathan Bailey's monolingual English dictionary, and many of his new entries are valuable idiomatic words and expressions such as *you hit the nail on the head*. The English-Spanish part was now no longer an appendage to the other side of the dictionary. Pineda's translations were short and concise, the parts of speech were designated systematically, and pronunciation of Spanish letters was indicated.

4.3. Joseph Giral Delpino

The publishers of Pineda's dictionary hired Hippolyto San José Giral Delpino to compile a new work brought out in 1763. Giral Delpino removed his predecessor's abusive definitions concerning the Spanish Academy and the Pope. He contributed several thousand original entries.

4.4. Joseph Baretti

A name that was to resound in lexicography for over a century was that of Dr. Johnson's friend and the compiler of an Italian and English bilingual dictionary, Giuseppe Marcantonio Baretti. His work was almost entirely editorial, but his edition of Giral Delpino's dictionary was reprinted word for word in 1786, in 1794, and in frequent later "editions", and it was pirated all over Europe.

5. A Turning Point: 1797—1802

Baretti 1778 was the culmination of a series of dictionaries each of which borrowed from its predecessor. Original lexicography entered the field in a four-volume work published in 1797 and 1798 under the aegis of the King of Spain, and continued its influence in a work derived from it under the supervision of London publishers in 1802.

5.1. Connelly and Higgins

The honor of compiling the first Spanish and English bilingual dictionary to be printed in Spain belongs to two Irish friars, Father Thomas Connelly and Father Thomas Hig-

SACRAMENT. s. An oath, any ceremony producing an obligation. *Sacramento, la obligacion y vínculo del juramento.*
SACRAMENT. An outward and visible sign of an inward and spiritual grace. *Sacramento, señal exterior y visible de gracia interior é invisible.*
THE SEVEN SACRAMENTS. *Los siete sacramentos.*
SACRAMENT. The Eucharist, the holy communion. *Sacramento del altar.*
TO RECEIVE THE SACRAMENT. *Comulgar.*
SACRAMENTAL. adj. Constituting a sacrament, pertaining to a sacrament. *Sacramental, lo que constituye sacramento, ó pertenece á él.*
SACRAMENTALLY. adv. After the manner of a sacrament. *Sacramentalmente, con modo y realidad de sacramento.*

Dictionary excerpt 308.2: Dictionary excerpt (from: Connelly/Higgins 1797)

gins. A vast dictionary of four volumes was printed at royal expense. For fourteen years Connelly and Higgins welded together Samuel Johnson's monolingual English dictionary and the Dictionary of the Spanish Academy to make a work that not only supplies the equivalent in the target language but a definition as well, and also supplies a definition of the headword in the source language. In a way, this dictionary can be considered three dictionaries in one: a monolingual English dictionary, a monolingual Spanish dictionary, and a bilingual dictionary (Steiner 1970, 93 ff.).

5.2. Henry Neuman

In the preface of his 1802 work, Henry Neuman admits his debt to Connelly and Higgins. He consistently copied their equivalents and translations verbatim after removing most of their definitions. It is remarkable that Neuman did not copy the Baretti dictionary since Vernor and Hood, who had published Baretti in 1794, were also two of Neuman's publishers. Neuman does adopt Baretti's method of indicating accent on the Spanish entry word: the accent is placed after the vowel, e.g., **SABOREA'R**. A subsequent edition of the Neuman copied the 1802 edition word for word, enlarged some of the entries, and added entirely new entries. The 1802 had had unequal parts: approximately 40 000 entries on the Spanish-English side to 25 000 entries on the English-Spanish side. The Neuman 1817 had a better balance with an approximate relationship of 50 000 to 42 000.

6. The Neuman and Baretti

The "partnership" of "Neuman and Baretti" started as late as 1823, thirty-four years after Baretti's death, in a work called the "fourth edition" (Neuman/Baretti 1823). The "third edition" in 1817 had had only Neuman's name on the title page but nevertheless was the same dictionary word for word. Hilliard, Gray, Little, and Wilkins, a Boston publishing house, secured the plates of the 1823 edition and reprinted the work several times under its Boston imprint. Meanwhile in England, the dictionary received further retouches from a Spanish émigré by the name of Mateo Seoane y Sobral in a "fifth edition" (Seoane 1831). Dr. Seoane practiced medicine in England and had the lexicographic help of fellow political refugees Vicenti Salvá, Pablo de Mendibil, and Joaquín Villanueva. It was Seoane's goal simply to add corrections and emendations. His dictionary was an enormous success with many reprintings, many of them pirated.

7. The Velázquez Dictionaries

In New York, Appleton & Co. hired Mariano Velázquez de la Cadena, professor of the Spanish language at Columbia and writer of pedagogical books, to put retouches on Seoane's Neuman and Baretti. The result was Velázquez 1852: *A Pronouncing Dictionary of the Spanish and English Languages*. After a number of reprintings, Appleton & Co. hired Juan S. Iribas and Edward Gray to produce a revision published in 1900. Most of the changes were on the English-Spanish side, and only half of the century-old text was remodeled. After occasional reprintings, another publishing house bought the work and later produced a scissors-and-paste job, the Velázquez 1959. A mere five thousand neologisms were substituted throughout for words removed to make place for them, and the pagination was kept. The publishers used at least 400 of the plates from 1900 unchanged, and over half of the material was at least 142 years old. Velázquez 1985 inserts 33 pages of neologisms in the middle of the book.

8. Other Nineteenth-Century Dictionaries

A pocket dictionary, Gattel 1803, was pirated in London in 1809. Fernández 1811, *The First Dictionary of Two Languages under a Single Alphabet,* eliminated the necessity of turning from one side of the dictionary to the other since Spanish-English entries and English-Spanish entries follow one another on the same page. Garnier Frères in Paris published the Lopes/Bensley 1878, which acknowledges its debt to Velázquez, the Spanish Academy, Terreros, Salvá, Domínguez, Seoane, Worcester, Clifton, and Webster. Garnier Frères also published in smaller format the Corona Bustamante 1878 with debts acknowledged to Seoane, Neuman and Baretti, Blanc, and Velázquez. The reprinting in 1959 is an example, along with the Velázquez 1959 (cf. 7), of the way in which some publishers take advantage of the buying public in publishing outdated dictionaries with updated blurbs.

9. The Cuyás Dictionaries

Responding to the American interest in Spanish after the War of 1898 with Spain, Appleton & Co. commissioned Arturo Cuyás to produce a "successor to the Velázquez", the Cuyás 1903. Many whole entries were copied from the Velázquez word for word. However, Cuyás radically changed the principle of compilation. No longer would the lexicographer give long explanations in English of the meaning of a Spanish word but would search for correct equivalents. The Cuyás 1940 was a complete revision and resetting by Antonio Llano, who added supplements of new words and equivalents.

10. The Influence of World War II

World War II brought an increased awareness to the Americas of the importance of foreign languages, and a consistent production of Spanish and English bilingual dictionaries began. The Cuyás was reprinted in 1942 and revised in 1953 (cf. 9). In Buenos Aires, Steinhardt 1944 was published. In Chicago the Follett Publishing Co. brought out the Fucilla 1943. Also in Chicago, two university professors compiled the Castillo/Bond 1948. The title, *The University of Chicago Spanish Dictionary,* proved an irresistible gimmick as millions of buyers conceived of the dictionary as emanating from austere conclaves of noted scholars and these purchasers put it on the "best sellers' list". However, Castillo/Bond 1948 is woefully lacking in neologisms and is not authoritative. The noted scholar D. Lincoln Canfield was not allowed to do a really thorough job of revision in 1972.

11. The Williams Dictionaries

David McKay, a Philadelphia publisher, who had adopted McLaughlin 1911, died too soon to finish his project of publishing an entirely original encyclopedic Spanish and English bilingual dictionary compiled by scholars at the University of Pennsylvania under the direction of Edwin Bucher Williams. Williams secured a contract with the Holt Company, which published Williams 1955. Using prime sources such as monolingual dictionaries, encyclopedias, books, media publications, and native informants, Williams produced one of the few bilingual dictionaries compiled according to a consistent plan. Some of the features are: (1) *User identification*. If the dictionary is bidirectional, it gives to the English-speaking user (a) the Spanish words needed to express thoughts in Spanish and (b) the English meanings of Spanish words needed to understand Spanish, and to the Spanish-speaking user (c) the English words needed to express thoughts in English and (d) the Spanish meanings of English words needed to understand English. A monodirectional or unidirectional dictionary serves only one of the foregoing language groups (*a & b* or *c & d*). The lexicographer must identify the users he or she wishes to serve, lay out a cogent plan, and execute it consistently. (2) *Reversibility*. If an entry is important on one side of the dictionary, then probably its translations should become headwords on the other side of the dictionary. (3) *Meaning discrimination*. Words are set apart in italics and between parentheses to guide the user in choosing the correct translation. (4) *Inclusiveness of lexical elements*. Provide not only literary words but words needed to read the daily newspaper: scientific words, neologisms, acronyms, colloquialisms, slang, etc. (5) *Ready translations rather than paraphrases or definitions*. Provide equivalents of the same caste and level of speech for the translator. (6) *No confusion of lexicographical style and orthography*. Capitalize words when that is the way they are spelled and not on account of the dictionary's system. (7) *A consistent arrangement and style of all elements.* This feature may include: consistency of alphabetization of entry words, run-on entries, examples, expressions, and abbreviations; a fixed order of parts of speech. The features listed above are not only characteristics of a Williams dictionary but also constitute a sampling of the principles that Williams used as he trained over a dozen students and colleagues in the art, craft, and science of lexicography. These lexicographers went on to compile and revise dictionaries. Williams revised his 1955 work in 1962 and expanded it in 1963. Another different work is Williams 1968, published by Bantam Books. Rarely has a publishing house shown the scholarly imagination, vision, and courage as that shown in the creation of a series of original bilingual dictionaries of which the Williams 1968 is a part and of which Edwin Bucher Williams was the general editor and Walter D. Glanze the Bantam editor. The Williams 1968 was not a reduced version of the others but rather a new and independent work. It was completely bidirectional with source-language meaning discrimination. Williams considered this work as the one most clearly demonstrating his method and theory. Bantam Books also publishes a special export edition, which contains an English grammar (Williams 1980).

12. Three American Dictionaries

(1) The Thomas Y. Crowell Co. commissioned Gillhoff 1963, and (2) the World Publishing Company brought out Pei 1968. (3) Much larger was the 1605-page 200 000 -entry Simon & Schuster's Gámez 1973, with its staff of 79 persons. It is a carefully prepared work with meticulous proof-reading, but contrary to its claims, it fails to "reflect the language of the historical moment" because its word list is swollen with derivative and uncommon words at the same time that it lacks many useful neologisms.

13. Dictionaries From England

Raventós 1953 is an original work and completely equipped with source-language meaning discriminations. Peers 1959, after undergoing reduction in Dutton 1969, was the subject of a version published in 1978 in New York by Macmillan, but this edition did not change very much; the dictionary still was not organized on a consistent plan developed on the basis of sound lexicographical principles. The Smith 1971, on the other hand, laid out a plan by which the user could be afforded some kind of a dictionary of construction by providing abundant usage examples for basic entries such as *have, haber, head, cabeza,* etc. Many Spanish-American regionalisms were entered by Manuel Bermejo Marcos and Eugenio Chang-Rodríguez, but the chief compiler, Colin Smith, used British words, expressions, and spellings throughout, with relatively few Americanisms. Because of the space limitations caused by the many examples, the compilers were not able to offer as long a word list as some competitors. Smith 1988 is over a third larger than Smith 1971, offers many new words, and uses a style of meaning discrimination comparable to that of other excellent dictionaries.

14. Dictionaries From France

The prestigious Larousse company secured Ramón García-Pelayo y Gross to create over 2000 pages using nesting, a compact style that prefers run-ons to headwords and leads to a high entry count. The dictionary is based upon Castilian Spanish and British English. García-Pelayo 1984a and 1984b are revisions of the original 1976. In 1986 the Larousse company and the Houghton Mifflin company published the first Larousse dictionary prepared outside of France: Senerth/Sola 1986. The English usage is that of the United States. A successful effort has been made to represent both "pan-Hispanic" usage and the diverse special forms and senses found in Spanish America. Meaning discrimination is a strong point: in multiple-sense entries, explanatory words or synonyms for each sense are given in the language of the entry word. A pioneering and commendable feature is the use of reference numbers that key many entries to appropriate grammar references in the introductory matter.

15. Dictionaries From Germany

The Langenscheidt company holds a position in Germany comparable to Larousse in France. Its *Standard Dictionary of the English and Spanish Languages* (Smith 1966) uses British English, but a revised version, MacDonald/Steiner 1988, uses American

English. MacDonald/Steiner 1985 is a smaller version of the Smith 1966. Duden, an important name in German monolingual dictionaries, published a dictionary (Duden 1963) that uses pen-and-ink drawings to represent the meanings of Spanish words, with English index.

16. Dictionaries From Spain

Four publishers in Barcelona brought out dictionaries: (1) Hymnsa published Cuyás 1936 (cf. 9). (2) Sopena published Martínez Amador 1946. Amador 1957 is a smaller edition. (3) Juventud was responsible for Maccragh 1963. (4) Biblograf published MacHale 1964. This bilingual "VOX" complements the well-known monolingual VOX. Both dictionaries are rich in Spanish-American regionalisms. In Madrid Julio Casares published the *Novísimo Diccionario*. The largest bilingual work from Spain was published in Madrid by EDAF, Ediciones-Distribuciones, S.A., the *Gran diccionario general* (EDAF 1977). There are 1500 pages in each of the two volumes and its well over 100 000 entries are not brief or abbreviated.

17. Conclusion

One can take especial note of three things in the history outlined herein: (1) the frequent dependence of one dictionary upon its predecessors; (2) the publication of dictionaries as a reflection of the political and social needs of the time; (3) the accelerating rate at which Spanish and English bilingual works have been published, particularly during the past quarter of a century.

18. Selected Bibliography

18.1. Dictionaries

Amador 1957 = Diccionario Manual Amador inglés—español y español—inglés. Barcelona 1957 [1267 p.].

Baretti 1778 = Giuseppe Marcantonio Baretti: A Dictionary Spanish and English, and English and Spanish. London 1778, 1786, 1794 [632 p.].

Biblograf 1969 = VOX Diccionario Manual inglés—español, español—inglés. 3d ed. Barcelona 1969 [1007 p.].

Casares n.d. = Julio Casares y Sánchez: Novísimo Diccionario inglés—español y español—inglés. Madrid n.d. [1456 p.; ed. 1925].

Castillo/Bond 1948 = Carlos Castillo/Otto F. Bond/Barbara M. García: The University of Chicago Spanish Dictionary Spanish—English, English—Spanish. Chicago·London 1948 [531 p.; ed. Pocket Books, New York 1950, 534 p.].

Castillo/Bond 1972 = Carlos Castillo/Otto F. Bond/Barbara M. García/D. Lincoln Canfield: The University of Chicago Spanish Dictionary. Rev. Chicago. London 1972 [494 p.; ed. Pocket Books, 1975].

Castillo/Bond 1987 = Carlos Castillo/Otto F. Bond/Barbara M. García/D. Lincoln Canfield: The University of Chicago Spanish Dictionary. 4th ed. Chicago. London 1987 [475 p.].

Connelly/Higgins 1797—8 = Thomas Connelly/Thomas Higgins: Diccionario nuevo de las dos lenguas española e inglesa. 4 vol. Madrid 1797—8 [4843 p.; III, IV 1797 Eng.—Sp. 1395 p.; I, II 1798 Sp.—Eng. 3448 p.].

Corona Bustamante 1878 = Francisco Corona Bustamante: Diccionario inglés—español y español—inglés. 2 vol. Paris 1878 [1250 p.; Garnier 1900, 1902, 1903; LaPlata 1942 Mundo Científico; Baltimore 1959].

Cuyás 1903 = Arturo Cuyás: Appleton's New Spanish—English and English—Spanish Dictionary. New York 1903 [1227 p.; 2d ed. 1928; 3d ed. New York. London 1940, 1179 p., ed. Antonio Llano; 4th ed. New York 1953: Eng.—Sp. 729 p., ed. Lewis E. Brett; Sp.—Eng. 592 p., ed. Helen S. Eaton/Walter Beveraggi-Allende].

Cuyás 1936 = Arturo Cuyás Armengol/Antonio Cuyás Armengol/Alberto del Castillo Yurrita: Gran Diccionario inglés—español. Barcelona 1936 [1359 p.; Pocket ed. 1927, 767 p.].

Duden 1963 = Duden Español. Diccionario por la imagen. 2d ed. Barcelona. Mannheim 1963 [911 p.].

Duden 1985 = The Oxford-Duden Pictorial Dictionary. Oxford 1985 [384, 112, 96 p.].

Dutton 1969 = Brian Dutton/L. P. Harvey/Roger M. Walker: Cassell's New Compact Spanish—English English—Spanish Dictionary. New York 1969 [444 p.].

EDAF 1977 = Ubaldo DiBenedetto et. al.: Gran diccionario general inglés—español, español—inglés. Madrid 1977 [3000 p.].

Fernández 1811 = Felipe Fernández; The First Dictionary of Two Languages under a Single Alphabet. London 1811 [2d ed. 1817].

Fucilla 1943 = Joseph G. Fucilla: The Follett Spanish Dictionary Spanish—English and English—Spanish. Chicago 1943 [652 p.; London 1948, N.Y. 1961].

Gámez 1973 = Tana de Gámez/Guido N. Forbath/Clive D. Page et al.: Simon and Schuster's International Dictionary. New York 1973 [1631 p.].

Gámez 1975 = Tana de Gámez/Guido N. Forbath/Clive D. Page et. al.: Simon & Schuster's Concise International Dictionary. New York 1975 [1405 p.].

García-Pelayo 1976 = Ramón García-Pelayo y Gross/Micheline Durand/Barry Tulett/Fernando

García-Pelayo: Diccionario Moderno español—inglés. Paris. Buenos Aires. Mexico City. New York 1976 [2101 p.].

García-Pelayo 1984a = Ramón García-Pelayo y Gross/Micheline Durand/Fernando García-Pelayo y Gross: Diccionario General español—inglés. Paris 1984 [977 p.].

García-Pelayo 1984b = Ramón García-Pelayo y Gross/Micheline Durand/Barry Tulett: Gran Diccionario Moderno español—inglés, English—Spanish Larousse. Marsella. Mexico 1984 [North American ed. 1562 p.].

Gattel 1803 = Claude Marie Gattel: Nuevo Diccionario portátil, español e inglés. Paris 1803 [908 p.; London 1809].

Gillhoff 1963 = Gerd A. Gillhoff: Crowell's Spanish—English and English—Spanish Dictionary. New York 1963 [1272 p.].

Giral Delpino 1763 = Hippolyto San José Giral Delpino: Diccionario, español e inglés e inglés y español. London 1763 [763 p.].

Las Casas 1570 = Cristóbal de Las Casas: Vocabulario de las dos lenguas toscana y castellana. Seville 1570 [247 p.].

Lopes/Bensley 1878 = José M. Lopes/Edward R. Bensley: Nuevo Diccionario inglés—español y español—inglés. Paris 1878 [1501 p.; Supplement 1910 ed. M. de la Torre/E. Troughton].

Maccragh 1963 = Esteban Maccragh: Nuevo diccionario inglés—español. Barcelona 1963 [768 p.].

MacDonald/Steiner 1985 = C. C. Smith/G. A. Davies/H. B. Hall/Gerald J. MacDonald/Roger J. Steiner: Langenscheidt's Pocket Spanish Dictionary. New York. Berlin. Munich. Vienna. Zurich 1985 [656 p.].

MacDonald/Steiner 1988 = C. C. Smith/G. A. Davies/H. B. Hall/Gerald J. MacDonald/Roger J. Steiner: Langenscheidt's New Standard Spanish Dictionary. New York. Berlin. Munich. Vienna. Zurich 1988 [1103 p.].

MacHale 1964 = Carlos F. MacHale: VOX Diccionario inglés—español español—inglés. Barcelona 1964 [1448 p.; 7th ed. 1975].

Martínez Amador 1946 = Emilio M. Martínez Amador: English—Spanish and Spanish—English Dictionary. Barcelona 1946 [1910 p.; 1951; London 1957].

McLaughlin 1911 = Arturo Angeli/J. McLaughlin: A New English—Spanish and Spanish—English Dictionary. Philadelphia n. d. [1349 p.; 1st ed. 1911].

Minsheu 1599 = John Minsheu: A Dictionarie in Spanish and English. London 1599 [391 p.].

Minsheu 1617 = John Minsheu: A Most Copious Spanish Dictionarie, with Latine and English. London 1617 [200 p.; an appendix to The Guide into the Tongues].

Nebrija 1492 = Elio Antonio de Nebrija Grammatici Lexicon ex sermone latino in hispaniensen. Salamanca 1492.

Neuman 1802 = Henry Neuman: A New Dictionary of the Spanish and English Languages. 2 vol. London 1802 [1262 p.; 3d ed. 1817, 1326 p.].

Neuman/Baretti 1823 = Henry Neuman/Joseph Baretti: Neuman and Baretti's Dictionary of the Spanish and English Languages. 2 vol. London 1823 [1326 p.; Boston 1827, 1832, 1845—7].

Peers 1959 = Edgar Allison Peers/José V. Barragán/Francesco A. Vinyals/Jorge Arturo Mora: Cassell's Spanish—English English—Spanish Dictionary. London 1959 [1491 p.; rev. New York 1978 by Anthony Gooch/Angel García de Paredes].

Pei 1968 = Mario A. Pei/Salvatore Ramondino: The New World Spanish—English and English—Spanish Dictionary. New York 1968 [584 p.].

Percyvall 1591 = Richard Percyvall: A Dictionarie in Spanish, English, and Latine. London 1591 [184 p.; II Bibliotheca Hispánica].

Pineda 1740 = Pedro Pineda: Diccionario, español e inglés e inglés y español. London 1740 [757 p.].

Raventós 1953 = Margaret H. Raventós: The English Universities Press Modern Spanish Dictionary. London 1963 [1230 p.].

Senerth/Sola 1986 = Diane Senerth/Mauricio Sola: The American Heritage Larousse Spanish Dictionary. Boston 1986 [1152 p.].

Senerth/Sola 1989 = Diane Senerth/Mauricio Sola: The Concise American Heritage Larousse Spanish Dictionary. Boston 1989 [616 p.].

Seoane 1831 = Mateo Seoane y Sobral: Neuman and Baretti's Dictionary of the Spanish and English Languages. London 1831 [ed. S. H. Blanc, Paris 1848].

Smith 1966 = C. C. Smith/G. A. Davies/H. B. Hall: Langenscheidt's Standard Dictionary of the English and Spanish Languages. Berlin. Munich. Zurich 1966 [1070 p.; Barcelona 1979, Berkeley 1982].

Smith 1971 = Colin Smith/Manuel Bermejo Marcos/Eugenio Chang-Rodríguez: Collins Spanish—English English—Spanish Dictionary. London. Glasgow 1971 [1280 p.].

Smith 1988 = Colin Smith et al.: Collins Spanish-English English-Spanish Dictionary. 2nd ed. London. Glasgow. Toronto 1988 [1579 p.; 1989, 1990].

Steinhardt 1944 = Steinhardt Diccionario inglés—español y español—inglés. Ed. Hemisferio. Buenos Aires 1944 [1456 p.].

Stevens 1705—6 = Captain John Stevens: A Dictionary English and Spanish. London 1705—6. 2 vol. [518 p.; 2d ed. 1726].

Velázquez 1852 = Mariano Velázquez de la Cadena: Seoane's Neuman and Baretti by Velázquez, A Pronouncing Dictionary of the Spanish and English Languages. New York 1852 [Ed. 1885].

Velázquez 1900 = Mariano Velázquez de la Cadena/Juan S. Iribas/Edward Gray: The New Revised Velázquez Spanish and English Diction-

ary. New York 1900 [1483 p.; Chicago · New York 1942, 1523 p., sup. by Carlos Toral; 1956].
Velázquez 1959 = Mariano Velázquez de la Cadena/Edward Gray/Juan Iribas/Ida Navarro Hinojosa: New Revised Velázquez Spanish and English Dictionary. Chicago·New York 1959 [1480 p.; rev. New York 1985 + supplement by R. J. Nelson].
Williams 1955 = Edwin B. Williams: Holt Spanish and English Dictionary. New York 1955 [1 277 p.; rev. 1962, 1277 p.].
Williams 1963 = Edwin B. Williams: Dictionary of Spanish and English, Expanded Edition. New York 1963 [1323 p.; 1972].
Williams 1968 = Edwin B. Williams: The Bantam New College Spanish and English Dictionary. New York 1968 [723 p.].
Williams 1980 = Edwin B. Williams: Diccionario inglés y español. New York 1980 [750 p.].

18.2. Other Publications

Fabbri 1979 = Maurizio Fabbri: A Bibliography of Hispanic Dictionaries. Imola 1979.

Martín-Gamero 1961 = Sofía Martín-Gamero: La Enseñanza del inglés en España (desde la edad media hasta el siglo XIX). Madrid 1961.
Steiner 1970 = Roger J. Steiner: Two Centuries of Spanish and English Bilingual Lexicography, 1590—1800. The Hague. Paris 1970.
Steiner 1985 = Roger J. Steiner: Lexicon in the First Spanish—English Dictionary. In: Hispanic Linguistics 2. 1985, 87—98.
Steiner 1986 = Roger J. Steiner: The Three-Century Recension in Spanish and English Lexicography. In: History of Lexicography. Ed. R. Hartmann. Amsterdam 1986, 229—240.
Williams 1959 = Edwin B. Williams: The Problems of Bilingual Lexicography Particularly as Applied to Spanish and English. In: Hispanic Review 27. 1959, 246—253.
Williams 1960 = Edwin B. Williams: Analysis of the Problem of Meaning Discrimination in Spanish and English Bilingual Lexicography. In: Babel 6. 1960, 121—125.

Roger Jacob Steiner,
Newark, Delaware (USA)

309. La lexicographie bilingue anglais-français, français-anglais

1. De Palsgrave à Cotgrave
2. Miège et Boyer
3. Le 20ᵉ siècle
4. Bibliographie choisie

1. De Palsgrave à Cotgrave

Pendant des siècles le dictionnaire français-anglais fut l'apanage de l'Angleterre qui désirait accéder à la langue française et non l'inverse. Le premier, John Palsgrave intègre dans sa grammaire française (1530) un dictionnaire anglais-français qui permet aux Anglais de s'exprimer en français (Stein 1985, Kibbee 1985, 1986). Bien que le vocabulaire soit divisé selon les parties du discours (Hausmann 1980), il s'agit d'un authentique dictionnaire alphabétique de 20 000 entrées, d'une richesse particulière dans la partie consacrée aux verbes. La traduction française de nombreuses phrases-exemples ne semble d'ailleurs pas encore avoir été mise à profit par la lexicologie française malgré la réédition commode de F. Génin en 1852.

Palsgrave 1530 précède, au 16ᵉ siècle, tous les autres dictionnaires reliant deux langues modernes, le dictionnaire gallois-anglais (1547) de W. Salesbury (Stein 1985), le dictionnaire italien-anglais (1550) de W. Thomas (Tancke 1984), le *Dictionnaire en françois et flameng ou bas allemand* (Anvers 1552) de Claude Luython (Claes 1980, 137), pour ne citer que les tout premiers.

Tant la naissance de l'intellectualisme moderne est liée à la Réforme, tant l'intolérance religieuse des 16ᵉ et 17ᵉ siècles a contribué à promouvoir la lexicographie bilingue. Parmi les premiers réfugiés huguenots figure Claude de Sainliens (Claudius Hollyband) qui, résidant en Angleterre depuis 1564 (Farrer 1908), publie sous son nom en 1580 un dictionnaire français-anglais fort ressemblant au *Dictionarie French and English* de 1571 qu'on a l'habitude d'attribuer à Lucas Harrison et que Hollyband a ou bien produit lui-même ou bien copié sans scrupule. Hollyband 1593, version élargie, reprend d'ailleurs le titre de Harrison 1571 (pour la comparaison des trois dictionnaires cf. Stein 1985, 245—272).

Abstraction faite de Veron 1552 où le français figure à côté de l'anglais derrière une nomenclature latine, on trouve encore des composantes françaises dans le dictionnaire anglais-latin-français de John Higgins (Huloet 1572) et surtout dans les dictionnaires anglais-latin-(grec-)français de John Baret (1573—1580) qui connaissent également un index français renvoyant à l'anglais moyennant de chiffres (Stein 1985, 273—295).

Toutefois le premier lexicographe digne de Palsgrave est Randle Cotgrave en 1611 avec son *Dictionarie* français-anglais qui compte parmi les dictionnaires les mieux étudiés qui soient (Anderson 1978, Naïs 1968, Rickard 1983, 1985, Schmidt-Küntzel 1984, Smalley 1948, Smith 1980). Cotgrave a pour seul souci de permettre aux Anglais la lecture des grands auteurs français du 16ᵉ siècle, d'où la richesse en unités lexicales absentes des dictionnaires français de l'époque. On comprend dès lors la notoriété de Cotgrave auprès des lexicologues francisants qui n'ont qu'à se féliciter d'un pareil instrument de travail. Accompagné depuis la seconde éd. de 1632 d'une partie anglais-français par Robert Sherwood, le dictionnaire de Cotgrave connaîtra quatre éditions jusqu'en 1672.

2. Miège et Boyer

Or, au cours du 17ᵉ siècle le vent linguistique a bien tourné en France. La cour ayant imposé la loi de la compréhension immédiate, la langue classique favorise l'usage nuancé d'un vocabulaire de base et rejette comme archaïque et ridicule tout le fatras lexicologique du siècle précédent. C'est pourquoi le calviniste suisse Guy Miège, né en 1644 et émigré en Angleterre en 1661, juge le moment venu de dépoussiérer Cotgrave pour publier en 1677 un *New Dictionary,* plus conforme à la réalité littéraire contemporaine. Mal lui en a pris. Le public anglais, habitué pour sa propre langue aux «hard word dictionaries» et fidèle à la prose française du 16ᵉ siècle, proteste de façon si énergique que Miège est obligé de livrer deux ans plus tard un supplément au titre coléreux de *Dictionary of barbarous French*.

Dans sa préface, Miège avoue s'être basé, pour la partie français-anglais, sur le *Dictionnaire Royal des langues françoise et latine* du père François Pomey (1664 ou 1671) et à l'instar de Pomey, qui avait produit en 1667 un *Petit Dictionnaire royal,* Miège publie en 1684 un *Short Dictionary*. Cette dépendance met par ailleurs en lumière le rôle des dictionnaires français-latin qui, au-delà de la naissance des dictionnaires français monolingues à partir de 1680, alimentent la lexicographie bilingue avec le français (cf. les titres étudiés par Bray 1986, 20—32 et Hausmann 1987; d'autres auteurs, comme Guy Tachard et Guillaume Lebrun, seraient dignes de l'attention des métalexicographes).

Sitôt Miège 1677 paru, commence la publication coup sur coup des trois grands dictionnaires monolingues du français classique de P. Richelet en 1680, de F. Furetière en 1690 et de l'Académie en 1694 (cf. art. 185). Comment ne pas en profiter pour la lexicographie bilingue? Celui qui s'en charge à Londres s'appelle Abel Boyer, né en 1667 à Castres, chassé par la révocation de l'édit de Nantes et arrivé en Angleterre en 1691 après un séjour à l'université hollandaise de Franeker (Gibbs 1978 ss.). Le dictionnaire «royal» de Boyer 1699, tout comme son abrégé de 1700, sera l'un des plus grands succès dictionnairiques de tous les temps et, cent cinquante ans plus tard, les dictionnaires français-anglais porteront encore le nom de Boyer. Si la qualité de la partie français-anglais y est pour quelque chose, le succès est plus encore dû à la partie anglais-français, doublée par rapport à celle de Miège. En l'absence d'un dictionnaire général monolingue de l'anglais, Boyer 1699 est la meilleure description du vocabulaire qui existe à l'époque; il alimentera non seulement le premier grand dictionnaire anglais-allemand (cf. Hausmann/Cop 1985) mais surtout celui de S. Johnson qui y puise un grand nombre de *phrasal verbs* (Osselton 1986).

La France du 17ᵉ siècle ne s'intéressait guère à l'anglais. Le 18ᵉ siècle, en revanche, versant dans une véritable anglomanie (mot attesté depuis 1754), profitera largement du dictionnaire de Boyer, qui dès le début du siècle paraît également à Amsterdam et depuis 1768 à Lyon. Le dictionnaire sera successivement augmenté et remanié, certaines éditions prenant le nom du remanieur. C'est ainsi que Louis Chambaud publiera en 1761 une nouvelle édition de la partie français-anglais à laquelle J. B. Robinet ajoutera en 1776 une partie anglais-français, le tout publié à la fois à Londres et à Paris. Les éditions les plus estimées, soit du Boyer, soit du Chambaud/Robinet sont celles de Garner 1802, de J. Th. H. Des Carrières (Chambaud 1805), de Fain 1817 et finalement l'immense dictionnaire de Fleming/Tibbins 1839—43 qui, s'il ne se pare plus du nom de Boyer, lui doit toujours une bonne partie de son contenu. Le rapport de forces culturel étant désormais renversé, le Fleming/Tibbins paraît chez F. Didot à Paris (dernière éd. en 1889).

3. Le 20ᵉ siècle

Il va de soi qu'un dictionnaire de près de deux cents ans a beau être révisé et remanié, il charrie les scories de l'histoire. Et pourtant celui de Boyer restera longtemps sans rival et, après son essoufflement, sans successeur. En attendant, le public se contente d'un grand nombre de dictionnaires de taille moyenne qui, eux aussi, connaissent souvent une longévité étonnante (Spiers 1846, Cassell's 1853, Bellows 1872 qui présente les deux parties sur la même page, Clifton/Grimaux 1872, Elwall 1895, Edgren 1901, Petit 1934).

Le vrai successeur de Boyer sera, juste avant la Seconde Guerre Mondiale, le *Harrap's Standard* de J. E. Mansion (1934/39), remplacé depuis par le *Harrap's New Standard* (Ledésert 1972/80). Ce dictionnaire, de facture peu sophistiquée, impressionne par le nombre d'expressions et d'exemples traduits en entier.

Seul peut prétendre au succès de vente le bilingue bipartiel en un volume. Harrap l'a compris dès les années quarante en dérivant du *Standard* un *Shorter* refondu en 1982 (Collin et al. 1982). Sans concurrent pendant vingt ans, le *Shorter* a vu naître un premier rival en 1960 (Dubois 1960), un deuxième en 1978 (Robert/Collins). Ce dernier s'est imposé avec panache (tout comme d'autres dictionnaires bilingues dont la maison Collins a entrepris la publication depuis 1971). L'édition 1987 de ce dictionnaire non seulement est ce qu'il y a de plus à jour mais encore séduit par la densité de son information en microstructure (très lisible à cause des nombreux alinéas et d'un heureux emploi de la typographie). Le Robert/Collins a raison d'opter résolument pour une description en profondeur du vocabulaire commun et de négliger les termes techniques dont le stock inépuisable et toujours en renouvellement a sa place dans les dictionnaires techniques spécialisés. Pour certaines caractéristiques le Robert/Collins demande un utilisateur averti, le système de marquage étant partiellement iconique et les dérivés et composés étant sous-lemmatisés (*touch wood* s.v. *touch*). Sans être complètement absent du paysage lexicographique en question, les États-Unis (Steiner 1972, honorable mais fort réduit) et le Canada (Vinay 1962, un nouveau projet semble en ce moment en chantier) ne se montrent guère entreprenants. A signaler le dynamisme de la lexicographie d'apprentissage (depuis les dictionnaires de Françoise Dubois-Charlier, cf. art. 305 et Girard et al. 1982) dont témoigne aussi le sympathique Tintin 1989.

A l'avenir, le dictionnaire anglais-français, français-anglais devra se trouver au centre de la politique linguistique française. La montée irrésistible de l'anglais vers un statut de langue internationale — le latin du troisième millénaire — fera de ce dictionnaire la pièce maîtresse dans l'architecture d'une politique de français langue étrangère. Le monde, après avoir appris l'anglais, apprendra le français via l'anglais. Or il est peu probable que la Grande Bretagne se chargera encore longtemps du poids principal de la lexicographie bilingue avec le français. La désaffection américaine est à cet égard de mauvaise augure. C'est donc à la France qu'il appartiendra de créer de véritables banques de données bilingues dont on pourra dériver des dictionnaires taillés sur mesure. La Francophonie (notamment le Canada) devrait aider la France dans cette tâche.

4. Bibliographie choisie

4.1. Dictionnaires

Baret 1573 = John Baret: An Alvearie or Triple Dictionarie, in Englyshe, Latin, and French. London 1573 [2ᵉ éd.: An Alvearie or Quadruple Dictionarie, Containing Foure Sundry Tongues, London 1580].

Bellows 1872 = John Bellows: Dictionary for the Pocket. French and English, English and French. Both Divisions on the Same Page. London 1872 [605 p.; New York. Paris jusqu'en 1951].

Boyer 1699 = Abel Boyer: The Royal Dictionary. In Two Parts. First, French and English. Secondly, English and French. London 1699 [644, 744 p.].

Boyer 1700 = Abel Boyer: The Royal Dictionary, Abridged. London 1700.

Cassell's = Cassell's French Dictionary. London 1853 [517 p.; éd. Jean-Louis de Lolme, 1881; éd. James Boïelle, autre titre: Heath's French and English Dictionary, Boston 1903, 595, 616 p.; éd. V. Payen-Payne, 1905, 1910; éd. E. A. Baker 1920; 8ᵉ éd. cf. Girard 1968].

Chambaud 1761 = Louis Chambaud: Dictionary French and English. London 1761.

Chambaud 1776 = Louis Chambaud: Nouveau Dictionnaire françois-anglois et anglois-françois. Ed. J. B. Robinet. Amsterdam. Rotterdam 1776 [744, 650 p. Nouvelle éd. revue, corrigée et augmentée du double par John Thomas Hérissant Des Carrières. 2 vol. London 1805].

Chevalley 1934 = Abel Chevalley/Marguerite Chevalley: The Concise Oxford French Dictionary Part 1. French-English. Oxford 1966 [XX, 908 p.; 1e éd. 1934; pour la partie anglais-français, cf. Goodridge 1940; cf. Oxford 1989].

Clifton 1872 = Ebenezer Clifton/Adrian Grimaux: A New Dictionary of the French and English Languages. Paris 1872 [éd. J. McLaughlin, 1906, 1341 p., jusqu' en 1929; éd. L. Dhaleine jusqu'en 1962; éd. John Bell, 1968].

Collin et al. 1982 = Peter Collin/Helen Knox/Margaret Ledésert/René Ledésert: Harrap's New Shorter French and English Dictionary. London. Paris 1982 [XVII, 983, 32, 798 p. 1e éd. 1940—1944].

Cotgrave 1611 = Randle Cotgrave: A Dictionarie of the French and English Tongues. London 1611 [sans pag. 1082 p.; Reprint 1950, Columbia, SCar. 2e éd. 1632 by Robert Sherwood; 3e éd. 1650; 4e éd. 1672].

Deletanville 1779 = Thomas Deletanville: A New French Dictionary: French and English, English and French. 2e éd. London 1779 [jusqu'en 1814].

Dubois 1981 = Marguerite-Marie Dubois: Dictionnaire français-anglais Saturne. English-French Dictionary Saturne. Nouv. éd. augmentée de 10 000 termes. Paris 1981 [XVI, 796, XVI, XVI, 782 p., 1e éd. 1960].

Dufief 1810 = Nicolas Gouin Dufief: New Universal and Pronouncing Dictionary of the French and English Languages. 3 vols. Philadelphia 1810.

Edgren 1901 = August Hjalmar Edgren/Percy B. Burnett: A French and English Dictionary. New York 1901 [1252 p.; depuis 1840/43; jusqu'en 1938].

Elwall 1895 = Alfred Elwall: Dictionnaire anglais-français. Paris 1895 [jusqu'en 1930].

Fain 1817 = A. Boyer/L. Chambaud/J. Garner/M. Des Carrières: Dictionnaire anglois-françois et françois-anglois. Nouv. éd., rev. et corr. par L.-F. Fain. 2 vol. Paris 1817.

Fleming/Tibbins 1839—43 = Charles Fleming/J. Tibbins: The Royal Dictionary, English and French and French and English. Vol. I: English and French. Grand Dictionnaire anglais-français, français-anglais. Tome II: Français-Anglais. Paris 1839—1843 [1234, 1104 p. jusqu'en 1889].

Garner 1802 = John Garner: Le nouveau dictionnaire universel françois-anglois et anglois-françois. 2 vol. Rouen 1802.

Girard 1968 = New French-English, English-French Dictionary. 8e éd. par Denis Girard et al. London 1968 [XVI, 762, 655 p.].

Girard et al. 1982 = Denis Girard/William B. Barrie/André Chaptal/Henri Yvinec: Dictionnaire de l'anglais d'aujourd'hui. Anglais-français/français-anglais. Paris 1982 [633 p.].

Goodridge 1940 = G. W. F. R. Goodridge: A Practical English-French Dictionary for English-Speaking Countries. Oxford 1940 [296 p.; 1942, 1963; cf. Oxford 1989].

Harrison 1571 = [Lucas Harrison]: A Dictionarie French and English. London 1571.

Hollyband 1580 = Claudius Hollyband [Claude de Sainliens]: The Treasurie of the French Tong. London 1580 [2e éd.: A Dictionarie French and English, London 1593; Reprint Menston 1970].

Huloet 1572 = Richard Huloet: Huloet's Dictionarie. Another Ed. of the Abecedarium Anglo-Latinum. By John Higgins. London 1572.

Kettridge 1986 = Julius Ornan Kettridge: French Dictionary. French-English. English-French. Completely revised ed. London 1986 [566 p.; 1e éd. 1936].

Ledésert 1972/1980 = J. E. Mansion: Harrap's New Standard French and English Dictionary. Rev. and Ed. by R. P. L. Ledésert/Margaret Ledésert. 1: French-English A—I. 2: French-English J—Z. 3: English-French A—K. 4: L—Z. 4 vol. London. Paris 1972, 1980 [XXIX, 2549 p.].

Mansion 1934/1939 = J. E. Mansion: Harrap's Standard French and English Dictionary. French-English. English-French. London 1934, 1939 [912, 1488 p.; F—E, rev. ed. 1940; Supplements 3e éd. 1962]

Miège 1677 = Guy Miège: A New Dictionary French and English, With Another English and French (...). London 1677 [860 + 452 p. 1679, 1688, 1700, autre titre: Great French Dictionary, 1688].

Miège 1679 = Guy Miège: A Dictionary of Barbarous French. London 1679.

Miège 1684 = Guy Miège: A Short Dictionary English and French, With Another French and English. London 1684 [456 + 340 p. jusqu'en 1703; autre titre: The Short French Dictionary, 1690].

Nugent 1767 = Thomas Nugent: A New Pocket Dictionary of the French and English Languages. London 1767.

Oxford 1989 = N. Ferrar/Joyce Hutchinson/Jean-Dominique Biard: The Concise Oxford French Dictionary. French-English. English-French. New Edition. Oxford 1989 [912 p. cf. Chevalley 1934 et Goodridge 1940].

Palsgrave 1530 = John Palsgrave: Lesclarcissement de la langue francoyse. London 1530 [Ed. F. Génin, Paris 1852, 889 p., Reprint of the original, Menston 1970].

Petit 1934 = Charles Petit: Dictionnaire anglais-français. Paris 1934 [1272 p. augm. par W. Savage/E. Renoir].

Pomey 1664 = François Pomey: Dictionnaire royal des langues françoise et latine. Lyon 1664 [éd. 1671, 1676, 1708, 1716; Petit dictionnaire royal, 1667, 1670, 1710, 1723].

Potier/Bovaird = L. Potier/A. Bovaird: Dictionnaire anglais-français, français-anglais. Moderne — pratique — idiomatique. Paris s.d. (1989) [559 p.].

Robert/Collins 1987 = Beryl T. Atkins/Alain Duval/Rosemary C. Milne et al.: Robert Collins Dictionnaire français-anglais, anglais-français/Collins. Robert French-English, English-French Dictionary. Nouv. éd. London. Glasgow. Toronto. Paris 1987 [768, 930 p. First ed. 1978, 717, 781 p.].

Sherwood 1632 = Robert Sherwood: Dictionnaire, Anglois et François (...). A Dictionarie English and French (...). London 1632 [2ᵉ éd. 1650; 3ᵉ éd. 1660; 4ᵉ éd. 1672].

Spiers 1846 = Alexander Spiers: General French and English Dictionary. 2 vol. Paris 1846—1849 [728 p.; jusqu'en 1882; sous le titre: Spiers' and Surenne's English-French Pronouncing Dictionary jusqu'en 1930].

Steiner 1972 = Robert J. Steiner: The New College French and English Dictionary. New York 1972 [XIV, 341, 379 p.].

Tarver 1845 = J. C. Tarver: The Royal Phraseological English-French, French-English Dictionary. London 1845 [jusqu'en 1867].

Tintin 1989 = Hélène Houssemaine-Florent/David Jones: Tintin au pays des mots. Tintin Illustrated Dictionary. Anglais-Français, Français-Anglais. Bromley 1989 [214, XIV, 215 p.].

Urwin 1968 = Kenneth Urwin: Langenscheidt's Standard Dictionary of the French and English Languages. London 1968 [1216 p.; autre titre: Dictionnaire pratique français-anglais, anglais-français, Paris 1968].

Veron 1552 = John Veron: Dictionariolum puerorum tribus linguis, Latina, Anglica & Gallica conscriptum. London 1552.

Vinay 1962 = Jean-Paul Vinay/P. Daviault/H. Alexandre: Everyman's French-English Dictionary. With Special Reference to Canada. London 1962 [XXVI, 862 p.; autre titre: The Canadian Dictionary French-English, English-French. Concise Ed.].

4.2. Travaux

Anderson 1978 = James David Anderson: The Development of the English-French, French-English Bilingual Dictionary. A Study in Comparative Lexicography. London 1978 (Supplem. to Word 28, 3, Dec. 1972, Monograph No. 6).

Bray 1986 = Laurent Bray: César-Pierre Richelet (1626—1698). Biographie et œuvre lexicographique. Tübingen 1986 (Lexicographica Series Maior 15).

Claes 1980 = Frans M. Claes: A Bibliography of Netherlandic Dictionaries. Amsterdam 1980.

Farrer 1908 = Lucy E. Farrer: Un devancier de Cotgrave. La vie et les œuvres de Claude de Sainliens alias Claudius Hollyband. Paris 1908.

Gibbs 1978 ss. = Graham C. Gibbs: Abel Boyer Gallo-Anglus Glossographus et Historicus, 1667—1729. In: Proceedings of the Huguenot Society of London 1978, 87—98; 1983, 46—59.

Hausmann 1980 = Franz Josef Hausmann: Louis Meigret. Humaniste et Linguiste. Tübingen 1980 (Lingua et traditio 6).

Hausmann 1987 = Franz Josef Hausmann: Sprachwissenschaft im Wörterbuchvorwort. Das französisch-lateinische Wörterbuch des Pierre Danet (1673—1691). In: Die Frühgeschichte der romanischen Philologie von Dante bis Diez. Hrsg. v. H.-J. Niederehe/B. Schlieben-Lange. Tübingen 1987 (TBL 303), 123—133.

Hausmann/Cop 1985 = Franz Josef Hausmann/Margaret Cop: Short History of English-German Lexicography. In: Symposium on Lexicography II. Ed. K. Hyldgaard-Jensen/A. Zettersten. Tübingen 1985, 183—198.

Kibbee 1985 = Douglas A. Kibbee: Progress in Bilingual Lexicography During the Renaissance. In: Dictionaries. Journal of the Dictionary Society of North America 7. 1985, 21—31.

Kibbee 1986 = Douglas A. Kibbee: The Humanist Period in Renaissance Bilingual Lexicography. In: The History of Lexicography. Ed. by R. R. K. Hartmann. Amsterdam. Philadelphia 1986 (Amsterdam Studies in the Theory and History of Linguistic Science III, 40), 137—146.

Klaar 1975 = R. M. Klaar: French Dictionaries. London 1975.

Naïs 1968 = Hélène Naïs: Le Dictionarie of the French and English Tongues. In: Verba et Vocabula. Ernst Gamillscheg zum 80. Geburtstag. München 1968, 343—357.

Osselton 1986 = Noel E. Osselton: Dr. Johnson and the English phrasal verb. In: Lexicography. An Emerging International Profession. Ed. R. Ilson. Manchester 1986, 7—16.

Rickard 1983 = Peter Rickard: Le «Dictionarie» franco-anglais de Cotgrave (1611). In: Cahiers de l'Association internationale d'études françaises 35. 1983, 7—22, 267—269.

Rickard 1985 = Peter Rickard: Les Essais de Montaigne et le Dictionnaire franco-anglais de Cotgrave (1611). In: Cahiers de Lexicologie 47. 1985, 121—137.

Schmidt-Küntzel 1984 = Michèle Schmidt-Küntzel: Cotgrave et sa source rabelaisienne. Diss. Köln 1984.

Smalley 1948 = Vera E. Smalley: The Sources of A Dictionarie of the French and English Tongues by Randle Cotgrave. Baltimore 1948.

Smith 1980 = P. M. Smith: Henri Estienne et Cotgrave. In: Le Français Moderne 48. 1980, 246—255.

Stein 1985 = Gabriele Stein: The English Dictionary Before Cawdrey. Tübingen 1985 (Lexicographica Series Maior 9).

Tancke 1984 = Gunnar Tancke: Die italienischen Wörterbücher von den Anfängen bis zum Erscheinen des «Vocabolario degli Accademici della Crusca» (1612). Bestandsaufnahme und Analyse. Tübingen 1984 (Beihefte zur Zeitschrift für romanische Philologie 198).

Franz Josef Hausmann, Erlangen
(République Fédérale d'Allemagne)

310. Bilingual Lexicography: English-German, German-English

1. Introduction
2. Layout
3. How Many Words
4. Pronunciation and Stress
5. Collocations
6. Syntax
7. Semantics
8. Conclusion
9. Selected Bibliography

1. Introduction

This article deals with bilingual English-German (= EG), German-English (= GE) dictionaries (= dicts.), mostly from the point of view of German-speaking users. It will look at the EG (decoding, passive) parts and particularly at the GE (encoding, active) parts to point out their strengths and weaknesses (for a corpus-based evaluation of bilingual GE-EG dicts. cf. Henke/Pätzold 1987, 110—137).

2. Layout

How easy is it for users to find the information they are looking for? Bilingual GE-EG dicts. have come a long way in the last decade in terms of clarity of print and lay-out. Now they usually strike a reasonable balance between the limited supply of space and the demand of the users who want to take in everything at one glance. Entries are split into individual sections, which moreover begin on new lines. The major divisions are, usually, first along syntactic lines and then according to meaning. Arabic and Roman numbers as well as capital and lower-case letters are used to distinguish the various meanings. Head words are displayed in bold, while different type faces and print sizes are used for style or field labels, illustrative phrases, translations, cross references and semantic or syntactic comments. Some dicts. also use pictorial symbols for various purposes. So users can find out very quickly how articles are structured, though there are still enormous differences between works, sometimes even from the same publishing house.

For example, Pons-Globalwörterbuch/Schöffler-Weis (= PGSW) and Pons-Globalwörterbuch (PGW), though bearing confusingly, if not misleadingly, similar titles, are as different as chalk and cheese. While PGW illustrates almost all the new virtues mentioned above (except the use of pictorial symbols to refer to subject areas), PGSW is in many ways a lexicographic fossil. Entries here still consist of monolithic blocks, with different senses and syntactic uses of the headword, and sometimes phrasal verbs, crammed into one run-on entry. Bold typeface is employed only for headwords, their compounds and derivations, and, sometimes, for the numbers for the different senses or syntactic uses of homonyms. Lack of indentation and bold type face thus combine to create eye strain, e.g. in finding the verbal, adverbial, adjectival and substantival uses of one and the same word form. With compounds and derivations, the tilde (and indeed the double tilde) is used to stand for (part of) the headword so that words can be truncated out of recognition (cf. S ~ e, s ~ en, S ~ er s.v. **Suchaktion**). The same comments apply to the two volumes from the Enzyklopädie publishers in Leipzig. While the Wörterbuch Englisch-Deutsch (= VEB1) is rather user-unfriendly (try finding the different syntactic uses of the word form *round*!), the Wörterbuch Deutsch-Englisch (VEB2) is easier on the eyes than PGSW2 as it uses only the single tilde, and that more sparingly, and employs bold numbering for different senses and word classes, though they do not begin on new lines. Harrap's Concise German and English Dictionary (= HCD) suffers from the same defects, but its layout is made more bearable through the use of spacing, bold print, Roman and Arabic numerals as well as lower case letters. Wildhagen Englisch-Deutsches Deutsch-Englisches Wörterbuch (= WH) divides its longer entries into indented sections, but it suffers from over-differentiation in that it employs three different types of brackets as well as single and double bars, thus creating what can only be called an optical confusion. WH2 is, moreover, bedevilled by a wealth of abbreviations of common German words, which sometimes have more than one meaning, such as the letter ⟨s⟩, which is used for *substantive, sein,* "[s] mit sein konstruiert" and "s. siehe".

The remaining dictionaries all have a good to excellent lay-out. Collins Concise German-English English-German Dictionary (= CCGD), Collins German-English English-German Dictionary (= CGD) and PGW start each syntactic use or sense group with a new line. Phrasal verbs follow directly on their simplexes, receive headword treatment and are highlighted by a special sign (◆). The Langenscheidt dicts. Langenscheidts Enzyklopädisches Wörterbuch der englischen und deutschen Sprache (= LEW) and Langenscheidts Großwörterbuch (= LGW) put fixed expressions in a separate paragraph ("Besondere Redewendungen"). Also, Langenscheidt has for many years used pictorial symbols like a steam engine to signal railway terms or crossed swords to refer to military language. Other signs may be less obvious, e.g. Mercury's caduceus for economic language or a pair of compasses for mathematics. Sadly, Langenscheidts Großes Schulwörterbuch (= LGSW) is the only Langenscheidt dictionary to keep these symbols. I would like to see pictographic symbols in all the dicts. and more of them (a chef's hat for cookery terms?). This would make a welcome change from meta-languages that consist of words only. In our ever more visually-oriented world lexicographers could thus be fashionable and increase the ease of reference of their dicts. at the same time.

3. How Many Words?

The bigger and older works are better in their coverage of archaisms and historical terms. In the EG parts, items like *heriot, multure* and *pannage* are found only in Cassell's German-English, English-German Dictionary (= Cas), LEW, LGW, and WH. Words and meanings from the pages of Shakespeare (e.g. *apothecary, ope, sirrah; still* = always) are best covered by the Langenscheidts and WH. The other dicts. under review have little to offer in this area, because they are too small (The Bantam New College German and English Dictionary (= BNCGED), Pons-Kompaktwörterbuch (PKW), CCGD) or concentrate on the modern English vocabulary. In specialist fields like the language of literary criticism LGW and LEW lead the field from WH, CGD and Cas. There is very little on the language of modern linguistics in any of the dicts., though LEW and LGW again offer the most. For its size, VEB1 has a surprising number of technical terms from medicine and the natural sciences. The language of computing and computers, though arguably among the most important specialist fields these days, is not well represented as yet. Dicts. divide here into two groups, those that do not even have "Computer" as one of the translations of *computer* (WH1, LEW1, Cas, PGSW1, VEB1), and those which include it. While LGW is the only work to list RAM and ROM, we find such items as "Laufwerk" (drive), "Festplatte" (hard disk) and "menügesteuert" (menu-driven) only in CCGD2, which offers perhaps the most up-to-date treatment. The modern, everyday English of novels and newspapers is not served well by Cas 2, LEW1, PGSW1, VEB1 and WH1. BNCGED also scores low, but HCD is better than its size would lead one to expect. The best Pons-Collins dicts. come into their own here, with CGD and PGW including as many items and illustrative examples, if not more, than LGW and LGSW.

In the GE parts, there are also great differences between dicts. in their coverage of modern, non-specialist German vocabulary as found in newspapers. The absence of *jdn. anmachen, Elefantenhochzeit, Entsorgung, Frührentner, Italowestern* or *jobben* from the pages of Cas1, LEW2, The Oxford-Harrap Standard German-English Dictionary (OHSGED), PGSW2 and WH2 must no doubt be put down to the fact that they were last revised many years ago, though Cas1 and PGSW2 came out in new editions as recently as 1978. LGSW2 and HCD2 list fewer items than LGW1, CGD, CCGD and PGW2. Despite its small size, CCGD manages to be up-to-date with *sich einbringen, GAU, hinterfragen* and *Ozonschicht*. Conversely, Cas1, WH2 and PGSW2 contain a number of old-fashioned items that few people will want to look up these days, cf. *Aftergelehrsamkeit, Markscheider, Studentenmädel* (all WH2). This type of word has its place in encyclopedic works like LEW and OHSGED, but is particularly out of place in modern, pocket-size dicts. like BNCGED, which lists *Hauptschriftleiter* and *Oberpostamt,* but does not include *Chefredakteur* and *Hauptpostamt.* For a general dict. of its size, PGSW2 includes a surprising number of military terms, while PKW2 has a special line in sexual language (cf s.vv. *blasen, Fakultät* and *kalt*). VEB2 is valuable for its numerous items current in (and often restricted to) the former German Democratic Republic. Examples are *Pionier, Plan* and *Plaste,* and compounds s.vv. *Arbeiter* and *Partei,* but also less obvious items, though similarly without regional label, like *Fremdsprachenkabinett, Platzkartenwagen* and *Theateranrecht*. It also offers a number of technical terms like *Melkkarussell, Rosarium, Rotlauf,* and *Rundstrickmaschine,* of which PGW and CGD have only *Rotlauf,* while even LEW does not list *Melkkarussell.*

4. Pronunciation and Stress

All dicts. put the information on how English words are pronounced and stressed only in the EG part, although it is perhaps even more needed in the GE part. No doubt they do it to save space, but by the same token further space could be saved if they also listed the lexical and syntactic combinations of lexemes only in the passive part. Thankfully, no dict. would dream of doing that, but it is difficult to see why this differential treatment should be continued in an age that attaches the greatest importance to speaking skills.

Most dicts. boast that they pay great attention to American English, and yet they consistently fail to list /d/ as the realization of medial ⟨t⟩ in words like *matter* and *letter*, even though LGW for instance usually records final /r/. Similarly, one looks in vain for the US variants in stress and pronunciation of the noun *cigarette*, adjectives like *agile, fertile* or *hostile*, and proper names like *Anthony, Bernard* or *Maurice*.

Again, none of the dicts. takes into account that in English polysyllabic words the stress shifts to an earlier syllable when the word is followed by another stress. Examples are *abso'lutely* vs *'absolutely 'wonderful* and *fif'teen* vs *'fifteen 'men*. Stress is, moreover, often not marked for adverbs, cf. LGW1, LHE1, WH1 and HCD1 s.v. *temporarily*. Dicts. are also poor at recording alternative stress in such items as *'ap'plicable, 'de'spicable* or *'ha'rass*. Finally, bilingual dicts., unlike some monolingual learners' dicts., do not mark stress in multi-word items, esp. fixed expressions, where the stress cannot be predicted, cf. *to get on like a 'house on fire; to keep body and 'soul together,* and *you can say 'that again*.

5. Collocations

Collocations are often unpredictable and are therefore extremely important for encoding. Generally speaking, coverage of collocations depends on the age and size of the dicts., and the modernity of their lexicographic conception. Neither BNCGED nor Cas list the English for *Ähnlichkeit haben*, though this seems to be for reasons of space in *BNCGED*'s case, while Cas is a dict. that has never been properly modernized. Again, VEB2 has about as many collocations as the much larger PGSW2, which is very old-fashioned in its approach. OHSGED and LEW, because they are the largest dicts. and also attach great importance to syntagmatic aspects, offer more collocations than the next biggest, LGW. Considering their price and size, the Pons-Collins works are remarkably rich in collocations. CGD and PGW list only slightly fewer items than LGW, and slightly more than LGSW and the vastly more voluminous WH.

Lexicographers have devised various ways of saving space in the listing of collocations. OHSGED does not give the German object, as in "einhalten ⟨...⟩ keep to (timetable, conditions, contract, fixed date, etc.)". This is fairly safe as the German-speaking users get the complete English collocation. It is certainly much more dangerous to leave something out in the target language, as is often done in CGD, PGW and CCGD. Under *verletzen*, CGD suggests that *schwer* in *er wurde schwer verletzt im Unfall* can be translated by "deeply" (s.v. *schwer*) plus a suitable form of *wound/injure/hurt*. But *deeply* can be used only in the figurative sense, while *badly, severely* or *seriously* are usually employed for the physical sense. Other dicts. leave out the verb, as with *ein Lippenbekenntnis ablegen,* where Cas, HCD, LGSW, PKW and VEB only give *lip service,* but not the verb *pay,* which cannot be guessed by the learner. Dictionaries should therefore list collocations in their entirety.

It is striking that adverb collocations are heavily under-represented. While we find the English translation of *kongeniale Übersetzung* in LEW, there is no English equivalent for *kongenial übersetzen,* and HCD is the only dict. to include the highly frequent *enjoy thoroughly*. In none of the works under review do we find *sehr bewundern, schrecklich verliebt, bei weitem vorziehen, ganz und gar/völlig zustimmen,* or double adverb constructions like *es hat mir ausgesprochen gut gefallen*. In the EG parts, no dict. lists *disagree violently, guard jealously* or *kick fiercely*.

There is even more room for improvement with larger constructions like *München führt mit zwei Punkten vor Hamburg (Munich leads by two points from Hamburg), das wird mir keine schlaflosen Nächte bereiten (I won't lose any sleep over this)* or *er ist verheiratet und hat zwei Kinder (he is married with two children)*. Dicts. are rarely aware of this syntagmatic challenge. No work includes the examples given above, though LEW and HCD offer translations of *sich jemanden zur Frau nehmen,* CGD lists "jemanden in etw schlagen" as well as "unsere Mannschaft schlug den Gegner (mit) 2:1", and LEW has "er stellte die Uhr um 10 Minuten vor".

6. Syntax

Many of the structures that will be discussed in this section cannot be found in the smallest dicts. (BNCGED, PKW, VEB). In other cases (Cas, PGSW) the reason is an old-fashioned approach to lexicography. While the biggest Collins dict., CGD, offers more constructions and illustrative examples than the works derived from it (PGW, CCGD) this is, surprisingly, not wholly true for the Langenscheidt family, where LGW has the edge not only on the smaller LGSW but also on the larger LEW.

In the EG parts, most dicts. list irregular forms of nouns and verbs as headwords (with cross-references) but WH1, HCD1, PKW1 and PGSW1 could be much better. PKW1 lists irregular verb forms and *mice*, but not *geese* and *hooves*, which are also missing from HCD1. In HCD1, *gone* and *was* are correctly analysed, while *left*, *made* and *taught* are described as past participles only. PGSW1's treatment is even more erratic and incomplete: although one finds *done*, *fell*, *gone*, *left* and *made*, the reader will look in vain for *geese*, *hooves*, *mice* and irregular *bought*, *meant*, *shone* or *wore*.

Dicts. use a simple, three-term classification for verbs as reflexive, transitive and intransitive. This needs to be further refined for the intransitive uses into at least intransitive proper and pseudo-intransitive uses with passive meaning, like *the cream beats well, the berries chill well* or *the beard never shaves off completely*. The latter are not formally marked, not very common in German, and sometimes deceptive (syntactic false friends), cf. *she bores easily* (not *sie ist ein Langweiler,* but *sie langweilt sich leicht*). Not enough of these uses are recorded in the dicts., nor have lexicographers begun to give users help with recognising and understanding them, for instance by regularly setting up separate readings for these verbs (only the Langenscheidt works do this). Moreover, none of the dicts. provide glosses (e.g. *mit passiver Bedeutung* or *can be beaten/chilled/shaved off* etc.) so that users are unlikely to gain an insight into the underlying form-meaning relationship. Finally, some dicts. provide illustrative examples for some entries, but not for others: while LGW and CGD both put *attach* into context, only LGW gives an example for *act* and *digest*, while only CGD has one for *bruise, reproduce, separate, switch on* and *unzip*.

In their EG parts, even quite big dicts. like WH, CGD, LEW or LGW do not pay enough attention to the structural possibilities of words, especially contrastively relevant ones. While many dicts. are good on preposition-noun constructions, they offer too little on adjective/noun plus preposition-constructions, such as *he made an effort at self-control* or *the Conservatives have a permanent majority over Labour*. German has impersonal constructions with adjectives like *unmöglich,* but English can have *the chronology of his works is impossible to fix* (neither CGD2 nor LGW2 list this). Other striking constructions that should be included are *I would hate/like/love you to go there,* of which CGD has two (*like* and *love*) while LEW, LGSW, WH only mention the *like*-construction (cf. also Herbst 1985, 308—331).

Similar gaps and inconsistencies can be found in the GE parts. Compare

in der Absicht zu, Antrag/Antwort/eifersüchtig auf, Auswahl aus, Dozent für, Forderung nach, froh über, Haß auf, Kritik an, Suche nach, verrückt sein auf

with the following list

Buch über, Dozent für, Fakultät für, Erfahrung mit, Methode zu, pünktlich zu, Schwierigkeiten haben zu, Spiel gegen, gut mit Kindern umgehen können, jdm bei etw unterstützen, jdn an jdn verraten.

The second list has a few verbs, but other than that the only difference between them is that the items in the first list are found in the majority of dicts., while no work under review handles the second list adequately. Only four have *nett von Ihnen daß...* [*nice of you to ...*; CGD, CCGD, PGW, HCD] and *vermeiden zu* [*avoid -ing*; LEW, LGW, CGD, PGW]. Only two dicts. help the user to decide between *have news of/from someone (Nachrichten haben von;* LGW, OHSGED), and only the Collins works mention both possibilities for *Lösung des Problems* (*solution to/of the problem;* CGD, PGW, CCGD).

Dicts. also rarely point out or illustrate syntactic restrictions. Nowhere can we learn that English has figurative *to break the ice* in both the active and the passive, while German uses it only in the passive. No dict. tells the German user that *everything* should be used in unmarked contexts instead of *all* in *er erzählte mir alles,* nor do they give illustrative examples. CGD, it is true, only lists *everything* as an equivalent, but LGW's entry runs like this: "all, everything, all things, the whole (of it), the lot ⟨...⟩". In the productive parts of dicts., where it is needed, we get no help on where to put the object of phrasal verbs, though the Collins dicts. provide information on this point at least in the EG part. While monolingual learners' dicts. often include this information (also on subject-verb concord and the correct choice of the simple or expanded form), their bilingual GE-EG counterparts are only just beginning to tackle these questions seriously.

7. Semantics

7.1. General Considerations

Dicts. set up far too many readings, particularly for such verbs as *kommen, machen, go,* or *take*. Compilers should at least marshal the many possible readings into major meaning groups, as CGD often attempts to do. Long strings of undifferentiated translations are equally pointless, and can be misleading, cf. the entry for *gering:* "⟨...⟩ slight, insignificant, negligible, trifling, minor, small, petty, unimportant (sum, difference, etc.)" (LGW). Not only the Langenscheidts, but all dictionaries commit this sin, with the exception of the small works (BNCGED, VEB), HCD and the Pons-Collins works, which latter try consciously to cut down on the number of translation equivalents. Translations should, moreover, be arranged in order of frequency, wherever that can be established. It is absurd to list the verbal uses of *water* before the noun (LGW, LGSW), or *Wählerschaft* before *Wahlkreis* (LGW s.v. constituency).

7.2. Glosses

Short semantic explanations are another means to help readers to find the right equivalent. For German-speaking users these should be in German, as they are in all the Langenscheidts as well as in PGSW, PKW, VEB, and WH. Cas and OHSGED, which use English and give next to no glosses anyway, are unhelpful. PGW, BNCGED, CGD, CCGD, and HCD are only useful in their active, GE parts, where they use German.

Glosses are particularly necessary in the many cases of divergence between two languages. An excellent, concise example is offered by LGW (s.v. *Nachricht*) for the phrase *Nachricht haben von:* "a) direkt: have heard from s.o., b) indirekt: have news of s.o." On the other hand, no dict. helps with the difference between *sorry* and *excuse me* for *Entschuldigung,* or *bucket* and *pail* for *Eimer*. There is some room for improvement here. Special mention should be made of *HCD*'s gloss "approx", e.g. s.v. *chip,* by which the German translation "der Apfel fällt nicht weit vom Stamm" is characterized as not in all respects equivalent to the English *a chip off the old block*. Similarly useful is the symbol " ≃ ", which CGD regularly employs for this purpose. The other works do not indicate whether the translations given are fully equivalent.

7.3. Labels

Labels to indicate stylistic levels or regional distribution of translations are perhaps the most important semantic help that dicts. can give in their active parts. Sadly, even good dicts. do not take enough trouble over this, cf. the entries for *abfassen:* "to draw up, draft, word, write (out) (agreement, report, letter, etc.) ⟨...⟩ to compose, pen (sermon etc.)" (OHSGED), and similarly in LEW and LGW: "1. *(verfassen)* write, compose, pen ...". Of these, *compose* and *pen* should be marked as formal and archaic respectively. For *sich besaufen* we find properly labelled slang expressions ("⟨...⟩ to get plastered (sl) or pissed (Brit sl)"; CGD), slang expressions without label ("to get plastered"; HCD), only a neutral expression ("get drunk"; Cas, LGSW, OHSGED, PGSW), to which LGW adds *tight* with stylistically fitting label, while WH lists, in addition, the stylistically adequate, but obsolete and unlabelled "to fuddle", which is current only in the passive *(he is fuddled).*

There are also a number of instances where the labels given are wrong because the items concerned have changed their stylistic status. This applies particularly to Cas, LEW, PGSW, VEB1, and WH, but in some cases also to LGSW and even LGW, which persist in labelling *bra* and *pram* in their GE parts as colloquial and, conversely, do not think *brassière* or *perambulator* formal and old-fashioned, as do most monolingual English dicts. Sometimes dicts. use regional labels that no longer apply, often because of the rapid traffic in words between the USA and other English-speaking parts of the world. This is the case with *take-home pay* (VEB: Am) and *bag lady* (LGW: Am colloq.). The converse is found in VEB2's "pink-collar jobs" for *Frauenberufe,* which seems to be restricted to the United States at present, though it is not marked as such.

Labels, though welcome in the passive part, are indispensable in the active part (cf. Kromann/Riiber/Rosbach 1984, 173). In the case of regional items, for instance, we need to know their provenance because American words or phrases often arouse strong feelings in Britain, ranging from admiration and slavish imitation (usually younger speakers) via amused or head-shaking dismissal, to open resentment. BNCGED has to be used with caution: it addresses an American audience and does not use the label US very often. While it includes almost exclusively American equivalents where there is a choice, the other dicts. try, on the whole successfully, to include both American and British English equivalents, though a division of labour between dicts. is not uncommon: for *Wahlpflichtfach* CGD1 offers only a British equivalent ("required optional subject") and LGW1 only an American one ("required elective"). Labelling is also often defective. *Full professor* (for *ordentlicher Professor*) with its US label only graces the pages of LGSW, LEW, Cas, PGSW, though the item is also found in VEB2, CGD, LGW. The British terms *afters* (LGW1, VEB2), *pudding* (PGW2, CCGD1) and *sweet* (PGW2, CCGD1, VEB2) are all found for *Nachtisch,* but the correct label is found only for *sweet* (HCD2, VEB2) and *afters* (VEB2).

7.4. Missing Meanings and Translations

In dicts. that have not been thoroughly revised, a category to which Cas, VEB1, PGSW and WH belong, one often notices translations that date them, even when the publishers try to conceal their real age. Thus, *Umwelt* und *Verschmutzung* for *environment* and *pollution* are absent from VEB1, as are *Computer, Hardware* and *Linguistik* for *computer, hardware* and *linguistics*. In addition, figurative expressions are often not given translations that capture their particular metaphorical and rhetorical flavour (cf. Hietsch 1980). *For a friend in need is a friend indeed* we find pedestrian paraphrases like "der wahre Freund zeigt sich erst in der Not" (LGW, LGSW) or "in der Not erkennt man seine Freunde" (Cas, WH). These miss the bipartite structure and the rhyme of the original, even though German does have an exact equivalent in *Freunde in der Not gehen tausend auf ein Lot* (CGD). Other omissions include numerical expressions like *in his mid-twenties, middle-thirties* etc., and *jeder zehnte Deutsche* or *10 % der Deutschen,* where English prefers to say *one in ten;* also terms from university life, like *Hausarbeit* (British *long essay,* American *term paper), Sitzung* (*session)* and *Sommerferien* (British *long vacation).* Only the Collins dicts. and PGW give *Ms.* for *Frau* (title), but this can hardly surprise when *Doktorin, Ärztin* (s.v. *doctor;* PGSW) and *Sekretärin* are not listed (s.v. *secretary;* LEW, PGSW), and LGSW and LGW fail to consider *Hochschullehrerin* s.v. *professor* 2, though they give *Professorin* s.v. *professor* 1. The new compounds ending in *-person* have also been slow to make their way into the passive parts: *chairperson* (in CGD, HCD, LGSW, but not in LGW) gets a better treatment than *spokesperson* (LGW, LGSW, HCD only *spokesman;* CGD has both *spokeswoman* and *spokesperson*).

Finally, dicts. could improve their treatment of discourse markers and situational idioms. We do not learn when *again* has the meaning *darüber hinaus* (cf. *again, we should consider the financial aspect);* HCD is the only work to list *right (then)* in the sense of "also gut!", although we are not shown a context in which it takes on that meaning. German *wir sprechen uns noch* means both the literal *"I'll be seeing you"* (LGSW; s.v. *sprechen*) and the figurative "you haven't heard the last of it" (CGD), but only LGW lists both.

7.5. Wrong Translations

There are many translations that are out of date in Cas, LEW, PGSW, VEB1 and WH (e.g. "Cowboy-, Texashose" in WH for *blue jeans*). Other translations contain bad German because they do not put the source-language items in context, cf. "bedeutungsmäßige Kategorien betreffend" (LEW1; for *notional*), or LGW's "von London abfahrend od. kommend: — train" (for *down train*). We find equally context-insensitive translations for *thirsty (work):* VEB's "durstmachend" or LGW's "⟨...⟩ (e-e) Arbeit, die Durst macht", where a little more context (as in *that is thirsty work*) would yield acceptable German *(das macht/da wird man durstig).* Similarly with *U-turn,* which occurs especially in *do a U-turn* and *No U-turns (wenden* or *eine Kehrtwendung machen, Wenden verboten),* though LGW only gives the noun *Wende.* No such excuse is available for LGW's *to put the question* "zur Abstimmung e-r Sache schreiten", instead of "zur Abstimmung über eine Sache schreiten" (LGSW), or CGD's "er wurde über mich befördert" *(he was promoted over me,* s.v. *over).* Cas2 offers the hilarious "als Mitglied der ersten Mannschaft erwählt werden" *(get one's blue,* s.v. *blue,* "das Heimatspiel" for *Heimspiel (home game)* and "ihn am Arsch lecken" for *jemandem in den Arsch kriechen (suck up to).* Cas2 as well as WH2 contain so many mistakes that one can really only use them as joke books, not serious dicts.

The same wrong syntactic analysis (infinitive instead of imperative) lies behind VEB1's "den Mut nicht verlieren" (for *never say die*) and Cas1's "⟨...⟩ not mince matters" for "sprich wie Dir der Schnabel gewachsen ist". A different mistake has caused PGSW's and PKW's "verzweifelte Hoffnung" for *hope against hope,* instead of "verzweifelt hoffen" (LGSW).

Lexical mistakes are even more frequent. English *meet a deadline* is *einen Termin einhalten,* not "erfüllen" (CGD2 s.v. *meet;* the correct collocation is found s.v. *deadline).* Conversely, LEW has "to be plagued by misfortune" *(vom Unglück verfolgt)* where *dogged by misfortune* is the established expression. "Blue-eyed" cannot translate the figurative meaning of *blauäugig (naive),* LGW notwithstanding; nor are its translations "there's a nut for every bolt" (for *jeder Topf findet seinen Deckel)* or "right-extremist" *(Rechtsextremist)* established English expressions. Sometimes we find lexicographers the victims of false friends, as in CGD's "direct mandate" *(Direktmandat)* or LGW's "excess(ive) mandate" *(Überhangsmandat).* LGW also gives (s.v. *clear)* "alles klar" (for *all clear)* instead of *alles frei (traffic), die Luft ist rein (war).* Finally, lack of correspondence between the stylistic levels of source and target language items is a frequent source of unsatisfactory translations. Thus, CGD, LGW and LGSW only give *Putzfrau, Raumpflegerin* etc. for colloquial *char,* and LGSW and LGW can only think of *hungrig* for colloquial *peckish.* In OHSGED's *Ei*-entry we find: "2 (e) *F:* Eier, money. 3 *P:* testicle", where the stylistically appropriate translations would be *bread* and *balls* respectively.

8. Conclusion

Publishers should not continue the bad habit of selling lexicographic fossils. They should revise their bilingual dicts. regularly so that the dead wood is cut out. Computers should help to achieve a uniform treatment and remove inconsistencies. Lexicographers, on the other hand, will have to make a more thorough analysis of structural differences between German and English. Most important of all, they should become more aware of users' needs, especially in language production. Above all, glosses, exact and plentiful labelling, and the provision of (examples in) context give users the help they need to speak and write correct and appropriate English.

(For the history of English-German lexicography see Hausmann/Cop 1985, Stein 1985, Hartmann, forthcoming.)

9. Selected Bibliography (K.-M.P./F.J.H.)

9.1. Dictionaries

Adelung 1783—96 = Johann Christoph Adelung: Neues grammatisch-kritisches Wörterbuch der englischen Sprache für die Deutschen; vornehmlich aus dem größeren englischen Werke des Hrn. Samuel Johnson nach dessen 4. Ausgabe gezogen, und mit vielen Wörtern, Bedeutungen und Beyspielen vermehrt. 2 vol. Leipzig 1783, 1796 [LXXII, 2016 p.].

Adler 1848 = Georg J. Adler: Dictionary of the German and English Languages (...). New York 1848 [852, 522 p. last ed. 1910].

Arnold 1736/39 = Theodor Arnold: Nathan Bailey's Englisches Wörterbuch (...). Verdeutscht und vermehrt von Th. A. Neues deutsch-englisches Wörter-Buch (...). 2 vol. Leipzig 1739 [4. ed. 1770 by Anton Ernst Klausing. 7. ed.: A Complete English Dictionary. Vollständiges deutsch-englisches Wörterbuch 1788: 958, 612 p. 9. ed. by Fahrenkrüger 1796. 12. ed.: Bailey-Fahrenkrüger's Wörterbuch der englischen Sprache by Adolf Wagner 1822: 1224, 953 p.].

BNCGED = The Bantam New College German and English Dictionary. Ed. by John C. Traupman. New York 1981 [German-English: X, 356 p. 1a—24a Grammatical explanations].

Buck 1990 = Timothy Buck: The Penguin German-English Dictionary. London 1990 [555 p.].

Cas 1+2 = Cassell's German-English (Cas1) English-German (Cas2) Dictionary. Completely revised by Harold T. Betteridge. London 1978 [XX, 1580 p. 1st ed. 1889].

Cassell's = E. Weir: Cassell's German Dictionary. London 1889 [= Heath's German Dictionary, Boston 1889. Ed. K. Breul 1906, 1936/1939. Ed. H. T. Betteridge, 1957, 1978, see Cas 1+2].

CCGD 1+2 = Collins Concise German-English (CCGD1) English-German (CCGD2) Dictionary. Peter Terrell, Horst Kopleck et al. London. Glasgow 1987 [CCGD1: XIX, 508 p.; CCGD2: 528 p.].

CGD 1+2 = Collins German-English (CGD1) English-German (CGD2) Dictionary. Ed. by Peter Terrell et al. London. Glasgow 1980 [CGD1: XVII, 792 p.; CGD2: 790 p.].

Duden-Oxford 1990 = Duden-Oxford Großwörterbuch Englisch-Deutsch, Deutsch-Englisch. Edited by the Duden Redaktion and Oxford University Press. General editors: Werner Scholze-Stubenrecht and John Sykes. Mannheim. Wien. Zürich 1990 [1696 p.].

Ebers 1793—99 = Johannes Ebers: Vollständiges Wörterbuch der englischen Sprache für die Deutschen. The New and Complete Dictionary of the German and English Languages Composed after the German Dictionary of Mr. Adelung and Mr. Schwan. 5 vol. Leipzig 1793—1799.

Ebers 1800/02 = Johannes Ebers: A New Hand-Dictionary of the English Language for the Germans and of the German Language for Englishmen. Neues Hand-Wörterbuch (...) 3 vol. Halle 1800, 1802 [1940, 1543 p.].

Fick 1802 = Johann Christian Fick: Vollständiges englisch-deutsches und deutsch-englisches Lexicon. A Complete (...) Dictionary. 2 vol. Erlangen 1802 [2. ed. by Heinrich Fick, 1823: 777, 570 p.].

Flügel 1830 = Johann Gottfried Flügel: A Complete Dictionary of the English and German Languages Containing All the Words in General Use. German-English Part by Johann Sporschil. Leipzig 1830 [3. ed. 1847—56 with a German-English Part by N. W. Meißner. Adapted to the English Student by C. A. Feiling/A. Heimann, London 1841].

Flügel 1839 = Felix Flügel/Johann Gottfried Flügel: Praktisches Wörterbuch der englischen und deutschen Sprache. Leipzig 1839 [877, 1184 p. 16. ed. 1895].

Flügel 1891 = Felix Flügel: Allgemeines englisch-deutsches und deutsch-englisches Wörterbuch. 4. gänzlich umgearb. Auflage von Dr. J. E. Flügels Vollständigem Wörterbuch. 3 vol. Braunschweig 1891 [XXXII, 1816, 923 p. Last edition 1912].

Flügel 1895 = Immanuel Schmidt/Gustav Tanger: Flügel-Schmidt-Tanger. Wörterbuch der englischen und deutschen Sprache für Hand- und Schulgebrauch. Unter besonderer Benutzung von Dr. Felix Flügels Allgemeinem (...) Wörterbuch. 2 vol. Braunschweig 1895 [4. ed. 1900: 968, 1006 p. Last ed. 1917].

Grieb 1842—47 = Christoph Friedrich Grieb: Englisch-deutsches und deutsch-englisches Wörterbuch. 2 vol. Stuttgart 1842, 1847 [1140, 1087 p. 9 eds. Continued by Schröer 1894—1902].

HCD 1+2 = Harrap's Concise German and English Dictionary. English-German (HCD1) German-English (HCD2). Robin Sawers. London 1982 [XX; HCD1: 499 p.; HCD2: 627 p.].

Héraucourt/Motekat 1952 = Will Héraucourt/Helmut Motekat: Brockhaus Illustrated Dictionary. Wiesbaden 1952 [8. ed. 1978, 680, 773 p.].

Hilpert 1828—45 = Johann Heinrich Hilpert: A Dictionary of the English and German Languages. 4 vol. Karlsruhe 1828—1845 [2756 p.].

James 1848 = William James: Vollständiges Wörterbuch der englischen und deutschen Sprache. Leipzig 1848. [Continued by Wildhagen/Héraucourt 1938/1953].

Köhler 1859—61 = Friedrich Köhler: Vollständigstes englisch-deutsches und deutsch-englisches Handwörterbuch. Leipzig 1859, 1861 [520, 594 p. Last ed. by H. Kißling 1946].

LEW 1+2 = Langenscheidts Enzyklopädisches Wörterbuch der englischen und deutschen Sprache. Teil I: Englisch-Deutsch (LEW1). Völlige Neubearbeitung 1962, edited by Otto Springer. Berlin 1962—63. Teil II: Deutsch-Englisch (LEW2). Völlige Neubearbeitung 1974, edited by Otto Springer. Berlin 1974—75 [LEW1: XXXVII, 1844 p.; LEW2: XXXVII, 2024 p.; 1st edition: 1891—1901, Muret/Sanders 1891—1901].

LGSW 1+2 = Langenscheidts Großes Schulwörterbuch. Teil 1: Englisch-Deutsch (LGSW1). Bearbeitet von Heinz Messinger. Berlin. München 1988. Teil 2: Deutsch-Englisch (LGSW2). Hrsg. v. Heinz Messinger. Berlin. München 1977 [LGSW1: 1437 p.; also published as Langenscheidts Handwörterbuch, 760 p. 1st ed. 1964; LGSW2: 1328 p. 1st ed. 1959].

LGW 1+2 = Langenscheidts Großwörterbuch. Deutsch-Englisch (LGW1) von Heinz Messinger und der Langenscheidt-Redaktion. Berlin. München 1982. Englisch-Deutsch (LGW2) von Helmut Willmann, Heinz Messinger und der Langenscheidt-Redaktion. Berlin. München 1985 [LGW1: 1296 p.; LGW2: 1200 p.; 1st ed. 1972].

Lucas 1854—68 = Newton Ivory Lucas: Englisch-deutsches und deutsch-englisches Wörterbuch (...) 4 vol. Bremen 1854—68 [4422 p].

Ludwig 1706 = Christian Ludwig: A Dictionary English, German and French. Leipzig 1706 [786 p. 2. ed. 1736: 739 p. 3. ed. by J. B. Rogler 1763: 1022 p. 4. ed. 1791].

Ludwig 1716 = [Christian Ludwig?]: Teutsch-Englisches Lexicon. Leipzig 1716 [1336 p. 2. ed. 1745. 3. ed. 1765. 4. ed. 1789].

Muret/Sanders 1891—1901 = Ernst Muret/Daniel Sanders: Encyklopädisches Wörterbuch der englischen und deutschen Sprache. 4 vol. Berlin 1891—1901 [XXXII,2460, XLVIII, 2368 pp. Continued by Springer 1962—1975, LEW 1+2].

Neubert/Gröger 1989 = Albrecht Neubert/Erika Gröger: Handwörterbuch Englisch-Deutsch. Leipzig 1989 [959 p.; 1st edition 1988].

OHSGED = The Oxford-Harrap Standard German-English Dictionary. Edited by Trevor Jones. A—R. 3 vol. Oxford 1963—1977 [511, 612, 484 p.].

PGSW 1+2 = Herbert Schöffler: Pons Globalwörterbuch Schöffler-Weis. Teil 1: Englisch-Deutsch (PGSW1). Bearbeitet von Erich Weis unter Mitwirkung von Heinrich Mattutat. Stuttgart 1978. Teil 2: Deutsch-Englisch. Bearbeitet von Erwin Weis und Erich Weis. Stuttgart 1978 [PGSW1: 1178 p. 1st ed. 1948; PGSW2: 1176 p. 1st ed. 1951].

PGW 1+2 = Pons Globalwörterbuch. Roland Breitsprecher et al. Stuttgart 1983. Englisch-Deutsch (PGW1). Bearbeitet von Jennifer Turner-Flechsenhar, Veronika Calderwood-Schnorr. Deutsch-Englisch (PGW2). Bearbeitet von Veronika Calderwood-Schnorr [PGW1: XVIII, 1390 p.; PGW2: XXIII, 1380 p.].

PKW 1+2 = Pons Kompaktwörterbuch Englisch-Deutsch; Deutsch-Englisch. Herausgegeben v. E. Weis. Stuttgart 1982. Englisch-Deutsch (PKW1) von E. Weis et. al. Deutsch-Englisch (PKW2). Neu bearbeitet und ergänzt von C. Nekvedavičius [PKW1: IX, 638 p.; PKW2: XX, 641 p.].

Prager 1757—60 = Johann Christian Prager: Neu eingerichtetes englisches Wörterbuch. Coburg. Leipzig 1757—60.

Schröer 1894—1902 = Arnold Schröer: Chr. Fr. Grieb's Dictionary of the English and German Languages. 10th ed. rearranged, revised and enlarged with special regard to pronunciation and etymology. 2 vol. Stuttgart 1894—1902 [1356, 1192 p. 11. ed. Berlin 1907. Continued by P. L. Jaeger].

Schröer/Jaeger 1937—70 = Arnold Schröer/P. L. Jaeger: Englisches Handwörterbuch in genetischer Darstellung aufgrund der Etymologien und Bedeutungsentwicklungen. 3 vol. Heidelberg 1937—1970 [XVI, 2066 p.].

Sheridan 1791 = Thomas Sheridan/Johann Ernst Gruner: Thomas Sheridan's Englisches Wörterbuch zur richtigen und festen Bestimmung der Aussprache. Für die Teutschen bearbeitet von Johann Ernst Gruner. Coburg 1791 [LII, 433 p.].

Thieme 1846 = F. W. Thieme: Neues vollständiges kritisches Wörterbuch der Englischen und Deutschen Sprache. Leipzig 1846 [740, 490 p. Ed. Emil Preußer. Hamburg 1860. Ed. Emanuel Wessely, Hamburg 1884. 236. Tausend 1903: 840, 763 p.].

VEB 1+2 = Wörterbuch Englisch-Deutsch (VEB1). Käthe Briese et. al. Leipzig 1986. Wörterbuch Deutsch-Englisch (VEB2) Erika Gröger. Leipzig 1986 [VEB1: 610 p. 1st edition 1955; VEB2: 556 p.].

VEB 3 = Jürgen and Karla Schröder: Wörterbuch Englisch-Deutsch. Leipzig 1989 [759 p.].

WH 1+2 = Karl Wildhagen: Englisch-Deutsches Deutsch-Englisches Wörterbuch. Englisch-Deutsch. 15. Aufl., neu bearbeitet und erweitert von Will Héraucourt. Wiesbaden 1963 (WH1). Deutsch-Englisch (WH2). Neu bearbeitet und erweitert von Will Héraucourt. Wiesbaden 1972 [WH1: XXX, 1144 p. 1st ed. 1938; WH2: XXXVIII, 1524 p. 1st ed. 1953].

9.2. Other Publications

Fabian 1985 = Bernhard Fabian: Englisch als neue Fremdsprache des 18. Jh. In: Mehrsprachigkeit in der deutschen Aufklärung. Hrsg. v. D. Kimpel. Hamburg 1985 (Studien zum 18. Jh. 5), 178—196.

Hartmann (forthcoming) = Reinhard R. K. Hartmann: 300 Years of English-German Language Contact and Contrast. In: Language and Civilization. Essays in Honour of Otto Hietsch (forthcoming).

Hatherall 1980 = Glyn Hatherall: Which Dictionary? In: Treffpunkt 12,3. 1980, 12—17.

Hatherall 1982 = Glyn Hatherall: Which Pocket Dictionary? In: Treffpunkt 14,2. 1982, 14—19.

Hausmann/Cop 1985 = Franz Josef Hausmann/Margaret Cop: Short History of English-German Lexicography. In: Symposium on Lexicography II. Ed. by Karl Hyldgaard-Jensen/Arne Zettersten. Tübingen 1985 (Lexicographica Series Maior 5), 183—198.

Henke/Pätzold 1987 = Käthe Henke/Kurt-Michael Pätzold: Englische Wörterbücher und Nachschlagewerke. In: E. Zöfgen (ed.), Wörterbücher und ihre Didaktik. Bad Honnef 1987 (= Bielefelder Beiträge zur Sprachlehrforschung 14. 1985), 98—180.

Herbst 1985 = Thomas Herbst: Das zweisprachige Wörterbuch als Schreibwörterbuch: Informationen zur Syntax in zweisprachigen Wörterbüchern Englisch-Deutsch/Deutsch-Englisch. In: H. Bergenholtz/J. Mugdan (eds.), Lexikographie und Grammatik, Tübingen 1985 (Lexicographica. Series Maior 3), 308—351.

Hietsch 1980 = Otto Hietsch: The Mirthless World of the Bilingual Dictionary. A Critical Look at Two German-English Examples, and a Glossary. In: Linguistica 20. 1980, 183—217.

Kromann/Riiber/Rosbach 1984 = Hans-Peder Kromann/Theis Riiber/Poul Rosbach: Überlegungen zu Grundfragen der zweisprachigen Lexikographie. In: Germanistische Linguistik 3—6/1984, 159—238.

Lehnert 1956 = Martin Lehnert: Das englische Wörterbuch in Vergangenheit und Gegenwart. In: Zeitschrift für Anglistik und Amerikanistik 4. 1956, 265—324.

Stein 1985 = Gabriele Stein: English-German, German-English Lexicography: Its Early Beginnings. In: Lexicographica 1. 1985, 134—164.

Traupman 1985 = John C. Traupman: Modern Trends in German-English Lexicography. In: Lexicographica 1. 1985, 25—31.

Kurt-Michael Pätzold, Bielefeld
(Federal Republic of Germany)

311. Bilingual Lexicography: English-Italian, Italian-English

1. William Thomas
2. John Florio
3. Giovanni Torriano
4. Ferdinand Altieri
5. Giuseppe Baretti
6. The Nineteenth Century
7. The Twentieth Century
8. Selected Bibliography

1. William Thomas

English and Italian had appeared side by side in early multilingual wordlists such as Sex Linguarum (Gamberini 1970, 49), but the first Italian-English dictionary (Thomas 1550) was one of the earliest of the Italian bilingual group to match Italian words with their equivalents in another modern language. The first Italian-French dictionary, for example, did not appear for another three decades (Van Passen 1981, 32). Thomas's dictionary, compiled in Padua at the request of an English friend (see Adair 1924, Griffith 1961, Rossi 1966, O'Connor 1990), consisted of a selection of c. 9000 words used by Dante, Petrarch, and Boccaccio, which Thomas took from Alunno 1543 and Acarisio 1543, and to which he added brief English translations. Most glosses were accurate (but: **crediti** "debts", **rame** "brasse", **stagno** "copper"), Italian weights and measures (e.g. **staio**) were given English equivalents, and Italian food items (e.g. **rauiuoli**) were explained (see dictionary excerpt 311.1). In the second half of the century, when foreign-language texts flourished in England, two reprints of the dictionary were published.

Staio, a certeigne measure, not mache different in quantitie from our buschell.

Rauiuoli, a certein kynd of meate made in little morsels of herbes and grated cheese, with a little rinde of paste.

Dictionary excerpt 311.1: Dictionary articles (from: Thomas 1550, s.v.)

2. John Florio

Florio's important contribution to Italian-English lexicography, as well as his life (1553—1625) and his other scholarly pursuits, have been studied in detail (Chambrun 1921, Yates 1934, Policardi 1947 & 1948, Rosier 1963, Starnes 1965, Rossi 1969, Gamberini 1970, O'Connor 1972 & 1990, Frantz 1979, Tancke 1984). His dictionary (Florio 1598) consisted of c. 44 000 entries gathered from 72 Italian books (listed at the front of the volume) whose titles included other dictionaries (Thomas 1550, Venuti 1564, Las Casas 1570, Fenice 1584), encyclopedias (Citolini 1561, Garzoni 1585), books on horsemanship, cookery, falconry, botany, zoology and history, and a selection of plays, poems, dialogues and letters by a variety of sixteenth-century writers. It is a little-known fact that the source he used most of all was a Latin-English dictionary deliberately omitted from the booklist: nearly every page of Thomasius 1592 was borrowed by Florio and transcribed word for word (Starnes 1937, O'Connor 1990, 34 f).

Florio made no attempt to compile a Tuscan wordlist. Rather, his aim was to collect the broadest variety of words possible, in-

Philtrum, i.n.g. & Philtra, orum, p.n. Ovid. Amorous potions, poyson of loue, or a medicine to make one loue: also the hollownes, or gutter in the vpper lips vnder the nostrils. Also the faire and comelie proportion of ones bodie and his courteous behauiour, which with the verie sight doth purchase loue and fauour.

Philura, vel Philyra, æ, f. g. Horat. A little thinne skinne, as parchments, a sheete of paper, that which is betweene the backe and the wood of the tree, and is called Tylia, wherupon in auncient time they were wont to write.

Dictionary excerpt 311.2: Dictionary articles (from: Thomasius 1587, s.v.)

Philtro, Philtri, amorous potions, poisons of loue, or medicines to make one loue. Also the hallownes or gutter in the vpper lips vnder the nostrils. Also the faire and comely proportion of ones bodie, and his curteous behauiour, which with the verie sight doth purchase loue and fauour.

Philura, a little thin skin as parchment, a sheete or leafe of paper, that which is betweene the barke and the wood of the tree, of some called Tylia, whereupon in old time they were wont to write.

Dictionary excerpt 311.3: Dictionary articles (from: Florio 1598, s.v.)

cluding regionalisms, archaisms, latinisms, contemporary colloquial expressions, and a wealth of words related to the animal, vegetable, and mineral world. Not content with this first effort, he compiled a second edition (Florio 1611), again Italian-English only, almost double the size, and preceded by 252 titles that he claimed to have consulted. This time the headwords carried stress accents, and open e and o were marked according to Tolomei's system. A curious feature of the dictionary was the inclusion of nearly 200 "difficult" headwords that had no definition, or were followed merely by the original Italian quotation (O'Connor 1973).

3. Giovanni Torriano

The manuscript of a third edition left by Florio was revised and published by Torriano, a teacher of Italian in London. Torriano 1659 was designed not only for the literati of the court (Florio's principal audience) but also for travellers to Italy and for English traders in the Levant where Italian was the recognised lingua franca. This time no list of sources was included, but in the preface Torriano stated that he had added words from the Vocabolario della Crusca "and severall others", and had "much corrected the English interpretations". Rossi (1969, 182) and O'Connor (1990, 50 f) have shown that he also used Cotgrave 1611. Additions included terms related to anatomy, medicine, exotic flora and fauna, astronomy and mythology, as well as derivatives of words already present in Florio 1611 (Messeri 1956, 109). Torriano made no attempt to compile a normative dictionary but merely reordered and enlarged the collection that Florio had prepared. He did, however, add the first English-Italian wordlist, which was no more than an English-Italian version of Sherwood 1632 (O'Connor 1977, 94). Neither Florio nor Torriano indicated the gender of Italian nouns in their lists. Paravicino 1662 went some way towards meeting this need by assembling c. 3000 Italian nouns ending in -e, with a label of the gender of each, and the English gloss.

4. Ferdinand Altieri

Torriano's dictionary was eclipsed by Altieri 1726/1727, which was compiled with "elegant and pure Tuscan diction" as its model, and Crusca 1691 as its main source. Little is known of Altieri, one of the most important figures in Italian-English lexicographical history, yet virtually forgotten until recently (Nibbi 1968, 40), partly because Baretti in his own dictionary three decades later virulently criticised his efforts (see 5. below). To stress the rigorous approach he had adopted, Altieri prefaced his dictionary with an abridged list of the Table of Authors in Crusca 1691, to which he added a few titles of his own (O'Connor 1990, 68 f). His Italian wordlist contained all the entries in Crusca 1691, as well as others, including odd exoticisms, taken (unacknowledged) from Torriano 1659. To some glosses (e.g. **amare**, **bisognare**, **dove**) he added a number of simple but useful illustrative phrases. Altieri's approach was remarkably modern: on the Italian side he indicated the part of speech beside each entry except verbs, supplied the gender of nouns, marked the stressed syllable on each headword, distinguished (as in Crusca) the open and closed tonic vowels of some homographs (e.g. **pesca**, **foro**), and used symbols to designate uncommon words, metaphors, and figurative speech. For the English-Italian side he used (unacknowledged) Boyer 1699, supplemented by Bailey 1721, and, occasionally, by the Italian glosses in Torriano (O'Connor 1977, 96 & 1990, 74 f). As in Bailey's first edition, the stressed syllable was not marked on the English entries.

5. Giuseppe Baretti

Inspired by the labours of his friend Samuel Johnson (Lubbers 1951, 56 f), Baretti compiled a dictionary based on Altieri, whom he acknowledged as the main source, but whom he condemned for his ignorance and inaccuracy, for his "love of obscene words and phrases", and for being "in the dark as to the beauties of his native language" (Baretti 1760, Preface). Despite this tirade, Baretti's dictionary was nonetheless in many places identical to Altieri's. To Altieri's Italian list he added some entries from Crusca 1729/1738 (Nibbi 1968, 43), made some orthographical improvements, and expunged the vulgar expressions that Altieri had copied from Crusca 1691 and from, on the English side, Bailey 1721. From the Italian list he also deleted most of the entries that Altieri had taken from Torriano, though a small number of exoticisms did survive (e.g. **alcatrozzo, alchiterano, aldarga**). Very few changes were made on the English side: he added some items from Johnson 1755 and, like Johnson, marked the stressed syllable on the English headwords. By the end of the century Altieri's name had disappeared from the title-page of Baretti's dictionary, destined to be forgotten even by modern scholars such as Praz (1942, 300) and Migliorini (1946, 144). Baretti 1760, greatly reduced, was used for the first Italian and English pocket dictionary (G. Graglia 1787). The revised edition (C. Graglia 1795 — with incorrect initial C), continued to be republished in various sizes and countries throughout the Nineteenth Century to satisfy a demand for bilingual pocket dictionaries that was to continue to the present day (O'Connor 1982 & 1990).

6. The Nineteenth Century

Baretti's dictionary went through numerous reprints and revisions, the last reprint as recently as 1928. The most radical revision was carried out in the final edition (Davenport/Comelati 1854): meaning discrimination was introduced into some of the glosses, irregular verb forms were included, diminutives, augmentatives, and irregular plurals were listed alongside nouns, and a much-needed selection of neologisms and idiomatic and colloquial expressions was added. A useful companion to Baretti's dictionary was Santagnello 1820, which was a list of c. 1500 English words with grammatical information about how the Italian equivalent should be used in context. It was the first English-Italian glossary to indicate which Italian prepositions should be used after selected verbs and adjectives.

The first large Italian and English dictionary to compete with Baretti was Petronj/Davenport 1824. On the Italian side the authors used D'Alberti 1797/1805, thus providing a good range of neologisms and scientific terms, but the English side still relied heavily on Baretti, and was only half the size of the Italian part. In the Italian list, for the first time since Florio 1611, both stress accent and open tonic e and o were marked. Furthermore, stress was indicated on the first person sing. pres. tense of polysyllabic verbs (e.g. **sbroccolare, sbrôccolo**), the present tense of irregular verbs was listed in full, and the irreg. plural of nouns was indicated. Meadows 1834, modelled on both Petronj/Davenport and Baretti, proved popular as a compact yet comprehensive volume, and was reprinted numerous times in the following decades.

The three most important dictionaries to be published in the middle of the Nineteenth Century, Millhouse 1849/1853, James/Grassi 1854, and Roberts 1867, all used Baretti as their main source. Millhouse also consulted Petronj/Davenport 1824 and similarly marked stress and open e and o on the Italian side. On the English side he was the first to incorporate into the English headword a system of italics and accents to indicate the pronunciation. James/Grassi, who borrowed from Millhouse as well as from Baretti, were the first to add full pronunciation alongside each Italian entry, including the distinction between voiced and unvoiced z, while Roberts, who followed James/Grassi almost to the letter, put the figurative pronunciation alongside each English entry. De Bermingham 1877 also relied on his predecessors, but attempted to update their work by adding a selection of neologisms (e.g. **communist, pudinga**). Melzi 1892 was the first to attempt to break away from the Baretti tradition: for the Italian part he used his own Italian-French dictionary (Melzi 1886/1887), and for the English part his sources included Elwall 1860 and Spiers 1846/1849. His work contained a conspicuous number of Americanisms and some previously unrecorded neologisms related to the sciences, but also an abundance of "false friends" and examples of near-translation (O'Connor 1990, 111 f). Indeed, inaccurate translation into the target language was to become one of the most noticeable shortcomings of the lexicographers who followed immediately after him.

7. The Twentieth Century

Bilingual lexicographers could no longer hope to include all the entries found in multi-volume monolingual vocabularies. They had now to choose from among such categories as archaisms, neologisms, Americanisms, regionalisms, literary, poetic, technical, scientific words, vulgarisms, colloquialisms, and slang. Furthermore, they had to decide how much space, if any, should be given to pronunciation, etymology, and grammatical information. Edgren 1901 and Enenkel 1909 chose to include both obsolete words and neologisms. Edgren added the etymology against the Italian headwords, gave pronunciation on both sides, and on the English side included a number of Americanisms (e.g.

elevator, **grizzly bear**, **sidewalk**). Between the two World Wars the most popular dictionaries were Lysle 1913/1915, Hoare 1915, and Spinelli 1929/1930. Lysle, designed specifically for Italians, contained a large English wordlist, but also numerous errors (O'Connor 1978, 341 & 1990, 123). Hoare, designed for English-speakers, contained a large Italian-English side, which also provided etymologies and considerable grammatical information. Spinelli, like Lysle before him, was guilty of inaccuracies in English, and of near-translations and "false friends" (Praz 1942, 302, Baldini 1955). Orlandi 1942 has been accused of similar inaccuracies and of a bias towards British English only (Melzi 1972, 338, O'Connor 1978, 345). Borgogni 1935, the last dictionary of note to appear before World War II, was an inexpensive medium-sized volume for Italian school-children, and reflected the economic difficulties of the period ("ho pensato anzitutto alle famiglie disagiate") (Borgogni 1935, vi). The dictionary is noteworthy for the care taken in discriminating the various meanings of the headword, a feature which would be insisted upon more and more in post-war dictionaries.

More Italian and English bilingual dictionaries have been published in the four decades since World War II than in the whole of the preceding four centuries, as the extensive bibliographies of Marin 1978/1979 and O'Connor 1990 show. The vast majority of the medium-sized and large dictionaries have been published in Italy, designed implicitly or explicitly for Italians, and so in cases of polysemy give meaning discriminations in Italian on both sides of the dictionary (e. g. Cambridge-Signorelli 1985). A major exception is Sansoni/Harrap (= S/H 1970/1975), which is intended for both Italian- and English-speaking users, and appropriately has discriminations in Italian on the Italian side, and in English on the English side. The few medium-sized to large dictionaries that have been published outside of Italy (e.g. Purves 1953, Cassell 1958, Cambridge 1962/1981) provide discriminations in English. Anglo-American publishers have generally preferred to issue small to medium-sized dictionaries (e.g. Bocchetta 1963, May 1970, Melzi 1976), perhaps with the tourist market in mind (Marello 1989, 165, O'Connor 1990, 132).

Hazon 1961, Cambridge 1962/1981 and Ragazzini 1967 are landmarks in modern Italian-English lexicography and have served as a point of reference for all subsequent dictionaries. Heeding the plea made by e.g. Praz (1942, 302), they used a group of specialists, some Italian, some English speakers, to compile far more comprehensive and accurate entries than those of their predecessors. Many contemporary dictionaries (e.g. Helder 1981) boast of the range of modern vocabulary, neologisms, and Americanisms they contain. Few, however, have been able to keep abreast of the times as a survey has shown (O'Connor 1979, 285). On the English side, dictionaries now usually employ IPA symbols to indicate pronunciation, and some also indicate syllabic division (e.g. Hutchings 1970, Sani 1974, S/H 1970/1975, Love 1985). On the Italian side, stress (at least) is usually marked, although this was deemed unnecessary in Skey 1978, which claimed to be the first bilingual dictionary "ad uso *esclusivo* del lettore italiano". Some dictionaries (e.g. Ragazzini 1967 and Cambridge 1962/1981) also provide the Latin name for words describing flora and fauna. Most contemporary dictionaries do not contain the numerous inaccuracies found in Cassell 1958 and Ciaramella 1966. "False friends" now rarely meet, except in an appendix included for didactic purposes (May 1954, Ragazzini 1984). Vulgar and taboo words not recorded since Florio have been restored by Skey 1978 and Cambridge 1962/1981. Dictionaries published in Italy usually provide some valuable grammatical assistance for students of English. For these users Paravia 1989 is exceptionally rich in this regard and has as yet no equivalent amongst dictionaries of similar size intended primarily for use by students of Italian.

8. Selected Bibliography

8.1. Dictionaries

Acarisio 1543 = Acarisio da Cento: Vocabolario, Grammatica, et orthographia de la lingua volgare. Cento 1543 [316 p.].

Altieri 1726/1727 = Ferdinand Altieri: Dizionario italiano ed inglese. 2 vol. London 1726/1727.

Alunno 1543 = Francesco Alunno: Le ricchezze della lingua volgare. Venice 1543 [225 f.].

Bailey 1721 = Nathaniel Bailey: An Universal Etymological English Dictionary. London 1721.

Baretti 1760 = Giuseppe Baretti: A Dictionary of the English and Italian Languages. 2 vol. London 1760.

Blount 1656 = Thomas Blount: Glossographia. London 1656 [691 p.].

Bocchetta 1963 = Victor Bocchetta: Follett vestpocket Italian dictionary. Chicago 1963 [288 p.].

Borgogni 1935 = Michele Borgogni: Nuovissimo vocabolario inglese per le scuole. Rome 1935 [556, 592 p.].

Boyer 1699 = Abel Boyer: The Royal Dictionary [...] French and English [...] English and French. London 1699.

Cambridge 1962/1981 = Barbara Reynolds (ed.): The Cambridge Italian Dictionary. Cambridge (vol. 1) 1962, (vol. 2) 1981 [899, 843 p.].

Cambridge-Signorelli 1985 = Cambridge Signorelli Dizionario italiano-inglese inglese-italiano dal Cambridge Italian Dictionary di Barbara Reynolds. Milan 1985 [2276 p.].

Cassell 1958 = Piero Rebora (with the assistance of Francis M. Guercio and Arthur L. Hayward): Cassell's Italian-English English-Italian Dictionary. London 1958 [1079 p.].

Ciaramella 1966 = Michele Ciaramella: Dizionario inglese-italiano italiano-inglese. Milan 1966 [1191 p.].

Cotgrave 1611 = Randle Cotgrave: A Dictionarie of the French and English Tongues. London 1611.

Crusca 1691 = Vocabolario degli Accademici della Crusca. 4 vol. 3. ed. Florence 1691 [1. ed. 1612].

Crusca 1729/1738 = Vocabolario degli Accademici della Crusca. 6 vol. 4. ed. Florence 1729/1738.

D'Alberti 1797/1805 = Francesco D'Alberti di Villanova: Dizionario universale critico enciclopedico della lingua italiana. 6 vol. Lucca 1797/1805.

Davenport/Comelati 1854 = John Davenport/Guglielmo Comelati: A New Dictionary of the Italian and English Languages. 2 vol. London 1854 [753, 797 p.].

De Bermingham 1877 = Alphonsus de Bermingham: New Dictionary of the English and Italian Languages. Paris 1877 [570, 376 p.].

Edgren 1901 = Hjalmar Edgren: An Italian and English Dictionary with Pronunciation and Brief Etymologies. London.New York 1901 [576, 452 p.].

Elwall 1860 = Alfred Elwall: Nouveau Dictionnaire Anglais-Français. Paris 1860.

Enenkel 1909 = Arturo Angeli Enenkel: A New Dictionary of the English and Italian Languages. London 1909 [520, 553 p.].

Fenice 1584 = Jean Antoine Fenice: Dictionnaire françois et italien. Paris 1584.

Florio 1598 = John Florio: A Worlde of Wordes, Or Most copious, and exact Dictionarie in Italian and English. London 1598 [462 p.].

Florio 1611 = John Florio: Queen Anna's New World of Words. London 1611 [690 p.].

C. Graglia 1795 = C. Graglia: The New Pocket Dictionary of the Italian and English Languages [...] corrected throughout by A. Montucci and J. Sivrac. London 1795 [377, 256 p.].

G. Graglia 1787 = Giuspanio Graglia: An Italian and English Pocket Dictionary. London 1787.

Hazon 1961 = Mario Hazon (ed.): Dizionario inglese-italiano italiano-inglese. Milan 1961 [2090 p.].

Helder 1981 = M. P. Helder: Il dizionario d'oggi. Italiano-inglese. Saluzzo 1981 [1439 p.].

Hoare 1915 = Alfred Hoare: An Italian Dictionary. Cambridge 1915 [633, 135 p.].

Hutchings 1970 = Geoffrey Hutchings: Vocabolario inglese-italiano italiano-inglese. Milan 1970 [1085 p.].

James/Grassi 1854 = William James/Giuseppe Grassi: Dizionario italiano-inglese e inglese-italiano. Leipzig 1854 [456, 356 p.].

Johnson 1755 = Samuel Johnson: A Dictionary of the English Language. 2 vol. London 1755.

Las Casas 1570 = Christobal De Las Casas: Vocabulario de las dos lenguas toscana y castellana. Seville 1570.

Love 1985 = Catherine E. Love (ed.): Giunti Marzocco Collins Dizionario inglese-italiano italiano-inglese. London. Florence 1985 [1005 p.].

Lysle 1913/1915 = Andrea de Roever Lysle: Nuovo Dizionario moderno-razionale-pratico inglese-italiano. 2 vol. Turin 1913/1915 [2052, 958 p.].

May 1954 = Isopel May: Collins Italian Gem Dictionary. London. Glasgow 1954 [676 p.].

May 1970 = Isopel May: Collins Contemporary Italian Dictionary, revised by Antonia Sansica Stott. London. Glasgow 1970 [448 p.].

Meadows 1834 = F. C. Meadows: New Italian and English Dictionary. London 1834 [664 p.].

Melzi 1886/1887 = Giovanni Battista Melzi: Nuovo dizionario francese-italiano e italiano-francese. Milan 1886/1887 [561, 539 p.].

Melzi 1892 = Giovanni Battista Melzi: Nuovo dizionario inglese-italiano italiano-inglese. Milan 1892 [607, 579 p.].

Melzi 1976 = Robert Charles Melzi: The Bantam New College Italian and English Dictionary. New York 1976 [364, 356 p.].

Millhouse 1849/1853 = John Millhouse: New English and Italian Pronouncing and Explanatory Dictionary. 2 vol. Milan 1849/1853 [534, 528 p.; 4. ed. Ferdinand Bracciforti, 1870].

Orlandi 1942 = Giuseppe Orlandi: Dizionario italiano-inglese inglese-italiano. Milan 1942 [2071 p.].

Paravia 1989 = Carlo Passerini Tosi (ed.): Dizionario italiano inglese Italian-English. Turin 1989 [2556 p.].

Paravicino 1662 = Peter Paravicino: A Short Italian Dictionary of all the words of the two Genders, which have the termination in the vowel E. London 1662 [63 p.].

Petronj/Davenport 1824 = Stefano Egidio Petronj/John Davenport: A New Dictionary English and Italian, Italian and English, with the equivalents in French. London 1824 [1050, 400 p.].

Purves 1953 = John Purves: A Dictionary of Modern Italian. Italian-English and English-Italian. London 1953 [833 p.].

Ragazzini 1967 = Giuseppe Ragazzini: Dizionario inglese-italiano italiano-inglese. Bologna 1967 [1864 p.].

Ragazzini 1984 = Giuseppe Ragazzini: Il Nuovo Ragazzini gigante. Bologna 1984 [2128 p.].

Roberts 1867 = J. P. Roberts: Dizionario italiano-inglese e inglese-italiano. Florence 1867 [525, 455 p.].

Sani 1974 = Luciano Sani: Vocabolario inglese-italiano italiano-inglese. Città di Castello 1974 [2315 p.].

Santagnello 1820 = M. Santagnello: A Dictionary of the Peculiarities of the Italian Language. London 1820 [311 p.].

S/H 1970/1975 = Sansoni-Harrap Standard Italian and English Dictionary. 4 vol. Florence. London 1970/1975 [1472, 1596 p.]. 1 vol. Florence. Rome 1975 [964, 772 p.; 3. ed. 1988].

Sherwood 1632 = Robert Sherwood: A Dictionary English and French. London 1632.

Skey 1978 = Malcom Skey (ed.): Dizionario inglese italiano italiano inglese. Turin 1978 [1894 p.].

Spiers 1846/1849 = Alexander Spiers: Dictionnaire général anglais-français. 2 vol. Paris 1846/1849.

Spinelli 1929/1930 = Nicola Spinelli: Dizionario italiano-inglese inglese-italiano. 2 vol. Turin 1929/1930 [1698, 1649 p.].

Thomas 1550 = William Thomas: Principal rules of the Italian Grammer, with a Dictionarie for the better understandynge of Boccace, Petrarcha, and Dante. London 1550 [291 p.].

Thomasius 1592 = Thomas Thomasius: Thomae Thomasii Dictionarium. 3. ed. Cambridge 1592 [1. ed. 1587].

Torriano 1659 = Giovanni Torriano: Vocabolario Italiano e Inglese [...] Formerly Compiled by John Florio. London 1659.

Venuti 1564 = Filippo Venuti da Cortona: Dittionario volgare e latino. Venice 1564.

8.2. Other Publications

Adair 1924 = E. R. Adair: William Thomas: A Forgotten Clerk of the Privy Council. In: R. W. Seton-Watson (ed.): Tudor Studies. London 1924, 133—160.

Baldini 1955 = Gabriele Baldini: Nicola Spinelli: Dizionario italiano-inglese. In: Rivista di Letterature Moderne e Comparate VIII. 1955, 298—301.

Chambrun 1921 = Clara Longworth De Chambrun: Giovanni Florio, un apôtre de la Renaissance en Angleterre à l'époque de Shakespeare. Paris 1921.

Citolini 1561 = Alessandro Citolini: La Tipocosmia. Venice 1561.

Frantz 1979 = David O. Frantz: Florio's Use of Contemporary Italian Literature in *A Worlde of Words*. In: Dictionaries 1. 1979, 47—56.

Gamberini 1969 = Spartaco Gamberini: I primi strumenti dell'italianistica in Inghilterra. In: Belfagor 24. 1969, 446—470.

Gamberini 1970 = Spartaco Gamberini: Lo studio dell'italiano in Inghilterra nel '500 e nel '600. Messina. Florence 1970.

Garzoni 1585 = Tommaso Garzoni: La piazza universale di tutte le professioni del mondo. Venice 1585.

Griffith 1961 = T. Gwynfor Griffith: Avventure linguistiche del Cinquecento. Florence 1961, 53—80.

Lubbers 1951 = C. J. M. Lubbers-Van der Brugge: Johnson and Baretti. Some Aspects of Eighteenth-Century Life in England and Italy. Groningen. Djakarta 1951.

Marello 1989 = Carla Marello: Dizionari bilingui con schede sui dizionari italiani per francese, inglese, spagnolo, tedesco. Bologna 1989.

Marin 1978/1979 = Marina Marin: La lessicografia italo-inglese. Tesi di laurea. Università degli Studi di Udine 1978/1979.

Melzi 1972 = Robert C. Melzi: A Critique of Several Modern Italian and English Dictionaries. In: Italica 49. 1972, 338—343.

Messeri 1956 = Anna Laura Messeri: Giovanni Torriano e il suo dizionario inglese-italiano. In: Lingua Nostra XVII. 1956, 108—111.

Migliorini 1946 = Bruno Migliorini: Che cos'è un vocabolario? Rome 1946.

Nibbi 1968 = Alessandra Nibbi: Il dizionario italiano-inglese e inglese-italiano di Giuseppe Baretti. In: Lingua Nostra XXIX. 1968, 40—46.

O'Connor 1972 = Desmond O'Connor: John Florio's Contribution to Italian-English Lexicography. In: Italica 49. 1972, 49—67.

O'Connor 1973 = Desmond O'Connor: Voci non spiegate nei dizionari di John Florio. In: Studi di Filologia Italiana XXXI. 1973, 207—246.

O'Connor 1977 = Desmond O'Connor: Ancora sui primi dizionari italiano-inglesi. In: Lingua Nostra XXXVIII. 1977, 94—98.

O'Connor 1978 = Desmond O'Connor: Italian-English Lexicography in the Twentieth Century. In: Italica 55. 1978, 338—358.

O'Connor 1979 = Desmond O'Connor: Neologisms in Modern Italian-English Dictionaries. In: Italica 56. 1979, 283—287.

O'Connor 1982 = Desmond O'Connor: A Survey of some Twentieth-Century Italian-English Pocket Dictionaries. In: Italica 59. 1982, 175—181.

O'Connor 1990 = Desmond O'Connor: A History of Italian and English Bilingual Dictionaries. Florence 1990.

Policardi 1947 = Silvio Policardi: John Florio e le relazioni culturali anglo-italiane agli albori del XVII secolo. Venice 1947.

Policardi 1948 = Silvio Policardi: I dizionari di Giovanni Florio. In: Lingua Nostra IX. 1948, 54—60.

Praz 1942 = Mario Praz: Machiavelli in Inghilterra e altri saggi. Rome 1942.

Rosier 1963 = James L. Rosier: Lexical strata in Florio's *New World of Words*. In: English Studies 44. 1963, 415—423.

Rossi 1966 = Sergio Rossi: Un 'italianista' nel Cinquecento inglese: William Thomas. In: Aevum XL. 1966, 281—314.

Rossi 1969 = Sergio Rossi: Ricerche sull'umanesimo e sul rinascimento in Inghilterra. Milan 1969.

Starnes 1937 = Dewitt T. Starnes: Bilingual Dictionaries of Shakespeare's Day. In: Publications of the Modern Language Association of America 52. 1937, 1005—1018.

Starnes 1965 = Dewitt T. Starnes: John Florio Reconsidered. In: Texas Studies in Literature and Language 6. 1965, 407—422.

Tancke 1984 = Gunnar Tancke: Die italienischen Wörterbücher von den Anfängen bis zum Erscheinen des "Vocabolario degli Accademici della Crusca" (1612). Bestandsaufnahme und Analyse. Tübingen 1984.

Van Passen 1981 = Anne-Marie Van Passen: Appunti sui dizionari italo-francesi apparsi prima della fine del Settecento. In: Studi di Lessicografia Italiana III. 1981, 29—65.

Yates 1934 = Frances A Yates: John Florio. The Life of an Italian in Shakespeare's England. Cambridge 1934.

Desmond O'Connor, Flinders University, Adelaide (Australia)

312. La lexicographie bilingue espagnol-français, français-espagnol

1. Introduction et délimitation du sujet
2. Dictionnaires bilingues généraux
3. Dictionnaires bilingues spécialisés
4. Dictionnaires bilingues des langues de spécialités
5. Bibliographie choisie

1. Introduction et délimitation du sujet

Tandis que la lexicographie hispano-anglaise et la lexicographie hispano-italienne ont déjà fait l'objet d'études d'ensemble (cf. art. 308 et art. 314), aucun travail de ce type n'a encore été consacré à la lexicographie hispano-française. Plus étonnant encore, les études partielles font, elles aussi, cruellement défaut, sauf en ce qui concerne la période initiale. Nous avons donc dû explorer un immense domaine resté pratiquement vierge jusqu'ici. Vu l'espace et le temps limités, il ne s'agit pour l'instant que d'une première reconnaissance du terrain, dans l'espoir de compléter cette étude par d'autres publications. — Dans cet aperçu de l'ensemble des ouvrages lexicographiques bilingues »Espagnol-Français« (E-F) et/ou »Français-Espagnol« (F-E) imprimés depuis le XVIe siècle jusqu'à nos jours, nous nous sommes imposé les restrictions suivantes: (a) Nous excluons de cet aperçu tous les dictionnaires plurilingues (c-à-d. trois langues et plus), excepté les trilingues où la troisième langue est le latin. (b) Parmi les dictionnaires bilingues (accompagnés ou non du latin) nous ne parlerons pas — si ce n'est de manière occasionnelle — des dictionnaires des langues de spécialités. (c) Nous éliminons aussi les dictionnaires de volume réduit. Ceux-ci sont, en effet, trop nombreux pour être tous mentionnés ici et leur intérêt lexicographique est d'ailleurs mineur dans le cadre de ce chapitre. — A l'intérieur des limites que nous venons de fixer, notre description du paysage dictionnairique sera plus poussée pour les XVIe, XVIIe et XVIIIe siècles que pour les XIXe et XXe siècles. Le foisonnement des dictionnaires bilingues F-E/E-F après 1800 est, en effet, tel qu'il nous contraint dans la plupart des cas à une simple énumération. Ajoutons encore que nous avons examiné personnellement chacun des dictionnaires dont nous parlons dans ce chapitre.

2. Dictionnaires bilingues généraux

2.1. Du XVIe au XVIIIe siècle

2.1.1. En France et en Belgique

Si nous tenons compte des restrictions susmentionnées, le premier dictionnaire général où apparaissent ensemble le français et l'espagnol est Hornkens 1599, qui paraît à Bruxelles, capitale des Pays-Bas espagnols. Il y a trente ans déjà, Colón (1956, 384) soulignait l'importance et l'originalité de cet ouvrage unidirectionnel Français-Espagnol-Latin, qui ne compte pas moins de 554 pages. Nous lui consacrerons donc toute l'attention qu'il mérite.

Verdonk (1979 et 1988 b) a examiné les raisons pour lesquelles ce premier véritable dictionnaire F-E surgit précisément à cet endroit et à ce moment-là. L'auteur, H. Hornkens, n'est pas un Espagnol, mais un «Flamenco», originaire de Bois-le-Duc (ville qui à l'époque faisait partie des Pays-Bas espagnols), qui a appris la langue espagnole en Espagne durant un séjour de plus de dix ans à la cour de Philippe II. Lorsqu'en 1596 l'Archiduc Albert, qui réside également à cette cour, est nommé gouverneur général des Pays-Bas, Hornkens fait partie de la suite qui l'accompagne à Bruxelles. Peu de temps avant sa mort, Philippe II décide de donner sa fille Isabelle en mariage à Albert et d'octroyer à ceux-ci une très large autonomie quant au gouvernement des Pays-Bas espagnols. Bruxelles voit ainsi surgir en son sein une véritable cour avec des souverains hispanophones. Les membres de l'aristocratie «belge», de même que les nombreux généraux et officiers étrangers, qui font partie de l'*Ejército de Flandes,* fréquentent cette cour et veulent apprendre la langue espagnole. C'est pour répondre à leur demande que Hornkens rédige son dictionnaire.

Comme l'a déjà indiqué Colón (1956, 384), ce n'est pas dans la nomenclature française, ni dans sa traduction en latin, qu'il faut en premier lieu rechercher l'originalité de Hornkens. En effet, celles-ci proviennent presque intégralement de l'édition »du Puys« (1573, 1584) du *Dictionnaire françois-latin* de R. Estienne. Toute l'originalité du lexicographe brabançon réside, par contre, dans la colonne espagnole. Comme il rédigeait le premier «véritable» dictionnaire franco-espagnol, il ne disposait en effet d'aucune source directe pour les équivalents espagnols. La réalisation, par Verdonk/Daulie (1983), d'un index exhaustif des occurrences espagnoles (il y en a 47.781), reclassées alphabétiquement par ordinateur, a permis à Verdonk (1988 b et 1990) de prouver le haut degré d'originalité du lexique espagnol contenu dans Hornkens 1599. Celui-ci innove largement par rapport à tous les dictionnaires monolingues et bilingues ayant paru avant lui. Il constitue une source inestimable pour connaître le vocabulaire espagnol du XVIe siècle tel qu'il se pratiquait à la cour de Madrid et, en plus, il reprend un certain nombre de néologismes empruntés au français (picard, wallon) des Pays-Bas, qui étaient devenus courants dans la langue espagnole pratiquée là-bas, et dont certains seront repris plus tard dans l'espagnol de la Péninsule. Même si le dictionnaire de Hornkens n'a connu qu'une seule édition (1599) — l'auteur est décédé un an plus tard — son influence, surtout à travers Oudin, sur la lexicographie franco-espagnole du XVIIe et du début du XVIIIe siècle a été très grande (cf. Colón 1956, 384).

Jean Palet, médecin français au service de Henri de Bourbon, prince de Condé, est l'auteur du premier dictionnaire bidirectionnel E-F/F-E (1604). Cooper (1962) a démontré que la partie F-E s'inspire largement de Hornkens 1599. En ce qui concerne la partie E-F, Gili Gaya (1951, 36 sq) affirme que Palet a tiré sa nomenclature espagnole du *Vocabulario* »Espagnol-Latin« de A. de Nebrija et du *Vocabulario* »Espagnol-Italien« de C. de las Casas; Cooper (1962), par contre, estime que c'est à nouveau Hornkens 1599 qui lui a servi de base. Un examen approfondi devrait permettre de trancher la question. Palet 1604 a été réédité en 1606/1607. Pour les différences entre la 1e et la 2e édition, nous renvoyons à Cooper (1962, 300 sq).

Nous en arrivons ainsi au fameux *Tesoro* de César Oudin, qui de par ses nombreuses éditions (échelonnées entre 1607 et 1675) domine toute la lexicographie franco-espagnole du XVIIe siècle. Même s'il doit beaucoup à ses prédécesseurs, Hornkens 1599 et Palet 1604, comme l'a démontré de manière convaincante L. Cooper (1962), il leur est très supérieur, tant quantitativement que qualitativement. Von Gemmingen a analysé récemment les différents mérites de Oudin 1607 et arrive à la conclusion suivante:

«In der Geschichte der zweisprachigen Lexikographie ist Oudin 1607, trotz mancher Mängel und Inkonsequenzen, einer der Marksteine, die eine Abkehr von den lexikographischen Traditionen des 16. Jahrhunderts signalisieren und zugleich auch neue Wege weisen. Oudin beschränkt sich nicht nur darauf, zwei Nomenklaturen gegenüberzustellen bzw. eine bloße Umkehrung von Makro- und Mikrostruktur vorzunehmen, sondern er bemüht sich, dem Benutzer zwei unterschiedliche Sprachstrukturen mit ihren jeweiligen Besonderheiten vor Augen zu führen. Zweifellos kann eine Reihe von Merkmalen seines lexikographischen Diskurses als vorbildhaft auch für die nachfolgende einsprachige Lexikographie angesehen werden» (von Gemmingen 1987 b, 233).

Von Gemmingen fait cependant remarquer que c'est surtout le vocabulaire français — et pas tellement le vocabulaire espagnol — qui dans Oudin frappe par sa richesse et sa variété. — L'édition de 1616 se trouve sensiblement augmentée par rapport à celle de 1607. Cooper (1960a et 1960b) a prouvé que C. Oudin a puisé pour ce faire dans deux sources: (1) Il a emprunté au *Tesoro* de Covarrubias mille entrées nouvelles et un nombre indéterminé d'acceptions servant à amplifier des entrées déjà existantes. (2) Il a repris les trois quarts des trois mille entrées nouvelles, ajoutées par Vittori à son *Tesoro* (1609) trilingue (ce dernier est fondamentalement un plagiat de Oudin 1607, auquel Vittori a ajouté la partie italienne). Ajoutons à cela que Oudin 1616 contient également en annexe le *Vocabulario de Germanía* de J. Hidalgo. — C. Oudin étant décédé en 1625, les éditions postérieures à cette date sont l'œuvre de son fils Antoine; après la mort de celui-ci en 1653, le *Tesoro* sera encore réédité à Bruxelles, Paris et Lyon. Sánchez Regueira (1982) a prouvé que l'apport d'Antoine Oudin a été considérable et linguistiquement pertinent, tant pour le vocabulaire espagnol que pour le vocabulaire français.

En plus de ses nombreuses rééditions, le succès du *Tesoro* de Oudin ressort également du fait que de nombreux autres lexicographes bilingues ou plurilingues l'ont pris comme source ou l'ont tout simplement plagié. C'est le cas, entre autres, de G. Vittori (cf. Cooper 1960a, 5sqq), L. Franciosini (cf. Gallina 1959, 271) et du *Grande dictionario y thesoro de las tres lenguas Española, Francesa y Flamenca*. Cet ouvrage a été imprimé plusieurs fois à Anvers entre 1639 et 1646 sur les presses de C.-J. Trognesius, sans nom d'auteur, et est connu en Espagne sous le nom de *Anónimo de Amberes* (cf. Peeters-Fontainas 1965, 163). Verdonk (1988 a) en a analysé et comparé les différentes éditions et a démontré que cet «Anónimo» se compose, en fait, de trois parties bien distinctes, dont il a établi la paternité comme suit: (1) La partie Espagnol-Français-Néerlandais (qui se trouve dans la 1e et la 2e édition): toutes les entrées espagnoles et leurs équivalents français sont un plagiat presque littéral de la 4e édition (Bruxelles, Mommart, 1625) de C. Oudin. Quant aux équivalents néerlandais, qui y ont été ajoutés (de manière très littérale d'ailleurs), ils sont l'œuvre, soit de l'imprimeur Trognesius lui-même, soit d'un de ses collaborateurs. (2) La partie Français-Espagnol (qui se trouve dans la 3e édition) est encore moins originale. Il s'agit à nouveau d'un plagiat de la 4e édition de C. Oudin, cette fois-ci dans sa partie «F-E». Trognesius a copié systématiquement toutes les entrées françaises de C. Oudin, sauf les sept premières, probablement pour donner l'impression qu'il s'agissait d'un dictionnaire différent. Les équivalents espagnols sont eux aussi plagiés littéralement de Oudin. Les seules différences consistent en quelques modifications de type graphique et des suppressions de l'un ou l'autre équivalent espagnol, lorsque Oudin en donne plusieurs. (3) La partie Néerlandais-Espagnol (qui se trouve dans la 2e, la 4e, la 5e et la 6e édition) n'a rien d'original non plus: c'est une simple réimpression du *Nieuwen Dictionaris om te leeren de Nederlantsche ende Spaensche Talen,* dont l'auteur est J. Fr. Rodríguez et qui avait été publié en 1634 à Anvers, précisément sur les presses de C. J. Trognesius (cf. Verdonk 1981, 273 sq). Après la mort de l'auteur, qui survint quelques années plus tard, l'imprimeur n'eut aucun scrupule à publier le *Nieuwen Dictionaris* sous un titre différent sans faire la moindre allusion à son auteur.

Au début du XVIIIe siècle paraît à Bruxelles un nouveau dictionnaire F-E/E-F, le *Dicionario nuevo de las lenguas española y francesa,* dont l'auteur est Fr. Sobrino, ancien officier de l'*Ejército de Flandes* et maître de langues à la cour de Bruxelles. La source principale du tome E-F n'est autre que le *Tesoro* de C. Oudin. Verdonk (1979, 335 sqq) a cependant démontré que Sobrino l'utilise de manière assez critique. D'une part, il supprime un grand nombre d'entrées (environ un quart) qui se trouvaient chez Oudin. Ces suppressions ont trait à: (1) des lexèmes qui étaient devenus des archaïsmes au début du XVIIIe siècle; (2) des lexèmes qui ne semblent jamais avoir été attestés chez les auteurs espagnols et pouvaient donc être considérés comme de pures inventions de Oudin; (3) les lexèmes de *germanía* qu'Oudin avait introduits dans son *Tesoro* à partir de la deuxième édition. — D'autre part, Sobrino ajoute un certain nombre d'entrées nouvelles par rapport à Oudin. Parmi ces additions, qui sont cependant moins nombreuses que les suppressions, Verdonk distingue plusieurs catégories: (1) des collocations pour des entrées figurant déjà chez Oudin; (2) des néologismes ayant surgi dans la langue espagnole de la Péninsule ou des Pays-Bas espagnols durant le XVIIe siècle; (3) des lexèmes qui existaient depuis bien avant le XVIIe siècle, mais qui ne figuraient pas chez Oudin. Ajoutons à cela que Sobrino intègre dans la macrostructure toute une série de toponymes et d'hydronymes (chez Oudin une liste plus restreinte de ceux-ci se trouvait en annexe). La partie E-F de Sobrino 1705 constitue donc une mise à jour de Oudin, une adaptation à l'évolution de l'espagnol tel qu'il s'utilisait au début du

XVIIIᵉ siècle. — En ce qui concerne la partie F-E du *Dicionario nuevo,* des recherches en cours, menées sous la direction de Verdonk, indiquent que c'est non seulement le *Tesoro* de Oudin, mais aussi le *Dictionnaire français* de Richelet et la créativité propre de l'auteur, qui sont à la base de la nomenclature française de Sobrino 1705. Les équivalents espagnols que Sobrino donne pour ces entrées françaises font en ce moment l'objet d'une étude approfondie — sur base d'un index exhaustif des occurrences espagnoles reclassées alphabétiquement par ordinateur (Verdonk/ Daulie 1989) — mais d'ores et déjà on peut affirmer que pour ceux-ci également, Sobrino fait preuve d'originalité. Le fait qu'un certain nombre de traductions de Sobrino soient des néologismes de la langue espagnole des Pays-Bas méridionaux, inconnus dans la Péninsule, tend à confirmer que Sobrino se basait sur sa propre compétence linguistique et celle du milieu dans lequel il vivait. — Le Sobrino 1705 a connu plusieurs rééditions (1721, 1734, 1744, 1751, 1760), mais ce n'est que celle de 1721 qui a été réalisée par l'auteur. Les quatre suivantes sont posthumes.

En 1749 paraît à Paris le *Nouveau Dictionnaire espagnol-françois et latin.* L'auteur, M. de Séjournant, avait été nommé en 1740 interprète du Roi de France, après un séjour de 34 ans en Espagne. La partie E-F-L de son dictionnaire est très volumineuse: elle contient deux fois plus d'articles que le Sobrino 1705. Cette richesse s'explique par le fait que presque toute la nomenclature espagnole est tirée du *Diccionario de Autoridades* de la *Real Academia española* (Madrid, 1726—1739, 6 vol.); les équivalents et définitions en français s'inspirent d'ailleurs largement de la même source. Pour les entrées de la partie F-E (sans latin), l'auteur s'est basé sur le dictionnaire de l'Académie française. Séjournant 1749 a connu un grand succès tout au long de la 2ᵉ moitié du XVIIIᵉ siècle. Il a été plusieurs fois réédité, et aussi copié. — Le plagiat le plus flagrant est l'œuvre de Cormon 1769, qui porte comme titre *Sobrino aumentado* et comme lieu d'édition Anvers. Il s'agit d'une double contre-vérité: d'une part, ce n'est pas à Anvers, mais à Genève qu'il a été édité et imprimé (cf. Bonnant 1981, 35); d'autre part, il usurpe le nom de Sobrino puisque c'est Séjournant qu'il plagie presque complètement. Hormis une série de suppressions (surtout dans la première partie du volume E-F), son unique apport consiste à avoir ajouté des équivalents latins dans le volume F-E de Séjournant. — Gattel 1790 se base également sur Séjournant, mais de manière beaucoup plus indépendante. Ce dictionnaire attire particulièrement l'attention par une longue introduction de 72 pages, qui constitue une réflexion approfondie à propos de l'ensemble des problèmes qui se posent aux traducteurs et lexicographes F-E/E-F. Il se distingue également par son système original de symboles pour toute une série de marques d'usage et par l'application systématique qu'il en fait dans la microstructure.

2.1.2. En Espagne

Il faut attendre jusqu'au XVIIIᵉ siècle (qui coïncide avec l'avènement des Bourbons) pour voir se publier des dictionnaires généraux F-E et/ou E-F. Le premier est Torre y Ocón 1728/1731. Il s'agit d'un ouvrage bidirectionnel qui, d'après son auteur (traducteur de profession), forme un tout avec sa double grammaire (l'une française, expliquée en espagnol et l'autre espagnole, expliquée en français), éditée la même année (Palau, 335645). Herrero 1744, unidirectionnel F-E, est un dictionnaire de décodage qui se propose de dépasser qualitativement et quantitativement Torre y Ocón et Sobrino. Son abondante nomenclature française est tirée du *Dictionnaire de Trévoux.* Non seulement Herrero traduit les définitions et marques d'usage de ce dictionnaire, mais il propose également une solution pour les nombreux proverbes, collocations et expressions qu'il y trouve: il donne soit une traduction ou un équivalent quand ceux-ci existent, soit, dans le cas contraire, une périphrase ou une définition. — Une vingtaine d'années plus tard paraît González de Mendoza 1761—63. Il s'agit d'un ouvrage bidirectionnel dont la partie E-F présente une structure particulière: l'auteur donne d'abord (pages 1 à 342) les unités lexicales qui ont une traduction directe dans l'autre langue; ensuite seulement (pages 343 à 356) viennent les expressions idiomatiques et les proverbes pour lesquels il n'existe que des équivalents approximatifs.

2.2. Du XIXᵉ au XXᵉ siècle

Pour les raisons mentionnées sous 1., nous nous bornons à énumérer ici les dictionnaires. Sauf indication contraire, il s'agit d'ouvrages bidirectionnels.

2.2.1. En France et en Belgique

Durant le XIXᵉ siècle on assiste en France à un véritable foisonnement de dictionnaires F-E/E-F.

Pas moins de neufs nouveaux ouvrages (sans compter les dictionnaires «portatifs»: cf. 2.3.) voient le jour entre 1812 et 1860: Núñez de Taboada 1812, Trapany/Rosily/Nodier 1826, Fonseca 1840 (dont la nomenclature est très largement redevable au précédent), Valdemoros Alvarez 1840, Martínez-López/Maurel 1841, Salvá/Guim (F-E) 1856 et Salvá/Noriega (E-F) 1856, Gildo 1858 et Blanc 1860. Ceux qui, parmi eux, ont incontestablement obtenu le plus grand succès sont Núñez de Taboada (18 éditions, rien qu'en France) et Salvá/Guim-Salvá/Noriega (14 éditions entre 1856 et 1893). Pour ce qui est du XIXe siècle, il faut encore mentionner Corona Bustamante 1882/1901. Durant le XXe siècle, la publication de dictionnaires F-E/E-F en France se poursuit à un rythme accéléré: Salvá/Toro Gómez 1900 (qui est le continuateur de Salvá/Guim et Salvá/Noriega et a connu — comme eux — de multiples rééditions), Delgado Campos 1948/1950, Salvá/Larrieu/García Morente 1951, Denis/Maraval (F-E) 1960 et Denis/Pompidou/Maraval (E-F) 1968 (ainsi que Maraval/Denis/Pompidou 1976, qui en est une réélaboration), Corbière/Lautier 1965 (E-F) (qui est une mise à jour de Delgado Campos 1950), García-Pelayo/Testas 1967.

2.2.2. En Espagne

Comme pour les siècles précédant l'année 1800, le bilan est quantitativement bien plus maigre qu'en France. Il y a d'abord Capmany 1805, unidirectionnel F-E, qui critique durement, dans son prologue, la qualité des dictionnaires F-E publiés en dehors d'Espagne et se propose d'y apporter une alternative. Domínguez 1845 est le plus étendu des dictionnaires bilingues publiés jusqu'alors: il peut être rangé parmi les dictionnaires universels à caractère encyclopédique. Fernández Cuesta 1885/1887 se situe dans la même lignée. En ce qui concerne le XXe siècle, il y a lieu de mentionner d'abord Reyes 1926. Ce dictionnaire a connu un grand succès en Espagne et en est actuellement à sa 41e édition. Ensuite il faut mentionner le Vox 1950 (suivi par le Vidal/Vox 1977, considérablement augmenté et actualisé), Martínez Amador 1950 (plusieurs fois réédité depuis), Valle Abad s. d., Puy-Costa 1966, García Navarro/Clerc 1976 et Larrieu/García Llorente 1981 (dont la nomenclature est identique à celle de Salvá/Larrieu/García Morente 1951).

2.3. Dictionnaires «portatifs» ou «de poche»

Dès la fin du XVIIIe siècle nous voyons surgir — en France d'abord et ensuite en Espagne — des dictionnaires bilingues appelés *portatifs (portátiles)* ou *de poche (de faltriquera)*. Ils ne contiennent que rarement des marques d'usage ou de la phraséologie et se limitent généralement à un ou deux équivalents par entrée. Les premiers dictionnaires de ce type que nous ayons relevés sont Godoy 1795, Gattel 1798 et Cormon 1800. Ils sont suivis de toute une série d'autres. Vu l'espace limité qui nous est accordé, il ne nous est pas possible de les énumérer.

3. Dictionnaires bilingues spécialisés

3.1. Dictionnaires d'apprentissage

3.1.1. Vocabulaires de base classés par centres d'intérêt

Le premier à mentionner ici est Robles 1615. La majeure partie de cet ouvrage est constituée par une liste de mots espagnols usuels classés par matières (pages 13 à 62), suivie de sept dialogues en espagnol, que Robles, originaire de Alcalá, a fait traduire par Jean Blanchet, à l'intention du public français. — Dans Luna 1625 (pages 211 à 260) on trouve également un vocabulaire unidirectionnel E-F classé par centres d'intérêt. Intitulé *Nomenclator,* il vient à la suite d'une longue série de *Dialogos familiares,* bilingues eux aussi, destinés à la compréhension de la langue espagnole par un public français. — Oudin 1647 porte le titre significatif de *Nomenclature françoise et espagnole.* Ses 348 pages y sont entièrement consacrées. Il est évidemment beaucoup plus exhaustif que Robles et Luna. Contrairement à ceux-ci, il est unidirectionnel F-E, destiné donc à l'apprentissage actif de l'espagnol par un public français. — En 1680 paraît la *Nouvelle Grammaire* de Ferrus, qui comprend également une nomenclature unidirectionnelle F-E. Celle-ci est de taille plus modeste (108 pages) que celle d'Oudin. Elle connaîtra plusieurs rééditions.

Mentionnons, pour le XIXe siècle, Hamonière 1815, qui, outre une série de dialogues et une liste d'idiotismes, comprend aussi une nomenclature unidirectionnelle E-F de 77 pages, intitulée «Vocabulaire de mots usuels», ainsi que Ochoa 1843, également E-F, plusieurs fois réédité jusqu'en 1881. — Vu le foisonnement de ce type d'ouvrages, nous nous bornons à citer quelques-uns d'entre eux, destinés au public scolaire français du dernier demi-siècle: Contamine/Novion 1930, Agnès/Viñas 1948, Cazes/Chicharro 1950, Labarde/Pau 1980, Collins 1983. Ils sont unidirectionnels E-F. En plus de la traduction des mots les plus fréquents, ils donnent aussi des équivalents pour un certain nombre de locutions et d'idiotismes.

3.1.2. Vocabulaires de base classés alphabétiquement

Ledel de Liaño 1565 contient un modeste répertoire d'environ 1500 mots français, avec leurs équivalents en espagnol.

D'après Flores Varela 1978, sa publication à Alcalá en 1565 s'inscrit dans le contexte du rapprochement politique entre la France et l'Espagne suite à la paix du Cateau-Cambrésis. En 1560, Philippe II, roi d'Espagne, épouse la princesse française Isabelle de Valois. Celle-ci vient s'installer à la Cour d'Espagne avec toute une suite de dames et de gentilhommes français. Le besoin d'intercompréhension explique la parution, non seulement du *Vocabulario* de Ledel de Liaño, mais aussi, la même année et chez le même éditeur, d'une grammaire française rédigée en espagnol, dont l'auteur est B. de Sotomayor.

Azorín (1985) a analysé le *Vocabulario* et est arrivé à la conclusion qu'il n'est pas original du tout: Ledel de Liaño s'est inspiré directement dans un des *dictionariola* appartenant à la lignée des Berlaymont, probablement le quadrilingue publié à Louvain en 1558 par B. Grave. Azorín estime d'ailleurs qu'il est inférieur à son modèle quant à l'efficacité didactique et l'orientation pragmatique. — Malgré son titre, l'*Espeio General de la Gramatica* 1614 de Salazar aborde également des problèmes lexicaux. Morel-Fatio passe en revue les différentes parties de cet ouvrage et conclut que «la plus instructive en même temps que la plus nouvelle partie du *Miroir* est le recueil de mots et d'expressions avec exemples à l'appui qui remplit la septième journée» (Morel-Fatio 1900, 65 sq). D'après Abouaf, «il s'agit en fait d'une des premières tentatives systématiques visant à compléter les dictionnaires de l'époque. Il y avait là une lacune à combler. Les auteurs des manuels se sentaient obligés de mettre en appendice les listes d'expressions traduites qui servaient à doubler les dictionnaires, voire à les rectifier» (Abouaf 1982, XX). — La première partie (pages 1 à 96) de Huillery 1661 présente un vocabulaire de base unidirectionnel E-F, qui, d'après l'auteur (qui a passé 22 ans de sa vie en Espagne) est destiné, de manière quelque peu grandiloquente, à «apprendre aysément et briévement à lire, escrire et parler la langue Espagnolle.» — Maunory 1701 paraît peu après l'avènement de Philippe V sur le trône d'Espagne et se veut un instrument pratique et efficace d'encodage pour les Français qui se rendent dans ce pays. La première partie (pages 1 à 80) est une grammaire espagnole expliquée en français et la seconde (pages 81 à 328) un dictionnaire unidirectionnel F-E, qui se limite à donner les équivalents espagnols sans autre indication que le genre des noms. Dans sa préface, Maunory signale — pour justifier son travail — que les mots et expressions contenus dans les ouvrages d'Oudin sont devenus caducs et ne permettent plus de se faire comprendre en Espagne. — En 1717, Fr. Sobrino fait suivre la troisième édition de sa *Grammatica nueva* (pages 290 à 461) d'un petit dictionnaire bidirectionnel E-F/F-E destiné aux écoliers, qui se limite à une nomenclature sèche. — Vu l'espace limité, il ne nous est pas possible de prêter attention aux très nombreux vocabulaires de base parus ultérieurement.

3.2. Dictionnaires syntagmatiques

3.2.1. Dictionnaires de phraséologie et d'idiotismes

Le premier ouvrage phraséologique à mentionner ici est Tejeda, publié à Paris en 1629. La seconde partie de sa *Méthode* (pages 208 à 361) ne contient pas moins de 1953 *frases de hablar difíciles de la lengua española,* classées alphabétiquement et accompagnées de leur traduction en français. Comme il s'agit d'un livre très rare, Collet Sedola (1984) a pris l'initiative de les rééditer dans la revue *Criticón*. Tejeda 1629 s'adresse essentiellement à un public francophone, qui désire comprendre la littérature espagnole contemporaine. Dans sa thèse de 3e cycle, Abouaf (1982) a étudié ces *frases* et en a réalisé une édition critique. Il loue l'élégance et l'exactitude des traductions de Tejeda et arrive à la conclusion que son œuvre peut être considérée comme l'ensemble phraséologique bilingue le plus important paru en France durant le premier tiers du XVIIe siècle. — Le second ouvrage phraséologique qui mérite d'être cité est Capmany 1776, publié à Madrid. C'est un ouvrage de décodage F-E qui s'adresse tant aux traducteurs qu'aux simples lecteurs hispanophones. Il se veut un complément indispensable des dictionnaires bilingues généraux F-E, où, d'après l'auteur, la phraséologie la plus élémentaire fait défaut. Même si cette affirmation nous semble quelque peu exagérée, la longue préface de Capmany constitue une réflexion intéressante sur les nombreux problèmes que posent la contrastivité des langues et la traduction.

Les deux dictionnaires suivants, Rotondo 1841 et Besses 1901, paraissent à Madrid et sont bidirectionnels. Le second est plus volumineux que le premier car il ne lance d'exclusive à l'encontre d'aucun niveau de langue (cf. Besses 1901, 6 sq). — Coïncidant avec la présence militaire française au Mexique, le *Tratado* de Trusson 1856 se veut un manuel sélectif d'encodage pour les Mexicains. Il approfondit 86 points d'ordre lexical et grammatical pour lesquels l'espagnol et le français présentent une structure différente. — Tout au long de la période considérée, les dictionnaires bilingues généraux présentent une moisson plus ou moins abondante de phraséologie et d'idiotismes caractéristiques des deux langues en question. C'est ce qui explique probablement la relative rareté d'ouvrages purement syntagmatiques E-F et/ou F-E. Mentionnons le plus récent et le plus copieux d'entre eux: il s'agit de Rongé-Dethier 1983, qui offre par ordre alphabétique plus de 2000 locutions et expressions idiomatiques espagnoles présentées en regard de tournures homologues — quant au contenu — en français et utilisées dans des phrases dont les versions espagnole et français sont également offertes en parallèle.

3.2.2. Dictionnaires de proverbes

Le premier recueil de proverbes espagnols traduits en français est Oudin 1608 (Morel-Fatio 1900, 108 date erronément la première édition de 1605), qui sera plusieurs fois réédité. Oudin y a rassemblé quelque 2000 proverbes espagnols tirés de diverses sources péninsulaires et les a traduits en français; la seule source qu'il mentionne explicitement est Alonso Guajardo Fajardo, dont une série de *proverbios morales* se trouvent réunis à la fin du volume (pages 233 à 256). — Ensuite il faut mentionner Ferrus 1680 qui a rassemblé à la fin de sa *Nouvelle Grammaire espagnolle* une série de 346 «sentences courtes, et proverbes pleins de sens tirez des plus excellens Auteurs, & de l'entretien ordinaire des Espagnols», qu'il a traduits en français. Cette série a été reprise intégralement dans Maunory 1704, qui ne mentionne pas sa source. — Les pages 179 à 215 de Hamonière 1815, intitulées «Recueil d'idiotismes, d'expressions familières et de proverbes» constituent une liste E-F fort hétérogène où les proverbes se trouvent mélangés à la phraséologie.

3.3. Dictionnaires de périodes historiques

Le seul ouvrage à mentionner est Sésé 1968. Il s'agit d'un dictionnaire de décodage E-F du vocabulaire des «siècles d'or», classé par centres d'intérêt et destiné aux étudiants universitaires français.

3.4. Dictionnaires d'images

Les dictionnaires d'images, qui se limitent nécessairement au vocabulaire concret, constituent un phénomène récent dans le paysage dictionnairique F-E/E-F. Il y a lieu de saluer ici la parution récente de l'excellent ouvrage de référence que constitue le Duden/Alvar/Moskowitz 1985, qui vient enfin combler une grande lacune.

3.5. Dictionnaires de «faux amis»

S'agissant de deux langues fort proches, les paronymes soulèvent pas mal de problèmes lors de l'apprentissage de la langue espagnole par les Français et vice versa. C'est pourquoi les dictionnaires de «faux amis» jouent un rôle important sur le plan didactique. Citons, à titre d'exemple, Dupont 1961, Dumont 1970 et Péan 1971.

3.6. Dictionnaires des dictionnaires

Gili Gaya 1947/1957, qui a eu un large écho parmi les spécialistes dont Alonso (1951) et Colón (1956), réunit la nomenclature contenue dans 93 dictionnaires espagnols (tant monolingues que plurilingues) publiés entre 1492 et 1726. Parmi ceux-ci ne se trouvent que cinq dictionnaires imprimés contenant notre paire de langues: Ledel de Liaño 1565, Palet 1604, Oudin 1607 et 1616 et Sobrino 1705. Il est en outre dommage que Gili Gaya ne reprenne que la partie E-F de ceux-ci, et non la partie F-E. A propos des inconvénients résultant de cette option, nous renvoyons à Colón (1956, 381) et Verdonk (1980, 207). Signalons aussi que le travail de Gili Gaya est resté inachevé: il ne va pas au-delà de la lettre E.

3.7. Dictionnaires de néologismes

Belot 1986 est un dictionnaire d'encodage F-E sélectif qui se propose d'offrir au public français le vocabulaire et la phraséologie de la langue espagnole récente ne figurant pas dans les dictionnaires courants. En regard des mots français, chaque équivalent espagnol donné est illustré par une citation-attestation, tirée de la presse espagnole des dernières années.

4. Dictionnaires bilingues des langues de spécialités

Les premiers dictionnaires bilingues E-F/F-E de ce type font leur apparition au début du XIXe siècle. Ils iront se multipliant rapidement, surtout au courant du XXe siècle, et embrassent les domaines les plus divers. Comme il est impossible de les énumérer ici, nous renvoyons aux bibliographies spécialisées telles que Quemada/Menemencioglu 1978 et Fabbri 1979. Il faut d'ailleurs noter que très souvent ces dictionnaires ne sont pas bilingues mais plurilingues.

5. Bibliographie choisie

5.1. Dictionnaires

Agnès/Viñas 1948 = J. Agnès/A. Viñas: Les mots espagnols et les locutions espagnoles groupées d'après le sens. Paris 1980 [311 p.; 1e éd. 1948].

Belot 1986 = Albert Belot: Lexique français-espagnol de la langue actuelle. Toulouse 1986 [325 p.].

Besses 1901 = Luis Besses: Novísimo diccionario fraseológico francés-español y español-francés formado de expresiones, modismos y locuciones familiares, vulgares y populares según los mejores diccionarios y autores más modernos. Madrid s. d. (1901) [912 p.].

Blanc 1860 = Saint-Hilaire Blanc: Novísimo diccionario francés-español y español-francés, con la pronunciación figurada en ambas lenguas [. . .] Revista y corregida la parte española por D. A. Jover. 2 Vol. Paris. Lyon 1860 [1158, 1286 p.].

Capmany 1776 = Antonio de Capmany: Arte de traducir del idioma francés al castellano, con el vocabulario lógico y figurado de la frase comparada de ambas lenguas. Madrid 1776 [XVI, 200 p.; dernière éd. 1839].

Capmany 1805 = Antonio de Capmany: Nuevo diccionario francés-español. En este van enmendados, corregidos, mejorados, y enriquecidos considerablemente los de Gattel, y Cormon [. . .] Madrid 1805 [XXIV, 794, 54 p.; 2e éd. 1817].

Cazes/Chicharro 1950 = Jean Cazes/J. Chicharro de León: Petit Vocabulaire Espagnol. Gap 1968 [94 p.; 1e éd. 1950].

Collins 1983 = Collins: Connaître et utiliser 5000 mots d'espagnol. s. l. 1983 [191 p.].

Contamine/Novion 1930 = E. Contamine de Latour/F. Novion: Palabras y modismos. Toulouse. Paris 1948 [VIII, 324 p.; dernière éd. 1955; 1e éd. 1930].

Corbière/Lautier 1965 = A. Corbière/D. Lautier: Dictionnaire espagnol-français. Paris 1965 [X, 1035 p.].

Cormon 1769 = Francisco Cormon: Sobrino aumentado, o nuevo diccionario de las lenguas española, francesa y latina. Compuesto de los mejores Diccionarios, que hasta ahora han salido a luz; dividido en tres tomos: los dos primeros contienen el Español explicado por el Francés y el Latín, y el tercero el Francés explicado por el Español y el Latín [. . .] 3 Vol. Amberes 1769 [IV, 589, II, 697, II, 613 p.; dernière éd. 1791].

Cormon 1800 = J. L. Barthelemi Cormon: Dictionnaire portatif et de prononciation espagnol-français et français-espagnol, à l'usage des deux nations, composé et rédigé fidèlement, d'après la dernière Edition du Dictionnaire de l'Académie Royale Espagnole, et les meilleurs Dictionnaires Français [. . .] 2 Vol. Lyon 1800 [VIII, 776, XII, 688 p.; 2e éd. 1803].

Corona Bustamante 1882/1901 = Francisco Corona Bustamante: Diccionario francés-español basado en la parte francesa sobre el gran diccionario de E. Littré y en la parte española sobre el diccionario de la lengua castellana [. . .] Diccionario español-francés [. . .] 2 Vol. Paris 1882/1901 [1374, 1459 p.].

Delgado Campos 1948/1950 = J. Delgado Campos: Novísimo diccionario francés-español y español-francés. 2 Vol. Paris 1948—1950 [XVI, 784, XII, 939 p.].

Denis/Maraval 1960 = Serge Denis/Marcel Maraval: Dictionnaire français-espagnol. Paris 1960 [VIII, 903 p.].

Denis/Pompidou/Maraval 1968 = Serge Denis/L. Pompidou/Marcel Maraval: Dictionnaire espagnol-français. Paris 1968 [XXI, 1750 p.].

Domínguez 1845 = Ramón Joaquín Domínguez: Diccionario universal francés-español [. . .] Diccionario universal español-francés [. . .] 2e éd. 2 Vol. Madrid, Paris 1853/1854 [II, 1804, 1586 p.; 1e éd. Madrid 1845].

Duden/Alvar Ezquerra/Moskowitz 1985 = Dudenredaktion/Manuel Alvar Ezquerra/Daniel Moskowitz: Oxford-Duden Bildwörterbuch Spanisch und Französisch. Mannheim. Wien. Zürich 1985 [677, 112, 104 p.].

Dumont 1970 = Maurice Alex Dumont: Espagnol-Français. Les fausses concordances lexicales. Louvain 1970 [180 p.].

Dupont 1961 = Louis Dupont: Les faux amis espagnols. Genève. Paris 1961 [166 p.].

Fernández Cuesta 1885/1887 = Nemesio Fernández Cuesta: Diccionario de las lenguas española y francesa comparadas, redactado con presencia de los de las Academias española y francesa, Bescherelle, Littré, Salvá y los últimos publicados [. . .] 4 Vol. Barcelona 1885/1886 [IV, 1078, 699, 759, 675 p.; dernière éd. Buenos Aires 1946].

Ferrus 1680 = Sieur Ferrus: Nouvelle grammaire espagnolle [. . .] avec un ample vocabulaire des choses les plus communes, et usitées dans les Discours familiers. Et un recueil de sentences et proverbes, dont les Espagnols se servent ordinairement dans leurs entretiens. 2e éd. Lyon 1695 [IV, 326 p.; 1e éd. 1680].

Fonseca 1840 = Joseph da Fonseca: Dictionnaire français-espagnol et espagnol-français avec la nouvelle orthographe de l'Académie espagnole rédigé d'après Gattel, Sobrino, Nuñes de Taboada, Trapani, etc.; l'Académie française, Boiste, Laveaux, etc. [. . .] 3e éd. Paris. Mexico. Buenos Aires 1852 [VIII, 485, II, 640 p.; 4e éd. 1858; 1e éd. 1840].

García Navarro/Clerc 1976 = Ana María García Navarro/J. Clerc: Diccionario francés I Francés-Español II Español-Francés. Barcelona 1976 [644 p.].

García-Pelayo/Testas 1967 = Ramón García-Pelayo y Gross/Jean Testas: Dictionnaire moderne français-espagnol. Dictionnaire moderne espagnol-français. Paris. Buenos Aires. México 1967 [XXIV, 783, XVI, 976 p.; dernière éd. 1987].

Gattel 1790 = Claude Marie Gattel: Dictionnaire françois-espagnol et espagnol-françois, avec l'interprétation latine de chaque mot [. . .] 2 Vol. Lyon 1803 [XXIV, 768, 903 p.; 1e éd. 1790].

Gattel 1798 = Claude Marie Gattel: Nouveau dictionnaire de poche françois-espagnol rédigé d'après les meilleurs lexicographes des deux Nations; enrichi des conjugaisons des verbes espagnols tant réguliers qu'irréguliers. Paris 1798 [294 p.].

Gildo 1858 = Domingo Gildo: Dictionnaire espagnol-français et français-espagnol augmenté de plus de 20.000 mots usuels de sciences, arts et métiers et de la prononciation figurée de chaque mot dans les deux langues. Paris 1860 [1097 p.; 1ᵉ éd. 1858].

Gili Gaya 1947/1957 = Samuel Gili Gaya: Tesoro lexicográfico 1492—1726. 4 Fasc. (A—E) Madrid 1947/1957 [XXXI, 1005 p.].

Godoy 1795 = Diego Antonio Godoy: Diccionario nuevo portátil, y manual francés-español [. . .] Bolonia 1795 [496 p.].

González de Mendoza 1761/1763 = Nicolás González de Mendoza: Diccionario general de las dos lenguas española, y francesa. Esta primera parte será de español en francés, y la segunda de francés en español. Es diferente en el methodo de todos los que hasta aora se han dado al Público [. . .] 3 Vol. Madrid 1761/1763 [VIII, 368, IV, 468, 566 p.].

Grande Dictionario 1639 = El Grande Dictionario y Thesoro de las tres lenguas Española, Francesa y Flamenca, con todos los nombres de los Reynos, Ciudades, y lugares del Mundo [. . .]. T'Hantwerpen 1639 [416 F.; dernière éd. 1646].

Hamonière 1815 = G. Hamonière: La nueva guía de la conversación en español y francés, en tres partes [. . .]. La première contenant un vocabulaire de mots usuels par ordre alphabétique; la seconde, quarante Dialogues sur différens sujets; et la troisième, un Recueil d'idiotismes, d'expressions familières et de proverbes. Paris 1815 [VI, 215 p.; dernière éd. 1823].

Herrero 1744 = Antonio María Herrero: Diccionario universal, francés, y español, mas copioso que quantos hasta ahora se han visto, el qual contiene todos los términos usados en la Lengua Francesa, con las frasses y locuciones proprias, y figuradas de todos estilos, y refranes, y todo lo necessario para la perfecta inteligencia de dicho Idioma [. . .] Madrid 1744 [XII, 977 p.].

Hornkens 1599 = Henricus Hornkens: Recueil de dictionaires francoys, espaignolz et latins [. . .]. Bruxelles 1599 [VI, 554 p.].

Huillery 1661 = François Huillery: Vocabulario para facilmente y brievemente deprender a ler, escrebir, y hablar la lengua Castellana con algunas curiosidades [. . .] Paris 1661 [XVIII, 171 p.].

Labarde/Pau 1980 = H. Labarde/F. Pau: Vocabulaire de base espagnol-français. Paris 1980 [222 p.].

Larrieu/García Llorente 1981 = Robert Larrieu/Manuel García Llorente: Diccionario maior francés-español español-francés diáfora. Barcelona 1981 [XXXV, 529, 815 p.].

Ledel de Liaño 1565 = Iaques Ledel de Liaño: Vocabulario de los vocablos que mas comunmente se suelen usar. Puestos por orden del Abecedario, en frances, y su declaracion en Español [. . .] Alcalá 1565 [64 F.].

Luna 1625 = Juan de Luna: Dialogos familiares [. . .]. Muy utiles, y provechosos para los que quieren aprender la lengua Castellana [. . .] con un Nomenclator Español y Frances. Bruxelles 1625 [264 p.; 1ᵉ éd. 1619 (sans *Nomenclator*)].

Maraval/Denis/Pompidou 1976 = Marcel Maraval/Serge Denis/L. Pompidou: Dictionnaire espagnol-français. Paris 1976 [1072 p.].

Martínez Amador 1950 = Emilio M. Martínez Amador: Diccionario Francés-Español Español-Francés revisado y puesto al día por Leopoldo Gimeno [. . .] Barcelona 1970 [1562 p.; 1ᵉ éd. 1950].

Martínez-López/Maurel 1841 = Pedro Martínez-López/Fr. Maurel: Dictionnaire français-espagnol et espagnol-français. Edition économique à l'usage des maisons d'éducation des deux nations [. . .] Paris 1844 [483, 620 p.; 1866; 1ᵉ éd. 1841].

Maunory 1701 = Guillaume de Maunory: Grammaire et dictionnaire françois et espagnol [. . .] suivant l'usage de la Cour d'Espagne. Paris 1701 [VI, 328 p.; dernière éd. 1704].

Núñez de Taboada 1812 = Melchor Manuel Núñez de Taboada: Diccionario francés-español y español-francés, más completo y correcto que todos los que se han publicado hasta ahora, sin exceptuar el de Capmany [. . .] 8ᵉ éd. 2 Vol. Paris 1840 [IV, 964, II, 1392 p.; dernière éd. 1886; 1ᵉ éd. 1812].

Ochoa 1843 = Eugenio de Ochoa: Guía de la conversación español-francés, al uso de los viageros y de los estudiantes [. . .] Paris 1843 [X, 367 p.; dernière éd. 1881].

Oudin 1607 = Cesar Oudin: Tesoro de las dos lenguas francesa y española. Thresor des deux langues françoise et espagnolle: auquel est contenue l'explication de toutes les deux respectivement l'une par l'autre: Divisé en deux parties [. . .] Paris 1607 [VIII, 272, 228 F.; dernière éd. 1675. Il existe une édition en facsimilé de la partie E-F de Oudin 1675, présentée par Bernard Pottier, Paris 1968. Il existe aussi une édition en microfiches de Oudin 1607 et 1645, présentée par Manuel Alvar Ezquerra, Barcelona, ETD Micropublicaciones.].

Oudin 1608 = Cesar Oudin: Refranes o proverbios castellanos traduzidos en lengua Francesa [. . .] 2. éd. Paris 1609 [XVI, 256 p.; 1ᵉ éd. Bruxelles 1608].

Oudin 1647 = Antoine Oudin: Nomenclature françoise et espagnole. Paris 1647 [IV, 348 p.].

Palet 1604 = Iean Palet: Diccionario muy copioso de la lengua Española y Françesa [. . .] Dictionaire tres-ample de la langue françoise et Espagnole [. . .] 2ᵉ éd. Bruxelles 1606/1607 [360 F.; 1ᵉ éd. Paris 1604].

Péan 1971 = F. Y. Péan: Les mots-pièges dans la version espagnole et leurs analogues français. Paris 1971 [320 p.].

Puy-Costa 1966 = Mariano Puy-Costa: Diccionario moderno Langenscheidt de los idiomas francés y español. 14ᵉ éd. Berlin. Munich. Viena. Zurich. Nueva York 1987 [512, 512 p.; 1ᵉ éd. 1966].

Reyes 1926 = Rafael Reyes: Diccionario francés-español y español-francés [...] Madrid 1926 [662 p.; 41e éd. 1979].

Robles 1615 = Lorenzo de Robles: Advertencias y breve metodo para saber leer, escrivir y pronunciar la lengua Castellana con buena ortografia [...]. Paris 1615 [77 p.].

Rongé-Dethier 1983 = Mady Rongé-Dethier: Dicho. Dictionnaire d'hispanismes. Liège 1983 [sans pag.].

Rotondo 1841 = Antonio Rotondo y Rabasco: Diccionario fraseológico español-francés y francés-español. Madrid 1841 [426 p.].

Salazar 1614 = Ambrosio de Salazar: Espeio general de la gramatica en dialogos para saber la natural y perfecta pronunciacion de la lengua Castellana. Servira tambien de Vocabulario para aprenderla con mas facilidad, con algunas Historias graciosas y sentencias muy de notar. Rouen 1627 [XX, 513 p.; 1e éd. 1614; dernière éd. 1659].

Salvá/Guim 1856 = Vicente Salvá/Juan Guim: Nuevo diccionario francés-español y español-francés, con la pronunciación figurada en ambas lenguas, arreglado con presencia de los materiales reunidos para esta obra por D. Vicente Salvá [...] por D.J.B. Guim. Paris. Méjico 1856 [X, 888 p.; 13e éd. 1890].

Salvá/Larrieu/García Morente 1951 = Vicente Salvá y Pérez: Diccionario moderno español-francés y francés-español. Nueva edición enteramente refundida y aumentada por Robert Larrieu y Manuel García Morente. Paris 1951 [XLI, 904, XVII, 591 p.; 12e réimpression 1980].

Salvá/Noriega 1856 = Vicente Salvá/Francisco de Paula Noriega: Nouveau dictionnaire espagnol-français et français-espagnol, avec la prononciation figurée dans les deux langues [...] rédigé d'après les matériaux rúnis par D. Vicente Salvá [...] par F. de P. Noriega. Paris 1856 [646 p.; 13e éd. 1890].

Salvá/Toro Gómez 1900 = Vicente Salvá/Miguel de Toro y Gómez: Nuevo diccionario francés-español con la pronunciación figurada por D. Vicente Salvá. Edición cuidadosamente revisada, corregida y aumentada con diez y ocho mil voces y acepciones nuevas, proverbios, locuciones etc. por Miguel de Toro y Gómez [...]. Nouveau dictionnaire espagnol-français avec la prononciation figurée par D. Vicente Salvá, édition soigneusement revue, corrigée et augmentée de plus de dix mille mots, acceptions nouvelles, proverbes, locutions etc. par Miguel de Toro y Gómez [...] Paris 1905 [XI, 1124, II, 910 p.; 1e éd. 1900; dernière éd. 1947].

Séjournant 1749 = M. de Séjournant: Nouveau dictionnaire espagnol-françois et latin, composé sur les Dictionnaires des Académies Royales de Madrid et de Paris [...]. Nouveau dictionnaire françois-espagnol [...] 2e éd. 2 Vol. Paris 1759 [VII, 1088, II, 520 p.; dernière éd. 1790; 1e éd. 1749].

Sesé 1968 = Bernard Sesé: Vocabulaire de la langue espagnole classique (XVIe et XVIIe siècles). 3e éd. 2 Vol. Paris 1971 [III, 529 p.; 1e éd. 1968].

Sobrino 1705 = Francisco Sobrino: Dicionario nuevo de las lenguas española y francesa. El más copioso y el mejor que ha salido a luz hasta ahora, en que se contiene la explicación del español en francés, y del francés en español, en dos partes [...] 2 Vol. Brusselas 1705 [XII, 376, IV, 430 p.; 6e éd. 1760].

Sobrino 1717 = Francisco Sobrino: Grammatica nueva española y francesa [...]. Corrigida y aumentada en esta tercera Edicion de un Pequeño Diccionario [...] Brusselas 1717 [VIII, 464 p.; 1e éd. 1697; 6e éd. 1745].

Tejeda 1629 = Hierosme de Tejeda: Methode pour entendre facilement les Phrases et difficultez de la langue Espagnolle [...] Paris 1629 [IV, 363 p.].

Torre Ocón 1728/1731 = Francisco de la Torre y Ocón: El maestro de las dos lenguas. Diccionario español, y frances; frances, y español. 2 Vol. Madrid 1728/1731 [XXIV, 531, IV, 500 p.].

Trapany/Rosily/Nodier 1826 = Domingo Gian Trapany/A. de Rosily/Charles Nodier: Nouveau dictionnaire français-espagnol et espagnol-français avec la nouvelle orthographe de l'Académie espagnole rédigé d'après Gattel, Capmany, Nuñez de Taboada, Boiste, Laveaux etc. [...] 2 Vol., Paris. New York. México 1826 [VII, 852, 1275 p.].

Trusson 1856 = J. E. Trusson: Tratado de modismos españoles y franceses. Méjico 1856 [229 p.].

Valdemoros Alvarez 1840 = Pedro de Valdemoros Alvarez: Dictionnaire général espagnol-français et français-espagnol. 2 Vol. Paris 1840 [XIII, 1000, 1200 p.].

Valle Abad s. d. = Federico del Valle Abad: Diccionario francés-español. Avila s. d. [852 p.].

Valle Abad s. d. = Federico del Valle Abad: Dictionnaire espagnol-français avec plus de 140.000 mots ou expressions. Granada s. d. [921 p.].

Vidal/Vox 1977 = Jean-Paul Vidal/Equipe lexicographique Vox: Vox Manual Dictionnaire Français-Espagnol Espagnol-Français. Barcelona, Paris 1977 [LIII, 514, XXIX, 626 p.].

Vox 1950 = Vox: Diccionario manual francés-español español-francés. 13e éd. Barcelona 1987 [514, 626 p.; 1e éd. 1950].

5.2. Travaux

Abouaf 1982 = Sylvain Abouaf: Contribution au vocabulaire du Siècle d'Or. Etude critique des *Phrases de Hablar dificiles de la lengua Española* de Jerónimo de Techeda (1629). Paris 1982 (thèse de 3e cycle).

Aguilar 1981/1986 = Francisco Aguilar Piñal: Bibliografia de autores españoles del siglo XVIII. 5 Vol. (A—M) Madrid 1981/1989.

Alonso 1951 = Amado Alonso: Reseña de Samuel Gili Gaya: Tesoro Lexicográfico 1492—1726. In: Nueva Revista de Filología Hispánica 5. 1951, 324—328.

Alvar Ezquerra 1981 = Manuel Alvar Ezquerra: Los diccionarios bilingües: su contenido: In: Lingüística Española Actual 3. 1981, 175—196.

Azorín 1985 = Dolores Azorín Fernández: Un capítulo de lexicografía hispánica. En torno al vocabulario bilingüe francés-español de Jacques Ledel: In: Lexis. Revista de Lingüística y de Literatura 9. 1985, 101—117.

Belot 1984 = Albert Belot: Pour un lexique français-espagnol de la langue actuelle. In: Les Langues néo-latines 78. 1984, 111—133.

Bonnant 1981 = Georges Bonnant: La librairie genevoise en Amérique latine au XVIIIe siècle. In: J. D. Candaux/B. Lescaze (ed.): Cinq siècles d'Imprimerie genevoise: Actes du Colloque international sur l'histoire de l'imprimerie et du livre à Genève. Genève 1981, 15—41.

Brunot 1966/1972 = Ferdinand Brunot: Histoire de la langue française des origines à nos jours, nouvelle édition sous la direction de Gérald Antoine, Georges Gougenheim et Robert-Léon Wagner. 23 Vol. Paris 1966/1972.

Collet Sedola 1984 = Sabina Collet Sedola: Las *Phrases de hablar difíciles de la lengua española* de Jerónimo de Texeda. In: Criticón 26. 1984, 81—142.

Colón 1956 = Germán Colón: A propos du Tesoro Lexicográfico de M. Gili Gaya. In: Zeitschrift für Romanische Philologie 72. 1956, 379—386.

Cooper 1960a = Louis Cooper: Girolamo Vittori y César Oudin. Un caso de plagio mutuo. In: Nueva Revista de Filología Hispánica 14. 1960, 3—20.

Cooper 1960b = Louis Cooper: Sebastián de Covarrubias: Una de las fuentes principales del *Tesoro de las dos lenguas francesa y española* (1616) de César Oudin. In: Bulletin Hispanique 62. 1960, 365—397.

Cooper 1962 = Louis Cooper: El *Recueil* de Hornkens y los diccionarios de Palet y de Oudin. In: Nueva Revista de Filología Hispánica 16. 1962, 297—328.

Fabbri 1979 = Maurizio Fabbri: A Bibliography of Hispanic Dictionaries. Imola 1979.

Fernández-Sevilla 1974 = Julio Fernández-Sevilla: Problemas de lexicografía actual. Bogota 1974.

Flores Varela 1978 = Camilo D. Flores Varela: Les deux premières méthodes de français pour Espagnols publiées en Espagne. In: Verba. Anuario galego de Filoloxía 5. 1978, 341—350.

Gallina 1959 = Annamaria Gallina: Contributi alla storia della lessicografia italo-spagnola dei secoli XVI e XVII. Firenze 1959.

Gemmingen 1987a = Barbara von Gemmingen: Das verborgene Kochbuch des Herrn Oudin oder: Untersuchungen zum kulinarischen Wortschatz im zweisprachigen Wörterbuch. In: Zeitschrift für Romanische Philologie 103. 1987, 491—499.

Gemmingen 1987b = Barbara von Gemmingen: Untersuchungen zu César Oudins Tesoro de las dos lenguas francesa y española (1607). In: Hans-Josef Niederehe (Hrsg.): Schwerpunkt siglo de Oro: Akten des Deutschen Hispanistentages Wolfenbüttel, 28. 2.—1. 3. 1985. Hamburg 1987, 215—234.

Gili Gaya 1947/1957 = Samuel Gili Gaya: Tesoro lexicográfico 1492—1726. 4 Fasc. (A—E) Madrid 1947/1957.

Gili Gaya 1951 = Samuel Gili Gaya: El primer diccionario español-francés. In: Clavileño 2,12. 1951, 36—37.

Lépinette 1988 = Brigitte Lépinette: Les définitions des émotions en français et en espagnol: Etude sémantique et lexicographique. In: Revue Québecoise de Linguistique 17,2. 1988, 95—131.

Morel-Fatio 1900 = Alfred Morel-Fatio: Ambrosio de Salazar et l'étude de l'espagnol en France sous Louis XIII. Paris. Toulouse 1900.

Niederehe 1987 = Hans-Joseph Niederehe: Les dictionnaires franco-espagnols jusqu'en 1800. In: Histoire Epistémologie Langage, 9,2. 1987, 13—26.

Palau 1948/1977 = Antonio Palau y Dulcet: Manual del Librero Hispanoamericano. 2e éd. 28 Vol. Barcelona 1948/1977.

Peeters-Fontainas 1965 = Jean Peeters-Fontainas: Bibliographie des impressions espagnoles de Pays-Bas méridionaux. 2 Vol. Nieuwkoop 1965.

Polo 1976 = José Polo: El español como lengua extranjera, enseñanza de idiomas y traducción. Tres calas bibliográficas. Madrid 1976.

Quemada 1967 = Bernard Quemada: Les dictionnaires du français moderne 1539—1863. Etude sur leur histoire, leurs types et leurs méthodes. Paris. Bruxelles. Montréal 1967.

Quemada/Menemencioglu 1978 = B. Quemada/K. Menemencioglu: Répertoire des dictionnaires scientifiques et techniques monolingues et multilingues 1950—1975. Paris 1978.

Sánchez Regueira 1982 = Isolina Sánchez Regueira: César et Antoine Oudin: étude comparative des éditions de son *Thrésor* et son importance dans le domaine de la lexicographie. In: Verba. Anuario galego de Filoloxía 9. 1982, 329—340.

Seco 1987 = Manuel Seco: Estudios de lexicografía española. Madrid 1987.

Suárez Gómez 1961 = G. Suárez Gómez: Avec quels livres les Espagnols apprenaient-ils le français (1520—1850)? In: Revue de Littérature comparée 35. 1961, 158—171.

Verdonk 1979 = Robert A. Verdonk: Contribución al estudio de la lexicografía española en Flandes en el siglo XVII (1599—1705). In: Boletín de la Real Academia Española 59. 1979, 289—369.

Verdonk 1980 = Robert A. Verdonk: La lengua española en Flandes en el siglo XVII. Contribución al estudio de las interferencias léxicas y de su proyección en el español general. Prólogo de Alonso Zamora Vicente. Madrid 1980.

Verdonk 1981 = Robert A. Verdonk: Het eerste woordenboek «Nederlands-Spaans»: De *Nieuwen Dictionaris* van Juan Francisco Rodríguez (Antwerpen, 1634). In: Handelingen der Koninklijke Zuidnederlandse Maatschappij voor Taal- en Letterkunde en Geschiedenis 35. 1981, 271—283.

Verdonk 1988 a = Robert A. Verdonk: El diccionario plurilingüe llamado *Anónimo de Amberes* (1639), reflejo de la lexicografía española en Flandes. In: Actas del Primer Congreso Internacional de Historia de la Lengua Española. Ed. M. Ariza/A. Salvador/A. Viudas. Madrid 1988, 995—1002.

Verdonk 1988 b = Robert A. Verdonk: Le *Recueil* de H. Hornkens. Premier dictionnaire français-espagnol. In: Actes du XVIIIᵉ Congrès International de Linguistique et Philologie Romanes. Ed. D. Kremer. T. 4. Tübingen 1988, 60—69.

Verdonk 1990 = Robert A. Verdonk: La importancia del „Recueil" de Hornkens para la lexicografía bilingüe del siglo de Oro. In: Boletín de la Real Academia Española 70. 1990, 69—109.

Verdonk/Daulie 1983 = Robert A. Verdonk en colaboración con Michel Daulie: Indice alfabético exhaustivo de las voces españolas contenidas en el *Recueil* de Hornkens (Bruselas, 1599). Amberes 1983.

Verdonk/Daulie 1989 = Robert A. Verdonk en colaboración con Michel Daulie: Indice alfabético exhaustivo de las voces españolas contenidas en la parte «francés-español» del *Dicionario nuevo* de Fr. Sobrino (Bruselas, 1705). Amberes 1989.

Viñaza 1893 = Conde de la Viñaza: Biblioteca Histórica de la Filología Castellana. 3 Vol. Madrid 1893.

Robert A. Verdonk,
Anvers/Louvain-la-Neuve (Belgique)

313. Die zweisprachige Lexikographie Spanisch-Deutsch, Deutsch-Spanisch

1. Geschichte und Gegenwart
2. Literatur (in Auswahl)

1. Geschichte und Gegenwart

1649 heiratet Philipp IV. von Spanien Maria Anna, die Tochter Kaiser Ferdinand III. 1665 übernimmt Maria Anna die spanische Regentschaft und überläßt die Regierung ihrem deutschen Beichtvater Johann Eberhard Neidhardt. Im Jahre darauf heiratet Philipps und Maria Annas Tochter Margarete Theresia ihren Onkel, Kaiser Leopold I. Der Wiener Hof wird nicht nur prächtiger denn je, sondern auch zweisprachig. Daraus erwächst das erste spanisch-deutsche Wörterbuch, das der kaiserliche Notar Nicolaus Mez von Braidenbach 1670 in Wien bei Johann Jacob Kürner publiziert, nachdem, wie er schreibt, „etliche Bekannte" ihn gebeten haben, „dergleichen Werck" zu verfertigen. Das Buch ist Kaiser Leopold I. gewidmet. Mez war 5 Jahre vorher bereits im gleichen Verlag durch eine französische Grammatik (Mez 1665) hervorgetreten.

Das Wörterbuch besteht nur aus dem spanisch-deutschen Teil, hergestellt durch Weiterübersetzung des spanisch-französischen Wörterbuchs von César Oudin von 1607 (vgl. Art. 312). Gegenüber Oudin zeichnet sich Mez durch strikt alphabetische Reihenfolge und durch Verzicht auf jegliche Verweisung aus. In den zahlreichen Fällen graphischer Variation (z. B. *zecear — cecear*) wiederholt Mez kurzerhand die Information und ersetzt dergestalt in radikaler Weise die Ökonomie des Drucks durch die Ökonomie des Nachschlagens. Im Vorwort meldet er denn auch ausdrücklich sein Patent für Benutzerfreundlichkeit an: „... indem ich dieses Werk in eine solche Ordnung gerichtet, daß ich dergleichen noch nicht gesehen, dieweilen du in demselbigen nicht vonnöten hast, ein Wort zwei- oder dreimal zu suchen, dann wirst du es also bald finden mit seiner Bedeutung".

Das Wiener Wörterbuch blieb ein Einzelfall und wurde prompt wieder vergessen. So kommt es, daß der „Wegbereiter der Hispanistik", F.J.J. Bertuch, im Vorwort zu Schmid 1795 dieses Wörterbuch als „das erste spanisch-deutsche Wörterbuch für Deutsche" bezeichnet. Bertuch (1747—1822, vgl. Heymann 1989) hatte im Anschluß an sein Handbuch der spanischen Sprache (1790) ein „kleines spanisch-deutsches Handlexikon" geplant, wurde aber von seinem Verleger gedrängt, ein vollständiges Wörterbuch zu liefern, das dann statt seiner der Weimarer Bibliothekar Ernst August Schmid auf der Basis des spanischen Akademiewörterbuchs, der spanisch-französischen Wörterbücher von Séjournant und Sobrino (vgl. Art. 312) sowie des spanisch-englischen Wörterbuchs von Stevens (vgl. Art. 308) erstellt. Für die an der Literaturgeschichte orientierte Sehweise von Bertuch ist bezeichnend, daß auch das alte „spanisch-holländische" Wörterbuch von Hornkens (vgl. Art. 312) noch hinzugezogen wird. Besonderes Verdienst kommt übrigens dem Leipziger Verleger Engelhard Benjamin

Schwickert zu, der Ende des 18. und Anfang des 19. Jhs. planvoll eine Serie bedeutender zweisprachiger Wörterbücher aufbaut, welche die deutsche Sprache mit nahezu allen wichtigen Sprachen Europas verbindet, so z. B. auch erstmalig und seither unüberboten mit dem Neugriechischen (Papachristos 1990).

Schmids deutsch-spanischer Teil erscheint 1805, zu spät, um hier den Premierenpreis zu gewinnen, denn inzwischen hat in Hamburg der Spanisch-(Portugiesisch- und Italienisch-)Lehrer J. D. Wagener ein Unternehmen abgeschlossen, das er eigener Aussage nach bereits 20 Jahre zuvor begründet hatte. Die 1750 Seiten Spanisch-Deutsch von 1800 (der deutsch-spanische Teil von 1801 ist nur halb so stark) mußten zwar durch spätere Lexikographen scharfe Kritik hinnehmen, sind aber ungeachtet mancher Fehler eine respektable Leistung. Dem Bedürfnis nach kompakterer Information kam Wagener acht Jahre später mit seinem Handwörterbuch nach. Nimmt man die Taschenwörterbücher von Braubach 1807 und Deranco 1829 sowie Wagener 1810 und Huber 1832 hinzu, so fällt auf, daß der Schwerpunkt des hispanistischen Interesses in den Hafenstädten (Hamburg und Bremen) liegt. Es verwundert deshalb nicht, daß auch die erste herausragende Leistung der hispano-deutschen Lexikographie, der dem späteren König Ludwig I. gewidmete *Diccionario* des Freiherrn Theresius von Seckendorff 1823—28 bei Perthes und Besser in Hamburg (und gleichzeitig bei Riegel und Wießner in Nürnberg) erscheint. Der Benutzerkreis dieser Wörterbücher ist nicht in erster Linie in der Philologie zu suchen, sondern im wachsenden Handels- und Emigrationsinteresse an Südamerika, das sich gerade von Spanien emanzipiert. Es traf sich, daß die Aufnahme diplomatischer Beziehungen zwischen Preußen und Spanien 1782 (Heymann 1989, 45) und die Reduktion des spanischen Akademiewörterbuchs auf einen Band (1780) zeitlich zusammenfielen. Ersteres machte zweisprachige Wörterbücher nötig, letzteres machte sie möglich. Der spanische Befreiungskampf gegen Napoleon hat daneben zum wachsenden Interesse beigetragen.

In dieser Situation muß es überraschen, daß ausgerechnet ein privatisierender mittelfränkischer Freiherr, nämlich der 1758 geborene Theresius von Seckendorff, die erste lexikographische Großtat hispanistischer Lexikographie vollbringt, doch ist hier zu bedenken, daß die Seckendorffs in allen Erdteilen zu Hause waren und daß ein Siegmund von Seckendorff (1744—1785) in Weimar mit Bertuch zusammen von 1780—1782 das *Magazin der spanischen und portugiesischen Literatur* herausgab, in dem er auch eigene Übersetzungen vorlegte (Heymann 1989, 39—41). Seckendorff nennt übrigens unter seinen Informanten auch Joh. Andr. Schmeller, der bekanntlich 1804—08 in Spanien war und später A. Ruiz de Padróns *Gutachten über die Inquisition* ins Deutsche übersetzte (Kohlheim 1985). Die eigentliche Initialzündung mag aber von Leys 1732 ausgegangen sein, den Seckendorff ausgeschlachtet hat.

Wenn man die Größenkategorien Großwörterbuch, Handwörterbuch und Taschenwörterbuch unterscheidet, so wird man Wagener 1800/01 und Seckendorff 1823—28 in ihren spanisch-deutschen Teilen als Großwörterbücher ansehen, hingegen Schmid 1795/1805 und Wagener 1808—09 als Handwörterbücher. Die Entwicklung aller drei Kategorien im 19. Jh. wird von Schlipf 1956—59 so ausführlich beschrieben, daß wir uns hier mit wenigen Andeutungen zufriedengeben können. Das Handwörterbuch wird weitergeführt von Franceson 1829/33 und Booch-Árkossy 1858. Vor allem letzterer legt besonderes Gewicht auf den literarischen Wortschatz früherer Jahrhunderte. Huber 1832 verwirklicht das interessante Projekt eines reinen Lesewörterbuchs, in dem die Wortbildungsdurchsichtigkeit des Wortschatzes für äußerste Knappheit der Darstellung genutzt wird. Das dritte Großwörterbuch in der Geschichte der spanisch-deutschen Lexikographie legt Tolhausen 1888/89 vor. Zum ersten Mal in einem Großwörterbuch ist nun der deutsch-spanische Teil gleichberechtigt. Nachfolger von Booch-Árkossy 1858 wird in der Kategorie der Handwörterbücher Stromer 1897/1900, der sich auf den Gegenwartswortschatz beschränkt.

Die Jahrhundertwende ist aber vor allem die große Zeit der Taschenwörterbücher, als Indiz dafür, daß die deutsch-hispanischen Beziehungen (vor allem zu Südamerika) auf ihrem Höhepunkt angekommen sind. Nach dem Taschenwörterbuch von Booch-Árkossy 1863 und dem Wörterbuch der Handelskorrespondenz von Kotzenberg 1875 erscheinen in rascher Folge Enenkel 1891, Ossig 1894, Moesch/Diercks 1895/96 und schließlich Paz 1903. Enenkel 1891 ist ein Produkt des Verlages Garnier in Paris und das erste auf den spanischen Benutzer zugeschnittene Wörterbuch. Ossig 1894 erscheint bei Reclam und ist revolutionär preiswert. Moesch/Diercks enthält die beste Glossierung und

Phraseologie und steht an der Grenze zum Handwörterbuch. Die beherrschende Marktstellung aber wird das erste von Langenscheidt verlegte spanisch-deutsche Wörterbuch (Paz 1903) erkämpfen. Die Qualität des spanischen Materials wird durch die Wahl eines angesehenen spanischen Gelehrten als Autor garantiert und erlaubt gleichzeitig den Verkauf in Spanien, doch darf das nicht darüber hinwegtäuschen, daß das Buch in erster Linie für das deutsche Publikum eingerichtet ist. Eine Vorstellung von den Werbemethoden vermittelt das am Anfang des Buches in zwei Sprachen abgedruckte Gutachten der Spanischen Akademie, in dem Paz y Mélia über den grünen Klee gelobt und alle Konkurrenten pauschal verdammt werden. Besonders stolz ist man bei Langenscheidt auf die Ausspracheangabe aller Wörter mit modernen Mitteln.

1920/22 bekommt das Langenscheidtsche Taschenwörterbuch Konkurrenz durch Le Boucher/Grossmann, in dem Rudolf Grossmann zum ersten Mal für eine angemessene Präsenz des südamerikanischen Wortschatzes sorgt (vgl. auch Schwauß 1977). Großer Beliebtheit erfreut sich daneben der bei Brockhaus verlegte Pfohl 1931. Zum würdigen Nachfolger des Tolhausen wurden dann die beiden Bände von Slabý 1932 und Grossmann 1938, die über verschiedene Neubearbeitungen bis heute bestehen. Der Slabý/Grossmann (vgl. Schlipf 1959, 101—114) ist mit Recht berühmt, doch leidet er einerseits unter seiner Bidirektionalität (die für den spanischen Benutzer wertvolle Information scheint dem deutschen Benutzer vielerorts als Platzverschwendung und umgekehrt) und erfolgen andererseits die Neubearbeitungen zu sehr mit fachsprachlichem Schwerpunkt. Außerdem merkt man dem Wörterbuch sein Entstehungsalter an. Statt Überarbeitung des alten, wäre es deshalb an der Zeit, ein völlig neues Wörterbuch zu schaffen.

Gemessen an der Qualität des Slabý/Grossmann ist das einzige größere spanische Wörterbuch, der Amador, rettungslos veraltet, da er seit seiner Entstehung 1931 (sein Autor, geboren 1881, starb 1951) nur einmal oberflächlich bearbeitet wurde (durch F. M. Biosca 1955), seither jedoch unverändert scheint. Hinzu kommt, daß der spanisch-deutsche Teil, der eigentlich auf den spanischen Benutzer zugeschnitten sein sollte, da das Wörterbuch in Deutschland gar nicht verkauft wird, in Wirklichkeit nahezu alle wesentlichen Charakteristika eines Herübersetzungswörterbuches trägt und folglich schon methodisch für den spanischen Benutzer völlig verfehlt ist. Zusätzlich muß man dem Verlag vorwerfen, daß er das Alter des Wörterbuchs systematisch vertuscht. Noch unverfrorener geschieht das übrigens mit dem Handwörterbuch des gleichen Autors (Amador man.), das 1986 auf 704 Seiten verkauft wird, ohne daß man erführe, daß diese Auflage textgleich ist mit einer von 1974 auf 1479 Seiten und ohne große Änderungen zurückgeht auf eine erste Auflage 1935. Zwischen Deutschland und der Hispanophonie besteht also ein nicht zu übersehendes Wörterbuchgefälle.

Die für den deutschen Benutzer empfehlenswertesten Wörterbücher sind wohl derzeit Müller 1987 und Alvarez-Prada 1985, die beide 1971 in erster Auflage erschienen. Das Taschenwörterbuch des gleichen Verlages Langenscheidt (Schoen/Noeli/Wiske 1941) kommt hingegen, trotz mancher Überarbeitung, inzwischen in die Jahre und sollte durch einen völlig neuen Text ersetzt werden. Der Konkurrenzverlag Klett verkauft in neuester Auflage 1988 ein Buch, das direkt auf 1977 (Haensch/Domínguez 1977) zurückgeht und als neubearbeitete Erweiterung von Haensch/Domínguez 1962 zu verstehen ist. Zur vergleichenden Wörterbuchkritik s. Werner 1986 (vor allem auch zu Beinhauer 1978) und 1987—88.

2. Literatur (in Auswahl)

2.1. Wörterbücher

Alvarez-Prada 1985 = Enrique Alvarez-Prada: Langenscheidts Handwörterbuch Spanisch. Teil II. Deutsch-Spanisch. Neubearbeitung v. Gisela Haberkamp de Antón. Berlin. München 1985 [640 S. 1. Aufl. 1971].

Amador = Emilio M. Martínez Amador: Deutschspanisches spanisch-deutsches Wörterbuch = Diccionario alemán-español español-alemán. Barcelona 1969 [1616 S.; ed. F. M. Biosca, 1955; 1. Aufl. 1931].

Amador man. = Emilio M. Martínez Amador: Diccionario manual alemán-español. Barcelona 1986 [704 S.; textgleich 1974, 1479 S.; 1. Aufl. 1935].

Beinhauer 1978 = Werner Beinhauer: Stilistisch-phraseologisches Wörterbuch spanisch-deutsch. München 1978 [1043 S.].

Booch-Árkossy 1858 = Friedrich Booch-Árkossy: Nuevo Diccionario de la Lenguas Castellana y Alemana, el más completo que se ha publicado hasta el día. Neuestes und vollständigstes (...). 2 Bde. Leipzig 1858 [1132, 704 S.; 7. Aufl. 1887].

Booch-Árkossy 1863 = Friedrich Booch-Árkossy: Neuestes und vollständigstes Taschenwörterbuch der spanischen und deutschen Sprache. 2 Bde. Leipzig 1863 [696, 526 S.; 7. Aufl. 1893].

Braubach 1807 = Daniel Braubach: Kurzgefaßtes spanisch-deutsches und deutsch-spanisches Taschenwörterbuch. Bremen 1807.

Deranco 1829 = P. Deranco: Spanisch-deutsches, portugiesisch-deutsches und deutsch-spanisches Taschenwörterbuch. Hamburg 1829.

Enenkel 1891 = Arturo Enenkel: Diccionario Español-Alemán y Alemán-Español. Paris 1891 [590, 500 S. Buenos Aires 1943].

Franceson 1829/33 = C. F. Franceson: Neues Spanisch-Deutsches und Deutsch-Spanisches Wörterbuch. 2 Bde. Leipzig 1829, 1833 [854, 760 S. —1906].

Grossmann 1938 = Rudolf Grossmann: Wörterbuch der spanischen und deutschen Sprache II. Deutsch-Spanisch. Leipzig 1938 [LII, 1316 S.].

Haensch/Domínguez 1962 = Günther Haensch/ José María Domínguez: Bertelsmann Wörterbuch Spanisch-Deutsch/Deutsch-Spanisch. Gütersloh 1962 [574 S.; 2. Aufl. 1968; Lizenzausgabe rororo 1969].

Haensch/Domínguez 1977 = Günther Haensch/ José María Domínguez: Diccionario alemán. Barcelona 1977 [Neubearb. Günther Haensch unter Mitwirkung von B. Lechner. Barcelona 1980. Auch als Pons Kompaktwörterbuch spanisch-deutsch, deutsch-spanisch. Stuttgart 1980, 684 S.].

Huber 1832 = Victor Aimé Huber: Spanisch-Deutsches Wörterbuch zu dem Spanischen Lesebuch. Bremen 1832 [118 S.].

Koch 1961—63 = Herbert Koch: Wörterbuch Deutsch-Spanisch. Spanisch-Deutsch. 2 Bde. Leipzig 1961, 1963 [512, 565 S.].

Kotzenberg 1875 = H.W.A. Kotzenberg: Deutsch-Spanisches und Spanisch-Deutsches Wörterbuch des Kaufmännischen Verkehrs und der Handelskorrespondenz. Bremen 1875 [268, 218 S.].

Le Boucher/Grossmann 1920—22 = Gastón Le Boucher/Rudolf Grossmann: Nuevo Diccionario de bolsillo de los idiomas español y alemán. Neues (...) Taschenwörterbuch. Leipzig 1920, 1922 [324, 328 S.; 1926—30].

Leys 1732 = Franz Jacob Leys: Nouveau Dictionnaire Espagnol-François. Nouveau Dictionnaire François-Espagnol. 5 Bde. (Manuskripte Nr. 1801—1803, 1805, 1806 der Universitätsbibliothek Erlangen; Span.-Frz. 3669 S.; Frz.-Span. 3721 S.).

Mez 1670 = Nicolás Mez de Braidenbach: Diccionario muy copioso de la lengua Española y Alemana hasta agora nunca visto (...). Wien 1670 [336 S.].

Moesch/Diercks 1895/96 = F. Moesch/G. Diercks: Taschenwörterbuch der spanischen und deutschen Sprache. Leipzig 1895, 1896 [D-Sp., 450 S.; Sp-D, 490 S.; Neuausg. A. Sardó y Vilar 1932, 2 Nachträge à 20 S.].

Müller 1987 = Heinz Müller/Günther Haensch: Langenscheidts Handwörterbuch Spanisch. I. Spanisch-Deutsch. Neubearbeitung 1987 durch G. Haensch. Berlin. München 1987 [656 S.; 1. Aufl. 1971].

Ossig 1894 = Hans Ossig: Taschenwörterbuch der spanischen und deutschen Sprache. Leipzig (1894) [544 S.].

Paz 1903 = Antonio Paz y Mélia: Diccionario manual de las lenguas Española y Alemana. Taschenwörterbuch (...). Berlin 1903 [528, 488 S. Taschenwörterbuch, 1927 ed. Eberhard Vogel].

Pfohl 1931 = Ernst Pfohl: Neues Wörterbuch der spanischen und deutschen Sprache für den Schul- und Handgebrauch. Leipzig 1931 [450, 595 S.].

Schmid 1795/1805 = Ernst August Schmid: Diccionario español y alemán oder Handwörterbuch der Spanischen Sprache für die Deutschen. 2 Bde. Leipzig 1795, 1805 [VI, 951, 942 S. Der dt-sp. Teil unter Mithilfe von L. H. Teucher].

Schoen/Noeli/Wiske 1941 = Theophil Schoen/ Teodosio Noeli/Friedrich Wiske: Langenscheidts Taschenwörterbuch der spanischen und deutschen Sprache. Berlin 1941 [512, 496 S. Spanisch-Deutsch Neubearb. 1980 v. Gisela Haberkamp de Antón, 544 S.; Deutsch-Spanisch, Neubearb. 1972 v. Hermann Willers, 545—1056 S.].

Schwauß 1977 = Maria Schwauß: Wörterbuch der regionalen Umgangssprache in Lateinamerika. Amerikaspanisch-Deutsch. Leipzig 1977 [692 S. 2. Aufl. 1986].

Seckendorff 1823—28 = Theresius Freiherr von Seckendorff: Diccionario de las lenguas española y alemana. 3 Bde. Hamburg. Nürnberg 1823, 1824, 1828 [XXIV, 832, 902; 936 S.; D—Sp vollendet von Christian Martin Winterling].

Slabý 1932 = Rudolf Jan Slabý: Wörterbuch der spanischen und deutschen Sprache I. Spanisch-deutsch. Leipzig 1932 [XLIV, 740 S.].

Slabý/Grossmann = Rudolf Jan Slabý/Rudolf Grossmann: Wörterbuch der spanischen und deutschen Sprache. Diccionario de las lenguas española y alemana. Bd. 1: Spanisch-Deutsch. Español-Alemán. 3. Aufl. völlig neu bearb. u. erw. v. José Manuel Banzo y Sáenz de Miera. Wiesbaden 1975. Nachtrag (Corrigenda Addenda). Zusammengestellt v. J. M. Banzo, A. Kučera u. H. Elsebach. 1978. Bd. 2: Deutsch-Spanisch. Alemán-Español. 4. Aufl. neubearb. u. erw. v. Carlos Illig. Wiesbaden 1989 [XXV, 1139 S.; XXVIII, 1319 S.].

Stromer 1897/1900 = Theodor Stromer: Neues Spanisch-Deutsches und Deutsch-Spanisches Wörterbuch. 2 Bde. Berlin 1897, 1900 [828, 812 S.].

Tolhausen 1888/89 = Louis Tolhausen: Nuevo Diccionario español-alemán y alemán-español. Neues (...) Wörterbuch. 2 Bde. Leipzig 1888, 1889 [764, 828 S.; 10. Aufl. 1928].

Wagener 1800/01 = Johann Daniel Wagener: Nuevo diccionario español-aleman y aleman-español. Neues und vollständiges Spanisch-Deutsches und Deutsch-Spanisches Wörterbuch. 3 Bde. Hamburg. Altona 1800, 1801 [843, 912, 467, 390 S.].

Wagener 1808—09 = Johann Daniel Wagener: Diccionario de faltriquera, o sea portátil (...). Spanisch-Deutsches, Deutsch-Spanisches Handwörterbuch. 2 Bde. Berlin 1808, 1809 [815, 613 S.].

Wagener 1810 = Johann Daniel Wagener: Allgemeines Warenlexikon in spanischer, portugiesischer, französischer, italienischer und englischer Sprache. Hamburg 1810 [Kurzfassung 1817].

2.2. Sonstige Literatur

Fabbri 1979 = Maurizio Fabbri: A Bibliography of Hispanic Dictionaries. Catalan, Galician, Spanish, Spanish in Latin America and the Philippines. Imola 1979.

Gimbernat 1807 = Carlos de Gimbernat: Manual del soldado espannol en Allemannia. München 1807.

Hausmann 1984 = Franz Josef Hausmann: Der Diccionario muy copioso des Nicolás Mez (1670). Ein frühes spanisch-deutsches Wörterbuch. In: Navicula Tubingensis. Studia in honorem Antonii Tovar. Festschrift zum 70. Geburtstag von Antonio Tovar, ed. F. J. Oroz Arizcuren. Tübingen 1984 (TBL 230), 167—171.

Hausmann 1988 = Franz Josef Hausmann: Les dictionnaires bilingues (et multilingues) en Europe au XVIIIᵉ siècle. Acquis et suggestions de recherche. In: La lexicographie française du XVIIIᵉ au XXᵉ siècle. Colloque international de lexicographie (...). Hrsg. B. v. Gemmingen/M. Höfler. Paris 1988 (Actes et Colloques 27), 11—32 (= In: Travaux de Linguistique et de Philologie 1 [= Travaux de Linguistique et de Littérature 26/1]. 1988, 11—32).

Heymann 1989 = Jochen Heymann: Ein Wegbereiter der Hispanistik: Friedrich Johann Justin Bertuch (1747—1822). In: Das Spanischinteresse im deutschen Sprachraum. Hrsg. v. Manfred Tietz. Frankfurt a. M. 1989, 34—49.

Kohlheim 1985 = Rosa Kohlheim: Schmeller und Spanien. In: Zeitschrift für bayerische Landesgeschichte 48. 1985, 195—223.

Marín 1987 = Rafael Marín: Los diccionarios bilingües Español/Alemán y Alemán/Español. Dos lenguas distintas y un mismo diccionario. Propósitos y resultados. In: Hispanorama 46. 1987, 160—166.

Mez 1665 = Nicolaus Mez von Braidenbach: Fontaine de la langue françoise (...). Brunnen der französischen Sprache. Wien 1665.

Papachristos 1990 = Evthymios Chr. Papachristos: Die deutsch-neugriechische Lexikographie von 1796 bis 1909. Tübingen 1990 (Lexicographica Series Maior 32).

Schlipf 1956—59 = Wolfgang Schlipf: Einige Bemerkungen zur Entwicklungsgeschichte des spanischen Wörterbuchs in Deutschland. In: Boletín de Filología (Santiago de Chile) 9. 1956/1957, 189—234; 10. 1958, 303—401; 11. 1959, 87—132.

Werner 1979 = Reinhold Werner: Formaler Vergleich einiger spanisch-deutscher und deutsch-spanischer Wörterbücher. In: Lebende Sprachen 24. 1979, 75—81.

Werner 1981 = Reinhold Werner: Umgangssprache im zweisprachigen Wörterbuch: lexikographische Probleme, aufgezeigt an zwei spanisch-deutschen Wörterbüchern. In: Zielsprache Spanisch 1/2. 1981, 69—75.

Werner 1986 = Reinhold Werner: Zum Stand der zweisprachigen Lexikographie Deutsch-Spanisch, Spanisch-Deutsch. In: Lexicographica 2. 1986, 127—161.

Werner 1987—88 = Reinhold Werner: Ein vergleichender Test dreier Wörterbücher Spanisch-Deutsch/Deutsch-Spanisch. In: Hispanorama 47. 1987, 159—171; 49. 1988, 151—167; 50. 1988, 167—175.

Franz Josef Hausmann, Erlangen
(Bundesrepublik Deutschland)

314. La lexicographie bilingue espagnol-italien, italien-espagnol

1. Histoire
2. Actualité
3. Bibliographie choisie

1. Histoire

1.1. L'histoire de la lexicographie Espagnol-Italien commence au début du 16ᵉ siècle avec la publication de petites nomenclatures plurilingues dans lesquelles, entre autres langues, l'espagnol et l'italien sont mis en parallèle, comme dans le *Vocabulista* de 1526. Plus tard, on trouve des listes de mots espagnols et italiens dans le dictionnaire d'Alunno 1543, dans Ulloa 1553 et Ulloa 1556. Avec le Calepino 1559 commence la série des dictionnaires plurilingues comprenant aussi l'espagnol et l'italien.

1.2. Le premier essai de lexique bilingue espagnol-italien est le Landucci 1562, qui ne présente cependant que la partie espagnol-italien. Ce petit vocabulaire, avec les deux autres parties qui l'accompagnent (espagnol-français et espagnol-basque), ne fut pas publié et le manuscrit est conservé dans la Biblioteca Nacional de Madrid. La partie espagnol-italien contient environ 7000 mots et locutions. Les mots espagnols sont tirés des mots espagnols correspondants de la partie espagnol-latin du dictionnaire de Nebrija 1495. La traduction italienne, originale, contient beaucoup d'erreurs, ce qui est d'ailleurs étrange si l'on considère que l'auteur est Italien.

1.3. Seulement huit ans après Landucci, parut le *Vocabulario de las dos lenguas Italiana y Castellana* de Cristóbal de Las Casas. La première édition fut imprimée à Séville en 1570, mais la plupart des éditions suivantes furent imprimées à Venise. Il s'agit d'un vrai dictiohnaire: ce n'est ni une nomenclature ni une traduction de mots latins, ni une aide à la compréhension d'un texte littéraire. Il comprend les deux parties italien-espagnol et espagnol-italien. C'est avec le Las Casas 1570 que commence véritablement la lexicographie bilingue espagnol-italien. Ce vocabulaire contient environ 15500 mots dans la

PRIMERA PARTE
DEL VOCABVLARIO DELA
LENGVA TOSCANA Y
CASTELLANA.

Bantico. Antiguamete.
Abada. En esperança, en tardança.
Abada. En entretenimiento.
Abastanza. Bastantemente.
Abbate. Abad.
Abbatessa. Abadessa.
Abbatia. Abadia.
Abbauare. Embeuecer.
Abbabato. Embeuescido.
Abbachista. Contador.
Abbachiera. Contadora.
Abbacinare. Encandilar, deslubrar.
Abbacinato. Encandilado.
Abbaco. Aparador.
Abbaco. Guarismo.
Abbagliare. Encandilar, deslumbrar.
Abbagliato. Encandilado.
Abbaiare. Ladrar.
Abbaiatore. Ladrador.
Abbalordire. Atronar.
Abbalordire. Entontescer.
Abbalordito. Atronado.
Abbalordito. Tonto.
Abbandonare. Desamparar.
Abbandonato. Desamparado.
Abbandono. Desamparo.
Abbarbagliare. Encandilar.
Abbarbagliato. Encandilado.
Abbarbicare. Arraygar.
Abbarbicare. Trauar
Abbarbicato. Arraygado, trauado.
Abbassare. Abaxar.
Abbassato. Abaxado.
Abbattere. Encontrar.
Abbattere. Llegar a caso.
Abbattere. Abatir, derribar.
Abbatuto. Encontrado.
Abbatuto. Abbatido, derribado.
Abbattimento. Encuentro.
Abbattimento. Abatimiento.
Abbattutamente. Abatidamente.
Abbellire. Hermosear.
Abbellito. Hermoseado.
Abbentare. Holgar.
Abbeuerare. Abreuar: dar a beuer.
Abbiccare. Amontonar.
Abbiccato. Amontonado.
Abbigliamento. Ornamento.
Abbocarsi. Iuntarse a vistas.
Abbocarsi. Verse, visitar se.
Abboccamento. Iunta, visita, vista.
Abbombare. Infundir, remojar.
Abbombato. Infundido, remojado.

B   Abbona

Extrait textuel 314.1: Début de Las Casas 1583

partie italien-espagnol et 10000 pour l'espagnol-italien. Il s'agit d'un vocabulaire riche, si nous considérons l'époque à laquelle il a été composé. Tout comme Landucci, Las Casas a utilisé le Nebrija de 1495 pour composer sa partie espagnol-italien, mais il l'a fait avec indépendance et intelligence. En effet, il a rejeté les mots les moins communs et a ajouté un grand nombre de mots opportuns pour une utilisation pratique du vocabulaire. De toute évidence son ouvrage a été composé pour un public moins instruit (probablement des commerçants) que celui qui consultait les dictionnaires latins. Plusieurs éléments indiquent qu'il s'agit d'un ouvrage encore élémentaire: il ne présente pas d'indications grammaticales; les synonymes y sont juxtaposés sans explications ou exemples qui aideraient à choisir la signification désirée; la phraséologie y est quasi inexistante. Cependant, parce qu'il était le premier, il a connu quinze éditions en l'espace d'un demi-siècle; quelques-unes d'entre elles apportèrent des additions et des améliorations.

Vittori 1609 contient une partie espagnol-français-italien où l'auteur traduit en italien le dictionnaire espagnol-français d'Oudin 1607. Vittori 1617, tout en reprenant cette partie, ajoute une partie italien-français-espagnol basée sur le dictionnaire de Politi (cf. art. 316, 2.3.). Du dictionnaire de Vittori (souvent appelé «Crespin» selon le nom de l'éditeur de 1617) le *Französisches etymologisches Wörterbuch* de W. v. Wartburg, comme la plupart des auteurs, croit connaître une édition de 1606. Gallina 1959, 231—3 prouve qu'il s'agit en réalité d'un cas de criminalité lexicographique, l'édition de 1606 étant celle parue en 1616/17, mais antidatée par l'éditeur.

1.4. Le *Vocabolario Italiano e Spagnolo* de Lorenzo Franciosini, qui parut en 1620 à Rome, remplaça celui de Las Casas et fut le seul à être imprimé pendant deux siècles. Il marque un grand progrès sur Las Casas 1570, qui néanmoins lui a servi de base en lui offrant la plus grande partie du matériel lexicographique. Franciosini l'a complété et corrigé avec l'aide d'autres vocabulaires; citons: Nebrija 1495, Covarrubias 1611 et Oudin 1607. Il a augmenté le nombre des lemmes, expliqué les différentes significations des mots et présenté une abondante phraséologie complétée par la citation de proverbes traduits littéralement et non par les proverbes correspondants de l'autre langue. Les quatorze rééditions de l'ouvrage, données en l'espace de cent quatre-vingts ans n'y ont apporté que des modifications mineures. Mais il est le premier dictionnaire bilingue espagnol-italien à avoir été conçu de façon moderne.

1.5. Le 18ᵉ siècle ne nous a pas donné de nouveaux dictionnaires: jusqu'en 1786 on a continué à imprimer le répertoire de Franciosini. Au début du 19ᵉ siècle, en 1805, paraît le *Diccionario de faltriquera* de J.L.B. Cormon et Vincente Manni. Bien qu'il s'agisse d'un ouvrage «de poche», comme l'indique le frontispice (cette indication disparaîtra des éditions ultérieures), son texte n'en est pas moins relativement riche. Il est curieux de noter qu'au 19ᵉ siècle la moitié des dictionnaires bilingues espagnol-italien est imprimée en France. Le Cormon/Manni 1805 est un ouvrage original qui présente des traductions précises, qui distingue clairement les différentes significations mais qui ne les explique pas. Le seul progrès sur le Franciosini 1620 est qu'il porte les indications grammaticales des lemmes, mais il manque presque complètement de phraséologie. Après deux réimpressions, il y a une édition (suivie par d'autres) «revista y aumentada par S. H. Blanc» qui corrigera l'ouvrage, lui ajoutera quelques entrées et l'enrichira de synonymes.

En 1853 est publié à Paris un anonyme *Nuevo diccionario Español-Italiano* qui est presque un plagiat du Cormon/Manni 1805. Les différences se bornent à la modernisation de l'orthographe et à quelques additions, très peu nombreuses. Le dernier dictionnaire imprimé en France au 19ᵉ siècle est celui de Caccia, publié en 1869, basé sur le *Nuevo diccionario* 1853, mais enrichi de mots, de synonymes et de phraséologie. L'auteur y a ajouté aussi la prononciation figurée, d'une façon très élémentaire, en se basant sur la prononciation de l'autre langue. Plus complet que ses prédécesseurs, Caccia 1869 ne marque pas un grand progrès sur ceux-là, parce qu'il donne encore la simple traduction des mots, sans expliquer les différentes significations: il distingue seulement les significations figurées.

Le premier dictionnaire bilingue du dix-neuvième siècle publié en Italie est le *Diccionario Español-Italiano* de Marco Antonio Canini: c'est un mélange du *Nuevo diccionario* 1853 et du Caccia 1869 qui n'apporte que peu de changements mais qui élimine la prononciation figurée. — Le *Nuevo diccionario Italiano-Español* publié à Milan en 1885 est anonyme. Lui aussi est fondé sur le *Nuevo diccionario* 1853 et sur le Caccia 1869, mais il est indépendant du Canini. Le *Nuevo diccio-*

nario de Felipe Linati y Delgado, imprimé à Barcelone en 1887, est supérieur aux précédents. Il a complètement remanié le matériel qu'ils lui offraient et a intégré de nouvelles informations: il ajoute des diminutifs et des augmentatifs et, surtout, il explique les différentes significations et indique les mots inusités et les termes commerciaux. En outre il accroît beaucoup la phraséologie. Avec ce dictionnaire, le dernier du 19e siècle, la lexicographie bilingue espagnol-italien marque un remarquable progrès.

1.6. Notre siècle voit s'accroître le nombre des dictionnaires bilingues espagnol-italien et c'est dans la première moitié que l'on publie les plus importants, surtout en Italie d'ailleurs. Les premiers sont le *Dizionario Spagnolo-Italiano* de Luigi Bacci et Agostino Savelli, imprimé en 1908—1916, et celui de Gaetano Frisoni 1917—1927. Le Bacci/Savelli est supérieur au Frisoni par la clarté des significations, souvent expliquées par un exemple. Cette supériorité du Bacci/Savelli n'empêche cependant le Frisoni 1917—27 d'être encore publié de nos jours. — Signalons ici le succès (une vingtaine d'éditions chez deux éditeurs) du Boselli 1900, un dictionnaire de poche remarquable par son exactitude. — Deux autres dictionnaires de poche, imprimés en Espagne, Moll 1939 et Ayala 1940, abrégés du Linati 1887, sont sans importance.

Le *Diccionario Italiano-Español* de José Ortiz de Burgos, imprimé à Barcelone en 1941, est un dictionnaire de dimension moyenne qui a eu et continue d'avoir un certain succès, mais qui est basé sur le vieux Caccia 1869 et sur le Frisoni 1917—27, auxquels il n'apporte que peu de changements.

Du dictionnaire de B. Melzi nous n'avons pu voir que l'édition de 1945, imprimée à La Plata, mais il y en a eu d'antérieures éditées en Italie par la maison Treves de Milan. Fabbri 1979 cite une édition de 1856: il s'agit probablement d'une erreur: B. Melzi, son auteur, ne naquit en effet qu'en 1844. La première édition est probablement celle de 1893. En 1940 Garzanti imprime une édition dans laquelle au nom de B. Melzi est ajouté celui de Carlo Boselli, qui a évidemment révisé l'ouvrage, mais les différences entre l'édition argentine et celle-ci ne sont pas importantes. Le texte du dictionnaire présente des ressemblances fréquentes avec le Bacci/Savelli 1908—16 et le Frisoni 1917—27 mais, puisque ceux-ci sont postérieurs à la première édition du Melzi, on peut affirmer que ce dernier est un ouvrage original. Il contient beaucoup de synonymes et significations qu'il distingue clairement. La phraséologie n'est pas abondante, mais exacte.

En 1949 Paravia publie à Turin le *Nuovo Dizionario Spagnolo-Italiano* de Lucio Ambruzzi. C'est le meilleur des dictionnaires bilingues espagnol-italien publiés jusqu'à maintenant. Il est beaucoup plus complet que tous ceux qui l'ont précédé et, quoique qu'il les ait utilisés, il se présente comme un ouvrage nouveau parce qu'il a profondément remanié le matériel, non seulement en augmentant les termes, mais aussi en supprimant ceux tombés en désuétude et en ajoutant de nombreux américanismes et mots d'argot. Les synonymes et la phraséologie sont abondants mais les différentes significations ne sont pas suffisamment expliquées, surtout dans la partie italien-espagnol. On doit signaler que les éditions postérieures sont toujours amendées et augmentées.

Le *Dizionario fraseologico* de Carbonell 1950—1953 est un dictionnaire en deux gros volumes (comme l'Ambruzzi 1949), qui utilise beaucoup le Frisoni 1917—27. Il élimine un grand nombre de synonymes, mais il ajoute aussi des mots. Les exemples qu'il donne sont souvent identiques à ceux du Frisoni, mais il les traduit différemment. Il distingue les différentes significations et donne quelquefois des exemples pour en expliquer l'usage. C'est un dictionnaire différent de l'Ambruzzi, mais il ne marque pas un progrès sur celui-ci, surtout dans la partie italien-espagnol.

Le dernier grand dictionnaire bilingue espagnol-italien publié jusqu'aujourd'hui est le *Diccionario Italiano-Español* de Martínez Amador, paru en Espagne en 1957. Il suit de près l'Ambruzzi 1949 et, quelquefois, utilise aussi le Frisoni 1917—27, mais Martínez Amador ne sépare pas les différentes significations et les explique rarement par un exemple. Parce que Martínez Amador ajoute souvent des synonymes, le lecteur ne voit qu'une liste de mots parmi lesquels il n'est pas à même de choisir celui qu'il cherche. Les traductions italiennes sont souvent inexactes ou inusitées. A cela il faut ajouter les très nombreuses coquilles qui, souvent, rendent le texte italien incompréhensible, réduisant encore la valeur de l'ouvrage.

2. Actualité

Les trente dernières années voient s'accroître le nombre des dictionnaires bilingues espagnol-italien, mais il s'agit presque toujours de dictionnaires de poche, comme le Bonelli 1956, le Herder 1970, le Ruiz de Arcaute 1971, etc. Seulement quatre, quoique de poche, ont un peu plus de prétentions: le *Piccolo Vocabolario spagnolo-italiano* de A. Alvisi 1959, le *Vox Diccionario Italiano-Español* 1980, le *Dizionario Spagnolo-Italiano* de Miglioli (1977) et le *Collins* 1985. Le premier, révisé par l'italianiste Joaquín Arce, est très exact et, bien que basé sur le Boselli 1921, a beaucoup d'éléments originaux. On en a récemment donné une nouvelle édition entièrement semblable à la première, mais en format plus grand. — Le Miglioli 1977 est basé sur Ambruzzi 1949; il choisit les mots les plus usuels, mais n'offre que très peu de néologismes. Le *Vox* 1980 suit de près l'Alvisi 1959, mais il ajoute la prononciation et indique les auxiliaires des verbes italiens. Il est, lui aussi, pauvre en néologismes. — Le *Collins* 1985 parut à Milan en deux éditions exactement égales, sauf pour le format. C'est un bon dictionnaire de poche qui donne la prononciation figurée, un peu de phraséologie, mais peu de néologismes. On continue d'imprimer le vieux Frisoni 1917—27, les trois dictionnaires majeurs: l'Ambruzzi, le Carbonell et l'Amador, et aussi Ortiz de Burgos, plus petit. — Dans le domaine des dictionnaires spécialisés on a publié en 1974 à Madrid un *Diccionario técnico e industrial italiano-español y español-italiano*, très utile, mais qui contient des erreurs (Técnico 1974); et, à Milan, un *Dizionario politico, economico, commerciale Spagnolo-Italiano/Italiano-Spagnolo*, premier dictionnaire bilingue espagnol-italien de ce type (Mursia 1986). Il est intéressant surtout pour le grand nombre de néologismes et l'abondante phraséologie qu'il présente.

Nous conclurons en remarquant que la lexicographie bilingue espagnol-italien de ces dernières années ne s'est pas enrichie beaucoup de publications nouvelles, de sorte qu'on dispose aujourd'hui de grands dictionnaires vieux de trente ou quarante ans et de beaucoup de dictionnaires de poche modernes, quelques-uns bien faits, mais tous pauvres en néologismes. Seulement en 1990 a paru à Milan un nouveau dictionnaire de dimension moyenne, le *Dizionario spagnolo-italiano, italiano-spagnolo*, très riche en significations, phraséologie et, ce qui le distingue surtout de tous les autres, de néologismes.

3. Bibliographie choisie

3.1. Dictionnaires

Alunno 1543 = Le Ricchezze della lingua volgare del M. Francesco Alunno. Aldus. Con priuilegio di N. S. Paolo III. Et della Illustris. Signoria di Vinegia. In Vinegia Nel M. D. XXXXIII [225 f.].

Alvisi 1959 = A. Alvisi: Piccolo Vocabolario Spagnolo-Italiano e Italiano-Spagnolo dell'uso moderno. Revisione speciale di J. Arce. Bologna 1959 [IX, 993 p. Autres éd. 1961, 1972, Barcelona 1982].

Ambruzzi 1949 = Lucio Ambruzzi: Nuovo Dizionario Italiano-Spagnolo. Torino 1949 [XX, 1100; XV, 1309 p. Autres éd. 1952, 1954, 1956, 1958, 1963, 1973].

Ayala 1940 = Fernando de Ayala: Vocabulario Italiano-Español, Español-Italiano revisado y puesto al día. Barcelona 1940 (Vocabularios Cuyás) [639 p.; autres éd. 1941, 1958].

Bacci/Savelli 1908/1916 = Luigi Bacci/Agostino Savelli: Dizionario Spagnolo-Italiano (...). Firenze 1908 [VIII, 856 p.]. Dizionario Italiano-Spagnolo (...) compilato da Luigi Bacci. Firenze 1916 [820 p. Autres éd. 1925—27, 1928, 1930, 1940, 1942].

Bonelli s. d. = M. L. Bonelli: Dizionario Italiano-Spagnolo e Spagnolo-Italiano. Bologna s. d. [365 p. Autres éd. 1956, 1985].

Boselli 1921 = Carlos Boselli: Nuevo diccionario portátil Español-Italiano y Italiano-Español. Parte 1ª Español-Italiano. Milán 1921 [411, 416 p. Autres éd. 1900, 1912, 1938, 1939. Carlo Boselli: Dizionario Spagnolo-Italiano e Italiano-Spagnolo. Nuova ed. corr. e aum. 1942. XXXIII, 479; XIX, 499 p. Autres éd. 1943, 1946, 1948, 1949, 1950, 1951, 1953, 1954, 1955, 1956, 1959, 1962, 1964, 1968, 1972].

Caccia 1869 = José Caccia: Nuevo diccionario Italiano-Español y Español-Italiano con la pronunciación figurada en ambas lenguas compuesto sobre los mejores textos contemporáneos italianos y españoles. Nueva ed. Paris 1869 [XVI, 528; XVI, 353 p. Autres éd. s. d.; 1874, 1882, 1885, 1905, Buenos Aires 1943].

Calepino 1559 = Ambrosii Calepini: Dictionarium (...) Adiecimus etiam Latinis Graecisque vocibus Italicas ac Hispanicas interpretationes (...). Lvgdvni. Apud Haered. Sebast. Gryphii 1559.

Canini 1875 = Marco Antonio Canini: Diccionario Español-Italiano con la pronunciación figurada, un compendio de gramática española y dos pequeños vocabularios que contienen los nombres propios geográficos los más en uso. Milano. Napoles 1875 [XXXVIII, 586; 544 p.].

Carbonell 1950—1957 = S. Carbonell: Dizionario fraseologico completo Italiano-Spagnolo e Spagnolo-Italiano (...). Parte Italiana-Spagnola. Milano 1950. [XV, 839 p.] Parte Spagnola-Italiana. Milano 1957 [XII, 1522 p. Autres éd. 1964—68, 1973—75, 1977—79, 1981—83, 1984—85, 1986—89].

Collins 1985 = Eleanor Londera: Collins Mondadori Dizionario Italiano-Spagnolo, Spagnolo-Italiano. Ed. speciale per studenti. Milano. Barcelona 1985 [VIII, 211, 416 p.].

Collins GEM = Eleanor Londera: Collins GEM. Dictionary Italiano-Spagnolo, Spagnolo-Italiano; Italiano-Español, Español-Italiano. London. Glasgow. Milano. Barcelona 1985 [IX, 325, 304 p.].

Cormon/Manni 1805 = J. B. Cormon/Vincente Manni: Diccionario de faltriquera Italiano-Español y Español-Italiano. Compuesto y fielmente recopilado según la última edición del Diccionario de la Academia Española y el Vocabulario de la Academia de la Crusca. Leon 1805 [X, 576 p. Autres éd. Leon 1821. Madrid 1833. Diccionario Italiano-Español y Español-Italiano. Nueva ed. rev. y aum. por S. H. Blanc. Leon. Paris 1843, XVI, 369; XI, 324 p. Autres éd. 1848, 1852, 1854].

Covarrubias 1611 = Tesoro de la Lengua Castellana o Española compuesto por el Licenciado Don Sebastian de Covarrubias Orozco. Madrid 1611 [212 f.].

Dicc. Esp. It. = Diccionario Español-Italiano. 1980 [sans pag. Autre éd. 1961].

Diz. it. sp. 1868 = Dizionario italiano-spagnolo e spagnolo-italiano. Milano 1868 [1040 p.].

Diz. it. sp. 1938 = Dizionario italiano-spagnolo, spagnolo-italiano. Milano 1938 [798 p.].

Diz. it. sp. 1987 = Dizionario italiano-spagnolo, spagnolo-italiano. Bologna 1987 [365 p.].

Espresso 1986 = Marina Pazzaglia/Rossella Tappino/Marco Gatti/Michele Magni: L'Espresso Dizionario Italiano-Spagnolo, Spagnolo-Italiano. 1986 [127 p.].

Franciosini 1620 = Lorenzo Franciosini Fiorentino: Vocabolario Italiano e Spagnolo non piv dato in luce ... Parte prima. In Roma, a spese di Gio. Angelo Ruffinelli, e Angelo Manni. Appresso Gio Paolo Profilio MDCXX. Vocabolario Español, e Italiano Aora nvevamente sacado a luz y compuesto Por Lorenzo Franciosini Florentin. Segunda parte. En Roma, A costa de Juan Angel Rufineli, y Angel Manni. MDCXX. Por Juan Pablo Profilio. [668, 784 p. Autres éd. Genevra 1636, s. l. 1637, Roma 1638, Venetia 1645, s. l. 1665, 1666, Genevra 1706, 1707, Venetia 1735, 1763, 1774, 1776, 1796].

Frisoni 1917—1927 = Gaetano Frisoni: Dizionario Moderno Italiano-Spagnuolo e Spagnuolo-Italiano (...) contenente oltre gli americanismi, le voci nuove, anche straniere, attinenti a tutto lo scibile. Parte italiana-spagnuola. Milano 1917. [XI, 1118 p.] Cayetano Frisoni: Diccionario moderno Español-Italiano e Italiano-Español (...) conteniendo además de los americanismos, los provincialismos aunque sean extranjeros, que se refieren a toda reciente innovación, los modos fundamentales de los verbos irregulares y la indicación del acento tónico de cada palabra del texto. Parte española-italiana. Milán 1927 [747 p. Autres éd. 1932, 1938, 1941, 1944, 1947, 1949, 1950, 1952, 1954, 1957, 1960, 1965, 1974, 1977, 1979, 1981—82, 1985].

Gallina 1990 = Anna Maria Gallina: Dizionario Spagnolo-Italiano, Italiano-Spagnolo. Milano 1990 [825 p.].

Garcia 1982 = Antonio Garcia: Italiano-Spagnolo, Spagnolo-Italiano. Italiano-español, español-italiano. Milano 1982 [XXX, 238, XXIV, 199 p. Autre éd. 1971].

Herder 1971 = Diccionario Universal Herder Español-Italiano, Italiano-Español. Barcelona. Munich 1971 [180, 258 p. Autres éd. 1970, 1972, 1981, 1984, 1985].

Ietti = Maria Luisa Ietti: Dizionarietto Italiano-Spagnolo, Spagnolo-Italiano. Roma s. d. [573 p.].

Iter = Diccionario Iter Italiano-Español. Español-Italiano (...). Barcelona 1978.

Landucci 1562 = Dictionarium Lingue Toscane. Anno M. D. LXII A Nicholae Landuchio ciuitatis Luçe regionis Toscanie suę vernacule Lingue Peritissimo. Ms. [f. 107].

Langenscheidt 1965 = Langenscheidt Dizionario Universale Italiano-Spagnolo, Spagnolo-Italiano. Berlino 1965 [384 p.].

Las Casas 1570 = Christoval de las Casas: Vocabulario de las dos lenguas Toscana y Castellana. (...) Vendese en Casa de Francisco de Aguilar mercader de libros. En Sevilla 1570 [496 p. Autres éditions: Venetia 1576, Sevilla 1579, Venetia 1582, Sevilla 1583, Venetia 1587, 1591, 1594, 1600, 1604, 1608, 1618, 1622].

Linati 1887 = Felipe Linati y Delgado: Nuevo Diccionario Italiano-Español (...) redactado en vista de los Diccionarios de la Academia de la lengua española, del de la italiana de la Crusca, y de los mejores textos contemporáneos italianos y españoles. Barcelona 1887 [677; 611 p. Autre éd. Milano s. d.].

Martínez Amador 1957 = Emilio M. Martínez Amador: Diccionario Italiano-Español y Español-Italiano. Revisado y ampliado por David Ortega Cavero (...). Barcelona 1957 [2069 p. Autres éd. 1967, 1973, 1983, 1985].

Melzi 1945 = B. Melzi: Nuevo diccionario Italiano-Castellano. La Plata 1945. [616, 478 p. Autres éd. Milano 1893]. B. Melzi/C. Boselli: Nuovo Dizionario Spagnolo-Italiano e Italiano-Spagnolo commerciale, scientifico, tecnico, militare, marinaresco, ecc. (...). 1940 [526, 624 p.].

Miglioli 1977 = Dizionario Spagnolo-Italiano, Italiano-Spagnolo. Firenze 1977 [660 p.].

Moll 1939 = Francisco de B. Moll C.: Diccionario manual Italiano-Español. Segunda ed. muy aum. Palma de Mallorca 1939 [VI, 331 p. Autre éd. 1938].

Mursia 1986 = Dizionario politico, economico, commerciale Spagnolo-Italiano, Italiano-Spagnolo. Milano. [Redazione di Annamaria Gallina]. 1986 [351 p.].

Nebrija 1495 = Dictionarium ex Hispaniensi in latinum sermonem. Interprete Aelio Antonio Nebrissensi. 1495 [104 f. n. ch.].

Nuevo dicc. 1853 = Nuevo diccionario Español-Italiano. Ed. muy aum. y mej. con un estado de los verbos regulares e irregulares en ambos idiomas. Paris 1853 [XXIV, 463 p. Autres éd. Paris 1860, Poissy 1863, Paris 1877].

Nuevo dicc. 1885 = Nuevo diccionario Italiano-Español y Español-Italiano con la pronunciación figurada en ambos idiomas. Edición mejorada y aumentada de los verbos regulares e irregulares en ambas lenguas. Milan 1885 [XXXII, 832 p. Autres éd. 1873, 1875, Guigoni 1890, 1898].

Nuevo dicc. 1907 = Nuevo diccionario español-italiano e italiano-español. Milano 1907 [XXXIII, 852 p.].

Ortiz 1943 = José Ortiz de Burgos: Diccionario Italiano-Español compilado con arreglo a las últimas ediciones de los Vocabularios de la Academia de la Crusca y filólogo P. Fanfani, con vista de la reciente Enciclopedia Italiana y ajustado a la nueva reforma ortográfica (...). Barcelona 1943 [544; 415 p.].

Oudin 1607 = César Oudin: Tesoro de las dos lenguas francesa y española. Thresor des deux langues françoise et Espagnole. Paris 1607.

Panorama 1987 = Dizionario Spagnolo-Italiano, Italiano-Spagnolo. Milano 1987 [152; 175 p.].

Roselli 1901 = Nuevo diccionario portátil español-italiano e italiano-español. Madrid 1901 [860 p.].

Rozzol 1927 = Arturo de Rozzol: Piccolo dizionario italiano-spagnolo (...). Paris 1927 [492 p.].

Ruiz 1971 = D. José Ruiz de Arcaute: Lexicón. Diccionario Italiano-Español y Español-Italiano (...). Barcelona 1971 [382 p. Autre éd. 1974].

Tam 1989 = Laura Tam: Dizionario Spagnolo-Italiano, Italiano-Spagnolo. Novara 1989 [328; 368 p.].

Técnico = Diccionario técnico e industrial Italiano-Español y Español-Italiano. Madrid 1974.

Ulloa 1553 = Introdutione del signor Alphonso di Vglioa (...) con una espositione da lvi fatta nella Italiana, di parecchi uocaboli Hispagnuoli difficili, contenuti quasi tutti nella Tragicomedia di Calisto e Melibea o Celestina. In Vinegia appresso Gabriel Giolito de Ferrari e fratelli MDLIII.

Ulloa 1556 = Exposicion de todos los lugares difficultosos que en el presente libro se hallan (...) por el S. Alonso Vlloa, con una exposicion por el hecha, de algunos vocablos Castellanos en lengua Thoscana. En Leon, en casa de Mathias Bonhomme en el año del s. M.D.L.VI. [16 f. n. ch.].

Vértice 1984 = Diccionario Everest Vértice. Diccionario Italiano-Español, Español-Italiano. S. d. [1984] [883 p. Autre éd. 1978].

Vittori 1609 = Gerolamo Vittori [Hierosme Victor]: Tesoro de las tres lenguas Francesa, Italiana, y Española. Genève 1609 [994 p.; partie Esp.-Français-It. et Français-It.-Esp.].

Vittori 1617 = Gerolamo Vittori: Le Thresor des trois Langves, Espagnole, Françoise, et Italienne. 3 vol. Cologny [Colonia Allobrogum] 1617 [570, 420, 504 p.; 1627, éd. revue 1637, 1644, 1671].

Vocabulista 1526 = Quinque linguarum utilissimus Vocabulista Latine Tusche Gallice Hyspanice et Alemanice Valde necessarius per mundum versari cupientibus (...). 1526 [36 ff. Autres éd. 1551, 1554, 1560, 1563, 1570, 1573, 1574, 1576, 1578, 1585].

Vox 1983 = Vox Diccionario Italiano-Español, Español-Italiano. Revisado por Giovanna Schepisi. Primera ed. Barcelona 1983 [XLIII, 366, XXIX, 333 p. Autres éd. 1984, 1985, 1986].

Vox 1987 = Il nuovo Vox: Dizionario Spagnolo Italiano, Italiano Spagnolo. Bologna 1987 [577 p.].

Vox abrev. 1980 = Vox Diccionario abreviado Italiano-Español, Español-Italiano. Primera ed. Barcelona 1980 [XXXVIII, 385, XXV, 350 p. Autres éd.: 1981, 1982].

Vox Turisti 1976 = Vox Spagnolo per Turisti di lingua italiana. Primera ed. Barcelona 1976 [304 p.].

3.2. Travaux

Fabbri 1979 = Maurizio Fabbri: A Bibliography of Hispanic Dictionaries. Imola 1979.

Gallina 1959 = Annamaria Gallina: Contributi alle storia della Lessicografia Italo-Spagnola dei secoli XVI e XVII. Firenze 1959.

Marello 1989 = Carla Marello: Dizionari bilingui. Bologna 1989.

Wiezell 1975 = Richard John Wiezell: Lexicographic Evidence from the Renaissance. Selected entries from the first Italian and Spanish bilingual dictionary, the cinquecento *Vocabulario de las lenguas toscana y castellana* by Christoval de Las Casas. Northwestern Univ. Ph.D. Diss. 1975 (Dissertation Abstracts 36, 7. 1976. 4458 A).

Annamaria Gallina, Padova (Italie)

315. Die zweisprachige Lexikographie Französisch-Deutsch, Deutsch-Französisch

1. Französisch und Deutsch in vielsprachigen Wörterbüchern vor 1600
2. Das erste französisch-deutsche und deutsch-französische Wörterbuch von 1596
3. Vielsprachige Wörterbücher im 17. Jh.
4. Das 18. Jh.: der Erfolg der zweisprachigen Konzeption
5. Entwicklungslinien im 19. und im 20. Jh.
6. Aktuelle Verlagsprogramme allgemeiner zweisprachiger Wörterbücher
7. Fragen der Makrostruktur
8. Fragen der Mikrostruktur
9. Literatur (in Auswahl)

1. Französisch und Deutsch in vielsprachigen Wörterbüchern vor 1600

Seit dem 15. Jh. macht der Buchdruck die größere Verbreitung lexikographischer Werke möglich. Das Sprachenpaar Französisch und Deutsch findet sich ab dem frühen 16. Jh. in dem damals häufigen Typus der vielsprachigen Wörterbücher mit mehr als zwei Sprachen.

Das erste Wörterbuch mit Französisch und Deutsch ist ein 1510 in Rom unter dem Titel *Introductio quaedam utilissima, sive Vocabularius quatuor linguarum* ... erschienenes sachlich geordnetes lateinisch-italienisch-französisch-deutsches Vokabular (Claes 1977, Nr. 188). Es basiert auf einem 1477 in Venedig gedruckten italienisch-deutschen Vokabular (Rottweil 1477; s. Claes 1977, Nr. 9), das seinerseits aus einem in drei Manuskripten erhaltenen italienisch-deutschen Sprachbuch von 1424 abgeleitet ist (Bray 1988, 314—315). Die *Introductio* von 1510 erfährt mehrere Neuausgaben und wird mit verschiedenen Sprachenkombinationen mehrfach neu bearbeitet (Claes 1977, Nr. 188, c; zur Filiation auch Bray 1988, 315—316 und 338).

Am Beginn eines zweiten Traditionsstranges steht das in Lyon erschienene und gleichfalls sachlich geordnete lateinisch-französisch-deutsche *Vocabularium* von 1514; auch zu diesem Werk sind zahlreiche Neuausgaben nachgewiesen (Claes 1977, Nr. 233).

Das erste alphabetische Wörterbuch mit Französisch und Deutsch dürfte der 1545 in Antwerpen veröffentlichte *Pentaglottos* sein, eine fünfsprachige lateinisch-griechisch-deutsch-flämisch-französische Ausgabe des berühmten lateinischen Wörterbuchs des Ambrosius Calepinus (Calepinus 1545; s. Labarre 1975, Nr. 68; vgl. Claes 1977, Nr. 402). Bearbeitungen des Calepinus mit bis zu elf Sprachen sind bekannt (Calepinus 1590; s. Labarre 1975, Nr. 152).

Ein anderes alphabetisches Wörterbuch humanistischer Gelehrsamkeit ist das kurz nach dem Antwerpener *Pentaglottos* 1548 in Zürich publizierte dreisprachige *Dictionariolum puerorum;* es ist die von Frisius um das Deutsche erweiterte Bearbeitung des lateinisch-französischen Werks von Robert Estienne (Frisius 1548; s. Claes 1977, Nr. 416).

In der zweiten Hälfte des 16. Jh. wird eine Reihe weiterer vielsprachiger Wörterbücher, vor allem auch sachlich geordneter „Nomenklatoren", mit Französisch und Deutsch veröffentlicht.

2. Das erste französisch-deutsche und deutsch-französische Wörterbuch von 1596

Das erste auf das Sprachenpaar Französisch und Deutsch beschränkte zweisprachige Wörterbuch, mit Alphabeten in den beiden Sprachen, wird 1596 von dem nach Deutschland ausgewanderten Flamen Levinus Hulsius in Nürnberg veröffentlicht (Hausmann 1984, 306—307).

Für das französische Alphabet legt Hulsius ein französisch-flämisches Wörterbuch zugrunde, dessen Bearbeitung durch Mellema kurz zuvor 1592 als *Dictionaire ou Promptuaire francois-flameng* in Rotterdam erschienen war. Hulsius ersetzt die flämischen Äquivalente und Übersetzungen durch deutsche (Hausmann 1984, 308).

Das deutsche Alphabet basiert auf dem deutsch-lateinischen Teil des seit 1536 mehrfach aufgelegten *Dictionarium latinogermanicum* von Dasypodius; statt der lateinischen werden französische Äquivalente beigefügt (Hausmann 1984, 311—312).

Weitere Auflagen des zweisprachigen Wörterbuchs von Hulsius erscheinen 1602 wieder in Nürnberg, stark überarbeitet 1607 in Frankfurt und 1614 in Oppenheim und in Frankfurt (Hausmann 1984).

3. Vielsprachige Wörterbücher im 17. Jh.

Das zweisprachige Wörterbuch von Hulsius wird bald von den Traditionen der Zeit eingeholt und zu drei- und viersprachigen Fassungen erweitert.

Zuerst 1610—1611 erscheint im Verlag von Iacob Stoer in Genf eine um das Lateinische erweiterte Ausgabe; ihre letzte Fassung wird 1663 bei den Erben von Ioseph Stoer in Genf verlegt (Hausmann 1984, 315).

Hulsius hat nach dem französisch-deutschen auch ein italienisch-deutsches Wörterbuch verfaßt (zuerst Frankfurt 1605). Beide Werke werden durch Ravellus zu einem dreisprachigen Werk zusammengeführt (Frankfurt 1616). Durch die Erweiterung um das Lateinische entsteht schließlich eine viersprachige Fassung (zuerst Frankfurt 1628) (Hausmann 1984, 315—316).

Die Genfer und die Frankfurter Ausgaben des Hulsius mit Latein haben, im Unterschied zu früheren vielsprachigen Wörterbüchern, aufgrund ihrer Herkunft aus einem zweisprachigen französisch-deutschen Werk ein französisches und ein deutsches Alphabet. Darin folgen ihnen andere Wörterbücher des 17. Jh. mit Französisch und Deutsch sowie Latein als dritter Sprache, diejenigen von Dhuez (auch: Duez; 1642), von Widerhold (1669) und von Pomey (1681); Originalität und Abhängigkeiten dieser Lexikographie bleiben zu klären (Hausmann 1984, 316).

Mit dem dreisprachigen Wörterbuch von Oudin 1674 entsteht, auf anderem Weg als Hulsius 1616, aus einem italienisch-französischen Wörterbuch (Oudin 1640) durch Hinzufügung des Deutschen ein weiteres dreisprachiges Wörterbuch ohne Latein (s. van Passen 1981, 39 und Bray 1988, 323—324).

Insgesamt bleibt die vielsprachige Lexikographie, auch in der Form von Nomenklatoren, im 17. Jh. dominierend.

4. Das 18. Jh.: der Erfolg der zweisprachigen Konzeption

Für die Jahre 1700—1767 verzeichnet Hausmann (1988, 30) noch 13 verschiedene Auflagen von drei- und viersprachigen Wörterbüchern mit Französisch und Deutsch und den weiteren Sprachen Latein und Italienisch. Jedoch rücken im 18. Jh. die zweisprachigen Wörterbücher klar in den Vordergrund. Nach der Aufstellung bei Hausmann (1988, 24—29) lassen sich zwischen 1711 und 1800 bisher 32 verschiedene Titeltypen nachweisen, wobei es von einem einzelnen Titeltyp noch mehrere Ausgaben geben kann, zum Beispiel 16 Ausgaben von Frisch 1716 bis 1793.

Daß die französisch-deutsche Lexikographie des 18. Jh. sich endgültig als zweisprachig etablieren kann, hängt einerseits mit dem Rückgang des Lateinischen und der, auch gegenüber dem Italienischen, immer größeren Bedeutung des Französischen als europäischer Kultursprache zusammen. Andererseits ist diese Entwicklung sicherlich aber durch die Herausbildung einer einsprachigen französischen Lexikographie zum Ende des 17. Jh. (Richelet 1680, Furetière 1690, Académie 1694) begünstigt. So nennt Rondeau 1711 als Quellen das Akademiewörterbuch und Richelet, Kramer 1712 zusätzlich Furetière. Die einsprachigen Wörterbücher setzen, vor allem bezüglich der Mikrostruktur, einen Informationsstandard, der die Möglichkeiten vielsprachiger Wörterbücher übersteigt und in gewisser Weise die Beschränkung auf ein einziges Sprachenpaar erzwingt.

Die Titelgebung einzelner Werke, die programmatischen Äußerungen des einen oder anderen Autors, die Ungleichgewichte zwischen französischem und deutschem Teil eines Wörterbuchs und nicht zuletzt die Vielzahl deutscher Verlagsorte sind Hinweise darauf, daß die zweisprachige Lexikographie in der ersten Hälfte des 18. Jh. vorrangig auf deutsche Benutzer orientiert ist. Zwar erklärt Frisch schon 1716, sein Werk sei im deutschen Teil so erweitert worden, „daß die Liebhaber beyder Sprachen dieses Buch mit großem Nutzen gebrauchen können" (Frisch 1716, Titelblatt), aber sein französischer Teil hat dennoch mehr als den doppelten Umfang des deutschen. Bei ausgeglichenem Umfang signalisiert als erstes das bei König in Straßburg 1762 veröffentlichte Wörterbuch mit dem Titelbestandteil ... à l'usage des deux nations eine zugleich auf französische Benutzer ausgerichtete Konzeption.

Nachdem König 1762 noch das Fehlen eines modernen deutschen Wörterbuchs bedauert, kann sich schon 1782 Schwan außer auf die französische Akademie auch auf das große deutsche Wörterbuch von Adelung beziehen (Rettig 1982, 105—106). Wie weitgehend Schwan durch die Übernahme von Definitionen auf diesem einsprachigen Werk aufbaut, zeigt Hausmann /1990/, 15—17.

In der zweiten Hälfe des 18. Jh. ist mit der Durchsetzung des zweisprachigen Typus neben den großen Projekten wie Schmidlin 1771—1779 (dazu: Höfler 1982a), Schrader 1771—1784 oder Schwan 1782—1793 und 1798 auch die Etablierung kleinerer Gattungen wie „dictionnaire portatif" und „dictionnaire de poche" zu beobachten.

Die Vielfalt der französisch-deutschen Lexikographie am Ende des 18. und zu Beginn des 19. Jh., in der Zeit zwischen französischer Revolution und Wiener Kongreß, wird in der bibliographischen Zusammenstellung von Baudrier 1970 dokumentiert. Als Besonderheit unter diesen Werken kann Catel 1800—1801 genannt werden, eine um deutsche Äquivalente erweiterte Ausgabe des französischen Akademiewörterbuchs (zu Catel und einer ähnlichen Bearbeitung von 1836—1840 s. auch Höfler 1983, 56—57).

5. Entwicklungslinien im 19. und im 20. Jh.

Wie zu Beginn des 19. Jh. Zielgruppenkonzeptionen — Wörterbuch für Schüler oder Fachwortschatz für „Kaufleute und Professionisten" — in Kollision geraten, zeigt Hausmann (1989, 42—44) am Beispiel der Publikationsgeschichte der Wörterbücher von Memmert 1800 und Memmert/Meynier 1800—1802 auf.

Mit Memmert/Meynier und anderen ähnlich dimensionierten und konzipierten Wörterbüchern der Zeit ist schon zu Beginn des 19. Jh. ein bis heute dominierender stark „enzyklopädischer", auch bei mittlerer oder kleinerer Dimension auf die Aufnahme von viel Fachwortschatz ausgerichteter Typ von Wörterbüchern vorhanden (Hausmann /1990/, 22).

Ein *Extrait* von Schwans großem Wörterbuch wird nur wenige Jahre nach seiner Veröffentlichung 1799—1804 im Verlag Cotta durch das Werk von Mozin abgelöst, welches bis in die zweite Hälfte des 19. Jh. hinein ein wichtiges Standardwerk sein wird (3. Auflage 1842—1846, Supplément 1859). Als Quellen für die 1. Auflage (1811—1813) werden zum Französischen insbesondere das Wörterbuch von Trévoux, die *Encyclopédie* und das Wörterbuch der Académie in der Ausgabe von 1802 (einer Bearbeitung durch Laveaux; s. Höfler 1983, 56—57) und für das Deutsche das Wörterbuch von Campe genannt (Mozin 1811 (F—D), II und VI).

Die dominierende lexikographische Leistung der zweiten Hälfte des 19. Jh. ist das im Verlag Langenscheidt veröffentlichte Wörterbuch von Sachs (1869—1874/1874—ca. 1880). Das Titelblatt nennt als Quellen für das Französische die Wörterbücher der Akademie und von Littré — ihm hat Sachs das Werk auch gewidmet — und für das Deutsche Grimm und Sanders.

Der „großen Ausgabe" des Sachs folgt unverzüglich eine verkürzte „Hand- und Schul-Ausgabe" (Sachs 1873/1881). Diese ursprünglich „kleine Ausgabe" des Sachs — auf dem Vorschaltblatt des zweiten Bandes firmiert sie bereits mit dem später durchgehend verwendeten Etikett „Sachs-Villatte" — ist über mehrere Stationen der Neubearbeitung die Basis für *Langenscheidts Großwörterbuch Französisch* und damit für das größte Anfang 1990 im Handel verfügbare französisch-deutsche Wörterbuch (Weis 1979/Gottschalk/Bentot 1968/Lange-Kowal 1979).

Textbeispiel 315.1: Artikel *français* bis *France* (aus: Sachs 1869—1874).

Ein zweiter aus dem großen Sachs abgeleiteter Titel der Zeit, das noch kleinere *Taschenwörterbuch* von 1884, befindet sich nach mehreren Neubearbeitungen ebenfalls aktuell noch im Handel (Lange-Kowal/Weymuth 1982).

Neben den großen Werken wie Mozin oder Sachs gibt es im 19. Jh. zahlreiche andere, zum Teil über Jahrzehnte hin wieder aufgelegte Titel. Zum Beispiel erscheint ein

Wörterbuch von Thibaut (Pseudonym für Johann Gottfried Haas, der seit 1786 unter diesem Namen verschiedene Wörterbücher publizierte; vgl. Hausmann 1989, 45) 1871 in 59. Auflage, 1908 in 150. Auflage. Dabei kommt es zur Herausbildung differenzierter Produktreihen auch verschiedener Autoren. So werden in einer Anzeige des „Wörterbücher-Verlags" George Westermann nebeneinander die folgenden französisch-deutschen Werke angeboten: Thibaut, *Wörterbuch* 59. Auflage; Molé, *Wörterbuch zum Gebrauche für alle Stände*, 27. Auflage; Molé, *Taschenwörterbuch zum Schulgebrauch*, 31. Auflage; Cousin, *Reise- und Conversations-Taschenwörterbuch*, 4. Auflage (Thibaut 1871, Vorschaltblatt).

Nur zögernd entsteht in der ersten Hälfte des 19. Jh. auch eine Pariser Wörterbuchproduktion mit kleineren Werken wie Henschel (zuerst 1836) und, bei Hachette verlegt, de Suckau (zuerst 1846), ansonsten wird der seit der Zeit der französischen Revolution offenbar stark expandierende Markt von den deutschen Verlegern beherrscht.

Die große Zahl der Titel im 19. und 20. Jh. ist ohne detailliertere Vorarbeiten kaum zu überblicken. Eine Recherche in einigen wenigen bibliographischen Quellen hat nur für die ersten 80 Jahre des 20. Jh. bereits eine Liste von ca. 600 Titeln allgemeiner und fachsprachlicher, hier oft vielsprachiger, Werke ergeben. Die Filiationen dieser zahlreichen Titel sind nur schwer zu ermitteln, auch weil aus kommerziellen Gründen über Alter und redaktionelle Konzeptionen eines Wörterbuchs oft keine hinreichenden Angaben gemacht werden (vgl. dazu auch Hausmann 1986).

Größere Werke der Mitte des 20. Jh., die für den aktuellen Stand eine Rolle spielen, sind die Wörterbücher von Bertaux/Lepointe 1941/1952 bei Hachette, Weis/Mattutat 1959/1967, Vorläufer zu einer ganzen Produktreihe von Klett, Lange-Kowal/Wilhelm 1963, Ergänzung der Langenscheidt-Serie zwischen Sachs-Villatte und Taschenwörterbuch, und Grappin 1963, größte Produktion von Larousse.

6. Aktuelle Verlagsprogramme allgemeiner zweisprachiger Wörterbücher

Im Februar 1984 sind 27 verschiedene Typen von Wörterbüchern der französischen und der deutschen Sprache im Handel, und dies unter 46 verschiedenen Titeln bei 16 verschiedenen Verlagen. Größere Produktreihen haben die Verlage Bordas (3 Texte in Lizenz von Klett), Garnier (3 Texte), Klett (3 Texte), Langenscheidt (6 Texte und 1 elektronisches Wörterbuch) und Larousse (5 Texte und 3 Texte in Lizenz von Langenscheidt) (Rettig 1985, 87—89 und 117).

In diesem Markt zeigen sich dynamische Weiterentwicklungen. Zum Beispiel ist nach dem Stand von Februar 1990 das Verlagsprogramm der „Pons"-Wörterbücher bei Klett von 3 auf 6 Texte erweitert worden. Die Abstufung des Umfangs läßt sich anhand der Satzfläche (Länge x Breite des Satzspiegels x Seitenzahl der beiden Alphabete) ungefähr ersehen:

Programm 1984:
Groß-/Globalwörterbuch 1978 (35, 2/25, 3 m^2)
Kompaktwörterbuch 1979 (14,7 m^2)
Taschenwörterbuch 1979 (3,9 m^2)

Programm 1990:
Großwörterbuch 1988 (39,0 m^2)
Globalwörterbuch 1978, 2. Aufl. 1985 (35,4 m^2)
Kompaktwörterbuch 1979 (14,7 m^2)
Standardwörterbuch 1989 (5,7 m^2)
Taschenwörterbuch 1979 (3,9 m^2)
Praxiswörterbuch 1988 (2,6 m^2)

Das größte Anfang 1990 im Handel befindliche zweisprachige Wörterbuch ist mit einer Satzfläche von 68,1 m^2 *Langenscheidts Großwörterbuch* (Weis 1979/Gottschalk/Bentot 1968/Lange-Kowal 1979), eine in den Jahren 1968 (D—F) und 1979 (F—D) abgeschlossene grundlegende Neufassung des zuletzt 1917 (F—D) und 1921 (D—F) revidierten Textes des „kleinen" Sachs-Villatte. Weitere umfangreichere Werke sind die Wörterbücher von Bertaux/Lepointe 1966/1968 bei Hachette, Grappin 1989 bei Larousse, Schlegelmilch 1985 im Verlag Enzyklopädie und, als *Großwörterbuch* der oben genannten Produktreihe, Weis/Mattutat 1988 bei Klett. Das kleinste Wörterbuch ist mit einer Gesamtsatzfläche von 1 m^2 das zweibändige *Lilliput-Wörterbuch* 1978 bei Langenscheidt.

Ein zweisprachiges elektronisches Wörterbuch mit ca. 8 000 Stichwörtern und einer extrem reduzierten Mikrostruktur wird 1983 von Langenscheidt veröffentlicht (Elektronisches Wörterbuch 1983). Die Neuausgabe von 1990 ist auf ca. 40 000 Stichwörter erweitert (Computer 1990). Sie konkurriert mit einer Reihe vielsprachiger elektronischer Wörterverzeichnisse, die bisher in drei verschiedenen Techniken angeboten werden: wie beim Computer 1990 feste Programmierung eines Gerätes im Taschenrechnerformat zum Beispiel beim fünfsprachigen Interpreter 1990 und beim sechssprachigen Hexaglot 1990; steckbare Programmkarte für einen Taschencomputer beim Translator 1988; Compact Disc als Datenträger für einen Personal Computer beim Videodizionario 1989.

Die Konzeption der Vielsprachigkeit und die Konzeption einer Gliederung nach Sachgruppen (beim Translator 1988) erinnern an frühe lexikographische Traditionen der gedruckten Wörterbücher.

Die Rückkehr zur Mündlichkeit („sprechender Hexaglot") ist angekündigt.

7. Fragen der Makrostruktur

7.1. Verhältnis von Makro- und Mikrostruktur

Wörterbücher sind „makrostrukturorientiert", wenn sie viele Stichwörter und vergleichsweise wenig Informationen zum einzelnen Stichwort enthalten. Als Beispiel eines größeren Wörterbuchs dieses Typs kann Pfohl 1960 genannt werden, der 1984 mit 26,5 m^2 nach der Satzfläche an 6. Stelle stand, nach der Auszählung der Stichwörter im Abschnitt *G-GAL*... beider Alphabete mit Einträgen wie *galactographie (/Beschreibung der Milch)* und *Galanteriedegen (/épée de parade)* aber den 1. Platz belegt (Rettig 1985, 93 und 105—106).

Wörterbücher mittlerer und kleiner Dimension sind durchweg mehr oder weniger „makrostrukturorientiert". Sie haben viele tausend Stichwörter und zum einzelnen Stichwort wenig Information, häufig nur die Angabe von Wortart oder Genus und ein Äquivalent.

7.2. Mehrwortige Lexeme

Mehrwortige Lexeme werden in vielen Wörterbüchern vernachlässigt. Soweit sie Berücksichtigung finden, werden sie bisher nur ganz sporadisch, wie *bon sens* bei Lange-Kowal 1976, als Elemente der Makrostruktur behandelt, sonst aber durchweg in der Mikrostruktur zu einem einwortigen Lemma abgehandelt. Sie werden dabei von bloßen Verwendungsbeispielen des Stichworts meistens nicht genügend abgegrenzt (vgl. Art. 52).

7.3. Lexeme des Nichtstandards

Die Berücksichtigung von Lexemen des Nichtstandards ist sehr uneinheitlich und oft ziemlich unvollständig. Im größten Wörterbuch fehlen Regionalismen wie *Jänner (/janvier)* und *Weck (/petit pain)*, die bei Weis/Mattutat 1988 berücksichtigt sind. Ein Regionalismus der DDR wie *Broiler (/poulet rôti)* fehlt in allen Wörterbüchern außer Olivier 1964/Liebold/Liebold 1983 (Rettig 1985, 107).

7.4. Anordnung der Stichwörter

Bei der Anordnung der Stichwörter können glatt-, nischen- und nestalphabetische Wörterbücher unterschieden werden (Rettig 1985, 109 nach Wiegand). Glattalphabetisch ist zum Beispiel Berlitz 1979: *Bau, Bauch* und *Bauholz* sind wie alle anderen Stichwörter am alphabetischen Ort ohne jede Zuordnung zu anderen Stichwörtern eingetragen. Nischenalphabetisch ist Weis/Mattutat 1988: Mit *Bau* wird ein typographisch zusammenhängender Abschnitt eröffnet, in dem nach dem Artikel *Bau* die semantisch zugehörigen Artikel *Bauabschnitt* bis *Baubüro* in einer „Nische" versammelt sind. Die Nische endet vor dem Stichwort *Bauch,* so daß die alphabetische Reihenfolge gewahrt bleibt. Der Artikel *Bauholz* folgt später in der Nische *Bauerwartungsland*. Nestalphabetisch ist im deutsch-französischen Teil Grappin 1989: Nach dem Artikel *Bau* eröffnet der Artikel *Bauabteilung* einen typographisch zusammenhängenden Abschnitt mit semantisch zugehörigen Artikeln bis zum Artikel *(Bau)-zeit*. Erst nach diesem die alphabetische Reihenfolge durchbrechenden „Nest" folgt der Artikel *Bauch*.

Die große Mehrzahl der aktuellen französisch-deutschen Wörterbücher ist nischenalphabetisch.

8. Fragen der Mikrostruktur

8.1. Ausführlichkeit der Mikrostruktur

Eine entwickelte Mikrostruktur mit ausführlicheren Angaben zu den Äquivalenten und auch zu mehrwortigen Ausdrücken haben nur größere zweisprachige Wörterbücher des Französischen und des Deutschen. Nach einer Tabelle zur Zahl der mehrwortigen Ausdrücke bei den Stichwörtern *nez* und *Nase* (Rettig 1985, 108) enthält das größte Wörterbuch 103 Ausdrücke, die 12 letztplazierten aber enthalten nur 0 bis 3 Ausdrücke.

8.2. Dimension der Äquivalente

Äquivalent zu einer einwortigen Stichwortform kann auch ein mehrwortiger Ausdruck der Zielsprache sein. Ein Äquivalent zu *billig* ist *bon marché*, ein Äquivalent zu *Schwarzmarkt* ist *marché noir*. Wie weit die Wortbildungsstruktur oder, bei mehrwortigen Ausdrücken, die syntaktische Struktur von Ausgangsform und Äquivalent einander ähnlich sind, ist nicht entscheidend. Zu *einen Meineid schwören* ist *se parjurer* trotz deutlicher Strukturverschiedenheit ein passendes Äquivalent, ebenso *la pierre philosophale* zu *der Stein der Weisen* (vgl. auch Rettig 1985, 96).

Manche Äquivalentangaben haben die Form einer mehrgliedrigen Definition und sind vom syntaktischen Status der Stichwortform so weit entfernt, daß man sie in Texten der Zielsprache nicht durchgehend in dieser Form verwenden kann. Das zu *gabion* gegebene Äquivalent *behelfsmäßige Hütte für die Jagd auf Wasserwild* (Lange-Kowal 1976/1982) kann in der Regel nur in einer ersten Verwendung in voller Länge erscheinen, bei anschließendem weiterem Vorkommen von *gabion* müßte die Übersetzung auf ein Äquivalent der Dimension *Hütte* beschränkt bleiben. Man könnte die Langform als „definitorische" Dimension und die Kurzform als „teildefinitorische" Dimension des Äquivalents bezeichnen. Allgemeinere Konventionen zur Kennzeichnung der verschiedenen Dimensionen eines mehrwortigen Äquivalents, zum Beispiel durch Klammerung von Bestandteilen, sind bisher nicht entwickelt.

8.3. Oberbegriff als Äquivalent

Eine Äquivalentangabe, die von vornherein auf eine Kurzform beschränkt ist, kann man auch als Angabe eines „Oberbegriffs" betrachten. Mit der Verwendung eines Oberbegriffs ohne differenzierenden Zusatz, wie *danse tyrolienne* für *Schuhplattler* (Lange-Kowal 1976/1982), wird im Text der Zielsprache eine größere Unschärfe der Bedeutung in Kauf genommen. Auch müssen dabei je nach Kontext spezifische Verwendungsbedingungen zum Beispiel beim Gebrauch des bestimmten oder unbestimmten Artikels beachtet werden. Für die Kennzeichnung dieser Art von Äquivalent, zum Beispiel drucktechnisch durch Kursivierung, fehlen allgemeinere Konventionen, ebenso für die im Hinblick auf die Übersetzung eines Textes notwendigen zusätzlichen Informationen.

8.4. Differenzierung mehrerer Äquivalente

Weil auch die typologisch ähnlichen Sprachen Französisch und Deutsch in vielen Teilen ihres Lexikons sehr verschieden strukturiert sind, gibt es sehr oft zu einem Ausdruck der Ausgangssprache mehrere Äquivalente der Zielsprache, die im Wörterbuch voneinander differenziert werden müssen.

Eine häufige Form der Differenzierung ist die Kommentierung in der Ausgangssprache. So werden die drei französischen Äquivalente von deutsch *Tee* bei Weis/Mattutat 1988 wie folgt kommentiert: ... (Teeblätter u. daraus bereitetes Getränk) *thé* ... (Aufguß von anderen Pflanzen) *infusion* ... (Krankentee) *tisane*.

Eine weitere häufige Form der Differenzierung ist die Zuordnung der Äquivalente zu einer Fachsprache (oder einem Sachgebiet) oder einem Diasystem der Sprache. Zum Beispiel gibt Weis/Mattutat 1988 für *Heidenangst* zwei Äquivalente und kennzeichnet dabei *peur bleue* als „fam" („vertraulich" — „familier") und *frousse* als „pop" („volkstümlich" — „populaire").

Die Differenzierung der Äquivalente ist oft unvollständig und auch innerhalb desselben Wörterbuchs heterogen.

8.5. Kollokationen

Eine mikrostrukturelle Information, die in vielen Wörterbüchern vernachlässigt ist, wird im *Kontextwörterbuch Französisch-Deutsch* (Ilgenfritz 1989) breiter dargestellt; in einem Alphabet französischer Substantive sind Kollokationen mit ihren deutschen Entsprechungen eingetragen.

Die Berücksichtigung von Kollokationen und dabei auch eine Abgrenzung von anderen Arten mehrwortiger Eintragungen (auf der einen Seite von semantisch spezifischen Phraseologismen, auf der anderen Seite von nicht spezifischen Textbeispielen) kann die Information der Benutzer in die syntaktische und auch stilistische Dimension hinein erweitern.

9. Literatur (in Auswahl)

9.1. Wörterbücher

(Bei der Angabe der Wörterbuchtitel wurde Groß- und Kleinschreibung standardisiert.)

Berlitz 1979 = Berlitz. Wörterbuch Französisch-Deutsch, Deutsch-Französisch Dictionnaire français-allemand, allemand-français. Revised edition. Lausanne 1979 [367 S.].

Bertaux/Lepointe 1941/1952 = Félix Bertaux/ Emile Lepointe: Dictionnaire allemand-français. Paris 1941. Dictionnaire français-allemand. Paris 1952 [Librairie française 1957—1958 (I)] [1442, 1314 S.].

Bertaux/Lepointe 1966/1968 = F. Bertaux/E. Lepointe: Dictionnaire français-allemand. Paris 1966. Dictionnaire allemand-français. Paris 1968 [1310, 1392 S.].

Calepinus 1545 = Ambr. Calepinus: Pentaglottos, Hoc est, quinque linguis, nempe Latina, Graeca, Germanica, Flandrica, & Gallica constans (...). Antuerpiae 1545 [Labarre 1975, Nr. 68; vgl. Claes 1977, Nr. 402. — 1460 S.].

Calepinus 1590 = Ambrosius Calepinus: Dictionarium undecim linguarum (...). Respondent autem Latinis vocabulis, Hebraica, Belgica, Graeca, Hispanica, Gallica, Polonica, Italica, Vngarica, Germanica, Anglica (...). Basileae 1590 [Labarre 1975, Nr. 152. — 1984 S.].

Catel 1800—1801 = Dictionnaire de l'Académie françoise (...). Nouvelle édition, enrichie de la traduction allemande des mots. Par S. H. Catel. 4 vol. Berlin 1800—1801 [XIV, 1716 S.].

Computer 1990 = Langenscheidts Wörterbuch Computer. Französisch. Alpha 40. München 1990 [Taschencomputer].

Cramer 1712—1715 = Matthias Kramer: Das recht vollkommen-königliche Dictionarium (...) Frantzösisch-Teutsch (auch: Matthias Cramer: Le vraiment parfait Dictionnaire roial (...) françois-allemand (...)). 4 vol. — Matthias Cramer: Nouveau & parfait Indice allemand-françois (...) (auch: Neuvollständiges teutsch-französisches Wörter-Register (...)). Nürnberg 1712—1715 [XLVIII, 2106, X, 478 S.].

Dasypodius 1536 = Petrus Dasypodius: Dictionarium Latinogermanicum (...) Argentorati 1536 [VI, 974 S. — Edition: Hildesheim. New York 1974].

Elektronisches Wörterbuch 1983 = Langenscheidts elektronisches Wörterbuch alpha 8, Französisch-Deutsch, Deutsch-Französisch. München 1983 [Taschencomputer].

Flathe 1798 = Philipp Jakob Flathe: Neues deutsch-französisches und französisch-deutsches Wörterbuch 5 Bde. Leipzig 1798 [5160, 1312 S.].

Frisch 1716 = Johann Leonhard Frisch: Nouveau Dictionnaire des passagers françois-allemand et allemand-françois, oder Neues frantzösisch-teutsches und teutsch-frantzösisches Wörter-Buch (...). Leipzig 1716 [XII, 1021, 446 S.; zuerst 1712].

Frisius 1548 = Joannes Frisius: Dictionariolum puerorum tribus linguis, Latina, Gallica et Germanica conscriptum. Zürich 1548 [Claes 1977, Nr. 416. — 613 (l. 853?) S.]

Gottschalk/Bentot 1968/1979 s. Weis 1979.

Grappin 1963 = Pierre Grappin: Dictionnaire français-allemand. Dictionnaire allemand-français. Paris 1963 [Edition 1983. — XVI, 848, XIV, 898 S.].

Grappin 1989 = Pierre Grappin: Grand Dictionnaire français allemand. Grosswörterbuch Deutsch Französisch. Paris 1989 [LVI, 1463 S.].

Haas 1786 = Jean Geofroy Haas: Dictionnaire des langues françoise et allemande accomodé à l'usage des jeunes gens. Leipzic 1786 [XII, 848 S.]. Johann Gottfried Haas: Neues deutsches und französisches Wörterbuch, der Jugend zum Gebrauch bequem eingerichtet. Leipzig 1786 [Hausmann 1989, 49n14. 1150 S.].

Henschel 1844 = G. A. Louis Henschel: Dictionnaire de langue française et allemande. 2 vol. Paris 1844 [1re édition 1836 (Lorenz 1867—1871 (II)].

Hexaglot 1990 = Hexaglot, by Dictiomatic. Englisch-Spanisch-Deutsch-Portugiesisch-Italienisch-Französisch. s. l. s. d. [1990. — Taschencomputer].

Hulsius 1596 = Dictionaire françois allemand et allemand françois (...) Dictionarium Teutsch Frantzösisch und Frantzösisch Teutsch (...) Noribergae, per Levinum Hulsium, 1596 [Hausmann 1984, 317; vgl. Claes 1977, Nr. 818. — 448, 172 S.].

Hulsius 1605 = Levinus Hulsius: Dictionarium Teutsch Italiänisch und Italiänisch Teutsch (...). Dittionario italian'-alemano et aleman'-italiano. Francfurt 1605 [Hausmann 1984, 317].

Ilgenfritz 1989 = Peter Ilgenfritz u. a.: Langenscheidts Kontextwörterbuch Französisch-Deutsch. Berlin usw. 1989 [320 S.].

Interpreter 1990 = Berlitz Interpreter. Deutsch-Englisch-Französisch-Italienisch-Spanisch. Minneapolis 1990 [Taschencomputer].

Introductio 1510 = Introductio quaedam utilissima, sive Vocabularius quatuor linguarum, Latinae, Italicae, Gallicae, Alamanicae (...). Romae, Jacobus Mazochius, 1510 [Claes 1977, Nr. 188. — 120 S.].

König 1762 = Nouveau Dictionnaire allemand-françois et françois-allemand, à l'usage des deux nations (...). Nouveau Dictionnaire françois-allemand et allemand-françois (...). 2 vol. Strasbourg 1762 [VIII, 774, II, 735 S.].

Kramer s. Cramer.

Lange-Kowal 1976/1982 = Ernst Erwin Lange-Kowal: Langenscheidts Handwörterbuch Französisch. I: Französisch-Deutsch. Berlin usw. 1976 (= Langenscheidts Großes Schulwörterbuch 1977). — Ernst Erwin Lange-Kowal: Langenscheidts großes Schulwörterbuch. II: Deutsch-Französisch. Berlin usw.1982 (= Langenscheidts Handwörterbuch 1983) [640 (= 1200), 1310 (= 670) S.].

Lange-Kowal 1979 s. Weis 1979.

Lange-Kowal/Weymuth 1982 = Ernst Erwin Lange-Kowal: Langenscheidts Taschenwörterbuch der französischen und deutschen Sprache (auch: (...) Langenscheidt. Dictionaire de poche des langues française et allemande (...). I: Französisch-Deutsch. Berlin usw. 1982. — Eduard Weymuth: Langenscheidts Taschenwörterbuch der französischen und deutschen Sprache. II: Deutsch-Französisch (...). Berlin usw. 1982 [1216 S. — 1. Auflage 1884].

Lange-Kowal/Wilhelm 1963 = Ernst Erwin Lange-Kowal: Langenscheidts Handwörterbuch Französisch. I: Französisch-Deutsch. — Kurt Wilhelm: (...) II. Deutsch-Französisch. Berlin usw. 1963 [656, 688 S.].

Laveaux 1784 = Jean-Charles Thibault de Laveaux: Dictionnaire françois-allemand, allemand-françois à l'usage des deux nations. Réd. par une Société de gens de lettres. 3 Bde. Berlin 1784, 1785 [2. Aufl. des Wb. v. Heinrich Friederich Roux 1779. Oft zit. unt. d. Namen des Verlegers Wever. 6 weit. Aufl. bis 1807].

Lilliput-Wörterbuch 1978 = Langenscheidts Lilliput-Wörterbuch. I: Deutsch-Französisch. II: Französisch-Deutsch. Berlin. München 1978 [576, 576 S.].

Mellema 1592 = Elcie Edouard Leon Mellema: Dictionaire ou Promptuaire francois-flameng (...) Rotterdam 1592 [Hausmann 1984, 319].

Memmert 1800 = J. F. Memmert: Neues deutsch-französisches und französisch-deutsches grammatisches Wörterbuch (...). Weimar 1800 [Baudrier 1970(-2), 106].

Memmert/Meynier 1800—1802 = Johann Friedrich Memmert: Dictionnaire françois-allemand à l'usage des écoles et de l'état bourgeois (...). Französisch-teutsches Handwörterbuch für die Schulen und den Bürgerstand (...) aufs neue durchgegangen und vermehrt von Johann Heinrich Meynier (...). Erlangen 1800. — Johann Heinrich Meynier: Dictionnaire allemand-françois à l'usage des écoles et de l'état bourgeois (...). Teutsch-französisches Handwörterbuch für die Schulen und den Bürgerstand (...). Erlangen 1802 [XVI, 1300, XIV, 1581 S.].

Mozin 1811—1813 = abbé Mozin (...): Nouveau Dictionnaire complet à l'usage des Allemands et des Français. Partie française. 2 vol. Stuttgart. Tubingue 1811—1812. — abbé Mozin (...): Neues vollständiges Wörterbuch der deutschen und französischen Sprache (...). Deutscher Theil. 2 vol. Stuttgart. Tübingen 1811—1813 [LXXXVI, 1675, 1656 S.].

Mozin 1842—1846 = abbé Mozin: Dictionnaire complet des langues française et allemande (...). 3e édition par A. Peschier. 2 vol. Stuttgart. Tubingue 1842. — Mozin's vollständiges Wörterbuch der deutschen und französischen Sprache. 3. Auflage von A. Peschier. 2 vol. Stuttgart. Tübingen 1844—1846 [VIII, 2373, 2580 S. — Supplément s. Peschier 1859].

Olivier 1964/Liebold/Liebold 1983 = René Olivier: Wörterbuch Französisch-Deutsch. 2. Auflage. Leipzig 1964 [Nachdruck 1983]. — Gisela Liebold/Harald Liebold: Wörterbuch Deutsch-Französisch. Leipzig 1983 [XVI, 708, 528 S.].

Oudin 1640 = Antoine Oudin: Recherches italiennes et françoises, ou Dictionnaire (...). Paris 1640. — Seconde partie des Recherches italiennes et françoises. Contenant les mots françois expliquez par l'italien. Paris 1642 [VI, 932, 587 S.].

Oudin 1674 = Nuovo et ampio dittionario di tre lingue, diviso in III parti: I. Italiano-francese-tedesco. II. Francese-italiano-tedesco. III. Tedesco-francese-italiano. Composto, prima in quelle due lingue da Antonio Udino (...) ed aumentato adesso della terza (...) Francoforte 1674 — (...) [s. van Passen 1981, 39; vgl. Bray 1988, 324].

Peschier 1859 = A. Peschier: Supplément au Dictionnaire complet des langues française et allemande de l'abbé Mozin. Stuttgart. Augsbourg 1859 [IV, 489 S.].

Pfohl 1960 = Ernst Pfohl: Brockhaus Bildwörterbuch Französisch-Deutsch, Deutsch-Französisch. 31., von Pierre Benoit neub. u. erw. Aufl. Wiesbaden 1960 [720, 610 S.].

Poëtevin 1754 = François Louis Poëtevin: Le nouveau dictionnaire suisse françois-allemand. Basel 1754 [1246 S.].

Rondeau 1711—1712 = Nouveau Dictionnaire françois-allemand (...). Neues frantzösisch-teutsches Wörter-Buch. Leipzig 1711. — Peter Rondeau: Neues teutsch-frantzösisches Wörter-Buch (...). Leipzig 1712 [VI, 611 (l. 591), IV, 678 S.].

Rottweil 1477 = Introito e porta de quele che voleno imparare e comprender todescho o italiano. (Venedig), Adam von Rottweil, 1477 [Claes 1977, Nr. 9. — 112 S.] (Edition: Vito R. Giustiniani: Adam von Rottweil. Deutsch-italienischer Sprachführer (...). Tübingen 1987).

Roux 1744 = François Roux: Dictionnaire nouveau françois et allemand, allemand et françois. Jena 1744 [763, 573 S. 11. Aufl. bis 1809].

Sachs 1869—ca. 1880 = Karl Sachs: Encyklopädisches französisch-deutsches und deutsch-französisches Wörterbuch (...). Grosse Ausgabe. I. Theil: Französisch-Deutsch (auch: Charles Sachs: Dictionnaire encyclopédique (...). Edition complète (...). Berlin 1869—1874. — Carl Sachs: Encyklopädisches französisch-deutsches und deutsch-französisches Wörterbuch (...) unter Mitwirkung von Cäsar Villatte (...). Große Ausgabe. II. Theil: Deutsch-Französisch (auch: Charles Sachs: Dictionnaire encyclopédique (...) avec le concours de César Villatte (...). Grande édition (...)). Berlin 1874(—ca. 1880) [XL, 1630, XXXII, 2119 S.].

Sachs 1873/1881 = Karl Sachs: Französisch-deutsches und deutsch-französisches Wörterbuch (...). Hand- und Schul-Ausgabe. Französisch-Deutsch. Berlin 1873 [2. Auflage 1878]. — Karl Sachs: Encyklopädisches französisch-deutsches und deutsch-französisches Wörterbuch (...). Hand- und Schul-Ausgabe. Deutsch-Französisch. Berlin 1881 [LVI, 738, 908 S.].

Sachs 1894 = Karl Sachs: Französisch-deutsches Supplement-Lexikon (...) (auch: Charles Sachs: Dictionnaire-supplément français-allemand (...)) unter Mitwirkung von Césaire Villatte. Berlin 1894 [XXXII, 329 S.].

Schlegelmilch 1985 = Aribert Schlegelmilch (ed.): Handwörterbuch Französisch-Deutsch. 2 Bde. Leipzig 1985 [1063 S.].

Schmidlin 1771—1779 = Johann Joseph Schmidlin: Catholicon ou Dictionnaire universel de la langue françoise. Catholicon oder Französisch-deutsches Universal-Wörterbuch der französischen Sprache (Buchstaben A—I). 9 vol. Hamburg 1771—1779 [Datierung nach Höfler 1982 a, 55. — XL, 4269 S.].

Schrader 1771—1784 = Christian Friedrich Schrader: Nouvel et complet Dictionnaire étymologique, grammatical et critique de la langue françoise ancienne et moderne. I: François-allemand. Halle 1771. — Vollständiges deutsches und französisches Wörterbuch. II: Allemand et françois (...) 2 vol. Halle 1781—1784 [II, 1284, VI, 1710 S.].

Schwan 1782—1793 und 1798 = Chrétien Frédéric Schwan: Nouveau Dictionnaire de la langue allemande et françois (...). 2 vol. Mannheim 1782—1784. — Chrétien Frédéric Schwan: Nouveau Dictionnaire de la langue françoise et allemande (...). 4 vol. Mannheim 1787—1793. — Chrétien Frédéric Schwan: Supplément au Dictionnaire de la langue allemande et françoise (...). Mannheim 1798 [XXVI, 2117, X, 3128, II, 288 S.].

Schwan 1799—1804 = Chrétien Frédéric Schwan: Nouveau Dictionnaire de la langue allemande et française (...). Extrait de son grand dictionnaire (...). 2 vol. Louisbourg 1799—1800 (Baudrier 1970 (—2), 103). — Chrétien Frédéric Schwan: Nouveau Dictionnaire de la langue françoise et allemande (...). Extrait de son grand dictionnaire (...). 2 vol. Tubingen 1802—1804 [XL, 2162 S.].

Stoer 1610—1611 = Dictionaire francois-alleman-latin (...). Geneve, Iacob Stoer, 1610. — Novum Germanico-Gallico-Latinum Dictionarium (...). Genevae, Iacobus Stoer, 1611 [Hausmann 1984, 318].

de Suckau 1859 = Wilhelm de Suckau: Dictionnaire classique français-allemand et allemand-français. 2 vol. Paris 1859 [1re édition 1846. (Lorenz 1867—1871 (IV))].

Thibaut 1871 = M. A. Thibaut: Vollständiges Wörterbuch der französischen und deutschen Sprache. 59. Auflage. Braunschweig 1871 [VI, 618, 587 S.].

Thibaut 1908 = M. A. Thibaut: Wörterbuch der französischen und deutschen Sprache. Neu bearbeitet von Otto Kabisch. 2 vol. 150. Auflage. Braunschweig 1908 [V, 874, V, 737 S.].

Translator 1988 = 8-Language Translator. English - French - German - Italian - Spanish - Swedish - Japanese-Chinese. Osaka 1988 [Programmkarte für Taschencomputer SHARP IQ-7100 M Electronic Organizer].

Videodizionario 1989 = CD-ROM 12 LINGUE. VIDEODIZIONARIO. Inglese-cinese, danese, finlandese, francese, giapponese, italiano, norvegese, olandese, spagnolo, svedese e tedesco. Bologna 1989 [Compact Disc für Personal Computer. — Zanichelli. Novità autunno inverno 1989/90. Bologna 1989, 9].

Vocabularium 1514 = Vocabularium Latinis, Gallicis et Theutonicis verbis scriptum. Lyon, Jehan Thomas, 1514 [Claes 1977, Nr. 233. — 68 S.].

Weis 1979/Gottschalk/Bentot 1968/Lange-Kowal 1979 = Erich Weis: Langenscheidts Großwörterbuch Französisch. Begründet von Karl Sachs und Césaire Villatte. Französisch-Deutsch. Berlin usw. 1979. — Walter Gottschalk/Gaston Bentot: (...). Deutsch-Französisch. Berlin usw. 1968 mit Nachtrag von Ernst-Erwin Lange-Kowal 1979 [XXIX, 1047, XXIX, 1080 S.].

Weis/Mattutat 1959/1967 = Erich Weis: Weis/Mattutat. Wörterbuch der französischen und deutschen Sprache. I: Französisch-Deutsch. Stuttgart 1959 [2. Auflage, 9. Druck 1973]. — Heinrich Mattutat: (...) II: Deutsch-Französisch. Stuttgart 1967 [4. Druck 1973. — XX, 1015, XII, 1169 S.].

Weis/Mattutat 1988 = Erich Weis: Pons Großwörterbuch Weis Mattutat. Französisch-Deutsch. — Heinrich Mattutat: (...) Deutsch-Französisch. Erweiterte Neubearbeitung. Stuttgart 1988 [XIV, 568, 754 S.].

9.2. Sonstige Literatur

Baudrier 1970 = P. Baudrier: Bibliographie des dictionnaires allemand-français et français-allemand de 1789 à 1815. In: Cahiers de lexicologie 16. 1970 (—1), 77—100. — 17. 1970 (—2), 100—127.

Beaulieux 1904 = Charles Beaulieux: Liste des dictionnaires, lexiques et vocabulaires français antérieurs au „Thresor" de Nicot (1606). In: Mélanges de philologie offerts à Ferdinand Brunot. Paris 1904, 371—398.

Bray 1988 = Laurent Bray: La lexicographie bilingue italien-allemand, allemand-italien du dix-septième siècle. In: International Journal of Lexicography 1. 1988, 313—342.

Claes 1977 = Franz Claes: Bibliographisches Verzeichnis der deutschen Vokabulare und Wörterbücher, gedruckt bis 1600. Hildesheim. New York 1977.

Hausmann 1977 = Franz Josef Hausmann: Einführung in die Benutzung der neufranzösischen Wörterbücher. Tübingen 1977.

Hausmann 1984 = Franz Josef Hausmann: Das erste französisch-deutsche Wörterbuch. Levinus Hulsius' *Dictionaire* von 1596—1607. In: Zeitschrift für romanische Philologie 100. 1984, 306—320.

Hausmann 1986 = Franz Josef Hausmann: Romanistische Wörterbuchforschung und Gesellschaft. Das Beispiel der Wörterbuchkriminalität. In: Herbert Christ (ed.): Romanistik: Arbeitsfelder und berufliche Praxis. Tübingen 1986, 73—83.

Hausmann 1988 = Franz Josef Hausmann: Les dictionnaires bilingues (et multilingues) en Europe au XVIIIe siècle. Acquis et suggestions de recherche. In: Travaux de linguistique et de philologie 26. 1988, 11—32.

Hausmann 1989 = Franz Josef Hausmann: Wörterbücher und Grammatiken durch Erlanger Hugenotten. In: Jürgen Eschmann (Hrsg.): Hugenottenkultur in Deutschland. Tübingen 1989, 37—52.

Hausmann /1990/ = Franz Josef Hausmann: Christian Friedrich Schwan und sein deutsch-französisch, französisch-deutsches Wörterbuch (1782—1798). — (Unveröffentlichtes Manuskript, 27 Seiten).

Höfler 1982 = Manfred Höfler (ed.): La lexicographie française du XVIe au XVIIIe siècle. Wolfenbüttel 1982.

Höfler 1982a = Manfred Höfler: Le *Catholicon ou Dictionnaire universel de la langue françoise* de Johann Joseph Schmidlin. In: Höfler 1982, 49—63.

Höfler 1983 = Manfred Höfler: Das Wörterbuch der Académie française von 1694—1935. In: Bernhard Fabian/Paul Raabe (ed.): Gelehrte Bücher vom Humanismus bis zur Gegenwart. Wiesbaden 1983, 51—61.

Höfler 1988 = Manfred Höfler: Le dictionnaire de Flick (1802), le *Nouveau Dictionnaire françois-allemand et allemand-françois à l'usage des deux nations* et les dictionnaires en lexicologie et en lexicographie. In: Travaux de linguistique et de philologie 26. 1988, 133—140.

Labarre 1975 = Albert Labarre: Bibliographie du Dictionarium d'Ambrogio Calepino (1502—1779). Baden-Baden 1975.

Librairie française 1957—1958 = La Librairie française. Catalogue général des ouvrages parus du 1er janvier 1946 au 1er janvier 1956. Tables décennales. I: Auteurs et anonymes. 2 vol. Paris 1957—(1958).

Lorenz 1867—1871 = Otto Lorenz: Catalogue général de la librairie française pendant 25 ans (1840—1865). 4 vol. Paris 1867—1871.

van Passen 1981 = Anne-Marie van Passen: Appunti sui dizionari italo-francesi apparsi prima della fine del Settecento. In: Studi di lessicografia italiana 3. 1981, 29—65.

Quemada 1967 = Bernard Quemada: Les dictionnaires du français moderne 1539—1863. Paris 1967.

Rettig 1982 = Wolfgang Rettig: Les dictionnaires bilingues des langues française et allemande au 18e siècle: Questions de méthode. In: Höfler 1982, 103—113.

Rettig 1985 = Wolfgang Rettig: Die zweisprachige Lexikographie Französisch-Deutsch, Deutsch-Französisch. Stand, Probleme, Aufgaben. In: Lexicographica 1. 1985, 83—124.

Wolfgang Rettig, Düsseldorf
(Bundesrepublik Deutschland)

316. La lexicographie bilingue français-italien, italien-français

1. Introduction
2. Période ancienne (XVIe—XVIIIe s.)
3. Période récente (XIXe—XXe s.)
4. Bibliographie choisie

1. Introduction

La liste complète des dictionnaires bilingues en français et italien et de leurs éditions jusqu'à nos jours n'a pas encore été établie. Les seuls travaux d'ensemble (Quemada 1967 et 1967 Ms) s'arrêtent à 1863 et ne concernent pas uniquement les dictionnaires en français et italien; en outre, ils sont incomplets et non dépourvus d'erreurs. On trouvera la bibliographie des éditions anciennes (XVIe—XVIIIe s.) dans Van Passen 1981, Zolli 1981, Bingen 1987. — Le problème le plus étudié a été celui des sources, mais essentiellement pour la période ancienne (cf. Emery 1947, Venuti 1950—1951, Gallina 1959, Cooper 1960, Van Passen 1981, Zolli 1981). L'étude quantitative et qualitative du lexique, l'organisation des microstructures, la conception du dictionnaire en fonction d'un public cible et bien d'autres questions n'ont pas encore été abordées pour la plupart des ouvrages. D'autres secteurs restent encore dans l'ombre, comme les rapports entre la lexicographie bilingue et la lexicographie monolingue; les rapports des grands dictionnaires bilingues avec les nomenclatures présentes dans les manuels scolaires dès la période la plus ancienne, les dictionnaires abrégés et les dictionnaires spécialisés; les rapports entre la lexicographie bilingue et les grands dictionnaires polyglottes, comme ceux de Calepin ou de Junius.

2. Période ancienne (XVIe—XVIIIe s.)

2.1. A l'origine, la lexicographie bilingue en français et italien ne concerne que l'aire francophone. Non que l'Italie n'ait eu une certaine participation à son élaboration: le Vochabuolista, petite nomenclature polyglotte dont dérive le premier dictionnaire bilingue conservé (Vocabulaire 1583), est né à Venise en 1477 en version allemand-italien et a reçu à Rome en 1510 sa première traduction française (Rossebastiano Bart 1984, 41; 71). Les premiers essais de dictionnaires bilingues (quelques feuillets seulement) se trouvent dans Alunno 1543 et dans Toscanella 1568

(Gallina 1959, 37 sq, 153 sq). Ces tentatives restèrent sans lendemain: le premier dictionnaire bilingue publié en Italie date de 1647, et encore est-ce une édition du dictionnaire Canal, d'origine genevoise. Notons cependant que la lexicographie bilingue naît dans les zones francophones à forte émigration italienne, Lyon et surtout Genève: les trois premiers lexicographes connus, Fenice, Canal et Vittori, sont tous liés à la diaspora des protestants italiens. La lexicographie en français et italien est tributaire à l'origine de deux grands filons lexicographiques: les ouvrages polyglottes qui dominèrent le XVIe siècle (Quemada 1967, 63 sq), dont le Vochabuolista, et les dictionnaires français-latin et italien-latin, sources de Fenice et de Canal. Destiné au début aux marchands (Vocabulaire 1583), le dictionnaire bilingue s'adresse ensuite à la noblesse (Fenice 1584) et puis aux studieux et aux érudits (Oudin 1640). Manuel pratique à l'origine, il devient un instrument de référence. Aussi son format se modifie: du petit in-16 de 1583, on passe à l'in-8 (Fenice 1584; Canal 1598), encore de poche mais déjà assez volumineux, pour aboutir au gros in-4 d'Oudin (1640) et de ses successeurs. Dès lors, on devra disposer, à côté du gros ouvrage de référence, de nomenclatures et de dictionnaires abrégés à visées plus pratiques. Ce phénomène culminera au XIXe siècle.

2.2. Le premier dictionnaire italien-français conservé est le Vocabulaire de 1583 paru à Lyon. D'après la Bibliothèque françoise de Du Verdier (éd. de 1772—1773, V, 267), il aurait été précédé par un dictionnaire bilingue édité à Lyon en 1578 par Roger de Brey. Cette indication est toutefois douteuse, car cet éditeur n'est connu par aucune autre publication et aucun exemplaire de ce vocabulaire ne nous est parvenu. Si la lexicographie bilingue en français et italien est assez tardive par rapport à celle du français avec d'autres langues vulgaires (Quemada 1967, 40), elle a été cependant précédée par des ouvrages polyglottes contenant conjointement le français et l'italien: le Vocabulaire des trois langues (latin-italien-français), publié à Paris probablement entre 1531 et 1545 (Bingen 1987), et le Vochabuolista, qui a connu à Lyon et à Paris au moins 9 éditions de 1542 à 1583 (Rossebastiano Bart 1984). Le premier livre du Vocabulaire de 1583 reprend la nomenclature du premier livre du Vochabuolista, sauf le chapitre 49 relatif à l'Eglise, censuré par le compilateur de l'ouvrage, certainement protestant. Le second livre contient un petit dictionnaire italien-français de 60 pages in-16, simple juxtaposition de mots (Bingen 1987). Ce Vocabulaire ne sera pas réédité.

2.3. Le premier dictionnaire bilingue digne de ce nom est celui de Fenice 1584, revu et augmenté considérablement par Canal en 1598 et en 1603. Fenice a utilisé comme sources diverses éditions des dictionnaires français-latin de Robert Estienne (surtout «Les mots françois... tournez en latin pour les enfants» et le «Dictionnaire françois-latin») et le «Dittionario di A. Calepino... ridotto da Lucillio Minerbi» de 1553 (Venuti 1950—1951). Canal reprend chez Estienne nombre de mots négligés par Fenice, mais il puise aussi aux «Ricchezze della lingua volgare» d'Alunno et au «Dittionario volgare et latino» de Filippo Venuti (dans l'édition de 1596), sa source principale, surtout pour la partie italien-français. A partir de 1614, la page de titre de cette partie portera d'ailleurs le nom de Filippo Venuti à la place de celui de Canal (Bingen 1987). Si Fenice réduit et simplifie ses sources dans le souci majeur de fournir un manuel de première initiation, Canal manifeste une plus claire conscience du travail lexicographique. Il augmente l'inventaire des mots et il cerne davantage les nuances, notamment en multipliant la phraséologie. Les exemples d'auteurs (Pétrarque, mais surtout Boccace), puisés dans Alunno, sont choisis et adaptés dans le dessein de décrire la langue vivante. Dans ce sens d'ailleurs, Canal recueille aussi des expressions de la langue de son temps. Il réalise en outre l'équilibre entre les deux parties du dictionnaire et une meilleure liaison entre elles du point de vue des traductions (Venuti 1950—1951). Les 11 éditions de son ouvrage attestent un succès mérité.

2.4. Le Thrésor des trois langues de Vittori, publié à Genève en deux parties (1609), puis en trois (1617—1616), est compilé à partir du Tesoro de las dos lenguas de César Oudin (1607) pour les entrées en espagnol (Cooper 1960), du Dittionario toscano... d'A. Politi (1614) pour les entrées en italien (Van Passen 1981) et du Dictionnaire françois-latin de J. Nicot (1573) pour les entrées en français (Bingen 1987). L'apport de Vittori dans le choix des lemmes ajoutés, dans l'adaptation de ses sources et dans son travail de traduction dans les diverses langues reste encore à étudier.

2.5. Les Recherches Italiennes et Françoises d'Antoine Oudin (partie italien-français seule: 1640; les deux parties: 1643—1642) constituent une étape importante de la lexicographie bilingue en français et italien. Par son souci d'indiquer ses sources et son attitude critique à leur égard, Antoine Oudin manifeste un esprit scientifique. Avec lui, la grammaire commence à s'introduire dans le dictionnaire: Oudin donne un abrégé de grammaire italienne, développe la partie syntaxique de certains lemmes (cf. usage des prépositions) et marque l'accent tonique sur certains mots. Cette «grammaticalisation» se renforce dans la troisième édition (1663—1662), revue par Ferretti: celui-ci introduit des remarques sur la conjugaison des verbes irréguliers et sur la prononciation de certains mots italiens. A l'heure où se consolide en Italie et en France la tendance puriste sous l'influence des Académies, Oudin maintient l'orientation de la lexicographie, tournée vers la langue vivante: il puise dans celle-ci des termes non enregistrés par les dictionnaires antérieurs (Baccetti Poli 1953; Prati 1940), accueille même des mots populaires, voire argotiques et dialectaux. Il rejette les archaïsmes et les latinismes, désormais marqués de l'astérisque. Mais, première concession à la bienséance, il marque aussi les mots vulgaires, sans les éliminer pour autant. Pour son inventaire italien, il recourt à Politi, mais surtout au New World of Words de J. Florio (1611[2]) (Van Passen 1981), rompant avec le filon Fenice-Canal. Pour la partie français-italien, encore à étudier, il se sert du dictionnaire français-espagnol de César Oudin. — L'ouvrage d'Antoine Oudin a connu un énorme succès aux XVIIe et XVIIIe siècles. Il a servi au dictionnaire de N. Duez (1659—1660), qui n'apporte rien d'original (Prati, 1951, 1077; Van Passen 1981, 53). D'autre part, revu par Veneroni (dès l'édition parisienne de 1680—1681, celle d'Amsterdam 1677 étant douteuse) et par d'autres correcteurs après lui, comme Louis de Lépine ou Filippo Neretti (éditions vénitiennes à partir de 1686), le dictionnaire d'Oudin, appelé désormais «dictionnaire Veneroni», connaîtra un très grand nombre d'éditions jusqu'en 1800 (Van Passen 1981, 56—61). Parues à Paris, à Venise, à Amsterdam, à Bâle, elles manifestent le souci croissant d'adapter l'ouvrage au public. Dans les éditions destinées aux francophones, la partie italien-français s'enrichit de nouveaux mots et les lemmes se gonflent de synonymes, de phraséologie et d'indications sur l'usage et la diffusion de certains termes (Van Passen 1981, 43—51). Du dictionnaire d'Oudin dérivent aussi des dictionnaires trilingues ou quadrilingues édités en Allemagne, comme le dictionnaire allemand-français-italien publié à Francfort en 1674 ou le dictionnaire impérial quadrilingue publié par Veneroni en 1700, revu par Nicolò di Castelli (1714) et par Carlo Placardi (1766).

2.6. Le Dictionnaire Antonini 1735 adopte une position puriste jusque-là étrangère à la lexicographie bilingue: les termes de l'usage vivant présents dans les dictionnaires antérieurs sont exclus au profit des seuls termes «consacrés» par les Académies de France et de la Crusca. En revanche, les microstructures ont pris une allure moderne: présence de notations grammaticales, distinction des diverses acceptions par un signe typographique et inclusion de la phraséologie qui se présentait auparavant comme une succession d'entrées indépendantes.

Dans le dictionnaire d'Antonini, les définitions, reprises telles quelles de celui de la Crusca, occupent une place plus grande que les équivalents français. De la sorte, Antonini est le fondateur d'une tradition «définissante» dans l'histoire de la lexicographie italo-française. En effet, la définition jouera encore un grand rôle dans Alberti 1771/72, Ferrari/Caccia 1874 et, récemment, dans Robert/Signorelli 1981.

2.7. Le Dictionnaire d'Alberti (1771—1772), qui a connu comme celui d'Antonini un grand nombre d'éditions (Zolli 1981), annonce la période récente. Malgré son respect pour l'œuvre accomplie par les Académies, Alberti dénonce les limites du critère du «bon usage» et critique les lacunes des dictionnaires dans les domaines des «Sciences, Arts et Métiers». Aussi introduit-il dans son ouvrage un nombre élevé de termes techniques recueillis auprès des gens de métier (Zolli 1981).

3. Période récente (XIXe—XXe s.)

3.1.1. La période récente se caractérise par la multiplication des dictionnaires bilingues, grands dictionnaires ou dictionnaires abrégés, et par le nombre très élevé de leurs éditions (cf. Ghiotti 1890, réédité pour la 99e fois en 1928; Aquenza: 34e réédition en 1897). L'amélioration des techniques d'édition contribue à ce phénomène qui s'explique principalement par l'accroissement du public cible, dû à l'intensification des voyages et des échanges commerciaux (d'où la prolifération des dictionnaires portatifs), mais surtout à l'apparition d'un public scolaire. La plupart des grands dictionnaires (Roujoux 1826; Sergent/Strambio/Tassi 1854—1860; Buttura/Piranesi 1832, revu par Renzi 1861; Barberi/Basti/Cerati 1838—1839; Ferrari/Caccia 1874, revu par Angeli 1916; Ghiotti 1890; Magnarapa 1934; Calogero 1948; Garzanti 1966; Ferrante/Cassiani 1973; Balmas/Wagner 1975; Boch 1978; Robert/Signorelli 1981; Sansoni/Larousse 1981) et des dictionnaires abrégés (Cormon/Manni 1802; Biagioli/Ronna 1836; Barberi/Ronna 1846; Ferrari s. d.; Ferrari/Angeli 1904—1905; Angeli [1929]) sont désormais destinés aux écoles et ce fait ne va pas sans répercussions sur leur économie interne (cf. 3.2.2.).

3.1.2. Le travail lexicographique devient un travail d'équipe: le dictionnaire n'est plus l'œuvre d'un seul lexicographe, enrichie éventuellement par des réviseurs ultérieurs, mais le résultat d'une collaboration entre plusieurs spécialistes de l'une et de l'autre langue.

3.1.3. Enfin, si la lexicographie bilingue se développe au début dans la zone francophone, elle se déplace progressivement vers la zone italienne: après un certain équilibre aux XVIIIe et XIXe siècles, le nombre de dictionnaires publiés en Italie s'accroît considérablement. Ces derniers temps cependant, éditeurs italiens et éditeurs français ont tendance à collaborer.

3.2.1. Du point de vue interne, la lexicographie bilingue est marquée par deux phénomènes. Le premier, caractéristique du XIXe siècle, est celui de l'intégration de la langue littéraire — telle qu'elle est présentée dans les dictionnaires des Académies — avec le lexique pratique des sciences et des arts (Vitale 1978, 346 sq). La tendance puriste l'emporte au début: les termes scientifiques non présents dans les «bons auteurs» sont relégués dans les lexiques spécialisés qui connaissent une floraison au XIXe siècle (Zolli 1973 et 1978). Mais malgré le rôle de frein joué par l'école, tournée vers les textes littéraires, le problème se résout progressivement en faveur de l'ouverture au vocabulaire technique (Melzi 1909; Rouède/Rossi [1957]). A cet égard d'ailleurs, les dictionnaires portatifs, poussés par leur nature pratique, se sont montrés plus modernes et n'ont pas craint de puiser des termes dans les dictionnaires non puristes, même si l'on trouve sur leur page de titre la référence obligée aux Académies (cf. Briccolani 1830).

3.2.2. Mais le phénomène qui a eu le plus d'influence sur la structure des dictionnaires bilingues est celui de leur liaison à l'école. Plus qu'un outil pour déchiffrer une langue étrangère, le dictionnaire bilingue devient dans la période récente un «outil à thèmes». En 1826 déjà, Roujoux se vante de fournir un instrument pour «de meilleures compositions»; les dictionnaires des années 1970 continuent à poursuivre le même but. Aussi ces dictionnaires récents, destinés à un public italien, développent-ils davantage les entrées en langue italienne (Debyser 1981, 40).

3.2.3. Même comme «outils à thèmes», les dictionnaires bilingues restent cependant fort imparfaits. Certes, au fil du temps, sont apparues des modifications importantes: on s'est rendu compte de la nécessité de fournir les explications dans la langue d'arrivée (Cormon/Manni 1802; Roujoux 1826); malgré certaines résistances (Roujoux 1826), on a introduit la prononciation (Cormon/Manni 1802; Garzanti 1966, premier dictionnaire en Italie à transcrire les entrées françaises en symboles phonétiques, selon les normes de l'Association Phonétique Internationale); on a réalisé de nets progrès dans le domaine de la phraséologie (Debyser 1981, 42). Toutefois la méthodologie est restée substantiellement inchangée et l'on peut regretter avec Debyser (1981, 41—42) que la lexicographie bilingue n'ait pas intégré les apports de la lexicologie: l'outil serait certainement meilleur s'il fournissait des tableaux de distribution comparée des synonymes, des indications sur les procédés de traduction par transposition et modulation et une plus grande information syntaxique.

4. Bibliographie choisie

4.1. Dictionnaires

Alberti 1771—72 = François Alberti de Villeneuve: Nouveau dictionnaire [...] composé sur les Dictionnaires de l'Académie de France et de la Crusca, enrichi de tous les termes propres des sciences et des arts [...]. Paris. Marseille. Naples 1771—72 [2 part./1 vol.: XVI. 946; XXII. 988 p.].

Alunno 1543 = Francesco Alunno: Le Ricchezze della lingua volgare [...]. Venezia 1543 [1 vol.: [1], 225, [1] f.].

Angeli [1929] = Arturo Angeli: Petit dictionnaire [...]. Paris [1929] [1 part.: [2] f., 353 p., [1] f.].

Antonini 1735 = Annibale Antonini: Dictionnaire italien, latin et françois contenant non seulement un abrégé du dictionnaire de la Crusca [...]. Paris 1735 [t. 1: XXVII, 698 p., 1 f.; Dictionnaire français, latin et italien. Paris 1743, 600 p.].

Aquenza 1897 = Giuseppe Aquenza: Nuovo dizionario tascabile [...]. 34e éd. Lipsia 1897 [2 part./2 vol.: XVIII, 524; XIV, 326 p.].

Balmas/Wagner 1975 = E. Balmas/R. L. Wagner: Vocabolario del francese moderno. Novara 1975 [2 part./1 vol.: 2526 p.; dernière éd. 1979].

Barberi/Basti/Cerati 1838—39 = Giuseppe Filippo Barberi/Nicolao Basti/A. Cerati: Grand dictionnaire [...]. Paris 1838—39 [2 part./2 vol.: XVI, 1062; XVI, 1328 p.].

Barberi/Ronna 1846 = Giuseppe Filippo Barberi/Antonio Ronna: Dictionnaire [...]. Paris 1846 [2 part./1 vol.: 4 f., 326 p.; 1 f., 446 p.].

Biagioli/Ronna 1836 = Giosafatte Biagioli/Antonio Ronna: Dictionnaire [...], à l'usage des maisons d'éducation [...]. Paris 1836 [2 part./1 vol.: [2] f., LVI p., 232 p.; [2] f., 308 p.].

Boch 1978 = Raoul Boch: Dizionario [...]. Bologna 1978 [2 part./1 vol.: 2178 p.; dernière éd. 1985].

Briccolani 1830 = A. Briccolani: Nouveau dictionnaire de poche [...]. Paris 1830 [2 part./1 vol.: XL, 339, [1]; XVI, 382 p.].

Buttura/Piranesi 1832 = Antonio Buttura/Pietro Piranesi: Dictionnaire [...]. Paris 1832 [2 part./2 vol.: XXXVI, 643; XXX, 764 p.].

Buttura/Renzi 1861 = Antonio Buttura/Angelo Maria Renzi: Dictionnaire général [...]. 2e éd. Paris 1861 [1re éd. 1850].

Calogero [1948] = Giorgio Calogero: Vocabolario [...]. Firenze [1948] [2 part./1 vol.: 1738 p.].

Canal 1598 = Pierre Canal: Dictionnaire françois et italien: recueilli premièrement par L. Antoine Phenice: & nouvellement reveu & augmenté [...]. Dittionario [...]. [Genève] 1598 [2 part./1 vol.: [338]; [248] f.].

Cormon/Manni 1813 = G. L. Bartolomeo Cormon/Vincenzo Manni: Dizionario portatile e di pronunzia [...]. 3e éd. Lione. Parigi 1813 [2 part./2 vol.: 14, 894; 16, 718 p.; 1re éd. Lione 1802; éd. revue par Carlo Chapellon. Parigi/Lione 1823; par Ange Lauri. Parigi/Lione 1830; par S.-H. Blanc. Paris. Lyon 1851; par Giuseppe Asti. Milano 1857; par Teodoro Algier. Milano 1858; par Gemello Gorini. Milano 1861; par Oreste Ferrario. Milano 1866; par Ciro Galpinozzi. Milano 1875].

Fenice 1584 = Giovanni Antonio Fenice: Dictionnaire [...] Profitable et Necessaire à ceux qui prenent plaisir en ces deux langues [...]. Morges 1584 [2 part./1 vol.: [304] f.].

Ferrante/Cassiani [1974] = Vincenzo Ferrante/Ernesto Cassiani: Dizionario moderno [...]. Torino [1974] [2 part./1 vol.: XIV, 2238 p.; 1re éd. 1973].

Ferrari s. d. = Costanzo Ferrari: Nouveau dictionnaire [...]. Paris s. d. [2 part./1 vol.: XI, [1], 568; XV, [1]], 372 p.].

Ferrari/Angeli 1904—1905 = Costanzo Ferrari/Arturo Angeli: Nouveau dictionnaire [...]. Paris 1904—1905 [2 part./1 vol.: XII, 590; XVIII, 402 p.].

Ferrari/Caccia 1874 = Costanzo Ferrari/Joseph Caccia: Grand dictionnaire [...]. Paris 1874 [2 part./1 vol.: XII, 778; XII, 1000 p.].

Ferrari/Caccia/Angeli [1921] = Costanzo Ferrari/Joseph Caccia/Arturo Angeli: Grand dictionnaire [...] étymologique, historique et géographique [...]. Paris [1921] [2 part./2 vol.: XII, 980; X, 1139 p.; 1re éd. [1916]].

Garzanti 1966 = Dizionario Garzanti [...]. Milano 1966 [2 part./1 vol.: [16], 2029 p.; dernière éd. 1974].

Ghiotti s. d. = Candido Ghiotti: Vocabolario comparativo [...]. 25e éd. Torino s. d. [2 part./2 vol.].

Ghiotti 1902 = Candido Ghiotti: Vocabolario scolastico [...]. 25e éd. Torino 1902 [2 part./1 vol.: 945; 655 p.; 1re éd. 1890].

Ghiotti/Chanoux 1928—31 = Candido Ghiotti/Antonio Chanoux: Vocabolario scolastico [...] 99e éd. Torino 1928—31.

Ghiotti/Chanoux 1964 = Candido Ghiotti/Antonio Chanoux: Il Piccolo Ghiotti [...] 53e éd. Torino 1964 [2 part./1 vol.: VI, 824 p.].

Ghiotti/Cumino 1973 = Candido Ghiotti/Giulio Cumino: Il novissimo Ghiotti. Vocabolario [...]. 36e éd. Torino 1973 [2 part./1 vol.: XVIII, 2387, [1] p.; 1re éd. 1960].

Grimod/Caselli 1972 = Francesco Grimod/G. Caselli: Vocabolario [...] 9e éd. Napoli. Città Di Castello 1972 [2 part./1 vol.: XII, 2215 p.].

Magnarapa 1934 = Celideo Magnarapa: Dizionario novissimo [...]. Milano 1934.

Mariotti [1964] = Scevola Mariotti: Vocabolario [...]. Milano [1964] [2 part./1 vol.: XIV, 2014 p., [1] f.].

Melzi 1909 = B. Melzi: Nuovo dizionario [...] Commerciale, Scientifico, Tecnico, Militare, Marinaresco, ecc. [...]. Milano 1909 [2 part./1 vol.: VIII, 540; [4], 562 p.].

Oudin 1640 = Antoine Oudin: Recherches Italiennes et Françoises, ou Dictionnaire [...] 1640 [dict. i–f uniquement]; [3] f., 932 p.].

Oudin 1643—42 = Antoine Oudin: Recherches [...] Augmenté de la Seconde Partie, & de plusieurs mots pour la Premiere. Paris 1643—42 [2 part./1 vol.: [3] f., 932 p., 59 p.; [1] p., 587 p., [1] p.].

Oudin/Ferretti 1663—62 = Antoine Oudin/Laurens Ferretti: Dictionnaire [...]. Paris 1663—62 [2 part./1 vol.: [4] f., 575 p.; 364 p.].

Oudin/Ferretti/Veneroni 1681—80 = Antoine Oudin/Laurens Ferretti/Giovanni Veneroni [Jean Vigneron]: Dictionnaire [...]. Paris 1681—80 [2 part./1 vol.].

Oudin/Ferretti/Veneroni/de Lépine 1686 = Antoine Oudin/Laurens Ferretti/Giovanni Veneroni/Louis de Lépine: Dictionnaire [...]. Venise 1686 [2 part./2 vol.: [8], 780; [4], 551 p.].

Robert/Signorelli 1981 = Robert & Signorelli Dizionario [...]. Milano. Paris 1981 [2 part./1 vol.: 3002 p.; dernière éd. [1983]].

Ronna [1853] = Antonio Ronna: Dictionnaire [...]. Paris [1853] [2 part./1 vol.: [4] f., 304 p.; [2] f., 414 p.].

Rouède/Lacombe [1930] = Pierre Rouède/A. Lacombe: Nouveau dictionnaire [...]. Paris [1930] [2 part./1 vol.: VIII, 654; VIII, 768 p.].

Rouède/Rossi [1957] = Pierre Rouède/Mario Rossi: Dictionnaire moderne [...]. Paris [1957] [2 part./1 vol.: II, 826; VIII, 748 p.].

Rouède/Rouède/Rossi [1969] = Pierre Rouède/Denise Rouède/Mario Rossi: Dictionnaire [...]. 3e tirage. Paris [1969] [2 part./1 vol.: XXXV, 1184 p.; 1er tirage 1965].

Roujoux/Morlino 1826 = Prudence-Guillaume de Roujoux/Morlino: Dictionnaire classique [...]. Paris 1826 [2 part./2 vol.: XXIX, 734 p.; [5] f., 528 p.].

Sansoni/Larousse [1982] = Claude Margueron/Gianfranco Folena: Dizionario Sansoni Larousse [...]. Firenze [1982] [2 part./1 vol.: XXXVIII, 714; L, 798 p.; 1re éd. 1981].

Sergent/Strambio/Tassi s. d. [ca 1854—1860] = Antonio Sergent/A. Strambio/L. Tassi: Grande dizionario [...] Grand dictionnaire [...]. Milano s. d. [ca. 1854—60]. [4 vol.].

Toscanella 1568 = Orazio Toscanella: Dittionario volgare et latino [...]. Venezia 1568 [1 vol.: [46], 248 f.].

Veneroni 1695 = Giovanni Veneroni [Jean Vigneron]: Dictionnaire [...]. Paris 1695 [2 part./1 vol.: 4 f., 785 p.; 2 f., 576 p.].

Veneroni/Neretti 1698 = Giovanni Veneroni/Filippo Neretti: Dittionario [...]. Venetia 1698 [2 part./1 vol.].

Veneroni/Placardi 1749 = Giovanni Veneroni/Charles Placardi: Dictionnaire [...]. Paris 1749 [2 part./2 vol.].

Vittori 1609 = Girolamo Vittori: Tesoro de las tres lenguas, francesa, italiana y española [...]. Genève 1609 [2 part./2 vol.: [318]; [240] f.].

Vittori 1617—16 = Girolamo Vittori: Le Thresor des trois langues, espagnole, françoise et italienne [...]. Le tout recueilli des plus celebres Auteurs [...] par César Oudin, Nicot, La Crusca & autres [...]. Cologny [Genève] 1617—16 [3 part./3 vol.: [24] f., 522 p., [1] f.; 424 p.; [248] f.].

Vocabulaire s. d. = Vocabulaire de trois langues cestassavoir latine italienne & francoyse de tant de noms qu'il cest peu trouver figure par Alphabet [...]. Paris s. d.

Vocabulaire 1583 = Vocabulaire en langue francoyse et italienne necessaire pour plus familierement comprendre l'une & laultre [sic] langue. C'est a-dire, Vocablario in Lingua Francese & Italiano [sic]. Lyon 1583 [1 vol.: 121 p., [1] p., [1] p., [3] f.].

4.2. Travaux

Baccetti Poli 1953 = Rossana Baccetti Poli: Saggio d'una bibliografia dei gerghi italiani. Padova 1953.

Barblan 1979 = Maria Clotilde Barblan: Biblioteca dell'Accademia della Crusca — Dizionari [1970—78]. In: Studi di Lessicografia italiana 1. 1979, 309—38.

Barblan 1980 = Maria Clotilde Barblan: Dizionari della lingua italiana, sec. XVI—XIX. In: ibid. 2. 1980, 303—45.

Barblan 1981 = Maria Clotilde Barblan: Dizionari della lingua italiana, sec. XIX—XX. In: ibid. 3. 1981, 191—281.

Barblan 1982 = Maria Clotilde Barblan: Dizionari della lingua italiana, sec. XX. In: ibid. 4. 1982, 387—92.

Baudrier 1895—1921 = Henri Baudrier: Bibliographie lyonnaise. Recherches sur les imprimeurs, libraires [...] de Lyon au XVIe siècle. Lyon 1895—1921 [12 vol.].

Bingen 1987 = Nicole Bingen: Le Maître Italien [1510—1660]. Bibliographie des ouvrages d'enseignement de la langue italienne destinés au public de langue française. Suivie d'un Répertoire des ouvrages bilingues imprimés dans les pays de langue française. Bruxelles 1987.

Cooper 1960 = Louis Cooper: Girolamo Vittori y César Oudin: un caso de plagio mutuo. In: Nueva Revista de Filologia Hispanica 14. 1960, 3—20.

Debyser 1981 = Francis Debyser: De meilleurs dictionnaires bilingues? In: Le Français dans le monde 159. 1981, 37—42.

Emery 1951 = Luigi Emery: Il dizionario di N. di Castelli e gli altri principali. In: Lingua Nostra 12. 1951, 35—39.

Emery 1947 = Luigi Emery: Vecchi manuali italo-tedeschi. Il Vochabuolista-Il Berlaimont-La Ianua Linguarum. In: Lingua Nostra 8. 1947, 3—39.

Gallina 1959 = Annamaria Gallina: Contributo allo studio della lessicografia italo-spagnola dei secoli XVI e XVII. Firenze 1959 (Biblioteca dell'Archivum Romanicum, I, 58).

Marini 1985 = Adriana Marini: Un classico della lessicografia italo-francese: il «Dictionnaire» di Cormon e Manni. In: Filologia moderna 7. 1985, 219—44.

Messi 1942 = Clara Messi: Contributi alla storia della più antica lessicografia italiana [a proposito di uno studio di Ornella Olivieri]. In: Atti del Reale Istituto Veneto di Scienze, Lettere ed Arti. Anno accad. 1942—43, Tomo CII, Parte II: Classe Scienze mor. e lett., 589—620.

Olivieri 1942 = Ornella Olivieri: I primi vocabolari italiani fino alla prima edizione della Crusca. In: Studi di Filologia italiana 6. 1942, 64—192.

Prati 1940 = Angelico Prati: Voci di gerganti, vagabondi e malviventi. Pisa 1940.

Prati 1951 = Angelico Prati: Vocabolario etimologico italiano. Torino 1951.

Quemada 1967 = Bernard Quemada: Les dictionnaires du français moderne, 1539—1863 [. . .]. Paris. Bruxelles 1967.

Quemada 1967 Ms = Bernard Quemada: Les dictionnaires du français moderne. Essai de bibliographie [. . .]. I: Auteurs et anonymes [. . .]. Besançon 1967 [Manuscrit dactylographié].

Rossebastiano Bart 1984 = Alda Rossebastiano Bart: Antichi vocabolari plurilingui d'uso popolare: la tradizione del «Solenissimo Vochabuolista». Torino 1984.

Table alphabétique 1758 = Table alphabétique des dictionnaires [. . .]. Paris 1758 [4 f., 90 p.].

Tancke 1984 = Gunnar Tancke: Die italienischen Wörterbücher [. . .] bis zum Erscheinen des «Vocabolario degli Accademici della Crusca» [1612]. [. . .]. Tübingen 1984 (Beihefte zur Zeitschrift für romanische Philologie Bd. 198).

Van Passen 1974—1975 = Anne-Marie Van Passen: I dizionari di Giovanni Veneroni. Contributo alla storia della lessicografia italo-francese nel Sei e Settecento. Mémoire de licence inédit. K U Leuven 1974—75 [198 p.].

Van Passen 1981 = Anne-Marie Van Passen: Appunti sui dizionari italo-francesi apparsi prima della fine del Settecento. In: Studi di Lessicografia italiana 3. 1981, 29—65.

Venuti 1950—1951 = Annamaria Venuti: Primo contributo alla storia della lessicografia italo-francese. L'opera lessicografica di G. A. Fenice e di P. Canal. Mémoire de licence inédit. Univ. di Padova 1950—51 [XII, 503 p.].

Vitale 1978 = Maurizio Vitale: La questione della lingua. Palermo 1978.

Zolli 1973 = Paolo Zolli: Bibliografia dei dizionari specializzati italiani nel XIX secolo. Firenze 1973 (Biblioteca di Bibliografia Italiana, vol. LXXIV).

Zolli 1978 = Paolo Zolli: Appunti linguistici e bibliografici sui dizionari specializzati italiani tradotti dal francese nel XVIII secolo. In: La ricerca dialettale 2. 1978, 35—55.

Zolli 1981 = Paolo Zolli: Innovazione e tradizione nel «Nouveau dictionnaire françois-italien» di F. Alberti de Villeneuve. In: Mélanges à la mémoire de Franco Simone. France et Italie dans la culture européenne, vol. II, XVIIe et XVIIIe siècles. Genève 1981, 589—627.

Nicole Bingen, Bruxelles/
Anne-Marie Van Passen, Anvers (Belgique)

317. Die zweisprachige Lexikographie Deutsch-Italienisch, Italienisch-Deutsch

1. Von den Anfängen bis 1800
2. 19. und 20. Jahrhundert
3. Literatur (in Auswahl)

1. Von den Anfängen bis 1800

Der erste, auf 1424 datierte, italienisch-deutsche Reisesprachführer in Sachgruppen hat zum Autor einen Georg von Nürnberg, Sprachlehrer in Venedig (Pausch 1972 sowie Holtus/Schweickard 1985). Dieses Manuskript beeinflußte alle Nachfolger, namentlich das erste (1477 in Venedig) gedruckte Sprachbuch des Adam von Rottweil mit dem Titel *Introito e porta* (Bart-Rossebastiano 1971, 1977; Giustiniani 1987) und dessen Nachfolger mit den Titeln *Solenissimo vocabuolista* oder *Libro utilissimo,* sowie die mehrsprachigen Sammlungen, welche das ganze 16. Jh. durchziehen (vgl. zu beiden Jh. Rossebastiano-Bart 1986 und Bray 1988).

Das erste alphabetische Wörterbuch moderner Prägung, das die italienische und deutsche Sprache in beiden Richtungen verbindet, erscheint 1605 in Frankfurt. Sein Autor, der universal interessierte Flame Levinus Hulsius aus Gent, hat als Glaubensflüchtling in Nürnberg bereits 1596 das erste französisch-deutsche und deutsch-französische Wörterbuch publiziert (Behrens 1910, 318—325, Merkel 1980, Hausmann 1984). Da Hulsius erst kurz vor der Drucklegung nach Frankfurt übergesiedelt ist, müssen auch die 500 Seiten seines italienisch-deutschen und deutsch-italienischen Wörterbuchs als ein Nürnberger Produkt aufgefaßt werden. Der stärkere italienisch-deutsche Teil zeigt laut Tancke 1984 Abhängigkeit von einem vorausgehenden italienisch-französischen Wörterbuch, doch wurden offenbar auch italienisch-lateinische und andere Quellen benutzt (Bray 1988, 320). Der deutsch-italienische Teil stammt eindeutig von Hulsius' deutsch-französischem Wörterbuch her, freilich wurde die bereits 1602 in der dortigen zweiten Auflage eingeleitete strikte Alphabetisierung in Hulsius 1605 vom Autor zum ersten Mal komplett verwirklicht. 1616 hat dann der Heidelberger Sprachmeister F. M. Ravelli die beiden Hulsianischen Wörterbücher in ein dreisprachiges zusammengegossen und erweitert, dessen italienische Komponente, die bis 1659 verlegt wurde, bislang nicht erforscht ist. (Das zweisprachige Wörterbuch existierte bis 1687). In Durlach erscheint 1625 das Wörterbuch des Straßburgers G. F. Messerschmid (Bray 1988 330—32), heute ein bibliothekarisches Rarum.

In den 70er Jahren des 17. Jh. folgt eine neue Wörterbuchgeneration. Das gilt zuerst für den wiederum in Abhängigkeit von der italienisch-französischen Lexikographie entstandenen dreisprachigen Oudin 1674, der die Frankfurter Tradition beendet, denn bis zum Ende des 18. Jh. wird die italienisch-deutsche Lexikographie nahezu ausschließlich in Nürnberg und Leipzig erscheinen.

Die Nürnberger Tradition wird zwischen 1676 und 1732 auf ihren Höhepunkt geführt, dank eines der bedeutendsten Lexikographen aller Zeiten, Matthias Kramer, der nicht nur für das Italienische in Deutschland Gewaltiges geleistet hat, sondern in nahezu gleicher Weise auch für das Französische, Spanische und Niederländische. Unter dem Einfluß der Stammwort-Lehre des Justus Georg Schottel und der wortschatzdidaktischen Schriften des Johann Joachim Becher (vgl. Bray 1988, 325 f.) unterscheidet Kramer zwischen dem striktalphabetischen Herverstehenswörterbuch, das er *Dictionarium* nennt, und dem nach den Stammwörtern geordneten *Lexicon*, das reiche Synonymik und Phraseologie integrieren muß. Nachdem bereits der Nürnberger Johann Güntzel 1648 in Augsburg ein solches nach Stammwörtern geordnetes und phraseologiereiches deutsch-italienisches *Lexicon* (mit italienisch-deutschem Index, also *Dictionarium*) publiziert hat, kommt diese Vorstellung bei Kramer für den italienisch-deutschen Teil zuerst 1676 und dann erweitert 1693 zur Entfaltung, zuletzt auf 3858 Spalten. Während der deutsch-italienische Teil von 1678 auf 2612 Spalten eine Art striktalphabetischer Index zum italienisch-deutschen Gegenstück, und somit ein *Dictionarium*, darstellt, liefert der deutsch-italienische Teil von 1700/1702 auf 7446 Spalten ein großartiges *Lexicon*, das vor allem durch seinen phraseologischen Reichtum besticht und für geraume Zeit die umfassendste Beschreibung des deutschen Wortschatzes bleiben wird (cf. Ising 1956).

Es versteht sich, daß die riesigen, teuren und wissenschaftlich ambitionierten Werke des Matthias Kramer einem breiten Publikum unzugänglich blieben. Hier springt nun zum ersten Mal ein Leipziger Verleger in die Bresche und publiziert 1700 eine Art in das strikte Alphabet gebrachten Auszug aus Kramer, den der Hallenser Sprachmeister Castelli vorlegt. Diese *Fontana della Crusca* wird bis 1771 acht Auflagen erleben, die jeweils neu bearbeitet werden, und muß deshalb der Wirkung nach, wenn auch nicht der lexikographischen Leistung nach, als der eigentliche Nachfolger von Hulsius angesehen werden.

Daneben ist Castellis Name mit einer Reihe weiterer Wörterbücher verbunden. Zuerst einmal mit dem viersprachigen *Kaiserlichen Wörterbuch,* das aus dem italienisch-französischen Wörterbuch des Giovanni Veneroni weiterentwickelt worden war und deshalb auch als Nachfolger des dreisprachigen Oudin 1674 betrachtet werden kann, und von dem zwischen 1700 und 1804 vier Auflagen erschienen, von denen Castelli die zweite von 1714 bearbeitet hat. In diesem Wörterbuch ging es in erster Linie darum, das Italienische, und in geringerem Maße das Französische, auf Französisch, Italienisch, Deutsch und Latein zu erklären. Der deutsche und der lateinische Teil haben vornehmlich Indexcharakter. Das Buch beweist durch das ganze 18. Jh. hindurch die nach wie vor starke Stellung des Latein als internationaler Wissenschaftssprache. Ab dem 19. Jh. sind derartige viersprachige Wörterbücher nicht mehr denkbar.

Des weiteren verbindet sich mit dem Namen Castelli ein wenig bekanntes italienisch-deutsches Wörterbuch, das er unter seinem italienischen Namen veröffentlicht hat (Anguselli 1710, vgl. Emery 1951, 38), ferner Kirsch 1718, dessen Verhältnis zu Castelli 1718 zu klären wäre, und schließlich ein dreisprachiges Taschenwörterbuch für die Reise, das die Sprachen besonders benutzerfreundlich nach Spalten verteilt (Veneroni 1713). Reisezwecken dient daneben das *Hand-Lexicon* von Graben 1731.

Die beinahe frenetische Wörterbuchaktivität des frühen 18. Jh. bringt es mit sich, daß nun noch drei bedeutende, wenn auch nicht erfolgreiche Wörterbücher genannt werden müssen. In Nürnberg inkorporiert der 3000 Seiten starke *Gran Dizionario universale e perfetto* von Erberg 1710 in das Kramer-Castellische Material umfangreiche Phraseologie des Handelswesens, sowie den internationalen Sprichwortreichtum. Ein Jahr später publiziert in Leipzig Johann Rädlein ebenfalls ein dreisprachiges Wörterbuch, das wiederum ohne Kramer und Castelli nicht denkbar ist, das aber einen besonderen Akzent auf das Deutsche legt. Aus dem von ihm geplanten, aber nie publizierten einsprachigen deutschen Universalwörterbuch übernimmt er z. B. reiches sprechsprachliches Material. Besondere metalexikographische und germanistische Aufmerksamkeit verdient daneben sein langes Vorwort.

Schließlich muß ein unpubliziertes Wörterbuch erwähnt werden, das in der Universitätsbibliothek Erlangen auf nahezu 6000 Folio-Seiten Manuskript schlummert. Der aus Antwerpen stammende Sprachmeister der Universität Altdorf, Franz Jacob Leys, hat es bei seinem Tode 1732 einer Nachwelt hinterlassen, die so undankbar war, es nicht zu drucken. Es muß zukünftiger Forschung vorbehalten bleiben herauszufinden, welchen Verlust dies für die italienisch-deutsche Lexikographie des 18. Jh. bedeutete.

Etwa gegen 1760 wird der alte Castelli zum Notbehelf. Die Nachfrage nach neueren Wörterbüchern wird daran sichtbar, daß 1760 in Leipzig eine Neuauflage des italienisch-französischen Wörterbuchs von A. Antonini verlegt wird, in der keinerlei deutsche Komponente erscheint und in der die französische Komponente sehr spärlich bleibt (Hausmann 1987, 212). Deshalb publiziert 1763 der Sekretär der Kursächsischen Staatskanzlei J. A. Lehninger eine deutsche Übersetzung des Antonini, der in Wirklichkeit eine Art Kurzfassung der 4. Aufl. des Crusca-Wörterbuchs darstellt. Im Unterschied zu Antonini, der sich für das Französische mit lexikalischen Äquivalenten begnügt, übersetzt Lehninger auch die italienischen Definitionen. Der Antonini/Lehninger 1763 ist bis 1802 in sechs Auflagen erfolgreich.

Etwa gleichzeitig wird auch noch einmal der traditionsreiche Verlagsort Nürnberg produktiv, wo 1764 der Erlanger Lektor Clemente Romani postum mit Hilfe von W. Jäger ein kompaktes Wörterbuch publiziert, dessen dritte und letzte Auflage noch knapp 60 Jahre später erscheinen wird.

Bevor der neuerliche Höhepunkt der italienisch-deutschen Lexikographie ab 1780 dargestellt werden soll, lohnt es sich, den Gründen nachzuspüren, welche die Lexikographen selbst für italianistische lexikographische Aktivität im deutschen 18. Jh. angeben. Neben der unbestrittenen Spitzenstellung des Französischen als internationaler Verkehrssprache hat das Italienische Gewicht durch seine Bedeutung im levantinischen Handel, als Sprache des bevorzugten Reiselandes, bedeutender Kunst-Literatur, politischer Literatur und Belletristik. Eine besondere Bedeutung kommt der italienischen Oper zu, die Europa im 18. Jh. erobert und die wesentlich zur starken Stellung des Italienischen am Wiener Hof beiträgt (Folena 1973). Lehninger meint 1763, allein Metastasio lohne bereits die Erlernung seiner Sprache. In einem Zeitalter, in dem ohnehin jeder, der etwas auf sich hält, Französisch kann, wird Italienisch zu einer Art Snob-Sprache, mit der zusätzliche Gesellschaftserfolge zu erzielen sind. Damit einher geht eine Art linguistischer Aufstand gegen französisches sprachliches Monopoldenken, wie es der Abbé D. Bouhours im 17. Jh. verkörpert. A. Antonini gelingt in einem linguistisch substantiellen Vorwort die Rehabilitation des von Bouhours geschmähten Italienischen, und etwa gleichzeitig lobt Graben 1731 das Italienische wegen seiner Artikulationsbasis (er nennt es Grundakzent) als ideale Schlüsselsprache für das weitere Erlernen des Spanischen und Französischen.

Vor dem Hintergrund dieser starken Position des Italienischen in Europa geht nun der unmittelbare Anstoß zu neuen Höhepunkten in der zweisprachigen Lexikographie auf italienischer Seite von dem italienisch-französischen Wörterbuch des Alberti di Villanuova von 1772 aus (vgl. Art. 316) und auf deutscher Seite von der Existenz des ersten allgemeinen einsprachigen Wörterbuchs, das Adelung von 1774—1786 vorlegt, wobei das auf Adelung aufbauende deutsch-französische Wörterbuch des Christian Friedrich Schwan (vgl. Art. 315) eine partielle Vermittlerrolle gespielt haben könnte. Der Ort des Geschehens ist nunmehr Leipzig. Zuerst läßt der Verlag Weidmann durch den Leipziger Lektor Ph. J. Flathe eine völlige Neubearbeitung des Castelli erstellen, die 1782 in großer Ausgabe und 1785 als *Dizionario manuale* erscheint. Sodann läßt der rührige Verleger Schwickert (vgl. Art. 313) durch K. H. Reich ebenfalls ein 2000 Seiten starkes Handwörterbuch erarbeiten. Indes, keines der beiden Wörterbücher hat weitere Auflagen erlebt. Für das im Zeitalter der französischen Revolution sich wandelnde Publikum sind diese Wörterbücher nicht kompakt genug. Der wahre Nutznießer der Situation und eigentliche Nachfolger von Castelli ist deshalb Chr. J. Jagemann (1735—1804), nach längerem Italienaufenthalt seit 1775 Bibliothekar in Weimar und bedeutender Italianist, dessen Wörterbuch von 1790—1838 in mehreren Auflagen und Bearbeitungen die lexikographische Szene beherrscht.

2. 19. und 20. Jahrhundert

Es entspricht dem italienisch-deutschen Kulturgefälle, daß bislang mit Ausnahme von Anguselli 1710 alle Wörterbücher in Deutschland erscheinen. Man lernt in Deutschland Italienisch, nicht umgekehrt. Wie in der deutsch-französischen Lexikographie auch, ändert sich dieses Verhältnis ab 1800 progressiv. Mit Borroni 1793—99 beginnt eine italienische Tradition, die allerdings im 19. Jh. über lange Strecken nur schmalbrüstige Werke hervorbringt (vgl. die Dokumentation von Bruna 1983) und deshalb hier nicht weiter gewürdigt werden kann. Auch Heucke 1806 visiert, obwohl in Augsburg erschienen, den italienischen Benutzer an. Während Schade 1820 die Jagemannsche Spitzenposition nicht erschüttern kann, bricht mit Valentini 1831—36 in der italienisch-deutschen Lexikographie ein neues Zeitalter an. Es ist das romantisch-beflügelte Streben nach neuer Wissenschaftlichkeit und thesaurierender Vollständigkeit. Nach Valentini wird es 65 Jahre dauern bis zu einem würdigen Nachfolger (Rigutini/Bulle 1900) und darauf wieder 70 Jahre (Macchi 1970/72).

In Wahrheit wird das 19. Jh. bis zum 1. Weltkrieg beherrscht von einer Fülle von Hand- und Taschenwörterbüchern von Valentini 1821—1906, Beretti 1825/1848, Weber 1840—1903, Feller 1851—1905, Feller 1855—1882, Michaelis 1879/81—1932, Enenkel 1892 (in Paris!), Hecker 1900—1913 und schließlich *Langenscheidts Taschenwörterbuch der italienischen und deutschen Sprache* von Gustav Sacerdote (LTWB 1905). Damit bricht die Produktivität auf deutscher Seite ab. Das LTWB wird den Markt 80 Jahre lang unangefochten beherrschen, während für sehr anspruchsvolle Benutzer das Wunderwerk des Rigutini/Bulle 1900 zur Verfügung steht, dessen mythisches Prestige in Italien gar 1981 zu einem Nachdruck führt (vgl. dazu Gervasi 1982). Zwischen beiden muß man in Deutschland für ein neues Handwörterbuch bis 1964 (Brockhaus Bildwörterbuch) bzw. 1965 (LHWB) warten.

Ganz anders Italien. Dieses Land entwickelt sich im 20. Jh. zu einem der größten Produzenten zweisprachiger Wörterbücher, weil das bedeutende Kulturland sie braucht, ihm jedoch wegen der geringen Verbreitung von Italienisch als Fremdsprache in der Welt die gesamte Last der Anfertigung dieser Wörterbücher zufällt. Folgende Wörterbücher mit rund 2000 Seiten sind im 20. Jh. in Italien erschienen: Lysle 1909, Lazzioli/Nemi 1938, Ciardi Dupré/Escher 1955, der an den Universitäten viel benutzte Bidoli/Cosciani 1957/59, Deidda 1971 und schließlich als Krönung 1970/72 das gewaltige Wörterbuch von Macchi, von dem 1975 eine immer noch beeindruckende Kurzfassung erschien, die in Deutschland als *Langenscheidts Großwörterbuch* verkauft wird.

Bei einer solchen Aktivität im Bereich der zweisprachigen Lexikographie ist es nicht verwunderlich, daß auch die einzige größere metalexikographische und deskriptive Arbeit, die es überhaupt über zweisprachige Wörterbücher gibt, aus Italien stammt (Marello 1989). Über die Qualität der heutigen italienisch-deutschen und deutsch-italienischen Wörterbücher aus italienischer Sicht kann man sich dort (211—234) ausführlich unterrichten. Insgesamt wird man beklagen, daß keines der genannten Werke aus einer originären deutsch-italienischen Zusammenarbeit entstanden ist. Vielmehr sind die Wörterbücher entweder, wie die meisten, in Italien entstanden und im deutschen Material unzuverlässig oder umgekehrt in Deutschland entstanden und im italienischen Material unzuverlässig. 1986 hat es seit langer Zeit wieder einmal eine deutsche Neuproduktion gegeben (Pons 1986), doch ist dieses Wörterbuch der Größenordnung nach eher als Konkurrent zu LTWB anzusehen, demgegenüber es deutlich bidirektionalere Züge trägt.

Für die Zukunft im geeinten Europa bedarf es vor allem eines zuverlässigen zweisprachigen Thesaurus der Gemeinsprache sowie zahlreicher hochspezialisierter Fachwörterbücher. Dazu müßten sich ein deutscher und ein italienischer Verlag von der Planung an zusammentun, anstatt, wie bisher üblich, das in dem einen Land angefertigte Wörterbuch lediglich in Lizenz zu übernehmen, oft unter Mißachtung seiner monodirektionalen Ausrichtung auf eine der beiden Sprechergruppen. Es ist auch nicht einzusehen, warum ein und dasselbe Wörterbuch, nämlich Macchi 1984a, in dem einen Land nur in zwei teueren Bänden, hingegen in dem anderen Land nur in einem Band und für den halben Preis zur Verfügung steht. Eine systematische Kritik der italienisch-deutschen und deutsch-italienischen Wörterbücher bleibt Desiderat.

3. Literatur (in Auswahl)

3.1. Wörterbücher

Anguselli 1710 = P. F. Biaggio Anguselli [Nicolò Castelli]: Reggia di Mercurio. 4 Bde. Venezia 1710 [Darin It-D Wörterbuch].

Antonini 1763 = Annibal Antonini/Giovanni Agosto Lehninger: Dizionario italiano-tedesco, tedesco-italiano il quale contiene non solamente un Compendio del Vocabolario della Crusca (...) migliorato e tradotto in tedesco. Lipsia [Leipzig] 1763 [840, 446 S.; weitere Aufl. auch in Wien, erw. durch Ludwig Heinrich Teucher, bis 1802].

Beretti 1848 = Carlo Beretti: Neues Wörterbuch der italienischen und deutschen Sprache. Neue Ausgabe. 2 Bde. Nürnberg 1848 [866, 900, 76 S. 1. Aufl. 1825].

Bidoli/Cosciani 1957/59 = Emilio Bidoli/Guido Cosciani: Dizionario italiano-tedesco tedesco-italiano. 2 Bde. Torino 1957, 1959 [1016, 1190 S.; 1970: 1096, 1281 S.].

Borroni 1793/99 = Bartolomeo Borroni: Nuovo vocabolario italiano-tedesco e tedesco-italiano ad uso de' principianti. 2 Bde. Milano 1793, 1799 [536, 487 S.; 2. Aufl. Venezia 1806: 725, 634 S.].

Brockhaus 1964 = Brockhaus Bildwörterbuch/Dizionario Illustrato Brockhaus-Longanesi It-D, D-It. 2 Bde. Wiesbaden 1964 [776, 826 S.].

Castelli 1700 = Nicolò Castelli: La Fontana della Crusca, Overo: Dizzionario italiano-tedesco e tedesco-italiano (...). Hrsg. v. Ferromontano. Leipzig 1700 [684, 420 S.; ed. J. Mühlmann 1709; ed. Castelli 1718: 1664 S.; 1730; ed. C. Coutelle 1749; 1759: 1024, 560 S.; ed. I. G. di Fraporta 1771].

Ciardi Dupré/Escher 1955 = Giuseppe Ciardi Dupré/Angelica Escher: Dizionario italiano-tedesco tedesco-italiano. Torino 1955 [1696 S.; 1970: 1762 S.].

Deidda 1971 = Armando Deidda: Vocabolario Tedesco-Italiano, Italiano-Tedesco. Ozzano Emilia 1971 [2454 S.].

Enenkel 1892 = Arturo Enenkel: Neues deutsch-italienisches und italienisch-deutsches Taschenwörterbuch für Literatur, Wissenschaft und Leben. Paris 1892 [493, 515 S.].

Erberg 1710 = Matthias von Erberg: Il gran dizionario universale e perfetto, diviso in III parti: I. Italiano-Francese-Tedesco. II. Francese-Italiano-Tedesco. III. Tedesco-Francese-Italiano. 3 Bde. Nürnberg 1710 [1231, 1248, 990 S.].

Feller 1851 = F. E. Feller: Nuovo dizionario portatile (...). Leipzig 1851 [941 S. —1905].

Feller 1855 = F. E. Feller: Handwörterbuch der italienischen und deutschen Sprache. Leipzig 1885 [1033 S. —1882].

Flathe 1782 = [Philipp Jacob Flathe:] Nuovo dizionario italiano-tedesco, e tedesco-italiano, Prima di Nic. di Castelli, ma ora esattamente corretto, ed a detta de'Dizionarij dell'Accademia della Crusca, e del Signor Abate Francesco de Alberti di Villanuova, arrichito (...) oder Neues Italienisch-Deutsches und Deutsch-Italienisches Wörterbuch (...) 4 Bde. Leipzig 1782 [1467, 2424 S.].

Flathe 1785 = Philipp Jacob Flathe: Nuovo dizionario manuale italiano-tedesco e tedesco-italiano. Secondo i novissimi Vocabolarj dell'Accademia della Crusca, e del Signor Abate Francesco de Alberti di Villanuova. Oder Neues Italiänisch-Deutsches und Deutsch-Italiänisches Wörterbuch Auf das genaueste berichtiget und ausgearbeitet. 4 Bde. Leipzig 1785 [1178, 1079 S.].

Graben 1731 = Otto von Graben zum Stein: Italiänisch-Teutsches und Teutsch-Italiänisches Hand-Lexicon (...). Leipzig 1731 [435, 71 S.].

Grande Diz. 1837/39 = Grande Dizionario italiano-tedesco, tedesco-italiano. Vollständiges (...). 2 Bde. Mailand 1837, 1839 [988, 1172 S.].

Güntzel 1648 = [Johann Güntzel:] A. M. A. D. Haubtschlüssel Der Teutschen und Italiänischen Sprache. Das ist: Vollständiges Wortbuch aller Teutschen und Italiänischen Stamm: und Beywörter, sambt derselben Gebrauch, Redarten und würcklichen Kunst:fügungen. La Chiave Maestra (....). Per Giovanni Alemanni. Augsburg 1648 [931, 451 S.].

Hecker 1905 = Oskar Hecker: Neues deutsch-italienisches Wörterbuch. 2 Bde. Braunschweig 1905 [405, 643 S. Die 1. Aufl. des dt.-it. Teils von 1900; 1911—1913].

Heucke 1806 = Johann Joachim Heucke: Nuovissimo dizionario italiano-tedesco e tedesco-italiano. Augsburg 1806 [1504, 1438 S.; 1818, 1836].

Hulsius 1605 = Levinus Hulsius: Dictionarium Teutsch-Italiänisch und Italiänisch-Teutsch. Zuvorn niemahl in druck außgangen. Frankfurt 1605 [35, 322 (It-D), 165 (D-It) S.; aufgelegt bis 1687: 488, 323 S.].

Hulsius/Ravelli 1616 = Levinus Hulsius/Francesco Martino Ravelli: Dictionarium Teutsch-Frantzösisch-Italiänisch: Frantzösisch-Teutsch-Italiänisch: Italiänisch-Frantzösisch-Teutsch. 3 Bde. Frankfurt 1616 [444, 627, 595 S.; ed. 1659; viersprachige Aufl. (mit Latein) 1628—1659].

Jagemann 1790 = Christian Joseph Jagemann: Dizionario italiano-tedesco e tedesco-italiano. 4 Bde. Weissenfels. Leipzig 1790, 1791 [Ed. nuova 4 Bde. 1803, 1804: 1272, 1458 S.; 1816: ed. J. v. Vogtberg/G. E. Kappherr; 1838: ed. J. B. Bolza, 4 Bde. 1636, 1362 S.].

Jagemann 1799 = Christian Joseph Jagemann: Nuovo vocabolario italiano-tedesco e tedesco-italiano disposto con ordine etimologico. 2 Bde. Leipzig 1799, 1800 [747, 786 S. 2. Aufl. 1816].

Kirsch 1718 = Adam Friedrich Kirsch/Nicolaus von Castelli: Il nuovo dizionario de viaggianti italiano-tedesco e tedesco-italiano. Neues Italiänisch-Teutsches und Teutsch-Italiänisches Wörterbuch, aus dem bekannten Vocabulario des Herrn Pergamini (...) gezogen (...). Nürnberg 1718 [766, 416 S.].

Kramer 1676/78 = Matthias Kramer: Das neue Dictionarium oder Wort-Buch in Italiänisch-Teutscher Sprach. (...) in Teutsch-Italiänischer Sprach. 2 Bde. Nürnberg 1676, 1678 [1858, 1306 S.].

Kramer 1693 = Matthias Kramer: Neuausgefertigtes herrlich-grosses und allgemeines Italiänisch-Teutsches Sprach- und Wörter-Buch. Nürnberg 1693 [1286 S. 2. Aufl. 1724].

Kramer 1700/02 = Matthias Kramer: Das herrlich Große Teutsch-italiänische Dictionarium oder Wort- und Red-Arten-Schatz. 2 Bde. Nürnberg 1700, 1702 [2482 S.; 2. Aufl. 1724; Nachdruck Hildesheim 1982].

Lazzioli/Nemi 1938 = Constante Lazzioli/Giuseppe Nemi: Novissimo dizionario delle lingue italiana e tedesca. Brescia 1938 [Ed. 1960: 1914 S.].

Leys 1732 = Franz Jacob Leys: Dizionario italiano-tedesco. Neues Teutsch-Italienisches Wörterbuch. 5 Bd. (Manuskripte Nr. 1807—1811 der Universitätsbibliothek Erlangen; It-D, 3575 S.; D-It, 2214 S.].

LHWB = Paolo Giovanelli/Herbert Frenzel/Walter Frenzel: Langenscheidts Handwörterbuch Italienisch-Deutsch, Deutsch-Italienisch. 2 Bde. 2. Aufl. Berlin 1972, 1982 [568, 656 S.; 1. Aufl. 1965. Milano 1982: Langenscheidt-Signorelli].

LTWB = Langenscheidts Taschenwörterbuch der italienischen und deutschen Sprache v. Gustav Sacerdote. Berlin 1905 [470, 480 S.; zahlr. Neubearb. durch E. E. Lange-Kowal, R. Stoff, W. Ross, P. Giovanelli, V. Macchi, W. Frenzel. 1978: 640, 606 S.].

Lysle 1909 = [Andrea de Roever] Lysle: Nuovo dizionario moderno razionale pratico tedesco-italiano italiano-tedesco. Venaria Reale 1909 [855, 1058 S.; ed. G. Pontevivo, 1939].

Macchi 1984 = Vladimiro Macchi (Hrsg.): Die großen Sansoni Wörterbücher/I Grandi Dizionari Sansoni: Wörterbuch der italienischen und deutschen Sprache/Dizionario delle lingue italiana e tedesca. Parte prima: Italiano-Tedesco. Zweiter Teil: Deutsch-Italienisch. 2. verb. u. erw. Aufl. 2 Bde. Florenz. Rom. Wiesbaden 1984 [XXII, 1532, XVIII, 1650 S. 1. Aufl. 1970, 1972].

Macchi 1984a = Vladimiro Macchi (Hrsg.): Dizionario Sansoni Tedesco-Italiano, Italiano-Tedesco. 2. Aufl. Firenze 1984 [972, 820 S.; 1. Aufl. 1975; textgleich in 2 Bd. als Langenscheidts Großwörterbuch].

Messerschmid 1625 = Georg Friedrich Messerschmid: Tutitalogia sive Vocabularium Italo-Germanicum et Germanico-italicum. Vocabularium, das ist: Wörterbuch, Teutsch-Italienisch (...). Durlach 1625 [478 S.].

Michaelis 1879/81 = Henriette Michaelis: Vollständiges Wörterbuch der italienischen und deutschen Sprache. Dizionario completo (...). 2 Bde. Leipzig 1879, 1881 [640, 719 S.; bis 1899, dann u. d. Titel: Praktisches Wörterbuch/Dizionario pratico, 1900: 878, 911 S.; bis 21. Aufl. 1932].

Oudin 1674 = Nuovo et ampio dittionario di tre lingue. Diviso in III parti: I. Italiano-Francese-Te-desco. II. Francese-Italiano-Tedesco. III. Tedesco-Francese-Italiano. Composto prima in quelle due lingue da Antonio Udino [Antoine Oudin] (...) ed aumentato adesso nuovamente della terza (...). Frankfurt 1674 [1005, 680, 591 S.].

Pons 1986 = Birgit Klausmann-Molter u. a.: Pons-Globalwörterbuch Italienisch-Deutsch, Deutsch-Italienisch. 2 Bde. Stuttgart 1986 [842, 838 S.; auch Bologna 1987].

Rädlein 1711 = Johann Rädlein [Giovanni Redlino]: Europäischer Sprachschatz oder (...) Wörter-Buch der vornehmsten Sprachen in Europa. Tesoro di lingue europeo overò Dizzionario delle più principali lingue dell'Europa. 3 Bde. Leipzig 1711 [D-It-F, 1127 S.; F-D-It, 869 S.; It-D-F, 502 S.].

Reich 1786/89 = [Karl Heinrich Reich:] Neues italienisch-deutsches Wörterbuch, bearbeitet nach dem Werke der Akademie della Crusca, und dem Wörterbuche des Abts Francesco de Alberti. = Dizionario italiano-tedesco (...). Erster Theil. Neues deutsch-italienisches Wörterbuch bearbeitet nach Adelungs deutschem Wörterbuche als zweyter Theil des neuen italiänischen Wörterbuchs (...). 2 Bde. Leipzig 1786, 1789 [872, 1172 S.].

Rigutini/Bulle 1900 = Giuseppe Rigutini/Oskar Bulle: Neues italienisch-deutsches oder deutsch-italienisches Wörterbuch. Nuovo Dizionario (...). 2 Bde. Leipzig. Mailand 1896—1900 [919 S.; 6. Aufl. 1920; Nachdruck in 1 Bd., Bologna 1981].

Romani 1764 = Clemente Romani/Wolfgang Jäger: Nuovo dizionario italiano-tedesco e tedesco-italiano (...). Oder Vollständiges Italiänisch-Deutsches und Deutsch-Italiänisches Wörter-Buch. Nach der Orthographie der Florentinischen Akademie und nach Anleitung ihres Wörter-Buchs (...). Nürnberg 1764 [616, 261 S.; 2. Aufl. 1786, 3. Aufl. 1820].

Schade 1820 = M. K. B. Schade: Nuovo dizionario manuale italiano-tedesco e tedesco-italiano. Neues vollständiges (...) Handwörterbuch. 2 Bde. Leipzig 1820 [874, 1118 S.].

Valentini 1821 = Francesco Valentini: Vollständiges deutsch-italienisches und italienisch-deutsches Taschenwörterbuch. Berlin 1821 [403, 600 S.; später Leipzig bis 1906].

Valentini 1831—36 = Franz Valentini: Vollständiges italienisch-deutsches und deutsch-italienisches grammatisch-praktisches Wörterbuch. Gran Dizionario grammatico-pratico (...). 4 Bde. Leipzig 1831—1836 [It-D, CIV, 1392 S.; D-It., C, 1414, 74 S.].

Veneroni 1700 = Giovanni di Veneroni [Jean Vigneron]: Il Dittionario imperiale. Frankfurt 1700 [It-F-D-L, 878 S.; F-It-D-L, 570 S.; D-F-It-L, 218 S.; L-F-It-D, 152 S.; bis 1804].

Veneroni 1713 = Giovanni di Veneroni/Nicolò Castelli: Neues Dictionarium oder Wörter-Buch in drey Abteilungen. It-F-D. F-L-D. D-F-L. (...) Sonderlich jungen Anfängern und Reisenden. Frankfurt. Leipzig 1713 [480 S.].

Weber 1840 = Ferdinand Adolf Weber: Neues vollständiges Wörterbuch der Italienischen und der Deutschen Sprache. Leipzig 1840 [568, 722 S. bis 1903].

3.2. Sonstige Literatur

Bart-Rossebastiano 1971 = Alda Bart-Rossebastiano: Introito e porta. Vocabulario italiano-tedesco. Compiuto per Meistro Adamo di Roduila 1477 adi 12 Augusto (Neolatina rariora. Lexicalia 1, 1). Turin 1971.

Bart-Rossebastiano 1977 = Alda Bart-Rossebastiano: Antichi vocabulari plurilingui d'uso popolare. Parte I: La tradizione del „Solenissimo Vochabuolista". In: Gulden Passer 55. 1977, 67—153.

Behrens 1910 = Dietrich Behrens: Beiträge zur französischen Wortgeschichte und Grammatik. Halle 1910.

Bray 1987 = Laurent Bray: La lexicographie bilingue italien-allemand et allemand-italien au dix-septième siècle. L'exemple des dictionnaires de L. Hulsius et de M. Kramer. In: Snell-Hornby 1987, 199—206.

Bray 1988 = Laurent Bray: La Lexicographie Bilingue Italien-Allemand, Allemand-Italien du Dix-Septième Siècle. In: International Journal of Lexicography 1. 1988, 313—342.

Brenner 1886 = Oskar Brenner: Italienisch-deutsche Vocabulare des XV. und XVI. Jahrhunderts. In: Germanica 31. 1886, 129—136.

Brenner 1895 = Oskar Brenner: Ein altes italienisch-deutsches Sprachbuch. In: Bayerns Mundarten 2. 1895, 384—444.

Bruna 1983 = Maria Luisa Bruna: La lessicografia italo-tedesca. Tesi di laurea. Università degli studi di Udine. Anno accademico 1982/1983 (thèse dactylographiée).

Emery 1949—51 = Luigi Emery: Vecchi manuali italo-tedeschi. In: Lingua Nostra 10. 1949, 80—84; 11. 1950, 43—45; 12. 1951, 35—39.

Folena 1973 = Gianfranco Folena: L'italiano in Europa. Turin 1973.

Gervasi 1982 = Teresa Gervasi: Problemi teorici della lessicografia bilingue: a proposito della ristampa del Rigutini-Bulle. In: Annali. Sezione Germanica. Studi Tedeschi 25. 1982, 259—269.

Giustiniani 1987 = V. R. Giustiniani: Adam von Rottweil. Deutsch-Italienischer Sprachführer. Màistro Adamo de Rodvila. Introito e porta de quele che voleno imparare e comprender todescho o latino, cioè italiano. Edito di sulle stampe del 1477 e 1500 e corredato di un'introduzione, di note e di indici. Tübingen 1987.

Hausmann 1984 = Franz Josef Hausmann: Das erste französisch-deutsche Wörterbuch. Levinus Hulsius 'Dictionaire' von 1596—1607. In: Zeitschrift für romanische Philologie 100. 1984, 306—320.

Hausmann 1987 = Franz Josef Hausmann: Les dictionnaires bilingues italien-allemand/allemand-italien au dix-huitième siècle. In: Snell-Hornby 1987, 207—216.

Hausmann 1988 = Franz Josef Hausmann: Les dictionnaires bilingues (et multilingues) en Europe au XVIIIe siècle. Acquis et suggestions de recherche. In: La lexicographie française du XVIIIe au XXe siècle. Colloque international de lexicographie (. . .). Hrsg. B. v. Gemmingen/M. Höfler. Paris 1988 (Actes et Colloques 27), 11—32 (= In: Travaux de Linguistique et de Philologie 1 [= Travaux de Linguistique et de Littérature 26/1]. 1988, 11—32).

Holtus/Schweickard 1985 = Günter Holtus/Wolfgang Schweickard: Elemente gesprochener Sprache in einem venezianischen Text von 1424: das italienisch-deutsche Sprachbuch von Georg von Nürnberg. In: G. Holtus/E. Radtke (eds.), Gesprochenes Italienisch in Geschichte und Gegenwart. Tübingen 1985.

Høybye 1964 = Poul Høybye: Glossari italiano-tedeschi del Quattrocento. Maistro Zorzi. In: Studi di filologia italiana 22. 1964, 167—204.

Ising 1956 = Gerhard Ising: Die Erfassung der deutschen Sprache des ausgehenden 17. Jahrhunderts in den Wörterbüchern Matthias Kramers und Kaspar Stielers. Berlin 1956.

Marello 1987 = Carla Marello: Linguistica contrastiva attraverso i dizionari bilingui italiano e tedesco. In: Parallela III. Atti de IV incontro italo-austriaco dei linguisti a Vienna 1986. Hrsg. v. W. U. Dressler et al. Tübingen 1987, 81—93.

Marello 1989 = Carla Marello: Dizionari bilingui con schede sui dizionari italiani per francese, inglese, spagnolo, tedesco. Bologna 1989.

Merkel 1980 = Ernst Merkel: Der Buchhändler Levinus Hulsius, gest. 1606 zu Frankfurt am Main. In: Archiv für Frankfurts Geschichte und Kunst 57. 1980, 7—18.

Pausch 1972 = Oskar Pausch: Das älteste italienisch-deutsche Sprachbuch. Eine Überlieferung aus dem Jahre 1424 nach Georg von Nürnberg. Wien 1972.

Rossebastiano-Bart 1986 = A. Rossebastiano-Bart: Alle origini della lessicografia italiana. In: Lexique 4. 1986, 113—156.

Simonsfeld 1893 = H. Simonsfeld: Italienisch-deutsche Reise-Sprachführer aus alter Zeit. In: Das Ausland 66/27. 1989, 417—424.

Snell-Hornby 1987 = Mary Snell-Hornby (ed.): ZüriLEX '86 Proceedings. Papers read at the Euralex International Congress, University of Zürich, 9—14 September 1986. Tübingen 1987.

Tancke 1984 = Gunnar Tancke: Die italienischen Wörterbücher von den Anfängen bis zum Erscheinen des 'Vocabolario degli Accademici della Crusca' (1612). Tübingen 1984.

Maria Luisa Bruna, Udine (Italien)/
Laurent Bray/Franz Josef Hausmann,
Erlangen (Bundesrepublik Deutschland)

318. Die zweisprachige Lexikographie mit Portugiesisch

1. Einleitung
2. Zweisprachige Lexikographie mit Portugiesisch von den Anfängen bis ins 18. Jahrhundert. — Fruchtbare und erloschene Linien
3. Das Aufkommen nationaler bis in die Gegenwart reichender Linien. Das genealogische Dickicht des 18., 19. und 20. Jahrhunderts
4. Glanz und Elend der deutschen Linie sowie ihrer englischen Seitenlinie
5. Welcher Linie gebührt heute die Krone?
6. Einfluß der modernen Sprachwissenschaft auf die zweisprachige Lexikographie mit Portugiesisch
7. Fachsprachliche Wörterbücher
8. Ausblick — Noch ist Portugal nicht verloren
9. Literatur (in Auswahl)

1. Einleitung

So bitter es einen lusophilen Genealogen auch ankommen mag, die zweisprachige Lexikographie mit Portugiesisch verfügt nur über eine bescheidene Stammtafel. Die keineswegs hehre Ahnengalerie ist rasch abgeschritten, die wenigen illustren Vorfahren sind schnell aufgezählt, und viele Altvordern werden lediglich der Kontinuität wegen überliefert. Die glücklich Überlebenden dieser Ahnenreihe, die vielfach allein durch ihr Überleben von Bedeutung sind, präsentieren sich nun den Zeitgenossen als wundersame Ergebnisse geheimnisumwitterter Parthenogenese (die Vorworte mancher Wörterbücher sollen oftmals systematisch Spuren verwischen), und sie werden auch in dem folgenden Beitrag die ihnen gebührende Anteilnahme erhalten. Unser Interesse gilt darüber hinaus auch den schwarzen Schafen der Ahnenreihe, Erbschleichern zumeist, die schamlos, aber offensichtlich gekonnt, Vorläufer plagiieren und auf ihre Weise den lexikographischen „Fortschritt" beförderten. Da es nicht Aufgabe des vorliegenden Beitrages sein kann, lexikographische Schmankerl (wie z. B. die Abgrenzung der Homonymie von der Polysemie) genußvoll für das Portugiesische wiederzukäuen, wird der Diachronie ein verhältnismäßig großer Raum eingeräumt, anschließend wird der nicht sehr befriedigende Zustand der zweisprachigen Lexikographie Deutsch-Portugiesisch und Portugiesisch-Deutsch beschrieben, und in einem kleinen Ausblick soll etwas optimistische Futurologie betrieben werden.

2. Zweisprachige Lexikographie mit Portugiesisch von den Anfängen bis ins 18. Jahrhundert. — Fruchtbare und erloschene Linien

2.1. Die portugiesisch-lateinische Linie

Ahnherr der zweisprachigen Lexikographie mit Portugiesisch ist der Humanist Jerónimo Cardoso (Hieronymus Cardosus), der in der zweiten Hälfte des 16. Jahrhunderts in Coimbra und Lissabon drei Wörterbücher des Sprachenpaares Portugiesisch/Latein veröffentlichte, deren Einfluß bis in unsere Tage reichen sollte: (a) Das allererste zweisprachige Wörterbuch des Portugiesischen ist eine Sammlung lateinischer Wörter, die — nach Sachgruppen geordnet — jeweils ins Portugiesische übersetzt werden und — wie es der Titel *Dictionarium iuventuti studiosae admodum frugiferum* verrät — didaktischen Zielen diente. Es enthält 4120 Stichwörter (Teyssier 1985, 246). Die Erstauflage von 1551 bleibt verschollen, den Forschern zugänglich ist die zweite Auflage von 1562 (Cardoso 1562). (b) Das zweite lexikographische Werk Cardosos ist ein alphabetisch geordnetes portugiesisch-lateinisches Wörterbuch (Cardoso 1562/1563) mit 12 076 Stichwörtern. (c) Die dritte lexikographische Arbeit Cardosos, postum veröffentlicht (Cardoso 1569/1570), vereinigt mehrere Teile, von denen ein lateinisch-portugiesisches Wörterbuch mit 26 863 Stichwörtern (Teyssier 1980, 26) sowie das kaum veränderte portugiesisch-lateinische Wörterbuch von 1562/63 erwähnenswert sind. Aus den zahlreichen Auflagen dieses Werkes (1588, 1592, 1601, 1613, 1619, 1630, 1643, 1677, 1694 und 1695) läßt sich sein nachhaltiger Einfluß auf die portugiesische Lexikographie ablesen. Wie Teyssier (1980 und 1985) gezeigt hat, sind diese frühen Arbeiten unter mehreren Gesichtspunkten beachtenswert: (a) Die zweisprachige Lexikographie des Portugiesischen entwickelt sich aus der Lexikographie des Lateinischen, sie ist in gewisser Hinsicht nur ein Nebenprodukt, hervorgegangen aus dem Bestreben, die unzulänglichen Lateinkenntnisse der portugiesischen Jugend im 16. Jahrhundert zu verbessern. Laus stultitiae! (b) Nicht zu leugnen ist die Abhängigkeit Cardosos 1569/1570 von dem lateinisch-spanischen Wörterbuch Nebrijas, trotz einiger Streichungen und Ergänzungen (Teyssier

1980, 28—30). (c) Besonders hervorzuheben ist die lexikographische Neuerung bei Cardoso 1569/1570, die Adagia des Erasmus von Rotterdam fast vollzählig (d. h. ca. 4000 Beispiele) aufzunehmen. (d) Die Wörterbücher Cardosos enthalten bereits zwei wichtige Anordnungskriterien (Sachfelder versus Alphabet) und sind für Weiterentwicklungen in beiden Richtungen offen. (e) Der Einfluß des Lexikographen Cardoso läßt sich in den wichtigsten Wörterbüchern des Sprachenpaares Portugiesisch/Latein noch im 17. und 18. Jahrhundert nachweisen, und, da das zehnbändige — ebenfalls von Cardoso beeinflußte — *Vocabulario Portuguez e Latino* von Raphael Bluteau (1712—1728) leicht umgearbeitet 1789 als einsprachiges portugiesisches Wörterbuch (Verfasser dieser Umarbeitung ist niemand anderer als António de Morais Silva, dessen Umarbeitung heute noch als der Morais aufgelegt wird (10. Auflage von 1949 bis 1959)) erschien, kann Cardoso mit Fug und Recht auch als Stammvater der einsprachigen portugiesischen Lexikographie gelten (vgl. Artikel 181). „Ainsi Jerónimo Cardoso est bien l'initiateur, l'ancêtre, le fondateur de la lexicographie portugaise. Par l'intermédiaire d'Agostinho Barbosa (1611), de Bento Pereira (1634) et de Bluteau (1712—1728), une chaîne ininterrompue conduit de lui à Morais (1789), et finalement à tous les dictionnaires modernes de la langue" (Teyssier 1985, 249).

2.2. Portugiesisch in Verbindung mit außereuropäischen Sprachen. Die portugiesisch-asiatische Linie

Weniger überschaubar präsentieren sich die zahlreichen lexikographischen Arbeiten, bei denen das Portugiesische, sehr oft neben Latein, mit einer Vielzahl asiatischer (und in geringerem Maße auch amerikanischer) Sprachen kombiniert wurde. Die Publikationsspanne dieser Wortlisten, Vokabularien und Wörterbücher erstreckt sich vom 16. Jahrhundert bis gegen Ende des 18. Jahrhunderts und sie erklärt sich aus der Bedeutung des Portugiesischen als lingua franca Asiens nach der Entdeckung des Seewegs nach Indien (Valkhoff 1975, 73—85). Für viele dieser *línguas exóticas* (Carvalhão Buescu 1983) stellen diese lexikographischen Werke gleichzeitig auch die erste Fixierung in einer europäischen Sprache dar. Lopes (1936/1969, 140—158) erwähnt in seiner Spezialuntersuchung ca. zwanzig derartige Wörterbücher, denen de Matos noch fast dreißig weitere hinzufügt (Lopes 1936/1969, 158—160). Aber auch diese Addenda sind nicht vollständig. Spezialbibliographien, wie z. B. die ersten sieben Bände der *Bibliotheca missionum* (Streit 1916—1931) lassen das Herz jedes Lexikographen höher schlagen. Hier finden sich — in einer kleinen alphabetischen Auswahl — Wörterbücher des Portugiesischen in Verbindung mit Annamitisch, Bengali, Chinesisch, Konkani, Malaiisch, Japanisch, Persisch, Singhalesisch und Tamil, um nur einige bekanntere Sprachen zu zitieren. Mit dem Verdrängen des Portugiesischen aus dem asiatischen Raum, zunächst durch das Niederländische, später durch das Französische und vor allem das Englische, kam diese fruchtbare zweisprachige Lexikographie zum Erliegen. Solche lexikographische Schätze aus Ali Babas Höhle verdienen es jedoch, für die Nachwelt geborgen zu werden (Vermeer 1969).

2.3. Portugiesisch in Verbindung mit modernen europäischen Sprachen

So bedeutend die Rolle des Portugiesischen auch in Asien sein mochte, in Europa bleibt es weiterhin eine wenig beachtete Randsprache. Die bekannten Spezialbibliographien verzeichnen bis zum Beginn des 18. Jahrhunderts keine zweisprachigen Wörterbücher mit Portugiesisch. Lediglich in den *Colloquia et Dictionariolum* des Noël van Berlaimont kommt das Portugiesische vor, aber ausschließlich in den achtsprachigen Ausgaben (Claes 1974, 36/37, 82 und 93 und Claes 1977, 178, 220). Selbst in den mehrsprachigen Ausgaben des schulebildenden *Dictionarium* von Ambrogio Calepino ist Portugiesisch nicht in Verbindung mit einer modernen europäischen Sprache vertreten, sondern nur einmal mit Latein und Japanisch (Labarre 1975, 81).

Nach Verdeyen 1926 lassen sich 13 Ausgaben der *Colloquia et Dictionariolum* mit Portugiesisch nachweisen: 1598 Delft (Nr. 44), 1605 Delft (Nr. 51), 1613 Vlissingen (Nr. 61), 1613 Den Haag (Nr. 62), 1613 Amsterdam (Nr. 63), 1622 Amsterdam (Nr. 73), 1623 Amsterdam (Nr. 74), 1630 Amsterdam (Nr. 78), 1631 Amsterdam (Nr. 80), 1631 Middelburg (Nr. 81), 1639 London (Nr. 85), 1646 Venedig (Nr. 90), 1656 Venedig (Nr. 95), 1622 Antwerpen (Nr. 96) und 1692 Bologna (Nr. 99). Obwohl diese achtsprachigen Ausgaben im 17. Jahrhundert kontinuierlich aufgelegt wurden und auch von den Druckorten her sich über mehrere europäische Länder erstreckten, scheint ihr Einfluß auf die Weiterentwicklung der zweisprachigen Lexikographie mit Portugiesisch doch von geringer Bedeutung gewesen zu sein.

3. Das Aufkommen nationaler bis in die Gegenwart reichender Linien. Das genealogische Dickicht des 18., 19. und 20. Jahrhunderts

Eine eigenständige zweisprachige Lexikographie europäischer Sprachen mit Portugiesisch bildet sich erst im 18. Jahrhundert und im 19. Jahrhundert heraus, bei den skandinavischen und slawischen Sprachen teilweise sogar erst im 20. Jahrhundert. Aber selbst in dieser Zeit findet sich das Portugiesische noch in Verbindung mit mehrsprachigen Wörterbüchern (Newman 1799, Nemnich 1799). Nicht wenige dieser zweisprachigen Wörterbücher mit Portugiesisch überbrücken mit ihren Neuauflagen größere Zeiträume, und vor allem Wörterbücher des 19. Jahrhunderts reichen bis in unsere Tage hinein. Für das Sprachenpaar Portugiesisch/Englisch lassen sich von 1773 bis 1840 zahlreiche Auflagen des Wörterbuches von Vieyra nachweisen. Französische Benutzer können heute noch die 4. Auflage des französisch-portugiesischen Wörterbuches von Azevedo (1952) erwerben, dessen Erstauflage auf die Jahre 1887—1889 zurückgeht, oder die 6. Auflage des portugiesisch-französischen Teils (neu gedruckt im Juni 1980). In ähnlicher Weise waren für die zweisprachige Lexikographie des Deutschen und Portugiesischen über fast ein Jahrhundert hinweg die Wörterbücher von Michaelis von beachtlicher Bedeutung. In einem notwendigerweise raschen und unprätentiösen Überblick aus der Vogelperspektive soll nur auf einige *dates-phares* dieser drei Jahrhunderte hingewiesen werden. Unser *tour d'horizon* beginnt mit dem Englischen, das wohl das erste zweisprachige Wörterbuch mit Portugiesisch kennt (A. J. 1701), das den Bibliographien nach zu urteilen auch hinsichtlich der Quantität führend ist und das schließlich schon über differenziertere Wörterbücher verfügt: Mascherpe 1968 (Faux amis), Chamberlain/Harmon (1983) (Brasilianisch), Magalhães 1964, Alfredo Estêves 1970 und Serpa 1972 (Redewendungen) sowie Fernandes Valdez 1875 (Aussprache). 1701 erschien in London *A Compleat Account of the Portugueze Language*, ein englisch-portugiesisches und portugiesisch-englisches Wörterbuch mit ca. 50 000 bis 55 000 Einträgen in einer etwas eigenwilligen alphabetischen Anordnung. Es weist eine starke Einzellemmatisierung auf, bringt im portugiesisch-englischen Teil erstaunlich viele Diminutive sowie Adverbien auf *-mente* und führt die regelmäßigen Adjektive in der femininen Form in Verbindung mit *cousa* (= Sache) ein (z. B. *maravilhósa cóusa: That is wonderful or admirable*). Großer Beliebtheit erfreute sich Vieyra 1773, wie die Auflagen von 1782, 1794, 1809, 1813, 1827 und 1840 zeigen. Seit 1958 wird Taylor mit ca. 60 000 Stichwörtern neuaufgelegt und 1964 kam — ebenfalls mit ca. 60 000 Stichwörtern — Houaiss/Avery heraus mit besonderer Berücksichtigung der brasilianischen Variante des Portugiesischen (Walford/Screen 1977, 73—75). Für das Niederländische erschien 1714 in Amsterdam ein portugiesisch-niederländisches Wörterbuch (Alewijn/Collé 1714) und 1742 ein Pendant in Lissabon (Folqman 1742). (Vgl. noch Claes 1980, 207/208). Seit der Mitte des 18. Jahrhunderts lassen sich zweisprachige Wörterbücher mit Französisch nachweisen (Marques 1758 und 1764). Zuweilen finden sich noch dreisprachige Ausgaben mit Latein (Costa e Sá 1794), die erst später zu zweisprachigen werden (Costa e Sá 1811). Für das 19. Jahrhundert kann man einige mehrfach aufgelegte Werke aufzählen: Solano Constancio 1820, 1828, 1834, 1842, 1852, 1856, 1859, 1864, 1867, 1874, 1877, 1887, Roquette 1841, 1850, 1853, 1855, 1856, 1857, 1858, 1860, 1862, 1863 und 1882 und Fonseca 1850, 1853, 1856, 1861 und 1878. Ab 1887—1889 geht Azevedo in Führung. Deutschsprachigen Benutzern steht erst zu Beginn des 19. Jahrhunderts das erste zweisprachige Wörterbuch mit Portugiesisch zur Verfügung (Wagener 1811/1812), Italiener müssen noch etwas länger warten (Bordo 1853/1854; für die neuere Zeit Spinelli/Casasanta 1983/1985), und auch die Spanier müssen sich gedulden (Canto e Castro Mascarenhas Valdez 1864/1866, Marques 1897 oder auch Monso 1900. Benutzer dieser beiden romanischen Sprachen können für die neuere Zeit Wörterbücher der Verlage Editôra Globo (Pôrto Alegre), Porto Editora (Porto) und Edições de Ouro (Rio de Janeiro) konsultieren. Innerhalb der slawischen Sprachen bilden das Russische (Gutman 1909, Starec/Feerštejn 1961, 1972 und Voinova/Starets/Verkhucha/Zditovetski 1975), das Polnische (Zdanowski 1905/1912) und das Tschechische (Hampl 1964, 1975, Hampl/Holšan 1976) relativ gesehen gewisse Schwerpunkte, während z. B. das Bulgarische noch über kein zweisprachiges Wörterbuch mit Portugiesisch verfügt. (Vgl. allgemein hierzu die Bibliographien von Grzegorczyk 1967, Aav 1977 und Lewanski 1973). Last not least muß das Ungarische Erwähnung finden, für das 1978 ein solide gemachtes, 45 000 Wörter umfassendes portugiesisch-ungarisches Wörterbuch publiziert wurde (Király 1978). Für alle diese Sprachen wären noch wörterbuchgeschichtliche Darstellungen mit Berücksichtigung des Portugiesischen zu erstellen.

4. Glanz und Elend der deutschen Linie sowie ihrer englischen Seitenlinie

Obwohl die deutsche Linie der zweisprachigen Lexikographie mit Portugiesisch im europäischen Kontext relativ spät beginnt, so ist ihr Debüt doch sehr vielversprechend. Klammert man die diachronisch bedingten Veränderungen des Wortschatzes aus, dann braucht der vierbändige Wagener 1811/1812, das erste Wörterbuch dieser Art, hinsichtlich der Zahl der Lemmata wie auch bei Berücksichtigung der Kollokationen und Redewendungen keinen Vergleich zu scheuen mit den heute allein noch zur Verfügung stehenden zweibändigen Taschenwörterbüchern. Später kommen Wollheim da Fonseca (1844) und Bösche (1858) hinzu. Mit Michaelis 1887 blüht diese Linie auf und erreicht so beachtliches Ansehen, daß fast ein Jahrhundert portugiesisch-deutscher und deutsch-portugiesischer Lexikographie davon zehren sollte. Michaelis wird zum Synonym für solide zweisprachige Lexikographie, wobei Henriette Michaelis sicherlich auch ein wenig von der Verwechslung mit ihrer Schwester Carolina Michaëlis de Vasconcellos, einer bekannten Lusitanistin, profitiert haben mag. Das zweibändige Handwörterbuch von Michaelis erlebt bis 1934 in Leipzig bei Brockhaus vierzehn Auflagen, wird dann in New York ohne Jahreszahl von der Frederick Ungar Publishing Company fotomechanisch nachgedruckt und war bis in die 70er Jahre im Handel erhältlich. Eine englische Adaptation des Michaelis erschien 1893 ebenfalls bei Brockhaus in Leipzig, erfreute sich bis 1932 insgesamt acht Auflagen, wurde dann wiederum von Ungar in New York vertrieben (1943) und mit einem Anhang neuer Wörter versehen 1945 und 1955 neu aufgelegt. Diese englische Ausgabe wurde vom brasilianischen Wörterbuchverlag Melhoramentos 1958/1961 überarbeitet und mit ca. 130 insgesamt 4000 Illustrationen umfassenden — im Grunde jedoch überflüssigen — Bildtafeln ausgestattet. Dergestalt „geliftet" wird das Wörterbuch der Henriette Michaelis als Brockhaus Picture Dictionary und gleichzeitig als Novo Michaelis von Melhoramentos für die beiden Amerikas vertrieben und von Brockhaus in Wiesbaden für Europa und den Rest der Welt. Die letzten Auflagen stammen aus dem Jahre 1976. Zu Beginn des 20. Jahrhunderts entwickelte sich die Filiation der Langenscheidt Taschenwörterbücher (Ey 1904/1909), die ebenfalls kontinuierlich aufgelegt wurden (1935, 13. Auflage des portugiesisch-deutschen Teils bzw. 12. Auflage des deutsch-portugiesischen). Nach dem Kriege wurden diese Wörterbücher von Beau bzw. Irmen 1953/1954 neubearbeitet, 1968/1969 nochmals von den beiden Autoren umgearbeitet und mit der A.P.I.-Lautschrift versehen, und die letzte Umarbeitung besorgte Irmen 1982 für den portugiesisch-deutschen Teil. Über eine eigenständige lexikographische Tradition verfügen auch die Wörterbücher des Verlages Porto Editora, dessen Dicionários 'Académicos' (DA 1976 und 1978) sowie die zuletzt erschienenen Handwörterbücher der Reihe Dicionários 'Editora' (DE 1983 Portugiesisch-Deutsch und 1986 Deutsch-Portugiesisch) vor allem für den portugiesischen Markt von Bedeutung sind. Seit 1963 ist auch die DDR mit eigenen Wörterbüchern vertreten: Meister/Laus 1963 und 1965 sowie die umfangreicheren Taschenwörterbücher von Klare 1984 und 1986. Einen Einblick in das kaum gestiegene Niveau soll eine stichprobenartige Synopse des Lemmas **spielen** ermöglichen.

5. Welcher Linie gebührt heute die Krone?

Versucht man die heute am meisten benutzten und auch im Handel noch erhältlichen zweisprachigen Taschen- und Handwörterbücher des Sprachenpaares Portugiesisch/Deutsch kritisch einander gegenüberzustellen, so läßt sich verständlicherweise kein Pauschalurteil fällen. Unter Rückgriff auf einen Beitrag (Ettinger 1987) können hier für die Wörterbücher von Beau 1969, Irmen 1982, DE 1983, 1986, Tochtrop 1984 sowie Klare 1984 und 1986 einige differenzierende Ergebnisse zusammengefaßt werden. Obwohl die Wörterbücher im Format verschieden sind (Tochtrop 1984 und DE 1983 bzw. 1986 sind Handwörterbücher, die übrigen lediglich Taschenwörterbücher), sind die Abweichungen untereinander hinsichtlich der vom Verlag angegebenen bzw. von uns grob geschätzten Stichwortzahl nicht so gravierend. Sie enthalten ca. 35 000 bis 45 000 Stichwörter, wobei lediglich die DE 1983 und 1986 nicht unbeträchtlich nach oben abweichen dürften. Da die Qualität eines Wörterbuches keineswegs allein von der Zahl der Stichwörter abhängt, soll daher vor allem die Makro- und Mikrostruktur verglichen werden: (a) Lediglich Beau 1969 und Irmen 1982 verwenden die A.P.I.-Lautschrift, die anderen Wörterbücher klammern die Aussprache aus. (b) Am vollständigsten sind Beau 1969 und Irmen 1982 bei den Genus- und Numerusangaben der Adjektive und Substantive, während bei den syntaktischen und grammatikalischen Angaben zu den Verben alle Wörterbücher zufriedenstellend sind. (c) Es ist nicht leicht, aus den Vorworten und aus den Angaben zu den Lemmata herauszufinden, für welche Sprachgruppe die Wörterbücher bevorzugt oder ausschließlich gedacht sind. Zuweilen ändert sich gar die Zuordnung von Auflage zu Auflage bei unverändert bleibendem Wortschatz (Tochtrop 5. Auflage 1968 „für Deutschsprachige zur Aneignung der Sprache Brasiliens", 6. Auflage 1984 „für Studierende des Deutschen"). Wohl eher für deutschsprachige Benutzer gedacht sind Klare 1984 und 1986 (Vorwort und Hinweis nur auf Deutsch), während der DE 1983 für Portugiesischsprachige bestimmt ist. Zweisprachige Vorworte und Benutzerhinweise bei Beau 1969, Irmen 1982 und beim DE

1986 lassen den Schluß zu, daß luso- und germanophone Sprecher gleichermaßen anvisiert werden. (d) Bei der Lemmatisierung von Homonymen und Polysemen greifen Tochtrop 1984, Klare 1984 bzw. 1986 und der DE 1986 stärker auf die wohl benutzerfreundlichere Mehrfachlemmatisierung zurück, während die übrigen Wörterbücher ausschließlich monolemmatisieren. (e) Recht konsequent wird bei der Zusammenziehung der Lemmata zu Absätzen die platzsparende Nesterbildung bei Beau 1969, Irmen 1982, Klare 1984 und 1986 angewandt, während Tochtrop 1984 sowie der DE 1983 und 1986 eine Mehrfachlemmatisierung bevorzugen. (f) Hinsichtlich der Kennzeichnung der Normabweichungen ist der DE 1983 für die diatopische Differenzierung innerhalb des Portugiesischen vorbildlich. Klare 1984 und 1986 berücksichtigen die bisher kaum behandelten Varianten des Portugiesischen in Afrika und Beau 1969 sowie Irmen 1982 differenzieren stärker im Deutschen. Besondere Berücksichtigung des Brasilianischen findet sich bei Tochtrop 1984. Insgesamt gesehen scheinen die im deutschen Sprachgebiet veröffentlichten Wörterbücher der Mikrostruktur größere Aufmerksamkeit zu schenken. Dehnt man diesen Vergleich auch auf einige inhaltliche Schwerpunkte aus, so läßt sich die Beurteilung noch weiter ausfächern. (g) Bei einem ausgewählten Bereich des Fachwortschatzes im weiteren Sinn (nämlich einer Wortliste Auto) schneiden bei den deutsch-portugiesischen Wörterbüchern Klare 1984 und der DE 1986 am besten ab, Tochtrop 1984 dagegen am schlechtesten. (h) Die Überprüfung einer Neologismenliste des Portugiesischen läßt — vorsichtig extrapoliert — die Schlußfolgerung nicht abwegig erscheinen, daß Klare 1986 den Neubildungen gegenüber aufgeschlossener ist als Irmen 1982. (i) Auch bei der Berücksichtigung der portugiesischen Phraseologie fällt ein Stichprobenvergleich zugunsten von Klare 1986 aus, gefolgt vom DE 1983 und Irmen 1982. (j) Am ausführlichsten berücksichtigten der DE 1983 und 1986 die Kollokationen ausgewählter Beispiele (Substantiv + Adjektiv, Substantiv + Verb, Verb + Substantiv), gefolgt von Klare 1984 und

Spielen, v. n. jogar, divertirse, recrearse, entreterse, folgar, gracejar, regocijarse, brincar, alegrarse. Mit etwas spielen, es nicht achten, abusar, profanar, user mal de alguma cousa. Mit einem spielen, spaßen, zombar, mofar, fazer zombaria, mofa de alguem; meter á bulha. it. ter a alguem sob seu dominio. Die Katze spielt mit der Maus, o gato não faz caso dos ratos. Das Glück spielt mit den Menschen, a fortuna faz zombaria dos homens. Das Pferd spielt mit dem Zaume, o cavallo está brincando com o freio. Mit den Händen spielen, jogar das mãos, brincar com as mãos. Eine Parthie spielen, jogar huma partida, hum lanzo. Pifet spielen, jogar aos centos. Eine Karte spielen, jogar, lanzar huma carta. Die Violine, die Laute spielen, tocar a viola, a guitarra. Eine Menuet, tocar hum minuete. Sich reich, arm spielen, enriquecerse, empobrecerse com o jogo. Einem einen Possen spielen, pregar huma peza, huma logração á alguem. Ein Stück auf der Bühne, representar. Heldenrollen spielen, representar no teatro, fazer o papel de heroes. Eine große Rolle spielen, fazer huma grande figura, representar hum grande papel no estado, na scena do mundo. Den Betrübten, den großen Mann spielen, fingirse, mostrarse asflicto; querer passar praza de homem de grande parte. Heute wird nicht gespielt, hoje não haverá comedia. Bankerot spielen, quebrar, falir, suspender os seus pagos. Den Krieg in ein Land, levar a guerra em hum pais.

Textbeispiel 318.1: Wörterbuchartikel (aus: Wagener 1812, 361/362)

Spielen, v. a. u. n. h. jogar; brincar, divertir-se, folgar, recreiar-se; corrér, saltar; jogar (artilharia); jogar (um jogo); tocar (fallando de instrumentos músicos e d'uma orchestra); voar, saltar (fallando de minas); Billard, Pifert, Kegel ꝛc. ~, jogar o bilhar, os centos, a bola etc.; ein Spiel ~ ob. zu ~ wissen, sabér jogar um jogo; eine Karte, Herzen ꝛc. ~, jogar um naipe ou uma carta, jogar copas etc.; mit einem Kinde ~, divertir um menino; hoch, niedrig ~, jogar forte, não jogar forte; hoch ~, aventurar-se a muito; falsch ~, enganar no jogo, fazér batota, gatunar, fazér trapaças no jogo; auf einem Instrumente ~, auf der Flöte, Harfe, Laute ꝛc. ~, tocar um instrumento, tocar a flauta, a arpa, o alaúde etc.; eine Rolle ~, desempenhar um papel; eine traurige Rolle ~, fazér triste figura; die Rolle des . . ~, fazér ou representar o papel de . . ; den Dummen ~, fazér papel de tolo; ein (Musik-)Stück ~, tocar, executar uma peça de música; nach Noten ~, tocar pelas notas ob. por música; vom Blatt ~, tocar á vista; aus dem Kopf ~, tocar de cór; den großen Herrn ~, fazér figura; fazér de gran senhor; jm. einen Streich ~, pregar uma peça a alg.; eine Mine ~ lassen, voar ob. fazér saltar a mina; (mil.) das Geschütz ~ lassen, mandar jogar a artilharia; ins Blaue, Gelbliche ꝛc. ~, tirar ao azul, a amarello; jm. etw. in die Hände ~, arranjar, grangear, procurar alg. c. a alg.; passar alg. c. para as mãos d'alg.; um Geld ~, jogar por dinheiro; das Stück spielt in Berlin, a scena passa-se em Berlim; er läßt nicht mit s. ~, não é para brincadeiras; não dá o seu braço a torcer; etw. ~b überwinden, vencér uma difficuldade com facilidade.

Textbeispiel 318.2: Wörterbuchartikel (aus: Michaelis 1920, 564/565)

spielen a) *intr* jogar 57; *Kinder* brincar 41; *Handlung* passar-se 1, desenrolar-se 4; falsch ~ fazer 72 batota; um Geld ~ jogar a dinheiro; diese Farbe spielt ins Blaue esta cor atira para o azul b) *tr Karten, Schach* jogar; *Instrument* tocar 56; *Theat Rolle* desempenhar 3, representar; die große Dame ~ armar 1 em grande senhora; den Dummen ~ fazer-se passar por lorpa, fingir-se 48; jmdm. einen Streich ~ pregar 54 uma partida a alg.; eine traurige Rolle ~ fazer triste figura

Textbeispiel 318.3: Wörterbuchartikel (aus: Klare 1984, 381)

sp·ielen, *v. i./v. t.* jogar; *(Kinder)* brincar; *(mús.)* tocar; *(teat.)* representar, desempenhar; *eine Rolle* —, *(teat.)* fazer (representar) um papel; ser importante; *(fig.)* salientar-se; *eine traurige Rolle*—, fazer triste figura; *(Handlung)* passar-se; desenrolar-se; *keine Rolle* —, não ter importância; *einen Streich* —, pregar uma partida; *(mús.) vom Blatt* —, tocar à primeira vista; *nach Noten* —, tocar por música; *falsch* —, fazer batota, batotar; *(mús.) desafinar; den Kranken* —, fingir-se doente; *den Dummen* —, fazer-se tolo; *er läßt nicht mit sich* —, ele não é para brincadeiras.

Textbeispiel 318.4: Wörterbuchartikel (aus: Dicionários Editora 1986, 841)

1986 sowie Beau 1969 und Irmen 1982. Tochtrop 1984 bringt hier die wenigsten Angaben. (k) Überraschend gut schneidet das — zum Vergleich noch zusätzlich herangezogene — ältere Wörterbuch von Michaelis 1920 bei der Berücksichtigung der Präfixverben ab, während die modernen Wörterbücher ziemlich gleichmäßige Ergebnisse aufweisen. Besondere Beachtung verdient jedoch Tochtrop 1984, da er beim Lemma eines Grundverbs jeweils mehrere Präfixverben zusammenstellt. (l) Die meisten Modifikationsformen (Diminutiv- und Augmentativbildungen) verzeichnen die Wörterbücher DE 1983 und 1986, wobei auch Michaelis 1920 sehr gut abschneidet. Beau 1969 und Irmen 1982 klammern dagegen solche Bildungen bewußt, aber nicht immer konsequent, aus. Nach dem hier Dargestellten dürfte es schwierig sein, einer Linie eindeutig den Vorzug zu geben. Vermutlich wird jede nationale Linie in ihrem jeweiligen Land die meisten Verehrer haben.

6. Einfluß der modernen Sprachwissenschaft auf die zweisprachige Lexikographie mit Portugiesisch

Da zweisprachige Wörterbücher des Sprachenpaares Portugiesisch/Deutsch zumeist entsprechende Bearbeitungen von Wörterbüchern anderer Sprachenpaare darstellen, ist es nicht weiter verwunderlich, daß die moderne Sprachwissenschaft zumeist nur indirekt und mit beträchtlicher zeitlicher Verzögerung auf die zweisprachige Lexikographie mit Portugiesisch einwirkt. Hierher gehört etwa der *Grund- und Aufbauwortschatz Portugiesisch* (Armorim-Braun 1972), der nach nicht näher erläuterten Frequenzkriterien 2000 Wörter des Grundwortschatzes in alphabetischer Reihenfolge und 2500 — nach Sachgruppen geordnete — Wörter des Aufbauwortschatzes bringt. Daneben erschienen einige Beiträge, die auf die Notwendigkeit der Semanalyse hinweisen (Ettinger 1981), ein Modell für die Einbeziehung der Modifikationsformen vorschlagen (Ettinger 1984 — konzipiert zwar für einsprachige Wörterbücher, aber auch auf zweisprachige Wörterbücher ausdehnbar) oder für eine linguistisch abgesicherte Darstellung der deutschen Präfixverben plädieren (Ettinger 1985). Eine nachahmenswerte Neuerung findet sich bei Klare 1984 bereits im Wörterbuch verwirklicht. Für Ausdrücke, die nur im soziokulturellen Kontext der deutschen Sprachgemeinschaft verwendet werden, bringt er einen — jeweils durch die Abkürzung ÜV gekennzeichneten — „Übersetzungsvorschlag" (Typ: *Geländespiel* = jogos de esconder e agarrar e de orientação pela bússola e pelo mapa (no campo)). Der potentielle Benutzer kann diese paraphrasierende Übersetzung verwenden, er kann aber auch — auf die fehlende Äquivalenz hingewiesen — eine selbständige Paraphrasierung versuchen. Einfluß der modernen Linguistik verrät eine Sammlung portugiesischer Verbalperiphrasen (Schemann/Schemann-Dias 1983), die als Lehr- und Übungsbuch konzipiert ebenso als selektives Teilwörterbuch benützt werden kann. Diese im Portugiesischen häufig vorkommenden Verbalperiphrasen sind alphabetisch geordnet, sie werden anhand zahlreicher Beispielsätze mit jeweils vollständiger deutscher Übersetzung illustriert und ermöglichen somit dem Benutzer eine genauere Verwendungsmöglichkeit als die knappen, isolierten und zuweilen irreführenden Angaben der traditionellen Wörterbücher. Besondere Beachtung verdient ein portugiesisch-deutsches idiomatisches Wörterbuch (Schemann/Schemann-Dias 1979). Es ist allein schon vom Umfang her (859 Seiten!) „monumental!" (Hausmann 1985, 383) und somit auch von der Beispielfülle her (ca. 8000 Idioms) beeindruckend. Anerkennen muß man aber vor allem die Sorgfalt der Autoren bei der Erarbeitung des gewaltigen Beispielmaterials (Überprüfung aller Beispiele durch native speakers zwecks Unterscheidung portugiesischer und brasilianischer Varianten und zur stilistischen Einordnung) sowie bei den Angaben zum Gebrauch der Redewendungen (z. B. besondere Kennzeichnung, wenn ein Idiom von einer Geste begleitet wird). Die idiomatischen Ausdrücke sind jeweils in einen Kontext eingebettet, und diese Beispielsätze — ergänzt durch zahlreiche syntaktische und grammatikalische Angaben — erleichtern das Verständnis und ermöglichen ihren richtigen Gebrauch. Nach dem Urteil zahlreicher positiver Rezensionen handelt es sich hier um eine Pionierleistung der portugiesischen Lexikographie, die vorbildhaft auch für andere Sprachen werden könnte.

7. Fachsprachliche Wörterbücher

Im Bereich der fachsprachlichen Lexikographie, die auch für das Portugiesische schon schwer überschaubar geworden ist, lassen sich — wiederum mit den üblichen Verallgemeinerungen — drei Feststellungen treffen:

(a) Ähnlich wie bei den allgemeinen Wörterbüchern erscheinen fachsprachliche Wörterbücher für das Sprachenpaar Portugiesisch/Deutsch mit beträchtlicher Verzögerung zu anderen Sprachen und können daher weder von der Konzeption noch von dem inzwischen teilweise veralteten Inhalt her lexikographische Originalität beanspruchen. So erschien Ernst 1948/1951 für das Sprachenpaar Deutsch/Englisch, 1963/1967 erst für Deutsch-Portugiesisch, und Závada/Eberle 1978 geht letztlich auf Závada 1965 zurück.

(b) Da aber andererseits die allgemeinsprachlichen Wörterbücher des Sprachenpaares Portugiesisch/Deutsch nur vereinzelt über das Format von Taschenwörterbüchern hinausgehen, füllen diese Fachwörterbücher selbst in bescheidener Aufmachung nicht nur eine schmerzlich empfundene Lücke, sondern sie stellen jeweils für ein Teilgebiet sogar die besseren Wörterbücher dar (Kick/Ehlers 1981 und 1982). Für die insgesamt mehr als 200 Millionen lusophoner und germanophoner Sprecher zeichnet sich hier eine erstaunliche Entwicklung ab. Die für den Wirtschaftsaustausch notwendigen Bereiche (Handel, Verkehr, Technik usw.) verfügen entsprechend den wachsenden Wirtschaftsbeziehungen der vergangenen 20 Jahre inzwischen über recht gute Wörterbücher, während die Publikation der allgemeinsprachlichen Wörterbücher hier nicht Schritt halten konnte. So enthält Ernst 1963 ca. 70 000 Stichwörter, Dora/Wein 1985 allein 15 000 Fachtermini und Pabst 1971 jeweils ca. 24 000 Einträge pro Sprachrichtung, während die allgemeinsprachlichen Wörterbücher etwa von Klare 1984 und 1986 lediglich ca. 40 000 Wörter aufweisen.

(c) Daß Portugiesisch für die fachsprachliche Lexikographie zunehmend an Bedeutung gewinnt, zeigt sich in seiner immer stärkeren Einbeziehung in mehrsprachige Fachwörterbücher (z. B. Vollnhals 1984). Eine Bibliographie (*Mehrsprachige Fachwörterbücher* 1983) umfaßt insgesamt 42 Titel, wobei die Fachwörterbücher der Gesellschaftswissenschaften mit 15 Beispielen vertreten sind.

8. Ausblick — Noch ist Portugal nicht verloren

Daß im Bereich der zweisprachigen Lexikographie mit Portugiesisch noch manche Lücke zu schließen wäre, kann nach den bisherigen Darstellungen wohl kaum als abgegriffener Allgemeinplatz abgetan werden. Vordringlichste Aufgabe wäre es, für die größeren europäischen Sprachen zweisprachige Wörterbücher mit jeweils ca. 80 000 bis 100 000 Einheiten pro Sprachrichtung zu erstellen. Darüber hinaus könnte sich die zweisprachige Lexikographie mit Portugiesisch beachtliche Meriten erwerben, wenn sie lexikographische Neuerungen anderer Sprachenpaare übernähme oder sogar selbst innovatorisch werden könnte, wie es etwa Schemann/Schemann-Dias 1983 im Bereich der Verbalperiphrasen gezeigt hat. Denkbar wären hier etwa Wörterbücher zu Teilbereichen des Wortschatzes, wie etwa zu den Adverbien, Präfixverben, Modifikationsformen oder auch Wörterbücher, die bewußt als Übersetzungswörterbücher konzipiert werden. Notwendig wäre auch eine stärkere diatopische Differenzierung, die letztlich zu einem eigenen Wörterbuch der Brasilianismen führen sollte. Im Bereich der fachsprachlichen Wörterbücher müßte konsequent die neueste technische Entwicklung lexikographisch verarbeitet werden und auch hier wären lexikographische Neuerungen, wie etwa ein Fügungswörterbuch, wünschenswert.

9. Literatur (in Auswahl)

9.1. Wörterbücher

A. J. 1701 = A. J.: A Compleat Account of the Portugueze Language. Being a Copious Dictionary of English with Portugueze and Portugueze with English together with an Easie and Unerring Method of its Pronunciation, by a distinguishing Accent, and a Compendium of all the necessary Rules of Construction and Orthography digested into a Grammatical form. London 1701 [522 S.].

Alewijn/Collé 1714 = Abraham Alewijn/Johannes Collé: Tesouro dos vocabulos das duas linguas Portugueze e Belgica. Woordenschat der twee taalen, Portugeesch en Nederduitsch. Amsterdam 1714 [XIV, 933 S.].

Amorim-Braun 1972 = Maria Luisa Amorim-Braun: Grund- und Aufbauwortschatz Portugiesisch. Stuttgart 1972 [207 S.].

Azevedo 1887 = Domingos de Azevedo: Grande Dicionário Francês-Português. Revista e actualizada por J.-J. Duthoy/J. Rousé. 4. Aufl. Lissabon 1952 [XV, 1489 S.; 1. Aufl. 1887].

Azevedo 1889 = Domingos de Azevedo: Grande Dicionário Português-Francês. Revista e actualizada por E. Cardoso/J. Rousé. 4. Aufl. Lissabon 1953 [1432 S.; 1. Aufl. 1889. Der Neudruck des Jahres 1980 enthält im Titelblatt die Angabe 6.ª edição].

Beau 1953 = Albin Eduard Beau: Langenscheidts Taschenwörterbuch der portugiesischen und deutschen Sprache. Zweiter Teil Deutsch-Portugiesisch. 1. Aufl. Berlin 1953 [XX, 545 S.].

Beau 1969 = Albin Eduard Beau: Langenscheidts Taschenwörterbuch der portugiesischen und deutschen Sprache. Zweiter Teil Deutsch-Portugiesisch. 1. Aufl. Berlin 1969 [641−1246 S.].

Bösche 1858 = Eduard Theodor Bösche: Neues vollständiges Taschenwörterbuch der portugiesischen und deutschen Sprache. Mit besonderer Rücksicht auf Wissenschaften, Künste, Industrie, Handel, Schifffahrt(!) etc. Erster Theil Portugiesisch−Deutsch. 4. Aufl. Hamburg 1888 [682 S.; 1. Aufl. 1858] Zweiter Theil Deutsch-Portugiesisch. 4. Aufl. Hamburg 1888 [644 S.; 1. Aufl. 1858].

Bösche 1897 = Eduard Theodor Bösche: Neues vollständiges Taschenwörterbuch der portugiesischen und deutschen Sprache. Mit besonderer Rücksicht auf Wissenschaften, Künste, Industrie, Handel, Schifffahrt(!) und die Umgangssprache. Erster Theil Portugiesisch-Deutsch. 6. Aufl. vollständig umgearbeitet und stark vermehrt von A. Dammann. Leipzig 1897 [784 S.] Zweiter Theil Deutsch-Portugiesisch. 6. Aufl. vollständig umgearbeitet und stark vermehrt von A. Dammann. Leipzig 1897 [740 S.].

Bordo 1853/1854 = Antonio Bordo: Diccionnario italiano-portuguez e portuguez-italiano. Zwei Bände. Rio de Janeiro 1853/1854.

Canto e Castro Mascarenhas Valdez 1864/1866 = Manuel do Canto e Castro Mascarenhas Valdez: Diccionario español-portugués, el primero que se ha publicado con las vozes, frases, refranes y lucuciones(!) usadas en España y Americas españolas, en el lenguaje comun antiguo y moderno [...]. Lissabon 1864/1866.

Cardoso 1562 = Jerónimo Cardoso: Dictionarium iuuentuti studiosae admodum frugiferum nunc diligentiori emendatione impressum. Coimbra 1562.

Cardoso 1562/1563 = Jerónimo Cardoso: Dictionarium ex lusitanico in latinum sermonem. Lissabon 1562/1563.

Cardoso 1569/1570 = Jerónimo Cardoso: Dictionarium latino-lusitanicum et vice versa lusitanicolatinum, cum adagiorum ferè omnium iuxta seriem alphabeticam perutili expositione [...]. Coimbra 1569/1570.

Chamberlain/Harmon 1983 = Bobby J. Chamberlain/Ronald M. Harmon: A Dictionary of Informal Brazilian Portuguese, with an English Index. Washington 1983 [XIX, 701 S.].

Costa e Sá 1794 = Joaquim José da Costa e Sá: Diccionario portuguez−francez e latino. Novamente compilado. Lisboa 1794 [555 S.].

Costa e Sá 1811 = Joaquim José da Costa e Sá: Dictionnaire françois-portugais. [...]. 2. Aufl. Paris 1811.

Dicionários 'Académicos' 1976/1978: Dicionário de português-alemão. Porto 1978 [576 S.] Dicionário alemão-português. Porto 1976 [767 S.].

DE = Dicionários 'Editora' 1983/1986: Dicionario de português-alemão. 1. Aufl. Porto 1983 [1069 S.] Dicionário de alemão-português. 1. Aufl. Porto 1986 [1088 S.].

Dora/Wein 1985 = Helmut Dora/Volker Wein: Ökonomisches Wörterbuch Deutsch-Portugiesisch. Berlin 1985 [207 S.].

Ernst 1948/1951 = Richard Ernst: German-English, English-German technical dictionary; a representation of the vocabulary of industrial technics including related fields of science and engineering. Hamburg 1948/1951.

Ernst 1963 = Richard Ernst: Wörterbuch der industriellen Technik einschließlich Hilfswissenschaften und Bauwesen. Band VII Deutsch-Portugiesisch, bearbeitet von Rolf R. Römer. Wiesbaden 1963 [955 S.].

Ernst 1967 = Richard Ernst: Wörterbuch der industriellen Technik einschließlich Hilfswissenschaften und Bauwesen, Band VIII Portugiesisch-Deutsch, bearbeitet von Rolf R. Römer. Wiesbaden 1967 [587 S.].

Ernst 1983/1986 = Richard Ernst: Wörterbuch der industriellen Technik unter weitgehender Berücksichtigung der neuzeitlichen Techniken und Verfahren. Band VII: Deutsch-Portugiesisch. Band VIII: Portugiesisch-Deutsch. Völlig neu bearbeitet von Franciso José Lǔdovice Moreira. 2. Aufl. Wiesbaden 1983/1986 [419, 355 S.!].

Estêves Sobrinho 1970 = Alfredo Estêves Sobrinho: Dicionário de expressões idiomáticas inglês-português. Rio de Janeiro 1970 [147 S.].

Ey 1904 = Louise Ey: Langenscheidts Taschenwörterbuch der portugiesischen und deutschen Sprache. Zweiter Teil Deutsch-Portugiesisch. 12. Aufl. Berlin 1935 [1. Aufl. 1904, XVI, 456 S.].

Ey 1909 = Louise Ey: Langenscheidts Taschenwörterbuch der portugiesischen und deutschen Sprache. Erster Teil Portugiesisch-Deutsch. 13. Aufl. Berlin 1935 [1. Aufl. 1909].

Fernandes Valdez 1875 = João Fernandes Valdez: A Portuguese and English pronouncing dictionary, newly composed from the best dictionaries of both languages [...]. Rio de Janeiro. Paris 1875 [851 S.].

Folqman 1742 = Carlos Folqman: Portugeese en Nederduitse Spraakkonst, met eene wydloopige naam-noeminge [...] t'zamenspraaken, en eene verzameling de uitgeleezenste spreekwoorden van beide talen. Lissabon 1742.

Fonseca 1850 = José da Fonseca: Dictionnaire français-portugais et portugais—français. Diccionario portuguez—francez e francez-portuguez [...]. Zwei Bände. 4. Aufl. Paris 1850.

Gutman 1909 = I. Gutman: Portugal'sko—russkij i russko-portugal'skij slovar', soderžaščij bolee 2000 slov, najbolee upotrebitel'nych v ežednevnoj žizni. Riga 1909 [111 S.].

Hampl 1964 = Zdeněk Hampl: Portugalsko-český a česko—portugalský kapesní slovník. Dicionário de bolso português-checo e checo-português. Prag 1964 [666 S.].

Hampl 1975 = Zdeněk Hampl: Portugalsko-český slovník. Dicionário português-checo. Prag 1975 [883 S.].

Hampl/Holšan 1976 = Zdeněk Hampl/Jiří Holšan: Portugalsko-český a česko-portugalský kapesní slovnik. Dicionário de bolso português-checo e checo-português. Prag 1976 [497 S.].

Houaiss/Avery 1964 = Antônio Houaiss/Catherine B. Avery: The New Appleton dictionary of the English and Portuguese languages. Zwei Bände. New York 1967 [XX, 636 S. und XX, 666 S.; 1. Aufl. 1964].

Irmen 1954 = Friedrich Irmen: Langenscheidts Taschenwörterbuch der portugiesischen und deutschen Sprache. Erster Teil Portugiesisch-Deutsch. 1. Aufl. Berlin 1954 [XXIV, 582 S.].

Irmen 1982 = Friedrich Irmen: Langenscheidts Taschenwörterbuch der portugiesischen und deutschen Sprache. Erster Teil Portugiesisch-Deutsch. 1. Aufl. Berlin 1982. Neubearbeitung der Auflage von 1968 [640 S.].

Jayme/Neuss 1990 = Erik Jayme/Jobst-Joachim Neuss: Wörterbuch der Rechts- und Wirtschaftssprache. Teil 1: Portugiesisch-Deutsch. Teil 2: Deutsch-Portugiesisch. München 1990.

Kick/Ehlers 1981 = Edel Helga Kick Ehlers/Gunter Ehlers: Dicionário alemão-português de economia e direito. Deutsch-portugiesisches Wörterbuch für Wirtschaft und Recht. São Paulo 1981 [424 S.].

Kick/Ehlers 1982 = Edel Helga Kick Ehlers/Gunter Ehlers: Dicionário português-alemão de economia e direito. Portugiesisch-deutsches Wörterbuch für Wirtschaft und Recht. São Paulo 1982 [505 S.].

Király 1978 = Rudolf Király: Portugál-magyar szótár. Dicionário português-húngaro. Budapest 1978 [728 S.].

Klare 1984 = Johannes Klare: Wörterbuch Deutsch—Portugiesisch. Leipzig 1984 [551 S.].

Klare 1986 = Johannes Klare: Wörterbuch Portugiesisch—Deutsch. Leipzig 1986 [606 S.].

Magalhães 1964 = Raymundo Magalhães: Dicionário de coloquialismos anglo-americanos: provérbios, idiotismos e frases feitas. A dictionary of Anglo-American colloquialisms: proverbs, idioms and clichés. Rio de Janeiro 1964 [240 S.].

Marques 1897 = Henrique Marques: Novo diccionario hespanhol-portuguez; contendo todos os vocabulos, phrases e locuções usados não só em Hespanha, mas ainda em toda a America hespanhola [...]. Lissabon 1897.

Marques 1758 = Joseph Marques: Nouveau dictionnaire des langues françoise et portugaise. 2. Aufl. Lissabon 1758.

Marques 1764 = Joseph Marques: Novo diccionario das linguas portugueza e franceza. Lissabon 1764 [763 S.].

Mascherpe 1968 = Mário Mascherpe: A tradução do inglês para o português; os falsos cognatos. São Paulo 1968 [100 S.].

Meister/Pereira Laus 1963 = Werner Meister/ Esaú Pereira Laus: Taschenwörterbuch Deutsch—Portugiesisch. 4. Aufl. Leipzig 1981 [312 S.; 1. Aufl. 1963].

Meister/Pereira Laus 1965 = Werner Meister/ Esaú Pereira Laus: Taschenwörterbuch Portugiesisch-Deutsch. 4. Aufl. Leipzig 1982 [380 S.; 1. Aufl. 1965].

Michaelis 1887 = Henriette Michaelis: Neues Wörterbuch der portugiesischen und deutschen Sprache mit besonderer Berücksichtigung der technischen Ausdrücke des Handels und der Industrie, der Wissenschaften und Künste und der Umgangssprache. Erster Teil Portugiesisch-Deutsch. 12. Aufl. Leipzig 1920 [737 S.; 1. Aufl. 1887]. Zweiter Teil Deutsch-Portugiesisch. 12. Aufl. Leipzig 1920 [767 S.; 1. Aufl. 1887].

Monso 1900 = Isidro Monso: Novo diccionario portuguez-hespanhol; contendo todos os vocabulos, phrases e locuções usados não só em Portugal, como no Brazil, colonias portuguezas da Africa e Asia [...]. Lissabon 1900 [1277 S.].

Nemnich 1799 = Philip Andrew Nemnich: The Universal European Dictionary of Merchandise, in the English, German, Dutch, Danish, French, Italian, Spanish, Portuguese, Russian, Polish and Latin Languages. London 1799.

Newman 1799 = Henry Newman: A Marine Pocket Dictionary of the Italian, Spanish, Portuguese, and German Languages [...] being a Collection of [...] the most useful Sea Terms in the above Idioms. London 1799.

Novo Michaelis 1958 = Novo Michaelis. Dicionário Ilustrado. Volume I Inglês-Português. Amplo vocabulário moderno. Frases idiomáticas. Grande número de pranchas com mais de 4000 referências [...]. 2. Aufl. São Paulo. Wiesbaden o. J. [XXXII, 1123 S.; 1. Aufl. 1958].

Novo Michaelis 1961 = Novo Michaelis. Dicionário ilustrado. Volume II Português-inglês. Amplo vocabulário moderno. Frases idiomáticas. Grande número de pranchas com mais de 4000 referências. 2. Aufl. São Paulo. Wiesbaden o. J. [LI, 1320 S.; 1. Aufl. 1961] (Ebenfalls englischer Titel auf der Rückseite des Einbandes: Brockhaus Picture Dictionary).

Pabst 1971 = Martin Pabst: Technologisches Wörterbuch Portugiesisch. Deutsch-Portugiesisch. Portugiesisch-Deutsch. Essen 1971 [550 S.].

Roquette 1841 = José Ignacio Roquette: Nouveau dictionnaire portugais-français composé sur les plus récents et les meilleurs dictionnaires des deux langues [...]. Paris 1841 [XVI, 1238 S.].

Schemann/Schemann-Dias 1979 = Hans Schemann/Luiza Schemann-Dias: Dicionário idiomático português-alemão. Portugiesisch-deutsche Idiomatik. As expressões idiomáticas portuguesas, o seu uso no Brasil e os seus equivalentes alemães. Die portugiesischen Idioms, ihr Gebrauch in Brasilien und ihre Entsprechungen im Deutschen. München 1979 [XLVII, 859 S.].

Schemann/Schemann-Dias 1983 = Hans Schemann/Luiza Schemann-Dias: Die portugiesischen Verbalperiphrasen und ihre deutschen Entsprechungen. Lehr- und Übungsbuch mit ausführlichen portugiesischen Beispielen und ihren deutschen Übersetzungen. Tübingen 1983.

Serpa 1972 = Oswaldo Serpa: Dicionário de expressões idiomáticas, inglês-português português-inglês. Rio de Janeiro 1972 [303 S.].

Solano Constancio 1820 = Francisco Solano Constancio: Novo Diccionario portatil das linguas portugueza e franceza. 2. Aufl. Paris 1820 [XXXII, 484 S.].

Solano Constancio 1828 = Francisco Solano Constancio: Nouveau Dictionnaire portatif des langues française et portugaise. Français-Portugais. Portuguez-francez. Zwei Bände. 3. Aufl. Paris 1828 [Weitere Auflagen bis 1887].

Spinelli/Casasanta 1983/1985 = Vincenzo Spinelli/Mario Casasanta: Dizionario completo. Italiano-Portoghese (Brasiliano) e Portoghese (Brasiliano)-Italiano con l'etimologia delle voci italiane e portoghesi (brasiliane) la loro esatta traduzione frasi e modi di dire. Erster Teil. Italiano-Portoghese (Brasiliano). Mailand 1983 [XXI, 895 S.]. Zweiter Teil. Portoghese (Brasiliano)-Italiano. Mailand 1985 [IX, 1035 S.].

Starec/Feerštejn 1961 = S. M. Starec/E. N. Feerštejn: Portugal'sko-russkij slovar'. 2. Aufl. Moskau 1972 [936 S.; 1. Aufl. 1961].

Taylor 1958 = James Lumpkin Taylor: A Portuguese-English dictionary. Stanford 1958 [XX, 655 S.].

Tochtrop 1943 = Leonardo Tochtrop: Dicionário alemão-português. 6. Aufl. Rio de Janeiro 1984 [LI, 686 S.; 1. Aufl. 1943, 672 S.].

Verdeyen 1926 = R. Verdeyen: Colloquia et dictionariolum septem linguarum. Antwerpen. 's Gravenhage 1926.

Vieyra 1773 = Antonio Vieyra: A dictionary of the Portuguese and English languages in two parts. Portuguese and English. English and Portuguese [...]. London 1773.

Vieyra 1840 = Antonio Vieyra: A dictionary of the Portuguese and English languages in two parts. Portuguese and English. English and Portuguese. A new ed., carefully cor., and very considerably improved, by A. J. da Cunha, with the Portuguese words properly accented to facilitate the pronunciation to learners [...]. London 1840.

Voinova/Starets/Verkhucha/Zditovetski 1975 = N. Voinova/S. Starets/V. Verkhucha/A. Zditovetski: Dicionário russo-português. Compreende cerca de 47000 palavras [...]. Moskau 1975 [922 S.].

Vollnhals 1984 = Otto Vollnhals: Elsevier's dictionary of personal and office computing. English - German - French - Italian - Portuguese. Amsterdam 1984 [504 S.].

Wagener 1811 = Johann Daniel Wagener: Novo diccionário protuguez-alemão e alemão-portuguez. Diccionário portuguez-alemão que contem muitas voces importantísimas, que não se achão nos diccionários até agóra publicados. Leipzig 1811.

Wagener 1812 = Johann Daniel Wagener: Neues Portugiesisch-Deutsches und Deutsch-Portugiesisches Lexikon. Erster Theil A bis J welcher das Deutsch-Portugiesische enthält. Leipzig 1812 [783 S.]. Zweyter Theil K—Z und Nachtrag welcher das Deutsch-Portugiesische enthält. Leipzig 1812 [704 S.].

Wollheim da Fonseca 1844 = Anton Edmund Wollheim da Fonseca: Diccionario portatil das linguas portugueza e alleman. 2 Bände. 2. Aufl. Leipzig 1856 [1. Aufl. 1844].

Závada 1965 = Dušan Závada: Česko-německý slovník obchodní korrespondence. Tschechisch-deutsches Wörterbuch der Handelskorrespondenz. Prag 1965 [485 S.].

Závada/Eberle 1978 = Dušan Závada/Krista H. Eberle: Satzlexikon der Handelskorrespondenz. Dicionário fraseológico comercial. Deutsch-Portugiesisch. Wiesbaden 1978 [XXIV, 435 S.].

Zdanowski 1905/1912 = Feliks Bernard Zdanowski: Słownik portugalsko-polski i polsko-portugalski podług najnowszych źródeł opracowany. Zwei Bände. Krakau 1905/1912 [468 S.; 280 S.].

9.2. Sonstige Literatur

Aav 1977 = Yrjö Aav: Russian Dictionaries. Dictionaries and Glossaries printed in Russia 1627—1917. Zug 1977 (Biblioteca Slavica 10).

Carvalhão Buescu 1983 = Maria Leonor Carvalhão Buescu: O estudo das línguas exóticas no século XVI. Lisboa 1983 (Biblioteca Breve 71).

Claes 1974 = Frans M. Claes: Lijst van Nederlandse woordenlijsten en woordenboeken gedrukt tot 1600. Nieuwkoop 1974.

Claes 1977 = Franz M. Claes: Bibliographisches Verzeichnis der deutschen Vokabulare und Wörterbücher, gedruckt bis 1600. Hildesheim. New York 1977.

Claes 1980 = Frans M. Claes (Comp.): A Bibliography of Netherlandic (Dutch, Flemish) Dictionaries. München 1980 [XVI, 314 S.].

Mehrsprachige Fachwörterbücher 1983 = Deutsche Staatsbibliothek. Bibliographische Mitteilungen. Band 28: Mehrsprachige Fachwörterbücher. Bestandsverzeichnis, Teil 1 Naturwissenschaften, Technik, Land- und Forstwirtschaft, Medizin. Berichtszeit 1960—1972, Nachtrag 1973—1980. Berlin 1983 [261 S.]. Teil 2 Gesellschaftswissenschaften. Berichtszeit 1956—1974, Nachtrag 1975—1980. Berlin 1983 [110 S.].

Ettinger 1981 = Stefan Ettinger: El análisis de componentes y la enseñza del portugués. Estudio de semántica estructural. In: Revista Portuguesa de Filologia 18. 1981, 97—115.

Ettinger 1984 = Stefan Ettinger: Die Modifikation in der Lexikographie. In: Theoretische und praktische Probleme der Lexikographie. 1. Augsburger Kolloquium. Hrsg. D. Götz/Th. Herbst. München 1984, 63—106.

Ettinger 1985 = Stefan Ettinger: Zur Problematik der Übersetzung deutscher Präfixverben ins Portugiesische. Ein Beitrag zur Integration der Wortbildung in der Lexikographie. 1985 (im Manuskript).

Ettinger 1987 = Stefan Ettinger: Einige ‚apontamentos' zur modernen zweisprachigen Lexikographie Deutsch—Portugiesich und Portugiesisch—Deutsch. In: Vox Romanica 46. 1987, 180—247.

Gold 1973 = David L. Gold: Raising the Standards of Portuguese-English Bilingual Lexicography. A Plea. In: Babel 19. 1973, 25—30.

Grzegorczyk 1967 = Piotr Grzegorczyk: Index lexicorum Poloniae. Bibliografia słowników polskich. Warschau 1967.

Hausmann 1985 = Franz Josef Hausmann: Lexikographie. In: Handbuch der Lexikographie. Hrsg. Chr. Schwarze/D. Wunderlich. Königstein/Ts. 1985, 367—411.

Labarre 1975 = Albert Labarre: Bibliographie du Dictionarium d'Ambrogio Calepino (1502—1779). Baden-Baden 1975 (Bibliotheca Bibliographica Aureliana 26).

Lewanski 1973 = Richard C. Lewanski: A Bibliography of Slavic Dictionaries. Band 1—4. 2. Aufl. Bologna 1973.

Lopes 1936/1969 = David Lopes: A expansão da língua portuguesa no oriente durante os séculos XVI, XVII e XVIII. 2.ª edição revista, prefaciada e anotada por Luís de Matos. Porto 1969.

Streit 1916—1931 = Robert Streit O.M.I.: Bibliotheca Missionum. Münster 1916—1931. Bd. 1—7 [reprographischer Nachdruck Darmstadt 1963—1969].

Teyssier 1980 = Paul Teyssier: Jerónimo Cardoso et les origines de la lexicographie portugaise. In: Bulletin des Etudes Portugaises et Brésiliennes 41. 1980, 7—32.

Teyssier 1985 = Paul Teyssier: Une source pour l'histoire du vocabulaire portugais: Les dictionnaries de Jerónimo Cardoso (1562, 1562—1563, 1569—1570). In: XVI Congrés Internacional de Lingüística i Filologia Romàniques. Actes. Tom II. Palma de Mallorca 1985, 245—256.

Valkhoff 1975 = Marius F. Valkhoff: Miscelânea Luso-Africana. Colectânea de estudos coligidos. Lisboa 1975.

Vermeer 1969 = Hans J. Vermeer: Das Portugiesische in Südasien. In: Aufsätze zur portugiesischen Kulturgeschichte 9. 1969, 136—226.

Walford/Screen 1977 = A. J. Walford/J. E. O. Screen: A Guide to Foreign Language Courses and Dictionaries. Third edition, revised and enlarged. Westport 1977.

Stefan Ettinger, Augsburg
(Bundesrepublik Deutschland)

319. Die zweisprachige lateinische Lexikographie seit ca. 1700

1. Lexika vor Scheller
2. Von Scheller zu Georges
3. Jüngste Unternehmungen
4. Literatur (in Auswahl)

1. Lexika vor Scheller

In der neueren Geschichte der zweisprachigen lateinischen (d. h. hier: lateinisch-muttersprachlichen) Lexika ist Immanuel Johann Gerhard Scheller (1735—1803), der langjährige Gymnasialrektor im schlesischen Brieg, die vergessene Zentralgestalt. — Die zahlreichen Lexika vor ihm — zu einem erheblichen Teil Bearbeitungen von Werken der beiden vorangegangenen Jahrhunderte — wenden sich an Benutzer (Schüler), für die Latein weniger Fremdsprache (geschweige denn „tote" Sprache) als zweite Verkehrssprache war. Dementsprechend haben sie fast alle, vom großen Faber (1571) bis zum simplen Elementarbuch des Cellarius (1689), lateinische Titel, sind ihre Vorreden fast ausnahmslos lateinisch, und erfolgen auch die sprachlichen und sachlichen Erläuterungen innerhalb der einzelnen Artikel vielfach in lateinischer Sprache. Wichtiger aber als diese Gemeinsamkeit im Äußerlichen ist die ebenfalls aus dieser ganz anderen Rolle des Lateinischen resultierende Gemeinsamkeit des Ziels: alle diese Lexika — die früheren mehr, die späteren weniger — sind nicht nur (z. T. nicht einmal in erster Linie) als Hilfsmittel zum besseren Verständnis lateinischer Texte konzipiert, sondern wollen und sollen auch (bzw. vor allem) die aktive Sprachbeherrschung fördern. Wer meint, so Faber (1571) in der Vorrede, dieses Werk sei dazu da, erst dann aufgeschlagen zu werden, wenn man die Bedeutung eines lateinischen Wortes nicht wisse, der sei völlig auf dem Holzwege; vielmehr müßten Lehrende wie Lernende, so fordert er (und andere Lexikographen nach ihm), gestützt auf Autoritäten wie Hieronymus Wolf, den Folianten immer wieder vom Anfang bis zum Ende mit größter Sorgfalt durchlesen! Diese uns so fremde Zielsetzung beeinflußt die Lexikongestaltung vor allem in folgenden Punkten:

(a) Wenn das Lexikon mit Gewinn durchgelesen, ja zum Vokabellernen herangezogen werden soll, ist eine streng alphabetische Anordnung aller berücksichtigten lateinischen Wörter nicht unbedingt ideal, vielmehr empfiehlt es sich unter diesem Gesichtspunkt, lediglich die nichtzusammengesetzten und nichtabgeleiteten Wörter alphabetisch zu reihen und ihnen dann jeweils Komposita und Ableitungen unterzuordnen. Dieser ordo mnemonicus (so Dentzler 1666, Praefatio), den vor allem die früheren Lexika favorisiert haben (u. a. Faber 1571, Cellarius 1689, Weismann 1725), bedingt allerdings, soll das Lexikon auch noch zum Nachschlagen taugen, zahlreiche Verweise (wer sucht schon **reconditus** sofort unter **dare**), evtl. sogar zusätzlich einen eigenen Index schwer zu findender Wörter (so Dentzler 1666, Cellarius 1689) — kein Wunder also, daß Kirsch (1714), Bayer (1724) und Hederich (1739) ganz auf das Alphabet setzen.

(b) Sprichwörter und dgl., womit man sein Latein wirkungsvoll aufputzen kann, spielen gerade in den älteren Lexika eine schier unglaublich große Rolle. Bei Faber (1571) geht das so weit, daß er reihenweise Zitate aus griechischen Autoren bringt, die zum Verständnis des lateinischen Wortes, bei dem sie gebracht werden, überhaupt nichts beitragen (so erscheint unter **color** eine Sentenz aus Stobaeus, Schamröte sei die schönste Farbe). So weit gehen die späteren Lexika nicht, doch erscheinen adagia, proverbia, usus proverbialis bei Bayer (1724), Dentzler (1666) und Weismann (1725) sogar im Titel, und umgekehrt hält es Kirsch (1714) für notwendig, in seiner Vorrede ausdrücklich zu begründen, warum er bei den proverbia Sparsamkeit habe walten lassen.

(c) Doch welches Latein soll der Benutzer des Lexikons schreiben und reden lernen?

Die humanistische Tradition legt dem Lexikographen die Beschränkung auf die klassischen Stilmuster nahe, die Realität dagegen fordert selbst die Einbeziehung des Gegenwartslateins, insbesondere der Sprache der verschiedenen Wissenschaftsdisziplinen. In der lexikographischen Praxis dominiert der Kompromiß (Puristen: Cellarius 1689, Weismann 1725): man berücksichtigt zwar auch unklassisches, insbes. modernes Latein (so vor allem Kirsch 1714, Bayer 1724 und Hederich 1739, der, zumindest was sein Autorenverzeichnis betrifft, auch das Mittelalter bei weitem am ausgiebigsten mit einbezieht), versucht aber, die verschiedenen Sprachstufen auseinanderzuhalten, indem man bei den einzelnen Wörtern und Ausdrücken entweder in großem Umfang die Quellenautoren angibt (so Faber 1571, Frisius 1750) oder den neueren Sprachgebrauch kennzeichnet (so Dentzler 1666, Bayer 1724; beide Möglichkeiten kombiniert Kirsch 1714). Den Bedürfnissen des um einen guten lateinischen Stil Bemühten war damit Genüge getan, einer genauen Angabe der Fundstellen bedurfte es dafür nicht — so unterblieb sie in der Regel.

(d) Vor allem aber hat die Ausrichtung auf die aktive Sprachbeherrschung bis gegen Ende des 18. Jhs. verhindert, daß das Hauptmanko aller frühen Lexika (vgl. Art. 180,3.) abgestellt wurde: die mangelnde Gliederung der einzelnen Artikel nach Bedeutungen. Wohl tauchen in den Vorreden gelegentlich Bemerkungen auf, die zeigen, daß das Problem natürlich nicht völlig übersehen worden ist (so Hederich 1739 über die Notwendigkeit, die ursprüngliche Bedeutung eines Wortes aufzuspüren). In der Praxis aber reihte man doch in erster Linie Ausdrücke, die man sich einprägen konnte; und wenn man tatsächlich Gruppen bildete und diese sogar noch bezifferte, so war das mehr ein Aufsetzen einer äußerlichen Ordnung als das Aufspüren eines in der Sache selbst liegenden Zusammenhangs und Beziehungsgeflechts: Gruppen werden in endloser Reihe präsentiert (bei Hederich 1739 ist **a/ab** in 27 durchgezählte Rubriken unterteilt), aber kaum je wird der Versuch gemacht, einzelne dieser Gruppen wieder zu größeren Einheiten zusammenzufassen und so zu einer sachlich gerechtfertigten und zugleich übersichtlichen Anordnung von Bedeutungen und Ausdrucksweisen zu kommen. Muster für die eigene Lateinpraxis zu bieten — dieses Ziel hatte eben einen allzugroßen Einfluß.

2. Von Scheller zu Georges

Scheller, ein Schüler Ernestis, verdankt seine besondere Rolle keiner auf einem genialen Einfall beruhenden umstürzenden Neuerung, sondern der konsequenten Fortführung, Verknüpfung und Verwirklichung von Tendenzen, Entwicklungen und Forderungen der vorangegangenen Jahrzehnte, wie sie sein großes Wörterbuch bietet (Scheller 1804; Ansätze schon bei Scheller 1780).

Von der Rücksicht auf das Latein als immer noch praktizierte Sprache ist hier kaum mehr etwas übriggeblieben: deutsch ist die „Verkehrssprache" des Lexikons, alphabetisch die Anordnung der Wörter, Sentenzen spielen keine Rolle mehr. Ziel des Wörterbuchs ist die „Erklärung der Alten" (s. Titel); deswegen beschränkt sich Scheller auf das Latein der Antike (das 8. Jh. n. Chr. mit Beda und Paulus Diaconus wird noch mit einbezogen), dieses Latein aber will er möglichst vollständig dokumentieren, und zwar sowohl was den Wortbestand als auch die Bedeutungen und den Gebrauch der einzelnen Wörter betrifft. Die einzelnen aus den antiken Autoren angeführten Belegstellen werden so genau bezeichnet, daß sie jeder Benutzer in der entsprechenden Textausgabe nachschlagen und kontrollieren kann; andererseits bemüht sich Scheller durch Anführung von Textvarianten und Erklärungsversuchen der Kommentare, ein solches Nachschlagen überflüssig zu machen (nach Scheller 1804, V ist bzw. soll ein Lexikon sein „eine Erklärung aller Autoren"). Zur Erklärung einer einzelnen Stelle gehört aber auch, daß man die gesamte Entwicklung eines Wortes überblickt; so legt Scheller größtes Gewicht darauf, die einzelnen sich aus den antiken Belegstellen ergebenden Bedeutungen eines Wortes in der Ordnung vorzuführen, die diese Entwicklung verständlich bzw. zumindest übersichtlich macht. Dieses mühselige Geschäft (Scheller 1804, XXI: „ich habe mit dieser Rangordnung allein ... oft bey einem einzigen Worte sechs bis acht Stunden zugebracht") konsequent betrieben zu haben, hat Scheller nicht zuletzt seinen hervorragenden Platz in der Geschichte der lateinischen Lexikographie verschafft. Es lohnt sich noch heute, sein großes Wörterbuch in schwierigen Fällen zu konsultieren.

Von Scheller und dem gut zehn Jahre älteren Forcellini (über ihn und die Frage, inwieweit Scheller selbst von Forcellini beeinflußt ist, Art. 180,3.) hängen fast alle späteren Lexika ab (genauer darüber Krömer 1978, 244—251). Scheller ist nicht nur für andere Sprachen bearbeitet worden; vor allem führt eine direkte Linie von seinem knapperen *Handlexicon* (Scheller 1796) über die Bearbeitungen von Lünemann (1831) und K. E. Georges (Einfluß auf Italien durch die Übersetzung von Calonghi 1950) zu H. Georges (1918), dem heute im deutschen Sprachraum meistbenutzten Wörterbuch. Trotz vernichtender Kritik, die das Werk zu Recht erfahren hat (Hofmann 1915), ist diese seine dominierende Rolle nicht ganz unbegründet, da es unter den neueren zweisprachigen Lexika insgesamt immer noch das reichhaltigste ist; allerdings ist es, ganz abgesehen von den vielen Fehlern, seit Scheller mit dem von seiner ursprünglichen Bestimmung für Schüler herrührenden schweren Manko behaftet, daß es vielfach nur summarische Autorenangaben statt genauer Stellenangaben bietet.

Auch die lexikographischen Aktivitäten von Freund sind ohne Schellers Wirken nicht denkbar. Zwar wurden die ersten Teile seines vierbändigen *Wörterbuchs der lateinischen Sprache* (Freund 1845) bei ihrem Erscheinen voreilig als epochale Leistung begrüßt, doch letzten Endes und vor allem in den späteren Teilen blieb das ganze Unternehmen wesentlich von Scheller abhängig, ohne jedoch mit seiner Akribie konkurrieren zu können. — Freund seinerseits hat einen besonders großen Einfluß auf den nichtdeutschsprachigen Raum ausgeübt: sein großes Lexikon hat nicht nur in französischem Gewand (s. Krömer 1978, 251 Anm. 34) Jahrzehnte weitergewirkt, sondern es ist vor allem 1850 von Andrews ins Englische übersetzt worden; diese Übersetzung ist dann von Lewis/Short (1879) bearbeitet worden, und in dieser Form ist das Lexikon ein Jahrhundert lang ein über den englischen Sprachraum hinaus geschätztes Hilfsmittel geblieben — nicht zuletzt wegen der darin gebotenen genauen Stellenangaben.

Genaue Stellenangaben bietet auch das Wörterbuch von Klotz (1857), das ebenfalls nicht ohne Scheller zu denken ist; insbesondere die von Klotz im Laufe der Arbeit herangezogenen Mitarbeiter haben Freund und Georges kräftig benutzt. Dieses Lexikon ist erst jüngst wieder im Ausland zu Ehren gekommen: Grilli (1974) legt es seinem neuen lateinisch-italienischen Lexikon zugrunde.

Natürlich haben sich auf der Grundlage der genannten großen Werke eine Fülle kleinerer Lexika etabliert (z. T. aus der Feder derselben Autoren, z. B. Freund und Georges), bei denen allerdings der wissenschaftliche Anspruch hinter der Sorge für das Elementarverständnis lateinischer Texte zurücktritt und die daher in einigen Punkten den Vertretern der früheren Epoche wieder näherstehen: sie verzichten natürlich mehr oder weniger auf genaue Stellenangaben und bringen dafür Wörter und Bedeutungen aus dem Bereich des Mittel- und Neulateins. Ein besonders gelungenes Exemplar dieser Gattung ist das Langenscheidt-Lexikon von Pertsch (1971).

3. Jüngste Unternehmungen

Neuere große zweisprachige Wörterbücher, die das gesamte antike Latein berücksichtigen, gibt es nicht. Schon im Lauf des 19. Jhs. hatte sich ja die Überzeugung durchgesetzt, für fundierte Aussagen über das Latein in seiner ganzen antiken Breite bedürfe es einer breiteren Basis, als sie die bisherigen Lexika hatten und sie ein einzelner überhaupt schaffen kann — eine Überzeugung, die schließlich zur Begründung des *Thesaurus linguae Latinae* geführt hat (s. dazu Art. 180, 4). In Sachen zweisprachiges Wörterbuch bedeutet dies: entweder warten, bis der Thesaurus fertiggestellt ist, oder selber für eine weit umfassendere Materialsammlung sorgen, als sie den früheren Lexika zugrunde lag.

Dieser letztere Weg ist bisher nur einmal beschritten worden (ob auch das spanische *Diccionario* 1984 hierhergehört, läßt sich noch nicht sagen): durch das *Oxford Latin Dictionary* (1982). Allerdings ist man (nur zu verständlich) auf halbem Wege stehengeblieben: berücksichtigt wurde nur die nichtchristliche Literatur bis etwa zum Jahre 200 n. Chr. Für diesen eingeschränkten Bereich ist ein durchaus respektables Hilfsmittel entstanden (s. Wieland 1983), das die Fortschritte der philologischen Wissenschaft berücksichtigt, z. T. tatsächlich mehr und bessere Belege bietet (insbes. auch aus dem Bereich der Epigraphik) und diese Belege alle durch genaue Stellenangabe der Überprüfung zugänglich macht. Ausgesprochen problematisch ist allerdings die Anordnung der Bedeutungen; das Bemühen, verschiedene Bedeutungen und Ausdrucksweisen bei einem Wort zu übergeordneten Gruppen zusammenzufassen, tritt zurück gegenüber dem unübersichtlichen und auch sachlich unbefriedigenden Prinzip der einfachen Reihung von keineswegs gleichrangigen Gruppen —

eine Form, die an die Zeit vor Scheller erinnert. — So bleiben daneben Georges, Lewis/ Short und auch Klotz einstweilen weiterhin unentbehrlich.

4. Literatur (in Auswahl)

4.1. Wörterbücher

Bayer 1724 = Paedagogus Latinus [...] sive Lexicon Germanico-Latinum et Latino-Germanicum [...] digestum [...] a Jacobo Bayer. Moguntiae 1724 [ungez., 778, 439 S.; oft gedruckt bzw. bearbeitet].

Calonghi 1950 = Ferruccio Calonghi: Dizionario della Lingua Latina, [...] 3ª edizione [...] del dizionario Georges-Calonghi. Torino 1950 [XVI S., 2960 Sp.; mehrere Drucke, 1. Aufl. 1891].

Cellarius 1689 = Christophori Cellarii [...] Latinitatis probatae et exercitatae Liber Memorialis [...] cura ac studio Ioan. Matthiae Gesneri [...]. Manhemii. Francofurti 1765 [ungez., 266 S.; zuerst 1689, oft gedruckt bzw. bearbeitet].

Dentzler 1666 = Clavis linguae Latinae [...] Authore Joh. Jacobo Dentzlero. Basileae 1666 [ungez., 739 S.; mehrere Aufl. u. Drucke].

Diccionario 1984 = Diccionario Latino, [...] redactado y compilado por C. Cantueso [u. a.]. Madrid 1984 ff. [bisher fasc. 0—1: A—acute 1984—1988, 112 S.].

Faber 1571 = Thesaurus Eruditionis Scholasticae [...] a Basilio Fabro Sorano. Lipsiae 1587 [ungez., 1110 S.; zuerst 1571, oft gedruckt bzw. bearbeitet].

Freund 1845 = Wörterbuch der lateinischen Sprache [...] von Wilhelm Freund. 4 Bde. Leipzig 1834—1845 [LXXXVIII, 1112, 1208, 1154, 1034 S.].

Frisius 1750 = Joannis Frisii Dictionarium Latino-Germanicum, nec-non Germanico-Latinum [...]. Editio nova [...]. Coloniae Agrippinae 1750 [754, 372 S.; ursprüngl. 1556 als Novum Dictionariolum puerorum, oft gedruckt bzw. bearbeitet].

Georges 1918 = Ausführliches Lateinisch-Deutsches Handwörterbuch [...] von Karl Ernst Georges. 8. Aufl. v. Heinrich Georges. 2 Bde. Hannover. Leipzig 1913—1918 [VIII S., 3108, 3576 Sp., mehrere Nachdrucke; zuerst 1837/38 als 8. Aufl. von Lünemann 1831].

Grilli 1974 = (Reinhold Klotz e) Alberto Grilli: Dizionario della lingua Latina. Brescia 1974 ff. [bisher 480 S.; vol. I fasc. 1: A-acquiesco 1974, fasc. 2: acquiesco-adnodo 1975, fasc. 3: adnodo-Aeolicum 1979].

Hederich 1739 = Beniamini Hederici [...] Lexicon manuale Latino-Germanicum [...]. 2 Bde. Lipsiae 1766 [ungez. S., 2970, 2966, 140 Sp.; zuerst 1739].

Hederich 1988 = Benjamin Hederich: Lexicon manuale latino-germanicum. Leipzig 1739. Promtuarium latinitatis probatae et exercitae, oder vollständigstes Teutsch-Lateinisches Lexicon. Leipzig 1729. Lexicon manuale graecum. Leipzig 1722. Auf Mikrofiches. Erlangen 1988 [66 Mikrofiches].

Kirsch 1714 = Abundans Cornucopiae linguae Latinae et Germanicae selectum [. . .] Adami Friderici Kirschii. Noribergae 1714 [ungez., 1298, 387 S., mehrfach gedruckt bzw. bearbeitet].

Klotz 1857 = Handwörterbuch der lateinischen Sprache [. . .] hrsg. v. Reinhold Klotz. 2 Bde. Braunschweig 1853—1857 [VIII, VI, 1718, 1844 S.; 3. Aufl. 1862, mehrfach nachgedruckt].

Lewis/Short 1879 = A Latin Dictionary founded on Andrews' edition of Freund's Latin Dictionary [. . .] by Charlton T. Lewis and Charles Short. Oxford 1969 [XIV, 2019 S., einer der zahlreichen Nachdrucke des ursprünglich 1879 unter etwas and. Titel erschienenen Werks].

Lünemann 1831 = Georg Heinrich Lünemann's [. . .] lateinisch-deutsches und deutsch-lateinisches Handwörterbuch nach Imm. Joh. Gerh. Scheller's Anlage [. . .]. Lateinisch-deutscher Theil. 2 Bde. 7. Aufl. Leipzig 1831 [XVI S., 1644, 1788 Sp.; Bearbeitung von Scheller 1796, 1. Aufl. 1807 unter etwas abweichendem Titel, spätere Bearb. s. Georges 1918].

Oxford Latin Dictionary 1982 = Oxford Latin Dictionary [hrsg. v. P.G.W. Glare]. Oxford 1968—1982 [XXIII, 2126 S.].

Pertsch 1971 = Langenscheidts Handwörterbuch Lateinisch-Deutsch, bearbeitet von Erich Pertsch [. . .]. Berlin. München. Zürich 1971 [652 S.; Erw. Neuausg. 1983].

Scheller 1780 = Imman. Jo. Gerh. Schellers kleines lateinisches Wörterbuch [. . .]. 2. Aufl. Leipzig 1781 [XVI, 314, ungez. S.; 1. Aufl. 1780, mehrfach bearbeitet].

Scheller 1796 = Imm. Joh. Gerh. Schellers lateinisch-deutsches und deutsch-lateinisches Handlexicon [. . .]. Erster [. . .] Theil. 2 Bde. 2. Aufl. Leipzig 1796 [XX S., 3214 Sp.; 1. Aufl. 1792, spätere Bearb. s. Lünemann 1831 und Georges 1918].

Scheller 1804 = Imman. Joh. Gerhard Schellers ausführliches und möglichst vollständiges lateinisch-deutsches Lexicon oder Wörterbuch zum Behufe der Erklärung der Alten und Übung in der lateinischen Sprache. 5 Bde. 3. Aufl. Leipzig 1804 [XXXX S., 12 562 Sp., 1. Aufl. 1783 unter etwas anderem Titel].

Weismann 1725 = Lexicon bipartitum, Latino-Germanicum, et Germanico-Latinum [. . .], Auctore Eryco Weismanno. 8. Aufl. Stuttgardiae 1725 [ungez., 752, 520 S.; später mehrfach gedruckt].

4.2. Sonstige Literatur

Hausmann 1988 = Franz Josef Hausmann: Altsprachliche Lexikographie im Zeitalter des Barock. Die Wörterbücher des Benjamin Hederich (1675—1748). In: Hederich 1988, 1—40.

Hofmann 1915 = Johann Baptist Hofmann: Rez. von Georges 1918. In: Berliner philologische Wochenschrift 33. 1913, 659—666; 35. 1915, 1542—1546.

Krömer 1978 = Dietfried Krömer: Grammatik contra Lexikon: rerum potiri. In: Gymnasium 85. 1978, 239—258.

Wieland 1983 = Hans Wieland: Rez. von Oxford Latin Dictionary 1982. In: Gnomon 41. 1969, 746—752; 49. 1977, 136—141; 52. 1980, 53—54; 55. 1983, 586—589.

Dietfried Krömer, München
(Bundesrepublik Deutschland)

320. Bilingual Lexicography With Dutch

1. Introduction
2. The Early Dictionaries: Sources and Methods of Compilation
3. Dutch and French
4. Dutch and English
5. Dutch and German
6. The Nineteenth Century and After
7. Selected Bibliography

1. Introduction

Bilingual lexicography with Dutch or Flemish (no further distinction between the terms is offered here) has developed to a high degree during the past four and a half centuries. The production of dictionaries involving Dutch and other languages can be seen to reflect the practical needs of a minor-language community which has at the same time always been a major trading nation with strong international ties, both cultural and political. The following selective list, based on Claes (1980), of dates for the earliest known bilingual dictionaries involving Dutch with other languages shows that geographical contiguity was far from being the main factor in determining the repertoire of foreign languages with which Dutch was combined:

Dutch with		
	French	1546
	Malaysian	1612
	Spanish	1617
	English	1647
	Yiddish	1710
	Italian	1710
	Portuguese	1714
	German	1719
	Russian	1813
	Danish	1826

Javanese	1827
Japanese	1855
Sranan	1855
Chinese	1882
Swedish	1907
Turkish	1971
Polish	1977

The early take-up of exotic languages is noteworthy. Claes records five items for Malaysian in the seventeenth century. Despite the long land frontier and all the language contacts this must entail, German is relatively late in the list — after Italian, and a century and a half later than French. The appearance only in 1971 of the first bilingual dictionary for Turkish and Dutch reflects new contacts resulting from the reverse flow from east to west of the twentieth-century migrant workers.

2. The Early Dictionaries: Sources and Methods of Compilation

The first bilingual dictionaries with Dutch, like those with other European languages, derived much in both form and content from the well-established tradition of bilingual works combining Latin with a vernacular which goes back to the middle ages; they also drew directly or indirectly on the very substantial renaissance polyglot compilations such as the Plantijn *Thesaurus* (1573) and Kiliaan (1599) with its 40,000 entries (Osselton 1973, 49; Claes 1977, 210—17). Thus in the earliest French-Flemish dictionary, Meurier 1557, 1563, the word-list is based on a French-Latin compilation of Estienne, while the other half of the combination (Flemish-French) uses a Dutch-Latin version of Dasypodius (Claes 1977, 207—8).

At a later stage the tendency was to take material from combinations of two vernacular languages, as when Hexham for his Dutch-English dictionary (Hexham 1647, 1648) drew on the Dutch-French list of Mellema 1618 (Osselton 1969, 358—62). The initial disinclination to use single-language dictionaries might seem surprising, though these were often used later for supplementary material, as for instance by Sewel (Osselton 1973, 79—80, 88). In the early stages suitable works were no doubt often not to hand; in many respects the evolution of monolingual dictionaries lagged behind that of bilingual ones, and in any case another man's list incorporating a different foreign language would be more likely to provide a suitable set of items. But the rather opportunistic borrowing that went on from various combinations of other foreign languages can be shown to have resulted at times in an initial imbalance between the two halves, from and into the native language (Riemens 1921, 17; Osselton 1973, 44—9).

This complex pattern of sources and inter-relationships between the early vernacular dictionaries of Europe (upon which much research still needs to be done) has resulted in striking similarities between the types of word-stock which many of them contain. The Dutch works share fully in this common tradition from the sixteenth century onwards.

3. Dutch and French

Combinations with French dominate the early history of Dutch bilingual lexicography, and not surprisingly the first volumes come from that area of the southern Netherlands where the two languages were (and still are) most forcibly in contact: the Dutch-French *Naembouck* (1546) was published in Ghent, and the dictionaries of Meurier 1557, 1563 and Sasbout 1576, 1579 in Antwerp. It was not until Waesberghe (1599) and the Mellema dictionary of 1618 that the scene shifted to what is now called Holland; the partially regional character of the vocabulary of early Dutch-French dictionaries is a matter of some scholarly interest (Sterkenburg 1984, 46; Tollenaere 1977, 222).

Meurier's dictionary (like that of Cotgrave 1611) contains some neologisms, and he could boast of a certain literary colouring to his vocabulary, with items from Marot and Ronsard (Riemens 1921, 11), but no such claim could ever be made for the productions going under the name of Mellema, which with their numerous editions between 1587 and 1641 may be regarded as the standard practical translation/decoding dictionaries of their time. The 47,000 Dutch entries in the 1636 edition nearly double the number to be found in his predecessors, though these are commonly single-line items, with little effort at structuring lemmata so as to distinguish main entries, derivatives, illustrative phrases, etc. Many of the seemingly redundant entries such as 'lam in een been, Ohie d'vne jambe' are of a type which has been shown to go back to Latin sources, and from which the vernacular dictionaries took centuries to free themselves (Osselton 1973, 49).

Other dictionaries in the seventeenth century continued much in the same tradition.

Van den Ende (Ende 1654, 1656) has been called «le premier "dictionnaire phonétique" destiné aux Hollandais» (Riemens 1919, 216), though the compiler was aiming primarily at warning his users against the vagaries of French spelling. The work of d'Arsy 1643 (with editions down to 1699) was little more than a reissue of Mellema, and he was also involved in revising Van den Ende (Tollenaere 1977, 221): the dictionary publishing world was still a small one.

As typical of the eighteenth century productions we may take Halma (1708, 1710) with its numerous editions down to 1784. With 1023 pages for Dutch-French and 774 pages for French-Dutch it is a very substantial work indeed «composée sur le modele des dictionaires de Richelet, Pomey, Tachard, et Danet, revû & considerablement augmenté sur le dictionaire & la grammaire de l'Academie Françoise». It is typographically much superior to Mellema, and there is by now a quite impressive coverage of technical terms (see Dictionary excerpt 320.1), and cautionary guidance is given after the fashion of Richelet on jocular words, archaic words and figurative meanings. The volumes no doubt kept their place in the market despite the rival works of the Frenchman Marin (1701, 1710) particularly on account of the wide range of idiomatic and illustrative phrases (there are for instance 22 for the verb *donner*), though these are by modern standards still somewhat haphazardly arranged.

Marin produced the first *Dictionnaire portatif* (Marin 1696) and up to a quarter of the 21 new Dutch and French dictionaries listed by Claes (1980) as being published in the eighteenth century appear to have been abridged or compact volumes: «un grand livre est un grand mal» as Des Roches observes in the interesting «Observations générales» prefixed to his handy volume (Roches 1769) — why have fifty phrases to illustrate the meaning of a word when your user may be satisfied with three? All this serves to highlight the dominant characteristic of the early Dutch and French dictionaries: they were of the market place, not of the scholar's study, and served the practical, everyday needs of a partly bilingual community.

4. Dutch and English

Dictionaries combining Dutch with English appear a century later than those with French. They are fewer in number (only three substantial works down to the end of the eighteenth century) and are to be associated with the needs of translators and readers of foreign books rather than with the schoolroom. Henry Hexham, who produced the first one, was, like the author of the first Dutch-Spanish dictionary (Rodriguez 1624), a soldier who had fought in the Spanish wars in the Netherlands. Hexham had stayed on in time of peace, and turned his hand to the translation of French, Latin and Dutch works into English. His dictionary (Hexham 1647, 1648) is heavily dependent on the sources he chose: an English-Latin dictionary (Rider 1589) for the English-Dutch half, and a Dutch-French one (Mellema 1618) for the Dutch-English half. His dictionary is said to be for 'divines, students and others', but Hexham generally kept clear of over-bookish terms, and added a number of contemporary idiomatic items of his own (Osselton 1973, 44—54). The 35,000 English and 47,000 Dutch entries commonly provide a single equivalent in the target-language, and there is a very extensive use of cross-reference ('a Banket, *Siet* banquet') which would no doubt be specially useful at a time when the instability of spelling in both languages could be a problem for the foreign reader. No grammatical information is given in the individual entries, but the Hexham dictionary is notable for its inclusion in all editions of an appended grammar of each language.

DIMINUTIF, *f. m.* (*Terme de Grammaire.*) Een verkleinwoordt, verkleinnaam, of verkleining.
DIMINUTION, *f. f.* Vermindering, verkleining, afneeming.
Diminution de crédit. Vermindering van geloof, van gezagh, of aanzien.
DIMISSION. (Mot inufité.) Voyez Demission.
DIMISSOIRE, *f. m.* (*Terme de l'Eglife Romaine.*) Zekere Biffchoppelyke brieven, volmagtbrieven.
DIMISSORIAL, *adj.* Lettres dimifforiales. Zekere volmagtbrieven van eenen Biffchop.
DINANDERIE, *f. f.* Allerhande geel koperwerk.
DINDON, *f. m.* Jeune poulet d'Inde. Een jonge kalkoen.
DINDONNEAU, *f. m.* Petit dindon. Een kieken van een kalkoen.
DINE, dincr, *f. m.* 't Middagmaal, de middagmaaltydt, (Brabantfch, De noen, of noenmaaltydt.)

Dictionary excerpt 320.1: Articles *diminutif-dine* (in: Halma 1717, 272)

Hexham's dictionary was totally replaced at the end of the seventeenth century by the famous and quite independently contrived work of Willem Sewel, the historian of the Quakers, who was also a formidable translator, philologist and literary journalist. Sewel (1691), like Hexham, draws too heavily on a Latin-English dictionary (Coles 1677) and a Dutch-French one (Ende 1654, 1656; rev. 1681). It is no bigger than Hexham, but it is generally better thought out, more up-to-date, and has more precise definitions (Osselton 1973, 72). Sewel's philological interests are reflected in his decision to include a treatise on Dutch spelling, and guides to the pronunciation of the two languages as well as grammars of them. He provides also more grammatical information in the text itself, for instance by placing the article before Dutch nouns to indicate gender. The presence of some characteristic items from Sir Thomas Browne *(to supererogate, testaceous)* shows the influence of Sewel's activities as a translator.

Sewel's dictionary was to remain the standard work throughout the eighteenth century. He devoted four years to a revision which appeared in 1708. He turned to a monolingual dictionary (Kersey/Phillips 1706) for many political, ecclesiastical and technical terms on which Dutch users might need fuller information. With meticulous editorial changes throughout, and a better typography, it is a greatly improved work.

There were further editions in 1727, 1735, 1749 and 1754, but it is in the two volumes of 1766 'more than the half part augmented' that we reach the high point in the cumulative tradition of eighteenth-century bilingual lexicography in Holland. The reviser Egbert Buys had himself produced a technical dictionary and, drawing especially on Boyer's English-French dictionary (Boyer 1764) he incorporated a vast amount of new material to improve the coverage of eighteenth-century usage. It is especially rich in current idioms (48 items under the verb *to grow*) and these two volumes, each with roughly a thousand pages in triple columns (see excerpt 320.2) are still valuable reference works even today for anyone working on eighteenth-century Dutch or English texts.

The dictionary of Holtrop (1789, 1801) is a somewhat condensed version of Sewel, with improvements to the arrangement of material, so that the compiler achieves something approximating to a modern pattern of lemmatization. He gives parts of speech, indi-

> To grow rich, *Ryk worden.*
> ☞ It grows day, *Het wordt dag.*
> It grows towards evening, *Het begint avond te worden, de avond begint te vallen.*
> To grow little, (*or* leſſer, to grow ſhort,) *Korter worden, inkrimpen.*
> The days begin to grow ſhort, *De dagen beginnen te korten.*
> ☞ To grow ſtronger and ſtronger, after a fit of ſickneſs; *Na een ziekte in kragten toeneemen, ſtèrker worden.*
> ☞ To grow young again, *Weder jong worden.*
> To grow dear; *Duur worden.*
> ‡ To grow weary of a thing, *Iets moede worden, een afkeer ergens van krygen.*
> ☞ To grow a ſcholar, *Een geleerde worden.*
> ☞ To grow tame, *Tam worden.*
> ☞ There grew a quarrel upon it, *Daar ontſtond een krakeel uit.*
> ☞ To grow INTO faſhion, *In 's gebruik komen, de mode worden.*

Dictionary excerpt 320.2: Extract from the article *to grow* (in: Sewel 1766, 323)

cates the stress-pattern of English words, and — rather late in the day — benefits from the Johnson and Bailey dictionaries for some of his new items. For the Dutch-English half he too appears to have turned to Marin (Osselton 1973, 100—107).

5. Dutch and German

It was not until the eighteenth century that the first dictionary of Dutch and German was published, and the late appearance of this combination has been plausibly explained (Tollenaere 1977, 224) on the ground that the two languages were sufficiently close for people to get on without feeling the lack of a lexicographical prop. Whatever the reason, the need for one was evidently felt first by German speakers, for the earliest dictionary combining the two languages (Kramer 1719) was published in Nürnberg. The compiler of this bulky work, Matthias Kramer, was a teacher of languages and a member of the Prussian Academy of Sciences. He was 78 when the dictionary came out, but, revised by others, his work held the market throughout the eighteenth century. Kramer's initial Dutch word list was based on the Halma Dutch-French dictionary (Vooys 1947, 266) and at times retains gratuitous French explanations ('*Onder-rok* ... Unter-rock/Unterrocklein. *gall.* sou-jupe, cotillon'). The Kramer dictionary is unusually strong on grammatical information, and is typographically more inventive than Halma. It was drastically cut down by J. D. Titius for the octavo second edition (Leipzig 1759) but extended again for the third (Leipzig/Amsterdam 1768), in which the spelling was revised and information inserted on gender by the Dutch reviser Adam van Moerbeek. In the Dutch-German half there are some 62,000 entries, and it is clear that much of the added material (including whole illustrative sentences) has been lifted from the 1766 edition of Sewel.

6. The Nineteenth Century and After

With the improved communications and expanding world trade of the nineteenth and twentieth century, production of bilingual dictionaries of all kinds has grown explosively. For Dutch, combinations with the three languages of the nearest neighbours have remained dominant. Illustration 320.1, based on the list of new publications for the seventeenth, eighteenth, nineteenth and twentieth century as recorded in Claes (1980) shows how French was in the lead from the start, and is totally dominant in the nineteenth century, when English lay third to German. It also shows the considerable levelling up which has taken place in the twentieth century.

Typical of the new productions of the nineteenth century are the dictionaries of Bomhoff. D. Bomhoff was of humble origins and worked his way up from paper-maker's apprentice to become a well-known translator and writer on spelling, grammar and literature. He first produced a dictionary of English and Dutch (Bomhoff 1822) which went through five editions, then one with French (Bomhoff 1835), and finally a German one (Bomhoff 1846). They are serviceable works, with for instance about 32,000 entries for English-Dutch (in the 1832 edn.) and some 67,000 in the companion Dutch-English volume — a discrepancy in bulk which he attributes in part to the need to include so many Dutch compound words. The new thing about them is that there should have been the three dictionaries from the single Bomhoff stable for what are still called the 'school languages' in Holland today: English, French and German. Whether Bomhoff himself was personally responsible for all three language combinations might be worth investigating. But the pattern of the triple two-volume series became firmly established: other nineteenth-century examples are those of Calisch and Servaas de Bruin (Claes 1980). Even in the highly commercialized world of twentieth-century bilingual dictionary production it is not hard to trace the same pattern of the basic three combinations of Dutch with the three dominant modern foreign languages. These often go with a monolingual dictionary as the 'flagship' of the series, and it has been shown (Sterkenburg 1983) that the bilingual dictionaries of Marin and Halma are the direct forefathers of the authoritative Van Dale monolingual dictionary of present-day Dutch (Dale 1984). Disparities between the volumes of such series will always occur. But it is a tradition well-placed to reap the full benefits of normalization which may now be achieved by the use of computerized data-bases.

7. Selected Bibliography

7.1. Dictionaries

Arsy 1643 = Jan Louis d'Arsy: Le Grand Dictionaire François-Flamen. Het Groote Woorden-Boek vervattende den Schat der Nederlantsche Taele, met een Fransche uit-legginghe. Rotterdam. Utrecht 1643 [298; 314 p.].

Bomhoff 1822 = Derk Bomhoff: New Dictionary of the English and Dutch Language. Nieuw Woordenboek der Nederduitsche en Engelsche Taal. Nijmegen 1822 [672; 1211 p.].

Bomhoff 1835 = Derk Bomhoff: Nouveau dictionnaire français-hollandais et hollandais-français Zutphen 1835 [1101; 720 p.].

Bomhoff 1846 = Derk Bomhoff: Vollständiges Deutsch-Holländisches und Holländisch-Deutsches Taschen-Wörterbuch ['s-Gravenhage 1846].

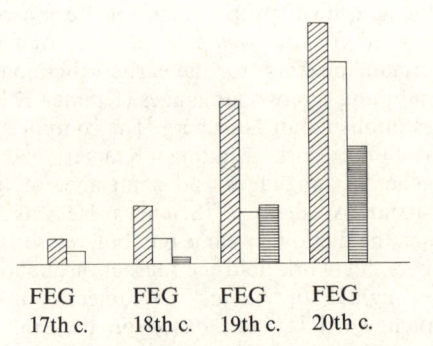

Ill. 320.1: Production of bilingual dictionaries with Dutch

Boyer 1764 = Abel Boyer: The Royal Dictionary, French and English, and English and French. London 1764 [1st ed. 1699].

Coles 1677 = Elisha Coles: A Dictionary, English-Latin, and Latin-English. London 1677 [335 p.].

Cotgrave 1611 = Randle Cotgrave: A Dictionarie of the French and English Tongues. London 1611.

Dale 1984 = Johan Frederik van Dale: Groot Woordenboek der Nederlandse Taal. 11th ed. 's-Gravenhage 1984 [3730 p. 1st ed. 1864].

Ende 1654, 1656 = Caspar van den Ende: Le gazophylace de la langue Françoise et Flamande. Schatkamer der Nederduytsche en Francoysche tale. Rotterdam 1654, 1656 [404 p.].

Halma 1708, 1710 = François Halma: Le Grand Dictionaire François & Flamend. Woordenboek der Nederduytsche en Fransche Taalen. Amsterdam. Utrecht 1708, 1710 [774; 1023 p. 3rd ed. 1717].

Hexham 1647, 1648 = Henry Hexham: A Copious English and Netherduytch Dictionarie. Het Groot Woorden-Boeck: Gestelt in 't Nederduytsch, ende in 't Engelsch. Rotterdam 1647, 1648 [560; 764 p.].

Holtrop 1789, 1801 = John Holtrop: A New English and Dutch Dictionary. Nieuw Nederduitsch en Engelsch Woorden-boek. Dordrecht. Amsterdam 1789, 1801 [932; 1012 p.].

Kersey/Phillips 1706 = Edward Phillips: The New World of Words: or, Universal English Dictionary. The Sixth Edition, Revised by J[ohn] K[ersey]. London 1706 [1st ed. 1658].

Kiliaan 1599 = Cornelis Kiliaan: Etymologicum Teutonicae Linguae. Antwerp 1599 [764 p. 1st ed. 1574].

Kramer 1719 = Matthias Kramer: Het Koninglyk Neder-Hoog-Duitsch, en Hoog-Neder-Duitsch Dictionnaire. Das Königliche Nider-Hoch-Teutsch, und Hoch-Nider-Teutsch Dictionarium. Nürnberg 1719 [548; 289 p.].

Marin 1696 = Pierre Marin: Dictionnaire portatif Hollandais et Français of Nederduitsch en Fransch woordenboekje. Amsterdam 1696 [842 p.].

Marin 1701, 1710 = Pierre Marin: Nieuw Nederduits en Frans Woordenboek. Compleet Fransch en Nederduitsch Woordenboek. Amsterdam 1701, 1710 [850; 1212 p.].

Mellema 1618 = Elcie Edouard Léon Mellema: Le grand dictionnaire François-Flamen. Den schat der Duytscher tale. Rotterdam 1618 [512; 632 p.].

Meurier 1557, 1563 = Gabriel Meurier: Vocabulaire François-Flameng. Dictionaire Flamen-François. Antwerp 1557, 1563 [272; 230 p.].

Naembouck 1546 = Naembouck van alle naturelicken, ende ongheschuumden vlaemschen woirden. Ghent 1546 [152 p.].

Plantijn 1573 = Christoffel Plantijn: Thesaurus theutonicae linguae. Schat der Neder-duytscher spraken. Antwerp 1573.

Rider 1589 = John Rider: Bibliotheca Scholastica. Oxford 1589 [600; 439 p.].

Roches 1769 = Jean des Roches: Nieuw Nederduytsch en Fransch Woorden-boek. Nouveau Dictionnaire François-Flamand. Antwerp 1769 [897; 587 p.].

Rodriguez 1624 = Juan Francisco Rodriguez: Nieuwen dictionaris om te leeren de Nederlandtsche ende Spaensche talen. Antwerp 1624 [314 p.].

Sasbout 1576, 1579 = Mathias Sasbout: Dictionaire Flameng-Francois tres-ample et copieux. Dictionaire Francois-Flameng tres ample et copieux. Antwerp 1576, 1579 [312; 928 p.].

Sewel 1691 = Willem Sewel: A New Dictionary English and Dutch. Nieuw Woordenboek der Nederduytsche en Engelsche Taale. Amsterdam 1691 [728; 431 p. 6th ed. 1766].

Waesberghe 1599 = Jean Waesberghe: Dictionnaire Françoise-Flameng, tres ample et copieux. Rotterdam 1599 [744 p.].

7.2. Other Publications

Claes 1977 = F. Claes: De lexicografie in de zestiende eeuw. In: D. M. Bakker/G. R. W. Dibbets: Geschiedenis van de Nederlandse taalkunde. 's-Hertogenbosch 1977, 205—17.

Claes 1980 = F. Claes: A Bibliography of Netherlandic (Dutch, Flemish) Dictionaries. Amsterdam 1980.

Collison 1982 = Robert L. Collison: A History of Foreign-Language Dictionaries. London 1982.

Osselton 1969 = Noel Edward Osselton: The sources of the first Dutch and English dictionary. In: Modern Language Review 64. 1969, 355—62.

Osselton 1973 = Noel Edward Osselton: The Dumb Linguists. A Study of the Earliest English and Dutch Dictionaries. Leiden. London 1973.

Quemada 1967 = Bernard Quemada: Les dictionnaires du français moderne 1539—1863. Paris. Brussels. Montreal 1967.

Riemens 1919 = K.-J. Riemens: Esquisse historique de l'enseignement du français en hollande du xvie au xixe siècle. Leiden 1919.

Riemens 1921 = K.-J. Riemens: Les débuts de la lexicographie franco-néerlandaise. Paris 1921.

Sterkenburg 1983 = P. G. J. van Sterkenburg: Johan Hendrik van Dale en zijn opvolgers. Utrecht. Antwerp 1983.

Sterkenburg 1984 = P. G. J. van Sterkenburg: Van Woordenlijst tot Woordenboek. Inleiding tot de geschiedenis van woordenboeken van het Nederlands. Leiden 1984.

Tollenaere 1977 = Félicien de Tollenaere: De lexicografie in de zeventiende en achttiende eeuw. In: D. M. Bakker/G. R. W. Dibbets: Geschiedenis van de Nederlandse taalkunde. 's-Hertogenbosch 1977, 219—27.

Voort van der Kleij 1977 = J. J. van der Voort van der Kleij: De studie van Nederlandse woordenboeken. In: P. G. J. van Sterkenburg (ed.): Lexicologie. Een bundel opstellen voor F. de Tollenaere. Groningen 1977, 287—93.

Vooys 1947 = C. G. N. de Vooys: Matthias Kramer als grammaticus en lexicograaf. In: C. G. N. de Vooys: Verzamelde Taalkundige Opstellen. Derde bundel, Groningen 1947, 259—67.

Noel Edward Osselton, Newcastle upon Tyne (Great Britain)

321. La lexicographie bilingue suédois-français, français-suédois

1. Histoire du dictionnaire suédois-français
2. Bibliographie choisie

1. Histoire du dictionnaire suédois-français

En Suède, à la fin du 17ᵉ siècle, le français était devenu une sorte de seconde langue maternelle pour les membres de la noblesse et de la haute bourgeoisie. Nombreux étaient même ceux qui employaient le français de préférence au suédois, aussi bien dans la conversation que dans leur correspondance. Le premier dictionnaire français-suédois et suédois-français ne parut pourtant qu'en 1745 (Möller 1745), plus d'un siècle, par exemple, après le premier dictionnaire entre le danois et le français (paru en 1628 selon Quemada 1967, 48—49). En ce qui concerne les dictionnaires bilingues du suédois avec d'autres langues, l'anglais et l'allemand précédèrent le français, même si ce ne fut que de quelques années: dictionnaire anglais-suédois-latin en 1734 par Jakob Serenius, dictionnaire allemand-suédois et suédois-allemand en 1738 par Olof Lind, et dictionnaire suédois-anglais-latin en 1741 par Jakob Serenius. Il est même probable que ce fut la publication de ces trois dictionnaires et le succès qu'ils obtinrent qui incitèrent l'éditeur Kiesewetter à publier enfin un dictionnaire français-suédois et suédois-français. Il en confia la rédaction à Levin Möller, professeur de philosophie et de mathématiques à Greifswald, en Poméranie suédoise, et futur doyen du chapitre de Linköping.

Rien ne semblait prédisposer Levin Möller à écrire un dictionnaire français-suédois et suédois-français. Pour avoir été le premier entre ces deux langues, son dictionnaire est cependant étonnamment bien fait et mérite notre attention pour plus d'une raison. Tout d'abord la préface, où l'auteur commence par avouer qu'il n'a jamais pris de plaisir à apprendre les langues et que jusque-là il ne s'est guère intéressé au français plus que nécessaire. S'il a accepté, dit-il, la tâche qui lui avait été confiée, c'était pour rendre service à ses compatriotes mais aussi à cause de la rétribution que lui avait promise l'éditeur! Et puis, ajoute-t-il, la rédaction de ce dictionnaire l'obligerait à perfectionner ses connaissances en allemand, ce dont il avait le plus grand besoin. Cette dernière remarque, qui peut surprendre, nous amène à la principale raison de l'intérêt de ce dictionnaire, à savoir la méthode suivie par l'auteur.

En effet, comme les connaissances de Möller en français étaient tout à fait insuffisantes pour créer à partir du néant un premier dictionnaire bilingue entre le français et le suédois, il décida d'adapter à ses besoins deux autres dictionnaires bilingues, l'un français-allemand (et c'est pour cela qu'il allait avoir l'occasion de se perfectionner en allemand), l'autre suédois-allemand.

Pour son lexique français-suédois, Möller choisit de traduire en suédois les traductions et explications allemandes qui se trouvaient dans le *Dictionnaire des Passagers* de J. L. Frisch, un des dictionnaires français-allemand et allemand-français les plus appréciés du 18ᵉ siècle (1ᵉʳᵉ éd. en 1712), ce qu'il fit en laissant inchangés les 9/10 du contenu même du texte allemand de Frisch. Möller explique son choix par le fait que le dictionnaire de Frisch est basé sur ceux de l'Académie française, de Richelet et de Danet. La traduction du texte allemand de Frisch étant presque littérale, on peut dire que les qualités du lexique français-suédois de Möller sont principalement dues à Frisch.

En ce qui concerne la partie suédois-français de son dictionnaire, Möller adopta la même technique de traduction mais, comme il était lui-même surchargé de travail, il confia à C. W. Victorin le soin de traduire en français la nomenclature suédoise du dictionnaire de Lind cité ci-dessus, paru quelques années auparavant. La nomenclature du dictionnaire suédois-anglais-latin de Serenius était bien meilleure, mais par l'intermédiaire des traductions allemandes de Lind, Möller pouvait se reporter au *Dictionnaire des Passagers* pour contrôler la traduction en français de sa nomenclature suédoise! Il est donc bien évident que le premier dictionnaire français-suédois et suédois-français s'est fait par l'intermédiaire de l'allemand et qu'il a été composé par un homme qui n'avait pas de bien grandes connaissances en français mais qui eut la sagesse, du moins en ce qui concerne son lexique français-suédois, de se baser sur un bon modèle et d'adopter une technique à laquelle on a encore recours aujourd'hui.

Avant de quitter Möller, arrêtons-nous encore à l'une de ces remarques singulières que contient la préface de son dictionnaire, à savoir le passage où il envisage que certaines fautes auraient pu se glisser dans son lexique suédois-français: L'inconvénient en sera d'autant moins grand, dit-il, que ceux qui savent bien le français se servent rarement de cette partie du dictionnaire et que les débutants pourront s'adresser à leurs professeurs pour obtenir de bonnes traductions françaises!

Möller eut plusieurs successeurs dans la seconde moitié du 18e siècle et au début du 19e siècle. Aucun d'eux ne mérite d'être mentionné dans ce bref aperçu, si ce n'est, à titre de curiosité, un dictionnaire de J. C. Dähnert paru en 1784, *Kurzgefasstes Deutsches und Schwedisches Hand-Lexicon mit angefügten Französischen Bedeutungen* (Dähnert 1784). Il s'agit en réalité d'un dictionnaire en trois parties: allemand-suédois-français, suédois-allemand-français, et un index français renvoyant aux pages des deux premières parties où le lecteur peut trouver les mots français. Dähnert constate dans sa préface le manque de bons dictionnaires suédois et déplore en particulier le grand nombre de fautes que contient selon lui le dictionnaire allemand-suédois et suédois-allemand de Lind. Malheureusement, il ne nous renseigne guère sur les raisons qui l'ont poussé à compléter les articles de son dictionnaire par une traduction française: «Ein Französisches Lexicon für beide Nationen zu schreiben und ins kurze zu fassen, war hier die Absicht nicht; dass man aber durch geringes Nachschlagen übersehen kann, wie die Französischen Wörter für sich allein, und in vielerley Redensarten einer und der andern Sprache zu deuten sind, wird sehr guten Nutzen haben.»

S'agit-il en réalité d'un projet de dictionnaire trilingue abandonné après la rédaction des deux premières parties? Quoi qu'il en soit, le dictionnaire de Dähnert peut être considéré comme un dictionnaire suédois-français autant que suédois-allemand, et nous savons que l'on s'en servait comme tel, puisque Nyström, auteur d'un dictionnaire suédois-français paru dix ans plus tard (Nyström 1794), cite Dähnert parmi ses sources.

Près de cinquante ans après Dähnert, en 1842—43, parut le dictionnaire français-suédois de Anders Fredrik Dalin (Dalin 1842). Dalin, qui était né en 1806, en était alors à son premier grand dictionnaire et devait devenir célèbre plus tard grâce à son grand dictionnaire monolingue suédois. Son dictionnaire français-suédois est par l'importance de sa nomenclature le plus grand dictionnaire français-suédois jamais publié en Suède (env. 90 000 entrées). C'est à tous points de vue un dictionnaire remarquablement complet puisqu'on y trouve aussi, comme l'annonce la page de titre, une phraséologie très détaillée, la prononciation des mots lorsqu'elle ne suit pas les règles générales, une section sur les synonymes de la langue française, une section sur les noms géographiques et ethniques, une liste des prénoms français et un registre étymologique pour la dérivation des mots. En ce qui concerne les termes techniques, il faut ajouter que Dalin est le premier (et aussi le dernier) à donner non seulement la traduction des mots, mais aussi une explication. Il est à regretter que Dalin n'ait pas aussi voulu nous donner un dictionnaire suédois-français de la même envergure que son dictionnaire français-suédois.

L'auteur à nommer immédiatement après est Ferdinand Schulthess, un Suisse né en France et qui, travaillant comme professeur de français à Moscou se maria avec une baronne suédoise. Installé en Suède, Schulthess publia dans les années 1880—90 des dictionnaires français-suédois et suédois-français en trois versions: en grand format (par ex. Schulthess 1885), bien moindre cependant que celui des deux grands volumes de Dalin, en format moyen dit ‹scolaire› (par ex. Schulthess 1891) et en format de poche. Depuis Schulthess, peu de choses ont vraiment changé en ce qui concerne les dictionnaires standard français-suédois et suédois-français. Son dictionnaire de poche français-suédois publié pour la première fois en 1891 en était en 1948 à sa neuvième réimpression (il faut bien lire ‹neuvième réimpression›, et non ‹dixième édition revue et corrigée›).

En 1936, la maison d'édition (Svenska Bokförlaget) remplaça les deux dictionnaires de Schulthess dits ‹scolaires› par ceux de Thekla Hammar (suédois-français, Hammar 1936) et de Johan Vising (français-suédois, Vising 1936). Vising (1855—1942) avait été professeur de langues romanes à l'université de Göteborg. Thekla Hammar (1872—1953), professeur de français au lycée, séjournait en France au moment où éclata la guerre de 1914—1918. Elle ne put quitter le pays, s'engagea comme infirmière dans l'armée française et resta jusqu'en 1938 à Paris où elle travailla dans un laboratoire médical. Plutôt que de nouveaux dictionnaires, les dictionnaires de Vising et de Hammar doivent être considérés comme des rééditions amplement revues des deux dictionnaires de Schulthess.

Depuis 1936, aucun grand dictionnaire français-suédois ou suédois-français n'a été publié en Suède. Ceux de Vising et de Hammar sont donc les seuls dictionnaires standard de quelque envergure que nous ayons aujourd'hui entre ces deux langues. À première vue il est difficile de reconnaître une page de l'édition de Hammar vendue en 1986 d'une page du Schulthess paru plus d'un siècle plus tôt. La typographie est la même et l'ordonnancement des articles aussi est resté tout à fait inchangé, ce qui semblerait montrer qu'il n'y a eu aucune discussion dans les milieux concernés quant à l'organisation du dictionnaire. Pour ce qui est du contenu même, qu'il nous suffise de dire que nos étudiants en français en sont réduits à se servir de dictionnaires écrits il y a plus d'un demi siècle, et que l'auteur d'un de ces dictionnaires a peut-être commencé ses études de français au temps de Napoléon III. Les dictionnaires de Vising et de Hammar, malgré tous les services qu'ils ont rendus dans le passé, sont plutôt de vénérables pièces de musée que des outils de travail adaptés à nos besoins. Il aurait fallu depuis longtemps les corriger, compléter leur nomenclature, les mettre à jour en ce qui concerne la phraséologie et le français parlé et familier, et moderniser la langue, aussi bien en ce qui concerne les entrées qu'à l'intérieur des articles.

À ce qu'il semble, la maison d'édition qui a repris les droits de ces deux dictionnaires (Esselte Studium) aurait l'intention de remplacer Vising et Hammar par de nouveaux dictionnaires. Est-on prêt à faire un travail original, ou, en reprenant la méthode de Möller, se contentera-t-on d'adapter avec plus ou moins de succès d'autres dictionnaires bilingues?

Ce bilan très négatif n'est heureusement valable que pour les dictionnaires généraux les plus importants entre le suédois et le français. Les dictionnaires spécialisés se portent mieux et nous avons vu il y a quelques années la parution d'un dictionnaire technique qui mérite d'être cité comme un modèle du genre (Lötmarker/Pioud 1984).

Pour l'allemand, il y a de bons dictionnaires, et pour l'anglais, qui est de très loin la première langue étrangère en Suède, nous avons même le premier grand dictionnaire général bilingue né du traitement automatique. Il faut espérer que les méthodes de l'informatique rendront bientôt possible la rédaction de bons dictionnaires, même pour une langue qui, comme le français, a perdu beaucoup de son importance en Suède.

2. Bibliographie choisie

2.1. Dictionnaires

Dähnert 1784 = Johann Carl Dähnert: Kurzgefasstes Deutsches und Schwedisches Hand-Lexicon mit angefügten Französischen Bedeutungen. Stockholm. Upsala. Åbo 1784 [Titre de la seconde partie: Schwedisch-Deutsch-Französisches Hand-Lexicon. Troisième partie: Alphabetische Nachweisung der Französischen Wörter die in den beiden ersten Abtheilungen vorkommen. VIII, 838 p.].

Dalin 1842 = Anders Fredrik Dalin: Nytt fransyskt och svenskt lexikon. Stockholm 1842—43 [564 + 642 p.].

Frisch 1712 = Johann Leonhard Frisch: Nouveau Dictionnaire des passagers françois-allemand et allemand-françois. Leipzig 1712.

Hammar 1936 = Thekla Hammar: Svensk-Fransk ordbok. Stockholm 1936 [VIII, 1086 p.].

Lind 1738 = Olof Lind: Teutsch-Schwedisches und Schwedisch-Teutsches Lexicon oder Wörter-Buch. Stockholm 1738.

Lötmarker/Pioud 1984 = Ruth Lötmarker/Gérard Pioud: Svensk-fransk fackordbok. Handel, ekonomi, juridik, förvaltning. Stockholm 1984 [320 p.].

Möller 1745 = Levin Möller: Nouveau dictionnaire françois-svedois et svedois-françois. En Ny Frantzösk och Swensk samt Swensk och Frantzöskt Lexicon eller Orda-Bok. Stockholm. Upsala 1745 [VIII, 754 + 158 p.].

Nyström 1794 = Barthold Nyström: Dictionnaire françois-suédois et suédois-françois. Fransyskt och Swenskt samt Swenskt och Fransyskt Lexicon. Stockholm 1794 [II, 300 p. pour la troisième partie de ce dictionnaire (français-suédois) qui seule est de Nyström, les deux premières (français-suédois) étant de Björkegren.].

Schulthess 1885 = Ferdinand Schulthess: Svensk-fransk ordbok efter de bästa källor och med biträde af sakkunniga män [. . .]. Stockholm 1885 [1737 p.].

Schulthess 1891 = Ferdinand Schulthess: Fransk-svensk ordbok — Skolupplaga. Stockholm 1891 [XXXIII, 740 p.].

Serenius 1734 = Jacob Serenius: Dictionarium anglo-svethico-latinum. Hamburg 1743.

Serenius 1741 = Jacob Serenius: Dictionarium suethico-anglo-latinum. Stockholm 1741.

Vising 1936 = Johan Vising: Fransk-svensk ordbok. Stockholm 1936 [VIII, 781 p.].

2.2. Travaux

Haugen 1984 = Eva L. Haugen: A Bibliography of Scandinavian Dictionaries. White Plains, New York 1984.

Kahlmann 1982 = André Kahlmann: Den första fransk-svenska och svensk-franska ordboken. In: Moderna Språk 76. 1982, 345—361.

Quemada 1967 = Bernard Quemada: Les dictionnaires du français moderne 1539—1863. Paris 1967.

André Kahlmann, Stockholm (Suède)

321a. Die zweisprachige Lexikographie Schwedisch-Deutsch, Deutsch-Schwedisch

1. Gliederung und Auswahl der Wörterbücher
2. Einleitung: Die Stellung der deutschen Sprache und Kultur in Schweden
3. Wörterbücher des 18. Jahrhunderts
4. Wörterbücher 1800—1871
5. Wörterbücher 1871—1945
6. Wörterbücher der Nachkriegszeit
7. Literatur (in Auswahl)

1. Gliederung und Auswahl der Wörterbücher

Der folgenden Übersicht zugrunde liegen die Bibliographien von Haugen 1984 und Braunmüller 1987, die freilich in vielen Fällen korrektur- und ergänzungsbedürftig sind. Die chronologische Gliederung ergibt sich aus der Einleitung. Es werden hauptsächlich die größeren bzw. mehrfach aufgelegten Wörterbücher registriert. Für weniger wichtige Taschen-, Miniatur- und Speziallexika siehe Haugen und Braunmüller.

2. Einleitung: Die Stellung der deutschen Sprache und Kultur in Schweden

Es empfiehlt sich, die Wörterbücher vor dem Hintergrund der Geschichte des schwedischen Deutschunterrichts und der kulturellen Beziehungen Schwedens zu Deutschland zu behandeln. Das 18. Jh. gilt in Schweden als das französische Jh. (Hammar 1980), aber gleichzeitig gingen von Schwedisch-Pommern (1648—1814), namentlich von der Universität Greifswald, wichtige Impulse aus (Seth 1956). Das um 1800 einsetzende Interesse an der deutschen Klassik und Romantik führt zu einer Neuorientierung. Die deutsche Sprache wird 1807 unter die Gymnasialfächer aufgenommen (Björn 1979). Um diese Zeit setzt auch ein stärkerer deutscher Kultureinfluß ein. 1859 wurde Deutsch erste Fremdsprache. Spätestens seit der Reichsgründung ist die deutsche Dominanz markant. Die deutsche Kultur hatte nun eine ähnlich starke Stellung wie heute die angloamerikanische (Schweden als „deutsche Kulturprovinz", Korlén 1987). Deutsch war die Sprache nicht nur der Geisteswissenschaften und der Theologie, sondern auch der Naturwissenschaften und der Medizin. Deutschland war für das schwedische Bildungsbürgertum zweifellos das Land der Dichter und Denker. Diese Lage änderte sich nach dem 1. Weltkrieg langsam, nach dem 2. radikal. Englisch wurde 1946 erste Fremdsprache statt Deutsch, das seit 1962 fakultativ mit Französisch Wahlfach ab Klasse 7 ist (wobei die Mehrzahl der Schüler Deutsch wählt). Für die neunziger Jahre ist mit einem verstärkten Interesse für Deutsch als „Sprache der europäischen Mitte" zu rechnen.

3. Wörterbücher des 18. Jahrhunderts

Lind, schw.-dt. und dt.-schw. 1738 und 1749 — Dähnert, schw.-dt. und dt.-schw. 1784 und 1796 — Möller, schw.-dt. und dt.-schw. 1782—90 und 1801—08.

Die Wörterbücher des 17. Jhs. waren multilingual (Hammar 1980). Als älteste bilinguale Wörterbücher verzeichnet Haugen 1984 die von Lind 1749. Aber wie der Verf., ein bekannter Pfarrer, im Vorwort mitteilt, handelt es sich um eine erweiterte Fassung eines von ihm 1738 anonym herausgegebenen „Dictionarium". Während Lind dies als „Nothilfe für unstudierte Leute und Jugendliche" vorstellt, erhebt er 1749 höhere Ansprüche, namentlich was die Phraseologie betrifft. Daß aber beide Wörterbücher erhebliche Mängel aufweisen, ergibt sich aus einem Vergleich mit Möller. Dieser war ein gebürtiger Deutscher, der nach zehnjährigem Aufenthalt in Schweden Professor für Geschichte in Greifswald und Mitglied der schwedischen Akademie der Wissenschaften wurde. Er war daher für die Aufgabe ganz anders qualifiziert. Sein Wörterbuch behauptete sich auch lange als das führende Wörterbuch. Ungefähr gleichzeitig gab ein anderer Greifswalder Professor, J. C. Dähnert, ein Handlexikon heraus. Als eine Spiegelung der französischen Kulturdominanz enthält Dähnert 1784 neben dem Schwedischen (Teil I) und dem Deutschen (Teil II) auch französische Übersetzungen, sowie in Teil III ein französisches Register. Die 1796 postum erschienene 2. Aufl. verzichtete aber auf die französischen Bestandteile. Das Vorwort beruft sich hier auf Möller, „dem an Genauigkeit, Richtigkeit, Vollständigkeit, Deutlichkeit und Zweckmässigkeit wenige Handwörterbücher irgendeiner Sprache gleich kommen".

4. Wörterbücher 1800—1871

Wikforss, dt.-schw. 1804 — Anonymus, dt.-schw. 1815 — Heinrich, schw.-dt. 1814 — Heinrich, schw.-dt. 1817, 1825, 1841 — Heinrich, dt.-schw. 1818, 1823, 1835 — Viereck 1825 — Heinrich, schw.-dt. 1828 — Deleen, schw.-dt. 1836 — Freese, schw.-dt. 1842 — Leffler, dt.-schw. 1844, 1873, 1876, 1885, 1893 — Anonymus (Leffler?), schw.-dt. 1844 — Dalin, schw.-dt. 1851.

Wikforss verzeichnet unter Verzicht auf Phraseologie gegenüber seiner Hauptquelle Möller allein für den Buchstaben A 3400 Wörter mehr. Das erste Schulwörterbuch ist das 1815 anonym erschienene „Handlexikon für die Schuljugend", das laut Vorwort an Wortreichtum sowohl Dähnert als auch Möller übertrifft. Über mehrere Dezennien verbreitet ist Leffler. Am produktivsten und erfolgreichsten in der ersten Hälfte des Jhs. war Heinrich. Deleen enthält nach eigener Angabe 60 000 Wörter mehr als die bisherigen Wörterbücher. Das besondere Kennzeichen von Freese ist, daß es „mit besonderer Rücksicht auf nordische Geschichte, Alterthumskunde und Mythologie, sowie Bergbau, Seefahrtskunde und Naturgeschichte zusammengetragen" ist. Es überrascht, daß Dalin nicht neu aufgelegt wurde, da der Verf. sich, u. a. mit seinem bis ins 20. Jh. maßgeblichen schwedischen Wörterbuch (1850—53), als der bedeutendste Lexikograph dieses Zeitraums ausgewiesen hat.

5. Wörterbücher 1871—1945

Helms, schw.-dt. und dt.-schw. 1872, 1885, 1887, 1893, 1904, 1923 — Hierta, schw.-dt. 1872 — Hierta, dt.-schw. 1873, 1876, 1885, 1893 — Widmark, dt.-schw. 1883—89 — Hoppe, schw.-dt. 1886, 1890, 1900, 1904, 1910, 1914, 1917, 1920, 1923, 1928, 1931 — Hoppe, dt.-schw. Schulwb. 1889, 1901, 1904, 1908, 1913, 1917, 1920, 1924 — Hoppe, schw.-dt. Schulwb. 1892, 1898, 1901, 1905, 1911, 1913, 1914, 1916 — Rosenberger, dt.-schw. 1894, 1911, 1913, 1919, 1927, 1954, 1956 — Hierta, dt.-schw. Schulwb. 1894 — Hierta, schw.-dt. Schulwb. 1898 — Morén, schw.-dt. 1901, 1905 — Klint, schw.-dt. 1906, 1910, 1915 — Auerbach, schw.-dt. 1907—16, 1918, 1967 — Wrede, schw.-dt. und dt.-schw. 1910—12 — Hoppe/Hildebrand, schw.-dt. 1916, 1919, 1922,1925, 1930, 1933, 1935, 1937, 1940, 1943, 1945, 1953, 1954 — Hoppe/Auerbach/Reutercrona, dt.-schw. 1927, 1933, 1937, 1939, 1942, 1945, 1950, 1955, 1959 — Kock, dt.-schw. 1929 — Auerbach/Holmberg/Reutercrona, dt.-schw. 1932, 1967 — Holmberg, dt.-schw. 1940, 1949, 1951, 1954, 1957, 1958, 1959, 1960, 1962, 1963, 1964, 1968.

Die deutsche Kulturdominanz führt, wie ersichtlich, zu einer markanten Zunahme an Wörterbüchern, namentlich für den Schulgebrauch. Wiewohl Helms laut Titelangabe „verpfl. Übersetzer und Dolmetsch bei den königl. Gerichten zu Leipzig" war, ist seine Beherrschung der schwedischen Sprache höchst mangelhaft, wie aus einer dem Ex. in der Königl. Bibliothek zu Stockholm beigefügten Zeitungsbesprechung zu ersehen ist. Von den Schulwörterbüchern war Klint von Anfang an verbreitet (Rez. E. A. Meyer und E. Rodhe in Moderna språk [Mspr.] 1906, 42—47) und hat sich, wie Rosenberger, in Neubearbeitungen (Klint-Lutze 1952) noch lange gehalten. Bis in die Nachkriegszeit dominierte aber Hoppe, zumal in den Bearbeitungen von Auerbach/Reutercrona bzw. Hildebrand (Rez. N. O. Heinertz, Mspr. 1918, 28—29). Bisher unübertroffen an Umfang und Qualität ist das klassische schwedisch-deutsche Wörterbuch von Auerbach (Rez. E. A. Meyer, Mspr. 1909, 29—30 und N. O. Heinertz, Mspr. 1918, 25—28). Als Hilfsmittel in der Abiturprüfung wurde es Mitte der 30er Jahre verboten, da nach Ansicht der Schulbehörden die reichhaltigen syntaktischen und phraseologischen Angaben die Übersetzung allzusehr erleichterten. Das deutsch-schwedische Pendant von Auerbach/Holmberg/Reutercrona enthält trotz des Umfangs von 2880 Seiten allzu viele Lücken (Tamsen 1954).

6. Wörterbücher der Nachkriegszeit

Holmberg/Reutercrona, dt.-schw. und schw.-dt. 1948—50, 1952, 1953, 1955, 1956, 1957, 1959, 1960, 1963, 1969, 1970 — Gerring/Johnson, dt.-schw. 1951, 1958, 1963, 1967, 1976 — Ahldén, schw.-dt. 1952, 1958, 1960, 1965 — Klint/Lutze 1952, 1956 — Kornitzky/Hellwig, dt.-schw. 1954, 1984—85 — STO, schw.-dt. 1957, 1963, 1978 — Kornitzky, schw.-dt. 1958, 1984—85 — TSO, dt.-schw. 1962, 1980 — Worgt/Sieber, dt.-schw. 1965, 1969, 1973, 1976, 1979, 1982, 1986 — Prisma, schw.-dt. 1974, 1980, 1987 — Prisma, dt.-schw. 1984 — Fachwörterbücher: Engström dt.-schw. 1949, 1959, 1965, 1970, 1976, 1982, 1987 — Engström, schw.-dt. 1951, 1955, 1959, 1971, 1976, 1983, 1988 — Parsenow, schw.-dt. und dt.-schw. 1975, 1985.

Von den ersten Nachkriegswörterbüchern waren Gerring/Johnson und Ahldén an Umfang und Qualität unzulänglich (Rez. M. Tamsen, Mspr. 1954, 123—139 und 1959, 432—436 bzw. G. Korlén, Mspr. 1954, 117—123). Auch Holmberg/Reutercrona, wiewohl wiederholt neu gedruckt, enthält zu wenig Phraseologie. Als Ersatz für Hoppe/Hildebrand und Hoppe/Auerbach/Reutercrona wurden STO (Rez. M. Tamsen, Mspr. 1958, 398—406 und G. Korlén, Mspr. 1978, 293—296) und TSO (Rez. G. Mellbourn, Mspr. 1980, 348—351) lanciert, die bis heute den Markt dominieren, obwohl sie natürlich schnell veralten (Rossenbeck 1985). Von den Konkurrenzunternehmen Prisma 1974 und 1984 war ersteres eine Katastrophe (Rez. K. Rossenbeck, Mspr. 1975, 21—34 und 316—333) und ist auch in der 2. Aufl. unbefriedigend (Rez. K. Rossenbeck, Germ. Bulletin 5, Linköping 1981, 75—103, positiver G. Mellbourn, Mspr. 1981, 357—361). Es überrascht, daß der Langenscheidt-Verlag das Wörterbuch für den deutschen Markt übernahm, da hier mit Kornitzky 1958 ein sehr brauchbares Wörterbuch vorlag (Rez. M. Tamsen, Mspr. 1959, 429—432, über Kornitzky/Hellwig 1954 Tamsen, Mspr. 1955, 395—400). Prisma 1984 war ein lexikographischer Fortschritt und wird von Rossenbeck als „passabel" eingestuft (Rez. Mspr. 1988, 211—225). Von den Fachwörterbüchern haben sich die von Engström (Technik) 1949 und 1951 über Dezennien bewährt, während Parsenow (Recht und Wirtschaft) 1975 ebenso katastrophal war wie Prisma 1974 (Rez. K. Rossenbeck, Mspr. 1977, 75—86) und in der 2. Aufl. ebenfalls höchst unbefriedigend ist (Rez. K. Rossenbeck, Mspr. 1987, 82—86 und Lexikographica 1989, 227—240).

7. Literatur (in Auswahl)

7.1. Wörterbücher

Ahldén 1952 = Tage Ahldén: Svensk-tyskt lexikon. Stockholm 1952 [VIII, 310 S., 5. Neudruck 1976].

Anonymus 1815 = Tyskt och Svenskt Hand-Lexicon för Skol-ungdom, Bd. 1—2. Jönköping 1815 [406, 436 S.].

Auerbach 1907—16 = Carl Auerbach: Svensk-tysk ordbok. Stockholm 1907—16 [X, 1529 S., 2. Aufl. 1918, 3. Aufl. mit Suppl. 54 S. 1959, 9. Druck 1967].

Auerbach/Holmberg/Reutercrona 1932 = C. Auerbach/J. Holmberg/H. Reutercrona: Tysk-svensk ordbok. Stockholm 1932 [VIII, 2880 S., Neudruck 1967].

Dähnert 1784 = J. C. Dähnert: Kurzgefasstes Deutsches und Schwedisches Hand-Lexicon mit angefügten Französischen Bedeutungen. Stockholm. Greifswald 1784 [VIII S., 1676 Sp., 2. Aufl. mit dem Titel „Schwedisch-deutsches und deutsch-schwedisches Wörterbuch" 1796, XIV, 274 S.].

Dalin 1850—53 = A. F. Dalin: Ordbok öfver svenska språket. Bd. I—II, Stockholm 1850—53 [897, 772 S., photomech. Neudruck 1964].

Dalin 1851 = A. F. Dalin: Nytt svenskt och tyskt handlexikon. Stockholm 1851 [492 S.].

Deleen 1836 = Carl Deleen: Tysk och svensk ordbok. Örebro 1836 [946 S.].

Freese 1842 = A. G. F. Freese: Schwedisch-deutsches Wörterbuch. Stralsund 1842 [442 S.].

Engström 1949 = Einar Engström: Tysk-svensk teknisk ordbok. Stockholm 1949 [498 S., 7. Aufl. 1976, Neudruck 1983, 1987, 774 S.].

Engström 1951 = Einar Engström: Svensk-tysk teknisk ordbok. Stockholm 1951 [477 S., 7. Aufl. 1976, Neudruck 1983, 1988, 758 S.].

Gerring/Johnson 1951 = Hugo Gerring/Gösta Johnson: Tysk-svenskt lexikon. Stockholm 1951 [XV, 367 S., 2. Aufl. 1958, Neudrucke 1963, 1973, 1976].

Heinrich 1814 = Carl Heinrich: Svenskt och tyskt lexicon. Bd. I—II. Christianstad 1814 [748, 596 Sp., 2. Aufl. Stralsund 1829, 592 S.].

Heinrich 1817 = Carl Heinrich: Svenskt och tyskt hand-lexicon. Stockholm 1817 [4 S., 960 Sp., 2. Aufl., Örebro 1825, 8, 592 S., 3. Aufl. von F. Eimele, Lund 1841, 4, 583 S.].

Heinrich 1818 = Carl Heinrich: Tyskt och svenskt hand-lexicon. Stockholm 1818 [6 S., 1004 Sp., 2. Aufl. Örebro 1823, 2, 837 S., 3. Aufl., 2 Bände, 1835, 2, 480 und 2, 528 S.].

Heinrich 1828 = Carl Heinrich: Nytt och fullständigt svenskt och tyskt lexicon. Stockholm 1828 [VIII, 1554 S.].

Helms 1872 = Svenn Henrik Helms: Neues vollständiges schwedisch-deutsches und deutsch-schwedisches Wörterbuch. Leipzig 1872 [XXVI, 494 und XXVIII, 456 S., 6. Aufl. 1923].

Hierta 1872 = Svenskt-tyskt handlexikon. Stockholm 1872 [492 S.].

Hierta 1873 = Tyskt och svenskt handlexikon. Stockholm 1873 [493 S., Neudrucke 1876, 1885, 1893].

Hierta 1894 = Tysk-svensk ordbok. Hiertas skolordböcker. Stockholm 1894 [712 S.].

Hierta 1898 = Svensk-tysk ordbok. Hiertas skolordböcker. Stockholm 1898 [768 S.].

Holmberg 1940 = John Holmberg: Tysk-svensk ordbok. Stockholm 1940 [VI, 218 S., 13. Neudruck 1968].

Holmberg/Reutercrona 1948—1950 = John Holmberg/Grete und Hans Reutercrona: Tysk-svensk, svensk-tysk ordbok. Stockholm 1948—50 [VI, 218 und IV, 220 S., 15. Neudruck 1970].

Hoppe 1886 = Otto Hoppe: Tysk-svensk ordbok. Stockholm 1886 [VI, 798 S., 2. Aufl. 1890, 3. Aufl. 1900, 9. Druck 1931].

Hoppe 1889 = Otto Hoppe: Tysk-svensk ordbok. Skolupplaga. Stockholm 1889 [vI, 536 S., 2. Aufl. 1901, 9. Druck 1924].

Hoppe 1892 = Otto Hoppe: Svensk-tysk ordbok. Skolupplaga. Stockholm 1892 [V, 391 S., 2. Aufl. 1901, 6. Druck 1916].

Hoppe/Auerbach/Reutercrona 1927 = Hoppe 1889, vollst. umgearb. 3. Aufl. von Carl Auerbach und Hans Reutercrona. Stockholm 1927 [VIII, 688 S., 4. Aufl. 1937, 7. Druck 1959].

Hoppe/Hildebrand 1916 = Hoppe 1892, 3. umgearb. und erw. Aufl. von Sune Hildebrand [VII, 563 S., 13. Druck 1954].

Klint 1906 = Axel Klint: Svensk-tysk ordbok. Stockholm 1906 [973 S., Neudruck 1910, 1915].

Klint/Lutze 1952 = Axel Klint/Dieter Lutze: Schwedisches Taschenwörterbuch, schwedisch-deutsch und deutsch-schwedisch. Berlin 1952 [576 S., 2. Aufl. 1956].

Kock 1929 = Ernst Albin Kock: Tysk-svensk ordbok. Stockholm 1929 [VIII, 423 S.].

Kornitzky/Hellwig 1954 = Hans Hellwig: Deutsch-schwedisches Taschenwörterbuch. Neubearbeitet von H. Kornitzky. Berlin 1954 [549 S., 7. Aufl. 1968].

Kornitzky 1958 = H. Kornitzky: Schwedisch-deutsches Taschenwörterbuch. Berlin 1958 [555 S., 5. Aufl. 1965, Neubearbeitung von E. Engbrant-Heider 1984—85 in einem Band mit Kornitzky/Hellwig 1954, 1006 S. Schwedische Ausgabe mit dem Titel „Den moderna tyska ordboken", Stockholm 1985].

Leffler 1844 = Otto Emanuel Leffler: Nytt tyskt och svenskt lexikon. Stockholm 1844 [494 S., 2. Aufl. mit dem Titel „Tyskt och svenskt handlexikon" 1873, 5. Aufl. 1893].

Lind 1738 = Olof Lind: Teutsch-Schwedisches und Schwedisch-Teutsches Dictionarium oder Wörterbuch. Stockholm 1738 [382, 229 S.].

Lind 1749 = Olof Lind: Teutsch-Schwedisches und Schwedisch-Teutsches Lexicon oder Wörterbuch. Stockholm 1749 [1919, 1015 Sp.].

Möller 1782—90 = Johannes Georg Möller: Teutsch-Schwedisches und Schwedisch-Teutsches Wörterbuch. Bd. I—III, Stockholm 1782—90 [14 S. 1300 Sp., 4 S. 1542, 8 S., 1984 Sp., 2. Aufl. Uppsala 1801—08].

Morén 1901 = C. G. Morén et al.: Svenskt-tyskt konstruktionslexikon. Stockholm 1901 [404 S.].

Parsenow 1975 = G. Parsenow: Fachwörterbuch für Recht und Wirtschaft. Schwedisch-deutsch und deutsch-schwedisch. Köln 1975 [XII, 504 S., 2. Aufl. 1985].

Prisma 1974 = Modern svensk-tysk ordbok. Stockholm 1974 [596 S., 2. umgearb. Aufl. 1980, 632 S., Neudruck 1987, 1990].

Prisma 1984 = Modern tysk-svensk ordbok. Stockholm 1984 [736 S., 1987, 1990].

Rosenberger 1894 = G. Rosenberger: Tysk-svensk ordbok. Stockholm 1894 [XV, 283 S., 2. rev. Aufl. von C. Auerbach 1911, 12. Neudruck 1956].

STO 1957 = Svensk-tysk ordbok. Stockholm 1957 [XVI, 755 S., 2. Aufl. 1963, 3. Aufl. 1978, 783 S. mit Supplement 28 S., 4. erw. Aufl. mit dem Titel „Stora svensk-tyska ordboken" 1989, 963 S.].

TSO 1962 = Tysk-svensk ordbok. Stockholm 1962 [866 S., 2. Aufl. 1980 mit Supplement 30 S.].

Viereck 1825 = Carl Friedrich Viereck: Tyskt och svenskt handlexikon med grammatiska upplysningar, jemte ett svenskt och tyskt ordregister. Stockholm 1825 [726 S.].

Widmark 1883—89 = Per Fredrik Widmark: Tysk-svensk ordbok. Stockholm 1883—89 [1548 S.].

Wikforss 1804 = Jonas Wikforss: Tyskt och svenskt lexikon. Bd. I—II, Stockholm 1804 [II, 1006 und 1094 S.].

Worgt/Sieber 1965 = Gerhard Worgt/Annemarie Sieber: Deutsch-schwedisches Wörterbuch. Leipzig 1965 [XXIV, 271 S., 7. Aufl. 1986].

Wrede 1910—12 = Ernst Wrede: Taschenwörterbuch der schwedischen und deutschen Sprache. Bd. I—II. Berlin 1910—12 [XIV, 646 und XXIV, 433 S.].

7.2. Sonstige Literatur

Björn 1979 = Gösta Björn: Deutsche Literatur in den Deutschbüchern des schwedischen Gymnasiums 1905—1970. Diss. Stockholm 1979.

Braunmüller 1987 = Kurt Braunmüller: Deutsch-Skandinavisch im Vergleich. Eine Bibliographie zur Linguistik und Lexikographie. Neumünster 1987.

Hammar 1980 = Elisabeth Hammar: L'enseignement du français en Suède jusqu'en 1807. — Méthodes et manuels. Diss. Stockholm 1980.

Hannesdóttir/Ralph 1988 = Anna Hannesdóttir/Bo Ralph: Early Dictionaries in Sweden: Traditions and Influences. In: Symposium on Lexicography IV. Ed. by K. Hyldgaard-Jensen/A. Zettersten. Tübingen 1988 (Lexicographica Series Maior 26), 265—279.

Haugen 1984 = Eva Haugen: A Bibliography of Scandinavian Dictionaries. New York 1984.

Korlén 1987 = Gustav Korlén: Über den deutschen Kultureinfluß in Schweden. In: Verstand zur Verständigung. Festschrift für Heinrich Pfeiffer. Berlin 1987, 64—68.

Malmgren 1991 = Göran Malmgren: German-Swedish Lexicography in 18th Century Pomerania.

In: Symposium on Lexicography V. Tübingen 1991 (Lexicographica Series Maior 41).

Rossenbeck 1985 = Klaus Rossenbeck: Zur gegenwärtigen Lage der schwedisch-deutschen und deutsch-schwedischen Lexikographie. In: Die Brüder Grimm — Erbe und Rezeption, hrsg. von Astrid Stedje. Stockholm 1985, 142—154.

Seth 1956 = Ivar Seth: Die Universität Greifswald und ihre Stellung in der schwedischen Kulturpolitik 1637—1815. Berlin (DDR) 1956.

Tamsen 1954 = Martin Tamsen: Über deutschschwedische Lexika. In: Moderna språk 48. 1954, 2—43.

Gustav Korlén, Stockholm (Schweden)

321 b. Bilingual Lexicography: Swedish-English, English-Swedish

1. Cultural Background
2. Dictionaries and Dictionary-Makers
3. Treatment of Grammar and Pronunciation
4. Bibliographical Note
5. Selected Bibliography

1. Cultural Background

1.1. Education

The position of English in the present Swedish school system is very strong. Starting at the age of 9 or 10, everybody studies English until the age of 16, and English is also a prominent subject in later education. However, this situation, which greatly favours the production of English general-purpose dictionaries, is a result of fairly recent developments. Modern languages in general were not taught in Swedish schools until late in the 18th century, and English hardly at all until towards the middle of the 19th century. In 1905, English was made obligatory in Swedish secondary schools, and since 1950 English has been a compulsory subject for all pupils in Sweden.

1.2. Emigration

Mainly during the latter half of the 19th century, about a million Swedes emigrated to the USA, thus temporarily creating a market for English dictionaries outside Sweden. Examples are Chils 1888 and Hill's 1907.

2. Dictionaries and Dictionary-Makers

2.1. The 18th Century

The first English-Swedish dictionary is Serenius 1734, which translates English words into both Swedish and Latin and includes footnotes with etymologies and lists of related words in other languages. A specialized part, "A Table of Terms of Trade and Navigation", indicates one reason why a dictionary was needed. Serenius 1757 is counted as the second edition of the previous work in spite of its new title and other modifications. Serenius also produced Sweden's first Swedish-English dictionary, Serenius 1741. In the spirit of the age, he describes English as a daughter-language of Swedish, although mixed with Norman French. — The first small-size dictionary, Sjöbeck 1774—75, praises Serenius and assures the reader that all basic words have been taken over from him. — The second major dictionary for English-Swedish is Brisman 1783, drawing on (the 2nd ed. of) Johnson 1755 and Serenius 1757, and for Swedish-English Widegren 1788. The latter work is also the source of a short Swedish-English dictionary appended to later editions of Brisman 1783 (1801, 1815).

2.2. 1800—1875

The first new English-Swedish 19th-century dictionaries are Delén 1806—07 and Granberg 1807. — The list of references in Delén 1806—07 includes specialized dictionaries on natural history, trade and navigation, whereas Granberg 1807 is too small to be able to accommodate specialized vocabulary. — Deleen (this is how Delén spelled his name from 1816) also produced a Swedish-English dictionary, Deleen 1829, based on Widegren 1788 but exceeding it in size by 6,000 entries, many of them terms from natural history and navigation.

The rest of this period is characterized by pocket dictionaries, some of them anonymous and all of them lacking information about source material. One and the same work is often ascribed to different authors or occurs under different publishers' names. For details, see Olofsson (forthcoming). Two pocket dictionaries with definable authorship are Jungberg 1856 (Swedish-English) and Jungberg 1875 (English-Swedish). — What started as plans to revise Deleen 1829 resulted in a new Swedish-English pocket dictionary, Öman 1872, featuring some typographical innovations, e.g. the abolishing of Gothic typeface.

2.3. 1875—1935

Two large English-Swedish dictionaries, Nilsson e.a. 1875 and Wenström/Lindgren 1889, appeared in such rapid succession that the preface of the latter includes an apologetic comment on the great activity of the time in the field of English lexicography. — Both Lindgren and Wenström made abridged versions, Lindgren 1891 (the first English-Swedish dictionary explicitly intended for schools) and Wenström 1894 (pocket-size). — Björkman 1889, the first Swedish-English work to appear in this period, complains of the scarcity of good previous works in Swedish-English lexicography. — The first major Swedish-English dictionary explicitly produced for use in schools, Wenström/Harlock 1904, is the result of team-work, whereas the next two dictionaries, Montgomery 1906 (English-Swedish) and Montgomery 1914 (Swedish-English), are the products of one person. The latter work has the secondary purpose of being a guide for English-speaking people in the study of Swedish.

Between 1914 and 1935, no major works appeared, but important preparation was going on.

2.4. 1935—1980

The next major English-Swedish work is Kärre e.a. 1935. Work on this dictionary, which was intended to replace Lindgren 1891, had been started as early as 1916. The main source is stated to be *A New English Dictionary on Historical Principles*. Different senses are organized in numbered groups. An abridged version of Kärre e.a. 1935 was made by one of the members of the team and appeared as Nöjd 1939. Nöjd also played an important part in Wenström 1941, the revised version of Wenström 1894. — A large-scale Swedish-English project was started by Harlock in 1919 but was never quite finished. A first volume (the letters A—K) was published as Harlock 1936. The second volume (L—R) appeared after Harlock's death (Harlock/Gabrielson 1951). No final volume was ever published. — Three small and medium-size Swedish-English dictionaries, all of them drawing on Harlock 1936 and Harlock's unpublished material, appeared in rapid succession: Tornberg/Ångström 1940, Ernolv/Petterson/Ångström 1942 and Harlock 1944.

Work on Harlock 1944, which was to replace Wenström/Harlock 1904 as a Swedish-English school dictionary, was started by Harlock and Gabrielson, but neither took part in the whole sequence of letters. — In English-Swedish lexicography, the next major work, Cronwall/Freudenthal 1943, was written in Finland on the basis of an English-Danish dictionary. After a decade, it was superseded by an extensively revised version, Freudenthal e.a. 1953. — The next Swedish-English dictionary, Reuter 1952, originated in Finland too. The author declares that he is indebted to Harlock's works and to other modern dictionaries, general and specialized.

The extension of English into the compulsory school created a market for even smaller and simpler dictionaries and study aids, some of them frequency-based, one of them, Lindén/Petti 1960, even for both English and Swedish. For details, see Olofsson (forthcoming).

The next major English-Swedish dictionary, Danielsson 1964, is based on an English-Dutch dictionary, but largely independent, particularly through later revisions. Meanings are grouped and numbered, with frequency as the guiding principle. Danielsson 1964 soon got a Swedish-English counterpart, Gomer/Morris-Nygren 1970, with 50,000 entries presented in a typographically compressed form. Though produced in Sweden and mainly for Swedes, it can also be used by learners of Swedish, since it includes information about Swedish pronunciation and grammar. — Harlock 1944, for many years regarded as the standard Swedish-English dictionary for advanced studies, was replaced by Svensk-engelsk 1968, largely a new work, with material from Harlock's different dictionaries taken into account but not used as a basis. An abridged version, Svensk-engelsk pocket 1973, has a new appendix dealing with e.g. the new British monetary system. — Bergström/Carlson/Ferm 1975 (English-Swedish, 40,000 words) concentrates on present-day English. It introduces some features that are new in English-Swedish lexicography, e.g. pictures to supplement definitions. Senses, grouped and numbered, are ordered according to frequency.

2.5. The 1980s

The dictionaries published in the 1980s fall into three fairly distinct classes in terms of size: (a) SESO 1980 (English-Swedish) and SSEO 1988 (Swedish-English), marketed as a pair, have about 120,000 items each, covering general and, to some extent, specialized vocabulary. (b) In the class with 50—60,000 entries there are three English-Swedish dictionaries but no Swedish-English ones first published in the 1980s. Engelsk-svenska 1983 is an abridged version of SESO 1980. Its Swedish-English counterpart dates from the 1970s (Svensk-engelsk pocket 1973). BESO 1987 (about 50,000 words and phrases) is not based on any previous English-Swedish dictionaries. Collins of Glasgow provided a complete set of English entries and Bonniers of Stockholm the Swedish translations. For the grouping of different senses, BESO 1987 uses a system of indicators (subject field, synonyms, specialist register etc.). BESO 1987 has no Swedish-English counterpart. Like BESO 1987, Prisma's Eng-Sw 1988 claims to be a completely new work. One of its characteristics is that non-technical explanations are preferred to grammatical terminology. It has a Swedish-English counterpart first published in the 1970s (Gomer/Morris-Nygren 1970), but revised as late as 1988. (c) Petti/Petti 1987, a two-way dictionary with roughly 30,000 words and phrases in each part, belongs to the same series as SESO 1980 and Engelsk-svenska 1983 and their Swedish-English counterparts.

3. Treatment of Grammar and Pronunciation

Despite the high degree of correspondence between parts of speech in English and Swedish, most dictionaries give this kind of information for every item. It is omitted in some small practical dictionaries like Hill's 1907, Goodwin 1928 and Lindén/Petti 1960, but also in the medium-size work Cronwall/Freudenthal 1943. A more flexible system, with information only in cases of multiple membership, is employed in Danielsson 1964 and Bergström/Carlson/Ferm 1975. For the classification of verbs, the older system of dividing them into active and neuter verbs was replaced by the transitive/intransitive dichotomy around 1890. — Notes on English grammar are to be found in Sjöbeck 1774—75 and Montgomery 1906, and on Swedish grammar in Montgomery 1914 and Gomer/Morris-Nygren 1970.

As for English pronunciation, the first English-Swedish dictionary, Serenius 1734, has no information, but in its Swedish-English counterpart, Serenius 1741, there is a four-page chapter on the subject. The first English-Swedish dictionaries to use transcription (in the Swedish alphabet) are Sjöbeck 1774—75 and Brisman 1783. In the 19th century, main stress was normally the only indication used until 1875, when Walker's system (with numbers above the vowel signs) was introduced in Nilsson e.a. 1875. It was also used in Wenström/Lindgren 1889 and in one of its abridged versions, Lindgren 1891. Distinctive placement of the accent sign in non-transcribed words (la'dy/lad'der) was first used in Wenström 1894 and the system was continued in e.g. Nöjd 1939 and Wenström 1941. The Toussaint-Langenscheidt notation occurs only in Montgomery 1906. Sturzen-Becker's system was used in some works produced in the USA, e.g. Hill's 1907. The IPA notation (including the vertical stroke) was introduced in Goodwin 1928, and a similar form occurs in Cronwall/Freudenthal 1943. With modifications involving e.g. the shape and placement of the accent, the IPA system was used in Kärre e.a. 1935, Freudenthal e.a. 1953, Lindén/Petti 1960 and Danielsson 1964. A later edition (1974) of Danielsson 1964 settled for the vertical stroke before the stressed syllable, and from 1975 all new English-Swedish dictionaries have used the current IPA system.

4. Bibliographical Note

The present account is the first to cover English-Swedish and Swedish-English general-purpose lexicography through the 1980s. For a general account of early Swedish lexicography up to 1850, see Hannesdóttir/Ralph 1988 (with references). English-Swedish and Swedish-English dictionaries published before 1905 are described in Bratt 1977 and Bratt 1982. The standard bibliography, Haugen 1984, which also contains a description of general developments, lists the full range of dictionaries, general and specialized, from the earliest days of Scandinavian lexicography until 1980. Full coverage of English-Swedish and Swedish-English general-purpose dictionaries 1734—1990 is given in Olofsson (forthcoming). Reviews in English of some recent dictionaries have appeared in Moderna språk (Gröndahl 1969, Seltén 1965, Wright 1981).

5. Selected Bibliography

5.1. Dictionaries

Bergström/Carlson/Ferm 1975 = Mats Bergström/Ingvar Carlson/Rolf G. E. Ferm: Engelsk-svensk ordbok. Stockholm 1975 [451, (4) p.].

BESO 1987 = Catherine E. Love/Gunnel Tottie (eds. in chief): Bonniers engelsk-svenska ordbok — English-Swedish dictionary. Glasgow. Stockholm 1987 [XVI, 512 p.].

Björkman 1889 = C. G. Björkman: Svensk-engelsk ordbok. Stockholm 1889 [(6), 1360 p.].

Brisman 1783 = Sven Brisman: Engelskt och Swänskt Hand-Lexicon [. . .]. Stockholm. Uppsala. Åbo 1783 [8, XII p., 724 cols.].

Chils 1888 = Otto Chils: Practical Swedish-English dictionary. 30,000 Swedish words translated to English [. . .]. New York 1888 [298 p.].

Cronwall/Freudenthal 1943 = Uno Cronwall/Fritiof Freudenthal: Engelsk-svenskt lexikon [. . .]. Stockholm 1943 [8, 371 p.].

Danielsson 1964 = Bror Danielsson (ed.): Modern engelsk-svensk ordbok — A Modern English-Swedish Dictionary. Stockholm 1964 [11, 393 p.].

Delén 1806—07 = Carl Delén: Engelskt och Svenskt Lexikon. Part I (A—L). Stockholm 1806 [32, 395 p.]. Part II (M—Z). Stockholm 1807 [(3), 330 p.].

Deleen 1829 = Carl Deleen: Swedish and English Pocket-Dictionary eller Swenskt och Engelskt Hand-Lexikon. Örebro 1829 [IV, 626 p.].

Engelsk-svenska 1983 = Bo Svensén (ed.): Engelsk-svenska ordboken. Solna 1983 [10, 758 p.].

Ernolv/Petterson/Ångström 1942 = Carl Ernolv/Anna C. Petterson/Margareta Ångström: Svensk-engelsk ordbok. Stockholm 1942 [VI, 570 p.].

Freudenthal e.a. 1953 = Fritiof Freudenthal/Uno Cronwall/Rudolf Löfgren e.a.: Engelsk-svenskt lexikon [. . .]. Stockholm 1953 [(8), 348 p.].

Gomer/Morris-Nygren 1970 = Eva Gomer/Mona Morris-Nygren: Modern svensk-engelsk ordbok. A modern Swedish-English dictionary [. . .]. Stockholm 1970 [XVI, 566 p. Later revised and (in 1988) re-named Prismas svensk-engelska ordbok — Prisma's Swedish-English dictionary].

Goodwin 1928 = Henry Buergel Goodwin: Svenskt-engelskt parlörlexikon [. . .]. Stockholm 1928 [XLVIII, 356 p.].

Granberg 1807 = Per Adolf Granberg: English and Swedish Pocket-Dictionary eller Engelskt och Swenskt Hand-Lexikon. Stockholm 1807 [6 p., 1276 cols.].

Harlock 1936 = Walter E. Harlock: Svensk-engelsk ordbok [. . .] (A—K). Stockholm 1936 [XV, 1230 p.].

Harlock 1944 = Walter E. Harlock: Svensk-engelsk ordbok. Skolupplaga [. . .]. Stockholm 1944 [VIII, 1048 p.].

Harlock/Gabrielson 1951 = Walter E. Harlock/Arvid Gabrielson: Svensk-engelsk ordbok (L—R). Stockholm 1951 [(4), pp. 1231—2096, 16 p.].

Hill's 1907 = Hill's Swedish-English and English-Swedish pronouncing dictionary — Svensk-engelsk och engelsk-svensk fick-ordbok. Philadelphia 1907 [98, 158 p.].

Johnson 1755 = Samuel Johnson: A dictionary of the English language [. . .]. London 1755.

Jungberg 1856 = Carl Gustaf Jungberg: Nytt svenskt och engelskt hand-lexicon [. . .]. Stockholm 1856 [4, 844 p.].

Jungberg 1875 = Carl Gustaf Jungberg: Engelskt och svenskt hand-lexikon med de engelska ordens uttal. Stockholm 1875 [524 p.].

Kärre e.a. 1935 = Karl Kärre/Harald Lindkvist/Ruben Nöjd/Mats Redin: Engelsk-svensk ordbok. Skolupplaga [. . .]. English-Swedish dictionary. School edition [. . .]. Stockholm 1935 [XV, 1023 p.].

Lindén/Petti 1960 = Niloés Engelsk-svenska och svensk-engelska lexikon. Utgivet under medverkan av Orvar Lindén, Vincent Petti m. fl. Stockholm 1960 [190, 252, (2) p.].

Lindgren 1891 = Erik Lindgren: Engelsk-svensk ordbok — skoluppl. — på grundvalen av Wenström-Lindgrens större engelsk-svenska ordbok. Stockholm 1891 [(4), 674, 50 p.].

Montgomery 1906 = Albert Montgomery: Engelsk-svensk ordbok. Stockholm 1906 [XII, 659 p.].

Montgomery 1914 = Albert Montgomery: Svensk-engelsk ordbok. Stockholm 1914 [14, 615 p.].

Nilsson e.a. 1875 = Lars Gabriel Nilsson/Per Fredrik Widmark/August Zacharias Collin e.a.: Engelsk-svensk ordbok, med Walkers uttalsbeteckning. Stockholm 1875 [(2), 1304 p.].

Nöjd 1939 = Ruben Nöjd: Engelsk-svensk ordbok. Stockholm 1939 [VIII, 248 p.].

Öman 1872 = Victor Emanuel Öman: Svensk-engelsk hand-ordbok. Örebro 1872 [IV, 470 p.].

Petti/Petti 1987 = Vincent Petti/Kerstin Petti: Lilla engelska ordboken. Engelsk-svensk. Svensk-engelsk. Solna 1987 [XX, 747 p.].

Prisma's Eng-Sw 1988 = Prismas engelsk-svenska ordbok — Prisma's English-Swedish dictionary. Stockholm 1988 [612 p.].

Reuter 1952 = Ole R. Reuter: Svensk-engelskt lexikon. Stockholm 1952 [(8), 395 p.].

Serenius 1734 = Jacob Serenius: Dictionarium Anglo-Svethico-Latinum [. . .]. Hamburg 1734 [44, 500 (unnumbered) p.].

Serenius 1741 = Jacob Serenius: Dictionarium Suethico-Anglo-Latinum [. . .]. Stockholm 1741 [26, 284 p.].

Serenius 1757 = Jacob Serenius: An English and Swedish Dictionary [. . .]. Printed at Harg and Stenbro 1757 [24, 632 (unnumbered) p.].

SESO 1980 = Bo Svensén (ed.): Stora engelsk-svenska ordboken. A comprehensive English-Swedish dictionary. Stockholm 1980 [XXVII, 1071 p.].

Sjöbeck 1774—75 = Johan Carl Sjöbeck: Engelskt och Swenskt samt Swenskt och Engelskt Hand-dictionaire [. . .]. Stockholm 1774—75 [96, 8 p.].

SSEO 1988 = Stora svensk-engelska ordboken. A comprehensive Swedish-English dictionary. Utarbetad av Vincent Petti [. . .]. Solna 1988 [XXVIII, 1108, (3) p.].

Svensk-engelsk 1968 = Rudolph Santesson (ed. in chief): Svensk-engelsk ordbok. Stockholm 1968 [XVI, 979 p.].

Svensk-engelsk pocket 1973 = Svensk-engelsk pocketordbok. Stockholm 1973 [XVI, 480 p. From 1983 re-named Svensk-engelska ordboken, without any changes involving content].

Tornberg/Ångström 1940 = Astrid Tornberg/ Margareta Ångström: Svensk-engelsk ordbok. Stockholm 1940 [IV, 220 p.].

Wenström 1894 = Edmund Wenström: Engelsk-svensk ordbok (English-Swedish dictionary). Stockholm 1894 [III, 464 p.].

Wenström 1941 = Edmund Wenström: Engelsk-svensk ordbok. Fullständigt omarbetad av Ruben Nöjd och Anna C. Petterson. Stockholm 1941 [VIII, 648 p.].

Wenström/Harlock 1904 = Edmund Wenström/ Walter E. Harlock: A Swedish-English Dictionary/Svensk-engelsk ordbok — skolupplaga. Stockholm 1904 [VI, 880 p.].

Wenström/Lindgren 1889 = Edmund Wenström/ Erik Lindgren: Engelsk-svensk ordbok. Stockholm 1889 [(6), 1758 p.].

Widegren 1788 = Gustaf Widegren: Svenskt och engelskt lexicon, efter kongl. secreteraren Sahlstedts svenska ordbok. Stockholm 1788 [898 p.].

5.2. Other Publications

Bratt 1977 = Ingar Bratt: Engelskundervisningens framväxt i Sverige. Tiden före 1850. Stockholm 1977 (Årsböcker i svensk undervisningshistoria 139).

Bratt 1982 = Ingar Bratt: Läromedel i engelska utgivna i Sverige 1850—1905. Lund 1982 (Studia Psychologica et Paedagogica 58).

Gröndahl 1969 = Eja M. Gröndahl: Friedländer, Langlet, Lindvall, Petti, Ninni Skjöldebrand m. fl., Svensk-engelsk ordbok [...]. In: Moderna språk 63. 1969, 73—77 (Review in English of Svensk-engelsk 1968).

Hannesdóttir/Ralph 1988 = Anna Hannesdóttir/ Bo Ralph: Early dictionaries in Sweden. Traditions and influences. In: Symposium on Lexicography IV [...]. Tübingen 1988 (Lexicographica Series Maior 26), 265—279.

Haugen 1984 = Eva L. Haugen: A Bibliography of Scandinavian Dictionaries. White Plains, New York 1984.

Olofsson (forthcoming) = Arne Olofsson: Continuity and competition. A short history of English-Swedish and Swedish-English dictionaries and dictionary-making 1734—1990. In: Moderna språk 85. 1991.

Seltén 1965 = Bo Seltén: Bror Danielsson (ed.), Modern engelsk-svensk ordbok [...]. In: Moderna språk 59. 1965, 361—365 (Review in English of Danielsson 1964).

Wright 1981 = David Wright: A comprehensive English-Swedish dictionary (CESD) — some points of comparison with other dictionaries. In: Moderna språk 75. 1981, 337—346 (Review of SESO 1980).

Arne Olofsson, Göteborg (Sweden)

322. La lexicographie bilingue avec le danois

1. Les besoins de communication linguistique
2. Les débuts (XVIIe et XVIIIe siècles)
3. Développement et croissance (XIXe siècle)
4. Les grands dictionnaires bilingues du XXe siècle
5. Dictionnaires de base
6. Théorie et pratique
7. Perspectives d'avenir
8. Bibliographie choisie

1. Les besoins de communication linguistique

La linguistique bilingue s'est développée au Danemark en étroite liaison avec les besoins de communication linguistique. A partir du XVIIe siècle, les langues modernes des grandes civilisations européennes s'imposent comme véhicules d'échanges entre le Danemark et les pays de langues allemande, française et anglaise. L'apprentissage de ces langues est favorisé aussi par le prestige culturel qui s'attache à la connaissance d'une langue étrangère moderne. A la cour royale de Danemark, l'allemand et le français sont, dans certaines périodes du XVIIe et du XVIIIe siècle, employés plus fréquemment que le danois, et l'habitude du parler étranger se répand progressivement dans la noblesse et la haute bourgeoisie. L'apprentissage d'une langue étrangère, qu'il se fasse par un «maître de langues» ou par des cours dispensés dans certaines institutions spécifiques, dont la plus célèbre fut l'«Académie nobiliaire» de Sorø, établie en 1623, requiert, dorénavant, non seulement des textes d'étude et des manuels de grammaire, mais aussi des dictionnaires.

L'anglais est encore et surtout réservé aux usages commerciaux, mais son emploi s'accroîtra dans le courant du XIXe siècle pour conquérir, à l'époque contemporaine, la première place, et les dictionnaires avec l'anglais dominent actuellement dans le public. Au XXe siècle, beaucoup de langues qui sont, au Danemark, d'un emploi moins fréquent, comme l'italien, le russe, le roumain, sont également enregistrées dans les dictionnaires, tandis que l'étude contrastive du vocabulaire des grandes langues exotiques, telles que l'arabe, le chinois et le japonais, doit encore aujourd'hui se faire à l'aide de dictionnaires bilingues avec l'anglais, le français ou l'allemand.

2. Les débuts (XVIIe et XVIIIe siècles)

La première publication qui porte le titre de dictionnaire (Matras 1628) est apparue au Danemark au début du XVIIe siècle, ce qui est relativement tôt par rapport aux pays scandinaves voisins. L'auteur, qui, dans le titre de l'ouvrage, se dit «Vendosmois de naissance, professeur des langues française et italienne à l'illustre Académie de Sore», a dû avoir une connaissance imparfaite de la langue danoise, car il déclare, dans un avis au lecteur, qu'il a composé son livre avec l'assistance d'un jeune Danois de ses amis.

Le répertoire des mots de son dictionnaire est organisé, dans une large mesure, par thèmes, et les listes de mots ont sans doute été destinées à être apprises par cœur. Une certaine tendance d'alphabétisation transparaît parfois, surtout pour les verbes, mais la logique de l'organisation laisse à désirer et les digressions et les associations fortuites sont nombreuses. Le vocabulaire représenté ne manque pas de réalisme, les termes crus n'étant pas, à cette époque, bannis par les règles de la bienséance.

Un vocabulaire anglais-danois (Bolling 1678 cf. Kabell 1988), publié en annexe à une grammaire anglaise du même auteur, témoigne de l'intérêt porté par un public spécialisé à suivre la production littéraire en langue anglaise, tendance qui est attestée aussi par un certain nombre de traductions danoises d'ouvrages philosophiques et théologiques anglais.

Le premier vrai dictionnaire avec le danois et une autre langue moderne ne voit le jour qu'au XVIIIe siècle. Il a été précédé d'une publication modeste en un volume (Aphelen 1754), un dictionnaire français-danois, muni d'un index des mots danois renvoyant aux entrées en français. Le même auteur achève quelques années plus tard un ouvrage en trois volumes in-quarto, portant le titre majestueux «Le Grand Dictionnaire Royal Français et Danois» (Aphelen 1759). On y trouve une réalisation de la plupart des principes de rédaction qui sont à la base des dictionnaires des siècles suivants en ce qui concerne les renseignements grammaticaux et les emplois d'un mot, y compris les collocations et les expressions phraséologiques. Dans une deuxième édition, «considérablement améliorée et augmentée» (Aphelen 1772—1775), le troisième tome, de 831 pages in-quarto, constitue un dictionnaire danois-français complet. Il se distingue par une élaboration soignée et par une grande richesse de mots-entrées. Dans la macrostructure, les substantifs prédominent, mais les autres classes de mots n'en sont pas pour autant négligées. Ainsi, le verbe «gaae» (= aller) occupe deux pages in-quarto de trois colonnes et la préposition «på» (= sur) presque une colonne entière. Les matériaux de Von Aphelen ont été utilisés par ses successeurs jusqu'au temps présent et la partie danoise est une source importante pour l'étude du vocabulaire danois de l'époque. Après son grand dictionnaire français, Von Aphelen publie, sur le même modèle, un dictionnaire danois-allemand et allemand-danois (Aphelen 1764), premier dictionnaire danois offrant cette combinaison de langues. Par l'étendue du plan et la compétence professionnelle, Von Aphelen peut être regardé comme le fondateur de la lexicographie bilingue danoise avec les langues modernes.

Cependant, les successeurs ne se font pas attendre. Un philologue et lexicographe célèbre, Jacob Baden, professeur d'éloquence à l'Université de Copenhague et qui avait déjà composé un dictionnaire latin-danois, est l'inspirateur et le maître d'œuvre d'un dictionnaire allemand-danois et danois-allemand (Baden 1787). Dans la préface de cet ouvrage, le dictionnaire allemand et danois de Von Aphelen est reconnu pour ses grands mérites mais qualifié d'incomplet puisqu'il n'avait pu se fonder sur des dictionnaires allemands récents. Les plus grands problèmes s'attachent, cependant, au vocabulaire danois, qui n'avait pas encore été répertorié de façon systématique. Baden dit avoir fréquenté les ateliers pour apprendre les termes danois des arts et métiers, procédé de travail qui n'était pas courant à l'époque. Pour le français aussi, un remplaçant du dictionnaire de Von Aphelen ne tarde pas à paraître (Wolff 1796). La préface de ce dictionnaire français-danois loue Von Aphelen pour avoir brisé la glace et facilité la tâche aux successeurs. L'auteur reconnaît aussi ses dettes envers les dictionnaires français-allemand et allemand-français de Roux. Les sources étrangères, essentiellement les dictionnaires bilingues allemands, ont longtemps offert des modèles tout indiqués aux lexicographes danois, et la partie danoise d'articles entiers était parfois traduite d'une langue étrangère.

L'anglais fait aussi son entrée dans les dictionnaires pendant la seconde moitié du XVIIIe siècle, mais les réalisations sont plus modestes en ce qui concerne le volume et la conception des ouvrages. Le premier dictionnaire anglais-danois est composé par un théologien norvégien et publié à Londres (Berthelson 1754). Un autre Norvégien, commerçant à Londres, complète le tableau par un dictionnaire danois-anglais (Wolff 1779). Il n'y a rien d'étonnant à voir des Norvégiens consacrer leurs efforts à la lexicographie bilingue avec le danois. A cette époque, la Norvège était incorporée, en effet, au royaume du Danemark, et la langue littéraire de la communauté était le danois. Un dictionnaire avec l'anglais et le danois qui eut beaucoup de succès à la fin du XVIIIe et dans la première moitié du XIXe siècle est une traduction du dictionnaire allemand et anglais de Theodor Arnold. Ce dictionnaire (Bay 1784) connaît de nombreuses éditions et le nom de l'auteur original disparaît de la page de titre à partir de la deuxième édition sans que l'apport personnel de l'adaptateur, à savoir quelques termes commerciaux et maritimes, cités en annexe, marque une notable augmentation par rapport à la première édition. A la fin du dictionnaire, on trouve une liste de 100 souscripteurs, ce qui donne une idée de la composition du public acheteur: 10 exemplaires pour le roi, 8 pour le dauphin, 10 pour un libraire, le reste destiné à des étudiants, des officiers, des fonctionnaires, des commerçants, des nobles. Il est symptomatique que, parmi les dictionnaires mentionnés jusqu'ici, ceux qui ont la langue étrangère comme langue source soient plus élaborés et apparaissent plus tôt que les dictionnaires à partir du danois. Ceux-ci ne comprennent souvent que la moitié des pages du dictionnaire en sens inverse. Cela tient d'abord au fait qu'il n'existe pas au XVIIIe siècle de bon dictionnaire monolingue danois qui puisse servir de point de départ. De plus, l'intérêt du public acheteur s'attache en premier lieu à la compréhension des textes écrits.

3. Développement et croissance (XIXe siècle)

Après les tentatives initiales, la lexicographie du XIXe siècle est caractérisée par la recherche d'un traitement lexicographique plus soigné et bien plus précis en ce qui concerne les équivalents de traduction proposés dans la langue cible. Une indication sommaire de niveaux stylistiques et la représentation d'expressions phraséologiques et de lexiques spécialisés deviennent peu à peu plus courantes, mais la distribution des sens d'un terme et l'exemplification des différents emplois sont, en général, insuffisamment élaborées. Les innovations méthodiques sont rares et la plupart des lexicographes se contentent de transmettre l'héritage de leurs prédécesseurs, en apportant des corrections et des ajouts aux matériaux existants. De fait, l'originalité se réduit le plus souvent à une spécialité de détail.

Sous une forme rudimentaire, le dictionnaire bilingue n'est, à cette époque, qu'une juxtaposition de deux vocabulaires. La conception d'une équivalence de principe entre la langue source et la langue cible s'exprime par le titre des dictionnaires, qui met les deux langues au même niveau (par ex. Dictionnaire allemand *et* danois). Cette coutume est remplacée dans le courant du XIXe siècle par l'emploi du tiret pour indiquer la direction du procédé de traduction.

3.1. Dictionnaires avec le français

La différenciation de l'emploi des dictionnaires résulte, au XIXe siècle, dans la production d'un certain nombre de dictionnaires dits «de poche». Les poches des vêtements de l'époque ont dû être assez larges pour contenir des dictionnaires d'un format souvent impressionnant. Un dictionnaire de poche typique (Hasse 1805), renfermant à la fois un vocabulaire français-danois et un répertoire de mots danois-français, se distingue par l'indication de certains niveaux stylistiques (par ex. «familier», «peu usité», «nouvelle création»). Les néologismes créés du temps de la Révolution française sont aussi distingués par une marque spéciale, et le vocabulaire révolutionnaire est abondamment représenté. Ainsi, le mot «sans-culotte» y figure avec de nombreux dérivés.

La mise à jour du vocabulaire est un argument de vente souvent employé. Les superlatifs ne manquent pas dans les titres, comme en témoigne un petit dictionnaire de poche danois-français et français-danois (Høst 1840—1842), qui se présente (en traduction) comme «Le dictionnaire le plus nouveau, le plus complet et le plus détaillé suivant les besoins du temps présent». Dans la préface, l'auteur déclare avoir soigneusement évité toutes les expressions plates et indécentes afin que son dictionnaire convienne à l'usage des dames, des jeunes gens et des écoliers. Le nombre d'entrées est considérable par rapport à l'espace limité, les matériaux étant présentés dans un texte continu, sans alinéas, ce qui rend la consultation de l'ouvrage malaisée. Dans certains cas, les emprunts aux prédécesseurs sont marqués de leurs initiales, signe de loyauté — ou de dégagement de responsabilité.

Une indication des sources se généralise peu à peu dans les dictionnaires pour souligner que l'auteur s'est efforcé de travailler méthodiquement. Dans la préface (en français) d'un autre dictionnaire abrégé (Borring 1853), l'auteur cite, en ce qui concerne la langue française, le dictionnaire de l'Académie française, et les dictionnaires de Boiste, de Raymond, de Napoléon Landais et de Bescherelle. Le but de l'ouvrage est d'«aplanir à la jeunesse les difficultés d'une langue indispensable à quiconque souhaite de se mettre au courant des progrès de la civilisation!» L'aspect pédagogique se traduit aussi dans des renseignements sur la prononciation des mots français (s final prononcé dans «vasistas»).

La transcription phonétique des mots-entrées français n'est pratiquée systématiquement que vers la fin du XIXe siècle. Elle est représentée dans un grand dictionnaire français-danois (Sick 1883), qui s'inspire des meilleurs lexicographes étrangers (Littré en ce qui concerne le français et Karl Sachs en ce qui regarde l'aspect contrastif avec une langue germanique). Cet ouvrage se propose de couvrir les besoins de l'enseignement, même au niveau supérieur, et de guider le lecteur cultivé dans la compréhension de textes en langue française. L'auteur se déclare d'accord avec Sachs pour rompre avec le principe étymologique dans la présentation des sens d'une entrée, en plaçant le sens le plus fréquent en premier. Ce principe, préconisé avec énergie au XXe siècle, est représenté chez Sick comme une tendance, mais pas d'une manière suivie. Malgré quelques imperfections méthodiques, ce dictionnaire a été longtemps, grâce à sa documentation consciencieuse, un excellent instrument de travail pour le public danois et norvégien.

Un travail parallèle a été réalisé à la même époque du danois/norvégien vers le français (Sundby/Baruël 1883). Les mots norvégiens y sont présentés comme des cas particuliers, marqués par un astérisque. L'auteur principal, Thor Sundby, professeur de langues romanes à l'Université de Copenhague, s'est allié avec un professeur de lycée, Euchaire Baruël, pour mener à bien cette grande tâche. Dans la préface, Sundby mentionne les obstacles qui rendent le travail difficile, notamment le retard de la lexicographie norvégienne et danois par rapport à l'évolution de la langue, ce qui a pour résultat que beaucoup de mots nouveaux et de changements de sens ne sont pas enregistrés. Une partie considérable des matériaux a été établie sur la base des recherches personnelles de Sundby. Il signale avoir rédigé 1300 notes personnelles pour la lettre S et avoir travaillé trois mois entiers aux termes botaniques.

Les avantages du dictionnaire de Sundby et Baruël sur les dictionnaires précédents sont l'utilisation critique des sources et le dépouillement de textes authentiques.

3.2. Dictionnaires avec l'allemand

Dans la première moitié du XIXe siècle, l'allemand est traité en combinaison avec le danois dans plusieurs dictionnaires assez volumineux. Le nombre des éditions successives de ces publications atteste qu'à cette époque, la langue allemande est la première langue étrangère au Danemark. L'auteur d'un dictionnaire allemand-danois (Reisler 1804—1807) se vante d'avoir essayé d'allier l'exhaustivité à la brièveté. Cependant, la macrostructure de son ouvrage ne donne pas l'impression qu'il s'agit vraiment d'un dictionnaire complet comme le titre le promet. Des mots allemands très courants n'y figurent pas et les remplissages occupent beaucoup de place. Par ex. le mot **Kutsche** y figure avec 20 mots composés ou dérivés, dont la création ne pose pas, dans la plupart des cas, de problèmes à un Danois. En plus, la représentation des mots ne semble pas bien équilibrée. Ainsi, les lettres A jusqu'à K remplissent 1123 pages; tandis que le reste de l'alphabet (L—Z) n'en occupe que 844, ce qui ne correspond pas aux proportions des autres dictionnaires allemands-danois de l'époque.

Un auteur contemporain de Reisler (Müller 1800 et 1807—1810) observe des proportions qui reflètent mieux le vocabulaire de l'usage réel. Dans son dictionnaire allemand-danois, il prétend servir aussi bien un public danois qu'un public allemand. Cette fonction est soulignée dans le titre d'un autre dictionnaire (Bresemann 1850—1855). Toutefois, les dictionnaires ne sont en général pas adaptés à l'usage actif des Allemands, les renseignements grammaticaux étant bien plus maigres pour les termes danois que pour les mots allemands. Des renseignements grammaticaux sommaires sont indiqués aussi dans un dictionnaire (Grønberg 1824—1826) qui s'est perpétué, dans des éditions remaniées, tout au long du XIXe siècle. La continuation de ce dictionnaire est un exemple typique de production par couches superposées. Le dictionnaire de Grønberg est réédité en 1836, 1846 et 1866 pour être remanié par J. Kaper (Kaper 1870 et 1878). Ce dernier, qui avait été élevé dans la langue allemande au Holstein, avait d'excellentes qualités pédagogiques pour améliorer la description lexicale et la présentation des matériaux. Son dictionnaire marque un progrès notable en adoptant un grand nombre de termes de la vie de tous les jours et des sciences naturelles. La démonstration de l'emploi d'un mot se fait par des exemples bien choisis et des indications grammaticales pertinentes (par ex. en ce qui concerne la construction des verbes allemands).

3.3. Dictionnaires avec l'anglais

Les progrès de la lexicographie bilingue avec l'anglais sont entravés pendant assez longtemps par le manque de prestige de l'emploi de la langue anglaise, celle-ci étant utilisée surtout par des commerçants et des officiers de marine à des fins pratiques. Il est caractéristique qu'un professeur titulaire de langue anglaise n'ait été institué à l'Université de Copenhague qu'en 1893, avec la nomination d'Otto Jespersen à la chaire d'anglais. Le statut essentiellement utilitaire de la langue anglaise est souligné par le fait que les dictionnaires bilingues avec l'anglais manquent souvent d'une préface raisonnée. C'est le cas d'un dictionnaire «danois et anglais» du début du XIXe siècle (Olsen 1802). Le titre annonce que cet ouvrage est composé d'après les meilleurs auteurs des deux langues, ce qui dénote une certaine ambition culturelle (respect du bon usage), mais la distinction sémantique des équivalents de traduction est le plus souvent laissée au choix du lecteur.

Un dictionnaire plus consciencieusement élaboré apparaît vers le milieu du siècle (Ferrall/Repp 1845). Cet ouvrage contient une préface de 28 pages, où les résultats des prédécesseurs sont passés en revue. Le concurrent immédiat (Bay 1784 et éditions suivantes), qui a maintenu sa position pendant longtemps, y est dépossédé de toute valeur et ses nombreuses fautes lexicales sont mises en évidence. En comparaison des ouvrages qui l'ont précédé, le dictionnaire de Ferrall et Repp représente un progrès important. Les réflexions exprimées dans la préface des deux auteurs prouvent que ceux-ci ont été conscients de problèmes lexicographiques qui ont peu préoccupé leurs contemporains.

Pour la langue danoise, les auteurs déclarent avoir suivi une autorité de l'époque (Molbech 1833) et ils gardent une certaine distance par rapport aux tendances réformatrices du grand linguiste contemporain Rasmus Rask, qui voulait rapprocher la norme orthographique de la prononciation. Un dictionnaire anglais-danois de base (Rosing 1853) est composé à la demande de la maison d'édition danoise Gyldendal, qui, au fur et à mesure des besoins du public, s'engage sérieusement dans la production de dictionnaires bilingues. Une innovation lancée par cet ouvrage consiste à se fonder sur le phonéticien anglais Smart pour faire accompagner un grand nombre de mots anglais d'un commentaire sur leur prononciation. On constate aussi un intérêt croissant pour les termes de certains métiers (exemple: référence à un ouvrage danois sur «l'apparence extérieure du cheval»).

Vers la fin du XIXe siècle, la coutume qui consiste à incorporer des mots norvégiens dans la partie danoise des dictionnaires devient de plus en plus fréquente. Cette tendance, qui permet un élargissement du public acheteur d'un dictionnaire, résultait souvent en une collaboration entre lexicographes norvégiens et danois. Le principe de la combinaison des deux langues scandinaves est annoncé dans le titre même d'un dictionnaire danois-norvégien-anglais (Larsen 1880). Cet ouvrage, révisé dans plusieurs éditions successives, reste en usage au Danemark jusqu'après la première guerre mondiale. Dans la préface de la 2e édition, l'auteur discute de deux systèmes d'organisation d'un dictionnaire: le système étymologique, qui place les mots dérivés et composés sous le mot-thème, et le système alphabétique. Il constate que l'ordre alphabétique gagne du terrain dans les dictionnaires bilingues, même dans les articles d'une certaine longueur, où un terme secondaire faisant collocation avec l'entrée peut servir de point de repère. L'auteur de ce dictionnaire aurait voulu indiquer la prononciation de tous les mots-vedettes, mais il y renonce faute de place, une notation précise demandant pour beaucoup de mots une transcription double (danoise et norvégienne).

4. Les grands dictionnaires bilingues du XXe siècle

L'accroissement de la communication entre les pays d'Europe avec les pays d'Amérique crée, à partir de 1900, la demande d'une maîtrise plus variée et plus approfondie des langues étrangères et d'une étude du vocabulaire de la vie quotidienne, culturelle, commerciale, scientifique et technique. En même temps, les sources lexicographiques à utiliser deviennent plus abondantes: grands dictionnaires monolingues nationaux et étrangers, ouvrages encyclopédiques universels ou spécialisés, etc. La communauté de publication dano-norvégienne, qui avait été courante jusqu'à la première guerre mondiale, est abandonnée, le norvégien ayant acquis maintenant une identité propre.

Cependant, c'est un Norvégien, John Brynildsen, qui peut être considéré comme l'initiateur du développement de la lexicographie bilingue danoise au XXe siècle. Non seulement il est l'auteur de deux grands dictionnaires bilingues, l'un avec l'anglais comme langue source (Brynildsen 1902—1907) et l'autre avec l'anglais comme langue cible et le norvégien comme langue source (Brynildsen 1913—17, 1927), mais il a rédigé, parallèlement à ces ouvrages, des dictionnaires avec le norvégien/danois et l'allemand (Brynildsen 1900 et 1926). Même ses dictionnaires qui ne tiennent pas explicitement compte de la langue danoise ont été beaucoup utilisés au Danemark, faute de grands dictionnaires analogues avec le danois. C'est le cas de ses dictionnaires norvégien-anglais (Brynildsen 1913—1917) et norvégien-allemand (Brynildsen 1926).

L'allemand fait par ailleurs la matière de deux grands dictionnaires, qui paraissent presque en même temps. Le premier en date (Mohr/Nissen 1900—1904) ne se distingue guère méthodiquement des dictionnaires de J. Kaper, mais les auteurs déclarent avoir cherché à introduire une plus grande précision et une plus grande richesse d'expressions phraséologiques et de termes techniques. Un dictionnaire d'un volume semblable (Ipsen 1906) vise le même public. L'auteur déclare s'être appuyé sur les travaux lexicographiques de Daniel Sanders et de Hermann Paul et affirme avoir innové en choisissant l'ordre strictement alphabétique. Par la citation de nombreux exemples, aussi bien des collocations que des expressions phraséologiques, ce dictionnaire apporte un surcroît de renseignements lexicaux. Ces deux tentatives de produire des dictionnaires avec l'allemand qui vont plus loin qu'un dictionnaire de base n'ont pas été suivies de réalisations nouvelles au XXe siècle. La lexicographie bilingue avec l'allemand n'a donc pas encore donné lieu à des ouvrages d'une envergure comparable à celle des grands dictionnaires qui ont été composés pour l'anglais et le français.

C'est pour la communication en langue française que des efforts d'innovation à grande échelle ont tout d'abord été déployés. Sur la base d'un fonds de fiches imposant, recueilli depuis le début du XXe siècle par la traductrice Margrethe Thiele, le professeur d'université Andreas Blinkenberg accepte de diriger l'entreprise lexicographique qui résulte dans la publication d'un dictionnaire danois-français (Blinkenberg/Thiele 1937, Blinkenberg/Høybye 1975—1976), le plus grand dictionnaire existant du danois vers une langue étrangère. La spécialité de Blinkenberg était la syntaxe, mais, à partir de la fin des années 1920, il consacre une large part de ses capacités de travail à la confection de plusieurs éditions de gros dictionnaires danois-français et français-danois. C'est avec lui que la lexicographie bilingue s'élève définitivement au-dessus du niveau artisanal en s'appuyant sur une conception linguistique qui combine érudition et passion du détail. Dans son travail, Blinkenberg s'était attaché l'assistance d'un autre romaniste syntacticien, Poul Høybye, qui allait faire de la lexicographie bilingue, non seulement avec le français, mais encore avec l'italien et le roumain, son domaine spécial.

L'ambition du grand dictionnaire danois-français était de couvrir le vocabulaire de domaines aussi vastes que possible des deux langues: langue générale et langues de spécialité, vie commerciale, juridique et technique, professions artisanales et disciplines scientifiques. La recherche d'exhaustivité faisait admettre les mots de tous les niveaux stylistiques ainsi que des formes dialectales et même des mots archaïques des XVIIe et XVIIIe siècles. La nomenclature en danois reposait essentiellement sur le fonds extrêmement riche d'un grand dictionnaire danois en cours de publication (ODS 1918—1956). Pour les dernières lettres de l'alphabet, l'ODS était en retard sur le dictionnaire de Blinkenberg de sorte qu'il put utiliser, au stade final, les exemples de vocabulaire danois présentés dans le dictionnaire danois-français.

L'ouvrage était destiné à satisfaire les besoins aussi bien des Danois que d'un public francophone, pour lequel ce dictionnaire était une porte ouverte sur la littérature danoise. Evidemment, il était impossible de servir également bien les intérêts des deux groupes d'usagers. Les francophones qui désirent obtenir une maîtrise de la langue parlée danoise regrettent, par ex., que la prononciation des entrées danoises ne soit pas du tout indiquée. L'innovation principale du dictionnaire danois-français porte sur la structure des articles. Les grands articles sont conçus sur un modèle qui répartit les matériaux en une «tête» et en une «queue». La «tête» sert de tableau d'ensemble, résumant le répertoire d'équivalents avec la distinction des différents sens, précisés par des marqueurs stylistiques et thématiques ou d'autres explications. La «queue» est formée d'exemples: collocations, expressions phraséologiques, phrases entières, rangées en ordre alphabétique en fonction du terme secondaire le plus marquant. L'innovation la plus intéressante est un système de renvois par chiffres, qui permet une économie de place. Dans les grands articles, les équivalents français qui figurent dans la tête sont couramment munis d'un chiffre qui peut remplacer le terme français dans les exemples cités dans la «queue».

Ce système, apparemment ingénieux, n'est cependant pas sans inconvénients. Dans la présentation du dictionnaire, le nombre de traductions enregistrées paraît souvent exagéré, les équivalents français proposés étant rarement synonymes. Ainsi, la richesse des matériaux risque de plonger l'usager dans l'incertitude. Un dictionnaire en sens inverse, à savoir du français vers le danois, avait été envisagé par Blinkenberg et Høybye parallèlement aux travaux lexicographiques danois-français. La publication de cet ouvrage (Blinkenberg/ Høybye 1964—1966) est le couronnement de leurs efforts. Les matériaux sont constitués en partie par le fichier de leur dictionnaire danois-français, complétés par une collection de termes puisés dans des dictionnaires bilingues et monolingues avec le français. Le dépouillement de textes français et de dictionnaires spécialisés a joué aussi un rôle considérable résultant en une représentation abondante des langues de spécialité. La structure des articles du dictionnaire français-danois est analogue à celle du grand dictionnaire danois-français, mais le système des renvois chiffrés est abandonné, ce qui s'explique par la fonction de ce dictionnaire, destiné principalement à la compréhension de textes français.

La mise à jour et la révision de ces grands dictionnaires ont occupé la fin de la carrière des deux éminents lexicographes. Après leur mort, une fondation qu'ils avaient créée s'emploie à poursuivre, de façon permanente, le travail lexicographique entre le danois et le français.

La même époque a vu un développement important de la lexicographie avec l'anglais. Le manque d'un grand dictionnaire moderne danois-anglais a été comblé par la publication d'un ouvrage (Vinterberg/Bodelsen 1954—1956), qui, comme les dictionnaires de Blinkenberg et Høybye, a fait date dans la lexicographie bilingue danoise. Ce dictionnaire danois-anglais est comparable, à maints égards, au grand dictionnaire danois-français. La sélection des entrées est presque la même et les exemples avec les mots danois en contexte sont, pour une large part, identiques, mais la structure des grands articles diffère sur un point essentiel, l'arrangement combinant la structuration grammaticale avec l'ordre alphabétique. Après une présentation des principaux équivalents de traduction, classés sur la base de critères sémantiques, suit une section d'exemples ordonnés selon la classe de mots avec laquelle le mot-vedette fait collocation. Cette disposition donne aux articles complexes une grande clarté qui facilite la consultation du dictionnaire. La documentation des possibilités d'emploi des équivalents de traduction est riche et variée, étant illustrée non seulement par des expressions parallèles dans les deux langues, mais aussi par des exemples cités dans la seule langue cible. Tout l'ouvrage se distingue donc par un souci évident de présentation pédagogique.

Un grand dictionnaire en sens inverse, anglais-danois (Kjærulff Nielsen 1964), est publié quelques années après par un lexicographe qui avait collaboré au grand dictionnaire danois-anglais. Son ouvrage, qui est composé avec beaucoup de conscience et de compétence, imite, dans une certaine mesure, la présentation des dictionnaires monolingues anglais, la distinction des sens des mots-vedettes étant souvent définie par des mots anglais synonymes ou apparentés par leur sens. Ce dictionnaire n'est donc pas simplement un dictionnaire «passif» de traduction, mais un ouvrage qui sert aussi à apprendre la langue anglaise pour l'usage «actif». La métalangue, qui est généralement l'anglais, contribue aussi à fixer l'attention sur la langue source. De cette façon, l'expérience linguistique gagnée par la compréhension et la traduction d'un mot anglais est destinée à pouvoir profiter plus tard à la production active.

Les dictionnaires avec l'espagnol n'apparaissent qu'à partir du XXe siècle. Les besoins d'apprendre l'espagnol ont longtemps été sporadiques, la langue espagnole n'obtenant statut de langue enseignée au niveau secondaire qu'à partir du milieu du siècle. Un besoin de se familiariser avec la langue espagnole s'impose d'abord pour les émigrants danois, qui, à partir des années 1890, s'établissent en grand nombre en Amérique du Sud, notamment en Argentine. Des glossaires élémentaires sont rédigés à leur intention, et un dictionnaire norvégien-danois-espagnol de taille moyenne (Bratli 1916) vient faciliter la communication avec les pays hispanophones. En misant sur la langue vivante «telle qu'elle se reflète dans la presse, la correspondance, les documents juridiques et les ouvrages techniques», l'auteur cherche à adapter son ouvrage aux besoins de l'époque. Ce dictionnaire est fondé sur des matériaux assez vastes, qui, toutefois, sont présentés d'une manière peu systématique. Les apports nouveaux sont, entre autres, des indications sur la construction des verbes et les marques pour distinguer certaines particularités latino-américaines, par ex. les formes chiliennes, argentines ou péruviennes.

Le même auteur fait paraître plus tard un dictionnaire espagnol-danois (Bratli 1947—1948), qui, surtout dans sa 2e édition, a puisé dans le fonds lexical du dictionnaire espagnol-allemand de Rudolf Grossmann. Par son enrichissement de la nomenclature et des équivalents fournis, le dictionnaire de Bratli atteint un niveau d'information qui ouvre l'accès à une grande variété de textes en langue espagnole.

5. Dictionnaires de base

Une réforme de l'enseignement secondaire, instituant, à partir de 1903, trois langues modernes: l'anglais, l'allemand et le français dans les lycées danois a entraîné un développement intense de la production de dictionnaires de base. Ceux-ci étaient destinés non seulement aux lycéens, mais encore aux élèves des cours postscolaires et en général, aux gens qui voulaient entretenir leurs connaissances des langues modernes par la lecture d'une littérature étrangère dans l'original ou par des contacts avec l'étranger. La maison d'édition Gyldendal, qui avait une longue tradition de publication de dictionnaires bilingues, s'est efforcée de répondre aux besoins nouveaux. Le but des dictionnaires Gyldendal était de couvrir les vocabulaires littéraire et quotidien fondamentaux et de présenter les renseignements d'une manière pédagogique. Les auteurs étaient pour la plupart des professeurs de lycée, qui, grâce à leur expérience des exercices de traduction, étaient conscients des pièges lexicaux qui se présentent dans une optique contrastive. Comme exemples de publications au début du siècle, on peut relever un dictionnaire français-danois/norvégien (Stigaard 1906) et un ouvrage parallèle danois/norvégien-français (Stigaard 1912). Les points forts de ces dictionnaires sont la séparation judicieuse des sens principaux des entrées et l'intérêt porté aux structures contextuelles (collocations et expressions phraséologiques). Grâce à leurs qualités, ces ouvrages d'un volume réduit ont pu influencer plus tard les grands dictionnaires de Blinkenberg et Høybye.

Au début du XXe siècle, la maison Gyldendal a publié aussi des dictionnaires avec l'allemand et avec l'anglais. Dans certains cas, il s'agit de continuations d'ouvrages dont les bases ont été jetées dès le début du XIXe siècle. La diffusion d'un dictionnaire de base permet, en effet, une réimpression et des remaniements à peu d'années d'intervalle, ce qui autorise, de façon permanente, corrections et innovations.

Le succès des dictionnaires Gyldendal ne s'est pas démenti de nos jours. La continuation des dictionnaires «rouges», comme on les apelle couramment à cause de la couleur de leur couverture, est souvent assurée par un lexicographe à vie ou bien par un assistant de rédaction qui prend la relève à la mort d'un rédacteur responsable. Les dictionnaires rouges bilingues existent maintenant dans des éditions contemporaines mises à jour pour les langues suivantes: anglais-danois et danois-anglais (Axelsen 1986 a—b); allemand-danois et danois-allemand (Bork 1986 a—b); français-danois et danois-français (Sørensen/Dalager 1985 a—b); espagnol-danois (Vater 1986) et danois-espagnol (Vater 1984); suédois-danois (Palmgreen Munch Petersen/Hartmann 1985); russe-danois (Harrit 1987). Ce dernier dictionnaire est intéressant en ce qu'il représente certaines tendances modernes d'économie lexicographique (par ex. l'indication du programme grammatical des termes russes au moyen d'un système de marques).

Une autre série de dictionnaires de base qui complétaient les dictionnaires Gyldendal a été lancée à partir des années 1930 par la maison «Berlingske Forlag». Dans cette série, il y a lieu de mentionner les dictionnaires avec l'italien (Høybye/Mengel 1956 et 1959), un dictionnaire anglais-danois (Haislund/Salling 1964), un dictionnaire danois-français (Sten 1950) et un dictionnaire allemand-danois (Siegler 1944). Ce dernier s'est attaché surtout à définir les possibilités de combinaisons des entrées, aussi bien les constructions grammaticales que les contextes.

Plus récemment, d'autres maisons d'édition se sont intéressées à produire des dictionnaires d'un format maniable. Ainsi, la maison d'édition Munksgaard a publié un dictionnaire danois-espagnol de taille moyenne (Christensen/Windfeld Hansen 1982), qui contient un assez large choix d'entrées et d'exemples. La nouveauté la plus récente dans le répertoire des dictionnaires bilingues est un dictionnaire danois-roumain (Høybye e. a. 1984), publié en coproduction avec une maison d'édition roumaine. Le rédacteur principal de cet ouvrage, Poul Høybye, y a adapté les méthodes suivies dans ses dictionnaires avec le français et a, en outre, innové dans un domaine particulier en présentant les entrées danoises avec une transcription phonétique.

6. Théorie et pratique

Au Danemark, comme ailleurs, les réflexions sur les principes de composition d'un dictionnaire ont été, traditionnellement, bien plus maigres dans la lexicographie bilingue que dans la lexicographie monolingue. Pendant longtemps, la production d'un dictionnaire bilingue a été considérée surtout comme une activité artisanale, qui demandait, certes, une parfaite maîtrise des langues concernées et une méthode rédactionnelle bien choisie, mais qui n'avait pas besoin d'être préparée par une définition des buts à poursuivre et des règles à observer. Par opposition à la lexicographie monolingue, qui s'intéressait à éclaircir l'étymologie et les changements de sens des mots, activité reconnue au XIXe siècle comme fondamentale pour la linguistique, la lexicographie bilingue n'avait pas acquis ses titres de noblesse. Il aura fallu des professeurs d'université réputés tels que les romanistes Sundby, Blinkenberg et Høybye, l'angliciste Bodelsen et, surtout, de nos jours, l'essor de la linguistique appliquée pour que la lexicographie bilingue fût considérée comme une activité méritoire pour un chercheur scientifique. Le plus souvent, les commentaires de méthode doivent être décelés dans les préfaces des dictionnaires ou bien dans un compte rendu du travail d'un collègue lexicographe. Blinkenberg expose quelques-uns de ses principes fondamentaux dans un article de journal (Blinkenberg 1954). Il s'oppose à une théorisation étroite de la présentation lexicographique, en recommandant l'emploi de plusieurs modèles de rédaction, qui doivent être adaptés au mot traité. En dernier lieu, c'est le jugement équilibré, qui doit, selon lui, guider le lexicographe. Un seul principe lui paraît incontestable: l'arrangement alphabétique, alpha et oméga de la lexicographie.

Høybye a souvent rendu compte des travaux que Blinkenberg et lui ont entrepris en commun. Dans un article intitulé «Un dictionnaire de traduction» (Høybye 1971), il parle des sources et des procédés utilisés pour les grands dictionnaires avec le français, donnant des renseignements sur la sélection de la nomenclature, les consultations de contrôle, le recours aux informateurs et la façon de les interroger, le traitement des expressions phraséologiques, etc. Pour lui comme pour Blinkenberg, les aspects pratiques de la production d'un dictionnaire: présentation typographique, sectionnement des matériaux complexes suivant un système détaillé de chiffres et de lettres, brièveté des explications, étaient des soucis constants. Selon eux, le dictionnaire bilingue devait être aussi facile à consulter qu'un annuaire téléphonique.

Un intérêt accru pour les problèmes théoriques de la lexicographie a abouti, ces dernières années, à la création de plusieurs centres et groupes de recherches s'occupant de la planification de travaux lexicographiques. Un échange fructueux avec des collègues et des lexicographes étrangers a favorisé le développement d'idées nouvelles. Ainsi, le Département d'anglais et le Département d'allemand de l'Université de Copenhague ont passé en revue, dans une série de colloques internationaux (Symposium 1983 et 1985), les idées et les expériences de lexicographes novateurs. D'autre part, la lexicographie et la terminologie constituent une branche privilégiée des activités de recherches conduites à la Faculté des Langues Modernes de l'Ecole des Hautes Etudes Commerciales de Copenhague, où un Centre de terminologie s'occupe de problèmes théoriques et pratiques du traitement de termes techniques. Au Département d'allemand de la même faculté, un groupe de recherches a contribué au développement d'une théorie globale de la lexicographie par la définition des règles rédactionnelles qui doivent présider à la composition d'un dictionnaire bilingue: distinction entre dictionnaire «actif» et dictionnaire «passif», présentation des équivalents de traduction, élaboration de dictionnaires sur la base d'un corpus, etc. (Kromann/Riiber/Rosbach 1984).

Finalement, l'intérêt pour le fonctionnement du dictionnaire bilingue a résulté dans des recherches sur les besoins des usagers (Rasmussen 1985), analyses qui doivent permettre de mieux adapter le travail lexicographique aux conditions de l'actualité.

7. Perspectives d'avenir

Les travaux en cours dans la lexicographie bilingue danoise (cf. Ordbøger 1987) comportent la préparation de dictionnaires avec des langues nouvelles, par ex. certaines langues slaves et certaines langues exotiques. Une autre tâche importante est la révision de dictionnaires existants, entre autres les grands dictionnaires avec l'anglais et avec le français. Pour ces travaux, la technologie nouvelle est mise en application. Ainsi, l'informatisation de la production d'un dictionnaire a été expérimentée notamment dans la réédition des dictionnaires avec le français de Blinkenberg et Høybye, qui sont passés par les stades suivants: lecture optique de la dernière édition, établissement d'une base de données à partir de laquelle se font les changements à apporter, enfin édition à l'aide de la base de données révisée (Nistrup Madsen/Engel 1986).

L'ordinateur permet de traiter des matériaux abondants, de mettre à jour le fonds lexical d'une façon permanente et de mieux utiliser les sources d'information des deux langues, condition essentielle pour produire des dictionnaires solidement documentés qui suivent l'usage de la langue avec un minimum de retard.

8. Bibliographie choisie

8.1. Dictionnaires

Aphelen 1754 = Hans von Aphelen: Dictionnaire abrégé, eller en Fransk og Dansk Ordbog (- - -). Kiøbenhavn 1754 [832 p. + registre de mots danois].

Aphelen 1759 = Hans von Aphelen: Le Grand Dictionnaire Royal Français et Danois. Kiøbenhavn 1759. I, Français et Danois [1120 p.] II, Dansk og Fransk [544 p.].

Aphelen 1764 = Hans von Aphelen: Kongelig Dansk ordbog oplyst med Exempler og Talemaader. Kiøbenhavn 1764. I, Dansk og Tydsk. II, Tydsk og Dansk [791 + 859 p.].

Aphelen 1772—1775 = Hans von Aphelen: Dictionnaire Royal [...]. Kiøbenhavn. I. Fransk og Dansk, A—K, 1772 [664 p.] II. Fransk og Dansk, L—Z, 1773 [635 p.] III. Dansk og Fransk, 1775 [831 p.].

Axelsen 1986a = Jens Axelsen: Engelsk-dansk ordbog. 10. udg. København 1986 [584 p].

Axelsen 1986b = Jens Axelsen: Dansk-engelsk ordbog. 8. udg. København 1986 [656 p.].

Baden 1787 = Jacob Baden: Fuldstændig Tydsk og Dansk Ordbog sammendragen af de nyeste og bedste Tydske Ordbøger, I—III: Kjøbenhavn 1787 [1536 + 1224 + 614 p.].

Bay 1784 = Christian Frideric Bay: A Compleat Vocabulary English and Danish. Fuldstændigt Engelsk og Dansk Haand-Lexicon, udgivet paa Engelsk og Tydsk af Theodor Arnold, nu på Dansk oversat, forbedret og forøget med en Samling af Søe-Termini og Talemaader. Kjøbenhavn 1784 [584 p.].

Berthelson 1754 = Andreas Berthelson: An English and Danish Dictionary. London 1754 [666 p.].

Blinkenberg/Thiele 1937 = Andreas Blinkenberg/ M. Thiele: Dansk-fransk Ordbog. København 1937 [1699 p.].

Blinkenberg/Høybye 1964—1966 = Andreas Blinkenberg/Poul Høybye: Fransk-dansk ordbog, I—II. 1. udg. København 1964—1966. 2. udg. København 1984 [1957 p.].

Blinkenberg/Høybye 1975—1976 = Andreas Blinkenberg/Poul Høybye: Dansk-fransk ordbog, I—II. Tredie reviderede og forøgede udgave. København 1975—1976 [1043 + 1039 p.].

Bolling 1678 = Friderici Bollingii Engelske Dictionarium af hvilcket kand læris Den Engelske Tale [. . .]. Kiøbenhafn 1678 [123 p.].

Borring 1853 = L.-S. Borring: Dictionnaire français-danois et danois-français. Kjøbenhavn 1853 [526 p.].

Bork 1986a = Egon Bork: Tysk-dansk ordbog. 12. udg. 1986 [608 p.].

Bork 1986b = Egon Bork: Dansk-tysk ordbog. 9. udg. 1986 [632 p.].

Bratli 1916 = Carl Bratli: Norsk/dansk-spansk Ordbog. Kristiania. Kjøbenhavn 1916 [517 p.].

Bratli 1947—1948 = Carl Bratli: Spansk-dansk ordbog, I—II. København 1947—1948 [1425 p.].

Bresemann 1850—1855 = Frederik Bresemann: Tydsk-dansk og dansk-tydsk Haand-Ordbog til Brug for begge Nationer. I, Tydsk-Dansk. Kjøbenhavn 1855 [421 p.]. II, Dansk-Tydsk. Kjøbenhavn 1850 (= 1852).

Brynildsen 1902—1907 = John Brynildsen: Engelsk-dansk-norsk Ordbog. I, København 1902 [727 p.]. II, København 1907 [1150 p.].

Brynildsen 1913—1917, 1927 = John Brynildsen: Norsk-engelsk ordbog. 2. udg. 1913—1917. 3. udg. Oslo 1927 [1228 p.].

Brynildsen 1926 = John Brynildsen: Norsk-tysk ordbog. Oslo 1926 [1078 p.].

Christensen/Windfeld Hansen 1982 = Palle Christensen/Johan Windfeld Hansen: Dansk-spansk ordbog. København 1982 [786 p.].

Ferrall/Repp 1845 = J. S. Ferrall/Thorl. Gudm. Repp: A Danish-English Dictionary. Copenhagen 1845 [436 p.].

Grønberg 1824—1826 = B. C. Grønberg: Tydsk-Dansk og Dansk-Tydsk Haand-Ordbog. I, Kjøbenhavn 1824 [824 p.]. II, Kjøbenhavn 1826 [672 p.].

Haislund/Salling 1964 = Niels Haislund/Aage Salling: Engelsk-dansk ordbog. 3. udg. København 1964 [563 p.].

Harrit 1985 = Jørgen og Valentina Harrit: Russisk-dansk ordbog. København 1985 [548 p.].

Hasse 1805 = Lauritz Hasse: Nouveau dictionnaire de poche français-danois et danois-français. Fridericia 1805 [456 p.].

Høst 1840—1842 = Joh. Nik. Høst: Nyeste, fuldstændigste og udførligste Fransk-dansk Ordbog efter Nutidens Tarv. Kjøbenhavn 1840 [399 p.]. — Dansk-fransk Ordbog. Kjøbenhavn 1842 [421 p.].

Høybye/Mengel 1956 = Poul Høybye/Johanne Mengel: Italiensk-dansk ordbog. København 1956 [434 p.].

Høybye/Mengel 1959 = Poul Høybye/Johanne Mengel: Dansk-italiensk ordbog. København 1959 [644 p.].

Høybye e. a. 1984 = Poul Høybye e. a.: Dansk-rumænsk ordbog. Dicţionar danez-român. Lyngby, Bucureşti 1984 [807 p.].

Ipsen 1906 = P. L. Ipsen: Tysk-dansk ordbog, I—II. København 1906 [1970 p.].

Kaper 1870 = J. Kaper: Dansk/Norsk-Tysk Haandordbog. Kjøbenhavn 1870 [554 p.].

Kaper 1878 = J. Kaper: Tysk-Dansk/Norsk Ordbog. Kjøbenhavn 1878 [643 p.].

Kjærulff Nielsen 1964 = B. Kjærulff Nielsen: Engelsk-dansk ordbog. 1. udg. København 1964. 3. udg. 1974 [1471 p.].

Larsen 1880, 1888 = A. Larsen: Dansk-Norsk-Engelsk Ordbog, 1. udg. Kjøbenhavn 1880. 2. udg. Kjøbenhavn 1888 [645 p.].

Matras 1628 = Daniel Matras: Le petit dictionnaire français-danois [. . .]. Kjøbenhavn 1628 [177 p.].

Mohr/Nissen 1900 = F. A. Mohr/C. A. Nissen: Tysk-Dansk Ordbog, I—II. Kjøbenhavn 1900 [609 p. + 957 p.].

Molbech 1833 = Chr. Molbech: Dansk Ordbog, I—II. Kjøbenhavn 1833.

Müller 1800 = G. H. Müller: Neues Dänisch-Deutsches Wörterbuch zum Gebrauch für Deutsche [. . .], I—II. Schleswig und Kopenhagen 1800 [592 p. + 644 p.].

Müller 1807—1810 = G. H. Müller: Tysk-Dansk Ordbog, I—II. Kiel 1807—1810 [748 + 804 p.].

ODS 1918—1956 = Ordbog over det danske sprog. I—XXVIII. København, 1918—1956.

Olsen 1802 = L. B. Olsen: Dansk og Engelsk Lexicon udarbejdet efter de bedste Forfattere i begge Sprog. Kiøbenhavn 1802 [712 p.].

Palmgreen Munch Petersen/Hartmann 1985 = Valfrid Palmgreen Munch Petersen/Ellen Hartmann: Svensk-dansk ordbog. 2. udg., 3. oplag. København 1985 [252 p.].

Reisler 1804—1807 = Carl Gottlieb Reisler: Fuldstændig Tydsk og Dansk Ordbog, I—II. Kjøbenhavn 1804—1807 [1123 + 844 p].

Rosing 1853 = S. Rosing: Engelsk-dansk ordbog. Kjøbenhavn 1853 [620 p.].

Sick 1883 = Chr. Sick: Fransk-dansk-norsk Haandordbog. Kjøbenhavn 1883 [1037 p.].

Siegler 1944 = J. J. Siegler: Dansk-tysk ordbog. København 1944 [430 p.].

Sten 1938 = Holger Sten: Dansk-Fransk Ordbog. København 1938 [326 p.].

Stigaard 1906 = Vilh. Stigaard: Fransk-dansknorsk Ordbog. København 1906 [368 p.].

Stigaard 1912 = Vilh. Stigaard: Dansk-norsk-fransk ordbog. København. Kristiania 1912 [380 p.].

Sundby/Baruël 1883 = Thor Sundby/Euchaire Baruël: Dansk-norsk-fransk Haandordbog, I—II. Kjøbenhavn 1883 [617 + 702 p.].

Sørensen/Dalager 1985a = N. Chr. Sørensen/Inge-Lise Dalager: Fransk-dansk ordbog. 8. udg., 5. oplag. København 1985 [496 p.].

Sørensen/Dalager 1985b = N. Chr. Sørensen/Inge-Lise Dalager: Dansk-fransk ordbog. 6. udg. København 1985 [520 p.].

Vater e. a. 1984 = Pia Vater e. a.: Dansk-spansk ordbog. København 1984 [536 p.].

Vater/Winding 1986 = Pia Vater/Ulla Winding: Spansk-dansk ordbog. København 1986 [680 p.].

Vinterberg/Bodelsen = Hermann Vinterberg/C. A. Bodelsen: Dansk-engelsk ordbog, I—II, 1. udg. 1954, 2. udg. 1966 [918 + 928 p.].

Wolff 1779 = Ernst Wolff: En Dansk og Engelsk Ord-Bog [. . .]. Kjøbenhavn 1779 [555 p.].

Wolff 1796 = Odin Wolff: Fuldstændigt Fransk og Dansk Lexicon efter de bedste Ordbøger udarbejdet, I—II. Kiøbenhavn 1796 [964 + 738 p.].

8.2. Travaux

Blinkenberg 1954 = Andreas Blinkenberg: Et nyt stort Ordbogsværk. In: Berlingske Aftenavis' Kronik, 8. 10. 54.

Høybye 1971 = Poul Høybye: En oversættelsesordbog. In: Danske opslagsværker. Redigeret af Axel Andersen. København 1971, 299—324.

Kabell/Lauridsen 1988 = I. Kabell/H. Lauridsen: The First English-Danish Dictionary: Frideric Bolling's «Engelske Dictionarium». In: Symposium on Lexicography III. Ed. K. Hyldgaard-Jensen/A. Zettersten. Tübingen 1988, 373—387.

Kromann/Riiber/Rosbach 1984 = Hans-Peter Kromann/Theis Riiber/P. Rosbach: Überlegungen zu Grundfragen der zweisprachigen Lexikographie; In: H. E. Wiegand (Hrsg.): Studien zur neuhochdeutschen Lexikographie, V. Hildesheim. Zürich. New York 1984 (Germanistische Linguistik 3—6/85), 159—238.

Nistrup Madsen/Engel 1986 = Bodil Nistrup Madsen/Gert Engel: Anvendelse af ny teknologi i ordbogsarbejdet. In: Festskrift til Jens Rasmussen, København 1986. 288—298.

Ordbøger 1987 = Ordbøger i Danmark. En oversigt. (Rapport polycopié). DANLEX-gruppen, Institut for Nordisk Filologi, Université de Copenhague 1987.

Rasmussen 1985 = Jens Rasmussen: Enquête sur l'emploi du dictionnaire danois-français de Blinkenberg et Høybye. In: CEBAL, no 7, København 1985, 130—154.

Symposium 1983 = Symposium zur Lexikographie. Proceedings of the Symposium on Lexicography September 1—2, 1982, at the University of Copenhagen. Hrsg. von Karl Hyldgaard Jensen/Arne Zettersten. Hildesheim 1983. In: Germanistische Linguistik 5—6/82.

Symposium 1985 = Proceedings of the Second International Symposium on Lexicography II, 16.—17. 5. 1984 at the University of Copenhagen. Ed. by Karl Hyldgaard Jensen/Arne Zettersten. Tübingen 1985. (Lexicographica Series Maior 5).

Jens Rasmussen, Copenhague (Danemark)

323. Die zweisprachige Lexikographie mit Polnisch

1. Einleitendes
2. Die Zeit bis zum Ende des zweiten Weltkrieges
3. Die Zeit nach dem zweiten Weltkrieg
4. Zur Bibliographie
5. Literatur (in Auswahl)

1. Einleitendes

Die Geschichte der polnischen Lexikographie, die übrigens von Anfang an zwei- oder mehrsprachigen Charakter hat, beginnt im 16. Jh. Es handelt sich zunächst natürlich um die klassischen Sprachen Latein und Griechisch.

Seit dieser Zeit sind viele zwei- bzw. mehrsprachige Wörterbücher mit Polnisch entstanden. Allein im Bereich der allgemeinen zweisprachigen Wörterbücher sind mehr als 500 Titel zu verzeichnen. Naturgemäß können hier nicht alle lexikographischen Werke besprochen werden. Wir befassen uns nur mit den allgemeinen Wörterbüchern, und zwar durchweg der nichtklassischen Sprachen. Ausführlicher ist nur die Zeit nach dem 2. Weltkrieg behandelt.

2. Die Zeit bis zum Ende des zweiten Weltkrieges

2.1. Gemeinsam ist der ganzen Periode ein negativ zu formulierendes Merkmal, nämlich das Fehlen einer systematischen, auf langfristiger Perspektive beruhenden lexikographischen Tätigkeit. Es sind Zeitabschnitte, die in 2.2. bis 2.4. summarisch behandelt sind.

2.2. Von den Anfängen bis zum Ausgang des 18. Jahrhunderts

Dieser Zeitraum ist gekennzeichnet durch die politische Unabhängigkeit des Königreichs Polen und den Anteil Polens an der Entwicklung der gemeinsamen westeuropäischen Zivilisation und Kultur. In dieser Zeit ent- und bestanden in mehreren größeren Städten private und institutionelle Druckereien, darunter auch solche, die man als königliche und/ oder staatliche bezeichnen könnte, z. B. die Drukarnia Jego Królewskiej Mości i Rzeczypospolitej (= Druckerei Seiner Königlichen Majestät und der Republik) in Wilna.

Von den in dieser Zeit erschienenen Wörterbüchern seien nur zwei genannt: Vollständiges deutsches und polnisches Wörterbuch (Trotz 1772) und Nouveau dictionnaire françois, allemand et polonais (Trotz 1744—1747).

In dieser Zeit konnte sich die lexikographische Tätigkeit relativ ungehindert entwickeln. Die Lage ändert sich aber gegen Ende des 18. Jhs. Im Jahre 1795 verliert Polen endgültig seine politische Unabhängigkeit. Dieser Komplex von Ereignissen hat natürlich seine negativen kulturpolitischen Folgen, darunter auch in der Lexikographie.

2.3. Vom Ausgang des 18. Jahrhunderts bis 1918

Das ganze 19. Jh. hindurch, bis zum Ende des 1. Weltkrieges, befindet sich Polen unter der Herrschaft der drei Nachbarmächte: Rußland, Preußen/Deutschland und Österreich. U. a. durch die Fremdherrschaft der drei Mächte kann die Tatsache erklärt werden, daß polnische lexikographische Werke vielfach in fremden Städten gedruckt werden, z. B. in Berlin, Wrocław bzw. Breslau, Leipzig, Königsberg, Wien, Kiew.

Von den wichtigeren Wörterbüchern seien genannt: Bandtkie 1806; Booch-Árkossy 1864—65; Konarski 1904—08 (alle mit Deutsch); Rykaczewski 1849—51 (mit Englisch).

Von den vielen französischen Wörterbüchern sei nur das erwähnt, das mehrere Ausgaben erlebt hat, nämlich das zweiteilige von Callier 1906.

2.4. Zwischen den zwei Weltkriegen

Die Periode von 1918 bis 1939 ist die Zeit einer recht regen lexikographischen Tätigkeit in dem nunmehr wieder unabhängigen Polen. Es entstehen jetzt neue, meist private, Verlage und Druckereien und das polnische Verlagswesen kann sich frei entwickeln. Zwei bedeutende Werke müssen erwähnt werden:

(1) das zweibändige polnisch-französische und französisch-polnische Wörterbuch von Kalina 1928—31;

(2) das ebenfalls zweibändige Wörterbuch Deutsch-Polnisch und Polnisch-Deutsch von Ippoldt 1937—41.

Die Periode der ungehinderten lexikographischen Tätigkeit hat aber lediglich 20 Jahre gedauert und ist mit dem Ausbruch des 2. Weltkrieges jäh unterbrochen worden. In den nun folgenden fünfeinhalb Jahren eines rücksichtslosen Kampfes gegen das polnische Kulturerbe und die kulturellen Einrichtungen konnte von einer offiziellen polnischen lexikographischen Tätigkeit keine Rede sein.

3. Die Zeit nach dem zweiten Weltkrieg

3.1. Es ist praktisch die Zeit von 1947 bis 1986. Infolge der neuen politischen Konstellation in Mittel- und Osteuropa wurden in Polen tiefgreifende innenpolitische, kulturpolitische u. dgl. Veränderungen durchgeführt. Die alten privaten Verlage und Druckereien wurden entweder nationalisiert oder abgeschafft. An ihrer Stelle wurden jedoch rasch staatliche bzw. genossenschaftliche Verlage gegründet. Dadurch erhielt die Verlagstätigkeit einen völlig anderen Charakter. Jetzt konnte man auch, zum ersten Mal in der Geschichte der polnischen Lexikographie, einen weitreichenden Plan von herauszugebenden Wörterbüchern entwerfen. Dies geschah in dem 1947 in Warschau gegründeten Staatlichen Verlag Wiedza Powszechna, der in wenigen Jahren die Herausgabe praktisch aller allgemeinen zweisprachigen Wörterbücher (mit Ausnahme der klassischen Sprachen) übernommen hat. Deswegen müssen wir uns im folgenden, besonders aber in 3.2., mit seiner lexikographischen Tätigkeit näher befassen.

Der Verlag hat mehrere Redaktionen, von denen eine ausschließlich zweisprachige Wörterbücher mit Polnisch zum Druck vorbereitet. Sie besteht seit 1955. Verfaßt aber werden die Wörterbücher außerhalb des Verlages, von hauptamtlich woanders tätigen Autoren.

In den ersten Nachkriegsjahren wurden Wörterbücher in verschiedenen Verlagen veröffentlicht. So wurde z. B. das deutsch-polnische und polnisch-deutsche Wörterbuch von Paweł Kalina im Verlag Czytelnik wiederaufgelegt. Bis zum heutigen Tag erscheinen sporadisch allgemeine Wörterbücher auch in anderen Verlagen. Quantitativ fällt das aber kaum ins Gewicht. Fach- und Spezialwörterbücher werden von verschiedenen, sachlich zuständigen Verlagen herausgegeben. Wörterbücher der klassischen Sprachen erscheinen im Państwowe Wydawnictwo Naukowe in Warschau.

3.2. Zur lexikographischen Tätigkeit des Verlages Wiedza Powszechna

3.2.1. In den rund 30 Jahren seiner lexikographischen Tätigkeit hat der Verlag Erstaunliches geleistet. Es wird nach einem langfristigen und differenzierten Plan gearbeitet, der systematisch realisiert wird. Der Plan sieht mehrere Wörterbuchserien vor, die im folgenden besprochen sind.

N. B.: (1) Für viele der im folgenden enthaltenen Informationen über die lexikographische Tätigkeit von Wiedza Powszechna, samt den meisten Zahlenangaben, habe ich dem Stellvertretenden Verlagsdirektor Herrn Józef Chlabicz zu danken.

(2) Die Zahlen der Wörterbuchtitel, der Ausgaben und der herausgegebenen Exemplare spiegeln den Stand vom 25. Juli 1986 wider.

(3) Vorliegender Artikel ist keine Bibliographie der zweisprachigen Wörterbücher mit Polnisch. Deswegen wurde bei deren Aufzählung bzw. Besprechung meist auf den polnischen Titel verzichtet.

3.2.2. Die Serie Große Wörterbücher (Słowniki wielkie)

Bisher sind in dieser Serie 13 Wörterbücher erschienen, mit einer Gesamtzahl der Exemplare (samt Supplementen) von 1 671 500. Es sind dies:

— Englisch-Polnisch von Jan Stanisławski, mit 9 Ausgaben seit 1964 und 360 000 Exemplaren;
— Polnisch-Englisch von Jan Stanisławski, mit 7 Ausgaben seit 1969 und 295 000 Exemplaren;
— Französisch-Polnisch von Stefania Ciesielska-Borkowska, Jerzy Dobrzyński, Jadwiga Gałuszka [...], in 2 Bänden, mit 3 Ausgaben seit 1980 und 90 000 Exemplaren;
— Deutsch-Polnisch von Jan Piprek und Juliusz Ippoldt, in 2 Bänden, mit 7 Ausgaben seit 1968 und 260 000 Ex.;
— Polnisch-Deutsch von Jan Piprek und Juliusz Ippoldt, in 2 Bänden, mit 6 Ausgaben seit 1971 und 230 000 Ex.;
— Russisch-Polnisch von Anatol Mirowicz [...], in 2 Bänden, mit 2 Ausgaben seit 1971 und 100 000 Ex.;
— Polnisch-Russisch von Dymitr Hessen und Ryszard Stypuła, mit 2 Ausgaben seit 1967 und 130 000 Ex.;
— Ungarisch-Polnisch von einem Autorenkollektiv. (Reychman 1968), mit 2 Ausgaben seit 1968 und 17 900 Ex.;
— Polnisch-Ungarisch von einem Autorenkollektiv (Csorba 1958), mit 2 Ausgaben seit 1958 und 8600 Ex.

Insgesamt sind es 10 Wörterbücher und 3 Supplemente.

Am Rande sei hier noch ein umfangreiches Wörterbuch erwähnt, das als Nachdruck erschienen ist, jedoch nicht im Verlag Wiedza Powszechna, sondern im Państwowe Wydawnictwo Naukowe. Es ist ein zweibändiges Wörterbuch in 8°: Bulas/Whitfield/Thomas 1959—1961. Vor dem Erscheinen des Großen Wörterbuches von Stanisławski war es das umfangreichste und wohl beste Wörterbuch des Englischen und Polnischen.

Die Großen Wörterbücher, im Verlag „wissenschaftliche Wörterbücher" genannt (wohl deswegen, weil sie vor allem für Wissenschaftler und Übersetzer bestimmt sind), enthalten jeweils (d. h. z. B. in dem fremdsprachlich-polnischen Teil) zwischen 120 000 und 200 000 lexikalische Einheiten. Sie werden meist in zwei Bänden herausgegeben.

Ein solches Wörterbuch ist z. B. das große deutsch-polnische Wörterbuch von Piprek und Ippoldt. Die Verfasser arbeiten hier mit wenigen Abkürzungen, Formeln und Verweisen. Das meiste wird ausdrücklich gesagt; die grammatischen Formen werden voll ausgeschrieben. Die Kenntnis der Aussprache wird vorausgesetzt. Die semantische Komponente aber ist ausführlich behandelt: In den meisten Fällen wird eine zielsprachliche lexikalische Einheit durch mehrere synonyme ausgangssprachliche Entsprechungen glossiert.

3.2.3. Die Serie Handwörterbücher (Słowniki podręczne)

Diese Serie ist noch zahlreicher vertreten als die der Großen Wörterbücher, sowohl hinsichtlich der Zahl der Fremdsprachen als auch der Zahl der herausgegebenen Exemplare. Die Gesamtzahl der aufgelegten Exemplare dieser Serie beläuft sich auf 3 168 000, darunter zwei Supplemente je 50 000 Exemplare. Hier die wichtigsten Handwörterbücher:

— Englisch-Polnisch von Jan Stanisławski, mit 6 Ausgaben seit 1971 und 440 000 Exemplaren;
— Polnisch-Englisch von Jan Stanisławski, mit 4 Ausgaben seit 1973 und 300 000 Exemplaren;
— Deutsch-Polnisch von Jan Chodera und Stefan Kubica, mit 6 Ausgaben seit 1966 und 400 000 Exemplaren;
— Polnisch-Deutsch von Andrzej Bzdęga, Jan Chodera und Stefan Kubica, mit 5 Ausgaben seit 1973 und 380 000 Ex.;
— Französisch-Polnisch von Kazimierz Kupisz und Bolesław Kielski, mit 6 Ausgaben seit 1968 und 250 000 Ex.;
— Polnisch-Französisch von Kazimierz Kupisz und Bolesław Kielski, mit 5 Ausg. seit 1969 und 190 000 Ex.;
— Polnisch-Russisch von Ryszard Stypuła und Halina Kowalowa, mit 4 Ausg. seit 1976 und 215 000 Ex.;
— Russisch-Polnisch von einem Autorenkollektiv, hrsg. von M. F. Rozwadowska, mit 6 Ausg. seit 1958 und 180 000 Ex.
— Französisch-Polnisch von Paweł Kalina, mit 4 Ausg. seit 1956 und 135 000 Ex. (Nachdruck);
— Polnisch-Französisch von Paweł Kalina, mit 4 Ausg. und 130 000 Ex. (Nachdruck);
— Deutsch-Polnisch von Paweł Kalina, mit 9 Ausg. und 136 000 Ex. (Nachdruck);
— Polnisch-Deutsch von Paweł Kalina, mit 10 Ausg. und 280 000 Ex. (Nachdruck);
— Spanisch-Polnisch von Stanisław Wawrzkowicz und Kazimierz Hiszpański, mit 1 Ausg. 1982 und 80 000 Ex.;
— Italienisch-Polnisch von Wojciech Meisels, mit 2 Ausg. und 50 000 Ex.;
— Polnisch-Italienisch von Wojciech Meisels, mit 1 Ausg. und 15 000 Ex.;
— Russisch-Polnisch [Hrsg. J. H. Dworecki], mit 7 Ausg. seit 1958 und 191 000 Ex.;
— Englisch-Polnisch und Polnisch-Englisch von Władysław Kierst mit 1 Ausg. 1957 und 40 000 Ex. (Nachdruck).

Insgesamt sind es 19 eigentliche Wörterbücher und 2 Supplemente.

Die Handwörterbücher enthalten jeweils (z. B. im deutsch-polnischen Teil) zwischen 50 000 und 70 000 lexikalische Einheiten der Stichwortsprache. Sie tragen einen stärker ausgeprägten linguistischen Charakter und haben deutlich eine phonetische, eine grammatische und eine semantisch-pragmatische Komponente. Die phonetische Komponente (die Angabe der Aussprache) ist kurz gefaßt, aber ausreichend. Die grammatische Komponente ist viel reichhaltiger; jedoch wird hier mit vielen Abkürzungen, Verweisen und konventionellen Formeln gearbeitet. Das verleiht dem Wörterbuch einen ziemlich abstrakten Charakter.

Die Menge der konventionellen Formeln, somit der Grad der Abstraktheit, variiert von Wörterbuch zu Wörterbuch. Wie weit der Gebrauch von Formeln gehen kann, ist im folgenden am Beispiel des Handwörterbuchs Deutsch-Polnisch von Jan Chodera und Stefan Kubica (Hrsg. Jan Czochralski) gezeigt.

Bei Adjektiven partizipialer Herkunft wurden beide grammatischen Hauptfunktionen (durch römische Zahlen) angegeben. Z. B.:

bestimmt I *part perf zob* (= siehe) *bestimmen* II *adj : adv pewn-y/-ie.*

Unter II sind also die adjektivische und die adverbielle Funktion signalisiert. Die polnischen Äquivalente sind in kurzer From notiert: Die Formel *pewn-y/-ie* steht für: *pewny* (Adjektiv) und *pewnie* (Adverb).

Die semantisch regulären deadjektivischen Substantive auf *-heit, -keit, -igkeit* werden nur durch die Formeln Sh, Sk, Si angedeutet, wobei hier S für „Substantiv" steht. Die Substantive auf *-heit, -keit, -igkeit* werden nicht ausgeschrieben. Die genannten Formeln stehen jeweils am Ende des adjektivischen Stichwortartikels.

Die deverbalen Substantive auf *-ung* werden, mit Ausnahme von Fällen einer vom Verb abweichenden Bedeutung, durch die Formel Su (= Substantiv auf *-ung*) signalisiert. Die Formel steht am Ende des verbalen Stichwortartikels.

In derartigen Fällen muß sich der Benutzer des Wörterbuchs selbständig das nicht ausgeschriebene Substantiv hinzubilden und die substantivische Bedeutung aus der adjektivischen bzw. verbalen ableiten.

Die semantische Komponente ist recht ausführlich behandelt, und zwar dadurch, daß eine lexikalische Einheit der einen Sprache vielfach durch mehrere Entsprechungen der anderen Sprache wiedergegeben wird.

3.2.4. Die Serie Kleine Wörterbücher (Słowniki małe)

Wörterbücher dieser Serie enthalten jeweils 20 000 bis 25 000 lexikalische Einheiten im fremdsprachlich-polnischen Teil und wieder so viel im polnisch-fremdsprachlichen Teil. Sie sind für weniger anspruchsvolle Benutzer bestimmt. Praktisch werden sie jedoch auch von Oberschülern und Studenten benutzt.

Der fremdsprachlich-polnische Teil enthält jeweils eine phonetische Komponente, die sich allerdings auf die Angabe des Hauptakzents der Stichwörter beschränkt. Analog sind auch die grammatischen Angaben auf das Notwendigste beschränkt. Die semantische Komponente ist ebenfalls kürzer gefaßt: Sie enthält wenige synonyme Entsprechungen. Dafür aber wird die stilistisch-emotionale Konnotation und die Verwendungssphäre der lexikalischen Einheiten durch entsprechende Abkürzungen präzisiert.

Bisher (Stand vom 25. Juli 1986) sind in dieser Serie Wörterbücher von 14 Sprachen mit Polnisch erschienen. Es handelt sich um folgende Sprachen: Englisch, Französisch, Deutsch, Spanisch, Esperanto, Schwedisch, Vietnamesisch, Portugiesisch, Russisch, Rumänisch, Serbo-Kroatisch, Suahili, Italienisch, Niederländisch.

Die Gesamtzahl der herausgegebenen Exemplare der Wörterbücher dieser Serie beträgt 3 Millionen. An der ersten Stelle rangiert das russische Wörterbuch von Andrzej Bogusławski mit 810 000 Ex.; ihm folgen: das englische von Tadeusz Grzebieniowski mit 800 000 Ex., das deutsche von Jan Czochralski und Stanisław Schimitzek [...] mit 600 000 Ex., die französischen von Ludwik Szwykowski und Jerzy Tomalak mit 160 000 Exemplaren.

3.2.5. Die Serie Taschenwörterbücher (Słowniki kieszonkowe)

Wörterbücher dieser Art enthalten in jedem Teil, z. B. dem deutsch-polnischen, zwischen 10 000 und 15 000 lexikalische Einheiten. Sie sind vor allem für Touristen bestimmt. Praktisch aber werden sie von sehr verschiedenen Interessierten benutzt. Denn sie weisen gegenüber Wörterbüchern anderer Serien bestimmte Vorzüge auf. Gerade in ihnen erschienen, zum ersten Mal in der Geschichte der polnischen Lexikographie, die polnischen Stichwörter in phonetischer Umschrift — gemäß den Festsetzungen der API. Die phonetische Transkription samt dem Akzent wurde von Jan Czochralski besorgt.

Dank der Angabe der Aussprache in phonetischer Umschrift können diese Wörterbücher mit Vorteil ebenfalls von Polnisch lernenden Ausländern benutzt werden.

Die grammatischen Informationen sind so knapp wie im Kleinen Wörterbuch.

Bisher erschienen in dieser Serie zweiteilige Wörterbücher mit 8 Sprachen: Deutsch, Russisch, Französisch, Bulgarisch, Tschechisch, Slowakisch, Ungarisch, Englisch. Die Gesamtzahl der aufgelegten Wörterbücher dieser Serie beträgt 1 310 000 Exemplare. Von der Beliebtheit dieser Wörterbücher zeugen u. a. die Auflagenhöhen. So wurde z. B. das polnisch-deutsche und deutsch-polnische Taschenwörterbuch von Czochralski und Schimitzek im J. 1984 in 200 000 Exemplaren neu aufgelegt.

3.2.6. Die Serie Minimalwörterbücher (Słowniki minimum)

Diese Wörterbücher enthalten jeweils ca. 5000 lexikalische Einheiten. Die grammatischen Angaben sind auf ein absolutes Minimum reduziert. Trotzdem ist die Nachfrage ungemein groß. Insgesamt wurden bisher 3 585 000 Exemplare von Wörterbüchern dieser Serie herausgegeben.

3.2.7. Phraseologische Wörterbücher

Viel seltener als die in 3.2.2. bis 3.2.6. dargestellten sind die phraseologischen Wörterbücher. Zu erwähnen sind drei Sammlungen:
(1) Phraseologisches Wörterbuch Französisch-Polnisch von Leon Zaręba (1969);
(2) Kleines idiomatisches Wörterbuch Polnisch-Deutsch von Jan Czochralski (1976);
(3) Phraseologische Wortverbindungen der russischen Sprache von Reginina/Tiurina/Szyrokowa (1980).

Sie enthalten jeweils 5000 bis 6000 Phraseologismen, die nach Möglichkeit durch phraseologische Einheiten der anderen Sprache wiedergegeben sind.

Die Auflagenhöhen sind, ungeachtet der großen Nachfrage, nicht gerade überwältigend. Von dem französisch-polnischen sind insgesamt 45 000 Exemplare erschienen, von dem polnisch-deutschen 35 000, von dem russisch-polnischen 30 000.

3.2.8. Illustrierte Wörterbücher

Es handelt sich um allgemeine Wörterbücher, in denen manche Stichwörter durch schematische realistische Zeichnungen (zusätzlich) erklärt sind. Bisher sind erschienen:
— Deutsch-Polnisch von Wanda Brzeska und Alojzy Brzeski;
— Englisch-Polnisch und Polnisch-Englisch von Tadeusz Grzebieniowski;
— Russisch-Polnisch und Polnisch-Russisch von Andrzej Bogusławski.

Außerdem wurden drei illustrierte Wörterbücher für Kinder herausgegeben:
— Französisch-Polnisch und Polnisch-Französisch von Anna Jedlińska;
— Russisch-Polnisch und Polnisch-Russisch von Iryda Grek-Pabisowa und Wanda Sudnik-Owczuk;

— Deutsch-Polnisch und Polnisch-Deutsch von Jerzy Jóźwicki.

Diese Wörterbücher sind insgesamt in 265 000 Exemplaren erschienen.

3.2.9. Schlußbemerkungen

Bis Juli 1986 hat der Verlag Wiedza Powszechna Wörterbücher mit einer Gesamtauflage von 13 906 200 Exemplaren herausgegeben, die 106 Titel repräsentieren. Davon entfallen ca. 13 Millionen auf allgemeine zweisprachige Wörterbücher. (Den Rest bilden zweisprachige Spezialwörterbücher.) Folgende Sprachen wurden bisher mit dem Polnischen konfrontiert: Deutsch, Englisch, Weißrussisch, Bulgarisch, Tschechisch, Dänisch, Esperanto, Finnisch, Französisch, Spanisch, Niederländisch, Portugiesisch, Russisch, Rumänisch, Serbo-Kroatisch, Slowakisch, Suahili, Schwedisch, Türkisch, Ungarisch, Vietnamesisch, Italienisch.

Zahlenmäßig an erster Stelle steht das Russische (Russisch war Pflichtsprache in den polnischen Schulen), an zweiter das Englische, an dritter das Deutsche; ihm folgt mit einem gewissen Abstand das Französische.

Obwohl Wörterbücher der vier wichtigen Sprachen oft und in großen Auflagen erscheinen, sind sie immer in wenigen Wochen vergriffen.

Der Begriff der wichtigen Sprachen ist relativ zu verstehen. Französisch war lange Zeit, bis zum 2. Weltkrieg, wichtiger als das Englische. Jetzt ist es umgekehrt, obwohl die polnische Lexikographie mit Englisch praktisch erst im 19. Jh. beginnt, also viel später als die mit Französisch und Deutsch. Einen hohen Rang erlangte nach 1945 das Russische. Die Popularität des Deutschen unterlag — aus politischen Gründen — Schwankungen. Immerhin sind alle vier Sprachen heute als wichtig zu bezeichnen, da sie — in unterschiedlichem Maße — übernationale Geltung erlangt haben.

Historisch sind in der Wichtigkeit der Fremdsprachen für das polnische Volk bzw. den polnischen Staat Verschiebungen zu beobachten. Aus politischen, kulturellen, konfessionellen und wirtschaftlichen Gründen waren in früheren Jahrhunderten andere Sprachen wichtig: aus mannigfachen Gründen Latein, aus politischen Gründen Litauisch, aus kulturellen und politischen Gründen Italienisch und Französisch, aus politisch-militärischen Türkisch.

Die historisch unterschiedliche Intensität der Beziehungen Polens zu anderen Völkern und die unterschiedlichen politischen Orientierungen sind z. T. in der polnischen zwei- bzw. mehrsprachigen Lexikographie sichtbar. So gibt es bisher keine oder keine nennenswerten zweisprachigen Wörterbücher z. B. des Chinesischen, Japanischen, Indonesischen, Arabischen, Hindi und Urdu, wohl aber des Vietnamesischen und des Suahili. Spanisch und Portugiesisch gehörten bis in die 60er Jahre des 20. Jhs. zu den halbexotischen Sprachen; heute ist es natürlich anders.

Die polnische Lexikographie mit Russisch beginnt bereits im 18. Jh. und entwickelt sich auch im 19. Jh. Eine Blütezeit erlebt sie aber erst nach 1945. In der Zeit zwischen den zwei Weltkriegen wurden polnisch-russische Wörterbücher praktisch nur in der UdSSR herausgegeben.

4. Zur Bibliographie

Eine annähernd vollständige Bibliographie der zweisprachigen Wörterbücher mit Polnisch enthält das wertvolle Werk: Index lexicorum Poloniae (Grzegorczyk 1967). Empfehlenswert sind auch Lewański 1959 und Bibliographie 1965—78 mit Angaben über Wörterbücher, die in sieben sozialistischen Staaten in den Jahren 1945—1961 herausgegeben wurden.

Zur Metalexikographie zweisprachiger Wörterbücher und zu den deutsch-polnischen Wörterbüchern vgl. Czochralski 1977, 1977/78 und 1981, sowie historisch Falkenhahn 1960 und Stankiewicz 1984, 45—60.

5. Literatur (in Auswahl)

5.1. Wörterbücher

Bandtkie 1806 = Jerzy S. Bandtkie: Słownik dokładny [...]. Vollständiges polnisch-deutsches Wörterbuch zum Handgebrauch für Deutsche und Polen. 2 Bde. Breslau 1806.

Bogusławski 1960 = Andrzej Bogusławski: Słownik rosyjsko-polski, polsko-rosyjski. Warszawa 1960.

Bogusławski 1978 = Andrzej Bogusławski: Ilustrowany słownik rosyjsko-polski i polsko-rosyjski. Warszawa 1978.

Booch-Árkossy 1864—65 = Friedrich Booch-Árkossy: Nowy dokładny [...]. Neues vollständiges poln.-dt. und dt.-poln. Wörterbuch. 2 Bde. Leipzig 1864—65.

Brzeska/Brzeski 1975 = Wanda Brzeska/Alojzy Brzeski: Ilustrowany słownik niemiecko-polski. Warszawa 1975.

Bulas/Whitfield/Thomas 1959—61 = Kazimierz Bulas/Francis J. Whitfield/Lawrance L. Thomas: The Kościuszko Foundation Dictionary English-Polish and Polish-English. New York [1959—1961].

Bzdęga/Chodera/Kubica 1973 = Andrzej Bzdęga/Jan Chodera/Stefan Kubica: Podręczny słownik polsko-niemiecki/Handwörterbuch Polnisch-Deutsch. Warszawa 1973.

Callier 1906 = Oskar Callier: Dictionnaire de poche français-polonais et polonais-français [...]. Leipzig 1906.

Chodera/Kubica 1966 = Jan Chodera/Stefan Kubica: Podręczny słownik niemiecko-polski/Handwörterbuch Deutsch-Polnisch. Warszawa 1966.

Ciesielska-Borkowska/Dobrzyński/Gałuszka 1980 = Stefania Ciesielska-Borkowska/Jerzy Dobrzyński/Jadwiga Gałuszka [...]: Wielki słownik francusko-polski. 2 Bde. Warszawa 1980.

Csorba 1958 = Tibor Csorba (Hrsg.): Lengyel-magyar szótár/Słownik polsko-węgierski. Budapest 1958 [2. Ausg. mit Supplement. Warszawa 1985.].

Czochralski 1964 = Jan Czochralski: Mały słownik polsko-niemiecki/Kleinwörterbuch Polnisch-Deutsch. Warszawa 1964.

Czochralski 1976 = Jan Czochralski: Mały słownik idiomatyczny polsko-niemiecki/Kleines idiomatisches Wörterbuch Polnisch-Deutsch. Warszawa 1976 [2. Ausg. 1986].

Czochralski/Schimitzek 1967 = Jan Czochralski/Stanisław Schimitzek: Kieszonkowy słownik niemiecko-polski i polsko-niemiecki/Taschenwörterbuch Deutsch-Polnisch und Polnisch-Deutsch. Warszawa 1967.

Czochralski/Schimitzek [...] 1968 = Jan Czochralski/Stanisław Schimitzek/Barbara Sypniewska/Magdalena Żurakowska: Mały słownik niemiecko-polski i polsko-niemiecki/Kleinwörterbuch Deutsch-Polnisch und Polnisch-Deutsch. Warszawa 1968. 9. Ausg. 1984.

Dworecki/Rozwadowska 1958 = I. H. Dworecki/M. F. Rozwadowska [Hrsg.]: Słownik rosyjsko-polski i polsko-rosyjski. 7. Ausg. 1958.

Grek-Pabisowa/Sudnik-Owczuk 1982 = Iryda Grek-Pabisowa/Wanda Sudnik-Owczuk: Ilustrowany słownik dla dzieci rosyjsko-polski, polsko-rosyjski. Warszawa 1982.

Grzebieniowski 1958 = Tadeusz Grzebieniowski: Mały słownik angielsko-polski i polsko-angielski. Warszawa 1958.

Grzebieniowski 1978 = Tadeusz Grzebieniowski: Ilustrowany słownik angielsko-polski i polsko-angielski. Warszawa 1978.

Hessen/Stypuła 1967 = Dymitr Hessen/Ryszard Stypuła: Wielki słownik polsko-rosyjski. 2 Bde. Warszawa 1967.

Ippoldt 1937—41 = Juliusz Ippoldt: Trzaski, Everta i Michalskiego słownik niemiecko-polski i polsko-niemiecki. 2 Bde. Warszawa [1937—41].

Jedlińska 1979 = Anna Jedlińska: Ilustrowany słownik dla dzieci polsko-francuski i francusko-polski. Warszawa 1979.

Jóźwicki 1984 = Jerzy Jóźwicki: Ilustrowany słownik dla dzieci niemiecko-polski, polsko-niemiecki. Warszawa 1984.

Kalina 1928—31 = Paweł Kalina: Słownik francusko-polski i polsko-francuski. 2 Bde. Warszawa [1928—31].

Kalina 1933—34 = Paweł Kalina: Słownik podręczny francusko-polski i polsko-francuski z wymową fonetyczną. [...]. 2 Bde. Warszawa 1933—34.

Kalina 1935 = Paweł Kalina: Nowy słownik podręczny niemiecko-polski i polsko-niemiecki z wymową fonetyczną. 2 Bde. Warszawa [1935].

Kalina 1963 = Paweł Kalina: Podręczny słownik polsko-niemiecki. 6. Ausg. Warszawa 1963.

Kalina 1963a = Paweł Kalina: Podręczny słownik niemiecko-polski. 6. Ausg. 1963.

Kierst 1957 = Władysław Kierst: Słownik podręczny angielsko-polski i polsko-angielski. 2 Bde. Warszawa 1957 [Nachdruck].

Konarski 1904—08 = Franciszek Konarski [...]: Dokładny słownik [...]. Vollständiges Handwörterbuch der dt. und poln. Sprache. 4 Bde. Wien 1904—08.

Kupisz/Kielski 1968 = Kazimierz Kupisz/Bolesław Kielski: Podręczny słownik francusko-polski. Warszawa 1968.

Kupisz/Kielski 1969 = Kazimierz Kupisz/Bolesław Kielski: Podręczny słownik polsko-francuski. Warszawa 1969.

Martens/Morciniec 1977 = Nico Martens/Elke Morciniec: Mały słownik holendersko-polski i polsko-holenderski. Warszawa 1977.

Marti Marca [...] 1961 = Antonio Marti Marca/Juan Marti Marca/Barbara Jardel: Słownik hiszpańsko-polski. Warszawa 1961.

Marti Marca [...] 1964 = Antonio Marti Marca/Juan Marti Marca/Barbara Jardel: Słownik polsko-hiszpański. Warszawa 1964.

Meisels 1964 = Wojciech Meisels: Podręczny słownik włosko-polski. Dizionario pratico italiano-polacco. Warszawa 1964.

Meisels 1970 = Wojciech Meisels: Podręczny słownik polsko-włoski. Warszawa 1970 [1028 S.].

Mirowicz 1971 = Anatol Mirowicz/I. Dulewicz [...]: Wielki słownik rosyjsko-polski. 2 Bde. Warszawa 1971.

Piprek/Ippoldt 1968 = Jan Piprek/Juliusz Ippoldt: Wielki słownik niemiecko-polski. Warszawa: Bd. 1 1968, Bd. 2 1970, Supplement 1974.

Piprek/Ippoldt 1971 = Jan Piprek/Juliusz Ippoldt: [...] Wielki słownik polsko-niemiecki. Warszawa: Bd. 1 1971, Bd. 2 1974.

Reginina/Tiurina/Szyrokowa 1980 = Kira W. Reginina/Galina P. Tiurina/Ljuksewa I. Szyrokowa: Frazeologiczne związki łączliwe w języku rosyjskim. Warszawa 1980.

Reychman 1968 = Jan Reychman [Hrsg.]: Słownik węgiersko-polski/Magyar-lengyel szótár. Warszawa 1968.

Rozwadowska 1958 = M. F. Rozwadowska (Hrsg.): siehe Dworecki/Rozwadowska 1958.

Rykaczewski 1849—51 = Rykaczewski: A complete dictionary English and Polish, and Polish and English. [. . .]. Berlin 1849—51 [2 Bde.].

Stanisławski 1964 = Jan Stanisławski: Wielki słownik angielsko-polski [. . .]. Warszawa 1964 [9 Ausg.].

Stanisławski 1969 = Jan Stanisławski: Wielki słownik polsko-angielski [. . .]. Warszawa 1969 [7 Ausg.].

Stanisławski [. . .] 1971 = Jan Stanisławski/Katarzyna Billip/Zofia Chociłowska: Podręczny słownik angielsko-polski. Warszawa 1971 [6 Ausg.].

Stanisławski/Szercha 1973 = Jan Stanisławski/Małgorzata Szercha: Podręczny słownik polsko-angielski. Warszawa 1973.

Stypuła/Kowalowa 1976 = Ryszard Stypuła/Halina Kowalowa: Podręczny słownik polsko-rosyjski. Warszawa 1976 [4 Ausg.].

Szwykowski 1962 = Ludwik Szwykowski: Słownik francusko-polski. Warszawa 1962.

Tomalak 1964 = Jerzy Tomalak: Słownik polsko-francuski. Warszawa 1964.

Trotz 1744—47 = Michał A. Trotz: Nouveau dictionnaire françois, allemand et polonais [. . .]. Leipzig 1744—47 [2 Bde.].

Trotz 1772 = Michał A. Trotz: Vollständiges dt. und poln. Wörterbuch [. . .]. Leipzig. Letzter Teil 1772.

Wawrzkowicz/Hiszpański 1982 = Stanisław Wawrzkowicz/Kazimierz Hiszpański: Podręczny słownik hiszpańsko-polski. Warszawa 1982.

Zaręba 1969 = Leon Zaręba: Słownik frazeologiczny francusko-polski. Warszawa 1969 [2. Aufl. 1973].

5.2. Sonstige Literatur

Bibliographie 1965—78 = Bibliografia słowników/Bibliographie der Wörterbücher/Bibliography of Dictionaries/Bibliografija słovarej. [Verlagslektoren: Mieczysław Boratyn/Danuta Rymsza-Zalewska]. Wydawnictwa Naukowo-Techniczne. 1. Bd. Warszawa, 1965.

Czochralski 1977 = Jan Czochralski: Deutsch-Polnische Wörterbücher in Volkspolen. In: Ulrich Engel (Hrsg.): Deutsche Sprache im Kontrast. Tübingen 1977, 198—205.

Czochralski 1977/78 = Jan Czochralski: Über das gegenseitige Verhältnis von Grammatik, Lexik und Lexikographie. In: Germanistisches Jahrbuch DDR — VRP. Warszawa 1977/78, 56—68.

Czochralski 1981 = Jan Czochralski: Zur theoretischen und praktischen Lexikographie. In: Kwartalnik Neofilologiczny 28./1981, 167—180.

Falkenhahn 1960 = V. Falkenhahn: Das polnische Wörterbuch von seinen Anfängen bis Michel Abraham Troc und die Wörterbuchtheorie des Grammatikers Onufry Kopczyński. In: Zeitschrift für Slawistik 5. 1960, 101—111.

Grzegorczyk 1967 = Piotr Grzegorczyk: Index lexicorum Poloniae. Bibliografia słowników polskich. Warszawa 1967.

Lewański 1959 = Richard C. Lewański: A Bibliography of Polish Dictionaries with a Supplement of Lusatian and Polabian Dictionaries. New York 1959.

Stankiewicz 1984 = Edward Stankiewicz: Grammars and Dictionaries of the Slavic Languages from the Middle Ages up to 1850. An Annotated Bibliography. Berlin. New York 1984.

Jan A. Czochralski, Warschau (Polen)

324. Die zweisprachige Lexikographie mit Russisch

1. Vorläufer der zwei- und mehrsprachigen Wörterbücher
2. Ausländische Gesprächswörterbücher und Lehrbücher des Russischen mit zwei- und mehrsprachigen Wörterbüchern
3. Erste gedruckte Wörterbücher
4. Einige handschriftliche zwei- und mehrsprachige Wörterbücher des 17. Jahrhunderts
5. „Europäisierung" und erster Aufschwung der zwei- und mehrsprachigen Lexikographie im 18. Jahrhundert
6. Das 19. Jahrhundert. Blüte der westeuropäischen und Beginn der slavischen zweisprachigen Wörterbücher
7. Das 20. Jahrhundert. Neue Sprachen und neue Konzeptionen
8. Literatur (in Auswahl)

1. Vorläufer der zwei- und mehrsprachigen Wörterbücher

Am Beginn der russischen Lexikographie stehen Wortlisten. Sie markieren zugleich den Anfang der zwei- und mehrsprachigen Lexikographie, da sie meistens zweisprachig-erklärend sind. In den Anfangsstadien der Lexikographie in Rußland muß man allerdings die Bezeichnung „russisch" eher territorialpolitisch als als Terminus für eine Sprach- und Sprechergemeinschaft verstehen. Wegen der von einem großen Teil der Forschung als Diglossie (vgl. z. B. Uspenskij 1987) bezeichneten Situation bei den Russen und den Ostslaven allgemein unterscheidet man bis zum ausgehenden 17. Jh. die Schriftsprache als kirchenslavisch, russisch-kirchenslavisch von der mündlichen Umgangssprache. Wenn im folgenden nicht gesondert darauf hingewiesen wird, ist also unter „russisch" bis zum 18. Jh. immer „russisch-kirchenslavisch" zu verstehen. Die ersten altrussischen Glossare oder Wortlisten enthielten Erklärungen schwer verständlicher kirchlicher griechischer, hebräischer, aber auch altkirchenslavischer Namen, Termini und Wörter. Das älteste russische Wörterbuch *Reč' židov'skago jazyka preložena na russkuju,* das in der 1280 oder 1282 für den Novgoroder Erzbischof Kliment geschriebenen *Kormčaja kniga* enthalten ist, umfaßte 174 Lemmata. Davon waren 115 Erläuterungen biblischer Personen- und Ortsnamen und 59 Erklärungen und Übersetzungen von Appellativa. In letzteren sieht Kovtun (1963, 392) Anfänge der zweisprachigen Lexikographie. In späteren Handschriften wurde diese Liste erweitert, bei der sich ein Ordnungssystem nur in Ansätzen erkennen ließ, das sowohl thematische als auch alphabetische und textuelle (die Glossen wurden nach ihrer Reihenfolge in bestimmten Texten, z. B. dem Psalter, angeordnet) Prinzipien zu enthalten schien. Wegen ihres vornehmlich an den onomastica sacra orientierten Aufbaus nennt man im Anschluß an Kovtun (1963) diese Wörterbücher Onomastika. Eine weitere Gruppe von Wörterbüchern erhielt die Bezeichnung Symbol- oder Gleichniswörterbücher, da in ihnen meistens die Symbolik der Gleichnisse aus den religiösen Schriften erläutert wurde. Hierzu zählten vornehmlich Erklärungen zu den Symbolwörtern des Psalters, die bereits in *Reč' židov'skago jazyka . . .* enthalten waren und in einem speziellen Wörterbuch des 13. Jhs., *A se imena židov'skaja rus'sky t-lkovana,* erläutert wurden. Sie fanden später Eingang in Wörterbücher des 16. und 17. Jhs., wobei Kovtun (1963, 155—215) in den späteren Azbukovniki (s. u.) eine deutlichere Unterscheidung zwischen realer und symbolischer Bedeutung der Wörter feststellt und ein größeres Interesse an der realen Bedeutung. Eine Art innerslavisches Wörterbuch wird mit dem im 14. Jh. entstandenen *Tolkovanie neudob' poznavaemom- rečem'* begründet, das sich meistens in der Übersetzung der Klimax des Johannes Sinaites findet und in seiner ältesten Version 61 Wörterbuchartikel umfaßt, in denen vornehmlich altbulgarische Wörter aus früheren Übersetzungen mit ihren russischen Entsprechungen versehen wurden. Diese altkirchenslavisch-russischen Wörterbücher (vgl. Kovtun 1963, 216—317) sind im Zusammenhang mit der Revision der religiösen Bücher im 16. Jh. zu sehen. Sie bildeten aber gleichzeitig die Grundlage der nationalen Wörterbücher der Ostslaven, die ab dem 17. Jh. entstanden. Die vierte große Gruppe der Vorläufer der mehrsprachigen Lexikographie bildeten nach Kovtun (1963, 313—389) die Gesprächs- oder Konversationswörterbücher, die in Rußland und im Ausland im 15.—17. Jh. entstanden. Bekannteste und z. T. mehrfach herausgegebene Beispiele in Rußland sind hier *Reč' tonkoslovija grečeskogo; Se tatarskij jazyk; Tolkovanie jazyka poloveckogo.* In *Reč' tonkoslovija grečeskogo* (ed. Vasmer 1922) gab es 2621 griechisch-russische bzw. russisch-griechische Entsprechungen, die wahrscheinlich von einem Nordgroßrussen im 15. Jh. auf dem Athos zusammengestellt worden waren, um die Kommunikation mit den Griechen zu ermöglichen. Es handelte sich um systematische Aufzählungen von Wörtern und ihren Entsprechungen zu bestimmten Themen bzw. um Listen von Wörtern und Ausdrücken zu Gesprächen über einzelne Themen, aber auch um zusammenhängende Texte (als Erzählung oder Dialog) aus dem Bereich des täglichen und klösterlichen Lebens. Dieses Wörterbuch bildete einen Bestandteil der sog. Azbukovniki, die im 16. und besonders im 17. Jh. in Rußland verbreitet waren. Die *Azbukovniki* oder auch *Alfavity inostrannych rečej* (vgl. Alekseev 1968) waren alphabetische Wortlisten mit ausführlichen Erklärungen, aber auch Sammelbände, die diese Listen enthielten, wurden so bezeichnet. Die Ersteller der Azbukovniki sammelten die Glossen und Fremdwörter, die in den religiösen Texten ohne Übersetzung geblieben waren, und gaben sie alphabetisch geordnet heraus. Die Ersteller beriefen sich dabei auf Maksim Grek. Dieser hatte mit seinen Schülern eine Reihe von religiösen Schriften im 16. Jh. neu übersetzt, Glossen dazu geschrieben und diese auch gesammelt herausgegeben. Auch diese Glossen enthielten Übersetzungen der griechischen, hebräischen, lateinischen, aber auch der serbisch- und bulgarisch-kirchenslavischen Namen, Termini und Wörter, die den Ostslaven nicht ohne weiteres verständlich waren. Das von Maksim Grek erstellte *Tolkovanie imenam- po alfavitu,* das in drei Redaktionen und 24 Hss. aus dem 16. und 17. Jh. erhalten ist, enthielt ursprünglich 250 Wörterbuchartikel, deren Zahl in der dritten Redaktion bis auf 434 anwuchs. Neben der Erklärung der biblischen Namen hatte das Wörterbuch das Ziel, die griechischen Wurzeln dieser Namen zu erläutern, verfügte also über einen wortbildenden Aspekt, war aber gleichzeitig auch ein zweisprachiges Übersetzungswörterbuch (griechisch-kirchenslavisch, lateinisch-kirchenslavisch, vgl. Kovtun 1975, 204). Die Ausgangssprache dieses Wörterbuches war das Griechische (lateinische und hebräische Namen und Wörter wurden erst ins Griechische und von diesem ins Kirchenslavische übertragen), doch war am wichtigsten nicht die nomenklatorische (griechische) Seite, sondern die erläuternde (kirchenslavische). Dieses Wörterbuch hatte großen Einfluß auf die Azbukovniki und auch auf das Wörterbuch von Polikarpov. Einfluß auf die Azbukovniki hatten auch die westeuropäischen lexikographischen Bemühungen eines Simon Roth, Konrad Gesner, Hieronymus Megiser und vieler anderer (vgl. dazu Alekseev 1968; Kovtun 1975). Die Azbukovniki wurden auch von Mönchen erstellt, die mit der Umarbeitung und Verbesserung der kirchlichen Bücher beschäftigt waren. Sie waren bestimmt für den „eifrigen Leser religiöser Schriften" (Kovtun 1975, 210). Es gab eine kürzere Redaktion mit ca. 2500 Lemmata, die um die Mitte des 16. Jhs. erstellt wurde, und eine ausführlichere Redaktion mit ca. 5000 Lemmata, die gegen Ende des 16. Jhs. (nicht später als 1596) verfaßt wurde.

2. Ausländische Gesprächswörterbücher und Lehrbücher des Russischen mit zwei- und mehrsprachigen Wörterbüchern

Aus den Jahren 1546 (vgl. Alekseev 1974) und 1551 sind ein hochdeutsch-russisches und Fragmente eines niederdeutsch-russischen Gesprächsbuches (Johansen 1955) übermittelt (zu anderen vgl. Alekseev 1968, 78). Weiters gibt es zwei niederländisch-russische Gesprächsbücher aus dem 17. Jh. von H. Newenburgk und J. von Heemer (vgl. Günther 1963 und 1965). In einigen dieser Gesprächsbücher finden sich auch zweisprachige Wörterverzeichnisse, so z. B. in dem Pariser *Dictionnaire moscovite* (Larin 1948), das von Jean Sauvage unter der Mithilfe einheimischer Dolmetscher bei einer Handelsexpedition in die Gegend von Archangel'sk erstellt wurde, und in dem *Russisch-englischen Wörterbuch-Tagebuch* des Engländers Richard James, der von 1618—1619 Aufzeichnungen über die russische Umgangssprache in Cholmogory und Archangel'sk machte, die Larin (1959) herausgab. Hier ist auch das 1607 von Tönnies Fenne in Pskov geschriebene Russisch-niederdeutsche Handbuch zu nennen (vgl. Hammerich/Jakobson eds. 1961 und 1970), das ein umfangreiches thematisches Wörterbuch der russischen Umgangssprache in kyrillischer Schrift und lateinischer Umschrift mit niederdeutschen Übersetzungen enthält sowie einen grammatischen Teil, Phraseologie, Konversationstexte, aber auch Sprichwörter, Rätsel und Redensarten. Eine einfache und sehr kurze lateinisch-deutsch-russische Wortliste ist auch in der russischen Grammatik von Heinrich Wilhelm Ludolf enthalten (Larin 1937, Unbegaun 1959).

3. Erste gedruckte Wörterbücher

Im Jahre 1596 erschien in Wilna das erste gedruckte russische Wörterbuch. Es steht in der Tradition der Azbukovniki und stammt von Lavrentij Zizanij Tustanovskij, der es als Ergänzung zu seinen grammatischen Werken des Kirchenslavischen unter dem Titel *Leksis, sireč' rečenija vkratce sobrany i iz slovenskogo jazyka na prosty russkij dijalekt istolkovany* verfaßt hatte. Dieses Wörterbuch enthielt auf 67 Seiten 1601 Wörter der kirchenslavischen Schriftsprache und einige Fremdwörter, die in den ostslavischen Sprachen Ukrainisch, Weißrussisch und Russisch erklärt wurden (Nimčuk ed. 1964). Das Wörterbuch Zizanijs hatte wiederum Einfluß auf die späteren Azbukovniki und auf das Wörterbuch des Ukrainers Pamva Berynda. Dessen *Leksikon slaveno rossijskij. Imen tolkovanie* erschien in zwei Ausgaben (Kiev 1627, Kuteinskij monastyr' 1653, vgl. Nimčuk 1961). Das Material zu diesem Wörterbuch hatte der Verfasser, ein Philologe, Schriftsteller und Buchdrucker, in 30jähriger Arbeit aus verschiedenen Quellen der geistlichen Literatur und aus anderen Wörterbüchern, deren Materialien er teilweise kritisch umarbeitete, gesammelt (Cejtlin 1958, 12 f.). Das Wörterbuch bestand aus zwei Teilen, deren erster 4980 altkirchenslavische Wörter enthielt, die vom Verfasser meistens in ukrainischer, aber auch in russischer, weißrussischer und polnischer Sprache erklärt wurden. Oft gab es auch Übersetzungen des altkirchenslavischen Wortes ins Griechische oder Lateinische, manchmal auch ins Serbische oder Tschechische. Der zweite Teil enthielt 2002 Fremdwörter, meistens Eigennamen, mit den entsprechenden Übersetzungen und Erklärungen. Wegen einer Reihe von Synonymen, die im ersten Teil angegeben wurden, läßt sich der erste Teil als Mischung aus Synonym- und Übersetzungswörterbuch charakterisieren, der zweite eher als Fremdwörterbuch.

Der Lexikograph und Direktor der Moskauer Buchdruckerei Fedor Polikarpovič Polikarpov-Orlov gab 1704 in Moskau ein *Leksikon trejazyčnyj, sireč' rečenij slavenskich, ellinogrečeskich i latinskich sokrovišče* ... (vgl. Keipert ed. 1988) heraus, an dessen Bearbeitung und Durchsicht griechische und ukrainische Kollegen von ihm mitgewirkt hatten. Es beruhte großenteils auf dem handschriftlichen griechisch-slavisch-lateinischen Lexikon von Epifanij Slavynec'kyj (s. u.) und war das erste russischkirchenslavisch-griechisch-lateinische Wörterbuch seiner Art in Rußland. Es enthielt 19 712 russischkirchenslavische Wortartikel, wobei vielen Wörtern mehrere Artikel gewidmet waren. Die Wörter stammten meistens aus dem geistlich-religiösen Bereich. Das Wörterbuch war vor allem „ein Übersetzungswörterbuch, das möglichst viele Äquivalente im Griechischen und Lateinischen bereitstellen sollte" (Keipert ed. 1988, XXIII), und diente vornehmlich schulischen Zwecken. Die Reihenfolge der Sprachen entspricht der Bedeutung, die ihnen beigemessen wurde.

Bereits 1700 waren in Amsterdam die beiden thematischen Wörterbücher des Il'ja Fedorovič Kopievskij (Kopievič, Kopiewitz), eines Polen oder Weißrussen, erschienen, die das Ziel hatten, die Russen die betreffenden Fremdsprachen zu lehren. Es waren dies ein *Nomenclator in lingua Latina, Germanica et Russica* und *Nomenclator in Lingua Latina, Hollandica et Russica,* die bis auf den deutschen bzw. holländischen Teil identisch waren. Sie waren in 47 thematische Kapitel untergliedert und enthielten auf der russischen Seite eine Reihe von Ukrainismen, Ausdrükken der weißrussischen und auch der russischen Volkssprache. Ein ähnlicher Typ von Wörterbuch wurde übrigens von F. Polikarpov unter dem Titel *Kratkoe sobranie imen* im Rahmen seines *Bukvar'* 1701 in Moskau herausgegeben (zum Vergleich dieser beiden thematischen Lehrwörterbücher s. Berezina 1980).

4. Einige handschriftliche zwei- und mehrsprachige Wörterbücher des 17. Jahrhunderts

Obwohl sie nur handschriftlich vorlagen, hatten doch die Wörterbücher von Epifanij Slavynec'kyj, einem Ukrainer, der 1649 nach Moskau kam, einen großen Einfluß auf die nachfolgenden gedruckten Wörterbücher. Außer einem philologischen Wörterbuch, in dem er in der Tradition seiner Vorgänger die schwer verständlichen Wörter und Namen der kirchlichen Literatur erklärte, stammen von ihm ein lateinisch-slavisches Wörterbuch, eine Übersetzung des lateinischen Wörterbuchs des Ambrosius Calepinus (wahrscheinlich der 1590 und in mehreren späteren Auflagen in Basel erschienenen elfsprachigen Ausgabe, die auch eine polnische Version enthielt, vgl. Birgegård 1985, 22) ins Kirchenslavische und Ukrainische, mit 27 000 Stichwörtern eines der umfangreichsten Wörterbücher der damaligen Zeit, und eine spätere strenger am Kirchenslavischen orientierte umgekehrte Ausgabe dieses Wörterbuchs, die er mit A. Korec'kyj-Satanovskyj (Nimčuk ed. 1973) in Moskau vorbereitete. Von ihm gibt es ferner eine *Kniga Leksikon grekoslavenolatinskij,* die später Polikarpov als Vorlage diente (Brailovskij 1890).

Vom Ende des 17. Jhs. ist eine in Wien aufbewahrte Handschrift eines umfangreichen Wörterbuchs überliefert, das als Russisch-Lehrbuch für Deutschsprechende angelegt war und mit Phraseologismen und Redensarten ca. 24 000 deutsch-russische (nach dem Deutschen alphabetisch geordnet) Einträge enthält, die von zwei Schreibern geschrieben wurden und im russischen Teil südgroßrussisch-ukrainischen Einfluß erkennen lassen und eine volkssprachliche Ausrichtung. Dieses Wörterbuch liegt inzwischen in einer vorbildlichen Ausgabe (Birkfellner ed. 1984) vor.

Von großer Bedeutung für die russische Lexikographie ist das handschriftliche *Lexicon Slavonicum* des Schweden Johan Gabriel Sparwenfeld, das dieser gegen Ende des 17. und Anfang des 18. Jhs. mit einer Reihe von Mitarbeitern erstellte, das aber eher ein slavisch-lateinisches Wörterbuch war, das den Zweck hatte, „die slavischen Länder und Völker für Westeuropa besser zugänglich zu machen" (Birgegård 1985, 104). Es enthielt 25 636 Einträge und berücksichtigte in hohem Maße die in den slavischen Ländern und vor allem in Rußland bis dahin erschienenen lexikographischen (auch handschriftlichen) Quellen. Inzwischen liegen die ersten drei Bände in einer gedruckten Ausgabe (Birgegård ed. 1987—1989, A—I, K—O und P—R) vor.

Auch in Polen hatte es im 17. Jh. einige lexikographische Bemühungen gegeben, polnisch-russischkirchenslavische Wörterbücher zu erstellen, die großenteils jedoch ebenfalls nur handschriftlich erhalten sind (vgl. dazu Witkowski 1961; Kochman 1967).

5. „Europäisierung" und erster Aufschwung der zwei- und mehrsprachigen Lexikographie im 18. Jahrhundert

Für das 18. Jh. hat Birkfellner (ed. 1984, 11) aufgrund der Angaben in Svodnyj katalog (1967) im Hinblick auf den Umfang von einer eher bescheidenen Produktion von zweisprachigen und polyglotten Wörterbüchern in Rußland gesprochen. Berücksichtigt man jedoch all die Grammatiken, Lehr- und Gesprächsbücher, die Wörterbücher enthalten, und dazu die terminologischen mehrsprachigen Verzeichnisse der Fachbücher und Fachwörterbücher, so ist, nicht nur auf dem Hintergrund der vorhergehenden Jahrhunderte, diese Produktion alles andere als bescheiden zu nennen. Vomperskij (1986) führt in seinem Verzeichnis der Wörterbücher des 18. Jhs. 277 Titel an. In Polikarpovs Lexikon von 1704 war noch das Griechische an erster Stelle der klassischen Sprachen geblieben. Im weiteren Verlauf des 18. Jhs. trat hier mehr das Lateinische in den Vordergrund. Neben dieser Ausrichtung an den klassischen Schulsprachen gewannen aber die westlichen Sprachen, vor allem das Deutsche und Französische mehr und mehr an Bedeutung. Hinzu kamen das Italienische und das Englische, und auch andere westliche Sprachen wurden berücksichtigt. Weniger stark ausgeprägt waren die innerslavischen lexikographischen Bemühungen (zur frühen Geschichte der Lexikographie der ostslavischen Sprachen vgl. Nimčuk 1980), wenn man vom Polnischen einmal absieht. Die Sprachen und Nachbarsprachen des russischen Imperiums fanden nur zögernd Berücksichtigung. Oft existieren frühe Wörterbücher nur in handschriftlicher Form (vgl. die Angaben zu russisch-georgischen, russisch-tatarischen und russisch-lettischen Wörterbüchern bei Vomperskij 1986, 6) oder man übersetzte (wie z. B. beim Türkischen) westeuropäische Vorlagen. Eine Ausnahme bildete das von Pallas gesammelte reichhaltige Material von 200 Sprachen für das *Vergleichende Wörterbuch aller Sprachen*. L. I. Bacmeister hatte mit der Sammlung des Materials aus aller Welt begonnen, und Katharina II. wollte ursprünglich selbst ein Wörterbuch aller Sprachen herausgeben, sie übergab diese Aufgabe dann aber dem Naturforscher P. S. Pallas, dem viele Gelehrte halfen und der 1787 und 1789 den ersten Teil dieses Wörterbuches aller Sprachen herausgab. Es enthielt in den beiden Bänden 130 und 155 Wörter, die nach Begriffsfeldern geordnet waren: Gott, Himmel, Vater, Mutter, Sohn...Verwandtschaftsbeziehungen, Körperteile usw., und berücksichtigte 51 europäische und 149 asiatische Sprachen, die alle in kyrillischer Schrift gedruckt wurden. Dabei unterliefen dem Nichtphilologen Pallas jedoch bereits bei der Umsetzung von Wörtern aus slavischen Sprachen mit lateinischen Alphabeten grobe Fehler (Jagić 1910, 71 f). Eine neue Ausgabe wurde von F. I. Janković de Mirievo 1790—1791 in vier Bänden herausgegeben. Sie berücksichtigte zusätzlich 4 europäische, 22 asiatische und 30 afrikanische und 23 amerikanische Sprachen. Doch waren die Wörter aller Sprachen diesmal in eine alphabetische Reihenfolge gebracht, wodurch das Werk sehr schwer benutzbar wurde. Das mag mit ein Grund gewesen sein, daß es nicht weiter fortgesetzt wurde. In diesem Werk fanden viele der handschriftlichen Aufzeichnungen und Wörterverzeichnisse und Gesprächsbücher Berücksichtigung, die von den ostasiatischen und orientalischen Sprachen an den Grenzen und innerhalb Rußlands gemacht worden waren (vgl. dazu Bulič 1904, 222 f und 365—520).

Gedruckt und mehrfach aufgelegt wurden in Rußland im 18. Jh. vor allem Schullehrbücher, Grammatiken und Gesprächsbücher der klassischen Sprachen und der westeuropäischen Sprachen, die meistens thematische Wörterbücher oder Verzeichnisse enthielten. Außerdem gab es Wortkonkordanzen zu bestimmten (oft religiösen) Texten, die unter dem Titel *Simfonija* erschienen. Die mehrsprachigen alphabetischen Wörterbücher sind oft Übersetzungen westlicher Werke, denen ein russischer Teil hinzugefügt wird. Zu den russisch-westeuropäischen, westeuropäisch-russischen lexikographischen Werken vgl. auch Biržakova (1977, 96 ff). Mit der Herausgabe des ersten russischen Akademiewörterbuches (1789—1794) beginnt jedoch eine stärkere Orientierung am Russischen bzw. vom Russischen zu den anderen Sprachen. Durch die Ausrichtung an den klassischen und westlichen Quellen gab es eine starke Tendenz zu Entlehnungen (vgl. Hüttl-Worth 1956), und auch die Zahl der Fremdwörterlexika stieg an. Das Akademiewörterbuch versuchte, dem mit z. T. überzogenem Purismus entgegenzuwirken. Die polyglotten Wörterbücher berücksichtigten bis zu sechs und mehr Sprachen. Aus der relativ großen Zahl der lexikographischen Werke des 18. Jhs. können im folgenden nur einige exemplarisch genannt werden. Die Zahlen hinter dem Ersteller des Verzeichnisses (Vomperskij 1986) beziehen sich nicht auf die Seiten, sondern auf die Nummern dieses Verzeichnisses. Der Nomenclator von Kopievskij erschien zu Beginn des Jhs. in mehreren Auflagen, z. T. erweitert und z. T. unter anderem Titel. Ein Unikum stellt das einzige russisch-niederländische Wörterbuch des 18. Jhs. von Jacob Bruce, das 1717 in Petersburg erschien, dar (Vomperskij 1986, 12; Alekseev 1968, 148 ff; Biržakova 1980). Bruce hatte auf Geheiß Peters d. Gr. die Grammatik der niederländischen Sprache von Willem Sewel übersetzt und dazu ein niederländisch-russisches Wörterbuch der dort vorhandenen Liste der Substantive erstellt. Diese Liste drehte er um und ergänzte sie durch Wörter aus dem englisch-niederländischen, niederländisch-englischen Wörterbuch von W. Sewel (Amsterdam 1708). Auf diese Weise erhielt er ein russisch-niederländisches Wörterbuch, bei dem die russische erklärende Seite alphabetisch geordnet links steht und die zu erklärende niederländische Seite rechts. Das Wörterbuch enthält hauptsächlich Substantive und Adverbien, aber auch einige Adjektive und Verben (die aus der „Umdrehung" resultieren).

1731 wurde zu dem deutsch-lateinischen Teil des urspr. lateinisch-deutschen Wörterbuches des Österreichers E. Weißmann eine russische Übersetzung angefertigt und in Petersburg herausgegeben. Dieses Wörterbuch erlebte mehrere Ausgaben (Vomperskij 1986, 32, 124, 269; Scholz ed. 1982—83) und hatte großen Einfluß auf die russische Lexikographie. Es war eine Art Gegenstück zu den Grammatiken mit lexikalischem Anhang, denn es war ein Lexikon mit grammatischem Anhang, einer kurzen in deutscher Sprache verfaßten Grammatik des Russischen. Es enthielt ca. 100 000 russische Entsprechungen, worunter viele Phraseologismen und Sprichwörter waren. Dieses Wörterbuch zog der Schriftsteller A. Kantemir auch zur Abfassung seines russisch-französischen Wörterbuches heran (Gradova 1987). An weiteren größeren russischen Wörterbüchern mit Deutsch sind zu erwähnen das russisch-deutsche und das deutsch-russische Wörterbuch von Jacob Rodde von 1784 (Vomperskij 1986, 139), das deutsch-russische, russisch-deutsche Wörterbuch von J. A. Heym von 1795—98, das mehrere Auflagen erlebte und dessen russisch-deutscher Teil dem russischen Akademiewörterbuch folgte (Vomperskij 1986, 254, 274), und das vollständige deutsch-russische Lexikon von 1798, das aus dem grammatisch-kritischen Wörterbuch von J. Chr. Adelung (Leipzig 1774—1786) erstellt wurde (Vomperskij 1986, 265). Auch im Bereich der Wörterbücher mit Französisch gab es neben einem umfangreichen dreibändigen handschriftlichen russisch-französischen Wörterbuch (Vomperskij 1986, 138) russische Übersetzungen des Wörterbuchs der französischen Akademie (Übers. der 4. Ausgabe von 1762; 1773 erschien nur der Buchstabe A, 1786 die vollständige Übersetzung, 1798 in zweiter, ergänzter Auflage, vgl. Vomperskij 1986, 91, 149 und 266) und 1799—1802 in drei Bänden von J. A. Heym eine französische Übersetzung des russischen Akademiewörterbuches (Vomperskij 1986, 272). Ein größeres englisch-russisches Wörterbuch erschien 1784 von P. I. Ždanov in Petersburg. Es gab aber auch Übersetzungen bzw. russische Ergänzungen von mehrsprachigen Wörterbüchern, wie die des 1703 in 3. Aufl. erschienenen „Nouveau dictionnaire du voyageur françois-aleman-latin et aleman-françois-latin", die S. S. Volčkov durchführte und die erstmals in zwei Teilen 1755 und 1764 erschien und dann noch zwei weitere ergänzte Auflagen erlebte (Vomperskij 1986, 50, 107, 148). Das deutsch-französisch-lateinisch-italienisch-russische Lexikon von M. G. Gavrilov wurde 1781 und 1789 in Moskau herausgegeben. Erwähnenswert sind die beiden Ausgaben des griechisch-russischen Wörterbuchs von 1783 und 1794 des Archimandriten Mefodij mit z. T. etymologischen Erklärungen der griechischen Wörter, aber auch mit einer Grammatik und einem russisch-neugriechischen Wörterbuch in der zweiten Auflage (Vomperskij 1986, 133 und 236) und das handschriftliche russisch-japanische Lexikon von A. Tatarin von ca. 1782, das 1962 (Petrova ed. 1962) herausgegeben wurde und ungefähr 1000 Wörter enthält.

In den vielen Grammatiken, Lehr- und Konversationsbüchern, die im 18. Jh. oft in mehreren Auflagen erschienen (die deutsche Grammatik von M. Schwanwitz mit einem orthographischen deutsch-russischen Wörterbuch erschien z. B. in fünf Auflagen, vgl. Vomperskij 1986, 30), waren die lexikalischen Teile zumeist nach thematischen Prinzipien aufgebaut. Das galt z. B. für die Italienisch-Grammatik von E. Bulatnickij von 1759, die Französisch-Grammatik von Teplov nach J. R. Des Pepliers von 1752, das Englisch-Lehrbuch von Krjažev von 1791, das Armenisch-Lehrbuch von Sarafova von 1788 u. a. (Vomperskij 1986, 53, 47, 207, 170). Viele Auflagen erlebten auch Gesprächsbücher mit Titeln wie „Škol'nye razgovory" (Colloquia scholastica) und „Domašnie razgovory" (die „Dialogues domestiques" von Georg Philipp Plats bildeten ihre Vorlage), die latein., französ., russ. und deutsche Paralleltexte und Wortlisten enthielten. Als Vorläufer der heutigen didaktischen Lexikographie (učebnaja leksikografija) stufen Jakimovič (1985, 54) und Keipert (1987) die in Rußland verwendeten und erstellten Versionen des Cellarius ein. Christoph Cellarius hatte ein in Deutschland mehrfach aufgelegtes Vocabularium latino-germanicum erstellt, das das Erlernen der Lateinvokabeln erleichtern sollte. Es war unter dem Kurztitel Liber memorialis bekannt. Außerdem hatte er den Thesaurus eruditionis scholasticae von Basilius Faber bearbeitet und neu aufgelegt. Beiden Werken war die Anordnung nach Wortfamilien, grammatische Kennzeichnungen und ein deutsches Wortregister für die Übersetzung ins Lateinische gemeinsam. Für den Wörterbuchtyp, „der die etymologische Anordnung des Wortmaterials mit einer sprachpädagogischen Zielsetzung verbindet" (Keipert 1987, 310), bildete sich der Oberbegriff Cellarius heraus. 1746 gab es eine russische Version des Liber memorialis, die erneut 1768, 1781, 1795 und 1810 aufgelegt wurde. Franz Hölterhof, Lektor der deutschen Sprache an der Moskauer Universität, gab 1765 einen deutschen Cellarius heraus. Das russ. Register dazu erschien 1767. Dem folgte 1769 eine russische Bearbeitung des französischen Cellarius von G. Philipp Plats für Russen, die ebenfalls mehrere Auflagen erlebte. Dann verfaßte er einen russ. Cellarius für Deutsche (1770), auf dem auch sein 1778 herausgegebenes alphabetisches russ.-deutsch-lateinisches Wörterbuch gründete. Im Cellarius waren jeweils die Fremdwörter gesondert erfaßt. Das kam der Tendenz zu Fremdwörterbüchern entgegen. Viele Auflagen erlebt hat die russische Grammatik *Pismovnik* von N. G. Kurganov, die im zweiten Teil eine Erläuterung und Übersetzung von hebräischen, griechischen, lateinischen, französischen, altkirchenslavischen u. a. Fremdwörtern enthielt (Vomperskij 1986, 193). Eine Sammlung der religiösen, kirchenslavischen und kirchlichen Terminologie stellte der *Cerkovnyj slovar'* von P. A. Alekseev dar, der 1773 erschien und später mehrere Ergänzungen erfuhr. Er ging weit über die Wortkonkordanzen zu einzelnen Schriften hinaus und vereinte die Arbeit seiner Vorgänger. Im 18. Jh. kamen auch die ersten zwei- und mehrsprachigen terminologischen Spezialwörterbücher zu Bereichen wie Architektur, Medizin, Mineralogie usw. (Vomperskij 1986, 9, 145, 267) auf, die auch die russischen Entsprechungen enthielten.

6. Das 19. Jahrhundert. Blüte der westeuropäischen und Beginn der slavischen zweisprachigen Wörterbücher

Am Beginn der lexikographischen Bemühungen im 19. Jh. steht der von Nikolaj Maksimovič Janovskij 1803—1806 in Petersburg herausgegebene *Novyj slovotolkovatel'*, ein Wörterbuch, das die Bemühungen der Fremdwörterbücher und der terminologischen Wörterbücher des 18. Jhs. vereinte und doch über sie hinausging und in seiner Konzeption grundsätzlich neu war. Es enthielt 10 000 Einträge von Entlehnungen aus den unterschiedlichsten Sprachen und Wissensgebieten, brachte aber deren phonetische, morphologische und orthographische Varianten, etymologische Erklärungen, funktionale Zuordnungen, Angaben der Gebrauchssphären und statt der wörtlichen Übersetzungen zumeist Erklärungen philologisch-enzyklopädischen Charakters. Es fand eine gute Aufnahme, und die hs. konzipierte zweite, 1825 geplante, wesentlich erweiterte Ausgabe unterblieb nur wegen des Todes des Verfassers 1826. Die Hs. der geplanten Neuauflage ist verschollen (Vojnova 1980, 48).

Während die einsprachige russ. Lexikographie für das 19. und 20. Jh. monographisch bereits relativ gut bearbeitet ist, steht eine zusammenfassende Darstellung für die zweisprachige Lexikographie noch aus. Hier muß man sich weitgehend mit (z. T. kommentierten) Bibliographien behelfen (Zaunmüller 1958, Lewanski 1973, Vinogradov ed. 1954, Aav 1977, Stankiewicz 1984) oder ist auf Arbeiten zu speziellen Problemen und Bereichen angewiesen, da auch in den Sprachgeschichten die zweisprachige Lexikographie für diese Zeit zumeist stiefmütterlich behandelt wird. Zunächst werden die großen deutsch-russischen und russisch-deutschen, aber auch die russisch-französisch-deutschen und französisch-russisch-deutschen Wörterbücher von Johann Heym neu herausgegeben. Letzteres, in zwei Bänden 1816—1817 in Petersburg erschienen, enthielt ca. 54 000 Lemmata, berücksichtigte in großem Umfang die Terminologie aus Technik und Wissenschaft und enthielt zusätzliche Verzeichnisse männlicher und weiblicher Eigennamen und geographischer Namen. Es gab aber auch das bislang umfangreichste englisch-russische Wörterbuch von M. A. Parenago und N. F. Grammatin, das diese auf der Grundlage der Wörterbücher von Johnson, Ebers und Robinet erstellten und 1808—1817 in Moskau in vier Bänden mit insgesamt ca. 49 500 Lemmata herausgaben. Das vollständige französisch-russische Wörterbuch von I. I. Tatiščev, das 1816 ebenfalls in zwei Bänden (1068 und 1194 Sp.) in Moskau erschien und in erster Linie auf den Wörterbüchern der jeweiligen Akademien beruhte, erlebte noch mehrere (z. T. überarbeitete) Auflagen. Es umfaßte über 34 000 Wörter und berücksichtigte in großem Umfang technische und wissenschaftliche Termini. Große Bedeutung hatte auch das umfangreiche lateinisch-russische Wörterbuch von I. Ja. Kroneberg, das in zwei Bänden (1446 und 1624 S.) 1819—1820 in Moskau erschien, eine veränderte Neuauflage 1824 und eine weitere Auflage 1870 erlebte. Es enthielt 60 000 lateinische Wörter mit russ. Äquivalenten, grammatischen Erläuterungen, Hinweisen auf die Herkunft von Wörtern aus dem Griechischen, teilweise Belegstellen und einen eigenen russ. Wortindex.

Das Interesse an der Erstellung eines universalen Glossariums, einer Darstellung und Erfassung aller Sprachen der Welt, findet eine Fortsetzung in der Arbeit Johann Christoph Adelungs und der seines Neffen Friedrich Adelung. Dieser veröffentlicht 1806—1817 zusammen mit S. Vater in vier Bänden das Werk seines Onkels *Mithridates oder allgemeine Sprachenkunde* und bringt 1820 in Petersburg seine *Übersicht aller Sprachen und ihrer Dialekte* heraus, die ca. 2000 bzw. 3064 Sprachen nennt. Im Rahmen des Plans einer „Bibliotheca glottica" sollten auch vergleichende Wörterbücher zu diesen Sprachen erscheinen. Weiter als bis zu dem 1830 in Petersburg herausgegebenen *Versuch einer Literatur der Sanskrit Sprache* ist dieses Vorhaben aber nie gediehen. Angeregt von Reiffs (s. u.) etymologischem Lexikon war das vergleichende Wurzelwörterbuch von F. Šimkevič, *Korneslov russkogo jazyka...*, in dem er 1378 russische Stammwörter und ihre Ableitungen mit den slavischen und 24 weiteren Sprachen verglich. Es kam 1842 in Petersburg in zwei Bänden heraus.

Mit der Romantik, der Beschäftigung mit der eigenen Geschichte und Sprachgeschichte begann innerhalb und außerhalb Rußlands eine Hinwendung zu historischen, historisch-vergleichenden und etymologischen Wörterbüchern. Außerdem nahm man die Erstellung von Dialektwörterbüchern in Angriff. Der Beginn der nationalen Wiedergeburt in den anderen slavischen Ländern und die Entdeckung der slavischen Gemeinsamkeiten förderten die Pläne zur Herausgabe innerslavischer mehrsprachiger Wörterbücher. A. Ch. Vostokov, von dem das bekannteste kirchenslavische Wörterbuch stammt, das 1858 und 1861 in Petersburg herauskam und 22 000 Wörter mit griechischen und lateinischen Entsprechungen und Belegstellen aus den altkirchenslavischen Texten enthielt, trug sich in den Jahren 1810—20 mit dem Plan, ein slaveno-russisches etymologisches, nach Wortnestern angeordnetes Wörterbuch herauszugeben, wovon hs. Aufzeichnungen erhalten sind (Bulič 1904, 994 ff). Es gab das Vorhaben eines Wörterbuches der slavischen Dialekte, und A. S. Šiškov trat 1822 mit dem Plan eines Wörterbuches aller slavischen Dialekte an die Öffentlichkeit (Bulič 1904, 1202). Zunächst wurde jedoch in langwieriger Arbeit eine Neuherausgabe des Wörterbuches der Akademie unternommen. Diesmal war die Anordnung alphabetisch, und ursprünglich hatte man auch lateinische, deutsche und französische Entsprechungen aufnehmen wollen (Bulič 1904, 716). Man entschied sich dann aber für ein „slaveno-russisches etymologisches Wörterbuch in alphabetischer Anordnung", das in 6 Bänden 1806 (1), 1809 (2), 1814 (3), 1822 (4—6) erschien, gegenüber der alten Ausgabe aber nicht grundsätzlich geändert war, wenn es auch 8131 Wörter mehr enthielt und die Anordnung jetzt alphabetisch war. Die Herausgabe eines Wortableitungswörterbuches blieb ein Torso (Bulič 1904, 964 ff). Die Sammlung von Dialektwörtern kam etwas besser voran, doch konnten auch hier die Vorhaben, slavisch-russische Wörterbücher herauszugeben, zunächst nicht realisiert werden. Die von Lobojko bereits 1824 beabsichtigte Herausgabe eines weißruss.-russ. Glossars verzögerte sich, bis dann Grigorovič 1851 einen Teil eines weißruss. Wörterbuchs herausgeben konnte (Bulič 1904, 1000 f.). Heute gibt es ein umfangreiches weißrussisch-russisches Wörterbuch bereits in 2. Auflage (Atrachovič ed. 1988—1989). Ein von der Akademie 1818 erworbenes hs. ukrainisch-russ. Wörterbuch ging offensichtlich verloren (Bulič 1904, 990 f.), und ein ebenfalls 1818 angekauftes Glossarium Illiricum, ein serbisch-lateinisches hs. Wörterbuch aus dem 18. Jh., das von Ozereckovskij bearbeitet und mit einem russischen Teil versehen wurde und von der Akademie zur Herausgabe vorgesehen war, ist nur hs. erhalten geblieben (Bulič 1904, 1180 f., 1190). Es hatte zwar bereits früher längere ukrainisch-russische Wortlisten zu einzelnen Werken und Sammlungen gegeben (so zu dem in Petersburg erschienenen Poem Ėneida von I. P. Kotljarev'skyj 1798 mit 972 Wörtern und bei den Neuauflagen 1808 und 1809 mit 1125 Wörtern), und O. P. Pavlov'skyj gab zu seiner ukrainischen Grammatik (Petersburg 1818) ein thematisch in vier Gruppen geordnetes Wörterverzeichnis heraus, das wegen einer Reihe von nicht gezählten Synonymen mehr als die angegebene Zahl von 1131 Wörtern enthielt, doch erschien das erste selbständige ukrainisch-russische Wörterbuch von I. V. Vojcechovyč erst 1823 in Moskau. Es enthielt 1173 alphabetisch angeordnete Wörter mit Betonungen und grammatischen Angaben. Erst in der zweiten Hälfte des 19. Jhs., als man das Ukrainische als selbständige Sprache betrachtete und nicht nur als russischen Dialekt, erscheinen umfangreichere ukrainisch-russische Wörterbücher und auch das erste russisch-ukrainische Wörterbuch von M. Levčenko (Moskau 1874, 188 S., ca. 9000 Wörter). Die zweisprachige Lexikographie Russisch-Ukrainisch ist in den Darstellungen von Moskalenko (1961) und Horeckyj (1963) berücksichtigt. Heute existieren an Standardwerken ein großes sechsbändiges ukrainisch-russisches Wörterbuch (Kiew 1953—1963, 506, 767, 528, 570, 591 und 618 S.), ein dreibändiges russisch-ukrainisches (Kiev 1970, 700, 756 und 727 S.) und ein einbändiges ukrainisch-russisches Wörterbuch (Kiev 3. Aufl. 1975, 944 S., ca. 65 000 Wörter).

Besser stand es bereits in der ersten Hälfte des 19. Jhs. um die russischen Wörterbücher mit Polnisch. Nachdem schon 1775 in Petersburg von K. Kondratowicz ein allgemeines und biblisches Wörterbuch ins Russische übersetzt worden war, erschien 1810 ebenda ein polnisch-russisches administrativ-juristisches Spezialwörterbuch von I. Buczyński, das einen russ.-poln. Index enthielt. Diese Art von Wörterbüchern mit dieser Form der Sprachenanordnung war offensichtlich für die Verwaltung notwendig, denn 1834 erschien ein ähnliches Wörterbuch von J. A. E. Schmidt in Breslau, und der *Słownik polsko-rosyjski administracyjny i sądowy* von P. P. Dubrovskij, Warschau 1847 (258 S.), erlebte 1867 eine zweite Auflage. Wichtiger jedoch für die zweisprachige russische Lexikographie mit Polnisch sind das russ.-poln. Wörterbuch von Antoni Jakubowicz, das dieser nach den beiden Ausgaben des russ. Akademiewörterbuches erstellte und um technische Ausdrücke ergänzte (2 Bände, Warschau 1825—28, 688 und 603 S., ca. 25 000 Lemmata), das poln.-russ. Wörterbuch von Stanisław Müller (er hatte zunächst ein poln.-französ. Wörterbuch 1826, 2. Aufl. 1847, erstellt), das 1829—30 in Wilna erschien (3 Bde., XVI + 623, 514, 502 S.), auf dem polnischen Wörterbuch von S. B. Linde und dem russ. Akademiewörterbuch aufbaute, 32 000 Wörter umfaßte und 1841 und 1854 jeweils neu aufgelegt wurde, und das in 3 Bänden in Warschau 1836—38 (489, 450, 372 S.) von F. Łubkowski herausgegebene „Neue polnisch-russische und russisch-polnische Wörterbuch". Von I. A. E. Schmidt erschien 1834 in Breslau ein polnisch-russisch-deutsches und 1836 ein russisch-polnisch-deutsches Wörterbuch. Das polnisch-russische und russisch-polnische Taschenwörterbuch von Schmidt (Leipzig 1845, XVI + 772 S., 30 000 Wörter) erlebte bis 1922 7 weitere Auflagen. In Wilna erschien 1838—40 anonym ein polnisch-russisch-französisches Wörterbuch in drei Bänden (IV + 540, 396, 394 S.), das nach dem Wörterbuch Lindes und den jeweiligen Akademiewörterbüchern erstellt war. Ein weiteres russisch-polnisches Wörterbuch, unter den Initialen A. R. (= Adam Rogalski) 1841 in Warschau erschienen, enthielt 80 000 Wörter (3 Bde., 556, 638, 938 S.). Andere Wörterbücher, wie das bis weit in das 20. Jh. genutzte zweibändige polnisch-russisch, russisch-polnische von D. Bartoszewicz (Warschau 1841—43, 539, 538 S., 50 000 Lemmata), fußen teilweise auf anderen Vorlagen, wie in diesem Fall dem polnisch-deutschen, deutsch-polnischen Wörterbuch von J. K. Troiański (4 Bde., Poznań 1835—1838). Die vielen Wörterbücher mit Polnisch, die dann vor allem in der zweiten Hälfte des 19. Jhs. folgen, können hier nicht alle genannt werden. Von S. B. Linde stammt der Plan eines auf seinem Wörterbuch fußenden vergleichenden russischen (eigentlich „slavischen") Wörterbuches, von dem aber nur ein Heft mit dem Buchstaben K 1845 in Warschau erschien.

Aus der Fülle der zwei- und mehrsprachigen Wörterbücher des 19. Jhs. sollen nur einige exemplarisch genannt werden, da sie mit ihren Verfassern für bestimmte Konzeptionen stehen. Das gilt zunächst für die Wörterbücher des Schweizers Carl Philipp Reiff, der als Hauslehrer nach Rußland gegangen war. Er vereinigte die später getrennten Funktionen von etymologischem und Übersetzungswörterbuch in seinem russisch-französischen Wörterbuch (2 Bände, Petersburg 1835—36, IV, 279, 8 S.), denn dieses gründete auf dem ersten Akademiewörterbuch und die russischen Wörter waren nach ihrer Herkunft angeordnet. Das Wörterbuch enthielt aber einen Index. Er bekam für dieses Wörterbuch einen Preis und widmete sich nun ganz der Wörterbucharbeit, von der er lebte. Ende der dreißiger Jahre ging er nach Karlsruhe, eröffnete eine Druckerei und plante eine Reihe von Wörterbüchern, mit denen er der russischen Jugend mehrere Fremdsprachen beibringen wollte. Zunächst waren das Taschenwörterbücher, die parallel das Russische, Französische, Englische und Deutsche berücksichtigten und jeweils in der Ausgangssprache wechselten. Sie erschienen ab 1843 und ab 1849 schon nicht mehr als Taschenwörterbücher, sondern wesentlich erweitert unter dem Titel *Parallel'nye slovari*.... Die verschiedenen Auflagen und Neudrucke (über 20) wurden in alle Welt verkauft, und in Rußland war es das populärste Wörterbuch des 19. Jhs. (Jakimovič 1985, 92). Allerdings war wegen der parallelen Anordnung von vier Sprachen der Platz begrenzt, und Redewendungen und Phraseologismen blieben weitgehend unberücksichtigt, ebenso wie der Bedeutungsumfang der Äquivalente oft nicht genau abgegrenzt werden konnte. Gegen diese Konzeption und für ausschließlich zweisprachige Wörterbücher trat N. P. Makarov ein, der mit seinen russisch-französischen und französisch-russischen Wörterbüchern zunächst Schwierigkeiten hatte, obwohl diese später bis weit ins 20. Jh. hinein viele Auflagen erlebten. Von ihm stammen nicht nur die französisch-russischen und russisch-französischen *Meždunarodnye slovari dlja srednich učebnych zavedenij* (Erstauflage Petersburg 1870, XII + 744 S., und 1873, XI + 746 S.) und der *Polnyj russko-francuzskij* bzw. *Polnyj francuzsko-russkij slovar'* (Erstauflage Petersburg 1867, XVIII, 394, 477 S., bzw. 1870, XIX, 512, 550 S.), sondern er gab zusammen mit V. V. Šeerer und A. N. Engel'gardt auch entsprechende deutsch-russische und russisch-deutsche Wörterbücher heraus, die von 1876 und 1877 bis 1917 in vielen Auflagen erschienen. Er legte Wert auf die Erfassung möglichst vieler Bedeutungen und Bedeutungsnuancen des Stichwortes und achtete darauf, daß die Phraseologie möglichst umfassend Berücksichtigung fand. Darin stand ihm ein anderer bedeutender Lexikograph des 19. Jhs., der eines der besten zweisprachigen Wörterbücher schuf, sehr nahe. Es ist dies I. Ja. Pavlovskij mit seinem *Vollständige(n) deutsch-russische(n) Wörterbuch* (2 Bände, Riga 1856, XX, 704, 564 S.) und *Russko-nemeckij slovar'* (2 Bände, Riga 1859—67, XII, 376, 470 S.). Beide Wörterbücher wurden mehrfach aufgelegt (4. Auflage 1911, bzw. 3. Auflage Leipzig 1900—1902) und zeichnen sich durch eine Konzeption aus, die uns erst im 20. Jh. wieder begegnet (Jakimovič 1985, 101 ff). Pavlovskij berücksichtigte in hohem Maße die Umgangssprache, die Terminologie vieler Bereiche, jeweils neueste Entwicklungen in der Lexik, faßte die Lexik als System auf und brachte auch die einzelnen Bedeutungen eines Wortes in systematischer, hierarchischer Anordnung. Außerdem gab er Beispiele mit kontextuell gebundenen Verwendungen der Wörter, führte Phraseologismen und Sprichwörter an, erklärte in der Zielsprache nicht vorhandene Realien, nahm auch in der Literatur gebräuchliche Dialektwörter auf und nannte auch Synonyme. Noch heute wird daher sein russisch-deutsches Wörterbuch von deutschen Übersetzern genutzt.

Viele und immer wieder verbesserte Auflagen haben auch das *Polnyj anglo-russkij* und das *Polnyj russko-anglijskij slovar'* erlebt, die zunächst in Petersburg (1878—79, IX, 608, 717, 15 S., bzw. 1879, X, 608, 718, 16 S.) erschienen und bis zur Revolution in Rußland (eine Ausgabe erschien bereits 1909 in New York) und in den 20er Jahren in New York herausgegeben wurden. Der Verfasser, der diesem Wörterbuch seinen Namen gab,

A. Aleksandrov, ist ein Pseudonym für ein Arbeitskollektiv. Mehrfach in Leipzig aufgelegt wurden auch die in den 30er und 40er Jahren entstandenen deutsch-russischen und russisch-deutschen Wörterbücher von J. A. E. Schmidt, die in den späteren Auflagen die Phraseologie stärker berücksichtigten und jeweils einen kurzen grammatischen Abriß der beiden Sprachen, Verzeichnisse der weiblichen und männlichen Vornamen, der geschichtlichen und der mythologischen Namen und ein geographisches Wörterbuch enthielten.

In der zweiten Hälfte des 19. Jhs., mit dem Eingreifen Rußlands in die Befreiungskämpfe auf dem Balkan und den Kriegen gegen die Türken, erschienen neben einem kurzen praktischen russisch-türkischen Wörterbuch für die russischen Soldaten auch verstärkt russisch-südslavische Wörterbücher. 1854 gibt Sava Filaretov in Petersburg sein „Taschenbuch für die russischen Soldaten, die sich auf Feldzügen gegen die Türken in den bulgarischen Ländern aufhalten", heraus, das das erste gedruckte russisch-bulgarische Wörterbuch enthält. Najden Gerov beginnt 1856 mit dem Druck eines russisch-bulgarischen Wörterbuches in Moskau. Die Anfänge der bulgarischen Lexikographie mit Russisch schildert Kjuvlieva-Mišajkova (1988). 1870 kam in Petersburg das erste serbisch-russische Wörterbuch (V, 806 Sp.) von P. A. Lavrovskij heraus, das nach dem Wörterbuch von Vuk Karadžić (Wien 1852) gearbeitet war. Lavrovskij drehte sein Wörterbuch um, und so folgte 1880 sein *Russko-serbskij slovar'* (II, 578 Sp.). Die zweisprachige Lexikographie russisch-serbokroatisch, serbokroatisch-russisch bis Ende der 60er Jahre des 20. Jhs. schildert Barsukova (1972). 1870—74 kam in Prag ein russisch-tschechisches Wörterbuch von J. V. Rank heraus (907 S.).

Im 19. und auch zu Beginn des 20. Jhs. wurden auch die zweisprachigen Wörterbücher der klassischen Sprachen in Rußland immer wieder aufgelegt. Neben den zahlreichen lateinisch-russischen Wörterbüchern, zu denen viele lateinisch-russische Spezialwörterbücher hinzukamen, verdient das griechisch-russische Wörterbuch von Kossovič (1848 Moskva, 1093, 904 S., und 1858) Erwähnung wegen seines großen Umfangs und auch das von A. D. Vejsman, das von 1879 (Sankt Peterburg, VIII S. + 1368 Sp.) bis 1899 fünf Auflagen erlebte und zu den Standardwerken gehörte. Es gab im 19. Jhundert weitere zweisprachige Wörterbücher westlicher Sprachen (Italienisch, Schwedisch u. a.), besonders groß aber wurde die Zahl der zwei- und mehrsprachigen Spezialwörterbücher mit Deutsch, Französisch und Englisch, an deren Anfang ja bereits 1795 das englisch-französisch-russische *Trejazyčnyj morskoj slovar'* (Sankt Peterburg, 6, VIII, 84, 41 S.) von A. S. Šiškov stand. Mehr und mehr bemühte man sich in Rußland selbst auch um Wörterbücher der Völker des eigenen Reiches und solche der unmittelbaren und mittelbaren Nachbarn mit Russisch. In Kazan' erschienen viele Wörterbücher der uralo-altaischen und anderer Sprachen des Nahen und Fernen Ostens mit Russisch. In China selbst wurde 1867 ein russisch-chinesisches Wörterbuch herausgegeben (Peking, 536 S.). Diesem folgten ein russisch-chinesisches 1879 (Sankt Peterburg, V, 743 S.) und ein chinesisch-russisches 1887 (Sankt Peterburg, XVI, 226 S.) in Rußland. Ein ainu-russisches Wörterbuch mit 76, 487, 92 S. und 11 000 Wörtern war bereits 1875 in Kazan' erschienen. Im folgenden werden nur kurz einige Wörterbücher mit Erscheinungsjahr genannt, um einen schwachen Eindruck von der reichhaltigen Wörterbuchproduktion in diesem Bereich zu vermitteln: russisch-japanisch (1857 und 1860); russisch-kalmückisch (1857, 1860 und 1899); russisch-kirgisisch, kirgisisch-russisch (1883); russisch-kirgisisch (1895, 1899); russisch-koreanisch (1874); russisch-lettisch (1877), lettisch-russisch, russisch-lettisch (1877); mandschurisch-russisch (1866 und 1875); mongolisch-russisch (1893—1896); tibetisch-russisch (1843); tungusisch-russisch (1859). Oft hatten diese Wörterbücher nur geringen Umfang, doch sind sie ein Indiz für das stärker werdende Interesse an den bislang „vernachlässigten" Sprachen in Rußland. Hierher gehört auch das Erscheinen von Wörterbüchern der Minderheiten im russischen Sprachgebiet selbst. So erschienen 1877 und 1900 z. B. Wörterbücher der Zigeunersprache mit Russisch (romani-russisch) und 1876 und 1869 ein russisch-jiddisches und ein jiddisch-russisches Wörterbuch, deren letzteres mehrere Auflagen (4. Auflage Žitomir 1886) erlebte.

7. Das 20. Jahrhundert. Neue Sprachen und neue Konzeptionen

Die großen Tendenzen, die im 20. Jahrhundert bestimmend werden für die Entwicklung der zweisprachigen Lexikographie mit Russisch innerhalb und außerhalb der Sowjetunion, lassen sich einteilen in vornehmlich gesellschaftspolitische und durch die Entwicklung der lexikographischen Theorie selbst bestimmte. Zu den gesellschaftspolitischen gehören die Notwendigkeit der Alphabetisierung und Akkulturation der oft schriftlosen Völker der Sowjetunion, die meistens über die Vermittlung des Russischen stattfand, die Notwendigkeit der verstärkten Kommunikation mit den Völkern der sog. Volksdemokratien nach dem Zweiten Weltkrieg und ab den 50er Jahren mit den Völkern in den Ländern der dritten Welt. Wörterbücher werden auch gebraucht im Gefolge der verstärkten ideologischen Auseinandersetzung in Ost und West. Mit dem sog. technischen Fortschritt, der Spezialisierung in allen Wissens- und Tätigkeitsbereichen und der Ausweitung der internationalen Beziehungen steigt auch der Bedarf an zweisprachigen Spezialwörterbüchern. Als Folge sprachpolitischer Tendenzen ist seit den dreißiger Jahren der Trend zum Zentralismus, zur Vereinheitlichung zu sehen, der im Bereich der Lexikographie zu Normativität und Präskription führt. Davon macht sich die sowjetische Lexikographie erst heute zögernd frei, und fast alle ein- und mehrsprachigen Wörterbücher sozialer Slangs sind seit jener Zeit im Ausland erschienen, was nicht ohne negativen Einfluß auf ihre Aktualität bleiben konnte. Gesellschaftspolitische Gründe haben auch die Entwicklung der Theorie im Bereich der pädagogischen oder didaktischen Lexikographie (učebnaja leksikografija) beschleunigt und zu einer beachtlichen Zahl zwei- und mehrsprachiger Lehr- und Lernwörterbücher des Russischen geführt. Einige Überlegungen der theoretischen Lexikographie selbst haben die Herausgabe bestimmter zweisprachiger Wörterbücher, ja bestimmter Typen von Wörterbüchern geprägt. Schließlich hat die lexikographische Theorie und Praxis in der Sowjetunion und einigen anderen Ländern zur Herausbildung der neuen Teildisziplin der Phraseographie geführt. Im folgenden können diese Punkte wiederum nur exemplarisch behandelt werden, ohne daß auch nur in Ansätzen der Fülle der Sprachen, die Gegenstand von zweisprachigen russischen Wörterbüchern sind, und der Fülle der Arten dieser Wörterbücher Rechnung getragen werden kann.

Der Trend zum Deskriptivismus, zur Aufnahme lexikalischer Einheiten aus allen Strata, besonders auch dem sozialen, der in der einsprachigen Lexikographie in Rußland zu Beginn des 20. Jhs. feststellbar ist (Baudouin de Courtenay bearbeitet in diesem Sinne das Wörterbuch von Dal', Šachmatov und seine Nachfolger versuchen, aus dem streng normativ angelegten Akademiewörterbuch von Grot in der Fortsetzung einen echten Thesaurus zu machen), läßt sich in der zweisprachigen Lexikographie nicht feststellen. Hier erscheinen die großen Wörterbücher des 19. Jhs. in neuen Auflagen: 1900 z. B. die 9. und 1916 die 13. Auflage von N. P. Makarovs „Vollständige(m) russisch-französische(m) Wörterbuch", das auch nach der Revolution 1918, allerdings grundlegend überarbeitet, in der 14. Auflage herauskommt.

Die Bemühungen um den Abschluß des von Grot begonnenen und Šachmatov fortgesetzten einsprachigen Akademiewörterbuches blieben trotz mehrerer neuer Redaktionen erfolglos und wurden 1936 abgebrochen. Statt dessen wurden drei Typen von normativen Wörterbüchern entwickelt (Ožegov 1952), die auf die Lexikographie der anderen Völker der Sowjetunion und auf die zweisprachige Lexikographie mit Russisch später großen Einfluß gewinnen sollten. Sie unterscheiden sich hauptsächlich dem Umfang nach: D. N. Ušakovs vierbändiges Wörterbuch von 1935—40, ca. 85 000 Wörter; später (1957—61, 2. Aufl. 1981—84) tritt an dessen Stelle das sog. „Kleine Akademiewörterbuch"; S. I. Ožegovs einbändiges erklärendes Wörterbuch (1949, ca. 53 000 Wörter; erst die 21. Auflage 1989, 924 S., wurde wesentlich überarbeitet und erweitert und enthält 70 000 Wörter) und das „Große Akademiewörterbuch" in 17 Bänden (1950—1965, ca. 120 000 Wörter). Besonders das nun sog. „mittlere" vierbändige und das „kleine" oder einbändige Wörterbuch wurden zur Leitschnur für viele russisch-nationalsprachliche Wörterbücher der Völker der Sowjetunion. Ožegovs einbändiges Wörterbuch wurde sogar 1953 in Peking nachgedruckt und diente dort neben dem Wörterbuch von Ušakov als Grundlage des 1956—58 herausgegebenen russisch-chinesischen Wörterbuches. Vor Schaffung dieser Wörterbücher stützte sich die zweisprachige Lexikographie mit Russisch oft auf das Wörterbuch von Dal' und andere Quellen, was der Tendenz zur Normativität nicht immer entgegenkam. Die zweisprachige Lexikographie mit Russisch nimmt in der UdSSR einen ungeahnten Aufschwung durch die Kodifizierung von Schriftsprachen der Völker, die bislang ohne eigene Schriftsprachen waren. Die Entwicklung war durch drei Phasen gekennzeichnet. Bei den islamischen Völkern in Zentralasien, im Kaukasus und an der Wolga hatte oft das Arabische die Funktion der Schriftsprache gehabt, so daß man zur Schaffung der eigenen Alphabete gleich nach der Revolution die modifizierten arabischen Schriftzeichen nutzte. In den 20er Jahren, beginnend mit dem Aserbeidschanischen 1922, ging man dann zum lateinischen Alphabet über, das bis zum Anfang der 30er Jahre alle zentralasiatischen Völker nutzten und das ab 1930 auch für die Völker des Nordens eingesetzt wurde, wobei man mit den Ewenken (Tungusen) begann. Das Kabardinisch-Tscherkessische, das 1923 ein Alphabet auf lateinischer Grundlage erhalten hatte, stellte bereits 1936 sein graphisches System auf eine kyrillische Basis. Dem folgten die anderen Völker mit neu geschaffenen lateinischen Alphabeten größtenteils in den Jahren 1937—40. Bei den zweisprachigen Wörterbüchern mit Russisch haben wir es also innerhalb eines relativ kurzen Zeitraums für gleiche Sprachen mit manchmal drei sehr unterschiedlichen graphematischen Systemen zu tun. In manchen Fällen wird zunächst auch das Russische mit arabischen Schriftzeichen transkribiert.

Als kurzes Beispiel für diese Entwicklung seien hier nur das Tatarische und das Krimtatarische genannt, die ja eine auf der arabischen Graphik beruhende schriftsprachliche Tradition hatten. So erschien das *Tatarsko-russkij slovar'* von M. Kurbangaliev et al. 1927 in Kazan' in arabischer Schrift und in der zweiten ergänzten Auflage mit orthographischen Regeln und kurzer Grammatik versehen 1931 in lateinischer Schrift. Ähnliches gilt auch für die russ.-tatar. Wörterbücher aus dieser Zeit. Und so ist es auch im Krimtatarischen. Das in Simferopol' 1924 im Rahmen eines Lehrbuches von A. Odabaš und I. S. Kaja herausgekommene tatarisch-russische Wörterbuch verwendet für den tatarischen Teil ebenfalls die arabische Schrift. Doch bereits 1928 gibt I. S. Kaja ein „Lehrbuch für die krimtatarische Sprache nach dem neuen Alphabet" heraus, in dem ein tatarisch-russisches und ein russisch-tatarisches Wörterbuch enthalten sind, in dem das Tatarische auf lateinischer Grundlage geschrieben wird. Seit 1939 wird für das Tatarische dann auch in den zweisprachigen Wörterbüchern eine Schrift auf kyrillischer Basis verwendet.

Es kommt zu einigen Besonderheiten, die nicht ohne Auswirkung auf die Lexikographie bleiben. Das Ossetische, das Udmurtische, das Kalmückische und einige andere Sprachen, die bereits vor der Revolution Alphabete auf kyrillischer Grundlage besaßen, müssen diese nun gegen eine lateinische auswechseln, um dann wieder zu ihr zurückzukommen. Andere Völker lehnen sich an die Schriftsysteme der Nachbarn an. Die Kurden, die in der Sowjetunion hauptsächlich in Armenien wohnen, verwendeten seit 1921 ein Alphabet auf armenischer Basis, dann seit 1929 auf lateinischer und ab 1945 auf kyrillischer. Die Abchasen, für die P. K. Uslar bereits 1862 ausgehend vom kyrillischen Alphabet ein Schriftsystem geschaffen hatte, kamen von der neuen lateinischen Grundlage (1928—1938) zu einer georgischen bis 1954, ehe auch sie zum Kyrillischen übergingen. Die Schriftsprachlichkeit einiger ganz kleiner Völker verschwand mit der Umstellung auf das Kyrillische ganz. Sie brauchten auch keine zweisprachigen Wörterbücher mit Russisch mehr, da sie ohnehin als zweisprachig geführt wurden und andere Sprachen für sie die schriftsprachlichen Funktionen übernahmen (Glück 1984, 550).

In die Zeit dieser „Umstellungen" fällt die Herausgabe und theoretische Begründung eines wichtigen zweisprachigen Wörterbuches, die für die gesamte zweisprachige Lexikographie in der Sowjetunion und nach dem 2. Weltkrieg auch in den Ländern der sog. Volksdemokratien bis heute große Bedeutung besitzt. Es ist die von L. V. Ščerba 1936 in seiner Einleitung zum russisch-französischen Wörterbuch, dessen Herausgeber er war, und 1940 in einer weiteren theoretischen Abhandlung begründete Auffassung, daß für jedes Sprachenpaar 4 zweisprachige Wörterbücher notwendig seien, ein jeweils passives zum Verstehen und ein jeweils aktives zum Übersetzen. Ein derart aktives Wörterbuch war das von Ščerba herausgegebene *Russko-francuzskij slovar'* (Moskva 1936, 491 S. und ca. 75 000 Wörter), das mehrere Auflagen erlebte. Es setzte die Kenntnis der „Grundlagen der Grammatik der gegebenen Sprache in ihrem aktiven Aspekt voraus" (Ščerba 1936, 302) und sollte weniger dem Franzosen ein vollständiges Verständnis der russischen Wörter erschließen als vielmehr dem russischen Benutzer die Übersetzung in die Fremdsprache in verschiedenen Kontexten ermöglichen. Diesem Zweck diente auch eine kurze dem Wörterbuch hinzugefügte „aktive" französische Grammatik. Ausgangsbasis für die nun erscheinenden russisch-nationalsprachigen Wörterbücher war aber der passive Wörterbuchtyp, der allerdings auch in Ščerbas Konzeption Elemente einer Didaktik der Ausgangssprache beinhaltete. Einen kritischen Bericht über die erste Serie der russisch-nationalsprachigen Wörterbücher (russisch-aserbeidschanisch 1—4, Baku 1940; -tadschikisch, Moskva-Stalinabad 1949; -kirgisisch, Moskva 1944; -kasachisch 1—2, Alma-Ata 1946; -usbekisch, Taškent 1941; -karakalpakisch, Moskva 1947; -baschkirisch, Moskva 1948; -tschuwaschisch, Moskva 1951) gibt A. K. Borovkov (1957), der z. T. auch das fünfbändige russisch-usbekische Wörterbuch (Taškent 1950—56, XXIV, 520; XI, 480; VIII, 582; VI, 720; VI, 736 S.) mit einbezieht, zu dem in der Beilage eine von ihm verfaßte kurze russische Grammatik in usbekischer Sprache geliefert wurde. Diese Wörterbücher waren in erster Linie als erklärende russische Wörterbücher für die Nationalsprachen gedacht und hatten das pädagogische Ziel, die Erlernung des Russischen zu festigen und zu befördern. Kritik gab es an Ščerbas Auffassung, daß ein allgemeines Wörterbuch spezielle Termini nur allgemein zu erklären brauche, da gerade für die Sprachen, für die das Russische in hohem Maße aufklärerische und bildende Funktion besaß, der Verzicht auf genaue Erklärungen von Termini als ein Mangel empfunden wurde. Trotz der generellen Ausrichtung auf den passiven erklärenden Wörterbuchtyp versuchten einige der Wörterbücher, in bescheidenem Umfange auch Übersetzungswörterbücher zu sein. Borovkov trat mit der Forderung nach zwei Typen von russisch-nationalsprachigen Wörterbüchern, einem großen (60—80 000 Wörter) erklärenden Wörterbuch und einem kleineren (25—30 000 Wörter), das vornehmlich didaktische Ziele haben sollte, auf. Diese Forderung wurde nach und nach realisiert. Es entstanden dann auch die entsprechenden nationalsprachig-russischen Wörterbücher in der Sowjetunion, und in der Nachkriegszeit folgten die größeren zweisprachigen Wörterbücher mit Russisch; außerhalb der Sowjetunion zunächst vornehmlich in den sog. Volksdemokratien. Aus den zahlreichen Beispielen für jeweils in ihrer Art vorbildliche passive Wörterbücher im Umfang von 50—60 000 Wörtern seien hier das russisch-deutsche Wörterbuch von H. H. Bielfeldt (Berlin 1958, letzte 14. Auflage 1982, XXIII, 1119 S.) und das bulgarisch-russische von S. B. Bernštejn (Moskau 1966, 3. Auflage 1986, 768 S.) genannt. Beide dienen dem Benutzer der Zielsprache als erklärendes Wörterbuch der Ausgangssprache und helfen ihm darüber hinaus durch ein System von grammatischen, prosodischen (Betonungsregeln), morphonologischen (Lautregeln) Kennzeichnungen (so Bielfeldt) bzw. durch einen kurzen Abriß der Grammatik der Ausgangssprache (so Bernštejn) ganz im Sinne Ščerbas beim Erlernen dieser Ausgangssprache. Als jüngere Beispiele großer paralleler passiver und aktiver Wörterbücher können das passive *Bol'šoj nemecko-russkij slovar'* unter der Leitung von O. I. Moskal'skaja (1—2, Moskva 1969, 2. Aufl. 1980, 760, 656 S., 165 000 Wörter, Ergänzungsband 1982, 352 S., 16 000 Wörter) und das aktive *Deutsch-Russische Wörterbuch* unter der Redaktion von R. Lötzsch (1—3, Berlin 1983—84, XXXI, 761; 706; 787 S., ca. 100 000 Stichwörter) gelten. In der Einleitung zu letzterem (VI—X) findet sich auch eine theoretische Begründung (vgl. dazu auch Duda 1986). Seit den 50er Jahren wächst die Zahl der innerslavischen zweisprachigen Wörterbücher mit Russisch, und seit Ende der 50er, Anfang der 60er Jahre werden in immer größerem Umfang die Sprachen des indischen Subkontinents, die afrikanischen Sprachen, die indonesischen Sprachen, das Vietnamesische, die Mon-Khmer-Sprachen, das Koreanische (es gibt eine koreanische Minderheit in der UdSSR), das Arabische, in jüngerer Zeit das Puschtu und Dari berücksichtigt. Es gibt bereits zweisprachige Wörterbücher der polynesischen Sprachen mit Russisch. Die Sprachen der Minderheiten mit wenigen Sprechern in der Sowjetunion finden größere Berücksichtigung. Daneben erscheint weiterhin eine Vielzahl von zweisprachigen Wörterbüchern der sog. Standardsprachen nicht nur in der Sowjetunion. Als Beispiele jüngeren Datums sind hier das *Oxford English-Russian* und *Russian-English Dictionary* (beide Oxford 1984) zu nennen, die beide in erster Linie für den Englisch sprechenden Benutzer konzipiert sind. Das 1990 in Amsterdam erschienene *Russian-English Dictionary* von P. Macura (4 Bde.) ist mit 3 264 S. und 240 000 Wörtern das bislang umfangreichste zweisprachige Wörterbuch mit Russisch. Die Zahl der zweisprachigen terminologischen Wörterbücher mit Russisch wächst gerade in diesen Standardsprachen ins Unermeßliche und nimmt auch für die übrigen Sprachen ständig zu. Seit den 60er

Jahren (Lukina 1966) steigt auch die Zahl der Lehr- und Lernwörterbücher unaufhaltsam. Auch hier gibt es neben einsprachigen ein ganzes Spektrum von zweisprachigen mit Russisch, die inzwischen im Rahmen einer eigenen Theorie behandelt werden (Red'kin ed. 1977, Denisov/Morkovkin eds. 1978).

Eine sprachwissenschaftliche Disziplin, die sich vornehmlich in der Sowjetunion, später aber auch in anderen Ländern, zunächst wiederum in den sog. Volksdemokratien, aus dem Bereich der Lexikologie entwickelt hat, ist die Phraseologie. In Analogie zur Lexikographie hat sich hier die Phraseographie herausgebildet, die sich „mit Fragen der Theorie phraseologischer Wörterbücher unterschiedlichen Typs und der Praxis ihres Aufbaus" (Umarchodžaev 1983, 3) beschäftigt. Inzwischen gibt es eine große Anzahl von zweisprachigen phraseologischen Wörterbüchern mit Russisch. Einige der wichtigeren großen (über 5000 Lemmata) seien hier genannt: französisch-russisch von Ja. I. Recker (Moskva 1963, 35 000 Einheiten); englisch-russisch von A. V. Kunin (2. Aufl. Moskva 1967, 25 000 Einheiten, 4. erg. Aufl. 1984); russisch-mongolisch von Č. Luvsanžav (Ulan-Bator 1970, 9580 Einheiten); ukrainisch-russisch und russisch-ukrainisch von I. S. Olejnik und M. M. Sidorenko (Kyjiv 1971, 7000 bzw. 5000 Einheiten); russisch-englisch von P. Borkowski (London 1973, 8600 Einheiten); russisch-aserbeidschanisch von M. T. Tagiev (Baku 1974, über 10 000 Einheiten); deutsch-russisch von L. È. Binovič und N. N. Grišin (2. Aufl. Moskva 1974, 14 000 Einheiten); bulgarisch-russisch von A. Košelev und M. Leonidova (Sofija-Moskva 1974, 9500 Einheiten); russisch-kroatisch oder serbisch von A. Menac (2 Bände, Zagreb 1979—80, 35 000 Einheiten); russisch-bulgarisch von S. Vlachov (Moskva-Sofija 1980, 5695 Einheiten). Der Umfang hängt in gewissem Maße von der Definition der phraseologischen Einheit und der Art ihrer Aufnahme ab. Da die phraseologische Einheit immer aus mehreren Wörtern besteht, sind das System der Anordnung und Verweise für die Benutzbarkeit von großer Bedeutung. Hier hat es sich eingebürgert, eine Kombination aus dem jeweiligen Buchstaben des Alphabets und einer Nummer vor die Lemmata mit Erklärungen zu stellen und alle anderen notwendigen Mehrfacheinträge darauf zu verweisen (so verfahren z. B. Binovič/Grišin und Košelev/Leonidova). Schwerer gestaltet sich die Suche im Wörterbuch von Menac, in dem die Leitwörter der Einheiten nach morphologischen Kriterien alphabetisch angeordnet sind und ein System von Verweisen zu diesen Leitwörtern führt, unter denen manchmal lange Serien von Phraseologismen stehen. Vlachov hat das System der Buchstabennummernkombination mit einem alle in den Phraseologismen vorkommenden Wörter enthaltenden alphabetischen Verzeichnis verbunden und so die Suche am leichtesten gestaltet. Obwohl es in der lexikographischen Praxis nur wenige allgemeine ideographische oder thematische Wörterbücher mit Russisch gibt (*Duden Bildwörterbuch Deutsch und Russisch.* Leipzig 1953; *K. Babov/A. Vărgulev/E. Rot: Tematičen rusko bălgarski rečnik.* Sofija 1961), berichtet Vlachov 1987 von der Erstellung eines ideographischen russisch-bulgarischen phraseologischen Wörterbuches.

Zum Schluß seien zwei Versuche der schöpferischen Überwindung des Schemas von Ščerba genannt, das die lexikographische Praxis innerhalb und außerhalb der Sowjetunion lange Zeit bestimmt hat. Es geht zunächst um V. P. Berkovs *Russko-norvežskij slovar'* (Moskva 1987, 936 S., 51 000 Wörter). Berkov, ein bekannter Theoretiker der zweisprachigen Lexikographie (vgl. Berkov 1973 und 1977), mußte aus ökonomischen Gründen zwei der von Ščerba geforderten Wörterbücher in einem vereinigen und hat diese Aufgabe hervorragend gelöst. Sein Wörterbuch ist für Russen und Norweger gleichermaßen verwendbar. Es enthält deshalb außer morphologischen Tabellen des Russischen auch einen kurzen Abriß der Phonetik und Grammatik des Norwegischen mit entsprechenden Angaben im Wörterbuch. Kollokationen sind für beide Sprachen nach einem ökonomischen System angegeben. Die Aufnahme der Termini berücksichtigt nationale Gegebenheiten und Erfordernisse. Geographische, mythologische und Personennamen werden ebenso wie gebräuchliche Pragmatonyme und Abkürzungen in die alphabetische Anordnung aufgenommen. Gleiches gilt für Phraseologismen, Redensarten, Sprichwörter und geflügelte Worte. Dafür waltet Ökonomie durch Weglassen von überflüssigen Kennzeichnungen wie z. B. „bot." bei offensichtlichen Pflanzennamen, und auch gruppenweise usuelle Gebundenheit von Wörtern wird durch ein Verweissystem ökonomisch gestaltet. Im Anhang findet sich ein russisch-norwegisches Verzeichnis der gebräuchlichsten russischen Familiennamen und der Werke der Weltliteratur unter Berücksichtigung der Lektürelisten sowjetischer Bildungsinstitutionen.

Eine andere äußere Notwendigkeit in der Sowjetunion selbst fordert eine weitere Überwindung des Schemas von Ščerba. Im Zuge zunehmender Zweisprachigkeit von Russen und vor allem Nichtrussen in der Sowjetunion werden die russisch-nationalen und die national-russischen Wörterbücher der 60er und 70er Jahre als unzureichend empfunden. Sie liefern keine realen Parallelen der Wörter der jeweiligen Sprachen, beschränken sich allenfalls auf den semantischen Kern, die „Grundbedeutung" der Wörter und können nicht ihre reale Bedeutung in der Rede wiedergeben, referiert Ščerbin 1988 die Klagen sowjetischer Sprachwissenschaftler. Er möchte nationalsprachig-russische und russisch-nationalsprachige Thesauri schaffen, die den aktiven Gebrauch der jeweiligen Sprachen besser ermöglichen sollen. Dieser Versuch, der zunächst im Bereich des Weißrussisch-Russischen unternommen wird, beruht auf der Annahme von Korrelationen der Beziehungen der Lexik im Text mit den Beziehungen der Lexik im System. Durch die Erfassung und systematische Klassifizierung der Lexik beider Sprachen in einem gemeinsamen ideographischen Schema und die dann folgende paarweise Abbildung der lexikalischen Einheiten in diesem Schema, auf das dann wiederum alphabetische Listen mit Indexierungen, d. h. Zuordnungen zu bestimmten Feldern und Unterfeldern folgen, hofft man, die reale Rolle der in beiden Sprachen korrelierenden Wörter in der Rede zu ermitteln. Diese Arbeit wird mit Hilfe der EDV beschleunigt. Was ein derartiger zweisprachiger Thesaurus für die Praxis bringt und wie es mit seiner Verwendbarkeit aussieht, bleibt abzuwarten.

8. Literatur (in Auswahl)

8.1. Wörterbücher

Adelung 1798 = Johann Christoph Adelung: Vollständiges deutsch-russisches Lexicon. Sankt Petersburg 1798. Teil 1 A—L [2 + X + 1048 S.], Teil 2 M—Z [4 + 1060 + 4 S.].

Alekseev 1773 = Petr Alekseevič Alekseev: Cerkovnyj slovar', ili Istolkovanie rečenij slavenskich drevnich... Moskva 1773 [26 + 396 + 2 S.].

Atrachovič ed. 1988—1989 = Kandrat Kandratovič Atrachovič (= Kandrat Krapiva) (ed.): Belaruska-ruski sloŭnik. 2. überarbeitete und erg. Aufl. 2 Bde. Minsk 1988—1989 [813, 748 S.].

Azbukovniki = Alfavity inostrannych rečej veröffentlicht u. a. in: I. Sacharov: Skazanija russkogo naroda, T. II, kn. 5 Sankt Peterburg 1849, 132—191 und in: Alekseev 1968, 107—151.

Birgegård ed. 1987—1989 = Ulla Birgegård (ed.): Johan Gabriel Sparwenfeld: Lexicon Slavonicum I, II und III. Uppsala 1987, 1988 und 1989.

Birkfellner ed. 1984 = Teutscher, Und Reussischer Dictionarium (Dictionarium Vindobonense). Das Wiener deutsch-russische Wörterbuch (Cod. Conv.FF.Minorum Vindobonensis XVI). Herausgegeben und eingeleitet von Gerhard Birkfellner. Berlin 1984.

Gavrilov 1781 = Matvej G. Gavrilov: Novyj leksikon, na nemeckom, francuzskom, latinskom, italianskom i rossijskom jazykach. Moskva 1781 [XV + 766 S.].

Grek = Maksim Grek: Tolkovanie imenam- po alfavitu 16—17. Jh. In: Kovtun 1975, 313—349.

Heym 1795—1798 = Johann (Ivan Andreevič) Heym: Deutsch-russisches und russisch-deutsches Wörterbuch. Riga 1795—1798 [Teil 1, 1570 Sp.; Teil 2, 2308 Sp.].

Heym 1799—1802 = Ivan Andreevič Gejm: Novyj rossijsko-francuzsko-nemeckij slovar', sočinennyj po Slovarju Rossijskoj akademii... 3 Bde. Moskva 1799—1802 [A—K, 12 + 502 S.; K—P., 2 + 652 S.; P—V., 2 + 398 S.].

Hölterhof 1778 = Franz Hölterhof (Goeltergof Franciscus): Russisches alphabetisches Wörterbuch mit deutscher und lateinischer Übersetzung. 2 Bde. Moskva 1778 [8 + 944 S.].

Janovskij 1803—1806: = Nikolaj Maksimovič Janovskij: Novyj slovotolkovatel', raspoložennyj po alfavitu... 3 Bde. Sankt Peterburg 1803—1806 [1577 S.].

Keipert ed. 1988 = F. Polikarpov: Leksikon trejazyčnyj. Dictionarium trilingue. Moskva 1704. Nachdruck und Einleitung von H. Keipert. München 1988 (= Specimina Philologiae Slavicae 79) [XXX + 806 S.].

Kopievskij 1700 = I. F. Kopievskij: Nomenklator na ruskom, latinskom i nemeckom jazyke. Amsterdam 1700 [127 S.].

Larin 1948 = Boris Aleksandrovič Larin: Parižskij slovar' moskovitov 1586 g. Riga 1948.

Larin 1959 = Boris Aleksandrovič Larin: Russko-Anglijskij slovar'-dnevnik Ričarda Džemsa (1618—1619 gg.). Leningrad 1959.

Mefodij 1783 = Mefodij (Smirnov): Leksikon prostago grečeskago jazyka. Moskva 1783 [120 + 6 S.].

Nimčuk 1961 = V. V. Nimčuk: Leksikon slovenoros'kyj Pamvy Beryndy. Kyjiv 1961.

Nimčuk ed. 1964 = V. V. Nimčuk (ed.): Leksys Lavrentija Zizanija. Synonima slavenorosskaja. Kyjiv 1964.

Nimčuk ed. 1973 = V. V. Nimčuk (ed.): Leksykon latyns'kyj Je. Slavynec'koho. Leksykon sloveno-latyns'kyj Je. Slavynec'koho ta A. Korec'koho-Satanovs'koho. Kyjiv 1973.

Pallas 1787—1789 = Sravnitel'nye slovari vsech jazykov i narečej, sobrannye desniceju vsevysočajšej osoby. Sankt Peterburg 1787—1789. Otdelenie 1, Čast' 1, 1787 [18 + 411 S.], Čast' 2 1789 [8 + 487 S.]. Überarbeitet von F. I. Jankovič de Mirievo. Sankt Peterburg 1790—1791. Čast' 1—4 [2 + 454; 2 + 499; 2 + 518 und 2 + 618 S.].

Petrova ed. 1962 = „Leksikon" russko-japonskij Andreja Tatarinova. Izd. teksta i predislovie O. P. Petrovoj. Moskva 1962.

Polikarpov 1701 = Fedor P. Polikarpov(-Orlov): Bukvar' slavenskimi, grečeskimi, rimskimi pismeny. Moskva 1701; enthält Kratkoe sobranie imen, po glaviznam raspoložennoe tremi dialektami.

Polikarpov 1704 = Keipert ed. 1988.

Reč' tonkoslovija grečeskogo = in: Vasmer ed. 1922.

Reč' židovskago jazyka preložena na russkuju 1280/1282 = in: Kovtun 1963, 399—420.

Rodde 1784 = Jacobus Rodde: Deutsch-russisches und russisch-deutsches Wörterbuch. Riga 1784 [758 S.].

Scholz ed. 1982—83 = Bernd Scholz (ed.): Weismanns Petersburger Lexikon von 1731, I—III. München 1982—1983.

Šimkevič 1842 = Fedor Spiridonovič Šimkevič: Korneslov russkogo jazyka, sravnitel'no so vsemi glavnejšimi slavjanskimi narečijami ... 2 Bde. Sankt Peterburg 1842 [160 S., 168 S.].

Tolkovanie neudob' poznavaemom- rečem' 14. Jh. = in: Kovtun 1963, 421—431.

Vojcechovyč 1823 = Ivan Vojcechovyč: Sobranie slov malorossijskago narečija. In: Trudy Obščestva ljubitelej rossijskoj slovesnosti. Moskva. 3. 1823, 264—326.

Volčkov 1755—1764 = Sergej Volčkov: Novoj leksikon na francusskom, nemeckom, latinskom i na rossijskom jazykach. 2 Bde. Sankt Peterburg 1755—1764 [2 + 1066 S.; 2 + 1282 S.].

Vostokov 1858—1861 = Aleksandr Christoforovič Vostokov: Slovar' cerkovnoslavjanskogo jazyka. 2 Bde. Sankt Peterburg 1858—1861 [255 S., 295 S.].

Ždanov 1784 = Prochor I. Ždanov: A new dictionary English and Russian. Sankt Peterburg 1784 [6 + 776 S.].

8.2. Sonstige Literatur

Aav 1977 = Yrjö Aav: Russian Dictionaries. Dictionaries and Glossaries Printed in Russia 1627—1917. Zug 1977.

Alekseev 1968 = Michail Pavlovič Alekseev: Slovari inostrannych jazykov v russkom azbukovnike XVII veka. Leningrad 1968.

Alekseev 1974 = Michail Pavlovič Alekseev: Thomas Schrowe und das „Russischbuch" von 1546. In: Ders.: Zur Geschichte russisch-europäischer Literaturtradition. Berlin 1974 (Neue Beiträge zur Literaturwissenschaft 35), 21—31, 344—348.

Barsukova 1972 = V. V. Barsukova: Obzor dvujazyčnych russko-serbochorvatskich i serbochorvatsko-russkich slovarej. In: R. Bulatova: Issledovanija po serbochorvatskomu jazyku. Moskva 1972, 353—362.

Berezina 1980 = O. E. Berezina: Dva tematičeskich leksikona načala XVIII v. (Sravnitel'naja charakteristika). In: L. L. Kutina/E. È. Biržakova (eds.): Slovari i slovarnoe delo v Rossii XVIII v. Leningrad 1980, 6—22.

Berkov 1973 = Valerij Pavlovič Berkov: Voprosy dvujazyčnoj leksikografii (Slovnik). Leningrad 1973.

Berkov 1977 = Valerij Pavlovič Berkov: Slovo v dvujazyčnom slovare. Tallin 1977.

Birgegård 1985 = Ulla Birgegård: Johan Gabriel Sparwenfeld and the Lexicon Slavonicum. His contribution to the 17th century slavonic lexicography. Uppsala 1985 (Acta Bibliothecae R. Universitatis Upsaliensis vol. XXIII).

Biržakova 1977 = E. È. Biržakova: Leksiko-grafičeskie istočniki i ich ispol'zovanie v Slovare russkogo jazyka XVIII v. In: Problemy istoričeskoj leksikografii. Leningrad 1977, 94—106.

Biržakova 1980 = E. È. Biržakova: Iz istorii russko-inojazyčnoj leksikografii XVIII v. „Russko-gollandskij leksikon" Jakova Brjusa. In: L. L. Kutova/E. È. Biržakova (eds.): Slovari i slovarnoe delo v Rossii XVIII v. Leningrad 1980, 23—37.

Borovkov 1957 = A. K. Borovkov: Iz opyta sostavlenija russko-nacional'nych slovarej. In: Leksikografičeskij sbornik. Vyp. I. Moskva 1957, 135—159.

Brailovskij 1890 = S. I. Brailovskij: Filologičeskie trudy Epifanija Slavineckogo. In: Russkij filologičeskij vestnik 12, 1 (23). 1890, 236—250.

Bulič 1904 = Sergej Konstantinovič Bulič: Očerk istorii jazykoznanija v Rossii. Sankt-Peterburg 1904.

Cejtlin 1958 = Ralja Michajlovna Cejtlin: Kratkij očerk istorii russkoj leksikografii. Moskva 1958.

Denisov/Morkovkin eds. 1978 = P. N. Denisov/ V. V. Morkovkin (eds.): Problemy učebnoj leksikografii i obučenija leksiki. Moskva 1978.

Duda 1986 = Walter Duda: Ein „aktives" russisch-deutsches Wörterbuch für deutschsprachige Benutzer? In: Beiträge zur Lexikographie slawischer Sprachen. Berlin 1986 (Linguistische Studien, A 147), 9—15.

Glück 1984 = Helmut Glück: Sowjetische Sprachenpolitik. In: Handbuch des Russischen. Herausgegeben von Helmut Jachnow. Wiesbaden 1984, 519—549.

Gradova 1987 = B. A. Gradova: A. D. Kantemir — sostavitel' pervogo russko-francuzskogo slovarja. In: Kratkie tezisy dokladov naučnoj konferencii „Rossija-Francija. Vek Prosveščenija" (po materialam vystavki v Pariže i Leningrade). Leningrad 1987, 16—18.

Günther 1963 = Erika Günther: Ein niederländisch-russsisches Gesprächsbuch aus dem 17. Jahrhundert. In: Zeitschrift für Slawistik 8. 1963, 485—496.

Günther 1965 = Erika Günther: Zwei russische Gesprächsbücher aus dem 17. Jahrhundert. Diss. Berlin 1965.

Hammerich/Jakobson eds. 1961 u. 1970 = Tönnies Fenne's Low German Manual of Spoken Russian. Pskov 1607. Edited by L. L. Hammerich/Roman Jakobson et al. Vol. I: Facsimile Copy. Copenhagen 1961. Vol. II: Transliteration and Translation. Copenhagen 1970.

Horeckyj 1963 = P. J. Horeckyj: Istorija ukrajins'koji leksykohrafiji. Kyjiv 1963.

Hüttl-Worth 1956 = Gerta Hüttl-Worth: Die Bereicherung des russischen Wortschatzes im XVIII. Jahrhundert. Wien 1956.

Jagić 1910 = I. V. (Vatroslav) Jagić: Istorija slavjanskoj filologii. Sanktpeterburg 1910.

Jakimovič 1985 = Julija Klavdianovna Jakimovič: Dejateli russkoj kul'tury i slovarnoe delo. Moskva 1985.

Johansen 1955 = P. Johansen: Fragment eines niederdeutsch-russischen Sprachführers (1551). In: Zeitschrift für slavische Philologie 23. 1955, 275—283.

Keipert 1987 = Helmut Keipert: Cellarius in Rußland. In: Russian Linguistics 11. 1987, 297—317.

Kjuvlieva-Mišajkova 1988 = Vesa Kjuvlieva-Mišajkova: Pǎrvite bǎlgarski prevodni rečnici prez vǎzraždaneto. In: Bǎlgarski ezik XXXVIII. 1988, kn. 3, 201—207.

Kochman 1967 = St. Kochman: Polsko-rosyjskie kontakty językowe w zakresie słownictwa w XVII wieku. Wrocław. Warszawa. Kraków 1967.

Kovtun 1963 = Ljudmila Stepanovna Kovtun: Russkaja leksikografija èpochi srednevekov'ja. Moskva. Leningrad 1963.

Kovtun 1975 = Ljudmila Stepanovna Kovtun: Leksikografija v Moskovskoj Rusi XVI-načala XVII v. Leningrad 1975.

Larin 1937 = Boris Aleksandrovič Larin: Russkaja grammatika Ludol'fa. Leningrad 1937.

Lewanski 1973 = Richard C. Lewanski: A Bibliography of Slavic Dictionaries I—IV. Bologna 1973 und 1972.

Lukina 1966 = G. N. Lukina: Novye perevodnye slovari dlja nerusskich. In: Sovremennaja russkaja leksikologija. Moskva 1966, 173—177.

Moskalenko 1961 = A. A. Moskalenko: Narys istoriji ukrajins'koji leksykohrafiji. Kyjiv 1961.

Nimčuk 1980 = V. V. Nimčuk: Staroukrajins'ka leksykohrafija v jiji zvjazkach z rosijs'koju ta bilorus' koju. Kyjiv 1980.

Ožegov 1952 = Sergej Ivanovič Ožegov: O trech tipach tolkovych slovarej sovremennogo russkogo jazyka. In: Voprosy jazykoznanija 1952, 2, 85—104.

Red'kin ed. 1977 = V. A. Red'kin (ed.): Aktual'nye problemy učebnoj leksikografii. Moskva 1977.

Ščerba 1936 = L. V. Ščerba: Predislovie k Russko-francuzskomu slovarju. Moskva 1936. In: Ščerba 1974, 304—312.

Ščerba 1940 = L. V. Ščerba: Opyt obščej teorii leksikografii 1940. In: Ščerba 1974, 265—304.

Ščerba 1974 = Lev Vladimirovič Ščerba: Jazykovaja sistema i rečevaja dejatel'nost'. Leningrad 1974.

Ščerbin 1988 = V. K. Ščerbin: K probleme postroenija russko-nacional'nogo tezaurusa. In: Ju. N. Karaulov (ed.): Slovarnye kategorii. Moskva 1988, 213—216.

Stankiewicz 1984 = Edward Stankiewicz: Grammars and Dictionaries of the Slavic Languages from the Middle Ages up to 1850. An Annotated Bibliography. Berlin 1984.

Svodnyj katalog 1962—1967 = Svodnyj katalog russkoj knigi graždanskoj pečati XVIII veka: 1725—1800. Moskva 1962—1967. T. 1—5. Dopolnenija 1975.

Umarchodžaev 1983 = Muchtar Isanchodžaevič Umarchodžaev: Osnovy frazeografii. Taškent 1983.

Unbegaun ed. 1959 = Henrici Wilhelmi Ludolfi Grammatica Russica. Oxoni A. D. MDCXCVI. Ed. B. O. Unbegaun. Oxford 1959.

Uspenskij 1987 = Boris Andreevič Uspenskij: Istorija russkogo literaturnogo jazyka (XI—XVII vv.). München 1987.

Vasmer ed. 1922 = Max Vasmer (ed.): Ein russisch-byzantinisches Gesprächsbuch. Beiträge zur Erforschung der älteren russischen Lexikographie. Leipzig 1922.

Vinogradov ed. 1954 = V. V. Vinogradov (ed.): Bibliografičeskij ukazatel' literatury po russkomu jazykoznaniju s 1825 po 1880 god. Vypusk II. Leksikologija i leksikografija. Moskva 1954.

Vlachov 1987 = Sergej Vlachov: K sostavleniju ideografičeskogo perevodnogo slovarja russkoj frazeologii (na materiale russkoj i bolgarskoj idiomatiki). In: A. S. Aksamitov (ed.): Frazeologizm i ego leksikografičeskaja obrabotka. Minsk 1987, 20—23.

Vojnova 1980 = L. A. Vojnova: „Novyj slovotolkovatel'" N. Janovskogo i ego istočniki. In: L. L. Kutina/E. È. Biržakova (eds.): Slovari i slovarnoe delo v Rossii XVIII v. Moskva 1980, 45—69.

Vomperskij 1986 = Valentin Pavlovič Vomperskij: Slovari XVIII veka. Moskva 1986.

Witkowski 1961 = N. Witkowski: Dwa rękopiśmienne słowniki polsko-cierkowno-ruskie z XVII w. In: Zeszyty naukowe Uniwersytetu Jagiellońskiego. Prace językoznawcze 4/8. 1961, 217—225.

Zaunmüller 1958 = Wolfram Zaunmüller: Bibliographisches Handbuch der Sprachwörterbücher. Stuttgart 1958.

Wolfgang Eismann, Graz (Österreich)

325. Bilingual Lexicography With Arabic

1. The Middle Ages
2. European Bilingual Arabic Dictionaries Based on Medieval Arabic Works (16th—19th C.)
3. The 19th and 20th Centuries: Handy Dictionaries in One or Two Volumes
4. Specialised Dictionaries and Vocabularies
5. Dictionaries of Colloquial Arabic
6. Selected Bibliography

1. The Middle Ages

In the medieval Islamic Empire, no pressing need was felt for bilingual dictionaries. Arabic was the language of religion, the reading of the Qur'an in the original language being mandatory. It was also the language of government. Wherever one travelled in the Islamic world, the educated were expected to understand Arabic. From the advent of the 'Abbasid Caliphate in 750, the government became increasingly non-Arab, positions of authority being often occupied by men of Iranian or Turkic origin. A semblance of unity under Arab caliphs was maintained until the sack of Baghdad by the Mongols in 1258. But from nearly four centuries previously, the Empire had gradually become divided into a number of principalities, independent de facto if not de jure, many ruled by non-Arab dynasties. A new Persian literature evolved, using Arabic script, and incorporating numerous Arabic loan-words. There were similar developments in Turkic languages. But it was the emergence later of Ottoman Turkish literature which gave prominence to the process. Yet, until the end of the Middle Ages, lexicographers from Iran and Transoxiana were content, by and large, to devote their energies to monolingual Arabic lexicography (cf. Art. 237).

1.1. The Middle East

In the Middle East, the earliest extant bilingual dictionary was Diwān lughat al-Turk, by [Maḥmūd ibn al-Ḥasan ibn Muḥammad al-] Kashgharī. Written in 1032, it is a Turkish-Arabic lexicon dedicated to the Caliph al-Muqtadī in Baghdad (Kashgarī 1333—5 AH). Kashgharī hailed from Central Asia, where he had travelled extensively studying several Turkic languages or dialects. He records their vocabularies in the Arabic script, according to a system which he explains in his Arabic Introduction. He justifies his work by stating that the Turks have been exalted by Allah to be numbered among the 'monarchs of the age'. He quotes an obviously spurious Tradition of the Prophet, which he had heard from experts in Bokhara and Nisapur, foretelling that the Turks would enjoy long rule, and that it therefore behoved Muslims to learn their language. He acknowledges his debt to Arabic lexicographers, naming only Khalīl (cf. Art. 237) from whom it would appear that he derived some of his phonological ideas. Unfortunately the Arab influence on Kashgharī's arrangement has created problems, and modern Turkish scholars have had to write many volumes, not merely changing the words defined into the modern Turkish Latin script, and Arabic definitions into Turkish, but also providing commentaries and indexes, thus placing the historical and dialectic evidence at the disposal of modern Turks unfamiliar with the Arabic script. The work is divided into eight books, based partly on the number of letters in the root, partly on the presence of weak or nasal consonants. In each book, nouns and verbs are treated in separate sections; and there are supporting citations from poetry and proverbs.

Nearly a century later, the earliest extant Arabic-Persian dictionary was compiled by Zamakhsharī (1075—1144) (Haywood 1959, 104 ff., 118 f.), entitled Muquaddimat al-adab (= introduction to culture). While Kashgharī's work was designed to help Arab speakers to learn Turkish, Zamakhsharī aimed to help Iranians to learn Arabic. Its arrangement is almost as complex as Kashgharī's. Its three main sections are devoted to nouns, verbs and particles respectively. Arabic nouns are listed according to their meanings, beginning with time, earth, sky and water, with Persian equivalents. Verbs are listed according to their measures and then in rhyme order (Wetzstein 1850).

1.2. Arab Spain (cf. Fück 1955, 10—34)

The Arabs conquered most of Spain and Portugal from 710 onwards. From the mid-8th. c. the rulers were independent of the caliphs in Baghdad, and their capital Cordoba was a brilliant culture centre, rivalling Baghdad in the arts and sciences, including lexicography. With the passage of time, Muslim Spain declined politically. The Christians of the North began a systematic reconquest of the country. Arab Spain split into a number of small principalities, and two waves of extremist Muslims from N. Africa, the Almoravides and the Almohades, successively dominated the country. Muslim rule ended in 1492, with the conquest of the Arab Kingdom of Granada by the armies of Ferdinand and Isabella of Castile. Against this background, it is easy to see why bilingual Arabic-Latin/Castilian lexicography should have developed. Between the 11th and the early 16th centuries, three such dictionaries have survived. Of particular note is their interest in the spoken language, whereas the major medieval Arabic monolingual dictionaries concentrated on the literary language. The first of the trio was the 11th C. Arabic—Latin *Glossarium Latino-Arabicum*, described by Fück (1955, 10) as "halb Wörterbuch, halb Reallexicon" (for the text, cf. Seybold 1900). The second dictionary, written c. 1275, was the *Vocabulista in Arabico* of Raimundus Martinus (Schiaparelli 1871). It consists of two parts, one Arabic-vulgar Castilian, the other Castilian-Arabic. Despite the colloquialisms, the Arabic words in both of the above works are in Arabic script. The same cannot be said of the third work, Pedro de Alcalá's *Vocabulista Aravigo en Letra Castellana* (Alcalá 1505). This was written for the Archbishop of Granada to assist his drive to convert the defeated Muslims to Christianity. It sheds light on the spoken language of Granada. But Alcalá's transliteration of Arabic words is so ambiguous as to render the identification of some words almost impossible (cf. Fück 1955, 30; Haywood 1965, 129; and Dozy 1881, I, 10).

2. European Bilingual Arabic Dictionaries Based on Medieval Arabic Works (16th—19th C.)

The development of Arabic lexicography in W. Europe was a by-product of the Renaissance and Reformation. From the religious viewpoint, the Arabic language was important for the light it sheds on Hebrew and other Semitic languages. Moreover there is substantial Arabic Christian literature, both Biblical and patristic. Again, events in Spain and — more important — the westward expansion of the Ottoman Empire, stimulated interest in Islam. On land, this Empire was to stretch as far as Hungary, and even Vienna was threatened: on sea, the Turks at times seemed likely to dominate the Mediterranean. Then there was the 'expansion of Europe' into Africa and Asia, which resulted in European powers first trading with, then occupying Muslim countries. Arabic departments were established in European universities, and scholars went to the Middle East to collect Arabic manuscripts. The lexicographical fruits of all this took two forms; firstly, polyglot dictionaries incorporating Arabic, usually with the Christian scriptures in mind; and secondly, bilingual dictionaries of general application, each based mainly on one of the major Arabic medieval monolingual dictionaries, re-arranged to suit Europeans, and with definitions translated into Latin or some modern European language.

2.1. Golius, Freytag, Lane

The compilers of these dictionaries faced daunting difficulties. They depended on MSS of dictionaries, mostly arranged in 'rhyme order' under roots, but with no regular system for listing words under these roots. Thus the translation of definitions, and citations (if any) was only half the work. Three major works stand out. The first was Jacobus Golius' *Lexicon Arabico—Latinum*, publ. in 1653 in Leiden (Golius 1653). In the important (but unpaginated) Preface, Golius lists the verb forms — root and 12 derived forms for the triliteral, root and three for the quadriliteral, that is, in the order in which they occur in the entries. Then he mentions his sources, beginning with his chief one, the Ṣaḥāḥ of Jauharī, then other dictionaries, the Qur'ān, a few literary works, and some obscure bilingual vocabularies each incorporating pairs of languages from Arabic/Persian/Turkish. The work is characterised by large clear print, and, like its main source, it is not prolix. It is a most useful basic lexicon for the Qur'ān and classical literature. For two centuries it remained the standard reference.

It was superseded by the *Lexicon Arabico-Latinum* of Georg Wilhelm Friedrich Freytag, publ. in Halle in 4 vv. (Freytag 1830—37), based primarily on the Qāmūs of Fīrūzābādī. Like Golius, its definitions are basic and succinct; but its vocabulary is fuller. The third dictionary was of a different kind, Edward William Lane's incomplete 8-volume *Arabic-English Lexicon* (Lane 1863—93). Lane paid three extended visits to Egypt, where he conceived the idea of compiling a large-scale Arabic dictionary with definitions in English, instead of the Latin of Golius and Freytag. He took as his prime source Zabīdī's Tāj al-'Arūs (cf. Art. 237) of which he found a MS. Compiled in Egypt in the 18th C., it is of all extant Arabic dictionaries the most copious in words defined (c. 120,000), though exceeded by others in fulness of citations. But Lane also used about 100 other sources, which he lists, with abbreviations, in his Preface (cf. Lane I, xxxi), and these include major dictionaries in three different arrangements — the phonetic-anagrammatical and the modern alphabetical arrangement as well as the rhyme order. Moreover, Lane aimed to give the fullest and most accurate English definitions, supported by citations from Arab lexicographers and literary quotations. Leaving Egypt finally, he returned to England, taking his MSS with him to complete the task, with financial support from the Duke of Northumberland. But, realising that he would not live to finish his work, he divided it into two parts, Pt. I being restricted to the commoner roots, thus omitting most quadri- and quinqueliteral roots. He completed Pt. I as far as the root q-d-d, q being the 21st of the 28 letters of the Arabic alphabet. V. 6 was published after his death, in 1877. His nephew, Stanley Lane-Poole, at first decided to complete the work from notes left by his uncle, but, finding these inadequate, he contented himself with rearranging them, and publishing them as vv. 7 & 8. They are, in fact, very sketchy. Nevertheless, Lane's Lexicon is considered one of the finest dictionaries in any language, even though it is incomplete, and omits the rarer roots, the knowledge of which is required for the understanding of much of the classical literature, both poetry and 'art prose'; and it is, of course, inadequate for Arabic of the 19th and 20th C. It lacks also words peculiar to peripheral areas of the Arab world of which the lexicographers failed to take note. Two supplementary dictionaries were written to fill these gaps, particularly so far as Arab Spain and North Africa are concerned. They are R. Dozy's *Supplément aux dictionnaires arabes* (Dozy 1881) and E. Fagnan's *Additions aux dictionnaires arabes* (Fagnan 1923).

2.2. The Project for a New Comprehensive Arabic Dictionary

The impact of Lane was tremendous, not only on European orientalists, but also on Arab scholars — and scant justice has been done to this impact so far. For example, would Zabidi's Taj al-'Arus have been published (Bulaq, Cairo, 1306—7 AH), had Lane not drawn attention to it? The Arabs themselves seemed unable to embark on a new dictionary comparable in scope with the OED, despite the Egyptian Royal Decree of 1932 calling for one. At that time, August Fischer was in Cairo collecting material for one. He left Egypt in 1939, and when he died 10 years later, he left behind him 360,000 pieces of paper containing material for the project. The International Congress of Orientalists called for the 'completion of Lane's Lexicon': but Fischer's objective was much more ambitious — no less than a comprehensive Arabic dictionary on etymological and historical lines, illustrating every word and meaning from actual use in literature, taking due note of syntax, phraseology and style. The project was commenced in Tübingen in 1954 by Jörg Kraemer and Helmut Gätje. The first fascicule appeared in Wiesbaden in 1954 as *Wörterbuch der klassischen arabischen Sprache* (WKAS 1970—). It starts with the letter $kāf$ (k), with the aim of deferring work on those parts of the work which are already covered — however imperfectly — by Lane, thus concentrating the effort where the need is greatest. (For an account of the scope and progress of WKAS, and discussion of the limitations of medieval Arabic dictionaries, see Gätje 1985). This dictionary has only roots in the Arabic script. All other words are in Latin transliteration, thus permitting the use of small print without undue loss of legibility. But this will be regretted by many Arabists and most Arabs. Detailed definitions and explanations are in German; but English definitions are included. So the work is not strictly bilingual: nevertheless so vital a research tool had to be discussed. It will take decades to complete: v. II appeared in 1983. During the same period work has been in progress on a somewhat similar project in France — *Dictionnaire arabe-français-anglais, langue classique et moderne,* ed. Blachère, Chouémi and Denizeau (DAFA 1967—), the first three volumes of which were published in 1967, 1970 and 1974. In the long run, it will partially duplicate WKAS, but it is distinguished by its inclusion of modern vocabulary. However, entries in the French work seem to be less full. One point in its favour is that all words defined are in Arabic script. It should be noted that it starts at the first letter of the alphabet, *alif.* But it certainly does not replace Lane, with his full and exact definitions of classical words and his numerous citations.

3. The 19th and 20th Centuries: Handy Dictionaries in One or Two Volumes

The Arabs themselves date their literary nahḍa (= renaissance) from Napoleon's Egyptian expedition of 1798. This turned Arabs' attention to the West. The Ottoman Sultans' hold over the Middle East was gradually weakened. Turkish influence was replaced by that of Europe, especially Britain and France. Western technology aided economic development. The introduction of printing and the press, plus the spread of education, brought the written language within the grasp of a greatly enlarged but less expert readership. New literary forms were adopted from the West — novel, short-story, drama, newspaper article. Arabic vocabulary was enlarged by foreign loan-words, especially for technology in its broadest sense. At the same time, the purists, through the great language academies (in Cairo, Damascus, Baghdad, etc.), were trying to stem the flood by coining new technical terms from genuine Arabic roots. The admissibility of colloquial words in literature was considered, and occasionally even the reform or replacement of the Arabic script was discussed, though with little enthusiasm. Meanwhile, cheap and handy bilingual dictionaries became necessary for both educated Arabs and Europeans working or trading in the Arab world, or studying its culture. It was difficult to compile works equally suitable for both these categories; but they had some common problems. For example, though it is generally agreed that Arabic words should be entered under their roots (e.g. **maktab** = office, under **kataba** = he wrote), it is sometimes hard to identify the root of an unfamiliar word, because (a) a weak radical may be omitted, (b) a doubled consonant may appear as one, and (c) the signs for short vowels are seldom shown, as also other orthographical signs, such as that for doubling a letter. Again, Arabic has so complex an array of plural forms ('broken plurals') that it is essential for non-Arabs to be given the plurals of a large proportion of nouns and adjectives. The medieval monolingual dictionaries always gave them, but for some reason, modern Arab bilingual lexicographers take them for granted. Another important point is that familiar Arabic words came to be used in new phrases, often almost literally translated from English or French idioms, and old words acquired new meanings.

3.1. General Bilingual Dictionaries, 19th Century

These are so numerous that only a few can be mentioned. In the early 19th C., French was the language most commonly paired with Arabic, but by the end of the century, English was supplanting it. The commonest centres of publication were Beirut, Cairo, London and Paris. Lexicographers faced the following problems: (1) How far should colloquial and literary words be mixed? (2) Should Arabic script only be used for 'literary' dictionaries, and Latin script only for colloquial dictionaries, or should both be used? (3) Should allowance be made for the difficulty in identifying roots of some words (vide supra) by listing them independently? (4) Should illustrations be included to clarify meanings of some words? A pioneer work was *Dictionnaire français-arabe,* by the Egyptian Ellious Bocthor, described as augmented and revised by the French orientalist A. Caussin de Perceval, published in Paris (Bocthor 1848). Colloquial words are included, such as Ottoman Turkish ōḍah (= room), then, as now, commonly used in Egypt for classical ḥujra/ ghurfa. This set the French pattern of including classical and colloquial words side-by-side. For example, Kazimirski (Paris 1860, Cairo 1875) included words used in Algeria and Morocco, and Beaussier (Paris 1931, Algiers 1887) words from Algeria and Tunis. Turning to English, Joseph Catafago's *Arabic Dictionary* was published in London in 1857. It is described as 'for travellers and students', and this may explain why in v. 1 words are entered not under their roots, but in alphabetical order as spelled, this being presumably considered simpler. Thus **mutabaṣṣir** (= observant) comes under m, whilst its root **baṣura** (= to see, perceive) comes under b, hundreds of pages earlier. However, as the first is a regular active participle of derived from verb V of **baṣura,** the root should be easily identified by a relative beginner in Arabic grammar. E. W. Newman's *Dictionary of Modern Arabic,* publ. London 1871, designed to show current usage, is oddly arranged. V. I, Eng.-Ar., is entirely in the Latin script. V. II, Ar.-Eng., is in two sections. The first lists Arabic words in Latin script in alphabetical order, irrespective of roots. Section 2 lists them under their roots, these roots only being in Arabic as well as Latin script. George Percy Badger's very substantial *English-Arabic lexicon* (Badger 1881) remained a favoured work for several decades. It is based on the Qāmūs, Busṭānī's Muḥīṭ al-Muḥīṭ and Lane, whose Lexicon Badger describes (p. vii) as the best dictionary in any language. Shortly afterwards, Francis Steingass' English-Arabic (1882) and Arabic-English (1884) dictionaries were published in London. In both, Arabic words are given in Latin as well as Arabic script. Steingass aimed at a wide readership, ranging from travellers to students — even those venturing on literature as difficult as pre-Islamic poetry! In the Ar.-Eng. dictionary, Arabic words are variously listed, partly under their roots, partly independently, with some duplication. The aim is to help the less expert user: but the advisability of this mixed arrangement is dubious, and the basis on which certain derivatives are singled out for this special treatment is not immediately clear. In the event, Steingass went on to achieve more lasting fame in Persian lexicography, whilst his Arabic dictionaries were soon neglected. The *Advanced Learner's Dictionary Arabic-English* of H. A. Salmoné (2 vv, London 1890) was more conservative in aim and arrangement, being intended as a 'comprehensive, handy and cheap' lexicon of the literary language (Salmoné 1890). V. 1 of 1200 p. is Ar.-Eng., in Arabic script. Space is saved by using, for the various forms of derivative under each root, a number of symbols which are listed at the end of the volume. V.II, in 179 p. only, is an 'English-Arabic Index'. Instead of giving Arabic equivalents for English words, it merely gives page references to v. I, indicating where they can be found. This work was soon superseded by the Jesuit J. G. Hava's *Arabic-English Dictionary* of 1899, published by the Catholic Press, Beirut, and frequently reprinted since. It is a comprehensive dictionary of classical Arabic, compressed into under 1000 pages, by the use of small print and succinct definitions, and the elimination of citations. Though not quite pocket-size, it occupies less shelf space than the average modern novel, and will enable the advanced student to understand quite abstruse classical literature. Hava follows European scholars like Lane in arranging derivatives under their roots, and uses abbreviations, both English and Arabic. He gives the origins of many foreign loanwords, and there is an etymological appendix listing many of them with their probable sources, language by language: — French-German-Greek-Hebrew-Italian-Latin-Persian-Syriac-Ottoman Turkish. Dialect words from Syria and Egypt are included and indicated, but on a modest scale, where they are liable to occur in print: but this is not in any sense a colloquial dictionary. Hava is a well-established tool for modern Western Arabists, occupying a place analogous with that of the Qāmūs among Arab scholars. There is also a French version by Jean Baptiste Belot (1911). Mention must also be made here of the *Arabic English Vocabulary of the Modern and Colloquial Language of Egypt*, by Socrates Spiro-Bey, in both Arabic and Latin script (Spiro-Bey 1895/7). V. I Ar.-Eng. is meant to cover ordinary conversation and even slang, but also the vocabulary of administration, finance, engineering and the armed forces, v. II, Eng.-Ar., is intended to assist foreigners in conversing intelligently with Egyptians, and is largely restricted to words and sentences serving this purpose. During the 19th C., German contributions to Arabic lexicography were limited after Freytag. For contemporary Arabic, the standard work was Adolf Wahrmund's *Handwörterbuch der neuarabischen und deutschen Sprache* (Wahrmund 1870—77). In a restricted classical Arabic area, Friedrich Dieterici's *Arabisch-deutsches Handwörterbuch zum Koran und Thier und Mensch* (Dieterici 1881) was highly regarded, despite the strange juxtaposition of horse, man and Qur'ān in its title and content.

3.2. The 20th Century

The use of English and Egyptian Higher Education under British influence bore fruit in lexicography, as can be seen in the *Arabic-English Dictionary for the use of schools,* by John Wortabet and Harvey Porter, published in Cairo (Wortabet 1913, reprinted in 1954 in New York, with a supplement of 'modern words and new meanings'). It could prove useful as a first dictionary for mature students. But the period from around the outbreak of the First World War to the end of the Second may justly be called the 'Elias Era' in Arabic lexicography, being dominated by the productions of the Egyptian Copt Elias Antoon Elias, which were published by his Modern Press in Cairo in progressively enlarged and amended editions (Elias 1913/1922).

> The 1st; ed. of his *Elias' Modern Dictionary English-Arabic* contained 32.000 words in 440 p.; the 13th of 1862 369.000 in 814 p. In the Preface of the 1st ed., he states that it is intended primarily to assist Arabic-speaking students of English, but

with the hope that it will also help English-speaking students of Arabic who have already "a fair degree of proficiency in that language". He adds: "The Arabic used ... is essentially modern, popular in Egypt and all other Arabic-speaking countries, and adopted by the best authorities of recent writers". It is thus a dictionary of contemporary written Arabic, though a few colloquialisms are admitted. There are special symbols for these, as also for Arabic equivalents for English words coined by the Egyptian Academy of the Arabic Language, and for other words not so approved, and rejected by purists, yet in daily use. Small illustrations in the text give visual clarification of some definitions. The greatest limitation of this dictionary in its various editions is that definitions are essentially word-for-word. And though different meanings of one and the same word are catered for, they are not clearly differentiated. An example is the English verb **to espouse**, with its rather antique meaning of 'to marry', and its figurative meaning 'to support, attach oneself to (a cause)'. Certainly both are given, but they could be more clearly differentiated. With all its defects, this dictionary served English-speaking users for 50 years, thanks to its copiousness, its being regularly brought up to date, and the lack of a comparable alternative.

Elias' Modern Dictionary Arabic-English was first published in 1922. By the 7th ed. of 1954, it contained 64,000 words in 972 pages, and there are illustrations not only in the text, but also in a classified selection at the end of the book (7th ed., 825—65). Obsolete words are avoided, the stress being on the language of the modern press and literature. Elias addressed himself to the difficulty in identifying the roots of many words by interspersing groups of such words at appropriate points in the text, and indicating the roots under which they can be found in brackets (see dictionary excerpt 325.1).

This was an improvement on previous solutions to the problem (vide Steingass supra), as it helped the inexpert without offending the purist. The failure to record 'broken plurals' is regrettable especially for non-Arab users. Elias' publications also included series of 'School dictionaries' and 'Pocket dictionaries', abridging the contents of the two main series. He died in 1952, but his work has been continued by his son Edward Elias Elias, whose obituary of his father will be found as a preface to the 6th & 7th eds. of the Ar.-Eng. Dict., 1953—4.

Reliance on Elias in the West has been drastically curtailed since the Second World War. This is chiefly due to two works: that of Hans Wehr (Ar.-Ger. 1952, with its Ar.-Eng. version, 1961); and the *Oxford Eng.-Ar. Dictionary,* (OEAD 1972). The former is devoted to 'modern written Arabic', the latter to 'current usage'. Hans Wehr's *Arabisches Wörterbuch für die Schriftsprache der Gegenwart* (Wehr 1952) was first published in 2 vv. in Leipzig, but publication was subsequently moved to Wiesbaden, where a *Supplement* appeared in 1959. An English version followed in 1961 with the support of the American Council of Learned Societies. The 4th ed. appeared in 1979. Its 1301 pages include c. 13,000 additions, including new entries, definitions, idiomatic phrases and compounds. This work is now a standard guide to the language of written Arabic since 1900. Arabic script is used throughout, but Latin transliterations also are given. There are compounds and idiomatic phrases, but the aim has been to include the greatest possible number of words. Definitions are brief but clear: thus no involved explanations are given to assist Arabic-speaking users, for whom this work is presumably not intended. The *Oxford English-Arabic Dictionary of current usage* (OEAD 1972) was edited by N. S. Doniach, with the co-operation of a team of assistants, many of them Arabic-speakers. The Preface

To jest; joke.	— : مَزَحَ
To be gross, *or* coarse.	— : غَلُظَ
Jesting; joking.	مُجُون : مَزَاح
Drollery; buffoonery.	— : مَزَاح سَمِج
Impudent; shameless; brazenfaced.	مَجَّان. ماجِن : قَلِيل الحَيَاء
Jester; joker.	— . . : مازِح
Free; gratuitous; free of charge.	‌. مَجَّانِيّ : بِلا مُقابِل
Gratis; for nothing; free (of charge); freely; gratuitously.	مَجَّانًا

° مجنون (في جنن) ° مجهر(في جهر)° مجوب(في جوب)
° مجوس (في مجس) ° مجون (في مجن) ° مح (في محح)
° محا (في محو) ° محابٍ (في حبو) ° محار (في حور)
° محال (في حول) ° محامٍ (في حمي) ° محتاج (و حوج)
° محتال (في حول) ° محتشد(في حشد)° محتنِد (في حند)
° محتشم (في حشم) ° محجر (في حجر) ° محجة (في حجج)

Worn-out; threadbare.	(محّ) مَحّ : بالٍ
Cream; choicest part; quintessence.	مُحّ : خَالِص كُلّ شَيْء
Yolk of egg; vitellus, (*pl.* vitelli.)	— البَيْض

Dictionary excerpt 325.1: Dictionary articles (in: Elias 1922, ed. 1954)

declares that it is "designed to meet the needs of those whose mother-tongue is English, and who are learning Arabic, and of those whose mother-tongue is Arabic, and who are learning English". Consequently the mere equating of words was not considered to be enough, in view of the wide gap between the two languages. The presence of long circumlocutions whose aim is to explain English words before — and sometimes instead of — giving equivalents which the translator might use, while it may well help the Arab user, is liable to irritate, and at times even mislead, the English-speaking user. But this is the inevitable result of trying to cater for both types of user. Where this work particularly shines is in the idiomatic usages, phrases and sentences, both English and Arabic which are included in many entries. Elias (Eng.-Ar.) cannot bear comparison, though it can sometimes provide the experienced Arabist with a speedy reminder of a half-forgotten Arabic word. The time is now ripe for a revised and enlarged edition of OEAD, to maintain its position as a fitting partner to Wehr. Other postwar English-Arabic dictionaries include Munir al-Ba'labaki's Al-Mawrid (1967; 100,000 entries) and Hasan S. Karmi's Al-Manar (1970; 40,000 entries), the latter catering for students at schools and colleges. Both are more suitable for Arabic- than English-speakers.

Dictionaries in German in this century have included Ernst Harder's *Deutsch-arabisches Wörterbuch* (1902), and his *Deutsch-arabisches und arabisch-deutsches Taschenwörterbuch* (1919—25). In Egypt, Riyad Gayed's *Das einzige Wörterbuch der deutschen und arabischen Sprache* (Germ-Ar.) was published in several undated editions by Elias' Modern Press, and the influence of Elias is clear. Tribute must also be paid to the work of Günther Krahl in E. Germany. In French, Léon Bercher's *Lexique arabe-français* (Algiers 1944) is useful for modern Arabic. Jean Baptiste Belot's *Dictionnaire français-arabe* (Beirut 1952) is highly regarded. His French version of Hava was republished as *Al Faraid dictionnaire arabe-français* (Beirut 1934). In the same year C. K. Baranov's *Arabic-Russian Dictionary of the Literary Language* appeared in Moscow. The 8th ed. (1976) contains c. 42,000 words. G. S. Sharbatov's *Russian-Arabic Dictionary* (Moscow 1964) is notable for its 139-page explanatory introduction. Lack of space precludes mention of dictionaries in other languages. The Arab world has for some time been at the centre of the international stage, with consequent world-wide interest in the Arabic language.

4. Specialised Dictionaries and Vocabularies

The specialised vocabulary was known to the medieval Arabic lexicographers. But in the 20th C., European influence gave it a new lease of life in bilingual form: bilingual because it was applied to western technical terms and concepts. And this was true of familiar fields like government and education no less than science and technology. In many, perhaps most, instances Arabic equivalents were formed from Arabic roots. And where foreign nouns were adopted, they were usually made to sound like Arabic by being given that typical Arabic feature, the broken plural; e. g. **lastīk** (from Fr. *élastique*) = tyre (of car, etc.), pl. lasātīk. Specialised vocabularies have so proliferated, especially since the 2nd World War, that only typical examples will be mentioned.

An early and very substantial one was M. Sharaf's *English-Arabic Dictionary of Medicine, Biology and Allied Sciences,* publ. Cairo 1926. It must now be partially out-of-date, but such is the usual fate of these dictionaries. However, the earliest subject of these dictionaries was government, administration, politics and diplomacy. Bernard Lewis' *Handbook of diplomatic and political Arabic* was published in London (1947). F. V. Martinez' *Glosario Español-Arabe* (Madrid 1980) is devoted to diplomacy, politics and international affairs. Ma'mun al-Hamawi's *Terms of International Relations,* Eng.-Ar. (Beirut 1968) may also be mentioned. The following works cover the field of business, trade, commerce and economics: M. A. Abdel Haleem/Ernest Kay, *English-Arabic Business Dictionary* (London 1984); Mustafa Henni, *Dictionnaire des termes économiques et commerciaux* (Fr.-Eng.-Ar., Beirut 1970); Hasan al-Najafī, *Dict. of trade & banking terms,* Eng.—Ar., Baghdad 1976, which gives long Arabic explanations as well as brief definitions of the English terms. In Jacques Schmidt's *Dictionnaire d'arabe moderne: économie—politique—actualité* (Fr.-Ar. 1979, Ar.-Fr. 1982), "actualité" covers many fields, including religion, with such words as 'incarnation'. For finance, there is Adnan Abdeen's *Eng.-Ar. Dictionary of Accounting and Finance* (Beirut, N.Y., etc. 1981. This has an Ar.-Eng. Glossary, and specimen formats of balance sheets, etc. In the actual dictionary, there are long explanations of terms in both English and Arabic. Among naval/maritime dictionaries is an Eng.-Ar. one of pocket size Qāmūs al-jaib al-baḥrī, by naval officers M. Kamāl Farīd and M. Ḥusain Aḥmad and Aḥmad Fu'ād 'Arab (Alexandria 1979). Rather fuller is M. Bechir al-Kefi's *Les termes techniques de la marine,* Fr.-Ar. & Ar.-Fr. (Beirut 1981). Somewhat wide in scope is Magdi Wahba's *An English-Arabic Vocabulary of Scientific, Technical and Cultural Terms* (Cairo

1968). More recently, bilingual lexicography has spread to education, witness M. Ali Alkhuli's *Dictionary of Education Eng.-Ar.* (Beirut 1981) and Tarik al-Nasiri's *Dictionary of Sport and Scouting Eng.-Ar.* (Baghdad 1982). In contrast to the narrowing of fields, we may refer to Shafi Shaikh's Dictionary of (sic) *English-Arabic for Professionals* (Delhi. Calcutta. Madras 1983). In his Preface, the author complains that the recent spate of Ar.-Eng. dictionaries from various parts of the world has been by and large confined to general works, failing to cater for the growing influx of professionals (managers, scientists, technicians, doctors, etc.). To cater for these he has produced a dictionary of the terminology of dozens of arts and sciences, ranging from astronomy and aeronautics to medicine, music and tailoring. A bold plan! But the risk is that such a work might be too general for the specialist yet too specialised for the general user. But let us leave the 'last word' in this section to a well-tried classic in its specialised field — *Faruqi's Law Dictionary Eng.-Ar.* (Faruqi 1970), published in Beirut.

5. Dictionaries of Colloquial Arabic

We have seen that some major general bilingual Arabic lexicons admitted colloquial words alongside the classical — particularly French works. But during the last 100 years numerous dictionaries devoted purely to the colloquial have appeared; however, some basic facts must be mentioned, to assist the non-specialist. First, there is essentially only one classical or written Arabic, whether it be in medieval poetry or modern newspapers. It is a highly inflected language, though some — and only some — of the inflection is hidden when, as is usual, short vowels above or below consonants are omitted. On the other hand, spoken Arabic has discarded most of the inflection (such as case endings of nouns), and simplified the syntax. But colloquial Arabic is not unified. It may, for convenience, be considered as divided into a number of regional dialects, equating very roughly with political, ethnic and cultural areas. Thus, for practical purposes, we may speak of Egyptian Colloquial Arabic, Sudan Colloquial, Iraqi Colloquial and so on; and it is on these lines that dictionaries of spoken Arabic have usually been compiled. These dialects may differ from each other in grammar, syntax and vocabulary, according to geographical and historical factors. There are also phonological differences. Certain letters may not be pronounced according to classical norms. Thus ḍābiṭ (= officer) may be so pronounced in Baghdad, but be heard as zābiṭ in Cairo or Khartoum. It therefore follows that many common colloquial words cannot be accurately reproduced in the Arabic script without being 'mis-spelt', and this has often proved unpalatable to Arabs and even Arabists. It seems preferable to use the Latin script. If it is desired to include Arabic script as well, the classical spelling may be retained, and regarded as etymological information rather than a key to pronunciation.

During the last hundred years, dictionaries of colloquial Arabic have often been compiled at the behest of governments or missionary societies. Works printed commercially have usually been at a lower level, for travellers or merchants. But pure scholarship is now playing an increasing part: the Western passion for linguistic sciences has now reached the Arabs. The dictionaries mentioned below have been selected as typical of different types of production, regions and dates.

Budget Meakin's *An Introduction to the Arabic of Morocco* was published in London and Tangier (1891), and was the result of years of field-work by the missionary author. In it, a short grammatical introduction is followed by a 200-page vocabulary, of which, he says, "every word has been culled from the lips of the people". It is not in alphabetical order, but divided into 305 groups of a few words each, arranged under nouns, adjectives, verbs and particles. In these main sections ('parts') words are classified according to meaning: e. g., for nouns, the universe, mankind, buying & selling, eating & drinking and so on. Similarly pronounced words form a special short part. There is an English index. In contrast, Valentin Beneitez Cantero's *Vocabulario español-arabe Marroqui* (2nd ed., Tetuan 1952) is an alphabetical Spanish-Arabic dictionary, with Arabic in both Arabic and Latin scripts. Belkassem ben Sedira's *Dictionnaire français-arabe de la langue parlée en Algérie* (Algiers 1886) is a 1000-page pocket-size dictionary Fr.-Ar., usually word for word, with a grammatical introduction. The tendency to regard the whole of former French NE Africa (Morocco/Algeria/Tunis) as a single dialect-region is reflected in Gilbert Colomer's *Lexique français-arabe de l'arabe parlé maghrébin,* claimed to contain "the most usual current words". There is a grammatical introduction. It is a pity that the work is lithographed from a handwritten MS (Colomer 1982). For Libya an early Italian-Arabic dict. published in Milan is Eugenio Griffini, *l'Arabo parlato della Libia* (Griffini 1913). Local dialect words are included in this essentially practical pocket dictionary. In Egypt, Elias' Modern Press published various colloquial vocabularies, arranged partly by subject matter, partly by parts of speech. A notable scholarly work is Kurt Munzel,

Ägyptisch-arabischer Sprachführer (Wiesbaden 1983) entirely in the Latin script. Sudan Arabic has been well served by two works, one superseding the other. Capt. H. F. S. Amery's *English-Arabic Vocabulary for the use of officials in the Anglo-Egyptian Sudan* was published in Cairo (Amery 1905). Arabic words are in both script and transliteration. Though an indispensible reference for 20 years, it is not sufficiently exact and scientific. It is not etymological, and rather short in local variants which are so interesting and important in a country which stands at the parting of the ways between Semitic, Hamitic, Bantu and West-African cultural and linguistic regions. The second work is Hillelson (1925), now regarded as the standard reference. For Palestine, the less said about a commercial production, *Cosmos' Palestinian Colloquial Arabic* (Jerusalem 1939) the better. Described as "specially prepared for the British Police and members of H. M. Forces in Palestine", it names no author. It is a mixture of grammar and vocabulary, but even the page-numbering defies comprehension. Turning to Syria and the Lebanon, we find Claude Denizeau's scholarly *Dictionnaire des parlers arabes de Syrie, Liban et Palestine* (Paris 1960), an Ar.-Fr. dictionary, the Arabic being in both scripts, and supported by source references. On a similar level is *A Dictionary of Iraqi Arabic*, by D. R. Woodhead, Wayne Beene and others (Woodhead 1982), publ. Washington D. C. Arabic words are in the Latin script. But where there is no exact English equivalent, the Arabic letter is used. The Arabic alphabetical order is followed. This is specifically a lexicon of Baghdad Arabic, and abounds in idiomatic expressions. Finally, in the Cosmos vein but somewhat superior is Naoumi B. Seresser of Mosul's *Mesopotamian Arabic,* for members of the British Expeditionary Forces, published in Bombay (Seresser 1918). An ambitious work of 550 pages, it gives Arabic equivalents for English words in both scripts. The arrangement, however, is too complex. There are four sections: I. Man, parts of the body, etc. II. The world and natural life. III. General terms. IV. Civil, military and naval terms. There are also nearly 100 pages of verb conjugation tables! The various early experiments in vocabulary arrangement appear to have high-lighted the greater convenience of the simple unified alphabetical order.

6. Selected Bibliography

6.1. Dictionaries

Abdeen 1981 = Adnan Abdeen: An English-Arabic Dictionary of Accounting and Finance. Beirut 1981 [226 + 40 p.].

Abdel Haleem/Kay 1984 = M. A. Abdel Haleem/ Ernest Kay: English-Arabic Business Dictionary. London 1984 [xxi, 263 p.].

Alkhuli 1981 = M. Ali Alkhuli: Dictionary of Education, English-Arabic. Beirut 1981 [537 p.].

Alcalá 1505 = Pedro de Alcalá: Vocabulista arávigo in letra castellana. Granada 1505. New ed., Paul Anton de Lagarde. Berlin 1883.

Amery 1905 = Capt. H. F. S. Amery: English-Arabic Vocabulary for the use of officials in the Anglo-Egyptian Sudan. Cairo 1905 [xiii, 451 p.].

Badger 1881 = George Percy Badger: An English-Arabic Lexicon. London 1881 [1244 p.].

Ba'labaki 1967 = Munir al-Ba'labaki: Al-Mawrid. Beirut 1967 [7th ed. 1972, 1115 p.; Abridged version: Al-Mawrid al-Muyassar, a simplified English-Arabic Dictionary, Beirut 1979, 575 p.].

Baranov 1976 = C. K. Baranov: [Arabic-Russian Dictionary] 8th ed. Moscow 1976 [942 p.].

Beaussier 1887 = Marcel Beaussier: Dictionnaire pratique Arabe-français. Algiers 1887 Paris 1931 [764 p.].

Belkassem ben Sedira 1886 = Belkassem ben Sedira: Dictionnaire français-arabe de la langue parlée en Algérie. Algiers 1886 [lxiv, 928 p.].

Belot 1911 = Jean Baptiste Belot: Vocabulaire arabe-français. Beirut 1911 [916 p.; 1. ed. 1883, Repri. as: Al-Faraid dictionnaire arabe-français classique, Beirut 1934].

Belot 1952 = Jean-Baptiste Belot: Dictionnaire français-arabe. Nouv. éd. refondue. Beirut 1952 [745 p.; 1. ed. 1890].

Bercher 1944 = Léon Bercher: Lexique arabe-français. 2. ed. Algiers 1944 [107, 244 p.; 1. ed. Paris 1938, 320, 44 p.].

Bocthor 1848 = Ellious Bocthor: Dictionnaire français-arabe. Paris 1848 [867 p.].

Cantero 1952 = Valentin Beneitez Cantero: Vocabulario español-arabe marroqui. Tetuan 1952 [516 p.].

Catafago 1857 = Joseph Catafago: Arabic Dictionary for travellers and students. London 1857 [V. 1: Ar.-Eng., 315 p. V. 2: Eng.-Ar., 1060 p.].

Colomer 1982 = Gilbert Colomer: Lexique français-arabe de l'arabe parlé maghrébin. Niort 1982 [429 p.].

Cosmos 1939 = Cosmos' Palestinian Colloquial Arabic. Jerusalem 1939 [?200 p.].

DAFA 1967— = Dictionnaire arabe-français-anglais (langue classique et moderne). Paris 1967 ff. [V. I, 1967, II, 1970, III, 1973, xxxvii, 2287 p., ed. Régis Blachère/Moustafa Chouémi/Claude Denizeau, and from v. III, Charles Pellat].

Denizeau 1960 = Claude Denizeau: Dictionnaire des parlers arabes de Syrie, Liban et Palestine. Paris 1960 [563 p.].

Dieterici 1881 = Friedrich Dieterici: Arabisch-deutsches Handwörterbuch zum Koran u. Thier u. Mensch vor dem König oder Genien. Leipzig 1881 [180 p.].

Dozy 1881 = Reinhart Dozy: Supplément aux dictionnaires arabes. Leiden 1881 [V. I, 864, II, 854 p.].

Elias 1913/1922 = Elias Antoon Elias: Elias' Modern Dictionary English-Arabic. Cairo 1913 [13th ed. 1962/3, 814 p.; Arabic-English 1922, 7/8th ed. 1954, 972 p.].

Fagnan 1923 = E. Fagnan: Additions aux dictionnaires arabes. Algiers 1923 [193 p.].

Farīd etc. 1979 = Muhammad Kamāl Farīd/Husain Aḥmad/Aḥmad Fu'ād 'Azab: Qāmūs al-jaib al-baḥrī. 2nd ed. Alexandria 1979 [181 p.].

Faruqi's Law Dictionary 1970 = Harith Sulaiman Faruqi: Faruqi's Law Dictionary English-Arabic. Beirut 1970 [758 p., Arabic-English, 1972, 288 p.].

Freytag 1830—37 = Georg Wilhelm Friedrich Freytag: Lexicon Arabico-Latinum. 4 vol. Halle 1830—37.

Gayed 1970 = Riyad Gayed: Das einzige Wörterbuch der deutschen und arabischen Sprache. 4. ed. Cairo 1970 [1214 p.].

Golius 1653 = Jacobus Golius: Lexicon Arabico-Latinum. Leiden 1653 [2200 p.].

Griffini 1913 = Eugenio Griffini: L'Arabo parlato della Libia. Milan 1913 [lii, 378 p.].

Hamawi 1968 = Ma'mun al-Hamawi: Terms of International Relations and Politics, Eng.-Ar. Beirut 1968 [218 p.].

Harder 1902 = Ernst Harder: Deutsch-arabisches Wörterbuch. Heidelberg 1902 [804 p.].

Harder 1919—25 = Ernst Harder: Deutsch-arabisches und arabisch-deutsches Taschenwörterbuch. Heidelberg 1919, 1925 [457, 804 p.].

Hava 1899 = J. G. Hava: Arabic-English Dictionary. Beirut 1899 [Frequently reprinted, 916 pages, in 1951].

Henni 1970 = Mustafa Henni: Dictionnaire des termes économiques et commerciaux, français-anglais-arabe. Beirut 1970 [250 p.].

Hillelson 1925 = Sigmar Hillelson: Sudan Arabic Vocabulary. London 1925 [341 p.].

Karmi 1970 = Hasan S. Karmi: Al-Manar Dictionary. London 1970 [903 p.].

Kashgharī 1333/5 = Mahmūd ibn al-Hasan ibn Muhammad al-Kashgharī: Dīwān lughat al-Turk. 3 vv. Istanboul 1333/5 AH [1106 p.].

Kazimirski 1875 = A. de Kazimirski-Biberstein: Dictionnaire arabe-français. 4 vol. Cairo 1875 [3800 p.].

Kefi 1981 = M. Bechir el-Kefi: Les termes techniques de la marine, Fr.-Ar., Ar.-Fr. Beirut 1981 [67, iv, 76 p.].

Krahl 1964 = Günther Krahl: Wörterbuch Deutsch-Arabisch. Leipzig 1964 [480, 27 p.; 6. ed. 1986, 508 p.].

Krahl/Gharieb 1984 = Günther Krahl/Mohamed Gharieb: Wörterbuch Arabisch-Deutsch. Leipzig 1984 [864 p.].

Krotkoff/Schukry/Humberdrotz 1976 = Langenscheidts Taschenwörterbuch der arabischen und deutschen Sprache. Erster Teil: Arabisch-Deutsch von Georg Krotkoff. Zweiter Teil: Deutsch-Arabisch von Kamil Schukry/Rudolf Humberdrotz. München 1976, 1967 [624, 440 p.].

Lane 1863—93 = Edward William Lane: An Arabic-English Lexicon. 8 vol. London 1863—93 [XXXIV, 3064 p.].

Lewis 1947 = Bernard Lewis: Handbook of diplomatic and political Arabic. London 1947 [72 p.].

Martinez 1980 = Fernando Valderrama Martinez: Glosario español-arabe. Madrid 1980 [210, 272 p.].

Meakin 1891 = Budget Meakin: An introduction to the Arabic of Morocco — English-Arabic Vocabulary, grammatical notes, etc. London. Tangier 1891 [xii, 256 p.].

Munzel 1983 = Kurt Munzel: Ägyptisch-arabischer Sprachführer. Wiesbaden 1983 [247 p.].

Najafi 1976 = Hasan al-Najafi: Dictionary of Trade and Banking Terms, Ar.-Eng. Baghdad 1976 [516 p.].

Nasiri 1982 = Tarik Nasiri/ed. Khalil al-Hamad: Dictionary of Sport and Scouting, Eng.-Ar. Baghdad 1982 [402 p.].

Newman 1871 = E. W. Newman: Dictionary of Modern Arabic. London 1871 [V. I, Eng.-Ar. 376 p. V. II, Ar.-Eng. 460 p.].

OEAD 1972 = The Oxford English-Arabic Dictionary. Oxford 1972 [1392 p.].

Reig 1983 = Daniel Reig: As-Sabil. Dictionnaire arabe-français, français-arabe. Paris 1983 [1450 p.].

Salmoné 1890 = H. A. Salmoné: Advanced Learners' Arabic-English Dictionary. London 1890 [V. I, Ar.-Eng., 1254 p. V. II, Eng.-Ar., Index, 179 p.].

Schiaparelli 1871 = Raimundus Martinus: Vocabulista in Arabica. Ed. Celestino Schiaparelli. Florence 1871 [643 p.].

Schmidt 1979 = Jean Jacques Schmidt: Vocabulaire d'arabe moderne, économie—politique—actualité. Paris 1979, 1982 [V. I, Fr.-Ar., 1979, 627 p. V. II, Ar.-Fr., 1982, 670 p.].

Schregle 1974 = Götz Schregle: Deutsch-arabisches Wörterbuch. Wiesbaden 1974 [1472 p.].

Schregle 1981ff. = Götz Schregle: Arabisch-deutsches Wörterbuch. Wiesbaden 1981ff.

Seresser 1918 = Naoumi B. Seresser of Mosul: Mesopotamian Arabic. Bombay 1918 [550 p.].

Seybold 1900 = Christian Friedrich Seybold: Glossarium latino-arabicum. Berlin 1900 (Semitische Studien 15—17) [XX, 574 p.].

Shaikh 1983 = Shafi Shaikh: Handbook of English-Arabic for professionals. Delhi. Calcutta. Madras 1983 [512 p.].

Sharaf 1926 = M. Sharaf: An Arabic-English Dictionary of Medicine, Biology and Allied Sciences. Cairo 1926 [971 p.].

Sharbatov 1964 = G. S. Sharbatov: [Russian-Arabic Dictionary]. Moscow 1964.

Spiro-Bey 1895/7 = Socrates Spiro-Bey: Arabic-English Vocabulary of the Modern Colloquial Language of Egypt. Cairo 1895, 1897 [V. I, Ar.-Eng., 1895, 661 p. V. II, Eng.-Ar., 1897, 602 p.].

Steingass 1884/7 = Francis Steingass: A Students' Arabic-English Dictionary. London 1884 [1242 p.; 1887, Eng.-Ar., 466 p.].

Wahba 1968 = Magdi Wahba: English-Arabic Vocabulary of scientific, technical and cultural terms. Cairo 1968 [250 p.].

Wahrmund 1870—7 = Adolf Wahrmund: Handwörterbuch der neuarabischen und deutschen Sprache. 3 vol. Gießen 1870—1877 [2. Ed. 1887. 3.Ed. 1898. Repr. Graz 1970; 1028, 1240, 560 p.].

Wehr 1952 = Hans Wehr: Arabisches Wörterbuch für die Schriftsprache der Gegenwart. Leipzig 1952 [986 p.; Supplement, Wiesbaden 1959, 144 p.].

Wehr 1961 = Hans Wehr: A Dictionary of Modern Written Arabic (Arabic-English). Ed. J. Milton Cowan. Wiesbaden 1961 [4th ed. 1979, 1301 p.].

Wetzstein 1850 = Johann Gottfried Wetzstein (ed.): Samachscharii Lexicon Arabicum-Persicum. Leipzig 1850 [300 p.].

WKAS 1970— = Wörterbuch der klassischen arabischen Sprache. V. I, ed. Jörg Kraemer und Helmut Gätje. V. II, ed. Manfred Ulmann. Wiesbaden 1970, 1983 [586, 673 p.].

Woodhead 1982 = D. R. Woodhead/Wayne Beene, etc.: A Dictionary of Iraqi Arabic. Washington D.C. 1982 [509 p.].

Wortabet 1913 = John Wortabet/Harvey Porter: Arabic-English Dictionary for the use of schools. Cairo 1913 [426, 397 p.; New York 1954].

6.2. Other Publications

Fück 1955 = Johann Fück: Die arabischen Studien in Europa bis in den Anfang des 20. Jahrhunderts. Leipzig 1955.

Gätje 1985 = Helmut Gätje: Arabische Lexikographie — ein historischer Überblick. In: Historiographia Linguistica 12. 1985, 105—147.

Harrell 1962 = Richard S. Harrell: Some notes on bilingual lexicography. In: Problems in Lexicography. Ed. F. W. Householder/S. Saporta. Bloomington 1962, 51—61.

Haywood 1965 = John A. Haywood: Arabic Lexicography, its history and its place in the general history of lexicography. 2nd. ed. Leiden 1965.

Lane-Poole 1925 = Stanley Lane-Poole: The Mohammadan Dynasties — chronological and genealogical tables with historical introductions. Paris 1925.

(Note: For the system used to transliterate Arabic words see Haywood 1965, viii.)

John A. Haywood, Lewes
(Great Britain)

326. Bilingual Lexicography on the Indian Subcontinent

1. Linguistic Picture of the Indian Subcontinent
2. Indian-Indian: National/Recognized Languages
3. Indian-Indian: Non-National/Unrecognized Languages
4. Indian-English/English-Indian
5. Foreign-Indian/Indian-Foreign
6. Special Dictionaries
7. Selected Bibliography

1. Linguistic Picture of the Indian Subcontinent

The Indian subcontinent consists of five sovereign states, viz. India, Pakistan, Bangladesh, Nepal and Bhutan, where a large number of languages belonging to four families, viz. Indo-Aryan, Austro-Asiatic, Dravidian and Tibeto-Burman, are spoken (cf. Chatterji 1963, 12—34). As per the 1981 census (Padmanabha 1987) 106 household languages with more than 10,000 speakers and 1652 mother-tongues as per the 1961 census (Pattanayak 1973 a) are spoken in India alone. Of these, 15 languages are recognized as national languages by the 8th schedule (under article 344 (1) and 351) of the Indian Constitution. They are Assamese, Bengali, Gujarathi, Hindi, Kannada, Kashmiri, Malayalam, Marathi, Oriya, Panjabi, Sanskrit, Sindhi, Tamil, Telugu and Urdu, all of which belong to the Indo-Aryan and Dravidian families only. Among these, Hindi is the official language. In addition, English is used as the alternate official language and language of higher and technical education, and taught as a second language in schools. Other languages spoken in India include languages like Konkani, Manipuri, Nepali, Tulu etc., spoken by major communities, and also a number of tribal languages, like Gondi, Gadaba, Santhali, etc. In Pakistan, Baluchi, Brahui, Pushto (Pashto or Pakhtu), Panjabi, Sindhi and Urdu (official) are the major languages spoken. English is also used as in India. In Bangladesh, Bengali is the official language, while Urdu and English are also used. In Nepal, Nepali is the national language. In addition, dialects of Hindi such as Maithili, Bhojpuri and Kumaoni are spoken. Besides these, Tibeto-Burman languages like Newari, Magarkun, Gurungkur etc., are also spoken. In Bhutan, Dzonghta, a Tibeto-Burman dialect, is the official language. Besides this dialect, other Tibetan dialects and Nepali are also spoken. An interesting point to note here is that many of the languages spoken in other sovereign states like Nepali, Panjabi, Sindhi and Urdu are spoken in India, thereby making the Indian subcontinent linguistically a single unit (cf. Chatterji 1963, 1). Bilingual lexicographic activity is mainly concentrated between the 8th schedule languages of India, Baluchi, Brahui, Nepali, Pushto and English, classical languages like Persian other than Sanskrit, and some foreign languages like Arabic, Burmese, French, Japanese, Portuguese etc., with some activity directed toward non-literary and tribal languages and dialects. Though numerically the linguistic picture is large, bilingual dictionary production between languages of the Indian subcontinent is very poor both quantitatively and qualitatively. Yet, it is interesting to note that samples for different types of projects such as general dictionaries, vocabularies, glossaries of technical terms, dictionaries of usages, proverbs and common vocabularies may be found. This article will concentrate on bilingual dictionaries meant for intercommunication between recognized national languages and touch upon other types. Because of this emphasis on intercommunication, dictionaries involving classical languages, Sanskrit, Latin and Persian, will not be considered in this article. Furthermore, because of the great number of languages involved this will be a survey article dealing mainly with the quantitative aspect of the bilingual dictionaries. The general dictionaries involving Indian national recognized languages (2), non-national unrecognized major and minor languages (3), Indian-English/English-Indian (4), foreign and Indian languages (5), and special dictionaries (6) will be studied in different sections. Here, 'Indian' refers to the whole subcontinent while 'India' refers to the single sovereign state, natively called 'Bhārat'.

2. Indian-Indian: National/Recognized Languages

2.1. Bilingual Lexicographic Picture

The major bilingual lexicographic activity on the Indian subcontinent is between the 14 national languages of India excepting Sanskrit (cf. 1). As observed in (1) some of them, viz. Bengali (Bangladesh), Panjabi, Sindi and Urdu (Pakistan), are recognized in other sovereign states also. Therefore dictionaries of these languages deserve detailed treatment. Of the 14 national languages, Hindi has been declared the official language or language of central administration in addition to its being spoken by the largest number of people (as per the 1981 census, Padmanabha 1987, 3). This situation has placed it in a favourable position while all other languages are in an equal situation. As a result, we find that the number of bilingual dictionaries with Hindi as Source Language (SL) or Target Language (TL) are greater in number than those with other languages. Hindi is the only language which is found coupled as SL with the other 13 languages. They are Assamese (Das 1965), Bengali (Cakravarti 1958a), Gujarathi (Śāha 1950), Kannada (Sabhā 1959), Malayalam (Nair 1981), Marathi (Nene/Jośi 1967), Oriya (Pātra 1951), Panjabi (B. Vibhag 1970), Sindhi (Nideśālaya 1984c), Tamil (Sabhā 1962), Telugu (O. V. Sharma 1966), and Urdu (Nideśālaya 1984b). It occurs with Kashmiri only in the common vocabulary series (Handoo/Handoo 1975). While this is the bright side, the bleak side is presented by Assamese, Kashmiri, Malayalam, Oriya and Sindhi. There are no bilingual dictionaries with Assamese and Kashmiri as SL coupled with any other national language. Malayalam occurs as SL with Hindi (Abdulla 1971) only. Oriya occurs as SL with Hindi, but only as part of a monolingual cum multilingual dictionary (Praharaja 1931/1940) along with Bengali and English. Sindhi occurs as SL with Urdu only (Baloc/Khan 1959). From this bleak side we find improvement in the case of Kannada, Marathi and Panjabi which occur as SL with two languages each. Kannada occurs as SL with Hindi (Dakshinamurthi 1971) and Marathi (Katgade 1969). Marathi occurs with Hindi (Nene 1971) and Tamil (R. Jośi 1961a). Panjabi is coupled with Hindi (H. Vibhag 1963) and Urdu (Ibadullah 1966) as SL. In the case of Urdu, it is a special dictionary of *Ādigranth*, the holy book of the Sikhs. The next level of improvement is achieved by Bengali, Gujarathi and Tamil which occur as SL with three languages each. Bengali with Hindi (Cakravarti 1958b), Marathi (Āpate 1952) and Urdu (Choudury 1966); Gujarathi with Bengali (Thakkara 1924), Hindi (Vidyapiṭh 1961) and Marathi (Dharmadhikari 1967); and Tamil with Hindi (H. Sarma 1962), Marathi (R. Jośi 1961b) and Telugu (Śeṣācāryulu 1939). Telugu shows the next level of improvement occurring as SL with four languages, viz. Hindi (Ayācit 1970), Marathi (Kirane 1879), Tamil (Ayyar 1925), and Urdu (Rāvu 1960). Other than Hindi, Urdu is the eighth schedule language having the highest number of bilingual dictionaries, combining with eight languages as SL. They are Bengali (Rabbani 1952), Gujarathi (Nuruddin 1912), Hindi (Anjuman Taraqquii 1982), Kashmiri (Academy 1967/1983), Marathi (Joshi/Gorekar 1970), Sindhi (Baloc/Khan 1960), Tamil (Kṛishṇayyar 1898), and Telugu (Raju 1962). The accompanying illustration (Fig. 326.1) shows the bilingual lexicographic picture of India.

Source Language (SL)	\multicolumn{14}{c}{TARGET LANGUAGE (TL)}

Source Language (SL)	ASSAMESE	BENGALI	GUJARATHI	HINDI	KANNADA	KASHMIRI	MALAYALAM	MARATHI	ORIYA	PANJABI	SINDHI	TAMIL	TELUGU	URDU
ASSAMESE														
BENGALI				/				/						/
GUJARATHI	/			/				/						
HINDI	/	/	/		/	/	/	/	/	/	/	/	/	/
KANNADA				/				/						
KASHMIRI														
MALAYALAM				/										
MARATHI				/								/		
ORIYA				/										
PANJABI				/										/
SINDHI														/
TAMIL				/				/					/	
TELUGU				/				/				/		/
URDU		/	/	/				/			/	/	/	

Fig. 326.1: Bilingual dictionaries of the national languages of India

From the illustration it is clear that as TL also Hindi occurs with the highest number of 10 languages, followed by Marathi 7, Urdu 5, Tamil 4, Bengali and Telugu 3 each, Gujarathi, Kashimiri and Sindhi 2 each, and Assamese, Kannada, Oriya and Panjabi 1 each. This is the overall picture emerging from the bilingual dictionaries published so far. Of the mathematically possible 196 bilingual dictionaries only 43 have been compiled, resulting in a gap of 153 possible dictionaries. But the real state of affairs becomes more bleak when the fact of the non-availability of many dictionaries is considered which is due to the lack of new editions or reprints of earlier works. Here also, only dictionaries with Hindi as SL or TL are reprinted or have new editions brought out or new dictionaries compiled. In the case of other languages such activity is absent. New editions like Hindi-Marathi (S. Jośi 1987, 3rd ed.), Hindi-Telugu (O. V. Sharma 1966, 8th ed.); reprints like Urdu-Hindi (Anjuman Taraqquii 1982); and new compilations like Hindi-Assamese (Nideśālaya 1985b), Hindi-Malayalam (Nair 1981), Hindi-Tamil (Nideśālaya 1986) are some examples. But, in the case of other languages, Marathi-Tamil (R. Jośi 1961a),

Tamil-Marathi (R. Jośi 1961b), Tamil-Telugu (Śeṣācāryulu 1939), etc., such works are not available as these dictionaries have been neither reprinted nor reedited. In the other sovereign states of the Indian subcontinent bilingual lexicographic activity is even less than in India. Among them Pakistan shows relatively greater activity. Even before the partition of India and Pakistan some dictionaries were produced. Baluchi-Urdu (Hitturāma 1881), Urdu-Pushto (Baksh 1892) are some examples. Hitturāma 1881 is a textbook of Baluchi with a dictionary part of 30 pages. Dictionaries published after partition include Baluchi-Urdu (Marri 1970), Urdu-Pushto (Haq 1970), and Pushto-Urdu (Kākakhel 1960) dictionaries. In Nepal, a Newari-Nepali (Vaidya 1956) dictionary was brought out. Activities in Bangladesh after separation from Pakistan and those in Bhutan are not known.

2.2. Efforts to Fill the Gaps

The gaps in the bilingual lexicographic situation of the Indian languages have been felt and steps have been taken by governmental and government supported cultural organizations, though in a small way. The recent best efforts have been made by the Central Hindi Directorate (Kendrīya Hindī Nideśālaya) established by the Ministry of Education and Culture, Government of India. As per one of its brochures (Nideśālaya 1986a) it has taken up bilingual dictionary preparation of Hindi and 13 recognized languages other than Sanskrit both as SL and TL as part of its efforts to bring Indian languages closer together. Trilingual dictionaries with English as one of the target languages and common vocabulary series (6.2) are part of this effort. Dictionaries entitled practical dictionaries (Vyavahārika laghu kośa) which contain about 10,000 entries given in the scripts of both SL and TL presented in tabular form are being prepared (See Dictionary excerpt 326.1).

Up to 1986 (as per the brochure) 11 dictionaries with Hindi as SL and 3 with other Indian languages have been prepared. Of these, with Hindi as SL and Assamese (Nideśālaya 1985b), Gujarathi (1984a), Marathi (1985a), Sindhi (1984c), Tamil (1986) and Urdu (1984b) as TL have been published. Another attempt has been that of the Maharashtra Government Board of Literature and Culture which published Gujarathi-Marathi (Dharmadhikari 1967) and Kannada-Marathi (Katgade 1969) and Urdu-Marathi (Joshi/Gorekar 1970) dictionaries. A big attempt was the publication of a twelve volume Urdu-Kashmiri dictionary (Academy 1967/1983) by the Jammu and Kashmir Academy of Arts, Culture and Languages. Earlier than these, Dakshin Bharath Hindi Prachar Sabha, established first at Madras with later branches at other places, started publishing bilingual dictionaries with Hindi and four major Dravidian languages, Kannada, Malayalam, Tamil, and Telugu both as SL and TL. A Hindi-Telugu dictionary was published as early as 1922 (O. V. Sharma). The Sabha's latest publication is *Navīna Hindi Malayalam Śabda Kośa* (Nair 1981). Again, many official or semiofficial attempts like those of the Bengal Mass Education Society (Hindi-Bengali, Cakravarti 1958a), Gujarath Vidya Pith (Desai 1956 (1939), Vidyapiṭh 1961), Hindi Sahitya Sammelan, Alahabad (Prayag), (Dakshinamurthi 1971, Ayācit 1970), Maharashtra Rashtra Bhasha Sabha, Poona (Keḷusakara 1961, Nene/Jośi 1967), were concerned with Hindi and Indian languages only. An official attempt in Pakistan is the Bengali-Urdu dictionary (Choudury 1966) by the Central Board for Development of Bengali, Dacca.

हिंदी-सिंधी व्यावहारिक लघु कोश

हिंदी शब्द	व्या. क्रो.	सिंधी लिप्यंतरण	सिंधी पर्याय	नागरी लिप्यंतरण
अंक	पुं.	اَڃُ	الڪُل (عدد ، اَلمار) الڃايُ (ڄرجي) ۽ مارڪ (امتحان ۾)	अंगु (अदद, निशानु), अंकु (नाटक जो), मार्क (इम्तिहान में)

Dictionary excerpt 326.1: Dictionary entry (from: Nideśālaya 1984c, 1)

3. Indian-Indian: Non-National/Unrecognized Languages

Bilingual dictionaries involving non-eighth schedule languages of India and non-official or non-national languages of other countries come under two classes: (1) those involving non-national, non-literary major languages spoken by larger groups, some of which are considered to be dialects of national languages, and (2) minor languages including tribal languages. This group includes dictionaries and vocabularies. In this group also Hindi is found to be coupled with a greater number of languages than any of the other languages. Another interesting feature of this group of dictionaries is that either the SL or TL is always one of the national or official languages, and no work involving two non-national or tribal languages can be found to have been compiled. The dictionaries belonging to the first group include many with Hindi as TL and different SLs like Bhojpuri (Bahri 1981, Tripathi/Dube 1983), Braj-Hindi (Caturvedi 1985), Garwali (Varma 1982), Khariya (Prasad 1985), and Rajasthani (Sakaria 1977/1982). Others involving languages other than Hindi are Bhili-Gujarathi (Acharya 1965), Kachi-Gujarathi (Pandya 1885), Konkani-Marathi (Desaya 1980), Kodagu-Kannada (Muthanna 1983), and Tulu-Kannada (Rao 1980). Though compilation of bilingual dictionaries involving national and tribal languages started in the 19th century with Bengali-Garo (Ramkhe 1888), the interest was renewed only in the seventies and eighties of the 20th century. Numerous publications of dictionaries and word lists especially by Nagaland Bhasha Parishad, Kohima edited by Kumara were brought out. They include the following with Hindi as SL and Bhoti (Kumara 1978), Ho (1982), Kurukh (1981), Manipuri (1977), Khasi (1974b), Hmar (1975d), Kom (1975c), Mao (1974c), Maram (1975e), Mering (1974a), Tripuri (1973), Vaipei (1975b), and Zou (1975a) as TL. But, Singh (1980, 174) points out the shortcomings of these publications as "Tones are not marked, transcription is faulty, grammatical categories are not indicated properly. Many difficult and uncommon Hindi words are given". Dictionaries with Bhili (N. Jain 1962), Khariya (Kullū 1981), Kurukh (Prasada 1979), and Manipuri (N. Sharma 1963) as SL and Hindi as TL are also found. Other non-Hindi national tribal language dictionaries include Telugu-Savara (Ramamurthi 1914), Urdu-Siraiki/Siraiki-Urdu (Dilshad 1979/1981), and Nepali-Tulung (Rai 1944) dictionaries. It has to be noted that only a small number of minor and tribal languages have been covered.

4. Indian-English/English-Indian

English has a special place in the communicative activities of the Indian sub-continent. Introduced during the British colonial period, it continues to be used as an alternative official language and medium of education, and it is taught as a second language in schools and colleges. Because of this, the number of bilingual dictionaries published with English either as SL or TL is quite large. A perusal of the available bibliographies (Library 1964, 1, 2, 6, 7, 22—28 etc.; Navalani/Gidwani 1972, 27—34, 44—47, 240—328 etc.) will show this. The publication of Indian-English dictionaries still continues (Pushto-English, Rahīmī 1979; Panjabi-English, Singha/Singha/Kaura 1981; English-Malayalam, Sheppard/Warier 1984), and earlier works have been edited and reprinted repeatedly (English-Tamil, Lifco 1966, 8th edition; English-Gujarathi, Ojhā 1970, 25th edition). English as SL and TL is coupled with all the recognized languages of the Indian subcontinent except with Kashmiri, with which it occurs as SL in a single volume two part dictionary (Elmslie 1872), and many minor languages. Of these, Indian-English dictionaries are of two types. One type is mainly intended to describe the lexical system of the Indian languages. Kittel 1894 (Kannada-English), Grierson 1916/1932 (Kashmiri-English), Molesworth/Candy/Candy 1857 (Marathi-English), etc. belong to this class. Non-literary languages like Garo (Macdonald/Madhunatha 1910) and Konkani (Francisco 1916) are also covered in such dictionaries. The second major type of dictionary is intended for the learners of both Indian languages and English. This aim is precisely stated in some earlier dictionaries. Upjohn (1793) states in the sub-title of his Bengali English dictionary: "An extensive vocabulary, Bengalese and English very useful to teach the natives English and to assist beginners in learning the Bengali language". English-Indian language dictionaries too were compiled with similar purpose. Grant/Colebrooke's (1850) English Urdu Handbook with dictionary part has the subtitle

"Strangers Self-Interpreter and Guide, to Colloquial and General Intercourse with the Natives of India". Chapman (1907), another such guide book, has given Urdu in Roman script in its dictionary part. Many of the later English-Indian bilingual dictionaries were meant to help Indian learners of different levels and are of different sizes like school and students' dictionaries (English-Assamese, Calihā 1910; English-Hindi, Ramnarainlal 1957); pocket dictionaries (English-Tamil, Srīmakal 1955); and big comprehensive dictionaries (English-Hindi, Bahri 1969). A special feature of certain English/Indian bilingual dictionaries is to incorporate a monolingual component in the same work, as Dāsa 1962, Oriya-Oriya-English, Ajanta 1970, English-English-Hindi, etc. Another type are two part works like Elmslie 1872, Kashmiri-English and English-Kashmiri. Varata 1881/1887 gives English-English-Bengali and Bengali-Bengali-English in one volume presented in three columns. Special dictionaries with English as SL or TL will be discussed in (6).

5. Foreign-Indian/Indian-Foreign

Bilingual dictionaries involving foreign languages (other than English) and Indian languages began being produced in the 17th century. In fact, the first bilingual dictionary with an Indian language was Tamil-Portuguese (Proenca 1679). See Dictionary excerpt 326.2. The incipit of Proenca (p. 3102). There was much activity before the twentieth century and in the early part of this century, mostly by foreign scholars. There was a lull from the twenties to the forties of the 20th century. Activities started in the fifties again which still continue. Leaving out classical languages like Latin, Persian, Sanskrit, etc., 20 foreign languages and 13 Indian languages are involved. Of these, 5 foreign languages (Arabic, French, Japanese, Portuguese and Russian), and 6 Indian languages (Bengali, Gujarathi, Hindi, Malayalam, Tamil and Urdu) are coupled either as SL or TL with more than two languages. Many others occur only with one or two languages. Of the foreign languages, Arabic occurs as SL with Bengali (Al-Azhari 1970), Malayalam (Kunjamu 1967), Tamil (Nāvalar 1902) and Urdu (Keranavi 1981), and as TL with Urdu (Hafiz 1954). French occurs as SL with Bengali (Bondopadhia/Chottopadhia n.d.) and with Tamil (Lap 1891), and as TL with Hindi (Garcin de Tassy 1849), and Tamil (Lap 1926). Japanese occurs as SL with Marathi (Gāngala 1951) in a small vocabulary book, and as TL with Gujarathi (Seṭhna n.d.) and Nepali (Terne 1965). Portuguese is coupled as SL with Gujarathi (Narbheramo 1916), Konkani (Dalgado 1905) and Tamil (Henrique 1731), and as TL with Bengali (Assumpcam 1931), Konkani (Dalgado 1913), Marathi (Rājadikṣa 1879), and Tamil (Proenca 1679). Russian occurs as SL with Bengali (Litton 1966), Hindi (Beskrovanii 1957), Tamil (Andronov 1965), and Urdu (Klieuv 1959), and as TL with Bengali (Bikova 1957), Hindi (Dymshits 1958), Panjabi (Rabinovich/Serebriakov 1961), Pushto (Zudin 1950), Tamil (Patigorskii/Rudin 1950), and Urdu (Birjuley 1964). Indian languages which occur as SL or TL with other foreign languages in addition to those listed above include Bengali as SL with German (Bannerjea n.d.), Gujarathi with Swahili (Sachedina n.d.) as SL, and as TL with Modern Persian (Nayak 1972/1974). Hindi occurs as SL with Chinese (University 1960) and as TL with Greek (Hooper/Katavarilāla 1878). Malayalam occurs as TL with German (Chacko 1972) and Syriac (Palakosha 1898). Panjabi occurs as TL with Malay (Singh 1887). Tamil occurs as SL with Burmese (Chettiar 1905) and Sinhalese (Katukolinhe 1960), and as TL with Malay (Samy 1962). Urdu occurs as TL with Italian (Tagliabue 1898) and Turkish (Sabir 1968) also. As in the case of Indian-Indian dictionaries (2.1.), but for the recently published ones and a few reprints (e.g. Lap 1926 (1984), Tamil-French) many of the earlier works are not available.

6. Special Dictionaries

6.1. Special dictionaries of different types and serving different purposes have also been produced in addition to the majority of general dictionaries. They include dictionaries of pronunciation, aspects of grammar, usage, varieties of language, authors, technical terms, proverbs, etc. Tamil-French (Martinet 1890/1897) and English-Tamil/Tamil-English (Wells 1932) are pronunciation dictionaries. Dictionaries of verb phrases (N. Joshi 1896, English-Marathi), grammatical vocabulary (Rāmasvāmi 1863, English-Kannada), usages (Keḷusakara 1961, Hindi-Marathi), and idioms (Dikshitar 1900, Tamil-English) cover aspects of grammar and usage. A historical and comparative dictionary of Hindi and Oriya (Pradhan 1985) is also available. Language varieties like newspaper vocabulary (Satyaprakāśa 1943, English-Hindi) and Muslim Bengali (Olsen 1967, Bengali-English) are also covered. Other special dictionaries include text dictionaries like Ibadullah's (1966) Panjabi-Urdu dictionary of *Gurugranth,* the holy book of the Sikhs, Māstara/Māstara's (1957) Hindi-Gujarathi dictionary of *Srirāmacarita mānasa* of Tulasidas, and Hooper/Katavarilāla's (1878) Greek-Hindi vocabulary of the New Testament. There is also an author dictionary of terms used by Sri Aurobindo (Ācārya 1969, English-Hindi). Dictionaries of proverbs are found between Hindi-Marathi (Jaina/Jaina 1959), Malayalam-English (Nāyar 1948) and Tamil-English (Lazarus 1894). Glossaries of technical terms from English to Indian languages covering different subjects either as a single volume (Raghuvīra 1952, English-Hindi) or as multiple volumes (Institute 1969/1970, 1969/1971, English-Malayalam) are quite numerous (cf. Navalani/Gidwani 1972, 248, 250, 251 (Bengali); 262—68, 276—277 (Hindi); 306—309 (Tamil)) and are published by governmental and other agencies. There are also a few Indian-Indian bilingual glossaries like Kothārī (1948) (Hindi-Gujarathi), and R. Śarma (1942) (Urdu-Hindi). There is also a Hindi-Latin glossary (S. K. Jain 1967) of botanical terms.

6.2. Common vocabularies are a unique class of bilingual dictionaries brought out exploiting the fact that Indian languages share vocabularies of common origin that are similar in form and whose words have the same or different meanings. These were published by the Central Hindi Directorate, Delhi; the Central Institute of Hindi (Kendriya Hindi Sansthan), Agra; and the Central Institute of Indian Languages, Mysore, all of these attached to the Government of India, Ministry of Education; the Maharashtra Rashtra Bhasa Sabha, Poona; and the Nagaland Bhasha Parishad, Kohima. While the first four institutions brought out works involving Hindi and another national language of India, the last one published a series involving Hindi and different tribal languages. The purpose of these vocabularies has been different. It was either "to evolve a standard uniform technical vocabulary for Hindi and other Modern Indian languages ... an excellent starting point for Hindi to develop into an all India language" (Ministry 1957, Introduction), or "to meet the initial needs of people engaged in the teaching of Indian languages and production of material" (Pattanayak, in Kumari 1973, iii). The national languages of India coupled with Hindi are Assamese (Reddi 1976), Gujarathi (R. K. Jośi 1985), Kannada (Upadhyaya 1973), Kashmiri (Handoo/Handoo 1975), Malayalam (Kumari 1973), Marathi (Directorate 1959), Oriya (Reddi 1974), Panjabi (Directorate 1960), Tamil (Rajaram 1973), and Telugu (Sastry 1980). Nagaland Bhasha Parishad publications cover Hindi with a number of tribal languages in mimeographed form (e.g. Kumara 1980, Hindi-Boro). The different

Dictionary excerpt 326.2: From Proenca 1679, 1

1. अंक-म् (सं)—अंक—नाटक् का अंक ।
   —अंग—अंग, विभाग; शरीर के अवयव । -त्तितर्-षदस्य ।
2. अंकुलम् (सं)—अंगुल—इं'च ।

Dictionary excerpt 326.3: Two entries (from: Jagannathan 1974, 37)

| खाली adj | க'ாலி | காலி adj | காலि | empty |
| खीर nf | கீ'ர் | கீர் n | கீர் | a sweet drink prepared with milk |

Dictionary excerpt 326.4: Hindi-Tamil common vocabulary (from: Rajaram 1973, 3)

works by different agencies show differences both in their pattern of presentation and content. While the Ministry of Education (later Central Hindi Directorate 1959, 5) and the Central Institute of Hindi, Agra (Jagannathan 1974, 37, see Dictionary excerpt 326.3) series use Devanagari script fully, the Central Institute of Indian Languages, Mysore series use the scripts of both the languages with transliterations in the other language scripts using diacritics wherever necessary (Rajaram 1973, 3, see Dictionary excerpt 326.4).

7. Selected Bibliography

7.1. Dictionaries

Abdulla 1971 = A. Abdulla: Sarala Malayalam koś. Kunnamkulam 1971 [322 p.].

Academy 1967/1983 = Jammu Kashmir Academy [...]: Urdū Kashmīrī farhang. 12 vols. Srinagar 1967/1983.

Ācārya 1969 = Keśavadesa Ācārya: Angreji-Hindi Śri Aravinda Śabda kośa [...]. Pondicherry 1969 [122 p.].

Acharya 1965 = Shantibhai Purusottam Acharya: Bhīli-Gujarāti śabdāvali. Ahmed-abad 1965.

Ajanta 1970 = Ajanta Comprehensive English-English- Hindi dictionary. Delhi 1970.

Al-Azhari 1970 = Muhammad Alauddin Al-Azhari: Arabī-Bamlā abhidhāna. Dacca 1970.

Andronov 1965 = M. S. Andronov: Russko-tamil'skij slovar. Moskow 1965 [1175 p.].

Anjuman Taraqquii 1982 = Anjuman Taraqquii: Urdu (Hind) Hindi Dictionary. New Delhi 1982 [738 p.; 1st ed. Aligarh 1955].

Āpate 1952 = Vasudev Govinda Āpate: Bangāli Marāṭhī koṣa. Poona 1952 [248 p.].

Assumpcam 1931 = Mancel da Assumpcam (ed. by S. K. Chatterji/P. Sen): Bengali grammar [...] Bengali-Portuguese vocabulary. Calcutta 1931 [254 p.].

Ayācit 1970 = Hanumacchāstri Ayācit: Telugu-Hindi Śabdakoś. Prayag 1970 [314 p.].

Ayyar 1925 = V. S. Kṛṣṇaswami Ayyar: Vidya mālika. Madras 1925 [61 p.].

Bahri 1969 = Hardev Bahri: Bṛhat Angreji-Hindi kośa. 2 vols. Varanasi 1969 [1234, 1235—2196 p.].

Bahri 1981 = Hardev Bahri: Bhojpuri śabda sampada: Bhojpuri [...] kośa. Ilahabad 1981 [238 p.].

Baksh 1892 = Karim Baksh: Kalid-e-Zudāni-Pasthu. Lahore 1892 [32 p.].

Baloc/Khan 1959 = Nabi Bakhsh Khan Baloc/Ghulam Mustafa Khan: Sindi-Urdu lughat. Hyderabad 1959 [866 p.].

Baloc/Khan 1960 = Nabi Bakhsh Khan Baloc/Ghulam Mustafa Khan: Urdu-Sindhi lughat. Hyderabad 1960 [591 p.].

Bannerjea n.d. = Biren Bannerjea: [...] Deutschen und Deutsch-Bengalischen Glossar. Leipzig s. d.

Beskrovanii 1957 = Vasili Matveevich Beskrovanii: [...] Rūsi-Hindi śabdokośa. Moscow 1957 [1376 p.].

Bikova 1957 = E. M. Bikova: Bengalsko Russkii Slovar [...]. Moskva 1957 [908 p.].

Birjuley 1964 = S. V. Birjuley: Urdu Russkij Slovar. Moscow 1964 [890 p.].

Bondopadhia/Chottopadhia = Romanatte Bondopadhia/Chochi Bouchone Chottopadhia: Dictionnaire français-bengali [...]. Chandernagor s. d. [72 p.].

Cakravarti 1958a = Gopālacandra Cakravarti: Hindi Bangla Abidhana. Calcutta 1958 [350, 10 p. 1st ed. 1950].

Cakravarti 1958b = Gopālacandra Cakravarti: Vangālā-Hindi śabdakoṣa. Calcutta 1958 [383 p.].

Calihā 1910 = Mākhanalāla Calihā: Students' English-Assamese Dictionary. Dibrugarh 1910 [474 p.].

Caturvedi 1985 = Dvāraka Prasāda Śarma Caturvedi: Sahityike Brajbhāṣā kośa (vol. 1). Lucknow 1985.

Chacko 1972 = V. C. Chacko: Deutsch-Malayalam Wörterbuch. Trivandrum 1972 [812 p.].

Chapman 1907 = Francis Robert Henry Chapman: English-Hindustani Pocket Vocabulary. London 1907 [126 p.].

Chettiar 1905 = K. Pullappa Chettiar: Tamiz Burma akarāti. Rangoon 1905 [56 p.].
Choudury 1966 = A. M. Faiz Ahmad Choudury: Bāngla Urdu Abhidāna. Dacca 1966.
Dakshinamurthi 1971 = N. S. Dakshinamurthi: Kannaḍ-Hindi Śabdakoś. Alahabad 1971 [432 p.].
Dalgado 1905 = Sebastio Rodolpho Dalgado: Diccionario Portugeez Konkani. Lisbon 1905 [Reprint: New Delhi 1986].
Dalgado 1913 = Sebastio Rodolpho Dalgado: Concani-Portugese Dictionary. Bombay 1913 [562 p.].
Das 1965 = Soneswar Das: Adarsh Hindi Assamia Sabdakosh. Kamrup 1965 [865 p.].
Dāsa 1962 = Sridhara Dāsa: Naba abhidhna. Kaṭaka 1962 [971 p.].
Desai 1956 = Maganbhāi Prabhudāsa Desai: Rāṣṭra bhāṣano Gujarāti kośa. 3rd ed. Ahmedabad 1956 [573 p.; 1st ed. 1939, 367 p.].
Desaya 1980 = Sripāda Raghunātha Desaya: Konkaṇi Śabdakośa. Pedanehoya 1980 [2 vols.].
Dharmadhikari 1967 = S. Dharmadhikari: Gujarati-Marathi Shabd Kosh. Bombay 1967 [436 p.].
Dikshitar 1900 = A. Ramasami Dikshitar: Tamil Idioms [. . .]. Madras 1900.
Dilshad 1979/1981 = Dilshad Kalānavī: Pākistān [. . .] sirāēki lughat-i Dilshā diyyah. Bhāvalpur 1979/1981 [2 vols.].
Directorate 1959 = Central Hindi Directorate: Hindi words common to other Indian Languages: Hindi-Marathi. New Delhi 1959 [158 p.].
Directorate 1960 = Central Hindi Directorate: Hindi words Common to Other Indian Languages: Hindi-Panjabi. New Delhi 1960 [71 p.].
Dymshits 1958 = Z. M. Dymshits: Saṁkṣīpta Hindi Rūsi Śabdakośa. Moscow 1958 [1080 p.].
Elmslie 1872 = William Jackson Elmslie: Vocabulary [. . .] Kashmiri-English and English-Kashmiri. London 1872 [264 p.].
Francisco 1916 = Aeixo Caetano/Jose Francisco: Dictionary of Concani into English. Bombay 1916 [114 p.].
Gāngala 1951 = D. D. Gāngala: Japānī Marāṭhi Śabda sangraha. Poona 1951 [98 p.].
Garcin de Tassy 1849 = J. H. Garcin de Tassy: Hindi Hindouimuntakhalat. Paris 1849 [144 p.].
Grant/Colebrooke 1850 = H. Grant/E. Colebrooke: Anglo-Hindoostani handbook [. . .]. Calcutta 1850 [934 p.].
Grierson 1916/1932 = G. A. Grierson: Dictionary of Kashmiri Language [. . .]. Calcutta 1916/1932 [4 vols.].
Hafiz 1954 = Abul Fadal Abdul Hafiz: Urdu-Arabi dictionary. Lucknow 1954 [480 p.].
Handoo/Handoo 1975 = Jawaharlal Handoo/Lalitha Handoo: Hindi-Kashmiri Common Vocabulary. Mysore 1975 [292 p.].
Haq 1970 = Anvarul Haq: Urdu Pashto lughat. Lahore (vol. 1) 1970.

Henrique 1731 = Henriquex Henrique: [. . .] Vocabulario em Portugeez e malabar. Tranquebar 1731.
Hitturāma 1881 = Hitturāma: Hiṣṣah Avval: Biluchi-Nāmah [. . .]. Lahore 1881 [147 p.].
Hooper/Katavarilāla 1878 = William Hooper/Katavarilāla: Naye Niyama Keliye Yavanabhāṣa kā Kośa Hindi mēm. Alahabad 1878 [435 p.].
Ibadullah 1966 = Ibadullah: Guru Granth aur Urdu. Lahore 1966 [209 p.].
Institute 1969/1970 = Kerala Bhasha Institute: Mānavika Śabdāvali (Humanities Glossary). Trivandrum (vol. 1) 1969, (vol. 2) 1970 [332, 458 p.].
Institute 1969/1971 = Kerala Bhasha Institute: Vijñāna Śabdāvali (Science Glossary). Trivandrum (vol. 1) 1969, (vol. 2) 1971 [657, 482 p.].
Jagannathan 1974 = V. R. Jagannathan: Hindi aur Tamil kī samāna srotīya bhinnārthī śabdāvali. 2nd ed. Agra 1974 [112 p.].
N. Jain 1962 = Nemichand Jain: Bhili-Hindi Kosh. Indore 1962 [120 p.].
S. K. Jain 1967 = S. K. Jain: Vanaspathi Kośa. Delhi 1967 [100 p.].
Jaina/Jaina 1959 = S. K. Jaina/Lilavati Jaina: Muhāvarā aura lokoktiyām. Sholapur 1959 [366 p.].
N. Joshi 1896 = Narayan Ballal Nam Joshi: English Verb phrases [. . .] Marathi equivalents. Poona 1896 [84 p.].
Joshi/Gorekar 1970 = Sripad Joshi/N. S. Gorekar: Urdu-Marathi dictionary. Bombay 1970.
R. Jośi 1961a = Ramabhai Jośi: Marāṭhi-Tamila laghu Śabdakośa. Madras 1961 [124 p.].
R. Jośi 1961b = Ramabhai Jośi: Tamila laghu Sabdakośa [. . .]. Poona 1961.
R. K. Jośi 1985 = Rajanīkānta Jośi: Hindī-Gujarāti kī Samānasrotīya Śabdāvali. Ahmadabad 1985 [106 p.].
S. Jośi 1987 = Sripada Jośi: Abhinava Śabdakośa. 3rd ed. Poona 1987 [673 p.; 1st ed. 1958, 299 p.].
Kākakhel 1960 = Zafar Kākakhel: Zafarul Lughāt. Pikhhāvar 1960 [1012 p.].
Katgade 1969 = Pundalikaji Katgade: Kannada Marāṭhi Śabda kośa. Bombay 1969 [644 p.].
Katukolinhe 1960 = Francis Katukolinhe: Gunasena Tamil-Sinhalese Dictionary. Colombo 1960 [1335 p.].
Kelusakara 1961 = B. V. Keḷusakara: Hindi Śabda prayoga kośa. Poona 1961 [184 p.].
Keranāvi 1981 = Vahiduzzamān Keranāvi: [. . .] Arabi-Urdu dictionary. Dihli 1981 [656 p.].
Kirane 1879 = Trimbaka Govinda Kirane: Upayukta Śabdasāra Sangraha. Bombay (vol. 1) 1879.
Kittel 1894 = Ferdinand Kittel: A Kannada English Dictionary. Mangalore 1894 [1752 p.].
Klieuv 1959 = B. I. Klieuv: Russko-Urdu Slovar. Moskva 1959 [1135 p.].

Kothārī 1948 = Viṭṭhaladāsa Magana lāla Kothārī: Artha Śāstra ki Paribhāṣā. Ahmedabad 1948 [65 p.].

Kriṣhṇayyar 1898 = N. S. Gopala Kriṣhṇayyar: Hindustani bhāṣa mañjari. Madurai 1898 [169 p.].

Kullū 1981 = Paulusa Kullū: Khaṛiya Vyākaraṇa evam Saṅkshīpta Śabda kośa. Ranci 1981 [160 p.].

Kumara 1973 = Braj Bihari Kumara: Hindi-Tripuri kośa. Kohima 1973.

Kumara 1974a = Braj Bihari Kumara: Hindi-Mering koś. Kohima 1974.

Kumara 1974b = Braj Bihari Kumara: Hindi-Khasi kośa. Kohima 1974.

Kumara 1974c = Braj Bihari Kumara: Hindi-Mao koś. Kohima 1974.

Kumara 1975a = Braj Bihari Kumara: Hindi-Zou kośa. Kohima 1975.

Kumara 1975b = Braj Bihari Kumara: Hindi-Vaipei kośa. Kohima 1975.

Kumara 1975c = Braj Bihari Kumara: Hindi-Kom koś. Kohima 1975.

Kumara 1975d = Braj Bihari Kumara: Hindi-Hmar kośa. Kohima 1975.

Kumara 1975e = Braj Bihari Kumara: Hindi-Maram koś. Kohima 1975.

Kumara 1977 = Braj Bihari Kumara: Hindi-Manipuri kośa. Kohima 1977 [294 p.].

Kumara 1978 = Braj Bihari Kumara: Hindi-Bhoti kośa. Kohima 1978 [228 p.].

Kumara 1980 = Braj Bihari Kumara: Common vocabulary: Hindi-Boro & Boro-Hindi. Kohima 1980 [52 p.].

Kumara 1981 = Braj Bihari Kumara: Kuṛukha kośa [...] Hindi. Kohima 1981 [378 p.].

Kumara 1982 = Braj Bihari Kumara: Hindi-Ho kośa. Kohima 1982 [395 p.].

Kumari 1973 = B. Syamala Kumari: Hindi-Malayalam Common Vocabulary. Mysore 1973 [80 p.].

Kunjamu 1967 = P. B. Kunjamu: Āl Faraidh Arabi-Malayalam nighantu. Edappilly 1967 [740 p.].

Lap 1891 = P. A. Lap: Vocabulaire français-tamoul. Pondicherry 1891 [812 p.].

Lap 1926 = M. A. Lap: Petit Vocabulaire Tamoul-Français [...]. 2nd ed. Pondicherry 1926 [286 p.; 1st ed. 1886 (Reprint New Delhi 1984)].

Lazarus 1894 = John Lazarus: Dictionary of Tamil Proverbs [...]. Madras 1894.

Lifco 1966 = Great Lifco Dictionary. English-English-Tamil. 8th ed. Madras 1966 [624 p., 1st ed. 1952].

Litton 1966 = Džek Litton: Russko Bengalesky Slovar. Moskva 1966 [759 p.].

Macdonald/Madhunatha 1910 = A. Macdonald/Momin Madhunatha: Garo-English Dictionary. Shillong 1910 [27 p.].

Marri 1970 = Mitthukhan Marri: Balūci-Urdu lughat. Quetta 1970 [322 p.].

Martinet 1890/1897 = Ernest Martinet: Dictionnaire de prononciation Tamoule Figure en Français. 2 vols. Pondicherry 1890/1897.

Māstara/Māstara 1957 = Phūlābhai Māstara/Dāhyābhai Māstara: Srirāmacarita mānasa kośa. 2nd ed. Ahmedabad 1957 [94 p.; 1st ed. 1933].

Ministry 1957 = Ministry of Education, Govt. of India: Hindi words common to other Indian Languages: Hindi-Tamil. New Delhi 1957.

Molesworth/Candy/Candy 1857 = J. T. Molesworth/George Candy/Thomas Candy: Dictionary of Marathi and English. 2nd ed. Bombay 1857 [921 p.; 1st ed. 1831].

Muthanna 1983 = I. M. Muthanna: Kodava Kannada Nighaṇṭu. Bangalore 1983 [188 p.].

Nair 1981 = P. K. Kesavan Nair: Navīna Hindi Malayalam Śabda kośa. Ernakulam-Cochin 1981 [784, 208 p.].

Narbheramo 1916 = M. Narbheramo: Portugues-Guzerate e vice-versa. Diu 1916 [162 p.].

Nāvalar 1902 = V. Gulām Qādir Nāvalar: Araputtamil akarāti. 4 vols. Karaikal 1902.

Nayak 1972/1974 = Choṭubai Ranchodji Nayak: Pārsi Sabdon Sārtha vyutpatti koś. Ahmedabad (vol. 1) 1972, (vol. 2) 1974 [357, 284 p.].

Nāyar 1948 = Karuṇākaran Nāyar: Malayala English pazañ sollukal. Kottayam 1948 [37 p.].

Nene 1971 = Gopal Paraśurām Nene: Bṛhat Marāṭhi Śabda koś. Poona 1971 [729 p.].

Nene/Jośi 1967 = Gopal Paraśurām Nene/Sripad Jośi: Hindī Marāṭhi Śabda kośa. 4th ed. Poona 1967 [597 p.; 1st ed. 1939].

Nideśālaya 1984a = Kendrīya Hindi Nideśalaya: Hindi Gujarathi Vyavahārika laghu koś. New Delhi 1984 [386 p.].

Nideśālaya 1984b = Kendrīya Hindi Nideśalaya: Hindi-Urdu Vyayahārika laghu koś. New Delhi 1984 [384 p.].

Nideśālaya 1984c = Kendrīya Hindi Nideśalaya: Hindi-Sindhi Vyavahārika laghu koś. New Delhi 1984 [554 p.].

Nideśālaya 1985a = Kendrīya Hindi Nideśalaya: Hindi Marāṭhi Vyavahārika laghu koś. New Delhi 1985 [384 p.].

Nideśālaya 1985b = Kendrīya Hindi Nideśalaya: Hindī-Asāmiyā Vyavahārika laghu koś. New Delhi 1985 [435 p.].

Nideśālaya 1986 = Kendrīya Hindi Nideśalaya: Hindi-Tamil Vyavahārika laghu koś. New Delhi 1986 [396 p.].

Nuruddin 1912 = Nijhamuddin Nuruddin: Urdu miśra Gujarāti koś. 1912 [215 p.].

Ohjā 1970 = Sāntilālā Sārābhāi Ohjā: Modern [...] English into English and Gujarati and Gujarati into English and Gujarati. Bombay 1970 [1015 p.].

Olsen 1967 = Viggo Bi Olsen: Muslim Bāṃlā-Imreji Abidhāna [...]. Chittagong 1967 [216 p.].

Palakosha 1898 = Abraham Palakosha: Dictionary Syriac-Malayalam. Mannanam 1898 [192 p.].

Pandya 1885 = Pandya: Kachhi-Gujarati Lexicon.

Pjatigorskii/Rudin 1950 = A. M. Pjatigorskii/S. G. Rudin: Tamilsko Russkii Slovar. Moskva 1950 [1384 p.].

Pātra 1951 = Nihāra Pātra: Hindī Odiyā śabda kośa. Cuttack 1951 [394 p.].

Pradhan 1985 = Appana Pradhan: Hindi and Oriya Vocabulary, an Historical and Comparative Linguistic Study. Bhubaneshwar 1985.

Praharaja 1931/1940 = Gopala Chandra Praharaja: Pūrṇachandra Odiya bhāṣā koś. Cuttack 1931/1940 [7 vols.].

Prasad 1985 = Svarṇalata Prasad: Khariya vārtālāpa nirdeśika. Ranchi 1985 [119, 93, 33 p.].

Prasada 1979 = Svarṇalata Prasada: Kuṛukh-Hindi Sabda kośa. Ranchi 1979 [428 p.].

Proenca 1679 = Antam De Proenca: Vocabulario Tamulico com a significacam Portugueza. Ambalakatta 1679.

Rabbani 1952 = Siraj Rabbani: Farhang-i-Rabbani. Calcutta 1952 [671 p.].

Rabinovich/Serebriakov 1961 = I. S. Rabinovich/ I. D. Serebriakov: Panjabsko-Russkii Slovar. Moscow 1961 [1039 p.].

Raghuvīra 1952 = Raghuvīra: Consolidated Great English Indian [...] technical terms. 3rd ed. Nagpur 1952 [1191 p.; 1st ed. 1950].

Rahīmī 1979 = Muhammad Hāshim Rahīmī: Puṣhto Inglīsi qāmus. Kābul 1979 [591 p.].

Rai 1944 = Agam Simga Davasā Rai: Asalacchi Śiksha. Darjeeling 1944.

Rājadikṣa 1879 = Sūryāji Ānanda Rājadikṣa: Maharaṣṭra Portuguese kośa. Goa 1879 [573 p.].

Rajaram 1973 = S. Rajaram: Hindi-Tamil common vocabulary. Mysore 1973 [70 p.].

Raju 1962 = B. Rama Raju: Urdu-Telugu Nighaṇṭuvu. Hyderabad 1962 [507 p.].

Ramamurthi 1914 = G. V. Ramamurthi: Telugu-Savara Dictionary. Madras 1914 [108 p.].

Rāmasvāmi 1863 = M. Rāmasvāmi: Grammatical Vocabulary in English and Kanarese [...]. 3rd ed. Bangalore 1863 [195 p.].

Ramkhe 1888 = Rev. M. Ramkhe: Vāṅgālā-Gāro abhidhān. Tura 1888 [888 p.].

Ramnarainlal 1957 = Ramnarainlal: Students' Practical dictionary [...]. 18th ed. Alahabad 1957 [1956 p.; 1st ed. 1901].

Rao 1980 = Panambur Sridhara Rao: Tuḷu terile: Tuḷu-teḷiyin. Mangalore 1980 [30 p.].

Rāvu 1960 = K. Gopalakṛṣṇa Rāvu: Telugu-Urdu Nighaṇṭuvu. Hyderabad 1960 [259 p.].

Reddi 1974 = Vijayaraghava Reddi: Samānasrota aur bhinna vartanī kī śabdāvali [...] Odiya Hindi aur Hindi Odiya. Agra 1974 [104 p.].

Reddi 1976 = Vijayaraghava Reddi: Samanasrota aur bhinna vartanī kī sabdavali Asāmiyā-Hindī aur Hindī-Asamiyā. Agra 1976 [162 p.].

Sabhā 1959 = Dakṣiṇa Bhārata Hindī Pracāra Sabhā: Hindi Kannada kośa. Madras 1959 [576, 6 p.; 1st ed. 1950].

Sabhā 1962 = Dakṣiṇa Bhārata Hindī Pracāra Sabhā: Hindi Tamila kośa. 7th ed. Madras 1962 [595 p.].

Sabir 1968 = Muhammad Sabir: Turkī-Urdū lughat. Karachi 1968.

Sachedina n.d. = A. J. Sachedina: Gujarathi Swahili Dictionary.

Śāha 1950 = Rasikalāla Śāha: Rāṣṭrabhāṣa kośa. Ahmedabad 1950 [1280 p.].

Sakaria 1977/1982 = Badri Prasad Sakaria: Rājasthani Hindi Śabda kośa. Jayapura (vol. 1) 1977, (vol. 2) 1982.

Samy 1962 = M. A. Samy: A Concise dictionary of Malay-Tamil. Madras 1962.

H. Sarma 1962 = Harihara Sarma: Tamil Hindi koś [...]. Madras 1962 [219 p.; 1st ed. 1926].

R. Śarma 1942 = Rāmanātha Śarma: Vyāvahārika Śabda kośa. Gwalior 1942 [45 p.].

Sastry 1980 = J. Venkateswara Sastry: Hindi-Telugu Common Vocabulary. Mysore 1980 [129 p.].

Satyaprakāśa 1943 = Satyaprakāśa: Sāmacārapatra Śabda-kośa. Alahabad 1943 [106 p.].

Śeṣācāryulu 1939 = Kandāḍi Śeṣācāryulu: Sampradaya akarādi anu Draviādāndhra nighaṇṭuvu. Grantur 1939 [488 p.].

Sethna = Ratenji Pharāmji Sethna: Japanese bhāṣānosōmiō. Bombay s.d. [96 p.].

N. Sharma 1963 = L. K. Narayana Sharma: Manipuri Hindi Shabda kosh [797 p.].

O. V. Sharma 1966 = Origanti Venkateswara Sharma: Hindī Telugu kośa. 8th ed. Madras 1966 [522, 23 p.; 1st ed. 1922].

Sheppard/Warier 1984 = C. A. Sheppard/M. I. Warier: Assissi Concise English-English-Malayalam Dictionary. 4th ed. Changanacherry 1984 [674 p.].

Singh 1887 = Sundar Singh: Singapore da tāpu ki boli. Amritsar 1887 [64 p.].

Singha/Singha/Kaura 1981 = Guracarana Singha/Sarana Singha/Ravindra Kaura: Panjabi-Angrezi Shabda Kosha. Amritsar 1981 [612 p.].

Srīmakal 1955 = Srīmakal: Pocket dictionary. Madras 1955 [512 p.].

Tagliabue 1898 = Camillo Tagliabue: Scolastica vol. 2. Manuele e glossario [...] Urdu. Napoli. Roma 1898 [288 p.].

Terne 1965 = Nakamun Terne: Suruko Nepali Japani kos. Nan 1965.

Thakkara 1924 = Devaji Govardhanadasa Thakkara: Gujarathi Bengali Sikṣaka ane sabdakośa. Bombay 1924 [118 p.].

Tripathi/Dube 1983 = Sarvendrapati Tripathi/Braj Kiśore Dube: Bhojpuri Sabdasagara. Patna 1983.

University 1960 = Peking University: Hindi-Chīni Śabda kośa. Peking 1960.

Upadhyaya 1973 = Sushila P. Upadhyaya: Hindi-Kannada Common Vocabulary. Mysore 1973 [134 p.].

Upjohn 1793 = A. Upjohn: Iṅgarāji Vaṅgāli vokebilari. Calcutta 1793 [455 p.].

Vaidya 1956 = Panna Prasad Jośi Vaidya: Saṁkṣīpta Nepal Bhāṣa Śabdakośa. Katmandu 1956.

Varata 1881/1887 = Trailokyanātha Varata: Pronouncing, etymological and pictorial dictionary of the English and of the Bengali language [...]. Calcutta 1881/1887.

Varma 1982 = Jayalāla Varma: Garwāli Bhāshā kā śabdakosha. Koṭadvan-Garhvala 1982 [70, 160 p.].

B. Vibhag 1970 = Basha Vibhag: Hindī-Panjabi Kosha. Patiala 1970 [1168 p.].

H. Vibhag 1963 = Hindi Vibhag: Panjabi-Hindi koś. Patiala 1963 [360 p.].

Vidyapiṭh 1961 = Gujarat Vidyapiṭh: Gujarathi Hindi kośa. Ahmedabad 1961 [552 p.].

Wells 1932 = W. G. B. Wells: Tamil English, English Tamil. A Concise New Style pronouncing [...]. Colombo 1932.

Zudin 1950 = P. B. Zudin: Kratkii Afgansko Russkii Slovar'. Moskva 1950.

7.2. Other Publications

Chatterji 1963 = S. K. Chatterji: Languages and Literatures of Modern India. Calcutta 1963.

James 1991 = Gregory James: Tamil Lexicography. Tübingen 1991 (Lexicographica Series Maior 40).

Library 1964 = National Library: A Bibliography of Dictionaries and Encyclopaedias in Indian Languages. Calcutta 1964.

Navalani/Gidwani 1972 = K. Navalani/N. N. Gidwani: Dictionaries in Indian Languages [...]. Jaipur 1972.

Nideśālaya 1986a = K. H. Nideśālaya: Kośa evam vārtālāpa-pustikā yojanā. New Delhi 1986.

Padmanabha 1987 = P. Padmanabha: Census of India 1981, Series I. Households and Household population by Language [...]. New Delhi 1987.

Pattanayak 1973a = D. P. Pattanayak: Preface. In: Central Institute of Indian Languages: Distribution of Languages in India [...]. Mysore 1973, III—X.

Pattanayak 1973b = Debi Prasanna Pattanayak: Foreword. In: Syamala Kumari: Hindi-Malayalam Common Vocabulary. Mysore 1973, I—III.

Singh 1980 = R. A. Singh: Dictionaries of Tribal Languages. In: Symposium on Perspectives in Lexicography (mimeo). Trivandrum 1980, 173—176.

*K. Balasubramanian, Telugu University,
Hyderabad (India)*

327. Bilingual Lexicography With Chinese

1. Introduction
2. Chinese as Source Language
3. Chinese as Target Language
4. Arrangement
5. Summary
6. Selected Bibliography

1. Introduction

For centuries, foreigners have been fascinated by things Chinese. Long before Marco Polo brought back to Europe stories of the wonders of China, China's neighbors had eagerly sought to engage her in diplomatic, commercial and economic relations. Until the mid-nineteenth century China conducted her foreign relations with all non-Chinese through a tribute system. Under this system, foreign countries and peoples agreed to enter into vassal-like relationships with China in order to tap her rich material and cultural resources. In the course of these relations knowledge of each other's language played an important role. For its part, China established language academies and translation bureaus to deal with the language problems inherent in foreign relations. At the same time, the foreign countries quickly became aware of the importance and advantages of learning Chinese. The tribute system began to crumble after China's defeat in the Opium War. The war ended with the signing of the Treaty of Nanjing (Nanking) in 1842, which marked the beginning of the so-called "unequal treaty system". In these treaties the foreign powers were given wide-ranging rights in China including the right to own property and travel into the hinterland. As the nature of diplomatic relations changed, foreign language learning became even more important. On the one hand, China, after suffering humiliating defeats at the hands of the foreigners, realized the necessity of learning about Western science and technology and about the conduct of relations in the new international community in order to protect her sovereign rights. On the other hand, the diplomats, merchants and missionaries who rushed to China were faced with the formidable task of communicating in Chinese. The renewed activity in China resulted in a proliferation of Chinese bilingual dictionaries and glossaries from the mid-nineteenth century to the 1920s. Another flurry of lexicographic activity occurred during World War II owing to the strategic importance of China. The current decade has witnessed an upsurge in bilingual lexicography with Chinese. The number of excellent dictionaries and glossaries attests to the healthy state of bilingual lexicography with Chinese.

2. Chinese as Source Language

The rich nature of Chinese lexicography notwithstanding (cf. Art. 263), it was not until 1978 and the publication of the Xiandai Hanyu Cidian (现代汉语词典, A Dictionary of Contemporary Chinese) (Xian Han 1978) that bilingual lexicographers had a reliable monolingual Chinese dictionary on which to base their work. Before 1978 Chinese monolingual dictionaries were in the European "hard word" tradition and often lacked basic information about an entry such as part of speech, pronunciation and level of usage. Despite the lack of monolingual works to serve as guides to entry selection, definitions and related lexicographic problems, there are many impressive bilingual dictionaries with Chinese as the source language. Until recently, the more noteworthy dictionaries have been compiled by non-Chinese lexicographers with Japanese, Russian, English and French as the target language.

2.1. Japanese lexicographers have produced some of the finest Chinese bilingual dictionaries. The most notable is Morohashi Tetsuji (诸桥辙次, 1883—1982) and his Dai Kan-Wa Jiten (大汉和辞典, An Encyclopedic Chinese-Japanese Dictionary) (Morohashi 1955). Dai Kan Wa Jiten is not only the most comprehensive bilingual dictionary of Chinese, but also was the most complete dictionary of the Chinese language until the publication of Zhongwen Da Cidian (中文大辞典, The Encyclopedic Dictionary of the Chinese Language) (Zhongwen 1962) in 1962 in the Republic of China (on the island of Taiwan or Formosa, hereafter ROC) and Hanyu Da Cidian (, An Encyclopedic Dictionary of the Chinese Language) (Han Da 1986) in 1986 in the People's Republic of China ("Mainland China", hereafter PRC). Japanese lexicographers have also compiled excellent medium-sized dictionaries. Of particular importance is Aichi University's Chu-Nichi Daijiten (中日大辞典, A Comprehensive Chinese-Japanese Dictionary) (Aichi 1968).

2.2. Russian scholars have been active in Chinese bilingual lexicography for more than a century. Early Russian lexicographers such as V. P. Vasiliev helped lay the foundation for Sino-Soviet studies with their dictionaries and Cyrillic transcription schemes for Chinese. In modern times, the center for Chinese-Russian bilingual lexicography has been the Far East Institute of the Academy of Sciences of the Soviet Union. The dictionaries published there under the editorship of I. M. Oshanin are among the most reliable Chinese bilingual dictionaries. Oshanin's first major dictionary *Kitaisko-Russkii Slovar* (Oshanin 1955) was published in 1955 and was one of the standard Chinese reference works for over twenty years. In 1983, after more than four decades of work, a team of Russian lexicographers headed by Oshanin published *Bolshoi Kitaisko-Russkii Slovar* (Oshanin 1983). The dictionary contains 250,000 entries and will likely remain the major Chinese-Russian dictionary for many years. In the PRC, Russian is, for obvious reasons, an important foreign language, so much so that the first bilingual dictionary based on Xiandai Hanyu Cidian was Han-E Cidian (汉俄词典, A Chinese-Russian Dictionary) (SIFL 1977).

2.3. Even though British and American lexicographers have yet to publish works to rival those of their Japanese or Russian counterparts, they have produced a number of good Chinese bilingual dictionaries. One of the earliest large-sized Chinese bilingual dictionaries in a Western language was Robert Morrison's (1782—1834) three-part Dictionary of the Chinese Language (Morrison 1815) published between 1815 and 1822. In the twentieth century, Herbert Giles (1845—1935) and Robert Mathews (1877—1970) are two names that have become synonymous with Chinese bilingual lexicography. Giles, one of the most respected Sinologists of his day, is best known for the Wade-Giles romanization system (cf. 4.2.), a revision of the system developed by Thomas Wade (1818—1895), and for A Chinese-English Dictionary (Giles 1892). The dictionary is still a valuable reference for those reading classical Chinese texts. Robert Mathews' *A Chinese-English Dictionary* (Mathews 1931) appeared in 1931 and was the main Chinese-English dictionary until the 1970s. In the 1970s, native Chinese scholars such as Liang Shiqiu (梁实秋) with his Zuixin Shiyong Han-Ying Cidian (最新实用汉英辞典 , A New Practical Chinese-English Dictionary) (Liang 1971) and Lin Yutang (林语堂 , 1895—1976) with his Chinese-English Dictionary of Modern Usage (当代汉英词典 , Dangdai Han-Ying Cidian) (Lin 1972) came to the forefront of Chinese-English lexicography. The premier Chinese-English dictionary is the Beijing Institute of Foreign Languages' Han-Ying Cidian (汉英词典 , A Chinese-English Dictionary) (BIFL 1978), which, like E-Han Cidian (cf. 2.2.), was based on Xiandai Hanyu Cidian. Han-Ying Cidian itself has been used as the basis for a number of recent Chinese-English general and technical dictionaries.

2.4. The timely coverage of current Chinese terminology has been the hallmark of Chinese-German lexicography. One of the first important Chinese-German dictionaries was Werner Rüdenberg's *Chinesisch-Deutsches Wörterbuch* (Rüdenberg 1924). The dictionary was highly regarded by Sinologists of the time because it was one of the first Chinese bilingual dictionaries in a Western language to reflect the changes in the Chinese language following the fall of the Chinese monarchy in 1911 (Franke 1967). In a situation somewhat analogous to Rüdenberg's dictionary, Han-De Cidian (汉德词典 , Chinesisch-Deutsches Wörterbuch) (BIFL 1959), compiled by the German Department of the Beijing Institute of Foreign Languages, was one of the first Chinese bilingual dictionaries in a Western language to include the new terminology of the PRC. Because of the lack of a similar bilingual or monolingual dictionary of contemporary Chinese, the United States Government translated Han-De Cidian into English under the title *Chinese-English Dictionary of Modern Communist Chinese Usage* (JPRS 1959). German lexicographers such as Helmut Martin with *Chinesisch-Deutscher Wortschatz. Politik und Wirtschaft der VR China* (Martin 1977) were also among the first to document the often confusing language that emerged from the Chinese Cultural Revolution (1966—1976).

2.5. The Jesuits have been involved in Chinese bilingual lexicography for several centuries, particularly Chinese-French lexicography. The first major Chinese bilingual dictionary printed in Europe was Chretien Louis Joseph De Guignes' (1759—1845) *Dictionnaire Chinois, Français et Latin* (De Guignes 1813), which was based on the Jesuits' "Manuscript Dictionaries" (cf. 4.2.). Dictionaries by the French Jesuit Seraphin Couvreur (1835—1919) were among the most respected Chinese bilingual works at the turn of the twentieth century. His *Dictionnaire Classique de la Langue Chinoise* (Couvreur 1904), like Giles' dictionary, is still a useful dictionary for students of classical Chinese. Jesuits have remained active in Chinese-French lexicography as witnessed in the publication of *Dictionnaire Français de la Langue Chinoise* (Institut Ricci 1976), by the Jesuit-sponsored Institut Ricci in Taizhong, Taiwan. *Dictionnaire Français de la Langue Chinoise* is of interest not only because it is a good dictionary, but also because it is the first tangible product of the ambitious project initiated by a team of Jesuits in 1949 in Macao to compile a series of five large Chinese bilingual dictionaries with French, Spanish, English, Latin and Hungarian as the target languages. In addition to the Jesuits, the Chinese have also compiled a valuable Chinese-French dictionary, namely Han-Fa Cidian (汉法词典 , Dictionnaire Chinois-Français) (Han Fa 1964).

3. Chinese as Target Language

Lexicographers compiling bilingual dictionaries with Chinese as the target language traditionally have had a decided advantage over those working with Chinese as the source language because the former generally have had reliable source-language monolingual dictionaries on which to base their work. The main difficulty facing compilers of dictionaries with Chinese as the target language has not been with the selection of headwords, but rather with the selection of accurate lexical equivalents in Chinese; a language whose structure is often the antithesis of the source language. It is perhaps because of this difficulty that the majority of the important dictionaries with Chinese as the target language have been compiled by native speakers of Chinese.

3.1. Historically, the compilation of target language-Chinese dictionaries has been influenced by shifting strategic or political concerns. Prior to the twentieth century, superb target language-Chinese dictionaries were produced by Asian nationalities, in part to enhance their relations with the Chinese. For instance, during the Qing (清) Dynasty (1644—1911), the last Chinese dynasty and one ruled by Manchus, a number of Manchu-Chinese dictionaries were compiled to help bridge the communication and cultural gap between the two peoples. The dictionaries Da Qing Quanshu (大清全书, A Comprehensive Dictionary of the Great Qing Dynasty) (Daqing 1683), Yuzhi Zengding Qingwenjian (御制增订清文鉴, The Enlarged Imperial Manchu Language Survey) (Yuzhi 1771) and Qingwen Zonghui (清文总汇, A Comprehensive Collection of the Manchu Language) (Qing Wen 1897) are excellent examples of Manchu-Chinese lexicography and remain valuable resources for Manchu studies (Ji 1982).

In the twentieth century, there have been hundreds of bilingual Chinese dictionaries published in scores of languages. Many of the dictionaries, until the last two decades, have been of the general language. There has been a dramatic shift of attention to the scientific and technical language since the 1960s, and especially since the implementation in the PRC of the Four Modernizations policy, a nation-wide effort initiated in 1975 to modernize China's agriculture, industry, national defense and science and technology. Interestingly, a similar emphasis on the scientific and technical language occurred almost exactly a century earlier as China, challenged by foreign encroachment, sought to modernize its military and industrial base (Li 1982).

3.2. Space does not allow a detailed discussion of the many noteworthy bilingual dictionaries with Chinese as the target language. The compilation of the more important of these dictionaries has been concentrated in two publishing houses in the PRC. The Commercial Press (商务印书馆) of Beijing (Peking), China's leading publishing house, has produced excellent dictionaries including Ri-Han Cidian (日汉词典, A Japanese-Chinese Dictionary) (Ri Han 1979) and E-Han Da Cidian (俄汉大辞典, A Comprehensive Russian-Chinese Dictionary) (E Han 1963).

The Translation Press (译文出版社) of Shanghai has also published several good dictionaries including De-Han Cidian (德汉词典, A German-Chinese Dictionary) (De Han 1983) and Fa-Han Cidian (法汉词典, A French-Chinese Dictionary) (Fa Han 1979). The Translation Press is also sponsoring the compilation of Ying-Han Da Cidian (英汉大词典, A Large English-Chinese Dictionary), which, when completed in the late 1980s, promises to be one of the largest Chinese bilingual dictionaries ever published.

3.3. English has long been the most popular foreign language in China. The popularity of English is reflected in the success of the Model English-Chinese Dictionary (英汉模范字典, Ying-Han Mofan Zidian) (Model E-C 1929). The dictionary was first published in 1929 and was reprinted more than one hundred times before it was revised in 1965. The compilation of English-Chinese dictionaries, glossaries and related language materials continues at a furious pace in the PRC and in the ROC. In the PRC, Ying-Hua Da Cidian (英华大词典, An English-Chinese Dictionary) (Ying Hua 1950) and Xin Ying-Han Cidian (新英汉词典, A New English-Chinese Dictionary) (Xin Ying Han 1975) are the principle English-Chinese general language dictionaries. In the ROC, Liang Shiqiu, well known for his Chinese-English works (cf. 2.3.), has also published a series of English-Chinese dictionaries. One of his latest efforts is the Far East English-Chinese Dictionary (远东英汉大辞典, Yuandong Ying-Han Da Cidian) (Liang 1975).

3.4. Although it has yet to receive widespread attention, Česko-Čínský Slovnik (CCS 1974) is perhaps the most lexicographically sound Chinese bilingual dictionary. The dictionary was compiled at the Oriental Institute of the Czechoslovak Academy of Sciences and was based on principles established by a group headed by Ladislav Zgusta and later by D. D. Heroldová. Česko-Čínský Slovnik is particularly valuable for its sensitivity to lexical equivalence, levels of usage and exemplification. The dictionary demonstrates the positive results when the skills of the lexicographer, the language scholar and the native informant are combined; a combination that is all too rare in Chinese bilingual lexicography. Unfortunately, the dictionary will perhaps remain more of a curiosity than the valuable

4. Arrangement

Bilingual dictionaries with Chinese as the target language are arranged according to the alphabetic, phonetic or graphic scheme of the source language, and a discussion of the various source languages is obviously beyond the scope of this essay. As with Chinese monolingual dictionaries (cf. Art. 263.4.), bilingual dictionaries with Chinese as the source language are arranged by either the sound or shape of a character.

4.1. Shape

The major shape-based arrangement system for Chinese bilingual dictionaries is the Kangxi radical system (cf. Art. 263.4.1.1.). Several dictionaries have also been arranged by the Chinese Standard Telegraphic Code, a four-number code used to transmit Chinese by telegraph and telex. The listing of the characters in the Standard Telegraphic Code is based on the Kangxi radical system. Russian lexicographers have devised a look-up system based on the way in which a character is stroked or written. The Russian graphic system has been used most prominently in the dictionaries compiled by Oshanin, but has yet to be used in a major Chinese bilingual dictionary published outside of Russia.

4.2. Sound

The most common method for arranging Chinese bilingual dictionaries is by an alphabetical listing based on the sound of a character. Matteo Ricci (1552—1610), an Italian Jesuit missionary to China, is thought to have been the first person to devise a scheme for rendering Chinese sounds using the roman alphabet (Yang 1960). Ricci's romanization system, based on Italian and Portuguese orthography, was used in *Dizionario portoghese-chinese* (Dizionario 1588?) compiled by Ricci and fellow Jesuit Michele Ruggieri (1543—1607). Later Jesuits developed romanization systems for French, German and English that were used in a series of dictionaries known as the "Manuscript Dictionaries". As Europeans became active in Chinese bilingual lexicography, especially during the late nineteenth century, the number of romanization systems proliferated. The confusion caused by the different systems became a cause for concern. In 1897 at the XIth International Conference of Orientalists held in Paris a committee was established to draft a unified romanization system for all to use. A scheme was developed and put before the XIIIth International Congress convened in Hamburg in 1902, but was not approved. Instead of a single system, the members of the Congress decided that each country should adopt its own romanization system for Chinese based on its national orthography (Legeza 1968). The various national romanization systems are still in use today, in addition to more than a dozen systems developed by individual scholars. Several countries such as Czechoslovakia and Hungary even have two romanization systems, one academic and one popular (Legeza 1968). In recent years, however, a number of countries have moved away from their own system in favor of pinyin (拼音, sound spelling), the romanization system used in the PRC (cf. Art. 263 section 3.2.1.). The pinyin system is becoming the most common method for arranging Chinese bilingual dictionaries. The following chart indicates some of the similarities and differences between the pinyin romanization system and the major Western romanization systems.

Pinyin	English (Wade-Giles)	French	German	Russian
a	a	a	a	а
ben	pen	pen	bën	бэнь
chi	ch'ih	tch'e	tschï	чи
ci	tz'u	ts'eu	tsï	цы
dai	tai	tai	dai	дай
er	erh	eul	örl	эр
fo	fo	fo	fo	фо
gong	kung	kong	gung	гун
he	ho	ho	ho	хэ
jiang	chiang	kiang	djiang	цзян
jue	chüeh	kiue	djüä	цзюе
ke	k'o	k'o	ko	кэ
lü	lü	liu	lü	люй
meng	meng	meng	mëng	мэн
nie	nieh	nie	nïa	не
ou	ou	ngeou	ou	оу
pian	p'ien	p'ien	piän	пянь
qu	ch'ü	ts'iu	tjü	цюй
re	je	jo	jo	жэ
si	ssu	sseu	sï	сы
tou	t'ou	t'eou	tou	тоу
wu	wu	wou	wu	у
xuan	hsüan	hiuan	hsüan	сюань
yi	i	yi	i	и
zi	tzu	tseu	dsï	цзы

Fig. 327.1: The Major Western-language Romanization Systems for Chinese (from: Legeza 1968)

5. Summary

Until the 1970s, the major bilingual dictionaries with Chinese as the source language were compiled by non-Chinese scholars. The most common method for arranging these dictionaries is by a romanization system for the Chinese headwords. Although there are several dozen romanization schemes for Chinese, pinyin is becoming the standard arrangement and transcription system for Chinese monolingual and bilingual dictionaries. Native Chinese scholars in the PRC and ROC have, with few exceptions, accounted for the major dictionaries with Chinese as the target language. Indeed, bilingual lexicography with Chinese had an interesting history and promises an exciting future.

6. Selected Bibliography

6.1. Dictionaries

Aichi 1968 = Aichi Daigaku (爱知大学, Aichi University): Chu-Nichi Daijiten (中日大辞典, A Comprehensive Chinese-Japanese Dictionary). Tokyo 1968 [Revised 1986.].

BIFL 1959 = Beijing Institute of Foreign Languages: Han-De Cidian (汉德词典, Chinesisch-Deutsches Wörterbuch). Beijing 1959. [Second edition Beijing 1960].

BIFL 1978 = Beijing Institute of Foreign Languages: Han-Ying Cidian (汉英词典, A Chinese-English Dictionary). Beijing 1978.

CCS 1974 = Lexicographical Group of the Oriental Institute of the Czechoslovak Academy of Sciences: Česko-Čínský Slovník. Prague 1974—1984.

Couvreur 1904 = Seraphin Couvreur: Dictionnaire Classique de la Langue Chinoise. Ho Kien [Fujian] 1904. [Other editions include: 1931; Taizhong, Taiwan 1966; Taibei 1966].

Da Qing 1683 = Shen Quilliang (沈启亮) et al.: Da Qing Quanshu (大清全书, A Comprehensive Collection of the Great Qing Dynasty). Beijing 1683.

De Guignes 1813 = Chretien Louis Joseph De Guignes: Dictionnaire Chinois, Francais et Latin [...]. Paris 1813.

De Han 1983 = De Han Cidian (德汉词典, A German-Chinese Dictionary). Shanghai 1983.

Dizionario 1588? = Matteo Ricci/Michele Ruggieri: Dizionario portoghese-chinese. n.p. 1588? [Manuscript in the Archives of the Society of Jesus, Rome.].

E Han 1963 = Liu Zerong (刘泽荣) et al.: E-Han Da Cidian (俄汉大词典, A Comprehensive Russian-Chinese Dictionary). Beijing 1963.

Fa Han 1979 = Fa-Han Cidian (法汉词典, A French-Chinese Dictionary). Shanghai 1979.

Giles 1892 = Herbert A. Giles: A Chinese-English Dictionary. London. Shanghai 1892 [Revised and enlarged edition 1912. Reprinted New York 1964].

Han Da 1986 = Hanyu Da Cidian. (汉语大词典, An Encyclopedic Dictionary of the Chinese Language). Shanghai 1986.

Han Fa 1964 = Beijing University: Han-Fa Cidian (汉法词典, Dictionnaire Chinois-Français). Beijing 1964 [Other editions include: Hong Kong 1969 and 1979].

Institut Ricci 1976 = Institut Ricci Centre D'Etudes Chinoises: Dictionnaire Français de la Langue Chinoise. Taibei. Paris 1976.

JPRS 1959 = U.S. Joint Publications Research Service: Chinese-English Dictionary of Modern Communist Chinese Usage. Arlington, Va. 1959 [Second edition no date].

Liang 1971 = Liang Shiqiu (梁实秋): Zuixin Shiyong Han-Ying Cidian (最新实用汉英辞典, A New Practical Chinese-English Dictionary). Taibei 1971.

Liang 1975 = Liang Shiqiu (梁实秋): Far East English-Chinese Dictionary (远东英汉大辞典, Yuandong Ying-Han Da Cidian). Taibei 1975.

Lin 1972 = Lin Yutang (林语堂): Chinese-English Dictionary of Modern Usage (当代汉英词典, Dangdai Han-Ying Cidian). Hong Kong 1972.

Martin 1977 = Helmut Martin et al.: Chinesisch-Deutscher Wortschatz. Politik und Wirtschaft der VR China. Berlin 1977.

Mathews 1931 = Robert H. Mathews: A Chinese-English Dictionary. Shanghai 1931 [Revised American edition: Harvard-Yenching Institute: Cambridge, Mass. 1943 and 1944].

Model E-C 1929 = Wang Yunwu (王云五) et al.: Model English-Chinese Dictionary (英汉模范字典). Shanghai 1929 [Revised Taibei 1965].

Morohashi 1955 = Morohashi Tetsuji (诸桥辙次): Dai Kan-Wa Jiten (大汉和辞典, An Encyclopedic Chinese-Japanese Dictionary). Tokyo 1955—1960.

Morrison 1815 = Robert Morrison: A Dictionary of the Chinese Language, in Three Parts. Macao 1815—1822.

Oshanin 1955 = J. M. Oshanin: Kitaisko-Russkii Slovar. Moscow 1955 [Third edition 1959].

Oshanin 1983 = J. M. Oshanin et al.: Bolshoi Kitaisko-Russkii Slovar. Moscow 1983.

Qing Wen 1897 = Zhikuan (志宽) et al.: Qingwen Zonghui (清文总汇, A Comprehensive Collection of the Manchu Language). Beijing 1897.

Ri Han 1979 = Chen Tao (陈涛) et al.: Ri-Han Cidian (日汉词典, A Japanese-Chinese Dictionary). Beijing 1979.

Rüdenberg 1924 = Werner Rüdenberg: Chinesisch-Deutsches Wörterbuch. Hamburg 1924 [Other editions: Rüdenberg and Walter Simon 1936, Rüdenberg and Hans O. Stange 1963].

SIFL 1977 = Shanghai Institute of Foreign Languages: Han-E Cidian (汉俄词典, A Chinese-Russian Dictionary). Beijing 1977.

Xian Han 1978 = Dictionary Compilation Office of the Institute of Linguistics of the Chinese Academy of Social Sciences 中国社会科学院语言研究所词典编辑室: Xiandai Hanyu Cidian (现代汉语词典, A Dictionary of Contemporary Chinese). Beijing 1978.

Xin Ying Han 1975 = Xin Ying-Han Cidian (新英汉词典, A New English-Chinese Dictionary). Shanghai 1975 [Other editions: Hong Kong 1975; Shanghai 1985].

Ying Hua 1950 = Zheng Yili (郑易里) et al.: Ying-Hua Da Cidian (英华大词典). Beijing 1950 [Other editions: Beijing 1957; Hong Kong 1957, 1965. Revised Beijing 1984].

Yuzhi 1771 = Fu Heng (傅恒) et al.: Yuzhi Zengding Qingwenjian (御制增订清文鉴, The Enlarged Imperial Manchu Language Survey). Beijing? 1771.

Zhongwen 1962 = Zhang Qiyun (张其昀) et al.: Zhongwen Da Cidian (中文大辞典, The Encyclopedic Dictionary of the Chinese Language). Taibei 1962—1968.

6.2. Other Publications

Franke 1967 = Wolfgang Franke: Chinesisch-Deutsches Wörterbuch. In: Harvard Journal of Asiatic Studies 27. 1967, 324—326.

Ji 1982 = Ji Yonghai (季永海): Manwen Cishu Shihua (满文辞书史话, The History of Manchu Lexicography). In: Cishu Yanjiu (辞书研究, Lexicographical Studies) 2. 1982, 148—156.

Legeza 1968 = Ireneus Laszlo Legeza: Guide to Transliterated Chinese in the Modern Peking Dialect. Leiden 1968.

Li 1982 = Li Nanqiu (黎难秋): Zhongguo Shuangyu Cidian Lishi (中国双语词典史话, A History of Chinese Bilingual Dictionaries). In: Cishu Yanjiu (辞书研究, Lexicographical Studies) 1. 1982, 166—172.

Yang 1960 = Paul Yang Fu-mien: The Catholic Missionary Contribution to the Study of Chinese Dialects. In: Orbis 1. 1960, 158—185.

Thomas B. I. Creamer, Takoma Park, Maryland (USA)

328. Bilingual Lexicography With Japanese

1. Introduction
2. Portuguese
3. Dutch
4. English-Japanese
5. Japanese-English
6. French, German, Russian, Italian, and Spanish
7. Selected Bibliography

1. Introduction

Lexicographically speaking, Japan may well claim to be one of the most advanced countries in the world. Besides those surveyed in the following sections, bilingual dictionaries of various sizes, as far as I have noticed, of the following languages are available now: Ainu, Arabic, Burmese, Cambodian, Ethiopian, (biblical and classical) Greek, Hausa, Hebrew, Hindi, Hungarian, Indonesian, Korean, Latin, Mongolian, Pali, Persian, Polish, Rumanian, Sanskrit, Swahili, Swedish, Tibetan, Turkish, and Vietnamese. But the most important dictionaries to the history and culture of Japan are those of the languages of advanced Western countries, and the present article will therefore be devoted to a historical sketch of them.

2. Portuguese

Apart from the introduction of Chinese characters in the second half of the fourth century, the most consequential event in the linguistic history of Japan is unquestionably the contact with European languages which started in the sixteenth century. The first language to arrive was Portuguese, brought by accident by a merchantman in 1543, then by Jesuit missionaries headed by Francis Xavier, who came in 1549 and succeeded in propagating Christianity rapidly until it was banned in 1587. Portuguese has left its mark in a few borrowings (e. g. Jap. **pan** "bread" from Port. **pān**), but its greatest linguistic heritage is Vocabulario 1603, a Japanese-Portuguese dictionary with more than 30,000 entries, produced by forty years' labour of several unknown Jesuit missionaries. Its importance for the study of the Japanese of the time is well attested by the fact that its facsimile was published in 1960, its Japanese version came out in 1980, and an Index (in the Japanese *kana* characters) of its headwords in 1989.

3. Dutch

In 1637, for religious reasons, the Tokugawa government closed Japan's doors to all foreign countries with the sole exception of the Netherlands. During this self-imposed isolation (1637—1855), the Netherlands enjoyed the exclusive privilege of trading with Japan; and, unlike the preceding period when the Japanese were only receptive linguistically, the new era saw enlightened Japanese begin working hard to study Dutch, producing a number of Japanese translations of Western science books. In the field of lexicography, two Dutch-Japanese dictionaries should be noted, both based on Halma 1729. The first to appear was Inamura 1796, which is a crude dictionary or rather a wordbook, though, with some 65,000 entries, giving for each headword only a few Japanese equivalents represented by Chinese characters — a vehicle of scholarship of the time — thus reflecting the character of the Dutch studies at Yedo [Tokyo]. An abridged version of this dictionary is Fujibayashi 1810, boiling down the original entries to approximately 30,000.

Although outstripped by about four decades lexicographically, Nagasaki had pride of place for Dutch studies in chronological priority and linguistic quality. Trade being the primary purpose, Dutch studies at Nagasaki tended markedly to practicality, and official Dutch-Japanese interpreters there had the decided advantage of learning the language under the capitão, the head of the Dutch factory. Hence the irrefutable superiority to Inamura 1796 of Doeff 1833, produced by several Dutch-Japanese interpreters under the guidance of H. Doeff. To give just an instance for comparison, for Dut. **opstand** Inamura gives only one Japanese equivalent, whereas under the same headword Doeff 1833 gives, besides two Japanese equivalents, six illustrative phrases and sentences with their Japanese translations, faithfully reproducing the base dictionary. A woodprint edition of Doeff 1833 is Katsuragawa 1858, in which is introduced a slight revision by eliminating too broad Nagasaki dialects.

4. English-Japanese

Dutch-Japanese interpreters at Nagasaki also made, at the command of the government, the first English-Japanese wordbook, Motoki/Narabayashi/Yoshio 1814, which is a revised and enlarged version of Motoki 1811. Both sets of manuscripts were kept secret in the government's library, so that they remained lone precursors having nothing to do with the dictionaries of English to be made in later years.

With the opening of doors in 1855 to advanced European countries and America, foreign language studies in Japan underwent a sweeping change, in which Dutch gave way to English which has since acquired the position of the first foreign language to be learned at middle and high schools. The flourish of English studies reached its first peak in 1872, which saw the publication of 57 titles (78 volumes) designed for learners of English.

If we may leave out of account Medhurst 1830 on the grounds that it was made by a foreigner and printed at Batavia in the Dutch East Indies, the first substantial English-Japanese dictionary is Hori 1862, with entries exceeding 35,000. Hori based his dictionary on the Dutch-English part of Picard 1857; but far more intriguing is the fact that in its Japanese equivalents it has extensively (more than 70 per cent) drawn on Katsuragawa 1858 (cf. 3), thus proving itself to be a connecting link between the sinking Dutch studies and the emerging English studies of the time. The next notable dictionary is Shibata/Koyasu 1873, illustrated with more than 500 woodcuts. It is based on Ogilvie 1863; but the most conspicuous feature of the book is its unrestrained predilection for Chinese characters, some of which are taken from Lobscheid 1866—69, a Japanese version of which is Lobscheid/Inouye 1884. Along with Hori 1862, Shibata/Koyasu 1873 continued to be reprinted, in revised and pirated editions, well down to the end of the 1880s.

The subsequent history may well be summarized by listing the more important dictionaries, with brief comments, where appropriate, on their noteworthy features. Seki 1889, based on Webster 1870 (?), is the first to adopt Western lexicographical techniques, discriminating the different meanings of each word systematically. Shimada 1887 declares in the preface that his book is based on *Webster's Unabridged Dictionary*, but it in fact is a faint imitation, and in its Japanese equivalents heavily depends on its predecessors. As with Shimada's, the pretentious title of Eastlake/Tanahashi 1888 should not be taken literally. In the preface Kanda 1911 mentions various sources, of which the Century, including its pictorial illustrations, seems to have provided the largest proportion. Kanda's dictionary was later revised and enlarged into Sanseido 1928. Iriye 1921 has again extensively drawn on the Century, but it is far more advanced linguistically than Kanda's in that nearly every word is provided with illustrative phrases and sentences, most of which are taken from the source book.

As is evident, the English-Japanese dictionaries so far surveyed have been influenced exclusively by American dictionaries, but the appearance of the *Concise Oxford Dictionary* (= C.O.D.) turned the tables by its immediate impact. Inouye 1915 is scarcely anything other than a Japanese version of the C.O.D. The author of Saito 1915, before launching into work, also made a minute scrutiny of the C.O.D.; but the outcome is not a mere imitation but a highly idiosyncratic book, embodying the author's peculiar theory of "idiomology". Later it was revised and enlarged into Saito 1922. Okakura 1927 was compiled on "bilingual principles", by which is meant the practice of providing each word or meaning with synonymous English equivalents, which are taken almost without exception from the C.O.D. Since its appearance Okakura's dictionary has occupied the throne of the English-Japanese dictionaries, the latest (fifth) edition of which, with more than 230,000 entries, is Koine 1980. Ichikawa/Kuroyanagi/Iijima 1931 distinguishes itself by including more than 8,000 personal and place names. Fujioka 1921—32 adopted for the first time "Jones's phonetic alphabet", a version of the IPA. Iwasaki 1941 is virtually the first learner's dictionary, devoting as much space as possible to the basic and grammatical words. Saito 1944 is in effect a reduced imitation of Okakura 1927.

During World War II, when English was banished as "an enemy's language", and for years after its end, the English dictionary in Japan inevitably fell into a low ebb, and it took two decades to revive. Otsuka 1964 is mainly based on Guralnik 1953. Nakajima 1970 is virtually a condensed version of the Oxford English Dictionary. As apparent in the title, Inamura/Stein 1973—74 is a Japanese version of an American dictionary, supplementing the original with an addition of approximately 10,000 words. The outstanding feature in the current trends of the English-Japanese dictionary is that small-sized learner's dictionaries (1,500 to 2,000 pages) have been appearing quickly one after another, and in those that have come out after 1980 the influence of the *Longman Dictionary* has been making itself more and more strongly felt. The more popular among them are: Kawamura 1954, Koine 1967, Kawamoto 1969, Shibata 1972, Konishi 1980, Nakajima/Oshitari 1981, Takebayashi/Kojima 1984, Kihara 1988, Konishi 1988.

5. Japanese-English

For obvious reasons the encoding dictionary comes after the decoding dictionary, and the first Japanese-English dictionary, putting aside Medhurst 1830 (cf. 4), did not materialize until Hepburn 1867. This dictionary went through the second (1872) to the third (1886) edition, each time with considerable revisions and enlargement, and finally reached more than 35,000 entries in the Japanese-English part and 15,000 entries in the English-Japanese part, the title of the later editions being accordingly revised. Hepburn's influence over the dictionaries that followed him was so overwhelming that the latter were nothing more than condensed, adapted or pirated versions of the former until the first decade of the present century.

The first Japanese-English dictionary produced independently of Hepburn is Inouye 1909, later revised and enlarged into Inouye 1921. In his analysis of the meanings of Japanese words and in other respects, Inouye superseded Hepburn indeed, but his arrogance is such that in the preface he declares: "In its compilation I have not consulted any foreigner; indeed I have hardly spoken to one during the years I have been engaged on it". Takenobu 1918 achieved an unprecedented success, going through twenty-six reprintings in ten months. Unlike Inouye, Takenobu was wise enough to solicit the collaboration of several competent experts, and the descendants of his dictionary have deservedly taken pride of place in the field concerned, the latest (fourth) edition being Masuda 1974. Alongside the Takenobu/Masuda dictionary, two large-sized dictionaries may be mentioned: Takehara 1924 pays special attention to idioms and connectives; Saito 1928 is the final and comprehensive accumulation of the author's "idiomological" studies of English, which led him to the belief that "the English of the Japanese must, in a sense, be Japanized."

Along with the larger encoding dictionaries, there have of course appeared smaller ones designed for high school and college students. In the following current dictionaries of this type, it should be noted, the dominant practice is to present headwords by and in the order of the Japanese *kana* syllabary instead of the once prevailing Roman alphabet: Yamada 1961, Nakajima 1975, Kojima/Takebayashi 1984, Kondo/Takano 1986, Hasegawa 1987.

6. French, German, Russian, Italian, and Spanish

Needless to say, English is not the sole language that has been studied in Japan: French began to be studied seriously in the first decade of the nineteenth century, German and Russian in the 1860s. After the Restoration (1868), the new government set up a school of foreign languages in Tokyo in 1873, which in the following year was divided into two: one specializing in English, the other in French, German, and classical Chinese. French has since been regarded as the language for fine arts, literature, and mathematics; German for philosophy, medicine, and political science; and Russian mainly for literature. As the history of these languages in Japan has not been studied as much as that of English, we have to content ourselves with the chronological lists of bilingual dictionaries of those languages which have been studied in Japanese colleges, usually as the optional second languages. The languages include, besides the above-mentioned, Italian and Spanish, which have been adopted rather recently as official subjects at schools. The following lists of early dictionaries of French, German, and Russian are therefore not as exhaustive as that of English dictionaries; and the early histories of the Italian and Spanish dictionary are still to be investigated, though presumably they do not go much further back in time than those listed below:

French: Murakami 1864, crude by the standards of today, but bears the honour of being the first French-Japanese dictionary, containing more than 35,000 words; Okada 1871, a Japanese version of M. Nugent's small French-English dictionary; Nakaye 1887; Raguet/Ono 1905; Fukuoka 1921, so excellent and comprehensive that for more than three decades it deterred the appearance of any rivals; Suzuki 1957; Suzuki 1970; Ibuki 1981; Ooga 1988.

German: Oda/Fujii/Sakurai 1872, Matsuda/Senokuchi/Murakami 1873, Teachers of German 1873, Tobari 1912, Kimura/Sagara 1940, Kimura 1952, Sagara 1958, Kunimatsu 1985.

Russian: Ogata 1873, Ministry of Education 1887, Igeta 1954, Yasugi 1965, Igeta 1966, Konrad 1971, Sato 1981, Togo 1988.

Spanish: Takahashi 1958, Nagata/Tai 1976, Miyagi/Contreras 1979, González/Isshiki 1986, Kawano 1990.

7. Selected Bibliography

7.1. Dictionaries

Century = William Dwight Whitney: The Century Dictionary. An Encyclopedic Lexicon of the English Language. 6 vol. New York 1889—91 [Cyclopedia of Names 1894; Atlas of the World 1897; Supplement 2 vol. 1909; new ed. rev. and enlarged by Benjamin E. Smith, 12 vol. 1911, 7046 p. excluding the last 2 supplementary vol.].

Concise Oxford Dictionary = Henry Watson Fowler/Francis George Fowler: The Concise Oxford Dictionary of Current English. Oxford 1911 [1041 p.; 8. ed. by R. E. Allen 1990, 1454 p.].

Doeff 1833 = Hendrik Doeff: Zufu-Haruma [Halma 1729 translated into Japanese under Doeff] or Nagasaki-Haruma [Halma 1729 translated at Nagasaki]. 8, 9 or 24 vol. in MS. Nagasaki 1833.

Eastlake/Tanahashi 1888 = Frederick Warrington Eastlake/Ichiro Tanahashi: Webster's Unabridged Dictionary. Translated into Japanese. Tokyo 1888 [1838 p.].

Fujibayashi 1810 = Taisuke Fujibayashi: Nederduitsche Taal. Yakken [A Key for Translation]. 2 vol. Kyoto 1810.

Fujioka 1921—32 = Katsuji Fujikoa: A Complete English-Japanese Dictionary. 2 vol. Tokyo 1921—32 [1638, 2120 p.].

Fukuoka 1921 = Ekinosuke Fukuoka/Katsuji Yanagawa/Tetsuji Hirose et al.: Nouveau Dictionnaire Français-Japonais. Tokyo 1921 [2176 p.].

Gonzáles/Isshiki 1986 = Vincente González/Tadayoshi Isshiki: Diccionario Español-Japonés. Tokyo 1986 [1547 p.].

Guralnik 1953 = David B. Guralnik: Webster's New Dictionary of the American Language, College Edition. Cleveland. New York 1953 [2. ed. 1970, 1692 p.].

Halma 1729 = François Halma: Woordenboek der Nederduitsche en Fransche Taalen/Dictionnaire Flamand et François. 2. ed. Amsterdam. Utrecht 1729.

Hasegawa 1987 = Kiyoshi Hasegawa/Katsuaki Horiuchi/Tsutomu Momozawa/Saburo Yamamura: Obunsha's Comprehensive Japanese-English Dictionary. Tokyo 1987 [1797 p.].

Hepburn 1867 = James Curtis Hepburn: A Japanese and English Dictionary, with an English and Japanese Index. Yokohama 1867 [696 p., reprinted Tokyo 1966; 2. ed. A Japanese-English and English-Japanese Dictionary 1872, 868 p., reprinted Tokyo 1970; 3. ed. Tokyo 1886, 962 p., reprinted 1980].

Hori 1862 = Tatsunosuke Hori: A Pocket Dictionary of the English and Japanese Language [sic]. Yedo [Tokyo] 1862 [953 p., reprinted 1973].

Ibuki 1981 = Takehiko Ibuki/Akimasa Watanabe/Toshiaki Goto et al.: Dictionnaire Général Français-Japonais. Tokyo 1981 [2652 p.].

Ichikawa/Kuroyanagi/Iijima 1931 = Sanki Ichikawa/Kunitaro Kuroyanagi/Kozaburo Iijima: Fuzambo's Comprehensive English-Japanese Dictionary. Tokyo 1931 [1855 p.].

Igeta 1954 = Sadatoshi Igeta: Sanseido's Concise Russian-Japanese Dictionary. Tokyo 1954 [4. ed. 1977, 1205 p.].

Igeta 1966 = Sadatoshi Igeta: Sanseido's Concise Japanese-Russian Dictionary. Tokyo 1966 [2. ed. 1976, 921 p.].

Ikeda 1983 = Kiyoshi Ikeda/Kanji Arisato/Jiro Aratani et al.: Dizionario Shogakukan Italiano-Giapponese. Tokyo 1983 [1735 p.].

Inamura 1796 = Sanpaku Inamura: Harumawage [Halma 1729 translated into Japanese] or Yedo-Haruma [Halma 1729 translated at Yedo] 27 vol. in MS. Yedo [Tokyo] 1796.

Inamura/Stein 1973—74 = Matsuo Inamura/Jess Stein: Shogakukan Random House English-Japanese Dictionary. 4 vol. Tokyo 1973—74 [2-vol. ed. 1975; 1-vol. ed. 1979, 3048 p.].

Inouye 1909 = Jukichi Inouye: Inouye's Japanese-English Dictionary. Tokyo 1909 [1872, 12 p.].

Inouye 1915 = Jukichi Inouye: Inouye's English-Japanese Dictionary. Tokyo 1915 [2326, 26 p.].

Inouye 1921 = Jukichi Inouye: Inouye's Comprehensive Japanese-English Dictionary. Tokyo 1921 [2913, 22 p.].

Iriye 1921 = Iwaye Iriye: A New English-Japanese Dictionary. Tokyo 1921 [1427, 255 p.; reprinted Tokyo 1985].

Iwasaki 1941 = Tamihei Iwasaki: Kenkyusha's Concise English-Japanese Dictionary. Tokyo 1941 [1819 p.].

Kanda 1911 = Naibu Kanda/Tokitaka Yokoi/Toyokichi Takamatsu et al.: Sanseido's English-Japanese Dictionary. Tokyo 1911 [2016 p.].

Katsuragawa 1858 = Hoshu Katsuragawa: Waranjii [A Dutch-Japanese Dictionary]. Yedo [Tokyo] 1858 [reprinted in 5 vol. Tokyo 1974, 3780 p.].

Kawamoto 1969 = Shigeo Kawamoto: The Kodansha English-Japanese Dictionary. Tokyo 1969 [2. ed. 1977, 1557 p.].

Kawamura 1954 = Jujiro Kawamura: The New Crown English-Japanese Dictionary. Tokyo 1954 [4. ed. 1977, 1664 p.].

Kawano 1990 = Kazuhiro Kawano/Masataka Hata/Naoshi Tsuzumi et al.: Diccionario Español-Japonés. Tokyo 1990 [2088 p.].

Kihara 1988 = Kenzo Kihara: The New Century English-Japanese Dictionary. Tokyo 1988 [1580 p.].

Kimura 1952 = Kinji Kimura: Großes Japanisch-Deutsches Wörterbuch. Tokyo 1952 [2633 p.].

Kimura/Sagara 1940 = Kinji Kimura/Morio Sagara: Kimura-Sagara Deutsch-Japanisches Wörterbuch. Tokyo 1940 [rev. ed. 1963; 1792, 17 p.].

Koine 1967 = Yoshio Koine/Kikuo Yamakawa/Shigeru Takebayashi et al.: Kenkyusha's New Collegiate English-Japanese Dictionary. Tokyo 1967 [5. ed. 1985, 1967 p.].

Koine 1980 = Yoshio Koine: Kenkyusha's New English-Japanese Dictionary. 5. ed. Tokyo 1980 [2477 p.].

Kojima/Takebayashi 1984 = Yoshiro Kojima/Shigeru Takebayashi: Kenkyusha's Lighthouse Japanese-English Dictionary. Tokyo 1984 [1757 p.].

Kondo/Takano 1986 = Ineko Kondo/Fumi Takano: Shogakukan Progressive Japanese-English Dictionary. Tokyo 1986 [1975 p.].

Konishi 1980 = Tomoshichi Konishi/Minoru Yasui/Tetsuya Kunihiro et al.: Shogakukan Progressive English-Japanese Dictionary. Tokyo 1980 [2. ed. 1987, 2101 p.].

Konishi 1988 = Tomoshichi Konishi: Taishukan's Genius English-Japanese Dictionary. Tokyo 1988 [2005 p.].

Konrad 1971 = Nicolai Konrad: New Japanese-Russian Dictionary. Tokyo 1971 [1411 p.].

Kunimatsu 1985 = Koji Kunimatsu: Großes Deutsch-Japanisches Wörterbuch. Tokyo 1985 [2715 p.].

Lobscheid 1866—69 = William Lobscheid: An English and Chinese Dictionary. 4 vol. Hongkong 1866—69 [2140 p.].

Lobscheid/Inouye 1884 = William Lobscheid/Tetsujiro Inouye: An English and Chinese Dictionary, Revised, Enlarged and Translated into Japanese. Tokyo 1884 [1270 p.].

Longman Dictionary = Paul Procter: Longman Dictionary of Contemporary English. London 1978 [1303 p.; new. ed. 1987, 1227 p.].

Masuda 1974 = Koh Masuda: Kenkyusha's New Japanese-English Dictionary. 4. ed. Tokyo 1974 [2110 p.].

Matsuda/Senokuchi/Murakami 1873 = Tametsune Matsuda/Takanari Senokuchi/Tsuneharu

Murakami: Deutsch-Japanisches Wörterbuch. Shanghai 1873 [719 p.].

Medhurst 1830 = Walter Henry Medhurst: An English and Japanese, and Japanese and English Vocabulary. Batavia 1830 [344 p.].

Ministry of Education 1887 = Ministry of Education: A Russian-Japanese Dictionary. Tokyo 1887.

Miyagi/Contreras 1979 = Noboru Miyagi/Enrique Contreras: Diccionario Japonés-Español. Tokyo 1979 [1239 p.].

Motoki 1811 = Shoyei Motoki: Angeria-kogaku-shosen [An English Vocabulary for Beginners]. 10 vol. in MS. Nagasaki 1811 [reprinted in 3 vol. Tokyo 1982].

Motoki/Narabayashi/Yoshio 1814 = Shoyei Motoki/Takami Narabayashi/Nagayasu Yoshio: Angeria-gorin-taisei [A Comprehensive Vocabulary of English]. 15 vol. in MS. Nagasaki 1814 [reprinted in 1 vol. Tokyo 1974; reprinted in 4 vol. Tokyo 1982].

Murakami 1864 = Hidetoshi Murakami: Futsugo-meiyo [A French-Japanese Dictionary]. 4 vol. Tokyo 1864.

Nagata/Tai 1976 = Hirosada Nagata/Yoshitaro Tai: Diccionario Manuel Japonés-Español. Tokyo 1976 [1471 p.].

Nakajima 1970 = Fumio Nakajima: Iwanami's Comprehensive English-Japanese Dictionary. Tokyo 1970 [2124 p.].

Nakajima 1975 = Fumio Nakajima: Sanseido's Concise English-Japanese Dictionary. Tokyo 1975 [2. ed. 1985, 1202 p.].

Nakajima/Oshitari 1981 = Fumio Nakajima/Kinshiro Oshitari: Iwanami's New English-Japanese Dictionary. Tokyo 1981 [2. ed. 1987, 1554 p.].

Nakaye 1887 = Tokusuke [Chomin] Nakaye: Dictionnaire Universel Français-Japonais. Tokyo 1887 [1290 p.].

Nogami 1964 = Soichi Nogami: Nuovo Dizionario Italiano-Giapponese. Tokyo 1964 [rev. ed. 1981, 1006 p.].

Oda/Fujii/Sakurai 1872 = Shinojiro Oda/Saburo Fujii/Yusaku Sakurai: Deutsch-Japanisches Taschen-Wörterbuch. Tokyo 1872 [1353, 13 p.].

Ogata 1873 = Koretaka Ogata: Rogosen [A Handbook of Russian Vocabulary]. Sapporo 1873.

Ogilvie 1863 = John Ogilvie: The Comprehensive English Dictionary. London 1863 [1294 p.].

Okada 1871 = Yoshiki Okada [Kojudo]: Nouveau Dictionnaire Français-Japonais. Shanghai 1871 [440 p.].

Okakura 1927 = Yoshitaro Okakura: Kenkyusha's New English-Japanese Dictionary on Bilingual Principles. Tokyo 1927 [2048 p.].

Ooga 1988 = Masaki Ooga: Shogakukan Robert Grand Dictionnaire Français-Japonais. Tokyo 1988 [2597 p.].

Otsuka 1964 = Takanobu Otsuka: Sanseido's College Crown English-Japanese Dictionary. Tokyo 1964 [2. ed. 1977, 2301 p.].

Oxford English Dictionary = James A. H. Murray/Henry Bradley/Charles T. Onions/William A. Craigie: The Oxford English Dictionary. 10 vol. Oxford 1884—1928 [15488 p.; corrected re-issue, 13 vol. 1933; 2nd ed. prepared by J. A. Simpson and E. S. C. Weiner, 20 vols., 1989; 21728 p.].

Picard 1857 = H. Picard: A New Pocket Dictionary of the English and Dutch Languages. 2. ed., rev. and enlarged by A. B. Maatjes. Zelt-Bommel 1857 [483 p.; 1. ed. 1843].

Raguet/Ono 1905 = Eugene Raguet/Tota Ono: Dictionnaire Français-Japonais. Tokyo 1905 [78, 1084 p.].

Sagara 1958 = Morio Sagara: Sagara Großes Deutsch-Japanisches Wörterbuch. Tokyo 1958 [1801 p.].

Saito 1915 = Hidesaburo Saito: Saito's Idiomological English-Japanese Dictionary. 2 vol. Tokyo 1915 [1594 p.; rev. by Minoru Toyoda 1936, 1 vol., 1786 p.].

Saito 1922 = Hidesaburo Saito: Saito's Vade Mecum English-Japanese Dictionary. Tokyo 1922 [632, 15 p.; reprinted 1982].

Saito 1928 = Hidesaburo Saito: Saito's Japanese-English Dictionary. Tokyo 1928 [4640 p.; reprinted 1979, 1160 p.].

Saito 1944 = Shizuka Saito: Fuzambo's English-Japanese Dictionary on Bilingual Principles. Tokyo 1944 [1918 p.].

Sakamoto 1988 = Tetsuo Sakamoto: Dizionario Giapponese-Italiano. Tokyo 1988 [1217 p.].

Sanseido 1928 = The Sanseido Editorial Board: Sanseido's Encyclopedic English-Japanese Dictionary. Tokyo 1928 [2680 p.].

Sato 1981 = Isamu Sato: Kodansha's Japanese-Russian Dictionary. Tokyo 1981 [1154 p.].

Seki 1889 = Shimpachi Seki: An English-Japanese Dictionary. Tokyo 1889 [1270 p.].

Shibata 1972 = Tetsuo Shibata: The New Anchor English-Japanese Dictionary. Tokyo 1972 [new ed. 1988, 1651 p.].

Shibata/Koyasu 1873 = Masayoshi Shibata/Takashi Koyasu: An English-Japanese Dictionary. Yokohama 1873 [1556 p.; reprinted Tokyo 1975; 2. ed. 1882; 3. ed. 1887].

Shimada 1887 = Yutaka Shimada: An English and Japanese Lexicon. Tokyo 1887 [932, 54 p.].

Suzuki 1957 = Shintaro Suzuki: Dictionnaire Standard Français-Japonais. Tokyo 1957 [rev. by Sueo Asakura 1987, 1191 p.].

Suzuki 1970 = Shintaro Suzuki: Dictionnaire Standard Japonais-Français. Tokyo 1970 [1391 p.].

Takahashi 1958 = Masatake Takahashi: A Spanish-Japanese Dictionary. Tokyo 1958 [rev. ed. 1979; 982, 33 p.].

Takebayashi/Kojima 1984 = Shigeru Takebayashi/Yoshiro Kojima: Kenkyusha's Lighthouse English-Japanese Dictionary. Tokyo 1984 [1711 p.; 1. ed. Kenkyusha's Union English-Japanese Dictionary 1972].

Takehara 1924 = Tsuneta Takehara: A Standard Japanese-English Dictionary. Tokyo 1924 [rev. ed. 1926, 1710 p.; reprinted 1983].

Takenobu 1918 = Yoshitaro Takenobu: Takenobu's Japanese-English Dictionary. Tokyo 1918 [2480 p.].

Teachers of German 1873 = Teachers of German at Middle Schools in Kyoto: Deutsch-Japanisches Wörterbuch. Kyoto 1873 [1228 p.].

Tobari 1912 = Shin-ichiro Tobari: Tobari Deutsch-Japanisches Wörterbuch: Muret-Sanders Enzyklopädisches Deutsch-Englisches Wörterbuch (Hand- und Schulausgabe) ins Japanische übertragen. Tokyo 1912 [2344, 12 p.].

Togo 1988 = Masanobu Togo: Kenkyusha Russian-Japanese Dictionary. Tokyo 1988 [2763 p.].

Vocabulario 1603 = Unknown Jesuit Missionaries: Vocabulario da Lingoa Iapam. Nagasaki 1603 [Suppl. 1604; reprinted Tokyo 1960; Japanese version translated by Tadao Doi/Takeshi Morita/Minoru Chonan, 1980, 845 p. (text); Index in the cursive *kana* characters by Takeshi Morita 1989].

Webster 1870 (?) = Webster's National Pictorial Dictionary [spine title]. Springfield. New York. Philadelphia 1870 (?) [996 p.].

Webster's Unabridged Dictionary = Noah Webster: An American Dictionary of the English Language. 2 vol. New York 1828 [thoroughly rev. and improved by Chauncey A. Goodrich and Noah Porter. Springfield 1864].

Yamada 1961 = Kazuo Yamada: The New Crown Japanese-English Dictionary. Tokyo 1961 [5. ed. 1986, 1236 p.].

Yasugi 1965 = Sadatoshi Yasugi: Iwanami's Russian-Japanese Dictionary. Tokyo 1965 [rev. ed. 1979, 1599 p.].

7.2. Other Publications

Nagashima 1970 = Daisuke Nagashima: Ranwa-Eiwa-Jisho Hattatsushi [A History of Dutch-Japanese and English-Japanese Dictionaries]. Tokyo 1970.

Ogasawara 1984 = Linju Ogasawara: Problems in Improving Japanese English-Learners' Dictionaries. In: LEXeter '83 Proceedings. Ed. R. R. K. Hartmann. Tübingen 1984 (Lexicographica Series Maior 1), 253—257.

Toyoda 1939 = Minoru Toyoda: Nihon Eigakushi no Kenkyu [Studies in the History of English Studies in Japan]. Tokyo 1939 [3rd impr. 1969].

Daisuke Nagashima, Osaka (Japan)

XXXVII. Lexikographie von Hilfssprachen und anderen Kommunikationssystemen
Lexicography of Auxiliary Languages and of Other Communication Systems
Lexicographie des langues auxiliaires et d'autres systèmes de communication

329. Lexikographie der Plansprachen

1.   Esperanto
1.1. Stationen des offiziellen Wortschatzes
1.2. Der Wortschatz Zamenhofs
1.3. Einsprachige Wörterbücher (Definitionswörterbücher)
1.4. Mehrsprachige Wörterbücher
1.5. Spezialwörterbücher
2.   Andere Plansprachen
2.1. Volapük
2.2. Ido
2.3. Occidental/Interlingue
2.4. Interlingua
3.   Literatur (in Auswahl)

(a) Verzeichnis abgekürzter Buchtitel
FdE Fundamento de Eo (1906)
FK   Fundamenta Krestomatio de la lingvo Eo (1903)
PIV Plena Ilustrita Vortaro de Eo (1970)
PV   Plena Vortaro de Eo (1930)
PVS Suplemento de PV (1954)
PVZ Iam kompletigota plena verkaro de L. L. Zamenhof (1973—1981)
UL   Unua Libro (1887)
UV   Universala Vortaro (1894)

(b) Verzeichnis abgekürzter Sprachennamen
Ar Arabisch; Bg Bulgarisch; C Chinesisch; Cs Tschechisch; D Deutsch; Da Dänisch; E Englisch; Eo Esperanto; Es Estnisch; F Französisch; Fi Finnisch; G Griechisch; He Hebräisch; Hu Ungarisch; I Italienisch; Ia Interlingua; Ie Interlingue (= Occidental); Is Isländisch; J Japanisch; Ko Koreanisch; La Latein; Le Lettisch; Li Litauisch; Nl Niederländisch; No Norwegisch, Pe Persisch; Pl Polnisch; Pt Portugiesisch; R Russisch; Ru Rumänisch; S Spanisch; Sh Serbokroatisch; Sk Slowakisch; Sn Slowenisch; Sv Schwedisch; Ur Urdu; Vp Volapük; X irgendeine Sprache; Yi Yiddisch.

1. Esperanto

1.1. Stationen des offiziellen Wortschatzes

1.1.1. Das Unua Libro (1887)

Vorbemerkung: Aus darstellungstechnischen Gründen werden im vorliegenden Beitrag zahlreiche Abkürzungen verwendet; diese sind in den voranstehenden Verzeichnissen aufgelöst.

Die Geschichte der Eo-Lexikographie beginnt mit der Veröffentlichung von Zamenhofs erstem Lehrbuch, dem sog. „Unua Libro" (UL), im Sommer 1887. Es enthielt im Anhang ein Faltblatt mit ca. 1000 Morphemen, aus denen mit Hilfe eines Affix-Systems das Eo ein Vielfaches an Wörtern bilden konnte. Eine genaue Analyse des Wortschatzes in den fünf Sprachen R, Pl, F, D und E sowie des Textteils des Buches steht bislang aus. Ciliga (1961/62, 38) spricht von insgesamt 931 Morphemen in den fünf Ausgaben.

1.1.2. Das Universala Vortaro (1894)

Diese schmale Basis wurde von Zamenhof selbst bald erweitert (vgl. 1.2.); er wollte damit dem Ruf nach einem umfangreichen Wörterbuch zur Handhabung der neuen Sprache gerecht werden.

Man darf nicht vergessen, daß viele Esperantisten vom Vp kamen, das bereits umfangreiche Wörterbücher kannte (vgl. 2.1.). Den Charakter eines Dokumentes erhielt allerdings erst 1894 das „Universala Vortaro" (UV). Es erschien, nachdem in einer Abstimmung in diesem Jahr ein Reformprojekt Zamenhofs verworfen wurde und damit eine neue Phase innerer Stabilisierung beginnen konnte, die bis 1906 dauerte. (Die dann erneut aufkommende Diskussion um Reformen endete schließlich mit der Veröffentlichung des Plansprachenprojekts Ido; vgl. 2.2.)

Das UV (Zamenhof 1894 c) ist als mehrsprachiges Wörterbuch angelegt; es benutzt die UL-Sprachen wie später (1905) das „Fundamento" (vgl. 1.3.), dessen Bestandteil es wird. Nach den Zählungen Waringhiens (1955) enthält es 2641 Morpheme, nach Ciliga (1961/62) 2644. Nach der Gründung der Eo-Akademie (1905) beginnt eine umfangreiche Revisionsarbeit, die vor allem die irrtümlichen Übersetzungen korrigiert. Sie findet ihren Niederschlag in mehreren Berichten der Oficiala Gazeto (Raporto...), kommt aber, bedingt durch die Kriegswirren, erst Anfang der 20er Jahre zum Abschluß (Cart 1922/23/24).

Cart hatte die Frage nach den Irrtümern und Widersprüchen schon früher (1907) aufgeworfen, und noch 1957/58 geht Gregor der Frage nach den Irrtümern im englischen Teil (von den fünf UL-Sprachen beherrschte Zamenhof E am wenigsten) nach. Albault hat in seiner FdE-Ausgabe von 1963 die Frage zum Abschluß gebracht.

Vorschläge, eine erweiterte Fassung des UV zu erarbeiten, wie sie Huet machte, wurden nie in die Tat umgesetzt. Die Akademie sah ihre Aufgabe primär darin, Nachträge (vgl. 1.1.4.) zusammenzustellen, während die ein- und zweisprachigen Wörterbücher schon früh über den Umfang des UV hinausgingen.

1.1.3. Das Fundamento de Esperanto (1905)

Um sich ganz seinen philosophisch-religiösen Arbeiten widmen zu können, wollte Zamenhof das Eo völlig unabhängig von seiner Person machen (vgl. die einschlägigen Biographien von Boulton 1960 und Maimon 1978). Die Verabschiedung einer Systemurkunde, des FdE (Zamenhof 1905), die er dem Kongreß von Boulogne-sur-Mer vorlegte, sollte dazu beitragen.

Es faßt drei ältere Werke zusammen: die Grammatik des Jahres 1887, das Übungsbuch „Ekzercaro" (1894 b), dessen Wortschatz Wackrill (1907) in einer Konkordanz erfaßt hat, und das UV. Ein Vorwort als integrierender Bestandteil erklärt die sprachlichen Prinzipien des Eo und die Rolle des FdE.

Für die Eo-Lexikographie stellt das Werk ein nicht unerhebliches Problem dar. Trotz der Tatsache, daß alle Morpheme des Werkes, gleichwohl, welchem Teil sie angehören, zum „fundamentalen" Wortschatz des Eo gehören, enthält das UV den Wortschatz nur zum Teil. Selbst die späteren Nachträge haben ihn nie richtig erfaßt. Waringhien (1955) hat mit diesem Mißstand gründlich aufgeräumt. Die von ihm erfaßten „vergessenen" FdE-Morpheme wurden 1958 im 7. Nachtrag von der Akademie als „offiziell" erklärt, u. a. (ein Kuriosum!) der Name der Sprache selbst: *Esperanto*.

1.1.4. Die Oficialaj Aldonoj

Die Arbeit der Eo-Akademie war lange Jahre vorwiegend beschränkt auf die Erweiterung des offiziellen Wortschatzes, die sich bislang in der Veröffentlichung von acht „Oficialaj Aldonoj" (1909—1975) vollzog, die (nach Ciliga) bis 1958 insgesamt 1761 Morpheme umfaßte.

Mehrere Sammlungen bilanzieren dieses Anwachsen des Wortschatzes in verschiedenen Phasen: Boirac (1911), Cart (1912, 1922, 1923), Devjatnin (1919), Wüster (1923), Grosjean-Maupin (1924), Grenkamp (1937), Ockey (1971, 1975) und Hukuta (1985).

1.2. Der Wortschatz Zamenhofs

Trotz seiner offiziellen Zurückhaltung in Sprachangelegenheiten (Schleyers Beispiel, das zum Ruin des Vp beitrug, darf hier nicht unterschätzt werden) wurde und wird Zamenhofs Œuvre in stilistischer, lexikologischer und grammatikalischer Hinsicht große Bedeutung beigemessen. Allerdings steht eine umfassende Zamenhof-Konkordanz bislang aus. (Vorarbeiten von Bailey blieben als Zettelmanuskript unveröffentlicht; Wüsters Wörterbuch (1923) blieb unvollendet.)

1.2.1. Wörterbücher

Zamenhof selbst hat folgende Wörterbücher verfaßt bzw. als Herausgeber oder Bearbeiter daran mitgewirkt:

1889 R-Eo. Dazu haben Kawasaki (1974, 1975a) und Itô (1976) Studien vorgelegt: Kawasaki (1975a) untersucht die Suffixbildungen, Itô die Wortstämme (Morpheme).

1889 Eo-D. Einen Vergleich mit den UV-Morphemen hat Haupenthal (1968) vorgenommen.

1894 D-Eo (nur bis „Ablativ").

1904 Eo-D (vgl. Jürgensen 1904) und D-Eo. Waringhien (1980) geht der Geschichte dieser beiden Wörterbücher und der damit verbundenen Polemiken nach. Schon 1904 erschien dazu eine Studie (Novaj vortoj...), und 1907 untersuchte Corret die jeweiligen Zweitauflagen der beiden Wörterbücher.

1905 Eo-Pl, Pl-Eo.

1906 Eo-Pl.

1907 D-Eo, Eo-D.

1909 Eo-R. Vgl. hierzu die Ausführungen von Kawasaki (1975 b).

1.2.2. Andere Quellen

Zamenhofs Originalwerke sind in zwei Sammlungen zusammengetragen: dem (philologisch unzuverlässigen) Originala Verkaro (1929) und dem PVZ (1973—1981), das auch die gesamte bekannt gewordene Korrespondenz enthält.

Hinzu kommen die Übersetzungen aus der Weltliteratur: La batalo de l'vivo (Dickens), Hamleto (Shakespeare), Fundamenta Krestomatio (1903), La revizoro (Gogol), La Malnova Testamento (1907—1914, 1926), La rabistoj (Schiller), Georgo Dandin (Molière), Ifigenio en Taŭrido (Goethe), Marta (Orzeszko), La gimnazio (Ŝalom-Alejĥem), La rabeno de Baĥaraĥ (Heine), und Fabeloj (Andersen).

1.2.3. Zur Erfassung des Wortschatzes

Die Fülle dieses Materials ist lexikologisch nur z. T. systematisch erfaßt. Die bedeutendsten Versuche zur Registrierung des Zamenhofschen Wortschatzes haben Wüster (1923, 1927) und Nomura (1987) unternommen. Vor allem Wüsters Zamenhof-Radikaro bleibt als Vorläufer einer Zamenhof-Konkordanz ein unerreichtes Modell esperantologischer Lexikographie.

Konkordanzen liegen vor zum Originala Verkaro (Stancliff), La Predikanto (Haupenthal 1968), Sentencoj de Salomono (Gate), Marta (Kidosaki), La gimnazio (Kocher) sowie zum Ekzercaro (vgl. oben 1.1.3.).

Werkübergreifende Wortschatzerfassungen haben vorgenommen: Wackrill (1908: Ekzercaro, Hamleto, FK, La Revizoro, La Rabistoj), Boulet (1909), und Kawasaki (1940, 1949). Einzelwerke wurden schon bald nach ihrem Erscheinen nach Neologismen durchforstet, so von Mencel und Esselin die FK, von Corret (1907) und Parisot der Hamleto, von Boulet der Revizoro (1907) und La Rabistoj (1908), von Butler (1927/31) die Bibelübersetzung.

1.3. Einsprachige Wörterbücher (Definitionswörterbücher)

Es dauerte über 20 Jahre, bis es zur Herausgabe einsprachiger Definitionswörterbücher in Eo kam. Den Anfang machte 1909 der damalige Rektor der Universität Dijon, E. Boirac. Sein Ziel war es, das damals existierende Wortmaterial zu erfassen, so wie es bereits in den relativ einheitlichen Wörterbüchern des Typs Eo-X vorlag, wie es sich in den bereits umfangreichen des Typs X-Eo abzeichnete (hier plädierte Boirac für die Erstellung von Dublettenverzeichnissen zur Vereinheitlichung des Wortschatzes), wie es in den ersten technischen Wörterbüchern sich darbot und schließlich in den Werken anerkannter Autoren vorkam. Seinen kurzen Definitionen fügte Boirac noch eine französische Übersetzung bei. So verfuhr auch ein Jahr später Verax für sein technisches Wörterbuch, das auf diesem Gebiet einen ersten Versuch zur Zusammenfassung der geleisteten fachsprachlichen Vorarbeiten darstellt. Den Brauch griff dann erst 1983 wieder Vatré in seiner Neologismen-Sammlung auf.

Boiracs Wörterbuch war jedoch kaum Breitenwirkung beschert. Zu einem ersten lexikographischen Standardwerk wurde 1910 das Wörterbuch des polnischen Ophthalmologen K. Bein. Vor allem durch seine Beispielsätze war es geeignet, zur Vereinheitlichung des Sprachgebrauchs beizutragen. Es spielte (wie die Neuauflagen von 1922 und 1925 dokumentieren) knapp zwei Jahrzehnte seine Rolle, bis ihm das 1930 erstmals erschienene PV den Rang ablief, das dann ab 1934 (Datum der seither unverändert erscheinenden Zweitauflage) den Sprachgebrauch nachhaltig bestimmte. Auf ihm basieren viele der späteren Eo-X-Wörterbücher. Die Hauptarbeit an dem Wörterbuch führte Grosjean-Maupin aus; auf die 2. Aufl. (kurz nach Grosjean-Maupins Tod erschienen) hatte Waringhien maßgebenden Einfluß. Im Rückblick konnte Waringhien (PIV, X) von diesem rund 7000 Stichworte umfassenden Wörterbuch feststellen:

„So wie es in seiner 2. Auflage beschaffen war, konnte das PV in der Tat seine beabsichtigte Rolle spielen: als Festlegung des Sprachgebrauchs und als diskreter Ratgeber der Sprachbenutzer. Obwohl es anfangs einige Rigoristen angriffen, wurde seine Autorität nach und nach allgemein anerkannt. Hinzu kam, daß wegen des unvollendet gebliebenen Enzyklopädischen Wörterbuches von Wüster und der nicht veröffentlichten Zamenhof-Konkordanz von Bailey viele ihm die Rolle eines sprachhistorischen Wörterbuchs auferlegten, die es nie in Anspruch nahm."

Es gewann weiter an Ansehen und praktischer Verwendbarkeit durch einen 1954 von Waringhien erarbeiteten Nachtrag (PVS), der ab der 4. Aufl. (1954) zusammen mit dem Hauptwerk erscheint.

Das PV wurde dann 1970 durch das PIV abgelöst. Trotz seines Titels ist es kein illustriertes Wörterbuch (wie der Petit Robert, der Pate gestanden hat), sondern eine auf den Stand gebrachte Neuauflage des PV. Es bleibt trotz der z. T. heftigen Kontroversen,

Koro. - **1.** Ĉefa, centra organo de la cirkulado de la sango : *La homa koro konsistas el kvar kavoj.* - **2.** Centro de la sentimentoj : *bona, nobla koro.* - **3.** Centro, ĉefa punkto : *Parizo estas la koro de Francujo.* **Kora.** Amika, sincera : *kora akcepto, kora saluto.* **Kore.** En kora maniero. **Kortuŝi.** Tuŝi la sentimentojn : *kortuŝanta sceno.*

✱ **Koro. 1** Muskola organo, kun formo de renversita konuso, kiu estas centro k ĉefa aganto de cirkulado de sango : *senti batojn ĉe l'* ∼*o ; la sango alfluas al la* ∼*o ; eĉ pinglo povas* ∼*on trapiki* ^{Z} *; tio premas la* ∼*on* (pro fizika aŭ morala angoro). **2** Tiu organo, konsiderata kiel sidejo de la sentoj (deziro, ĝojo, sufero) : *havi, kiom la* ∼*o deziras* ^{Z} *; frakasi, rompi* ^{Z}*, ŝiri* ^{Z}*, trabori* ^{Z}*, fendi* ^{Z}*, mueli ies* ∼*on* ^{Z} *; kio iras al* ∼*o, venas al* ∼*o* ^{Z} (konfido naskas konfidon) *; se okulo ne vidas,* ∼*o ne avidas* ^{Z} *; malŝarĝi la* ∼*on* ^{Z} *; se la* ∼*o tiras vin* ^{Z} (se tio plaĉas al vi) *; alpreni ion al la* ∼*o* ^{Z} (tutkore interesiĝi pri io) *; ami* ^{Z}*, ĝoji, ridi* ^{Z}*, labori el (per* ^{Z}*) la tuta* ∼*o* ^{Z} *;* ∼*o aroganta, ĝoja, kontenta, malica, malmola, milda, prudenta, saĝa, suferanta* ^{Z} *; mia* ∼*o neniel emas al rido* ^{Z} *; peza ŝarĝo falis al mi sur la* ∼*on* ^{Z} *; havi* ∼*on* (kuraĝon aŭ kompatemon) *; ĉu vi havas iomete da* ∼*o k konscienco* ^{Z} *? ; homoj sen* ∼*o* ^{Z} *; havi bonan* ∼*on* ^{Z} (kompatemon)*, puran* ∼*on* ^{Z} *;* ∼*o el oro* ^{Z} *;* ∼*amato* ^{Z} *;* ∼*inklinoj* ^{Z} *;* ∼*ĝojiga* ^{Z}*,* ∼*ŝira,* ∼*kreviga spektaklo.* (Kp ANIMO, KAPO SENTOKAPABLO). **3** Tiu organo, konsiderata kiel sidejo de amo, de pasio : *belecon taksas ne okulo, sed* ∼*o* ^{Z} *; edziĝi laŭ* ∼*o* ^{Z} *; doto* ∼*on ne varmigas* ^{Z} *; for de l' okuloj, for de la* ∼*o* ^{Z}*.* **4** Centro, ĉefa punkto : *pom*∼*o ; li loĝas ĉe la* ∼*o de la urbo ; penetri ĝis la* ∼*o de la temo* ^{Z} *; Parizo estas la* ∼*o de Francujo* ^{B} (Kp KERNO). ∼**a.** Venanta el ∼*o* ; amika, sincera, favora : ∼*a akcepto, saluto, danko ;* ∼*a sindona amiko ; mi salutas vin tut*∼*e ; preĝu* ∼*e k laboru fervore* ^{Z}. ∼**favori** (tr). Bon∼e kompati iun. (Kp FAVORA). ∼**tuŝi** (tr). Eksciti ies sentojn ; emocii : ∼*tuŝa rakonto.* **Bon**∼**a.** Kompatema. **Sen**∼**a.** Senkompata, kruela.

✱**kor/o 1** ♥ Muskola kava organo, kiu per siaj kontrahiĝoj pumpas la sangon tra la korpon k prezentas la centran organon de la sangocirkuliga sistemo (*cor*): *la homa* ∼*o estas dividita je du paroj da kavoj: atrioj k ventrikloj; senti batojn ĉe l'* ∼*o; la sango alfluas al la* ∼*o; eĉ pinglo povas* ∼*on trapiki* ^{Z}*; tio premas la* ∼*on* (pro fizika aŭ morala angoro); *li havis la senton, kvazaŭ pro malgoj tuj krevos al li la* ∼*o* ^{Z}. ☞ *angino, endokardio, perikardio, sistolo, diastolo, valvoj, palpitacio.* **2** (f) Tiu sama organo, rigardata kiel sidejo de la sentoj (deziro, ĝojo, sufero): *havi, kiom la* ∼*o deziras* ^{Z}; *frakasi, rompi* ^{Z}*, ŝiri* ^{Z}*, trabori* ^{Z}*, fendi* ^{Z}*, mueli ies* ∼*on* ^{Z}; *kio iras el* ∼*o, venas al* ∼*o* ^{Z} (konfido naskas konfidon); *se okulo ne vidas,* ∼*o ne avidas* ^{Z}; *malŝarĝi la* ∼*on* ^{Z}; *se la* ∼*o tiras vin* ^{Z} (se tio plaĉas al vi); *alpreni ion al la* ∼*o* ^{Z} (tutkore interesiĝi pri io); *ami* ^{Z}*, ĝoji, ridi* ^{Z}*, labori el (per* ^{Z}*) la tuta* ∼*o* ^{Z}; ∼*o aroganta, ĝoja, kontenta, malica, malmola, milda, prudenta, saĝa, suferanta* ^{X}; *mia* ∼*o neniel emas al rido* ^{Z}; *peza ŝarĝo falis al mi sur la* ∼*on* ^{Z}; *havi* ∼*on* (kuraĝon aŭ kompatemon); *ĉu vi havas iomete da* ∼*o k konscienco?* ^{Z}; *homoj sen* ∼*o* ^{Z}; *havi bonan* ∼*on* ^{Z} (kompatemon), *puran* ∼*on* ^{Z}; ∼*o el oro* ^{Z}; ∼*amato* ^{Z}; ∼*inklinoj* ^{Z}; ∼*ĝojiga* ^{Z}, ∼*ŝira,* ∼*kreviga spektaklo.* ☞ *animo, kapo, sentokapablo.* **3** (f) Tiu sama organo, rigardata kiel sidejo de amo, de pasio: *belecon taksas ne okulo, sed* ∼*o* ^{Z}; *edziĝi laŭ* ∼*o* ^{Z}; *doto* ∼*on ne varmigas* ^{Z}; *for de l' okuloj, for de la* ∼*o* ^{Z}. **4** (f) Karesnomo de amata persono: *mia* ∼*o, iru paroli kun via filino* ^{Z}; *mia plej kara* ∼*o* ^{Z}; *frata* ∼*o, mi vin sekvos!* ^{Z}. **5** (f) La plej interna parto de io: *la* ∼*o de la tero, de pomo; li loĝas ĉe la* ∼*o de la urbo; penetri ĝis la* ∼*o de la temo* ^{Z}; *Parizo estas la* ∼*o de Francujo* ^{B}. ☞ *kerno.* **6** ♣ Meza parto de planto, ekz. la plej juna parto de ŝoso (∼*ŝoso*), medolo de trunko: ∼*putro* (putro de ekz. ∼*ŝoso* aŭ de la meza parto de tubero). ∼**a 1** ♥ ♥ Apartenanta al la ∼o: ∼*aj valvoj;* ∼*a blokado.* ☞ *kardia.* **2** ♥ Efikanta sur la ∼on: ∼*a drogo.* **3** (f) Venanta el la ∼o: *per* ∼*a movo etendi la manon por manpremo* ^{Z}; ∼*an dankon!* ^{Z}; *amo pli* ∼*a, disiĝo pli dolora* ^{Z}; ∼*a akcepto;* preĝu ∼e k *laboru fervore* ^{Z}; *ami plej* ∼*e* ^{Z}. ∼ **eco.** El ∼o venanta bonvolo, afablo: *neniam mi premis al iu la manon kun pli sincera estimo k* ∼*eco* ^{Z}. ∼**premi** (tr). Fizike k morale premi ies ∼on: *malgaja k* ∼*premata, ŝi iom revigliĝadis ekvidante la patrinon* ^{Z}; ∼*premanta vidajo* ^{Z}. ∼ **tuŝi** (tr). Emocii: *profunde* ∼*tuŝis min la malĝoja novaĵo* ^{Z}; *legu al mi la historion pri . . . Jozefo! ĝi ĉiam tiel* ∼*tuŝadis min* ^{Z}; *mi rememoras* ∼*tuŝite pri la unuaj pioniroj* ^{Z}; *venkante sian* ∼*tuŝitecon, ŝi turnis sin al Marta* ^{Z}. **antaŭ**∼**a** ♥ Troviĝanta antaŭe de la ∼o: *antaŭ*∼*a regiono de la torako.* **sen**∼**a 1** ♥ Ne posedanta ∼on. **2** Senkompata, nesentema: *ho sen*∼*a pastro!* ^{Z}; *vi paroladas kiel sen*∼*ulo* ^{Z}. **tut**∼**e.** El la tuta ∼o: *ŝi pentis tut*∼*e pri sia peko* ^{Z}; *mi estas tut*∼*e via* ^{Z}. **bon**∼**a.** Kompatema, sentema: *ili agis kun mi kiel bon*∼*aj friponoj* ^{Z}; *bon*∼*aj penoj* ^{Z}; *bon*∼*a, varmiga rigardo* ^{Z}; *la dioj donu al vi rekompencon pro via bon*∼*eco!* ^{Z}. **favor** ∼**a.** Indulga, inklina favori: *kun favor*∼*ulo vi estas favor*∼*a* ^{X}; *tiel same favor*∼*e, kiel mi agis kun vi, vi agos kun mi* ^{X}; *kiamaniere vi havas la eksteraĵon de besto k tamen estas plena de favor*∼*eco?* ^{Z}; *mi favor*∼*os tiun* ^{X}. ☞ *korfavori.* **mol**∼**a.** Facile emociita, influebla. **plen**∼**a.** Tute sincera; ne havanta ian retenon: *liaj okuloj brilis per plen*∼*a gajeco* ^{Z}; *plen*∼*e petadi Dion* ^{Z}.

Textbeispiel 329.1: Artikel *koro* aus drei verschiedenen Wörterbüchern (Bein 1910, 85; PV² 1934, 260; PIV 1970, 565)

die es sowohl im fachsprachlichen wie im allgemeinsprachlichen Teil ausgelöst hat (hier insbesondere wegen der belletristischen Neologismen, die seither von modernen Übersetzern, vor allem den Repräsentanten eines „naturalistischen" Eo, in verstärktem Maße gebraucht werden), das Standardwerk, das heute den Sprachgebrauch regelt. (Daß dem so ist, zeigt u. a. ein im Iran angefertigter Raubdruck.)

Die Entwicklung der Definitionswörterbücher sei am Beispiel des Wörterbucheintrags **kor** (Herz) in Beins „Vortaro", dem PV und dem PIV aufgezeigt.

1.4. Mehrsprachige Wörterbücher

1.4.1. Zweisprachige Wörterbücher

Die Gesamtheit des Materials entfalten die Bibliographien von Stojan und Ockey, die italienischen Wörterbücher analysiert Rizzo. Umfangreichere Wörterbücher liegen für die Mehrzahl der europäischen Sprachen (vgl. Tab. I u. II, Abb. 329.1 u. 2) vor.

Von den außereuropäischen Sprachen sind lediglich C, J und Ko (aufgrund der relativen Verbreitung des Eo in diesen Ländern) gut vertreten, in neuerer Zeit auch Ar und Pe. Für viele andere Sprachen liegen lediglich kleine Wortverzeichnisse (sog. „ŝlosiloj") vor.

1.4.1.1. Wörterbücher vom Typ Eo-X (vgl. Tab. I, Abb. 329.1)

Sieht man von unbedeutenden Vorläufern im 19. Jh. ab, so gilt, daß den Wörterbuchtyp Eo-X die beiden wegweisenden Werke von Beaufront (1902) und Jürgensen (1904), beide von Zamenhof mitbeeinflußt, geprägt haben. An ihnen orientieren sich die Vorkriegswörterbücher. Nie mehr wieder erreichten Modellcharakter erhielt in der Zwischenkriegsperiode das Wörterbuch von Wüster (1923), das im Buchstaben *K* abbricht (zu seiner Geschichte vgl. Schwarz und Plehn). Es ist der bislang einzige Versuch, auch Belegstellen (für Zamenhof-Texte) aufzuführen. Waringhiens Wörterbuch von 1957 basiert auf den Vorarbeiten des PV und PVS; an ihm orientieren sich in der Nachfolge die anderen Eo-X-Wörterbücher, z. B. Hu (1959), Bu (1963) und Ru (1974). Bislang liegt nur ein Wörterbuch vor (I), das das PIV-Material verarbeitet.

Alle Wörterbücher sind nach den Eo-Morphemen angeordnet, also nicht streng alphabetisch; eine Ausnahme bildet das Wörterbuch von Pechan (Eo-Hu), dem eine strenge Alphabetisierung zugrunde liegt. Sieht man von dem Beispiel Wüsters ab, so wird nirgends in größerem Umfange die Phraseologie berücksichtigt.

1.4.1.2. Wörterbücher vom Typ X-Eo (vgl. Tab. II, Abb. 329.2)

Dieser Mangel macht sich bei den Wörterbüchern des Typs X-Eo noch mehr bemerkbar. Auch sie beschränken sich in der Regel auf Vokabelgleichungen und lassen den Benutzer bei allen komplizierten Sachverhalten im Stich.

So fällt z. B. das Wörterbuch von Wingen (D-Eo) hinter den Stand von Bennemann (1926) zurück, dessen Niveau erst 1983 durch Krause wieder erreicht wird. Für die bekannteren Sprachen (E, F, S ...) liegen heute keine den Bedürfnissen entsprechenden Wörterbücher vor. Eine Ausnahme bildet das 1982 erschienene Wörterbuch von Miyamoto (J-Eo).

Die X-Eo-Wörterbücher kranken auch daran, daß sie das vorhandene Material nicht hinreichend einbeziehen bzw. gewollte Lösungen bieten.

1.4.2. Vielsprachige Wörterbücher

Sieht man vom UV und den in seiner Nachfolge entstandenen Verzeichnissen (vgl. 1.1.2. u. 1.1.4.) sowie einem Teil der Fachwörterbücher (vgl. 1.5.6.) ab, so lassen sich nur wenige allgemeinsprachliche Beispiele nennen, z. B. Hecker (1907) und Hrynkiewicz (1972); beide sind nach Sachgebieten geordnet. Hierher gehört trotz seines irreführenden Titels auch das „etymologische" Wörterbuch von Bastien (1950). Ein wirkliches etymologisches Wörterbuch hat erst 1989 Vilborg vorgelegt.

1.5. Spezialwörterbücher

Systematisch erfaßt wird lediglich das monographische Schrifttum. Auf Zeitschriftenliteratur und kleinere Wörterverzeichnisse (z. B. im Anhang zu Fachbüchern) kann nicht eingegangen werden.

1.5.1. Redensarten, Sprichwörter

Die bedeutendste Sammlung stammt von Zamenhof selbst (1910, 1961); sie fußt auf einer mehrsprachigen Phraseologie seines Vaters, die Holzhaus (1980) in allen Auflagen wieder zugänglich gemacht hat.

Die Geschichte der Sammlung beschreibt Waringhien im Vorwort der Ausgabe von 1961. Bearbeitungen stammen von Butler (1926; E), Minor 1922; D) und Couto Fernandes (Pt). Ein weit über die Sammlung Zamenhofs hinausgehendes Verzeichnis von Redensarten haben Csiszár/Kalocsay vorgelegt.

1.5.2. Bildwörterbücher

Der Versuch, eine Eo-Fassung des Bilder-Dudens (1. Aufl.) vorzulegen, wurde nach Vorarbeiten (Esperanta bildvortaro...) 1988 (Eichholz 1988) abgeschlossen. Nützlich, da auf die Alltagssprache bezogen, ist das Praktika Bildvortaro.

1.5.3. Homonymiken und Paronymiken

Nur vier Sammlungen verdienen Erwähnung: Loy (1921) hat mehrsinnige deutsche Wörter in Eo zusammengestellt, Bernard/Ribot (1971) gehen dem Problem der „faux amis" nach, Gjivoje (1979) hat Antonyme, Homonyme, Paronyme, Synonyme und Wortspiele erfaßt. Ojalo hat eine Synonymensammlung vorgelegt.

1.5.4. Reimwörterbücher

Reimwörterbücher haben in Eo eine lange Tradition: sie reichen in die Anfänge des Jh. zurück: Parisot, Rhodes (1905) und Thomson (1918). 1932 veröffentlichten Kalocsay und Waringhien ihr Parnasa Gvidlibro, das sowohl ein Reimwörterbuch als auch ein Neologismenverzeichnis (vgl. 1.5.5.) enthält.

Es hat — trotz mancher Anfechtungen — seine Stellung bis heute behauptet. Einen ersten Versuch eines rückläufigen Wörterbuchs (auf dem PV basierend) hat Schlüter (1972) vorgelegt; ihm folgte Pabst (1989).

1.5.5. Neologismen

Daß sich die Entwicklung des Eo über den Weg von Archaismen und Neologismen vollzieht, hat Zamenhof 1905 im FdE festgeschrieben. Seit dieser Zeit verfolgt die Eo-Bewegung ein Zwiespalt: auf der einen Seite die Verfechter eines sprachlichen Minimalismus, der den Schematismus der Wortbildung ausnutzen will, auf der anderen Seite die Befürworter eines sprachlichen „Naturalismus" (hierzu zählen alle namhaften Literaten), die für die Benutzung eines elaborierten Wortschatzes eintreten.

Kalocsay/Waringhien haben in ihrem Parnasa Gvidlibro schon früh (1932) die belletristischen Neologismen erfaßt. 1983 legte Vatré eine Neologismensammlung vor, die 1000 im PIV nicht registrierte Morpheme enthält. Eine 3. Aufl. fügt weitere 1000 Wortwurzeln hinzu (Vatré 1987). Cherpillod (1988) erfaßt sogar 6800 Wortstämme, die das PIV nicht kennt.

1.5.6. Fachwörterbücher (vgl. Tab. III, Abb. 329.3)

Das Material ist erfaßt bei Haferkorn (1962, 1964), Carlevaro und Ockey (1982). Nach der Statistik Carlevaros (1974, 282) soll es bis Ende 1964 127 Fachwörterbücher gegeben haben, von denen jedoch nur 36 mehr als 75 Seiten umfassen.

Hier sind alle Wörterbuchtypen vertreten: einsprachige Definitionswörterbücher, zwei- und mehrsprachige, Wörterbücher in ABC-Folge und nach Sachgebieten geordnete. Am besten vertreten sind folgende Disziplinen: Botanik, Elektrotechnik, Eisenbahnwesen, Chemie, Handel, Mathematik, Medizin, Religion, Rundfunk und Technik.

Da das Eo eine nur geringfügige fachwissenschaftliche Literatur aufweist, gilt dieser Teil der Sprache als nach wie vor unterentwickelt. Erst in jüngster Zeit gibt es wieder Versuche, die Fachsprache systematisch anzugehen und Normungsgrundsätze auszuarbeiten (vgl. Dehler 1986a; 1986b). Dabei wird bewußt an die Arbeit des lange maßgeblichen Normungsspezialisten Wüster angeknüpft (vgl. Wüster 1931).

1.5.7. Namenwörterbücher

Hier lassen sich zwei große Gruppen unterscheiden: Personennamen und Länderbezeichnungen.

Auf die Darstellung der geschichtlichen Entwicklung (auch der Transkriptionsprobleme) muß hier verzichtet werden. Wörterbuchartig erfaßt sind Heiligennamen (Wannemakers 1963; Propraj nomoj...) und Ländernamen (Poŝatlaso...). Eine Sammlung von 400 japanischen Ethnonymen hat Nakamura (1969) erarbeitet.

1.5.8. Abkürzungen

Ein erstes Verzeichnis legte 1982 Haupenthal vor.

1.5.9. Frequenzwörterbücher

Es gibt bislang nur unzureichende Häufigkeitswörterverzeichnisse, geschweige denn daran sich orientierende Lehrbücher. Vatré (1986) legte eigene, an literarischen Texten orientierte Untersuchungen vor.

Seit Ende der 20er Jahre liegen jedoch einige Verzeichnisse vor: Danneil, Sadler (1958/59) und Harry (1967). Eine Statistik von 50 000 Textwörtern hatte Blaas (1949/55) veröffentlicht.

Neuen und z. T. didaktischen Zwecken dienend sind die Verzeichnisse von Albault (1975), Tišlar (1982) und Dietze (1989).

Tabelle I: Wörterbuchtyp Eo-X

Sprache		Zeitraum			Sprach-gruppe
		I. bis 1918	II. bis 1939	III. ab 1945	
= 20	E	1908 Millidge	1921 Fulcher/Long	1967 Butler, 1973 Wells	Germanische Sprachen
= 30	D	1904 Jürgensen	1923 Bennemann, Wüster, 1924 Minor	1952 Butin/Sommer	
= 393.1	Nl		1928 Veer, 1936 Straaten		
= 395.9	Is				
= 396	No			1948 Rian	
= 397	Sv	1905 Ahlberg	1919 Backman 1933 Nylén		
= 398	Da				
= 40	F	1902 Beaufront 1910 Grosjean-Maupin		1957 Waringhien	Romanische Sprachen
= 50	I		1931 Tellini	1959 Tellini 1984 Brocatelli	
= 60	S	1905 Inglada		1967 Paluzie-Borrell	
= 690	Pt	1919 Leite			
= 82	R	1909 Zamenhof		1974 Bokarev	Slawische Sprachen
= 84	Pl	1916 Grabowski		1959 Michalski	
= 850	Cs	1908 Čejka		1947 Filip, 1969 Ĥromada	
= 854	Sk				
= 861 / 862	Sh		1934 Zivanović	1959 Zivanović	
= 863	Sn			1959 Avsec, 1970 Seemann	
= 867	Bg		1939 Nikolov	1963 Vortaro ...	
= 882	Li			1988 Puodenas	Baltische Sprachen
= 883	Le			1979 Jaunvalks/Gūtmanis	
= 915.5	Pe			1983 Saminy	Semitische Sprachen
= 924.6	He				
= 924.61	Yi			1966 Fineman, 1969 Rusak	
= 927	Ar			1968 Isaac	
= 945.11	Hu		1923 Tomán	1958 Pechan	Ural-Altaische Sprachen
= 945.41	Fi			1963/1982 Vilkki	
= 945.45	Es		1927 Vo-Ko	1957 Sepamaa	
= 951	C			1980 Uang, 1987 Eo-C	Asiatische Sprachen
= 956	J			1963 Okamoto	
= 957	Ko			1969 Hajpin	

Abb. 329.1: Die zweisprachigen Wörterbücher mit Esperanto als Ausgangssprache

329. Lexikographie der Plansprachen

Tabelle II: Wörterbuchtyp X-Eo

Sprache		I. bis 1918	II. bis 1939	III. ab 1945	Sprach-gruppen
= 20	E	1908 Rhodes		1973 Wells	Germanische Sprachen
= 30	D	1904 Zamenhof 1910 Christaller	1923 Christaller 1926 Bennemann	1954 Wingen 1983 Krause	
= 393.1	Nl	1916 Haak	1936 Straaten	1971 Middelkoop	
= 395.9	Is			1965 Skaftfell	
= 396	No			1963 Rian	
= 397	Sv		1921 Backman		
= 398	Da		1940 Frey		
= 40	F	1903 Cart, 1910 Grosjean	1936 Grosjean-M.	1961 Léger/Albault	Romanische Sprachen
= 50	I			1981 I-Eo	
= 60	S			1966 Tudela F.	
= 690	Pt	1913 Leite	1936 Conto F.	1954/1965 Gomes Braga	
= 82	R	1889 Zamenhof		1966 Bokarev	Slawische Sprachen
= 84	Pl	1910 Grabowski		1969 Guterman, Tymiński	
= 850	Cs	1914 Kühnl		1949 Filip	
= 854	Sk			1970 Seemann	
= 861/862	Sh			1966 Gjivoje	
= 863	Sn			1963 Petriĉ	
= 867	Bg		1931 Grigorov	1981 Bg-Eo	
= 882	Li			1988 Puodenas	Baltische Sprachen
= 883	Le			1979 Jaunvalks/Gūtmanis	
= 914	Ur			1987 Eo-Ur	Semitische Sprachen
= 915.5	Pe			1981 Saminy	
= 924.6	He				
= 924.61	Yi			1966 Fineman	
= 927	Ar				
= 945.11	Hu		1927 Tomán	1958 Pechan	Ural-Altaische Sprachen
= 945.41	Fi		1923 Setälä	1963/1982 Vilkki	
= 945.45	Es			1957 Sepamaa	
= 951	C			1980 Uang	Asiatische Sprachen
= 956	J		1935 Okamoto	1957 Kaji, 1982 Miyamoto	
= 957	Ko			1983 Hajpin	

Abb. 329.2: Die zweisprachigen Wörterbücher mit Esperanto als Zielsprache

Tabelle III: Fachwörterbücher

DK-Zahl	Fach	Autor (Jahr: Sprache(n))
1	Philosophie	Kamaryt (1934: Eo-Cs-D)
282	Katholizismus	Flammer (1963: D-Eo), Wannemakers (1963a: Eo-La), Claramunt (1964: Eo-S), Roosen (1965: Eo-Nl; 1972: Nl-Eo)
294.3	Buddhismus	Sadler (1962: Eo)
34	Recht	Liebeck (1931: D-Eo), Mildwurf (1946: Eo)
335	Armee	Durrant (1940: Eo), Militista vortareto (1955: Eo-F-E-D-I)
362.191	Rotes Kreuz	Uhlmann (1913: D-Eo)
369.4	Pfadfinder	Hammer (1974: Eo)
38	Handel	Eiselin (1925: Nl-Eo), Kreuz/Mazzolini (1927: Eo), Munniksma (1975: E-Eo-D-S-F-I-Nl-Pt-Sv)
51	Mathematik	Bricard (1905: Eo), Bean (1954: Eo), Hilgers/Yashovardhan (1980: Da-Eo, D-Eo, F-Eo, I-Eo, Nl-Eo, Pt-Eo), Kiselman (1985: Eo-E-F-Sv)
526	Geodäsie	Geodezia fakterminaro ... (1976-81: E-Eo-F, D-Hu-R)
527	Aeronautik	Armon/Archdeacon (1913: F, E, D, S, I, Eo), Durrant (1941: Eo)
54	Chemie	Esperanta nomenklaturo ... (1913: Eo-E-F-D-I), Dellian (1948: Eo), Pióro (1966: Eo), Westermayer (1981: Eo-E-D)
551.5	Meteorologie	Lewin (1961: Eo)
581.5	Bäume	Markheden (1982: Sv-Eo-La, Eo-Sv-La)
595	Insekten	Steinmann (1987: Eo-La-C)
598.2	Vögel	Stojan (1911: La-F-E-D-I-Pl-R-Eo), Bossong (1971: La-Eo), Mészáros (1980: La-Eo-Hu-D-E-Cs-Pl-R)
61	Medizin	Briquet (1932: Eo), Hradil (1982: Eo, passim F, D, Gr, La)
611	Anatomie	Anatomia ... (1906: La, F, E, Eo), Anatomia nomenklaturo (1989: La, E, F, Eo)
615	Pharmazie	Rousseau (1911: Eo-E-F-D-S-Nl-Sv-La)
62	Technik	Verax (1907: F-Eo), Haferkorn (1956: Eo, passim: F, E; 1967: D-Eo), Moberg (1958: Sv, Eo, E, Da, Fi, D, S, I, Nl, P, R)
621	Maschinen	Wüster (1923: Eo-D, D-Eo)
621.22	Hydraulik	Rybář (1982: Eo-E-Cs-D-R)
621.3	Elektrotechnik	Alexandersson (1953: Eo-Sv), Siwicki (1963: Eo-Pl), Internacia elektroteknika ... (1965: Eo-Pl-E-F-D-I-Sv)
621.396	Radio	Venture (1960: Eo)

DK-Zahl	Fach	Autor (Jahr: Sprache(n))
621.93	Sägen	Plehn (1934: D-E-F-I-Eo)
621.96	Stanzen	Mizeruña (1973: Eo)
625.1	Eisenbahn	Habellok (1923: D-Eo), Rosher (1953: Eo-E), Ritterspach (1966: D-Eo, Eo-D), Engen (1968: No-Eo, Eo-No), Bengtsson (1976: Sv-Eo, Eo-Sv), Fervoja ... (1989: Eo)
625.7/.8	Straßenbau	Broise (1959: Eo-E-F-D)
629.1	Auto	Eyama (1969: Eo-J-E, J-Eo-E)
629.12	Nautik	Rollet de L'Isle (1908: Eo), Clissold (1950: Eo-E-D-Sp)
635	Hortikultur	Neergaard (1938: Eo-E-Da-Sv-D-F)
642	Gastronomie	Urban (1958: Eo-E-Cs-F)
656.835	Philatelie	Lemaire (1903: F-Eo), Scott (1928: Eo-E-F-D)
677	Nähen	Green (1947: Eo)
681.177	Datenverarbeitung	A vállatirányitasi ... (1972: Hu, D, E, R, Eo)
72	Architektur	Azorin (1932: S-Pt-I-F-E-Pl-Sv)
78	Musik	Ménil (1908: Eo), Butler/Merrick (1944: Eo), Briano (1972: I), Hill (1980: Eo)
796	Sport	Uljaky-Nagy (1972: Eo)
796	Kinderspiele	Terminaro ... (1960: Eo)
929.6	Heraldik	Klement (1979: D-E-F-I-R-Cs)

Abb. 329.3: Die Fachwörterbücher des bzw. mit Esperanto

2. Andere Plansprachen

Die große Mehrzahl der Plansprachen ist über kurze Entwürfe nicht hinausgekommen (vgl. die Gesamtdarstellungen von Couturat/ Leau (1903), Drezen (1931) und Blanke (1985)). Praktische Bedeutung im internationalen mündlichen und schriftlichen Verkehr erlangten im wesentlichen nur fünf Projekte: Vp (1880), Eo (1887), Ido (1908), Occidental (1922, ab 1947: Ie) und Ia (1951). Diese wurden von Wüster (1931, ³1977) und Manders (1947) eingehend analysiert, auch bezüglich ihres Wortmaterials.

2.1. Volapük

Wie kaum ein anderes Projekt wurde Vp von Schleyer dirigistisch gelenkt. Seine Grammatiken und Wörterbücher (Schleyer 1880, 1882) erhoben Anspruch auf Verbindlichkeit. Die 3. Auflage enthielt im Teil D-Vp 12 570 Wörter, die 4. (1888) sogar 20 000 Lexeme. Nachdem Vp bereits seinem Niedergang zustrebe, ließ Schleyer in Fortsetzungen ein noch größeres Wörterbuch erscheinen, das jedoch unvollendet blieb (Schleyer 1898).

Weitere nennenswerte Wörterbücher liegen in folgenden Sprachen vor: D (Pflaumer, Walther), E (Scherzinger, Wood), F (Kerckhoffs), I (Mattei, Tommasi) und Sv (Liedbeck). Das umfassendste, allerdings in reformiertem Vp verfaßte Wörterbuch stammt von de Jong.

Die Gesamtheit des Materials — u. a. die kleineren Fachwörterbücher Schleyers — erfaßt Haupenthal (1982b).

2.2. Ido

Das sich als Reform des Eo verstehende Ido kennt zwei Phasen der Wörterbuchproduktion: die des Anfangs (1908) und die nach der von der Ido-Akademie beschlossenen Stabilisierungsphase zu Beginn der 20er Jahre.

Nennenswerte Wörterbücher liegen ausschließlich in den Sprachen D (Beaufront 1908, Couturat 1919, Feder 1919), E (Beaufront/Couturat 1908, Dyer 1922) und F (Beaufront 1908/11, 1915) vor. Daneben hat Ido einige kleinere Fachwörterbücher vorzuweisen für Biologie (Boubier 1911), Handel

(Hugon 1909), Mathematik (Couturat 1910), Photographie (Pfaundler 1914) und Rundfunkwesen (Feder/Nordin 1924). Ein einsprachiges Definitionswörterbuch hat Pesch (1964) vorgelegt.

2.3. Occidental/Interlingue

Dem vom Vp, Eo und Idiom Neutral kommenden de Wahl ging es darum, einen Kompromiß zu schaffen zwischen Natürlichkeit (d. h. Imitation romanischer Sprachen) und Regelmäßigkeit. Das schlägt sich im Wortschatz des Occidental nieder. Zu den bedeutendsten Wörterbüchern zählen:

De Wahl (1925: D, E, F, I, Nl, Pt, R, Sp), Gär (1928, D-Ie), Berger (1947: Ie) und Kemp (1958, E-Ie).

2.4. Interlingua

Interlingua ist das Kollektivprodukt der International Auxiliary Language Association (IALA; Literatur bei Blanke 1985, 167—173). Es blieb im wesentlichen bei dem Wörterbuch von Gode, mit dem das Projekt 1951 startete. Dazu hat Wüster (1973) umfangreiche Marginalien ausgearbeitet.

3. Literatur (in Auswahl)

3.1. Wörterbücher

Ahlberg = P. Ahlberg: Esperanto-svensk ordbok. Stockholm 1905 [XI, 162 S.].

Albault 1975 = A. Albault: Baza radikaro oficiala. In: Aktoj de la Akademio. II. 1968—1975. Rotterdam. Paris 1975, 28—54.

Alexandersson = S. Alexandersson: Elektroteknika terminaro esperanta-sveda. Stockholm 1953 [10 Bl.].

Anatomia = Anatomia vortaro kvarlingva. Paris 1906 [IV, 76 S.].

Anatomia nomenklaturo. Trad. kaj komp. de Li Kexi kaj A. Albault. Pekino 1989 [697 S.].

Armon = R. d'Armon/E. Archdeacon: Lexique aéronautique en 6 languages. Paris 1913 [212 S.].

A vállatirányítási = A vállatirányítási számítógépalkalmazás fogalmainak több nyelvü szótára. Budapest 1972 [464 S.].

Avsec = O. Avsec: Esperanto-slovena kaj slovenaesperanta vortaro. Ljubljana 1958 [301 S.].

Azorin = F. Azorin: Universala terminologio de la arkitekturo. Madrid 1932 [215 S.].

Backman 1919 = G. H. Backman: Esperantosvensk ordbok. Stockholm 1919 [IV, 166 S.].

Backman 1921 = G. H. Backman: Svensk-Esperanto ordbok. Stockholm 1921 [V, 214 S.].

Bastien = L. Bastien: Naúlingva etimologia leksikono de la lingvo Esperanto. London 1950 [XVII, 317 S.; 1. Aufl. Paris 1907].

Bean = C. M. Bean: Matematika terminaro. Heronsgate 1954 [39 S.].

Beaufront 1902 = L. de Beaufront: Dictionnaire Esperanto-Français. Paris 1902 [XII, 209 S. — 18. Tsd. 1907].

Beaufront 1908 a = L. de Beaufront/L. Couturat/ P. D. Hugon: English-international dictionary. London 1908 [271 S.].

Beaufront 1908 b = L. de Beaufront/L. Couturat: International-English dictionary. London 1908 [XXII, 230 S.].

Beaufront 1908 c = L. de Beaufront/L. Couturat/ R. Thomann: Deutsch-internationales Wörterbuch. Stuttgart 1908 [376 S.].

Beaufront 1908 d = L. de Beaufront/L. Couturat/ R. Thomann: International-deutsches Wörterbuch. Stuttgart 1908 [XXIV, 294 S.].

Beaufront 1908 e = L. de Beaufront/L. Couturat: Dictionnaire Français-International. Paris 1908 [240 S. Supplément 1911. 24 S.].

Beaufront 1915 = L. de Beaufront/L. Couturat: Dictionnaire Français-Ido. Paris 1915 [XIII, 586 S.].

Bein = K. Bein: Vortaro de Esperanto. Paris 1910 [175 S.; 2. Aufl. 1922; 3. Aufl. 1925; Nachdr. d. 2. Aufl. Seoul 1977].

Bengtsson = H. Bengtsson: Fervoja terminaro. Lund 1976 [VI, 167 S.].

Bennemann = P. Bennemann: Esperanto HandWörterbuch. Leipzig 1923—1926. 1. Teil: Eo-D. 1923 [XIV, 159 S.], 2. Teil: D-Eo. 1926 [XX, 555 S.].

Berger 1929 = R. Berger: Dictionnaire FrançaisOccidental. Chapelle 1929 [315 S.].

Berger 1947 = R. Berger: Fundamental vocabularium. Cheseaux 1947 [164 S.].

Bernard = R. Bernard/A. Ribot: Falsaj amikoj en Esperanto. Marmande 1971 [39 S.].

Blaas = L. Blaas: Statistiko de 50 000 tekstvortoj. In: Esperatnologio 1. 1949/55, 107—32, 160—200.

Boirac 1909 = E. Boirac: Plena vortaro Esperantoesperanta kaj Esperanto-franca. Dijon 1909 [XIX, 430 S.].

Boirac 1911 = E. Boirac: Vortaro de la oficialaj radikoj de Esperanto laŭ Universala Vortaro kaj Unua Oficiala Aldono. Paris 1911 [27 S.].

Bokarev 1966 = E. A. Bokarev: Rusa-esperanta vortaro. Moskvo 1966 [536 S.].

Bokarev 1974 = E. A. Bokarev: Esperanta-rusa vortaro. Moskvo 1974 [488 S.; ²1982].

Bossong = R. H. Bossong: Komunlingva nomaro de eŭropaj birdoj. Cardiff. Ontario 1971.

Boubier = M. Boubier: Internaciona biologial lexiko. Jena 1911 [V, 73 S.].

Boulet 1909 = P. Boulet: Du mil novaj vortoj. Paris 1909 [XI, 75 S.].

Briano = J.-B. Briano: Esperanto-lingva muzika leksikono. Milano 1972 [95 S.].

Bricard = R. Bricard: Matematika terminaro kun krestomatio. Paris 1905 [59 S.].

Briquet = M. Briquet: Esperanta teknika medicina vortaro. Bruxelles 1932 [358 S.].

Broccatelli = U. Broccatelli: Vocabolario Esperanto-Italiano. Milano 1984 [XVI, 482 S.].

Broise = A. Broise: Teknika terminaro pri ŝoseoj kaj pontoj. In: Jarlibro de UEA. 1959. 2. Teil, 101—268.

Bulgara = Bulgara-esperanta vortaro. Sofia 1981 [426 S.].

Butin = M. Butin/J. Sommer: Wörterbuch Esperanto-Deutsch. Limburg 1952 [244 S.; Nachdr. Hildesheim. New York 1981].

Butler 1926 = M. C. Butler: Proverbs in Esperanto and English. London 1926 [159 S.].

Butler 1927/29 = M. C. Butler: Kelkaj vortoj kaj esprimoj en la zamenhofa traduko de la Malnova Testamento. In: Kristana Revuo 1. 1927/29: Nr. 6—15.

Butler 1944 = M. C. Butler/F. Merrick: Muzika terminaro. Heronsgate, Rickmansworth 1944 [35 S.; Oakville, Ontario ^{2}1960.].

Butler 1967 = M. C. Butler: Esperanto-English Dictionary. London 1967 [450 S.].

Cart 1903 = Th. Cart/M. Merckens/P. Berthelot: Vocabulaire Français-Esperanto. Paris 1903 [XII, 252 S.; ^{2}1903; ^{3}1905; ^{4}1906; ^{5}1907].

Cart 1912 = Th. Cart/E. Robert: Plena klasika libro de Esperanto. Paris 1912.

Cart 1922 a = Th. Cart: Vortaro de la oficialaj radikoj de Esperanto. Paris 1922 [16 S. als Ms. gedr.].

Cart 1922 b = Th. Cart: Vortaro de la oficialaj radikoj de Esperanto laŭ „Universala Vortaro" kaj la tri Oficialaj Aldonoj. Paris 1922 [32 S.].

Cart 1922/23/24 = Th. Cart: Korekto de la eraraj tradukoj en „Universala Vortaro". 1. Franca Parto. Paris 1922. 2. Angla Parto. London 1922. 3. Germana Parto. Berlin 1923. 4. Rusa Parto. Berlin 1924. 5. Pola Parto. Berlin 1923 [je 4 S.].

Cart 1923 = Th. Cart: Vortaro de la oficialaj radikoj de Esperanto laŭ „Universala Vortaro" kaj la tri oficialaj aldonoj. Berlin 1923 [32 S.].

Čejka = Th. Čejka: Slovník esperantsko-český. Bystřice-Hostýn 1908 [XVI, 179 S.].

Cherpillod = A Cherpillod: Nepivaj vortoj. Listo de 6800 vortoj ne troviĝantaj en PIV. o. O. 1988 [179 S.].

Christaller = P. Christaller: Deutsch-Esperanto Wörterbuch. Berlin 1910 [XXVI, 516 S.; 2. Aufl. Berlin. Dresden 1923. 22, 660 S.].

Ciliga = P. Ciliga: Statistika tabelo de l'esperanta vortaro (radikoj, afiksoj, finaĵoj, literenomoj). In: Scienca Revuo 12. 1961/62, 38—44.

Claramunt = J. M. Claramunt: Katolika Terminaro Esperanto-Español. Tilburg 1964 [56 S.].

Clissold = P. Clissold: Marista terminaro. Rickmansworth 1950 [62 S.].

Couto Fernandes 1936 = A. Couto Fernandes/C. Domingues/C. Porto/C. Neto: Diccionário Português-Esperanto. Rio de Janeiro 1936 [XVIII, 488 S.].

Couto Fernandes 1964 = A. Couto Fernandes: Esperanta-portugala proverbaro. Rio de Janeiro 1964 [168 S.].

Corret 1907 a = P. Corret: Novaj vortoj en la dua eldono de la Esperanta-germana vortaro. In: Lingvo Internacia 12. 1907, 120—125.

Corret 1907 b = P. Corret: Novaj vortoj en la dua eldono de la Germana-Esperanta vortlibro. In: Lingvo Internacia 12. 1907, 264—267.

Corret 1907 c = P. Corret: Vortoj ĉerpitaj el „Hamleto". In: Lingvo Internacia 12. 1907, 315—316.

Couturat 1910 = L. Couturat: Internaciona matematikal lexiko. Jena 1910 [IV, 36 S.].

Couturat 1919 = L. Couturat: Großes Wörterbuch Deutsch-Ido. Lüsslingen 1919 [XVIII, 823 S.].

Csiszár = A. Csiszár/K. Kalocsay: 600 frazeologiaj esprimoj hungaraj-esperantaj. Budapest 1975 [188 S.].

Dellian = C. Dellian: Racia kaj internacia kemia nomenklaturo. München 1948.

Dietze = J. Dietze: Frequenzwörterbuch Esperanto-Deutsch. Halle 1989 [67 S.].

Durrant 1940 = E. D. Durrant: Armea terminaro. In: Jarlibro de Internacia Esperanto-Ligo 1940. 2. Teil, 21—47.

Durrant 1941 = E. D. Durrant: Aeronaŭtika terminaro. Rickmansworth 1941 [41 S.].

Dyer 1924 a = L. H. Dyer: English-Ido dictionary. London 1924 [XI, 392 S.].

Dyer 1924 b = L. H. Dyer: Ido-English dictionary. London 1924 [XXVI, 408 S.].

Eichholz = R. Eichholz: Esperanta bildvortaro. Bailieboro, Ont. 1988 [880 S.].

Eiselin = J. B. Eiselin: Nederlandsch-Esperanto Handelstermen benevens 1500 Spreekworden en Uitdrukkingen. 's-Hertogenbosch 1925 [100 S.].

Engen = P. Engen: Fervoja terminaro. Løten 1968 [81 S.].

Esperanta bildvortaro = Esperanta bildvortaro. Bailieboro, Ontario 1979 [672 S.].

Esperanta nomenklaturo = Esperanta nomenklaturo de kemio kaj vortaro de kemio. Paris 1913 [14 S.].

Esperanto-ĉina = Esperanto-ĉina vortaro. Peking 1987 [1035 S.].

Esperanto-urdu = Esperanto-urdu vortaro. Islamabad 1987 [484 S.].

Eyama = T. Eyama: Aŭta terminaro. Tokio 1969 [141 S.].

Feder 1919 = K. Feder/F. Schneeberger: Vollständiges Wurzelwörterbuch Ido-Deutsch. Lüsslingen 1919 [XX, 161 S.].

Feder 1924 = K. Feder/J. Nordin: Radio lexiko. Stockholm 1924 [259 S.].

Fervoja = Fervoja terminaro en Esperanto. Supl. al Lexique général des termes ferroviaires. o. O. 1989 [127, 100 S.].

Filip 1947 = J. Filip/K. Filip: Granda vortaro esperanta-ĉeĥa. Přerov ²1947 [446 S.].

Filip 1949 = J. Filip/K. Filip: Granda vortaro ĉeĥa-esperanto. Přerov 1949 [654 S.].

Fineman = H. Fineman: Plena Esperanto Juda vortaro kaj Plena Juda Esperanto vortaro. Montreal 1966 [149, 316 S.].

Flammer = W. Flammer: Katolika terminaro. Tilburg 1963 [44 S.].

Frey = P. Frey u. a.: Store Esperanto-dansk ordbok. Ringsted 1940 [377 S.; Aabyhøj ³1969. 268 S.].

Fulcher = F. Fulcher/B. Long: English-Esperanto dictionary. London 1921 [X, 346 S.; ²1925; ³1949].

Gär = J. Gär: Deutsch-Occidental Wörterbuch. Reval 1928 [XXXI, 460, 16 S.].

Gate = W. A. Gate: Konkordanco de La Sentencoj de Salomono. London 1910 [63 S.].

Geodezia fakterminaro = Geodezia fakterminaro en ses lingvoj. Budapest 1976—1981 [322, 388, 374, 343 S.].

Gjivoje 1966 = M. Gjivoje: Kroatoserba-esperanta vortaro. Zagreb 1966 [369 S.].

Gjivoje 1979 = M. Gjivoje: onimoj. — Listo de antonimoj, homonimoj, paronimoj, sinonimoj kaj vortludoj. Pisa ²1979 [117 S.].

Gode = A. Gode: Interlingua-English. New York 1951.

Gomes Braga 1954 = I. Gomes Braga: Dicionário Português-Esperanto. Rio de Janeiro 1954 [300 S.].

Gomes Braga 1965 = Dicionário Português-Esperanto. Rio de Janeiro 1965 [362 S.].

Grabowski 1910 = A. Grabowski: Granda vortaro Pola-Esperanta. Warszawa 1910 [553 S.].

Grabowski 1916 = A. Grabowski: Słownik Języka Esperanto. Esperanto-Polska. Warszawa 1916 [411 S.].

Green = M. Green/W. Green: Kudra kaj trika terminaro. Heronsgate, Rickmansworth 1947 [22 S.; Oakville, Ontario ²1960.].

Grenkamp = S. Grenkamp: Oficiala vortaro de Esperanto. Paris 1937 [249 S.].

Grigorov = A. Grigorov: Bulgara-Esperanta vortaro. Sofia 1931 [189 S.].

Grosjean-Maupin 1910a = E. Grosjean-Maupin: Dictionnaire complet Esperanto-Français. Paris 1910 [XXVIII, 255 S.; ²1921, ³1924].

Grosjean-Maupin 1910b = E. Grosjean-Maupin: Dictionnaire complet Français-Esperanto. Paris 1910 [XVI, 656 S.; ³1924; ⁵1937; ⁶1947; Supplément 1936. VIII, 179 S.].

Grosjean-Maupin 1924 = E. Grosjean-Maupin: Oficiala klasika libro de Esperanto. Paris 1924 [120 S.].

Guterman = M. Guterman: Słownik polsko-esperancki. Warszawa 1969 [357 S.].

Haak = W. J. v. d. Haak/M. J. Wessel/L. Wit: Woordenboek Nederlandsch-Esperanto. Rotterdam 1916 [302 S.].

Habellok = G. Habellok: Eisenbahn-Wörterbuch. Breslau 1923 [49 S.; Köln ²1954].

Haferkorn 1956 = R. Haferkorn/K. Dellian/F. J. Belinfante: Scienca kaj teknika terminaro. Tokio 1956 [X, 248 S.].

Haferkorn 1967 = R. Haferkorn: Technisches Wörterbuch. Cardiff, Ont. 1967 [84 S.].

Hajpin 1969 = L. Hajpin: Esperanto-korea vortaro. Seoul 1969 [677 S.].

Hajpin 1983 = L. Hajpin: Korea-Esperanta vortaro. Seoul 1983 [478 S].

Hammer = J. K. Hammer: Skolta kaj tenduma terminaro. o. O. 1974 [44 S.].

Haupenthal 1968a = R. Haupenthal: Konkordanco de „La Predikanto". In: Scienca Revuo 19. 1968, 77—94.

Haupenthal 1982 = R. Haupenthal: Listo de mallongigoj. Saarbrücken 1982 [17 S.].

Hecker = O. Hecker: Systematisch geordneter Wortschatz Deutsch-Französisch-Englisch-Esperanto. Berlin 1907 [324 S.].

Hilgers = R. Hilgers, Yashovardhan: EG-Wörterbuch mathematischer Begriffe. Alsbach 1980 [161 S.].

Hill = D. G. Hill: Alfabeta indekso de la Muzika Terminaro de M. C. Butler kaj F. Merrick. Harlow 1980 [24 S.].

Holzhaus = A. Holzhaus: Proverboj de Marko Zamenhof kaj de Lazaro Zamenhof (13 155 proverboj). Helsinki 1980 [704 S.].

Hradil = J. Hradil: Esperanta medicina terminaro. Praha 1982 [63 S.].

Ĥromada = R. Ĥromada: Esperanta-ĉeĥa ĉeĥa-esperanta poŝvortaro. Praha 1969 [349, 37 S.].

Hrynkiewicz = A. Hrynkiewicz: Laŭtema vortaro Esperanto-angla-franca-hispana. Buenos Aires 1972 [234 S.].

Huet = H. Huet: Pri la preparo de nova kaj pli plena eldono de Universala Vortaro. Paris 1911 [42 S.].

Hugon = P. D. Hugon: International Commercial Lexicon. London 1909 [79 S.].

Hukuta = M. Hukuta: Fundamenta vortaro naŭlingva. Tokio 1985 [820 S.].

Inglada = O. V. Inglada/A. L. Villanueva: Vocabulario esperanto-español y español-esperanto. Barcelona 1905 [XIX, 364 S.].

Internacia elektroteknika = Internacia elektroteknika vortaro. Warszawa 1965 [174 S.].

Isaac = N. Isaac: Esperanto-araba poŝvortaro. Cairo 1968 [285 S.].

Itô = K. Itô: Malnudaj vortoj el no 17. In: Hebreo el la geto. De cionismo al hilelismo. Kioto 1976, 171—223.

Jaunvalks = E. Jaunvalks/A Gūtmanis: Esperanto gramatiko. Esperanta-latva vortaro. Latva-esperanta vortaro. Riga 1979 [577 S.].

Jong = A. de Jong: Wörterbuch der Weltsprache. Leiden 1931 [XV, 494 S.].

Jürgensen = H. Jürgensen: Wörterbuch Esperanto-Deutsch. Berlin 1904 [VII, 220 S.; [2]1906; [5]1912].

Kaĵi = H. Kaĵi: Japana-Esperanta vortaro. Tokio [2]1966 [VI, 425 S.].

Kalocsay = K. Kalocsay/G. Waringhien: Kiel farĝi poeto aŭ Parnasa gvidlibro. Budapest 1932. [2. Aufl. mit R. Bernard: Warszawa 1968; Pisa [3]1984].

Kamaryt = S. Kamaryt: Filozofia vortaro. Olomouc 1934 [170 S.].

Kawasaki 1974 = N. Kawasaki: Historia signifo de Zamenhof, Plena Vortaro Rusa-Internacia, 1889. Nagoya 1974 [3 Bl.].

Kawasaki 1975 a = N. Kawasaki: Sufiksitaj vortoj el Zamenhof, Plena Vortaro Rusa-Internacia, 2-a eldono 1896. Oosaka 1975 [9 S.].

Kemp = Ch. Kemp/F. R. Pope: English-Interlingue dictionary. Warndon, Worcester 1958 [422 S.].

Kerckhoffs = A. Kerckhoffs: Dictionnaire Volapük-Français et Français-Volapük. Paris 1887 [319 S.].

Kidosaki = M. Kidosaki: Konkordanco de Marta. Tokio 1979 [18, 245 S.].

Kiselman = Ch. O. Kiselman: Matematika terminaro. Uppsala 1985 [30 S.].

Klement = J. Klement: Heraldiko, Veksikologio. České Budějovice 1979 [80, 131 S.].

Kocher = H. Kocher: Konkordanco de „La Gimnazio". In: Literatura Kajero 1. 1968, 7—8, 15—16.

Krause = E.-D. Krause: Wörterbuch Deutsch-Esperanto. Leipzig 1983 [594 S.].

Kreuz = R. Kreuz/A. Mazzolini: Komerca vortaro en Esperanto. S. Vito al Tagliamento 1927 [XI, 93 S.].

Kühnl = E. Kühnl/K. Procházka: Slovník česko-esperantský. Praha 1914 [284 S.].

Léger = R. Léger/A. Albault: Dictionnaire Français Esperanto. Marmande 1961 [672, LVI S.].

Leite 1910 = T. Leite: Vortaro esperanta-portugala. Rio de Janeiro. Paris 1910 [176 S.].

Leite 1913 = T. Leite: Diccionario Portuguez-Esperanto. Rio de Janeiro. Paris 1913 [XX, 417 S.].

Lemaire = R. Lemaire: Vocabulaire Français-Esperanto. Paris 1903 [21 S.].

Lewin = M. Lewin: Meteologia terminaro. In: Jarlibro de UEA 1961, 2, 129—89.

Liedbeck = G. Liedbeck: Volapük-svensk ordbok. Svensk-volapük ordbok. Stockholm 1887 [108, 127 S.].

Liebeck = S. Liebeck: Juristisches Wörterbuch. Berlin 1931 [86 S.].

Loy = K. J. Loy: Mehrsinnige deutsche Wörter in Esperanto. Berlin 1921 [78 S.].

Markheden = M. Markheden: Svedaj arboj kaj arbedoj. Sjöhagen 1982.

Matejka = A. Matejka: Wörterbuch Occidental-Deutsch und Deutsch-Occidental. Chapelle 1945 [XVII, 133 S.].

Mattei = C. Mattei: Dizionario Volapük-Italiano e Italiano-Volapük. Milano 1890 [XX, 204 S.].

Mencel = R. Mencel: Vortoj ĉerpitaj el „Fundamenta Krestomatio" de la lingvo Esperanto. In: Lingvo Internacia 12. 1907, 554—556.

Ménil = F. de Ménil: Muzika terminaro. Paris 1908 [20 S.].

Mészáros = B. Mészáros: Oklingva nomaro de eŭropaj birdoj. Debrecen 1980 [180 S.].

Michalski = T. J. Michalski: Esperanta-pola vortaro. Warszawa 1959 [XX, 265 S.].

Middelkoop = A. J. Middelkoop: Nederlands-Esperanto-Nederlands. Utrecht. Antwerpen 1971 [481 S.].

Mildwurf = A. Mildwurf: Leĝa terminaro. Heronsgate. Rickmansworth 1946 [11 S.].

Militista vortareto = Militista vortareto. Ricksmansworth 1955 [53 S.].

Millidge = E. Millidge: The Esperanto-English Dictionary. Washington 1912 [480 S.; London [2]1913; [5]1924].

Minor 1922 = K. Minor: Deutsche Redensarten in Esperanto. Berlin 1922 [56 S.; Nachdr. Saarbrücken 1975; [2]1983].

Minor 1924 = K. Minor: Esperanto-Deutsches Handwörterbuch. Berlin. Dresden 1924 [VII, 71, 216 S.].

Miyamoto = M. Miyamoto: Vortaro japana-esperanta. Tokio 1982 [VI, 1083 S.].

Mizeruña = S. Mizeruña: Esperanta ŝtancila terminaro. Tel Aviv 1973 [14 S.].

Moberg = K. J. Moberg: Konstruteknika terminaro sveda-esperanta. Malmö 1958 [99 S.].

Munniksma = F. Munniksma: International Business Dictionary in nine languages. Deventer. Antwerpen 1975 [XVI, 535 S.].

Nakamura = T. Nakamura: Enciklopedieto Japana. Osaka 1969 [217 S.].

Neergaard = P. Neergaard: Terminaro hortikultura seslingva. Paris 1938 [29 S.].

Nikolov = A. Nikolov: Plena Esperanto-Bulgara Vortaro. Sevlievo 1939 [488 S.].

Nomura = R. Nomura: Zamenhofa ekzemplaro. Nagoya 1987 [XXI, 568 S.]. Neue Ausg. Nagoya 1989 [XXI, 512 S.].

Nova vortaro = Nova vortaro Esperanta-ĉina. Peking 1980 [VI, 327 S.].

Novaj vortoj = Novaj vortoj Esperantaj donitaj aŭ aprobitaj de L. Zamenhof. Bystřice-Hostýn 1904 [12 S.].

Nylén = P. Nylén: Esperantisk-Svensk ordbok. Stockholm 1933 [231 S.].

Ockey 1971 = E. Ockey: Leksikono de oficialaj vortoj. Banstead 1971 [20 S.].

Ockey 1975 = E. Ockey: Fundamenta Vortaro-Radikaro. Banstead 1975 [127 S.].

Oficiala aldono 1909—1975 = ... Oficiala aldono al Universala Vortaro. — 1. Paris 1909 [31 S.]; 2. Paris 1919 [16 S.]; 3. In: Oficiala Gazeto Esperantista 8. 1921/22, 153—164; 4. In: Oficiala Bulteno de la Esperantista Akademio 1929, 4—8; 1930, 25—29; 5. In: Oficialaj Sciigoj de la Akademio. 1934: 4; 6. In: Oficialaj Sciigoj de la Akademio 1935: 9; 7. o. O. 1958 [4 S.]; 8. In: Aktoj de la Akademio. II. 1968—1974. Rotterdam. Paris 1975, 11—27.

Ojalo = J. Ojalo: Esperantaj sinonimoj. Vilnius. Tallinn. Kaunas 1985 [79 S.].

Okamoto 1935 = J. Okamoto: Nova vortaro Japana-Esperanta. Tokio 1935 [XII, 800 S.].

Okamoto 1963 = J. Okamoto: Nova vortaro Esperanto-Japana. Tokio 1963 [380 S.].

Pabst = B. Pabst: Inversa vortaro de Esperanto. Paderborn 1989 [91 S.].

Paluzie-Borrell = J. Paluzzie-Borrell: Diccionario Esperanto-Español y Español Esperanto. Barcelona 1967 [381 S.].

Parisot 1904 = J. Parisot/Th. Cart: Esperanta versfarado. Paris 1904 [15 S.; ²1909. 41 S; Nachdr. Saarbrücken 1990].

Parisot 1907 = J. Parisot: Pri la vortoj ĉerpitaj el „Hamleto". In: Lingvo Internacia 12. 1907, 365—366.

Pechan 1958a = A. Pechan: Eszperantó-magyar szótár. Budapest 1958 [448 S.; ²1961; ³1963; ⁴1968; ⁶1988].

Pechan 1958b = A. Pechan: Magyar-Eszperantó szótár. Budapest 1958 [544 S.; ²1961; ³1964; ⁴1968; ⁶1988].

Pesch = M. Pesch: Dictionario de la 10 000 radiki di la linguo universala Ido. Genève. New York. Paris 1964 [631 S.].

Petrič = M. Petrič: Slovena-esperanta vortaro. Ljubljana 1963 [588 S.].

Pfaundler = L. Pfaundler: Internaciona fotografala lexiko. Jena 1914 [XII, 30 S.].

Pflaumer = W. Pflaumer: Wörterbuch des Volapük. Halle 1888 [XVI, 447 S.].

Pióro = J. Pióro: Kemiaj afiksoj internaciaj. Warszawa 1966 [36 S.].

Plehn 1934 = H. J. Plehn: Sägen-Wörterbuch. Wien 1934 [32 S.].

Plena Ilustrita vortaro = Plena Ilustrita vortaro de Esperanto. Paris 1970 [XXXVII, 1299 S.; ²1977; Nachdr. 1981. — Suplemento. Paris 1987. 45 S.].

Plena vortaro esperanta-ĉina = Plena vortaro de esperanto-ĉina. Peking 1984 [915, 7 S.].

Plena vortaro de Esperanto = Plena vortaro de Esperanto. Paris 1930 [XV, 517 S.; ²1934; ³1947; ⁴1953; ⁵1956; ⁶1960; ⁷1964; ⁸1971].

Poŝatlaso = Poŝatlaso de la mondo. Prago 1971 [Karten, 55 S.].

Praktika Bildvortaro = Praktika Bildvortaro de Esperanto. Oxford 1979 [96 S.].

Propraj nomoj = Propraj nomoj de sanktuloj kaj sanktulinoj. Tilburg 1962 [33 S.].

Puodenas = K. Puodenas: Esperanto-lietuvių ir Lietuvių-esperanto kalbų zodynas. Vilnius 1988 [288 S.].

Rhodes 1905 = J. Rhodes: Vortaro de esperantaj rimoj. Keighley 1905 [23 S.; Nachdr. Saarbrücken 1984].

Rhodes 1908 = J. Rhodes: The English-Esperanto dictionary. London 1908 [XXII, 547 S.].

Rian 1948 = R. Rian: Esperanto-norsk ordbok. Oslo 1948 [174 S.].

Rian 1963 = R. Rian/E. A. Haugen: Norsk-Esperanto ordbok. Oslo 1963 [374 S.].

Ritterspach = G. Ritterspach: Kleines Eisenbahn-Fachwörterbuch. Frankfurt 1966 [80 S.].

Rollet de l'Isle = M. Rollet de l'Isle: Provo de marista terminaro. Paris 1908 [VI, 74 S.].

Roosen 1965 = H. Roosen: Katolika terminaro. Esperanto-Nederlands. Tilburg 1965 [56 S.].

Roosen 1972 = H. Roosen/H. G. Wannemakers: Katolika terminaro. Nederlands-Esperanto. Tilburg 1972 [96 S.].

Rosher = E. M. Rosher: Fervoja terminaro. Heronsgate. Rickmansworth 1953 [67 S.].

Rousseau = C. Rousseau: Poliglota vademecum de internacia farmacio. Paris 1911 [285 S.].

Rusak = H. Rusak: Enciklopedia vortaro Esperanta-jida. Jerusalem 1969—1973 [670 S.].

Rybář = J. Rybář: Terminaro de hidraŭlaj meĥanismoj. Praha 1982 [52 S.].

Sadler 1962 = V. Sadler: Budhisma terminaro. Kandy, Ceylon 1962 [11 S.].

Saminy 1981 = B. Saminy: Persa Esperanta vortaro. Teheran 1981.

Saminy 1983 = B. Saminy: Plena Esperanto-persa vortaro. Teheran 1983 [745 S.].

Scherzinger = J. A. Scherzinger: A complete English Dictionary of the roots of the world-language Volapük. Konstanz 1897 [VI, 343 S.].

Schleyer 1882 = J. M. Schleyer: Wörterbuch der Universalsprache für alle gebildeten Erdbewohner. Überlingen ²1882 [256 S.; 1. Aufl. in Schleyer 1880]; 3. Aufl.: Wörterbuch der Universalsprache Volapük. Konstanz 1885; 4. Aufl.: Großes Wörterbuch der Universalsprache Volapük. 1888 [XXII, 646 S.].

Schleyer 1898 = J. M. Schleyer: Mittleres Wörterbuch der Universalsprache Volapük. 11. sehr verm. Aufl. Konstanz 1898—1907 [1056 S.].

Schlüter = K. Schlüter: Inversa vortaro. Nürnberg 1972 [37 S.].

Scott = H. M. Scott: Filatela terminaro. Horrem 1928 [47 S.].

Seemann = St. R. Seemann: Esperanta-slovaka kaj slovaka-esperanta terminaro. Bratislava 1970 [834 S.].

Sekelj = A. Sekelj: Serbkroata-esperanta vortaro. Beograd 1967 [706 S.].

Sepamaa = H. Sepamaa: Väike Esperanto-Eesti ja Eesti-Esperanto Sõnaraamat. Tallinn 1957 [159 S.].

Setälä = V. Setälä: Plena vortaro Finna-Esperanta. Otava 1923 [831 S.].

Siwicki = K. Siwicki: Internacia elektroteknika vortaro Esperanta-pola. Warszawa 1963 [41 S.].

Skaftfell = B. B. Skaftvell: Islanda-esperanto vortaro. Reykjavík 1965 [X, 479 S.].

Stancliff = F. Stancliff: Konkordanco al la Originala Verkaro de Zamenhof. Rockford, Ill. 1937 [50 S.].

Stojan 1911 = P. E. Stojan: Ornitologia vortaro oklingva de birdoj Eŭropaj. St. Peterburg 1911 [216 S.].

Straaten = A. G. J. van Straaten: Beknopt Esperanto-woordenboek. Zutphen 1936 [715 S.].

Tellini 1931 = A. Tellini: Vocabolario completo Esperanto-italiano. S. Vito al Tagliamento 1931 [VIII, 509 S.].

Tellini 1959 = A. Tellini/C. Grazzini: Vocabolario Esperanto-italiano. S. Vito al Tagliamento 1959 [VIII, 509, 64 S.].

Terminaro por infanludoj = Terminaro por infanludoj. Oakville, Ont. ²1960 [28 S.].

Thomson = A. W. Thomson: Rimvortaro Esperanta. London 1918 [V, 34 S.].

Tišlar = Z. Tišlar: Frekvencmorfemaro de parolata Esperanto. Zagreb 1982 [41 S.].

Tomán = J. Tomán: Kompleta poŝvortaro de la mondlingvo Esperanto. Budapest. I. Esperanta-hungara parto. 1923 [164 S.]; II. Hungara-esperanta parto. 1927 [366 S.].

Tommasi = M. Tommasi: Vocabolario italiano-volapük e volapük-italiano. Milano 1889 [1000, IV S.].

Tudela = E. Tudela Flores: Vocabulario español-esperanto. Valencia 1966 [527 S.].

Tymiński = K. Tymiński: Malgranda vortaro pola-esperanta. Warszawa 1968 [XVI, 431 S.].

Uang = M. Uang Bu-jung: Ĉina-Esperanta vortaro. Taipei 1980 [749, 69, II S.].

Uhlmann = F. Uhlmann: Deutsch-Esperanto-Wörterbuch für das Rote Kreuz. Schussenried 1913 [43 S.].

Újlaky-Nagy = T. Újlaky-Nagy: La sporta lingvo en Esperanto. Budapest 1972 [V, 303 S.].

Urban = E. Urban: Gastronomia terminaro. In: Jarlibro de UEA 1958, 2, 97—221.

Vatré 1989 = H. Vatré: Neologisma glosaro. Postrikolto al PIV. 3. eld. Kun laŭ-tema Klasifiko Kaj rimaro en suplemento. Saarbrücken 1989 [87 S.]. [¹1983].

Veer = C. L. de Veer: Schidhof's Zakwoorden boekje. 1. Esperanto-Nederlandsch. 2. Nederlandsch-Esperanto. Amsterdam 1931 [298, 275 S.].

Venture = A. Venture: Radio-terminaro. Oakville. Ont. ²1960 [33 S.].

Verax 1907 = Ch. Verax: Vocabulaire Technique et Technologique Français-Esperanto. Paris 1907 [X, 130 S.].

Verax 1910 = Ch. Verax: Enciklopedia Vortareto Esperanta. Paris 1910 [XV, 249 S.].

Vilborg = E. Vilborg: Etimologia vortaro de Esperanto. Malmö 1989 [T. 1 A—D. 104 S.].

Vilkki 1963 = J. Vilkki: Suomi Esperanto Suomi. Osakeyhtiö 1963 [XII, 204 S.].

Vilkki 1982 = J. Vilkki/H. Favén: Suomi Esperanto suomi taskusanakirja. Porvoo. Helsinki. Juva 1982 [449 S.].

Vocabolario = Vocabolario Italiano-Esperanto. Verona 1981 [XVIII, 494 S.].

Vo-Ko = Vo-Ko: Esperanto eesti sõnastik. Tallinn 1927 [239 S.].

Vortaro Esperanto-Bulgara = Vortaro Esperanto-Bulgara. Sofia 1963 [441 S.].

Wackrill 1907 = A. E. Wackrill: Konkordanco de Ekzercaro de L. L. Zamenhof. Paris 1907 [95 S.].

Wackrill 1908 = A. E. Wackrill: Zamenhofaj vortoj netroveblaj en la Universala Vortaro. Paris 1908.

Wahl = E. de Wahl: Radicarium directiv del lingue international (Occidental). Tallinn 1925 [125 S.].

Walther = E. Walther: Dictionnaire der ... internationalen Handels- und Verkehrssprache Volapük. Ansbach 1888 [V, 217, 217 S.].

Wannemakers 1963a = H. G. Wannemakers: Katolika terminaro Esperanto-Latine. Tilburg 1963 [53 S.].

Wannemakers 1963b = H. G. Wannemakers: Propraj nomoj en la Nova Testament. Tilburg 1963 [30 S.].

Waringhien 1954 = G. Waringhien: Plena vortaro de Esperanto. Suplemento. Paris 1954 [63 S.].

Waringhien 1957 = G. Waringhien: Grand Dictionnaire Espéranto-Français. Paris 1957 [367 S.; ²1976, 367, 16 S.].

Wells = J. C. Wells: The E.U.P. concise Esperanto and English dictionary. London 1969 [IX, 419 S.].

Westermayer = M. Westermayer: Internacia kemio-vortaro. Tübingen 1981 [71 S.].

Wingen = H. Wingen: Wörterbuch Deutsch-Esperanto. Limburg 1954 [176 S.]; Nachdr. Hildesheim. New York 1981 [176 S.].

Wood = M. W. Wood: Dictionary of Volapük. New York. London 1889 [VIII, 389 S.].

Wüster 1923a = E. Wüster: Maschinentechnisches Esperanto-Wörterbuch der Grundbegriffe. Leipzig 1923 [89 S.].

Wüster 1923b = E. Wüster: Enciklopedia vortaro Esperanta-germana. Leipzig 1923—29 [66, 4, 576 S.].

Wüster 1923c = E. Wüster: La oficiala radikaro. Berlin. Dresden 1923 [69 S.; Suplemento 1932, 3 S.].

Wüster 1927 = E. Wüster: Zamenhof-Radikaro. Leipzig 1927 [84 S.].

Zamenhof 1889a = L. L. Zamenhof: Plena vortaro rusa-internacia. Warszawa 1889 [XV, 232, 3 S.]. ²1896; ³1900; ⁴1905; ⁵1910; ⁶1921 [VII, 232 S.].

Zamenhof 1889b = L. L. Zamenhof: Meza vortaro internacia-germana. Warschau 1889 [73 S.].

Zamenhof 1894a = L. L. Zamenhof: Granda vortaro germana-esperanta. Odeso 1894 [16 S.; Nachdr. Saarbrücken 1968].

Zamenhof 1894c = L. L. Zamenhof: Universala Vortaro de la lingvo internacia Esperanto. Varsovio 1894 [52 S.]; ²1898; ⁴1904; Paris ⁵1906; ⁶1907.

Zamenhof 1904 = L. L. Zamenhof: Wörterbuch Deutsch-Esperanto. Berlin 1904 [277 S.]; ²1906; ³1907; ⁴1911; ⁵o. J.

Zamenhof 1905 = L. L. Zamenhof: Słownik esperancko-polski i polsko-esperancki. Warszawa 1905; ³1906 [58 S.].

Zamenhof 1906b = L. L. Zamenhof: Fundamenta vortaro Esperanto-pola. Warszawa 1906 [50 S.].

Zamenhof 1907 = L. L. Zamenhof: Taschenwörterbuch Deutsch-Esperanto und Esperanto-Deutsch. Berlin 1907; ²1908; ³1910 [137 S.]; ⁴1912; ⁵1921; neu bearb. Aufl. v. P. Christaller, H. Böbs. Berlin 1928 [120 S.].

Zamenhof 1909 = L. L. Zamenhof: Vortaro esperanto-rusa. Moskva 1909 [151 S.]; ²1911.

Zamenhof 1910 = L. L. Zamenhof: Proverbaro Esperanta. Paris 1910 [82 S.]; ²1925 [³ = Zamenhof 1961].

Zamenhof 1961 = L. L. Zamenhof: Proverbaro Esperanta. Alfabete ordigita kaj provizita de indeksoj analiza kaj sinteza de C. Rogister. La Laguna 1961 [167 S. ²1974].

Živanović = St. Živanović: Esperanto-serbkroata vortaro. Beograd 1934 [VIII, 168 S.]; ²1955 [VII, 177 S.]; ³1959 [238 S.].

3.2. Sonstige Literatur

Albault 1963 = A. Albault: Akademiaj korektoj de la Universala Vortaro. In: L. L. Zamenhof: Fundamento de Esperanto. Marmande ⁹1963, 239—283.

Andersen = H. Chr. Andersen: Fabeloj. Plena kolekto. Übers. v. L. L. Zamenhof. Paris (4: Bruxelles) 1923—1963 [Bd. 1 1923, 152 S., 2. Aufl. 1926, 3. Aufl. Bruxelles 1965, 236 S.; Bd. 2 1926, 154 S.; Bd. 3 1932, 153 S.; Bd. 4 1963, 240 S.]. Fabeloj de Andersen. 1—4. Kioto 1990.

Blanke = D. Blanke: Internationale Plansprachen. Berlin 1985.

Boulet 1907 = P. Boulet: Pri „La Revizoro". In: Lingvo Internacia 12. 1907, 505—507.

Boulet 1908 = P. Boulet: Pri „La Rabistoj". In: Lingvo Internacia 13. 1908, 446—470.

Boulton = M. Boulton: Zamenhof, creator of Esperanto. London 1960. ²1980.

Butler 1930/31 = M. C. Butler: Lingvaj notoj pri la „Malnova Testamento". In: Kristana Revuo 2. 1930/31: Nr. 1—11.

Carlevaro = I. Lapenna/U. Lins/T. Carlevaro: Esperanto en Perspektivo. London. Rotterdam 1974.

Cart 1907 = Th. Cart: Ĝenerala raporto pri la demando rilata al „Vortoj el la Universala Vortaro, kies tradukoj ŝajnas ĉu kontraŭdiraj, ĉu malĝustaj, ĉu malkorektaj". In: Lingvo Internacia 12. 1907, 210—213.

Couturat 1903 = L. Couturat, L. Leau: Histoire de la langue universelle. Paris 1903 [Nachdr. Hildesheim. New York 1979].

Danneil = H. Danneil: Esplorado pri vortofteco en Esperanto kaj aliaj lingvoj. In: Internacia Pedagogia Revuo 7. 1928, 8, 1—15.

Dehler 1986a = W. Dehler: Nova ŝanco por terminologio. In: der esperantist 22. 1986, 1—4.

Dehler 1986b = W. Dehler: Multlingva mondo kaj fakvortara normigado. In: Esperanto 79. 1986, 207—208.

Devjatnin = V. N. Devjatnin: Plena oficiala radikaro de Esperanto. Leipzig 1919.

Dickens = Ch. Dickens: La batalo de l'vivo. London. Paris 1910 [Nachdr. Saarbrücken 1982].

Drezen = E. Drezen: Historio de la mondolingvo. Leipzig 1931 [Nachdr. Oosaka 1967].

Esselin = A. Esselin: Pri la vortoj ĉerpitaj el „Krestomatio". In: Lingvo Internacia 13. 1908, 357.

Goethe = J. W. v. Goethe: Ifigenio en Taŭrido. Übers. v. L. L. Zamenhof. Paris. Berlin 1908 [Nachdr. Saarbrücken 1982. ²1921. ³1929].

Gogol = V. N. Gogol: La revizoro. Übers. v. L. L. Zamenhof. Paris 1907 [²1928; Nachdr. Tokyo 1978].

Gregor = D. B. Gregor: Kio estas erara en la angla sekcio de la UV. In: Scienca Revuo 9. 1957/58, 113—15.

Haferkorn 1962 = R. Haferkorn: Scientific technical and other special dictionaries in Esperanto. London 1962 [20 S.; Supplementary list 1964. 3 S.].

Harry = R. Harry: Relativaj oftecoj de lingvaj elementoj en Esperanto. In: Scienca Revuo 18. 1967, 49—63.

Haupenthal 1968b = R. Haupenthal: Komparo inter EGM kaj UV. In: Scienca Revuo 19. 1968, 71—72.

Haupenthal 1982b = R. Haupenthal: Volapük-Bibliographie. Hildesheim. Zürich. New York 1982.

Heine = H. Heine: La rabeno de Baĥaraĥ. Übers. v. L. L. Zamenhof. Paris 1924 [Nachdr. Saarbrücken 1984; ²1929].

Kawasaki 1940 = N. Kawasaki: Fremdlingvaĵoj en Zamenhofaj Verkoj. Oosaka 1940.

Kawasaki 1949 = N. Kawasaki: Goŝei-go ziten. Osaka 1949.

Kawasaki 1975 b = N. Kawasaki: Historia signifo de Zamenhof, Plena Vortaro Esperanta-Rusa, 1909. o. O. 1975.

Maimon = N. Z. Maimon: La kaŝita vivo de Zamenhof. Tokio 1978.

Malnova testamento = La sankta biblio. Malnova kaj nova testamento. London. Edinburgh. Glasgow 1926.

Manders = W. J. A. Manders: Vijf kunsttaalen. Purmerend 1947.

Molière = Molière: Georgo Dandin. Übers. v. L. L. Zamenhof. Paris 1908 [Nachdr. Saarbrücken 1984; ^{2}1924; ^{3}1930].

Ockey 1982 = E. Ockey: Bibliography of Esperanto Dictionaries. Banstead 1982.

Orzeszko = E. Orzeszko: Marta. Übers. v. L. L. Zamenhof. Paris 1910 [^{2}1924; ^{3}1928 (Nachdr. Tokio 1979); Marmande ^{4}1968. 213 S.].

Plehn 1985 = H. J. Plehn: Biografio de duona vortaro aŭ Kial Esperanto perdis sian gvidantan Esperantologon. Saarbrücken 1985.

Raporto = Raporto pri la dubaj tradukoj en Universala Vortaro. In: Oficiala Gazeto Esperantista. Angla parto. 4. 1911/12, 363—375, 400—401; Germana parto. 5. 1912/13, 64—73; Franca parto. 5. 1912/13, 210—211; Rusa parto. 5. 1912/13, 226—231; Pola parto. 5. 1912/13, 81—89.

Rizzo = P. Rizzo: Lineamenti di lessicographia dell' esperanto. Pisa 1983.

Ŝalom-Alejĥem = Ŝalom-Alejĥem: La gimnazio. Übers.v. L. L. Zamenhof. Paris 1924 [65 S.; ^{2}1929].

Sadler 1958 = V. Sadler: Relativaj oftecoj de kelkaj lingvaj elementoj en Esperanto. In: Scienca Revuo 10. 1958/59, 67—72.

Schiller = F. Schiller: La rabistoj. Übers. v. L. L. Zamenhof. Paris 1908 [144 S.; ^{2}1928].

Schleyer 1880 = J. M. Schleyer: Volapük. Die Weltsprache. Sigmaringen 1880 [Nachdr. Hildesheim. Zürich. New York 1982. 2. Aufl. u. d. T.: Grammatik der Universalsprache ... Überlingen 1882; ^{3}1884; Konstanz ^{5}1885; Mittlere Grammatik der Universalsprache Volapük. ^{6}1886; ^{7}1887; ^{8}1887; ^{9}1888].

Schwarz = A. Schwarz: El la laborejo de la Enciklopedia Vortaro de Eugen Wüster. In: Literatura Informilo 6. 1930, 7—11.

Shakespeare = W. Shakespeare: Hamleto, reĝido de Danujo. Übers. v. L. L. Zamenhof. Nürnberg 1894 [Paris ^{2}1902; ^{3}1904; ^{5}1909; ^{6}1924; ^{7}1929; Marmande ^{8}1974].

Stojan 1929 = P. E. Stojan: Bibliografio de internacia lingvo. Genève 1929 [Nachdr. Hildesheim. Zürich. New York 1973].

Vatré 1986 = H. Vatré: Vort-statistikaj esploroj. Saarbrücken 1986.

Waringhien 1955 = G. Waringhien: Inventaro de la fundamenta kaj oficiala vorttrezoro. In: Scienca Revuo 7. 1955, 137—143.

Waringhien 1980a = G. Waringhien: 1887 kaj la sekvo... Eseoj IV. Antwerpen. La Laguna 1980 [293 S.].

Waringhien 1980b = G. Waringhien: Polemiko ĉirkaŭ vortaroj. In: Waringhien 1980a, 155—185.

Wüster 1931 = E. Wüster: Internationale Sprachnormung in der Technik, besonders in der Elektrotechnik. Berlin 1931 [Bonn ^{2}1966; ^{3}1977].

Wüster 1973 = E. Wüster: Notas marginal al dictionnario „Interlingua-English", 1951. Wieselburg 1973.

Zamenhof 1894b = L. L. Zamenhof: Ekzercaro de la lingvo internacia Esperanto. Varsovio 1894 [43 S.]. ^{2}1898; ^{3}1900; ^{4}1904; Paris ^{5}1906; ^{7}1907; ^{7}1910.

Zamenhof 1903 = L. L. Zamenhof: Fundamenta krestomatio de la lingvo Esperanto. Paris 1903.

Zamenhof 1905 = L. L. Zamenhof: Fundamento de Esperanto. Paris 1905; 9. Aufl. hg. v. A. Albault. Marmande 1963.

Zamenhof 1929 = L. L. Zamenhof: Originala Verkaro. Leipzig 1929 [604 S.; Nachdr. Osaka 1983].

Zamenhof 1973 = L. L. Zamenhof: Iam kompletigota plena verkaro. Kioto 1973—1981. 13 Bde.

Reinhard Haupenthal, Saarbrücken (Bundesrepublik Deutschland)

330. Lexikographie der Kurzschriften

1. Typen von Kurzschriftwörterbüchern
2. Funktion der Kurzschriftwörterbücher
3. Gestaltung der Kurzschriftwörterbücher
4. Auswahlgrundsätze
5. Zur Geschichte der Kurzschriftwörterbücher
6. Kurzschriftwörterbücher in der Gegenwart
7. Literatur (in Auswahl)

1. Typen von Kurzschriftwörterbüchern

Es gibt zwei Typen von Kurzschriftwörterbüchern: erstens vollständige Wörterbücher, die das Nachschlagen jedes Wortes ermöglichen sollen, und zweitens Spezialwörterbücher mit begrenztem Verwendungszweck und entsprechender Auswahl (Fachausdrücke, Fremdwörter, Kürzungen oder dgl.). Ein dritter Typ stenographischer Lexika wären Enzyklopädien, die unter alphabetisch angeordneten Stichwörtern das Gesamtwissen über Stenographie zusammenfassen wollen. Zweimal wurde versucht, ein Werk dieser Art zu schaffen. Von Theodor Goluboff in Bulgarien sind 1931/32 die Buchstaben A—E erschienen. Karl Heck in Deutschland kam über ein paar Seiten Probedrucke in den 1950er Jahren nicht hinaus. Dieser Typ stenographischer Lexika soll hier nicht weiter berücksichtigt werden.

Linie andere Personen, die beruflich oder privat stenographieren. Diese zweite Gruppe benötigt Wörterbücher deshalb weniger, weil sie nicht so viel Wert auf Fehlerlosigkeit legt. Es gibt Argumente für und gegen Kurzschriftwörterbücher, mit denen im Konkurrenzkampf der Systeme gearbeitet wird: Die Vertreter des einen Systems heben hervor, daß Wörterbücher verfügbar sind, die das Anwenden des Systems leicht und bequem machen. Die Gegner behaupten, ihr System sei so leicht, daß man, wenn man es erlernt habe, keine Wörterbücher zum Nachschlagen mehr brauche.

2. Funktion der Kurzschriftwörterbücher

Kurzschriftwörterbücher können natürlich nur für ein bestimmtes Stenographiesystem gelten. Für fast jede Sprache gab oder gibt es mehrere, sehr stark voneinander abweichende Systeme. Die Systeme stehen miteinander in einem Konkurrenzkampf, der manchmal erbitterte Formen annimmt. In manchen Ländern entstanden Einheitssysteme; diese konnten sich aber oft nicht vollständig durchsetzen.

Ein Kurzschriftwörterbuch gibt dem Benutzer die Möglichkeit, nachzuschlagen, wie ein Wort geschrieben wird oder wie ein Wort gekürzt werden kann. Die Benutzer sind in erster Linie Lehrer und Schüler, in zweiter

3. Gestaltung der Kurzschriftwörterbücher

Manche Systeme sind in mehrere Stufen unterteilt, andere nicht. Nicht unterteilt ist z. B. das französische Stenographiesystem Prévost-Delaunay:

Man erkennt immer ein stenographisches Wortbild, dem alle Bedeutungen, die es haben kann, in Druckschrift beigefügt sind. Verweisungen erleichtern die Benutzung. Weil *l'ample* wie *l'humble* geschrieben wird, wird auf dieses Stichwort verwiesen. Weil *l'an* auch *l'en* bedeuten kann, steht acht Seiten später, wo *l'en* nach dem Alphabet hingehört, ein Hinweis. — Wenn ein System in mehrere Stufen unterteilt ist, muß das Wörterbuch zwei- oder dreispaltig angelegt sein.

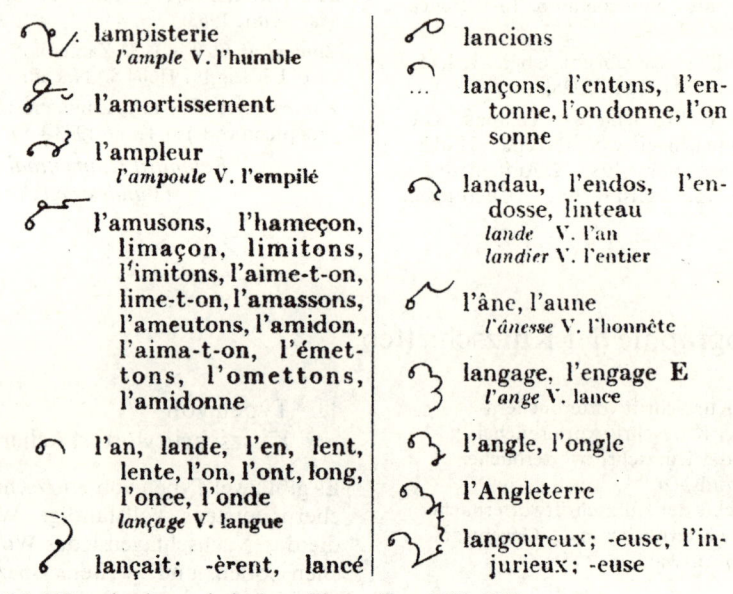

lampisterie
  l'ample V. *l'humble*

l'amortissement

l'ampleur
  l'ampoule V. *l'empilé*

l'amusons, l'hameçon, limaçon, limitons, l'imitons, l'aime-t-on, lime-t-on, l'amassons, l'ameutons, l'amidon, l'aima-t-on, l'émettons, l'omettons, l'amidonne

l'an, lande, l'en, lent, lente, l'on, l'ont, long, l'once, l'onde
  lançage V. *langue*

lançait; -èrent, lancé

lancions

lançons, l'entons, l'entonne, l'on donne, l'on sonne

landau, l'endos, l'endosse, linteau
  lande V. *l'an*
  landier V. *l'entier*

l'âne, l'aune
  l'ânesse V. *l'honnête*

langage, l'engage E
  l'ange V. *lance*

l'angle, l'ongle

l'Angleterre

langoureux; -euse, l'injurieux; -euse

Textbeispiel 330.1: Wörterbuchausschnitt (aus: Fleury/Roy 1900, 188)

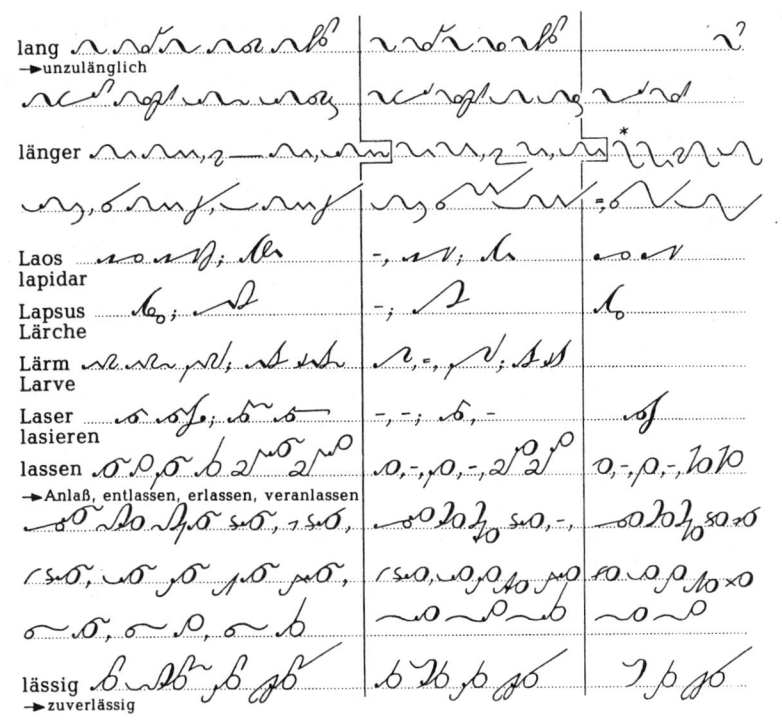

330. Lexikographie der Kurzschriften

lang
→unzulänglich

länger

Laos
lapidar
Lapsus
Lärche
Lärm
Larve
Laser
lasieren
lassen
→Anlaß, entlassen, erlassen, veranlassen

lässig
→zuverlässig

Textbeispiel 330.2: Wörterbuchausschnitt (aus: Haeger/Lambrich 1973, 132)

So zeigen Haeger/Lambrich 1973 die drei Stufen der Deutschen Einheitskurzschrift in drei Spalten, links Verkehrsschrift, in der Mitte Eilschrift, rechts Redeschrift:

Nicht jedes Wort wird in Druckschrift und Kurzschrift nebeneinander gezeigt, sondern unter einem Stichwort werden mehrere, oft sogar sehr viele Kurzschriftbeispiele zusammengefaßt.

Man erkennt z. B. unter dem Stichwort **lang** die Beispiele *lang, längste, lange, langsam, langfristig, langweilig, Längsschnitt, verlangen, Verlangsamung*.

Ganz vorn enthält das Buch „Hinweise für den Benutzer", aus denen er z. B. entnimmt, warum er *Unterführung* unter dem Stichwort **führen,** dagegen *Lebensführung* unter dem Stichwort **leben** suchen muß. Ein einfacher kurzer Strich bedeutet, daß die Schreibweise der niedrigeren Systemstufe unverändert bleibt; ein Doppelstrich bedeutet, daß die Kürzung mit der unmittelbar vorhergehenden identisch ist.

4. Auswahlgrundsätze

Auch ein „vollständiges" Kurzschriftwörterbuch kann nicht alle Wörter der Sprache enthalten. Der Verfasser muß eine Auswahl treffen und tut das unter drei Gesichtspunkten: (a) Auf seltene Wörter wird verzichtet; (b) einfache Wörter, die sich so problemlos stenographieren lassen, daß niemand sie nachschlagen wird, werden weggelassen; (c) zusammengesetzte Wörter werden nur in Ausnahmefällen aufgenommen; normalerweise muß der Benutzer jeden Bestandteil einzeln nachschlagen.

Im Textbeispiel 330.2 findet man hintereinander die fünf Wörter *Laos, laotisch, lapidar, Lapsus, Lärche*. Der Duden (Band 1, 19. Aufl.) enthält zwischen *Laos* und *Lärche* 43 Wörter. Von den 38 Wörtern, die im Kurzschriftwörterbuch fehlen, sind z. B. (a) *Laparoskop* und *Lapislazuli* wegen Seltenheit, (b) *Lappen* und *Lar* wegen Problemlosigkeit, (c) *Lapidarschrift* und *Lapidarstil* als Zusammensetzungen nicht aufgenommen worden (*Schrift* und *Stil* findet man an anderer Stelle). Ähnlich ist es im Französischen. Aus dem Textbeispiel 330.1 ergibt sich, daß unter den mit *lamp*- beginnenden Wörtern z. B. *lampique, lampyre* und *l'amplitude* fehlen. Die Gründe sind die gleichen.

Bei den Spezialwörterbüchern bestimmt der Zweck die Auswahlgrundsätze. In der Bundesrepublik werden u. a. folgende Spezialwörterbücher angeboten: „Fremdwörterkürzungen für die kaufmännische Praxis", „Redewendungen aus Politik und Wirtschaft", „Fachkürzungen aus der Berufspraxis der Medizin". Auch die alphabetisch geordneten Bücher „Beispielsammlung zur Eilschrift" und „Beispielsammlung zur Redeschrift" sind als Spezialwörterbücher anzusehen. Ein völlig andersartiges Spezialwörterbuch schrieb Strassner (1931). Es umfaßt und erläutert alle Fachausdrücke, die man beim Erlernen und Anwenden der Kurzschrift braucht.

5. Zur Geschichte der Kurzschriftwörterbücher

Das älteste Kurzschriftsystem sind die lateinischen „Tironischen Noten". Die Verzeichnisse dieser Noten können wohl als die ältesten Kurzschriftwörterbücher bezeichnet werden. Solche Verzeichnisse, die man *Kommentare* nannte, gab es schon im Altertum. Der älteste erhaltene Kommentar stammt aus dem 8. Jh. n. Chr. Die Kommentare ordnen die Noten weder alphabetisch noch systematisch, sondern die Reihenfolge ist völlig willkürlich. In der Neuzeit gibt es Stenographiesysteme seit 1588, aber Wörterbücher sind mit Ausnahme von Feutry 1775 erst seit der Mitte des 19. Jh. erschienen. Ihre Blütezeit erlebten sie in den ersten Jahrzehnten des 20. Jh. — Das erste deutsche stenographische Wörterbuch verfaßte Förster (1849) nach dem System Gabelsberger. Ihm folgten Fischer (1862) und Ruess (1896). Sie fanden keineswegs allgemeine Zustimmung. Über Ruess schreibt Heck (1902, II, 303):

„Um auch ein ziemlich überflüssiges Werk zu erwähnen, das einzig wegen seines Umfangs Beachtung verdient, sei das stenographische Wörterbuch von Dr. Ruess genannt, das durch seine Existenz lediglich geeignet ist, den Gegnern unnötigerweise eine Waffe [...] in die Hände zu spielen."

Im Jahre 1924 wurde die Deutsche Einheitskurzschrift eingeführt. Jetzt stellte nicht nur Ruess sein Wörterbuch um (Ruess 1926), sondern es erschienen Wörterbücher von Brandenburg (1925) und noch 4 weitere, die bei Johnen (1930, 38) aufgezählt werden. Als 1936 das System reformiert wurde, wurde nur ein Wörterbuch umgearbeitet und neu aufgelegt (Brandenburg 1925); dazu erschien neu Baier (1937). Nach der abermals geänderten Systemform von 1968 erschien nur ein Wörterbuch: Haeger/Lambrich (1973). Eine Anzahl kleinerer Spezialwörterbücher gab und gibt es weiterhin. In der DDR wird seit 1970 eine abweichende Systemform gelehrt. Hier gibt es das Wörterbuch 1958, auf dessen Titelblatt kein Verfassername genannt wird. —

Im französischen Sprachgebiet gibt es 3 Stenographiesysteme, aber nur für Prévost-Delaunay erschien ein Lexikon: Fleury/Roy (1900). Es wurde bis heute immer wieder neu aufgelegt. — Für die englische Sprache gibt es vor allem die Systeme Pitman (seit 1837) und Gregg (seit 1888). Obgleich beide Systemerfinder längst gestorben sind, erscheinen die Dictionaries (Pitman in London, Gregg in New York) immer noch unter ihrem Namen. — Für das russische Einheitssystem GESS haben der Systemerfinder Sokolov im Jahre 1946 und Frau Bessonova (mit 3 Mitautoren) 1952 einige Wörterbücher herausgegeben. Von Zeit zu Zeit erscheinen Neuauflagen, sind aber, wie fast alle Bücher in der Sowjetunion, immer ganz rasch vergriffen. — In Italien sind 4 Systeme für den Unterricht zugelassen. Nur für das verbreitetste System (Gabelsberger-Noe) gibt es Lexika: Greco (1902), Molina (1908) und Pico (o. J.). — Für die spanische Stenographie gibt es ein Lexikon, für die japanische nicht. In China ist die Stenographie selbst noch fast unbekannt. — Für Sprachgebiete von geringerer Größe sei als Beispiel die Tschechoslowakei herausgegriffen. Für dieses Land zählt Petrásek (1973, 185 ff.) in seinem bibliographischen Anhang 6 Wörterbücher nach dem System Gabelsberger auf und nach dem 1920 eingeführten Einheitssystem 20 tschechische und 6 slowakische Wörterbücher. Aber nur Krondl (1885) und Herout/Mikulik (1923) schufen vollständige Wörterbücher, die übrigen 30 Titel sind Spezialwörterbücher für Kürzungen.

6. Kurzschriftwörterbücher in der Gegenwart

Die Stenographie der Gegenwart kehrt zu den Funktionen zurück, für die sie im 16.—19. Jh. erfunden wurde: Sie ist als Notiz- und Konzeptschrift für jeden nützlich, der viel zu schreiben hat, sei es privat, sei es beruflich. Außerdem dient sie der wörtlichen Aufnahme von Reden. Um 1900 gewann sie eine zusätzliche Funktion; sie wurde in den Büros als Diktatschrift benutzt. Diese zusätzliche Verwendungsart verliert seit etwa 1950 an Bedeutung; hier — aber nur hier! — wird die Stenographie z. T. durch die Technik verdrängt. Das verleitet viele zu der irrigen Annahme, die Stenographie sei generell überholt. So geht z. Z. die Zahl der Lernenden zurück, und die Nachfrage nach Lehrmitteln, auch nach Lexika, wird geringer. Zwar gibt es für fast alle Systeme Kürzungsverzeichnisse, aber ausführliche Lexika nur noch für die deutsche Sprache (eins in der BRD, eins in der DDR), ferner für Italienisch (nur noch ein Lexikon), Französisch, Russisch und Spanisch. Auch englische Lexika sind noch im Handel, aber der Bedarf ist gering, zumal viele Berufsstenographen in den USA Stenographiermaschinen mit Computer-Übertragung benutzen.

7. Literatur (in Auswahl)

7.1. Wörterbücher

Baier 1937 = Max Baier: Wörterbuch der Deutschen Kurzschrift. Darmstadt 1937 [IV, 416 S.].

Bessonova 1952 = O. A. Bessonova: Stenograficheskij slovar'. Moskau 1952 [296 S.].

Brandenburg 1925 = Josef Brandenburg: Wörterbuch der Deutschen Einheitskurzschrift. Wolfenbüttel 1925 [140 S., Neubearb. 1936].

Brousse 1980 = Guy Brousse: Dictionnaire Foucher de sténographie. Système Prévost-Delaunay. Paris 1980 [346 S.].

Byers 1977 = E. E. Byers: Gregg's medical shorthand dictionary. Maidenhead 1977 [400 S.].

Feutry 1775 = A. A. J. Feutry: Manuel tironien ou Recueil d'abréviations faciles et intelligibles de la plus grande partie des mots de la langue française, rangés par ordre alphabétique. Ouvrage utile aux personnes qui ont beaucoup d'écritures à expédier et qui connoissent la valeur du temps. Paris 1775 [485 S.].

Fischer 1862 = Robert Fischer: Stenographisches Wörterbuch nach Gabelsbergers System. Glauchau 1862 [5. Aufl. Altenburg 1877, 290 S.].

Fleury/Roy 1900 = Paul Fleury/Ernest Roy: Dictionnaire de Sténographie. Paris 1900 [364 S.].

Förster 1849 = Karl Förster: Handwörterbuch der deutschen Stenographie. Leipzig 1849 [126 S.].

Greco 1902 = Oscar Greco: Lessico della stenografia. o. O. 1902.

Gregg 1955 = John Robert Gregg: Gregg's shorthand dictionary simplified. New York 1955 [328 S.; 1. Aufl. 1901, 146 S.].

Haeger/Lambrich 1973 = Fritz Haeger/Hans Lambrich: Winklers Wörterbuch der Deutschen Einheitskurzschrift. Darmstadt 1973 [304 S.].

Herout/Mikulik 1923 = Alois Herout/Svojmir Mikulik: Slovník nového těsnopisu československého [Wörterbuch der neuen tschechoslowakischen Stenographie] 1923.

Krondl 1885 = Antonin Krondl: Těsnopisný slovniček [Stenographisches Wörterbuch] 1885.

Molina 1908 = Enrico Molina: Dizionario etimologico stenografico. Milano 1908.

Ruess 1896 = Ferdinand Ruess: Ausführliches stenographisches Wörterbuch nach Gabelsbergers System. Neustadt 1896.

Ruess 1926 = Ferdinand Ruess: Stenographisches Wörterbuch für die Deutsche Einheitskurzschrift. Neustadt 1926.

Strassner 1931 = Paul Strassner: Kurzschriftliches Taschenlexikon. Wolfenbüttel 1931 [152 S.].

Wörterbuch 1958 = Stenografisches Wörterbuch. (Ost-)Berlin 1958, 8. Aufl. 1986.

7.2 Sonstige Literatur

Haeger 1972 = Fritz Haeger: Geschichte der Einheitskurzschrift. 2. Aufl. Wolfenbüttel 1972 [168 S., 1. Aufl. 1960].

Heck 1902 = Karl Heck: Geschichte der Schule Gabelsberger. 2. Bde. Wolfenbüttel 1901/02 [VI, 294 u. VIII, 548 S.].

Johnen 1930 = Christian Johnen: Die Deutsche Einheitskurzschrift. Berlin 1930 [324 S.].

Mentz/Haeger 1974 = Arthur Mentz/Fritz Haeger: Geschichte der Kurzschrift. Wolfenbüttel 1974 [152 S.].

Petrásek 1973 = Jan Petrásek: Dějiny těsnopisu [Geschichte der Stenographie]. Prag 1973 [200 S.].

Fritz Haeger (†), Bad Vilbel
(Bundesrepublik Deutschland)

331. Dictionaries of Deaf Languages

1. Introduction
2. History
3. Structure of Lexicons
4. Manual Alphabets
5. Selected Bibliography

1. Introduction

Linguistic research into the sign languages used by deaf people generated little interest before 1960, because most linguists did not accept the hand signals used by deaf people as representations of a language distinct from the spoken form (Schein 1984). Sign languages, when they were considered at all, were regarded as codes for the native language of the country or for a pidgin, as in the case of the American Indian Sign Language (Tomkins 1969). This attitude changed after publication of *A Dictionary of American Sign Language* (Stokoe/Casterline/Croneberg 1960). This seminal document, along with an earlier publication on the structure of sign language (Stokoe 1960), convinced most linguists that American Sign Language is not "English on the hands" but a separate language complete in itself, with a unique vocabulary and grammar. After this revelation, interest in sign languages has burgeoned, with many countries initiating studies of the manual languages used by their deaf citizens and discovering, as in the United States, that these manual languages are inherently different from spoken forms.

2. History

Some anthropologists argue that manual communication preceded spoken communication in human pre-history. However, from at least the time of Aristotle, born-deaf people have been regarded as intellectually subnormal. Society generally held that, since they did not speak, deaf-mute persons (die Taubstummen) were intellectually inferior. Aristotle's followers, confusing speech and language, concluded that those who did not speak did not have language and, hence, existed at an animal level. Accordingly, born-deaf children received no formal education until the 16th century (Schein 1984). The first recorded success in teaching deaf children by the Spanish monk Pedro Ponce de Leon has been lost, but it was followed by that of another Spanish cleric, Bonet (1620), whose teaching methods included signs and a manual alphabet.

Manual alphabets represent each letter and number with a distinct hand-motion configuration. They have been used by silent religious orders from at least the Middle Ages, but not for communication with deaf people. The earliest surviving publication of a one-handed manual alphabet is in a book of prayers, one for each letter of the alphabet (Yerba 1593); the author attributed the handshapes to St. Bonaventure. Dalgarno (1661) presented a manual alphabet that is somewhat like that used today in England, i.e. it is two-handed. He elaborated his alphabet into an educational system, which also included some signs (Dalgarno 1680).

The first pictorial dictionary of signs was prepared by a deaf teacher and poet at the National Institute for the Deaf, in Paris (Pélissier 1856). It contained 400 signs, with motions indicated by dotted lines, and further explication in the text.

Signs have also been used to represent speech sounds being employed in teaching speech to deaf children (Periere 1750).

One of the most influential dictionaries in the education of deaf children was written by the Abbé de l'Epée (1784) for use in the first public school open to deaf students. Vocabulary and grammar are described, with no illustrations to assist readers in making the so-called "Methodical Signs". His disciple Abbé Sicard followed with a version ordering vocabulary entries ideationally rather than by French words in alphabetical order (Sicard 1808).

Sign languages vary as much as spoken languages. Today, sign dictionaries can be found for Brazil, Bulgaria, Denmark, England, Finland, Germany, Haiti, Israel, Japan, Poland, Spain, Sweden, Thailand, U.S.A., U.S.S.R., and more. The myth of a "universal sign language" persists, though non does *naturally*. A committee of the World Federation of the Deaf (Commission 1975) has created "Gestuno", a compilation of signs, borrowed from various sign languages, and having no particular grammar. It is now used in international meetings of deaf people.

3. Structure of Lexicons

No single format distinguishes sign dictionaries. The fundamental distinctions rest upon how signs are represented, the order in which they are presented, and the choice of entries.

3.1. Mechanical Problems

How can motion in three-dimensional space be represented on the two-dimensional page of a dictionary?

3.1.1. Representing Signs

At first, signs were only described; however, for complex two-handed configurations, such verbal formulae become long and difficult to follow. Line drawings, usually with some supplementary instructions, have most often been used, though conventions must be established to indicate the sequence and direction of movements. Watson (1964) employed color to indicate the movement on cartoons illustrating the signs. Photographs have been less satisfactory, since they must be retouched to show the movement. Klima/Bellugi (1979) used photos of a hand holding a light to create an impression of movement. A third approach uses a notational system. Sutton (1977) has designed pictographs that can be combined to write sign sentences, as well as to represent signs. Cohen/Namir/Schlesinger (1977) adapted a system designed for recording dance steps; it is, however, too complex for general use. The most efficient system was designed by Stokoe/Casterline/Croneberg (1960). It breaks signs into three basic elements: *tabula*, 12 symbols indicating places where the sign is made in relation to the body; *designata*, 19 shapes of the hands; and *significata*, 24 motions made by the hands. These 55 symbols can be easily memorized, and when combined, they can depict virtually all signs.

Some collections of signs have been recorded on videotape. These television displays can be stored on videodiscs and accessed by computers, which would be a major advance in sign dictionaries.

3.1.2. Order of Entries

Users seeking a particular entry in Stokoe/Casterline/Croneberg (1960) can enter by the designate, an advantage for decoding an unfamiliar sign. An alphabetical list of word-equivalents is also provided. Most sign dictionaries order the signs in accordance with the spoken-language's alphabet. Some dictionaries group signs into conceptual units: foods, time concepts, etc. The latter two systems do not enable the reader to determine the meaning of a sign; they assume that the reader will be determining the sign equivalent of a spoken word, not the obverse.

3.2. Selection of Entries

Do sign dictionaries for any particular manual language represent the complete range of its expressions? Probably not. What requires three or four spoken words — good, better, best, for example — can be expressed with small variations in the same basic sign. Also, facial expressions prove to be important modifiers of many signs (a fact long overlooked by most lexicographers) thus greatly increasing the linguistic range. It has been suggested that to inquire as to the size of a sign vocabulary, in terms of the number of signs, misses the critical question: To what extent can thoughts and feelings be expressed in the target language? The correct test of a language's power resides in the answer to that question and not to some arbitrary number, an answer that dictionaries alone cannot provide. However, as living languages, natural sign languages must grow to accommodate the introduction of new concepts. Rather than await native development of signs, efforts have been made to create them. This trend has been especially evident in technical areas (Jamison 1983; Kannapell/Hamilton/Bornstein 1969).

3.3. Grammars

Visual languages appear to use different strategies than auditory languages to accomplish essential linguistic functions, such as denoting time. The failure to credit sign languages with true linguistic status led earlier lexicographers to conclude that these features were simply missing, and so systems were developed to impose the grammar of the spoken language on the signs of the natural manual language. That was the strategy employed by Epée (1784). Others have followed to the present day; e.g., Michaels (1923) provides markers for various tenses 'missing' from American sign language; Paget/Gorman (1968) offer a complete manual analog of British English; Gustason/Pfetzing/Zawolkow (1972) add to and modify American sign language to develop a manual mirror of spoken American English.

Only recently have efforts been made to elicit and publish the grammars of natural sign languages. These studies have reinforced the point made by comparative studies of spoken languages: all languages solve the same basic problems but in different ways. Thus, American sign language, like spoken English, has a strategy for establishing tense, but that strategy differs between the spoken and manual forms (Schein 1984).

3.3.1. Sign Codes vs. Sign Languages

As noted in the preceding section, many sign codes have developed to permit the encoding of spoken language in a manual form. The majority of dictionaries catalogue the codes, not the natural sign languages. Increasingly, however, this situation is changing: the newer dictionaries attempt to capture the language, rather than a sign code used as a pidgin for deaf-hearing communication (e.g., Hoemann/Oates/Hoemann 1981; Vasishta/Woodward/Santis 1985).

3.3.2. Etymologies

Etymologies are an expected feature of dictionaries, but because recording of signs has not been systematic and has taken place only in the last few hundred years, the origins of signs cannot be determined without serious doubts. Nonetheless, many dictionaries offer as facts speculations about the origins of signs. Working within a limited time span of seventy years, Frishberg (1975) demonstrated that the evolution of signs follow principles such as least effort. Thus, over time, signs tend to become simpler in execution. Studies of this nature render as poetry, not fact, most pronouncements about the origins of particular signs.

3.3.3. State of Syntactical Research

Among trends in ongoing sign research, the role of facial expression as a modifier of the manual expression excites much attention. Regional variations in signs of the same country provide another area of continuing interest to lexicographers (Shroyer/Shroyer 1984).

4. Manual Alphabets

By means of various handshapes, every letter of any alphabet can be represented. Countries differ as to whether the signs for a letter are made with one or both hands. The manual alphabets also vary from nation to nation (Carmel 1982).

5. Selected Bibliography

Bonet 1620 = Juan Pablo Bonet: Reducción de las letras y arte para ensenar a ablar los modus. Madrid 1620. Simplification of the letters of the alphabet and method of teaching deaf-mutes to speak. Translated from the original Spanish by H. N. Dixon, with an historical introduction by A. Farrar. Harrogate 1890.

Carmel 1982 = Simon J. Carmel: International hand alphabet charts. Rockville, Maryland 1982.

Cohen/Namir/Schlesinger 1977 = Einya Cohen/Lila Namir/I. M. Schlesinger: A New Dictionary of Sign Language. Paris 1977.

Commission 1975 = Unification of Signs Commission, World Federation of the Deaf: Gestuno. International Sign Language of the Deaf. Carlisle, England 1975.

Dalgarno 1661 = George Dalgarno: Ars signorum vulgo character philosophica. London 1661.

Dalgarno 1680 = G. Dalgarno: Didascalocophus, or the deaf and dumb man's tutor. Oxford, England 1680 [Reprinted in the American Annals of the Deaf 9. 1857, 14—64].

Epée 1784 = Charles-Michel de l'Epée: La veritable manière d'instruire les sourds-muets, confirmée par une longue éxperience. Paris 1784 [Parts I and II reprinted in American Annals of the Deaf 12. 1860, 1—132].

Frishberg 1975 = Nancy Frishberg: Arbitrariness and iconicity: Historical changes in American Sign Language. In: Language 51. 1975, 676—710.

Gustason/Pfetzing/Zawolkow 1972 = Gerilee Gustason/D. Pfetzing/E. Zawolkow: Signing Exact English. Rossmoor, California 1972.

Hoemann/Oates/Hoemann 1981 = Harry W. Hoemann/Eugene Oates/Shirley A. Hoemann (Eds.): The sign language of Brazil. Mill Neck, New York 1981.

Jamison 1983 = Steven L. Jamison: Signs for computing technology. Silver Spring, Maryland 1983.

Kannapell/Hamilton/Bornstein 1969 = Barbara Kannapell/Lillian B. Hamilton/Harry Bornstein: Signs for instructional purposes. Washington, D.C. 1969.

Klima/Bellugi 1979 = Edward Klima/Ursula Bellugi: The signs of language. Cambridge, Massachusetts 1979.

Michaels 1923 = J. W. Michaels: Handbook of the sign language of the deaf. Atlanta 1923.

Paget/Gorman 1968 = Richard Paget/Pierre Gorman: A Systematic Sign Language. London 1968.

Pélissier 1856 = Pierre Pélissier: Iconographie des Signes. Paris 1856.

Periere 1750 = Jacob Rodriguez Periere: Observation sur les sourds-muets et sur quelques endroits du mémoire de M. Ernaud. In: Mémoires de mathématique et de physique présentés a l'Académie Royale des Sciences par Divers Savants. Paris 1750—1786, 5, 500—530.

Schein 1984 = Jerome D. Schein: Speaking the language of sign. New York 1984.

Shroyer/Shroyer 1984 = Edgar H. Shroyer/Susan P. Shroyer: Signs across America. Washington, D.C. 1984.

Sicard 1808 = Roch-Ambroise Cucurron Sicard: Théorie des signes pour l'instruction des sourds-muets. Paris 1808.

Sternberg 1981 = Martin L. A. Sternberg: American Sign Language. A Comprehensive Dictionary. New York 1981 [XLV, 1132 pp.].

Stokoe 1960 = William C. Stokoe: Sign language structure. Buffalo 1960. (Studies in Linguistics. Occasional Papers 8.)

Stokoe/Casterline/Croneberg 1960 = William C. Stokoe/Dorothy Casterline/Carl G. Cronenberg: A Dictionary of American Sign Language on Linguistic Principles. Washington 1965. 2nd edition, Silver Spring, Maryland 1976.

Sutton 1977 = Valerie Sutton: Sutton Movement Shorthand. Irvine, California 1977.

Tomkins 1969 = William Tomkins: Indian sign language. New York 1969.

Vasishta/Woodward/Santis 1985 = Madan Vasishta/James Woodward/Susan de Santis: An Introduction to the Bangalore Variety of Indian Sign Language. Washington, D.C. 1985.

Watson 1964 = David O. Watson: Talk with your hands. Winnecone, Wisconsin 1964.

Yerba 1593 = Melchor Yerba: Libro llamado refugium infirmorum. Madrid 1593.

Jerome D. Schein, New York University, Gallaudet University, Washington, D.C. (USA)

332. Dictionaries in and of Braille

1. Introduction
2. Definition of Braille
3. Braille as a Communication System
4. Dictionaries in Braille
5. Dictionaries of Braille
6. Selected Bibliography

1. Introduction

A discussion of "Dictionaries in and of Braille" must be preceded by a brief explanation of the communication systems known as braille. Contrary to the beliefs of many people, there is not a single braille system. Instead, there are numerous braille systems in use throughout the world. Basically, a braille system exists for almost all major languages or language groups. These codes include literary braille, braille for mathematics, music, foreign languages, and computer braille codes. However, many systems are not standardized to the extent that they could be classified as codes. All standardized systems would have dictionaries "of" their braille code and most would have dictionaries "in" their braille code.

It is not possible in this brief article to include a discussion of all standardized braille codes. Therefore, only English literary braille will be discussed. It should be noted, however, that the methods of preparing most dictionaries in and of all braille codes are basically the same. Therefore, the discussions in this article related to English braille will apply to almost all standardized braille codes.

2. Definition of Braille

Braille is a system of touch reading for the blind which employs embossed dots evenly arranged in quadrangular letter spaces or cells. In each cell, it is possible to place six dots, three high and two wide. By selecting one or several dots in characteristic position or combination, 63 different characters can be formed. To aid in describing these characters by their dot or dots, the six dots of the cell are numbered 1, 2, 3, downward on the left, and 4, 5, 6, downward on the right thus:

    1 .. 4
    2 .. 5
    3 .. 6

English braille as officially approved by the Braille Authority of North America (BANA) and the Braille Authority of the United Kingdom (BAUK) is comprised of two grades. Grade 1 braille is in full spelling and consists of the letters of the alphabet, punctuation, numbers, and a number of composition signs which are special to braille and have no print counterpart. Grade 2 braille consists of all of Grade 1 braille and numerous contractions and short-form words, and is known as "English Braille". Therefore, the uncontracted braille code is designated as "English Braille, Grade 1". (This definition is taken from English Braille American Edition 1959 [1987], pp. 1—2.)

3. Braille as a Communication System

English braille, Grade 2 is a unique communication system. As stated in the definition above, it consists of all of Grade 1 braille plus numerous contractions. The resulting Grade 2 braille consists of 63 configurations of dots which are derived from the 6 dot cell described above. To these configurations, 263 meanings have been assigned. From this, it can be seen that there is not a one-to-one braille correspondence with English print. For that reason, English braille can best be described as a "mixed" code. Some elements of this "mixed" code are *alphabetic* in nature in the sense that braille symbols (or dot configurations) which represent the English alphabet do exist and words written in full alphabetic spelling would be spelled exactly the same as in English print spelling. Some examples would be:

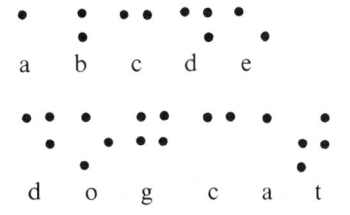

a   b   c   d   e

d   o   g   c   a   t

These same elements could also be described *logograms* because 24 of the alphabetic configurations also represent complete English words. Some examples of these logograms are:

but   can   do   every   from   go

Other logograms are formed by using two or more of the alphabetic letters to represent English words. These logograms may contain the initial two or three letters of a word, or they may form a consonant framework which contains all or some of the consonants in an English word. Examples of these logograms are:

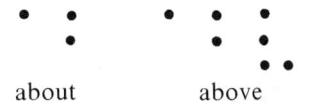

about   above

could   would

Still other elements of English braille bear no resemblance to the letters or words in English print which they are intended to represent. Some are syllabic in nature, for example:

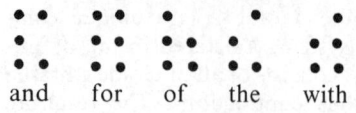

and   for   of   the   with

Others could be classified as phonograms. Examples of these might be:

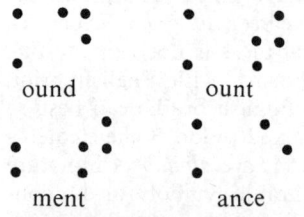

ound   ount

ment   ance

Many other examples and descriptions of the "mixed" nature of English braille could be given, but space does not permit a more extensive discussion here. These examples should serve as a background upon which the descriptions of the dictionaries in and of braille can be understood.

In spite of the fact that English braille is a "mixed" code, persons who use it as their reading medium are constantly required to consider it in relation to English print. For that reason, dictionaries "in" braille could be described as simply transliterations of dictionaries originally written in print. Dictionaries "of" braille contain the meanings, or definitions, of the dot configurations in the code as well as the rules to be used in reading and writing it. The remaining sections of this article will, therefore, decribe these two aspects of braille dictionaries separately.

4. Dictionaries in Braille

Dictionaries "in" braille are published primarily by those organizations which specialize in the publication of materials for the blind. The major publishing house of this kind in the United States is the American Printing House for the Blind in Louisville, Kentucky. The major publishing house of this kind in Great Britain is the Royal National Institute for the Blind in London, England. Both publishing houses select dictionaries which are used most widely in their educational programs and produce those dictionaries in braille. As stated above, these dictionaries can best be described as transliterations of English print dictionaries. The diacritical markings and pronunciation keys used in the print dictionaries are used in the braille dictionaries. An attempt is made to approximate the English print as nearly as possible in the braille dictionaries. However, since there is not a one-to-one correspondence between braille and English print, some differences do exist between them.

The most notable difference is in the initial presentation of the words being defined. These words appear in three forms for each entry. First the word is written in the highly contracted English braille, Grade 2; next it is written in fully spelled out English braille, Grade 1 and divided into syllables; and finally it is written in English braille, Grade 1 and divided into syllables with the accents, pronunciation symbols and diacritical markings included. Because of the nature of the braille code, such things as capital letters, pronunciation symbols, accent marks, and diacritical marks must be written separately from the word itself. This results in a rather long and complicated presentation of the word before its definition is given. An example of a typical entry would be:

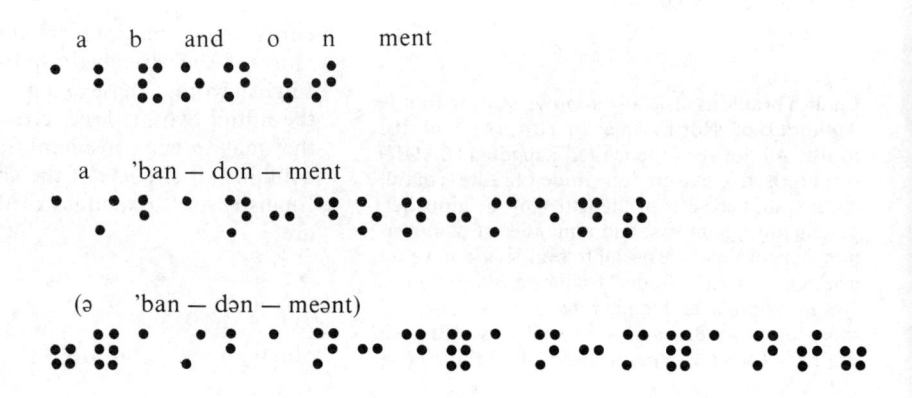

a   b   and   o   n   ment

a   'ban — don — ment

(ə   'ban — dən — meənt)

The definition of the word then follows in correct English braille, Grade 2.

5. Dictionaries of Braille

Dictionaries of braille consist of presentations of the various dot configurations (contractions) along with their meanings, the rules for their correct usage, and some examples of both correct and incorrect usage. The following is an example of such a presentation from the publication English Braille American Edition 1959 (1987).

Rule XIII — Lower Signs

Sign	Contraction		Punctuation
⠰	ea	⠰	(comma)
⠆	be bb	⠆	
⠒	con cc	⠒	(semicolon)
⠲	dis dd	⠲	(period)
⠢	en enough	⠖	(exclamation mark)
⠖	to ff		
⠶	were gg	⠶	(parentheses)
⠦	his	⠦	(opening quotation marks and question marks)
⠔⠆	into		
⠶	was by	⠴	(closing quotation mark)
⠤	com	⠤	(hyphen)

Rules with examples (Underlined words in examples are contractions)

1. The lower signs which represent the words "be", "enough", "were", "his", "in", and "was" may be preceded by the capital and or italic sign, but must not be in contact with any other letter, contraction, word, or punctuation sign. Example:
   It may be.
   Was it as you th/ought it was?

2. Two or more lower signs must not follow one another when they are not in contact with an upper sign containing a dot 1 or a dot 4.
   Was that his?

These examples illustrate only a small part of a dictionary of English braille, but they do illustrate what such a dictionary would contain. As the initial paragraphs of this article explained, almost all standardized braille codes would have dictionaries of this kind. Some more lengthy and complex than others, of course. No attempt will be made to provide a listing of all those available. It is doubtful that such a list exists. For those who might be interested in such a list, it is suggested that the National Library Service for the Blind and Physically Handicapped, 1291 Taylor Street, NW, Washington, DC 20542, USA, be contacted.

6. Selected Bibliography

6.1. Dictionaries in Braille

Common Usage Dictionary 1956 = Ralph Weiman: Common Usage Dictionary: French-English, English-French. Crown 1956 [10 vol., 958 p.].

Dorland's 1965 = Dorland's Medical Dictionary. 24. Ed. Saunders 1965 [49 vol., 13,069p.].

Follett 1962 = Richard Switzer: Follett Vest-Pocket Dictionary: French-English, English-French. Chicago 1962 [10 vol., 830p.].

Instant Spelling Dictionary 1964 = M. Dougherty, et al.; Instant Spelling Dictionary. Career Institute 1964. Louisville [8 vol., 602 p.].

Latin 1962 = Sidney Woodhouse: Latin-English, English-Latin Dictionary. McKay 1962 [22 vol., 2187p.].

Scott, Foresman 1979 = Edward Thorndike/Clarence Barnhart: Scott, Foresman Beginning Dictionary. Little Brown, Glenview, Ill. 1979 [15 vol., 3305p.].

Standard German Vocabulary 1937 = C. Purin: Standard German Vocabulary. Lexington, I.a. 1937 [4 vol., 649p.].

University of Chicago 1961 = Carlos Castillo/Otto Bond: University of Chicago Spanish-English, English-Spanish Dictionary. Louisville, Ky 1961 [27 vol., 2187p.].

Webster's 1956 = Webster's Students Dictionary. Louisville, Ky 1956 [36 vol., 8518p.].

Webster's 1970 = David Guralnik: Webster's New World Dictionary of the American Language. 2nd College Ed. Louisville, Ky 1970 [72 vol., 19,446p.].

6.2. Dictionaries of Braille

BANA 1987 = Provisional Guidelines for Literary Linear Braille Format. BANA. Louisville, Ky 1987.

Dorf 1984 = Marine Dorf et al.: Instruction Manual for Braille Transcribing. 3. Ed. Washington, D.C. 1984.

English Braille American Edition 1959 = English Braille American Edition. Louisville, Kentucky 1959. (Revised 1962, 1966, 1968, 1970, 1972; BANA changes 1980, 1987.).

Heinz 1972 = Adam Heinz: German Braille Contractions. Louisville, Ky 1972.

Introduction to Braille Mathematics = Helen Roberts et al.: Introduction to Braille Mathematics. Washington, D.C., Library of Congress 1972.

Introduction to Braille Music Transcription = Mary DeGarmo: Introduction to Braille Music Transcription. Louisville, Ky 1970.

Jenkins 1971 = Edward Jenkins: Primer of Braille Music. Louisville, Ky 1971.

Key to Grade Three Braille = Key to Grade Three Braille, a revision of Alphabetical Key to Grade Three, 1926 Ed. based on Louis Rodenberg: Revised Braille for Reading and Writing Grade Three. Louisville, Ky 1945.

Manual for Spanish Braille = Dorthea Goodlin: Manual for Spanish Braille. Lehigh Valley Braille Guild. Louisville Ky [1 vol.].

Nemeth 1972 = AAWB-AEVH Braille Authority: Nemeth Braille Code for Mathematics and Science Notation, 1972 revision. Louisville, Ky 1972.

Spanner 1956 = H. Spanner: Revised International Manual of Braille Music Notation. World Council for the Welfare of the Blind. Louisville, Ky 1956.

World Braille Usage 1999 = National Library Service for Blind and Physically Handicapped. Washington, D.C., U.S.A.

Hilda Caton, University of Louisville, Louisville, Kentucky (USA)

333. Wörterbücher zu Bildsymbolen

1. Bildzeichen-Definitionen
2. Historische Vorformen von Bildsymbolwörterbüchern
3. Zur Typologie und Morphologie von Wörterbüchern zu Bildsymbolen
4. Literatur (in Auswahl)

1. Bildzeichen-Definitionen

In Wörterbüchern zu Bildsymbolen (WzB) begegnen sich mittels Schrift visualisierte Sprache und Bilder, also zwei sehr unterschiedliche menschliche Mitteilungsformen. Daraus ergeben sich besondere theoretische Probleme, die es sinnvoll erscheinen lassen, einige pragmatisch angelegte Begriffserklärungen voranzustellen.

Dabei können weder die teils kontroversen Forschungsstandpunkte diskutiert noch die Detailprobleme differenziert abgehandelt werden (vgl. Eco 1972, 197ff.; Eco 1977; Nöth 1985). Auch die besonderen zeichentheoretischen Aspekte höher organisierter Bilder müssen hier unberücksichtigt bleiben.

Im folgenden geht es um Wörterbücher zu Bildzeichen, die wie Wörter oder Sätze als künstliche visuelle Zeichen in kommunikativer Absicht verwendet werden. Sie sind konventionell (Eco 1972, 64f.) und ihre Codes lassen sich nach Strukturtypen (Nöth 1985, 197ff.) oder nach der Art ihrer Verwendung unterscheiden.

Der deutsche Ausdruck *Bild* faßt zwei Aspekte zusammen, die etwa im Englischen durch die Begriffe *picture* (visuell wahrnehmbares, materielles Abbild eines Objekts) und *image* (mentale Repräsentation, Vorstellung, kognitives Konzept) unterschieden werden. Damit sind auf der einen Seite das Gebiet der visuellen Kommunikation einschließlich Formfragen angesprochen, auf der anderen Seite Gebiete der Kognitionspsychologie, Erkenntnistheorie und Semantik (Nöth 1985, 409). Beide Aspekte sind stets zu berücksichtigen.

Bei der folgenden vereinfachten Klassifizierung sollen nur drei — für die hier interessierenden Wörterbücher wesentliche — Zeichen-„Stufen" (Eco 1972, 225) unterschieden werden: (1) Einfaches Ikon, (2) ikonographisches Symbol und (3) freies Symbol.

1.1. Einfache Ikone (oder „Gleichbilder", so Breysig 1830, XXVIII)

Bei ihnen stehen die Objektebene und die Bildzeichenebene in einer Similaritätsbeziehung. Nach Peirce ist ein Ikon dementsprechend ein Zeichen, das infolge „Ähnlichkeit" (so auch bereits Breysig 1830, XX) auf ein Bezugsobjekt verweist (Peirce 1932, 275 u. 299; Morris 1946, 190 ff. u. 349; Nöth 1985, 111 ff.). Eco hat deutlich gemacht, daß es sich hierbei zunächst um ein wahrnehmungspsychologisches Problem handelt:

„Wenn das ikonische Zeichen mit irgendetwas Eigenschaften gemeinsam hat, dann nicht mit dem Gegenstand, sondern mit dem Wahrnehmungsmodell des Gegenstandes." (Eco 1972, 213)

Solch ein Ikon hat also bestimmte eigene „konfigurationelle" Merkmale (Eco 1977, 140), die ein Perzipient beim Vergleich mit dem Objekt als beiden gemeinsam identifizieren könnte. Eine Fotografie hat in diesem Sinn ein sehr hohes Maß an Ikonizität und nähert sich dem Idealtypus eines einfachen Ikons (Peirce 1932, 281).

Zeichen, die zu den Ikonen gezählt werden können, sind gekennzeichnet durch einen hohen Grad an Motiviertheit (geringe Arbitrarität).

Festgelegt sind dadurch sowohl die Zeichenform — aufgrund objektanaloger oder -imitativer Gestaltung — als auch die Semantik. In der Terminologie de Saussures ausgedrückt: Signifikant und Signifikat sind durch den Referenten festgelegt.

Dementsprechend kommen — von Phantasieprodukten als Sonderfall einmal abgesehen — als Objekte nur optisch wahrnehmbare Gegenstände der physischen Welt in Betracht.

Um Ikone zweifelsfrei als solche erkennbar zu machen, bedarf es eines Objekt-Denotation anzeigenden Kontextes. Das ist etwa bei Bildwörterbüchern der Fall (vgl. Art. 108), in denen Ikone ein Grundelement sind.

1.2. Ikonographische Symbole

Sie haben sich schon in frühen Stadien der Menschheitsgeschichte vor und neben freien Symbolen (vgl. 1.3.) behauptet. Offenbar sind sie wahrnehmungspsychologisch besonders wirkungsvoll (Krampen 1983, 199 ff.) sowie als nonverbale Informationsvermittler rationell und leistungsfähig. Die ikonographischen Symbole entsprechen in etwa der Symbol-Definition de Saussures (Krampen 1983, 200) und sind der Hauptgegenstand von WzB.

Der ältere, noch in der Umgangssprache lebende Symbolbegriff, mit dem Vorstellungen von

Adler, als Symbol-Tier sehr weit verbreitet, meist mit der ↗Sonne u. dem ↗Himmel gelegentl. auch mit dem ↗Blitz u. dem ↗Donner in Zshg. gebracht. Symbolprägend waren vor allem seine Kraft u. Ausdauer u. sein dem Himmel zustrebender Flug. In mehreren indian. Kulturen wird der A., als sonnen- u. himmelverwandt, dem chthonischen ↗Jaguar gegenübergestellt. Seine Federn wurden als Symbole der Sonnenstrahlen zu kult. Schmuck verwendet. — Der A. gilt als „König" der Vögel u. war bereits im Altertum ein Königs- u. Götter-Symbol. In der griech.-röm. Antike war er Begleiter u. Symbol-Tier des Zeus (Jupiter). In der röm. Kunst verkörpert oder trägt ein auffahrender A. die Seele des Herrschers, die nach Verbrennen der Leiche zu den Göttern aufsteigt. Die röm. Legionen hatten den A. als Feldzeichen. — In der Bibel begegnet der A. als Sinnbild für Gottes Allmacht oder auch für die Stärke des Glaubens. — Der ↗Physiologus schreibt dem A. die gleichen legendären Eigenschaften wie dem ↗Phönix zu, daher ist er im MA auch ein Symbol für Neugeburt u. Taufe sowie gelegentl. Symbol Christi u. (auch wegen seines Fluges) Symbol für dessen Himmelfahrt. Die Mystiker verglichen den auffliegenden A. verschiedentl. mit dem Gebet. Da der A. angebl. (nach Aristoteles) beim Aufsteigen direkt in die Sonne blickt, galt er auch als Symbol der Kontemplation u. spirituellen Erkenntnis. Mit Bezug darauf wie auf seinen Höhenflug ist er auch Attribut des Evangelisten Johannes (↗Evangelistensymbole). — Unter den sieben Todsünden symbolisiert der A. den Hochmut, unter den vier Kardinaltugenden die Gerechtigkeit. — C. G. Jung sieht in ihm ein väterl. Symbol. — Der A. war in Fortführung der röm. Tradition dt. Reichsadler, heute ist er dt. Bundesadler; als Zeichen der Souveränität steht er auch in vielen anderen Staatswappen.

Adler

Einköpfiger Reichsadler des Mittelalters

Doppelköpfiger Reichsadler seit 1401

Adler als Symbol des Geistes; aus: Hermphroditisches Sonn- und Mondskind, 1752

Adler: Symbol des Evangelisten Johannes; Kapitell im Kloster Saint Trophime, Arles; 12. Jh

Textbeispiel 333.1: Wörterbuchartikel (aus: Oesterreicher-Mollwo 1978, 11)

Sinnfälligkeit und Sinnbildlichkeit verknüpft sind, bezieht sich auf sie.

Mit welchen Merkmalen ikonographische Symbole in WzB auftreten, soll am Beispiel des Eintrags **Adler** im 'Herder Lexikon Symbole' (Oesterreicher-Mollwo 1978) erläutert werden (vgl. Textbeispiel 333.1).

Der ikonographische Code baut sich zwar auf der Grundlage des ikonischen Codes auf (Eco 1972, 243), ist aber durch größere Arbitrarität resp. verminderte Objektmotiviertheit gekennzeichnet. Die Zeichenform (Signifikant/Ausdrucksseite) ist zunächst noch erkennbar vom ursprünglichen Bezugsobjekt festgelegt.

So sind die wichtigsten Grund- oder Erkennungsmerkmale des ursprünglich motivierenden Vogels bei den vier abgebildeten Adlern noch vorhanden. Die größere Arbitrarität gegenüber dem Ikon 'Adler', das in einem Bildwörterbuch ebenfalls unter dem Lemma **Adler** geführt würde, zeigt sich aber in der Möglichkeit freierer graphischer Stilisierung und im Hinzutreten von nichtikonischen (objektfremden) graphischen Varianten (z. B. Doppelköpfigkeit) oder Attributen (z. B. Szepter und Reichsapfel).

Die Bedeutung (Signifikat/Inhaltsseite) ist nur noch in Konnotationen motiviert. Im Kommunikationsprozeß sollen ikonographische Symbole ihre Interpreten nämlich nicht veranlassen, sich wie beim Ikon das ursprünglich motivierende Objekt vorzustellen, sondern infolge irgendeiner Konvention bestimmte Abstrakta, Ideen, metaphysische Größen, Denkfiguren o. ä. (Resnikow 1968, 178 ff.; Jones 1978, 53). Nach Breysig (1830, XVI) ist die „Symbolik" in diesem Sinne „eine Bild- oder Zeichenkunst für Außersinnliches", weil man bei ihr „Sinnliches mit Nichtsinnlichem zu vergleichen hat" (Breysig 1830, V).

Die in den jeweiligen Gruppencodes festgelegten Bedeutungen können in der Regel auf einfaches Analogiedenken zurückgeführt werden (z. B. Höhenflug des Adlers → Christi Himmelfahrt). Die Merkmale des ursprünglich motivierenden Objekts treten als (erläuternde, verstärkende) Konnotate hinzu.

So sollen etwa beim Adler die natürlichen Eigenschaften des Tieres mitgedacht werden. Welche Bedeutung im Einzelfall gemeint ist, legen entweder die spezifischen graphischen Varianten fest (z. B. Doppelköpfigkeit des Adlers → Deutsches Reich u. a.), oder der einem bestimmten Code verpflichtete Kontext (Adler in einem Evangeliar → Evangelist Johannes). Dabei können völlig gegensätzliche Bedeutungsaspekte abgerufen werden: „Unter den sieben Todsünden symbolisiert der Adler den Hochmut, unter den vier Kardinaltugenden die Gerechtigkeit." (Oesterreicher-Mollwo 1978, 11).

1.2.1. Gebrauchsformen

Ikonographische Symbole treten ebenso als alleinstehende Bildzeichen auf (z. B. als staatliche Hoheitszeichen) wie als Bestandteile höher organisierter Bilder (z. B. als Attribute von Figuren in Gemälden oder als Bestandteile von emblematischen oder allegorischen Bildkompositionen).

Ikonographische Symbole werden heute in allen Bereichen des kulturell-gesellschaftlichen Lebens verwendet, teilweise nur noch in Form von „semiotischen Minimaleinheiten" (Nöth 1985, 215) wie bei Ikonogrammen (Eco 1977, 55) oder Piktogrammen (Nöth 1985, 215). Als Verwendungsbereiche sind u. a. zu nennen:

Verkehrswesen (Flughafenpiktogramme, Verkehrszeichen, Wegmarken); Sport (olympische Piktogramme); Militär, Politik und Verwaltung (Feld- und Militärzeichen, Staatsembleme, Flaggen, Hoheitszeichen, Wappen, Rang- u. Ehrenzeichen, Siegel, Stempel); Wirtschaft, Werbung (Handwerkszeichen, Warenzeichen, Pflegekennzeichen für Textilien, Fabrikmarken, Firmenzeichen, Brandmarkungen); Buch-, Kunst- und Bauwesen (Wasserzeichen, Signets als Druck- und Verlagszeichen, Wappen und Bauschmuck) sowie verschiedene Bereiche des religiösen Lebens. Hinzu kommen Bezirke der Alltagskommunikation, in denen Abzeichen oder Vereinssymbole, aber auch Sonderformen wie gestische Codes u. a. eine Rolle spielen.

In Wörterbüchern bzw. Lexika sind diese Symbole erst teilweise erfaßt.

1.3. Freie Symbole

Sie entsprechen der Symbol-Definition von Peirce (Nöth 1985, 40), d. h. sie sind nicht oder nicht mehr ohne weiteres erkennbar motiviert. Bei einer gedachten Stufenfolge von Zeichen, mit dem Ikon als am wenigsten arbiträr am Beginn, steht das freie Symbol als am meisten abiträr und konventionell am Ende.

Zu den freien Symbolen sind u. a. zu rechnen: Zahlen, Buchstaben und Schriften (Faulmann 1880; Gessmann 1899), Monogramme (Nagler 1858—65), Farben (Prange 1782) und Farbkombinationen, wie sie etwa in der Heraldik eine Rolle spielen, aber auch symbolisch-geometrische Figuren (wie Pentagramm oder Hexagramm und ähnliches) (Nöth 1985, 211).

2. Historische Vorformen von Bildsymbolwörterbüchern

Die Geschichte der WzB läßt sich in zwei historische Phasen gliedern. In der ersten, älteren Phase entstehen gebrauchsorientierte Vorstufen; in der zweiten Phase, ab dem 18. Jh., entwickeln sich die Wörterbücher im modernen Sinn.

Am Anfang stehen handschriftliche Vorformen von „Bildwörterbüchern" (vgl. Art. 108) zu naturkundlichen Gegenständen wie z. B. dem Wiener Dioskurides (Codex med. gr. 1) vom Beginn des 6. Jh. oder dem Berliner Codex Hamilton 407 vom Beginn des 14. Jhs.

Sie waren für den medizinisch-naturkundlichen Gebrauch bestimmt und fanden früh gedruckte Nachfolger. Bei beiden Codices lassen sich schon bildlexikonartige Strukturen feststellen. Die einzelnen „Artikel" (sie sind beim Berliner Codex bereits alphabetisch geordnet) weisen folgende Elemente auf: (1) Lemma, (2) Definition/Explikation in unterschiedlichem Umfang und (3) Bild (Illustration).

Ein ebenfalls nur der Naturkunde dienendes Werk scheint auf den ersten Blick der vielfältig überlieferte 'Physiologus' (2./3. Jh.) zu sein.

Er besteht in der Regel aus 55 nichtalphabetisierten Artikeln zu naturkundlichen Gegenständen, vor allem Tieren. Versteht man die Explikationen jedoch — wie im Mittelalter geschehen — auch als Anleitung zur Bildkunst, dann liegt hier eines der ältesten Beispiele für eine bewußte geistlich-allegorische Semantisierung von Ikonen, mithin die bewußte Herstellung eines ikonographisch-symbolisch verwendbaren Lexikons vor.

Mittelalterliche Bestiarien und neuere, alphabetisch angelegte Wörterbücher zur Tiersymbolik wie das von Clébert (1971) stehen in direkter Nachfolge des 'Physiologus'.

Auf mittelalterliche Vorläufer gehen auch Sonderformen von neueren Werken zurück.

Erwähnt seien Lexika zu Traumsymbolen (Kurth 1976, Textbeispiel 333.2) mit ihren Wegbereitern (Grenzmann 1980), zu Gebärden (vgl. Art. 109) mit ihren älteren Entsprechungen (Jarecki 1981) sowie zur Heraldik (z. B. Neubecker 1985).

Zwischen reiner Gelehrsamkeit und praktischem Bezug zur bildenden Kunst und Moraldidaxe sind die seit 1531 verbreiteten Sammlungen von Emblemen (Heckscher 1967) angesiedelt, deren ungeheuer reiche Tradition Henkel/Schöne (1967) dokumentieren.

Adler
— sehr kühne, tollkühne Gedanken und Taten können erfolgreichen und gefährlichen Ausgang haben.
— lebend: Gewinn und Nutzen.
— sitzend oder stehend: Tod großer Herren.
— auf dem Haupt befindlich: Unglück und Tod.
— in großer Höhe: mit einem besonders großen Glücksfall ist zu rechnen.
— schwarz: baldiger Tod eines guten Freundes.
— weiß: mögliche große Erbschaft.
— schießen oder fangen: Verlust und Gram.
— besitzen: Ehre, im Handel Vorteil.

Textbeispiel 333.2: Wörterbuchartikel (aus: Kurth 1976, 86)

Im Prinzip findet sich auch bei den „Artikeln" dieser Werke die erwähnte Trias von Lemma, Definition und Bild. Da das Lemma jedoch in der Regel ein sentenzartiges Motto ist, kann man nicht von Wörterbüchern reden. Das gilt auch für die Impresenbücher, in denen Devisen, Familiensymbole oder persönliche Symbole von Würdenträgern gesammelt wurden (z. B. Typotius 1601—03).

Als direkte Vorläufer der modernen WzB sind am ehesten die Renaissance-Hieroglyphiken (Volkmann 1923) und die Ikonologien (z. B. Boschius 1702) in Nachfolge Cesare Ripas (1603) anzusehen (Textbeispiel 333.3), bei denen es sich um bereits alphabe-

Textbeispiel 333.3: Ikonologie (aus: Ripa 'Iconologia' 1603; Abb. n. d. frz. Version, Paris 1644, 3)

tisch lemmatisierte Verzeichnisse von Emblemen oder *Allegorien* (Held 1937) handelt.

Werke dieser Art (Boudard 1766; Ramler 1788; Pinnock 1830) erschienen noch bis ins 19. Jh. neben den gleichzeitig auftretenden WzB im strengeren Sinn.

Bereits die Untertitel der frühen, teils mit wissenschaftlicher Akribie zusammengestellten WzB zeigen, daß sie wie die Allegorie-Lexika der Zeit vor allem für den Gebrauch der bildenden Künstler gedacht waren (Lacombe de Prezel 1779; Ikonologisches Lexikon 1793; Breysig 1830). Erst die Werke des 20. Jh. sind vornehmlich gelehrsamen Interessen gewidmet.

3. Zur Typologie und Morphologie von Wörterbüchern zu Bildsymbolen

Wörterbücher zu Bildsymbolen werden heute zumeist unter dem Namen *Lexikon* geführt. Da aber eine strikte Trennung von Sprachlexikographie und Sachlexikographie nicht möglich ist (Hausmann 1985, 370; Wiegand 1985, 24f.), tauchen auch Titel wie 'Wörterbuch der Symbolik' (Lurker 1983) auf.

Die im deutschen Sprachraum üblich gewordene terminologische Abgrenzung von sachlich informierendem Nachschlagewerk *(Lexikon)* und sprachlich informierendem *(Wörterbuch)* wird im englischen und französischen nicht in gleicher Weise nachvollzogen. Dort kann jede Art verbal lemmatisierten Nachschlagewerks *dictionary* bzw. *dictionnaire* heißen. Bei der im Deutschen üblich gewordenen Benennungskonvention entnimmt der Benützer dem Namen *Lexikon* zunächst, daß das Nachschlagewerk Sachen erklären will und nicht Wörter. Tatsächlich aber sind solche im Gegenstandsbereich eingegrenzten Lexika in gewissem Maße zugleich onomasiologische Wörterbücher. Denn jeder Lexikon-Artikel beginnt gewöhnlich mit einem Wort als Lemma, auch wenn es vom Verfasser nur auxiliär als Ordnungs- oder Auffindungshilfe gedacht ist.

Für die hier in Frage stehenden Wörterbücher werden darum die Namen *Lexikon* und *Wörterbuch* synonym gebraucht.

3.1. Wörterbücher zu besonderen Codes und Symbolfamilien

WzB im modernen Sinn entstanden, als das Wissen um bestimmte ikonographische Gruppencodes nicht mehr lebendiges Alltagswissen war. Tervarent (1958—64) gibt seinem Werk deshalb den Untertitel „Dictionnaire d'un Langage perdu". An seine Stelle trat gelehrt-antiquarischer Sammeleifer im Dienste der Erklärung und Anregung für weitere historisierende Verwendung.

Zunächst betraf das die hauptsächlich antikmythologisch geprägten Allegorien und Personifikationen, die in den bereits genannten Werken wie Ripas 'Iconologia' (Textbeispiel 333.3) gesammelt wurden. Nach der Aufklärung entstanden zur Symbolik der mittelalterlichen und spezifisch christlichen Kunst zahlreiche wissenschaftliche Überblickswerke (z. B. Chapeaurouge 1984) und Lexika (z. B. Corblet 1877; Beigbeder 1969; Heinz-Mohr 1974; Forstner 1982). Mit einem wirklich strengen methodischen Anspruch treten dabei allerdings nur die großen Werke zur christlichen Ikonographie von Aurenhammer (1959-67) und Kirschbaum (1968-76) auf.

Hilfsmittel zur Entschlüsselung von Symbolen in ganz bestimmten Wissensdisziplinen sind etwa die Lexika zur bildenden Kunst im 20. Jh. (Wilhelmi 1980), zur Staatsheraldik (Smith/Neubecker 1981), zur Religions- und Kulturgeschichte (Lurker 1974; Williams 1931), zur Politik und Massenkommunikation (Rabbow 1970) sowie zur Sexualwissenschaft und Psychoanalyse (Doucet 1971).

Werke mit Piktogrammen (z. B. AdV 1974; Modley 1976) oder anderen freien Symbolen (z. B. Arnell 1963; Robinson 1972; Schwarz-Winkelhofer 1972) sind zumeist anwendungsbezogen konzipiert.

3.2. Makrostruktur allgemeiner Bildsymbolwörterbücher

Die Darstellung des Standards heute geläufiger WzB soll anhand der allgemeinen Bildsymbolwörterbücher (wie z. B. dem von Droulers 1950) erfolgen, in denen Artikel zu diversen Codes und Sachbereichen vereinigt sind. Für sie gilt generell, daß ihre Artikel im Informationsgehalt stark voneinander abweichen und daß die Wörterbücher untereinander im wissenschaftlichen Niveau sehr differieren.

Herausragend sind nur wenige Lexika, wie z. B. die von Lanoë-Villène (1927—30) und Chevalier (1969). Wissenschaftlich unbrauchbar sind Werke wie das von Kurth (1976; Textbeispiel 333.2).

Bei einer Analyse ihrer „Makrostruktur" (vgl. Hausmann 1985, 372 und Art. 38) geht es um die Frage, nach welchen Kriterien die Artikel insgesamt in ihrer Abfolge organisiert sind. Das betrifft die formale Anordnung der Artikel (3.2.1.) und die behandelten Sachbereiche (3.2.2.).

3.2.1. Aufgrund der Eigenart der hier in Frage stehenden Symbole wäre ein Zusammenwirken bildlicher und verbaler Elemente bei den Einzelartikeln denkbar. Als Bestandteile kämen dann in Betracht: (1) Lemma: (a)

AGRICULTURE

Farm Structures and Lands *(continued)*

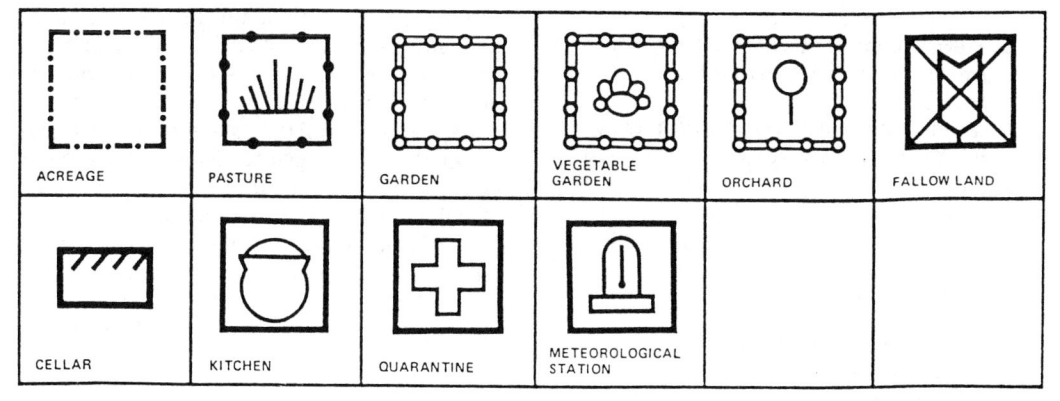

ACREAGE	PASTURE	GARDEN	VEGETABLE GARDEN	ORCHARD	FALLOW LAND
CELLAR	KITCHEN	QUARANTINE	METEOROLOGICAL STATION		

Textbeispiel 333.4: Artikelausschnitt (aus: Dreyfuss 1972, 44)

Verballemma; (b) Bildsymbol-Lemma; (2) Definition/Explikation: (a) verbale Explikation; (b) bildliche Explikation (Illustration).

Da aber für Bildsymbole kein dem Alphabet vergleichbares, allgemein anerkanntes Bild-Ordnungssystem existiert, gibt es nur ganz selten nach Bildsymbol-Lemmata geordnete Wörterbücher (z. B. von Kapff 1957). Jedoch kann auch in ihnen nicht auf Findewörter verzichtet werden, weil mit ihrer Hilfe die nötige Gruppensystematik der Zeichen vorgenommen werden muß (vgl. Textbeispiel 333.4). Die Verf. der allgemeinen Bildsymbolwörterbücher machen sich deshalb bei den Einträgen konsequent die Vorteile der durchgängig alphabetischen Gliederung nach Verballemmata zunutze (zum Terminus *Lemma* vgl. Wiegand 1983).

Bei den Speziallexika findet sich in Ausnahmefällen eine Kombination von Sachgruppensystematik (zur Großgliederung) und kapitelinterner alphabetischer Lemmatisierung (Forstner 1982).

Selten tritt eine Großgliederung nach alphabetischen Stichwörtern, aber ohne kapitelinterne alphabetische Lemmatisierung auf (Dreyfuss 1972; Textbeispiel 333.4; Neubekker 1985). Lexika zu technischen Zeichen sind zumeist nichtalphabetisch nach systematischen Gruppen geordnet (Arnell 1963; DIN-Fachbericht 1986).

Im Prinzip besteht die Möglichkeit, mittels Lemmata entweder nur die Zeichenformen (z. B. „Adler") oder nur die Bedeutungen (z. B. 'Deutsches Reich') anzuzeigen. In der Praxis findet aber — wohl zum Vorteil der Benutzer — nirgendwo eine klare Trennung statt, was dadurch verstärkt wird, daß sich keines der allgemeinen Wörterbücher als reines Symbolverzeichnis versteht (vgl. 3.2.2.). Zeichenform-Lemmata und Bedeutungs-Lemmata stehen also gemischt, werden jedoch zumeist durch Querverweise innerhalb der Artikel in Beziehung gesetzt, seltener durch Gesamtregister. Gewöhnlich überwiegen aber die zeichenform-bezogenen Lemmata.

Bei ihrer Formulierung macht sich eine Neigung zur ökonomischen Vereinfachung bemerkbar.

Nach Möglichkeit werden nämlich nur die Namen der ursprünglich motivierenden Objekte resp. ihrer Ikonen gewählt (vgl. *the generic term,* de Vries 1984, Preface). Doch es gibt Abweichungen davon.

Bei Breysig (1830) findet sich eine Art Mehrfachlemma-Verfahren, wobei nur das Eingangslemma ausgedruckt und die folgenden durch Spiegelstriche angezeigt sind (Textbeispiel 333.5).

Auch das erste Wort eines Satzes kann bei ihm als Lemma dienen („**Geschändet** ward die hl. Pelagia"). Lanoë-Villène (1927—30) arbeitet mit einer Nestlemma-Variante und Ronchetti (1922) verwendet Nebenlemmata; so stehen bei ihm nach **Aquila** [Adler]: **Aquila a due teste, Aquila che porta un sasso** und **Aquila pigargo.**

3.2.2. Das Gros der Artikel verzeichnet ikonographische Symbole einschließlich Allegorien, Attributen von Figuren o. ä. sowie freie Symbole wie Monogramme, Buchstaben *(Alpha)* und Wörter *(Amen).* In allen Wörterbüchern bzw. Lexika sind aber noch zahlreiche andere Sachbereiche mit Artikeln vertreten.

Vor allem sind das den visuellen Symbolen benachbarte Gegenstände wie religiös-literarische Figuren aus Bibel *(Adam)* und Mythologie *(Achilles),*

Adler: von einem brennenden Scheiter-
haufen emporsteigend: Vergötterung
d. Fürsten (a. r. M.).
—: von einem flammenden Altare sich
aufschwingend: Vergötterung d. Fürsten
(a. r. M.).
Adler auf einer Kugel bereit zu fliegen:
Vergötterung (a. r. M.)
— anstatt der Fahne, s. Romulus.
— mit Blitzen hat Frankreich.
— — — und einem Oelzweige:
Gnade (a. röm. M.).
— mit Blitzen in den Klauen: röm.
Reich (a. M.).
— auf Blitzen ruhend u. ein Oelzweig:
Clementia, Gnade.
— mit einem Sacke, in welchem das
Haupt des heil. Lupentius.
—: verjüngtes langes Leben; s. Arznei-
kunst.
—: Tapfere stammen von Tapfern.

Textbeispiel 333.5: Artikelausschnitt (aus: Breysig 1830, 11)

symbolträchtige Materialien *(Asche)*, symbolische Handlungen *(Astraltänze)*. Häufig werden auch fachsystematische und theoretische Begriffe *(Archetypus, Alchemie)* oder literarische Motive und Metaphern *(Aladin's lamp, Blaue Blume)* sowie Begriffe zu Heraldik und Ländersymbolik *(Africa)* mit aufgenommen. De Vries (1984) weist auch auf psychoanalytisch gedeutete Traumsymbole *(Aeroplane)* hin; Hall (1979) verzeichnet zusätzlich bestimmte Heilige *(Agnes)*, literarhistorische Kategorien *(Ars moriendi)* und Motti *(Ad Majorem Dei Gloriam)*.

Am weitesten greifen Breysig (1830) und Lurker (1983). Lurker möchte alle wichtigen Sachbereiche der Disziplin „Symbolik" erfassen und verzeichnet auch einschlägige Termini diverser Nachbarfächer: Psychoanalyse *(Abwehrmechanismus)*, Religion und Volkskunde *(Ahnenkult, Allah)*, Biographik *(Alciatus)*, historische Ethnologie *(Ägypten)*.

Ein ähnlich umfassendes Werk wollte wohl auch schon Breysig mit den Mitteln seiner Zeit zu Beginn des 19. Jhs. schaffen (Textbeispiel 333.5). Manchem seiner 50 000 Kurzeinträge merkt der Benutzer jedoch an, daß er unreflektiert(?) aus dem Zettelkasten übernommen wurde (z. B. **„Abenteuerliches:** Theuerdank. Deutsche Architektur."). Als Lemmata treten bei ihm auch Prädikate wie *aasfressend* auf.

3.3. Mikrostruktur allgemeiner Bildsymbolwörterbücher

Bei der folgenden Analyse der Mikrostruktur geht es um die Frage, welche Informationen die Wörterbücher innerhalb der Einzelartikel auf welche Weise vermitteln. Um es kurz machen zu können, sollen nur die nach Zeichenformen lemmatisierten Artikel in Betracht gezogen werden. Da keines der Wörterbücher alle Möglichkeiten ausschöpft, wird bei der Darstellung eine Art Idealtypus mit 10 Elementen zugrunde gelegt. Dabei betreffen die ersten fünf Elemente die Struktur, die letzten fünf den Umfang der Informationen:

(1) Lemmatisierte Binnengliederung (Sublemmata): In alphabetisierter Form tritt solch eine Gliederung nicht auf, sondern nur in Abwandlung nach systematischen Stichwörtern. Insgesamt ist sie selten.

Lurker (1983) etwa führt *Doppeladler* nicht als Sublemma unter *Adler*, sondern eigenständig. Lanoë-Villène (1927—30) gliedert seine umfangreichen Artikel, von teils monographischem Charakter, mittels Überschriften zu einzelnen Bedeutungs- und Verwendungskreisen. Systematische Stichwörter verwendet auch de Vries (1984), die mit Großbuchstaben alphabetisch indiziert sind. Sie betreffen Bedeutungen, korrespondierende Symbole und Gebrauchsweisen (bei **eagle** finden sich: *A. general; B. majesty, power; C. spirit; D. sun, fire; E. heavens, air; F. character-traits; H. correspondences; I. special meanings; J. alchemy; K. psychology; L. heraldry; M. combinations; N. part* [z. B. Kopf des Adlers]; *O. folklore)*. Cooper (1978) gliedert seine Artikel mit Stichwörtern zu den Codes.

(2) Verweisstichwörter: Fast alle Lexika arbeiten mit Querverweisen, allerdings oft recht willkürlich.

(3) Illustrationen: Bereits Breysig (1830) hat zahlreiche Tafeln mit insgesamt 3119 graphischen Darstellungen angefügt. Cairo (1922) gibt den Pflanzen-Artikeln ikonische Zeichnungen bei und Cooper (1978) Fotos zu Bildquellen. Ganz vereinzelt treten Illustrationen bei Cirlot (1962) und Hall (1974) auf. Dem Ideal einer repräsentativen Bilddokumentation zu den Symbolvarianten bei jedem Artikel kommt trotz der Kürze noch am ehesten das 'Herder Lexikon Symbole' (Textbeispiel 333.1) entgegen.

(4) Quellenangaben. Regelmäßige Belegnachweise oder gar besondere Quellenkapitel wie in einigen Speziallexika (Kirschbaum 1968—76) sind selten. Relativ vorbildlich für den Quellenbereich des griechisch-römischen Altertums sind Lacombe de Prezel (1779) und Lanoë-Villène (1927—30). In den meisten Lexika finden sich jedoch nur relativ beliebig angeführte Autoren- oder Werknamen in Klammern. Selbst zusammenfassende Quellenüberblicke (wie etwa bei Hall 1974 in der

Einleitung) fehlen gewöhnlich oder sind spärlich.

(5) Literaturhinweise: Bei den allgemeinen WzB findet sich nur bei Lurker (1983) jeweils konsequent ein bibliographischer Artikelbestandteil. Lanoë-Villène (1927—30) hat aber immerhin Anmerkungen.

(6) Codes: Abgesehen von Einzelfällen (vgl. Kurth 1976; Textbeispiel 333.2) benennen alle Lexika verschiedene Codes in den Artikeln. Jedoch gibt es teils Beschränkungen zeitlicher (z. B. nur Altertum) oder geographischer Art (z. B. nur westliche Welt). Die Codes werden oft als internes Gliederungsprinzip herangezogen (vgl. Textbeispiel 333.1), am klarsten bei Cooper (1978), der sie fortlaufend mit Stichwörtern indiziert:

bei **eagle:** *Alchemic, Amerindian, Australian aboriginal, Aztec, Buddhist, Celtic, Chinese, Christian, Egyptian, Greek, Hebrew, Hindu, Mithraic, Roman, Scandinavian, Sumero-Semitic.*

(7) Bedeutungen: Bei der Angabe der verschiedenen Codes werden zumeist auch die jeweiligen Bedeutungsaspekte erläutert. Lanoë-Villène (1927—30) läßt auf das Lemma zunächst eine code-übergreifende Kurzdefinition folgen, dann einen Abschnitt „Généralités" und schließlich Sonderbedeutungen. Dieser Weg vom Allgemeinen zum Besonderen wird auch von den meisten anderen Autoren beschritten. Chevalier (1969) handelt jede Bedeutung gesondert, mit einer Ordnungszahl versehen ab. In den meisten Lexika sind die Angaben jedoch so summarisch oder ausschnitthaft, daß sie für wissenschaftliche Zwecke kaum verwendbar sind (vgl. Textbeispiel 333.6 mit den oben unter Punkt (1) genannten Differenzierungen von de Vries 1984).

(8) Bedeutungsätiologien: Der Nachzeichnung von Bedeutungsursprüngen und -entwicklungen mit genauer Angabe der verschiedenen Zeitstufen wird aus Platzgründen zumeist keine besondere Aufmerksamkeit geschenkt (vgl. Textbeispiel 333.6). Allerdings kann der Benützer oft aus den verschiedenen Hinweisen einen Entwicklungsgang rekonstruieren.

Wenn Rückführungen auf Bedeutungsursprünge vorgenommen werden, dann nicht selten spekulativ und unter Verzicht auf genaue Belege (Textbeispiel 333.1). Eine vorbildliche Ausnahme stellt das Speziallexikon von Kirschbaum (1968—76) dar.

(9) Pragmatik (Gebrauch des Symbols): In die meisten Artikel sind Hinweise auf die Verwendungsweisen der Symbole eingestreut. Das 'Dizionario' Cairos (1922) hebt sich insofern ab, als in ihm mehr als bei anderen der literarische Gebrauch von Symbolen mit Zitaten dokumentiert ist.

(10) Beziehungs- und Oppositions-Symbole: Nur de Vries (1984) hat jeweils ein eigenes Artikelstichwort **correspondences**, unter dem verwandte oder oppositionelle Symbole oder Bedeutungsbereiche genannt werden. Aber auch die meisten anderen Lexika erwähnen derartige Symbole gelegentlich (vgl. Textbeispiel 333.1). Jedoch gilt auch hier, daß die Autoren häufig willkürlich verfahren.

4. Literatur (in Auswahl)

4.1. Wörterbücher/Lexika

AdV 1974 = Arbeitsgemeinschaft Deutscher Verkehrsflughäfen (Hrsg.): Piktogramme zur Orientierung auf Flughäfen. Pictographs for Orientation at Airports. Stuttgart 1974 [Loseblattsammlung].

Arnell 1963 = Alvin Arnell: Standard Graphical Symbols. A Comprehensive Guide for Use in Industry, Engineering, and Science. New York. Toronto. London 1963 [X, 543 S.].

Aurenhammer 1959—67 = Hans Aurenhammer: Lexikon der christlichen Ikonographie. Wien 1959—67 [640 S.; nicht mehr erschienen].

Eagle. Sacred to JUPITER and his attribute, sometimes with a thunderbolt in its claws; GANYMEDE was borne to heaven by Jupiter's eagle. A young goddess with a jug, an eagle beside her, is HEBE. An eagle sent by Jupiter pecks the liver of PROMETHEUS. The eagle was an ancient symbol of power and victory and was represented on the standards of the Roman legions. In the same sense it has since been adopted in the armorial bearings of numerous nations. It was a medieval symbol of Christ's Ascension. It is the attribute of JOHN THE EVANGELIST, perhaps with a pen or inkhorn in its beak, and is one of the four 'apocalyptic beasts' (FOUR EVANGELISTS; APOCALYPSE, 3, 9). An eagle utters cries of woe as the last trumpet sounds (APOCALYPSE, 11). In allegory the eagle is an attribute of PRIDE (with lion, peacock), and of Sight, one of the FIVE SENSES. It is an *impresa* of the Gonzaga family of Mantua, patrons of the arts in the Renaissance.

Textbeispiel 333.6: Wörterbuchartikel (aus: Hall 1974, 109)

Beigbeder 1969 = Olivier Beigbeder: Lexique des Symboles. St. Léger 1969 [435 S.].

Boschius 1702 = R. P. Jacobus Boschius: Symbolographia sive De Arte Symbolica. 2 Teile. Augsburg. Dillingen 1702.

Boudard 1766 = Giovanni B. Boudard: Iconologie. Vienna 1766. Repr. New York 1976 [208 S.].

Breysig 1830 = Adam Breysig: Wörterbuch der Bildersprache oder kurzgefaßte und belehrende Angaben symbolischer und allegorischer Bilder und oft damit vermischter konventioneller Zeichen. Zugleich Versuch eines Zierathwörterbuchs. Leipzig 1830 [XXX S., 54 Tafeln, 973 S.].

Cairo 1922 = Giovanni Cairo: Dizionario ragionato dei Simboli. Milano 1922. Repr. Bologna 1967 [XIII, 365 S.].

Chevalier 1969 = Jean Chevalier/Alain Gheerbrant (Hrsg.): Dictionnaire des Symboles. Mythes, Rêves, Coutumes, Gestes, Formes, Figures, Couleurs, Nombres. Paris 1969 [XXXII, 844 S.].

Cirlot 1971 = Juan-Eduardo Cirlot: A Dictionary of Symbols. (Orig. span.: Diccionario de Simbolos Tradicionales) London 2. Aufl. 1971 [LV, 419 S.; 1. Aufl. 1962).

Clébert 1971 = Jean-Paul Clébert: Bestiaire Fabuleux. Paris 1971 [455 S.].

Cooper 1978 = Jean C. Cooper: An Illustrated Encyclopaedia of Traditional Symbols. London 1978. Repr. 1984 [207 S. Dt. Ausg. Leipzig 1986].

Corblet 1877 = Jules Corblet: Vocabulaire des Symboles et des Attributs employés dans L'Iconographie chrétienne. Paris 1877 [107 S.].

DIN-Fachbericht 1986 = Graphische Symbole nach DIN 30 600. Teil 1: Bildzeichen. Übersicht. Berlin. Köln 5. Aufl.1984 [108 S.].

Doucet 1971 = Friedrich W. Doucet: Taschenlexikon der Sexualsymbole. München 1971 (Mensch und Sexualität 21) [172 S.].

Dreyfuss 1972 = Henry Dreyfuss: Symbol Sourcebook. An Authoritative Guide to International Graphic Symbols. New York etc. 1972 [292 S.].

Droulers 1950 = Eugène Droulers: Dictionnaire des Attributs, Allégories, Emblèmes et Symboles. Turnhout 1950 [VIII, 281 S.].

Faulmann 1880 = Carl Faulmann: Das Buch der Schrift, enthaltend die Schriftzeichen und Alphabete aller Zeiten und aller Völker des Erdkreises. Wien 1880. Repr. Nördlingen 1985 [XII, 286 S.].

Forstner 1982 = Dorothea Forstner: Die Welt der christlichen Symbole. 4. Aufl. Innsbruck. Wien. München. 1982 [461 S.; 1. Aufl. 1961].

Gessmann 1899 = Gustav W. Gessmann: Die Geheimsymbole der Chemie und Medicin des Mittelalters. Graz 1899. Repr. 1972 [67 S., 120 Tafeln, 36 S.].

Hall 1979 = James Hall: Dictionary of Subjects and Symbols in Art. 2. Aufl. New York etc. 1979 [XXIX, 349 S.; 1. Aufl. 1974].

Heinz-Mohr 1974 = Gerd Heinz-Mohr: Lexikon der Symbole. Bilder und Zeichen der christlichen Kunst. 3. Aufl. Düsseldorf. Köln. 1974 [319 S.; 1. Aufl. 1971].

Henkel/Schöne 1967 = Arthur Henkel/Albrecht Schöne (Hrsg.): Emblemata. Handbuch zur Sinnbildkunst des XVI. und XVII. Jahrhunderts. Stuttgart 1967 [LXXXI, 2196 S.].

Ikonologisches Lexikon 1793 = Ikonologisches Lexikon oder Anleitung zur Kenntnis allegorischer Bilder auf Gemälden, Bildhauerarbeiten, Kupferstichen, Münzen und Vergleichen. Ein Handbuch. Sowohl für Künstler insbesondere als für jeden Liebhaber der bildenden Künste überhaupt. Nürnberg 1793 [382 S.].

Jarecki 1981 = Signa loquendi. Die cluniacensischen Signa-Listen eingeleitet und hrsg. v. Walter Jarecki. Baden-Baden 1981 (Saecvla Spiritalia 4).

v. Kapff 1957 = Taktische Zeichen von Wehrmacht und Bundeswehr (NATO) in Gegenüberstellung. (Bearbeitet v. von Kapff). Heidelberg 1957 [19 S.].

Kirschbaum 1968—76 = Engelbert Kirschbaum/ Wolfgang Braunfels (Hrsg.): Lexikon der christlichen Ikonographie. 8 Bde. Rom. Freiburg. Basel. Wien 1968—76.

Kurth 1976 = Hanns Kurth: Lexikon der Traumsymbole. 2300 Begriffe, 6250 Symbolbedeutungen. Zahlreiche Abbildungen. Genf 1976 [322 S.].

Lacombe de Prezel 1779 = Honoré Lacombe de Prezel: Dictionnaire Iconologique, ou Introduction a la Connaissance des Peintures, Sculptures, Estampes, Médailles, Pierres Gravées, Emblemes, Devises, & C. Avec des Descriptions tirées des Poetes anciens & modernes. Nouvelle édition, revue & considérablement augmentée. Tome 1. 2. Paris 1779. Repr. Paris 1972 [XX, 310 S.].

Lanoë-Villène 1927—30 = Georges Lanoë-Villène: Le livre des symboles. Dictionnaire de Symbolique et de Mythologie. 4 Teile. Paris 1927—30 [mehr nicht erschienen].

Lurker 1974 = Manfred Lurker: Götter und Symbole der alten Ägypter. Einführung und kleines Lexikon. 2. Aufl. Bern. München. Wien. 1974 [219 S.; 1. Aufl. 1964].

Lurker 1983 = Manfred Lurker: Wörterbuch der Symbolik. 2. Aufl. Stuttgart. 1983 [XVI, 800 S.; 1. Aufl. 1979].

Modley 1976 = Rudolf Modley: Handbook of Pictorial Symbols. 3.250 Examples from International Sources. New York 1976 [XIV, 143 S.].

Nagler 1858—65 = Georg Kaspar Nagler: Die Monogrammisten und diejenigen bekannten und unbekannten Künstler aller Schulen, welche sich zur Bezeichnung ihrer Werke eines figürlichen Zeichens, der Initialen des Namens, der Abbreviatur desselben & c. bedient haben. Mit Berücksichtigung von Buchdruckerzeichen, der Stempel von Kunstsammlern, der Stempel der alten Gold- & Silberschmiede, der Majolicafarben, Porcellan-

Manufacturen usw. 4 Bde. München 1858—65. Register 1920.

Neubecker 1985 = Ottfried Neubecker: Großes-Wappen-Bilder-Lexikon. München 1985 [1147 S.].

Oesterreicher-Mollwo 1983 = Herder Lexikon Symbole. Bearbeitet von Marianne Oesterreicher-Mollwo. Freiburg 6. Aufl. 1983 [192 S.; 1. Aufl. 1978].

Pinnock 1830 = W. Pinnock: Iconology: or Emblematic Figures Explained; in Original Essays on Moral and Instructive Subjects. London 1830 [414 S.].

Prange 1782 = Christian F. Prange: Farbenlexikon. Halle 1782 [XXXII, 572 S. u. 48 Farbtafeln].

Rabbow 1970 = Arnold Rabbow: dtv-Lexikon politischer Symbole A—Z. München 1970 [269 S.].

Ramler 1788 = Karl Wilhelm Ramler: Allegorische Personen zum Gebrauche der bildenden Künste. Berlin 1788 [82 S.].

Ripa 1603 = Cesare Ripa: Iconologia o vero Descrittione di diverse Imagini cauate dall'antichità, & di propria inuentione. Roma 1603. Repr. Hildesheim. New York 1970. [527 S.; 1. Aufl. 1593] Frz. Version von Jean Baudouin: Iconologie. Paris 1644. Reprint New York. London 1976 [204, 196 S.].

Robinson 1972 = L. J. Robinson: A Dictionary of Graphical Symbols. London 1972.

Ronchetti 1922 = Guiseppe Ronchetti: Dizionario illustrato dei Simboli. 2 Bde. Milano 1922. Repr. Milano 1985 [1009, XCI S.].

Schwarz-Winkelhofer 1972 = Inge Schwarz-Winkelhofer/Hans Biedermann: Das Buch der Zeichen und Symbole. Graz 1972 [XI, 281 S.].

Smith/Neubecker 1981 = Whitney Smith/Ottfried Neubecker: Wappen und Flaggen aller Nationen. München 1981 [263 S.].

Tervarent 1958—64 = Guy de Tervarent: Attributs et Symboles dans L'art profane 1450—1600. Dictionnaire d'un Langage perdu. 2 Teile. Genève 1958—64 [482 S. u. div. Abb.].

Typotius 1601—1603 = Jacobus Typotius: Symbola divina et humana pontificum imperatorum regum. 3 Bde. Prag 1601—1603. Repr. Graz 1972.

de Vries 1984 = Ad de Vries: Dictionary of Symbols and Imagery. Amsterdam. London 3. Aufl. 1984 [515 S.; 1. Aufl. 1974].

Wilhelmi 1980 = Christoph Wilhelmi: Handbuch der Symbole in der bildenden Kunst des 20. Jhs. Frankfurt. Berlin 1970 [542 S.].

Williams 1931 = Ch. A. Speed Williams: Outlines of Chinese Symbolism. Peiping 1931 [XXV, 423 S.].

4.2. Sonstige Literatur

Chapeaurouge 1984 = Donat de Chapeaurouge: Einführung in die Geschichte der christlichen Symbole. Darmstadt 1984.

Eco 1972 = Umberto Eco: Einführung in die Semiotik. Autorisierte deutsche Ausgabe von Jürgen Trabant. München 1972 (UTB 109).

Eco 1977 = Umberto Eco: Zeichen. Einführung in einen Begriff und seine Geschichte. Frankfurt 1977.

Grenzmann 1980 = Ludger Grenzmann: Traumbuch Artemidori. Baden-Baden 1980 (Saecvla Spiritalia 2).

Hausmann 1985 = Franz Josef Hausmann: Lexikographie. In: Christoph Schwarze/Dieter Wunderlich (Hrsg.): Handbuch der Lexikologie. Königstein 1985, 367—411.

Heckscher 1967 = William S. Heckscher/Karl August Wirth: Emblem, Emblembuch. In: Reallexikon zur deutschen Kunstgeschichte V. Stuttgart 1967, 85—228.

Held 1937 = Julius Held: Allegorie. In: Reallexikon zur deutschen Kunstgeschichte I. Stuttgart 1937, 346—65.

Jones 1978 = Ernest Jones: Die Theorie der Symbolik und andere Aufsätze. Mit einem Vorwort von Peter Krumme. Frankfurt. Berlin. Wien 1978.

Krampen 1983 = Martin Krampen: Zur Ontogenese von visuellen Symbolen und verbalen Zeichen. In: Martin Krampen (Hrsg.): Visuelle Kommunikation und/oder verbale Kommunikation? Hildesheim. Zürich. New York 1983 (Semiot. Stud. z. Kommunik. 1), 199—224.

Morris 1946 = Charles Morris: Signs, Language, and Behaviour. Englewood Cliffs 1946.

Nöth 1985 = Winfried Nöth: Handbuch der Semiotik. Stuttgart 1985.

Peirce 1932 = Collected Papers of Charles Sanders Peirce. Vol. 2. Ed. by Charles Hartshorne and Paul Weiss. 3. Aufl. Cambridge, Mass. 3. Aufl. 1965 [1. Aufl. 1932].

Resnikow 1968 = Lasar Ossipowitsch Resnikow: Erkenntnistheoretische Fragen der Semiotik. Berlin 1968.

Volkmann 1923 = Ludwig Volkmann: Bilderschriften der Renaissance. Hieroglyphik und Emblematik in ihren Beziehungen und Fortwirkungen. Leipzig 1923.

Wiegand 1983 = Herbert Ernst Wiegand: Was ist eigentlich ein Lemma? Ein Beitrag zur Theorie der lexikographischen Sprachbeschreibung. In: Studien zur neuhochdeutschen Lexikographie III. Hrsg. v. Herbert Ernst Wiegand. Hildesheim. Zürich. New York 1983 (Germanistische Linguistik 1—4/82), 401—474.

Wiegand 1985 = Herbert Ernst Wiegand: Eine neue Auffassung der sog. lexikographischen Definition. In: Symposium on Lexicography II. Ed. by Karl Hyldgaard-Jensen and Arne Zettersten. Tübingen 1985 (Lexicographica. Series Maior 5), 15—100.

Joachim Knape, Tübingen
(Bundesrepublik Deutschland)

334. Probable Future Developments in Lexicography

1. Introduction
2. Linguistic Research
3. Research in the Application of the Computer
4. Adjacent Areas
5. Conclusion
6. Selected Bibliography

1. Introduction

At the end of a book that gives thousands of pages to the consideration of lexicography's past and present, a few pages may be allotted to its future; and by the same token, after thousands of pages of most meticulously documented accuracy, a few lines may be spent on a fling of imagination if necessarily a nebulous one. In the last two decades, lexicography as an activity that results in publishing dictionaries has flourished, and the study of its theory and methodology even more so; indeed, the dictum is that this is the 'Golden Age of Lexicography'. This is both true and good; however, similar classifications of various epochs (in the history of literature, culture, etc.) as the Golden Age usually entail an epoch of stagnation or even decay that follows the culminating point. What do we, then, suppose the future development of lexicography to be? Recession, stagnation, or further growth?

2. Linguistic Research

As any other discipline or subdiscipline, lexicography also is interconnected with other fields, irrespective of whether they are conceived of as adjacent, or overlapping, or hierarchically superposed: in particular, lexicography is connected with linguistics and with computer science. As far as linguistics is concerned, the research undertaken in the last decade was most useful. Without going into detail, one can say that problems of the lexicon have attracted more attention than in the preceding decades. While it is true that some schools of linguistic thought never failed to be interested in semantics and lexis (traditional historical and comparative linguistics, anthropological or culturally-oriented linguistics, philologically-oriented linguistics, as well as functional structuralism manifested in studies of valences, lexical fields or lexical relations, among others), there is no denying that descriptivist structuralism, particularly in its American variety, and the transformational-generative theories were much more interested in phonology and syntax than in anything else. The last decade or so has brought a most welcome change in this respect; most important for lexicography are such areas of research as the intertwining of syntactic, semantic, and lexical classes and rules in a sentence and in a text; psychologically-oriented cognitive studies; and derivational or componential studies of semantics and the lexicon, such as the research connected with the explanatory-and-combinatory model. Since all of this research moves on paths which, if not completely untrodden, then are through areas previously neglected, and since the results of this research may be of long-lasting value both in theory and in practice, one can suppose that developments which already feed valuable data to lexicography will continue to do so in the future.

A better understanding of lexical meaning and of its representation also is an area of necessary research. The prototype theory brought back and stressed the assumption that denotata (classes of 'things') have fuzzy boundaries; that some members of a class are more (proto)typical for it. This conception certainly is right in as far as general language is concerned. On the other hand, there is a trend towards the development of defined terms in each technical or administrative register; the terms themselves enter, in their turn, the general language, although with a less precise meaning. Much research will be necessary to determine the relation of the prototypes to the terminologization.

What linguistic research will supply to lexicography is self-evident, at least in general terms: an increasingly detailed description of the lexicon both in the paradigmatic and in the syntagmatic dimension. One can, for instance, expect that bilingual dictionaries, above all the 'active' ones (those used in the production of texts in the target language by speakers of the source language), and learner's dictionaries will be refined through linguistic research (which, of course, can be undertaken by the lexicographer himself, if he has time for it, and within a lexicographic project as well): the refinement of valences, of the syntactic-semantic classes, of all the other collocational restrictions, and, last not least, the study of limited, even idiosyncratic properties of lexical units in all respects (paradigmatic *valeurs,* connotations, collocations) can and will lead to better advice which the dictionary can give the user; the greater finesse of linguistic description will, however, make itself felt in any type of dictionary, perhaps with the exception of the simplest word lists, glossaries, etc.

3. Research in the Application of the Computer

If it is true that the usefulness of linguistics to lexicography will increase, then the same can be expected from computer science, to wit an increasingly rapid development and growth of its usefulness. (See a particularly useful survey in Walker 1989.) As far as the involvement of lexicography with what usually is somewhat simplistically called 'the computer' is concerned (see Art. 173), we can discern several levels, or areas, of it. The shallowest of them (because it consists of mere technicalities), is that of the gadgetry. The electronic dictionary, even its smallest, portable variety, already has an advantage over any printed dictionary of whatever size: it can give pronunciation viva voce, in real sound. Similarly, one can easily imagine that not only will the electronic dictionary give pictorial illustrations (see Art. 66), but that it will be able to surmount the main limitation of such pictorial representations since the *Orbis pictus* of Comenius, namely their static character: there is no theoretical and no grave technical reason why it should in the future be difficult to give electronic representations of actions and processes in order to illustrate, for instance, the verbs, or a noun such as, e.g. 'ambler'. As far as gadgetry is concerned, we can expect rapid and multifarious developments.

As opposed to what was called 'gadgetry', the editing of dictionaries (with all the preparatory steps) will need at least as much progress in the linguistic part of the enterprise as in the computational area. As of now, the main advantage of the computer to the lexicographer consists in its ability to organize data quickly, to keep them in order, and to reorganize them into subsets (and their unions, intersections etc.) by Boolean algebra. Also, computer programs can help in the conversion of bilingual dictionaries (that is, converting the pair of languages A—B into the new pair B—A), if the partial equivalents are well delimited and glossed; the technical terminology is particularly easy to treat in this way (Art. 293) because the stylistic level of the partial equivalents is identical. One can with confidence expect that in the near future, mechanical scanners will help much more than now with the collection of data, and refined lemmatization programs with their organization. As of now, the situation already is such that amassing huge quantities of data (contexts, occurrences, whatever) causes less difficulty than the classification and digestion of all these data. A mere increase in the amount of data collected and in the speed with which they are accumulated could cause severe problems. Programs for the recognition of classificatory properties and for classification (in the broadest sense of the word) are at least as necessary (if not more so) than data collecting programs. However, it is hard to imagine that the computer will soon (say, within a decade) be able to cope with metaphorical or metonymical extensions of meaning (already the mere vagueness, or generality of meaning, may prove a difficult obstacle), or that it will be able to make inferences from the semantic richness or redundancy of a context as to the hitherto unrecognized meaning of a lexical unit that is a part of it. The task of recognizing social or geographical dialects or a technical register from the formal properties of the context (such as some key-words, morphological markers, etc.) is perhaps somewhat easier, but one cannot expect such classifications to be performed by the computer soon. And the task of establishing hitherto unrecognized syntactic and semantic classes and patterns will also remain outside the domain of mechanical computing, apart from the amassing of colligational and collocational evidence contained in contexts. Given a very elaborate algorithm, the computer may at some point in time be able to organize the material, particularly the illustrative contexts, for the entry in a regular if flexible pattern; but the fine grain interpretative and classificatory preparation of the contexts will not be done mechanically anytime soon, if ever. Thus, with all the huge but mostly quantitative help of the computer, the creative part of the preparation of databases will largely remain the task of the (sub-)editors. In this area, the immediate progress, or improvement of the lexicographic enterprise crucially depends on the linguistic part of the undertaking. It is the finesse of the linguistic description mentioned above that is decisively important, the recognition of as many restricted, fine-grained, semantic and syntactic classes as are necessary to capture all minute syntactic and collocational differences, even if such classes have a small membership; or the recognition of minute differences in valences within the polysemy of a lexical unit: these are examples of necessary linguistic (in this case, descriptive) information. No need to go into details in this respect since everybody knows them; may it suffice to say that any aspect of linguistic description should be incorporated into the classification of the material present in the database by proper flags, tags, box codes, subject codes, pattern codes, labels, or whatever. However, it should be stressed that the help of the computer will be fully exploited only if purely lexicographic classifications also are marked for retrieval. For instance, everyone knows that one of the biggest helps the computer can offer consists in the easy possibility of checking huge quantities of data as to the consistency of their treatment. If, e.g., the lexicographer wishes to be able at a later stage of the project to check whether all the ostensive definitions, or generic definitions etc. are homogeneously treated, these classes of definitions must be indicated in the database and each definition's class properly (retrievably) marked as well; the same is true of, say, treatment of atypical collocations by explanatory glosses, or of exemplification of typical collocations with insertible members: if the lexicographer wishes to check on the homogeneity of the treatment of such groups, or classes of information, the respective classes and each of their members must be retrievably marked. The same holds, of course, in bilingual lexicography: if the lexicographer decides to differentiate, say, absolute equivalents and partial ones, and translational equivalents and explanatory ones (these four classes variously overlap), he must make their respective classes and each of their members retrievable if he wishes to have the homogeneity of their treatment extensively checked in the course of editorial work. In short, in this area the improvement, or progress, seems to be largely dependent on how energetically the linguist-cum-lexicographer will rise to the opportunities already offered by the computer (the extent and multifarious character of which certainly will keep increasing in the future). Much work has already been done in the area of conversion of existing dictionaries first into a machine-readable form and then into a database.

When all the knowledge accumulated in present dictionaries is converted into database form, the gain will be great because, e.g., the syntactic patterns given in English learner's dictionaries are rich and accurate. There is no doubt, however, that future databases will have to go far beyond that, because they will have to contain a richer vocabulary, and the accuracy of description (i.e., of the syntactic-semantic classes, style-levels, etc.) will have to be even more fine-grained. Furthermore, still more encyclopedicity (both technical and cultural) will be required, not only for the user's benefit, but also for various problems of disambiguation of meaning and of bilingual equivalence. All this will require much research. No need to say, either, that the creation of database management systems and the handcrafting of entries in the database will require an effort similar to that expected from the editor of a large dictionary. It will perhaps be useful to recall at this juncture an experience from the history of lexicography: A mere increase of not digested data does not strikingly improve the quality of a dictionary. When the original edition of the *Thesaurus linguae Graecae* by Henricus Stephanus, dating from 1572 (see Art. 178) was enlarged at the end of the 18th century by several English scholars who simply multiplied the number of contexts quoted without any further work, the second edition proved to be a failure. The real improvement came only in the third edition of 1830 when the mass of data was not only increased but digested: this edition has been used to this very day. It will not be different with databases. Without a useful organization (that is, classification in the first line), masses of contexts will remain 'indigesta moles'. (See also Cannon 1989 strongly advocating the principle that innovation is the requirement for each new edition of any dictionary.)

The usefulness of the computer in the area of publishing dictionaries is manifold. The material side of production, particularly setting and printing by computer is a technicality the details and possibly the principles of which certainly will keep improving. As far as the compilation of dictionaries is concerned, the trend of development undoubtedly is such that the foundation of the entire lexicographic undertaking is a comprehensive database out of which published dictionaries (whether in the form of printed books or in computer-readable form, which as of now are CD-ROM disks or smaller electronic dictionaries in their own apparatus) are created by the selection of one or more of the subsets of the lexical material, and in the case of bilingual dictionaries, by correlating the chosen material to corresponding (sub)set(s) from the database of the target language. This has again to do with the classification of each entry in the database according to anticipated future needs and intentions. Once a rich database with well classified material is available, the creation of special dictionaries by selecting subjects from the material is a technically trivial task; this is one of the reasons why highly specialized dictionaries have proliferated in recent years. (There is, perhaps no need particularly to stress the self-evident fact that a database must constantly be kept up-to-date, because language also changes constantly. If constant collecting — if only of the gleaning type — and editing of new data is stopped, the database will start getting obsolete.) Somewhat more delicate is the determination of which special dictionaries are necessary: some of the types of dictionaries were created a long time ago (terminology, hard words, grammatical difficulties, etc.), and some only recently (learner's dictionary). The number of such (sub-)types can be confidently expected to grow. Empirical, market-oriented studies of the purposes for which various consumer groups use dictionaries will be necessary to make that further growth as effective as possible. It is not only necessary to determine the groups (by age, education, profession, purposes pursued), but also to find out what they expect to find: as opposed to what they objectively need: both points of view are necessary.

Much more difficult is the search for the most effective, useful dictionary style; that is, of the ways and manners in which information is presented in the dictionary: that optimal styles may vary with the type of dictionary goes without saying. This is an area of research that overflows into other disciplines; for instance, a better knowledge of the psychology of learning will be the decisive element in determining the style of the learner's dictionary (taking into consideration both foreign and mother-tongue learners).

Whatever the outcome of this research, it may be taken for granted that the users' preferences as to style will not be fully uniform. For instance, in the domain of the (foreign) learner's dictionary, some students seem to prefer to get the examples of syntactic patterns first and their abstract expression in a rule afterwards, whereas other students prefer the reverse order; and concerning the rules themselves, the students' preferences vary as to the desired degree of abstractness in their formulation. A printed book can only partly offer a style that takes into consideration all of these sometimes contradictory preferences; or, if it does consider all preferences, the length of the entries grows and becomes unwieldy.

Another circumstance brings a similar result: the requirements on a good dictionary grow as to the amount and type of information offered and as to the degree of its detail, and this entails the concomitant growth of the dictionary's bulk. If a learner's dictionary were to indicate all the valences of verbs and all the collocational possibilities of nouns, for instance, can we imagine how much that would increase the dictionary's bulk? On another occasion, (Āsatyakośyam, Zgusta 1989, 4) I mentioned that improvements in a dictionary usually are accompanied by or consist in an increase in the amount of information offered; which, in its turn, tends to make the dictionary too large. The usual way out of this impasse lies either in the selective reduction of entries (the principles of such reduction are not always easy to find), or in an increased succinctness of presentation which in its turn makes the text of the dictionary difficult to consult, and often negatively affects the dictionary's style. I have discussed this in relation to the learner's dictionary, but the same can be said about other types of dictionaries as well. This would lead either to the compilation of always bulkier (and more expensive) dictionaries, or to the compilation of small dictionaries with a highly limited scope or range of entries (so that ultimately, the user would have to buy more of them). That various users seem to have various preferences as to style, and that to pander to all the possible modes of presentation would have the same consequences has already been mentioned.

It would seem that this is a situation in which 'the computer' could be particularly useful. We can confidently suppose that the computer's capacity and the finesse and multifarious character of its programs will continue to increase rapidly without any particular increase in its physical bulk. In this case, one can suppose that electronic dictionaries will be constructed that will contain much information of diversified types and that the user will be able to activate selectively that block of information in which he is interested; for example, the definitions of all the senses of an entryword; or all the examples pertaining to one of the senses; or some usage advice; or first the syntactic pattern and then the examples, or vice versa; etc.

Naturally, one can continue this line of thought: an electronic dictionary of the modular type envisaged here could contain much more cultural information, which is so sorely needed in learner's dictionaries, because language is embedded in culture. (It goes withouth saying that this will raise a host of questions parallel to those connected with the perceived descriptivism, prescriptivism, and normativity in the presentation of language material: which 'level' of culture should be presented? Should subcultural behavior be illustrated and if yes, how should it be labeled? Endless possibilities of clashes of opinion in this area.) Even encyclopedic information could be included in such an electronic dictionary on a larger scale than is now possible. Optimally, one can easily assume that all these types of information should be retrievable in different degrees of detail and density, from the barest skeleton of the indispensable indications over more detailed blocks of information to a more or less exhaustive treatment. To reach this stage in the development of on-line electronic dictionaries is not so much a problem of computer science: huge capacities and very fine software are already normal. Quick, easy retrievability in general and simple access to the single blocks or types of information in particular is the main desideratum here. Naturally, a cordless connection of the terminal with its database would be most useful. To collect and digest all the linguistic (cultural, etc.) information and create the modes of its presentation in such an electronic dictionary would seem to be more difficult tasks than coping with the technicalities of the computer; it may be, however, that this is the linguist-cum-lexicographer's, not the computer scientist's judgement.

The on-line dictionary is by now no rarity. The only possible expectation is that it will become more and more the usual mode of consultation. Its competitor, the CD-ROM disk (Art. 35), has many advantages over the printed book (as of now, particularly the little space it takes). but it shares one of the book's disadvantages: it is the final product; to change it, to improve it, to insert new data into it entails making a new edition of it. A database can be modified as need be, so the on-line dictionary can more easily be kept constantly up-to-date.

As of this writing (Fall, 1990), electronic dictionaries can be perceived as falling into three broad categories. First, the small portable dictionaries; second, CD-ROM disks containing huge dictionaries; and last, terminological and similar data banks connected to terminals. There are vast lexicographic undertakings that result in huge printed dictionaries; typically, the *Thesaurus linguae latinae* (Art. 180), the *Chicago Assyrian Dictionary* (Art. 175), etc. However, some new editions of the *Oxford English Dictionary* and of its *Supplement* are available both as printed books and in the form of CD-ROM disks. Similarly, while work on the *Trésor de la langue française* (Art. 173 a, 186) undoubtedly will bring this printed dictionary to completion, the counterparts of this huge dictionary that deal with the older stages of French will not be printed. Similar other developments of this type can be expected in the near future. All this shows that the electronic form of publication is gaining ground in the area of very large dictionaries that are prepared for scholarly purposes. The immediate reason for this switch is, of course, the huge cost of printing spread over the few copies usually printed. There is, however, yet another advantage to the electronic form of publication: a scholarly dictionary that is as exhaustive as can be should register every important new context or attestation, every new interpretation, emendation, or athetesis; or else, in the case of a living language, every new development in the lexis: in short, it should accurately reflect the current scholarship in its entirety. Whereas a printed book can be changed only when a new edition (if there is any) is published with the scholarship scattered in various publications in the meantime between the editions, the electronic form allows easy insertion of new text and alterations of the old one. As of now, the intermediary stage of the CD-ROM disk still dominates, so that a new version must be bought or rented (the latter possibility being more advantageous in cases of frequent new 'editions' of the disk), but some terminological data banks already operate on the on-line principle; if technical developments such as those discussed above take place, the on-line mode of drawing on a database (that will, optimally, have the form of a fully-edited dictionary) will become quite normal. Such a database-dictionary could, then, have the modular architecture to accommodate all the various types of information, as discussed above.

This does not mean that I would expect the printed dictionary to disappear. It has certain advantages, traditional aesthetic values being not the last among them (Art. 35). However, when one extrapolates the trend that brought us to a situation in which a relatively cheap typewriter already contains a spelling dictionary and a thesaurus, in which every type of information in any type of enterprise, administration, or research is handled electronically, and in which, last not least, children have no difficulty whatsoever in pushing buttons on their various electronic gadgets for complicated sequences of commands, one cannot but expect 'electronic lexicography' to spread.

4. Adjacent Areas

Up to now we have discussed undertakings and projects in which the lexicographic component is central. However, lexicography may play an important if somewhat ancillary role in other types of endeavor that are connected with the study of language or with handling language data, and with the whole area of what is called 'language industry' in general.

One of these is the highly practical but ill-fated area of what is called 'machine translation' (a by now traditional misnomer). After a period of optimistic expectation, this endeavor ran into deep trouble in the late sixties and the early seventies, largely (as I believe and as I perceived it then) because of the lack at that time of suitable software programs, and because of the syntax-only orientation of linguistic research. Since much improvement has taken place in both of these areas and since we can expect more of it, it would seem that fully (or nearly fully) mechanical translation of texts in technical, scientific, and administrative registers written in non-innovative, non-figurative, matter-of-fact and rather monotonous language (all these being properties of which most texts in these registers can boast, anyhow) will be possible in the not distant future. In any such project, the lexicon will be one of the main components, with rich indications of valences and of bilingual lexical equivalences, (most of them partial and whenever possible discriminated by some collocation, colligation, or another formal feature of the context): hence I suppose that lexicography will be of prime importance in this endeavor. Since, however, emotions seem to be running quite high concerning this field and unfavorable judgements are sometimes made on the basis of uninformed assumptions, let us make the following two remarks. First, what is said above is an expression of limited optimism only; I do not expect that metaphors, metonymies and other changes and extensions of meaning, and creative, innovative language and style in general will admit of automatic translation soon, if ever. Even new derivations, that is, lexical items not listed as such in the program, should provide a strong obstacle to automatic translation, because even if they are regularly, predictably formed as to their morphology, their meaning is not necessarily predictable. (The only exception to this are normatively, or rather prescriptively safe-guarded terminological open sets, such as, e.g., chemical nomenclature, in which each derivational morpheme has its prescribed, predictable effect on the meaning of the new derivation: this seems to be the only area in which a 'morphological' [or rather 'derivational'] 'generator' could have an immediate practical usefulness.) Second, one occasionally hears the objection that automatic translation would have an undue influence on the style of the text as written by its original author. I think that this is true but that it is not a real objection. In the same way as my handwriting changes when I know that a typist, poor thing, will have to produce a copy, or an author's style varies when he is writing for his learned colleagues and when for the broad public, so can the text of some circular letters, bulletins, and memoranda produced, e.g., by the European Community bureaucracy be couched, at least in the future as I imagine it, with consideration of the fact that it will be automatically translated into several languages.

In a similar way, one can assume that the presently existing terminological banks will grow into multilingual institutions on the one hand, and on the other that they will be enriched by normative rules concerning future terminological coinages: there is a constant need for new terms in the rapidly developing sciences, so a terminological bank should contain also the productive suffixes and morphemes in general, together with the derivational rules, in order to be capable of offering normatively-admissible candidates for membership in a nomenclature.

In the preceding paragraphs, we have discussed various avenues of research connected with theoretical and practical application of the computer in lexicography. The bulk of research and its specificity is such that the area is sometimes called 'computational lexicography' (undoubtedly on the model of 'computational linguistics'). Besides the types of research already mentioned, there are also other types of problems investigated; they sometimes extend beyond lexicography in its narrower sense. Such are, for instance, lexicological studies of semantic relations (in the broadest sense of the word) within the lexicon. Another series of problems arising in computational coping with meaning has been partly mentioned above; for instance, disambiguation of meaning by context (i.e., by compatibilities of syntactic-semantic classes) et sim.

There persists, however, the not yet sufficiently researched problem of the generality, or vagueness of meaning and of the applicability of a lexical unit to new referents without any perceivable change in the lexical meaning. It would seem that ideally, a program, or dictionary-plus-sense resolution algorithm, should be capable of extending its power also over collocations that are not 'itemized' or listed as such in the dictionary. Or, considered from another point of view: to what extent is it advantageous to have such a program based on the assumption of many restricted senses of the headword? Or will it prove operationally more useful to have few, broad senses and allow for a vagueness of meaning? If we envisage a future possibility of automatic disambiguation of meaning (or, put in another way, recognition of the sense of the polysemous word that applies for a given context) by diagnostic means that derive from a 'knowledge-of-the-world database', is it useful to continue the linguistic tradition of separating 'the language' and the 'knowledge of the denotata', (i.e., encyclopedicitiy, 'the world'), or do the two fuse; and if so, do they fuse only ultimately or are they completely intertwined?

It goes without saying that one could proceed to questions and problems even more remote from the core of lexicography, such as the construction of information-handling devices that would be able directly to handle natural language, giving, e.g., answers to questions asked in natural language etc.

However, this Encyclopedia tells the reader in the first sentence of the Preface that its subject is lexicography of (natural) language: therefore, we shall stop our survey here. Two remarks should, however, be made. First: since the whole flow of information in any of its aspects and in any area of life, and all aspects of handling the information flow are connected with (natural) language, one can safely expect lexicography to have an important role in all future developments of this field. Second, as of now, there seems to exist a certain gap between computational lexicography and lexicography without any attribute. There is every reason to believe that the distance between the two will grow smaller as the computer will become everyone's everyday tool and as the creation of huge databases and their full exploitation will require expertise that is lexicographic, linguistic, and computational combined. Be this as it may, one can safely expect lexicography to remain important in this whole field, and increasingly so.

5. Conclusion

So far we have considered only the possible or probable future developments within the field of lexicography. If we turn our attention outside of lexicography, to the cultural situation in which it is and will be embedded, we come to the same conclusion: lexicography will be increasingly important. Monolingual and pedagogical lexicography, because of the educational (in the broad sense of the word) needs of a constantly growing number of people, caused not only by the population explosion, but also by the broadening availability of education and by the constantly greater demand of skilled as opposed to unskilled labor; bilingual lexicography, because of the constantly closer contacts between speakers of different languages and because of the fading importance of linguistic and political boundaries. One remark in this connection; occasionally one hears the opinion that the rapidly growing use of English in the Third World will diminish the lexicographic output there. This will hardly prove to be the case; only in the first stage, there will be more bilingual dictionaries with pairs such as English — Language X, English — Language Y (or vice versa, Language X, Y — English) than with pairs such as Language X — Language Y. The same can be said, if to a limited extent, about the Francophone areas.

To return to the point from which we started: no stagnation of lexicography is to be expected, but on the contrary further flourishing.

6. Selected Bibliography

Abate 1985 = Frank R. Abate: Dictionaries past and future: Issues and prospects. In: Dictionaries 7. 1985, 270—283.

ACL 1988 = Association for Computational Linguistics: Second conference on applied natural language processing. Proceedings of the conference. Morristown, New Jersey 1988.

ACL European Chapter 1987 = Third conference of the European Chapter of the Association for Computational Linguistics, Copenhagen. Proceedings of the conference. Morristown, New Jersey 1987.

Ahlswede/Evens 1988 = Thomas Ahlswede/Martha Evens: A lexicon for a medical expert system. In: Evens, ed. 1988, 97—111.

Ahlswede et al. 1986 = Thomas Ahlswede et al.: Building a lexical database by parsing *Webster's Seventh Collegiate Dictionary*. In: UW Centre 1986, 65—78.

Akkerman 1989 = Eric Akkerman: An independent analysis of the LDOCE grammar coding system. In: Boguraev/Briscoe, eds. 1989, 65—83.

Akkerman et al. 1985 = Erik Akkerman/Pieter Masereeuw/Willem Meijs: Designing a computerized lexicon for linguistic purposes. Amsterdam 1985.

Alshawi 1987 = Hiyan Alshawi: Processing dictionary definitions with phrasal pattern hierarchies. In: Computational linguistics 13. 1987, 195—202.

Alshawi 1989 = Hiyan Alshawi: Analysing the dictionary definitions. In: Boguraev/Briscoe, eds. 1989, 153—169.

Alshawi et al. 1989 = H. Alshawi/B. Boguraev/D. Carter: Placing the dictionary on-line. In: Boguraev/Briscoe, eds. 1989, 41—63.

Amsler 1984a = Robert A. Amsler: Lexical knowledge bases. In: COLING 1984, 458—459.

Amsler 1984b = Robert A. Amsler: Machine-readable dictionaries. In: Annual review of information science and technology 19. 1984, 161—209.

Bailey 1986 = Richard W. Bailey: Dictionaries of the next century. In: Lexicography: An emerging international profession. Ed. by Robert F. Ilson. Oxford 1986, 123—136.

Ballard 1988 = Bruce W. Ballard: A lexical, syntactic, and semantic framework for TELI: A user customized natural language processor. In: Evens, ed. 1988, 211—236.

Barnett et al. 1986 = Brigitte Barnett/H. Lehmann/M. Zoeppritz: A word database for natural language processing. In: COLING 1986, 435—440.

Bátori et al., eds. 1989 = István S. Bátori/Winfried Lenders/Wolfgang Putschke, eds.: Computational linguistics: An international handbook on computer oriented language research and applications. Berlin 1989.

Beale 1988 = Andrew David Beale: Lexicon and grammar in probabilistic tagging of written English. In: 26th Annual meeting of the Association for Computational Linguistics, Buffalo, New York. Proceedings of the Conference. Morristown, New Jersey 1988, 211—216.

Boas 1988 = Hans Ulrich Boas: The internal structure of lexical entries: Structural and/or 'definitional' semantics. In: Hüllen/Schulze, eds. 1988, 50—61.

Boguraev/Briscoe 1987 = Bran Boguraev/Ted Briscoe: Large lexicons for natural language processing: Utilising the grammar coding system of LDOCE. In: Computational linguistics 13. 1987, 203—218.

Boguraev/Briscoe 1989 = Bran Boguraev/Ted Briscoe: Utilising the LDOCE grammar codes. In: Boguraev/Briscoe, eds. 1989, 85—116.

Boguraev/Briscoe, eds. 1989 = Bran Boguraev/Ted Briscoe, eds.: Computational lexicography for natural language processing. London. New York 1989.

Boguraev et al. 1987 = Branimir Boguraev/David Carter/Ted Briscoe: A multi-purpose interface to an on-line dictionary. In: ACL European Chapter 1987, 63—69.

Boitet/Nedobejkine 1986 = Ch. Boitet/N. Nedobejkine: Toward integrated dictionaries for M(a)T: Motivations and linguistic organisation. In. COLING 1986, 423—428.

Bosch 1988 = Peter Bosch: On representing lexical meaning. In: Hüllen/Schulze, eds. 1988, 62—72.

Brugman/Lakoff 1988 = Claudia Brugman/George Lakoff: Cognitive topology and lexical networks. In: Small et al., eds. 1988, 477—508.

Bukowski 1986 = Jedrzej Bukowski: Indexage lexical au geta. In: COLING 1986, 429—431.

Byrd 1989 = Roy J. Byrd: Discovering relationships among word senses. In: UW Centre 1989, 67—79.

Byrd et al. 1987 = Roy J. Byrd et al.: Tools and methods for computational lexicology. In: Computational linguistics 13. 1987, 219—240.

Calzolari 1984 = Nicoletta Calzolari: Machine-readable dictionaries, lexical data bases and the lexical system. In: COLING 1984, 460.

Calzolari 1988 = Nicoletta Calzolari: The dictionary and the thesaurus can be combined. In: Evens, ed. 1988, 75—96.

Calzolari/Picchi 1986 = Nicoletta Calzolari/Eugenio Picchi: A project for a bilingual lexical database system. In: UW Centre 1986, 79—92.

Calzolari/Picchi 1988 = Nicoletta Calzolari/Eugenio Picchi: Acquisition of semantic information from an on-line dictionary. In: COLING 1988, 87—92.

Calzolari et al. 1987 = Nicoletta Calzolari/Eugenio Picchi/Antonio Zampolli: The use of computers in lexicography and lexicology. In: The dictionary and the language learner: Papers from the EURALEX Seminar at the University of Leeds. Ed. by Anthony P. Cowie. Tübingen 1987, 55—77.

Calzolari et al. 1990 = N. Calzolari/C. Peters/A. Roventi: Computational model of the dictionary entry. Preliminary report. ACQUILEX. Esprit Basis Research Action No. 3030. Pisa 1990.

Cannon 1989 = Garland Cannon: Review of *Loanwords Dictionary* by Laurence Urdang and Frank Abate (Detroit 1987). In: American Speech 64. 1989, 261—270.

Carroll/Grover 1989 = John Carroll/Claire Grover: The derivation of a large computational lexicon for English from LDOCE. In: Boguraev/Briscoe, eds. 1989, 117—133.

Carter 1989 = David Carter: LDOCE and speech recognition. In: Boguraev/Briscoe, eds. 1989, 135—152.

Chaffin/Herrmann 1988 = Roger Chaffin/Douglas Herrmann: The nature of semantic relations: A comparison of two approaches. In: Evens, ed. 1988, 289—334.

COLING 1984 = Proceedings of the 10th International Conference on Computational Linguistics, Stanford, California. Morristown, New Jersey 1984.

COLING 1986 = Proceedings of the 11th International Conference on Computational Linguistics, Bonn. Bonn 1986.

COLING 1988 = Proceedings of the 12th International Conference on Computational Linguistics, Budapest. Budapest 1988.

Collins/Smith, eds. 1988 = Allan Collins/Edward E. Smith, eds.: Readings in cognitive science: A perspective from psychology and artificial intelligence. San Mateo, California 1988.

Cruse 1988 = D. Alan Cruse: Word meaning and encyclopedic knowledge. In: Hüllen/Schulze, eds. 1988, 73—84.

Daelemans 1987 = Walter M. P. Daelemans: A tool for the automatic creation, extension and updating of lexical knowledge bases. In: ACL European Chapter 1987, 70—74.

Domenig 1987 = Marc Domenig: Entwurf eines dedizierten Datenbanksystems für Lexika: Problemanalyse und Software-Entwurf anhand eines Projektes für maschinelle Sprachübersetzung. Tübingen 1987 (Sprache und Informationen 17).

Domenig 1988 = Marc Domenig: Word Manager: A system for the definition, access and maintenance of lexical databases. In: COLING 1988, 154—159.

Domenig/Shann 1986 = Marc Domenig/Patrick Shann: Towards a dedicated database management system for dictionaries. In: COLING 1986, 146—150.

Elia/Mathieu 1986 = Annibale Elia/Yvette Mathieu: Computational comparative studies on Romance languages: A linguistic comparison of lexicon-grammars. In: COLING 1986, 91—96.

Engel/Madsen 1984 = Gert Engel/Bodil N. Madsen: From dictionary to database. In: LEXeter '83 proceedings. Ed. by Reinhard R. K. Hartmann. Tübingen 1984, 339—344.

Engelkamp 1988 = Johannes Engelkamp: Nouns and verbs in the mental lexicon. In: Hüllen/Schulze, eds. 1988, 303—313.

Evens, ed. 1988 = Martha Walton Evens, ed.: Relational models of the lexicon. Cambridge. New York 1988.

Fass 1988 = Dan Fass: An account of coherence, semantic relations, metonymy, and lexical ambiguity resolution. In: Small et al., eds. 1988, 151—177.

Fox 1988 = Edward A. Fox: Improved retrieval using a relational thesaurus for automatic expansion of extended Boolean logic queries. In: Evens, ed. 1988, 199—210.

Fox et al. 1988 = Edward A. Fox et al.: Building a large thesaurus for information retrieval. In: ACL 1988, 101—108.

Frawley 1988 = William Frawley: Relational models and metascience. In: Evens, ed. 1988, 335—372.

Gazdar/Mellish 1989a = Gerald Gazdar/Christopher Mellish: Natural language processing in LISP. Wokingham, England. New York 1989 [Particularly ch. 7: Features and the lexicon, and ch. 8: Semantics].

Gazdar/Mellish 1989b = Gerald Gazdar/Christopher Mellish: Natural language processing in POP-11. Wokingham, England. New York 1989 [Particularly ch. 7: Features and the lexicon, and ch. 8: Semantics].

Golan et al. 1988 = I. Golan/S. Lappin/M. Rimon: An active bilingual lexicon for machine translation. In: COLING 1988, 205—211.

Grimes 1988 = Joseph E. Grimes: Information dependencies in lexical subentries. In: Evens, ed. 1988, 167—181.

Gross 1986 = Maurice Gross: Lexicon-Grammar: The representation of compound words. In: COLING 1986, 1—6.

Hüllen/Schulze, eds. 1988 = Werner Hüllen/Rainer Schulze: Understanding the lexicon: Meaning, sense and world knowledge in lexical semantics. Tübingen 1988.

Hutchins 1986 = W. J. Hutchins: Machine translation: Past, present, future. Chichester, England 1986.

Isoda/Aiso 1986 = Michio Isoda/Hideo Aiso: Model for lexical knowledge base. In: COLING 1986, 451—453.

Jensen/Binot 1988 = Karen Jensen/Jean-Louis Binot: Dictionary text entries as a source of knowledge for syntactic and other disambiguations. In: ACL 1988, 152—159.

Jones 1986 = K. Sparck Jones: Synonymy and semantic classification. Edinburgh 1986.

Karius 1988 = Ilse Karius: Aspects of lexical categorization. In: Hüllen/Schulze, eds. 1988, 344—354.

Katz/Levin 1988 = Boris Katz/Beth Levin: Exploiting lexical regularities in designing natural language systems. In: COLING 1988, 316—323.

Kawamoto 1988 = Alan H. Kawamoto: Distributed representations of ambiguous words and their resolution in a connectionist network. In: Small et al., eds. 1988, 195—228.

Kay 1984a = Martin Kay: The dictionary of the future and the future of the dictionary. In: The possibilities and limits of the computer in producing and publishing dictionaries: Proceedings of the European Science Foundation Workshop. Ed. by Antonio Zampolli and Amedeo Cappelli. Pisa 1984, 161—174.

Kay 1984b = Martin Kay: The dictionary server. In: COLING 1984, 461.

Klavans 1988 = Judith Klavans: COMPLEX: A computational lexicon for natural language systems. In: COLING 1988, 815—823.

Kučera/Vollnhals 1986 = Antonín Kučera/Otto Vollnhals: Compact mit dem Computer: Maschinelle Umkehr eines zweisprachigen Fachwörterbuches. Lexicographica 2. 1986, 120—126.

Kučera 1986 = Henry Kučera: Uses of on-line lexicons. Information in Data. 1986, 7—10.

Lenders 1990 = Winfried Lenders: Gebrauchswörterbücher und maschinelle Wörterbücher. Prospektiven der maschinellen Lexikographie. In: Muttersprache 10. 1990, 211—222.

Nagao 1989 = Makoto Nagao: Machine translation: How far can it go? Trans. by Norman D. Cook. Oxford. New York. Tokyo 1989.

Neff et al. 1988 = Mary S. Neff/Roy J. Byrd/Omneya A. Rizk: Creating and querying hierarchical lexical data bases. In: ACL 1988, 84—92.

Neuhaus 1986 = H. Joachim Neuhaus: Lexical database design: The *Shakespeare Dictionary* model. In: COLING 1986, 441—444.

Newman 1988 = Paula S. Newman: Combinatorial disambiguation. In: ACL 1988, 243—252.

Nirenburg 1989 = Sergei Nirenburg: Lexicons for computer programs and lexicons for people. In: UW Centre 1989, 43—65.

Nirenburg/Raskin 1986 = Sergei Nirenburg/Victor Raskin: A metric for computational analysis of meaning: Toward an applied theory of linguistic semantics. In: COLING 1986, 338—340.

Nirenburg/Raskin 1987 = Sergei Nirenburg/Victor Raskin: The subworld concept lexicon and the lexicon management system. In: Computational linguistics 13. 1987, 276—289.

Papegaaij et al. 1986 = B. C. Papegaaij/V. Sadler/ A. P. M. Witkam: Experiments with an MT-directed lexical knowledge bank. In: COLING 1986, 432—434.

Parsaye et al. 1989 = Kamran Parsaye et al.: Intelligent databases: Object-oriented, deductive, hypermedia technologies. New York 1989.

Rieger/Schraeder, eds. 1990 = B. Rieger/B. Schraeder, eds.: Lexikon und Lexikographie. Hildesheim. Zürich. New York 1990 [= Linguistische Datenverarbeitung, Bd. 10/1].

Ritchie et al. 1987 = Graeme D. Ritchie et al.: A computational framework for lexical description. In: Computational linguistics 13. 1987, 290—307.

Rosch 1978 = Eleanor Rosch: Principles of categorization. In: Cognition and categorization. Ed. by E. Rosch and B.B. Lloyd. Hillsdale, New Jersey 1978, 27—48. Reprinted in: Collins/Smith, eds. 1988, 312—322.

Schaeder 1986 = Burkhard Schaeder: Die Rolle des Rechners in der Lexikographie. In: Studien zur neuhochdeutschen Lexikographie VI. Hrsg. v. Herbert Ernst Wiegand. Hildesheim 1986, 243—277.

Sebastiani et al. 1986 = Gabrizio Sebastiani/Giacomo Ferrari/Irina Prodanof: A conceptual dictionary for contextually based structure selection. In: UW Centre 1986, 127—146.

Seuren 1988 = Pieter A. M. Seuren: Lexical meaning and presupposition. In: Hüllen/Schulze, eds. 1988, 170—187.

Sinclair, ed. 1987 = John M. Sinclair, ed.: Looking up: An account of the COBUILD Project in lexical computing. London. Glasgow 1987.

Small et al., eds. 1988 = Steven L. Small/Garrison W. Cottrell/Michael K. Tannenhaus: Lexical ambiguity resolution: Perspectives from psycholinguistics, neuropsychology, and artificial intelligence. San Mateo, California 1988.

Staib 1988 = Bruno Staib: Extralinguistic knowledge and semantic analysis. In: Hüllen/Schulze, eds. 1988, 216—227.

Starosta 1988 = Stanley Starosta: The case for lexicase: An outline of lexicase grammatical theory. London. New York 1988.

Tanaka/Yoshida 1986 = Yasuhito Tanaka/Sho Yoshida: Acquisition of knowledge data by analyzing natural language. In: COLING 1986, 448—450.

Tompa 1989 = Frank Wm. Tompa: What is (tagged) text? In: UW Centre 1989, 81—93.

Tsurumaru et al. 1986 = H. Tsurumaru/T. Hitaka/ S. Yoshida: An attempt at automatic thesaurus construction from an ordinary Japanese language dictionary. In: COLING 1986, 445—447.

Turing 1950 = A. M. Turing: Computing machinery and intelligence. In: Mind 59. 1950, 443—460. Reprinted in: Collins/Smith, eds. 1988, 6—19.

UW Centre 1986 = Advances in lexicology: Proceedings of the second annual conference of the UW Centre for the *New Oxford English Dictionary*. Waterloo, Canada 1986.

UW Centre 1989 = Dictionaries in the Electronic Age: Proceedings of the fifth annual conference of the UW Centre for the *New Oxford English Dictionary,* Oxford, England. Waterloo, Canada 1989.

Vossen et al. 1989 = P. Vossen/W. Meijs/M. den Broeder: Meaning and structure in dictionary definitions. In: Boguraev/Briscoe, eds. 1989, 171—192.

Walker 1989 = Donald E. Walker: Developing lexical resources. In: UW Centre 1989, 1—22.

Weiner 1987 = Edmund S. C. Weiner: The *New Oxford English Dictionary:* Progress and prospects. In: Dictionaries of English: Prospects for the record of our language. Ed. by Richard W. Bailey. Ann Arbor, Michigan 1987, 30—48.

Weiner 1989 = Edmund S. C. Weiner: Editing the OED in the Electronic Age. In: UW Centre 1989, 23—31.

Werner 1988 = Oswald Werner: How to teach a network: Minimal design features for a cultural knowledge acquisition device or C-KAD. In: Evens, ed. 1988, 141—166.

White 1988 = John S. White: Determination of lexical-semantic relations for multi-lingual terminology structures. In: Evens, ed. 1988, 183—198.

Wilks et al. 1988 = Yorick Wilks et al.: Machine tractable dictionaries as tools and resources for natural language processing. In: COLING 1988, 750—755.

Wilks et al. 1989 = Yorick Wilks et al.: A tractable machine dictionary as a resource for computational semantics. In: Boguraev/Briscoe, eds. 1989, 193-228.

Wolski 1988 = Werner Wolski: Zu Problemen und Perspektiven des Prototypen- und Stereotypenansatzes in der lexikalischen Semantik. In: Hüllen/Schulze, eds. 1988, 415—425.

Woods 1975 = William A. Woods: What's in a link: Foundations for semantic networks. In: Representations and understanding: Studies in cognitive science. Ed. by D. G. Bobrow and A. Collins. New York 1975, 35—84. Reprinted in: Collins/Smith, eds. 1988, 102—125.

Yokoyama/Hanakata 1986 = Shoichi Yokoyama/Kenji Hanakata: Conceptual lexicon using an object-oriented language. In: COLING 1986, 226–228.

Zgusta 1989 = Ladislav Zgusta: Āsatyakośyam: Vaticinations on the Learner's Dictionary. In: Learner's Dictionaries. Ed. by M. Tickoo. Singapore 1989, 1—9.

Ladislav Zgusta, University of Illinois, Urbana, Illinois (USA)

XXXVIII. Bibliographischer Anhang und Register
Bibliographic Appendix and Indexes
Annexe bibliographique et index

335. Bibliography of Dictionary Bibliographies

This is a selected list of the most important dictionary bibliographies including the published catalogs of major library collections and publishers/booksellers. For a more comprehensive listing with annotations see M. Cop: Babel unravelled. An annotated world bibliography of dictionary bibliographies 1658—1988. Tübingen: Niemeyer, 1990.

The symbol * is used to designate bibliographies which are reproduced directly from typewritten copy. ∅ indicates items which I have not seen. Generally, these were sent to me by librarians in response to a worldwide questionnaire on dictionary bibliographies. The transcription of non-Latin scripts such as Hebrew, Chinese, Japanese and Arabic is reproduced here as it was found in my sources.

(1) *Aav, Yrjö:* Russian Dictionaries. Dictionaries and glossaries printed in Russia 1627—1919. Zug: Inter Documentation Co. AG, 1977. 196 p. (Bibliotheca Slavica; vol. 10).

(2) *Almeida, Horácio de:* Catálogo de dicionários portugueses e brasileiros [Catalog of Portuguese and Brasilian dictionaries]. [Rio de Janeiro]: Coleção Horácio de Almeida (printed by Companhia Brasileira des Artes Gráficas), 1983. 132 p.

(3) *Alston, Robin Carfrae:* A bibliography of the English language from the invention of printing to the year 1800. A systematic record of writings on English, and on other languages in English, based on the collections of the principal libraries of the world. Leeds and others: privately printed, 1966—. Vols. 13—17 do not appear to have been published yet. Each vol. is limited to 500 copies. OTHER EDS.: A bibliography of the English language... A corrected reprint of volumes I—X reproduced from the author's annotated copy with corrections and additions to 1973. Including cumulative indices. Ilkley, Yorkshire: Janus Press, 1974. The facsimile pages included in each separately published volume are excluded from this edition. See also (56) Kennedy.

(4) *Ayer, Edward Everett (Collection)/Butler, Ruth Lapham:* A bibliographical check list of North and Middle American Indian linguistics in the Edward E. Ayer Collection; 2 vols. Vol. 1: A—M; vol. 2: N—Z. Chicago: Newberry Library, 1941. Vol. 1: ±240 l.; vol. 2: ±200 l.*.

(5) *Azerbaijan, Akademija Nauk Azerbaidžanskoj SSR/Sa'diiev, Sh. M./Pashaieva, Sh. R./Abdullaiev, B. T. (eds.):* Lŭghätlarin bibliografiłasy. Bibliografija slovarej [Bibliography of dictionaries]. Baku: ELM, 1970. 55 p. ∅.

(6) *Bart Rossebastiano, Alda:* Antichi vocabolari plurilingui d'uso popolare: La tradizione del "Solenissimo Vochabuolista". [Early multilingual vocabularies in popular use. The tradition of the "Solenissimo Vochabuolista"]. Alessandria: Edizioni dell'Orso, 1984. 379 p. (Lessicografia e lessicologia). OTHER EDS.: pp. 9—97 of this work (covering the period from 1477—1522) first appeared under the title Antichi vocabolari plurilingui d'uso popolare. Parte I: La tradizione del "Solenissimo Vochabuolista", in: De Gulden Passer 55. 1977, 67—153.

(7) *Basuki, Sulistyo:* Perkamusan bahasa nusantara dalam kepustakaan: sebuah bibliografi perkamusan Indonesia antara tahun 1960—1976 [Dictionaries of Nusantara languages: a bibliography of Indonesian dictionaries from 1960 to 1976]. Jakarta: Lonceng Ignatius, 1977. 123 p. ∅.

(8) *Baudrier, Paul:* Bibliographie des dictionnaires allemand-français et français-allemand de 1789 à 1815. In: Cahiers de lexicologie 16/1. 17/2. 1970, 77—100; 100—127.

(9) *Beaulieux, Charles:* Liste des dictionnaires, lexiques et vocabulaires français antérieurs au "Thresor de Nicot (1606). In: Mélanges de philologie offerts à Ferdinand Brunot. Paris: Société Nouvelle de Librairie et d'Édition, 1904, 371—398. OTHER EDS.: reprint, Genève: Slatkine, 1972; for a supplement see (65) Levy.

(10) *Benhacine, Djamal:* Bibliografia de los inventarios lexicográficos del español de América [Bibliography of lexicographical inventories of the Spanish of America]. Bogotá: Instituto Caro y Cuervo, forthcoming.

(11) *Berlin-East, Deutsche Staatsbibliothek/ Schüler, Gisela/Schindler, Ulrike/Schlademann, Regina/Strahl, Irmgard:* Mehrsprachige Fachwörterbücher. Bestandsverzeichnis. Teil 1: Naturwissenschaften, Technik, Land- und Forstwissenschaft, Medizin. Berichtszeit 1960—1972. Nachtrag 1973—1980. Teil 2: Gesellschaftswissenschaften. Berichtszeit 1956—1974. Nachtrag 1975—1980. Berlin-East: Deutsche Staatsbi-

bliothek, 1983, viii, 261 p.; v, 110 p. (Bibliographische Mitteilungen; 28) OTHER EDS.: 1963, 3rd rev. and enl. ed., by Barbara Jenisch, 165 p.; 1957, 2nd ed., by Kurt Gassen, 56 p.; 1954, 1st ed., by Kurt Gassen, 32 p.

(12) *Bhaṭṭacarya, Yatīndramohana:* Bāmlā abhidhāna granther paricaya 1743—1867 [Bibliography of Bengali Dictionaries]. Calcutta: Calcutta University, 1970. xxxvi, 298 p.

(13) *Bowker, R. R. Company (Publisher):* World dictionaries in print 1983. A guide to general and subject dictionaries in world languages. Subject index, title index, author/editor/compiler index/ language index. New York. London: R. R. Bowker Company, 1983. 1st ed. xii, 579 p. OTHER EDS.: published at regular intervals.

(14) *Bowker, R. R. Company (Publisher)/Sader, Marion (ed.):* General reference books for adults. Authoritative evaluations of encyclopedias, atlases, and dictionaries. New York. London: R. R. Bowker Company, 1988 a. xvi, 614 p. (The Bowker Buying Guide Series).

(15) *Bowker, R. R. Company (Publisher)/Sader, Marion (ed.):* Reference books for young readers. Authoritative evaluations of encyclopedias, atlases, and dictionaries. New York. London: R. R. Bowker Company, 1988 b. xii, 615 p. (The Bowker Buying Guide Series).

(16) *Braunmüller, Kurt/Stropnicky, Sabine:* Deutsch-skandinavische Wörterbücher. In: Braunmüller: Deutsch-skandinavisch im Vergleich. Eine Bibliographie zur Linguistik und Lexikologie (1945—1985). Neumünster: Karl Wachholtz Verlag, 1987, 81—143 (Kieler Beiträge zur deutschen Sprachgeschichte; Bd. 9). OTHER EDS.: an earlier bibliography is Braunmüller, Kurt: Kontrastive Linguistik im Rahmen der Skandinavistik (mit einer Bibliographie deutsch-skandinavischer Arbeiten). In: Skandinavistik 7. 1977, 81—105.

(17) *Brewer, Annie M./Browne, Marie:* Dictionaries, encyclopedias, and other word-related books. A classed guide to dictionaries, encyclopedias, and similar works, based on Library of Congress Catalog Cards, and arranged according to the Library of Congress Classification System. Including compilations of acronyms, Americanisms, colloquialisms, etymologies, glossaries, idioms and expressions, orthography, provincialisms, slang, terms and phrases, and vocabularies in English and all other languages. 3 vols. Vol. 1: English books, xix, 519 p.; vol. 2: Multiple languages (with English as one language), xvi, 462 p.; vol. 3: Non-English books, xix, 695 p. Detroit, Michigan: Gale Research Co., 1987. 4th ed. OTHER EDS.: 1988, 4th edition in 2 vols., with a subject index; 1983, suppl. to the 3rd ed., xvi, 236 p.; 1982, 3rd ed.; 1979, 2nd ed.; 1975, 1st ed. published under the title Dictionaries, encyclopedias, and other word-related books, 1966—1974.

(18) *Calcutta, National Library/Mulay, Y. M.:* A bibliography of dictionaries and encyclopaedias in Indian languages. Calcutta: National Library, Government of India, Ministry of Education, 1964. x, 165 p.

(19) *Canada, Secretary of State/Translation Bureau:* Liste par sujet des dictionnaires, encyclopédies, glossaires, et vocabulaires répertoriés dans DOTT (DOcumentation pour la Traduction et la Terminologie; catalogue collectif de la documentation au Bureau des traductions). List by subject of dictionaries, encyclopedias, glossaries and vocabularies entered in DOTT (DOcumentation for Translation and Terminology; union catalogue of the documentation available in the Translation Bureau). Ottawa: Translation Bureau, 1980. 2nd ed. 971 p. OTHER EDS.: new cumulations originally appeared every 6 months; later on they began appearing on a quarterly basis under the title "ACQUI/DOTT"; a number of cumulations have appeared monthly.

(20) *Chalabī, Samīr, 'Abd al-Rahīm:* A bibliography of translation and dictionaries: with special reference to the Arab World with a preface by Peter Newmark. Bibliyūghrāfīyā al-tarjamah wa-al-ma 'ājim lil-waṭan al-'Arabī. Baghdad: Al-Hahidh Press, 1979. 1st ed. 130, 4 p. ∅.

(21) *Chien, David:* Lexicography in China: Bibliography of dictionaries and related literature. 2 vols. in one. Vol 2: Language dictionaries. Exeter: University of Exeter, 1986, 125—237 (Exeter Linguistic Studies; vol. 12).

(22) *Chinese-English Translation Assistance Group/ Creamer, Thomas/Hixson, Sandra (comps.)/ Mathias, James (managing ed.):* Chinese dictionaries. An extensive bibliography of dictionaries in Chinese and other languages. Compiled and edited by the Chinese-English Translation Assistance (CETA) Group. Westport, Conn. London, England: Greenwood Press, 1982. 1st ed. xvi, 446 p. OTHER EDS.: an earlier list was published by Hixson and Mathias in 1975.

(23) *Claes, Frans M.:* Lijst van Nederlandse woordenlijsten en woordenboeken gedrukt tot 1600 [List of Netherlandic wordlists and dictionaries printed up to 1600]. Niewkoop: B. de Graaf, 1974. 104 p. (Bibliotheca Bibliographica Neerlandica; vol. iv). OTHER EDS.: first appeared in: De Gulden Passer 49. 1971, 130—229; supplement in: De Gulden Passer 54. 1976, 49—63.

(24) *Claes, Frans M.:* A bibliography of Netherlandic dictionaries. Dutch-Flemish. Amsterdam: John Benjamins B. V., 1980, xvi, 314 p. (World Bibliography of Dictionaries; vol. v).

(25) *Claes, Frans M./Kramer, P./Veen, B. van der:* A bibliography of Frisian dictionaries. In: Us wurk 33/1. Grins/Groningen: Frysk Institut RU, 1984. 24 p. ∅.

(26) *Claes, Franz M.:* Bibliographisches Verzeichnis der deutschen Vokabulare und Wörterbücher, gedruckt bis 1600. Hildesheim. New York: Georg Olms Verlag, 1977. xxxii, 256 p.

(27) *Collison, Robert Lewis Wright:* Dictionaries of foreign languages. A bibliographical guide to the general and technical dictionaries of the chief foreign languages, with historical and explanatory notes and references. New York. London: Hafner, 1955. xviii, 209 p. OTHER EDS.: 1971, 2nd ed., much rev. and updated, under the title Dictionaries of English and foreign languages: A bibliographical guide to both general and specialized dictionaries, with historical and explanatory notes and references. 303 p.

(28) *Cordell, Warren N. and Suzanne B. (Collection)/Koda, Paul Stephen:* A descriptive catalogue of the Warren N. Cordell Collection of Dictionaries. 3 parts in 2 vols. Bloomington, Indiana. Ann Arbor, Michigan: doctoral dissertation; University Microfilms, 1974. lix, 514 p.

(29) *Cordell, Warren N. and Suzanne B. (Collection)/Koda, Paul Stephen:* A short-title catalogue of the Warren N. and Suzanne B. Cordell Collection of Dictionaries, 1475—1900. With a foreword by Warren N. Cordell. Terre Haute, Indiana: Cunningham Memorial Library, Indiana State University, 1975. 210, 2 p. Addenda. 500 copies.

(30) *Cordell, Warren N. and Suzanne B. (Collection)/O'Neill, Robert Keating:* English language dictionaries, 1604—1900: The catalog of the Warren N. and Suzanne B. Cordell Collection. New York. Westport, Connecticut. London: Greenwood Press, 1988. xxiv, 480 p. (Bibliographies and Indexes in Library and Infomation Science, no. 1).

(31) *Craig, Hardin Jr./Craig, Raemond Wilson (completed by):* A bibliography of encyclopedias and dictionaries dealing with military, naval and maritime affairs 1577—1971. Houston, Texas: Department of History, Rice University, 1971. 4th ed., rev. and corrected. 134, xiii p. *. OTHER EDS.: 1965, 3rd ed., enl. and corrected (timespan 1577—1965), 101, xi p.; 1962, 2nd ed. (timespan 1577—1961), 70 p.; 1959, 1st ed. (timespan 1626—1959), 45 p. 1st—3rd eds. were published in Houston by The Fondren Library, Rice University.

(32) *D'Elia, Alberto L.:* A bibliography of Italian dialect dictionaries. Chapel Hill, North Carolina: University of North Carolina, 1940. 98 p. (Studies in the Romance Languages and Literatures; no. 1).

(33) *Dhamotharan, Ayyadurai:* Tamil dictionaries: a bibliography. Wiesbaden: Franz Steiner, 1978. 185 p. (Beiträge zur Südasienforschung; Bd. 50).

(34) *Durey de Noinville, Jacques Bernard:* Table alphabétique des dictionnaires, en toutes sortes de langues, & sur toutes sortes de Sciences & d'Arts. Paris: Hug. Chaubert; Herissant, 1758. 87 p.

(35) *Fabbri, Maurizio:* A bibliography of Hispanic dictionaries. Catalan, Galician, Spanish, Spanish in Latin America and the Philippines. Appendix: A bibliography of Basque dictionaries. Imola: Galeati, 1979. xiv, 381 p. (Biblioteca di "Spicilegio Moderno"; Collana bibliografica; 1).

(36) *Fabri, Johannis Alberti:* De lexicis graecis exercitatio [Exercise on Greek lexicons]. In: Fabri: Decas Decadum sive plagiariorum & pseudonymorum centuria, accessit exercitatio de lexicis Graecis, eodem auctore. Lipsiae (Leipzig): Sumptibus hered. Frid. Lanckischii Halis Saxonum Literis SALFELDIANIS, 1689. 29 p.

(37) *Food and Agriculture Association of the United Nations, Terminology and Reference Section:* Dictionaries and vocabularies in the Terminology and Reference Library, 1966—1981. Dictionnaires et vocabulaires à la Bibliothèque de terminologie et références. Diccionarios y vocabularios de la Biblioteca de Terminología y Referencias. Al-maʻāǧim wa l-qawāmīs al-mauǧūda bi-maktabat al-muṣṭalaḥāt wa l-marāǧiʻ. Ci hui can kao tu shu shi zi dian he ci hui biao. Rome: FAO, 1983. 6th ed. viii, 224 p. (GIP:Bib/8). OTHER EDS.: the catalog is issued on a regular basis. Some other editions: 1986, 66 p. (supplement covering 1982—1985). 1978, 170 p. 1970, 101 p. 1968, 93 p. 1967, 51 p.

(38) *Franolić, Branko:* A bibliography of Croatian dictionaries. Paris: Nouvelles Editions Latines, 1985. 139 p.

(39) *Freiberg, Bergakademie/Schmidmaier, Dieter:* Fachwörterbuch-Bibliographie: Bergbau: ein- und mehrsprachige Wörterbücher und Lexika des Bergbaus von 1700 bis 1965. Freiberg/Sachsen: Bergakademie, 1966. 27 p. ∅ (Veröffentlichungen der Bücherei der Bergakademie Freiberg, 17).

(40) *Freiberg, Bergakademie/Fircks, Barbara von:* Fachwörterbuch-Bibliographie: Geowissenschaften. Ein- und mehrsprachige Wörterbücher und Lexika der Geowissenschaften von 1700—1968. Freiberg/Sachsen: Bergakademie, 1968. 40 p. (Veröffentlichungen der Bibliothek der Bergakademie Freiberg; 27).

(41) *Freiberg, Bergakademie/Braun, Gerlinde:* Fachwörterbuch-Bibliographie. Metallurgie. Ein- und mehrsprachige Wörterbücher und Lexika der Metallurgie von 1700—1969. Freiberg/Sachsen: Bergakademie, 1970. 24 p. (Veröffentlichungen der Bibliothek der Bergakademie Freiberg, Nr. 38).

(42) *Ġālī, Waǧdī Rizq:* ʻal-muʻǧamāt al-ʻarabīya. bibliyūǧrāfiya šāmila mašrūḥa. Arabic dictionaries, an annotated comprehensive bibliography. Cairo, 1971. 252 p.

(43) *Grzegorczyk, Piotr:* Index lexicorum poloniae. Bibliografia słowników polskich [Bibliography of Polish dictionaries]. Warszawa: Panstwowe Wydawnictwo Naukowe, 1967. 286 p.

(44) *Halász de Beky, I[van] L[eslie]:* Bibliography of Hungarian dictionaries, 1410—1963. Toronto: University of Toronto Press, 1966. xiv, 190 p.

(45) *Haugen, Eva Lund:* A bibliography of Scandinavian dictionaries. With an introduction by Einar Haugen. White Plains, N.Y.: Kraus International Publications, 1984. xxii, 387 p.

(46) *Hendrix, Melvin K.:* An international bibliography of African lexicons. Metuchen, New Jersey. London: Scarecrow Press, 1982. xxi, 348 p.

(47) *Heslop, Oliver (Collection)/Mitchell, William Smith:* Catalogue of the Heslop Collection of Dic-

tionaries in the Library of King's College, Newcastle upon Tyne. Newcastle upon Tyne: King's College Library, 1955. 24 p. (King's College Library Publications, No. 2).

(48) *Heumann, Johann:* X. Specimen bibliothecae glotticae [Example from the library of languages]. In: Heumann: Opuscula quibus varia iuris germanici itemque historica et philologica argumenta explicantur. Norimbergae (Nuremberg): Sumtibus Iohannis Georgii Lochneri, 1747, 480—672.

(49) *Horn, Alexander (International Bookseller):* Wörterbuchkatalog 1987. Allgemeine Wörterbücher und Fachwörterbücher. Wiesbaden: Horn, 1987 (September 1986). 12th ed. 232 p. OTHER EDS.: appears periodically; some earlier editions: catalog no. 10, 1981; catalog no. 9, 1974; catalog no. 8, 1966.

(50) *Indonesia, Pusat Pembinaan dan Pengembangan Bahasa Departemen Pendidikan dan Kebudayaan:* Bibliografi perkamusan Indonesia [Bibliography of Indonesian dictionaries]. Jakarta: Pusat Pembinaan dan Pengembangan Bahasa, 1976. 71 p.

(51) *International Food Information Service/Lück, Erich/Kalbskopf, Günther:* Bibliography of dictionaries and vocabularies on food, nutrition and cookery. Frankfurt am Main. Shinfield: IFIS, 1985. 139 p. (FSTA [Food Science and Technology Abstracts] Reference Series, No. 4).

(52) *International Information Centre for Terminology/Wüster, Eugen (initiated by)/Felber, Helmut/ Krommer-Benz, Magdalena/Manu, Adrian:* International bibliography of standardized vocabularies. Bibliographie internationale de vocabulaires normalisés. Internationale Bibliographie der Normwörterbücher. München. New York. London. Paris: K. G. Saur, 1979. 2nd enl. and completely rev. ed. xxiv, 540 p. (Infoterm series 2 (UDC 016:006.72)). OTHER EDS.: 1955—59, 1st edition, see (106). Supplements to this ed. were published between 1959 and 1973 in the periodical Babel; from 1958 onwards they appeared in Lebende Sprachen, and from 1959 till 1967 in DIN-Mitteilungen. Since 1987, supplements to the second edition have been appearing as a quarterly current awareness journal issued by Infoterm, called StandardTerm (STT) (ISSN 0258—837X).

(53) *Israel, Academy of the Hebrew Language/ Va'ad ha-lashon ha-'ivrit be-Erets — Yisrael:* Munaḥim 'ivriyim le-mikts 'otehem. Jerusalem: Academy of the Hebrew Language, [1969] 16 p.

(54) *Kahn, Louis E. (Collection)/Hamer, Jean:* A catalog of dictionaries. English language, American Indian and foreign languages. The Louis E. Kahn Collection in the Department of Rare Books and Special Collections. Cincinnati: Public Library of Cincinnati and Hamilton County, 1972. xi, 94 p. *.

(55) *Kaufman, Isaak Michajlovič:* Terminologičeskie slovari. Bibliografija [Terminological dictionaries. Bibliography]. Moskva: Izdatel'stvo Sovetskaja Rossija, 1961. 419 p.

(56) *Kennedy, Arthur Garfield:* A bibliography of writings on the English language from the beginning of printing to the end of 1922. Cambridge, Massachusetts. New Haven, Connecticut: Harvard University Press, 1927. OTHER EDS.: reprint, New York: Hafner, 1961. Additions and corrections can be found in Arvid Gabrielson's review: Prof. Kennedy's Bibliography of writings on the English language: A review, with a list of additions and corrections. In: Studia Neophilologica 2. 1929, 117—168. The bibliography by (3) Alston originally set out to be a supplement to Kennedy but became a work of its own because of the volume of material involved.

(57) *Kirkness, Alan:* Zur germanistischen Fremdwortlexikographie im 19./20. Jh.: Bibliographie der Fremd- und Verdeutschungswörterbücher 1800—1945. In: Wiegand, Herbert Ernst (ed.): Studien zur neuhochdeutschen Lexikographie IV. Hildesheim. Zürich. New York: Olms, 1984, 113—174 (Germanistische Linguistik 1—3/83).

(58) *Kroeger, Alice Bertha:* Guide to the study and use of reference books. See (94) Sheehy.

(59) *Kühn, Peter:* Deutsche Wörterbücher. Eine systematische Bibliographie. Tübingen: Niemeyer, 1978. 266 p. (Reihe Germanistische Linguistik; 15).

(60) *Kyoto, Gaikokugo Daigaku/Fuzoku Toshokan:* Bibliotheca lexicographica: a catalogue of pre-twentieth century dictionaries and encyclopaedias in the collection of the University Library. (Spine title: Kojisho jitenrui mokuroku) Kyoto: University Library, Kyoto University of Foreign Studies, 1981. xxv, 468 p. ⌀.

(61) *Kytomaa, Sinikka/Martin, Elmikaarina:* Sanakirjat: valikoi luettelo [Wordbooks: a selective list]. Helsinki: Kirjastopalvelu, 1982. 64 p. ⌀.

(62) *Labarre, Albert:* Bibliographie du Dictionarium d'Ambrogio Calepino (1502—1779). Baden-Baden: Éditions Valentin Koerner, 1975. 125 p. (Bibliotheca Bibliographica Aureliana; XXVI).

(63) *Leipzig, Deutsche Bücherei/Müller, Karl-Heinz/Müller, Rita U./Termette, Elena:* Bibliographie der Fachwörterbücher mit deutschen und russischen Äquivalenten. Vol. 1: Naturwissenschaften, Landwirtschaften, medizinische Wissenschaften. Vol. 2: Technische Wissenschaften: Technik insgesamt. Allgemeintechnische Disziplinen. Automatisierungstechnik. Energiewirtschaft. Elektrotechnik. Leipzig: Verlag für Buch- und Bibliothekswesen, 1966—1978. 254 p. 516 p. (Sonderbibliographien der Deutschen Bücherei, 42; 61).

(64) *Lengenfelder, Helga/van Hoof, Henri/ Ahlborn, Ilse:* International bibliography of specialized dictionaries. Fachwörterbücher und Lexika. Ein internationales Verzeichnis. München. New York. London. Paris; Saur; R. R. Bowker, 1979. 6th ed. xxi, 470 p. (Handbook of International Documentation and Information, vol. 4). OTHER EDS.: 1972, 5th rev. ed. under the title Fachwörterbücher und Lexika. Ein internationales

Verzeichnis. International bibliography of dictionaries, xxvi, 511 p.; 4th—1st eds., see (93) Saur.

(65) *Levy, Raphael:* Répertoire des lexiques du vieux français. New York. London: Modern Language Association; Oxford University Press, 1937. x, 64 p. See also (9) Beaulieux.

(66) *Lewanski, Richard Casimir:* A bibliography of Slavic dictionaries. 4 vols. Bologna: Editrice Compositori, Istituto Informatico Italiano, 1972—1973. 2nd rev. and enl. ed. (The Johns Hopkins University Bologna Center Library Publications, nos. 7, 5, 4, 7; World Bibliography of Dictionaries). OTHER EDS.: vol. I was first issued in 1959 under the title A bibliography of Polish dictionaries with 57 p.; vol. II, 1962, xviii, 366 p.; vol. III, 1963, xlii, 400 p. had Russian dictionaries and addenda to vols. I and II. The first ed. was issued by the New York Public Library.

(67) *Lozovan, E.:* La lexicologie roumaine. 2 parts. In: Revue de linguistique romane 22/janvier—juin, 1958, 120—140, 324—356 (dictionaries on p. 128—140).

(68) *Lyngby, Danmarks Tekniske Bibliotek/Andersen, Ejvind/Malmtorp, Inger:* Dansk fagterminologie 2. Bibliografi over ordboger, handboger m.m. til brug ved oversættelsesarbejde. Danish technical, scientific, and professional terms 2. A bibliography of dictionaries, reference works, etc. compiled for the purpose of translating from or into Danish. A continuation and partial revision of the publication Dansk fagterminologi, 1975. Lyngby: Danmarks Tekniske Bibliotek, 1981. 67 p. * (DTB Publikation Nr. 68). OTHER EDS.: 1975, 73 p. (DTB Pub. no. 35); 1979, 60 p. (DTB Pub. no. 56).

(69) *Lyons, Rev. Ponsonby Annesley:* Dictionary. In: Encyclopaedia Britannica. 9th ed., Vol VII. 1877, 179—193 (bibliography p. 182—193). OTHER EDS.: the 10th ed. article is signed by Benjamin E. Smith; the 11th ed. article of 1910 is unsigned: it incorporates the salient features of Lyons's and Smith's articles and also includes the bibliography on p. 190—200.

(70) *Marsden, William:* A catalogue of dictionaries, vocabularies, grammars, and alphabets. In two parts. Part I: Alphabetic catalogue of authors, 82 p. II: Chronological catalogue of works in each class of language, p. 85—154. London: privately printed, 1796. 154 p., 60 copies.

(71) *Moskva, Vsesojuzna Gosudarstvennaja Ordena Trudovogo Krasnogo Znameni/Biblioteka Inostrannoj Literatury/Kajgorodov, A. M.:* Sinologičeskie slovari v krupnejšich bibliotekach Sovetskogo Sojuza. Annotirovannyj ukazatel' [Sinological dictionaries in the major libraries of the Soviet Union. Annotated guide]. Moskva: VGBIL, 1976. 399 p.

(72) *Mudge, Isadore Gilbert:* Guide to reference books. See (94) Sheehy.

(73) *Navalani, K./Gidwani, N. N.:* Dictionaries in Indian languages; a bibliography. Jaipur: Saraswati Publications, 1972. 1st ed. iv, 370 p.

(74) *New York, Public Library:* List of grammars, dictionaries, etc. on the languages of Asia, Oceania, and Africa in the New York Public Library. New York: New York Public Library, 1909. 201 p. OTHER EDS.: this is a reprint from the Library's Bulletin (May—August 1909).

(75) *Noltenius, Johann Friedrich:* Bibliothecae Latinitatis restitutae. In: J. F. Noltenius: Lexici latinae linguae antibarbari quadripartiti tomus posterior, ed. Johann Andreas Noltenius. Leipzig: 1758, 1—512.

(76) *Parlement européen; Direction de la traduction et de la terminologie; Bureau de terminologie:* Catalogue systématique des dictionnaires se trouvant à la Bibliotheque et à la Direction de la traduction et de la terminologie et liste alphabétique des périodiques disponibles au Bureau de terminologie. 2 vols., suppl. Luxemburg: Parlement européen, 1978—1983. 3rd ed. xiv, 200 p.; v, p. 201—545; 87 p. * (PE 48.167). OTHER EDS.: 1974, 2nd ed.; regular updates are published: Répertoire des ouvrages récemment acquis par la Bibliothèque, published by the Library; and Informations terminologiques, published by the Bureau of Terminology.

(77) *Pentland, David H./Wolfart, H. Christoph:* Bibliography of Algonquian linguistics. Winnipeg: University of Manitoba Press, 1982. xix, 333 p. OTHER EDS.: 1974, by Pentland, Ellis, Simpson, and Wolfart. It is planned to update this bibliography on a regular basis. See also (80) Pilling.

(78) *Pergamon Press (Publisher):* Encyclopedias and dictionaries of the world. New York: Pergamon Press, 1983. 154 p. ∅.

(79) *Petrounias, Evangelos:* Ta lexika tis neas Ellinikis, oi Etymologies tous kai oi etymologies tou lexikou tou Idrymatos Triantafyllidi [Dictionaries of modern Greek, their etymologies and the etymologies of the dictionary of the Triantafyllides Institute]. In: Studies in Greek linguistics. Proceedings of the third annual meeting of the Department of Linguistics, Faculty of Philosophy, Aristotelian University of Thessaloniki, 26—28 April 1982. Thessaloniki: Aristotelian University, 1985, 324—355: part 3 of the article.

(80) *Pilling, James Constantine/Smithsonian Institution. Bureau of Ethnology:* Bibliographies of Indian languages, nine parts. Washington, D.C.: Government Printing Office, 1887—1894. 100 copies of each vol. of the original edition were issued. (U.S. Bureau of American Ethnology. Bulletin, no. 1—5—6, 9, 13—16, 19). OTHER EDS.: reprint, New York: AMS Press, 1973 in 3 vols. Vol. 1: parts I—IV; vol. II: part. V; vol. III: parts VI—IX. These publications are based on Pilling's Proof-sheets of a bibliography of the languages of the North American Indians printed by the Government Printing Office, Washington in 1885 in 110 copies (xl, 1135 p. + 1091 p. of plates) and distributed only to collaborators of the Bureau of Ethnology. (77) Pentland/Wolfart continues Pilling's bibliography for Algonquian languages (part V), covering from 1891—1981.

(81) *Platzmann, [Karl] Julius:* Verzeichnis einer Auswahl amerikanischer Grammatiken, Wörterbücher, Katechismen usw. Leipzig: K. F. Köhler's Antiquarium (printed by F. A. Brockhaus), 1876. 38 p.

(82) *Praha, Státní Knihovna ČSR:* Informativní literatura: slovníky [Reference works: dictionaries]. Praha: Státní Knihovna v Praze, 1966—.∅ (Novinky literatury: Prehledy informativní literatury). OTHER EDS.: this list is issued annually.

(83) *Praha, Státní Knihovna ČSR; Sektor Bibliografie a informace/Kubásková, E.:* Soupis encyklopedií a slovníků z fondů Universitní Knihovny. Díl 1: Soupis cizojazyčných encyjklopedií a slovníků 1945—1972 [List of encyclopedias and dictionaries in the University Library. Part 1: List of foreign language encyclopedias and dictionaries 1945—1972]. Praha: Státní Knihovná ČSR v Praze, 1973. 238 p. OTHER EDS.: for parts 2 and 3, see (84) and (85).

(84) *Praha, Státní Knihovna ČSR; Sektor Bibliografie a informace/Kubásková, E.:* Soupis encyklopedií a slovníků z fondů Státni Knihovny ČSR. Díl 2 [List of encyclopedias and dictionaries in the State Library of the Czechoslovak Socialist Republic. Part 2]. Praha: Státní knihovna ČSR, sektor bibliografie a informace, 1979. OTHER EDS.: for part 1 and 3, see (83) and (85).

(85) *Praha, Státní Knihovna ČSR; Sektor bibliografie a informace/Kubásková, E.:* Soupis encyklopedie a slovníků z fondů Universitní knihovny. Díl 3: Soupis českých a slovenských encyklopedií a slovníků vydané v letech 1977—1981 [List of encyclopedias and dictionaries in the University Library. Part 3: List of Czech and Slovak encyclopedias and dictionaries published 1977—1981]. Praha: Státní knihovna ČSR v Praze, 1984. 104 p. OTHER EDS.: for parts 1 and 2, see (83) and (84).

(86) *Prati, Angelico:* I vocabolari delle parlate italiane [Vocabularies of Italian dialects]. Bologna: Arnaldo Forni [1931]. Ristampa anastatica dell'edizione di Roma, 1931. 69 p. OTHER EDS.: Roma: [Caponera & figlio] 1931. 68 p.; reprint, Bologna 1965.

(87) *Princi Braccini, Giovanna/Vecchio Kevorkian, Emanuelita:* Glossario dei glossari a testi italiani anteriori al quattrocento. Bibliografia [Glossary of glossaries to pre—15th century Italian texts. Bibliography]. Firenze: Presso L'Accademia della Crusca, 1986. xi, 200 p.

(88) *Québec, Office de la langue française/Banque de terminologie du Québec/Bedard, Constant/Algardy, Françoise/Goulet, Pierre/Willems, Martine:* Inventaire des travaux en cours et des projets de terminologie [List of work in progress and projects in terminology]. Montréal: Office de la langue française, 1987. 115 p.∅. OTHER EDS.: 1974, 1st ed.; 1975, 2nd ed., 92 p.; 1983, 3rd ed.; autumn 1988, another ed.; 1989 another planned ed.; May, 1989 an Inventaire des travaux de terminologie parus depuis 1986 was scheduled to appear. This publication began in 1974 and was published by the Régie de la langue française between 1974 and 1977.

(89) *Québec, Office de la langue française/Banque de terminologie du Québec:* The Olf has issued a large series of bibliographies of terminological dictionaries in various fields. For individual titles see Cop: Babel unravelled. Tübingen, 1990.

(90) *Quemada, Bernard:* Les dictionnaires du français moderne 2. Essai de bibliographie générale des dictionnaires, vocabulaires et glossaires français I: Auteurs et anonymes. Liste provisoire. Besançon: Centre d'Etude du Vocabulaire Français CEVF (unpublished), 1967. 568 l. *.

(91) *Quemada, Bernard/Menemencioglu, K.:* Répertoire des dictionnaires scientifiques et techniques monolingues et multilingues 1950—1975. Paris: Conseil international de la langue française; Haut Comité de la langue française, 1978. ix, 590 p. (Trésor des langues et parlers français. Centre National de la Recherche Scientifique ILF).

(92) *Sági, István:* A magyar szótarak es nyelvtanok könyveszete [Bibliography of Hungarian dictionaries and language books]. In: Magyar könyvszemle 28—29. 1921—1922, 96—116; 72—156 (dictionaries are listed up to p. 91). OTHER EDS.: also published separately: Budapest: Kíadja a Magyar Nyelvtudományi Társaság Kiadványai 18, sz.; 105 p.

(93) *Saur, Karl Otto/Gringsmuth, Grete:* Technik und Wirtschaft in fremden Sprachen. Internationale Bibliographie der Fachwörterbücher. Fachwörterbücher und Lexika. Ein internationales Verzeichnis. Techniques, science and economics in foreign languages. International bibliography of dictionaries. München: Verlag Dokumentation, 1960—62 (Handbuch der technischen Dokumentation und Bibliographie, 4. Bd.). OTHER EDS.: 1963, 2nd enlarged ed., lxxxiv, 338 p.; 1966, 3rd ed., cxlvi, 304 p.; 1969, 4th ed. under the title Technik, Wissenschaft und Wirtschaft in fremden Sprachen. Techniques, science and economics in foreign languages, ed. by Helga Lengenfelder; 5th—6th eds., see (64) Lengenfelder.

(94) *Sheehy, Eugene Paul/Keckeissen, Rita G./McIlvaine, Eileen:* Guide to reference books, section AD: General reference works. language dictionaries. English language. Foreign languages, p. 109—160 (Section AD was prepared by R. Keckeissen). Chicago: American Library Association, 1976. 9th ed., rev., expanded and updated. OTHER EDS.: 1986, 10th ed. with added title science, technology, and medicine compiled by Richard J. Dionne et al., xiv, 1560 p.; 1980, 1st supplement to 9th ed.: 1974—1978, ix, 305 p.; 1982, 2nd suppl. to 9th ed.: 1978—1980, ix, 243 p.; 1967, 8th ed., and 1951, 7th ed., both by Constance Winchell. 1936, 6th ed., 1929, 5th ed., 1923, 4th ed., and 1917, 3rd ed., by Isadore Gilbert Mugde. 1908, 2nd ed. and 1902, 1st ed., by Bertha Kroeger.

(95) *Shuppan Nenkan Henshûbu (Publisher):* Jiten jiten sôgô mokuroku [General catalog of diction-

aries and encyclopedias]. Tokyo: Shuppan Nyusu Sha, 1985. 470 p. ∅. OTHER EDS.: this list is published on a regular basis.

(96) *Skeel, Emily Ellsworth/Carpenter, Edwin H., Jr. (ed.):* Dictionaries. In: A bibliography of the writings of Noah Webster. New York: New York Public Library, 1958. 225—264. 500 copies.

(97) *Sofija, Narodna Biblioteka "Kiril i Metodij"/ Davidova, Teodora (comp.)/Vlachov, Sergej/Velinova, Liljana (eds.):* Rečnici, izdadeni v Bălgarija, i čuždi izdanija s bălgarski tekst 1944—1980. Bibliografski ukazatel [Dictionaries published in Bulgaria and foreign publications with Bulgarian text, 1944—1980. Bibliographic guide]. Sofija: Narodna Biblioteka "Kiril i Metodij", 1981. 79 p. OTHER EDS.: 1988, supplement, under the title Priturka kăm bibliografskija ukazatel na rečnici [1981] za godinite 1981—1986. In: Căjuz na prevodačite v Bălgarija; Vlachov, Sergej (ed.): Leksikografski problemi na prevoda. Materiali ot tvorčeskata crešča na prevodači i leksikografi [z Juni 1986 godina]. Sofija, 1988, 186—196. 200 copies.

(98) *Sōgō, Masaaki/Asakura, Haruhiko (eds.):* Jisho kaidai-jiten [Annotated dictionary of dictionaries]. Tokyo: Tôkyôdô Shuppan Co., Ltd., 1977. 538 p. ∅.

(99) *Soviet Union, Akademija Nauk SSSR; Institut Russkogo Jazyka/Veselitskij, Vladimir Vladimirovič/Debec, N. P. (eds.):* Slovari, izdannye v SSSR. Bibliografičeskij ukazatel' 1918—1962 [Dictionaries published in the USSR. Bibliographic guide 1918—1962]. Moskva: Izdatel'stvo Nauka, 1966. 232 p.

(100) *Spain, Instituto Nacional del Libro Español/ Ministerio de Cultura:* Diccionarios españoles [Spanish dictionaries]. Madrid: INLE, 1980. 207 p.

(101) *Streit, Robert O.M.I./Dindinger, P. Johannes O.M.I./Rommerskirchen, P. Johannes O.M.I./Kowalsky, P. Nikolaus O.M.I./Metzler, P. Josef O.M.I.:* Bibliotheca missionum. Münster i. W. Aachen. Freiburg. Rome. Vienna: Verlag der Aschendorffschen Buchhandlung; Aachener Missionsdruckerei; Herder, 1916—1974. 30 vols., many of which list a large number of dictionary titles for Australian, African, and North American Indian languages (Veröffentlichungen des Internationalen Instituts für missionswissenschaftliche Forschung).

(102) *Tatár, Béla:* Russkaja leksikografija. Odnojazyčnye filologičeskie slovari [Russian lexicography. Monolingual philological dictionaries]. Budapest: Tankönyvkiadó Vállalat, 1985. 355 p.

(103) *Tonelli, Giorgio:* A short-title list of subject dictionaries of the sixteenth, seventeenth and eighteenth centuries as aids to the history of ideas. London: Warburg Institute, University of London, 1971. 63 p. (Warburg Institute Surveys; IV).

(104) *Unión Latina; Instituto de Información y Documentación en Ciencia y Tecnologia/Santos, Elena/Pérez, Javier:* Catálogo de recursos terminológios en lengua española (España) 1987 [Catalogue of terminological resources for the Spanish language (Spain) 1987]. [Madrid]: C.S.I.C, 1987a. 1st ed. 168 p. OTHER EDS.: yearly updates are planned.

(105) *Unión Latina:* Catálogo de recursos terminológicos en língua portuguesa 1987 [Catalogue of terminological resources in the Portuguese language 1987]. [Madrid:] C.S.I.C., 1987b. xiii, 86 p.

(106) *United Nations Educational, Scientific and Cultural Organization/Wüster, Eugen:* Bibliography of monolingual scientific and technical glossaries. 2 vols. Vol 1: National standards (1955). Vol. 2: Miscellaneous sources; glossaries published privately (1959). Paris: UNESCO, 1955—1959. 219 p.; 146 p. (Documentation and terminology of science). OTHER EDS.: for supplements and 2nd ed., see (52); the multilingual counterpart to this bibliography, first pub. in 1951, was (107).

(107) *United Nations Educational, Scientific and Cultural Organization/Holmstrom, John Edwin:* Bibliography of interlingual scientific and technical dictionaries. Bibliographie de dictionnaires scientifiques et techniques multilingues. Bibliografía de diccionarios scientíficos y técnicos plurilingües. Paris: UNESCO, 1969. 5th ed. 250 p. (Documentation and terminology of science). OTHER EDS.: 1965, suppl. to 4th ed.; 1961, 4th ed., rev. and enl. xxxvi, 236 p.; 1953, 3rd ed. xlvii, 178 p.; 1952, 2nd ed.; 1951, 1st ed. 220 p. The first edition was "an expansion and improvement of that originally appended to a report entitled Interlingual scientific and technical dictionaries compiled for Unesco in 1949 by Dr. J. E. Holmstrom". The report contained 500 dictionaries. The monolingual counterpart to this volume was (106).

(108) *Valpola, Aarne:* Luettelo suomalais-ruotsalaisista ja ruotsalais-suomalaisista sanakirjoista ja sanastoista [A list of Finnish-Swedish and Swedish-Finnish dictionaries and wordlists] [Helsinki: privately printed, 1976]. 29 p. *. ∅.

(109) *Vicenza, Biblioteca Bertoliana:* Catalogo dei dizionari ed enciclopedie nella Biblioteca Bertoliana di Vicenza [Catalog of dictionaries and encyclopedias in the Biblioteca Bertoliana of Vicenza]. Vicenza: Rumor, 1908. 137 p. ∅.

(110) *Vietnam, Nha Văn-Khố và Thu'-Viện Quốc-Gia/Nguyễn Khắc Kham:* Thu'-tịch tuyển-trạch vễ danh-tù' chuyển-môn. A selected bibliography on scientific and technical terminology in Vietnamese. Saigon: Nguyễn Khắc Kham, 1967. 211. ∅.

(111) *Viñaza, Cipriano Muñoz y Manzano, Conde de la:* Del diccionario [on the dictionary]. In: Biblioteca histórica de la filología castellana; obra premiada por voto unánime en público certamen de la Real Academia Española, tomo tercero. [Historical bibliography of Castillian Philology, vol. 3]. Madrid: Imprenta y fundición de Manuel Tello, 1893, 721—1018 (cols. 1441—2030) and 1060—1080 (cols. 2118—2154). OTHER EDS.: reprint, Madrid: Ediciones Atlas, 1978.

(112) *Vomperskij, Valentin Pavlovič:* Slovari XVIII veka [Dictionaries of the 18th century]. Moskva: Nauka, 1986. 135 p.

(113) *Wajid, Mohammad:* Oriental dictionaries; a select bibliography. Karachi: Library Promotion bureau, 1967. xii, 54 p. (Library Promotion bureau publication, no. 2).

(114) *Walford, Albert John/Rider, K. R./Taylor, F. R.:* Guide to reference material. 2 vols. Vol. 1: Science and technology (1966); vol. 2: Philosophy and psychology, religion and social sciences, geography, biography and history (1968). London: The Library Association, 1966—68. 2nd ed. vii, 483 p.; vii, 543 p. OTHER EDS.: 1980, 4th ed. 3 vols., vol. 3: Generalia, language and literature, the arts; 1966, 2nd ed.; 1963, suppl.; 1959, 1st ed.

(115) *Walsh, James Patrick:* Home reference books in print. Atlases, English language dictionaries, and subscription books, compiled by S. Padraig Walsh. New York: R. R. Bowker, 1969, 3—98, English language dictionaries in print. OTHER EDS.: 1965. English language dictionaries in print was also published separately, New York: Reference Books Research Publications, 1965. 55 p.

(116) *Wartburg, Walther von/Keller, Hans-Erich/ Geuljans, Robert:* Bibliographie des dictionnaires patois galloromans (1550—1967). Genève: Droz, 1969. Nouvelle éd., entièrement revue et mise à jour. 376 p. (Publications romanes et françaises CIII). OTHER EDS.: 1934, 1st ed. under the title Bibliographie des dictionnaires patois; 1955, suppl. Genève: Droz and Lille: Giard (these two without the collaboration of Geuljans).

(117) *Washington, Library of Congress/Dunn, Robert:* Chinese-English and English-Chinese dictionaries in the Library of Congress: an annotated bibliography. Washington: Library of Congress, 1977. vii, 140 p.

(118) *Washington, Library of Congress, Reference Department, General Reference and Bibliography Division/Carpenter, Gladys R.:* Foreign language-English dictionaries. Vol. 1: Special subject dictionaries with emphasis on science and technology; vol. 2: General language dictionaries. Washington: Library of Congress, 1955. vi, 246 p.; vi, 239 p. OTHER EDS.: 1942, 1st ed. compiled by Grace Hadley Fuller under the direction of Florence Hellman, 1 l., 132 p.; 1944, a supplementary list of references, 1 l., 42 p.

(119) *Weinberg, Elyakim/Polani, Hanah:* Bibliografia mueret shel milonim ivriim [A bibliography (annotated) of: Hebrew-Hebrew, Hebrew-bilingual and multilingual dictionaries published since 1948 in Israel and abroad]. In: Bulletin of the Council on the Teaching of Hebrew 7, 1975. 116 p. ∅.

(120) Wen-shih-che kungchü shu chien chieh [Dictionary of dictionaries]. Nanking 1980. (Kungchü shu).

(121) *Winchell, Constance Mabel:* Guide to reference books. See (94) Sheehy.

(122) *Wydawnictwa Naukowo-Techniczne (Publisher)/Rymsza-Zalewska, Danuta/Siedlecka, I. (eds.):* Bibliographie der Wörterbücher erschienen in der Deutschen Demokratischen Republik, Rumänischen Volksrepublik, Tschechoslowakischen Sozialistischen Republik, Ungarischen Volksrepublik, Union der Sozialistischen Sowjetrepubliken, Volksrepublik Bulgarien, Volksrepublik China, Volksrepublik Polen, 1945—1961. Bibliography of dictionaries published in Bulgarian People's Republic, Chinese People's Republic, Czechoslovak Socialist Republic, German Democratic Republic, Hungarian People's Republic, Polish People's Republic, Rumanian People's Republic, Union of Soviet Socialist Republics, 1945—1961. Title also appears in Polish and in Russian. Warszawa: Wydawnictwa Naukowo-Techniczne, 1965—1981. Volume one in a series. xxxii, 248 p. OTHER EDS.: supplements were originally scheduled to appear every 5 years. In actual fact, subsequent volumes appeared as follows: Vol. 2 (1962—1964), 1968, xxxii, 166 p.
Vol. 3 (1965—1966), 1969, xxviii, 110 p.
Vol. 4 (1967—1968), 1970, xxviii, 100 p.
Vol. 5 (1969—1970), 1972, xxviii, 132 p.
Vol. 6 (1971—1972), 1974, xxviii, 117 p.
Vol. 7 (1973—1974), 1976, xxviii, 133 p.
Vol. 8 (1975—1976), 1978, xxviii, 141 p.
Vol. 9 (1977—1978), 1981, xxviii, 155 p.

(123) *Wynar, Bohdan S./Patterson, Anna Grace/ Kelminson, L.:* American Reference Books Annual (ARBA). Littleton, Colorado: Libraries Unlimited, 1970—. OTHER EDS.: appears yearly; vol. 16 appeared in 1985.

(124) *Wynar, Bohdan S./Cameron, Heather/ Dority, G. Kim:* ARBA guide to subject encyclopedias and dictionaries. Littleton, Colorado: Libraries Unlimited, 1986. xxi, 570 p.

(125) *Yamagiwa, Joseph K.:* Bibliography of Japanese encyclopedias and dictionaries. Ann Arbor, Michigan: The Panel on Far Eastern Language Institutes of the Committee on Institutional Cooperation, 1968. ix, 139 p. ∅.

(126) *Yang, Paul Fu-mien:* Chinese lexicography. In: Yang: Chinese lexicology and lexicography. A selected and classified bibliography. Part II, p. 205—299. Hong Kong: Chinese University Press, 1985. xlvi, 361 p.

(127) *Zalewski, Wojciech:* Russian-English dictionaries with aids for translators. A selected bibliography. New York: Russica, 1981. 2nd ed. 101 p. ("Russica" Bibliography Series; No. 1). OTHER EDS.: 1976, 1st ed., sponsored and published by Stanford University Libraries, iii, 51 p.

(128) *Zaunmüller, Wolfram:* Bibliographisches Handbuch der Sprachwörterbücher: Ein internationales Verzeichnis von 5600 Wörterbüchern der Jahre 1460—1958 für mehr als 500 Sprachen und Dialekte. An annotated bibliography of language dictionaries. Bibliographie critique des dictionnaires linguistiques. New York. London. Stuttgart: Hafner; Anton Hiersemann, 1958. xvi p., 496 cols.

OTHER EDS.: the subject dictionary counterpart to Zaunmüller is (129) Zischka.

(129) *Zischka, Gert A.:* Index lexicorum: Bibliographie der lexikalischen Nachschlagewerke [Index lexicorum: Bibliography of lexical reference works]. Wien. New York. London: Verlag Brüder Hollinek; Hafner, 1959. xliii, 290 p.
OTHER EDS.: the language dictionary counterpart to Zischka is (128) Zaunmüller.

(130) *Zolli, Paolo:* Bibliografia dei dizionari specializzati italiani del XIX secolo [Bibliography of specialized Italian dictionaries of the 19th century]. Firenze: Leo S. Olschki, 1973. 149 p. (Biblioteca di bibliografia italiana; 74).

Margaret Cop, Erlangen
(Federal Republic of Germany)

336. Sachregister/Subject Index/Index des matières

1. Aufbau der Registereinträge

Der alphanumerische Ausdruck

,Mikrostruktur 328, 371 f., 409 ff.'

ist ein Registereintrag.

Jeder Registereintrag besteht aus dem Registereingang (hier: ,Mikrostruktur') und aus der Registerinformation (hier: ,328, 371 f., 409 ff.').

1.1. Registereingänge

Die Registereingänge sind Ausdrücke, die entweder zur deutschen oder englischen oder französischen Sprache gehören. Von dieser Regelung gibt es zwei Ausnahmen:

(a) bei interlingual homographen Wortformen wurde eine Homographentrennung vorgenommen, die zu zweisprachigen Registereingängen der folgenden Art führt:

microstructure [engl.], microstructure [franz.]

(b) Wörterbuchkennzeichnungen können auch in anderen Sprachen auftreten, insbesondere in Latein.

Als Registereingänge treten auf:
— Termini; bei Mehrworttermini wurde meistens eine Mehrfacheintragung vorgenommen, so daß z. B. für den Terminus *analytische Definition* zwei Registereingänge vorliegen: ,analytische Definition' und ,Definition, analytische'.
— Sprachen- und Dialektnamen; diese sind unterstrichen, um ein schnelleres Auffinden zu ermöglichen.
— geordnete Paare von Sprachennamen (z. B. ,Deutsch-Englisch'). Registereingänge dieser Art bezeichnen ein zweisprachiges Wörterbuch oder mehrere (vgl. unten 5.).
— Ausdrücke, mit denen Textabschnitte zusammengefaßt werden (z. B. ,Artikelpositionen des Sprachstadienwörterbuches'); diese Ausdrücke gehören immer zur gleichen Sprache, zu der auch der Text gehört, dessen Inhalt sie zusammenfassen.
— Wörterbuchkennzeichnungen (z. B. ,Wörterbuch der deutschen Gegenwartssprache', vgl. unten 4. u. 5.).

Personennamen werden nicht als **selbständige** Registereingänge geführt. Es gibt jedoch Registereingänge, in denen Personennamen auftreten (z. B. ,Lexikographie Adelungs').

1.2. Registerinformation

Eine Registerinformation folgt auf den Registereingang. In Registereinträgen, welche keinen Verweis enthalten (vgl. hierzu unten 3.), ist die Registerinformation eine geordnete Menge von Ziffern (z. B.: 328) und/oder alphanumerischen Ausdrücken wie 371 f. und 409 ff. Die Ziffern verweisen auf die Seiten der drei Teilbände; „f." bedeutet soviel wie *und die folgende Seite,* „ff." soviel wie *und die folgenden Seiten.* Zu weiteren Arten von Registerinformationen vgl. unten 3.

2. Alphabetisierung

Die Alphabetisierung der Registereingänge wurde mit Hilfe eines Computerprogramms vorgenommen. Diakritische Zeichen zu den Buchstaben — wie z. B. die Umlautkennzeichen im Deutschen — wurden bei der Alphabetisierung nicht berücksichtigt. Die Alphabetisierung ist striktalphabetisch über dem gesamten Registereingang. Das Alphabet, nach welchem alphabetisiert wurde, hat als erstes Zeichen einen Blank (= Zwischenraum zwischen zwei Wortformen), als zweites Zeichen ein Komma und als drittes Zeichen „A/a" (usw. bis „Z/z"). Es ergibt sich daher z. B. folgende Anordnung von Registereingängen:

Wörterbuch
Wörterbuch als Autorität
Wörterbuch, allgemeines
Wörterbuchartikel

3. Registerinterne Verweise

Zur Registerinformation kann auch ein registerinterner Verweis oder mehrere zählen, z. B.:

access profile 333
    s. Zugriffsprofil

oder

active dictionary 2715, 2719, 2784 ff.
    s. aktives Wörterbuch,
    s. Hinproduktionswörterbuch,
    s. Hinübersetzungswörterbuch.

Verwiesen wird von Termini auf synonyme oder quasisynonyme Termini der gleichen Sprache sowie auf terminologische Äquivalente bzw. Quasiäquivalente aus den beiden anderen Sprachen. In wenigen Fällen wird auch auf über- oder untergeordnete Termini verwiesen.

Für die Bezeichnung von Wörterbuchtypen wurden reine Verweiseinträge aufgenommen. In diesem Fall enthält die Registerinformation keine Ziffer(n), z. B. ‚dictionnaire de citations, s. Zitatenwörterbuch'.

4. Verweise vom Sachregister in das Namenregister

In Registereinträgen, deren Registereingang eine Wörterbuchkennzeichnung ist, wird häufig explizit auf das Namenregister verwiesen, z. B.:

Wörterbuch der deutschen Gegenwartssprache 333, 382, ..., 2170
    s. NR: R. Klappenbach; H. Malige-Klappenbach; W. Steinitz.

„s. NR:" ist zu lesen wie *siehe im Namenregister unter*. Als Verweisziel im Namenregister werden die Namen von Herausgebern und/oder Bearbeitern angegeben sowie in einigen Fällen zusätzlich auch die Namen von Wörterbuchforschern, die über das entsprechende Wörterbuch geschrieben haben.

Manche Wörterbuchkennzeichnungen, die als Registereingänge auftreten, enthalten den Namen des Lexikographen, z. B.:

Wörterbuch der deutschen Umgangssprache von H. Küpper.

In solchen kann der Name als impliziter Verweis auf das Namenregister gelesen werden. Nur in begründeten Ausnahmefällen wurde in solchen Registereinträgen zusätzlich die Verweisbeziehungsangabe „s. NR." gesetzt.

5. Hinweise zur Benutzung des Sachregisters

Das Sachregister soll den Wert des Handbuches als Nachschlagewerk erhöhen. Es ist vor allen Dingen für Handbuchbenutzer gedacht, die
— schnell unter einer bestimmten Suchfrage punktuelle Informationen zu Sachen und/oder Termini benötigen
— zu einer Fragestellung verschiedene Informationen systematisch zusammenstellen möchten, die in verschiedenen Handbuchartikeln auftreten.

In allen Benutzungssituationen, welche zu den beiden charakterisierten Klassen gehören, empfiehlt sich zunächst der Zugriff auf die Informationen in den drei Teilbänden über das Sachregister.

Die Sprachen- und Dialektnamen im Sachregister ermöglichen dem Benutzer u. a. das Auffinden auch solcher Textstellen, in denen Sprachen behandelt werden, die nicht im Inhaltsverzeichnis in den Artikeltiteln auftreten und deren Zugehörigkeit zu einer Sprachfamilie oder Sprachenregion er nicht kennt. Wer sich z. B. über die Lexikographie des Gelbuigurischen informieren will und nicht weiß, daß es sich um eine der älteren in China gesprochenen Turksprachen handelt, kann auch nicht wissen, daß er im Artikel 232. „Die Lexikographie der Turksprachen II: Sonstige Turksprachen" suchen muß. Der Weg über den Registereintrag ‚Gelbuigurisch 2411' führt ihn direkt zur gesuchten Information. In den meisten Fällen findet er auf der Seite, zu der er geführt wird, auch wenigstens eine Literaturangabe in Form eines Kurztitels. Von diesem gelangt er dann direkt ins Literaturverzeichnis des Artikels.

Die Wörterbücher zu Sprachen und Dialekten findet man also über die Sprachennamen im Sachregister. Zweisprachige Wörterbücher findet man direkt über die Registereinträge, deren Registereingänge ein Sprachenpaar bezeichnen. Die wichtigsten Textstellen zu großen bedeutenden Wörterbüchern oder zu solchen, die besonders ausführlich behandelt werden, findet man entweder über Registereinträge, deren Registereingänge Wörterbuchkennzeichnungen sind, oder — wenn man die/den Herausgeber und/oder Bearbeiter kennt — über deren Namen im Namenregister.

---

1. Structure of Index Entries

The alphanumerical expression

'Mikrostruktur 328, 371 f., 409 ff.'

is an index entry.

Each index entry consists of the index head (here: 'Mikrostruktur') and the index information (here: '328, 371 f., 409 ff.').

1.1. Index Heads

The index heads are expressions in German, English, or French. There are two exceptions to this rule:

(a) interlingually homographic words have been separated as bilingual index heads of the following type:

microstructure [engl.], microstructure [franz.]

(b) names of dictionaries in other languages, particularly in Latin, also occur.

There are various kinds of index heads:
— technical terms; in the case of technical terms comprising more than one word usually more than one entry has been made; e.g. for the term 'analytische Definition' there are two index heads: 'analytische Definition' and 'Definition, analytische';
— names of languages and dialects; they are underlined in order to facilitate access;
— ordered pairs of language names (e.g. 'Deutsch-Englisch'). Index heads of this kind refer to one or more bilingual dictionaries (see 5. below);
— expressions which summarize sections of the text (e.g. 'Artikelpositionen des Sprachstadienwörterbuchs'); expressions of this kind always belong to the same language as the text which they summarize;
— names of dictionaries (e.g. 'Wörterbuch der deutschen Gegenwartssprache', see 4. und 5. below).

Personal names are not listed as s e p a r a t e index heads. There are, however, index heads that contain personal names (e.g. 'Lexikographie Adelungs').

1.2. Index Information

The index head is followed by the index information. In index entries not containing any reference (see 3. below), the index information is an ordered sequence of figures (e.g.: 328) and/or alphanumerical expressions such as 371 f. and 409 ff. The figures refer to the pages of the three volumes, with "f." meaning *and the following page,* and "ff." meaning *and the following pages*. For further kinds of index information see 3. below.

2. Alphabetical Arrangement

The alphabetical arrangement of the register heads was carried out by computer. Diacritical signs belonging to specific letters — as for example the two dots denoting the German *Umlaut* — have not been taken into consideration for the alphabetical arrangement. The alphabetical arrangement is strictly alphabetical for the whole of the index head. Spaces and commas influence the alphabetical arrangement in the way exemplified by the following sequence:

Wörterbuch
Wörterbuch als Autorität
Wörterbuch, allgemeines
Wörterbuchartikel.

3. References Within the Index

The index information may also consist of one or more references within the index, e.g.:

access profile 333
    s. Zugriffsprofil

or:

active dictionary 2715, 2719, 2784 ff.
    s. aktives Wörterbuch,
    s. Hinproduktionswörterbuch,
    s. Hinübersetzungswörterbuch.

The reader is referred from technical terms to synonymous or near synonymous terms of the same language as well as to terminological equivalents or near equivalents from the other two languages. In a few cases reference is also made to superordinate or subordinate terms.

For the indication of dictionary types cross-references have been used. In such a case the index information does not contain any figure(s), e.g.:

'dictionnaire de citations, s. Zitatenwörterbuch'.

4. References From Subject Index to Name Index

In index entries the index head of which is a dictionary title, an explicit reference to the name index frequently occurs; e.g.:

Wörterbuch der deutschen Gegenwartssprache 333, 382, ..., 2170
    s. NR: R. Klappenbach; H. Malige-Klappenbach; W. Steinitz.

"s. NR:" means *see in name index under*. This reference is used for names of editors and/or collaborators as well as in some cases for the names of scholars who have written about this particular dictionary.

Some dictionary names appearing as index heads also include the name of the lexicographer, e.g.:

Wörterbuch der deutschen Umgangssprache von H. Küpper.

In such cases the lexicographer's name may be read as an implicit reference to the name index. Only exceptionally does the index entry also include the abbreviation "s. NR.".

5. Remarks on how to Use the Subject Index

The purpose of the subject index is to increase the usefulness of the Encyclopedia as a reference manual. It has mainly been devised for readers who
— need quick access to specific information on a specific subject matter and/or technical terms;
— want to systematically collect specific information on the same subject from different articles.

In all such usage situations the best procedure is to start by looking for the information through the subject index.

For example, the language and dialect names in the subject index enable the user to find those sections of the text where languages are dealt with that are not mentioned in the titles of articles listed in the table of contents and of which the reader does not know the language family or region they belong to. For instance, a reader interested in the lexicography of Gumuz who does not know that it is a Nilo-Saharan language cannot know that information is to be sought in article 275. On the other hand, the index entry "Gumuz 2642" gives direct access to the relevant passage. In most cases, the passage to which the reader is referred will also contain some reference to secondary literature in the form of an abbreviated title. This reference in turn will lead him straight to the bibliography of the article.

It follows that dictionaries of languages and dialects can be found through the language names in the subject index. Bilingual dictionaries may be found directly through index entries, the index heads of which denote a language pair. The most important sections of the text dealing with particularly important dictionaries or with dictionaries which have been dealt with in great depth, may be found either through index entries, the index heads of which are dictionary names, or — if the user knows the editor(s) or the collaborator(s) — through the names of these persons in the index of names.

---

1. Structure des entrées d'index

La séquence alphanumérique

›Mikrostruktur 328, 371 f., 409 ff.‹

est un exemple d'entrée d'index. L'entrée se compose d'une adresse (ici: ›Mikrostruktur‹) et d'une information (ici: ›328, 371 f., 409 ff.‹)

1.1. Les adresses d'index

Les entrées d'index sont des séquences faisant partie des langues allemande, anglaise ou française. Il y a cependant deux exceptions:

(a) Les formes lexicales homographes dans deux langues différentes ont été séparées, ce qui produit des adresses bilingues, par ex.:

microstructure [engl.], microstructure [franz.]

(b) Les titres de dictionnaires ont naturellement été conservés dans leur langue originale.
Les adresses d'index appartiennent essentiellement aux sous-ensembles suivants:
— les termes; les termes polylexicaux bénéficient souvent d'un adressage multiple, par ex.: *analytische Definition* connaît deux adresses: ›analytische Definition‹ et ›Definition, analytische‹.
— les noms de langues et de dialectes; pour être plus facilement repérables, ils sont soulignés.
— les paires de noms de langues (par ex. ›Deutsch-Englisch‹ ou ›Français-Italien‹). Ce genre d'adresse se réfère aux dictionnaires bilingues (cf. infra 5.).
— les expressions résumant certains paragraphes du texte (par ex. ›Artikelpositionen des Sprachstadienwörterbuches‹); ces expressions appartiennent à la langue du texte résumé.
— les titres de dictionnaires (par ex. ›Petit Robert‹, cf. infra 4. et 5.).

L'index des matières ne connaît pas d'adresses pour les noms de personnes. Certains noms font cependant partie d'adresses (par ex. ›Lexikographie Adelungs‹).

1.2. L'information d'index

L'adresse est suivie d'une information d'index. A moins de contenir un renvoi (cf. infra 3.), les entrées présentent l'information d'index sous forme d'un ensemble ordonné de chiffres (par ex.: 328) et/ou de séquences alphanumériques (par ex.: 317 f. et 409 ff.). Les chiffres indiquent les pages des trois tomes; »f.« signifie *et à la page suivante,* »ff.« signifie *et aux pages suivantes.* Pour d'autres types d'informations indexicales cf. infra 3.

2. Alphabétisation

Pour alphabétiser les adresses on a eu recours à un logiciel. Le logiciel opère sur l'ensemble de l'entrée, les signes diacritiques des lettres — comme par ex. les accents français — n'étant pas pris en compte. L'alphabet utilisé a comme premier signe un blanc (c'est-à-dire l'espace entre deux formes lexicales), comme second signe une virgule et comme troisième signe »A/a« (etc. jusqu'à »Z/z«). Il s'ensuit par ex. l'ordre suivant d'adresses:

Wörterbuch
Wörterbuch als Autorität
Wörterbuch, allgemeines
Wörterbuchartikel.

3. Renvois internes

L'information d'index peut se présenter sous forme de renvoi(s) interne(s), par ex. :

access profile 333
   s. Zugriffsprofil

ou

active dictionary 2715, 2719, 2784 ff.
   s. aktives Wörterbuch,
   s. Hinproduktionswörterbuch,
   s. Hinübersetzungswörterbuch.

On renvoie aux termes synonymes ou quasi-synonymes d'une même langue ainsi qu'aux équivalents ou quasi-équivalents terminologiques des deux autres langues de publication, rarement aux termes hyponymes ou hyperonymes.

Certaines entrées ne consistent qu'en renvoi(s) interne(s) et ne présentent de cette façon aucun chiffre. C'est le cas, notamment, des renvois concernant la dénomination des types de dictionnaires, par ex.

›dictionnaire de citations, s. Zitatenwörterbuch‹.

4. Renvois de l'index des matières à l'index des noms

Dans les entrées dont l'adresse est un titre de dictionnaire, on renvoie souvent à l'index des noms, par ex. :

Wörterbuch der deutschen Gegenwartssprache 333, 382, ..., 2170
   s. NR: R. Klappenbach; H. Malige-Klappenbach; W. Steinitz.

»s. NR:« signifie *voir l'index des noms à l'entrée*. De cette façon le lecteur est renvoyé aux noms d'auteurs et/ou de rédacteurs de dictionnaires, parfois à des métalexicographes qui en ont fait la critique.

Certaines adresses concernant les titres de dictionnaires contiennent également le nom du lexicographe, par ex. :

Wörterbuch der deutschen Umgangssprache von H. Küpper.

Dans ces cas, le nom propre est à prendre comme renvoi implicite à l'index des noms. Ce n'est qu'exceptionnellement qu'on trouvera de façon supplémentaire l'indication »s. NR«.

5. Comment utiliser l'index des matières?

L'index des matières a pour but de faciliter la consultation de l'encyclopédie. Il s'adresse avant tout aux utilisateurs

— qui cherchent une information rapide, ponctuelle et précise concernant certains faits et certains termes
— qui voudraient rassembler de façon systématique différentes informations concernant un même problème mais réparties sur plusieurs articles de l'encyclopédie.

Dans ces deux situations d'utilisation le lecteur a intérêt à accéder à l'information contenue dans les trois tomes à partir de l'index des matières.

Les adresses de langues et de dialectes se justifient par le grand nombre de langues peu connues traitées dans l'encyclopédie. C'est ainsi que l'entrée »*Gelbuigurisch* 2411« renvoie à l'article 232 »Lexicographie des langues turques II: autres langues turques« où on apprend qu'il s'agit d'une langue turque parlée en Chine. Dans la plupart des cas on trouvera également une information bibliographique concernant notamment la lexicographie de la langue en question. Quant à la lexicographie bilingue, on y accède par les entrées d'index dont les adresses désignent des paires de langues, à moins, évidemment, de connaître l'auteur du dictionnaire et de passer par l'index des noms. De la même façon, les dictionnaires bénéficiant d'une description privilégiée peuvent être repérés soit par leurs titres à l'index des matières, soit par les noms de leurs auteurs à l'index des noms.

A

à alphabet droit 336
A Table Alphabeticall 1943ff.
　　s. NR: R. Cawdrey
a tergo dictionary
　　s. rückläufiges Wörterbuch
Abaza 2418
Abaza-Russian 2419
Abbildung 1103, 2795
　　s. Bild,
　　s. Illustration,
　　s. illustration
abbreviation 1509, 2816
　　s. Abkürzung,
　　s. abréviation,
　　s. acronym
abbreviations item 348
　　s. Abkürzungsangabe
Abdeckung, lexikographische 336, 396
—, makrostrukturelle 2133
　　s. coverage in breadth
abécédaire 1835
Abecedarium anglico-latinum 2912
abgeschlossener lexikographischer Prozeß 2101
Abipón 2708
Abkhaz 2418
Abkhaz-English 2419
Abkhaz-Georgian 2420
Abkhaz-Russian 2420
Abkhazians 2415
Abkürzung 649, 963
　　s. abbreviation,
　　s. abréviation,
　　s. acronym
Abkürzungsangabe 433, 468
Abkürzungsauflösungsangabe 433, 455, 468
Abkürzungswörterbuch 1100, 1261ff.
Ableitung s. dérivé
— in den Wörterbüchern des Niederländischen 2015
Ableitungssuffix 869
　　s. Wortbildungsmittel
Abor-Miri 2559
Abor-Miri-Dafla 2555
abrégé 323
abréviation 675, 2863
　　s. abbreviation,
　　s. Abkürzung,
　　s. acronym
Abrogans 2037
Absicht, normative 2286
absolut obligatorische Angabe 455
— Mikrostruktur 456
absolutely obligatory microstructure 346

abstract hierarchical microstructure 345f.
— microstructure 344
abstraction lexicale 2869
abstrakte hierarchische Basisstruktur 470ff.
— hierarchische Kernstrukturen 471ff.
— hierarchische Mikrostruktur 466, 473
— hierarchische Mikrostruktur, Definition 467
— hierarchische Teilstrukturen von Mikrostrukturen 469ff.
— lineare Mikrostruktur 415
— Mikrostruktur 412ff., 415, 440
— partitive Mikrostruktur, Definition 467
— präzedentive Mikrostruktur, Definition 467
Abtönungspartikel 805ff., 823, 1221
　　s. Modalpartikel
academic dictionary criticism 225
　　s. Wörterbuchkritik
— principle of Danish lexicography 1913f.
Académie Française 10, 1089
academy-function of dictionaries 29f.
Accademia della Crusca, its dictionaries 147
　　s. Crusca
accentuation 506f.
accès aux données 1674
access profile 333
　　s. Zugriffsprofil
— structure 328, 337ff.
　　s. Zugriffsstruktur
— structure of indexes 339
　　s. Registerzugriffsstruktur
—, typology 339
Ače 2704
Achang 2559
Aché-Guayaki 2701ff.
Achi 2661, 2664
Achinese 2566
acronym 1159, 1509, 2816
　　s. abbreviation,
　　s. Abkürzung,
　　s. abréviation
acte de consultation 1096
　　s. Nachschlagehandlung
active dictionary 2715, 2719, 2784ff.
　　s. aktives Wörterbuch,
　　s. Hinproduktionswörterbuch,
　　s. Hinübersetzungswörterbuch
active translatory dictionary 2776
　　s. Übersetzungswörterbuch

Adamawa-Eastern 2647
Adare 2452
addád 2440
additives flächiges Suprasegment 375
— lineares Suprasegment 375
addressing 349
　　s. adressage,
　　s. Adressierung
— procedure 328
— structure 329, 346
　　s. Adressierungsstruktur
adjectif composé 179
adjuvant 909
— contextuel 909f.
— différenciateur 909
— distributionnel 913f.
— spécificateur 909, 914
— stylistique 912f.
adressage 349, 507
　　s. Adressierung,
　　s. addressing
— zéro 350
　　s. Nulladressierung
adresse 180, 1096, 1563, 2817
Adresse 445f., 2729f.
Adressierung 328, 349, 2729ff.
　　s. addressing
—, hierarchische 2730
—, infralemmatische 2729f.
—, lemmatische 446f.
　　s. lemmatic addressing
—, nichtlemmatische 446f., 537
　　s. non-lemmatic addressing
—, sublemmatische 446
　　s. sublemmatic addressing
—, vollständige lemmatische 446
　　s. full lemmatic addressing
Adressierungsbeziehung 445
Adressierungsrelation 445
Adressierungsstruktur 329, 440, 445ff.
　　s. addressing structure
adverbe composé 179
advertising and dictionaries 89
—, misinformation by publishers 98ff.
advisory panel for dictionaries 76
Afar 2462
Affade 2457
Affix 869ff., 1225
Affixe in deutschen Wörterbüchern 870ff.
Affixoid 869ff., 1224
　　s. Wortbildungsmittel
Affixoide in deutschen Wörterbüchern 875ff.
affixoides Kompositum 869
African lexicons 3171
africanisme 1500
Afrikaans 2010
—, Wörterbuch 2019

Agaw 2452, 2461
age of dictionaries, manipulations by publishers 98f.
agglutination and headwords 300
Aguakatek 2661
Aguaruna 2703
Ägyptisch-Arabisch 3094
Ahi 2560
Ailei 2643
Aiki-French 2643
Ainu 2621, 2628
Ainu-Japanisch 2621
Ainu-Portugiesisch 2621
Aja 2644
Akademielexikographie des 16./17. Jhs. 10
— des 20. Jhs. 2129ff.
   s. Wörterbuch der deutschen Gegenwartssprache
Akademiewörterbuch, russisches 3079
akannie 2336
Akatek 2661
Akha 2559
Akkadian 1682
Akkadian lexicography 1682ff.
akkadische Keilschrift 1686
Aklanon 2571
Akzentsilbenangabe 433, 468, 2144, 2163
aktives Wörterbuch 2779f.
   s. active dictionary,
   s. Hinproduktionswörterbuch,
   s. Hinübersetzungswörterbuch
Akzentumsprung 509
Alaba 2463f.
Alacalufe 2709
Albanisch-Deutsch 2362f.
Albanisch-Englisch 2363
Albanisch-Italienisch 2363
Albanisch-Neugriechisch 2365
Albanisch-Serbokroatisch 2292
Algic 2691
Algonquian 2691, 3173
Aljutor 2628
Allbuch 989
   s. encyclopaedic dictionary,
   s. enzyklopädisches Wörterbuch
Allbuch als Terminus 989
Allbuch, fachliches 1254
   s. Fachwörterbuch
allemand-créole 2871
allemand-français 2046, 2051, 3040, 3053
allemand-italien 3007
allemand-suédois 3040f.
Allentiak 2709
allgemeine Theorie der Lexikographie 258ff., 1639
   s. systematische Wörterbuchforschung,
   s. theoretical lexicography
Allgemeiner Deutscher Sprachverein 1232
allgemeines Strukturbild 470
— für einfache Mikrostrukturen 474
— für einfache integrierte Mikrostrukturen 489
— für einfache nichtintegrierte Mikrostrukturen 489
— für extern vollständig erweiterte integrierte Mikrostrukturen 493
— für integrierte Mikrostrukturen mit binnenerweiterter Basisstruktur 493
— für integrierte Mikrostrukturen mit linkserweiterter Basisstruktur 494
— für linkserweiterte Mikrostrukturen 474
— für linkserweiterte Mikrostrukturen mit links- und rechtserweiterter Basisstruktur 497
— für Mikrostrukturen mit binnenerweiterter Basisstruktur
— für Mikrostrukturen mit linkserweiterter Basisstruktur 476
— für Mikrostrukturen mit rechtserweiterter Basisstruktur 477
— für rechtserweiterte Mikrostrukturen mit binnenerweiterter Basisstruktur 497
— zu vollständig erweiterten Mikrostrukturen 479
allgemeines Wörterbuch 680ff., 970
— Wörterbuch und Fachwörterbuch 842
— einsprachiges Wörterbuch 329ff., 462ff., 518ff., 525ff., 530ff., 588ff., 593ff., 599ff., 614ff., 628ff., 635ff., 640ff., 649ff., 657ff., 662ff., 673ff., 680ff., 688ff., 693ff., 700ff., 704ff., 726ff., 732ff., 749ff., 761ff., 772ff., 779ff., 788ff., 797ff., 805ff., 814ff., 822ff., 830ff., 835ff., 842ff., 849ff., 855ff., 862ff., 869ff., 882ff., 888ff., 893ff., 899ff., 905ff., 917ff., 931ff., 937ff., 946ff., 956ff., 2105ff.
   s. Bedeutungswörterbuch,
   s. Definitionswörterbuch,
   s. dictionnaire monolingue,
   s. general monolingual dictionary
alltägliches enzyklopädisches Sachwissen 560
alltags- und fachsprachliche Bedeutung 550
Alltagsdialog und Bedeutungsparaphrasenangabe 553
Alltagssprache 1184
   s. Umgangssprache
Alltagswissen und Fachwörter 680f.
Alltagswortschatz im Wörterbuch des 16./17. Jhs., Zwecke 11
Allusion 1055
allusion 912
Allzweckwörterbuch 1301f.
Alphabet 374ff.
   s. Cyrillic alphabet,
   s. Japhetic alphabet,
   s. Schrift,
   s. script,
   s. Zugriffsalphabet
Alphabet als Terminus 478
alphabetexterner Buchstabe 375
alphabetic organization of dictionaries 297
   s. Anordnungsform
alphabetical vs. topical arrangement bilingual learner's dictionaries 2889f.
alphabetinterner Buchstabe 376
alphabetische Lexikographie des 15. Jhs. 2040
— Lexikographie des 16. Jhs. 2044
— Makrostruktur 373ff.
   s. Anordnungsform
— vs. thematische Anordnung 2922
alphabetisches Schriftsystem 374
Alphabetisierung 2790
   s. alphabetization
—, exhaustiv mechanische 379
—, partielle mechanische 379
Alphabetisierungsmethode 376, 383
—, exhaustive mechanische 375
—, nicht-mechanische 379
alphabetization 1944, 2590, 2953
   s. Alphabetisierung
alphabets, types of 297
   s. Alphabet
Alphabetschrift 374
Altaitürkisch 2408
Altbulgarisch 2259, 2304
Altdeutsch 1419
Altenglisch-Altfranzösisch 2937
Alternation 735
alteuropäisch als Terminus in der Gewässernamenforschung 1285
Altfranzösisches Wörterbuch 1459
   s. NR: E. Lommatzsch A. Tobler

Altfriesisch 2023
Altfriesisch-Neuhochdeutsch 2024
altgriechische Lexikographie 1694ff.
Althochdeutsch 154
althochdeutsche Lexikographie 2087f., 2104
altiranische Lexikographie 2470ff.
Altirisch 2339
altirische Lexikographie 2339ff.
Altisländisch 1928
Altkirchenslawisch 2304
altkirchenslawische Lexikographie 2255ff.
Altlettisch 2359
Altniederdeutsch 1418
Altniederfränkisch 1419
Altniederländisch 1419
Altnordisch 1928
Altnorwegisch 1928
Altprovenzalisch 1892ff.
Altsächsisch 1418
Altslawisch 2304
Alttürkisch 2412
Alutiiq 2631
Amahuaca 2703
Amaqua 2655
Amdang 2643
aménagement linguistique 46
An American Dictionary of the English Language 1958ff., 1989ff.
  s. NR: N. Webster
American dictionary, expectations of users 30f.
— English 2963
American Heritage Usage Panel 30
— Indian sign language 3141
American lexicography 763f., 1958, 1987ff.
— lexicography, attitudes towards usage 30
— lexicography, conservative tendencies 30
amerikanische Lexikographie,
  s. American lexicography
amerikanisches Spanisch 1751
Amharic 2448
Amharic-English 2451
Amharic-French 2451
Amharic-Italian 2451
Amharic-Latin 2451
Amharic-Russian 2451
Ammonite 1690
Amorite 1690, 2425
amount of information 3161
Anagramm 1144
Anagramm-Wörterbuch 1144

analogical information 1976
analogie 635ff., 1096
Analogie 2795
analogisches Wörterbuch 1100, 1144
analytische Definition 551, 851
Analytizität 851
Anatolisch 1686
Aneityum 2574
Anekdotenwörterbuch 1054, 2177
Anfangsalphabetisierung 379
  s. Alphabetisierung
Angabe 412, 427, 433, 468, 961, 2729
  s. Information ,
  s. item,
  s. lexikographisches Textsegment
Angabe als Terminus 428f.
Angabe der Kontaktvarietät 2204f.
— der pejorativen Bedeutung 2139
— des obligatorischen Objektes 2164
— des semantisch relevanten Kontextes 2145
— eines lexikalsemantischen Netzteils 2161
— und Kommentar 432ff.
— zum Entlehnungsweg 670
— zum obligatorischen Objekt 2164
— zum Satzakzent 515
— zum semantischen Übergang 468
— zum Varietätenkontakt 2204f.
— zur Bedeutungsgleichsetzung 2119
— zur Bennenungsmotivik 2204f.
— zur Grammatik 2164
— zur Herkunft 2126, 2144
— zur Herkunftsform 2144
— zur Neologismenkennzeichnung 2143
— zur Satzphonetik 515
—, absolut obligatorische 455
—, äquivalenzdifferenzierende 2732
—, enzyklopädische 430, 839f.
  s. encyclopaedic information
—, etymologische 103f., 525ff.
  s. etymological information
—, —, Form und Position 528f.
—, —, Kritik 527f.
—, —, Reichweite 527f.
—, —, Zwecke 526f.
—, explizite 430f.
—, glossierte 397
—, grammatische 468
—, implizite 429ff.
—, kommentierende 432ff.

—, linguistische 430
—, morphologische 2147
  s. grammatische Angabe,
  s.information on inflectional morphology
—, natürlichsprachliche 429
—, nichtkommentierende 432ff.
—, nichtsprachliche 429ff.
—, nichtstandardisierte 431
—, normative 2157, 2159
  s. normativer Kommentar
—, phonetische 508ff.
  s. Ausspracheangabe
—, — bei Fremdwörtern 514
—, — Doppeltranskription 512f.
—, — Geschichte 509f.
—, — im zweisprachigen Wörterbuch 510ff.
—, — Klammerkonvention 512
—, — Norm 513
—, — Nutzen 510ff.
—, — Position 512
—, — Prinzipien 511
—, — Typen 509
—, — Typographie 513
—, — Umfang der Transkription 514
—, pragmatisch-semantische 2109, 2138
—, pragmatische 623, 691, 963, 2139
  s. pragmatische Markierung
—, relativ obligatorische 455
—, rhematische 949f.
—, skopusbeschränkende 435
—, skopuseröffnende 449
—, sondersprachliche 429
—, sprachliche 429f.
—, standardisierte 431
—, vollständig standardisierte 431
—, wortgeschichtliche 840
Angabe-Thema 953
Angabeklasse 429ff., 466, 467ff.
Angabestruktur 440, 445ff., 447
  s. item structure
—, rhematische 950
Angabesymbol 363, 429, 495, 963, 2845, 2851
—, positionsspezifisches 390, 440
  s. Platzhaltersymbol
—, rechtsadressiertes 491
Angami 2558
Angkola Batak 2564
anglais-allemand 2957
anglais-danois 3058
anglais-français 2795, 2956ff.
anglais-italien 2808
anglicism in Norwegian 1923
Anglizismus 1168, 1183
Anglo-Saxon glosse 1437

anisomorphism 2718ff., 2856
Anlautmutationen 2344
Annäherung an Wortfamilienwörterbücher 1146
Annamite 2584
Annamitisch 2913
Annex 482, 2749f., 3139
annexe 1376
annexierte hierarchische Mikrostruktur 2138f.
— Mikrostruktur 482, 2162
Anordnung nach Morphemen 3124
— von Zugriffsstrukturen 397
— von Angaben,
  s. Mikrostruktur
— von Lemmata,
  s. Anordnungsform,
  s. Makrostruktur
Anordnungsform 373
  s. arrangement,
  s. Sortierung
—, artikelalphabetische 2748
—, einfachalphabetische 1144
—, finalalphabetische 384
  s. rückläufige Anordnung
—, glattalphabetische 383, 385, 2137, 2746, 2748
—, initialalphabetische 380ff.
—, itemalphabetische 1100, 2748
—, kombinationsalphabetische 1144
—, nestalphabetische 391ff., 2746
—, nischenalphabetische 386f., 2746f.
—, positionsalphabetische 1144
—, schwach nischenalphabetische 390
—, stark nischenalphabetische 390
—, striktalphabetische 383f.
Anordnungsmethode 376, 380
— in Metatexten 377
Anordnungsprinzip 376
Anthroponym 1267, 1276
anthroponyme 1258
antiphrase 912
Antisprichwort 1036
antonyme [franz.] 218, 635ff.
— item 348
  s. Antonymenangabe
Antonym, morpholexikalisches 629
Antonym, als Teil der Bedeutungserklärung 629ff., 880
Antonymenangabe 433, 468
Antonymengruppenangabe 468
Antonymenwörterbuch 1081ff.
— des Deutschen 2177ff.
Antonymie 2794f.
antonymie 635, 1096
Antonymik 1076, 2177, 2795

antonymische Triade 629
Anwendungsbeispiel 2731
  s. Beispiel,
  s. Beispielangabe,
  s. example,
  s. exemple,
  s. Kompetenzbeispielangabe
Ao 2558
Ao Naga 2558
Apabhramśa 2498
Apatani 2559
Apiacá 2671
appareil de lecture 324
application of the computer 3159
  s. computer and lexicography,
  s. ordinateur
apprentissage 1386
Äquabilia 1335
Äquate 1335
—, ihre Rolle für die Rekonstruktion 1336
Äquivalent 154, 2730, 2744ff.
  s. equivalent,
  s. équivalent
Äquivalent im phraseologischen Wörterbuch 1022
Äquivalentangabe 3002
  s. Wortäquivalentangabe
Äquivalentdifferenzierung 3003
  s. meaning discrimination
Äquivalentsurrogat 2738
Äquivalenttypen 2746
Äquivalenz 2796ff.
— als Problem im zweisprachigen Fachwörterbuch 1630, 2943
— im Translationsprozeß 172
— und Komposita 2779
äquivalenzdifferenzierende Angaben 2732
Äquivalenzdifferenzierung 2730ff., 2738
  s. meaning discrimination
Äquivalenzkumulation 622
Äquivalenzproblematik im gruppenbezogenen Wörterbuch 1527
arabe-français 3092
Arabian 1690
Arabic 2438, 3086
Arabic ditionaries 2171
— lexicography 2438ff.
Arabic-Armenian 2370
Arabic-Bengali 3101
Arabic-English 2445, 3087ff.
Arabic-French 2445, 3089
Arabic-Hebrew 2431
Arabic-Latin 3087
Arabic-Malayalam 3101
Arabic-Persian 2444, 2477, 2711, 3086
Arabic-Russian 3092

Arabic-Tamil 3101
Arabic-Urdu 3101
Arabisch 2919
Arabisch-Deutsch 3090, 3092
Aramaic 2425
Aramaic lexicography 2424ff.
— script 2475
Aramaic-German 2428
Aramaic-Latin 2431
Aranda 2639
Aranda-English 2639
Araona 2703
Araucanian 2709
Arawak 2702
Arbore 2463f.
archaische und untergegangene Wörter, in verschiedenen Wörterbuchtypen 1157
archaisches Wort 1153
Archaismenwörterbuch 25
  s. Wörterbuch archaischer und untergegangener Wörter
Archaismus 25, 690, 1154, 2412
— im etymologischen Wörterbuch 1327
Archaizität 1153f.
Archi 2422
archilexème 635
Ardhamāgadhī 2498
Argobba 2448
Argot 912, 1184, 1524, 1534
  s. Slang,
  s. slang
Argotwörterbuch 1100, 1184, 1777
Arin 2628
Arikem 2671
Arleng Alam 2559
Armenian lexicography 2367ff.
Armenian-Arabic 2370
Armenian-Azerbaijani 2369
Armenian-English 2369f.
Armenian-French 2369f.
Armenian-German 2369
Armenian-Greek 2369
Armenian-Italian 2369f.
Armenian-Kurdish 2369
Armenian-Latin 2368, 2370
Armenian-Russian 2369
Armenian-Turkish 2369f.
Armeno-Kiptschakisch 2412
arrangement 1315
  s. Anordnungsform
—, phonetical-anagrammatical 2440
Arten der lexikographischen Datenbasis 1641
  s. Wörterbuchbasis
— von Bedeutungsparaphrasenangaben 562
— von Mikrostrukturen 462ff.

article 306
  s. entry,
  s. Wörterbuchartikel
  — structure in Swedish lexicography 1936
  — structure in the Ordbog over det danske Sprog 1915
  — structure of the Svenska Akademiens Ordbok 1941
article, their structure in early Danish dictionaries 1913
artikelalphabetische Anordnung 2748
Artikelaufbau 2116, 2791
  s. Artikelstruktur,
  s. Mikrostruktur
  — des textsortenbezogenen Wörterbuches 1543
  — im allgemeinen einsprachigen Wörterbuch 340ff., 415ff., 462ff., 2106ff.
  — im Wörterbuch archaischer und untergegangener Wörter 1155
Artikelbildungsangabe 2844
Artikelgestaltung des gesamtsprachbezogenen Wörterbuches 1404
  — im gruppenbezogenen Wörterbuch 1527
Artikelgliederung 3031
  s. Artikelaufbau,
  s. Artikelposition,
  s. Mikrostruktur
artikelinterne Adressierung 446
  — Ordnungsstruktur 441f.
artikelinterner Blank 438
Artikelkopf 2749
  s. Formkommentar
Artikelkörper 2749
Artikelpositionen des Sprachstadienwörterbuches 1421
  — des Wörterbuchs von Tier- und Pflanzenbezeichnungen 1256
  — deutscher Sprachstadienwörterbücher 1426
Artikelstrecke 335
  s. Lemmareihe
Artikelstruktur 2056
  s. Artikelaufbau,
  s. Artikelgliederung
—, hierarchische 440, 442f.
—, partitive 442f.
—, präzedentive 443
—, vollständige 441, 452f.
Ashaninca 2702
Ashanti 2648
Ashkhagrabas 2368
Ashkharabar-Grabar 2368
asiatische Sprachen 3021
Assamese 2509, 3096

Assamese-English 2509
Assan 2628
Assaorta 2466
Association Phonétique Internationale (API) 510
Assoziationswörterbuch 2320
astérisque 932, 2863
ästhetischer Aspekt des Wörterbuches 20
Asuriní 2704
Atacameño 2706
Athabaskan 2691
atlas linguistique 1469
Atsi 2560
attestation 938, 944f.
Atticistic lexica 1697
attitudinales Ausdrucksmittel 810
Auffindungsproblem 392
Aufgabentypen der Lexikographie 5f.
aufgespaltene rechte Kernstruktur, Definition 478
aufgespaltete linke Kernstruktur, Definition 477
auflistende Mikrostruktur 2112ff., 2116, 2157
  — Mikrostruktur mit linkserweiterter Basisstruktur 2116f., 2158
Aufwand als Kritierium der Korpusbildung 1643
/ ʔauni 2650
Aurelião 1732, 1734f.
Ausdrucksmittel, attitudinales 810
—, einstellungsregulierendes 810
Ausgangsbegriff, onomasiologischer 1059
Ausgangssprache, lexikographische 2729, 2845
Ausgangszeichen im onomasiologischen Wörterbuch 1057
ausgelagerter Subkommentar 2151
Auskunftslexikographie 8
Auslagerung 447, 449, 2837
  s. Verfahren der Textverdichtung
  — des Formkommentars 450, 471
Auslassungsangabe 468
Ausspracheangabe 429, 433, 468, 2732, 2845
  s. phonetische Angabe,
  s. Wortakzentangabe
Aussprachelexikographie 2093
  — des Deutschen 2090
Aussprachenorm 513
Aussprachevariante 513f.
Aussprachewörterbuch 509, 511, 513, 1293
  s. dictionary of pronunciation,

  s. dictionnaire de prononciation
Australian lexicography 2638
Auswahlexzerption 2262
Auswahlgrundsätze 3139f.
  s. selection,
  s. sélection,
  s. Selektion
Auswahlproblem für das Wortfamilienwörterbuch 1147
Auswahlwörterbuch 1551
  s. selektives Wörterbuch
Außenkommunikation 836
Außentext 331, 2124
  s. outside matter
äußere lernzielorientierte Selektion 2172
  — Selektion 373, 396
  s. Auswahlgrundsätze,
  s. headword selection
  — Selektion der Wortbildungsmittel 2153
  — Vollständigkeit 1592, 2124, 2133
  — Wörterbuchgeschichte 2101f.
  — Zugriffsstruktur 373, 2106, 2209
  s. outer access structure
äußeres Zugriffsprofil 373
Authentizität der Daten des Fachwörterbuchs 1627
author's dictionary 1446, 1452
  s. Autorenwörterbuch
author-specific Danish lexicography 1920
authorship of dictionaries, manipulations by publishers 98
automatic disambiguation of meaning 3164
automatische Paradigmatik 2794
autonyme 306, 600, 931, 2859
Autonymie 421
Autoren-Bedeutungswörterbuch 1549, 1590
  s. Autorenwörterbuch
Autorenangabe 2138
Autorenlexikographie 1549ff.
  s. Textlexikographie
—, Eigennamen 1556
—, Geschichte 1556
Autorenwörterbuch 157, 1777, 2268, 2380, 2386, 2915
  s. author's dictionary
—, semantischer Kommentar 1554
—, Typologie 1549
—, Wörterbuchfunktion 1552
Autorität des Wörterbuches 22
Autosemantika vs. Synsemantika 1222
auxiliary languages 3120
Avañe'ẽ 2670

Avar 2421
Avestisch 2471
Avestisch-Pahlavi 2471
avis de normalisation 49
— de recommandation 49
Awa 2636
Awetí 2671
Ayachucho Quechua 2681
Ayacucho 2705
Ayiwo 2636f.
Aymara 2684, 2705
Aymara lexicography 2684ff.
Aymara-Spanish 2685ff.
Aymellel 2452
Azeri 2408, 2412
Aztec 2697

B

Baagandji 2639
back matter 331, 640, 762, 2004
   s. Nachspann
Bactrian 2473
Badaga 2529
Bagirmi 2642
Bahamas 1493
Bahasa Indonesia 2563
Bahasa Malaysia 2563
Bahdīnānī 2483
Bahnar 2591
Bai 2558
Baic 2555
Baka 2644
Balearisch 1773
Balearisch-Spanisch 1773
Balinese 2564
Balkanisierung 2304
Balkanismen 2304
Balkansprachbund 2304
Balōčī 2481
Balōčī-English 2484
Baluchi 3096
Baluchi-Urdu 3099
Bandangabe 2138
banque de données 86, 326
   s. base de données,
   s. Datenbank,
   s. lexical database
Bandjalang 2639
Bao'an 2626
Baraba 2409
Barbacoan 2706
Barbarismen 2365
Bare'e 2564, 2566
Barea 2643
Bari 2644, 2704
Bartangi 2481
Baschkirisch 738, 745, 2408
Baskarisch-Russisch 745

base de données 2806
   s. banque de données,
   s. Datenbank,
   s. lexical database
— dictionnairiques 2807
— relationnelle 2811
— textuelles 1673
base de la collocation 1010
— du dictionnaire 337
   s. Wörterbuchbasis
base form 2813f.
   s. canonical form,
   s. forme canonique,
   s. Nennform,
   s. Zitierform
— structure 353
   s. Basisstruktur
basic vocabulary,
   s. Grundwortschatz
basisexterne Kernstruktur 481f.
basisexterner semantischer Kommentar 2143
Basislemma 365, 389
Basisstruktur 470f.
   s. base structure,
   s. Teilstrukturen von Mikrostrukturen
—, einfach überdachte 480f.
Basiswortschatz 1353
Baskisch 2913
Basque lexicography 2371ff.
Basque-French 2373
Basque-Spanish 2373f.
Batak 2566, 2571
Batsbi 2422
Bauan 2573
Bauteile von Wörterbuchartikeln,
   s. component parts of general monolingual dictionaries
Bayso 2464
bearbeitete Einheit und Lemma 397
Bearbeitungseinheit 328, 972, 2729
   s. treatment unit
—, zweisprachige 2729, 2732ff.
bebildertes Wörterbuch 1365
   s. illustriertes Wörterbuch
Bedeutung, lexikalische 609f., 810, 850
   s. lexical meaning
—, operative 864
Bedeutungsangabe 534, 2792
   s. Bedeutungserläuterung,
   s. Bedeutungsparaphrasenangabe,
   s. définition,
   s. lexikographische Definition,
— im phraseologischen Wörterbuch 1022
— und nichtintegrierte Mikrostruktur 2147f.

Bedeutungsdifferenzierung,
   s. meaning discrimination,
   s. sense discrimination
Bedeutungsentwicklung 1688
Bedeutungserklärung 629ff.
   s. lexikographische Definition
Bedeutungserklärung als Terminus 540
Bedeutungserläuterung 608ff., 621
— im gesamtsprachbezogenen Wörterbuch 1405
— im Sprachstadienwörterbuch 1423
— im textsortenbezogenen Wörterbuch 1545
— vs. Remotivierung 596
—, generisch-ausgliederndes Prinzip 1405
—, lexikographische 621
—, narrativ-lineare Züge darin 1405
—, Reihungsprinzip 1405
Bedeutungsgleichheit 616
Bedeutungsidentifizierungsangabe 473
Bedeutungsnuancierungsangabe 487, 2154
Bedeutungsparaphrase und Handlungssemantik 557
Bedeutungsparaphrasenangabe 534ff., 550, 2109, 2839
— aus der mehrere Bedeutungsparaphrasen erschließbar sind 2139
— in allgemeinen einsprachigen Wörterbüchern des Deutschen 534f., 2109ff.
— mit Interglossat 484
— und Alltagsdialog 553
— und enzyklopädisches Sachwissen 562
— und Explikation 542
— und Handlungssemantik 552
— und klassische Definition 546f.
— und Merkmalsemantik 543
— und Redundanz 550
—, einsetzbare 563f.
—, nichteinsetzbare 563f.
—, nichtverdichtete 570
—, um eine Monosemierungskennzeichnung binnenerweiterte 2161
—, verdichtete 535, 537, 570
Bedeutungsspezifizierungsangabe 487, 2145
Bedeutungs- und Sachwissen 846
Bedeutungsunterschied zwischen Synonymen 618
Bedeutungswissen, enzyklopädisches 559

—, gegenstandskonstitutives 554ff., 561
—, nichtenzyklopädisches 559
Bedeutungswörterbuch 608, 1104, 1109, 1172
   s. allgemeines einsprachiges Wörterbuch,
   s. Definitionswörterbuch
   s. general monolingual dictionary
— vs. Formwörterbuch 1567
Bedja 2461ff.
Beğa 2448
Begriff als Terminus im onomasiologischen Wörterbuch 1057
Begriffsgeschichte 1428
Begriffsnorm DIN 2342
Begriffsnormung 318f.
Begriffsrepräsentation im onomasiologischen Wörterbuch 1057
Begriffstypen im onomasiologischen Wörterbuch 1059
Begriffswörterbuch 157, 1077, 1100
   s. onomasiologisches Wörterbuch,
   s. thesaurus
Beispiel 608f., 2731, 2734, 2877
   s. Beispielangabe,
   s. example,
   s. exemple
— im normativen Wörterbuch 68
— im phraseologischen Wörterbuch 1025
— in den Wörterbüchern des Niederländischen 2016
—, lexikographisches 426, 607ff., 903f., 964
—, prototypisches 812
Beispielangabe 426, 437, 2734ff.
   s. example,
   s. exemple,
   s. Kompetenzbeispielangabe
—, aus der mehrere Beispiele erschließbar sind 2138
Beispielbeleg zur Ausschaltung lexikographischer Willkür 1614
Beispielgruppenangabe 437
—, verdichtete 437
Beispielparaphrase 624, 807
Beleg 608
   s. citation,
   s. Zitat
— im Fachwörterbuch: Art und Umfang 1626
— im gesamtsprachbezogenen Wörterbuch 1407
— im textsortenbezogenen Wörterbuch 1547
Belegangabe 433, 468, 2139
Belegauswahl als Problem 1643

— im Fachwörterbuch: Kriterien 1627
Belegbeispielangabe 437
—, um eine Auslassungskennzeichnung binnenerweiterte 2138
Belegformenwörterbuch, rückläufiges 1135
Belegnutzung 1607
Belegsammlung in der Lexikographie, Probleme 1619
— und Gewinnung lexikographischer Daten 1618
Belegstellenangabe 433, 447, 468, 2138, 2851
   s. Stellenangabe,
   s. Textstellenangabe
Belegstellenwörterbuch 1567
   s. Index,
   s. index,
   s. indexe
   s. Stellenhinweiswörterbuch
Belegteil in Namenartikeln 1278
Belegtextwörterbuch 1567ff., 2851
   s. concordance,
   s. Konkordanz
Belegzettel, Muster 1607
belgicisme 1500
belles-lettres and dictionary,
   s. dictionary and literature 146
Belorussian lexicography 2335ff.
Benennungskontext, usueller 556, 618
Bengali 2509, 3096, 3170
Bengali-English 2509f., 3102
Bengali-German 3101
Bengali-Hindi 3098
Bengali-Marathi 3098
Bengali-Portuguese 3101
Bengali-Russian 3101
Bengali-Urdu 3098f.
Benue-Congo 2647
Benutzbarkeit von Indices und Konkordanzen 1568
Benutzer 680ff., 2789
   s. user
— des textsortenbezogenen Wörterbuches 1540
— und Wörterbuch 772
— von Indices und Konkordanzen 1568
— von Ortsnamenwörterbüchern 1280
—, kundiger 2114
—, wissenschaftlicher 129
Benutzeradäquatheit 130
Benutzerfreundlichkeit 130
Benutzergruppe 114, 972
Benutzerinteresse an diachronischen Markierungen 650
benutzerorientierte Wörterbuchforschung 1007

Benutzerverständis und fachsprachliches Bedeutungswissen 846
Benutzung einsprachiger Wörterbücher 132f.
— zweisprachiger Wörterbücher 132
Benutzungsanlässe textsortenbezogener Wörterbücher 1540
Benutzungsanlaß 128
Benutzungsanleitung 983
   s. Benutzungshinweis
— graphische 983
Benutzungsart 115
Benutzungsarten von Wörterbüchern bei der Translation 173
Benutzungsaspekte des Fachwörterbuches und Datenselektion 1625
— des Fachwörterbuchs und Wörterbuchumfang 1626
Benutzungsdauer 386, 391, 954
Benutzungsforschung 128
   s. user research
—, Methoden 106ff., 1631
—, Operationalisierung 1632
—, Probandenauswahl 1633
Benutzungshandlung, nichtusuelle 568
Benutzungshinweise 750ff., 2118
   s. user's guide
Benutzungsmöglichkeiten 115ff.
— der Sprachstadienwörterbücher des Deutschen 1427
— des onomasiologischen Wörterbuches 1063
Benutzungszweck des Wörterbuches archaischer und untergegangener Wörter 1155
— und Wörterbuchtypen 115
berbère 2455
Berta 2642
Berufsbezeichnung im Wörterbuch 1248
—, sprachliche Interpretation 1249
Berufsschelte 1191
Beschreibungsmethode der Integration 483f., 2108
Beschreibungssprache, lexikographische 424, 531, 1551
   s. métalangage,
   s. métalangue
—, metalexikographische 438
—, semantische 161
Beslamar 2574
Bestandsaufnahme rückläufiger Wörterbücher 1136f.
bêtisier social 1348
Betonungsangabe 2849
Bewertungskontext, usueller 557
Bewußtsein, metasprachliches 1417

Beygo 2644
Bezeichnung für Tiere und Pflanzen 1254
Bezeichnungslehre, Wörterbuch der vergleichenden 1412
Beziehungsgefüge 414
Bezug diachronischer Markierungen 660
Bezugsregel 812
Bhili 3100
Bhili-Hindi 3100
Bhojpuri 3096
Bhojpuri-Hindi 3100
Bibelgotisch 1908
bible, its role in Swedish lexicography 1935
Biblia poliglotta Complutense 2915
bidirectional 2742, 2952f.
bidirektionale Wörterbuchteile 2742f.
Bidirektionalität 2989
— in der zweisprachigen Lexikographie 7, 2742
bifunctional translation dictionary 2713
   s. Übersetzungswörterbuch
bifunktionale Wörterbücher 2841
— Wörterbuchteile 2742
Bikol 2571
Bikol-Spanish 2571
Bilateralität des sprachlichen Zeichens 1058
Bild 1365, 3065
   s. Abbildung,
   s. Illustration,
   s. image
— und Sprache 714
— und Text 707f
Bildbedeutung 2792
Bildergruppe im Sprach-Brockhaus 2107
Bildsymbolwörterbuch 3148ff.
Bildtafel 1365
Bildtafelwörterbuch 1365
Bildungsbürgertum 1233
Bildungslexikographie, ihr Erbwortbezug 1235
Bildungswesen und Lexikographie 2
Bildungswörterbuch 2399
Bildwörterbuch 186f., 767, 1103ff., 1365, 2307, 2921
   s. pictorial dictionary
Bilin 2463
bilingual and quasi-bilingual dictionary 304
bilingual dictionary 100, 1506, 2784
   s. dictionnaire bilingue,
   s. zweisprachiges Wörterbuch
— of Norwegian 1925

— of Swedish 1938
bilingual item 2729
bilingual lexicography
   s. lexicographie bilingue,
   s. zweisprachige Lexikographie
— on the Indian subcontinent 3096ff.
— with Arabic 3086ff.
— with Chinese 3107ff.
— with Dutch 3034ff.
— with Japanese 3113ff.
— with new Indo-Aryam languages 2507ff.
— with the Chadic languages 2457ff.
—, main principles 2717ff.
bilingual learner's dictionaries 2888ff.
bilinguales Konstruktionswörterbuch 1002
bilingue enrichi 2867
Biltine 2643
binnenerweiterte Lemmazeichengestaltangabe 2123, 2158, 2163
Binnenkommunikation 836
Binnenstruktur, textuelle 2106
   s. textual word list structure
Birhor 2538
Birhor-English 2538
biskopal 2740
biskopales zweisprachiges Wörterbuch 2740f.
Bislama 1494
Black English 1394
Blank, artikelinterner 438
Bodo 2558
Bodo-Garo 2555
Bolaang Mongondow 2564
Bonda 2543
Bongo 2644
Bongu 2636
Boni 2464
Bontok 2571
Bora 2703
Borana 2464
borrowing 1159
Boscheman 2655
Boshies-man 2655
Bosjeman 2655
Bosnisch-Türkisch 2399
bound morpheme as a headword 302ff.
Brahmi script 2476
Brahui 2521, 3096
braille 3145
brasilianische Lexikographie 1723, 1731ff.
brasilica lingua 2670
Brazil 2706
Breitenabdeckung 982f.
   s. coverage in breadth

Bretonisch 2347f.
Bretonisch-Englisch 2344
Bretonisch-Französisch 2344, 2348
British university education and lexicography 1448
brochures d'accompagnement 176
Brockhaus-Wahrig 331, 364, 376ff., 414ff., 447ff., 486ff., 511, 531ff., 536, 565, 622, 630, 663, 669, 682, 686, 694, 750, 777, 788, 806, 817, 829, 858, 871, 2130ff., 2137, 2146, 2188, 2770
   s. NR: G.Wahrig
browsing 24, 970
browsing function 1071
Brunei-Malay 2569
Bruu 2591
Buchkunst im Wörterbuch 20
Buchstabe 374
—, alphabetexterner 375
—, alphabetinterner 376
Buchstabeninstanz 374
Buchstabenklasse 376
budgeting of lexicographical projects 89
Budukh 2422
Bugis 2564
Buin 2636
Bukidnon Manobo 2571
Bulgarian 3175
Bulgarisch-Deutsch 2307
Bulgarisch-Englisch 2306
Bulgarisch-Französisch 2306
Bulgarisch-Griechisch 2305
Bulgarisch-Russisch 2305f., 3078
bulgarische Lexikographie 2304ff.
Bündnerromanisch 1895
   s. Rätoromanisch
Burgenländische Kroaten 2292
Burji 2464
Burmese 2550
Burmese lexicography 2550ff.
Burmese-Chinese 2552
Burmese-English 2551f., 2556
Buryat 2626
Bwe Karen 2559
Byzantine Greek 1705
Bžedugh 2419

C

Caddoan 2691
Caffra 2655
Čaha 2452
Caha-English 2452
Cakchikel 2661

Callahuaya 2705f.
Callawaya 2706
Callighari 2655
Camacã 2707
Cambodian 2592
Canaanite 1690, 2452
Candoshi 2703
Canoeiro 2671
canonical equivalents 2786
— form 518
　s. kanonische Form,
　s. Nennform
— form of the headword 299
canonicity 2786
cant 1524, 1533
— language of Swedish, their lexicography 1940
career aspect of lexicographical work 93f.
caribbean languages 2702
cartographie 1583
Cashinahua 2703
Casiguran Dumagat 2571
Casiguran Dumagat-English 2571
Castilian-Arabic 3087
Castilian Spanish 2953
catch phrase 1054
catchword 1055
Catholicon 2038f.
Caucasian-Russian 2421f.
Cavina 2703
Cayapa 2706
CD-ROM 2809, 3160ff.
Cebuano 2571
Cebuano-Bisayan 2571
Cebuano-Bisayan-Spanish 2571
Cebuano-English 2571
Cellarius 3074
censure 80
Centrafrique 1502
Chakassisch 2409
Chakhesang 2558
Chaladsch 2407, 2412
Cham 2591f.
Chamacocos 2708
chamito-sémitique 2455
Chamling 2558
Chamorro 2574
Chanca 2705
Chané 2674
Chaneabal 2661
Chang 2558
Chaplino 2632
character dictionaries 2599
Chatino 2698
Chauces Society 1448
Chayahuita 2704
Chechen 2421
Chepang 2558

Cheremis 2395
Cherokee 2692
Cherokee-English 2692
Chibcha 2700, 2706
Chicahuaxtla Triqui 2698
Chikomuseltck 2661
children's dictionary
　s. Kinderwörterbuch
Chimbu 2636
Chin 2559
China 3170
Chinese 3176f.
— dictionaries 3170
— lexicography 2595ff.
— simplified characters 2598
Chinese-English 2556, 3108, 3176
Chinese-French 3108f.
Chinese-German 2725, 3109
Chinese-Hungarian 3109
Chinese-Japanese 3108
Chinese-Latin 3109
Chinese-Malay 2563
Chinese-Russian 3108
Chinese-Spanish 3109
Chinese-Tibetan 2548f.
Chinese-Vietnamese 2583
Chinesisch 2826
Chinesisch-Kasachisch 2410
Chinesisch-Russisch 3078
Chipaya 2705f.
Chippewa 2692
Chiriguano 2674
chiriguano-español 2674
Chiripá 2671
Chleuh 2456
Chol 2661, 2698
Ch'ol 2661, 2698
Chon 2710
Chorasantürkisch 2409
Chorasmisch 2473
Choroti 2708
Chorti 2661
Chontal 2661
Chrau 2591
chronological dictionary
　s. chronologisches Wörterbuch
chronologisches Wörterbuch 1342ff.
Chufi 2481
Chuh 2661
Chukchi 2628
Chukchi-Russian 2630
Chukotian languages 2628
Chuvan 2628
Circassian 2418
circularité 935
circularity 899f.
　s. lexikographischer Zirkel
citation 84, 93, 177, 219, 306, 600, 637, 728, 1161, 1979

　s. Beleg,
　s. Zitat
citation d'auteur 1820
citation form 518, 2694
— in dictionaries, manipulations by publishers 99f.
citation référencée 1829
citation, its role in US-American lexicography 35
classement 1470
classificateur 2864
classification sémantique arborescente 1822
classologie 1823
clauses 2783
cliché 1054
cluster concordance 1565
co-édition 2862
co-occurence 1565
Cocama 2671, 2703
Cocamilla 2671
code de marque 678
　s. label
　s. Markierung
Codex Argenteus Upsaliensis 1908
— Cumanicus 2479
codification typographique 141
　s. Typographie
cohyponyme 635, 1096
coin 2788
coining of examples 2788
collecte 1469
　s. Datenerhebung
collecting 1160
college dictionaries 1998ff.
Collins COBUILD English Language Dictionary 553, 1379ff., 1971ff.
　s. NR: J. Sinclair
collocability 2857
collocatif 1010
collocation [engl.] 1508ff., 1948, 2114, 2121, 2775ff., 2783, 2963
collocation [franz.] 179, 219, 308, 601, 636, 909f., 1010ff., 1387
　s. Kollokation
— légitime 909
—, base 1010
—, orientation 1010
collocational analysis 1071
collocations in bilingual dictionaries 2775ff., 2783
collocator 2776, 2785
Colloquia et Dictionariolum 3021
colonne 139
Colorado 2706
combinaison libre 1010
comment 328, 2720
　s. Rhema
— on form 345ff.
　s. Formkommentar

— on lexical meaning 354
    s. Kommentar zur lexikalischen Bedeutung
— on lexical partial meaning 354
    s. Kommentar zur lexikalischen Teilbedeutung
— on semantics 345ff.
    s. semantischer Kommentar
commentaire normatif 700
    s. normativer Kommentar
commercial aspect of lexicography 291
commercialisation 1576, 2862
commercialism 763
communicative intention of dictionaries 291f.
comparative word lists 2704
comparison of dictionaries: OED, DWB and Littré 228
    s. Wörterbuchvergleich
complementation 588
complete obligatory microstructure 346
    s. vollständige obligatorische Mikrostruktur
component parts of general monolingual dictionaries 328ff.
composé 636, 937ff. 1011
    s. Kompositum,
    s. Kompositumangabe
composition 937ff.
    s. Wortbildung,
    s. Zusammensetzung
— au carré 140
— en débord 139
— en renfoncement 140
compound as a headword 301f.
— word 1509
compte rendu 217
Comprehensive Pronouncing and Explanatory Dictionary of the English Language 1991ff.
    s. NR: J. E. Worcester
computational lexicography 3164
— linguistic and Swedish lexicography 1938
computer 1160, 1511, 2724
    s. ordinateur
computer and lexicography 1645
    s. maschinelle Lexikographie
    s. ordinateur
—, algorithmic method 1647
—, computational analysis of dictionary definitions 1664
—, computational analysis of the lexicographical process 1664
—, computational control of lexicographical consistency 1664
—, computational definitions of *word* and *sentence* 1650
—, computational identification of multi-word units 1651

—, computational identification of compound words 1652
—, computational identification of collocations 1652
—, computational internal analysis of dictionaries 1664
—, computer assistance in dictionary definitions 1654
—, computer assistance in the core activities of dictionary-making 1653
—, computer-assistance in creating a new dictionary 1650
—, computer-assistance in revising editions of dictionaries 1649
—, computer-assistance in the post-lexicographical phase 1648
—, computer-assistance in the pre-lexicographical phase 1648
—, computer-assisted lemmatisation 1651
    s. Lemmatisierung
—, computer-assisted text segmentation 1650
—, computer-controlled sub-editing and printing 1648
—, computer-generated concordances 1650
    s. concordance,
    s. Konkordanz
—, computer-generated word frequency studies 1650
—, computer output microfilm 325
—, corpus linguistics 1650
—, data capture 1648
    s. Datenerfassung
—, database management system 1655
—, dictionary software for the computerised office 1659
—, electronic information era and dictionaries 1665
—, expert systems 1664
—, fundamental computing concepts 1646
—, general functions of the computer 1646
—, generalised mark-up languages 1648
—, generic mark-up codes 1649
—, hardware 1647
—, information retrieval systems 1660
—, information science and terminology 1660
—, lexical databases 1655
    s. Datenbank,
    s. banque de données

—, lexical databases, retrieval options 1657
—, lexical databases, retrieval strategies 1655
—, lexical databases, their ergonomic design 1658
—, lexical databases, zooming method 1658
—, machine and machine-aided translation lexicography 1658
—, MATER 1663
—, methods of ordering entries 1656
—, optical character recognition (OCR) 1648
—, programming languages 1647
—, questions of usefulness 1646
—, reutilization of pre-existing lexicographical material 1649
—, software 1647
—, terminography, definition 1660
    s. Terminographie
—, terminography, examples of terminographical networking 1663
—, terminography, examples of computerised thesauri 1663
—, terminography, feature sets for classifying technical lexis 1662
—, terminography, methods of data capture 1661ff.
—, terminography, terminological data-bases 1662
—, terminological lexicography
    s. terminography 1660
—, terminology 1645
    s. Terminologie
—, types of computer-based dictionaries 1658
—, user interests 1656
—, word and text processing 1660
Computereinsatz und rückläufige Lexikographie 1133
computergerechte Transliteration 2260
Computerisierung 473
    s. informatisation
computerization in historical English lexicography 1454
— in Old English lexicography 1443
computerized dictionaries 292
concordance 1562f., 1874
    s. Belegtextwörterbuch,
    s. Konkordanz
concrete hierarchical microstructure 345, 347
    s. konkrete hierarchische Mikrostruktur

— precedentical microstructure
   348
   s. konkrete präzedentive Mikrostruktur
condition d'emploi 913
confrontative linguistics 2855
Congo-Kordofanian 2646
connotation 2819
   s. Konnotation
consistency of treatment 3160
construction [engl.] 2770ff., 2964
construction [franz.] 177f., 178,
   601, 702, 1370, 1387
   s. Konstruktion
— verbale 218
constructions, idiosyneratic 271
consultabilité 136
consultation 40, 177
   s. Nachschlagen
consultation-lecture 1673
contexte 1387
— notionnel 2864
— phrastique 2864
contrainte sélectionnelle 913
contraintes de contenu contextuel
   2862
contraire 635, 1370
contrastive linguistics 2854ff.
contrastivité 2866ff.
— des langues 2981
controlled defining vocabulary
   531
   s. defining vocabulary
convergence 2718
conversion 937, 941ff.
cooccurrents 2864
Copainalá Zoque 2698
copying 99
— as a possible form of lexicographical deception 99
copyright date of dictionaries,
   manipulations by publishers
   98
Coranna 2652ff.
Corans 2655
core lexeme 1509
— structure 354
   s. Kernstruktur
coreén-français 2615
Cornish 2343
corps de l'article 2817
corpus 604, 606
   s. Korpus,
   s. lexikographisches Korpus
— de référence 2804
Corpus des textsortenbezogenen
   Wörterbuches 1543
corpus in Danish lexicography
   1913
Corpusprobleme, quantitätsbestimmte 1598
Corpussprache 1589, 2470

correction 1583
costs of dictionaries, their distribution 89
Côte d'Ivoire 1502
Cotoque 2661
courant 912
coverage in breadth 982
   s. Breitenabdeckung
— in depth 982
Creole 1477
créole 2870f.
créole-français 2874
Crimea Tartar 2408
criminalité lexicographique 2993
   s. Wörterbuchkriminalität
criminality and lexicography 97ff.
criterium of lexicographical data
   selection 289ff.
   s. Selektionskriterien
critical reception of the Deutsches
   Wörterbuch 226
Croatian 3171
cross-reference 344, 728, 931
   s. lexikographischer Verweis,
   s. renvois,
   s. Verweisangabe
Crusca 10, 1089, 1854, 2971
   s. Accademia della Crusca
Crusca-Tradition in Spanien 10
Crusca-Wörterbuch 148, 1852
Cuicatec 2698
Cuiva 2701
Čulymtürkisch 2409
cultural dictionary 2587
— heritage and study of language
   226
— languages and lexicography
   71
— susceptibilities 2687
culture 2818, 2865
— dictionnairique 43
cumulative thesaurus 1083f.
—, microstructure 1086
cuneiform script 297f.
Cunza 2706
customer 754
Čuvašisch 2407
Cyrillic alphabet 764
Czech 3110
Czechoslovak-Chinese 3110

D

Dachstruktur 481
Dafla 2558
Daghestanian languages 2423
Daghur 2626
Dairi-Pahpah Batak 2564
Daju 2644
Dakota-English 2692

Dalecarlian dialect 1939
Dalmatisch 1903
Damara 2653
Danakil 2461
Dangaléat 2458
Dänisch 2913
Dänisch-Deutsch 2780
Dänisch-Friesisch 2026
Dänisch-Isländisch 1929
Danish lexicography 1913ff.
— Society for Language and
   Literature 1914, 1920, 1921
Danish-English 1926, 2772, 2787
Danish-German 1926, 2719, 2772
Dano-Norwegian 1925
Dano-Norwegian standard 1923
danois 3051
danois-allemand 3058
danois-anglais 2807, 3057ff.
danois-espagnol 3057f.
danois-français 3057, 3059
danois-italien 3056, 3058
danois-roumain 3056, 3058
Dansk Dialect-Lexikon 1918
— Glossarium eller Ordbog over
   formaeldede danske Ord 1916
— Ordbog for Tolket 1915
Dansk-Engelsk 2714
danske Sprog-og Litteraturselskal
   1914
Dargi 2421
Dari 2477, 2481
Dari-Russisch 3081
Darstellungsfunktion 616
Darstellungsmodalität im etymologischen Wörterbuch 1324
Das neue deutsche Wörterbuch
   von Matthias 2111f.
Das treffende Wort. Wörterbuch
   sinnverwandter Ausdrücke
   von Peltzer und von Normann
   2180f.
Dasenech 2463
data bases 3160
data collection 93, 3159
   s. Datenerhebung
— processing 3159
   s. Datenverarbeitung
—, oral sources 93
—, written sources 93
database, terminological 168f.
   s. terminological banks
datation 1828
Daten, metalexikographische
   1631
—, primäre 1591
—, sekundäre 1590
—, Vollständigkeit 1592
Datenauswertung 1640
Datenbank 987, 1733
   s. banque de données,
   s. data bases

Datenbasis als Stichprobe 1642
—, ihre Gewinnung 1642
—, lexikographische 1641
  s. Wörterbuchbasis
Datenbereitstellung 1640
Datenerfassung 1640
Datenerhebung 1590ff.
  s. data collection
— als Bestandteil einer Theorie der Spracherforschung 1639
— für das mehrsprachige Fachwörterbuch 1630
— für Fachwörterbücher 1625
— für gegenwartsbezogene synchronische Wörterbücher 1611
— für historische Wörterbücher 1588
—, Fehlformen 1602
—, lexikographische 2202
—, Praxisformen 1600
—, quantitative 1638
—, Thesen dazu 1603
Datenexemplifzierung 973
Datenpräsentation 1640
Datentarnung, lexikographische 2204
Datenverarbeitung 1640
  s. data processing,
  s. informatique
Datierungsangabe 433, 468
Daumenregister 335
Dauro 2462
Dayak 2566
DDR-Deutsch 2962
de poche 323
deaf languages 3141
Decke, makrostrukturelle 373
  s. lexikographische Abdeckung
décodage 905, 1369, 1387, 1673, 2820, 2859
  s. Dekodierung
decoding 2717
— dictionary 2786, 2841
découpage d'un article 2863
Definiendum 1100
Definiens 1100
defining thesaurus 1083f.
— vocabulary 530ff., 900f., 917ff.
définisseur 80
Definition 531, 1050, 1100, 1196, 1366, 1381, 1727, 1947, 1978
Definition als Terminus 539
Definition des Sprachstadienwörterbuches 1418
— fachsprachlicher Lexik 846ff.
— im phraseologischen Wörterbuch 1022
—, analytische 551
—, chronologische Reihenfolge 920f.

—, distributionsorientierte Anordnung 923
—, etymologische Reihenfolge 920f.
—, frequenzorientierte Reihenfolge 921f.
—, hierarchische Anordnung 924ff.
—, historisches Anordnungsprinzip 920f.
—, implizite 612
—, Kriterien für die Reihenfolge 920ff.
—, Lemma 363
—, lexikographische 531, 533, 850, 896
—, Probleme der Anordnung 917ff.
  s. Bedeutungsangabe,
  s. Bedeutungserklärung,
  s. Bedeutungserläuterung,
  s. Bedeutungsparaphrasenangabe
—, Reihenfolge nach logischen Beziehungen 922f.
definition 219, 309, 1087, 2445f., 2785
— in Johnson's dictionary 225
— in the Deutsches Wörterbuch 226
définition 82, 286, 602, 637, 639, 914, 942ff., 2860
— humoristique 1349
— synonymique 83, 1374, 1375, 1387, 1833
definitional dictionary
  s. allgemeines einsprachiges Wörterbuch,
  s. Definitionswörterbuch
définitions analytiques 2864
Definitionsanalyse 545
Definitionsanordnung, Typographie 927f.
Definitionslemma 1100
Definitionsproblem 541
Definitionsreihenfolge und strukturelle Semantik 922
Definitionssprache 848
Definitionsstil 570
Definitionsverfahren, klassisches 555
Definitionsvokabular 531, 900f.
Definitionswörterbuch 981ff., 1100, 3122ff.
  s. allgemeines einsprachiges Wörterbuch,
  s. Bedeutungswörterbuch,
  s. general monolingual dictionary,
  s. dictionnaire monolingue
dégroupement 914, 1376, 1832
deinflection 2813

Deklinationsangabe 433, 468
Dekodierung 2741
  s. decoding,
  s. décodage
délemmatisation 308
Demoskopie und Erhebung von Sprachdaten 1611
demotic 1707f.
Demotisch 1679
Dendi 2643
Deng 2559
Denotatsbezug diachronischer Markierungen 659
derivation and headwords 300f.
dérivé 85, 602, 937ff., 1372
descriptive Danish lexicography 1915
— dictionary and standard language 74
Dese 2644
desí (provincialism) 2498
desk dictionaries 1997f.
Deskription und Methode 1639
deskriptive Lexikographie 199
— Norm 194f.
deskriptives Wörterbuch 198ff.
dessin 1583
deśya 2525
Deutlichkeit als Terminus der Aufklärung 1232
Deutsch als "HaubtSprache" 2051ff.
— und Französisch in vielsprachigen Wörterbüchern 2998
Deutsch-Arabisch 3092
Deutsch-Bulgarisch 2307
Deutsch-Dänisch 2780
Deutsch-Engadinisch 1898
Deutsch-Englisch 2714, 2716, 2719ff., 2732, 2740ff., 2790, 2880, 2961, 3026
Deutsch-Französisch 2733, 2737, 2795, 2797, 2939, 2997ff., 3015f.
Deutsch-Friesisch 2029ff.
Deutsch-Gotisch 1910
Deutsch-Isländisch 1929
Deutsch-Italienisch 1847, 2041ff., 2053, 2802, 2907, 3013ff.
Deutsch-Katalanisch 1776
Deutsch-Latein 2039, 3073, 3079
Deutsch-Lettisch 2354ff., 2359
Deutsch-Niederländisch 2714
Deutsch-Niedersorbisch 2275
Deutsch-Obersorbisch 2275
Deutsch-Polnisch 3062f., 3077
Deutsch-Portugiesisch 3020, 3022ff.
Deutsch-Rätoromanisch 1899
Deutsch-Romanisch 1896
Deutsch-Rumänisch 1883, 1886f., 2745

Deutsch-Rumantsch Grischun 1900
Deutsch-Russisch 2714, 2780, 2800, 2939, 3071ff., 3081
Deutsch-Schwedisch 3043ff.
Deutsch-Slowenisch 2298, 2939
Deutsch-Spanisch 2734, 2743ff., 2790, 2797ff., 2905, 2987ff.
Deutsch-Surselvisch 1898
Deutsch-Tschechisch 2280, 2282, 2939
Deutsch-Ungarisch 2376ff.
Deutsch-Unterengadinisch 1896
Deutsch Walachisch 1883
deutsche einsprachige Lexikographie 2037ff., 2049ff., 2078ff., 2100ff.
   s. allgemeines einsprachiges Wörterbuch
— Lexikographie und Sprachgesellschaften 2051
— Phraseologie 2174ff.
— Standardsprache, Entstehungshypothese 1233
Deutsches Rechtswörterbuch 1392
deutsches Sprachstadium, Soziologie 1419
— Sprachstadium, Sprachraum 1418
Deutsches Wörterbuch von G.Wahrig 330, 339, 356, 377, 382f., 389f., 488, 531, 541, 550, 669, 694, 742, 777, 806, 838, 858, 947, 958, 2147, 2160, 2170
— von Jacob Grimm und Wilhelm Grimm 509, 644, 801, 805, 859, 863, 1395, 2079ff.
   s. NR: J.Grimm, W.Grimm
— von M. Heyne 2084f.
   s. NR: M. Heyne
— von L. Mackensen 339, 531, 694, 734, 2106, 2115ff., 2170
   s. NR: L. Mackensen
— von H. Paul 2084f.
   s. NR: H. Paul
—, Fremdwortschatz 1397
Deutungsteil in Namenartikeln 1278
dhimotiki 1707
diachrones Wortfamilienwörterbuch 1146
diachronic identifying information 341
— markedness 1974
diachronisch (als Markierung) 651
diachronische Markierung 690
— Stufung 658
— Veränderung 1417
diaconnotative markedness 1974
diacritic sign 297

diaevaluativ (als Markierung) 651
diafrequent (als Markierung) 651
diafrequente Markierung 688ff.
diafrequential markedness 1975
diaintegrativ (als Markierung) 651
diaintegrative markedness 1974
dialect 1477
dialect dictionary (Danish) 1918, 1921
— dictionary in the USA 36
— dictionary of Swedish 1939
dialectologie 1468
dialektbezogenes etymologisches Wörterbuch 1328
Dialektlexikographie des Deutschen 2059f., 2198ff.
Dialektstadium 1419
Dialektwörterbuch 1100, 1777
   s. dialect dictionary,
   s. dictionnaire dialectal,
   s. Mundartwörterbuch
— des Deutschen 239f., 2198ff.
— des Friesischen 2027
—, französisches
   s. dictionnaire dialectal français
—, niederländisches 2018
diamedial (als Markierung) 651
dianormativ (als Markierung) 651
dianormative markedness 1975
dianormative Markierung 1777
diaphasisch (als Markierung) 651
Diyari 2638
Diyari-German 2639
diastratic markedness 1974
diastratisch (als Markierung) 651
diastratische Markierung 688
   s. marque diastratique
diasystem and lexicography 294
Diasystem, ranghöchstes, mit Norm 1392
diasystematic information 1974f.
diatechnisch (als Markierung) 651
diatechnische Markierung 680ff.
diatextuell 651
diatopic markedness 1974
diatopisch (als Markierung) 651
diatopische Markierung 662ff.
— und Dialektgeographie 666
—, engl. Wörterbücher 665
—, franz. Wörterbücher 665
diatopische Markierungspraxis 665f.
diatopisches Gebietswörterbuch 2198
Diccionario de autoridades 10, 1742
— de construcción y régimen 1331, 1768
   s. NR: R. J. Cuervo

— de la lengua española de la Real Academia Española 1742ff.
— del Español de México 1754
— enciclopédico 1746
   s. encyclopaedic dictionary,
   s. enzyklopädisches Wörterbuch
Dichter und Gelehrte im 18. Jh. 237
Dichtung und Lexikographie 2
   s. Autorenlexikographie
dictionnairique,
   s. computer and lexicography
dictionaries dealing with languages of specific groups
   s. gruppenbezogenes Wörterbuch
— and translation 90, 100
— of secret languages
   s. Wörterbuch von Geheimsprachen
— in and of braille 3145ff.
— of colloquial Arabic 3093f.
— of deaf languages 3141ff.
— of texts by single authors
   s. Autoren-Bedeutungswörterbuch
Dictionariolum puerorum 1791f., 2912
Dictionarium Britannicum 1943f.
   s. NR: N. Bailey
— iuventuti studiosae ad modum frugiferum 3020
— Latino-Epiroticum 2361
— Latino-Lusitanicum, ac. Iaponicum 2610
— Latino-Ungaricum 1882
— puerorum 2912, 3014
— sex linguarum 2910
— Scoto-Celticum 2346
— sive Thesauri Linguae Iaponicae Compendium 2619
— trium linguarum germano-latino et daco-romanum
— turgo-latinum 2400
— valachico-latinum 1881f.
Dictionarius trium linguarum, Latinae, Teutonicae et Boemicae potiora vocabula continens 2913
dictionary and foreign-language learning 183f.
— and foreign-language teaching 181ff.
— and lexicon, distinction 290
— and literary study 146
— and literature 146
   s. Dichtung und Lexikographie

— and standard language 70ff.
— and standard language, typology 70
— and terminological glossary 169
dictionary and writers 146
— in France 147
— in Italy 147
—, Gabriele d'Annunzio 149
dictionary article 328, 345
   s. entry,
   s. Wörterbuchartikel
—, misunderstandings by users 32f.
—, order of entries 32
   s. Artikelaufbau,
   s. Mikrostruktur
dictionary as a commodity 88ff.
— as a help for active expression 90
— as arbiter of correctness in the USA 34f.
— as a label 290
— as linguistic authority 29, 31f.
— automation
   s. computer and lexicograpy
— basis 337
   s. Wörterbuchbasis
— bibliographies 3168ff.
— criminaltity 97ff.
   s. Wörterbuchkriminalität
dictionary criticism 225
   s. dictionnaire critique,
   s. Wörterbuchkritik
— and dictionary research 229
— in the 18th century 225
— in the 19th century 226, 288
— in the 19th century, user interest and the OED 228
—, Deutsches Wörterbuch 226
—, its professionalization 229
—, its shortcomings 229
—, Johnson's dictionary 225
—, the Oxford English Dictionary 228
—, Woordenboek der Nederlandsche Taal 227
dictionary culture 100
— dealing with specific parts of speech
   s. wortklassenbezogenes Wörterbuch
— dealing with the whole language system
   s. gesamtsystembezogenes Wörterbuch
— for foreign language teaching 1379ff.
   s. dictionnaire pour l'enseignement de la langue étrangère
— in standardization 170

— of abbrebviations
   s. Abkürzungswörterbuch
Dictionary of American Regional English 1394
A Dictionary of the English Language 1943ff., 1954
   s. NR: S. Johnson
dictionary of antonymes
   s. Antonymenwörterbuch
— of archaic and obsolete words
   s. Archaismenwörterbuch,
   s. Wörterbuch archaischer und untergegangener Wörter
— of basic vocabulary
   s. Grundwortschatzwörterbuch
— of catchwords
   s. Schlagwörterbuch
— of collocation
   s. dictionnaire de collocation
— of constructions 2858
   s. Konstruktionswörterbuch
— of difficulties
   s. dictionnaire de difficultés
— of doublets
   s. dictionnaire de doublets
— of eponymes
   s. dictionnaire d'éponymes
— of false friends 2882ff.
— of foreign words 1920
   s. Fremdwörterbuch
— of gestures
   s. dictionnaire de gestes
— of hard words
   s. Wörterbuch der schweren Wörter
— of homonyms, homophones and paronyms
   s. Wörterbuch der Homonyme, Homophone und Paronyme
— of idioms 2858
— of individual texts and text types (Danish) 1917
   s. textsortenbezogenes Wörterbuch
— of inflection
   s. Flexionswörterbuch
— of insults
   s. Schimpfwörterbuch
— of internationalisms
   s. Internationalismenwörterbuch
— of levities
   s. dictionnaire humoristique
— of names of professions
   s. Wörterbuch der Berufsbezeichnungen
— of native words in German
   s. erbwortbezogene Wörterbücher im Deutschen
— of neologisms 1159ff.
   s. Neologismenwörterbuch

The Dictionary of Old English 1444
dictionary of onomatopoeic expressions
   s. Onomatopöienwörterbuch
— of personal names
   s. Personennamenwörterbuch
— of place-names
   s. Ortsnamenwörterbuch
— of plant and animal names
   s. Wörterbuch der Tier- und Pflanzenbezeichnungen
— of pronunciation 2857
   s. Aussprachewörterbuch,
   s. dictionnaire de prononciation
— of proverbs
   s. Sprichwörterbuch
— of quotations
   s. Zitatenwörterbuch
— of regionalisms
   s. Wörterbuch des landschaftlich markierten Wortschatzes
— of river names
   s. Gewässernamenwörterbuch
— of set expressions and idioms
   s. phraseologisches Wörterbuch
— of sexual vocabulary
   s. Wörterbuch des sexuellen Wortschatzes
— of spoken vocabulary
   s. Wörterbuch der Sprechsprache, des Argot und des Slang
— of synonyms 2857
   s. Synonymenwörterbuch,
   s. Synonymik
— of synonyms: cumulative synonymy 1076ff.
   s. kumulative Synonymik
— of syntactic patterns
   s. Konstruktionswörterbuch
— of the Older Scottish Tongue 1395
— of transplanted varieties of languages: English 1475ff.
— of word families
   s. Wortfamilienwörterbuch
— of word formation elements
   s. Wörterbuch der Wortbildungsmittel
— skills 210f.
— skills, teaching 211f.
— style 3161
style lexicographique
   s. Wörterbuchstil
— typology 103
   s. Wörterbuchtypologie,
   s. Typologie
— use 102
   s. Benutzung
— use and foreign-language teaching 182f.

- use, reasons 208
- user 102ff.
  s. Benutzer,
  s. Wörterbuchbenutzer
- user profile 106
- war 763, 1991f.
-, attitudes of the public 28ff.
-, bilingual 100, 1506, 2784
-, — and quasi-bilingual 304
-, definition 293
-, education of the user 32f., 100
  s. Wörterbuchdidaktik
-, electronic 109

dictionary, encyclopedic (als Terminus) 989
dictionary, ethnological 2698
-, hypostatization by users 29
-, influence of scripts and morphological language types on its structure 296ff.
-, its prestige in the UK and USA 28ff.
-, its prevalence in the UK and USA 29
-, misunderstandings by users 32
-, onomasiological 167
  s. onomasiologisches Wörterbuch
-, translatory bilingual 2776f.
-, user expectations 31, 32
-, — and marketing aspects 31

dictionnaire 306, 507, 1875
  s. dictionary,
  s. Wörterbuch
- actif 2821
  s. active dictionary,
  s. aktives Wörterbuch
  s. Hinproduktionswörterbuch,
  s. Hinübersetzungswörterbuch

Dictionnaire alphabétique et analogique 639, 730, 932ff., 1827
  s. NR: P. Robert

dictionnaire analogique 635ff., 1094ff.
- bilingue 178, 217, 220, 1226
  s. bilingual dictionary,
  s. zweisprachiges Wörterbuch
- bilingue électronique 2809
- bilingue et divergences culturelles 2865ff.
- chronologique,
  s. chronologisches Wörterbuch
- complet 1500
- correctif 1210
- critique 1218
  s. dictionary criticism,
  s. Wörterbuchkritik
- d'abréviations
  s. Abkürzungswörterbuch

- d'africanismes 1502
- d'amour 1195
- d'antonymes
  s. Antonymenwörterbuch
- d'apprentissage 1386, 1673
- d'écriture 1673
- d'épithètes 1011
- d'éponymes 1258ff.
- d'homonymes, d'homophones et de paronymes
  s. Wörterbuch der Homonyme, Homophone und Paronyme
- d'hydronymes
  s. Gewässernamenwörterbuch
- d'image
  s. Bildwörterbuch
- d'injures
  s. Schimpfwörterbuch
- d'internationalismes
  s. Internationalismenwörterbuch
- d'onomatopées
  s. Onomatopöienwörterbuch
- d'orthographe
  s. Orthographiewörterbuch
- de choses 307, 988
  s. Sachglossar,
  s. Sachlexikon,
  s. Sachwörterbuch
- de citations
  s. Zitatenwörterbuch
- de collocations 1010ff.
  s. Kollokationswörterbuch
- de conjugaison et de déclinaison,
  s. Flexionswörterbuch
- de construction
  s. Konstruktionswörterbuch
- de contraires 637f.
- de correction 1210
- de définitions
  s. allgemeines einsprachiges Wörterbuch,
  s. Definitionswörterbuch,
  s. general monolingual dictionary
- de difficultés 1210, 1218
  s. Wörterbuch der Sprachschwierigkeiten
- de familles de mots
  s. Wortfamilienwörterbuch
- de fautes 1219
- de fréquences
  s. frequency dictionary
- de gestes 1112ff.

Dictionnaire de l'Académie française 994, 1798
dictionnaire de l'anglais exporté
  s. dictionary of transplanted varieties of languages: English

- de la langue parlée
  s. Wörterbuch der Sprechsprache, des Argot und des Slang
- de langue 280ff., 307, 2859
  s. Sprachwörterbuch,
  s. Wörterbuch
- de lecture 1673
- de locutions
  s. phraseologisches Wörterbuch
- de mots 307
- de mots difficiles
  s. Wörterbuch der schweren Wörter
- de mots du fonds germanique
  s. erbwortbezogene Wörterbücher im Deutschen
- de mots étrangers
  s. dictionary of foreign words,
  s. Fremdwörterbuch
- de néologismes
  s. dictionary of neologisms,
  s. Neologismenwörterbuch
- de noms de lieux
  s. Ortsnamenwörterbuch
- de noms de métiers
  s. Wörterbuch der Berufsbezeichnungen
- de noms de personnes
  s. Personennamenwörterbuch
- de noms de plantes et d'animaux
  s. Wörterbuch von Tier- und Pflanzenbezeichnungen
- de noms propres 1267ff.
- de patois 1468
- de périodes historiques
  s. period dictionary,
  s. Sprachstadienwörterbuch
- de phrases 1370
  s. Satzwörterbuch
- de poche 2809
- de production 909, 1011
  s. Produktionswörterbuch
- de prononciation 1304ff.
  s. Aussprachewörterbuch
- de proverbes (espagnol-français) 2982
  s. Sprichwörterbuch
- de régionalismes 1471
  s. Wörterbuch des landschaftlich markierten Wortschatzes
- de rimes 1125
  s. Reimwörterbuch
- de synonymes 637f.
  s. dictionary of synonyms,
  s. Synonymenwörterbuch,
  s. Synonymik
- de thème 220, 2716
- de version 220, 2716
- des arts et des sciences 990
- des jeux de mots 1349

— des éléments formants
  s. Wörterbuch der Wortbildungsmittel
— des lieux communs 1348
— des mots vieillis et disparus
  s. Archaismenwörterbuch,
  s. Wörterbuch archaischer und untergegangener Wörter
— des mots-clés d'une époque donnée
  s. Schlagwörterbuch
— dialectal 1467, 1876
  s. Dialektwörterbuch
— dialectal français 1467ff.
— différentiel 1500
Dictionnaire du français contemporain 13, 175, 310, 352, 784, 1369, 1832
  s. NR: J. Dubois
— du français langue étrangère 718
dictionnaire du vocabulaire sexuel
  s. Wörterbuch des sexuellen Wortschatzes
— électronique 325f., 1674, 2812
  s. electronic dictionary
— encyclopédique 220, 280ff., 284f., 988f., 1574
  s. Allbuch,
  s. encyclopaedic dictionary,
  s. enzyklopädisches Wörterbuch
dictionnaire encyclopédique als Terminus 989
dictionnaire étymologique des langues à informateurs ou à corpus
  s. etymologisches Wörterbuch von Informanten- und Korpussprachen
— étymologique des langues reconstruites
  s. etymologisches Wörterbuch rekonstruierter Sprachen
Dictionnaire général 995, 1822
  s. NR: A. Darmesteter
dictionnaire grammatical 1004, 1218ff.
— historique 988, 1819
  s. historisches Wörterbuch
— humoristique 1348f.
  s. humoristische Wörterbücher des Deutschen
— idéologique 1094
  s. Begriffswörterbuch,
  s. thesaurus
— informatisé 1672
— inversé 2808
  s. Umkehrwörterbuch
— linguistique 282

— monolingue 178
  s. allgemeines einsprachiges Wörterbuch,
  s. general monolingual dictionary
— normatif 1471
  s. normatives Wörterbuch
— onomasiologique
  s. onomasiologisches Wörterbuch
— Dictionnaire onomasiologique de l'ancien gascon 1893
— Dictionnaire onomasiologique de l'ancien occitan 1893
dictionnaire par ordre de matières 2880
— paradigmatique 1057ff., 1096
  s. paradigmatische Spezialwörterbücher
— parodique 1349
— passif 2821
  s. passive dictionary,
  s. passives Wörterbuch
— pour enfants 1834
  s. Kinderwörterbuch
— pour l'enseignement de la langue étrangère 1386ff.
  s. dictionary of foreign language teaching
— scolaire 175, 1369
  s. Schulwörterbuch
— se limitant à certaines parties du discours
  s. wortklassenbezogenes Wörterbuch
— syntagmatique 1000ff.
— topographique 1276
— traitant l'ensemble du système
  s. gesamtsystembezogenes Wörterbuch
Dictionnaire universel 10, 990, 1800
— universel de Commerce 165
dictionnaire-gigogne 80
dictionnaires d'images 2982
— de définitions se limitant aux textes d'un seul auteur
  s. Autorenbedeutungswörterbuch
— de langues de groupes
  s. gruppenbezogenes Wörterbuch
— de langues cryptées
  s. Wörterbücher von Geheimsprachen
— portatifs 2980
— se limitant au traitement de certaines sortes de textes
  s. textbezogenes Wörterbuch
dictionnariste 905
Didaktik 2795

Diḍayi 2536
Diḍei 2536
Didinga 2643
différenciation des significations 905ff.
different kinds of semantic information 342
differentiation of Chinese 2598
differentia specifica 548f.
differential linguistics 2855
diffusion 2862
digestion of data 3160
diglossia 1707
— and lexicography 73
diglossie 2872
Diglossie 2347
digraph 297
Diminutivangabe 433, 468
Diminutivgruppenangabe 433, 468
Dinka 2642
DIN-Normen zur Lexikographie und Terminographie 317f., 2922
directionality 2857
Direktion des Wörterbuchs 2742
Direktionalität 2742
Direktionsbestimmung 2744
discours lexicographique 309ff., 675
  s. Wörterbuchartikel als Text
discours métalexicographique 41, 673ff.
discussion to explain function words 1977
diskontinuierliches Lemma 364
Diskriminierungsfunktion 2798
dispositif de marquage 678
dispositif de marque 676
Dispositionsplan für Konjunktionen 866
disque compact 326
disquette 326
distinktive Synonymik 2086, 2794
  s. Synonymenwörterbuch
— Synonymiken des Deutschen 2181ff.
distribution de marques 677, 678
Distributionalismus und Konstruktionswörterbuch 1002
Disziplin, ihr Status 254
divergence 2718
divergences culturelles et dictionnaire bilingue 2865ff.
Divergenz 2716
Dizionario della lingua italiana 150, 1857
  s. NR: B. Bellini N. Tommaseo
— Enciclopedico Italiano 1869
— etimologico sardo 1903

Dobrudschatatarisch 2408
documentaliste 1582
documentation 1581f.
— informatisée 1829
Dogon 2648
Dokumentation von Textcorpora des Deutschen 1641
Dokumentationslexikographie 5f., 2049
— des Deutschen 2053
Dolomitenladinisch 1895, 1900
domaine 1824
— sémantique 2864
domaines 2861
Dongxiang 2626
Doni 2643
Doppeltranskription phonetischer Angaben 512f
double barre 1820
— définition 910
— macrostructure 636f, 933, 936
doublet 1241
doublon 935
Dravidian lexicography 2521ff.
Druckraum 386
Druckraumeinsparung 383, 391, 958
   s. Platzproblem,
   s. Primat der optimalen Platzverwendung
Dublettenwörterbuch
   s. dictionnaire de doublets
Duden-Orthographiewörterbücher 1301f., 2082f., 2191ff.
   s. NR: K.Duden
Duden-Universalwörterbuch 328, 333, 364f., 383, 386ff., 458, 493, 498, 522, 531, 537, 568, 593, 609, 646, 694, 733, 750, 777, 817, 845, 966, 2146ff., 2152f.
   s. NR: G.Drosdowski
Duden-Wörterbücher 186, 328ff., 382ff., 458, 493ff.
   s. NR: G.Drosdowski K.Duden P.Grebe W.Müller W.Scholze-Stubenrecht
Duden, Großes deutsches Wörterbuch 331, 352, 365, 368, 378, 382, 389, 391ff., 404, 447, 458, 480, 493, 501, 528, 531, 563, 572, 593, 598, 623, 631, 659, 663ff., 669, 681, 694, 751, 777, 797, 803, 828, 838, 843, 947, 965, 1013, 2102, 2130ff., 2167
   s. NR: G. Drosdowski
Dulong 2558
Dullay 2464
Dumagat 2571
Dume 2463
Dumi 2558

Dutch 3034, 3114
Dutch-English 2716, 3036f., 3114
Dutch-French 2716, 2771, 3035f.
Dutch-German 2716, 2771, 3037f.
Dutch-Japanese 3114
Dyirbal 2639
Dyirbal-English 2639
Dzonghta 3096

E

The Early Modern English Dictionary 1453
early modern English lexicography 1437, 1451
Easter Island language 2574
écriture 1304
éditeur 221
édition 2862
edition 98
Edition, kritische, als Textgrundlage für Indices und Konkordanzen 1569
Edomite 1690
educated public and dictionaries in the USA 34
Egyptian-Akkadian 1682
Eigenname 788, 1291, 1300, 2257
   s. Name,
   s. name,
   s. nom propre,
   s. proper name
— in der Autorenlexikographie 1556
—, geographischer in mehrsprachigen Wörterbüchern 2991
Eigennamenlexikon 988, 992
Ein-Buchstaben-Alphabet 378
Einbettung 864
Einbettungsstruktur, prädikative 883
einfach subintegrierte Mikrostruktur 2145f., 2154
— überdachte Basisstruktur 481
einfachalphabetisch 1144
einfache Dachstruktur 481
— auflistende Mikrostruktur 2114
— hierarchische Mikrostruktur, Definition 470
— integrierte hierarchische Mikrostruktur 2120
— integrierte Mikrostruktur 2108, 2119, 2137f., 2154, 2160
— Mikrostruktur 469f., 473f., 482
Eingangslemma 1077, 2747
Einheit, bearbeitete 397
   s. Bearbeitungseinheit
Einschub 331
   s. insert,
   s. middle matter

einsetzbare Bedeutungsparaphrasenangabe 563
Einsetzbarkeit 564, 568
einsprachige lateinische Lexikographie des Mittelalters 9
— Lernlexikographie für den Ausländer 15
   s. pedagocical lexicography
einsprachiges Wörterbuch
   s. allgemeines einsprachiges Wörterbuch,
   s. general monolingual dictionary
— als Hilfsmittel der linguistischen Forschung 160ff.
Einstellung 810
Einstellungskonstellation 810
Einstellungspartikel 810
einstellungsregulierendes Ausdrucksmittel 810
Einteilung des Stichwortartikels 2258
   s. Artikelaufbau,
   s. Artikelstruktur,
   s. Mikrostruktur
Einwanderersprache 1928
Einwegwörterbuch 394
   s. monoakzessives Wörterbuch
Einzeltradition deutscher Lexikographie 1233
Eipo 2636
Ekagi 2636
ekavisch 2288
Elamite 1691
electronic dictionary 109, 3159, 3161
   s. dictionnaire électronique
elegantiae 1051
élément (als Lemma) 1374, 1834
— de repérage 338
Ellipse, nicht-natürliche 570
Emok-Toba 2708
emotive Interjektion 823f.
Empfindungs-Paraphrasetechnik 824f.
Empfindungslaut 825
empirischer Gegenstandsbereich der Wörterbuchforschung 262
emploi 177, 701
   s. usage
emplois figurés 677
emprunt 86
Enciclopedia 1747
encodage 1369, 1387, 1673, 2820, 2859
   s. Enkodierung
encoding 2717, 2896
— dictionary 2786, 2841
   s. dictionnaire de production,
   s. Produktionswörterbuch
— with the help of dictionaries 90

encyclopaedic dictionary 989,
    1920, 1960, 2004
  s. dictionnaire encyclopédi-
    que,
  s. enzyklopädisches Wörter-
    buch
— feature 1084
— information 290, 1956
— material in outside matter 763
Encyclopaedia Britannica 219
encyclopedia 1505
Encyclopédie 219
  s. NR: J. Le Rond d'Alembert
    D. Diderot
encyclopédie 280ff., 306, 307,
    640, 1068, 1821
— alphabétique 1580
encyclopédique 1574, 1869
Encyclopédisme 604f.
Endegeň 2452
endozentrische Konstruktion
    1061
Enets 2395
enfant et dictionnaire 176ff.
enfants, dictionnaire pour 1834
Enga 2636
Engadinisch-Deutsch 1899
Englisch 3022
Englisch-Bulgarisch 2306
Englisch-Deutsch 2714, 2716,
    2719ff., 2740ff., 2795, 2797,
    2937
Englisch-Französisch 2795
Englisch-Friesisch 2027
Englisch-Gälisch 2346
Englisch-Gotisch 1910
Englisch-Irisch 2346
Englisch-Isländisch 1929, 2794
Englisch-Italienisch 1848f.
Englisch-Katalanisch 1776
Englisch-Kornisch 2348
Englisch-Lateinisch 2912
Englisch-Lettisch 2357, 2359
Englisch-Niederländisch 2937f.,
    3073
Englisch-Pašto 2484
Englisch-Polnisch 3062f.
Englisch-Portugiesisch 3022
Englisch-Russisch 3073, 3075ff.
Englisch-Serbokroatisch 2292
Englisch-Tschechisch 2282
Englisch-Ungarisch 2377, 2380
englischer Familienname, Aus-
    sprachewörterbuch 1293
English 2949, 3108ff.
— Dialect Dictionary 1394
English lexicography 1943ff.,
    1953ff., 1967ff.
—, Britain-American differences
    90, 91
—, German influences 1446
—, patriotism 1440

—, Tudor and Stuart words 1452
English-Amharic 2451
English-Arabic 3089ff.
English-Armenian 2369f.
English-Assamese 2509, 3101
English-Balōčī 2484
English-Bengali 2509f.
English-Burmese 2552
English-Chinese 3110
English-Danish 1926, 2772, 2788,
    3048
English-Dutch 2777
English-Estonian 2394
English-French 2883, 2893f.
English-Gafat 2452
English-Ge'ez 2450
English-German 1507, 2711,
    2719ff., 2772, 2786, 2815,
    2883, 2961ff.
English-Gorum 2544
English-Gujarathi 3100
English-Gujarati 2508, 2511f.
English-Gurage 2452
English-Gutob 2543
English-Harari 2453
English-Hausa 2458f.
English-Hebrew 2431
English-Hindi 2512, 3101f.
English-Ho 2540
English-Indian 3097, 3100f.
English-Italian 2970ff.
English-Japanese 2620, 3114ff.
English-Juang 2542
English-Kannada 2524, 3101
English-Kashmiri 3101
English-Kharia 2542
English-Khmer 2593
English-Korean 2616
English-Korku 2537
English-Latin 2711
English-Malayalam 3100, 3102
English-Marathi 2514, 3101
English-Norwegian 1926
English-Oriya 2515
English-Panjabi 2515
English-Remo 2543
English-Russian 3081
English-Sabaot 2644
English-Sanskrit 2492
English-Santali 2541f.
English-Sindhi 2516
English-Somali 2464
English-Sora 2533, 2544
English-Spanish 2949ff.
English-Swedish 3047ff.
English-Tamil 3100f.
English-Telugu 2527
English-Tibetan 2549f.
English-Tigré 2450
English-Urdu 2516
English-Vietnamese 2588
English-Yiddish 2250f.

Enkodierung 2741
  s. encodage,
  s. encoding
Ennemor 2452
enseignement 174ff., 3010
entlehnte Wortbildungsmittel
    1225
Entnazifizierung, lexikographi-
    sche 2106f.
entrée 139ff., 306, 308, 905, 1375
  s. Lemma
entries, their components 90, 91
entry 1160, 2720
— in dictionary, misinformation
    by publishers 99f.
— structure 2961
  s. Artikelstruktur,
  s. Mikrostruktur
— system 759
— word 1315, 2783, 2813, 2953
entryword
  s. headword,
  s. Lemma
Entstehungsgeschichte der Fami-
    liennamenbücher 1271
entwicklungsbezogenes Wörter-
    buch und Sprachstadienwör-
    terbuch 1431
Enzyklopädie 988, 992, 1779
  s. encyclopédie
enzyklopädische Angabe 430, 839
— Erklärung 2257
enzyklopädischer Kommentar
    1172
enzyklopädisches Bedeutungs-
    wissen 559
— Merkmal 550
— Wissen 554
— Wörterbuch 11, 705, 988ff.,
    992, 1747, 2661
  s. Allbuch,
  s. encyclopaedic dictionary
enzyklopädisches Wörterbuch als
    Terminus 988f.
enzyklopädisches Wörterbuch,
    Anfänge 10
episodisches Wissen 554
épithète 218, 1011
éponyme 1258
Eponymenwörterbuch
  s. dictionnaire d'éponymes
épreuve en placards 1586
équipe éditoriale 1583
equivalence 2717f.
équivalence 220, 2717, 2817,
    2865, 2869
  s. Äquivalenz
equivalence discrimination 2730
  s. meaning discrimination
équivalences de signes 2860
equivalent 2719, 2730, 2784f.
équivalent 2730, 2859

erbwortbezogenes Wörterbuch im Deutschen 1231ff.
Erbwortbezug im allgemeinen einsprachigen Wörterbuch 1236
Erbwortschatz 1231
Erenga 2643
Ergänzungswörterbuch 1206
Erhebung metalexikographischer Daten 1631
Erhebung von Daten 1590
　s. data collection,
　s. Datenerhebung
Erhebungslücke 1592
Erkenntniskurve, lexikographische 1596
Erklärung, enzyklopädische 2257
Erklärungswörterbuch 2776
　s. Definitionswörterbuch
Erläuterungsparaphrase 624, 807
erroneous definition, charges of 225
erschöpfende Stellenangabe 2258
Ersetzungsoperation 389
Erstbeleg 671, 1202
— im etymologischen Wörterbuch 1326
erste rechte Teilkernstruktur 2149
— Stufe der Textverdichtung 449, 2837
Erwartung, normative 193
erweiterte Mikrostruktur 474ff., 490ff.
Erwerbswörterbuch 132
　s. Spracherwerbswörterbuch
Erźa 2395
Erzählung, lexikographische 1365
Eskimo-Aleut 2628, 2691
Eskimo-Aleut-Danish 2632
Eskimo-Aleut-English 2632
Eskimo-Aleut-French 2632
Eskimo-Aleut-Russian 2632
Eskimo-Danish 2632
Eskimo-English 2632
Eskimo-French 2632
espagnol 2991, 3057
espagnol-allemand 3057
espagnol-basque 2991
espagnol-danois 3057f.
espagnol-français 2976ff., 2991
espagnol-italien 2977
espagnol-latin 2977, 2991ff.
Esperanto 3120
Esse-Essencia-Glossar 2039
Estonian 2392
Estonian lexicography 2392ff.
Estonian-English 2394
Estonian-Finnish 2393f.
Estonian-French 2394
Estonian-German 2392ff.
Estonian-Russian 2393
état de langue 1417

ethnische Schelte 1191
ethnological dictionary 2698
ethnologie 2866
Etikette 649
　s. label,
　s. Marker,
　s. Markierungsprädikat,
　s. marque
étiquetage 2830
— métalinguistique 2823
etymological dictionary of English 1440
— dictionary of informant and corpus languages
　s. etymologisches Wörterbuch von Informanten- und Korpussprachen
— dictionary of modern Greek 1710f.
— dictionary of reconstructed languages
　s. etymologisches Wörterbuch rekonstruierter Sprachen
— dictionary of Swedish 1938
etymological information 525ff.
　s. etymologische Angabe
—, criticism 527f.
—, European history 525f.
—, presentation 528f.
—, purposes 526f.
—, scope 527f.
Etymologicum Magnum Romaniae 1885
Etymologie 1171, 1535
　s. etymology
étymologie 83, 218, 1370, 1471
Etymologie des Gotischen 1909
— im gesamtsprachbezogenen Wörterbuch 1404
— und Arbitrarität 25
—, Hinweis im Sprachstadienwörterbuch 1423
—, interne 1336
—, zur Geschichte 1323
etymologische Angabe 103f., 433, 468, 525ff.
　s. etymological information
—, Form und Position 528f.
—, Kritik 527f.
—, Reichweite 527f.
—, Zwecke 526f.
etymologische Lexikographie 1234, 1589
— des Deutschen 2088, 2193ff.
etymologischer Postkommentar 2108f., 2140, 2144, 2159, 2200
etymologisches Wörterbuch 120, 1778, 2054
— des Altirischen 2340f.
— des Deutschen 2193ff.
— des Niederländischen 2017
— des Polnischen 2271
— des Rumänischen 1885f.

— des Russischen 2318
— einer rekonstruierten Sprache: Außerindogermanisch 1338
— rekonstruierter Sprachen 1335ff.
— von Informanten- und Korpussprachen 1323
—, Lesung als onomasiologisch-sprachübergreifend 1411
etymology 1069, 1948, 1957, 1974, 1988
　s. Etymologie
—, interest for 2570
euphémisme 912
Euphemismenwörterbuch 976
Euphemismus 1196
Europäismus 1168, 1179, 1237
　s. Internationalismus
Euskara 2371
evaluation in dictionary entries 293
evaluative Markierung, deutsche Wörterbücher 694
—, englische Wörtebücher 695
—, französische Wörterbücher 694f.
— und Wörterbuchbenutzung 697f.
Ewe 2648
example 1382, 2771, 2782ff.
　s. Beispiel,
　s. Beispielangabe,
　s. Kompetenzbeispielangabe
— sentence 903f.
exemple 84, 308f., 637, 638f., 639, 1370, 1373ff., 1471, 1833
— cité 600f.
— construit 600
— de dictionnaire 638f.
— en tête 1375
— fabriqué 600
— fonctionel 1833
— forgé 308, 600
— lexicographique 599ff.
— liminaire 1832
— neutralisé 1833
— signé 308
—, fonction 601ff.
exemple-phrase 308
exemples-contextes 2863
exemplification 1977
exhaustive mechanische Alphabetisierung 379
— funktional-positionale Segmentation 438
— funktionale Segmentation 438
— mechanische Alphabetisierungsmethode 375
exhaustivité 85
exozentrische Konstruktion 1061
expansion 1977
Expansionsform 962

explanation 1976, 2785
explanatory bilingual dictionaries 2776
— chart 984f.
  s. graphische Benutzungsanleitung
— information 341
— principle of lexicography 288
Explikation als Terminus 539
explizite Angabe 430f.
— Norm 194f.
expliziter Synonymieverweis 622
expression 179
expressions figées 2822
extension 336
  s. Abdeckung
extension du sens 702
extern erweiterte Mikrostruktur 490ff.
— vollständig erweiterte Mikrostruktur 475, 492f.
— vollständig erweiterte Mikrostruktur mit linkserweiterter Basisstruktur 495f.
— vollständig erweiterte Mikrostruktur, Definition 475
externe Erweiterung von Wörterbuchartikeln 474
— Norm 194
Externkommentar 475
extraction 1674
Exzerpieren 1606f.
—, Kostenaspekte 1592
Exzerption 2109
  s. Auswahlexzerption
Exzerptionsbasis 2256, 2262
Eyiguayegi 2708
Eža 2452

F

fachenzyklopädisches Sachwissen 560
Fächerfixierungsmodell 947f.
Fachgebietsangabe 433, 468, 535
  s. special field item
fachinterne Wörterbuchkritik 2211
Fachjargon 2941
Fachjargonismus 843
Fachlexikographie 2909ff., 2937ff.
—, Feldmethode 1630
—, Informantenbefragung 1628
—, Kulturwissen 1630
—, sprachplanerische Aspekte 1628
—, sprachwissenschaftliche 2207
—, zweisprachige 2275, 2937ff.
fachliches Allbuch 1254
— Sachwörterbuch 1254

— Sprachwörterbuch 1254
Fachsprache 680ff., 1523, 2939ff.
— der Lexikographie 312ff.
—, Funktion der 312
Fachsprachenwörterbuch 2054
  s. Fachwörterbuch
fachsprachliche Markierung 680ff.
— Markierung und gemeinsprachliche Lexik 842f.
fachsprachliches Bedeutungswissen und Benutzerverständis 846
— Wörterbuch 1103, 3026
Fachstilistik im textsortenbezogenen Wörterbuch 1546
Fachterminus 843
Fachtextkorpus 1625
Fachumgangssprache der Lexikographie 315
Fachwort in den Wörterbüchern des Niederländischen 2016
Fachwörterbuch 1052, 1100, 1169, 1207, 1512, 1777, 2937
— und allgemeines Wörterbuch 842
—, Aktualität von Fachausdrücken als Selektionskriterium 1627
—, Beleg: Art und Umfang 1626
—, Belegauswahlkriterien 1627
—, Benutzungsaspekte und Datenselektion 1625
—, — und Wörterbuchumfang 1626
—, Datenauthentizität 1627
—, Konventionalität von Fachausdrücken als Selektionskriterium 1627
—, latentes 2922
—, mehrsprachiges, Datenerhebung 1630
—, Neologismus als Lemma 1627
—, sprachwissenschaftliches 2207ff.
—, Subjektivität der Lemmaauswahl 1625
—, Textsortenberücksichtigung 1627
—, Zielgruppen 1626
—, zweisprachiges, Äquivalenz als Problem 1630
Fachwörterbücher, Typen 118
Fachwortglossare, mehrsprachige 2915
Fachwortlexikographie, Repräsentativität 1626
Fachwortschatz im enzyklopädischen Wörterbuch 991
— im gesamtsprachbezogenen Wörterbuch 1396
— und Wortart 844

Fachwortschatzinventare 2922
Fadijja 2643
Fahnenwort 1200
faisabilité 1576
Falashan 2452
falsche Freunde 2941
  s. faux amis
false friends 2857, 2882
familier (als Markierung) 912, 2797
Familiennamenbuch 1271
famille de mots 635ff., 1371, 1388
  s. Wortfamilie
Fante 2648
Färöisch 1930
Farsi 2477
Faszination durch das Wörterbuch 19
fausses variantes 934
faux amis 1157
  s. falsche Freunde
— bilingues 2860, 2866
Fehlformen der Datenerhebung 1602
Feldmethode in der Fachlexikographie 1630
feminine forms 2814
(festland)nordfriesische Standardsprache 2030
Feuerländisch 2710
fiche documentaire 1582
field 2864
file des lemmes 336
  s. Lemmabestand
Filipino 2569
finalalphabetische Ordnung 379
  s. Anordnungsform
financial calculation of lexicographical projects 89
Finland, Swedish dialect 1939
Finnisch-Schwedisch 2384
Finnish-Estonian 2393f.
Finnish-Swedish 3175
fixed collocation 2816
flächiges Suprasegment 375f.
Flemish-French 3035
Flexion im normativen Wörterbuch 68
Flexionswörterbuch 1311ff.
Flurname 1277
Flurnamenbuch 1277f.
folk classification systems 2698
folk taxonomics 2698
For 2643
Fore 2636
foreign language 2719
— and Swedish lexicography 1935
form, canonical 518
  s. Nennform
Form, homonymische 2270
Format 137

format 98, 136, 323, 2807
formatage des données lexicales 2810ff., 2829
forme 1563
— abrégée 934
— canonique 1563
  s. Nennform
forme-entrée 1820
Formen von diafrequenten Markierungsprädikaten 688f.
Formenverzeichnis, rückläufiges 1132
Formkommentar 434f., 470, 471
  s. Artikelkopf,
  s. comment on form
—, ausgelagerter 471
Formulierung und Idiomatizität 2877
Formvariantenangabe 433, 468
Formwörterbuch vs. Bedeutungswörterbuch 1567
Forschung, linguistische 159ff.
foundation of lexicography 288
Fox 2691
Fox-English 2695
Fragebogen, lexikographischer 2202
fragmentation alphabétique 1580
frame 1060
Frame 573, 893f.
Frame-Theorie 573, 893ff.
— und lexikographische Definition 893ff.
framebasierter Wörterbuchtext 573
français 3040
français fondamental 1356
— hors de France 1500
— régional 1500
— standard 1500
français-algonquin 2692, 2695
français-allemand 1024, 1796, 2046, 2051, 2808, 3040, 3053
français-arabe 3089, 3092
français-anglais 2956ff.
français-créole 2871
français-danois 3056f.
français-espagnol 1796, 2976ff.
français-italien 3007ff.
français-latin 1792, 1795f., 1801, 2957ff., 2977, 3008
français-néerlandais 2808
français-persan 2479
français-suédois 3040ff.
Französisch 3022
Französisch-Bulgarisch 2306
Französisch-Bretonisch 2348
Französisch-Deutsch 1848, 2795, 2938, 2997, 3013
Französisch-Englisch 2795, 2797, 2937
Französisch-Lateinisch 1739, 2938

Französisch-Niederländisch 2911, 2938
Französisch-Polnisch 3062f.
Französisch-Portugiesisch 3022
Französisch-Provenzalisch 1895
Französisch-Rumänisch 1883f., 1887
Französisch-Russisch 3073, 3075ff., 3080
Französisch-Serbokroatisch 2292
Französich-Tschechisch 2282
Französisch-Türkisch 2399
Französisch-Ungarisch 2378
Französisch-Wayapi 2675
Französische Revolution 1054
freie Symbole 3150
freies Platzhaltersymbol 430
Fremdsprache/Tochtersprache, Zusammensetzung ihrer Lexika 1335
Fremdsprachenpurismus 5
fremdsprachiges Präfix 872
fremdsprachlicher Laienbenutzer 132f.
Fremdwort
  s. mot étranger
—, phonetische Angabe 514
Fremdwortauffassung der Aufklärung 1232
Fremdwörterbuch 1100, 1168, 1172, 1207
  s. dictionary of foreign words
Fremdwörterlexikon 2400
fremdwortfeindliche Tradition der deutschen Bildungslexikographie 1236
Fremdwortlexikographie 2049
— des Deutschen 2062
Fremdwortschatz 1231
— im Deutschen Wörterbuch 1397
— im gesamtsprachbezogenen Wörterbuch 1397
French 3109, 3116
— lexicography 764, 1788ff., 1818ff.
French-Amharic 2451
French-Armenian 2369
French-Bengali 3101
French-Chinese 3110
French-Danish 1926
French-Dutch 2777, 3036
French-Flemish 3035f.
French-English 2786, 2883, 3116
French-Eskimo 2632
French-Gafat 2452
French-Gurage 2452
French-Hausa 2458
French-Hebrew 2431
French-Japanese 3116
French-Korean 2615
French-Latin 3035

French-Somali 2464
French-Swedish 1939
French-Tamil 3101
French-Vietnamese 2584f.
Frenswegener Vokabular 2039
fréquence 938ff.
frequency 1314, 2891
frequency dictionary 1314ff.
  s. Frequenzlexikographie,
  s. Häufigkeitswörterbuch
— of Swedish 1938
frequency measure 1315
Frequenz im Konstruktionswörterbuch 1001
— von Wörtern 1594
Frequenz-Lexikographie 1353
Frequenzangabe,
  s. Häufigkeitsangabe,
  s. indication de fréquence
Frequenzwörterbuch
  s. frequency dictionary
Friaulisch 1895, 1901
friesische Lexikographie 2022ff.
Friesisch-Dänisch 2026
Friesisch-Deutsch 2029ff.
Friesisch-Englisch 2027
Friesisch-Niederländisch 2026f.
Friesland 2022
Frisian 3170
front matter 330, 761, 1944, 2004
  s. Vorspann
Fruchtbringende Gesellschaft 10
frühe historische Lexikographie des Deutschen 2079
Frühmittelniederländisches Wörterbuch 1431
Fryske Academy 2026
Fügungswörterbuch 1011
  s. Kollokationswörterbuch
full lemmatic addressing 349
  s. vollständige lemmatische Adressierung
function of the dictionary 103
  s. Funktion der Wörterbücher
Fundierung des Valenzbegriffes 1003
Fünf-Sprachen-Wörterspiegel 2625
Funktion der Wörterbücher 2010, 2256
— des Wörterbuches 23
— des Wortfamilienwörterbuches 1146
— einer lexikographischen Datenbasis 1641
— von Fachsprache 312
— von Wörterbüchern 5f., 172
— zweisprachiger Wörterbücher 2741
—, mnemotechnische 1044
funktional-positionale Segmentation 438, 464

funktionale Segmentation 366
— Wortklasse 1221
funktionales Textsegment 425, 961
  s. Angabe,
  s. Strukturanzeiger
Funktionen der Konstruktionswörterbücher 1001f.
— der Sprache 1232
— des gesamtsprachbezogenen Wörterbuches 1400f.
Funktionsbestimmung 2744
Funktionssprache 836
Funktionsverbgefüge 882ff.
Funktionswort und Synonymie 623
Fur 2643
Futunan 2574

G

Gaam 2643
Gad(a)ba 2543
Gadaba 3096
Gadba 2521
Gafat 2448
Gafat-English 2452
Gafat-French 2452
Gagausisch 2409
Galician 1736
Galician-Spanish 1736
Galizisch 2919
Gälisch 2346
Gälisch-Englisch 2346
Galla 2462
Gallenna 2448
Gallicismus 227
Gallizismenpurismus in Lateinamerika 65
Gallizismus 1168
gallois-anglais 2956
Gallong 2558
galloroman 3175
G//ana 2654
G//ana-khoe 2654
Gandhari 2498
Garo 2558
Garo-English 3100
Garwali-Hindi 3100
Gaskognisch 1893
Gaunersprache 1535, 2271
Gayo 2564ff.
gazetteer 1277
Ge'ez 2448
Ge'ez-Amharic 2450
Ge'ez-English 2450
Ge'ez-French 2450
Ge'ez-Latin 2449
Gê 2700
Gebietswörterbuch, diatopisches 2198

gebildete Öffentlichkeit und Wörterbuchbenutzer 19ff.
Gebrauchslexikographie 5f.
— des Deutschen, ihr Erbwortbezug 1235
—, Probleme ihrer Verbesserung 14
Gebrauchsregel 617
Gebrauchstheorie der Bedeutung 609f., 618
Gebrauchswörterbuch 981
gebundenes Platzhaltersymbol 430
Gefühlswort 851
Gegenfeldwort 629
Gegenstand des gesamtsprachbezogenen Wörterbuches 1395, 1401
— deutscher Sprachstadienwörterbücher 1418
— lexikographischer Normierung 67f.
gegenstandskonstitutives Bedeutungswissen 554, 556, 561
gegenwärtiger Status der Lexikographie 246
gegenwartsbezogenes synchronisches Wörterbuch, Datenerhebung 1611
Gegenwort 629
  s. Antonym
Gegisch 2361
Gegisch-Ripuarisch 2361
Geheimsprache, Definition 1532ff.
Geheimsprachenwörterbuch 1532
Geländename 1277
Gelbuigurisch 2411
Geltungsbereich von Angaben 448
Geltungsbeziehung, standardisiert regulierte 450
Gemeinsprache 681
gemeinsprachliche und fachsprachliche Lexik 842f.
gemeinsprachliches Wörterbuch 970
gemischte Erweiterung von Wörterbuchartikeln 479
gemischt erweiterte Mikrostruktur 495ff.
Gende 2636
general dictionary of Swedish 1937
general monolingual dictionary 328, 1956ff., 1967ff.
  s. allgemeines einsprachiges Wörterbuch,
  s. dictionnaire monolingue
generische Struktur 463
genormte lexikographische Terminologie 319

genre prochain 914
Gentoo 2526
genuiner Zweck 426
genus proximum 548f., 1100
Genusangabe 433, 468, 2847
  s. item giving gender
Genuswörterbuch 1313
geographical criterion of lexicographical data selection 289
Geonym 1277
  s. Ortsnamen
Georgian 2415
Georgian lexicography 2415ff.
Georgian-German 2417
Georgian-Russian 2416f.
German 3109, 3116
— cognate in English lexicography 1439
— influence on Danish lexicography 1920
— influences on English lexicography 1446
German-Amharic 2451
German-Armenian 2370
German-Chinese 2725, 3110
German-Danish 1926, 2719, 2772, 2783
German-Dutch 2771, 2777
German-English 1507, 2711, 2719, 2723, 2772, 2786, 2961ff.
German-Estonian 2392ff.
German-French 2894
German-Greek 1699
German-Ik 2643
German-Ket/Kolt 2628
German-Krongo 2643
German-Malayalam 3101
German-Norwegian 1926
German-Nubian 2643
German-Old Prussian 2353
German-Pāli 2502
German-Român 2844ff.
German-Russian 2369, 2894
German-Ukrainian 2330
German-Yiddish 2249f.
Germanicismus 227
germanistische Neologismenlexikographie 2187
— Sprachstadienlexikographie 2105
— Wörterbuchpflege 2213ff.
Gesamtprozeß, lexikographischer 2128, 2167ff.
gesamtsprachbezogen 1392
gesamtsprachbezogenes onomasiologisches Wörterbuch 1064
gesamtsprachbezogenes Wörterbuch 1394
—, Artikelgestaltung 1404
—, Basis 1400
—, Bedeutungserläuterung darin 1405

—, Belege darin 1407
—, Etymologie darin 1404
—, Fachwortschatz 1396
—, Fremdwortschatz 1397
—, Funktionen 1400f.
—, Gegenstand 1395, 1401
—, Gruppensprache 1396
—, historischer Wortschatz 1399
—, kulturpädagogische Funktion 1403
—, Lemmaform 1404
—, Mundartwortschatz 1398
—, nationale Identifikationsfunktion 1402
—, nationalliterarische Erziehungsfunktion 1403
—, Nutzungsmöglichkeiten 1400f.
—, paradigmatische Wortschatzvernetzung 1408
—, Reihenfolge der Einzelbedeutungen 1406
—, situationsgebundener Wortschatz 1399
—, sozialschichtiger Wortschatz 1399
—, Symptomwertangaben 1408
—, Syntagmatik 1408
gesamtsystembezogen als Terminus 1391
gesamtsystembezogenes Wörterbuch 1391ff.
Gesamtwerkwörterbuch 1549
Gesamtwörterbuch 970, 981, 2053
— zu Varietäten 1392, 1393
Geschichte der Autorenlexikographie 1556ff.
— der deutschen Lexikographie 2027ff., 2049ff., 2078ff., 2100ff.
— der Gewässernamenwörterbücher 1284
— der gotischen Lexikographie 1909ff.
— der Lexikographie von Tier- und Pflanzenbezeichnungen 1254f.
— der Wortfamilienwörterbücher 1149
— des Konstruktionswörterbuches 1004ff.
— des Wörterbuchs einer rekonstruierten Sprache 1337f.
— lexikographischer Programme in Deutschland 230ff.
— phonetischer Angaben 509f.
— rückläufiger Wörterbücher 1132ff.
geschichtlicher Text, Verstehbarkeit 1417
Gesellschaft und sexuelles Vokabular 1194

— und Wörterbücher 1ff.
—, Fruchtbringende 10
gesellschaftliche Relevanz der Lexikographie 5ff.
— Voraussetzung für Erbwortlexikographie 1231
Gesprächsanalyse und Hecken 856
Gesprächsbücher 2910, 2915, 2918, 3070
s. phrase books
Gesprächsformel 1054
Gesprächswort als Terminus 822
Gesprächswörterbücher 3070
geste 1112
Gestenwörterbuch
s. dictionnaire de gestes
Gewässername 1277
—, Definition 1286
Gewässernamenbuch 1277
Gewässernamenforschung, Prinzipien 1285
Gewässernamenlexikographie, allgemeine Prinzipien 1285
Gewässernamenlexikon, Typen 1286
Gewässernamenraum, historischer 1285
Gewässernamenwörterbuch 1284ff.
Gewerbebürgertum 1233
Gewohnheiten vs. Normen 195
ghost words 2475
Giddole 2464
Gilaki 2481
Gilani 2481
Gilbertese 2574
Gilyak 2628
Gilyak-Russian 2630
Gimirra 2463
Giriquas 2655
glattalphabetisch 336, 383, 1076, 3002
glattalphabetische Anordnungsform 383, 385
— Zugriffsstruktur 396
glattalphabetisches Wörterbuch 385f., 2748
Glavda 2458
Gliederungspartikel 823
—, illokutionstransformierende 823f.
Gliederungszeichen, lexikographisches 437
s. Strukturanzeiger
glose 350, 1820, 1832, 2865, 2868f.
— contextuelle 2818
— définitionnelle 2860
gloss 350, 2785, 2788
s. Glossat
glôssai 1696
Glossaire des patois de la Suisse romande 1897

Glossar 1629, 1680, 1844ff., 2339, 2921, 2937, 2940
Glossare, mehrsprachige, des späten Mittelalters 1411
glossarist 1476
Glossarium Ansileubi 1714
— Bernense 2040
— juridico-danicum 1916
— Latino-Arabicum 3087
— mediae et infimae latinitatis 1719
— Norvagicum 1924
— Palaeo-Persicum 2471
glossary 1696, 2367
— style dictionary 1164
—, terminological 167
Glossat 350, 447, 457, 534, 2843, 2847
Glosse, semantische 653
Glossen 1738, 2339
— im zweisprachigen Wörterbuch 2737ff., 2798
glosses 2783, 2965
glossierte Angabe 397
Glossierung 2794
Glossierungstechnik 447
glossing 1437
Glossographie 1788
— des Früh- und Hochmittelalters 2037f.
—, deutsche, des 14. Jhs. 2038
glossographie 1788f.
Gni 2559
Goethe-Lexikographie 1558
Gogot 2452
Gondi 2521, 3096
Gonga 2462
Gorum 2544
Gorum-English 2544
gotische Lexikographie 1908ff.
Gotisch, methodische Zugänge zu seinem Wortschatz 1908
Gotisch-Englisch 1910
Gotisch-Lateinisch 1909
Gotland, its dialect and lexicography 1939
Grabar 2368
Grabar-Ashkharabar 2368
Gradierungsangabe 433, 468
Gradierungsbeschränkungsangabe 433, 468
Gradus ad Parnassum 1011, 1051, 1076
Graged 2566
grammage du papier 137
grammaire 178, 3009
grammaire alphabétique 1218, 1219
grammaire-lexique 310, 1218
grammar 2722f., 2963
grammar and the dictionary 2773
s. Grammatik und Wörterbuch

grammatical dictionary
   s. dictionnaire grammatical,
   s. grammatisches Wörterbuch
— constructions in the bilingual dictionary 2770ff.
— information 756ff., 2720
   s. grammatische Angabe
— morpheme as a headword 304
— properties 2783
— supplement 764
Grammatik 160
— als Stütze für die Gewinnung lexikographischer Daten 1612
Grammatik und Wörterbuch 732
—, Unterschiede ihrer normativen Wirkung 63
Grammatikangabe 433, 468
grammatische Angabe 1026, 2110f., 2847
— Kategorisierung im zweisprachigen Wörterbuch 2824ff.
grammatisches Wörterbuch 1004, 2880
   s. dictionnaire grammatical
Grammatisch-kritisches Wörterbuch der Hochdeutschen Mundart 2054ff.
   s. NR: J. Ch. Adelung
grāmya 2525
Gran Enciclopèdia Catalana 1776, 1779
Grand Dictionnaire encyclopédique Larousse 940, 1574
   s. NR: Cl. Dubois
Grand Larousse de la langue française 940
Grande Dizionario della lingua italiana 1870
Graphie 1297
graphie phonétique 1470
graphische Benutzungsanleitung 983, 2118
— Nische 2747
Grebo 2648
Greek 3173
Greek-Armenian 2369f.
Greek-English 1710
Greek-German 1699
Greek-Hindi 3101f.
Greek-Latin 1698
Griqua 2651
Griechisch-Gotisch 1910
Griechisch-Katalanisch 1776
Griechisch-Kirchenslawisch 3070
Griechisch-Koptisch 1680
Griechisch-Lateinisch 1714, 2039
Griechisch-Rumänisch 1883
Griechisch-Russisch 3069, 3073, 3078
Griechisch-Türkisch 2402
Grigrikwaas 2655
Grikwa 2655

grille de marques 678
Griqua 2655
Grönländisch 2916
Groot Woordenboek der Nederlandsche Taal 2012f.
   s. NR: G. Geerts H. Heestermans
Großcorpus 1593
Größenklassen 2127f.
   s. size
Großwörterbuch 2988, 3063
Grundbedeutung und Einzelbedeutung 922
Grundform 2813
— im etymologischen Wörterbuch, historische Tiefe 1331
Grundkommentar 434, 470
Grundprinzip der Lexikographie 806
Grundsatz quantitativer Datenerhebung 1641
Grundschema für den Artikelaufbau 458
Grundsprache 1335
—, Probleme der Rekonstruktion 1335
Grundwortschatz 161f., 1353
Grundwortschatzbuch, Typen 1358f.
Grundwortschatz-Lexikographie 1353ff.
Grundwortschatzwörterbuch 1050, 1353ff., 2032
Gruppe und Heterogenität von Sprachen 1523
Gruppe, Typen 1523
Gruppenarchaismus 1154
gruppenbezogenes Wörterbuch 1523ff.
—, Äquivalenzproblematik 1527
—, Artikelgestaltung 1527
—, Typen 1525f.
gruppenspezifischer Wortschatz 1524
Gruppensprache 1523, 1532
Gruppensprache im gesamtsprachbezogenen Wörterbuch 1396
Gruppensprachenbezeichnungen 1524
Gruppensprachen-Lexikographie 1524
Gruppierung 390, 393, 398, 923
   s. regroupement
— und Typographie 389
Gruppierungsmotiv 393
Gta' 2536
Guahiban 2704
Guajajara 2671
Guajiro 2703
Guana 2708
Guaraní 2703
Guarani-Spanish 2673

Guarayo 2674
Guayakí 2704
Guaykuru 2708
Gude 2458
Guerrero 2659
/Gui-khoe 2654
guiding element 338
   s. Leitelement
Gujarathi 3096
Gujarathi-Japanese 3101
Gujarati 2511
Gujarati-English 2508, 2511f.
Gula 2644
Gule 2643
Gullah 1394
Gumuz 2642f.
Gununa Kune 2710
Gupta alphabet 2548
Gur 2647
Gurage 2448
Gurani 2481
Gurung 2558
Gurungkur 3096
Gutnic, its lexicography 1939
Gutob 2543
Gutob-English 2543
G/wi 2654
Gyeto 2452

H

Habitualisierung 195f.
Hadiyya 2463
Hadza 2650
Hakaltek 2661
Halbaffix 1224
Halbterminus 844
Hamer 2463
Hamgyong 2614
Han (Chinese studies) 2587
Handel und Lexikographie 4
Handelskorrespondenz, Phraseologie 1052
Handwörterbuch 2988, 3064
Handwörterbuch der deutschen Gegenwartssprache 339, 345, 354, 382, 389, 397, 412ff., 428, 432, 437, 458, 464, 471, 485ff., 491, 533ff., 541, 563ff., 571, 593, 608, 619, 659, 697, 749, 775, 777, 827, 832, 838, 845, 867, 964, 2102, 2146, 2159, 2170
   s. NR: G. Kempcke
hapax 1736, 1830
— legomenon 1627
Haquearu 2705
Harari 2448
Harari-English 2453

Harari-French 2453
Harari-Italian 2453
hard word 1168, 1950, 3108
　s. schweres Wort
— dictionary 89
　s. Schwerwörterbuch
Hasada 2539
Hatraean 2431
Hattisch 1687
Häufigkeit als lexikalisches Merkmal 1640
— und Selektion 690
Häufigkeitsangabe 433, 468
　s. Frequenzangabe
Häufigkeitswörterbuch 1353, 2358
　s. frequency dictionary
Hauptbasismenge 463
Hauptlemma 364
Hauptzugriffsstruktur 398, 2110
Hausa 2457
Hausa-English 2458f.
Hausa-French 2458
Hausa-German 2458
Hausa-Japanese 3113
Hausa-Russian 2459
Haute-Volta 1502
Hawaii-Pidgin 1394
Hawaiian 2573
Hawaiian-English 2573
headword 296, 2783, 2813
　s. entry word,
　s. Lemma
— from isolating languages 302
— inclusion 89f.
— inclusions, misinformation by publishers 99f.
— selection from Chinese 302
— selection from Turkish 300
—, its canonical form 299
　s. Nennform
—, its morphology 299
—, its paradigms 299
—, type: token relation 299
Hebräisch 2913
Hebräisch-Deutsch 2428
Hebräisch-Ladino 1906
Hebrew lexicography 2424ff.
Hebrew-Arabic 2431, 2712
Hebrew-English 2431
Hebrew-French 2431
Hebrew-Japanese 3113
Hebrew-Russian 2431
Heckenausdrücke (hedges) 855ff.
Hecken und Gesprächsanalyse 856
Heiligennamenlexikon 1267
helvétisme 1500
Herders Sprachbuch 331, 377, 742, 3890, 389, 391, 2124ff.
hermeneutischer Zirkel 1020
Herstellung von Indices und Konkodanzen 1567ff.

Herübersetzung 2741
Herübersetzungswörterbuch 2716, 2840ff., 2989
　s. passive dictionary,
　s. passives Wörterbuch
heterogenes Ortsnamenbuch 1277
heteroglottes Wörterbuch 1431
Heterogramm 1687
heterograms 2475
Heteronym 619
Hethitisch 1686
hethitische Lexikographie 1686ff.
Hexaglotton geminum, docens linguas 2916
Hidalgo 2659f.
hidden glossaries 2921
hierarchical integrate 355
　s. Integrat
hierarchisch einfach überdachte Mikrostruktur, Definition 481
hierarchische Artikelstruktur 440, 442f.
— basisexterne Kernstruktur, Definition 482
— Basisstruktur, Definition 471
— binnenerweiterte Basisstruktur 475
— binnenerweiterte Basisstruktur, Definition 476
— binnenerweiterte Mikrostruktur, Definition 475
— Dachstruktur, Definition 481
— hintere linke Kernstruktur, Definition 477
— hintere rechte Kernstruktur, Definition 478
— integrierte Mikrostruktur, Definition 483
— linke Interstruktur, Definition 477
— Mikrostruktur 393, 443ff., 464ff., 806
— Mikrostruktur mit linkserweiterter Basisstruktur, Definition
— Mikrostruktur mit rechtserweiterter Basisstruktur, Definition 477
— mittlere Interstruktur 476
— partiell integrierte Mikrostruktur, Definition 482
— rechte Interstruktur, Definition 478
— rechtserweiterte Basisstruktur, Definition 478
— überdachende Mikrostruktur, Definition 481
— vordere linke Kernstruktur, Definition 477
— vordere rechte Kernstruktur, Definition 478
hierarchisches Integrat, Definition 484

hieratische Schrift 1679
Hieroglyphenluwisch 1687
hieroglyphische Schrift 1679
Hilfsbasismenge 463
Hilfssprachen 3120ff.
Himalayish 253,3
Hindi 2512, 3096
Hindi-Assamese 3098f.
Hindi-Bengali 3098f.
Hindi-Bhojpuri 3100
Hindi-Bhoti 3100
Hindi-Chinese 3101
Hindi-English 2512
Hindi-French 3101
Hindi-Gujarathi 3098f., 3102
Hindi-Hmar 3100
Hindi-Ho 3100
Hindi-Japanese 2512, 3113
Hindi-Kannada 3098
Hindi-Kashmiri 3098
Hindi-Kharia 2542
Hindi-Khasi 3100
Hindi-Kom 3100
Hindi-Kurukh 3100
Hindi-Latin 3102
Hindi-Malayalam 3098
Hindi-Manipuri 3100
Hindi-Mao 3100
Hindi-Maram 3100
Hindi-Marathi 3098ff.
Hindi-Mering 3100
Hindi-Mundari 2539
Hindi-Oriya 3098
Hindi-Russian 2512, 3101
Hindi-Sindhi 3098f.
Hindi-Tamil 3098f.
Hindi-Telugu 3098f.
Hindi-Tripuri 3100
Hindi-Urdu 3098f.
Hindi-Vaipei 3100
Hindi-Zon 3100
Hinproduktionswörterbuch 2840
　s. aktives Wörterbuch
hintere linke Kernstruktur 476
— rechte Kernstruktur 477
hinterer Formkommentar 476
— semantischer Kommentar 477
Hinterintegrat 484
—, Definition 485
Hinübersetzung 2741
Hinübersetzungswörterbuch 117, 132, 2716, 2840ff.
　s. active dictionary,
　s. aktives Wörterbuch
Hinweis zur Etymologie im Sprachstadienwörterbuch 1423
—, lexikographischer 428
Hinweisangabe 433, 468
hispanoamerikanische Lexikographie 1752
historical Danish lexicography 1916

historical dictionary 1736, 1984
  s. historisches Wörterbuch,
  s. Sprachstadienwörterbuch
—, methodological problems 229
historical English lexicography,
  computerization 1454
—, sense ordering 1451
—, transferred sense 1450
historisch-etymologisches Interesse an Vornamen 1268
historische Lexikographie 2078ff.
  s. Sprachstadienlexikographie
Historische Lexikographie nach
  den Grimms 2084
— Sprachstufen, Personennamenwörterbuch 1267
— Wörterbuchforschung 262, 2050
historischer Beruf, Sachinformation 1249
— Text, Verfügbarkeit 1593
— Wortschatz im gesamtsprachbezogenen Wörterbuch 1399
historisches Prinzip in der deutschen Lexikographie 2078
— Sprachstadienwörterbuch 432
— Wörterbuch 1342, 1750
  s. historical dictionary
— Wörterbuch, Datenerhebung 1588
— Wörterbuch, Informationspositionen 1594
— Wörterbuch, Vollständigkeit 1599
history of dictionary use 103
— of Norwegian lexicography 1924f.
Hmong 2591
Ho 2534
Ho-English 2533, 2540
Hochdeutsch als Problem 236
Hochdeutsch-Vaterländisch 2028
hochsprachliche Variation und Lexikographie 14
Hokan 2691
Holländisch
  s. Niederländisch
Holländisch-Japanisch 2619
homogenes Ortnamenbuch 1277
homoglott einsprachiges/zweisprachiges Wörterbuch 1430
homographe 507, 640
Homographenwörterbuch 1123
Homographie 1120
Homoionymenangabe 2161
— aus der mehrere Homonyme erschließbar sind 2161
Homoionymengruppenangabe 2161
Homonym 1120

homonyme 507, 703
Homonymenindex 380, 450
Homonymenlexikographie des Deutschen 2090
Homonymenwörterbuch 1120ff., 2270
Homonymie 640, 1120, 1832f.
  s. homonymy
— im deutschen Wörterbuch 783
— im englischen Wörterbuch 782f.
— im spanischen Wörterbuch 782
— in den Wörterbüchern des Niederländischen 2017
— in italienischen und französischen Wörterbüchern 783f.
— und Polysemie im allgemeinen einsprachigen Wörterbuch 779ff.
homonymie interne 914
homonymische Form 2270
Homonymisierung 380
homonymy 167f., 2814
  s. Homonymie
Homophone 640f., 1120
Homophonenwörterbuch 1121
Homophonie 1120
homophonie 640f.
Hörbeleg 1619
horizontal parallellaufende Zugriffsstruktur 398, 400, 404
Hottentot 2650
Hsi-hsia 2560
Huasteca 2660
Huastek 2661
Huautla 2659
Huave 2698
Huichol 2698
Huitoto 2703
Humanismus und deutsche Lexikographie 2042
Humanisten, niederländische und gotische Lexikographie 1909
humanistische Onomastica 2043
humoristische Wörterbücher des Deutschen 2197
humoristisches Wörterbuch
  s. dictionnaire humoristique
Hungarian 3174
Hungarian-Japanese 3113
Hurrian 1691f.
Hurrisch 1687
Hurritisch 1687
hybrid sequence in the organization of dictionaries 299
Hydronomia Europaea 1287
— Germaniae als Typ des Gewässernamenwörterbuches 1286
hyperbole (als Markierung) 912

hypernorvagization 1925
hyperonyme 635, 914, 2864
Hyperstruktur 425, 947
—, standardisierte 948
Hyperthema-Progression 947, 949
hyphenated words 2815
hypocoristique (als Markierung) 912
hyponyme 635, 914
Hyponymie 1076
Hypothetisches im etymologischen Wörterbuch 1325

I

Ianua Linguarum, Vokabulare dazu 2376
Iban 2564, 2566
Iban-English 2566
iconographie 1583
ideal dictionary user 209ff.
— user 209
ideale Textsorten des textsortenbezogenen Wörterbuches 1540
Identifikationsfunktion, nationale, des gesamtsprachbezogenen Wörterbuches 1402
identity of dictionaries, manipulations by publishers 97ff.
Ideogramm 1687
ideogram 2475
ideographic script 297
idéologie 79ff., 605f.
Ideologie in der Vornamenlexikographie 1269
Ideologiesprache 836
idéologique 1821, 1470
ideologisches Wörterbuch 1777
  s. Begriffswörterbuch
Ideologisierung der Lexikographie 27, 2058f., 2111, 2131ff.
idiom 1098, 2721, 2783ff.
  s. Phrasem
— as a headword 302
Idiomatik 1184, 2790, 3025
  s. Phraseographie
  s. Phraseologie
— und Wörterbuch 25
—, mehrsprachige 2920f.
Idiomatikforschung 1019
Idiomatizität 1026, 2877
Idiomatizitätstyp, lexikographisch relevanter 596
idiosyncrasy 2787
idiosyncratic phrases 2722
Idiotika des 18. Jhs. 1394
Idiotikenprogramm der 2. Hälfte des 18. Jhs. 1233
Idiotikensammlung als Programm im 18. Jh. 237
Idiotikographie 2049

— des Deutschen 2059
idiotismes 2981
Ido 3129
Igbo 2648
Ignaciano 2703
ijekavisch 2288
Ik 2643
ikavisch 2288
Ikon 3158
ikonisches Zeichen 3148
ikonographische Symbole 3149
Il nuovo Zingarelli 757
　　s. NR: N. Zingarelli
Illokution 815
illokutionsvollziehende Sprechhandlungspartikel 823f.
illustration [engl.] 1084, 1508, 1976, 1988, 2785
illustration [franz.] 284, 1376, 1470, 1826
Illustration 704ff., 992, 1105, 1383, 1836, 1947, 1976, 2906
　　s. Abbildung,
　　s. Bild
Illustrationstyp 710ff.
illustrierte zweisprachige Wörterbücher mit Polnisch 3065f.
illustriertes Wörterbuch 1103, 2106, 2202f., 3065
Illyrisch 2288
illyrische Wiedergeburtsbewegung 2290
Ilokano 2571
image 1387, 1836
　　s. Bild,
　　s. Illustration
image of dictionaries in the USA 34ff.
— of the dictionary 103 f.
implicit material 2720
Implikation 615
implizite Angabe 429ff., 446
— Definition 612
— Norm 194f.
inclusion 1972
indentation of lemmas 1087
index 339, 1085, 1127, 1563, 1567, 1874
　　s. Belegstellenwörterbuch,
　　s. Index 1567,
　　s. Wortformenindex
index cumulatif final 1675
— général 636
Index und Konkordanz, Benutzbarkeit 1568
—, Benutzer 1568
—, Herstellung 1567
—, Herstellungsprobleme 1569
—, kritische Edition als Textgrundlage 1569
—, Nutzung 1568
—, Textbasis 1569

—, Veröffentlichung 1568
—, Veröffentlichungsformen 1571
Index, lemmatisierter 1567
　　s. Wortindex
—, philologische Bearbeitung 1571
—, Vollständigkeit 1569
Indexarbeit, Programme 1572
Indexerstellung, Lemmatisierung als Problem 1571
—, Textzerlegung 1570
—, Wortbegriff der Lexikographie 1570
Indian-English 3097, 3100
indication de fréquence 701
　　s. Frequenzangabe
— syntaxique 1373
indicator 2785
Indikatoren für partikelbezogene Textsegmente 807f.
individuelle vs. institutionelle Lexikographie 1601
Individuum und Team in normativer Lexikographie 65f.
Indizierung als Terminus für Markierung 649
Indonesian 2563
Indonesian dictionaries 3172
Indonesian-Japanese 3113
industrie de la langue 1673
inflection and headwords 300
inflectional information, individual articles 521ff.
inflectual morphology, information 518ff.
　　s. grammatische Angabe
—, model paradigms 520f.
—, types of information 519
inflectual paradigm, variants and gaps 523f.
influence of dictionary on usage 1951, 2685
infolio 323
Informanten- und Corpussprache, 1323
Informantenbefragung in der Lexikographie, Probleme 1616
—, Fachlexikographie 1628
—, Typen 1615
Informantenbeleg und Gewinnung lexikographischer Daten 1615
Informantensprache 1323, 1589
information morphoétymologique 943
information and computer 1646ff.
— on inflectional morphology 518ff.
— on syntactic constructions 588ff.

— program 340
　　s. Informationsprogramm,
　　s. Mikrostrukturenprogramm
— types 341ff.
—, amount of 2787
—, diachronic identifying 341
—, different kinds of semantic 342
—, etymological 525ff.
—, —, criticism 527f.
—, —, European history 525f.
—, —, presentation 528f.
—, —, purposes 526f.
—, —, scope 527f.
—, explanatory 341
—, grammatical 756ff.
—, inflectional, individual articles 521ff.
—, paradigmatic 342
—, synchronic identifying 341
—, syntagmatic 341f., 1975
Information, lexikographische 427
Informationen zum Lemma im Wörterbuch einer rekonstruierten Sprache 1336
Informationsdichte 982
Informationskern eines Wörterbuchs 417
Informationspositionen des onomasiologischen Wörterbuches 1062
—, interpretative 1597
— des historischen Wörterbuches 1594
Informationsprogramm 417, 420, 457
　　s. information program,
　　s. Mikrostrukturenprogramm
—, lexikographisches 416
Informationssprache, nicht-homologe 6
Informationstypen
　　s. Angabeklassen
— des onomasiologischen Wörterbuches 1058
— in Vornamenbüchern 1270
— textsortenbezogener Wörterbücher 1542
informatique 180, 1673, 1873
　　s.computer and lexicography,
　　s. data processing,
　　s. Datenverarbeitung
informatisation 1215, 1587, 3059
infralemmatisch 2729
infralemmatische Adresse 2729f., 2747
　　s. nichtlemmatische Adressierung,
　　s. non-lemmatic addressing
Inga 2705
Ingessana 2643

Ingrisch 2383
Ingush 2421
initialalphabetische Anordnungsform 380ff.
initialalphabetische Makrostruktur 382
— und Zugriffsstruktur 393ff.
inner access structure 329, 338
   s. innere Zugriffsstruktur
— rapid access structure 338
   s. innere Schnellzugriffsstruktur
— selection 337
innere Selektion 2121, 2159, 2207
— Vollständigkeit 1592, 2124
— Wörterbuchgeschichte 2101f.
— Zugriffsstruktur 393, 2172
inselnordische Lexikographie 1928ff.
insert 331
   s. Einschub,
   s. intertext
Instabilität, semantische 837
institutionelle vs. individuelle Lexikographie 1601
instruction for the user of dictionaries 92
   s. Benutzerhinweis,
   s. user's guide
instructive purpose of dictionaries 289
Instrumentalität des Wörterbuches 21
intégrat 355
Integrat 484, 535, 2748
   s. Teilstrukturen von Mikrostrukturen
—, präzedentives 484, 2120
—, vollständiges präzedentives 484
integrated microstructure 354
   s. integrierte Mikrostruktur
integratives lineares Suprasegment 375f., 428
— flächiges Suprasegment 375
Integratkern 484
—, Definition 485
integrierte linkserweiterte Mikrostruktur 490f.
integrierte Mikrostruktur 435, 483ff., 2137ff., 2748
— Mikrostruktur mit binnenerweiterter Basisstruktur 493f., 2154
— rechtserweiterte Mikrostruktur 491f., 2109, 2150, 2206
Intensity of the microstructure 2892
intentionelle Paradigmatik 2794
interaction langagière 678
Interglossat 447, 469
Interjektion 823

—, emotive 823, 824
—, schallnachahmende 823
Interlingua 3130
interlingual dictionaries 2854
— hyperonymy 2718
— hyponymy 2718
— synonyme 2718
Interlingue 3130
intern erweiterte Mikrostruktur 493ff., 2140
— vollständig erweiterte Mikrostruktur 478
— vollständig erweiterte Mikrostruktur, Definition 478
internationalisms 2723
Internationalismenwörterbuch 1179ff.
Internationalismus 1168, 1179, 1225
   s. Europäismus
interne Erweiterung von Wörterbuchartikeln 475
— Etymologie 1336
— Norm 194
Internkommentar 475
interpretative Informationsposition 1597
Interstruktur, linke 476
intertexte 331
   s. Einschub,
   s. insert
Intertextualität und Zitatenwörterbuch 1044
Introspektion und Gewinnung lexikographischer Daten 1613
— und Qualität des Wörterbuches 1614
—, ihre Zuverlässigkeit 1613
Intuition in der Lexikographie 1614
— und Methode 1638
Inuit 2631
inventaire lexicographique 1469
Inventar als Terminus 374
inventory 1509
inverted microstructure 1088
Irisch-Deutsch 2344
Irisch-Englisch 2339
Irisch-Französisch 2344
Iroquoian 2691
Irula 2521
Iselardic sagas, their lexicography 1935
Iškāšmī-Sanglēčī 2481
Isländisch 1928
—, Grundzüge der Sprachgeschichte 1925
—, historische Sprachstufen 1928
Isländisch-Dänisch 1929
Isländisch-Englisch 1929
Isländisch-Lateinisch 1929
Isländisch-Niederländisch 1929

Isländisch-Russisch 1929
Isoglosse 1337
Isomorphie von Teilstrukturen
— von Mikrostrukturen 354, 2163
isomorphisme 2863
Italian 3116, 3174
Italian lexicography and the works of Dante 148
—, its history 147
Italian-Amharic 2451
Italian-Armenian 2369f.
Italian-English 2950, 2970ff.
Italian-French 2970, 2972
Italian-Harari 2453
Italian-Me'en 2643
Italian-Nubian 2643
Italian-Somali 2464
Italian-Tigrinya 2450f.
Italian-Urdu 3101
italien 2991
italien-anglais 2956
italien-espagnol 2591ff.
italien-français 3007ff.
italien-latin 3008
Italienisch 1844, 3015, 3022
Italienisch-Deutsch 2795, 2802, 2907, 2910, 3013ff.
Italienisch-Englisch 1848f.
Italienisch-Französisch 1846, 2999, 3013, 3015
Italienisch-Friaulisch 1901
Italienisch-Katalanisch 1776
Italienisch-Kroatisch 2289, 2938
Italienisch-Kurdisch 2483
Italienisch-Lateinisch 1313
Italienisch-Polnisch 3064
Italienisch-Rumänisch 1882
Italienisch-Sardisch 1902
Italienisch-Spanisch 1848
Italienisch-Ungarisch 2378
italienische Lexikographie des 16./17. Jhs. 10
Itbayaten 2571
Itelmen 2628
item 905
   s. Angabe
— giving the declination 345
   s. Deklinationsangabe
— giving the form of the lemma sign 345
   s. Lemmazeichengestaltangabe
— giving the gender 345
   s. Genusangabe
— giving the plural form 346
   s. Pluralbildungsangabe
— giving the singular form 346
   s. Singularbildungsangabe
— structure 346
   s. Angabestruktur
itemalphabetisch 1100, 2748
itemalphabetisches Prinzip 2748

Itonama 2703
Itza 2661
Ixil 2661

J

Jacaranda 2637
Jaqi languages 2684
Jakutisch 2407
Jamaica 1492
jambage 142
Janjero 2462
Japan 3172
Japanese 3108, 3113, 3176
Japanese-Ainu 3113
Japanese-Arabic 3113
Japanese-Burmese 3113
Japanese-Cambodian 3113
Japanese-Chinese 3110
Japanese-English 2620, 3115
Japanese-Ethiopian 3113
Japanese-German 3116
Japanese-Greek 3113
Japanese-Hausa 3113
Japanese-Hebrew 3113
Japanese-Hindi 3113
Japanese-Hungarian 3113
Japanese-Indonesian 3113
Japanese-Korean 3113
Japanese-Latin 3113
Japanese-Marathi 3101
Japanese-Mongolian 3113
Japanese-Pali 3113
Japanese-Persian 3113
Japanese-Polish 3113
Japanese-Portuguese 3113
Japanese-Rumanian 3113
Japanese-Russian 3116
Japanese-Sanskrit 3113
Japanese-Spanish 3116
Japanese-Swahili 3113
Japanese-Swedish 3113
Japanese-Tibetan 3113
Japanese-Turkish 3113
Japanese-Vietnamese 3113
Japanisch-Katalanisch 1776
Japanisch-Portugiesisch 2619, 3021
Japanisch-Russisch 2619
Japanisch-Slowenisch 2299
japanische Lexikographie 2617ff.
Japhetic alphabet 2420
Jaqaru 2684
Jaqi 2684
Jargon 1184, 1524
javanais 1532
Javanese-English 2562
Javanese lexicography 2561ff.
Javanisch-Bahasia Indonesia 2800

Jebel 2643
Jenjero 2462
jeu de mot, dictionnaire 1349
Jiddisch-Russisch 3078
Jieng 2642
Jingpho 2558
Jingpho-Nung 2558
Jinuo 2559
Jirel 2558
Jirru 2644
Jivaroan 2703
Jiwarli 2639
Jo'rai 2593
Juang 2536
Juang-English 2542f.
Juárez Zapotec 2698
Judenspanisch-Bulgarisch 1906
Judenspanisch-Englisch 1906
Judenspanisch-Französisch 1906
Junktor 1221
Jurak 2398
Juray 2544

K

Kaba 2644
Karbadian-Russian 2420
kabyle 2455
Kachin-Nung 2555
Kado 2642
Kadugli 2643
Kadugli-English 2643
Kaffa 2462
Kafir 2651
Kaike 2558
Kaingang 2707
Kaíwá 2671
kajkavisch 2288
Kalahari 2655
Kalam 2636
Kalenjin 2642
Kalmückisch 2626
Kalmückisch-Russisch 2625
Kamano 2636
Kamarupan 2555
Kamassian 2395
Kamayuara 2671
Kambera 2564
Kamchadal 2628
Kamilaraay 2639
Kana 2617
Kanakuru 2457
Kanbera 2566
Kanembu 2642
Kanhobal 2661
kanji 2617
Kannaḍa 2521, 3096
Kannaḍa-English 2524f., 3100

Kannaḍa-Hindi 3098
Kannaḍa-Malayalam 3098
kanonische Form 365, 736, 2625
 s. canonical form,
 s. forme canonique,
 s. Zitierform
Kanuri 2642
Kapampangan 2571
Kapampangan-Spanish 2571
Kapauku 2636
Kara 2644
Karachanidisch 2410
Karaimisch 2409
Karagass 2395
Karakalpakisch 2408
Karelisch 2383
Karen 2555, 2559, 2591
Karenic 2556
Karitiana 2704
Karo Batak 2564
Kartvelian 2415
Kartvelian lexicography 2415ff.
Kasachisch 2408
Kasachisch-Chinesisch 2410
Kashmiri 2513, 3096
Kashmiri-English 3100f.
Kashmiri-Persian 2513
Kashmiri-Sanskrit 2513
Kassite 1692
Kassite-Babylonian 1692
Katalanisch 1770, 2917, 2938
Katalanisch-Deutsch 1776
Katalanisch-Englisch 11776
Katalanisch-Italienisch 1776
Katalanisch-Japanisch 1776
Katalanisch-Portugiesisch 1776
Katalanisch-Spanisch 1775
Kâte 2636
Kategorie als Terminus in der Linguistik 2824f.
kategoriell-alphabetische Sortierung 2749
kategoriell-semantisch-alphabetische Sortierung 2749
Kategorisierungsmodifikatoren 857ff.
katharevusa 1707
Kauderwelsch-Sprechführer 2906
 s. Typologie der Reisewörterbücher
Kawahyb 2671
Kawesqar 2709
Kawi 2561
Kawki 2684
Kawurna 2639
Kayabí 2671
Kayah 2559
Kayardild 2639
Kayardild-English 2639
Kazakh 2408

Kechwa 2705
Keilschrift, akkadische 1686
Keilschriftluwisch 1687
Kekchi 2661
Kemant 2463
Kembata 2463f.
Kennwortforschung 1428
Kenzi 2643
Kera 2539, 2458
Kerek 2628
Kerkük 2408
Kernstruktur 471ff.
   s. core structure
—, linke 471f.
—, linke konkrete hierarchische 2162
—, rechte 472f., 2114, 2119, 2141, 2146, 2158, 2164, 2206
—, — basisexterne 2143
—, vordere linke 2158
Kernwortschatz 1353
Ket 2628
Kewa 2636
keyword (in a thesaurus) 1087
Khaling 2558
Khalkha 2626
Kham 2558
Khanty 2395
Kharia 2534
Kharia-English 2542
Kharia-German 2542
Kharia-Hindi 310
Khazara 2481
Kheza 2558
Khmer 2590
Khmu' 2591
Khoe-Kowap 2655
Khoi-khoin 2654
Khoisan 2650ff.
Khorasan Turk 2408
Khufi 2481
K(h)ung 2650
Khwarezmian 2473, 2476
Kiche 2661
Kičua 2705
kiLuba 2648
Kinderwörterbuch 1050, 1365ff.
   s. dictionnaire pour enfants
Kiptschakisch 2407, 2625
Kirgisisch 2408
Kirgisisch-Russisch 3078
kiRundi 2648
Klamath 2695
Klammerkonvention bei phonetischen Angaben 512
Klassen von funktionalen Textsegmenten 426ff.
Klassifikation 968f.
— von Makrostrukturen 382ff.
klassisches Definitionsverfahren 555

Kleincorpus 1593
Kleine Idiomatik der deutschen Sprache von Görner 2175ff.
Kleines Hessisches Wörterbuch von Friebertshäuser 2200f.
— vogtländisches Wörterbuch von Bergmann u. Hellfritzsch 2199f.
— Wörterbuch des DDR-Wortschatzes von Kinne u. Strube-Edelmann 2187f.
Kleinwörterbuch 3064
KLT-Dialekt 2347
Kluges etymologisches Wörterbuch 2193f.
   s. NR: F. Kluge
Knaurs Deutsches Wörterbuch 331, 338
— etymologisches Wörterbuch 2195f.
— Großes Wörterbuch der deutschen Sprache 378, 380, 387ff., 531, 2108, 2156, 2159, 2162ff. 2170
Kodagu 2521
Kognate 1335
Kognatreihe 1335
Kohärenz 452, 609, 947f.
Kohäsion 452
Koiné 1697
Kolami 2521
Kollokation 608, 612, 777, 892, 1052, 2743, 3003
   s. collocation
— fachsprachlicher Art 1625
— in den Wörterbüchern des Niederländischen 2016
Kollokationsangabe 2121, 2137
Kollokationspartner 2736
Kollokationssammlung 1081
Kollokationswörterbuch 979, 1076, 2878
   s. dictionnaire de collocations,
   s. Fügungswörterbuch
Kollokationswörterbücher des Deutschen 2177
Koman 2642f.
kombinationsalphabetisch 1144
Kombinem 1224ff.
Komi 2395
Kommentar als Terminus für die Verzeichnisse von älteren Kurzschriftsystemen 3140
Kommentar zur Komposition 482, 2139
— zur lexikalischen Bedeutung 488, 2147f.
   s. comment on lexical meaning
— zur lexikalischen Teilbedeutung 482
   s. comment on lexical partial meaning

—, basisexterner semantischer 2143
—, enzyklopädischer 1172
—, lexikographischer 432
—, lexikographischer, im textsortenbezogenen Wörterbuch 1547
—, normativer 199
   s. commentaire normatif
—, offener lexikographischer 434
—, semantischer 434, 621, 1423, 2113, 2149
—, semantischer basisexterner 2143
—, semantischer, im Autorenwörterbuch 1554
—, sprachreflexiver 807
Kommentarsprache im etymologischen Wörterbuch 1324
kommentierende Angabe 432ff.
kommentierendes Wörterbuch 1045
Kommentierungsvokabular 806
kommerzielles Wörterbuch des heutigen Niederländischen 1433
Komo 2643
komparatives Prädikat 431
Kompatibilität, internationale, der Berufsbezeichnungen 1249
kompetente Körperschaft und normative Lexikographie 67
Kompetenz des Translators in Arbeitskulturen 171
Kompetenzbeispielangabe 437, 535, 2114, 2150
   s. Beispiel,
   s. example,
   s. exemple
Kompetenzbeispielangabe, verdichtete 431, 568
Komplexbildung, Prinzipien der 864
komplexe Namenstruktur 1268
Komposita 2116, 2134
   s. mot composé
— im zweisprachigen Wörterbuch 2779ff.
— und Äquivalenz 2781f.
Kompositaangabe 2116, 2118, 2162
Kompositaangaben als Beispielangaben 2142
Kompositagruppenangabe 433, 468
Kompositanester 2795
Kompositumangabe 490, 2117, 2148
Konda 2521
Kondensat 449, 958, 2837
— und Leittext 960f.

— und Volltext 959f.
Kondensierung 366
  s. Textverdichtung 958
Kondensierungsprozeß 366
Konferenz für Sicherheit und Zu-
  sammenarbeit in Europa
  (KSZE) 1
Konfix 869, 1225
Kongruenz 2716
Konjugationsangabe 433, 468
  s. information on inflectional
  morphology
Konjugationsmusterangabe
  2162f.
Konjugationswörterbuch 1312
Konjunktion 862ff., 1221
Konkani 3096
Konkani-English 3100
Konkani-Portuguese 3101
Konkordanz 1567
  s. Belegtextwörterbuch,
  s. concordance
— mit rückläufigem Formenver-
  zeichnis 1132
Konkordanz und Index, Benutz-
  barkeit 1568
—, Benutzer 1568
—, Herstellung 1567
—, Herstellungsprobleme 1569
—, kritische Edition als Textgrundlage 1569
—, Nutzung 1568
—, Textbasis 1569
—, Veröffentlichung 1568
—, Veröffentlichungsformen
  1571
konkrete hierarchische linke
  Kernstruktur 2162
— hierarchische Mikrostruktur
  464ff.
  s. concrete hierarchical microstructure
— hierarchische Mikrostruktur,
  Definition 465
— Mikrostruktur 412ff., 440
— partitive Mikrostruktur, Definition 466
— präzedentive Mikrostruktur
  466
  s. concrete precedential
  microstructure
— präzedentive Mikrostruktur,
  Definition 466
Konnektor 864
Konnotation 618, 653
  s. connotation
Konso 2463f.
Konstruktion 2828
  s. construction
—, endozentrische 1061
—, exozentrische 1061
Konstruktionsangabe 2732

Konstruktionswörterbuch
  1000ff., 1768
  s. Valenzwörterbuch
—, bilinguales 1002
—, Frequenzen 1001
—, Funktionen 1001
—, Geschichte 1004ff.
—, kontrastives 2878
—, makrostrukturelle Unterschiede 1001
—, mikrostrukturelle Merkmale
  1001ff.
Konstruktlemma 365, 1422
Kontaktdatierungsangabe 2204f.
Kontext, semantisch relevanter
  2142
Kontextkommentar, semanti-
  scher 2149
Kontextrestriktionen 2793
Kontextwörterbuch 2879
Kontinuant als Teil von Kognat-
  reihen 1335
  s. Äquat
kontinuierliches Lemma 364
kontrastive Synonymik 2879
kontrastives Lokalwörterbuch
  2201
Konua 2636ff.
Konventionalität von Fachaus-
  drücken als Selektionskriterium für das Fachwörterbuch
  1627
Konvergenz 2716
Konversationslexikon 1206
— des 18./19. Jhs. 12
Konyak 2558
Koon 2656
Koordination 864
Koptisch 1679
Koptisch-Arabisch 1680
Kora 2651
Korean 2611
Korean-English 2615f.
Korean-Japanese 2615, 3113
Korean lexicography 2611ff.
Korku 2537
Kornisch 2348
Kornisch-Englisch 2348
Korpus
  s. corpus,
  s. Corpus
— als Grundlage für die lexiko-
  graphische Datenerhebung
  1619
— von Fachtexten, seine Aus-
  wertung in der Fachlexikogra-
  phie 1628
—, lexikographisches 2131
  s. Wörterbuchbasis
Korpusgröße in der Lexikogra-
  phie 1621
Korpusprinzip 2131, 2176, 2184

Korpuswörterbuch 774
Korrana(h) 2655
Korrekturhandbuch, Konstruk-
  tionswörter als 1001
Korwa 2538
Koryak 2628
Kōta 2521, 2529
Kotextangabe 2734ff.
Kotextkategorisatoren 2736
Kott 2628
Kott-German 2628
Kōya 2521
Kräuterbuch 1254
Kresh 2644
Kreuzworträtsellexikographie
  1144
Kreuzworträtselwörterbuch 1100
Krimtatarisch 2408
Krio 1494
Kriterien für alteuropäische Ge-
  wässernamen 1285
kritische Edition als Textgrund-
  lage für Indices und Konkor-
  danzen 1569
— Wörterbuchforschung 262
  s. dictionary criticism,
  s. Wörterbuchkritik
Kroatisch-Lateinisch 2289
Kroatoserbisch 2288
Krongo 2643
Kru 2647
Kui 2521, 2591
Kuki 2558
Kuki-Chin-Naga 2555
Kuliak 2642
Kultur und Lexikographie 1f.
kulturell definierte Syntagmatik
  1054
kulturelle vs. sprachliche Infor-
  mation in Wörterbüchern 173
kulturhistorische Information
  und Bedeutungserläuterung
  1426
— Lexikographie 2175
kulturpädagogische Funktion des
  gesamtsprachbezogenen Wör-
  terbuches 1403
— Funktion des textsortenbezo-
  genen Wörterbuches 1540
— Zwecke deutscher Wörter-
  buchprogramme 241
Kultursensitivität von Wörterbü-
  chern und Lexika 171
Kultursprache (Friesisch) 2026
Kulturwissen in der Fachlexikographie 1630
Kulturwörterbuch 1054
Kuman 2638
Kumaoni 3096
Kumükisch 2409

kumulative Synonymenexplikation 621
  s. Synonymengruppenangabe
kumulative Synonymik 1076ff., 1081, 2086f.
—, Benutzbarkeit 2180
kumulative Synonymiken des Deutschen 2177ff.
kumulatives Zitatenwörterbuch 1045
Kunama 2642
!K(h)ung 2650
Kunsa 2706
Kunstsprache (nach Adelung) 312
Kunstwort 1232
Kur 2590
Kurdisch 2481
Kurdisch-Englisch 2483
Kurdisch-Französisch 2483
Kurdisch-Russisch 2483
Kuṟukh 2521
Kuṟukh-Hindi 3100
Kurzschriften 3137
Kurzschriftenwörterbücher 3137ff.
Kuvi 2521
Kuyonon 2571
Kwa 2647
Kwama 2643
Kwegu 2643
Kymrisch 2347
Kyonggi 2614
Kyongsang 2614

L

Laaz 2247
label 649, 1384, 1948, 2785, 2965
  s. Markierung
Ladino 1906
Lagowa 2644
Lahu 2559
Laienbenutzer 128ff.
—, Typen 129
Laienbenutzung, fremdsprachliche 130f.
—, muttersprachliche 130f.
Laienwörterbuch 2911
Lak 2421
Lakandon 2661
Lakher 2559
Lamé 2458
landschaftlich markierter Wortschatz 1166
landschaftliches Idiotikon im 18. Jh. 237ff.
Landschaftsname 1277
landsmål (Neo-Norwegian) 1925f.
Langenscheidts Deutsches Wörterbuch 2114ff.

Langeweile durch das Wörterbuch 20f.
language change and lexicography 74
— change and the user of dictionaries 76
— development and lexicography 70
—, definition 294
langue cible 2817, 2860, 2863
— de description 2861
  s. lexikographische Beschreibungssprache
— morte 2866
— orale 604
— source 2817, 2864
Languedokisch 1895
langue-Lexikographie und Datenerhebung 1592
langues auxiliaires 3120
  s. Hilfssprachen
langues-objets 2861
Lappisch 2916
Lappisch-Deutsch 2389
lateinamerikanische Lexikographie 1751
Lateinisch 1771, 1844, 3020
Lateinisch-Altenglisch 2348, 2937
Lateinisch-Deutsch 2037f., 2045, 2939, 3073
Lateinisch-Englisch 2734
Lateinisch-Französisch 2794, 2998
Lateinisch-Gotisch 1910
Lateinisch-Griechisch 1714
Lateinisch-Italienisch 3032
Lateinisch-Katalanisch 1739, 1771
Lateinisch-Kirchenslawisch 3070
Lateinisch-Kroatisch 2289
Lateinisch-Niederländisch 2939
Lateinisch-Portugiesisch 1725f., 3020f.
Lateinisch-Rumänisch 1882, 1884
Lateinisch-Russisch 3075, 3078
Lateinisch-Slowakisch 2284f.
Lateinisch-Spanisch 1738f., 1741, 1771
Lateinisch-Türkisch 2402
Lateinisch-Ungarisch 2375ff.
Lateinisch-Wayapi 2675
lateinische Lexikographie 1713ff., 3030ff.
— Wortäquivalentangabe 2144
Latin data bank 1719
Latin in the Deutsches Wörterbuch 227
Latin-Armenian 2367, 2370
Latin-English 1950, 2711, 2970
latin-français 1788f.
Latin-Ge'ez 2449
Latin-Japanese 3113

Latin-Spanish 2697, 2950
Latin-Swedish 1934
Latin-Vietnamese 2583f.
Lau 2574
Lawa 2591
Laz 2415
layout 1365, 2961
Laz 2415
learned society and Swedish lexicograph 1934
learner's dictionary 184, 1219, 1379, 1972, 2888
  s. Lernerwörterbuch
learning by heart as lexicographic medium 2498
— dictionaries 2883
left core structure 354
  s. linke Kernstruktur
— partial core structure 356
  s. linke Teilkernstruktur
legal terminology in Danish lexicography 1916f.
legibility 2961
Lehnbildung 1920
Lehnwort 1168
Lehnwörterbuch 2193
  s. Fremdwörterbuch
Lehnwortschatz 1231
Lehrbuch 1106, 1109, 3070
Leistung des Wörterbuchs einer rekonstruierten Sprache 1337
Leitadresse 2747ff.
Leitbegriff 2176
Leitelement 338, 363, 372, 445, 2749
  s. guiding element
Leitelementträger 372, 380, 450, 2175
—, registerinterner 394
Leitform 41
Leittext und Kondensat 960f.
Leitvarietät 2104
Leitwort 1200, 2790
Leitwörterbuch 960, 2102, 2140, 2170
Lemma 328, 360ff., 397, 949, 1057, 1946, 2112, 2720, 2730, 2816
  s. entrée,
  s. entry,
  s. headword,
  s. lemme,
  s. mot vedette,
  s. Stichwort
— als Konstrukt 1422
  s. Konstruktlemma
— im Sprachstadienwörterbuch 1421
— im Wörterbuch einer rekonstruierten Sprache 1336
— und bearbeitete Einheit 397
— und Schrift 2617

—, Definition 363
—, diskontinuierliches 364
—, kontinuierliches 364
lemma file 336
   s. Lemmareihe
lemma-clustering 336
lemma sign 329
   s. Lemmazeichen
Lemmaansetzen 365
Lemmaauswahl
   s. äußere Selektion
Lemmabestand 1076
— von Ortsnamenbüchern 1278
lemmaexterner Nesteingang 365, 391
Lemmaform im gesamtsprachbezogenen Wörterbuch 1404
Lemmalücke 386
Lemmaposition 364, 368
Lemmaregister zu rückläufigen Wörterbüchern 1132
Lemmareihe 336
   s. Artikelstrecke,
   s. lemma file
—, vertikale 385
Lemmataanzahl, Berechnung der 2117, 2127
Lemmataaufnahme
   s. Selektion, äußere
Lemmateil 365
Lemmateil und Teillemma 368
lemmatic addressing 349
   s. lemmatische Adressierung
lemmatisation 308, 507, 1564
   s. Lemmatisierung,
   s. lemmatization
lemmatisch adressierte Bedeutungsparaphrasenangabe 538
lemmatische Adressierung
— Adressierung, vollständige 446
— Vollständigkeit 1592
Lemmatisieren 365
lemmatisierter Index 1567
— Wortindex 153
Lemmatisierung 380, 858f., 919, 1101
   s. lemmatization
— als Problem 1422
— als Problem bei der Indexerstellung 1571
— von Verben 2109
—, motivationelle 646
Lemmatisierungsaufgabe 366
Lemmatisierungskonvention 365
Lemmatisierungsverfahren 366
lemmatization 337, 518, 2723, 2813ff.
   s. Lemmatisierung
Lemmatyp 360ff.
Lemmawahl im etymologischen Wörterbuch 1330

Lemmawörterbuch, rückläufiges 1135
Lemmazeichen 329, 363, 364, 445
   s. lemma sign
Lemmazeichengestaltangabe 376, 429, 434, 445, 2116, 2123
   s. item giving the form of the lemma sign
—, binnenerweiterte 2123, 2158, 2163
—, rechtserweiterte 2123
—, um eine Silbentrennungsangabe binnenerweiterte und um eine Wortakzentangabe unten erweiterte 2158
—, unten erweiterte 2158, 2163
Lemmazeichenparadigma 431, 446
Lemmazeichentyp 453
lemme 1563
   s. entry word,
   s. head word,
   s. Lemma,
   s. mot vedette,
   s. Stichwort
Lepcha 2558
Lernerwörterbuch 132, 745
   s. learner's dictionary
Lernfunktion 2741, 2795
Lernlexikographie, einsprachige für Ausländer 15
Lernwörterbuch 129, 2160, 2852
Lesebuchfunktion 3031
Lesewörterbuch 184, 2716, 2988
Lettgalisch-Russisch 2358
Lettisch-Deutsch 2357
Lettisch-Englisch 2357, 2359
Lettisch-Französisch 2357
Lettisch-Litauisch 2357
Lettisch-Russisch 57, 2357, 3078
Lettisch-Schwedisch 2359
lettrine 138
Lexem 642ff., 1224, 2779
—, Definition 642f.
—, einfaches und komplexes 642
Lexembildungslehre, Aufgaben 643
Lexemdefinition, sprachbezogener Ansatz 642
Lexemverbindungen 2779
lexical database 2724
   s. base de données,
   s. Datenbank
— information in dictionaries, definition 290
— meaning 3158
   s. lexikalische Bedeutung
— meaning, its determination in dictionaries 292
lexicalisation 938
lexicographer 1980
   s. Lexikograph

—, academic instruction 95f.
—, his qualifications 92f.
—, his training 93
—, on-the-job instruction 95
—, requirements for editional positions 95
—, training through in-house programs 96f.
lexicographic evidence 1979
lexicographical category 2784
— coverage 336, 2962
   s. Abdeckung
— label and convention, misunderstandings by users 33
— principles 287ff.
   s. Grundprinzip der Lexikographie
— programmes in English lexicography 1436
— project, problems of consistency 227
— style 2952
   s. Wörterbuchstil
lexicographie automatique
   s. computer and lexicography
— bilingue 2711
— bilingue avec le danois 3051ff.
— computationnelle
   s. computer and lexicography
— d'apprentissage 2958
— espagnole
   s. spanische Lexikographie
— française 1788ff.
   s. French Lexicography
— italienne 1863ff.
lexicography and laws of language 287
— and terminology 72, 167f.
— as a purposeful humen activity 287
— as act of communication 291
— as an academic discipline 95
   s. Lexikographie und andere Disziplinen
— of Ancient Greek 1694ff.
— of Byzantine and modern Greek 1705ff.
— of Colonial Quechua 2676ff.
— of Indonesian 2563ff.
— of New Indo-Aryan 2507ff.
— of Nilo Saharan 2642ff.
— of Old Indo-Aryan 2487ff.
— of Old Prussian 2351ff.
— of scots 1983ff.
— of the Eskimo-Alent languages 2631ff.
— of the Khoisan languages 2649ff.
— of the languages of New Guinea 2636ff.
— of the languages of the Andian indians 2704ff.

- of the languages of the Indians of the Orinoco and Amazon area 2700ff.
- of the languages of the Mesoamerican indians 2697ff.
- of the languages of the North American indians 2691ff.
- of the Munda languages 2533ff.
- of the Near East 1690ff.
- of the Niger-Kordofanian languages 2646ff.
- of the Palaesiberian languages 2627ff.
—, bilingual 2854ff.
 s. zweisprachige Lexikographie
—, commercial aspects 88ff.
—, distribution of costs 89
—, English: German influences 1446
—, English: patriotism 1440
—, English: Tudor and Stuart words 1452
—, historical English: computerization 1454
—, historical English: sense ordering 1451
—, historical English: transferred sense 1450
—, ideological aspects 32
 s. Ideologisierung der Lexikographie
—, interests of users 89
—, its function in society 1f., 100
—, market research 88, 92
—, Old English: computerization 1443
—, Old English: phonological principles 1442
—, organizational aspects 89
lexicological categories 2784
lexicology 1071
Lexicon 2912, 3014
- in Veteris Testamenti libros 2428
- Novi Testamenti Graeco-Latino-Belgicum
- novum herbarium tripartitum 2916
- Poeticum 1929
- rei herbaricae trilingue 2915
- Slavonicum 3071
- Syriacum 2432
- palaeoslovenico-graeco-latinum emendatum auctum 2261
 s. NR: F. Miklosich
- Tetraglotton 1088
- trilingue, ex Thesauro Roberti Stephani et Dictionario Joannis Frisii collectum 2912

lexie 602
Lexik der Sprache als System 1639
lexikalische Bedeutung 543ff., 810
 s. lexical meaning
- Einheit 971
- Kategorisierung im zweisprachigen Wörterbuch 2824ff.
- Liste 1680
- Paraphrase 620, 807
 s. Bedeutungsparaphrasenangabe
- Relation im onomasiologischen Wörterbuch 1061
- Synonymie 618
 s. Synonymie,
 s. synonymie,
 s. synonymy
lexikalsemantischer Wandel 2197
Lexikograph 266ff.
 s. lexicographer
- und Datenerhebung 1589
Lexikographenjargon 2123
Lexikographie Adelungs 2054ff.
Lexikographie als Terminus 246ff.
Lexikographie als wissenschaftliche Praxis 253
- archaischer und untergegangener Wörter 1234
- Baileys 1944ff.
- Campes 491, 2057f.
- der deutschen Standardsprache 2104ff.
- der deutschen Umgangssprache 2201ff.
- der Fremdsprache 6ff.
- der Grimms 2079f.
 s. Deutsches Wörterbuch
- der Kurzschriften 3137ff.
- der Mayasprachen 2661ff.
- der Mundarten des späten 19. und 20. Jhs. 1233
- der neukeltischen Sprachen 2343ff.
- der Plansprachen 3120ff.
- des Althochdeutschen 1418ff., 2087f., 2104
- des Altpersischen 2471f.
- des amerikanischen Spanisch 1751ff.
- des Avestischen 2471
- des Calepinus 1715f.
- des Deutschen, Geschichte 2101ff.
- des Esperanto 3120ff.
- des Forcellini 1716f.
- des Frühneuhochdeutschen 1418ff., 2104
- des Larousse 1820f.
- des Manx 2346f.
- des Mittelhochdeutschen 1420ff., 2088, 2104, 2197

- des Stephanus 1715f.
- des Tupī-Guaranī 2670ff.
- deutscher Verben 2189ff.
- Etiennes 1792ff.
- Furetières 1800f.
- Heynes 2084f.
- Heyses 2079
- historischer Sprach- und Varietätenstadien 1234
- in der Lehre 270
- Johnsons 1954f.
- Klappenbachs 2129ff.
 s. Wörterbuch der deutschen Gegenwartssprache
Komenskýs 2279ff., 2914
 s. NR: Comenius
- Kramers 2053
- Küppers 2201ff.
- Littrés 1818ff.
- Mackensens 2115ff.
- Meninskis 2401
- Murrays 1962f.
- Nicots 1792f.
- Pauls 2085
- Richardsons 1957
- Richelets 1796ff.
- Rogets 2086
- Sanders 382, 492, 494, 496, 2083f.
- Steinbachs 2053
- Stielers 2052
- und andere Disziplinen 257
- und angewandte Sprachwissenschaft 249
- und Gesellschaft, Konflikte 12ff.
- und Ideologie 79f., 835ff., 2093f., 2131ff.
- und Lexikologie 247
- und Staatsorganisation 3
- und Tourismus 4
- und Wirtschaft 4
- Wurms 2083
- zu historischen Fachvarietäten 1235
—, afghanische 2483f.
—, afrikaanse 2011ff.
—, ägyptische 1679ff.
—, albanische 2361ff.
—, alt- und mitteltürkische 1412f.
—, altiranische 2470ff.
—, altirische 2339ff.
—, altkirchenslawische 2255ff.
—, altpreußische
 s. lexicography of Old Prussian
—, amerikanische
 s. American lexicography
—, arabische
 s. Arabic lexicography
—, aramäische
 s. Aramaic lexicography

—, armenische
  s. Armenian lexicography
—, australische
  s. Australian lexicography
—, autorbezogene 1590
  s. Autorenlexikographie,
  s. Textlexikographie
—, baskische
  s. Basque lexicography
—, berberische
  s. lexicographie berbère
—, brasilianische 1723
—, bretonische 2347f.
—, bulgarische 2304ff.
—, chinesische
  s. Chinese lexicography
—, dalmatische 1891ff.
—, dänische
  s. Danish lexicography
—, deskriptive 199
—, deutsche 2037ff., 2049ff., 2078ff., 2100ff.
—, drawidische
  s. Dravidian lexicography 2521
—, englische
  s. English lexicography
—, estnische
  s. Estonian lexicography
—, etymologische 1234, 1589
—, Fachsprache der 312
—, Fachumgangssprache der 315
—, färöische 1930
—, finnische 2383ff.
—, französische
  s. lexicographie française
—, friesische 2022ff.
—, georgische
  s. Georgian lexicography
—, gotische 1908ff.
—, hebräische
  s. Hebrew lexicography
—, hispanische: Cuervos Wörterbuch 1767ff.
—, hispanoamerikanische 1752ff.
—, historische 2078ff.
—, individuelle vs. institutionelle 1601
—, indonesische
  s. lexicography of Indonesian
—, inselnordische 1928ff.
—, Intuition 1614
—, irische 2345f.
—, isländische 1928ff.
—, italienische 1844ff.
—, japanische 2617ff.
—, javanische
  s. Javanese lexicography
—, judenspanische 1906ff.
—, kartvelische
  s. Kartvelian lexicography
—, katalanische 1770ff.

—, keltische 1686ff.
—, koptische 1679ff.
—, koreanische
  s. Korean lexicography
—, korelische 2386ff.
—, kornische 2347
—, kulturhistorische 2175
—, kurdische 2481f.
—, kuschitische
  s. lexicography of the Cushitic Languages
—, lappische 2388ff.
—, lateinamerikanische 1751
—, lateinische 1713ff., 3030ff.
—, lettische 2354ff.
—, litauische
  s. Lithuanian lexicography
—, livische,
  s. Livonian lexicography
—, lusitanische 1723
—, makedonische 2302ff.
—, mittelindoarische
  s. lexicography of Middle Indo-Aryan
—, mitteliranische
  s. Middle Iranian lexicography
—, mongolische 2623ff.
—, neuindoarische
  s. lexicography of New Indo-Aryan
—, neuiranische
  s. Iranian lexicography
—, neusprachlich-lateinische 9
—, niederländische 2010ff.
—, nornische 1930f.
—, norwegische
  s. Norwegian lexicography
—, onomasiologische 1057ff., 1083ff., 1590
—, onomastische 1267ff.
—, osmanisch-türkische 2399ff.
—, ossetische 2484
—, persische
  s. Persian lexicography
—, polabische 2271
—, polnische 2268ff.
—, portugiesische 1723ff.
—, provenzalische 1891ff.
—, rätoromanische 1891ff.
—, rumänische 1880ff.
—, russische 2309ff.
—, sardische 1891ff.
—, schottisch-gälische 2346
—, schottische
  s. lexicography of scots
—, schwedische
  s. Swedish lexicography
—, serbokroatische 2288ff.
—, slowakische 2284ff.
—, slowenische 2296ff.
—, sorbische 2274ff.

—, spanische 1738ff.
—, sprachübergreifende semasiologische 1410
—, sumerische und akkadische
  s. Sumarian and Akkadian lexicography
—, terminologisch orientierte 4, 317ff., 1505ff., 1512ff., 2206ff.
—, Theoriesprache der 314
—, Traditionsvermittlung 14
—, tibetische
  s. Tibetan lexicography
—, tschechische 2278ff.
—, ukrainische
  s. Ukrainian lexicography
—, ungarische 2375ff.
—, vedische 2487ff.
—, vietnamesische
  s. Vietnamese lexicography
—, walisische 2347
—, wissenschaftliche 263
lexikographiehistorische Darstellungen, Arten von 2101ff.
— Periodisierung 2103
lexikographiezentrierte Wörterbuchgeschichte 2101
lexikographische Abdeckung 336, 396
  s. coverage
— Angaben, Übersichten 433, 468f.
— Ausgangssprache 2729, 2845
— Bearbeitungseinheit 328, 972, 2729
— Bedeutungserläuterung 621
  s. lexikographische Definition
— Beschreibungssprache 424, 438, 1551, 2051
  s. métalangage,
  s. métalangue
— Datenbasis 1641
  s. Wörterbuchbasis
— Datenerhebung 1588ff., 2202
  s. data collection
— Datentarnung 2204
— Datenverarbeitung
  s. computer and lexicography,
  s. ordinateur
— Definition 531, 533, 850, 896
  s. Bedeutungsangabe,
  s. Bedeutungserklärung,
  s. Bedeutungsparaphrasenangabe,
  s. definition,
  s. définition
lexikographische Definition als Terminus 539
lexikographische Definition und Frame-Theorie 893ff.
— Definition, Anordnung 917ff.
— Entnazifizierung 2106f.
— Erkenntniskurve 1596

— Erzählung 1365
— Information 427
— Nomination 790
— Praxis 251, 681
— Prozesse, Verflechtung der 2122f.
— Regelformulierung 621
— Synonymie 568, 620
— Textsegmente, Übersichten 432f., 468f.
— Textverdichtung 386, 390, 431, 440, 447ff., 534, 807, 956ff., 2114, 2130, 2156, 2837 s. Kondensat
— Theoriesprache 428
— Werkstattsprache 428, 2209
— Wörterbuchpflege 2213ff.
— Zielsprache 2729, 2847
lexikographischer Fragebogen 2202
— Gesamtprozeß 2128, 2167ff.
— Gesamtprozeß bei den Wörterbüchern der deutschen Standardsprache, Übersicht vgl. Faltblätter nach 2188, 2197f.
— Hinweis 428
— Kommentar 432
— Kommentar im textsortenbezogenen Wörterbuch 1547
— Prozeß 2123
— Prozeß, abgeschlossener 2101
— Textbaustein 607
— Verweis 428, 964, 1027f.
  s. cross reference,
  s. renvois,
  s. Verweisangabe,
  s. Verweiskommentar
— Zirkel 161
  s. circularity
lexikographisches Beispiel 426, 607ff., 903f., 964
  s. Beispielangabe,
  s. example,
  s. exemple,
  s. Kompetenzbeispielangabe
— Gliederungszeichen 437
  s. structural indicator,
  s. Strukturanzeiger
— Informationsprogramm 416, 420, 457
  s. information program,
  s. Mikrostrukturenprogramm
— Korpus 2131
  s. corpus,
  s. Wörterbuchbasis
— Programm 419
— Qualitätsprofil 2136
— Textsegment 806
  s. Angabe,
  s. Strukturanzeiger
Lexikon 159f.

— der deutschen Sprachlehre von Ludewig 2146
— der Fachsprache: Einheiten, Kombinationen und Markierungen 1629
— der grammatischen Terminologie von Bohusch 2209f.
— der sprichwörtlichen Redensarten von Röhrich 1035, 2174ff.
— der Sünde von Weiss 2177
— und Wörterbuch 159, 3152
—, wirtschaftskundliches 164ff.
Lexikondefinition als Terminus 532
Lexikoneintrag und Wörterbucheintrag 160
Lexikostatistik 1638
lexique 1469, 1790, 1874
— construit 941
lexiques occultes 2921
Lezghi 2421
Liangmai 2558
Liber ordinis rerum 2039
Limbu 2558
limited word in US-American lexicography 36
Limosinisch 1895
lineares Suprasegment 375
Lingala 2919
lingo 1524
liNgombe 2648
lingua brasílica 2670
— geral 2670
linguicide 2330f.
linguistic degeneration and US-American lexicography 36
— information and outside matter 764
— innovation and US-American lexicography 36
— norm and Danish lexicography 1914
— research and future developments in lexicography 3158ff.
— standard and US-American lexicography 35
Linguistik 159ff.
linguistische Angabe 430
link word 1054
linke hierarchische Kernstruktur, Definition 471
— hierarchische Randstruktur, Definition 474
— Interstruktur 476
— Kernstruktur 471f., 2162
  s. left core structure
— Randstruktur 474, 493, 495ff.
— Teilkernstruktur 488, 2117, 2148, 2158
linker Zwischenkommentar 476, 496

— zur Etymologie 2116
links laufende Zugriffsstruktur 402
Linksauslagerung 450f., 485
linkserweiterte hierarchische Basisstruktur, Definition 477
— hierarchische Mikrostruktur, Definition 474
— Basisstruktur 476
— hierarchische Basisstruktur 477
— Mikrostruktur 474, 490f.
— Mikrostruktur mit links- und rechtserweiterter Basisstruktur 496
— Mikrostruktur mit linkserweiterter Basisstruktur 496
lisibilité 136, 311, 1823
liste des abréviations 2862
Liste, lexikalische 1680
listing 1509
Lisu 2559
Litauisch-Lettisch 2357
Literalismus 1908
literarisches Zeugnis über Wörterbücher 19
Literary Welsh 2347
Literaturangabe 2211
— im Wörterbuch einer rekonstruierten Sprache 1336
Literaturhinweis im etymologischen Wörterbuch 1324
literatursprachbezogenes Wörterbuch 236f.
Literatursprache 1154
Lithuanian lexicography 2351ff.
Lithuanian-Old Prussian 2530
littéraire 912
Livisch 2357, 2383
Livonian 2392
Livonian lexicography 2394
livre de poche 323
loanword in Norwegian 1923
Loba 2559
local order of glosses 1696
locution 635, 935, 1010, 1112, 1388, 2860
  s. Phrasemangabe,
  s. Redewendung,
  s. Sprichwort,
  s. Sprichwortangabe
— figuré 1098
— idiomatique 179, 218
  s. Phraseologismus
Lödäi 2636
Logbara 2644
logical sense-ordering in historical English lexicography 1451
logiciel 1674
Logogramm 1687
logogram 3145
logographisches Schriftzeichen 375

Lokalwörterbuch, kontrastives 2201
—, syntopisches 2198
Lolo 2555, 2559
loMóngo 2648
Longman Dictionary of Contemporary English 1379ff., 1967ff.
Loshn-koydesh 2249
Losung 1200
Lotha 2558
loucherbem 1532
Luchuan 2621
Luchuan-English 2621
Lücke in der Datenerhebung 1592
Lule 2708
Lule-Vilela 2708
Luo 2642
Lur 2481
Lushai 2559
lusitanische Lexikographie 1723
Luwisch 1687
Lydisch 1687
Lykisch 1687

M

Mabe, Maban 2642
Mabuyag 2639
Macassarese 2564
Machchaj-juyai 2706
machine lexicography
 s. computer and lexicography
machine translation 3163
— and lexicography
 s. computer and lexicography
Macro-ge 2707
macro-texte lexicographique 136
macrostructure [engl.] 288, 328, 336, 1943f., 1973, 2889
macrostructure [franz.] 307, 931, 1096, 1211, 1243, 1259, 1470
 s. Makrostruktur
macrostructure [franz.] als Terminus 371
macrostructure of thesauri 1084ff.
Madagasisch 2913
Madurese 2564ff.
Magadhi 2498
Magari 2558
Magarkun 3096
Maguindanao 2571
Maguindanao-Spanish 2571
Maharastri 2498
Mailänder Paulusfragmente 1909
Maithili 3096
Majang 2643
Makassara 2566
Makedonen 2302
makedonische Lexikographie 2302ff.

Makedonisch-Russisch 2302
Makrostruktur 328, 371ff., 396f., 1553, 2106f., 2133ff., 2790, 2922, 3002
 s. macrostructure [engl., franz.]
— allgemeiner Bildsymbolwörterbücher 3152ff.
— bei monoakzessiven Wörterbüchern 384
— bei Sprachstadienwörterbüchern romanischer Sprachen 1461f.
— der drei sechsbändigen Wörterbücher der deutschen Gegenwartssprache 2133ff.
— der Wörterbücher von Tier- und Pflanzenbezeichnungen 1255f.
— der Wortfamilienwörterbücher 1146
— des Bildwörterbuchs 1104f.
— des gegenwärtigen deutschen Fremdwörterbuchs 1170f.
— des onomasiologischen Wörterbuches 1058
— des Orthographiewörterbuchs 1299ff.
— des Ortsnamenwörterbuches 1279
— des Schlagwörterbuchs 1201f.
— und Zugriffsstruktur, initialalphabetische 393ff.
— zweisprachiger Fachwortschatzinventare 2941f.
— zweisprachiger Wörterbücher 2746ff., 3002
—, alphabetische 373ff.
—, Definition 372
—, initialalphabetische 382
—, Klassifikation 382f.
—, striktalphabetische 383ff.
makrostrukturelle Abdeckung 2133
 s. coverage in breadth
— Decke 373
— Unterschiede des Konstruktionswörterbuchs 1001
makrostrukturelles Profil 373
makrostrukturlastiges Wörterbuch 2124
Makrostrukturlastigkeit 2212
Malaiisch 2913
Malay 2563
Malay-Dutch 2563
Malay-English 2563
Malay-French 2563
Malay-Russian 2563
Malayalam 2521, 3096
Malayalam-English 2528f., 3102
Malayalam-Hindi 3098
Malayalam-Italian 2528

Malayalam-Portuguese 2528
Mallorkinisch 1773, 1776
Malto 2521
Mam 2661
Mamluk-Kiptschakisch
Mamluk-Osmanisch
mamotrect 296
Manchu 3110
Manchu-Chinese 3110
Manda 2521
Mandaic 2432
Mandar 2564ff.
Mande 2647
Mandschurisch-Russisch 3078
Mangarevan 2574
Mangbetu 2644
Mangbutu 2644
Manggarai 2564ff.
maniabilité 136ff.
manipulation of dictionary data 97ff
— by publishers 98f.
Manipuri 2555, 3096
Manipuri-Hindi 3110
Mansi 2395
manual alphabets 3142
— languages 3142
Manx 2346
Manx-Englisch 2346
Mao 2558
„Mao" 2643
Maori 2573f.
Mapuche 2709
maquette 1586
Mara 2559
Maranao 2571
Marathi 2514, 3096
Marathi-Engish 2514, 3100
Marathi-Hindi 3098
Marathi-Portuguese 3101
Marathi-Tamil 3098
marché 41
marges 138f.
Mari 2395
Mari-Russian 2397
Marind 2636
Marinewortschatz 2918
Marker 649ff.
 s. label,
 s. Markierungsangabe,
 s. marques
marketing and lexicography 88
— aspect of lexicography, manipulations by publishers 98
Markierung 649ff., 1077, 1196, 1535, 2796
 s. labelling,
 s. marquage
— der Neologismen 659f.
— des inneren Lehngutes 670
— fachsprachlicher Lexik 845f.

— im zweisprachigen Wörterbuch 2796ff.
— von direkten Entlehnungen 669
— von Entlehnungen 668ff.
— von nicht-direkten Entlehnungen 669f.
—, diafrequente 688ff.
—, dianormative 1777
—, diastratische 688
—, diatechnische 680ff.
—, diatopische 662ff.
—, evaluative 694ff.
—, fachsprachliche 680ff.
—, Makromodell der 650ff.
—, stilistische 693ff., 2130
Markierungsangabe 430, 433, 468, 2732, 2738, 2796, 2799ff.
s. label,
s. Marker,
s. marque
Markierungsausdruck 697
Markierungsausdruck, Probleme 695ff.
Markierungsdifferenz 650
Markierungsetikette 649
Markierungskennzeichnungen im zweisprachigen Wörterbuch 2802
Markierungsprädikat 649, 794
Markierungspraxis in Benutzungshinweisen 689
—, diatechnische 681
—, diatopische 665f.
—, evaluative 696f.
Markierungsraum 650
Markierungsschema 650
marquage 673, 694
s. labelling,
s. Markierung
—, dispositif de 675
—, programme de 678
marque 81, 649
s. label,
s. Marker
— d'usage 673
— diastratique 701
s. diastratische Markierung
— stylistique 673ff.
—, échelle de 675
Marquisan 2574
Marshallese 2574
Mas?an 2452
Masa 2458
Masai 2644
maschinelle Lexikographie
s. computer and lexicography
— Sortierung von Wörtern, Probleme 1570
Mascoi 2708
mass media and lexicography in the USA 34ff.

Mataco 2708
Mataguayo 2708
material aspect of lexicography 291
— form of dictionary 292
Materialgrundlage
s. Wörterbuchbasis
Matlatzinca 2697
Mator 2395
Matrix 969f.
Maué 2671
Maya-Spanisch 2663
Mayan 2698
Mayaner 2664
Māzandārānī 2481
Mbyá 2671, 2675
Me'en 2643
Me'en-Italian 2643
meaning 2785
— discrimination 2715, 2720, 2730, 2783ff., 2794, 2857, 2952
s. äquivalenzdifferenzierende Angabe,
s. sense discrimination
meaning discrimination als Terminus 2730
meaning identification 2720f.
Mecayapan 2660
médias et lexicographie 38ff.
Medieval Greek 1705ff.
Mediostruktur 2172, 2748
Mehr-Wort-Adresse 2729
Mehr-Wort-Annex 2749
Mehr-Wort-Einheit 2731
s. multi-word lexical unit
Mehrfachlemma 364, 367f.
Mehrfachlemmatisierung 919
s. Oligolemmatisierung
mehrsprachige Glossare des späten Mittelalters 1411
— Lexikographie 2909ff.
— Wörterbücher 1088f., 1682, 1690ff., 1711, 1726, 1739, 1741f., 1773, 1776, 1792, 1849f., 1882ff., 1906, 1929f., 1934f., 1997, 2030, 2042, 2044, 2046, 2249ff., 2257, 2262, 2268, 2285f., 2289ff., 2297ff., 2302, 2305, 2341, 2346, 2351, 2354f., 2368ff., 2373ff., 2380, 2384, 2389ff., 2396, 2401, 2410, 2422, 2427ff., 2449ff., 2462f., 2479ff., 2500, 2510ff., 2523, 2529ff., 2534ff., 2548ff., 2561, 2574, 2578, 2583, 2591ff., 2615, 2621, 2625, 2643ff., 2658, 2686, 2688ff., 2711, 2950, 2957, 2976, 2978f., 2993, 2998f., 3008f., 3014, 3021f., 3040f., 3055ff., 3062,

3070ff., 3075, 3078
s. vielsprachige Wörterbücher
— Wörterbücher, Titel 2912
mehrsprachiges Fachwörterbuch, Datenerhebung 1630
mehrsprachiges Wörterbuch 1104, 2920
—, Äquivalenzprobleme 2924
—, Typologie 2920ff.
mehrsprachiges/sprachvergleichendes Vornamenbuch 1270
Mehrwegwörterbuch 394
s. polyakzessives Wörterbuch
mehrwortige Lexeme 3002
Mehrwortlexem 397, 2779
Mehrwortsyntagmen 2779
Meinungsgruppenbezogenheit der politischen Lexik 837f.
Meinungssprache 836
Meiteiron 2559
Meithei 2555
Melghat 2537
mélioratif (als Markierung) 912
Memoriale della lingua 217
s. NR: G. Pergamini
Menba 2559
Menominee 2692, 2695
Menorkinisch 1773
Meo 2590f.
Merarit 2643
Merkmal, enzyklopädisches 550
—, semantisches 544, 546
s. sème
Merkmalsemantik 544f., 617
Merkmaltypologie der Mikrostrukturen von Konstruktionswörterbüchern 1002
Meroitic 2642
Mesalit 2643
métagraphie 504
métalangage 305ff., 675, 2859
s. Kommentarsprache,
s. lexikographische Beschreibungssprache
metalanguage and objectlanguage 294
métalangue 305ff., 504, 2859ff.
s. lexikographische Beschreibungssprache
— dans les dictionnaires bilingues 2859ff.
metalexicographical theory, its function 287
metalexicography, its tasks 295
—, principles 287
metalexikographie 216ff., 258
Metalexikographie 257ff.
Metalexikographie als Terminus 258
Metalexikographie und Autorenlexikographie 1558

— und Wörterbuchforschung
258f.
—, spanische 1750
metalexikographische Daten 1631
— Wörterbuchpflege 2213ff.
Metapher 797ff.
metaphrase 2857
metasprachliches Bewußtsein
1417
metatext 331
Metatext 425, 447, 453, 947, 950,
955, 1367, 2126, 2173, 2212
—, Anordnungsmethode im 377
Methode der funktionalen Segmentation 438
s. textual segmentation
— der funktional-positionalen
Segmentation 438ff.
— der Integration
s. Beschreibungsmethode
— der summierten Information
beim Einzelstichwort 2159
— zur Segmentation von standardisierten Wörterbuchartikeln 438ff.
méthode éditoriale 1822
Methode, integrierte grammatisch-semantische 2160
Methoden der Benutzungsforschung 106ff., 1631
methodical index 1087
Methodik der deskriptiven Lexikographie 1638
— der Ortsnamenlexikographie
1279
Metonymie 2793
Michif 2695
Micro Robert 1373
micro- and macrostructural interrelations 289
micro-context 2788
micro-ordinateur 326, 2809
micro-texte 136
microfiche 322ff., 1566
microfilm 324
microforme 324
microstructure [engl.] 328, 340,
344, 2892
microstructure [franz.] 218, 308,
311, 1096f., 1211f., 1243f.,
1259, 1470, 2830, 2863ff.,
2874
s. Mikrostruktur
microstructure [franz.] als Terminus 371
microstructure in defining thesauri 1087f.
— of cumulative thesauri 1086
— of the frequency dictionary
1315ff.
Middelnederlandsen Woordenboek 2011

Middle Ages 3086
— Iranian lexicography 2473ff.
— English lexicography 1437,
1446ff.
— matter 761f.
s. Einschub,
s. insert
— Norwegian 1923
Middle Persian-Sogdian 2476
Migration von Arbeitskräften
und Lexikographie 4
Mikir 2559
Mikrostruktur 328, 371f., 409ff.,
440f., 443, 1554, 2138ff., 2748,
2791, 3002
s. Artikelaufbau,
s. Artikelgestaltung,
s. Artikelgliederung,
s. microstructure [engl., franz.]
Mikrostruktur als Terminus 410ff.
Mikrostruktur allgemeiner Bildsymbolwörterbücher 3154f.
— bei Sprachstadienwörterbüchern romanischer Sprachen
1462ff.
— der drei sechsbändigen Wörterbücher der deutschen Gegenwartssprache 2137ff.
— der Wörterbücher von Tier-
und Pflanzenbezeichnungen
1256
— der Wortfamilienwörterbücher 1147
— des allgemeinen einsprachigen Wörterbuchs 462ff., 982,
2108ff.
— des Bildwörterbuchs 1104f.
— des Fachwörterbuchs für den
Laien 1520ff.
— des gegenwärtigen deutschen
Fremdwörterbuchs 1171f.
— des Konstruktionswörterbuchs 1001ff.
— des Orthographiewörterbuchs
1300f.
— des Schlagwörterbuchs 1201
— des Wörterbuchs der Wortbildungsmittel 1227f.
— des Wörterbuchs des sexuellen
Wortschatzes 1196f.
— des Wörterbuchs von Geheimsprachen 1534ff.
— des zweisprachigen Wörterbuchs 2732ff., 2748ff.
— eines polyinformativen Wörterbuches 453ff.
— eines standardisierten Wörterbuches 453
— eines Wörterbuches als Teilstruktur 456
— im Ortsnamenwörterbuch
1278

— mit aufgespaltener Kernstruktur 494f.
— mit binnenerweiterter Basisstruktur 475, 493f., 2140
— mit linkserweiterter Basisstruktur 494, 2127
— mit rechtserweiterter Basisstruktur 494
— onomasiologischer Wörterbücher 1060f.
— und Informationsprogramm
415ff., 418
— zweisprachiger Fachwortschatzinventare 2942f.
— zweisprachiger Wörterbücher
3002
—, abstrakte (lineare) 415
—, abstrakte 412ff., 415, 440
—, annexierte 2162
—, — hierarchische 2138f.
—, auflistende 2112ff., 2116,
2157f.
—, — mit linkserweiterte Basisstruktur 2116f., 2158
—, einfach subintegrierte 2145f.,
2154
—, einfache integrierte 2108,
2119, 2137f., 2154, 2160
—, — integrierte hierarchische
2120
—, — vollständig erweiterte
492f.
—, extern vollständig erweiterte
mit linkserweiterter Basisstruktur 495f.
—, hierarchische 393, 443ff., 806
—, integrierte 435, 2137ff., 2748
—, — mit binnenerweiterter Basisstruktur 2154
—, — rechtserweiterte 491f.,
2147ff.
—, intern erweiterte 2140
—, konkrete 412ff., 440
—, linkserweiterte mit links—
und rechtserweiterter Basisstruktur 496
—, mehrsprachiger Wörterbücher
2924f.
—, nichtintegrierte 488ff., 2147,
2748
—, partiell auflistende 2114
—, — integrierte 482f., 2137ff.,
2748
—, partitive 444
—, präzedentive 444f., 950
—, rechtserweiterte 2108, 2142,
2144, 2151, 2159, 2200
—, — integrierte 2109, 2150,
2206
—, — mit binnenerweiterter Basisstruktur 496f.
—, — nichtintegrierte 2149

—, rudimentäre 383, 456
—, überdachende 2137
—, — nichtrudimentäre 2140, 2143
—, — partiell rudimentäre 2140f.
—, — vollständig rudimentäre 2140
—, semiintegrierte 2749
—, zusammengesetzte 2140
—, zweifach partiell integrierte 2163f.
—, — subintegrierte 2146, 2154
mikrostrukturelle Profile zweisprachiger Wörterbücher 2748ff.
Mikrostrukturenprogramm 2108, 2112, 2124ff., 2130, 2146, 2172, 2192, 2194, 2208
s. Informationsprogramm
Militärwortschatz 2918
„Mimi" 2643
Mingrelian 2415
miniformat 324
Minimalwörterbücher 3065
Minimalwortschatz 1353
minority languages in Norwag 1926
Minorkinisch 1776
Minorkinisch-Spanisch 1776
Miri 2555
mise en page 136, 1583
Misiiri 2643
Mission und Lexikographie 2
Mitarbeiter und Datenerhebung 1589
mittellateinische Wörterbücher 1719f.
Mittel(west)friesisch 2025
Mittelniederländisch 1432
Mittelniederländisches Wörterbuch 1431
Mitteltürkisch 2412
Mittelwalisch 2447
mittlere Interstruktur 475
mittlerer Zwischenkommentar 475, 493, 2140
Mixe 2697
Mixtec 2697
mnemotechnische Funktion des Zitatenwörterbuchs 1044
Moabite 1690
Mocha 2464
Mocho 2661
Modalpartikel 805ff., 827
s. Abtönungspartikel
— und Synonymie 625
model role of an older dictionary 2697
modèle de communication 1822
modélisation de l'exemple 309
modern Greek 1705

— Swedish lexicography 1934ff.
Moderne 913
Moderne deutsche Idiomatik von Friederich 2175f.
modernizing dictionary 72ff.
Modewort 1200
Modifikation 3025
— von Phraseologismen 598
Modo 2644
Moesogotisch 1909
Moghol 2626
Mokša 2395
Molbech's dictionary 1914
s. NR: Chr. Molbech
Momgodow 2566
Mon 2591ff.
Mon-Khmer 2590
monème lié 1834
s. morphème lié
Mongo 2644
Mongolian wordlist in Armenia 2368
Mongolian-Japanese 3113
Mongolian-Tibetan 2548
mongolische Lexikographie 2623ff.
Mongolisch-Arabisch 2625
Mongolisch-Chinesisch 2410, 2625
Mongolisch-Persisch 2625
Mongolisch-Russisch 3078
Monguor 2626
monoaccessible dictionary, outer access structure 339
monoakzessives Wörterbuch 382ff., 400, 2108, 2135, 2180
s. Einwegwörterbuch
monodirectional 2949, 2952
monodirektional als Terminus 2742
Monodirektionalität in der zweisprachigen Lexikographie 7
monofunctional translation dictionary 2713
s. Übersetzungswörterbuch
monofunktionale zweisprachige Wörterbücher 2841
monofunktionales Textelement 426
monolingual dictionary, definition 294
s. Definitionswörterbuch
— lexicography, principles 287
monoskopal 2740
monoskopales zweisprachiges Wörterbuch 2740f.
monotonia 1706
Monpa 2558
monstration 602
Monumbo 2636
Mooringer Friesisch 2030

Mopan 2661
Mopan-Spanisch 2663
Mordva 2395
Mordvinian 2395
Morelos 2659
Morphem, derivationelles in den Wörterbüchern des Niederländischen 2017
morphème lié 936
Morphemwörterbuch 119
morpholexikalisches Antonym 629
morphological structure 2421
Morphologie im textsortenbezogenen Wörterbuch 1544
morphologische Angabe 2147
s. Grammatikangabe
morphologisches Wörterbuch 1311
morphology and headwords 301
—, inflectional, information 518ff
—, —, types of information 519
Mosetene 2703
Moso 2555, 2559
mot 1563
s. Wort
— analogique 1096
— complexe 937
— composé 507
s. Komposita,
s. Kompositaangabe
— construit 937ff.
— de base 1371
— de départ 1096
— disponible 1318
— étranger 1168
— non complexe 937
— propre 1010, 1076
— simple 179
mot-analogue 1096
mot-centre 635, 1096
mot-cible 1096
mot-clef 1563
mot-entrée 2859
mot-thème 1096
mot-valise 1350
mot-vedette 506, 1094, 1563
s. entrée,
s. entry word,
s. headword,
s. Lemma,
s. Stichwort
Moth's dictionary 1913
s. NR: M. Moth
motivationelle Lemmatisierung 646
Motivationsstruktur komplexer Wörter 642
Motive der Gruppensprachenlexikographie 1524

Motiviertheit/Durchsichtigkeit als Ordnungskriterium in der Lexikographie 1146
Motozintlek 2661
Motto 1054
Movima 2703
Mpi 2559, 2591
Muher 2452
Muhso 2559
Muisca 2706
Mukrī 2483
multi-language dictionary of Swedish 1935
multi-word lexical unit 2785
   s. Mehr-Wort-Einheit,
   s. Wortgruppenlexem
multicolonage 139
multilingual dictionary 2909ff.
   s. mehrsprachiges Wörterbuch,
   s. vielsprachiges Wörterbuch
multimédia 507
multivergence 2857
Munda 2533
Mundari 2534, 2538
Mundari-English 2538
Mundari-Hindi 2539
Mundartenwörterbuch in Frankreich 26
Mundartlexikographie des Deutschen 2059, 2198ff.
Mundartwörterbuch 122
   s. dialect dictionary,
   s. Dialektwörterbuch
Mundartwortschatz im gesamtsprachbezogenen Wörterbuch 1398
Mundurukú 2671, 2704
Mundžī-Yidgha 2481
Muong 2588
Muqaddimat al-adab 2476
Murik 2636
Murinypata 2639
Murle 2643
Mursi 2643
Murui 2703
Muskogean 2691
Musterartikel für Partikelwörterbuch 812
muttersprachlicher Laienbenutzer 131f.
Mycenaean Greek 1694, 1696

N

Nabataean 2425, 2431
Nachi 2555, 2559
Na-khi 2559
Nachdruck von deutschen Wörterbüchern 2213f.
nachgestellte Registerzugriffsstruktur 403
— Zugriffsstruktur 403, 2125
Nachkriegslexikographie, frühe deutsche 2106ff.
Nachschlagebedürfnis 8, 1169
Nachschlagehandlung 1101
   s. acte de consultation
Nachschlagen 970, 1063, 2790
— onomasiologischer Wörterbücher 1063
Nachschlagewerk 988, 1106
   s. ouvrage de référence
— mit etymologischer Information 1323
Nachschlagewerke, nichtlexikographische 2207
Nachschlagewörterbuch 1110
Nachspann 331, 398, 767
   s. back matter,
   s. post texte,
   s. Register
Naga 2559
Nahuatle lexikography 2657ff.
Nahuatle-Spanish 2658f.
Naiki 2521
Nakh-Daghestanian languages 2421
Nama 2650
Namaqua 2652
Nambiquara 2707
Namen im Wörterbuch 775, 1267, 2133
   s. Eigenname,
   s. Name,
   s. name,
   s. nom propre,
   s. proper name
Namenartikel 1278
—, Beispiel für 1278
—, seine Teile 1278
Namengebung 1269
namenkundliche Abhandlung 1279
Namennachschlagewerk 1279
Namenstruktur, komplexe 1268
Namenvolumen von Ortsnamenbüchern 1278
Namenwörterbuch 1267ff., 1779
   s. Onomastikon
—, Typen 1267ff., 1291ff.
name 2816
   s. Eigenname,
   s. Name,
   s. nom propre,
   s. proper name
nanartha als Terminus 2522
Nandi 2644
Naro(n) 2650
narrativ-lineare Züge in der Bedeutungserläuterung 1405
national orientiertes Wörterbuch des 19. Jhs. 12

nationale Identifikationsfunktion des gesamtsprachbezogenen Wörterbuches 1402
nationalkulturelle Rolle von Wörterbüchern 1402
nationalliterarische Erziehungsfunktion des gesamtsprachbezogenen Wörterbuches 1403
nationalsprachliches Wörterbuch, Reduktionsformen 12
native susceptibilities 2687
natürlichsprachliche Angabe 429
Naukan Yupik 2632
Navajo 2694
Naxi 2555, 2559
Nazifizierung von Wörterbüchern 2111
Ndjébbana 2639
Ndjébbana-English 2639f.
Nebenlemma 364
néerlandais-allemand 2808
néerlandais-espagnol 2978
néerlandais-français 2808, 2810
negerhollands 2871
Nenets 2395
Nemiqua 2655
Nennform 365
   s. canonical form,
   s. forme canonique,
   s. kanonische Form,
   s. Zitierform
Neo-Norwegian 1923, 1925
— standard 1925
neologism 1159, 1508, 2393
— in Norwegian 1926
— in US-American lexicography 36
néologisme 1211, 1868, 2982
Neologismenlexikographie, germanistische 2185ff.
Neologismenwörterbuch 25, 1169, 1777, 2185ff.
   s. dictionary of neologisms
Neologismus 25, 690, 1232, 2130, 2185, 2344f., 2348, 2394
— als Lemma des Fachwörterbuchs 1627
—, seine Markierung 659
Nepali 2517, 3096
Nera 2643
Nest 391
—, Definition 391
—, nichtalphabetisches 391
nestalphabetisch 336, 1076, 3002
nestalphabetische Anordnungsform 391ff.
— Zugriffsstruktur 395
nestalphabetisches Wörterbuch 336, 2746
Nestartikel 391, 2119, 2140
Nestbildung 336, 965

s. nesting,
s. regroupement
Nesteingang, lemmaexterner 365, 391
Nesteingangslemma 2747
nesting 336
s. Nestbildung,
s. nichification
Nestlemma 364f., 365, 391, 2116, 2135
Netzexzerption 2262f.
s. Auswahlexzerption
Neubedeutung 2130, 2186
Neues Deutsches Wörterbuch 2156f.
— Großes Wörterbuch der deutschen Sprache 240f.
Neugriechisch-Albanisch 2361
neuhochdeutsche Sprichwörtersammlung 1034ff.
Neuhochdeutsch-Altfriesisch 2024
Neupersisch-Pašto 2484
Neuprägung 2130, 2186
neusprachlich-lateinische Lexikographie 9
neutralisation 600
Neuuiguirisch 2410
Neuwestfriesisch 2025
Neuwort 2130, 2186
new word 1159
Newari 2555, 2558, 3096
Newari-Nepali 3099
newspaper and lexicography in the USA 34
Ngaju Dayak 2564
Ngadju Dayak-German 2567
Nganasan 2395
Ngbaka 2648
Ngbandi 2648
Ngeq 2590f.
Nggela 2574
Ngiyampaa 2639
Nharo 2650
Nheengatú 2670
nichification 336
s. Nischenbildung
niching 336
nicht-homologe Informationssprache 6
nicht-mechanische Alphabetisierungsmethode 379
nicht-natürliche Ellipse 570
nichtalphabetisches Nest 391
nichteinsetzbare Bedeutungsparaphrasenangabe 563f.
nichtenzyklopädisches Bedeutungswissen 554, 559
nichtfunktionale Textsegmente 425
nichtintegrierte Mikrostruktur 488, 2147ff.

— und Bedeutungsangabe 2147f.
—, einfache 489
—, rechtserweiterte 2148f.
nichtkommentierende Angabe 432ff.
nichtlemmatische Adressierung 446f., 537
s. non-lemmatic addressing
nichtlexikographische Nachschlagewerke 2207
nichtsprachliche Angabe 429f.
nichtstandardisierte Angabe 431
nichttypographischer Strukturanzeiger 428, 512, 927, 2157, 2180
s. lexikographisches Gliederungszeichen
nichtverdichtete Bedeutungsparaphrasenangabe 570
Nickname 1055
nickname 1292
Niederdeutsch als Varietät des Deutschen 1419
Niederländisch 1430, 3022
—, heutiges, kommerzielles Wörterbuch 1433
—, heutiges, Wörterbuch 2012
—, Situation nach 1830 1402
—, Sprachstadienwörterbücher 1431
Niederländisch-Deutsch 2714, 2780, 2918, 2939
Niederländisch-Englisch 2939, 3073
Niederländisch-Französisch 2918, 2939
Niederländisch-Friesisch 2026f.
Niederländisch-Gotisch 1910
Niederländisch-Isländisch 1929
Niederländisch-Javanisch 2800
Niederländisch-Portugiesisch 3022
Niederländisch-Russisch 3073
Niedersorbisch-Deutsch 2275
Ngzim 2458
Niger abbas 2039
Nilagiri languages 2529
Nische 365, 388, 2747
—, Definition 388
Nischen- und Nestbildung 645
nischenalphabetisch 336, 2746, 3002
nischenalphabetische Anordnungsform 386f.
nischenalphabetisches Wörterbuch 2746
Nischenartikel 365, 388, 2119
Nischenbildung 336, 965, 2747
s. nichification,
s. niching
— mit Teillemmata 389
Nischeneingangslemma 365, 390, 2730, 2747

Nischenlemma 365, 388, 389, 390, 2118f., 2146, 2150
niveau de langue 179, 674, 912, 1370
Nivkh 2627
Nobiin 2643
Nobiin-German 2643
Nocte 2558
nôm (demotic script) 2583
nom composé 179
— propre 1211, 1258, 1305, 1580
s. Eigenname,
s. Name,
s. name
Nomenclator Aquatilium Animantium 2915
— Hadriani Junii, ad scholarum usum 2044
— in Lingua Latina, Germanica et Russica 3071
— in Lingua Latina, Hollandica et Russica 3071
— Latino-Saxonicus 2044
— omnium 1088, rerum 2043, 2912
s. NR: H. Junius
Nomenclatura rerum deomesticarum 2043
nomenclaturae 2912
nomenclature [engl.] 1509, 1944
s. Wörterverzeichnis
nomenclature [franz.] 283, 307, 1372, 1676, 2865
s. Wörterverzeichnis
Nomenklatoren 2998
Nomenklatur Linnés 1255
Nominaldefinition 541
Nominalisierung 882, 886, 957
Nominalisierungsverbgefüge 882f.
Nomination, lexikographische 790
Nomos-These 1057
non-alphabetic sequence 297
non-base forms 2816
non-lemmatic addressing 349
s. nichtlemmatische Adressierung
Nordfriesisch 2028, 2031
Nordgegisch-Italienisch 2363
Norm 189, 513f., 1197, 1297, 1930
Norm als Terminus 189f.
norm in Swedish lexicography 1936f.
Norm phonetischer Angaben 513
— und Gewohnheit 195
—, deskriptive 194f.
—, explizite 194f.
—, externe 194f.
—, implizite 194f.
—, interne 194f.
—, präskriptive 194f.

—, Grundzüge der Sprachgeschichte 1930
Normalisation 309ff.
normative Absicht 2286
— Angabe 2157, 2159
— Erwartung 193
normative dictionary 2393
  s. präskriptives Wörterbuch
normative Lexikographie in Lateinamerika 65
— Wirkung deskriptiver Wörterbücher 189ff.
normativer Kommentar 199
  s. commentaire normatif
normatives Wörterbuch 63ff., 198ff., 2055, 2191f., 2270
  s. normative dictionary
Normativität und Deskriptivität, Grenzprobleme 63, 202f.
normativité 700
Normdeskription 194
norme 46f., 501, 1304, 2867f., 2873
  s. Norm
— socio-culturelle 81
Normen und Gewohnheiten 195f.
— und Regeln 194f.
— und Sanktionen 192
Normenwörterbuch 2206, 2941
  s. terminological dictionary
Normexplikation 194
Normkennzeichnung im Wörterbuch des sexuellen Wortschatzes 1197
Normung lexikographischer Fachsprache 317ff.
Normwörterbuch 318
  s. Normenwörterbuch,
  s. Terminographie
Norsk 1926
North Frisian 1441
Norwegian 1923
Norwegian Language Council 1923
Norwegian-English 1926
Norwegian-German 1926
Norwegian-Serbo-Croatian 1926
Norwegian-Vietnamese 1926
Notationskonvention für Angabeklassen 469
notes 342
  s. usage note
Novo dicionário compacto da língua portuguesa 1731
Nu 2558
Nuancierungslücke 1428
Nubian 2643
Nubisch 1680
Nudansk Ordbog 1916
Nukuoro 2574
Nulladressierung 350
  s. adressage zéro

Nulläquivalenz 2943f.
numérotation 1822, 2830
Numismatik 2918
Nunggubuyu 2639
Nutzen von Wörterbüchern 1ff., 115ff., 128ff., 146ff., 152ff., 159ff., 163ff., 167ff., 171ff., 174ff., 181ff.
Nutzung von Belegen 1607
— von Indices und Konkordanzen 1568
Nutzungsmöglichkeiten des gesamtsprachbezogenen Wörterbuches 1400f.
Nutzungswert 955
Nyah 2590
Nyala 2644
Nyalgulgule 2644
Nyangi 2643
Nyangumarta 2639
Nyanja 2648
Nyanja-English 2648
Nyima 2643
Nymylan 2628
Nynorsk 1925, 1926
Nyungar 2639

O

Oberadresse 2731
obere Zugriffsstruktur 400
Oberengadinisch 1896
Obersorbisch-Deutsch 2275
obligatorische Mikrostruktur 456
obligatory microstructure 346
Obugrian 2395
Obwaldisch 1895
Ocaina 2703
Occidental 3130
occitan als Terminus 1892
  s. provençal
occurence 1563
Odul 2627
offener lexikographischer Kommentar 434
Öffentlichkeit und Diachronie 24f., 25
— und Onomasiologie 25
Oghusisch 2407, 2411
Ogom-Inschriften 2340
Oiratisch 2626
Ojibwa 2692, 2695
Ökonomie des Nachschlagens 2987
okzitanisch als Terminus 1892
Old Danish lexicography 1921
Old English lexicography 1436f.
—, computerization 1443
—, phonological principles 1442
Old English, special purpose dictionaries 1444

Old Frisian 1441
Old Icelandic lexicography 1934
Old-Javanese-English 2561
Old Norwegian 1923
Old Saxon 1441
Old Swedish lexicography 1934
Oligolemmatisierung 365
  s. Mehrfachlemmatisierung
Ollari 2521
Oluta Popoluca 2698
Omagua 2671
Ometo 2463
Omok 2628f.
Omotic 2461
onglets 138
onomasiological dictionary 167
  s. onomasiologisches Wörterbuch
—, its purpose 291
onomasiological principle in Danish dialect lexicography 1919
Onomasiologie im textsortenbezogenen Wörterbuch 1546
onomasiologique 636, 1470
onomasiologische Lexikographie, Datenerhebung 1590
— Vernetzung des Wortschatzes 1408
— Vernetzung im Sprachstadienwörterbuch 1424
onomasiologischer Ausgangsbegriff 1059
— Charakter von Wörterbüchern als Ergebnis der Interpretation 1058
— Teil des semantischen Kommentars 621
onomasiologisches Paradigma 612
— Register zu semasiologischen Wörterbüchern 1065
— Spezialwörterbuch 1081
  s. Antonymenwörterbuch,
  s. Synonymenwörterbuch
— Vermögen 1063
— Wörterbuch 26, 767, 1057ff., 2089
  s. Synonymik,
  s. Synonymenwörterbuch
— Wörterbuch zu mehreren Sprachen 1411
onomastic dictionaries 1267ff.
Onomastikon 1680
  s. Namenwörterbuch
onomatopoeic words 2615
Onomatopöienwörterbuch 1245f.
Operationalisierung in der Wörterbuchbenutzungsforschung 1632
operative Bedeutung 864
Opo 2643
Oppositum 1081

Oraon 2529
Oraon-English 2529
Orbis sensualium pictus 2914
Orbis pictus 1365, 2914ff.
Ordbog over det danske Sprog 1914
    s. NR: V. Dahlerup
Ordbog til det aeldre danske Sprog 1917
    s. NR: O. Kalkar
Ordensdeutsch 2353
order of entries in sign dictionaries 3143
— structure 344
    s. Ordnungsstruktur
ordering devices 344
— structure 1509, 1978
    s. Ordnungsstruktur
ordinateur 311, 507, 1829, 1834, 1873, 1874, 2804ff.
    s. computer and lexicography
ordinateur et dictionnaire bilingue 2804ff.
Ordnung, alphabetische 297ff., 376ff.
    s. Anordnungsform,
    s. Alphabet
—, finalalphabetische 379
    s. rückläufiges Wörterbuch
Ordnungsprinzip ägyptischer Wörterbücher 1679
Ordnungsproblem in der onomasiologischen Lexikographie 1059
Ordnungsrelation 441
— strukturprägende 472
Ordnungsstruktur 372, 379, 464
—, artikelinterne 441f.
ordo mnemonicus 3031
ordonnateur 335, 1097
    s. Gliederungszeichen,
    s. ordering devices,
    s. Strukturanzeiger
Ordos 2626
ordre 310f.
— alphabétique 1096f.
    s. Anordnungsform
organization of dictionaries 296
Orientalistisches Wörterbuch 2401
orientation de la collocation 1010
Oriya 2515, 3096
Oriya-English 2515
Oriya-Hindi 3098
Orma 2464
Ōrmurī 2481
Oromo 2462
Orošōrī 2481
orthographe 177, 218, 501ff., 701, 1581, 2873
    s. spelling and dictionaries,
    s. Rechtschreibung

Orthographie 380, 1297
— und Orthoepie im normativen Wörterbuch 67
Orthographienormierung mittels Lexikographie 11
Orthographiewörterbuch 1297ff.
    s. Rechtschreibwörterbuch,
    s. spelling dictionary
orthographische Angabe
    s. Rechtschreibangabe
orthography and dictionaries 90
orthotypographie 504
Ortslexikon 1277
Ortslexikon, Definition 1277
Ortsname 1277
Ortsnamenwörterbuch 1276ff.
Ortsnamenbuch, Definition 1277
Ortsnamenwörterbuch als Terminus 1276
Ortsnamen-Lexikon 1277
Ortsnamenlexikographie für England 1281f.
— für Frankreich 1282
—, für das deutsche Sprachgebiet 1280f.
Ortsschelte 1191
Ösbekisch 2408
Ossetisch 744
Ossetisch-Russisch 2484
Ostfriesisch 2027
Ostyak 2395
Ostyak-Samoyed 2395
Otchipwe 2692
Otomí 2658, 2697
outer access structure 329, 337f.
    s. äußere Zugriffsstruktur
outer rapid access structure 338
    s. äußere Schnellzugriffsstruktur
outer selection 337
    s. äußere Selektion,
    s. Auswahlgrundsätze,
    s. sélection
outside matter 331, 761
    s. Außentext
— and commercial factors 762
— in popular dictionairies 769
— in metalexicography 764
ouvrage de référence 1819
    s. Nachschlagewerk
Oxford Advanced Learner's Dictionary of Current English 1379ff., 1968ff.
    s. NR: A. S. Hornby
Oxford English Dictionary 1395, 1436, 1962f., 1967ff.
    s. NR: H. Bradley; R. Burchfield; W. A. Craigie; J. A. H. Murray; C. T. Onions
Oyampi 2703
Özbekisch 2408

P

Pa'a 2457
P'yongan 2614
Pacoh 2590f.
Pädagogisch mnemotechnisches Wörterbuch 2399
Páez 2706
page rose (Petit Larousse) 761, 764
Paī 2671
Paisaci 2498
Pajapan 2659
Pakhtu 3096
Palaisch 1687
Paläologismus zu umrissenen Zeiten 659
—, seine Markierung 654
Palauan 2574
Pali 2498
Pāli-Burmese 2550f.
Pāli-English 2501
Pāli-French 2500
Pāli-Japanese 3113
Palimpsest
Palmyrenian 2431
Pama-Nyungan 2638
Pampa 2710
Pampango 2569
Pamphletwörterbuch 1054
panel of advisors in US-American lexicography 35
Pangasinan 2569ff.
Pangasinan-Spanish 2571
Panjabi 2515, 3096
Panjabi-English 2515, 3100
Panjabi-Hindi 3098
Panjabi-Russian 3101
Panjabi-Urdu 3098
Pano 2703
Panoan languages 2703
Panyjima 2639
Papantla Totonac 2698
papiamentu 2871
Pappa Pueroum 2043
    s. NR: J. Murmellius
Papua New Guinea 1494
Parāčī 2481
paradigm and headword 299
—, inflectional, variants and gaps 523f.
Paradigma, onomasiologisches 612
paradigmatic dictionaries 1057ff.
— information 342
paradigmatique 1821
Paradigmatik im zweisprachigen Wörterbuch 2794ff.
paradigmatische Relation 888
paradigmatische Spezialwörterbücher 1057ff.

— des Deutschen 2177ff., 2184
—, zweisprachige 2879f.
paradigmatische Wortschatzvernetzung im gesamtsprachbezogenen Wörterbuch 1408
paradigme fermé 283
Parallelisierung im zweisprachigen Wörterbuch 2750
Paraphrase, lexikalische 620, 807
   s. Bedeutungsparaphrasenangabe
Paraphrasierbarkeit 546
Paraphrasierung und Übersetzungsvorschlag 3025
parasynonymie 1211
Parecis 2703
Parenga 2544
Parengi 2544
Parengi-English 2544
parenthèse morpho-étymologique 943
Parintintin 2675, 2703
Parintintin-Português 2675
Parji 2521
Parole vs. Schlagwort 1200
parole straniere 1168
Parömiographie 1033
—, vergleichende 1036ff.
Parömiologie 1033
Paronym 1120
paronyme 640f., 703
Paronymenwörterbuch 1122f.
Paronymie 1120
paronymie 640f., 1211
part-of-speech abbreviation 1315
Parthian 2473
partially integrated microstructure 354
   s. partiell integrierte Mikrostruktur
partiell auflistende Mikrostruktur 2114
— integrierte Mikrostruktur 482f., 2137ff., 2748ff.
partielle Äquivalente 2738
— mechanische Alphabetisierung 379
Partikel und Relationsprädikat 962
Partikelnwörterbuch 1221, 2880
partitive Artikelstruktur 442f.
— Mikrostruktur 444, 466
— Relation 428
Pashto 3096
passive dictionary 2715, 2719, 2776, 2786
passive Funktionen 2741
passives Wörterbuch 2779, 2800, 2840
   s. Herübersetzungswörterbuch,
   s. Rezeption und zweisprachiges Wörterbuch

Pašto 2481
Pašto-English 2483f.
Pašto-Neupersisch 2484
Pašto-Russisch 2484
pàthaanúkrom als Terminus 2579
patois 1471
patriotism in English lexicography 1440
pattern code 1383
Pauserna 2671
paysage dictionnairique 43
Payungu 2639
pedagogical aspect of lexicography 292
   s. learner's dictionary
— lexicography 2888
   s. Lernlexikographie
Pehuelche 2709
péjoratif (als Markierung) 912
Pemón 2702
Pengo 2521
Penutian 2691
Perfektbildungsangabe 2164
pericope 1700
period dictionary 1985
   s. Sprachstadienwörterbuch
— of English 1436
Periodisierung der isländischen Sprachgeschichte
— des Deutschen, Kriterien 1417
—, lexikographiehistorische 2103
periodization in English lexicography 1436
peripherer Wortschatz 1100
périphrase 2861
Pero 2457
Persian lexicography 2479ff.
Persian-Armenian 2368f.
Persian-English 2479
Persian-Japanese 3113
Persian-Pashto 2480
Persisch-Türkisch 2399
Personengruppe als Gegenstand der Lexikographie 1271
—, zugehörige Wörterbücher 1294
Personennamenlexikon 1267
Personennamenwörterbuch 1267ff.
Personenschelte 1190
Petit Larousse 41, 713, 1821
Petit Robert 349, 590, 674, 683, 987, 1828
petite main 932
Pflanzenbezeichnung 1254
Philological Society of London 1446
philologische Bearbeitung von Indices 1571
— Wörterbuchbenutzungssituation 152, 155
Phoenician 1690, 2425

Phom 2558
phonemische Transkription 513
Phonemsystem in Benutzungshinweisen 512
phonetical-anagrammatical arrangement 2440
phonétique 1305
phonetisch-semantisches Feld 643
phonetische Angabe 508ff.
   s. Ausspracheangabe
— bei Fremdwörtern 514
— im zweisprachigen Wörterbuch 510ff.
—, Doppeltranskription 512f.
—, Geschichte 509f.
—, Klammerkonvention 512
—, Norm 513
—, Nutzen 510ff.
—, Position 512
—, Prinzipien 511
—, Typen 509
—, Typographie 513
—, Umfang der Transkription 514
phonetische Transkription 513
— und Silbengrenzenangabe 513
phonograms 3145
phonological principles in Old English lexicography 1442
phonology and headwords 301
phótcanàanúkrom als Terminus 2579
photocomposition 1586, 2806
photographie 1583
Photographie und Zeichnung 708
   s. Illustration
phrase as a term 2721
phrase books 2915
   s. Gesprächsbücher
phrase figée 179
—, dictionnaire scolaire 1370
phrase-exemple 1375
   s. Beispiel,
   s. example,
   s. exemple
Phrasem 397, 537f., 983
   s. idiom,
   s. Phraseologismus,
   s. Redensart
Phrasemangabe 433, 468, 537, 2120, 2147, 2149, 2151, 2850
—, aus der zwei Phrasemvarianten erschließbar sind 2151
—, um einen Verweis binnenerweiterte 2151
Phraseographie 1046
   s. Idiomatik
— des Deutschen 2064f., 2174ff.
phraseological verb as a headword 302
Phraseologie 1045, 1051f., 1776, 2258, 2750, 2789ff.

phraséologie 909, 2981
Phraseologie als Terminus 2159
Phraseologie bei J. Maaler und G. Henisch 2046
— der Handelskorrespondenz 1052
— im zweisprachigen Wörterbuch 2789ff.
— und Wörterbuchbenutzer 594
—, deutsche 2174ff.
Phraseologiemisere 2121, 2127, 2150
phraseologische Einheit, Präsentierung 1022
—, Zusammenhang 1027
phraseologische Verbindung 1019
Phraseologische Wörterbücher des Deutschen 2174ff.
— mit Polnisch 3065
phraseologischer Postkommentar 492, 2150f., 2206
phraseologisches Synonymenwörterbuch 2178f.
 s. NR: H. Schemann
phraseologisches Wörterbuch 593, 1019ff., 2174, 2270, 2315, 2878
—, Umfang 1021
Phraseologismus 593ff., 608, 2150
 s. Phrasem
—, Anordnung 594f.
—, artikelinterne Position 595
—, Bedeutungserläuterung 596f.
—, externe Valenz 597
—, Lemmatisierung 595
—, Nennform 595f.
—, morphosyntaktische Restriktionen 597f.
—, Uneinheitlichkeit der Aufnahme ins Wörterbuch 1020
phrases 2783
Physis-These 1057
pictographic symbols 2962
pictorial dictionary
 s. Bildwörterbuch
— of signs 3141
pictorial illustration 342
 s. Bild,
 s. Illustration
picture dictionary 294
 s. Bildwörterbuch
pidgin 1477, 2870ff.
pidgins 2870
Pilagás 2708
Pilbara 2639
Pilipino 2569
pinyin 299, 311
Pipil 2657
plagiarism 2006
—, charges of 225
Plagiat 2912
plaisanterie (als Markierung) 912

Plansprachen 3120ff.
Platzhaltersymbol 389f., 948, 964
 s. Angabesymbol,
 s. repetition symbol
—, freies 430
—, gebundenes 430
Platzproblem 2779
 s. Druckraumeinsparung
Pluralbildungsangabe 433, 468, 2116
 s. item giving plural form
Pluraletantumangabe 433, 468, 2161
plurifunktionale Wörterbuchteile 2742
plurilingual dictionaries 2909
 s. mehrsprachige Wörterbücher
plurilingue 2864ff.
plurilinguisme 2864
Pochury 2558
poetic-language dictionary of English 1442
poétique (als Markierung) 912
Pokomam 2661
Pokomchi 2661
Polabian-English 2271
polabische Lexikographie 2271
Polish-Japanese 2271
political aspect of Danish lexicography 1913
Politik und Lexikographie 3, 2131f.
 s. Ideologie der Lexikographie
politique langagière 46ff.
Polnisch 2268, 3022, 3061
Polnisch-Bulgarisch 3065
Polnisch-Deutsch 3063ff., 3076f.
Polnisch-Englisch 3065
Polnisch-Esperanto 3065
Polnisch-Französisch 3062f., 3065
Polnisch-Italienisch 3064
Polnisch-Kirchenslawisch 3072
Polnisch-Niederländisch 3065
Polnisch-Portugiesisch 3062, 3065
Polnisch-Rumänisch 3065
Polnisch-Russisch 3063ff., 3076
Polnisch-Schwedisch 3065
Polnisch-Serbo-Kroatisch 3065
Polnisch-Slowakisch 3065
Polnisch-Spanisch 3065
Polnisch-Suahili 3065
Polnisch-Tschechisch 3065
Polnisch-Ungarisch 2380, 3063, 3065
Polnisch-Vietnamesisch 3065
polyaccessible dictionary, outer access structure 339
polyakzessives Wörterbuch 394, 402, 2172, 2204
 s. Mehrwegwörterbuch,
 s. Zweigwegwörterbuch

polyäquivalent 2877
Polyäquivalenz 2730
polyfunktionale Wörterbuchteile 2741f.
polyfunktionales Textelement 426
polyglot dictionaries 2854
 s. mehrsprachige Wörterbücher
polyglott 2909
Polyglotta Africana 2647
polyinformative dictionary 344
polyinformatives Wörterbuch 467, 2159
Polylemmatisierung 365
polylexie 2863
Polynesian and Melanesian lexicography 2573ff.
Polyrektionsangabe 2163f.
polysème 507
polysémie 311, 909ff., 1832
Polysemie 918
polysémie d'acceptions 914
— de sens 914
— externe 914
Polysemie im deutschen Wörterbuch 783
— im englischen Wörterbuch 782f.
— im spanischen Wörterbuch 782
— in italienischen und französischen Wörterbüchern 783f.
polysémie interne 914
Polysemie von Tier- und Pflanzenbezeichnungen 1255
Polysemieangabe 433, 437, 450, 468, 2109, 2119, 2127, 2138, 2206, 2843
 s. polysemy item
Polysemierung 380
Polysemiestruktur 1366, 2748
polysemistischer Sprachzeichenbegriff 449
polysemy 167f., 2965
— item 355
 s. Polysemieangabe
Polyvalenz 1104
Ponape 2574
ponctuation 2830
Popoluca 2698
populaire (als Markierung) 912, 2797
popular approach in neologistic dictionaries 1163
— commentator on language in the USA 34
— magazine and lexicography in the USA 34
Porta als Terminus 2912
portatif 323
portmanteau word 1350
Portugiesisch 3020

Portugiesisch Afrikas 1733
Portugiesisch-Deutsch 2802, 3020, 3022ff.
Portugiesisch-Englisch 3022
Portugiesisch-Italienisch 3022
Portugiesisch-Japanisch 2619, 3021
Portugiesisch-Lateinisch 1725f., 3020f.
Portugiesisch-Niederländisch 3022
Portugiesisch-Polnisch 3022
Portugiesisch-Tschechisch 3022
Portugiesisch-Ungarisch 3022
Portugiesische Lexikographie 1723ff.
Português-Tembé-ténêtéhar 2675
Portuguese 3113
Portuguese-Gujarathi 3101
Portuguese-Japanese 3113
Portuguese-Konkani 3101
Portuguese-Nyanja 2648
Portuguese-Tamil 3101
Portuguese-Vietnamese 2584
Position diachronischer Markierungen 660
— phonetischer Angaben 512
Positionen des onomasiologischen Wörterbuches 1057
positionsalphabetisch 1144
positionsspezifisches Angabesymbol 390, 440
possible words 2698
Postglossat 447, 469, 490
Postintegrat 482, 2139
Postkommentar 397, 474, 491, 2138, 2206
—, etymologischer 2108f. 2140, 2144, 2159, 2200
—, phraseologischer 2150f., 2206
posttexte 331
  s. Nachspann
Potiguara 2671
practical constraints on lexicographical work 291
Prädikat, komparatives 431
Prädikation, sprachreflexive 431
prädikative Einbettungsstruktur 883
Prädikator 807
Prädikatorenklassen als funktionale Wortklassen 702f.
prädizieren 618
Präfix 869ff.
—, fremdsprachiges 872
—, seine Behandlung in deutschen Wörterbüchern 646
präfixoides Kompositum 870
Präfixverben 3025
Präglossat 469
pragmatic criterion for lexicographical data selection 289

— principle of lexicography 291
Pragmatik 160
pragmatisch-semantische Angabe 433, 468, 2109, 2138
pragmatische Angabe 433, 468, 623, 691, 693, 2139, 2845
— Markierung 850f.
Präintegrat 482, 2164
Prakrit 2502
Prakrit-English 2502
Präkommentar 383, 474, 490ff.
Präposition 1221
Präsentierung phraseologischer Einheiten 1022
Präskription 1298
  s. Norm
präskriptive Norm 194
präskriptives Wörterbuch 2054ff.
  s. normative dictionary,
  s. normatives Wörterbuch
präzedentives Integrat 484, 2120
pratique de marquage 678
  s. Markierung,
  s. Markierungspraxis
— morpho-étymologique 945
Praxisformen der Datenerhebung 1600
präzedentive Artikelstruktur 443
— Mikrostruktur 444f., 465, 950
präzedentives Subintegrat 487
— Vorderintegrat 449
Präzedenzrelation 465
pré-texte 330
  s. front matter,
  s. Vorspann
preface 99, 216f., 220f., 754ff., 1951
préface 673ff., 700, 2783, 2862
  s. Vorwort
préfixation 937
prefixation and headwords 300
préformée 1387
prérédaction 1585
prescriptive lexicography, its criticism in the 19th century 226
  s. Norm,
  s. Präskription
presentation 2723
présentation 2828
presentation and format of dictionaries 90
— of lexicographical data 288
pretheoretical notion of dictionary 294
primäre Daten 1591
primary learning dictionaries 2889
Primat der optimalen Platzverwendung 2779f.
  s. Druckraumeinsparung
Prinzip der Gewässernamenforschung 1285

— des semantischen Kommentars 434, 2142
Prinzipien phonetischer Angaben 511
privilegierte Zugriffsstruktur 2181
Probandenauswahl in der Wörterbuchbenutzungsforschung 1633
Problemkommentar 434
production 1069
Produktion fremdsprachlicher Texte 2741
Produktionsfunktion 2795
Produktionsnorm 191
Produktionswörterbuch 2157
  s. dictionnaire de production,
  s. encoding dictionary
produktives Wortbildungsmittel 871
Produktnorm 191
Professionalisierung der Lexikographie als Problem 13
Profil, makrostrukturelles 373
—, mikrostrukturelles bei zweisprachigen Wörterbüchern 2748f.
  s. Arten von Mikrostrukturen
Programm für Indexarbeit 1572
Programm, lexikographisches 419
—, —, in Deutschland 230ff.
Programmdiskussion 2052
programme du dictionnaire 1581
Progression, thematische 949f.
Prominentenvorwort in Wörterbüchern 19
Promtuario 2917
prononciation 218, 1218, 1304, 2863, 3010
pronouncing dictionary 1921, 1955
  s. Aussprachewörterbuch,
  s. dictionary of pronunciation
pronunciation 1384, 1948, 1973, 1995, 2962
proper name 2816
propos 328
  s. Rhema
propositionale Dichte 2838, 2845
Protohattisch 1687
Prototyp 969
Prototypensemantik 611
Prototypentheorie 573
prototypical dictionary 293
prototypisches Beispiel 812
provençal als Terminus
  s. *occitan*
Provenzalisch 1891ff.
provenzalisch als Terminus
Provenzalisch-Französisch 1894
proverbe [engl.] 2822
  s. Sprichwort,
  s. Sprichwortangabe

proverbe [franz.] 2982
Provinzialismus 1155, 1167, 1232
— im 18 Jh. 238
— im etymologischen Wörterbuch 1327
Prozeß, abgeschlossener lexikographischer 2101
—, lexikographischer 2123
pseudo-construit 937
Pseudonym 1292
Pseudonymenwörterbuch 1292
public criticism of US-American lexicography 35
publication data, manipulations by publishers 98f.
   s. Wörterbuchkriminalität
publicité 38ff.
publisher and mass media in the USA 34
Puebla 2659
puissance onomasiologique 1096
Pumi 2560
Punic 1690
purism 2438
— in Danish lexicography 1915
— in Norwegian lexicography 1925
— in Tagalog 2569
purisme 1212, 1213, 3009
Purismus 5, 64, 1173, 2403
— des 19. und 20. Jhs. 1232
— im Färoischen 1930
— in der historischen Lexikographie des Deutschen 1155
— in der russischen Lexikographie 3073
Puschtu-Russisch 3081
Pushto 3096
Pushto-English 3110
Pushto-Russian 3101
Pushto-Urdu 3099
Putér 1896

Q

Qabena 2464
Qašqa' i-Aynallu 2408
Qawasqar 2709
Qiang 2560
Qiangic 2555
Qualitätsprofil, lexikographisches 2136
Quantität als lexikalisches Merkmal 1640
quantitative Datenerhebung 1638ff.
— Feststellungen in der Lexikographie 1641
quantitativer Wörterbuchvergleich 2118

Quantitäts- und Qualitätsdifferenz zwischen der semasiologischen und onomasiologischen Lexikographie 1064
quantitätsbestimmte Corpusprobleme 1598
quasi-renvoi 932
quasi-synonyme 635
Quasiäquivalenz 2943
Quasisynonym 624
québécisme 1500
Quechua 2684, 2705
Quechua-Spanish 2678, 2682
Quechumaran 2705
Quellenangabe 433, 468, 1045, 2139
Quellennachweisprinzip 2131
Quellenverzeichnis im Wörterbuch 2115
Quellenwert von Wörterbüchern 2110, 2115, 2184, 2208, 2214
Querübersetzung 173
Queshwa 2705
Quichua 2705
quotation 1949
— 1957, 1979
— in Johnson's dictionary 225
— in the Deutsches Wörterbuch 226
— in the Oxford English Dictionary 228
quotations and examples in bilingual dictionaries 2783f.
quote 1508

R

Radê 2591
radical 1834
Rahmenartikel 2125
Rahmenstruktur
   s. textuelle Rahmenstruktur
—, textuelle 2106f., 2112, 2153, 2165, 2178, 2199
   s. textual book structure
Rajasthani 3100
Rajasthani-Hindi 3100
rallying cry 1056
Raluana 2574
Randspalte 1367
Randstruktur, linke 474, 493, 495ff.
—, rechte 2144, 2149, 2151, 2206
   s. right border structure
range 1318, 2777
ranghöchstes Diasystem mit Norm 1392
rapid access structure 335
   s. Schnellzugriffsstruktur
rappel 933

Rarámuri 2699
rare 912
Rarotongan Maori 2574
Rätoromanisch 1895
Raumarchaismus 1154
Raumsynonym 619
Raumvarietätenangabe 2175
Rayón Zoque 2698
readability 1071
Real Academia Española 1742
Real- und Nominaldefinition 541
Realdefinition 1172
Realwörterbuch 988
reception 1069
Recht von Einzelsprachen auf Lexikographie 15
rechte basisexterne Kernstruktur 2143
— hierarchische Kernstruktur, Definition 472
— hierarchische Randstruktur, Definition 475
— Interstruktur 477
— Kernstruktur 472ff., 2114, 2119, 2141, 2146, 2158, 2164, 2206
   s. right core structure
— Randstruktur 474, 492, 2144, 2149, 2151, 2206
   s. right border structure
— Teilkernstruktur 488, 2157f.
   s. right partial core structure
rechter Zwischenkommentar 477, 494
rechts laufende Zugriffsstruktur 402
Rechtsauslagerung 485
Rechtschreibangabe 429, 433, 446, 468
   s. ortographe,
   s. Ortographie,
   s. spelling and dictionaries
Rechtschreibgrundwortschatz 2191f.
Rechtschreiblexikographie 2091ff.
Rechtschreiblexikographie des Deutschen 2090
Rechtschreibung 1297
   s. ortographe,
   s. Ortographie,
   s. spelling and dictionaries
Rechtschreibwörterbuch 1777, 2155, 2157
   s. Ortographiewörterbuch
— des Deutschen 2190ff.
—, amtliches 2192
   s. Duden-Ortographie-Wörterbuch
—, verstecktes 2112
rechtserweiterte Basisstruktur 477
— hierarchische Mikrostruktur 474

— integrierte Mikrostrukturen 2147ff.
— Lemmazeichengestaltangabe 2123
— Mikrostruktur 474, 491f., 2108, 2142, 2144, 2151, 2159, 2200
— Mikrostruktur mit binnenerweiterter Basisstruktur 496f.
— nichtintegrierte Mikrostruktur 491
   s. right-expanded unintegrated microstructure
Rechtswörterbuch, Deutsches 1392
   s. NR: H.Speer
rédacteur 1582
rédacteur en chef 1583
Redensart 1054
Redewendung 1052, 1054, 1098
   s. locution,
   s. Phrasem,
   s. Phraseologismus
Redukt 442, 466
— vs. Substruktur 443
Reduktionsform 962
Redundanz und Textverdichtung 966
Redundanzverdikt 550f.
référence 912, 931
— bibliographique 728
— croisée 931
— d'exemples 1674
— numérique 1563
reference skill 105
   s. Benutzer
référentiel 2860
referenzunterstellendes Relationsprädikat 807
referieren 618
refinement of dictionaries 3158
refonte 1586
Reformation und Lexikographie 2
Reformwörterbuch 1302
Regel 610
Regel als Terminus 189
Regel und Norm 189ff., 194ff.
Regelformulierung 610
—, lexikographische 621
régional 912
regional, function of the label 289
regional variety and lexicography 71f.
régionalisme 86, 1500, 1837
regionalism 2733, 2953
Regionalismus 2798
Regionalwörterbuch 1894, 2198
Register 339, 394, 404, 767ff., 1076, 1106, 1948, 2176, 2179, 2181, 2204, 2923
   s. index,

   s. Nachspann,
   s. Wörterbuchregister
register and lexicography 72f.
— dictionary 2698
— marking 1974
Register und Computer 770
—, Form und Funktion 767f.
Registereintrag 394
registerexterne Zugriffsstruktur 396, 2115
Registerinformation 394
registerinterne Zugriffsstruktur 394
registerinterner Leitelementträger 394
Registertradition 769
Registerzugriffsstruktur 393
   s. access structure of indexes
registre 674
— de langues 912
regroupement 1371, 1373, 1376, 1388
   s. Gruppierung
— de mots 933
— morphologique 1833
Reichtum als Terminus der Stammwortdiskussion 232, 238
Reichtum der Sprache 1232
Reihenfolge der Einzelbedeutungen im gesamtsprachbezogenen Wörterbuch 1406
Reihungsprinzip in der Bedeutungserläuterung 1405
Reimlexikographie 2049
Reimlexikographie des Deutschen 2066
Reimlexikon 1126, 2410
Reimwörterbuch 26, 978, 1126, 1127, 1771, 1778, 2270
   s. dictionnaire de rimes
Reinheit als Terminus der Stammwortdiskussion 232
Reinheit der Sprache 1232
Reiseführer 2904
Reisesprachführer 3013
Reisewörterbuch 2740, 2878, 2903ff.
—, Typen 2906ff.
rekonstruierte Sprache: Wörterbuch, Geschichte 1337
—, Informationen zum Lemma 1336
—, Literaturangaben darin 1336
rekonstruierte Vokabel 1335
Rekonstrukt 1336
Rekonstruktion von Vokabeln, Beispiel 1336
Rektion 2258
— im normativen Wörterbuch 68
Rektionsangabe 433, 468
Relation, paradigmatische 888

—, partitive 428
—, skopusbezogene 447
—, syntagmatische 888
Relationsprädikat 807, 812, 962
— zur Einstellungsbekundung 807
—, bei Partikel 962
—, referenzunterstellendes 807
relativ obligatorische Angabe 455
relative äußere Vollständigkeit 373
Relevanz, gesellschaftliche, der Lexikographie 5ff.
Religion und Lexikographie 2
remarque 700
Remo 2543
Remo-English 2543
Renaissancewörterbuch 9
Rendille 2464
Rengma 2558
renvoi 82, 507, 931ff., 1372, 1581
   s. cross reference,
   s. lexikalischer Verweis,
   s. Verweisangabe
— analogique 1373, 1376
— bibliographique 726ff.
— externe 728
— interne 728
repérage 139
répertoire général de normes 1581
Repertorium als Sammlung von Familiennamen 1271
repetition symbol 344
   s. Platzhaltersymbol
—, representation 344
Repräsentativität eines Textkorpus 1642
— in der Fachwortlexikographie 1626
— und Korpus 200
representation of lexical meaning 3158
— of signs 3142
repression of the Belorussian language 2336
research approach in neologistic dictionaries 1163
Resígaro 2702
restbildende Linksauslagerung 452
restfreie Linksauslagerung 452
retrogrades Wörterbuch des Friesischen 2026
rétrotraduction 2823
reversa alphate Fization 2590
reverse-order dictionary of Swedish 1938
reversibility 2952
review of dictionaries in the USA 34
revival of languages and lexicography 71

Revolution, Französische 1054
Rezeption der gotischen Lexikographie 1920
— und zweisprachiges Wörterbuch 2741
Rezeptionsfunktion 2795
Rhade 2593
Rhema 328, 945ff.
Rhemafixierung 948
rhematische Angabe 949f.
— Angabestruktur 950
Rhodanisch 1894
rhyme arrangement 2441ff.
rhyming dictionary
   s. dictionnaire de rimes,
   s. Reimwörterbuch
right border structure 356
   s. rechte Randstruktur
— core structure 354
   s. rechte Kernstruktur
— partial core structure 356
   s. rechte Teilkernstruktur
— word 1069
right-expanded unintegrated microstructure 356
   s. rechts erweiterte nichtintegrierte Mikrostruktur
riksmål (Norwegian) 1925
rimari 1125
rimario 1127
rime 1125
Rio de la Plata Region 2706
Ripuarisch 2361
Ritwan 2691
Robert méthodique 646, 1374
   s. NR: J. Rey-Debove
Rogets Thesaurus 1081, 1083ff.
Rohindex 1567
Român-German 2844ff.
Romanisch-Deutsch 1896
Romanisch, Bündner 1895
Romany and Swedish criminals cant 1940
Ron 2457
Ronge 2643
root dictionary 2697
Rottinese 2564ff.
Rotuman 2574
roumaine 3173
Routineformel 830ff.
Royal Academy of Sciences in Stockholm 1934
— Society of Sciences in Uppsala 1934
rubrique morphétymologique 942
rückläufige Anordnungsform 379
rückläufiges Belegformenwörterbuch 1135
— Formenverzeichnis 1132
— Lemmawörterbuch 1135
rückläufiges Wörterbuch 1131ff., 1779

— des Deutschen 2184
— des Russischen 2319f.
—, Abgrenzung 1131
—, Aufbau 1134
—, Aufgabe 1134
—, Definition 1131
—, Typen 1131
Rückmeldungsfunktion, von Partikeln 828
Rückmeldungspartikel 823
rudimentäre Mikrostruktur 383, 456, 469
   s. rudimentary microstructure 354
— Wörterbuchgrammatik 2107, 2126
rudimentärer Subartikel 2140
rudimentary microstructure 354
Rumanian-Japanese 3113
Rumänische Lexikographie 1880ff.
Rumänisch-Deutsch 1883, 1886f.
Rumänisch-Französisch 1883f., 1887
Rumänisch-Ungarisch 2380
Rumantsch Grischun-Deutsch 1900
run-in entry 2000
run-on entry 2953, 2961
Runeninschrift 1908
Runga-Kibet 2643
russe-danois 3058
Russian 3108, 3116, 3175
Russian lexicography 764
Russian-Amharic 2451
Russian-Arabic 3092
Russian-Archi 2422
Russian-Armenian 2369
Russian-Belorussian 2336f.
Russian-Bengali 3101
Russian-Budukh 2422
Russian-Caucasian 2421f.
Russian-Chinese 3110
Russian-English 3081, 3176
Russian-Estonian 2393f.
Russian-French 2715
Russian-German 2896
Russian-Gilyak 2630
Russian-Hindi 3101
Russian-Somali 2464
Russian-Tamil 3101
Russian-Ukrainian 2330
Russian-Urdu 3101
Russian-Yiddish 2249ff.
russification 2393
Russisch 3022, 3068
russische nationalsprachliche Wörterbücher 3081
Russisch-Arabisch 3081
Russisch-Aserbeidschanisch 3081
Russisch-Baschkirisch 3081
Russisch-Bulgarisch 2305ff., 3078

Russisch-Chinesisch 3078f.
Russisch-Dari 3081
Russisch-Deutsch 2714, 2845, 3073, 3075, 3077f., 3081
Russisch-Englisch 3070, 3081
Russisch-Französisch 3073, 3077, 3079f.
Russisch-Georgisch 3072
Russisch-Griechisch 3069
Russisch-Italienisch 3078
Russisch-Japanisch 2619, 3073, 3078
Russisch-Kalmückisch 3078
Russisch-Karakalpakisch 3081
Russisch-Kasachisch 3081
Russisch-Katalanisch 1776
Russisch-Kirchenslawisch 2304, 3069
Russisch-Kirgisisch 3078, 3081
Russisch-Koreanisch 3078
Russisch-Kurdisch 2483
Russisch-Lettisch 2357f., 3072, 3078
Russisch-Neugriechisch 3073
Russisch-Neukirchenslawisch 2265
Russisch-Niederländisch 3073
Russisch-Norwegisch 3082
Russisch-Ossetisch 2484
Russisch-Pašto 2484
Russisch-Polnisch 3063ff., 3076
Russisch-Puschtu 3081
Russisch-Rumänisch 1883
Russisch-Schwedisch 3078
Russisch-Serbokroatisch 3078
Russisch-Slowakisch 2286
Russisch-Tadschikisch 3081
Russisch-Tatarisch 3072, 3080
Russisch-Tibetisch 3078
Russisch-Tschechisch 2282, 3078
Russisch-Tschuwaschisch 3081
Russisch-Türkisch 2408f., 3078
Russisch-Ukrainisch 3076
Russisch-Ungarisch 2380
Russisch-Usbekisch 3081
Russisch-Vietnamesisch 3081
Russisch-Weißrussisch 3076
Rusticanus terminorum 2042
Ryukyu 2621

S

Sa'a 2574
Sabaot 2644
Sabaot-English 2644
sabir als Terminus 2871
Sach- und Bedeutungswissen 846
Sachbeschreibung im enzyklopädischen Wörterbuch 991

Sachglossar des Früh- und Hochmittelalters 2037ff.
— des späten Mittelalters und der frühen Neuzeit 1061
Sachgruppenwörterbuch, zweisprachiges 1088, 1792f., 2795, 2880
　s. dictionnaire par ordre de matières,
　s. Thesaurus
Sachlexikographie 11f., 989
— und Erbwortbezug 1233
Sachlexikon 1106
Sachlich geordnetes Wörterbuchverzeichnis des Mittalters 2038
Sachschelte 2202
Sachwissen, fachenzyklopädisches 560
Sachwörterbuch 1203, 2042f.
— und philologische Benutzungssituation 156
— zu Berufsbezeichnungen 1248
—, fachliches 1254
Sachwörterbuch: Stottern und Poltern von Scholz und Eckert 2211
SAE-Sprachen 2344
Sag es treffender von Textor 2180f.
　s. kumulative Synonymik
Saharan 2642
Saho 2462
saisie als Terminus 2806
Saka 2473
Sakapulas 2664
Sakapultek 2661
Salarisch 2408, 2411
Salishan 2691
samanartha als Terminus 2522
Sambal 2569
Samoan 2573
Samoan-English 2574
Samogitian 2352
Samoyed 2395
San 2654
Sandawe 2650
Sangirese 2564ff.
Sango 2648
Sangtam 2558
Sani 2559
sanscrit-français 2492
Sanskrit 2487, 3096
　s. lexicography of Old Indo-Aryan
Sanskrit-English 2490ff., 2528
Sanskrit-French 2491
Sanskrit-German 2492
Sanskrit-Japanese 3113
Sanskrit-Kannada 2524
Sanskrit-Tibetan 2548

Santa Cruzan 2636
Santali 2534, 2541
Santali-English 2541
Santhali 3096
Saora 2544
Saphre 2655
Sápmi 2388
Šapsugh 2419
saramaccan 2871
Sardisch 1901
Sardisch-Italienisch 1902
Sarikoli 2481
Saterfriesisch 2028
Satzakzent, Angabe 515
Satzäquivalent im phraseologischen Wörterbuch 1025
Satzbauplan 2173
Satzbildung und Konstruktionswörterbuch 1000f.
Satzlexika, mehrsprachige 2920f.
Satzmusterangabe 433, 468, 2136
— für Verben 2145
Satzphonetik 515
Satzwörterbuch 1050ff., 2879
— des Deutschen 2177
— und Synonymenwörterbuch 1051
Śaurasenī 2498
Savara 2527
scanning 140
scene 894
　s. frame,
　s. Frame
schallnachahmende Interjektion 823
Scheinarchaismus 1154
Scheinkognate 1335
Schelte, ethnische 1191
Schema-F-Kodifikation 424
Scherz- und Spottname, zugehörige Wörterbücher 1294
Schichtarchaismus 1154
Schichtung der fachsprachlichen Lexik 843f.
Schimpfwort 1190, 1294
Schimpfwörterbuch 1190ff.
— des Deutschen 2188
schottisch-gälische Lexikographie 2346
Schlagwort 1221
— vs. Parole 1200
Schlagwörterbuch 1045, 1199ff.
— des Deutschen 2188
"Schmökern" im Wörterbuch 24
Schnellzugriffsstruktur 335, 2150
　s. rapid access structure
scholarly aspect of lexicography 292
— dictionaries 2003
— dictionary vs. popular dictionary, outside matter 765

Schottisch-Gälisch 2346
Schreibtischwort 2345
Schreibungsangabe 433, 468
Schreibvariantenangabe 468
Schreibwörterbuch 184, 1001, 1044, 2716
Schrift 374
　s. akkadische Keilschrift,
　s. Alphabet,
　s. script
—, arabische 2625
—, chinesische 2625
—, kyrillische 2226
—, nigurische 2625
—, oriatische 2625
—, hieratische 1679
—, hieroglyphische 1679
Schriftenwechsel in der U.S.S.R. 3080
Schriftkultur, Süd-Nord-Gefälle 1419
Schriftsprache 1154
— Europas 2255
Schriftsystem 372, 373f.
—, alphabetisches 374
Schrifttyp 374
Schriftzeichen 374
—, logographisches 375
Schülerwörterbuch 2213
　s. dictionnaire scolaire
Schulvokabular des 16. Jhs. 2043
Schulwörterbuch 1365, 1778, 2054
schwach nischenalphabetisches Wörterbuch 390
— teildistinktive Synonymik 2181
Schwedisch 2916
Schwedisch-Deutsch 3043ff.
Schwedisch-Finnisch 2384
Schwedisch-Isländisch 1929
Schwedisch-Lettisch 2359
schweres Wort 1100, 1206
　s. hard word
Schwerwortwörterbuch 1207
Schwierigkeitswörterbuch
　s. dictionnaire de difficultés
scolaire 1386
Scot 1983
scotticism 1983
Scrabble-Wörterbuch 1144
script 297ff., 894
—, cuneiform 297f.
—, ideographic 297
　s. Schrift
Scythian 2471
Sechsbänder der deutschen Standardsprache 2130ff.
secondary dictionary function 2777
— learning (learner's dictionaries) 2893
secrétaire général de rédaction 1583

Sedang 2591
Segmentation 423ff.
— von standardisierten Wörterbuchartikeln 437ff.
—, exhaustive funktional-positionale 438
—, — funktionale 438
—, funktional-postitionale 438
—, funktionale 366
segmentation textual 330
Segmentationsmethode 437f.
Seitenangabe 2138
sekundäre Daten 1590
Sekundärsuffixoid 870
selection 1160, 2723, 2891f.
sélection 1835
selection of entries 3143
— of lexicographical data 288
selectivity 1069
Selektion der Phraseme 2155
— von Komposita 2134f.
— von Wortbildungsmitteln 2135
—, äußere 373, 396, 2106f., 2110, 2114, 2121ff., 2129ff., 2147, 2150, 2152, 2159, 2165, 2171, 2182, 2192f., 2201, 2203, 2207, 2209f., 2213
 s. macrostructure [engl., franz.],
 s. Makrostruktur,
 s. outer selection,
 s. selection,
 s. sélection
—, — der Wortbildungsmittel 2153
—, — lernzielorientierte 2172
Selektion, innere 2121, 2159, 2207
 s. inner selection
Selektionskriterien 3139
 s. criterium of lexicographical data selection
— für Komposita 644
Selektionsproblematik in der onomasiologischen Lexikographie 1059
— bei der Fachlexik im gesamtsprachbezogenen Wörterbuch 1396
selektives Wörterbuch 1551
Selepet 2636
Selkup 2395
Selti 2452
Sema 2558
semantic bridge 1699f.
— comment on context 355
— paraphrasing item 355
 s. Bedeutungsparaphrasenangabe
— prototype and lexicography 292

— subcomment 354f.
 s. semantischer Subkommentar
— subdivision 2785
Semantik im textsortenbezogenen Wörterbuch 1542
semantisch relevanter Kontext 2142
semantische Beschreibungssprache 161
— Form von Sprachzeichen 790
— Glosse 653
— Instabilität 837
— Nische 2747
 s. Nische
— Vereinbarkeitsrelationen 888ff.
semantischer basisexterner Kommentar 2143
— Kommentar 434, 470, 621, 1423, 2113
 s. comment on semantics 345
— Kommentar im Autorenwörterbuch 1554
— Kotextkommentar 488ff., 2149
 s. semantic comment on context 355
semantischer Subkommentar 435, 2109, 2137, 2142
 s. semantic subcomment
— zur Komposition 2117, 2157f.
— 2. Stufe 2145
semantisches Merkmal 544, 546
— Wissen vs. Weltwissen 992
semasiological dictionary, its purpose 291
semasiologische Lexikographie, sprachübergreifend 1410
semasiologischer Teil des semantischen Kommentars 621
semasiologisches Wörterbuch
 s. allgemeines einsprachiges Wörterbuch
sematische Subkommentare zweiter und dritter Stufe 486
sème 281
 s. semantisches Merkmal
sémème 1820
Semgallisch 2358
semiintegrierte Mikrostruktur 2749
Semiotaktisch 2877
Semnānī 2481
sens 702
— figuré 906
— propre 906
sense discrimination 1978
 s. Äquivalenzdifferenzierung
— ordering in historical English lexicography 1451
sentence introducer 1054

sentential dictionary,
 s. Satzwörterbuch
séquence 1387
sequence, non-alphabetic 297
Šera Yõgur 2626
Serbisch-Lateinisch 3076
Serbisch-Russisch 3078
serbokroatische Lexikographie 2288ff.
Serbokroatisch-Albanisch 2292
Serbokroatisch-Englisch 2292
Serbokroatisch-Französisch 2292
Serbokroatisch-Italienisch 2292
Serbokroatisch-Neugriechisch 2292
Serbokroatisch-Polnisch 2292
Serbokroatisch-Russisch 2292, 3078
session de consultation 2812
set phrase 2785
sexueller Wortschatz 1193
Shabo 2643
Shatt-Liguri 2644
Shemya 2644
Sherpa 2558
Shilluk 2644
Shinasha 2463
Shona 2648
Shona-English 2648
Shuar 2703
Siamese 2576
Sidamo 2463f.
Siedlungsname 1277
sigle 934, 1211
Siglit 2632
sign and symbol 762
— codes 3143
— dictionaries 3142
— languages 3141
signes, équivalences de 2860
Sila 2644
Silbenalphabet 378
Silbenangabe 433, 468, 2144, 2163
Silbengrenze 513
Silbengrenzenangabe und phonetische Transkription 79
Silbentrennungsangabe 429, 433, 468, 2144, 2847
 s. syllabification
Silesiazismus 1155
Similia 1335
simple microstructure 353
 s. einfache Mikrostruktur
Simplified characters (Chinese) 2606
Sindhi 2516, 3096
Sindhi-English 2516
Sindhi-Urdu 2516, 3098
Singularbildungsangabe 433, 468, 2116
 s. item giving singular form 346

Singularetantumangabe 433, 468
Sinngruppe im phraseologischen
    Wörterbuch 1028
Sinnspruch 1054
Sinyar 2644
Siouan 2691
Sipakapa 2661
Sirenik 2631
Sirianó 2701
Sirionó 2674, 2704
sisamu als Terminus 2525
situationsgebundener Wortschatz
    im gesamtsprachbezogenen
    Wörterbuch 1399
Situationswörterbuch 2905
size 1943, 1972
    s. Größenklassen
Skopus 449, 450, 485, 2740
— und Geltungsfeld 450
— von Angabesymbolen 2110
skopusbeschränkende Angabe
    435
Skopusbeschränkungsrelation
    452
Skopusbeziehung, Vertextung der
    2137
skopusbezogene Relation 447
skopuseröffnende Angabe 449
Skopusrelation 451
Skythisch 2471
Slang 1184, 1524
slang 1477, 1532
— dictionary and glossary of
    Swedish 1940
— in American lexicography 36
slogan 1054
Slogan 1200
Slovinzisch 2270
Slowakisch 2284
Slowakische Lexikographie
    2284ff.
Slowakisch-Russisch 2286
Slowakisch-Tschechisch 2282
Slowenisch 2913
slowenische Lexikographie
    2296ff.
Slowenisch-Deutsch 2298, 2745
So 2643
So 2590
sobriquet 1055
sociolinguistic criterion of lexi-
    cographical data selection 289
sociolinguistique 673
Soddo 2452
Sogdian 2473, 2475
Solenissimo vocabuolista 1088
Solomek 2661
Solomon Pijin 1494
Somali 2462f.
Somali-English 2463f.
Somali-Italian 2464

Sondersprache 1523, 1532
Sondersprachenlexikographie des
    Deutschen 2061f.
sondersprachliche Angabe 429
Songay 2642
Sonqori 2408, 2411
Sora 2534, 2544
Sora-English 2533, 2544
Sorbisch 2274f.
sorbische Lexikographie 2274ff.
Sortierung, kategoriell-alphabeti-
    sche 2749
—, kategoriell-semantisch-alpha-
    betische 2749
—, maschinelle, von Wörtern,
    Probleme 1570
    s. Anordnungsform
sottisier 1348
source language 2719
    s. lexikographische Ausgangs-
    sprache
— of reference, manipulations
    by publishers 99
sous-adresse 350
    s. Subadresse,
    s. Unteradresse
sous-entrée 308, 507, 636, 638,
    933ff., 2865
    s. Subartikel,
    s. sub-lemma
South America 2708
soziale Norm 191
sozialschichtiger Wortschatz im
    gesamtsprachbezogenen Wör-
    terbuch 1399
soziokulturell orientierte Wörter-
    buchgeschichte 2103
Soziolekte, ihre Merkmal in den
    Wörterbüchern des Nieder-
    ländischen 2016
soziolektbezogenes etymologi-
    sches Wörterbuch 1329
Soziologie deutscher Sprachsta-
    dien 1419
Spanisch 3022
—, amerikanisches 1751
Spanisch-Arabisch 1742
Spanisch-Cakchike 2661
Spanisch-Deutsch 2730, 2733f.,
    2741ff., 2797ff., 2905, 2987ff.
Spanisch-Französisch 2745, 2987
Spanisch-Holländisch 2987
Spanisch-Italienisch 1848
Spanisch-Japanisch 1741
Spanisch-Katalanisch 1776ff.
Spanisch-Lateinisch 1849, 2661
Spanisch-Polnisch 3064
Spanisch-Portugiesisch 1726
Spanisch-Serbokroatisch 2292
Spanisch-Tschechisch 2283
spanische Lexikographie 1738ff.
— Metalexikographie 1750

Spanish 1736, 2949, 3116
Spanish-Armenian 2370
Spanish-Aymara 2685, 2688
Spanish-Aztec 2697
Spanish-Chiriguano 2674
Spanish-English 2715, 2949ff.,
    2987
Spanish-Galician 1737
Spanish-Guaraní 2673f.
Spanish-Latin 2657, 2697
Spanish-Mixtec 2697
Spanish-Mopan 2663
Spanish-Nahuatl 2658
Spanish-Quechua 2678, 2682
Spanish-Tarascan 2697
Spanish-Zapotec 2697
Spanish lexicography
    s. spanische Lexikographie
special dictionary, future 3161
— dictionary of Swedish 1938
— field item 355
    s. Fachgebietsangabe
special-purpose dictionary of Old
    English 1444
spécialement 912
specialist dictionary (Danish)
    1920
spécificateur 2817
Specimen lexici comparativi om-
    nium linguarum europearum
    2918
spelling and dictionaries 90
    s. Orthographie,
    s. Rechtschreibung
— dictionary 2587, 2857
    s. Ortographiewörterbuch,
    s. Rechtschreibwörterbuch
— dictionary (Danish) 1916
Speziallexikographie, germanisti-
    sche Desiderata 2184
Spezialwörterbuch 970, 973f.,
    1679
— des Deutschen 2171ff.
— und gebildete Öffentlichkeit
    24ff.
—, paradigmatisches des Deut-
    schen 2177f., 2184
—, syntagmatisches des Deut-
    schen 2171ff., 2177
—, zweisprachiges 2877ff.
Spezialwörterbücher 2877ff., 3139
—, paradigmatische 1057ff.
—, syntagmatische 1000ff.
Spezifizierung des Bezugsberei-
    ches 536
Spitz- und Schimpfname, ethni-
    scher 1293
Spitzname 1292
spoken language in Danish dic-
    tionaries 1913
Sprach- und Sachlexikographie
    der Ortsnamen 1276

Sprach-Brockhaus 331, 390, 430, 531, 705, 721, 742, 806, 963, 2106ff., 2128, 2135
Sprachbildung 2093f.
Sprachdatum 972
Sprache als Identifikationsinstrument 1403
— und Bild 714
—, deutsche: Probleme ihrer Bestimmung in der Lexikographie 1410
—, rekonstruierte: Wörterbuch 1335ff.
Spracheinheit 2093f.
— des Niederländischen 1402
Sprachenidentifizierungsangabe 433, 468, 2144
Sprachenpaare der Erde 8
Sprachenvergleichsangabe 433, 468
Spracherwerbswörterbuch 184
s. Erwerbswörterbuch
Sprachgebrauchstradition des 17.-20. Jhs. 1233
— im Deutschen 1236
Sprachgesellschaft des 17. Jhs. 232
—, Textkanon 1540
Sprachglossar des 14. Jhs. 2039
— des 15. Jhs.. 2041
Sprachglosse 2176
Sprachhandlungsmuster 816
Sprachkultur 2132
sprachliche Angabe 429f.
Sprachnorm 189
s. Norm,
s. norme,
s. Präskription
—, Gefahren 197f.
—, Prager Schule 190
Sprachpflege 2111
— und Lexikographie 4
Sprachplanung und Lexikographie 4
Sprachpolitik in der USSR 2408
sprachpolitische Bedeutung des zweisprachigen Wörterbuches 7
Sprachprestige und zweisprachige Lexikographie 6
Sprachproblemsituation 131
Sprachraum deutscher Sprachstadien 1418
sprachreflexive Prädikation 431
sprachreflexiver Kommentar 807
Sprachrichtigkeit 2093f.
Sprachstadienlexikographie des Deutschen 1416ff., 2087
— des Deutschen, Textsorten 1419
—, germanistische 2105
Sprachstadienwörterbuch 1157, 1393, 1416ff.

—, Artikelpositionen 1421
—, Definition 1430
—, Hinweis zur Etymologie 1423
—, historisches 432
—, Lemma 1421
—, onomasiologische Vernetzung 1424
—, Standardisierung 1426
—, Symptomwerte 1424
—, synchrone Wortschatzstruktur 1430
—, Syntagma 1425
—, Wortartangabe 1423
—, Wortbildung 1425
—, Wortvariante 1422
Sprachstadienwörterbücher des Deutschen, Benutzungsmöglichkeiten 1427
— des Deutschen, Zeitansatz 1420
— des Katalanischen 1777
— des Niederländischen 1431
Sprachstadium 1417
—, Bestimmungsprobleme 1430
—, deutsches: Soziologie 1419
—, — : Sprachraum 1418
Sprachstatistik 1638
Sprachstufe des Friesischen 2022
sprachstufenbezogenes etymologisches Wörterbuch 1328
sprachübergreifende semasiologische Lexikographie 1410
sprachübergreifendes Wörterbuch 1392, 1410
— von Varietäten 1410
— zu Varietäten 1392
Sprachvariation und Wörterbuch 1553
Sprachwissen und Wörterbuch 20
Sprachwissenschaft und Lexikographie 5
sprachwissenschaftlich orientierte Wörterbuchgeschichte 2103
sprachwissenschaftliche Fachlexikographie 2207ff.
sprachwissenschaftliches Fachwörterbuch 2207ff.
— von Knobloch et al. 2208
—, Adressaten 2213
Sprachwörterbuch 171, 988, 993
—, fachliches 1254
Sprachzeichen, semantische Form von 790
Sprachzeichenbegriff, polysemistischer 449
Sprechaktrestriktion im phraseologischen Wörterbuch 1025
Sprechakttheorie 814
Sprechhandlungspartikel 823
—, illokutionsvollziehende 823f.
Sprechsprache 1184

Sprechsprachenwörterbuch, zweisprachiges 2880
s. Wörterbuch der Sprechsprache
Sprichwort 3031
s. proverbe
Sprichwortangabe 433, 468
Sprichwörterbuch 1033ff., 2174
s. dictionnaire de locutions
— und Wörterbuchforschung 1038f.
—, Anordnung 1034
—, besondere Typen 1036
Sprichwörterlexikographie 1033f.
Sprichwörtersammlung 1033, 2915, 2917f.
—, mehrsprachige 2915ff.
—, neuhochdeutsche 1034ff.
Staatsorganisation und Lexikographie 3
Stammwortauffassung 231f.
— der Barockzeit 1232
Stammwörterbuch 2052
Stammwörterbuchprogramm in Deutschland 231ff.
Stammwortlexikographie 2053
Stammwortprinzip 2052, 2088, 2090
Standard Average European 2344
— Danish 1913, 1915
standard language 289
s. Standardsprache
— and lexicography 70ff., 294
— and lexicography, antiquating (archaizing) dictionairies 73
— and lexicography, influences on the user 75
— and lexicography, modernizing dictionaries 72
— and lexicography, regional varieties 71
— and lexicography, revival of languages 71
— and lexicography, standard-creating dictionaries 70ff.
— and lexicography, standard-descriptive dictionaries 74
standard of Norwegian 1923ff.
Standardfriesisch 2026
standardisiert regulierte Geltungsbeziehung 450
standardisierte Angabe 431
— Hyperstruktur 948
standardisierter Wörterbuchartikel 423ff., 946ff., 959
Standardisierung und Textverdichtung 957ff.
— von Sprachstadienwörterbüchern 1426
Standardisierungsmerkmal 431, 432, 434
Standardisierungstradition 424, 487

Standardsprache 662
    s. standard language
—, (festland)nordfriesische 2030
—, Westfriesisch 2026
standardsprachliche Variation 662
stark nischenalphabetisches Wörterbuch 390
— teildistinktive Synonymik 2181
statistisches Wörterbuch 163
Stellenangabe 2736
    s. Belegstellenangabe
Stellenhinweiswörterbuch 2851
Stenographiesysteme 3140
stenographische Lexika 3138
stéréotype 84
Stereotypensemantik 572
Stichwort 363, 1057, 2257
    s. entrée,
    s. entryword,
    s. headword,
    s. Lemma,
    s. lemme,
    s. mot vedette
— im phraseologischen Wörterbuch 1027
Stilebenenangabe 2733
Stilschichtangabe 433, 468
Stilschichtenkennzeichnung 2798
Stilwörterbuch 1012, 2037
— des Deutschen 2177
Štokavisch 2288
straight-alphabetical 336
    s. striktalphabetisch
Strichartikel 368, 480, 964, 965
striktalphabetisch 383f.
striktalphabetische Makrostruktur 383ff.
structural indicator 335
    s. Gliederungszeichen,
    s. Strukturanzeiger
— lexicography (Danish) 1919
— principle of lexicography 288
structuralism 1069
structuralisme 280ff., 1369
structuration de mot 942
structure and outward form of dictionaries 288
structure d'accès rapide 335
    s. Schnellzugriffsstruktur
— de mot 938ff., 941ff.
Struktur als Terminus 409f.
Strukturanzeiger 335, 375, 427f., 948, 950, 961, 965
    s. funktionales Textsegment,
    s. Gliederungszeichen,
    s. ordonnateur,
    s. structural indicator
— und Interpunktionszeichen 428
—, nichttypographischer 428, 512, 927, 2157, 2180, 2810

—, Polyfunktionalität 959
—, typographischer 375, 428, 512, 595, 927, 2119
Strukturart 441, 463
Strukturbegriff 372
Strukturbild, allgemeines 470
—, —; für einfache Mikrostrukturen 474
—, —; für einfache integrierte Mikrostrukturen 489
—, —; für einfache nichtintegrierte Mikrostrukturen 489
—, —; für extern vollständig erweiterte integrierte Mikrostrukturen 493
—, —; für integrierte Mikrostrukturen mit binnenerweiterter Basisstruktur 493
—, —; für integrierte Mikrostrukturen mit linkserweiterter Basisstruktur 494
—, —; für linkserweiterte Mikrostrukturen 474
—, —; für linkserweiterte Mikrostrukturen mit links- und rechtserweiterter Basisstruktur 497
—, —; für Mikrostrukturen mit binnenerweiterter Basisstruktur
—, —; für Mikrostrukturen mit linkserweiterter Basisstruktur 476
—, —; für Mikrostrukturen mit rechtserweiterter Basisstruktur 477
—, —; für rechtserweiterte Mikrostrukturen mit binnenerweiterter Basisstruktur 497
—, —; zu vollständig erweiterten Mikrostrukturen 479
Strukturdiagramme von Mikrostrukturausschnitten und Mikrostrukturen 348, 354ff., 453f., 456, 465f., 470ff., 535f., 2114ff., 2119ff., 2138ff., 2143ff., 2148f., 2151, 2154, 2158, 2161ff., 2205
stufenweise Segmentation von Wörterbuchartikel 439
style 1821, 1948
— lexicographique 1211
    s. dictionary style
    s. Wörterbuchstil
sub-addressing 329
sub-entry 2783ff., 2787
sub-lemma 2784f.
    s. sous-entrée
subaddress 349
Subadresse 349, 2730, 2747

Subadressierung 329
Subartikel 365, 481, 2119, 2141
— mit rudimentärer Basisstruktur 2142
—, rudimentärer 2140
Subinha 2661
Subintegrat 487, 2145f., 2740, 2748
Subintegratseingang 2749
Subkommentar, ausgelagerter 2151
—, semantischer 435, 2109, 2137, 2142
    s. Kommentar zur lexikalischen Bedeutung
—, —; zur Komposition 2117, 2157
—, —; 2.Stufe 2145
Sublemma 365, 2112, 2117, 2730, 2747
—, verstecktes 447
sublemmatic addressing 349
sublemmatische Adressierung 447
Substandard 1535
Substruktur 443, 466
— vs. Redukt 443
Subsystembezogenheit 836
Suchausgang 1076f.
Süd-Nord-Gefälle der Schriftkultur 1419
südamerikanisches Spanisch 2989
Sudanic 2642
Südhessisches Wörterbuch 2200
Südsibirisch 2407
suédois 3040
suédois-allemand 3040
suédois-danois 3058
suédois-français 3040ff.
Suffix 869, 873ff.
suffixation 937
Suffixoid 869ff., 876
suffixoides Kompositum 870
Šughnī-Rošānī 2481
Sumerian 1682
Sumerian and Akkadian lexicography 1682ff.
Sumerian-Akkadian 1682f.
Summarium Henrici 2038
Sundanese 2564ff.
Sungor 2643
Sunwari 2558
support 322ff.
— électronique 324
— réel 1674
Suprasegment 375
—, additives flächiges 375
—, — lineares 375
—, flächiges 375f.
—, integratives flächiges 375
—, — lineares 376, 428
—, lineares 375
Suprasegmentklasse 375

sur-équivalence 2823
surface 1585
Surin Khmer 2591
Surmic 2643
Sumerisch 1895
surrogate equivalents 2718
Surselvisch 1895
Surselvisch-Deutsch 1899
Suruí 2671
susceptibilities, cultural 2687
—, native 2687
Sutselvisch 1895
Svan 2415
Svan-English 2418
Svan-Russian 2417
Svenska Akademiens Ordbok 1940
Swahili-Japanese 3113
Swedish Academy 1934
— Centre for Technical Terminology 1939
— dialect of Finland and Estonia 1939
Swedish-English 2783, 3047ff.
Swedish-Estonian 2394
Swedish-Finnish 3175
Swedish-French 1939
Swedish-Japanese 3113
Swedish lexicography 1933ff.
syllabe 506f.
syllabification 1973
   s. Silbentrennungsangabe
sylva als Terminus 2912
Symbol 758
symbole de représentation 344
   s. Platzhaltersymbol,
   s. repetition symbol
Symbole, freie 3150
—, ikonographische 3149
symboles non langagiers 2863
Symptomfunktion sprachlicher Einheiten 1059
Symptomwert im Sprachstadienwörterbuch 1424
— im textsortenbezogenen Wörterbuch 1544
Symptomwertangabe 433, 468
— im gesamtsprachbezogenen Wörterbuch 1408
synchrone etymologische Kompetenz 1146
— Wortschatzstruktur als Gegenstand des Sprachstadienwörterbuches 1430
synchrones Wortfamilienwörterbuch 1146
synchronic identifying information 341
Synchronie vs. Diachronie im phraseologischen Wörterbuch 1023

synonym 2785
— dictionary of Swedish 1938
Synonym in onomasiologischer Position und Bedeutungsparaphrasenangabe 571
— in semasiologischer Position 571
synonym item 348
   s. Synonymenangabe
—, Danish dictionary of 1916
synonyme 219, 635, 800, 1370, 1877
Synonyme, ihre Bedeutungsunterschiede 618
Synonymen- und Thesauruslexikographie des Deutschen 2086f.
Synonymenangabe 433, 468, 534, 2117, 2159, 2211
   s. synonym item
— und andere funktionale Textsegmente 621
—, an die Phrasemangabe adressierte 2149
—, ihr Status 620f.
Synonymenexplikation, kumulative 621
Synonymengruppenangabe 2138
Synonymenlexikographie 2049
— des Deutschen 2058f.
Synonymenparonymie 1123
Synonymenunterscheidungsangabe 2178, 2181
   s. meaning discrimination
Synonymenwörterbuch 769, 2180
— der deutschen Redensarten von Schemann 2178ff.
— des Deutschen 2177ff.
— und Satzwörterbuch 1051
— von Görner u. Kempcke 2181f.
—, Typologie 2182
synonymie 218, 1833
Synonymie 598, 614ff., 2794f.
synonymie cumulative 1011
Synonymie von Modalpartikeln 625
— von Tier- und Pflanzenbezeichnungen 1255
—, lexikalische 618
—, lexikographische 568, 620
Synonymieverweis, expliziter 622
Synonymik der Idiomatik 1028
—, distinktive 1067ff.
—, kontrastive 2879
—, kumulative 1076, 1081
—, schwach teildistinktive 2181
—, stark teildistinktive 2181
Synonymiken, distinktive des Deutschen 2181ff.
—, kumulative des Deutschen 2177ff.

—, teildistinktive des Deutschen 2181ff.
Synonymkontrolle 615
Synonymwörterbuch 1051, 1777, 2182, 2378, 2794, 2879
   s. Synonymenwörterbuch
synonymy 168, 1076
synoptisches Lokalwörterbuch 2198
Synsemantika 569
— vs. Autosemantika 1222
syntactic construction, information 588ff.
— information, codes 589
— restrictions 2964
syntagm 1508, 2783
Syntagma 2779
— im Sprachstadienwörterbuch 1425
— im textsortenbezogenen Wörterbuch 1547
syntagmatic information 341f., 1975
   s. syntactici information
Syntagmatik im gesamtsprachbezogenen Wörterbuch 1408
—, kulturell definierte 1054
—, linguistisch definierte 1054
syntagmatique 1821
syntagmatische Relation 888
— Spezialwörterbücher 1000ff., 1054ff., 2878ff.
— Spezialwörterbücher des Deutschen 2171ff., 2177
syntagme 913
— codé 2860
syntagmes 933ff.
syntagmes-types 913
Syntax 608
syntax in English pedagogical dictionaries 589f.
— in monolingual English dictionaries 588f.
— in monolingual French dictionaries 590
syntopisches Lokalwörterbuch 2198
Syriac 2431
Syriac-Arabic 2427
Syriac-English 2432
Syriac-Latin 2432
Syriac-Malayalam 3101
Syriac script 2475
Systemäquivalente 2745
systematische Wörterbuchforschung 262
   s. allgemeine Theorie der Lexikographie
système de marquage 678
— de marques 678

T

Ta'e 2566
Tabassaran 2421
Tabelle zu Mikrostrukturen 2126
Tabi 2643
table 762, 1087
— d'abréviations 675
tableau 1370
— annexe 1375
taboo word in dictionaries 32
— in US-American lexicography 36
tabou 85f.
Tabu 1194
Tacanan languages 2703
tadbhava 2524
Tadžikisch 2477, 2481
Tag 2568
Tagalog 2568
Tagalog-English 2568f., 2733
Tagalog-French 2568
Tagalog-German 2568
Tagalog-Spanish 2568
Tagalog lexicography 2568ff.
Tahaggart 2456
Tahitian 2574
Taigi 2395
Tajik 2477, 2481
Takana 2703
Tališi 2481
Tama 2643
Tamil 2521, 3096, 3171
Tamil-Burmese 2524
Tamil-English 2523f., 3101f.
Tamil-French 2524, 3101
Tamil-Hindi 2524, 3098
Tamil-Malayalam 3098
Tamil-Portuguese 2524, 3101
Tamil-Russian 2524, 3101
Tamil-Sanskrit 2524
Tamil-Sinhalese 2524
Tamil-Telugu 2524, 3098
Tangkhul Naga 2559
Tangut 2555
Tankhur Naga 2558
Tanoan 2691
Tapiete 2671
Tapirapé 2671
Tarahumar 2699
Tarascan 2697
target language 2719
    s. lexikographische Zielsprache,
    s. Wörterbuchzielsprache
target word 1096
Tarma Quechua 2705
Tartarisch-Russisch 3080
Taschenwörterbuch 2988, 3065
Tasmanian languages 2638

Tātī 2481, 2485
tatsama als Terminus 2524
Tausug 2571
Tausug-English 2571
Tavgi 2395
taxinomie 2865
taxonomic principle of lexicography 288
taxonomy 1509
Tày-Nùng 2588
Tboli 2571
Tcheretch Agow 2452
teaching of dictionary use 208ff.
Teamarbeit vs. Einzelarbeit in der Lexikographie 242
technical dictionary 1505
— of Swedish 1939
technologie 326
Technosoziolekt 2941
Teda 2642
teilbereichsbezogenes Wörterbuch 1591
teildistinktive Synonymiken des Deutschen 2181ff.
Teilintegrat 2146, 2154, 2161
Teilkernstruktur, erste rechte 2149
—, linke 2117, 2148, 2158
—, rechte 2157f.
—, zweite rechte 2149
Teillemma 365, 369, 389, 2117, 2135, 2146
— und Lemmateil 368
teilparallelisiert 2750
Teilstandardsprache 662
Teilstrukturen von Mikrostrukturen 443ff., 469ff.
    s. Basisstruktur,
    s. Dachstruktur,
    s. Integrat,
    s. Interstruktur,
    s. Kernstruktur,
    s. Randstruktur
Teiltext 425f.
Teis-umm-Danab 2644
Tekniska nomenklaturcentralen 1939
Teko 2661
Telefol 2636
Telelcingo Aztec 2697
télématique 1674
Telugu 2521, 3096
Telugu-Hindi 3098
Telugu-English 2526ff.
Telugu-French 2526
Telugu-Marathi 3098
Telugu Savara 2527
Telugu-Tamil 3098
Telugu-Urdu 3098
Tembé 2675
Tembé-ténêtéhar 2676

Tembé-ténêtéhar-Português 2675
Temein 2643
Temirgoi-Russian 2420
Tenor 983
Tepes 2643
term banks
    s. computer and lexicography,
    s. Datenbank
terme vedette 907
Terminographie 2206
    s. computer and lexicography
Terminolgie 2783
terminological banks 3163
— data base 168f., 292
— dictionary 2393
    s. Normenwörterbuch
— glossary 167
Terminologie 49, 2865, 2940
— für Textsegmente 427
Terminologiebildung in der Ortsnamenlexikographie 1277
Terminologienormung 318
terminologique 1820
terminologisch orientierte Lexikographie 4
terminologische Wörterbuchbenutzungssituation 169f.
terminology and lexicography 72, 167f.
— of Norwegian 1927
—, lexicographical 2782
Terminus 843
Territorialwörterbuch 2198
tertium comparationis 2737, 2854
Teso 2644
Tesoro de la lengua castellana o española 1740
    s. NR: S. de Covarrubias
Tesouro da Língua Portuguesa 1726
    s. NR: B. Pareira
test 43
tête 2830
Tetelcingo 2659
Tetzcoco 2660
Teuthonista vulgariter dicendo der Duytschlender 2041f.
Text in Situation 171
— und Bild 707f.
—, beschreibender 366
—, historischer, Verfügbarkeit 1593
—, usueller 617
—, Wörterbuchartikel 946ff.
Textbasis 1549
— von Indices und Konkordanzen 1569
Textbaustein 425, 426, 431, 806
—, lexikographischer 607, 1227
Textbegriff 947
Textblock 376
Textblockbildung 386, 390, 2173

Textcorpus als lexikographische
    Datenbasis 1642
    s. Corpus,
    s. Wörterbuchbasis
texte de stockage 139
— externe 331
    s. Außentext
Textelement 425f., 806
—, monofunktionales 426
—, polyfunktionales 426
Textexegese und Wörterbuch
    1552
Texthaftigkeit 946, 953
Textkanons einer Sprachgesell-
    schaft 1540
Textkohärenz 609
    s. Kohärenz
Textkonstituentenstruktur 465
Textkonstituentenstrukturbäume
    470
Textkorpus und Lexikographie,
    Bezüge 1620
Textlänge in lexikographischen
    Korpora 1643
Textlexikographie 1234, 1590,
    2212
    s. author's lexicography,
    s. Autorenlexikographie
— und etymologisches Wörter-
    buch 1328
Textproduktion 117
Textrezeption 116f.
Textsegment 425, 432
    s. Angabe,
    s. Strukturanzeiger
—, funktionales 366, 425, 961
—, lexikographisches 806
—, nichtfunktionales 425
Textsorte im textsortenbezogenen
    Wörterbuch 1542
— in der Sprachstadienlexiko-
    graphie des Deutschen 1419
—, ihre Berücksichtigung im
    Fachwörterbuch 1627
textsortenbezogenes Wörterbuch
    des Deutschen 1539
—, Artikelaufbau 1543
—, Bedeutungserläuterung darin
    1545
—, Belege 1547
—, Benutzer 1540
—, Corpus 1543
—, Fachstilistik 1546
—, ideale Textsorten 1540
—, Informationstypen 1542
—, kulturpädagogische Funktion
    1540
—, lexikographischer Kommen-
    tar darin 1547
—, Morphologie 1544
—, Onomasiologie 1546
—, Semantik 1542

—, Symptomwerte 1544
—, Syntagmen 1547
—, Wortbildung 1544
Textstellenangabe 2138
    s. Belegstellenangabe
textual book structure 328, 330
    s. textuelle Rahmenstruktur
— condensation 336
— segmentation 330
    s. Methode der funktionalen
    Segmentation
— word list structure 328, 333
textuelle Binnenstruktur 2106
    s. textual word list structure
— Rahmenstruktur 2106f., 2112,
    2153, 2165, 2178, 2199
    s. textual book structure
Textumfang und Ergiebigkeit von
    Korpora 1643
Textverdichtung 386, 390, 431,
    440, 447ff., 534, 570, 807,
    2114, 2130, 2156, 2837ff.
— im zweisprachigen Wörter-
    buch 2837ff.
— und Redundanz 966
— und Standardisierung 957ff.
— und Textverständnis 966
— und Vereinheitlichung 958
—, erste Stufe 2837
—, zweite Stufe 449, 2837f.
—, lexikographische 956ff.
—, Verfahren 961ff.
Textverdichtungsgrad 2137, 2839,
    2845
Textverdichtungsverfahren
    2837ff.
Textverständlichkeit 953, 955,
    2839
Textverständnis und Textverdich-
    tung 966
Textwörterbücher des Russischen
    2319
Textzerlegung und Indexerstel-
    lung 1570
Thai-English 2578
Thakali 2558
Thalanyji 2639
Thema 328
    s. thème
Themaangabe 433, 468
Thema-Rhema-Einheit 950ff.
Themafach 948
thematisch orientierte Zugriffs-
    struktur 955
thematische Progression 949f.
— vs. alphabetische Anordnung
    2922
Themavariation 953
thème 328, 2821, 2859, 2862
    s. Thema
Themenwechsel 447

theoretical lexicography
    s. allgemeine Theorie der Le-
    xikographie,
    s. metalexicography,
    s. systematische Wörterbuch-
    forschung
Theorie der Lexikographie, allge-
    meine 258ff., 1639
— der zweisprachigen Lexiko-
    graphie 2979
théorie lexicale 937f.
Theorie lexikographischer Texte
    462
Theoriesprache der Lexikogra-
    phie 314, 458
—, lexikographische 428
thesaurus 1083ff., 1698, 1827,
    2912
    s. dictionnaire idéologique,
    s. Sachgruppenwörterbuch
Thesaurus 1077, 1550f., 1769,
    1771, 2268, 2279
— Artificiosae Memoriae 1088
— Ciceronianus 2915
— elegantiarum 1051
— Graecae Linguae
    s. NR: H. Stephanus
— linguae bohemicae 2279f.
— linguae Dravaenopolabicae
    2271
— linguae latinae 151, 1717f.
— linguae tschuvaschorum 2408
— philologicus criticus 2428
— Polono-Latino-Graecus 2268
— puerilis 1771
— und Weltauffassung 1065
thesaurus-dictonary 1094
    s. dictionnaire idéologique
Thesen zur Datenerhebung 1603
threshold level 1357
Thresor de la langue francoyse
    1974
    s. NR: J. Nicot
Thulung 2558
thumb index 335
Tibetan 2548
Tibetan-Chinese 2550
Tibetan-English 2549f.
Tibetan-German 2550
Tibetan-Japanese 3113
Tibetan-Russian 2550
Tibetan-Sanskrit 2548
Tibetan lexicography 2548ff.
Tibetisch-Russisch 3078
Tiddim Chin 2559
Tiefenabdeckung 982f.
    s. coverage in depth
Tierbezeichnung 1254
Tiername, zugehörige Wörterbü-
    cher 1294
Tiernamenwörterbuch 1294
Tifal 2636

Tigre 2448
Tigré-French 2450
Tigré-Italian 2450
Tigrinya 2448
Tigrinya-Amharic 2451
Tigrinya-English 2451
Tigrinya-French 2450
Tigrinya-Italian 2450f.
tilde 344
    s. Platzhaltersymbol,
    s . repetition symbol
Tilde 369, 948
Timbaro 2463f.
time-scheduling of lexicographical projects 89
Tironische Noten 3140
Titel mehrsprachiger Wörterbücher 2912
title of dictionaries, manipulations by publishers 98
titres du dictionnaire 2861
    s. Wörterbuchtitel
Tiwi 2639
To Raja Ta'e 2564
Toaripi 2636
Toba Batak 2564
Toba 2708
Tochtersprache 1335
Toda 2521, 2529
Toholabal 2661
Tojiki 2477
Tojolobal 2698
Tok Pisin 1494, 2574, 2637
token 1563
Tolosanisch 1895
Tongan 2573
Tongan-English 2574
Tongan-French 2574
Tonocoté 2708
Tontemboan 2564ff.
topic 328
topographisches Wörterbuch 163
Toponomastik, zur Terminologie 1276
Toponym 1276, 1277
toponymisch woordenboek 1276
Toradja 2566
torlakisch 2288
Totius latinitats lexicon 1716
    s. NR: E. Forcellini
Totonac 2698
Totontepec Mixe 2697
Touareg 2457
Tourismus und Lexikographie 4
Tourkokratia 1697
Tradition der Erbwortlexikographie 1232
Traditionsvermittlung durch Lexikographie 14
traduction 2817
    s. Translation,
    s. translation

traduisants 2730
traduisibilité 284
transcodage 2860
transcription phonétique 3054
    s. phonetische Transkription
transferred sense in historical English lexicography 1450
Transkription, phonemische 513
—, phonetische 513
—, volkstümliche 511, 512f.
—, wissenschaftliche 511, 512f.
Transkriptionsalphabet 510
Transkriptionssystem 511, 512f., 734
— Toussaint-Langenscheidt 510, 514
Translat 171
Translation 171, 1977, 2717
    s. traduction
translation 2785
— and dictionaries 90, 100
— equivalents 2783
— manuals 2678
Translation, Begriffsbestimmung 171
translator 1506
Translator 171
translatory bilingual dictionaries 2776f.
    s. Übersetzungswörterbuch
Transliteration, computergerechte 2260
Transliterierung des Ägyptischen 1679
transparent words 2720
treatment unit 328
    s. Bearbeitungseinheit
Trennzeichen 428, 442
    s. Strukturanzeiger
Trésor de la langue française 600ff., 674, 906ff., 1457, 1501, 1672, 1829
    s. NR: P. Imbs
Trévoux 10, 1801
Triade, antonymische 629
trilingue 2867
Triqui 2698
trivial (als Markierung) 912
trobar 1125
Trübners Deutsches Wörterbuch 2085f.
Trukese 2574
Tsakhar 2626
Tschechisch 745, 2278, 3022
tschechische Lexikographie 2278ff.
Tschechisch-Arabisch 2282
Tschechisch-Chinesisch 2282
Tschechisch-Deutsch 745
Tschechisch-Englisch 2282
Tschechisch-Portugiesisch 3022
Tschechisch-Russisch 2282

Tschechisch-Slowakisch 2286
Tschechisch-Ungarisch 2380
Tschechisch-Vietnamesisch 2282
Tscherkessisch 2418
Tschuwaschisch 2408
Tshu-Khwe San 2650
Tuamotuan 2574
Tübinger System von Textverarbeitungsprogrammen 1572
Tubu 2643
Tucanoan 2702
Tudor and Stuart words in English lexicography 1452
Tulishi 2643
Tulu 2521, 3096
Tulu-English 2529
Tumak 2457
Tungus 2628
Tungisch-Russisch 3078
Tupi 2703
tupí-français 2673
Tupí-Portugiesisch 2672
Tupinambá 2670, 2703
Tupiniquim 2671
Türkisch-Bulgarisch 2403
Türkisch-Deutsch 2400
Türkisch-Finnisch 2403
Türkisch-Georgisch 2403
Türkisch-Griechisch 2402
Türkisch-Holländisch 2400
Türkisch-Lateinisch 2400
Türkisch-Neugriechisch 2403
Türkisch-Niederländisch 2403
Türkisch-Polnisch 2403
Türkisch-Rumänisch 1883
Türkisch-Russisch 2403, 2408f.
Türkisch-Schwedisch 2400, 2404
Turkish-Arabic 3086
Turkish-Armenian 2369f.
Turkish-Japanese 3113
Turkish-Norwegian 1926
Turkish-Urdu 3101
Turklexikographie Chinas 2410f.
— der UdSSR 2408ff.
— Irans 2411f.
Turkmenisch 2411
Ṭūrōyō 2432
TUSTEP 1572
Twampa 2643
Twi 2648
type 1563
— of dictionaries, manipulations by publishers 100
— of dictionary and user interest 293
— of information inside the microstructure 343
— of microstructure 353
    s. Arten von Mikrostrukturen
Typen des Familiennamenbuches 1271

— des gruppenbezogenen Wörterbuches 1525f.
— des Sprichwörterbuches 1036
— des Synonymenwörterbuchs 2182
— diatopischer Markierung 663f.
— phonetischer Angaben 509
— von Fachwörterbüchern 118
— von Gewässernamenlexika 1286
— von Gruppen 1523
— von Informantenbefragungen 1615
— von Kurzschriftwörterbüchern 3137ff.
— von Laienbenutzern 129
— von Namenwörterbüchern 1267ff., 1291ff.
— von Vornamenbüchern 1269
— von Wörterbüchern nach dem Kriterium der Translationsrelevanz 171
Typenkombination 978
Typenkritik 978
typenspezifisches Datensortiment 455
types de collocations 1010f.
— de dictionnaires 180
   s. Typologie,
   s. Wörterbuchtypologie
types of dictionaries 29, 75
— of information in dictionaries 290
   s. Angabe
— of bilingual learner's dictionaries 2888
typographical device 1947
   s. typographischer Strukturanzeiger
typographical display 1087
typographie 136, 143, 311, 1822, 2830
Typographie 385, 424
— im phraseologischen Wörterbuch 1028
— phonetischer Angaben 513
typographischer Strukturanzeiger 375, 428, 512, 595, 927, 2119
typographisches Zeichen 2258
typography 2961
   s. Typographie,
   s. typographie
Typologie 968f.
— der Autorenwörterbücher 1549
— der Reisewörterbücher 2906ff.
— der Wörterbücher nach Benutzungsmöglichkeiten 115ff.
— der zweisprachigen Spezialwörterbücher 2877ff.
— mehrsprachiger Wörterbücher 2920ff.

— normativer Wörterbücher 63
— von funktionalen lexikographischen Textsegmenten 432
— von kumulativen Synonymiken 1076ff.
— von Synonymenwörterbüchern 2182
— zweisprachiger Wörterbücher 2877ff.
typologie du dictionnaire bilingue 2829f.
typology of access structures 339
— of neologistic dictionaries 1163f.
— of thesauri 1085
— of Yiddish dictionaries 2248f.
Typusprädikat 431
Tzeltal 2661
Tzeltal-Spanish 2663
Tzotzil 2661, 2698
Tzutuhil 2661

U

überdachende Mikrostruktur 481, 2137
— nichtrudimentäre Mikrostruktur 2140, 2143
— partiell rudimentäre Mikrostruktur 2140f.
— vollständig rudimentäre Mikrostruktur 2140
Überflüssigkeitsverdikt 825
Übersetzung 117
Übersetzungsäquivalent 2285, 2745
   s. Äquivalenz
Übersetzungsvorschlag und Paraphrasierung 3025
Übersetzungswörterbuch 118, 154, 2285f., 2776
Ubykh 2418
Ubykh-French 2419
Udmurt 2395
Udora 2396
Uduk 2643
Ugaritic 1690, 2425
Uigurisch 2407
Ukhrul 2559
Ukrainian-French 2332
Ukrainian-German 2330
Ukrainian-Hungarian 2333
Ukrainian-Polish 2332
Ukrainian-Russian 2330
Ukrainian lexicography 2329ff.
Ukrainisch-Russisch 3076
Ulathian 2574
Ulawa 2574
Ullstein Lexikon der deutschen Sprache 2159ff.

Ulubú 2671
Umfang phraseologischer Wörterbücher 1021
Umgangssprache 2201f.
   s. Alltagssprache
—, ihre Wortgeographie 1166
Umkehrprobe 620
Umkehrwörterbuch 1100ff., 1144
   s. dictionnaire inversé
— des Deutschen 2184
Umlautangabe 433, 468
Umlautbuchstabe 374
Umschreibung 2801
— im phraseologischen Wörterbuch 1022
unaccessibility of lexicographical data 291
Ungarinjin 2639
Ungarisch 3022
Ungarisch-Albanisch 2380
Ungarisch-Bulgarisch 2380
Ungarisch-Deutsch 2376ff., 2939
Ungarisch-Englisch 2378ff.
Ungarisch-Finnisch 2378
Ungarisch-Französisch 2377f.
Ungarisch-Hebräisch 2378
Ungarisch-Hindi 2380
Ungarisch-Holländisch 2380
Ungarisch-Italienisch 2380
Ungarisch-Koreanisch 2380
Ungarisch-Lateinisch 2376
Ungarisch-Polnisch 2380, 3063
Ungarisch-Portugiesisch 2380, 3022
Ungarisch-Rumänisch 2378
Ungarisch-Russisch 2378ff.
Ungarisch-Schwedisch 2380
Ungarisch-Serbokroatisch 2378
Ungarisch-Slowakisch 2378
Ungarisch-Spanisch 2378
Ungarisch-Türkisch 2377
Ungarisch-Ukrainisch 2378
Ungarisch-Vietnamesisch 2380
Ungarische Lexikographie 2375ff.
unidirectional 2952
unified Yiddish spelling 2251
Unifizierung der Gemeinsprache 2270
unilingue 2866
unintegrated microstructure 354
   s. nichtintegrierte Mikrostruktur
unité centrale 1583
— de traitement 328
   s. Bearbeitungseinheit
Universae Naturae Theatrum 1088
Universalwörterbuch 3015
university training in lexicography, advantages 96
—, in Europe 96
—, in the USA 95f.

unrepresentability of lexicographical data 291
unten erweiterte Lemmazeichengestaltangabe 2158, 2163
Unteradresse 2731
   s. subaddress,
   s. sous-adresse
untere Zugriffsstruktur 400
untergegangenes Wort 1153
Unterlassungsangabe 2175
Untertextblock 392
Urartaean 1691f.
Urbegriff 1059, 1234
— bei J. Grimm 1232, 1404
Urdu 2516, 3096
Urdu-Arabic 3101
Urdu-Bengali 3098
Urdu-English 2516
Urdu-Gujarathi 3098
Urdu-Hindi 3098
Urdu-Kashmiri 3098
Urdu-Marathi 3098
Urdu-Pushto 3099
Urdu-Russian 3101
Urdu-Sindhi 2516, 3098
Urdu-Tamil 3098
Urdu-Telugu 3098
Urteil über Wörterbücher 19ff.
usage 674, 1315, 1477, 2005
— and standards in US-American lexicography 35
usage label 1996
— in US-American lexicography 35
usage note 76, 342, 1161, 1383, 2002
— of words, its documentation in Danish dictionaries 1913f.
Usbekisch 2408
Usbekisch-Russisch 3081
user 2713f.
   s. Benutzer
— identification 2952
— interest and the presentation of headwords 299f.
— interest in dictionaries 291, 292
— interest in dictionaries in the USA 35
— of dictionaries, his interests 89
— research in lexicography 92
   s. Benutzungsforschung
user's guide 754ff.
   s. Benutzungsanleitung,
   s. Benutzungshinweis
Uspantek 2661
usuel (als Markierung) 912
usueller Benennungskontext 556, 618
— Bewertungskontext 557
— Text 617
utilisation du dictionnaire 177f.

Uto-Aztecan 2691
Uvean 2574

V

Vagheit 1200
valency 2770
Valenzbegriff und Konstruktionswörterbuch 1002
—, Fundierung 1003
Valenzforschung 1003
Valenzianisch 1777
Valenzwörterbuch 1005
— des Deutschen 2171ff.
—, Benutzung des 2173
Vallader 1896
value judgements in dictionaries 290
Variabilitätsdimension 1391
Variante 513
Variation, standardsprachliche 662
Varietät im gesamtsprachbezogenen Wörterbuch 234
varietätenbezogenes Gesamtwörterbuch 1392
Varietätenlexikographie des Deutschen 2198ff.
Varietätenpurismus 5
Varietätenstadienwörterbuch 1430
Varietätenstadium 1417
variété nationale 1500
variety in the dictionary, marketing aspects 89
varukka-kkōvai 2522
Venetian-German 1088
ventes de dictionnaires 41
Veracruz 2659
veraltend, Bestimmungsprobleme 659
Veränderung, dichronische 1417
verb pattern 589, 2964
verbe composé 179
Verben in Feldern. Valenzwörterbuch zur Syntax und Semantik deutscher Verben 2172ff.
   s. NR: H. Schumacher
Verbindung, phraseologische 1019
verbum-de-verbo-Praxis 1908
Verbvalenzangabe 433
Verbwörterbuch 1001f., 1221, 1313
verdeckt normatives Wörterbuch 198, 203
Verdeutschungswörterbuch 1172f.
verdichtete Bedeutungsparaphrasenangabe 537, 570

— Beispielgruppenangabe 437, 469
— Kompetenzbeispielangabe 431
Verdichtungsgrade 2839
Vereinbarkeitsrelationen, semantische im allgemeinen einsprachigen Wörterbuch 888ff.
Verfahren der Textverdichtung 961ff.
Verfügbarkeit historischer Texte 1593
Vergleichbarkeit von Markierungen 650
vergleichende Bezeichnungslehre, Wörterbuch 1412
— Parömiographie 1036ff.
vergleichendes etymologisches Wörterbuch 1329
— Wörterbuch aller Sprachen 3072
Verlagstätigkeit 3062
verlegerische Wörterbuchpflege 2213ff.
Vermögen, onomasiologisches 1063
Vernetzung, onomasiologische, des Wortschatzes 1408
—, —, im Sprachstadienwörterbuch 1424
Veröffentlichung von Indices und Konkordanzen 1568
Veröffentlichungsform für Indices und Konkordanzen 1571
version 2821, 2859, 2862
verstecktes Rechtschreibwörterbuch 2112
— Sublemma 447
— Wörterbuch 2155
Verstehbarkeit geschichtlicher Texte 1417
Verteilersprache, lexikographische 316
Verteilung von Wörtern im Text 1595
vertikal parallellaufende Zugriffsstruktur 398, 402, 2183
vertikale Lemmareihe 385
Verweis im phraseologischen Wörterbuch 1027
—, lexikographischer 365, 428, 964
   s. cross reference,
   s. renvois
Verweisangabe 428, 433, 468, 2114, 2137, 2141, 2144, 2147, 2211
Verweisartikel 365, 383, 2180
Verweisbeziehungsangabe 2141
Verweisbezugszeichen 365
Verweiskommentar 2141
   s. Verweisangabe

Verweislemma 365, 400, 1077, 1422
Verweissymbol 365
Verweiszielangabe 2141
Verwendungstyp von Modalpartikeln 810
Verzeichnis 988
Vestibulum 2912
Videnskabernes Selskabs Ordbog 1913
vieilli 912
vielsprachige Wörterbücher 2998, 3124
   s. mehrsprachige Wörterbücher
Vietnamese 2590, 3175
Vietnamese-Chinese 2587
Vietnamese-English 2588
Vietnamese-French 2584f., 2587
Vietnamese-German 2587
Vietnamese-Japanese 3113
Vietnamese-Latin 2583f.
Vietnamese-Portuguese 2583
Vietnamese lexicography 2583ff.
vieux 912
— français 3173
vignette 1822, 2863
visual languages 3143
Vocabula rerum 2043
vocabulaire 1469
— de base 2980
   s. Grundwortschatz
vocabulaires cachés 2921
Vocabulario de romance en latin 1739, 1742
— degli Accademici della Crusca 10, 217, 1852, 1865
   s. Crusca
— marino e militare 150
— nuovo 2913
Vocabularium 2912
— Catherinae 2916
— Cornicum 2348
— Germanico-Curlandicum 2355, 2358
— latino-sveco-germinico-finnicum 2914
— Latinum, Hispanicum, et Congense 2647
— Latinum 2913
— Nebrissense ex sicilience sermone in Latinum 2911
— Syrianicum 2432
Vocabularius Brevilogus 2039
— de significacione nominum 2039
   s. NR: J. Twinger vom Königshofen
— Ex quo 2040ff.
— fundamentarius 2041
— gallicus-belgico-latinus 2911
— incipiens teutonicum ante latinum 2042

— Lucianus 2039
— optimus 2038
— praedicantium 2041
— Principaliter 2041
— quadriidiomaticus 2039
   s. NR: D. Engelhus
— quattuor linguarum scilicet Latine, Italice, Gallice, Alimanice 2046
— Sancti Galli 2038, 2041
— saxonicus 2039
— theutonicus 2042
vocabulary of Norwegian 1923
— selection 2891
vocabulista 2912
vogue word 1160
Vogul 2395
Vokabel, rekonstruierte 1335
Vokabelrekonstruktion, Beispiel 1336
Vokabelsammlung des Mittelalters 2037
Vokabular des Alten Schulmeisters 2040
Vokal- und Konsonantenqualität 509
Vokalquantität 509, 514
Vokalquantitätsangabe 433, 468, 2126, 2158
Volapük 3129
Volkssprache in der Lexikographie des 16. Jhs. 2044
Volkssprachenvergleich in der Lexikographie des 16. Jhs. 2046
volkstümliche Transkription 511, 512f.
Volläquivalenz 2943
Vollemma 364, 2116, 2150
vollständig erweiterte Mikrostruktur 478f.
— erweiterte Mikrostruktur, Definition 478
— standardisierte Angabe 431
vollständige Artikelstruktur 441, 452f.
— lemmatische Adressierung 446
   s. full lemmatic addressing
— obligatorische Mikrostruktur eines Wörterbuches 456f.
vollständiges präzedentives Integrat 484
Vollständigkeit bei Indices 1569
— der Daten 1592
— im historischen Wörterbuch 1599
— von Wörterbüchern 2124
—, äußere 1592, 2124, 2133
—, innere 1592, 2124
—, lemmatische 1592
—, relative äußere 373
Volltext 958

— und Kondensat 959
— zu Wörterbuchartikeln 449
vorangestellte Zugriffsstruktur 2125
Voraussetzung gotischer Lexikographie 1908
vordere linke Kernstruktur 476, 2158
— rechte Kernstruktur 477
vorderer Formkommentar 476
— semantischer Kommentar 477
Vorderintegrat 484f.
—, Definition 484
—, präzedentives 449
Vorgeschichte deutscher Lexikographie 2037
Vorkommenshäufigkeit von Wörtern 1594
Vorname als Subkategorie der Anthroponyme 1268
Vornamenbuch 1268f.
Vornamengebung, Motivationen 1268
Vornamenstatistik 1270
Vorspann 330, 398, 767
   s. front matter,
   s. pré-texte,
   s. Wörterbuchvorwort
Vorwort 750
   s. preface,
   s. préface
Vorwort-Praxis 750f.
Vorwortgliederung 751
Votyak 2395
vox obscura 2261
vulgaire (als Markierung) 912

W

Wa 2591
Wahgi 2636ff.
Wahlspruch 1054
Wajapi 2704
Wakashan 2691
Walachisch 1883
Walachisch-Deutsch 1883
Walisisch 2347, 2913
Walisisch-Englisch 2347
Wandel, lexikalsemantischer 2197
Wangeroogisch 2028
Warlpiri 2639
Warlpiri-English 2639
Wata 2464
Watindega 2654
Waxī 2481
Wayan 2573
Wayãpi 2675
Wayãpi-Französisch 2675
Webster's Third Controversy 30

Webster-Worcester dictionary
  war 763
Weißrussisch-Russisch 3076, 3083
Weiterübersetzung von Wörter-
  büchern 7
Welamo 2462
Wellerismus 1033
Welsh 2347
Weltbildthese 282
Weltwissen und semantisches
  Wissen 992
Wendisch 2275
Wepsisch 2383
Werkangabe 2736
Werkgruppenwörterbuch 1549
Werkstattsprache der Lexikogra-
  phie 315
—, lexikographische 428, 2209
Werkwörterbuch 1549
Weskos 1494
West-Atlantic languages 2647
westfriesische Standardsprache
  2026
Wiradjuri 2639
Wirtschaft 2918
— und Lexikographie 4
wirtschaftskundliches Lexikon
  164
— Wörterbuch 164
Wissen, enzyklopädisches 554
—, episodisches 554
wissenschaftliche Lexikographie
  263
— Transkription 511, 512f.
— Wörterbuchkritik 162
wissenschaftshistorisch orientierte Wörterbuchgeschichte
  2102f.
Wolane 2452
Wolfenbütteler Paulusfragmente
  1909
Woordenboek der Nederlandsche
  Taal 1395, 2010ff.
  s. NR: M. de Vries L.A. te
    Winkel
  — van die Afrikaanse Taal 2019f.
    s. NR: P. C. Schoonees
      F. J. Snijman
word classes of Indian linguistics
  2488
— dictionaries in Chinese 2600
— finding list 1078
— form 2813
— list 331, 2704
— list section 335
word-supplier 1076
Wordbildungsmittel 1223ff.,
  2153f.
Worora 2639
Wort 2779
—, archaisches 1153
—, schweres 1100, 1206

—, untergegangenes 1153
—, zusammengesetztes 1054
  s. mot composé
wort-finding list 1076
Wort: sprachmögliches vs. textbe-
  legtes vs. sprachübliches 643
Wortableitungswörterbuch 3075
Wortakzent 514
Wortakzentangabe 433, 509,
  2126, 2144, 2851
  s. Ausspracheangabe,
  s. phonetische Angabe
Wortäquivalentangabe 433, 468
  s. Äquivalenz,
  s. équivalence
Wortäquivalentangabe, lateinische 2144
Wortart 788ff., 1221
— und Fachwortschatz 844
Wortartangabe 433, 468, 1423,
  2163
  s. part of speech
— im Sprachstadienwörterbuch
  1423
Wortarten 2826
wortartenbezogenes Wörterbuch
  1221
— des Deutschen 2188ff.
Wortartikel 749
  s. dictionary article,
  s. Wörterbuchartikel
Wortbegriff der Lexikographie
  und Indexerstellung 1570
Wortbildung 2779
— im Sprachstadienwörterbuch
  1425
— im textsortenbezogenen Wörterbuch 1544
— im zweisprachigen Wörterbuch 2795f.
— in den Wörterbüchern des
  Niederländischen 2015
Wortbildungsbaustein (Konfix)
  877f.
wortbildungsbezogene historische
  Lexikographie 1234
Wortbildungsdurchsichtigkeit
  2988
Wortbildungselement 869
Wortbildungseuropäismus 1397
Wortbildungsmittel 404
—, produktives 871
Wortbildungsstrich im rückläufigen Wörterbuch 1135
Wortbildungssyntagma 642
—, Definition 643
Wortbildungszusammenhang im
  allgemeinen einsprachigen
  Wörterbuch 642
Worteigenschaften, Frequenzpro-
  bleme 1595
Wörter und Gegenwörter von Ch.
  u. E. Agricola 2184

Wörterbuch als Autorität 21ff.
— als Dokumentation gesellschaftlichen Wissens 20
— als Gegenstand der Verehrung
  22ff.
— als Mikrofiche 2215
— als Stütze für die Gewinnung
  lexikographischer Daten 1612
— archaischer und untergegangener Wörter 1153ff.
— der Anspielungen 1054
— der Berufbezeichnungen
  1248ff.
— der deutschen Gegenwartssprache 333, 382, 389, 424,
  458, 488, 510, 531, 537, 540,
  548ff., 593, 624, 631, 645, 659,
  663, 669, 681, 686, 689, 693,
  697, 741, 751, 773, 777, 797,
  802, 805, 817, 827, 837, 843,
  870, 891, 963, 2117, 2129ff.,
  2138, 2160, 2185, 2170
  s. NR: R.Klappenbach H.Ma-
    lige-Klappenbach W.Steinitz
— der deutschen Sprache 2057f.
  s. NR: J. H. Campe
— der deutschen Sprache 2083f.
  s. NR: D. Sanders
— der deutschen Sprache von
  Hoffmann 2109ff.
— der deutschen Umgangssprache von Küpper 2202ff.
— der Fremdsprachendidaktik
  s. dictionary for foreign
    language teaching,
  s. dictionnaire pour l'enseig-
    nement de la langue étrangère
— der Homonyme, Homophone
  und Paronyme 1120ff.
— der Liebe 1195
— der schweren Wörter 1206ff.
— der Sprachschwierigkeiten
  2188
— der Sprechsprache, des Argot
  und des Slang 1184ff.
— der Synonyme und Antonyme
  von E. u. H. Bulitta 2182ff.
— der Technik im 19. Jh. 2918
— der vergleichenden Bezeichnungslehre 1412
— der Wortbildungsmittel
  1223ff.
— der Zigeunersprache mit Russisch 3078
— des deutschen Gefühlswort-
  schatzes 853
— des Deutschen, allgemeines
  einsprachiges 2105ff.
— des landschaftlich markierten
  Wortschatzes 1166ff.
  s. dictionnaire de régionalis-
    mes

- des Neuhochdeutschen von Pekrun 2115ff.
- des sexuellen Wortschatzes 1193ff.
- einer rekonstruierten Sprache, Geschichte 1337
—, —; Informationen zum Lemma 1336
—, —; Leistung 1337
—, —; Literaturangabe darin 1336
- fiktionaler Eigennamen 1293f.
- für Bei- und Übernamen 1292
- nach frames 1060
- nach Sachgruppen 1144
  s. Begriffswörterbuch
- und Benutzer 772
- und Grammatik 732
  s. grammar and the dictionary
- und Ideologie 2132
- und Lexikon 3152
- und Sprachvariation 1553
- und Sprachwissen 20
- und Textdatierung 156f.
- und Texterklärung 153ff.
- und Testexegese 1552
- und Textherstellung 152
- und Textinterpretation 157f.
- und Textlokalisierung 156f.
- und Übersetzung 153
  s. translation and dictionaries
- von Geheimsprachen 1532ff.
- von Tier- und Pflanzenbezeichnungen 1254ff.
- zu Bildsymbolen 3148ff.
- zu fremdsprachigen Eigennamen 1293
- zur Valenz und Distribution deutscher Verben 2171
—, allgemeines 680ff.
—, analogisches 1100
—, bebildertes 1365
—, bifunktionales 2845
—, biskopales 2740
—, deskriptives 198ff., 2318f.
—, deutsches Nachdruck von 2213ff.
—, einsprachiges 160ff.
—, entwicklungsbezogenes und Sprachstadienwörterbuch 1431
—, enzyklopädisches 11, 705, 988ff., 992, 1747
—, etymologisches 1323, 1335ff., 1778, 2054, 2318
—, —, Lesung als onomasiologisch-sprachübergreifend 1411
—, —, von einer rekonstruierten Sprachen: Außerindogermanisch 1338
—, — des Deutschen 2193ff.

—, fachsprachliches 1103
—, gegenwartsbezogenes synchronisches, Datenerhebung 1611
—, gesamtsprachbezogenes 1394
—, —, Artikelgestaltung 1404
—, —, Basis 1400
—, —, Bedeutungserläuterung darin 1405
—, —, Belege darin 1407
—, —, Etymologie darin 1404
—, —, Fachwortschatz 1396
—, —, Fremdwortschatz 1397
—, —, Funktionen 1400f.
—, —, Gegenstandsbereiche 1395, 1401
—, —, Gruppensprache 1396
—, —, historischer Wortschatz 1399
—, —, kulturpädagogische Funktion 1403
—, —, Lemmaform 1404
—, —, Mundartwortschatz 1398
—, —, nationale Identifikationsfunktion 1402
—, —, nationalliterarische Erziehungsfunktion 1403
—, —, Nutzungsmöglichkeiten 1400f.
—, —, paradigmatische Wortschatzvernetzung 1408
—, —, Reihenfolge der Einzelbedeutungen 1406
—, —, situationsgebundener Wortschatz 1399
—, —, sozialschichtiger Wortschatz 1399
—, —, Symptomwertangaben 1408
—, —, Syntagmatik 1408
—, glattalphabetisches 385f.
—, grammatisches 1004
—, gruppenbezogenes 1523ff.
—, —, Äquivalenzproblematik 1527
—, —, Artikelgestaltung 1527
—, —, Typen 1525f.
—, heteroglottes 1431
—, Hilfsmittel 159ff.
—, historisches 1342, 1750
—, —, Datenerhebung 1588
—, —, Informationspositionen 1594
—, —, Vollständigkeit 1599
—, homoglott einsprachiges/ zweisprachiges 1430
—, homonymisches 2270
—, humoristisches des Deutschen 2197
—, Hyperstruktur 947
—, ideologisches 177
—, illustriertes 1103, 2106, 2202f.

—, Informant 160ff.
—, kommentierendes 1045
—, kommerzielles, des heutigen Niederländischen 1433
—, kumulatives 1045
—, literatursprachbezogenes 236f.
—, makrostrukturlastiges 2124
—, mehrsprachiges 1104, 2920
—, —, Äquivalenzprobleme 2924
—, —, Typologie 2920
—, monoakzessives 382, 400, 2108, 2135, 2180
—, monoskopales 2740
—, morphologisches 1311
—, Namen im 775
—, nationalkulturelle Rolle 1402
—, normatives 198ff., 2270
—, onomasiologisches 26, 767, 1057
—, —, zu mehreren Sprachen 1411
—, phraseologisches 593, 1019, 2270
—, —, Umfang 1021
—, polyakzessives 394, 402, 2172, 2204
—, polyinformatives 2159
—, präskriptives 2054ff., 2313f.
—, rückläufiges 1131, 1779
—, — des Deutschen 2184
—, — des Russischen 2319f.
—, schwach nischenalphabetisches 390
—, seine Beurteilung durch Käufer 19
—, sprachübergreifendes 1392, 1410
—, —, von Varietäten 1410
—, —, zu Varietäten 1392
—, stark nischenalphabetisches 390
—, statistisches 163
—, teilbereichsbezogenes 1591
—, textsortenbezogenes 1539ff.
—, —, Artikelaufbau 1543
—, —, Bedeutungserläuterung darin 1545
—, —, Belege 1547
—, —, Benutzer 1540
—, —, Corpus 1543
—, —, des Deutschen 1539
—, —, Fachstilistik 1546
—, —, ideale Textsorten 1540
—, —, Informationstypen 1542
—, —, kulturpädagogische Funktion 1540
—, —, lexikographischer Kommentar darin 1547
—, —, Morphologie 1544
—, —, Onomasiologie 1546
—, —, Semantik 1542

—, —, Symptomwerte 1544
—, —, Syntagmen 1547
—, —, Wortbildung 1544
—, topographisches 163
—, verdeckt normatives 198, 203
—, verstecktes 2155
—, wirtschaftskundliches 164
—, wortartenbezogenes 1221
—, —; des Deutschen 2188ff.
—, zweisprachiges 745, 1100, 2711f.
—, —; grammatische und lexikalische Kategorisierung 2824ff.
—, zwischengrundsprachliches 1337
Wörterbuchartikel 328, 749, 2119, 2123, 2211
   s. dictionary article,
   s. Wortartikel
— als Teiltext 947
— als Text 946ff.
—, Hyperthemaprogression 947
—, Kohärenz und Kohäsion 947f.
—, standardisierter 423ff., 946ff., 959
—, stark standardisierter 947
—, Texthaftigkeit 946, 953
—, Thema-Rhema-Einheit 950ff.
—, Thema-Rhema-Struktur 946ff.
—, Themavariation 953
—, Verständlichkeit 953, 955
Wörterbuchausgangssprache 2741
   s. lexikographische Ausgangssprache
Wörterbuchbasis 337, 373, 396, 455, 2108, 2112, 2130ff., 2147, 2162, 2167, 2184, 2197, 2211ff., 2851
   s. lexikographische Datenbasis
Wörterbuchbenutzer 772, 2789
— und gebildete Öffentlichkeit 19ff.
— und Wörterbuchtypen 113ff.
Wörterbuchbenutzung 131, 159, 560, 948, 2178, 2213
   s. Benutzung,
   s. dictionary use
— im Forschungsprozeß 119, 2214
— und diafrequente Markierung 691
— und Kulturniveau 22
—, Möglichkeiten 121
—, psychische Voraussetzungen 21
Wörterbuchbenutzungsforschung 112f., 262, 1631
   s. Benutzungsforschung
—, Operationalisierung 1632
—, Probandenauswahl 1633

Wörterbuchbenutzungssituation 104, 812, 948, 1226f.
—, philologische 152, 155
—, terminologische 169f.
Wörterbuchdefinition als Terminus 532
Wörterbuchdidaktik 130
Wörterbucheinleitung 749
   s. Metatext,
   s. Vorspann,
   s. Wörterbuchvorwort
Wörterbucheintrag und Lexikoneintrag 160
Wörterbücher des Englischen außerhalb Großbritaniens
   s. dictionary of transplanted varieties of languages: English
— des Französischen außerhalb Frankreichs
   s. dictionnaires du français hors de France
—, mittellateinische 1719f.
Wörterbuchform 2109, 2118f., 2130, 2156, 2210, 2212
Wörterbuchforschung 14, 257
   s. dictionary research
— als akademische Disziplin 266
— und Metalexikographie 258f.
—, benutzerorientierte 1007
—, historische, 262
—, kritische 262
—, Perspektiven 259
—, systematische 262
Wörterbuchfunktion 159 ff., 2840, 3138
— bei Autorenwörterbüchern 1552
— und Textverdichtung 2841ff.
Wörterbuchgegenstand 2102, 2109, 2135ff., 2147, 2150
Wörterbuchgegenstandsbereich 2102
Wörterbuchgeschichte 1366
—, äußere 2101f.
—, innere 2101f.
—, lexikographiezentrierte 2101
—, Quellen der 2101f.
—, soziokulturell orientierte 2103
—, sprachwissenschaftlich orientierte 2103
—, wissenschaftshistorisch orientierte 2102f.
Wörterbuchgrammatik 732ff., 2114, 2152
— im Duden-Universalwörterbuch 2152f.
— und Pragmatik 741
— und Semantik 740
— und Sprachgeschichte 742
— und sprachliche Varietäten 741f.
—, Aufgaben 732f.

—, Flexion 736f.
—, Graphemik 734f.
—, Morphophonemik 735
—, Phonetik und Phonologie 733f.
—, rudimentäre 2107, 2126
—, Syntax 738ff.
—, Terminologie 743f.
—, Wortarten 735f.
—, Wortbildung 737f.
Wörterbuchherstellungsitutation 948
Wörterbuchinformatik
   s. computer and lexicography
Wörterbuchintention 680, 684
Wörterbuchkriminalität 14
   s. criminalité lexicographique
Wörterbuchkritik 225, 978, 2106, 2115, 2129, 2131, 2135, 2176, 2182, 2191f., 2194, 2206, 2208, 2210, 2213
   s. dictionary war,
   s. kritische Wörterbuchforschung
—, fachinterne 2211
—, wissenschaftliche 162
Wörterbuchkultur 2192
—, Verbesserungsmöglichkeiten 13
Wörterbuchnachspann 749
   s. back matter
Wörterbuchpflege, germanistische 2213ff.
—, lexikographische 2213ff.
—, metalexikographische 2213ff.
—, verlegerische 2213ff.
Wörterbuchplan 2133
Wörterbuchprogramme in Deutschland 230ff.
Wörterbuchregister 767ff.
   s. Register
Wörterbuchstil 572, 2130, 2138, 2175, 2194, 2206
   s. dictionary style,
   s. style lexicographique
— der frühen deutschen Nachkriegslexikographie 2110
Wörterbuchtext, framebasierter 573
Wörterbuchtitel 974
   s. titres du dictionnaire
Wörterbuchtyp 680
Wörterbuchtypen und Wörterbuchbenutzer 113ff.
Wörterbuchtypologie 111ff., 968ff.
   s. types de dictionnaires,
   s. types of dictionaries
Wörterbuchvergleich, quantitativer 2118
Wörterbuchvorspann 749
   s. front matter

Wörterbuchvorwort 680, 684, 749ff.
   s. Metatext,
   s. Vorspann
— und Laienbenutzer 752
— und wissenschaftlicher Benutzer 752
—, Bestandteile 749f.
—, funktionsgerechte Gestaltung 752f.
—, Probleme 751
Wörterbuchwerbung 2124
Wörterbuchzielsprache 2741
   s. lexikographische Zielsprache,
   s. target language
Wörterbuchvergleich 2130ff.
   s. comparison of dictionaries
Wörterverzeichnis 328, 331, 749
   s. nomenclature [engl., franz.]
Wortfamilie 1366
   s. famille de mots
Wortfamilienlexikographie, Probleme 1150
Wortfamilienwörterbuch 1145ff.
— als Gegenstand der Wörterbuchforschung 1148
— des Deutschen 2184
—, diachrones 1146
—, synchrones 1146
Wortfeldtheorie 895
Wortfindungsschwierigkeit 2180
Wortform 2813
Wortformenangabe 433, 468, 472
Wortformenindex 153, 1567
   s. Index,
   s. index,
   s. indexe
Wortformenwörterbuch 1313
wortgeschichtliche Angabe 840
Wortgruppenlexem 858
   s. multi-word lexical unit
Wortindex 1567
   s. lemmatisierter Index
—, lemmatisierter 153
Wortintonation 514
Wortinventar historischer Varietäten des Deutschen 1421
Wortklasse, funktionale 1221
wortklassenbezogenes Wörterbuch 1221ff., 2880
wörtlich / übertragen (als Markierung) im phraseologischen Wörterbuch 1023
Wortnest 3075
Wortneutralität im Wörterbuch 838f.
Wortschatz, gruppenspezifischer 1524
—, historischer, im gesamtsprachbezogenen Wörterbuch 1399
—, onomasiologische Vernetzung 1408

—, peripherer 1100
—, situationsgebundener, im gesamtsprachbezogenen Wörterbuch 1399
—, sozialschichtiger, im gesamtsprachbezogenen Wörterbuch 1399
Wortschatzmenge 972
Wortschatzstruktur, synchrone als Gegenstand des Sprachstadienwörterbuches 1430
Wortschatzvernetzung, paradigmatische im gesamtsprachbezogenen Wörterbuch 1408
Wortsynonym 571
   s. Synonym,
   s. synonym
Wortsyntagmen 2779
Wortvariante im Sprachstadienwörterbuch 1422
Wortvorkommenshäufigkeit 1594
Wortwahlwörterbuch 1076
Wortzeichen 1687
Wortzusammensetzungen 2779
Wotisch 2383
Wurdboek fan de Fryske taal 2027
Wurzel 1335
Wurzelerweiterung 1336
Wurzelkognate 1335
Wurzelvariante 1336

X

Xalitla 2659
/Xam 2654
/Xam-ka.!-k'e' 2654
Xazara 2481
Xetá 2671
Xicotepec Totonac 2698
Xixia 2555
!Xo 2656
!Xóõ 2650
!Xu 2655
Xufi 2481

Y

Yachaycusunchi 2705
Yagan 2709
Yagaria 2636
Yaghnōbī 2481, 2485
Yakut 2408, 2628
Yamana 2710
Yamana-English 2709f.
Yaminahua 2703
Yanomamɨ 2704
Yao 2590

Yaqui-Mayo 2698
Yawyin 2559
Yazgulāmī 2481
Yenisei-Ostyak 2627
Yenisei-Samoyed 2395
Yi 2555, 2559
Yiddish-English 2250f.
Yiddish-French 2251
Yiddish-German 2249f.
Yiddish-Russian 2249f.
Yiddish-Spanish 2251
Yidiny 2639
Yimchungru 2558
Yindjibarndi 2639
Yivo spelling 2251
Yocotan 2661
Yolngu 2639
Yolngu-English 2639
Yucatec Mayan 2698
Yucpa 2701
Yukagir 2628
Yukatek 2661
Yulu 2644
Yupa 2702
Yurak 2395
Yupik 2631

Z

Zacapoaxtla 2659
Zagawa 2643
Zaiwa 2560
Zamuco 2708
Zapotec 2697f.
Zāzā 2481
Zeichen, ikonisches 3148
—, typographisches 2258
Zeichenbegriff 780
Zeichengestaltangabe 433, 468
Zeichnung und Photographie 708
Zeitansatz für Sprachstadienwörterbücher des Deutschen 1420
Zeitarchaismus 1154
Zeitungswörterbuch 1207
Zeliang 2558
Zentraltürkisch 2407
Zerlegen von Texten und Indexerstellung 1570
Zerma 2643
zero addressing 350
   s. Nulladressierung
Zhemaitish 2352
Zielgruppen des Fachwörterbuchs 1626
Zielsprache, lexikographische 2729, 2847
Zielwort 1096, 1100
Ziffernlautschrift 509
Zigeunersprache 2378

Zinancantan 2698
Zirkel, hermeneutischer 1020
—, lexikographischer 161
Zirkelsynonymität 622
Zirkularität 547, 899f.
— bei der Gewinnung von Datenbasen 1642
Zitat 612
    s. citation
Zitatenwörterbuch 1044ff.
Zitierform 365, 736
    s. canonical form,
    s. forme canonique,
    s. kanonische Form,
    s. Nennform
Zivilisationsterminologie 2290
Zoque 2698
Zugriffsalphabet 380, 382, 2125
    s. access structure,
    s. Alphabet
Zugriffsaspekt, 394
Zugriffsprofil 382, 398, 400, 404
    s. access profile
—, äußeres 373, 2108, 2112, 2114f., 2125, 2182
Zugriffsstruktur 328, 393, 394, 954f., 2729
    s. access structure
—, allgemeines einsprachiges Wörterbuch: Übersicht 394
—, aufeinanderfolgende 398
—, äußere 373, 2106, 2209
    s. outer access structure
—, glattalphabetische 395f.
—, horizontal parallellaufende 398, 400, 404
—, innere 393, 2172
    s. inner access structure
—, links laufende 402
—, nachgestellte 403, 2125
—, nestalphabetische 395

—, obere 400
—, privilegierte 2181
—, rechtslaufende 402
—, registerexterne 396, 2115
—, registerinterne 394
—, thematisch orientierte 959
—, untere 400
—, vertikal parallellaufende 398, 402, 2183
—, vorangestellte 2125
Zukunftsaufgabe der Lexikographie 14f.
Žu/'hōasi 2654
Zulu 2648
Zuordnungsangabe 2139, 2162
zusammengesetzte Mikrostruktur 480ff., 2140
zusammengesetztes Wort 1054
Zusammenhang phraseologischer Einheiten 1027
Zusammenordnungszeichen 428
Zusammenrückung 2838
Zusammensetzung in den Wörterbüchern des Niederländischen 2015
Zusatzangabe 534, 2852
    s. Glossat
Zusatzbuchstabe 375, 376
Zway 2452
Zweck rückläufiger Wörterbücher 1133
— übersetzungsrelevanter Wörterbücher 172
—, genuiner 426
Zwei-Buchstaben-Alphabet 378
zweifach partiell integrierte Mikrostruktur 2164
— subintegrierte Mikrostruktur 2146, 2154
zweisprachige Bearbeitungseinheit 2732ff.

— Fachlexikographie 2937ff.
— lateinische Lexikographie 3030ff.
zweisprachige Lexikographie 2711ff.
    s. bilingual lexicography,
    s. lexicographie bilingue
— mit Esperanto 3124ff.
— mit mongolischen Sprachen 2625
— mit Polnisch 3061ff.
— mit Portugiesisch 3020ff.
— mit Russisch 3068ff.
— und Sprachprestige 6
zweisprachige phraseologische Wörterbücher mit Portugiesisch 3025
— mit Russisch 3082
zweisprachiges Fachwörterbuch, Äquivalenz als Problem 1630
— Wörterbuch 1100, 2741
    s. bilingual dictionary,
    s. dictionnaire bilingue
— Wörterbuch und gebildete Öffentlichkeit 26f.
zweite rechte Teilkernstruktur 2149
— Stufe der Textverdichtung 449, 2837f.
Zweiwegwörterbuch 1100
    s. polyakzessives Wörterbuch
Zwischengrundsprache 1335
Zwischengrundsprachliches Wörterbuch 1337
Zwischenkommentar, linker 476, 496
—, —, zur Etymologie 2116
—, mittlerer 2140
—, rechter 477, 484
Zyrian 2395

F. J. H./O. R./ H .E. W./L. Z.
unter Mitarbeit von Thorsten Roelcke

337. Namenregister/Index of Names/Index des noms

Das Namenregister wurde mit Hilfe eines Computerprogramms erstellt. Die Alphabetisierung richtet sich nach den Grundzeichen; Diakritica (wie die französischen Akzente) und sprachspezifische Buchstaben (wie Khoisan !, ǂ) blieben unberücksichtigt. Bei mehrteiligen Namen setzt die Alphabetisierung nach dem ersten Blank neu ein.

Die Leitlinie für die Einträge bildet die Schreibung im Artikeltext bzw. in den Literaturangaben. Verweise auf die dadurch auftretenden Namenvarianten (wie z.B. deutsches *ch* für den russischen velaren Frikativ im Gegensatz zu engl. *kh*) werden nur in Ausnahmefällen gegeben. Namen mit den Bestandteilen *de, la, van, von* (usw.) können unter diesen Zeichenketten sowie unter dem darauf folgenden Namenbestandteil erscheinen.

The alphabetic sequence of the names was established by a computer program. Diacritics (such as the French accents) and language-specific letters (such as Khoisan !, ǂ) are not taken into consideration. On the other hand, space between words influences the sequence (e.g. *de Saussure* precedes *Deak*).

Names are indexed in the form used in the text. This is one of the main reasons for some names to occur in different variants (e.g., the Russian velar fricative being transcribed as *ch* in German but as *kh* in English). In most cases, there are no cross-references to such variants. Names containing elements such as *de, la, van, von* may be alphabetized either by them or by the following name itself.

Pour alphabétiser les noms on a eu recours à un logiciel. Les signes diacritiques (accents ou lettres spécifiques à certaines langues, cf. Khoisan !, ǂ etc.) n'ont pas été pris en compte. En revanche, l'alphabet repart à zéro après un blanc (*de Saussure* devant *Deak*).

A divers endroits de l'encyclopédie le même nom peut être écrit de façon différente (par ex. le même son russe est transcrit *ch* en allemand et *kh* en anglais). En règle générale on a renoncé à renvoyer d'une variante à l'autre. Les noms comportant des particules du genre *de, la, van, von,* etc. sont susceptibles de figurer tant à l'ensemble du nom qu'à la particule.

A

Aaron, F. 1883, 1889
Aars, J. 1925
Aarsleff, H. 219, 223, 226, 229, 1700, 1704, 1951f., 1966, 2936
Aarts, J. 1623, 1650, 1666
Aasen, I. 1923-1925, 1927f.
Aav, Y. 2325, 3022, 3029, 3075, 3084, 3169
Aavik, J. 2394
Abaev, V.I. 744, 747, 2484f.
Abate, F.R. 1031, 1037, 1044, 1056, 1169, 1177, 1209, 3165
Abbadie, A. d' 2450f., 2453
Abbé d'Olivet, s. Thoulier
Abdeen, A. 3092, 3094
Abdel Haleem, M.A. 3092
Abdul Hag 2521
Abdul Majid 2521
Abdulla, A. 3097, 3103
Abdullaev, S.N. 2422f.
Abdullaiev, B.T. 3169
Abe, Ch. 2621, 2623
Abel Hallem, M.A. 3094
Abel, C. 1069, 1074
Abel, F. 1892
Abel, L. 1691, 1694
Abels, K. 272, 258, 405, 574, 747, 2222
Abelson, P. 2250f., 2253
Abelson, R. 539, 575
Abelson, R. P. 893f., 899
Abenaim, R. 61
Abend, H. 2751, 2908
Abercrombie, D. 509, 517
Abhyankar, K. V. 2494-2496
Abikian, M. 2370
Ablancourt, N. P. d' 1797
Abondolo, D. 2398
Abouaf, S. 2981, 2085
Abraham, R. C. 2459, 2464f.
Abraham, W. 655, 698f., 797, 804, 835, 1258, 2207, 2211, 2215, 2237, 2751
Abrahamian, R. 2369
Abrahamowicz, Z. 2401, 2407
Abrahamyan, R. 2475f.
Abramov, N. 1128
Abramov, N.A. 2317, 2322
Abramowicz, D. 2253

Abregú Virreira, C. 2707, 2709
Abū 'Ubaid 2445, 2447
Abū-l-Ḥasan bar Bahlūl 2427, 2433
Abuladze, I. 2418
Abu-l-Walīd, s. Yona ibn Ǧanah
Acarisio da Cento 2970, 2973
Ācārya, K. 3102f.
Acero, I. 1739, 1764
Acevedo y Huelves, B. 1755
Achard, C.-F. 1895, 1903
Acharisio, A. 10, 1848, 1851, 1858
Acharya, P. K. 2496
Acharya, S.P. 3100, 3103
Achmanova, O.S. 2224, 2318, 2322, 2325
Achmerov, K. Z. 738, 747
Ackermann, P. 1081f., 1803, 1808, 1841
Ackermann, R. W. 1293f.
Acosta, J. de 2682
Acson, V. Z. 2533
Acuña, R. 2661, 2665
Adair, E.R. 2970, 2975
Adam von Rottweil 1093, 1847, 1860, 2041, 2047, 3005
Adam, J. H. 1517f., 1520, 1522
Adam, J.-M. 42, 45
Adam, M. T. 2513, 2518
Adam, R. 1440
Adamescu, G. 1886, 1888f.
Adamo de Rodvila 1847, 1850
Adams, E. N. 1456
Adams, G. R. 102, 109, 110
Adams, J. N. 1195, 1197
Adelaar, W. F. H. 2705
Adelberg, E. 1414, 1608, 2220
Adeline, J. 1747, 1755
Adelung, F. 3075
Adelung, J. Chr. 10, 15, 139, 143, 155, 158, 225, 231, 236f., 241f., 312, 498, 509, 526, 529f., 626, 630, 634, 656, 694, 698, 750, 753, 800f, 803, 813, 825, 829, 858, 860, 868, 880, 892, 966, 1073, 1157, 1173, 1219, 1232, 1235, 1238, 1240, 1596, 1608, 2050f., 2054f., 2057f., 2060, 2063, 2066f., 2070, 2072-2074, 2076f., 2079, 2081, 2083f., 2091-2095, 2098, 2115, 2119, 2214f., 2217, 2376, 2918, 2925, 2967, 2999, 3015, 3018, 3073, 3075, 3083
Adhwani, R. N. (alias Pandit Rao) 2514, 2519
Adjarian, H. 2370
Adler, A. 997, 1704
Adler, G.J. 2967
Adodorov, V.E. 2310
Adorno, R. 2683
Adrados, F. R. 591, 1696, 1701, 1702, 1704, 2751

Adrian, K. 2659f.
Adriani, M. J. 1308
Adriani, N. 2566f.
Adrienne 1186
Advani, B. M. 2516, 2520
Aebersold, W. E. 2566f.
Aelianus 1699
Afgānī, 'A. 2485
Afghānī-navīs, 'Abdullah 2480
Afzelius, J. A. 1308
Ağakay, M.A. 2404
Aganin, R.A. 2399, 2404, 2407
Agarwal, R. C. S. 2505
Ageenko, F. L. 1304, 1308, 2316, 2322
Ágel, V. 243, 245, 1429
Ageno, F. 1194, 1198
Aghayan, E. 2369f.
Agnès, J. 2980, 2982
Agoireitês, Z. 2402, 2404
Agostini, F. 2464f., 2468
Agricola, Chr. 631, 634, 1081f., 2215
Agricola, E. 78, 274f., 406, 544f., 548, 575, 578, 580, 584, 626, 634, 648, 655, 779, 832, 834, 854, 868, 881f., 892f., 1011-1013, 1019, 1028, 1031, 1036, 1039, 1081f., 1230, 1258, 1652, 1666, 1671, 2130, 2183, 2184, 2215, 2232, 2238, 2243
Agricola, J. 1034, 1039, 1042, 2065, 2067, 2215
Agricola, M. 2386
Aguilar M., J. de 2681, 2683
Aguilar P. R. 2683
Aguilar Piāl, F. 2985
Aguilera, Ó. 2709
Aguiló i Fuster, M. 1774, 1777, 1779
Agusti, Fra Miguel 1779
Agustí, F. M. 2925
Agustí, M. 2938
Agustín, M. 1741, 1755
Ahlbäck, O. 1939, 1941
Ahlberg, P. 3126, 3130
Ahlborn, I. 3172
Ahldén, T. 3044f.
Ahlheim, K.-H. 1100f., 1171f., 1175f., 2184, 2188, 2215
Ahlin, M. 2299, 2301
Ahlswede, Th. E. 1669, 3165
Aḥmad, M.Ḥ. 3092
Ahmed Vefik, P. 2404
Ahmed, H. 1668
Ahmed, S. 2517
Ahmed, Vefik, F. 2403
Ahrends, M. 2185, 2186, 2216
Ahterî, K.M.b.S. 2399, 2404
Aicardo, J. M. 1743, 1764
Aihara, S. 1132, 1142
Aijmer, K. 856, 861

Aik, L. T. 2506
Aintābī, Ahmad Āṣim 2446
Aisenstadt, E. 892, 1016
Aiso, H. 3166
Aistleitner, J. 1693
Aitchison, J. 1661, 1666
Aitken, A. J. 327, 653, 1017, 1414f., 1456, 1595, 1598, 1600, 1603, 1605, 1607, 1609, 1967, 1982, 1984-1987
Aitzetmüller, R. 1133, 1138, 1142, 1337, 1341, 2259f., 2263, 2266f.
Aizkibel, J.F. 2373, 2375
Akhmanova, O. S. 2224 (s. Achmanova)
Akisina, A. 1119
Akkerman, E. 3165
Aksamitov, A. S. 3085
Aksoy, Ö.A. 2404
Aktaş, A. 2895, 2899
Akulenko, V. V. 2885
Akurgal, E. 1686, 1689
Akyüz, K. 2399, 2404, 2407
al Mutarrizi = Abul-Fath Nasir 2444f.
Al, B. 210, 213, 2728, 2752, 2762, 2767, 2771, 2775
Al, B. P. F. 1319f., 1621, 1624, 2716, 2726, 2751, 2777, 2805-2807, 2809, 2812f., 2816f., 2829-2831, 2836f., 3038
al-Abyārī, Ibrāhīm 2447
Al-Azhari, M.A. 3101
al-Azharī, Manṣūr Muḥammad ibn Aḥmad 2441
al-Busṭānī, Butrus 2445, 2447
al-Fārābī 2410
al-Fārābī, Isḥāq ibn Ibrāhīm 2441, 2445, 2447
al-Fīrūzābādī, Majd al-Din Muhammad 2443, 2445, 2447
al-Ḥajjāj b. Yū'suf 2438
al-Hamawi, s. Hamawi
al-Jauharī, Ismā'il ibn al-Hammād 2441f., 2445, 2447
al-Jawālīqī = Maūhub b. Aḥmad al Jawālīqī 2444
Al-Kasimi, A. 1671, 2783, 2789
Al-Kasimī, A. M. 132f., 246, 273, 722, 724, 2716, 2726, 2752, 2770, 2774, 2829, 2836
Al-Khlil 2712
al-Khalīl, ibn Aḥmad 2440f., 2443, 2445, 2447, 2698
al-Laith b. Sajyār 2440
al-Malīk, 'Abd 2438
al-Muṭarrizī = Abū l-Fatḥ Nāsir 2447
al-Rāġib, al-Isfahānī 2444, 2447
al-Rāzī, Muḥammad ibn Abī Bakr 2442, 2447

al-Ṣaghānī, Ḥasan Maḥmūd
    2442f., 2447
al-Shaibānī, Abū 'Amr 2444f.,
    2447
al-Shurṭūnī, Sa'id 2446
Āl-Yāsīn, Muḥammad Ḥasan
    2447
al-Zabīdī, Murtadā 2443, 2447
Al-Zamakhshari 2711f.
al-Zamakhshari, Abū l-Qāsim
    2444, 2447
al-Zamaxšari, Abu 'l-Qasim
    Maḥmud ibn 'Umar 2476
al-Zinjānī, Maḥmūd ibn Aḥmad
    2442, 2447
Aladern, J. 1775, 1779
Aland, B. 1700, 1702
Aland, K. 1137f., 1700, 1702
Alasia [da Sommaripa], G. 2297,
    2300
Alatyrev, V.I. 2398
Alba, R. de 1743, 1755
Albaigés, J. M. 1271
Albaigès Olivart, J. M. 1779
Albano Leoni, F. 1874, 1928, 1932
Albault, A. 3121, 3125, 3127,
    3130, 3133, 3136
Albeck, U. 1078
Albers, W. 166
Albert Torrellas, A. 1779
Albert, Archiduc 2977
Alberti de Villanova, F. 1089
Alberti de Villeneuve, F. 1863,
    3009f., 3013
Alberti di Villanova, F. 11, 15
Alberti di Villanuova, F. 1845,
    1859, 3017f.
Albertí i Gubern, S. 1776, 1780
Alberti, H. J. v. 165f.
Albertoni, A. 67, 69
Alberus, E. 9, 15, 978, 980, 1126,
    1128, 1132, 1137f., 1143, 2046,
    2066f.
Albisetti, C. 2707
Albrand, H. 2220
Albrecht, E. 574
Albrecht, J. 219, 223, 410, 459,
    499, 649, 652f., 1146, 1151
Albrecht, J.-H. C. 1068, 1071
Albrecht, K. 2215f. 2216
Albuquerque, S. G. de 2707
Alcalá Venceslada, A. 1755
Alcalá, P. de 1739f., 1755, 3087,
    3094
Alcalay, R. 2436
Alcaly, R. 2431
Alcedo, A. de 1751, 1755
Alcina, J. 1128
Alcorn, J. 2664f.
Alcover, A. M. 1775, 1780, 1787
Alcover, M. 1779, 1787
Alderete, B. 1755

Aldrete, B. 1755
Aldrete, B. de 1741, 1766
Alegre i Urgell, M. 1780
Alegret i Sanromà, S. 1778, 1780
Alehseev, P. A. 3083
Alejandre, M. 2664f.
Aleksandrov, A. 3078
Aleksandrov, P.S. 2317, 2321,
    2325
Aleksandrova, Z. E. 1078, 2317,
    2321f., 2325f.
Aleksandrovič, A.A. 2337
Alekseev, D.I. 2317, 2322, 2326
Alekseev, M. P. 3069, 3070, 3073,
    3084
Alekseev, P. 2264, 2266
Alekseev, P. A. 2311, 2322, 3074
Alekseev, P. M. 249f., 273, 1316f.,
    1320, 1322, 1641, 1643f., 1668,
    2321, 2326
Aleksić, R. 2293, 2295
Alektorova, L.P. 2316, 2322
Alemand 1212
Alemanni, G. 3017
Alemany y Bolufer, J. 1755
Alembert, J. Le Rond d' 219-221,
    223, 652f., 726, 731
Aler, P. 1011, 1013
Alessio, G. 1325, 1331, 1875, 1903
Alewijn, A. 3022, 3026
Alexander the Great 1697
Alexander, C. 1989, 2007
Alexander, R. 1031
Alexandersson, S. 3128, 3130
Alexandre, H. 2960
Alexandre, P. 2647, 2649
Alexandre, R. 1046f.
Alexandridês, D. 2402, 2404
Alexeew, P. M. 1320, 1322
Alfaro, A. 1757
Alfaro, R. J. 1176
Alfes, L. 1146, 1151, 1953
Alfieri, V. 1855
Alfonso el Sabio, P. 1761
Alfonso, L. 1311
Algarotti, F. 1855
Algary, F. 3174
Algeo, J. 30, 33, 34, 37, 38, 2009
Algier, T. 3011
Alibert, L. 1892, 1894f., 1903
Aliko H. 2366
Alinei, M. 1090, 1093, 1873f.,
    1878
Alinei, M. L. 1138
Alishan, Gh. 2369
Alkhuli, M.A. 3093f.
Allan, R. 1984f.
Allard, I. R. 2695f.
Allen, E. A. 1242, 1244
Allen, F. S. 1071
Allen, H. B. 214, 277, 1949, 1952
Allen, N. J. 2558

Allen, R. E. 1964, 1966
Allén, St. 362, 1138, 1270f., 1320,
    1650, 1666, 1668, 1933, 1938,
    1941f.
Allen, W. H. 2495
Alletz, P. A. 1164
Allin, T. R. 2702
Allodoli, E. 67, 69
Allott, A. 2552, 2554
Allsopp, R. 653
Allwood, M. S. 1360
Almeida, H. de 1735, 3169
Almela i Vives, F. 1778, 1780
Almerich Sellarés, L. 1780
Almirante, J. 1747, 1755
Alnaes, I. 1308f.
Alonso Estravis 1737
Alonso Hernández, J. L. 1157,
    1533, 1536f.
Alonso Pedraz, M. 1748, 1755
Alonso y de los Ruyzes de Fonte-
    cha, J. 1741, 1755
Alonso, A. 1750, 1764, 2982, 2985
Alonso, J. 2661, 2664
Alonso, M. 1071, 1078
Alsdorf-Bollée, A. 1138, 1341
Alshawi, H. 1669, 3165
Alsina Bofill, Cl. 1778, 1780
Alsina, R. 1312
Alsonso, J. 2665
Alsted, J. H. 1089
Alster, B. 1033, 1039, 1042
Alston, R. C. 1943, 1950, 1952,
    3169
Alston, W. P. 852f.
Altamira, R. 1755
Altenkirch, G. 1192
Altermann, R. 1066
Althaus, H. P. 125, 374, 406, 459,
    581, 587, 628, 822, 1230, 1283,
    1429, 1531, 2075, 2214, 2238
Altheim, F. 2437
Althuysen, J. 2025
Altieri, B. 1195, 1197
Altieri, F. 1849, 2971-2973
Altmann, G. 1644, 1671
Altmann, H. 2211, 2234
Alton, J. 1901, 1903
Altrocchi, R. 2885
Altuna, P. 2373, 2375
Alunāns, J. 2355, 2360
Alunno, F. 10, 217, 222, 1089f.,
    1845, 1848, 1850-1852, 1858,
    1860, 1867, 2970, 2973, 3007f.,
    3010
Alunno, M.F. 2991, 2995
Alvar Ezquerra, M. 1742, 1744,
    1748-1750, 1764, 2752, 2936,
    2982-2985
Alvar López, M. 1738, 1751, 1764
Alvar, M. 654, 1764
Alvarado L., M. 2664f.

Alvarado, F. de 2697, 2699
Alvarado, L. 1753, 1755
Álvarez, C. 2698, 2700
Alvarez Carracedo, F. 1737
Alvarez, D. 1737
Alvarez de la Brana, D. R. 1261, 1263
Alvarez del Real, M. E. 1758
Alvarez, M. C. 2664f.
Alvarez-Prada, E. 2793, 2989
Alvarus, E. 2376, 2380
Alvisi, A. 2995
Alwis Wijesekera, O. H. de 2506
Alzugaray Aguirre, J. J. 1176
Amadeo, J. 1778, 1785
Amades, J. 1113, 1119, 1778, 1780
Amador, E.M.M. 2989
Aman, R. 1191-1193, 1197, 1199
Amara 2489
Amarasiṃha 2499
Amassiatsi, A. 2368
Amatuni, S. 2370
Amberg, H. Chr. 221f.
Amborn, H. 2464, 2466
Ambrosoli, S. 2918, 2925
Ambruzzi, L. 2994f.
Amelio, S. 1881, 1889f.
Amelot de la Houssaye, A. N. 1815
Amengual, J. J. 1774, 1780
Amery, C.H.F.S. 3094
Ames, D. W. 2459
Amet, E. 1051f.
Amet, G. de 2067
Amélineau, É. 1680, 1682
Amiel, Ph. 679, 1836
Amiguet, J. 1771, 1780
Amīnī, Amīrqulī 2479
Amirova, G.S. 2317, 2322
Amkreutz, J. J. 1261, 1263
Ammon, F. von 1506, 1511
Ammon, U. 207, 275, 580, 1429
Amor, R. 1755
Amoral, B. de 2584
Amorim-Braun, L. 1030
Amorim-Braun, M. L. 1360, 2895, 2899, 3027
Amos, A.C. 327, 1445, 1454, 1456
Amsalu Aklilu 2451, 2453
Amsler, R. 1656, 1665f., 2661
Amsler, R.A. 3165
Ānandāsagarasūri 2502, 2504
Anastasi, A. 1755
Anchieta, P. J. de 2670f., 2676
Anchorani, J. 2925
Andelin, A. 2391
Anders, W. 269
Andersen, A. 3061
Andersen, D. 2501
Andersen, E. 3173
Andersen, H. 1305, 1090
Andersen, H.Chr. 3122, 3130, 3136

Anderson, A. J. O. 2660
Anderson, H. 1308
Anderson, J. D. 34, 2752, 2758, 2957, 2960
Anderson, J. G. 2885
Anderson, K. N. 1198
Anderson, M. 2360
Anderson, R. 2698f.
Anderson, R. R. 265, 272f., 364, 369f., 380, 406, 460, 582, 612f., 627, 656, 728, 731, 771, 918f., 926f., 930, 1065f., 1238, 1241, 1414, 1418, 1422, 1428f., 1435, 1544, 1548, 1571f., 1608, 2221, 2240, 2727
Anderson, T. 2644
Andersson, J.-G. 644
Andersson, S.-G. 648
Andersson, Th. 1940, 1942
Andler, P. 1841
Andolz, R. 1755
Andrade, M. 2663-2666
Andreev, M. S. 2485
Andreeva, L. 2307
Andreeva-Georg, V.P. 1006f.
Andreev, M. S. 2485
Andrejčin, L. 1138, 2307f.
Andresen, K. G. 1244
Andrews, D. 2663, 2666
Andrews, E. A. 3032
Andrews, J. R. 2659f.
Andrews, L. 2573f.
André, J. 1334
Andréini, L. 1186
Andrés y Rodriguez, E. 1746, 1755
Andrés, M. F. 1078
Andrésson, G. 1929, 1931
Andrianov, S. N. 2752
Andrić, D. 2292f.
Andriotis, N. P. 1710-1712
Andrjuščenko, V.M. 2320f., 2326
Andronov, M.S. 3101, 3103
Andrusyshen, C.H. 2331-2333
Andry, J. 1900, 1903
Andrzejewski, B. W. 2464f., 2468
Angel Rivas, R. 2702
Angel, F. 2664, 2666
Angel, F. 2666
Angeli, A. 3010f.
Angelis, J. de 2621
Angelis, V. de 1721
Angere, J. 2628, 2630
Angione, H. 1215
Anglés, P.M. 1772, 1780, 1787, 2917, 2925
Ångström, M. 3048, 3050f.
Angus, W. 1308
Anguselli, P. F. B. 3014, 3016
Anhalt-Köthen, L. von 231
Anjuman Taraqquii 3097f., 3103
Anker-Moller, S. 1186

Ánna, J. við 1930, 1932
Annandale, Ch. 1960, 1963-1965, 1993, 2007
Anpilogova, B.G. 1360
Anreiter, P.P. 1138
Anshl, R. 2251, 2253
Ansted, A. 1505, 1511
Antal, L. 1149, 1151
Antelava, G.I, 2404
Antoine, E. 1802, 1804
Antoine, G. 1810, 1843, 2986
Antoinette, J.-Chr. 603
Antolín y Sáez, F. 1743, 1755
Antolín, F. 1215
Antolini, F. 1126, 1128, 1130
Antonescu, G.M. 1885, 1888
Antonini, A. 221f., 1846, 1858, 2917f., 2925, 3009, 3011, 3015, 3017
Antonoff, A. 2925
Antons, G. 957
Antonsen, E. H. 461, 500
Antony, H. 158, 361, 370
Antor, H. 2752
Antos, G. 960, 967
Anwyl, J.B. 2347, 2349
Aoki, T. 2623
Āpate, V.G. 3097, 3103
Apeldoorn, C. G. L. 1261, 1263
Apelt, W. 185, 188
Aphelen, H. v. 1926, 3062, 3059
Apherdianus, P. 1014
Apianus, P. 1261, 1263, 2215f.
Apin, S. J. 15, 1011, 1218f.
Apinus, S. J. 11, 1014
Apostel, A. 2297
Apostel, L. 273
Apovnik, P. 2299
Appel, K. 1893
Apperson, G.L. 1036, 1039
Apresjan, J. 889, 892
Apresjan, J. D. 575, 1002, 1006f., 2321, 2326
Aprings, A.2641
Apte, V. G. 2514
Apte, V. K. 2517
Apte, V. S. 2493, 2495, 2497, 2519
Aquarone, St. 1803, 1810
Aquensis, J.2284
Aquenza, G. 3009, 3011
Aquin, Th. d' 1788
Aquistapace, J.-N. 1517f., 1520, 1522
Ara, D. de 2663f., 2666
Aramon i Stein, N. 1778, 1784
Arana, E. 2698f.
Araoz, F. X. 2659f.
Arapov, M.V. 1644
Arat, R.R. 2412f.
Aratani, J. 3117
Arazzola, L. 1747, 1755
Arbatskij, D. I. 645, 648, 2326

Arbeo von Freising 2049
Arbor, A. 2623
Arbuleau, J. 1273
Arcais, P. F. d' 1868
Arce, J. 2995
Arcère de l'Oratoire, A. 2400, 2404
Archdeacon, E. 3128, 3130
Ard, J. 106, 108, 110, 208, 213, 1632, 1637, 2752
Arenas, P. de 2659f.
Arens, H. 2221
Arensen, T. 2644
Arfsten, R. 2031, 2033
Argani Villanueva, T. E. 2690
Argent, J. 1123
Arghezi, T. 1887
Argirov, St. 2305
Argote de Molina, D. 1740, 1755
Arguedas, J. M. 2683
Århammar, N. 2024f., 2027-2033, 2035f.
Arias de la Cruz, M. A. 1752, 1755
Aribau, B. C. 1773
Arimany, M. 923, 928, 1776f., 1779f.
Ariola, J. L. 1755
Ariost, L. 1851
Arioste 1125
Arisato, K. 3117
Ariste, P. 2394
Aristophanes 1696f.
Aristoteles 251, 274, 539, 547, 573, 992, 1699, 1873, 3142
Arizzi, S. 2836
Arlìa, C. 1216, 1867, 1878
Armalleda, C. de 2702
Armbruster, Ch. H. 1680, 2451, 2453, 2643f.
Armentia, N. 2703
Armogathe, J.-R. 2752
Armon, R. d' 2542, 2547, 3128, 3128
Armstrong, E. 1810
Armstrong, S. L. 575
Arn, M.-J. 1304
Arnal Cavero 1755
Arnaldi, F. 1721
Árnason, M. 1930f.
Arnaud, D. 324, 327
Arnaudov, J. 2307
Arndt, E. M. 2131
Arndt, M. 1053
Arndt, W. F. 1700, 1702
Arnedo, C. de 1746, 1756
Arnell, A. 3152f., 3155
Arnheim, R. 708, 715, 724
Arnim, B. von 2131f.
Arnim, L. A. von 2131
Arnold ter Hoernen 2041
Arnold, Chr. 1051f.
Arnold, D. I. 653, 853

Arnold, Th. 2967, 3053, 3060
Arnold, Th. K. 1073
Arntz, R. 170, 1660, 1666
Aro, J. 1684f.
Arona, J. de 1752, 1755
Aronoff, M. 1670
Arora, S. 1036, 1039
Arrebo, A. 1918
Arrivabene, G. 1088f., 1091
Arrivé, M. 1219
Arronches, J. de 2672, 2675
Aršba, N.V. 2420
Arsen'eva, M. G. 2181f., 2216
Arsy, J. L. d' 1795, 3036, 3038
Artells, E. 1776, 1780
Arthur, W. 1269, 1271
Artiles y Calero, F.N. 1755
Artin, E. 512
Artsakhetsi, H. 2368
Arumaa, P. 2394
Ārzū, Sirāj ul-din 2478
Asachi, G. 1884
Asadī, yi-Ṭūsī 2446f.
Asakune, S. 2925
Asakura, H. 2620, 2623, 3175
Asakura, S. 3118
Asar, J. A. K. 2517
Asbach-Schnitker, B. 980
Aschmann, E. D. 2699
Aschmann, H. P. 2698f.
Ascoli, W.I. 2340f.
Ash, J. 509, 1955f., 1965
Asher, R. E. 517
Ashkenazi, S. 1261, 1263
Âsim, A. 2399, 2404
Asimov, I. 1616
Asinovskij, A.S. 2321, 2326
Askedal, J. A. 822
Askedal, J. O. 585, 628, 2244
Askedal, O. 628
Askjani, M. 2690
Aslanov, M G. 2484f.
Ašmarin, N.I. 2408f.
Asoka, K. 2518
Asselineau, Ch. 223, 1800, 1810
Asser, G. 574
Assumpcam, M. da 2509, 3101, 3103
Asti, G. 3011
Astius, F. 1558
Ašukin, N.S. 2322 š
Ašukina, M.G. 2322 š
Asylbaev, A.A: 2397
Atanacković, L. 2292, 2294
Atanasova, V. 2307f.
Atanassian, Kh. 2370
Atibbā, Nāzimu'l- 2479
Atkins, B. 1030
Atkins, B. T. 106, 108, 110, 184, 188, 208, 213, 2751f., 2796, 2816f., 2824, 2836, 2856, 2858, 2860, 2864, 2959

Atkinson, R. 2340-2343
Atlatis, J. E. 654
Atrachovič, K. K. 3083
Atrakhovič, K.K. 2337
Atrián y Salas, M. 1743, 1764
Atteslander, P. 1634, 1636f.
Atzori, M. T. 1901-1903
Aubin, G. F. 1339
Aubin, N. 2938, 2944
Auden, W. H. 1967
Auderska, H. 2271
Auer, E. 1813
Auerbach, C. 3044-3046
Aufenanger, H. 2636f.
Aufrecht, Th. 2494, 2496
Aufrecht, W. A. 1693
Aufrecht, W.E. 2437
Auger, C. 1761
Auger, Ch. P. 1259f.
Auger, P. 49, 62
Augé, C. 64, 69, 1821-1826, 1831
Augé, P. 1826
Augier, Y. 1885
Augst, G. 119, 123, 269, 897f., 1146-1152, 1234, 1238, 1303, 1525f., 1529, 1616, 1622f., 2184, 2191f., 2216, 2233, 2241
Auguselli, P. F. G. 3017
Augusta Félix, J. de 2709
Augustin, Chr. F. B. 2062, 2067
Aulete, F. J. C. 1728-1733
Aulie, E. 2663f., 2666
Aulie, E. W. 2698f.
Aulie, W. 2663, 2666, 2698f.
Aulnaye, St. de 1195, 1197
Aurbacher, L. 2058, 2067
Aurenhammer, H. 3152, 3155
Auroux, S. 1067, 1069, 1074, 1813
Aurre, J. 2374f.
Aust, H. 1303, 2233
Austen, J. 1067
Austerlitz, R. 2628, 2631
Austin, D. 1664, 1666, 1668
Austin, H. S. G. 2513
Austin, J. 814f., 821
Austin, P. 2639-2641
Autenrieth, G. 1698, 1704, 2215f.
Auvray, J. 1838
Avalle, A. S. 1871, 1879
Avanchers, L. des 2462
Avanesov, R. I. 511, 515, 1305, 1308, 2316, 2322
Avdal, A. 2483, 2485
Avegrian, M. 2368
Avellana, M. del C. 1777, 1780
Avello Valdés, J. de 1741, 1755
Avenel, P. 604
Aventinus 1284
Averçó, L. de 1771, 1780
Avermaet, E. van 2648
Averna, G. 1197
Avery, C. B. 3022, 3028

Avetikian, G. 2368, 2370
Avgerian, M. 2370
Avilova, N.S. 2326
Avis, W. S. 641
Avramović, D. 2299f.
Avramović, Th. 2290, 2293
Avsec, O. 3126, 3130
Awagon, Ch. 2621
Axelsen, J. 2726, 3058, 3060
Ayācit, H. 3097, 3103
Ayala Manrique, J. F. 1741, 1755
Ayala, M. de 1755
Ayer, E. E. 2660, 3169
Aylward, W.W. 1446, 1448
Aymonier, E. 2591-2593
Aynī, Sadriddin 2480
Ayrosa, P. 2671f., 2675
Ayto, J. R. 133, 524, 532, 544, 552, 575, 747, 897f., 902f.
Ayyar, V.S.K. 3097, 3103
Aze, F. R. 2545, 2547
Azevedo, D. de 3022, 3027
Aziza, Cl. 1294
Azizbekov, Chr.A. 2409
Azkúe, R.M. 2373-2375, 2919, 2925
Azorín, F. 3129f.
Azorín Fernández, D. 2981, 2985
Azzaretti, M. 1261, 1263
Azzocchi, T. 1847, 1858

B

Ba Han 2552, 2554
Ba, J. 2542
Ba, M. 2505
Babault, M. 1258, 1260
Babič, St. 2752
Babinger, F. 2399, 2407
Babkin, A. M. 370, 764f., 980, 2312f, 2315f., 2318f., 2321f., 2326, 2328
Babnik, J. 2298, 2300
Babor, K. 3082
Babos, K. 2378, 2380
Babuik, J. 2939, 2944
Babukica, V. 2293
Baccetti Poli, R. 3009, 3012
Baccherius, J. 1011, 1014
Bacci, L. 2995
Bach, A. 1279f., 1283f., 1290
Bachelard, G. 1678
Bachellery, É., 2339-2342
Bacher, B.Z. 2434
Bachhaus-Gerst, M. 2466
Bachmann, H. 1138
Bachofer, W. 231, 243, 245, 407, 767, 770, 1136-1138, 1143, 1429, 2104, 2216, 2233
Bächtold, J.M. 1100-1102, 2198, 2232

Baci, L. 2994
Back, O. 249, 274
Bäcker, N. 1168, 1178
Backes, H. 1017, 2234
Backhausen, N. 1107, 1109f., 2921, 2925
Bäcklund, U. 1016
Backman, G.H. 3127
Backmann, G.H. 3126, 3130
Bacmeister, L. I. 3072
Bacon, F. 1089, 1949
Bacovia, G. 1887
Bacri, R. 1350
Badaev, C. X. 2483
Badakhshi, S. A. 2485
Baden, J. 221, 1612, 1622, 1920f., 3052, 3060
Badenas, R. 1702
Badens, J. 223
Bader, M. 2925
Badger, G.P. 3089, 3094
Badger, K.M. 1014
Badia i Margarit, A. 1755, 1772, 1777f., 1780, 1787
Badings, A. H. L. 2918, 2925
Badiola, R. 2374f.
Badten, L. W. 2632f.
Baecker, E. 1296
Baer, P. 2225
Baermann, N. G. 2067, 2091, 2094
Baeteman, J. 2451, 2453
Baetke, W. 1929, 1931
Bagaev, N. K. 2484f.
Baganz, L. 2752
Bagaty, N. (= Bagaev, N. K.) 2485
Bagdan, F. 2332
Bagder, K.M. 1012
Baggioni, D. 2872-2876
Bahder, K. von 124, 2085, 2098
Bahl, K. Ch. 2536, 2545
Bahlow, H. 1269, 1271f.
Bahmet, A. 2332
Bahner, W. 530, 598, 614, 841, 882, 1205, 1230, 1549
Bähr, D. 662f., 667
Bahr, J. 247, 274, 591, 770f., 849, 853, 1236, 1236, 1415, 1595f., 1604f., 1607, 1609, 2081f., 2098f., 2220
Bahrdt, H. P. 191, 196, 206
Bahri, H. 2512, 2518, 3100, 3103
Baier, M. 3140f.
Bailey 3121f. (= folgender?)
Bailey, B. 2528, 2531
Bailey, D. C. 2618f., 2623
Bailey, H. W. 2476
Bailey, N. 29, 509, 526, 528f., 720, 723, 1159, 1943-1951, 1954-1956, 1958, 1988, 2008, 2950, 2967, 2971, 2973, 3037

Bailey, R. W. 33, 325, 327, 653, 662, 665, 667, 1454, 1456f., 1600, 1603, 1605, 1607-1609, 3165, 3168
Baillairgé, Ch. 1122f.
Bailly, A. 1388
Bailly, M. A. 1699, 1702
Bailly, R. 1069, 1071
Bails, B. 1747, 1755
Bajkow, M. 2336f.
Bakaev, Č. Ch. 2483, 2485
Bakaya, R.M. 1360
Bakel, J. van 2021
Baker, E.A. 2958
Baker, G. 610, 613
Baker, Ph. 2872-2875
Baker, W.M. 1144f.
Bakker, D. 2021f.
Bakker, D. M. 3039
Bakonyi, H. 1320, 1354f., 1358, 1360
Bakos, F. 249, 274, 2380, 2383
Bakró-Nagy, M. 2398
Baksh, K. 3099, 3103
Ba'labaki, M. al 3092, 3094
Balari i Jovany, J. 1774, 1777, 1780f.
Balasescu, N. 1884
Balassa, J. 2380
Balasubramanian, K. 3107
Balázs, S.F. 2375, 2382
Balbastre y Ferrer, J. 1776, 1778, 1781
Balbi, G. 136, 143, 996
Balbi, J. 1739
Balbigny, A. 1215
Balbus, J. 994, 996, 1788f., 1810 (s. Jo(h)annes)
Balčikonis, J. 2352f.
Bald, W.-D. 1183f., 1813
Baldauf, I. 2412
Baldegger, M. 183, 188
Baldelli, I. 1360, 1844, 1859, 1861
Baldinger, K. 17, 281, 286, 372, 406, 614, 626, 663, 667, 1066, 1090, 1093, 1192f., 1331, 1343f., 1347f., 1412, 1415, 1596, 1609, 1756, 1792, 1795, 1810, 1816, 1837, 1842f., 1893, 1903, 1905, 2716, 2726, 2752, 2886
Baldini, G. 2973, 2975
Balducci, G. 70
Balg, G. H. 1910f.
Balgden, C. O. 2565
Balhorn, H. 1146, 1150
Balin, V. I. 1360
Bálint, S. 2382
Balkan, K. 1692, 1694
Balker, G. P. 575
Balkevičius, J. 2357, 2359
Balkevičs, J. 2359

Ball, C. J. E. 1445
Ball, R. H. 1529
Ball, W. J. 1054f., 1219, 1221f.
Ballagi, M. 2377, 2380
Ballard, B.W. 3165
Ballarin Cornel, A. 1756
Ballassa, J. 2377
Ballentyne, D. W. G. 1259f.
Ballmann, A. 2290, 2295
Ballmer, Th. T. 162, 163, 815-816, 818, 820-822, 894, 897f., 2177, 2181, 2188, 2189, 2190, 2216
Ballweg, J. 123, 439, 459, 821, 1007
Ballweg-Schramm, A. 123, 278, 408, 460, 499, 575, 585, 2236, 2243
Bally, Ch. 888, 892, 1016, 1031, 1090-1092, 1429
Balmas, E. 3010f.
Baloc, N.B.K. 3097, 3103
Baloch, N. B. K. 2516, 2520
Balzac, H. de 147, 1343, 1534
Bammesberger, A. 229f., 1334, 1454, 1572f., 1610, 2242, 2342
Banchet, J. 2886
Bandeira, M. 1732
Bandhauer, W. 654
Bandhyopadhyaya, H. 2517
Bandtkie, J. S. 3062, 3066
Bandyopadhyaya, H. 2510
Banerjee, G. 2510, 2517
Banerjee, M. 2504
Bang, I. 1920f.
Bang, J. 1920f.
Banker, E. 2591, 2593
Banker, J. 2591, 2593
Bannerjea, B. 3101
Bantaş, A. 2752, 2887
Banti, G. 2469
Banzo y Sáenz de Miera, J. M. 2803, 2990
Bapat, V. R. 2514, 2519
Bar, E. D. 1011, 1014, 1078
Bar-Hillel, Y. 1617, 1623
Baraga, F. J. 2692f., 2696
Baraibar y Zumarraga, F. 1756
Baralt, R. M. 65, 69, 1176
Baranger, C.-M. 1362
Baranov, C.K. 3092, 3094
Baranyai Decsi, J. 2380
Barat, Chr. 2873, 2875
Barat, T. N. 2510, 2517
Barata, M. da G. T. 1735
Barbeau, A. 1306, 1308
Barber, E. A. 1700, 1702
Barber, H. 1272
Barberi, G. F. 3010f.
Barbé, J.-M. 1269, 1272
Barbi, M. 1870, 1879
Barbier de Meynard, A.C. 2402-2404

Barbier, J. 2925
Barbier, V. 2584, 2588
Barbina, A. B. 1874
Barblan, M.-C. 2947, 3012
Barbon Rodriguez, J. A. 1743, 1764
Barbosa, A. 1726, 1733, 2584, 3021
Barbosa, O. 1071
Barbu, I. 1887
Barbut, M. 410, 459
Barc, B. 1680f.
Bárcena, A. de 2707f.
Barchudarov, S. G. 2324, 2328, 2751
Barchudarova, L. S. 2752, 2754, 2756, 2760, 2767
Barcia, J. 1756
Barcia, R. 1071, 1746f., 1756
Barcianu, S. 1883, 1888
Barclay, J. 1944, 1951, 1955f., 1965
Bárczi, G. 2382
Bardhi, F. 2361
Bardhi, M. 2295, 2365f.
Bardosi, V. 1066
Bardovič, A.M. 2337
Bardsley, Ch. W. 1272
Baret, J. 1793, 2925, 2957f.
Baretti, G. 64, 69, 1849, 1862, 2971, 2973, 2975
Baretti, G. M. A. 1855, 1858
Baretti, G.M. 2954
Baretti, J. 2950-2952, 2955
Bargery, G. P. 2459
Barić, H. 2292f., 2363, 2365
Barisone, E. 1533, 1536
Barit, G. 1884
Barit, O. 1884
Baritz, G. 1883, 1888
Bark, M. van den 1186f., 1526, 1529
Barker, M. A. R. 2692, 2695f.
Barlough, J. E. 1157
Barlow, A.C. 1029
Bärmann, N. 1123
Barnadas, J. M. 2681, 2683
Barnard, A. 2650, 2653
Barner, W. 1200
Barnes, J. 2220
Barnes, M. 1931f.
Barnett, B. 3165
Barney, St. A. 1444, 1454
Barnhart, C.L. 31, 33, 77, 106, 110, 131, 133, 249, 274, 530, 606, 1164f., 1166, 1331, 1535f., 1967, 1982, 1988, 1994, 1997-2000, 2003f., 2007f., 3147
Barnhart, D. K. 2007
Barnhart, R. K. 1164, 1166, 1535f., 2004, 2007f.
Barnier, J. 1388, 2889f., 2899f.

Barnils, P. 1785
Barnoud-Maisdon, M. 1367f.
Baron, D. E. 1444, 1456
Baron, E. 43
Barone, J. M. 2221
Barone, R. 208, 213
Barons, K. 2355
Baróti, S.D. 2382
Barr, J. 2433
Barragán, J.V. 2955
Barraine, R. 1516, 1518, 1522
Barrera M., A. 2663, 2666
Barrera V., A. 2663, 2666
Barrera, F. 2662, 2664, 2666
Barrera-Vidal, A. 779, 787, 905, 1363, 2789, 2901, 2903
Barreteau, D. 2648f.
Barreti, G. 2972
Barré, L. 217, 223, 641, 1081f., 1129, 1206, 1208, 1798, 1803f., 1810, 1822
Barrère, A. 1186
Barrie, W.B. 2959
Barrowman, J. 1984f.
Barseghian, H. 2369
Barsov, A.A. 2319, 2322
Barsov, N.P. 2315, 2322
Barsukova, V. V. 3078, 3084
Bart Rossebastiano, A. 1088, 1090, 1093, 1860-1862, 3013, 3019, 3169
  cf. Rossebastiano
Barta, P. I. 1416, 1562, 1610, 2242, 2245
Bartas, G. de S. du 1823
Bartel, A. 2300
Bartels, K. 2216
Barth, E. 239, 243
Barth, H. 2642, 2645, 2657f., 2460
Barthe, R. 1894f., 1903
Barthel, M. 1292, 1294
Barthelemi, M. 1130
Barthes, R. 23f., 707f., 716, 724
Bartholomae, Chr. 1133, 1137f., 2471f., 2492
Bartholomew, D. A. 71, 77, 2698, 2700, 2752
Bartlett, J. 1045-1047
Bartlett, J.R. 1137f.
Bartoletti Colombo, A.M. 1872, 1878
Bartoli, D. 1089, 1091
Bartoli, M. G. 1903, 1905
Bartolomeus von Chlumec 2279
Bartoszewicz, D. 3076
Bartra, E. 2682f.
Bartsch, J. 1029
Bartsch, K. 1551, 1558
Bartsch, R. 191, 194, 198, 206, 575
Bartschat, B. 2217
Barua, H. 2509, 2517
Barua, M. K. 2517

Baruël, E. 3054, 3061
Baruffaldi, G. 1128
Barzizza, G. 1844f.
Barzun, J. 1216
Bas, C. 1778, 1781
Bas, P. 49
Basavaradhya, N. 2525, 2533
Baseggio, L. 1855
Bashakov, N. A. 2752
Bašić, P. 2289
Basil'ev, V.M. 2397
Baskakov, N.A. 2411, 2414
Baskervill, W.M. 1442, 1455
Basler, O. 405, 458, 771, 1011, 1014, 2064, 2068, 2072, 1106, 1110f., 1139, 1149, 1151, 1174f., 1177, 2216, 2218
Basnage de Beauval, H. 1801, 1806
Bassano, F. da 2451, 2453
Bassegoda, B. 1778, 1781
Basset, A. 2457
Basseta, D. de 2662, 2664, 2666
Bassols de Climent, M. 1771, 1777, 1781
Basta, P. I. 1241
Bastardas Parera, J. 1721, 1771, 1777, 1781
Bastarrachea, J. 2663, 2666
Bastarrachea, J. R. 2698, 2700
Bastert, U. 862, 868
Basti, N. 3010f.
Bastien, L. 3124
Basto, C. 1114, 1119
Basu, R. 2517
Basuki, S. 3169
Batalla, J. 1780
Batalova, R.M. 2395, 2397
Batchelor, J. 2621
Bate, J. D. 2512, 2518
Bately, J. M. 1950, 1952
Baten, L. 2765
Bathe, W. 2925
Batlle, L. C. 1776, 1781
Bátori, I.S. 1573, 3165
Batres Jauregui, A. 1752, 1756
Batres Jáuregui, A. 65, 69
Battaglia, S. 149, 149, 151, 1393, 1413, 1857f., 1868, 1870, 1878, 1880
Battig, W. F. 1672
Battisti, C. 1325, 1331, 1875, 1903
Bauche, H. 1185f.
Bauché, R. 1207f.
Baucom, K. 2650, 2654
Baudelaire, Ch. 24, 147
Baudeneau, J. 1841
Baudot, A. 1207f.
Baudot, J. 1674, 1678
Baudouin de Courtenay, J. 734, 748, 2312
Baudrier, P. 2999, 3005f., 3012, 3169

Baudry, H. 1263
Bauer, B. 1078, 2179f., 2182, 2216
Bauer, E. 1134, 1137f., 1571f.
Bauer, K. 2215f.
Bauer, K.H. 1044, 1047
Bauer, L. 127, 170, 409, 1671
Bauer, R. 1284, 1290
Bauer, W. 1205, 1700, 1702f.
Bäuerle, R. 2887
Bauga, A. 2357, 2359
Baugh, A. C. 1071
Baulies Cortal, J. 1778, 1781
Baum, H. 2199, 2201, 2216
Baum, J. 2064, 2067
Bauman, I. 1885
Baumann, H. 1186, 1527, 1529
Baumann, O. 2463, 2466
Baumbach, L. 1696, 1703
Baumgarten, A. G. 1873
Baumgarten, R. 2351
Baumgartner, H. M. 459, 580
Baumgartner, W. 2428, 2434f., 2437
Bäuml, B. J. 1118f.
Bäuml, H. H. 1118f., 1136-1138
Baunebjerg Hansen, G. 2726, 2749, 2752, 2824, 2832, 2836, 2841, 2853, 2898, 2901
Baur, G. W. 239, 243, 2199, 2233
Baurley, G. L. 1110
Baurmann, J. 189
Bausch, K.-H. 321
Bausch, K.-R. 1066, 2752
Bausinger, H. 42, 45, 850, 853
Baxter, J. 106, 108, 110, 2752, 2888, 2901
Baxter, J. H. 1722
Baxton, A. 1776, 1785
Bay, Chr. F. 3053, 3055, 3060
Bayer, E. 163, 166
Bayer, J. 3031, 3033
Bayle, P. 216f., 223, 988f., 996, 1796, 1800
Bayley, N. 1952
Bayliss, B. 1741, 1764
Baylon, Chr. 1217
Bayo, C. 1753, 1756
Bazerque, A. 2875
Bazin, H. 1350
Bazzarini, A. 996
Bazzetta de Vemenia, N. 1532, 1536
Beach, D. M. 2651f., 2654
Beale, A.D. 3165
Beale, P. 1055
Beam, M. S. 2643f.
Bean, C.M. 3128, 3120
Beaton, A. G. 2643, 2645
Beattie, J. 1983, 1985
Beattie, N. 182, 187, 188, 208, 209, 211, 213, 2752
Beau, A. E. 3023, 3025, 3027

Beaucourt, M. 2823
Beaufront, L. de 3124, 3126, 3129f.
Beaugrande, R. de 1671
Beaugrande, R.-A. de 947f., 955
Beaujean, A. 66, 69, 141, 143, 1837, 1841
Beaujean, J. 1826
Beaujot, J.-P. 83, 86f.
Beaulieux, Ch. 1790, 1793, 1795, 1798, 1800, 1810, 3006, 3169
Beauquier, Ch. 1329, 1331
Beaussier, M. 3089, 3094
Beauvais, A.E. 1052
Beauvoir, J. M. 2710
Beauzée, N. 906, 1071f., 1079
Bec, I.V. 2323
Bec, P. 1892, 1903, 1905
Becerra, M. 2664, 2666
Becher, J. J. 3014
Bechert, H. 2500, 2506
Bechhaus-Gerst, M. 2467, 2467, 2664, 2666
Bechtel, G. 1045, 1047
Bechtermünze, N. 2040
Beck, F. A. 1558
Beck, J. W. 1074
Beck, R. 1516-1518, 1520, 1522
Beck, Th. 1388
Bečka, J. V. 1321, 1669, 2281, 2283
Becker, D. 1138
Becker, D. A. 213
Becker, H. 1011, 1014, 1016
Becker, H. 2177, 2216
Becker, K. 1261, 1263
Becker, R. K. 2216
Becker, R. Z. 2077
Becker, W. W. 1261, 1263
Becker-Carns, C. 123
Beckerath, E. v. 166
Beckers, H. 269, 2211, 2233
Beckhoven, B. van 1320
Beckwith, Y. 1208
Beda Venerabilis 3032
Bedard, C. 3174
Bédard, E. 62, 78, 88, 680, 704
Bedevian, A.K. 2402, 2404
Bedford, E. 852f.
Beebe, J. F. 2631
Beeching, C. L. 1259f.
Beekman, E. 2663, 2666
Beekman, J. 2663, 2666
Beene, W. 3094, 3096
Beer, E. 1173, 1176
Beersmans, F. 1623, 2782
Beeston, A. F. L. 1651, 1666, 1690, 1693
Beg, M. Q. 2516, 2520
Began Lotsawa 2548f.
Bégué, C. 1841
Behaghel, O. 1242, 1244, 1619, 1623

Behrens, D. 3013, 3019
Beigbeder, O. 3152, 3156
Beil, J. 2918, 2925
Beilharz, R. 2207, 2224
Bein, K. 3122-3124, 3130
Beinhauer, W. 1012, 1014, 1021, 1027f., 1030, 1038f., 2776, 2989
Bejarano, A. 1078
Bejta, M. 2365
Béjoint, H. 106, 108, 110, 115, 124, 128, 132f., 208f., 213, 215, 532, 575, 653, 698, 1383, 1385, 1630, 1637, 1975, 1982
Beke, Ch. T. 2452, 2462, 2466, 2469
Bektaev, K. B. 1644, 1671
Bektaev, Qu. B. 1139
Bel'čikov, J.A. 2322
Belemnon 1349
Belèze, G. L. G. 1269, 1272
Bélèze, G. 1838
Bělič, J. 2284
Belik, J. 2761
Belinfante, F.J. 3132
Belkassem ben Sedira 3093f.
Bell, C. L. M. 1652, 1667
Bell, Ch. A. 2549f.
Bell, J. 2959
Bell, M. 1962
Belle, A. 1123
Bellefroid, P. 2939, 2944
Bellengardus, St. 1051f.
Beller, R. 2659f.
Bellew, H. W. 2484f.
Belli, G. G. 1874
Bellin, J. 2215f.
Bellini, B. 149, 151, 1857f., 1860, 1862-1866, 1870, 1879
Bellini, T. 150
Bello, A. 1768f.
Bellows, J. 2958
Bellucci, A. 1302
Bellugi, U. 3142, 3144
Bellvitge, J. 1773, 1783
Bellvitges, J. 2928
Belon, P. 2915, 2925
Belostenec, J. 2289, 2293, 2296
Belot, A. 2982
Belot, J.B. 3090, 3082, 3094
Belsare, M. B. 2512, 2518
Beltramo, A. 1361
Beltrán, P. 2663, 2666
Beltz, W. 1522
Bembe, M. 2626
Bembo, P. 1125, 1850-1852, 1854
Bemmerlein, A. 1767
Bénac, H. 84, 86, 1069, 1071, 1314
Bénard, Th. 1825, 1839f.
Ben-Hayyim, Z. 2427, 2429f., 2433, 2435f.
Ben-Yehuda, Ehud 2436

Ben-Yehuda, Eliezer 66, 69, 2430, 2436
Benbow, T. 106, 108, 110, 1655, 1666
Bencsics, N. 2292f.
Bender, F. J. 1304, 1308f.
Bender, M. L. 1339, 2642-2645, 2461, 2464, 2466, 2469
Bender, T. K. 1566
Bendiks, H. 2358f.
Bendsen, B. 2029, 2033
Benecke, F. 1405, 1413
Benecke, G. F. 242, 1149f., 1234, 1238, 1418-1420, 1424-1426, 1428, 1434, 1539, 1548-1551, 1557f., 1601, 1608-1610, 2088, 2090, 2094, 2096, 2215, 2216
Benedict, P. K. 1339, 2557f.
Benedicto, P. 1734
Benediktsson, H. 1928, 1932, 2761
Benediktsson, J. 1929, 1932
Benedum, J. 1230
Beneken, G. W. F. 1268, 1272
Beneš, E. 947, 955, 957, 967, 1353, 1356, 1363
Benešić, J. 2292f.
Benês, J. 1110
Benfey, Th. B. 2471f., 2490f., 2495
Bengtsson, H. 3129f.
Benhacine, D. 3169
Benham, W.G. 1046f.
Benhamou, S. 87
Beni, P. 217f., 223, 652f., 1854, 1859
Benizeau, C. 3094
Benkö, J. 1882
Benkö, L. 1559, 1561, 2381f.
Benn, G. 2131
Bennemann, P. 3124, 3126f., 3130
Bennett, E. L. 1696
Bennett, E. L. Jr. 1704
Bennett, P. A. 168, 170, 1669
Bennewitz, I. 1140
Bennewitz-Behr, I. 1139, 2232
Benoist, A. de 1270, 1272
Benoit, P. 3005
Benoliel, J. 1907
Benot y Rodriguez, E. 1128
Benot, E. 1014, 1089, 1091
Bense, M. 2207, 2216
Benseler, G. E. 1699, 1703
Bensley, E.R. 2938, 2946, 2952, 2955
Benson, E. 1007, 1014, 1385, 1652, 1666, 1967, 1975, 1982
Benson, M. 96, 892, 1006f., 1012-1014, 1016, 1385, 1652, 1666, 1967, 1975, 1982, 2292f., 2316, 2322
Benson, Th. 1440, 1442, 1454
Bensoussan, M. 106, 109, 110, 209, 213, 1632, 1637

Bentolila, A. 2872-2875
Bentot, G. 2803, 3000f., 3006
Benveniste, E. 1334, 2485
Benware, W. A. 2136, 2233
Benz, F. L. 1693
Benzing, B. 2460
Benzing, J. 2476f.
Berberi Squarotti, G. 1868
Berca, O. 1131
Bercher, L. 3092, 3094
Berckel, J. A. Th. M. van 1321
Bercy, L. de 1187
Berednikov, J. I. 2267
Bérésine, E. 2483, 2485
Beretti, C. 3016f.
Berezina, O. E. 3071, 3084
Berg, B. van den 1139
Berg, D. 2039, 2047
Berg, P.C. 1163f.
Berg, St. 1938
Berg, W. 804
Bergantini, G. P. 1846f., 1856, 1859
Berganza, F. de 1742, 1756
Bergenholtz, H. 111, 127, 130, 133-135, 181, 184, 188, 199-201, 206f., 214, 251, 274, 317, 391, 393, 406, 461, 500, 518, 522, 524, 564, 575, 586, 591f., 614, 642, 644, 648, 736, 739f., 747-749, 774-779, 788-790, 796, 814, 851, 853, 868, 880, 892, 904f., 921, 923, 930, 955, 1009f., 1016-1018, 1322, 1595, 1609, 1611, 1613-1615, 1621-1625, 1631, 1638, 1644f., 2106, 2130, 2136, 2150, 2152, 2207, 2233, 2235, 2237, 2241, 2244, 2722, 2726, 2728, 2752, 2757, 2760, 2770, 2774f., 2783, 2789, 2903, 2969
Berger, D. 123, 369, 1362, 2218, 2219, 2234
Berger, G. 273
Berger, H. 732, 748
Berger, J. E. 1155, 1157
Berger, R. 1272, 3130
Berger, V. K. 2763
Bergerot, E. 1839
Berghe, Chr. L. van den 1247
Bergin, O. 2343
Bergin, O.J. 2342
Bergin, Th. G. 1874
Bergius, R. 123
Bergmann, G. 1310, 2198-2201, 2216
Bergmann, K. 1149, 1151 1234, 1238, 2086, 2090, 2095
Bergmann, R. 157-159, 780, 782, 784, 786, 1132, 1143, 1147, 1152, 1241, 2037, 2047, 2104, 2233

Bergsdorf, W. 1204f.
Bergsland, K. 2632f.
Bergsträsser, G. 2432, 2437
Bergström, M. 3048f.
Berkhout, C. T. 1456
Berkov, V. P. 1929, 1931, 2715, 2717, 2726, 2753, 3082, 3084
Berkowitz, L. 1701, 1704
Berlaimont, N. de 2910f., 2915f., 2925, 2927, 2929, 2935
Berlaimont, N. van 3021
Berlan, F. 1011, 1017, 1219f., 1810
Berlan-Lacourt, F. 1068, 1074
Berlaymont, N. de 2981
Berlin, A. 1100f., 1186
Berlin, B. 2664, 2666, 2698, 2700
Berlin, G. T. 1296
Berlitz, Ch. 1169, 1177
Berloquin, P. 1349f.
Bermejo, M. 2953, 2955
Bermond, D. 38, 41, 43, 45
Bernabé, J. 2874f.
Bernado da Parigi, M.R.P.F. 2404
Bernard, J. R. L. 1090f.
Bernard, R. 3125, 3130
Bernardoni, G. 1847, 1859
Berndt, J.G. 237f., 242
Berneker, E. 1337, 1339
Bernet, Ch. 1260
Berning, C. 1201, 1204, 2188, 2216
Berni-Canani, M. 2753
Bernolák, A. 2285, 2287, 2377, 2380
Bernot, D. 2552, 2554
Bernstein, I. 1033, 1042
Bernstein, Th. M. 1101
Bernstejn, S. B. 2260, 2306f., 3081
Berold, K. 2890-2893, 2900
Béronie, N. 1895, 1903
Berrár, J. 2382
Berrey, L.V. 1090, 1186f., 1526, 1529
Berry, J. 2645, 2648
Berry, Th. 2934
Berry-Rogghe, G.L.M. 1017
Berset, F. 2921, 2925
Berström, M. 3049
Bersuire, P. 1790
Berta 2643
Bertaud du Chazaud, H. 1078, 1837, 1839
Bertaux, F. 2793, 3001, 3003f.
Bertaux, P. 2753, 2793
Berthelin, P.-Ch. 1802, 1804
Berthelot, M. 1825
Berthelot, P. 3131
Berthelsen, Chr. 2632f.
Berthelson, A. 1926, 3053, 3060
Berthier, P.-V. 1123, 1210-1212, 1215
Berthold, L. 242, 719, 722, 1035, 1042, 2036

Berti, L. 1855, 1861
Bertinin, G.M. 1762
Bertoni, G. 67, 1308f., 1864, 1877f.
Bertonio, L. 2685-2690
Bertrand, J. 1122f., 1314
Bertsch, A. 1529
Bertuch, F.J.J. 2987f., 2991
Berty, A. 2937, 2944
Berual Leongomez, J. 1220
Berulfsen, B. 1308f.
Berynda, P. 2264-2266, 2310, 2322, 2329, 2332f., 2335, 3070
Berzoli de Gubbio, P. 1845
Besch, W. 18, 111, 124-127, 135, 158, 224, 244, 278, 359, 408, 461, 500, 517, 582, 585, 627, 652f., 655, 662, 666f., 814, 821, 842, 980f., 998, 1031, 1067, 1143, 1152, 1158, 1241, 1283, 1284, 1291, 1415f., 1429, 1435, 1531, 1546, 1548f., 1562, 1572f., 1608-1610, 1645, 2074-2976, 2098, 2100, 2130, 2136, 2233, 2235, 2238, 2240, 2244
Bescherelle, L.-N. 99-101, 139, 144, 220-222, 224, 606, 1311-1313, 1746, 1768, 1802-1804, 1839, 2983, 3054
Beschi, s. Father Beschi
Beses, L. 1187
Beskrovanii, V.M. 3101, 3103
Besnard, Ph. 1270, 1272
Besselaar, J.J. van den 1735
Bessenyei, G. 2376
Besses, L. 2981, 2983
Bessé, B. de 62
Bessinger, J.B. 1443f., 1454
Bessonova, O.A. 3140f.
Best, R. I. 2342, 2351
Betancourt, G. 2659
Bétant, E.-A. 1558
Betanzos, P. de 2669
Bethe, E. 1703
Bethel, J.P. 2008
Béthune, E. de 1789
Bettarini, R. 1874
Betteridge, H. T. 2725, 2967
Bettinger, J.-B. 1219
Betts, L. 2674-2676
Betts, L. V. 2703
Betz, W. 69, 144, 158, 1146, 1151, 1204, 1234-1236, 1239f., 243, 406, 459, 499, 670, 672, 731, 753, 804, 826, 830, 2098, 2192, 2194, 2215f., 2222, 2231-2233
Beucheler, F. 1337, 1339
Beumann, H. 1905, 2049
Beurard, J.B. 2939, 2944
Bever, Th. G. 1617, 1623
Beveraggi-Allende, W. 2954

Bevilacqua, A. 2451, 2453
Bevilacqua, L. A. 1845, 1852, 1859
Bevington, J. 1367
Bevzenko, S. P. 1139
Beyer, A. 42, 44f., 1036, 1039, 2174, 2216
Beyer, H. 42, 44f., 1035, 1039, 2174, 2216
Beyer, K. 2429, 2431, 2436, 2437
Beyhl 1126
Bezerque, A. 2872
Bezlaj, F. 1285f., 1289, 2299f.
Bezold, C. 1683f.
Bezzenberger, A. 1337, 1340, 1342, 2341f.
Bezzola, R. 1898f.
Bezzola, R. R. 1903
Bhaduri, M. Bh. 2538, 2545
Bhagavat, S. 2518
Bhakta, T. K. 2511, 2518
Bhaldraithe, T. de 2344-2346, 2348
Bhandarkar, R. G. 2490, 2496
Bhanja, V. 2515, 2520
Bhāskara, B. J. 2504
Bhaskara-raya 2490
Bhat, D. N. S. 2558
Bhattacarya, Y. 3170
Bhattacharya, B. N. 2509, 2517
Bhattacharya, S. 2509, 2530, 2532, 2543, 2547
Bhayani, H. C. 2499, 2506
Bhide, V. V. 2514, 2519
Biagioli, G. 3010f.
Bialik Hubermann, G. 1764
Bianchi, P. 1854, 1861
Bianchi, T.X. 2402, 2405
Biard, J.-D. 2959
Bibel, W. 899
Bibolotti, B. 2703
Bichatk, F. 2277
Bickmann, H.-J. 615f., 618, 626
Bidoli, E. 3016f.
Bieber, F. 2463, 2466
Bieber, F.J. 2466
Biedermann, H. 3157
Biehlfeldt, H. H. 172f.
Bielefeldt, H. H. 1139
Bieler, K.H. 1051f.
Bielfeldt, H. H. 1138, 2276-2278, 2714f., 2725-2727, 2753, 2761, 2782, 2850, 2853, 3081, 2319, 2322
Biella, J.C. 1690, 1693
Bienenthal, T.J.H.R. 2434
Bierbach, M. 1011, 1017, 1054f., 1206, 1209, 1795, 1804, 1810
Bierbaumer, P. 1444, 1454
Bierce, A. 251f., 272, 290, 293, 296, 1349f.
Biere, B.U. 123, 551, 575
Bierhorst, J. 2659f.

Bierwisch, M. 539, 575, 629, 634, 804, 809f., 813
Biesterfeld, W. 158
Bietenhard, R. 2198, 2221
Biette, L. 1825
Biezais, H. 2354, 2360
Bigelow, Ch. 142, 145
Biggs, B. 2636f.
Bigot, Ch. 2884f.
Bihari, F. 2376, 2382
Bikova, E. M. 2510, 2517, 3103
Bilabel, F. 1140
Bilec'kyj-Nosenko, P. 2331-2333
Bilek, F. 1029, 2224f.
Biligiri, H. S. 2542, 2546
Billip, K. 3068
Billmeier, G. 1644
Bilodid, I.K. 1139, 2332
Binchy, D.A. 2340, 2342f.
Binder 2191, 2216
Bingen, N. 1861, 3007f., 3012
Binot, J.-L. 3166
Binovič, L. E. 3082
Binowitsch, L.E. 1028
Biondelli, B. 1534, 1537
Biosca, F.M. 2989
Birbrajer, J. 2885
Birdwhistell, R.L. 172, 174
Birgegård, U. 3071, 3072, 3083f.
Birjukov, V.G. 903f.
Birjuley, S.V. 3101, 3103
Birkenhauer, K. 2753
Birkenhauer, R. 1030, 2188, 2217, 2229, 2753
Birket-Smith, K. 2633
Birkfellner, G. 3071f., 3083
Birks, R. O. 2751
Birlinger, A. 2215f.
Birnbaum, H. 2193, 2217
Birnbaum, S. A. 2246, 2254
Biržakova, E. E. 3072f., 3084f.
Bischoff, B. 2215
Bischoff, E. 1529
Bischoff, J.M. 1016
Bischoff, K. 2198, 2217
Bisenieks, V. 2357, 2359
Bishop, R. 2698f.
Biswas, B. 2511, 2517
Biswas, S. 2509
Bittle, W.E. 305
Bivar, A. 1098
Bivens, L. 228, 230
Bjelke, J. 1924, 1927
Bjerrum, A. 1919, 1921
Bjerrum, M. 1919, 1921f.
Björkegren, J. 3042
Björklund, St. 1939, 1942
Björkman, C. G. 3048, 3050
Björn, G. 3043, 3046
Blaas, L. 3125, 3130
Blachère, R. 2919, 2925, 3088, 3094

Black, G.F. 1272
Black, P. 2464-2466
Blackall, E.A. 236, 243
Blaga, L. 1887
Blagdeu, C. O. 2563
Blair, E. H. 2565
Blair, R. 2663, 2666, 2670
Blaise, A. 1720
Blake, B. J. 2639-2641
Blana, H. 330, 359
Blanar, V. 274
Blanc, E. 1089, 1091, 1110, 1839
Blanc, L.G. 1549-1552, 1554, 1557f.
Blanc, S.-H. 2952, 2955, 2980, 2983, 2993, 2996, 3011
Blancardus, St. 2916, 2925
Blanchet, J. 2980
Blanchus, R.D.F. 2361, 2365
Blancpain, M. 21, 27
Blancquaert, E. 1308f.
Blandford, F.G. 1310
Blanke, D. 3129f., 3136
Blasi, N. De 2754
Blasi, S. di 1361
Blasius, R. 1985
Blass, A. 1028, 1360, 2890, 2900
Blatt, A. 1669
Blatt, F. 1721
Blau, J. 2428, 2435, 2485f.
Blau, O. 2290, 2295
Blav, J. 2483
Blavier, E. 2919, 2925
Bláhová, E. 2260
Bledy, G. 1889
Bleek, D. F. 2651, 2653f.
Bleek, W. H. 2650
Bleek, W. H. I. 2650,
Bleek, W. H. J. 2652-2655
Bleiweis, J. 2298
Bleske, H. 2218
Blériot, J. 2823
Bliese, L. 2469
Blinkenberg, A. 2835, 3056-3060
Blinkenberg, G. 3061
Blinova, C.I. 2319, 2322
Bliss, A.J. 1169, 1176
Bloch, B. 1999
Bloch, M. 213
Bloch, O. 1325, 1332, 1344, 1347, 1795, 1803, 1810, 1827, 1839
Block, M. 631, 634, 2110-2112, 2115, 2128, 2223
Bloise Campoy, P. 1128
Blom, G. 2027, 2033
Blondeau, N. 1195, 1197
Bloomfield, L. 1999, 2691-2693, 2695f.
Blount, Th. 719, 723, 1162, 1944, 1946-1951, 2971, 2974
Bloy, L. 1349f.
Blöndal, S. 1929, 1931

Blum, S. 2104, 2215, 2233
Blumenthal, A. 423, 428, 459, 964, 967
Blumenthal, P. 956, 967, 2753
Blumgarten, S. 2252f.
Blumrich, Chr. 598, 1017
Bluntschli, J.C. 166, 2069
Bluteau, D.R. 1733f.
Bluteau, R. 217, 223, 1011, 1014, 1019, 1075, 1726f., 3021
Blutner, R. 575
Blümner, H. 1249, 1253
Bo, D. 1551, 1558
Bo, L. L. de 2019f.
Boag, J. 1958f., 1965
Boas, H.-U. 2753
Boas, H.M. 3165
Boatner, M.T. 1028
Bobb, I. 1882f., 1888, 2377, 2381
Bobbio, G. 1128
Bobrik, E. 2918, 2925
Bobrow, D.G. 898, 3168
Boccaccio, G. 10, 22, 147, 149, 995, 1846, 1850-1852, 1859f., 2970
Boccace, G. 218, 1125, 1874, 3009
Bocchetta, V. 2973f.
Boch, R. 2753, 2836, 3010f.
Bochmann, K. 1889
Bochnarskij, M.S. 2322
Bock, J.G. 242
Bocthor, E. 3089, 3094
Bodding, P. O. 2537f., 2540f., 2545f.
Bodelsen, C. A. 2714, 2726, 2789, 2807, 2813, 3057f., 3061
Boden, M.A. 893, 898
Bödiker, J. 233, 236, 243, 2053, 2074, 2090, 2099
Bodin, J. 1088, 1091
Bodmer, J.J. 1551, 1558
Bodmer, Th. 2220
Bodouèn de Kourtené, J. A. [Baudouin de Courtenay] 2752
Bodra, L. 2535, 2537, 2539, 2545
Bodrogligeti, A. J. E. 2467
Bödvarsson, A. 1939, 1931
Boeck, L. B. de 2647, 2649
Boehncke, H. 1349f., 2185, 2197, 2217
Boekenoogen, G. J. 2019f., 2027
Boelcke, J. B. 2753, 2947
Boerio, G. 1876
Boersma, J. 2027
Boesch, B. 1280f., 1283
Boeschoten, H.E. 2412
Bogaards, P. 2753
Bogacki, K. 1004f., 1008
Bogatova, G.A. 2315, 2318, 2321, 2326
Bogdan, F. 2332
Bogdanov, A. I. 2620, 2622

Bogdanović, D. 2266
Boggiani, G. 2708
Boggs, R.A. 1137, 1139, 1569, 1572
Boggs, R.S. 1756
Bogin, G. J. 2753
Bogoraz, V. G. 2630
Bogorov, I. A. 2304-2307
Bogrea, V. 1889
Boguraev, B. 1666, 1669, 3165
Bogus, R.J. 2007
Boguslawski, A. 598, 2753, 2793, 3065f.
Bohle, B. 1047
Böhm, G. 715f., 724, 2652, 2655
Böhmer, E. 1896
Bohn, H. 1036f., 1039
Bohn, H.G. 1046f., 1991, 2918, 2925
Böhnke, R. 629, 634
Bohorič, A. 2297
Böhtlingk, O. 2490-2492, 2495f.
Bohusch, O. 2207, 2208, 2209, 2210, 2211, 2217
Boileau, E. 1249, 1253
Boileau-Despréaux, N. 40
Boillot, F. 2885
Boinvilliers (= Forestier, J.-E.-J.) 1071, 1128, 1802, 1804
Boirac, E. 3121f.
Boissière, J.-B.-P. 1816
Boissière, J.B. 1804
Boissière, P. 26, 175, 220, 635f., 638, 640, 1058, 1065, 1095-1099, 1194, 1197, 1819, 1828, 1839
Boiste, C. 1213
Boiste, P.-C.-V. 640f., 656, 764f., 1071, 1081, 1128, 1215, 1745, 1802, 1804-1806, 1808f., 1817, 1822, 1839, 2983, 2985, 3054
Boisvert, L. 656
Boitet, Ch. 3165
Boïelle, J. 2958
Bojadžiev, T. 2306, 2308
Bojäte, A. 2357, 2359
Bokarev, E.A. 1339, 3126f., 3130
Böke 2626
Bokher, E. 2249-2251, 2253
Bolc, L. 899
Bolea, S. de 1765
Bolelli, T. 1876
Bolinger, D. 575f., 856, 861, 1017, 1617, 1623, 2002
Bolinger, D.L. 1180, 1183 2887
Böll, H. 2131
Bollée, A. 2871, 2875
Bollifant, E. 2950
Bolling, F. 3052, 3060f.
Bolocan, G. 2263f., 2266
Bolton, R. 2684
Bolza, G.B. 1331f.

Bolza, J. B. 3017
Bombaci, A. 2405
Bomhard, A.R. 1338f.
Bomhoff, D. 3038
Bommatei 1854
Bomser, M. 1110
Bonaparte, L. L. 2925
Bonaventura, St. 3142
Bond, O. 3147
Bond, O.F. 1363, 2952, 2954
Bondarčuk, N.S. 2318
Bondopadhia, R. 3101, 3103
Bondy, S.A. 1128
Bondzio, W. 250, 274, 615, 620, 626
Bonelli, L. 2403f.
Bonelli, M.L. 2994f.
Bonet, F. 1778, 1781
Bonet, J. 2584, 2588
Bonet, J.P. 3142, 3144
Bongers, D. 1637
Bonhomme, M. 2997
Boniface, A. 1302
Böning, H. 2028
Bonnaffé, E. 1176
Bonnaire, A. 1804
Bonnant, G. 2979, 2986
Bonnard, H. 61, 786, 1005, 1007, 1215, 1829
Bonnardot, F. 1253
Bonnaud, P. 1895, 1903
Bonne, A. 1214
Bonnet, A. 1664, 1666
Bonnet, C. 1810
Bonnevie, P. 180, 679, 1378, 1836
Bonnonzio, O. 1128
Bono, M. 44f.
Bonser, W. 1033, 1042
Bont, A. P. de 2019f.
Booch-Árkossy, F. 2988f., 3062, 3066
Boodt, A. B. de 2935
Boogart, P.C. nit den 1668
Boom, D. J. 2918, 2925
Boons, J.-P. 1006, 1009
Booth, A.D. 1650, 1666
Booth, D. 1091, 1957-1959, 1965
Bopp, F. 1767, 2496
Bopp, F. B. 2490, 2495
Bor, N. L. 2558
Borao y Clemente, J. 1747, 1756
Boratyn, M. 3068
Borba, F. da S. 1005, 1007
Borch, O. 217, 223
Borchard, W. G. 1035f., 1039, 2065, 2067
Borchardt 2217
Borchling, C. 1418, 1420-1422, 1424-1426, 1428
Borcila, M. 1889
Borden, A.R. jr. 1444f.
Bordier, E. 2753

Bordo, A. 3022, 3027
Borek, H. 1286, 1289, 2271, 2273
Borel, P. 1157, 1812, 2900
Borelli, J. 2463, 2466
Boretzky, N. 2365
Borger, R. 1684f.
Borges, J.L. 24
Borgogni, M. 2973f.
Borhani, M. 1305
Boriac, E. 3130
Bork, E. 747, 2753, 2789, 3058, 3060
Borko, H. 1669
Borkovskij, V. J. 2761
Borkowski, P. 3082
Bornäs, G. 648, 722, 724, 784, 786, 942, 946, 1389, 1842
Bornemann, E. 119, 775, 778, 1090, 1193f., 1196f., 2062, 2067, 2188, 2217, 2753
Bornet, P.A. 1016
Bornstein, H. 3143f.
Borovkov, A. K. 2753, 3081, 3084
Borrás, J. 1046f.
Borrichius, O. 217, 223
Borring, L. S. 3054, 3060
Borroni, B. 3016f.
Borrot, A. 1210, 1215
Borsdorf, W. 1650, 1666, 2753
Borsodi, R. 539, 576
Bortolini, U. 1320, 1874, 1878
Bortolini, V. 1668
Bortz, J. 1631f., 1634-1637, 1882, 1888
Borvenich, A. 2926
Boryś, W. 2271
Bosch, P. 573, 576, 851, 853, 3165
Bösche, E. Th. 3032, 3037
Boschius, R.P.J. 3151, 3156
Bosco, U. 996
Boselli, C. 2994-2996
Bosque, I. 532, 576, 1139
Bossert, A. 1388
Bossong, R.H. 3128, 3130
Bossuet, J.B. 1824
Bostantzoglou, Th. 1089, 1091
Boswell, J. 225, 1983
Bosworth, J. 1437, 1441-1446, 1454, 1456
Botero, G. 1849
Botev, Chr. 1549f., 1553, 1557f., 2306
Botha, R.P. 1671
Botifall, E. 1781, 1778
Bott, H. 1110
Bott, St. 1110
Bottarelli, F. 323, 326, 2925
Böttcher, K. 1047
Bottequin, A. 1215
Botterweck, G.J. 2428, 2434
Bottéro, J. 304
Boubier, M. 3129f.

Boučev, A. 2265
Boucher, J. 1984f.
Boudard, G.B. 3152, 3156
Boudin, M. H. 2674, 1676
Bouffartigue, J. 1229
Bougard, P. 1272
Bouhours, D. 221, 3015
Boukar, B. L. G. 2644
Boulanger, J.-C. 49, 51-53, 55, 61f., 85, 87, 653, 1842
Boulet, P. 3122, 3130, 3136
Boulifa, A. 2456f.
Boulton, M. 3121, 3130, 3136
Bounfour, A 2457
Bouquiaux, L. 2648f.
Bourbaki, N. 331, 359, 372, 406f., 410, 440f., 457, 459, 463, 469, 499
Bourdieu, P. 679, 1577, 1588
Bourdon, M.-F. 41, 45
Bourgoing, J. 1845, 1859
Bourguignon, A. 1839
Bourlet de Vauxcelles, S.-J. 1804
Bourquin, J. 1131, 1804, 1810
Bourquin, W. 1339
Bouscaren, Chr. 2885
Boussinot, R. 1081f.
Bouttaz, J.L. 1302
Bouvard, Ph. 1349f.
Bouverot, D. 653, 1804, 1810
Bouvet, F. 1841
Bouvier, B. 1812
Bouvier, J.-C. 1893f., 1904f.
Bovaird, A. 2959
Bovary, Ch. 21
Bovier-Lapierre, G. 1840
Bowen, E. 36f.
Bowker, R.R. 3170, 3172, 3176
Bowman, W.P. 1529
Bowring, L. B. 2513, 2519
Boyce, M. 2475f.
Boyd-Bowman, P. 1756
Boyenval, R. 1271f.
Boyer de Petit Puy, P. 9, 15, 978, 980, 1128, 1206, 1208, 1795f., 1804
Boyer, A. 175, 218, 222, 2956-2960, 2971, 2974, 3037f.
Boyer, P. 1126
Boyle, R. 1946
Božkov, St. 2307
Bozkurt, M.F. 2412
Bra sti dge bshes rin chen don grub 2548
Braasch, A. 2753
Braccifort, F. 2974
Brachet, A. 1242-1244
Brack, W. 2039, 2043
Brackenier, R. 1563, 1566
Brackmann, K.-H. 2188, 2217
Bradac, J.J. 1617, 1623
Bradley, D. 2559

Bradley, D.B. 2577-2580, 2582
Bradley, D.F. 2578
Bradley, H. 228-230, 667, 868, 1414, 1436f., 1441, 1446-1449, 1453f., 1456, 1609, 1623, 1962, 1966, 1986, 3118
Bradly, H. 928
Brady, J.H. 1078
Bragonier jr., R. 1110
Bragonier, R. 1103, 1105, 1109
Brahmer, M. 517
Brailovskij, S. I. 3071, 3084
Brajmohan 2512, 2519
Brambila, D. 2697, 2699
Branca-Rosoff, S. 677, 679, 1219f., 1802, 1804, 1810
Brancus, G. 1889
Brand, J. F. 698f., 835, 1258, 2237
Brandenburg, J. 3140f.
Brandenstein, W. 2472
Brandis, M. 2041
Brandl, T. 835
Brandl, V. 1235, 1238
Brandon, E.E. 792-1794, 1810f.
Brands, H.W. 2408, 2410, 2414
Brandsma, W. L. 2025, 2036
Brandstetter, R. 1342
Brandt, dit Grierin 2938, 2944
Brandt Corstius, H. 1321
Bransiet, Ph.-M. 1805
Brant, S. 1399
Braren, E. 2032
Brassat, B. 2226
Brasseur de Bourbourg, É. 2664, 2666
Brasseur, I. 1320
Brassius, J. 1011, 1016
Brater, K. 166, 10, 13, 136-138, 145, 17, 217, 223, 41, 45
Bratkov, J. 2308
Bratli, C. 3057, 3060
Bratt, I. 3049, 3051
Bratus, B. V. 1012, 1014, 2776
Braubach, D. 2988, 2990
Bräuer, H. 2316, 2322
Braun, E. 1516f., 1520, 1522, 2029, 2035, 2198, 2217
Braun, G. 3171
Braun, H. 2058, 2067, 2091, 2095
Braun, J. 1778, 1781
Braun, J. R. 273, 2224
Braun, P. 653, 837, 841, 1179, 1183, 2192, 2233
Braun, S. 2222
Braun, W. 1253, 2081, 2099, 2220, 2233
Braunfels, W. 3156
Bräunling, P. 2173, 2233
Braunmüller, K. 3043, 3046, 3170
Brause, U. 551, 2232
Braußke, U. 575f., 2770, 2775
Bräutigam, K. 2199, 2217

Bravo, B. 1741, 1756
Bravo, D. 2705
Brawand, A. 2664, 2666
Brawand, J. 2664, 2666
Bray, D. 2529, 2531
Bray, L. 731, 1125f., 1131, 1185f., 1189, 1206, 1209, 1795-1798, 1801f., 1811, 1818, 2753, 2957, 2960, 2998f., 3005f., 3013f., 3019
Bréal, M. 1242, 1244, 1388f., 1814
Breasted, J.H. 1683
Breban, V. 1888f.
Brechenmacher, J.K. 1271f.
Brecher, Ch. M. 2428, 2433, 2435
Brecht, B. 2131
Bredemeier, J. 578, 1066, 1093f.
Brederode, T. v. 1017
Breedlove, D. 2667
Breedlove, D. E. 2698, 2700
Breen, J. G. 2639
Breffny, B. de 1272
Breitkopf, A. 541, 547, 579
Breitkreuz, H. 1389
Breitsprecher, R. 524, 747, 2726, 2751, 2789, 2817
Brekle, H.E. 779, 980
Bremer, E. 2038, 2047
Bremer, O. 2024
Bremmer, R. 2025
Bremmer, R. H. 2023, 2036
Brence, M. 2355, 2360
Brender, F. 2353
Brennenstuhl, W. 162f., 815f., 818, 820-822, 897f., 2177, 2181, 2188-2190, 2216
Brenner, E. 357, 405, 2106, 2112-2114, 2127f., 2155, 2167, 2217
Brenner, O. 3019
Brennert, H. 2062, 2067
Brentano, C. 2131
Bresemann, F. 3054, 3060
Breskovny, B. N. 2512, 2519
Breton, N. 1453
Breton, R. 217
Brett, L.E. 2954
Breuer, H. 1326, 1332
Breul, K. 2725, 2967
Brewer, A.M. 1204f., 2006, 2008, 3170
Brewer, E.C. 1054f., 1258, 1260
Brewer, F. 2659f., 2697, 2699
Brewer, J. G. 2659f., 2697, 2699
Brewer, R.F. 1128
Brewster, K.G. 1071, 2007
Breysig, A. 3148-3150, 3152-3154, 3156
Breznik, A. 2297, 2301
Br̥haspati 2487
Briano, J.-B. 3129, 3131
Bricard, R. 3128, 3131

Bricchetti-Robecchi, L. 2453
Briccolani, A. 3010f.
Brickenkamp, R. 1632, 1637
Bricker, H. 1207f., 1253
Bridges, Th. 2709f.
Briese, K. 2969
Briggs, A. 273
Briggs, Ch.A. 2428, 2434
Briggs, L. Th. 2684, 2685, 2790
Briguiel, J. 2708
Brijbhukhandas, B. 2511, 2518
Brijbhukhandas, C. 2511, 2518
Brill, E. J. 2562, 2567
Brinckmeier, E. 1235, 1238
Bring, S.C. 1089, 1091
Brink, L. 1305, 1308
Brinkley, J. 2920, 2925
Brinkman, J.A. 1694
Brinkmann, H. 822, 830
Briquet, M. 3128, 3131
Briscoe, E. 1669
Briscoe, T. 1666, 3165
Brisman, S. 3047, 3049f.
Brison, S.J. 716, 725
Brito 2040
Brito Sansores, W. 2663, 2667
Brito, R. 1753, 1756
Britten, J. 1255f.
Brocatelli, U. 3126, 3131
Brocense, El 1740
Broch, J. 1756, 1772, 1781, 2917, 2926
Brockelmann, C. 2432, 2437
Brockhaus, F.A. 15, 990, 995f., 2495, 3174
Broderick, G. 2346, 2349
Brodführer, E. 821
Brodin, D. 1321, 1361, 1643, 1669
Brodovskij, M. 1128
Brodovskis, J. 2351
Broeder, M. den 3168
Broek, M.A. van den 582, 930, 2048
Broekman, J.M. 410, 459
Broglio, E. 1858f., 1866, 1879
Broise, A. 3129, 3131
Bronson, M. 2509, 2517
Bronstein, A.J. 509, 512, 517, 1311, 1948, 1952
Brooke, K. 2104, 2230
Brossard, S. de 2917, 2926
Brosse, S. de la 42f., 45
Brosses, Ch. de 1247
Brou, A. 1802, 1811
Brousse, G. 3141
Broussous, M. 2885
Brouwer, J. H. 2024f., 2027
Brouwers, L. 1089, 1091
Brower, R. H. 2621, 2623
Brown, A.F. 1139
Brown, C. P. 2527
Brown, Ch. Ph. 2526f., 2531

Brown, F. 2428, 2434
Brown, G. 894, 898
Brown, H. 2636f.
Brown, Th. 1984f.
Brown, W. 2526f., 2531
Browne, M. 3170
Browne, Th. 1949, 3037
Browning, D.C. 1044, 1047
Brownson, R.C. 1139
Brownstein, S.C. 1207f.
Broz, I. 2291, 2294
Brozović, D. 77
Bröger, A. 1367
Bruant, A. 1185
Bruant, M. 1187
Bruce, J. 2452, 2455, 2461, 2466, 3073
Bruce, R. 2664, 2667
Brucioli, A. 1851, 1859
Bruckner, G. 2917, 2926
Bruder, A. 167
Bruderer, H.E. 1670
Brueckner, J.H. 1012, 1014
Brugère, V. 42f., 45
Brugger, J.D.C. 1173, 1176, 2064, 2067
Brugman, C. 861, 3165
Brugmann, K. 17, 223f., 1561, 1704, 2208
Brugsch, H. 1679f.
Bruguera, J. 1777, 1781, 1787
Bruhn, K. 2503, 2506
Bruin, S. de 2920, 2926, 3038
Bruining, G. 1068, 1971
Brulé, M. 1164, 1176
Brun, Th. 1117, 1119
Bruna, M. 2938, 2947
Bruna, M. L. 3016, 3019
Bruneau, Ch. 1306, 1800, 1802, 1804, 1811
Brunet, E. 1569-1572
Brunet, J. 1313f.
Brunneau, Ch. 1828
Brunner, H. 725
Brunner, L. 1338f.
Brunner, O. 117, 123, 166, 841, 854, 1058f., 1065, 1539f., 1548
Brunner, Ph. 2092, 2096
Brunner, R. J. 2061, 2074
Brunner, T. 1701
Brunner, Th. F. 1701f.
Bruno, G. 1089, 1873
Bruno, L. 2708
Brunot, F. 221, 223, 1795f., 1798, 1804, 1810f., 1827f., 1842, 2986, 3006, 3169
Bruns, F. 1111
Brunsch, W. 1681
Brunt, R.J. 1169, 1176
Brustkern, J. 275, 407, 459, 1571, 1573, 1657, 1667, 2233, 2236
Brutel de la Rivière, J. 1801, 1806

Brutzer, H. 2918, 2926
Bruun, E. 1012, 1014
Brückner, A. 1205, 2271
Brückner, T. 1137, 1139, 1643, 1655, 1666, 2184, 2217
Brüel, S. 1176, 1920f., 2789
Brüllmann, R. 1044, 1047
Brünnow, R.E. 1683f.
Bryan, M. A. 2642, 2645ff., 2649
Bryant, A. T. 2648
Brynildsen, J. 1926f., 3055f., 3060
Bryson, B. 1207f., 1215
Brzeska, W. 3065f.
Brzeski, A. 3065f.
Buarque de Holanda Ferreira, A. 920, 928
Bublitz, W. 810, 813
Bucă, M. 1082, 1098, 1888
Bucca, S. 2708
Buccellini, J. 1011, 1014
Buchanan, J. 509, 1308f.
Buchanan, M.A. 1355, 1361, 1756
Buchanan-Brown, J. 1176
Buchda, G. 1592
Buchheit, R. 1637
Buchholz, O. 747, 2365
Buchlerus, J. 1011, 1051-1053
Büchmann, G. 1045-1047, 2066f., 2094f.
Buchmann, O. 848
Büchner, A. 1261-1263
Büchner, G. 2131
Buchoz, P. 2938, 2944
Buck, C.D. 1059, 1065, 1132-1135, 1137, 1139, 1412f.
Buck, T. 43, 45, 1612, 1623, 2130, 2234
Bučkina, B.Z. 2316
Bücking, J. 1034, 1039
Bücking, Y.J.H. 2065, 2067
Buckley, W.F. Jr. 2002
Bucksch, H. 2753
Buckwalter, A. S. 2708
Buczyński, I. 3076
Budaev, C. B. 2626
Budagov, L. 1339, 2404
Budagov, L.Z. 2413
Budai, E. 2376
Budai-Deleanu, I. 1882, 1890
Buddhadatta, A. P. 2505
Budenz, J. 2377, 2382
Budé, G. 1698
Budkowska, J. 2270f.
Bues, M. 773, 778
Bufano, A. 1874
Būga, K. 1285, 1290, 2351-2353
Buhl, F. 2428, 2434
Buhl, I. 2885
Bühler, G. 2504
Bühler, H. 2793
Bühler, K. 577
Buhofer, A. 599, 831, 834, 1020, 1031, 1042

Buhr, K. 206
Buhr, M. 579, 848
Bührer, V.M. 2064, 2067
Bùi Phụng 2588
Bùi Ý 2588
Bui, D. L. 2284
Buitenrust Hettema, F. 2024, 2026, 2036
Bujas, Ž. 106f., 110, 2292f., 2753
Bukčina, B.Z. 2322
Bukowcowa, Z. 2274
Bukowski, J. 3165
Bulas, K. 3063, 3066
Bulatnickij, E. 3074
Bulatova, R. 3084
Bulbena i Tosell, A. 1776, 1781
Bulcke, C. 2519
Büld, H. 1035f., 1039
Bulgar, Ch. 1078
Bulič, S. K. 2310f., 2313, 2321, 2326, 3072, 3075f., 3084
Bulitta, E. 1081f., 1361, 2182-2184, 2217
Bulitta, H. 2182-2184, 2217
Bulke, C. 2512
Bulle, O. 3016, 3018f.
Bullock, A. 1204
Bullokar, J. 1943f., 1946f., 1950f.
Bulmer, R. 2636f.
Bülow, F. 164, 166
Bulst, W. 1551, 1553, 1558
Buma, W. J. 2024, 2026f., 2036
Bunc, St. 2300
Bunganič, P. 2286f.
Bungart, H. 2041
Bungarten, Th. 201, 206, 321, 581, 955, 967, 1317, 1322, 1642, 1644
Bungert, G. 1192
Büngül, N.R. 2404
Bunlọ, Ch. 2506
Bünting, K.-D. 1219, 1617, 1623, 2207, 2213, 2217
Buonarroti, M. 149
Buonmattei, B. 1854
Buradz, J.M. 1528
Burchfield, R.W. 32f., 35-37, 71, 77, 95, 99f., 110, 226, 228-230, 582, 652-657, 661, 667, 672, 753, 766, 929, 1164f., 1333, 1456, 1609, 1966
Burchiello, D. 149
Bureus, J. 1934
Burfeind-Moral, H. 1052
Burger, A. 1550f., 1553, 1558
Burger, H. 531, 537, 564, 576, 594-599, 716, 724, 830-834, 1020, 1031, 1039, 1042, 1044, 1090f., 1596, 1609, 2130, 2136, 2234
Burger, H.G. 208, 212
Burgi, Chr. 245

Bürgisser, M. 2193, 2223
Burgos, M. de 1747, 1756
Burguet, M. 1803, 1805
Buridant, C. 2, 9, 17, 407, 1788, 1790, 1811, 2047
Buriel, A.M. 1742
Burjacok, A.A. 1128
Burján, M. 2763
Burke de Ott, R. 2702
Burkett, E.M. 100, 1987f., 2000
Burkhardt, A. 531, 576, 809f., 813, 823, 830, 860f.
Burling, R. 2558f.
Burnadz, J. M. 1529, 2185, 2198, 2217
Burnett, P.B. 2959
Burney, P. 1314
Burnouf, E. 2491, 2495, 2500
Burr, I. 1138, 1341
Burriel, A.M. 1763
Burriel, P. A. M. 2917, 2926
Burrow, Th. 1338f., 2524, 2528-2532
Burrows, L. 2534, 2545
Burtch, S. 2703
Burton, D.M. 1563, 1566f., 1572
Burton, J. 2759, 2778
Burton, R. F. 2453
Burton, S.K. 1573
Burton, T. L. 2759, 2778
Burvenich, A. 2920
Busa, G. 1739, 1771, 1781
Busa, R., S. J. 1137, 1139, 1563f., 1566, 1874, 1878, 2813
Busch, W. 2131
Buscha, J. 796, 863, 867, 883, 887, 1221f., 2188f., 2217
Buschmann, S. 1737
Bush, F.W. 1693
Buss, K. M. 2199, 2217
Busse, A. 358, 405, 2114f., 2155, 2168, 2217, 2225
Busse, W. 1002f., 1005, 1007, 1009
Bussy, Ch. de 2937, 2944
Busto, E. 1752, 1756
Bußmann, H. 2207f., 2210f., 2213, 2217, 2234
Buti, F. da 149
Butin, M. 3126, 3131
Butler, Chr. 1644, 1650, 1666
Butler, Chr. S. 2902
Butler, M.C. 3122, 3124, 3126, 3129, 3131, 3136
Butler, R.L. 3169
Butler, S. 299, 305, 327, 1142
Butor, M. 86
Buttafava, V. 2366
Buttler, D. 2270f.
Büttner, Th. 2687, 2689, 2705f.
Buttress, F.A. 1261, 1263
Buttura, A. 3010f.
Bửu Cân 2587f.

Buwalda, H. S. 2026, 2033
Buxtorf, J. 2427f., 2433
Buys, E. 2937f., 2945, 3037
Buyssens, E. 715, 724
Buzandatsi, N. 2369f.
Buzon, Chr. 85, 87, 915f., 1835, 1842
Bwakolo, P. 2636-2638
Bybee, J.L. 737, 748
Byck, J. 1889
Byers, E.E. 3141
Byra, R.J. 3165
Byrd, R. J. 1670, 2808, 2813, 3167
Byrne, J.H. 1207f.
Byron, J. 2363, 2367
Bysshe, E. 1126, 1128
Bzdęga, A. 746, 3064, 3067

C

Caballero, J. 1746, 1756
Caballero, R. 1028
Cabanes, J. 1778, 1781
Cabanes, S. 1759
Cabaton, A. 2591-2593
Cabdulgaadir, F. B. 2464f.
Cabduraxmaan Ciise Oomaar 2464, 2466
Cabej, E. 2363, 2365
Cabral, T. 1028
Cabrera, L. 1755f.
Cabrera, R. 1747, 1756
Caccia, J. 2993-2995, 3009-3011
Cáceres, M.L. 1756
Cadogan, L. 2674, 2676
Cadovius Müller, J. 2028, 2033
Caesar, C. Iulius 1285
Caetano, D.M. 1253
Caf, O. 2298
Cagaeva, A. D. 2484f.
Çağatay, S. 2399, 2404, 2407
Cagout, A. 305
Cailleux, A. 1229
Caillot, A. 1185, 1187
Caillot, N. 1071
Cairo, G. 3154-3156
Caitucoli, C. 2458, 2460
Cakravarti, G. 3097, 3103, 3099
Calagius, A. 1011, 1014, 1078, 2926
Calame-Giraule, G. 2648
Calandrelli, M. 1746, 1756
Calani, E. 1052
Calbris, G. 1113, 1119
Caldarini, E. 1812
Caldas Tibiriçá, L. 2704
Calder, G. 2340
Calder, W. 2342
Calderwood-Schnorr, V. 524, 747, 2726, 2751, 2789, 2817, 2968
Calepino, A. 1847, 1849f., 1853, 1860, 2991, 3007f., 3021, 3030

Calepinus, A. 9, 15, 1715f., 1720, 1790-1792, 1805, 1814, 1848, 1850, 1859, 2045f., 2375, 2381, 2910, 2913-2916, 2926, 2936, 2995, 2998, 3004, 3007, 3071, 3172
Calihā, M. 3101, 3103
Calisch, I. M. 2918, 2926, 3038
Callebaut, B. 653f., 1179, 1183
Calleja, S. 1746, 1756
Callender, J.Th. 226
Calleri, D. 2754
Callier, O. 3062, 3067
Calogero, G. 3010f.
Calonghi, F. 3032f.
Calvino, I. 1873
Calvo, T. 2664, 2667
Calzolari, N. 576, 1670, 2753, 2813, 3165
Câmara Cascudo. L. da 1114, 1119
Cambray, Ph.G. 1055, 1201, 1205
Cambry, J. 2918, 2926
Cameron, A. 327, 1437, 1444f., 1451, 1456
Cameron, H. 3176
Cameron, K. 1281, 1283
Camhy, O. 1906
Caminiti, L. 27, 1351
Camion, J. 1121, 1123
Cammarota, F. 1756
Camp, E. 2703
Campanile, E. 2341, 2348, 2350
Campano, L. 1746, 1756
Campart de Kostine, M. 2946
Campbell, A. 1441f., 1454, 2024, 2541, 2546
Campbell, L. 1339, 2664, 2667
Campbell, R. J. 2658-2660
Campbell, W. H. 2526f., 2531f.
Campe, J. H. 72f., 77, 231, 237, 241f., 395, 405, 458, 498, 634, 694, 697f., 750, 753, 768, 770, 801, 803, 825, 829, 880, 892, 966, 1172f., 1176, 1232, 1235f., 1238, 1596, 1608, 2055, 2057f., 2063, 2067f., 2070, 2076, 2081, 2084, 2214f., 2217, 2376, 3000
Camperio, M. 2450, 2453
Campi, G. 1862
Campion, L. 1349f.
Campos, L. 1535f.
Camps Cardona, M.D. 1781
Campuzano, R. 720, 724, 1746, 1756
Camus, A. 637
Cañada, F. 2938, 2945
Canal, J. de la 1078
Canal, P. 1845, 1859, 3008f., 3011, 3013
Canavan, J. 1014, 1972
Candaux, J.D. 2986

Candel, D. 653f., 1389
Candeland, R. 1670
Candeo, G. 2462, 2466
Candey, G. 2520
Candey, Th. 2520
Candé, R. de 1778, 1781
Candrea, I.A. 1886, 1888
Candy, G. 2514, 3100, 3105
Candy, Th. 2514, 3100, 3105
Canellada, M.J. 1756
Canello, U.A. 1243f.
Cañes, F. 1742, 1756
Caney, J. Ch. 2464f., 2469
Canfield, D.L. 2952
Canger, U. 2660
Canini, M.A. 2993, 2995
Cankor, A. K. 2305, 2307
Cankov, D. K. 2305, 2307
Cannon, G. 1165, 3160, 3166
Cano, T. 1756
Cantacuzino, C. 1882
Cantagalli, R. 1196f.
Cantemir, D. 1889
Cantero, V.B. 3093f.
Cantineau, J. 2427, 2431, 2437
Cantini Guidotti, G. 1872
Canto e Castro Mascarenhas Valdez, M. de 3022, 3027
Canto, F. del 2683, 2689
Cantueso, C. 3033
Čanturišvili, D. S. 2754
Canyameres, F. 1778, 1781
Caomhánach, S. 2341
Capell, A. 1339, 2573f.
Capella, M. 154
Capelle, C. 1550f., 1556, 1558
Capelle, G. 1360, 1388
Capeller, C. 2492, 2495
Capidan, T. 1885
Capmany i Palau, A. de 1742, 1772, 2980f., 2983-2985
Capomazza, I. 2462, 2466
Cappelli, A. 111, 1261, 1263, 3167
Cappello, T. 1294, 1533, 1536
Capponi, G. 1857
Cappuccini, G. 66, 69, 1866, 1878f.
Caprile, J.-P. 2457, 2460
Capus, G. 2485
Caput, J. 1005, 1007, 1313f.
Caput, J.-P. 1005, 1007, 1314
Caradec, F. 1185, 1187, 1529, 1534, 1536
Caragiale, M. 1882
Carassou, M. 1192
Carayol, M. 2873, 2875
Carbone, G. 1086, 1091, 1558
Carbonell Relat, L. 1778, 1784
Carbonell, J. 1783
Carbonell, S. 2994f.
Cárcer de Sobies, E. 1776, 1781
Carciotto, P. 1196f.

Cardarelli, V. 1874
Carden, G. 1617, 1623
Cárdenas Nannetti, J. 1761
Cardinal, M. 38, 45
Cardinale, U. 1164, 1868
Cardinali, F. 1856, 1859
Cardona, G. R. 2468
Cardona, O. 1778, 1781
Cardoso, E. 3027
Cardoso, J. 1725, 1735, 3020f., 3027, 3030
Cardosus, H. 1725, 1733, 3020
Carducci, G. 1875
Carena, G. 1083, 1085, 1087, 1089-1091, 1867
Caressa, F. 2463, 2466
Careta i Vidal, A. 1777f., 1781
Carey, W. 2509, 2514, 2517-2519
Carhart, P.W. 2007
Carigiet, B. 1896, 1903, 1905
Carion, J. 1273
Carisch, O. 1896f., 1903
Carl, H. 1257
Carl, W. 1261, 1263
Carletti, E. 1904
Carlevaro, T. 3125, 3131, 3136
Carlier, R. 22, 27, 1045, 1047
Carlos, C. 3147
Carlson, I. 3049
Carmel, S.J. 3144
Carnap, R. 372, 422, 440, 459, 543, 582
Carney. M. 2341
Caro, M.A. 1768
Carochi, H. 2658-2661
Carol I. 1885
Caron, Ph. 1811
Carpenter, E. 2864
Carpenter, E.H. jr. 3175
Carpenter, G.R. 3176
Carpenter, W. 1078
Carpentier, L.J.M. 1011, 1014, 1126, 1128
Carradori, F.A. de 2400, 2404
Carranza, Á. J. 2708
Carrasco, F. 2682
Carrasco, V. 2706
Carreño, F. 1755
Carreras i Marti, J. 1782
Carreras Pons, A. 1785
Carré Alvarellos, L. 1736f.
Carrère, M. 1163, 1185, 1189, 1530
Carrière, J.-C. 1045, 1047
Carrin-Bouez, M. 2537, 2541
Carrión, J. 1071
Carroll, J. 3166
Carroll, J.B. 1318, 1320, 1322, 1617, 1623
Carroll, L. 306
Carruth, G. 515, 1145, 2000
Carson, I. 3048

Carstairs, A. 521, 524
Carstensen, B. 670, 672, 732, 748, 1017, 1169, 1178, 2754
Cart, Th. 3121, 3127, 3131, 3134, 3136
Carter, C.W. jr. 1320
Carter, D. 3165f.
Carter, H.H. 1724f., 1733
Carus, C. 1738
Carvalhão Buescu, M. L. 3021, 3029
Carvajal, F. 1756
Cary, H.N. 1196f.
Casacuberta, J.M. de 1781, 1788
Casagrande, G. 218, 1859
Casagrande, J.B. 299, 305, 553, 555, 576
Casalis, D. 524, 703, 746, 916, 1832
Casalis, J. 524, 746, 1832
Casanovas y Ferran, J. 1215
Casares (y Sanchez), J. 67, 69, 77, 96, 222f., 247, 274, 917f., 930, 1743, 1750, 1764f., 1777, 1867, 1090f., 1093f., 1096-1099, 2954
Casas Homs, J.M. 1125, 1131, 1771, 1780, 1787
Casas, Chr. de las 1859
Casas, N. 1747, 1756
Casasanta, M. 3022, 3029
Casati, L. 61
Cascorbi, P. 1271, 1273
Caselli, G. 3011
Casiri, M. 1742, 1756
Cassandre, D.C.S.D.S.S. 1206, 1208
Cassandre, F. 1797f., 1805
Cassiani, E. 3010f.
Cassidy, F.G. 37, 654, 1413, 1967, 2000, 2004, 2007
Cassius, Bartholomaeus, s. Kašić, Bartol
Cassola, C. 1873
Castagnola, M. 1028
Castelbajac, B. de 1054f.
Casteleiro, J.M. 1727, 1735
Castell, E. 2327
Castellani, A. 1845, 1850, 1861
Castellanos Llorens, C. 1776, 1781
Castellanos, J. de 1764
Castelli, N. 3014f., 3017
Castellini, N. 3019
Castellus, E. 2405, 2433
Casterline, D. 3141-3144
Castiglione, B. 1851, 1854
Castiglione, C.O. 1909
Castillo Mantilla, G. de 1128
Castillo, C. 2952, 2954
Castrén, M. A. 2396f., 2628, 2630
Castro, A. 1738, 1756, 1765
Castro, A. de 1746, 1756, 2697

Castro, A.F. de 1532, 1536
Casullo, F.H. 1187, 1756
Catach, N. 501, 503f., 506-508, 1054f., 1795, 1811
Catafago, J. 3089, 3094
Catalán, D. 274
Catel, S.H. 2999, 3004
Caterina da Siena, St. 1855
Catherinot, N. 1242, 1244
Catineau, P.M.S. 1802, 1805
Cato, O. 1047
Caton, H. 3148
Catricala, M. 1872
Cattunar, P. H. 2674, 2676
Caturangabalāmacca 2500, 2504
Caturvedi, D.P.Ś. 3100, 3103
Caubulina, D. 2357, 2359
Causse, J.-P. 2885
Caussin de Perceval, A. 3089
Cauzin, M. M. 2511
Cavada, F.J. 1753, 1756
Cavallin, Chr. 1939, 1942
Cavigneaux, A. 1682, 1685
Cawdrey, J. 726
Cawdrey, R. 95, 224, 1055, 1943f., 1946-1948, 1950f., 2711, 2728, 2926, 2960
Caxton, W. 2866
Cayotte, L. 1128
Cayrou, G. 1157f.
Cazacu, B. 1889
Cazes, J. 2980, 2983
Ceachir, M. 2412
Ceballos, E. 1742, 1756
Cecchi, A. 2462, 2466
Cecil, E.I. 1438
Cecil, W. 1438
Cejador y Frauca, J. 1756
Cejka, Th. 3126, 3131
Cejtlin, R. M. 2260, 2310f., 2313-2315, 2318f., 2321, 2326, 3070, 3084
Cel'cova, L.K. 2316, 2322
Cela, C.J. 1196f.
Célérier, P. 1005, 1007
Celeyrette-Pietri, N. 1099, 1126f., 1131
Celi-Kresling, V. 2908
Celier, P. 1800, 1811
Cellard, J. 43, 45, 679, 740, 743, 748, 1029, 1054f., 1164, 1185, 1187, 1229, 1525, 1529, 1534-1536, 1837, 1839
Cellarius, Chr. 2381, 2387, 3030f., 3033, 3074
Cellarius, J. 1011, 1014
Celmrauga, I. 2357, 2359
Celorio, M. 1029
Cenepo Sangama, V. 2705
Cense, A. A. 2566f.
Cepas, J. 1757
Ceplītis, L. 2357, 2359

Ceppelini, V. 1215, 1219
Ceppi, M. 1309
Cerati, A. 3010f.
Čerdanceva, T. Z. 2896, 2900
Cereli, K.G. 2437
Čeremisov, K. M. 2626
Čerfas, R.A. 746, 1622
Čerkasova, E.T. 2326
Cerkevich, K. 2333
Čermák, F. 2281, 2283
Černjavskaja, T.N. 2321f.
Černý, J. 1680
Černyj, A.I. 1660, 1667
Černyšev, V.I. 2320, 2322
Černyševa, I.I. 1032
Cerrón-Palomino, R. 2683, 2705
Cerruti, F. 1866, 1878
Cerulli, E. 2437, 2449, 2451-2453, 2455, 2463f., 2466
Cervantes, M. de 1757f.
Cervenka, E.J. 1117, 1119
Cesana, G. 1071
Cesari, A. 1846, 1847, 1856, 1859
Cestre, Ch. 2823
Cevallos, D.J. 1752, 1757
Cevel, J. 2626
Ch'oe Hak-kŭn 2614, 2616
Ch'oe Hyŏn-bae 2614
Chaballe, L.Y. 1507, 1511
Chabanel, J. de 1311, 1314
Chabat, C.G. 1757
Chabbert, R. 1903
Chablo, E.P. 1014, 2323, 2316
Chačikjan, M.L. 1693
Chacko, V.C. 3103
Chadwick, J. 1696, 1703
Chafe, W. L. 2692, 2696
Chaffin, R. 3166
Chagmagchian, H. 2370
Chaince, S. 2761
Chajdakov, S.M. 1339
Chako, V.C. 3101
Chakrabarti, G. 2510, 2518
Chalabī, S. 'Abd al-Rahīm 3170
Chalmers, A. 1991
Chambaud, L. 2957-2959
Chamberlain, B. H. 2621
Chamberlain, B.J. 1187, 3022
Chamberlain, J. 3027
Chambers, E. 994, 996, 1847
Chambers, F.M. 1294
Chambille, L. 1015
Chambreau [= Chamereau], N. 2926
Chambrun, C.L. de 2970, 2975
Chamereau, N. 2916, 2926
Chamisso, A. von 2131
Champion, S. 1036f., 1039
Champollion, J.F. 1679, 1681
Chandaburinarünathah, K. K. 2506
Chande, R.H. 1754, 1766

Chang Chi-yŏng 2614, 2616
Chang-Rodríguez, E. 1321, 1361, 1643, 1669, 2953, 2955
Changuion, A. N. E. 2019f.
Channell, J. 1672
Chanoux, A. 3011
Chantepie de la Saussaye, J.R.S.C. 2939, 2945
Chantraine, P. 1326, 1332, 1334, 1699, 1702, 1837, 1839
Chantreau, P.N. 1054f.
Chantreau, S. 1021, 1023, 1030, 1837, 1841
Chao, E. 1746, 1757
Chao, J. A. 2917, 2926
Chao, Y.-R. 2868, 2870
Chapeaurouge, D. de 3152, 3157
Chapelain, J. 1798, 1815
Chapellon, C. 3011
Chapman, C.O. 1293, 1295
Chapman, F.R.H. 3101, 3103
Chapman, R.L. 30, 33f., 36f., 1066, 1092f., 1186f., 1524-1526, 1528f., 1997, 2008
Chapman, R.W. 588, 591
Chapny, P. 1272
Chapsal, Ch.-P. 80, 87, 1803, 1808f.
Chaptal, A. 2959
Char, R. 24
Charakoz, P.I. 1643, 2322
Charbit, G. 1349, 1352
Charencey, H. de 2664, 2667
Charpentier, F. 39
Charrassin, F. 1149, 1151
Chartchai Phromjakgarin 2593
Chartier, R. 146, 1533, 1537
Charvet, G. 1895, 1904
Chassant, A.A.L. 1054f.
Chassant, L.-A. 1261, 1263
Chastelain, C. 1269, 172, 1333
Chastillon, N. 1011, 1014
Chateaubriand, F.R. de 25, 147
Chatterji, S.K. 3096, 3103, 3107
Chaturvedi, D. P. 2513, 2519
Chaturvedi, M. 2512, 2519
Chaucer, G. 2, 1157, 1451, 1455, 1949
Chaudenson, R. 2872f., 2875
Chaudhuri, T. 2496
Chautard, E. 1185, 1187, 1196, 1198
Chavarría Mendoza, M. C. 2703
Chaves, A. de 1740
Chaves, C. de 1741, 1757
Chazanovič, A. P. 2216
Chávez, A. 2705
Châlons,P. de 2347, 2349
Chen Bingzhao 2595, 2598, 2601, 2611
Chen Penguian 2610
Chen Yi Sein 2552, 2554

Chen, J. 1305, 1308f.
Chen, T. 3112
Chenu, J.-F. 1803, 1805
Chereau, O. 1533, 1536
Cherezli, S.I. 1906
Cherkesi, E. 2417f.
Cherubim, D. 813, 815, 821, 2093f., 2099
Cherubini, F. 1876
Chesapčieva-Maleškova, C. 2308
Chettiar, K.P. 3101, 3104
Chettuphon, S. S. 2506
Chevalier, J. 3152, 3155f.
Chevalier, J.-C. 1068, 1075
Chevalley, A. 2958f.
Chevalley, M. 2958f.
Chevreuil 1839
Cheydler, F. 1320
Chésurolles, D. 641, 1805, 1840
Chiari, A. 150
Chiarini, G. 2462, 2466
Chicharro de León, J. 2980, 2983
Chidiroglou, P. 2399, 2402, 2404, 2407
Chien, D. 3170
Childers, R. C. 2500-2502, 2504
Chilendarskij, P. 2304
Chils, O. 3047, 3050
Chince, F. 2761
Chiomo, G. 2466
Chirac, J. 40, 45
Chiri, M. 2621
Chisholm, G.G. 1308f.
Chivescu, R. 2754
Chlabicz, J. 3063
Chlôros, I. 2402, 2404
Chmielnicki, B. 2249
Chocitowska, Z. 3068
Chodera, J. 746, 3064, 3067
Chodorow, M. S. 1670, 2813
Cholinus, P. 2045
Chombeau, Chr. 42, 45
Chomsky, N. 1614, 1621, 1623, 2824
Chomsky, W. 2433
Chomutov, D.S. 2322
Chonan, M. 3119
Chorochorin, L. G. 2754
Chottopadhia, Ch.B. 3101, 3103
Choudury, A.M.F.A. 3097, 3099, 3104
Chouémi, M. 3088, 3094
Choul, J.-C. 2754, 2824
Chouvenc, J. M. 2705
Choux, J. 1197
Chranov, D. V. 2307
Christ, G.E. 1078
Christ, H. 101, 2757, 3006
Christ, I. 1359, 1363
Christ, J.F. 1145
Christaller, P. 3127, 3131
Christensen, Chr. 585, 628, 822, 2244

Christensen, P. 3058, 3060
Christian, D. R. 2704
Christmann, E. 1281f., 1608
Christmann, H.H. 1144f.
Christmann, K. 1016, 2754, 2776
Christophorides, K. 2362, 2365
Christy, R. 1037, 1039
Chrulev, T. T. 2307
Chu, Run 634
Chu, Y. 305
Chubinskij, P. 2333
Church, C. 2664, 2667
Church, K. 2664, 2667
Church, M. 40
Churchward, C. M. 2574f.
Chytraeus, N. 2044, 2046
Ciakciak, M. 2368, 2371
Cianfione, G. 88
Ciaramella, M. 2973f.
Ciardi Dupré, G. 3016f.
Ciardi, J. 1207f.
Ciba, W. 1176
Cicero, M. Tullius 10, 1081
Ciesielska-Borkowska, St. 3063, 3067
Cieslik, H. 2621
Cigale, M. 2298, 2300
Cignoni, L. 1018
Cihac, A. de 1329, 1332, 1886, 1888
Čikobava, A.S. 1339, 2417f.
Ciliga, P. 3120f., 3131
Cilujko, K.K. 1286, 1290, 2332f.
Cimino, A. 2450, 2453
Cingularius, H. 1078
Cinti, D. 1078, 1207f., 1877f.
Cintra, L.F.L. 1735
Cioranescu, A. 1888
Cipariu, T. 1889
Čirkova, E.K. 2326
Cirlot, J.-E. 3154, 3156
Čirrilov, I. 1164
Citolini, A. 1851, 2970, 2975
Civera Sormani, J. 1776, 1781
Civil, M. 1682, 1684-1686
Claes, A. 908
Claes, F. (M.) 1047, 1050, 1169, 1178, 1214, 1217, 1367f., 1434f., 1790, 1792, 1795, 1811, 2018, 2021, 2023, 2036, 2039-2047, 2911, 2916, 2928, 2934, 2936-2938, 2947, 2956, 2960, 2998, 3004-3006, 3021f., 3029, 3034-3036, 3038f., 3170
Clair-Vasiliadis, Chr. 2706
Clairac y Sáenz, P. 2918, 2926
Clairis, Chr. 2709
Claramunt, J.M. 3128, 3131
Clare, J.Chr. 2392
Clark, A. H. 2565
Clark, E. W. 2558
Clark, L. E. 2698f.

Clarke, H. 1959f., 1964f.
Clarke, J.F. 1292, 1295
Clason, S. 1204f.
Clauson, G. 1339, 2412f.
Claussen, R. 276
Clavería, C. 1750
Clavijero, X. 2658f.
Cleasby, R. 1929, 1931
Clebert, J.-P. 3156
Cleishbotham 1984f.
Clemens, A. 1883
Clemens, P. M. 2029
Clement, K. J. 2029
Clepitis, L. 2359
Clerc, J. 2980, 2983
Clerck, R. de 652-654, 667
Clerck, W. de 295f.
Cleri, A. 1129
Cleveland, A.D. 1660, 1666
Cleveland, D.B. 1660, 1666
Clébert, J.-P. 3151
Clédière, J. 1110
Clément, J.M.B. 1349f.
Clément-Janin, M.-M. 1192, 1294f.
Clifford, J.L. 1068, 1075, 1949f., 1952
Clifton 2952
Clifton, E. 2958f.
Clinton, K. 1701
Clissold, P. 3129, 3131
Clodius, J.Chr. 2401, 2404
Closener, F. 2039f., 2042, 2048
Clough, B. 2500, 2504
Clyne, M.G. 186, 188
Cnapius, G. 2272, 2913
Coate, H. H. J. 2639, 2641
Cobarruvias, S. de 281, 186
Coblin, W. S. 2558
Cocchia, E. 1308f.
Cochojil, R. 2670
Cock, A. de 1036, 1039
Cockeram, H. 1101f., 1943f., 1950f.
Cocquempet, J.-B. 1123
Codicillus, P. 2913, 2926
Codrescu, T. 1884, 1888
Coelho, F.A. 1244
Coester, M. 1273
Coetsem, F. van 1142
Coglievina, L. 1852, 1861
Cohen, D. 305, 1339, 1342, 2427, 2433
Cohen, E. 3142, 3144
Cohen, I. 1038f.
Cohen, J.M. 1047
Cohen, M. 61, 405, 601f., 606, 641, 653f., 672, 679, 686, 765, 924, 928, 1052, 1147, 1149, 1151, 1339, 1378, 1588, 1833, 1839, 2452f., 2464, 2466
Cohen, M.J. 1047

Cohn, L. 2, 17, 221, 223, 1557, 1561, 1698, 1700, 1704
Col de Villars, E. 2938, 2945
Col, J. O. de 2660
Čolakova, K. 2307f.
Colbert, J.-B. 1796
Colby, F.O. 1308f.
Colby, K.M. 1670
Cole, P. 1667
Colebrooke, E. 3100, 3104
Coledridge, H. 1962
Coleman, L. 573, 576
Coleman, S.S. 1139
Colenso, J. W. 2648
Coleridge, H. 1446, 1454
Coles, E. 1943, 1946-1949, 1951, 3037, 3039
Colignon, J.-P. 1123, 1210-1212, 1215
Colin, J.-P. 606, 1187, 1207f., 1210-1212, 1215, 1217
Colitz, H. 2216
Colizza, G. 2462, 2466
Collado, D. 1741, 1757, 2619, 2621
Collantes, A.E. 1747, 1757
Collet Sedola, S. 2981, 2986
Collé, J. 3022, 3026
Colli, Ch. 1874
Colliander, P. 1006, 1009. 1616, 1622
Collignon, L. 136, 145, 212, 213, 605f., 700, 703, 917, 989, 991f., 997, 1842
Collin, A. Z. 3048, 3050
Collin, P. 2789, 2823, 2958f.
Collin, P.H. 1517-1520, 1522, 2853
Collinder, A. 2391
Collinder, B. 1338f., 2389f.
Collinot, A. 1800, 1802, 1811
Collins, A. 3166, 3168
Collins, R. 2529, 2532
Collins, V.H. 1029
Collinson, W. E. 2754, 2879, 2881
Collison, R.L. 1, 17, 526, 530, 724, 989, 994, 997, 1031, 1671, 2936f., 2947, 3039
Collison, R.L.W. 3171
Collocott, T.C. 1511
Colmeiro, M. 1747, 1757
Colmenares del Valle, E. 1757
Colom Mateu, M. 1777, 1782
Colomb, A. 2574f.
Colombo, J.R. 1295
Colomer, G. 3093f.
Colomer, J. 1776, 1782
Colón, G. 603, 1538, 1739, 1761, 1771f., 1774f., 1777, 1787f.
Colon, Germà 1771, 1773, 1775, 1779, 1783, 1786
Coloşi, V. 1883

Colón i Domenech, G. 2916, 2927, 2930
Colón, G. 2976f., 2982, 2986
Colpron, G. 1176
Colussi, G. 1873, 1878
Comas, A. 928
Combe McBride, N. 1001, 1005, 1008
Combet, L. 1029
Comelati, G. 2972, 2974
Comenius, J. A. 719, 721f., 726, 1052, 1089f., 1105, 1110, 1365, 1367, 2376, 2381f., 2914, 2916, 2920, 2927, 3159 (s. Komenský)
Comes, J. 1778, 1782
Commelin, P. 1839
Commynes, Ph. de 1346, 1918
Companys, F. 1389
Comrie, B. 737, 740, 748, 1389, 2398, 2628, 2631
Condamin, J. 1046f.
Conde de La Viñaza (= Muñoz y Manzano, C.) 2937, 2948 (s. Viñaza)
Condillac, E.B. de 218f., 1068, 1071, 1075, 1212, 1813
Condon, J.C. 172, 174
Condori Cruz, D. 2688f., 2706
Conev, B. 2305
Coneys, Th. de V. 2346, 2348
Confield, D.L. 2954
Confucius 1350
Congleton, E.C. 225, 230, 1947, 1950, 1952
Congleton, J.E. 33f., 225, 230, 517, 655, 1816, 1947, 1950, 1952, 2009
Coninck, R.H.B. 1308
Connelly, Th. 2950f., 2954
Connesson, R. 1798, 1811
Conrad, J. 164, 166, 1011, 1014
Conrad, R. 250, 274, 2207f., 2212f., 2217
Conradi, M. 1896, 1903
Conrady, K.O. 1241
Conrath, K. 2198, 2217
Consiglio, A. 1534, 1536
Constâncio, F. Solano 1728, 1734
Constantin, Th. 1192, 2185, 2217
Constantinescu, N.A. 1888
Constantiono, E. 2572
Consuelo de Rivera, M. 2703
Contamine de Latour, E. 2980, 2983
Conti Rossini, C. 2463f., 2467
Conti Rossini, K. 1690, 1693
Contini, G. 1844, 1861
Conto Fernandes, A. 3124, 3127, 3131
Contreras, E. 3116, 3118
Conze, W. 117, 123, 166, 841, 854, 1058f., 1065, 1539f., 1548

Cook, J. 2573
Cook, N.D. 3167
Coolsma, S. 2566f.
Cooper, J.C. 3154-3156
Cooper, L. 1741, 1765, 2977f.,
    2986, 3007f., 3012
Cooper, M. 1344, 1347, 2623
Cooper, Th. 1793, 1955
Cop, M. 7, 17, 181, 183, 188, 767,
    1075, 2711, 2727, 2754, 2757,
    2775f., 2778, 2800, 2803, 2957,
    2960, 2967, 2969, 3169, 3177
Copana, B. 2690
Copomazza, I. 2462
Copperud, R.H. 1163
Coppin, J. 1091
Coquelin, Ch. 166
Corachan, M. 1778, 1782
Corazzini, F. 1085, 1090f.
Corazzini, S. 1874
Corbea, T. 1882
Corbeil, J.-C. 46, 61, 62, 170, 1110
Corbera i Pou, J. 1777, 1782
Corbière, A. 2980, 2983
Corbin, D. 81, 86f., 675, 677, 679,
    938, 942f., 945f.
Corbin, P. 81, 85, 87, 98, 101,
    673-675, 678f., 941, 944-946,
    1389
Corblet, J. 1329, 1332, 3152, 3156
Cordell, S.B. 3171
Cordell, W.N. 33f., 517, 1816,
    2009, 3171
Cordes, G. 1428
Cordier, G. 2584, 2588
Cordignano, F. 2365
Cordoso, J. 1726
Cordova (s. Juan de Córdoba)
    2683f.
Corell, W.N. 655
Corgnali, G.B. 1904
Cormon, F. 2983
Cormon, J.L.B. 1802, 1805, 1809,
    2979f., 2983, 2993, 2995,
    3010f.
Cornagliotti, A. 1771f., 1787
Corneille, P. 1824
Corneille, Th. 990, 994, 996, 1206,
    1208, 1798f., 1805, 1817, 1822
Cornejo, A. 1742, 1757
Cornelissen, G. 2199, 2201, 2218,
    2234
Cornelissen, P. J. 2019f.
Cornell, A. 2883f., 2886
Cornide, J. 1736
Cornu, A.-M. 2765
Cornu, J. 1325
Čoroleeva, M. 2308
Corominas, J. 1325, 1332, 1345,
    1347, 1750, 1757, 1778, 1782
Coromines, J. 1778f., 1787
Corona Bustamante, F. 1757,
    2952, 2954, 2980, 2983

Corradini, F. 1721
Corrales Zumbado, C. 652, 654
Correas, G. 1029, 1741, 1757
Correia, J. da S. 1194, 1198
Correnti, S. 1868
Corret, P. 3121f., 3131
Corripio, F. 1078, 1096, 1098,
    1215
Corsini, L. 1747, 1757
Corso, R. 1198
Corson, D. 1168, 1178
Corson, H. 1446
Corson, R. 1196
Cortelazzo, M. 1164, 1199, 1325,
    1332, 1535, 1537f., 1862f.,
    1868, 1875f., 1903
Cortès, F. 1778, 1782
Cortiella i Martret, A. 1777, 1782
Cortina, J. Gómez de la 1071
Coryn, A. 2708
Cosciani, G. 3016f.
Coseriu, E. 190, 206, 223, 281f.,
    286, 680, 787, 804, 889, 892,
    1090, 1093, 1843, 1889, 2224,
    2921, 2936
Cosijn, P.J. 227
Cossa, P. 149
Costa e Sá, J. J. da 2917, 2927,
    3022, 3027
Costa, A. 1078
Costa, A.C. 1774, 1782
Costa, J. Almeida 1731, 1734
Costa, P. 1856, 1859
Costas Rodríguez, C.I. 1138
Costaz, L. 2432, 2437
Costinescu, I. 1884
Costinescu, M. 1888
Coston, H. 1292, 1295
Cotarelo y Mori, E. 1743, 1765
Cotarelo, A. 1743, 1765
Cotari, D. 2706
Coteanu, I. 1887, 1889
Coté-Préfontaine, G. 180, 1367,
    1835, 1840
Cotgrave, R. 1818, 1849, 1949,
    2956, 2957, 2959f., 2971, 2974,
    3035, 3039
Coto, Th. de 2661, 2665, 2667
Cotta, J. F. 2079
Cotteret, J.-M. 1315, 1322
Cottez, H. 85f., 304, 1149, 1151,
    1168, 1176, 1228f., 1828, 1837,
    1839
Cottle, B. 1271f.
Cotton, R. 1439
Cottrell, G.W. 3167
Coulbeaux, P. S. 2450, 2453
Coulmas, F. 379, 407, 830f., 834,
    1031
Coulson, J. 524, 687, 821, 929
Courchêne, R. 249, 274
Courdier, G. 2130, 2234

Courouve, C. 1197
Courtat, F.-T. 1798, 1800, 1811
Courtenay, J.B. de 734, 748, 2312
Courtés, J. 1066
Courtillon-Leclerq, J. 1223
Courtnay, B. de 3079
Courtney, R. 1026, 1028f., 1385
Cousin d'Avallon, Ch.-Y. 1350
Cousin, Ch.-Y. 1349
Cousin, E. 3001
Cousin, P. H. 2751, 2754
Cousins, N. 1099
Coustenoble, H. 1308f.
Coutelle, C. 3017
Couto, A.M. do 1123
Couturat, L. 3129-3131, 3136
Couvreur, D. 43, 45
Couvreur, S. 3109, 3112
Covarrubias Orozco, S. 9, 15,
    1323, 1325, 1332, 1740f., 1743,
    1745, 1757, 1765, 1796
Covarrubias, S. de 2978, 2986,
    2993, 2996
Cowan de Beller, P. 2659f.
Cowan, J.M. 3096
Cowan, M. 2664, 2667
Cowie, A. 725, 2728, 2757, 2766,
    2770, 2775, 2901, 2903
Cowie, A.P. 43, 45, 78, 109f.,
    181f., 184, 187-189, 208, 212f.,
    357, 405, 523, 525, 588f., 589,
    591f., 606, 692, 746f., 753, 785,
    1012, 1014, 1017, 1029, 1379,
    1385, 2754, 3166
Cowles, E.N. 1757
Cox, H. 653
Cox, H.L. 667, 1319f., 1623, 2233,
    2781, 2725, 2751, 2774, 2780,
    2782, 2813, 2817, 2836, 3039
Coxe, R.S. 1308f.
Coyaud, M. 1671
Cozianul, M. 2264-2666
Crabb, G. 1068, 1071
Craig, H. jr. 3171
Craig, R.W. 3171
Craigie, J.H. 1966
Craigie, W.A. 95, 97, 667, 929,
    1414, 1430, 1435, 1437, 1446,
    1449, 1451-1453, 1456, 1608f.,
    1623, 1931, 1958, 1962, 1965,
    1985f., 1999, 2007, 3118
Cramer [Kramer], M. 2999, 3004
Cramer, Th. 2099
Cramer, W. 1015
Crato, A. 2913, 2927
Crawford, J. C. 2696
Crazzolara, J. P. 2644f.
Creamer, Th. 2754, 3170
Cregeen, A. 2344, 2346, 2349
Creider, J. T. 2644
Creixell, L. 1776, 1782
Cremmins, E.T. 1660, 1666

Crescenzio, P. de 150
Crespin, J. 2927, 2993
Crespin, S. 1845, 1859
Crespo Pozo, J.S. 1737
Creswell, Th.J. 31, 33, 76, 77f., 703, 1217, 2002, 2009
Creteli, K. 2432
Crețu, G. 1881, 1888f., 2266
Creutz Lechleitner, W. J. 2918, 2927
Crews, C.M. 1906f.
Créqui-Montfort, G. de 2681f., 2684, 2690
Criado de Val, M. 1197
Cridlaud, A. E. 2643f.
Criqui, F. 1098
Crisp, S. 2422f.
Croce, B. 1848, 1861, 1865
Croft, H. 225
Croft, K. 208, 213
Crofts, M. 2704
Cronan, U. 1762
Croneberg, C.G. 3141-3144
Cronia, A. 2289, 2295
Cronquist, M. 1261, 1263
Cronwall, U. 3048-3050
Crooke, W. 2536, 2545
Crosbie, J.S. 1349f.
Crosby, O. T. 2463, 2467
Crowell, Th.Y. 2953
Crowley, E.T. 1100f., 1261-1263, 1295
Crowley, T. 2638, 2641
Crönert, W. 1699, 1703
Crum, W.E. 1680f.
Cruse, D.A. 576, 3166
Crusius, G.C. 1558
Cruz Aufrere, J. 1081f., 1124, 1765
Cruz, J. de la 2664, 2667
Crystal, D. 208f., 213, 249, 272, 1973, 1982
Csiszár, A. 3131
Csorba, T. 3063, 3067
Csúcs, S. 2398
Csüry, B. 2381f.
Cuapius, G. 2926
Cuartas, A. 1216
Cubber, W. de 1623, 2782
Čubinov (Čubinašvili), D. 2416, 2418
Cubuat 2594
Cuervo, H. 1763
Cuervo, R. 1747f., 1750, 1765
Cuervo, R.J. 930, 1005, 1007, 1221, 1331f., 1743, 1750, 1752, 1767, 1769f.
Cuesta y Kerner, J. 1747, 1757
Cui Zhichao 2559
Čukalov, S. K. 2306f.
Cumino, G. 3011
Cuncliffe, R.J. 1454

Cunha, A. J. da 3029
Cunliffe, R.J. 1451, 1558
Ćupić, D. 77, 277, 2301, 2765
Čupovski, D. 2302
Curl, M. 1144f.
Cusihuamán Gutiérrez, A. 2705
Cuthbertson, J. 1558
Cuveiro Piñol, J. 1736f.
Cuyás, A. 2952, 2954
Cuychens, H. 573, 576
Cuyer, E. 1113, 1119
Cürvers, H. 2199, 2218
Cvilling, M.J. 746, 1622
Cydendambaev, C. B. 2754
Cyffer, N. 2643f.
Cyganenko, G.P. 2318, 2322
Cyganov, N.F. 2395, 2397
Cyvin, A.M. 980, 2321, 2326
Czisar, A. 3125
Czochralski, J. 252, 274, 3067
Czochralski, J. A. 2754, 3064-3066, 3068
Czuczor, G. 2381

D

da Assumpcan, M. 2518
d'Abbadie, A. 2462f., 2467, 2469
d'Alberti di Villanova, F. 1090, 1846f., 2972, 2974
d'Alembert, J. Le Rond 147, 307, 720, 723, 988f., 994, 996f., 1068, 1522
da Milano, G.B. 1130
D'Annunzio, G. 149-151, 1875
D'Ans, A.-M. 2703
da Palermo, G. M. 2462, 2465
d'Arpino, L. 2463, 2467
da Sale, F. 1896, 1904
da Thiene, G. 2463, 2465
da Trento, G. 2467
Daan, J. 2027
Dabeva, M. E. 2307
Daelemans, W.M.P. 3166
Dag Naud, A. 1044, 1047
Dagenais, G. 1215
Dagenais, L. 532, 576
Daghbashian, H. 2369, 2371
Dagnaud-Macé, P. 1215
Dahl, B.T. 1915, 1920f.
Dahl, F.V. 1920f.
Dahl, H. 1320, 1668, 1915, 1920f.
Dahl, J.P.F.D. 1920f.
Dahlberg, I. 269, 682, 686f., 1090, 1671
Dahlerup, V. 512, 515, 1414, 1915, 1922
Dahlgren, F.A. 1937, 1942
Dahlström, 2922, 2932
Dahmen, W. 269
Dähnert, J.C. 238, 247, 2060, 2068, 2215, 2218, 3041-3045

Dai Qingxia 2558f.
Daiches, D. 1986
Daire, L.F. 1011, 1014
Daire, R.P. 1017
Dakin, K. 2659-2661
Dakshinamurthi, N.S. 3097, 3099, 3104
Dal', V.I. 68f., 2312f., 2315, 2319, 2322
Dalager, I.-L. 3058, 3061
Dalametra, I. 1888
Dalbiac, Ph.H. 1048
Dalby, B.A. 1721
Dalby, D. 1235, 1238, 1529, 1543, 1545, 1548, 2104, 2198, 2218
Dalcher, P. 269f.
Dale, J. F. van 2771, 2774, 3038f.
Dalechamps, J. 2913, 2916, 2927, 2937, 2945
Dalgado, S.R. 3101, 3104
Dalgarno, G. 3142, 3144
Dali Morel, J. 1761
Dali, V. I. 3079
Dalin, A.F. 1069, 1072, 1937, 1942, 3041f., 3044f.
Dalitz, G. 2754
Dallenbach, K.M. 142, 145
Dallet, J.-M. 2456f.
Dalman, G. 2429, 2435
Dalmatin, J. 2297
Daly, B.A. 1788, 1811
Daly, L.W. 373, 407, 1721, 1788, 1811
Dalziel, J. M. 2459f.
Damaskin, D. S.-R. 2398
Damet, P. 217
Damé, F. 1886-1889
Damköhler, E. 2215, 2218
Dammann, A. 3027
Damme, R. 2039, 2042, 2047
Dănăilă, I. 1889
Danay, K. 2644
Danby, H. 2431, 2436
Dančetović, V. 2363
Danck, G.F. 1268, 1272
Daṇḍādinātha, I. 2489, 2496
Dandaron, B. D. 2550
Dandin, G. 3137
Daneš, F. 218, 221-213, 754, 949, 955, 1795, 1813, 2281, 2283
Danet, P. 2917, 2927, 2960, 3036, 3040
Đặng Chuān Liêu 2588
Dang, J. S. 2199, 2218
Dangitsis, K. 1710, 1712
Daničić, B. 2291
Daničić, D. 2264, 2266, 2293
Daniel Adam von Weleslawin 2044
Daniel, A. 2279
Daniels, K. 882, 887
Danielsson, B. 3048-3051

Daniil, M. A. C. 2305
Danilenko, V.P. 1671
Daninos, P. 1349f.
Danker, F.W. 1700, 1703
Dankoff, R. 2412f.
Dankovszky, G. 2377, 2381
Danneil, H. 3125, 3131, 3136
Dansel, M. 1259f.
Dante Alighieri 10, 22, 147-149, 218, 754, 995, 1125, 1851f., 1860, 1873f., 2970
Dantzig, B. van 1308f.
Danzer, F. 1110
Đào Đăng Vỹ 2585, 2587f.
Đào Duy Anh 2584f., 2587f.
Đào Văn Tập 2585, 2587f.
Đào Văn Tiēn 2588
Daoust, D. 48, 62
Darbelnet, J. 2754, 2831, 2836, 2887
Darbelnet, J. L. 2855, 2858f.
Darbois, L.-F. 1302, 1805
Dard, F. 40, 45
Dardano, M. 654, 1868, 1875, 1878, 2234
Dariault, P. 2768
Darmesteter, A. 66, 69, 222, 606, 916, 996, 1326, 1332, 1344, 1347, 1822f., 1839
Darms, G. 1900, 1903
Darwish, A. 2446f.
Das Gupta, D. 2542f., 2546
Das Gupta, K. 2558
Das, B. 2513
Das, B. P. 2542, 2547
Das, Ch. 2550
Das, J. M. 2510, 2518
Das, S. 2519, 3097, 3104
Das, S. C. 2549
Dāsa, S. 3101, 3104
Dästa Täklä Wäld 2451, 2433
Dasypodius, P. 9, 15, 139, 144, 1698, 1703, 1949, 2043, 2045f., 2049f., 2068, 2077, 2214, 2279, 2283, 2376, 2927, 2998, 3004, 3035
Date, C.J. 1658, 1666
Date, T. R. 2514, 2519
Dati, C.R. 1854
Daube-Schackat, R. 276
Daulie, M. 2977, 2987
Daum, E. 1006f., 1110, 1312-1314, 2322
Daurella de Nadal, J. 1783
Dautry, J. 1801, 1811
Dauzat, A. 731, 1215, 1269-1272, 1280, 1282f., 1286, 1289, 1291, 1295, 1325, 1332, 1347, 1533, 1537, 1804, 1810f., 1827, 1838
Davary, G. D. 2476
Davau, M. 61, 405, 601f., 606, 641, 672, 679, 686, 765, 924, 928, 1052, 1151, 1378, 1833, 1839
Dave, N. S. 2511, 2518
Davenport, J. 2972, 2974
Davias-Baudrit, J. 2591, 2593
Daviault, P. 2960
David Ben Abraham al-Fasi 2434
David, J. 945, 1837, 1839
Davidoff, H. 1037, 1039
Davidova, T. 3175
Davidovitch, C. 1321, 1362, 1643, 1669
Davidsen-Nielsen, 2760
Davidson, B. 2428, 2434
Davidson, G. 1090, 1092
Davidson, G.W. 1080
Davidson, Th. 1964f.
Davies, G.A. 2955
Davies, J. 2347, 2349
Davies, P. 326, 515, 1320
Davies, T.R. 1272
Davis, Ch.H. 1660, 1666
Davis, I. 1339
Davis, M. 1112, 1119
Davitz, J.R. 849, 853
Davoust, E. 2885
Dawkins, J. 588, 591
Dawson, J.L. 1563, 1566, 1652, 1666
Dawson, L.H. 1131, 1293
Dawson, R.H. 1295
Day, Chr. 2663, 2667, 2700
Day, D. 142, 145
Dayre, J. 2292f.
Dazat, O. 1044, 1047
de Aguilar, F. 2996
de Alencar, M. 1128
de Almeida, H. 1197
de Amaral, V.B. 1214
De Armond, R. 2543
de Averco, L. 1125, 1131
de Ayala, F. 2994f.
De Backer, G. 1029
de Balzac, H. 1534
de Bercy, A. 1533, 1538
de Berlaimont, N. 1088, 1091
De Bermingham, A. 2972, 2974
De Blasio, A. 1534, 1536
de Boor, H. 1310
de Brey, R. 3008
de Cantalausa, J. 1895, 1903
de Capol, J. 1896, 1903
de Castilho, A.F. 1128
de Castillo Mantilla, G. 1126
De Colle, A. 1242, 1244
de Colombier 2937, 2945
De Coninck, R.H.B. 1309
de Covarrubias, S. 2978, 2986, 2993, 2996
De Felice, E. 140, 144, 357, 1194, 1197, 1272, 1875f., 1878
de Ferrai, G.G. 2997
De Ferrari, R. 1078
de Fourvières, X. 1904
De Gaulle, Ch. 1315
de Gámez, T. 2953f.
De Gorog, R. 1346f.
De Gregorio, G. 1845, 1861
De Guignes, C.L.J. 3109, 3122
De Han, C. 3112
De Jong, E.D. 1320
De Jorio, A. 1114, 1119
De Körös, A. C. 2549f.
De la Court, J.F.H.A. 1320
de La Noue, O. 1125, 1127, 1129
de la Torre, M. 2955
de La Touche, F. 1212, 1216
de Landes, L. 1195, 1198
de Las Casas, C. 2949, 2955
De las Casas, Chr. 1848, 2993
de Laveaux, J.Ch.Th. 3005
de Lépine, L. 3009, 3012
D'Elia, A. L. 3171
D'Ewes, S. 1439
De Lollis, C. 1865, 1879
De Lormes, Th. 1815
de Lucca D., M. 2687
De Man, L. 1088, 1093
De Maria, R. 1949f.
De Maria, R. jr. 225, 230, 1952
De Martino, G. 2754
De Mauro, T. 1196, 1198
De Mello Vianna, F. 1077f.
de Mendibil, P. 2951
de Nebrija, E.A. 2949, 2955
de Ochoa, C. 1129
de Oliveyra, S. 1906
de Penalver, J. 1126, 1130
de Ponton d'Amécourt, A. 1092
De Rienzo, G. 1874
De Rivarol, A. 225
De Robertis, D. 1871, 1879
de Roujoux, P. G. 3012
de Rozzol, A. 2997
de Saint-Maurice, R.-A. 1004, 1008
De Saluste, G. 1015
De Sanctis, F. 149
de Saussure, F. (see Saussure) 342, 888, 893
De Silva, J. W. P. 2505
De Silva, M. W. S. 2503, 2506
De Silva, W. A. 2505
De Smet, G.A.R. 667, 813, 1091, 1094
de Sola, A. 1091
de Sola, R. 1261f., 1265
de Sylva, V. 2949
De Titta, C. 1007
De Tollenaere, F. 293, 296, 531, 583, 1090, 1094, 1165 (s. Tollenaere)
de Valdés, P. 2949
de Vaugelas, C.F. 1213, 1217 (s. Vaugelas)

De Vriendt-de Man, M.-J. 1314, 1320
De Vries, L. 1507, 1510f.
De-Vit, V. 1720f.
Deak, E. 1187, 2920, 2927
Deak, S. 1187
Deanović, M. 2292f.
DeArmond, R. 2546
Deb, P. C. 2515
Debec, N.P. 3175
Debrunner, A. 2491
Debus, F. 1276, 1283
Debus, G. 849, 852f.
Debyser, F. 2754, 3010, 3012
Decimator, H. 1088, 1791, 1850, 1859, 2912-2914, 2916, 2927
Decsi, B. 2376
Decurtins, A. 1897-1899, 1905
Decurtins, C. 1896, 1905
Dedenbach, S. 2705
Dedenbach-Salazar Sáenz, S. 2681-2683
Deeney, J. 2533f., 2537, 2539, 2546
Dees, A. 18, 1814
Deeters, G. 1342
Defner, M. 1711f.
Defoe, B.N. 1950f.
DeFrancis, J. 2602, 2611
DeGarmo, M. 3148
Degliotti, M. 766
Degubol, H. 1931
Dehler, W. 3125, 3131, 3136
Dei, B. 1851, 1861
Deidda, A. 3016f.
Deighton, L.C. 508
Deimel, A. 1683f.
Deines, H. von 1680f.
Dejanova-Makedonska, A. 2308
Del Bocca, E. 1874
del Castillo, A. 2954
Del Olmo Lete, G. 1693
Delacour, J. 1044, 1048, 1349f.
Delacroix, J. 2400, 2405
Delafosse, M. 2871, 2875
Delage, E. 1388, 2889f., 2899f.
Delahaye, M. 2765
Delahaye, V. 1308f.
Delamarre, X. 1338f.
Delaporte, R. 2344, 2350
Delas, D. 1096-1098
Delas-Demon, D. 1098
Delatte, L. 1137, 1139
Delattre, M. 1306
Delattre, P. 2855, 2858
Delboulle, A. 1823
Delbridge, A. 2005, 2009
Delbrück, E. 1068
Delbrück, F. 2059, 2068
Delbrück, J.F.G. 1072
Delbrun, P. 1795
Delcros, H. 2591, 2593

Deleen, C. 3044f., 3047, 3050
Delesalle, G. 1185, 1187
Delesalle, S. 80, 83-85, 87f., 1125, 1830, 1843
Deletanville, Th. 2959
Delén, C. 3047, 3050
Delfosse, H.P. 1568, 1572
Delgado Campos, J. 2980, 2983
Delgaty de Osorio, J. 2702
Delgaty, A. 2663f., 2667
Delgaty, A. H. viuda de 2698f.
Delgaty, C. 2667
Delheure, J 2456f.
Delion-Baruffa 1123
Delisle, L. 1800, 1811f.
Delitzsch, F. 1683f.
Delius, N. 2502, 2504
Dell, F. 2558
Della Bella, A. 2289, 2293
Dellepiane, A. 1752, 1757
Dellian, C. 3128, 3131
Dellian, K. 3132
Delrieu, A.-M. 1229
Delsalle, S. 1121
Delvau, A. 1185, 1187, 1195, 1197
Demaizière, C. 48, 62, 1793, 1812
Demauny, Ch. 1124
Deme, L. 2381
Demidova, A.K. 1006f.
Democritus 1696
Dempwolff, O. 1339, 2463, 2467, 2650, 2652, 2654f.
Denecke, L. 245, 1240, 1415
Denis, S. 2980, 2983f.
Denis-Papin, M. 1100f.
Denisov, P. 2768
Denisov, P.N. 361f., 370, 980, 1006f., 1012, 1014, 1018, 1652, 1666, 1668, 2316, 2319-2322, 2326, 2328, 2759, 2842, 2853, 2892, 2896, 2902, 3082, 3084
Denisova, M.A. 2321f.
Denizeau, C. 3088, 3094
Denniston, J.D. 1221f.
Denooz, J. 1137, 1139
Densușianu, A. 1890
Densusianu, O. 1881, 1886, 1888, 1890
Dent, R. 1036, 1039
Dentzler, J. J. 3031, 3033
Denux, R. 508, 1055
Deny, J. 2404, 2407
Denys de Montfort, P. 2918
Depecker, L. 61, 1164, 1176
Depkin, L. 2355
Depping, G.-B. 1253
Deranco, P. 2988, 2990
Derchi, F. 2462, 2467
Deribas, V.M. 2316, 2322
Derocquigny, J. 2884f.
Derval, B. 1572
Des Carrières, J.T.H. 2957f.

Des Carrières, M. 2959
Des Pepliers, J. R. 3074
Desai, D. M. 2511, 2518
Desai, M.P. 3099, 3104
Desaya, S.R. 3100, 3104
Descamps, J.-L. 132f., 208, 211. 213, 915f., 1052, 1632f., 1637, 1839
Descartes, R. 1089, 1873
Deschanel, E. 1244f.
Deschler, J.-P. 2264-2266
Desfeuilles, A. 1558
Desfeuilles, P. 1126f., 1129, 1558
Desfontaines, P.-F.G. 1164f.
Desgranges, J.C.L.P. 1185, 1187, 1804f., 1813
Desgrouais 1212, 1215
Deshpande, M. K. 2514, 2519
Deslandes, G. 1286, 1289, 1295
Deslongschamps, L. 2496
Desplanques, G. 1270, 1272
Despodova, V. 2263, 2266, 2303f.
Desproges, P. 1349f.
Destaing, E. 2456f.
Destro, A. 174
Detering, K. 2756
Detter, F. 2089f., 2095
Dettler, F. 2086
Dettmer, H. A. 2621, 2623
Deutschmann, O. 1017f., 1765, 1813, 2887
Deva, R. 2493
Devaux, P. 1185, 1188
Devedjian, K. 2402, 2404f.
Devellioğlu, F. 2404f.
Devi, V. 1776, 1786
Dević, L.M. 1329, 1332
DeVinne, P. 2007
Devjatnin, V.N. 3121, 3131, 3136
Devlamminck, B. 1910f.
Devlin, J. 1078, 1997, 2008
Devloo, E. 2610
Devos, M. 2021
Devoto, G. 66, 69, 687, 692, 706, 724, 982, 987, 1179, 1183, 1325, 1331f., 1865, 1871, 1875f., 1878, 1880
DeWolf, P. P. 2647, 2649
Dewora, V.J. 1124
Déchelette, F. 1185, 1187
Décsy, G. 2398
Dégardin, F. 1121, 1124
Désirat, C. 679, 1072
Dhadphale, M. G. 2499, 2506
Dhaleine, L, 2959
Dhamotharan, A. 3171
Dhanan Chantrupanth 2590f., 2593
Dhanapāla 2498f., 2504
Dharmadhikari, S. 3097, 3099, 3104
Dheralde, L. 1895, 1903

Dhombres, D. 40, 45
D'Hombres, M. 1895, 1904
Dhuez, N. 2999
d'Hulster, L. 1308f.
Di Benedetto, U. 2954
di Boerio 1199
di Castelli, N. 3009
Di Cesare, D. 1067, 1075
di Falco, B. 1126, 1129
Di Nola, L. 1198
di Paolo Healey, A. 327, 1142, 1445, 1454
Di Pietro, R. J. 2856, 2858
Di Stefano, G. 1029
Di Virgilio, P.S. 1795, 1812
Diakonoff, I.M. 1692f.
Díaz del Castillo, B. 1764
Diaz Rengifo, J. 1126, 1129
Diaz-Retg, E. 1215
Dibbets, G. 2021f.
Dibbets, G. R. W. 3039
Dickel, G. 1410, 1415, 2218
Dickenmann, E. 1285f., 1289
Dickens, Ch. 3122, 3131, 3136
Dickson, P. 1207f.
Diculescu, C. 1885
Diderot, D. 147, 184, 219, 223f., 307, 653, 720, 723, 906, 996, 1068, 1149, 1515, 1518f., 1522, 1802, 1805, 1813
Didier, M. 1210, 1215, 1367, 1378, 1836
Didot, A.F. 1704, 1790, 1812
Didot, F. 2957
Dieckhoff, H.C. 2345f., 2349
Dieckmann, W. 551, 576, 837, 841f., 1200, 1205
Diederich, P.B. 1361
Diefenbach, L. 1411, 1414, 1539, 1548, 1910f., 2041, 2047, 2084, 2088, 2095
Dielitz, J. 1054f.
Diels, H. 1700f.
Diem, W. 2444, 2447
Diemer, A. 248, 274, 583
Diener, G. W. 2199, 2218
Diercks, G. 2988, 2990
Diesner, H.-J. 17, 997
Dieterici, F. 3090, 3094
Dietherr, M. 1036, 1040, 2065, 2069
Dietrich, K.F. 1124
Dietrich, M. 122, 124, 239, 243, 1690
Dietrich, R.-A. 816, 821
Dietrich, W. 648, 787, 881, 1230, 1731, 1735, 2673, 2676
Dietz, Ph. 1235, 1238, 1557, 1559
Dietze, J. 3125
Dietze, W. 1562
Điêu Chinh Nhim 2591, 2593
Díez Quijano, D. 1778, 1782

Diez, F. 1329, 1332, 1337, 1339, 1728f., 1812f., 1883, 1897, 2960
Diez, T. 1325
Diffloth, G. 2541, 2545
Dihkhudā, 'Ali Akbar 2479
Dijk, T.A. van 893, 898, 959, 967
Dijkhoff, M. 2871, 2873-2875
Dijkstra, W. 2025f., 2033
Dikshitar, A.R. 3101, 3104
Dil, A. S. 2870
Dill, Chr. 250, 265, 272, 574, 1549, 1553f., 1559, 1561, 2104, 2218
Dillmann, A. 2449ff., 2453
Dillon, M. 1671
Dilshad Kalānavī 3100
Dilthey, W. 1020
Dimaras, K.Th. 1713
Dimitrakos, D. 1708, 1712
Dimitrescu, F. 1164, 1888-1890
Dimitrie Cantemier 1882
Dimitrov, B. 2308
Dimitrova, M. 2308
Dimitrovski, T. 2303f.
Dimmendaal, G. J. 2644f.
Dimova, A. 2307
Dinçol, A.M. 1692f.
Dindinger, P.J. 3175
Dindorf, L. 1698
Dindorf, W. 1559, 1698
Dindorfius, G. 1559, 1698
Dineen, P.S. 2344
Dinekov, P. 2265
Ding Du 2603, 2610
Dingel, I. 1842
Dingeldein, H. J. 79, 126, 237, 243f., 461, 581, 586, 1066, 1416, 2198, 2235, 2243, 2245
Dinglinge, G.F. 1272
Dinguirard, J.-C. 653f.
Dinh Hoa Nguyen 96 (s. Nguyen)
Dinkelacker, W. 2241
Dinneen, P.S. 2345f., 2348
Dinner, K. 1011, 1014
Diogenianos 1697f.
Dion, A. de 1825
Dionisotti, A.C. 1714, 1722
Dionne, R.J. 3174
Dios Yapita, J. de
Dioscorides 2946
Dirks, M. 2633
Dittel, F. 2524
Ditten, H. 2754
Dittmar, N. 207, 275, 580, 1429, 2222
Dittmer, A. 2754, 2794
Dittmer, E. 991, 997
Dittrich, H. 1029, 2174, 2176, 2218
Diwetrich, W. 2704
Dixon, R. M. W. 2638-2641
Díez Mateo, F. 2802

D'jakonov, I. M. 1692f., 2427 (= Diakonoff)
Djajadinigrat, H. 2566f.
Djuvernua, A. L. 2305-2307
Dmitiev, N.K. 2414
Dobbie, E.V.K. 1443, 1456
Dobel, R. 1044, 1048
Doble, M. 2636f.
Doblin, J. 714, 724
Dobrotvorskij, M. M. 2621
Dobrovie-Sorin, C. 1812
Dobrovol'skij, V.N. 2336f.
Dobrovský, J. 2279f., 2283
Dobrzyński, J. 3063, 3067
Dobson, E.J. 1948, 1952
Dobson, J. 1259f.
Doce, J.M. 1747, 1757
Dochez, L. 1803, 1805
Dockx, W. 2939, 2945
Dodd, R. 1038, 1041
Dodd, W. St. 2828, 2836
Doderer, H. von 20
Dodoens, R. 2916, 2928
Doederlein, L. 1069, 1072
Doeff, H. 2619, 2622. 3114, 3116
Doerfer, G, 2410, 2412, 2414
D'Offay, D. 2872, 2874f.
Dogliotti, M. 66, 930
Doherty, M. 810, 813
Dohna, L. Graf zu 1571f.
Doi, K. 2512, 2519
Doi, T. 2623, 3119
Doillon, A. 1185, 1187
Doke, C. M. 2647-2649, 2651, 2653, 2655
Dokulil, M. 190, 206
Dolamore, C. E. J. 2887
Dolby, J.L. 1139
Dolce, L. 1011, 1014, 1129
Dolcino, M. 1196f.
Dolet, E. 1011, 1014
Dolezal, F. 10, 17, 99, 101, 1090, 1093, 1704, 1944, 1952
Dolgopol'skij, A. B. 2465, 2467
Dollmayr, V. 242, 826
Domenig, M. 1571f., 3166
Domingues, C. 3131
Domínguez, J. 1029
Domínguez, J.M. 2989f.
Domínguez, R.J. 1746, 1757, 2952, 2980, 2983
Domokos, P. 2396, 2398
Donà dalle Rose, M.C. 1029
Donadiu y Puignau, D. 1773, 1782
Donaldson, D. 1139, 1455, 1984-1986
Donaldson, J. 2591, 2593
Donegan, P. 2542-2545
Doniach, N.S. 3091
Donner, H. 2428f., 2431, 2433-2435, 2437

Donner, K. 2629f., 2395, 2397f.
Donner, O. 1339
Dony, Y. P. de 1019, 1027, 1029, 2920, 2928
Dooley, R. A. 2674, 2676
Doornbos 2643f.
Doornkaat Koolman, J. ten 2028
Dopatka, U. 1294
Doppagne, A. 1176
Dora, H. 3026f.
Dorais, L.-J. 2633f.
Dorf, M. 3148
D'Oria, D. 87, 1196, 1198, 1812
Doria, M. 1139, 1207f.
Doritsch, A. 2307f.
Dority, G.K. 3176
Dornmeyer, A.J. 1011, 1014, 1221f.
Dornseiff, F. 114, 123, 125, 162, 769, 771, 898, 1058-1061, 1065, 1090f., 1093, 1140, 1194, 1197, 1867, 2087, 2095, 2177, 2182, 2193, 2218
Doroszewski, N. 274
Doroszewski, W. 246, 1139f., 1671, 2270-2273
Dorsch, F. 118, 123
Dorsey, J. O. 2696
Dose, M. 123, 1362, 2219
Dośi, B. J. 2504
Dossi, C. 149
Dostal, K. A. 1078, 2179, 2180, 2182, 2218
Dotter, F. 1290
Dotter, M. 1290
Doucet, F.W. 3152, 3156
Doucet, M. 2942, 2945
Douceur, D. 1794
Dougherty, M. 3147
Douglas, Ch.N. 1046, 1048
Douglas, G. 1986
Douglas, G.H. 1090, 1093
Doujat, J. 1895, 1904
Dournon, J.-Y. 1047f., 1210-1213, 1215
Doutrelepont, Ch. 1572
Doutrepont, G. 1258, 1260
Dove, K. 2653f.
Downer, J.W. 1456
Downes, L. S. 2885
D'Oylie, Th. 2949
Dozon, A. 2362
Dozy, R. 1329, 1332, 3087f., 3094
Dölling, J. 539, 576
Dpal khang lo tsaa ba 2549
Dpal sgang lo tsa ba 2548
Drach, P. 2041f.
Drach-Eiswolke, P.R. 206, 2223
Drăganu, N. 1881, 1885
Drage, H. 1019
Drake, R. 2949
Drati geshe rinchen döndrup 2548

Dravinš, K. 2354f., 2360
Dravnieks, J. 2357
Draye, H. 1275
Dressel, G. 2355
Dressler, W. U. 591, 653f., 947f., 955, 2191, 2234, 3019
Dreux du Radier, J.-F. 1195, 1197
Drew, D. 2636f.
Drewek, R. 270, 1572
Drewes, J. B. 2020
Drews, J. 1349, 1351, 2218
Dreyfus, J. 146
Dreyfuss, H. 3153, 3156
Drezen, E. 3129, 3131, 3136
Driem van, G. L. 2558
Drijvers, H.J.W. 2431, 2433, 2437
Drimba, V. 1890
Drini, S. 2295
Drisler, H. 1700, 1703
Driver, G.R. 2433
Driver, S.R. 2428, 2434
Drizari, N. 2363, 2366
Drljić, R. 2290, 2295
Drobnić, J. D. 2291, 2293
Droege, G. B. 2023, 2036
Drosdowski, G. 17, 27f., 68f., 111, 123, 127, 131, 134f., 144, 158, 162f., 174, 201, 203, 206, 272, 274, 278, 320, 358f., 369, 405, 458, 460, 499, 500, 516, 524, 529, 574, 585, 613f., 626, 647, 661, 667, 672, 687, 692, 731, 746, 753, 773, 778f., 786, 795-797, 799, 803-805, 813, 820, 822, 830, 834, 841, 848f., 853f., 868, 892, 899, 928, 955, 966, 980, 989, 997, 999, 1011, 1013f., 1017, 1064f., 1177, 1238, 1269f., 1272, 1303, 1364, 1414, 1608, 1611, 1619, 1622f., 2020, 2048, 2075, 2092, 2099, 2130, 2133, 2135, 2147, 2188, 2191, 2218-2220, 2234, 2236, 2244
Droste-Hülshoff, A. von 2131
Droulers, E. 3152, 3156
Drower, E.S. 2432, 2437
Droz 3176
Drozd, L. 315, 321, 848
Druart 2542
Drumbl, J. 174
Drummond, D.A. 2323
Drummond, s. Father Drummond
Drumond, C. 2675, 2702
Druon, M. 1826
Drvodelić, M. 2292f.
Drysdale, P.D. 527, 530, 606, 641, 1031
Du Bartas, G.d.S. 1015, 1018
Du Bellay, J. 1793
Du Cange, Ch. d. F. 1252, 1346f., 1719f., 1897

Du Chazaud, H.B. 137, 144
Du Fresne 1126
Du Gran, C. 1101f.
Du Marsais, 533
Du Ryer, A. 2400, 2405, 2407
Du Verdier, A. 3008
Duan Yucai 2598, 2610
Duarte i Montserrat, C. 1777f., 1780, 1782
Duarte, P. 2918, 2928
Dube, B.K. 3100, 3107
Dubislav, W. 539, 576
Dubler, C. E. 2930, 2946
Dubois, C. 180, 222f., 280, 286, 361, 364, 370, 459, 590f., 606, 609, 613, 700, 703, 783f., 786, 917f., 920f., 930, 989, 991, 997, 1194, 1198, 1588, 1827, 1831, 1835, 1842
Dubois, J. 15, 44, 61, 77f., 104, 110, 129, 134, 144, 180, 222f., 280, 286, 311, 361, 364, 370, 459, 515, 524, 590f., 606, 609, 613, 640f., 647, 661, 678f., 700, 703, 731, 746, 766, 780, 783f., 786, 903f., 916-921, 923, 928, 930, 945f., 989, 991, 997, 1050-1052, 1078, 1157f., 1194, 1198, 1218f., 1325, 1332, 1347, 1361, 1369, 1378, 1388f., 1575, 1588, 1827, 1832, 1834, 1837, 1842, 2836, 2894, 2900, 2902
Dubois, M. 1262f.
Dubois, M.-M 1021, 1029, 2823, 2885, 2958f.
Dubois-Charlier, F. 678f., 903f., 1361, 1388, 2795f., 2893, 2900, 2958
Dubost, J.-P. 1002f., 1005, 1007
Dubray, G. 2884f.
Dubrovskij, P. P. 3076
Dubský, J. 2282f.
Dubuc, R. 169f.
DuCange, S. 1705f., 1712
Ducati, B. 2463, 2467
Ducet, M. 1215
Duchastel, P. 714, 724
Ducker, A.R. 664
Duckert, A.R. 33, 79, 111, 275, 517f., 579, 582, 655, 667f., 703, 861, 2009
Dückert, E. 591
Dückert, H. 1217
Dückert, J. 231, 243, 1215, 1240, 1253, 1398f., 1415, 1600, 1609, 2081, 2083, 2099f., 2188, 2218, 2220
Duckett, G. 2918, 2928
Duckett, W. 224
DuCloux, L. Ch. 2894, 2900
Ducoeurjoly, S. J. 2871, 2875
Duculot 1214

Duda, W. 736, 745, 748, 2715, 2725f., 2754f., 2776, 2778, 3081, 3084
Dud'huit, A. 1469, 1473
Duden, K. 16, 67, 69, 123, 1301-1303, 2091f., 2095, 2192-2196, 2219
Duez, N. 1195, 1795f., 1845, 1859, 2928, 2999, 3009
Dufief, N.G. 2959
Dufour, J.E. 1282
Duft, J. 2215
Dugas, J.-Y. 1295
Dugast, D. 1644, 1671
Dugdale, W. 1439
Dugué, B. 1308f.
Duhamel du Monceau 2938f., 2945
Duhamel, G. 24
Dühmer, A. 1044, 1048
Dülberg, P. 1207, 1209
Dulewicz, I. 1139, 2264, 2266, 2319, 2323, 3067
Dulong, G. 1210, 1215
Dultz, W. 1100, 1102, 1175f., 2188, 2219
Duma, J. 1290, 2273
Dumarsais, C.Ch. 219, 223
Dumas, D. 517
Dumcke, J. 1216
Dumonceaux, P. 1812
Dumont, M.-A. 2885, 2982f.
Dumstorf, H. 2033
Duncan, A. 1983, 1986
Dungdung, M. 2542, 2546
Dunger, H. 1173f., 1176, 2215, 2219
Dungworth, D. 1660, 1667
Dunkling, L.A. 1269, 1272
Dunn, R. 3176
Dunnebier, W. 2566f.
Dunoyer, J.-M. 43, 45
Dupiney de Vorepierre, J.F.M.B. 1805, 1839
Duplais, L. 1803, 1812
Dupont, L. 2885, 2982f.
Dupont, P.F. 1052
Dupont-Sommer, A. 2432, 2437
Dupré, P. 1045, 1047f., 1215, 1217
Dupuis, H. 1081f.
Dupuys, J. 1792f., 1806, 1808
Duraffour, A. 1812, 1828
Durand, M. 2955
Durand, R.-H. 718, 724
Duranteau, J. 43, 45
Đurđević, B. 2289
Durey de Noinville, J.B. 217, 223, 1812, 3171
Durga 2490
Durgāprasāda 2496
Duridanov, I. 1286, 1289
Düringsfeld, I. von 1037, 1039, 2066, 2068

Durlin 1302f.
Duro, A. 140, 144, 357, 687, 922, 924, 928, 992, 995f., 1194, 1197, 1325, 1333, 1572, 1609, 1869-1871, 1874f., 1877-1880
Durrant, E.D. 3128, 3131
Dürrenmatt, F. 2131
Durrerus, A. 1221f.
Durrieu, L. 1215
Dutch, R.A. 1092
Duthoy, J.-J. 3027
Dutourd, J. 1349, 1351
Dutton, B. 2953f.
Duttweiler, C.G. 1051f.
Duval, A. 2751, 2755, 2796, 2816, 2824, 2830f., 2836, 2861, 2864, 2959
Duval, R. 2427, 2433
Duviols, P. 2683
Düwell, H. 2895, 2902
Dwelly, E. 2344, 2349
Dworecki, I. H. 3064, 3067f.
Dwyer, F.M. 708, 724
Dwyer, R. 1141
Dybowski, B. 2630
Dyche, Th. 509, 1206, 1208, 1308f., 1802, 1805, 1944, 1948, 1951
Dyer, L.H. 3129, 3131
Dyhr, M. 101, 127, 279, 461, 500, 586, 2239, 2245, 2760
Dykstra, A. 2026, 2033
Dykstra, M. 1664, 1666
Dykstra, W. 2026
Dymshits, Z.M. 3101, 3104
Džanašia, B. 2418, 2420
Dzierżanowska, H. 1015, 1652, 1666
Dzokanga, A. 732, 748
Dzul Poot, D. 2663, 2667

E

Eagleson, R.D. 1560, 1617, 1623
Eastlake, F.W. 3115f.
Eaton, H.S. 1320, 1361, 1668, 2954
Ebbing, J. E. 2686, 2689, 2706
Ebbinghaus, E.A. 1912
Ebbitt, W. 764, 767
Ebbitt, W.R. 30, 34f., 38, 1995, 2005, 2009
Ebel, A. 1191f.
Ebel, H. 2339, 2342f.
Ebeling, E. 1684f., 2475, 2477
Ebeling, H. 1549f., 1559
Eberhard, J. A. 126, 135, 769, 801, 1062-1065, 1068f., 1072f., 1075, 2059, 2068, 2070, 2076, 2078, 2086f., 2100, 2215, 2220
Eberhard, U. 576, 582

Eberhard-Wabnitz, M. 1273
Eberle, K. 3026
Eberle, K. H. 1053, 3029
Ebers, J. 2967f., 3075
Ebert, F. A. 2066, 2074
Ebert, K. H. 2458, 2460
Ebert, Th. 251, 374
Ebert, W. 274
Ebner, J. 123, 1362, 2220
Ebneter, Th. 1900, 1904f.
Echegaray, E. de 1747, 1758
Echeverría Reyes, A. 1753, 1758
Echeverría, V. 2663, 2667
Echols, J. 2563, 2565
Echols, J.M. 78, 2870
Eckart, R. 1035, 1039
Eckert, R. 616, 616, 2207, 2211, 2229, 2853
Eckes, Th. 573, 576
Eckey, W. 272, 358, 405, 574, 1622, 2219
Eco, U. 551f., 576, 926, 930, 992, 997, 3148-3150, 3157
Edalji, S. 2511
Édel'man, D. I. 2485
Edelweiss, F. G. 2670, 2672, 2676
Edgar, J. 2643-2645
Edgerton, F. 2493, 2495, 2499, 2504
Edgeworth, M. P. 2513, 2519
Edgren, A.H. 2958f.
Edgren, H. 2972, 2974
Edmonds, C. J. 2483, 2486
Edmondston, Th. 1984, 1986
Edmonson, M. 2661-2663, 2667
Edmont, E. 719, 723
Edouard, R. 1191f., 1535f.
Edwards, E. D. 2563, 2565
Edwards, P. 575, 1321
Edwards, P.M.H. 1361, 1669, 1889
Edwards, R.J. 1144f.
Eeg-Olofsson, M. 1938
Eegholm-Pedersen, S. 1920, 1922
Efremova, T.F. 1229, 1312-1314, 2317, 2326
Efron, D. 1117, 1119
Egan, R.F. 1068, 1075
Egede, P. 2632f., 2916, 2928
Egel, M.J. 2390f.
Egenolff, Chr. 1034, 1039, 1042
Egger, J. 2938, 2945
Eggermont, J.L. 1361
Eggers, H. 162f., 277, 584, 769, 771, 774, 778, 956f., 967, 1017, 1059, 1066, 1089, 1093, 1573, 1651, 1666, 2087, 2098, 2177, 2182, 2232, 2234, 2243, 2887
Egilsson, S. 1929, 1931
Egli, J. J. 1284f., 1291, 2215, 2220
Eguílaz y Yanguas, L. de 1329, 1332, 1747, 1758

Ehegötz, E. 2755
Ehlers, G. 3026, 3028
Ehlich, K. 830
Ehnert, R. 1364
Ehrentraut, H. G. 2028, 2033f.
Ehret, Chr. 1340, 2464f., 2466, 2642, 2645
Ehrich, S. 1104, 2184, 2227
Ehrismann, O. 1140
Ehrlich, E. 515, 2008
Ehrlich, R. 1177, 2223
Ehrlich, S. 1111
Ehrmann, Th. 323, 327
Ehrsam, Th.C. 1016
Eib, A. von 1399
Eibl, K. 2055, 2074
Eichbaum 2436
Eichelberger, U. 1047f.
Eichert, O. 1559
Eichhoff, J. 619, 626, 1167
Eichhorn, O. 2094f.
Eichler, E. 1035, 1042, 1279f., 1282f., 1286, 1289, 2276f.
Eichler, W. 1219, 2207, 2213, 2217
Eichmann, J. 2041
Eichner, W. 1046, 1048
Eick, J. 574
Eickmans, H. 2039, 2041f., 2047, 2199, 2201, 2234
Eickmeyer, H.-J. 573
Eiffel, G. 1825
Eikmeyer, H.-J. 163, 576
Eimele, F. 3045
Einarsson, St. 1928, 1932
Eis, G. 1294, 1294
Eiselein, J. 1034f., 1039, 2064f., 2068
Eiselin, J.B. 3128, 3131
Eisenberg, P. 373, 407, 796, 883, 887
Eisenhart, J. F. 2065, 2068
Eisler, R. 577, 581
Eismann, W. 1042f., 2755, 3085
Eissfeldt, O. 1693
Ėjjubi, K. R. 2483, 2486
Ek, J.A. van 183, 189, 741, 748, 1357, 1363
Ekbo, S. 1942
Ekmann, P. 853
Ekwall, E. 1280-1282
Elbert, S. H. 2573-2575
Elderkin, E. D. 2461
Eldrige, R.C. 1361
Elert, P. 2928
Eley, L. 539, 576
Elezović, G. 2292f.
Elfenbein, J. 2484f.
Elger, G. 2355, 2359f.
Elger, R.P.G. 2359
Elgozy, G. 1349, 1351, 1673, 1678
Elgueta, M. 2664, 2667
Elia, A. 3166

Elia, E. 2755
Elias, E.A. 3090-3092, 3095
Elias, Ph. 1340
Elíes i Busqueta, P. 1776, 1782
Eliyā bar Šīnāyā 2427, 2434
Elizaga, L. 1758
Elkin, A. P. 2639, 2641
Elkins, R. E. 2573
Ellendt, F. 1551, 1559
Elliot, G. 1868
Elliot, W.Th. 1302f.
Elliott, H. 2664, 2667
Elliott, J. 1989, 2007
Elliott, N.D. 1617, 1623
Elliott, R. 2664, 2667
Ellis, A. 1962, 2347, 2349
Ellyson, L. 1124
Elmaleh, A. 2431
Elmslie, W. J. 2513, 2519, 3100f., 3104
Elovin 1187
Elphinstone, M. St. 2483, 2486
Elsebach, H. 2803, 2990
Elster, L. 166
Elvers, C. 2355
Elwal, A. 2972, 2974
Elwall, A. 2958f.
Elwell-Sutton, L. P. 2477, 2479f.
Elwert, W.Th. 1891, 1905
Elyot, Th. 9, 1368
Emanuel, H. 2347, 2351
Emblen, D.L. 1093
Emden, J. v. 1216
Emeneau, M. B. 1339, 2524, 2528-2530, 2532f.
Emerich de Judy, J. 2703
Emery, D.W. 508
Emery, H.G. 1071, 2007
Emery, L. 3007, 3012, 3014, 3019
Eminescu, M. 1549f., 1557, 1559, 1882
Eminian, S. 2917, 2928
Emmelen, Van A. 2537
Emmelius, H. 1791, 2910, 2912, 2928
Emmerick, R. E. 2476f.
Emons, R. 269
Enard, J.-P. 25, 27
Enckell, P. 1185, 1187
Ende, C. van den 3036f., 3039
Endepols, H. J.E. 2019
Enders, H.W. 576
Endicott, J.G. 509, 517, 902, 905, 1305, 1311
Endler, D. 2307
Endres, E. 2220
Endriß, A. 1571f.
Endt, E. 1187
Endzelins, J. 2350, 2355, 2357-2360
Enenkel, A.A. 2972, 2974, 2988, 2990, 3013, 3016

Engbraut-Heider, E. 3046
Ėngel'gardt, A. N. 3077
Engel, E. 1173f., 1176, 2220
Engel, G. 3059, 3061, 3166
Engel, U. 114, 123, 796, 1002-1007, 1009, 1017, 1622, 2130, 2171, 2188, 2220, 2234, 2754, 2770, 2774
Engel, V. 789f.
Engelen, B. 180, 882f., 887, 1006, 1009
Engelhus, D. 2039f., 2047
Engelkamp, J. 573, 577, 716, 724, 3166
Engelmann, G. 78, 2755
Engelmann, W.H. 1329, 1332, 1747, 1758
Engels, L.K. 1320
Engelstoft, L. 2035
Engen, P. 3129, 3131
Engeroff, K. 1029, 1038f.
Enggink, H. 2567
Engler, R. 855, 893, 1429
Engström, E. 3045
Engwall, G. 1563, 1566
Enria, U. 1305, 1308, 1309
Enrile, J. M. 2918, 2928
Entick, J. 509
Enzensberger, H. M. 1142, 2230
Eöllis 3173
Epkema, E. 2025, 2033
Epstein, B. 1650, 1666
Eraslan, K. 2413
Erasmus von Rotterdam, D. 1036, 1039, 1726, 3021
Erb, T. 158, 1252f.
Erbe, K. 2092, 2095
Erben, J. 195, 197, 206f., 796, 802
Erben, K. J. 2280, 2283
Erberg, M. von 3014, 3017
Erbse, H. 1697, 1703f.
Erdélyi, I. 2396-2398
Erdélyi, J. 2377, 2381
Erdmann, E. 1362, 2230
Erevantsi, O. 2368
Erichsen, W. 1680f.
Eringa, F. S. 2566f.
Erize, E. 2708f.
Erk, H. 768f., 771, 1146-1149, 1151, 1620, 1622, 1643, 1668, 2220
Erlitz, W. 2064, 2068
Erman, A. 1141, 1681, 1683
Erman, G. A. 2629, 2631
Ermann, H. 1048
Ermanyte, I. 1290
Ernaud, M. 3144
Ernault, E. 2347f., 2350
Ernesti, J. A. 3032
Ernesti, J.Chr.G. 1068, 1072
Ernolv, C. 2885, 3048, 3050
Ernout, A. 1146, 1151, 1324, 1326, 1332, 1334, 1837, 1839

Ernst, G. 1322
Ernst, R. 1510f., 3026f.
Es'ad, M. 2400, 2405
Esar, E. 1044, 1048, 1351
Eschbach, A. 577
Esche, A. 2552-2554
Escher, A. 3016f.
Eschmann, J. 3006
Escobar Risco, G. 2682f.
Escobar Zambrano, A. 2705
Escobar, C. de 2911f., 2914, 2928
Escobar, L.C. de 1740, 1758, 1849, 2683 (s. Scobar)
Escobar, W. 1758
Escrig, J. 1773, 1782
Eseverri Hualde, C. 1758
Esnault, G. 1185, 1187, 1529, 1534-1536, 1827
Espe, H. 709, 724
Espergaard, A. 1919, 1921
Espersen, J.C.S. 1918, 1921
Espinosa, F. 1740, 1758
Esquerra, R. 1765
Esselin, A. 3122, 3131, 3136
Essen, O. von 2651, 2655
Essler, W.K. 539, 543, 576f.
Estapé, F. 1522
Ester, H. 2048
Esteve, J. 1051f., 1771, 1773, 1783, 2917, 2928
Estêves Sobrinho, A. 3027
Estêves, A. 3022
Estienne, H. 13, 16, 1563, 1698, 1794, 2960 (s. Stephanus)
Estienne, R. 9, 16, 48, 61f., 139, 144, 146, 151, 501, 1101f., 1715, 1739, 1791-1793, 1795, 1805f., 1810-1812, 1817f., 1845, 2045, 2864, 2928, 2932, 2977, 2998, 3008, 3035 (s. Stephanus)
Estler, H. 2762
Estorch, P. 1774, 1783
Estrada, A. 2664, 2667
Estreicher, St. 2272
Estrela, E. 1215
Etcheverri, J. de 1742, 1758, 2917, 2928
Etienne, R. 2910, 2912
Ettinger, S. 126, 274, 584, 648, 881, 997, 1031
Ettinger, St. 1017, 2755f., 2768, 2824, 2936, 3023, 3025, 3030
Ettmüller, E.M.L. 1442, 1454
Etz, A. 2223
Eurén, G.E. 2384, 2387
Europaeus, D.E.D. 2384, 2387
Evans, B. 1047f., 1215
Evans, C. 1215, 2350
Evans, H. 2886
Evans, H.M. 2347, 2349
Evans, I.H. 1055

Evans, N. 2639-2641
Evans-Prichard 2643
Eveleth, F. H. 2554
Even-Shosham, A. 2428, 2430, 2433f., 2436
Evens, M.W. 579, 1671, 3166
Evensen, A.C. 1930, 1932
Evgen'eva, A.P. 661, 764f., 1069, 1072, 2317, 2323, 2326
Evolceanu, D. 1885
Evrard, É. 1137, 1139
Evremova, T.F. 2324
Ewald, H. von 2467
Ewald, P. 1303
Ewart, N. 1054f.
Ey, L. 3023, 3027
Eyama, T, 3129, 3131
Eyering, E. 2065, 2068
Eyes Cody, I. 1118f.
Eymery, A. 1072
Eyüboğlu, E.K. 2404f.
Ezawa, K. 517, 2755

F

Fabbri, M. 1047, 1050, 1765, 1787, 2927, 2936f., 2947, 2956, 2982, 2986, 2991, 2994, 2997, 3171
Fábchich, J. 2376, 2381
Faber, B. 3030f., 3033, 3074
Faber, K.-G. 2101, 2234
Fabian, B. 1814, 2969, 3007
Fábián, P. 2381
Fábián, Z. 2755
Fabra, P. 69, 511, 516, 761, 766, 1775-1777, 1779, 1783, 1787
Fabras, P. 64
Fabre, A. 1798, 1800, 1812
Fabre, F. 1758
Fabre, J.-C. 1801
Fabre, P. 1774
Fàbregas, E. 1777, 1783
Fabri, J.A. 3171
Fabricius, J.P. 2523, 2532
Fabricius, O. 2633
Fabritius, H. 1121, 1124
Fabula, K. 2755
Facciolati, J. 1221, 1716, 1720
Faeries, R. 2692, 2696
Faggin, G. 1901, 1904
Fagiuoli, G.B. 149
Fagnan, E. 3088, 3095
Fagniez, G. 1249, 1253
Fahning, W. 2234
Fähnrich, H. 1340
Fahrenkrüger 2967
Faidit, H. 1125, 1127, 1129
Fain, L.-F. 2957, 2959
Faine, J. 2871, 2875
Fairbanks, G. 2533

Faitelson-Weiser, S. 1139
Fakhrī, Sams-i 2477
Falbi, L. 2942, 2945
Falc'hun, F. 2348
Falconnet, G. 87
Falgueras, A. 1783
Falk, A. 1644
Falk, H. 1337, 1340, 1342, 1393, 1414
Falkenhahn, V. 3066, 3068
Falletti, F. 2917, 2928
Fallon, S. W. 2512, 2519
Fallone, E.-M. 1136-1138
Fallows, S. 641, 1078
Fanfani Bussolini, G. 1861
Fanfani, G. 1854
Fanfani, P. 1072, 1085, 1090f., 1216, 1308f., 1851, 1861, 1866f., 1878f., 2997
Fantapié, A. 1164, 1176
Fantom, I.D. 1670
Farell, J. 1778, 1783
Farfán, J. M. B. 2686, 2689
Fargher, D.C. 2346, 2349
Faria, E. de 1728, 1734
Farīd, M.K. 3092, 3095
Farina, D.M.T.G. 280, 409, 462, 587, 1645, 2246
Farina, L. 1902
Farizov, I. O. 2483, 2485
Farkas, D. 725, 1982
Farkas, J.G. 1193
Farmer, J. St. 1186-1188, 2920, 2928
Farrell, R. B. 767, 771, 2181, 2182, 2220
Farrell, R.A. 1196, 1199
Farrer, L.E. 2956, 2960
Faruqi, H.S. 3093, 3095
Fasmer, M. (Vasmer) 2325
Fass, D. 3166
Faßke, H. 2275, 2278
Father Beschi 2523, 2531
Father Drummond 2511, 2518
Fatio, J.-B. 1796
Fauconnier, A. 1569f., 1572
Fauconnier, G. 1569f., 1572
Faulkner, R.O. 1680f.
Faulmann, C. 3150, 3156
Faulmann, K. 2089, 2095
Faust, M. 648, 715, 725, 1290
Favén, H. 3135
Favre, P. E. 2565
Favre, L. 1308f., 1720
Favre, P. E. 2563
Fay, E.A. 1874
Faydel, G. 1800
Fázsy, S. 2412
Febrés, A. 2709
Fecia, A. 1084, 1091
Feddersen, F. 2029
Feder, K. 3129-3131

Federhart, P. 1671
Federspiel, G. 1078
Fedorov, A.V. 1552, 1561, 2755
Fédry, J. 2458, 2460
Feeling, D. 2692, 2696
Feerštejn, E. N. 3022, 3029
Feijóo, B.G. 1742, 1758
Feilberg, H.F. 1919, 1921
Feiling, C.A. 2968
Feist, S. 1329, 1332, 1908, 1910-1912
Feitsma, A. 2026
Feitsma, S. K. 2026
Feixó Cid, X.G. 1737
Felber, H. 119, 124, 317, 321, 460, 585, 1660, 1666, 2206, 2234, 2921, 3172
Feldman, D. 1245
Feldman, J. 87, 1196, 1199
Feldmann, A. 213
Feldmann, J. 1195
Fel'dmann, N. J. 2755
Félibien, A. 1817
Felice, E. de 687, 922, 924, 928, 992, 995f.
Felici, L. 647
Felicyna, V.P. 2323
Féline, A. 1306, 1308f., 1821
Felipe II 2681
Feller, F. E. 3016f.
Femmis, J. 1801
Fenby, Th. 1072
Fendel, G. 2828
Feneis, H. 1110
Fénelon, F. de Salignac de la Mothe 25, 27, 1800, 1812
Feneyrol, Ch. 269
Fenice, G. A. 3008f., 3011, 3013
Fenice, J.A. 1845, 1859, 2970, 2974
Fenne, T. 3070, 3085
Fennell, Ch.A.M. 1176
Fennis, J. 1812
Fenske, H. 652, 654, 667, 2130, 2192, 2234
Fenzl, R. 1350
Feoktistov, A.P. 2396, 2398
Féraud, F. 654
Féraud, J.-F. 11, 16, 501, 607, 1004, 1007, 1009, 1056, 1074, 1131, 1208, 1212, 1216, 1218-1220, 1803-1806, 1810-1812, 1814-1817
Ferdinand III (Kaiser) 2987
Ferdinando III. (Großherzog der Toskana) 1856
Ferdinandy, M. de 1193
Fergar, F.E. 1129
Ferguson, J. 1351, 2512, 2519
Ferguson, R. 1284f., 1291
Fergusson, R. 1037, 1039, 1126f., 1129

Ferişteoğlu, A. 2399, 2405
Ferm, R. G. E. 3048f.
Fernald, J.C. 1072
Fernandes Valdez, J. 3022, 3027
Fernandes, F. 1005, 1007, 1078
Fernandes, T. 1738
Fernández Armesto, F. 1737
Fernández Castro Andrade, P. 1751
Fernandez Cosgaya, L. 2571, 2573
Fernández Cuesta, N. 996, 1746, 1758, 2980, 2983
Fernández de Oviedo y Valdés, G. 1751, 1758
Fernández del Riego, F. 1737
Fernández Ferraz, J. 1752, 1758
Fernández Gómez, C. 1758
Fernández Ramírez, S. 1750
Fernández Sevilla, J. 989, 997, 1738, 1750, 1765, 2986
Fernández y Fernández, M. 1755
Fernandez, F. 2543, 2547
Fernández, F. 2952, 2954
Fernández, J. 2664, 2667
Fernández, M. 2928
Ferraguto, P. 2400, 2405
Ferrall, J. S. 3055, 3060
Ferran i Serafini, J. 1777, 1786
Ferrante, V. 3010f.
Ferrar, N. 2959
Ferrari, C. 3009-3011
Ferrari, G. 3167
Ferrario, O. 3011
Ferreccio Podesta, M. 1754, 1758
Ferreira dos Santos Azevedo, F. 1091
Ferreira, A. 641
Ferreira, A. Buarque de Hollanda 1732, 1734f.
Ferreira, F. 1089
Ferreiro, M. 2931
Ferrer del Río, A. 1743, 1765
Ferrer i Pastor, F. J. 1776, 1778, 1783
Ferrer y Parpal, J. 1774, 1783
Ferrer, M. 1773, 1783
Ferrero, E. 1534, 1536, 1868
Ferretti, L. 1845f., 1859, 1861, 3009, 3011
Ferromontano 3017
Ferrus, S. 2980, 2982f.
Festus, S.P. 1714, 1720
Fetus, G.H. 2578, 2582
Feuchtwanger, L. 2131
Feutry, A.A.J. 3140f.
Feydel, G. 1812
Ficino, M. 1873
Fick, A. 1144f., 1337f., 1340, 1342
Fick, H. 2968
Fick, J.Chr. 2968
Fiedler, W. 747, 2365
Field, J. 1281f.

Fiellström, P. 2389, 2391
Fiennes, J.B. de 2400, 2405
Fifshits, Y. M. 2254
Figge, U. L. 2755
Figueiredo, C. de 1729, 1734
Figuera, A. 1774, 1783
Figueras, E. 1777, 1783
Figulus, S. 1011, 1014
Filaretov 3078
Filgueira Valverde, J. 1736, 1738
Filičeva, N.I. 746, 1622
Filin, F.P. 2311, 2314f., 2318f., 2321, 2323, 2326f.
Filip, J. 3132
Filip, J. und K. 3126f.
Filip, K. 3132
Filipec, J. 78, 190, 206, 252, 274, 621, 626, 844, 848, 2281-2284, 2755
Filipova-Bajrova, M. 2755
Filipović, R. 1165, 1179, 1183, 2292, 2294
Filippov, A.V. 2315, 2324
Fillauer, W. 2230
Fillmore, Ch.J. 557, 573, 616, 626, 714, 725, 893f., 899, 1624, 1976, 1982
Finály, H. 1072
Fincati, L. 2938, 2945
Finck, F.N. 2344, 2348
Findler, N.V. 1664, 1666, 1670
Findley, C.V. 2402, 2407
Findreng, Å. 585, 628, 822, 2244
Fineman, H. 3126f., 3132
Finifter, G. 679, 1367
Fink, G. 1361
Finka, B. 2293
Finkenstaedt, Th. 768, 770f., 1343f., 1347
Finkielkraut, A. 1349-1351
Finzi, G. 1046, 1048
Fiorelli, P. 1305, 1310, 1872, 1878, 1880
Fioretti, B. 1130
Fircks, B. von 3171
Firth, J.R. 299, 889, 892, 1012, 1017f.
Fischer, A. 2445, 3088
Fischer, H. 1157f., 1239, 1609
Fischer, J.E. 2408
Fischer, J.L. 242
Fischer, K.G. 1074, 2058
Fischer, M.W. 883, 887
Fischer, P. 1235, 1238, 1550, 1557, 1559
Fischer, R. 1280-1282, 3140f.
Fischer, R.E. 1281f.
Fischer, W. 1052, 1361, 2885, 2890, 2895, 2900
Fischer, W.-D. 2766
Fisher, D. 1103, 1105, 1109f.
Fisher, R. J. 2027, 2033

Fishman, D. E. 2250, 2254
Fishman, J. A. 2246f., 2254
Fissi, A. 1872
Fitz-Gerald, A. 1049
Fitzmyer, J.A. 2437
Fix, H. 1573, 2887
Fîrûzâbâdî, M.b.Y. 2399, 2405
Flachskampf, L. 1115, 1119
Flacius, M. 1154f., 1158, 2296
Flaherty, M.C. 208, 213
Flajšhans, V. 2278f., 2283
Flammarion, C. 1839
Flammer, W. 3128, 3132
Flandin, M. 1189
Flasche, H. 1771, 1787
Flashar, H. 276
Flathe, Ph. J. 3004, 3015, 3017
Flaubert, G. 21, 26f., 290, 296, 1349, 1351, 2197, 2220
Flavell, L.M. 1217
Flavell, R.H. 1217
Flämig, W. 887, 2828
Fleck, K.E.W. 143, 145, 2942, 2945
Fleckenstein, Chr. 1053, 2881
Flegon, A. 2323
Fleischer, H. 1051f.
Fleischer, U. 1704
Fleischer, W. 274, 596-599, 830f., 834, 837, 841, 1031, 1205, 1671, 2051, 2074, 2237
Fleischner, J.M. 1270-1272
Fleming, Ch. 2795f., 2957, 2959
Fleming, D. 1532, 1537
Fleming, H. C. 2461, 2464, 2467, 2643, 2645
Fleming, L.A. 1078
Fleming, M.L. 709, 725
Flemming, P. 2071
Fletcher, P. 1645
Fletcher, P.J. 1073
Fleury, J. 83, 87, 990, 997, 1824f., 1841
Fleury, P. 3138, 3140f.
Flevriot, L. 2341, 2348, 2350
Flexner, St.B. 36f., 515, 1186, 1189, 1530, 2004, 2008
Flick, S. 3007
Flierl, W. 2636f.
Flines, Q. de 2939, 2945
Flodin, J.J. 1129
Flood, W.E. 901, 904
Floor, H. 2534, 2542, 2546
Flores Varela, C.D. 2980, 2986
Florescu, St. 1098
Flórez, L. 1753, 1758
Florian, U. 1029
Floriato, M. 1741, 1758, 2915, 2928
Florinus, H. 2384, 2387, 2914, 2928
Florio, G. 2975f.

Florio, J. 1162, 1845f., 1849, 1859f., 2970-2976, 3009
Flórez, L. 2925
Fluck, H.-R. 321, 682, 687, 1660, 1666
Fluegel, G. 2448
Flutre, L.-F. 1293, 1295
Fluvià, A. de 1778, 1783
Flügel, E. 1436, 1446-1450, 1454
Flügel, F. 2968
Flügel, J.G. 2968
Flydal, L. 680, 1311
Fodor, I. 62, 2469
Foerste, W. 239, 244
Foerster, W. 1326, 1332, 1551, 1559
Fogarasi, J. 2381
Fogel, E. 1035, 1040
Fohrer, G. 2428, 2434
Fokkema, D. 2027, 2033
Fokos-Fuchs, D.R. 2395-2397
Folch y Capdevila, R. 1778, 1783
Folena, G. 1092, 1333, 1844, 1851, 1861, 1866, 1870, 1879f., 2836, 3012, 3015, 3019
Foley, D. 2346, 2348
Follett, W. 35, 37, 1216
Follmann, M. F. 1233, 1238, 2215, 2220
Folomkina, S. K. 2896, 2900
Folqman, C. 3022, 3027
Folz, J. 272, 405, 574, 1622, 2219
Fonfrías, E.J. 1758
Fonseca, J. da 1073, 3022, 3028
Fonseca, J. de 2980, 2983
Fonseca, M.A. da 1735
Fonseca, P.J. da 1727
Font, A. 1772, 1783
Font, M.T. 1758
Fontaine, C.-F.-J. 1302f.
Fontane, Th. 858, 2131
Fontanillo Merino, E. 8, 16, 143, 1755f., 1783, 2919, 2928
Fontecha, C. 1157f., 1758
Fonteneau, M. 1367
Fontseré Iriba, E. 1778, 1783
Fonvizin, D.I. 2317, 2323
Foot, E. C. 2463, 2465
Forbath, G.N. 2954
Forbes, D. 2686, 2690
Forcellini, A. 1715-1717, 1720
Forcellini, E. 151, 1716, 3032
Forestier, J.-E.-J., s. Boinvilliers
Forgays, D.G. 140, 145
Forgue, G.J. 934, 937
Formigari, L. 1090, 1093
Fornander, A. 1338, 1340
Fornari, P. 1084f., 1091
Fornas Prat, J. 1776, 1783
Forner, J.P. 1742, 1765
Forni, A. 3174
Forni, J. 604

Forssman, B. 1342
Förstemann, E. 1268, 1271f., 1280, 1238f., 1291, 2215, 2220
Forster, K. 1275, 1281, 1283, 1293, 1295, 1308f.
Förster, K. 3140f.
Forster, L. 2759
Förster, W. 2776
Forstinger, J. 2377, 2381
Forstner, D. 3152f., 3156
Fort, M. C. 2028, 2033
Fortia de Piles, A.T.J.A.M.M. de 1806
Foscolo Sguazzini, U. 1052
Foscolo, U. 148
Fossum, L. O. 2483, 2486
Foster, B. 1165
Foster, J. 1451, 1454, 1550, 1552, 1559
Foth, A. 1036, 1042
Foucauld, Ch. de 2, 16, 2456f.
Fouché, P. 513, 517, 1306
Fougeroux 2945
Foulché-Delbosc, R. 1762
Fournier, E. 1046, 1048
Fournier, E.E. 2345f., 2348
Fournier, M.-A. 1272
Fournier, N. 652, 654, 1812
Fourré, P. 1835, 1840
Fowler, F.G. 405, 524, 753, 928, 1622, 1964f., 3116
Fowler, H.W. 405, 524, 687, 753, 821, 928f., 1216, 1622, 1964f., 3116
Fox, E.A. 3166
Fox, J. 2667
Fox, M.S. 187f.
Fozilov, M. 2480
Fradin, B. 577
Fraenkel, E. 2359
Frajzyngier, Z. 2457, 2460
France, A. 24
France, H. 1188
Franceson, C.F. 2988, 2990
Franciosini, L. 1088, 1091, 1848, 1859, 2978, 2993, 2996
Francis, W.N. 1320f., 1643
Francisco, A.C.J. 3100, 3104
Franciscus Xavier, St. 3113
Francisque-Michel, X. 1534, 1537
Franck, J. 2018, 2020
Franck, S. 1034, 1040, 1043, 2215, 2220
Franco Bahamonde, F. 1770, 1774
Franco García, G.E. 1758
Franco Grande, X.L. 1737
Franco Inojosa, M. 2686, 2689f.
Franco, C. 1188
Franco, F. 1776
François, A. 1212, 1217, 1798, 1800, 1804, 1812

François, D.J. 1157f., 1456
François, J. 784, 786, 1372, 1378, 2755f.
François, P. 1663, 1666
François, 1er 48
Frank 3129
Frank, B. 24f., 27
Frank, H. J. 2090, 2099
Frank, R. 1445f., 1456
Frank, Th. 1089f., 1093
Franke, D. 2027, 2033
Franke, L. 1357, 1363
Franke, R. O. 2498, 2506
Franke, Th. 2092, 2095
Franke, W. 2756, 3109, 3113
Frankena, W.K. 196, 206
Franklin, A. 1251f.
Franklin, B. 1987
Franklin, J. 2636f.
Franklin, K. 2636f.
Franklyn, J. 1127, 1129, 1186, 1188, 1293, 1295
Franolić, B. 2289, 2295, 3171
Franquesa, M. 1777, 1783
Franquin, A. 40
Frantz, D.O. 2970, 2975
Franz, G. 1245
Franz, S.K. 580
Fraporta, I. G. di 3017
Frappat, B. 44f., 1044
Fraschery, Ch.S.-B. 2402f., 2405
Fraser, D. 1047f.
Fraser, J. O. 2559
Fraser, P.M. 1699, 1703
Fratzke, U. 1235f., 1240, 1397, 1415, 2220
Frauenstädt, J. 1058, 1065
Frawley, W. 33, 78, 551, 577, 2009, 3166
Freddi, G. 1362
Freeman, H.G. 171, 173
Freeman, J.W. 1293, 1295
Freeman, W. 1029, 1189
Freese, A. G. F. 3044f.
Frege, G. 541, 2134, 2150
Frei, H. 1052
Freidhof, G. 274, 2321, 2327
Freie, M. 1293
Freigang, K.-H. 1669
Freij, W. 2359
Freiligrath, F. 2131
Freind, J.H. 1988
Freire, F.J. 1129
Freire, L. 1732, 1734
Freitag, R. 1200, 1205
Freixedo Tabarés, X.M. 1737
Frencel, A. 2275-2277
French Allen, V. 209, 213
French, N.R. 1320
French, W. T. 2559
Frenzel, E. 2106, 2111, 2112, 2125, 2168, 2227

Frenzel, H. 1029, 1052, 3018
Frenzel, H. A. 2106, 2111, 2112, 2125, 2168, 2227
Frenzel, I. 583
Frenzel, M. 748, 2715, 2725f., 2754, 2776, 2778
Frenzel, W. 3018
Fresne, Ch. du 1705, 1712
Freu, J.-B. 1311, 1314
Freud, S. 848
Freudenstein, R. 2222
Freudenthal, F. 3048-3050
Freund, F. 1217
Freund, W. 3032-3034
Frey, Chr. 2174, 2221
Frey, E. 2726
Frey, P. 3127, 3132
Frey, U.H. 1044, 1048, 1054f.
Freyer, H. 2099
Freytag, G.W. 2445-2447
Freytag, G.W.F. 3087, 3090, 3095
Freytag, K. 1175f.
Frémont d'Ablancourt, N. 1125, 1127, 1129
Friebertshäuser, H. 79, 126, 239, 242-246, 269, 461, 581, 586, 657, 1066, 1416, 1639, 1644, 2036, 2061, 2074, 2198-2201, 2221, 2235, 2243, 2245
Fried, J. 1078
Friedemann, F.T. 1016
Friederich, G. 2990
Friederich, W. 1005, 1008, 1011, 1014, 1021, 1025f., 1028f., 1036, 1040, 1360f., 1972, 2174-2176, 2221, 2879f., 2890, 2900
Friederici, G. 1752, 1755, 1758, 2989
Friedländer, H. 1079, 1938
Friedrich, A. 1059, 1066, 2038, 2047, 2229
Friedrich, H. 2230
Friedrich, J. 407, 1688f., 1692-1694, 2437
Friedrichsen, G.W.S. 929, 1333
Friend, J.H. 101, 1987, 1989, 2008f.
Fries, Ch.C. 1453, 1456, 1999
Fries, N. 780, 786
Fries, N.M. 1456
Fries, P.H. 1456
Friis, J.A. 2389-2391
Frînculescu, O. 1005, 1008
Frings, Th. 1334, 1428, 1548, 2132, 2170, 2215
Frisch, J.L. 233-236, 242, 244, 800, 803, 995f., 2053f., 2068, 2074, 2076, 2090, 2099f., 2999, 3004, 3040, 3042
Frisch, L. 243
Frisch, M. 26f., 2131

Frischbier, H. 1035, 1040, 2215, 2221
Frischlin, N. 2928
Frishberg, N. 3143f.
Frisius, J. 1791, 2045, 2047, 2912, 2928f., 2998, 3004, 3031, 3033
Frisk, H. 1326, 1332
Frisoni, G. 1776, 1783, 2994-2996
Friswell, J.H. 1046, 1048
Fritsche Closener 2038
Fritzner, J. 1925, 1927, 1929, 1931
Fritzsche, P. 2225
Frizzi, G. 1072, 1085, 1090f.
Frobisher, M. 2631, 2633
Frohn, K. W. 2234
Fröhler, H. 251, 274, 2191, 2235
Fröhlich, E. 2111, 2155, 2167, 2169, 2221
Frölen, R. 1261, 1264
Frollo, G.L. 1884
Fromaigeat, E. 1052
Fromm, W.-D. 1668
Frommann, G. K. 243, 1239, 1290, 1414, 2072
Fronto, C. 1067, 1072
Fronzaroli, P. 305, 1342, 1693, 2433
Froschauer, Chr. 2043, 2045
Frösell, E. 2180, 2221
Frost, C. 2226
Frumkina, R.M. 1317, 1322, 1671
Fu Maoji 2559
Fu, H. 3113
Fucci, F. 1207f.
Fuchs, C. 1068, 1075
Fuchs, H. 1142
Fuchs, J.W. 1721
Fuchs, O. 634
Fuchs, P. I. 1234, 1238, 2090, 2095
Fuchs, R. 2062, 2069
Fuchs, V. 2756
Fucilla, J.G. 2954
Fück, J. 3086f., 3096
Fuentes Estañol, M.-J. 1690, 1693
Fujibayashi, T. 3114, 3116
Fujii, S. 3116, 3118
Fujioka, K. 3115f.
Fukuoka, E. 3116
Fulcher, F. 3126, 3132
Fulcilla, J.G. 2952
Fulda, F.C. 237f., 242, 1394, 1414, 2060, 2069, 2076, 2088, 2095, 2215, 2221
Fulda, F.K. 1912
Fulda, M. 2066
Fullana Llompart, M. 1777f., 1783
Fullana Mira, L. 1783
Fullat, O. 1778, 1783
Fuller, E. 1046, 1048, 1054f.
Fuller, G.H. 3176
Fumagalli, G. 1046, 1048, 1877f.

Fumel, Y. 2753
Funk and Wagnalls 2919, 2929
Funk, Ch.E. 1029, 1993, 2007
Funk, H. E. 2871, 2875
Funk, I.K. 1992-1994, 1997f., 2000, 2007
Funke, H. G. 2727, 2764
Fürecker, C. 2355
Furetière, A. 10f., 16, 39f., 43, 45, 143f., 216f., 222f., 312, 525, 528f., 688, 994 996, 1206, 1208, 1743, 1795-1798, 1800-1802, 1806, 1810-1812, 1814-1818, 1838, 2957, 2999
Fùrnari, M. 1534, 1536
Furnivall, F.J. 1446, 1448, 1961f.
Fürst, J. 2428, 2434, 2712, 2726
Fürstenberg, F. von 1796
Furuya, A. 305
Fusanoshin, A. 2614
Fusella, L. 2451, 2453
Fusius, A. 1081f.
Fustier, G. 1187
Fynning, A. 1183

G

Gabain, A. V. 2413
Gabamadjian, S. 2369, 2371
Gabaraev, N. J. 2484f.
Gabelentz, H.C. von der 1909-1911
Gabelsberger, F. X. 3140f.
Gabelsberger-Noe 3140
Gabinski, M. 1888f.
Gabka, K. 1672
Gabler, A. 1191f., 1297, 1304
Gabler, E. 2939, 2945
Gabler Th. 164, 166
Gablingen, J. von 2048
Gabriel, G. 539, 541-543, 547, 577, 581
Gabrielli, A. 1078, 1098, 1216, 1220-1222, 1312, 1314, 1877f.
Gabrielson, A. 3048, 3050, 3172
Gadamer, H.-G. 724
Gâdei, C. 1312-1314, 1889
Gadet, F. 1219
Gadola, G. 1896, 1905
Gadžiev, M.M. 2422f.
Gaffiot, F. 718, 723, 990, 997
Gagini, C. 1752f., 1758
Gagnon, G. 65, 69, 1163, 1168, 1177, 1837, 1841
Gaidoz, H. 1257
Gaiger, J. A. 2297
Gailer, J.E. 1367
Gailums, K. 1142
Gainey, J.W. 2593
Gak, V. G. 1672, 2314, 2321, 2327, 2715, 2717, 2726, 2756, 2832, 2836, 2900

Gălăbov, K. 1021, 1030, 2307
Galand, L. 2457
Galante, H. 2683
Galanus, C. 2368
Gáldi, L. 1560, 1882, 1889f., 2377, 2380f., 2383
Gale, J. S. 2615f.
Galeano L., L. G. 2705
Ġālī, W.R. 3171
Galilei, G. 1873
Galinsky, H. 1165
Galisson, R. 104, 106, 108, 110, 131, 134, 213, 1012, 1014, 1019, 1029, 1348-1352, 1389, 1637
Galland, A. 2400, 2405
Gallardo, A. 78
Gallée, J.H. 1418-1421, 1426, 1428
Galler, M. 2323
Gallet, F. 1302f.
Galletti Di Cadilhac, A. 2527, 2532
Galli de 'Paratesi, N. 1194, 1199
Gallina, A. 1088, 1090, 1093, 1765, 1845, 1847-1850, 1861, 2756, 2911f., 2914-2916, 2932f., 2935f., 2978, 2986, 2993, 2996f., 3007f., 3012
Gallina, F. 2451, 2453
Galling, K. 167
Gallisson, R. 1387
Gallmann, P. 374f., 385, 407, 428, 459
Gallo, C. 1758
Gallois, L. 1046, 1048
Galmiche, M. 1219
Galon, 2938, 2945
Galpinozzi, C. 3011
Galtier, Ch. 1269, 1272
Galtier-Boissière, J. 1188
Galtung 193
Gambarellius, A. 1081f.
Gamberini, Sp. 2970, 2975
Gamble, W. 1319f.
Gamboa, S.F. de 1741, 1758
Gamillscheg, E. 1324f., 1327, 1332, 1827, 1840, 1889, 2960
Ganander, Chr. 2384, 2387
Gaṇapawarupuwēnukaṭakawi 2525, 2531
Gandhi, M. K. 2511
Gāndzaketsi, K. 2368
Gāngala, D.D. 3101, 3104
Gangopadhyaya, V. 2509, 2518
Gangutia Elicegui, E. 1702, 1704
Gani, K. 2511
Ganivet, A. 1768
Gann, Th. 2663, 2667
Gans, R. de 1273
Ganschow, G. 2398
Gantzel, A. 2032, 2034

Ganz, P. 1169, 1176, 1402, 1415
Ganz, P.F. 1066
Gao Huanian 2559
Gaon, Saadia 2441, 2447
Gär, J. 3130, 3132
Garbe, B. 2220
Garbe, H. 2199, 2221
Garbell, I. 2437
Garcia Bellsola, D. 1129
García de Cabañas, M.J. 1758
García de Diego, V. 1247, 1330, 1332, 1759
García de León, A. 2659, 2661, 2698f.
García de Palacio(s), D. 1740, 1759
García Hidalgo, M.I. 1754, 1766
García Hoz, V. 357, 405, 1759
García Icazbalceta, I. 1752
García Larragueta, S. 1738, 1759
Garcia Llorente, M. 2980, 2984
Garcia Morente, M. 2980, 2985
García Navarro, A.M. 2980, 2983
García Oliveros, A. 1129
García Riera, G. 2702
García Serrano, J. 1759
Garcia, A. 2664, 2667, 2955, 2996
Garcia, B.M. 2954
Garcia, C. 1737, 2699
García, F. 1759
García, H. de 1733
García, J.L. de Tomas 1758
García-Lomas, G.A. 1759
García-Pelayo y Gross, R. 923, 928, 1748, 1759, 1761, 2980, 2983
García-Pelayo, F. 2955
García-Pelayo, R. 2953
García-Rey, V. 1759
Garcin de Tassy, J.H. 3101, 3104
Gard, R.M. du 26
Garde, G. A. van de 2782
Gardin-Dumesnil, J.B. 1068, 1072
Gardiner, A.H. 1680f.
Gardos, I. 1033, 1042
Garin, E. 1873
Garner, J. 2957, 2959
Garon, F. 2911, 2929
Garonus [= Garon], F. 2910
Garscha, K. 28
Garside, R. 1670, 2805, 2813
Gärtner, K. 119, 124, 153, 158, 1134, 1136, 1143, 1567, 1572f., 2066, 2074, 2104, 2235
Gärtner, L. 2276f.
Gartner, Th. 1895f., 1905
Garvin, P.L. 1670
Gary, J.-M. 1800, 1812
Garzanti 2994
Garzón, T. 1753, 1759
Garzoni, M. 2483, 2486
Garzoni, T. 1251f., 2970, 2975

Gasanova, S.M. 1340
Gasca Queirazza, G. 1851, 1861
Gašparíková, Ž. 2282f.
Gasparini, A. 2464f.
Gassen, K. 3170
Gate, W.A. 3122, 3132
Gatenby, E.V. 524, 589, 591, 746, 2900
Gates, J.E. 33, 95-97, 106f., 110, 251, 274, 1816, 1988, 2003, 2009
Gates, N. 2667
Gates, W. 2663
Gätje, H. 3088, 3096
Gattel, C.-M. 221, 223, 506, 766, 1802, 1805f., 1808f., 2952, 2979f., 2983, 2985
Gattell, C.M. 2955
Gatti, M. 2996
Gatuszka, J. 3063, 3067
Gatzlaff, M. 2756
Gaudemar, A. de 43, 45
Gaudin, J. 1795
Gaudin, R. P. 2929
Gaudray, F. 1029
Gauger, H.-M. 616, 626, 881, 1066, 1068f., 1075, 1230, 2752, 2887
Ğauharî, Abû Naṣr Ismâ'îl
Gaukin, E. 2451, 2453
Gause, J.T. 1072, 1096, 1099
Gauthier de Tournay 1816
Gauthier, H. 1680f.
Gautier, Th. 25, 147
Gauvenet, H. 1223
Gavare, R. 1938
Gavrilov, M. G. 3073, 3083
Ğawaliki = Mauhūb b. Aḥmad al-Jawālīqī 2447
Gay, P. 1247
Gayayan, H. 2369
Gayed, R. 3092, 3095
Gaymann, P. 273, 2228
Gazdar, G. 3166
Gazier, A. 1825, 1840
Gazier, A.L. 1079
Gàzulli, N. 2363, 2366
Gburek, H. 269
Geary, J. A. 2691, 2696
Gebauer, J. 2281, 2283
Gebert, M. 2756
Gebhardt, K. 1344, 1347
Geck, E. 1112
Geckeler, H. ,581f., 629,633f.,648, 780, 786f., 881, 1090, 1093, 1230
Gedney, W. 2726
Gee, R.D. 1661, 1668
Geel, J. van 2647
Geens, D. 1318, 1320
Geeraerts, D. 288, 292, 296, 562, 573, 577, 765f., 980f., 988,
1316, 1322, 1367f., 1978, 1982, 2010-2012, 2014, 2019, 2021, 2756
Geerts, G. 929, 1435, 2020
Geffroy, A. 1054, 1056, 1804, 1812
Gégou, F. 1798, 1800, 1812
Gehle, H. 2221
Geiger, Th. 1290
Geiger, W. 2471f., 2484, 2486
Geigern, A. 1017
Geißler, E. 979
Gejm, I. A. 3083
Gelb, I.J. 247, 274, 1683f., 1690, 1693, 2433
Geldner, K. F. 2471f.
Gelenius, S. 2279, 2913, 2929 (s. Zikmund Hrubý)
Gel'gardt, R.R. 2318, 2321, 2327
Gelhaus, H. 1623
Gellert, Chr. F. 2055
Gellert, W. 848
Gelli, J. 1054f.
Gémar, J.-C. 1674, 1678
Gemert, G. van 2048, 2762
Gemmingen, B. von 1219f., 1796, 1804, 1810-1813, 1815, 1817f., 2757, 2977, 2986, 2991, 3019
Gemmingen-Obstfelder, B. von 269, 652, 654, 1743, 1765, 1812
Genadieva, Z. 2307
Gendron, J.-D. 48, 54, 62
Gênes, J. de 1789
Genest, E. 1046, 1048
Genette, G. 1247
Genetz, A. 2390f.
Geng Shimin 2411
Genibrel, J. F. M. 2584, 2588
Génin, F. 2956, 2959
Genius, A. 1173, 1176
Gennep, A. van 1532, 1537
Genouvrier, E. 679, 1069, 1072, 1837, 1840
Genovard Rosselló, C. 1778, 1783
Genthe, A. 1186, 1188, 2059, 2062, 2069
Genthe, F.W. 1072, 2069
Gentile, P. 1865
Geoffroy, E.F. 165
Georg von Nürnberg 1847, 1860, 2048
Georgacas, B. 1713
Georgacas, D.J. 1704, 1710, 1712f.
George, J. 1840
George, K.E.M. 1185, 1188, 1262, 1264
George, St. 2131
Georges, H. 3032f.
Georges, K.E. 151, 369, 1133, 1313f., 1716, 3032-3034
Georgescu, M. 1881, 1888, 1890

Georgiev, L. 2307
Georgiev, V. 2307f.
Georgieva, E. 2308
Georgievich, B. 2293
Georgin, R. 1211f., 1216
Gerard van der Schueren 2041, 2043 (= Gerd)
Géraud, H. 1252
Gerber, A. 1549, 1551, 1559
Gerber, B.L. 1029
Gerd van der Schueren 2042 (= Gerard)
Gerdel, F. L. 2663, 2669, 2706
Gerdes, K. 1632, 1637
Gerhardt, C.J. 1291
Gerhardt, D. 1132-1134, 1136, 1142f.
Gerhardt, L. 1340
Gerhart, E.C. 1047f.
Gericke, B. 835
Gericke, J. F. C. 2561f.
Gerighausen, J. 173f.
Gérin Roze, M. de 2945
Gerlanc, B. 2300
Germa, P. 1054f.
Germa Ṣeyon Mäbrahtu 2451, 2453
Germain, R. 2872, 2875
Gerov, N. 2305-2307, 3078
Gerring, H. 3044, 3045
Gerritsen, J. 1304
Gersbach, B. 1142
Gershuny, H.L. 87
Géruzet, J.B. 2939, 2945
Gervasi, T. 784, 786, 3016, 3019
Gerzymisch-Arbogast, H. 366, 947-949, 955f., 2206, 2235
Gesenius, W. 2428, 2434
Geshe Chödrak 2549f.
Gesner, C. 1715
Gesner, J.M. 1716
Gesner, K. [= Gesnerus, C.] 2915, 3070
Gesner, M. 3033
Gesnerus, C. 2913, 2929
Gessinger, J. 233, 244
Gessmann, G.W. 3150, 3156
Geuljans, R. 3176
Geurtjens, H. 2636f.
Geus, C.H.J. de 2433
Gevorgian, V. 2369
Geyr, H. 1039, 1042
Geysen, R. 1180f., 1183
Gharibian, A. 2369
Gharieb, M. 3095
Ghatage, A. M. 2494f.
Ghazarian, B. 2370
Gheerbrant, A. 3165
Gherardini, G. 1847, 1856, 1859, 1863
Gherman, M.A. 1882
Gheţie, I. 1890

Gheysens, V. 2542, 2546
Ghijsen, H. C. M. 2019f.
Ghinassi, G. 1859
Ghiotti, C. 3009-3011
Gholston, H.D. 1261, 1264
Ghoshal 2517
Ghul, M.A. 1693
Giannecchini, P. D. 2674
Giannesini, M. 43, 45
Giannoli, P.X. 1204
Gibbs, G.C. 2957, 2960
Gibson, H. 1940, 1942
Gide, A. 26, 1213
Gidwani, N. N. 2517, 3100, 3102, 3107
Gierach, E. 1281, 1283
Gigli, G. 1854f., 1859, 1862
Gignoux, Ph. 2473, 2476
Gil, J. 1014
Gilanor, S. M. 2920, 2929
Gilbereti, M. 2697
Gilbers, C. 269
Gilbert, L. 524, 1567, 1573
Gilbert, P. ,606, 653f., 667, 672, 945, 1164, 1676, 1678, 1795, 1798, 1804, 1813, 1837, 1840
Gilberti, M. 2697, 2699
Gilbertson, G. W. 2484f.
Gilchrist, A. 1666
Gilchrist, J. 2512, 2519
Gildo, D. 2980, 2984
Giles, H.A. 3108f., 3112
Gili Gaya, S. 66, 69, 1072, 1738, 1740, 1742f., 1750, 1759, 1764f., 2936, 2982, 2984-2986
Gili, J. 732, 748
Giljarevskij, R.S. 1660, 1667
Gillard de Nujac 1124
Gilles, N. 1794
Gillespie 1293
Gillhoff, G.A. 2953, 2955
Gilliéron, J. 1343
Gillot, H. 2894, 2900
Gilman, S. 1034, 1042
Gilmour-Bryson, A. 1572
Gil'tebrandt, P. A. 2264-2267, 2319, 2323, 2327
Gimbernat, C. de 2991
Gimson, A.C. 357, 405, 511-513, 516f., 692, 753, 785, 1309
Gingold, K. 1263
Gingrich, F.W. 1700, 1702f.
Ginsberg, H.L. 2431
Ginschel, G. 2208, 2220, 2236
Ginzburg, R.S. 247, 274
Ginzburg, R.Z. (= S.) 1651, 1666
Gioan, P. 1832
Gioberti, V. 149
Giorgini, G. 1858f., 1866, 1879
Giovanelli, G. 1126, 1129
Giovanelli, P. 1361, 2895, 2900, 3018

Giovanni Balbi von Genua 9
Gipper, H. 634, 1222f., 1623
Girace, A. 2451, 2453
Giral Delpino, H.S.J. 2955
Giral Delpino, J. 2950
Girard de Propiac, C.-J.-F. 1195, 1198
Girard, B. 2535f., 2545
Girard, D. 2958f.
Girard, G. 1219, 1360, 1388, 1068f., 1071f., 1074f., 1081, 2058
Girard, V. 1340
Girardin, Ch. 80, 85, 87, 653f., 1813
Giraud, J. 946, 1164
Giraud, R. 719, 723, 1100, 1102, 1185, 1188
Giraud, Y. 1189, 1789, 1813
Girault-Duvivier, Ch.-P. 1212, 1217
Girke, W. 2327
Girodet, J. 144, 676, 679, 703, 766, 945, 1214, 1216, 1836, 1840f.
Giry-Schneider, J. 180
Gisbert, M. 2896, 2900
Giuglea, G. 1890
Giusti, G. 1857
Giustiniani, V.R. 1088, 1093, 2041, 2047, 2933, 3005, 3013, 3019
Givanel i Mas, J. 1777, 1783
Gjevori, M. 2363, 2366
Gjini, N. 2365f.
Gjivoje, M. 3125, 3127, 3132
Gjurin, V. 2297, 2301
Glaap, A.-R. 1038, 1042
Gladow, F. 1177, 2072
Glanville, A.D. 142, 145
Glanze, W. D. 2756, 2953
Glare, P. G. W. 2751, 3034
Glas, R. 1642, 1644
Gläser, R. 1039, 1042
Glastetter, W. 166
Glatigny, M. 136, 145, 212, 213, 605f., 700, 703f., 917, 989, 991f., 997, 1069, 1075, 1795, 1810f., 1813-1817, 1842
Glättli, H. 592, 1093
Glehn, P. von 2628
Gleiss, A. 2221
Gleitmann, H. 575
Gleitmann, L.R. 575
Glinz, H. 821, 1066, 2209
Glonar, J. 2299f.
Glover, J. 1282f.
Gloy, K. 191-193, 197, 202, 207
Glück, H. 3080, 3084
Gluski, J. 1038, 1040, 2920, 2929
Gmelin, J.F. 2939, 2945
Gneuss, H. 1446
Gnutzmann, K. 269

Gobello, J. 1188, 1759
Gobuloff, Th. 3138
Gociman, A. 2887
Goclenius, R. 1011, 1014, 1081f.
Godabole, N. B. 2496
Godart, L. 1703
Godbole, R. B. 2514, 2519
Gode, A. 3130, 3132
Gode, P. K. 2493, 2495
Godefroy, F. 1819f., 1823-1825, 1827, 1840
Godel, R. 780, 786
Godfroy, C. 1302f.
Godin, M.A.F. von 2363, 2366
Godiveau, R. 1216
Godman, A. 1513, 1516, 1518, 1520, 1522
Godoy, D.A. 2980, 2984
Godwin Austin, H. S. 2519
Goebel, U. 265, 272f., 364, 369f., 380, 406, 460, 582, 612f., 627, 656, 728, 731, 771, 918f., 926f., 930, 1065f., 1238, 1241, 1414, 1416, 1418, 1422, 1428f., 1435, 1544, 1547f., 1562, 1571f., 1608, 1610, 2221, 2235f., 2240, 2242, 2245, 2727
Goedecke, W. 1261, 1263f.
Goethe, J.W. von 14, 22, 155, 157f., 753, 2131f., 1235, 1549f., 1554, 1557-1559, 2218, 2221, 3122, 3132, 3136
Goetschalckx, J. 1311, 1670, 2728, 2767, 2775, 2813
Goetz, D. 18, 101, 127, 133-135, 269, 274, 648f., 1953, 2756
Goetz, G. 1714, 1721
Goetz, W. 1205
Goetze, A. 1240, 1418-1420, 1426-1428
Goetze, D. 881
Goff, H. 2648f.
Gogol, V.N. 3122, 3132, 3136
Goicoechea, C. 1047f., 1759
Golan, I. 3166
Gold, D.L. 653f., 670, 672, 2726, 2756, 3030
Goldast, M. 232
Goldbeck, K. 1446, 1455
Goldenberg, G. 2469
Goldenson, R.M. 1198
Goldin, Z.D. 519, 525, 736, 748
Goldman, A.I. 815, 821
Goldman, L. 1110
Goldsmith, U.K. 1137, 1139
Goldstein, M. C. 2550
Goldstücker, Th. 2491, 2495
Golescu, I. 1884
Golfand, J. 508, 1055
Golias, J. 2299f.
Golius, J. 2401, 2405, 3087, 3095
Golius, Th. 1091, 2044, 2047

Göller, A. 213, 1829, 1842, 2756
Golobardes, G. 1776, 1783
Golovaščuk, S. I. 2715, 2726
Golte, J. 2683
Gombert, A. 199, 206, 1198
Gombocz, Z. 2381
Gombrich, E.H. 716, 725
Gomer, E. 3048-3050
Gomes Braga, I. 3127, 3132
Gómez Carillo, E. 1091
Gómez de Silva, G. 1759
Gómez Perasso, J. A. 2704
Gonçález Holguín, D. de 2677-2679, 2681-2684
Gonçalves Viana 67, 69
Gonfroy, G. 1894f., 1904
Gönnenwein, O. 2218
Gonza 2619, 2622
González de la Rosa, M. 720, 724, 1746, 1759
González de Mendoza, N. 2979, 2984
González de Pérez, M. S. 2706
González Hermoso, A. 1312-1314
González Salas, M. 1759
González, A. 1759
Gonzalez, A. B. 2569f.
Gonzalez, Marimon, B. 2885
González, V. 3116
Gooch, A. 2955
Gööck, A. 1019, 1029, 2174, 2221
Good, C. 2130, 2235
Good, C. 2698f.
Good, C.H. 274, 577
Goodlin, D. 3148
Goodner Nellis, J. 2699
Goodrich, Ch.A. 1072, 1958, 1990f., 2007, 3119
Goodridge, G.W.F.R. 2959
Goodwin, H. B. 3049f.
Goosse, A. 86f., 277, 606, 1803, 1813
Goossens, J. 207, 1429, 2018f., 2021, 2077
Gorbačevič, K.S. 613, 2316f., 2323, 2327
Gorbačevič, L.S. 1012, 1014
Gorbahn, A. 1380, 1382, 1385
Gorbahn-Orme, A. 2888
Gorcy, G. 907, 909, 917, 1017, 1674f., 1678
Gordon, C.H. 1139, 1690, 1693
Gordon, E. 1033, 1040
Gordon, I.A. 71, 77
Gordon, P. R. T. 2509
Gordon, S. W. 2520
Gorekar, N.S. 3097, 3099, 3104
Goria, M. 1114
Gorini, G. 3011
Gorkij, M. 1556-1558, 2313, 2319
Görlach, M. 269, 406, 834, 1058, 1065, 1079, 2174-2176, 2181f., 2221, 2232

Gorman, P. 3143f.
Görner, H. 1028f.
Górnowicz, H. 1286, 1289f., 2272
Gorodeckij, B.J. 2320, 2327
Gorog, L. de 1139
Gorog, R. de 1100, 1102, 1139
Górski, K. 2270, 2272
Gorys, E. 1102
Göschel, J. 1429
Göseken, H. 2392, 2394
Goshen-Gottstein, M.H. 2428, 2430, 2433, 2436
Gosling, W. 1272
Gosselin, M. 1367f.
Gossen, C.Th. 592, 1324, 1538
Gossing, G. 2756
Gotfredsen, L. 1919, 1921
Gothot-Mersch, Cl. 1351
Gothus, J.P. 1934, 1942, 2929
Goto, T. 3117
Gottfried von Straßburg 1558
Gotti, A. 1088, 1091
Gottlieb, K. H. 2885, 2887
Göttling, H. 1262, 1264
Gottschald, M. 821, 1252f., 1271f., 2221
Gottschalk, W. 1021, 1025, 1030, 1036, 1038, 1040f., 1531, 2803, 2879f., 3000f., 3006
Gottsched, J.Chr. 114, 123, 128, 133, 231, 233f., 236, 238, 244, 574, 1068, 1072, 1075, 1232, 1240, 2052, 2053f., 2056, 2058, 2063, 2069, 2074-2076, 2090f., 2093, 2095, 2099f.
Gottskálksson, O. 1929
Gottzmann, C. 1400, 1415
Götz, D. 181, 188f., 575, 584, 725, 905, 997, 999, 1017, 1112, 1385, 1765, 2243, 2903, 3030
Götz, H. 2215
Götze, A. 124, 731, 821, 966, 1323, 1530, 2085, 2088, 2095, 2098, 2193, 2223
Götze, L. 1006, 1009
Gougenheim, G. 679, 718, 724, 903f., 945, 1318, 1321, 1355f., 1361, 1363, 1388f., 1668, 1804, 1813, 1835, 1839f., 2891, 2900, 2986
Gougeroux 2938
Gouin, E. 2588
Goulart, S. 1011, 1014, 1018
Goulet, J.-G. 2703
Goulet, P. 3174
Goulin, J. 1803, 1806
Govaerts, S. 1137, 1139
Gove, Ph.B. 78, 213f., 311, 517, 524, 530f., 536, 552, 562, 577, 588, 591f., 612, 614, 640, 653f., 661, 667, 672, 747, 763, 766f., 778, 821, 930, 934, 937, 1334, 1623, 1994, 2007f.

Gover, J.E.B. 1281, 1283
Goyvaerts, D. 2644f.
Gozman, I.G. 2317, 2322
Gozzano, G. 1874
Grabar, B. 2262
Graben zum Stein, O. von 3014f., 3017
Grabes, H. 518, 672
Grabias, S. 2271f.
Grabis, R. 2359
Grabowski, A. 3126f., 3132
Grachow, J. 2939, 2945
Gradenwitz, O. 1133, 1137, 1139f.
Gradova, B. A. 3073, 3084
Graefe, J. 1560
Graf, A. 149, 2349
Graf, E. 1036, 1040, 2065, 2069
Graf, H.-J. 1529
Graf, R. 1142
Grafenauer, I. 2298, 2301
Graff, E.G. 120, 124, 242, 771, 1147, 1149, 1151, 1234, 1238, 1418, 1420f., 1423, 1425-1428, 2088f., 2095
Gragg, G. B. 2464f., 2469
Graglia, C. 2972, 2974
Graglia, G. 2972, 2974
Graham Bailey, T. H. 2515, 2520
Graham, E.C. 901, 904
Graham, G.F. 1072
Graham, W. 1446, 1985f.
Graichen, J. 123
Grambs, D. 1351
Grammatin, N. F. 3075
Grammont, M. 1306
Granada, D. 1752, 1759
Granberg, P. A. 3047, 3050
Grande, B.M. 2431, 2436
Grandgagnage, Ch. 1329, 1332
Grandpre, J. 2917, 2929
Granell, L. 1778, 1782
Granger, S. 2886f.
Grangier, L. 2884f.
Grannis, O. 269
Grant, H. 3100, 3104
Grant, W. 1415, 1985f.
Granta, K. 2357, 2359
Granville, W. 1530
Grapaldus Parmensis, F. 1725
Grapow, H. 1141, 1680f.
Grappin, P. 2747, 2751, 2795f., 3001f., 3004
Grass, G. 114, 127, 2131
Grassi, G. 1072, 2972, 2974
Gräßli, J. 2073
Grassmann, H. 1133, 1135, 1137, 1140, 2493, 2495
Gratet-Duplessis, P. 1033, 1042
Grau, H.-D. 1034, 1042
Grauberg, W. 2902
Graudina, L.K. 691, 693, 2323
Graumann, C. F. 2222

Graur, A. 1363, 1887, 1890
Grauwe, L. de 2044, 2047
Grave, B. de 2910f., 2929, 2981
Graves, B. 2185, 2229
Graves, E.V.T. 2348, 2351
Grawe, Chr. 1293, 1295
Gray, A. 2007
Gray, E. 2951, 2956
Gray, I. 2592f.
Grazzini, C. 3135
Grazzini, G. 1856f., 1861
Greaves, J. 1293, 1295
Grébaut, S. 2449, 2453
Grebe, P. 69, 123, 198, 207, 405, 458, 889, 892, 967, 1011, 1015, 1069, 1072, 1238, 1310, 1362, 2218f., 2234
Gréciano, G. 596, 599, 1020, 1031, 2756, 2760, 2778
Greco, O. 3140f.
Greco, S. 718, 724
Greef, A. 1549, 1551, 1559
Green, J. 1044, 1048
Green, M. 3132
Green, M. und W. 3129
Green, W. 3132
Greenbaum, S. 31, 33, 37, 106f., 110, 763, 766, 862, 1017, 1186, 1188, 1530, 1616-1618, 1620f., 1623, 1632, 1637
Greenberg, J. 2463, 2469
Greenberg, J. H. 2642f., 2645f., 2649
Greene, B.B. 1670, 1672
Greene, D. 2340, 2342
Greene, D.J. 1950, 1952
Greene, R. 1453
Greenfield, C.C. 1670
Greenslade, S.L. 2433
Greet, W.C. 1293, 1295, 1299
Gregersen, E. A. 2642, 2645
Gregerson, K. 2584, 2589
Gregg, J.R. 3140f.
Gregg, R.J. 641
Gregor, B. 2193, 2223
Gregor, D.B. 3121, 3132, 3136
Gregor, W. 1984, 1986
Gregory, C.R. 1563, 1566
Gregory, J. 1296
Gregory, T. 1873
Greh, M. 3083
Greidanus, T. 2756
Greiffenhagen, M. 1205
Greimas, A.J. 281, 286, 635, 640
Grein, Chr.W.M. 1442, 1454
Greisman, J. 1080
Greive, A. 1179, 1183
Grek, M. 3069
Grek-Pabisowa, I. 1139, 2264, 2266, 2323, 3065, 3067
Grenand, F. 2675f.
Grenier, J. 1351

Grenkamp, S. 3121, 3132
Grente, G. 1811
Grenzmann, L. 2241, 3151, 3157
Grétsy, L. 1244
Greule, A. 1277-1281, 1283f., 1286, 1290f.
Greve, R. 1138, 1142, 2319, 2323
Grevisse, M. 859, 861, 1211-1213, 1216
Grewendorf, G. 160, 163, 804, 821, 853, 855
Grey, G. 2651, 2655
Greyerz, O. von 2198, 2221
Grgić, B. 2294
Gribble, Ch.E. 2323
Grieb, Chr. F. 2968f.
Grienberger, Th. von 1910f.
Griera i Gaja, A. 1777f., 1783f., 1787
Griera, A. 1125, 1131, 1781, 1784, 1787
Grierson, G. 2545
Grierson, G. A. 2499, 2504, 2513, 2519, 2558, 3100, 3103
Griesbach, H. 796, 1029, 2174, 2221, 2229
Griesheim, I. von 1030
Griffin, P.J. 186-188, 208, 212f.
Griffini, E. 3093, 3095
Griffith, F.L. 1680, 1682
Griffith, T.G. 2970, 2975
Grignard, A. 2529
Grigorian, V. 2370
Grigorov, A. 3127, 3132
Grigorovič, I. I. 3076
Griguard, A. 2532
Grijalbo, J. 20
Grilli, A. 3032f.
Grillot, F. 1691, 1693f.
Grillparzer, F. 2131
Grimaux, A. 2958f.
Grimblot, L. 1096, 1099
Grimes, J. 2664, 2667
Grimes, J. E. 2698f., 3166
Grimes, L.M. 1199
Grimm, H.-J. 1222, 2221
Grimm, J. 11f., 16, 21, 24, 27, 119, 122f., 158, 199, 206, 219, 225-229, 231, 241f., 245, 270, 393, 461, 500f., 508f., 516, 526, 529, 586f., 591, 591f., 644f., 647, 750, 753, 801, 803, 818, 820, 826, 829, 853, 853, 859-861, 863, 867, 1065, 1071, 1126, 1157f., 1232, 1235, 1238, 1240f., 1284, 1291, 1397-1400, 1402-1408, 1414f., 1431, 1434, 1522, 1601, 1608f., 1865, 1872, 1897, 1912, 2020, 2026, 2042f., 2049-2051, 2054, 2057f., 2062, 2064-2066, 2069, 2074-2076, 2078f., 2081-2084, 2089-2091, 2095, 2098-2100, 2110, 2118, 2214, 2220, 2237, 2242-2245, 3000

Grimm, W. 12, 16, 21, 24, 27, 119, 122f., 158, 199, 206, 225-229, 231, 241f., 245, 270, 461, 500f., 508f., 516, 526, 529, 587, 591f., 645, 647, 750, 753, 801, 803, 820, 826, 829, 859-861, 862, 867, 1065, 1126, 1157f., 1238, 1240f., 1398, 1400, 1403, 1414f., 1431, 1434, 1522, 1601, 1608, 1865, 1872, 1897, 2020, 2049-2051, 2057f., 2064, 2066, 2069, 2074-2076, 2078f., 2081-2084, 2095, 2098-2100, 2118, 2214, 2237, 2242f., 2245, 3000
Grimod, F. 3011
Grin'ov, S.V. 2940, 2947
Grīnberga, E. 2358, 2360
Grindsted, A. 2756
Gringsmuth, G. 3174
Grinó Garriga, D. 1778, 1784
Gris, N. 2251, 2253
Grisc-Allard, J. 1270
Grisch, M. 1899, 1904
Grischin, N.N. 1028
Grisé-Allard, J. 1272
Grišin, N. N. 3082
Gröber, G. 1905
Groeben, G. F. von der 2062, 2069
Groeben, N. 966f.
Groenewolt, L. van 't 1102
Gröger, E. 2969
Grønberg, B. C. 3054, 3060
Gröndahl, E. M. 3049, 3051
Gröndahl, F. 1693
Groote, E. von 2361
Gros, A. 1282f.
Gros, J. 2344, 2348, 2350
Groschopp, F. 1442, 1455
Grose, F. 1186, 1188, 1530, 1536
Grosjean-Maupin, E. 3121f., 3126f., 3132
Gross, G. 180, 1389, 1842
Gross, H. 1661, 1667, 2753
Gross, J. 1044, 1047f.
Gross, M. 179f., 1005f., 1009, 1389, 1837, 3166
Grosse, R. 2215 (= Große, R.)
Große, R. 239, 244, 2104, 2235
Grosse, S. 135
Grosse, W. 1263f.
Großkopf, J. A. 2062, 2069
Grossmann, R. 1771, 1787, 2431, 2798-2801, 2803, 2982, 2989f., 3057
Grot, J. K. 4, 16, 2312f., 2323, 3079
Grotjahn, R. 1671
Grover, C. 3166

Grubb, N. 1934, 1942
Grube, W. 2628, 2630
Grübel, J. V. 2064, 2069
Gruber, J.G. 1062f., 1065. 1072., 2059, 2068, 2086, 2220
Gruber, J.S. 577
Grubitzsch, S. 1632, 1637
Grubmüller, K. 8, 10, 17, 269, 510, 517, 1624, 1715, 1721, 1788, 1813, 2037-2040, 2042, 2045, 2047-2049, 2215
Gruhle, U. 2221
Grümwald, M. 2069
Grun, P.A. 1261, 1264
Grunau, S. 2353
Grünbaum, M. 1906f.
Grundström, H. 2390f., 2919, 2929
Gruner, J.E. 2969
Grüner-Nielsen, H. 1922
Grünhoff, H. 1183
Grunow, P. 2094f., 2227
Grunst, G. 1152
Grünwald, M. 2066
Grünwedel, A. 2556, 2558
Grunzel, J. 1340
Grüssner, E. J. A. 2556, 2559
Gruterus, J. 2065, 2069, 2915, 2929
Gruzberg, A.A. 2320, 2323
Gryphius, A. 2071
Grzebieniowski, T. 3065, 3067
Grzegorczyk, P. 2274, 3022, 3030, 3066, 3068, 3171
Grzegorczykowa, R. 1139f., 2268f., 2272
Grzyb, G. 581
Grzybek, P. 1033, 1042f.
Gsell, O. 629, 634
Gspann, L. 1029
Guacci, C. 1085, 1087, 1090. 1092
Guadix, F.D. de 1740, 1759
Guajardo Fajardo, A. 2982
Guamán Poma de Ayala, F. 2678, 2683
Guàrdia, M. 1784
Guàrdia, R. 1776, 1784
Guardian, R. 1778
Guarnieri, J.C. 1759
Guasch, A. 2674, 2676, 2704
Guckler, G. 1670
Gudeler, G. 2756
Gudjedjiani, C. 2418
Guđmundsson, S. 1929, 1931
Gudschinsky, S.C. 1340
Gueintz, Chr. 231f., 244, 2074, 2052
Guérard, E. 1054f.
Guérard, F. 44, 61, 180, 766
Guérard, M. 1842
Guercio, F.M. 2974
Guérin, P. 326f., 1820. 1823f., 1840

Guérios, R. F. M. 2707
Guerlac, O. 1046, 1048
Guertler, N. 2917, 2929
Guessard, F. 1129
Gueth, A. 2505
Gueunier, N. 49, 62
Guglielmotti, A. 150
Guha, Ch. Ch. 2510, 2518
Guhrauer, G. E. 2076, 2099
Guidi, I. 2449, 2451, 2453, 2455
Guignes, Chr. L. J. de 2917, 2929
Guilbert, L. 61, 327, 590f., 606, 647, 661, 667, 679, 786, 942, 945f., 980, 989, 997, 1343, 1575, 1588, 1827, 1829, 1833, 1842
Guilelmus Brito 2038
Guillain, Ch. 2462, 2467
Guillaumin, G.U. 166
Guillén de Segovia, P. 1125, 1129
Guillermou, A. 1213
Guillet, A. 1006, 1009
Guillevic, A. 2347, 2350
Guillot, H. 1207f., 1124
Guillot, R. 1367
Guim, D.J.B. 2985
Guim, J. 2980, 2985
Guinard, M. 679, 1079, 1123, 1314
Guiraud, P. 1168, 1178, 1185, 1189, 1193, 1196-1199, 1318, 1322, 1332, 1334, 1595f., 1610, 1644, 1837
Guiter, H. 1644
Guizot, F.P.G. 1068f., 1073, 1075
Güldenstädt, J. A. 2483, 2486
Gülensoy, T. 2407
Gulevska, D. 2359
Gülich, E. 814, 821, 831, 834, 959, 967, 2222
Guljaev, E.S. 2397
Gullberg, I.E. 1939, 1942, 2789
Gulsoy, J. 1786f.
Gumbuxani, H. M. 2516
Gundersen, D. 1079, 1925, 1927f.
Gundert, H. 2528, 2532
Gunnarsson, F. 1929, 1931
Gunning, J. G. H. 2562
Günther, A. 2360
Günther, E. 580, 2327, 2755f., 2763, 2769, 2776, 3070, 3085
Günther, H. 359, 372, 374f., 378, 407, 428f., 438, 459
Günther, K. 1133, 1142f.,
Günther, K.B. 407
Günther, L. 1531
Günther, W. 2871, 2875
Güntzel, J. 3014, 3017
Guralnik, D.B. 211f., 517, 530, 577, 2004, 2008, 3115f., 3148
Gurin, I.I. 1128
Gurkenbiehl, H.L. 206
Gursky, K.-H. 1340

Gurst, G. 17, 995, 997, 2223
Gurumūrtiśāstri, R. 2527, 2532
Gushina, N. 1743, 1765
Gusmani, R. 1687, 1689
Gustaf II. Adolf 1934
Gustaf III. 1934
Gustason, G. 3143f.
Gustavson, H. 1939, 1942
Gutenberg, J. 1788
Güterbock, B.G. 2341f.
Güterbock, H.G. 1688f.
Guterman, M. 3127, 3132
Gütersloh, A.P. 156, 159
Guthrie, A. M. 2647, 2649
Guthrie, M. 1340, 2647, 2649
Gutiérrez S., M. 2702
Gutjahr, S. 2192, 2235
Gutknecht, Chr. 648
Gutman, I. 3022, 3028
Gūtmanis, A. 3126f., 3133
Gutschmidt, K. 893, 2756, 2763
Gutschow, H. 2222
Gutslaff, J. 2392, 2394
Gutsmann, O. 2298, 2300f.
Gutstuff 2578
Gutzkow, K. 27
Guyonarc'h, Chr.-J. 2350
Guyonvarc'h, Chr.J. 2348
Guyot, J. 1802
Gûys, H. 2367
Guzmán Betancourt, I. 2661
Guzmán y Raz Guzman, J. 1759
Guzmán, A. de 2664, 2667
Guzman, M. O. de 2570
Guzmán, P. de 2664, 2667
Gvarjaladze, Th. 2417f.
Gymnick, J. 2046
Gysseling, M. 1140, 1277, 1283, 1286, 1289, 1431f., 1435, 1593, 1610

H

Hà Thành 2587f.
Haack, F.W. 2351, 2353
Haak, F. van der 2593f.
Haak, W.J. v.d. 3127, 3132
Haake, W. G. H. 2653
Haan Hettema, M. de 2024, 2034
Haarmann, A.-L.V. 2398
Haarmann, H. 2366, 2397f.
Haas, J.G. 3001, 3004
Haas, K. 1692, 1694
Haas, M.R. 102, 105, 110, 130, 132, 134, 2756
Haas, V. 1694
Haas, W. 1233, 1240, 2233
Haaschka, Ch. 2883
Haase, A. 1353, 1355f., 1361, 1363, 2890, 2900
Habdelić, G. 2289, 2294, 2296

Habel, Chr. 551, 554, 577
Habel, E. 1720f.
Habellok, G. 3129, 3132
Habenstein, E. 1361
Haberkamp de Antón, G. 2989f.
Haberkamp, G. 2793, 2922, 2929
Haberkern, E. 163, 166
Habermann, A.M. 2429, 2433, 2435
Habermann, B. 2429
Habermann, S. 2215
Habermas, J. 836, 841
Hachette 1214
Häcker, H. 123
Hacker, P.M.S. 575
Hacking, 564
Hadjadj-Pailler, D. 1813
Hadrovics, L. 2380f.
Hadži P. Daniil 2917, 2929
Hae, R. de 2344, 2348
Haebler, C. 407
Haefs, G. 2220
Haeger, F. 3139-3141
Haemmerle, A. 1252
Haenisch, E. 2626
Haensch, G. 126, 247, 269, 274, 584, 662, 667, 762, 765f., 787, 930, 988f., 991, 997, 999, 1031, 1741f., 1750, 1752, 1754, 1759, 1765, 1767, 1776, 1781, 1787f., 2756, 2768, 2803, 2854, 2909, 2922, 2929, 2936f., 2945f., 2948, 2989f.
Haeringen, C. B. van 2018, 2020
Haferkorn, R. 3125, 3128, 3132, 3136
Haffmans, G. 2220
Hafid, M. 2400, 2405
Hafiz, A.F.A. 3101, 3104
Hafner, St. 2301
Hag, A. 2516
Haga, Y. 2622
Hagan, S.F. 1122-1124
Hagège, C. 23, 44, 48, 53, 62, 2469, 2647, 2649
Hageman, H. 1011, 1015
Hagen, G. 2220
Hager, A. 2070
Hagerup, E.H. 1919
Hagman, R. S. 2651f., 2654f.
Hagos Täkästa 2451, 2454
Hagspihl, A. 2172, 2242
Hagström, B. 1929, 1931
Hahmann, H. 273, 804, 2231
Hahn, G. von 2366
Hahn, H. 273, 2224
Hahn, J.G. von 2362
Hahn, Th. 2655
Hahn, W. von 313, 321, 770, 893, 899, 1136-1138, 1143, 2104, 2216
Hailund, N. 3058

Haiman, J. 280, 286, 290, 577, 992, 296, 551, 997
Hain, M. 2215, 2220
Haipus, M. 1669, 2385, 2386f.
Hair, P. E. H. 2460, 2469
Hais, K. 2282f.
Haislund, N. 3060
Hajdú, M. 1270, 1272
Hajdú, P. 2396-2398
Hajpin, L. 3126f., 3132
Hakamies, R. 1720
Hakulinen, L. 2384, 2388
Hāla 2503
Halász de Beky, I.L. 3171
Halász, I. 2389-2391
Halāyudha 2489, 2496
Halbach, W. 2201
Halbertsma, J. H. 2025f., 2034f.
Halbertsma, T. 1395, 1414, 2034
Hald, K. 1308f., 1916
Haldorson, B. 2917, 2929
Hale, B. 2558
Hale, K. 299, 305, 553, 555, 576, 2639-2641
Hale, S. 1368
Halem, F.W. von 2939, 2945
Halici, M. 1881
Halīmī, Lutfullāh 2478
Hâlis, Y. 2399, 2406
Halit, M. 2404f.
Hall, C. 1134, 1137, 1143
Hall, H.B. 2955
Hall, J. 3154-3156
Hall, J.R.C. 1443f., 1455
Hall, R. A. jr. 1245, 2871f., 2876
Hallager, L. 1924, 1927
Halldórsson, B. 1929, 1931
Halldórsson, H. 1929, 1931
Haller, H. 1138, 1572
Haller, J. 1033, 1042, 2281, 2283
Halliday, M.A.K. 1672
Halliday, R. 2591, 2593
Hallig, R. 282, 286, 293, 296, 1059, 1066, 1090f., 193, 1672, 1777, 1827, 1867, 1893, 1969, 1982, 2281, 2922, 2936
Halliwell, J.O. 1394, 1414, 1448, 1452, 1455
Halm, W. 1029
Halma, F. 2619, 3036, 3038f., 3114, 3116f.
Halma, H. 3038
Halpern, A. 2665
Haltaus, Chr.G. 1235, 1239
Halthof, B. 575
Halyn, M. 2331f.
Hamad, Kh. al- 3095
Hämäläinen, S. 2386f.
Hamawi, M. al- 3092, 3095
Hamer, J. 3172
Hamesse, J. 1670
Hamilton, L.B. 3143f.

Hamilton-Smith, N. 327
Hamm, F. 160, 163
Hamm, J. 2290, 2293, 2295
Hammar, E. 3043, 3046
Hammar, Th. 3041f.
Hammarlöw, A. 1129
Hammer, H. 1915, 1921
Hammer, J.K. 3128, 3132
Hammer, P. 2885, 2887
Hammerich, L. L. 3070, 3085
Hammerl, P. 1322
Hammershaimb, V.U. 1932
Hamoche, L.A. 1126f., 1129
Hamonière, G. 2980, 2982, 2984
Hamp, E.P. 2367
Hampares, K.J. 87
Hampel, H. 1351
Hampl, Z. 3022, 3028
Hamre, H. 1924, 1927f.
Hamst, O. 1295
Hamsun, K. 1923
Hanakata, K. 3168
Hand, F. 1221f.
Handjéri, P.A. 2402, 2405
Handoo, J. 3097, 3102, 3104
Handoo, L. 3097, 3102, 3104
Handrik, M. 2275, 2278
Haneda, K. 2411
Hänger, H. 2041, 2048
Hanka, V. 2283
Hanke, A. 2636f.
Hanks, P. 330, 357, 405, 515, 524, 529, 553, 557, 562, 564, 570, 572, 577, 588f., 591, 672, 1271f., 2007
Hanna, J.F. 543, 578
Hannaas, T. 1924, 1927
Hannan, M. 2648
Hannemann, J. 725
Hannesdóttir, A. 3049, 3051
Hannover, D. 2225
Hanon, S. 1563f., 1566f.
Hanotaux, G. 1825
Hanover, N. 2250, 2253f.
Hansberger, O. 1054f.
Hanse, J. 41f., 44, 1210f., 1213, 1216, 1218, 1220
Hansen, A. 1920, 1922
Hansen, B. 1133, 1137, 1140, 1146, 1149, 1152
Hansen, C. P. 2029
Hansen, J. 2029
Hansen, J. P. 2030
Hansen, K. C. 2639-2641
Hansen, L. E. 2639-2641
Hanson, O. 2558
Hanssen, F. 1752
Hansson, I.-L. 2559
Hao Yixing 2598, 2610
Happ, H. 1002, 1004, 1009
Haq, A. 3099, 3104
Harbeck, H. 1129

Harbottle, Th.B. 1046, 1048
Harcum, E.R. 140, 145
Hardaway, R. T. 2756
Hardelandt, A. 2565, 2567
Harder, E. 3092, 3095
Harder, H. 2355
Harding, G.L. 1690, 1693
Hardman, M. J. 2684f., 2690
Hardman-de-Bautista, M. J. 2690, 2706
Hardt, D. 224
Hare, E. M. 2502, 2505
Hare, R.M. 852f.
Harel, F.A. 1349, 1351
Harell, R.S. 3096
Hares, W. P. 2515, 2520
Harff, A. von 2361, 2367
Harfst, G. 251, 272, 1525, 1528, 1530, 1536, 2185, 2198, 2221
Haridas Bhat, K. S. 2529
Harig, L. 114
Harkavy, A. 2250, 2253
Harkavy, A.E. 2434
Harkin, D. 1319, 1322, 1355, 1363
Harlez, C. de 2471f.
Harlock, W. E. 3048, 3050f.
Harmaon, R. M. 3027
Harmatta, J. 2472f.
Harmer, L. C. 2885
Harmon, R. M. 1187, 3022
Harnack, A. 244, 2075, 2081, 2099
Harras, G. 17f., 163, 269, 279, 359, 371, 408, 459, 461f., 500, 531, 552, 574, 57, 586, 614, 654, 821, 850f., 854, 955, 967, 988, 1165, 1207f., 1221, 1223, 2202, 2217, 2236, 2240, 2245
Harrassowitz, O. 2495
Harrebomée, P. 1036, 1040
Harrell, R. S. 2726, 2756
Harriet, M. 2373, 2375
Harrington, D.J. 2437
Harris, J. 40, 45, 720, 723, 994, 997, 1946, 1951
Harris, M. 1534, 1537
Harris, M.R. 1140
Harris, R.L. 2428, 2435
Harris, W.T. 1994, 2007
Harris, Z.S. 180
Harrison, H. 1273
Harrison, J.A. 1442, 1455
Harrison, L. 1792, 2956, 2959
Harrison, M. 2698f.
Harrison, R. 2698f.
Harrit, J. 3058, 3060
Harrit, V. 3058, 3060
Harry, R. 3125, 3132, 3137
Harsdœrffer, G. Ph. 231f., 244, 644, 2065f., 2069, 2074
Harte, G. 2221
Harte, J. 2221
Hartenstein, K. 274, 2316, 2320, 2327

Hartgenbusch, R. 1053
Harti, L. 2395
Hartmann von Aue 1139, 2075
Hartmann, D. 553, 582, 2211, 2235
Hartmann, E. 2886, 3058, 3061
Hartmann, H. 272f., 405, 574, 804, 1622, 2219, 2231
Hartmann, L. M. von 2880f.
Hartmann, M. 2411
Hartmann, P. 2881
Hartmann, R. 1058, 1065, 1355, 1363, 1552, 1559, 2235, 2887
Hartmann, R.R.K. 31, 33f., 78, 88, 96f., 99, 101f., 110f., 113, 115, 120, 124, 126, 132-135, 145, 170, 174, 181f., 184, 186, 188f., 208f., 212-214, 267f., 274f., 277f., 287, 305, 359, 500, 517, 525, 575-577, 579, 581, 583-585, 591, 607, 653-656, 661, 699, 749, 767, 787, 892, 898f., 905, 1009, 1066, 1093f., 1183, 1189f., 1304, 1311, 1512, 1624, 1630, 1637, 1648, 1667, 1811, 1814, 1952, 1966, 1980, 1982, 2009, 2235, 2714, 2716, 2722, 2726, 2728, 2752, 2757, 2760-2764, 2766, 2768, 2773, 2775, 2813, 2824, 2836, 2854, 2858f., 2870, 2881, 2888, 2899, 2902f., 2956, 2960, 2967, 2969, 3119
Hartshorne, C. 704, 725, 3157
Hartung, L. 2398
Hartung, W. 191, 194f., 197f., 207, 248, 275, 2237
Hartzenbusch, J.E. 1760
Harutjunjan, N.V. 1692, 1694
Harvey, L.P. 2954
Hasan, F. 1353, 1363
Hasan, R. 1672
Haschka, Chr. 2887
Hasdeu, B.P. 1881, 1885-1888, 1890
Hasegawa, K. 3116f.
Hasenohr, G. 1790, 1813
Hashimoto, M.J. 305
Haslam, G.W. 1530
Haß, U. 3, 17, 574, 1066, 1076, 1080, 1207f., 1221, 1223, 2058, 2072, 2074, 2217
Hassán, I.M. 1906f.
Hassan, S. 2412
Hasse, L. 3053, 3060
Hasselbrink, G. 2389, 2391
Hassell, E. A. L. 2871, 2875
Hassell, J. 1036, 1040
Hastings, F.E. 1149, 1151
Hata, M. 3117
Hatfield, W.W. 37

Hatherall, G. 31, 33, 108, 110, 133f., 1304, 1631f., 1637, 2191, 2235, 2969
Hattori, S. 2621f., 2636, 2638
Hatzfeld, A. 66, 69, 222, 606, 916, 996, 1326, 1332, 1344, 1347, 1822f., 1825, 1839
Häublein, G. 1361, 2891, 2895, 2900
Hauck, L.C. 2008
Haugen, Einar 514, 516, 1169, 1178, 1924-1928, 1932-1934, 1942, 3043, 3046, 3171
Haugen, E. 1933f., 1942
Haugen, E.A. 3134
Haugen, E.L. 1920, 1922, 1928, 1932, 2913f., 2926, 2928, 2931, 2947, 3042, 3049, 3051, 3171
Haupenthal, R. 3121f., 3125, 3129, 3132, 3137
Hauptmann, G. 2131
Hauptová, Z. 2260, 2262, 2267f.
Hauschka, E.R. 1047f.
Hauser, A. 1036, 1040
Häusler, F. 2881
Hausmann, F.-R. 854
Hausmann, F.J. 4, 7, 17, 38, 40, 42, 45, 96f., 101, 112, 115, 118, 120, 122, 125, 132, 134, 181, 183, 188, 208, 212f., 217, 221, 223, 256, 258, 267, 269, 275, 359, 362, 370f., 383, 407, 421f., 459, 513, 517, 606, 608, 614, 616, 626, 641, 644, 648, 652-654, 657, 662, 666-668, 673, 675, 679, 682, 687f., 693f., 696, 698, 700, 703, 705, 723, 725, 754, 765f., 772, 777f., 784, 786, 817, 821, 834, 860f., 889f., 892, 917-923, 926, 930, 970, 974, 980f., 983, 988-992, 997, 1011f., 1017-1019, 1031, 1039, 1042, 1050, 1053, 1056, 1068, 1068f., 1071, 1075, 1080f., 1083, 1089f., 1093, 1099f., 1102, 1120, 1125, 1145, 1149, 1152, 1174f., 1178, 1184, 1186, 1189f., 1209f., 1220, 1223, 1241, 1247, 1276f., 1283, 1311, 1314, 1352, 1360, 1363, 1365, 1368, 1372, 1375, 1378-1380, 1382, 1385, 1388-1390, 1515, 1520, 1522, 1673, 1678, 1765, 1795, 1804, 1813, 1829-1831, 1842, 1967f., 1974, 1980, 1982, 2016, 2021, 2046, 2048, 2051, 2074, 2130f., 2136, 2175f., 2185, 2215, 2222, 2235, 2239, 2711, 2716, 2720, 2725-2727, 2749, 2757, 2768, 2770f., 2775-2778, 2796, 2809, 2813, 2829, 2831-2836, 2840f., 2845,

2853f., 2877, 2881, 2888f.,
  2891, 2893, 2898, 2902, 2956f.,
  2960, 2967, 2969, 2991,
  2998-3001, 3004-3007, 3013,
  3015, 3019, 3025, 3030, 3152,
  3157
Hausmann, M. 2131
Hautel 1185, 1188
Hauzenberga, E. 2357, 2359
Hauzenberga-Šturma, E. 2224, 2357
Hava, J.G. 3090, 3092, 3095
Havas, L. 2757
Haverkamp, A. 804
Havlik, E.J. 1246f., 2188, 2221
Havlová, E. 2267
Havránek, B. 190, 207, 2281-2284
Hawke, A. 1967, 1972, 1982
Hawkes, H. 2757
Hawkins, J. A. 2858
Hawkins, J.D. 1687, 1689
Hawkins, J.M. 515, 2008
Hayakawa, S.I. 1069, 1073, 2000
Hayashi, T. 993, 998, 1943, 1952, 1955, 1966
Haydar, Ch.K. 2412
Hayeková, M. 2287
Hayes, F. 1112, 1119
Hayward, A.L. 515, 1293, 1295, 2974
Hayward, D. 2464f.
Hayward, R. 2645
Hayward, R. J. 2464, 2467
Hayward, T. 2887
Haywood, J. A. 2087, 2440, 2442, 2444-2448, 2711f., 2727, 3096
Hazai, G. 2413
Hazlewood, D. 2573, 2575
Hazon, M. 2974
Hazuka, W. 1102
He Jiren 2559
He Rong 2599, 2610
Headley, R. 2591, 2593
Healey, A. 2636f.
Healey, A. di Paolo 327, 1142, 1445, 1454
Healey, P. 2636f.
Heasty, J. A. 2644
Heath, D. 132, 134, 182, 184, 186-188, 208, 211-213, 592, 1383, 1385
Heath, J. 2638-2641
Heberth, A. 119, 124, 1164, 2185, 2186, 2187, 2222
Hecht, W. 245, 1241, 2077
Heck, H. 3138
Heck, K. 3140f.
Hecker, O. 3016f., 3124
Heckmann, H. 2222
Heckscher, W.S. 3151, 3157
Hederich, B. 2215, 2222, 3031, 3033

Hediger, H. 1759
Heemer, J. von 3070
Heepe, M. 518
Heerdegen, F. 17, 221, 223, 1716, 1722
Heeschen, V. 2636f.
Heestermans, H. 1018, 1435, 2010, 2020-2022
Heffner, R.-M.S. 153, 158
Hegel, G.W.F. 850, 854
Heger, K. 617, 626, 786, 1392, 1415, 1419, 1429, 1593f., 1610, 1644
Heggstad, K. 1924, 1927
Hego, J.M. 38, 41, 43, 45
Heid, U. 2757
Heidegger, M. 1020
Heidolph, E. 887
Heidolph, K.-E. 792, 796, 2828
Heidorn, G.E. 1660, 1667
Heike, G. 2222
Heimann, A. 2968
Heimbach, E.E. 2590f., 2593
Heine, B. 1340, 2464, 2467, 2469, 2643, 2645, 2649
Heine, H. 2131, 3122, 3132, 3137
Heinemann, M. 2185, 2186, 2222
Heinemann, W. 831, 834, 2217,
Heinertz, N. O. 3044
Heinimann, S. 2224
Heinisch, G. 2045
Heinle, E.-M. 269
Heinrich, A. 2091, 2095
Heinrich, C. 3044f.
Heinrichs, W. 2199, 2222
Heinse, G. H. 2063, 2069
Heinsius, J. 1910f.
Heinsius, Th. 1235, 1239, 2058, 2069
Heintze, A. 1011, 1015, 1271, 1273
Heinz, A. 3148
Heinz, W. 2155, 2166, 2168, 2222
Heinz-Mazzoni, M. L. 2901
Heinz-Mohr, G. 3152, 3156
Heinze, A. 2938, 2945
Heinze, S. 2761
Heinzmann, F. 1644
Heißenbüttel, H. 127, 159
Heisser, U. 1043
Heister, R. 1261, 1264
Hejzlarová, L. T. 2284
Helbig, G. 114, 124, 531, 578, 739f., 747, 789, 796, 810, 813, 883, 887, 1001, 1004f., 1008f., 1221f., 1615, 1622, 2171-2173, 2188f., 2207, 2211, 2222, 2235, 2237, 2243, 2770, 2774
Held, G. 2234
Held, J. 3152, 3157
Helder, M.P. 2973f.
Helel, M. 2284
Helgorsky, F. 701, 703

Heliade, I. 1884
Heliade-Rădulescu, I. 1885
Heller, K. 1165, 2185, 2187, 2235
Heller, L.G. 527f., 530
Heller, R. 2215
Heller, W. 1516f., 1520, 1522
Hellerer, H. 273, 358, 405, 459, 499, 574, 804, 2224
Hellevik, A. 1927
Hellfritzsch, V. 2198, 2199, 2220, 2201, 2216
Hellgardt, E. 1624
Helliwell, M. 2883-2885
Hellmann, F. 3176
Hellmann, M.W. 1640, 1644, 2192, 2236, 2241
Hellquist, E. 1286, 1289, 1936, 1938, 1941f.
Hellweg, P. 1351
Hellwig, Chr. 2939, 2945
Hellwig, G. 1035, 1040, 1047f., 2185, 2188
Hellwig, H. 1044, 3045f.
Hellwig, P. 366, 370, 948, 950, 955, 959, 967
Helms, S. H. 3044f.
Helsingius, E.P. 1934, 1942
Helsingius, O. P. 2913, 2929
Helsloot, N. 2919, 2929
Heltai, P. 2757
Helten, W. L. van 2024, 2036
Hemacandra 2489, 2497-2500, 2503f.
Hemme, A. 2215, 2222
Hemmer, J. 1232, 1240
Hemon, R. 2345, 2347f., 2350f.
Hempel, F. F. 582, 2073 (s. Syntax)
Hemshaw, Th. 1440
Hencke, J. J. 3017
Henderson, B.L.K. 1029
Henderson, E.J.A. 517, 2559
Hendrickson, R. 1259, 1260
Hendrickson, R.H. 78, 577
Hendrickx, R. 1358, 1363
Hendrix, M.K. 3171
Heng, E. 2920, 2929
Henisch, G. 800, 804, 2045-2047, 2052, 2065, 2069, 2215, 2929
Henke, K. 1054, 1056, 1982, 2757, 2961, 2969
Henkel, A. 3151, 3156
Henkel, N. 2038, 2048
Henley, W. E. 1187f., 2920, 2928
Henmon, V.A.Chr. 1321, 1361
Henne, D. 2663, 2667
Henne, H. 17, 22, 27, 102, 110f., 115, 122, 125, 127, 134f., 174, 206, 222f., 231-235, 240, 242, 244, 250-252, 275, 278, 359, 361, 370, 405f., 408, 458-460, 498-500, 531f., 542-544, 547,

552, 562, 575, 578, 581, 585, 587, 609, 614, 617, 626, 628, 770, 778f., 800, 804, 813, 822-825, 829f., 849, 853f., 861, 868, 892, 899, 922f., 930, 966, 980, 991, 997-999, 1017f., 1068f., 1075, 1178, 1207, 1209f., 1217, 1230, 1238, 1283, 1298, 1304, 1364, 1415, 1429, 1524, 1530-1532, 1537f., 1562, 1608, 1611, 1623, 1672, 2014, 2021, 2042, 2048, 2050-2052, 2054-2056, 2058f., 2067f., 2073, 2075f., 2090, 2093, 2099, 2103, 2185, 2193, 2214f., 2234-2236, 2238, 2243f.
Henni, M. 3092, 3095
Hennicke, F. 2937, 2945
Hennig, B. 2104, 2233
Hennig, D. 2099
Henning, H. 1034, 1042
Henning, W. B. 2473, 2476f.
Henri de Bourbon 2977
Henri IV 912
Henrion 1093
Henrique, H. 3101, 3104
Henríquez, B. 1741, 1759
Henry, F. 1674, 1678
Henry, L. 2462, 2465
Henry, V. 2341, 2348, 2350
Henscheid, E. 272, 1349, 1351, 2219, 2229
Henschel, G.A.L. 3001, 3004
Henschelmann, K. 269
Henschen, J. 1204
Henson, J. 1368
Hentschel, E. 808, 810, 813, 1221, 1223
Henzen, W. 634, 2055, 2075
Heo, H. 2751
Hepburn, J.C. 3115, 3117
Hérail, R.J. 1186, 1188, 1190
Héraucourt, W. 2968f.
Hérault, G. 2647, 2649
Herbau, S. 2917, 2929
Herberg, D. 359, 532, 544, 578, 652, 654, 690, 693, 751f., 754, 849, 854, 1165, 2130, 2135, 2150, 2185f., 2232, 2235f.
Herbst, J. 209
Herbst, Th. 18, 101, 127, 132-135, 181f., 184, 186-189, 208, 211-213, 274, 531, 575, 578, 584, 590, 592, 648f., 725, 881, 901, 905, 997, 999, 1000f., 1006, 1009, 1112, 1381, 1383, 1385, 1765, 1953, 2243, 2756f., 2768, 2903, 2964, 2969, 3030
Herdan, G. 1318, 1322, 1644, 1650, 1667
Herden, R. 1362
Herfurth, M. 2225

Herg, E. 1038, 1040
Hergemöller, B.-U. 1267
Heringer, H.J. 180, 197, 207, 781, 785, 786, 815, 821, 882f., 887, 2172, 2236
Herlitz, B. 2220
Herman, L.J. 1149, 1151, 1183
Hermann, K.A 2393
Hermann, P. 1198
Hermann, Th.M. 1263
Hermann, U. 273, 320, 358, 405f., 459, 499, 574f., 786, 804, 1240, 2224, 2231
Hermann, V. 2886
Hermanns, F. 117, 125, 578, 607f., 611f., 614, 653f., 793, 796, 837f., 840f., 849-851, 854, 1204f.
Hermanns, W. 2199, 2222
Heřmanová, Z.T. 2284
Hermant, A. 1214
Hermes, E. 1361
Hermes, L. 2758
Hernández, C. 2665
Hernández, H. 2898, 2902
Hernandez-Aquino, L. 1755, 1759
Herodes, St. 2260
Herok, Th. 591
Heroldová, D. 2284
  (= Štovíčková, D.)
Heron, W. 140, 145
Herout, A. 3140, 3141
Herrás, J. 1761
Herrera, G.A. de 1741, 1859
Herrero, A.M. 2979, 2984
Herrieu, A.M. 2350
Herrlitz, W. 883, 887
Herrmann, D. 3166
Herrmann, R. 1361, 2890, 2895, 2900
Herrmann, Th. 853
Herschberg-Pierrot, A. 1352
Herte, R. de 1272
Hertel, L. 2215, 2222
Herthum, P. 2231, 2232
Hertz, R. 2341
Hervás y Panduro, L. 2929
Hervás, L. 2916, 2918
Hervé, F. 2225
Herzfeld, M. 2908
Herzog, A. 1035, 1042, 1052, 2221
Herzog, E. 220, 224, 2758
Herzog, M. 1522
Herzog, M.I. 850, 854
Hesche, W. 2412
Hesiodus 1701
Heslop, O. 3171
Hess, K. 1657, 1667
Heß, K. 275, 371, 407, 459, 1571, 1573
Heß, K.-D. 2234, 2236
Hess-Lüttich, E.W.B. 687

Hesse, H. 2132, 2192
Hesselmann, B. 1933, 1935, 1942, 2934
Hessen, D. 3063, 3067
Hessen, H. 2341
Hessky, R. 576, 1039, 1042, 2234, 2758, 2794
Hestermann, F. 2652
Hesychius 1697, 1703
Hetherington, M.S. 1439, 1456
Hetherwick, A. 2648
Hetzel, S. 1186, 1188
Hetzer, A. 2361, 2366f.
Hetzron, R. 2461, 2464, 2467, 2469
Heubeck, A. 1687, 1689
Heucke, J. J. 3016
Heuer, G.F. 1522
Heuer, H.M. 1261, 1264
Heukels, H. 1255f.
Heumann, J. 3172
Heupel, C. 1355f., 1458f., 1361, 2207f., 2211f., 2222, 2895, 2900f., 2930
Heupold, B. 2063, 2069
Heurlin, K. 1361
Heuvel, G. van den 1816f.
Hewitt, B.G. 2418
Hexham, H. 1949, 3035-3037, 3039
Hey, K. F. G. 2275, 2277
Hey, O. 1242, 1244
Heyd, W. 1036, 1040
Heyden, S. 2043, 2048
Heydenreich, T. 223, 1813, 1184
Heydrich, W. 578, 854
Heym, J. 2917, 2929, 3075, 3083
Heym, J. A. 3073
Heymann, J. 2987f., 2991
Heymann, W. 1813
Heymans, R. 2805, 2813
Heynatz, J.F. 1068, 1073, 1216, 2093, 2095
Heyne, M. 124, 634, 731, 801, 804, 825f., 880, 1147, 1235-1237, 1239, 1268, 1273, 1522, 1912, 2078, 2081, 2084f., 2095, 2100, 2214
Heyse, J.Chr.A. 64, 69, 630f., 634, 801, 804, 871, 873-876, 880, 1173, 1176, 1234-1236, 1239, 2063, 2070, 2079, 2091, 2096, 2215, 2222
Heyse, K.W.L. 199, 206, 804, 1176, 2079, 2096
Hidalgo, C. 2683
Hidalgo, J. 1741, 1757, 2978
Hīdāyat, Ridā qulī Khan 2478
Hiddemann, H. 186, 188, 2758
Hiersche, R. 1234, 1239, 1589, 1608, 2193, 2196f., 2208, 2214, 2222, 2236

Hiersemann, A. 3176
Hietsch, O. 1039, 1042, 2719, 2727, 2758, 2966, 2969
Higgins, J. 2957, 2959
Higgins, Th. 2950f., 2954
Hildebrand, R. 127, 826, 1398, 1402, 1415, 2050, 2056, 2075, 2081, 2216, 2245
Hildebrand, S. 3044-3046
Hildebrandt, M. 1759, 2703
Hildebrandt, R. 17, 279, 359, 408, 461, 500, 576, 586, 619, 626-628, 688, 849, 1237, 1429, 1523, 1617, 1623, 2038, 2047-2049
Hilders, J. H. 2644
Hilferding, A. 2270
Hilgendorf, B. 2106, 2220, 2222
Hilgers, R. 3128, 3132
Hill, A.A. 129, 134, 656, 703, 1616f., 1623f., 2002, 2009
Hill, C.P. 1093
Hill, D.G. 3132
Hill, G. 1883, 1889
Hill, H.W. 1144f.
Hill, J. 1073
Hill, J.M. 1739, 1766
Hill, L.A. 1006, 1008, 1368
Hill, P. C. 2649
Hill, R.H. 1207f.
Hill, R. J. 2883-2885
Hill, St.P. 747
Hill, W.G. 3129
Hillebrand, J. H. 2065, 2070
Hillelson, S. 3095
Hiller, H. 250, 272
Hilpert, J.H. 2968
Hiltrop, J. 2934
Hilty, G. 275
Hindelang, G. 815f., 821
Hinderdael, M. 883, 887
Hinderling, R. 1132-1135. 1138, 1140, 1143, 1402, 1415, 2083, 2099
Hindmarsh, R. 1321, 1361, 2891, 2900
Hindoglu, A. 2402, 2405
Hinrichs, G. 1415
Hinrichsen, N. 2031
Hinske, N. 1573
Hinst, P. 539, 578
Hintze, F. 2270, 2272
Hinüber, O. von 2501, 2506
Hinz, W. 2471, 2472
Hinze, F. 2761
Hiorth, F. 557, 578
Hiorth, K. 118
Hippocrates 1696
Hippolytus, P. 2297
Hirachand, H. 2511, 2518
Hirai, K. 1338, 1340
Hirayama, T. 1306, 1308f.

Hirche, P. 2938, 2945
Hirmer, M. 1686, 1689
Hirose, T. 3116
Hirsch, R. 2690
Hirschbold, K. 1216
Hirschmann, R. 1567, 1573
Hirt, H. 124, 248, 273, 1157, 1240, 2062, 2075, 2085, 2098
Hirte, W. 2188, 2229
Hirth, H. 2062
Hirzel, S. 2081
Hiszpański, K. 3064
Hitaka, T. 3167
Hitler, A. 2086, 2106
Hitturāma 3099, 3104
Hitzenberger, L. 1140
Hixon, S. 3170
Hjelmslev, L. 361, 367, 411, 419, 544, 616, 1090, 1093
Hjort, K. 125, 989, 998
Hjorth, E. 1667, 1918, 1922, 2754
Hjorth, F. 552
Hjorth, P.L. 1922
Hlebka, P. 2337
Ho Giac, Th. 2506
Ho Yüan-chieh 2410
Hoad, T.F. 1571, 1573
Hoàng Thúc Trâm 2587f.
Hoàng Xuân-Hān 2588
Hoare, A. 2973f.
Hobar, D. 33f., 653, 656, 767, 998, 1816, 2009, 2728, 2758, 2767
Hoberg, R. 131, 134
Hochfelder, G. 1093
Hochleitner, F. 2802
Hochmuth, H. 2758
Hockett, Ch. F. 2696
Hockey, S. 1572f., 1646, 1667
Hocquart, É. 1803, 1806, 1840
Hodek, B. 2282f.
Hodges, F. 1271-1273
Hødnebø, F. 1927, 1929, 1931
Hoefer, E. 1036, 1040, 1186, 1188
Hoefer, F.A. 2939, 2946
Hoekema, T. 2027, 2034
Hoekstra, J. 2024
Hoekstra, S. 1361
Hoeller, A. 2674, 2676
Hoemann, H.W. 3143f.
Hoemann, S.A. 3143f.
Hoeppner, W. 899
Hoeufft, J. H. 2018, 2020
Hoey, M. 1672
Höfer, A. 1816f.
Höfer, J. 167
Hofer, M. 1513, 1517f., 1522
Hoff, B. J. 2702
Hoffer, B.L. 275
Hoffman, J. 2536-2538
Hoffman, L. 1320
Hoffmann von Fallersleben, H. 2029, 2131

Hoffmann, H.G. 1363
Hoffmann, I. 2533
Hoffmann, J. 2545
Hoffmann, K. 2471f.
Hoffmann, L. 321, 681f., 686f., 848, 1322, 1353, 1359, 1363, 1593, 1595f., 1610, 1644, 1661, 1667, 1669, 2891, 2902
Hoffmann, P.F.L. 631, 634, 1073, 1069, 1173, 1176, 2086, 2096, 2106, 2109-2112, 2115, 2128, 2222
Hoffmann, W. 106f., 110, 1234, 1240, 1334, 2083, 2096, 2195, 2236
Hoffmannswaldau, Chr. 2071
Hoffner, H.A. 1688f.
Hofland, K. 1315-1318, 1321, 1643, 1669
Höfler, M. 17, 145, 312, 654-656, 1017, 1169, 1177f., 1220, 1343f., 1347f., 1800, 1802, 1804, 1810-1813, 1815-1818, 1837, 1840, 1842f., 2757, 2765, 2864f., 2991, 2999f., 3006f., 3019
Hofmann, D. 2024f., 2028, 2031f., 2034, 2036
Hofmann, E. 2360
Hofmann, J. 2643f.
Hofmann, J.B. 1324, 1326, 1334, 2207f., 2223, 3032, 3034
Hofmann, R. 122, 125
Hofmann, W. 1036, 1042
Hofmannsthal, H. von 2131
Hofmeister, J. 854
Höfner, M. 2450, 2454
Hofstadter, D.R. 893, 899
Hofstetter, J.B. 1052
Hoftijzer, Ch.-F. J.-J. 2429, 2431f., 2434f., 2437
Hoftijzer, J. 1690, 1693
Höftmann, H. 2647f.
Hogan, E. 2341f.
Högg, G. H. 2091, 2096
Hohendorf, G. 1035, 1042
Hohenwart-Gerlachstein, A. 2643, 2645
Hohmann, H.-O. 1054f., 1189, 1359, 1363
Höhn-Ochsner, W. 1257
Höhne, St. 2124, 2236
Hohnerlein, M. 2096
Hohnhold, I. 173f.
Hohulin, E. L. 2758, 2824, 2870
Hoijer, H. 2693f., 2696
Hokama, S. 2621f.
Hoke Sein, U. 2552, 2554
Holberg, L. 1920, 1923
Holder, A. 1285, 1289, 2497
Hölker, K. 532, 539, 546, 551f., 578, 850, 854

Holladay, W.L. 2428, 2435
Holland, J. 327, 1547f.
Holland, R. 1255f.
Hollander, E. von 2124, 2155, 2166, 2167, 2169, 2185, 2188, 2223, 2226
Hollier, D. 1818
Hollmann, R. 2199, 2231
Hollunder, S. J. 2034
Holly, W. 393, 407, 531, 578, 643-645, 648, 815-817, 820-822, 881, 1152, 1230, 2052, 2075, 2082, 2099, 2130, 2135f.
Hollyband, C. (= Sainliens, C. de) 2956, 2959f.
Holm, G. 1929, 1931, 1936, 1942, 2758
Holm, K. 1632, 1637
Holm, L. 1933f., 1942f.
Holma, H. 1684f.
Holmberg, J. 3044-3046
Holmes, O.W. 24, 27
Holofcener, L. 1129
Holoskevych, H. 2332f.
Holovaščuk, S. J. 2758f.
Holšan, J. 3022, 3028
Holstrom, J.E. 3175
Hölterhof, F. 3074, 3083
Holthausen, F. 1328, 1332, 1418-1420, 1426-1428, 1442-1444, 1455, 1908, 1910f., 1929, 1931, 2024f., 2029, 2034
Holtrop, J. 3037, 3039
Holtsmark, A. 1925, 1927
Holtus, G. 269, 653, 656, 668, 1199, 1538, 1905, 3013, 3019
Holtz, W. 1261, 1264
Holtzmann, O. 2924, 2929
Holub, J. 2282f.
Holz-Mänttäri, J. 171, 174
Holzhaus, A. 3124, 3132
Holzinger, H. 1193
Holzmann, A. 2058, 2070
Homberg, W. 165
Homberger, D. 2207, 2213, 2223
Homerus 2, 148, 296, 1696, 1701, 1708
Homs i Guzman, A. 1779, 1784
Honemann, V. 2048
Honig, W. 2757, 2809, 2813
Honnen, P. 2199, 2201, 2234
Honnorat, S.J. 1893f., 1904
Honsa, V. 2690
Hoock, J. 167
Hood, Th. 1129, 2951
Hooft, P. C. 2010
Hooght, E. van der 2933
Hookoomsing, V. Y. 2872-2875
Hooper, W. 3101f., 3104
Hope, E. 2559
Hope, R.Ch. 1308f.

Hopf, Chr. 1632, 1637
Hopkins, K. 816, 822
Hopkins, N. 2663f., 2667
Hoppe, G. 276, 321, 648, 881, 1171f., 1175, 1178, 1230, 1234, 1240, 2218
Hoppe, O. 189, 3044-3046
Hoppe, P. 3044
Hoppe, S. 2271f.
Hoppe, U. 251, 272, 1349, 1351, 1530, 1532, 1537, 2185f., 2197, 2223
Horák, G. 2287
Horálek, K. 206f., 274, 2282f.
Horatius 146
Horbach, O. 2333f.
Horbatsch, O. 2271f., 2316, 2319, 2323, 2327
Horcasitas, F. 2661
Hordé, T. 679, 1072
Horecký, J. 576, 2287
Horeckyj, P. J. 3076, 3085
Hořejší, V. 2282f.
Hori, T. 3114, 3117
Horiuchi, K. 3117
Hörmann, H. 804
Horn, A. 3172
Horn, E. 1321
Horn, P. 2447, 2477, 2480
Horn, U. 2220
Hornbostel, W. 2228
Hornby, A.S. 160, 184, 187, 208, 212, 357, 405, 511f., 515-517, 524, 589-592, 692, 723, 746, 753, 785, 1110, 1017f., 1362, 1379, 1383, 1385, 1968, 2889f.
Hornby, R. 1273
Horne, E. 2562
Horne Tooke, J. 1956f., 1966
Hornig, C.A. 1551, 1559
Hornkens, H. 1817, 2929, 2976f., 2984, 2986f.
Hornung, W. 185, 188
Horovitz, J. 2378, 2381
Horst, P. 1791, 2044
Horstkotte, G. 551, 557, 578
Horta Massanes, J. 1129
Horukens, H. 1792
Horvat, V. 2289f., 2295
Hosák, L. 2282f.
Hoskison, J. T. 2458, 2460
Hôsô Kyôkai, N. 1306, 1308f.
Hospers, J.H. 1693, 2433
Hospitaler, J. 1774, 1784
Høst, J.N. 1920, 1922, 3053, 3060
Hotten, J.C. 1186, 1188
Hottinger, H. 2427
Hottinger, J.H. 2433
Houaiss, A. 1732-1734, 3022, 3028
Hough, G. H. 2552, 2554
Houghton, F.T.S. 1283
Houis, M. 2649

Householder, F.W. 33, 78f., 102, 110, 128, 133f., 274, 277, 584, 656, 668, 779, 980, 998, 1032, 1617, 1621, 1624, 1968, 1982, 2407, 2411, 2715, 2726f., 2756-62, 2767, 2896, 2902, 3096
Houssemaine-Florent, H. 2960
Houtman, F. de 2913f., 2930
Houttuyn, M. 2917, 2930
Hovad, P. 1286, 1289
Hovdenak, M. 1928
Hovis, M. 2647
Howard-Hill, T.H. 1566, 1573
Howardy, G. 1683f.
Howatt, A.P.R. 181, 188
Howe, D.R. 1655, 1667
Howell, J. 1088, 1092, 2914, 2916, 2030
Howes, D.A. 1321
Howlett, D.R. 1721
Høybye, R. 2835, 3019, 3056-3060
Hoyer, W. M. 2871f., 2875
Hoyt, J.K. 1046, 1048
Hrabec, St. 2272
Hradil, J. 3128, 3132
Hradský, L. 2283
Hraste, M. 2292, 2294
Hrinchenko, B. 2331f., 2334
Hristea, T. 1890
Hromada, R. 3126, 3132
Hryhorovych (Gregorovich), A. 2334
Hrynkiewicz, A. 3124, 3132
Hsaya, K. 2504
Hu Mujing 2597
Huang Borong 2611
Huarte Tejada, F. 1759
Hubad, F. 2300
Huber, A. 1139, 2081f., 2099, 2220
Huber, G.L. 1632, 1637
Huber, O. 2810, 2813
Huber, V.A. 2988, 2990
Hubig, Chr. 251, 275
Hübler, A. 856, 861
Hübner, A. 244
Hübner, F. 405, 2155, 2166, 2169, 2179, 2182, 2223
Hübner, J. 1129, 2062, 2066, 2070
Hubschmid, J. 269, 1348
Hudson, G. 2464f.
Hudson, K. 1529f.
Hudson, R.A. 102, 110
Hué, G. 2584, 2588, 2919, 2930
Huehnergard, J. 1690, 1693
Huerta, J. López de la 1068, 1073
Huesca, F. 1747, 1759
Huet, H. 3121f.
Hufeland, K. 135
Huffman, F. 2590f., 2593
Huffmann, F. E. 2558
Huffmon, H.B. 1690, 1693

Hügel, F. S. 2215, 2223
Hughes, A. 1645
Hughes, J.J. 1572f.
Hugo, V. 25-27, 603, 729, 911, 1044, 1184f., 1534, 1824
Hugon, P.D. 1099, 3130, 3132
Hugucio 2042
Hugucio de Pise 1788f.
Hugucio von Pisa 2038 (s. Uguccione)
Hugutio von Pisa 9, 1715
Huguet, E. 1157f., 1827, 1840
Huillery, F. 2981, 2984
Huình-Tịnh, P. Cua 2587f.
Huitu, M. 2385, 2388
Hukuta, M. 3121, 3132
Hulbert, J.R. 97, 527, 530, 588, 592, 1943, 1952, 1960, 1965f., 1987, 2007, 2009
Huld, M.E. 2363, 2366
Hull, V.E. 2341
Hüllen, W. 188, 580, 587, 1093, 1363f., 1944, 1952, 2895, 2902, 3166
Huloet, R. 1793, 2912, 2930, 2957, 2959
Hulsius, L. 43, 45, 1792, 1847f., 1860, 2046, 2048, 2051, 2053, 2070, 2074, 2913f., 2930, 2998f., 3004, 3006, 3013f., 3017, 3019
Hulstaert, G. 2648
Hultin, N.C. 326f.
Humbach, H. 2471f.
Humberdrotz, R. 3095
Humbert, J. 1029
Humbley, J. 1183, 1814
Hume, D. 551, 1983, 1986
Hume, M.A.S. 1048
Humec'ka, L.L. 2332f.
Humières, L. J. P. d' 2930
Hundsnurscher, F. 383, 393, 407, 1146, 1150, 1152, 1234, 1240
Hunger, W. 1527, 1530
Hunn, E. S. 2698, 2700
Hunold, G. 1196, 1198, 2188, 2223
Hunsberger, I.M. 1207f.
Hunsinger, W.W. 1054f.
Hunt, C. 1259f.
Hunt, J. 1048
Hunt, R.W. 1721
Hunter, G. G. R. 2535
Hunter, R. 1964f.
Hunter, S.C. 1144f.
Huot, C. 1313f.
Hupel, A.W. 2392, 2394
Hupka, W. 101, 269, 704, 706, 708f., 711, 714, 716, 718, 720, 722, 725, 988, 991f., 994f., 998f., 1105, 1112, 1383, 1385, 2915, 2936

Hurd, J.C. 2437
Hurley, A. 2699
Hurm, A. 2292, 2294
Hurt, J. 2393
Hurtado y Mendoza, M. 1747, 1759
Hurtaut, P.-Th.-N. 1121, 1124
Hüsejnov, H, 2409
Husen, T. 189
Hüsnü 2403, 2405
Hustad, T. 524
Huston, N. 1199
Hut Cin 2505
Hutchings, G. 2973f.
Hutchins, W.J. 1659, 1667, 1671, 3166
Hutchinson, J. 2643f., 2959
Huth, J. 2092, 2096
Hutterus, E. 2915, 2930
Hüttl-Folter, G. 2327
Hüttl-Worth, G. 2631, 3073, 3085
Huvāji Uskūfī, M. 2290
Huygens, Ch. 2010
Huygue, G. 2457
Hyams, Ph.J.E. 1190
Hyamson, A.M. 1054f.
Hyde, S. 2703
Hyldgaard-Jensen, K. 17, 127, 135, 188, 213, 223, 278f., 359f., 371, 408, 460f., 499f., 575, 583-587, 628, 656, 693, 749, 754, 787, 814, 855, 868, 893, 930, 981, 999, 1165, 1178, 1304, 1415f., 1549, 1987, 2236, 2239f., 2243-2245, 2726, 2753f., 2756-2761, 2764, 2770, 2775, 2778, 2836, 2853f., 2902, 2960, 2969, 3061
Hyman, R. 1047, 1049
Hymes, D.H. 305f.
Hyurmuzian, E. 2368, 2371
Hyvärinen, I. 2172, 2237

I

Iannelli, R. 1349, 1351
Iannucci, J.E. 1979, 1982, 2715, 2719f., 2727
Ibadullah 3097, 3102, 3104
Ibel, R. 2223
Iben Manzur 12
Ibn 'Abbād, al-Ṣāḥib 2441, 2443f., 2447
Ibn al-Muhannā 2625
Ibn al-Nadīm, Fihrist 2440, 2448
Ibn Duraid, Muḥammad ibn al-Ḥasan 2441, 2447
Ibn Fāris, al Mujmal fi l-Lugha 2447
Ibn Farīs, Maqāyīs al-Lugha 2444, 2447

Ibn Janâh, A.-W. M. 2712
Ibn Manzūr, Muḥammad ibn Mukarram 2442, 2445, 2447
Ibn Muhannā 2411
Ibn Qūṭiyya 2445
Ibn Sīdāh = 'Ali b. Ibrāhīm b. Sīdah 2441, 2445, 2447
Ibrahim, A. 1389
Ibrahim, A.H. 41, 45, 2753, 2881
Ibsen, H. 1923
Ibu Ilyas 2520
Ibuki, T. 3116f.
Icchāsaya 2504
Ichikawa, S. 3115, 3117
Ickler, Th. 13, 17, 115, 119f., 125, 129, 131-134, 184, 187f., 957, 967, 1069, 1075, 1359f., 1363, 2237
Ickovič, V. 693, 2323
Ietti, M.L. 2996
Igeta, S. 2622, 3116f.
Ignatius, M.A. 1361
Ihayer, J. E. 2645
Ihre, J. 1909, 1911, 1934, 1936, 1942
Ihwe, J. 462
Iijima, K. 3115, 3117
Ikeda, K. 3116f.
Ilarion, M. 2331, 2333
Ilčev, St. 2307f.
Ilg, G. 2920, 2930
Ilgenfritz, P. 2776, 2881, 3003f.
Iliescu, M. 269, 1361, 1890, 2758
Iliev, St. P. 2305, 2307
Illič-Svityč, V.M. 1338, 1340
Illig, C. 2803, 2990
Illing, K. 2038, 2048
Ilnytzkyj-Zankowytsch, J. 2332f.
Ilson, R. (B.) 32-34, 94, 97, 99, 101, 143, 145, 210, 212-215, 275f., 296, 350, 359, 367, 370, 517f., 525, 532f., 552, 562, 576ff., 581, 607, 649, 704, 714, 725, 882, 892, 905, 1007, 1009, 1014, 1016, 1093, 1183, 1367f., 1385, 1389, 1624, 1652, 1666, 1672, 1843, 1952, 1967, 1969, 1975, 1982f., 1988, 2008f., 2021, 2752, 2756, 2758, 2824, 2864, 2902, 2960
Ilson, R. F. 181, 188f., 524, 588, 592, 747, 3165
Imami, S. 2295
Imbert, P. 42, 45
Imbs, P. 62, 145, 222, 224, 229, 277, 311, 327, 342, 359, 517, 544, 579, 601, 604-606, 635, 640, 653f., 667, 672, 674, 679, 681, 684, 687, 703, 778, 906, 910f., 914, 916f., 929f., 946, 997, 1588, 1609, 1623, 1673, 1677f., 1814

Imjarekov, A.K. 2396, 2398
Imme, Th. 1531
Immelmann, J. 1803, 1814
Imnaišvili, I. 2417f.
Imre, S. 2379, 2381
Imura, J. 1800, 1814
Inamura, M. 3115, 3117
Inamura, S. 2619, 2622, 3114, 3117
Inėnlīkėj, P. I. 2630
Ingen, F. van 2074
Ingendahl, W. 804
Ingenkamp, K. 1632, 1637
Inglada, O.V. 3126, 3132
Inglés, M. 1778, 1784
Īnjū, Jamālu'l-dīn Husayn 2478
Innes, Ch. 1368
Innes, G. 2647-2649
Inoue, Y. 2622f.
Inouye, J. 3115, 3117
Inouye, T. 3114, 3117
Insler, St. 2471f.
Insley, J. 1275
Ioanid, G. 1884
Ionchère, C. la 2917, 2930
Iordan, I. 579, 1887, 1890
Iorga, N. 1884
Iosif, Ė. V. 2484
Ippel, E. 853
Ippoldt, J. 746, 3062f., 3067
Ipsen, G. 2224
Ipsen, P. L. 3056, 3060
Iriarte, T. de 1742, 1764
Iribarren, J.M. 1759
Iribas, J.S. 2951, 2956
Iris, M.A. 579
Iriye, I. 3115, 3117
Irmandades da Fala 1737
Irmen, F. 3023-3025, 3028
Irvine, A.H. 1079
Irvine, Th.U. 1293, 1295
Irwin, G. 1525, 1530
Irwin, R. 43, 45
Isaac, N. 3126, 3132
Isabelle de Valois 2981
Isabelle, Infante 2977
Isačenko, A. V. 2286f.
Isaeva, Z. G. 2484f.
Isajlović, D. 2291, 2294
Isbâşescu, M. 1889, 2759, 2853
Isbell, Ch.D. 2432, 2437
Isella, D. 151
Isenberg, Ch. W. 2451, 2454, 2462, 2465
Ishaq, Y. 2437
Ishikawa, M. 2619, 2622
Isidor von Sevilla 8f., 148, 280, 994, 1323, 1332, 1714, 1721, 1789, 2038
Ising, E. 78, 206, 274, 2208, 2236
Ising, G. 233, 242f., 804, 830, 956f., 960, 967, 2052f., 2070, 2073, 2075, 2215, 3014, 3019

Işitman, I,R. 2403-2405
Iskandar, T. 2563, 2565
Iskos, A. 250, 275
Isoda, M. 3166
Isola, F. 1804, 1814
Israel, F. 1690, 1693
Isser, A. 1883, 1888
Isshiki, T. 3116
Issing, L.J. 716, 725
Issler, G. 2229
Itkonen, E. 2385-2387, 2391
Itkonen, T.I. 2391
Itô, K. 3121, 3132
Iustinianus 1878
Ivančev, S. 1129
Ivánescu, G. 1890
Ivanov, D. L. 2485
Ivanov, V.V. 2324
Ivanova, A.F. 2323
Ivanova, E. 2853
Ivanova, E. A. 2896, 2900
Ivanova, V.A. 2317, 2327
Ivanova-Mirčeva, D. 2266f.
Ivanová-Šalingová, M. 2286f.
Ivarra, M. 1771, 1784
Iveković, F. 2291, 2294
Iversen, R. 1550f., 155
Ivir, V. 2759, 2776, 2778
Iwanowa, E. 1361
Iwasaki, T. 3115, 3117
Iyyäsus, Y. G. 2450
Ižakevič, G.P. 2320, 2323
Izjumov, O. 2331, 2333

J

Jaba, A. 2483, 2485
Jaberg, K. 1331f.
Jablonski, D.E. 231, 233-236, 244, 2053, 2056, 2061, 2075, 2093, 2099
Jablonski, St. 1259f.
Jacevič, L. St. 2484f.
Jachnov, H. 274, 308, 2310, 2321, 2327, 2329
Jachnow, W. 274
Jachontov, S. E. 2826, 2828
Jacks, L. 2664, 2667
Jackson, A. V. W. 2471f.
Jackson, Chr.E. 1257
Jackson, F. 2667
Jackson, H. 522, 525, 1975, 1982, 2759
Jackson, K. 2341f.
Jackson, K.P. 1690, 1693
Jacob, G. A. 2496
Jacob, G. S. 2494
Jacobi, H. G. 2502
Jacobs, J. 247, 277
Jacobsen, B. 2029
Jacobsen, J. 2761, 2783, 2786, 2789, 2841, 2854

Jacobsen, J. R. 1667, 2754
Jacobsen, L. 1916f., 1922
Jacobsen, M.A. 1930, 1932
Jacobsen, R. 1657
Jacobsen, S. 1083
Jacobsen, W.M. 1982
Jacobson, St. A. 2632-2634
Jacobsson, U. 662, 668
Jàcono, A. 1867, 1879
Jacopo di Calcinia 1844
Jaeger, P.L. 2969
Jafar Ali Khan Asar 2521
Jäfärov, J.M. 2410
Jagannathan, V.R. 3102-3104
Jagemann, Chr. J. 3015-3017
Jäger, L. 269, 531, 552, 557, 579, 849f., 853-855
Jäger, S. 197, 207
Jäger, W. 223, 3015, 3018
Jagić, V. 3072, 3085
Jago, F.W.P. 2348, 2350
Jahn, F.L. 1232
Jahn, J.F.L.Chr. 1068, 1073, 2059, 2070
Jähns, M. 1294
Jain, M.P. 132-134, 2776, 2778
Jain, N. 3100, 3104
Jain, S.K. 3102, 3104
Jaina, L. 3104, 3192
Jaina, S.K. 3102, 3104
Jainas, D. 2498
Jaini, J. L. 2502, 2504
Jakimovič, J. K. 3074, 3077, 3085
Jakob Twinger von Königshofen 2038, 2040, 2048
Jakobi, A. 2644
Jakobsen, J. 1930-1932
Jakobson, R. 716, 725, 1093, 1538, 2628, 2631, 3070, 3085
Jakolev, N.F. 2420
Jakovlev, N.F. 2420
Jaksche, H. 598, 834, 1031, 1044
Jakubaite, T. 1669, 2358, 2360
Jakubajtis, T.A. 1671
Jakubaš, F. 2276f.
Jakubowicz, A. 3076
Jal, A. 2918, 2930
Jamālzāda, M. 'A. 2479
Jamaspji, H. 2475, 2477
Jambrešić, A. 2289, 2296
Jambressich, A. 2294
James, C. 2857f.
James, G. 1704, 2902
James, J. 1196, 1199
James, R. 1439, 2396, 3070
James, W. 2968, 2972, 2974
James, W. I. 2823
Jameson, A. 899
Jamieson, J. 1448, 1455, 1984-1986
Jamison, S.L. 3141, 3144
Janceneckaja, M.N. 2319, 2323

Jančovič, S. 2285, 2287
Jandebeur, F. 2066, 2075
Jané, A. 1777, 1782, 1784
Janelle, C. 1044, 1049
Janežić, A. 2298, 2300
Janggya röbe dorje 2548
Janhunen, J. 1340, 2395, 2397f.
Janitza, J. 1219f.
Jankovič de Mirievo, F. I. 2932, 3072, 3084
Jankuhn, H. 1254
Jannen, R. 2029
Jannet, M. 1804, 1806
János, M. 2378
Jánošik, A. 2285
Janovskij, M. 2315, 2323
Janovskij, N. M. 3074, 3083
Janow, J. 2332
Janowowa, W. 1274
Jansen, G. P. 2871, 2875
Jansen, H. 2092, 2096
Jansen, Hild. 2222
Jansen, Hub. 2192, 2223
Jansen, L.M. 1066, 1084, 1093
Jansens, G. 2010, 2019
Janssen, H. 275
Janssen, O. 1140
Janssens, G. 765f., 1367f., 2021
Janua, J. de 1788f.
Janucci, J. E. 2758
Japicx, G. 2025
Jarancev, R.I. 2323
Järborg, J. 1938
Jarceva, V. N. 2328, 2752
Jardel, B. 3067
Jarden, D. 1261, 1263
Jarecki, W. 3151, 3157
Jarivier, L. 2515, 2520
Jarnik, C. 2298
Jarosseau, A. 2463, 2465
Jarring, G. 2412
Jarvie, J.N. 1985f.
Jaschke, H. A. 2549f.
Jaspers, G.J. 582, 930, 2048
Jastrow, M. 2429, 2435
Jastrzembski, J.E. 141, 145
Jaubert, A. 1252
Jaugin, E. 1814
Jaunvalks, E. 3126f., 3133
Jawaliki = Mauhub b. Ahmad al-Jawaliqa 2444
Jayadevan, V. 2533
Jean, G. 1351
Jean-Paul II 1112
Jeddore, R. 2634
Jedlička, A. 2281, 2283f.
Jedlińska, A. 3065, 3067
Jefferson, Th. 1159
Jefremov, S. 2331, 2333
Jelinek, F. 1235, 1239, 1539, 1543, 1548, 2088, 2096
Jelínek, J. 1669, 2283

Jelinek, M. 1321
Jellinek, M.H. 1146, 1152
Jellinghaus, H. 1280, 1283, 1289, 2220
Jellissen, H. 1624
Jember, G.K. 1444, 1455
Jenč, H. 2276-2278
Jenč, R. 2275-2278
Jenisch, B. von 2401
Jenish, B. 3170
Jenkins, E. 3148
Jenkins, R. 1361, 2891, 2895, 2900
Jenness, D. 2634
Jenni, E. 2428, 2435
Jensen, E. 1919, 1922
Jensen, H. 1186
Jensen, H.J. 1915
Jensen, K. 1660, 1667, 3166
Jensen, P. 2030, 2034
Jenssøn, Chr. 1924, 1927
Jentsch, H. 2275, 2278
Jerabek, G. 1219f.
Jernej, J. 1018, 2292f.
Jespersen, O. 732, 748, 3055
Jessen, Chr. H. von 2271, 2274
Jessen, H. 816, 821, 2880f.
Jevy, J. 2434
Jhalkikar, B. 2496
Ji, Y. 3110, 3113
Jiang Zhuyi 2559
Jiménez Girón, E. 2698, 2699
Jin, B. 2410
Jinavarasirivadhana 2504
Jinavijaya 2504
Jireček, J. 2302
Joachimsohn, P. 1076, 1080
Joannes Balbus 1721 (s. Balbus)
Joannes Paulus II 1112
Joannes, J. 1302f.
Joannes, N. 2931
Job, M. 2196, 2236
Jobinus 1791
Jochelson, W. 2629f.
Jodlowski, S. 1303
Jodogne, O. 1275
Joffe, J. A. 2252
Johann von Gablingen 2041
Johann, E. 2237
Johann, E.D. 1263
Johannes Balbus von Genua 2038 (s. Balbus)
Johannes Januensis 1715, 1721
Jóhannesson, A. 1929, 1931
Johannison, T. 1012, 1015
Johannsen, A. 2030f.
Johansen, Chr. 2029, 2034
Johansen, P. 2354, 2360, 3070, 3085
Johansson, St. 1315-1318, 1321, 1643, 1669
Johnen, Chr. 3140f.
Johnson, A. 1029, 2698, 2700

Johnson, B. 1129
Johnson, Ch. 1722
Johnson, Ch.B. 1188
Johnson, D.B. 1147-1149, 1151, 2325
Johnson, E. L. 2471f.
Johnson, M. 856, 861, 1670
Johnson, R. 1293, 1295
Johnson, R.L. 170, 1669
Johnson, S. 10, 16, 29f., 139, 144, 219, 224-230, 509, 526, 528f., 720, 722f., 726, 754f., 761, 860f., 1068, 1093, 1159f., 1348, 1452, 1803, 1815, 1822, 1865, 1872, 1943f., 1946-1959, 1961f., 1965, 1983, 1985, 1988-1991, 2002, 2004f., 2007, 2950f., 2957, 2960, 2967, 2971f., 2974f., 3037, 3047, 3050, 3075
Johnson, S. jr. 1998, 2007
Johnson, W. 1207f.
Johnson-Laird, Ph.N. 899
Johnsson, G. 3044f.
Johnston, B. 2695f.
Johnston, H. H. 1340, 2647, 2649
Johnston, M. C. 2887
Johnston, W. 509, 1308f.
Johnstone, W. 2428
Joki, A. 1338, 1340
Joki, A. J. 2385-2387, 2395, 2397, 2630
Joly, Ph.-L. 1798, 1814
Jomard, F. 2462, 2469
Jóna, E. 2285, 2287
Jonama, S. 1073
Jónasson, J. 1929, 1931
Jones, D. 509, 513, 516, 1293, 1295, 1305, 1308-1311, 2823, 2960
Jones, D.R. 2433
Jones, E. 3150, 3157
Jones, G.F. 1137, 1139f.
Jones, H.P. 1046, 1049
Jones, H.St. 1700, 1702
Jones, J. D. Rh. 2653, 2655
Jones, K.P. 1652, 1667
Jones, K.S. 3166
Jones, L.V. 1321
Jones, M.L. 140, 145
Jones, R. B. 2559
Jones, R.L. 1134, 1142, 1567, 1573, 1910, 1912
Jones, S. 1018, 1652, 1667
Jones, T. 1622, 2578, 2582, 2759, 2853, 2968
Jones, W. 526, 1169, 1178, 1440, 2063f., 2075, 2490, 2493
Jones, W.J. 1169, 1172, 1175, 1177
Jong, A. de 3129, 3133
Jong, E. de 1669
Jonghe, A. de [= Junius, H.] 1850, 2912

Jongkindt, A. M. C. 2930
Jonke, L. 2289, 2296
Jonker, J. C. G. 2566f.
Jonson, B. 1453
Jonsson, H. 1943
Joos, A. 2019f.
Joos, M. 579
Jordan, J. 2751
Jordan, R. 1255, 1257
Jordan, R.R. 211, 214
Jørgensen, J. 1919, 1922
Jørgensen, J.N. 1305, 1308
Jørgensen, M. W. 2759, 2770, 2775
Jørgensen, P. 2029
Jörgensen, V. T. 2030-2032, 2034
Jorif, R. 24, 28
Joscelyn, J. 1438f.
Joseph i Mayol, M. 1778, 1784
Joshi, L. 2496
Joshi, N.B.N. 3101, 3104
Joshi, P. N. 2514, 2519
Joshi, S. 3097, 3099, 3104
Joshi, V. 2496
Jośi, R. 3097-3099, 3104
Jośi, R.K. 3102, 3104
Jośi, S. 3097-3099, 3104
Josif, E. V. 2485
Josselson, H.H. 1321, 1666, 1669, 2320, 2323
Josserand, J. K. 2661
Jost, D. 1450, 1456
Josten, D. 232, 244
Jostsone, A. 2359
Jouette, A. 1303
Jourdain, E. 2871, 2875
Joustra, M. 2567
Jouy, M.E. de 1805
Jovanović, G. 2263, 2267
Jovanović, R. 2292, 2294
Jovellanos, G.M. de 1742, 1766
Jover Peralta, A. 2676
Jover, D.A. 2983
Jóvgan, s. Ánna
Joxel'son, V. 2629 (s. Jochelson, W.)
Joyce, P.W. 2341
Joynt, M. 2342
Jóźwicki, J. 3066f.
Juan de Córdoba, Fray 2683f., 2697, 2699
Juan Manuel, D. 1740
Jucht, V. A. 2885
Jucquois, G. 1911
Jud, J. 1327, 1331f., 1343
Judson, A. 2552, 2554, 2556
Judy, R. 2703
Juglà i Font, A. 1773, 1783, 2928
Juhász, G. 1550, 1554f., 1557, 2380f.
Juhász, J. 197, 207, 2381, 2396f.

Juilland, A. 77, 296, 304, 509, 516, 1132, 1134f., 1138, 1140, 1244f., 1306, 1308f., 1315, 1318, 1321, 1357, 1361, 1643, 1650, 1667, 1669, 1889f., 2887
Juilland, I. 1321, 1361, 1669, 1889
Juker, B. 1550, 1552, 1559
Jukes, A. 2520
Jump, J.R. 1759
Jung, F. W. 2066, 2070
Jung, U.H. 1262, 1264
Jung, W. 796
Jungberg, C. G. 3047, 3050
Jungclaussen, G. 1652, 1667
Jungmair, O. 2223
Jungmann, E. 117, 125, 214
Jungmann, J. 2279f., 2283
Jungraithmayr, H. 1340, 2457, 2460
Junius, A. 2914
Junius, F. 1436, 1440f., 1455, 1909, 1911f.
Junius, H. [= Jonghe, A. de] 1088, 1092, 1094, 1791, 1806, 1845, 1847f., 1850, 1860, 1948, 1954, 2043f., 2046f., 2916, 2930, 3007
Junker, H. F. J. 2475, 2477
Juquois, G. 1910
Jurevič, A.L. 2337
Jürgensen, H. 3121, 3124, 3126, 3133
Jurin, J. 2290
Jurišić, B. 2292, 2294
Jurkatam, J. 2393
Jusayú, M. A. 2703
Jusenius, D. 2916, 2930
Juška, A. 2351, 2353, 2357
Juskevič, A. 2353
Juslenius, D. 2384, 2387
Jussien, A. de 165
Justi, F. 2471f., 2485
Justinien 1873
Jusupova, Z. A. 2483, 2485
Jütte, R. 1530, 1532, 1538
Jütting, W.U. 1550, 1552, 1559
Jüttner, F. 575
Juynboll, H. H. 2561f.
Jyhlarz, E. 2646

K

Kaasik, I.-R. 2801f.
Käbbäda Dästa 2451, 2453
Kabelka, J. 2357, 2359
Kabell, I. 3052, 3061
Kabisch, O. 3006
Kabuli, J. 1906
Kačala, J. 2286f.
Kachlak, T. 746
Kachru, B.B. 71, 78

Kacori, Th. 2363
Kaczmarek, L. 2271f.
Kadagidze, D. 2422f.
Kadagidze, N. 2423
Kaddari 2428
Kade, O. 174, 2759
Kadri, H.K. 2404f., 2413
Kaeding, F.W. 119, 124, 1141, 1317, 1319, 1321, 1353-1356, 1361, 1595, 1608, 1643, 1650, 1666
Kaempfert, A.M. 1206
Kaesri, S. 2506
Kafka, F. 1142
Kafker, F.A. 17, 1817
Kagaine, E.K. 2358, 2360
Kaganoff, B.C. 1271, 1273
Käge, O. 78, 369, 653, 655, 741, 748, 2130, 2219, 2237
Kagine, E.K. 2360
Kahane, H. and R. 78
Kahle, G. 849, 851, 853-855
Kahlmann, A. 1078, 1080, 3043
Kahn, L. 2252, 2254
Kahn, L.E. 3172
Kahn, M. H. 2521
Kaindl, J. E. 2088f., 2096
Kaiser, E. 1217
Kaiser, K. 2060, 2075
Kaiser, St. 122, 125, 1093
Kaisersberg, G. von 1399
Kaja, I. S. 3080
Kajgorodov, A.M. 3173
Kaji, H. 3127, 3133
Kajiga, B. 2648
Käkakhel, Ẓ. 3099, 3104
Kakati, B. K. 2509
Kalajdović, P. 2317, 2323
Kalakuckaja, L. P., 2316, 2322
Kálal, K. 2285, 2287
Kálal, M. 2285, 2287
Kalānavī, D. 3104
Kalašev, A.I. 2437
Kalbskopf, G. 3172
Kalgren, B. 1308
Kalima, J. 2359f.
Kalina, P. 3062-3064, 3067
Kalinin, A. V. 2312-2320, 2327
Kalinin, W.M. 1322
Kalkar, O. 1917, 1922
Kallio, A.H. 2384
Källquist, E. 1207f.
Kálmán, B. 2396f.
Kalnciems, O. 2360
Kalnyn', L.E. 2327
Kalocsay, K. 3125, 3131, 3133
Kalonymus, I.N. ben 2434
Kaltschmidt, J. 2939, 2946
Kaltschmidt, J.H. 1234, 1239, 2064, 2070
Kaltz, B. 748
Kalveram, C. 1759

Kalverkämper, H. 681, 685-688, 947, 955, 1517, 1519, 1522f., 2947
Kamaryt, S. 3128, 3133
Kambartel, F. 410, 459
Kaminska, M. 2271
Kamiš, A. 2282f.
Kamlah, W. 539, 547f., 579
Kammenhuber, A. 1687-1689
Kämper-Jensen, H. 1532, 1538, 2076, 2193, 2236f.
Kanapell, B. 3144
Kanda, N. 3115, 3117
Kandler, G. 1149
Kane, Th. L. 2451, 2454f.
Kaneshiro, V. O. 2633
Kangrga, J. 512, 516, 2292, 2295
Kangxi 2598, 2610
Kaniz, F. 2224
Kann, K. 511, 516
Kannapell, B. 3141
Kannas, C. 679, 945, 1367, 1378, 1835
Kannenberg, A. 2463, 2467f.
Kanngießer, S. 580
Kannisto, A. 2381
Kano, Ch. 1119
Kano, M. 2459
Kant, I. 541-543, 551, 556, 579, 1545, 1873, 2059
Kant, K. 124, 2085, 2098
Kantemir, A. 2319, 2323
Kantemir, A. D. 3073, 3084
Kany, Ch.E. 1194, 1199
Kāpaḍiā, H. R. 2502, 2504
Kapeller, L. 120, 124, 1192
Kaper, E. 747
Kaper, J. 3054, 3056, 3060
Kapff, von 3153, 3156
Kappherr, G.E. 3017
Kaplan, L. D. 2634
Kapr, A. 142, 145
Kapur, B. N. 2512, 2519
Karadžić, V.St. 2290f., 2293f., 2298, 2305, 2307, 3078
Karanastasis, A. 1712
Karapetian, P.Z. 2370f.
Karaś, M. 527, 1308f., 2270-2272
Karasaev, A.T. 2422f.
Karaulov, J.N. 1665f., 1669, 1672, 2320f., 2323, 2327, 3085
Kardanov, B.M. 2420
Karg-Gasterstädt, E. 1428, 1548, 2215
Karinus, I. 3166
Karjalainen, K.F. 2396f.
Karker, A. 1079, 1916
Karl, I. 575, 2716f., 2727, 2943, 2947
Karl, J. 2759
Karlgren, B. 1305, 1309
Karlgren, H. 1671

Karlins, J. 1142
Karłowicz, J. 2268, 2271f.
Karmi, H.S. 3092, 3095
Károly, S. 2382
Karow, O. 2587f., 2618, 2623
Karpjuk, G.V. 2313, 2315f., 2318f., 2327
Karpova, O.M. 1556, 1561
Karpovič, A.E. 312, 314, 321, 362, 370, 2327
Kärre, K. 3048-3050
Karsandas Mulji 2518
Karskij, Je.F. 2336
Karsten, G. 2027
Karttunen, F. 71, 77f., 2659-2661
Karttunen, K. 2385, 2387
Karuṇāratna, T. 2505
Karve, C. G. 2493, 2495
Kasai, S. 2925
Kashgharī, M. al- 3086, 3095
Kašić, Bartol (Bartholomaeus Cassius) 2289
Kaširina, M.E. 1668
Kask, A. 2395
Kasovsky, B. (= Kosovsky) (= Q'sswsqy) 2429
Kasovsky, Ch.Y. (= Kosovsky) (= Q'sswsqy) 2429f.
Kasovsky, M. (= Kosovsky) (= Q'sswsqy) 2429
Kasowski, Ch.J. 2435f.
Kaspjarovič, M.I. 2336f.
Kasprowicz, E. L. 2918, 2930
Kassai, J. 2376, 2381
Kasser, R. 1680f.
Kastelec, M. 2297
Kasten, L.L. 1756
Kastner, F. 1261, 1264
Kastner, G. 1036, 1040
Kastovsky, D. 583f., 779, 1368, 1624, 1953
Kastūri Ranga Kawi 2525
Katančić, M. P. 2290
Katanov, N.F. 2410
Katavarilāla 3101f., 3104
Kate Hermansz, L. ten 2018, 2020
Katgade, P. 3097, 3099, 3104
Katharina II. 3072
Katičić, R. 2288, 2296
Katlinskaja, L.P. 693, 2323
Katre, S. M. 2497, 2500, 2867, 2870
Katre, W. M. 2506
Katsuragawa, H. 3114, 3117
Katukolinhe, F. 3101, 3104
Kātya 2489
Kātyāyana 2488
Katz, B. 3166
Katz, D. 2247, 2254
Katz, J.J. 544
Katzschmann, M. 2397
Kauczor, J. 1152

Kauczor, Joh. 2193, 2232
Kaufhold, M. 245
Kaufman, I.M. 3172
Kaufman, T. 2664, 2666f.
Kaufmann, G. 1357, 1363
Kaufmann, H. 1272, 1280, 1283
Kaufringer, H. 1142, 1573
Kaul Grünwald, G. 1760
Kaura, R. 3100, 3106
Kausalyāyana, Ā. B. 2505
Kaushik, J.N. 1669
Kavakli, E. 1692f.
Kavalliotis, Th.A. (= Kaballiotes) 2361, 2366
Kavi, M. R. 2496
Kawamoto, A.H. 3167
Kawamoto, S. 3115, 3117
Kawamura, J. 3115, 3117
Kawano, K. 3116f.
Kawasaki, N. 3121f., 3133, 3137
Kawase, K. 2623
Kawi, K. R. 2532
Kay, Chr.J. 1090, 1093
Kay, E. 3092, 3094
Kay, M. 1665, 1667, 1671, 3167
Kay, M.W. 1077, 1079, 1164
Kay, P. 573, 576, 861
Kayser, K. 2655
Kazár, L. 1340
Kazimirski-Biberstein, A. de 2938, 2946, 3089, 3095
Keast, W.R. 1951f.
Keckeissen, R.G. 3174
Kedilaya, A. S. 2525, 2533
Keegan, J. 2644
Keen, D. J. 2823
Keenadiid Yaasiin Cismaan 2465
Keesing, R.M. 286
Kefi, M.B. el- 3092, 3095
Kehr, K. 269
Kehrein, F. 2062, 2070
Kehrein, J. 120, 124, 1059, 1173f., 1177, 1233f., 1239, 1592, 2062, 2064, 2070, 2088, 2096, 2215, 2223
Keil, H. 1072
Keil, K. 1703
Keil, R.-D. 1320, 1322
Keipert, H. 1142f., 2319, 2327, 3071, 3074, 3083, 3085
Kelekian, D. 2402, 2405
Kelemen, B. 2378, 2381, 2727, 2759
Kelemen, J. 2378, 2383
Kelle, J. 1551, 1559
Kelleher, J.V. 2343
Keller, A. 1840
Keller, G. 728
Keller, H.E. 1894, 1905, 3176
Keller, H.H. 1147-1149, 1151f., 2184, 2223
Keller, R. 804

Keller, S. 2592f.
Keller-Bauer, F. 799, 804
Kellner, L. 1551
Kellow, S.E. 199, 206, 2185, 2223
Kelly, E. 1651, 1667
Kelly, J. 2346, 2349
Kelly, L.G. 722, 725, 2936
Kelly, P. 1271, 1273
Kelly-Bootle, St. 1349, 1351
Kelm, A. 2683
Kelminson, L. 3176
Kelusakara, B.V. 3099, 3101, 3104
Kemble, J.M. 1284, 1291
Kemivé, J. 2885
Kemme, H.-M. 810, 813
Kemp, Ch. 3130, 3133
Kemp, J.A. 749
Kempcke, G. 130, 134, 144, 273, 275, 320, 358, 405, 458, 499, 510, 516, 532, 574, 579, 592, 596, 599, 613, 626, 661, 672, 681, 684, 687, 697f., 747, 753, 778, 785, 787, 834, 841, 848f., 868, 881, 966, 1031, 1058, 1064f., 1078-1080, 1215, 1235, 1239, 2130, 2150, 2181, 2182, 2188, 2218, 2221, 2223, 2232, 2237
Kemper, H. 1257
Kemper, Th.D. 853f.
Kemper, W. 1257
Kempler, D. 1624
Kenaʻani (= Ycqb kuʻny) 2436
Kenin, R. 1045, 1050
Keniston, H. 1319, 1321, 1361, 1756
Kennedy, A.G. 1449f., 1455, 1966, 3172
Kenrick, W. 509, 1308f., 1955, 1965
Kent, A. 1566
Kent, R. G. 2471f.
Kent, R.K. 1073
Kenyon, J.S. 78, 1308f.
Keppler, K. 2759, 2887
Keranāvi, V. 3101, 3104
Keraševa, Z.I. 2420
Kerbrat-Orecchioni, C. 653, 655, 912, 917
Kerckhoffs, A. 3129, 3133
Kerestedjian, B.E. 2402, 2404f.
Keresztes, K. 2382
Keresztes, L. 2396, 2398
Kerger, A. 1205
Kerimova, A. A. 2485
Kerketta, J. 2542
Kerler, R. 2921, 2930
Kerling, J. 2, 17, 655, 1946f., 1949, 1952
Kern, H. 2024, 2500, 2506
Kerner, S. 2251, 2253
Kernycʼkyj, I.M. 2332f.

Kerobian, G. 2369
Kersey, J. 1162, 1943f., 1946-1951, 3037, 3039
Kerviler, R. 1800, 1814
Kēśirāja 2524, 2532
Kesselring, W. 269, 770, 1347f.
Ketelius, R. 1053
Kettner, B.-U. 1286, 1289f.
Kettridge, J. O. 2920, 2930, 2959
Kettunen, L. 2393f.
Key, H. 2659f.
Key, M. R. 1340, 2700, 2702f., 2705, 2707, 2709
Keyser, S. 2027
Keysser, Chr. 2636f.
Khajdakov, S.M. 2422f.
Khalīl 3086
Khan, G. 2521
Khan, G. M. 2516, 2520, 3097
Khan, G. U. 2517
Khan, G.W. 3103
Khan, M. 2512
Khan, M. H. 2517
Khan, M. M. 2517, 2521
Kharma, N. N. 2759, 2896, 2902
Khatanov, A.A. 2420
Khātir Bey, Mahmūd 2442, 2447
Khažinskaja, M.S. 1670
Khestlová, D. 2284
Khetagurov, K. 2484
Khidekel, S.S. 274, 1651, 1666
Khudāydede, Ibrāhīm ibn 2478
Khursro, A. 2512
Kibbee, D. A. 1814, 2759, 2956, 2960
Kibbermann, E. 516, 2394
Kibbermann, F. 516
Kibrik, A.E. 2422f.
Kiçi, G. 2365f.
Kick Ehlers, E. H. 3026, 3028
Kidanä Wäld K fle 2450, 2454
Kido, F. 616, 627
Kidosaki, M. 3122, 3133
Kidrič, F. 2297, 2301
Kiefer, F. 539, 575, 813
Kieffer, Ch.M. 2412
Kieffer, J.D. 2402, 2405
Kieft, C. van de 1721
Kiel, M. W. 2247, 2254
Kielhorn, L. F. 2496
Kielmayer, C. 2462, 2467
Kielski, B. 3064, 3067
Kielten, K. 2387
Kiener, F. 1193
Kienle, K. 2091, 2096
Kienle, R. von 1175, 1177, 2185, 2188, 2223
Kienpointer, M. 584
Kierst, W. 3064, 3067
Kiesewetter, L. 1173f., 1177, 3040
Kieuv, B.I. 3104
Kihara, K. 3115, 3117

Kiliaan, C. 1433f., 2017f., 2020, 2047, 3035, 3039
Kiliaan, H. N. 2566f.
Kilianus, C. 2930
Killer, W.K. 1104, 1110
Killy, W. 1241
Kim Pyŏng-je 2617
Kim Tu-bong 2614, 2616
Kim Yun-gyŏng 2614
Kim, S. S.-D. 2759
Kimchi, D. 2434
Kimpel, D. 1210, 1240, 2969
Kimpel, R. 1199
Kimura, D. 140, 145
Kimura, K. 3116f.
Kindaichi, H. 1306, 1308f., 2622
Kindaichi, K. 2622
Kindberg, L. 2702
Kinderling, J. F. A. 2063, 2070
Kindermann, U. 1722
Kindlam, M. 2394
King, A. 1049
King, A. V. 2459
King, W.F.H. 1046f., 1049
Kingdom, W. 1046, 1049
Kingon, J. R. L. 2654
Kingsburg, St. 1034, 1042
Kinne, M. 1201, 1204, 2185-2187, 2223, 2237
Kintana, X. 2374f.
Kiparski, P. 2494
Kiparsky, V. 1336f., 1340, 2359f.
Kipfer, A. 320f.
Kipfer, B.A. 208, 212, 214, 531, 579, 582, 652, 655, 766, 1620, 1622, 1624, 1644
Kipp, H. 2883-2885
Kipšidze, I. 2417
Királyföldy, E. 2377, 2381
Király, R. 3022, 3028
Kirane, T.G. 3097, 3104
Kirchberger, J.H. 1047, 1049
Kirchert, K. 2038f., 2041, 2047f.
Kirchhofer, M. 1035, 1040
Kirchner, G. 1134, 1143,
Kirchner, H. 1261, 1264
Kirk-Green, Chr. W. E. 2885
Kirkness, A. 131, 134, 226f., 230-232, 234, 244f., 276, 405, 458, 671f., 771, 881, 1139, 1149, 1151, 1169, 1173, 1175f., 1178, 1207, 1209, 1230-1232, 1235f., 1240f., 1399, 1408, 1415f., 2064, 2075f., 2079, 2081-2083, 2091, 2099f., 2104—2106, 2110, 2130, 2197, 2218, 2237, 2243, 3172
Kirkpatrick, B. 208, 214, 761, 901, 905, 1092, 2010, 2021
Kirkpatrick, E.M. 212, 515, 589-591, 667, 687, 746, 765f., 786, 904, 1385

Kirkpatrick, W. 2512, 2519
Kiro, H. 2542
Kirotar, S. 516, 2394
Kirsch, A. F. 2376, 3014, 3017, 3031, 3034
Kirsch, E. 835
Kirschbaum, E. 3152, 3154-3156
Kirschstein, B. 1548, 1609, 2232
Kirwin, W.J. 77
Kis-Viczay, P. 2376, 2381
Kisch, G. 1592
Kiselevskij, A. I. 2327, 2337
Kiselman, Ch.O. 3128, 3133
Kisidze, I. 2418
Kiskū, P. C. 2534, 2546
Kispi, H. G. 2688, 2690
Kiss, J. 2379, 2381
Kiss, L. 1334, 2381
Kisser, G. 1140
Kissling, H. 1389
Kißling, H. 2968
Kister, K.F. 31, 33, 98, 101, 136-138, 145, 765f., 1145, 1169, 1178, 1217, 1266, 1367f., 2006, 2009
Kistner-Deppert, K. 173f.
Kitchen, P.C. 1071
Kittel, F. 2524f., 2532, 3100, 3104
Kivi, A. 2384
Kivimies, Y. 1079, 2385, 2387
Kjær, A. L. 594, 597—599, 1031, 2130, 2237
Kjærulff Nielsen, B. 2789, 3057, 3060
Kjellmann, H. 1262, 1264
Kjuvlieva-Mišajkova, V. 3078, 3085
Klaar, R.M. 2960
Klaarbergen, B. W. van 2024
Klaiber, L. 1771, 1787
Klaić, B. 2293f.
Klappenbach, R. 158, 206, 273, 320, 358, 370, 406, 459, 499, 510, 516f., 575, 626, 647, 653, 655, 661, 667, 672, 681, 684, 686f., 692, 696-699, 747, 753, 778, 782, 786f., 796, 804, 813, 821, 834f., 841, 848, 856, 858f., 861, 887, 889, 892, 966, 1018, 1039, 1042, 1151, 1240, 1415, 1623, 2130, 2133, 2232, 2237, 2239
Klaproth, J. von 2483f., 2486
Klar, H. 2502, 2504
Klare, J. 542, 579, 1031, 1343, 1348, 3023-3026, 3028
Klaret 2278f.
Klasov, G. 1129
Klatzkin, J. 2436
Klaudi, K. 2759
Klaus, G. 539, 549, 579, 848, 1334
Klausing, A.E. 2967

Klausmann-Molter, B. 3018
Klavans, J. L. 1670, 2813
Klaviňa, S. 1142
Klavina, S. 2358
Klavins, J. 3167
Klecha, G. 2220
Klees, H. 1257
Kleiber, G. 573, 579, 1031
Kleiber, W. 1277, 1283
Kleij, V.D. 408
Kleij, van der 228
Klein, A. von 238, 242
Klein, D. 2041, 2048
Klein, E. 1328, 1332
Klein, H. 1038, 1040
Klein, H. E. M. 2684, 2690, 2702, 2704f., 2707-2710
Klein, H.-W. 607, 719, 724, 779, 787, 905, 1012, 1015, 1029, 1039, 1042, 1217, 2759, 2789, 2879-2885, 2887
Klein, J. 269
Klein, S.v.Micu 1882
Klein, W. 460, 499
Kleineidam, H. 269, 779, 1012, 1018, 2879f., 2881, 2901
Kleinknecht, R. 539, 579
Kleinmayr, J. 2300
Kleinpaul, R. 1254, 1257, 1294f.
Kleinschmidt, E. 2757
Kleinschmidt, S. P. 2632, 2634
Kleivan, I. 2633
Klement, J. 3129, 3133
Klenz, H. 1192, 1531, 2062, 2070
Klett, E. 2192
Kletzel, C. 726
Klien, H. 1110, 1111, 1175, 1177
Klieuv, B.I. 3101
Klima, E. 3142, 3144
Klimaszewska, Z. 883, 887
Kliment 3069
Klimeš, L. 2281, 2283
Klimov, G.A. 1340
Klimpert, R. 165f.
Klincksieck, C. 2495
Klingenheben, A. 2451, 2454
Klingenschmitt, G. 2471f.
Klinkenberg, J.M. 652, 655
Klinkert, H. C. 2563, 2565
Klint, A. 3044, 3046
Klinzing, G. 1140
Kljueva, V.N. 1073, 2317, 2323, 2327
Klockow, R. 856f., 861
Kloosterziel, U. 1079, 2179, 2181, 2182, 2223
Klopsch, P. 1722
Klopstock, F.G. 236, 245
Klosener, F. 2047
Kloss, H. 1417, 1429
Klosterboer, J. 2018
Klotz, R. 3032f.

Kluge, F. 728, 731, 769, 771, 1174, 1234, 1236, 1239, 1323, 1329, 1333, 1524, 1526, 1530, 2062, 2070, 2089, 2096, 2193-2198, 2223, 2240, 2242
Kluge, W. 2227
Klyška, M.K. 2337
Kmicykevych, B. 2331, 2333
Knapiusz, G. 2268
Knapp, H. 2199, 2201, 2223
Knapp, W.I. 1766
Knapp-Potthoff, A. 1358, 1363
Kneen, J.J. 2346, 2349
Knežević, A. 2293f.
Knight, H. 1111
Knight, P. 1030
Knittel, F.A. 1909, 1912
Knobloch, C. 277, 321, 881, 2130, 2147, 2237
Knobloch, J. 2041, 2207, 2208, 2224
Knoop, U. 17, 125f., 244f., 627, 655, 980, 1415, 1429, 1608f., 2048f., 2060f., 2074-2076, 2235, 2238
Knopp, K. 1530, 1532, 1537
Knorr, K.D. 275
Knorr, St. 2177, 2224
Knott, E. 2342
Knott, T. 517
Knott, Th.A. 1309, 1447, 1450, 1994, 2007
Knowles, F. 768, 770f., 1570, 1573
Knowles, F.E. 1646, 1659, 1667, 1669f., 1672, 2817
Knox, H. 2789, 2823, 2959
Knudsen, G. 1268, 1271, 1273, 1275
Knudsen, K. 1925, 1927
Knudsen, T. 532, 579, 1927f.
Knusi, M. 1033
Knuttel, J.A.N. 1435
Knyazeva, G.J. 274, 1651, 1667
Knyght, Th.E. 16
Köbert, R. 2432, 2437
Köbler, G. 1337f., 1340, 1444, 1455, 1910, 1912, 2024, 2034, 2104, 2224
Koblischke, H. 1263f., 2188, 2224
Kobmann, G. 2092, 2096
Kobrina, N. B. 2896, 2900
Kobyljans'kyj, J. 2331, 2333
Kočetov, I. S. 2267
Koch, G.A. 1016
Koch, H. 2640f., 2990
Koch, H.-J. 1191f.
Köchel, D. 43, 45
Kocher, H. 3122, 3133
Kochman, St. 3085
Kochmann, St. 3072
Kochs, Th. 2220
Kock, E. A. 3044, 3046

Kocka, J. 166
Koda, P.St. 3171
Ködderitzsch, R. 2342
Kodzasov, S.V. 2423
Koehler, L. 2428, 2435, 2437
Koelle, S. W. 2457, 2460, 2642, 2647
Koelle, W. 2645
Koenen, M. J. 2013f., 2016f., 2020
Koenig, E. 2462, 2467
Koenig, W. jr. 1320
Koerber, Chr. 1221f.
Koerner, E. F. K. 2208, 2237
Koerner, V. 3172
Koessler, M. 2884f.
Kogotkova, T.S. 2327
Köhler, A. 1389
Köhler, C. 1040
Köhler, F. 2968
Köhler, G. 581f.
Köhler, J.J. 1255, 1257, 1442, 1455
Köhler, K.F. 3174
Köhler, O. R. A. 2650, 2652, 2655
Köhler, R. 1261, 1264, 1644
Köhler, W. 1036
Kohler, W. 2115, 2224
Kohlheim, R. 2988, 2991
Kohring, H. 1907
Köhring, K. H. 2207, 2224
Kohrt, M. 194, 197, 207, 2237
Kohut, A. 2428, 2434
Koine, Y. 3115, 3117
Kojima, Y. 3115-3118
Kokona, V. 2366
Kokwaro, J. O. 2644
Kolas, Ja. 2337
Kolasa, J. 929
Kolatch, A.J. 1269, 1273
Kolb, A. 1811
Kolb, G. 10, 18, 606
Kolb, G.J. 1943, 1949f., 1952f.
Kolb, R.A. 606, 1949, 1952
Kolbe, K.W. 1232
Kölbel, A. 1258-1260
Kolde, G. 186, 188, 531, 579, 861f.
Kolegova, M.A. 2398
Kolers, P.A. 716, 724-726
Kolesnikov, N.P. 1081, 1083. 1124, 2317f., 2323, 2327
Koljadenkov, M.N. 2395, 2397
Kolk, J. van de 2636f.
Koller, W. 596, 599, 1031
Köller, W. 804
Kollicker, P. 2039
Kolsrud, S. 1927
Komenský (Comenius), J. A. 1089, 1091, 2278f., 2914
Komisarčik, C. J. 2885
Komorn, J. 1229
Konadrovskij, M. A. 2484f.
Konarski, F. 3062, 3067

Kondakow, N.I. 574
Konder, R. W. 2886
Kondō, H. 2622
Kondo, I. 3116f.
Kondor, R. 1972
Kondratovič, K.A. 2310
Kondratowicz, K. 3076
Koneczna, H. 1560, 2270, 2272
Konerding, K.-P. 440, 452, 459, 462, 499
Koneski, B. 2302-2304
König, E. 2028, 2759, 2880
König, F.W. 1692, 1694
König, R. 1638
König, W. 2207, 2224
Konishi, T. 3115, 3117
Konjuchov, N.P. 1140
Kononov, A.N. 2408, 2413
Konoshi, T. 3115
Konow, St. 2503, 2506, 2535
Konrad von Mure 2040
Konrad, N. 3116f.
Konstanciak, F.-J. 1715, 1720, 1722
Konsugi, O. 2623
Konzog, K. 2077
Koolwijk, J. van 1632, 1637
Kooy, T. van der 2027, 2034
Kopeckij, L. V. 2282f., 2715, 2717, 2727, 2759
Kopečný, F. 1337, 1340, 2282f.
Kopf, L. 2440
Köpf, St.E. 1351
Kopievskij, I. F. 3071, 3073, 3083
Kopitar, B. 1883, 2290
Kopitar, J. 2298
Kopleck, H. 2967
Kopp, J. 2938, 2946
Kopp, R. 1538
Köppe, I. 2215
Koppel, P. 2394
Koppelmann, H. 1338, 1340
Koppenburg, R. 1179, 1183, 2887
Korać, T. 2294
Koreć'kyj Satanovs'kyj, A. 2329, 2334, 3071
Korhonen, E. 2464, 2467
Korhonen, J. 118, 125, 592, 599, 835, 1031f., 2237, 2240, 2727, 2760
Korhonen, M. 2390, 2392, 2396, 2398
Korlén, G. 778, 2237, 3043, 3045-3047
Korlétjanu, M. G. 2759
Kornelius, J. 269
Körner, G. 2276f.
Körner, K.-H. 2222
Korneslov, R. 1149
Korninger, S. 1573
Kornitzky, H. 1044, 1045, 3046
Korosadowicz-Strużyńska, M. 2778

Körösi Crisan, St. 1882
Korsakov, G. M. 2630
Körte, W. 1034f., 1040, 2065, 2070
Körting, G. 1324, 1329, 1333, 1337, 1340
Kortt, I.R. 2397
Korubin, B. 2304
Košak, S. 1140
Kosaras, I. 1358, 1361
Kosarik, M.A. 1143
Koşay, H.Z. 2403-2405
Košelev, A. 3082
Koselleck, R. 117, 123, 166, 841, 850, 853f., 1058f., 1065, 1539f., 1548
Koshimizu, N. 2622
Koskinen, K.E. 1338, 1341
Kosnyreva, R.I. 2397f.
Kosowski, B. 2435
Kosowski, M. 2435
Kossovič, I. A. 3078
Kossovič, K. A. 3078
Kossowicz, C. 2471, 2473
Kostakis, Th. 1711, 1713
Kostallari, A. 2363, 2366
Köster, R. 272f., 405, 574, 804, 1622, 2219, 2230f., 2237
Kostomarov, V.G. 1314
Kostov, N. 2307
Kostovsky, D. 634
Kostrenčić, M. 1721
Koşula, A. 1884
Kosuth, J. 38f.
Kotelova, N.Z. 1165, 2315, 2323, 2327f.
Kothārī, V.M. Lála 3102, 3105
Kotlarevskyj, I. 2330
Kotljarev'skyj, I. P. 3076
Kotljarev'skyj, J. 2333
Kotmann, J. 2038
Kotnik, J. 747
Kotschi, Th. 856, 861, 1003, 1009
Kott, F. Št. 2280, 2283
Kötz, W. 810, 813
Kotzenberg, H.W.A. 2946, 2988, 2990
Koubourlis, D.J. 1565f.
Koumanoudis, St.A. 1711, 1713
Kourmoules, G.I. 1140
Kouyoumdjian, M. 2370f.
Kovačić, I. G. 2293
Koval'ov, V. P. 2759
Kovtun, L.St. 1549-1551, 1553-1555, 1559, 1561, 2310, 2321, 2328, 3069f., 3085
Kowalowa, H. 3064, 3068
Kowalski, K. 715, 725
Kowalsky, P.N. 3175
Koyasu, T. 3114, 3118
Kozak, A.S. 1147-1149, 1151, 2325
Kozielewski, I. 2886

Kozłovskij, V. 2319, 2323, 2327
Kozlowska, Chr. D. 1012, 1015, 1652, 1666
Kozyrev, I.S. 2315-2320, 2328
Kozyrev, V.A. 2318, 2328
Krack (Pseud.) 1195, 1198
Krack, K. E. 2174, 2224
Kraemer, J. 3088, 3096
Kraemer, R. 251f., 273, 2155, 2166, 2169, 2224
Kraetsch, E. 273
Kraft, Ch. H. 2457, 2460
Krahe, H. 1285, 1287-1291, 2223
Krahl, G. 3092, 3095
Krahl, S. 2207f., 2224
Král', Á. 511, 516, 1308f.
Král, J. 2276f.
Králik, J. 2281, 2284
Krallmann, D. 1146, 1152, 1644
Kramer, G. 1560
Krämer, H. 272, 357, 369, 405, 458, 498, 515, 574, 626, 661, 667, 672, 687, 753, 778, 786, 795, 803, 820, 834, 848, 860, 1238, 1608, 1622, 2217
Kramer, J. 1714, 1721, 1894f., 1900f., 1904f.
Krämer, J. 242, 1600, 1608, 2224
Kramer, M. 217, 222, 233-236, 242, 1195, 2046, 2053f., 2070, 2075, 3014f., 3018f., 3037-3039
Kramer, P. 2028, 2034, 3170
Kramer, W. 245, 1290
Krampen, M. 714, 725, 3149, 3157
Krámský, J. 1650, 1667
Kranzmayer, E. 242
Krapf, J. L. 2462, 2465, 2467
Krapf, L. 2454, 2647
Krapiva, K.K. 2337
Krapp, A. 1513, 1517f., 1522
Krapp, G.Ph. 1443, 1456, 1988, 1990f., 2004, 2009
Krašeninnikov, St. P. 2629, 2631
Krasnoff, G.D. 1261, 1264
Kratochvil, P. 2602, 2611, 2759, 3110
Kratschmer, Th. 2192, 2224
Kratzer, A. 460, 499
Kraus, C. von 1542, 1548
Krause Morales, R. 2751
Krause, A. 2939, 2946
Krause, E.D. 1149, 1151, 3124, 3127, 3133
Krause, G. 244f., 2074
Krause, K.C.F. 1232
Krauß, E. 2936
Krauss, F. 2224
Krauss, W. 28, 2761
Krebs, J.Ph. 1220
Krech, E.-M. 1308f.
Krecher, J. 1684f.
Kredel, E. 1201, 1204f.

Kreezer, G.L. 142, 145
Kreindler, I. T. 2254
Krejnovič, E. A. 2631
Krelj, S. 2296
Kremer, D. 656, 1209, 1252-1254, 1268, 1273f., 1810, 1812, 1814, 1817, 1910, 1912, 2757, 2768, 2987
Kremnitz, G. 1891f., 1905
Kremsier, J.F. 1234, 1239, 2089, 2096
Krender, H.-D. 2211f., 2237
Krenn, H. 576, 582
Kresznerics, F. 2376, 2381
Kretov, A. 2759
Kretschmer, A. 1167
Kretschmer, P. 1140, 1700, 2187, 2224
Krett, J.N. 2331-2333
Kreussler, O. 1703
Kreutzer, G. 2036
Kreuz, R. 3128, 3133
Kreuzer, H. 687, 1522
Kreuzer, P. 2185, 2224
Kreviski, J. 1302f.
Krey, P. 2226
Kriaras, E. 1705, 1713
Kridalaksana, H. 2563, 2565
Krikmann, A. 1036, 1040
Krimpel, D. 243
Krindler, I.T. 2423
Krings, H. 459, 580
Krings, H.-P. 106, 108, 110, 185, 189
Krippendorff, K. 1672
Krishnamurti, B. 2521, 2530f., 2533
Krishnayyar, N.S.G. 3097, 3105
Křístek, V. 2284
Kristensen, M. 1268, 1271, 1273, 1918, 1922
Kristeva, J. 1044, 1050
Kristinus, H. 1005, 1008
Kristoforidhis, K. (Christophorides) 2362f.
Kristol, A.M. 1245
Kristophson, J. 2366
Kristovska, D. 1669, 2360
Krivoščekova-Gantman, A.S. 2395, 2397
Kriz, J. 1632, 1637
Krjažev, V. S. 3074
Krjučkov, S.E. 2325
Kroeber, A.L. 410, 459
Kroeger, A.B. 3172
Kroeger, B. 3174
Kroehndorf, P. 2938
Kroenlein, J. G. 2652-2654
Kroesche, B. 1138, 1142, 2319, 2323
Krogmann, W. 2033f.
Krohmer, U. 269

Krohn, R. 275
Kroihndorf, P. 2946
Kröll, B. 2225
Kröll, H. 1194, 1199, 1536, 1538
Kromann, H.-P. 102, 110, 117f., 125, 131f., 134, 172, 174, 278, 408, 460, 499, 519, 525, 575, 585, 592, 745, 748, 777f., 1032, 1531, 2236, 2244, 2713, 2716, 2720, 2725, 2727, 2760, 2773, 2775f., 2778, 2780, 2782, 2794, 2829, 2831, 2836, 2840, 2842, 2853, 2857f., 2896, 2902, 2947, 2965, 2969, 3059, 3061
Krömer, D. 1716f., 1722, 3032, 3034
Kromer-Benz 3172
Kromrey, H. 1632, 1637
Kron, R. 1186, 1188
Krondl, A. 3140f.
Kroneberg, I. J. 3075
Kronow, S. 2545, 2558
Kropáček, L. 2282f.
Krothoff, G. 2432, 2437, 3095
Krötzsch-Viannay, M. 87
Kroupas, J. 2352f.
Krstić, K. 2296
Kru That 2578
Krueger, J.R. 1140
Krüger, G. 2879f., 2894, 2900
Krüger, M. 1152
Krüger, W. 1268, 1273
Krüger-Lorenzen, K. 1024, 1027, 1029, 1035f., 1040, 2174, 2176, 2224
Kruisinga, E. 589, 592, 732, 748
Krumbacher, K. 1700
Krumnack, U. 1152
Krumova, L. 2308
Krünitz, J.G. 165f.
Kruopas, J. 2352
Krupnik, B. 2436f.
Krüss, J. 1366f.
Kruyskamp, C. 296, 929, 1036, 1040, 1435
Kruyskamp, C.H.A. 227, 1435, 2021
Krylova, G. V. 2755
Kryms'kyj, A. 2331, 2333
Kryński, A. A. 2272
Krysin, L.P. 1617, 1624, 2323
Krytenko, A. P. 2760
Krzyżanowski, J. 1036, 1040
Kubásková, E. 3174
Kubczak, H. 804
Kubica, St. 746, 3064, 3067
Kubitscha, H. 1139
Kucala, M. 2274
Kučera, A. 247, 251, 275, 279, 371, 373, 383, 409, 422, 449, 462, 501, 563f., 587, 668, 751, 754, 1507, 1509, 1511, 1628,

1630, 2131, 2133, 2135-2137, 2142, 2160, 2170, 2185, 2246, 2803, 2990, 3167
Kučera, H. 1320f., 1643, 2002
Kuchař, J. 190, 206f., 274
Kück, E. 244, 1233, 1239
Kudela, J. 2883, 2887
Kuen, H. 1322
Küffner, G. 1037, 1040
Kufner, H. L. 2855, 2858
Küfner, R. 406, 834, 1176, 2232
Kuhberg, W. 1154f., 1157f.
Kühl de Mones, U. 1752, 1766
Kühlwein, W. 955, 1067, 1364, 1443, 2234, 2765
Kuhn, H. 2031
Kuhn, K.G. 1140, 2429, 2435
Kuhn, M. 327
Kühn, P. 102, 104, 106f., 110, 112-116, 118-120, 122-127, 130f., 134, 153, 158, 186, 189, 208, 214, 238f., 245, 531, 547, 552, 564, 579, 596, 599, 622, 627, 652, 698f., 769, 771, 823, 830f., 833, 835, 837f., 841, 980, 989, 998, 1032, 1038f., 1042f., 1064-1066, 1069, 1075, 1078, 1080, 1083, 1090, 1092f., 1134, 1136, 1143, 1169, 1175, 1178, 1204f., 1241, 1276, 1283, 1355, 1357-1360, 1363f., 1368, 1398, 1415f., 1430, 1435, 1531, 1567, 1573, 1672, 2010, 2021, 2054, 2056, 2059-2061, 2065f., 2074-2077, 2082, 2087, 2092, 2094, 2099f., 2104-2106, 2110, 2130f., 2174, 2177, 2180-2182, 2191f., 2197-2199, 2229, 2235, 2237f., 2243, 2936f., 2947, 3172
Kuhn, S.M. 579, 1442, 1450f., 1455f., 1609
Kühn, U. 655
Kühne, P. 2051
Kühnel, H. 2886f.
Kühnel, P. C. J. 2276f.
Kühnert, H. 1032
Kühnl, E. 3127, 3133
Kuhs, E. 1145
Kuiper, F. B. J. 2499, 2506
Kuipers, A.H. 1341, 2419f.
Kujola, J. 2386f.
Kūkai 2618
Kulamandana Gani 2518
Kulkarni, K. P. 2515, 2519
Kull, R. 2394
Kullavanijaya, P. 2582
Kullū, P. 2542, 2546, 3100, 3105
Kumār, B. B. 2546, 2867
Kumara, B.B. 3100, 3102, 3105
Kumari, B.B. 3102
Kumari, B.S. 3105

Kumerdej, B. 2298
Kumoi, S. 2506
Kundu, A. 2511
Kungurov, R.K. 1140
Kunihiro, T. 3117
Kunimatsu, K. 3116f.
Kunin, A. V. 3082
Kunitsch, M. 1121f., 1124, 2070, 2091, 2096
Kunitskaya-Peterson, Chr. 1198
Kunjamu, P.B. 3101, 3105
Kunoss, E. 2377, 2381
Künßberg, E. Freiherr von 1609, 2218
Kunst, A.E. 1573
Kupisz, K. 3064, 3067
Küpper, H. 69, 706, 723, 726, 1039f., 1100, 1102, 1186, 1188, 1190, 1192f., 1528, 1530, 2109, 2119, 2134, 2185, 2188, 2198, 2202-2204, 2206, 2224f., 2238
Küpper, M. 1530, 2185, 2225
Küppers, H. 68, 719
Kuraszkiewicz, W. 1140, 2268
Kurath, H. 327, 654, 668, 703, 1447, 1449-1451, 1455f., 1609
Kurbangaliev, M. 3080
Kurcz, I. 2270, 2272
Kurdeov, K. K. 2483, 2485f.
Kurganov, N. G. 2315, 2323f., 3074
Kuri, E. 1176
Kuri, E. F. 2222
Kurka, A. 2272
Kurka, E. 1309
Kurkiev, A.S. 2422f.
Kurkowska, H. 2270, 2272
Kurmins, J. 2355, 2358
Kürner, J.J. 2987
Kuroyanagi, K. 3115, 3117
Kurschat, A. 2351, 2353
Kurschat, F. 2351, 2353
Kurschildgen, E. 269
Kürschner, J. 2919f., 2930
Kurth, H. 2225, 3151f., 3155f.
Kurutsch, R.D. 2391
Kuryłowicz, J. 2224
Kurz, G. 804
Kurz, J. 2207, 2208, 2224, 2265-2267
Kurzowa, Z. 1139, 2271f., 2274
Kussmaul, P. 269
Küstner, H. 2223
Küther, C. 1531
Kutina, L. L. 3084f.
Kutova, L. L. 3084
Kutscher, E.Y. 2433
Kutschera, F. von 539, 541, 547, 549, 579, 896, 899
Kuusi, M. 1037f., 1040, 1043, 2384, 2388, 2933
Kuvalayanada, S. 2496

Kuzela, Z. 2331, 2333f.
Kuznecov, N.G. 2317
Kuznecova, A.I. 1229, 2318, 2324
Kuznecova, R.D. 2326
Kvaran, G. 1290
Kwauka, P. 2359f.
Kwech, D. 1110
Kyaw Aung Sanda Sadaw 2505
Kyaw Yan 2505
Kyaw Zaw 2554
Kyber, D. 2915, 2930
Kylstra, A.D. 1335, 1341
Kyosaku, M. 2614
Kyōson 2619
Kyoto, G.D. 3172
Kyrychenko, I.M. 2331, 2333
Kytomaa, S. 3172

L

La Barre, W. 2686, 2688, 2690
La Bruyère, J. de 25, 28
La Chartre, M. de 603, 724, 1814
La Combe de Prézle, H. 1860 (s. Lacombe)
La Curne de Saint Palaye, J.-B. de 603
La Farge, O. 2664, 2667
La Fontaine, J. de 25, 1823
La Grasserie, R. de 2709
La Lande, J. de 2938, 2946
La Noue, P. de 1011, 1015, 1051f.
La Pointe 1349
La Polla, R. J. 2558
La Porte, M. de 9, 16, 146, 1011, 1013, 1015, 1206, 1208f., 1792, 1795, 1807, 1810
La Rosa, R. 1243f.
La Rue, J. 1185, 1188
La Stella, E. 1259f.
La Touche, F. de 1218, 1220
Laan, K. ter 1036, 1040, 2028
Laas d'Aguen, E.M.P. 1126, 1129
Labarde, H. 2980, 2984
Labarre, A. 9, 17, 1790f., 1814, 2911, 2936, 2998, 3004, 3007, 3021, 3030, 3172
Labbat, E. 1187
Labèrnia y Esteller, P. 1773, 1779, 1784, 2917, 2930
Labernia, P. 1745f., 1760
Laborde, L. de 1157f.
Laborde, R. 1904
Laboulaye, C. 1252
Labov, W. 850, 854, 1614f., 1617, 1624
Labrousse, P. 2563, 2565, 2868
Lacal, L. 1747, 1760
Lacassagne, J. 1185, 1188, 1530
Lacavalleria, A. 1772, 1784, 2913, 2930

Lacea, C. 1885
Lachâtre, M. 1804, 1806, 1840
Lachmann, K. 242, 1126, 1158, 1422, 1559, 2066
Lacombe de Prezel, H. 3152, 3154, 3156
Lacombe de Prézle, H. 1846, 1860
Lacombe, A. 3012
Lacombe, F. 1157f.
Lacombe, H. 1860
Lacombe, J. 1802
Lacroix, P. F. 2647, 2649
Lacroix, U. 1012, 1015
Lacurne de Sainte-Palaye, J.B. de 1819, 1840
Ladendorf, O. 163, 166, 838, 841, 1200f., 1203, 1205, 2062, 2070
Ladó, J. 1270, 1273
Laet, J. de 1439
Lafaye, P.B. 1068f., 1073f., 1819, 1840
Laffal, J. 1092
Lafleur, B. 1021, 1023f., 1026, 1029, 1036, 1040
Lafon, P. 1670
Lafone Quevedo, S. A. 2708
Lafont, R. 1892
Lagadeuc, J. 1789, 1814, 2347, 2350, 2911, 2930
Lagaffe, G. 39f.
Lagane, R. 61, 180, 327, 524, 667, 679, 703, 746, 786, 916, 928, 945, 1158, 1212, 1216-1218, 1220, 1378, 1800, 1814, 1829, 1832, 1836
Lagarda, A. 1895, 1904
Lagarde, P. de 2427, 2434
Lagarde, P.A. de 3094
Lagercrantz, E. 2389, 2391
Lagneau, Ph. 1271, 1273
Lägreid, A. 2297, 2301
Laguna, A. 1740, 1760, 2913, 2915, 2930, 2938, 2946
Laine, J. 2385, 2387
Laird, Ch. 1076, 1079
Laitenberger, H. 2888
Laitos, N. 2387
Lajnert, J. 2275, 2277
Lakalendola, A. 2366
Lakhana Daoratanahong 2593
Lako Bodra 2540
Lakó, G. 2381
Lakoff, G. 247, 275, 855-859, 861, 3165
Laksmanakawi, P. 2531
Lal Shankar 2518
Lalas, S. 2513, 2519
Lalević, M. S. 2292, 2294
Lallemand, M. 61, 405, 601f., 606, 641, 672, 679, 686, 765, 924, 928, 1052, 1151, 1378, 1833, 1839

Lallot, J. 1334
Lalou, A. 1129
Lamano y Beneyte, J. de 1760
Lamb, G.F. 1046, 1049
Lambarde, W. 1438f.
Lambert, E. 1282f.
Lambert, M. 1684
Lambert, P.-Y. 2339-2342
Lamberti, L. 1856
Lamberti, M. 2464, 2469
Lambertz, M. 2363, 2366
Lamblin, S. 1367
Lambrich, H. 3139-3141
Lamizet, B. 915f., 1078, 1080
Lämmert, E. 1241
Lammertz, J. 2111
Lampe, G.W.H. 1700, 1703
Lamy, M.-N. 209, 214, 312, 590-592, 1389, 1843, 1977, 1982, 2751, 2888, 2902
Lanao, M.E. 1760
Lancaster, F.W. 1084, 1093
Lancour, H. 1566
Landa, J. 1126f., 1129
Landais, N. 501, 504, 508, 640f., 1081f., 1129, 1208, 1802, 1804-1807, 1813, 1821, 1840, 3054
Landau, I. 706, 722, 725
Landau, J.M. 1669
Landau, M. 2434
Landau, M.J. 2428
Landau, O. 1696, 1703
Landau, S. 350, 359, 958-960, 1367
Landau, S.I. 31, 33, 36f., 95, 97, 247, 275, 362, 370, 526f., 530, 552, 562, 564, 579, 588, 592, 622, 627, 652, 655, 761, 765f., 780, 787, 967, 989, 994, 998, 1368, 1993, 2004, 2006f., 2009
Landauer, S.I. 407
Landerman, P. 2681, 2683, 2705
Landeroin, M. 2458, 2460
Landes, G.M. 2435
Landheer, R. 2760, 2813
Landin, D. 2704
Landois, N. 1804
Landré, G.N. 1074
Landrieux, N. 1355, 1364
Landsberger, B. 1682, 1684f., 1688
Landucci, N. 1848, 2991f.
Landuchi, N. 2913
Landuchio, N. 2992, 2996
Landy-Houillon, I. 1814
Lane, A. 173f.
Lane, E.W. 2443, 2447, 3087f., 3090, 3095
Lane, T. O'Neill 2348
Lane-Poole, St. 2447, 3087, 3096
Lanfranco, G.M. 1016, 1129

Lang, A. 2636f.
Lang, E. 163, 275, 531, 533, 546, 580, 629, 634, 810, 813, 862-865, 868, 2207, 2210f., 2225, 2238
Lang, F. 460, 585
Lang, S. 123
Langacker, R.W. 1339, 1624
Lange, Chr. 2235
Lange, J. 2355
Lange, O. 2091, 2096
Lange-Kowal, E. E. 1890, 3000-3004, 3006, 3018
Langen, A. 158f., 2055, 2060, 2076
Langen, H. 166
Langenbacher, J. 703
Langendorf, D. 1313
Langer, B. 2215
Langhans, F.-P. 1253
Langius, J. 2355
Langlois, E. 1125, 1129, 1293, 1295
Langosch, K. 1568, 1573
Lankenau, K. 206
Lanman, Ch. 2490, 2496
Lanneau de Marey, P.A.V. de 1802, 1807, 1809
Lanneau, P.A. 1127, 1129
Lanoë-Villène, G. 3152-3156
Lanszweert, R. 1341
Lantsheer, H. W. 2918, 2931
Lanusse, M. 1794, 1814
Lanza, V. 1902, 1904
Laomonen, A. 2759
Laoust, E. 2456f.
Lap, M.A. 3101, 3105
Lap, P.A. 3101, 3105
Lapa, A. 1188
Lapenna, I. 3131, 3136
Lapesa, R. 1744, 1750, 1766
Lapi, D. 1847
Lapi, J. I. 2638
Lapidus, B.A. 524, 747, 2896, 2901
Lapli, J. I. 2636
Lappin, S. 3166
Laptukhin, V. 2459f.
Lara, J. 2705
Lara, J.J. de 1751, 1766
Lara, L.F. 71, 77f., 1754, 1760, 1766
Larajasse, E. de 2463, 2465
Larbaud, V. 602
Larchey, L. 1185, 1188
Larin, B. A. 1553, 1561, 2319, 2324, 2328, 2760, 3070, 3083, 3085
Larive 83, 87, 990, 997, 1824f., 1841
Laroche, E. 1686, 1688f., 1692, 1694
Larochette, J. 2644f.

Larousse, P. 11, 80f., 86, 140, 144, 175, 220, 222, 508, 528, 703, 724, 764, 766, 995, 1054f., 1081, 1141, 1210, 1213f., 1574, 1588, 1819-1825, 1829, 1838, 1840f.
Larramendi, M. de 1742, 1760, 2373, 2917, 2931
Larramenti, M. 2375
Larreula, F. 1784
Larrieu, R. 2980, 2984f.
Larrucea de Tovar, C. 2700, 2702, 2705, 2707, 2709
Larsen, A. 3055, 3060
Larsen, H. V. 2758, 2760
Larsen, J. 2644
Larsen, R. 2663, 2668
Larson, M. L. 2703
Larthomas, B. 652
Larthomas, P. 653, 1017, 1219, 1804, 1814
Las Casas, Chr. de 2970, 2974, 2992, 2996f.
Lasch, A. 1418, 1420-1422, 1424-1426, 1428
Lasch, R. 1532, 1538
Lasnier, P. 1100, 1102
Lass, A.H. 1308f.
Lassen, Chr. 2471, 2473, 2490, 2496, 2502, 2507
Lasso, F. 2683
Last, J. 2647
Lastra de Suárez, Y. 2661
Latendorf, F. 2220
Latham, E. 1044, 1049, 1261, 1264, 1295
Latham, R.E. 1721f.
Latham, R.G. 1950f., 1954
Latif, A. 2516
Latiri, D. 2864
Latour, B. 2131, 2134, 2136-2238
Latte, K. 1697, 1703
Laua, A. 1142, 2359f.
Laučiute, Ju.A. 2359f.
Laučka, A. 2352f.
Laude, Cirtautas, I. 2410
Laudy-Houillon, I. 1219f.
Lauer, B. 2099
Lauffer, H. 2211, 2234
Lauffs, D. 1551f., 1559
Laughams, F.-P. 1249
Laughlin, R. 2661f., 2668
Laughlin, R. M. 2698f.
Laughren, M. 2639-2641
Laukkanen, K. 1033, 1043
Laumane, B.E. 2358, 2360
Launay, L. 1569, 1572
Laur, W. 1281, 1283
Laures, J. 2619, 2623
Lauri, A. 3011
Laurian, A.T. 1885, 1889
Lauridsen, H. 3061

Lauriol 49
Lautier, D. 2980, 2983
Lautin, R. 2222
Lautmann, R. 192, 207
Lava, A. 2357
Laveaux, Ch. 2983, 2985
Laveaux, J.Ch. 1005, 1008, 1210-1214, 1216
Laveaux, J.-Ch.Th. de 1073, 1802-1809, 3000
Laverdure, P. 2695f.
Lavigne, Ch. 1216
Lavine, I. 1261, 1264
Lavrov, P. 2305
Lavrovskih, P. A. 3078
Lavy, J. 524
Law, A.G. 109, 111
Lawrance, J. C. P. 2644
Lawson, V. 1667
Laycock, D. C. 2636f.
Layme Pairumani, F. 2688-2690
Lazar, M. 1906f.
Lazard, G. 2477, 2480
Lăzărescu, I. 2853
Lázaro Carreter, F. 88, 1742f., 1750, 1766
Lazarus, J. 3102, 3105
Lazić, G. 2291, 2294
Lazova, M.V. 1138, 1140
Lazzati, S. 1124, 1312, 1314
Lazzioli, C. 3016, 3018
Lcang skya rol pa'i rdo rje 2548
Lê Bá Kông 2588f.
Le Bidois, R. 1018
Le Boucher, G. 2989f.
Le Breton, A. 1185, 1188
Le Brun, L. 1011, 1015
Le Comte, E.S. 1552, 1559
Le Dû, J. 2348, 2350
Le Gai, E. [= Passard, F.-L.] 1351
Le Gal, E. 1216
Le Gaygnard, P. 1125, 1129
Le Goffic, P. 1001, 1005, 1008
Le Guern, M. 1801, 1814
Le Huche, J.-M. 2887
Le Men, R.F. 1789, 1814
Le Menn, G. 1269, 1273
Le Mesurier, H.G. 1622
Lê Ngọc Trụ 2587, 2589
Le Pennec, M.-F. 1196, 1198
Le Rond d'Alembert, J. 1805
Le Roux de Lincy, A. 1036, 1040
Le Roux, Ph.-J. 1185f., 1188f., 1798, 1811, 1813
Le Roux, T.H. 1309
Le Roy, G. 1071
Le Soyeur 1124
Le Tellier, P. 2911
Lê Văn Dúc 2587, 2589
Lê Văn Hùng 2588f.
Le Ver, F. 1789f., 1815
Leach, I. M. 2703

Leake, W. 2362
Leake, W.M. 2365, 2367
Lean, V. 1036, 1040
Learmonth, T. 1966, 2936, 2947
Leau, L. 3129, 3131, 3136
Léautaud, P. 22
Leauthier, A. 43, 45
Leavitt, J. 1650, 1667
Leavitt, R.K. 763, 766, 1067, 1075, 1990, 2009
Lebedev, K. A. 2480, 2484f.
LeBerre, Y. 2348, 2350
Lebrecht, F. 2434
Lebrun, G. 2957
Lebrun, Y. 276
Lebsanft, F. 2879, 2881
Lechin, I.V. 2315, 2324
Lechner, B. 2990
Leclair, P. 1187
Leclerc, G. 1230
Leclercq, R. 2066, 2076
Leclère, Chr. 1006, 1009
Leclerq, R. 1126f., 1131f., 1143
Ledel de Liaño, I. 2980-2982, 2984
Ledel, J. 2986
Leder, Z. 2301
Ledésert, M. 2789, 2823, 2958f.,
Ledésert, R. 2823, 2959
Ledésert, R.P.L. 2958f.
Lee, A. van der 582, 855, 930, 1429, 2048
Lee, S.-H. 1664, 1666
Lee, T.H. 1209
Lee, W.R. 1090, 1092
Leech, G. 862, 1670, 2805, 2813
Leech, G.N. 737, 748
Leed, R. L. 2533
Leem, K. 1924, 1927, 2389, 2391, 2916, 2931
Leèmets, Ch. D. 2760
Leenders, Th. 1320
Leer, J. 2632, 2634
Lefaucheur, N. 87
Lefebvre, G. 2871
Lefebvre, T. 2462, 2467
Lefevre, J. 1125, 1127, 1129
Leffler, O. E. 3044, 3046
Legaré, R. 1082
Leger, L.P.M. 1149, 1151
Léger, R. 3127, 3133
Legeza, I.L. 3111, 3113
Legissa, L. 1030
Legner, W.K. 154, 158, 1561
Légoarant, B. 1803, 1807
LeGoff, P. 2347, 2350
LeGonidec, J.-F. 2347, 2350
Legrand, É. 2367
Lehfeldt, W. 273, 1644, 2290, 2296
Lehmacher, W. 2341
Lehman, D. 36f., 814, 821
Lehman, P.V. 1456

Lehmann, Chr. 1034, 1040, 1043, 1065, 1070
Lehmann, H. 3165
Lehmann, M.A. 82f., 87
Lehmann, W.P. 854, 1910, 1912
Lehnert, M. 509, 517, 1138, 1140, 1361, 1966, 2969
Lehninger, G. A. 3017
Lehninger, J. A. 3015
Lehr, R. 2199, 2201, 2225
Lehr-Splawiński, T. 2274
Lehtisalo, T.V. 2396f.
Leibniz, G.W. 231, 233-236, 245, 460, 551, 564, 1284, 1291, 2053, 2056, 2060-2063, 2075f., 2088, 2093, 2099, 2650, 2655
Leineweber, A. 2070
Leineweber, H. 2065, 2070
Leinfellner, W. 542f., 580
Leino, P. 1034, 1043
Leirbukt, O. 585, 628, 822, 2244
Leiris, M. 1349, 1351
Leisering, H. 273, 358, 405, 459, 499, 574, 804, 1255, 1257, 1273, 2188, 2224f.
Leisi, E. 544, 580, 770, 789, 796, 888, 892, 990f., 998, 1168, 1178, 1347, 1531, 2716, 2727, 2760, 2855, 2859
Leisinger, H. 1005, 1007, 1215
Leistner, G. 1261, 1264
Leite de Vasconcelhos, J. 1114, 1119, 1736, 1738
Leite, T. 3126f., 3133
Lejeune, J. 2238, 2760
Lejeune, M. 1132, 1137, 1140, 1696, 1703
Lekens, B. 2648
Lekov, I. 2307f.
Leland, Ch.G. 1186
Lello, E. 1734
Lello, J. 1734
Lemaire, R. 3129, 3133
Lemare, P.-A. 1129, 1131, 1810
Lembke, R. 1349, 1351, 2225
Lemery, N. 165
Lemke, H. 1367
Lemle, M. 2704
Lemmens, M. 592, 739, 748, 1975, 1982, 2770, 2775
Lemmer, M. 1204f.
Lemnitzer, L. 248, 276, 423, 428, 459, 964, 967
Lemoine, G. 2692, 2695f.
Lemon, G.W. 1436, 1455
Lempicka, Z. 2271
Lemus y Rubio, P. 1760
Lenders, W. 275, 371, 407, 459, 1067, 1571, 1573, 1623, 1657, 1667, 1670, 2236, 3165, 3167
Lengenfelder, H. 1204f., 3172, 3174

Lenin, V.I. 2313, 2319
Lenkersdorf, C. 2663, 2668, 2698f.
Lenkowa, A. 250, 275
Lenoble-Pinson, M. 1176
Lenschen, W. 157, 159, 838, 841, 2238
Lentz, R. 716, 725
Lenz, R. 1329, 1333, 1752, 1755, 1760, 2872, 2876
Lenz, W. 19, 28
Leo XIII 1824
Leo, H. 1442, 1455
Leon, A.L. 1126, 1129
Leon, C. 2660
León, J. de 2664, 2668
Leon, V. 1188
Leonard, St.A. 31, 33
Leonard, W. 1199
Leone, A. 1861
Leonhard, K. 1119
Leonhardi, A. 1005, 1008, 1011, 1015
Leonidova, M. 3082
Leont'ev, A.A. 2320, 2324, 2328
Leony, F. A. 2754
Leopardi, G. 148, 1857, 1874
Leopold I 2987
Leopold, M. 820
Leotti, A. 2363, 2366
LePage, R. 1967
L'Epée, Ch.-M. de 3142-3144
LePelletier, D.L. 2347, 2350
Lépinette, B. 1795, 1814, 2760
Leping, A. A. 2848, 2853
Leping, E.I. 746, 1622, 2845, 2853
Lepinoy, P. 2131, 2238
Lepointe, E. 2793, 3001, 3003f.
Lepp, F. 1201, 1205
Leppin, R. 2225
Lepsius, R. 2462, 2469
Lerat, P. 1179, 1184
Lerch, H.-G. 1529f.
Lerchner, G. 249, 276, 2131, 2238
Lereboullet, J. 1261, 1264
Lerman, Y.-Y. 2251, 2253
Lermina, J. 1185, 1188
Lerner, I. 1157f.
Lerond, A. 61, 1158, 1305f., 1308f., 1313f., 1829
Leroux, J.-P. 1195, 1198
LeRoux, R. 2350
Leroy de Flagis, J.-B. 1073
Leroy, Ch. 1302f., 1807, 1841
Leroy, J. 1340
Lescallier, D. 2937f., 2946
Lescaze, B. 2986
Leschka, St. 2377, 2381
Lesclache, Ch. de 1124
Lesk, M. 1980, 1982
Leška, O. 2282f.
Lesko, L.H. 305, 1680f.
Leslau, W. 2450-2455, 2464f., 2467

Leslie, J. 1101f., 1984, 1986
Lespinasse, R. de 1249, 1253
Lessay, J. 1814
Lessenich-Drucklieb, C. 532, 546, 548, 580, 850f., 854
Lesser, P. 1044, 1046, 1049
Lessing, F. 2623, 2626
Lessing, G.E. 236f., 242, 715, 725, 1154-1158, 1550, 1552, 1558f., 2132
L'Estrange, R. 225
Letellier, Ch.-C. 1802f., 1807
Letellier, L. 2917, 2931
Letellier, P. 2928
Lettinga, J.P. 1693
Leuchs, J.M. 165
Leupol, L. 2495
Leuschner, B. 585, 2244
Leuschner, K. 1800, 1814
Leutsch, E.L. 1033, 1040
Levander, L. 1939, 1942
Levašov, E.A. 2313f., 2328
Levčenko, S. P. 2760
Levchenko, M. 2330, 2333, 3076
Levée, J.-B. 1011, 1015
Levenston, E. 2431
Levenston, E.A. 2436
Lévèque, H. 1185, 1188
Levi, J.N. 1651, 1667
Levie, W.H. 716, 725
Levin, B. 3167
Levin, I. 1033, 1043
Levins, P. 9, 16, 978, 980, 1126, 1129
Levinsohn, St. H. 2705
Levita, E. 2427, 2434
Leviţchi, L. 1888
Levitskij, V.V. 2320, 2324
Levitt, J. 1212, 1217
Levitzky, L. D. 2727, 2760
Levy, B. 1068, 1075, 1093
Levy, E. 1892f., 1904f.
Levy, J. 2436
Lévy, P. 1271, 1273
Levy, R. 3173
Lewandowska-Tomaszczyk, B. 862
Lewandowski, Th. 2207, 2211-2213, 2225, 2233, 2238
Lewański, R. C. 1169, 1178, 2289, 2296, 2301, 2306-2308, 3022, 3030, 3066, 3068, 3075, 3085, 3173
Lewanskij, R.C. 2328
Lewicka, H. 1004f., 1008
Lewin, M. 3128, 3133
Lewis 269
Lewis, B. 3092, 3095
Lewis, Ch. T. 3032, 3034
Lewis, Ch.Th. 151
Lewis, D. 544, 580
Lewis, G.L. 1652, 1667

Lewis, H. 2341f., 2347, 2349
Lewis, J.W. 511, 746, 1308, 1310
Lewis, M. A. 2751
Lewis, N. 1099
Lewis, P. 2559
Lewis, R.A. 1455
Lewis, R.E. 1450
Lewkowskaja, X.A. 247, 252, 276
Lexell, L.J.L. 1129
Lexer, M. 153, 158, 242, 574, 768, 770, 1138, 1234, 1418-1422, 1424-1428, 1430, 1434, 1600, 1608, 2050, 2081, 2088, 2096, 2215f., 2225
Lexer, M. von 825f., 2076
Leyn, K. 2853
Leys, F. J. 2990, 3015, 3018
Leyser, J. A. 2058, 2076
Leyton, J. 2895, 2901
Lhande, P. 2374f.
L'Huillée, C. 2946
Li Deng 2603
Li, David Chen-ching 2598, 2611
Li, N. 3110, 3113
Liang, Sh. 3109f., 3112
Liaño, J. 1792
Liberatore, R. 1864
Liburnio, N. 10, 1851, 1853, 1860
Liccardi, M. 2703
Lichtenstein, H. 2651
Liddell, H.G. 1133, 1699f., 1702f.
Lidzbarski, M. 2437
Lieb, H.-H. 276, 1417, 1424, 1429
Liebeck, S. 3133
Lieberman, St. 1684f.
Liebich, B. 1059, 1065, 1147-1151, 1234, 1239, 2089f., 2096
Liebknecht, W. 1173, 1177
Liebold, G. 3002, 3002
Liebold, H. 249, 276, 2760, 3002, 3005
Liebsch, H. 1035, 1043
Liedbeck, G. 3128f., 3133
Lienert, G.A. 1632, 1637
Lierow, C. 272, 2219
Liétard, A. 2559
Liewehr, F. 2224
Lifshits, Y. M. 2249f., 2253
Liger, L. 1801, 1807
Ligeti, L. 2412, 2625f.
Lilič, G. A. 2755
Limet, H. 1684f.
Lin, Y. 3109, 3112
Lin, Z. 3112
Linati, F. 2994, 2996
Lincoln, N.J. 1341
Lind, O. 1935, 1942, 3040-3043, 3046
Lindahl, E. 2389, 2391, 2916, 2931
Lindberg, L. 2917, 2931
Linde, S. B. 1139, 2268, 2272, 2280, 2283, 3076f.

Lindemann, F. 1011, 1015
Lindemann, H. 1011f., 1015
Lindemann, M. 9, 17, 269, 1788f., 1804, 1814
Lindén, O. 3048-3050
Lindenbrog, F. 1439
Lindfors, A.O. 1939, 1942
Lindgren, E. 3048-3051
Lindgrün, G. 580
Lindkvist, H. 3050 (s. Lindquist)
Lindow, W. 2198, 2225
Lindquist, H. 2760, 3050
Lindsay, W.M. 1261, 1264, 1332, 1714, 1720f.
Lindskoog, C. A. 2706
Lindskoog, J. N. 2706
Lindstrom, N. 2761
Lindvall, L. 1190
Linfield, J.L. 1303
Lings, K. K. 2660
Link, E. 258, 276, 321, 363, 366, 368-370, 405, 458, 881f., 1175, 1178, 1230, 1240, 2218
Linke, A. 1031
Linnartz, K. 1271, 1273
Linné, C. von 1255
Lins, E. 119, 124, 2199, 2225
Lins, V. 3131, 3136
Linschoten, J. 1321
Lionnet, A. 2698f.
Lionnet, G. 2872, 2874f.
Liperovskaja, N. 1361, 2843, 2853, 2896, 2900
Lipka, L. 573, 580
Lipperheide, F. Frhr. von 120, 124, 1046, 1049, 2094, 2096, 2215, 2225
Lippert, W. 2761
Lipshits, D. Y. A. 2251, 2253
Lisch, R. 1632, 1637
Liskenne, L. 1130
Lisowsky, G. 2428, 2435
Lissance, A. 2753, 2761, 2870
List, F. 2091, 2096
Litowitz, B.E. 579
Little, W. 524, 687, 821, 929, 1966
Littmann, E. 1329, 1333, 2450, 2454f.
Litton, D. 3101, 3105
Littré, (M. P.) É. 12, 16, 38, 42, 66, 69, 75-77, 128, 133, 137, 143f., 147, 151, 225, 228f., 230, 311, 323, 327, 501, 503, 508, 512, 515f., 526, 529, 601, 603-607, 638, 681, 687, 698, 701, 703, 820, 905-907, 916f., 1141, 1213, 1408, 1414, 1768f., 1789, 1803f., 1807, 1812-1829, 1836, 1838, 1841, 1872, 2305, 2795f., 2983, 3000, 3054
Liu Lu 2558
Liu Xi 2601, 2609f.

Liu, J.J. 2611
Liu, J.J.L 2603
Livaditu, I.H. 1884
Liver, R. 1035, 1038, 1043
Livet, Ch.-L. 1550, 1557, 1559, 1798, 1815
Livisca, R. 2359
Livius, T. 1846
Livoy, Th. de 1076, 1079
Livšic, V. A. 2485
Livšica, R. 2359
Lizarralde, R. 2704
Lizot, J. 2704
Ljapunov, B. 2305
Ljěč, R. 2761 (s. Lötzsch)
Ljubenov, L. 1129
Ljubimov, J.V. 2320, 2328
Ljung, M. 1314, 1322, 1669
Ljunggren, K.G. 1015, 1934
Llano, A. 2952, 2954
Llave, P. de la 2938, 2946
Llorach, E.A. 930
Llorente, O. 1778, 1781
Lloshi, X. 2761
Lloyd, A. L. 2104, 2220, 2225, 2239
Lloyd, B. 296
Lloyd, B.B. 3167
Lloyd, L. C. 2654
Lloyd, S.M. 1065, 1092
Lloyd, W. 10, 1093, 1944, 1951
Lloyd-Jones, J. 2347, 2349
Llull Martí, A. 1777, 1784
Llull, R. 1770
Loban, M.P. 2337
Lobelius, M. 2916, 2931, 2938, 2946
Lobojko, I. N. 3076
Lobscheid, W. 3114, 3117
Locke, J. 219, 720, 725
Locker, E. 1133, 1137, 1140
Lockwood, L.E. 1559
Loderecker, P. 2289, 2294, 2931
Loebe, J. 1909-1911
Loewe, H. 1052f., 2086, 2089, 2096
Loewenstamm, S.E. 2428, 2435
Loewenthal, R. 2413
Löffler, R. 1031
Löfgren, R. 3050
Löfstedt, E. 2025, 2031, 2036
Logan, H.M. 326f.
Logau, F. von 237, 1155
Lohenstein, D. C. 2071
Lohmann, J. 2224
L'okhin, I. V. 2332f.
Lokotsch, K. 2193, 2226
Lokšina, S.M. 2324
Loliée, F. 1825
Lolliot, Y. 1885
Lolme, L. de 2958
Loman, B. 1933, 1942

Lomanto, V. 1137, 1141
Lombard, A. 1312-1314, 1889
Lombard, S.J. 2590, 2593
Lombarde, G. 1124
Lomholt, A. 1922
Lommatzsch, E. 603, 606, 1343, 1561, 1820, 1842
Lommel, H. 1429
Lomonosov, M.V. 2310, 2312
Londera, E. 2995
Long, B. 3126, 3132
Long, G. 2704
Long, H. 2704
Long, Th. H. 524
Longacre, R. E. 1341, 2705
Longmin 1131
Longmuir, J. 1455, 1984, 1986
Lönnrot, E. 2384, 2387, 2391
Loof, F. W. 2064, 2070
Loos, J. 2285, 2287
Lope Blanch, J.M. 1753, 1760, 1766
Löpelmann, M. 2232
Lopes da Silva, B. 2871, 2876
Lopes, D. 3021, 3030
Lópes, J.M. 2938, 2946, 2952, 2955
López de Mendoza, I. 1762
Lopez Facal, J. 1700, 1702, 1704
López García-Molins, A. 1079
López Martínez, M. 1757
López Morales, H. 1752f., 1760, 1766
López Tamarid, F. 1740, 1760
Lopez Torral, F. 1747, 1760
López Vázquez, C. 2699
Lopez, J.M. 1184
Lorain, P. 1803, 1807
Lorck, J.E. 1844, 1859
Lorentz, F. 2270, 2272
Lorenz, O. 3006f.
Lorenzen, J. 2031, 2034
Lorenzen, P. 539, 547f., 579
Lorenzo, J. 2918, 2931
Lorenzo, R. 1737f.
Loretz, O. 1690
Lorez-Brunold, Chr. 2198, 2226, 2229
Lorez-Brunold, T. 2198, 2226, 2229
Lorge, I. 1321, 1669, 1998f., 2009
Lörinczy, É. 2382
Loring, A. 1129
Loriquet, J.-N. 1807
Lorrain, I. H. 2559
Lorrain, R. A. 2559
Lörscher, W. 188, 580
Lot, G. 1351
Loth, J. 2341, 2349
Lothholz, K. 269
Lötmarker, R. 3042
Lötscher, A. 1295

Lotter, M. 2043
Lottner, C. 2469
Lottner, Ch. 2462
Lötzsch, R. 172f., 893, 2714f., 2719, 2726f., 2761, 2763, 2779, 2781f., 2829, 2831, 2836, 2840, 2842, 2845, 2848, 2853, 3081
Lougheed, W.C. 79
Lounsburg, Th.R. 228
Lounsbury, F. 2678, 2683
Louw, J.P. 1700, 1703, 2429
Lovatt, E.A. 607, 1186, 1188, 1190, 2761
Love, C. E. 2973f., 3050
Lovelace-Käufer, C. 1029, 1038f.
Lovera, L. 1874
Lovett, D.R. 1259f.
Loving, A. 2636f.
Loving, R. 2636f.
Löwe, J. 1068, 1073
Lowe, J. B. 2558
Lowe, J.D. 1505, 1511
Lowe, P. 2761
Lowe, R. 2632-2634
Lowes, R. H. G. 2708
Löwi, M. 1079, 2179, 2181f., 2223
Lowie, R. H. 2692, 2696
Loy, K.J. 3125, 3133
Loyson, E. 1846
Lozachmeur, G. 1804, 1810
Lozovan, E. 3173
Lu Erkui 2601, 2610
Lu Fayan 2603
Lu Feikui 2599, 2611
Lu Shaozun 2559f.
Lü Shuxiang 2826, 2828
Lü To Kyin Sin Kyan 2505
Lubaś, W. 2271
Lübben, A. 1418-1420, 1422, 1424-1426, 1428, 1559, 2088, 2096f., 2215, 2226
Lubbers-Van der Brugge, C.J.M. 2975
Lübke, D. 120, 126, 1389, 2881, 2888, 2890-2892, 2901f.
Lubkowski, F. 3076
Luboteni, G. 2295
Lucas, A. 1187
Lucassen, W. 2419f.
Lucca D., M. de 2689
Luce, G. H. 1341, 2558
Luciani, L. 1310, 1877, 1879
Lück, E. 3172
Luckhardt, H.-D. 1651, 1666
Lüddeckens, E. 1680f.
Ludewig, G. 2226
Ludewig, W. 738, 741, 748, 2146, 2207f., 2226
Lüdi, G. 544f., 580, 804, 992, 998
Ludolf, H. 2449, 2453f., 2461, 2469, 3070, 3085
Lůdovice Moreira, F. J. 3027

Ludovici, C.G. 165
Lüdtke, J. 1787, 2755, 2824
Ludwig I (König) 2988
Ludwig von Anhalt-Köthen 2052
Ludwig, Chr. 181f., 188, 2711, 2968
Ludwig, K.-D. 78, 575, 649, 653, 655, 693, 697, 699, 850, 854, 2131, 2233, 2238
Ludwig, O. 374, 407
Ludwig, W. 1219f.
Ludwikowski, W. 2272
Luelsdorff, P. 525
Luft, C.P. 1078
Lugo, S. de 1747, 1760
Lugones, L. 1760
Luhmann, N. 192f., 198, 207
Luhn, H.P. 1565, 1567
Luidl, Ph. 138, 145
Luik, G. 1209
Luk'janova, E.M. 1657, 1667
Lukan, W. 2297f., 2301
Lukas, J. 2457, 2460
Lukina, G. N. 3081, 3085
Lukoschik, A. 251, 273, 2185, 2226
Lukstinš, G. 2360
Luling, V. 2464f.
Lull, R. 1089
Lumbroso, J. 1906
Luna, F. 10, 1851
Luna, J. de 2980, 2984
Lunačarskij, A.V. 2313
Lund, G.F.V. 1917, 1922
Lund, J. 1305, 1308
Lunel, B. 1054f.
Lünemann, G. H. 3032-3034
Lunt, H.G. 1190
Lurati, O. 1532, 1535, 1537f.
Luria, M.A. 1907
Lurker, M. 3152, 3154-3156
Lurquin, G. 1311
Lusignan, G. 2369, 2371
Lusitano, C. 1011, 1015, 1019, 1129
Luther, M. 145, 232, 406, 459, 499, 516, 830, 1154f., 1157, 1268, 1273, 1552, 2043, 2072, 2079, 2084, 2215, 2226
Lutz, F. 1141
Lutz, L. 166, 953, 955
Lutze, D. 3044, 3046
Lutzeier, P.R. 162f., 544, 551, 580, 611, 614-617, 627, 780, 782, 787, 992, 998
Luvsanžav, Č. 3082
Lux, A. 2188, 2226
Lux, S. 2919, 2931
Luython, C. 1792, 2956
Luzán, I. de 1742
L'vov, M. R. 1082f., 2317, 2324
Lyberis, A. 2353

Lye, E. 1440-1442, 1455, 1909, 1912
Lyford, E. 1268, 1273
Lyngby, K.J. 1919
Lyon, J. E. 2886
Lyon, O. 1072, 2222
Lyons, A. 219f.
Lyons, J. 544, 580, 615, 627, 780-782, 787, 796, 1672, 2824, 2828
Lyons, P.A. 19, 28, 224, 3173
Lysaght, Th. A. 2259, 2266f.
Lysenko, P. 2332
Lysenko, P.S. 2333
Lysle, A. de R. 2973f., 3016, 3018
Lyth, R. E. 2645
Lytkin, V.I. 2397f.

M

Ma Xueliang 2559
Maak, H.-G. 2220
maalaj cansăncaj 2577, 2582
Maaler, J. 800, 804, 813, 824f., 829, 1154, 1158, 2042f., 2045-2047, 2050, 2070
Maalouf, L. 2445, 2447
Maas, G. 1261, 1264
Maas, H. 1192f.
Maas, H.-D. 1650f., 1666f., 2222
Maaß, J.G.E. 1062f., 1065, 1072, 2059, 2068, 2220
Maatjes, A.B. 3118
Mabire, J.-L. 1046, 1049
Mac Cuilennáin, C. 2339
Mac Hale, C. 1743, 1766
Macafee, C. 1987
Macarie 1882
MacArthur, T. 1368
Macary, J. 1802, 1814
Macaulay, Th.B. 225
MacAuslane, J.A. 1145
MacCarthy, P.A.D. 1308, 1310
Macchī, V. 1111, 2751, 2803, 3016
Macchini, V. 3018
MacDavid, R.J. 518
Macdonald, A. 3100, 3105
MacDonald, A. M. 2020
MacDonald, G.J. 1761, 2661, 2699
Macdonell, A. A. 2492
Macdonnel, D.E. 1046, 1048f.
Macdonnell, A. A. 2495
Macé, P.-A. 679, 1077, 1079
MacFarquhar, P.D. 531, 580
Machado, D.B. 1735
Machado, J.P. 1345, 1347, 1731, 1734f.
Mache, U. 2074
Machek, V. 2282f.
Machiavelli, N. 1858

Machoni de Cerdeña, P. A. 2707f.
Maciev, A.G. 2422f.
Mackay, Ch. 1984, 1986
MacKay, M.St. 1310
Mackensen, L. 138f., 144, 247, 273, 358, 405, 574, 634, 687, 694, 698, 734, 743f., 747, 802, 804, 848, 880, 982, 987, 989, 997, 1030, 1035, 1041, 1049, 1176f., 1207, 1209, 1231, 1234f., 1239, 1269f., 1273, 1362, 1513, 1522, 1610, 2106, 2113, 2115-2119, 2121-2125, 2128, 2130, 2133, 2147, 2155, 2165-2170, 2174, 2177, 2181f., 2185, 2188, 2191-2193, 2220, 2223, 2226
MacKenzie, D. N. 2475f., 2483, 2486
MacKenzie, K. 1874
Mackevič, Ju.F. 2337
Mackey, M.G. 1295
Mackey, M.S. 1293, 1295
Mackey, W.F. 1321, 1356, 1364
Mackie, A. 1983, 1986
Mackin, R. 208, 212, 747, 1014, 1018, 1029, 1385
Maclean, A.J. 2432, 2437
Maclean, E. A. 2632, 2634
MacLeod, I. 1987
MacMahon, M.K.C. 1962, 1966
Macphail, R. M. 2540f., 2546
Macrea, D. 1887, 1890
Macrobe, A. 1185, 1188, 1195, 1198
Mactaggart, J. 1984, 1986
Macuch, R. 2432, 2437
Macura, P. 3081
Macwilliam, St. 1966
Mączyński, J. 1140, 2268, 2272
Madano-pāla 2489
Madejowa, M. 517, 1309
Mader, E. 2300
Mader, M. 1183
Mādhava-Kara 2489
Madhunatha, M. 3100, 3105
Madsen, B. N. 2754, 3166
Madsen, H. 1657
Maduro, A. J. 2875
Maes, V. 2648
Maffla Bilbao, A. 2705
Magalhães, R. 3022, 3028
Magalotti, L. 1854
Magay, T. 275, 1308, 1310, 2380f., 2753, 2761, 2778, 2836, 2881
Mager, A. 2092, 2096
Mager, E. 1560
Mager, J. F. 2567
Maggiora, G. de 2450, 2454
Magier, D. 2546
Mägiste, J. 2394
Magnarapa, C. 3010f.

Magni, M. 1209, 1216
Magni, P. 1872
Magnus, J. 1261, 1264
Magnússon, H. 1932
Magometov, A. A. 2423, 2761
Magri, D. 1008
Mahamane, I. 2459f.
Mahapatra, B. P. 2535, 2543f., 2546f.
Mahapatra, Kh. 2535, 2543, 2546f.
Mahapatra, R. 2544, 2547
Mahāprajña, Y. 2505
Mahdī Xān, M. 2411
Mahendra 2497
Maheshawar, N. 2517
Maheśvara 2490
Mahler, M.A. 1266
Maḥmūd (al-Kāšğari) 2410
Mahn, E.A.Ph. 64, 69, 224
Mahn, K.A.F. 1990f., 2007
Mahomed Cauzin Mirza 2518
Mai, A. 1721
Mai, E. 575, 2761
Mai, J. 2761
Maid, V. 2074
Maier, E. 78, 703, 1814
Maier, J. 2044
Maillard, J.-P. 1005, 1007
Maillot, J. 2883, 2887
Maimon, N.Z. 3121, 3133, 3137
Maingard, L. F. 2650, 2652f., 2655
Maino, M. 2464f.
Mainwaring, G. B. 2556, 2558
Maior, G. 1882
Maior, P. 1883
Mair, W. 1184
Mair, W.N. 1199
Maistre, J. de 602
Maixner, R. 2292f.
Majda, T. 2399, 2407
Majid, A. 2517
Major, G 2043, 2048
Majtinskaja, K. E. 2761
Makarov, N. P. 3077, 3079
Makkai, A. 897, 899, 1028, 1516f., 1520, 1522
Makkzūmī 2447
Maksimov, S. 2324
Malachi, A.R. 2433
Malachovskij, L.V. 917, 920, 924, 930
Malagoli, G. 1308, 1310, 1877, 1879
Malakhovskij, L.V. 1659, 1667
Malaret, A. 1752f., 1760, 1766
Malblanc, A. 2855, 2859
Maldonado, J. 2663, 2668
Maletzke, E. 272, 2219
Malherbe, F. 1068, 1775
Malhotra, V. 2541, 2546

Malige-Klappenbach, H. 4, 18,
  27f., 101, 206, 652, 655, 835,
  1235, 1241, 1258, 2103, 2130f.,
  2134f., 2238f., 2727, 2761
Malik, A. A. 2643f.
Malíková, O. 2761
Malina, A. 2761
Malizia, E. 1536f.
Malkhassiants, S. 2369, 2371
Malkiel, Y. 30f., 33, 65, 70, 78,
  249, 276, 528, 530, 732, 748,
  854, 972, 980, 982f., 988f., 998,
  1152, 1245, 1334, 1766
Mallarmé, St. 23
Mallery, G. 1119
Malmtorp, I. 3173
Malone, J. L. 2887
Malone, K. 517, 1999, 2761
Maloux, M. 1036, 1041, 1044,
  1049
Malov, S.E. 2411
Mamani M., M. 2689f.
Mamedzade, A. K. 2485
Man, L. de 2046
Man, O. 2761
Manarini, A. 1329
Mancelius, G. 2354f., 2358, 2360
Mancheño, J.F. 1747, 1760
Manchon, J. 1188
Mancourt, J. 917
Mandelkern, S. 2428, 2433-2435
Manders, W.J.A. 3129, 3133, 3137
Manderström, Chr. 1130
Mandl, H. 1632, 1637
Maneca, C. 1888, 1890
Maneikis, Ch. 1777, 1784
Manekeller, W. 1216
Manes, J. 553, 580, 2254, 2690
Manessy, G. 1338, 1341, 2647,
  2649
Manfrino de Monferrato 1847
Mang, D. 272, 358, 574, 1622,
  2219
Mangada, J. 1216
Mangenot, E. 1563, 1567
Manger, M. 2044
Mangold, M. 509f., 517, 1308,
  1310f., 1623, 2198, 2217, 2219
Mangoldt, U. von 2185, 2226
Mani, C. 1899, 1904
Maniet, A. 1137, 1141
Maníková, Z. 2286f.
Mańkha 2489
Manley, J. 2761, 2783, 2786, 2789,
  2841, 2854
Mann, A. 119
Mann, St.E. 1338, 1341, 2363,
  2366
Mann, Th. 2176
Männer, A. 2529, 2532
Mannheim, B. 2677f., 2681f., 2684
Manni, D.M. 1855, 1860

Manni, V. 3010f.
Manning, E.O. 1912
Männling, J. Chr. 1011, 1015,
  2066, 2071
Manrique, V.G. 1768f.
Manser, M. 1054f.
Manser, M.H. 1030, 1086, 1090,
  1092
Mansion, J.E. 26f.
Mantey, J. 2220
Manthey, F. 2761
Mantilla Ruiz, L.C. 1767
Manu, A. 124, 317, 321, 2206,
  2234, 3172
Manuel, J. 1759
Manutius, A. 1051, 1053
Manutius, P. 1715
Manuzzi, G. 1856, 1860
Many, D. 405
Manzano, C. de la 3175
Manzoni, A. 148, 151, 1090, 1814,
  1857f., 1866, 1871
Mao Zedong 2601
Maquet, Ch. 1095, 1097, 1099
Maran, L. 2558
Marazzi, M. 1688f.
Marbach, G. O. 2065, 2071, 2174,
  2227
Marc, J. 1771, 1784
Marcel, G. 2709
Marcello, B. 1855, 1861
March, F.A. 1096f., 1099
March, J. 1073, 1125, 1131, 1784
Marchand, F. 180, 1367f., 1835
Marchand, H. 779
Marchand, J.W. 461, 500, 1912
Marchio Sessa 1847
Marcillac, J. 1102, 1185, 1188,
  1525, 1530
Marcks, M. 2227
Marckwardt, A.H. 78f., 208, 214,
  654f., 668, 703, 1456, 2000
Marcotorchino, F. 1078, 1080
Marcoux, Ch.-M. de 1805
Marcu, F. 1888
Marčuk, J.N. 2328
Marcus, J. 2683
Marcus, S. 532, 580
Mardarie Cozianul 1889
Mardarie von Cozia 1881
Marden, C.C. 1760
Maréchal, P.-S. 1195, 1198
Marello, C. 532, 580, 722, 725,
  1090, 1093f., 1880, 2729f.,
  2738, 2748-2750, 2754, 2761f.,
  2794-2796, 2828, 2831, 2834,
  2836, 3016, 3019
Mareš, F. W. 2256, 2258, 2261f.,
  2267f.
Margalits, E. 2378, 2381
Margani, G. 1089, 1092
Margoliouth, P. 2437

Margueron, C. 2836, 3012
Marguess, H.E. 2323
Maria, B. V. 2300
Máriafi, I. 2382
Mariano, M. 1088, 1090, 1092
Mariappa Bhat, M. 2532
Mării, I. 1889
Marimoutou, C. J. Cl. 2873, 2876
Marin, P. 3036-3039
Marin, R. 2762
Marinello, G. 1011, 1015, 1089,
  1092
Marini, A. 3012
Marinoni, A. 1844, 1849, 1861
Marione, N. 1141
Mariotti, S. 3011
Mark, Y. 2252f.
Markheden, M. 3128, 3133
Markov, J. 2324
Markovkin, V.V. 2322
Markowitz, J. 580
Marks, G. 1670
Marks, G.A. 1186, 1188
Markus, Š. 1906f.
Marmontel, J.Fr. 1212
Marot, C. 3035
Marouschek, H.v. 1111
Marques, H. 3022, 3028
Marques, J. 3022, 3028
Marquet i Ferigle, L. 1778, 1784
Marquez Villegas, L. 1189
Marr, N.J. 2417f., 2420f.
Marri, M. 3099, 3105
Marrison, G. E. 2559
Marsá, F. 786, 1749, 1760
Marsden, W. 2563, 2565, 3173
Marshall, E. 1144f.
Marshall, J.H. 1129
Marshall, L. 2653f.
Marsigli, L.F. 1881f.
Marston, E. W. 2484, 2486
Martelli, V. 1902, 1904
Martellotti, G. 1878
Martem'janov, J. S. 2762
Martens, F. 1051, 1053
Martens, N. 3067
Martí, F. A. 2927
Martí i Castell, J. 1776, 1785
Marti Marca, J. 3067
Marti Marca, M. 3067
Marti y Gadea, J. 1776, 1784
Martignoni, G.A. 1087, 1089,
  1092, 1867
Martin 582
Martin, B. 720, 723, 1944,
  1946-1949, 1951
Martin, Ch. 1004, 1008, 1213,
  1803, 1807
Martin, E. 3172
Martin, H. 3109, 3112
Martin, H.-J. 146, 1816
Martin, J. 1189, 1572f.

Martin, J.M. 1198, 1310
Martín, L. 1006, 1009
Martin, L.W. 1617, 1623
Martin, R. 607, 917, 1843
Martin, S. E. 2762
Martin, W. 1316-1319, 1321f., 1670, 2222, 2540, 2546, 2716, 2728, 2751, 2762, 2767, 2771, 2775, 2805, 2813, 2829, 2830f., 2836, 3039
Martin, W.J.R. 1621, 1624, 2805, 2813
Martin-Berthet, F. 1814
Martín-Gamero, S. 2956
Martinello, G. 10
Martinet, A. 274, 283, 286, 505, 513, 516, 715, 725, 1125, 1304-1308, 1310f., 1334, 1369, 1378, 1828, 1834, 1836, 1843, 2876
Martinet, E. 3101, 3105
Martinet, J. 1305, 1308, 1310
Martínez Amador, E. M. 120, 1216, 2744, 2751, 2800f., 2803, 2955, 2984, 2994, 2996
Martínez de Espinosa, J. J. 2938, 2946
Martínez de Sousa, J. 1264, 1743, 1766
Martínez de Waucquier, M. 2931
Martínez Moles, M. 1753, 1760
Martínez Virgil, C. 1760
Martínez, E. 1757, 1763
Martínez, F. 1029
Martínez, F.A. 1766, 1768, 1770, 1766
Martinez, F.V. 3092
Martínez, J. 1303, 2668, 2683
Martínez-Barbeito, C. 1736, 1738
Martínez-Hidalgo y Terén, J.M. 1778, 1784
Martínez, A. de 2682
Martini, F. de 1842
Martinon, Ph. 1126f., 1130, 1306
Martins-Baltar, M. 704, 725, 1090, 1092, 1221, 1223
Martinus, R. 3087, 3095
Martius, K. F. Ph. von 2707
Márton, J. 2376, 2381, 2376
Marty y Caballero, L. 1743, 1760
Marty y Caballero, D.E. 1746, 1760
Marty-Laveaux, M.Ch. 1008, 1549, 1552, 1559f.
Martynow, V.V. 2337
Marvan, J. 1141
Marwick, H. 1931f.
Maryniak, I. 1139, 2264, 2266, 2323
Marzell, H. 1059, 1064f., 1255-1257, 1393, 1414, 1590, 1609

Marzys, Z. 652, 655, 1803, 1815
Mas i Solenc, J.M. 1778, 1784
Masamune, A. 2622f.
Mascherpe, M. 2886, 3022, 3028
Mascis, A. 2400, 2405
Masclans i Girvés, F. 1778, 1784
Masereeuw, P. 3165
Masing, O.W. 2393
Masini, A. 1854, 1861
Masjuan i Buxó, M.D. 1778, 1784
Maslova-Lašanskaja, S. S. 2762
Mass, P. 1702
Massa, J.-M. 1733
Massariello Merzagora, G. 989, 991, 998
Masse, F. 40, 45
Masser, A. 2077
Massieu, Abbé 1804
Massim, I. 1885, 1889
Massmann, H.F. 768, 771, 1126, 1130, 1147, 1909f., 1912
Masso i Rubi, M.L. 1779
Massolini. C.B. 2366
Masson, A. 1092, 1807
Masson, J.-R. 1745, 1760, 1803, 1807
Masson, R. 1983, 1986
Massot i Muntaner, J. 1775, 1785, 1787
Māstara, D. 3102, 3105
Māstara, P. 3102, 3105
Mastermann, K.Ch. 1362
Mastrelli, C.A. 1871
Mastrofini, M. 1312, 1314
Masucci, F. 1351
Masuda, K. 3115, 3117
Maß, J. G. E. 2086
Matallana, M. 1747, 1760
Matekaja, A. 3133
Mateo, F. 1313
Mater, E. 1131, 1134, 1137, 1141f., 1221, 1223, 1643, 2184, 2188f., 2227
Matešić, J. 2292, 2294, 2764
Mathews, M.M. 208, 214, 1943, 1952, 1958, 1966, 2007, 2902
Mathews, R.H. 3108f., 3112
Mathias, J. 305, 3170
Mathieu, Y. 3166
Matignon, J. 1047, 1049
Matisoff, J. A. 2556f., 2559f.
Matons, A. 1778, 1784
Matoré, G. 18, 222, 224, 277, 679, 718, 724, 945, 989, 991, 994, 998, 1353, 1362, 1388f., 1796, 1815, 1820f., 1835, 1841, 1843
Matos, D. 3021
Matos, L. de 3030
Matras, Chr. 1930, 1932
Matras, D. 3052, 3060
Matson, D. 2542, 2546
Matsuda, T. 3116f.

Matsuda, Y. 1165
Matsui, K. 2620, 2623
Matsushita, Sh. 2643, 2645
Mattausch, J. 616, 627, 849, 854, 1542, 1548, 1554-1556, 1561f., 2131, 2135, 2239
Mattei, C. 3129, 3133
Mattes, B. F. 2566
Matteson, E. 1341, 2704, 2706
Mattheier, K.J. 207, 275, 580, 1429
Matthes, B. F. 2566f.
Matthes, H.C. 1443
Matthews, E. 1699, 1703
Matthews, P.H. 518, 520, 525
Matthews, W. K. 2628, 2631
Matthias, Th. 1239, 2097, 2106, 2109, 2111f., 2125, 2128, 2168, 2227
Mattioli, P.A. 1847
Mattutat, H. 1051, 1053, 1353, 1356, 1362, 1669
Matušević, M. I. 2765
Mätzner, E. (A. F.) 1436, 1446-1449, 1455
Mau Tsai, L. 1012, 1015
Mauchon, J. 1186
Maucroix, F. de 1797
Mauersberger, A. 1550, 1560
Maung Tin, P. 2506
Maurais, J. 48, 50, 62, 78, 88, 680, 704
Maurer, D.W. 1196, 1199, 1536f.
Maurer, F. 672, 1240, 2230
Maurer, K. 2069
Mauriac, F. 84
Mauro, T. de 43, 45
Mauser, H. 1385
Mauser, M.H. 359
Maußer, O. 1531, 2072
Mauvillon, E. de 2884, 2886
Mawer, A. 1281, 1283
Mawson, C.O.S. 1092, 1099, 1169, 1177
Maxamed Cabdi Maxamed 2464f.
Maximilian II 2069
Maxwell, Chr. 1302f.
Maxwell, J. 225
May, J.K. 165
Mayáns y Siscar, G. 1742, 1760
Mayenowa, M. R. 2270, 2272
Mayer, E. 2684
Mayer, H. 1067, 1075
Mayer, J. 2452, 2454, 2462, 2467
Mayer, J.B. 1073
Mayer, R. 1842
Mayers, M. 2663, 2668
Mayeux, F.-J. 1124, 1807, 1809
Mayhew, A.L. 1436, 1447f., 1452f., 1455
Maynard, G. 2662f., 2670

Mayo, P.J. 2337
Mayr, E. 1261, 1264
Mayrhofer, C. 2503, 2507
Mayrhofer, M. 1142, 1334, 2470-2473, 2494f.
Mazaudon, M. 2558
Mažejka, N.S. 2337
Mazière, F. 1800, 1802, 1811, 1815
Mažiulis, V. 2353
Mazochius, J. 1806, 2046
Mazon, A. 1581, 1588
Mažuranić, I. 2291, 2294
Mažuranić, V. 2291, 2294
Mazzarello, A. 1874
Mazzetti, A. 1360
Mazzolini, A. 3128, 3133
Mbogho, K. 2762
McArthur, J.K. 1696, 1703
McArthur, T. 1, 18, 185, 188, 266, 276, 1030, 1066, 1083-1085, 1090, 1092f., 1672, 1960, 1966
McC.Gatch, M. 1456
McCaig, I. 208, 212
McCaig, I.R. 747, 1385
McCarthy, E. 1616
McCarus, E. N. 2483, 2486
McCawley, J. D. 2762
McClaran, M. 2664, 2668
McCracken, D. 1947, 1952
McCraig, I.R. 1014, 1029
McCulloch, J.R. 166f.
McCune, 2617
McDavid, R.I. (Jr.) 29, 33, 37f., 79, 111, 275, 517, 579, 582, 655, 662, 664, 666-668, 703, 861, 1217, 2009
McDavid, V. 31, 33, 37, 76, 78, 655
McDavid, V.G. 668, 2002, 2009
McDonald, P.C. 1660, 1667
McDougall, D. 327
McDougall, I. 327
McElhanon, K. 2636f.
McElhanon, N. 2636f.
McFarland, C. D. 2568, 2570
McFarland, S.G. 2578, 2582
McGill, M.J. 1671
McGlynn, P. 1560
McGregor, Ch. 94
McIlvaine, E. 3174
McIntosh, E. 753, 1622
McKaskill, St.G. 1216
McKay, G. R. 2639-2641
McKenzie, D. N. 2477-2480
McKenzie, R. 1703
McKinnon, A. 1569, 1572
McLendon, S. 1341
McLeod, W.T. 357, 405, 1076, 1079, 1979, 1982
McLintock, D.R. 153
McMillan, J.B. 33, 37, 667f.
McMillan, J.B. 2000, 2003, 2008f.

McNaught, J. 170, 1662, 1667-1669
McPhee, C. 1047, 1049
McPheron, E. 1047, 1050
McQuown, N. 2664, 2666, 2668, 2670
Meakin, B. 3093, 3095
Mealue, J. 2636, 2638
Mecklenburg, L. F. 2029
Medhurst, W. H. 2620, 2622, 3114f., 3118
Medici, L. de 1854
Medici, M. 1252
Medina, A. 2670
Meech, St.B. 1450, 1456
Meeks, D. 1679, 1681
Meer, G. van der 2025, 2036
Meerburg, G. (A. G.) 2026f., 2033f.
Meertens, P.J. 1271, 1273
Meeussen, A.E. 1341
Mefodij 3073
Mège, A. 1124
Megen, J. van 2048f., 2762, 2782
Meggle, G. 853, 855
Meghretsi, E. 2368, 2371
Megiser, H. 2297f., 2300f., 2400f., 2405, 3070
Mehling, F. 273, 804, 2231
Mehlman, I. 1669
Mehta, K. M. 2511, 2518
Mei Yingzuo 2599, 2605, 2610
Meibauer, J. 816, 821f.
Meid, W. 591
Meier, H. 1321, 1353, 1355f., 1362, 1595, 1610, 1643, 1650, 1667, 1731, 1735, 2191f., 2227
Meier, H.H. 249, 276
Meier, J. 1124
Meier, P.G. 1800, 1815
Meier-Brügger, M. 1704
Meier-Pfaller, H.-J. 1037, 1041
Meijer, G. 1617, 1624
Meijering, H. D. 2024
Meijs, W. 1623, 1650, 1666, 3165, 3168
Meil, K. 1051, 1053
Meili, R. 855
Meillet, A. 1146, 1151, 1324, 1326, 1332, 1342f., 1837, 1839
Meinel, G. 2175
Meinert, F. 2217
Meinhard, H.-J. 573, 580
Meinhof, C. 2652 (= Meinhof, K.)
Meinhof, K. 2463, 2467
Meini, G. 1857f.
Meininger, H. 1191f.
Meisels, W. 3064, 3067
Meisser, U. 1034
Meissner, B. 1683-1685
Meißner, R. 2085, 2099

Meister, W. 3023, 3028
Meiszner, R. 820
Mejía, J. 2706
Mejía, S. 1115f., 1119, 1197f.
Mejlanova, U.A. 2422f.
Majsner, E. 2065, 2071
Melber, J. 2041, 2048
Melcher, F. 1897
Melchers, P. 1275
Melcior, C.J. 1747, 1760
Mel'čuk, I. A. 208, 212, 270, 310f., 520, 525, 599, 732, 748, 917, 1006, 1008, 1012f., 1015, 1018, 1657, 1665-1667, 1837, 1841, 2316, 2324, 2698, 2700, 2715, 2727, 2833f., 2836
Meldan, R. 2181, 2227, 2879, 2881
Meliá, B. 2670, 2676
Melich, J. 2376, 2381, 2383
Melikišvili, G.A. 1692, 1694
Mellado de Hunter, E. 1760
Mellbourn, G. 778, 3045
Mellema, E. E. L. 3035f., 3039
Mellish, Chr. 3166
Mellon, A.S. 1450
Mellor, Ch.J. 643f., 648
Mel'ničenko, G.G. 2328
Mel'nychuk, O.S. 2331, 2333
Melo, A. Sampaio e 1731, 1734
Melo, A.L.P. de 1079
Melo, G.Ch. de 1735
Melzer, F. 2227
Melzi, B. 3010f.
Melzi, G.B. 721, 724, 990, 995, 997, 1866, 1879
Membreño, A. 1752, 1760
Memmert, J.F. 221f.
Menac, A. 2292, 2294, 3082
Ménage, G. 218, 1158, 1323, 1333
Menahem ben Saruq 2427, 2447
Ménard, N. 653, 655
Menarini, A. 1196-1198, 1333, 1532, 1537
Menas Orea 2539
Mencel, R. 3122, 3133
Mencken, H.L. 34, 37, 1046, 1049
Mendelssohn, S. 2651, 2653-2655
Méndez Carrasco, A. 1760
Mendez, B. 1165
Mendoza Pérez, D. 1220
Meneghino, A. 1195, 1197
Menemencioglu, K. 3174
Menéndez Pidal, R. 66, 69, 1328, 1333, 1738, 1744, 1750, 1766, 1768
Meneses Díaz, C. 2699
Menetrier, E. 2506
Meng, H. 2227
Mengel, J. 3058, 3060
Menges, K.H. 2411, 2414
Mengin, E. 2668
Ménil, F. de 3129, 3133

Meninski, F. à M. 2400f., 2402f., 2405, 2407
Menne, A. 539, 580
Menovshchikov, G. A. 2632, 2634
Mensch, G. 2091, 2097
Mensel, J. G. 2095
Mensing, O. 242, 1233, 1239, 2031, 2033, 2061, 2076
Mentrup, W. 131, 134f., 206, 240, 244, 276, 278, 460, 576, 578, 583, 585, 619, 627f., 796, 813, 817, 821f., 830, 842, 849, 853f., 861, 1121, 1124, 1178, 1207, 1209, 1217, 1302-1304, 2014, 2021f., 2192, 2227, 2235f., 2239, 2243f.
Mentz, A. 3141
Mentz, F. 769, 1294, 1296
Menut, A.D. 1244
Menzel, H.-B. 1261f., 1266
Meo Zilio, G. 1112, 1114-1116, 1118f., 1760, 1197f.
Merbach, F. 1560
Mercier, L.-S. 1165, 1815f.
Merckens, M. 3131
Merenciano, F. 1778, 1784
Merguet, H. 1549f., 1554, 1560
Meriggi, P. 305
Meritt, H.D. 1443f., 1455
Merk, Y. 2253
Merkel, E. 3013, 3019
Merker, E. 1550, 1553f., 1560
Merkin, R. 607
Merkle, E. 1269, 1273
Merkle, L. 1269, 1273
Merle, P. 1186, 1189
Merlet, L. 1294f.
Merlette 1824
Merlin, L. 1185, 1189
Merlino, J. 1349, 1351
Merlo, C. 67, 1865
Merriam, Ch. 1990f.
Merriam, G. 1990f.
Merrick, F. 3131
Merrilees, B. 9, 18, 1789f., 1815
Merten, K. 1632, 1637
Merz, G. 1361
Meschonnic, H. 524, 703, 746, 1247, 1832
Mesgnien, F. à (s. Meninski) 2401
Messelaar, P.A. 781, 783-785, 787, 2762
Messeri, A.L. 1849, 1861
Messerschmid, G. F. 3014, 3018
Messi Sbugo, C. 1872
Messi, C. 1844, 1861, 3012
Messina, G.L. 1536f.
Messinger, H. 182, 188, 516, 2751, 2793, 2853
Messner, D. 1183, 1344f., 1347f., 2886
Mestica, E. 1866, 1879
Mestres i Guadreny, J. 1778, 1784
Mészáros, B. 3128, 3133
Métayer, R. P. M. 2632, 2634
Meter, H. 1199
Metrich, R. 2239, 2762
Mettas, O. 1795, 1811
Mette, H.J. 1704
Metteson, E. 2702
Metz, C. 715, 725
Metzeltin, M. 269, 1199, 1538
Metzler, P.J. 3175
Meurier, G. 1792, 3035, 3039
Meursius, I. 1705, 1713
Meusel, J.G. 1234, 1239, 2221
Mewaram, P. 2516, 2520
Meyer de Schauensee, R. 1761
Meyer, C. H. 1065, 1072, 2059, 2068, 2220
Meyer, Ch.F. 31, 33, 106f., 110, 763, 766, 1632, 1637
Meyer, Chr. F. 1069, 1073, 2059, 2071
Meyer, E. A. 3044
Meyer, E.H. 1240
Meyer, G. 998, 1324, 1333, 2362f., 2366
Meyer, G.A. 1030
Meyer, H. 1104, 1111, 2184, 2227
Meyer, I. 2762
Meyer, J. 16, 995, 997
Meyer, K. 2227
Meyer, K. H. 2259f., 2267
Meyer, L. 1920
Meyer, R. 2428, 2434f.
Meyer, R.M. 1201, 1203, 1205
Meyer, Th. 1362
Meyer, W. 1102, 2185, 2188, 2227
Meyer-Hermann, R. 821
Meyer-Lübke, W. 1323, 1329f., 1333, 1337, 1341, 1347, 1756, 1827, 1841, 1875, 1885, 1904f., 1908, 1912
Meyer-Pfaller, H.-J. 2174, 2227
Meyer-Riefstahl, R. 1189
Meyers, R.B. 816, 822
Meyersteen, R. S. 276, 2727, 2762
Meynier, J.H. 221f.
Mez de Braidenbach, N. 221f.
Mez, N. 223, 1766
Mézáros, B. 3128
Mezger, F. 1066
Mézières, A. 1825
Mičátek, L. A. 2285, 2287
Michaelides-Novaros, M.G. 1712f.
Michaëlis de Vasconcellos, C. 1328, 1333, 3023
Michaelis, C. 369, 1244, 1269, 1273
Michaelis, H. 509, 516, 1305f., 1308, 1310, 3016, 3018, 3022-3025, 3028
Michaelis, J. 1221, 1223
Michaelis, J. E. 2071
Michaels, J.W. 3143f.
Michaels, L. 33
Michałk, S. 2275f., 2278
Michalski, T.J. 3133
Michalus, Š. 2286f.
Michatsch, F.J. 1771, 1787
Michaud, G. 273
Michaux, H. 24
Michéa, R. 1321, 1353, 1356, 1362-1364, 1835
Michel, A. 2221
Michel, F. 1184, 1189
Michel, G. 653, 655, 699
Michel, J.-F. 1185, 1189
Michelangelo 1854
Michelena, L. 2374
Michell, E.B. 2577, 2582
Michell, G. 530
Michelon, O. 2668
Michiels, A. 901, 905, 1018, 1670
Michel'son, M.I. 2315, 2324
Michler, M. 1230
Mickiewicz, A. 1549-1551, 1557, 1560, 2270f.
Micu Moldovanu, I. 1884
Micu-Klein, S. 1882f., 2377
Middelkoop, A.J. 3127, 3133
Middleton, Th.H. 36, 38
Midzuno, K. 2506
Miedema, H. Th. J. 2026, 2036
Mieder, W. 1033-1038, 1041, 1043f., 1351, 2065f., 2071, 2076f., 2239
Miège, G. 1796
Miethaner-Vent, K. 18, 373, 378f., 407, 1788, 1815, 2039f., 2048
Miežinis, M. 2357
Mighetto, D. 1141, 1766
Migliorini, B. 66, 69, 151, 222, 224, 989, 998, 1165, 1179, 1184, 1258, 1260, 1305, 1308, 1310, 1325, 1333, 1362, 1845, 1855, 1862, 1866-1869, 1871, 1875-1880
Mihăescu, H. 1890
Mihăilă, G. 1888, 1890, 2264, 2267
Mihajlović, V. 2293f.
Mihalic, F. 2637
Mijinguini, A. 2459f.
Mikailov, Š. 2422f.
Mikalja, J. 2289, 2294
Mikhailov, M.S. 2404f.
Mikhajlov, A.I. 1660, 1667
Mikkonen, P. 2385, 2388
Miklavz, A. 2298
Miklosich, F. 1337, 1341, 2260f., 2263f., 2267 (Miklošič), 2298
Mikó, M. 2887
Mikola, T. 2396, 2398

Mikuckij, S.P. 2336
Mikulik, S. 3140f.
Milanian, H. 1305
Milano, P. M. da 2454
Mildwurf, A. 3128, 3133
Mīlenbahs, K. 2357
Milev, A. 2308
Miličik, V. 1141, 2303f.
Militz, H.-M. 1030, 1032
Mill 541
Millares, A. 1760
Millares, L. 1760
Miller, E. 2762
Miller, G.M. 1304, 1308, 1310
Miller, L.A. 1660, 1667
Miller, V. F. 2484-2486
Miller, W.R. 1338, 1341
Miller, W.S. 1207, 1209
Millidge, E. 3126, 3133
Mills, A.D. 1281, 1283
Milne, R. C. 2751, 2796, 2816, 2824
Milner, G. 2574
Milner, G. B. 2575
Milton, J. 1451, 1453, 1949, 1960
Minamoto, S. 2618, 2622
Minaty, W. 41, 46
Minckwitz, M.-J. 1815
Mineemi, M. 2754
Minerbi, L. 1845, 1849ff., 1860, 3008
Minerophilus Freibergensis (Pseudonym) 2062
Minina, G. F. 2552, 2554
Minio, M. 2289, 2296
Minjung Sorin 2616
Minkova, G. 2307f.
Minor, K. 3124, 3126, 3133
Minotto, F. 1881
Minozzi, M. T. 2464f.
Minsky, M. 893f., 899
Minssen, J. F. 2028f., 2034
Miot, B. 1247
Miotto, L. 1877, 1879
Mir y Noguera, J. 1046, 1049, 1051, 1053, 1760
Miracchi, R. 1130
Miracle Montserrat, J. 1776, 1784
Miracle, J. 1783, 1787
Miram, H. 2664, 2668
Miranda, P. 2686, 2690
Mirandas, P. 2706
Mirčeva, D. 2265
Miret i Güell, J. 1772, 1784
Miri, H.F. 1761
Mirò, A. 1778, 1784
Miron, P. 1882, 1889, 1891, 2851, 2853
Mirowicz, A. 3063, 3067
Mirza Khan 2519
Misail 1882
Mischlich, A. 2458, 2460

Mish, F.C. 37, 672, 1164f., 1999, 2004, 2008
Mishkin, M. 140, 145
Misra, B. G. 2533
Misra, D. 2515
Mistler, J. 1213
Mistral, C.-F. 1803, 1807
Mistral, F. 66, 69, 1892-1895, 1904f.
Mistrík, J. 2287
Mitaš, A. 2276f.
Mitchel, L.A. 2435
Mitchell, E. 106, 109, 111, 208-211, 214, 1632, 1637
Mitchell, P.M. 244, 1240, 2069, 2099
Mitchell, T.F. 1018
Mitchell, W.S. 3171
Mitra, S. 2510, 2517f.
Mitre, B. 2709
Mitrović, B. 2293f.
Mittelstraß, J. 276, 574, 796
Mitter, P. 2539
Mitterand, H. 731, 1325, 1332, 1347, 1575, 1588, 1827, 1843
Mittermann, H. 1571, 1573
Mitzka, W. 239, 242, 244f., 771, 821, 1323, 1333f., 2035, 2075, 2085, 2098, 2223
Mivátek, L. A. 2285
Miyagi, N. 3116, 3118
Miyamoto, M. 3124, 3127, 3133
Mizeruňa, S. 3129, 3133
Mladenov, St. 2305, 2306, 2308
Mo' 2593
Moayyad, H. 2479f.
Moberg, K.J. 3128, 3133
Möbius, Th. 1929, 1931
Mochet, M.-A. 704, 725
Möcker, H. 305, 374-376, 407, 2191, 2239
Modest, A. 1092, 2089, 2097
Modglin, N. 1130
Modi, J. J. 2471, 2473
Modley, R. 3152, 3156
Moeller, B. 2048
Moerbeek, A. van 3038
Moerdijk, A. 276
Moerdijk, F. 2011, 2021
Moers, J. 2887
Moesbach, P. E. W. de 2709
Mogensen, H. 1918
Mogensen, K.K. 1362
Moggallāna Thera 2499, 2504, 2551, 2554
Mogiluitski, Y. 2251, 2253
Mohamed Haaji Cosman 2464, 2466
Mohammed Meerza Mohazzab 2517, 2521
Möhlig, W. J. G. 2647, 2649

Möhn, D. 134, 206, 240, 244, 321, 686f., 770, 830, 853, 1136-1138, 1143, 1209, 1523, 1531, 2104, 2216, 2236
Mohr, F. A. 3056, 3060
Möhren, F. 219, 224, 990, 998, 1344, 1348
Moirand, S. 704, 725, 1223
Moisan, A. 1293, 1295
Moitier, R. 406, 459
Mok, Q.I.M. 782, 784, 787, 938, 946, 2752
Mokken, R.J. 1321
Molard, E. 1185, 1189, 1210, 1216
Molas, J. 1787
Molbech, C. 2035(= Molbech, Chr.)
Molbech, Chr. 1394, 1414, 1914-1918, 1922, 2035, 3055, 3060
Molde, B. 1165, 1937, 1942
Molema, H. 2019, 2021, 2028
Moles, A.A. 714, 725
Molesworth, G. 2514, 2519f.
Molesworth, J.T. 3100, 3105
Molho, M. 1906f.
Molière 1824
Molière, J.-B. 729
Molière, J.B.P. 3133
Molina (el Cuzqueño), C. de 2684
Molina, A. de 1740, 1761, 2657-2660, 2697, 2699
Molina, C. de 2678
Molina, E. 3140f.
Molina, J.A. de 1741, 1766
Moliner, M. 286, 692, 918, 920f., 929, 936, 1748, 1761, 1767
Molino, G. 2400, 2405
Molins, M. de 1743, 1766
Moll Marqués, A. 1785
Moll Marqués, N. 1776
Moll, A. 1775
Moll, F. de B. 1771, 1775f., 1778-1781, 1784f., 1787
Moll, O. 1033, 1043
Moll, T. A. 2630
Mollay, K. 231, 245, 1592
Molle, F. 1252
Möllemann, St. 2044
Möllencamp, R. 2028, 2034
Möller, B. P. 2030, 2034
Møller, E. 278, 408, 460, 499, 575, 585, 787, 2236, 2244, 2762, 2780, 2782
Möller, J. G. 3043f., 3046
Möller, L. 1935, 1942, 3040-3142
Møller, N. 1922
Molnar Albertus S. 1882
Molnár, A. 2381
Molnár, A.S. 2375
Molotkov, A.I. 2315, 2324, 2328
Moltke, E. 1917, 1922

Molza, F.M. 1125
Momozawa, T. 3117
Moṅ Krī, L. tī 2505
Moncayo Rosales, L. 2702
Mondon-Vidailhet, F. M. C. 2452, 2454
Monelli, P. 1867, 1879
Monesi, A. 1177
Monet, Ph. 39, 140f., 144, 1795, 1807, 1816
Mongelli, G. 1126
Monier-Williams, M. 2492, 2494f., 2497
Monlau, F. 1216 (= Monlau, P. F.)
Monlau, P.F. 1324, 1333, 1747, 1761
Monna, M. C. 2471, 2473
Monniot, A. 1351
Monod, M. J. 2885, 2887
Monroy Ocampo, B. 1092
Monso, I. 3022, 3028
Monson, S.C. 79
Montag, S. 2703
Montale, E. 149, 1874
Montandon, G. 2463, 2467
Montbrand, D. 2872-2875
Monteil, V. 2411
Montemerlo, G.S. da 10
Monterde, F. 144, 1754, 1762
Montero, E. 1194, 1199
Montes Giraldo, J.J. 1753, 1761
Montgolfier, P. de 2458, 2460
Montgomery, A. 3048-3050
Montgomery, H. 1054f., 1201, 1205
Montgomery, R. 2511, 2518
Montherlant, A. de 24
Montherlant, H. de 1841
Monti, V. 148, 1846, 1856f., 1863
Montméran, A. de 1011, 1015
Montoliu, M. de 1779, 1781
Montoya, A. R. de 2671, 2673-2676
Montredon, J. 1113, 1119
Montreynaud, F. 1047, 1049
Montsià, B. 1777, 1785
Moon, R. 532, 580. 917
Moor, J.C. de 1693
Moore, B. R. 2706
Moore, H. 1046, 1049
Moore, S. 1449f., 1452f., 1456
Moore, T.E. 582
Mora, I. 1507, 1511
Mora, J.J. de 1073
Morais, A. de 3021
Morais, siehe Silva 1727f., 1734
Moral-Arroyo, J.A. 1052
Morales Pettorino, F. 1754, 1757
Morales, E. 1778, 1781
Morán, F. 2664, 2668
Morán, P. 2664, 2668

Morandini, F. 1130
Moravia, A. 1873
Morawski, J. 1036, 1041
Morciniec, E. 3067
Mordechai, R.N. 1563
Moreau, G. 1822
Moreau, R. 1315, 1322
Morehead, A.H. 1099
Morehead, Ph.D. 1099
Morel, H.V. 1761
Morellet, Abbé 165
Morén, C. G. 3044, 3046
Moreno Pacheco, M. 1029
Moreno, A. 1735
Moreno, A.J. 1124
Moreno, M. 2463f., 2467
Moréri, L. 988, 991, 997
Moreto, F.P. 1125, 1130
Morgan, B.Qu. 1353-1355, 1362
Morgan, R. 2876
Morgan, R. jr. 2871f.
Morgan, W. 2692, 2694-2696
Morganwg, I. 2347
Morgenstierne, G. 2484-2486
Morgenthaler, R. 1669
Morin, B. 1073
Moríngio, M.A. 1752, 1761
Morita, T. 3119
Moritz, K.Ph. 1220
Moritz, Ph. 2063, 2071
Morkovkin, V. V. 1006f., 1014, 1018, 1099, 1652, 1666, 1668, 1671, 2316, 2320, 2324, 2326, 2328, 2759, 2762, 2902, 3082, 3084
Morlet, M.-Th. 1268, 1272f., 1275, 1282, 1284
Morlino 3012
Mormile, M. 599, 607, 1165, 1815
Morohashi Tetsuji 2601, 2610
Morohashi, T. 2620, 2622, 3108, 3112
Moroškin, M. 2315, 2324
Morottaja, M. 2391
Morpurgo-Davies, A. 1324, 1333, 1689, 1696, 1703
Morris, Ch. 3149, 3157
Morris, J. C. 2527, 2532
Morris, M. 1216
Morris, W. 37, 69, 211, 213, 515, 529, 667, 778, 1216, 1331, 1622, 2002, 2007
Morris, W. V. A. 524, 747, 2726, 2751, 2817
Morris, W. W. A. 2789
Morris-Nygren, M. 3048-3050
Morrison, R. 3108, 3112
Morscher, E. 196, 207
Morse, C. F. 2305, 2306, 2308
Mortara Garavelli, B. 1089
Mortet, Ch. 1789, 1815
Mortier, R. 1077, 1079

Morvan, R.G. 1230
Morvay, K. 2755
Mosback, G. P. 2451, 2453
Moschopolites, D. 2362, 2366
Mosdra 2395
Moser, H. 110, 1067, 1310, 2727, 2763f.
Mošin, V. A. 2256, 2261, 2268
Moskalenko, A. A. 2334, 3076, 3085
Moskal'skaja, O. I. 746, 1622, 2848, 2853, 3081
Mosqua, F. W. 2063, 2071
Mossé, F. 1912
Mossman, J. 1295
Mossy, G. 1846
Moszyński, L. 2262f., 2268
Moth, M. 1913f., 1916, 1918, 1922, 1924
Motherby, R. 1984, 1986
Motoki, S. 3114, 3118
Motsch, W. 645, 648, 774, 778, 813, 879, 881, 887, 967, 1230, 2828
Motter, T.H.V. 1071
Moulin, A. 653, 655, 2887
Moulis, A. 1895, 1904
Mountain, K. 2702
Moura, F. 1312, 1314
Moussay, G. 2591-2593
Moya, J. de 1740, 1761
Moŷiy̱a, M. 2636-2638
Mpaayei, T. O. 2646
Mra-toṅ Charā-tō 2551, 2554
Mran-ma Sasana Aphavai 2551, 2554
Mran-mā-cā Aphavai 2551, 2552, 2554
Mran-ma-ca Aüjvao 2554
Mrâo Ênao-Mrô, Y. 2593
Mrazovic, P. 2292, 2294
Mück, H. 1137, 1140
Mück, H.-D. 1137, 1140
Mucke, E. 2275, 2278
Muckenhaupt, M. 716, 725
Mudersbach, K. 573, 580, 947f., 950, 955
Mudge, I.G. 3173f.
Mueller, O.M. 1016
Mufwene, S.S. 531, 580
Mugand, J. 646
Mugdan, J. 111, 127, 130, 133-135, 181, 184, 188, 200f., 206, 214, 251, 269, 274, 317, 391, 393, 406f., 461, 500, 518-525, 564, 575, 586, 591f., 614, 642, 644f., 648, 734, 736f., 739f., 747-749, 774-779, 814, 868, 880f., 892, 905, 921, 923, 930, 955, 1009, 1010, 1018, 1596, 1610-1615, 1621-1625, 1638, 2106, 2131, 2135f., 2150,

2152, 2207, 2233, 2235, 2237,
2239, 2241, 2244, 2722, 2726,
2728, 2752, 2757, 2760, 2770,
2774f., 2903
Mughini, G. 1868
Mugica, P. 2374f.
Muhammad, as-S. 2399, 2405
Mühlau, F. 1068, 1075
Mühle, Chr. 2460
Mühlen, H. v. zur 2360
Mühlenbach, K. 2360
Mühlhäsler, P. 2637
Mühlmann, J. 3017
Mühlner, W. 580
Muhr, R. 2191, 2239
Muide, J. 2393
Mu'īn, Muhammad 2479
Mujika, L.M. 2374f.
Muka, E. 2275-2278
Mukarovsky, H. 1341
Mukriāni, W. 2483, 2486
Mulagk, K.-H. 269
Mulako, L. 2295
Mulay, Y. 3170
Mulc, I. 2262
Mulch, R. 2230
Mulch, Roland 242
Mulch, Rudolf 242
Mülhause, R. 1019, 1028, 1030
Muljačić, Ž. 1179, 1184
Mulji, K. 2511
Müller, A. 1293, 1296, 1308, 1310, 2636f.
Müller, A.W. 251, 276
Müller, B. 663, 668, 1345, 1348, 1430, 1434, 2715, 2754f., 2763, 2887
Müller, B. [Bärbel] 2726
Müller, B.-D. 173f.
Müller, C. 1766
Müller, C.F. 1552, 1560
Müller, Ch. 86f., 704, 1316, 1318, 1322, 1563, 1567, 1644, 1671, 1815, 1829, 1843
Müller, F. 1337, 1341, 2567
Müller, G. 1334, 2215
Müller, G. H. 3054, 3060
Müller, G.C. 1124
Müller, H. 2218
Müller, J. 242, 2216
Müller, K. 856f., 861, 2220, 2239, 2276, 2278, 2755, 2726
Müller, K.-H 3172
Müller, M. 188, 2054, 2056, 2076, 2490, 2651
Müller, O. 892, 1130, 2066, 2071, 2763
Müller, P.E. 1068, 1073
Müller, R.V. 3172
Müller, St. 3076
Müller, T. 2568
Müller, U. 1137, 1139f., 2232

Müller, W. 123, 144, 242, 247,
272, 276, 405, 540, 564, 574,
580, 620, 622, 627, 634f., 646,
648, 654, 740, 748, 768, 771,
849, 854, 882, 1017, 1028,
1030, 1069, 1072f., 1075-1077,
1079, 1123f., 1165, 1169,
1175f., 1178, 1230, 1234, 1238,
1362, 1596, 1608-1610, 1622,
1638, 1644, 1813, 2088, 2090,
2094, 2096, 2105f., 2109, 2114,
2123, 2131, 2135, 2147, 2159,
2175f., 2180-2182, 2184f.,
2219, 2227, 2234, 2239, 2887
Müller, W.W. 1693
Müller, Wi. 1149f., 1276, 1283,
1405, 1413, 1418-1420,
1424-1426, 1428, 1539, 1548,
1601, 1610
Müller-Fraureuth, K. 2215, 2227
Müller-Marzohl, A. 2192, 2239
Müller-Thurau, C.P. 574, 1034,
1043, 1351, 1528, 1530, 2185,
2198, 2227
Müllich, H. 1386, 1389
Mulon, M. 1275
Mumprecht, V. 1038, 1043
Mun Se-yŏng 2614, 2617
Munari, B. 1114, 1119
Munch, V. 2886
Muncker, F. 1158f.
Mundy, P. 2396
Mungard, N. 2030, 2034
Muni, V. 2504
Munier, F. 1216
Munkácsi, B. 2396f.
Munker, F. 243
Munkha 2489
Munniksma, F. 3128, 3133
Muñoz y Manzano, C. (= Conde de La Viñaza) 1767
Munshī, Shams-i 2477
Munske, H.H. 127, 245, 279, 322, 359, 408, 461, 500, 576, 586, 626, 628, 688, 849, 999, 1146, 1152, 1258, 1523, 2035, 2245
Munson, K.A. 1703
Munson, R. 856, 860f.
Munster, S. 2434
Munteanu, D. 1762, 1766
Munteanu, G. 1883, 1888
Munzel, K. 3093, 3095
Munzinger, W. 2450, 2454
Murakami, H. 3116, 3118
Murakami, T. 3116f.
Murav'ev, V. L. 2886
Murayama, S. 2620, 2622
Murdoch, B.O. 1137, 1143
Murdoch, J. 1124
Muret, E. 1612, 1619, 1623, 2771, 2774
Muret, M.A. 1011, 1015

Murison, D.D. 1985-1987
Murith, J. 1261, 1264
Murke, A. 2300
Murkelinskij, G.B. 2422f.
Murko, A. 2298
Murmellins, J. 2043
Murmū, Bh. 2546
Murnu, G. 1890
Murphy, J. D. 2648f.
Murphy, M. 1439, 1456
Murphy, M.G. 1017
Murra, J. V. 2681, 2683
Murray, A. 2452, 2455
Murray, A. H. 2010, 2021
Murray, D. 1987
Murray, G.W. 1680f.
Murray, J. 103, 110, 766
Murray, J.A.H. 229f., 529, 644f., 647, 667, 786, 821, 868, 929, 1414, 1436f., 1454, 1609, 1623, 1872, 1943, 1952, 1961-1963, 1966, 1984-1986, 1990, 2001, 2004, 2009, 3118
Murray, J.H. 1966
Murray, K.M.E. 225, 228, 230, 1962, 1966
Murrison, D. 1415
Murtonen, A. 2435f.
Musaev, K.M. 2414
Musanić, R. 2292, 2295
Muss-Arnolt, W. 1683, 1685
Mussafia, A. 1847, 1862
Müssener, H. 778
Musset, A. 912, 1044
Musulin, St. 2289, 2290, 2296
Muthanna, I.M. 3100, 3105
Muthmann, G. 374, 379, 406, 1134-1137, 1141, 1643, 2184, 2227
Mutschmann, H. 1362
Muuk, E. 2394
Muzzo, G. 1902, 1904
Myataung, S. 2506
Mykhal'chuk, K.P. 2331, 2333
Mylius, K. 2763
Myller, Chr.H. 1601, 1610

N

Naci, M. 2400, 2405
Nadeljaev, V.M. 2412f.
Naden, T. 1967, 1982
Nadžip, È.N. 2411
Naess, A. 539, 580
Näf, A. 2233
Nafīsī, Sa'īd 2477f., 2480
Nagao, M. 3167
Nagashima, D. 3119
Nagata, H. 3116, 3118
Nagler, G.K. 3150, 3156
Nagpur, Ch. 2535

Nagy, G.O. 1075, 1079, 2381f.
Nahir, M. 79
Nai Muang 2578
Nail, N. 1429
Nair, P.K.K. 3097-3099, 3105
Naïs, H. 1789, 1815, 2957, 2960
Naj Muang 2578
Najafī, H. al- 3092, 3095
Najlis, E. 2708
Nakahara, Z. 2621f.
Nakajima, F. 3115f., 3118
Nakajima, H. 2619, 2622
Nakamoto, M. 2621f.
Nakamoto, S. 2621f.
Nakamura, T. 3125, 3133
Nakamura, Y. 2622
Nakano, A. 2454, 2464f.
Nakao, K. 2763
Nakashima, H. 2763
Nakaye, T.(Ch.) 3116, 3118
Nakhjavāni, Muḥammad ibn Hendushqh-e 2447
Nakhprathip, S. 2506
Nam Yong-sin 2616f.
Nama 2653
Namboodiripad, K. V. 2532
Nametak, A. 2290, 2296
Namir, L. 3142, 3144
Nanabhai Rustomji Remina 2518
Naṇatilaka 2504
Nance, R.M. 2348, 2350
Nanda Sharma, G. 2515, 2520
Nandadāsa 2512
Náñez, E. 1008
Nanni, U. 1192f., 1535, 1537
Nanobhasatissa 2504
Nanov, L. 2306, 2308
Nanova, A. 2308
Ñāṇuttara, S. 2506
Napier, A.S. 1455
Napoleon 1856, 3089
Narabayashi, T. 3114, 3118
Narbheramo, M. 3101, 3105
Nares, R. 1436, 1452, 1455
Narumov, B.P. 1143
Nascentes, A. 1030, 1325, 1333, 1732, 1734
Nascentes, O.A. 1073
Nash, D. 2639-2641
Nash, R. 1179, 1184, 2886
Nasiri, T. 3093, 3095
Nasody, A.A.P. 1882
Nathan ben Kalonymus 2428
Nathan ben Yeḥiel 2427, 2434
Nathan, D. 2641
Nathan, M. 2434
Naum, T. 1885
Naumann, H. 1280, 1282
Naumova, M. 2307
Nauta, G. A. 2024, 2034
Navalani, K. 2517, 3100, 3102, 3107

Nāvalar, V.W.Q. 3101, 3105
Navarrete, P.F. de 1741, 1761
Navarrete-Luft, A. 1157f.
Navarro Tomás, T. 1750
Navarro, I. 2956
Navarro, J. 2895, 2901
Navarro, J.M. 1767, 2766
Nayak, Ch.R. 3101, 3105
Nayak, S. 2515, 2520
Nāyar, K. 3102, 3105
Nazor, A. 2262, 2266, 2268
Ndreca, M. 2365f.
Neagu, V. 1762, 1766
Neal, E. 1051, 1051
Neaman, J.S. 976, 980
Neander, M. 1011, 1015
Nebrija, A. de 63, 69, 1771, 1788, 2657, 2659, 2661, 2668, 2697, 2699
Nebrija, E.A. 1725, 1845, 1848
Nebrija, E.A. de 9, 16, 1739-1743, 1761, 1764, 1849, 2911, 2938, 2946, 2949, 2955, 2992f., 2966 (Nebrissensis), 3020
Nebrixa, A. de 63, 69 (s. Nebrija)
Nečas, J. 2939, 2946
Neck, M. G. van 2886
Nedil's'kyj, S. 2331, 2333f.
Nedobejkine, N. 3165
Nedobity, W. 119, 124, 317, 321, 2206, 2234
Neergaard, P. 3129, 3133
Neff, M. 2810
Neff, M. S. 2813, 3167
Negreira, M. 1738
Negulici, I.D. 1889
Nehama, J. 1907
Nehring, J.Chr. 1172, 1177, 2063, 2071
Neidhardt, J.E. 2987
Neikens, J. 2357
Neilson, W.A. 1994, 2007
Nekraševič, S. 2336f.
Nekvedavicius, C. 2968
Nelde, P.H. 1183
Nellessen, H. 629, 634
Nellis, N. 2698f.
Nelson, A. 1368
Nelson, R. J. 2763, 2956
Németh, J. 2400, 2407
Nemi, G. 3016, 3018
Nemikorpi, A. 1669
Nemnich, Ph.A. 2917f., 2932, 2939, 2946, 3022, 3028
Nemoto, M. 2131, 2240
Nemser, I. 2857
Nemser, W. 2857, 2859
Nencioni, G. 151, 580, 1089, 1093, 1869-1872, 1876, 1880
Nepokupnyj, A.P. 1286, 1290, 2332f.
Neretti, F. 3009, 3012

Nerius, D. 1299f., 1303f., 2055, 2076, 2099, 2131, 2240
Nersesovich, A. 2368
Neruda, P. 22f., 28
Nesheim, A. 1926f.
Neske, F. 1169, 1177, 1516, 1522, 2185, 2193, 2228
Neske, I. 1169, 1177, 2185, 2193, 2228
Nesselmann, G.H.F. 2351, 2353
Neto, C. 3131
Netsvetov, J. 2632, 2634
Neu, E. 1692, 1694
Neubauer, F. 113, 115, 126, 128, 133, 135, 161-163, 531, 542, 552, 581, 818, 822, 900f., 903, 905, 1360, 1364, 1632, 1637, 1672, 1978, 1982, 2131, 2240
Neubecker, O. 3151-3153, 3157
Neubert, A. 172, 174, 2756, 2763, 2776, 2778
Neubert, G. 304, 1230, 1661, 1667, 1672, 2240, 2753
Neue, G.P. 3097, 3099, 3105
Neuendorff-Fürstenau, J. 1560
Neufeldt, V. 2001, 2004, 2008
Neufeldt, V.E. 641
Neugaard, E. 1777, 1784
Neuhaus, H.J. 1590, 1610, 2887, 3167
Neuhaus, J.H. 1573
Neuhäusler, A. 1516f., 1522
Neuland, E. 183, 189
Neumann, G. 79, 269, 1687, 1689
Neumann, H. 2951f., 2955
Neumann, I. 269, 1273f., 2871, 2876
Neumann, J. 2282f.
Neumann, M. 2393
Neumann, R. 1084, 1094
Neumann, W. 893, 1549
Neurath, R. 79, 579, 583f., 655f., 699, 2768
Neuß, E. 1255, 1257
Nevenswander, H. 2669
Neves, A. 1752, 1761
Newald, R. 2207-2209, 2228
Neweklowsky, G. 2300
Newell, J. E. 2575
Newenburgk, H. 3070
Newhouse, D. 1124
Newman, E. 35
Newman, E.W. 3089, 3095
Newman, H. 3022, 3028
Newman, P. 1341, 2457, 2459f., 2762, 2766
Newman, P.S. 3167
Newman, R. M. 2457, 2459f.
Newmark, P. 3170
Newmeyer, F.J. 1027, 1032
Newton, D. 1367
Newton, E. P. 2515, 2520

Newton, I. 1951
Nguyễn Dinh-Hoà 96, 2583f., 2588f., 2727, 2763, 2869f., 2898, 2902
Nguyễn Quang Xỹ 2587, 2589
Nguyễn Trân Mô 2587, 2589
Nguyễn Văn Khôn 2587-2589
Ngyen X. C. 2284
Nibbi, A. 1862, 2971, 2975
Niborski, Y. 2251, 2253
Niccoli, A. 1875, 1879
Niccoli, M. 1878
Niceforo, A. 1196, 1199
Ničev, A. 2305, 2307f.
Ničeva, K. 2307, 2308
Nichols, J. 2423
Nicholson, M. 1216
Nicholson, R.A. 2438, 2448
Nicholson, V. 2704
Nickel, G. 883, 887, 1632, 1638, 2222
Nickolaus, G. 1353, 1355, 1359, 1362, 1364, 2890, 2895, 2901
Nicolai, F. 21
Nicolai, J. 1261, 1263f.
Nicolai, R. 2643, 2645
Nicolas, A. 653, 655, 1185, 1190
Nicolet, J. 3008
Nicot, J. 9, 16, 39, 146, 218, 1792, 1794f., 1801, 1806, 1808, 1810-1814, 1816-1818, 2864, 2866, 3006, 3012
Niculescu, A. 1890
Nida, E.A. 544, 581, 917, 1672, 1700, 1703, 2429, 2868
Niderehe, H.-J. 2928
Nideśālaya, K.H. 3098
Niebaum, H. 238f., 242, 245, 581, 652, 655, 662-666, 668, 2027, 2036, 2131, 2136, 2240
Niederehe, H.-J. 9, 18, 62, 269, 653, 655f., 754, 1739, 1766, 1815, 2936, 2960, 2986
Niedermann, M. 2353
Niedźwiedzki, W. 2272
Niehl, P. 135
Niel, R.L. 376, 406
Nielsen, B. K. 2725f.
Nielsen, F. 2633
Nielsen, H. 1918, 1922
Nielsen, K. 1926f., 2389-2391, 2714, 2919, 2932
Nielsen, K.M. 1917
Nielsen, N.A. 1176
Niemann, P. 1100, 1102
Niemann, R.-F. 1388, 2899
Niemeyer, J. 576, 582
Niemikorpi, A. 2385-2387
Nienaber, G. S. 2651, 2655
Niermeyer, J.F. 1346f., 1720f.
Nießen, J. 1256f.
Nieto Jiménez, L. 1755

Nieto, R. 1757
Nieuwborg, E.R. 1141
Nieuwstadt, M. van 293, 296
Nijhoff, M. 2562f., 2567f.
Nikelov 3126
Nikifarowski, M. 2336
Nikitevič, V. M. 2763
Nikkila, E. 2759
Nikolov, A. 3133
Nikolov, B. 2308
Nikolova, C. 2306, 2308
Nikolova-Gălăbova, Z. 1021, 1030, 2307
Nikonov, V.A. 2316, 2324
Nikula, H. 531, 581, 608, 614, 2898, 2902
Nilkanth, M. R. 2512, 2518
Nilles, J. 2636, 2638
Nilson, A.P. 87
Nilsson, J. 2660
Nilsson, L. G. 3048-3050
Nilsson, N.J. 893, 899
Nimchuk, V.V. 2332-2334
Nimčuk, V. V. 2266, 3070-3072, 3083, 3085
Nin'ovs'kyj, V. 2332f.
Niobey, F. 1829
Niobey, G. 61, 327, 524, 667, 679, 703, 746, 786, 916, 945, 1096-1099, 1832
Nir, R. 79
Nirenburg, S. 3167
Nirmutanus, Ch. 2932
Niselovič, I. 2359
Nishida, T. 2560
Nisieli, U. 1126, 1130
Nisiello, U. 1079
Nissen, C. 1112
Nissen, C. A. 3056, 3060
Nissen, M. M. 2028f., 2034
Nistrup Madsen, B. 3059, 3061
Nitti, L. 2492
Nixon, R. 36
Nizolius, M. 1014
Nižskij, V. A. 2896, 2900
Nizzoli, M. 2915, 2932
Njock, P.E. 1353, 1355, 1364
Nobel, P. 1789, 1815
Nobel, V. 1296
Nobis, H.M. 539, 541f., 547, 581
Nobl, S. 2252-2254
Nobre, E. 1189, 1535, 1537
Noci, C. 1126, 1130
Noctuel 1351
Nodier, Ch. 1081, 1184, 1247, 1745, 1799f., 1802-1805, 1808f., 1814f., 1817, 1821, 1841, 2980, 2985
Noël, A.P. 80
Noël, F. 1011, 1015, 1197
Noël, F.J. 1803, 1808f.
Noël, J. 901, 905, 1018

Noël, J.-F.M. 87
Noël, L. 1102
Noeli, T. 2989f.
Nogami, S. 3113, 3118
Nogle, L.E. 532, 553, 581
Nogueira, J. 2896, 2901
Nogueira, R. de Sa 1216
Nöjd, R. 3048-3050
Noldius, Chr. 1221, 1223
Nolten, J.A. 224 (= Noltenius)
Nolten, J.F. 217, 224, 1051, 1053, 1080
Noltenius, J.F. 224, 1068, 1075f., 1081, 1083, 3173
Nonahan, B. 1119
Nonius Marcellus 1714, 1721
Noory, S. 1308, 1310
Nopitsch, Chr. 1033, 1043
Nopitsch, Chr. C. 2076
Nopitsch, S. 2066
Norback, C. 1207, 1209, 1302f.
Norback, P. 1207, 1209, 1302f.
Norden, E. 1717
Nordin, J. 3130f.
Noreen, A. 1933, 1943
Noreng, H. 1928
Norganwg, I. 2349
Noriega Varela, A. 1736f.
Noriega, F. de P. 2980, 2985
Norling-Christensen, O. 2754
Nørlund, P. 1922
Norman, F. 1066
Norman, K. R. 2499, 2502, 2507
Normann, R. von 1047, 1049, 1079, 1102, 2180-2182, 2228
Norstett, I. 2916, 2932
Northrup, C.S. 1449
Nortmeyer, I. 276, 405, 458, 881f., 1178, 1230, 2218
Norton, Ch.L. 841
Nosovič, I.I. 2336f.
Noszkó, A. 2377, 2382
Noter, R. de 1078f., 1185, 1189
Nöth, W. 715f., 725, 3148f., 3157
Notker III. von St. Gallen 154
Nougayrol, P. 2643f.
Nouguier, E. 1185, 1189
Novak, F. 2299, 2300
Novarro Tomás, T. 1766
Novikov, L.A. 2316, 2321, 2326, 2328
Noviliers Clavel, G.A. de 1088, 1092, 2914, 2916, 2932
Novion, F. 2980, 2983
Novo Mier, L. 1761
Novotná, Z.T. 2759
Novotny, J.L. 1030
Novotny, M. 2224
Nowell, L. 1438-1440, 1455
Nowikowa, I. 1321
Noydens, B.R. 1757
Noyes, G. 8, 18, 224, 1068, 1075

Noyes, G.E. 225, 230, 722, 726, 993f., 998, 1943f., 1948-1950, 1952f., 1988, 2006, 2009, 2896, 2903
Nudurupāṭi Wenkanna 2526
Nugent, M. 3116
Nugent, Th. 2959
Nunberg, G. 2002
Nunez y Taboada, M.M. 1745, 1761
Nunn, A.D. 1201, 1204f., 2188, 2228
Nunnesius, P.J. 1011, 1015
Núñez de Taboada, M.M. 2918, 2932, 2980, 2983-2985
Núñez, C.H. 2946
Nuparian, M. 2371
Nuparian, P. 2369
Nurm, E. 2394
Nürnberg, G. von 3013, 3019
Nurnberg, M. 1269, 1274
Nurse, D. 2647, 2649
Nuruddin, N. 3097, 3105
Nurul Hasan, N. 2517, 2521
Nüssler, O. 276, 1273
Nutki, S. 2404f.
nuuencan 2577, 2583
Nyāyālan Kara, B. 2515, 2520
Nybakken, O.E. 1230
Nyberg, H. S. 2475, 2477
Nyberg, M. 1919, 1922
Nylén, P. 3126, 3133
Nyrop, K. 1244f., 1306
Nyström, B. 3041f.

O

Oates, E. 3143f.
Oates, J. 1701
Obalk, H. 1532, 1537
Oberländer, S. 2939, 2946
Oberlin, J.J. 1601, 1609
Obhāsa, A. Ū. 2551, 2554
Objartel, G. 250-252, 275, 361, 370, 531, 575, 581, 770, 1234, 1241, 1334, 1429, 1524, 1530, 1532, 1538, 2062, 2067, 2073, 2076, 2193, 2215, 2236, 2240
Oblak, V. 2297, 2301
Oblitas Poblete, E. 2706
Obrębska-Jabłońska, A. 1139, 2266
Obregón, H. 2702
O'Brian, M.A. 2341, 2343
Obrien, S. 2516, 2520
O'Brien, T. 211, 214
Obugrian 2395
Ochey, E. 3137
Ochiai, N. 2620, 2622
Ochoa, D. de 2918, 2932
Ochoa, E. de 2980, 2984

Ockey, E. 3121, 3124f., 3134
O'Cleary, M. 2339
O'Connor, D. 1862, 2970-2973, 2975
Oda, S. 3116, 3118
Ó'Dálaigh, P. 2345, 2348
Odabaš, A. 3080
O'Daly, M. 2341
O'Davoren, D. 2339
Oddy, R.N. 1671
Odelman, E. 1721
Odend'hal, P. 2593
Odhner, E. 1130
Ó'Dónaill, N. 2346, 2348
O'Donnell, H. 2751
O'Donovan, J. 2341f.
Ó'Duirinne, S. 2345, 2348
Oehler, H. 185, 188, 1355f., 1358f., 1362, 1364, 2032, 2895, 2901, 2930
Oehler, J. 2763
Oehler, K. 276
Oehlschager, A. L. 2462, 2465
Oellers, N. 1415, 2099
Oelrichs, P. A. 2029, 2034
Oelschläger, V.R.B. 1761
Oertel, E.F.Chr. 1173, 1177, 1349, 1351
Oesch, E. 2180, 2228
Oesterreicher-Mollwo, M. 3149f., 3157
Ófeigsson, J. 1929, 1932
Ogata, K. 3116, 3118
Ogden, C.K. 1968
Ogienko, I.I. 2320, 2324
Ogier, R. 1221, 1223
Ogilvie, J. 720, 723, 1959f., 1965f., 1993, 2007, 3114, 3118
Ogle, L. 1111
O'Grady, G. N. 1341, 2638, 2641
Ohienko, I. 2331, 2333
Ohjā, S.S. 3105
Öhler, K. 724
Öhlschläger, G. 194, 207
Ohly, S. 1548, 1609, 2232
Öhmann, E. 1172, 1177, 2071
Öhrling, J. 2389, 2391
Öhrling, J. J. 2916
Õim, H. 582
Ojha, S.S. 3100
Okada, Y. 3116, 3118
Okakura, Y. 3115, 3118
Okami, M. 2622
Okamoto, J. 3126f., 3134
Okamura, S. 592
O'Kane, E. S. 1758
O'Keefe, J. W. 2342
Okell, J. 2552-2554
Okoma, S. 2755
Okopenko, A. 28, 1351
Ólafsson, M. 1929, 1932
Ölberg, H.M. 584

Oldendorp, Chr. G. A. 2871
Olderogge, D. A. 2459f.
Olea 1736, 1738
Olejnik, I. S. 3082
Olesch, R. 1140, 2271f., 2274, 2277, 2292, 2294
Oli, G.C. 66, 69, 687, 692, 706, 724, 982, 987, 1875, 1878
Oliva, S. 1776, 1785
Olivares Oviedo, P. 2700
Olive, P.M. de 1073
Oliver, Fra Antonio 1772, 1785
Oliver, J.M. 1189
Oliver, R.A. 1800, 1804, 1815
Olivet (= Thoulier, P.J.) 1798, 1814f.
Olivet, P.J.Th. d' 1212
Olivier, J.-P. 1696, 1703f.
Olivier, R. 1030, 3002, 3005
Olivieri, Cl. 1294
Olivieri, D. 1327, 1330, 1333, 1875
Olivieri, O. 1844, 1850f., 1862, 3012
Olmedo, F.G. 1766
Olmo Lete, G. del 1772, 1787
Olmos, A. de 2658, 2661
Olofsson, A. 3047-3049, 3051
Olovjannikova, I.P. 2423
Olpp, J. 2652, 2654
Olšanski, I.G. 247, 276, 1018, 1066, 2131, 2240
Ol'šanskij, J. G. 2763
Olschki, L.S. 3177
Olsen, H. 1130
Olsen, J. 101, 127, 279, 461, 500, 586, 2239, 2245, 2760
Olsen, L. B. 3055, 3060
Olsen, V.B. 3102, 3106
Olshausen, W. von 1560
Olson, D.R. 724f.
Olson, R. 2674, 2704
Olson, R. D. 2706
Olt, R. 1531
Olza Zubiri, J. 2703
Öman, V. E. 3047, 3050
Omang, J. 37f.
O'Mulconry, J. 2339
Onatsky, E. 2333
O'Neill, R. K. 3171
Onelli, O. 2886
Onions, C.T. 516, 524, 667, 821, 929, 1325, 1333, 1347, 1414, 1451, 1455, 1557, 1560, 1609, 1623, 1962, 1966, 1986, 3118
Ono Toru 2552, 2554
Ono, T. 3116, 3118
Onofre, Frei 2672, 2675
Onofri, A. 149
Onvlee, L. 2566f.
Ooga, M. 3116, 3118
Oomen, I. 1358, 1364
Oosterhout, M. G. 2024

Oosting, J. 2918, 2932
Oovi, M. 2633
Opdycke, J.B. 1073, 1207, 1209
Opitz, K. 104, 111, 1512, 1625, 1630f.
Opitz, M. 235, 2066, 2071
Oppenheim, A.L. 1683, 1685
Oppertshäuser, O. 1353, 1355, 1364
Oraham, A.J. 2437
Oranskif, I. M. 2480f., 2486
Ordoño, C. M. 2660
Ordoño, M. 2657, 2659
Orea, A. 2545
Orefice, G. A. 2919f., 2932
O'Reilly, E. 1308, 1310, 2339, 2342, 2346, 2348
Orel, A. 2332f.
Orellana, F.J. 65, 69
Oresme, N. 1790
Oreszko, E. 3122
Orezeszko, E. 3134
Orlandi, G. 2973f.
Orlando, S. 1874
Ornemann, E. 123
Ornstein, J. 653, 655
Oroz Arizcuren, F.J. 223, 2991
Oroz, R. 1761
Orr, C. 2705
Orsat Ponard, G. 1099
Orsman, H.W. 71, 77
Országh, L. 2378, 2380, 2382f., 2763
Ortale, R. 1532, 1537
Ortega Cavero, D. 1079, 2996
Ortega Ricaurte, C. 2702
Ortega y Gasset, J. 581
Ortiz, F. 1753, 1761, 2704
Ortiz, J. 2664, 2668, 2994f., 2997
Ortmann, R. 2093, 2097
Ortmann, W.D. 1123f., 1137, 1141, 1146f., 1149, 1151, 1357, 1643, 1669
Ortner, H. 956, 967, 1230
Ortúzar, C. 1752, 1761
Ortvay, T. 1285
Orudžev, A. A. 2763
Orwell, G. 27f.
Ory, P. 85, 87, 1820, 1843
Orzeszho, E. 3137
Osagawara, L. 3119
Osaniu, J. M. 2761
Osbern von Gloucester 1714f., 1721, 2038
O'Scanlan, T. 2918, 2932
Osgood, Ch.E. 1615, 1624
Oshanin, I.M. 3108, 3111f.
Oshershon, D.W. 573
Osherson, D.W. 581
Oshitari, K. 3115, 3118
Osing, J. 1682
Osman, N. 119, 124, 214, 661, 1154-1158, 2193, 2228

Osselton, N.E. 652f., 655, 661, 943, 1302, 1304, 1946-1953, 2763, 2957, 2960, 3035-3037, 3039
Ossiannilsson, S. 2886
Ossig, H. 2988, 2990
Ossoveckij, I.A. 2324
Ost, J.M. 1165
Östberg, H.O. 1260
Oster, P. 1045, 1047, 1049
Östergren, O. 510, 516, 1937, 1942
Ostler, G. 1964, 1966
Ostrá, R. 13, 18, 28
Ostwald, H. 1530, 2071
Ostyn, P. 1672
Osuna, T. 2676
Oswald, H. 2062
Otero Alvarez, A. 1737f.
Otfried von Weissenburg 1155, 1158
Ōtomo, H. 2619, 2622
Otsuka, T. 3115, 3118
Ōtsuki, F. 2620, 2622
Ott, H. 167
Ott, W. 1136f., 1141, 1571, 1573, 2702
Otten, D. 1623, 2782
Otto, A. 1033, 1041
Otto, B. 1269, 1274
Otto, E. 2215
Otto, G. 716, 725
Ottonelli, G. 1854, 1861
Ottsen, M.B. 1919, 1922
Otzoy Cutzal, F. 2664, 2668
Ouatsky, J. 2331
Oubine, I. 2766
Oud, A. G. 2027, 2034
Oudin, A. 1030, 1184f., 1189, 1795f., 1808, 1845f., 1851, 1859-1861, 2978, 2980f., 2984, 2986, 2999, 3005, 3008f., 3011, 3014, 3018
Oudin, C. 1741, 1743, 1765, 1796, 1813, 2912, 2932, 2977f., 2982, 2984, 2986f., 2993, 2997, 3008, 3012
Ouseg, H. L. 2919, 2932
Outes, F. F. 2709
Outzen, N. 2029, 2035
Ouyang Jueya 2559
Oviedo, F. de 2683
Owen, M. 2663f., 2668
Oxenvad, E. 1916
Oyon 1824
Ozanam, F. 604
Ozdoeva, F.G. 2422
Ožegov, S.I. 510, 516, 658f., 661, 691f., 750, 753, 764, 766, 1147, 1308, 1310, 2314-2316, 2322, 2324, 2328, 3079, 3085
Ozereckovskij, J. 3076
Ozodeva, F.G. 2423

Ozola, V. 1669, 2360
Ozolin, E. 2359f.
Ozolina, N. 2359
Ozolinš, E. 2357
Ozols, A. 2355, 2361
Ozols, J. 2360
Özön, M.N. 2400, 2404, 2406

P

Paacaan thát 2578
Paardekooper, P.C. 1308, 1310
Paasonen, H. 2397f.
P"axsi Limachi, R. 2688, 2690
Pabst, M. 3026, 3028
Pachalina, T. N. 2486
Pacheco, J.M.F. 1765
Pacheco, S. 2663f., 2668f.
Pacnerová, L. 2260
Padhi, B. 2515, 2520
Padmanabha, P. 3096f., 3107
Paepcke, F. 174, 2763
Paffen, K. A. 1052f., 2879, 2881
Paganini, A. 1084, 1092
Page, C.D. 2954
Pagès, A. 61, 1164, 1176, 1348, 1352, 1748, 1761
Paget, R. 3143f.
Pagliaro, A. 1876
Paikeday, Th.M. 2004, 2008
Paikkala, S. 2388
Paivio, A. 716, 725
Pajot, Ch. 1795
Pajot, R. P. 2932
Pakalin, M.Z. 2404, 2406
Pakalka, K. 2355, 2360
Palakosha, A. 3101, 3106
Palamarčuk, L. S. 2334, 2759, 2763
Palander, H. 1255, 1257
Palau y Dulcet, A. 2979, 2986
Palay, S. 1895, 1904
Palazzi, F. 1090, 1092, 1866, 175, 1879
Palazzolo-Nöding, B. 653, 656
Palen, F. 1703
Palencia, A. de 16, 63, 69, 1738f., 1761, 1766
Palet, I. 2982, 2984
Palet, J. 2977, 2986
Palevskaja, M.F. 2315, 2324
Pálfy, M. 2763
Páll, E. 1002, 1006f.
Pall, V. 2394
Pallas, P. S. 2330, 2333, 2396, 2398, 2408, 2484, 2486, 2916, 2918, 2932, 3072
Pallegoix, D. 2917, 2932
Pallegoix, J.B. 2577f., 2582
Pallhausen, V. von 2067
Pallioppi, E. 1896f., 1904

Palm, J.J. 221
Palma, R. 1743, 1752, 1754, 1761, 1766
Palma, St. 1085, 1088, 1090, 1092
Palmaitis, L. 2418
Palmer, A. 1044, 1049
Palmer, A.S. 976, 980, 1333
Palmer, H. 1967, 1975
Palmer, H.E. 589, 592, 1005f., 1008, 1308, 1310, 1362
Palmér, J. 1079, 1938, 1942
Palmer, V. 1044, 1049
Palmgreen Munch Petersen, V. 3058, 3061
Palmireño, J.L. 1740, 1761, 1785
Palmireño, L. 1771
Palomo, F. 2663, 2669
Palovskij, I. J. 3077
Palsgrave, J. 1791, 2712, 2956f., 2959
Paludanus, J. 2932
Paluzie-Borrell, J. 3126, 3134
Pamart, P. 946, 1164
Pampe, E. 2357, 2359
Pamphilos 12, 1697
Pamukciyan, K. 2399, 2406f.
Pan Zaiping 276, 337, 359, 394, 407, 449, 459, 2725, 2728, 2749, 2751, 2764, 2834, 2836
Panagopoulos, A.Ch. 141, 144
Pančev, T. 2305, 2307
Pancoucke, Ch.J. 1808
Pandit, B. V. 2514, 2519
Pandit, S. 2513, 2519
Pando Villaroya, J.L. de 1752, 1761
Pandya 3100, 3106
Panejko, O. 2333
Panganiban, J.V. 301, 304, 2569f.
Pangyong, J. 1016
Panikkar, N. 2529, 2532
Pāṅini 2488-2491, 2494f.
Paṅis, A. 2886
Panjuševa, M.S. 2322
Pankevych, I. 2332
Pankhurst, R. 2461
Pankrac, Ju.G. 523, 525
Pannamoltissa, T. 2504
Pannonius, G. 1792, 1845, 1860
Panoussi, E. 2437
Pansner, L. von 1192
Pantiyesīlavaṃsa 2504
Panzini, A. 1165, 1216, 1867f., 1879
Paññālaṅkāra 2504
Paññāsīha, M. 2505
Paoli, C. 1261f., 1264
Papachristodoulou, Chr.I. 1712f.
Papachristos, E.Chr. 2764, 2988, 2991
Papadopoulos, A.A. 1711, 1713
Papahagi, T. 1887, 1889f.

Pápai Páriz, F. 2382
Pápai, K. 2397
Papasteriju, N. 2292, 2294
Papazahariu, G. 2290
Pape, W. 1132, 1141, 1699, 1703
Papegaaij, B.C. 1672, 3167
Paper, H.H. 747
Papias 9, 1714f., 1721, 1739, 1788f., 1844, 2038
Papp, F. 1135, 1141, 2382
Pappenheim, S. 1068, 1073
Paquali, G. 1865
Paque, E. 1257
Paquot, A. 1137, 1141
Paracelsus, Th. B. 2041
Paradis, J.-M. de V. de 2455, 2457
Paradis, J.N. 1208
paramaanúchitchi2noorót 2577f., 2583
Paravicino, P. 2971, 2974
Parčić, D. A. 2291, 2294
Pardo Asso, J. 1761
Pardo, N.J. 1906
Pardon, W. 1944, 1948, 1951
Paredes, I. 2658f., 2661
Parenago, M. A. 3075
Pareus, Ph. 1015, 1051, 1053, 1221, 1223
Parfionovich, J. M. 2550
Parigi, B. da 2400
Paris, C. 2419, 2421
Paris, G. 217, 224, 1815, 1819, 1823, 1843
Parisot, J. 3122, 3134, 3215
Parisot, V. 1130
Páriz, F.P. 2376
Páriz, P. 2376, 2383
Park, M. 2705
Parker, E. 2464f.
Parker, E. M. 2469
Parker, G. J. 2677, 2684, 2705
Parker, H. H. 2574
Parker, M. 1438-1440
Parkes, G. 2883f., 2886
Parmentier, Th. 2938, 2946
Parnassi, R. 147
Parnwell, E.C. 1368
Parodi, S. 1858, 1862
Paros, L. 1198
Parra, F. de la 2662, 2669
Parsaye, K. 3167
Parsenow, G. 2765, 3045f.
Partnow, E. 1047, 1049
Parton, J. 35
Partridge, E. 1054f., 1146, 1151, 1186, 1188f., 1194, 1196, 1198f., 1216, 1259f., 1264, 1367f., 1529f., 1532-1534, 1536-1538, 1965
Partridge, H.B. 1341
Partyc'kyj, O. 2330, 2333
Părvev, Chr. 2308

Părvev, H. 1310
Pasch, R. 249, 276, 868, 2764
Pasche, A. 1532, 1537
Pascoe, G. 2883f., 2886
Pascoe, H. 2883f., 2886
Pascoli, G. 1875
Pascu, G. 1889f.
Pascual, J.A. 1325, 1332, 1347, 1757, 1782
Pascual, P. 1906f.
Pasek, J.Chr. 1550, 1553, 1557, 1560, 2270
Pashai'eva, Sh.R. 3169
Paska, Chr. 2273
Pasolini, P.P. 149
Pasoń, A. 2273
Pasoni 2270
Pasor, G. 2915, 2933
Pašov, P. 1310, 2308
Pasquali, G. 1870, 1880
Pasques, L. 1815
Passen, A.-M. van 1846, 1862, 2999, 3005, 3007
Passerini Tosi, C. 1871, 1875, 1879, 2974
Passerini, G.L. 1875
Passos, J.A. 1220
Passow, F. 217, 219, 224, 301, 305, 369, 1404f., 1414, 1699, 1701-1704
Passy, P. 509, 516, 1305f., 1308, 1310
Pastor, E. 1036, 1041
Pat Pingua, B. 2540
Páta, J. 2284
Patačić, A. 2289, 2296
Patañjali 2487f.
Patel, J. J. 2518
Patel, J. T. 2511
Patel, T. G. 2511, 2518
Patela, S. G. 2511, 2518
Paterson, D.G. 138, 145
Pathak, P. B. 2502, 2504
Patigorskii, A.M. 3101, 3106
Patkar, M. M. 2496
Pātra, N. 3097, 3106
Patrick, G.Z. 1149, 1151, 1362
Patru, O. 1797
Patsis, Ch. 1709, 1713
Pattanayak, Ch. 2515, 2520
Pattanayak, D.P. 3097, 3102, 3107
Pattanayak, J. 2515
Pattanayaka, J. 2520
Pattermann, W. 1030
Patterson, A.G. 3176
Patyal, H. Ch. 2764
Patze, H. 2048
Pätzold, K.-M. 214, 1056, 1982, 2757, 2961, 2969
Pau, F. 2980, 2984
Paul, H. 66, 69, 114f., 124, 140, 144, 155, 158, 578, 644, 728,

731, 750, 753, 826, 830, 863, 867, 960, 1146, 1151, 1234-1236, 1239, 1257, 1323, 1333, 1417, 1429, 2078, 2085, 2097, 2099f., 2193, 2240, 3056
Paul, J. 26
Paul, R. 231, 243, 245, 1429, 1594, 1610
Pauli-Żegota, I. 2330, 2333
Pauli, J. 1399
Paulian, A.-H. 1802
Paulitschke, Ph. 2463, 2467
Paulus Diaconus 1714, 3032
Pausch, O. 1847, 1860, 2048, 3013, 3019
Pausner, J. 2938, 2946
Pautex, B. 1089, 1092, 1800, 1815
Pauvert, J.-J. 1828
Pavić, M. 1351, 2290, 2296
Pavlica, J. 2300
Pavlov-Šiškin, V.D. 2324
Pavlov, V. M. 2782
Pavlovskij, A. 2330, 2333
Pavlovskij, I. J. 3077
Pavlov'skyj, O. P. 3076
Pawis, R. 1813
Pawley, A. 2636f., 2573, 2575
Pawlowski, K. 510, 517f., 2106, 2131, 2240
Pawlowski, T. 539, 543, 552, 581
Paxton, J. 1261, 1263f.
Payḍipāṭi Lakṣmaṇakawi 2525
Payen-Payen, V. 2958
Payfūn M. 2411
Payne, A. 2636f.
Payne, D. 2707
Payne, E.M.F. 1513, 1516, 1518, 1520, 1522
Payuttō, P. 2506
Paz y Mélia, A. 2988-2990
Pazzaglia, M. 2996
Peacock, F. W. 2634
Péan, F. 2886
Péan, F. Y. 2886, 2982
Peano, G. 1362
Pearse, A. S. 2663, 2669
Peate, W. F. 2465
Pebesma, H. 2027, 2035
Pécan, F.Y. 2984
Péch, A. 2939, 2946
Pechan, A. 3124, 3126f., 3134
Péchoin, D. 1832
Pechon de Ruby 1533
Peciar, Št. 510, 516, 2285, 2287
Peck, Ch. 2764
Pedersen, H. 2341-2343
Pedersen, V. H. 2761, 2764, 2783, 2786f., 2789, 2841, 2854
Pederson, L. 2002
Pedrell, F. 1747, 1761
Peek, W. 1560
Peer, O. 1899, 1904

Peers, E.A. 2953, 2955
Peeters-Fontainas, J. 2978, 2986
Pef 1350f.
Pei, M. 1616
Pei, M.A. 2953, 2955
Peigné, M.A. 1802, 1808
Peindl, J. von de 2401
Peirce, Ch.S. 704, 725, 3149f., 3157
Pekrun, R. 273, 358, 405f., 574, 631, 634, 2114-2118, 2121, 2125, 2128, 2155, 2165-2170, 2217, 2225, 2228
Pelissier, H.J.F.E. 217, 224
Pélissier, P. 3142, 3144
Pelka, R. 321, 686f., 1523, 1531
Pell, G. 2933
Pellat, Ch. 3095
Pellegrini, G. 1333
Pellegrini, S. 1862
Pellen, R. 1573
Pelleschi 2708
Pellissier, E. 1146f., 1151
Pellisson, P. 1798, 1815
Peltola, R. 2387
Peltz, R. 2247, 2254
Peltzer, K. 1047, 1049, 1079, 1130, 2180-2182, 2188, 2228
Pelzer, A. 1263
Peña, C. 1078
Peñalver, J. de 1745, 1761
Penavin, O. 2382
Penders, C. 2647, 2649
Pendlebury, B.J. 1130
Peñe Alvarez, J. 1757
Peng Chunan 2826, 2828
Penicaut, N. 41f., 46
Penkethman, J. 1268, 1270, 1274
Pennachietti, F.A. 2437
Pennance, F.G. 1516-1518, 1522, 1763
Pensado, J.L. 1736, 1738
Pensinger, B. J. 2698f.
Pentland, D.H. 3173
Penttinen, A. 2386f.
Penzenkuffer, Chr. W. 221, 224
Penzl, H. 244, 2069
Peorwadarminta, W. J. S. 2562
Pepłowski, F. 2272
Peralta, M. 1747, 1761
Peralta-Osuna, J. 2674
Péras, J. 2938, 2946
Percivall, R. 2933
Percyvall, R. 2949, 2955
Perego, G.A. 1101f.
Pérégo, P. 2871, 2876
Pereira Laus, E. 3023
Pereira, B. 1726f., 3021
Perelmuter, J. 2328
Perera, J. 2505
Pereyra, B. 1726, 1734
Perez Castro, F. 1907

Pérez Hervas, J. 1130
Pérez Mozún, D. 1742, 1761
Pérez Sánchez, A. 1759
Pérez, J. 3175
Pérez, J. P. 2663f., 2669
Perez-Bustamante, C. 1755
Pergamini, G. 10f., 16, 217, 222, 1796, 1851f., 1860, 3018
Periere, J.R. 3142, 3144
Perin, J. 1721
Perkins, G. 2323
Perl, M. 2764, 2871, 2876
Permjakov, G. 1033, 1038, 1041, 1043
Pernis, H. D. van 2563, 2565
Pernon, L.-D. 1094, 1096, 1099
Peroncel-Hugoz, J.-P. 43, 46
Perramon, S. 1776, 1785
Perret, P. 1185, 1189
Perrochon, H. 1011, 1018
Perrot d'Ablancourt, N. 1815
Perrot, J. 1211f., 1216
Perrot, J.-C. 165, 167, 1801, 1815
Perroud, P. C. 2705
Perry, D.J. 1302f.
Perry, W. 509, 1077, 1079, 1988, 2008
Persson, I. 883, 887
Pertsch, E. 3033f.
Peščereva, E. M. 2485
Pesch, M. 3130, 3134
Peschier, A. 1125, 3305
Pesendorfer, F. J. 1130, 2071
Pešikan, M. 2263, 2268
Pestalozzi, K. 1031
Pestelli, L. 1157f.
Pesthi, G. 2913, 2933
Petasch-Molling, G. 2183, 2184, 2228
Peter der Große 3073
Peter, F. 1703
Peter, L.J. 1047, 1049
Petermann, H. 774, 779, 2220
Petermann, J. 1032, 2764
Peters, A.M. 1672
Peters, C. 1018
Peters, F. W. 2112, 2191, 2227f.
Peters, R. 269
Petersen, A. 2030
Petersen, C. 36, 38
Petersen, E. 2030, 2032, 2035
Petersen, J. 2632, 2634
Petersen, P.R. 672
Petersen, R. 2633
Petersen, U. 206
Petersen, W. 1074, 1132-1135, 1137, 1139, 2058
Peterson, A. 1258, 1260
Petiot, G. 311
Petit, Ch. 2958f.
Petit, K. 1047, 1049
Petitot, E. 2632, 2634

Petković, S. 2264, 2267
Petöfi, J.S. 161, 163, 576, 578, 581, 891, 893, 1066, 1084, 1093f., 1650, 1666
Petöfi, S. 1549f., 1553, 1557, 1560, 2380, 2382
Petov, P. 2764
Petr, J. 2281, 2284
Petrarca 10, 22, 147, 149, 218, 995, 1125, 1566, 1850f., 1858, 1860, 1871, 1874, 2970, 3008
Petrásek, J. 3140f.
Petré, F. 2296, 2301
Petreius, J. 2043
Petri, F. 1034, 1041, 1043, 2065, 2071
Petri, F.E. 1121, 1123f., 1173, 1177, 2071, 2091, 2097
Petrič, M. 3127, 3234
Petrikovits, H. von 1252, 1254
Petrocchi, P. 406, 1308, 1310. 1858, 1860, 1866, 1879
Pétroff, A. 606
Petronius 1720
Petronj, St.E. 2972, 2974
Petrounias, E. 3173
Petrov, F.M. 2315, 2332f.
Petrov, F. N. 2324
Petrov, F.P. 2324
Petrova, O. P. 3073
Petrovici, E. 2751
Petrovoj, O. P. 3084
Petrovskij, N.A. 2316, 2324
Petrovský, A. 2286f.
Petruškov, V. P. 2751
Petschenig, M. 524, 2751
Petterson, A. C. 3048, 3050
Petti, K. 3049f.
Petti, V. 2764, 3048-3051
Pettigrew, W. 2559
Pettinato, G. 1683, 1685
Pétursson, M. 1928, 1932
Petuškov, V.P. 2314, 2321, 2328
Peuchet, J. 166f., 1801, 1808
Peuckert, R. 206
Pewters, C.R. 1145
Pey i Estrany, S. 1777, 1785
Pey, S. 1079
Peyron, A. 1091, 1681
Peyser, A. 1261, 1264
Peytard, J. 43, 46, 704, 725
Pezenas, E. 1208
Pezenas, R.P.E. 1805
Pfaundler, L. 3130, 3134
Pfeffer, A. 1358
Pfeffer, A. J. 2764
Pfeffer, J.A. 767f., 771, 1321, 1353, 1355f., 1362, 1364
Pfeffinger, J. F. 2271
Pfeifer, G. 2217, 2220
Pfeifer, W. 526, 530, 1257f., 2146, 2195, 2220, 2240

Pfeiffer, O.E. 591, 1137, 1142
Pfeiffer-Rupp, R. 269
Pfetzing, D. 3143f.
Pfister, M. 1324, 1327, 1330, 1333f., 1342, 1815, 1847, 1862f., 1876f., 1895, 1904f.
Pflaumer, W. 3129, 3134
Pfleiderer, W. 1158, 1239, 1609
Pfohl, E. 718, 723, 2989f., 3002, 3005
Pfuhl, Chr. T. 2277
Phee taalalāk 2579
Phạm Xuân Tín 2591, 2593f.
Phantharangsi, S. 2506
Phayao Memanas 2593
Phelps, W.H. 1761
Phenice, A. 1859, 3011
Phikulthong Ruchirapha 2593
Philibert, Chr. 2464f.
Philipon de la Madelaine, L. 1121, 1124, 1126, 1130 (s. Philippon)
Philipp IV 2987
Philippe II 2977
Philippe V 2981
Philippide, A. 1885, 1890
Philippon de la Madelaine, L. 1802, 1808 (s. Philipon)
Phillips, E. 1162, 1943-1951, 3037, 3039
Phillips, M. 269, 1036, 1043
Philomusus, P. 1011, 1015, 1081, 1083
Phinney, F. D. 2554
Photios 1697
phráyaa paríyátthamthadaa 2579
Phrynichus 73, 1697
Phyfe, W.H.P. 1308, 1310
Phyongs ston rin chen bkra shis 2549
Phythian, B.A. 1177, 1186, 1189, 1216, 1536f.
Phythian, E. 1216
Pialat, M. 1144f.
Pianigiani, O. 1328, 1333, 1875
Picabia, L. 592
Picard, H. 3114, 3118
Picatoste, F. 1746, 1761
Picchi, E. 3165
Piccillo, G. 1881, 1889
Piccirille, T. 2463, 2450f., 2454, 2468
Piccitto, G. 1877, 1879
Pichardo, E. 1751f., 1761
Pichette, J.-P. 1192
Pichl, R. 2751
Picht, H. 170, 1660, 1666
Picken, E. 1984, 1986
Pico 3140
Picoche, J. 989, 992, 998
Picón Febres, G. 1753, 1761
Piel, J.M. 1268, 1274, 1737, 1910, 1912

Pieper, U. 1644
Pierer, H.A. 990, 997
Pierrugues, P. 1195, 1198
Pierson, R.M. 2003, 2009
Piesarkas, B. 2352f.
Piestre, J.L. 1073
Pieters, A. A. 2615f.
Pietro d'Abbavilla, P.F. 2404
Pietro Leopoldo 1855
Pietsch, R. 2359f.
Pigafetta, A. 2563, 2565
Pigeaud, Th. 2561f.
Pigneau de Behaine, P. 2584, 2589
Pignon, J. 1575, 1588, 1827
Piirainen, I.T. 269
Pijnenburg, W. 230, 277, 408, 654, 1165, 2018, 2022, 2301
Pijnenburg, W.J.J. 358, 919, 921, 929, 988, 1319, 1321, 1431f., 1434f., 1593, 1610, 2020
Pike, J. G. 2515, 2520
Pike, K. L. 2686, 2697
Pilch, H. 1610, 1614, 1624, 2342
Pilch, K. 1644
Pillai, S. K. 2529, 2532
Pillai, S. P. 2529, 2532
Pilling, J.C. 3173
Pillon, A. 1073
Pilovski, A. L. 2247, 2254
Pilz, K. 2915f., 2936
Pilz, K.D. 593, 599, 831, 835, 1020-1022, 1032, 1035, 1038f., 1043, 1672, 2174, 2240
Pinana, I. 1532, 1537
Pinchon, J. 1800, 1815
Pineda, P. 2950, 2955
Pineda, V. 2664, 2669
Pinedo Peydro, F.J. 1115, 1119
Pingua, B.P. 2537, 2539
Pinkal, M. 780, 787, 856, 861
Pinkerton, E.C. 1243, 1245
Pinloche, A. 718, 723, 1104, 1106, 1111, 1147-1149, 1151, 1234, 1239, 2089, 2097
Pinnock, W. 3152, 3157
Pinnow, H.-J. 1339, 1341, 2537, 2542, 2546
Pino Saavedra, Y. 1761
Pinoteau, H. 1273
Pintos, J.M. 1736
Pióro, J. 3128, 3134
Piotrovskaja, A.A. 1644, 1651, 1667, 1671
Piotrovskij, R.G. 1661, 1667, 1670f.
Piotrowski, R.G. 1322, 1593, 1595f., 1610, 1644
Piotrowski, T. 581, 2764
Pioud, G. 3042
Piozzi, H.L. (Mrs. Thrale) 1068, 1073, 1075
Pipano, A.D. 1906

Piper, P. 154, 159
Piper-Andresen, H. 2220
Piprek, J. 746, 3063, 3067
Piranesi, P. 3010f.
Pireira Laus, E. 3028
Pirejko, L. A. 2485f.
Pirona, G.A. 1901, 1904
Pirona, J. 1876, 1901, 1904
Pisani, V. 1334, 1338, 1341
Pisant, E. 2919, 2933
Pisarčik, A. K. 2485
Pisárčiková, M. 2286f.
Pischel, R. 2502, 2504
Piskunov, F. 2330, 2333
Pistorius, G. T. 2065, 2071
Pitman, M. de 2703, 3140
Pitou, S. 1798, 1815
Pitré, G. 1114, 1119
Pitt, W. 1950
Pittaluga, M.G. 1801, 1815f.
Pittano, G. 1868
Pitteri, F. 1856
Pittmann, R. 2568, 2570
Pivot, B. 41, 45
Piyatissa, V. 2505
Pizzinini, A. 1901, 1904
pleek sŏnthí Prak 2582
Pla y Torres, C. 1745, 1761
Placardi, C. 3009, 3012
Places, É. des 1551f., 1554, 1560
Plākis, J. 2359-2361
Planas, J. 1778, 1785
Planatscher, F. 2228
Plangg, G. 1904
Planta, R. von 1897
Plantijn, Chr. 3035, 3039
Plantin, Chr. 1791, 1811, 2933
Plantinus, Chr. 1806, 2043
Platania d'Antoni, R. 1130
Plato 1067, 1696
Plats, G. Ph. 3074
Platt, J. 1441, 2512
Platt, J. jr. 1437, 1444, 1456
Platteau, F. 2805, 2813
Plattner, Ph. 1219f.
Platts, J. 1079, 2519
Platzmann, J. 2672, 2675, 2709f., 2674, 3174
Plautus, T. Maccius 726, 1141, 1715
Plaza Martinez, P. 2705
Plazikowsky-Brauner, H. 2465
pleek sonthí Prak 2582
Plehn, H.J. 3124, 3129, 3134, 3137
Plēsuma, A. 2359
Pleteršnik, M. 2298, 2300
Plezia, M. 1721, 2268, 2274
Plickat, H.-H. 1358, 1362
Ploeg, D. T. E. van der 2027, 2033
Ploetz, K. 2894, 2901
Plomley, N. J. B. 2638, 2641
Plomteux, H. 2762

Ploompuu, J. 2393
Plössel, G. 1207, 1209
Plum, S. 531, 552, 557, 579, 854f.
Plumier, Ch. 1801
Poal 1776
Pobłocki, W. 2270
Počchua, B. 1141
Poch, R. 1777, 1783
Poenar, P. 1883, 1889
Poerio, A. 149
Poerwadarminta, W. J. S. 2562f., 2565
Poëtevin, F.L. 3005
Poethe, H. 2192, 2240
Poeticus (Pseudonym) 2066, 2071
Poggi Salani, T. 1851f., 1857, 1862
Poghirc, C. 1890
Pogorelova, R. V. 2885
Pöhl, E. 2753, 2757, 2760, 2764-2766, 2768, 2775
Pohl, Chr. 835
Pohl, H.D. 1291, 1296, 2289, 2296
Pohl, L. 214
Pohlin, M. 2298, 2301
Poincaré, R. 1825
Poinsotte, J.-P. 1261, 1265
Pointon, G.E. 1293, 1296
Poirié, H. 1367
Poirier, C. 71, 77, 327, 331, 1825, 1843
Poisson, R. 1302f.
Poitevin, P. 99, 100f., 140, 144, 221, 224, 1124, 1803, 1808
Poittier, B. 544
Pokorny, J. 294, 296, 1338, 1341f., 1393, 1412, 1414f., 1443, 2341f.
Pokrovskij, M.M. 2313
Polac, M. 1351
Polacco, L. 1130
Polák, V. 2283
Polani, H. 3176
Polánski, K. 1005, 1008, 2271, 2273f.
Poldauf, I. 2282f., 2287
Poldauf, J. 2775
Polenz, A. von 2076
Polenz, P. von 127, 180, 197, 207, 279, 359, 408, 461, 500, 531, 581, 586, 626, 628, 688, 788f., 792-794, 796, 819f., 822, 840f., 849, 882-887, 956f., 967, 1169, 1175, 1178, 1230f., 1241, 1429, 1523, 2055, 2062, 2076, 2093, 2099, 2245
Poletti-Turbini, C. 2464f.
Policardi, S. 2970, 2976
Polidori, G. 2917, 2933
Polikarpov, F. 3070-3072, 3083f.
Polikarpov-Orlov, F. P. 3071
Politi, A. 1845, 1854f., 1860f., 3008f.

Polizu, G.A. 1889
Poljakova, G.P. 2320, 2324
Pollack, Ch.R. 1617, 1623
Pollak, W. 2886
Polle, F. 1550, 1561
Pollmann, F. 1353, 2890, 2892f., 2901
Pollmann-Laverentz, C. 2901
Pollux, Iulius 1697
Polo, J. 2887, 2986
Polo, M. 3107
Polomé, E. C. 2647, 2649
Polon, D.D. 1261, 1265
Poltoratzky, M.A. 1147, 1149, 1151
Polycarpius, Th. 2917, 2933
Polydeukes, Ioulios 1697
Polzer, W. 1530
Pomai, F. 2913, 2917, 2933
Pomay, F. 2795f.
Pomey, F. 1795 , 2957, 2959, 2999
Pomey, F.-A. 3036
Pomis, D. de 2913, 2933
Pompidou, L. 2980, 2983f.
Ponce de León, N. 2938, 2946
Ponce de Leon, P. 3142
Ponce Villanueva, T. 2700
Ponette, P. 2537, 2545
Ponge, F. 23
Pons, A.C. 1778
Pons, J.A. 1839
Pons, R. 1778, 1785
Pontbriant, R. de 1884, 1889
Ponten, J.-P. 1018, 2727, 2764
Pontevivo, G. 3018
Pontoppidan, E. 1924, 1927f.
Poole, D. A. 2683
Poortinga, Y. 2026, 2033, 2035
Pope, A. 1949, 1957
Pope, F.R. 3133
Popelar, I. 652, 656, 1796, 1798-1800, 1816
Popescu, V. 1885, 1889
Popma, A. 1068f., 1073
Popov, V.M. 2323
Popova, M. 2306, 2308
Popović, D. 2291, 2294
Popovič, J. S. 2301
Popovič, J. Ž. 2297
Popović, M. 2294
Popowitsch, J.S.V. 112, 126, 2060, 2071, 2075
Popowska-Taborska, H. 2270, 2274
Poppe, N. 2414, 2623, 2625f., 2414
Póra, F. 1089, 1092, 2378, 2382
Porcacchi, T. 10, 1852, 1860f.
Porcher, L. 1349-1351
Porep, R. 1230
Porīte, T. 2359
Pörksen, U. 269

Porras Barrenechea, R. 2681f., 2684
Porru, V. 1902, 1904
Pors, H. 1571, 1573
Porte, M. de la 1017
Porter, H. 3090, 3096
Porter, N. 1958, 1991, 1994, 2007, 3119
Porter, N.A. 1445, 1456
Porthan, H.G. 2384
Portilla, M. L. 2697, 2699
Portitor, H. 2884, 2886
Portmann, P. 1035, 1041
Porto Dapena, J.-A. 592, 917f., 920, 930
Porto, C. 3131
Porto, J.A. 1768, 1770
Porto-Dapena, A. 1750
Porzig, W. 888f., 893
Posner, R. 254, 256-258, 260, 267, 276
Post, V.W. 1795, 1816
Postlethwaite, T.N. 189
Postlethwayt, M. 165, 167
Potanin, G.N. 2411
Potapkin, S.G. 2396, 2398
Potapova, M.D. 2328
Potebni, O.O. 929
Potebnia, A. 2331
Poth, Ch. 2219, 2229
Pothan, H.G. 2384
Pothorn, H. 1368
Poticha, Z.A. 1149, 1151, 2324
Potier, L. 2959
Pott, A.F. 1534, 1537
Potter, S. 228, 230
Potthoff, K. 442f., 460, 499
Pottier, B. 22, 550, 581, 890, 893, 915-917, 2984
Pou, O. 1771, 1785, 1788
Poucha, P. 1141
Pougens, Ch. 605, 1157f., 1814
Poulin, J. 24, 26, 28
Poullet, H. 2872-2875
Poulovsky, L. H. 2886
Poulsen, J.H.V. 1932
Pourret, L. 1841
Pousland, E. 1165
Pouvreau, S. 2373, 2375
Powell, D. 1124
Powell, F.V. 214
Powell, J.E. 1560
Powers, M. D. 2764
Powitz, G. 233-235, 242, 803, 2041, 2048, 2050, 2054, 2069, 2076, 2088, 2100, 2215
Poza, A. de 1740, 1761
Prada 2989
Pradez, E. 1030, 2920, 2933
Pradhan, A. 3102, 3106
Prado, J. del 1737
Prado, M. 2881

Prager, J.Chr. 2969
Praharaja, G.C. 3097, 3106
Praharay, G. C. 2515
Prahray, W. Ch. 2520
Prange, Chr.F. 3150, 3157
Prasad, N. 2535
Prasad, R. 2503
Prasad, S. 2536f., 2545, 3100, 3106
Prasada, S. 3100, 3106
Prasert Sriwises 2591, 2593
pràsìt kàapkloon 2582
Prat Turu, C. 1776, 1785
Prati, A. 1329, 1333, 1534f., 1537, 1875f., 3009, 3013, 3174
Prats, M. 1788
Pratt, G. 2574f.
Pratt, J. 1188
Praum, I. 2591
Pravdin, B. 2394
Prawer, S. S. 2759
Praz, M. 151, 2972, 2973, 2976
Prazeres Maranhão, Frei 2672, 2675
Preda, D. 1884
Predetis, A.A. 1882
Préfontaine, G. 1835
Préfontaine, R. 180, 1367
Préfontaine, R.R. 679
Pregel, D. 1525, 1527, 1530
Preindl, J. von de 2406
Preiss, B. 1349, 1351
Prell, S. 1513, 1517f., 1522
Premk, F. 2301
Premoli, P. 721, 724, 1867
Preobraženskij, A. 2318, 2324
Presa, G. 1126f., 1131
Prešern, F. 2300
Press, I. 2348, 2351
Preston, D.R. 172, 174, 653, 656
Preti, D. 1199
Pretzel, U. 2225, 2233
Preuß, G. 1111
Preußer, E. 2969
Prévost (= Exiles, A.F. d') 1802, 1808
Prevost, A. 2886
Prévost, A.-F. 1206, 1209
Prévost-Delaunay 3138, 3140f.
Prévot, A. 1351
Pride, G.L. 1984, 1986
Pride, K. 2698f.
Pride, L. 2698f.
Priese, O. 1910, 1912
Prieto, R. 1349, 1351, 1743, 1766
Prilutski, N. 2249
Primon, C.F. 1920, 1922
Primorac, R. 2292, 2294
Princi Braccini, G. 3174
Prinz, Ch. 524
Priscianus 1789
Pristípino, P. 2753
Probst, A. 2185, 2187, 2228

Procházka, K. 3133
Prochorov, J.E. 2323
Procter, P. 208, 213, 524, 588-591, 692, 747, 753, 902, 904, 1969, 3117
Proctor, P. 1385
Prodanof, I. 3167
Prodicos 1067, 1071
Proença, A. de 2523, 2532, 3101, 3106
Profilio, G.P. 2996
Profous, A. 2282f.
Prokopovič, N.N. 2316, 2324
Proschwitz, G. 1816
Prosinger, W. 251, 273, 1351, 2185, 2197, 2228
Prost, R. P. A. 2642, 2645
Protopopescu, E. 1885, 1889
Protze, H. 274
Proudhon, P.J. 1824
Proum, I. 2593
Proust, M. 25, 28
Provenzal, D. 1216
Prunč, E. 2301
Prūse, R. 2360
Prüss, J. 2041
Pruvost, J. 1096, 1099, 1804, 1816
Pryse, R.J. 2349
Puchmajer, A.J. 1130, 2283
Puchner, K. 1279, 1281, 1283f.
Puertas, A. 1758
Pugh, E. 1261, 1265
Pugh, J.M. 170
Pughe, W.O. 2347, 2349
Puhvel, A. 1333
Puhvel, J. 1324, 1688f., 2794
Puig, M. 1778, 1784
Pujan, S. 2536
Pujol i Serra, J. 1785
Pujol y Vallés, F. 1776
Pujol, F. 1778, 1785
Pujulá y Vallés, F. 1776, 1785
Pukui, M. K. 2573-2575
Pulci, L. 149, 1533, 1844, 1853
Pulěvski, D. M. 2302, 2304
Pulliam, T. 1144f.
Pulte, W. 2696
Puntsch, E. 1047, 1049
Puoti, B. 1847, 1860
Purdy, K. K. 2226
Pures, M. de 218
Puri, B. 2516, 2520
Puriu, C. 3147
Purty, D. S. 2537
Purusottamadeva 2489
Purves, J. 2973, 2975
Puryear, J.R. 1910, 1912
Puşcariu, S. 1333, 1885f., 1889f.
Puscarius, S. 1330
Pusch, L.F. 88, 860, 862, 2240
Püschel, U. 26, 28, 102, 104, 106f., 110, 113-116, 118, 123, 126,

131, 134f., 245, 398, 552, 557,
 581, 596, 617, 622, 627, 652f.,
 655f., 693f., 699, 818, 822, 849,
 854, 889, 893, 1018, 1032,
 1066, 1068, 1075, 1094, 1415,
 2010, 2021, 2051, 2054-2056,
 2058-2060, 2076f., 2081, 2087,
 2092f., 2099f., 2102, 2131,
 2180, 2191f., 2240, 2895, 2902
Puschkin, A.S. 1549-1551,
 1556-1558, 1560
Puškin, A.S. 2313f.
Püsküllüoğlu, A. 2404, 2406
Puṣpadanta 2503
Pusztay, J. 2397
Putanec, V. 2290, 2292, 2294, 2296
Putnam, H. 556, 572f., 579-581,
 584, 587
Putschke, W. 125, 244, 627, 655,
 980, 1415, 1429, 1573, 1608f.,
 1623, 2074-2076, 2235, 2238,
 3165
Pütulainen, M. L. 2764
Putz, K. 1352
Puxley, E. L. 2540, 2546
Puy-Costa, M. 2980, 2984
Puzynina, J. 1139f., 2269, 2272
Pye, V. 2506
Pyles, T. 1311
Pyles, Th. 656, 1989, 2009
Pynte, J. 141, 145

Q

Qimhi, D. 2427
Quarantotto, C. 1868
Quasthoff, U. 553, 582
Queixalos, F. 2704
Quellet, H. 1557, 1562
Quemada, B. 18, 55, 62, 138, 145,
 151, 222, 224f., 227, 229f., 247,
 249, 258, 276f., 280, 286, 323,
 327, 506, 508-510, 518, 602f.,
 605, 607, 679, 703, 764, 767,
 780, 787, 905f., 916f., 946,
 973f., 980, 989, 994, 998,
 1121f., 1125, 1141, 1149, 1152,
 1210, 1213f., 1217, 1264, 1311,
 1344, 1346, 1348f., 1352, 1573,
 1670, 1791, 1793f., 1796, 1800,
 1802-1804, 1816, 1819, 1821,
 1843, 2764, 2804f., 2813, 2895,
 2902, 2909, 2912, 2914, 2917,
 2926, 2934-2938, 2947, 2982,
 2986, 3007f., 3013, 3039f.,
 3043, 3174
Quenzel, K. 2111, 2112, 2128,
 2227
Queri, G. 1198, 2215, 2228
Quesada C., F. 2705
Quicherat, L. 1011, 1015

Quijano, A. 1743, 1766
Quilis, A. 1311
Quillet, A. 1826, 1831
Quin, W. 2341
Quinault, R.J. 1029
Quine, W.v.Orman 551, 582f., 853
Quintero, R.T. 930
Quirk, R. 29, 31, 33, 106f., 111,
 128, 131, 135, 588f., 592, 695,
 699, 858, 862, 996, 998, 1617,
 1624
Quiroga, M. A. 2705
Quiróz Mejias, O. 1757
Quiroz V., A. 2705
Quitard, P.-M. 1036, 1041, 1130
Qvigstad, J. 2390-2392

R

Raab, H. 1030, 2174, 2176, 2228
Raabe, P. 1814, 3007
Raasch, A. 269, 315, 321,
 1355-1358, 1362f., 2234
Raasch, W. 1364
Rabbani, S. 3097, 3106
Rabben, E. 1530
Rabbi, C.C. 1011, 1015
Rabbow, A. 3152, 3157
Rabe, H. 1052f.
Rabelais, F. 1346, 1793
Raben, J. 1670
Rabin, Ch. 2430, 2433, 2436
Rabinovich, I.S. 3101, 3106
Rabone, St. 2574f.
Rachel, B. 2276f.
Rachmanova, L.I. 2324
Racine, J. 1824
Rackebrandt, R. 78, 2755
Raday, Z. 2430, 2436
Radermacher, H. 1516f., 1520,
 1522
Radford, A. 160, 163
Radhakanta Deva 2495
Radhakrishna, B. 2531, 2533
Radiguel, A. 1311, 1314
Radion, St. 2332f.
Rädlein, J. 221f., 2917, 2933,
 3015, 3018
Radliński, I. 2629f.
Radloff, J.G. 231, 245, 1234, 1241
Radloff, W. 2404, 2406, 2413
Radó, A. 2378, 2382
Radonvilliers, J.-B.R. 1165
Radovich, N. 2260, 2267
Radszuweit, S. 1079, 2224
Radtke, D. 615, 627
Radtke, E. 652f., 656, 668,
 1193-1197, 1199, 1532,
 1534-1536, 1538, 3019
Rădulescu-Pogoneanu, I.A. 1885
Raether, M. 224

Raevski, N. 1888f.
Ragazzi, G. 1857, 1862
Ragazzini, G. 2834, 2836, 2973,
 2975
Rage, S.K. 2358, 2360
Raghavan, V. 2496
Raghuvīra 2512, 2519, 3102, 3106
Raguet, E. 3116, 3118
Raguse, J. de 1563
Rahīmī, M.H. 3100, 3106
Rahmatī, Yūsuf 2479
Rahnenführer, H. 2220
Rai, A.S.D. 3100, 3106
Raible, W. 959, 967
Raiet, E. 2394
Rainer, F. 269
Rainis, J. 2359
Rājadikṣa, S.A. 3101, 3106
Rajaram, S. 3102f., 3106
Rājaśekhara 2503
Rakhubo, N.P. 1670
Rall, D. 1005, 1008
Rall, M. 1005, 1008
Ralph, B. 3049, 3051
Raluy Poudevida, A. 144, 1754,
 1762
Ramalho, É. 1030
Ramamurti, G. V. 2527,
 2532-2534, 2537, 2543f., 2547,
 3100, 3106
Ramanujaswami, P. V. 2504
Ramaraju, B. (= Raju) 3097, 3106
Rāmasvāmi, M. 3101, 3106
Rāmayya, J. 2528
Rambach, C. 1195, 1198
Rambaud, A. 1825
Rambelli, G. 1085, 1090, 1092
Rameau, M. 1081, 1083
Ramée, P. de la 1089
Ramina, N. R. 2511
Ramírez Sánchez, C. 2709
Ramírez, C. 2659f.
Ramkhe, M. 3100, 3106
Ramler, C.W. 1559
Ramler, K.W. 3152, 3157
Ramnarainlal 3101, 3106
Ramon, J. 1776, 1785
Ramón, L.P. de 1746, 1762
Ramondino, S. 2955
Ramos y Duarte, F.I. 1752, 1762
Ramos, A. 1757
Ramovš, F. 2296, 2301
Ramsay, A. 1983, 1986
Ramsay, E. W. 2535, 2545
Ramseger, G. 2240
Ramsey, E. 2636, 2638
Ramułt, S. 2270, 2273
Ramus, P. 1089
Ranade, N. B. 2520
Ranconnet, A. de 1794, 1808
Rancoule, L. 2886
Randall, R.A. 816, 822

Rando, G. 1868
Ranganathan, S.R. 1671
Rank, J. V. 3078
Ranke, H. 1680f.
Ranna 2524
Ranson, H. M. 2887
Rao, J. 2515, 2520
Rao, P.S. 3100, 3106
Raphael, B. 1670
Raphael, L.J. 517
Raphael, S.J. 653, 656
Rapp, E. L. 2458, 2460
Raquette, G. 2411
Rasamaya 2517
Räsänen, M. 1341, 2404, 2406, 2413
Rashin, V. 573
Rask, R. 526, 2035, 2631, 3055
Rask, R.K. 1929
Raske, R. 2029
Raskii, R. K. 2929
Raskin, V. 582, 3167
Rasmussen, J. 106, 111, 2760, 2764, 2883, 2887, 3059, 3061
Rasmussen, K. 2634
Rasmussen, K.W. 1196, 1199
Raspall de Cauhé, J. 1777, 1785
Raspall i Juanola, J. 1776, 1785
Rastorgueva, V. S. 2485
Rat, M. 1030
Rath 2653
Rath, J.C. 1341
Rath, M. 2515, 2520
Rathmayr, R. 2764
Ratnachandra 2502, 2504
Rato y Hévia, A. de 1747, 1762
Rattay, D. 2007
Rātwǭramuni, P. 2506
Raub, J. 1035, 1041
Rauch, K. 1037, 1041
Rauch, R. 1361, 2890, 2895, 2900
Rauh, H.L. 1193
Raum, N. 273, 320, 358, 406, 459, 499, 575, 2231
Raumer, R. von 2050, 2060f., 2076, 2091, 2096, 2100
Raun, A. 2394
Raupach, M. 779, 2901
Rauschenbach, E. 2218
Raveling, I. 1268f., 1274
Ravelli, F. M. 3014, 3017
Ravellus, F.M. 2998
Raven, F. 2228
Raven, P. H. 2698, 2700
Raventós, M.H. 2953, 2955
Raverty, H. G. 2483, 2486
Ravila, P. 2398
Ravisius Textor, J. 1011
Ravisy, J.T. de 1015
Ravius, Chr. 2933
Rāvu, K.G. 3097, 3106
Rawlinson, H. C. 2471, 2473

Rawson, H. 976, 980
Ray Vidyanidhi, Y. C. 2510, 2518
Ray, F.R. 1453
Raymond, A. 1030
Raymond, F. 140, 145, 1206, 1209, 1802, 1804f., 1808, 3054
Raymond, J.C. 33, 37, 2009
Raynolds, L. 137
Raynouard, F. 1891f., 1904f.
Read, A.W. 29f., 33f., 36, 38, 79, 96, 518, 607, 653, 656, 668, 1949, 1952, 1987f., 1990-1992, 2003, 2009
Reagan, R. 1118
Reaney, P.H. 1271, 1274
Réaumur, R.A.F. de 2938, 2946
Rebora, P. 2974
Rebreanu 1882
Recker, J. I. 3082
Recker, Ja. I. 2764
Recktenwald, H.C. 164f., 167
Rector, M. 1115, 1119
Redard, G. 2412
Redard, P. 1230
Redd, J. 2666
Reddi, V. 3102, 3106
Reddy, G. N. 2531, 2533
Rédei, K. 1341, 2398
Redhouse, J.W. 2402f., 2404, 2406
Redi, F. 1854f.
Redin, M. 3050
Red'kin, V. A. 2327f., 2763f., 2853, 3082, 3085
Reed, C.E. 276, 748, 2764
Reed, J.A. 764, 767
Reed, L. 1130
Reehorst, K. P. F. 2918, 2933
Reenen, P. van 1322
Reenen-Stein, K.H. van 1322
Reershemius, P.F. 1268, 1274
Rees, N. 1296
Rees, P.A. van 2937, 2946
Reeve, W. 2524, 2532
Regan, B.T. 1910, 1912
Reginina, K. W. 3065, 3067
Reginina, K.V. 2324
Regnier, A. 1560
Regnier, H. 1551f., 1560
Régnier-Desmarais, F. 1799
Reguant i Serra, S. 1778, 1785
Regula, M. 2224
Régulo, J. 1764
Reh, M. 2643, 2645
Rehbock, H. 813, 823, 830
Rehder, P. 2267
Reibel, D.A. 269
Reich, H.W. 1261, 1265
Reich, K. H. 3015, 3018
Reich, P.A. 655
Reichan, J. 2271f.
Reichard, E. C. 2050, 2077
Reichardt, K. 1342

Reichardt, L. 1278f., 1281, 1283f.
Reichardt, R. 1816f.
Reichel, E. 1550-1552, 1557, 1560
Reichelt, H. 2475, 2477
Reichenberg, J. 273, 2224
Reichensperger, A. 1201, 1205
Reichert, P. 1141
Reichhardt, R. 1056, 1804
Reichling, A. 2224
Reichmann, O. 12, 14, 18, 103, 111f., 114f., 119f., 122, 124, 126f., 158, 224, 232f., 245f., 265, 269, 272f., 275, 278f., 359, 364, 366, 369f., 380, 406, 408, 432, 434, 460f., 500, 517, 531, 542, 552, 562, 576, 582, 585f., 612f., 620, 622f., 625-628, 653, 656, 667, 688, 728, 731, 770f., 814, 821, 842, 849, 855, 918f., 926f., 930, 969, 978-981, 989, 998, 1031, 1064-1067, 1143, 1152, 1157f., 1232, 1235, 1238, 1241, 1283f., 1291-1394, 1397, 1399, 1401f., 1405, 1407, 1414, 1416, 1418-1424, 1428-1430, 1435, 1523, 1531, 1542, 1544-1549, 1562, 1571-1573, 1589, 1592, 1596, 1598, 1600, 1604, 1608, 1610f., 1645, 2074, 2082, 2098, 2100, 2104, 2221, 2235f., 2240, 2242, 2244f., 2715, 2727, 2778, 2851, 2854
Reicke, S. 2218
Reid, A. A. 2698f.
Reid, L. A. 2573
Reidy, J. 78, 668, 703, 1450, 1455, 1630
Reif, J. A. 2889f.
Reifer, M. 1163, 1165
Reiff, C. Ph. 2917, 2933, 3075, 3077
Reiffenberg, F.A. de 1790, 1816
Reiffenstein, I. 221, 224
Reig, D. 3095
Reim, R. 1198
Reimer, E. 1693
Reimer, K. 2079, 2081
Reinecke, J. E. 2871, 2876
Reineggs, J. 2484, 2486
Reineke, W.F. 1141, 1681
Reiner, E. 1242, 1244f., 1691, 2883f., 2887
Reinhard, W. 1230
Reinhardt, W. 304, 1672
Reinhart, J. M. 2256, 2261, 2267f.
Reinheimer, M. 2886
Reinhold, C. L. 2059, 2071
Reinisch, L. 2463-2466
Reinius, J. 1260
Reinsberg-Düringsfeld, O. von 1037, 1039, 1041, 2066, 2068
Reinwald, W.F.H. 243, 1909, 1912

Reis, M. 126f., 279, 578f., 586, 599, 614, 835, 1067, 2076, 2235, 2238, 2244, 2760, 2767, 2902
Reis, W. 1261, 1265, 1617, 1624
Reischauer 2617
Reisler, C. G. 3054, 3061
Reiss, M. 408
Reissner, A. 1198
Reissner, P.A. 88
Reiß, K. 171, 174
Reißner, E. 1067
Reitsma, J. 2026, 2033
Reitterer, H. 2751
Reitterer, Th. 1030
Rekēna, A.St. 2358, 2360
Remacle, L. 719, 724
Remizova, S.Ju. 722, 725
Rémy, J. 1004, 1008, 1313f.
Rémy, M. 679, 945, 1841
Renan, E. 2462, 2469
Renck, G. 2636, 2638
Renda, U. 1854, 1862
René, A. 1840
Rennefahrt, H. 1592
Renner, J. 44, 46
Renner, R. 2942, 2946
Renoir, E. 2959
Renooij, D.C. 166
Renov, L. 2490, 2492, 2494f.
Rensch, K.H. 517
Renvall, K. 2384, 2387
Renzi, A. M. 3010f.
Repp, Th. G. 3055, 3060
Requardt, S. 2880
Réquédat, F. 1006, 1009
Requejo, V. 1742, 1762
Reques, M. 1789
Resa, H.J. de 1776, 1785
Reschelius, Th. 2279, 2283
Resden, M. 2406
Rešetar, M. 2289, 2296
Resmeriță, A. 1886
Resnikoff, H.L. 1139
Resnikow, L.O. 3150, 3157
Restivo, P. P. 2670, 2673-2676
Rétat, P. 137, 145, 1816
Réti, A. 2763
Rétif, A. 24, 28, 151, 1820-1822, 1843
Rettig, W. 101, 260, 269, 276, 383, 407, 642-645, 648f., 880-882, 1178, 1230, 1800, 1816, 1843, 2716, 2727, 2748, 2764f., 2841, 2854, 2857, 2859, 2863f., 2999, 3001-3003, 3007
Reuchlin, A. 2434
Reuchlin, J. 1715, 2039, 2427
Reule, G. 582
Reum, A. 979, 1011, 1015f., 2776
Reuss, Chr.F. 2939, 2946
Reuss, F. 2917, 2933

Reuter, B. 269
Reuter, O. 1242, 1244f.
Reuter, O. R. 3048, 3050
Reutercrona, G. 3045f.
Reutercrona, H. 3044-3046
Reuther, J. 2639
Reuther, T. 599, 1018, 2765
Rexilius, G. 1632, 1637
Rey, A. 1, 5, 12, 18, 26, 28, 44, 47f., 51, 54f., 61f., 79, 81, 84-86, 88, 93-97, 144, 167, 170, 180, 246, 267, 275, 277, 286f., 311, 411, 460, 516, 524, 529, 532, 544, 582, 590, 592, 614, 638-641, 652, 656, 661, 674, 679f., 682, 687f., 700, 703f., 731, 784, 787, 861, 916f., 929, 936, 945f., 972f., 980, 989, 998, 1021, 1023, 1030, 1032, 1039, 1043, 1083, 1090, 1094, 1099, 1149, 1151, 1185, 1187, 1247, 1294, 1296, 1374, 1378, 1525, 1529, 1534-1536, 1588, 1672, 1678, 1800, 1803, 1816, 1819, 1828, 1830, 1833, 1837-1839, 1841-1843, 2765, 2865, 2868, 2870, 2878
Rey, G. 573, 582
Rey-Debove, J. 44, 62, 65, 69, 78, 87, 136, 144-146, 180, 222, 224, 277, 282, 284, 286f., 306, 308, 310-312, 340f., 359, 361, 370f., 406f., 409-424, 453, 459f., 524, 529, 532-534, 540f., 550, 552, 557f., 562, 564, 580, 582, 584, 600, 602-605, 607, 637, 640f., 647f., 661, 676, 679-681, 703, 715f., 722, 725, 731, 784, 786f., 917, 929, 936f., 939, 945f., 989f., 992, 998, 1032, 1099, 1147, 1149, 1151, 1163, 1168, 1177, 1368, 1378, 1588, 1816, 1828, 1834, 1836f., 1841-1843, 2012, 2014, 2022, 2860, 2864
Reychman, J. 3067
Reyes, A. 1762
Reyes, R. 2980, 2984
Reyherus, A. 1011, 1016
Reynolds, B. 67, 69, 2974
Reynolds, J. 1440
Reynolds, L. 138f., 146
Reynoso, D. de 2664, 2669
Rězak, F. 2276f.
Rézeau, P. 653, 656, 1837, 1841
Rhamba, J. 2044
Rheims, M. 1207, 1209, 1244f.
Rhodes, A. de 2583f., 2589, 2913, 2933
Rhodes, J. 3125, 3127, 3134
Rhodes, R. A. 2692, 2695f.
Rhys Davids, T. W. 2500-2502, 2504

Rian, R. 3126f., 3134
Riba, O. 1778, 1785
Ribarova, Z. 2263, 2266, 2304
Ribarova-Kurzova, Z. 2263
Ribeiro, J. 1220
Riber Petersen, P. 1165
Ribot, A. 3125, 3130
Ricardo, A. 2682-2684
Ricart, A. 1778, 1784
Ricci, L. 2643, 2645
Ricci, M. 3111f.
Rich, A. 1008
Rich, E. 1670
Richard, J.F. 1375
Richard, P.-M. 1189
Richards, A. 2566f.
Richards, J. 1318, 1321f.
Richards, J.C. 531, 580, 1356, 1364
Richards, Th. 2347, 2349
Richardson, Ch. 226, 229, 1954, 1957-1959, 1961f., 1966
Richardson, H.B. 1756
Richaudeau, F. 141-143, 146
Richelet, C.-P. 139, 143, 145, 312, 501, 525, 528f., 603, 861, 1189, 1809
Richelet, P. 10, 13, 16, 43, 217, 322f., 327, 729, 731, 766, 860, 988, 994, 997, 1125-1127, 1129f., 1185f., 1189, 1743, 1795-1798, 1801f., 1809-1812, 1814-1816, 1818, 1853, 2957, 2979, 2999, 3036, 3040
Richey, M. 237f., 243, 2060f., 2071, 2215, 2228
Richey, W. 1036, 1041
Richman, B. 1320
Richter, A. 2290, 2295
Richter, E. 2550
Richter, F. 2193, 2228
Richter, G. 2217
Richter, H. 1610, 1644
Richter, M. 531, 542, 582, 837-839, 841, 2131, 2134, 2240
Richthofen, K. Freiherr von 2023f., 2035
Rickard, P. 2957, 2960
Ricken, U. 1165, 1804, 1816
Ricker, L. 1251, 1154
Rickheit, G. 1525, 1527, 1530
Rickmeyer, J. 1005, 1008
Ricks, Chr. 33
Riddell, J.A. 30, 34, 1947, 1953
Rider, J. 3036, 3039
Rider, K.R. 3176
Ridolfi, L. 1125, 1130
Ridpath-Klien, M. 1110f.
Riedel, H. 315, 321, 1052, 1638, 1644
Rieffel, Ch. 1053
Rieger, B. 200, 207, 576, 1642, 1644, 3167

Rieger, J. 1286, 1290, 2273
Riegler, R. 1257
Riehme, J. 2184, 2229
Riemens, K.-J. 3035f., 3039
Riemer, G.C.L. 1551, 1560
Riemschneider, K. 78, 280
Riera i Sans, J. 1777, 1785
Riera, A. 1780
Riesel, E. 1353, 1364
Riesen, I. 2220
Riesenfeld, B. 1557, 1562
Riesenfeld, H. 1562
Riesenfeldt, B. 1704
Riesenfeldt, H. 1704
Rieser, H. 163
Riessner, K. 9, 18
Rietz, J.E. 1939, 1942
Riev, Ch. 2496
Rigaltius, N. 1705, 1713
Rigaud, L. 1185, 1189, 1349, 1352
Rigby, Chr. P. 2462, 2468
Riggs, St. R. 2692, 2696
Righi, A. 1193
Rigler, J. 2296, 2301
Rigutini, G. 1308, 1310, 1866f., 1879, 3016, 3018f.
Rihel, W. 2045
Riiber, Th. 102, 110, 117f., 125, 132, 134, 519, 525, 745, 748, 1032, 1531, 2713, 2716, 2720, 2725, 2727, 2760, 2836, 2840, 2842, 2853, 2857f., 3059, 3061
Rijsbergen, Chr.J. van 1671
Rilke, R.M. 24, 1138
Rilski, N. 2304f., 2308
Rimon, M. 3166
Rincón, A. del 2659, 2661
Ringger, K. 1905
Ringgren, H. 2428, 2434
Rinnen, H. 1257
Riofrío, M. 1752, 1762
Ripa, C. 3151f., 3157
Ripfel, M. 112, 128, 135, 182, 189, 192, 207, 258, 260, 277, 498f., 1632, 1638, 2131, 2202, 2241, 2765
Rippmann, W. 1130
Riquer, M. de 1332, 1757
Rischel, J. 2633
Riss, P. F. 2485f.
Ristić, S. 512, 516, 2292, 2295
Ristovski, B. 2302, 2304
Ristow, B. 2207-2209, 2228
Risueño, C. 1747, 1762
Ritchie de Key, M. 2659f.
Ritchie, G.D. 3167
Rittendorf, M. 1532, 1537, 2185, 2197, 2229
Ritter Obradors, M. 1784
Ritter, E. 1803, 1816
Ritter, G.A. 166
Ritter, H. 2432

Ritter, J. 577, 581, 855
Ritter, K. 163, 167
Ritter, M. 1776
Ritterspach, G. 3129, 3134
Rittier, E. 1839
Rius Vidal, A. 1776, 1785
Rivalto, G. da 1855
Rivarol, A. 225, 1081, 1814
Rivenc, P. 1321, 1356, 1363, 1835
Riverain, J. 946, 1164
Rivers, W.M. 1386, 1389, 2765
Rivet, P. 2681f., 2684, 2686, 2690, 2705
Rivodó, B. 1743, 1752, 1762, 1766
Rivola, F. 2368, 2371
Rix, H. 1286, 1290
Rizk, O. A. 2813, 3167
Rizzo, P. 3124, 3137
Roback, A.A. 1037, 1041, 1192f.
Robbe, P. 2634
Robbins, C.D. 1054-1056
Robecchi-Bricchetti, L. 2462, 2468
Robelo, C.A. 1755, 1762
Robert, C. 1349, 1352
Robert, C.M. 1242, 1245
Robert, E. 3131
Robert, P. 12, 16, 20, 22, 28, 44, 61f., 128, 133, 144, 220, 222, 286, 358, 405f., 458f., 508, 516, 524, 526, 528f., 590f., 606, 638-640, 648, 653, 661, 667, 672, 679, 687, 692, 703, 731, 821, 861, 916, 929, 945f., 988, 1096, 1099f., 1214, 1294, 1296, 1345, 1347, 1588, 1676, 1827f., 1842f., 2816, 2836
Roberti, G. 1196f.
Roberts, A.H. 1314, 1322, 1644, 1669
Roberts, H. 3148
Roberts, J.P. 2972, 2975
Robertson, H.R. 1800, 1816
Robertson, J. A. 2565
Robertson, St.E. 1671
Robertson, Th. 1089, 1092
Robespierre, M. de 1081
Robinet, J.B. 2957f., 3075
Robins, R.H. 532, 582
Robinson, Ch. H. 2458, 2460
Robinson, D.F. 1141, 2765
Robinson, F. 1446
Robinson, J. 208, 214, 312, 314, 320, 539, 582
Robinson, J.L. 325, 327, 1456
Robinson, L.G. 3152, 3157
Robinson, M. 761, 1985
Robinson, R. 552, 582
Robles, C. 2664, 2669
Robles, L. de 2980, 2984
Robolsky, H. 1124
Roborero, E. 2647

Roca Cerdà, A. 1773, 1785
Roca, G. 1772
Roceric, A. 1650, 1667
Rocha Nogueira, A. 2702
Rocha, A. 2708
Roche, C. 1691, 1693
Rochefort, C. de 1809
Rochefort, J.B.B. de 1157f.
Rocher, D. 1110
Roches, J. des 3036, 3039
Rochet d'Héricourt, Ch. E. X. 2462, 2468
Rock, J. F. 2559
Rodale, J.I. 1012, 1014, 1016, 1076f., 1079
Rodde, J. 3073, 3084
Rode, E. 1931
Rode, M. 1078, 2765
Rodegem, F. M. 2648
Rodenberg, L. 3148
Rodgers, B. 1196, 1198
Rodhe, E. 1306, 1308f., 3044
Rodić, N. 2263, 2268
Röding, J. H. 2917, 2933
Rodoni 1054f., 1121, 1125
Rodrigo, L. 1758
Rodrígues, A. D. 2704
Rodríguez Bou, I. 1762
Rodríguez Castellano, L. 1762
Rodríguez Castelo, H. 1196, 1198, 1762
Rodríguez González, E. 1737
Rodríguez Marín, F. 1743, 1766
Rodríguez Marín, S. 1746, 1762
Rodríguez, J.F. 1736f., 2986, 3036, 3039
Rodríguez, Z. 1752, 1762
Rodríguez-Navas, M. 1746, 1762
Rodvila, A. de 1860 (s. Rottweil)
Roe, K. 763, 765, 767, 989, 994, 998, 1946, 1953
Roegele, O.B. 1201, 1205
Roelcke, Th. 1545, 1549
Roerisch, N. 2550
Roever, A. de 3018
Roey, J. van 1019
Rogalski, A. 3076
Rogby, O. 2031, 3036
Roger, P. 1789
Rogers, W.T. 1261, 1265
Roget, J.L. 1092
Roget, P.M. 26, 98, 168, 220, 636, 640, 754-756, 761, 769, 1059, 1065, 1068, 1077, 1081, 1083, 1085, 1087-1090, 1092-1094, 1186, 1867, 1879, 1944, 1952, 1969, 2086
Roget, S.R. 1092
Roggen, C. 2027, 2035
Roggenhofer, J. 980
Rogler, J.B. 2968
Rogov, N. 2398

Rogožnikova, R.P. 2321, 2328f.
Rohan-Chabot, G. de 1349, 1352
Röhl, E. 2229
Rohlfs, G. 1274, 1333, 1711-1713, 1762, 1766, 1788, 1876f., 1879, 1893, 1905
Rohlfsen, G. 1328
Rohr, B. 848
Rohr, J. 2112
Rohr, K.I. 1189
Rohracher, H. 855
Rohrbacher, L. 1052
Röhrborn, K. 2412f.
Röhrich, L. 1019, 1021, 1024f., 1027, 1030, 1034-1036, 1043, 2066, 2077, 2174f., 2229
Rohwedder, E. 2765
Roig, E. 1780
Rojo Sastre, A.J. 1313
Roland, P. 1189
Rolland, E. 1255-1257
Rollet de L'Isle, M. 3129, 3134
Röllig, W. 2429, 2431, 2334, 2337
Rolling, L. 1311, 1670, 2728, 2767, 2775, 2813
Roloff, H.-G. 1594, 1610
Rolshoven, J. 269
Roma, G. de 1788
Román, M.A. 1753, 1762
Roman, V.S. 2367
Romani, C. 220, 222, 3015, 3018
Romani, G. 1073, 1075
Romano, P. S. 2674, 2676
Romano, S. 1906
Romanova, G.J. 2326
Romanski, St. 2306, 2308
Rombach, H. 576
Römer, G. P. A. G. H. 2918, 2933
Römer, R. 269
Römer, R. R. 3027
Romera-Navarro, M. 1762
Romero C., M. 2663, 2669
Romero F., L. 2663
Romero, C. A. 2684
Romero, F. L. 2669
Romeu Jover, X. 1777, 1785
Romey, M. Ch. 2660
Rommerskirchen, P.J. 3175
Romportl, M. 1308, 1310
Ronchetti, G. 3153, 3157
Ronciglione, P. A. da 2454
Rondeau, G. 168, 170, 1672
Rondeau, P. 2999, 3005
Rongé-Dethier, M. 2982, 2985
Rongus, O. 1261, 1263, 1265
Ronna, A. 3010-3012
Ronner, M.M. 1049
Ronsard, P. 3035
Ronsard, P. de 1794
Rood, N. 2648
Room, A. 1054f., 1073, 1123, 1125, 1281, 1283, 1292, 1296

Roorda van Eysinga 2561, 2562
Roorda, T. 2561, 2562
Roos, E. 1018, 2765
Roosen, H. 3128, 3134
Rooyen, M. van 1274
Roper, J.P.G. 1670
Roques, G. 653, 656, 1795, 1804, 1816f.
Roques, M. 1812, 1816, 2365
Roquette, J. I. 1073, 3022, 3029
Roquette-Pinto, E. 2708
Rorriano, G. 2971
Ros, C. 1772, 1785
Rosa, V. 2278-2280
Rosal, F. del 172, 1019, 1030, 1741
Rosamani, E. 1877, 1879
Rosas, J. M. de 2710
Rosasco, G. 1126, 1130
Rosbach, P. 102, 110, 117f., 125, 132, 134, 519, 525, 745, 748, 1032, 1531, 2713, 2716, 2720, 2725, 2727, 2760, 2775, 2836, 2840, 2842, 2853, 2857f., 2902, 2947, 2965, 2969, 3059, 3061
Rosch, E. 292f., 296, 573, 582, 3167
Rose, H.J. 1966
Rosembach, J. 1771f., 1785, 1787
Rosen, H.B. 1669
Rosenberg, A. 1261f., 1265,
Rosenberg, G. 3044, 3046
Rosenberger, G. 3044
Rosenblat, A. 1753f., 1762
Rosenblum, M. 1269, 1274
Rosenfeld, H. 719, 725
Rosenfeld, H. F. 2229
Rosengren, I. 585, 819, 822, 830, 1136f., 1141, 1321f., 1621, 1624, 1643, 1669
Rosengren, P. 1141
Rosenhoff, A. 1219f.
Rosenstein, R. 1795, 1817
Rosensthiel, A. 1247
Rosenthal, D. 1216
Rosenthal, F. 2431, 2433, 2437
Rosetti, A. 1890, 2751
Rosher, E.M. 3129, 3134
Rosiello, L. 66, 766, 930
Rosier, J.L. 1440, 1456, 2970, 2976
Rosily, A. de 2980, 2985
Rosing, S. 3055, 3061
Rosmini, A. 1873
Rospond, S. 2271, 2273
Ross, E. M. 2686f., 2690, 2706
Ross, H. 1925, 1928
Ross, J.R. 1617, 1624
Ross, W. 3018
Ross, W.W. 1800, 1817
Rossebastiano Bart, A. 18, 1847, 1850, 1861f., 3007f., 3013 (s. Bart)
Rossell, L. 1778, 1784

Rosselli, C. 1088, 1092
Rossenbeck, K. 101, 251, 277, 999, 2765, 2772, 2775, 3045, 3047
Rossetti, C. 2886
Rossetti, M. V. 2886
Rossi, A. 1872
Rossi, M. 3010, 3012
Rossi, P. 1088, 1090, 1094
Rossi, S. 2970f., 2976
Rossi, V. 1865
Rossich i Vidal, C. 1775
Rossignol 1185, 1189
Rossipal, H. 693, 778
Rössler, G. 653, 656
Rossner, R. 208, 214
Rost, V.Chr.F. 369, 1699, 1703
Rostagno, L.A. 1866, 1878
Rostaing, Ch. 1280, 1282, 1286, 1289, 1291, 1295, 1838
Rostand, E. 911
Rosten, L. 1190
Rostgaard, F. 1913
Rostok, M. 2275, 2278
Rostrenen, G. de 2350
Rostrenen, W. de 2347
Rößler, R. 661
Rot, E. 3082
Rot, S. 1170, 1172f., 1177
Roth, E. 24, 28
Roth, J. F. 2071
Roth, K.-H. 269
Roth, R. 2490f., 2495
Roth, S. 1177, 1209, 2050, 2062f., 2071, 2220, 3070
Rothacker, E, 1059, 1066
Rothe, R. 2216
Rother, K. 1035, 1041
Rothkegel, A. 370, 967, 1573
Rotondo y Rabasco, A. 2981, 2985
Rotteck, C. von 166f., 841
Rottland, F. 1341, 2644f.
Rottler, J. P. 2523, 2532
Rottweil [= Rodvila di], A. von 1790, 1860, 2911, 2914, 2928, 2933, 3013, 3019
Rouaix, P. 1094, 1096-1099
Roubaud, P.J. 1068f., 1074f.
Roucel, F. 2938, 2947
Rouède, D. 3012
Rouède, P. 3010, 3012
Roujoux 3010
Roura, J. 1780
Rourret, R. 1894, 1904
Rousé, J. 3027
Rousseau, C. 3128, 3134
Rousseau, J.-J. 25, 1572
Rousset, J.H. 1209
Roussin, A. 1044
Rouvroy, F. von 2938, 2947
Rouvroy, J. de 1790

Roux, E. de 43, 46
Roux, F. 3005, 3053
Roux, H.F. 3005
Roux, J. 1904
Roventi, A. 3166
Rovira i Virgili, A. 1776, 1785
Rowan, O. 2703
Rowan, P. 2703
Rowley, A. 1136, 1140, 1143
Roy, E. 3138, 3140f.
Roy, K. K. 2510, 2518
Roys, R. 2663f., 2669
Rozanova, V.V. 2320, 2324
Rozanovoj, V.V. 524
Roze 1206, 1209
Roze, G. 2938
Roze, K. 2357, 2359
Roze, L. 2355, 2357-2359, 2361
Rozenbaha, H. 2359
Rozenc'vejg, V. Ju. 1006, 1009, 2762
Rozental', D. È. 1006, 1008, 1308, 2317, 2324, 2896, 2901
Rozoy, A. 1842
Rozwadowska, M. F. 3064, 3067f.
Rozwadowski, J. 1285, 1291, 2268
Rozyki, W. 1141
Ruano, A. 2664, 2669
Rubenbauer, H. 2207f., 2223
Rüber, Th. 2775, 2902, 2947, 2965, 2969
Rubin, D.L. 1075
Rubin, G.M. 1670, 1672
Rubinyi, M. 2378, 2382
Rubió i Lluch, A. 1787
Rubio y Bel, M. 1747, 1762
Rubió, M. 1778, 1781
Rubtsova, E. S. 2632-2634
Ruby, P. de 1187
Rück, H. 653, 656
Rücker, H. 159
Ruddiman, Th. 1983, 1986
Rudenberg, W. 2828, 3109, 3113
Rudin, S.G. 3101, 3106
Rudnicki, N. 2274
Rudnyckyj, J.B. 2329-2334
Rudolph, L. 1235, 1239, 1552, 1560
Ruduicki, M. 2270
Rudzka, B. 1672
Ruess, F. 3140f.
Ruff, G. 2059
Ruff, J.G. 1072
Ruffinelli, G.A. 2996
Ruffner, F.G. 1056, 1098f.
Ruffner, J.A. 1260
Rüger, H.-P. 2429, 2435
Ruggieri, M. 3111f.
Ruh, K. 2048f.
Ruhe, E. 787
Ruhlen, M. 2642, 2645
Rühme, K. 2231

Ruhnken, D. 1716
Ruhs, R. 1286
Ruigys, P. 2351
Ruiter, V. de 881
Ruiz Calonja, J. 1079
Ruiz Cárdenas, A. 1079
Ruiz de Montoya, A. 2670
Ruiz de Padron, A. 2988
Ruiz León, J. 1092
Ruiz Sánchez, A. 2698f.
Ruiz, A. 2663, 2667, 2675
Ruiz, D.J. 2994, 2997
Rūke-Dravina, V. 2357, 2359-2361
Ruland, M. 1051, 1053, 2933
Rulandus, M. 1079
Rüme, K. 273, 320, 358, 406, 459, 499
Rümme, K. 575
Rumpel, I. 1560
Runck, G. 1192
Ruoff, A. 1135, 1137, 1142, 1321, 1643
Rupp, H. 1031
Ruppert, F. 1261, 1265
Ruppert, H. 2907f.
Rusak, H. 3126, 3134
Ruscelli, G. 1011, 1016, 1126, 1130, 1850, 1852, 1860
Ruse, Chr. 2900
Rush, J.E. 1660, 1666
Rush, R. 1290
Russell, D. 2703
Russell, I.W. 33, 37, 1163, 2009
Russell, R. 2703
Russu, I.I. 1890
Rust, F. 2652-2655
Rutten, A. 2019, 2021
Ruus, H. 2754
Ružička, J. 2287
Ruzicka, R. 813
Ruzsiczky, E. 615f., 622, 627, 1079, 2382
Ryan, W.M. 79
Ryba, B. 2279, 2284
Rybakin, A.I. 1270, 1274
Rybakova, P.G. 2397
Rybář, J. 3128, 3134
Rybicki, St.A. 1100, 1102, 1262, 1265
Rybnikova, M.A. 2324
Ryckeboer, H. 2021
Ryckmans, J. 1693
Rygh, O. 1286, 1290
Rykaczewski, E. 3062, 3068
Ryle, A. 1209
Rymsza-Zalewska, D. 3068, 3176
Rymut, K. 1291, 2271, 2274
Rypins, St. 225, 230, 1950, 1953
Rypka, J. 2480
Rysiewicz, Z. 2270, 2273
Ryssel, V. 2726

Rzepka, J. 1252
Rzetelska-Feleszko, E. 1290, 2273

S

Sa^cadya 2427, 2434
Saagpakk, P. 2394
Saalfeld, G.A. 1174, 1177, 1296
Saareste, A. 2394f.
Saba Orbeliani, S. 2416, 2418
Sabar, Y. 2432, 2437f.
Sabek, J. 2919, 2933
Sabio, St. da 1705, 1713
Sabir, M. 3101, 3106
Sabrino, F. 2934
Såby, V. 1917, 1922
Sacchetti, F. 149f.
Sacerdote, G. 3016, 3018
Sacharov, G.V. 2317, 2322
Sacharov, I. 3083
Sachau, E. 2447
Sachedina, A.J. 3101, 3106
Sachella, B. 1844, 1861
Šachmatov, A. A. 2313, 3079
Sachnine, M. 2458
Sachs, Ch. 3005
Sachs, G. 1328, 1333
Sachs, H. 1251, 1253, 1552
Sachs, K. 514, 516, 2751, 2795f., 2802, 3000, 3005f., 3054
Sachuine, U. 2460
Saciid Narsame Xirsi 2464, 2466
Sacy, S. de 1803, 1817
Sadasivam, M. 1054f.
Saddhammakitti 2500, 2504
Sadeanu, F. 1890
Sader, M. 3170
Sa'dii'ev, Sh. M. 3169
Sadler, V. 1672, 3125, 3128, 3134, 3137, 3167
Sadnik, L. 1133, 1138, 1142, 1337, 1341, 2259, 2263, 2266
Saeki, S. 2622
Saenz, C. 2663, 2669
Sáez Godoy, L. 2706, 2709
Saf'jan, J.A. 1668, 2320, 2322, 2324
Šafařík, P. J. 2280, 2284, 2302
Safire, W. 34, 38, 841, 1201, 1204f.
Sagalongos, F. T. E. 2570
Sagara, M. 3116-3118
Sagarin, E. 1194, 1199
Sager, J. 1670
Sager, J.C. 169f.,1084. 1094, 1660, 1662, 1666-1668, 1670
Sager, N. 1670
Sági, I. 3174
Šagirov, A.K. 1341
Sagroi, S.C. 88
Sågvall, A.-L. 1651, 1668
Šāha, R. 3097, 3106

Sahani, A. T. 2516, 2520
Saheb, G. 2516
Šähidi, B. 2410
Şâhidî, I. 2399, 2406
Sahlgren, J. 1308, 1310
Sahlstedt, A. 217, 224, 1934, 1936, 1939, 1942
Saidov, M. 2422f.
Sailer, J. M. 2065, 2072
Sainean, L. 1331, 1333f.
Şăineanu, L. 1886, 1889, 1891
Sainéau, L. 1184f., 1189f., 1532f., 1538
Sainliens, C. de (= Hollyband) 1848
Saint Joseph, A. de 2933
Sainte-Beuve, Ch.A. 84
Saint-Francois de Sales 1350
Saint-Gérand, J.-Ph. 653, 656, 1802, 1804, 1817
Saint-Joseph, A. de 2913
Saint-Maurice, R.A. de B. 1302f.
Sáinz de Robles, F.C. 1079
Saínz Rodríguez, P. 1765
Saito, H. 3118
Saito, S. 3115f., 3118
Saitz, R.L. 1117, 1119
Sajkowski, A. 2401, 2407
Sakakura, A. 2622
Sakamato, T. 3116, 3118
Sakamoto, Y. 2591, 2593
Sakari, A. 2765
Sakaria, B.P. 3100, 3106
Śākaṭāyana 2488
Sakharova, M.A. 2397f.
Šakhovskaja, L. 1130
Šakun, L.M. 2337
Sakurai, Y. 3116, 3118
Sala, M. 1754f., 1762, 1766, 1907
Salâhî, M.S. 2400, 2406
Salas, A. 1743, 1766
Salas, P. de 1011, 1016, 1742, 1762
Salas, R. 1216
Salazar García, S. 1753, 1762
Salazar, A. de 1762, 2981, 2985f.
Salazar, E. de 1741, 1762
Salemann, C. 2485
Salesbury, W. 2347, 2349, 2956
Salillas, R. 1762
Salinari, C. 141, 145
Salinkow, N. 269
Sallager, E. 1184
Salling, A. 3058, 3060
Salmoné, H. A. 2896, 2901, 3090, 3095
Šalom-Alejhem 3122, 3137
Salonen, A. 1685
Salonen, E. 1684f.
Salt, H. 2453f., 2461, 2468
Salton, G. 1671
Saltveit, C. 2244
Saltveit, L. 585, 628, 822

Saltzmann, Ph. 1155
Saluveer, M. 573, 582
Salvá y Pérez, V. 2985
Salvá, D.V. 2985
Salva, K. 2285, 2287
Salvá, V. 1745f., 1762, 2951f., 2980, 2983, 2985
Salvadó i Rovira, G. 1778, 1785
Salvador Rosa, A. 653, 656, 1751, 1767
Salvador, C. 1785
Salvador, G. 1762
Salvador, J. 2664, 2669
Salvador, T. 1189
Salvadore, C. 1777
Salviati, L. 1852-1854
Salvini, M. 1692, 1694
Salys, A. 2352f.
Samani, S. 1877, 1879
Samarin, W.J. 1615f., 1624
Sambor, J. 1671
Samedov, D.S. 2423
Saminy, B. 3126f., 3134
Sammallahti, P. 2391
Sampson, G. 1670, 2805, 2813
Šamšalović, G. 2292, 2295
Samson, G. 1220
Samuels, M.L. 228, 230, 1967, 1983
Sāmurrā'ī 2447
Samy, M.A. 3101, 3106
San Buenaventura, P. de 2568, 2570
San José, D. de 1741, 1762
Sánchez de la Ballesta, A. 1740, 1762
Sánchez de las Brozas, F. 1740, 1756
Sánchez Ladero, L. 786, 1749, 1762
Sanchez Pérez, A. 516, 786
Sánchez Regueira, I. 2978, 2986
Sánchez Somoano, J. 1752, 1762
Sánchez, J. 1778, 1785
Sánchez, M. 1312, 1314
Sanchez, R. 1030
Sánchez-Labrador, J. 2708
Sánchez-Monge y Parellada, E. 2924, 2933
Sanchis Guarner, M. 1775, 1788
Sancho, M. 2659f., 2698, 2700
Sandberg, G. 2916, 1927, 2931
Sander, Chr. L. 1074, 2058
Sanders, Chr. 1931
Sanders, D. 140, 145, 226f., 231, 242f., 245, 406, 427, 455, 459, 499, 512, 516, 630f., 634, 728, 731, 752-754, 771, 801, 804, 826, 830, 870, 872, 875, 880, 1046, 1049, 1063, 1065, 1069, 1074f., 1083, 1085, 1087, 1089, 1092-1094, 1173f., 1177, 1216,

1235f., 1239, 1241, 1418 1619, 1623, 2063f., 2066, 2072, 2075, 2078, 2081-2084, 2086f., 2092, 2094, 2097, 2099f., 2178, 2215, 2229, 2771, 2774, 2968, 3000, 3056
Sanders, W. 1429
Sanderson, D. 2532
Sandesara, B. J. 2499, 2505
Sandfeld, K. 1918, 1922
Sandhu, B. S. 2520
Sandig, B. 370, 693, 699, 967
Sandness, G.D. 109, 111
Sandru-Olteanu, T. 1762, 1766
Sandry, G. 1163, 1185, 1189, 1530
Sands, D. B. 2131, 2150, 2241
Sanelo, M.J. 1772f., 1785
Sáñez Reguart, A. 1742, 1763
Sanford, G. 1252, 1254
Sangers, A.G. 1321
Sanguinetti, E. 43, 46
Sani, L. 2973, 2975
Šanidze, A. 2417f.,
Sankaranārāyaṇa, P. 2528, 2532
Sankin, A.A. 274
Sanna, C. 1534, 1537
Sannazaro, I. 150, 1854
Sanneg, J. 1132, 1142
Sanoff, A.P. 36, 38
Sanskaja, T.V. 2324
Šanskij, N.M. 2315, 2318, 2324
Sansome, R. 653, 656, 1368
Sansone, M.T. 1079
Santacreu Sirvent, A. 1778, 1786
Santacruz Pachacuti Yamqui Salcamaygua, J. de 2678, 2680, 2684
Santagnello, M. 2972, 2975
Santamaría, A. 1079, 1216
Santamaría, F.J. 1752, 1753, 1762
Santandrea, St. 2644f.
Santesson, R. 3051
Santholzer, R.W. 1263
Santiago, B. de 2682
Santillana, M. de 1740, 1762
Santini, L. 1099
Santis, S. de 3143f.
Santo Domingo, T. de 2664, 2669
Santo Tomás, D. de 2678, 2681-2684
Santos Coco, F. 1763
Santos, E. 3175
Santos, V. C. 301, 304, 2569, 2570
Sanz, R. 1742, 1763
Šaov, Ž.A. 2420f.
Sapan 2436
Sapeto, G. 2462, 2468
Sapir, E. 1331, 2869
Šapiro, A.B. 1147, 1310, 2316, 2324
Šapiro, F.L. 2431, 2436

Saporta, S. 33, 78f., 110, 133f., 274, 277, 584, 656, 668, 779, 980, 998, 1032, 1968, 1982, 2715, 2726f., 2756-2758, 2761f., 2767, 2902, 3096
Sapper, K. 2664, 2669
Sappler, P. 1134, 1137, 1142, 1573
Saraiva, C. (Luiz, F. de S.) 1019, 1074f.
Saraṇankara, B 2504
Sarasola, I. 2374f.
Sarauw, Chr. 2341, 2343
Sarčević, S. 2765
Sardó y Vilar, A. 2990
Sardou, A.-L. 1005, 1008, 1074, 1809, 1842
Sarfsteyn, s. Scharfstein
Särkkä, H. 519, 525, 737, 748
Sarles, H. 2663f., 2669
Sarma, H. 3097, 3106
Śarma, R. 3102, 3106
Sarmiento, F.M. 1736, 1738, 1742, 1767
Saroyan, W. 28
Sarpraserith, N. 2504
Sarrazin, G. 1452
Sarrazin, O. 1173f., 1177
Sartorius, J. B. 2215, 2229
Sartre, J.-P. 20, 28
Sarv, I. 1036, 1040
Sasanaratana, M. 2505
Sasbout, M. 3035, 3039
Sasse, H. J. 1341, 2461, 2464, 2466, 2468f.
Sassu Frescura, M. 2886
Sastry, J.V. 3102, 3106
Šāsvata 2489
Šatèrnik, M.V. 2336f.
Sathirasut, L. 2506
Sato, I. 3116, 3118
Satō, K. 2623
Satta, L. 1216, 1868
Sattler, J.R. 1011, 1016, 1051, 1053, 1079, 2091, 2097
Satyaprakāśa 3102, 3106
Sauer, Chr. 359
Sauer, G. 2398
Šauer, V. 2283
Sauer, W. W. 11, 18, 2092, 2100f., 2191f., 2241
Sauger-Préneuf, F. 1803, 1806, 1809
Saukkonen, P. 1669, 2385-2387
Saulnier, V.-L. 62, 1812
Saur, K.G. 1261, 1265, 3172
Saur, K.O. 3174
Saura, S. 1773, 1786
Saussure, F. de 318, 342, 411, 419, 501, 617, 749, 850, 855, 888, 893, 991, 1045, 1075, 1093, 1144, 1146f., 1429, 1700, 3149
Saussy, G.St. 1207, 1209

Sauter, Chr. 1137, 1139, 1643, 2184, 2217
Sauvage, J. 3070
Sauvageot, A. 1018, 1321, 1356, 1363, 1835, 2378, 2382
Sauvagerd, K. 2199, 2201, 2229
Savage, St. 2574f.
Savage, W. 2959
Savard, J.-G. 1321, 1356, 1364
Savary des Bruslons, J. 165, 167, 1801, 1809, 1816
Savatkova, A. 2397
Savel'eva, V. N. 2630f.
Savelli, A. 2994f.
Säves, C. 1939, 1942
Säves, P.A. 1939, 1942
Savidis, Chr. 1125
Savigneau, J. 41, 46
Savigny, E. von 539, 541, 582, 853, 855
Savigny, F.C. von 539, 541, 582, 853, 855
Savin, E. 1002, 1004, 1007, 2770, 2774, 2853
Savonese, G.B. 1844
Savukynas, B. 1286, 1290
Savvaitov, P.I. 2395, 2398
Sawers, E.-M. 2853
Sawers, R. 2853, 2968
Saxild, P. 2029
Sāyana 2490
Sazoṅova, I. 2324
Scafoglio, D. 88
Scaglione, A. 79
Scapula, J. 13, 16, 1698, 1703
Scargill, M.H. 641
Scarry, R. 1368
Scatori, S. 2887
Scavnicky, G.E.A. 1142
Ščepkin, V. 2305
Ščerba, L. V. 112, 118, 126, 132, 172, 174, 980, 1562, 2313, 2321, 2328, 2715f., 2728, 2765, 2829, 2836, 2840, 2854, 2896, 2903, 3080-3083, 3085
Ščerbak, A.M. 2410
Ščerbin, V. K. 3083, 3085
Schaal, R. 1261, 1265
Schaar, J. van der 1270, 1274
Schade, M. K. B. 3016, 3018
Schade, O. 1395, 1414, 1418, 1420, 1423, 1426, 1428, 2088, 2097
Schade, W. 2765f., 2824
Schadeberg, Th. 2645
Schadeberg, Th. C. 2647, 2649
Schaden-Turba, R. 1140
Schadewaldt, W. 1562
Schaechter, M. 2249f., 2252, 2254
Schaeder, B. 115, 126, 199, 200f., 206-208, 211, 214, 246, 249-252, 258, 269, 277, 312f.,

321, 371, 407, 460, 614, 688, 693, 868, 921, 930, 988f., 991, 995, 998, 1017, 1322, 1531, 1573, 1595f., 1609f., 1624, 1631, 1639-1645, 1672, 2101, 2131, 2134, 2191, 2192, 2233, 2241, 3167
Schaefer, G.H. 1132, 1142
Schäfer, A. 2908
Schäfer, C. 245
Schäfer, G.H. 1130
Schäfer, J. 8, 18, 229f., 1206, 1209, 1452, 1456f., 1532, 1537, 1946, 1950, 1953, 1963, 1966, 2229
Schäfer, W. 2751
Schäfers, B. 206
Schaldach, H. 848
Schallman, L. 1763
Schank, G. 815, 822
Schank, R.C. 893f., 899, 1670
Schanski, N. 1362
Schapera, J. 2650, 2655
Scharfenberger, W. 2636, 2638
Scharfstein, S. (= Šarfšṭeyn) 2430, 2436
Scharnhorst, J. 78, 206, 274, 653, 656, 694, 696, 699
Schatz, J. 1560
Schatz, L. 1352
Schauer, G.K. 407
Schaufelbüel, A. 2920, 2933
Schauffler, W.G. 1906
Schaw, A. D. 2468
Schay, H. 269
Schebeck, B. 2639-2641
Scheel, W. 2222
Schéfer, P. 1079, 1221, 1223
Schei, J.D. 3144
Scheidt, B. 1155
Schein, J.D. 3141-3144
Scheingraber, G. 1261, 1265
Scheitz, E. 1261, 1265
Schelbert, D. 2766
Schelbert, T. 582
Scheler, A. 1198, 1328, 1333
Scheler, M. 1168, 1178, 1245, 1597, 1610
Schellbach-Kopra, I. 1023f., 1030, 1038, 1041
Scheller, I. J. G. 1717, 2376, 3030, 3032, 30?
Scheller, M. 1702
Schellhorn, A. 1034, 1041
Schellingius, D. 1791, 2928
Schemann Dias, L. 1025, 1030, 2817, 3025f., 3029
Schemann, H. 269, 1020f., 1025, 1030, 1032, 2174, 2176, 2178, 2179, 2182, 2229, 2816f., 2834, 3025f., 3029
Schenck, M. 2044
Schenckius, M. 2047

Schendels, E. 1353, 1364
Schendl, H. 1571, 1573
Schenk, W. 1006f., 1110,
    1312-1314, 2322, 2896, 2900
Schenkel, W. 114, 124, 739f., 747,
    1001, 1004, 1088, 1615, 1622,
    2171, 2172, 2173, 2222, 2237,
    2243, 2770, 2774
Schepisi, G. 2997
Scheppelmann, Th. 1110f.
Schepping, M.-Th. 162f., 583,
    2880f.
Scherber, P. 2300f.
Scherer, A. 2473
Scherer, W. 2091, 2100
Scherfer, P. 186, 189, 716, 726,
    1357f., 1364
Schermair, A. 2674, 2676, 2704
Scherner, M, 554, 583, 947, 955
Schertel, A. 1261, 1265
Scherwinsky 1125
Scherzinger, J.A. 3129, 3134
Scherzius, J.G. 1235, 1239, 1601,
    1609
Scheuch, E. 1632, 1638
Scheuerl, Chr. 1572
Scheuermann, U. 245
Schewe, W.H.U. 321
Schiaffini, A. 1867
Schiaparelli, C. 3087, 3095
Schieb, G. 1549-1551, 1554, 1556,
    1560
Schieder, Th. 2241
Schiefelbein, H. 1102, 1294, 1296
Schiefenhövel, W. 2636f.
Schiefner, A. 2396f., 2630
Schieke, H. 1352, 2185, 2229
Schiendorfer, M. 1573
Schierholz, St. 2160, 2241
Schiff, M. 1047, 1049
Schifko, P. 544, 546, 583
Schildt, J. 78, 127, 163, 174, 274f.,
    278, 321, 359, 408, 460, 500,
    578, 580, 584, 599, 614, 626f.,
    655, 699, 779, 782, 787, 835,
    854, 868, 881f., 893, 1009,
    1019, 1031, 1230, 1645, 1671,
    2237f., 2243, 2727, 2760, 2766,
    2853
Schiller, E. 2546
Schiller, F. 22, 1237, 3122, 3137
Schiller, Fr. 1044
Schiller, K. 1418-1420, 1422,
    1424-1426, 1428, 2088, 2097
Schiller, K. M. 1130, 2184, 2230
Schils, G. H. 2652, 2654
Schimitzek, St. 3065, 3067
Schimpff, J.W. 1368
Schincke, J.Chr.G. 1269, 1274
Schindler, U. 3169
Schindler, V. 2427, 2433
Schinke-Llano, L. 214

Schippan, Th. 79, 247, 277, 653,
    656, 693, 699, 1531, 1672
Schirmer, A. 69, 821, 1323, 1333,
    2062, 2072, 2217, 2223
Schirokauer, A. 2045, 2048, 2050,
    2077
Schischkoff, A. 2918, 2933
Schischkoff, G. 118, 124
Schlachter, W. 2391, 2398
Schlademann, R. 3169
Schlaefer, M. 543-545, 583,
    1132-1135, 1143, 1147, 1149,
    1152, 1234, 1241, 1600, 1605,
    1610, 2091, 2100, 2104, 2241
Schläfer, W. 2748
Schlanbusch, A. 2660
Schlandt, H. 2378, 2382
Schlauch, M. 517
Schlaug, W. 1268, 1274
Schlechta-Wessehrd, O. de 2402,
    2406
Schlee, G. 2464, 2468
Schleef, W. 2198, 2229
Schlegelmilch, A. 3005
Schlegelmilch, H. 5, 16
Schleicher, A. 1337
Schleiermacher, F. 1020
Schlepper, W. 269
Schlerath, B. 2471f.
Schlesinger, I.M. 3142, 3144
Schlessing, A. 1089, 1092, 2086f.,
    2094, 2098
Schleyer, J.M. 3121, 3129, 3134,
    3137
Schlick, W. 1356, 1364
Schlieben-Lange, B. 269, 687,
    754, 1054-1056, 1121, 1125,
    1522, 1817, 1892, 2960
Schlimmer, L. 2479
Schlimpert, G. 1268, 1274
Schlipf, W. 2766, 2988f., 2991
Schlobinski, P. 2199, 2229
Schlueter, F. 2058
Schlüter, F. 1074, 3125, 3134
Schmalz, J.H. 17, 223, 1220, 1722
Schmarsow, A. 245
Schmeja, H. 584
Schmeller, J.A. 221, 223, 239,
    242f., 1234, 1239, 1284, 1290,
    1393, 1414, 2060, 2072, 2074,
    2988, 2991
Schmid, A. 1287, 1289f., 2766
Schmid, E.A. 2987f., 2990
Schmid, H. 1288, 1900, 1905
Schmid, J. 1563, 1567
Schmid, J. Chr. 2061, 2072
Schmid, M.J.Chr. 238f., 243
Schmid, W.P. 1285, 1288-1291
Schmidlin, J.J. 2999, 3005, 3007
Schmidmaier, D. 3171
Schmidt, A. 1436, 1452, 1455,
    1457, 1549f., 1553, 1557, 1560,
    2192, 2224

Schmidt, Ch. 1393, 1414
Schmidt, D. 1290
Schmidt, E. 117, 125
Schmidt, G.D. 276, 881f., 1178,
    1230, 2241
Schmidt, H. 118, 124, 532, 534,
    540, 550, 553, 557, 562, 583,
    773, 779, 843, 848f., 882, 1402,
    1416, 1540, 1549, 2031, 2035,
    2220, 2241
Schmidt, I. 2968
Schmidt, I. A. E. 3076
Schmidt, J. 186, 188, 1103f., 1111,
    2219, 2492, 2636, 2638, 2917,
    2933
Schmidt, J. A. E. 3078
Schmidt, J.H.H. 1074
Schmidt, J.J. 3092, 3095
Schmidt, K.Chr.L. 238, 243
Schmidt, K.H. 1341, 2340, 2342f.
Schmidt, K.M. 1066
Schmidt, L. 1047, 1049
Schmidt, M. 1703, 2229
Schmidt, P. 269, 1548
Schmidt, R. 868
Schmidt, S.J. 426, 460
Schmidt, V. 661, 837, 841, 882,
    887
Schmidt, W. 250, 273, 836, 841,
    843, 849, 1353, 1364, 2638
Schmidt, W. P. 2272
Schmidt-Hidding, W. 1038, 1041
Schmidt-Joos, S. 2185, 2229
Schmidt-Küntzel, M. 2957, 2960
Schmidt-Petersen, J. 2030, 2035
Schmidt-Radefeldt, J. 2756
Schmiedel, F. L. 2058, 2072
Schmitson, A. 10734
Schmitt, A. 407, 2224
Schmitt, Chr. 652f., 656, 662f.,
    665, 668, 1195, 1199
Schmitt, E. 214, 1056, 1816f.
Schmitt, H. 2199, 2229
Schmitt, J. 2059, 2072
Schmitt, L.E. 127, 239, 245, 279,
    322, 359, 408, 461, 500, 576,
    582, 586, 626, 628, 688, 849,
    999, 1258, 1334
Schmitt, P. 1609, 2035f., 2039,
    2047, 2075, 2214, 2232, 2245
Schmitt, P.A. 313, 321
Schmitt, R. 1142, 1347,
    2470-2473, 2495
Schmitter, P. 2211, 2230
Schmitthenner, F. 2079, 2085,
    2097f.
Schmitz, B. 1052f.
Schmitz, K.D. 1651, 1668f.
Schmitz, S. 2766, 2856, 2859
Schmitz, U. 1266
Schmuck, A. 2766, 2809, 2813
Schmutz, J. F. 2276f.

Schneeberger, F. 3131
Schneider, F. 1056, 2880f.
Schneider, G. 188, 2776
Schneider, J.G. 1698f., 1703
Schneider, L. 2632-2634
Schneider, M. 1074
Schneider, Th. 1139
Schneidewin, F.W. 1033, 1040
Schnell, B. 18, 1813, 2038, 2040, 2047f.
Schnelle, H. 412, 428, 460, 547, 583
Schnellenbach, E. 1532, 1538
Schnerrer, R. 2235
Schnitzler, S. 2188, 2229
Schnorr, V. 214, 2718, 2728, 2766, 2824, 2841, 2854, 2870
Schober, J. 2185, 2229
Schoen, Th. 2989f.
Schoenhals, A. 2697f., 2700
Schoenhals, L. C. 71, 77, 2697f., 2700, 2752, 2766
Schoensleder, W. 1011, 1016
Schoeps, H.-J. 1046, 1049
Schöffer, P. 2048
Schöffler, H. 2968
Schogt, H.G. 780, 787
Schokker, H.N. 2937, 2939, 2947
Scholart, L. 2462, 2468
Scholfield, Ph. 208-210, 214
Scholfield, Ph.J. 105, 111, 552, 583
Scholl, Ch. 1052f.
Scholler, H. 78, 668, 703, 1630
Scholz, A. 245, 2050, 2061, 2077
Scholz, B. 3073, 3084
Scholz, F. 1334
Scholz, H. 547, 583
Scholz, H.-J. 2207, 2211, 2229
Scholze-Stubenrecht, W. 123, 1112, 2751
Schön, J. F. 2458, 2460
Schon, P.M. 592
Schönberger, F.X. 1157
Schöne, A. 101, 134f., 279, 408, 578f., 586, 599, 1031, 1102, 1241, 1562, 1573, 2100, 2235, 2238, 2244, 2760, 2767, 2782, 3151, 3136
Schöne, M. 1823
Schonell, F. 1315
Schönfeld, E. 1530
Schönfeld, M. 1286, 1290, 1294, 1296
Schönfeldt, A. 1251, 1254
Schoonees, P. C. 2019-2022
Schophaus, R. 2061, 2077
Schoppe 2217
Schöpper, J. 1059, 1065, 1076, 1079f., 2058, 2072
Schopper, K. 1103f., 1108f., 1111
Schorer, Chr. 1177

Schorr, G. 2766
Schorus, A. 1011, 1016, 1051, 1053, 1081, 1083
Schott, G. 1149f., 1152
Schottel, G. 2052f.
Schottel, J. G. 644, 2051, 3014
Schottelius, J.G. 231-234, 245, 1149, 1151, 1232, 1241, 2065, 2077
Schrader, Chr.F. 2999, 3066
Schrader, H. 1036, 1041
Schraeder, B. 3167
Schraffl, I. 1053
Schramm, F. 1205
Schramm, K. 2199, 2229
Schranka, E.M. 1294, 1296
Schregle, G 3095, 2766
Schreiber, H. 178, 180, 1005, 1008, 2171, 2230, 2242, 2770, 2774
Schreiber, J. 2450, 2453
Schreier-Hornung, A. 1531
Schrenck, L. von 2628, 2630
Schrenke, J. 2327
Schröder, F. E. 2486
Schröder, J. 1221, 1223, 2188, 2229
Schröder, K. 115, 126, 181, 185, 188f., 214, 1359, 1364, 2895, 2903
Schröder, R. 1609, 2218
Schröder, W. 1572f., 1905, 2049
Schroderus Vpsaliensis, E.J. 1933, 1935, 1942,
Schroderus, E. 2384, 2387, 2913, 2933
Schröer, A. 119, 126, 220, 224, 2766, 2968
Schröer, M.M.A. 1293, 1296, 1308, 1310
Schroeter, W. 652, 656
Schröpfer, J. 171, 173, 1059, 1063, 1065-1067, 1392, 1412-1414
Schröter, D. 2220
Schröter, T. 2220
Schröter, U. 1400, 1416, 2081, 2100
Schröter, W. 804, 2053, 2072, 2077
Schrowe, Th. 3084
Schrupp, Ch. 272, 358, 405, 574, 1622, 2219
Schubert, A. 668, 2192, 2241
Schubert, K. 1262f., 1265, 2188, 2229
Schubert, W. 1562
Schubring, W. 2503, 2507
Schuchardt, H. 732, 749, 1343, 1767, 2871
Schuchhard, H. 1242f., 1245
Schuck-Wersig, P. 277, 408, 627
Schueren, G. van der 2047, 2072
Schuermans, L. W. 2018, 2021

Schuh, R. G. 2458, 2460
Schukry, K. 3095
Schulenburg, S. von der 2060, 2077
Schüler, G. 3169
Schulte-Kemminghausen, K. 1065, 1076, 1079f.
Schulthess, F.P. 1939, 1942, 2437, 3041
Schultz, F. 1074
Schultz, G. 1294, 1296
Schultz-Lorentzen, C. W. 2632, 2634, 2692, 2696
Schultze-Jena, L. 2662, 2664, 2669
Schulz, D. 796, 1029, 2174, 2221, 2229
Schulz, H. 405, 458, 770, 1139, 1149, 1151, 1174f., 1177, 2068, 2218
Schulz, W. 2766
Schulze, B. 2398
Schulze, C. 1033, 1036, 1041
Schulze, E. 1909f., 1912
Schulze, H. 2064
Schulze, H.H. 266, 273, 1516f., 1519f., 1522
Schulze, J. P. 2271
Schulze, R. 188, 580, 587, 3166
Schulze, U. 1539, 1544, 1548f., 1609, 2104, 2232, 2241
Schulze, W. 362, 370, 407
Schulze-Busacker, E. 1036, 1041
Schumacher, H. 114, 123, 273, 278, 408, 460, 499, 575, 585, 771, 1001, 1004f., 1007, 1009, 1067, 1221, 1223, 1355, 1364, 1620, 1622, 1624, 2171, 2220, 2236, 2242, 2770, 2774
Schumann, B. 2150, 2242
Schumann, Ch. L. 2871
Schumann, H.-G. 841, 1205
Schumann, H.B. 653, 656f.
Schumann, O. 2663f., 2669
Schunck, P. 787
Schupp, V. 135
Schur, N.W. 1207, 1209
Schüren, G. van der 2050
Schurmann, H.F. 2412
Schuster-Šewc, H. 2275-2277
Schütz, A. 269, 592
Schütz, G. 1770
Schütz, I. 2366
Schütze, G. 1155
Schütze, J. F. 2061, 2072
Schütze, R. 1230, 1672, 2221
Schützeichel, R. 154, 158f., 1253, 1272, 1281, 1284, 1418-1420, 1422, 1426, 1428, 1539, 1544, 1548, 2104, 2229, 2242
Schuver, J. M. 2463, 2468
Schvaneveldt, J.D. 102, 109f.
Schwabe, B. 2092, 2096

Schwake, H.-P. 269, 1343, 1348
Schwan, Chr.F. 2737, 2751, 2999f., 3006f., 3015
Schwanwitz, M. 3074
Schwartz, R.J. 1262f., 1265
Schwartze, R. 1817, 2936
Schwartzenbach, L. 3, 1060f., 1066, 1076, 1080, 2050, 2058, 2072, 2074
Schwarz, A. 2217, 3124, 3137
Schwarz, C.M. 1080, 1092
Schwarz, H. 2886
Schwarz, J. A. T. 2566f.
Schwarz, J.C.P. 1144f.
Schwarz, J.K. 1221
Schwarz, W. 1137, 1142
Schwarz-Mackensen, G. 687, 747
Schwarz-Winkelhofer, I. 3152, 3157
Schwarzbard, J. 2253
Schwarze, C. 189, 726, 997f.
Schwarze, Chr. 125, 275, 407, 577, 580, 583, 627, 654, 668, 858, 862, 980, 1031, 1093, 1283, 1311, 1364, 2222, 2235, 2257, 2879, 2881, 1887, 3030
Schwarzer, Chr. 573
Schwauß, M. 1752, 1763, 2989
Schweickard, W. 3013, 3019
Schweikle, G. 152, 157, 159
Schweikle, I. 159
Schweizer, J. C. 2215, 2229
Schwenck, K. 2089, 2097
Schwertner, S. 1261, 1265
Schwickert, E. B. 2988, 3015
Schwitalla, J. 815, 822
Schwob, M. 1533, 1538
Schwyzer, E. 1695, 1704
Sciarone, A.G. 1321, 1362, 2766
Scobar, s. Escobar 1849
Scobar, L.Chr. 9, 16, 1845, 1849, 1860f., 1862
Scobare Bethico, Chr. 1740, 1758
Scoppa, L.G. 1862
Scoppa, L.I. 1845, 1860
Scott, D. C. 2648
Scott, G. 2636, 2638
Scott, H.M. 3129, 3134
Scott, I.N. 1159
Scott, J.N. 720, 7231946, 1952, 1988, 2008
Scott, R. 1133, 1699f., 1702f.
Scott, W. 754, 1984
Screen, J. E. O. 3030
Scriban, A. 1886, 1889
Sctrick, R. 1294
Seabra, M. de 1776, 1786
Seaman, W. 2400, 2406
Searle, J.R. 813-816, 818-820, 822
Searle, W.G. 1274
Sears, B. 1089, 1092
Seaton, A. 1090, 1092

Seaton, M.A. 1076, 1080
Sebastatsi, M. 2368
Sebastiani, G. 3167
Sebastiatsi, M. 2371
Sebeok, Th. A. 230, 276, 972, 980, 1766, 2009, 2395, 2398, 2433, 2533, 2641, 2686, 2690, 2706
Séchan, L. 1699, 1702
Seche, L. 141, 145, 1080, 1888
Seche, M. 141, 145, 1881-1884, 1886, 1888, 1890
Sechehaye, A. 1429
Sechia, B. 1896, 1904
Seckendorff, Th. von 2988, 2990
Seco, M. 88, 921, 930, 1216, 1348, 1352, 1738, 1741, 1743, 1745f., 1748-1750, 1763, 1767, 1770, 2986
Sedaj, E. 2365
Sedat, G. 2663, 2669
Sedelow, S.Y. 1573
Sedláček, J. 2282f.
Seebold, E. 115, 126, 530, 1334, 1337, 1341, 2106, 2131, 2136, 2159, 2193, 2195, 2223, 2242
Seel, P.C. 174
Seemann, St. R. 3126f., 3135
Šeerer, V. V. 3077
Seetzen, U. J. 2457, 2461, 2468
Seewald, P. 2358, 2361
Segal, M.H. 2431, 2436
Segar, M. 1943, 1953
Segebade, J. 1561
Segert, St. 1690, 1693f., 2427, 2431, 2433, 2437f., 2467
Segeth, W. 539, 583
Seghers, P. 1207, 1209
Sègneri, P. 1854
Segovia, L. 1753, 1763
Segoviano, C. 1767, 2766
Seguier, J. de 1734
Seguin, G. 1812, 1817
Seguin, J.-P. 80, 83, 88, 652, 1802, 1804, 1812
Séguin, R.-L. 1193
Sehnert, J. A. 2271, 2274
Sehrt, E.H. 154, 158f., 1418-1420, 1425, 1428, 1551, 1561
Sehwers, J. 2357, 2361
Seibicke, W. 321, 1147, 1152, 1166f., 1184, 1191-1193, 1268, 1271, 1275, 1296, 1556, 1562, 2062, 2077, 2135, 2187, 2229, 2242
Seidel, A. 2463, 2468
Seidel, K.O. 159
Seidel-Slotty, I. 1363
Seidensticker, P. 2104, 2242
Seidl, H. 1036, 1043
Seidler, M. 835
Seidner-Weiser, M. 2885
Seiler, F. 1034, 1036, 1041, 1043, 2065f., 2077

Seiler, G.A. 119f., 124
Sèité, V. 2350
Sējēja, K. 2359
Sejong 2611
Séjournant, M. de 2917, 2934, 2979, 2985, 2987
Seka, J. 2293
Sekaninová, E. 2286
Sekelj, A. 3135
Seki, S. 3114, 3118
Sel'kov, N.N. 2397f.
Seldon, A. 1516-1518, 1522, 1763
Seligman, E.R.A. 165f.
Sell, E. 2394
Səllase, T. 2450
Seltén, B. 3049, 3051
Semenov-Rudnev (Damaskin), D. 2396
Semichov, B. V. 2550
Sen, N. 2497
Sen, P. 3103
Sen, R. K. 2510, 2518
Sen, S. 2510, 2518
Sen, Y. 2516, 2521
Šendecov, V.V. 764f., 2315, 2322
Senerth, D. 2953, 2955
Sengebusch, M. 1699, 1703
Senisio, A. 1844, 1849, 1861f.
Senn, A. 2352f.
Senokuchi, T. 3116f.
Seoane, M. 2951f., 2955
Sepamaa, H. 3126, 3135
Sephila, H.V. 1906f.
Šepić, A. 2292
Šepić-Tomin, A. 2295
Seppänen, L. 551, 583
Sequin, J.-P. 657
Serain, D. 1670
Šěrakowa, I. 2276, 2278
Séré, A. 1115, 1119
Serébrennikow, B. A. 2828
Serebriakov, I.D. 3101, 3106
Serenius, J. 1935, 1942, 2916, 2934, 3040, 3042, 3047, 3049f.
Seresser, N.B. 3094f.
Sergeev, V.N. 2315, 2321, 2328
Sergent, A. 3010, 3012
Sergievsky, N.N. 2325
Serguine, J. 1349, 1352
Serianni, L. 1865, 1880
Serís, H. 1743, 1751, 1767, 2936f., 2947
Sermain, J.-P. 607, 1817
Serpa, O. 1030, 3022, 3029
Serra Estruch, J. 1778, 1786
Serra, F. 1011, 1016
Serra-Caraccioli, P. 2462, 2468
Serralonga y Guasch, L.G. 1778, 1783
Serrano Aybar, C. 1698, 1702, 1704
Serrano, N.M. 1746, 1763

Serranus, J. 1080
Serraris, P.A. 2939, 2947
Serre, R. 2766
Serrey, J. 2934
Servilius, J. 2913f., 2934
Servortjan, E.V. 2409
Serzisko, F. 2466f., 2469
Seşācāryulu, K. 3106, 3097, 3099
Sese, B. 1763
Sésé, B. 2982, 2985
Sessa, M. 1855, 1862
Setälä, V. 3127, 3135
Seth, I. 3043, 3047
Seṭhna, R.P. 3101, 3106
Sethupillai, R. P. 2530, 2532
Šetka, J. 2293, 2295
Seton-Watson, R.W. 2975
Seufert, G. 976, 980
Seura, S.K. 2387
Seuren, P.A.M. 3167
Seux, M.-J. 1684f.
Ševčenko, T. 1550f., 1553, 1557, 1561
Ševcova, S. V. 524, 747, 2896, 2901
Sève, A. 1211f., 1216
Ševeleva, M.S. 2319, 2325
Séville, I. de 1789 (s. Isidor)
Sevortjan, Ė.V. 1341, 2404, 2406, 2413f.
Seward, R. D. 2886
Sewel, W. 2934f., 3037-3039, 3073
Seybold, Chr. F. 2674f., 3087, 3095
Seybold, J. G. 2065, 2072
Seydel, S. 1703
Seydewitz, G. von 2076
Sezemana, D. V. 126, 2728
Sezgin, F. 2445, 2448
Sferrazzo, A. 1008
Sfirlea, L. 1890
Shadily, H. 2563, 2565
Shafer, R. 2558
Shahidullah, M. 2510, 2518
Shaikevich, A. 2766
Shaikh, S. 3093, 3095
Shaked, Y. 1669
Shakespear, J. 2512, 2519
Shakespeare, W. 22, 1044, 1451, 1455, 1949, 1960, 3122, 3137
Shalu chögyong sang bo 2548
Shāmlū, Ahmad 2479
Shanker, U. 1669
Shann, P. 3166
Shapiro, M. 2251, 2253
Shapur, Edalji 2518
Sharaf, M. 3092, 3095
Sharbatov, G.S. 3029, 3095
Sharma, B. C. 2517
Sharma, B. R. 2496
Sharma, L.K.N. 3106
Sharma, N. 3100

Sharma, O.V. 3097-3099, 3106
Sharma, S. M. 2504
Sharp, H.S. 1296
Sharpe, P. A. 2766
Shastre, D. 2504
Shastri, V. B. 2495
Shaw, A. D. 2463
Shaw, H. 1216
Shaw, M. 2664, 2669
Shaw, R. 2411
Shaw, W. 2346, 2348
Sheehy, E.P. 3174
Sheffield, A.D. 1080
Sheikian, M. 709, 725
Shejkovs'kyj, K. 2330, 2334
Sheldon, E.A. 1874
Sheldon, E.K. 509, 518,
Shell, O. 2703
Shen, Q. 3112
Shenker, I. 31, 34f., 38. 2004, 2009
Shepherd, V. M. 2480
Sheppard, C.A. 3100, 3106
Sheppard, H.E. 1100, 1002, 1263, 1265
Sheridan, Th. 29, 509, 1308, 1310, 1955, 1966, 1988, 2004, 2008, 2969
Shertl, M. 2251, 2253
Sherwood, P. 2766
Sherwood, R. 2957, 2959f., 2971, 2975
Sheth, H. D. T. 2505
Shevelov, G.Y. 2334
Shiaty, A.E. 61
Shibata, M. 3114, 3118
Shibata, T. 3115, 3118
Shimada, Y. 3114f., 3118
Shimbo, M. 2104, 2229
Shimizu, K. 1340-1342
Shimmura, I. 2620, 2622
Shimonaka, Y. 2621
Shintani, T.L.A. 2591, 2593
Shipley, J.T. 1333
Shipp, G.P. 1711, 1713
Shirt, G. 2516, 2520
Shitnikov, B.N. 2410, 2414
Shiv Pujan 2538
Shney, B. 2823
Shōjū 2618, 2623
Short, Ch. 151, 3032, 3034
Short, D.D. 1573
Shorto, H.L. 2591, 2593
Shriyan, R.N. 2499, 2503, 2505
Shroyer, E.H. 3144
Shroyer, S.P. 3144
Shu Xincheng 2601, 2610
Shukurov, M. 2480
Shulman, M. 2251, 2253
Şiadbei, I. 1891
Sialm, A. 599, 831, 834, 1020, 1031, 1042, 1044
Sibbald, J. 1983, 1986

Siber, A. 2044, 2047
Sibermann. A.M. 2436
Sicard, R.-A.C. 3142, 3144
Sicilia, M.J. 1074
Sick, Chr. 3054, 3061
Sickel, K. E. 2055, 2077
Siddhattha, V. 2504
Sidorenko, M. M. 3082
Sidorenko, M.I. 2315, 2325
Sieb, Th. 2030
Siebelis, J. 1550, 1561
Siebenmann, G. 1759
Siebenschein, H. 747, 2282f., 2727, 2761
Sieber, A. 3045f.
Siebs, B. E. 2028
Siebs, Th. 1308, 1310, 2029f., 2035, 2093, 2097
Siebzehner-Vivanti, G. 1561
Siedhof, K.F.W. 1011, 1016
Siedlecka, I. 3176
Siegert, R. 2061, 2077
Siegl, E. A. 2191, 2242
Siegler, J. J. 3058, 3061
Siegrist, L. 2855, 2859
Siekmann, J. 899
Siepmann, H. 854
Siesso y Bolea, J. de 1742, 1763
Sievers, E. 157, 159, 510, 518
Sigalés, J.M. 1778, 1786
Sigmundsson, S. 1931
Sigurd, B. 1933, 1942f.
Sīka, N. 2360
Silbermann, A. 1520, 1522
Siliakus, H.J. 1356, 1364, 1631
Silin, V.L. 616, 627
Sillner, L. 2174, 2176, 2229
Sills, D.L. 166
Silva Fuenzalida, I. 2664, 2669
Silva, A. de Moraes 1723, 1727, 1729-1732, 1734f.
Silva, E. 1312, 1314
Silva, E.C. da 1189
Silva, I.F. da 1728, 1735
Silvagni, U. 1867, 1879
Silve, C.G. 980
Silveira, Bueno, F. da 2704
Silverthorn, J.E. 1302f.
Silvester, G. 2185, 2230
Silvet, J. 2394f.
Silzer, E. 1111
Sim, D. 106, 109f., 213, 1632, 1637
Simai, K. 2376f., 2382
Simard, C. 1368
Simčenko, J.B. 2397
Simcox, C.E. 1044, 1049
Simeon, R. 2293, 2295
Siméon, R. 2658-2661
Šimhevič, F. S. 3075, 3084
Simmons, R.F. 1670
Simões, G.A. 1030
Simon 1842

Simón, F.P. 1751, 1767
Simon, I. 1946, 1953
Simon, I. M. 2559
Simon, R. 1801
Simon, W. 1341, 3113
Simone, F. 1863, 3013
Simonescu, D. 1891
Simoni, Z. 2365f.
Simonin, A. 1185, 1189
Simonis, J. 2434
Simonsen, V.L. 1922
Simonsfeld, H. 3019
Simonyi, Z. 2382
Simpson 3173
Simpson, A.S. 1609
Simpson, J. 1080, 1092, 1670
Simpson, J.A. 1414, 1548, 1966
Simpson, J.B. 1049
Simrock, K. 1034f., 1041
Simrock, K. J. 2065, 2072
Šimunović, P. 2292, 2294
Sinaites, J. 3069
Sinapian, K. 2402, 2406
Şincai, G. 1882
Sinclair, J. 96f., 904, 1367, 1385, 1387, 1389, 1621, 1624
Sinclair, J.M. 267, 270, 277, 578, 580, 917, 1018, 1670, 2805, 2813, 3167
Sinclair, J.McH. 1652, 1667
Sinclair, L. A. 2751
Sindou, R. 1282, 1284
Sinesis, Ph. 2615, 2617
Singer, S. 1038, 1041
Singh, B. K. 2516, 2520
Singh, B. M. 2515, 2520
Singh, R. A. 2521, 3107
Singh, S. 3100f.
Singh, T. 2515
Singha, G. 3100, 3106
Singha, S. 3100, 3106
Sinha, N. K. 2545
Šink, F. 2301
Sinnemäki, M. 2385, 2387
Sinor, D. 1141, 2398, 2413
Sintenis, C.H. (Sintenisius) 1011, 1016
Sintes Pros, J. 1047, 1049f., 1352
Sipma, P. 2024, 2026, 2035
Sîrbu, R. 1891
Sircar, D. Ch. 2503, 2505
Sirinelli, J.-F. 85, 87
Sirisaka, A. 2378, 2382
Sirisumedha, K. 2505
Siro, P. 2398
Širokova, L.J. 2324
Širvydas, K. 2351, 2353, 2360
Šiškov, A. S. 3075, 3078
Sisson, A.F. 1076, 1080
Sitapati, G. 2528
Sītārāmācāryulu, B. 2527, 2532
Sitta, H. 1623

Sivan, R. 2431, 2436
Sivrac, J. 2974
Siwicki, K. 3128, 3135
Six, B. 573, 576
Sjöbeck, J. C. 3047, 3049f.
Sjöberg, Å.W. 1684f.
Sjögreen, Chr. 1938
Sjögren, A. J. 2484, 2486
Sjögren, J.A. 2394f.
Sjölin, B. 2024f., 2032, 2035f.
Skačinskij, A. 2319, 2325
Skaftfell, B.B. 3127, 3135
Skála, E. 277
Škaljić, A. 2293, 2295
Skandasvāmin 2490
Skarbek, A. 1274
Skarđi, J. av 1930, 1932
Skautrup, P. 1918f., 1921f.
Skeat, W.W. 1245, 1328, 1333, 1436, 1444, 1447f., 1452f., 1455, 1910, 1912, 1962
Skeel, E.E. 3175
Skene, J. 1983, 1986
Skey, M. 2973, 2975
Skinner, A. N. 2459f.
Skinner, M. G. 2457, 2460
Skinner, St. 1440, 1455, 1948-1950, 1952, 1954
Skjærvø, P. O. 2470, 2473, 2476f.
Skljarov, M. 2294
Škljarov, V.T. 2315, 2325
Skok, P. 2293, 2295
Sköld, H. 2486
Skopina, M.A. 2316, 2328
Skorik, P. J. 2630f.
Skorokhod'ko, E.F. 1671
Skorupka, S. 1080, 2269f., 2273
Skrefsud, L. O. 2541
Skripecz, S. 2382
Skubalanka, T. 2271f.
Skupien, J. 1119
Skupy, H.-H. 1044, 1047, 1050
Skutsch, F. 2751
Skvorcov, L.I. 2323
Slaby, H. 1092, 1362, 2177, 2182, 2230
Slabý, R. J. 2798-2801, 2803, 2989f.
Slaby, W.A. 1138
Sladek, A. 269
Slangen, J.H. 236, 244f., 574
Slater, W.J. 1550f., 1561
Slatka, D. 43, 46
Slavíčková, E. 1134, 1138, 1142, 2281, 2284
Slavynec'kyj, E. 2329, 3071
Slavynec'kyj, J. 2334
Sławski, F. 1337, 1341, 2271, 2273
Sledd, J. 30f., 34f., 38, 764, 767, 1439, 1457, 1951, 1995, 2005, 2009
Sledd, J.H. 10, 18, 518, 1943, 1950, 1952f.

Sletsjöe, L. 1311
Slevogt, Chr.A.A. 1349,1352
Sloan, H.S. 1516f., 1520, 1522
Slocum, M. 2663, 2669
Slocum, M.C. 2706
Slotte, P. 1939, 1941
Slotty, F. 1342
Smailović, I. 2399, 2407
Smailus, O. 2664, 2669
Smal'-Stoc'kyj, R. 2334
Small, St. 1665, 1668
Small, St.L. 3167
Smalley, V.E. 2957, 2960
Smart, B.H. 1308, 1310, 3055
Smee, T. 2462, 2468
Šmeleva, I.N. 653, 657, 694, 699
Smet, G.A.R. de 653, 804, 830, 978, 980, 1132, 1138, 1158, 2042f., 2046f., 2048-2050, 2055, 2068, 2071, 2077, 2214f., 2233
Smetánka, E. 2281, 2283
Miešková, E. 2286f.
Smijters, A. 1011, 1016, 1019
Šmilauer, V. 2281, 2283f.
Smirnova, I. A. 2483, 2486
Smith, A. 165, 225, 1444, 1455
Smith, A. D. 2463, 2468
Smith, A.H. 1281, 1283
Smith, B.E. 1162, 1165, 2007, 3116, 3173
Smith, C. 2953
Smith, C.C. 2953, 2954f.
Smith, Ch.J. 1074, 1080f., 1083
Smith, D. 1367
Smith, E. 1054f.
Smith, E.C. 1269, 1271, 1273-1275
Smith, E.E. 573, 581, 3166
Smith, H. 2485f., 2501
Smith, H.P. 1074
Smith, J.P. 2432, 2437
Smith, J.W. 1217
Smith, K.D. 2591, 2593
Smith, L. 2918, 2934
Smith, N. 740, 748
Smith, P.M. 2957, 2960
Smith, Ph.H. 1142
Smith, R. 1046, 1050, 2590f., 2593
Smith, R. N. 2766
Smith, R.P. 2432, 2437
Smith, S.J. 2577, 2582
Smith, W. 3152, 3157
Smolik, W. 2715, 2728
Snegirev, M.I. 2325
Snell, B. 1700-1702, 1704
Snell-Hornby, M. 17f., 184, 189, 223, 275, 321, 359, 370, 581f., 1667, 1815, 2728, 2753, 2757, 2760f., 2764-68, 2775, 2857, 2859, 2880f., 2898, 2903, 3019
Snijman, F. J. 2022
Snow, C. 1617, 1624

Snyckers, A. 1110f., 1021, 1025, 1031
Snyder, W.H. 1290
Snyman, J. W. 2651, 2653-2655
Soares, A.J. de Macedo 1723, 1731, 1735
Soares, E. 1735
Sobeira, F.J. 1736
Sobejano, G. 1018
Soberanas i Lleó, A.-J. 2916, 2927, 2930, 2936
Soberanas, A.H. 1761
Soberanas, A.J. 1739, 1771f., 1773-1775, 1779, 1781, 1784, 1786-1788
Sobreira, F.J. 1738
Sobrino, F. 2917, 2978f., 2981-2983, 2985, 2987
Socin, A. 1268, 1274, 2061, 2077, 2481, 2486
Soden, W. von 1683-1685
Söderwall, K.F. 1934, 1942
Soeffner, H.G. 1152
Soergel, D. 1090, 1094, 1661, 1668, 1671
Soffritti, M. 174
Sog po lo tsaa ba mgon po skyobs 2549
Soglian, G. 1903, 1905
Sōgō, M. 2620, 2623, 3175
Söhns, F. 1186, 1189
Soida, E. 1142, 2358
Šojat, A. 2293
Sokoll, A.H. 1261, 1265
Sokolov 3140
Sokolov, P. 2311
Sokolov, P.I. 2325
Sokolova, V. St. 2485f.
Sola, M. 2953, 2955
Solano Constancio, F. 3022, 3029
Soldán y Unanue, P.P. 1755
Soldt, W. van 1694
Solé, C. 1767
Soler i Janer, J. 1779, 1786
Soler, S. 1778, 1786
Solf, K. D. 186, 188, 1103f., 1111, 2219
Solganik, G.J. 2320, 2324
Solin, H. 1268, 1274
Solís, E. 2663, 2669
Sölken, H. 2457
Söll, L. 653, 657, 663, 668
Solms, H.-J. 1423, 1429
Solnit, D. 2559
Solomon, R.C. 853, 855
Solon 3
Solschenizin, A. 25
Soltau, D. W. 2058, 2072
Soltész Katalin, J. 2382
Som, O. V. 2908
Somābhīsīrī, S. 2506
Somer, W. 1948

Somers, H.L. 170
Somis, G. 1859
Sommant, M. 1164, 1206f., 1209
Sommaville, A. de 1860
Sommer, E. 1055, 1074, 1130
Sommer, J. 3126, 3131
Sommer, M. 1055
Sommer, U. 1139
Sommerfeldt, K. E. 178, 180, 956, 967, 1005, 1008, 2770, 2774, 2171, 2207, 2213, 2230, 2242, 2767
Sommerfelt, A. 532, 579, 1928, 2342
Sommerhoff, J.Chr. 2939, 2947
Somner, W. 1439f., 1442, 1455
Sonder, A. 1899, 1904
Sonderegger, St. 18, 111, 124, 126f., 154, 158f., 224, 243, 270, 278, 359, 408, 461, 500, 517, 582, 585, 667, 814, 821, 842, 981, 998, 1031, 1067, 1143, 1152, 1158, 1241, 1283f., 1291, 1416, 1435, 1531, 1549, 1562, 1572f., 1610, 1645, 2074, 2098, 2100, 2215, 2235, 2240, 2244,
Sondrup, St.P. 1567, 1573
Sontheimer, W. 158
Sonthirak, P. 2506
Sopher, G. 2043
Sophocles, E.A. 1706, 1713
Sora, F. 2767
Soral, A. 1532, 1537
Sorel, G. 1829
Soren, D. 2546
Soren, K. R. 2534, 2546
Soreng, J. B. 2542
Sörensen, A. 1127, 1130
Sørensen, F. 2760
Sørensen, I. 2901
Sørensen, J. 1664,1668
Sørensen, J.K. 1286, 1290
Sørensen, N. Chr. 3058, 3061
Sørensen, P.M. 1932
Sorensen, S. 2490, 2496
Sörenson, S. 1929, 1932
Sorin, R. 40, 45
Sorkin, M. 1349, 1351
Sornig, K. 697, 699
Sorokin, J.S. 2314f., 2321, 2323, 2328
Sorokina, Y.S. 1165
Sorokoletov, F.P. 2309-2311, 2313-2315, 2318f., 2328
Sorokoletov, V. P. 2751
Sorrento, L. 1849
Sosenko, Ė.J. 2316, 2328
Soto Ruiz, C. 2705
Sotomayor, B. de 2981
Soukup, J. 1763
Soule, R. 1080
Soulice, Th. 1004f., 1008, 1217, 1842

Soulkhanov, A. 2917, 2934
Sourvinou, C. 1703
Souto, M. 1535, 1537
Soy, N. 2536, 2545
Spada, G.B. 1011, 1016
Spagnol, E. 1047, 1050
Spagnola, Fr. L. 2644
Spalding, K. 1019, 1030, 2104, 2230, 2242, 2683
Spalier, M. 1079, 2224
Spang, R. 1290
Spangenberg, K. 242, 1531, 2234
Spanner, H. 3148
Spano, G. 1902, 1904
Sparkes, I.G. 976, 980, 1221, 1223
Sparkes, J.J. 515
Sparmann, H. 2242
Sparnaay, H. 1068, 1075
Sparwenfeld, J. G. 3071, 3083
Spasova, A. 2308
Spasova-Michailova, S. 2307
Spat, C. 2563, 2565
Spatuy, F. 2939, 2947
Spaulding, J. 2643f.
Spears, R.A. 214, 1535, 1537
Specht, G. 406
Spechtler, F.V. 1137, 1140
Speer, H. 1235, 1241, 1410, 1415f., 2206, 2218, 2242
Spegel, H. 1935f., 1942, 2916, 2934
Speidel, W. 1137, 1142
Speier, H.-M. 2763
Speiser, E.A. 1694
Spelman, H. 1439
Spencer, A. 1012, 1016
Spencer, H. 137-139, 142, 146
Spencer, N.J. 1617, 1624
Spenser, E. 1451
Spenter, A. 2024, 2027, 2036
Sperander (Pseudonym) 1172, 1177, 2063, 2072
Sperber, H. 838, 841
Sperber, R. 1290
Speroni, Ch. 1036, 1041, 2976
Spevack, M. 1564-1567
Spiegel, F. 2471, 2473, 2500
Spiegel, H.-R. 321
Spiers, A. 1308, 1310, 2938, 2947, 2958, 2960, 2972
Spies, G. 1258
Spiewok, W. 2207f., 2213, 2230
Spillner, B. 562, 583
Spillner, P. 1261f., 1264f.
Spinelli, N. 2973, 2975
Spinelli, V. 3022, 3029
Spinoza, B. 1873
Spiro-Bey, S. 3090, 3095
Spitler, H. 2464, 2466
Spitler, K. A. 2464, 2466
Spitzer, C. 1099
Spitzer, L. 21f., 28, 1020, 1032

Spivak, E. 2251, 2253
Spivak, K. 2252f.
Splett, J. 269, 1146, 1150, 1152, 1234, 1241, 2037, 2049, 2104, 2242
Splettstößer, W. 2155, 2157, 2166, 2168, 2230
Spohn, W. 581
Spohr, O. M. 2653, 2655
Spooner, A. 1368
Sporon, B.G. 1068, 1074
Sporschil, J. 2968
Sporta, S. 2407
Spranger, U. 1261, 1265
Sprengel, K. 544f., 583, 1813
Springer, O. 1623, 2220, 2226, 2853, 2968f.
Springhetti, A. 1243, 1245
Sprissler, M. 955, 1522
Sprudzs, A. 1261, 1265
Spurrell, W. 2347, 2349
Spyrka, I. 653, 657, 699, 2150, 2242
Squarotti, G.B. 692
Squitier, K. 1704
Šraaten, A.G. J. van 3126
Šrámek, R. 1556, 1562, 2282f.
Sreznevskij, I. I. 2264, 2267, 2309, 2318f., 2325
Sriharsa 2525, 2532
Srīmakal 3101, 3106
Srinuan 2556, 2559
Srinvan Duanghom 2591, 2593
Srivastav, K. P. 2513, 2519
St. Bonaventure 3142
St. Thomas 1874
Stabej, J. 2298, 2301f.
Stabenow, K. 1052f.
Stack, G. 2516, 2520
Stackmann, K. 2048, 2241
Stade, D. von 1155, 1557, 1561
Stadler, F. J. 2060, 2072
Stahl, F.A. 1142
Stahl, H. 2392, 2395
Stahl, H.-J. 1813, 2040, 2049
Staib, B. 3167
Staicu 1881
Stairs, E. 2698, 2700
Stairs, G. 2698, 2700
Stalder, F. J. 2061
Stalin, J. 2132
Stallybrass, O. 1204
Stamatakos, I. 1708f., 1713
Stamati, T. 1885, 1889
Stamatoski, T. 2304
Stamm, F.L. 1910, 1912
Stamm, J.J. 2428
Stammerjohann, H. 275, 1362, 2050, 2077, 2222, 2891, 2903
Stammler, W. 1203, 1205, 1861, 2076
Stampe, D. 2542, 2544f.

Stancliff, F. 3122, 3135
Standley, P. 2663, 2669
Standop, E. 132, 135, 182, 189, 269, 365, 370, 408, 706, 726, 1069, 1075, 1090, 1094, 1379, 1384f., 1973-75, 1983, 2191, 2242, 2767, 2841
Stange, H.O. 3113
Stanisławski, J. 3063f., 3068
Stankiewicz, E. 2289, 2296, 2302, 2310f., 2313, 2328, 2334, 3066, 3068, 3075, 3085
Stankov, V. 2308
Stanley, E. 1446
Stanley, G. E. 2650, 2655
Stanzel, F.K. 1541, 1549
Stapelkamp, Chr. 2025
Stapf, K.H. 123
Starčevskij, A. V. 2264, 2267
Starck, T. 154, 158f., 1418, 1420, 1426, 1539, 1543, 1548, 1561, 2104, 2230, 2243
Starec, S. M. 3022, 3029
Stark, D. 2759, 2880
Stark, L. A. 2684
Stark, L. R. 2702, 2704-2707, 2709
Stark, S. 2698, 2700
Starke, G. 796
Starkey, S. C. 2515, 2520
Starnes, D.T. 8, 18, 221, 224f., 230, 722, 726, 993f., 998, 1793, 1795, 1817, 1943, 1948-1950, 1988, 2006, 2009, 2895f., 2903
Starobinski, J. 1144f.
Starosta, M. 2276f.
Starosta, St. 3167
Starostin, S.A. 1692f.
Starreveld, A. 2419f.
Stati, S. 1891
Staub, F. 242
Staub, W. 2664, 2669
Staupitz, J. von 1572
Stavrovski, N.V. 1671
Stchoupak, N. 2492
Stebnickij, S. N. 2630
Steche, Th. 2132
Stechow, A. von 460, 499, 550, 580, 583
Stede, W. 2501f., 2504
Stedje, A. 592, 648, 1322, 2765, 3047
Steegmüller, B. 1189
Steel, B. 1748, 1767
Steel, R. 1389
Steele, J. 1018
Steen Due, O. 1720
Steen, E.B. 1261, 1265
Steensen, Th. 2028, 2036
Stéfanini, J. 1219f., 1804, 1817
Stefanović, M. 2300
Stefanovskij, P.A. 2324
Stefenelli, A. 25, 28, 652, 657, 1157f., 1179, 1184, 1797, 1817

Steffens, D. 2233, 2235
Stegentritt, E. 1573
Steger, H. 680, 1280, 1284, 1355, 1362, 1531, 2110, 2127, 2242
Stegmann, H. 1140
Stegmüller, W. 539-541, 549, 557, 583
Stehlík, O. 2737, 2751
Steiger, A. 2192, 2242
Stein, G. 8, 18, 29, 31, 34, 79, 120, 126, 181, 189, 213, 226, 230, 588, 592, 648f., 882, 978, 980, 993, 998, 1131, 1366, 1368, 1381, 1385, 1615, 1624, 1793, 1817, 1948, 1950, 1953, 2711f., 2728, 2757, 2767, 2895, 2897, 2903, 2936f., 2947, 2956f., 2960, 2967, 2969
Stein, J. 516, 529, 667, 766, 2007f., 3115, 3117
Stein, J.M. 1130
Stein, P. 2871, 2876
Steinacker, E. 2242
Steinbach, Ch. E. 9, 242, 2046f., 2215
Steinbach, Chr. E. 16, 800, 804, 1149, 1151, 2029, 2053f., 2072, 2077
Steinbauer, F. 2637f.
Steinbock, U. 2104, 2214, 2242
Steiner, E. 1018
Steiner, J. 88
Steiner, R. 33, 78, 2009
Steiner, R. J. 32, 34, 96, 577, 653, 657, 1862, 2713, 2719, 2724, 2728, 2758, 2767, 2841f., 2854, 2947, 2951, 2954-2956, 2958, 2960
Steinfeldt, E. 1362, 1669
Steingass, F. 2479, 2896, 2901, 3090f., 3096
Steinhöwel, H. von 1399
Steinitz, W. 158, 206, 273, 320, 358, 370, 406, 459, 499, 510, 516f., 575, 626, 647, 652f., 661, 667, 672, 681, 684, 686f., 692, 694, 698f., 747, 753, 778, 786, 796, 804, 813, 821, 834, 841, 848, 861, 887, 892, 966, 1151, 1240, 1415, 1532, 1538, 1623, 2129, 2131-2133, 2170, 2232, 2242, 2396, 2398
Steinke, K. 2308
Steinkeller, P. 1684f.
Steinkrauss, W. 2636f.
Steinmann, E. 2225
Steinmeier, E. von 2215
Steinmetz, H. 1111
Steinmetz, S. 1164, 1535f., 2004, 2007
Steinmeyer, E. von 153, 157, 159
Steinthal, H. 1362

Štejnfel'd, E.A. 2320, 2325
Steller, G. W. 2630f.
Steller, K. G. F. 2566f.
Steller, W. 2024
Stellmacher, D. 115, 126, 239, 245, 2061, 2077, 2198f., 2243
Steltenpool, J. 2636, 2638
Stemshaug, O. 1269, 1275
Sten, H. 3058, 3061
Stenberg, Th. 1949, 1953
Stender, A. 2355
Stender, G.F. 2355, 2358
Stengrevica, M. 2359
Stenton, F.M. 1281, 1283
Stenzel, B. 2071
Stenzel, Th. 1242, 1245
Stenzler, A. F. 2490, 2497
Stepanchenko, D. I. 2464, 2466
Stepankowsky, W.J. 2332
Stepanova, E.M. 2325
Stepanova, M.D. 789, 796, 1032, 1230
Stepanowsky, W.J. 2334
Stephan, H. 2063
Stéphan, L. 2350
Stephan-Gabinel, N. 2776
Stephanus, H. 151, 301, 304, 1698f., 1702, 1704f., 3160 (s. Estienne)
Stephanus, J. 1783
Stephanus, R. 9, 13, 16, 151, 1715f., 1721, 1792, 2045, 2912, 2928 (s. Estienne)
Stephens, R. 1269, 1275
Steputat, W. 1126, 1130, 2066, 2073, 2184, 2230
Sterkenburg, P. G. J. van 227f., 230, 305, 361, 370, 408, 919, 921, 929, 988, 1401, 1416, 1572, 1607, 1610, 1621, 1624, 2011, 2022, 2020, 2046, 2716, 2728, 2767, 2771, 2775, 2805, 2812f., 2835f., 3038f.
Stern, M. 1031
Sternbeck, H. 1892, 1905
Sternberg, M.L.A. 3144
Sternefeld, W. 160, 163
Stetter, Ch. 269
Steube, A. 2217
Steudel, W.-I. 1230
Steuerwald, K. 510, 517
Steuerwald, K. 2403, 2406
Steven, E.M. 1343, 1348
Stevens, C.J. 2955
Stevens, Cj. 517
Stevens, J. 2950, 2987
Stevens, P. 2767
Stevenson, B. 1044, 1046, 1050
Stevenson, J.A.C. 1414, 1985
Stevenson, R. C. 2643, 2645
Stewandt, J. A. 2552, 2554
Stewart, G.R. 1275

Stewechius, G. 1221, 1223
Stichel, K. 822, 860, 1892, 1905
Stickel, G. 2222
Stieber, Z. 2761
Stiehl, R. 2437
Stiehl, U. 1052f.
Stieler, C. (oder K.) 9, 16, 114, 124, 128, 133, 233, 235, 242f., 768, 771, 800, 804, 824f., 830, 860f., 1147, 1149, 1191, 1234, 1240, 2052, 2063, 2073, 2075, 2077, 2215, 3019
Stiernhielm, G. 1909, 1912, 1934, 1942
Stigaard, V. 3058, 3061
Stigliani, T. 1130
Stiles, N. 2660
Stiller, H. 2074
Stillman, F. 1126f., 1130
Stimm, H. 703, 1253, 1348, 2875
Štindlová, J. 297, 305, 408, 1143, 1670
Stock, E. 1309
Stock, P.F. 787
Stock, W. 1337
Stocker, B. 2087, 2098
Stockfleth, N.V. 2389, 2392
Stoer, J. 1845, 1850, 1860, 2913, 2934, 2998, 3006
Stoett, F.A. 1036, 1041, 1432
Stoff, R. 3018
Stohoe, W.C. 3141-3144
Stojan, P.E. 3124, 3128, 3135, 3137
Stojkov, St. 2306-2308
Stokes, W. 1340, 1342, 2339-2343
Stokhamerum, S. 1733
Stoks, F. 2049, 2762
Stoks, F. C. M. 1623, 2782
Stoll, J. 2199, 2201, 2230
Stoll, O. 2664, 2669
Stolt, B. 778, 1018
Stoltze, F. 1191
Stoltze, R. 1193
Stolz, F. 17, 223, 1722
Stolze, F. 1704
Stolze, R. 2767
Stölzel, G. 2050
Stone, G. 2276f.
Stone, Ph. 1651, 1667
Stopa, R. 2651, 2655
Storaci, E. 2463, 2468
Storck 2934
Storey, C. A. 2478, 2480
Störig, H.J. 6, 18, 247, 276f., 405, 499, 989, 998
Storni, B. 2886
Storrer, A. 423, 428, 459, 964, 967, 2131, 2172f., 2243
Story, G.M. 71, 77, 79
Storz, G. 2231
Storzer, G.H. 1029

Stosch, S. J. E. 1068f., 1074, 2058, 2073
Stott, A.S. 2974
Stötzel, G. 274, 278, 586, 1152, 2077, 2147, 2234, 2237, 2243f.
Stötzer, U. 1309
Šťovíčková, D. 2759 (= Heroldová, D.)
Stowasser, J. M. 2749, 2751
Straaten, A.G.J. van 3127, 3135
Straberger, M. 1290
Strachan, J. 2339, 2343
Strachova, N. P. 746, 1622, 2845, 2848, 2853
Strackerjan, K. 2091, 2098
Stradelli, E. 2673, 2676
Strahl, I. 3169
Strahlenberg, Ph.J. von 2396
Straka, G. 1343, 1348, 1676, 1678
Strambio, A. 3010, 3012
Strand-Juchansen, E. 2767
Strasbach, M.-O. 1680f.
Strassmaier, J.N. 1683, 1685
Strassner, P. 3140f.
Straßner, E. 1573, 2061, 2077
Stratmann, F.H. 1436, 1446-1449, 1453-1455
Straub, B. 2947
Strauchius, J. 1221, 1223
Strauss, H. 2636f.
Strauß, G. 117, 126, 405, 458, 531, 552, 574, 583, 617-620, 627, 788, 790-793, 796, 836-840, 842, 849, 850-852, 855, 1200, 1205, 1207-1209, 1221, 1223, 2017, 2022, 2104, 2217, 2218, 2243
Stray Jorgensen, P. 1186
Strecker, B. 207, 816, 822
Strehle, D. 1141
Strehlke, F. 1552, 1561
Streit, R. 3021, 3029, 3175
Streitberg, W. 1908, 1910-1912
Stresser-Péan, G. 2663
Streuber, A. 1051, 1053
Strevens, P. 591, 1308, 1310
Strich, Chr. 1352
Strich, M. 1036, 1041
Strilbiţchi, M. 1883
Strižak, O.S. 1286, 1290
Strodtmann, J. Chr. 2061, 2073
Stroh, F. 672, 2105
Strohbach, M. 2056f., 2077
Strohl-Goebel, H. 583, 881
Strömberg, A. 1080
Stromer, Th. 2988, 2990
Stroomer, H. 2464, 2468
Stropnickey, S. 3170
Strub 2166, 2169, 2188, 2230
Strube-Edelmann, B. 1201, 1204f., 2185-2187, 2223
Strunk, H. 1303, 1312-1314, 2191, 2233

Strutyński, J. 2271, 2274
Stryzhak, O.S. 2332
Stubenberg, J.W. von 2350
Stubenrauch, H. 1350, 2185, 2197, 2217
Stucke, G. 1147, 1149, 1151, 1234, 1240, 2090, 2098
Stulli, J. 2289, 2291, 2295
Stupin, L.P. 1556, 1561, 2767
Štúr, Ľ. 2285
Stürenburg, C. H. 2028
Sturm-Schnabl, K. 2302
Sturmius, J. 2047, 2934
Sturzen-Becker 3049
Sturzenegger, Joh. J. 2232
Stussi, A. 1857, 1862
Stutchkoff, N. 2430, 2436
Stutshkov, N. 2252f.
Stutz, E. 1912
Stutz, J. E. 1220, 2071
Styputa, R. 3063, 3064, 3067f.
Suali, L. 2502, 2507
Suárez Gómez, G. 2986
Suárez, C. 1743, 1767
Suárez, L. de 2660
Suarez, T.M. 184, 189
Subatnieks, V. 2357, 2359
Subbayyaśāstri, K. 2528
Sube, R. 249, 264, 273, 1263
Subhūti, W. 2504
Subra, J. 2593
Sucharowski, W. 2756
Suchsland, P. 2237
Suci, G.J. 1615, 1624
Suciu, C. 1891
Suckau, W. de 3001, 3306
Şu'ûrî, H. 2399, 2406
Suda 994, 997, 1704
Sudassana, U. 2506
Sudnik, M.R. 2337
Sudnik-Owczuk, W. 3065, 3067
Sudrabkalns, J. 2359
Sudre, L. 1823
Sue, E. 1184, 1187, 1534, 1536
Suescún, G. 1763
Suffel, J. 1351
Sugareva, T. 2307f.
Sugawara, T. 2622
Sugawara, Y. 305
Suhadolnik, St. 2300, 2302
Suhonen, S. 2359f.
Suidas 994, 997 (s. Suda)
Suijman, F. J. 2019, 2021
Suits, G. 2394
Suyūtī = Jatal al-Dīn al-Sūutī 2442
Sukalenko, N. J. 2717, 2728, 2767
Sukhānanada-nātha 2493, 2495
Sukhumawadee Khamhiran 2593
Sukiassian, A. 2369, 2371
Sükûn, Z. 2399, 2406
Sulaka, H. 2387

Šulek, B. 2291, 2295
Sullivan, Th. D. 2661
Sumangala, M. 2505
Sumarán, J. A. 2914-2916, 2934
Sumaran, J.A. 1088, 1092
Summers, D. 1385, 1969
Sun Hongkai 2558-2560
Sunaga, K. 2767
Sundby, B. 1305, 1311
Sundby, Th. 3054, 3058, 3061
Sundén, D.A. 1937, 1942
Suolahti, H. 1255, 1257
Supple, J. 2667
Suprun, A.Ja. 23337
Surenne, G. 1310
Sūri, V. 2499
Suringar, W. 1036, 1043
Suriya Ratanakul 2591, 2593
Surūrī, Muhammad Qāsim 2478
Sušnik, B. 2704, 2708
Sussanneau, H. 1011, 1016
Suter, R. 2198, 2230
Sutton, A. 2515, 2520
Sutton, V. 3142, 3144
Suvorin, A. S. 2267
Suwilai Premsrirat 2592f.
Suzuki, S. 3116, 3118
Suzzarini, F. 1099
Svabo, J.Chr. 1930, 1932
Svāmī, J. 2504
Svartvik, J. 862, 1617, 1624
Svecevičius, B. 2353
Švedova, N.Ju. 661, 753, 766, 2326f.
Svensén, B. 277, 652, 657, 1926, 1928, 2770, 2775, 3050
Svoboda, J. 2282-2284
Svoboda, V. 2332
Svobodová-Chmelová, J. 1184, 2887
Swadesh, M. 2659f., 2663, 2669, 2697-2700
Swainson, Ch. 1036, 1041, 1257
Swallow, H. 2886f.
Swan, M. 1219f.
Swann, H.K. 1257
Swanson, D.C. 774, 779, 1142, 1293, 1296, 2767
Swedberg, J. 1933-1936
Sweet, H. 589, 592, 732, 749, 1328, 1333f., 1436, 1442-1444, 1455, 1962
Swift, J. 1957
Swift, L.B. 1652, 1668
Swiggers, P. 1004, 1009, 1804, 1817f.
Switzer, R. 3147
Šwjela, B. 2276f.
Swótlik, Y. H. 2276f.
Syamsudardas, S. 2513
Syaqi, M.D. 2447
Sychta, B. 2270, 2273

Syed Ahmed 2521
Sykes, J. 2751
Sykes, J.B. 1622, 405, 515, 524, 529, 588f., 591, 672, 901, 904, 928
Sylnès, G. 1215
Symmachus, A. 1141
Syntax, P. 1130, 1142, 2066, 2073, 2215, 2230
Sypniewska, B. 3067
Syurmelian, Kh. 2368, 2370
Syv, P. 1916, 1922
Sywulka, E. 2664, 2669
Szabó, T.A. 2382
Szaitz, L.M. 2377, 2382
Szalai, L. 243, 245, 1429
Szamota, I. 2382, 2932
Szana, A. 1261, 1265
Szapszal, S. 2411
Szarvas, G. 2382
Szende, T. 2753
Szendy, G.L. 1507, 1511
Szercha, M. 3068
Szily, K. 2382
Szimay, Chr. [Simai] 1131
Szinneyei, J. 2381
Szirmay, A. 2382, 2377
Szkiłądź, H. 2273
Szklarczyk, L. 1361
Szmidt, D. 1776, 1786
Szober, S. 2270
Szwedek, A. 1368, 1624, 1953
Szwykowski, L. 3065, 3068
Szymczak, M. 2269f., 2273
Szyrokowa, L. I. 3065, 3067
Szyrwid, C. 2355

T

Ta'ati, Abd'd Ali 2447
Taberd, J. L. 2589
Tabourot, E. 1127, 1129
Tabrīzī, Muhammad Husayn 2478
Tachard, G. 1795, 2957, 3036
Tachibana, T. 2618, 2623
Tacla, A. 1189
Taggert, J.E. 1294, 1296
Tagiev, M. T. 3082
Tagliabue, C. 3101, 3106
Tagliavini, C. 1126f., 1269, 1275, 1294, 1305, 1310, 1320, 1668, 1874, 1878, 1881, 1889, 1891f., 1895, 1901f., 1905, 2381
Tai, Y. 3116, 3118
Tailleur, O. G. 2629, 2631
Takahashi, M. 3116, 3118
Takamatsu, T. 3117
Takano, F. 3116f.
Takebayashi, S. 2767, 3115f., 3117f.

Takehara, T. 3119, 3155
Takenobu, Y. 3115, 3119
Taksami, Č. M. 2630f.
Tal, A. 2430
Talibov, V. 2422f.
Tallemant 39
Tallgren-Tuulio, O.J. 1037, 1043
Talor, N.W. 140
Tamás, G. 539, 583
Tamás, L. 1889, 2363, 2366
Tammemägi, J. 2393, 2395
Tammu, J. 2568
Tampucci, H. 1131
Tams Jørgensen, V. 2027
Tamsen, M. 2886, 3044f., 3047
Tamura, J. 2410
Tanahashi, I, 3115f.
Tanaka, J. 2650, 2653f.
Tanaka, Y. 3167
Tancke, G. 9f., 18, 652, 657, 994, 998, 1089, 1094, 1845, 1848f., 1851f., 1858, 1862, 2895, 2903, 2911, 2936f., 2948, 2956, 2960, 2970, 2976, 3013, 3019
Tandioy Chasoy, D. 2705
Tange, E.G. 1349, 1352
Tanger, G. 1293, 1296, 2968
Tanigawa, K. 2623
Tannenbaum, P.M. 1615, 1624
Tannenhaus, M.K. 3167
Tanocki, F. 2293, 2295
Tăntu, K. 2853
Tanzlinger-Zanotti, J. 2289
Tanzmeister, R. 654
Tapia Zenteno, C. de 2664, 2669
Tappert, W. 2197, 2230
Tappino, R. 2996
Taraman, S. 172, 174
Taranto, F. 1085, 1087, 1090, 1092
Tarasova, E.M. 1668
Tardy, Abbé 1308, 1310
Tardy, Ch.H. 1617, 1623
Tarnanidis, I.C. 2258, 2268
Tarnočzi, L. 1353, 1364
Tarongí, J. 1774, 1786
Taroni, N. 1131
Tarski 582
Tarvainen, K. 2243
Tarver, J.C. 2960
Täsämma Habtä Mika'el 2451, 2454
Tascón, L. 1753, 1763
Tassi, L. 3010, 3012
Tasso, T. 1854
Tassoni, A. 1854, 1862
Taszycki, W. 1303, 2271, 2273f.
Tatár, B. 3175
Tatarin, A. 3073
Tătaru, A. 1308, 1310
Tatevin, P. C. 2672f., 2676
Tatilon, C. 1208
Tatiščev, I. I. 3075

Tatišvili, Ju. G. 2767
Tatlock, J.S.P. 1449f., 1455
Tattavī, 'Abdu'l-rashīd 2478
Tauber, W. 1551, 1561
Taubert 2310
Taulí, A. 2644f.
Tavares, A. 1314
Tavema, F. 2229
Taver, F. 2478, 2480
Taylor, A. 1036, 1041, 2066, 2077
Taylor, A.M. 1163, 1165
Taylor, D. S. 2518
Taylor, F.R. 3176
Taylor, G. 2683, 2705
Taylor, I. 2888
Taylor, J. 31, 33, 106f., 110, 763, 766, 1632, 1637
Taylor, J.L. 65, 70, 3022, 3029
Taylor, N.W. 146
Taylor, P.A. 78, 577
Taylor, R. 1021, 1025, 1030, 1038
Taylor, S. 2511
Taylor, W. 1068, 1074
Tayyä, G.M. [=Tayyä, A.] 2450, 2455
Techeda, J. de 2985
Techtmeier, B. 893
Tedsen, J. 2031
Teeuw, A. 2563, 2565
Teichert, F. 2064, 2073
Teichmann-Nadiraschwili, Ch. 2767
Teichroew, F.J.M. 573, 583
Teirlinck, I. 2019, 2021
Tejavantābhivaṃsa, P. kyo 2506
Tejeda, D.G. 2985
Tejeda, H. de 2981
Tejera, M.J. 1754, 1763
Tekin, T. 2409
Telchid, S. 2872-2875
Telenkova, M.A. 2324
Telford, J. H. 2559
Tellenbach, E. 882, 1230, 2150, 2233, 2243
Teller, W. A. 1154f., 2058, 2073
Tellez, B. 2461, 2469
Telling, R. 2193, 2231
Tellini, A. 3126, 3135
Tello, M. 3175
Temler, Ch. F. 2290
Tendahl, H. 2226
Tenišev, È.R. 2411
Teodori, A. 1883
Teodorov-Balan, A. 2305
Teodorovici, I. 1883
Teplov, V. E. 3074
Teppe, J. 1211, 1213, 1217
Terajima, R. 2619, 2623
Terentius 726, 1715
Tereščenko, N.M. 2398
Tereškin, N.I. 2396, 2398
Terkelsen, P. 1720

Termer, F. 2664, 2669
Termette, E. 3172
Terne, N. 3101, 3106
Ternes, E. 511, 518, 2343, 2351, 2855, 2857, 2859
Terrace, H. 140, 146
Terrell, P. 524, 747, 2726, 2751, 2789, 2817, 2856, 2858, 2967
Terreros y Pando, E. 11, 16, 1742, 1763, 2917, 2934, 2938, 2947, 2952
Terry y Rivas, A. 1747, 1763
Ters, F. 180, 1367, 1835
Tersis, N. 2645
Tervarent, G. de 3157
Terwen, J. H. 2018, 2021
Terzian, P. 2370
Tesch, G. 670, 672
Těšitelová, M. 1321, 1669, 1671, 2281, 2283f.
Teske, R. 1309
Tesnière, L. 1005f., 1009
Testas, J. 2980, 2983
Tetzner, F. 1080, 2086, 2089, 2098
Teubert, W. 1655, 1668
Teucher, L.H. 3017
Teuchert, H. 239, 242, 245, 1233, 1240
Tevarent, G. de 3152
Texeda, J. de 2986
Textor, A.M. 1080
Textor, J. 1795
Teyssier, P. 1725, 1733, 1735, 3020, 3030
Tezcan, S. 2412
Tha Din, M. 2505
Thaker, J.P. 2499, 2505
Thakkara, D.G. 3097, 3107
Thakur, M. P. 2510, 2515, 2518, 2520
Thakur, S. 2511
Thal, H. 124, 1192f.
Thanh-Nghị 2587, 2589
Thani Nayagam, X. S. 2532
Tharp, J.A. 2591, 2593
Thayer, J. E. 2644
Thelwall, R. 2645
Theocharopoulos, G. 2917, 2934
Theraphan L. Thongkum 2591, 2593f.
Thérond, M. 1019, 1030
Theureau, S. 1367
Theurel, J. S. 2584, 2589
Thevenet 2535
Thibault-Laulan, A.-M. 725
Thibaut, M.A. 3001, 3006
Thiele, J. 2767
Thiele, M. 3056, 3060
Thiele, P. 2753, 2947
Thiele, S. 573, 580
Thicmc, F.W. 2969
Thiemer, E. 2888

Thienemann, T. 2381
Thierry, J. 1793, 1806, 1809
Thiers, S. 1142
Thiêù Chùù 2587, 2589
Thilo, G. 1717
Thirion, J.-B. 1349, 1352
Thissen, H.-J. 1681
Thổ Sang Luc 2594
Thoburn, T. 1111
Thody, Ph. 2886
Thoma, H. 2038, 2049
Thoman, R. 3130
Thomas v. Aquin 1874, 1878
Thomas, A. 66, 69, 996, 1326, 1332, 1344, 1347, 1822f., 1839, 2094, 2098
Thomas, A.-V. 68, 70, 1210-1213, 1217
Thomas, David 2591, 2594
Thomas, Dorothy 2591, 2594
Thomas, E. 1131
Thomas, J. 1791, 1809
Thomas, J. M. C. 2647, 2649
Thomas, K. 39, 46
Thomas, L. L. 3063, 3066
Thomas, P. 1204
Thomas, R. H. 2759
Thomas, Th. 1955
Thomas, W. 1848, 2956, 2970, 2975f.
Thomas, W.O. 2347, 2349
Thomasius, J. 1221, 1223
Thomasius, Th. 2970, 2975
Thompson, B.B. 1030
Thompson, E. 2663, 2669
Thompson, G. 2767
Thompson, P.A. 1445, 1456
Thompson, S. A. 2767
Thomsen, E. 1242, 1245
Thomsen, V. 1918
Thomson, A.W. 3125, 3135
Thomson, D.S. 2346, 2349, 2351
Thomson, R.L. 2346f., 2349, 2351
Thondam, P. C. 2559
Thongkum, Th.L. 2582
Thor Helle, A. 2392, 2395
Thorin, A. 2886
Thorkelin, G. 1984
Thorn, A.Chr. 1254
Thorndike, E. 3147
Thorndike, E.L. 136, 145, 221, 223, 1321, 1353, 1355, 1362, 1365, 1367f., 1388f., 1669, 1971, 1997-1999, 2004, 2008
Thorne, R. 139
Thorsson, Ö. 1931
Thoulier, P.J. (= Abbé d'Olivet) 1810
Thrale, H. 1068
Threadgold, T. 1389
Thumb, A. 17, 1561, 1704
Thun, H. 1019, 1032

Thunmann, J. 2361, 2366f.
Thureau-Dangin, F. 1691, 1694
Thürmann, E. 2222
Thurmayr, J. 1284
Thurneisser zum Thurn, L. 2041
Thurneysen, R. 2339, 2341-2343
Thurow, J. 2342
Thvan Mran, U. 2506
Tibbins, J. 2795, 2957, 2959
Tibirica, E. 1352
Tichonov, A.N. 1140,1147, 1149, 1151, 2317, 2320, 2325, 2328
Tick Twon 2505
Tickoo, M. 3168
Tickoo, M. L. 2764
Tieck, L. 728
Tiefenbach, H. 2104, 2243
Tietz, M. 2991
Tietze, A. 79, 2399, 2407
Tiitula, L. 2767
Tiktin, H. 1094, 1882, 1887, 1889, 2841, 2850f., 2853
Tilho, J. 2458, 2460
Tiling, E. 237f., 243, 2060, 2073
Tilley, M. 1036, 1041
Tilley, M.P. 1454f.
Tillotson, E. 1949
Timm, St. 1680, 182
Timmermann, E. 1078
Timmermans, A. 1185, 1189, 1247
Timusev, D.A. 2398
Tindall, H. 2650, 2652, 2654
Tindi, R. M. 2566f.
Tinghir, A.B. 2402, 2406
Tinker, M.A. 138f., 142, 145f.
Tischler, J. 1688f.
Tišlar, Z. 3125, 3135
Tissier, J. 1795
Titius, J. D. 3038
Titova, L. N. 2768
Titz, J. P. 1126, 1131, 2066, 2073
Tiurina, G. P. 3065, 3067
Tivadar, O. 1290
Tiwari, B. N. 2512, 2519
Tixier de Ravisy, J. 1795
Tjurina, G.P. 2324
Tjurina, L. 2359
Tobar, C.R. 1753, 1763
Tobari, S. 3116, 3119
Tobler, A. 603, 606, 1343, 1820, 1842
Tobler, L. 242
Tochtrop, L. 3023-3025, 3029
Todd, H.J. 1950-1952, 1954, 1991
Tōdō, A. 2620, 2623
Todoran, R. 1889
Todorov, C. 2307
Todrys, K.W. 1982
Togan, Z. V. 2476f.
Toget, P. M. 2097
Toglia, M.P. 1672
Togo, M. 3116, 3119

Togores, J. 1772
Toin, K. 2623
Toivonen, Y.H. 2385-2387f., 2396f.
Tokarski, J. 737, 749, 2270, 2273
Toki, Y. 2621
Tolgsdorf, H. 2354
Tolhausen, A. 2918, 2934
Tolhausen, L. 2795f., 2988f.
Tolksdorf, U. 269
Toll, H. J. 2199, 2231
Tollenaere, F. de 227, 230, 247, 277, 408, 654, 1067, 1134, 1142, 1431, 1435, 1572, 1610, 1910, 1912, 2010, 2012, 2018, 2022, 2301, 3035-3037, 3039 (s. de Tollenaere)
Toller, Th.N. 1437, 1441-1446, 1456
Tolmačeva, V.D. 1006f.
Tolmán, H. C. 2471f.
Tolomei, Cl. 2971
Tölpel, L. 1349, 1352
Tolstoj, I. 2292, 2295
Tomalak, J. 3065, 3068
Tomán, J. 3126f., 3135
Tomaszczyk, J. 106, 111, 181, 189, 856, 862, 1638, 2728, 2768, 2829, 2836, 2841, 2854, 2870, 2888f., 2896-2899, 2903
Tomback, R.S. 1693
Tomhins, W. 3144
Tomikawa, M. 2645
Tomimori, N. 1305, 1311
Tominc, I. 2299, 2301
Tomkins, W. 1118f, 3141.
Tomlin, J. 2918, 2934
Tommaseo, N. 149-151, 1068, 1074, 1090, 1857f., 1860, 1862-1866, 1870, 1872, 1877, 1879
Tommasi, M. 3129, 3135
Tommasi, P. 1855f.
Tommaso, S. 1880
Tompa, F.W. 3167
Tomsa, F. 2280, 2284
Tonelli, G. 1090, 1094, 3175
Tönjachen, R.O. 1898f., 1903
Tono, Y. 106, 109, 111, 208f., 212, 214, 1632, 1638
Tooke, J.Horne 1956f., 1966
Toorn-Piebenga, G.A. van der 1929, 1932
Toporov, V.N. 1286, 1290, 2353f.
Tops, G. 1318f., 1321
Tops, G. A. J. 2751, 2836, 3039
Toral, C. 2956
Torero, A. 2677, 2684
Toreza, M. 2762
Tornberg, A. 3048, 3051
Toro y Gisbert, M. de 1743, 1746, 1752, 1759, 1761, 1763, 1767

Toro y Gómez, M. de 2980, 2985
Toro, M. de 1817
Török, J. 2289
Torover, G. I. 2896
Torp, A. 1337, 1340, 1342, 1393, 1414
Torra, P. 1772, 1786, 1788
Torre Crespo, J. de 1747, 1763
Torre y Ocón, F. de la 2979, 2985
Torrellas, A. 1776
Torres i Graell, A. 1776, 1786
Torres Martínez, J.C. de 1753, 1763
Torres Quintero, R. 1770
Torres Rubio, D. de 2678, 2682f., 2686, 2690
Torres, C.P. 1745, 1763
Torriani, G. 1849, 1860f.
Torriano, G. 2975f.
Torro, F.A. 1696, 1704
Torsellino, O. 1221, 1223
Toscan, J. 1196, 1198
Toscanella, O. 1011, 1016, 1081, 1083, 2914, 2934, 3007, 3012
Toselli, G. 2468
Tošev, K. 2303f.
Toshkhani, S. K. 2513, 2519
Toshokan, F. 3172
Tottie, G. 3050
Tougard, A. 1800, 1817
Toulou, E. 1839
Tournefort, J.P. de 165
Tournes, J. A. de 2934
Tournes, S. de 2934
Tournier, M. 85, 88
Toury, G. 2768
Tovar, A. 223, 1766, 2670, 2676, 2700, 2702, 2705, 2707-2709, 2991
Tovar, E. de 1753f., 1763
Towell, J.E. 1100, 1102, 1265
Townley, H.M. 1661, 1668
Toyoda, M. 3119
Trabant, J. 223, 576, 648, 930
Trabant-Rommel, Chr. 576, 930
Tracia, A. [A.] 1131
Trager, G.L. 1342
Trail, A. 2650f.
Traill, A. 2653, 2656f.
Train, J. K. von 2062, 2073
Tramonti, N. 1261, 1265
Tran, X. D. 2284
Tranchedino, N. 1845
Trapani, F. 1845, 1862
Trapany, D.G. 2980, 2983, 2985
Traub, W. 1005, 1007, 1215
Traupman, J.C. 2967ff.
Trautmann, R. 1337, 1342, 2353f.
Traversa, V. 1321, 1361, 1669
Trávníček, F. 2267, 2281, 2284
Traxel, W. 852, 855
Trebecki, St. 1131

Trébuchet, A. 1187
Treccani, G. 1869, 1878f.
Trediakovskij, V.K. 2310
Tregar, E. 2574
Trejo Dueñes, A. 1763
Trench, R.C. 225f., 228f., 230, 1157f., 1961f., 1966
Trenckner, V. 2500-2502, 2505
Trenev, I. 1129
Trepica, H. 2938, 2947
Treves 2994
Treyer, H. 2091
Triandafyllidis, M. 1709
Tribbins, J. 2796
Tribouillois, E. 1206, 1209
Trier, J. 850, 855, 1331, 1334, 1425, 1429, 1700, 2018
Trim, E. 2251
Trima, E. 2254
Trimborn, H. 2683
Trinta, A.R. 1115, 1119
Tripāṭhī, Ch. B. 2503, 2506f.
Tripathi, S. 2513, 2519, 3100, 3107
Tripp, R.Th. 1046f., 1050, 1090
Trissinos, G.G. 1851
Trittschuh, T. 838, 841
Troc [Trotz], M. A. 2268, 2273, 2917, 2934
Troebes, O. 835, 1011, 1016, 2754, 2776
Trofimkina, O. J. 2755
Trognesius, C.-J. 2978
Trogney, J. 2911, 2935
Troiański, J. K. 3077
Troll, Th. 1193
Tropea, G. 1877, 1879
Trotz [Troc], M. A. 2934, 3062, 3068
Troude, A.E. 2347, 2350
Troughton, E. 2955
Trousset, J. 1842
Trüb, R. 383, 394, 408, 1067, 1100, 1102, 2232
Trubačev, O.N. 1286, 1290, 1337, 1342
Trubar, P. 2296
Trubetzkoy, N.S. 1342
Trübner, K. 2085, 2098
Trübner, K. J. 2495, 2497
Trübner, R. 1173, 1204
Truchot, C. 1183
Trujillo, O. 2702
Trummert, W. 1261, 1264
Trumpp, E. 2516
Trümpy, H. 2061, 2077
Trunk, M. 272
Trunk-Nußbaumer, M. 272, 358, 405, 574, 1622, 2219
Trunz, E. 158
Trường Vĩnh Ký, P. 2584, 2589
Trusler, J. 1068, 1074, 1131
Trusson, J.E. 2981, 2985

Tryjarski, E. 2273
Tsaholci, J. 2376, 2382
Tsanin, M. 2251, 2253
Tschauder, G. 581, 2756
Tschenkéli, K. 2417f.
Tscherning, A. 2071
Tschopik 2686
Tschumpert, M. 1897
Tsumaru, H. 3167
Tsutomu Sugimoto 2622
Tsuzumi, N. 3111
Tuaillon, G. 1817
Tubina, J. 2468
Tucker, A. N. 2642, 2644f.
Tudela Flores, E. 3127, 3135
Tuerlinckx, J. F. 2019, 2021
Tugendhat, E. 540, 584, 790, 796
Tuggy, J. 2703
Tugov, V.V. 2419, 2421
Tuksam, G. 2394
Tulard, G. 165, 167
Tuldava, J. 2395?
Tulett, B. 2955
Tumanovič, O. B. 2485f.
Tumans'kyj, F. 2330, 2334
Tuomi, T. 1142, 2385, 2387
Tupikov, N.M. 2315, 2325
Turabaev, A. 2768
Turima, Z. 2292, 2295
Turing, A.M. 3167
Turkina, E. 2357, 2359f.
Turner, G. W. 71, 77, 2759, 2778
Turner, R. 2494
Turner, R. L. 1337, 1342, 2497, 2505, 2517, 2521
Turner-Flechsenhar, J. 2968
Turover, G. I. 2901
Tursellinus, H. 1221
Turskiej, H. 1131
Turton, N.D. 359, 1030
Turunen, A. 2386f.
Tūsī, Asadī 2477
Tutschek, K. 2462, 2466
Tuuk, H. N. van der 2561, 2563, 2566f.
Tuulio, O.J. 1129
Tvaṅ:-saṅ: -tuik-van 2551, 2554
Tvrdý, P. 2285, 2287
Twent, A. C. 2918, 2931, 2935
Twinger von Königshofen, J. 2038, 2040, 2048
Twyman, M. 714, 726
Tymchenko, J. 2331, 2334
Tymiński, K. 3127, 3135
Typotius, J. 3151, 3157

U

Uboldi, A. 1131
Ubrjatova, E.I. 2414
Učaev, Z. 2397

Udino, A. 2935, 3005
Udolph, J. 1285, 1291
Udora 2396
Ueno, K. 1132, 1142
Ugarte Chamorro, M.A. 1751, 1753, 1763, 1767
Uglioa, A. di 1860
Ugolini, F. 1217, 1847, 1860, 1867, 1879
Ugolini, F.A. 1309, 1877f.
Ugrinova-Skalovska, R. 2263, 2266
Uguccione da Pisa 148, 151, 1844 (s. Hugucio)
Uhlenbeck, Chr.C. 1910, 1912
Uhlenbruck, G. 1044, 1047, 1050
Uhlisch, G. 747, 2365
Uhlmann, F. 3128, 3135
Ukrainka, L. 2332
Ulbricht, E. 1286, 1290, 2215
Ulhart, Ph. 2046
Uljaky-Nagy, T. 3129
Ullendorff, E. 2433
Ullmann, Chr. 2192, 2243
Ullmann, St. 247, 277, 281, 287, 780, 785, 787, 804
Ulloa, A. (di) 1848, 1860f., 2991, 2997
Ullstein, B. 106, 111
Ulmann, C.Chr. 2357
Ulmann, M. 3096
Ulner, H. 1051, 1076, 1080 (= Ulnerus)
Ulrich, M. 2663f., 2670
Ulrich, R. 2663f., 2670
Ulrich, W. 2207, 2211, 2212, 2213, 2231, 2237
Ulvestad, B. 1612, 1614f., 1624f.
Umanec', M. 2330, 2334
Umarchodžaev, M. I. 2768, 3082, 3085
Umbach, H. 584, 805, 1554f., 1562
Umbral, F. 1763
Umdike, D.B. 142
Umeshacandra, S.G. 2497
Unamuno, M. de 1551, 1561
Unbegaun, B.O. 3070, 3085
Underhill, A. 184, 187, 189, 208, 210, 214
Unseth, P. 2643, 2646
Unterberger, R. 1556, 1562
Untermann, J. 79, 1285, 1291
Up John 2509, 2518
Upadhayaya, U. P. 2529, 2533
Upadhyaya, S.P. 3102, 3107
Upasak, Ch.S. 2505
Updike, D.B. 141, 146
Upjohn, A. 3100, 3107
Urban, E. 3129, 3135
Urbanao, A. 2658
Urbańczyk, St. 2270, 2272-2274
Urbano, A. 2660

Urbin, J. d' 2450, 2453
Urbjatova, E.I. 2410
Urdang, L. 524, 529, 584, 667, 766, 1031, 1037, 1044, 1054, 1056, 1076, 1080, 1090, 1092, 1098f., 1169, 1177, 1207, 1209, 1228, 1229, 2001, 2004, 2008
Urfé, H. d' 1346
Uribe, R. 1752, 1763
Ursello da Roccantica, I. 1844
Ursu, N.A. 1891
Urteaga, H. 2684
Urwin, K. 2960
Usai, A. 1902, 1905
Ušakov, D.N. 68, 70, 692, 733, 735, 741, 744, 747, 750, 753, 764, 766, 1147, 2314, 2325, 3079
Ušakov, V.E. 2325
Usharani, T. 2526, 2533
Üsküfî, M.H. 2399, 2406
Uslar, P.K. 2420f., 2423, 3080
Uspenskij, B. A. 3068
Art. 316-324, 3085
Utatnaq, A. 2634
Uterhark, E. 2031
Uthe-Spencker, A. 1038, 1041
Utsi, E. 2390f.
Užarević, J. 2291, 2294

V

Vaarnas, K. 1261, 1265
Văcărescu, I. 1883
Văcaspati, T. T. 2495
Vaccari, L. 1856
Vaccaro, G. 1868
Vachek, J. 207
Vaidya, P.P.J. 3099, 3107
Vaillant, J. 1883, 1889
Vaisbord, A.S. 1143
Vaiyapuripillai 2533
Vakar, N.P. 1362
Vakhrušev, V.M. 2396, 2398
Val.lès, E. 1776f., 1786
Valbuena, A. de 1743, 1767
Valbuena, M. de 1742, 1763
Valda de Jaimes Freyre, L. 2705
Valdemārs, K. 2355, 2358
Valdemoros Alvarez, P. de 2980, 2985
Valderrama Martinez, F. 3095
Valdés, J. de 1740
Valdivia, L. de 2709
Valdman, A. 2872-2875
Valencia, A. 1754, 1763
Valensi, L. 80, 83, 87
Valente, A.L. dos Santos 1728
Valentin, Ch. 2917, 2935
Valentini, F. 221, 223, 3016, 3018
Valéry, P. 1677
Valette, T.G.G. 2919, 2935

Valkhoff, M.F. 3021, 3030
Valla, L. 1051, 1053
Valla, N. 1845, 1861f.
Valladares Núñez, M. 1736, 1738
Valle Abad, F. del 2980, 2985
Valle y Caviedes, J. del 1756
Vallée, F. 2344, 2347, 2350
Vallès, J. 603
Valles, M.P. 1740, 1763
Vallot, P.G. 2584, 2589
Valpola, A. 3175
Valuev, P. 2330
Valverde, B. 1741, 1763
Vámbéry, A. 2400, 2406
Vámbéry, H. 1342
Van Dale, J.H. 1620, 1623
Van den Ende, G. 1795
Van der Elst, G. 816, 822, 1429, 2880f.
Van der Voorst 228
Van der Voort van der Kleij, J.J. 1433-1435
Van der Wijk, W. 1798
Van Dijk, T.A. 331, 359
Van Emmelen, A. 2545
Van Ewijk, P.A.H.J. 2871, 2875
Van Goor 2919, 2935
Van Hoecke, W. 1817f.
Van Hoof, H. 3172
Van Passen, A.-M. 2970, 2976, 3007-3009, 3013
Van Roey, J. 2768, 2882-2884, 2886, 2888
Van Sterkenburg, P.G.J. 358, 1319, 1321f., 1432, 1434ff.
Văn Tân 2587, 2589
Van Vloten, J. 227
Van Volxem, D. 2221
Vanacker, V.F. 653, 667, 2233
Vanagas, A. 1286, 1290
Vandame, R.P.Ch. 2644, 2646
Vandendorpe, J. 1671
Vander Beke, G.E.(I.) 1318, 1321, 1355, 1362
Vanderhaege, M. 2923, 2931
Vanerius, J. 1011
Vang Bu-jung, M. 3127, 3135
Vangeois, D. 61
Vanierius, J. 1016
Vankuli, M.b.M. 2399, 2406
Vannier, V.-A. 1807
Vanoverbergh, M. 2571-2573
Vanparijs, J. 2765
Vanquli 2446
Van't Hul, B. 269
Vanvik, A. 1308, 1310
Váquez y Rodríguez, L. 1747
Varata, T. 3101, 3107
Varchi, B. 150, 1852, 1854
Varea, F. de 2661, 2664, 2670
Vargas Ugarte, R. 2682, 2684
Vărgulev, A. 3082

Varini, G. 2935
Varma, J. 3100, 3107
Varma, R. 2519, 2521
Varma, R.C. 2513
Varma, R.V. 2517
Varney-Pleasants, J. 1308, 1310
Varnhagen, F.A. de 2674
Varnhagen, F.A. von 2673, 2675
Varvaro, A. 1876
Váša, P. 2281, 2284
Vasič, S. 277
Vasilevskaja, I.A. 1209, 2310, 2329
Vasiliev, C. 2308
Vasiliev, V.P. 3108
Vasishta, M. 3143f.
Vaslet, D. 2881
Vasmer, M. 1138, 1142, 1285, 1290, 2315f., 2318, 2325, 2471, 2473, 3069, 3085
Vasnani, J. N. 2516, 2520
Vasseur, J. 1270, 1275
Vasu, V. 2495
Vater, J. 2462, 2925
Vater, L. S. 2468
Vater, P. 3058, 3061
Vatré, H. 3122, 3125, 3135, 3137
Vaugelas, C.F. de 1068, 1075, 1212, 1775, 1798f., 1815 (s. de Vaugelas)
Vaulchier, H. de 1247, 1802, 1804, 1817
Vaunaize, P. 132f., 208, 211, 213, 1632f., 1637
Vázquez y Rodríguez, L. 1763
Vázquez, G. 2901
Vecchio Kervorkian, E. 3174
Večerka, R. 2260
Veda, K. 2620, 2623
Vedder, H. 2652-2655
Vedernikov, N.V. 2325
Veen, B. van der 3170
Veen, H. van der 2568
Veen, K. van der 2027
Veen, P.A.F. van 2021
Veenhof, K.R. 1693
Veenker, W. 1142, 2413
Veer, C.L. de 3126, 3135
Veer-Bertels, E.T. van der 2920, 2935
Veeresatingam, K. 2531
Vega, V. 1047, 1050, 1054, 1056
Vegamián, F. M. de 2702
Vehara, K. 2621, 262
Vehbî, S.M. 2399, 2406
Veinbergs, A. 2359
Veinerte, B. 2359
Veith, G. 2084
Veith, H. 2062, 2073
Veith, W.H. 2091f., 2100
Vejle, Chr.O. 1916, 1922
Vejsman, A. D. 3078

Vekene, E. van der 1811
Velázquez Gallardo, P. 2697, 2700
Velázquez, M. de la Cadena 2951f., 2955f.
Velčeva, B. 2263
Veldeken, H. van 1560
Veldtrup, J. 1530, 1532, 1537
Veleslavín, D.A. 2279, 2280, 2284
Vélez de Aragón, Z. 1746, 1764
Velie, D. 2702
Velie, V. 2702
Velinova, L. 3175
Velleman, A. 2919, 2935
Vellīgs, A. 2355
Vellón, N. 1742, 1763
Velloso, Frei 2672
Vemura, S. 305
Venator, M. 2918, 2935
Vendell, H. 1939, 1942
Vendler, Z. 852, 855
Vendoti, G. 2916, 2935
Vendryes, J. 2341f.
Venegas, A. 1740, 1764
Veneroni, G. 1195, 1846, 1861, 2912, 2914, 2916, 2935, 3011-3014, 3018
Veneroni, G. di 3018f.
Veneziani, A. 1198
Venezky, R.L. 1142
Venkata Rao, N. 2528
Venkata Ratnam, M. 2531
Venkatasubbiah, G. 2525, 2533
Veṅkatamādhava 2490
Venkayya, M. 2526, 2531
Vennemann, Th. 247, 277, 575
Ventris, M. 1696
Venture, A. 3128, 3135
Venturelli, A. J. 2707
Venturin, R. 2294
Venturino, B. 2464, 2466
Venuti, A. 3007f., 3013
Venuti, F. 1845, 1847, 1852, 1861, 2970, 2975, 3008
Veny, J. 1772, 1777, 1788
Venzac, G. 66, 69, 1841
Vera y González, E. 1746, 1764
Verantius, F. (Veranzio) 2289, 2295, 2382, 2913, 2935
Verax, Ch. 3122, 3128, 3135
Verbinc, F. 2300f.
Verbraeken, R. 1817
Vercoullie, J. 2018, 2021
Verdaguer i Puigdemont, X. 1778, 1786
Verdam, J. 1411, 1414f., 1432-1435, 2021, 2041, 2047
Verdams, J. 2012
Verdelho, E. 1011, 1019, 1075
Verdeyen, R. 3021, 3029
Verdier, V. 1664, 1668
Verdonk, R.A. 1792, 1817, 2977f., 2982, 2986f.

Verdu, B. 1352
Verdugo, N. 1740, 1764
Verelius, O. 1934, 1942
Vergara y Martin, G.M. 1080, 1764
Vergara, G.M. 1743, 1767
Verger, V. 640f., 1803, 1808f.
Vergilius 149, 1141, 1717, 1986
Verheijen, J. A. J. 2568
Verhofstadt, E. 653, 667, 2233
Verikatamadhava 2490
Verini, G. 10, 1851f., 1861
Verkhrats'kyj, I. 2330, 2334
Verkhucha, V. 3022, 3029
Verlée, L. 1321, 1353, 1356, 1362, 1364
Vermeer, H.J. 171, 174, 2207, 2243, 3021, 3030
Vermont, R. 2663, 2666, 2670
Vernay, H. 1184, 1816
Vernon, J. 2912, 2928
Vernor 2951
Veron, J. 1793, 2957, 2960
Véron, P. 1349, 1352
Veroni, G. 3009
Verri, S. 2643, 2646
Verrius Flaccus 1714
Verschueren, J. 816, 819, 822
Versegi, F. 2376, 2382
Verstegan, R. 1948
Vertel, E.V. 2321, 2329
Vertel', V.A. 2321, 2329
Vertenten, P. 2636f.
Vervliet, J.B. 2019f.
Verwey, G. 166
Verwijs, E. 1411, 1414f., 1432, 1434, 2021
Veselić, R. 2290f., 2295
Veselitskij, V.V. 2316, 2329, 3175
Veselytskyi, V.V. 2768
Vesikansa, J. 2385, 2387
Veski, J.V. 2393-2394
Veslot, H. 2886
Vestring, S.H. 2392
Vey, J.L. 2577, 2583
Vial, P. 2559
Viala, A. 1796, 1818
Viallanueva, B. 2690
Vialle, J.-A. 1903
Vian, B. 84
Vian, R. 2901
Viani, P. 1217, 1847, 1861
Vianini, G. 1261, 1265
Vibhag, B. 3097
Vibhag, H. 3097, 3107
Vickery, A. 1671
Vickery, B.C. 1671
Vico, D. de 2661, 2664, 2670
Vico, G. 1873
Victor, H. 2912, 2916, 2935
Victor-Rood, J. 1567, 1573
Victorin, C.W. 3040

Vicuña Cifuentes, J. 1764
Vidal de Battini, B.E. 1764
Vidal, Fra Albert 1773, 1786
Vidal, J.-P. 2980, 2985
Vidocq 1184, 1187
Vidović, R. 2293, 2295
Vidyanidhi, P. 2519
Vidyapith, G. 3097, 3099, 3107
Vidyāvāgīsa R. Ch. 2510, 2518
Viehbeck, F.W. 1268, 1275
Viehweger, D. 78, 127, 163, 173f.,
   274f., 278, 321, 359, 408, 460,
   500, 532f., 539, 542-546, 548,
   550-552, 573, 578, 580, 584,
   599, 609, 614, 616-618, 626f.,
   699, 777, 779, 787, 831,
   833-835, 849, 854f., 868, 881f.,
   889, 891, 893, 956, 967, 1009,
   1019, 1031, 1230, 1645, 1671,
   2131, 2150, 2238, 2243, 2727,
   2760, 2766, 2853
Vieira, F.D. 1728, 1735
Vieli, R. 1898f., 1905
Vienney, R. 917
Viereck, W. 662-664, 668, 1183f.,
   2219
Viethen, H.W. 1813
Vietor, H. 2043
Viëtor, W. 1308, 1310, 2093, 2098
Vietze, H.-P. 1142, 2404, 2406,
   2768
Vieyra, A. 3022, 3029
Vigfússon, G. 1929, 1931
Vignans de 1125
Vignati, M.A. 2709f.
Vigner, G. 1031
Vignuzzi, U. 1844, 1860
Vigón, B. 1747, 1764
Vigué i Vinas, J. 1782
Viguier, P.F. 2401
Vijayarājendra, M. 2502, 2505
Vilborg, E. 3124
Vilikazi, B. W. 2648
Vilkki, J. 3126f., 3135
Vilkuna, K. 2385, 2388
Villamañán, A. de 2704
Villamayor, L.C. 1764
Villamizar Jaimes, M. 1758
Villamor, G.G. 2686, 2690
Villanova, A. di 11
Villanueva, A.L. 3132
Villanueva, J. 2951
Villanuova, A. di 3015
Villarin, J. 1189
Villatte, C. 514, 516, 1185, 1189,
   2751, 2802, 2920, 2935, 3005
Villemain, A.F. 1804
Villers, M.-E. de 61
Villiers, P. de 1310
Villon, F. 1533
Vilmar, A. F. Chr. 2215, 2231
Vimalabuddhitissa, T. 2505

Vinay, J.-P. 2768, 2855, 2858f.,
   2958, 2960
Viñas, A. 2980, 2982
Viñaza, C.Muñoz y Manzano
   Conde de la 1767, 2936f.,
   2948, 2987, 3175
Vincendon, S. 43, 46
Vincent, C. 1217
Vincenz, I. 2859
Vinci, L. da 1844
Vinguier, P.F. 2406
Vinja, V. 1903, 1905, 2292, 2295
Vinnikov, I.N. 2431, 2437
Vinogradov, N. 2323
Vinogradov, V.V. 2266,
   2309-2315, 2321, 2325, 2329,
   3075, 3085
Vinogradova, V.L. 2318f., 2321,
   2325, 2329
Vinokur, T.G. 2321, 2329
Vinteler, O. 1082, 1888
Vinterberg, H. 2714, 2726, 2789,
   2807, 2813, 3057, 3061
Vinyals, F.A. 2955
Vinyoles i Vidal, J.J. 1777, 1786
Vias, A. 2980, 2982
Violette, L. 2575
Virgil 149, 1141, 1717, 1986
Virkkunen, S. 2385, 2388
Virmaître, Ch. 1185, 1189
Virtaranta, P. 2387f.
Viscardi, A. 216, 224
Viscarra, V.H. 1764
Visconti, F.M. 1844
Vising, J. 3041f.
Visner, A. 1895, 1904
Višnjakova, O.V. 1125, 2317,
   2324f.
Visser, W. 2026, 2033, 2035
Vissian, M. 2938, 2947
Visuddhābhivamsa 2504
Viśva-Bandhu 1137, 1142
Viswas Sailendra 2518
Vit den Boogaart, P.C. 1321
Vitale, M. 1853-1856, 1862, 3010,
   3013
Vitebsky 2537
Viterbo, E. 2462, 2466
Vitezović, P. 2289
Vitkauskas, V. 1290
Vito, L. de 2455
Vittmann, G. 1681
Vittori, G. 2978, 2986, 2993, 2997,
   3008, 3012
Vittorio Emanuele II. 1857
Vivas, R. 2702
Vivre, G. de 1051, 1053
Vizetelly, F.H. 1308, 1311, 1993,
   2007
Vjlaky-Nagy, T. 3135
Vlachos, I. 1705, 1713
Vlachov, S. I. 2768, 3082, 3085

Vlachus, P. 2935
Vlačić, M. 2296
Vlajkov, T. 2305
Vlasits, J. 2293
Vlataris, M. 1880
Vlček, J. 2768
Vlloa, A. 2997
Vloten, J. van 227
Vo-Ko 3126, 3135
Vodnik, V. 2298
Vodňanský, J. 2279
Voelkel, M.J.A. 2094, 2098, 2358
Voetz, L. 1258, 2037, 2049
Vogel, A. 358, 405, 1776, 1786,
   2113, 2129, 2225, 2231
Vogel, C. 1120, 1125, 2498f., 2507
Vogel, E. 2990
Vogel, V.H. 1536f.
Vogelmann, G. 1011, 1016, 1081,
   1083
Vogt, E. 2428, 2437
Vogt, E.-M. 1704
Vogt, H. 2419, 2421
Vogt, H.L. 231, 246
Vogt, H.O. 1362, 2895, 2901
Vogtberg, J. v. 3017
Voiculescu, V. 1887
Voigt, Chr.F.T. 2058, 2073
Voigt, H. 124
Voigt, W. 14, 18, 101, 131, 135,
   773, 779, 1613, 1625, 2766,
   2768, 2809, 2813
Voinova, N. 3022, 3029
Voitl, H. 1275, 1293
Vojcechovyč, I.V. 3076, 3084
Vojnova, L. A. 3074
Vokoun-David, M. 305
Volchkov, S. 2917, 2935
Volckmann, E. 1254
Volčkov, S. S. 3073, 3084
Völkel, P. 2276f.
Volkmann, L. 3151, 3157
Volkmar, N. 1411, 1415
Volkov, S.S. 2329
Vollbeding, J.Chr. 1155, 1220,
   2071, 2091, 2098
Vollmann [Pseudonym = Johannes Gräßli] 2062, 2073
Vollmöller, K. 224, 2758
Vollnhals, O. 2807, 2813, 3026,
   3029, 3167
Volodin, A.P. 2629, 2631
Volos, R. 2294
Volostnova, M.B. 2316, 2325
Volpi, A. 1126, 1130
Volpi, G. 1844, 1855, 1860, 1863,
   1866, 1879
Voltaire, F.M.A. de 25, 1212
Voltić, J. 2289, 2295
Volz, H. 2111, 2112, 2128, 2227
Vomperskij, V.P. 2310f., 2329,
   3072-3074, 3085, 3176

von Kutschera, F. 539, 541, 547, 549, 579, 896, 899
Vondel, J. van den 2010
Vondrák, W. 2265
Voorhoeve, J. 1340
Voort van der Kleij, J.J. van der 3039
Voort, J.V.D. 408
Vooys, C.G.N. de 1011, 1019, 3038f.
Vopisco, M. 1844, 1861f.
Vorenc, G. 2297, 2301
Vorepierre, B.-D. de 1805
Vormann, F. 2636, 2638
Vosokov, A. Ch. 3075
Voss, H. 2058
Voss, K. 1038, 1041
Vossen, P. 3168
Vossen, R. 2644, 2646
Vossius, L. 2916, 2935, 2938, 2947
Vostokov, A.Chr. 2261, 2264, 2267, 2312, 2318, 2325
Vostoleov, A. Chr. 3084
Vosylyte, V. 1290
Voß, J.H. 2060
Voßen, R. 1342
Votila, T.E. 2396, 2398
Vovelle, M. 165, 167
Voyuova, L. A. 3085
Vrančić, F. 2289, 2296
Vreede, A. C. 2562
Vreese, W. de 2012, 2022
Vries, A. de 2026, 3153-3155, 3157
Vries, A. H. de 2035
Vries, J. de 294, 296, 1929, 1932, 2018, 2021, 2027
Vries, M. de 227, 229, 296, 1231, 1241, 1397-1400, 1402f., 1405, 1415, 1432, 1609, 2010, 2021, 2029, 2033
Vries, O. 2024f.
Vries, T.G. de 2035
Vrioste, J. 2683
Vũ Văn Kính 2587, 2587
Vujaklija, M. 2293, 2295
Vừờng Hoàng Tuyên 2591, 2594
Vusin, K. 2280, 2284
Vvedenskaja, L.A. 1081, 1083, 2317, 2325
Vvre, G. de 1080
Vyádi 2489
Vyasa, V. 2511, 2518
Vycichl, W. 1680f.

W

Waanders, J. G. B. 2926
Wacha, I. 1562
Wachter, J. G. 2088, 2098
Wächter, O. E. S. von 2073
Wächtler, J.Chr. 768, 771, 1172, 1177
Wackernagel, J. 2491
Wackernagel, W. 2088, 2098, 2215, 2231
Wackrill, A.E. 3121f., 3135
Wade, C. 1198
Wade, Th. 3109
Waesberghe, J. 3035, 3039
Wagener, H. 166f.
Wagener, J.D. 2988, 2990, 3022, 3024, 3029
Wagnalls, A.W. 1993f., 1997f., 2000
Wagner, A. 2967
Wagner, E. 2452f., 2455
Wagner, F. 1011, 1016, 2376, 2382
Wagner, H. 1390, 1843, 2786
Wagner, J. 2094, 2098
Wagner, K. 413, 438, 460, 499
Wagner, M.L. 1197, 1328, 1334, 1535, 1538, 1845, 1849, 1863, 1876, 1902f., 1906, 1907
Wagner, R. 2230
Wagner, R.-L. 43, 46, 222, 224, 602, 607, 907f., 917, 930, 1216, 1797, 1818, 1828, 1833, 1843, 2986, 3010
Wahba, M. 3092, 3096
Wahby, T. 2483, 2486
Wahl, E. de 3130, 3135
Wåhlin, St. 1270f.
Wahlster, W. 893, 899
Wahrmund, A. 3090
Wahrig, E. 277, 584, 855, 2243
Wahrig, G. 138-141, 143, 145, 163, 272, 277, 315-317, 320, 355, 357f., 369f., 405f., 458f., 498f., 508, 515, 532, 541, 574f., 584, 626, 634, 637, 640, 648, 661, 667, 672, 687, 698, 747, 750, 753, 778, 786, 795f., 802-804, 820f., 828, 832-834, 848f., 855, 858-861, 880, 919, 929f., 955, 966, 983, 987f., 1019, 1170, 1177, 1220, 1235, 1238, 1240, 1608, 1622, 1638, 1645, 1672, 2014, 2119, 2123, 2130f., 2142, 2146f., 2152f., 2155f., 2160, 2162, 2165-70, 2185, 2188, 2215, 2217, 2231, 2243, 2246
Wahrig, R. 277, 584, 2243
Wahrig-Burfeind, R. 273, 320, 358, 406, 459, 499, 575, 2231
Wahrmund, A. 3096
Wailly, E.-A. de 1803-1806, 1809
Wailly, N.-F. de 1803-1806, 1809
Wajid, M. 3176
Wakefield, H. 524, 589, 591, 746
Wakelin, M.F. 653, 657
Wakenfield, H. 2900
Walczak, W. 2272
Walde, A. 1324, 1326, 1334, 1338, 1341f., 1393, 1412, 1415, 2341f.
Waldmann, K. 2068
Waldmeier, Th. 2462, 2466
Waldschmidt, E. 2506
Walford, A.J. 3030, 3176
Walker, A. 2036
Walker, A. G. H. 2028, 2031f., 2035f.
Walker, C. H. 2455
Walker, D.C. 1143
Walker, D.E. 1666, 1670f., 3159, 3168
Walker, G. D. 2559
Walker, J. 509, 1126f., 1131, 1308, 1311, 1955, 1959, 1966, 1988, 1991, 2004, 2008
Walker, L.E.Q. 1260
Walker, R.M. 2954
Walker, W. 1221, 1223
Wall, R. 439, 460, 465, 499
Wallace, M. 209, 214
Wallach, J.F. 163, 166
Waller, R. 714, 724
Wallis, D.L. 575
Wallis, J. 737, 749
Wallmann, J.C. 2650, 2652, 2654
Wallnig, G. 1105, 1111
Wallraf, A. J. 2087, 2098
Wallraff, G. 773f., 779
Walsh, J.P. 3176
Walsh, R. 1199
Walsh, S.P. 3176
Walsh, W.S. 1046, 1050
Walshe, M. O. 2193, 2231
Walter, H. 513, 516, 1304-1308, 1310f., 1532, 1538, 2305
Walther, Chr. 1428, 2096, 2226
Walther, E. 2207, 2216, 3129, 3135
Walther, H. 1033, 1042, 1282, 1877, 1879, 2276f.
Walther, I.L. 1261, 1265
Walton, I. 1946
Waltz, N. E. 2702
Wamser, H. 1269f., 1275
Wamsleben, J. M. 2454
Wander, K.F.W. 27, 1035f., 1042f., 1601, 1609, 2065, 2073
Wandres, C. 2652-2654
Wandruszka, M. 1184, 2726, 2752, 2883, 2887f.
Wang Niansun 2598, 2611
Wang Yunwu (= Wong, Y.W.) 2606
Wang, W.S.-Y. 1624
Wang, Y. 1012, 1016, 3112
Wang, Y.-C. 1671
Wangensteen, B. 1927
Wängler, H.-H. 1321, 1362, 1669
Wannemakers, H.G. 3125, 3128, 3134f.
Wannenmacher, W. 1206
Wapnewski, P. 43, 46

Warczyk, R. 634
Ward, A.L. 1046-1048
Ward, J.H. 2572f.
Ward, S.R. 2509, 2517
Warder, A.K. 2501, 2507
Ware, J.R. 1163, 1186, 1189
Wares, A.C. 1342
Warfel, H.R. 277, 1989, 2009
Warhol, A. 1109
Warier, M.I. 3100, 3106
Waringhien, G. 3121f., 3124-3126, 3133, 3135, 3137
Warmer, Chr. 2935
Warnant, L. 506, 1126f., 1131, 1304-1306, 1308, 1311
Warnesson, I. 1080
Warnke, I. 1142, 2404, 2406
Warnke, K. 1242, 1245
Warrack, A. 1985f.
Warren, N. 582
Wartburg, W. von 282, 286, 293, 296, 672, 731, 1059, 1066f., 1090f., 1093, 1177, 1185, 1323-1325, 1327, 1330, 1332, 1334, 1342, 1343f., 1347f., 1414, 1430, 1435, 1531, 1672, 1777, 1827, 1839, 1867, 1893f., 1904f., 1969, 1982, 2281, 2922, 2936, 3176
Wason, P.C. 899
Wasserzieher, E. 120, 124, 1234, 1240, 1269f., 1275, 2090, 2094, 2098, 2100, 2193f., 2231f.
Wassileff, Chr. 1242, 1245
Wassink, T. 1366, 1368
Waters, Th. 2598, 2611
Watkins, C. 1331, 1334
Watkins, E. A. 2696
Watkins, R. 2949
Watnabe, A. 3117
Watson, D.O. 3142, 3144
Watson, G. 1987
Watson, H.D. 1985
Watson, O. 687
Watson, R. 2590f., 2594
Watson, S. 2590f., 2594
Watters, D. 2558
Watts, J.D.W. 2428
Wawra, F. 1242, 1245
Wawrzkowicz, St. 3064, 3068
Waxman, M. 2433
Weadley, R. 2592
Weathers, K. 2663, 2670
Weathers, N. 2663, 2670
Webb, G. I. 2641
Weber, A. 1100-1102, 2198, 2231f.
Weber, E. 165, 167
Weber, F. 2488
Weber, F.A. 3016, 3019
Weber, H.J. 787
Weber, N. 2705
Weber, P. F. 2174, 2232

Webster, D. 1993
Webster, D. H. 2634
Webster, N. 29f., 37, 98, 128, 133, 225f., 503-505, 511, 526, 723, 750, 763f., 783, 1072, 1162, 1326, 1334, 1768, 1951, 1954, 1958-1960, 1963-1966, 1989-1991, 1993f., 1996, 2000, 2004f., 2008, 2952, 3119, 3175
Webster, W. 1207, 1209
Weck, J. 2923, 2935
Wedewer, R. 715, 726
Wedl, R. 1052f.
Weekly, E. 1258, 1260
Weeren, J. van 1002, 1005, 1008, 2886
Weerman, F. 1017
Wegener, G. 1268, 1273, 2226
Wegener, H. 2173, 2243
Wegener, I. 573, 850, 855
Wegera, K.-P. 1423, 1429, 1610, 2048
Wegner, I. 584, 893f., 896, 898f., 1060, 1067, 1094, 1692, 1694
Wegner, J. 532, 540
Wegstein, W. 2038, 2048f.
Wehle, P. 119, 124
Wehr, H. 2445, 2766, 3091f., 3096
Wehrle, H. 162f., 769, 771, 1059, 1066, 1089, 1092f., 2087, 2097f., 2177, 2182, 2232
Weiers, M. 2625f.
Weigand, E. 581, 1157, 2756
Weigand, F.L.K. 112, 124, 248, 273, 1064, 1066, 1069, 1074, 1234-1237, 1240, 2059, 2064, 2073, 2079, 2081, 2083, 2085, 2095, 2098
Weigand, G. 2307f., 2366
Weigel, H. 1349, 1352, 2232
Weijnen, A. 2021
Weijters, T. 1144f.
Weiland, P. 1068, 1074
Weiman, R. 3148
Wein, V. 3026f.
Weinberg, E. 3176
Weinberg, F. 1752, 1767
Weinberger, Chr. 547f., 552, 584
Weinberger, O. 547f., 552, 584
Weinbrot, H.D. 34, 606, 767, 1944, 1952f.
Weiner, E. 326f., 1655, 1666, 1668, 1670
Weiner, E.S.C. 1414, 1609, 3168
Weiner, M. 1208
Weiner, S.C. 1548
Weingart, M. 2265, 2268
Weingarten, E. 1632, 1637
Weinheimer, H. 2428, 2435
Weinhold, K. 2091
Weinhold, N. 269
Weinmaier 2191, 2216

Weinreich, M. 2247, 2249-2254
Weinreich, U. 66, 277, 294, 296, 532f., 552, 564, 584, 652, 850, 854, 991, 998, 1032, 1615, 1625, 2247, 2249, 2250, 2253f., 2791, 2794
Weinrich, H. 10, 14, 18, 24, 28, 43, 46, 102, 110, 122, 125, 134, 206, 231, 240, 244, 611f., 614, 797, 805, 830, 853, 989, 998, 1157f., 1207, 1209, 1304, 1515, 1517, 1523, 2222, 2236
Weinsberger, Chr. 539
Weinsberger, O. 539
Weinstock, H. 509, 518
Weinzinger, E. 2454
Weir, C.J.M. 1684, 1686
Weir, E. 2967
Weis, Erich 1053, 1363, 2750f., 2794, 2796, 2803, 2890, 2895, 2901, 2965, 3000-3003, 3006
Weis, Erwin 2968
Weise, G. 2225
Weiser, H. 2896, 2900
Weisgerber, L. 282, 287, 848, 1146, 1150, 1152, 2208, 2224
Weismann, E. 3031, 3034
Weiss, F. 1125
Weiss, H. 1532, 1537, 2177, 2185, 2229, 2232
Weiss, P. 704, 725, 3157
Weiss, R. 106, 109f., 213, 1632, 1637
Weiss, W. 126f., 279, 408, 578f., 586, 599, 614, 835, 2076, 2235, 2238, 2244, 2902
Weiß, W. 1067
Weiss, W. E. 2760, 2767
Weißmann, E. 3073
Weitenauer, I. 2916, 2936
Weitershaus, F.W. 387, 408
Weith, O. 1110f.
Weizsäcker, W. 2218
Wekker, H. 592, 739, 748, 1975, 1982, 2770, 2775
Welcker, C. 166f., 841
Wełzcewa, B. 2268
Weleslawin, D. A. de 2936
Welke, K. 79, 579, 583, 584, 655f., 699, 2768
Wellby, M.S. 2463, 2468
Weller, F.-R. 1019, 1038, 1042
Wellmann, H. 269, 531, 552, 562, 584, 1623, 2105, 2131, 2136, 2243
Wells, D.A. 1137, 1143
Wells, E. 1270, 1275
Wells, J.C. 518, 1418, 1420, 1426, 1428, 1539, 1543, 1548, 1974, 1983, 2104, 2230, 2243, 3126f., 3135

Wells, R.A. 30, 34, 652, 657, 704, 993, 999, 1217, 1951, 1953, 2005, 2009
Wells, S.W. 1363
Wells, W.G.B. 3101, 3107
Welsh, B.W.W. 1005, 1008
Welsh, C. 573, 584
Welte, W. 2207, 2211, 2232
Welter, E. G. 119, 124, 2198, 2232
Wemmers, J. 2449, 2455
Wendt, H.F. 1891
Wenig, Chr. 629f., 634, 874, 880
Weniger, D. 584
Wenkanna, N. 2531
Wennrich, P. 1261, 1265
Wenström, E. 3048f., 3051
Wentholt, L.R. 1107, 1111
Wentworth, H. 36, 1186f., 1189, 1530
Wenzel, W. 2276, 2278
Wepman, J.M. 1321
Werdena, M. de 2043
Wergeland, H. 1923, 1925
Werlich, E. 1011, 1016
Werlin, J. 1262, 1266, 2188, 2232
Wermser, R. 768, 771
Werner, F.C. 1228-1230
Werner, G. 1126, 1131
Werner, M. 1047, 1050
Werner, O. 1932, 3168
Werner, R. 87, 118, 126f., 274, 363, 370, 532, 551f., 557, 562f., 584, 657, 704, 706, 713f., 722, 726, 765, 767, 782, 919-922, 927, 930, 991, 997, 999, 1031, 1112, 1119, 1178, 1751f., 1754f., 1765, 1767, 2643, 2646, 2728, 2756, 2768f., 2797f., 2800, 2803, 2829, 2832, 2835-2837, 2841, 2854, 2864, 2908, 2936, 2989, 2991
Werny, P. 1021, 1025, 1031
Wersig, G. 168, 170, 277, 394, 408, 460, 585, 615, 627
Weseen, M.H. 1125
Wesemann, M. 2752
Wesle, C. 820
Wesley, J. 1209, 1944, 1950, 1952
Wessel, M.G. 3132
Wessely, E. 2969
Wessén, E. 1935
Wessman, V.E.V. 1939, 1942
West, G.D. 1293, 1296
West, M. 133, 135, 901-905, 1316, 1322, 1353, 1362f., 1967f., 2891, 2895, 2901
West, M. L. 1702
West, M. P. 509, 517, 1669
West, M. Ph. 1305, 1311
Weste, E.W. 1939, 1942
Westendorf, W. 1680f.
Westerbergh, U. 1721

Westergaard, N. L. 2473
Westermann, C. 2428, 2435
Westermann, D. 1342, 2642, 2646-2649
Westermann, K. 2199, 2217
Westermayer, M. 3128, 3135
Westkolle, P. 199, 206, 2185, 2223
Weston, J. 1368
Westphal, E.O.J. 2650f., 2654, 2656
Wetekamp, S. 2045, 2049
Wetzel, C. 719
Wetzel, Chr. 2225
Wetzel, R. 1571f.
Wetzstein, J.G. 3096
Wetzstein, J.I. 3086
Wexler, P. 2246, 2254
Wexler, P.J. 1803, 1818, 2769
Wey, F. 1800, 1818
Weydt, H. 808, 810, 813, 823, 830, 862, 1221, 1223, 1624, 2759
Weymuth, E. 3000, 3004
Weyssenhoff-Brożkowa, Chr. 1721
Wharton, L.C. 1437
Whately, E.J. 1074
Whatmough, J. 1342
Wheatley, H.B. 1129
Wheeler, A. 2702, 2706
Wheeler, M. 2769
Wheeler, P. 1659, 1668
Wheelock, A. 1439
Wherpster, Z. 1145
Whitaker, R.E. 1693
Whitcut, J. 31, 34, 88, 115, 127, 208f., 214, 704, 1980, 1983
White, A.C. 1874
White, J.S. 3168
White, L. 2769
Whitehall, H. 512, 1450, 1456
Whiteley, W.H. 2647, 2649
Whitfield, F. J. 3066
Whitfield, F. T. 3063
Whitfield, J.S. 1130f.
Whitford, H.C. 1125
Whiting, B. 1034, 1036, 1041f.
Whitley, R. 275
Whitling, R. B. 2879, 2881
Whitney, W.D. 11, 17, 220, 223, 1133, 1135, 1137, 1143, 1162, 1166, 1958, 1966, 1992, 2003f., 2007, 2490, 2497, 3116
Whorf, B. L. 1342, 2869
Whyte Ellis, F. 2529
Wiarda, T.D. 2023, 2035
Wicelius, G. 1275
Wichen-Schol, M. van 2027, 2035
Wichmann, Y. 2378, 2381, 2396, 2398
Wichter, S. 787, 837, 842
Wick, St. 2663, 2670
Widding, O. 1929, 1932

Widdowson, J.D.A. 77
Widegren, G. 3047, 3051
Widerhold, J.H. 1795f., 2999
Widłak, St. 1194, 1199
Widmann, G. 2199, 2232
Widmark, P.F. 3044, 3046, 3048, 3050
Widmer, W. 1219f.
Wiechmann, H. A. 2191, 2232
Wiecynsky, J.L. 167
Wieczorkiewicz, B. 2271, 2273f.
Wiedemann, B. 1074
Wiedemann, F.G. 2393
Wiedemann, F.J. 2394f., 2398
Wiegand, H.E. 7, 17-19, 24, 28, 45, 78f., 99, 101f., 104-106, 108-119, 124, 126-128, 130f., 133-135, 171f., 174, 181f., 189, 206f., 209, 214, 216, 224, 239f., 244, 246, 248-253, 257-260, 262, 265, 267-269, 271, 273-280, 287, 314, 316, 321, 330f., 333-339, 341, 344-347, 350, 353, 356, 359-376, 379-383, 386, 388-391, 393f., 396-398, 400, 404, 406-410, 412f., 416-435, 437f., 440f., 445-453, 455f., 458-472, 480f., 485, 488-491, 493, 495, 497-501, 518, 522, 525, 530-534, 537-545, 550-564, 566, 568, 570-572, 575f., 578-581, 585-587, 591f., 599, 607, 613-629, 634f., 645, 648f., 652-657, 668, 671f., 688f., 691, 693, 697-699, 733, 736, 740f., 745, 747-749, 751, 754, 761, 767f., 771f., 777-779, 788, 791, 793, 796, 804-806, 812-814, 817-819, 821f., 830, 834f., 837, 840-842, 846f., 849-851, 854f., 863, 868, 881, 896f., 899, 930, 947f., 950, 955f., 958f., 961f., 964-967, 970, 977, 979-981, 988f., 992, 998f., 1001, 1009, 1032, 1043, 1064, 1067, 1146, 1152, 1178, 1230, 1236, 1240f., 1254, 1258, 1275, 1283, 1360, 1364, 1394, 1415f., 1428-1430, 1435, 1513, 1515f., 1518, 1521, 1523, 1531, 1540f., 1548f., 1551, 1557, 1562, 1567, 1569, 1572f., 1590-1592, 1608-1611, 1613, 1620, 1623-1625, 1632f., 1638f., 1644f., 1656, 1668, 1704, 1966, 2021, 2048, 2051, 2074-2077, 2085, 2099f., 2102-2106, 2108, 2110, 2112-2114, 2118f., 2112-2124, 2126f., 2131, 2133, 2135-2138, 2140, 2142, 2146f., 2150, 2155, 2157, 2159f., 2163, 2165, 2170,

2172f., 2175, 2178, 2180,
2185f., 2189, 2191, 2193-2195,
2197f., 2202, 2206, 2208, 2212,
2233-46, 2773, 2714, 2717,
2722, 2725, 2727f., 2750, 2757,
2760, 2764, 2767, 2769, 2774f.,
2778, 2789, 2836-2840, 2841f.,
2851, 2853, 2902, 2939, 2947f.,
3061, 3153, 3157, 3172
Wieger, L. 1165
Wieken-Mayser, M. 1632. 1637
Wieland, Chr.M. 236f., 246, 2055
Wieland, H. 3034
Wiele, H. 848
Wierlacher, A. 1066, 1364, 2243
Wierzbicka, A. 161, 163, 292, 296,
531, 544, 546, 587, 1672, 2640,
2889
Wiese, G. 719, 726
Wieselgren, P. 2394
Wiesemann, U. 2707
Wiesinger, P. 2191, 2240
Wießner, E. 1551, 1561, 2104,
2215, 2232
Wießner, J. 1219f.
Wiezell, R.J. 2997
Wijk, N. van 2018, 2020
Wijk, W. van der 1818
Wijnands, P. 1165
Wijngaarden, A. van 1321
Wikforss, J. 3044, 3046
Wiklund, K.B. 2390, 2392
Wilczynska, V. 2881
Wild, Chr. 459, 580
Wilde, J. 1257
Wildhagen, K. 2968f.
Wilensky, R. 1670
Wilhelm, G. 1694
Wilhelm, J. 2888
Wilhelm, K. 3001, 3004
Wilhelmi, Chr. 3152, 3157
Wilhelmsen, I. 1360
Wilke, J. 1207, 1210
Wilken, E. 2216
Wilkending, G. 26, 28
Wilkins, E.H. 1874
Wilkins, J. 10, 1089, 1093, 1944,
1951
Wilkinson, R.J. 2563, 2565
Wilks, Y. 3168
Wilks, Y.A. 1671
Will, H.-G. 2643f.
Wille, M. 315, 321, 1638, 1644
Willée, G. 362, 370f., 407
Willems, M. 3174
Willers, H. 1029, 1038, 1042, 2990
Williams, A.M. 1964, 1966
Williams, Ch.A.S. 3152, 3157
Williams, E.B. 2715f., 2725, 2728,
2769, 2952f., 2956
Williams, G.S. 2515
Williams, H.W. 2574f.

Williams, J. 1964, 1966
Williams, J.L. 1669, 2345,
2347-2349
Williams, M.J. 1450
Williams, R. 2350
Williams, St. 1665, 1668f., 1671
Williams, W. 2574f.
Williamson, K. 1342, 2648
Willinsky, J. 2006, 2009
Willis, W.H. 1701
Willmann, H. 516, 2853, 2968
Willnat, H. 2769
Wilmanns, W. 2092
Wilmeth, D.B. 1530
Wilske, L. 1168, 1178
Wilson, F.P. 1036, 1042
Wilson, H.H. 2490, 2492, 2496,
2509, 2528
Wilson, K.G. 78, 577, 2006, 2009
Wilson, R.M. 1274
Wilß, W. 2222
Wilts, O. 79, 2028, 2031f.,
2034-2036
Wimmer, Chr. 592
Wimmer, L. 1918
Wimmer, R. 195f., 207, 613, 788,
796, 1276, 1284, 2074, 2234
Wimsatt, M.H. 1949, 1953
Wimsatt, W.K. 1949, 1953
Winchell, C. 3174
Winchell, C.M. 3176
Winckler, H. 1691, 1694
Winder, M. 2231
Windfeld Hansen, J. 3058, 3060
Windfuhr, G.L. 2479f.
Winding, U. 3061
Windisch, E. 2340, 2343
Windisch, Z. 835
Wing, J. van 2647, 2649
Wingen, H. 3124, 3127, 3135
Winiecki, J. 1764
Winkel, L.A. te 296, 1241, 1415,
1609
Winkler 3141
Winkler, Chr. 1310, 1623
Winkler, H.J. 1102
Winkler, J. 2026
Winkler, L. 1036, 1042
Winkler, P. 2065
Winkler, W. 2751
Winograd, T. 893, 898, 1651,
1668, 1671
Winslow, M. 2523f., 2533
Winston, P.H. 1671
Winter, C. 2495, 2496
Winter, C.F. 2561, 2563
Winter, E. 2199, 2232
Winter, G. 1050
Winter, St. 1147, 1149, 1152
Winter, W. 2480, 2558
Winterling, Chr. M. 2990
Winther, A. 1217

Wintle, J. 1045, 1050
Wippel, J.J. 243, 2074, 2099
Wippich, W. 716, 726
wiPsit phutthiPbandit 2577, 2583
Wirsing, P. 2664, 2670
Wirth, K.A. 3157
Wirtjes, H. 1304
Wisbey, R.A. 1126, 1134, 1136f.,
1143, 1609
Wisdom, Ch. 2664, 2670
Wise, M. R. 2702
Wiske, F. 2989f.
Wissemann, H. 599
Wissmann, W. 1065, 1255, 1257,
1414, 1609
Wit, L. 3132
Withals, J. 2895, 2901
Withers, Ph. 225
Withycombe, E.G. 1274
Witkam, A.P.M. 1672, 3167
Witkowski, N. 3072, 3085
Witsen, N. 2396, 2398, 2408
Witt, R. 2177, 2224, 2754
Witte, H. 2155, 2166, 2199, 2232
Wittek, J. 2087, 2098
Wittels, H. 1080
Wittgenstein, L. 407, 541, 577,
716, 726, 850, 852, 855
Wittig, M. 1195, 1198
Wittig, S. 1566f.
Wittmer, L. 1090, 1093
Wittstock, O. 1152, 2193, 2232
Witty, M.B. 1261, 1265
Witzel, E. 2939, 2947
Witzel, G. 1268
Witzmann, A. 1230
Wjela-Radyserb, J. 2275, 2278
Wodak, R. 653f., 2191, 2234
Woetzel, H. 537, 544, 587, 617,
628, 653, 657, 798, 805, 851,
855, 2131, 2246
Wohlauer, E.M. 1264
Wohlauer, G.E.M. 1261
Wohlgemuth-Berglund, G. 1050,
1053, 1363
Wohlgenannt, R. 248, 279, 543,
587
Wohlwend, M. 1080
Wójcik, A. 746
Wójtowicz, A. 746
Wolf, A.A. 2298, 2300
Wolf, E.M. 1143
Wolf, F.A. 1700, 1717
Wolf, H. 3031
Wolf, H.J. 1296, 1344, 1348
Wolf, L. 47, 62, 126, 274, 584, 649,
835, 997, 1031, 1344, 1348,
1816, 1847, 1863, 2756, 2768,
2936
Wolf, S.A. 1529, 1531-1535, 1537
Wolf, U. 584
Wolfart, H. Chr. 3173

Wolff, A. 185, 188
Wolff, D. 768, 770f., 1347
Wolff, E. 1926, 2469, 2649, 3053, 3061
Wolff, J.U. 2572f.
Wolff, J.W. 2573
Wolff, O. 3052, 3061
Wolff, R.A. 1167
Wölfflin, E. 1717
Wolfram von Eschenbach 1558
Wolfrum, G. 2215
Wolfson, N. 2254, 2690
Wolgemuth, C. 2660f.
Wolk, A. 76, 79
Wolkonsky, C.A. 1147, 1149, 1151
Woll, D. 269, 1730, 1732, 1735
Wollemann, A. 1293, 1296
Wöller, E. 748, 2715, 2725f., 2754, 2769, 2776, 2778
Wollheim da Fonseca, A.E. 3023, 3029
Wollmann, F. 2191, 2246
Wollmanov, F. 2267
Wolnicz-Pawłowska, E. 1286, 1290, 2273
Wolski, W. 101, 114, 126f., 174, 321, 363, 370f., 389, 409, 424, 430, 432, 434, 462, 501, 531, 533, 544f., 552, 556f., 559, 562, 564, 569, 573, 587, 614, 616f., 623-625, 628f., 635, 648f., 657, 699, 793, 796, 800, 805-812, 814, 823, 825-827, 830, 851, 855, 857, 862f., 868, 956, 958, 960-962, 965, 967, 980f., 1210, 1562, 1621, 1625, 2102, 2131, 2207, 2246, 2321, 2326-2329, 2728, 2769, 2836, 2839, 2853f., 2903, 3168
Wolter, I. 2155, 2166, 2168, 2222
Wolters, G. 574
Wolters, J.B. 2562f., 2565
Wong, H.T. 408, 1142
Wong, Y.W. (= Wang Yunwu) 2606
Wood, C. 1131
Wood, F.T. 1006, 1008, 1031, 1217, 1219
Wood, J. 1046, 1050
Wood, M.W. 3129, 3135
Woodhead, D.R. 3094, 3096
Woodhouse, S. 3147
Woods, A. 1645
Woods, R.L. 1047, 1050
Woods, W.A. 3168
Woodward, F.L. 2502, 2505
Woodward, J. 3143f.
Wooldridge, T.R. 19, 136, 146, 328, 360, 652, 657, 1032, 1100, 1102, 1145, 1792f., 1794, 1818, 2860, 2864

Woolf, H.B. 35, 37, 1164, 2008
Worcester, J.E. 224, 358, 720, 723, 763, 766, 1958, 1988, 1990-1992, 2004, 2008, 2952
Worchester, J.E. 1966
Worchester, J.W. 29
Worgt, G. 3044
Worrall, A.J. 1031
Worst, G. 3046
Worstbrock, F.J. 2039, 2047
Wortabet, J. 3090, 3096
Worth, D.S. 1147-1149, 1151, 2325, 2628, 2631
Worth, S. 716, 726
Wortig, G. 1044
Wortig, K. 1050
Wossidlo, R. 242, 1233, 1240, 2076
Wothke, K. 1655, 1668
Wotjak, G. 545, 587, 2883, 2886, 2888
Woulfe, P. 1275
Wouters, A. 1720
Woykos, B. 2593f.
Wrangell, M. 2394
Wrede, A. 1393, 1415, 1600f., 1609
Wrede, E. 3044, 3046
Wrede, F. 1912
Wright, A. 1261, 1266, 1367
Wright, D. 3049, 3051
Wright, J. 860, 1414, 1608, 1962, 1966, 1984, 1986
Wright, Th. 719, 723, 1452, 1455
Wrisley, B. 2705
Wu, J. 298f., 303f.
Wu, Ying 2769
Wuite, E. 2751
Wülcker, E. 820, 1411, 1414, 2084, 2088, 2095
Wülfing, E. 634
Wülfing, W. 1200, 1203f., 1206
Wumkes, G.A. 2026, 2035
Wun, M. 2551f., 2554
Wunderli, P. 654, 1017, 1144, 1813, 2887
Wunderlich, D. 125, 189, 275f., 407, 410, 462, 533, 541, 577, 580, 587, 627, 654, 668, 726, 862, 896, 899, 980, 997f., 1031, 1093, 1283, 1311, 1364, 2235, 2757, 3030
Wunderlich, G. 2066, 2073, 2094, 2098
Wunderlich, H. 2081
Wunderlich, P. 1765
Wunsch, K. 2233
Wuras, C.F. 2651f., 2654
Wurm, Chr.F.L. 226f., 2078, 2081-2084, 2098-2100
Wurm, F. 2218
Wurm, St.A. 2636-2638

Wurms, R. 2225
Wüst, W. 2496
Wüster, E. 118, 127, 170, 318, 322, 372, 407, 409, 460, 585, 955f., 1067, 1660, 1668, 1838, 2206, 2246, 2921, 3121f., 3124-3126, 3128-3130, 3135-3137, 3172, 3175
Wustmann, G. 207f., 1035f., 1039, 2065, 2067, 2090, 2099, 2217
Wyld, H.C. 512f., 517, 526, 528, 530, 1162, 1965, 1968
Wyle, N. von 1399
Wynar, B.S. 3176

X

Xat'iašvili, T. 2417f.
Xavier, F. 3113
Xec, P. 2662f., 2670
Xhuvani, A. 2363, 2366
Xu Lin 2558
Xu Shen 2597, 2599, 2605, 2611
Xucišvili, O. 2417f.
Xue Shigi 2598f., 2611
Xulin de Lluza 1764
Xuriguera Parramona, J.B. 1776, 1778
Xuriguera, J.B. 1776, 1781, 1787
Xylander, J. Ritter von 2362, 2367

Y

Y-Bham Buon-Ya 2593
Yaasiin, K. 2464
Yabu, S. 2560
Yac Sam, S. 2667
Yadava-prakāśa 2489
Yaguello, M. 88
Yamada, B. 2620, 2623
Yamada, K. 3116, 3119
Yamagiwa, J.K. 3176
Yamakawa, K. 3117
Yamamoto, F. 1972, 1983
Yamamura, S. 3117
Yamasaki, K. 2299, 2301
Yan Xi Xiang 2594
Yanagawa, K. 3116
Yanagiwa, J. K. 2620, 2623
Yang Fu-mien, P. 3111, 3113
Yang Xiong 2602, 2610
Yang, P.F. 3176
Yapita Moya, J. de Dios 2685, 2688-2690
Yar-shater, Ehsau 2479
Yasen 'Isman Kenadid 2465
Yashovadhan 3128
Yasin 'Isman Kenadid 2464
Yāska 2488
Yasugi, S. 3116, 3319

Yasui, M. 3117
Yates, F.A. 1088, 1090, 1094, 2970, 2976
Yen-Ngvan 2506
Yerba, M. 3142, 3144
Yermoloff, A. 1036, 1042
Yi Chae-wŏn 2615
Yi Chae-won 2617
Yi Hŭi-sŭng 2614, 2616
Yi Sang-ch'un 2614, 2616
Yi Yun-jae 2614
Yofe, Y.A. 2252f.
Yohanan, A. 2437
Yoḥannəs Gäbrä Egzi'abəḥer 2451, 2455
Yokoi, T. 3117
Yokoyama, S. 3168
Yona ibn Ğanah (= Abū-l-Walīd) 2427
Yona ibn Ğavāh 2434
Yônâh, R. 2712
Yöpusë, F. B. 2636, 2638
Yoshida, K. 2623
Yoshida, S. 2622, 3167
Yoshio, N. 3114, 3118
Younes, G. 1069, 1074, 1217, 1220
Young, R. W. 2692, 2694-2696
Yousef, F. 172, 174
Yu Ch'ang-don 2614, 2616f.
Yu, Dao-chu 2550
Yuan, Jiahua 2560
Yule, G. 894. 898
Yve-Plessis, R. 1190
Yvinec, H. 2959
Yvon, H. 1083

Z

Zabidi, 3088
Zaborski, A. 2461, 2469
Zachariae, Th. 2497
Zacher, H.H. 1052
Zacher, J. 2066, 2077
Zachrisson, B. 139, 142, 146
Zaehme, V. 1266
Zagajewski, K. 1551, 1561
Zahn, J.Chr. 1912
Zaicz, G. 2398
Zainqui, J.M. 1069, 1074
Zajączkowski, W. 2412
Zajmi, A. 2292, 2295, 2365f.
Zaleman, K. G. (Salemann, C.) 2485
Zalewski, W. 3176
Zaliznjak, A. A. 1132, 1134f., 1138, 1143, 2316, 2319, 2325, 2896, 2900f.
Zalokar, J. 2298
Zamakhsharī 3086
Zambaldi, F. 1328, 1334, 1875
Zamčuk, D. B. 2216

Zamenhof, L.L. 3120f., 3124, 3126f., 3136f.
Zamora Munné, J.C. 1755, 1764
Zamora Vicente, A. 929, 1749, 1764, 1767, 2986
Zamora, A. 1080
Zamora, A. de 2427, (A. Zamorensis) RN 2434
Zamora, J. 1284
Zampolli, A. 111, 305, 626, 899, 1137, 1139, 1141, 1320, 1666, 1668, 1670, 1871, 1874, 1878, 1880, 2813, 3166
Zandt Cortelyou, J. van 1255, 1257
Zandvoort, R.W. 1166
Zang, Q. 3113
Zannetti, L. 2690
Zante, V. 2359
Zantema, A. 2027, 2035
Zantema, J. W. 2026, 2033, 2035
Zapf, H. 408
Zapp, F.J. 1363f.
Zaręba, L. 3065, 3068
Zarechnak, M. 577
Zarncke, F. 242, 1149f., 1234, 1238, 1405, 1413, 1418-1420, 1424-1426, 1428, 1434, 1539, 1548, 1601, 1608-1610, 2088, 2090, 2094, 2096,
Zarubin, I. I. 2485f.
Zarva, M.V. 2316, 2322
Zasorina, L.N. 1643, 1669, 1671, 2320, 2325, 2329
Zaunmüller, W. 1, 19, 1204, 1206, 2910f., 2937, 2948, 3075, 3085, 3176
Zaupser, A. 238, 243, 2060, 2073
Zauzich, K.-Th. 1681
Závada, D. 1052f., 3026, 3029
Zavala, M. 2664, 2670
Zavetu, N. 2266
Zavra, M.V. 1308
Zawolkow, E. 3143f.
Zbijowska, B. 1274
Zbiniowska, J. 1274
Ždanov, P. I. 3073, 3084
Zdanowski, F. B. 3022, 3029
Zditovetski, A. 3022, 3029
Zecchini, St.P. 1074
Zedler, G. 1818
Zedler, J.H. 217, 223
Zegers, T. N. 2915, 2936
Zehetmayr, S. 1412, 1415
Zeig, S. 1195, 1198
Żelazko, K. 2270, 2073
Zelders, N.L. 1290
Żelechovs'kyj, E. 2331, 2333f.
Zelinskij, V.A. 1149, 1151
Zeller, A.P. 1100, 1102
Zemach, E.M. 573, 587
Zemb, J.-M. 277, 1123, 1125, 1179, 1181, 1184

Zemzare, D. 2355, 2357f., 2361
Zeninger, C. 2042
Zenker, J.Th. 2402f., 2406
Zenker, L. 1142, 2404, 2406
Zeno, A. 1855, 1861
Zeps, V.J. 2359f.
Zerolo, E. 1746, 1764
Zesen, Ph. von 235, 1126f., 1131, 2066, 2074
Zetkin, M. 848
Zetterstéen, K.V. 2400, 2407
Zettersten, A. 17, 127, 135, 188, 213, 278f., 359f., 371, 408, 460f., 500, 583f., 586f., 628, 656, 693, 749, 754, 787, 814, 822, 855, 893, 930, 981, 999, 1165, 1178, 1304, 1415f., 1549, 1669, 1987, 2236, 2240, 2243-2245, 2726, 2753f., 2756-2759, 2761f., 2764, 2770, 2775, 2778, 2836, 2853f., 2902, 2960, 2969, 3061
Zeuner, H. 1142
Zeuschner, O. 1046, 1050, 2066, 2074
Zeuss, J.K. 2341-2343
Zgaraon, F. 1888
Zgółkowa, M. 2270, 2274
Zgusta, L. 18, 33, 72f., 77-79, 87, 96, 99, 101, 131, 135, 208, 215, 222, 224, 257, 275, 278, 280, 283, 287f., 296, 305, 360-362, 367, 371, 373, 406, 408-410, 460, 461f., 499f., 519, 521, 523, 525, 532, 557, 575, 577, 579, 581f., 585, 587f., 614, 620-622, 628, 652, 657, 693, 696, 699, 780, 782, 805, 861, 899, 905, 917f., 930, 989, 991, 999, 623, 1206, 1210, 1275, 1283, 1334, 1407, 1416, 1613, 1616, 1618, 1625, 1638, 1644f., 1672, 1698-1700, 1704, 1966, 2206, 2244, 2246, 2471, 2473, 2492, 2497, 2712, 2715, 2718, 2727f., 2752, 2759, 2763f., 2769f., 2775, 2778, 2783, 2789, 2824, 2829, 2831, 2837, 2854, 2858-2860, 2865, 2867, 2869f., 2937, 3110, 3161, 3168
Zgustová, M. 1776, 1786
Zhang Jichuan 2559
Zhang Jing 2597, 2611
Zhang Qiyon 2611
Zhang Qiyun 2601
Zhang Yi 2601
Zhang, Yi-sen 2550
Zhao Gao 2597
Zhao Yansun 2558
Zheng, Y. 3133
Zholkovskij, A. K. 2469, 2469, 2698, 2700 (s. Žolkovskij)

Zhou Zhi Zhi 2591, 2594
Zhukov, V.K. 1044
Zhukov, V.P. 1039
Zhwa lu chos skyong bzang po 2548
Zhwa lu mchod dpon you tan 'byung guas 2549
Zhylko, F.T. 2332
Zhytec'kyj, P. 2334
Zibell, W. 2634
Zide, A. 2544, 2546f.
Zide, N. 2535, 2542f., 2545-2547
Ziegelmeyer, P. 1349, 1352
Ziegler, E. 1008
Ziegler, K. 158
Ziehen, Th. 360, 371
Ziemann, A. 1601, 1609
Zierer, E. 1767
Zierhoffer, K. 2271
Ziesemer, W. 242
Zifonun, G. 117, 126, 552, 583, 617-620, 627, 790, 796, 836-838, 842, 849-852, 855, 1200, 1205, 1207, 1209
Zigány, J. 275, 2753, 2778, 2836, 2881
Zikmund Hrubý z Jelení 2279, 2284 (s. Gelenius)
Zikmund, H. 1137, 1143, 2828
Zimin, I. 2325
Zimin, V.I. 2315, 2324
Zimmer, D.E. 43, 46, 130, 135
Zimmer, H. 2339f., 2343
Zimmer, H.D. 708, 726
Zimmer, R. 2769, 2879, 2881
Zimmer, St. 2349
Zimmermann, G. 2663f., 2670
Zimmermann, H. 272, 357, 369, 405, 458, 498, 515, 574, 626, 661, 667, 672, 687, 753, 778, 786, 795, 803, 820, 834, 848, 860, 1238, 1361, 1608, 1622, 1660, 1668, 1671, 2217, 2222

Zimmermann, H. H. 109, 111
Zimmermann, K. 1220
Zimmermann, M. 1019
Zimmermann, O.T. 1261, 1264
Zimmermann, T. 748, 2725f., 2754, 2776, 2778
Zimmermann, V. 2220
Zimmermann, W. 2229
Zinder, L. R. 2765
Zingarelli, N. 66, 70, 141, 145, 359, 511-513, 515, 517, 648, 685, 687, 705, 721, 724, 761f., 766, 918, 930, 988, 1863, 1866, 1875, 1879
Zingerle, I. 2065, 2074
Zingref, J. W. 2065, 2074
Zinknan 3112
Zinn, R. 2670
Zips, V.J. 2395, 2398
Žirkov, L.I. 242-2423f.
Zischka, G.A. 1, 19, 988, 999, 1204, 1206, 2937, 2948, 3176
Ziszpanski, K. 3068
Žitnik, J. 2299, 2302
Živanović, St. 3126, 3136
Ziwès, A. 1533, 1538
Zizanij Tustanovskij, L. 2325, 2335, 3070 (s. Zyznij)
Zlatagorskoï, E. 1125
Zoder, R. 1271, 1275
Zoëga, G.T. 1929, 1932
Zoeppritz, M. 1671, 3165
Zoetmulder, P. J. 2561, 2563
Zöfgen, E. 109, 111, 115, 120, 126f., 131, 135, 215, 607, 777, 779-781, 784f., 787, 904f., 1001, 1007, 1009f., 1390, 1614, 1618, 1625, 1638, 2172, 2240, 2783, 2878, 2888f., 2897f., 2903, 2969
Zola, E. 1185
Žolkovskij, A.K. 1006, 1008, 1015, 3216, 2324 (s. Zholkovskij)
Zolli, P. 1090, 1094, 1166, 1168, 1178, 1217, 1325, 1332, 1845, 1847, 1856f., 1863, 1875-1877, 1880, 1903, 3007, 3009f., 3013, 3177
Zolnai, G. 2382
Zolotova, G.A. 740, 749, 2316, 2329
Zoltán, G. 2378
Zonneveld, W. 1017
Zoozmann, R. 1046f., 1050
Zorc, D. R. 2870 (= Zorc, R.D.)
Zorc, R. D. (P.) 2570, 2639-2641, 2769
Zorell, F. 2428, 2435
Zorrilla, O. 1005, 1008
Zorzi de Nurmbergo 1847
Zribi-Hertz, A. 592
Zudin, P. B. 2484, 2486, 3101, 3107
Zuidema, R. T. 2678, 2684
Žukov, V.P. 2315, 2325
Žukova, A. N. 2630f.
Žukovskaja, L. P. 2266
Zumthor, P. 1266
Zúñiga, D. de 2664, 2670
Zupitza, J. 1438, 1456
Zúquete, A. 1730, 1734
Żurakowska, M. 3067
Zurcher, A.J. 1516f., 1520, 1522
Zvonarich, St. 2293
Zwahr, J. G. 2278
Zwanenburg, W. 649, 784f., 787, 1833, 1843
Zwang, G. 1196, 1198
Zwarp, E.C. 1145
Zwirner, E. 517, 1311, 1610
Zwolinski, P. 1286, 1290
Zymberi, A. 2363, 2367
Zyzanij, L. 2310, 2329, 2332-2334 (s. Zizanij)

F. J. H./O. R./ H. E. W./L. Z.
unter Mitarbeit von Jenifer Brundage und Gisela Schmidt